February 15–19, 2014
Baltimore, Maryland, USA

Association for
Computing Machinery

Advancing Computing as a Science & Profession

CSCW 2014

CSCW'14

Proceedings of the 17th ACM Conference on Computer Supported Cooperative Work & Social Computing

Sponsored by:

ACM SIGCHI

Supported by:

NSF, Facebook, Microsoft Research, Grand NCE, IBM Research, Drexel University, Google and UMBC

Association for
Computing Machinery

Advancing Computing as a Science & Profession

The Association for Computing Machinery
2 Penn Plaza, Suite 701
New York, New York 10121-0701

Notice to Past Authors of ACM-Published Articles
ACM intends to create a complete electronic archive of all articles and/or other material previously published by ACM. If you have written a work that has been previously published by ACM in any journal or conference proceedings prior to 1978, or any SIG Newsletter at any time, and you do NOT want this work to appear in the ACM Digital Library, please inform permissions@acm.org, stating the title of the work, the author(s), and where and when published.

ISBN: 978-1-4503-2752-7 (Digital)

ISBN: 978-1-4503-3164-7 (Print)

Additional copies may be ordered prepaid from:

ACM Order Department
PO Box 30777
New York, NY 10087-0777, USA

Phone: 1-800-342-6626 (USA and Canada)
+1-212-626-0500 (Global)
Fax: +1-212-944-1318
E-mail: acmhelp@acm.org
Hours of Operation: 8:30 am – 4:30 pm ET

Printed in the USA

Welcome from the Conference Chairs

We warmly welcome you to Baltimore, Maryland, USA, for the 2014 ACM Conference on Computer Supported Cooperative Work and Social Computing! In keeping with previous years, CSCW 2014 presents premier research on computer-mediated collaboration, social computing, and social media, from the design of technical systems for collaboration to ethnographic studies of use in the wild. The mission of the conference is to share the novel research that will advance the state of our art. The conference program embraces a variety of perspectives, reflecting how collaboration permeates different aspects of people's work, social, and civic lives. This diversity of perspectives is mirrored by geographic diversity among contributors.

The CSCW 2014 program retains the richly articulated structure of previous conferences in this series including a robust program of workshops, papers, panels, demonstrations, videos, and interactive posters. This year, we also introduce CSCWhat's Next, a selection of forward-looking research-in-progress papers intended to foster discussion. Another innovation this year is the option for demos, videos and poster presenters to give short talks about their work immediately preceding Monday night's reception.

Special highlights this year include our opening plenary talk, **"Making a Difference In and Through Playful Design,"** by Mary Flanagan of Dartmouth University and our closing plenary, **"Next Generation Humanitarian Computing,"** by Patrick Meier of Qatar Computing Research Institute. We will also present the inaugural CSCW Lasting Impact Award to Jonathan Grudin for his groundbreaking 1988 paper "**Why CSCW applications fail: Problems in the design and evaluation of organizational interfaces**."

Interest in CSCW'14 is as high as ever, including a record number of paper submissions. The welcome message from our technical program chairs highlights the modifications to the review process this year as we continue to optimize our new revise and resubmit system.

Putting together CSCW'14 was a team effort. We first thank the authors for providing the content that is the core of our dynamic program. We are grateful to the program committee, who worked hard in reviewing papers and providing detailed feedback for authors. We heard from many about how this process truly helped improve the final papers. We thank our entire hard-working conference committee, from the papers chairs to the treasurer to the webmasters, an incredible group of people who donated countless hours of their time. We also thank Lisa Tolles at Sheridan Communications, Yvonne Lopez at RegOnline, and Ashley Cozzi and Stephanie Sabal from ACM for all of their assistance with arrangements, registration, and publications. Special thanks go out to John and Joanne Lateulere for their invaluable help with conference planning and management. Finally, we thank our sponsors ACM and SIGCHI, and generous sponsors, Facebook, Microsoft Research, National Science Foundation, Grand NCE, IBM Research, the iSchool at Drexel University, Google, and Information Systems at UMBC.

We hope that you find this program interesting and thought provoking and that the conference provides you with a valuable opportunity to share ideas with other researchers and practitioners from institutions around the world. Take time to enjoy all that Charm City has to offer.

Susan Fussell
Conference Co-Chair
Cornell University, USA

Wayne Lutters
Conference Co-Chair
UMBC, USA

From the Program Chairs

The CSCW research community is expanding at a tremendous pace. This year, we received a record 497 submissions – an increase of 27% from last year. Authors from 38 countries on 6 continents submitted papers. We accepted 134 papers for an acceptance rate of 27%. The growth in the number of submissions speaks to the increasing interest in CSCW. The papers range from traditional topics of interest to the CSCW community such as collaboration in work settings to newer topics such as crowdsourcing and social computing. The papers presented in this year's conference highlight the intellectual diversity of research in CSCW.

This was also the third year for the revise and resubmit (R&R) process for the conference. Similar to the process last year, we did not have page limits for the submissions, nor did we have a separate submission category for "notes" (short papers); rather, research contributions of any length were considered for the papers category. Out of the 497 papers submitted to the conference, 43% were invited to be revised and resubmitted. The overall response to the R&R process has been very positive. Many of the accepted papers were greatly improved through the revision process.

We would especially like to thank the external reviewers and Program Committee (PC) members. The revise and resubmit process would not be possible without the dedicated work of the reviewers and PC members. We had one of the largest PCs for CSCW with 64 members representing both the intellectual and geographical diversity of our community. This was a particularly challenging year for reviewing because of the record number of submissions and the reduced time frame for the review process. Without the amazing efforts of the PC members and external reviewers, we would not have been able to present the outstanding set of papers in the conference. Enjoy!

Meredith Ringel Morris
Program Co-Chair
Microsoft Research, USA

Madhu Reddy
Program Co-Chair
Penn State University, USA

Table of Contents

CSCW 2014 Organization xvi

CSCW'14 Additional Reviewers xx

CSCW 2014 Sponsor & Supporters xxiv

Session Order 1: Keynote Address

- **Making a Difference in and Through Playful Design** 1
  Mary Flanagan *(Dartmouth College)*

Session Order 2: Friendsourcing

Session Chair: Sharoda A. Paul *(GE Global Research)*

- **Help Is on the Way: Patterns of Responses to Resource Requests on Facebook** 3
  Cliff Lampe *(University of Michigan)*, Rebecca Gray *(Michigan State University)*, Andrew T. Fiore *(Facebook)*, Nicole B. Ellison *(University of Michigan)*
- **To Search or to ask: The Routing of Information Needs Between Traditional Search Engines and Social Networks** 16
  Anne Oeldorf-Hirsch *(University of Connecticut)*, Brent Hecht *(University of Minnesota)*, Meredith Ringel Morris, Jaime Teevan *(Microsoft Research)*, Darren Gergle *(Northwestern University)*
- **What Do Teens Ask Their Online Social Networks? Social Search Practices Among High School Students** 28
  Andrea Forte, Michael Dickard, Rachel Magee, Denise E. Agosto *(Drexel University)*

Session Order 3: Crowdfunding: "Show me the Money!"

Session Chair: Michael Bernstein *(Stanford University)*

- **Coordinating Donors on Crowdfunding Websites** 38
  Rick Wash, Jacob Solomon *(Michigan State University)*
- **The Language that Gets People to Give: Phrases that Predict Success on Kickstarter** 49
  Tanushree Mitra, Eric Gilbert *(Georgia Institute of Technology)*
- **Understanding the Role of Community in Crowdfunding Work** 62
  Julie S. Hui, Michael D. Greenberg, Elizabeth M. Gerber *(Northwestern University)*

Session Order 4: Telepresence

Session Chair: Gina Venolia *(Microsoft Research)*

- **Smart Face: Enhancing Creativity During Video Conferences Using Real-Time Facial Deformation** 75
  Naoto Nakazato, Shigeo Yoshida, Sho Sakurai, Takuji Narumi, Tomohiro Tanikawa, Michitaka Hirose *(The University of Tokyo)*
- **Towards a Questionnaire for Measuring Affective Benefits and Costs of Communication Technologies** 84
  Svetlana Yarosh *(AT&T Research Labs)*, Panos Markopoulos *(Eindhoven University of Technology)*, Gregory D. Abowd *(Georgia Institute of Technology)*
- **How Social Cues Shape Task Coordination and Communication** 97
  Allison Sauppé, Bilge Mutlu *(University of Wisconsin, Madison)*,

Session Order 5: Blinding me with Science

Session Chair: Jackie O'Neill *(Xerox Research Center Europe)*

- **Planet Hunters and Seafloor Explorers: Legitimate Peripheral Participation Through Practice Proxies in Online Citizen Science** 109
  Gabriel Mugar, Carsten Østerlund, Katie DeVries Hassman *(Syracuse University)*, Kevin Crowston *(National Science Foundation)*, Corey Brian Jackson *(Syracuse University)*

- **Study of Electronic Lab Notebook Design and Practices That Emerged in a Collaborative Scientific Environment** 120
  Gerard Oleksik *(Dovetailed Ltd)*, Natasa Milic-Frayling *(Microsoft Research)*, Rachel Jones *(Instrata Ltd)*
- **Reconciling Rhythms: Plans and Temporal Alignment in Collaborative Scientific Work** 134
  Stephanie B. Steinhardt, Steven J. Jackson *(Cornell University)*

Session Order 6: Building Communities and Relationships

Session Chair: Vanessa Evars *(University of Twente)*

- **Building Loyalty to Online Communities Through Bond and Identity-Based Attachment to Sub-Groups** 146
  Yla R. Tausczik, Laura A. Dabbish, Robert E. Kraut *(Carnegie Mellon University)*
- **Ethnography of Scaling, Or, How to fit a national research infrastructure in the room** 158
  David Ribes *(Georgetown University)*
- **Enabling Relationship Building in Tabletop-Supported Advisory Settings** 171
  Peter Heinrich, Mehmet Kilic, Felix-Robinson Aschoff, Gerhard Schwabe *(University of Zurich)*

Session Order 7: Filter Bubbles & News

Session Chair: Kate Starbird *(University of Washington)*

- **Can You Hear Me Now? Mitigating the Echo Chamber Effect by Source Position Indicators** 184
  Q. Vera Liao, Wai-Tat Fu *(University of Illinois at Urbana-Champaign)*
- **Deep Twitter Diving: Exploring Topical Groups in Microblogs at Scale** 197
  Parantapa Bhattacharya *(IIT Kharagpur & Max Planck Institute of Software Systems)*,
  Saptarshi Ghosh *(Bengal Engineering and Science University Shibpur)*,
  Juhi Kulshrestha, Mainack Mondal, Muhammad Bilal Zafar *(Max Planck Institute of Software Systems)*,
  Niloy Ganguly *(IIT Kharagpur, India)*, Krishna P. Gummadi *(Max Planck Institute of Software Systems)*
- **Characterizing the Life Cycle of Online News Stories Using Social Media Reactions** 211
  Carlos Castillo *(Qatar Computing Research Institute)*, Mohammed El-Haddad *(Al Jazeera English)*,
  Jürgen Pfeffer *(Carnegie Mellon University)*, Matt Stempeck *(Massachusetts Institute of Technology)*

Session Order 8: Performing Crowd Work

Session Chair: Dan Cosley *(Cornell University)*

- **Being A Turker** 224
  David Martin, Benjamin V. Hanrahan, Jacki O'Neill *(Xerox Research Centre Europe)*,
  Neha Gupta *(University of Nottingham)*
- **The Motivations and Experiences of the On-Demand Mobile Workforce** 236
  Rannie Teodoro *(Rutgers University)*, Pinar Ozturk *(Stevens Institute of Technology)*, Mor Naaman *(Cornell Tech)*,
  Winter Mason *(Stevens Institute of Technology)*, Janne Lindqvist *(Rutgers University)*
- **Information Extraction and Manipulation Threats in Crowd-Powered Systems** 248
  Walter S. Lasecki *(University of Rochester)*, Jaime Teevan, Ece Kamar *(Microsoft Research)*

Session Order 9: Work in Hospitals

Session Chair: Aleksandra Sarcevic *(Drexel University)*

- **How Physicians 'Achieve Overview': A Case-based Study in a Hospital Ward** 257
  Claus Bossen, Lotte Groth Jensen *(Aarhus University)*
- **Privacy Practices in Collaborative Environments: A Study of Emergency Department Staff** 269
  Alison R. Murphy, Madhu C. Reddy, Heng Xu *(The Pennsylvania State University)*
- **Institutional Logics of the EMR and the Problem of 'Perfect' but Inaccurate Accounts** 283
  Kathleen Pine *(Intel Labs)*, Melissa Mazmanian *(University of California, Irvine)*

Session Order 10: Craft, Repair, and DIY

Session Chair: David Randell *(University of Siegen)*

- **"It's in Your Spinal Cord, It's in Your Fingertips": Practices of Craft in Building Software** 295
  Jessa Lingel, Tim Regan *(Microsoft Research)*
- **Cultivating Practice & Shepherding Technology Use: Supporting Appropriation Among Unanticipated Users** 305
  Pablo-Alejandro Quiñones *(University of Michigan)*
- **Designing for Repair? Infrastructures and Materialities of Breakdown** 319
  Daniela K. Rosner *(University of Washington)*, Morgan G. Ames *(UC Irvine)*

Session Order 11: Q&A

Session Chair: David McDonald *(University of Washington)*

- **Fast, Functional, and Fitting: Expert Response Dynamics and Response Quality in an Online Newcomer Help Forum** 332
  Hon Jie Teo *(Virginia Polytechnic Institute and State University)*, Aditya Johri *(George Mason University)*
- **How Social Q&A Sites Are Changing Knowledge Sharing in Open Source Software Communities** 342
  Bogdan Vasilescu *(Eindhoven University of Technology & University of California, Davis)*,
  Alexander Serebrenik *(Eindhoven University of Technology)*,
  Prem Devanbu, Vladimir Filkov *(University of California, Davis)*
- **Collaborative Problem Solving: A Study of MathOverflow** 355
  Yla R. Tausczik, Aniket Kittur , Robert E. Kraut *(Carnegie Mellon University)*

Session Order 12: Social Media in the Enterprise

Session Chair: Jennifer Thom *(Amazon)*

- **Creepy But Inevitable? The Evolution of Social Networking** 368
  Hui Zhang *(University of Washington)*, Munmun De Choudhury, Jonathan Grudin *(Microsoft Research)*
- **Understanding Employee Social Media Chatter with Enterprise Social Pulse** 379
  N. Sadat Shami, Jiang Yang, Laura Panc *(IBM)*, Casey Dugan, Tristan Ratchford *(IBM T.J. Watson Research)*,
  Jamie Rasmussen *(IBM Research)*, Yannick Assogba *(IBM T.J. Watson Research)*, Tal Steier *(IBM Research, Israel)*,
  Todd Soule *(IBM T.J. Watson Research)*, Stela Lupushor *(IBM)*, Werner Geyer *(IBM T.J. Watson Research)*,
  Ido Guy *(IBM Research, Israel)*, Jonathan Ferrar *(IBM)*
- **Most Liked, Fewest Friends: Patterns of Enterprise Social Media Use** 393
  Gloria Mark *(University of California, Irvine)*, Ido Guy, Shiri Kremer-Davidson, Michal Jacovi *(IBM Research, Israel)*

Session Order 13: Values & Social Norms

Session Chair: Ingrid Erickson *(Rutgers University)*

- **Understanding Individuals' Personal Values from Social Media Word Use** 405
  Jilin Chen *(IBM Almaden Research Center)*, Gary Hsieh *(University of Washington)*,
  Jalal U. Mahmud, Jeffrey Nichols *(IBM Research)*
- **Cursing in English on Twitter** 415
  Wenbo Wang, Lu Chen, Krishnaprasad Thirunarayan, Amit P. Sheth *(Wright State University)*
- **How to See Values in Social Computing: Methods for Studying Values Dimensions** 426
  Katie Shilton, Jes A. Koepfler *(University of Maryland)*,
  Kenneth R. Fleischmann *(The University of Texas at Austin)*

Session Order 14: Social Media: Online and Off

Session Chair: Andrea Forte *(Drexel University)*

- **De-Virtualizing Social Events: Understanding the Gap Between Online and Offline Participation for Event Invitations** 436
  Ai-Ju Huang, Hao-Chuan Wang *(National Tsing Hua University)*,
  Chien Wen Yuan *(Cornell University)*

- **Awkward Encounters of an "Other" Kind: Collective Self-Presentation and Face Threat on Facebook** 449
  Eden Litt *(Northwestern University)*, Erin Spottswood *(Cornell University)*, Jeremy Birnholtz *(Northwestern University)*, Jeff Hancock *(Cornell University)*, Madeline E. Smith *(Northwestern University)*, Lindsay Reynolds *(Cornell University)*
- **"You Can't Block People Offline": Examining How Facebook's Affordances Shape the Disclosure Process** 461
  Jessica Vitak, Jinyoung Kim *(University of Maryland)*

Session Order 15: Family

Session Chair: Erika Poole *(Penn State University)*

- **Family Matters: Control and Conflict in Online Family History Production** 475
  Heather Willever-Farr, Andrea Forte *(Drexel University)*
- **"Our Life Is the Farm and Farming Is Our Life": Home–Work Coordination in Organic Farm Families** 487
  Gilly Leshed *(Cornell University)*, Maria Håkansson *(Chalmers University of Technology)*, Joseph 'Jofish' Kaye *(Yahoo! Research)*
- **Account Sharing in the Context of Networked Hospitality Exchange** 499
  Airi Lampinen *(Microsoft Research & Helsinki Institute for Information Technology (Finland))*

Session Order 16: Concurrency Control

- **Achieving Convergence in Operational Transformation: Conditions, Mechanisms and Systems** 505
  Yi Xu, Chengzheng Sun, Mo Li *(Nanyang Technological University)*
- **Exhaustive Search of Puzzles in Operational Transformation** 519
  Chengzheng Sun, Yi Xu, Agustina *(Nanyang Technological University)*
- **A Partial Replication Approach for Anywhere Anytime Mobile Commenting** 530
  Huanhuan Xia, Tun Lu *(Fudan University)*, Bin Shao *(Microsoft Research, China)*, Guo Li,Xianghua Ding, Ning Gu *(Fudan University)*

Session Order 17: Group Dynamics

Session Chair: Ido Guy *(IBM Haifa Research Lab)*

- **Monitoring Email to Indicate Project Team Performance and Mutual Attraction** 542
  Sean A. Munson *(University of Washington)*, Karina Kervin, Lionel P. Robert *(University of Michigan)*
- **Editing Beyond Articles: Diversity & Dynamics of Teamwork in Open Collaborations** 550
  Jonathan T. Morgan *(Wikimedia Foundation)*, Michael Gilbert, David W. McDonald, Mark Zachry *(University of Washington)*
- **Playing Well with Virtual Classmates: Relating Avatar Design to Group Satisfaction** 564
  Rabindra Ratan *(Michigan State University)*, Béatrice S. Hasler *(Interdisciplinary Center Herzliya, Israel)*

Session Order 18: Reflective Research

Session Chair: Steve Sawyer *(Syracuse University)*

- **The Kernel of a Research Infrastructure** 574
  David Ribes *(Georgetown University)*
- **The Policy Knot: Re-Integrating Policy, Practice and Design in CSCW Studies of Social Computing** 588
  Steven J. Jackson, Tarleton Gillespie, Sandy Payette *(Cornell University)*
- **Can Plans and Situated Actions Be Replicated?** 603
  John Rooksby *(University of Glasgow)*

Session Order 19: Social Technologies and Well-Being

Session Chair: Michael Massimi *(Microsoft Research)*

- **Social Structure and Depression in TrevorSpace** 615
  Christopher M. Homan *(Rochester Institute of Technology)*,
  Naiji Lu, Xin Tu, Megan C. Lytle, Vincent M. B. Silenzio *(University of Rochester)*
- **Characterizing and Predicting Postpartum Depression from Shared Facebook Data** 625
  Munmun De Choudhury, Scott Counts, Eric J. Horvitz, Aaron Hoff *(Microsoft Research)*
- **Books as a Social Technology** 639
  Annika Hupfeld, Tom Rodden *(The University of Nottingham)*

Session Order 20: Shopping and Collecting

Session Chair: Moira Burke *(Facebook)*

- **Framing the Conversation: The Role of Facebook Conversations in Shopping for Eyeglasses** 652
  Karim Said, Michele A. Williams, Amy Hurst, Shaun K. Kane *(University of Maryland, Baltimore County)*
- **Remote Shopping Advice: Enhancing In-Store Shopping with Social Technologies** 662
  Meredith Ringel Morris, Kori Inkpen, Gina Venolia *(Microsoft Research)*
- **Specialization, Homophily, and Gender in a Social Curation Site: Findings from Pinterest** 674
  Shuo Chang, Vikas Kumar *(University of Minnesota)*,
  Eric Gilbert *(Georgia Institute of Technology)*,
  Loren Terveen *(University of Minnesota)*

Session Order 21: ICT4D

Session Chair: Susan Wyche *(Michigan State University)*

- **Making IT "Pay a Bit Better": Design Challenges for Micro Rural Enterprise** 687
  Andy Crabtree, Alan Chamberlain *(The University of Nottingham)*
- **The Role of Data in Aligning the 'Unique Identity' Infrastructure in India** 697
  Aditya Johri *(George Mason University)*,
  Janaki Srinivasan *(Virginia Polytechnic Institute and State University)*
- **Enriching the Distressing Reality: Social Media Use by Chinese Migrant Workers** 710
  Jingjing Liu *(University of Siegen)*,
  Alexander Boden *(Fraunhofer Institute für Applied Information Technology)*,
  David William Randall, Volker Wulf *(University of Siegen)*

Session Order 22: Leadership

Session Chair: Gilly Leshed *(Cornell University)*

- **The Role of Founders in Building Online Groups** 722
  Robert E. Kraut *(Carnegie Mellon University)*, Andrew T. Fiore *(Facebook, Inc.)*
- **The Communication Patterns of Technical Leaders: Impact on Product Development Team Performance** 733
  Kate Ehrlich *(IBM Research)*, Marcelo Cataldo *(ConnReperio, LLC)*
- **Ensemble: Exploring Complementary Strengths of Leaders and Crowds in Creative Collaboration** 745
  Joy Kim, Justin Cheng, Michael S. Bernstein *(Stanford University)*

Session Order 23: Technology and Information Workers

- **The Perception of Others: Inferring Reputation from Social Media in the Enterprise** 756
  Michal Jacovi, Ido Guy, Shiri Kremer-Davidson, Sara Porat,
  Netta Aizenbud-Reshef *(IBM Research—Haifa)*

- **Supporting Task Resumption Using Visual Feedback** ... 767
  Yikun Liu, Yuan Jia, Wei Pan, Mark Pfaff *(Indiana University, Indianapolis)*
- **Geographical and Organizational Commonalities in Enterprise Crowdfunding** ... 778
  Michael Muller, Werner Geyer *(IBM T.J. Watson Research),*
  Todd Soule *(IBM Research),* John Wafer *(IBM)*

Session Order 24: Collaborative Search and Sharing

- **Teammate Inaccuracy Blindness: When Information Sharing Tools Hinder Collaborative Analysis** ... 797
  Ruogu Kang *(Carnegie Mellon University),* Aimée Kane *(Duquesne University),*
  Sara Kiesler *(Carnegie Mellon University)*
- **Collaborative Web Search in Context: A Study of Tool Use in Everyday Tasks** ... 807
  Ryan Kelly, Stephen J. Payne *(University of Bath)*
- **Modeling Search Processes Using Hidden States in Collaborative Exploratory Web Search** ... 820
  Zhen Yue, Shuguang Han, Daqing He *(University of Pittsburgh)*

Session Order 25: Romance

- **Romantic Partnerships and the Dispersion of Social Ties: A Network Analysis of Relationship Status on Facebook** ... 831
  Lars Backstrom *(Facebook, Inc.),* Jon Kleinberg *(Cornell University)*
- **Facebook Makes the Heart Grow Fonder: Relationship Maintenance Strategies Among Geographically Dispersed and Communication-Restricted Connections** ... 842
  Jessica Vitak *(University of Maryland)*
- **"Real, but Glossy" – Technology and the Practical Pursuit of Magic in Modern Weddings** ... 854
  Michael Massimi, Richard Harper, Abigail Sellen *(Microsoft Research)*

Session Order 26: Crowds in Crises

- **Digital Mobilization in Disaster Response: The Work & Self-Organization of On-Line Pet Advocates in Response to Hurricane Sandy** ... 866
  Joanne I. White, Leysia Palen, Kenneth M. Anderson *(University of Colorado, Boulder)*
- **Collaboration Surrounding Beacon Use During Companion Avalanche Rescue** ... 877
  Audrey Desjardins, Carman Neustaedter *(Simon Fraser University),* Saul Greenberg *(University of Calgary),*
  Ron Wakkary *(Simon Fraser University)*
- **Designing for the Deluge: Understanding & Supporting the Distributed, Collaborative Work of Crisis Volunteers** ... 888
  Camille Cobb, Ted McCarthy, Annuska Perkins, Ankitha Bharadwaj, Jared Comis, Brian Do,
  Kate Starbird *(University of Washington),*

Session Order 27: Supporting Communities

- **Beyond End User Content to Collaborative Knowledge Mapping: Interrelations Among Community Social Tools** ... 900
  Tara Matthews *(IBM Research—Almaden, San Jose),*
  Steve Whittaker *(University of California at Santa Cruz),*
  Hernan Badenes *(IBM, Argentina),* Barton A. Smith *(IBM Research—Almaden, San Jose)*
- **Think Globally, Act Locally: A Case Study of a Free Food Sharing Community and Social Networking** ... 911
  Eva Ganglbauer, Geraldine Fitzpatrick, Özge Subasi, Florian Güldenpfennig *(Vienna University of Technology)*
- **From Rookie to All-Star: Professional Development in a Graphic Design Community of Practice** ... 922
  Jennifer Marlow, Laura Dabbish *(Carnegie Mellon University),*

Session Order 29: Locations and Maps

- **Mind the Map: The Impact of Culture and Economic Affluence on Crowd-Mapping Behaviours** 934
  Giovanni Quattrone *(University College London)*, Afra Mashhadi *(Alcatel-Lucent)*, Licia Capra *(University College London)*
- **Aesthetic Capital: What Makes London Look Beautiful, Quiet, and Happy?** 945
  Daniele Quercia, Neil O'Hare *(Yahoo Labs, Barcelona, Spain)*, Henriette Cramer *(Yahoo! Labs, Sunnyvale, USA)*
- **Leveraging the Contributory Potential of User Feedback** 956
  Mikhil Masli *(IBM)*, Loren Terveen *(University of Minnesota)*

Session Order 30: Promoting Participation and Engagement

Session Chair: Mark Handel *(The Boeing Company)*

- **A Comparison of Social, Learning, and Financial Strategies on Crowd Engagement and Output Quality** 967
  Lixiu Yu, Paul André, Aniket Kittur, Robert Kraut *(Carnegie Mellon University)*
- **Motivating Contribution in a Participatory Sensing System via Quid-Pro-Quo** 979
  Anthony Tomasic, John Zimmerman, Aaron Steinfeld, Yun Huang *(Carnegie Mellon University)*
- **Crowd Synthesis: Extracting Categories and Clusters from Complex Data** 989
  Paul André, Aniket Kittur, Steven P. Dow *(Carnegie Mellon University)*

Session Order 31: Building on Others

Session Chair: Steven Dow *(Carnegie Mellon University)*

- **Standing on the Schemas of Giants: Socially Augmented Information Foraging** 999
  Aniket Kittur, Andrew M. Peters, Abdigani Diriye, Michael R. Bove *(Carnegie Mellon University)*
- **The Antecedents of Remix** 1011
  Giorgos Cheliotis *(National University of Singapore)*, Nan Hu *(University of Wisconsin)*, Jude Yew *(National University of Singapore)*, Jianhui Huang *(Singapore Management University)*
- **Remixers' Understandings of Fair Use Online** 1023
  Casey Fiesler, Amy Bruckman *(Georgia Institute of Technology)*

Session Order 32: Identifying Opportunities for Collaboration

Session Chair: Jeremy Birnholtz *(Northwestern University)*

- **Unsupervised Classification and Visualization of Unstructured Text for the Support of Interdisciplinary Collaboration** 1033
  Lisa J. Miller, Rich Gazan, Susanne Still *(University of Hawaii at Mānoa)*
- **Pair Research: Matching People for Collaboration, Learning, and Productivity** 1043
  Robert C. Miller *(Massachusetts Institute of Technology)*, Haoqi Zhang *(Northwestern University)*, Eric Gilbert *(Georgia Institute of Technology)*, Elizabeth Gerber *(Northwestern University)*
- **Supporting Group Interaction in Museum Visiting** 1049
  Peter Tolmie, Steve Benford, Chris Greenhalgh, Tom Rodden, Stuart Reeves *(The University of Nottingham)*

Session Order 33: The Office

Session Chair: Melissa Mazmanian *(University of California, Irvine)*

- **Trustworthy By Design** 1060
  Bran Knowles, Mike Harding, Lynne Blair, Nigel Davies *(Lancaster University)*, James Hannon *(InTouch Ltd.)*, Mark Rouncefield *(Lancaster University)*, John Walden *(In Touch Ltd)*
- **Tracking Serendipitous Interactions: How Individual Cultures Shape the Office** 1072
  Chloë Brown, Christos Efstratiou *(University of Cambridge)*, Ilias Leontiadis *(Telefonica Research, Barcelona)*, Daniele Quercia *(Yahoo! Labs, Barcelona)*, Cecilia Mascolo *(University of Cambridge)*
- **Capturing the Mood: Facebook and Face-to-Face Encounters in the Workplace** 1082
  Gloria Mark *(University of California, Irvine)*, Shamsi Iqbal,Mary Czerwinski, Paul Johns *(Microsoft Research, Redmond, WA)*

Session Order 34: Collaborative Software Development

Session Chair: Jim Herbsleb *(Carnegie Mellon University),*

- **Social Influences on Secure Development Tool Adoption: Why Security Tools Spread** 1095
  Shundan Xiao, Jim Witschey, Emerson Murphy-Hill *(North Carolina State University)*
- **"Figure Out How to Code with the Hands of Others": Recognizing Cultural Blind Spots in Global Software Development** 1107
  Stina Matthiesen *(IT University of Copenhagen),*
  Pernille Bjørn *(The IT University of Copenhagen & University of California, Irvine),*
  Lise Møller Petersen *(The IT University of Copenhagen)*
- **Articulation Spaces: Bridging the Gap Between Formal and Informal Coordination** 1120
  Alexander Boden *(Fraunhofer Institute for Applied Information Technology (FIT)),*
  Frank Rosswog, Gunnar Stevens, Volker Wulf *(University of Siegen)*

Session Order 35: Mobile Apps for Enhancing Connectedness

- **Everyday Dwelling with WhatsApp** 1131
  Kenton O'Hara, Michael Massimi, Richard Harper *(Microsoft Research, Cambridge),*
  Simon Rubens, Jessica Morris *(New Experience)*
- **Enhancing Community Awareness of and Participation in Local Heritage with a Mobile Application** 1144
  Kyungsik Han, Patrick C. Shih, Mary Beth Rosson, John M. Carroll *(The Pennsylvania State University)*
- **GEMS: The Design and Evaluation of a Location-Based Storytelling Game** 1156
  Jason Procyk, Carman Neustaedter *(Simon Fraser University, Surrey)*

Session Order 36: MOOCS

Session Chair: Anne Marie Piper *(Northwestern University)*

- **VidWiki: Enabling the Crowd to Improve the Legibility of Online Educational Videos** 1167
  Andrew Cross, Mydhili Bayyapunedi, Dilip Ravindran, Edward Cutrell, William Thies *(Microsoft Research India)*
- **Should Your MOOC Forum Use a Reputation System?** 1176
  Derrick Coetzee, Armando Fox, Marti A. Hearst, Björn Hartmann *(University of California, Berkeley)*

Session Order 37: Mobilizing for Action

Session Chair: Carsten Osterlund *(Syracuse University)*

- **Integrating On-Demand Fact-Checking with Public Dialogue** 1188
  Travis Kriplean *(University of Washington & Invisible College LLC),*
  Caitlin Bonnar, Alan Borning *(University of Washington),* Bo Kinney, Brian Gill *(Seattle Pacific University)*
- **Tweet Acts: How Constituents Lobby Congress via Twitter** 1200
  Libby Hemphill, Andrew Roback *(Illinois Institute of Technology)*
- **Catalyst: Triggering Collective Action, with Threshholds** 1211
  Justin Cheng, Michael S. Bernstein *(Stanford University)*

Session Order 38: Volunteering and Doing Good

Session Chair: Aniket Kittur *(Carnegie Mellon University)*

- **Competing or Aiming to be Average? Normification as a Means of Engaging Digital Volunteers** 1222
  Chris Preist, Elaine Massung, David Coyle *(University of Bristol)*
- **Capturing Quality: Retaining Provenance for Curated Volunteer Monitoring Data** 1234
  S. Andrew Sheppard *(University of Minnesota & Houston Engineering, Inc.),*
  Andrea Wiggins *(University of New Mexico & Cornell University),* Loren Terveen *(University of Minnesota)*
- **Understanding Factors of Successful Engagement Around Energy Consumption Between and Among Households** 1246
  Tawanna R. Dillahunt *(University of Michigan),* Jennifer Mankoff *(Carnegie Mellon University)*

Session Order 39: Parents and Children

Session Chair: Svetlana Yarosh *(AT&T Research)*

- **Adolescent Online Safety: the "Moral" of the Story** 1258
  Pamela Wisniewski, Heng Xu, Mary Beth Rosson, John M. Carroll *(The Pennsylvania State University)*
- **Social Networking Site Use by Mothers of Young Children** 1272
  Meredith Ringel Morris *(Microsoft Research)*
- **TalkBetter: Family-Driven Mobile Intervention Care for Children with Language Delay** 1283
  Inseok Hwang, Chungkuk Yoo, Chanyou Hwang *(KAIST (Korea Advanced Institute of Science and Technology))*, Dongsun Yim *(Ewha Womans University)*, Youngki Lee *(Singapore Management University)*, Chulhong Min, John Kim, Junehwa Song *(KAIST (Korea Advanced Institute of Science and Technology))*

Session Order 40: Civic Participation

Session Chair: Andrés Monroy-Hernández *(Microsoft Research)*

- **Giving Is Caring: Understanding Donation Behavior Through Email** 1297
  Yelena Mejova *(Yahoo! Labs)*, Venkata RK Garimella, Ingmar Weber *(Qatar Computing Research Institute)*, Michael C. Dougal *(University of California, Berkeley)*
- **Civic Action Brokering Platforms: Facilitating Local Engagement with ACTion Alexandria** 1308
  Derek L. Hansen *(Brigham Young University)*, Jes A. Koepfler *(University of Maryland & Intuitive Company, Philadelphia, PA)*, Paul T. Jaeger, John C. Bertot *(University of Maryland)*, Tracy Viselli *(Brookings Institution)*
- **MyPosition: Sparking Civic Discourse by a Public Interactive Poll Visualization** 1323
  Nina Valkanova *(TU Berlin & Universitat Pompeu Fabra)*, Robert Walter *(Telekom Innovation Laboratories, TU Berlin)*, Andrew Vande Moere *(KU Leuven - University of Leuven)*, Jörg Müller *(Alexander von Humboldt Institute for Internet and Society & Telekom Innovation Laboratories, TU Berlin)*

Session Order 41: Gaming

- **How Players Value Their Characters in World of Warcraft** 1333
  Ian J. Livingston *(Ubisoft Divertissements, Inc.)*, Carl Gutwin, Regan L. Mandryk, Max Birk *(University of Saskatchewan)*
- **The Effects of Consistency Maintenance Methods on Player Experience and Performance in Networked Games** 1344
  Cheryl Savery, Nicholas Graham *(Queen's University, Canada)*, Carl Gutwin *(University of Saskatchewan)*, Michelle Brown *(York University)*
- **The Identification of Deviance and Its Impact on Retention in a Multiplayer Game** 1356
  Kenneth Shores, Yilin He *(University of Minnesota)*, Kristina L. Swanenburg *(University of Pittsburgh)*, Robert Kraut *(Carnegie Mellon University)*, John Riedl *(University of Minnesota)*

Session Order 42: Multiple Dimensions and Displays

- **Quick and Dirty: Streamlined 3D Scanning in Archaeology** 1366
  Jarrod Knibbe *(University of Bristol)*, Kenton P. O'Hara *(University of Bristol & Microsoft Research, Cambridge)*, Angeliki Chrysanthi *(University of Southampton)*, Mark T. Marshall, Peter D. Bennett *(University of Bristol)*, Graeme Earl *(University of Southampton)*, Shahram Izadi *(Microsoft Research, Cambridge)*, Mike Fraser *(University of Bristol)*
- **Support for Deictic Pointing in CVEs: Still Fragmented After All These Years?** 1377
  Nelson Wong, Carl Gutwin *(University of Saskatchewan)*
- **Photoportals: Shared References in Space and Time** 1388
  André Kunert, Alexander Kulik, Stephan Beck, Bernd Froehlich *(Bauhaus-Universität Weimar)*

Session Order 43: Social Media and Politics

Session Chair: Gloria Marks *(University of California, Irvine)*

- **Managing Political Differences in Social Media** 1400
  Catherine Grevet *(Georgia Institute of Technology)*, Loren Terveen *(University of Minnesota)*, Eric Gilbert *(Georgia Institute of Technology)*
- **Social Media Supporting Political Deliberation Across Multiple Public Spheres: Towards Depolarization** 1409
  Bryan Semaan, Scott P. Robertson, Sara Douglas, Misa Maruyama *(University of Hawai'i at Mānoa)*
- **Hybrid Media Consumption: How Tweeting During a Televised Political Debate Influences the Vote Decision** 1422
  Misa Maruyama, Scott P. Robertson, Sara Douglas, Bryan Semaan , Heather Faucett *(University of Hawai'i at Mānoa)*

Session Order 44: Crowdsourcing Complexity

Session Chair: Karrie Karahalios *(University of Illinois)*

- **Voyant: Generating Structured Feedback on Visual Designs Using a Crowd of Non-Experts** 1433
  Anbang Xu, Shih-Wen Huang, Brian P. Bailey *(University of Illinois, Urbana)*
- **Reviewing Versus Doing: Learning and Performance in Crowd Assessment** 1445
  Haiyi Zhu, Steven P. Dow, Robert E. Kraut Aniket Kittur *(Carnegie Mellon University)*
- **AskSheet: Efficient Human Computation for Decision Making with Spreadsheets** 1456
  Alexander J. Quinn, Benjamin B. Bederson *(University of Maryland)*

Session Order 45: Personal Health Management

Session Chair: Helena Mentis *(University of Maryland, Baltimore County)*

- **Cancer Navigation: Opportunities and Challenges for Facilitating the Breast Cancer Journey** 1467
  Maia Jacobs, James Clawson, Elizabeth D. Mynatt *(Georgia Institute of Technology)*
- **Craving, Creating, and Constructing Comfort: Insights and Opportunities for Technology in Hospice** 1479
  Robert Douglas Ferguson *(McGill University)*, Michael Massimi *(Microsoft Research, Cambridge)*, Emily Anne Crist, Karyn Moffatt *(McGill University)*
- **Life Transitions and Online Health Communities: Reflecting on Adoption, Use, and Disengagement** 1491
  Michael Massimi *(Microsoft Research, Cambridge)*, Jackie L. Bender *(University Health Network, Toronto)*, Holly O. Witteman *(Université Laval)*, Osman Hassan Ahmed *(University of Otago)*

Session Order 46: Geographic Distance

Session Chair: Pernille Bjorn *(IT University Copenhagen)*

- **City, Self, Network: Transnational Migrants and Online Identity Work** 1502
  Jessica Lingel *(Microsoft Research, Cambridge)*, Mor Naaman *(Cornell Tech)*, danah boyd *(Microsoft Research)*
- **Twitter Ain't Without Frontiers: Economic, Social, and Cultural Boundaries in International Communication** 1511
  Ruth García-Gavilanes *(Universitat Pompeu Fabra)*, Yelena Mejova, Daniele Quercia *(Yahoo! Labs)*
- **Inferring the Origin Locations of Tweets with Quantitative Confidence** 1523
  Reid Priedhorsky *(Los Alamos National Laboratory)*, Aron Culotta *(Illinois Institute of Technology)*, Sara Y. Del Valle *(Los Alamos National Laboratory)*

Session Order 47: Distributed Teams

Session Chair: Daniele Quercia *(Yahoo Research)*,

- **Exploring the Social-Technological Gap in Telesurgery: Collaboration Within Distributed OR Teams** 1537
  Pieter Duysburgh, Shirley A. Elprama, An Jacobs *(iMinds-SMIT-VUB)*

- **How Beliefs about the Presence of Machine Translation Impact Multilingual Collaborations** 1549
  Ge Gao, Bin Xu, Dan Cosley, Susan R. Fussell *(Cornell University)*
- **Sounds of Silence: Exploring Contributions to Conversations, Non-Responses and the Impact of Mediating Technologies in Triple Space** 1561
  Joon-Suk Lee *(Virginia State University),* Deborah Tatar *(Virginia Polytechnic Institute and State University)*

Session Order 48: Keynote Address

- **Next Generation Humanitarian Computing** 1573
  Patrick Meier *(Qatar Computing Research Institute (QCRI))*

Author Index 1574

CSCW 2014 Organization

General Chairs: Susan Fussell, *Cornell University*
Wayne Lutters, *UMBC*

Treasurer: N. Sadat Shami, *IBM*

Papers Chairs: Meredith Ringel Morris, *Microsoft Research*
Madhu Reddy, *Penn State University*

Interactive Posters Chairs: Rogerio de Paula, *IBM Research*
Erika Poole, *Penn State University*

Workshops Chairs: Eric Gilbert, *Georgia Tech*
Jacki O'Neill, *Microsoft Research India*

Panels Chairs: Hideaki Kuzuoka, *University of Tsukuba*
Charlotte Lee, *University of Washington*

Demonstrations Chairs: Stephan Lukosch, *Delft University of Technology*
Hao-Chuan Wang, *National Tsing Hua University*

Videos Chairs: Katie Derthick, *University of Washington*
Scott McCrickard, *Virginia Tech*

Doctoral Colloquium Chairs: Claus Bossen, *Aarhus University*
Darren Gergle, *Northwestern University*

CSCWhat's Next Chairs: Mark Handel, *The Boeing Company*
Susan Wyche, *Michigan State University*

Industry Liaison Chairs: Sean Goggins, *University of Missouri*
Steve Poltrock

Student Volunteers Chairs: Victoria Schwanda Sosik, *Cornell University*
Kathy Weaver, *UMBC*

Webmasters and Graphic Design Chairs: Serena Hillman, *Simon Fraser University*
Pablo Quinones, *University of Michigan*

Social Media Chairs: Irina Shklovski, *ITU Copenhagen*
Sarita Yardi Schoenebeck, *University of Michigan*

Social Interaction Chairs: Jofish Kaye, *Yahoo Research*
Michael Massimi, *Microsoft Research*

Publications Chairs: Yong Ming Kow, *City University of Hong Kong*
Bryan Semaan, *University of Hawaii*

Accessibility Chairs: Jennifer Rode, *Drexel University*
Amy Hurst, *UMBC*
Shaun Kane, *UMBC*
Ravi Kuber, *UMBC*

Local Arrangements Chairs: Anita Komlodi, *UMBC*
Jessica Vitak, *University of Maryland, College Park*

PC Meeting Local Arrangements Chairs: Andrea Forte, *Drexel University*
Aleksandra Sarcevic, *Drexel University*

Program Committee Chairs: Meredith Ringel Morris, *Microsoft Research*
Madhu Reddy, *Penn State University*

Program Committee: Paul M. Aoki, *Google Inc.*
Louise Barkhuus, *Stockholm University*
Michael Bernstein, *Stanford University*
Mary Beth Rosson, *Penn State University*
Jacob Biehl, *FX Palo Alto Laboratory*
Jeffrey P. Bigham, *Carnegie Mellon University*
Jeremy Birnholtz, *Northwestern University*
Pernille Bjørn, *IT University of Copenhagen*
Marcos Borges, *UFRJ - Universidade Federal do Rio de Janeiro*
A.J. Bernheim Brush, *Microsoft Research*
Moira Burke, *Facebook*
Jack Carroll, *Penn State University*
Ed Chi, *Google Inc.*
Dan Cosley, *Cornell University*
Ed Cutrell, *Microsoft Research India*
Steven Dow, *Carnegie Mellon University*
Ingrid Erickson, *Rutgers University*
Vanessa Evers, *University of Twente*
Morten Fjeld, *Chalmers University of Technology*
Andrea Forte, *Drexel University*
Eric Gilbert, *Georgia Tech*
Carl Gutwin, *University of Saskatchewan*
Ido Guy, *IBM Research Haifa*
Mark Handel, *The Boeing Company*
James Herbsleb, *Carnegie Mellon University*
Karrie Karahalios, *University of Illinois at Urbana-Champaign*
Wendy Kellogg, *IBM Research*
Niki Kittur, *Carnegie Mellon University*
Joseph Konstan, *University of Minnesota*
Robert Kraut, *Carnegie Mellon University*
Hideaki Kuzuoka, *University of Tsukuba*
Gilly Leshed, *Cornell University*

Program Committee (Continued):

Myriam Lewkowicz, *Troyes University of Technology*
Christopher Lueg, *University of Tasmania*
Gloria Mark, *UC Irvine*
Michael Massimi, *Microsoft Research Cambridge (U.K.)*
Melissa Mazmanian, *UC Irvine*
David McDonald, *University of Washington*
Helena Mentis, *UMBC*
Andrés Monroy-Hernández, *MSR FUSE Labs*
Les Nelson, *Palo Alto Research Center, Inc.*
Jacki O'Neill, *Xerox Research Centre Europe*
Andrea Grimes Parker, *Northeastern University*
Sameer Patil, *Helsinki Institute for Information Technology*
Sharoda Paul, *GE Global Research*
Anne Marie Piper, *Northwestern University*
Daniele Quercia, *Yahoo! Labs Barcelona*
Erika Poole, *Penn State University*
Dave Randall, *University of Siegen*
Aleksandra Sarcevic, *Drexel University*
Steven B. Sawyer, *Syracuse University*
m. c. schraefel, *University of Southampton*
Kate Starbird, *University of Washington*
Gunnar Stevens, *University of Siegen*
Jennifer Thom, *IBM Research*
Max Van Kleek, *University of Southampton*
Gina Venolia, *Microsoft Research*
Daniel Wigdor, *University of Toronto*
Max L. Wilson, *University of Nottingham*
Volker Wulf, *University of Siegen*
Susan Wyche, *Michigan State University*
Naomi Yamashita, *NTT Communication Science Lab*
Svetlana Yarosh, *AT&T Research Labs*
Chen Zhao, *Microsoft*

Best Paper Award Chairs:

Joseph Konstan, *University of Minnesota*
Helena Mentis, *UMBC*

Best Papers Committee:

Pernille Bjorn, *IT University Copenhagen*
Carl Gutwin, *University of Saskatchewan*
Niki Kittur, *Carnegie Mellon University*
Hideaki Kuzuoka, *University of Tsukuba*
Jenn Thom, *IBM Research*

Ninja Review Team Chair:

Aaron Genest, *Solido Design Automation*

2014 Lasting Impact Award Committee:

Saul Greenberg, *University of Calgary* (CSCW 1998 & 2006 Papers Chair)
Irene Greif, *IBM Research* (CSCW 1986 Papers Chair)
Sara Kiesler, *Carnegie Mellon University* (CSCW 2000 Papers Chair)
Cliff Lampe, *University of Michigan* (CSCW 2013 Papers Chair)
Meredith Ringel Morris, *Microsoft Research* (CSCW 2014 Papers Chair)
Gary Olson, *UC Irvine* (CSCW 1996 Papers Chair)
Madhu Reddy, *Penn State University* (CSCW 2014 Papers Chair)
Tom Rodden, *University of Nottingham* (CSCW 2002 Papers Chair)
Loren Terveen, *University of Minnesota* (CSCW 2013 Papers Chair)
Steve Whittaker, *UC Santa Cruz* (CSCW 2010 Papers Chair)

CSCW 2014 Reviewers

Reviewers whose names appear in **bold** are being recognized by the Associate Paper Chairs for one or more excellent reviews.

Mark Aakhus
Margunn Aanestad
Joanna Abraham
Mark Ackerman
Lada Adamic
Bram Adams
Eytan Adar
Ana Afonso
Elena Agapie
Leila Alem
Florian Alt
Brian Amento
Morgan Ames
Kenneth Anderson
Paul André
Craig Anslow
Judd Antin
Ana Paula Appel
Jorge Aranda
Gabriela Avram
Leif Azzopardi
Naveen bagalkot
Brian Bailey
Saeideh Bakhshi
Eytan Bakshy
Ramnath Balasubramanyan
Rebecca Balebako
Elizabeth Bales
Stinne Ballegaard
Amartya Banerjee
Wolmet Barendregt
Scott Bateman
Benjamin Bederson
Ben Bedwell
Andrew Begel
Fabrício Benevenuto
Steve Benford
Edward Benson
Nicola Bidwell
Matthew Bietz
Christian Bird
Staffan Björk
Florian Block
Bridget Blodgett
Sara Bly
Alexander Boden
Marcela Borge
Sebastian Boring
Alan Borning
Christophe Bortolaso
Nina Boulus
Stacy Branham
Deana Brown
Barry Brown
Jed Brubaker
Amy Bruckman
Merijn Bruijnes
A.J. Brush
Michael Brzozowski
Martin Burkhard
Béatrice Cahour
Chris Callison-Burch
Maria Luiza Campos
Heloisa Candello
Jose Canos
Yiwei Cao
Xiang Cao
Robert Capra
Carlos Castillo
Marcelo Cataldo
Grevet Catherine
Daniel Cernea
Xiang ´Anthony´ Chen
Weiqin Chen
Nicholas Chen
Jilin Chen
Yunan Chen
Zhiyuan Cheng
Karen Cheng
Justin Cheng
Zhiyuan Cheng
Marshini Chetty
Lydia Chilton
Alvin Chin
Lars Rune Christensen
Hao-Hua Chu
Justin Chung
Luigina Ciolfi
Benjamin Collier
Tommaso Colombino
Rob Comber
Gregorio Convertino
Eric Cook
Dan Cosley
Lisa Cowan
David Coyle
Crabb Crabb
Henriette Cramer
Kevin Crowston
Mary Czerwinski
Laura Dabbish
Peng Dai
Elizabeth Daly
Catalina Danis
Antonella De Angeli
Munmun De Choudhury
Cleidson de Souza
Roelof de Vries
Morteza Dehghani
Katie Derthick
Prasun Dewan
Nicholas Diakopoulos
E.Ilana Diamant
Michael Dickard
Dominic DiFranzo
Tawanna Dillahunt
Xianghua Ding
Carl DiSalvo
Betsy DiSalvo
Morgan Dixon
Tao Dong
Brian Dorn
Andre Doucette
Sebastian Draxler
Honglu Du
Nicolas Ducheneaut
Andy Echenique
Dean Eckles
Hal Eden
Kate Ehrlich
Gunnar Ellingsen
Nicole Ellison
Niklas Elmqvist
Jenny Englert
Dmitry Epstein

Thomas Erickson
Chris Esposito
Jerry Fails
Shelly Farnham
Rosta Farzan
Haakon Faste
Jesus Favela
Jennifer Fernquist
Bruce Ferwerda
Megan Finn
Andrew Fiore
Scott Fleming
Fred Fonseca
Benjamim Fonseca
Laura Forlano
Marcus Foth
Mike Fraser
Chris Frisina
Wai-Tat Fu
Michael Gamon
Ge Gao
R. Kelly Garrett
Nadia Gauducheau
Rich Gazan
Aaron Genest
Elizabeth Gerber
Darren Gergle
Marco Gerosa
Werner Geyer
Elisa Giaccardi
Lorna Gibson
Sean Goggins
Jennifer Golbeck
Scott Golder
Jorge Goncalves
Victor Gonzalez
Roberto González-Ibáñez
Visda Goudarzi
Eric Graham
Raphael Grasset
Antonietta Grasso
Rebecca Gray
Mary Gray
Michael Greenberg
Beki Grinter
Miria Grisot
Diane Gromala
Jens Grossklags
Jonathan Grudin
Shion Guha
Jamie Guillory
Philip Guo
Frode Guribye
David Gurzick
Joerg Haake
Eija Haapalainen Ferreira
Eben Haber
Joshua Hailpern
Julia Haines
Maria Håkansson
Kayla Hales
Michael Haller
Kim Halskov
Christine Halverson
Martin Halvey
Keith Hampton
Kyungsik (Keith) Han
Jeff Hancock
Mark Handel
Alexander Hanna
John Hannon
Benjamin Hanrahan
Preben Hansen
Derek Hansen
Kotaro Hara
Richard Harper
Franklin Harper
Steve Harrison
Drew Harry
Mark Hartswood
Ari Hautasaari
Kirstie Hawkey
Gillian Hayes
Steven Haynes
Mike Hazas
Brent Hecht
Eric Hekler
Libby Hemphill
Morten Hertzum
Benjamin Mako Hill
Serena Hillman
Starr Roxanne Hiltz
Ken Hinckley
Jon Hindmarsh
Joanne Hinds
Christina Hochleitner
Lichan Hong
Hwajung Hong
Jason Hong
Alexis Hope
Michael Horn
Andrew Howes
James Howison
Yuheng Hu
Yun Huang
Shih-Wen Huang
Jeff Huang
David Huffaker
Amanda Hughes
Jina Huh
Christian Huitema
Jonathan Hurlock
CJ Hutto
Marleen Huysman
Ebba Thora Hvannberg
Inseok Hwang
Ioanna Iacovides
Kori Inkpen
Joshua Introne
Panos Ipeirotis
Shamsi Iqbal
Pourang Irani
Lilly Irani
Germaine Irwin
Petra Isenberg
Corey Jackson
Steven Jackson
Mohit Jain
Timo Jakobi
Jacek Jankowski
Mohammad Hossein Jarrahi
Rasmus Jensen
Carlos Jensen
Aditya Johri
Adam Joinson
Michiel Joosse
Elisabeth Joyce
Malte Jung
Sasa Junuzovic
Sanjay Kairam
Denis Kalkofen
Santosh Kalwar
Matthew Kam
Shaun Kane
Bridget Kane
David Karger
Hirokazu Kato
Andrea Kavanaugh
Joseph 'Jofish' Kaye
Brian Keegan
Caitlin Kelleher
Patrick Kelley
Ryan Kelly

Logan Kendall
Emad Khazraee
Andrea Kienle
Julie Kientz
Sara Kiesler
Taemie Kim
SeungJun Kim
Juho Kim
John King
David Kirk
Funda Kivran-Swaine
Predrag Klasnja
Mark Klein
Bart Knijnenburg
Stefan Knoll Knoll
Michael Koch
Yong Ming Kow
Adam Kramer
Jennifer Kraschnewski
Sven Kratz
Travis Kriplean
Per Ola Kristensson
Chinmay Kulkarni
Ranjitha Kumar
Andreas Kunz
Takeshi Kurata
Raja Kushalnagar
Diana Kusunoki
Lynette Kvasny
Ioanna lacovides
Richard Ladner
Mounia Lalmas
Nicolas LaLone
Shyong Lam
Cliff Lampe
Airi Lampinen
Jonas Landgren
Joel Lanir
Andreas Larsson
Walter Lasecki
Celine Latulipe
Eric Laurier
Yann Laurillau
Shaun Lawson
Robert Layton
Christopher Le Dantec
Matthew Lease
Michael Lee
Jinha Lee
Adam Lee
Ilias Leontiadis
Gilly Leshed
Na Li
Daniel Liebling
Rhema Linder
SiÃ¢n Lindley
Jessica Lingel
Yefeng Liu
Claudia López
Weiquan Lu
Stephan Lukosch
Kurt Luther
Kris Luyten
Rui Madeira
Charlotte Magnusson
Scott Mainwaring
Julie Maitland
Lena Mamykina
Clara Mancini
Regan Mandryk
Osama Mansour
Gabriela Marcu
Tiago Marino
Jennifer Marlow
Paul Marshall
David Martin
Christopher Mascaro
Afra Mashhadi
Winter Mason
Masood Masoodian
Tara Matthews
Stina Matthiesen
Michelle Mazurek
Nora McDonald
Poppy McLeod
Donald McMillan
Yevgeniy Medynskiy
Johanna Meurer
David Millen
Robert Miller
Andrew Miller
Tanushree Mitra
Karyn Moffatt
Sue Moon
Claudia Motta
Vicki Moulder
Martin Muehlpfordt
Ruth Mugge
Ingrid Mulder
Michael Muller
Heiko Müller
Sean Munson
Kyle Murray
Dave Murray-Rust
Elizabeth Mynatt
Mor Naaman
Miguel Nacenta
Hideyuki Nakanishi
Bonnie Nardi
Lisa Nathan
Carman Neustaedter
Dong Nguyen
Jeffrey Nichols
Jeffrey Nickerson
Sylvie Noël
Blair Nonnecke
Maria Normark
Oded Nov
Diarmuid Ó Séaghdha
Kieron O'Hara
Kenton O'Hara
Aisling O'Kane
Michael O'Mahony
Rosalie Ocker
Anne Oeldorf-Hirsch
Corinna Ogonowski
Alice Oh
Jonice Oliveira
Gary Olson
Tihomir Orehavacki
Myle Ott
Heather Packer
Xinru Page
Aditya Pal
Joshua Palay
Leysia Palen
Karljohan Palmerius
Katherine Panciera
Katrina Panovich
Nadia Pantidi
Katrina Paovich
Hugo Paredes
Tapan Parikh
Praveen Paritosh
Sun Young Park
Souneil Park
Sun Young Park
Shwetak Patel
Daniel Patel
Rupa Patel
Celeste Paul
James Pennebaker
Mark Perry

Daniel Perry
Anicia Peters
Helen Petrie
Tamara Peyton
Mark Pfaff
Martin Pielot
Jacqueline Pike
Fabiano Pinatti
Kathleen Pine
Niels Pinkwart
Volkmar Pipek
John Pollak
Nathan Prestopnik
Reid Priedhorsky
Michael Prilla
Kermit Purdy
Yan Qu
Alexander Quinn
Pablo-Alejandro Quinones
Emilee Rader
Rebecca Randell
Nimmi Rangaswamy
Dennis Reidsma
Katharina Reinecke
Philippe Renevier Gonin
Paul Resnick
Lindsay Reynolds
Rebecca Reynolds
Laurel Riek
Lionel Robert
Scott Robertson
Christine Robson
John Rooksby
Daniela Rosner
Chiara Rossitto
Mary Beth Rosson
Mattias Rost
Mark Rouncefield
Daniel Russell
Ian Ruthven
Jeffrey Rzeszotarski
Alan Said
Antti Salovaara
Nithya Sambasivan
Pedro Sanches
Christian Sandvig
Vagner Santana
Flavia Santoro
Stephanie Santoso
Christopher Scaffidi
Florian Schaub
Holger Schnädelbach
Oliver Schneider
Niko Schönau
Victoria Schwanda Sosik
Lauren Scissors
Stacey Scott
Kate Sellen
Bryan Semaan
Shilad Sen
Lauren Sessions Goulet
Leslie Setlock
Orit Shaer
Chirag Shah
Dafna Shahaf
N. Sadat Shami
Bin Shao
Sarika Sharma
Nikhil Sharma
Aaron Shaw
Haifeng Shen
S. Andrew Sheppard
Patrick Shih
Katie Shilton
Irina Shklovski
Garth Shoemaker
Leif Singer
Manya Sleeper
Nedim Slijepcevic
Daniel Smith
Madeline Smith
Ole Smørdal
Jaime Snyder
Emma Spiro
Ann Steele
Aaron Steinfeld
Stephanie Steinhardt
David Stillwell
Jennifer Stromer-Galley
H. Colleen Stuart
Fred Stutzman
Norman Su
Bongwon Suh
Nicole Sultanum
Chengzheng Sun
S. Shyam Sundar
Anthony Tang
Charlotte Tang
John Tang
Andrea Tapia
Yla Tausczik
Nick Taylor
Jaime Teevan
Loren Terveen
Alexander Thayer
William Thies
Elizabeth Thiry
John Thomas
Peter Tolmie
Stephanie Tong
Tammy Toscos
Zachary Toups
W. Ben Towne
Christoph Trattner
Jason Tsay
Jennifer Turns
Murray Turoff
Michael Twidale
Judith Uchidiuno
Kalle Ulvstig
Nancy Van House
Jos van Leeuwen
Sander van Splunter
Kami Vaniea
Radu-Daniel Vatavu
Sarah Vieweg
John Vines
Erik Vinkhuyzen
Thomas Visser
Jessica Vitak
Adriana Vivacqua
Juergen Vogel
Daniel Vogel
Amy Voida
Patrick Wagstrom
Jim Wallace
Yi-Chia Wang
William Yang Wang
Taowei Wang
Jing Wang
Hao-Chuan Wang
Jamie Wardman
Rick Wash
Nic Weber
Ingmar Weber
Carolyn Wei
Nadir Weibel
Astrid Weiss
Justin Weisz
Ryen White
Mark Whiting
Jason Wiese
Andrea Wiggins

Lauren Wilcox
Wesley Willett
Amanda Williams
Matt Willis
Mathew Wilson
Pamela Wisniewski
Donghee Yvette Wohn
Maria Wolters
Allison Woodruff
Shaomei Wu
Leslie Wu
Eugene Wu
Yan Xu
Kim Xu
Anbang Xu
Huahai Yang
Mika Yasuoka
Jude Yew
Daisy Yoo
Alyson Young
G. Michael Youngblood
Lixiu Yu
Nicola Yuill
Mark Zachry
Qiping Zhang
Jun Zhang
Haoqi Zhang
Dejin Zhao
Xiaomu Zhou
Mengxiao Zhu
Haiyi Zhu
Juergen Ziegler
Roshanak Zilouchian Moghaddam
John Zimmerman
Thomas Zimmermann
Arkaitz Zubiaga

CSCW 2014 Sponsor & Supporters

Sponsors: SIGCHI

Champion: NSF

Benefactors: Facebook, Microsoft Research

Contributors: GRAND (Graphisme, animation et nouveaux médias / Graphics, Animation and New Media), IBM Research

Drexel University College of Computing & Informatics

Friends: Google, information systems UMBC

Making a Difference In and Through Playful Design

Mary Flanagan
Sherman Fairchild Distinguished Professor in Digital Humanities
Dartmouth College
http://www.maryflanagan.com/

ABSTRACT
How can design (broadly thought) and creative thought in technology, "make a difference" empirically and conceptually from the point of view of design practice? In the world of social impact design, how do designers know if they have the right approach for the best outcomes? In this talk, Tiltfactor laboratory director and Dartmouth professor Mary Flanagan shares strategies for design, focusing on cooperative interactions and the unintended consequences of designers' actions. Urging designers to ask big questions about where our technology is heading and how we might improve it from a social justice perspective, Flanagan offers actionable approaches to these questions through design examples and case studies of specific projects from her innovative game design work at http://www.Tiltfactor.org.

Author Keywords
Games, values in design, values at play, evidence-based design, psychology, biases and stereotypes, STEM

ACM Classification Keywords
H.5.3 Group and Organization Interface: Computer-supported cooperative work

BIO
Mary Flanagan (@criticlaplay) -- founder of the Tiltfactor research lab as well as an artist, writer, and scholar -- will share recent research on how games can influence and change attitudes, opinions, and behaviors. Flanagan expands the boundaries of medium, discipline, and genre across writing, visual arts, computer science, psychology, and design to innovate in these fields with a critical play-centered approach. She is interested in collaboration, social impact, and creating paradigms for productive social interaction based on our inherent capacity for play-- while highlighting and prioritizing human values in the design of new technologies and systems. As an artist, her collection of over 20 major works range from game-inspired systems to computer viruses, embodied interfaces to interactive texts; these works are exhibited internationally.

CSCW'14, February 15–19, 2014, Baltimore, MD, USA.
ACM 978-1-4503-2540-0/14/02.
http://dx.doi.org/10.1145/2531602.2556855

As a scholar interested in how human values are in play across technologies and systems, Flanagan has written more than 20 critical essays and chapters on games, empathy, gender and digital representation, art and technology, and responsible design. Her recent books include *Critical Play* [1] and *Values at Play in Digital Games* with Helen Nissenbaum [2].

Flanagan's work has been supported by grants and commissions including The British Arts Council, the National Endowment for the Humanities, the Robert Wood Johnson Foundation, the ACLS, and the National Science Foundation. Flanagan is the Sherman Fairchild Distinguished Professor in Digital Humanities at Dartmouth College.

Web: http://www.maryflanagan.com.

SYNOPSIS
Flanagan's research in game-based environments over her career revealed bias in the design of technical systems, and has revealed ways that technical systems and games can be designed to support human values.

Flanagan's recent work has shown that well-designed, interdisciplinary game activities can effectively diminish the strength and impact of negative stereotypes about learners' capabilities in STEM fields. Specifically, Flanagan and her team have produced and studied several games that are experimentally proven to combating stereotypes. One game with particular relevance to the proposed project, *Awkward Moment*, poses embarrassing or stressful academic and social scenarios, to which players must select appropriate reactions. Many of the game's "moments" put players in the perspective of being a witness to gender bias – or being a target themselves. A series of experimental studies revealed that *Awkward Moment* doubles the percentage of players' association between "female" and "scientist" and, and it was associated with a higher level of assertiveness in response to hypothetical occurrences of bias, compared to participants assigned to a control group (who completed the measures of bias before playing the game).

Follow-up studies showed that the game also: (1) shifted players' away from the belief that STEM pursuits were for boys to these subject being viewed as equally appropriate for boys and girls and (2) enhanced players' general perspective-taking abilities. Importantly, these effects were produced only when the game presented fewer bias-related than neutral moments (as opposed to all neutral or a majority of bias-related moments) and when the game was framed in neutral language (i.e., described as a game that deals with social *situations* versus social *stereotypes*).

This pattern confirms that the game's power lies in its ability to engage players with issues of STEM bias in a subtle, non-didactic fashion.

Innovative Methods.

These results are informed by the design approach developed by Flanagan and her team at Tiltfactor. Tiltfactor has refined several unique game design methodologies that lead to innovation, making games that are particularly suited to explore social issues and education with distinct psychological approaches to be used for societal benefit, such as altering stereotypes and biases against women and girls in STEM, or increasing quality data tags in crowdsourcing through what they call 'Outlier Design.'

Our bias work, for example, is based on the psychological principles of social identity complexity and self-identification: one of Tiltfactor's games, *Awkward Moment*, triples associations of women in STEM among players and helps players assertively stop bias; another game reduces prejudice measures by a statistically significant margin in under 20 minutes of play. The technique used is called the 'Intermix Effect': psychological or learning content is mixed in with whimsical or playful content to achieve strongest results in an optimal ratio. Creating the perfect conditions for the Intermix Effect relies on heavy iteration and weekly playtesting with outside groups of the target audience.

Flanagan's team is producing a set of principles and methods for others to follow in the production, implementation, and assessment of games using these methods. Recently, Tiltfactor developed a new scale to assess gender bias, showing how framing games explicitly as games dealing with a social issue such as social bias actually *reduced* their effectiveness at reducing bias. We also assess how taking on the role of a game character impacts the player's perception of self, and more.

Flanagan returns to her idea of fostering "Critical Play" among players [1]: ***Critical*** because the play can enter territory that explores crucial, difficult to get to issues, and ***Play*** because fun and games can allow us the openness we need change thinking and foster truly innovative thinking. Critical Play is to Flanagan a productive paradox that distills the essential important elements from a tricky subject or topic, and puts them into play to produce something surprising and transformative. It is imperative that Critical Play games allow players the freedom to fail, the room to experiment, the benefits of cooperation, and the right to interpret. Critical Play starts at home: relies on team diversity: cultural, ethnic, SES, and disciplinary diversity, as well as a team with a range of play preferences and experience, from casual to hard core gamers.

Using the method, the team works in an iterative fashion, prioritizing the values of the target player group is essential. Critical Play incorporates fundamental human values and psychological principles to promote learning, attitude change, and behavior change.

By creating greater understanding of the factors that contribute to stereotypes and biases, and by harnessing new forms of knowledge to increase global awareness, Tiltfactor aims to revolutionize new technology design for a better world.

As their findings suggest, the team has established its ability to craft games that provide a fun, entertaining experience for players and, at the same time, stimulate significant changes to their attitudes, beliefs, and behaviors in important social contexts, such as with biases and stereotypes in STEM.

Moreover, the essential features that contributed to the success of recent games *Buffalo* and *Awkward Moment* – specifically, the instructive balance of bias-related and "neutral" narrative content; the positioning of users in a variety of perspectives (including the target, observer, and responder to occurrences of bias); and the employment of an informal, accessible tone and sense of humor – can directly inform other's work in this domain.

REFERENCES

1. Flanagan, M. (2009). *Critical play: radical game design*. Boston, MA: The MIT Press.
2. Flanagan, M. & Nissenbaum, H. (in press). *Values at Play in Digital Games*. Boston, MA: The MIT Press.

Help is on the Way: Patterns of Responses to Resource Requests on Facebook

Cliff Lampe
University of Michigan
School of Information
105 S. State St
Ann Arbor, MI 48109
cacl@umich.edu

Rebecca Gray
Michigan State University
409 CommArts Building
East Lansing, MI 48824
rebecca.a.gray@gmail.com

Andrew T. Fiore
Facebook
Menlo Park, CA
atfiore@fb.com

Nicole B. Ellison
University of Michigan
School of Information
105 S. State St
Ann Arbor, MI 48109
enicole@umich.edu

ABSTRACT

Research suggests that social network sites can support social capital exchanges, which are often triggered by requests for assistance, such as seeking recommendations or asking for favors. Responsiveness to these requests for help is important to study because these interactions have the potential to affect users' overall satisfaction with the experience of using SNSs, signal social grooming functions that are an essential part of relationship maintenance, and affect social capital processes. In this paper, we study a corpus of public status updates posted to Facebook (N=7,466) in order to identify the pattern of responses to status updates that attempt to mobilize resources from the poster's Facebook network. Findings suggest that mobilization requests are treated differently than other kinds of posts; posts that attempt to mobilize help receive more comments than non-mobilization attempts. Additionally, responses occur more quickly and are shaped by the type of support requested (e.g., a recommendation vs. a favor). These findings help us better understand the role of help-seeking behaviors in the social capital conversion process as it unfolds via social media.

Author Keywords

Social Search, Facebook, Social Network Sites, Social Capital, Mobilization, LIWC.

ACM Classification Keywords

H.5.2 [Information Interfaces and Presentation]: User Interfaces - Interaction styles.

INTRODUCTION

People engage in a wide range of activities on social network sites (SNSs) like Facebook. One of those activities is using the status update feature of the site to broadcast requests for help from their network. Related to studies of "Social Search" [1], we examine how users use SNSs to mobilize resources, including emotional support, opinions, social coordination and physical assistance with tasks. While recent research has examined various types of mobilization requests – requests for help, information, or other kinds of support – broadcasted via Facebook, in this paper we examine the *patterns of responses* to mobilization attempts. One rough measure of the effectiveness of using social network sites as a platform to receive help is whether requests receive any responses at all, and if so how many and when do they receive them. Requests for help on Facebook are important to study because they instantiate *social capital in action*. Social capital describes the benefits that people receive from social interactions with others, and research shows that levels of perceived social capital are related to SNS use [6, 11, 16, 25].

Using a large collection of public status updates from Facebook, we show that responsiveness to mobilization attempts differs significantly in a number of ways from responsiveness to posts that are not mobilization requests: responses differ in prevalence, in how quickly they are contributed, in the extent to which they are contributed by the original posters themselves, and in their linguistic composition. The heightened level of engagement associated with these mobilization requests suggests that successful identification of these posts may eventually lead to systems that better facilitate the exchange of resources between individuals online – and the social capital accrual embodied in these exchanges.

LITERATURE REVIEW

Previous studies have shown that receiving comments or other forms of feedback in online interactions is important for sustained participation in social media and online communities. For example, Usenet researchers found that almost a third of posts received no responses at all, which had negative effects on future posting behavior [3]. On Slashdot, receiving either replies or votes as feedback was highly predictive of both whether someone posted in the future and how quickly they did so [15]. Additionally, feedback from other users has been found to be important for sustained interaction in Wikipedia [2] and other user generated content sites [23].

CSCW'14, February 15–19, 2014, Baltimore, Maryland, USA.

http://dx.doi.org/10.1145/2531602.2531720

Whether or not a user receives feedback is perhaps even more salient in a sociotechnical system like Facebook – especially when the post is an explicit request for help – where "other users" are typically people with whom one has a pre-existing relationship [14] and the exchange is archived, visible, and associated with users' real names (as opposed to pseudonyms). Given the above research, in the case of SNSs, we assume that receiving replies to posts requesting help or action is useful to the poster and generative of the reciprocal exchanges that create social capital. Additionally these exchanges can be understood as forms of social grooming, helping to maintain and develop interpersonal relationships between site users. In the next section, we review the literature on social capital, social grooming, and social search, which helps us understand why individuals would turn to social media for variable information needs but does not generally focus on the interpersonal dimensions of these exchanges.

Social search

"Social Search" research examines how people use online tools to seek information from others, as opposed to use of a formalized resource like a search engine [1]. Much of this work examines social search via SNSs like Facebook or Twitter. Past research has identified higher levels of trust between known contacts and expected personalization of responses as motivations for posting questions to friends on SNSs as opposed to other Q&A sites where responses come from unknown others [20]. Additional motivations found by Morris et al. [20] for asking questions via SNSs were: the belief that search engines wouldn't work to answer subjective questions, the desire to connect socially with responders, the feeling that results are already "filtered" and relevant, and, in some cases, the consequence of search engine queries that had not yielded useful results. Social search via social network sites is also generally associated with positive outcomes, such as fast turn-around time for receiving support, by those who seek information in these ways [22, 24]. Compared with other media, such as the telephone, SNSs enable individuals to broadcast their needs to large portions of their social networks with one action [10].

Conversely, there are many reasons why people might be reluctant to share some kinds of information needs with their social networks, such as privacy concerns. Individuals may be reticent to broadcast information or other needs to their network because of the personal information this invariably discloses, which can present barriers to accessing social capital in these online contexts [30]. Balancing the desire to share information and concerns about controlling one's disclosures can be executed via strategies such as Friending behaviors, using privacy settings to manage the audience, and selective disclosures [12]. Stutzman et al. [24] found that privacy attitudes and behaviors affected disclosure behaviors and that disclosure activities affected perceptions of social capital. Second, individuals may not wish to burden their network with multiple requests or appear, in the words of one participant in a related study, too "needy" [26]. Third, people may not seek information or help regarding topics that are at odds with one's self-presentational goals. For example, Newman et al. [21] found that people were unwilling to post messages about health-related issues on Facebook because they were considered potentially embarrassing. Finally, individuals may question the sincerity of support responses to messages broadcast through public channels such as Facebook [26].

More recently, researchers have broadened the focus from how people use SNSs to meet information needs via question asking to the more general question of how individuals mobilize their online networks to access a broader set of resources. An analysis of several thousand public status updates on Facebook by Ellison et al. [9] confirmed the presence of multiple types of mobilization requests beyond information-seeking attempts. As adapted from Morris et al. [22], these fell into the following categories: Recommendation, Factual Knowledge, Social Coordination, Favor/Requests, and Opinion/polls. Past research has demonstrated that response patterns can vary based on characteristics of the post as well as of the poster himself or herself. For example, Wang et al. [27] found that the topics of status updates on Facebook were related to the number of responses they received. Liu and Jansen [19] studied responses to posts on the popular Chinese SNS Sina Weibo, examining factors like network sizes of posters and content of the post. They found that posters with more followers tended to receive more comments to their posts, that mentioning people in the post garnered more comments, and that topics like "Entertainment" negatively affected whether the post would receive comments.

From the work reviewed above, we have an understanding of why people might turn to their social networks as opposed to a traditional search engine or another less personalized forum when in need of information or support. But the social search literature is less clear about why individuals expend the time and effort to respond to these requests. For insight into this issue, we turn to the literature on social capital and social grooming.

Social capital and social grooming

Sustained social interactions generate resources that can be considered from a social capital framework. Social capital as a theoretical construct provides insights into social processes, such as reciprocity expectations, that help explain why people attend to the requests of those in their network. Social capital [5, 7] describes the ability of individuals or groups to access resources embedded in their social relationships and interactions within a network. Specifically, Lin et al. [18] defines social capital as the "investment in social relations with expected returns in the marketplace" (p. 19). These "expected returns" speak to the reciprocal nature of social capital exchanges. Facebook use and perceptions of social capital have been linked in the research literature [6, 11, 16, 25]. Within the context of Facebook, we see asking for help via a status update as an explicit signal meant to start the reciprocal exchanges that drive social capital accrual.

Beyond serving to connect individuals with the kinds of support or information they need, posting and responding to questions on SNSs can also serve important social grooming functions [8] because they signal that individuals are paying attention to those in their network [11]. For instance, Burke et al. [6] found that certain kinds of communication on Facebook were more closely related to social capital than others; specifically, engaging in directed communication with Facebook Friends (e.g., sending and receiving messages) was related to increases in social capital, whereas lurking and broadcasting activities (e.g., posting status updates and sharing photos) were not. The latter behaviors do not serve as signals of attention in the way that directed messages do.

Drawing from the social grooming literature, Ellison et al. [10] recently proposed a variable they call Facebook Relationship Maintenance Behaviors ('FRMB,' called Signals of Relational Investment (SRI) in earlier work such as Lampe et al. [17]). FRMB activities include responding to requests expressed via status updates, presumably with provisions of social, informational, or emotional support, or wishing a Facebook Friend 'Happy Birthday' on their Timeline. In a system like Facebook, where non-verbal attention cues such as eye contact or nodding in assent are not visible, social grooming activities such as "liking" a comment or answering a question may serve relationship maintenance purposes. Ellison et al.'s [10] findings highlight: "… the importance of actively managing, grooming, and maintaining one's network, suggesting that social capital is not generated simply by the existence of connections on a SNS, but rather is developed through small but meaningful effort on the part of users as they engage in relationship maintenance behaviors such as responding to questions, congratulating or sympathizing with others, and noting the passing of a meaningful day."

The social aspects of answering requests are noted in other work as well. Gray et al. [13] found that individuals on average rated the comments they received in response to Facebook posts as satisfying (7.5 on a scale of 1-10). In fact, close ties' responses were associated with lower usefulness ratings but still very high satisfaction ratings, suggesting that just the sheer contribution of a response – irrespective of how "useful" the information was – was meaningful to the person seeking help or information.

In light of the literature reviewed above, we believe the examination of response patterns to mobilization requests is important for several reasons. First, whether or not a request for help receives any responses from one's network may significantly affect the ways in which people experience the efficacy of seeking help through their online social connections and thus has implications for their future behavior (as well as potentially affecting those who witness the exchange). Second, examining responsiveness to requests may help us better understand the mechanism behind social capital exchanges via social media, representing "social capital in action." As described above, responding to requests for help may play a broader social role than the immediate fulfillment of a request for help by offering a type of "social grooming" [8] that enables relationship development. Finally, although research has demonstrated an empirical link between social capital and Facebook use, the specific mechanisms behind social capital generation via Facebook are less understood. While we don't measure social capital directly, if there is no response to requests for help on Facebook, that would have serious consequences for the value of social capital generated on the site.

Given the above literature on social search, social capital, and social grooming, we ask:

RQ1: What are the differences between mobilization and non-mobilization status updates in terms of user characteristics, the level of response to these posts, and characteristics of the responders?

RQ2: How do response levels to mobilization requests vary by the a) subtype of mobilization and b) the cost level of mobilization?

RQ3a: What user and post characteristics predict whether or not a post will receive a response?

RQ3b: What user and post characteristics – as well as mobilization subtypes – predict whether or not a mobilization post will receive a response?

METHODS

In order to address the questions raised above, we first developed a coding scheme to identify status updates that were mobilization attempts and then coded them into sub-categories. Subsequently, we trained a classifier on the coded status updates and used it to obtain a larger sample of these updates as well as their associated response/comment data and anonymized characteristics of the actors involved in the conversations. We analyzed this dataset comparing mobilizations to non-mobilizations across various characteristics of users and thread engagement.

Sampling and coding of posts

For the initial coding, a total of 40,000 status updates were drawn from two samples of Facebook posts with "Public" privacy settings, meaning they were visible to anyone with a Facebook account, made in August 2012. The first was a random sample of 20,000 status updates stratified by their posters' recent activity to ensure representation of less active users.

Status updates in this sample were hand-coded as mobilization requests (1) or non-mobilization requests (0) using a coding scheme developed by Ellison et al. [9], who

Mobilization category	Functional definition *Examples (created for this research based on observed patterns)*
RECOMMENDATION	A subjective, open-ended request for suggestions, or, in the case of referrals/social connections, a request to be referred or introduced to a specific person. *"What movie should I watch tonight?"* *"Can anyone recommend a good local plumber?"*
FACTUAL KNOWLEDGE	A question posed that assumes and expects a correct answer; objective as opposed to subjective. *"Does anyone know where "Grease" is playing in town?"* *"What's the weather going to be like for the game tomorrow?"*
SOCIAL COORDINATION	A search for others with similar agendas or motives or for company (an invitation), with an assumed goal of collaboration or meeting. *"Who wants to get together after the conference for some drinks?"* *"Where should we meet before the concert Saturday?"*
FAVOR/REQUEST	A request for help or action from one's network for any number of things including physical assistance, needed items, or emotional support. *"I need to get to the airport tomorrow morning and my car is on the fritz. Who can give me a ride pretty please?"* *"Can anyone loan me their copy of Romeo and Juliet this weekend? I need to read it for class."*
OPINION/POLL	A request for an opinion to be given in reaction/response to a status update, a vote or a choice between two alternatives to be made, or a general solicitation of what people are doing. *"What do people think of Proposition 4?"* *"Chicken pot pie or beef stew for dinner?"*

Table 1: Mobilization categories from Ellison et al. [9]

defined a mobilization request as "a request for action related to provisions of social, informational, or other forms of support or assistance." Two coders were trained on a subset of 2,000 status updates and reached 90% agreement before moving on to code the rest of the posts as mobilizations or non-mobilizations. Within the first sample, 6.2% of status updates were coded as mobilization requests. The second sample of 20,000 status updates was drawn by oversampling on likely mobilization requests as determined by a preliminary logistic regression text classifier trained on the coding of the first sample. This sample was subsequently coded using the same scheme as the first sample, with 21.5% of status updates determined by human coders to be mobilization requests.

For the posts in these samples, we used scripts to collect additional data about the responses, including "likes" and comments, accumulated as of April 2013 (approximately 8 months after the original postings). We filtered out posts that were removed by user or administrative actions between the original sampling and the subsequent data collection because information about responses to them could not be retrieved. These constituted approximately 14% of posts. Next, we used a refinement of the coding scheme to differentiate mobilization requests from linguistically similar yet conceptually distinct "lightweight" pseudo-mobilizations that did not seek meaningful support and thus could be considered unconnected to social capital (e.g., "Like my status"). These pseudo-mobilization posts (N = 1175) were excluded from analysis.

We then constructed from the remaining posts a sample approximately balanced between mobilization and non-mobilization status updates. To do so, we started with all available mobilization requests from both samples (N = 3589) and then drew an approximately equal-sized random sample of non-mobilization status updates (N = 3877), yielding a final dataset with 48.1% of status updates coded as mobilization requests and 51.9% as non-mobilization.

Explanatory variables

For the present analysis, we collected the following explanatory variables for each post in our balanced sample. Unless otherwise noted, the data are derived from Facebook server logs.

- Whether the post was a mobilization request (human-coded)
- Level of effort ("cost") required to fulfill the request (human-coded), ranging from 1 (lowest) to 3 (highest)
- Type or category of the mobilization (human-coded): Recommendation, Factual knowledge, Social coordination, Favor/request, and/or Opinion/poll
- Age of the poster and commenters
- Gender of the poster and commenters

Variable	*t* statistic (df)	Mobilization *M* (*SD*)	Non-mob. *M* (*SD*)
Poster's age	–.972 (7430)	33.02 (15.31)	32.67 (15.45)
Poster's num. of Facebook Friends	–3.775 (7259) ***	582.47 (750.10)	518.01 (712.38)
Poster's Facebook visitation frequency (# days of 28)	–1.063 (7337)	22.29 (7.99)	22.08 (8.01)
Num. of comments (not incl. original poster comments)	–12.686 (6418) ***	2.34 (4.24)	1.26 (3.00)
Num. of commenters	–11.516 (6830) ***	1.61 (2.81)	.94 (2.22)
Num. of likes	6.396 (6934) ***	2.34 (4.85)	3.22 (6.98)
Fraction of commenters living within 20 mi of poster†	–.4178 (3091)	.511 (.428)	.505 (.440)
Num. of comments made by original poster	–11.236 (6214) ***	.91 (1.99)	.47 (1.33)
Num. of comments "liked" by original poster†	–.830 (3023)	.79 (2.11)	.72 (2.44)
	Mann-Whitney *U*	**Mobilization median**	**Non-mob. median**
Minutes to first response†	1560441 ***	16.25	25.43
Median minutes between comments†	902653.5 ***	18.80	28.75

Table 2: *T*-tests and Mann-Whitney *U* tests comparing user characteristics and responses to mobilization requests and non-mobilization requests. For *t* and *U* statistics, * = $p < .05$, ** = $p < .01$, *** = $p < .001$. † indicates that only posts with at least one

- Friend count of the poster and commenters
- Facebook visitation of the poster and commenters (number of days out of 28 that the user visited Facebook around the time of the original post)
- Time between original post and first comment (minutes)
- Number of comments made on the post
- Number of distinct people commenting on the post
- Number of people who liked the post
- Distance between the poster's city-level home location and each commenter's city-level home location
- Counts of words in the post and comments matching selected categories from the Linguistic Inquiry and Word Count software [22]

Individuals who posted status updates were on average 32.84 years old (median = 27), 52.19% female, had an average of 549.10 Friends on Facebook (median = 317), and logged into Facebook an average of 22.18 days out of the most recent 28 days (median = 27).

To classify the kinds of mobilization requests, we applied a typology adapted from Morris et al. [20] and used by Ellison et al. [9], which categorizes mobilizations as one or more of the following: recommendation, factual knowledge, social coordination, favor/request, and opinion/poll. (See Table 1 for an appropriated set of definitions and examples of the categories.) We also utilized the coding scheme utilized in Ellison et al. [9] to categorize mobilization requests by the amount of effort required on the part of potential post-viewers to respond to the request. Two human coders applied a cost code to each status update identified as a mobilization. They coded a subset of the same 400 mobilization requests first, and upon reaching 90% agreement, divided and coded the remaining mobilization requests independently. The amount of effort required to respond has been divided into three levels (1, 2, and 3) and differentiates the cost of mobilization by how easily others can respond to the original poster's need. A question that can be answered directly on the post thread would be a 1, a response by another mediated channel or elsewhere within the Facebook platform would be a 2, and a request that necessitates responders to perform an offline action would be a 3.

RESULTS

Our first research question (*RQ1*) asked about the differences between mobilization and non-mobilization status updates in terms of user characteristics, the level of response to these posts, and characteristics of the responders. Table 2 shows comparisons between mobilizations and non-mobilizations across these characteristics. While there was no difference in the age of Facebook users who posted mobilization requests in our sample or how active they had been in the past month on the site, they had slightly more Friends on average than the authors of the non-mobilization status updates. Mobilization posts had significantly more comments, more unique commenters per post, and fewer Likes than non-mobilization posts. The percentages of people who lived within 20 miles of the poster were no different between different types of posts. Facebook status updates that were mobilization requests not only received more comments on average than non-mobilization requests, but also there was a shorter median time to receive the first comment for these posts. Mobilization posts that received more than one comment also had shorter median times between comments than non-mobilization posts. (We used median times for these measurements to manage outlying response times.) Lastly, posts differed in the degree of engagement of the status update posters themselves within the comment threads. Mobilization threads included more comments from the status posters themselves; however, mobilizations and non-mobilizations did not significantly differ in the number of comments that were liked by the original posters.

Linguistic features of mobilization posts and comments

Table 3 contains comparisons of linguistic differences in the original posts and responses across these mobilization and non-mobilization status updates. As described above, these differences are detected using comparisons of word frequencies with the Linguistic Inquiry and Word Count (LIWC) text analysis software. LIWC has a variety of dictionaries (word lists) that contain words whose presence in text has been shown to signify different emotions expressed in the text [22]. We used LIWC to provide some insight into the content of the responses to requests for help. While LIWC only provides a very high-level view of word prevalence in responses, it does give some sense of the general types of words used when responding.

For this analysis, we chose five LIWC dictionaries:

- SOCIAL: This dictionary includes both nouns and verbs that indicate social processes. Examples include *mate, talk, they,* and *child.*
- POSEMO: Short for "Positive Emotion" and a subset of "Affective Processes," this dictionary contains words like *love, nice,* and *sweet.*
- NEGEMO: Short for "Negative Emotion" and a subset of "Affective Processes," this dictionary contains words like *hurt, ugly,* and *nasty.*
- TIME: A subset of the "Relativity" dictionary, this group of terms includes *end, until,* and *season.*
- ASSENT: This set of words includes terms commonly used to signal agreement. Examples include *agree, OK,* and *yes.*

The Social dictionary was selected because requests for help might include more words pertaining to social relationships, such as in a recommendation request seeking advice about a particular relationship. Given that requests for help can not only be used to mobilize resources, but also to signal the need for emotional support, we expected more Positive Emotion and Negative Emotion words in mobilization status updates and comments. For example, a mobilization request that expresses a problem may contain more negative emotion words, whereas the responses received from Friends may either echo the negative sentiments or respond using positive words in attempt to comfort the poster. We included "Time" words because mobilization attempts might be more likely to include urgency or the need to perform an action within a specified time period (e.g., "I need a dog sitter Saturday!"). Assent was selected because the words in this dictionary are

LIWC category	*t* statistic (df)	Mob. *M*	Non-mob. *M*
ORIGINAL POST TEXT			
Social	−14.340 (7436) ***	9.7%	6.8%
Posemo	8.560 (6238) ***	3.3%	4.6%
Negemo	5.209 (6352) ***	1.3%	1.8%
Time	3.949 (7027) ***	4.1%	4.7%
Assent	2.500 (6612) *	0.7%	0.9%
Word count	1.365 (7054)	29.0	30.6
COMMENT TEXT (EXCLUDING ORIGINAL POSTER)			
Social	2.587 (2847) **	8.6%	9.4%
Posemo	6.661 (2447) ***	6.2%	9.1%
Negemo	3.386 (2814) **	1.7%	2.4%
Time	1.022 (2762)	3.2%	3.4%
Assent	1.200 (2733)	3.1%	3.5%
Word count	−5.234 (3521) ***	60.8	42.7

Table 3: *T*-tests comparing linguistic attributes of mobilization requests and non-mobilization requests. Mean word counts and percentages of words belonging to each

closely associated with providing opinions or answering questions. The word "yes," for example, is typically the response to a question and would be more expected in response to a mobilization request/question than a non-mobilization status update.

Occurrences of words in the selected LIWC dictionaries were measured as a percentage of all words in the text of each status update and in the combined text of all comments on each update. For example, a 25-word status update with 5 of its words in the Social dictionary would receive a score of 20% for that category. Because for the present work we are primarily interested in qualities of comments and commenters in the aggregate, for the comment text LIWC analysis, we applied the LIWC dictionaries to the combined text of all comments on a status update rather than applying them to comments individually.

The original mobilization status updates were much more likely to include words in the social dictionary. However, comments to mobilization status updates were less likely than comments to other types of status updates to include Social words. Both original mobilization updates and comments to them were significantly less likely to include either Positive or Negative Emotion words compared to other types of status updates. This might be because these posts are more likely to be filled with words that are more factual, presenting the need, than emotional. Or it could be that interacting around a need is already making oneself vulnerable, so less emotion words mitigate that vulnerability. Mobilization updates had slightly lower percentages of both Assent and Time words, but there were no differences in the appearance of these words in responses. There were no overall differences in the number of words per status update for these mobilization status updates compared to other types of status updates, but responses to mobilization updates included quite a few more words, commensurate to our finding that they had more posts overall.

While we did not conduct a detailed analysis of the content of the responses to mobilization requests, LIWC analysis sheds some light on some of the tone of these posts compared to non-mobilization updates. While differences in the words used by responders to mobilization and non-mobilizations updates are only modest (a few percentage points different), there is a trend where responders use fewer social and emotion words in responses. At a high level, this shows there are content differences between posts that request help, not just a difference in amount or speed of posting.

Differences between types of mobilizations

As described above, previous research has categorized status updates that request help according to the type of resource mobilized and the costliness to respondents of fulfilling the request [9]. Tables 4a and 4b show the prevalence of the category and cost labels in our data.

Mobilization category	Including those labeled as multiple categories	Excluding those labeled as multiple categories
Recommendation	171 (4.8%)	160 (4.6%)
Social coordination	364 (10.1%)	315 (9.1%)
Favor request	1374 (38.3%)	1259 (36.5%)
Opinion/poll	1324 (36.9%)	1233 (35.7%)
Factual knowledge	496 (13.8%)	484 (14.0%)
TOTAL	3589 (100%)	3451 (100%)

Table 4a: Frequencies of Mobilization Categories

Cost Level	Frequency
1	2487 (69.3%)
2	540 (15.0%)
3	562 (15.7%)

Responses by type of mobilization

We examined how responses to mobilization requests vary by category (*RQ2a*) and cost level (*RQ2b*) of the request. To this end, we conducted analyses of variance, or the analogous Kruskal-Wallis non-parametric test for variables with highly skewed distributions, on posts that were assigned to only one category of mobilization (N = 3451). We found that mobilizations of different categories vary significantly in the number of comments they receive, $F(4, 3446) = 14.92$, $p < .001$, in the number of commenters who participate in the thread, $F(4,3446) = 14.68$, $p < .001$, and in the receipt of likes on a post, $F(4, 3446) = 4.902$, $p < .05$ (see Table 5 for Bonferroni post-hoc corrections showing how the categories differed across these kinds of engagement).

Among posts that received at least one comment, mobilization subtypes did not differ significantly from one another with regard to the median distance between commenters and the original poster, Kruskal-Wallis χ^2 (4) = 8.985, *n.s.* They did vary significantly, however, in the median time that passed between comments, Kruskal-Wallis χ^2 (4) = 15.066, $p < .01$, with post hoc Mann-Whitney tests revealing a significant difference only between social coordinations (median = 10.4 min) and favor/requests (median = 25.8 min). Factual knowledge, opinion/poll, and recommendation requests did not differ significantly from each other or from social coordination or favor/request posts in median time between comments. Mobilization subtypes also differed in how quickly they received their first comments, Kruskal-Wallis χ^2 (4) = 14.337, $p < .01$. Bonferroni-corrected post hoc Mann-Whitney tests revealed that favor/request posts received first responses significantly later (median = 24.1 min) than factual knowledge requests (median = 12.1 min). There was no pairwise significant difference between any two of opinion/polls (median = 15.2 min), recommendations (median = 22.5 min), social coordinations (median = 15.8), and the other subtypes in time to first response.

Number of Comments *M(SD)*		Number of Commenters *M(SD)*		Number of Likes *M(SD)*	
Recommendation$_a$	4.06(5.45)	Recommendation$_a$	2.81(3.94)	Opinion/poll$_a$	2.70(5.78)
Factual knowledge$_b$	2.80 (4.18)	Factual knowledge$_b$	2.33(2.72)	Social coordination$_{ab}$	2.60(3.66)
Opinion/poll$_b$	2.51(4.53)	Opinion/poll$_b$	1.73(2.88)	Favor request$_{ab}$	2.26(4.69)
Social coordination$_b$	2.44(3.53)	Social coordination$_{bc}$	1.46(1.84)	Factual knowledge$_{ab}$	2.00(4.17)
Favor request$_c$	1.74 (3.90)	Favor request$_c$	1.26(2.77)	Recommendation$_b$	1.16(2.90)
Cost level 1$_a$	2.74(4.62)	Cost level 1$_a$	1.92(3.14)		
Cost level 3$_b$	2.08(3.83)	Cost level 3$_b$	1.26(1.99)		
Cost level 2$_c$	0.67(1.78)	Cost level 2$_c$	0.48(1.11)		

Table 5: Means of engagement metrics across mobilization subcategories and cost (effort) levels. *Note.* Means having no letter in common in their subscripts differ significantly at $p < .05$ after adjustment with Bonferroni's procedure.

Predictors	Block 1	Block 2
	EST. (S.E.) O.R.	EST. (S.E.) O.R.
Gender	–.077 (.048) .926	–.070 (.048) 0.932
Age	.010 (.002) *** 1.010	.009 (.002) *** 1.009
# Friends	.000 (.000) 1.000	.000 (.000) 1.000
Freq. of site visits	.036 (.003) *** 1.037	.037 (.003) *** 1.037
Post word count		.002 (.001) *** 1.003
Constant	–1.22 (.097) *** .294	–1.26 (.098) *** .283
Likelihood ratio test vs. null model	χ^2(4) = 183.82 ***	χ^2(5) = 206.15 ***
Likelihood ratio test vs. previous model	—	χ^2 (1) = 22.32 ***
Prediction accuracy (vs. null model)	57.5% (+5.2%)	58.2% (+5.9%)

Table 6: Binary Logistic Regression Predicting Response Instance among Mobilization and Non-Mobilization Posts. Coefficient estimates, standard errors, and odds ratios are

Response by cost of mobilization

Engagement with mobilization requests also varied significantly with the level of effort required to complete the requests (RQ2b). The number of comments (excluding those made by the original poster) differed significantly by cost level, $F(2, 3448) = 53.46$, $p < .001$ as did the number of commenters on posts, $F(2, 3448) = 62.93$, $p < .001$(see Table 5 for means and Bonferroni post-hoc significance tests). When examining the relationship between cost levels and timing of comments on those posts that received at least one, we found no significant difference between cost levels and the median time between comments, Kruskal-Wallis χ^2 (2) = 4.763, *n.s.* However, posts of different cost levels did differ significantly in terms of time to the first comment, Kruskal-Wallis χ^2 (2) = 16.568, $p < .001$, with post hoc Mann-Whitney tests using Bonferroni's correction showing a significant difference between cost levels 1 (median = 14.7 min) and 2 (median = 34.0 min). Cost level 3 (median = 22.0) did not differ significantly from the other levels. Finally, the median distance between status posters and respective commenters did not vary significantly by cost, Kruskal-Wallis χ^2 (2) = 1.622, *n.s.*

Response by user characteristics

Our next research question considered whether users' characteristics and the content of the status updates were related to whether or not the post receives a response/comment from another Facebook user, regardless of its identification as a mobilization request or not (*RQ3a*). To answer this question, we coded all the original posts that received zero responses with "0" and those that received one or more comments with "1" and conducted a binary logistic to see which characteristics increased our ability to predict this response outcome. The user characteristics included in the first block of the model were the poster's age, gender, friend count, and site use. The second block added a characteristic of the status updates, the word count of each post. The overall percentage of responses that the model was able to predict accurately was 58.2% with the inclusion of these personal and post characteristics, as compared to 52.3% with the null model. Table 6 summarizes the impact of the various predictors of receiving a response in the model and also provides likelihood-ratio tests of model fit. Odds ratios are given to characterize the increase or decrease in the odds of receiving a response associated with an increase in a predictor; these show that a one-year increase in age is associated with a 1% greater likelihood of receiving a comment on a status update, while each additional day on which the poster visits Facebook predicts a 3.7% greater likelihood of his or her post receiving a comment.

We then ran a binary logistic regression to predict whether or not a post would receive at least one response among mobilization posts only and added mobilization categories as predictors in the third block of the regression (*RQ3b*). The overall percentage of response vs. no-response outcomes that this mobilization-specific model was able to accurately predict with user characteristics, post characteristics, and mobilization categories was 62.8%, as compared to 56.4% for the null model (see Table 7). The five mobilization categories were entered into the model using deviation contrasts; thus, their coefficient estimates and odds ratios represent the difference in response between posts with the category in question and the mean of category mean responses with other IVs held at their base levels. Of interest: the chance of getting a response was substantially higher for factual knowledge and recommendation requests, and the chance for favor/requests substantially lower, as compared to mobilizations overall.

DISCUSSION

This paper explores a specific slice of Facebook activity – patterns of responses to broadcasted communications that request resources from one's network. We believe that these interactions can offer insight into social capital dynamics on SNSs and other online contexts where individuals are engaging with large numbers of primarily known ties. Our dataset of public post content and user characteristics allows us to document and describe the dynamics of resource requests and provisions in this specific online context. Because Facebook is a common platform used by over one billion individuals, we assume some of the behaviors witnessed on Facebook will

Predictors	Block 1	Block 2	Block 3
	EST. (S.E.) O.R.	EST. (S.E.) O.R.	EST. (S.E.) O.R.
Gender (M)	–.179 (.070) * .836	–.170 (.071) * .844	–.202 (.072) ** .817
Age	.009 (.002) *** 1.009	.008 (.002) *** 1.008	.007 (.002) ** 1.007
Number of Friends	.000 (.000) 1.000	.000 (.000) 1.000	.000 (.000) 1.000
Frequency of site visits	.033 (.004) *** 1.034	.034 (.005) *** 1.034	.027 (.005) *** 1.028
Post word count		.002 (.001) 1.002	.004 (.001) ** 1.004
Factual knowledge†			.207 (.093) * 1.230
Favor/request†			–.754 (.069) *** .470
Opinion/poll†			–.113 (.069) .893
Recommendation†			.603 (.154) *** 1.828
Social coordination†			— — 1.059
Constant	–.691 (.143) ***	–.728 (.144) ***	–.342 (.152) *
Likelihood ratio test vs. null model	$\chi^2(4) = 75.434$ ***	$\chi^2(5) = 79.827$ ***	$\chi^2(9) = 209.234$ ***
Likelihood ratio test vs. previous model	—	$\chi^2(1) = 4.393$ *	$\chi^2(4) = 129.407$ ***
Prediction accuracy (vs. null model)	57.2% (+0.8%)	58.0% (+1.6%)	62.8% (+6.4%)

Table 7: Binary logistic regression predicting whether or not mobilizations would receive at least one comment. Coefficient estimates, standard errors, and odds ratios are provided for each term. † Deviation contrasts with social coordination as the base level.

propagate to other sites, as users see positive outcomes and then replicate them through a social learning process.

This work differs from early work in this area in that we study a specific kind of activity, not overall use. In contrast to early scholarship on the effects of Internet use, researchers have moved from global measures of Internet use (e.g., minutes online) and have instead focused on specific kinds of behaviors that are more strongly correlated with outcomes of interest. For example, Bessière et al. [4] found that overall use of the Internet was associated with higher levels of self-reported depression, but when they examined different kinds of use, other patterns emerged. Specifically, communicating with friends and family online had a negative relationship with depression, while communicating with weaker ties such as those met online was positively related to depression. Research examining Facebook use and social capital reveals similar patterns. Ellison et al. [11] identified three "connection strategies" and find that social information-seeking, where people are using the site to learn more about people with whom they share some offline connection, is more predictive of social capital that other uses such as meeting new people. Similarly, Burke et al. [6] found that directed communication had a stronger relationship with social capital than broadcasted communication or passively consuming content on the site.

Taken as a whole, this stream of research suggests that access to a particular site or the Internet in general is not as meaningful as the specific kinds of activities and interactions that are taking place. This is true for Facebook as well. We believe that asking and answering resource requests on SNSs represent a kind of activity that may be critical for social capital development and maintenance. Earlier work has documented that these requests take place [10]. However, for social capital exchanges to occur, it is critical for the network to respond. Are requests for help being answered or not? Our findings show that Facebook updates that are seeking to mobilize resources within social networks do indeed lead to different types of interactions than other kinds of broadcasted posts.

Number and kind of responses

For mobilization posts in our sample, 56% received at least one comment. We found that mobilization posts received more comments than non-mobilization posts and, similarly, received comments from more unique users. This suggests that users do attend to posts that request resources differently than they attend to posts that do not contain evidence of need.

Taken in conjunction with other work in this area, our findings suggest productive avenues for future research seeking to determine the relationship between different kinds of actions on Facebook and higher-level concepts such as social capital. For instance, Burke et al. [7] find that directed communication is more predictive of social capital than broadcasting or lurking, suggesting that interaction (as indicated by comments and other responses) is critical for social capital accrual and maintenance. Future work building on these two streams of research could examine the social capital implications of broadcasting a request that doesn't receive any responses (as happened with 44% of the mobilization requesters in our sample).

Interestingly, non-mobilization posts did receive more likes than mobilization requests. One explanation is that users may be less inclined to "like" the post of a friend who is expressing a need or asking for help, as this may be perceived as unhelpful or even inappropriate when posters are seeking more meaningful support or sharing negative news. Non-mobilization posts, such as those sharing updates or good news, may be more appropriate to "like" as opposed to a time-intensive comment.

Although recommendation posts were the least prevalent subcategory of mobilization posts, they received more responses than any other type of mobilization request and over two times the number of responses of non-mobilization posts. Previous work has suggested, in keeping with our finding, that recommendations may be less prevalent because they require specific shared characteristics to answer [10], limiting the potential respondent pool. The low number of potential respondents may be related to the high number of responses, in that feeling like one is part of a smaller, more exclusive group of those who could help diminishes the by-stander effect and increases the chances that one will help. In this way, a recommendation request may help activate particular nodes of a network that have expertise in an area, helping them realize the value of their response. Recommendation requests may receive more responses in part because they typically require only a relatively low-effort written response, as opposed to promises of material items or offline assistance. Favor requests, which demand more commitment from the responder, received the fewest comments, perhaps because an early commenter met the need, eliminating the need for additional responses. Unlike recommendations, where "more is better," many favor requests may only need one person to provide assistance. Interaction around some types of requests may have moved to a different channel, like private message or email, which our methods do not enable us to assess.

Receiving at least one response

In assessing the probability that a mobilization status update would receive any responses, we found that both user characteristics and request characteristics were important. Being a male mobilization requester was associated with a lower likelihood of receiving a response to requests. The biggest drivers of receiving responses were characteristics of the post itself – specifically: what *kind* of resources the post attempted to mobilize. In alignment with the analyses of variance, posts that were categorized as recommendations or factual knowledge requests increased the predictive accuracy of the model, ultimately enabling the prediction of receiving responses with accuracy well over chance. Whether or not posts receive responses has implications for both the ability of individuals to meet their resource needs as well as implications for the overall SNS user experience and perceived utility of posting requests in these spaces.

Time to receive responses

Mobilization threads are also notably different from non-mobilization threads with regard to the speed with which Friends of posters respond to the requests. Friends of mobilization posters respond more quickly, and less time passes between the comments received on the threads. At the surface level, this suggests that users are sensitive to the needs of their Facebook Friends and more likely to respond quickly to a call for help than to other kinds of posts.

Future Research and Implications for Theory

This work helps to forward our understanding of social capital processes in SNSs, but more work is needed to build upon this and other work in this area.

Our data do not allow us to discern whether these responses are, in fact, meeting the expressed or implied needs of the posters, and this is an important step future research should take. Interviewing or surveying help-seekers about the support they receive, similar to the methods used in Gray et al. [13], or examining data that may serve as proxies for satisfaction, such as the extent to which posters "like" the comments that others have provided, could help determine the extent to which requests are successful. We assume that most individuals posting a question would like an answer to that question in addition to the other benefits (such as emotional support) they might receive.

Social capital theory does acknowledge that support can come in different forms [19], and it may be that messages that do not address the explicit need of posters likely perform other interpersonal functions, such as provisions of social support, and are conducive to social capital processes. Given the lack of other signals of attention (such as gaze) in the online environment, responses to requests can serve as a way to signal attention and engage in social grooming with one's ties, and research suggests that users are satisfied with responses regardless of their instrumental utility [13]. As Gray et al. [13] note, "asking a question acts as an invitation for a social exchange that may not happen on its own. In other words, answering a question on Facebook gives individuals an excuse to interact and to signal they are paying attention to their ties on the site."

One way in which comments to a public Facebook post differ from other channels through which support may occur (e.g., a phone call to a friend) is the increased visibility and persistence of these messages. This has implications for social capital dynamics and suggests that second-order effects need to be considered – the ways in which network members are affected by witnessing successful and unsuccessful mobilization attempts. Similarly, future work could examine the extent to which individuals change their behavior after receiving (or not receiving) assistance in response to a post, given that these failed attempts are visible in their history.

Of course, these visible and persistent social capital exchanges may lead to other interactions that are not visible or persistent. Past research suggests that posts may be triggers for phone calls, face-to-face meetings, or other interactions [26]. Any responses that are made through channels other than Facebook would not be captured here, and future methods should consider actions taken through channels other than Facebook in response to mobilization posts, through surveys or other methods.

Limitations

We do not include data about impressions (how many people saw a post), and past research shows that the degree to which others view a post is unequivocally linked with the amount of responses the post receives. Wang et al. [27] found that Facebook posts that received more views received more comments, even though the number of Friends the posters had was a negative predictor, which they attribute to the interplay between views and the Facebook News Feed algorithm that controls who sees which posts. There may be elements of the News Feed algorithm that privilege certain kinds of posts in a way that impacts the analyses we present here regarding engagement metrics. We do not know that all kinds of posts get equal visibility upon being broadcasted and furthermore how the visibility of posts may change after Friends begin to interact with them. Future work should attempt to use the number of impressions (views) of posts as a control.

The fact that we used only public updates may affect the patterns we identify here, in that some kinds of exchanges are more likely to occur with restricted audiences. Because we hand-coded broadcasted status updates and were directly interacting with user-generated content via Facebook, we were limited to public updates to protect user privacy. Future work would ideally explore these questions using automated methods applied to private updates to look for any substantive empirical differences that may exist between limited-audience and public posts.

The deleted content mentioned in the description of our sample also presents problems for the generalizability of our study. We do not know if the deletions from the data set are due to user or to administrative actions; they may not be randomly distributed. For example, it may be that some user-deleted posts were removed because they received no responses and represented unsuccessful mobilization attempts, a potentially ego-threatening situation. As a recent Pew study found, "'likes' specifically seem to be a strong proxy for social status, such that teen Facebook users will manipulate their profile and timeline content in order to garner the maximum number of 'likes,' and remove photos with too few 'likes'"[21].

Broader implications

We find that people do respond more to mobilization status updates than they do to other types of updates on Facebook. We see this core finding as having multiple implications both for understanding Facebook and online interactions more generally.

Mobilization status updates and their responses may be an important factor by which Facebook users determine the usefulness of the site, and thus what their participation on the site should be. Consequently, SNSs where mobilization activity is occurring could explicitly support these activities through design decisions that highlight signals of social grooming, allow for better management of attention to requests for help, or enable new ways of responding to these requests.

People seek help in many different types of sociotechnical systems, such as discussion forums, Q&A sites, and SNSs. Our findings extend previous research showing that receiving responses is an important form of feedback in these systems. Besides encouraging future contributions, receiving responses may be an important form of social grooming that increases feelings of connectedness in an online community or social media site. However, we also show that different types of requests have different outcomes in how they receive responses. User characteristics can shape how likely a person is to receive responses to their requests. Given the different outcomes for types of help we've found, more attention to what type of resource is being requested could lead to more effective ways for people to engage in this important type of online activity. In other words, focusing on responses to requests for help is applicable to many online systems where users have few cues about whether others are paying attention to them. Given the heterogeneity of responses to requests we found on Facebook, other sites may consider how requests for interactions by users are or are not being met.

CONCLUSION

Social network sites support a wide range of activities for participants, including ways to access and foster their relationships with other people. As people post in these sites, receiving feedback and acknowledgment from other users is an important mechanism by which people measure both their success and satisfaction. This is especially true for posts that are intended by people to mobilize resources from their networks online. By examining a large set of status updates that both intended to mobilize resources, and those that didn't, we found that mobilization requests get more responses than other kinds of posts. Additionally, we found there were significant differences in the likelihood that a mobilization update received a response based on the type of resource the person was asking for.

This work contributes to our knowledge of how people engage with one another in Facebook interactions and provides some initial insight into the responsiveness to requests for help that may exist in social network sites. This insight is important not only for understanding the role of Facebook as a space where people seek help, but also how these behaviors facilitate the social grooming that is key to maintaining relationships and generating social capital.

ACKNOWLEDGMENTS

This work was supported by the National Science Foundation (HCC 0916019).

REFERENCES

1. Ackerman, M., Adamic, L., Ellison, N., Gergle, D., Hecht, B., Lampe, C., Morris, M.R. and Teevan, J. Social media question asking workshop *Proceedings of the 2013 conference on Computer supported cooperative work companion*, ACM, San Antonio, Texas, USA, 2013, 297-298.
2. Antin, J., Cheshire, C. and Nov, O. Technology-mediated contributions: editing behaviors among new wikipedians *Proceedings of the ACM 2012 conference on Computer Supported Cooperative Work*, ACM, Seattle, Washington, USA, 2012, 373-382.
3. Arguello, J., Butler, B.S., Joyce, E., Kraut, R., Ling, K.S., Rose, C. and Wang, X. Talk to me: foundations for successful individual-group interactions in online communities *Proceedings of the SIGCHI Conference on Human Factors in Computing Systems*, ACM, Montreal, Quebec, Canada, 2006, 959-968.
4. Bessiere, K., Kiesler, S., Kraut, R. and Boneva, B.S. Effects of Internet use and social resources on changes in depression. *Information, Community & Society, 11* (1). 47-70.
5. Bourdieu, P. Forms of Capital. in Richardson, J.G. ed. *Handbook of Theory and Research for the Sociology of Education*, Greenwood Press, New York, 1983.
6. Burke, M., Kraut, R. and Marlow, C. Social capital on facebook: differentiating uses and users *Proceedings of the 2011 annual conference on Human factors in computing systems*, ACM, Vancouver, BC, Canada, 2011, 571-580.
7. Coleman, J.S. Social Capital in the Creation of Human Capital. *American Journal of Sociology, 94*. S95-S120.
8. Donath, J.S. Signals in social supernets. *Journal of Computer Mediated Communication, 13* (1). 12.
9. Ellison, N., Gray, R., Vitak, J., Lampe, C. and Fiore, A., Calling All Facebook Friends: Exploring requests for help on Facebook. . in *7th annual International Conference on Weblogs and Social Media*, (Washington, DC, 2013), Association for the Advancement of Artificial Intelligence, forthcoming.
10. Ellison, N., Vitak, J., Gray, R. and Lampe, C. Cultivating Social Resources on Social Network Sites: Facebook Relationship Maintenance Behaviors and Their Role in Social Capital Processes. *Journal of Computer Mediated Communication.*
11. Ellison, N.B., Steinfield, C. and Lampe, C. Connection Strategies: Social Capital Implications of Facebook-enabled Communication Practices. *New Media & Society, 13*. 873-892.
12. Ellison, N.B., Vitak, J., Steinfield, C., Gray, R. and Lampe, C. Negotiating Privacy Concerns and Social Capital Needs in a Social Media Environment. *Privacy Online: Perspectives on Privacy and Self-disclosure in the Social Web*. 19.
13. Gray, R., Ellison, N.B., Vitak, J. and Lampe, C. Who wants to know?: question-asking and answering practices among facebook users *Proceedings of the 2013 conference on Computer supported cooperative work*, ACM, San Antonio, Texas, USA, 2013, 1213-1224.
14. Lampe, C., Ellison, N. and Steinfield, C., Changes in Use and Perception of Facebook. in *ACM Conference on Computer-Supported Cooperative Work (CSCW)*, (San Diego, CA, 2008), ACM Press.
15. Lampe, C. and Johnston, E., Follow the (Slash) dot: Effects of Feedback on New Members in an Online Community. in *International Conference on Supporting Group Work, GROUP '05*, (Sanibel Island, FL, 2005), ACM Press.
16. Lampe, C., Vitak, J. and Ellison, N. Users and nonusers: interactions between levels of adoption and social capital *Proceedings of the 2013 conference on*

Computer supported cooperative work, ACM, San Antonio, Texas, USA, 2013, 809-820.

17. Lampe, C., Vitak, J., Gray, R. and Ellison, N., Perceptions of Facebook's Value as an Information Source. in *CHI - Conference on Human Factors in Computing*, (Austin, TX, 2012), ACM Press.

18. Lin, N., Cook, K.S. and Burt, R.S. *Social capital: theory and research.* Aldine de Gruyter, 2001.

19. Liu, Z. and Jansen, B.J. Factors influencing the response rate in social question and answering behavior *Proceedings of the 2013 conference on Computer supported cooperative work*, ACM, San Antonio, Texas, USA, 2013, 1263-1274.

20. Morris, M.R., Teevan, J. and Panovich, K. What do people ask their social networks, and why?: a survey study of status message q&a behavior *Proceedings of the 28th international conference on Human factors in computing systems*, ACM, Atlanta, Georgia, USA, 2010.

21. Newman, M.W., Lauterbach, D., Munson, S.A., Resnick, P. and Morris, M.E. It's not that i don't have problems, i'm just not putting them on facebook: challenges and opportunities in using online social networks for health *Proceedings of the ACM 2011 conference on Computer supported cooperative work*, ACM, Hangzhou, China, 2011, 341-350.

22. Pennebaker, J.W., Francis, M.E. and Booth, R.J. Linguistic inquiry and word count: LIWC 2001. *Mahway: Lawrence Erlbaum Associates.*

23. Sarkar, C., Wohn, D.Y. and Lampe, C., Predicting length of membership in online community everything2 using feedback. in *Proceedings of the ACM 2012 conference on Computer Supported Cooperative Work Companion*, (2012), ACM, 207-210.

24. Stutzman, F., Vitak, J., Ellison, N.B., Gray, R. and Lampe, C., Privacy in Interaction: Exploring Disclosure and Social Capital in Facebook. in *Sixth International AAAI Conference on Weblogs and Social Media*, (2012).

25. Valenzuela, S., Park, N. and Kee, K.F. Is there social capital in a social network site?: Facebook use and college students' life satisfaction, trust and participation. *Journal of Computer-Mediated Communication, 14.* 875-901.

26. Vitak, J. and Ellison, N.B. "There's a network out there you might as well tap": Exploring the benefits of and barriers to exchanging informational and support-based resources on Facebook. *New Media & Society*, *15* (2). 243-259.

27. Wang, Y.-C., Burke, M. and Kraut, R.E., Gender, topic, and audience response: an analysis of user-generated content on facebook. in *Proceedings of the SIGCHI Conference on Human Factors in Computing Systems*, (2013), ACM, 31-34.

To Search or to Ask: The Routing of Information Needs Between Traditional Search Engines and Social Networks

Anne Oeldorf-Hirsch[1], Brent Hecht[2], Meredith Ringel Morris[3], Jaime Teevan[3], Darren Gergle[4]

[1]University of Connecticut
Storrs, CT
anneo@uconn.edu

[2]University of Minnesota
Minneapolis, MN
bhecht@cs.umn.edu

[3]Microsoft Research
Redmond, WA
{merrie,teevan}@microsoft.com

[4]Northwestern University
Evanston, IL
dgergle@northwestern.edu

ABSTRACT

In status message question asking (SMQA), members of social networking sites make use of status messages to express information needs to friends and contacts. We present findings from a laboratory study that examined 82 participants' SMQA behaviors in the broader context of online information seeking. When given the option of using a search engine and/or a social network, participants leveraged SMQA for 20% of their information needs, most often posing a question to their network in addition to issuing a query. We show the important roles played by the specificity of the information need and the perceived audience of a given network on routing decisions. We then demonstrate that routing decisions have varied effects on participants' satisfaction, information value, and trust of outcomes. In addition to highlighting the complementary advantages and disadvantages of search and SMQA, our findings suggest that search engines can better address a meaningful portion of people's information needs by integrating SMQA capabilities into their systems.

Author Keywords

Social media question asking; information seeking; social networks; Web search; social search.

ACM Classification Keywords

H.5.m [Information Interfaces and Presentation]: Miscellaneous

General Terms

Human Factors

INTRODUCTION

A new information seeking approach that has received attention from both researchers and practitioners is *status message question asking* (SMQA) [1, 12, 20, 23, 24, 31, 32, 37]. In SMQA, users of social networking sites like Facebook and Twitter co-opt the status message field to pose questions to their friends and contacts [24]. While researchers are beginning to develop an understanding of SMQA behavior in isolation, little is known about how this behavior fits into people's broader online information seeking strategies. For instance, although we have some understanding of users' motivations when they ask status message questions (e.g., [20, 24, 37]), the same cannot be said for when they purposely eschew their networks (e.g., by self-censoring Facebook posts [7, 30]) and instead route an information need to search engines. Similarly, while status message questions in Facebook and Twitter have been examined separately (e.g., [24, 26]), the process by which question askers choose a network to express a given information need has not been investigated. In addition, the relationship of these routing decisions to the type of information need is not well understood.

Developing a clear picture of the routing of information needs between traditional search engines and social networks has implications not only for our understanding of SMQA behavior but also for the design of systems that integrate the two, such as Bing's "Social Sidebar" [5], Google's "Search, plus Your World" [29], and research systems like SearchBuddies [15] and MSR Answers [17]. Because search engines and SMQA each bring unique benefits and costs for different types of information needs [4, 8, 23], a deeper knowledge of routing behavior has the potential to guide further development of such technologies.

In this paper, we present findings from a laboratory study designed to answer three questions about participants' SMQA behaviors in the broader context of online information seeking: 1) Which needs go where? 2) Why (and why not)? and 3) What was successful?

By asking, "*Which needs go where?*" we engage in the first examination of how people route information needs to search engines and social networks. When given the option of using a search engine or SMQA, our participants preferred to use a search engine, although they used SMQA for a meaningful portion of their needs (20%). The overall preference for search engines still exists for types of information needs that have been shown to be most prevalent in status message questions (e.g., recommendations), but it is weaker. We also found that when status message questions were asked, it was more often as a complement to issuing a query to a search engine than as a replacement. These results suggest that search

CSCW'14, February 15 - 19 2014, Baltimore, MD, USA
Copyright 2014 ACM 978-1-4503-2540-0/14/02…$15.00.
http://dx.doi.org/10.1145/2531602.2531706

engines may be able to better address a portion of information needs by integrating SMQA capabilities.

By exploring the question, "*Why (and why not)?*" with regard to routing decisions, we uncover new motivations for searching and asking. We show that the specificity of the information need and the perceived audience in a given network play an important role in participants' choices. Our findings suggest that these factors not only guided decisions with regard to searching and asking, but also figured into selecting the correct social network to ask.

Finally, in addition to examining routing decisions, we also look at the outcomes of these decisions by asking, "*What was successful?*" We show that no one strategy received universally better responses than another. Instead, each strategy had complementary advantages and disadvantages. Our findings show that overall, greater trust and value was placed on search engines as an information source than on social networks. However, ratings of individual responses received from SMQA were more trusted and satisfying than those received from search results. Although SMQA occurs less often than search engine use, there are clear benefits to the behavior that are worth understanding and supporting.

RELATED WORK

Since Morris et al. [24] identified that as many as 50% of Facebook and Twitter users engage in SMQA behavior, SMQA has become the focus of an increasing number of studies [1, 12, 20, 23, 24, 31, 32, 37]. Follow up work [22] has confirmed that 50% of Facebook users have tried SMQA, with lower numbers turning to other social networks (33% of Twitter users, 25% of Google+ and LinkedIn users). We extend this research by placing SMQA into a broader framework of online information seeking that includes both SMQA (on multiple networks) and search engine use.

In addition to establishing the popularity of SMQA, Morris et al. [24] found that the most popular information needs sent to social networks are requests for recommendations and opinions, primarily due to greater trust in friends' opinions, need for subjective information, and the belief that a search engine would not work well in such cases. Additional SMQA studies have built on this typology. In an exploration of 420 information-seeking status updates on Facebook, Gray et al. [12] identified similar question types but in very different proportions. Rhetorical questions were most common, followed by requests/favors and opinion/polls. When studying SMQA on Twitter, Paul et al. [26] found that rhetorical questions, requests for factual knowledge, and polls were particularly prevalent.

Researchers have examined the answers to status message questions, primarily by scoring friends' and contacts' responses on various measures of quality (e.g., [11, 12, 24, 26, 31]). Morris et al. [24] rated responses to information needs routed to social networks by whether or not they were helpful and if a response came as quickly as expected. Paul et al. [26] coded responses to question tweets as related or unrelated. Gray et al. [12] developed a more elaborate measure that examined both the satisfaction and usefulness of responses. In an assessment of the effects of tie strength on answer quality, Panovich et al. [25] developed a multi-faceted measure of answers including various informational and trust aspects of the information and the source. Building on this work, our experimental design enables us to assess the quality of an answer on various dimensions, depending on information need and routing decision.

The literature on answer quality in SMQA also contains the only other studies that simultaneously considered search and SMQA [11, 23]. In Morris, et al. [23], 12 information needs were issued as queries and status message questions, and the responses were compared for speed and quality. Evans et al. [11] compared usefulness of responses to specific information requests for problem-solving tasks in traditional search to several social search approaches to assess differences in learning scores. Our work, on the other hand, is focused on how people route information needs across SMQA and search, as well as on the entire question and answer pipeline.

Recent work has also started to consider the social costs of using one's network as an informational resource. Ellison et al. [8] categorized requests posted on Facebook into cost levels, finding that individuals use up more social capital with requests that require more effort from their friends. Other work has begun to examine instances in which users choose not to post information to their online social networks [7, 30], or to post only to a select audience within those networks [18, 21]. Our work complements such studies by examining the circumstances under which users prefer to route information needs to search engines rather than social sources, or combine these methods.

Evans and Chi [10] presented a model of social search in which a user interacted with others before, during, and/or after search engine use. Their model, developed before social networks achieved mass penetration, did not account for alternative social information seeking approaches, such as SMQA. Nor did it explore how users chose to route specific types of information needs to either social or non-social sources. Our work expands the "during search" phase of the Evans and Chi model, enriching our understanding of users' reasoning regarding social interaction while seeking information.

METHOD

We conducted a laboratory study to assess when people with information needs turn to a search engine versus when they ask their social networks. We examined what types of needs were directed to which services and why, and assessed how the participants felt about the answers and results they received in response. Participants considered both self-directed information needs and a set of prompted needs based on common status message question and query types identified in the literature [16, 19, 24, 28, 35].

Participants completed the study over two sessions one to five days apart to allow time for responses from social networks. In the first session, they used a custom designed web application to attempt to fulfill the prompted and unprompted information needs and completed questionnaires regarding their information seeking strategies. In the second session, participants rated the search engine results and answers to the questions that were posted to their social networks. Participants completed a pre-questionnaire that asked if they were familiar with and how often they used a variety of websites and apps – including the four used in the study (Google, Bing, Facebook and Twitter) – and others such as Wikipedia, YouTube, Instagram, and Quora (1 = *No, have never used it* to 5 = *Yes, currently use it often*). The questionnaire also contained Hargittai and Hsieh's 10-item web use skill measure [13]. At the conclusion of the first session they completed a post-questionnaire that measured how often they used each of the same services to ask for information (1 = *Never* to 6 = *Several Times a Day*). Demographic information was also collected in this survey and our study software collected numbers of Facebook friends and Twitter followers.

Participants

Participants (N = 82) were recruited from the geographic area surrounding a mid-sized Midwestern university. They were required to be regular users of the Internet and social media (self-defined) and have at least a Facebook account. The sample ranged in age from 18 to 64 (M = 24, SD = 10.10) and was 64% female. The majority of the participants (84%) were students. Fifty-one percent were Caucasian/White, 28% Asian/Pacific Islander, 11% African American/Black, and 10% multi-racial.

Participants were moderately skilled in their web use [13] (M = 3.53, SD = .82) and all but two participants stated they were familiar with all four of the services used in the study. All participants indicated that they seek information online daily, with issuing queries to Google being the most popular strategy. Facebook was used to seek information at least a few times per month by 67% of participants and Twitter by 33%. Participants' Facebook networks ranged widely in size from just one friend to 1,645 (*Median* = 511, SD = 394). For those who used Twitter in the study (24%), their number of followers ranged from 7 to 1,007 (*Median* = 122, SD = 214).

Procedure

The web application (Figure 1) allows users to type in a query or question and send it to (up to) two search engines (Google and Bing) and (up to) two social networks (Facebook and Twitter), by pressing each button separately. The layout order of these four service buttons was randomized. After selecting one service, the query remains in the textbox so that another service can be selected for the same text or the text can be modified or removed for another query. The first page of query results was displayed in a frame below the question box. Participants were informed that questions routed to Facebook and Twitter were recorded but not posted, and that only one would be randomly selected for each service at the end of the study and posted to their Facebook Timeline or Twitter news feed. This was done to prevent concerns about spamming one's network with too many questions in quick, unnatural succession [38] from interfering with participants' routing decisions. This allowed participants to send questions for which they would most want to use Facebook or Twitter to those services, rather than turning to search engines only to avoid the cost of asking their networks many artificial questions. In this study our goal was to understand routing decisions outside of cost constraints, as discussed in more detail below. The web application logged all questions, search results (including post-query interactions), and answers to Facebook and Twitter questions.

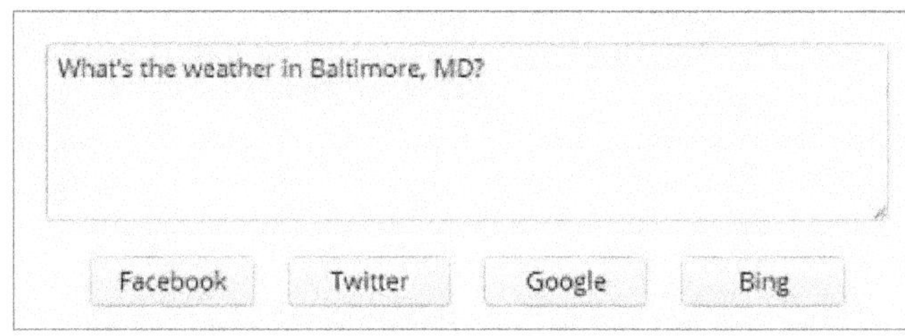

Figure 1. The primary interface to the web application used in the study.

Information Seeking Phase

The information seeking phase of the study began by giving participants five minutes to write down "anything you've been meaning to ask someone, information you have been seeking, anything you want to know more about, or want to understand better." Afterward, participants were instructed on how to use the web application and given 10 minutes to explore their own information needs. During this stage, they were allowed to enter as many questions or queries as they wanted using any of the available services.

Participants were then instructed to consider a number of prompted information needs (Table 1). Each participant saw 10 of the 30 prompted needs created for the study – one from each of the types discussed in the section that follows – selected and displayed in random order. Participants were required to use at least one service to investigate a prompted information need before they could move on to the next one. They had 20 minutes to complete this process. While the prompted approach is less natural than intrinsically motivated questions, it ensures coverage over a wide range of information need types.

At the conclusion of the *information seeking phase*, participants were shown each of their routing choices and were asked to complete the following open-ended items: "Why did you choose to use [service] to ask this question?" and "What [answers/results] were you expecting from [service]?"

Participants then completed a final questionnaire indicating how often they use each of the four services for seeking information on a six-point scale ranging from *Never* to *Several Times a Day.* At the end of this session, participants were partially compensated and instructed not to delete or edit any status message questions or any responses before their follow-up session.

Response Assessment Phase
Participants returned for a second session one to five days after the information seeking phase to rate the responses to their information needs. This allowed time for responses to SMQA information needs to be posted. In this response assessment phase of the study, participants were shown each of their previous information needs along with the results/answers they received. For search queries, they were shown the same results they had previously received, with those they had clicked highlighted in gray. If the question was posted to Facebook or Twitter and received any answers, that question was displayed with accompanying responses. Participants were instructed to select which result/answer they thought was best, which loaded a questionnaire about that answer, and then they rated it on dimensions of satisfaction, information value, and trust [25]. Upon finishing the answer-rating questionnaires, they were compensated for their second session.

Prompt Development
The prompted types used in the information seeking phase are presented in Table 1 and were based on typologies from the social media question asking and information retrieval literatures. The objective was to capture a wide range of query and question types and examine how they were routed between search engines and social networking sites. The bulk of the prompted types were based on the schema from Morris et al. [24] that includes eight types of questions: recommendation, opinion, factual knowledge, rhetorical, invitation, favor, social connection, and offer. However, due to our broader scope, it was also necessary to consider types of information needs not typically seen in SMQA but common in traditional search. In doing so, we identified two additional need types not captured by Morris et al.'s schema: 1) navigational information needs [16, 28], which are typically expressed by queries such as "cscw 2014" and "gmail", and 2) exploratory information needs [19, 35], which are defined by their open-ended and multifaceted nature. Taxonomies of traditional web search queries typically include information need types in addition to navigational and exploratory (e.g., transactional [6] and casual-leisure [9, 36]), but these have extensive overlap with Morris et al.'s question types.

Three prompts were written for each of the ten types. Wording was constructed so as not to bias participants toward any particular service. For example, the word "find" was used consistently across all prompts rather than the words "ask" or "search," and the use of the word "network" was avoided.

Recommendation
Find a good place to get food right after this study.
Find a good birthday present that you could buy online now for a specific relative.
Imagine a trip you'd like to take in the future and find out what others recommend as the best sights to see.
Opinion
Think of a certain place you are interested in seeing and find out whether it's worth traveling there.
Think of the next tech product you'd like to buy and find out what people think of it.
Think of a TV show that you plan to watch during your next free hour and find out what others think of the show.
Factual Knowledge
Find out what might be causing symptoms you have been having recently.
Find out what traffic will be like for your commute to your next destination after this study.
Find out what the weather is like outside right now.
Rhetorical
Contemplate something that's always confused you. See what others think.
Think of something that's frustrating you right now. See what others think.
Think of a strong opinion you have about a current issue. See what others think.
Invitation
Plan an activity you would like to do this weekend and find out who is interested in joining you.
Find out if someone in the area is interested in meeting up for your next meal.
Think of something you would like to do after this study and find out if anyone else would be interested too.
Favor
Think of a project you'd like to do or a task you need to finish for which you don't have the right tool or gadget. Find someone local who has this particular item you can borrow.
Think of a task at home you could use help with today, and find someone who would be willing and available to help.
Think of an errand that needs to get done today. Find someone else who can take care of it right now.
Social Connection
Find someone who can help you learn more about a new hobby you'd like to take up.
Find someone who would be a good person to know for finding a job in [local city] for you or someone else.
Find someone to teach you a new skill while you're online right now.
Offer
Think of a skill or particular area of knowledge you have. Find someone who could benefit from this skill/knowledge.
Think of an item you have at home that you no longer use. Find someone else who could use it.
Think of something you can offer to do in your next free hour that would be useful within your group of friends or local community.
Navigational
Find the website for the main gym at your university or alma mater.
Find Nike's website.
Find [local library] website.
Undirected / Exploratory
Find a current event you are interested in keeping up with (one you aren't already keeping up with).
Find an idea for a new hobby (a hobby you haven't considered before).
Find a new activity to do this week.

Table 1. Prompt by prompt type.

Data Preparation

Participants initially submitted a total of 1,728 information needs. Exact duplicates within each service were removed. Similarly, fixed typos and rephrasing strategies within the same service (i.e., query reformulation) were collapsed into a single information need (e.g., "Breaking Bad next season date" and "Breaking Bad season date 2013"). For prompted information needs, those that did not address the prompt were marked and excluded from further analyses. This left a total of 1,397 valid information needs, of which 584 (42%) were the participants' own needs (user-defined) and 813 (58%) were prompted.

All unprompted information needs were coded using our typology developed for prompts (Table 1). There were no unprompted needs expressed for two of the types (offer and social connection) and an additional type was added – polls – to capture needs that did not fit into our initial schema. This coding process was performed by two independent coders. Initial inter-rater agreement was low (Cohen's Kappa = .67, $p < .001$) due to conflicts in the categorization of navigational needs. The navigational type definition was clarified, questions were recoded, and acceptable inter-rater agreement was reached (Kappa = .81, $p < .001$).

WHICH NEEDS GO WHERE?: ROUTING DECISIONS

Because little is known about how people route their information needs between status message questions and search engines, our first series of analyses addresses the question of "which needs go where?"

A clear theme emerges from our participants' routing decisions: when given the option of issuing a query to a search engine or posing a question to their social networks, information seekers prefer search engines but utilize SMQA for a meaningful portion of their needs. Overall, 80% of unprompted information needs and 76% of prompted information needs were routed exclusively to search engines (Table 2).

Focusing on the more naturalistic distribution of information needs from the unprompted dataset, we found that when status message questions were asked, they were more often accompanied by a query to a search engine than not. While 7% of all unprompted information needs were expressed solely through status message question asking, 13% were expressed in combination with a search query (Table 2).

As discussed above, recent work has established that status message questions reflect a unique distribution of information needs. Requests for recommendations,

Type	Search	SMQA	Both
Unprompted Needs	80% (344)	7% (27)	13% (54)
Prompted Needs	76% (522)	20% (134)	4% (30)

Table 2: The final routing choices for unique prompted and unprompted information needs.

opinions, and factual knowledge are the most common. Our unprompted and prompted results show that even for these types of information needs, search engines remain dominant, although to a somewhat lesser degree. Figure 2 depicts participants' routing decisions by type of information need. Fifty-six percent of unprompted opinion needs went only to search engines, with the analogous numbers for recommendations and factual knowledge being 77% and 81%, respectively. The results for prompted information needs were similar, with a trend towards a higher percentage of search engine queries. Moreover, as with the results for the entire dataset, status message questions were accompanied by queries a majority of the time. For instance, only 3% of unprompted recommendation information needs were routed solely to social networks and 20% went to both.

We also found that the two types of information needs drawn from the information retrieval literature and not yet considered in the context of SMQA – navigational needs and exploratory needs – were routed almost exclusively to search engines. The navigational result is to be expected as search engines are known to excel at navigational queries

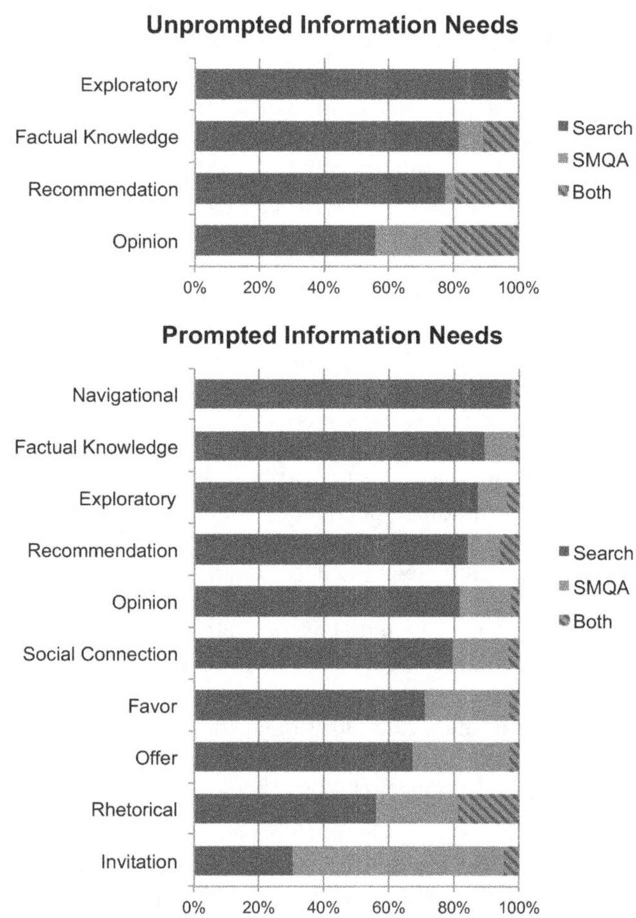

Figure 2: The routing decisions of participants by type of information need. Only types with 10 or more expressed information needs are shown.

[35]. The same is not true of exploratory queries, however, which are widely recognized as a weakness of modern search technology [34, 35]. Moreover, the rich conversational environment in which SMQA takes place would seem well-suited to exploratory information needs, which are open-ended, multifaceted, and typically fulfilled iteratively [35]. We address participants' motivations for routing exploratory needs away from their social networks and the implications of this finding for the development of new exploratory search technologies later in the paper.

WHY (AND WHY NOT?): MOTIVATIONS

For each information need, participants were asked to explain why they chose the service they did and what they were expecting. These open-ended responses were gathered for 1,195 of the expressed information needs and were analyzed for themes that compare and contrast the use of the two available service types: search and social. Participants' quotes are presented in their original wording.

Why SMQA?

Participants turned to social networks for their information needs for reasons that were largely consistent with previous findings [24]. We found that participants routed information needs to Facebook because they trusted their friends' opinions, were asking for subjective information, were seeking a specific audience, or hoped for better personalization and contextualization. That said, some previously documented reasons for routing needs to social networks were not observed in this study. Notably, participants rarely mentioned turning to Facebook because of a belief that a search engine would not work for the information need, although this was a common motivation in earlier work [24]. Connecting socially is another motivator missing in the present study. Participants may have routed some information needs to Facebook for this reason, but it was not explicitly expressed. Answer speed (social networks being *faster*), failed previous search, and social networks as an easier option were also common motivations in past literature not mentioned by participants in the present study. Conversely, we found that speed and ease sometimes drove participants to search.

Differentiating Use of Twitter and Facebook

Past research has focused either on social networks as an undifferentiated category or on a single network at a time, but the ability to choose between networks or use more than one in this study allowed for a comparison of differential routing behavior among networks. Gathering opinions from friends was a commonly cited motivation for asking a question on Twitter, as it had been for Facebook. However, Twitter users also took advantage of the site's broader network in different ways than they did of their more personal Facebook networks. Information needs often went to Twitter when they required a more personal audience, but were deemed inappropriate for Facebook. For instance, one participant used Twitter to ask what she felt was a very personal question, but one that she did not want her Facebook friends to know:

"I think the people in the Twitter could be a little bit smart and there isn't too many real-world friend in the Twitter, and interest in bible is a very personal thing, I don't want my friend know it."

Similarly, another participant wanted to gather a subset of friends for an event, but did not want to include all of his friends in the area:

"I know some people in [town] on Twitter and I would be curious to see if they'd be interested (a friend who is also on Twitter and in [town] had brought up the idea of going). I didn't post this to Facebook because I have a different set of [local] friends there and I didn't want them to see this post."

Twitter was also used for questions deemed too controversial for Facebook, such as political discussions:

"It is a platform that I generally use (and I know is commonly used) to follow political and social issues, as well as to interact with the opinions of my friends. I tend [not] to post political content on Facebook at all."

Twitter users were also aware of the potential for broader network audiences. One participant was frustrated about a local situation and was seeking others in the area that might have similar opinions:

"[Information about new campus construction] is something that a search engine probably won't be able to answer because it's a more under-the-wraps issue. I'm also looking more for people who feel the same way about me and to instigate a discussion."

Twitter's public network was described by one participant as having a benefit over other venues for gathering opinions specifically because of its potentially broader audience:

"Not only to get my question answered, I like that the fact someone replied to my answer pops up both on my page and the other person's page. The conversation becomes public therefore can engage other people in."

These examples show that social networks cannot be compared unilaterally to search engines; each service provides unique benefits. Specifically, it appears that Twitter serves as a unique middle ground between search at one end of the information-seeking spectrum and Facebook at the other. Participants can use the service to get subjective information not accessible from search engines, but with fewer social costs and a broader audience than routing information needs to Facebook.

Why Not SMQA?

While motivations for routing information needs to SMQA largely confirmed previous work [24], the structure of our experiment allowed us to examine for the first time motivations for routing information needs *away* from SMQA. We found that the three most common of these motivations were (1) information needs being either too specific or not specific enough for SMQA, (2) concerns about the limited information available in one's social networks, and (3) hesitation about disrupting one's networks.

Needs Were Too Specific, Or Not Specific Enough

Search engines were utilized most often when individuals had a very specific information need or when they had one that was quite abstract. The first indication of this U-shaped relationship between the specificity of an information need and search engine use came with our quantitative observation that navigational (very specific) and exploratory (very unspecific) needs are almost always sent to search engines. Participants also provided support for this relationship when discussing the motivations behind their routing decisions.

At the narrow end of the specificity spectrum, Bing and Google were most often chosen when users felt they were asking a "simple" or "straightforward" question to which they could quickly and easily find an answer. In the words of one participant, *"[The search engine] has a straightforward answer and would give me the fastest results."* On the other hand, when faced with very unspecific information needs, participants turned to a search engine because "it seemed like a good place to start" or because they were unsure what to ask their network. One participant explained, *"I felt that Google would help me direct my search through the results I'd get from this initial search, especially since I wasn't sure exactly what I was hoping to find."* Similarly, another participant stated, *"Since I wasn't sure exactly how to phrase the question, perhaps Google's results would help me do that."*

Limited Information in Networks

A common motivation for eschewing SMQA in favor of search was a belief by participants that the people in their networks would not have sufficient knowledge about the topic to answer their question. For instance, in seeking opinions on a new smartphone, a participant wrote, "*don't know anyone who has it yet, but I know it is being released soon and I imagined tech reviewers may already have their hands on it.*"

Although we (and others, e.g., [24]) found that participants often routed needs to SMQA because they believed their friends had a greater knowledge of the relevant context, we also saw the inverse occur. That is, some participants avoided using SMQA because they thought their friends and contacts knew very little about the relevant context. For instance, referring to a search for a new restaurant, one participant wrote, "*I did not want to use Facebook to ask this because people on Facebook do not know my specific taste in food. Instead I would like to use a search engine to check out menus and possibly see pictures.*"

Even for highly personal types of needs like invitations, there were a moderate number of cases in which participants searched for Meetup groups for a specific activity because they did not have the right group of friends for that activity. One participant wanted to start doing martial arts in her community, but her network was limited: *"I don't know of anyone in my networks that does this and lives in this area, so Google would be best for a primary search."*

In many cases, participants believed that searching for opinions and recommendations gave them a much wider variety of information than their friends could. To find tips for exploring the large city in which he currently resides, one participant routed his information need to search rather than his network "*because a lot of more people worldwide may have already done this before.*" Likewise, another participant decided that while her audience had some expertise, she wanted a different audience: "*As much as I know some friends have traveled extensively, I was more curious to see what cultural Francophiles had to say about the overrated tourist spots.*"

Disruptive to Network

Participants actively avoided SMQA for information when they were afraid of disrupting their networks. This was particularly true for controversial topics for which opinions were desired, but for which the social cost of posting to Facebook or Twitter was believed to be too high. One participant specifically sought a discussion about gun control from the comments in response to an opinion piece, stating, *"I know that using Facebook to discuss strong political issues can be a very tricky thing that can invite heated unpleasant arguments."* Similarly, another participant wrote, "*I would NOT use Facebook for this question because I already know my friends' opinions, and even if I didn't I'd be wary of asking political questions on Facebook.*"

A different form of disruption avoidance occurred when participants wanted to keep their activities out of the networks so as not to cause tension between contacts, such as when using search to find information related to an exclusive event: "*I'm going to a party there on Saturday. Thought I could get dinner before hand. didn't want to announce the party to everyone on Facebook or Twitter because I know people who are not invited.*"

Avoiding SMQA Completely

Twenty-two (27%) participants did not send any questions to Facebook or Twitter, despite all participants having social media accounts. While most did not mention purposely avoiding their networks, a few participants indicated that they did not want anything posted to their Facebook Timeline, a finding that is consistent with results that show that many Facebook users carefully curate their account [38]. More specific motivations matched those described above for routing information needs away from social networks. The majority of these 22 participants indicated that they were most comfortable using search engines for information or felt that a search was adequate or most relevant. As one participant who sent all her information needs to search indicated: "*I thought it would be unnecessary to wait for a response from Facebook friends when I could easily search it.*"

Merging SMQA and Search

Eighty-four information needs were sent to both SMQA and search engines. Two broad motivations emerged for this behavior: complementing friends' opinions with search and using social responses to interpret search results. With regard to the former, one participant asked his network for their "*passionate responses*" and then sent the question to search engines, doing so because "*a search engine would be better than asking my friends through Facebook where everyone ...has biased opinions.*" Similarly, one participant first asked her network because "*i want to know what all my smart friends are using to study [for the GRE],*" but then issued a query to Google because "*I thought google would give me less biased answers than my friends.*"

In contrast, sometimes friends' knowledge was expected to help clarify factual information found via search engines. For instance, one participant wanted to learn about a topic both on Wikipedia and then on Facebook because "*My friends might be able to summarize the answer to this question in a way that would be easier for me to understand.*"

WHAT WAS SUCCESSFUL?: RESPONSE OUTCOMES

Of the 1,397 information needs studied, 1,142 (82%) received responses. Thirty-nine percent of information needs posted to social networks received responses, ranging from one to ten in number, with a median of three. The median response time for the first response on social networks was five hours and 55 minutes, with the fastest response coming in one hour and 34 minutes after the information need was posted. All search queries received at least ten results in our study.

Participants selected the best response received for each information need and rated it on three dimensions using 7-point Likert-type scales: information value, satisfaction, and trust. These ratings were received for 1,036 (91%) of responses. Information value was measured using three items, which asked participants to rate to what extent the response contributed to existing knowledge, provided new information, and verified information already known. One item was used to measure their satisfaction with the response. Trust in the response was assessed in terms of their trust in the answer itself, trust in the source (e.g., the specific friend on Facebook or website from Google that provided the answer), and trust in the service (e.g., Bing or Twitter).

We used a mixed-effects regression model to analyze the information value, satisfaction, and trust scores. The independent variables include participants' web skill, age, gender, question type (categorical), and search (vs. SMQA). Because observations were not independent, participant was modeled as a random effect. Full results of these models can be found in Appendix 1.

Search vs. SMQA

Response ratings were compared for information needs routed to search engines and SMQA on the dimensions of information value, satisfaction, and trust.

Information Value

Overall, responses from search engines provide greater information value than those from social networks. Information needs routed to search engines were rated significantly higher for contributing to knowledge (M = 4.85) than those routed to social networks (M = 3.73), $F(1, 950.1) = 9.49$, $p < .01$. Search engine responses were also rated higher for providing new information (M = 4.78) than social media responses (M = 2.94), $F(1, 952.9) = 24.51$, $p < .001$. It is likely that responses from search engines more directly answer the question, while those from social networks may offer other content not necessarily relevant to the information need.

Satisfaction

While participants felt that information from search engines contributed more new knowledge than social networks, they were marginally more satisfied with responses to questions posted to social networks. The effect of routing on satisfaction shows a trending effect, with responses to information needs routed to social media rated as more satisfactory (M = 5.86) than those routed to search engines (M = 5.2), $F(1, 968.4) = 3.06$, $p = .08$. This indicates that satisfaction has a social component; users may rate responses that do not answer the question as satisfactory because of other factors (e.g., humor and tie building).

Trust

Trust varied significantly by routing decision. Participants trusted search engines (M = 5.78) more than social networks (M = 3.78) as a general resource for information, $F(1, 939.8) = 86.51$, $p < .001$. However, when rating the specific source of the information (a particular friend in the case of social networks or a specific website linked to by a search engine), participants placed greater trust in responses from social sources (M = 6.19) than search sources (M = 5.27), $F(1, 952.2) = 11.39$, $p < .001$. These results present an interesting contradiction whereby individuals generally perceive search engines as more trustworthy sources of information, but end up placing greater trust in the information provided by their friends.

Question Type

Ratings of responses in terms of information value, satisfaction, and trustworthiness also varied significantly by question type.

Information Value

Question types had a significant effect on contributing to knowledge, $F(10, 950.1) = 6.54$, $p < .001$, and on providing new information, $F(10, 953.4) = 5.52$, $p < .001$. For both outcomes, responses were rated highest for factual knowledge and exploratory information needs. In contrast, responses were rated significantly higher in verifying existing information for navigational needs, which are targeted and easily fulfilled, than for factual knowledge, social connections, invitations, favors, and offers ($F(10, 944.2) = 5.76, p < .001$).

Satisfaction

Question type also had a significant effect on satisfaction with responses, $F(10, 968.8) = 11.28, p < .001$. Navigational, recommendation, and factual knowledge information needs lead to the most satisfying results, while offers, favors, and invitations garner the least satisfactory result.

Trust

Finally, question type had a significant effect on trust in the source of the response, $F(10, 953.2) = 11.11, p < .001$, and trust in the content of the response, $F(10, 953) = 12.10, p < .001$. For both, responses to navigational needs are rated highest, whereas favors, offers, rhetorical questions and polls are rated lowest.

DISCUSSION

The results above contribute to our understanding of SMQA behavior and can inform the design of the growing number of technologies that seek to bridge traditional search and social networks. This section discusses both of these topics and also covers our work's limitations.

SMQA Behavior

Our findings related to the question "Which needs go where?" highlight both the potential of SMQA and its limitations. With regard to SMQA's potential, the fact that participants entirely ignored search engines in favor of SMQA for 7% of unprompted information needs means that SMQA can serve as a search engine alternative in special cases. Moreover, SMQA's utility as a complement to web search was highlighted by the 13% of information needs that went to both search and SMQA.

On the other hand, we also saw that search engines were used exclusively for a large majority of information needs, even those that are decidedly social (offers, favors, and social connections). It is possible that these needs are being routed to search engines to avoid the costs of asking one's social network for information [8], such as expectations of reciprocity [33, 37] or a desire to portray a highly curated persona [38]. Users may also route information needs away from their social networks despite the potential for more satisfactory answers in order to respect norms and etiquette surrounding social networks as personal spaces rather than as resources for information-seeking [8]. Overall, our findings suggest that SMQA has an important role to play as both an alternative and complement to web search, but that this role is somewhat constrained.

The trade-offs between search and social are captured in the motivations, which show not only when to route to, but also when to route away from or merge with SMQA. While motivations for turning to SMQA were consistent with previous work (e.g., [24]), our findings shed light on information seeking strategies for actively avoiding SMQA. We introduce the U-shaped curve of specificity, indicating that SMQA is deemed appropriate within a spectrum bound by needs that are believed to be too exploratory to be successful in SMQA and too specific to be necessary in SMQA. A desire to merge SMQA and search is evident in the various ways users employ both in their information routing needs: comparing both for a wider variety of information, using search to verify friends' opinions, and turning to friends to clarify search results.

Finally, when examining "what was successful?", we found a nuanced answer in which search and SMQA act differentially on various facets of success. In line with our findings about the large percentage of information needs that are sent to search engines, we discover that information seekers perceive search to provide more valuable information than SMQA. However, SMQA provides more satisfying answers, indicating that success goes beyond informational content, and information seeking potentially fulfills a more holistic, partly social need. That information-seekers place greater trust in search engines as a whole for information, but greater trust in their friends than web results found in search, corroborates the complementary roles that can be played by search and SMQA.

Implications for Design

At a high level, our results add to the growing body of work advocating for technologies that merge the searching and asking experience. Twenty percent of unprompted information needs in our study were routed to social networks, suggesting that search engines can better address a meaningful portion of information needs by integrating SMQA capabilities into their systems. Social networks, on the other hand, could increase the information value of asking a status message question by incorporating search engine technology into the conversations around status message questions.

Our work also presents the possibility of developing technologies that automatically route information needs to the appropriate service. We saw above that distinct patterns exist in people's routing choices and the motivations behind those choices. Using these patterns, a model could be developed that would allow, for instance, a search engine to know when to suggest posting a status message question in addition to – or instead of – continuing with a search. Working towards this model is a direction of future work.

Another important implication for design arises from our finding that exploratory information needs are almost always are routed to search engines, at least in part due to a tendency to avoid posing open-ended questions to one's social networks. Exploratory information needs are a well-known weakness of current search engines and are, accordingly, an active area of research (e.g., [3, 14]). Our research suggests that despite the conversations around status message questions having many properties conducive to the open-ended, multifaceted, and iterative process that is exploratory search [35], use of SMQA for exploratory search is not common. One interpretation of this finding is that SMQA has little value for exploratory search; an alternative interpretation is that further research is needed to develop novel approaches to make SMQA more amenable to exploratory information needs.

Limitations

Although this paper is the first to examine the routing of information needs across SMQA and search engines, we did not consider the effect of other social search strategies such as IM, email, SMS, and face-to-face discussion, whose relationships with traditional search has been a subject of several studies (e.g., [10, 27]). We also do not analyze the influence of network properties, such as size, which likely have an effect on the success of SMQA. Understanding routing in this more diverse ecology is a subject of future work.

Our research is also limited by potential sampling biases. Although the distribution of web skills among our participants was not abnormal, our sample had an overrepresentation of women and students. Participants also had a substantially higher median number of friends on Facebook than active Facebook users overall [2]. By recruiting those who consider themselves regular Facebook users, we may have also biased the sample toward Facebook use rather than regular use of Twitter or other social media. The sample was also relatively young, which does not allow us to assess the potential systematic effects of age on social media use for question asking. Additionally, our sample was drawn from a specific geographic area and an urban setting. Query sampling biases may also exist, and certain type of queries (e.g., navigational), may be under-sampled in this study.

Another issue not addressed here is the potential saturation effect present in SMQA, in terms of social capital costs [8]. In order to understand routing behavior at the information need level, we necessarily restricted the number of status message questions that would actually be posted to participants' networks. Our current work involves taking a longitudinal perspective in order to shed light on the relationship between the number of status message questions posted in a given timeframe and the likelihood of asking another question.

Finally, there is a possibility that our results related to prompted information needs are biased towards search engines due to participants being reluctant to post artificial information needs to their friends and contacts. While very few participants indicated that this was a concern in their questionnaires, this effect may still exist. This bias could exist more generally for information needs due to the experimental setting, in which the costs of posing questions to one's social network become more salient. Throughout the paper, we have attempted to mitigate this bias by using only the unprompted information needs or presenting the results separately when this issue could have affected our conclusions.

CONCLUSION

In this paper, we presented the results of an 82-participant laboratory study on SMQA, a form of information seeking in which social network users pose questions to their friends and contacts. We placed SMQA behavior in the context of more traditional search engines by identifying what types of information needs go to SMQA instead of, or in addition to, search engines. We also investigated why users are motivated to route information needs to or away from social networks and which routing decisions are most successful in terms of information value, levels of trust, and satisfaction. This work presents evidence that users combine routing strategies, providing support for new technologies that aim to merge search and social information seeking approaches.

ACKNOWLEDGEMENTS

This research was supported by a grant from Microsoft Research and completed while the first author was a Postdoctoral Fellow at Northwestern University. We thank Khalid Aziz and Irsal Alsanea for building the application used by participants in this study, Alison Ho and Jennifer Suh for helping with data collection, and members of the CollabLab for their insightful feedback.

REFERENCES

[1] Ackerman, M., Adamic, L., Ellison, N., Gergle, D., Hecht, B., Lampe, C., Morris, M.R. and Teevan, J. 2013. Social media question asking workshop. *Proc. of CSCW 2013*, ACM Press, 297-298.

[2] Backstrom, L. 2011. Anatomy of Facebook. *Facebook Blog.* http://www.facebook.com/notes/facebook-data-team/anatomy-of-facebook/10150388519243859

[3] Bozzon, A., Brambilla, M., Ceri, S. and Fraternali, P. 2010. Liquid query: Multi-domain exploratory search on the web. *Proc. of WWW 2010*, ACM Press, 161-170.

[4] Brady, E.L., Zhong, Y., Morris, M.R. and Bigham, J.P. 2013. Investigating the appropriateness of social network question asking as a resource for blind users. *Proc. of CSCW 2013*, ACM Press, 1225-1236.

[5] Bringing your friends to Bing: Search now more social. 2010. *Facebook Blog.* http://www.facebook.com/notes/facebook-data-team/anatomy-of-facebook/10150388519243859

[6] Broder, A. 2002. A taxonomy of web search. *ACM SIGIR Forum*, 3-10.

[7] Das, S. and Kramer, A. 2013. Self-censorship on Facebook. *Proc. of ICWSM 2013*, 120-127.

[8] Ellison, N.B., Gray, R., Vitak, J., Lampe, C. and Fiore, A.T. 2013. Calling all Facebook friends: Exploring requests for help on Facebook. *Proc. of ICWSM 2013*, 155-164.

[9] Elsweiler, D., Wilson, M.L. and Harvey, M. 2012. Searching for fun: Casual-leisure search. *ECIR 2012 Workshop Proposals.*

[10] Evans, B.M. and Chi, E.H. 2008. Towards a model of understanding social search. *Proc. of CSCW 2008*, ACM Press, 485-494.

[11] Evans, B.M., Kairam, S. and Pirolli, P. 2010. Do your friends make you smarter?: An analysis of social strategies in online information seeking. *Information Processing & Management, 46*, 6, 679-692.

[12] Gray, R., Ellison, N.B., Vitak, J. and Lampe, C. 2013. Who wants to know?: Question-asking and answering practices among Facebook users. *Proc. of CSCW 2013*, ACM Press, 1213-1224.

[13] Hargittai, E. and Hsieh, Y.P. 2012. Succinct survey measures of web-use skills. *Social Science Computer Review, 30*, 1, 95-107.

[14] Hecht, B., Carton, S., Quaderi, M., Schöning, J., Raubal, M., Gergle, D. and Downey, D. 2012. Explanatory semantic relatedness and explicit spatialization for exploratory search. *Proc. of SIGIR 2012*, ACM Press, 415-424.

[15] Hecht, B., Teevan, J., Morris, M.R. and Liebling, D. 2012. SearchBuddies: Bringing search engines into the conversation. *Proc. of ICWSM 2012*, 138-145.

[16] Jansen, B.J., Booth, D.L. and Spink, A. 2008. Determining the informational, navigational, and transactional intent of Web queries. *Information Processing & Management, 44*, 3, 1251-1266.

[17] Jeong, J.-W., Morris, M.R., Teevan, J. and Liebling, D. 2013. A crowd-powered socially embedded search engine. *Proc. of ICWSM 2013*, 263-272.

[18] Kairam, S., Brzozowski, M., Huffaker, D. and Chi, E. 2012. Talking in circles: Selective sharing in Google+. *Proc. of CHI 2012*, ACM Press, 1065-1074.

[19] Kules, B. and Capra, R. 2008. Creating exploratory tasks for a faceted search interface. *Proc. of HCIR 2008*, 18-21.

[20] Lampe, C., Vitak, J., Gray, R. and Ellison, N.B. 2012. Perceptions of Facebook's value as an information source. *Proc. of CHI 2012*, ACM Press, 3195-3204.

[21] Marwick, A.E. and boyd, d. 2011. I tweet honestly, I tweet passionately: Twitter users, context collapse, and the imagined audience. *New Media & Society, 13*, 1, 114-133.

[22] Morris, M.R. 2013. Collaborative search revisited. *Proc. of CSCW 2013*, 1181-1192.

[23] Morris, M.R., Teevan, J. and Panovich, K. 2010. A comparison of information seeking using search engines and social networks. *Proc. of ICSWM 2010*, 291-294.

[24] Morris, M.R., Teevan, J. and Panovich, K. 2010. What do people ask their social networks, and why?: A survey study of status message Q&A behavior. *Proc. of CHI 2010*, ACM Press, 1739-1748.

[25] Panovich, K., Miller, R. and Karger, D. 2012. Tie strength in question & answer on social network sites. *Proc. of CSCW 2012*, ACM Press, 1057-1066.

[26] Paul, S., Hong, L. and Chi, E. 2011. Is Twitter a good place for asking questions? A characterization study. *Proc. of ICWSM 2011*, 578-581.

[27] Paul, S.A. and Reddy, M.C. 2010. Understanding together: Sensemaking in collaborative information seeking. *Proc. of CSCW 2010*, ACM Press, 321-330.

[28] Rose, D.E. and Levinson, D. 2004. Understanding user goals in web search. *Proc. of WWW 2004*, ACM Press, 13-19.

[29] Singhal, A. 2012. Search, plus Your World. *Google Inside Search Blog.* http://googleblog.blogspot.com/2012/01/search-plus-your-world.html

[30] Sleeper, M., Balebako, R., Das, S., McConahy, A.L., Wiese, J. and Cranor, L.F. 2013. The post that wasn't: exploring self-censorship on Facebook. *Proc. of CSCW 2013*, ACM Press, 793-802.

[31] Teevan, J., Ringel Morris, M. and Panovich, K. 2011. Factors affecting response quantity, quality, and speed for questions asked via social network status messages. *Proc. of ICWSM 2011*, 630-633.

[32] Thom-Santelli, J., Helsey, S.Y., Matthews, T.L., Daly, E.M. and Millen, D.R. 2011. What are you working on? Status message Q&A in an enterprise SNS. *Proc. of ECSCW 2011*, 313-332.

[33] Uehara, E.S. 1995. Reciprocity reconsidered: Gouldner's "moral norm of reciprocity" and social support. *Journal of Social and Personal Relationships, 12*, 4, 483-502.

[34] White, R., Muresan, G. and Marchionini, G. 2006. Evaluating exploratory search systems. *SIGIR 2006 Workshop on Evaluating Exploratory Search.*

[35] White, R. and Roth, R. 2009. *Exploratory search: beyond the query-response paradigm.* Morgan & Claypool.

[36] Wilson, M. and Elsweiler, D. 2010. Casual-leisure searching: The exploratory search scenarios that break our current models. *Proc. of HCIR 2010*, 8-31.

[37] Yang, J., Morris, M.R., Teevan, J., Adamic, L.A. and Ackerman, M.S. 2011. Culture matters: A survey Study of social Q&A behavior. *Proc. of ICWSM 2011*, 409-419.

[38] Zhao, X., Salehi, N., Naranjit, S., Alwaalan, S., Voida, S. and Cosley, D. 2013. The many faces of Facebook: Experiencing social media as performance, exhibition, and personal archive. *Proc. of CHI 2013*, ACM Press, 1-10.

APPENDIX 1.

	Satisfaction	Contribute Knowledge	Provide Information	Verify Information	Trust Answer	Trust Service	Trust Source
	Estimate (SE)	*Estimate (SE)*	*Estimate (SE)*	*Estimate (SE)*	*Estimate (SE)*	*Estimate (SE)*	*Estimate (SE)*
Age	.0070 (.0076)	.0160 (.0108)	.0091 (.0106)	.0181 (.0124)	.0069 (.0076)	.0135 (.0082)	.0069 (.0075)
Female	-.0042 (.0898)	-.0329 (.1284)	-.0430 (.1259)	.0312 (.1478)	-.0285 (.0908)	.0711 (.0975)	.01780 (.0892)
Web Skill	-.0504 (.1030)	-.1679 (.1463)	-.0870 (.1434)	.1626 (.1680)	.1027 (.1035)	.0262 (.1108)	.1400 (.1016)
Search (vs. social)	-.3304 # (.1890)	.5621 ** (.1825)	.9200 *** (.1858)	-.1538 (.1708)	-.1942 (.1398)	1.003 *** (.1078)	-.4612 *** (.1367)
Question Types (vs. avg. others)							
Exploratory	.3124 # (.1632)	.6073 *** (.1576)	.5743 *** (.1604)	.2216 (.1474)	.3567 ** (.1205)	.0596 (.0932)	.2756 * (.1178)
Factual Knowledge	.6593 *** (.1343)	.5445 *** (.1301)	.5986 *** (.1324)	.2153 # (.1222)	.5190 *** (.0997)	-.0421 (.0772)	.4649 *** (.0976)
Favor	-.5127 * (.2242)	-.7857 *** (.2180)	-.3214 (.2204)	-.5337 ** (.2025)	-.1713 (.1659)	-.2549 * (.1288)	-.2106 (.1621)
Invitation	-.9318 ** (.3187)	-.2608 (.3083)	-.1614 (.3140)	-.3670 (.2889)	-.0584 (.2362)	-.3520 # (.1859)	.0191 (.2309)
Navigational	1.458 *** (.1911)	-.0748 (.1840)	-.3927 * (.1874)	.8572 *** (.1722)	1.343 *** (.1411)	.1689 (.1087)	1.249 *** (.1379)
Offer	-.5022 * (.2361)	-.4804 * (.2273)	.0860 (.2316)	-.6517 ** (.2126)	-.2292 (.1743)	-.1001 (.1342)	-.2663 (.1703)
Opinion	.3480 # (.1914)	.4224 * (.1846)	.5216 ** (.1880)	.3324 # (.1727)	.0474 (.1415)	-.0956 (.1090)	.0834 (.1383)
Poll	-1.269 (.8526)	-1.083 (.8230)	-1.697 * (.8381)	-.9006 (.7712)	-2.094 *** (.6313)	.5256 (.4865)	-2.042 ** (.6170)
Recommendation	.7248 *** (.1575)	.5846 *** (.1521)	.4858 ** (.1551)	.2410 # (.1427)	.4790 *** (.1166)	-.0011 (.0901)	.4899 *** (.1141)
Rhetorical	-.4343 # (.2467)	.2724 (.2364)	-.2233 (.2407)	.6045 ** (.2214)	-.3309 # (.1853)	-.0354 (.1397)	-.2664 (.1770)
Adj-R^2	.192 n = 1,006	.302 n = 1,008	.294 n = 1,008	.384 n = 1,009	.302 n = 1,007	.430 n = 1,007	.302 n = 1,008

*Notes: Significance levels are the following: #p < .10; *p < .05; **p < .01; *** p < .001.*
For ease of exposition only fixed effects are reported in this table.

What Do Teens Ask Their Online Social Networks? Social Search Practices among High School Students

Andrea Forte, Michael Dickard, Rachel Magee, Denise E. Agosto
College of Computing and Informatics
Drexel University, Philadelphia, PA, USA
aforte@drexel.edu, m.dickard@drexel.edu, rachelmagee@drexel.edu, dea22@drexel.edu

ABSTRACT
The majority of American teens use social network sites (SNSs) but little is known about how they leverage their online social networks to find information. As part of a larger study on social media and information behaviors, we surveyed 158 high school students to learn about their online question asking and answering practices. We describe which teens are most likely to ask and answer questions, what they ask about, on which sites they ask questions, and how useful they perceive SNSs to be as information sources. When possible, we draw comparisons with findings in the literature about adult populations. We contextualize these findings using early insights from interviews and focus groups with 80 teens and discuss how perceptions of audience, privacy concerns, and self-presentation all play a role in teens' use of SNSs to ask and answer questions.

Author Keywords
Social Search; Q&A; Social Media; Youth; Teens; Information Seeking

ACM Classification Keywords
H.3.3 Information Search and Retrieval: Search process

INTRODUCTION
Teenagers are notoriously active users of social media: in 2012, 95% of American teens were online and 81% of them used social network sites (SNSs) [25]. Ito et al. [21] demonstrated that young people use social media not only for identity exploration and socialization (friendship-driven activities), but also to engage in learning and exploration about the world around them (interest-driven activities). Simultaneously, research on question asking has begun to explore how people make use of their online social networks to find information, who is likely to engage in such practices, how question asking fits into their lives and what the benefits are. Yet we are aware of little work to date that has examined these questions in the context of teen life. In an ongoing study of American high school students, we are exploring how the increasing reach of online social networks and other social media into their daily lives plays a role in teens' online social information seeking practices.

CSCW'14, February 15 - 19 2014, Baltimore, MD, USA
Copyright 2014 ACM 978-1-4503-2540-0/14/02...$15.00.
http://dx.doi.org/10.1145/2531602.2531723

Recent work by Lampe et al. [22] found that the likelihood of adults using Facebook to ask questions was negatively correlated with age—in other words, younger adult participants were more likely to use Facebook to ask questions than older adult participants. Yang et al. [37] found this same trend among adults from four different cultures (India, China, the United Kingdom, and the United States) who use a variety of SNS platforms to ask questions. These studies point to teenagers as a group likely to ask questions using social media, yet researchers don't know much about what teenagers' online Q&A behaviors are like. We have begun to address this gap through a survey of 158 teens in two different regions of the United States. In our discussion of findings, we examine the ways that teenage life provides a unique context for question asking and answering online by drawing comparisons to literature on adult practices.

RELATED LITERATURE

The Work of Asking and Answering Questions Online
The ways information resources are collectively created and curated online are of interest to CSCW researchers who wish to better understand and support these processes. Because of this, question asking and answering has attracted a great deal of attention from the CSCW community. Once a question has been asked online and answers have been publicly posted, ranked and/or refined by interested parties, these socially constructed artifacts can become a resource for future information seekers. For this reason, research on question asking and answering has often focused on identifying and encouraging high quality questions and answers. Some researchers have developed algorithms to identify questions that are likely to have high informational value [20] and to predict the best answers [2, 19]. Others have examined how people assess answerers' authority and reputation [29], and have investigated linguistic features of posts that elicit responses in online forums [9]. Much of this existing work has investigated behaviors in contexts like Usenet forums and, more recently, services that are dedicated to supporting asking

and answering like Yahoo! Answers, the now-defunct Google Answers, and Quora, a Q&A site that integrates features of a SNS.

In the past few years, many researchers have shifted their focus to asking and answering in the context of SNSs that are not dedicated Q & A platforms, such as Facebook and Twitter. boyd [7] has examined SNSs as "networked publics" characterized by persistence, searchability, replicability, and invisible audiences. We view these four characteristics of networked publics as a compelling framework for understanding question asking activity on SNSs. When informal social exchanges are persistent and searchable online, they become information resources long beyond the timeframe of utility for the initial participants. Because they are replicable, such exchanges can also be broadcast and amplified across many social groups. Finally, invisible audiences may contribute to the sense that asking a question is a useful behavior in the first place: "I can't think of who, but someone must know about this."

One response to this information-centric view of question asking and answering is to problematize expertise finding. This thread has long been present in research on social search behaviors in the enterprise, where knowing who to ask within an organization can be a barrier to productive interaction and finding help or information [1, 38].

In a study of 624 Microsoft employees that was among the first to explore question asking in the context of SNSs, Morris et al. [28] found that about half of the respondents had asked a question on a SNS and, based on example questions, constructed a taxonomy of question types that people ask their online social networks. They also found that people sometimes preferred asking questions on SNSs rather than social Q&A sites or search engines, particularly when subjective information was requested and when questions required answers tailored to the asker. Teevan et al. [34] investigated the quality of responses to questions posted on SNSs and identified strategies for eliciting better, faster responses; for example, by including a question mark and scoping the question well. Conversely, Lampe et al. found that many Facebook users do not view the site as an appropriate venue for seeking information or asking favors [22]. Ellison et al. [11] examined requests for help (not just information) in 20,000 public Facebook status messages and discovered that help seeking was a relatively infrequent occurrence that appeared in less than 5% of their sample.

It is important to note that question asking and answering does not only serve as a vehicle for finding information or getting help. Participants in Morris et al.'s 2010 study [28] reported secondary benefits of asking questions of their online social networks such as emotional support, creating social awareness, or having fun. Thom et al. examined Q&A within the enterprise context—that is, using special, dedicated SNS platforms that are only accessed by other employees—and discovered that even in this context where work-related topics can be expected to dominate Q&A, 14% of questions were categorized as personal or social [35]. Paul et al. [30] found that rhetorical questions are the most common type of question posted on Twitter. When viewed as an archival resource, the presence of rhetorical questions, conversation starters, and social banter diminishes the utility of social media Q&A as an information resource; however, these studies suggest that the purpose of question asking is not always to meet an information need.

Teens' Lives as a Context for Social Media Q&A

The studies discussed in the section above draw from data on adults or do not differentiate between adults and minors. Teenage life is different from adult life. Different kinds of social, cultural and biological constraints and needs give rise to different experiences, expectations, and behaviors. Livingstone and Helsper found that young people differ from adults in their reasons for using or not using the Internet [24]; however, explanations for these differences are not yet robust. Developmental psychologists have described identity exploration as a critical feature of the teenage years [12, 36], and social scientists have examined the ways that young peoples' activities and relationships with technology are influenced, structured by and subject to monitoring and regulation by adults and institutions [5, 7]. The simultaneous experience of growth and vulnerability that characterize "teenagerhood" make youth experiences of mediated social interaction an object of widespread interest.

Some research on how teenagers look for information has focused on specific task contexts that are viewed as socially or developmentally important, such as homework [13, 14] or finding health information [16]. A large and growing body of research has also examined teens' practices as they encounter information needs in diffuse contexts sometimes referred to in aggregate as "everyday life." For example, Rieh has studied young people seeking information from their homes [31], and Gasser et. al. note that young people encounter information needs in diverse contexts outside of school that elicit unique search and assessment strategies [15]. Ito et al. [21] also suggest that the kind of activities youth are engaged in at a given time has a profound effect on the ways they communicate online and what they communicate about; friendship-driven participation on sites such as MySpace and Facebook largely involved learning about the opinions and values of peers, whereas interest-driven participation involved the development of specialized forms of expertise within niche knowledge communities. Agosto and Hughes-Hassell [3, 4] developed an empirically grounded taxonomy of youth information needs, including 28 discrete categories, which we use as a starting point for capturing the breadth of questions teens ask and answer in SNSs.

Teens Asking Questions Online

Between the interest in asking questions online, the widespread use of SNSs among teenagers and the interest in how teens find, assess, and use information, there has been surprisingly little work on SNSs as sites of information seeking among teenagers. Takahashi's ethnographic work on SNS use among Japanese youth found that SNSs served as information sources via browsing or passive reception but did not investigate question asking or answering as a practice [33].

We know little about how and when young people leverage their online social networks to satisfy information needs and in what contexts they are likely to do so. We don't know what kind of work question asking on SNSs might do for teens that goes beyond satisfying specific information needs, such as having fun or obtaining emotional support as observed by Morris et al. [28].

As a first step toward understanding these issues, we ask:

- How prevalent is question asking and answering using SNSs among teens?
- What demographic characteristics are correlated with online asking and answering?
- What kinds of questions do teens ask their online social networks?
- What are teens' perceptions of social media as sources of information?

METHODS

The data we used to answer these questions were collected as a part of a larger study on teens' social media use and information behaviors, including a survey of high school students, focus groups and interviews with a subset of survey participants, and a survey of libraries that provide youth services. In this paper, we focus primarily on data from the survey of high school students, which was designed to help us answer the four questions above. Survey data were collected from December 2012 through May 2013 and 158 students have participated. Once requisite permission had been obtained from parents and the surveys were completed, students became eligible to participate in interviews and focus groups. Surveys were administered online and could be completed by the students any place they could access the Internet. Our interview and focus group data collection effort was completed in June 2013 with 80 participants, 50 in focus groups and 30 in interviews. We offer some preliminary insights from interviews and focus groups where they help contextualize findings from the survey and explain how findings from the survey inform our ongoing study; however, analysis of these data are in progress.

Survey Instrument

In order to collect a dataset that builds on existing knowledge about question asking and answering, we integrated features from other surveys. First, we borrowed techniques from Morris et al.'s study of Microsoft employees [27] to collect a sample of real questions by asking teens to provide us with an example of a question they had recently asked on an SNS, answers they'd received, and an explanation about which answer was the best one. We also asked them to provide an example of a question they'd answered, the answer they provided, and why they had answered it. Although they were encouraged to copy-and-paste examples and some of them clearly did so, other students paraphrased questions and answers in part because they completed the survey using school computers where sites such as Facebook were blocked; thus, issues with participant recall may have affected the quality of some example questions.

We used Agosto and Hughes-Hassell's [3, 4] 28 categories of teens' information needs to collect data on the topics that respondents have asked questions about, would ask about, or would not ask about. Because they were sometimes based on constructs from the literature (i.e. "self-actualization"), the categories were modified to make them more understandable and distinct from one another. In the end, we retained 26 of the 28 original categories. The survey was piloted with undergraduate students to assess whether it was understandable. In addition, respondents were prompted to provide an example of a question for each category, which helped us assess their interpretations of the categories we asked about and ensure validity of the results.

Finally, we adapted a question about the usefulness of SNSs as information sources from Lampe et al. [22] and measured Web-use skill level using Hargittai and Hsieh's validated 10-item survey instrument [18], which was originally created by comparing people's actual online abilities in searching for information with their responses to survey questions about knowledge of Internet concepts [17]. Respondents were asked "How familiar are you with the following computer and Internet-related items?" with prompts for 10 Internet-related concepts (Advanced Search, Spyware, Wiki, JPG, Weblog, Cache, Malware, Tagging, Phishing, PDF). These items were coded using a 5-point Likert scale to assess the respondents' understanding of each item. The resulting index variable in our study ranges from 10 to 50, which exhibits high internal consistency with a Cronbach's alpha of .88. We will refer to this construct as "Web-use skill" and "skill" to be consistent with the literature [16].

We included two bogus terms in the skills scale (Proxypod and Fitibly) as well as a question to assess whether respondents were attending to the survey or simply checking off answers. Surveys that failed two of these three checks were discarded from the dataset, which comprised 6% of the original data set.

Sites and Participants

Our survey data were collected from two populations of American high school students. One population attends an urban public science and engineering magnet high school that we refer to as SciCentral High. SciCentral is known for its award-winning integration of technology throughout the curriculum and 1:1 laptop program. The school enrolls

	Facebook	Twitter	Google+*	Tumblr	Instagram**	Pinterest	MySpace
Several times a day	44.3%	34.4%	11.5%	20.4%	22.8%	1.3%	0.0%
About once a day	21.5%	7.0%	5.1%	5.1%	3.2%	2.5%	0.0%
3-5 days a week	7.6%	2.5%	7.7%	6.4%	1.3%	0.6%	0.0%
1-2 days a week	6.3%	3.8%	5.1%	3.8%	0.6%	3.2%	0.0%
Every few weeks	5.1%	2.5%	9.0%	5.7%	0.6%	3.8%	1.3%
Less often	6.3%	10.8%	20.5%	14.6%	0.0%	10.1%	18.4%
Total Users	**91.1%**	**61.1%**	**59.0%**	**56.1%**	**28.5%**	**21.5%**	**19.6%**
Total Non-Users	**8.9%**	**38.9%**	**41.0%**	**43.9%**	-	**78.5%**	**80.4%**

Table 1: Frequency of participants' social media use.
*** Focus group data suggests that teens may have confused Google+ with other Google products.**
**** Instagram was not included as an option but was the most frequently written in response for "other"; thus, it may be underrepresented relative to other sites and we have no data for non-use**

		School	
		Devens High N = 98	SciCentral High N = 60
Age	14	4.1%	13.3%
	15	3.1%	26.7%
	16	9.2%	23.3%
	17	17.3%	11.7%
	18	66.3%	25.0%
Sex	Male	43.9%	43.3%
	Female	56.1%	56.7%
Parent's Highest Level of Education	Don't Know	13.3%	6.7%
	Some high school	31.6%	11.7%
	High school diploma	19.4%	28.3%
	College degree	27.6%	26.7%
	Advanced graduate degree	8.2%	26.7%
Race	Asian	16.3%	5.0%
	Black	21.4%	33.3%
	White	12.2%	31.7%
	Hispanic or Latino	44.9%	13.3%
	Other	5.1%	16.7%

Table 2: Demographics of survey respondents by field site.

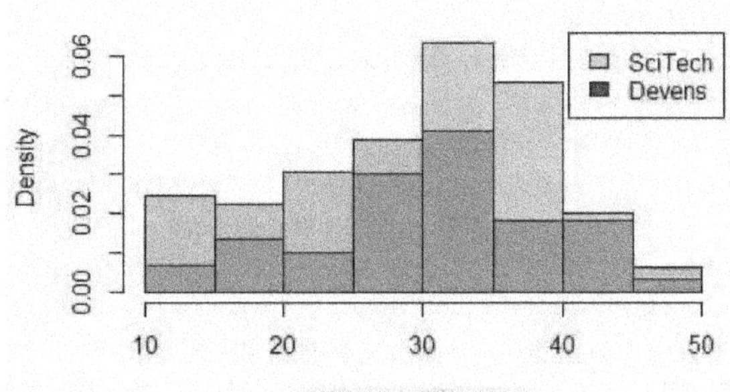

Figure 1: Overlaid distribution of skills by field site.

about 500 students, about 30% of which are economically disadvantaged and 65% of which are minority students. Our sample includes a diverse set of students (Table 2); note that the permission/assent protocol for minors presented a significantly higher barrier for participation than for 18-year-olds as we were required to make in-person or telephone contact with a parent or guardian of each survey taker who was under 18. Since many students had birthdays during the months of the study, some 17-year-olds reported waiting to participate until they turned 18.

The second population attends a suburban public high school that we call Devens High, located outside of a major metropolitan area in a different region of the country. Devens High also supports a science and engineering magnet program within its total student body of about 2500. Our sample from Devens includes both magnet and non-magnet students, although due to last minute changes, we were not aware of the magnet program until after the study had begun and did not collect data about which students participate in the program. About 55% of Devens students are economically disadvantaged and 75% are minorities. A disproportionately high number of older students participated at Devens not only because of the comparative ease of consent but also because school staff appeared to target senior-level classes for reminders about the study, which inflated the number of both 17- and 18-year olds. Three of the authors visited Devens for two days to conduct focus groups and interviews and to facilitate the consent process. Consent and assent for many students was obtained prior to the visit by providing the school with forms and self-addressed stamped envelopes. Receipt of forms was followed up by a phone call with parents.

Participants from SciCentral reported higher levels of parental education with over 25% of parents holding advanced degrees compared with 8% of Devens parents. Over 30% of Devens participants' parents had not completed high school. Students from SciCentral also reported a significantly greater understanding of Internet-related terms, $t(156)=-3.1$, $p=.002$, with a mean difference of 4.62, indicating they are more skilled and knowledgeable in their use of the Web than students at Devens (Figure 1 overlays the distribution of skills in each school).

Participants were overwhelmingly social media users and reported more frequent use of Facebook than any other site (See Table 1), consistent with recent literature on teen social media use [25].

In terms of demographics, our sample is not representative of the general U.S. teen population; however, we were careful to choose culturally and geographically diverse field sites in order to capture a diverse set of practices. One clear limitation of our site selection is that all our participants attend high school. All students in the schools were invited to participate. Participants were given $10 for their time.

FINDINGS

Our first research question aimed simply to establish the prevalence of asking questions using SNSs. In order to ensure they understood what we meant by SNS, we asked participants to indicate whether they had ever posted a question on several of the most trafficked SNSs and those we believed would be recognizable (i.e. Twitter, Facebook, MySpace) with the option of "No, I have not" and then prompted them to list any other sites where they had posted questions. We found that most of our participants had asked questions in SNSs and over half had answered questions (Table 3), higher than Morris et al.'s finding that 50% of adult Microsoft employees had asked a question on a SNS.

Who are the question askers and answerers?

Prior research has indicated that socioeconomic status and Web-use skills are predictive of certain online behaviors; in particular, higher Web-use skills have been associated with online activities that enhance social capital [17]. We believed that Q&A behaviors could be construed as capital-enhancing and were interested in whether higher levels of Web-use skills were also associated with asking questions online. We found that whether or not teens asked questions of their online social networks did not significantly differ by demographic characteristics, Web-use skills or by school. We found a marginal difference in skills between teens who have asked questions on SNSs (M=30.7) and those who have not (M=27.5), with question askers having slightly higher skills, t(156) = -1.78, p=.077). We do not know if reasons for asking questions or success in getting answers varies by skill level; future research could benefit from examining such questions.

On the other hand, our data shows that teens who *answer* questions have significantly higher skills (M=31.1) than those who have not answered questions (M=28.1), t(156)=-2.02, p<.05. Looking at the correlation between answering questions and skill level, we found a weakly significant correlation between answering questions and skills, *r*(156)=.16, p<.05, and a stronger correlation between answering questions and parental education *r*(156)=.24, p<.01. Answering questions of others in ones' network may be a more powerful relational investment than asking questions. These findings provide some support that Web-use skills are associated with teens' Q&A behavior, but further research and more nuanced measures of such behavior are needed to make more substantive claims.

	Total (158)	Devens (98)	SciCentral (60)
Ever asked a question	77% (122)	74% (72)	83% (50)
Ever answered a question	61% (97)	60% (59)	63% (38)

Table 3: Prevalence of question asking and answering.

		Total (122)	Devens (98)	SciCentral (60)
Asked on	Facebook	93% (114)	90% (65)	98% (49)
	Twitter	49% (60)	43% (31)	58% (29)
	MySpace	18% (22)	19% (14)	16% (8)
	Google+*	11% (14)	11% (8)	12% (6)
	Tumblr	11% (14)	7% (5)	18% (9)
	Instagram**	9% (11)	13% (9)	4% (2)
	Other	16% (20)	8% (6)	28% (14)
	None	23% (36)	27% (26)	17% (10)

Table 4: Top sites where participants had asked questions. *Focus groups suggest teens may not know what Google+ is. ** Teens explained that they asked questions on Instagram either by using the app Instatext or in comments.

Participants were asked where they ask questions, and most reported asking questions on Facebook, followed by Twitter, MySpace, and Other (Instagram was a popular response in the "Other" category, and since it wasn't included as an original option, it may under report the prevalence of asking questions on Instagram relative to other sites) (see Table 4). Question asking on specific sites did not differ significantly by demographic characteristics. The perceptions of a site as a useful source of information and frequency of using a site were both positively correlated with asking questions on those sites (p<.001), which makes intuitive sense.

What do teens ask their online social networks?

We collected data on what teens ask about in two different ways. First, we emulated the technique used by Morris et al. [26] to collect a sample of real questions by asking teens to provide us with examples of questions and answers they had posted themselves. Second, we used Agosto and Hughes-Hassel's categories of teens' everyday information needs [3] to find out whether participants ask questions of their online social networks to meet a broad set of information needs.

	Teens	Morris et al. [26]	Ellison et al. [10]
Factual Knowledge	39%	17%	7%
Opinion	25%	22%	40%
Invitation	11%	12%	7%
Rhetorical	7%	14%	--
Favor	10%	4%	47%
Recommend	9%	29%	4%

Table 5: Distribution of question types in our sample of teens compared to that of [27] and [11]

Category	YES has asked.	NO but would.	NO and would not.
School	76.6%	17.7%	5.7%
Social Activities	56.1%	27.4%	16.6%
Entertainment	50.6%	36.7%	12.7%
College	41.7%	46.2%	12.2%
Shopping	40.5%	35.4%	24.1%
Club or Org	35.3%	41.7%	23.1%
Daily Life	34.2%	41.1%	24.7%
Work	30.4%	47.5%	22.2%
Fashion	28.2%	32.7%	39.1%
Self Appearance	27.8%	22.8%	49.4%
Current Event	26.5%	42.6%	31.0%
Pop Culture	26.1%	43.3%	30.6%
Career	24.4%	48.1%	27.6%
Creative	22.8%	51.9%	25.3%
School Culture	21.8%	41.7%	36.5%
Romantic	19.6%	22.2%	58.2%
Family	19.6%	39.9%	40.5%
Norms	16.6%	46.5%	36.9%
Laws or Rules	16.6%	48.4%	35.0%
Philosophy	15.8%	33.5%	50.6%
Health	14.7%	44.9%	40.4%
Religion	12.0%	28.5%	59.5%
Public Safety	9.6%	40.1%	50.3%
Culture	8.9%	46.5%	44.6%
Sexual Identity	7.6%	21.0%	71.3%
Safe Sex	7.0%	20.4%	72.6%

Table 6: Occurrence of question asking to meet each information category. Ordered from most to least common.

We collected 118 examples of questions that teens had asked and coded them using the types of questions identified in [27] and also used by [11]. The first and second authors independently coded the corpus with a primary and secondary code if necessary. To test for consistent interpretation of the coding constructs, we used simple percent-agreement to check interrater reliability and found that coders agreed 85% of the time on the primary code alone and 97% of the time on at least one of the codes. The coders discussed the few discrepancies to come to a resolution on the final coded set.

We found that teens were far more likely to report asking questions about factual knowledge than either of the two studies that examined adult behaviors or, in the case of Ellison et al. [10], may have included but did not specifically differentiate teen behavior (see Table 5). Our data stands in contrast to Ellison et al.'s finding that factual information was sought less often by younger posters than by older ones [10]. Many of the factual questions in our corpus involved information about school; for example, "Do we have school tomorrow?" or "What were the homework pages for math?" We observed in both survey and interviews/focus group data that many teens interact online with peers from school; because their lives are structured by the same institutions there is a high level of homogeneity in the kinds of information they need and this gives rise to plenty of opportunities for factual knowledge sharing.

Participants reported asking questions to satisfy all 26 categories of information needs but the influence of school as a shared life experience with their online networks was again apparent. (Table 6) Some surveys were completed at the schools and this may have influenced students to recall school-related questions; however, we do not expect this to impact their responses when prompted to report actual or potential use of social media to ask questions about school relative to social activities, entertainment, news, fashion, or other topics. To assess the validity of the information needs categories, we prompted participants to provide an example question for each category they had asked about. Two authors coded the example questions as representative of the information category, not representative, or too little context to tell. Overall, the two coders agreed 88% of the time and found that students provided example questions that were representative of the category 93% of the time. This suggests that participants interpreted the categories in the same way as the researchers. The categories for which students were least likely to provide representative questions were "Popular Culture such as celebrities, sports figures, musicians, etc." and "Creative Activities, such as dancing, singing, writing, etc." each with 79% representative examples.

What are teens' perceptions of social media as information sources?

We asked participants to assess the usefulness of different SNSs as sources of information using a scaled response to the prompt "I feel I get useful information from…" With the exception of MySpace, $r(154)=.15$, $p=.06$, site use is significantly positively correlated with perceptions of that same site having useful information. See Table 7 for average assessment of SNSs as information sites. Our respondents assessed Facebook as having the same level of usefulness as those in Lampe et al.'s 2012 study of university staff [21], from which the survey question was adapted, albeit with a higher standard deviation.

An indirect way to assess the utility of different sites as information sources is to look at the correlations between what students are asking about and where they are asking questions. To identify associations between SNS and topics asked about, we utilized Cramer's V correlation coefficient, which is designed to test the correlation between two nominal or dichotomous variables (see Table 8). Interview data bolsters our confidence in these numbers; for example, note the correlation between asking questions on Instagram and asking questions about Shopping, Fashion, and Self-Appearance. Some teens we interviewed mentioned sharing pictures of outfits that they were wearing or thinking of buying; others described using Instagram to search for pictures related to fashion.

	N	Min/ Max	Mean	StDev
Facebook	157	1/5	3.55	1.26
Lampe et al. [21]			*3.54*	*.89*
Twitter	156	1/5	2.83	1.65
Tumblr	152	1/5	2.77	1.80
Google Plus	154	1/5	2.73	1.86
Pinterest	156	1/5	2.53	1.99
MySpace	156	1/5	2.40	2.03

Table 7: Assessment of SNSs as useful sources of information on a 5-point scale where 5 indicates the most useful.

	Facebook	Twitter	Instagram
Romantic			.303**
Daily Life	.241**	.195*	
School	.279**	.222*	
School-Culture		.258**	
Club/Org	.216*		
Shopping		.314**	.231*
Pop Culture	.231*	.210*	
Fashion	.286**	.237*	.191*
Social Norms		.244**	
Family		.227*	.210**
Self-Appearance	.233*	.229*	.340**
Work		.277**	

Table 8: Correlations between what participants have asked about and where they ask questions. *$p < 0.05$; **$p < 0.01$

Twitter is significantly correlated with the highest number of question topics (10) followed by Facebook (6). Because Twitter is used as a general communication channel at SciCentral, its utility as an all-purpose question-asking venue may be exaggerated in our dataset. Many interviewees indicated that their networks on Facebook included a greater range of relationship types, including family members, acquaintances, and in some cases co-workers and teachers. As a consequence, interviewees mentioned avoiding personal topics on Facebook to minimize drama or awkwardness. These narratives substantiate correlations in Table 8, which suggest that Facebook is used more frequently for low-risk information sharing about school, clubs, culture, and less for personal content.

DISCUSSION

We introduced SNSs as useful question asking venues using boyd's characteristics of networked publics: persistence, searchability, replicability, and invisible audiences. To quickly recap, social exchanges that are *persistent* and *searchable* can become information resources long after the original exchange. Because they are *replicable*, the informational content of such exchanges can be broadcast, copied and reused. Finally, we suggested that *invisible audiences* may contribute to the sense that asking a question on SNSs is a useful behavior in the first place based on the perception that "someone out there" may have useful information to share. We discuss our findings in light of these characteristics and, in particular, the concept of audience, invisible, real, and imagined.

The idea that people may perceive "invisible audiences" as a potential resource is a paradoxical idea; it is, after all, precisely one's inability to perceive it that renders much of her online audience invisible. Bernstein et al. found that social media users consistently underestimate the size of their audience on Facebook – believing it to be just 27% of its actual size on average [6]. Yet, despite the fact that they misjudge audience, there is also evidence that people understand that their perception of audience may be faulty and take measures to mitigate the risk of unintended disclosures on SNSs [8, 10]. Perception of audience, real or imagined, is a critical aspect of social media Q&A: without an audience, one can't expect an answer.

On Privacy and Audience

Our data suggest that when participants post questions online, they do so not as an effort to "crowdsource" their information needs to a vast unknown mob of potential answerers, but instead intend to direct their questions to specific audiences they believe to have the information they need. In interviews and focus groups, it was clear that switching between private messages, text, Facebook, Twitter and other communication channels was common. Even a single channel can provide access to different audiences depending on how and whether privacy settings are used. Teens report a high degree of confidence in their ability to manage privacy settings and most make an effort to control the audience for content they share [25]. On Facebook, the most frequented site among our participants, privacy settings are increasingly complex and used increasingly frequently [32]. Asking a question through a status update can be done in a way that has the potential to be seen by millions or restricted to just a few individuals;

however, only about 18% of teens customize privacy settings to tailor audiences for specific posts [25], so this fine-grained control is not likely a common practice among our participants. During interviews, teens indicated that they had different networks on different SNS sites, and this differentiation between audiences helped dictate which site to use for what purposes.

The prevalent use of privacy settings and awareness of audience on different SNSs may also help explain the apparent contradiction between our finding that teens asked more questions related to factual information compared with adult or mixed populations and the finding of Ellison et al. [11], that requesters of factual knowledge in public Facebook posts tended to be older, not younger. If teens are limiting their status updates to friends or groups of friends, these would not surface in a corpus of public posts.

Norms and Rules

Our survey data demonstrated that school-related information was regularly sought and provided by our participants as they used SNSs to ask and answer questions. Since they were all high school students, our participants spent a lot of time in school and completing school-related tasks. In interviews and focus groups it became clear that the composition of online social networks and the potential audience for questions depended on the policies in place at the different schools, for example, it was difficult for students at Devens High to connect online with teachers and administrators because of the strict rules in place regarding teacher/student friending.

In contrast, SciCentral students reported that it was common to friend teachers and administrators online. Some examples of context collapse surfaced in interviews and focus groups when SciCentral students described instances of teachers and administrators observing posts. These included episodes that were perceived as distressing, such as being asked to meet with the principal to discuss inappropriate posts, but also included playful and unexpected episodes such as tweeting that one is "starving" during class and having the principal show up with a snack.

Self-Presentation: Asking Means you Don't Know

Audience is also connected to identity management. Recent theoretical and empirical work has examined how social media users manage invisible or imagined audiences [23] and "context collapse," which is the experience of sharing information or behaviors across multiple audiences that would normally evoke different performances [26]. Such concepts often emerge in discussions of performed identity or presentation of self. Manipulating privacy settings and switching networks can be used as strategies to re-segregate audiences and manage others' perceptions. Critical for question asking: if people see you asking, they may realize that you *don't* know about something, and/or, perhaps equally revealing, that you *want* to.

One obvious explanation for school-related questions being the most frequently asked type of question, aside from the perception of a knowledgeable audience, is that being assigned homework and attending school functions are so common and generally socially sanctioned that they carry less social risk if asked about than, for example, questions about sexual identity, health or religion.

Our survey data demonstrated both that school-related topics were common and that they were equally prevalent at both field sites, which indicates that the mere presence of teachers in SNSs did not encourage or discourage asking questions about school. Yet, the possibility of teachers and administrators encountering questions online took on qualitative differences when discussed in interviews and focus groups. Some students suggested that if teachers saw them asking questions of one another online, they might be perceived as cheating, whereas others seemed to think the practice was as unremarkable as raising one's hand in class.

We have noted that school-related questions were the most frequently asked and we observed that they were usually mundane requests for information like reading assignments or schedules; unsurprisingly, in interviews and focus groups, students often provided examples of such questions, but were not interested in reflecting on them. The richer discussions happened around less common question types and reasons students wanted to avoid certain topics, which is difficult to capture in scaled survey questions. In other words, school is ubiquitous but not very interesting. As we continue analyzing interviews, we aim to develop a more robust understanding of the relationship between the perception of audience, self-presentation, and the kinds of information behaviors teens engage in on SNS.

Limitations

Although we were careful to collect data from diverse field sites and our sample represents a broad swath of ages, ethnicities and socio-economic backgrounds, it is not representative of the general United States teen population. We have described how the consent/assent protocol for minors that is required by our institution introduced considerably higher barriers to participation for younger high school students. In addition, because we conducted the research at high schools, our sample is limited to those students who attend school. The presence of science and engineering magnet programs at the schools may also have introduced a bias in our sample toward teens who are interested in science, technology, engineering and math and the common use of Twitter at one of the schools for communication among students, teachers and administrators may have introduced practices that are not common in high schools. Finally, the fact that many respondents completed the survey at school meant that they were unable to copy and paste questions from Facebook or other SNSs because these sites were typically blocked by the school district; these students had to rely on memory and paraphrase their remembered interactions.

We think it is worth noting the difficulty of capturing something as slippery as social media practices. Sites can become terrifically popular in a short period of time and, similarly, fall out of favor among specific groups. We witnessed this in our own data; we neglected to anticipate Instagram would be an important question-asking venue, yet it was written in many times as an "other." One methodological response to this problem is to use interviews as a source for constructing survey instruments. Because we conducted interviews and surveys in parallel, we had to rely on the literature to inform survey design rather than craft an instrument that was responsive to the practices we observed in the field.

SUMMARY

Our survey data have laid a foundation for understanding teen Q&A behaviors on social media. We found that teens' practices differ from adult practices documented in the literature in that they asked more questions related to factual information and that this stems in part from the shared life context of attending school. We found that answering questions is correlated with higher levels of Web use skills and parental education and suggest that question answering may be a more powerful social capital building activity than asking. We discussed these findings in the context of perceived audience, privacy and self-presentation. These findings begin to illustrate teen Q&A activities and raise questions for further research about what motivates teens to ask and answer questions and how they perceive different sites that could support Q&A.

ACKNOWLEDGMENTS

This material is based on work supported by the National Science Foundation Graduate Research Fellowship Grant #2011121873 and the Institute for Museum and Library Services Grant LG-06-11-0261. Thanks to our anonymous reviewers and Brian Dorn for their detailed feedback.

REFERENCES

1. Ackerman, M.S. and McDonald, D.W. Answer Garden 2: merging organizational memory with collaborative help. Proceedings *of Computer supported cooperative work*. ACM Press (1996), 97-105.
2. Adamic, L.A., Zhang, J., Bakshy, E., and Ackerman, M.S. Knowledge sharing and yahoo answers: everyone knows something. Proceedings *of the 17th international conference on World Wide Web*. ACM Press (2008), 665-674.
3. Agosto, D.E. and Hughes-Hassell, S., Toward a model of the everyday life information needs of urban teenagers, part 1: Theoretical model: Research Articles. *J. Am. Soc. Inf. Sci. Technol.*, *57*, 10 (2006), 1394-1403.
4. Agosto, D.E. and Hughes-Hassell, S., Toward a model of the everyday life information needs of urban teenagers, Part 2: Empirical model: Research Articles. *J. Am. Soc. Inf. Sci. Technol.*, *57*, 11 (2006), 1418-1426.
5. Ames, M.G., Go, J., Kaye, J.J., and Spasojevic, M. Understanding technology choices and values through social class. *Proceedings of the ACM Conference on Computer Supported Cooperative Work (CSCW)*. ACM Press (2011), 55-64.
6. Bernstein, M.S., Bakshy, E., Burke, M., and Karrer, B. Quantifying the invisible audience in social networks. *Proceedings of SIGCHI Conference on Human Factors in Computing Systems (CHI)*. ACM Press (2013), 21-30.
7. boyd, d., Why youth [heart] social network sites: The role of networked publics in teenage social life, in *Youth, identity, and digital media*, D. Buckingham, Editor, MIT Press, Cambridge (2008), 119-142.
8. boyd, d.m., *Taken out of context: American teen sociality in networked publics. PhD Dissertation.* University of California, Berkeley (2008).
9. Burke, M., Joyce, E., Kim, T., Anand, V., and Kraut, R. Introductions and Requests: Rhetorical Strategies That Elicit Response in Online Communities. *Proceedings of Communities and Technologies* (2007), 21-40.
10. Ellison, N., Vitak, J., Steinfield, C., Gray, R., and Lampe, C., Negotiating Privacy Concerns and Social Capital Needs in a Social Media Environment, in *Privacy Online*, S. Trepte and L. Reinecke, Editors., Springer Berlin Heidelberg (2011), 19-32.
11. Ellison, N., Gray, R., Vitak, J., Lampe, C., and Fiore, A. Calling All Facebook Friends: Exploring requests for help on Facebook. *Proceedings of the International Conference on Weblogs and Social Media (ICWSM)*. AAAI, (2013).
12. Erikson, E.H., *Identity, youth and crisis.* W. W. Norton Company, New York, (1968).
13. Fidel, R., Davies, R., Douglass, M., Holder, J., Hopkins, C., Kushner, E., Miyagishima, B., and Toney, C., A Visit to the Information Mall: Web Searching Behavior of High School Students. *Journal of the American Society for Information Science*, *50*, 1 (1999), 24-37.
14. Forte, A. and Bruckman, A., Citing, writing and participatory media: wikis as learning environments in the high school classroom. *International Journal of Learning and Media*, *1*, 4 (2009), 23-44.
15. Gasser, U., Cortesi, S., Malik, M., and Lee, A., Youth and Digital Media: From Credibility to Information Quality, Report, (2012), Berkman Center for Internet and Society.
16. Hansen, D.L., Holly A Derry, Resnick, P.J., and Richardson, C.R., Adolescents Searching for Health Information on the Internet: An Observational Study. *Journal of Medical Internet Research*, *5*, 4 (2003).
17. Hargittai, E. and Hinnant, A., Digital Inequality: Differences in Young Adults' Use of the Internet. *Communication Research*, *35*, 5 (2008), 602-621.
18. Hargittai, E. and Hsieh, Y.P., Succinct survey measures of web-use skills. *Social Science Computer Review*, *30*, 1 (2012), 95-107.

19. Harper, F.M., Raban, D., Rafaeli, S., and Konstan, J.A. Predictors of answer quality in online Q&A sites. *Proceedings of the SIGCHI Conference on Human Factors in Computing Systems (CHI).* ACM Press (2008), 865-874.

20. Harper, F.M., Moy, D., and Konstan, J.A. Facts or friends?: distinguishing informational and conversational questions in social Q&A sites. *Proceedings of the SIGCHI Conference on Human Factors in Computing Systems (CHI).* ACM Press (2009), 759-768.

21. Ito, M., Baumer, S., Bittanti, M., boyd, d., Cody, R., Herr-Stephenson, B., Horst, H., Lange, P., Mahendran, D., Martinez, K., Pascoe, C.J., Perkel, D., Robinson, L., Sima, C., and Tripp, L., *Hanging out, messing around, and geeking out : kids living and learning with new media.* MIT Press, Cambridge, Mass., (2010).

22. Lampe, C., Vitak, J., Gray, R., and Ellison, N. Perceptions of facebook's value as an information source. *Proceedings of the SIGCHI Conference on Human Factors in Computing Systems.* ACM (2012), 3195-3204.

23. Litt, E., Knock, Knock. Who's There? The Imagined Audience. *Journal of Broadcasting & Electronic Media 56*, 3 (2012), 330-345.

24. Livingstone, S. and Helsper, E., Gradations in digital inclusion: children, young people and the digital divide. *New Media & Society*, *9*, 4 (2007), 671-696.

25. Madden, M., Lenhart, A., Cortesi, S., Gasser, U., Duggan, M., and Smith, A., Teens, Social Media, and Privacy. Report Pew Internet and American Life. (2013)

26. Marwick, A.E. and boyd, d., I Tweet Honestly, I Tweet Passionately: Twitter Users, Context Collapse, and the Imagined Audience. *New Media & Society*, (2010), 114-133.

27. Morris, M.R., Teevan, J., and Panovich, K. What do people ask their social networks, and why?: a survey study of status message: a behavior. *Proceedings of the 28th international conference on Human factors in computing systems.* ACM Press (2010), 1739-1748.

28. Morris, M.R., Teevan, J., and Panovich, K. What do people ask their social networks, and why?: a survey study of status message q&a behavior. *Proceedings of SIGCHI Conference on Human Factors in Computing Systems (CHI).* ACM Press (2010), 1739-1748.

29. Paul, S., Hong, L., and Chi, E.H. Who is Authoritative? Understanding Reputation Mechanisms in Quora. in *Proc. Collective Intelligence Conference (CI)*, (2012).

30. Paul, S.A., Hong, L., and Chi, E.H. Is Twitter a Good Place for Asking Questions? A Characterization Study. *Proceedings of International Conference on Weblogs and Social Media (ICWSM).* AAAI. (2011).

31. Rieh, S.Y., On the Web at home: Information seeking and Web searching in the home environment. *Journal of the American Society for Information Science and Technology*, *55*, 8 (2004), 743-753.

32. Stutzman, F., Gross, R., and Acquisti, A., Silent Listeners: The Evolution of Privacy and Disclosure on Facebook. *Journal of Privacy and Confidentiality*, *4*, 2 (2012).

33. Takahashi, T., MySpace or Mixi? Japanese engagement with SNS (social networking sites) in the global age. *New Media & Society*, *12*, 3 (2010), 453-475.

34. Teevan, J., Morris, M.R., and Panovich, K. Factors Affecting Response Quantity, Quality, and Speed for Questions Asked via Social Network Status Messages. in *International Conference on Weblogs and Social Media (ICWSM)*, AAAI (2011).

35. Thom, J., Helsley, S., Matthews, T., Daly, E., and Millen, D., What Are You Working On? Status Message Q&A in an Enterprise SNS, in *ECSCW 2011: Proceedings of the 12th European Conference on Computer Supported Cooperative Work (ECSCW), 24-28 September 2011, Aarhus Denmark*, S. Bodker, et al., Editors., Springer, London (2011) 313-332.

36. Turkle, S., Adolescence and Identity: finding yourself in the machine, Siman and Schuster, 1984, 137-162.

37. Yang, J., Morris, M.R., Teevan, J., Adamic, L.A., and Ackerman, M.S. Culture Matters: A Survey Study of Social Q&A Behavior. in *Fifth International AAAI Conference on Weblogs and Social Media (ICWSM)*, AAAI (2011).

38. Yarosh, S., Matthews, T., and Zhou, M. Asking the right person: supporting expertise selection in the enterprise. *Proceedings of the SIGCHI Conference on Human Factors in Computing Systems (CHI).* ACM Press (2012), 2247-2256.

Coordinating Donors on Crowdfunding Websites

Rick Wash
Michigan State University
wash@msu.edu

Jacob Solomon
Michigan State University
solomo93@msu.edu

ABSTRACT

Crowdfunding websites like Kickstarter, Spot.Us and Donor's Choose seek to fund multiple projects simultaneously by soliciting donations from a large number of donors. Crowdfunding site designers must decide what to do with donations to projects that don't reach their goal by the deadline. Some crowdfunding sites use an all-or-nothing *return rule* in which donations are returned to donors if a project doesn't meet its goal. Other sites use a *direct donation* structure where all donations are kept by the project even if the total is insufficient.

We simulated a crowdfunding site using a threshold public goods game in which a set of donors tries to fund multiple projects that vary in riskiness. We find that the return rule mechanism leads to a marginal improvement in productivity of a site – more money is donated in total – by eliciting more donations. However, the return rule also leads to a potential loss in efficiency (percentage of projects funded) because donations become *spread* across too many projects and are not coordinated to achieve the maximum possible impact. The direct donation model, though, encourages donors to coordinate to creates a more efficient but slightly less productive marketplace.

Author Keywords

Crowdfunding; Quantitative; Experiment; Public Goods; Crowdsourcing

ACM Classification Keywords

H.5.m. Information Interfaces and Presentation (e.g. HCI): Miscellaneous

INTRODUCTION

Raising money to do a project is difficult; projects are inherently risky because they might not succeed in achieving their goals. When a project needs money to succeed, convincing people to contribute money to the project is challenging because potential donors see a lot of risk. Crowdfunding websites attempt to help by publicizing projects that need money and allowing many contributors to each make a small contribution toward the larger project. By aggregating many small donations, crowdfunding websites can fund large and interesting projects of all kinds. For example, the movie writer Charlie Kaufman and his associates raised over $400,000 from over 5,000 donors to fund the creation of an animated movie[1]. Kickstarter, Spot.Us, and Donors Choose are all examples of crowdfunding websites targeted at specific types of projects (creative, journalism, and classroom projects respectively).

Crowdfunding websites are two-sided matching marketplaces: they seek to match donors with projects that need money. However, crowdfunding websites introduce a second type of risk to projects: they allow people to contribute less money than the amount needed for the project, with no guarantee that the project will ever receive sufficient funds. For a project to receive its needed total, donors must coordinate. Crowdfunding websites do not use an algorithmic mechanism to achieve coordination, but instead provide an open marketplace for project creators and potential donors to match themselves. However, crowdfunding sites can be designed to enforce rules and mechanisms that help this coordination. Thus, crowdfunding site designers face important design questions that impact how well the site coordinates donation activity to fund projects.

One such design question is what to do when a project receives some donations, but these donations are insufficient to completely fund the project. Many crowdfunding websites have chosen a marketplace-enforced *return rule*: if a project does not receive sufficient funding by a pre-specified deadline, then all donations to that project are returned to the donors. The return rule formalizes a structure already present in donor preferences: donations to projects complement each other. Each donation is itself insufficient to fund a project, and therefore each donor prefers to donate to projects that are receiving donations from others, so that the project receives enough funds to succeed.

Other crowdfunding websites use a more traditional *direct donation* rule: all donated funds (minus the marketplace cut) are delivered to the project, regardless of whether they total up to the pre-specified goal of the project.

We ask two questions. First, how does this return rule affect the donation decisions of individuals who visit a crowdfunding site? Second, given the effects on individual donors, what are the consequences of the return rule for a site as a whole when these individual donations are aggregated? Specifically, does the return rule affect the ability of a site to fund projects and the efficiency with which this is accomplished?

CSCW'14, February 15–19, 2014, Baltimore, Maryland, USA.

http://dx.doi.org/10.1145/2531602.2531678

[1] `http://www.kickstarter.com/projects/anomalisa/charlie-kaufmans-anomalisa`

In this paper, we show that the return rule increases donors' willingness to donate. We also show that the return rule leads donors to donate according to their preferences rather than focusing on the projects that are more likely to be funded. These effects on individual donors have two consequences for a crowdfunding site. The increase in donations helps the site produce more projects. However, the return rule simultaneously reduces donor coordination, causing donations to become spread out among more projects, including those with little chance of being completed. This *spread* largely offsets the gains in site productivity obtained from increased donations

We contribute to crowdfunding site design by experimentally demonstrating that the decision to use either a return rule or direct donation model affects both individual and site-level behavior and outcomes on a crowdfunding site. We also demonstrate the importance of designing crowdfunding sites not only to solicit more donations from the crowd, but also designing to facilitate coordination among the crowd.

BACKGROUND

Crowdfunding

Crowdfunding is the act of soliciting, via an open call, resources from a wide variety of contributors in order to realize a new idea. Crowdfunding can be done in many ways – via an open call on one's webpage, through posting a notice in a public place, or through an organized online marketplace called a crowdfunding website. It is these online marketplaces that we are concerned with in this article.

A crowdfunding website is an online marketplace where users – who we call project creators – can post ideas for projects (art projects, businesses, bands, classroom exercises, etc.) and other users – donors – can contribute small amounts of money toward funding those projects. By aggregating large numbers of small-amount contributions, these sites enable project creators to raise funding for a wide variety of projects.

Crowdfunding websites are a relatively new phenomenon; Modern Internet technologies enable crowdfunding because they permit low-cost, centralized advertising of project ideas, secure and trustworthy contribution to those projects, and simultaneous solicitation by a large number of projects. Recent years have seen the rise of a wide variety of crowdfunding websites [8], including Kickstarter (which funds creative projects), IndieGoGo (which funds a wide variety of ideas and new businesses), Spot.Us (which funds investigative journalism), Sellaband (which funds musicians) and Donors Choose (which funds K–12 classroom projects).

Project creators sometimes solicit purely altruistic donations, but often creators offer something in exchange for donation. These exchanges fall into three categories: rewards, product pre-orders, and equity. Rewards are usually small tokens of appreciation that are attached to different levels of contribution, such as an acknowledgement at the end of a crowdfunded movie, or thank you letters from students who used crowdfunded supplies in their classroom. Product pre-orders are contributions that effectively "pre-order" a product, to be delivered at a later date. Product pre-orders are an effective way to raise initial capital to create a new product. Equity is currently relatively rare as a crowdfunding exchange in the US, though the recent JOBS act (H.R. 3606, 2012) explicitly legalized using crowdfunding for equity exchanges. The various crowdfunding websites have differing levels of support for each of the types of exchange.

In addition to the explicit exchange, crowdfunding almost always includes some amount of public good being funded. For product pre-orders, the public good being funded is the ability to purchase a product on the open market, as the product won't exist without startup capital. For example, the TikTok iPod Nano wristwatch that was famously funded on Kickstarter needed a minimum order size for the factory to be able to produce the watches. In more altruistic marketplaces like Donors Choose or Spot.Us, the public good is a more traditional public good such as news or education. Indeed, Belleflamme et al.[5] argue that in the absence of any public good aspect, crowdfunding theoretically "yields exactly the same outcome as seeking money from a bank or equity investor." In other words, the primary reason that someone would prefer crowdfunding as a method of raising capital is because of the public good aspects of what is being produced.

Project creators choose to use crowdfunding websites to raise capital for a number of reasons. Gerber et al. [7] identify six reasons beyond the obvious reason of needing capital: expanding awareness of one's work, maintaining creative control over the outcome, measuring supporter interest in the project, making longer-term connections with customers, gaining approval and confidence in the project, and to learn more about business and fundraising. Belleflame et al. [5] find that, at least when offering product pre-orders via crowdfunding, it is the high-value customers that are most likely to contribute to a crowdfunding project, thus suggesting that the connections made with customers through crowdfunding are likely to be high-value.

Many crowdfunded projects are discrete goods, for which there is no or little value if insufficient funds are raised. Products cannot be manufactured without enough capital to fund a production run. Films cannot be made without necessary equipment. Classroom projects cannot be completed without supplies for all students. The design of many crowdfunding sites may be appealing to these types of projects because they are focused around achieving target amounts. There has been some speculation that these type of discrete goods that can't use partial funds are better for sites that use a return rule, while more continuously funded goods like operating capital for a charity are better funded on sites that use a direct donation model.

Projects posted on crowdfunding websites have a surprisingly high likelihood of being funded. 43–47% of projects on Kickstarter are fully funded [12, 10]; 43.5% of projects on Spot.Us are fully funded [9], and almost 70% of projects on Donors Choose are fully funded [20]. Mollick [12] uses data from Kickstarter to find that projects are more likely to be successful if they ask for smaller amounts of money, they are created by someone with a large social network, are higher quality projects to start with (as indicated by the presence of a video), and fit in with the culture of the city the creator lives in (such as music projects in Nashville, TN or film projects in Los Angeles, CA).

People donate to crowdfunding projects irrespective of geography [1], though friends and family are often the initial donors that provide the first contributions [18]. Using qualitative interviews, Gerber et al. [7] find five motivations for people who contribute to crowdfunding projects: collecting rewards, helping others achieve their goals, supporting like-minded people, being part of a community, and supporting a cause. Confirming this with empirical data, Shin and Jian [18] find that people who find contributing fun, or who like contributing to friends and family contribute the most money to crowdfunded projects.

Complementarities and Coordination

Coordinating the decisions and actions of a large group of people is an important challenge in the design of crowdfunding, as well as many other forms of socio-technical systems. One of the things that complicates coordination in socio-technical systems is the presence of *complementarities* in the preferences or interests of individuals within the crowd. A complementarity occurs when an individual has a preference for some decision or outcome that depends on the preferences or decisions of others. For example, a visitor to a crowdfunding site may prefer a project and want to donate only if there are enough others that donate that the project can be completed. If the project cannot be completed, the visitor may prefer not to donate.

Complementarities can make it difficult for a group to successfully coordinate their actions to produce the best possible outcome. Economists studying Market Design have worked to develop algorithms that effectively coordinate the preferences of many individuals [15]. For example, this work has been used to design an algorithm that matches medical interns to hospital positions, taking into account both the preferences of the hospitals and the interns [16].

Complementarities can disrupt coordination by such algorithms. For example, when couples began graduating from medical school together, the individuals in these couples preferred positions near wherever their partner received a position. This created a complementarity in the preferences of the interns that led to an unraveling of the medical intern market [14]. The algorithm became unable to match interns to positions such that nobody wanted to ignore the decision of the algorithm. That is to say, the algorithm was no longer able to produce *stable* matches of interns to hospitals. However, Roth and Sotomayor [17] demonstrated a solution to this problem that works as long as complementarities are the exception rather than the norm in the market.

Socio-technical systems, including crowdfunding systems, often involve complementarities. For example, a person may only be interested in participating in an online community if she thinks others will also participate. Or a person may not want to provide an answer to a crowdsourced question if he thinks that there are many others who can provide the answer, but if nobody else will answer, he would prefer to answer the question. Additionally, many socio-technical systems are designed for self-coordination, where users make the best decisions they can about what to do or how to contribute based on the information they have. This is logical given that the number of complementarities in such systems likely makes the algorithmic approach to coordination excessively difficult.

We are interested here in whether the design of the rules of a socio-technical system, in this case a crowdfunding site, can influence the ability of users to self-coordinate. The nature of most crowdfunding projects as threshold goods creates complementarities in the preferences of users of that site. For example, a visitor to the site who sees a project for a new product she is interested in would only want to donate as long as the there are enough others who donate that the product can be produced. In order to achieve the goal of producing the product, all donors with similar preferences must coordinate their actions.

Threshold Public Goods

Many crowdfunding projects are examples of threshold public goods as described by Bagnoli and McKee [4]. A public good is anything that benefits everyone (no one can be excluded from benefits) and also does not get completely used up when it is used (i.e. its use is non-rivalrous). Most public goods grow in size and benefit with additional funds; additional funding to the army helps everyone be better protected. Threshold public goods, though, have a minimum threshold of funding necessary to receive any benefit. For example, if a bridge project has insufficient funding, then no bridge is built.

Threshold public goods are frequently studied using experimental economics and game theory. Threshold public goods games ask subjects to make donations to a group account, and if donations exceed a given threshold, all members of the group earn an additional payout. Bagnoli and Lipman [3] prove that in a threshold public goods game, any outcome where the sum of all contributions is exactly equal to the threshold required for producing the good is both a Nash Equilibrium and a Pareto Efficient outcome of the game, suggesting that it can be rational for individuals to contribute to threshold public goods. Unfortunately, other equilibria also exist which are not efficient. Particularly, there exists a strong free-riding equilibrium in threshold public goods games wherein nobody contributes to the good and therefore the good is not created. This multiplicity of equilibria means it is difficult to predict from theory alone what outcomes to expect when a group of individuals has an opportunity to contribute to a threshold public good.

Cadsby and Maynes [6] conducted a series of threshold public goods experiments which varied the size of the threshold for the good, the size of the reward for funding the good, the type of contribution allowable (continuous vs. discrete), and whether or not contributions would be refunded if the threshold was not met. In their experiments, higher rewards and allowing continuous contributions led to higher donations and more frequent funding of the public good. They also found that goods with a higher threshold received less contribution. However, they found that offering refunds when the threshold was not met increased the likelihood of reaching the threshold, particularly when the threshold was high.

This refund mechanism is analogous to the return rule in crowdfunding sites, so we expect that crowdfunding websites using the return rule will be more successful at generating contributions to projects. But crowdfunding websites are markets for multiple public goods that are simultaneously soliciting contributions from potential donors who visit the site. The presence of multiple goods simultaneously introduces a necessity for coordination that has not been examined in the existing literature on threshold public goods.

A BRIEF THEORY OF CROWDFUNDING SITE DESIGN

Crowdfunding markets are not guaranteed to have a stable match. Consider a market with 3 donors A, B, and C, and three projects 1, 2, 3. Each project has the the same preference: It needs donations from any two donors to succeed, but weakly prefers zero donors to having only one contribute. This is a complementary preference; one donor is not valued unless accompanied by another and therefore donors are complements. Now, assume the donors have the following preferences over projects:

$$\begin{aligned} A&: \quad 1 > 2 > 3 \\ B&: \quad 2 > 3 > 1 \\ C&: \quad 3 > 1 > 2 \end{aligned}$$

Given the preference against having only one donor contribute, only one project can possibly be matched to donors. However, no matter which project is matched to the donors, the two donors who don't list that project as their top choice have an incentive to defect and fund a different project. This means that no matter which project is matched to donors, the match is not stable. Thus, **crowdfunding websites do not always have a stable outcome**, and certainly there does not exist any mechanism that always produces a stable matching.

The presence of multiple simultaneous threshold public goods also creates new inefficiencies not seen in previous threshold public goods. In the example above, each donor might choose to contribute only to his or her top choice, hoping someone else will follow their lead. In that case, even though 3 people contributed, no project is funded because the donors spread out their donations among too many projects. Therefore, **crowdfunding websites can fail to fund projects even when there are sufficient donations and donor interest**. Designing a crowdfunding website to increase contributions isn't enough; donations need to be *coordinated* to fund as many projects as possible.

EXPERIMENT SETUP

The return rule is an innovation from industry that may or may not help crowdfunding websites overcome these theoretical challenges. To understand how the return rule affects contributions and funding of projects on crowdfunding sites, we simulated a crowdfunding site using a threshold public goods game similar to the games reported by Bagnoli and Lipman [4] and Cadsby and Maynes [6].

The public goods in our game were presented as projects on a crowdfunding site which were each requesting a minimum of 400 credits. Unlike previous threshold public goods experiments, our simulation involved multiple projects which simultaneously requested contributions from the public.

Table 1. The payout structure for each participant for each project

Subject	Low Risk	Medium Risk	High Risk	Unfundable
1	200	150	100	50
2	50	200	150	100
3	100	50	200	150
4	150	100	50	200
5	200	100	150	50
6	50	150	100	200

The experiment was designed to simulate three important tensions that can exist in a crowdfunding market. First, projects generally need more than one donor to achieve their funding goal. Second, not all projects can be funded and each donor has separate preferences; this simulates the coordination problem faced by the site as a whole. Third, projects differ in the risk of not being funded; donors who must choose between donating according to their preferences and donating according to the funding risk. These three tensions are all sources of potential inefficiency in a crowdfunding market.

Crowdfunding game

The crowdfunding simulation involved six players simultaneously making contributions to four fictional projects. Each player was given an endowment of 150 credits which could be allocated in any way among the four projects. Players could also keep some or all of the credits.

Subjects receive the payout described in Table 1 for each of the projects if that project receives its goal of 400 credits donated. Subjects receive their payout regardless of whether they contributed to the project; this reflects the public goods nature of the projects, and also provides an incentive to free-ride. At the end of the experiment, subjects exchange credits for cash.

Donors on real crowdfunding sites can have many reasons to prefer some projects over others, including an explicit reward, personal relevance, or a feeling of warm glow. In this experiment, we use the payouts to represent and induce preferences over the projects. Vernon Smith showed that in an experimental setting, paying subjects different amounts of real money for acquiring fake goods can induce those subjects to prefer one good over another, with the higher-payout good being more highly preferred [19]. His Induced Value theory [19] suggests that payouts such as ours can induce preferences in public goods experiments, even when the differences in payouts are very small. Since we are only interested how donors behave once they have formed their preferences, and not in the process of forming preferences for crowdfunding projects, we chose our payouts based on Induced Value Theory such that subjects will prefer the project they are supposed to prefer by being offered a higher payout for its completion.

All projects requested 400 credits. However, in order to simulate variation in risk between different crowdfunding projects,

Table 2. Details of the four different projects

	Amount Needed	Seed Funding	Probability of Being Funded
Low Risk	400	300	88%
Medium Risk	400	200	72%
High Risk	400	100	13%
Unfundable	400	0	0%

The different seed levels induced different levels of risk. In the experiment, the projects were given uninformative names. The probability of being funded is the frequency that each project was funded in the experiment.

we seeded varying amounts into the projects. This created four types of projects; a low-risk project, a medium risk project, a high risk project, and an unfundable project (Table 2). The seed funding did induce different levels of risk, as represented by the actual probability of being funded in Table 2.

Projects vary in riskiness, and donors vary in which projects they prefer. This creates a tension for donors, and the best decision isn't obvious. Even though the collective potential payouts for each project are equal (750 credits), some donors prefer high risk projects and must choose between donating according to their preferences, risking failure, and donating to low risk projects for a lower payout.

Experimental Conditions

The crowdfunding game is played under two conditions. In the direct contribution condition, all donations to projects are final and participants lose their contribution regardless of whether the project to which it was made reaches the funding threshold. In the return rule condition, any contributions made to a project that does not reach its funding threshold are refunded to participants.

These two conditions result in two different payoff functions of the game. P is the set of all contributions (including contributions of zero) made by a player to each project. F is the set of contributions made by the player to projects which were funded. R is the set of rewards earned by the player from funded projects. ϵ is the initial endowment of 150 credits given to each player. Equation 1 gives the function for the payoff (π) in the direct donation condition, in which donations to all projects are subtracted from the total payout. Equation 2 gives the function under the the return rule, where only contributions to funded projects are subtracted.

$$\pi = \epsilon + \sum_{r \in R} r - \sum_{p \in P} p \qquad (1)$$

$$\pi = \epsilon + \sum_{r \in R} r - \sum_{f \in F} f \qquad (2)$$

Participants

We recruited a random sample of undergraduate students from our university through an email from the registrar to participate in the study.

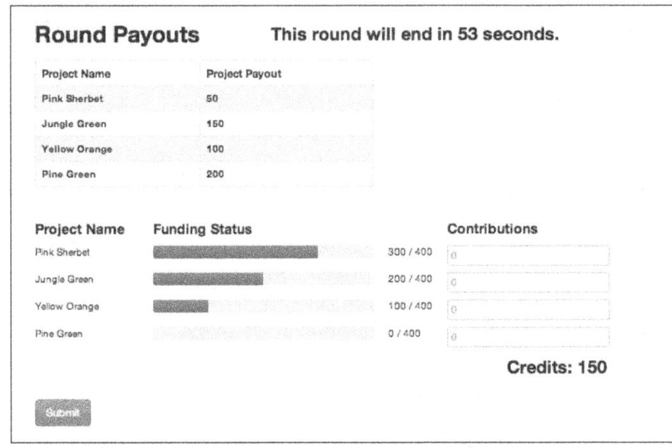

Figure 1. Crowdfunding simulation donation screen

The email promised $5 for signing up and showing up to the study, and an additional reward based on their performance and the performance of others in the experiment, with an expected average of $20 for participating. 4% of students contacted responded to the email, and a total of 168 participants were scheduled to participate in 14 experimental sessions (8 sessions under the return rule and 6 under direct donation).

Participants were 48% female with a median age of 20. This is equivalent to the demographics of the undergraduate population at our university from which we recruited participants, and so we do not suspect that our recruiting methods were biased.

Only 18% of participants had ever visited a crowdfunding website before, and only one participant had ever created a project on a crowdfunding site before. Because participants were generally unfamiliar with crowdfunding, we do not suspect that previous experience with crowdfunding sites would have influenced participants' behavior in the game.

Experiment Procedure

Each experimental session involved 12 players playing under a single experimental condition (return rule or direct donation). Each session consisted of 18 rounds of the game. In each round, the 12 players were randomly divided into two groups of six, and players were never aware of which other players were in their group in a given round. This follows the procedure used by [2] to prevent players from learning their partners' strategies in a public goods game.

In each round, participants were given a different set of preferences (see Table 2). Over the 18 rounds, each participant was assigned each of the six unique preferences three times.

Figure 1 shows the interface for the crowdfunding simulation. The interface provided participants with all necessary information and enforced the rules and timing of the game. All donors make their donations simultaneously. To help players learn the game, a detailed summary was provided at the end of each round that displayed the outcome of the round and a detailed calculation of the player's payout (see Figure 2).

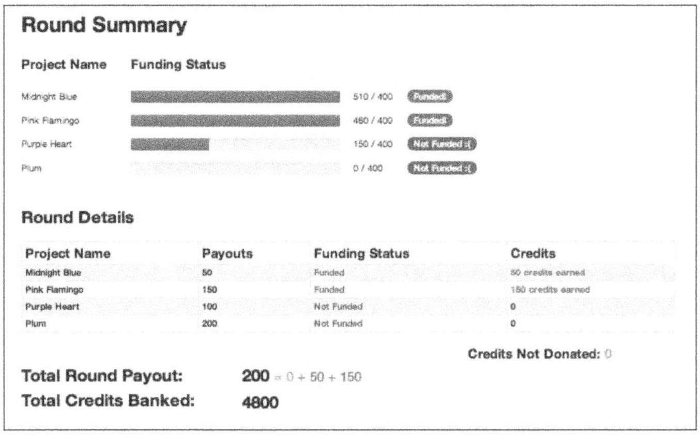

Figure 2. Crowdfunding simulation round summary screen

Table 3. Perceptions of risk for each project

	Return Rule		*Direct Donation*	
Project	Mean	(SD)	Mean	(SD)
Low risk	1.97	(1.36)	1.64	(0.83)
Medium risk	3.43	(1.00)	3.33	(0.80)
High risk	4.82	(1.08)	5.40	(0.80)
Unfundable	5.89	(1.99)	6.82	(0.78)

Manipulation Checks

After the game, we verified participants' understanding of the rules of the game in a short questionnaire.

20% of participants gave at least one incorrect answer. 10% did not understand the return rule (or lack of return rule). 12% did not know how many other donors were in their group. 7% of participants did not understand that others had different preferences for projects. Overall, participants appeared to understand the rules of structure of the game at the end, but there was not perfect comprehension of the game and it is possible that some results are skewed as a result.

We further verified in the questionnaire that participants interpreted the variation in seed credits among the four projects as variation in risk as was intended. Participants clearly interpreted projects with fewer seed credits as being more risky in both conditions (see Table 3). Thus, we are satisfied that the seed credits created the desired perception of risk for the projects.

RESULTS

Return Rule Increases Donations to High-Risk Projects

Table 4. Donations Decisions

	Direct Donation	*Return Rule*
Donation Amount	91	122
Donated Budget	27%	59%
# Projects Donated To	1.87	2.37

Donation amount is the average number of credits donated in a round by a subject. Donated budget is the proportion of donations decisions where the subject donated all 150 credits they were allocated.

Table 6. Donations Correlations

	Direct Donation	*Return Rule*
Payouts and Donations	0.34	0.50
Risk and Donations	0.41	0.16

Donor's average correlation between donations to projects and either payouts or riskiness of projects. Wilcoxon rank sum tests found that both differences between conditions were statistically significant ($p < .001$).

Logically, the return rule should reduce the risk to donors involved in contributing to crowdfunding projects. If a project doesn't receive enough funding, then your money is returned and you are no worse off than if you hadn't donated. Taken to its logical extreme, this argument predicts that subjects will donate all of their 150 credits in the return rule condition.

On average, people donated approximately 30 credits more under the return rule (Table 4). However, subjects in the return rule condition only donated an average of 121 out of their 150 credit budget, and only 60% of the time did they donate their full budget.

Even under the return rule, there is some risk; credits donated above what was requested are effectively lost. Also, because the return rule reduces risk, high-risk projects will seem less risky. For these two reasons, we expected more and larger donations to higher-risk projects.

The return rule had very little effect on the low-risk and medium-risk projects. However, it over doubled the total contributions made to the high-risk and unfundable projects, and over doubled the number of people donating to those projects (Table 5). When people donate, however, they donate similar amounts in both the direct donation and return rule conditions.

We also found that each donor on average donated to about 0.5 more projects under the return rule. The return rule caused donors to spread their donations out among a larger percentage of projects on the site. A Wilcoxon rank sum test confirmed that this difference was statistically significant.

The Return Rule Favors Individual's Preferences

The experiment created a tension for each donor between their personal preferences for projects (as induced by the payouts) and the amount of risk involved in donating (as manipulated by the seed credits). This tension was particularly evident when subjects had higher preferences for riskier projects.

We calculated the average correlation coefficient for each donor between his or her payouts for each project and donations to each project. We wanted to see if donors would generally donate more to projects with higher payouts and less to projects with lower payouts, and whether this would differ for return rule donors from direct donation donors. Table 6 describes these results. We found that under the return rule, there was a higher correlation between payouts and donations than under direct donation.

Similarly, for each donor we calculated the average correlation coefficient between donations and the amount of risk in

Table 5. Contributions to Each Project

	Total Contributions			Number of Donors			Average Donation		
	Direct Donation		Return Rule	Direct Donation		Return Rule	Direct Donation		Return Rule
Low Risk	166		161	4.07		4.13	41.5		39.5
Medium Risk	245		237	4.39		4.55	56.3	*	52.9
High Risk	102	*	226	1.75	*	3.69	62.7		62.2
Unfundable	33	*	108	0.71	*	1.84	48.1	*	60.3

Statistically significant differences ($p < 0.01$) from a Wilcoxon rank sum test between experimental conditions are marked with a *.

projects, as operationalized by the number of seed credits. Higher donations to projects with more seed credits would indicate stronger risk-based donating behavior. There was a higher correlation between risk and donations under direct donation than under the return rule.

Together, these findings show that direct donation leads crowdfunding donors to coordinate; they base their donation choices more on the relative risk between projects than on their actual preferences for projects. On the other hand, the return rule leads users to donate more in line with their own preferences with less adherence to the riskiness of projects. The riskiness of projects is a shared characteristic– all donors see the same risk in projects. Preferences are an individual characteristic– each donor has unique payoffs. Thus, by emphasizing the importance of the projects shared characteristic, direct donation leads users to coordinate around that characteristic.

Site-Level Outcomes are Mixed

Crowdfunding by definition aggregates the behavior and money of many individuals to fund multiple projects. As we illustrated above, simply receiving more donations doesn't necessarily lead to more projects being funded. The aggregate effects of the return rule on the marketplace are complicated, but important for site designers. In Table 7, we evaluate four market-level effects of the return rule.

Donors funded an average of 0.17 more projects per round under the return rule than under direct donation. While this difference is statistically significant, it is nonetheless a fairly modest increase given that contributions to the higher risk projects doubled under the return rule. As a result, there was a loss in efficiency under the return rule: Donations provided an 83% return on investment to donors for each credit donated under the return rule, compared to a 126% return on investment for direct donation.

This lack of efficiency can be characterized in two other ways. As noted above, donors individually *spread* their donations to more projects under the return rule. We operationalize spread using the Gini coefficient. The Gini coefficient is normally used to measure income inequality in a population, but here we use it to measure donation inequality across projects. A market is more spread out if the contributions to projects are more equal. Collectively, we found that the aggregated donations were more evenly spread out among projects under the return rule; the Gini coefficient is much smaller (0.16) under the return rule than under direct donation.

Table 7. Site-level outcomes

	Direct Donation	*Return Rule*
# Projects Funded	1.63	1.80
Gini Coefficient	0.39	0.23
Return on Investment	126%	83%
Uncoordinated Rounds	30%	60%

For the Gini coefficient, 0 means equal contributions to all projects, and 1 means all of the money is concentrated on a single project. Uncoordinated rounds are the percentage of rounds where the total donations to unfunded projects were enough to fund at least one more project. All comparisons are statistically significant ($p < 0.02$) from a Wilcoxon rank sum test.

This loss in efficiency when a site uses the return rule is due to a lack of coordination among donors. Under the return rule, in 60% of all rounds, the donations made to unfunded projects were sufficient to fund at least one more project had the donors coordinated their donations on a single project rather than spreading them among multiple projects. Under direct donation, only 30% of rounds could have funded additional projects. This lack of coordination offsets much of the gain made by the return rule through increased total donations.

The overall effect of the return rule is difficult to determine. First, subjects might be donating anew to higher risk projects, but not changing their low-risk donations. This basically means that the return rule only affects the likelihood of donation, but not the amount of donation. Second, subjects may spread all their money out across more projects, but choose to increase the total donated, offsetting the changes in donation amounts to existing projects. Both effects of the return rule — increased total donation amount and decreased donations due to spread — affect donation amounts. Our experiment is not able to distinguish between these two explanations.

Without the Return Rule, People Learn to Only Fund Low Risk Projects

Our experiment asked subjects to play this simulated crowdfunding game repeatedly. This allows us to examine how subjects learned what strategies were effective. Subjects' ability to learn over repeated rounds and collectively improve performance is another indicator of coordination on a crowdfunding site.

The return rule condition did not exhibit much learning; the number of donors to each project and the average amount

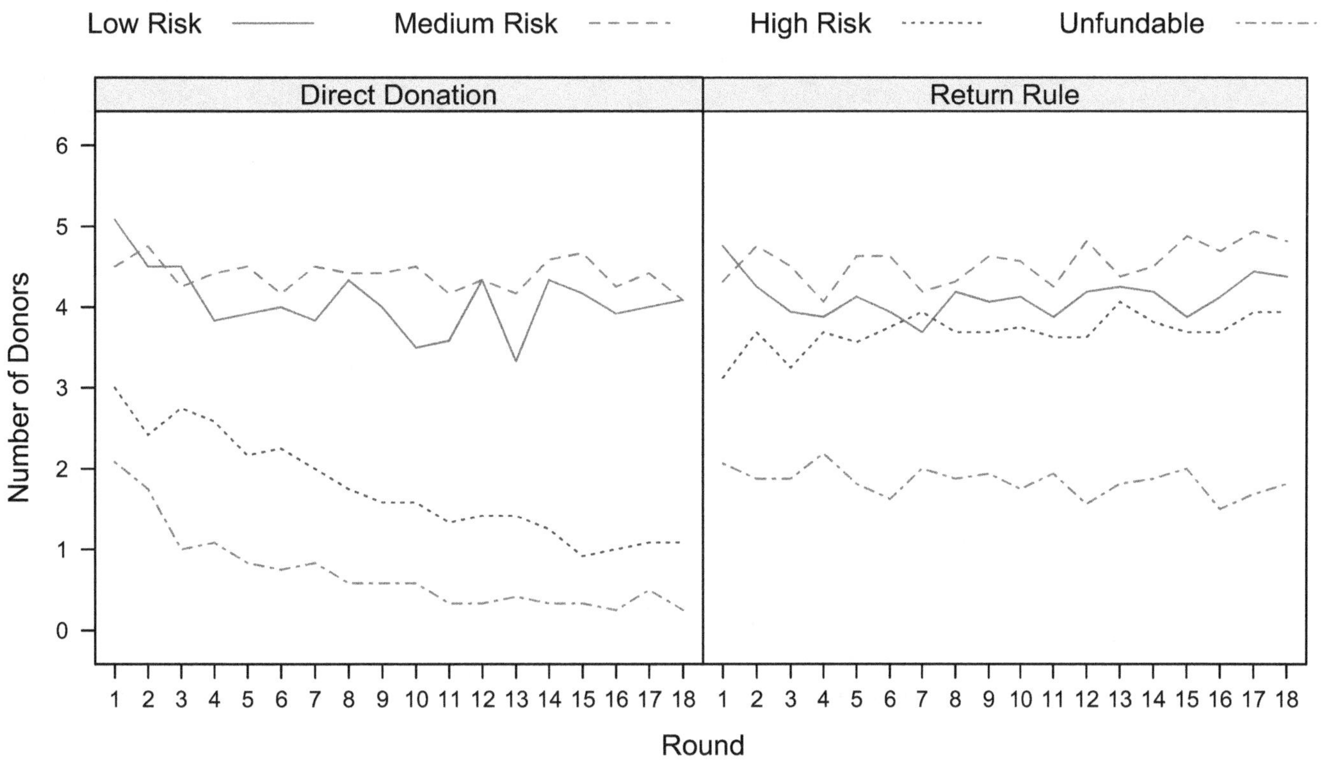

Figure 3. Number of donors who contribute to each project, by round. The left panel is for the Direct Donation condition. The right panel is for the Return Rule condition.

contributed to each project remained fairly stable over the course of the 18 rounds. The right sides of Figures 3 and 4 show little trend over time. Subjects did appear to learn to contribute more to the high-risk project, with the average contribution increasing from 25.8 in the first round to 40.6 in the last.

However, the direct donation condition did exhibit noticeable learning. Subjects appear to be learning not to donate to the high risk and unfundable projects. The number of subjects donating to the high risk project averages 3.0 in the first round, and decreases to 1.08 in the last round. Likewise, the number of subjects donating to the unfundable project averages 2.08 in the first round, and decreases to 0.25 in the last round. Average contribution amount shows a similar decrease.

We conclude that the direct donation condition helped donors learn over time to coordinate their donations on only those projects with a high likelihood of being funded. Under the return rule, donors did not learn to coordinate as the experiment went on and generally maintained a consistent behavior throughout.

DISCUSSION

The main goal of this study was to examine the effect that the all-or-nothing return rule has on a crowdfunding marketplace, relative to a direct donation model. We found that this rule has two distinct effects on the way individual donors make contributions to projects. These two individual-level effects lead to two important market-level outcomes that influence the efficiency of the market in opposite directions.

First, under the return rule, individual donors are more willing to contribute money to projects, and in particular high-risk projects, leading to an overall increase in donations. Second, the available donations are more spread out over more projects. Increased spread in the market makes it more difficult for each project to achieve its goal, and can potentially lead to fewer projects being funded. These two effects appear to approximately offset in our experimental setting, leading to a very small efficiency gain when using the return rule.

When donors use a direct donation system, they seem to learn to coordinate on low-risk projects that are highly likely to be funded. This implicit coordination makes it relatively easy to fund low-risk projects and also leads to a higher return (in terms of the value of the newly produced public good) on each donation. In this experiment, the risk inherent in the projects, largely due to complementarities inherent in projects that need a certain amount of funding to succeed, appears to have served as a coordination device.

On the other hand, in a return rule system, there was much less coordination among donors. Donors seem to feel like it is safe to donate to any project, since they get their money back if the project doesn't achieve its funding goal. The return rule, therefore, eliminated much of the incentive to coordinate with other donors about which projects are being funded. This is

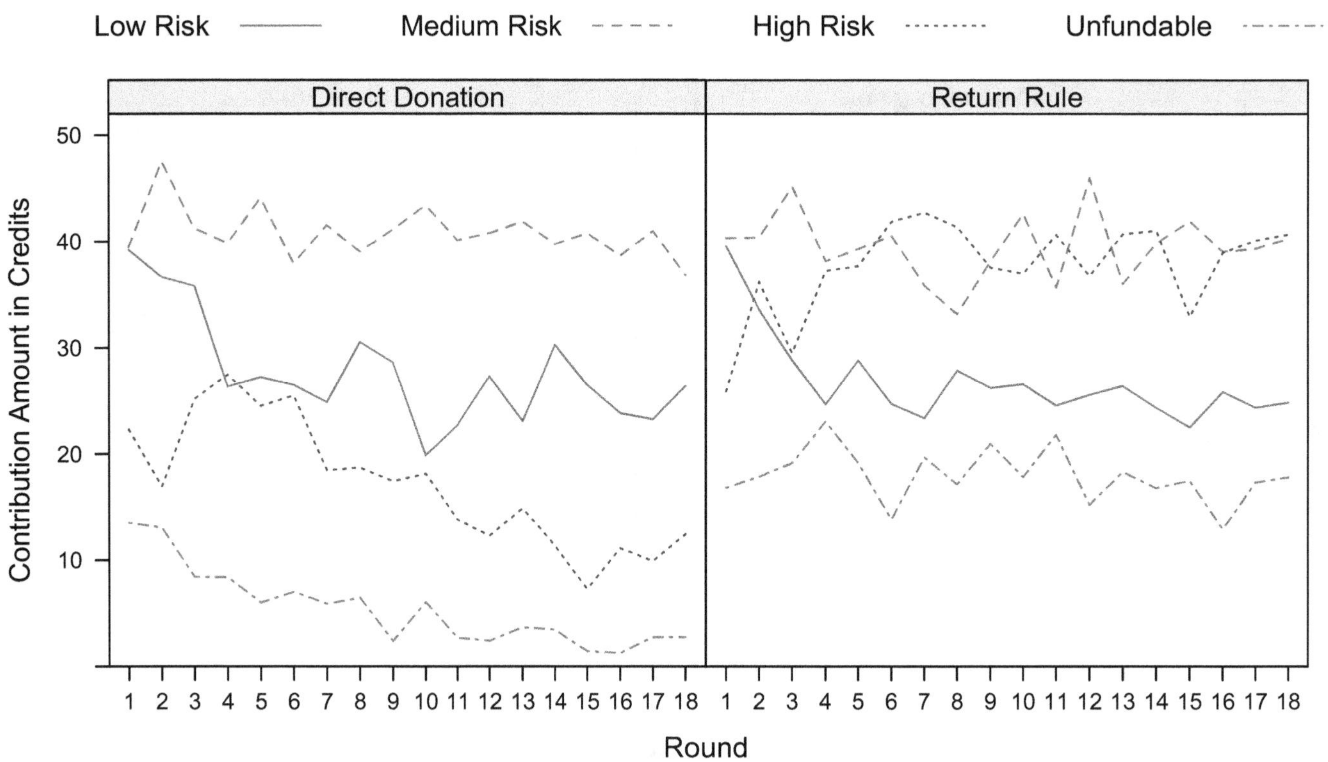

Figure 4. Average contribution to a project by round.The left panel is for the Direct Donation condition. The right panel is for the Return Rule condition.

why we saw an increased spread in donations; donors were focused more on the projects they preferred and less on solving the coordination problem.

These findings have implications for market designers working to design better crowdfunding systems. First, they suggest that there isn't a clear answer whether using an all-or-nothing return rule or using a direct donation rule is better. If the marketplace has a large number of projects simultaneously seeking support, the return rule has the risk that donors will spread out their donations, leading to many donations but low funding rates for projects. On the other hand, if projects are largely undifferentiated (so there is nothing to coordinate on) or if many projects are seen as high risk, then the increased donations that result from the return rule might enable the market to fund more projects.

Additionally, if the goal of the marketplace is to fund high-risk high-reward projects, the return rule is more likely to succeed. If the goal of the marketplace is to weed out high-risk projects and focus donor attention on projects with a high likelihood of success, using a direct donation mechanism might work better.

On a crowdfunding website, whether a project is able to successfully raise the funds it needs is a complex proposition. Mollick [13] suggests that project success is largely a function of the team of people working on the project, much like how venture capitalists fund traditional startup companies. Both Shin and Jian [18] and Gerber et al. [7] suggest that how hard a project's creator works to fund the project also plays an important role. Our results suggest that the marketplace also has a surprisingly strong influence; other projects available on the crowdfunding website can draw money away, and the structure of the website (return rule vs. direct donation) can also affect the likelihood of being funded.

Increasingly we are seeing crowdfunding websites that offer project creators a choice — on the same website, they can either offer their project as a direct donation project or as a return rule project. For example, IndieGoGo recently changed from a direct donation marketplace to one where each project gets to choose. Our results would suggest that higher risk projects should choose to be offered under a return rule. On the other hand, projects that can benefit from coordination and a strong word-of-mouth should probably choose direct donation, as that provides a stronger incentive for donors to coordinate and spread the word.

Our work also highlights an interesting tension that appears in the design of many groupware systems. There are design options like the return rule that can help people work more independently; these designs are a double-edges sword. By making the work easier, it encourages people to do more work overall. But they also remove the incentive to coordinate their work with others, which may lead to groups failing because the work didn't fit together well enough. This is sometimes seen on Wikipedia, for example. Wikipedia makes independent editing of articles easy, which encourages editors to work. However, sometimes that means that the articles feel disjointed and are written in different styles or tones, or are self-contradictory [11].

Limitations

There are a few important limitations to this study that should be considered. First, not all crowdfunded projects are necessarily threshold goods. Some projects could still benefit from even insufficient donations, and may be better classified as continuous goods. However, we believe such projects are generally the minority of crowdfunded projects. If continuous goods represented a strong majority of crowdfunded projects, we would expect that there would be little reason to even consider a return rule mechanism.

A second limitation is that the simultaneous nature of donations in our experiment differs from real crowdfunding sites, where donations are made sequentially. We did this to adhere to the public goods game framework and to avoid an additional variable that would have added complexity to the experiment. However, we believe this is an important variable that demands further research. The risk involved in donating to a crowdfunding project may be different depending on how much time is left for the project to meet its goal. It may be riskier, for instance, to donate on the first day than the last because the likelihood of the target being successful is less clear. Thus, the return rule could have the effect of soliciting more donations early in a project's timeline. We hope to explore this question in future extensions of this research.

CONCLUSION

Crowdfunding websites like Kickstarter, IndieGoGo, Donors Choose, and Spot.Us pose an interesting challenge for system designers. They are matching marketplaces, matching people who have ideas for projects with donors willing to contribute money to those projects. But they have a strong inherent complementarity in the market structure: multiple donors are needed to fund a project, and the project often cannot succeed without full funding. Complementaries such as this cause theoretical problems for market designers; matching markets with complementarities frequently do not have stable equilibria, and regularly have problems with market failure or market inefficiency.

There are two major strategies that existing crowdfunding websites have used to deal with this problem: allow direct donations to projects (used by IndieGoGo), or use an all-or-nothing return rule that returns donations if a project doesn't achieve its goal (used by Kickstarter). We conducted an experimental study of these two mechanisms to better understand how these strategies enable matching markets with complementaries to function.

We find that each of these two mechanisms has distinct strengths and weaknesses. Direct donations provide an incentive for donors to coordinate to solve the complementarity problem, and are more likely to fully fund projects even when total donations in the marketplace are small. The return rule encourages people to donate to more projects and to higher risk projects, but has the potential of spreading out contributions among too many projects, causing few of them to reach their goal. Both mechanisms appear to be viable means for partially solving the complementarity problem in matching marketplaces.

ACKNOWLEDGEMENTS

The authors would like to thank Kyle Safran for his help designing and running this experiment. The authors would also like to thank Jan Boehmer and the whole BITLab Lab Group for feedback. This material is based upon work supported by the National Science Foundation under Grant No. CCF-1101266.

REFERENCES

1. Agrawal, A., Catalini, C., and Goldfarb, A. The geography of crowdfunding. NBER Working Paper #16820, February 2011.
2. Andreoni, J. Why free ride?: Strategies and learning in public goods experiments. *Journal of Public Economics 37*, 3 (1988), 291 – 304.
3. Bagnoli, M., and Lipman, B. L. Provision of public goods: Fully implementing the core through private contributions. *The Review of Economic Studies 56*, 4 (1989), pp. 583–601.
4. Bagnoli, M., and McKee, M. Voluntary contribution games: Efficient private provision of public goods. *Economic Inquiry 29*, 2 (April 1991), 351—366.
5. Belleflamme, P., Lambert, T., and Schwienbacher, A. Crowdfunding: Tapping the right crowd. Tech. Rep. 1578175, Social Science Research Network (SSRN), April 2012.
6. Cadsby, C. B., and Maynes, E. Voluntary provision of threshold public goods with continuous contributions: experimental evidence. *Journal of Public Economics 71*, 1 (1999), 53 – 73.
7. Gerber, E., Hui, J., and Kuo, P.-Y. Crowdfunding: Why people are motivated to participate. Tech. Rep. 12-02, Northwestern University Segal Design Institute, 2012.
8. Greenberg, M., and Gerber, E. Crowdfunding: A survey and taxonomy. Tech. Rep. 12-03, Northwestern University Segal Design Institute, 2012.
9. Jian, L., and Usher, N. Crowd-funded journalism. *Journal of Computer Mediated Communication* (2013). (Forthcoming).
10. Kickstarter. Statistics. `http://www.kickstarter.com/help/stats`, December 2013.
11. Kittur, A., and Kraut, R. Harnessing the wisdom of crowds in wikipedia: Quality through coordination. In *Proceedings of Computer Supported Cooperative Work (CSCW)*, ACM Press (New York, New York, USA, 2008).
12. Mollick, E. The dynamics of crowdfunding: Determinants of success and failure. Tech. Rep. 2088298, Social Science Research Network (SSRN), July 2012.

13. Mollick, E. Swept away by the crowd? crowdfunding, venture capital, and the selection of entrepreneurs. Tech. rep., Social Science Research Network (SSRN), March 2013.

14. Roth, A., and Xing, X. Jumping the gun: Imperfections and institutions related to the timing of market transactions. *American Economic Review 84* (1994), 992–1044.

15. Roth, A. E. The Economist as Engineer: Game Theory, Experimentation, and Computation as Tools for Design Economics. *Econometrica 70*, 4 (2002), 1341–1378.

16. Roth, A. E., and Peranson, E. The redesign of the matching market for american physicians: Some engineering aspects of economic design. *American Economic Review 89*, 4 (September 1999), 748–780.

17. Roth, A. E., and Sotomayor, M. A. O. *Two-Sided Matching: A Study in Game-Theoretic Modeling and Analysis*. Cambridge University Press, 1990.

18. Shin, J., and Jian, L. Driving forces behind readers' donation to crowd-funded journalism: The case of spot.us. Working paper, University of Southern California, 2012.

19. Smith, V. L. Experimental economics: Induced value theory. *American Economic Review 66*, 2 (May 1976), 274–279.

20. Wash, R. The value of completing crowdfunding projects. In *International Conference on Weblogs and Social Media (ICWSM)*, AAAI Press (July 2013).

The Language that Gets People to Give: Phrases that Predict Success on Kickstarter

Tanushree Mitra
School of Interactive Computing
Georgia Institute of Technology
Atlanta, GA, USA
tmitra3@cc.gatech.edu

Eric Gilbert
School of Interactive Computing
Georgia Institute of Technology
Atlanta, GA, USA
gilbert@cc.gatech.edu

ABSTRACT
Crowdfunding sites like Kickstarter—where entrepreneurs and artists look to the internet for funding—have quickly risen to prominence. However, we know very little about the factors driving the "crowd" to take projects to their funding goal. In this paper we explore the factors which lead to successfully funding a crowdfunding project. We study a corpus of 45K crowdfunded projects, analyzing 9M phrases and 59 other variables commonly present on crowdfunding sites. The language used in the project has surprising predictive power—accounting for 58.56% of the variance around successful funding. A closer look at the phrases shows they exhibit general persuasion principles. For example, *also receive two* reflects the principle of *Reciprocity* and is one of the top predictors of successful funding. We conclude this paper by announcing the release of the predictive phrases along with the control variables as a public dataset, hoping that our work can enable new features on crowdfunding sites—tools to help both backers and project creators make the best use of their time and money.

Author Keywords
Crowdfunding; CMC; natural language processing (NLP)

ACM Classification Keywords
H.5.3. Group and Organization Interfaces; Asynchronous interaction; Web-based interaction

INTRODUCTION
Kickstarter is a crowdfunding website, a site where artists and entrepreneurs alike look to the internet for capital. At the time of this writing, a small startup called Pebble[1] is Kickstarter's most-funded project. An e-paper watch, Pebble only asked for $100K, but more than 18,000 people flocked to the idea and pledged a staggering $2.6M in just three days [31]. Yet, for every success story like Pebble, there is a failure like Ninja Baseball[2]. A PC game, Ninja Baseball was appealing enough to generate press attention [29], yet only attracted one-third of its requested $10K. As per Kickstarter's "all-or-nothing" funding rules, the Ninja Baseball team received no money.

Successful projects like Pebble have already raised over $300M on Kickstarter [30]. Furthermore, crowdfunding sites seem poised to rise to greater prominence soon. With President Obama's signing of the JOBS Act and its subsection the CROWDFUND ACT [7], industry observers expect several new crowdfunding sites to emerge very soon [13]. They will join prominent ones already on the internet, like StartSomeGood[3] and Flattr[4], in addition to crowdfunding platforms like Kickstarter, IndiGoGo and RocketHub.

While research in crowdfunding has recently gained attention in the HCI and CSCW communities [17, 21, 27, 35], we still know very little, for example, about what drives the "crowd" to take projects to their funding goals. What makes some projects like Pebble succeed while others, like Ninja Baseball, fail? In this paper, we look to answer this question. Results from our statistical model show that several project attributes (e.g., duration, presence of a video, etc.) have substantial predictive power, yielding a model with fairly high accuracy: 17.03% error under 10-fold cross-validation. We find, however, that the error-rate drops to 2.4% when we include the phrases used in the project's pitch—a non-random improvement over a strong null, controls-only model. This suggests that the language used by creators to pitch their project plays a major role in driving the project's success, accounting for 58.56% of the variance around success.

Adopting a corpus of 45K Kickstarter projects and natural language methods, we closely study 20K phrases, filtered from a corpus of 9M phrases. The aim is to see how they affect success on Kickstarter. Simultaneously, we control for 59 other variables commonly present on crowdfunding sites, like a project's goal amount, its duration and whether it has an associated video. Applying penalized logistic regression, we demonstrate the predictive power of phrases relative to these controls. Next, by comparing our phrase set with the Google 1T Corpus [5], we surface a more generalizable subset of phrases (i.e., phrases not specific to Kickstarter).

Taking a closer look at the words and phrases used in project pitches, we see general persuasion principles at work [10].

[1] `http://kck.st/OuioZA`
[2] `http://kck.st/Rb8ToC`
[3] `http://startsomegood.com`
[4] `http://flattr.com/`

CSCW'14, February 15–19, 2014, Baltimore, Maryland, USA.

ACM 978-1-4503-2540-0/14/02...$15.00.
http://dx.doi.org/10.1145/2531602.2531656

For example, the phrase *also receive two* (predicting a funded project), offers a favor in return for donating. In other words, this reflects *reciprocity* from the persuasion literature [10]. Reciprocity says that people tend to return a favor (donate money) after receiving one (gifts and offers). Another example is the phrase *given the chance*, promising something *scarce* to the funders. We are releasing these 20K phrases and their associated β weights as a public dataset.

We believe that the phrases dataset may enable new features on crowd-funding sites, such as tools to help backers and project creators make the best use of their time and money. For instance, a crowd-funding site might analyze the content of a project pitch while a project creator types it and notifies her whenever the words and phrases shift towards negative predictors. We see this work as particularly timely and important because crowdfunding provides small businesses a new way to access capital. Moreover, project creators can craft their language any way they see fit, as opposed to other indicators over which they have relatively little control, like social connections to influential people.

RELATED WORK

Here we provide an overview of related work in crowdfunding. Next we discuss work that adopts text analysis approaches similar to ours. Finally, we conclude this section by laying out work from the persuasion literature which we use to interpret our findings.

Dynamics of crowdfunding

Recent enthusiasm around crowdfunding startups has sparked some research to understand their properties. A qualitative study of the motivations behind crowdfunding shows that project creators use crowdfunding to spread awareness of their work and to receive online validation of their creativity [17]. This is in accordance with theories of self-efficacy which states that people's perception of their ability increases on receiving public recognition [2]. Other factors associated with crowd-funding initiatives are incentives to establish long-term relationships with funders, enjoyment in being part of a community [17] and an urge to keep control over one's projects [17, 24]. Similar results have also been reported by Ordanini et al.'s study of crowd-funding participants [36]. They found that for some participants the driving factor is social participation, or extending financial help and encouragement, while for others the motivation comes from the expectation of a monetary payoff [36] (see also [3]). These findings echo work on distinguishing intrinsic (e.g., enjoyment, involvement) and extrinsic (monetary rewards) motivations for funding [52].

Research on crowd-funding has also been extended to the enterprise level. Recent work on enterprise crowd-funding found that crowd-funding leads to enhanced inter-departmental collaboration and supports collective concerns over individual self-interest [35]. Other parallel studies using quantitative approach have found that higher funding goals and longer project durations lead to lower chances of successful funding on crowd-funding platforms like Kickstarter [34, 35]. Inclusion of a video in a project pitch increases the likelihood of full funding [34]. Additionally, one's social network has strong association with a project's success [34]. While these studies examined the determinants of successful funding and the motivating factors behind crowdfunding, they did not take into account the actual content in the project's description. The present work specifically examines the predictive power of content, and more precisely the words and phrases project creators use to pitch their projects.

A recent study used machine learning classifiers to predict the chances of successfully funding a Kickstarter project [21]. Similar to earlier work [34], the researchers used several attributes of a crowd funded project and surprisingly found that their accuracy hit an upper bound of 67%. The authors acknowledge that they were possibly ignoring additional factors, like the content of the project pitch. We build on their prior work and extend it by taking into account the language of the project pitch along with additional project attributes.

Analyzing Text for Social Information

Social scientists have studied the links between language and social behavior for decades. By analyzing the words and language people use in everyday life, they have developed tools like LIWC [38], a dictionary for inferring cognitive styles and social behavior from unstructured text. Using machine learning techniques, researchers have built SentiWordNet: a lexical resource to determine if text is opinionated by attaching valence scores to terms [37]. Positive and negative valence dictionaries have also been used to detect emotions during text-based CMC [23]. Emotions expressed via language even act as good predictors of future stock market prices, where emotions were estimated from blog posts [19]. In fact, research on tapping emotions and sentiment from language has grown enormously in the past few years [37]. Studies have shown, for example, that a Twitter user's personality (influential or not) is linked to the type of words he uses while tweeting [40], and that MySpace users express grief via certain words and linguistic styles [8].

More recently, researchers have demonstrated that certain words and phrases predict whether a corporate email will be sent up or down the organizational hierarchy [18]. Using statistical techniques, they built and announced the release of a reusable dictionary of power and hierarchy: one that can predict the direction of message flow from the raw text of the email. Following in their footsteps, our work looks to build a dictionary of phrases which signal successful crowdfunding. We base our study on statistical techniques, drawing inferences from analysis and visualizations of language usage. The interpretive framework we use is borrowed from the persuasion literature [10]. Next we provide a brief overview of this framework.

Theories of Persuasion

Theories of persuasion have played an important role in several spheres of scholarly research— advertising, marketing, consumer behavior research (see [44] for an overview) and more recently persuasive design [14]. Extensive work in this area has determined the basic principles that govern getting compliance from people [9, 10]. One of these principles is the rule of reciprocity, a widely studied idea among social psychologists [6, 20, 39, 41, 56]. Reciprocity is the sense of obligation to return a favor after receiving one [10]. Thus often requestors offer a gift in return for their requests [10].

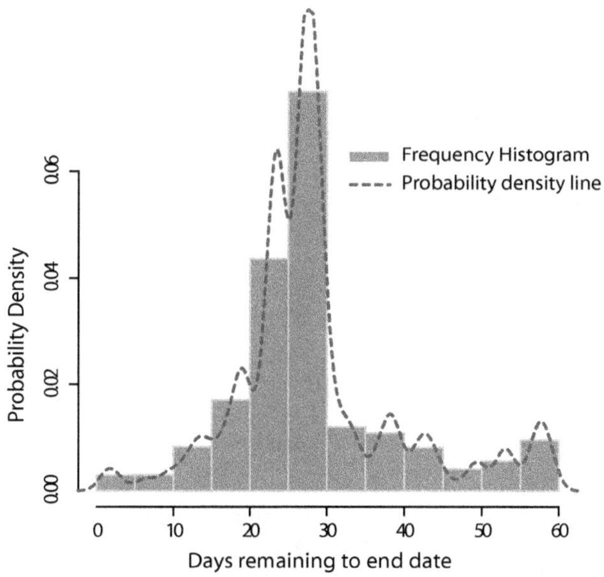

Figure 1. Histogram showing the days remaining for projects to reach their end date. The peak at around 30 days depicts that most projects were scheduled to finish collecting funds in the next 30 days.

They also exploit the power of scarcity principle—the tendency to attach more value to an item as soon as it becomes rare. Another factor which has been found to influence people's decision is whether others are also making that same choice, called social proof [1, 11]. Along similar lines, social identity theory posits that people identify themselves with a group when they perceive they have attributes in common [26]. These perceptions can then influence later decisions and choices [49]. Additionally, people often defer to expert opinions, an authority [10]. Moreover, liking for the requester can increase chances of compliance towards his request [10].

Using this interpretive framework of persuasion we delve into the qualitative explanation of our findings, looking for evidence of these theories in our predictive variables.

METHOD

We work from a list of 45,815 Kickstarter project URLs originally collected by Appsblogger [28] that includes all projects launched as of June 2, 2012. We scraped these project URLs on August 3, 2012 (when we performed our analysis) restricting our dataset to only those projects which had reached their last date of fund collection. We discuss our collection process in more detail in our next section. For reference and overview, Figure 2 illustrates the steps of our method.

On Kickstarter, you can fund creative projects in various categories. Table 1 lists the complete set of categories (13 in total) and sub-categories. A project creator pitches her project idea by providing a project description. She often uploads a video to substantiate the description. Every project on Kickstarter has a funding goal and an end date by which the goal needs to be reached. Kickstarter works on the "all-or-nothing" funding principle, whereby a project receives pledged money only if it meets or exceeds its funding goal by its end date.

Unit of Analysis: End-Dated Projects

The units of analysis in this paper are all projects which have reached their last date for collecting money. This ensures that our dataset contains only those projects which have reached their end date and thus have a clear outcome: *funded* or *not-funded*. This process eliminated 5 projects, and we were left with a dataset of 45,810 projects. Such a small number of eliminations might look strange at first, but recall that there is a lag between collection of project URLs (June 2, 2012) and scraping the project's page (August 3, 2012). When we plot the histogram of the days remaining for projects to reach their end date as of June 2nd, we obtain a unimodal distribution with a clear hump at 30 days (Figure 1). In other words, when we scraped data from the project's page, most projects had already reached their end date. In our final dataset of 45,810 projects, 51.53% (23,604) were successfully funded while 48.47% (22,206) not funded. Thus we had a fairly balanced dataset to do our statistical analysis.

Response Variable (dependent measure)

Our dependent variable is a binary response variable representing whether the project is *funded* or *not funded*.

Predictive Variables: Phrases

For each project, we scrape its textual content from its Kickstarter homepage. This includes scraping both the project's textual description and the promised rewards published by the project creator. We used Beautiful Soup[5] for scraping. It is a widely used Python library for scraping web content and allowed us to only select the text on the page related to pitches. Next, we convert all text to lowercase and tokenize text to every possible unigram, bigram and trigram, following the conventional bag of words model. Thereafter, we remove all phrases solely comprised of stop words. Finally, we end up with a corpus of 9,071,569 unique phrases.

However, including all phrases in our model will likely subtract information and produce poor results. This is because our collection of 9,071,569 phrases includes several obscure ones: those which would not matter in other domains or on other sites. We did not want our model to take into account these edge-case phrases and cloud our results. Rather, we wanted our model to reflect more general phrases. Hence we decided to build our model around relatively common English phrases. We throw away any phrase which occur less than 50 times in the corpus.

Moreover, some phrases might be specific to certain project categories. For example, the phrase *game credits* has a considerable presence in the entire corpus (140 occurrences), but unsurprisingly appears most often in projects belonging to the Games category. The phrase *our menu* has a large presence in the 'Food' category, but rarely appears in other categories. Because of this, we need a way to guard against phrases that uniquely identify categories and threaten generalizability. So, we keep only those phrases which are present in all thirteen categories. To summarize, by restricting phrases which occur at least 50 times and in all project categories, we ensure that we only build our model around relatively common English

[5] `http://www.crummy.com/software/BeautifulSoup`

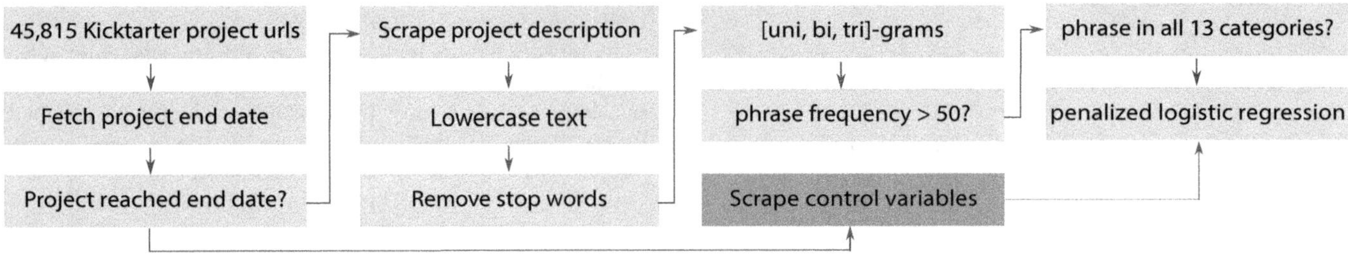

Figure 2. A flowchart of steps taken to extract predictive variables for modeling. We employ a series of filters to build our set of words and phrases. All phrases and control variables are fed into the penalized logistic regression model.

phrases and mitigate concerns associated with bias towards Kickstarter specific language. After these steps, we are left with 20,391 phrases, all of which are used as predictive features in our model.

Predictive Variables: Controls

In addition to these phrases, we include a set of 59 other Kickstarter variables as potential predictors of *funding*. This step is shown as a dark shaded box ("Scrape control variables") in Figure 2. Certain Kickstarter features—funding goal, project duration, project category, presence of a video in the project pitch, being featured on Kickstarter, and stating Facebook connections—can predict whether a project will be funded or not [34]. These variables are not just specific to Kickstarter. Most crowdfunding platforms (e.g., IndiGoGo, RocketHub) allow the project creators to mention their monetary goals, time line by which they plan to achieve their goal, category of the project, etc [17]. We control for these variables by adding them into the model's feature space (Table 1).

Project Goal: The amount of money (in USD) the project creator wants to raise for a project.

Project Duration: The time limit set by the project creator, up to which the project can accept funds.

Number of Pledge Levels: Project creators publish different levels of pledge amounts to seek donations from potential backers. They can be as small as $1, or as large as $10,000. For each pledge tier, they also promise rewards to backers in exchange for pledging.

Minimum pledge amount: The lowest tier amount.

Featured in Kickstarter: A project is said to be "Featured" in Kickstarter if it appears on any of these Kickstarter pages: *Staff Picks, Popular, Recently Launched, Ending Soon, Small Projects, Most Funded, Curated Pages.* Being featured is a strong indicator of successful funding [34].

Video Present: Creators often include a video explaining their project. Kickstarter claims that projects with a video report higher success rates than those without [6].

Video Duration: Since videos are often claimed to make projects compelling on Kickstarter, we wanted to test if the duration of videos actually has an effect. However, this is a coarse measure that does not reflect a video's quality.

[6]http://kck.st/UhMwge

Control Variables

Project Goal	Featured	No. of Updates
Project Duration	Video Present	No. of Comments
No. Pledge Levels	Video Duration	FB* Connected
Min. Pledge	Categories	

List of **Categories** & Sub-Categories

Art	**Music**	**Publishing**
Conceptual Art	Classical Music	Art Book
Crafts	Country & Folk	Children's Book
Digital Art	Electronic Music	Fiction
Illustration	Hip-Hop	Journalism
Painting	Indie Rock	Nonfiction
Performance Art	Jazz	Periodical
Mixed Media	Pop	Poetry
Public Art	Rock	**Technology**
Sculpture	World Music	Open Hardware
Design	**Film & Video**	Open Software
Graphic Design	Animation	**Dance**
Product Design	Documentary	**Theater**
Games	Narrative Fim	**Photography**
Board & Card Games	Short Film	**Food**
Video Games	Webseries	
Fashion	**Comics**	

Table 1. List of 59 control variables in our statistical model. Of these 59 controls, 49 are category and sub-category names. The 13 bolded items are the category names with their corresponding sub-categories listed below them. We include dummy variables for each of these in our model. FB stands for Facebook.

Number of updates: Project creators have the option to post updates stating the progress of the project to current backers and also to inspire new backers to donate.

Number of comments: Current and potential backers can use comments to ask questions to the project creator, which are then publicly visible.

Facebook connected: An entrepreneur's social ties influence the decisions of potential investors [43, 53]. We wanted to check if integrating Facebook connections to a Kickstarter project (an affordance the site offers) affects the likelihood of funding. We thus include a binary predictive variable to indicate whether the project creator has linked their Facebook account to the project page.

Project Categories: Kickstarter provides a list of categories and sub-categories for a new project. A project can be assigned either, but not both. Table 1 shows the full list of 49 categories and sub-categories. We include all as predictive variables.

Model Limitation

One potential confound with this approach is that the project's page might be updated during the lifetime of the project. For example, the project creator may add the names of the backers in the 'Backers' page, post updates in the 'Updates' page or even change the project description in the project 'Home' page. We made sure to guard against this by only crawling the content of the 'Home' page, ignoring any updates that have been made in the other pages. While this does not give us the exact mirror image of the project as it was first launched, we see it as a reasonable first-order estimate of the original project pitch. Follow-up work may find traction studying how dynamics affect funding success.

Statistical Technique

We employ penalized logistic regression [16] to predict the dependent variable *funded*. Penalized logistic regression is well-suited for our purposes because it guards against collinearity and sparsity, both of which are prevalent in our phrase dataset. Collinearity is a well-known property of English phrases. Consider an example from our phrase dataset: the phrase *week* will follow *every* more often then *fashion*. The regression technique handles this by moving the coefficient's weight to the most predictive feature. A parameter α determines how the weights will be moved among the predictive variables. $\alpha = 0$ includes all correlated terms but shrinks the weights towards each other (known as Ridge regression), while $\alpha = 1$ (Lasso regression) does both shrinkage and variable selection. In other words, Lasso includes only one variable per correlated cluster of variables by shrinking the coefficients of other variables to zero. We opted for a parsimonious model, letting our $\alpha = 1$.

A common problem with a large number of predictive variables is overfitting – a phenomenon where the statistical model fits the data under study too closely, explaining minor fluctuations but sacrificing overall predictive power. Cross-validation is a common technique to guard against overfitting. Thus we use an R implementation of penalized logistic regression with ten fold cross-validation, `cv.glmnet`[7] to handle phrase collinearity and guard against overfitting. `glmnet` also takes care of sparsity, another feature associated with texts, where a single project description spans only a small percentage of all possible phrases. Taking a predictive feature vector as input, `glmnet` predicts a binary response variable (*funded* or *not funded*), and upon fitting the data it associates β coefficients with the predictive variables. These β coefficients determine the relative power of the variables (both controls and phrases) in predicting whether the project will be *funded* or not. As our first step in building the predictive model we included only the control variables to measure model performance and the explanatory power of these variables. Next, we expand our feature list to include our set of phrases to see if there is any substantial gain in explanatory power..

[7] `http://cran.r-project.org/web/packages/glmnet`

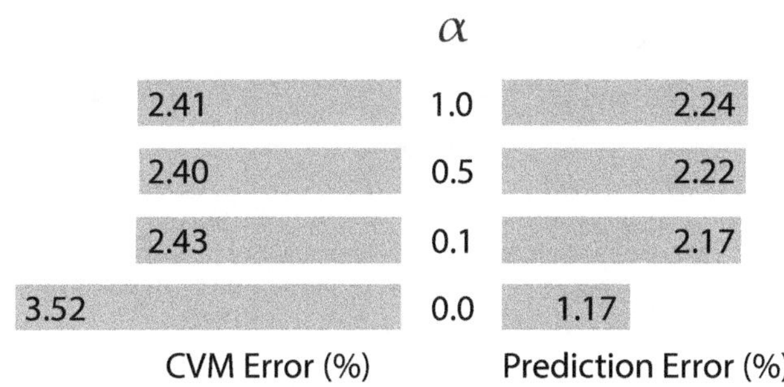

Figure 3. Percentage cross validation error and prediction error for different values of α. α=0 denotes ridge regression, while α = 1 is lasso regression. Prediction error is measured on an 80/20 train/test split.

Model	Dev	df	χ^2	p	Error
Null	63.4K	0			
Controls-only	37.5K	58	25.9K	$< 10^{-15}$	17%
Phrases + Controls	363.4	5.4K	37.2K	$< 10^{-15}$	2.4%

Table 2. Summary of different model fits. *Null* is the intercept-only model. *Dev* denotes deviance which measures the goodness of fit. Error is the cross validation error rate reported by the model.

RESULTS

Using a Controls-only model as our baseline model (instead of an intercept-only model), we compare the deviance reported by our Phrases + Controls model. The deviance is related to the log-likelihood of the model and is a useful measure of goodness of fit. Standalone comparisons with the null model will fail to expose the relative power of phrases in contrast to the other control variables. While the null model has a deviance of 63,463.47, the addition of control variables reduced the deviance to 37,525.52, suggesting that they have considerable explanatory power. However, a dramatic reduction in deviance happens upon addition of phrases to the model, going from 37,525.52 to 363.42. Table 2 summarizes these results.

The difference between the deviances of two models approximately follows a χ^2 distribution, with degrees of freedom equal to the number of additional predictors in a model. By comparing the deviances (Table 2), we see that the information provided by the control variables has significant predictive power: $\chi^2(58, N{=}45{,}810) = 63{,}463.47 - 37{,}525.52 = 25{,}937.95$, $p < 10^{-15}$. The cross validation error reported by the control only model is 17.03%. Adding phrases results in another massive reduction of deviance (58.56% drop), suggesting the substantial predictive power of the phrases: $\chi^2(5{,}427 - 58, N{=}45{,}810) = 37{,}525.52 - 363.42 = 37{,}162.1$, $p < 10^{-15}$. There is also a dramatic reduction in error rate, with cross-validation error being only 2.4%. The low cross validation errors ensure that our models are guarded from excessive overfitting.

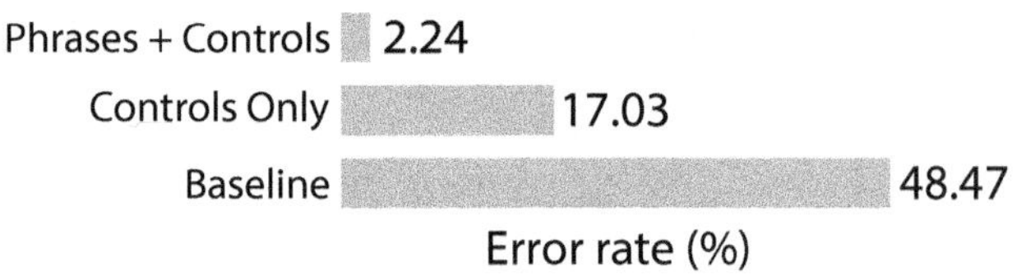

Figure 4. Comparison of error rates between the baseline, controls-only and phrases+controls model. The control variables alone result in a fairly high accuracy model. Addition of phrases gives an additional boost of about 15%.

The low error rate at first might imply that phrases are solely dominating the prediction results. However, recall that the control variables alone result in a fairly high accuracy model (cross validation error rate = 17.03%). Adding phrases gives an additional boost of about 15%. Figure 4 shows a comparison between the error rates of the baseline, Controls-only and Phrases + Controls model. The accuracy of the baseline model corresponds to picking the most likely class (*not funded*) every single time. To further gain confidence in our results we repeated our regression technique varying the parameter α and comparing two heuristics: 1) cross-validation error rate and 2) prediction accuracy on an 80/20 train/test split. Figure 3 shows the comparison. Lasso regression ($\alpha = 1$) performs better than ridge ($\alpha = 0$), and there is negligible difference among the other settings of α.

Looking at the β weights generated by our Phrases + Controls model we find that the top 100 positive and negative β predictors are solely comprised of phrases. Table 3 lists the 100 phrases with the most positive β weights. These are the ones which predict that a project will be funded *(F)*. Conversely, Table 4 presents 100 phrases with the most negative β weights, strongly predicting that a project will not be funded *(NF)*.

Can these phrases be grouped under meaningful categories? We turn to the LIWC (Linguistic Inquiry and Word Count) program [38] to find an answer to our question. LIWC is a text analysis technique based on a hand-built dictionary of words and word stems, assembled into categories. It matches the words from input text to words and stems of the dictionary, generating the percentage of words that match these categories. We tested against all 82 LIWC categories. Since LIWC performs simultaneous tests, we apply a Bonferroni correction, letting $\alpha = 0.05/82 = 0.0006$. We find that there is significant difference in 74 categories. Figure 5 shows the membership in seven of these 74 language dimensions (p-values $< 10^{-15}$). We interpret these results further in our Discussion section.

To get a glimpse of the structure of the predictive phrases, we present Word Tree visualizations [55] in Figure 6. We used the online site Many Eyes [54] to build these visualizations. Here we present the searches for the phrases *pledgers will* and *even a dollar* in the *funded* and *not funded* parts of the corpus, respectively. We see that *pledgers will* is often used to convey the gifts one would receive after funding the project. On the other hand, *even a dollar* perhaps reads as groveling for money and is less appealing.

How do these phrases map to more general text? In other words, are there phrases which occur fifty times and in all

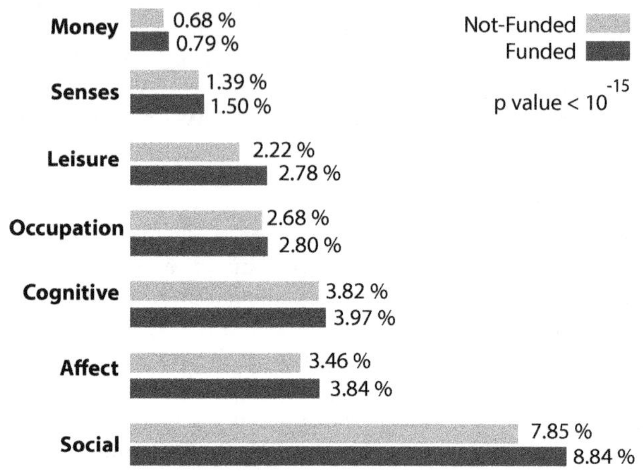

Figure 5. Testing for groupings of predictive phrases. We use LIWC to find membership of predictive phrases in 82 language dimensions. We have shown seven categories here. Phrases which predict that the project will be funded exhibit more social, cognitive, affective or emotional, and sensory or perceptual processes. They also have higher presence in 'Person Concern' categories (e.g., occupation, leisure, money and financial issues).

categories, but still only matter to Kickstarter alone? A cursory glance through the non-zero β weights pointed us to these phrases: *kickstarter goal, [via, of their, our, on, using] kickstarter*. All of them are specific to Kickstarter's culture and yet were not discarded by our filtering steps. To present a more generalizable set of phrases, we turn to the Google 1T corpus [5], a vast database of the frequency of n-grams Google has seen on the web. We made this choice because both Kickstarter and Google 1T corpus correspond to web text. Scanning the Google corpus, we look for all non-zero β phrases that our model generated from Kickstarter. We note their frequencies in the Google corpus. Next, we perform χ^2 tests of independence between the frequencies of phrases in Google and Kickstarter corpus. Since we performed simultaneous tests against the sets of Google unigrams, bigrams and trigrams, we apply Bonferroni correction, letting $\alpha = 0.05/5.4K$. Finally, we search for phrases with significant statistical differences and whose membership is higher in Google's 1T corpus. This discarded 4,440 phrases from our set of 5.4K phrases with non-zero β weights, yielding a rather small phrase set of 494 positive and 453 negative predictors. We mark (in gold) the occurrence of these phrases in our list of top 100 β predictors (Tables 3 and 4).

DISCUSSION

We find that among 59 control variables and 20,391 phrases, the top 100 predictors of *funded* and *not funded* are solely comprised of phrases. 29 of the 59 control variables had non-zero, non-random predictive power: presence of a video, number of updates, Facebook connected, number of pledge levels, and eleven categories and sub-categories (Graphic Design, Theater, Food, Games, Documentary, Art, Board & Card Games, Webseries, Fashion, Periodical, Animation) had positive β weights (Figure 5). Project duration was associated with *not funded* (β = -0.0129). This matches reports from recent research that longer project durations lower the chances of funding [34]. Additionally, thirteen categories and subcategories had negative β weights (Figure 6).

Figure 6. Word Tree visualizations showing membership of phrases in two sets of our dataset. The top visualization shows the occurrence of *pledgers will* (positive β weight) in the *funded* dataset. It occurs 70 times in the corpus. The visualization shows phrases that fork off from *pledgers will* in this part of the corpus. The font size of a phrase is proportional to its frequency of occurrence. We see that the most commonly occurring trigram is *pledgers will receive*. The visualization at the bottom depicts the search for the phrase *even a dollar* (negative β weight) in the *not funded* dataset. It occurs 56 times in this part of the corpus. The visualization shows that the most likely phrases are *even a dollar short*, *even a dollar will*, *even a dollar can*, perhaps reading as groveling for money.

(F) phrases	β	(F) phrases	β
project will be	18.48	difference for	5.60
has pledged	5.42	pledged will	4.01
pledged and	3.98	december of	3.21
we can afford	2.94	trip in	2.83
used in a	2.82	par	2.79
around new	2.78	trash	2.75
their creative	2.71	given the chance	2.69
mention your	2.69	your continued	2.65
to build this	2.65	cats	2.64
option is	2.59	inspired me	2.57
workshop and	2.56	project will allow	2.56
the coming	2.55	dollar pledged	2.54
we have chosen	2.53	accessible to the	2.52
and an invite	2.51	christina	2.51
all supporters	2.48	from the past	2.44
pledgers will	2.44	finding out	2.43
lane	2.39	plus recognition	2.37
want them to	2.31	farm	2.31
got you	2.31	atlantic	2.30
and encouragement	2.28	some help with	2.26
that exists	2.25	as people	2.25
in this new	2.22	projects will	2.21
would greatly	2.20	we are fully	2.20
dates and	2.15	a national	2.14
conception	2.14	problem of	2.12
and added	2.11	kind to	2.08
unveiling	2.07	good karma and	2.04
commemorating the	2.04	shows that	2.02
girl and	2.00	il	1.99
two friends	1.96	secure the	1.95
future is	1.94	testament	1.93
that i feel	1.91	the meaning	1.91
fundraising goal	1.89	their thoughts	1.89
nv	1.88	support at	1.87
a personal tour	1.86	are raising money	1.85
the brooklyn	1.85	good as	1.84
administration	1.83	and develop	1.83
also receive two	1.83	the inside of	1.81
upfront	1.81	to play the	1.79
looking for your	1.77	as a small	1.77
for two years	1.76	changed my	1.76
gain a	1.76	our social	1.76
answering	1.74	design elements	1.74
funding will help	1.73	guarantee a	1.73
company for	1.72	all previous rewards	1.72
thanks a	1.72	a detailed	1.71
sharing with	1.71	the correct	1.71
be called	1.70	and share it	1.70
of hot	1.70	a lot about	1.70
message and	1.70	poster of your	1.69

Table 3. The top 100 phrases signaling that the project will be funded. The phrases obtained after comparison with the Google 1T corpus are marked in gold. All phrases are significant at the 0.001 level.

(NF) phrases	β	(NF) phrases	β
pledged	-7.12	dressed up	-4.64
not been able	-4.02	trusting	-3.91
all the good	-3.89	based in the	-3.87
models of	-3.84	school that	-3.75
information at	-3.65	kids of all	-3.55
of the leading	-3.53	on a larger	-3.44
new form of	-3.43	that uses	-3.42
we have lots	-3.24	to enjoy a	-3.20
way for us	-3.18	room on	-3.18
an honorable mention	-3.17	panel of	-3.17
is time for	-3.14	even a dollar	-3.10
nm	-3.08	be followed	-3.02
easy and	-2.97	later i	-2.96
and to provide	-2.91	will surely	-2.90
word out about	-2.87	picture in	-2.87
logo on it	-2.84	also work	-2.83
location of the	-2.80	people into	-2.78
you message from	-2.76	blanket	-2.76
provide us	-2.76	every time you	-2.73
need one	-2.69	help support our	-2.68
the culture of	-2.68	us from the	-2.67
unseen	-2.67	in school	-2.65
a door	-2.59	a masters	-2.59
a blank	-2.57	discretion	-2.57
volunteers to	-2.56	we raise will	-2.55
to the cost	-2.54	reusable	-2.53
the profits	-2.52	hand made by	-2.52
educate and	-2.51	get to pick	-2.48
based upon the	-2.47	will soon	-2.47
unified	-2.46	illustration	-2.46
to identify	-2.45	the production costs	-2.45
product will be	-2.43	refined	-2.43
space at	-2.41	continue with	-2.41
hope to get	-2.39	no extra	-2.39
present in	-2.37	definitely a	-2.35
occur in	-2.34	you start	-2.34
the needed	-2.34	addition to being	-2.33
decide what	-2.32	tuning	-2.32
deeper into	-2.30	help to bring	-2.29
known and	-2.28	underway	-2.27
campaign will help	-2.25	for decades	-2.23
goes in	-2.23	notoriety	-2.22
get to vote	-2.22	make you an	-2.21
air and	-2.20	an alternative	-2.19
be creative	-2.19	shows the	-2.19
post card with	-2.19	website for more	-2.19
signed postcard	-2.18	varies	-2.18
on different	-2.16	left my	-2.16
of their choice	-2.16	who like	-2.15
name or logo	-2.14	piggy	-2.14

Table 4. The top 100 phrases signaling that the project will not be funded. The phrases obtained after comparison with the Google 1T corpus are marked in gold. All phrases are significant at the 0.001 level.

Control Variables	β	Control Variables	β
Graphic Design	1.35	Video Present	0.60
Theater	0.57	Food	0.48
Games	0.33	Documentary	0.32
Updates Count	0.25	Art	0.13
FB* Connected	0.13	Board & Card Games	0.12
Webseries	0.11	Fashion	0.05
Pledge levels	0.05	Periodical	0.04
Animation	0.01		

Table 5. The 15 control variables which have non-zero predictive power to signal that the project will be *funded*. All control variables are significant at the 0.001 level.

Taking a closer look at Tables 3 and 4, we find an intriguing view of words and phrases providing cues of *funded* and *not funded*. As is perhaps to be expected, phrases which exude negativism (*not been able*), or lack assurance (*later i*, *hope to get*) are predictors of *not funded*.

> i have **not been able** (β = -4.07) to finish the film because none of my editors will see the project through to the end.

> i can't take size orders and possibly **hope to get** (β = -2.47) them all made in time for christmas.

Perhaps unsurprisingly, phrases which signal lucrative offers to potential backers (*also receive two*, *mention your*) are positive predictors of successful funding.

> i'll thank you by name in each and every one of season one's episodes, and **mention your** (β = 2.69) own project or message at the top of one of them.

> add $40 and you will **also receive two** (β = 1.83) vip tickets to the premiere screening.

In more formal terms, these positive predictors reflect the principle of *reciprocity* [10] from the persuasion literature. We next illustrate how the usage of certain phrases exhibit subtle hints of persuasion, possibly motivating people to donate [10, 12, 15]. Finally, we conclude with the design and theoretical implications of our findings.

Reciprocity

Reciprocity is the tendency to return a favor after receiving one [10]. Social psychologists have studied the norms of reciprocity for many years [6, 20, 39, 41, 56]. People often use persuasive appeals when reflecting norms of reciprocity (i.e., "If you grant the request, I will reward you") [12]. We see similar phenomena in our phrase dataset: *mention your*, *also receive two*, *we can afford*, *pledged will* are among the top 100 positive predictors. Taking a closer look, we see that these phrases are often used to offer a reward or a gift in return for donation funds: *mention your name* in the [film, program, introduction, thank you section, acknowledgment section, credits of the film], *pledgers will* have [their pick, a special credit], *pledgers will* [get, also receive, have], *also receive two* [free, full passes, tickets, copies of].

> everyone who **has pledged** (β = 5.42) $xx [or more] will get ...

> if i make or exceed my goal then you will be charged what you **pledged and** (β = 3.98) you will get your fantastic rewards

Control Variables	β	Control Variables	β
Illustration	-2.55	Journalism	-1.12
Pop	-0.79	Rock	-0.5
Performance Art	-0.46	Film & Video	-0.44
Children's Book	-0.40	Mixed Media	-0.35
Country & Folk	-0.2	Music	-0.11
Public Art	-0.09	Electronic Music	-0.08
Short Film	-0.04	Project Duration	-0.01

Table 6. The 14 control variables which have non-zero predictive power to signal that the project will be *not funded*. All control variables are significant at the 0.001 level.

> we'll **mention your** (β = 2.69) name in the sleeve of our full length album (which you'll get the download code for) and you get our summer darling ep with additional never before released bonus track

A particularly interesting top predictor for *funded* projects was *good karma and* (β = 2.04).

> i will thank you on my website, send you **good karma and** (β = 2.04) give you a free digital download of the big spoon ep.

> you'll get an mp3 of a previously unreleased song delivered to you via email before anyone else hears it. i also trust that you'll accrue some **good karma and** i'll be truly grateful to have you on the team.

However, not all offers are alluring enough to attract backers. Low offers are often rejected [22, 42]. For example, the phrase *dressed up* is one of the top negative predictors in our dataset. On searching the corpus of *not funded* projects, the phrase usage reveals offers which are perhaps too low to attract backer attention.

> you get a physical copy of the ep, a rigoletto shirt, a rigoletto sticker, and a skype date with us **dressed up** (β = -4.52) as celebrities.

> **extremely limited** you will be our vip victim! we'll get you all **dressed up** in period clothing and have you be a victim in one of the paranormal crime scene set ups! (you are responsible for transportation and accommodations in utah. don't worry, i'll get you a deal with a hotel!) now that's killer!

Another dimension of reciprocity is 'personalization', a tactic often used by recommendation systems [33] and web personalization engines [50], whereby the person trying to persuade offers products and services that appeal to people.

> but we are going to ask that you send us a photo of yourself to be **used in a** (β = 2.82) collage featured in a piece of selfless season artwork.

> your vocal will be **used in a** similar way as a line or two of lead vocal - not just a faded background vocal.

Scarcity

People attach more value to products and opportunities which are rare, distinct, limited in supply or are available for a limited time [10]. For example, the following excerpt from a successful project pitch emphasizes limited time availability:

> for anyone who comes by and was thinking of pledging, the **option is** (β = 2.59) still there until 5:04 pm on 17 october. if you want the lower calendar price and no shipping charges, or if any of the rewards tickle your fancy, they're still available through kickstarter until monday afternoon.

Additionally, exclusivity is often harnessed while making offers, leading to higher chances of acceptance [10, 11].

> this custom color **option is** (β = 2.59) exclusive to kickstarter and will not be available at product launch!

> donating to this project is an opportunity contribute to something really special.first and foremost you are being **given the chance** (β = 2.69) to become part of something at its earliest stages.

> also, you will be **given the chance** to purchase our small batch pieces before the public domain.

> blast **from the past** (β = 2.44) – pledge and receive one of only ten remaining copies of the johnny starlings "aiming too high", my first ever cd release, long since out of print.

Social Proof

Social proof is the idea that people depend on others for cues on how to act [10]. Persuasive tactics use this principle by making people aware of what others are doing to increase their likelihood to follow along [11]. We see traces of social proof in the language of *funded* projects, often signaling the attention the project has already received.

> [name] **has pledged** (β = 5.42) some gas money.yay! thank you! so, you can see that i already have people willing to support my art.

> we've hit the 50% mark! huge thanks to everyone who **has pledged** so far. it is truly inspiring!

> dennis mckenna eethnopharmacologist): "now this is a worthy kickstarter project to support! i have **pledged and** (β = 3.98) suggest you do too! this is a possibility to change policy with respect to the use of ayahuasca in addiction treatment. support it if you can and tell your friends.

Social Identity

Social identity is an individual's knowledge that he belongs to a social group, in which individuals have common attributes and identify themselves in similar ways [25, 46]. They adopt the group member's attitudes as their own and their decisions are influenced by the group's majority opinion [47, 48, 57].

> collect is dedicated to making the arts **accessible to the** (β = 2.52) community, creating work and events that enhance and celebrate culture within the civilization of new york city

> a large portion of our community has come together **to build this** (β = 2.65) project.

Perhaps there are deeper underlying questions of whether funding efforts are driven by the group's interest. Our current work does not answer these; we hope future researchers can explore these questions.

Liking

People are more likely to comply with a person or product if they like them. Positive remarks about another person's attitudes and performance increases liking [4].

> with your help, this **project will be** (β = 18.48) a success, and you'll be able to enjoy our movie at a festival near you! thanks very much.

> thank you for your support **and encouragement** (β = 2.28)

Additionally, the two most important factors to increase liking are similarity and praise [10]. People use similarities to create bonds, which are later leveraged to garner support [10]. For instance, the following example shows how the project pitch leverages on the fan community and also extends appreciation—perhaps an attempt to draw other fans to fund the project.

> the support from the disney fan community and everyone who **has pledged** (β = 5.42) so far has been amazing. thank you all so much.

Authority

People often resort to expert opinions for making efficient and quick decisions [10]. Many of the top predictive phrases were used to portray the expertise of project creators and developers:

> that means having the best-quality exhibition master **we can afford** (β = 2.94), attending the film festivals in person to meet with potential buyers, and even hiring a professional publicist and graphic designer to help promote the film.

> the **project will be** (β = 18.48) sag certified and meet all union standards ensuring the highest level of professionalism.

> the **project will be** produced by dove award winning producer rusty varenkamp

> music development for the **project will be** coordinated by platinum-selling recording artist morten kier and supervised by gmcla artistic director e. jason armstrong.

However, research shows that people rely on experts more when they have to decide matters of low personal relevance, but engage in more thoughtful personal consideration when the matter is highly personal to them [57]. Unsurprisingly, higher thought process is associated with successfully funded projects, which we will discuss shortly in our LIWC results. Our study does not examine how the personal relevance of a project effects its success. We believe this is an interesting direction for future research.

LIWC and Sentiment

Our LIWC results in Figure 5 reveal some interesting findings: successfully funded projects demonstrate more active thinking (*Cognitive Process*), a higher degree of *Social Process*, higher perception rates (*Senses*), higher levels of emotions (*Affect*) and exhibit *Personal concerns* via references to Money, Occupation, Leisure and Home. We also examined the sentiment of the phrases, by performing sentiment analysis using the Natural Language Text Processing API provided by `text-processing.com`. Results reveal that *funded* projects have higher positive and negative sentiment compared to *not funded* projects, though the difference is not statistically significant. As is perhaps expected, LIWC results show that the membership in *Death* category (not shown in Figure 5) is significantly different in *funded* and *not funded* parts of the corpus, with higher presence in *not funded*. However, all of these differences are relatively minor and likely only show statistical significance because of our sample size.

Other phrases

While many of the top phrases relate to persuasion, others fell outside this framework, yet had high predictive power. As is perhaps to be expected, some phrases were used in the context of incentivizing donations.

> if you can't make a larger contribution, you can still contribute by telling all your friends about this. if ten people **mention your** (β = 2.69) name when they make a donation, you will get a free download of the film, a thanks in the credits"

A particularly interesting phrase is: *december of* (β = 3.21). *december of* mostly talks about projects and products scheduled to be released by December of a particular year. Despite our attempts to control for specificity, some phrases (e.g., *december of*) might be specific to Kickstarter's culture. That said, perhaps these projects subtly signal the tax exemptions people can take in the U.S. by donating by December 31 – a possible way to incentivize donations.

Another perplexing finding was the occurrence of phrases like *christina* ($\beta = 2.51$) and *cats* ($\beta = 2.64$) in our top predictors. While *christina* ($\beta = 2.33$) mostly referred to famous celebrity (i.e., Christina Aguilera), we had no clear explanation for the occurrence of *cats*—except for the commonly accepted wisdom that the internet loves them.

General Phrases

To map the phrases captured in the Kickstarter platform to more general text, we used Google's 1T corpus [5]. Their presence in the top 100 phrase predictors is marked in gold in Tables 3 and 4. Phrases like *and encouragement* ('Liking'), *given the chance* ('Scarcity'), *as people* ('Social Proof') make a reappearance. Additionally, pitching a completely *new form of* expression is associated with *not funded* projects, while drawing inspiration from something *that exists* seems to work better. We note the following examples to put this in context.

> it was to play educational games allowing students to experience a *new form of* (β = -3.33) discovery, curiosity, and mystery.

> we have one remaining trip to japan, where we hope to cover the creation of home video technology, as well as the extremely unique direct-to-video market **that exists** (β = 2.25) there.

Other intuitively positive predictors include *secure the* (β = 1.95), *gain a* (β = 1.76), *guarantee a* (β = 1.73).

> in exchange we offer the chance to **secure the** extremely limited special edition of the album and other items

> so pledging $10 is the only way to **guarantee a** copy!

Again, explicit groveling for money is less appealing as depicted by the phrases *provide us* (β = -2.87), *need one* (β = -2.69).

> we **need one** (β = -2.80) thing we don't have is money

Not surprisingly, more forward-looking phrases (*next step is*, *in the upcoming*,*will be published*, *to announce*), phrases indicative of ongoing project work (*and published*, *are preparing*, *working on a*, *worked in*, *teamed up with*), phrases exhibiting 'Authority' (*with a professional*) and phrases with positive sentiment (*wow*, *good for*) are predictors of *funded*. We have released the set of all non-zero positive and negative beta weights with membership in Google 1T corpus [8,9].

Phrase + Control Variables Dataset

Additionally we have also released all the predictive variables that form the core of our penalized logistic regression[10]. It consists of all possible phrases available to the regression model, in addition to the control variables. Each entry in the file lists predictive variables followed by their associated β weights, sorted in decreasing order. We also include entries with zero β weights, so that researchers can examine phrases which do not affect funding.

[8] http://cc.gatech.edu/~tmitra3/data/Gg.KS.pos

[9] http://cc.gatech.edu/~tmitra3/data/Gg.KS.neg

[10] http://cc.gatech.edu/~tmitra3/data/KS.predicts

Theoretical Implications

Despite advances in multi-media, computer mediated communication (CMC) systems mostly generate text [32]. Content analysis of CMC text can lead to meaningful inferences about human behavior in different social contexts, something we believe is demonstrated in this research. To our surprise, language has a strong effect on funding success, and many of these results seem to fit squarely within existing persuasion literature. We hope that this work stimulates new research in the CSCW and HCI community on crowdfunding. By releasing the model's predictive phrases and control variables, we inform two bodies of research: work on computerized text analysis to draw inferences of real-world behaviors [18, 51], and an emerging class of crowdfunding sites.

Though these phrases are associated with *funded* and *not funded* projects in very distinct ways, we do not claim that using these phrases guarantees success. Neither do we claim that using these phrases is the only means of successful funding. One should also note the importance of other project attributes, like certain project categories, the number of project updates and the number of pledge levels, all of which have substantial effect on the project's success. There could well be several other intervening variables which ultimately control a project's funding—perhaps they only manifest as language. We see this as a rich area for further study.

Design Implications

We foresee that our work may enable new features on crowdfunding sites—tools which can help both backers and project creators make best use of their time and money. Commentators have attached importance to observing both successful and failed projects before starting a new one [45]. With this as a backdrop, imagine the design of a "Help Center" or "FAQ" page on a crowdfunding site. The page lists words, phrases and language-style guides for project pitches: those which are associated with successful funding and those which are not. Moreover, perhaps while a project creator types her project pitch on the funding website, the site alerts her whenever the words and phrases shift toward negative predictors. It could perhaps also provide her with alternative language to increase the chances of success.

Study Limitations

Like many large-scale analysis of observational data, we cannot make any causal claims, such as whether the project's pitch was able to persuade people to donate money. Our work shows the factors which relate to successful funding and surprisingly found that along with some project attributes, the language used in the project pitch has a strong effect. Secondly, our study is a quantitative analysis followed by observations from our phrase dataset. While our approach is meaningful in describing what happens, without an accompanying qualitative analysis we can only speculate on the why. We hope our findings will motivate future researchers to address these limitations.

FUTURE WORK & CONCLUSIONS

The successful startup Pebble from the beginning of the paper has faced repeated problems delivering its product to market. There is certainly more work to do looking for traits like this—what some might call "over-promising and under-delivering."

Also, there is almost certainly additional predictive information outside the text of project pitches and our list of control variables. Future work could build on our results by exploring other attributes. For example, we saw that 'Facebook Connected' is a positive predictor of *funded*, but we did not explore the rich space of social network predictors.

Overall, our findings indicate a fundamental force which drives the "crowd" to fund crowd-projects: language. In this paper, we uncover the phrases which signal whether a project will be crowdfunded and announce the public release of a set of persuasive phrases. These phrases highlight the interesting ways in which raw CMC text can expose real world social behaviors. We hope our work motivates future researchers to delve deeper into the dynamics of crowdfunding, viewing it both through the lens of linguistic style and other traits of crowdfunding. Our results may also lead to a new class of applications, such as systems which can help project creators craft pitches with the best chances of success.

ACKNOWLEDGEMENTS

We would like to thank our reviewers, the comp.social lab at GeorgiaTech and Michael Muller for their valuable comments that improved this work. We also thank DARPA for supporting this research.

REFERENCES

1. Aronson, E., Wilson, T. D., and Akert, R. M. Social psychology. 5th, 2005.
2. Bandura, A. The explanatory and predictive scope of self-efficacy theory. *Journal of Social and Clinical Psychology 4*, 3 (1986), 359–373.
3. Belleflamme, P., Lambert, T., and Schwienbacher, A. Crowdfunding: Tapping the right crowd. In *International Conference of the French Finance Association (AFFI)* (2011), 11–13.
4. Berscheid, E., and Hatfield, E. Interpersonal attraction (2nd ed.). MA: Addison-Wesley (1978).
5. Brants, T., and Franz, A. Web 1T 5-gram Version 1. *Linguistic Data Consortium, Philadelphia* (2006).
6. Brehm, J. W., and Cole, A. H. Effect of a favor which reduces freedom. *Journal of Personality and Social Psychology*, 3 (1966), pp. 420–426.
7. Brown, Merkley, and Bennet. Crowdfund Act (S. 2190). Tech. rep., 2012.
8. Brubaker, J. R., Kivran-Swaine, F., Taber, L., and Hayes, G. R. Grief-stricken in a crowd: The language of bereavement and distress in social media. In *Proc. ICWSM'12* (2012).
9. Cialdini, R. B. *Influence (rev): The Psychology of Persuasion*. HarperCollins, 1993.
10. Cialdini, R. B. In *Influence: Science and practice*, Boston: Allyn & Bacon (2001).
11. Cialdini, R. B., and Goldstein, N. J. Social influence: Conformity and compliance. *Annual Review of Psychology. 55* (2004), 591–621.
12. Danet, B. The language of persuasion in bureaucracy: "modern" and "traditional" appeals to the israel customs authorities. *American Sociological Review 36*, 5 (1971), pp. 847–859.
13. Empson, R. Ready, set, crowdfund: President obama to sign jobs act tomorrow. http://tcrn.ch/hmhj67. retrieved sep. 19, 2012. (2012).
14. Fogg, B. J. Persuasive technology: using computers to change what we think and do. *Ubiquity 2002*, December (2002), 5.
15. French Jr, J. R., and Raven, B. The bases of social power. In *Group dynamics*, D. Cartwright and A. Zander, Eds., New York: Harper and Row (1960), 607–23.
16. Friedman, J., Hastie, T., and Tibshirani, R. Regularization paths for generalized linear models via coordinate descent. *Journal of Statistical Software* (2010).
17. Gerber, E., Hui, J., and Kuo, P. Crowdfunding: Why people are motivated to post and fund projects on crowdfunding platforms. In *CSCW Workshop* (2012).
18. Gilbert, E. Phrases that signal workplace hierarchy. In *CSCW* (2012), 1037–1046.
19. Gilbert, E., and Karahalios, K. Widespread Worry and the Stock Market. In *Proc. ICWSM* (2010).
20. Goranson, R. E., and Berkowitz, L. Reciprocity and responsibility reactions to prior help. *Journal of Personality and Social Psychology*, 3 (1966), 227–232.
21. Greenberg, M. D., Pardo, B., Hariharan, K., and Gerber, E. Crowdfunding support tools: predicting success & failure. CHI EA '13 (2013).
22. Güth, W., Schmittberger, R., and Schwarze, B. An experimental analysis of ultimatum bargaining. *Journal of Economic Behavior &; Organization 3*, 4 (1982), 367 – 388.
23. Hancock, J., Landrigan, C., and Silver, C. Expressing emotion in text-based communication. In *Proc. CHI* (2007), 929–932.
24. Harms, M. What drives motivation to participate financially in a crowdfunding community?
25. Hogg, M. A., Abrams, D., Otten, S., and Hinkle, S. The social identity perspective. *Small Group Research 35*, 3 (2004), 246–276.
26. Hogg, M. A., and Turner, J. C. Intergroup behaviour, self-stereotyping and the salience of social categories. *British Journal of Social Psychology 26*, 4 (1987), 325–340.
27. Hui, J., Greenberg, M., and Gerber, E. Understanding crowdfunding work: implications for support tools. CHI EA '13 (2013).
28. Jeanne, P. Kickstarter failures revealed! What can you learn from Kickstarter failures? http://www.appsblogger.com/kickstarter-infographic. Retrieved Sep. 19, 2012. (2012).
29. Jensen, K. The best kickstarter projects. http://www.ugo.com/web-culture/best-kickstarter-projects-ninja-baseball. retrieved sep. 19, 2012. (2012).

30. Kickstarter. http://kickstarter.com/help/stats. retrieved sep. 19, 2012. (2012).

31. Kosner, A. Pebble watch for iphone and android, the most successful kickstarter project ever. http://onforb.es/pp6dpw. retrieved sep. 19, 2012. (2012).

32. Lee Rainie, Kristen Purcell, A. S. The Social Side of the Internet. Tech. rep., Pew Internet & American Life Project, 2011.

33. Li, T., and Tsekouras, D. Reciprocity in effort to personalize: examining perceived effort as a signal for quality. Proc. ICEC '12, 1–8.

34. Mollick, E. The dynamics of crowdfunding: Determinants of success and failure. SSRN scholarly paper, Social Science Research Network, Rochester, NY, July 2012.

35. Muller, M., Geyer, W., Soule, T., Daniels, S., and Cheng, L.-T. Crowdfunding inside the enterprise: employee-initiatives for innovation and collaboration. Proc. CSCW'13, ACM (2013), 503–512.

36. Ordanini, A., Miceli, L., Pizzetti, M., and Parasuraman, A. Crowd-funding: transforming customers into investors through innovative service platforms. *Journal of Service Management 22*, 4 (2011), 443–470.

37. Pang, B., and Lee, L. Opinion mining and sentiment analysis. *Foundations and Trends in Information Retrieval 2*, 1-2 (2008), 1–135.

38. Pennebaker, J. W., and Francis, M. E. *Linguistic Inquiry and Word Count*. Lawrence Erlbaum, August 1999.

39. Pruitt, D. G., and Drews, J. L. The effect of time pressure, time elapsed, and the opponent's concession rate on behavior in negotiation. *Journal of Experimental Social Psychology*, 5 (1969), 43–60.

40. Quercia, D., Ellis, J., Capra, L., and Crowcroft, J. In the mood for being influential on twitter. In *Privacy, security, risk and trust (passat), 2011 IEEE SocialCom)* (2011), 307 –314.

41. Regan, D. T. Effects of a favor and liking on compliance. *Journal of Experimental Social Psychology*, 1 (1971), 621–639.

42. Roth, A. Bargaining experiments. In *Handbook of Experimental Economics.*, J. Kagel and A. Roth, Eds., vol. 3, Princeton University Press (1997), 253–348.

43. Shane, S., and Cable, D. Network ties, reputation, and the financing of new ventures. *Management Science* (2002).

44. Shrum, L., Liu, M., Nespoli, M., and Lowrey, T. M. Persuasion in the marketplace.

45. Steinberg, S., and DeMaria, R. In *The Crowdfunding Bible: How to Raise Money for Any Startup, Video Game or Project*, J. Kimmich, Ed., read.me (2012), 14–47.

46. Tajfel, H. Social categorization. In *Introduction à la psychologie sociale*, S. Moscovici, Ed., vol. 1, Paris: Larousse. (1972), 272–302.

47. Tajfel, H. In *Human Groups and Social Categories: Studies in Social Psychology.*, Cambridge, UK: Cambridge Univ. Press (1981).

48. Tajfel, H. Social psychology of intergroup relations. *Annual Review of Psychology 33*, 1 (1982).

49. Tajfel, H., and Turner, J. C. An integrative theory of intergroup conflict. *The social psychology of intergroup relations 33* (1979), 47.

50. Tam, K. Y., and Ho, S. Y. Web personalization as a persuasion strategy: An elaboration likelihood model perspective. *Info. Sys. Research 16*, 3 (2005), 271–291.

51. Tausczik, Y. R., and Pennebaker, J. W. The psychological meaning of words: Liwc and computerized text analysis methods. *Journal of Language and Social Psychology 29*, 1 (2010), 24–54.

52. Van Wingerden, R., and Ryan, J. Fighting for funds: An exploratory study into the field of crowdfunding. Tech. rep., Lund University School of Economics and Management, 2011.

53. Venkataraman, S. The distinctive domain of entrepreneurship research: An editor's perspective. In *Advances in entrepreneurship, firm emergence, and growth*, J. Katz and R. Brockhaus, Eds., vol. 3, Greenwich, CT: JAI Press (1997), 119–138.

54. Viegas, F., Wattenberg, M., Van Ham, F., Kriss, J., and McKeon, M. Many Eyes: a site for visualization at internet scale. In *InfoVis*, Published by the IEEE Computer Society (2007), 1121–1128.

55. Wattenberg, M., and Viégas, F. The Word Tree, an interactive visual concordance. In *InfoVis* (2008), 1221–1228.

56. Wilke, H., and Lanzetta, J. T. The obligation to help: The effects of amount of prior help on subsequent helping behavior. *Journal of Experimental Social Psychology*, 6 (1970), 488–493.

57. Wood, W. Attitude change: Persuasion and social influence. *Annual Review of Psychology 51*, 1 (2000), 539–570.

Understanding the Role of Community in Crowdfunding Work

Julie S. Hui
Segal Design Institute
Northwestern University
Evanston, IL USA
juliehui@u.northwestern.edu

Michael D. Greenberg
Segal Design Institute
Northwestern University
Evanston, IL USA
mdgreenb@u.northwestern.edu

Elizabeth M. Gerber
Segal Design Institute
Northwestern University
Evanston, IL USA
egerber@u.northwestern.edu

ABSTRACT

Crowdfunding provides a new opportunity for entrepreneurs to launch ventures without having to rely on traditional funding mechanisms, such as banks and angel investing. Despite its rapid growth, we understand little about how crowdfunding users build ad hoc online communities to undertake this new way of performing entrepreneurial work. To better understand this phenomenon, we performed a qualitative study of 47 entrepreneurs who use crowdfunding platforms to raise funds for their projects. We identify community efforts to support crowdfunding work, such as providing mentorship to novices, giving feedback on campaign presentation, and building a repository of example projects to serve as models. We also identify where community efforts and technologies succeed and fail at supporting the work in order to inform the design of crowdfunding support tools and systems.

Author Keywords

Crowdfunding; community; support tools; entrepreneurship; crowd work; distributed work.

ACM Classification Keywords

H.5.3 [Group and Organization Interfaces]: Design

General Terms

Design

INTRODUCTION

Entrepreneurship is often collaborative work—sharing information, resources, and connections in order to exploit new opportunities [43]. Such collaborations have accelerated over the past few decades as the Internet has created new opportunities for exchange, especially among geographically distributed collaborators.

Crowdfunding has emerged as the most recent Internet based technology to support community in entrepreneurship. Crowdfunding–the online request for resources from a distributed audience often in exchange for a reward [16]—provides a new way for entrepreneurs to solicit financial support from a distributed network that can range in size from dozens to thousands of supporters.

CSCW'14, February 15 - 19 2014, Baltimore, MD, USA

http://dx.doi.org/10.1145/2531602.2531715

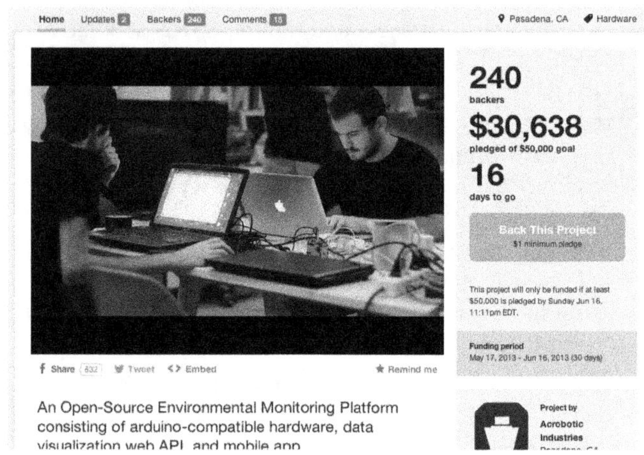

Figure 1: A campaign page on the crowdfunding platform, Kickstarter.

Crowdfunding platforms, such as Kickstarter, invite entrepreneurs to bring "projects big and small to life" by launching a fundraising campaign on their platform [24]. They herald successful examples on their websites, such as the team that raised more than $10,000,000 in a month from 60,000 supporters to manufacture and distribute a video game console [53] and another team that raised over $30,000 from 2,000 supporters to design and produce an eco-friendly pencil [54]. Entrepreneurs, particularly novices with limited networks and proven track records, have accepted the invitation, launching more than 1 million projects in 2011 [13].

Despite the popularity of crowdfunding, our empirical understanding of the cooperative work practices involved in this system is limited. As researchers of computer supported cooperative work (CSCW), we aim in this paper to understand the collaborative efforts and day-to-day activities of crowdfunding users to design and improve crowdfunding support tools [36]. We began our study by asking the question:

- **What is the work of crowdfunding?**

Once we identified a growing theme of community, we added the question:

- **What role does community play in crowdfunding work?**

In order to understand existing technologies that support the work involved [47], we asked:

- **What current technologies support crowdfunding work? And how can they be improved?**

Through a qualitative study of 47 crowdfunding users, we found that they carry out five main types of work—*preparing* the campaign material, *testing* the material, *publicizing* the project, *following through* with project goals, and *reciprocating* resources to the community. During each stage of work, they collaborate with others -- soliciting and giving advice based on their crowdfunding experience, engaging donors in online conversation, and encouraging their social network to spread the word [30]. In addition to using general computer mediated planning and creative tools, such as email, group calendars, and video editing software, users have also started using crowdfunding-specific tools, such as crowdfunding project search websites and supporter management platforms. By understanding how these community efforts and technologies succeed and fail at supporting crowdfunding work, we can identify how to better design tools that support collaboration within the crowdfunding community.

We organized the paper into three sections. The first section introduces crowdfunding work and related research. The second section presents our findings, identifying and describing crowdfunding work, the role of community, and existing technologies used. The third section discusses design implications and the need for tools and systems that facilitate the work practices.

CROWDFUNDING

The first crowdfunding platform was launched in 2001 [52] and has grown to over 452 platforms worldwide [13]. These platforms use existing systems to facilitate the exchange of resources between entrepreneurs and supporters, such as web-based payment systems (e.g. Amazon Payments), messaging systems (e.g. comment threads), social media (e.g. Facebook) and video sharing platforms (e.g. YouTube) to raise awareness about the project. Unlike traditional fundraising methods, such as applying for funds from banks or foundations, crowdfunding allows creators, people who request resources, to appeal for funds directly from supporters, people who give resources, without giving up project ownership [16].

In order to start a crowdfunding campaign on an online platform, creators develop a project profile, which typically includes a title, video, description of planned use of funds, funding goal, campaign duration, and reward descriptions. Creators fill out these recommended and required fields online, and if the project is approved, the crowdfunding platform posts their work in a pre-formatted public page where supporters can choose to donate (see Figure 1).

RELATED WORK

We found that crowdfunding is a type of entrepreneurial work that relies heavily on community building, distributed work, and crowd work. We review relevant literature in these related areas.

Entrepreneurial Work

Entrepreneurial work involves the discovery, evaluation, and exploitation of opportunities to introduce novel products, services, and organizations [42,43,48]. Entrepreneurs assess opportunities through psychological and environmental factors such as one's risk aversion and employment status [43]. When obtaining resources, scholars find that the majority of entrepreneurs use their own savings either out of necessity or to maintain control [3]. Entrepreneurs then exploit opportunities by creating a new firm or market mechanisms [43] through the organization of equipment, employees, production processes, and legal obligations [48].

Although scholars argue that the act of discovering entrepreneurial opportunities is a solitary endeavor, the exploitation of the entrepreneurial opportunity is often collaborative [43]. Entrepreneurs work in teams or form alliances with partnering organizations to benefit from other people's skillsets and to ease the workload [20,27,29,39]. However, entrepreneurs primarily collaborate to maintain a competitive advantage over other entrepreneurs, and therefore rarely share their best practices with the public [43]. This competitive environment makes it difficult for entrepreneurs to engage with communities in an open manner, which is considered a common practice in crowdfunding. Therefore, while crowdfunders also coordinate efforts and exploit opportunities to follow through with their project goals, they are more open about their process and interact more closely with their community to achieve their work.

Online Communities

Online communities are any virtual space where people interact to converse, exchange information or resources, learn, or play [38]. In these spaces, members can contribute to the community growth by performing menial tasks, such as voting, or coordinating content production, such as managing a forum. Kraut identifies five main design challenges to create and maintain online communities, including starting up the community, attracting members, motivating commitment, motivating contributions, and regulating community health and wellness. Similar to crowdfunding project creators, community designers overcome these challenges by deciding what content to post, communicating with members, and offering feedback and rewards to members [38].

To motivate people to join, scholars stress that community leaders should reach out to potential members personally

[32,33], send clear and easy to act on messages, get high status or a critical number of people to join the cause [19,33], give evidence that membership will make a difference on community wellbeing [31], and show that there is an urgency to join [31]. Crowdfunding project creators accomplish these tasks by sending personalized emails, asking friends and news media to publicize their project, show member contribution through a funding bar, and express the need to raise funds by a certain deadline.

Distributed Work and Crowd Work

Distributed and crowd work involve the collaborative efforts of many people to achieve a common goal. Distributed work involves collaborating with a known but physically distributed group of individuals [37], while crowd work involves many distributed anonymous workers performing online tasks [26].

In distributed work, to address the challenges of working distantly and online, workers must establish a mutual understanding of the work and determine the most effective mode of online communication [37]. By interacting regularly and often using communication technologies, workers with an ill defined task can quickly gain a mutual understanding of project goals and responsibilities [37]. Workers take into account the nature of the task to determine the extent and mode of communication, such as whether to work synchronously or asynchronously, through e-mail or group conferencing [37]. The effectiveness of using such technologies depends on the pre-established culture of worker collaboration [37].

Unlike distributed work [37], requestors of crowd work have limited information about workers and assign tasks through a mediated online platform (e.g. Amazon Mechanical Turk). Crowd work can be voluntary or paid [26]. To create well-designed crowd work tasks, requestors must take into account the order of tasks, the pairing of tasks with workers, and ways to enable collaboration [26]. Creating tasks that follow these guidelines supports an environment where crowd workers produce better quality work and have a greater role in the entire process [26].

Crowdfunding creators perform distributed work by managing team efforts, outsourced labor, and supporters whom they personally know. Concurrently, they perform crowd work by motivating people outside their social network to join the cause and spread the word about one's project [30]. However, unlike distributed and crowd work, crowdfunding supporters primarily contribute funds rather than labor.

Research on Crowdfunding

Economics, management, and business scholars initiated research into crowdfunding because of the potential disruption to the economy. Economists strive to understand how crowdfunding can be used as a mechanism to gather data on consumer willingness to pay [6]. Economists find that crowdfunding has market advantages such as increasing consumer awareness and disseminating product information [6]. Management scholars study how crowdfunding can overcome offline barriers to financial transactions [1]. They find that crowdfunding mainly eliminates the effects of distance from supporters whom creators did not previously know [1]. Business scholars strive to understand how crowdfunding can provide insight into the experience goods market [49]. They find that crowdfunding support is mainly controlled by peer effects [49].

However, few scholars have examined crowdfunding from a community standpoint in order to understand how communities of creators and supporters interact with each other to accomplish crowdfunding goals. Those who do have only studied "enterprise crowdfunding" where employees give money to projects of other employees to improve within-company collaboration and innovation [35]. The study on "enterprise crowdfunding" was done in a closed environment of one company, while the crowdfunding community that we study is open.

As designers and CSCW researchers, we strive to understand why people choose to use and interact within this new type of online platform. In a previous study of crowdfunding, researchers uncovered creator and supporter motivations and deterrents to crowdfund [16]. They found that creators were not only motivated to raise funds, but also to expand awareness of their work, establish connections, gain approval, maintain control, and learn new skills. Supporters were not only motivated to collect rewards, but also to help others, be part of a community, and support causes in which they believe strongly. However, creators were also wary of attracting negative public exposure, the time commitment, and how project creators would use the funds [17].

During the study of motivations for participation, creators routinely expressed concerns about the disparity between the perceptions of crowdfunding work in the popular press and what they actually experienced. While the press publishes sensational articles about former "nobody's" raising millions of dollars through social media marketing [55], project creators whom we interviewed described the difficulties creating a campaign and communicating and coordinating with a large online audience. These findings inspired the current research we present.

METHODS

Interview Participants

We interviewed 47 crowdfunding project creators from three crowdfunding platforms—Kickstarter, IndieGoGo, and Rockethub—the most popular and successful platforms in the US [4]. Projects included Art (7), Comics (1), Dance (1), Design (15), Education (1), Fashion (2), Film & Video (7), Food (4), Games (10), Music (3), Photography (3), Publishing (6), Science (4), Technology (1), and Theater (3). Approximately 50% of project creators met their fundraising goal on at least one of their projects, which is similar to the success rate of Kickstarter, the largest crowdfunding platform that we studied [56].

Most creators maintained full time professional day jobs – spending between 30 minutes and 7 hours a day on weeknights or weekends working on their crowdfunding project. Three informants relied on crowdfunding as their primary source of income. Participant ages ranged from 20 to 52 years old and raised between $71 and $313,371. Thirteen creators launched more than one campaign, ranging between one to nine campaigns per creator interviewed. Interviewees were not compensated for their participation. We found that our sample of participants is representative of the crowdfunding population based on success rate and spread of project types [56].

Procedure

We recruited interview participants through random and snowball sampling, which allowed us to identify typical and atypical participants from the crowdfunding population. Our semi-structured interview protocol was divided into two sections. In the first section, we asked participants about their professional background and how they learned about and became engaged in crowdfunding. During the second phase, we asked participants to describe the work involved - both collaborative and independent. We began each interview by explaining that we were researchers not affiliated with any crowdfunding platform and that personal information would remain anonymous.

Interview data collection lasted for 11 months with an average interview length of 30 minutes. Interviews were conducted over video conferencing, phone, and in person. Interviews were conducted during and after the creators' campaigns. Advantages of this research approach include collecting both reflective and in situ data. Disadvantages include biases from self-report [44].

Analysis

We used selective coding and analysis [44] to understand the work involved in crowdfunding. First, we flagged each instance describing work. After identifying all of the instances, we clustered tasks into conceptual categories. Initial data analysis for the semi-structured interviews began after 10 interviews, while the remaining interviews were used to gather data pertaining to emergent themes [34].

CROWDFUNDING WORK

We identified five main types of crowdfunding work: (1) *preparing* campaign content and initial prototypes, (2) *testing* the campaign material, (3) *publicizing* the crowdfunding project to potential supporters, (4) *following through* with project goals, and (5) *reciprocating* resources to the crowdfunding community. In each of these stages, we identify how community and support tools facilitate or hinder the work process.

Prepare the Campaign Material

Preparing the campaign material includes all crowdfunding related efforts prior to the campaign launch, which typically includes creating a video, project description, funding goal, campaign timeline, and reward descriptions to be posted on the campaign page (see Figure 1). From our initial data, we found that creators had difficulties learning the technologies and skills needed to perform these preparation tasks, such as using video editing software or writing a convincing description. In order to gain the necessary knowledge and skills, project creators relied on the community by using similar existing projects as models for their own, and reading blog posts and soliciting advice from experienced project creators.

Based on our interviews, preparing these materials can last three to six months before the campaign during which time the creators spend extensive efforts understanding the process and learning new skills. A creator of a science project described challenges with preparation:

"It was enveloping in terms of taking up time and emotion and overall effort. Creating a video, obviously, is difficult. I felt like it was a good opportunity and a good experience, but nonetheless, it takes a lot of time developing a script, collecting all the videos, editing, etc." -p11

To facilitate learning from others, crowdfunding platforms provide project search capabilities, such as finding projects based on location and category. Investigating other projects helps creators decide on reward ideas, video ideas, project description language, and nature of communication with supporters. A creator of a publishing project explained:

"It's always good to see what works for these projects and what doesn't work. How they're promoting, [performing] backer updates...All of those different parts of it, you kind of take those as inspiration and figure out how to adapt that to your own voice." -p6

However, Kickstarter, IndieGoGo, and Rockethub do not offer the ability to search for others people's projects by failed projects or by funding goal, number of supporters, or campaign duration, campaign features that project creators cite as ways to compare and contrast to their own campaign to others. In response, frustrated creators have started to create their own tools, such as the project search platforms Kickspy [57] and The Kickback Machine [58]. These platforms allow creators to find projects similar to theirs based on various project attributes in order to learn from the experiences of others.

Creators also reported reading advice blogs, where other creators have documented their crowdfunding experience, as a useful way to prepare for their own campaign. One creator of a photography project described how he got inspiration from a related project:

"I was reading somebody's Tumblr...It was another photo project...That's how I came up with a lot of my rewards...I kind of was trying to take a little from a lot of people [to] come up with rewards that people are kind of into." -p20

Some creators also described relying on experts with certain skillsets within the community to prepare campaign material. A creator of a children's food project described how she

Crowdfunding Work	Definition	Role of Community
Prepare	Prepare campaign materials	Provide example projects as models Provide general advice blogs Give one-on-one advice Offer specialized skill expertise
Test	Test campaign materials	Give feedback on campaign materials Provide opinion on design direction
Publicize	Market the project by using campaign materials	Spread the word Build an audience
Follow Through	Follow through with project goals and send rewards	Provide manufacturing or shipping support Offer specialized skill expertise
Reciprocate	Reciprocate resources back to the crowdfunding community	Provide advice Provide financial resources

Table 1: Table of crowdfunding work, including definitions and summary of the role of community throughout the work process.

relied on the free counseling of a film expert to help make her project video:

"The girl who helped us with the film...she gave us tips on script and stuff like that. We had a couple meetings with her, and she did it in her spare time too. So, that was part of the challenge because we were depending on other people who were kind of giving their time for it."-p17

Novice crowdfunders have begun to turn to self-proclaimed "crowdfunding consultants" who have made a name for themselves as expert crowdfunders in the crowdfunding community. One project creator explained how she agreed to give 7.5% of her post-campaign profits to a consultant who had successfully ran several of his own crowdfunding campaigns in exchange for his advice. Because the campaign material is the initial touch point between creators and potential supporters, some creators decide to spend extra money to seek their advice. The topic of crowdfunding mentors will be discussed further in the Reciprocate Resources section.

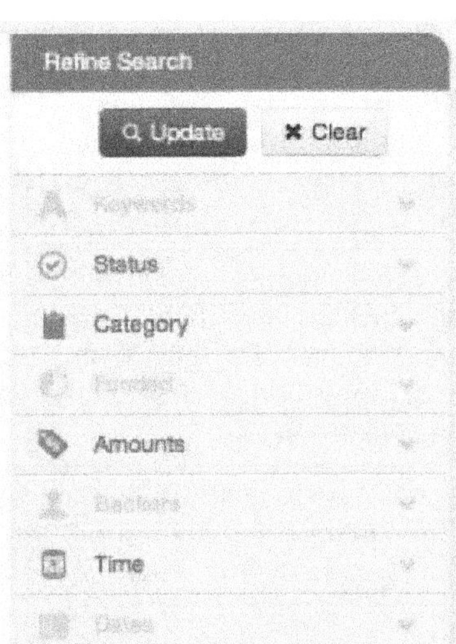

Figure 2: Kickspy's project search bar, which allows creators to search for crowdfunding projects based on keywords, campaign status, project category, amount raised, number of backers, campaign duration and what months the campaign was live.

In addition, all three platforms provide tutorial/information pages to explain crowdfunding responsibilities. But, few creators cited using these tutorials as a major method of preparing for their campaign. Rather they preferred to follow advice blogs or look at other projects for ideas. This suggests that more research is needed to understand what makes crowdfunding-specific tools useful or not useful.

Overall, creators described the usefulness of tools that support learning from analogy [15], such as reading advice blogs and searching for inspirational projects, and rely on other people's skillsets to accomplish the work. While participants described the usefulness of search tools, they expressed difficulties learning more complicated technologies, such as video editing software.

Test the Campaign Material

Creators test their campaign material by asking for feedback from their personal network and community of supporters. The amount of testing varies from creator to creator, some getting feedback from as many people as possible while others producing their work without input from others. We find that creators who actively seek feedback before and during the campaign tend to be more successful, which is consistent with research on the importance of getting feedback during the design process [21].

Creators first look to their personal network, such as friends and family, to give initial feedback. Creators preferred to be judged in a private setting with close friends rather than sharing materials with a public audience that could reject their work. A professor and creator of a science project described how he felt when showing his video publicly to his undergraduate class to get feedback:

"I was nervous because it's one thing to be sitting in front of a computer, and it's quite another thing to show a video to an audience where you can actually hear their reaction...Are they actually going to find this funny? When you haven't done something like that before, it's a little intimidating."-p31

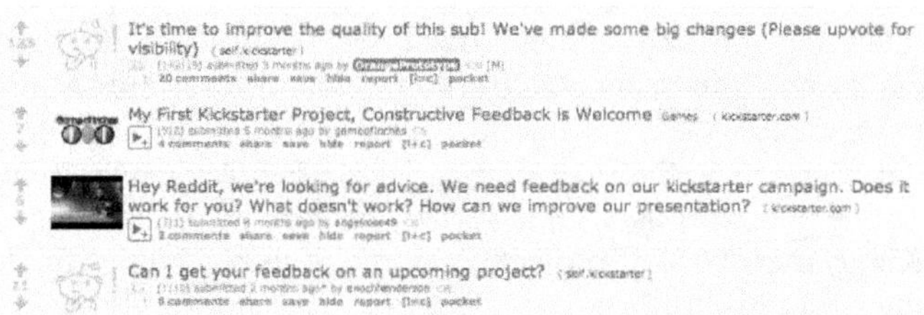

Figure 3: Posts on the Kickstarter Subreddit where project creators seek advice on their campaign material prior to launching.

Other creators reported turning to their supporters during the campaign to get feedback on project direction and design. One creator of a poetry book project posted daily poems and used his audience to gauge the quality of his writing:

"Some of the backers have been emailing me that they like the different poems, like, 'Oh, the poem today was great,' others are telling me, 'They're okay."-p24

Another creator of a snowshoe design project let his supporters decide the color of the shoe straps. Unlike traditional company-consumer relationships, such as buying a product on Amazon, crowdfunding project creators are able to involve the supporters in the design process by polling for their opinions or conversing with them on a discussion board throughout the design process.

Recognizing the need to incentivize giving and getting feedback, Rockethub's SciFund Challenge requires creators to give feedback to other creators in the platform community wiki page. One creator described how she used this platform-based support network to improve her campaign material:

"I did have the help of the other SciFund people. We had a wiki. We all put up our projects, and people would comment on them, so I got a lot of good feedback from the other people who were also putting up projects, and I commented on their projects."-p3

Currently there exists no online mechanism specifically for getting feedback on crowdfunding materials from the crowd in a private setting. Creators are able to gather feedback publicly through social media platforms, such as Facebook and Reddit, to gauge how the online crowd will react to their campaign.

Testing campaign material and project prototypes before the campaign acts as type of soft launch, releasing a product or service early to a limited audience, while testing the material after the campaign launches allows creators to iteratively improve their page to during the campaign.

Creators often emphasized the importance of editing their material prior to launch because they will be preoccupied publicizing their work and communicating with supporters during the campaign. Those who did not test their campaign material expressed difficulties finding an audience to solicit quick and honest feedback. People who turned to their community of friends and family expressed that their opinions were often not representative of the public as shown by their campaign success or failure. Participants also expressed worries that asking for help before the campaign would use up social capital [10,12] that they had hoped to save for publicity efforts later on.

Publicize the Project

Creators market their project by publicizing their idea through social media, contacting people individually through email, and sending press releases to news media outlets to reach a wider audience. Although creators reported relying on community efforts to help them publicize their project, they still expressed difficulties building an audience, getting people to spread the word, and managing discussions with supporters. One creator of a food project described the time commitment during a live campaign:

"It's honestly, like, it's a full time job. If you're going to launch a Kickstarter, you have to be prepared to devote 4-5 hours a day just making sure that you are promoting it or following up on it, you know, or anything like that." -p8

Creators reported spending 2-11 hours a day marketing during a live campaign that usually lasts 0.5-2.0 months, which often leads to a pay to time-spent ratio less than minimum wage.

In an effort to harness the power of their social network, creators ask their friends and family to spread the word [14]. For instance, a creator of another food project described:

"Help I get from my good friends is just reposting it...echoing it out on onto their networks and their Facebook or LinkedIn or Twitter accounts." -p18

Others reach out to existing online niche communities, such as Subreddits, in order to contact people that are interested in the specific project topic. For example, the creators of the game project, Planetary Annihilation, on Kickstarter, raised over $2 million from over 40,000 supporters and maintain an active Subreddit of 2,800 followers in which they keep supporters updated on the campaign and game progress.

Not only must creators act as their own publicist, they must also perform public relations by addressing questions and concerns from hundreds or thousands of supporters. By addressing questions and posting regular updates, creators maintain supporter relations and uphold a reputation of being responsible and trustworthy. A creator of a game project described how he keeps his supporters informed on progress:

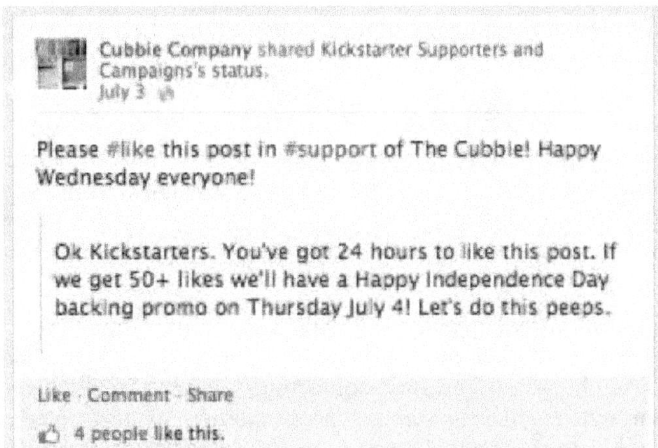

Figure 4: A post by a crowdfunding project creator asking Facebook friends to spread the word about the campaign.

"I will make sure that I send updates on how it's going... I'm able to share real time videos of how I lay out a book design, and so I can share the process as it goes through. The backers appreciate that, and that seems to kind of build up trust that I can fulfill on these projects, which is one big question mark early on."-p27

However, not all creators realize that supporters want to engage in the project creation process, and therefore fail to write enough project updates or respond to their comments. Some of our participants cited not interacting with their supporters enough as a major reason for why their campaign did not gain widespread publicity.

In order to continuously gain traction with personal connections, creators reported sending emails once or twice a week to remind people to support the campaign.

"I was emailing people individually asking for support...I would say, hey person's name, I am doing this project. It's really cool, and give them like a description of it, and at the end of it, I would say, I know that this project will be very successful on Kickstarter because of supporters like you." -p1

While some reported their project going viral, leading to a boost in support:

"I posted on Google+. I posted on Twitter. I posted on my blog...It was picked up on twitter by a British science journalist...and then CNN covered it, and Forbes covered it, and then everything just went crazy after that."-p3

Others had trouble making any impact in the online space:

"I've reached out to dozens and dozens of blogs and newspapers and entertainment sites...And I've just gotten a couple of mentions, which really surprises me. It's been very difficult getting the word out there... I have good friends that I haven't been able to get to the site. It's very shocking. It kind of shows you who your real friends are." -p24

Such comments suggest that creators do not have an accurate understanding of their social network or crowdfunding community, and may need further guidance in learning how to leverage their connections. The majority of failed project creators cited the inability to successfully leverage an online audience as a main reason for failing. According to Kickstarter, 56% of project creators fail to reach their funding goal [56].

Creators who reported having previous experience publicizing their work tended to be more successful. For instance, we found that creators with an established career in the arts had less trouble marketing their work than creators of science research projects. Because art project creators described having experience organizing public fundraising efforts throughout their career, they felt more comfortable asking their friends and family for support and had already developed an interested audience prior to launching their campaign.

By regularly interacting with an online audience through marketing efforts, participating in discussions, sending updates, and inquiring for supportive efforts, creators build an ad hoc community of supporters. While the work of maintaining this community takes public relations skills and is very time consuming, creators are able to create a following that lasts throughout their campaign and possibly for future projects.

Follow Through with Project Goals

Creators follow through with their campaign by carrying out project goals and delivering rewards. Creators who make it to this stage of crowdfunding find the public commitment of manufacturing and shipping rewards to be overwhelming because they must answer to hundreds or thousands of supporters [9]. In an effort to ease their responsibilities, some creators describe tapping into communities of skilled labor to outsource some of the work.

A creator of a board game project described how he and others collaborate with people with needed skillsets in a resource exchange of funds and labor:

"Say you do layout or you do editing, there's sort of this relationship now that you get with project creators where you can sort of agree handshake deal to work on their project on the condition that it be funded first...So, though no money has exchanged hands, and no one's really contractually obliged to...you can still come to agreements that are mutually beneficial."-p27

However, many project creators are not part of an existing community whom they can call on for project support. People with less community connections and fundraising experience describe being ill prepared for this stage of the crowdfunding process. A first-time creator of a publication project described how she was unprepared to produce on a large scale:

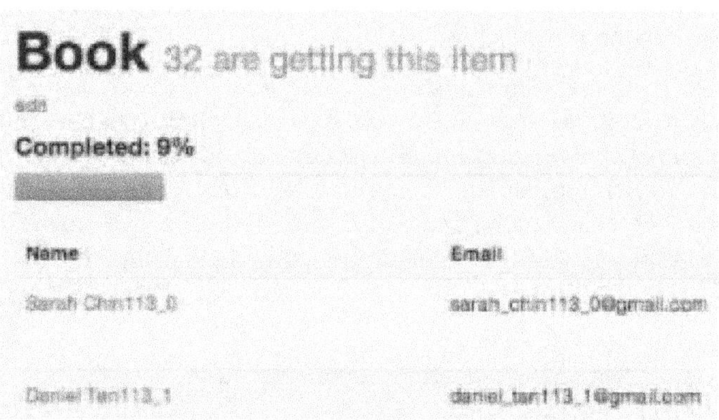

Figure 5: Screenshot of the BackerKit interface, a platform that was started by experienced crowdfunders, to help project creators keep track of supporters and rewards after the campaign ends.

"We're a one person company for the most part. I'm the only full time person working on this over here...It's just a lot to get all these things out to that many people." -p7

To the dismay of her supporters, p7 could not send her rewards out until months after her promised deadline. Sending out rewards after the proposed shipping date has become a prominent issue in popular press [50]. Of the 47 people we interviewed, creators reported having to manage between 3 and 3,258 supporters.

Those with extra funds often decide to hire outside help. For example, a creator of a dance project explained:

"I was very lucky in that I didn't handle the mailing myself. My assistant did. But, I think she wanted to throttle me and the postal service by the end." -p15

In response to difficulties during campaign follow through, project creators and other companies have begun to develop tools to support the organization of supporter information and reward shipment (see Figure 5) [59,60,61].

Creators reported the use of general planning and communication tools, such as Excel, email, and Google Calendar to manage orders and collaborate with others. Many expressed difficulties knowing how to use these technologies to accomplish the work since simply knowing how to use Excel does not mean that one has budget management experience. Although there has been an increase in the number of crowdfunding-specific tools, few of the creators interviewed knew of their existence.

Reciprocate Resources

While some would consider the previous four types of work to fully describe crowdfunding, we also take into account reciprocating resources, including providing crowdfunding advice and funds back to the community. Creators consider contributing as a critical task to maintaining a sustainable ecosystem that supports collaboration rather than competition. Creators contribute back knowledge by posting relevant online resources, such as blogs on their experience, or offering one-on-one help in person or though email or video chat. Creators also contribute back funds to support other creators the way the crowdfunding community first supported them. For instance, one film creator explained:

"There's a kind of etiquette in [my film program]. If someone funded me, then I'm supposed to fund them back. Otherwise, it would be a little awkward." -p30

Another creator of a publishing project described how this work was about more than just giving money:

"The funny thing is I probably gave other people as much money as I've just made on this Kickstarter campaign... I could have kept that money in my pocket, but the whole thing is like, a load of confidence." -p32

She described how crowdfunding served as public validation for her work, something that creators cannot measure when being funded by a single investor.

Creators also support each other by sharing crowdfunding advice with novice creators. One board game creator explained how he created a Pinterest board (see Figure 6) where he posts links to articles that answer commonly asked questions:

"I've put [advice] on a Pinterest board that I try to share when people come to me now and ask, 'How do I do a Kickstarter?'...Kickstarter itself actually documents some of these answers, but I think people just look at it and kind of get a little, I don't know, glassy-eyed? And so, to an extent, they're just looking for, 'Well, where do I start trying to figure out what I want to do here,' and that's what the pin board was for." -p33

Experienced creators provide advice at different stages of the campaign. Another mentor described giving more feedback on people's campaign material rather than advice before they started planning for the campaign:

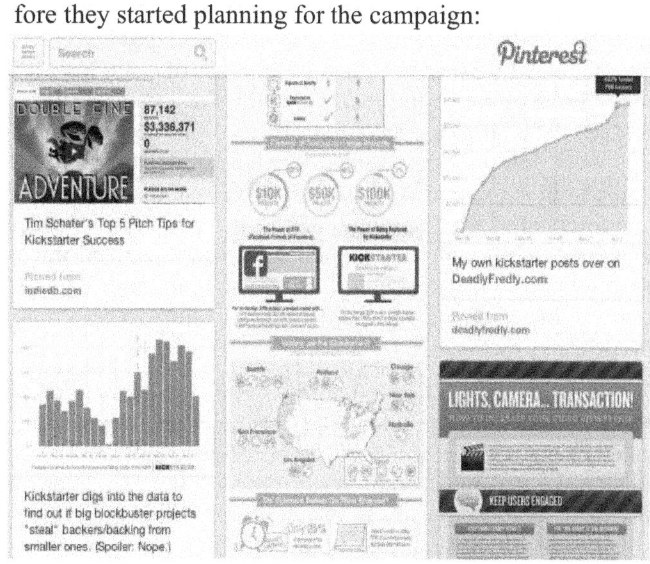

Figure 6: Screenshot of a creator's Pinterest advice board that he made to help mentor novice project creators.

"Every week or so, somebody emails me asking questions about Kickstarter, like, 'My project got rejected by Kickstarter, how do I redo it?' And I'm like, 'You need to change this, this, and this."-p6

Another successful crowdfunding team created public Google Documents templates of how to format a supporter email, press email, media management spreadsheet, supporter management spreadsheet, and update description.

While some creators have become well known in the crowdfunding community as mentors because they post advice blogs and actively seek out ways to support others, most project creators contribute back by helping out one or two people who reach out to them. For instance, a high school student who launched a crowdfunding citizen science project described:

"The other day I was approached by a 14 year old who was in medical school in Guatemala, and I gave her some help on [her project] and she helped me back. So, I'm not sure if I'm a mentor because she helped me as much as I helped her. But, I like to think that I will be helping other people as much as they helped me."-p47

Project creators feel a sense of responsibility for giving back to the community that supported them, whether that is financially or as a mentor. These practices have created an environment that is more supportive and less competitive compared to certain entrepreneurial practices, such as innovation competitions where entrepreneurs must maintain information asymmetry to get the resources that they need. We find that contributing knowledge and financial resources back to the community is critical for the growth of crowdfunding as a cooperative community.

DISCUSSION

The ongoing relationship that crowdfunders maintain with their community of creators and supporters sets it apart from typical entrepreneurial work. Scholars studying entrepreneurship find that less than 30 percept of entrepreneurs maintained direct or indirect ties with investors or customers [7]. This stands in contrast to crowdfunding creators who are advised to maintain regular contact with their community of supporters through project updates and discussion boards. Our findings suggest the community aspect of crowdfunding, including publicizing to the general Internet audience and managing hundreds or thousands of supporters, introduces unique difficulties to the typical entrepreneurial process.

Although the campaign duration is limited, many project creators are motivated to build lasting relationships with supporters, other creators, and resource providers long after their campaign ends. To do this, creators follow community building practices, such as engaging with supporters personally by explaining the value of their support [32], recruiting supporters to spread the word about the campaign in order to reach a critical mass of members [19,30,33], as well as extrinsically motivating people to contribute by promising rewards [28,40].

Unlike in entrepreneurship, crowdfunding creators describe their relationship with the public as a supportive rather than competitive relationship. Shane stresses that the act of identifying entrepreneurial opportunities is not a collective act, but the work of an individual formulating a new means-ends framework [43]. While he explains that the entrepreneurial process involves collaboration with teammates and other firms, he emphasizes that entrepreneurs aim to maintain information asymmetry in order to have a competitive advantage. This is different from crowdfunding where project creators feel responsible for helping other project creators by sharing advice and feedback. To support the mentorship and vicariously learning from other, project creators seek help on online forums and use search features to support researching campaigns [57,58].

Similar to entrepreneurship, the evaluation of crowdfunding projects relies on a socio-cultural environment where society ultimately makes the decision on what projects should or should not be funded [43]. In this case, the heavy reliance on community is beneficial for crowdfunding creators because their work is constantly being assessed by the consumers throughout the campaign. Creators acknowledge the usefulness of getting feedback from the crowd [21], but few attempt to do it on a large scale for fear of public rejection [9]. Those that want to test their materials with the crowd face difficulties in finding enough motivated people to give detailed feedback outside of their personal network.

We found that crowdfunding work relies on a mix of distributed work and crowd work since creators may work with distributed team members and supporters to organize campaign efforts while soliciting publicity help from hundreds of people that they have never met before. Similar to crowd work, creators must tailor their requests to the supporter community to motivate contributions [26]. Similar to distributed work, context still matters [37] in communicating with crowdfunding supporters (e.g. by social media, blog posts, etc.). Creators also use various web-based technologies, such as video, email, and personal blogs, to achieve common ground with their supporters when explaining their project idea and value. Unlike crowd and distributed work, crowdfunding supporters mainly contribute money while crowd workers typically contribute services in exchange for money.

Creators also express difficulties spreading the word about their project and mobilizing interest, which could be explained by creators having less business, marketing, and management experience [41], as well as lower social status [45] and fewer social ties [2,11,18]. Lescovec, Adamic, and Huberman's research in viral marketing has also shown that there exists a saturation point to the number of recommendations a person can receive to purchase a product [30]. We observe similar activity in the crowdfunding consumer space where creators who market their project too often become ignored by their social network, which may contribute to their inability to publicize their project effectively. This suggests that more research needs to be done on finding ways to gage community willingness to help.

The practice of relying on others for outsourced help, mentorship, and feedback has created a community where the crowd funds the work and creators collaborate with helpful individuals through a mutually beneficial partnership. During follow through, creators have begun to form connections with companies and people with specific skillsets to perform certain tasks. Similarly, entrepreneurial work emphasizes the usefulness of teams [27,39] and forming alliances [23] to help ease work responsibilities.

While both entrepreneurship and crowdfunding rely on collaboration to achieve project goals, crowdfunding inherently relies more on community support for project success. We find that creators rely on community efforts to overcome difficulties of getting advice, designing one's campaign, getting feedback, publicity, and shipping rewards. We call for the creation of systems tailored to the needs of crowdfunding project creators.

DESIGN IMPLICATIONS FOR SUPPORT TOOLS

Based on our findings, we provide an overview of current crowdfunding support tools, and how they do or do not support coordination and collaboration throughout the crowdfunding work process. We identify opportunities for improvement in the areas of feedback and mentorship. We also acknowledge that tool adoption is a primary issue as there may need to be better mechanisms that assist in new technology visibility or cheaper and easier ways to onboard.

Support campaign preparation

During the preparation stage, project creators described searching for example projects, reading advice blogs, seeking one-on-one advice, and outsourcing preparation tasks. Because many crowdfunding platforms, including Kickstarter, IndieGoGo, and Rockethub, do not allow project creators to search for failed projects or by certain attributes, platforms such as The Kickback Machine [58] and Kickspy [57] were designed to help project creators find crowdfunding projects from which creators can learn strategies to follow or avoid. Although crowdfunding articles and blogs stress the need to research other campaigns before launching one's own, most of our participants said they did not research enough, and few knew of the existence of these search tools. This suggests that extra steps must be taken to get the crowdfunding support tools into the hands of novice creators perhaps through establishing partnerships between crowdfunding platforms and independent crowdfunding support tools. From initial interviews, there appeared to be a disconnect between creators of crowdfunding support tools and managers of crowdfunding platforms, as the former say that platform managers have never reached out to them, while the latter describe having little time to partner with other websites.

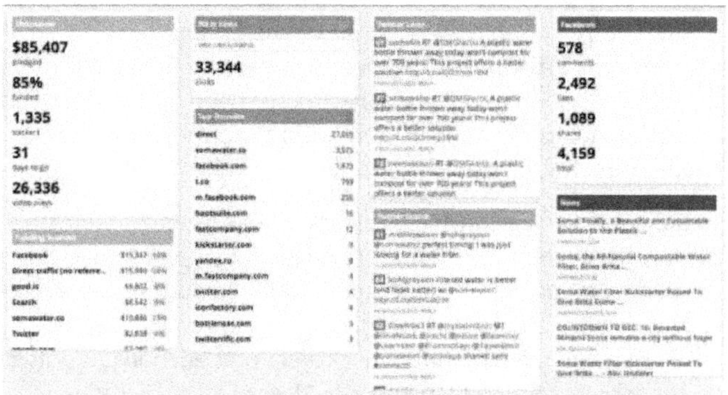

Figure 7: Screenshot of the Kickstarter Status Board, which allows creators to track who is posting about their campaign on which social media sites, and which of those links drives the most traffic to the crowdfunding campaign page.

Support campaign material testing

There are also no platforms dedicated to providing crowdfunding advice or feedback. Rather, creators find feedback providers mentors through word of mouth or online forums that serve as meeting places for people who give and seek advice. However, these forums offer mainly one-time interactions, and more general crowdfunding advice rather than more useful one-on-one feedback. Most of the project creators described seeking feedback from a few close friends or family members. Project creators described being unwilling to show their campaign material to a wider audience, such as weak ties on social media sites, prior to launch fearing they would use up social capital [10]. Because feedback provides insights on how to improve project quality [46], one potential design solution is to create a service that helps creators test their work with an anonymous crowd, such as on Amazon Mechanical Turk. As Mechanical Turk becomes an increasingly popular testing ground for new ideas in research [25], we could employ similar methods to help creators systematically collect and synthesize feedback about their project from an online crowd. Currently, crowdfunding researchers are beginning to develop tools that allow project creators to seek large amounts of feedback in a private setting from an anonymous crowd [51], which would allow them to test their ideas without wasting social capital.

Support publicity management

We have also identified a number of tools that support publicity and supporter management. Project creators describe publicizing the campaign as one of the most difficult stages of crowdfunding. However, because many of these tools were launched in the past year, few of the people we interviewed were able to use them for their campaign or were unaware of their existence.

To support the workload of running a campaign, creators could use personal virtual assistants provided by platforms, such as Zirtual [62], which allows people to hire online assistants to help with publicity efforts or community management. However, many of our participants described having little to no extra funds to hire an assistant, especially one they had never met before, as is the case with Zirtual. Instead most attempt to perform social media marketing on their own, finding that posting on their Facebook wall or Twitter feed quickly reaches its impact limit before the project is close to reaching its funding goal.

In an effort to help project creators better organize their publicity efforts, people in the crowdfunding community have created publicity tracking support tools, including the Kickstarter Status Board [5], which allows project creators to track all posts made about their project on Facebook, Twitter, and news media. Participants also described difficulties contacting their community of supporters on a large scale. One tool that supports this feature is Nationbuilder [63], which allows campaign managers to collect, organize, and contact large amounts of supporters personally. While Nationbuilder offers a wide variety of features that support crowdfunding work, it is not free and is marketed towards more intensive campaigns, such as running a nonprofit company or a political campaign, that may last many months or years. Learning to use its system may take too much extra time and money, especially for people who are crowdfunding for only a few weeks in addition to their daytime jobs.

Support campaign follow through

Tools have also been launched to support crowdfunding follow through work, including Backerkit [59], which allows project creators to organize supporter and reward information, Teelaunch [60], which prints and ships t-shirt rewards for crowdfunding campaigns, and Fullfillrite [61], which manages crowdfunding reward shipping efforts. In an effort to strengthen the "meta-economy" already being formed, HCI designers could design a matchmaking service in an effort to build a community between project creators who lack skills and people with skills but in need of employment. There exist search agencies that find people with specialized skillsets, such as Odesk [64], which directly connects people in search of help to people who can provide it. However, the dynamic of crowdfunding where creators cannot pay outsourced help until after having a successful campaign, may affect who is willing to offer their services as not all creators are able to guarantee payment if the project falls through. This suggests that there may be a need for trust-based connection services for crowdfunding where creators and people who provide skilled labor mutually understand the tenuous payment situation.

Support reciprocating resources

In terms of reciprocating resources, project creators have posted on blogs and personal websites, participated in crowdfunding online forums, created advice boards (see Figure 2), and responded to questions through email. However, participants described hearing about advice and mentors through word of mouth, which means that much advice goes unheard, and people with more ties to the crowdfunding community are more likely to find help. While online forums, such as the crowdfunding Subreddit, bring together mentors and people in search of advice, the relationship is not personal because users are anonymous, and very brief because people can come and go without being responsible for following up. While any advice is helpful, creators preferred more personal one-on-one advice from mentors with whom they could maintain a long-term trusting relationship. This suggests that creators would benefit from a mentorship service where novices are paired with experienced crowdfunders who are willing answer questions throughout the campaign.

While there has been a growth in the number of crowdfunding support tools in the past years, many project creators have not started using them or even know of their existence. This adoption failure could be a factor of cost, visibility, or onboarding effort. Many of these tools have already begun to address crowdfunding difficulties identified in this study, such as project search, publicity tracking, and reward fulfillment. However, there still exist many opportunities for improvement, such as ways to get crowd feedback prior to campaign launch or easier ways to connect crowdfunding mentors to novice creators. By building on relevant research in HCI and online communities, we take the opportunity to create design solutions that help creators accomplish crowdfunding work.

FUTURE RESEARCH

Our findings present many new questions for future research. First, we seek to discover why some people meet their goal and others do not. Possible explanations may include time management, team size, position in network, and the ability to use social media effectively. When considering future attempts to crowdfund, one creator said he would do the same work, but allocate his time differently – spending more time on marketing prior to the launch of his campaign. Another creator said he might expand his team to include members with needed skillsets. Believing that crowdfunding is the quantification of one's social capital, another creator suggested that he would build his network offline before attempting a crowdfunding project with a larger fundraising goal. This perspective is consistent with research that finds that network position influences access to resources [8].

We also intend to study how prior experience influences crowdfunding work. In this study, we found that creators of artistic projects tended to report less difficulties crowdfunding than creators of science projects. Creators of artistic projects reported having had to rely on other forms of crowdfunding (e.g. holding fundraisers) before online crowdfunding platforms existed. They reported finding it easy to ask people to give funds or to promote their project to as many people as possible. Scientific researchers on the other hand, who typically solicit funds from a single contact through government and private foundation grants, found this work more difficult.

While we hope to better understand factors leading to success, it is important to note that it is not our goal to get all creators to succeed. We acknowledge that in order for a sustainable funding economy to exist, some must succeed and some must fail. Rather we hope to make the path to success more transparent.

Lastly, we hope to study the role of emotion in crowdfunding work. As crowdfunding is a public action, creators have expressed reservations about sharing their work with the public, fearing idea theft, public rejection, and having to ask for help publicly [16]. By drawing from work on costly public action [9] and failure aversion [22], we hope to further uncover how the public aspect of crowdfunding and emotion affect this new type of entrepreneurial work.

CONCLUSION

We must seek to understand how the involvement of community support is changing the entrepreneurial work process. In this qualitative study of crowdfunding work, we find that many people underestimate the work involved and find themselves overwhelmed with the responsibilities of coordinating and answering to a large crowd of supporters. To overcome such obstacles, a community of collaboration has evolved where creators rely on mentorship, support tools, and outsourced help to accomplish their goals. We hope to build on this environment of mutual support by calling for CSCW researchers and designers to create crowdfunding support tools and systems that will help the community continue to grow and prosper.

ACKNOWLEDGMENTS

We are grateful to our informants who provided insights into this work. We thank our colleagues for their helpful comments on previous versions of this document and for transcribing the interviews.

REFERENCES

1. Agrawal, A., Catalini, C., and Goldfarb, A. *Offline Relationships, Distance, and the Internet: The Geography of Crowdfunding*. National Bureau of Economic Research,, Cambridge, MA, 2011.
2. Aldrich, H., Rosen, B., and Woodward, W. The impact of social networks on business foundings and profit: a longitudinal study. *Frontiers of entrepreneurship research 7*, (1987), 154–68.
3. Aldrich, H. *Organizations Evolving*. Sage, London, 1999.
4. Alexa.com. .
5. Allia, Z. Kickstarter Status Board. https://chrome.google.com/webstore/detail/kickstarter-status-board/pbbbkenlhfhdgjjjnkjkgibfkbnmflnj?hl=en-US.
6. Belleflamme, P., Lambert, T., and Schwienbacher, A. Crowdfunding: An Industrial Organization Perspective. *Prepared for the workshop Digital Business Models: Understanding Strategies', held in Paris on June*, (2010), 25–26.
7. Bhide, A. *The origin and evolution of new businesses*. Oxford University Press, 2000.
8. Burt, R. Structural Holes and Good Ideas. *American Journal of Sociology 110*, (2004), 349–399.
9. Cialdini, R.B. *Influence: The psychology of persuasion*. HarperBusiness, 2006.
10. Coleman, J.S. Social capital in the creation of human capital. *American journal of sociology*, (1988), S95–S120.
11. Denison, D., Swaminathan, A., and Rothbard, N. Networks, founding conditions, and imprinting processes: Examining the process of organizational creation. *Academy of Management Meetings, Dallas, Texas*, (1994).
12. Ellison, N., Vitak, J., Gray, R., Lampe, C., and Brooks, B. *Cultivating Social Resources on Facebook: Signals of Relational Investment and their Role in Social Capital Processes iCS-OII 2011 "A Decade in Internet Time" Symposium*. Oxford, UK, 2011.
13. Esposti, C. Crowdfunding Industry Report (Abridged Version): Market Trends, Composition and Crowdfunding Platforms. 2012. http://www.crowdsourcing.org/document/crowdfunding-industry-report-abridged-version-market-trends-composition-and-crowdfunding-platforms/14277.
14. Frenzen, J. and Nakamoto, K. Structure, Cooperation, and the Flow of Market Information. *Journal of Consumer Research 20*, 3 (1993).
15. Gentner, D., Loewenstein, J., and Thompson, L. Learning and transfer: A general role for analogical encoding. *Journal of Educational Psychology 95*, 2 (2003), 393.
16. Gerber, E.M., Hui, J.S., and Kuo, P.-Y. Crowdfunding: Why People are Motivated to Participate. http://www.segal.northwestern.edu/media/pdf/2012/May/29/segal_report_12-02.pdf.
17. Gerber, E.M. and Hui, J.S. Crowdfunding: Motivations and Deterrents for Participation. http://www.segal.northwestern.edu/media/pdf/2012/May/29/segal_report_12-02.pdf.
18. Granovetter, M.S. The Strength of Weak Ties. *American Journal of Sociology 78*, 6 (1973), 1360–1380.
19. Guadagno, R. and Cialdini, R. Online persuasion and compliance: Social influence on the Internet and beyond. *The social net: Human behavior in cyberspace*, (2005), 91–113.
20. Hansen, E.L. and Allen, K.R. The creation corridor: Environmental load and pre-organization information-processing ability. *Entrepreneurship Theory and Practice 17*, (1992), 57–57.
21. Hattie, J. and Timperley, H. The power of feedback. *Review of educational research 77*, 1 (2007), 81–112.
22. Kahneman, D., Slovic, P., and Tversky, A. *Judgment under uncertainty: Heuristics and biases*. Cambridge University Press, Cambridge, 1982.
23. Katila, R. and Mang, P.Y. Exploiting technological opportunities: the timing of collaborations. *Research policy 32*, 2 (2003), 317–332.
24. Kickstarter.com. .
25. Kittur, A., Chi, E., and Suh, B. Crowdsourcing User Studies With Mechanical Turk. *CHI 2007: Proceedings of the ACM Conference on Human-factors in Computing Systems*, ACM Press (2008).

26. Kittur, N., Nickerson, J., Bernstein, M., et al. The Future of Crowd Work. *Conference on Computer Supported Cooperative Work and Social Computing*, (2013).

27. Klepper, S. Employee startups in high-tech industries. *Industrial and Corporate Change 10*, 3 (2001), 639–674.

28. Kraut, R. and Resnick, P. Encouraging contributions to online communities. In *Evidence-baed social design: Mining the social sciences to build successful online communities*. MIT Press, Cambridge, MA, in press.

29. Larson, A. Network dyads in entrepreneurial settings: A study of the governance of exchange relationships. *Administrative science quarterly*, (1992), 76–104.

30. Leskovec, J., Adamic, L.A., and Huberman, B.A. The dynamics of viral marketing. *ACM Transactions on the Web (TWEB) 1*, 1 (2007), 5.

31. Locke, E.A. and Latham, G.P. Building a practically useful theory of goal setting and task motivation: A 35-year odyssey. *American psychologist 57*, 9 (2002), 705.

32. Markey, P.M. Bystander intervention in computer-mediated communication. *Computers in Human Behavior 16*, 2 (2000), 183–188.

33. Milgram, S. Behavioral study of obedience. *The Journal of Abnormal and Social Psychology 67*, 4 (1963), 371.

34. Mintzberg, H. An Emerging Strategy of "Direct" Research. *Administrative Science Quarterly 24*, (1979), 580–589.

35. Muller, M., Soule, T., Daniel, S., Geyer, W., and Cheng, L.-T. Crowdfunding Inside the Enterprise: Employee-Initiatives for Innovation and Collaboration. (2013).

36. Norman, D. *The Design of Everyday Things*. Doubleday, New York, NY, 1988.

37. Olsen, G.M. and Olsen, J.S. Distance Matters. *Human-Computer Interaction 15*, (2000), 139–178.

38. Resnick, P. and Kraut, R. Evidence-based social design: Introduction. In *Evidence-based social design: Mining social sciences to build online communities*. MIT Press, Cambridge, in press.

39. Roberts, E.B. *Entrepreneurs in high technology*. Oxford University Press New York, 1991.

40. Ryan, R.M. and Deci, E.L. Intrinsic and Extrinsic Motivations: Classic Definitions and New Directions. *Contemporary Education Psychology 25*, (2000), 54–67.

41. Shane, S., Khurana, R., and Hall, M. Career Experiences and Firm Foundings. (1999).

42. Shane, S. and Venkataram, S. The Promise of Entrepreneurship as a Field of Research. *Academy of Management Journal 25*, 1 (2000), 217–226.

43. Shane, S. *A General Theory of Entrepreneurship: The Individual-Opportunity Nexus*. Edward Elgar Publishing Limited, Northampton, MA, 2003.

44. Spradley, J.P. *Participant Observation*. Rinehart and Winston, New York, 1980.

45. Stuart, T.E., Hoang, H., and Hybels, R.C. Interorganizational endorsements and the performance of entrepreneurial ventures. *Administrative science quarterly 44*, 2 (1999), 315–349.

46. Thomke, S.H. *Experimentation matters: unlocking the potential of new technologies for innovation*. Harvard Business Press, 2003.

47. Trist, E. The evolution of socio-technical systems. In *Perspectives on Organizational Design and Behavior*. Wiley Interscience, 1981.

48. Venkataram, S. The Distinctive Domain of Entrepreneurship Research: An editor's perspective. In *Advances in Entrepreneurship, Fim, Emergence, and Growth*. JAI Press, Greenwich, CT, 1997, 119–138.

49. Ward, C. and Ramachandran, V. Crowdfunding the next hit: Microfunding online experience goods. *Computational Social Science and the Wisdom of Crowds*, (2010).

50. Wortham, J. Success of Crowdfunding Puts Pressure on Entrepreneurs. *The New York Times*, 2012. http://www.nytimes.com/2012/09/18/technology/success-of-crowdfunding-puts-pressure-on-entrepreneurs.html?_r=2&.

51. Xu, A., Huang, S.-W., and Bailey, B. Voyant: Generating Structured Feedback on Visual Designs Using a Crowd of Non-Experts. *CSCW 2014, (to appear)*.

52. Can You Spare a Quarter? Crowdfunding Sites Turn Fans into Patrons of the Arts. *Knowledge @ Wharton*, 2010. http://knowledge.wharton.upenn.edu/article.cfm?articleid=2647.

53. Ouya: A New Kind of Video Game Console. http://www.kickstarter.com/projects/ouya/ouya-a-new-kind-of-video-game-console?ref=live.

54. Sprout: a pencil with a seed. http://www.kickstarter.com/projects/democratech/sprout-a-pencil-with-a-seed?ref=live.

55. The iPod Nano Watch Raises $941,718 On Kickstarter. http://www.businessinsider.com/the-ipod-nano-watch-kickstarter-2010-12#.

56. Kickstarter Stats. *Kickstarter*. http://www.kickstarter.com/help/stats. Accessed 2012-09-17.

57. KickSpy. http://www.kickspy.com/.

58. The Kickback Machine. http://www.thekickbackmachine.com/.

59. BackerKit. https://www.backerkit.com/.

60. Teelaunch. teelaunch.com.

61. Fullfillrite. http://fulfillrite.com/.

62. Zirtual. http://zirtual.com/.

63. Nation Builder. http://nationbuilder.com/.

64. Odesk. https://www.odesk.com/.

Smart Face: Enhancing Creativity During Video Conferences using Real-time Facial Deformation

Naoto Nakazato
Graduate School of Information Science and Technology,
The University of Tokyo
7-3-1 Hongo, Bunkyo-ku,
Tokyo, 113-8656 Japan
nakazato@cyber.t.u-tokyo.ac.jp
81-3-5841-6369

Shigeo Yoshida
Graduate School of Interdisciplinary Information Studies,
The University of Tokyo
7-3-1 Hongo, Bunkyo-ku,
Tokyo, 113-8656 Japan
shigeodayo@cyber.t.u-tokyo.ac.jp
81-3-5841-6369

Sho Sakurai
Graduate School of Engineering,
The University of Tokyo
7-3-1 Hongo, Bunkyo-ku,
Tokyo, 113-8656 Japan
sho@cyber.t.u-tokyo.ac.jp
81-3-5841-6369

Takuji Narumi
Graduate School of Information Science and Technology,
The University of Tokyo
7-3-1 Hongo, Bunkyo-ku,
Tokyo, 113-8656 Japan
narumi@cyber.t.u-tokyo.ac.jp
81-3-5841-6369

Tomohiro Tanikawa
Graduate School of Information Science and Technology,
The University of Tokyo
7-3-1 Hongo, Bunkyo-ku,
Tokyo, 113-8656 Japan
tani@cyber.t.u-tokyo.ac.jp
81-3-5841-6369

Michitaka Hirose
Graduate School of Information Science and Technology,
The University of Tokyo
7-3-1 Hongo, Bunkyo-ku,
Tokyo, 113-8656 Japan
hirose@cyber.t.u-tokyo.ac.jp
81-3-5841-6369

ABSTRACT

This study develops a method for improving creativity by changing the facial appearance of people during video conferences. We focus on enhancing creativity during human interactions, especially cooperative work situations such as video conferences. Psychological studies have revealed that the facial appearance of people can affect creativity, i.e., "emotion can affect creativity" and "the appearance of others can affect the emotions." Based on the knowledge, we hypothesized that the media technology which modifies the facial appearance of people appropriately can enhance our creativity during cooperative work. Therefore, we develop a method to affect creativity by changing the facial appearance in real-time, such as facial expressions and facial resemblance. We test the effectiveness of this method by building a system for collaborative video conferences. The user study show that the proposed method could enhance creativity.

Author Keywords

Creativity; Cooperative Work; Emotion; Facial Expression;

INTRODUCTION

The main objective of this study is to establish a method that enhances the ability to perform cooperative work without any concerted effort. In particular, this study aimed to improve video conference outcomes by applying real-time facial deformation to the faces of users during video conference calls. Previous studies of video conferences have focused on improving the quality of the video images and voice sounds, as well as introducing other interaction techniques to reproduce the atmosphere of a remote place. These studies aimed to reproduce a realistic atmosphere because the sensation of reality is enhanced if the users share the same location.

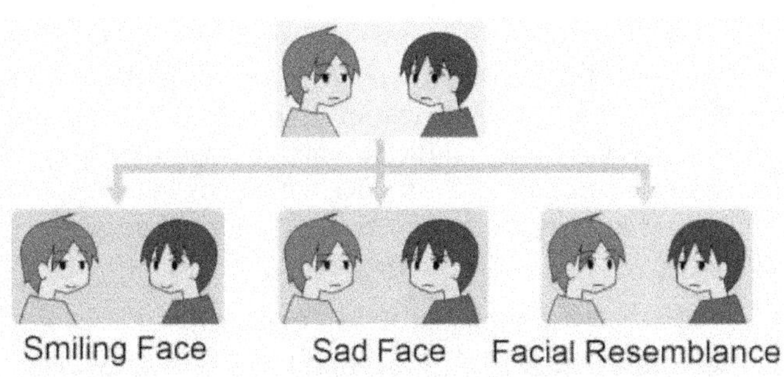

Figure 1. Enhancing creativity by changing the facial appearance in real-time.

However, a realistic atmosphere is not always beneficial for conference call outcomes. Different atmospheres can have huge effects on creativity and other behaviors [1]. For example, we do not perform to the best of our ability if we are in a nervous situation such as an interview. Thus, video conference systems that reproduce a realistic atmosphere may not improve the quality of the outcomes in all cases. In other words, this type of system cannot replace face-to-face conferences in terms of efficiency. However, an appropriate atmosphere can enhance our performance in some areas.

Thus, we hypothesized that our collaborative creativity could be enhanced by modifying the atmosphere during a video conference in an appropriate manner. This enhanced creativity will improve the outcomes of conference calls. Therefore, we aimed to improve the outcomes of conference calls by modifying the atmosphere in streaming video conference data, such as video images. This type of modulated video conference may be more efficient than face-to-face conference calls.

Many researchers have investigated the enhancement of an individual person's creativity [2]. Poor communication when working in a group represses the creativity of the team, even if each person has a high level of personal creativity. Many studies have also investigated the provision of cooperative working support using a computer to address this problem. However, the application of these techniques to the cooperative work in a group can disrupt communication, thereby preventing any improvement in the collective creativity of the team.

Meanwhile, positive affect has been shown to improve the quality of communication [1, 3, 4], i.e., the quality of work can be improved by removing feelings of tension and displeasure that may arise from communication when performing cooperative work with several people. Therefore, it may be possible to develop a technique to improve the level of creativity during cooperative work by evoking a positive affect without any actual effort.

In previous studies, the stimuli used to evoke positive affect were not appropriate for the cooperative working context. However, it is known that the smiles of other people evoke a positive affect during conversations [5], while a facial resemblance enhances trust [6]. Facial expressions can reflect the atmosphere during conversations. Thus, we hypothesized that it may be possible to allow the user to evoke a positive affect unconsciously by changing the facial appearance of partners during cooperative work, instead of using stimuli that do not consider the context of the work. This method may enhance creativity during cooperative work.

In this study, we developed a system to enhance creativity during cooperative work by slightly modifying the facial appearance of others so they has sad or smiling faces, as well as making the other person's face resemble the user's face. The basic concept of this system is shown in Figure 1. We evaluate the validity of this system in exploratory studies.

RELATED WORK ON THE IMPROVEMENT OF CREATIVITY

Creativity

According to Amabile [7], creativity is the ability to discover a new and useful solution to a given problem, which is a very important ability. Therefore, many studies have investigated the improvement of creativity.

Richard et al. [2] developed and evaluated various training methods for improving creativity. However, these training methods required that the participants expend considerable effort and time because these methods were intended for the education of children. Each of these training methods was also directed mainly at improving the creativity of a single person.

However, creativity is not limited solely to the work of an individual. Thus, it is necessary to develop techniques that improve creativity during collaborative work involving multiple people, where the collective creativity of the team is not simply the sum of the creativity of each individual in the team. This is because communication among team members is an important factor that promotes creativity during collaborative work. Furthermore, avoiding the disruption of communication with others is also an important issue when improving creativity during collaborations.

In the area of computer-supported cooperative work (CSCW), many studies have aimed to enhance communication and creativity during collaborations. For example, one study aimed to generate an artificial third-party opinion to stimulate conversations and brainstorming [8]. Another study developed a system that suggested a new direction to move the conversation to a given topic [9]. A method of facilitating communication using an avatar has also been proposed, where the computer graphics characters moved in response to the speaker's voice during video chat [10]. Thus, the users could communicate with each other using words and bodily expressions via the avatars [11].

However, cooperative work support using a computer may inhibit direct communication between users or degrade the outputs because the computer is too involved with interactions. There is also the problem that the information in the database might lack creativity.

Creativity and Emotion

Many studies have tried to improve creativity based on emotional aspects.

For example, Amabile et al. showed that there is a linear correlation between emotions and creativity [1]. Isen et al. also showed that the positive affect evoked by a short comedy film or a bag of candies improved performance in tasks that required creativity [3]. In addition, Lewis et al. conducted experiments to make participants think about new uses for a "Brick" or a "25 cent coin," and drew an image associated with a given circle to represent the images that evoked various emotions [4]. The experiments showed that images that evoked positive emotions improved the creativity of the answers.

Thus, many studies have improved creativity based on the positive feelings evoked by external stimuli. However, stimulation with external images such as pictures is not appropriate for tasks that require creativity. Thus, the use of this type of stimulation is unnatural in an actual work setting because it may disrupt communication with others.

The stimulus used to improve creativity during collaborative work should consider the context of communication in the work. Therefore, we believe that a useful approach should increase creativity by evoking positive emotions with an unconscious stimulus that can be presented without inhibiting the work context.

Facial Appearance and Emotions

There are various methods of changing emotions such as watching a comedy movie or showing an image of a laughing baby. These techniques provide explicit stimuli from the outside that affect the user's emotional state.

By contrast, Yoshida et al. proposed a method for unconsciously evoking pleasant/unpleasant feelings where visual feedback was used to display a deformed facial expression in real time [12].

Furthermore, DeBruine showed that if the face of another participant is similar to the user's faces, the creativity is increased compared with cases that lack any resemblance [6]. Most of these types of studies use still images, but some systems can change the user's face and transform them into another person's face interactively in real-time.

The use of stimuli such as images or movies to evoke positive emotions, as mentioned earlier, could not be considered in this study, which actually required the enhancement of creativity. However, the methods developed by Yoshida et al. and the effect explored by DeBruine evoked a positive affect without requiring the user's awareness. It is also known that changes in one's facial expression can affect the expressions of other participants in the same conversation [5].

Thus, we developed a method to enhance creativity during conversations with others, which evoked positive emotion by modifying the appearance of others during face-to-face work interactions.

FACE CHANGING TECHNIQUE FOR IMPROVING CREATIVITY

Thus, we developed two methods to enhance creativity during collaborative work by changing the facial appearance of others in real-time.: a method that modifies the user's facial expression and another that blends another person's facial features with those of the user's face.

Changing Facial Expressions

We developed a method for virtually deforming a user's facial expressions and transforming the user's facial expression in real-time using image deformation techniques.

To obtain accurate eye, nose, mouth, etc. features from an image of the user's face, we used the FaceTracker library developed by Saragih et al. [13]. Next, we deformed the face image using a rigid moving least squares (MLS) method [14]. This algorithm allowed us to deform the appearance of a user's face easily and naturally based on over three control points. The rigid MLS method seldom generates artifacts. This algorithm deforms the whole image, so there is a possibility of deforming the background as well as the face, and this deformed background might be considered to be an artifact.

Using these techniques, we generated two facial expressions, i.e., "smiling face" and "sad face," which represented the positive-negative affect dimension based on the knowledge of previous studies on facial expression and emotion [15] (Figure 2) (see the video figure). We

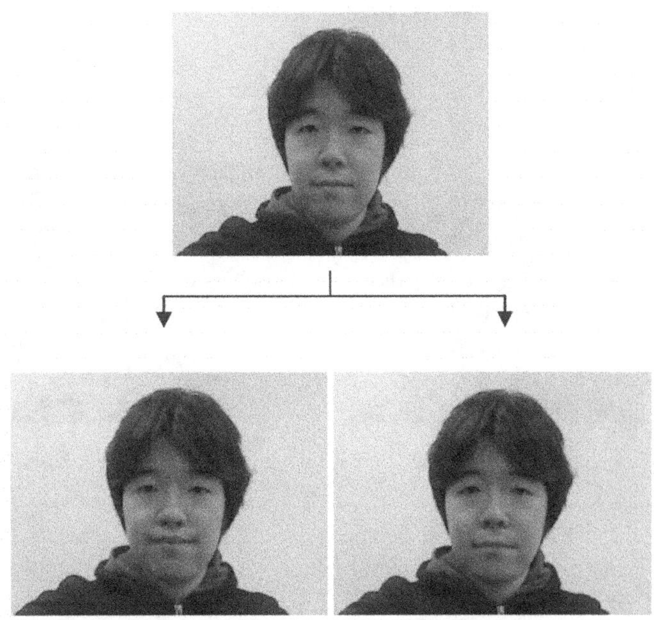

Figure 2. Deformation of two types of facial expressions: "smiling face" and "sad face."

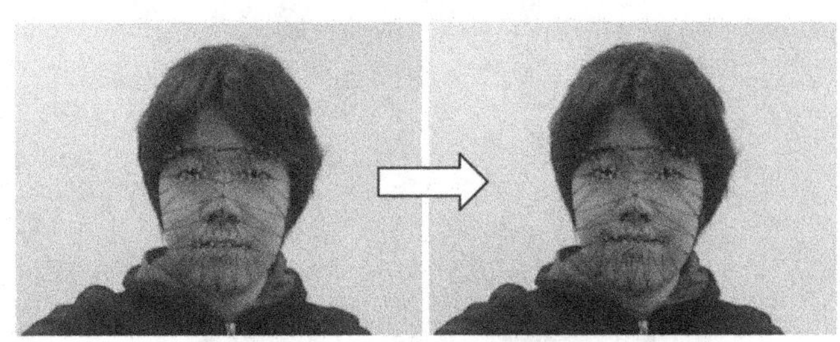

Figure 3. Deformation using a rigid MLS method (smiling face).

deformed the face image to create a "smiling face" by raising the corners of the mouth and the cheek while lifting the lower eyelids. For the "sad face," we deformed the face image by lowering the corner of the mouth while lifting the inside of the upper eyelid and the inside of the eyebrow. We determined the parameters used to produce these facial expressions based on a previous study [12]. Figure 3 shows an example of the modified facial expression. According to a previous study [15], the change applied to the user's facial expression was fixed, regardless of the user's attributes.

Blending Different People's Facial Features

We constructed a method for blending the facial image of the user with that of a different person. This method required that images of the users were provided in advance as the material images.

The FaceTracker library described above was used to obtain features from the camera image captured in real-time and the material image. Next, these images were scaled by the affine transformation, depending on the distance between the eyes. Then the material image was deformed to fit the feature points of the face in the camera image using a rigid MLS method.

After performing the transformation and deformation process, the material image was blended semi-transparently

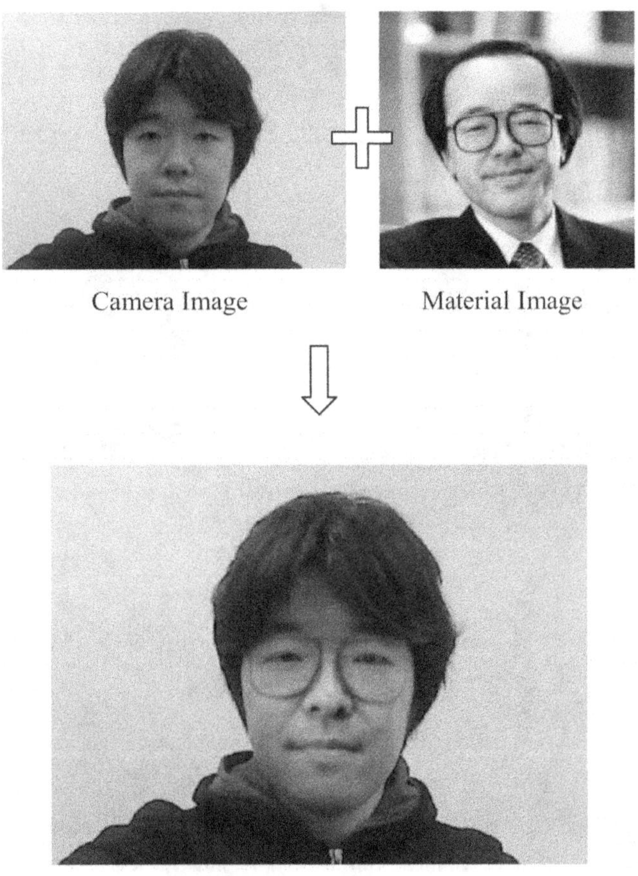

Figure 4. Blending two people's faces.

with the camera image. We used the alpha blending to ensure translucent blending. Instead of blending the image uniformly, we used an alpha value (opacity) of 0.0 in the contour of the face, 1.0 at the center of gravity, and a linear interpolation of the mean.

Figure 4 shows an example obtained after combining with the face of another person. This method blends the faces naturally although the facial expressions and poses in these images differ owing to the transformation and deformation process (see the video figure). We refer to this blended face as "facial resemblance."

According to the DeBruine [6], a face where the material's texture is blended and deformed to meet the material's outline is more trustful and attractive. However, in this study, the material was a still image whereas the real face was a moving image. Thus, it was unnatural to deform the camera image using the material image in the same way as that used in DeBruine's study because it caused background distortion. Therefore, the real face's outline was used as the material's outline in this system.

If a crucial matching error occurred during face tracking, the face was blended at an inappropriate position. This type of crucial matching error might occur if the user moved quickly or violently, but the users don't move quickly or violently in tele-conference settings. Therefore, artifacts were unlikely to occur due to this type of error.

USER STUDY OF CREATIVITY IMPROVEMENT DURING VIDEO CONFERENCES

We examined the effects of modifying the other user's facial appearance with our system on creativity during cooperative work. We selected brainstorming as the cooperative work that required creativity and we applied our method to the video conference system.

Experimental Overview

We used brainstorming to measure creativity. Brainstorming is one of the best-known techniques for creative problem solving [16].

In general, brainstorming is used during a face-to-face meeting in a meeting room. However, we constructed a remote brainstorming environment via a video conference to test our image processing techniques with the users.

In this experiment, we investigated the changes in the number of brainstorming responses to validate how this system affected the level of creativity by reference to previous studies on brainstorming because of high correlations between quantity and quality [17].

Hypotheses

We hypothesized that if the expressions of the conversation partners appeared to be smiling at each other, their positive emotions would be enhanced, thereby improving creativity, and the number of brainstorming responses would increase.

By contrast, we hypothesized that if the faces of the partners appeared sad, their negative emotions would be increased, thereby reducing creativity, and the number of responses would decrease.

We also hypothesized that if the face of the conversation partner resembled that of the user, positive emotions would be evoked and the number of responses would increase.

Experiment

System Configuration

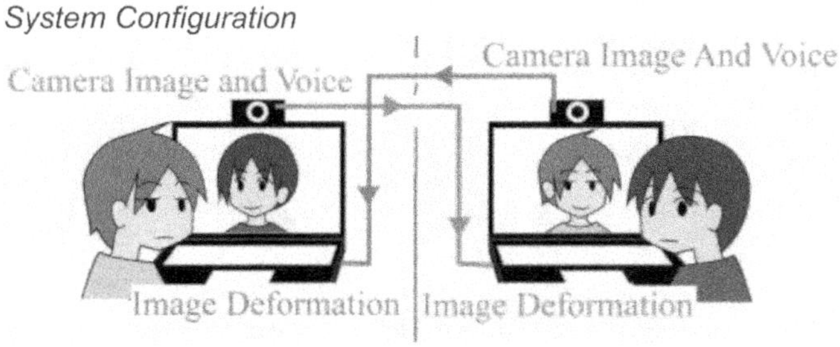

Figure 5. System configuration.

We configured a video conference environment without the internet using two web cameras with microphones and two computers (Figure 5). A camera connected to computer C1 was placed on the top of computer C2 and another camera on top of computer C1 was connected to computer C2. Thus, it was possible to perform the video conference without using the internet. This was because the use of the internet can cause displacements in the movements of the face and voice due to the communication lag over the internet, which might have affected factors other than facial expressions during a conversation.

The experiment was performed in one room but a video conference situation was required, so we placed both computers in booths that were sufficiently distant to prevent the two users from hearing their conversation partner. The participants entered white booths and there was nothing in the booths except the computers. In addition, the background behind the participants was white to reduce the tracking noise. To prevent the voice of the conversation partner from entering the ear directly, we used noise-canceling earphones. Thus, the participants could not hear each other across the room.

The user's own camera image was not displayed like a normal video conference, so there was a possibility that the face was outside the camera's field of view during the experiment. Therefore, we fixed the positional relationship between the computer and the chair, and we confirmed that participants were sitting correctly in front of the camera at the beginning of the experiment.

Procedures

In this experiment, we asked the two participants to engage in brainstorming. First, we asked them to test the communication capacity of each computer. We captured their facial images to blend their features with each other. Next, we explained brainstorming and its subjects. We prepared four subjects, i.e., "hunger," "broom," "pot," and "rubber band," and the users were asked to think of new uses for them based on Guilford's Alternative Uses Task and the AC test of creative ability [18]. We chose these four subjects because the participants recognized them intermediately but had never considered their new uses.

Brainstorming was conducted for 5 min on each subject. The brainstorming sessions in this experiment were conducted four times. The repetition of these tasks could exhaust the participants and reduce their performance over time if the duration of the brainstorming is long, so the overall time of the experiment was preferable less than 30 min to avoid the effects of weariness. This is why we decided to set the time limit at 5 min.

Each participant performed four sets of brainstorming task sessions and evaluation sessions. During each brainstorming task session, the participants were presented with one of four facial expression: "normal face" (no deformation), "smiling face," "sad face," and "facial resemblance." "Facial resemblance" blended the faces of both participants.

Figure 6. Brainstorming during a video conference.

To eliminate any effects on the presentation order of the facial expressions and the brainstorming subjects, the presentation order was assigned randomly and counterbalanced between participants using a Latin-square design. Given the fixed deformation of the facial expressions, some differences were apparent within the facial expressions that depended on the size of the participant's face. Thus, we adjusted the distance between the display and the participant to make the size of each participant's face uniform before the experiment.

In addition, we considered that the results of the experiment might depend on the emotional state of the participants, so we conducted a questionnaire before starting the experiment to determine whether the participants felt "very pleased" or "very displeased" a few days before this experiment. The experiments were only carried out with participants who were in a normal emotional state.

Participants

The study had 20 participants (20 males; mean age = 22.3 years, range = 22–25). To ensure that the conversations passed smoothly, the two participants in each pair were already acquainted with each other. The participants were not informed of the actual purpose of the study. The experimental setting is shown in Figure 6.

Evaluation Method

The most commonly used techniques for measuring creativity assess the originality, feasibility, elaboration, and flexibility of an answer and count the number of responses [19]. In this experiment, we used the increase in the number of responses during brainstorming as a measure of the creativity improvement because brainstorming aims to generate a large number of ideas. In fact, many previous studies used the number of responces for the measurement of the productivity of brainstorming [17] because of high correlations between quantity and quality [20, 21]. Therefore, we investigated the effects of the facial appearance on creativity by measuring the number of responses during each brainstorming task.

The participants were asked to rate their emotional state before the experiment and after each task. We evaluated the emotional state of the participants using the Japanese version of the Positive and Negative Affect Schedule (J-PANAS) [22, 23, 24]. The J-PANAS comprises two 11-item scales that measure the positive and negative affect. Each item was answered using a seven-point scale (1 = strongly disagree; 7 = strongly agree). Positive affect means the degree that person feels enthusiastic, active, and alert. Negative affect means the degree that person feel subjective anger, contempt, disgust, guilt, fear, and nervousness. In addition, it is assumed that positive affect and negative affect have a relationship of the orthogonal dimensions, and positive affect and negative affect are independent [25].

At the end of the experiment, we asked the participants to record their views of the experiment and checked whether the participants were aware of the actual purpose of the experiment.

Experimental Results

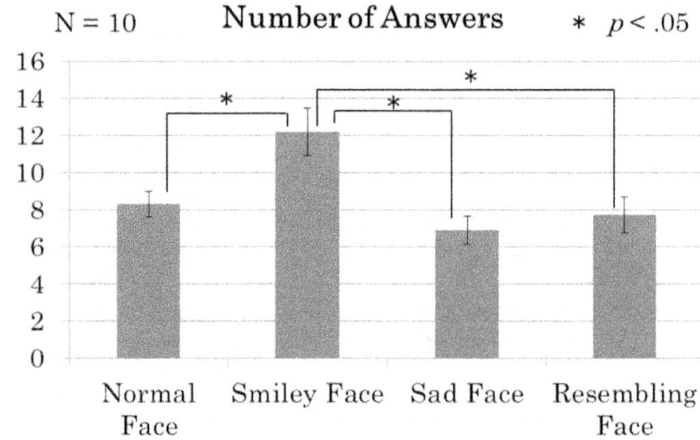

Figure 7. Mean number of answers.

Figure 7 shows the number of responses in the brainstorming task with each facial appearance. The error bars represent the standard error.

The mean and standard error for the brainstorming responses was 8.3 ± 0.8 answers with no deformation, 12.2 ± 1.3 answers with a smiling face, 6.9 ± 0.7 answers with a sad face, and 7.7 ± 1.0 answers with the facial resemblance.

A multiple comparison using the Benjamini-Hochberg (BH) method showed that there were significant differences between the smiling face condition and the no deformation condition, between the smiling face condition and the sad face condition, and between the smiling face condition and facial resemblance condition ($p < .05$). These results suggest that the creativity during brainstorming was improved if the conversation partner appeared to be smiling. However, the sad face condition and the facial resemblance condition were not significantly different from the no deformation condition.

Figures 8 and 9 show the average differences in the positive and negative affect scores before and after the conversation in each condition. The error bars represent the standard error. The figures represent the average evaluation values attached to each of 11 results that corresponded to the positive and negative affects.

The multiple comparisons using the BH method showed that there were significant differences in the pleasantness between the facial resemblance condition and the no deformation condition, between the facial resemblance condition and the smiling face condition, and between the facial resemblance condition and the sad face condition ($p < .05$). Furthermore, there was a significant difference in the unpleasantness between the facial resemblance condition and the smiling face condition. Therefore, the

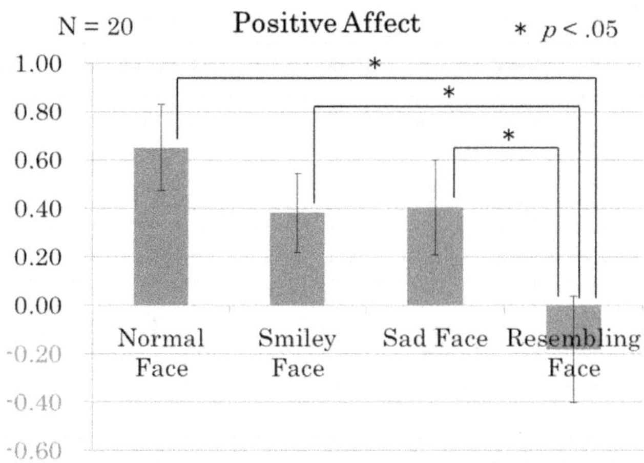

Figure 8. Mean positive affect scores.

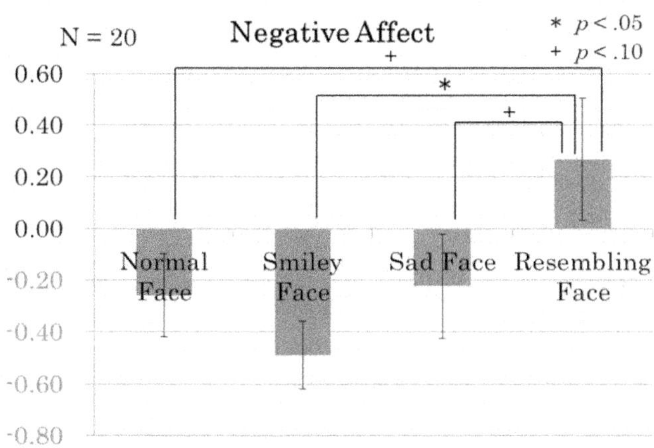

Figure 9. Mean negative affect scores.

participants felt discomfort when they looked at another person who shared their features.

In the post-experiment questionnaire, some participants pointed out that the difficulty varied among the brainstorming tasks. However, the difference in difficulty was not reflected in the experimental results.

In addition, only three subjects noted the change in the other participant's face in the facial deformation condition, so most participants were unaware of the changes in the conversation partner's facial expressions. Six participants were aware of the facial blending and they noted that it looked unnatural. The reason why is that the faces were not blended correctly because they moved quickly or violently. In addition, the reason why more participants were aware of facial blending than those who were aware of facial deformation was that the mismatched blending with a white background was more obvious than the mismatched deformation with a white background.

Discussion

The proposed system had a significant effect on improving creativity based on the increased number of brainstorming responses with smiling faces using our system.

However, the number of brainstorming responses with a sad face was not reduced compared with the no deformation condition, so the sad face did not reduce creativity in our experiment.

In addition, the number of brainstorming responses did not increase as predicted by our hypothesis with the facial resemblance/blending condition. This was because the participants felt discomfort with the facial resemblance condition, according to the results of the comfort-discomfort rating using J-PANAS. Based on the free descriptions of the participants, we consider that they felt strong discomfort because the participants were acquaintances. The blended face differed from the faces of their acquaintances, which was very unsettling.

According to Zajonc, the "mere exposure effect" also occurs with real people in everyday scenes [26], where the real face of a friend may look friendlier than a blended face. In addition, Giang et al. showed that the effects of facial resemblance on trust and cooperation were small and negligible compared with the strong effects of other cues on facial likability and facial trustworthiness [27]. In addition, we considered that the face blending did not function properly when the facial tracking failed, which was another problem. We observed that the tracking failed infrequently and the position of the tracking point was shifted as previously mentioned, which made the other participant look unpleasant.

These experiments used subjects who were already acquainted, so different results may have been obtained if we performed the same experiment using two subjects who were not mutual acquaintances.

In addition, positive or negative affects might not have been observed if they had viewed smiling or sad faces. The free descriptions indicated that the facial expressions looked unnatural to a few people, which was uncomfortable. Thus, it is necessary to improve the method to generate better facial expressions.

Some participants pointed out in their free descriptions that the difficulty varied among the brainstorming tasks. However, these differences in difficulty were not reflected in the experimental results. Thus, it is possible that the system affected the sense of difficulty. Therefore, the system might have affected the perceived difficulty of the collaborative task and avoided a loss of motivation when the problems appeared difficult.

CONCLUSION

We proposed a method for changing the facial appearance of subjects, thereby improving their creativity, especially during collaborative work. Based on previous reports that the facial appearance can affect creativity, and that "emotions can affect creativity" and "the appearance of others can affect the emotions," we developed a method to enhance creativity by changing the facial appearance in real-time, including facial expressions and facial resemblance.

We built a creativity improvement system for cooperative work situations such as video conferences using the proposed method. We focused on brainstorming to test whether our system helped to generate creative solutions to problems by facilitating more effective communication with others. Next, we evaluated the effects of the proposed system on the brainstorming ability of participants to measure the improvement in creativity. The user study showed that our method could enhance the creativity by showing a modified smiling face. However, it was not possible to improve creativity by showing a blended face (the facial resemblance condition). The technique used to make faces each other needs further consideration. In summary, these results suggest that we can augment creativity without changing the circumstances and the actions of users. We believe that this study contributes to the field of CSCW.

Our proposed method was applied to a video conference system where the facial characteristics of a single partner were changed in the experiment. However, brainstorming and other types of cooperative work are usually performed in face-to-face situations with several participants. Thus, we should consider how to apply this system in face-to-face situations.

In addition, we used the facial blending system to increase the facial resemblance, but we did not allow the user to evoke a positive emotion by changing their partner's face. By combining these methods, we could expand the potential applicability of our proposed system.

In this study, we focused only on creativity. We also plan to focus on other abilities such as communication with unfamiliar subjects, presenting a good speech, and concentrating on the speech of other people. We could construct a more effective system by changing the way a user hears another person's voice, or by changing gestures such as nods.

This system could be used to practice for interviews so the user will be less nervous about answering the interviewer correctly. In particular, the user can practice with their friend using a blended interviewer's face.

Finally, this method could be applied to communication assistance such as understanding others, psychotherapy for depression, and entertainment technology. This type of HCI techniques may be helpful for promoting social health and expanding the field of CSCW.

ACKNOWLEGEMENT

This work was partially supported by JSPS KAKENHI Grant-in-Aid for Challenging Exploratory Research (Grant Numbers: 80418657) and Core Research for Evolutional Science and Technology (CREST) Program "Creation of Human-Harmonized Information Technology for Convivial Society" of Japan Science and Technology Agency(JST).

REFERENCES

1. Amabile, T., Barsade, S., Mueller, J. and Staw, B., Affect and Creativity at Work. *Administrative Science Quarterly 50*, (2005), 367-403.
2. Mansfield, R.S., Busse, T.V. and Krepelka, E.J. The effectiveness of creativity training. *Review of Educational Research 48*, 4 (1978), 517-536.
3. Isen, A., Daubman, K. and Nowicki, G.P. Positive Affect Facilitates Creative Problem Solving. *Journal of Personality and Social Psychology 52*, (1987), 1122-1131.
4. Lewis, S., Dontcheva, M. and Gerber, E., Affective computational priming and creativity. *Proceedings of the 2011 annual conference on Human factors in computing systems*, (2011), 735-744.
5. Dimberg, U., Facial reactions to facial expressions. *Psychophysiology 19*, 6 (1982), 643-647.
6. DeBruine, L.M., Facial resemblance enhances trust. *Proceedings of the Royal Society of London. Series B: Biological Sciences 269*, 1498 (2002) 1307-1312.
7. Amabile, T., The social psychology of creativity: A componential conceptualization. *Journal of Personality and Social Psychology 45*, (1983), 357-376.
8. Nishimoto, K. and Sumi, Y. and Mase, K., Toward an outsider agent for supporting a brainstorming session-an information retrieval method from a different viewpoint. *Knowledge-Based Systems 9*, 6 (1996), 377-384.
9. Nishimoto, K., Sumi, Y. and Mase, K., Enhancement of creative aspects of a daily conversation with a topic development agent. *Coordination Technology for Collaborative Applications*, (1998), 63-76.
10. Watanabe, T., Okubo, M. and Danbara, R., InterActor for human interaction and communication support. *Proceedings of the International Conference on Human-Computer Interaction*, (2003), 113-120.
11. Ishii, Y. and Watanabe, T., E-VChat: A video communication system in which a speech-driven embodied entrainment character working with head motion is superimposed for a virtual face-to-face scene. *RO-MAN, 2012 IEEE*, (2012), 191-196.
12. Yoshida, S., Sakurai, S., Narumi, T., Tanikawa, T. and Hirose, M., Manipulation of an emotional experience by real-time deformed facial feedback. *Proceedings of the 4th Augmented Human International Conference*, (2013), 35-42.

13. Saragih, J.M., Lucey, S. and Cohn, J.F., Deformable model fitting by regularized landmark mean-shift. *International Journal of Computer Vision 91*, 2 (2011), 200-215.

14. Schaefer, S., McPhail, T. and Warren, J., Image deformation using moving least squares. *ACM Transactions on Graphics (TOG) 25*, 3 (2006), 553-540.

15. Ekman, P. and Friesen W., Unmasking the Face. *Prentice Hall, Inc*, Englewood Cliffs (1975).

16. Clark, C., Rona, G. and Patrel, P., Brainstorming. *Dunod*, (1971).

17. Isaksen, Scott G. *A review of brainstorming research: Six critical issues for inquiry*. Creative Research Unit, Creative Problem Solving Group-Buffalo, (1998).

18. Meadow, A. and Parnes, S.J., Evaluation of training in creative problem solving. *Journal of Applied Psychology 43*, 3 (1959), 189.

19. Bao, P., Gerber, E., Gergle, D. and Hoffman, D. Momentum, getting and staying on topic during a brainstorm. *In Proc. CHI 2010*, ACM (2010), 1233-1236.

20. Diehl, M., and Wolfgang S. "Productivity loss in brainstorming groups: Toward the solution of a riddle." Journal of personality and social psychology 53.3 (1987): 497.

21. Parnes, Sidney J. "Effects of extended effort in creative problem solving." Journal of Educational psychology 52.3 (1961): 117.

22. Clark L.A. and Watson D., Mood and the mundane: Relations between daily life events and self-reported mood. *Journal of Personality and Social Psychology 54*, (1988), 296-308.

23. Watson D., Clark L.A. and Tellegen A., Cross-cultural convergence in the structure of mood: A Japanese replication and comparison with U. S. findings. *Journal of Personality and Social Psychology 47*, (1984), 127-144.

24. Clark, L.A., and Watson, D., The Japanese Positive and Negative Affect Schedule: Factor-based scales for the assessment of mood. *Unpublished manuscript*, University of Iowa (1989).

25. Watson D., Clark L.A. and Tellegen A., Development and Validation of Brief Measures of Positive and Negative Affect: The PANAS Scales. *Journal of Personality and Social Psychology 54*, (1988), 1063-1070

26. Zajonc, R.B., Attitudinal effects of mere exposure. *Journal of personality and social psychology 9*, 2 (1968), 1.

27. Trang G., Raoul B. and Axel B., Does facial resemblance enhance cooperation? *PloS one 7*, 10 (2012), e47809.

Towards a Questionnaire for Measuring Affective Benefits and Costs of Communication Technologies

Svetlana Yarosh
AT&T Research Labs
Florham Park, NJ, USA
lana@research.att.com

Panos Markopoulos
Eindhoven University of Technology
Eindhoven, The Netherlands
p.markopoulos@tue.nl

Gregory D. Abowd
Georgia Institute of Technology
Atlanta, GA, USA
abowd@cc.gatech.edu

ABSTRACT
As CSCW creates and investigates technologies for social communication, it is important to understand the emotional benefits and costs of these systems. We propose the Affective Benefits and Costs of Communication Technologies (ABCCT) questionnaire to supplement traditional qualitative methods of understanding communication media. We discuss the pilots of this survey with 45 children and 110 adults measuring the inter-item reliability of this instrument. We present the results of interviews with 14 children and 14 adults, which help confirm that the ABCCT measures the same constructs that may emerge through interview investigations. Finally, we demonstrate that the ABCCT is sensitive enough to discriminate between different communication technologies and has shown promise in some of its early adoption. Though the ABCCT is not without limitations, it may provide a way to compare technologies in field deployments, draw findings across investigations, and quantify the impact of specific design decisions.

Author Keywords
Questionnaire; CMC; communication; affect; evaluation.

ACM Classification Keywords
H.5.3 [Information Interfaces and Presentation]: Group and Organization Interfaces – *Evaluation/Methodology*.

1. INTRODUCTION
Social communication frequently relies on generic communication media originally intended for work- and task-related purposes. Communication for most families relies on the telephone, text messaging, and videoconferencing [21]. At CSCW, interest has been growing in technologies that are aimed specifically at supporting affect-oriented communication (e.g., [27]). Relevant innovations may involve off-the-shelf technologies like tablets (e.g., [35]) or browsers or special purpose devices that enable informal social interaction (e.g., [43]). As the field progresses from early design explorations to robust technologies intended to address specific separation contexts, empirical evaluation of the emerging user experience can benefit from opportunities to triangulate findings from both qualitative and quantitative measures. In this work, we present the initial design and validation of a quantitative instrument that may supplement the existing qualitative approaches.

CSCW'14, February 15–19, 2014, Baltimore, Maryland, USA.

Field deployments of interactive systems allow for "exploring user understandings, practices and the eventual uses" of the novel system [7]. Typically, researchers log systems use (e.g., messages sent through the system) and interview the users post deployment. This approach provides rich qualitative data about contextualized user experiences, usage patterns, and appropriation of the technology, prompting and guiding subsequent improvements of the system. However, relying exclusively on qualitative methods presents some problems for this domain. One of the main problems is that a lack of agreed-upon metrics makes it difficult to draw conclusions across investigations, deployments, and systems (as discussed in [27,51]). It is difficult to compare systematically a specific technology either to earlier technologies or to alternate versions with different subsets of features. We propose that some of these challenges can be addressed by adopting a common approach for measuring the costs and benefits of communication systems, in addition to the commonly used qualitative methods.

We present the Affective Benefits and Costs of Communication Technologies (ABCCT) questionnaire as one such potential approach to the problem of evaluating communication technologies, which provides the following benefits:

- It addresses a specific technology in question, rather than connectedness or relationship quality in general.
- It is applicable to both synchronous and asynchronous communication technologies.
- It has less than 30 items and takes less than 10 minutes to complete.
- It can be used with both children and adults, with preliminary reliability and validity metrics provided.
- It highlights both emotional benefits and emotional costs that a system may introduce.
- It is sensitive enough to show differences between two communication systems.

The goal of this paper is to describe the process of developing and testing the ABCCT, as well as its early adoption in research. We developed the ABCCT questionnaire by building extensively on previous work, though collaborations with experts in the field, and through an analysis of interviews with separated parents and children (Section 4). In Sections 6 and 7, we describe our method of validating the survey and our findings, which show that the ABCCT is reliable and valid according to several metrics taken in piloting the questionnaire. In Section 8, we share early uptake of this instrument in the HCI and CSCW communities.

If you are an investigator considering the ABCCT for your own work, Section 5 contains a description of the scales of the ABCCT, Table 2 contains the full text of the questions, and Section 9 contains guidelines for analyzing the ABCCT, its appropriate use, and its limitations.

2. MOTIVATING AND RELATED WORK

We provide a review of current evaluation approaches for communication systems and briefly discuss previous efforts to develop validated metrics in this space.

2.1. Evaluations of Social Communication Technologies

We identified 35 papers published in archival HCI venues (e.g., CHI, CSCW) that presented and evaluated novel communication technologies for families, friends, or couples. As criteria for selecting papers, we looked at work published between 2000 and 2011 that presented a novel social communication technology and some form of evaluation. Here, we present the conclusions from this literature survey on the current practices in evaluating novel social communication technologies.

A significant proportion of papers in the HCI domain present novel communication technology ideas (e.g., [11,43]) or even novel systems (e.g., [45,47]) but do not provide any sort of evaluation. In this analysis, we included only those papers that provide a discussion of a system evaluation. Of the 35 papers we identified that provided an evaluation, 10 papers (29%) reported lab study evaluations. Most papers used passive observations and interviews in the evaluation, though 2 papers [34,54] also employed structured observation using specific validated criteria. Eleven papers (32%) involved field deployments of 1–4 weeks. All of these collected logs of system use and conducted periodic interviews with participants. Thirteen papers (38%) involved field deployments of 5–12 weeks. Most of these collected logs of system use and interviews with participants; two of these also collected diaries of participants' experiences. This demonstrates the prevalence of qualitative methods for evaluation in this field.

Only five of the studies we found included structured pre- and post-deployment questionnaires to understand the impact of system's use on the social relationships of the study participants. This is surprising, because investigations of family communication in the social science domain quite frequently involve the use of validated questionnaires in addition to other methods [28]. Kaye et al. stated that “participants were asked to subjectively rate the effectiveness and level of intimacy of their current methods of communication” [20]. No other detail was provided on the questions used or the effectiveness of these metrics. Rowan & Mynatt [38] “attempted to measure changes of perceived awareness and connectedness by asking [participants] to rank these indicators using a Likert scale daily in their diary.” Unfortunately, this metric did not yield useful results as they saw a ceiling effect. Khan et al. took measures before the introduction of their experimental system to support intra-family awareness, after a week of use, and a week after the end of this intervention [22]. They did not apply any validated instrument for the evaluation. Romero et al. report a two week deployment of an experimental system in which they compared measures prior to and after a week of using their system [37]. For the quantitative evaluation they used the Affective Benefits and Costs questionnaire (ABC-Q), a predecessor to the instrument presented here, that was developed for the purposes of that study [19]. Subsequent applications of the ABC-Q have shown it to be difficult to understand and to apply in relation to diverse technologies, making its revision necessary. We present a reworking of the affective benefits and costs questionnaire, validating the resulting questionnaire with a more rigorous quantitative approach, and extending it for use with children.

We do not advocate that qualitative methods should be replaced or abandoned, but rather support a mixed methods approach. We agree with Brown et al. that field trials present inherent challenges that could be ameliorated through diversifying the methods and approaches used in understanding system use [7]. Qualitative methods provide rich descriptions of system use and point to potential areas of improvements. On the other hand, collecting quantitative and structured data about how the system is perceived through the use of questionnaires better supports comparison between pre- and post-deployment experiences, between multiple novel systems, and between different versions of the same technology. This may be particularly important in the field of communication technology, since participant numbers tend to be fairly small in these evaluations (with two recent notable exceptions [24,35]). In order to be able to draw meaningful conclusions across systems and deployments, and eventually allow generalization of conclusions, it is helpful to use standard methods that would allow combining and comparing data across investigations. Our hope is that the ABCCT can provide one such standardized approach.

2.2. Questionnaire Instruments for Evaluating Communication Technologies

There are a number of survey instruments in social science that one might consider using to evaluate affective costs and benefits of communication technologies. Noller & Feeney provide a review of validated questionnaires for measuring characteristics of family communication [28]. A person's general positive and negative affect can be measured using the Positive and Negative Affect Schedule [46]. Further, there are a number of metrics for assessing the quality of any specific relationship, such as the Quality of Relationships Inventory [33]. Such measures could be taken before and after the introduction of a novel technology to evaluate its impact. However, these instruments measure characteristics that remain fairly stable over time. There is no evidence that any of these instruments are sensitive enough to detect a subtle change in a relationship, communication pattern, or personal affect that may be caused by a 1–12 week usage of a novel communication system, which is typical for field-tests in this domain.

There have been attempts within HCI literature to design survey instruments specifically aimed at evaluating communication technologies. Traditionally these focus on synchronous media, especially those intending to emulate and substitute physical co-presence. Validated inventories have been developed by Short, Williams, and Christie [42] and more recently the Networked Minds Social Presence questionnaire [15]. The limitations of such instruments pertain to the operationalization of social presence, which is not applicable for asynchronous systems. The Social Connectedness Questionnaire (SCQ) was developed to measure social connectedness as one particular benefit of communication technologies [3]. The SCQ can be used for comparing pre- and post- measures to reveal potential benefits of using a newly introduced communication technology. However, SCQ only evaluates one specific benefit of a new technology and is silent about potential downsides, which are crucial to understanding a design. Recognizing this need, IJsselsteijn et al. developed the Affective Benefits and Costs Questionnaire (ABC-Q) which provides the initial inspiration for the ABCCT [19]. However, the only validation of the ABC-Q was the measurements collected from 11 participants in a single case study deployment of novel technology [37]. Though its results were not in conflict with the qualitative data collected through diaries and interviews, no quantitative measure of agreement was provided. ABC-Q has been used in several research groups and industry projects; however, it is challenging for both respondents and designers. For example, the ABC-Q consists of 60 items, which makes it too long for most studies; and ABC-Q mixes questions regarding specific technologies with general contact questions, making it difficult to use it to compare specific technologies.

These early efforts at developing and validating surveys in HCI highlight that currently available instruments from the social science domain frequently do not meet the needs of HCI researchers. The testing of novel instruments in HCI is frequently limited to inter-item reliability statistics gathered from fairly small deployments. One of our goals in this paper is to provide an evaluation of a questionnaire that instead focuses on its convergent validity with qualitative metrics and its sensitivity to detecting changes between alternative communication media.

3. QUESTIONNAIRE DESIGN REQUIREMENTS

We wanted to design a questionnaire that could meet the needs of a designer in the field. Several requirements drove the design process of the ABCCT. The ABCCT must:

- Measure both the emotional benefits and emotional costs of communication technologies
- Be quick to administer, taking participants less than 15 minutes to answer
- Refer to a specific communication medium, since most of the time it will be used to compare technologies
- Demonstrate reliability and validity on multiple metrics
- Be sensitive enough to detect differences between communication technologies
- Be applicable to both synchronous and asynchronous communication technologies

For our own work in studying families, we had one additional requirement that the ABCCT must be validated for use with children as well as adults, since children are frequently partners in social communication but their voices are often excluded from the evaluation. In the next section, we describe our process in creating the ABCCT.

4. QUESTIONNAIRE DESIGN

We give an overview of the process used to generate and pilot the initial draft of the ABCCT.

Table 1. Original ABCCT Scales and Support for Each Scale in Previous Literature

Scale	Evidence for Scale Inclusion
Emotional Expressiveness	[2][12][17][23][30][36][53]
Engagement & Playfulness	[1][2][9][10][11][32][37][49][53]
Presence-in-Absence	[1][18][26][36][37][39][43][53]
Opportunity for Personal Effort	[17][23][36][37][41][44]
Opportunity for Social Support	[9][13][23][26][30][36][41][53]
Feeling Obligated	[17][37][39][44][47][53]
Unmet Expectations	[8][36][39][47][50]
Threat to Privacy	[5][8][26][37][44][47][53]

4.1. Generating the Scales

We created the children's ABCCT first and then adapted it for use by adults. Creating a survey appropriate for children forced us to simplify wording and make the questions more clear. Four types of previous work were used to draft ABCCT scales and questions: the ABC-Q [19], the theoretical background provided in related literature (see Table 1) re-coding of the interviews from a previously conducted study of parent-child communication in divorced families [53], and brainstorming by two social connectedness experts. This process yielded 12 scales with a total of 90 items. Review and discussion of the resulting measure by 2 experts lead to eliminating 23 questions and rewriting a significant portion of the remaining questions. This resulted in a draft of the survey with 8 scales and 55 items. Table 1 lists these scales and literature consulted at the time of the instrument's creation that supports the inclusion of each scale. We used Borger & Hox's [6] recommendations to choose a Likert-type scale that focused on frequencies of events in a specific period, rather than agreement (e.g., "never" to "always," rather than "strongly disagree" to "strongly agree"). This guideline let the questionnaire to remain more concrete and avoided advanced vocabulary (e.g., "neutral" is considered a 5th grade-level reading word) therefore allowing the ABCCT to be more appropriate for use with children.

4.2. Piloting the Questionnaire

We followed Bell's guidelines in designing and testing the children's questionnaires, by conducting comprehensive pretesting, including cognitive interviewing [4]. To pilot the survey with children, 3 nine- and ten-year-old boys were asked to complete the ABCCT-Child one-on-one with the researcher while reasoning out loud. By observing when the children became restless while taking the survey, we noted that it needed to be cut in size by half. The next draft of the survey restructured two of the scales and eliminated 9 questions that the children found unclear. The resulting measure was piloted with another four children using a think-aloud protocol. From this pilot, the next draft had most questions refined and redundant ones eliminated, resulting in an 8-scale, 32 item questionnaire. Following, an additional deployment (see Section 6.1), factorial analysis was done on the survey results leading to one item being moved to a different scale and to the merging of two closely-related scales. Ten questions were omitted in an effort to shorten the survey and remove confusing questions. The resulting draft consisted of the 7-scale, 22-item ABCCT-Child questionnaire (Table 2).

A pilot was conducted with 8 adults, asking them to complete the draft ABCCT-Child one-on-one with the researcher while reasoning out loud. This led to a number of changes that resulted in the adult version of the questionnaire:

- Reciprocity items were added to appropriate scales, as suggested by [19].
- Questions were reworded and used more nuanced vocabulary, on the suggestion of the participants.
- One question was removed, as it was the only negatively phrased question, frequently leading adult participants to mark the opposite answer.

This resulted in a 7-scale, 26-item ABCCT-Adult (Table 2).

5. ABCCT SCALES AND QUESTIONS

Through this design process, the ABCCT was focused and refined to measure the 4 major affective benefits and 3 major affective costs of communication technologies.

Benefit 1: Emotional Expressiveness. One benefit of a communication technology may be the ability to share emotional states with a partner. This includes both being able to express one's own feelings and being able to perceive the feelings expressed by the partner.

Benefit 2: Engagement & Playfulness. Social communication is frequently characterized by playful exchanges and other attempts at making the communication more engaging for both partners. The ABCCT asks whether the communication via a certain medium is fun and exciting to the participant. Adults may also be sensitive as to whether the communication is engaging to their partner, so the adult version includes a reciprocity item.

Benefit 3: Presence-In-Absence. Presence-In-Absence is defined as the "subjective sense of social others whilst separated from them by time or space" [18]. Some communication technologies may be more suited to fostering feelings of "closeness" or "connectedness" to a partner, as well as better supporting specific behaviors like remembering a contact or frequently thinking about each other.

Benefit 4: Opportunity for Social Support. One of the benefits of communication technologies is the opportunity to provide social support without being physically present. This includes a general sense of the other person "being there" for you, reducing negative affect (such as soothing anxiety), and increasing positive affect (such as feeling "special" or loved). This may also include more instrumental forms of support such as giving advice or helping make a decision. The ABCCT-Adult includes items about both providing and about receiving social support, while the children's version focuses on receiving support.

Cost 1: Feeling Obligated. A communication technology may introduce an unwanted obligation to connect. This may include feeling compelled to communicate or respond when you would rather not do so and even feelings of guilt over not maintaining adequate communication. The adult version of the questionnaire also includes a reciprocity item, since adults are often sensitive of situations where they might be creating obligations for others.

Cost 2: Unmet Expectations. A communication technology may increase expectations for communication. When these expectations are not met, participants may experience negative affect. Expectations may include the frequency of contact, how quickly a person returns a missed contact, and how much attention is devoted to the communication. The ABCCT asks about the situations where unmet expectation result in negative affect. The adult version of this scale also includes a reciprocity item, as negative affect may result if one feels one is not meeting the partner's expectations.

Cost 3: Threat to Privacy. This scale includes three major aspects: concerns over your communication partner being able to see or hear something you may want to keep secret, concerns over others in the environment overhearing the communication, and concerns that the communication may be invading the partner's privacy.

Table 2. ABCCT scales and questions. <X> is the relationship and <M> is the medium being investigated. Participant should respond on a 5 point Likert-type frequency scale (never, rarely, sometimes, usually, or always)

Scale	ABCCT-Adult Questions	ABCCT-Child Questions
Emotion. Express.	Communicating with <X> using <M> helps me tell how <X> is feeling that day.	I could tell over <M> how <X> was feeling that day.
	Communicating with <X> using <M> helps me let <X> know how I am feeling.	I could let <X> know how I was feeling over <M>.
	Communicating with <X> using <M> helps me see how much <X> cares about me.	I could tell over <M> how much <X> cares about me.
Engagement & Play	-	It was boring to use <M> with <X>. *[reverse score this item]*
	I feel that contact with me using <M> is engaging for <X>.	-
	I am excited about using <M> with <X>.	I was excited about using <M> with <X>.
	I have fun with <X> while using <M>.	I had fun with <X> while using <M>.
Presence-in-Absence	Communicating with <X> using <M> helps me feel closer to <X>.	I felt closer to <X> after using <M> together.
	After we are done communicating, I still keep thinking back to something <X> shared using <M>.	After we were done, I still kept thinking back to something <X> shared using <M>.
	Communicating with <X> using <M> helps me feel more connected to <X>.	I felt more connected to <X> after our contact using <M>.
Opportunity for Social Support	Communicating with <X> using <M> helps me provide <X> with social support.	-
	<X> makes me feel special in our contact using <M>.	<X> made me feel special in our contact using <M>.
	Communicating with me using <M> helps <X> be there for me when I need them.	<X> was there for me over <M> when I needed them.
	Communicating with <X> using <M> when I am having a bad day helps me feel better.	Using <M> with <X> when I was having a bad day helped me feel better.
	Communicating with <X> using <M> helps me feel less worried about something.	I felt less worried about something after using <M> with <X>.
Unwanted Obligations	I worry that <X> feels obligated to contact me using <M>.	-
	I have to talk to <X> using <M> even if I don't want to.	I had to talk to <X> using <M> even if I didn't want to.
	I feel guilty if I don't answer a contact <X> makes using <M>.	I felt guilty if I didn't answer a contact <X> made using <M>.
	I have to answer when <X> tries to contact me using <M> even if I don't want to.	I had to answer when <X> tried to contact me using <M> even if I didn't want to.
Unmet Expectations	I feel sad when <X> isn't around when I try to contact <X> using <M>	I felt sad when <X> wasn't around when I tried to contact <X> over <M>.
	I feel sad when <X> takes too long to respond when I try to contact <X> using <M>.	I felt sad because <X> took too long to respond when I tried to contact <X> using <M>.
	I worry that I am not meeting <X>'s expectations for our contact using <M>.	-
	I feel sad when <X> doesn't pay enough attention to me when we use <M>.	I felt sad because <X> didn't pay enough attention to me when we used <M>.
Threat to Privacy	I worry that <X> might learn something using <M> that I want to keep secret.	I worried that <X> might learn something over <M> that I want to keep secret.
	I worry about my privacy while <X> and I are using <M> together.	I worried about my privacy while <X> and I were using <M> together.
	I worry that others may overhear or see something that <X> and I share using <M>.	I worried that others would overhear or see something that <X> and I shared using <M>
	I worry that I am violating <X>'s privacy during our contact using <M>.	-

The full text of the scales and questions are presented in Table 2.

6. METHODS

We conducted three studies to gather reliability and validity measures of the ABCCT. In this section, we describe the procedures of all three studies: (1) we deployed the child version survey and discussed it in focus groups with 45 children; (2) we deployed the adult version of the survey online with 110 adult participants; (3) we conducted interviews and deployed the survey with 14 adults and 14 children in families where a parent travels frequently for work. The findings of all three studies and what these findings say about the reliability, validity, and sensitivity of the ABCCT are related in the results section.

6.1. Deployment and Focus Groups with Children

We tested the ABCCT with a larger group of children to gather reliability statistics and continue refining the question set. The study was conducted at a school in Preston, England with 45 eight- to ten-year-old children participating in testing the survey. The survey was read aloud by the researcher to groups of 6 children as they filled it out. They were asked to complete the survey for a relationship and medium of their choosing. The majority of the children discussed using the telephone with a family member (grandparent and cousin were the most common). The chil-

Table 3. Sample interview prompts and sample coded phrases for each interview scale.

Scale	Sample Interview Prompt	Sample Coded Phrase
Emotional Expressiveness	How can you tell how you son is feeling when you talk to him on the phone?	"I have to see them to really know. But sometimes it depends on what they are saying. If they get in trouble, yeah, usually."
Engagement & Playfulness	Tell me about a time that you and your mom had fun while using telephone together.	"Usually I act pretty goofy. Like we'll say something like an inside joke, and she'll laugh. And my brother, he'll say something weird. We don't what he be saying, but we just laugh."
Presence-in-Absence	How does exchanging MMS messages affect your sense of connection to your daughter?	"I have their pictures that I look at ... if I'm in the middle of wherever, I can just pop open my cell phone and look at the pictures."
Social Support	Tell me about a time that talking to you mom over videochat made you feel better when you were having bad day.	"We might joke around. Like I'm feeling blue and just kind of make a face and show her ... and you know, a lot of the negative stuff, kind of like dissipates."
Feeling Obligated	Give me an example of a situation where you didn't feel like talking to your mom on IM. What did you do?	"One time, my mom responded, and I didn't really want to, so I just ignored it."
Unmet Expectations	Give me an example of an expectation that you have of your daughter in term of responding to you on the phone.	"Yes. I expect her to return my calls, and I expect her to definitely respond to my texts or phone calls, because otherwise I get very concerned."
Threat to Privacy	Give me an example of a situation where you worried that somebody else might hear your phone conversation.	"Yes, that's why I like going home. Like, some certain things, I don't mind saying that in front of my friends. But some stuff I like to keep in the house."

dren were observed as they completed the survey and confusing questions were noted. After completing the survey, each group of six was led by the researcher to discuss which questions seemed to be most problematic. From the focus group responses, the authors identified questions that needed to be reworded or removed from the survey. The survey responses were analyzed quantitatively to gather metrics of inter-item reliability.

6.2. Deployment with Adults

To pilot the ABCCT with adults, we created an online version of the questionnaire. A link to the questionnaire was circulated using social networking media and posted in the craigslist.com "Volunteer" section. Each participant was asked to fill out the ABCCT for a relationship and communication technology of their choosing. A total of 113 participants completed the questionnaire. Two entries were removed from the analysis as the participants rated multiple communication technologies in a single survey instead of selecting one specific technology. One entry was removed because the participant gave the same answer to all questions and took less than 1 minute to complete the survey, suggesting he or she did not read the questions. The remaining 110 questionnaires were analyzed quantitatively to gather metrics of inter-item reliability and to gauge the questionnaire's sensitivity to different media.

6.3. Interviews and Surveys with Parent-Child Pairs

To continue rigorously measuring the reliability and validity of the questionnaire, we conducted a follow-up study with a smaller number of participants that allowed us to see how the results of the ABCCT corresponded to other measures of affects and benefits of communication technologies and see whether the results on the ABCCT remained stable over time for each participant.

6.3.1. Procedure

We recruited families who frequently used communication technologies and who were willing to participate in in-depth interviews. We interviewed parent-child pairs from 14 different families, where the parents and children (ages 7-13) frequently used communication technologies to stay in touch. Recruiting was done through word-of-mouth, ads on craigslist.org, and local military support organizations. We conducted hour-long semi-structured interviews with each participant. The questions focused on the participants' general experiences with the separation, how they manage contact during separation, and how they use technology to stay in touch. We also asked about their experiences with the two most common technologies they use, specifically what they see as the costs and benefits of each technology. In addition to the interview, each parent and child responded to ABCCT questionnaires for the two technologies they used most frequently to stay in touch. We also asked each adult to fill out a Social Connectedness Questionnaire [3] specific to his or her relationship with the child interviewed (unfortunately, no child version of the Social Connectedness Questionnaire is available). Finally, all study participants were contacted again two weeks after the interview and asked to again fill out the ABCCT questionnaire for the same technologies they had previously discussed.

6.3.2. Analysis

All interviews were audio-recorded and transcribed by the lead author. The interview transcripts were analyzed by creating thematic connections using a data-driven approach [40]. With each pass through the interview data, themes were refined until a set of distinct themes emerged. In addition to this data-driven approach, for each participant, we examined all interview statements corresponding to any of the ABCCT scales. Based on these interview statements, each participant was assigned a score of either "low," "medium," "high," or "insufficient information" for each ABCCT scale. For three randomly selected participants, the lead author and an independent coder scored interview statements for each scale. The agreement (Cohen's Kappa) between the two coders was for 0.80 ("excellent") over the 42 codes. Any disagreements on codes were discussed until consensus was reached. In order to be able to quantitatively compare the results of the interview coding and the ABCCT questionnaire responses, we also rated each participant's responses on the ABCCT according to the same scheme. If a participant averaged between 1.00 and 2.33 on a particular scale, he or she was classified as "low" on that scale; between 2.34 and 3.66 was classified as "medium" on that scale; and between 3.67 and 5.00 was classified as "high" on that scale. Thus, for each of the 14 adult and 14 child participants, for each scale of the ABCCT, we recorded two values: one as indicated by the participant through his or her ABCCT responses and one as coded by the researcher based on the participant's interview responses. We treated these two values as two sources of ratings and conducted inter-rater reliability analysis (Cohen's K) to understand the level of agreement between the two measures. Participant scales coded as "insufficient information" in the interviews were dropped from this analysis.

Lastly, we conducted a quantitative analysis of the surveys administered to these participants to get measures of convergent validity and test-retest reliability. To get a measure of convergent validity, we compared the average benefits of communication technologies as reported on the ABCCT with the Specific Social Connectedness metric of the SCQ [3]. We hypothesized that a participant that reports high level of benefits in using the group of communication technologies with a specific family member would also report having high levels of social connectedness with this family member. To get a measure of test-retest reliability, we compared two ABCCT measures taken 2 weeks apart.

6.4. Limitations

This evaluation of the ABCCT is meant to provide the first steps towards a final instrument. Though we provide several components of typical questionnaire validation, the number of participants in each part of the analysis is significantly lower than in a typical psychometrics study. For example, the PANAS affect schedule [46] was tested with an initial study of 407 participants and with a retest study of 163 (compared to 110 test and 27 retest for this ABCCT investigation). While the ABCCT approach exceeds the typical validation provided for other instruments in the HCI domain (e.g., SCQ tested with 215 participants, and provided no test-retest [3]; AttrakDif with 33 participants without test-retest [16]), it may not provide as thorough a validation as a true psychometric approach. However as a tradeoff, our work provides a metric of convergent validity with qualitative data that is rarely presented in psychometrics work but valued in HCI investigations. As HCI investigations utilize this instrument, the community may come to better understand the specific limitation it presents and which cases may require modifications of the instrument.

7. RESULTS

We present the results of the three studies described in the previous section, as related to the inter-item and test-retest reliability and convergent validity metrics of the ABCCT. We also show that the ABCCT is sensitive enough to detect differences between communication media.

Table 4. Inter-item reliability metrics for ABCCT scales.

Scale	Cronbach's α (Children)	Cronbach's α (Adult)
Benefits	**0.88**	**0.88**
Emotional Expressiveness	0.65	0.74
Engagement & Play	0.74	0.75
Presence-in-Absence	0.71	0.75
Social Support	0.86	0.75
Costs	**0.80**	**0.85**
Feeling Obligated	0.64	0.61
Unmet Expectations	0.78	0.70
Threat to Privacy	0.72	0.80

7.1. Inter-Item Reliability

We gathered inter-item reliability metrics of the ABCCT questionnaire by piloting with 45 children and 110 adults (see Table 4). Overall, the Benefits and the Costs dimensions both achieve internal consistency classified as "good." The scales for Engagement & Playfulness, Presence-in-Absence, Opportunity for Social Support, Unmet Expectations, and Threat to Privacy all achieve Cronbach's Alphas in the "acceptable" to "good" range. However, the Emotional Expressiveness scale on the child version and the Feeling Obligated scale on both versions have a Cronbach's alpha in the "questionable" range. Since lower values are acceptable for scales with a smaller number of items [29] and one of our goals was achieving a shorter questionnaire, these scales are within reasonable parameters to warrant their use. This reflects the design decision to focus on creating a shorter questionnaire rather than focusing on the internal consistency of each individual scale. If internal consistency is of particular concern to the researcher, we recommend administering and reporting results along the entire Benefits and Costs dimensions rather than splitting the results into each specific scale.

7.2. Test-Retest Reliability

One way of demonstrating the reliability of the ABCCT is by showing that two measures of the same partner-medium interaction taken from the same participant will yield simi-

Table 5. Agreement between the interview coding and the questionnaire responses for adults and children.

Scale	Cohen's K (Adults)	Cohen's K (Children)
Overall Agreement	**0.793**	**0.612**
Emotional Expressiveness	0.85	0.63
Engagement & Play	0.78	0.29
Presence-in-Absence	0.76	0.68
Social Support	0.62	0.50
Feeling Obligated	0.71	0.60
Unmet Expectations	0.65	0.71
Threat to Privacy	0.84	0.60

lar results when separated by a fairly short period of time. In this case, it would be reasonable to expect that the measures of benefits and costs of a medium for a particular relationship would stay largely the same when taken two weeks apart. All of the adult interview participants responded to the ABCCT retest request, allowing us to compare the measures for 27 ABCCT surveys total (13 participants responded about 2 communication media each, 1 participant responded about 1 medium). For adults, the correlation (Pearson *r*) of the average reported benefits and costs of each communication technology on the two surveys given two weeks apart was 0.951 which is statistically significant ($p < 0.001$). This shows that for adults, the ABCCT is a stable metric over a time period of two weeks and this contributes to the argument that the ABCCT is a reliable instrument.

Gathering an ABCCT retest measure from the children required more effort on the adult participants' parts (since the questionnaire needed to be administered verbally), so not all parents responded to the request to collect these measures from their children. We collected a total of 10 ABCCT retest surveys (5 participants responded about 2 communication technologies each). However, even with the reduced sample size, the correlation (Pearson *r*) of the average reported benefits and costs of each communication technology on the two surveys given two weeks apart was 0.686 which is statistically significant ($p = 0.001$). This shows that for children, the ABCCT is also a stable metric over a time period of two weeks and contributes to the argument that the ABCCT is a reliable instrument.

7.3. Convergent Validity with SCQ

We asked each of the 14 adult participants to fill out a Social Connectedness Questionnaire [3] to describe their sense of connection to their child. The Social Connectedness questionnaire is neither suitable nor validated for use with children so we could only collect this metric for adults.

It would stand to reason that participants who reported receiving higher benefits from each of the communication technologies they used to maintain contact with the child remotely on the ABCCT would also report a higher level of social connectedness with the same child on the Social Connectedness Questionnaire. Indeed, the correlation (Pearson *r*) between the average benefits reported on all technologies used by each adult participant and the SC score was 0.652 for the 14 adult participants, which is statistically significant ($p = 0.012$). This correlation confirms the expected relationship between the benefits dimension of the ABCCT and the construct of Social Connectedness.

7.4. Convergent Validity with Qualitative Data

Interviewing a person about the costs and benefits of a communication technology should produce roughly the same responses as asking that person to take the ABCCT. We conducted hour-long semi-structured in-depth interviews with 14 parents and 14 children. Several of the questions in the interview were explicitly designed to draw out responses related to certain ABCCT scales in an open-ended manner. Table 3 shows some of the questions that we asked in the interview to get insight into specific scales, as well as phrases from the interview that were coded as being relevant to that scale. We also coded phrases from the other parts of the interview that provided insight into specific costs and benefits of communication technologies. Since the interviewer did not pose the same questions as the survey and asked the participant to relate specific stories and experiences rather than data on frequency of particular events, not all participants addressed each scale in the interviews. If there was insufficient evidence in the interview to code a participant as "low," "medium," or "high" on a specific scale, that scale was dropped from the analysis (7.4% of scale-medium pairings for adults, 16.6% of scale-medium pairing for children).

On the child version, the overall agreement Cohen's Kappa was 0.612 (over 146 codes), which is statistically significant ($p < 0.001$). Table 5 shows the Cohen's Kappa for each scale on the survey. The "Engagement & Playfulness" scale stands out as having the lowest level of agreement. The interview coding almost always predicted a lower response than the one that appeared on the survey. The interview asked children to recall a time that they had fun with their parent while using a certain communication technology together. Many of the children could not recall a single instance of "having fun." Yet, on the survey the same children reported that talking to their parent was "never" boring and "sometimes" or "frequently" fun. There could be two possible reasons for this observation. First, it's possible that

Table 6. Comparing different communication technologies using the ABCCT, in the adult pilot deployment. All comparisons were done using 2-tailed Wilcoxon rank sum tests. Values in square brackets are not statistically significant, but show a trend.

	Phone (n=43) vs. Video (n=20)			IM (n=19) vs. Text (n=16)			Video (n=20) vs. Text (n=16)		
Scale	Phone	Video	M.-Wh.	IM	Text	M.-Wh.	Video	Text	M.-Wh.
Emotional Expressiveness	3.86	4.02	not sig.	3.67	3.15	p = 0.023	4.02	3.15	p < 0.001
Engagement & Play	3.42	3.84	p = 0.044	3.54	3.14	p = 0.047	3.84	3.14	p = 0.004
Presence-in-Absence	3.84	4.30	p = 0.027	3.51	3.17	not sig.	4.30	3.17	p < 0.001
Social Support	3.57	3.68	not sig.	3.54	3.50	not sig.	3.68	3.50	not sig.
Feeling Obligated	2.22	1.79	p = 0.049	2.32	2.03	[p = 0.160]	1.79	2.03	[p = 0.170]
Unmet Expectations	2.36	2.14	not sig.	2.51	2.22	not sig.	2.14	2.22	not sig.
Threat to Privacy	1.81	2.04	not sig.	1.89	1.39	p = 0.013	2.04	1.39	p = 0.038

the children were simply not very capable of recalling specific past examples, but may in fact have had a better gestalt impression of their engagement with their parents. Alternatively, it is possible that children experienced greater demand characteristics with the survey—a child may not want to say that talking with their parent was boring for fear of hurting their parents' feelings. In this situation, it is difficult to know whether the interview or the survey response is closer to the ground truth. With children, it seems that one may have to triangulate evidence from multiple sources in order to get an accurate understanding of their engagement. However, it seems that on the other scales, the interview and the ABCCT responses corresponded significantly for each participant—evidence that the ABCCT-Child measures what it intends to measure.

On the adult version, the overall agreement Cohen's Kappa was 0.793 (over 175 codes), which is statistically significant ($p < 0.001$). Table 5 shows the Cohen's Kappa for each scale on the survey. The adult version of the ABCCT showed significant agreement on all scales between the experiences related in the interview and the responses given on the written ABCCT. These results provide strong evidence that the ABCCT-Adult measures the same construct as gleaned from independently coded interviews.

7.5. Sensitivity to Differences between Technologies

One of our goals in this undertaking was creating a questionnaire that is sensitive enough to detect differences in emotional benefits and costs between different communication media. We used the data from the ABCCT administered online to 110 adults to address this concern. Unfortunately, we could not conduct a similar analysis for ABCCT-Child because there were fewer than 5 responses addressing any technology other than the telephone in the Preston pilot, so we could not make a meaningful quantitative comparison. Since the adult pilot gathered a number of responses for a fairly diverse set of communication technologies, we could conduct three comparisons. First, we compared two synchronous and two asynchronous communication technologies most frequently described in the online surveys.

We used a two-tailed Wilcoxon Rank Sum Test to compare telephone vs. videoconferencing, IM vs. texting, and texting vs. videoconferencing on each of the 7 ABCCT scales. Table 6 shows the results of these comparisons. As could be expected, videoconferencing scored significantly higher on the Engagement & Playfulness and Presence-in-Absence scales. This is consistent with previous qualitative findings in the field (e.g., [1,2]). Participants also felt more unwanted obligations with the telephone. Though there was no statistically significant difference between telephone and videoconferencing on Emotional Expressiveness and Threat to Privacy scales, both were trending in expected directions. Comparing IM and Texting showed that IM scored higher on measures of Emotional Expressiveness and Engagement & Playfulness. Interview data suggests that this might be due to IM's support for images, emoticons, and ability to link to other media (e.g., YouTube clip) [52]. There is a trend (through not statistically-significant) for IM introducing more unwanted obligations, which is consistent with Grinter et al.'s qualitative work examining IM and SMS [14]. Also as expected, IM introduced significantly more threats to privacy than texting, due to the fact that IM conversations can easily be saved and passed along to others. Lastly, we compared videoconferencing and texting, because these two media have been previously compared on social presence measures in the lab [15]. These two media are quite different and we expected to see differences on a number of scales. Indeed, we found that videoconferencing was significantly better at supporting emotional expression, engagement & playfulness, and presence-in-absence. Also, as can be expected, videoconferencing introduces significantly greater concerns over privacy. Texting showed a non-statistically significant trend for more obligations to communicate than videoconferencing, which is consistent with interview findings that users are often expected to answer their texts in a timely manner (e.g., [52]). It is likely that there was significant noise in this data, since the survey was administered online with very little guidance for participants. For example, participants may have used the same medium label (e.g., "IM") for two different experiences (e.g., Facebook messenger vs. Pidgin). It is encouraging that the ABCCT was able to highlight some statistically significant differences between communication technologies even with this significant noise, a relatively low number of responses, and data collected between (rather than within) participants.

8. EARLY QUESTIONNAIRE UPTAKE

The success of the ABCCT depends on community uptake. Though this paper presents the first archival publication of the ABCCT validation, we made early versions of the questionnaire available to other researchers. There are three independent examples of early uptake of this questionnaire prior to this paper. One project used the ABCCT to understand the ecosystem of communication tools available to users for sharing information and support in dealing with chronic health conditions [31]. The ABCCT helped these researchers articulate a problem space for novel technology and the different roles that synchronous and asynchronous communication media play in health-related communication. Another group of researchers, incorporated the ABCCT into their methodology to understand the role that telepresence robot can play in connecting separated family members [48]. In the third project, the ABCCT was used to evaluate a novel communication technology for connecting separated parents and children. The ABCCT was able to demonstrate the specific scales where the novel technology performed better than the previous communication media used by the families in an A-B field deployment [56]. These initial forays may be representative of the community's interest in incorporating validated questionnaires as one of the sources of evidence in understanding the emotional costs and benefits of communication technologies.

9. DISCUSSION

We provide guidelines for scoring and use of the ABCCT, discuss its limitations, and offer directions for future work.

9.1. ABCCT Questionnaire Scoring and Analysis

The ABCCT uses Likert-type frequency scales with the assumption of equal interval between items. The investigator should assign numbers from 1 to 5 for each item (i.e., "never" = 1, "always" = 5). One question on the child version (marked in Table 2) is to be scored negatively (i.e., assign score of 6 - response). Once scores for each question are obtained, the score for each scale can be computed by averaging those responses. The score for each dimension can be calculated by averaging the scores for each composing scale. With descriptive investigations, scores on each scale and/or dimension can be aggregated across participants and presented as descriptive statistics (average and standard deviation/error). With hypothesis-driven work, sets of data can be compared using standard statistical tests for paired (within subjects design) and non-paired (between subject design) data. A t-test or paired t-test is sufficient when the data is normally distributed. In cases where the normality assumption does not hold, we recommend the Wilcoxon rank sum and the Wilcoxon signed-rank tests as alternatives.

9.2. Guidelines for ABCCT Questionnaire Use

The ABCCT can be administered to adults on paper or online. The pilot deployment with 110 adults was completed online with minimal instruction for participants. In administering the child version of the questionnaire, we recommend following Borgers & Hox's guidelines [29]: the questionnaire should be clearly explained, the questions should refer to the opinions and behaviors of a recent time period (e.g., past 2 weeks), and all options on the survey should be labeled (e.g., "Never," "Rarely," etc.). When possible, we recommend that the survey be administered as a structured interview to children (i.e., read out loud to the child), as this helps ameliorate individual differences in reading level and comprehension. Additionally, this allows the researcher to verbally make the substitutions for the "person" and "medium" being investigated.

The main value of the ABCCT is in allowing the investigator to make comparisons between different technologies. Here are several potential scenarios for appropriate use of the ABCCT:

- **Within-Subject Comparison of Two Tech Versions**: Two versions of a communication technology (with and without an experimental feature) are deployed one-after-another in a series of homes. Each participant fills out the ABCCT for each technology after the deployment. A pairwise comparison is used to investigate how the feature affected the benefits and costs of the technology.
- **Between-Subject Comparison of Two Tech Versions**: One version of a communication technology (either with or without an experimental feature) is deployed in the home. After the deployment, each participant fills out the ABCCT for the technology version they used. Scores on each scale or dimension are compared between the control and experimental groups to investigate how the feature affected the benefits and costs of the technology.
- **Within-Subject Comparison of Prototype Tech with Existing Tech**: A technology is deployed to replace a particular current technology (e.g., better IM client). Before the study, the participant is asked to fill out the ABCCT for the current technology. After the deployments, the participant is asked to fill out the ABCCT for the novel system. A pairwise comparison is used to point out how the novel system differs from the status quo system (e.g., [56]).
- **Within-Subject Pre-Post Deployment Tech Ecosystem Comparison:** A technology that is meant to supplement the currently used communication systems is deployed in the field. Before and after the deployment, the participants fill out ABCCT questionnaires for each of the communication media they use. An analysis can show whether the new system filled a need different from the other systems, whether previous systems were now used differently because of the introduction of the novel technology, and how the novel system compares to the previously used systems on each of the ABCCT dimensions.
- **Meta-Analysis Regarding a Particular Feature:** An investigator wants to conduct a meta-analysis showing that adding a particular feature (e.g., asynchronous video messaging) to a communication system has a predicted effect on a specific ABCCT scale. He or she gathers all papers that investigated relevant systems with this feature and all papers that investigated relevant systems without this feature. Assuming these papers presented ABCCT scores (or made these metrics available by request), the investigator can use standard meta-analysis techniques to draw comparisons and conclusions.
- **Meta-Analysis Regarding a Particular Population:** An investigator wants to conduct a meta-analysis of ABCCT scores for systems supporting a particular population (e.g., remote couples). He or she gathers all papers that included this population. Assuming these papers presented ABCCT scores (or made these metrics available by request), the investigator can use standard meta-analysis techniques to draw comparisons and conclusions about the types of communication technologies that may be of most value to this population.

While this is not an exhaustive list of acceptable study designs, it provides some examples of how the ABCCT may be used. We caution investigators against making between-study comparisons when only a small number of other studies are available on a particular issue of interest. Particularly, **drawing favorable or unfavorable comparisons against a technology in one previous investigation is more likely to be misleading than informative**. Brown et al. point out the incredible difficulties in attempting to generalize from single-case field deployments, as even small variations in participants and methods can lead to drastically different interpretations of the same technology [5]. However, as similar technologies are deployed in a variety of contexts, there may be a large enough sample to compensate for this variability and allow for between-study comparisons.

9.3. Limitations

Researchers should understand the inherent limitations of the ABCCT questionnaire before using it. Most importantly, **this questionnaire should not be used as the only evaluation metric for a novel communication technology**. The emotional aspects of communication are inherently nuanced. While the ABCCT provides a good way to compare systems and synthesize findings across investigations, qualitative methods are still the best way of understanding the contextual factors that play into the adoption and use of a novel system for communication. However, triangulating data from rich qualitative metrics and the structured data from the ABCCT would lead to more valuable results than using either method alone.

Second, **the adoption and use of communication technologies is influenced not just by emotional factors but also by pragmatic time/effort-related factors and even basic usability issues**. For example, videochat is frequently not used by families because of the complex work required to set up a session [1] and because of the undivided attention demanded by this medium [52]. On the other hand, communication media that have low time and effort costs to compose and send a message may be compelling even if they do not provide a rich channel for communication (e.g., [10]). Measuring the costs of initiating contact, the costs of composing or maintaining the contact, and the opportunity provided for demonstrating personal effort are all meaningful metrics for communication technologies but outside of the scope of the ABCCT. To gain a more complete understanding of the technology being investigated, the **ABCCT may be combined with other validated metrics** (e.g., usability metrics).

Lastly, the ABCCT questionnaire has the same limitations as other questionnaire methods appropriate for field evaluations. The participants fill out the ABCCT some time after events of interests occur, so **(1) participants may forget important issues or have trouble estimating the frequency of particular events**. **(2) Participants may be biased to present themselves in a positive light to the investigator** and therefore choose responses that may not accurately reflect their experiences with the technology. Additionally, **(3) participants may respond to the demand characteristics of the investigator**, especially when the expected results easy to deduce (e.g., within-subjects design where the experimental system is obvious). This may be especially true of children, who often worry about providing the adult with "the right answer." Triangulating the results from multiple methods and multiple sources of data can mitigate these shortcomings. Additionally, taking care to equalize power between the child and the researcher using classic participatory design methods can address some inequalities that exacerbate demand characteristics with children (e.g., [25]).

9.4. Future Directions

There are a number of future directions that emerge from this work: (1) designing a methodology for measuring the "pragmatic" costs and benefits of a communication technology, (2) using the ABCCT in the field and iterating on the design when necessary, (3) creating alternative versions of the ABCCT that may be useful for experience sampling methodologies.

The ABCCT does not provide a complete picture of a participant's experience with a communication technology. Understanding the pragmatic costs and benefits of communication technologies, such as the time and effort expanded during use, may help complete this picture. It may be possible to gather some of this data using survey methodologies, but it may be impractical due to the difficulty that users have recalling the exact amount of time spent on a particular interaction. Logging methodologies may be most valuable in this domain, perhaps in combination with some appropriate self-response data (for example, getting a participant to reflect on specific log data in an interview).

One of the potential benefits of the ABCCT is in supporting synthesis and comparison across technologies in multiple studies. However, in order for this to be possible, investigators must include the ABCCT in their methods and report (or make available upon request) the results of these deployments. As the ABCCT is utilized in diverse contexts, it is quite likely that shortcomings will emerge that will need to be addressed in future iterations. As such, we greatly encourage any investigators who chose to use the ABCCT to share their experiences with the authors of this instrument. We also encourage investigators to modify the ABCCT to suit the needs of a particular research project, though with the caution that some modification may need to be re-validated before use.

One of the limitations of the ABCCT is that it asks participants to reflect upon past experiences, potentially leading to recall bias. Ideally, the survey could be adopted to pose appropriate questions to the participants immediately after an event of interest has occurred. For example, immediately after receiving a message from a loved one or terminating a synchronous communication session, the participant can be asked to answer 2–3 questions about their experience. While it would be impractical to administer the entire ABCCT after each session with the technology, a system may be designed to ask a random subset of relevant questions. Collecting such responses over the course of a long deployment may contribute to an understanding of the system with less recall bias. Such a method would not only involve rewording the questions to be relevant in the moment, but also designing the system that would provide the participant with the questions at the appropriate time.

10. CONCLUSION

This work presents the design and initial validation of a questionnaire instrument for measuring the Affective Benefits and Costs of Communication Technologies (ABCCT). We discuss the pilots of this survey with 45 children and 110 adults, leading to the preliminary conclusion that the ABCCT has acceptable inter-item reliability. We discuss the results of interviews with 14 children and 14 adults, which help confirm that the ABCCT measures the same constructs that may emerge through an interview investigation. We show that the ABCCT has high test-retest reliability and convergent validity with the Social Connectedness metric. Finally, we demonstrate that the ABCCT is sensitive enough to discriminate between different communication technologies and has shown promise in some of its early uptake. Though the ABCCT is not without limitations, it provides a step towards a reliable and valid way to compare communication technologies in field deployments.

ACKNOWLEDGMENTS

We would like to acknowledge Janet Read for helping us set up the Preston trial. We would also like to thank the many participants who shared their time and honesty with us during this project.

REFERENCES

1. Ames, M.G., Go, J., Kaye, J., and Spasojevic, M. Making Love in the Network Closet: The Benefits and Work of Family Videochat. *Proc. of CSCW*, (2010), 145–154.
2. Ballagas, R., Kaye, J. "Jofish," Ames, M., Go, J., and Raffle, H. Family communication: phone conversations with children. *Proc. of IDC*, ACM (2009), 321–324.
3. Bel, D.T. van, Smolders, K.C.H.J., IJsselsteijn, W.A., and Kort, Y.A.W. de. Social connectedness: concept and measurement. *International Conference on Intelligent Environments*, IOS Press (2011), 67–74.
4. Bell, A. Designing and testing questionnaires for children. *Journal of Research in Nursing 12*, 5 (2007), 461–469.
5. Bonner, J.V.H. Adding critical sensibilities to domestic communication technologies. *Intl J of Human Computer Studies 67*, 2 (2009), 215–221.
6. Borgers, N. and Hox, J.J. Reliability of Responses in Questionnaire Research with Children. *International Conference on Logic and Methodology*, (2000).
7. Brown, B., Reeves, S., and Sherwood, S. Into the Wild: Challenges and Opportunities for Field Trial Methods. *Proc. of CHI*, (2011), 1657–1666.
8. Caughlin, J.P. and Petronio, S. Privacy in Families. In *Handbook of Family Communication*. Lawrence Erlbaum Associates, Mahwah, NJ, 2004, 379–412.
9. Dalsgaard, T., Skov, M.B., Stougaard, M., and Thomassen, B. Mediated intimacy in families: understanding the relation between children and parents. *Proc. of IDC*, ACM (2006), 145–152.
10. Dalsgaard, T., Skov, M.B., and Thomassen, B.R. eKiss: Sharing Experiences in Families Through a Picture Blog. *Proc. of British HCI*, (2007), 67–75.
11. Feltham, F., Vetere, F., and Wensveen, S. Designing tangible artefacts for playful interactions and dialogues. *Designing Pleasurable Products and Interfaces*, ACM (2007), 61–75.
12. Fitness, J. and Duffield, J. Emotion and Communication in Families. In *Handbook of Family Communication*. Lawrence Erlbaum Associates, Mahwah, NJ, 2004, 473–494.
13. Gardner, K.A. and Cutrona, C.E. Social Support Communication in Families. In *Handbook of Family Communication*. Lawrence Erlbaum Associates, Mahwah, NJ, 2004, 495–512.
14. Grinter, R.E., Palen, L., and Eldridge, M. Chatting with teenagers: Considering the place of chat technologies in teen life. *ACM ToCHI 13*, 4 (2006), 423–447.
15. Harms, C. and Biocca, F. Internal consistency and reliability of the networked minds social presence measure. (2004), 246–246.
16. Hassenzahl, M., Burmester, M., and Koller, F. AttrakDiff: Ein Fragebogen zur Messung wahrgenommener hedonischer und pragmatischer Qualität. *Mensch & Computer: Interaktion in Bewegung*, (2003), 187–196.
17. Hindus, D., Mainwaring, S.D., Leduc, N., Hagström, A.E., and Bayley, O. Casablanca: designing social communication devices for the home. *Proc. of CHI*, (2001), 325–332.
18. Howard, S., Kjeldskov, J., Skov, M., Garnoes, K., and Grünberger, O. Negotiating presence-in-absence: contact, content and context. *Proc. of CHI*, (2006), 909–912.
19. IJsselsteijn, W., Van Baren, J., Markopoulos, P., Romero, N., and de Ruyter, B. Measuring Affective Benefits and Costs of Mediated Awareness: Development and Validation of the ABC-Questionnaire. In *Awareness Systems*. 2009, 473–488.
20. Kaye, J. "Jofish," Levitt, M.K., Nevins, J., Golden, J., and Schmidt, V. Communicating intimacy one bit at a time. *Proc. of CHI*, ACM Press (2005), 1529–1529.
21. Kennedy, T.L.M., Smith, A., Wells, A.T., and Wellman, B. *"Networked Families." Pew Internet & American Life Project Report.* Washington, D.C., 2008.
22. Khan, J.V., Markopoulos, P., Eggen, B., and Metaxas, G. Evaluation of a pervasive awareness system designed for busy parents. *Pervasive and Mobile Computing 6*, 5 (2010), 537–558.
23. Khan, V.-J. and Markopoulos, P. Busy families' awareness needs. *Intl J of Human Computer Studies 67*, 2 (2009), 139–153.
24. Lindley, S.E., Harper, R., and Sellen, A. Designing a technological playground: a field study of the emergence of play in household messaging. *Proc. of CHI*, ACM (2010), 2351–2360.
25. Markopoulos, P., Read, J.C., MacFarlane, S., and Hoysniemi, J. *Evaluating Children's Interactive Products: Principles and Practices for Interaction Designers*. Morgan Kaufmann, Amsterdam, 2008.

26. Mynatt, E., Rowan, J., Jacobs, A., and Craighill, S. Digital family portraits: supporting peace of mind for extended family members. *Proc. of CHI*, ACM Press (2001), 333–340.
27. Neustaedter, C., Brush, A., and McDonald, D.W. Designing for Families. *Ext. Abst. of CSCW*, (2008).
28. Noller, P. and Feeney, J.A. Studying Family Communication: multiple methods and multiple sources. In *Handbook of Family Communication*. Lawrence Erlbaum Associates, Mahwah, NJ, 2004, 31–50.
29. Nunnally, J. and Bernstein, I. *Psychometic Theory*. McGraw-Hill, 1994.
30. Olivier, P. and Wallace, J. Digital technologies and the emotional family. *Intl J of Human Computer Studies 67*, 2 (2009), 204–214.
31. Pang, C.E., Neustaedter, C., Riecke, B.E., Oduor, E., and Hillman, S. Technology preferences and routines for sharing health information during the treatment of a chronic illness. *Proc. of CHI*, (2013), 1759–1768.
32. Petersen, M.G. Squeeze: designing for playful experiences among co-located people in homes. *Ext. Abst. of CHI*, ACM (2007), 2609–2614.
33. Pierce, G.R. Quality of Relationships Inventory: Assessing the Interpersonal Context of Social Support. *Commun. of Social Support*, (1991), 246–266.
34. Raffle, H., Ballagas, R., Revelle, G., et al. Family Story Play: Reading with Young Children (and Elmo) Over a Distance. *Proc. of CHI*, ACM (2010).
35. Raffle, H., Revelle, G., Mori, K., et al. Hello, is Grandma there? Let's Read! StoryVisit: Family Video Chat and Connected E-Books. *Proc. of CHI*, (2011), 1195–1204.
36. Romero, N., van Baren, J., Markopoulos, P., de Ruyter, B., and IJsselsteijn, W. Addressing Interpersonal Communication Needs through Ubiquitous Connectivity: Home and Away. *Ambient Intelligence*, (2003), 419–429.
37. Romero, N., Markopoulos, P., van Baren, J., de Ruyter, B., IJsselsteijn, W., and Farshchian, B. Connecting the family with awareness systems. *Personal and Ubiquitous Computing 11*, 4 (2007), 299–312.
38. Rowan, J. and Mynatt, E.D. Digital Family Portrait Field Trial: Support for Aging in Place. *Proc. of CHI*, ACM (2005), 521–530.
39. Saslis-Lagoudakis, G., Cheverst, K., Dix, A., Fitton, D., and Rouncefield, M. Hermes@Home: supporting awareness and intimacy between distant family members. *Proc. of OZCHI*, ACM (2006), 23–30.
40. Seidman, I. *Interviewing as Qualitative Research: A Guide for Researchers in Education And the Social Sciences*. Teachers College Press, New York, 1998.
41. Sellen, A., Harper, R., Eardley, R., et al. HomeNote: Supporting Situated Messaging in the Home. *Proc. of CSCW*, (2006), 383–392.
42. Short, J., Williams, E., and Christie, B. *The social psychology of telecommunications*. Wiley, London, 1976.
43. Strong, R. and Gaver, W.W. Feather, Scent, and Shaker: Supporting Simple Intimacy. *Proc. of CSCW*, (1996).
44. Tee, K., Brush, A.J., and Inkpen, K.M. Exploring communication and sharing between extended families. *Intl J of Human Computer Studies 67*, 2 (2009), 128–138.
45. Teh, J.K.S., Cheok, A.D., Peiris, R.L., Choi, Y., Thuong, V., and Lai, S. Huggy Pajama: a mobile parent and child hugging communication system. *Proc. of IDC*, (2008), 250–257.
46. Thompson, E.R. Development and Validation of an Internationally Reliable Short-Form of the Positive and Negative Affect Schedule (PANAS). *Journal of Cross-Cultural Psychology 38*, 2 (2007), 227–242.
47. Tollmar, K., Junestrand, S., Torgny, O., Boyarski, D., and Kellogg, W.A. Virtually living together. *Proc. of DIS*, (2000), 83–91.
48. Tsui, K., Desai, M., and Yanco, H. Towards measuring the quality of interaction: Communication through telepresence robots. *Proc. Workshop on Performance Metrics for Intelligent Systems*, ACM (2012).
49. Vetere, F., Davis, H., Gibbs, M., and Howard, S. The Magic Box and Collage: Responding to the challenge of distributed intergenerational play. *Intl J of Human Computer Studies 67*, 2 (2009), 165–178.
50. Vetere, F., Gibbs, M.R., Kjeldskov, J., et al. Mediating intimacy: designing technologies to support strong-tie relationships. *Proc. of CHI*, ACM (2005), 471–480.
51. Visser, T., Dadlani, P., van Bel, D., and Yarosh, S. Designing and Evaluating Affective Aspects of Sociable Media to Support Social Connectedness. *Ext. Abst. of CHI*, (2010), 4437–4440.
52. Yarosh, S. and Abowd, G.D. Mediated Parent-Child Contact in Work-Separated Families. *Proc. of CHI*, ACM (2011), 1185–1194.
53. Yarosh, S., Chew, Y.C., and Abowd, G.D. Supporting Parent-Child Communication in Divorced Families. *Intl J of Human Computer Studies 67*, 2 (2009), 192–203.
54. Yarosh, S., Inkpen, K.M., and Brush, A. Video playdate: toward free play across distance. *Proc. of CHI*, (2010), 1251–1260.
55. Yarosh, S. and Markopoulos, P. Design of an instrument for the evaluation of communication technologies with children. *Proc. of IDC*, ACM (2010), 266–269.
56. Yarosh, S., Tang, A., Mokashi, S., and Abowd, G. "Almost Touching:" Parent - Child Remote Communication Using the ShareTable System. (2013), 181–192.

How Social Cues Shape Task Coordination and Communication

Allison Sauppé, Bilge Mutlu
Department of Computer Sciences, University of Wisconsin–Madison
1210 West Dayton Street, Madison, WI 53706 USA
{asauppe, bilge}@cs.wisc.edu

ABSTRACT
To design computer-supported collaborative work (CSCW) systems that effectively support remote collaboration, designers need a better understanding of how people collaborate face-to-face and the mechanisms that they use to coordinate their actions. While research in CSCW has studied how specific social cues might facilitate collaboration in specific tasks, such as the role of gestures in video instruction, less is known about how a range of communicative cues might facilitate activities across many collaborative settings. In this paper, we model the predictive relationships between facial, gestural, and vocal cues and collaborative outcomes in three different tasks, drawing conclusions on how each cue might contribute to these outcomes in a given task and how such relationships generalize across tasks. The resulting models provide a quantitative understanding of the relative importance of each type of social cue in predicting collaborative outcomes, as well as a more thorough understanding of how the role of each social cue changes across tasks. Additionally, our results provide confirmation and illumination of prior findings in face-to-face and computer-mediated communication research.

Author Keywords
Computer-supported collaborative systems (CSCW); computer-mediated communication (CMC); face-to-face communication; social cues; design

ACM Classification Keywords
H.5.3. **Information Interfaces and Presentation**: Group and Organization Interfaces—*collaborative computing, computer-supported cooperative work, computer-mediated communication*

INTRODUCTION
Successful collaboration requires effective communication and coordination of actions and intentions. Individuals engaging in collaboration make use of shared knowledge, such as visual or verbal common ground, to predict how their partners in collaboration will behave and to modify their own behaviors in response to that prediction [43]. This ability to predict others' behaviors during the collaboration requires paying attention to their *social cues*—implicit behaviors that express thoughts or intentions. For example, in the absence of utterances, physical positioning and gaze cues facilitate communication by directing the partners' attention to referents [19].

CSCW'14, February 15 - 19 2014, Baltimore, MD, USA
Copyright 2014 ACM 978-1-4503-2540-0/14/02\$15.00.
http://dx.doi.org/10.1145/2531602.2531610

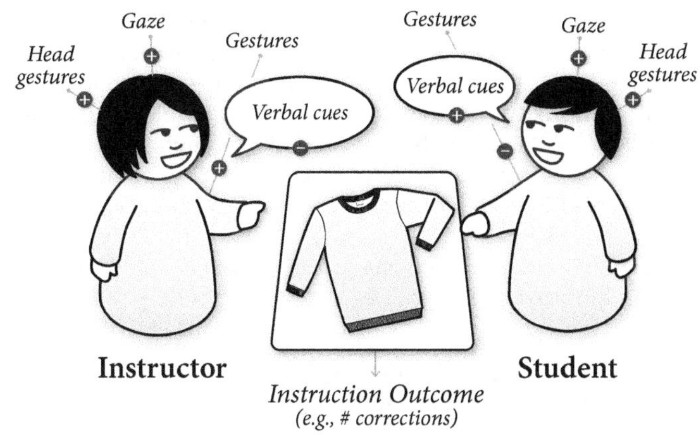

Figure 1. An illustration of the instructional scenario used in this work, highlighting the four categories of social cues we studied: head gestures, gaze, arm and hand gestures, and verbal cues.

In face-to-face collaborations, partners utilize each other's social cues to establish common ground. Individuals who are unable to meet face-to-face, on the other hand, rely on communication and collaboration technologies establish such common ground and collaborate at a distance. While these technologies enable participants to collaborate when the opportunity would not otherwise exist, they lack the level of social presence afforded in face-to-face interactions due to the limited number of *channels*—mediums that convey a subset of cues—that they convey (e.g., a telephone only mediates communication via the audio channel) [49, 51].

Previous research in CSCW has explored the role of specific social cues on collaboration in specific tasks as supported by specific communication channels, such as how gestures might support collaboration over the video channel in physical tasks [18]. However, a more comprehensive understanding of the role of social cues in collaboration, particularly how the broader range of social cues shape objective and subjective outcomes in collaboration across different roles and tasks, might inform the design of collaboration tools that provide support for a wider range of social cues and that adapt to the changing priorities of communication across different tasks.

To provide recommendations for designers of CSCW systems, we chose to study dyadic collaboration in its natural context, focusing on face-to-face dyadic communication. This approach allowed us to study the range of cues participants produced and was thereby not restricted by the channels available in a given CSCW system. While CSCW research has long been informed by studies of face-to-face communication, our work presents a more comprehensive perspective by examining how a wide range of social cues presented by all collaborators shapes interactions and how these interactions vary across contexts.

Based on the face-to-face interactions studied, we present a set of models that provides a holistic understanding of how numerous social cues impact communication in a variety of contexts. More specifically, these models describe the relationship between social cues, such as gaze, gestures, and verbal cues, and collaborative outcomes, such as task performance, perceived task success, and social outcomes, across three common collaborative activities: cooperation, instruction, and negotiation (Figure 1). These models are derived from a regression-based analysis of video data collected from eight human-human dyads in a laboratory setting. From these models, we draw the following contributions to CSCW:

- A quantitative understanding of the relative importance of each type of social cue in predicting collaboration outcomes.
- A better understanding of the variability in the role that each type of social cue plays in predicting these outcomes across different scenarios of collaboration.
- Confirmation and illustration of prior findings in face-to-face and mediated communication.

The remainder of this paper provides a review of related work, describes the methods of data collection, analysis, and results of the analysis, discusses the theoretical and design implications of these findings, and acknowledges some of the limitations of this work.

BACKGROUND

While remote collaboration draws on many of the same communicative cues and mechanisms as face-to-face communication [26], technologies that mediate such collaboration do not always support the channels necessary to perceive them, as audio and video communication restrict social cues that are commonly used in face-to-face interactions, such as gaze and nodding behaviors and shared view of gestures, respectively. These behaviors are crucial to the effectiveness of communication and collaboration; for example, gaze plays a particularly important role as it adds information to the dialogue [42] and indicates where attention is directed [19].

The mismatch between the range of behaviors people use to communicate and coordinate and the channels that CSCW systems support has been acknowledged by various theories of computer-mediated communication (CMC) [49, 51]. *Bandwidth theory*, initially implemented in more traditional media of the 1970s, discussed the effectiveness of a system in terms of the number of cues a system could convey (i.e., the system's *bandwidth*) and how it helped establish the perception of co-location between participants [44]. Previous work has shown that when the bandwidth of the system was increased, for example, by adding video to an audio-only system, participants' feelings of co-location would also increase [44]. An extension of bandwidth theory for collaboration systems is the *cues-filtered-out model*, which proposed a one-to-one attribution of cues to communicative functions [8]. According to this model, any decrease in the number of cues present in a system would directly decrease communicative function, since less information was communicated and social presence was lowered [8]. A third theory of CMC, *media richness theory*, aimed to explain the degree of communicativeness of the system as a function of the number, i.e., the richness, of cues communicated relative to the system task [9]. Based on this theory, systems that communicated a larger number of cues were better suited to more complicated tasks, such as explaining how to perform a surgical procedure, while systems that communicated a smaller number of cues were better suited to simpler tasks, such as setting up an appointment.

One challenge for CSCW system designers is to prioritize the cues most necessary for a given task, similar to the perspective presented by media richness theory that a more complex task will require that more cues are communicated [29]. While prior work has highlighted the superfluousness of video in many contexts [39], including simple tasks that require no spatial information [34], elimination of the visual channel in complex tasks or tasks that require spatial information can lead to degradation in task outcomes in remote collaboration. For example, instructional compliance during remote assistance for surgical procedures slows when the video screen is not visible to collaborators [32]. Many channels that enable the communication of social cues in face-to-face communication have been explored in the context of CSCW systems in an effort to increase the efficiency of future designs. The paragraphs below review previous work on how visual and audio channels support the communication of social cues.

Visual Channel

Gaze, one of the most important social cues in face-to-face interactions, has similar repercussions in remote collaboration that are enabled by CSCW systems. One of the most important functions of gaze is grounding, which improves communication, particularly in the execution of complex or spatial tasks [19]. Synchronized gaze can have additional positive effects on task performance and can also reduce overlap in conversational turn-taking [48]. Communicators also use head movements to direct attention and pass the floor in conversations [33]. Head movements also include nodding behavior, which communicators can use to signal that they are engaged in the conversation [27]. Nods can also take the place of verbal feedback, similarly indicating agreement with a speaker [46].

Although the region of the head is essential in conveying many of the important social cues, hands and arms also produce gestures that augment communication. Gestures can be used to replace speech turns [17] or achieve quicker grounding, reducing the number of speech overlaps [30]. Prior work shows that providing visual access to the gestures of remote collaborators in spatial tasks improves task outcomes as compared to audio-only communication by enabling participants to more precisely communicate spatial goals and thus make better decisions [14]. Past research also includes a number of systems that have been developed to augment visual channels to better capture and communicate the various gestures that occur in collaboration [7, 35].

Audio Channel

The use of the audio channel in the design of CSCW systems enables collaborators to use language in order to compensate for social cues that cannot be perceived due to design or technical limitations. Prior work that compared the use of audio-only and audio and video communication in spatial tasks has shown that the absence of a video feed cause participants to query their partner more for status updates [34], while the addition of a visual channel lead to the modification of dialogue structure to incorporate visual feedback [17]. Even in tasks that do not require spatial reasoning, the presence of video results in more fluent negotiations, enabling participants to revisit information more due to the reduced overhead of conversational turn-taking. The improvements in dialogue flow result in more mutually beneficial negotiations [10].

While these findings highlight the importance of social cues in specific collaborative activities and offer some guidelines for design, less is known about how the broader range of social cues contribute to these activities and how these relationships might generalize. Previous work provides only a limited understanding of this design space due to their focus on the role of social cues in the context of specific collaborative activities that are supported by specific technologies, limiting our ability to make comparisons across the findings of different studies. Our work seeks to investigate the knowledge gap in understanding the relationships between social cues and the outcomes of collaboration activities by building predictive models across a wider range of social behaviors and collaborative activities. A better understanding of these relationships will inform future theoretical explorations and designs of collaboration technologies.

METHOD

In this work, we collected data from dyads engaged in face-to-face collaboration and built regression-based models of the relationships between their social cues and the outcomes of their collaboration to inform future research and design in CSCW. To better understand how these relationships changed across different types of collaborative tasks, we studied three different tasks. For each task, we considered an objective measure of the effectiveness of the collaboration and a measure of the perceived success of the collaboration by the participants. At the conclusion of the study, we also collected a set of measures for social outcomes, such as the participants' perceptions of how much rapport was formed between themselves and their partner. The model for each outcome offers insight into which cues are significant predictors of the outcome and therefore should be supported by a CSCW system designed to improve task outcomes.

This section discusses the selection of the collaborative activities that are considered in this work, provides information on the specific instantiations of these activities for data collection, and describes the data corpus, measures, and the statistical modeling approach.

Approach

Our choice of studying face-to-face communication instead of remote interactions mediated by a CSCW system was motivated by our desire to explore the dynamics of the wider range of social cues across multiple collaborative contexts. The design of CSCW systems is informed either by studies of face-to-face communication or studies of communication using a specific collaboration technology. However, both types of studies are typically situated in a specific collaborative context, such as instruction, cooperation, or negotiation, and focused on specific communicative cues, such as gaze or gestures, making it difficult to identify how a wider range of social cues jointly affect collaboration outcomes and compare findings across contexts. Additionally, studies that use a specific collaboration technology to provide further design recommendations necessarily limits the number of social cues available to the parties in the interaction. Prior work has shown that users adapt their use of communicative cues to the channels supported by the technology used [20, 42]. Thus, it is difficult to discern what social cues the users would have naturally employed, what adaptations they would have made when these cues are not supported by the specific system used, and how future designs might support or deter such adaptations.

In contrast, studying face-to-face interactions provides the opportunity to gain a holistic understanding of how social cues shape collaboration without restricting the cues available for study. Furthermore, studying interactions in multiple contexts allows us to understand how these relationships vary across different forms of collaboration. From these studies, we can draw conclusions about which social cues are most important, the relative contributions of cues to collaboration outcomes, the tradeoffs between objective and subjective outcomes, and how participant behavior might change across tasks. These conclusions can inform the design of future CSCW systems as to which channels should be prioritized and enable predictions about how the elimination of particular channels might affect task and interaction outcomes.

Collaborative Tasks

Collaborative work encompasses a wide range of tasks. For instance, employees of a company might receive training and instruction on a regular basis, members of work teams might frequently cooperate on creative or physical tasks, and company representatives might engage in negotiations with clients or partners. As these tasks become increasingly distributed, it is increasingly important that the technologies facilitating such tasks are as effective as possible. In this study, we consider three common collaborative tasks: *instruction*, *cooperation*, and *negotiation* [3, 52]. The paragraphs below provide a brief review of prior work in CSCW that has explored collaboration in these tasks.

Instruction

Previous work has explored remote instruction in training and instruction contexts and has studied how specific cues and

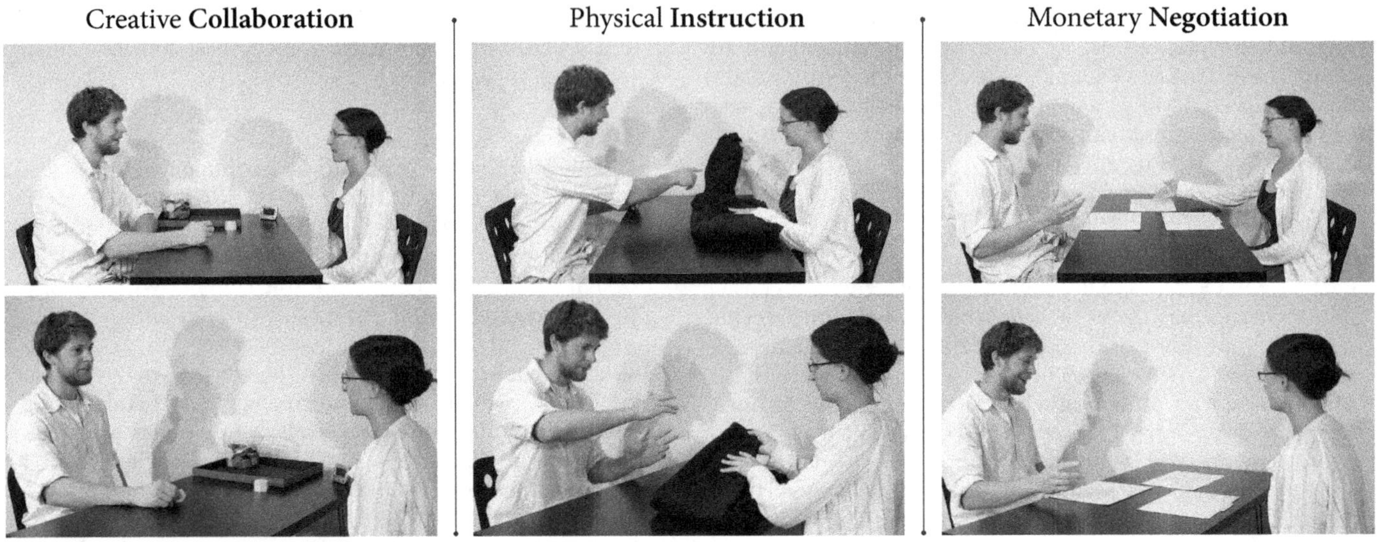

Figure 2. The three collaborative tasks used in our study: brainstorming a packing list in the creative *cooperation* task; learning to fold a pair of pants in the physical *instruction* task; and negotiating prices for two travel packages in the monetary *negotiation* task.

affordances affect instruction [16, 18, 21]. For instance, studies of video communication for surgical training in a hospital setting highlighted the importance of and increased need for a shared visual space among participants [32].

Cooperation
Cooperation has been explored in formal work contexts such as managing the London Underground [23] and air traffic control [5], as well as in informal cooperations such as brainstorming [36] and play dates [28]. These CSCW systems tend to display the person via video, the context via video, or both. Previous work has developed guidelines to help future development of cooperative systems [50]. This work emphasizes the need to carefully select a medium for communication based on the goals of the system. Developing a stronger understanding of the importance of significant behavioral cues in cooperative systems will better inform future developers as they choose a medium on which to focus for a particular application.

Negotiation
Negotiation has been well-studied in CSCW research, ranging from implicit negotiations that arise in face-to-face interactions [1] to explicit negotiation tasks [4]. Preliminary research into interaction patterns undertaken during negotiations that use collaboration systems shows that these patterns change when using text, audio, or video to perform the negotiation. For example, participants negotiating over video trade smaller pieces of information during a turn than those negotiating over text or audio [10]. A preliminary model of negotiation addresses the high-level structure of how computer-mediated negotiation differs from face-to-face negotiation [37].

Participants and Data Corpus
A total of 48 participants from a university campus participated in this study. The participants studied a diverse range of fields and were aged between 19 and 60 (M = 23.02, SD = 6.70). All participants were native English speakers. Participants were assigned into dyads of two participants who were unfamiliar with one another to jointly perform the experimental tasks. We assigned dyads, conversational roles, and task orderings so that each was fully stratified by gender, creating an equal number of female-female, male-male, and female-male dyads.

The experimental design stratified participants by gender to reflect earlier findings on gender effects in collaborative work and other social situations. For example, gender has been shown to affect participant behaviors in face-to-face negotiation [47], self-esteem [31], and approach to leadership [12].

In our experimental setup, the members of the dyads sat across from each other at a table, as illustrated in Figure 2. The data collection equipment included three high-definition cameras at 1080p resolution and 30p frame rate. Two of the cameras were positioned across from each participant, capturing their upper torsos as visible from across the table. The third camera captured the speech and nonverbal behaviors of both participants from the side using a wide-angle lens. The final data corpus consisted of 72 recorded tasks, with three tasks for each dyad and three angles for each task. These 72 tasks amounted to 4 hours and 17 minutes of audio and video data, and across tasks participants interacted for an average of 14 minutes and 11 seconds. The average video length for the instruction, cooperation, and negotiation tasks were 3 minutes and 4 seconds, 5 minutes, and 6 minutes and 7 seconds, respectively.

Procedure
Following informed consent and an overview of experimental procedures, both participants were seated across from one another at a table. Since the participants were strangers, an acclimation task was performed before starting the experimental tasks. During the acclimation task, participants were given three minutes to discuss their school or work life with one another. Participants then performed in each of the three experimental tasks—instruction, cooperation, and negotiation—in a stratified order. Following each experimental task, participants were asked to complete a questionnaire regarding their perceptions of themselves, the other participant, and their joint collaboration in completing the task. Upon completion of

all three tasks, participants completed a longer questionnaire that evaluated group characteristics and dynamics, as well as demographic information. The experimenter then debriefed the participants. All three tasks and questionnaires, as well as the post-experiment questionnaire, took between 45 minutes to an hour to complete. This variation arose from individual differences in completion times for tasks, particularly in the negotiation task. Participants were paid $10 for their time.

Experimental Task

We created the three collaborative activities considered in this study as part of a higher-level collaboration concerned with planning a trip abroad. The following sections describe the design of each of these experimental tasks.

Instruction

In the *instruction* task, one participant taught their partner how to fold a pair of pants, reflecting the theme of preparing for a trip abroad. One participant took on the role of the *instructor*, while the second participant took on the role of the *student*. To simulate the knowledge disparity that is often found in instructional tasks, the instructor learned how to fold the pants using a non-traditional set of steps prior to teaching it. To reflect the context disparity found in remote collaboration, the instructor was not allowed to touch the pants while teaching the student.

To introduce the folding technique to the instructor, the student was asked to leave the room while the instructor watched a video that explained the pant-folding procedure. The instructor was allowed to fold the pants along with the video and was given as much time as necessary to review the video. When the instructor felt that they had memorized the necessary steps to folding the pants, the student was brought back into the room. The instructor then taught the student how to recreate the steps necessary to reproduce the folds shown in the video.

Cooperation

In the *cooperation* task, participants worked together to identify items to pack for their trip abroad through brainstorming, following the structure of a common "creativity task" to build a cooperative atmosphere by creating a temporary problem-solving group [22]. The development of this task built on the definition of cooperation as "a style for direct interaction between at least two co-equal parties voluntarily engaged in shared decision-making as they work toward a common goal" [6]. During the cooperation task, participants were on equal ground as they worked to complete their packing list and built off of one another's ideas and experiences.

For this task, participants were told that the items must be able to fit in luggage that they can take on a plane. They were instructed not to count quantities (e.g., "three pairs of pants" would be reduced to "pants") to encourage them to rely on their creativity when identifying items. Participants were asked to think of as many items as possible in five minutes. One participant was given a bucket of counter chips. Each time the participants agreed upon a new item to pack, the assigned participant was instructed to move one of the counter chips into a second bucket, indicating that they wished to add this item to their packing list.

Negotiation

Participants in the *negotiation* task were given opposing roles in a business transaction. We strove to create a task that encouraged participants to follow a traditional argumentation-based negotiation model in which participants' goals conflict and cooperation cannot be assumed, forcing participants to use a series of arguments to persuade their partner to pursue some action [45]. Additionally, similar to many negotiation tasks, participants were not completely aware of their partner's goal. We chose money as the basis for our negotiation task so that we could quantify an objective measure of task success often not available in negotiation tasks. Participants were offered the chance at a small prize (a candy bar) in addition to their monetary compensation to help offset a lack of motivation to negotiate in the laboratory.

Participants were assigned to a role as either a *travel agent* or a *traveler*. The experimenter explained that each participant would be working within their respective role to negotiate prices for two different travel packages. Each participant was given a folder containing their price limits for each travel package. For the travel agent, this price was the *lowest* price the travel agent was willing to sell the travel package for. For the traveler, this price was the *highest* price the traveler was willing to pay for the travel package. The prices were chosen such that the travel agent's limit was substantially lower than the traveler's limit. The goal for the travel agent was to maximize how much they could convince the traveler to spend on the package over the travel agent's limit, while the goal for the traveler was to maximize how much they could save on the package by convincing the travel agent to sell the package for less than the traveler's limit.

Participants were given their instructions individually by the experimenter while their partner was outside of the room, and they were told not to share the information in their folder with the other participant. To further motivate an authentic negotiation, each participant was told that if they were able to minimize the amount of money they lost beneath a certain threshold, at the end of the experiment they would be given a small prize in addition to their monetary compensation. The "winning" participant received a candy bar at the end of the experiment. Participants would barter on one package at a time and were required to come to an agreement on both packages. When the participants agreed on a price, the travel agent would write the price on a sticky note and affix it to the back of that travel package.

Measurements

Our dependent variables reflected both objective and subjective outcomes. For each task, one objective measure described the effectiveness of the two participants at achieving the task goal. Participant responses to questionnaires on seven-point rating scales measured perceived task effectiveness for the participant, their partner, and their ability to work as a team (cooperation: 19 items, Cronbach's α = .837; instruction: 9 items, Cronbach's α = .793; negotiation: 16 items, Cronbach's α = .855). Additionally, participants answered a larger set of questions at the conclusion of all three tasks. These questions measured several group outcomes including rapport (24 items, Cronbach's α = .920), teamwork (7 items, Cronbach's α = .811), collaborativeness (4 items, Cronbach's α = .701), empathic concern (7 items, Cronbach's α = 764), perspective-taking (7 items, Cronbach's α = .820), interpersonal solidarity (14 items, Cronbach's α = .774), and homophily (9 items, Cronbach's α = .812).

Our objective measures varied based on task. In the instruction task, we measured the number of times the instructor offered a correction to the student ("No, unfold that part. You need to angle it more to the right when you fold it."). The objective measure for the cooperation task was the total number of unique items that were generated by participants in brainstorming. In the negotiation task, we measured the total discrepancy between the actual selling price and the median of the high point (how much the traveler was allowed to spend on a package) and the low point (the lowest amount for which the travel agent was allowed to sell a package).

In order to compare the relative importance of behaviors across tasks, we transformed our data so that a positive trend in the outcome measure indicated a more effective performance of the task. For example, in the cooperation task, the higher the objective measure (i.e., number of items brainstormed) was, the better the participants did at completing the task. The opposite is true for the instruction and negotiation tasks, however. The lower the number of corrections in the negotiation task and the lower the price discrepancy in the instruction task, the better participants did at completing the task, according to the transformed data. As we did with the measures for the cooperative task, we transformed our objective measures for the instruction and negotiation tasks. The negotiation measure was transformed so that the outcome that was most beneficial to both participants had the highest number, and the outcome which had the least beneficial outcome was given the lowest transformed number. Likewise, the measure for the instruction task was transformed so that the highest number reflected the fewest number of corrections, while a lower number reflected more corrections. Under the transformations of objective measures across tasks, the number associated with the most beneficial outcome became the highest number, and the number associated with the least beneficial outcome became the lowest number. For example, in a data set where $p_0 = 5$, $p_1 = 7$, and $p_2 = 11$, the transformation would result in $p_0 = 11$, $p_1 = 9$, and $p_2 = 5$.

Based on findings from prior work and a preliminary analysis of our data set, we identified 10 types of behavioral cues to serve as dependent variables requiring further analysis: gazing at one's partner, gazing at the shared context, iconic gestures, metaphoric gestures, deictic gestures, beat gestures, head nods, smiling, verbal filler, and laughter. All variables were coded in a binary manner—0 for *not occurring* and 1 for *occurring* events—every 33.3 milliseconds. The data was coded by two coders such that there was a 10% overlap with which to evaluate inter-coder reliability. One coder was responsible for creating a detailed description of each code, such as examples of the code, counter-examples of the code, and minimum requirements for the code (e.g., a participant must gaze away for at least 100 ms to count as a shift in gaze). This coder then trained the second coder with the given description, providing examples. The inter-rater reliability showed substantial agreement for all attributes; participant gazing at their partner (84% agreement, Cohen's κ = .69), participant gazing at the shared context (82% agreement, Cohen's κ = .65), head nods (89% agreement, Cohen's κ = .74), smiles (83% agreement, Cohen's κ = .67), filler speech (76% agreement, Cohen's κ = .65), laughter (75% agreement, Cohen's κ = .63), iconic gestures (82% agreement, Cohen's κ = .66), metaphoric gestures (78% agreement, Cohen's κ = .64), deictic gestures (78% agreement, Cohen's κ = .63), and beat gestures (76% agreement, Cohen's κ = .62).

Our resulting data set consisted of 15 data tables. Each row in a data table took the following form:

$$< \boldsymbol{y}\boldsymbol{x}_1\boldsymbol{x}_2 \ldots \boldsymbol{x}_n >$$

where $\boldsymbol{y}$ represents the *response* variable, and $\boldsymbol{x}_i$ represents a single *predictor* variable—one (of possibly many) variables that can be used to predict $\boldsymbol{y}$. We discuss the data tables for each dependent variable below.

Objective Measures

For each objective measure, the analysis considered the predictors x_i as the aggregate occurrences of each behavior for each *dyad* during that task. We chose to initially consider the individual roles of a dyad separately, compiling one data table for each participant, resulting in two data tables for each task, each data table with 24 tuples of 10 values each. After constructing models for each role, we then considered the significant predictors of each role in a single model to measure the relative importance of *both* participants' cues on the overall outcome of the task. This combined model considered 24 tuples for each task, with the number of variables varying with the task. In this model, it is possible for each value to appear twice, once for each participant in the dyad. Our final data corpus contained three data tables for objective measures, with one data table for each task.

Task Perception Measures

For the task perception measures, the analysis considered the predictors as the aggregate occurrences of each behavior for each *participant* during that task. We chose to consider the participants of a dyad individually since each participant had their own perception of the task outcome. This resulted in tuples which contained 10 values; one for each of the 10 behaviors of a single participant.

The dependent variable for the task perception measures was dependent on the task under analysis. For the cooperative task, participants had equal roles since both had an equal responsibility to brainstorm ideas. Thus, we chose to consider all participants in a single data table, resulting in 48 tuples for the cooperative task.

However, both the instruction and negotiation tasks split participants into different roles: instructor and student for the instruction task, and travel agent and traveler for the negotiation task. Because participants in one role may have had different perceptions of task outcome than participants in the other role, we chose to consider roles in both the instruction and negotiation task separately. This resulted in four data tables (two for instruction and two for negotiation), each of which had 24 tuples.

Subjective Measures

For the subjective measures, the analysis considered the predictors as the aggregate occurrences of each behavior for each *participant* across all three tasks. We chose to consider the participants of the dyad individually, as each participant had their own perception of task success. This consideration resulted in tuples that contained 10 values, one for each of the 10 behaviors of a single participant. The outcome variable for the subjective measures was the average of the scale items for that particular participant.

The tuples for all three of the outcomes discussed above were normalized across each tuple by dividing the values of the tuple by the length of the video for that task or, in the case of the final subjective measures, the aggregate time of all three tasks. Finally, each variable (i.e., each column) was normalized to vary between 0 (least frequent) to 1 (most frequent).

Analysis

Our analysis took a two-step approach. First, we analyzed our data using *stepwise multiple linear regression* to model the relationships among the independent and dependent variables. We then discovered significant themes of findings by combining an examination of these models and observations of the video data. This approach has been utilized in past HCI research to better understand how a range of behaviors shape task outcomes [2, 24].

Each analysis in Stepwise Multiple Linear Regression followed the formulation below:

$$y = (\beta_0 + \beta_1 x_1 + \beta_2 x_2 + \ldots + \beta_n x_n) + e$$

Where β_0 is a constant that represents the y-intercept, whereas $\beta_1 \ldots \beta_n$ are coefficients for each of the n predictors. The values of each predictor for a given situation are represented by $x_1 \ldots x_n$. The error for the model is represented by e.

In its simplest form, Linear Regression models the relationship between one predictor variable x and one outcome variable y with some error e. Given a set of x, y data points, a line is fitted to the data such that the sum of squared residuals is minimized. The resulting model provides a β value (measured in standard deviations) for x, which describes the change in y for a one unit change in x. A positive β indicates that the corresponding predictor has a similar trend with the outcome variable (e.g., an increase in the occurrence of the predictor x increases the outcome variable y), whereas a negative β indicates that the corresponding predictor has an inverse relationship with the outcome variable. The larger $|\beta|$ is, the more important x is in predicting y.

To expand regression modeling to more than one predictor variable requires Multiple Linear Regression. While there are numerous approaches to constructing Multiple Linear Regression models, we discuss our particular approach below, called Forward Stepwise Multiple Linear Regression. Here, the final model is constructed by gradually including predictors in the model according to their contribution to the model [13]. For the purposes of our study, at each step we included any predictor with a p-value below .250. The final model is then comprised of predictors which are statistically significant ($p < .100$). Because the β coefficients are measure in standard deviations, each β_k provides the relative contribution of each independent variable x_k in predicting the dependent variable y.

With the final models, we returned to the original video data collected from the study to offer explanations for the results in our models. Videos were reviewed in conjunction with the models to discover themes in the data. These themes focused on a number of different results, ranging from the importance of one cue across tasks, to the importance of multiple cues within a single task to produce a particular effect.

RESULTS

Our analysis resulted in a total of 13 models that characterized the relationship between observed cues and task outcomes. Figure 3 details the models and statistical tests of the significance of these relationships. Drawing on the quantitative findings from these models and qualitative observations from the video data, we constructed four themes under which these findings fell. Below, we provide examples from the videos and results from our models and, where appropriate, discuss the findings in the context of prior work for each theme.

Theme 1: Rapport in Negotiation

Prior work suggests that rapport can be an important component in mutually beneficial negotiation outcomes [11, 38]. Our data from the negotiation task showed that dyads that successfully negotiated a fair price also displayed behaviors that are associated with rapport. For example, in the exchange below, the traveler highlights his or her monetary situation as a student in an attempt to establish more rapport and increase the travel agent's empathy for him or her. When the travel agent rejects that attempt, the traveler laughs, acknowledging that the negotiation strategy would likely prove futile. Figure 4, Left illustrates both the traveler and the travel agent laughing during negotiation.

> **Traveler:** You know, as a student, I don't have much money. Can you give me a lower price?
> **Travel Agent:** Unfortunately, I really can't go any lower than that, with cutbacks and everything...
> **Traveler:** [laughter from traveler] OK, OK. It was worth trying.

Exhibited behaviors that are associated with an increase in rapport included a greater use of gazing toward the partner for both the traveler, $\beta = .116$, $t(23) = 2.66$, $p = .057$, and the travel agent, $\beta = .473$, $t(23) = 7.83$, $p = .016$, and—in the case of the traveler—laughing, $\beta = .323$, $t(23) = 5.73$, $p = .039$, as shown in Model 3 in Figure 3. The use of cues associated with rapport, particularly gazing toward the partner, was also a significant predictor of empathy between the participants, as shown in Model 8, $\beta = .761$, $t(47) = 4.10$, $p = .036$.

These behaviors help the participants in the negotiation to develop a relationship with each other, which results in more

#	Outcome (y)	Function ($\beta_0 + \beta_1 x_1 + \ldots + \beta_n x_n + \varepsilon$)	R_A^2	Significance
Objective Collaborative Task Outcomes				
1	Cooperation *# creative solutions*	$-.472 + .567\boldsymbol{E}_p^{\,l} - .322\boldsymbol{E}_t^{\,l} + .842\boldsymbol{G}_d^{\,l} - .307\boldsymbol{G}_b^{\,l} + .578\boldsymbol{H}_n^{\,l} + .575\boldsymbol{S}_f^{\,l} + .552\boldsymbol{G}_b^{\,r} + .441\boldsymbol{H}_n^{\,r} - .231\boldsymbol{S}_f^{\,r} + .758\boldsymbol{S}_l^{\,r} + .036$	.737	E_p^l $p < .001^{***}$ E_t^l $p = .005^{**}$ G_d^l $p = .017^{*}$ G_b^l $p < .001^{***}$ H_n^l $p = .004^{**}$ S_f^l $p = .001^{**}$ G_b^r $p = .012^{*}$ H_n^r $p = .013^{*}$ S_f^r $p = .011^{*}$ S_l^r $p = .091^{\dagger}$
2	Instruction *# corrections*	$.019 + .268\boldsymbol{G}_d^{\,s} + .210\boldsymbol{H}_n^{\,s} - .427\boldsymbol{S}_l^{\,s} + .201\boldsymbol{E}_p^{\,i} + .079\boldsymbol{G}_i^{\,i} + .314\boldsymbol{G}_d^{\,i} + .326\boldsymbol{H}_n^{\,i} + .048$	.826	G_d^s $p = .061^{\dagger}$ H_n^s $p = .015^{*}$ S_l^s $p = .019^{*}$ E_p^i $p = .017^{*}$ G_i^i $p = .047^{*}$ G_d^i $p = .014^{*}$ H_n^i $p = .023^{*}$
3	Negotiation *Monetary agreement*	$.109 + .473\boldsymbol{E}_p^{\,a} - .465\boldsymbol{G}_d^{\,a} + .323\boldsymbol{S}_l^{\,a} + .116\boldsymbol{E}_p^{\,t} - .247\boldsymbol{G}_d^{\,t} + .493\boldsymbol{H}_s^{\,t} + .512$	.364	E_p^a $p = .057^{\dagger}$ G_d^a $p = .026^{*}$ H_l^a $p = .005^{**}$ E_p^t $p = .016^{*}$ G_d^t $p = .045^{*}$ H_s^t $p = .039^{*}$
Perceived Collaborative Task Outcomes				
4	Cooperation *Perceived success*	$.700 - .611\boldsymbol{G}_i^{\,l} + .708$	.315	G_i $p = .016^{*}$
5	Instruction *Perceived success*	Instructor — *No significant model* Student — *No significant model*	N/A N/A	N/A N/A
6	Negotiation *Perceived success*	Travel Agent — *No significant model* $.567 - .392\boldsymbol{G}_i^{\,t} - .532\boldsymbol{H}_n^{\,t} - .647\boldsymbol{S}_l^{\,t} + .901$	N/A .431	N/A G_i^t $p = .038^{*}$ H_n^t $p = .041^{*}$ S_l^t $p = .008^{**}$
Social Outcomes				
7	Collaborativeness	*No significant model*	N/A	N/A
8	Empathy	$.638 + .761\boldsymbol{E}_p - .683\boldsymbol{E}_t + .844$	.064	E_p $p = .036^{*}$ E_t $p = .030^{*}$
9	Homophily	$.411 - .402\boldsymbol{G}_d + .740$	.129	G_d $p = .028^{*}$
10	Interpersonal Solidarity	*No significant model*	N/A	N/A
11	Perspective-taking	*No significant model*	N/A	N/A
12	Rapport	$.601 - .341\boldsymbol{E}_p - .407\boldsymbol{H}_n + .281\boldsymbol{S}_f + .634$	.322	E_p $p = .025^{*}$ H_n $p = .010^{*}$ S_f $p = .048^{*}$
13	Teamwork	$.679 - .266\boldsymbol{E}_t + .318\boldsymbol{G}_i - .446\boldsymbol{H}_n + .604$	.332	E_t $p = .036^{*}$ G_i $p = .018^{*}$ H_n $p = .003^{**}$

Figure 3. Models for the objective collaborative outcomes of each task, the perceived collaborative outcomes of each task, and the social outcomes overall. The variables represented are gazing toward the participant (E_p), gazing toward the shared context (E_t), iconic gesture (G_i), metaphoric gesture (G_m), beat gesture (G_b), deictic gesture (G_d), head nodding (H_n), smiling (H_s), verbal filler (S_f), and laughter (S_l). Superscripts l and r, i and s, and a and t denote the left and right participants in the collaboration scenario, instructor and student in the instruction scenario, and travel agent and traveler in the negotiation scenario, respectively.

empathy between the participants toward each other's position and working towards a more mutually beneficial agreement.

Theme 2: Establishing Procedural Grounding Using Gaze

Previous research has highlighted the importance of gaze in monitoring attention and understanding toward achieving procedural grounding in collaboration [15, 41]. The excerpt below illustrates how collaborators might use gaze to assess understanding, where the instructor monitors the student after issuing an instruction:

> **Instructor:** Put it to your left at a 90 degree angle. [watches student's face]
> **Student:** [performs the instruction correctly]

Our models showed visual monitoring of a partner to predict task success across tasks. The roles that demanded gazing toward one's partner included the instructor, $\beta = .201$, $t(23) = 7.25$, $p = .017$, in the instruction task (see Model 2), the traveler, $\beta = .116$, $t(23) = 2.66$, $p = .057$, and the travel agent, $\beta = .473$, $t(23) = 7.83$, $p = .016$ in the negotiation task (see Model 3), and the left participant in the cooperation task (see Model 1), $\beta = .567$, $t(23) = 11.82$, $p < .001$. Findings from the instruction task are contrary to prior work, which found little importance of monitoring in instruction [16]. On the other hand, gaze was shown to be more important for both participants in the negotiation task, which is consistent with prior work that has shown the addition of video to provide important benefits in negotiation and conflict resolution [10].

In the instruction task, monitoring seemed to play a particularly important role; instructors monitoring the actions and behaviors of their students when giving instructions and students offering feedback on their understanding of the instruction were both strong predictors of success in task outcomes as shown in Model 2. Predictors of task success included students who offered nonverbal feedback such as head nods $\beta = .210$, $t(23) = 8.12$, $p = .015$. While laughter can serve as a form of feedback, our models showed that laughter by students had a significant negative effect on the overall outcome of the task, $\beta = -.427$, $t(23) = -6.90$, $p = .019$, which might indicate students that are not taking the task seriously or not attending to the instructor's commands.

In tasks such as instruction, the introduction of a shared visual context requires participants to split their attention between their partner and the shared context. Visual monitoring enables participants to maintain the necessary level of awareness of

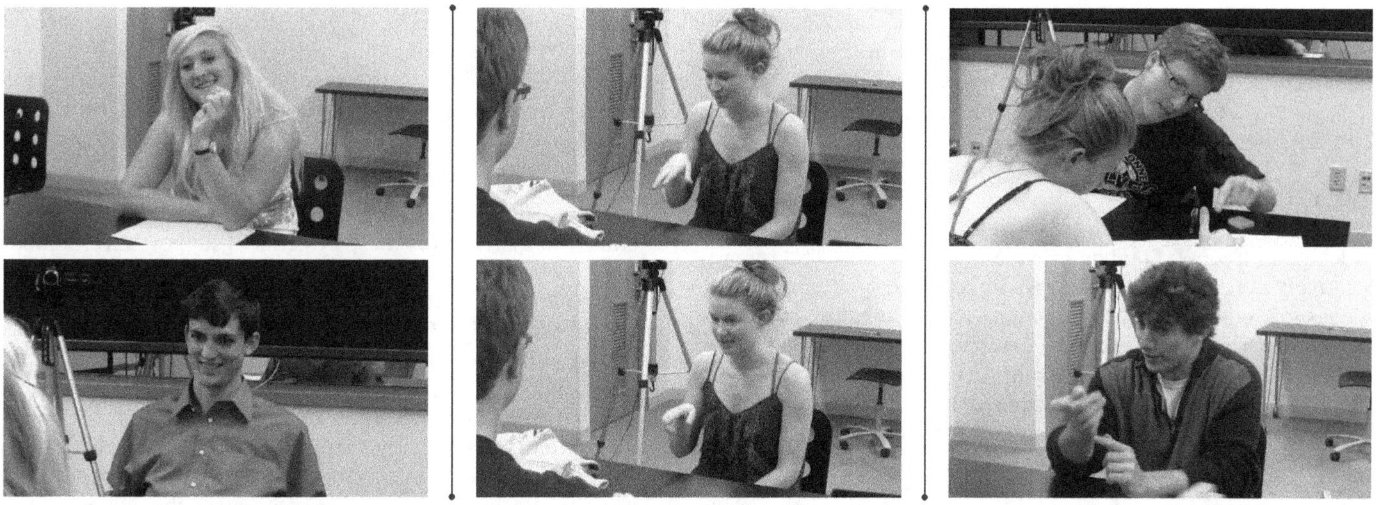

Figure 4. *Left*: An example of the agent rejecting a compromise proposed by the traveler. The traveler then laughs about the attempt, building rapport with the agent despite the failed negotiation. *Middle*: An example use of gaze for establishing procedural common ground. The instructor first uses her gaze combined with a deictic gesture aimed at the workspace to indicate the next step and then gazes at the student to monitor the student's face for indications of understanding. *Right*: Examples of the differential use of deictic gestures in the cooperative and negotiation tasks. Pointing was found to be a positive predictor of task success during cooperation, but to negatively predict task success in negotiation.

the shared context and their partner. Figure 4, Middle illustrates the instructor shifting her gaze to direct attention toward and/or monitor the task space and then to monitor her student's understanding while providing instruction. This process is further facilitated by nonverbal feedback from partners whose understanding and actions are being monitored.

Theme 3: Deictic Gestures in Shared Contexts

Speakers frequently use deictic gestures either in place of or in conjunction with verbal utterances [17] in order to facilitate their communication of spatial goals in tasks that involve a shared visual context [14]. The excerpt below from the instruction task illustrates the instructor using a deictic gesture to provide the student with the spatial information necessary to complete the next step of the task:

> **Instructor:** Now bring that piece in your hand to here [points].

In both the instruction and cooperation tasks, increased use of deictic gestures resulted in better task performance. In the instruction task, deictic gestures were used to disambiguate locations and objects by both the instructor, $\beta = .314$, $t(23) = 8.47$, $p = .014$, and the student, $\beta = .268$, $t(23) = 3.01$, $p = .061$ as shown in Model 2. In the cooperative task, the participant who controlled the counting chips pointed to emphasize a particular concept (see Model 1), $\beta = .842$, $t(23) = 12.75$, $p < .001$, as their hands often held the counting chips and were therefore unable to perform other gestures. Deictic gestures were also frequently used in the negotiation task, for instance, to highlight components of the written package description. However, we found that an increased use of deictic gestures lowered task outcomes (see Model 3), regardless of whether the gesture was performed by the travel agent, $\beta = -.247$, $t(23) = -2.94$, $p = .057$, or traveler, $\beta = -.465$, $t(23) = -3.20$, $p = .045$.

Across all tasks in our study, we observed deictic gestures to be regularly used to replace or augment verbal utterances. Particularly in tasks that demanded communication of spatial information, deictic gestures played a key role in conveying complex information or instructions that may be difficult or impossible to verbally describe. Communicators might also use deictic gestures to save the energy that they would put into providing complex verbal descriptions or to provide sufficient redundancy in their language to prevent misunderstandings. In negotiation, however, gestures pointed toward partners might be perceived as a sign of an aggressive strategy for negotiation. Figure 4, Right illustrates deictic gestures directed toward the task space in the cooperation task and toward the partner in the negotiation task.

Theme 4: Nonverbal Feedback to Avoid Interruption

Throughout all three tasks, nonverbal feedback positively predicted task performance. Such feedback can be used to provide input without interrupting the speaker [27, 46]. The example below from the cooperation task illustrates this behavior:

> **Participant 1:** We could bring a passport, cash, ...
> **Participant 2:** [nods]
> **Participant 1:** ...traveler's checks.

Here, Participant 1 is listing off items to pack for the trip, and Participant 2—not wanting to interrupt—nods to indicate their agreement with the items that Participant 1 listed thus far.

Head nods were a common form of nonverbal feedback observed in both the instructor, $\beta = .326$, $t(23) = 6.02$, $p = .023$, and the student (see Model 2), $\beta = .210$, $t(23) = 2.32$, $p = .061$, as well as both participants in the cooperation task (see Model 1), $\beta = .578$, $t(23) = 8.97$, $p = .004$ and $\beta = .441$, $t(23) = 7.28$, $p = .013$. Additionally, laughter was a significant predictor of task success for the left participant in the cooperative task (see Model 1), $\beta = .758$, $t(23) = 2.56$, $p = .091$, and the traveler in the negotiation task (see Model 3), $\beta = .323$, $t(23) = 4.73$, $p = .039$.

We observed participants to use nonverbal feedback to express their understanding or agreement with their partner's utterances without causing disruption. These cues enabled participants to provide feedback while maintaining the fluidity of the interaction.

DISCUSSION

Our findings make three main contributions to research and design in CSCW: (1) they provide a set of models that quantitatively characterize the relative importance of a set of social cues in predicting specific outcomes for a number of collaboration scenarios; (2) they enable comparisons of these predictive relationships across collaboration outcomes and scenarios; and (3) they confirm and further detail prior findings from face-to-face and mediated communication. The paragraphs below discuss the research and design implications of each type of contribution. Additionally, we discuss some of the key limitations of our study.

Relative Importance of Social Cues

The models presented in the previous section inform the design of technologies to support particular collaboration scenarios. For example, in the instruction task, deictic gestures were weighted more heavily than gaze, suggesting that if designers must choose a single channel to display, such as choosing between displaying either a partner or the workspace, choosing the workspace would provide greater benefits to task outcomes, as suggested by findings reported in Theme 3. However, these weights might vary across different outcomes within the same task, which are tradeoffs designers must consider. For instance, although our data did not show student gaze to affect task outcomes in instruction, it showed gazing toward one's partner to have a positive impact on empathy and gazing toward the shared workspace to decrease empathy.

While technologies would ideally make all essential channels simultaneously available to the user, this goal can be difficult to achieve due to technical, cost, or design constraints, such as limited screen space or the challenges of arranging multiple sources of channels in a useable layout. Designers might alleviate these limitations by providing users with control over how video feeds are displayed, allowing overlaying of channels, such as the ClearBoard design that involved a shared workspace for sketching that overlaid the partner's video [25], or mechanisms for quickly switching between channels to view the channel that best supports the current needs of the communication.

Change of Relative Importance of Cues Across Scenarios

Our models also inform designers about how the role each type of social cue plays in collaboration changes across different forms of collaboration. While the tasks considered in this study were each carried out and analyzed independently of the other tasks, real-world use of collaboration technologies might involve more fluid transitions in tasks. For example, a sales manager might use a collaboration tool to create a sales plan with another manager at a satellite branch and then later use the same system to negotiate product pricing with a distributor. In the cooperation task, the combination of a large number of verbal, facial, and gesture cues are equally important, while the negotiation task relies heavily on deictic gestures and gaze (see Theme 1). While a face-only video feed combined with a view of the shared visual context may be sufficient to support the negotiation task, a successful cooperative task might require a broader view of each participant that includes their hands and arms to support the communication of gestures.

The potential use of CSCW systems across different forms of collaboration requires these systems to support several modalities of communication, such as a view of the partner and their workspace and audio of the primary speech channel and of verbal feedback. All channels may not be necessary at all times, either because the social cues communicated in that channel do not affect task outcomes or because a channel is not currently available or useful. Future systems should consider dynamically prioritizing their support for channels based on the ongoing task. This goal might be achieved by providing users with a set of task-based profiles, such as "negotiation" or "instruction," to enable them to easily adapt their use of channels to the demands of the specific task at hand. Future systems might also detect the type of task users are engaged with in order to automatically adapt their support for different channels to specific task requirements.

Confirmation of Prior Results

Our work confirms a number of findings from previous research, demonstrating that our tasks are representative of collaboration scenarios explored in prior work. We corroborate findings from both face-to-face and computer-mediated communication studies, suggesting that our work might have implications for future design of CSCW systems.

Gaze has often been identified as an important cue in communication. In face-to-face interaction, gaze can be used to disambiguate or reinforce references to objects in instruction tasks [40]. Similar results have been found in mediated communication, where gaze synchronization between partners results in an increase in task performance [48]. As seen in Theme 2, across all three tasks, gaze was repeatedly one of the most significant predictors of objective outcomes. Participants' gaze was also a significant predictor of outcomes such as increased empathy, leading to an improvement in communication effectiveness in cooperative tasks. However, our findings contradict work that found that instructors do not use gaze towards their partner as an integral part of their communication during teaching tasks [16]. We found deictic gestures to be important predictors of objective outcomes when a shared workspace was in use, confirming prior work concerning the role of deictic gestures in augmenting communication, leading to a decrease in task time and an increase in task comprehension in instructional tasks [18]. Additionally, feedback behaviors such as nodding and verbal backchannels were found to be significant predictors of task outcomes in the instruction and cooperation tasks, as shown in Theme 4. This result is consistent with prior work concerning the role of backchannels in communicating acknowledgement and understanding of a partner's utterances [17], as well as work indicating that backchannels can improve task performance and communicate task engagement [27].

Limitations

Our investigation offers many insights into the role of social cues in collaboration, although the study and the research approach presented here have a number of limitations. First, our regression-based approach used aggregate counts of social cues to characterize their use in the entire duration of the task, which does not offer insight into the temporal characteristics of these behaviors and their implications for collaboration. Therefore, we are able to draw only high-level conclusions about the importance of each of these behaviors.

Second, while we expect our findings to inform the design of CSCW systems, we also anticipate limitations in how much findings from face-to-face interactions can predict outcomes of mediated interactions, as previous work has shown that communicators often adapt their behaviors to the limitations and opportunities introduced by remote collaboration technologies in order to achieve effective communication [20, 42].

Finally, as mentioned previously, additional factors such as the dialogue content or the environment in which the collaboration is carried out may serve as additional predictors of the objective and subjective outcomes for the tasks considered in this study. Our work is not an exhaustive exploration of additional factors, as it focuses only on visible or audible behaviors in a distraction-free laboratory environment. Future work should include a more nuanced exploration of factors such as discourse markers and thematic shifts in dialogue in noisy environments, which may offer a richer understanding of how social cues, features of dialogue, and environmental factors work together to shape collaboration.

CONCLUSION

With the increasing use of technologies that support remote collaboration, future technologies must be designed to facilitate a wide range of collaborative activities and support transitions between these activities. To help guide the development of such future systems, we conducted a study of face-to-face collaborations to better understand what communicative behaviors significantly predict task and social outcomes and thus might serve as important features that designers must seek to support in remote collaboration. Using a regression-based approach, we modeled the predictive relationships between facial, gestural, and vocal cues and collaborative outcomes in cooperation, instruction, and negotiation tasks. Our models provide a quantitative understanding of how each type of social cue contributes to shaping collaborative outcomes in each task and insights into how such relationships generalize across tasks. Our results also provide confirmation and illumination of prior findings from face-to-face and computer-mediated communication research. These findings will inform the design of future CSCW technologies by providing designers with an understanding of the role of social cues in collaboration.

ACKNOWLEDGMENTS

We would like to thank Brandi Hefty and Jilana Boston for their assistance in data collection and analysis, Catherine Steffel for her help with the editing of the paper, and our anonymous reviewers for their comments and suggestions. National Science Foundation award 1149970 supported this work.

REFERENCES

1. Birnholtz, J., Grossman, T., Mak, C., and Balakrishnan, R. An exploratory study of input configuration and group process in a negotiation task using a large display. In *Proceedings of the SIGCHI conference on Human factors in computing systems*, ACM (2007), 91–100.
2. Brendgen, M., Bowen, F., Rondeau, N., and Vitaro, F. Effects of friends. characteristics on children.s social cognitions. *Social Development 8*, 1 (1999), 41–51.
3. Carnevale, A. Workplace basics: The skills employers want. *Community, Technical, and Junior College Journal 59*, 4 (1989), 28–33.
4. Carnevale, P., and Isen, A. The influence of positive affect and visual access on the discovery of integrative solutions in bilateral negotiation. *Organizational behavior and human decision Processes 37*, 1 (1986), 1–13.
5. Conversy, S., Gaspard-Boulinc, H., Chatty, S., Valès, S., Dupré, C., and Ollagnon, C. Supporting air traffic control collaboration with a tabletop system. In *Proceedings of the ACM 2011 conference on Computer supported cooperative work*, ACM (2011), 425–434.
6. Cook, L., and Friend, M. Principles for the practice of collaboration in schools. *Preventing School Failure: Alternative Education for Children and Youth 35*, 4 (1991), 6–9.
7. Cornelius, C. J., Nguyen, M. A., Hayes, C. C., and Makena, R. Supporting virtual collaboration in spatial design tasks: Are surrogate or natural gestures more effective? *Human-Machine Systems, IEEE Transactions on 43*, 1 (2013), 92–101.
8. Culnan, M., and Markus, M. *Information technologies.* Sage Publications, Inc, 1987.
9. Daft, R., and Lengel, R. Information richness. a new approach to managerial behavior and organization design. Tech. rep., DTIC Document, 1983.
10. Dong, W., and Fu, W.-T. One piece at a time: why video-based communication is better for negotiation and conflict resolution. In *Proceedings of the ACM 2012 conference on Computer Supported Cooperative Work*, ACM (2012), 167–176.
11. Drolet, A. L., and Morris, M. W. Rapport in conflict resolution: Accounting for how face-to-face contact fosters mutual cooperation in mixed-motive conflicts. *Journal of Experimental Social Psychology 36*, 1 (2000), 26–50.
12. Eagly, A., and Johnson, B. Gender and leadership style: A meta-analysis. *Psychological bulletin 108*, 2 (1990), 233.
13. Efroymson, M. Multiple regression analysis. *Mathematical methods for digital computers 1* (1960), 191–203.
14. Farmer, S. M., and Hyatt, C. W. Effects of task language demands and task complexity on computer-mediated work groups. *Small Group Research 25*, 3 (1994), 331–366.
15. Fernald, A., Zangl, R., Portillo, A. L., and Marchman, V. A. Looking while listening: Using eye movements to monitor spoken language comprehension by infants and young children. *Language Acquisition and Language Disorders 44* (2008), 97.
16. Fussell, S., Setlock, L., and Parker, E. Where do helpers look?: gaze targets during collaborative physical tasks. In *CHI'03 extended abstracts on Human factors in computing systems*, ACM (2003), 768–769.
17. Fussell, S. R., Kraut, R. E., and Siegel, J. Coordination of communication: Effects of shared visual context on collaborative work. In *Proceedings of the 2000 ACM conference on Computer supported cooperative work*, ACM (2000), 21–30.
18. Fussell, S. R., Setlock, L. D., Yang, J., Ou, J., Mauer, E., and Kramer, A. D. Gestures over video streams to support remote collaboration on physical tasks. *Human-Computer Interaction 19*, 3 (2004), 273–309.

19. Gergle, D., and Clark, A. T. See what i'm saying?: using dyadic mobile eye tracking to study collaborative reference. In *Proceedings of the ACM 2011 conference on Computer supported cooperative work*, ACM (2011), 435–444.
20. Gergle, D., Kraut, R. E., and Fussell, S. R. Language efficiency and visual technology minimizing collaborative effort with visual information. *Journal of Language and Social Psychology 23*, 4 (2004), 491–517.
21. Gergle, D., Rosé, C., and Kraut, R. Modeling the impact of shared visual information on collaborative reference. In *Proceedings of the SIGCHI conference on Human factors in computing systems*, ACM (2007), 1543–1552.
22. Grawitch, M., Munz, D., Elliott, E., and Mathis, A. Promoting creativity in temporary problem-solving groups: The effects of positive mood and autonomy in problem definition on idea-generating performance. *Group dynamics: Theory, research, and practice 7*, 3 (2003), 200.
23. Heath, C., and Luff, P. Collaborative activity and technological design: Task coordination in london underground control rooms. In *Proceedings of the second conference on European Conference on Computer-Supported Cooperative Work*, Kluwer Academic Publishers (1991), 65–80.
24. Huang, C.-M., and Mutlu, B. Evaluating narrative gestures for humanlike robots. In *Robotics: Science and Systems 2013* (2013).
25. Ishii, H., and Kobayashi, M. Clearboard: a seamless medium for shared drawing and conversation with eye contact. In *Proceedings of the SIGCHI conference on Human factors in computing systems*, ACM (1992), 525–532.
26. Jonassen, D., and Kwon, H. Communication patterns in computer mediated versus face-to-face group problem solving. *Educational Technology Research and Development 49*, 1 (2001), 35–51.
27. Jung, M. F., Lee, J. J., DePalma, N., Adalgeirsson, S. O., Hinds, P. J., and Breazeal, C. Engaging robots: easing complex human-robot teamwork using backchanneling. In *Proceedings of the 2013 conference on Computer supported cooperative work*, ACM (2013), 1555–1566.
28. Junuzovic, S., Inkpen, K., Blank, T., and Gupta, A. Illumishare: sharing any surface. In *Proceedings of the 2012 ACM annual conference on Human Factors in Computing Systems*, ACM (2012), 1919–1928.
29. Karsenty, L. Cooperative work and shared visual context: An empirical study of comprehension problems in side-by-side and remote help dialogues. *Human-Computer Interaction 14*, 3 (1999), 283–315.
30. Kirk, D., Rodden, T., and Fraser, D. S. Turn it this way: grounding collaborative action with remote gestures. In *Proceedings of the SIGCHI conference on Human factors in computing systems*, ACM (2007), 1039–1048.
31. Kling, K., Hyde, J., Showers, C., and Buswell, B. Gender differences in self-esteem: a meta-analysis. *Psychological bulletin 125*, 4 (1999), 470.
32. Koschmann, T., LeBaron, C., Goodwin, C., and Feltovich, P. The mystery of the missing referent: Objects, procedures, and the problem of the instruction follower. In *Proceedings of the 2006 20th anniversary conference on Computer supported cooperative work*, ACM (2006), 373–382.
33. Kraut, R. E., Fussell, S. R., and Siegel, J. Visual information as a conversational resource in collaborative physical tasks. *Human-computer interaction 18*, 1 (2003), 13–49.
34. Kraut, R. E., Gergle, D., and Fussell, S. R. The use of visual information in shared visual spaces: Informing the development of virtual co-presence. In *Proceedings of the 2002 ACM conference on Computer supported cooperative work*, ACM (2002), 31–40.
35. Kuzuoka, H., Kosuge, T., and Tanaka, M. Gesturecam: a video communication system for sympathetic remote collaboration. In *Proceedings of the 1994 ACM conference on Computer supported cooperative work*, ACM (1994), 35–43.
36. Laufer, L., Halacsy, P., and Somlai-Fischer, A. Prezi meeting: collaboration in a zoomable canvas based environment. In *Proceedings of the 2011 annual conference extended abstracts on Human factors in computing systems*, ACM (2011), 749–752.
37. Munier, M., Baïna, K., and Benali, K. A negotiation model for cscw. In *Cooperative Information Systems*, Springer (2000), 224–235.
38. Nadler, J. Rapport in negotiation and conflict resolution. *Marq. L. Rev. 87* (2003), 875.
39. Ochsman, R. B., and Chapanis, A. The effects of 10 communication modes on the behavior of teams during co-operative problem-solving. *International Journal of Man-Machine Studies 6*, 5 (1974), 579–619.
40. Ou, J., Oh, L. M., Yang, J., and Fussell, S. R. Effects of task properties, partner actions, and message content on eye gaze patterns in a collaborative task. In *Proceedings of the SIGCHI conference on Human factors in computing systems*, ACM (2005), 231–240.
41. Peters, C., Pelachaud, C., Bevacqua, E., Mancini, M., and Poggi, I. A model of attention and interest using gaze behavior. In *Intelligent Virtual Agents*, Springer (2005), 229–240.
42. Schober, M. Spatial perspective-taking in conversation. *Cognition 47*, 1 (1993), 1–24.
43. Sebanz, N., Bekkering, H., and Knoblich, G. Joint action: bodies and minds moving together. *Trends in cognitive sciences 10*, 2 (2006), 70–76.
44. Short, J., Williams, E., and Christie, B. *The social psychology of telecommunications*. John Wiley and Sons Ltd, 1976.
45. Sierra, C., Jennings, N., Noriega, P., and Parsons, S. A framework for argumentation-based negotiation. *Intelligent Agents IV Agent Theories, Architectures, and Languages* (1998), 177–192.
46. Stivers, T. Stance, alignment, and affiliation during storytelling: When nodding is a token of affiliation. *Research on Language and Social Interaction 41*, 1 (2008), 31–57.
47. Stuhlmacher, A., and Walters, A. Gender differences in negotiation outcome: A meta-analysis. *Personnel Psychology 52*, 3 (1999), 653–677.
48. Vertegaal, R., and Ding, Y. Explaining effects of eye gaze on mediated group conversations:: amount or synchronization? In *Proceedings of the 2002 ACM conference on Computer supported cooperative work*, ACM (2002), 41–48.
49. Walther, J., and Parks, M. Cues filtered out, cues filtered in: Computer-mediated communication and relationships. *Handbook of interpersonal communication 3* (2002), 529–563.
50. Weiseth, P., Munkvold, B., Tvedte, B., and Larsen, S. The wheel of collaboration tools: a typology for analysis within a holistic framework. In *Proceedings of the 2006 20th anniversary conference on Computer supported cooperative work*, ACM (2006), 239–248.
51. Whittaker, S. Theories and methods in mediated communication. *The handbook of discourse processes* (2003), 243–286.
52. Zimmermann, P. Negotiation in the workplace. *Emergency nurse: the journal of the RCN Accident and Emergency Nursing Association 11*, 6 (2003), 12.

Planet Hunters and Seafloor Explorers: Legitimate Peripheral Participation Through Practice Proxies in Online Citizen Science

Gabriel Mugar,* Carsten Østerlund,* Katie DeVries Hassman,*
Kevin Crowston, Corey Brian Jackson***
*Syracuse University, School of Information Studies; 337 Hinds Hall, Syracuse, New York, 13244
{gmugar, costerlu, klhassma, cjacks04}@syr.edu
**National Science Foundation; 4201 Wilson Boulevard Room 1125, Arlington, Virginia, 22230
kcrowsto@nsf.gov

ABSTRACT
Making visible the process of user participation in online crowdsourced initiatives has been shown to help new users understand the norms of participation [2]. However, in many settings, participants lack full access to others' work. Merging the theory of legitimate peripheral participation [18] with Erickson and Kellogg's theory of social translucence [10, 11, 16] we introduce the concept of practice proxies: traces of user participation in online environments that act as resources to orient newcomers towards the norms of practice. Through a combination of virtual [14] and trace ethnography [12] we explore how new users in two online citizen science projects engage with these traces of practice as a way of compensating for a lack of access to the process of the work itself. Our findings suggest that newcomers seek out practice proxies in the social features of the projects that highlight contextualized and specific characteristics of primary work practice.

Author Keywords
Situated Learning; Social Translucence; Legitimate Peripheral Participation; Socialization; Citizen Science

ACM Classification Keywords
H.5.2 [Information Interfaces and Presentation]: User Interfaces - Interaction styles.

General Terms
Human Factors; Design; Measurement.

INTRODUCTION
To sustain a group over time, its newcomers must learn to become effective participants. In some groups, new members go through formal educational or orientation activities in order to learn group practices. However, researchers have argued that formal education alone does not convey the necessary tacit knowledge about work practices needed for good performance. Such tacit knowledge can be conveyed instead through informal learning experiences, such as through legitimate peripheral participation (LPP), a process of situated learning whereby newcomers initially engage in simple practices while observing the work practices and behavior of more experienced members of a community [18].

Online groups present more challenges to newcomer orientation. Many online groups are composed of members who are not part of a single formal organization and who contribute only in their free time, reducing or eliminating the possibility of formal training. However, the affordances of the technologies used to support group interactions often make it possible for distributed volunteers to observe work in progress, thus enabling a form of LPP. For example, Bryant et al. [2], studied new Wikipedia participants and suggested that new editors begin by reading articles before they make their initial contributions.

In this paper, we examine newcomer learning in online citizen science projects: non-temporary groups in which large numbers of distributed volunteers collaborate with domain scientists to collect, annotate, identify and analyze items in large data sets to fulfill scientific goals. These projects are an intriguing example of distributed learning and knowledge production supported by public engagement in scientific research processes [15, 26]. Specifically, we examined two projects developed as part of Zooniverse[1]: Planet Hunters (PH) and Seafloor Explorer (SE), in which members of the general public are asked to annotate scientific data (identifying evidence of possible planets and marine organisms, respectively). To be effective over time, the projects must facilitate the orientation of new users to the goals and work practice of the project. However, unlike other online projects like Wikipedia, PH and SE participants are not able to see the work other users have done, in this case, the primary annotations they have made.

CSCW'14, February 15 – 19, 2014, Baltimore, MD, USA.
Copyright 2013 ACM 978-1-4503-2540-0/14/02...$15.00.
http://dx.doi.org/10.1145/2531602.2531721

[1] https://www.zooniverse.org/

The scientific task was deliberately designed with this restriction to ensure independent responses by eliminating the possibility that one user's response to an image could affect responses by other users.

Given that project participants cannot observe other participants' primary work practices, we inquire how informal experiential learning such as LPP might work in such a setting. To address this question, we extend Erickson and Kellogg's work on social translucence and social proxies [10, 11, 16] to consider "practice proxies." We define practice proxies as system features that make visible the socially salient aspects of people's unfolding work practices rather than aspects of the practices directly. In doing so, we maintain Erickson and Kellogg's focus on design features in online environments that allow newcomers to observe traces of others' activities, but emphasize the aspects of social translucence that relate to work practices instead of social norms. By reflecting on the design implications of the project as they relate to LPP and access to practice proxies, we ask how characteristics of practice proxies support new users given their lack of access to other participants' primary project work practices.

We conclude by reflecting on how our analysis of practice proxies in Zooniverse applies to other open online collaborative communities. While deliberately limited access to other people's work is a unique characteristic of these Zooniverse projects, setting them apart from many open online collaborative communities, this design feature offers us the opportunity to explore practice proxies and the ways in which access to observing practice is made possible in online collaborative environments. On further reflection, it is clear that even in settings where the work products are shared, such as free/libre open source software (FLOSS) development or Wikipedia, many details of the work practices remain private (e.g., design, testing and debugging in FLOSS). Through our analysis, we will demonstrate the ways in which practice proxies in Zooniverse, which appear primarily in discussions about work, provide access to practice in the same ways that talk page conversations and edit histories in Wikipedia, or release notes and bug reports in FLOSS projects, or conversations between Xerox machine repair men [22] provide access to practice.

THEORY

The concept of legitimate peripheral participation (LPP) describes the process in a community of practice of moving from being a newcomer and outsider to becoming an insider in regard to a set of practices. Lave and Wenger [15] coined the term to describe learning among apprentices in a range of different fields from tailors in Liberia, Mayan midwives in the Yucatan, U.S. navy quartermasters, non-drinking alcoholics, and U.S. supermarket meat cutters. Newcomers start out by participating in a practice that makes them legitimate but peripheral members of the community. Socially, they move towards the center of the community, as they become *sustained participants*, that is, active participants increasingly fluent in the tasks, vocabulary and organizational principles of the community.

Legitimate peripheral participation articulates two areas of practices in which newcomers gradually become acculturated to the community: 1) their own participation and 2) the participation of others. First, as indicated by the concept, newcomers gradually gain access to participate in the practices of the community. The new apprentices described in Lave and Wenger's study begin by engaging in low-risk practices. If they stumble and fail as they learn the norms and practices, there is little impact on the community. Gradually they gain access to more elaborate forms of participation. For example, apprentice tailors start out detailing the nearly finished garment such as sewing on buttons. Following the production process in reverse they gradually move from detailing, to sewing to finally cutting cloth.

Second, LPP highlights the role of newcomers' access to other people's practices. If novices can observe more experienced participants in their daily work they can develop an understanding of the context and the various activities, process and activities central to becoming a full, sustained participant. Lave and Wenger offer an iconic counter-example of apprentice butchers in a supermarket where the physical layout of the space does not give them access to the work of expert meat cutters. They are literally stuck in a corner performing menial work. There is a lack of transparency. That is, the learners have limited access to the *context* and *specificity* of other people's unfolding work [25]. To put it differently, access to the other's practices does not happen through instructions or teaching *about* the practice, but only through specific and contextualized discussions and stories told *within* practice [18]. The context only comes to life in all its specificity when newcomers experience others conducting meaningful tasks (e.g., using the tools of the trade, bringing about coordination, negotiating disagreements or addressing uncertainties).

We find a number of studies that use LPP to understand participation in online environments [2, 7, 23, 24]. Notably, in a study of Wikipedia, Bryant, Forte and Bruckman [2] describe participant movements from newcomer to sustained user in regard to their access to 1) participate in the community and 2) to other participants' practices. Based on interviews with nine Wikipedia participants they find that newcomers perceive no technical barriers to full participation. Neither do they articulate a lack of access to other people's practices. The very design of Wikipedia gives anybody access to the articles produced by other participants, access to discussion boards for articles, and access to the history of changes to an article.

Experiences in Wikipedia and other online communities such as open source software development (i.e., FLOSS) raise the questions: what types of transparency and thus access to other people's participation facilitates newcomers' learning? In other words, what practices need to be readily observable for newcomers to learn?

There are several streams of research that address the ways in which participants in online collaborative environments benefit from access to work by other participants. For example, research on activity awareness (e.g. [6];[19]) describes how certain features in online collaborative environments support the work practices of a distributed collaborator base by keeping them up to date on the respective contributions of participants. In doing so, such features help collaborators make sense of each other's work, effectively tailor their respective contributions and so better coordinate the process. Similar research on FLOSS has focused on how the visibility of completed work and the visibility of decisions behind such work acts as a critical component for coordinating FLOSS projects [5].

While these studies focus on the coordination of work, the literature on social translucence (e.g. [10, 20]) looks at features in online environments that specifically help participants learn normative behaviors. As with activity awareness, social translucence refers to design characteristics of online environments that help promote coherent behavior among participants by making their actions visible to each other [8-10]. However, the focus in this case elaborates on Lave and Wenger's second type of access in LPP (i.e., transparency of other's practices), not in apprenticeship arrangements, but in online environments. By making the actions of participants visible, system design that provides social translucence allows people to draw on each others' experience to learn to make sense of the social setting [10].

But, what part of the social setting does a system make translucent? As McDonald et al. (2013) explain, any interaction with a system is a case for social translucence. The question is how the architecture of the system is designed to represent such participation [20]. For instance, article edit histories in Wikipedia make some aspects of Wiki work transparent, as do the reputation systems on eBay by displaying the history of a particular member's participation. In both cases however, there are other aspects of participant contributions that are not transparent but could bring more contextual salience to the work being done [20, 21].

As illustrated in Erickson's notion of social proxies, systems can also strive to make social norms translucent. Social proxies are system features that visualize the socially salient aspects of online interactions, where the concept of 'socially salient' implies the prominent normative behaviors that shape and define the activities of a particular social setting.

Erickson and Kellogg explore the visualization of group behavior by creating tools that visualize the placement of individuals in a space with both placement in the space and indicators of who is speaking as proxies that provide cues regarding the norms of interaction. In Erickson's words: "By making social cues visible, and allowing visible traces to accumulate over time, we create a public resource that allows people – especially those familiar with the interactive context – to draw inferences about what is happening that can inform the ways in which they participate, and, in turn, may ultimately shape the collective activities of the participants." [8]

In Wikipedia the type of transparency newcomers experience in Bryant's et al study [2] relates not only to norms of interaction, but to norms of practice, or what we refer to as *practice proxies*: that is, system features that make visible the socially salient aspects of people's unfolding work practices. Where social proxies emphasize normative expectations for interactions, we explore the aspects of social translucence that act as practice proxies, providing cues for people's unfolding practices by illuminating other people's unfolding work activities through online traces. This perspective leads us back to the questions raised by LPP: what types of transparency or social illumination facilitate the movement from newcomer to sustained participant? To be more specific, what are the characteristics of proxies emphasizing practice that matter for newcomers in a particular community? The practice proxies called for by newcomers in Wikipedia may not match practice proxies needed by learners in FLOSS teams or new citizen science participants. Answering these questions requires that we pay careful attention to the particular communities of practice and what activities contribute to the production and reproduction of the community [17, 18]. In our study, we address these questions inductively, allowing us to explore the role of practice proxies.

METHODS

The empirical data for this study were collected over the past nine months as part of a multi-year NSF funded action research collaboration [1], working closely with developers and designers of a collection of online citizen science projects hosted on the Zooniverse website. Each Zooniverse project (fourteen at the time of this writing) is developed around a large data set provided by different science teams. The sites are designed in collaboration with scientists, web developers and educators. Our action research project strives to enhance participants' learning and motivation through system enhancement of Zooniverse's existing sociotechnical system.

Descriptions of Research Site

As stated above, the research and findings presented in this article focus on two Zooniverse projects: Seafloor Explorer (SE) and Planet Hunters (PH). Both projects help scientists analyze large corpora of data by involving participants in annotating data objects. Participants in the PH project are asked to identify transiting planets in light curve images of the Cygnus constellation in order to help scientists to identify the presence of previously unknown orbiting planets (see Figure 1). At the time of this writing, PH participants have contributed around 17.6 million classifications that just recently contributed to the discovery of the project's first planet. Based on analysis of participant annotation data, we find that PH contribution follows a power law distribution common to crowdsourced initiatives where many users contribute a little and a few users contribute a lot.

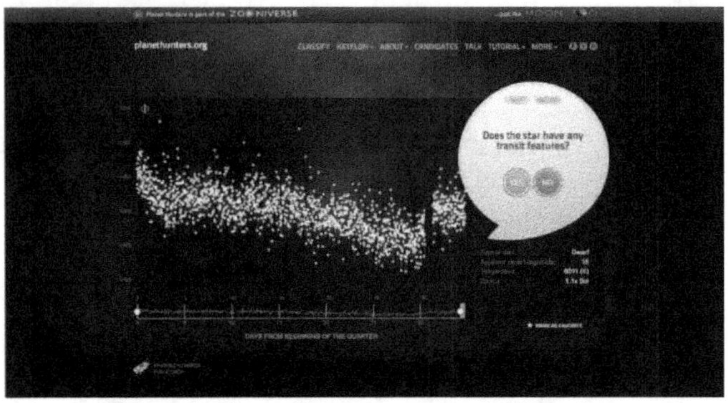

Figure 1. Planet Hunters annotation interface

In SE, participants identify and annotate the presence of marine specimens in images of the sea floor to help scientists better understand the continental shelf ecology off the Northeastern coast of the United States (see Figure 2). Since the project was officially launched early in the Fall of 2012, SE participants have annotated over 1.4 million image objects and, according to the project's blog, the participants have also helped to discover a potential candidate for a new species, currently referred to as the 'convict worm' because of its black and white striped body.

Description of Data Collection and Analysis

Combining the methods of virtual ethnography [14] and trace ethnography [12] the research team collected traces of user participation in PH & SE, engaged in nine months of participant observation, and conducted 10 semi-structured and focus group interviews. Virtual and trace ethnography supplement one another. Where virtual ethnography emphasizes the participation in the online environment as well as analyzing user produced text as evidence of activity, trace ethnography focuses on participant activity as it appears in the system logs of the online platform.

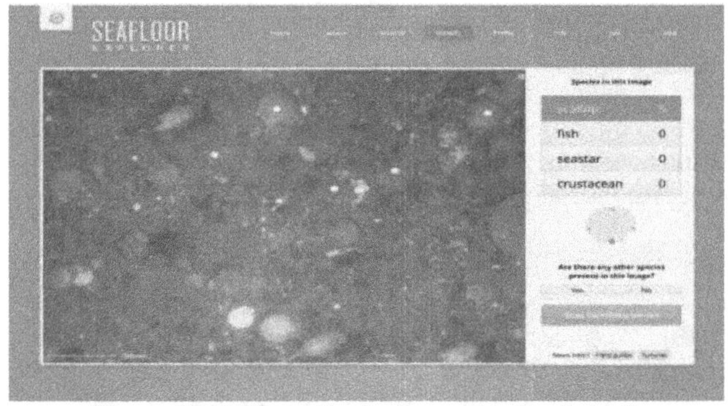

Figure 2. Seafloor Explorer annotation interface

By combining virtual and trace ethnography, researchers can identify and trace practices as they emerged based on visible participant comments, comment timestamps and other user created traces and resources within the talk and discussion features of each of the two sites. The traces left by participants' practices (e.g., comments on talk pages) within the PH and SE online citizen science sites were used to "capture the lived experience" of participants that interact with each of the projects [12,14]. Trace data such as talk comments were not only analyzed as evidence of past practice, but were also analyzed as resources available to assist and guide participant engagement and coordination within the projects [12]. Participant log data collected from participant interactions and made available to us by Zooniverse was used to contextualize our findings. While log data may be considered traces of participant practice, we do not consider them practice proxies, as they are not made available to general Zooniverse participants.

Second, we engaged as participant observers in both the PH & SE projects, which enriched our understanding of participation, helped us better understand how traces of participation are left, and how they are made meaningful throughout participants' interactions within the projects. As participants, we signed up for individual user accounts and completed new participant tutorials that all new users are prompted to complete prior to their first interaction with the projects. As participant observers, conducting and completing primary annotation activities, and eventually participating in the talk and discussion forum with other participants allowed us to explore the relationships between participation and site features and social resources. In short, our participation provided opportunities for reflexive analysis of user participation otherwise inaccessible through traces left on the site [14].

Finally, we conducted semi-structured interviews with project developers, members of the PH and SE science teams, moderators of the social features on the projects and PH and SE participants in order to better understand the role of the projects' interface, systems and structures. The science teams for each project are composed of working scientists and academics in charge of the data corpus around which each of the projects are structured. Aside from managing the project, members of the science team often interact with participants on the talk forum by providing feedback in response to their questions. Similarly, moderators provide feedback on questions to the best of their knowledge and ensure that conversations remain civil. More peripheral PH & SE participants tend to engage in primary annotation practices and engage talk and discussion features infrequently, whereas more sustained participants may perform question asking and answering practices similar to that of the moderators. Each interview lasted approximately one hour and included questions that addressed the perceived role of talk and discussion features for the overarching goals of the project. There were no direct questions relating to how newcomers learn to participate, however follow up questions prompted further discussions about participants' experiences as newcomers within the projects.

Using the theoretical framework of practice proxies and LPP as an analytical lens, we conducted a qualitative analysis of the interviews, participant observations and trace data. Data from the interview transcripts, participant observations and trace data were all independently analyzed by two doctoral students and then compared to identify themes relating to types of practice proxies and evidence of their use by newcomers. These emerging findings were discussed at weekly research meetings where the results from trace data, participant observation, and interviews were triangulated.

FINDINGS

The findings section explores the two types of practices that newcomers gradually gain legitimate access to: 1) their own participation and 2) the participation of others. First, by describing how newcomers' participation in the project and with system features changes we develop a sense of their general learning trajectory. Second, analysis of newcomers' access to fellow participants' practices opens the door to a description of practice proxies and how they promote newcomers' general learning trajectory. We outline a number of practice proxy attributes and discuss the importance of contextual detail and specificity in effective practice proxies. Finally we demonstrate how practice proxies perpetuate and support accurate citizen science work.

Access to Participating

Participants have access to four modes of participation: primary annotation, user generated annotations, user generated queries, and user generated analysis. First, the most common mode of participation within the PH & SE projects involves primary annotation of data objects. This practice is supported by the system that prompts participants with multiple questions about whether or not particular characteristics are present in the data object. In PH, for example, data is presented as a time series of points on a graph called light curves representing Kepler Telescope observations of a star (see Figure 1). Dips in the agglomeration of points may be due to transiting planets and so represent areas of interest to the scientists. Because of the noise and variability of the curves, computers are not adept at identifying patterns and aberrations in the light curves. Instead, participants are presented the images and asked to identify overall features of the light curves (e.g., variability) and dips in light curves that may indicate transiting planets. SE works in a parallel fashion, with participants identifying and annotating photographs of the sea floor for overall ground cover typology—sand, shell, gravel, cobble, boulder—and the presence of specimens from four species—sea scallops, sea stars, fish and crustaceans. Aside from annotating the presence of species, SE participants are also asked to measure each identified scallop, sea star, fish and crustacean with a measuring tool designed into the interface.

Second, after a participant has completed a primary annotation, they are presented with an option to discuss the object further. By selecting this option, participants are brought to an object talk page where they can view annotations and queries left by past participants (see Figure 3). They are also presented with the option to start or view an ongoing discussion related to the object. Third, participants can generate queries and ask questions about data objects by accessing talk/discussion pages for objects at the project website (talk.planethunters.org or talk.seafloorexplorer.org). There, a participant can view objects that are either trending with a high number of annotations or queries, or objects that have received the most recent annotations or queries. In addition to viewing recent or trending objects, the URL for the talk pages also provides access to collections, featured discussions, recent discussions, and trending keywords.

Finally, participants can engage in higher-level analysis, a practice that often exceeds the basic participation goals of the project. High-level analysis typically takes place on the talk pages of objects or on the discussion boards. This type of analysis is often stimulated by a hypothesis or observations about data objects made by one or more participants and then communicated through the discussion forum. For example, a user might download data about a light curve and analyze it to determine characteristics of the orbit of a hypothesized planet.

The four modes of participation are also representative of a trajectory of participation that reflects a movement from the periphery to more impactful engagement with the project [13]. For example, where making primary annotations can be performed by anyone contributing to the project for the first time, making informed contributions to the Talk or Discussion pages requires a degree of understanding about project terminology and procedure [13]. High-level analysis, in the case of PH, reflects modes of contribution that can have serious implications for scientific work and discovery [13]. Indeed, it is the contribution of members conducting high-level analysis that have led to the discovery of new planets.

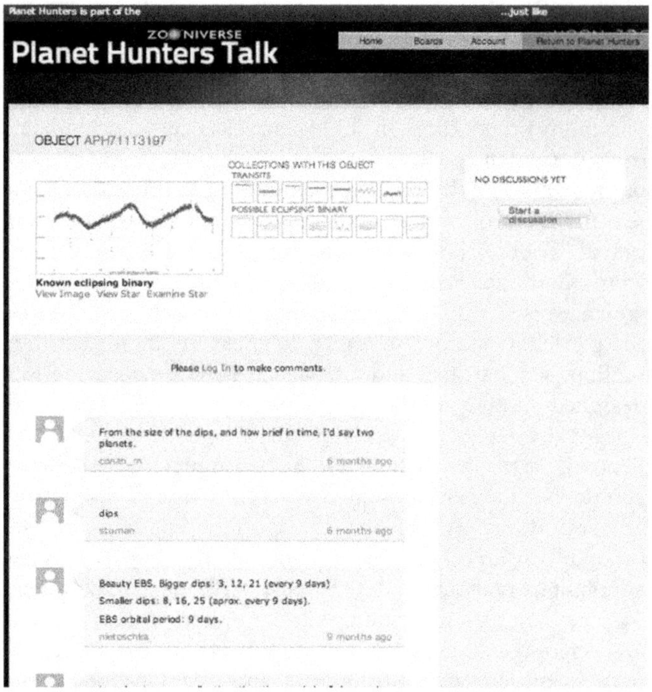

Figure 3. Talk interface for Planet Hunters

Access to Others' Participation via Practice Proxies

The traces of the first mode of participation, primary annotation, are not accessible to participants in PH and SE. According to members of the teams that manage Zooniverse projects, the reason for this restriction is to avoid bias in participants' annotation decisions (i.e., if participants learn in an uncontrolled manner from each other, there is a fear that they may learn and propagate incorrect data annotation practices). With the exception of primary annotations, all other practices are accessible to any participant that looks at the talk pages of data objects or the discussion forums. It is the traces of user generated annotation, queries, and higher level analysis that we define as the practice proxies of Planet Hunters and Seafloor Explorer. They can serve as a stand-in for the primary work.

Traces of annotations and queries include participants' notes about characteristics they marked in the primary annotation practice, or comments and questions seeking clarification about the presence of particular characteristics they just engaged. In either case, such annotations and queries indicate how participants are thinking about the data objects they encounter in primary annotation practice and what aspects they think are relevant to the goals of the project. As such, annotations and queries can help newcomers learn what characteristics are relevant to either primary or broader scientific objectives of the project. In doing so, practice proxies reflect resources that can support participant movement away from a peripheral position of primary annotation to more engaged positions of user generated annotation and querying.

Practice Proxy Attributes

In analyzing the annotations and queries, we identified three common practice proxy attributes. Practice proxies appear to be particular relevant to newcomers if they draw attention to 1) general characteristics of the data objects, 2) specific characteristics, or 3) ask questions about the data object. We provide examples of each feature below.

General characteristics

Some practice proxies outline general characteristics of the data object without making any detailed observations. For example, in PH we see annotations like *"looks like some surface activity"* or *"I also don't see evidence of planet. All downspikes are consistent with the main pulsating plot."* Similarly, in SE we see annotations like, *"Also, a funny shaped seastar,"* or *"It looks like there is something in the right bottom corner. Cannot identify it."* Such practice proxies help point out general characteristics that are important to consider when analyzing data objects, but do not make any detailed observations. By conveying the general description of characteristics that are relevant to the goals of the project, such practice proxies that draw attention to general descriptions in data objects help to establish a broad contextual framework for the goals of analyzing data in the primary practice process.

Specific characteristics

Other practice proxies draw attention to specific points in the data objects. In PH we see one participant leaving the annotation "There appears to be a dip at day 16," and in another example, *"possible transit at 29.25."* Similarly, in SE a participant notes, *"I believe there is a sponge growing on a scallop It looks like there is a small fish, red hake, on the upper side The image quality isn't the best though to be absolutely sure of this."* In all of these examples we see traces of specific points in the data objects that represent what participants pay attention to when engaged in the primary practice of annotation. In addition to highlighting specific points in the data, such traces act as examples of the characteristics that are important to project goals.

Questioning characteristics

Practice proxies also represent questions that participants have about the presence of characteristics in data objects. In an example from PH we see someone asking about the presence of a characteristic at a specific point in the data, *"Something at 19,"* and in another example someone appears to be questioning the presence of a phenomenon they have not seen before, *"Possibly transits at days 28,29,30, but what truncated the peak at days 6 and 7?"* As with the other examples, these types of practice proxies demonstrate what aspects of the data object are important to participants and how they engage them in the process of working on the primary goals of the project. Additionally, these examples reveal questions that come up for participants as they work on the goals of the project.

Having insight into the questions that other participants have about their work help newcomers make sense of the project. Identifying questions similar to their own or that reflect their own confusion can potentially help newcomers to pay attention to particular characteristics in the data, thus supporting an aspect of practice in the project.

Context and Specificity

Moving beyond the specific attributes, the effectiveness of practice proxies appears to hinge on how well they articulate the context and specificity of a particular practice. For instance, one moderator in the PH project related a story of telling a new volunteer of the value of being more specific when writing and creating comments. In other words, practice proxies vary in how well they bring the context of a practice and the specifics of the activity to life through discussions and stories told *within* meaningful tasks (e.g., using the tools of the trade, bringing about coordination, negotiating disagreements or addressing uncertainties).

Drawing on empirical analysis we explore specificity, as an orienting capacity of practice proxies within online communities. We present empirical examples below and highlight proxy characteristics that impact differences in proxy specificity.

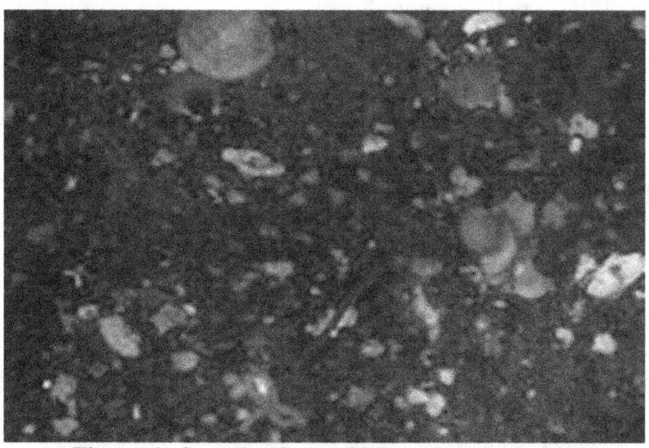

Figure 4. Sample photo of SE project data object.

In the SE project, the data object, image ASF0000k9g, (see Figure 4) is one of the thousands of images presented to participants during primary annotation activities. Scattered amongst sea scallops (orange shells), a lonely sea star, gravel, and sand are thin brown snake-like fish. The three comments below were left by SE participants in reaction to image ASF0000k9g. User B's inquiry, an example of the third type of proxy and representative of reflective practice, is directed at the presence of the snake-like creatures within the image. The description of the characteristic as "sea worms or sea snakes," adds specificity, however for peripheral participants, this comment may be less valuable because it only specifies that the objects in question look like worms, but does not direct participants to particular locations or coordinates within the image (e.g. sea snakes in the upper left quadrant and lower half). More sustained participants however may find this level of specificity valuable as they may already be familiar with the characteristics identified in this practice proxy.

[User A] "#sand-lance #asterias #shrimp"
[User B] "Are these sea worms or sea snakes"
[User C] "These are a fish called a sand lance."

User A's comment is valuable as a practice proxy to new users because it is a trace of the hashtagging practice, and it also adds specificity by indicating additional data characteristics (in this example additional species names) found in the images. If a peripheral participant does not know what sand-lance, asterias and shrimp look like, they will not know which of the characteristics mentioned in comment refer to which species objects within the image. Like User B's comment, the hashtags do not point or refer to any specific characteristic or objects within the image and thus provides a lesser amount of specificity. User C's comment also provides additional specificity, but because his comment refers to User B's previous comment, the specificity of User C's comment is only valuable relative to the specificity of User B's previous comment.

In the following example from PH we see an annotation on object APH71113197 (see Figure 5) where User A provides precise coordinates for the location of the characteristics in the data object that represent the presence of an eclipsing binary star or EBS as it is described in the talk comment below.

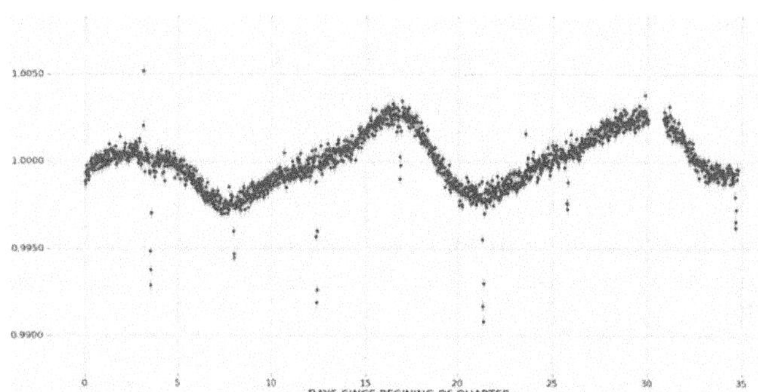

Figure 5. Planet Hunters object APH71113197

[User A] "Beauty EBS. Bigger dips: 3, 12, 21 (every 9 days). Smaller dips: 8, 16, 25 (aprox. every 9 days). EBS orbital period: 9 days."

Eclipsing binary stars (EBS) are defined as two stars orbiting around each other. Because each star has different levels of brightness, the brightness of the two stars will register accordingly in the data object. The above annotation leaves a level of detail that helps a user understand why the characteristics in the data object represent an eclipsing binary by not only indicating the location of the dips in the light curve, but also noting that the two groups have different levels of brightness. Given the detailed justification provided and the precise coordinates noted for each of the identified characteristics, this comment has a high level of specificity. The specificity of this proxy is useful for new participants as a resource for identifying and analyzing eclipsing binaries. The specificity in this case may also be valuable to more sustained participants in the PH projects, as it provides details justifying the participant's analysis, allowing other participants an opportunity to quickly review the comment for accuracy.

Based on participant observation, we found that added levels of detail are valuable for orienting new users towards more structured understanding of the characteristics in the data object that are relevant to the goals of the project. Highly contextual and specific practice proxies help participants become more skillful and engaged participants by immersing them in terminology and reasoning practices valuable for user generated annotations, queries, and higher-level analysis.

Task depth and complexity varies across projects. The level of detail required for identifying the presence of transiting planets in light curves is far greater than that required for identifying the presence of marine animals in the images of the seafloor. As such, annotations and queries in PH often necessitate a great amount of specificity and detail when pointing out the presence of a characteristic as compared to what is required in SE.

How Practice Proxies Perpetuate Practice

New project participants appear to interact with practice proxies in three ways. First, practice proxies help newcomers orient their own practices. A science team member noted that annotations and queries were left by participants on the object talk pages *"help improve classification, because it gives you education."* In other words, the practice proxies on data object talk pages help new participants learn what characteristics in the data they should pay attention to.

Similarly, a moderator for Planet Hunters pointed out that, when they were new to the project, they actively referenced the annotations and queries left by other users on the talk pages of objects in order to learn what characteristics were important and what they looked like in the data objects.

"New users, when they are becoming acclimated, can look at the work other users have posted and get tips on what is a transit...I know it helped me a lot when I was first doing it, to hear some of this discourse."

This strategy of using the traces of other users in order to learn more about the practice of the project was also used by both of our participant observers as they attempted to make sense of the practice in the project.

Second, participants reference the work of others in order to assess the quality of their own work. One forum moderator noted that the forums are a valuable place for new participants to see if they are doing their work correctly:

"If there wasn't a forum, it would feel like you are doing the project on your own, you don't know if anyone else is doing it, you don't know if you are doing it right, so I think that the role of the forum is there to act as a community resource, but also to act as a backup for people when they need it."

An active user of PH similarly noted that early on in their engagement with the project, they actively compared the decisions they had made with the comments made on the object talk pages:

"...most of the threads that have people posting targets to them, they are already vetting from other targets that other people found, so instead of just going to the very small, basic tutorial you get through the interface there, you can actually go check and see, "Oh this is what a bigger transit looks like, oh this is what a smaller transit looks like, oh this is what a not-transit looks like." And just kind of figuring out, with examples if what you found is something worthy or not..."

Additionally, we also know that the option to discuss data objects in PH is mostly used for referring to others' work, as 69% of participants access discussions, but only 22% of those actually leave at least one comment (see Table 1). The difference between the percentage of people who visit the object talk pages on PH but do not leave a comment may suggest that participants who click on the option to discuss mostly do so with the intention of seeing traces of other participant's practice.

Zoo	Annotation	Posts to Talk	Talk Visits	Posts to Discussion	Discussion Visits
PH	17.6M	389K	3.1 M	18K	673K
SE	1.4 M	29K	167K	511	18K

Table 1. Count of contributions and views in PH and SE

Third, participants benefit from questions left by other participants that are similar to their own questions. Traces of queries and conversations allow newcomers to map their own exploratory practice to those of others. As such they are not only seeking answers to specific questions but can attain valuable insights into the reasoning process of both fellow newcomers and more experienced participants.

How Practice Proxies Support Accurate Work

By being a resource for learning how to perform basic tasks in the projects, proxies support accurate and correct annotation of data objects. Where some citizen science projects will ensure accurate work by pairing citizen scientists with trained professionals [3], the distributed and large-scale nature of projects like PH and SE rules out expert oversight as a feasible model. It would simply be too taxing for the science team if participants sought their feedback at every turn. Instead, practice proxies act as important resources, facilitating the accurate and correct annotation of data objects. As our interviews suggest, participants often sought out the comments of other participants to see if they were doing their work correctly. In the case of projects like PH and SE, after having annotated the data object, a participant is always presented with the option to discuss the object further on the objects talk page. Here, participants can see if their choices match those of other participants based on the annotations other participants may have left. This practice of checking to see if work had been done correctly was noticed in our interviews and participant observations. In an interview with a participant, the respondent pointed out that she actively sought out annotations left by more experienced users, using the traces of their practice as a resource to learn how to accurately identify the characteristics relevant to project goals.

In summary, by representing the traces of others' practices, practice proxies act as a resource for newcomers to learn how to perform basic tasks in the projects. In particular, practice proxies support new users as they learn what characteristics in the data are relevant to project goals and how to identify such characteristics. Despite the presence of tutorials, interviews with science team members, moderators and project participants reveal that reviewing the comments on the data object talk pages is the most valuable means of learning about relevant data characteristics and how to identify such characteristics. As one science team member stated, the tutorials show the most ideal example of what annotating a data object might look like. More often than not, they do not relate to the data objects that participants are likely to encounter. The situated nature of annotations and queries on the talk pages or collections allows new participants to see what parts of the data objects people looked at and what characteristics they believed were present. Each trace of practice is thus a resource upon which new participants can draw as they learn how to identify the presence of important characteristics in the data. Examples from the findings demonstrate practice proxies on data objects highlighting general concepts related to the project goals, specific descriptions of data characteristics, as well as questions related to conducting practice.

DISCUSSION

We have found that the object-oriented discussions on PH and SE Talk Pages provide a degree of context and specificity around the descriptions of work being done that newcomers find useful as they acclimate to the practice of the projects. Practice proxies support newcomers' peripheral participation in the basic annotation practices and facilitate their gradual movement towards more engaged and skillful participation in the community involving user-generated annotation, queries and ultimately independent analysis. At the same time, the relative permanence of the practice proxies on the online site become an important part of the ongoing production and reproduction of the community.

Our findings have design implications for open online communities seeking to educate newcomers to become productive participants. At first glance, the lack of access to the work practices of others found in Zooniverse and other citizen science project may appear as an anomaly. However, the same characteristic applies to a greater or lesser degree in most online communities. Taking Wikipedia as an example [2, 23], while a newcomer has access to the primary practice of other participants (article edits) as well as the edit history and talk pages for an article, not all article talk pages or edit histories provide context and specificity to describe the reasoning behind the practice of participation. The work leading up to a page edit could be a few seconds to correct a typo, or hours of research and fact checking. Similarly, in Free/Libre Open Source projects [4] participants can see the code contributed, they cannot observe the work that led to that code, be it a few seconds to fix a trivial bug or hours of design and implementation for a new feature. Viewed in this light, most online communities may benefit from high quality practice proxies to support learning and knowledge sharing.

To improve newcomer learning, designers for open online communities might consider ways in which to effectively insert richer practice proxies into the newcomers' experience to help them orient themselves to the norms of practice. Considering how the production of context and specificity via practice proxies might work in other open online communities has the potential to impact the way we conceptualize the experience of newcomers and support their continued participation in open online communities of practice. The object-oriented discussion feature of Zooniverse projects such as PH and SE projects has parallels in Wikipedia talk pages oriented to a particular page, or FLOSS discussions associated to particular bug reports. Designers might consider presenting lists of popular subjects that have a high frequency of practice proxies to participants at predetermined times throughout their sessions. In doing so, researchers might explore how presenting practice proxies to newcomers at different moments relates to their growth in self-efficacy, learning, and motivation. Arguably even if PH and SE were to show the products of primary annotation, the question might be whether or not simply displaying decisions, for example Wikipedia's edit history feature, would provide as rich a practice proxy as those we have described in PH and SE.

More broadly, our research contributes to the theoretical work on social translucence by extending the conversation beyond a focus on normative behavior to a focus on practice. Online community design promoting social translucence might seek to support practice proxies rich in contextual detail and specificity about participants' practice. Simply providing access to the decisions made by a participant may not be sufficient to create social translucence in system design. By having practice proxies that emphasize context and specificity, a system has the potential to embed a richer description of community practice norms, thus helping a newcomer gain a deeper understanding of how to be a full and valuable member. Moving forward, we plan to further explore the question of context and specificity in the design of practice proxies. Additionally, we believe that future research would benefit from a comparison between the design of social proxies and practice proxies and their relative approaches to context and specificity.

CONCLUSION

In this paper we explored how new users orient themselves towards the goals and practices of massively distributed online collaborative projects. By combining the theories of legitimate peripheral participation [18] and social proxies [8, 9] we focused on the relationship between access to participate and access to others' participation in online environments. Empirically we examined two citizen science projects where the traces of primary practice are not accessible, yet where new users find ways to work around this lack of access.

Our findings suggest that, while newcomers lack access to the traces of primary community practices (i.e., primary annotations of data objects), they appear to compensate for this lack of transparency by taking advantage of traces of participation on the talk and discussion pages of data objects as a way to build their own understanding. In other words, the projects possess a rich resource of practice proxies that exist on the talk and discussion pages of the projects data objects. There, users have engaged in what we describe as user generated annotations and queries. They ask questions or make comments on the presence of particular characteristics in the data objects that are relevant to the primary annotations and broader project activities and goals. These annotations and queries are what we define as practice proxies in that they represent the traces of how users are thinking about both the primary annotations and broader project activities. The presence of such practice proxies serves as resources for new users as they learn how to become participants in the project.

By combining the concepts of social proxy and LPP we can seek out design approaches that better orient new users towards the goals and practices of online crowdsourced projects. To further this particular design approach to online crowdsourced work, future research should consider design interventions that test the relationship between practice proxies and learning opportunities for new users. Building on rich qualitative and trace data, such experiments might involve testing the degree of access to practice proxies and measuring the impact this has on continued participation.

ACKNOWLEDGMENTS

Without the Zooniverse volunteers working on the projects and taking the time to answer our questions there would be no paper. Many thanks to Stuart Lynn and the Zooniverse team for access to PH and SE data. Several colleagues and the anonymous reviewers offered invaluable feedback. This material is based on work supported by the National Science Foundation under Grant No. IIS 12-11071.

Kevin Crowston is supported by the National Science Foundation. Any opinions, findings, and conclusions or recommendations expressed in this material are those of the author(s) and do not necessarily reflect the views of the National Science Foundation.

REFERENCES

[1] Baskerville, R. and Myers, M.D. 2004. Special Issue on Action Research in Information Systems: Making IS Research Relevant to Practice--Forward *MIS Quarterly*. 28, 3 (2004), 329–335.

[2] Bryant, S.L. et al. 2005. Becoming Wikipedian: transformation of participation in a collaborative online encyclopedia. (Nov. 2005).

[3] Cohn, J.P. 2008. Citizen Science: Can Volunteers Do Real Research? *BioScience*. 58, 3 (2008), 192.

[4] Crowston, K. and Fagnot, I. 2008. The motivational arc of massive virtual collaboration. (2008), 1–35.

[5] Crowston, K. et al. 2011. Work as coordination and coordination as work: A process perspective on FLOSS development projects. (2011), 1–26.

[6] Dourish, P. and Bellotti, V. 1992. Awareness and Coordination in Shared Workspaces. (Dec. 1992), 107–114.

[7] Ducheneaut, N. 2005. Socialization in an Open Source Software Community: A Socio-Technical Analysis. *Computer Supported Cooperative Work (CSCW)*. 14, 4 (Jul. 2005), 323–368.

[8] Erickson, T. 2004. Designing Online Collaborative Environments: Social Visualizations as Shared Resources. (Rutgers University, New Brunswick, NJ, Jun. 2004), 143–158.

[9] Erickson, T. 2009. "Social" Systems: Designing Digital Systems that Support Social Intelligence. *Ai & Society*. 23, 2 (2009), 147–166.

[10] Erickson, T. and Kellogg, W.A. 2000. Social Translucence: An Approach to Designing Systems that Support Social Processes. *ACM Transactions on Computer-Human Interaction*. 7, 1 (Mar. 2000), 59–83.

[11] Erickson, T. et al. 2002. Social Translucence. *Communications of the ACM.*

[12] Geiger, R.S. and Ribes, D. 2011. Trace Ethnography: Following Coordination through Documentary Practices. (2011), 1–10.

[13] Hassman, K.D. et al. 2013. Learning at the Seafloor, Looking at the Sky: The Relationship Between Individual Tasks and Collaborative Engagement in Two Citizen Science Projects. (2013), 1–2.

[14] Hine, C. 2000. *Virtual Ethnography*. Sage Publications.

[15] Jason Reed, M.J.R.A.L.K.C. 2012. An Exploratory Factor Analysis of Motivations for Participating in Zooniverse, a Collection of Virtual Citizen Science Projects. (Dec. 2012), 1–10.

[16] Kellogg, W.A. and Erickson, T. 2002. Social Translucence, Collective Awareness, and the Emergence of Place. (2002), 1–6.

[17] Lave, J. 1988. *Congition in Practice: Mind, mathematics, and culture in everyday life*. Cambridge University Press.

[18] Lave, J. and Wegner, E. 1991. *Situated learning*. Cambridge University Press.

[19] Marlow, J. and Dabbish, L. 2013. Activity Traces and Signals in Software Developer Recruitment and Hiring. (2013), 145–155.

[20] McDonald, D.W. et al. 2013. Building for Social Translucence: A Domain Analysis and Prototype System. (2013), 637–646.

[21] McDonald, D.W. et al. 2009. System Design for Social Translucence in Socially Mediating Technologies. (2009), 1–7.

[22] Orr, J.E. 1986. Narratives at work: story telling as cooperative diagnostic activity. (1986), 62–72.

[23] Preece, J. and Ben Scheiderman 2009. The Reader to Leader Framework: Motivating Technology-Mediated Social Participation. *Transactions on Human-Computer Interaction*. 1, 1 (2009), 13–32.

[24] Schlager, M.S. and Fusco, J. 2003. Teacher Professional Development, Technology, and Communities of Practice: Are We Putting the Cart Before the Horse? *Information & Management*. 19, 3 (2003), 203–220.

[25] Wenger, E. 1998. *Communities of Practice: Learning, meaning, and identity*. Cambridge University Press.

[26] Wiggins, A. and Crowston, K. 2011. From Conservation to Crowdsourcing: A Typology of Citizen Science. (2011), 1–10.

Study of an Electronic Lab Notebook Design and Practices that Emerged in a Collaborative Scientific Environment

Gerard Oleksik
Dovetailed Ltd
23 Kings St., Cambridge, UK
gerard@dovetailed.com

Natasa Milic-Frayling
Microsoft Research
21 Station Rd., Cambridge, UK
natasamf@microsoft.com

Rachel Jones
Instrata Ltd
12 Warkworth St., Cambridge, UK
racheljones@instrata.com

ABSTRACT
Prolific adoption of digital media across scientific fields has led to inevitable transformation of a traditional lab book into an *electronic lab notebook* (ELN). Research so far has focussed on designing ELN prototypes and learning from their limited deployments. At the same time, a variety of commercially available ELNs have been adopted by industrial and academic laboratories. That provides opportunities for situated research and a deeper understanding of the role that ELNs assumes as an integral part of a scientific environment. In this paper we present a study of ELN design that has emerged as scientists appropriated commercial off-the-shelf note-taking software and adapted it to their work. Through in-situ observations we analysed the interplay between the technology and emerging practices. Our study reveals a tension that is intrinsic to the digital nature of ELNs: a conflict between the flexibility, fluidity, and low threshold for modifying digital records and the requirement for persistence and consistency. This led to refined requirements and design considerations for ELNs.

Author Keywords
Electronic lab notebook; content organization; practice; linking; tagging; pivots

ACM Classification Keywords
H5.m. Information interfaces and presentation: Misc.

INTRODUCTION
A scientist's lab notebook is a lynchpin of scientific record keeping. Scientists use it to keep daily records of the research progress, the developing thoughts, the findings, and the experiments they have run [15]. Traditionally a paper artifact, the lab notebook has been destined to undergo considerable transformations as the digital technology penetrated many aspects of the scientific work.

CSCW '14, February 15–19, 2014, Baltimore, Maryland, USA.
Copyright 2014 ACM 978-1-4503-2540-0/14/02...$15.00.
http://dx.doi.org/10.1145/2531602.2531709

Designers and HCI researchers have produced prototypes of the *electronic lab notebook* (ELN) to study implications of these transformations [7, 12, 15]. Kolkmose and Zander [3] gathered an exhaustive list of requirements for the future ELNs based on a series of workshops and discussions with a community of physicists. Studies of the developed ELN prototypes have considered the ways the electronic version of the lab notebooks can foster collaboration [15], create affinities between electronic and paper resources [5, 17], introduce semantics [16], and streamline data gathering and analysis workflows [12]. In many instances these studies involved a limited deployment of the prototype. While they led to valuable insights about the potential use of the prototypes, they also ascertained the need to extend the research inquiry through observation studies of ELNs that have been adopted as an integral part of a scientific environment.

In recent years, we have seen a steady rise in a variety of ELN solutions offered by commercial vendors. Rubacha et al. [10] provide a market survey of 35 commercially available ELNs grouped into 5 categories based on the primary audience: two categories related to the scientific fields of biology and chemistry, two categories focused on the functional objectives such as support for research and development (R&D) and support for quality assurance and compliance (QA/QC), and a class of ELNs with cross-disciplinary offerings.

Several publications from the practitioners describe the advantages of deployed solutions measured by the productivity, compliance, and quality assurance metrics [9, 18]. Recent work by Iyer and Kudrle [2] reports on the use of ELN to support a course curriculum in a bioanalytical laboratory. Although these papers provide accounts of adopted commercial ELN solutions, none of them follow observational and situated research methodology and, thus, offer no deeper insights into the role that ELNs play in the work of individuals and teams.

Our research fills this gap by observing the ELN design and practices that emerged within a fully operational scientific environment as a means of supporting cutting edge research and graduate level education in nanotechnology. We conducted a two-week observation study of a team of 8 scientists at the Nanophotonics Research Centre (NRC) who created and used ELNs in their everyday work. The NRC scientists adopted tablet PCs and generic, commercial,

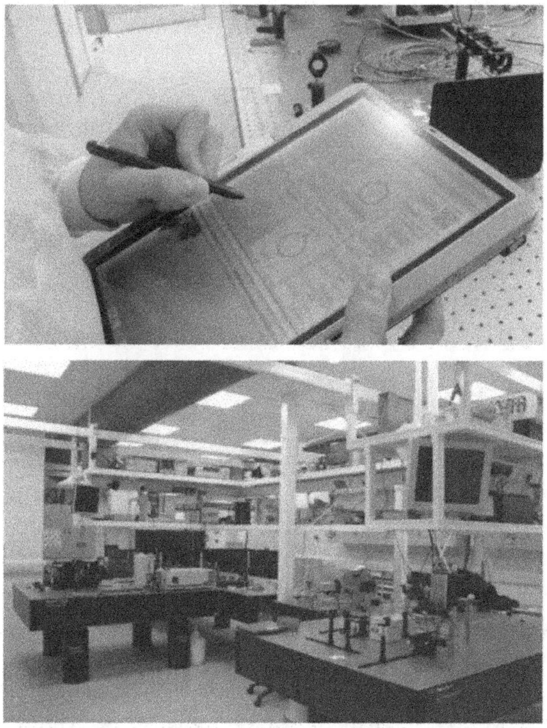

Figure 1: Use of the ELN in the NRC lab (above). The laboratory environment that ELN is interfacing with (below).

off-the-shelf software for note taking and turned them into ELNs. By closely following scientists' activities, we analyzed the use of ELNs for conducting experiments, processing data, sharing insights, and coordinating work. We captured interactions with ELNs and organizational structure of the created records. Based on the collected data, we gained valuable insights about the emerging practices and the influence of the organizational culture and the technology infrastructure on the use of ELNs.

Our research confirms most of the findings from the studies of ELN prototypes such as Prism by Tabard et al. [15], and the ELN design requirements that were solicited from the physics scientists by Klokmose & Zander [3]. However, situated research of adopted ELNs enables us to take a step further and understand the issues that arise in practice from the intrinsically digital nature of ELNs. First, we observe the tension between the flexibility, fluidity, and low threshold for modifying digital artifacts and the requirements for persistence and consistency of scientific records across individuals. Second, we uncover how these two aspects have a ripple effect on the collaborative work. The flexibility of digital media enables personalization and optimal support for needs of individual scientists while the conformity and consistency in the scientific record increases the capacity for sharing and leveraging each other's work.

Designing ELNs to achieve a desired balance between these opposing forces is critical for the practical deployment of ELNs and a sustained use to support scientific work. Constraining the format of data representation and record keeping in ELNs is commonly promoted by the commercially available solutions through features such as templates for data entries and fixed workflows [10]. That may be suitable for routine and well defined experimental work. However, for a wider spectrum of usage scenarios, where flexibility is preferred, we propose an alternative approach that applies computing technologies, such as text mining and natural language processing techniques, to extract information from free-form or semi-structured scientific records and present it into a consistent and unified view.

In the rest of the paper we first provide an overview of the research on ELNs and scientific record keeping. We then follow with a detailed description of the study method and observations. We discuss the implications of the findings for the design and conclude with a summary of presented research and future directions.

RELATED WORK

From a broader perspective, our research can be situated within two distinct strands of investigation, both concerned with the role of computing technologies as a support and a catalyst for discovery and innovation.

First, our methodology is inspired by the ethnographic studies of science and technology that contextualize science and consider "institutional circumstances of scientific work" as promoted by Latour and Woolgar [4] and Lynch [5]. Our analysis of the ELNs adoption was part of a broader effort to understand the NRC work environment and characterize the ways the computing technologies support scientific activities. Through in-situ observations, we captured the social interactions and the intricate digital ecology that evolved from the practices and supported the scientific discovery [6]. We used this deeper understanding as a backdrop for the analysis of the practices around the ELNs use.

Second, our attention was particularly drawn to the design of ELNs adopted at the NRC by the fact that the scientists appropriated and adapted generic note-taking software for their purposes in novel and innovative ways. This provided a unique opportunity to confirm in practice the position by Silverstone and Haddon [14] that "innovation requires to be seen as a process which involves both producers and consumers in a complex interweaving of activities". The observed behavior and attitude towards note-taking technology by the scientists are aligned with the notion of technology *domestication* where consumers of technology are involved "in appropriation, in taking technologies and objects home, and in making, or not making, them acceptable and familiar" [14]. More importantly, this frame of thought led us to reason about the interrelationship of software design and software appropriation in a way that enable us to identify specific features that give rise to the extended use. In effect, our work illustrates and confirms that the innovation does not stop with the technology design; instead, it evolves through appropriation and use over time.

In order to gain deeper insights about the characteristics of ELNs designs and practices, we focus our literature review on two research areas. First, we consider the studies of scientific record keeping and information management that investigate the role of the paper lab notebooks in the scientific practices. We then discuss the literature about research prototypes, ranging from augmented paper lab notebooks to full ELN applications, and the insights provided by that body of work. At the end, we reflect upon the state of the commercial solutions and outline the research questions that underpin our study.

Paper lab notebook and scientific record keeping

The lab notebook is a cornerstone of the scientific record keeping and often serves as a legal document and proof of discovery in patent claims [3, 16]. The work by Yeh et al. [17] and Mackay et al. [7] draws attention to the heterogeneous information types that scientists physically paste into lab notebooks, in some instances including X-ray images, photographs and computer printouts. In particular, Mackay et al. [7] describe the paper lab notebooks created by biologists as 'extremely multi-media documents'.

Schraefel et al. [10] observed the use of paper lab notebooks by chemists in their day to day work within chemistry labs and devised an ELN that was practical and useful for data entry and access. Tabard et al. [15] studied the use of paper notebooks in a biology lab, alongside electronic folders. Despite the ubiquity of electronic files, many participants continued to use paper lab notebooks. Indeed, due to the diligence required to complete these paper records and their fixed, un-editable nature, these paper artifacts continue to play an essential role in record keeping: 'paper lab notebooks serve as a formal repository for information that can be treated as a stable point in an evolving world' [15].

The chronological structure of a lab notebook enabled participants to find easily recently entered information. However, over time, the reliance on the chronological memory broke down and a project level categorization became more desirable. Investigating models for organizing the data and records throughout the lab, Tabard et al. [15] found that chronology and project based organization are, indeed, the two dominant strategies.

Augmented paper and electronic lab notebooks

While paper notebooks provide a rich body of contextual information, they are, unfortunately, not broadly accessible and shareable [16]. Furthermore, a highly personal style of information keeping in some instances, and a lack of *a priori* information about the content they include, may hinder search and reuse of paper notebooks by others [11]. In order to address these and other issues, a body of research has sought to augment the paper notebooks or replace them entirely with electronic versions.

Schraefel et al. [10] identified four main approaches to designing ELNs, i.e., those seeking to replicate, supplement, replace, or augment paper lab notebooks. Systems and applications that aim to replicate paper notebooks typically enable notebook pages to be scanned directly into searchable databases (e.g., software systems by SCRIP-SAFE deployed to support intellectual property claims [13]). Those that supplement the paper notebooks may focus on supporting some parts of the scientific process, such as entry of experiment planning data. For example, the software may produce a printed output which is then pasted into the paper notebooks (e.g., Labscape Lab Assistant by Borriello et al., [1]). The a-book (short for augmented notebook), designed by Mackay et al. [5] extends the reach of the traditional paper notebook by allowing the user to associate digital artifacts with handwritten notes via magic lens interaction.

Tabard et al. [15] conducted a longer term study of Prism, a hybrid paper electronic notebook aimed at gathering data from distributed information stores that biologists use in their work. The Prism prototype consists of Anoto paper notebook which tracks user handwriting and stores digital entries into an electronic lab notebook. The users can then tag ELN pages, send email and Web content, and link to documents and images. The digital pages can be shared through RSS feeds, thus increasing the visibility and reach of information. The prototype was used by 6 biologists in their daily work for 9 months. The authors found that tagging, although well used, was of limited benefit since scientists found it hard to recall the meaning of tags as time passed. On the other hand, the use of the tool was extended with sharing bibliographic references and calendar events.

While Mackay et al. [7], Yeh et al. [17], and Tabard et al. [15] pursued the augmentation of paper notebook, Schraefel et al. [10] have produced a wholly electronic lab notebook prototype. They developed a tablet based ELN and designed the software to mimic various affordances of the paper notebooks. Talbott et al. [16] sought to enhance ELNs with semantic features. They implemented the information architecture and described the integration of the lab notebook software with semantic services. However, they did not report on the system performance and user evaluation.

Research objectives

The discussed research literature illustrates a great interest in providing scientists with an effective means of creating rich lab records. The available commercial solutions now include a broad range of features, from general to domain specific support for record keeping activities [10].

For example, Kalabie ELN, a product of Agilent Technologies, supports scientists in creating experiment records through predefined experiment templates, copying and pasting of data between experiment records, providing alerts for signatories, and enabling rich text and media management. CERF-Notebook by Rescentris promotes both general features for R&D and specific support for biology research. It has built-in ontologies to support customization of the scientific data models, templates, and business policies. As R&D functions, it enables creating, viewing, analyzing, and annotating research records, enforcing the intellectual property protection, and integrating scientific records with existing systems and data. For biology research, it offers content management, search using full-text index, metadata, and controlled vocabularies, and features to enforce compliance with templates and forms for protocols and data capture. These two examples of ELN products are illustrative of features that are typically offered by bespoke ELN solutions.

The NRC has made a conscious decision not to use specialized ELN products for two reasons. First, to reduce the risk of software obsolescence since the market is volatile and the providers may not be able to guarantee software support for a long time. Second, most of the commercial ELNs' functionality is supporting mainstream processes and operations which are not relevant for the academic environments where the focus is on investigative research and innovative approaches. Interestingly, during the study the NRC researchers had to consider the upgrade from OneNote 2007 to OneNote 2009 which caused concerns about the backward compatibility and possible implications for their work.

The opportunity to conduct in-situ study of NRC has proven invaluable because we could study the emergent ELN design as the participants adopted the technology to support their scientific work. That enabled us to compare the observed ELN functions with the bespoke ELN prototypes and commercial solutions. More importantly, we began to understand the impact of ELNs on the individual's and collective work. Our research covered three main areas:

- Properties and practices enabled by the ELN in use at NRC
- Constraints of the NRC design of ELNs, as observed through workarounds and interviews with the scientists
- Design requirements and principles that can address the observed issues.

STUDY PLAN

Over a period of two months, we conducted three one-week observations within the scientific lab at the Nanophotonics Research Centre (NRC). The broad objective was to understand the entire work environment and characterize the ways the computing technologies support scientific activities [6]. Our observation centered on the work practices and movement of 8 study participants (P1–P8, Table 1). However, we also observed and investigated other aspects of the lab life such as group meetings and general interaction among the staff. During the first week we

Part.	Profile	At the Lab
P1	Professor. Founder of the Centre	18 months
P2	Post Doc – multiple projects	18 months
P3	Post doc – multiple projects	18 months
P4	PhD Student – Nano group	10 months
P5	PhD Student – Nano group	6 months
P6	PhD Student – Nano group	10 months
P7	PhD Student – Engineering group	10 months
P8	PhD Student – Nano group	18 months

Table 1: Study participants

conducted initial interviews with all the participants and started observations of the meetings and experiment procedures. This provided a detailed overview of the Centre, its organization, spatial layout and IT infrastructure for storing data and managing information.

During observations of meetings, the researcher video recorded the proceedings with a static camera and took notes throughout. The lab observation of experiments (Figure 1) was also video recorded, encouraging the participants to 'speak aloud' about their tasks and reasoning behind their activities. The researcher also asked the participants occasional questions to clarify the context or motivation for a particular activity, e.g., a reason for recording a particular piece of information into the ELN

Alongside observations, we conducted up to 3 in-depth interviews with each participant. Interviews lasted between 60 and 90 minutes and covered a broad range of aspects of the participants' work. We asked participants how and where they stored information, what collaborative and communication methods they used, how they ran the experiments in the lab, and how they used and managed their ELNs. We also gathered entire electronic lab notebooks from the participants and analyzed their structure and content.

We analyzed the collected data by applying the Thematic Coding method (Miles & Hubermann [8]) and using the software package Atlas.ti to aid the data processing. The analysis involved 15 hours of recorded and transcribed interviews and 5 hours of video footage of meetings and lab observations. Throughout the coding process, two researches discussed and refined the emerging codes. Over several sessions, the codes were clustered to identify the emerging research themes, concepts, and categories. During the analysis, samples of OneNote workbooks were viewed in order to understand the information structuring practices of the participants.

THE FIELD SITE AND STUDY PARTICIPANTS

The Nanophotonics Research Centre (NRC) is a nimble and active research environment, hosting a wide range of inter-connected and collaborative projects. The Center is oriented towards high impact science and exploration of new approaches in the field. The group is headed by a professor with many years of experience in industry and academia (P1). He is the founder of the Centre. At the time of the study the Centre employed 5 Post Docs, 11 PhD research students, and 5 support staff who were involved in 5 major research initiatives, comprising 12 sub-projects in total.

The staff applies highly sophisticated lab equipment to material samples that have been specially produced to facilitate scientific experiments. Furthermore, each scientist is provided with a tablet PC running Microsoft Operating System and Microsoft Office applications. MS OneNote 2007 was adopted as a lab notebook to create records of research activities. However, it also served as a means of collaboration and general information management. The use of Tablet PC provided the required mobility because the researchers conducted work both in the Lab and at their desk in the common research room. Furthermore, they needed access to their ELNs in meetings that took place in the professor's office and during discussions with their peers.

While OneNote is not bespoke lab notebook software, its functions have been co-opted to this purpose. Each scientist maintains a personal ELN, daily recording notes on the experiments and analyses, and importing supporting materials such as key graphs and Web resources to produce an account of progress for themselves and for discussions with others. As a collaboration tool, the lab notebook pages are shared back and forth between research staff to gather feedback and comments. In addition, the professor creates shared MS OneNote files to support discussion and note taking during meetings and project level notebooks to store information from sub-projects into a central repository. The latter are intended as a detailed record of the scientific work conducted in the Centre.

Both the experiment data and all OneNote files are stored on the networked servers in the lab and all the research files are accessible to everyone in the Centre. Most of the data analysis is performed by using Igor, a specialized signal processing and visualization software.

Microsoft OneNote. MS OneNote 2007 software is designed based on a notebook paradigm. The top level concept is a binder of notebooks. Each notebook supports a three level organization (Figure 2): section list (on the left), sub-sections tabs (on the top) and list of individual pages (on the right). Unfolding the hierarchy enables the user to switch between pages, sections, and notebooks.

MS OneNote on the Tablet PC supports both handwritten and typed input and maintains editing history. Most of the content formats can be imported by the standard drag&drop and copy&paste facilities. This includes the embedded files, represented as file icons or displayed fully in the pages, and files referenced by the file paths or URLs in case of Web pages. The user can annotate and tag pages and parts of pages through handwriting as well as recorded voice. The content within each notebook can be accessed by browsing, searching for tags, or through keyword search.

OneNote is integrated with other Office applications, allowing the user to direct content to OneNote from MS Word, MS Outlook (email client) and MS Internet Explorer (Web browser) through a 'send to' command. Furthermore, the user can link notebooks and individual pages from different notebooks. Most of these technical aspects of OneNote were articulated in the ELN requirements collected from physics scientists by Klokmose & Zander [3] and can be found in the specifications of the commercially available ELNs.

FINDINGS

We group the study findings into two broad categories: (1) the frameworks that participants applied to organize content within their personal ELNs and how effectively that organization supports their work, and (2) the ways that the participants use their ELNs throughout their research practice. Our analysis did include the usage of specific application features by the participants but we report on the intentions of the participants and achieved results rather than the mechanics of the technical features. We will, however, refer to them when discussing the users' workarounds. As it turned out, some of the OneNote features fell short in supporting the user. For example, the search is focused on the page content and not specifically on annotations. Second, the structure of section headings provides a fixed organization and does not support pivoting around specified headings to enable alternative views.

Information management

With the encouragement of the research leader (P1), the staff has adopted a naming convention of ELN records that includes the date, material sample, and experiment name. However, the organization of ELNs is largely under the control of individual scientists and varies considerably.

ELN Record Organization

From the interview data and analysis of the lab notebooks, we observe a fundamental tension between the content organization based on chronology, as suggested by the lab-wide convention, and the organization by semantic sections that some of the staff found useful.

Topical organization. Participants used OneNote sections to create areas in their notebook for recording notes and data about specific subjects, sub-projects, meetings, and other aspects of their work. While semantically consistent sections provide a structure for recording data, this approach has proven problematic due to the nature of the collected data. In their initial months at the Centre, the participants P2, P3 and P6 attempted to organize ELN content solely by subject such as sub-project, meeting notes, material samples or equipment used in the experiments.

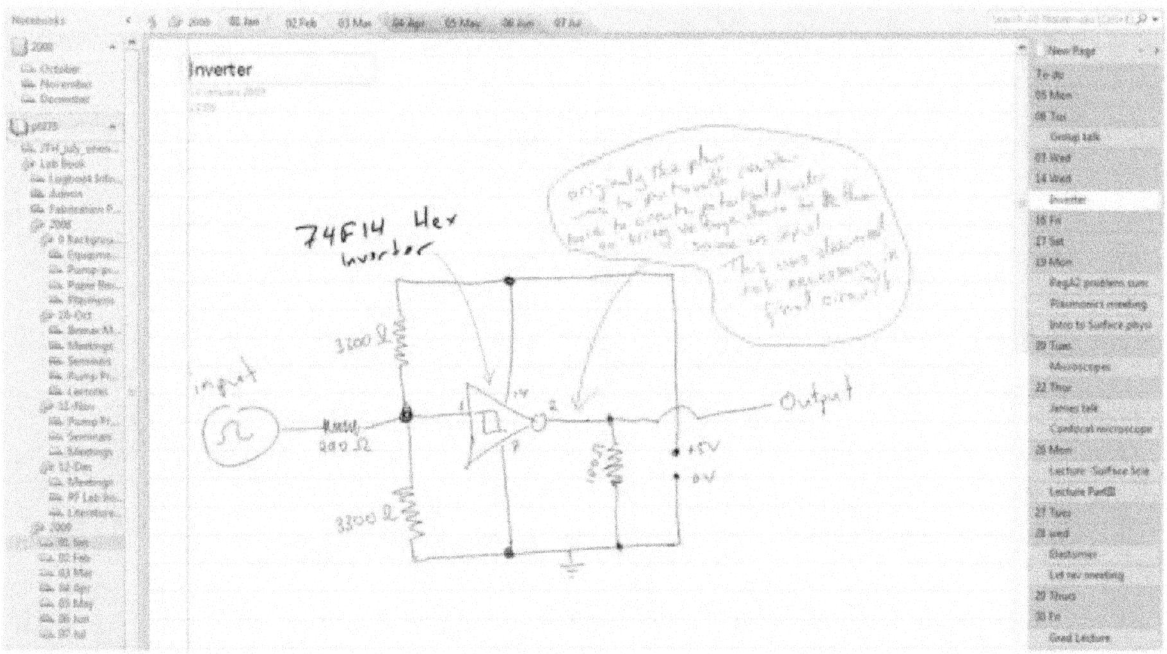

Figure 2: Example OneNote ELN page. Left pane displays open notebooks; upper tabbed pane displays sections; right hand pane displays individual pages.

While that helped with finding pages, each of them abandoned this approach due to the overhead it imposes when gathering information. The diversity of information grew and its classification became more difficult with a larger number of categories. The only participant who operated a fully topical organization of the ELN records at the time of the study was P5. He organized his data according to the material samples and experimental procedures. Significantly, he was the newest PhD student, having been with the group for only 6 month, and was already considering a change to the chronological structure as his data became more diverse.

Chronological organization. At the time of the study, chronology was the most prevalent organizational principle used by the participants (Figure 3). Chronology imposes a low overhead, allowing the users to record information without concern for categorization and, thus, without disrupting the experimental or analytic work.

Mixed approach. Similarly to the findings by Tabard et al. [15], we found that chronology was effective for searching recent information but not so for revisiting information that was recorded long ago. P2 stated that the transition point occurs around 2 weeks after which project and topic based information would be more useful for searching. Participants P3, P4, P6 and P7 attempted to overcome the issues of the sole chronological approach by replacing the date with keywords that describe the content, e.g., the name of the material sample, the name of the experiment, etc. (Figure 3). During the interview, participants stated that such a method helped when revisiting information since they preserved the chronological order of pages and more easily ascertained their contents based on the title. Furthermore, the date of creation is revealed on mouse hover, providing more specific chronological information where necessary.

This was very important to P8 who was applying a very loosely structured chronological approach, recording only the date of each page. P8's research was highly unstructured, engendering high degrees of uncertainty, and that was mirrored in the organization of his ELN:

"Everything I do is just exploratory. It's trying, 'oh, I wonder what will happen is I take this measurement or that measurement'... So it's a lot harder to keep a rigid structure of how you store everything... I don't really produce large amounts of data yet, I don't do systematic scans... When this experiment starts working, then it will be more systematic and you'll get a nice method of doing it."

Tagging Strategies

Tags were used to resolve a tension between organizing data by chronology and subject categories. OneNote's tagging functionality enables the user to tag their notes using a list of predefined tags or icons to which they can assign labels. While tags can be added at various levels of granularity, from individual sentences to paragraphs or entire pages, the majority of tags were added at the sentence level. Of the two participants who used tags, P2 was more prolific, creating a total of 21 different tags and applying them to over 200 objects within his ELN. Nearly half (45%) of tagged items were related to specific projects while just over a quarter (27%) referred to issues around laboratory equipment or computing. About 18% of tags were used to highlight key ideas and issues to return to and the remaining 10% were assigned to meetings or miscellaneous items.

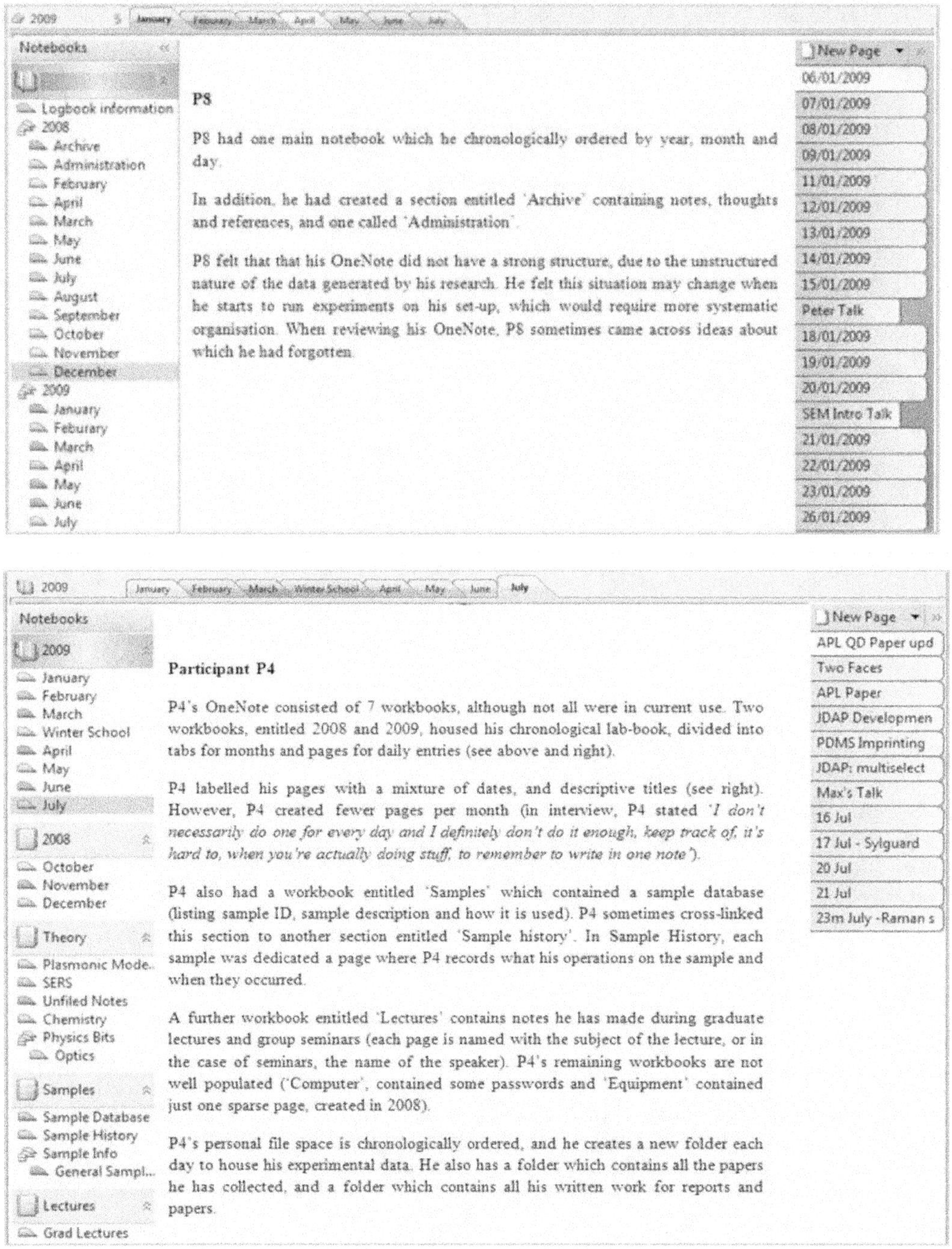

Figure 3: Examples of the chronological (top) and mixed chronological and topical organization of the ELN (bottom).

The high proportion of project tags tallies with P2's comments about his use of tags. He felt the need to split the chronological flow of records into projects categorization to help with revisitation after a longer time period, when the time based clues fade from his memory. While discussing his ELN structure, P2 stated:

"In OneNote one of the problems we have when you're doing it day by day if you're working in multiple projects its quite tough... I'll go back in time to last year when I was working on multiple projects... One of the problems you have is that you really don't know what, ... you know what you've done on a certain day, but you don't know when was the last time you were working on a certain type of project."

In the end, P2 was let down by the tag search features of OneNote which do not scale well nor offer sufficient options to filter results. Consequently, P2 had ceased to use tags except for the 'to do' tag to indicate required or planned actions.

P7's use of tags was quite different. He introduced them to increase the 'readability' of his lab notebook. Tags enable him to scan pages quickly and see what types of

Tag category	Tag name	Symbol	Applied
Actions	To do		500+
Highlighting / surfacing	Idea		23
	Important		140
	Question		32
	Critical		1
	Highlight		6
Contacts	Contacts		99
Other	Address		3
	Topic		1

Table 2: Tags applied by the participant P7.

information they contain (see Table 2). He used 9 different OneNote tags. Eight of these tags were applied in 305 instances. In two third (66%) of cases, the tags were used to highlight information such as research questions raised by the experiments, or to surface important details, such as password information. The remaining third (33%) designated contacts. The ninth, most frequent, was 'to do' tag, applied over 500 times to denote tasks and to keep track of progress.

Linking Strategies

Participants also used links to add structure to ELNs and connect to external resources. They created links to ELN pages, web pages, experimental data, local resources, and pages from another researcher's ELN. Table 3 shows the frequency and types of links included in OneNote by 6 participants. For each reviewed ELN we extracted and categorized all the links from OneNote pages. The analysis included OneNote sections with high concentrations of links, such as lists of links to material samples.

Half of the considered notebooks contained links within or between ELN pages. In the majority of instances, these links pointed to notes on previous experiments or operations relevant to the experiment currently being documented. This enabled researchers to reflect on previous relevant findings in the context of current research. In some instances, links were grouped and nested into tight clumps to pull together related information and provide an overview of a particular area. For example, P3 produced an ELN section entitled 'Summary' which, akin to bookmarks, contained a collection of links to key pages in the previous year. In the interview, P3 remarked that having a central access to these links saves him an effort of continually re-finding these important pages. This Summary page contained links to 36 ELN pages and 5 key data sets on the lab's servers.

P7 maintained an ELN section titled "Sample List" which contained a list of material samples that he had used in experiments. Each time P7 used a material sample, he

Area	Link to	P2	P3	P4	P5	P7	P8	Tot.
Web	Web info sources	17	13	2	6	4	4	**46**
	Web info on equip.	18	5	4	2		8	**37**
Samples	Samples list			52		20		**72**
Data	Raw data on server	12	23		3	10		**48**
	From other researcher		6					**6**
OneNote	Other pages	16	14			10		**40**
Meta-summary	Multiple pages		41					**41**
Shared resources	Manuals					2		**2**
	Shared document	11			1			**12**
	Scripts, commands					6		**6**
	Other's document				2			**2**
	Embedded program	6						**6**
Own docs	Locally stored PDF	1			1	6		**8**
	Own document	1	4					**5**
	Embedded Word doc	4	1					**5**
Summary	Own summary	5			1			**6**
	Other's summary	3						**3**
	Total	**94**	**107**	**58**	**16**	**58**	**12**	**358**

Table 3: Linking practices of six study participants.

created a link from the ELN record to the sample list and vice versa. This enabled him to keep track of all his activities related to a particular material sample.

The most frequently linked information sources within ELNs were webpages. Some links were auto-generated by OneNote when the participants pasted text or images from a Web site. Others were directly dropped from the Browser into the page by the user. Four participants created links between ELN pages and raw data such as data files, images, videos, etc., stored on the lab's servers. Linking to another researcher's ELN was rare; P3's ELN provided the only example of this.

Figure 4: A meeting setting where the shared ELN is shown on the large screen and accessed from the shared network drive. Participants can interact with the shared OneNote from their Tablet PCs.

Desire for Structure

While the participants already applied structure to record keeping through ELN using section tabs, tags, and links, they all wanted more means of structuring the data. Ability to pivot on specific entities or attributes was a desire consistently expressed by the participants. For example, due to inter-related nature of projects, material samples were often reused across projects, thus creating a natural association among experiments that shared the same sample but considered different aspects.

Each participant spoke of the wish to be able to access all the information related to a particular lab item, for example a specific material sample, and immediately gather all the information relevant to it—experiments that had been run with it, by whom, when, and with what results. The value of aggregating this information in meta-summaries was highly praised and widely supported amongst the participants.

Interestingly, the aspect of alternative representations and pivot views emerged in another context of the study. Reflecting on the flexibility of the ELN and the ease with which data may be moved within, P6 stated that the software negatively affected the diligence with which he kept his notebook and his overall attitude towards the ELN records that were meant to be comprehensive and fixed snapshots of the research process. In effect, the ELN's flexibility interfered with the lab notebook as an ongoing and stable chronicle of work and disturbed the intrinsic context which arises from it. When asked what may help to reinstate this context, P6 replied:

"I guess if each piece of information was related to something, so if someone saw this and immediately knew that this was linked to this experiment on this sample, then that would bring all the context you need basically, because if someone looks at this and has no idea what I was doing here.. But if this was linked to the experiment, the sample and the original data, then someone can completely make sense of it, you'd get all the context you need."

ELN use in collaborative scientific work

By observing lab activities, we identified how participants used the ELN during data collection, analysis and group interpretation of data. Here we illustrate the benefits and shortcomings of the adopted ELN in supporting collaborative work.

Management of collective information resources

The common practice was to create a shared OneNote workbook for each project. A project workbook contains the notes that the research leader P1 keeps for all meetings on behalf of the group members, plus the sections for collaborative activities, such as drafts of papers that were written as a group effort. The Plasmonics workbook, for example, also had sections for individual experiments, which had been part of an effort *to pool information by experiment across the group. However, these sections were not well populated and had become defunct. P8 explains some of the reasons for this:*

"I think we did try... a shared logbook for each experiment... It seems like a very good idea on paper but it didn't catch on. I think it's because people felt that they're writing all the information in their personal logbook then why is there a need to reproduce that information again just to write in the general logbook?"

Thus, while there was a collective desire to capture, as a team, all the information related to their experiment, the practicalities of recording information in two places proved too costly relative to the perceived benefit of individuals.

Group communication and feedback

Analysis of the group meetings and ELNs contents revealed that researchers used ELNs to collaborate synchronously and asynchronously with group members. Participants reported cases when they wished to gain rapid feedback on a particular analysis and had sent links to note pages to the research leader P1 who then made additional notes and annotations. This was easily facilitated since both the experiments and the ELNs are stored on the lab servers that are used as common computational resources. Coupled with the open access policy, this meant that the ELN pages become shared collaborative documents. They enable rapid circulation of information, improving the speed at which ideas are circulated and assistance and feedback are provided between a researcher and the lab leader. Similar ideas were promoted by the ELN architecture implemented by Talbot et al. [16].

A shared OneNote notebook was used for synchronous collaboration during group meetings. Tablets with ELNs and a large display for viewing the shared notebooks enabled efficient running of the meetings (Figure 4). All the participants had an opportunity to contribute to the meeting and share notes while updating their individual ELNs. The common ELN notes served as a record of discussions, conclusions, and plans for further actions. Participants used this resource to remind themselves of the tasks they needed to perform between meetings.

Group tagging and summarization

P4 described OneNote tags as being '*pretty useless... for what we want to do*', but felt that the notion of tagging could be highly beneficial to the collective organization of information and collaboration within the lab if correctly implemented. He felt that tagging would be best served through a '*central tag system*' which would support standardization in information management and, thus, efficient pooling of information. Reflecting on the usefulness of this, P4 stated that, when working with a new chemical or substance, he would like to see immediately who had worked on the chemical, what results they had derived, which experiments the chemical had been used in, etc. He felt that the time and date would also be important information to turn into tags since that information was relevant to the everyday work in the Centre.

Tagging could be a possible facilitator of meetings. We noted a recurrent desire for easy access to a summary of information related to an entity, e.g., a project, a process, and similar. All the participants stated that it would be beneficial to have a quick access to the entirety of information related to a particular item, for example a material sample used in the experiments. P4 spoke very clearly about this issue and wished to be able to access summaries for samples which pull together experimental results, prepared notes, images, people who had worked on it, relevant papers, associated projects, etc. This information could then be viewed on any of these pivots.

Alongside group level summaries, there was also a desire for 'personal' summaries. For example, P4 stated that he would like to have a daily summary of all the information he had used during a day:

"*What would be nice is something which helps bring all this together at the end of the day because we use lots of different machines in a day and lots of different programs and what would be nice is to have for One Note page which automatically collects things you've done.*"

DISCUSSION

We compare the observations of the ELNs created by NCR researchers with the design recommendations by Klokmose & Zander [3] that were based on the input from physicists. Table A, in the Appendix, provides details of the requirements that were relevant and fulfilled by the ELNs implemented at the NRC. In summary, most of the requirements related to interlinking, structuring, and aggregation of data, accessing and sharing of content, browsing, and history search were achieved through the adopted ELN. At the same time, the requirements for automation and control of instruments were not so prominent in the NRC lab. As noted in the previous sections, the NRC researchers dealt with very sensitive equipment that required careful manual calibration. Thus, automated calibration and control of parameters was not considered. However, the automation of data capture and generation of graphs were archived through the adoption of Igor software. Furthermore, the lack of the privacy concerns is an artifact of the NRC primary mission as a teaching research organization where knowledge sharing and collaboration is the key.

With regards to the observed practices, we compare them with the usage patterns of the Prism ELN which was designed and deployed by Tabard et al. [15] as a technology probe to investigate support for individual and collaborative work of biologists. In Table B (Appendix) we list the main aspects of the user practices in the Prism study and show how they relate to the observed behavior of the NRC researchers. Overall, the NRC researchers and the Prism users were supported in similar activities, from sharing, summarization, to review and reflection. While the Prism study participants practiced conformant data entries in the paper form, such requirements were not imposed in the NRC case. In fact, the researchers were encouraged to set exploratory experiments as they are inspired, without being constrained by formal planning and recording of the experiments. This practice was supported by the facilities to capture experiment data and metadata automatically or copy them easily into the notebooks from other software.

Two aspects that were not mentioned in the requirements from Klokmose & Zandar [3] and Tabard et al. [15] pertain to the exploitation of semantics and pro-active exposure of data by the system, both of which were articulated by the NRC study participants. In their work Talbot et al. [16] explore integration of ELN with SAM, a layered set of components and services for managing annotations and semantic relationships between data. NRC researchers, on the other hand, repeatedly expressed the desire for tools to drill and slice through the space of topics, projects, ideas, and experiments. At the moment, the search support is restricted to OneNote's keyword and tag search and desktop search.

Furthermore, Sarini et al. [11] propose to capture work patterns and provide suggestions during scientists' work, to lead them towards the fulfillment of their goals. Researchers at NRC did not express a need for automated guidance. They acquire their skills through communication with peers and the professor. However, they expressed a desire for a system that recommends relevant documents, experiments, data, and material samples as they use the ELN and other applications to plan, analyze, and summarize experiments.

RECOMMENDATIONS

The observed workarounds and expressed needs of the participants emphasize several fundamental issues of ELNs, some of which were hinted in the requirements and recommendations of previous studies but fully revealed in the practices of NRC. The very flexibility of the digital media raises concerns and calls for design considerations to

- Achieve a level of expected fixity of the digital records and consistency in practice.
- Support transitions in the organization of the project records over time as the role and activities of scientists evolve
- Enable integration of multiple ELNs with potentially diverse organizational structures.

The last two points speak eloquently to the conflicting requirements that arise in practice. They demonstrate the need to balance the support for diversity that is essential to achieve productivity of individuals in the team and the support for uniform and integrated view of the collective work that enables collaboration. We here reflect on techniques and design principles that could be suitable to achieve the outlined objectives.

Fixity vs. flexibility of the digital records and practices. Flexibility and fluidity are the assets of the digital media. However, the practice shows that in content organization, they can cause disconnect between the individual preference and needs and the institutional policies for record keeping that aim to ensure long term value to the team. In practice, that is reflected through rather simple and apparently inconsequential features, such as the ability to rename records and add information at a later time. However, this has a knock of effect by leading to much less thought and commitment to precision during record keeping. The consequences are often not foreseeable or fully appreciated at the time. This may need to be addresses with features and practices that go beyond the simple management of the edit history. It may require the ability to "freeze" specific views of the record so that they can be replicated at any time with full authenticity. The use of templates and data entry prompts, as suggested by Schraefel et al. [12], could be useful in counteracting the lack of diligence that some users felt arose from the use of the digital medium. Most of the commercial products, in fact, offer capabilities for creating data entry templates, with compliance enforcement, and devising workflow support to streamline the practices.

Evolving and heterogeneous structures vs. unified views. The study revealed different approaches to content organization across individuals and a practice of changing the organizational structure of the captured content over time. This was illustrated through the tension between topical and chronological record keeping and through the observed use of tagging and linking among ELN pages to support access to relevant information.

Making an up-front decision about the content organization is difficult in its own right. But, the situation is far more complex. The nature of the work changes over time, e.g., from initial experiments where chronological records may be suitable, to aggregation of findings where maintaining topical records is more natural. Early stages of research may require participants to work in unstructured ways, which may benefit from more open ended 'thinking spaces'. Similar conclusions were arrived by observing the use of 'master lab notebook' in the deployment of Prism by Tabard et al. [15]. Thus, the organization needs to change over time and it is of critical importance to provide flexibility in restructuring the content.

In order to fully embrace this diversity we recommend enhancing the ELNs with technologies that can deal with unstructured and multi-structured data. The ELN environments need to incorporate automatic or semi-automatic features that are supported by sophisticated technologies from text mining, natural language processing, information retrieval, schema integration, and similar in order to extract relevant entities and relations from the ELNs content. The extracted structure can be then be used by various applications and services to provide flexible search and pivot views.

CONCLUDING REMARKS

Through a detailed observation study, we arrive at insights into practices that naturally emerged around the ELN system adopted by a scientific research laboratory. Our work provided the means of comparing commercially available and prototype systems that were subjects of previous studies and the ELNs adopted by the NRC as fully operational and essential for the scientific work. Based on the workarounds and needs of the study participants, we expanded the set of requirements and design guidelines to mediate seamlessly conflicting aspects that arise from the digital nature of ELNs: the flexibility, fluidity, and low threshold for modifying digital records and the requirements for persistence and consistency. Addressing these issues is critical. That was reflected in a number of related requirements, including the migration of the content structure and providing alternative views to support specific analysis through pivoting, filtering, and aggregation. We suggest that this apparent tension can be mediated through the use of sophisticated digital technologies to deal with unstructured data and, thus, reconcile the need for both the personalization of record keeping practices and the conformity to enable collaborative work.

While our study is limited to the observation of a single research laboratory, we expect that our findings will inform future situated research of ELNs and expand the scope of inquiry to practices that emerge across various scientific domains as a result of ELN adoption.

ACKNOWLEDGMENTS

We thank Professor Jeremy Baumberg, Director of the Nanophotonics Centre at the University of Cambridge, England, and his team of researchers for their invaluable input and generous help with conducting the study.

REFERENCES

1. Borriello, G., Consolvo, S., and Su, J., Labscape: A Smart Environment for the Cell Biology Laboratory, *Intel Research Tech. Report*, IRS-TR-02-016, (2002).
2. Iyer, R. and Kudrle, W. Implementation of an Electronic Lab Notebook to Integrate Research and Education in an Undergraduate Biotechnology Program. *Technology Interface Int. J.* 12 2, (2012).
3. Klokmose, C. N. and Zander, P.O. Rethinking Laboratory Notebooks. In *Proc. Int. Conf. on Cooperative Systems* (2010).
4. Latour, B. and Woolgar, S. *Laboratory Life: The Construction of Scientific Facts*, Princeton University Press, (1979, 1986).
5. Lynch, M. *Art and artifact in laboratory science: A study of shop work and shop talk in a research laboratory*, Routledge and Kegan Paul (1985).
6. Oleksik, G., Milic-Frayling, N., and Jones, R. Beyond data sharing: artifact ecology of a collaborative nanophotonics research centre. In *Proc. of CSCW 2012*. ACM Press (2012), 1165-1174.
7. Mackay, W. E., Pothier, G., Letondal, C., Begh, K. and Srensen, H. E. The Missing Link: Augmenting Biology Laboratory Notebooks. In *Proc. UIST 2002*. ACM Press (2002), 41-50.
8. Miles, M. B., and Huberman, M. A. Qualitative Data Analysis, Second Edition. *SAGE,* (1994).
9. Rajarao, J. and Weiss S. Using E-WorkBook Suite to implement quality control in real time: expanding the role of electronic laboratory notebooks within a bioanalysis laboratory. *Bioanalysis* 3, 13, (2011), 1513-1519.
10. Rubacha M, Rattan A. K. and Hosselet S.C. A review of electronic laboratory notebooks available in the market today. *J. Lab Automation* 16, 1, (2010) 90–98.
11. Sarini, M., Blanzieri, E., Giorgini, P. and Moser, C. From actions to suggestions: Supporting the work of biologists through laboratory notebooks. In *Proc. Int. Conf. on Design of Cooperative Systems*, (COOP2004), (2004), 131-146.
12. Schraefel, M. C., Hughes, V. G., Mills H. R., Smith, G., Payne, R. T. and Frey, J G. Breaking the book: translating the chemistry lab book into a pervasive computing lab environment. In *Proc. CHI 2004*, ACM Press (2004), 25-32.
13. SCRIP-SAFE, PatentPad. http://www.scrip-safe.com/laboratory_notebooks.htm.
14. Silverstone, R. and Haddon, L. Design and the Domestication of ICTs: Technical Change and Everyday Life. In Silverstone, R. and Mansell, R (eds), *Communication by Design. The Politics of Information and Comm. Tech.*, Oxford Univ. Press (1996).
15. Tabard, A., Eastmond, E., and Mackay, W. E. From Individual to Collaborative: The Evolution of Prism, a Hybrid Laboratory Notebook. In *Proc. CSCW 2008*, ACM Press (2008), 569-578.
16. Talbott, T., Peterson, M., Schwidder, J., Myers, J.D. Adapting the electronic laboratory notebook for the semantic era. In *Proc. Int. Symp. on Collaborative Tech. and Systems,* (2005), 136-143.
17. Yeh, R., Liao, C., Klemmer, S., Guimbretière, F., Lee, B., Kakaradov, B., Stamberger, J., Paepcke, A. ButterflyNet: a mobile capture and access system for field biology research. In *Proc. SIGCHI 2006,* ACM Press (2006), 571-580.
18. Zeng, J., Hillman, M. and Arnold, M. Impact of the implementation of a well-designed electronic laboratory notebook on bioanalytical laboratory function. *Bioanalysis* 3, 13, (2011), 1501-1511.

APPENDIX

VISION OF FUTURE ELN (Klokmose & Zander, 2010)

Aim: Laboratory notebook system to support fusion of documentation, equipment control and data analysis in the same user interface.

Broken work cycle is a consequence of using the paper-based laboratory notebook together with computer applications for data collection and analysis.

CONFIGURATION		**NRC**
Automatic logging	Notebook should be configurable to document relevant information automatically and to support (or force) the researchers to document what had to be observed manually.	YES
Automatic pre-analysis of data	Produce intermediate graphs from data directly in the notebook.	N/A

ORGANIZATION		**NRC**
Interlinked data	Support structures that resemble Wiki, where all data could be interlinked. Abandon the forced chronology of the bound notebooks and have something that resembles the loose-leaf system.	YES
INTERACTION		**NRC**
Access and sharing	Access to notebook by multiple people from multiple devices – including mobile devices.	YES
Natural interaction	Multi-modal interaction and support for handwriting	YES
ARCHITECTURE		**NRC**
Common programming assets	Instruments and governors—interaction logic and application logic—could easily be programmed and shared. Support for programming through dynamic scripting language or visual programming language to enable automation of simple tasks.	N/A
Automation	Collecting and processing data in the laboratory notebook could be handled through data-flow programming. Should be able to continuously work from configuring data collection and data analysis to configuring governors to translate the data into publication quality figures and graph in the documentation part of the notebook environment.	YES
Instrumental interaction	Software architecture that enables ubiquitous instrumental interaction where there is no distinction between object for documentation (text and graphics) and objects for control (widgets). E.g., to document the angle of a laser, copy the control widget into the documentation part of the laboratory notebook and potentially use these objects to re-load the settings.	N/A
Cross platform use of ENL	Bring parts of the laboratory notebook interface to mobile devices, e.g., PDA.	N/A
DATA FLOW SUPPORT		**NRC**
Summaries	System should support either manual or automatic generation of summary pages that could be loaded on an interactive whiteboard in the meeting room.	YES
Structure	Structure, categorize, and access entries in ELN in multiple ways, e.g., by activity, chronology, or particular piece of equipment.	YES
Privacy	Support personal version of entries, where notes and annotations are not intended to be read by others, but could be made public through interaction with a simple instrument.	N/A
Forms for data input	Support for generating templates comprising fields and layout for documentation, comments, etc., that could include controls relevant for a given experiment.	N/A
History	Enable browsing the editing history (without cluttering the interface). History backed up in a secure way.	YES
Access to related content & controls	Hypermedia ways of clicking content to see associated data and controls.	YES
Aggregation	Need to support integration of digital content and data in different formats. Special facilities may be needed to enable integration or imbedding.	YES

Table A: Comparison of the recommendations for ELN by the physics scientists and the properties of the OneNote ELNs in use by the NRC scientists.

PRISM (Tabard et al., 2008)	
Aim: Support evolving work practices that involve paper and electronic lab notebooks. Support biologists in integrating activity streams and sharing information with colleagues. **NRC:** All the research assets are in the digital form, except for the material samples used in the Lab. There is no use and no concern about paper artifacts.	
SHARING	
Time factor	Two types of sharing: (1) over time, to preserve traces of activity for successors and (2) among colleagues, to share acquired knowledge and knowhow. **NRC:** Sharing among colleagues is achieved through open access to ELNs and regular meetings and presentations of findings. Projects level ELNs, created and curated by the professor, support archiving and preservation of knowledge.
Control	Adaptable information sharing. A fine grain control over what is shared, with whom, and when. **NRC:** n/a
Access	Enabling Prism for the Web made it into a central notification point, and the means of reciprocal sharing of bibliographic references and calendar events with each other. **NRC:** Shared OneNote ELNs support real time and asynchronous collaboration. Email is used for communication and calendar.
ORGANIZATION	
Common vocabulary	Development of the common vocabulary to support future reflection on work. Common tags: to do, important, and done; color coded content surrounded activities within the notebook and added meta-notes to comment on and synthesize existing notes. **NRC:** Common tags and annotations in OneNote facilitate planning and distribution of work.
Access and sharing	Access to notebook by multiple people from multiple devices—including mobile devices. **NRC**: The Center practices an open data access policy. All the data is stored on networked desktop PCs, Tablet PCs, and servers.
Dynamic organization	Organize data dynamically—mark things to do, develop, copy or move depending on what is done. **NRC**: OneNote ELN provided flexibility for adding new pages as the researcher decided to investigate a new direction. Re-assembling information can be easily done through copy&paste.
OVERVIEWS AND REFLECTIONS	
Master Lab Notebooks	All the participants created reference points, or master notebook, to organize the diverse strands of their personal activity. **NRC:** Summary and overview pages were used by a number of participants. The professor created master documents for projects that involve multiple team members.
Review and reflection	Prism enables review of information from diverse sources and comment on it, providing a series of ongoing reflections over time. **NRC:** OneNote ELN enables hybrid content to be collected and viewed within pages, allowing for annotations and comments.
Redundancy	Prism users welcome redundancy as a resource of reflection is welcome. Redundant information helps to reflect creatively about previous activities. Re-appearance of the item, in a different form means it is important. **NRC**: At NRC, redundancy in observations of the same phenomena is perceived as important signal for discovery. Redundancy in repeated experiments was undesirable if done because the students were not aware of each other's work.

Table B: Comparison of the recommendations for ELN by the physics scientists and the properties of the OneNote ELNs in use by the NRC scientists.

Reconciling Rhythms: Plans and Temporal Alignment in Collaborative Scientific Work

Stephanie B. Steinhardt
Department of Communication
Cornell University
sbg94@cornell.edu

Steven J. Jackson
Information Science
Cornell University
sjj54@cornell.edu

ABSTRACT
Plans and planning assume a central role and challenge of collaborative scientific work, bridging and coordinating often discordant rhythms and events emanating from the organizational, infrastructural, biographical and phenomenal dimensions of collaborative life. Plans align rhythms embedded in local practice with those operating at larger institutional levels, and establish shared temporal baselines around which local choice and action may be calibrated. This paper develops these arguments through ethnographic study of the Ocean Observatories Initiative, a prominent U.S.-based large-scale long-term collaborative research program in the ocean sciences. We emphasize the intersection between rhythms and plans at two crucial moments: formation ('plans-in-the-making'), and enactment ('plans-in-action') across complex fields of practice. Our findings hold important implications for CSCW research and practice around scientific and large-scale collaborative efforts, and for federal science policies meant to support productive forms of cooperation and discovery.

Author Keywords
Science, collaboration, policy, collaborative tools, cyberinfrastructure, rhythm, temporal factors.

ACM Classification Keywords
H.m. Miscellaneous.

I. INTRODUCTION
A growing body of CSCW work has advanced the proposition that "time matters" in the study of distributed collective practice in scientific and other workplace settings [8, 16, 23, 24]. From the micro level of an experiment's run time in the laboratory to the macro level of grant deadlines at a funding agency, aligning the heterogeneous forms of time that structure and constitute distributed work activities represents a central and arguably growing challenge of effective collaboration in the sciences – and undoubtedly many other sites of distributed collective practice.

CSCW'14, February 15–19, 2014, Baltimore, Maryland, USA.

http://dx.doi.org/10.1145/2531602.2531736

From the standpoint of understanding the real world of collaborative work, time is both an unwieldy abstraction and a tough object of study. While chronologies, schedules and timelines are powerful tools we regularly employ, and the design of specific time-management artifacts has attracted the periodic interest of CSCW scholars [18, 22, 33], explicit attention to temporality as such often fades into the background, in our work both as researchers and as practical actors in the world. Because of this, we often recognize it only in the breech: at moments when conflict between discrepant temporal orders is brought to (painful!) awareness through breakdowns in expectation and action that may delay or derail larger collaborative efforts. For this reason, with some important exceptions treated below, understandings of time in collaborative practice and CSCW scholarship occupies an important hole or lacuna at the center of the field, at once centrally present and conspicuously absent: or to paraphrase Coleridge's ancient mariner, "time, time, everywhere, and ne'er a drop to drink" [4, 13].

Our own way into this problem is through the language of "rhythms": roughly, the temporal patterns and regularities that stem from and in turn help to frame and support ongoing forms of action in the world. From the standpoint of large-scale distributed work in the sciences, rhythms have a number of important roles to play. Rhythms support regularities of practice, allowing work to unfold in predictable and routinized ways across spatially and temporally distributed sites. Rhythms establish structures of convention and expectation, allowing actors to mesh and coordinate otherwise disparate temporal flows. And rhythms organize time itself, ensuring that the temporal forces that shape and frame our working (and indeed personal) lives come to us in some form of navigable order. In all these ways, rhythms are 'circumstantial' to collaborative action in the sciences, in philosopher Michel Serres' [30] quite literal usage of the term: that which 'stands around', supporting and giving structure to flows of human activity in the world.

But rhythms – especially at their points of intersection – can just as often *fail*, limiting or derailing rather than supporting the cooperative flow of scientific life. Rhythms emanating from the biographical or organizational spheres may contradict those found in the infrastructure or the natural world. Rhythms at local levels of practice may fail to mesh with those emanating from larger scales and institutions. Rhythms may intersect in unpredictable ways with events: single-point occurrences that can accelerate or retard, disrupt or redirect, and sometimes set in motion new kinds of rhythm. The sheer variability in these results calls attention to the active and strategic quality of human interactions with the forms of time we engage. To echo a point suggested by Orlikowski and Yates [21], while we work in and through time, we also work *on* it: bending its structures and flows to accommodate the activities we set for ourselves (and others) in the world, while amending our actions to coordinate with temporal forms and structures coming to us as given or "found" (a category that may certainly include the structures and flows that other strategic actors seek to promote, but also the forms of time we find encoded in the built and natural worlds around us). Such forms of "alignment" work [16] constitute central and under-theorized elements within the coordination of collaborative work and life more generally.

Within this work, plans and planning take on special role and importance. Plans and planning (and its associated artifacts and practices) are a key moment or technology of alignment work. Plans bridge and coordinate rhythms and events emanating from the organizational, infrastructural, biographical and phenomenal dimensions of collaborative scientific life. Plans gather and align rhythms across scale, linking temporalities embedded in local practice with those operating at larger institutional levels. And plans establish shared temporal baselines around and against which local choice and action may be calibrated.

This paper extends recent CSCW approaches to the study of large-scale collaborative science in three ways. First, we link the two literatures of planning and of time to demonstrate a gap in our understanding of rhythm as an object of study. We begin by connecting collaboration studies literatures that have previously placed time and rhythm in the margins and draw this together with literature on plans and planning.

Second, we establish plans as an important site for unearthing practices of temporal alignment and identifying discordant rhythms. Following the seminal work by Suchman [31] and colleagues in other contexts, we explore how plans are actively deployed, negotiated, enforced, and adjusted as a site or mechanism of temporal alignment within the complex and 'heterochronic' (many-timed) worlds of large-scale collaborative science today.

Lastly, we demonstrate the ways in which rhythm emanates from both top-down and bottom-up scales of influence, where both directions are shaping and shaped by formalized plans. We explore how plans and planning gather and align separate rhythms at scales ranging from the small to the large and mediate between the temporalities embedded in local practices and those emanating from larger institutions of science planning and policy (e.g., NSF and Congress).

Through empirical examples of plans in-the-making and plans-in-action we detail how a large U.S. research network, the Ocean Observatories Initiative (OOI), moved into and through a planning process imposed by the U.S. National Science Foundation (NSF). Drawing from ethnographic field research within the OOI and other time-series oceanographic research initiatives, we identify forms of alignment work that attempt to reconcile conflicts in rhythms through plans and planning. We conclude with implications for research, design and policy.

II. LITERATURE REVIEW

II.A. TIME & RHYTHM

CSCW has long considered the design and use of specific collaborative artifacts with affordances that draw awareness to time, such as systems built for temporal orientation, reminders, archiving events and reflecting on activity patterns [2, 7, 17, 22, 33, 34]. This work often conceives of time as a discrete object that can be captured, represented, and designed around (e.g. as timeline [34] or trace history [25]). While these studies depict time as a depersonalized, divisible object within a design frame, others have adopted a more embedded approach, exploring time as it is experienced by individual users or as reflected and enacted through organizational form and practice. This body of work has included attention to time-sensitiveness and synchronicity, with special interest in the way that temporal factors may shape collaboration through verbal communication [17] or interaction with electronic information spaces [2, 7, 23]. Others have investigated the relationship between synchronous and asynchronous work, often with focus on a particular built environment and its affordances [3, 11, 35]. Still others have explored the design of information tools that are used to coordinate temporal structures and the mobile, changing nature of rhythm [20, 23].

Such artifact- or design-centered approaches are broadly paralleled by a wider reassessment of time currently underway within the social sciences more generally. Sociologist Eviatar Zerubavel has explored the significance of time as a neglected parameter of social life, arguing that social phenomena from institutions like hospitals [38] and monasteries [39] to revolutionary movements and religious communities [37] are best understood as "sociotemporal orders," established through carefully produced temporal regularities which constitute the foundation of collective action, meaning, and identity. Central to Zerubavel's account are the key temporal artifacts of schedules and calendars, and their role in bringing the potentially infinite sprawl and diversity of time into more coherent and collectively shared regularities.

Writing from an organizational science perspective, Orlikowski and Yates [21] have argued that social science approaches have tended to represent time in one of two ways: either as a subjective and socially-constructed abstraction (e.g. time-sensitiveness, synchronicity) or as an objective and substantive form existing outside of human action (e.g. clock time, age). Orlikowski and Yates seek to reconcile these perspectives through the language of 'temporal structuring', arguing that the temporal dimensions of organizational life are best approached as a process both shaped by and shaping of human actions. For example, when a team of programmers works toward releasing their application by a collectively established deadline, they reify calendar-time, imbuing a specific date with meaning. Yet, the deadline is subject to contingency and the same meaning could be reorganized around another date, time, or phenomena. The authors offer 'temporal structuring' as the social process that establishes and reinforces the temporal rhythms that shape ongoing practice. Im et. al. [12] extends this analysis to the assemblage of tools and communication strategies for aligning temporal structures, which provides understanding of the social problems of coordination. Collective action requires the alignment of rhythms in order to develop standards, routines, and associations of human action and calendar time.

Complementing this blended understanding of our interactions with time, Jackson et. al. [16] identify "collaborative rhythms" as evolving, durable, and active *objects* of collective life (p. 252). Rhythms establish temporal structures within our social lives, often fixed or recurring as part of convention like calendar time, seasons, deadlines, and holidays [37]. Rhythms can be episodic, tied to specific events, or emanate from complex and long-term factors like climate change.

The authors provide a heuristic to map collaborative rhythms to ongoing forms of work and agency. Organizational rhythms are regularities within institutional forms found in academic calendars or the grant review process. Biographical rhythms emanate from the flows of human life, including identity and role shifting, or changing relationships emanating from life events such as death and disease. Phenomenal rhythms emanate from an event such as a tsunami or earthquake. And rhythms can be infrastructural, emanating from the built environment (e.g., timelines of maintenance and decline associated with legacy systems of scientific equipment). Rhythms can represent hybridizations of these categories, and intertwine in variable and complex ways. And they can also conflict: for example, when an instrument deployment is scheduled for a date conflicting with a lead scientist's tenure review, organizational and infrastructural rhythms may be prioritized over the biographical rhythm of the scientist's ascension from associate to full professorship. The manner in which such tensions are resolved may be deeply embedded in the structures of authority that govern collaborative life: or as Jackson et. al. argue, "the question of which rhythms are adjusted to which (and *whose* rhythms to *whose*) turns out to be an important site for the exercise of power and control" [16].

The language of rhythm provides a vocabulary to describe some of the central temporal processes and challenges at the root of cooperative work. The authors demonstrate that discrepant rhythms are brought into coherence through many under-recognized forms of alignment work in a creative process of temporal alignment that requires efforts to bend pre-existing structures to fit environmental and collaborator needs into one reconciled trajectory. Collaborators reorganize resources, schedules and priorities; build or reorient instruments and facilities; shift their personal time and trajectories. Rhythm provides a structure to capture temporal factors as well as conflicts of a dynamic and complex nature, but leaves very few indications of its existence. However, many technologies and documentations act as archives of collaborative work (calendars, trace histories, edit logs, version control systems) that unmask new opportunities for identifying rhythms. In the following section, we emphasize the unique central role of plans as one technology for identifying rhythms and practices which reconcile conflicts of rhythm.

II.B. PLANS & PLANNING

An important contribution to the understanding of plans comes from ethnomethodological traditions within sociology and CSCW scholarship. These studies consider the role of plans as resources in (rather than mechanical executors in) coordinating work. Within these works plans can mean any structured or informal delineation of a set of temporally organized actions poised to achieve a goal. Our investigation focuses on the relationship between formalized plans and local culture.

In particular, Suchman's canonical research [32] offers the flagship example of this perspective; she defines "plans and situated actions" to argue against the formalist fallacy in which sequential tasks delineated within plans invoke a specific, determined set of sequential actions. She removes any fully determinative relation between plans and action and power vis-à-vis worlds of situated practice. Suchman instead emphasizes the blended quality of plans and situated action, providing a better account of how plans and planning meet the real world of practice.

In consonance with Suchman's theories on planning, Scott [26] provides powerful examples of the kind of error (and hubris!) that formalist approaches to plans and planning can lead us to. Scott's examples emphasize the relationship between plans and local circumstances, particularly of plans enacted *without* reference to local circumstances and the significant losses resulting from those top-down infrastructural changes. Scott's examples are drawn largely from state attempts to silo dynamic or nomadic populations, such as Le Corbusier's geometrically standardized cities, Stalin's Soviet collectivization and the Tanzanian "forced villagization." The plans within Scott's stories were developed without acknowledging the ongoing problems in the realities of implementation, shifting markets, labor economies, weather and soil, regimentation and collectivization. The failed attempts of Lenin to categorize and control without regard to the social and cultural standings of the people under that control, alongside the failed attempts of Tanzania to restrict nomadic populations to specific geometries, teach us that plans are subject to local human change and are not controllers of local human action themselves.

Scott draws on the notion of "metis" to describe forms of knowledge that are different from and in some sense in opposition to the models of top-down planning by Stalin and Tanzania. Metis is the "deep knowledge" that allows local people to respond to the complexities in their environment. Scott employs metis to explain that the state's success measures for a plan can overlook the negative effects on local culture. This discrepancy between local customs and state concerns can lead to economic and social failure as well as individual psychological harm, diminishing the self-perceived value of those who work within its constraints. For these reasons, Scott asserts that plans need to be flexible enough to react to local human change, adopt contingency, and provide room for emergence.

In Suchman's conception, in the real world, plans provide a structure that guides the continued actions of an organization, but are not strictly adhered to, blindly acted upon, or necessarily sequential. Plans are representative of a rational course of action and common practices and procedures, which are subsumed by the more organic, emergent and ad hoc world. Suchman's argument relocates the locus of control in purposeful human action, not in formalized procedures. Much of the mutual adjustment between plans and local culture may in fact have to do with the way in which plans and planning, as a temporal process or artifact, meet the real-world process of collaborative activity, including the different and potentially discordant rhythms embedded in specific features of the local collaborative landscape or situational context.

Suchman reveals the same kind of give and take found within Scott's accounts. According to Suchman, plans aid in making sense of these aforementioned complexities in the transient nature of cooperative work. Suchman characterizes plans as rhetorical devices for representing action and language, in the form of documentation and conversation. In this way, plans leave an identifiable trace of how collaborators perceived time, and are a resource for decision-making around actions. She describes plans as providing a pathway that offers a sense of stability as emergent changes become explicit. Garfinkel [9] similarly identifies that our tacit use of documentary method (such as generating plans) allows us to find standards, uniformities, and patterns that provide shared understanding of complex actions.

According to Suchman's characterization, plans are carried out through a blending of local circumstances, the internal common sense and knowledge of the actor, and interactions with the material world. Suchman offers that plans are interpreted in situ, where both the local circumstances within which they are to be enacted and an application of local knowledge (not literalistic following of the plan) are necessary to respond to unforeseen changes and adapt appropriately.

Across these literatures, plans are sites of negotiation. Plans represent the top-down decisions and assumptions of the stakeholders involved in the achievement of a goal that is also often also imposed from the top-down. Plans dictate the project goals, value and scope to its constituents, assign relations between resources and responsible parties, and provide a baseline of expectation during its execution via deadlines and deliverables. Once established, plans act as a standard for execution and control, often identifying protocols and hierarchical structures related to the achievement of tasks in pursuit of the goal.

But as Suchman and Scott also emphasize, plans may function as *resources* and sites of *negotiation*, places where disparate interests and understandings are brought together. As per Suchman and Scott, no matter the level of detail, plans are always incomplete and fail to reflect the depth and diversity of the worlds they attempt to put in order. Therefore, other forms of knowledge and action (Scott's metis, or Suchman's situated action) are always threatening to push through, disrupt, and reorient the plan.

Viewed historically, these separate literatures around timing and planning, rhythms and the plan, have made important contributions to CSCW research and practice. Attention to the multiple and often discrepant dynamics of time and rhythm have shed new light on an area of complexity and frequent tension in the design and deployment of CSCW systems. The work that actors do to overcome, work around, and calibrate action across the multiplicity of rhythms embedded in the worlds around them (named here as "alignment work") also constitutes an important and under-recognized element within broader CSCW processes of "articulation" [31] and "coordination" [27] work. For their part, CSCW literatures on plans and planning (including the seminal work of Suchman and colleagues at Xerox PARC) have produced richer and more satisfying accounts of how the formalism of plans meets the contingencies and resistances of "situated practice," with implications for the (in)sufficiency of plans and planning as a final guide or arbiter of collective action. This in turn has opened up new recognition around the modes of action available to participants in collaborative efforts, adding languages like bricolage, contingency, and improvisation to CSCW's arsenal of terms.

We argue that these insights gain additional force and clarity when put together, and that their connections have yet to be fully explored within CSCW scholarship. From this perspective, plans stand as agents of temporal alignment *par excellence*, gathering and aligning separate rhythms at scales ranging from the small to the large, and mediating between temporalities embedded in local forms of practice and those emanating from larger institutions of planning and policy. Plans call attention to (or sometimes render invisible) specific temporal conflicts that may directly impact the timing and completion of work. And plans establish common baselines of expectation around and against which local choice and action (including around the dispensation of local times and rhythms) can unfold. In the sections that follow we work out these arguments by reference to a case of considerable complexity and importance: the forms of planning and temporal alignment endemic to large-scale infrastructure development in the ocean sciences today.

III. RHYTHM, PLANS AND LARGE-SCALE SCIENCE

Growing investments in scientific infrastructure have increased pressure on policymakers and researchers alike to understand how to design, operate and maintain large-scale, long-term, and multidisciplinary scientific collaborations. Synthesizing these broader shifts, in 2003 the U.S. National Science Foundation published a blue ribbon panel report, "Revolutionizing Science and Engineering Through Cyberinfrastructure," which pointed to growing computational investments in the sciences as leading to a "new age" of science and engineering, marked by the growing complexity and scope of grand challenge scientific questions; the hardware, software and organizational capabilities centered around new scientific tools and methodologies; and new modes of high performance computing providing distributed knowledge across cultures, disciplines, and nations. Since the mid-1990s, investments in large-scale science and technology development from the NSF have been funded through a separate funding category called the Major Research and Facilities Competition (MREFC) account, intended to carry the weight of large-scale infrastructure builds that exceed the budgetary capacity of any single disciplinary line.

The high level of MREFC cost is matched with a proportionately high level of scrutiny, imposing a cascade of plans including a layered timeline and series of planning documentation. The five-year MREFC planning process prepares the champions of the initiative to tackle questions of scope and scale, solidify the science and technology requirements, and mobilize resources. This includes risk and contingency plans in order to prepare for the construction of the facilities.

And such formal planning processes represent just the tip of the iceberg. Subtending the list of formal MREFC requirements noted above are a wide variety of other planning activities – for example, individual investigators reorienting their research program, graduate students selecting their dissertation projects, and vendors positioning themselves for contracts – that are interwoven into large-scale scientific collaboration.

Our empirical work moving forward centers around one such NSF MREFC, the Ocean Observatories Initiative (OOI). In the case of the OOI, as well as other MREFC winners, its conscientious planning and documentation serves as passageway into the forms of alignment that reconcile the many rhythms of ocean science. We performed fieldwork at laboratories affiliated with the OOI at Woods Hole Oceanographic Institute, University of California San Diego, Rutgers University, Oregon State University, and University of Washington as well as unaffiliated offices in New Jersey and at Cornell University. We toured laboratories as well as both formal and informal workspaces (offices, conference rooms, docks, and museum spaces), capturing photographs and writing field notes as well as recording audio of our participants' presentations of each instrument and space. We conducted 31 in-person (23) and remote (8) semi-structured interviews with interview length between one and two hours. Interview questions centered on the kinds of work that led each participant to the OOI; the kinds of work they perform in their current roles; their involvement in OOI planning processes to date; and key temporal patterns and conflicts that affect their current work. We also traced and analyzed the informal and formal planning left within the iterations of documentation as the OOI came to be. We additionally mapped U.S. science policies around oceanographic research against OOI timelines and schedules, and further contextualized the OOI through histories of oceanography and time-series research found in the oceanography, science policy, and history of science literatures. On the basis of this data, and following grounded theory principles first established by Strauss and Glaser [6, 10] we developed memos around emergent themes (including around the themes of rhythm and planning explored here), which fed in turn into the ongoing course of the fieldwork. Memos were then written up into more substantive texts and findings that eventually fed into the text of this paper. The following sections report on this empirical work and develop arguments around the complex relationship between rhythms and planning as a key facet and complication of scientific collaboration and infrastructure development in the oceanographic research community.

III.A. PLANS IN-THE-MAKING

Historians often trace the rise of modern oceanography to a period during and immediately following World War II. While the U.S. Navy has a long history of supporting deep water and oceanographic scientific research, military patronage during wartime increased in volume significantly and helped to define the role of oceanography as a critical interest of the state. The practice of ocean science became inextricably linked to the operations of national military concerns, moving with changes in the political climate. This role was solidified with critical research expeditions in Bikini Island and Guantanamo Bay [19] where underwater sonar and acoustics were employed as powerful tools for submarine discovery and amphibious warfare.

In postwar oceanography, research was typically carried out through short-term soft money grants funded by the Navy where a single investigator or small research team would drop an instrument they had built into water off of a research vessel. The principal investigator or small team would then analyze and publish on the data collected by the instrument, largely structured by the rhythms of the academic calendar, tenure process and publication deadlines. In some cases these research teams would set sail multiple times, generally offset by 6 months to a full year between cruises. This period of oceanographic work was structured and determined by the time it took to develop, test and evaluate tools; determine areas of interest in which to position and deploy the tools; Navy ship availability and sponsoring; crew availability; fisherman and fishery involvement in the area; and phenomenal events in nature. This form of research only captured a series of snapshots about that area of water, often within a multi-week period. While critical to the understanding of Earth processes, only by luck would a configuration like this happen upon a hydrothermal vent or volcanic activity on the seafloor, as these events are unpredictable and difficult to capture.

In the late 1980s and early 1990s, growing concerns around the contributions of oceanic processes to wider processes of climate change sparked new interest and attention to the long-term coordination of ocean research. This period also marked a dissipation of the longstanding relationship between oceanographic research and the Navy. Visionaries in oceanography began to hold NSF-funded (not Navy-funded) symposiums to identify approaches to collecting data that would overcome previously held issues of transience and unpredictability. The underlying concerns of defense that were threaded into ocean initiatives funded by the Navy were shifted to concerns regarding climate [5]. Connecting through a common desire to address temporal concerns in long-term ocean observatories, a grassroots network of scientists and engineers involved themselves in the initial symposiums across the globe.

The U.S. efforts were primarily championed and led by a senior oceanographer at a large west coast university, backed by both national and international interest. Following an extended series of symposiums and discussions, the decision was taken to develop an initiative to wire and instrument an entire tectonic plate, building a long-term cabled observatory covering the entirety of the Juan de Fuca Plate off the coasts of Oregon and Washington in the U.S. and British Columbia in Canada. Funding from the NSF and the project leader's home institution supported the drafting of what would be one of the OOI's earliest plans, "The Feasibility of the Northeast Pacific Time-Series Undersea Networked Experiment Project (NEPTUNE) Project." At the same time, a corresponding feasibility document was developed for "NEPTUNE Canada" through investment by the Canadian government's ocean science funding body, Ocean Networks Canada. Together the Natural Sciences and Engineering Research Council of Canada and the U.S. National Science Foundation held workshops and symposiums together to address critical issues of engineering and science goals for the regional cabled observatory.

Many of our participants detailed the ways in which the international NEPTUNE project would turn the postwar characterization of oceanographic research on its head: introducing larger collaborative networks, industry-purchased instruments, real-time public data, and long-term and continuous maintenance and data collection without the need for research cruises (substitute maintenance cruises). While some rhythms of ocean science would remain primary (seasons and seasonal migration or mating patterns, temporal disruptions emanating from natural phenomena like hurricanes or tsunamis), many traditional rhythms of ocean science were not encompassed within the plans of NEPTUNE, such as the organizational rhythms of Navy funding cycles and field-wide ship scheduling, biographical rhythms of private data ownership, and infrastructural rhythms of short-term specific use instruments. At the same time the planning of the cabled network also unearthed a series of new concerns rhythms, which had little precedent in prior ocean science work, including the relation between research responsibilities and facility building for the MREFC planning process, activities related to managing the public attention and scrutiny of the initiative, and the long-term funding brought by a facility build unlike the predominant soft money structure of the field.

Through the initial development and continued construction of NEPTUNE we find organizational rhythms integrated into the planning of the facilities, such as the implementing organizations' semester schedules, teaching obligations for faculty, departmental requirements, expeditions unrelated to OOI, and publication timelines (AAAS, American Geophysical Union). Plans served to integrate these traditional organizational rhythms with the previously unseen infrastructural rhythms of the MREFC: iterations of the formalized planning documents (Feasibility, Conceptual, Preliminary, Final); the milestones of the construction process; the specific engineering requirements and evaluation practices for large-scale deployments; the release cycles of the cyberinfrastructure; software design and development; and the production of educational materials and tools affiliated with the new observatory.

The first cracks in this productive and collaborative relationship appeared in the early 2000s, and were identified by our participants as variations in timing and funding associated with federal investments and interest on either side of the bi-national relationship. While NEPTUNE Canada began construction in 2003, the U.S. was still hovering over central ideas and initiating the planning process. Participants speculated that the fiscal cutbacks associated with U.S. funding of the Afghan and Iraqi wars, the Bush administration's relatively lukewarm attitude towards science funding especially in areas associated with questions around climate change, and later the timing of U.S. economic slowdown of the 2000s drew significant federal scrutiny on science and ultimately delayed the U.S. efforts. This rift was further exacerbated by a brewing concern in Washington D.C. about NEPTUNE's distinct affiliation to its champion and his university, culminating in the decision to rebrand the U.S. side of the project as the 'Ocean Observatories Initiative' (OOI).

At this point the Consortium for Ocean Leadership was formed within the NSF, acting as a "unified voice in the nation's capital for oceanographic research", and as a liaison between OOI, Congress and the White House. As such Consortium of Ocean Leadership was tasked to oversee the planning process of the OOI, as a distinct entity from Canada's NEPTUNE. The OOI expanded its reach from the regional cabled observatory at the Juan de Fuca plate to additional coastal and global scale infrastructure largely formed by gliders and moorings implemented within U.S. waters as well as at the Irminger Sea offshore Southern Greenland, and Southern Ocean west of Chile.

In 2006, the construction of the "Ocean Observatories Initiative" became a line item in the U.S. President's budget, marking the start of the MREFC Conceptual Design, the OOI's first formal definition of plans including schedules, costs and contingencies. By this time, NEPTUNE Canada had not only completed the planning process but had become fully constructed and was collecting production quality, real-time data in its full operation: fully realizing the introduction of the unprecedented rhythms forecasted by our participants and generating new national and institutional policies surrounding their open data policies and publicly available instruments.

In 2008, more than $100 million from President Barack Obama's American Recovery and Reinvestment Act (the "Obama stimulus package") was awarded to the OOI, instantaneously accelerating its move into construction and prompting another reorganization and another iteration of the Conceptual Design plan. To cater to the climate change priorities of the stimulus package, a global node at the Argentine Basin was added to capture additional air-sea sampling and the budget was reorganized to accommodate this change. Multiple participants lamented the addition of the global node, as it forced the removal of a portion of the planned instrumentation from the original cabled observatory at what was once called NEPTUNE and was now renamed "Regional Scale Nodes."

A system engineer detailed for us the reorganization of his daily work that resulted from the removal of nodes. His original cooperation with Canada had led to the design of a circular architecture resembling a "big ring with the two leaves that became NEPTUNE and NEPTUNE Canada". The new resource constraints forced the engineer to collaboratively build a new architecture for the Southern leaf that no longer paralleled the circular configuration of its Canadian counterparts and rather employed a star-like architecture. Here we see the intertwining of the top-down rhythms of governing bodies at a larger, national scale, such as the NSF funding cycles built into milestones, the imposed MREFC five-year planning process detailed across the set of planning documents, the stimulus package and its corresponding reorganization of the OOI, the Afghan and Iraqi wars and financial crisis and their rescheduling of original timelines from the early documentation.

In November 2008, the OOI's Final Design plan was reviewed and accepted. By 2009, the construction funding for the OOI began, just as its Canadian counterparts became wholly operational. The separation between national efforts appears to be exaggerated if looking at only the plans (as Canada starts to drop out of the official documentation), but the stories of the participants reveal that on the ground the two countries remained very much cooperative, though at an informal level. Canada and U.S. hope to eventually connect their infrastructure, and each time the U.S. OOI plans change within the cyberinfrastructure or Regional Scale Nodes, their Canadian counterparts are informed and adjust their own plans accordingly.

Despite the seemingly increased separation between the two efforts, Canada still appeared within the lower-level (not MREFC-mandated) documentation of the OOI, as well as within the everyday activities of its affiliates. There remained an envisioned interchange between the U.S. and Canada where OOI would obtain NEPTUNE Canada data but also would move OOI data to Canadian repositories. While the two systems are not identical nor did Canada or the U.S. financially support their cooperation, there remained an interpersonal connection between the initiatives and our participants described the many regular collaborative efforts established at the local level: weekly phone meetings, laboratory visits, dinners at conferences and regular email exchange. In 2010, this connection was formally re-established when the U.S. Consortium for Ocean Leadership approached NEPTUNE Canada with a new Memorandum of Understanding, pledging to work together to manage and operate ocean observing systems.

The lag between NEPTUNE Canada and the OOI's Regional Scale Nodes greatly influenced the local adherence to the plans that would be detailed in the Final Design plan, and highlighted a disconnect between the operation of the OOI on the ground and the plans coming from the Consortium of Ocean Leadership. Some participants described that the extended time for any process to pass through Ocean Leadership slows operation to a point where they must consider breaking protocol in order to retain momentum. One participant described Ocean Leadership's desire to follow a strict MREFC process as sometimes being at odds with the local culture within one of the implementing organizations: "Because of this, at some point there were some rivalries in the program in terms of not wanting to be bound by Ocean Leadership restrictions or deal with them. It's been a constant problem with all of the implementing organizations about working together as a team versus running off and doing your own thing." In order to circumvent the long MREFC process of procurement, one implementing organization would "go rogue" then reconcile the 'damages' after the diversion from the plans. In this case, human action superseded the adherence to the top-down plans coming from Ocean Leadership and the system adapted to incorporate the effects from those self-governing actions. As one participant noted, "Ocean Leadership has had times of more and less leadership… There's a plan, the overarching plan, and then there is putting out the fire of the day… Sometimes the plan goes out the window." However, this autonomous dynamic was not found in all of the implementing organizations, and was reported as promoting tension and at times conflict.

We see here how the work of planning (plans in-the-making) changes, reorients, and aligns rhythms across the broad range of temporal kinds (organizational, infrastructural, biographical, and phenomenological) and scales that characterize the ongoing work of ocean science. Through juxtaposing plans with human action, we reveal a shifting loci of control, prioritizing and valuation at different scales within the organization, and locations and human actors within the organization that are more and less autonomous within the planning process. We are able to dissect the initial local, more grassroots rhythms emanating from the ground up in the long-term biographical rhythm of the OOI's champion from his conceiving of the idea for time-series instrumentation on the sea floor, to mobilizing the field around that idea, to becoming the nucleus of a self-organized group, then eventually leading to a formalized organization in which the high-level decisions came from government bodies, not the champion himself.

III.B. PLANS IN-ACTION

The work of plans and planning in aligning ongoing collaborative work hardly stops with the formulation of the final plan; nor, per Suchman, is the impact of such plans fully determinative of the forms of activity that follow. A complex reconciling of rhythms at many scales led to the creation of the final MREFC plans, and plans continue to shape and be shaped by rhythms after their formalization.

One requirement of MREFC planning is the definition of a detailed Work Breakdown Structure (WBS) that attempts to bridge the diffuse goals of the individuals within the initiative and steer them toward grand project goals. The WBS is imposed by the NSF to manage the complexities of a nonlinear, large-scale project. The WBS defines the integration of team organization with primary responsibilities, scheduling and success measures. The WBS document contains the high-level tasks for the whole field program, each ship, and each robotic vehicle, for example. It is divided firstly by OOI components (coastal, global and regional scale nodes, cyberinfrastructure, education and outreach) and subdivided by responsibilities and milestones mapped to each implementing organization (university and institute affiliates), then accountable roles within the implementing organizations (project scientist, technician, lead engineer, project manager, etc.). This is representative of the hierarchical relationships between entities with the NSF and Consortium of Ocean Leadership at the top level. Rather than around collaborating teams, the WBS is built around deliverables, such as final requirements, instrument or resource procurements, and building schedules. The project manager of each OOI component is responsible for their own WBS.

The WBS also includes a very detailed Cost Estimating Plan and progress reporting; a dictionary of the physical components, all deliverables, subsystems; R&D; design; prototyping; fabrication; assembly; installation; acceptance testing; administration; system engineering; purchasing; reporting not directly related to a product; hierarchies; major contracts; and specific products and labor (manager, engineer, scientist, technician, secretary, construction worker, etc.) including considerations of sick or vacation days and employee rates [29].

The WBS acts as a plan that addresses dissonance between rhythms in developing large-scale infrastructure: vendor schedules for procuring instruments and industrial spin-off, communication time between implementing organizations, varying funding cycles and academic calendars, prior investment histories of each implementing organization (and how this affects going forward into the initiative), cycles of technology development and ability for involvement in the initiative within each implementing organization, varying scientific interests and biographical rhythms of the individuals enacting the plans, and the level of debate and deference to hierarchy within an implementing organization's culture (wrapped up in time to complete tasks through formalized or informal processes). The WBS is also a plan embedded in other plans, and is formally mapped to both higher-level science goals and to national concerns as well as lower-level execution protocols, intermediary documents and informal collaborative structures.

The ability to adhere to and enact the WBS milestones is dictated by the effectiveness of low level coordination and alignment activities. One engineer explained the intermediary alignment steps between WBS milestones that reconcile the many moving parts of the collaborative OOI construction. He explained, "The implementing organizations are supposed to be inch people. We are supposed to making things happen and things happen by inches, not by miles." He particularly emphasized the usefulness of calendaring in defining and completing each WBS milestone. One participant noted over 20 Google Calendars are set up to manage right down to the hour the kinds of work that will go into this summer's infrastructure build. These calendars are lower-level and informal breakdowns of the formal WBS, including team events, specific instrument builds, cyberinfrastructure development, and an out of office calendar.

Each piece of the infrastructure has its own cost; as one OOI project scientist described, if any project scientist needs to move money from ship time to buying a sensor, for example, a change review board needs to be advised and must approve the shifted allocations at the level of the implementing organization. The Consortium of Ocean Leadership also has a high level change control board for issues that cross OOI components or affect more than one of the components. Upon approval of the change, the WBS is formally adjusted by an NSF program manager or officer at the Consortium for Ocean Leadership. The WBS is in this way a living but carefully managed document, responding to changes in the various project sub-units while still trying to hold them to a tight and highly regulated schedule.

In the course of one of our interviews, a project scientist received an Engineering Change Request in his email and was tasked to review and send comments to its author (a project scientist at another implementing organization). The change request detailed the original plan for the initial infrastructure build in the regional scale nodes, positioned for a series of cruises to lay cables and core instruments over the course of three months in summer 2013 with the cooperation of two other implementing organizations.

The infrastructure build set for summer 2013 was predicated on reconciling traditional, more predictable rhythms of ship-based ocean science such as ship time, crew availability, academic calendars, and fishery operation off the coasts. However, these cruises are distinct from the common research cruise, as their mission was deployment, not research itself. Therefore, this removes the rhythms of developing research questions, determining a locale, and building or procuring a tool in any traditional sense.

The request alerted the project scientist to changes needed to be made in infrastructure build's cruise plan, stemming from a significant delay on laying the 17km cable that connects one of the primary nodes to the shelf site on the seafloor at the Juan de Fuca Plate. The delay arose from what the scientists and engineers deemed as an unreasonable bid from the cable company, to which the OOI was forced to renegotiate with the vendor.

Various actors negotiate the WBS to address the change emanating from the unforeseen changes in prioritization by the vendor, and leading to an inability to lay the cable during the agreed upon schedule. Harmonizing the now muddled plans required a negotiation process between engineers and technicians to assess the ability for continued operation and development of all related technologies, including power availability, data flow range, and stereo or analog inputs. Additionally, project managers were involved to ensure the continued availability of human labor in the event of a changed schedule. Project scientists were consulted to assess new measures to reach science goals and requirements and a subject matter expert advised.

The resulting collaborative decision was to move the procurement and laying of cable to the following year, setting back the schedule significantly and rearranging priorities for the summer infrastructure build. Once all comments on this decision are gathered, the original author of the change request will synthesize all comments and considerations into the final Engineering Change Request then submit to his implementing organization's formalized change review board. The board will then collectively approve or disapprove the suggested changes and adjust the WBS accordingly.

At one level this change culminated in a formalized reorganization of efforts through the Engineering Change Request and WBS. At another level we find the more personal, biographical effects of removing ship time. Some of the scientists and engineers expressed a "restlessness" to get out to sea, citing damaging effects on morale, frustration with the vendor, and a humbling of the members in realizing that while their work was a top national priority to them, a cable company might not agree.

The phenomenal, emergent event of the cable company deprioritizing the OOI resulted in many local changes and shifts not only in the formalized plans but also in the lives of those within the OOI. The change in WBS impacts across scale, down to the individual, biographical rhythms of the project scientist who received the change request to review. The project scientist was responsible for a number of instruments set to be wired during the cruise this summer, but those procurements will now be instrumented next year. As a result, not only will the whole deployment schedule need to be reorganized (and ship time removed: affecting ship crews, fishermen, the Coast Guard, and the OOI itself) but also each individual's work plan that was involved in the summer cruises for the next full calendar year, and the WBS milestones which followed the anticipated instruments in production at the regional scale nodes. The delay in work must also be addressed by the OOI's Canadian collaborators, detailed in the previous section, who are awaiting the production-ready data from these seafloor instruments.

IV. DISCUSSION

As we have seen, plans and planning occupy a central position in the work of large-scale collaborative science, especially (though not exclusively) in their start-up phases. Viewed in a certain way, almost everything our informants do is about planning. The OOI's champion developed a series of plans to mobilize the community, develop a network and gain funding by the NSF. The NSF developed a series of plans to structure the construction of the OOI, manage funding cycles and budgetary restrictions, and situate and reorganize the effort to fit within a broader society-state context. And the project scientist was required to integrate an unforeseen change in vendor relations into new plans for both his team and his own personal trajectory.

But as we have also seen, the same phenomena were also centrally about *time*. OOI organizers were subject to (and tried to influence) temporal rhythms emanating from a whole host of sources: NSF and MREFC funding schedules; the timing of their Canadian counterparts, cycles of interest (and disinterest) emanating from science funders in Washington; and arguably the rhythms of public concern around the central concerns, including climate change, that the new observatory was meant to address. Plans and planning – large and small, formal and informal – represented key technologies by which actors tried to manage, control or amend these varying temporalities, attempting to bring otherwise discrepant rhythms into more and less workable *alignment*. We believe that the structure and outcome of collaborative work, in this and many other contexts, is deeply bound to the success of precisely such alignment efforts.

In exploring the deep connections between rhythm and planning across the collaborative contexts, setting and scales of the OOI, our paper also seeks to frame a number of larger contributes to CSCW theory and research. First, we identify plans and reconciling conflicts in rhythm as a central and critical challenge of collaborative work. Rhythms act as a substrate for classic notions of alignment work, yet are difficult to tease apart and analyze. We offer that planning and the formalization of plans act as an important site for making visible this temporal work, particularly in reconciling conflicting rhythms across scale and prioritizing and valuing rhythms in the process. The analytical power we gain from uncovering rhythms lets us look at how work evolves, rather than capturing only a snapshot in a dynamic, socially and historically embedded scientific practice. Rhythms and plans provide insight on how emergent changes (such as someone is fired or tenured, a hierarchy is re-organized, a hurricane forms, etc.) reconfigure the way we perform scientific work. Plans can lead to an ossification problem: once a plan is frozen-in-time it becomes brittle and stale, unable to withstand the dynamic natural world. Much has been written about the need for flexibility in plans and planning [1, 21, 36] but little is known about the rhythms embedded in the plans and their relations to human labor and life.

Second, we recognize that rhythms are relational. The rhythms of a scientific campaign, such as described within our plans in-the-making example, with its fits and starts and long waiting pauses, looks very different from those of a political campaign, of the turnover of a new presidential administration or of the maintenance of an in-production real-time data-producing infrastructure. Yet, we see these disparate rhythms align to establish the OOI's plans. Rhythms are called out, elevated or de-emphasized by plans, pointing to actors and resources that are being served or are underrepresented by the plans. The prioritizing and valuation of rhythms gives us a better understanding of power dynamics that might be invisible otherwise. This notion is similar in part to Star and Ruhleder's [28] assertion of the relational nature of infrastructure: as changes (in infrastructure, in plans) become formalized, the meaning of those changes will be unique to each individual and will highlight power relations in the adoption and resistance to different rhythms.

Third, we see that both rhythms and events can disrupt, shape and reorient plans. Despite the efforts entrenched in the work breakdown structure and its web of documentation in attempting to account for complexity. Phenomenal events like the Gulf Oil Spill, financial crisis, or even the stimulus package change the course of a plan unexpectedly and in emergent forms that are then crystallized within the next iterations of the plans. Often at these points of breakdown and change, we prioritize (like the stimulus package call for climate change led to more global scale nodes and less regional scale nodes). On the surface, these rhythms may seem external to the OOI, yet in practice posed a distinct and integral change to the initiative's plans and rhythms.

Fourth, plans link temporalities embedded in local practice with those operating at larger institutional levels. The specific relationship between local culture and the state can shed light on a number of concerns at a policy level. Science at the large-scale is politically essential to the operations of the state and is itself fundamentally dependent on the state. We have learned from scholars such as Suchman and Scott that any change to the way in which work is completed must at the very least reference the existing social and material arrangements that would be engaged in that work. Suchman teaches us that plans need feedback and iteration, attention to local circumstances and need to be dynamic in order to withstand emergent or phenomenal changes. Suchman asserts breakdown occurs when machines don't support local actions. This is true of plans (as a parallel to machines and automation) in organizing scientific work, and is a useful consideration in the development of policies that support plans and planning scientific endeavors. More broadly, this point echoes the assertion to take policy processes more fully into account in CSCW work [15].

Lastly, we note that rhythm and time more generally is methodologically difficult to study empirically for the challenges of visibility and emergence we've detailed. We often default to the formal structure of plans and take the work they detail too literally, not considering the emergent properties of action [14]. Additionally, informants find it difficult to reflect on time and rhythm directly. Often a rhythm is called out only in moments of difficult temporal coordination, such as the realignment of work spurred by the shifting priorities at the cable company in our previous example. We offer plans as a productive artifact for the study of time and rhythm, but encourage alternative representations that might make practices of temporal alignment.

V. CONCLUSION

Our study has emphasized the role of plans and planning as a key site or modality for the alignment of the multiple temporalities that go into and shape large-scale collaborative infrastructure projects in the sciences. We have argued for the role of plans and planning in coordinating discrepant rhythms across multiple scales of collaborative action. We have emphasized the work of plans in calling out (or sometimes obscuring) specific points of temporal conflict that may undermine or derail larger collaborative processes. And we have argued for the role of plans in establishing common baselines of expectation around which local and timely action can be coordinated. As our empirical case has also demonstrated, the challenges of rhythm typically show up in blended form, caught up in other kinds of problems and tensions that confront and limit infrastructure development efforts, and never fully captured or contained within the formalized confines of formal planning processes: rhythm can emanate from top-down broad fiscal, political, or institutional entities, as well as bottom-up biographical changes or organic phenomenal events. Plans play a central but rarely uncontested role in negotiating these collaborative dynamics.

VI. ACKNOWLEDGMENTS

We would like to thank our participants for their time and their feedback on this research. This work is supported under NSF grant #0847175.

VII. REFERENCES

[1] Agre, P.E. Planning and improvisation. in *Computation and Human Experience (Learning in Doing: Social, Cognitive and Computational Perspectives)*. Cambridge University Press, Cambridge, 1997, 142–159.

[2] Begole, J. and Tang, J. Work rhythms: analyzing visualizations of awareness histories of distributed groups. *in Proc. of CSCW '02, (New Orleans, LA, 2002), ACM, 230.*

[3] Churchill, E. and Bly, S. "It's all in the words: Supporting work activities with lightweight tools." *in Proc. of GROUP'99*, (Phoenix, AZ, 1999), ACM, 40–49.

[4] Coleridge, S.T. Rime of the Ancient Mariner. Acturus Publishing, London, 1768.

[5] Committee on Major U.S. Oceanographic Research Programs, National Research Council. *Global Ocean Science: Toward an Integrated Approach.* The National Academies Press, Washington, D.C., 1999.

[6] Corbin, J.M. and Strauss, A. *Basics of Qualitative Research: Techniques and Procedures for Developing Grounded.* Sage Publications, Thousand Oaks, CA, 2007.

[7] Egger, E. and Wagner, I. "Negotiating Temporal Orders – The Case of Collaborative Time Management in a Surgery Clinic." *JCSCW*, 1 (4), 255-275.

[8] Fisher, D. and Dourish, P. "Social and Temporal Structures in Everyday Collaboration." *in ACM Proc. of CHI '04*, (Vienna, Austria, 2004). ACM, 551-558.

[9] Garfinkel, H. Studies in Ethnomethodology. Polity, Cambridge, 1967.

[10] Glaser, B. and Strauss, A. *The Discovery of Grounded Theory: Strategies for Qualitative Research.* Aldine Transaction, Chicago, 1967.

[11] Handel, M. and Herbsleb, J.D. "What is Chat Doing in the Workplace?" *in Proc. of CSCW '12*, (Seattle, WA, 2002), ACM, 1-10.

[12] Im, H-G., Yates, J., Orlikowski, W.J. "Temporal Coordination through Genres and Genre Systems," Information, Technology and People, 18 (2), 89-119.

[13] Maiden, I. Rime of the Ancient Mariner: Full Length. Retrieved October 30, 2013 from Cornell University: http://www.youtube.com/watch?v=t7zk4as9kzA

[14] Jackson, S.J., Buyuktur, A. "Who Killed WATERS? Mess, Method, and Forensic Explanation in the Making and Unmaking of Large-Scale Science Networks," Science Technology and Human Values, 39 (1).

[15] Jackson, S.J., Steinhardt, S.B., and Buyuktur, A. Why CSCW needs science policy (and vice versa). *in Proc. of CSCW '13,* (San Antonio, TX, 2013), ACM, 1113.

[16] Jackson, S.J., Ribes, D., Buyuktur, A., and Bowker, G.C. Collaborative rhythm: temporal dissonance and alignment in collaborative scientific work. *in Proc. of CSCW '11*, (Hangzhou, China, 2011), ACM, 245–254.

[17] Landgren, J. "Making action visible in time-critical work." *in Proc. of CHI '06*, (Quebec, Canada, 2006), ACM, 201-210.

[18] Lee, H. Your time and my time: a temporal approach to groupware calendar systems. *Information & Management, 40* (3), 159–164.

[19] Mukerji, C. A Fragile Power: Scientists and the State. Princeton University Press, Princeton, 1990.

[20] Nilsson, M. and Hertzum, M. "Negotiated Rhythms of Mobile Work: Time, Place, and Work Schedules." *in Proc. of GROUP '05*, (Sanibel Island, FL, 2005), ACM, 148-157.

[21] Orlikowski, W.J. and Yates, J.A. It's About Time : Temporal Structuring in Organizations. *Organization Science*, 13 (6), 684–700.

[22] Palen, L. and Grudin, J. Discretionary Adoption of Group Support Software: Lessons from Calendar Applications. in Implementing collaboration technologies in industry. Springer-Verlag: London, UK, 2003, 159-179.

[23] Reddy, M.C., Dourish, P., and Pratt, W. Coordinating Heterogeneous Work: Information and Representation in Medical Care. in Proc. of ECSCW ''01, (Bonn, Germany, 2001), 239–258.

[24] Ribes, D. and Finholt, T.A. The Long Now of Technology Infrastructure: Articulating Tensions in Development. *Journal of the Association for Information Systems, 10 (5)*, 375–398.

[25] Rosner, D.K. The material practices of collaboration. *in Proc. of CSCW '12*, (Seattle, WA, 2012), ACM, 1155.

[26] Scott, J.C. Seeing Like a State. Yale University Press, New Haven, 1998.

[27] Schmidt, K. and Bannon, L. Taking CSCW Seriously: Supporting Articulation Work. *Computer Supported Cooperative Work,* 1 (1), 7–40.

[28] Star, S.L., and Ruhleder, K. "Steps Toward an Ecology of Infrastructure: Design and Access for Large Information Spaces." Information Systems Research 7(1), 111-134.

[29] Sanders, G. "Complex Projects." in Project Science Workshop Annual Meeting, (Ft. Lauderdale, FL, 2012).

[30] Serres, M. and Schehr, L.R. (tr). The parasite. University of Minnesota Press, Minneapolis, 2007.

[31] Strauss, A. Work and the Division of Labor. *The Sociological Quarterly, 26* (1), 1–19.

[32] Suchman, L. Human Machine Reconfigurations: Plans and Situated Actions. Cambridge University Press, Cambridge, 2006.

[33] Thayer, A., Sirjani, B., and Lee, C. Recalibrating the ratio: enacting accountability in intimate relationships using shared calendars. *in Proc. of CSCW '13*, (San Antonio, TX, 2013), ACM, 203–213.

[34] Thiry, E., Lindley, S., Banks, R., Regan, T. Authoring Personal Histories: Exploring the Timeline as a Framework for Meaning. *in Proc. of CHI '13*, (Paris, France, 2013), ACM, 1619-1628.

[35] Tyler, J. R. and Tang, J. C. "When Can I Expect an Email Response? A Study of Rhythms in Email Usage." *in Proc. of ECSCW'03*, (Helsinki, Finland, 2003), 239-258.

[36] Weick, K.E., Sutcliffe, K.M., and Obstfeld, D. Organizing and the Process of Sensemaking. *Organization Science, 16* (4), 409–421.

[37] Zerubavel, E. Hidden rhythms: schedules and calendars in social life. University of California Press, Berkeley and Los Angeles, 1985.

[38] Zerubavel, E. Patterns of Time in Hospital Life: A Sociological Perspective. University of Chicago Press, Chicago, 1979.

[39] Zerubavel, E. "The Benedictine Ethic and the Modern Spirit of Scheduling: On Schedules and Social Life," Sociological Inquiry, 50, 157-169.

Building Loyalty to Online Communities Through Bond and Identity-based Attachment to Sub-groups

Yla R. Tausczik
Human-Computer Interaction Institute
Carnegie Mellon University
ylataus@cs.cmu.edu

Laura A. Dabbish
Human-Computer Interaction Institute
Carnegie Mellon University
dabbish@cmu.edu

Robert E. Kraut
Human-Computer Interaction Institute
Carnegie Mellon University
robert.kraut@cmu.edu

ABSTRACT
Researchers and theorists have proposed that feelings of attachment to subgroups within a larger online community or site can increase users' loyalty to the site. They have identified two types of attachment, with distinct causes and consequences. With bond-based attachment, people feel connections to other group members, while with identity-based attachment they feel connections to the group as a whole. In two experiments we show that these feelings of attachment to subgroups increase loyalty to the larger community. Communication with other people in a subgroup but not simple awareness of them increases attachment to the larger community. By varying how the communication is structured, between dyads or with all group members simultaneously, the experiments show that bond- and identity-based attachment have different causes. But the experiments show no evidence that bond and identity attachment have different consequences. We consider both theoretical and methodological reasons why the consequences of bond-based and identity-based attachment are so similar.

Author Keywords
online communities; commitment; social attachment; group identity; computer-mediated communication; Mechanical Turk

ACM Classification Keywords
H.5.3. Information Interfaces and Presentation: Group and Organizational Interfaces.

INTRODUCTION
Many communities form online around common interests or goals, such as sharing pictures, creating an encyclopedia, playing a game, or co-writing music. However, once someone gets involved, even the most compelling interest or project may not be enough to retain participants. Survival of a site then depends on creating engaging experiences that keep members committed.

CSCW'14, February 15–19, 2014, Baltimore, Maryland, USA.

ACM 978-1-4503-2540-0/14/02...$15.00.
http://dx.doi.org/10.1145/2531602.2531688

A growing body of evidence shows that both mere social awareness that others are participating and direct communication among visitors to a common site can increase retention. For example, when players of a single-person game on Facebook were assigned to nominal groups and given tools to see the activity of other group members or other groups, they remained active members longer than if they weren't aware of others [6]. In a different site, users who were encouraged to communicate with others on the site were also more likely to return [4]. The rationale is that both social awareness and communication help people form social connections and attachment to each other or their groups, which in turn keeps them engaged and committed to the larger site. Theorists have proposed two distinct theoretical pathways mediating the effect of social awareness and communication on loyalty to a larger community or website [15, 19]. Bond-based attachment occurs between individuals, while identity-based attachment is the connection to a group as a whole.

In this paper we experimentally test whether these are two distinct pathways driving attachment. We assess whether we can differentially create bond and identity attachment and whether they have different downstream effects. In addition, we attempt to replicate previous work by experimentally testing whether adding social awareness and communication to a site will increase loyalty to the site. Our results have implications for designers and managers of online communities and suggest that interaction plays an important role in retaining members

RELATED WORK
Early research by Prentice and colleagues first proposed and demonstrated differences in the types of attachment students have to groups on campus; students were either attached to group members or the group as a whole [15]. They argued that this difference arose from two fundamentally different pathways to creating groups. Groups could arise either through interpersonal attraction, which would lead to common-bond groups, or through social identity processes, which would lead to common-identity groups.

These attachment differences were replicated among online groups that formed in IRC channels [19]. Sassenberg found that people had higher attachment to group members (or bond-based attachment) in IRC channels that focused on interaction among members without a common topic, whereas they had higher attachment to the group as a whole (or identity-based attachment) in channels that focused on a shared interest. In addition Sassenberg found that these differences in bond and identity attachment had different downstream effects in the groups. People in identity-based groups used more homogeneous online idioms, presumably because identity groups have stronger group norms. However, Sassenberg also found a high correlation between bond-based and identity-based attachment, suggesting that the distinct types of attachment may have a common component.

While early research was correlational, focusing on differences among naturally occurring groups, later research used experiments to create bond or identity attachment by introducing tools to increase social awareness and interaction. In general this research shows that manipulations designed to increase either bond-based or identity-based attachment increased people's behavioral loyalty to a site or an encompassing online community [4, 6,17]. Yet demonstrating that they have different pathways for producing behavioral loyalty has been difficult. For example, Farzan and colleagues varied social awareness in a Tetris™ game. Players were assigned to teams and either viewed other team members' scores to induce bond-based attachment or their group's score relative to other groups to induce identity-based attachment [6]. They found that both types of social awareness increased the number of sessions people played compared to players without social awareness. Although both types of attachment had the same behavioral consequences, mediation analyses suggested that the two types of awareness increased game-playing through different routes. However, research did not include self-reports about attachment type to corroborate this interpretation.

A longer-term field experiment in a movie-recommender site varied design features, such as individual, profiles, information about other people, and pairwise communication to induce bond-based attachment or group profile pages, information about groups and group-oriented communication to induced identity-based attachment [17]. Users in both bond and identity conditions increased behavioral loyalty to the site compared to a control condition. However, evidence was ambiguous about whether the manipulations increased participation though different types of attachment. Manipulations designed to induce group identity increased self-reported identity-based attachment, but also increased self-reported bond-based attachment although not as strongly. Manipulations designed to induce bonds increased self-reported identity-based attachment, but not attachment to particular other people. The authors argued that bond-based attachment was more difficult to generate than identity attachment, because users did not use the communication tools provided to them, which should have been most useful for developing interpersonal relationships. Further, when they conducted a mediation analysis, attachment type only partially mediated the effect of including communication tools on loyalty to the site.

In a study of loyalty to teams in an online game, when confederates initiated communication, particularly socio-emotional communication, players' willingness to continue playing with their team increased [4]. Presumably players remained with their teams longer because they formed a connection to teammates or the team. However this research did not clearly demonstrate this connection because it did not measure self-reported attachment type.

The current project focuses on testing the theoretical mechanisms thought to cause specific social design features to increase behavioral loyalty to a website or community. In particular, we focus on two goals:

1. To show compelling evidence that attachment to subgroups underlies the effect of social design features on site loyalty. Past work has been unable to establish this causal mechanism because either the manipulations of attachment were only partially successful [17] or attachment to subgroups was not measured directly through self-reports [4,6].
2. To evaluate whether there are two distinct types of attachment that can form to subgroups, bond and identity attachment, by attempting to create each in isolation and observing downstream effects. Past work has either not made use of experimental manipulations [15,19], had manipulations of attachment that were only partially successful [17], or failed to measure attachment type directly through self-reports [6].

EXPERIMENT 1

Previous research has demonstrated that inclusion of either social awareness of participation or direct communication among visitors to an online site can increase behavioral loyalty to a site [4, 6,17]. However, this research has not fully tested the underlying mechanisms. In Experiment 1 we attempt to demonstrate that including specific social design features increases site loyalty by creating psychological attachment to subgroups. Attachment to a subgroup is defined as feelings of attraction and identification with the group or its members and as a desire to continue interacting with the group or members. Attachment is defined broadly to encompass both bond and identity attachment, which we discuss in more detail below. Although we use the psychological vocabulary of attachment [9], our usage is equivalent to what organizational scholars refer to as affective commitment [1].

To test the causal mechanisms, Experiment 1 was designed to replicate previous findings in a new environment, Mechanical Turk (MTurk), which is an online labor market where requesters pay Turkers, as the workers are known, to do small tasks. A typical task on Mechanical Turk is structured to be short-term and done independently [10]. The

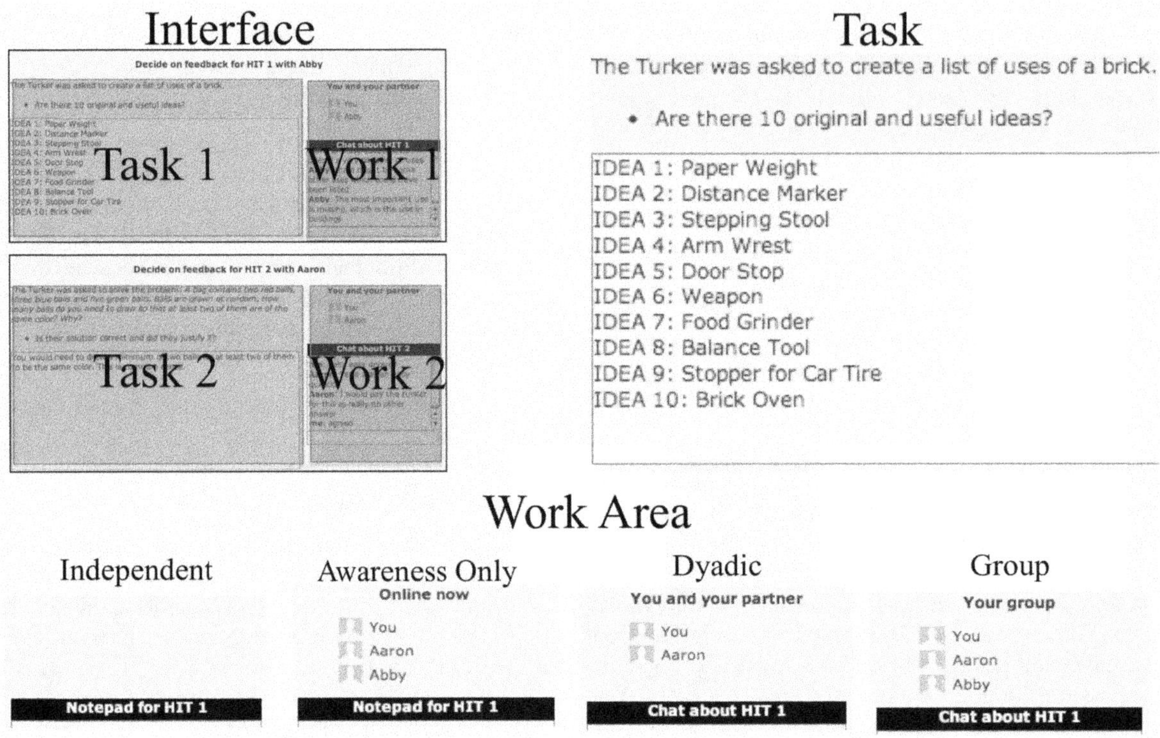

Figure 1: Example of the interface layout, a task used, and work area for the different experimental conditions.

primary motivation of a majority of Turkers is to earn money [7].

In this experiment, three-person work groups were recruited from MTurk to complete a set of tasks. Level of interaction within a work group was manipulated by including or excluding social features. Some workers got no information about other group members (independent). Others were shown group members' names (awareness). And others worked together and had tools to communicate (communication). Those workers who were made aware of their work group were expected to begin becoming attached to their work group, which in turn should translate into greater behavioral loyalty to MTurk and to the experimenters as employers. We predicted that compared to Turkers in the independent and awareness-only conditions, those who worked together in the communication conditions would feel greater attachment to MTurk as a community, as measured by beliefs that MTurk was a community, stronger self-reported identification with other Turkers, and beliefs that maintaining MTurk standards was important. We also predicted that these Turkers would want to complete more tasks for us and be more likely to recommend us to other Turkers, measures of loyalty to us as employers.

Hypothesis 1: Assigning Turkers to communicating groups will increase their loyalty to Mechanical Turk and their employer by increasing feelings of attachment to work groups.

Based on the prior literature, we expected that one could induce two distinct types of attachment to work groups, bond and identity attachment, through two different pathways. Bond attachment is thought to form from interpersonal attraction to specific individuals, while identity attachment is thought to form from identification with a social group or category. We tried to induce these types of attachment by assigning Turkers to work in the three-person group in pairs, to promote attachment between group members (bond attachment), or to work with everyone in their group simultaneously, to promote attachment to the group as an entity (identity attachment).

In the experiments we focus on the early-stages of attachment formation to have better control over how attachment forms and to tease the two processes apart. Both interpersonal and social identity processes can be studied in short-term interactions (e.g. [16,14,5]).

Hypothesis 2: Structuring group work and communication in pairs or as a group as a whole will differentially create bond or identity-based attachment respectively.

IV: Level of Interaction	IV: Small Group Attachment Type	Condition Interface	DVs
Independent		Independent	
Awareness		Awareness	Bond Attachment
	Bond	Dyad-Dyad	Identity Attachment
Communication	Identity	Group-Group	Community Orientation
	Hybrid	Dyad-Group	Employer Commitment
		Group-Dyad	

Table 1: Experiment 1 conditions and relevant independent and dependent variables.

METHOD

Participants

A total of 606 participants were recruited from Mechanical Turk and randomly assigned to groups of three people. Of those participants 509 (85.0%) completed the Experiment. 52% of participants were female; they ranged in age from 18 to 68 (M = 31.5, SD = 10.5). Most were from the United States (76%), followed by India (19%); the remained were from many other countries. Participants were asked to select their main motivation for Turking from a large range of possible options. The majority, 83%, reported that their main motivation for Turking was for money. Participants were paid 75 cents for participating.

A total of 202 three-person groups were formed and randomly assigned to one of the six conditions. Of these, 123 groups in which no group members dropped out were retained for analysis. The dropout rate did not vary by condition ($\chi^2(5) = 4.51, p = 0.48$).

Procedure

Participants were asked to evaluate work products created by other Turkers in other experiments [2, 21]. They evaluated a variety of work products, including brainstorms, limericks, and product reviews (see Figure 1 for an example). Within each product category, items for evaluation differed in quality. After being recruited participants practiced an evaluation task alone for one minute before agreeing to complete the experiment.

Once participants were placed in the experiment they were randomly assigned to a group of three people, and each group was randomly assigned to one of six interaction conditions. Participants took part in two sessions (Session 1 & Session 2). In each session they evaluated two articles that previous Turkers's had created. Each session lasted 5 minutes, they were prompted to *"Discuss how the Turkers could improve their work, and should it be rejected, accepted, or accepted with a bonus."* Each participants either evaluated the work individually or with others. Participants evaluating the work individually were asked to write down their thoughts as if they were discussing it with others. Participants evaluating the work with others were asked to jointly decide what feedback to give. Participants filled out questionnaires at the mid-point (i.e. between Session 1 and Session 2) and at the end.

Depending on condition, participants worked independently (independent), worked independently but were made aware of their group (awareness), or communicated with others (communication) either in pairs or as a group. When participants worked alone they typed notes into an entry box; when they worked together they were given chat boxes to communicate (see Figure 1).

Design

Three types of conditions were created to manipulate whether participants felt a part of a social group. In the independent condition participants worked alone and were not told they were part of a group. In the awareness condition participants were made aware of their group but could not communicate. Group awareness was created by telling the participants they were part of an evaluation team and displaying their group members' nicknames during the task. In the other four conditions the group members worked together and directly communicated (see Figure 1, Table 1).

There were two communication protocols to differentially promote bond or identity attachment. During each session, participants in the communication conditions either worked in pairs or as an intact group. The communication protocols were counterbalanced across sessions. The Group-Group condition was created to promote identity attachment; Dyad-Dyad condition was created to promote bond attachment; and Group-Dyad, and Dyad-Group conditions were hybrids to examine the process of attachment formation in more detail. However, detailed analysis of attachment formation using the hybrid conditions was not possible because the differences between bond- and identity-attachment were too small (see Results for more detailed discussion).

With the pairs protocol, both the tasks and communication was structured so that groups of three worked on two tasks at a time, one with each partner. This arrangement meant that there were three pairs total (AB, BC, AC), but each individual only saw the two pairs they were a part of (e.g. A only saw pairs AB, AC). To ensure that all conditions were balanced, participants in all conditions were given two evaluation tasks at a time and instructed to work on both simultaneously, which was reinforced by automated reminders if participants focused only on one task at a time (see Figure 1). Conditions were created so that participants

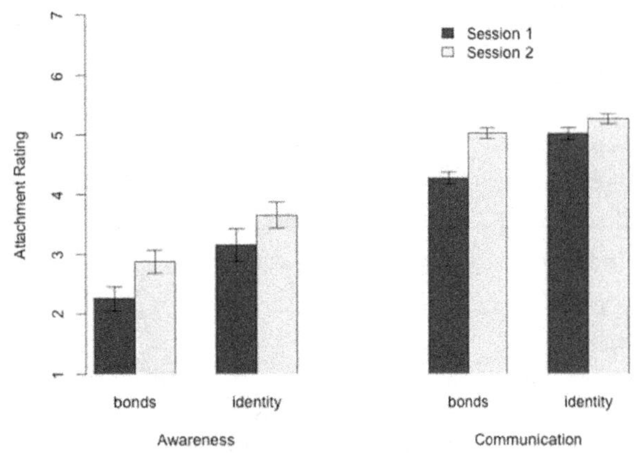

Figure 2: Turkers's mean (S.E.) ratings of bond and identity attachment in the group awareness only and group communication conditions. Bond and identity attachment were rated after Session 1 and 2 on a 7-point Likert scale.

could be assigned to work in one way in Session 1 and work in another way in Session 2 to allow for hybrid conditions.

Dependent measures

Participants separately rated the strength of their attachments to the individuals in their group (bond attachment) and to the group as a whole (identity attachment). After Session 1 we used agreement with a single item to measure bond attachment to each group member (*'I was starting to develop a bond with [partner's name].'*) [19]. Participants' rating of their two group members were averaged to create a composite score for strength of bond attachment ($\alpha = 0.86$). After Session 2 we measured bond attachment by combining this same item with an additional statement about willingness to work with each group member again. These four items, two item of two group members, were combined into a single composite bond attachment score ($\alpha = 0.94$).

Similarly, after Session 1, a single item was used to measure identity attachment (*'I was starting to identify with my evaluation team.'*). After Session 2, the measure of identity attachment was expanded to a modified version of a highly reliable four item measure of social identification [13] ($\alpha = 0.95$). All the attachment measures were rated on 7-point Likert scales from Strongly disagree to Strongly agree.

Community attachment was measured using 5 items, which included perception of MTurker as a community, social identification with the community, and beliefs about the importance of maintaining MTurk standards ($\alpha = 0.92$) [8]. Two aspects of employer commitment were measured, whether the participant would do another task from the same employer and whether the participant would write a review recommending the employer to other Turkers. These two measures of employer commitment, measured on 7-point Likert scales, were combined ($\alpha = 0.67$). To ensure Turkers were answering accurately, Turkers were asked to provide an email address to be contacted in the future and to write a review of us as employers which might be distributed to other Turkers. Self-reported measures of organizational commitment, similar to these measures of commitment, correlate with behavioral measures commitment [11].

We did not predict that social interaction would affect the quality of work. However because of the practical importance of work quality, we constructed a crude measure of it. Task materials had been selected because they were of low, medium, and high quality, as judged by one of the authors. Correlations between ratings given by each participant and the authors' gold standard ratings were used as a measure of a participant's evaluation accuracy and represent quality of work at the evaluation task.

RESULTS

Hypothesis 1: Small-group Attachment and Site Loyalty

We first evaluated whether social awareness and/or communication could create psychological attachment to work groups. We conducted a multi-level regression analysis in which, level of interaction (awareness only, communication), time (session 1, session 2), attachment type (bond, identity) and interactions were used to predict Turkers's ratings of the strength of attachment to their group. Turkers were nested within their group, to control for dependencies between group members. Because group attachment could only be measured if participants were aware they were part of a group, we include in the analysis only conditions with at least minimal social awareness (i.e. the awareness only and communication conditions).

We were able to promote attachment by allowing communication. However social awareness by itself was not sufficient to create psychological attachment to the groups. There was a main effect of level of social interaction on the strength of attachment ($t(105) = 9.06, p < 0.001, d = 1.77$; see Figure 2). On average participants in the communication conditions agreed with statements such as *"I was starting to identify with my evaluation team"* (as indicated by a mean score above 4 on the 7-point Likert scale), whereas those in the awareness only condition disagreed with these statements (as indicated by a mean score below 4).

A more detailed examination examining attachment type showed that identity and bond attachment exhibited distinct patterns. There was a main effect of attachment type ($t(918) = 7.81$, $p < 0.001$, $d = 0.52$). Participants formed stronger identity attachment than bond attachment. There was also an interaction between attachment type and communication ($t(918) = -2.70$, $p = 0.007$, $d = 0.18$). Groups that communicated had stronger bond attachment relative to identity attachment compared to groups with only social awareness. Attachment strengthened over time for both types of attachment ($t(918) = 10.33, p < 0.001, d = 0.68$), but bond

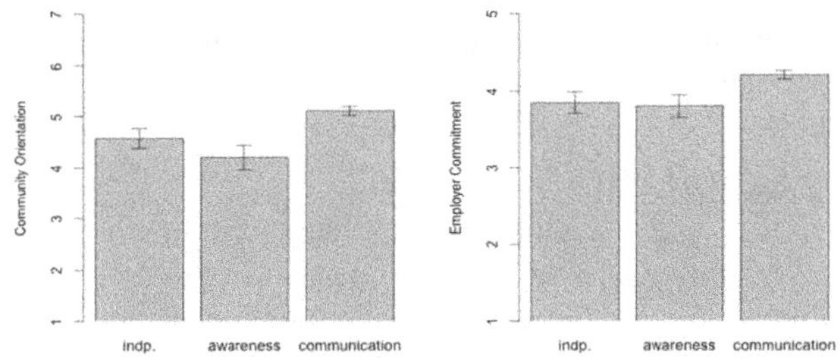

Figure 3: Reported mean (S.E.) community attachment and employer commitment for Turkers in the independent, group awareness only, and group communication conditions. Community orientation and employer commitment were measured on 7- and 5-point scales respectively.

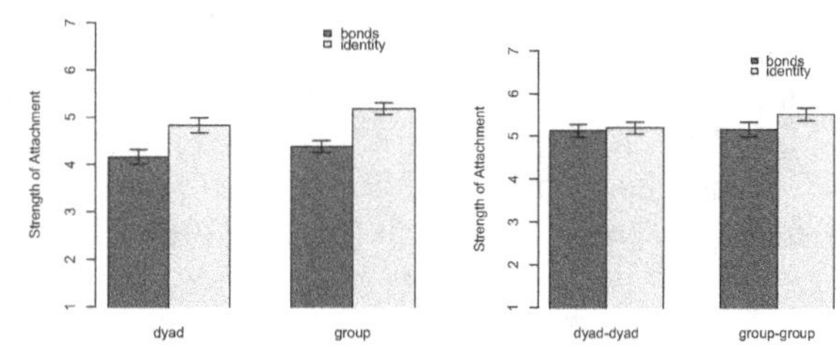

Figure 4: Mean (S.E.) ratings of bond and identity attachment for Turkers in groups that communicated as dyads or as a group at the midpoint (left) and by the end of the experiment (right) in Experiment 1.

attachment strengthened more than identity attachment did ($t(918) = -4.49, p < 0.001, d = 0.30$).

Next we examined whether social awareness and/or communication could increase community loyalty. Two multi-level models were constructed to test the effect of level of social interaction—independent, group awareness only, or group communication—on two measures of loyalty to Mechanical Turk as a community and to the employer.

Group communication, but not social awareness alone, increased loyalty to the Turker community. There was a main effect of communication on community loyalty ($LR = 18.1$, $p < 0.001$; see Figure 3). Participants in the communication conditions reported more attachment to MTurk as a community than those in either the group awareness only or independent conditions ($t_{comm.VSawareness}$ (120) = 3.95, $p < 0.001$, $d = 0.72$; $t_{comm.VSindp}$ (120) = 2.26, p =0.03, $d = 0.41$). There was also a main effect of communication on employer commitment ($LR = 12.4$, $p = 0.002$; see Figure 3). Participants in the communication conditions were more likely to agree to do another of our HITs than those in either the awareness only or independent conditions ($t_{comm.VSawareness}$ (120) = 2.88, $p = 0.005$, $d = 0.52$; $t_{comm.VSindp}$ (120) = 2.47, p =0.01, $d = 0.45$).

We did not expect that communication would influence the quality of work, and indeed found no differences ($LR = 0.51$, $p = 0.78$).

Hypothesis 2: Bond vs. Identity Attachment

Finally we examined whether structuring the way group members communicated differentially created bond and identity attachment. Two multi-level models were constructed to test whether communication type, dyads or group communication, had a differential effect on the strength of bond and identity attachment. After Session 1, there was no significant interaction between communication type and attachment type on the strength of attachment ($t(125) = 0.93$, $p = 0.35$), indicating that 5 minutes of interaction did not differentially influence bond or identity attachment. However, by the end of the experiment, after Session 2, there was a significant interaction between the communication type and the attachment type on the strength of attachment ($t(135) = 2.38$, $p = 0.02$, $d = 0.41$; see Figure 4). Participants who communicated as pairs within a group had roughly equal bond and identity attachment, whereas participants who communicated with the whole group simultaneously had stronger identity attachment than bond attachment.

Together, these results show that communication increased both attachment to participants' work groups and their loyalty to MTurk as a community and their employers. We used Structural Equation Models (SEMs) to evaluate whether the link between communication and loyalty to MTurk as a community and their employers was better explained by differentiating types of attachment to work groups—bond versus identity—or if it was better explained by positing an undifferentiated general attachment to Turkers' work group. We compared two models. Model A differentiated bond and identity attachment while Model B represented undifferentiated general attachment. Model B, with general attachment to a Turkers' work group (CFI = 0.82, RMSEA = 0.21, AIC = 3364), explained the data as well as Model A, with differentiated, bond and identity attachment (CFI = 0.84, RMSEA = 0.21, AIC = 3342) as indicated by equally good fit indices for Model B as Model A. Thus, there was no advantage to making a distinction between bond and identity attachment in explaining increases in loyalty to the larger community and employers.

Having established that undifferentiated general attachment to a Turker's work group was the most parsimonious representation of attachment, we conducted an analysis to show that this attachment was actually mediating the increase in loyalty. This analysis tested whether small group attachment mediated the increase in loyalty among Turkers in the group communication condition compared with those in the group awareness only condition. Individually, both communication ($t_{comm}(105) = 3.90$, $p < 0.001$) and work group attachment ($t_{attachment}(105) = 13.2$, $p < 0.001$) were significant predictors of attachment to MTurk as a community. When included in a model together, work group attachment completely explained the effect of communication on attachment to MTurk as a community ($t_{attachment}(212) = 12.5$, $p < 0.001$, $t_{comm}(105) = -1.35$, $p = 0.18$). Similarly both communication ($t_{comm}(105) = 2.91$, $p < 0.001$) and work group attachment ($t_{attachment}(105) = 10.2$, $p < 0.001$) were significant predictors of employer commitment. When included in a model together, work group attachment completely explained the effect of communication on employer commitment ($t_{attachment}(212) = 9.78$, $p < 0.001$, $t_{comm}(105) = -1.44$, $p = 0.15$). These results together show that undifferentiated work group attachment mediates the effect of social elements on the increase in loyalty to the Turker community and to the employer.

DISCUSSION

Experiment 1 was designed to test whether specialized social design features, such as social awareness and communication among work groups, would increase overall community loyalty by creating attachments with subgroups within the community.

We hypothesized that inducing Turkers to form attachments to their work groups would increase their loyalty to MTurk and to employers. The results partially confirmed this hypothesis: assigning Turkers to work groups and allowing communication within the groups caused Turkers to demonstrate more loyalty to MTurk and their employer, two measures of community loyalty. However, awareness of their group and its membership by itself did not create subgroup attachment; only work groups given tools to communicate formed subgroup attachment. Moreover, we were able to show that the increase in loyalty to the Turker community and employer was fully mediated by Turkers' increased attachment to their work groups. Our findings are an advance over previous research, which has failed to show that subgroup attachment fully mediates increased community-level loyalty either because this research did not collect self-reported attachment data [6, 4] or did not strongly induce distinct types of attachment to subgroups [17]

We expected that communicating in a subgroup would increase loyalty to Mechanical Turk and to employers through two different pathways, either by creating attachment to group members (bond attachment) or by creating attachment to the group as an entity (identity attachment). The experiment showed that when Turkers worked and communicated as pairs within a work group, bond and identity attachment were equally strongly. But when Turkers worked and communicated as an intact group, identity attachment formed more strongly than bond attachment. This difference demonstrates the presence of two distinct pathways for creating social attachment in groups. However results also showed that working as pairs, which was intended to promote the formation of bond attachment, also promoted identity attachment. Working as a group, which was intended to promote identity attachment, promoted bond attachment as well, although to a lesser extent. Although the results support distinct causes of bond and identity attachment the effect sizes were small and the results also suggest considerable overlap between the two types of attachment.

EXPERIMENT 2

Researchers and theoreticians have proposed two separate pathways through which attachment to groups form. Experiment 2 was designed to investigate whether these pathways are distinct, by testing whether they have distinct causes and consequences. Experiment 1 showed that the way that groups worked together and communicated had some distinct effects on how identity and bond attachment formed. Communicating as a group caused identity attachment to form more strongly than bond attachment. However, working and communicating in pairs, which should have primarily stimulated bond attachment, actually caused both bond and identity attachment to increase equally.

One possible explanation for this paradox is that working and communicating as an intact group versus as pairs were not a strong enough design intervention to isolate the social identity and interpersonal processes that are thought to independently drive identity and bond attachment respectively. Therefore, in Experiment 2 we developed what should be stronger manipulations to encourage greater bond attachment to work groups.

Bond attachment is based on interpersonal attraction [15]. Social psychological research has identified several ways to increase interpersonal attraction including longer exposure to someone [16], mutual self-disclosure [3], and perceived similarity [18, 12]. In order to promote bond-based attachment we manipulated all of these elements in addition to structuring communication among groups to differentially create bond and identity attachment.

Hypothesis 2 extended: Structuring group work and communication in pairs and including other manipulations to increase interpersonal attraction will stimulate bond-based attachment while structuring work and communication as a group as a whole will stimulate identity-based attachment respectively.

One of the main reasons the distinction between bond and identity attachments has received so much attention is because their root causes, interpersonal attraction or group identification respectively, should have large downstream consequences, in areas such as member retention or effort expended on behalf of a group [15, 19, 18].

Hypothesis 3: Bond and identity attachment should have different observable downstream consequences.

For example, bond-based attachment to a group, which is based on interpersonal ties, should lead people to be more interested in individual members of group [15]. In the context of work groups on MTurk, this implies that Turkers with bond-based attachment to their group should be more willing

IV: Small Group Attachment Type	Condition: Interface	Condition: Turnover Event	DVs
Bond	Dyad-Dyad	None	Bond Attachment Identity Attachment Continue Relationship Equal Bonus Disagreement
Identity	Group-Group		
Hybrid	Dyad-Group		
	Group-Dyad		
Bond	Dyad-Dyad	1 person forced to drop at mid-point	Resilience to Turnover
Identity	Group-Group		
Hybrid	Dyad-Group		
	Group-Dyad		

Table 2: Experiment 2 conditions and relevant independent and dependent variables.

to stay in contact with group members or talk with them after completing their paid task.

Hypothesis 3a: Bond-based attachment to a work group will increase Turkers' desire to stay in contact with work group members.

Identity attachment is based on group identification. Stronger group identification results in seeing individuals in a group as homogeneous and valuing the group and its members because of what the group represents and not because of individual group members' contributions [18]. On MTurk this might lead to individuals ignore differences in individual members contributions to the group. As a result, individuals might distribute a bonus equally among members of their work group despite differences among members in their output.

Hypothesis 3b: Identity-based group attachment will lead Turkers to distribute benefits equally among group members.

Similarly because in an identity-based group, the members are not as important as the group as whole, individuals may treat each other as interchangeable. Thus, we would expect that their loyalty to the group should be robust to members' leaving.

Hypothesis 3c: Identity-based group attachment will lead Turkers to remain in the group when another group member leaves.

Group identification also results in greater normative conformity pressure and greater influence from other group members [14]. One consequence on MTurk is that group members may influence each other's judgments more and disagree with each other less.

Hypothesis 3d: Identity-based group attachment will lead to great conformity and subsequently less disagreement among Turkers in a work group.

METHOD

Participants

A total of 801 participants were recruited from Mechanical Turk and randomly assigned to a group of three people. Of those participants 684 (85%) completed the Experiment. 47% of participants were female; they ranged in age from 18 to 74 (M = 32.0, SD = 12.8). The largest number of participants were from the United States (74%); followed by India (23%); the remained were from many other countries (2%). Participants were asked to select their main motivation for Turking from a large range of possible options. The majority, 78%, reported that their main motivation for Turking was for money. Participants were paid $1.20 for participating.

A total of 267 three-person groups were formed and randomly assigned to one of the eight conditions. Two samples were retained for analysis. The first sample included 182 groups in which no members dropped out during the first session. The dropout rate did not vary by condition during the first session ($\chi^2(3) = 2.67, p = 0.45$). The second sample included 85 groups in which no members dropped out or were forced to dropout during the entire experiment. The dropout rate also did not vary by condition during the entire experiment among groups in which no one was forced to dropout ($\chi^2(3) = 0.41, p = 0.94$). The samples had to be separated to distinguish natural turnover from cases where turnover was created artificially to test prediction 3d (see Table 2 and Design section).

Procedure

The procedure was very similar to the one in Experiment 1. However in this experiment participants answered questions in the waiting room, while waiting to be matched with a group. They either answered questions from each other using a chat room in the bond conditions or they answered questions by themselves in the identity conditions (see Design section). As in Experiment 1 participants reviewed other people's work; this time they were told they were reviewing work done by university students, to eliminate any personal bias associated with reviewing other Turkers' work. Finally, following completion of the experiment and questionnaires, participants were given the option to stay extra time for no additional pay to socialize with their group members. Those opting to stay were placed in a chat room with others who had also elected to stay.

Experimental design

As in Experiment 1 there were four communication conditions to manipulate bond and identity attachments (see Table 2). During the task participants in the communication conditions either worked in pairs or as an intact group. The Group-Group condition was created to promote identity attachment; Dyad-Dyad condition was created to promote bond attachment; and Group-Dyad, and Dyad-Group conditions were created as hybrids to examine the formation of attachment in more detail (the hybrid conditions turned out not to be necessary).

We changed some procedures from Experiment 1 to strengthen the induction of bond attachment in this experiment: groups assigned to the bond condition in session 1 communicated for longer, disclosed more personal information, and were told that they were matched with their group because they were similar to other group members. While supposedly waiting for group members to arrive, participants were put in a waiting room with their future group members and asked to chat. This meant that at least two group members communicated for between 1.5 and 5 minutes and all group members communicated for at least 1.5 minutes before the main task began. During the waiting room period, participants were asked to disclose personal information to each other by telling each other answers to personal questions such as "What's the most unique skill you have?" (modified from [20]).

Those participants assigned to group communication in Session 1 spent equal time in the waiting room and answered the same questions, but they were told that they were answering the questions so that we could find a group that would be a good fit for them. They were not given tools to communicate with group members during this time, nor were they aware that their future group was also waiting. These participants were told that they were matched with their group because they were a good fit.

In addition, to test the effect of turnover on group retention and attachment, in half the groups one member was randomly chosen and removed from their group between Sessions 1 and 2. The remaining group members were told this member had dropped out.

Dependent measures

The same measures of attachment from Experiment 1 were used in Experiment 2. Participants rated bond and identity attachment after Session 1 and Session 2. Additional measures were included to evaluate other outcomes of interest. As in Experiment 1 after jointly discussing what they believed to be students' work products, participants independently rated the quality of the work they were reviewing. They gave each product a letter grade from A to F. Instructions explained the grading scale. Letter grades were converted to standard grade point values and the average pairwise absolute difference among group members for each task was calculated as a measure of disagreement. Following the main tasks, participants were invited to exchange email addresses with each group member and to stay extra time for no addition pay to socialize with individual group members; agreeing to do either with at least one group member was considered a measure of relationship continuation. Finally, participants were told they had receive a 60-cent bonus for good group work and were asked to divide it among their group members (including themselves); whether they divided it evenly was considered a measure of equality.

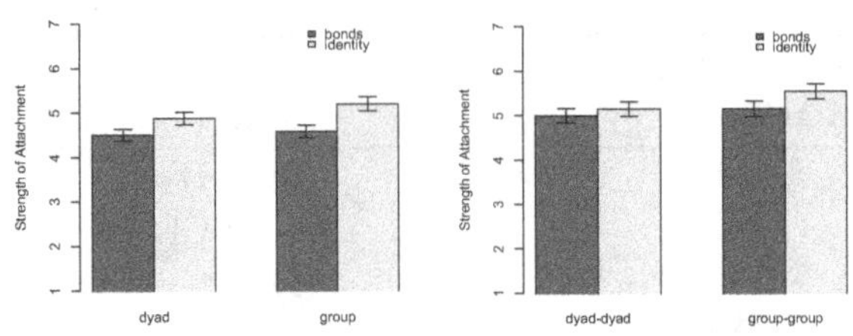

Figure 5: Mean (S.E.) ratings of bond and identity attachment for Turkers in groups that communicated as dyads or as a group at the midpoint (left) and by the end of the experiment (right) in Experiment 2.

RESULTS

Hypothesis 2: Bond vs. Identity Attachment Formation

In Experiment 2 we tried to get Turkers to form bond and identity attachment independently by increasing interpersonal attraction in the bond condition in addition to differences in the communication structure. We evaluated whether these changes increased relative differences in bond and identity attachment. Two multi-level models were constructed to test whether communication type (dyadic or group communication) had a differential effect on the strength of bond and identity attachment. Results in Experiment 2 were similar to those from Experiment 1. At the midpoint of the experiment there was a marginally significant interaction between communication type and attachment type on the strength of attachment ($t(244) = 1.76, p = 0.08, d = 0.23$; see Figure 5). The difference increased through the end of the experiment; there was a significant interaction between the communication type and the attachment type on the strength of attachment ($t(124) = 1.96, p = 0.05, d = 0.35$; see Figure 5). Turkers in groups that communicated as pairs with manipulations to enhance interpersonal attraction formed bond and identity attachment equally. Turkers in groups that communicated as a group formed stronger identity attachment than bond attachment.

Hypothesis 3: Impact of Bond vs. Identity Attachment

We examined whether the differences in relative bond and identity attachment had a downstream impact on aspects of group dynamics. Multi-level models tested whether type of communication influenced each outcome of interest. Participants were nested in groups to control for dependencies among group members (242 participants in 85 groups in the sub-sample with no turnover and 461 participants in 182 groups in the larger sample with and without turnover).

Turkers in groups that communicated dyadically with manipulations to increase interpersonal attraction were expected to have greater bond attachment and thus express more interest in contacting members after the task had ended. This prediction was not supported. They were no more likely to exchange emails or to stay and socialize with specific group members than were Turkers in the group communication condition ($\chi^2(3) = 3.43$, $p = 0.33$; see Table 3).

Turkers in groups that communicated as a group were expected to have greater group identification and identity attachment and, as a result, see all group members as homogeneous. Thus, these participants were expected to distribute the bonus more equally among their group members. This prediction was not supported. They were no more likely to distribute the bonus evenly ($\chi^2(3) = 4.93$, $p = 0.18$; see Table 3). Participants that communicated as a group were also expected to drop out at a lower rate following a turnover event. Again, this prediction was not supported; there was no significant interaction between communication condition and turnover on dropout rates ($\chi^2(3) = 2.75$, $p = 0.43$; see Table 3).

Outcome	Dyad-Dyad	Group-Group	Dyad-Group	Group-Dyad
Continue Relationship	21%	35%	25%	22%
Equal Bonus	71%	83%	74%	64%
Disagreement	0.57 (0.43)	0.50 (0.31)	0.64 (0.56)	0.59 (0.36)
Dropout	6.5%	5.6%	2.3%	2.3%

Table 3: Measures of group outcomes of interest across the communication conditions. Gives means (S.D.) or percent of participants as appropriate.

Finally, because of conformity effects associated with greater group identification, participants in groups that communicated as a group were expected to disagree less. This prediction was not supported; there was no significant difference in disagreement between communication conditions ($LR = 1.40$, $p = 0.71$).

DISCUSSION

Experiment 2 was designed to investigate whether there are distinct pathways through which attachment forms in a group by testing whether bond and identity attachment have distinct causes and consequences. This experiment found evidence of distinct causes of bond and identity attachment, but not distinct consequences. Experiment 2 replicated findings from Experiment 1 that bond and identity attachment could be formed to different degrees depending on how social interaction was structured. When social interaction was structured to promote interpersonal attraction bond and identity attraction formed equally and when interaction was structured to promote social identity processes identity attachment formed more strongly than did bond attachment. These results provide some evidence that bond and identity attachment have different causes and are created by distinct processes. However, there was considerable overlap between bond and identity attraction, that is when interaction was structured to promote identity attachment it led to the formation of both identity and bond attachment to some extent and the other way around. Either the way we structured social interaction did not cleanly promote interpersonal attraction and social identity processes independently or there is a more complicated relationship between these underlying processes and the two types of attraction.

The distinction between bond and identity attachment is thought to be important in part because their distinct causes are thought to lead to different downstream consequences. Although we found evidence of bond and identity attachment having distinct causes we found was no evidence that this resulted in different downstream consequences. Again one explanation is that our manipulations were not strong enough. Alternatively, there is a more complicated relationship between these underlying processes and the two types of attraction than suggested by prior theory.

GENERAL DISCUSSION

Previous work has shown that both mere social awareness and direct communication among visitors to a common site can increase retention [4, 6, 17]. In Experiment 1 we were able to partially replicate this finding on Mechanical Turk, a work environment in which Turkers do short-term tasks mainly by themselves. Turkers who were assigned to work in a group and given tools to communicate reported being more attached to MTurk and more likely to work for their employer again, two measures of loyalty on MTurk. We were able to extend previous work by showing that the effect of group communication on community loyalty was completely mediated by attachment to the assigned work group. This experiment provides compelling evidence that loyalty is mediated by attachment to the social entities present. However, unlike previous work only direct communication and not mere social awareness increased site loyalty on MTurk. This finding suggests that including social awareness and communication features only increase loyalty to the site to the extent that they crease attachment among subgroups.

Experiment 1 and 2 were designed to create attachment to Turkers' work groups in two distinct ways—through interpersonal attraction to promote bond attachment and through social identity processes to promote identity attachment. The results of the two experiments provide some evidence that these two different processes cause different degrees of bond and identity attachment. However, bond and identity attachment remain highly correlated in spite of the manipulations to promote one processes over the other. Interpersonal processes and social identity processes, the theorized underlying causes of bond and identity attachment, are expected to have very different downstream effects, Experiment 2 was designed to test differences in these downstream effects. However, we found no differences in downstream effects.

There are two compelling explanations for why bond and identity attachment remain so highly correlated and we observed no downstream effects. First, our manipulations to promote interpersonal processes and social identity independently may not have cleanly separated the two. Interpersonal attraction builds over time [16]; 25 minutes may not be long enough to feel close to specific group members. While we thought we were promoting interpersonal attraction in the bond condition, in a short-term task with complete strangers we may have actually been predominantly promoting weaker group identification. With longer periods of communication, there might behave been downstream differences in conformity between bond and identity groups as other research as shown in IRC channels [19].

Second, there may be a more complicated relationship between bond and identity attachment, and their root causes interpersonal and social identity processes. In particular, both bond and identity attachment may share a common factor – overall attachment to a social group. This may arise because bond attachment induces identity attachment and identity attachment induces bond attachment. For example, feeling attached to a group as an entity may spread and induce positive feelings toward individuals in the group. It could also be that bond and identity attachment both induce a general attachment to the group that cannot be differentiated. For example, feeling attached to a group as an entity may induce general positive feelings toward anything having to do with the group. These two mechanisms are conceptually equivalent. This explanation is supported by the strong correlation between bond and identity attachment, even when they are differentiated in these two studies as well as others [15, 17].

Design Implications

There is now growing evidence that social interaction can promote community loyalty and therefore should be integrated into online communities to enhance their survival. How to integrate and build social awareness and interaction into an online community is less clear. In other online communities, social awareness alone has been enough to increase loyalty. On MTurk, however, only direct interaction increased loyalty. Future work should explore the level of social interaction needed in a variety of online communities to increase loyalty. Although there was no decrease in the quality of the work in these experiments, there may be tradeoffs associated with introducing more social interaction than necessary.

The results of these studies do not provide a conclusive recommendation as to whether differences in bond and identity attachment should be considered when building social interaction. If bond and identity attachment share a strong common factor it may not matter which type of attachment social tools support. In the latter case designers should create tools to support identity attachment which seems to be easier to promote [17]. On the one hand, if the failure to observe downstream consequences from bond and identity attachment, occurred because interpersonal attraction and bond attachment are difficult to promote in short-term settings with strangers, designers should design tools to promote identity attachment when people first join a site and be concerned about bond attachment only later. Alternatively, they can build bond attachment by importing existing friendships.

ACKNOWLEDGMENTS

Preparation of this manuscript was aided by funding from the National Science Foundation (OCI-0943168). We would also like to thank Tom Postmes for his help.

REFERENCES

1. Allen, N. J., and Meyer, J. P. The measurement and antecedents of affective, continuance, and normative commitment to the organization. *Journal of Occupational Psychology 63,* (1990), 1-18.
2. André, P., Kittur, A., & Kraut, R. E. Utilizing multiple workers in small group collaboration: Effects of simultaneous and sequential work. *Unpublished Manuscript* (2013).
3. Collins, N. L., & Miller, L. C. Self-disclosure and liking: A meta-analytic review. *Psychological Bulletin 116,* (1994), 457-475.
4. Dabbish, L., Kraut, R. E., & Patton, J. Communication and commitment in an online team. In *Proc. CSCW 2012*, ACM Press (2012), 879-888.
5. Diehl, M. The minimal group paradigm: Theoretical explanations and empirical findings. *European Review of Social Psychology 1,* (1990), 263-292.
6. Farzan, R., Dabbish, L., Kraut, R. E., Postmes, T. Increasing Commitment in Online Communities via Building Social Attachment. In *Proc. CSCW 2011*, ACM Press (2011), 321-330.
7. Ipeirotis, P. G. Demographics of Mechanical Turk. *Working Paper,* (2010)
8. Kaufmann, N., Schulze, T., & Veit, D. More than fun and money. Worker motivation in crowdsourcing-A study on Mechanical Turk. In *Proc. Americans Conference on Information Systems*. (2011).

9. Lawler, E. Affective attachments to nested groups: A choice-process theory. *American Sociological Review 57,* (1992), 327-339.

10. Mason, W., & Suri, S. Conducting behavioral research on Amazon's Mechanical Turk. *Behavior Research Methods 44,* (2012), 1-23.

11. Meyer, J. P., Stanley, D. J., Herscovitch, L, and Topolnytsky, L. Affective, continuance, and normative commitment to the organization: A meta-analysis of antecedents, correlates, and consequences. *Journal of Vocational Behavior 61,* (2002), 20-52.

12. Montoya, R. M., Horton, R. S., & Kirchner, J. Is actual similarity necessary for attraction? A meta-analysis of actual and perceived similarity. *Journal of Social and Personal Relationships 25,* (2008), 889-922.

13. Jans, L., Postmes, T., & Van der Zee. The induction of shared identity: The positive role of individual distinctiveness for groups. *Personality and Social Psychology Bulletin 37,* (2011), 1130-1141.

14. Postmes, T., Spears, R., & Lea, M. Intergroup differentiation in computer-mediated communication: Effects of depersonalization. *Group Dyanamics: Theory Research and Practice 6,* (2002), 3-16.

15. Prentice, D. A., Miller, D. T., & Lightdale, J. R. Asymmetries in attachments to groups and to their members: Distinguishing between common-identity and common-bond groups. *Personality & Social Psychology Bulletin* 20 (1994), 484-493.

16. Reis, H. T., Maniaci, M. R., Caprariello, P. A., Eastwich, P. W., & Finkel, E. J. Familiarity does indeed promote attraction in live interaction. *Journal of Personality and Social Psychology 101,* (2011) 557-570.

17. Ren, Y., Harper, F. M., Drenner, S., Terveen, L., Kiesler, S., Riedl, J., & Kraut, R. E. Building member attachment in online communities: Applying theories of group identity and interpersonal bonds. *MIS Quarterly* 36 (2012), 841-864.

18. Ren, Y., Kraut, R. E., & Kiesler, S. Applying common identity and bond theory to design of online communities. *Organization Studies 28,* (2007) 377-408.

19. Sassenberg, K. Common bond and common identity groups on the Internet: Attachment and normative behavior in on-topic and off-topic chats. *Group Dynamics: Theory and Practice 6*, (2002), 27-37.

20. Sedikides, C., Campbell, W. K., Reeder, G., & Elliot, A. J. The Relationship Closeness Induction Test. *Representative Research in Social Psychology 23,* (1999), 1-4.

21. Zhu, H., Kittur A., & Kraut R. E. The impact of crowd reviewing on learning and the effectiveness of review strategies. *Manuscript Under Review,* (2013).

Ethnography of Scaling

Or, How to fit a national research infrastructure in the room

David Ribes
Communication, Culture & Technology (CCT)
Georgetown University
3520 Prospect St. NW, Suite 311
Washington, DC, 20057
dr273@georgetown.edu

ABSTRACT

Ethnographers have traditionally studied people in particular times and places. However, sociotechnical systems are often long-term enterprises, spanning the globe and serving vast communities. Drawing from three cases of research infrastructure development, this paper demonstrates a methodology in which the ethnographer examines *scalar devices*: actors' techniques and technologies for knowing and managing large-scale enterprises. Such devices are enacted in and across concrete times and places; for the ethnographer they are observable as activities of scaling. By examining the enactment of scale we can better investigate diverse kinds of size and growth within sociotechnical systems.

Author Keywords

Ethnography, large-scale, methodology, grounded theory, actor-network theory, infrastructure

Categories and Subject Descriptors

J.4 [**Social and Behavioral Sciences**] Sociology

K.4.3 [**Organizational Impacts**] Computer-supported cooperative work

General Terms

Management, Design, Human Factors, Theory

INTRODUCTION

As an ethnographer who has dedicated his career to the investigation of "large" sociotechnical systems, such as research infrastructures, I am often asked (accompanied by a puzzled look): "how can you study large-scale things using ethnography?"

This paper outlines a methodological approach I have adopted throughout my ethnographic investigations, what I call *ethnography of scaling*. Rather than seeking to investigate the large-scale thing itself, the ethnographer asks of the actors: how do you know your enterprise? *The key insight in this method is the recognition that anytime there is a "large" endeavor you will find actors tasked with managing the problems associated with its scale.*

In an ethnography of scaling the ethnographer turns her or his analytic attention to the techniques and tools actors employ as they go about knowing and managing the scale of their enterprise: administrative actors such as project managers or principal investigators; actors trained in social sciences serving to map the size of such activities; or, technical actors who scale the capacity of servers, monitor bandwidth usage, or design architectures with an eye to extensibility.

All of these people, and many more, are concerned with representing and coping with the size of their endeavor. In order to understand how they manage size and scaling, the ethnographer need only follow in their footsteps. Whether "social" or "technical," all of their work remains observable to the well-placed ethnographer in the form of practical activities, techniques and tools that I will call *scalar devices*.

Scholars within the ethnographic tradition have innovated additional approaches to investigate large-scale endeavors. For example, by traveling to a selection of targeted key sites, ethnographers have sought to "sample" geographically distributed enterprises, generating an understanding of the whole by assembling studies of its parts. Other approaches have sought to "scale-up" ethnography itself by adding more investigators to the research team. These are valuable and promising approaches that I have engaged in throughout my career, but this is not the approach I will describe in this paper. An ethnography of scaling turns these approaches on their head.

Rather than attempting to somehow match the scale of the object of investigation, in ethnography of scaling the investigator focuses on the work of actors as they go about knowing and managing that large-scale object. Observing scaling activities does not require a radical new approach.

CSCW'14, February 15 – 19, 2014, Baltimore, MD, USA.

http://dx.doi.org/10.1145/2531602.2531624

Instead, it demands the sustained application of an ethnographic sensibility that takes scaling as its object of investigation. We need never change the framework or the mode of analysis, regardless of what we, or our actors, consider to be the scale of the enterprise. All the activities of scaling are observable on what sociologist Bruno Latour has called a "flatland" [25].

In order to elucidate this methodology, I will draw from three past ethnographic studies of the development of research infrastructure: GEON, WATERS, the Open Science Grid (OSG). Research infrastructures are sociotechnical assemblies of information technologies, resources and services that support the doing of science, today often called Cyberinfrastructure or eResearch [36]. These endeavors are large in many ways [8]: they are geographically distributed across nations or the globe; they are ambitious, promising to change how science is done; they are significant financial investments; they target many users from many disciplinary backgrounds; they develop national or international computational networks; and so on.

I will focus on three scalar devices I have observed that have been present in all my investigations of research infrastructure: the All-Hands Meeting, surveys and descriptive statistics, and benchmark metrics – each of these scaling activities seek to represent and manage the size and growth of these sociotechnical systems.

Beyond a methodological contribution to ethnography, this paper is also a substantive contribution to understanding infrastructure development, and sociotechnical systems more generally. Such enterprises bristle with scalar devices: surveys, requirements collections, social network analyses, benchmarks, metrics, evaluations and "meetings all the way down." Developers are never satiated with one, two or even three results of such operations: they are forever seeking more, and new, handles on the scale of their enterprises. In the discussion section I will illustrate how multiple scalar devices are gathered together by actors in order to stich together representations of their endeavors.

ETHNOGRAPHY: Copresence, Artifacts and Practices of Representation

Ethnography is a long and varied tradition. In its most basic form, the observer is a participant in the activities of interest. By observing and participating, the ethnographer can recount, theorize or intervene on a rich array of possible themes of interest such as shared meanings and diverging understandings; practices and artifacts; collaborations and conflicts, and many more.

Rather than traversing a potted history of ethnography – from its roots in anthropology and sociology to its current use in infrastructure development [38] – I will jump straight to the approaches that inform this methodology:

i- those that emphasize the production of *copresence* rather than requiring colocation;

ii- in which *archival or trace evidence* can serve as ethnographic data; and,

iii- that focus on *material artifacts* and *practices of representation*.

Traditionally, for the ethnographer, investigation occurs at a common *site* that is shared with the actors, enabling a rich interactional environment for participant observation. However, it is easy to recognize that many interactions occur in a manner that is neither collocated nor synchronous; the internet is the current exemplar of distributed, asynchronous activity, but there are many others, such as love affairs by correspondence or business meetings held on conference phones. Anne Beaulieu has offered the concept of copresence as a corrective to the emphasis on colocation in ethnography. The concept "opens up the possibility that co-presence might be established through a variety of modes, physical co-location being one among others." [1]. In short, her argument is that today we achieve copresence in multifarious ways: by commenting on the same news feeds as our colleagues, through the "thin data" of an instant message, as well as by sharing a cup of tea at a café. Citing sociologist Erving Goffman, Beaulieu notes that "physical presence is not equivalent to availability for interaction."[1]. The ethnographer can generate a sense of copresence by listening in on a conference call, by joining a feed, by reading conversations on a message board or reconstructing activities from a detailed archive.

Ethnography need not be "live," it can be based on data generated in the past. In her study of the *Challenger Launch Decision*, Diane Vaughan [41] used the term historical ethnography to describe her practice of delving into the wealth of secondary data that NASA itself had produced through its investigation of the space shuttle explosion. What made her approach ethnographic, rather than historical alone, was her sensitivity to ongoing interaction (and copresence) in NASA.

My own investigations of Wikipedia [11, 12] and the Open Science Grid [35] have been based on archival traces documented in logs and in ticketing systems. In contrast to the thick description of classical ethnography [10], such traces are thin data. However, because the actors themselves in these online and distributed projects only have these same traces to make sense of distanced activities, the ethnographer and the actors are in symmetrical positions. In other words, in these two cases, actors and ethnographers both relied on thin data to go about their "thick activities" – though for different purposes.

Finally, material artifacts are important. In observing activities of scaling, practices of representing and representations themselves are central. "Large objects" are made available to interaction and practice by representing them at a human scale. For example, in a study of architectural practice, Albena Yaneva [46] focused on how designers work on scaled physical models of a building. Yaneva describes the use of a design tool called a "modelscope," a miniature periscope that is inserted into the architectural model, generating a viewpoint within its model space. A *small* model can thus be momentarily inhabited at the *human* scale, informing *large* design.

Different kinds of scaling activities are accompanied by their associated practices and tools: some of these tools are common across many spheres (e.g., the summative methods of descriptive statistics) and some are endogenous to only a few domains, such as the modelscope in architecture.

I will call an assembly of techniques, tools and representational conventions that are used to know and manage scale, a *scalar device*. In the empirical portions of this paper I will explore three specific scalar devices that I have seen used in all infrastructure development projects: meetings and agendas; surveys and descriptive statistics; and computational metrics and benchmarks.

A note on terms

I will use the term *observable* to refer to that which is visible (or audible, as with a conference call) to the ethnographer, whether through unassisted observation or through the use of digital traces, fieldnotes, audio and video recordings or other documentary materials. I will use the term *actors* to refer to those people the ethnographer is observing: they are actors in the sense that they are engaged in the *enactment* [43] of the scale or growth of their enterprise. My empirical topic is research infrastructure and so I will also call the actors infrastructure developers. I will use the term *object of investigation*, or *object*, to denote the target of scaling activities. Objects can be large or small (e.g., a group, an institution, a global network) as defined and worked-over by actors, but in a strict ethnography of scaling, large objects are only available as that which can be inspected in interaction as talk, practice, and inscription.

Large-Scale Objects in Ethnography

In the brief literature review that follows, I distinguish three approaches to ethnography of large objects: sampling, scaling-up ethnography and ethnography of scaling. I demarcate these approaches for heuristic reasons but in practice I have always used them together: I have always travelled to the distributed sites of my actors, and I have always had collaborators in the study of infrastructure, whether advisors, colleagues or research assistants. I focus on ethnography of scaling here, in order to add it to our repertoire of techniques.

Sampling in Ethnography

A popular approach to studying large-scale objects has been what anthropologist George Marcus has called multi-sited ethnography [29], but which in this paper I will refer to as *sampling in ethnography*. In studying a global scale object, such as colonialism, market regimes, state formation, or nation-building, the ethnographic investigator "moves out from the single sites and local situations of conventional ethnographic research designs to examine the circulation of cultural meanings, objects, and identities in diffuse time-space"[29]. Thus, in order to investigate, say, a globalized restaurant corporation, an ethnographer may travel across nations to synthesize, contrast and compare that restaurant's venues. Or, rather than literally traveling to sites, the investigator may use documentation to trace the movement of, for example, hamburger meat as it travels from farm, to processing plant, to restaurant, in order to arrive on a plate. As anthropologist Ulf Hannerz notes, "multi-site ethnography almost always entails a selection of sites from among those many which could potentially be included." [14].

One of the earliest ethnographic sampling approaches for the study of large sociotechnical systems is rooted in CSCW: Susan Leigh Star and Karen Ruhleder's classic study of the Worm Community System (WCS) infrastructure [39]. With a healthy travel budget in hand, Star [38] described flying from one site of implementation to another. At each site her ethnography would, in part, begin anew as she got to know the people, their scientific interests, the arrangement of their lab, and how (if at all) they were using the WCS.

The advantage of this method is its scope. At each site it is possible to observe, first hand, practices and discourse, material arrangements, or conflicts and cooperation. The "large," or "global," qualities of the object become specific by observing concrete connections and settings. As Marcus put it, in this approach "the global is an emergent dimension of arguing about the connection among sites" [29].

The disadvantages are: potentially thin ethnographies, cost, time, exhaustion of the investigator, and a healthy dose of ongoing awkwardness as each site poses new relations for the ethnographer. In ethnography the investigator must demonstrate that she or he has spent enough time engaged in interaction (collocated or not) to be able to faithfully relate actors' categories or practices. The grounded theory tradition that informed Star's work focuses on *theoretical sampling* (rather than representative sampling as with statistical methods [13]) in which it is important to return to the field site and target the elaboration of a concept: i.e., has sufficient sampling occurred to *saturate* the emerging theory? In any method that relies on sampling, saturation is a challenge.

Recently, scholars have displayed an interest in combining ethnography with other methods so as to better investigate large-scale objects. For example, there has been a recent spurt of papers using network analytic approaches in combination with ethnography [7, 18]. In such approaches, the network analyst assembles relational traces (such as co-authorship or citation data) to produce an image of the object; then, by identifying certain focal nodes an ethnographer can be dispatched to investigate this site in richer detail, i.e., sampling.

Scaling-Up Ethnography

In a second style, the approach is to scale-up the ethnography so as to match the scale of the object of investigation. This means assembling a team of investigators who will tackle the same object. If the object of investigation is geographically distributed, then the team may also be.

Williams and Pollock's study of enterprise resource planning software is an excellent example of a scaled-up study in which they investigated their object for extended periods, and in different settings of development and use [44].

The advantages are numerous. Having multiple eyes on different facets of the same object is invaluable. A classic danger in ethnography is providing an excessively unified view of the object ("a culture," "a community," or "shared meanings")[9]. Multiple collaborators engaged in participant observation can better ensure a complex understanding of contradictions or competing definitions.

The disadvantages of scaling-up ethnography are shared with all forms of team-based and/or geographically distributed research [17, 21]. Coordinating the work of multiple colleagues is a challenge of its own, including working to harmonize the data collection and analysis of the team. Because ethnography is a methodology that can be associated with highly heterogeneous theoretical commitments, working with multiple collaborators can make investigating common objects challenging.

Ethnography of Scaling

Ethnography of scaling inverts the above approaches to large-scale objects. Rather than reconstructing the object by sampling it, or by scaling ethnography to match it, the key methodological recognition is that *knowing and managing the size of the enterprise is a concern for the actors.* The object of analysis for the ethnographer then becomes the methods, techniques and technologies used by actors to know and manage their enterprise.

This approach is similar to past ethnographic analyses focused on centers of coordination or calculation. For example, classic CSCW studies have focused on crisis and airplane control centers [15, 40]. Work-practice studies of centers of coordination are often engaged with the question: how do members practically manage the complexity and diversity of their enterprise? More recently, Karin Knorr-Cetina has examined global financial markets as they occur on the computer screens of distributed trading room floors [23]. Investigators execute these studies by turning their ethnographic gaze to those concrete places and times where such activities are occurring.

However, in order to study scaling we must also track-back, or "open the black box," of scalar indicators themselves. For instance, in examining scaling, when the investigator is confronted with a statistic indicating the size of the object, the goal of the ethnographer is to uncover how this statistic was generated. An indicator of scale often hides the enormous organizational and technical work to produce it.

For example, the statement "we have 2341 members in our organization," renders invisible the activities that went into compiling this number. If this was done through a survey, then literally dozens of collaborators and hundreds of hours of work may have gone into the design, implementation, dissemination, harrying of respondents and then collating, analyzing and visualizing the resulting data to produce that single number.

An ethnography of scaling does not end at the indicator itself, it also tracks the course of indicators as they are deployed in managing the enterprise. The trajectory of the indicator "2341 members" does not end with its presentation as a finding, it goes on to be enacted in future organizational activities: the indicator may be used to decide funding allocations, to identify a needed growth in the organization, or to estimate server capacity required to support a website.

Ethnography of scaling sits at the intersection of the ethnomethodological insistence on the inspection of concrete circumstances [16] and the actor-network sensibility to trace concrete trajectories that weave across circumstances [6]. In broad stroke, ethnography of scaling involves a three part investigative focus on:

- i- the development and deployment of a scalar device;
- ii- the resulting indicator and its reception; and
- iii- the down-stream consequences of indicators as they are wrapped into organizational action or design.

It is across the trajectory of these activities that the scale of an enterprise comes to be represented, known and then managed.

A key methodological prescription in this approach is maintaining a *scalar agnosticism.* The investigator must bracket any preconception of the size of the object [6]. Whether the object is large or small (or something else – see the Discussion) is a concern for the actors. It is they who are engaged in knowing and managing scale, not the ethnographer. The concern for the ethnographer is being at the right place, at the right time, to observe activities of scaling, or, to gain access to the trace materials of those activities.

For example, in the statement "our website gets 12,485 hits a day," the ethnographer should consider the methodological difficulties that actors encountered in generating such a distinct count. What debates went into determining hits to a website: Do crawlers and bots count? What about multiple visits from the same browser? Should organic search arrivals (by a search engine) be treated differently than links from websites? This work of debating what does and does not count [30] is all but erased in the final indicator. In an ethnography of scaling these must be recovered in order to understand how the "size" of the website (its hits per day) came to be known.

Most difficult is that many scaling activities are fully automated and algorithmic. Unpacking how such figures are produced may require a kind of *code spelunking* that is outside the traditional skillset of the ethnographer. This is an example of *infrastructural inversion* [5], where the ethnographic investigator must take a "black-boxed" indicator of scale and actively seek to "open it up" by examining the, often highly technical, work that went into its production. The third empirical example in this paper (the Open Science Grid), demonstrates this spelunking by focusing on the actors that innovate and revise such automated scalar devices.

REFLECTIONS ON FIELDWORK IN GEON

I initially adopted the methodology described in this paper while doing the fieldwork for my Ph.D. dissertation [32]. For my thesis I investigated GEON: the geosciences network[1]. GEON was a very ambitious endeavor, with the goal of implementing an umbrella organization drawing together informational resources in the broader earth sciences e.g., geology, geophysics, paleobotany and many other geoscience disciplines [22]. The mandate for this project was to link the scientific data, mapping tools and computing resources of the geosciences in a single unified information infrastructure spanning the U.S.

During the first years of my fieldwork, I did not have a team of colleagues collectively inspecting this object (scaling-up) or the funds to travel to the sites of the nationally distributed team (sampling) [2]. One advantage of an ethnography of scaling (if you are fortunate enough to be where scaling happens, as I was) is that it does not require a team of investigators or vast travel funds. It is an ideal method for the modestly funded graduate student.

In this first case, I focus on how actors engaged in scaling by using the well-worn activity of meetings and taking of minutes; these meetings were preceded by meetings and followed by meetings. Notably, scaling activities need not be esoteric: they are often mundane. In the section after, I turn to the more technical practices of generating descriptive statistics.

"GEON, like the turtles, is meetings all the way down"

The organizational core of GEON was at the San Diego Supercomputer Center (SDSC) on the University of California San Diego campus. The sociology department was in the next building over, and so, to conduct fieldwork I needed only to cross a slim walking path. While names like GEON and Supercomputer Center may evoke grand imagery of towering servers and vast computing resources, the majority of this fieldwork was conducted in one of two rooms: an auditorium that never housed more than sixty participants, and a small conference room on the third floor.

Twice a year, protected from the racket of computers and servers by the fabric-covered walls of the SDSC auditorium, the GEON members engaged in a genre of meeting I saw enacted again and again, and thereafter in many other cyberinfrastructure projects: the All-Hands Meeting. These gatherings sought to bring together "all members" of the enterprise, such as geoscientists, computer scientists, and educational specialists. The hope was that such a meeting would help in formulating a unified vision across their heterogeneous activities.

The concern in large endeavors is, for example, that the social ties of members will dissipate, that geographic distribution will be an impediment to collaboration, or that a lack of coordination will lead to duplicate efforts. In short, running a large sociotechnical organization is hard and those who are doing so know it.

Meetings are a common, and mundane, method that actors use to ameliorate such problems [4]. Meetings are gatherings that (re)familiarize participants with each other and with their heterogeneous work. In a distributed organization, they are an opportunity to recount recent accomplishments to far off colleagues. In a multidisciplinary enterprise, explaining scientific topics and methods face-to-face can help members overcome the balkanization of technical specialization. In GEON, the technical topics included: earth science, its various objects and methods of investigation, as well as the promised information technologies of cyberinfrastructure, such as computational ontologies and grid computing – none of these are self-explanatory.

GEON had twelve principal investigators (PIs) at eight universities across the U.S. Each of these PIs had a local team at their institution working on aspects of the project: over one hundred computer scientists, information technologists, earth scientists, and administrators regularly participated in GEON. The All-Hands Meetings were one occasion that would bring a large proportion of these specialists together (but never truly all). Meetings served

[1] Now defunct, the GEON portal can still be accessed at geongrid.org

[2] In the later years of this investigation my study was wrapped into a comparative investigation of cyberinfrastructure – see interoperability.ucsd.edu – which used sampling methods and scaled-up the ethnography.

to render visible the distributed activity of participants as a local observable performance.

Meetings are like Russian dolls, nested. In advance of an All-Hands Meeting, PIs and administrative staff at the SDSC would arrange other meetings to write an agenda and settle the order of presenters (and to be sure that lunch and coffee would arrive on time!).

An agenda is a mundane little model for how a meeting will go. They are scalar devices. Without an agenda, or an equivalent of the work it does, attendees at the All-Hands Meetings would not know when they were presenting, and would constantly badger their hosts about coffee breaks and lunch.

The order of presenters on an agenda is meaningful, and it can even be touchy. Usually each of GEON's two lead-PIs were at the top of the agenda, inaugurating the day – one from geoscience and one from computer science, for balance. Then came the National Science Foundation (NSF) program officers, speaking in the name of the agency that had funded GEON. Then followed brief presentations by the other PIs and Co-PIs, and, occasionally, a young ethnographer to speak about community and interdisciplinarity [33]. Agendas map out these arrangements in advance, making the All-Hands Meetings easier to navigate by adding a little bit of order.

In a single morning of presentations a keynote speaker from NSF would outline the agency's plans to build a national cyberinfrastructure; next, in a ten-minute presentation, a programmer would outline his detailed work over the past six months of capturing earth science knowledge in an ontology; and, then, a geoscientist would report her work on the crustal structure of the Western U.S. These presentations sought to summarize the organization of GEON, its environment or technical advances, bringing everyone "onto the same page."

While GEON sought to implement high-end computing resources and experimental technologies, its meetings were no more high-tech than any contemporary conference presentation. At the first All-Hands, in 2002, one absent principal investigator did telecommute and showed up projected on-screen; but, technical difficulties delayed his appearance and eventually poor sound quality forced the reappearance of a rather old-fashioned looking conference phone, placed discretely in a corner of the room within reach of a jack. This little story should surprise no one who studies or does distributed work.

Throughout such meetings multiple participants were capturing the details of the meeting in notes and audio recordings:

> Who's doing what? I always write everything down, if I don't I'll never remember what to say when someone asks me what we are up to in GEON (PI, interview).

> I record the whole thing so I can go back and be sure what we decided (administrative assistant, interview)

Highly mobile, but hardly immutable, such notes circulate widely and in various forms, creating a short-lived archive of daily activity. GEON's project managers, administrative assistants, and lead-PIs transformed some of these notes into "meeting minutes" or lists of "action items," and sent them across the project email lists.

What is small and what is large here?

- A single presentation of a participant would last only ten minutes, but that presentation was an attempt to summarize and communicate the hundreds of hours of work done by many actors, conducted over the last six months.
- A small meeting helped to plan a larger meeting. At the larger meeting there were multiple note-takers working away who eventually summarized their observations into a short list of action items.
- GEON was one small part of the NSF's larger vision to *revolutionize the sciences through cyberinfrastructure*. But GEON was also one of largest concerted investments in information technology in the earth sciences thus far. The NSF geoscience Assistant Director told us all of this by using slides he projected on a fifteen-foot screen.

I attended the first meeting of GEON in 2002. At the end of my research I attended my last meeting in 2006. That first day, before they had built anything, I was able to look across ten meters (rather than the country) and see "all of GEON" in its days of simple composition: geoscientists, laptops, computer scientists and coffee. In the intervening time GEON members developed a plethora of information technologies for the earth sciences and built out its collaborations with other institutions: computational ontologies, integrative mapping tools, an affiliation with NASA, and innumerable computing cycles donated by the TeraGrid. But when I looked across the room during the 2006 All-Hands Meeting, three years later and after all these developments, even then I still saw geoscientists, computer scientists, and slides projected on-screen.

For the ethnographer watching presentations at a meeting, these were all observable as activities of scaling. Bruno Latour, in his studies of scientific laboratories and representations, reminds us that whether the object of investigation is a microscopic bacterium or a vast stellar constellation, in the end they must all be rendered available to the manipulation of scientists' eyes and hands as print-outs or images on a screen [24]. Similarly, in the work of building national, interdisciplinary infrastructures, meetings are the laboratories of their size: agendas, slides and notes are their scalar devices helping to fit the geosciences and their future information technologies into the room for all to see.

THE LITTLE TECHNOLOGIES OF COMMUNITY

Ultimately, the developers of a large infrastructure, such as GEON, still number in the scores or, at most, hundreds. But the target communities of such enterprises – the future users of an infrastructure – are an order of magnitude larger. To know and manage their size, different scalar devices are needed.

This section explores the more esoteric scalar device of surveys. Surveys seek to investigate either an existing community or the future users of an infrastructure, in order to inform the design of that infrastructure. Surveys are "esoteric" in the sense that there is an art and a science involved in their design that seeks to reveal the phenomena of, for example, "community opinion" or "user requirements." Often, the technical work of enacting a survey is delegated to those trained in social scientific methods who create and administer the survey, as well as analyze and represent findings. In an investigation of scaling practices, the analytic gaze of the ethnographer turns toward social scientists and their techniques. Such is the case with WATERS, which employed social scientists to help them make sense of a sudden growth and increased diversity in their targeted users.

The recent visions of research infrastructure, such as cyberinfrastructure, has targeted very large user bases: "Rather than supporting teams or groups, [developers] speak in terms of communities, disciplines and domains." [36]. A successful research infrastructure must support the activities of these broad and diverse constituencies. But how to know what these users want?

It is rarely possible to have "all of the future users" of a domain infrastructure in a single room, as it was possible to have "all the developers" in the rooms of GEON. In the U.S., even a small domain of practicing scientists will number in the thousands – not to mention their technicians, information managers, and other staff so crucial to the functioning of infrastructure [28]. Even if such a vast gathering were possible, the cacophony of voices that would ensue would help no one resolve the issue of how to build better information technologies. But a crafted survey can target just those issues of interest to developers and then summarize findings in tidy bar charts and pie graphs. In doing so, a survey, by its design, will shape findings, intentionally or unintentionally, and may also altogether leave out topics that are of less interest to developers.

Nicholas Rose has called the survey, along with many other such scalar devices, the "little technologies of community":

> Over the second half of the twentieth century, a whole array of little devices and techniques have been invented to make communities real. Surveys of attitudes and values, market research, opinion polls, focus groups, citizens' juries and much more have mapped out these new spaces of culture, brought these values and virtues into visibility and injected them into the deliberations of authorities. [37]

The survey is perhaps the most commonly employed "little technology of community" within the development of large sociotechnical systems. All the research infrastructures I have investigated have at some point commissioned a survey of their own membership or constituencies. Because within systems design it is often considered that "the community should drive development," surveys can serve to demonstrate that the community is being given voice in design decisions. The size, complexity and diversity of community – a multitude of heterogeneous users – can be accounted and summarized through descriptive statistics.

Surveys are tools of governance in that they empower a small group of people to speak in the name of a larger one. In some cases, a survey successfully assuages fears by assuring users that their interests are represented in the design of the future infrastructure; in other cases, surveys infuriate, as users feel silenced, underrepresented or misrepresented [19]. This is one feature of interest to the ethnographer of scaling. This should also be of the utmost importance to those developing infrastructure and to the constituency an infrastructure intends to serve, because, as with any scalar device, indicators will play a role in downstream design [45]. In the case of WATERS, survey findings were used to allocate resources in the planned development of the infrastructure.

The WATERS Event

WATERS, like GEON, had ambitious goals to develop cyberinfrastructure, but targeted the disciplines concerned with the environments of water: rivers, rainfall, sewers and estuaries. Unfortunately, it was inaugurated with much more fractious beginnings than GEON. WATERS was born out of the top-down matrimony of two cyberinfrastructures for the domains of hydrology and environmental engineering[3]. Because both research fields seek to understand the environments of water, officers at the National Science Foundation decreed that a single infrastructure would avoid unnecessary duplication of resources. Through WATERS, both fields would develop a single interoperable set of observatories and information resources for the unified domain. I will not further recount how this merger came to be, which in past writings I have called "the WATERS event" [34]. Instead I will focus on the consequences and responses of participants.

---

[3] WATERS was the Water and Environmental Research Systems Network. It sought to bring together previous efforts in hydrology led by CUAHSI (Consortium of Universities for the Advancement of Hydrologic Science) and environmental engineering's CLEANER (Collaborative Large-Scale Engineering Analysis Network for Environmental Research). WATERS and CLEANER are now defunct, but CUAHSI continues its information systems efforts on several fronts.

The initial reaction by both groups of researchers to the merger was heated – polemic even. It should surprise no one that the WATERS event was a controversy: there was a great deal at stake for all parties. Both sides felt that the rug had been yanked from beneath their vision of research infrastructure. At the heart of the matter was the question of resource distribution: what disciplinary groups would get funding? From the forthcoming observatories, what institutions would hold new troves of rich data? Most contentiously, what would those data be about? And thus, at the very kernel of designing research infrastructure: what disciplinary objects of investigation would be made easily researchable and which would receive less, or no attention?

From the perspective of the leadership of this newly merged cyberinfrastructure, WATERS was clearly a much larger endeavor than the two initial projects individually: but what kind of large? And how would it affect plans to develop research infrastructure? For an ethnographer who was well positioned to observe the action, the WATERS event led to a self-conscious and observable activity of scaling.

Questions about *scaling-up* in WATERS were of three kinds:

i. *Scaling-up users:* WATERS would serve two domain communities. Did this mean doubling the user base? Probably not, since it was known that hydrologists and environmental engineers overlap in many ways. So then, how big was the future user community of WATERS?

ii. *Scaling-up of objects of investigation*: A common phrase that emerged within WATERS was that "environmental engineers care about water quality while hydrologists care about water quantity" or, in other words, engineers are concerned with, for example, whether water can be used to safely irrigate crops, whereas hydrologists care about how fast water will erode a riverbank based on its flow. What this little shorthand indicated was that these communities are concerned with different objects of research. A single research infrastructure would have to support both, and, thus, would have to collect more kinds of data, would have to develop more instruments to collect those data, and hire more information managers familiar with those data. But how much more data, and what kinds? These specifics remained an open question.

iii. *Scaling-up of the institutional resources to be integrated*: Environmental engineers and hydrologists are already enmeshed within their existing funding agencies, scientific societies, and disciplines. They have vast extant data archives and distinct software they use to do their work. The promise of cyberinfrastructure is to interoperate databases and support sharing of software tools. Would WATERS mean a doubling of such resources to be integrated? Again, probably not, since the communities overlap; but again, how much?

In order to make sense of these diverse forms of growth, and to help clarify the fuzzy boundaries between environmental engineering and hydrology, a key strategy in WATERS was to commission surveys of these communities.

I was fortunate that as I began to study WATERS, it was my new post-doctoral advisor, Thomas Finholt, and his previous postdoc, Katherine Lawrence, who had recently conducted one of these surveys [27]. Once again, I did not need to travel any further than up the hall at the University of Michigan iSchool, in order to observe these scaling activities. From my inquiries, I garnered all kinds of informal details about how the survey had been conducted, such as the "incentivization" of participation in the survey by including a two-dollar bill in the envelope with the questionnaire. However, the basic methodology of the survey was *pro forma*: Lawrence and Finholt sent a questionnaire to three hundred randomly selected people from each of two scientific societies that stood-in for the two domain communities of WATERS [27].

The survey revealed a landscape of relatively clear differences and commonalities between and across these two communities, defining the boundaries of each field while also pointing to promising avenues for developing a common research infrastructure. As had been expected, environmental engineering and hydrology overlapped in many respects, while diverging in others:

> each group has very different needs for data sources. For example, [hydrologists] are substantially more reliant on streamflow data [while] engineers had a substantially greater interest [.] in the USGS and EPA water quality databases. [27]

These findings matched what was already known about these communities (i.e., quality vs. quantity), but now in the precise numbers of descriptive statistics and by identifying specific databases. Commonalities also emerged. For example, to the horror of developers, but to the surprise of no one, the most commonly used data storage format for all groups was the *Excel* spreadsheet.

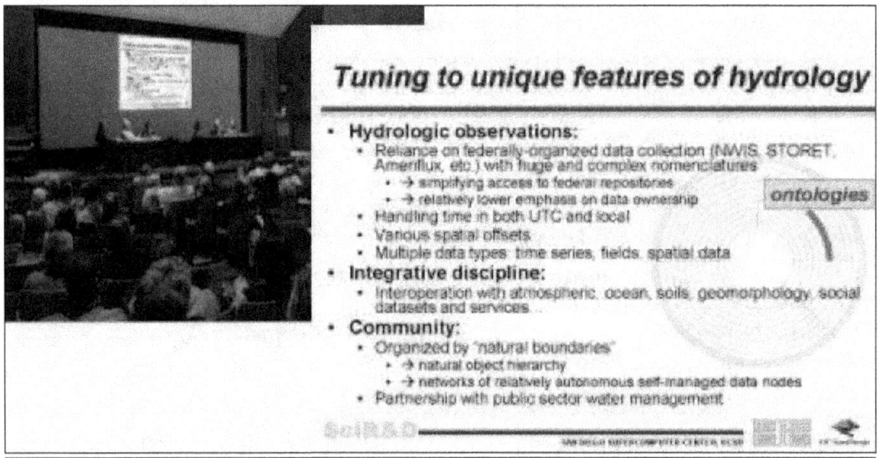

Figure 1: Displayed at a WATERS meeting (left), this image (right), scales the field of hydrology to a single slide that encapsulates its science, interdisciplinarity and culture.

Surveys reveal disciplinary difference as ordered preference and heterogeneous practice but they also point to shared goals, widespread objects of interest and commonly desired computing resources. The results of the survey translated the future users of WATERS into the precise language of descriptive statistics and rendered findings in colorful and easily readable charts. The boundaries of engineering and hydrology, once intuited but ephemeral, were buttressed by such findings, constituting a detailed statistical reality of what was formerly impressionistic disciplinary difference.

The trajectory of these findings did not conclude with the publication of the survey. This is merely a mid-point in the life of these new indicators. As I continued my investigations, these charts and graphs would reappear continuously, projected on screens as I attended the meetings of WATERS. *Figure 1* is a photograph (taken by me) of a slide that summarizes the cultural qualities of hydrology as a discipline, i.e., as the slide claims: hydrologists have a "lower emphasis on data ownership" and are an "integrative discipline."

Techniques such as surveying do not automatically compel users or developers to believe their findings. In principle, whether findings are representative of a community can be a matter of debate. The objectivity or competence of the survey can come under fire. However, I have never observed such a debate questioning a survey itself (though, see the outcome of the OSG survey in the next section).

What I have observed are debates over whether survey findings have been properly incorporated into the design of the infrastructure. For example, at the same meeting as the slide in *Figure 1* was displayed, during the question period, a self-identified hydrologist stood up and made the statement:

> We are all here deciding what WATERS will look like. And from what I see it's all quality and no quantity. And hydrology just isn't going to stand behind that. (field notes)

Referring to the shorthand I described above – that hydrology is concerned with quantity of water – the scientist argued that the interests of his discipline, in the form of plans to develop observatories and sensors, had not been properly reflected in the design for WATERS he was hearing discussed at that meeting.

A great deal of ink has been spilt demonstrating how surveys produce findings that are tidier than the sentiments of their respondents [20]: opinions held by individuals in shades of grey are captured for the aggregate in black and white. This is certainly the case. But we should also keep in mind that this is also the strength of the technique: the survey is a scalar device to reduce the cacophony of the crowd to a manageable diversity of voices. The full range of dissent and eccentricities in the domain are lost: Laura, the environmental engineer who insists on recording her data on paper; Bob, the hydrologist who checks for strychnine in river water by counting the average number of eggs in a bird's nest. Descriptive statistics do not capture such individual practices very well – granularity is lost. What is gained from a survey is a representation of community rendered as discrete groups and well-defined stakeholders. Each scalar device only preserves particular relations as it redescribes an object in its distinct representational form.

SCALABILITY: A design virtue in the metric

The two examples above could be characterized as cases of organizational scaling – they are about the number and qualities of people involved in projects. Lest the misconception be allowed to stand that scaling is a matter of *the social*, narrowly construed as only about humans, this last section will focus on a technical outcome: scaling computing capacity. This is perhaps the most common use of the term "scaling-up" within cyberinfrastructure development. Correspondingly, one of the greatest virtues in the design of infrastructure, and information systems more generally, is that they be scalable (can support growth), or the related virtues of extensibility (can expand into new capacities) and modularity (the use of common protocols that make discrete components interchangeable). Scalability, extensibility and modularity are the triumvirate gold standards of good design for today's technical architecture development efforts concerned with future growth. These too can be observed as a matter of scaling activities as long as the ethnographer is willing to spelunk into code, algorithms and esoteric metrics.

Here I will briefly explore activities within the Open Science Grid (OSG) as they planned to support the reopening of the Large-Hadron Collider (LHC) in 2009, which would demand a significant scaling-up of the computing power they were offering[4]. The kernel of the OSG is to make available processing power "on tap" to geographically distributed scientists. In sweeping (and not altogether accurate) terms, the OSG is an instantiation of the infrastructure-as-a-service (IAAS) model of cloud computing. *Figure 2* shows a chart of usage within OSG, and its projected future growth. How was such a projection made and what was concluded from it?

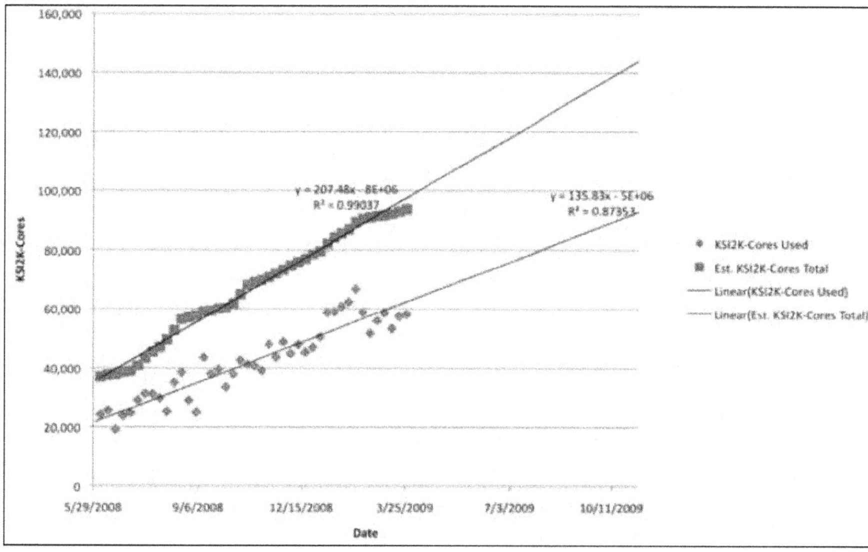

Figure 2: Will OSG scale-up to manage the reopening of the Large Hadron Collider in 2009? To answer this question, this chart projects its future growth [2].

In order to know its scale OSG must be instrumented with tools specific to computing. We are used to seeing metrics of computing use, and we tend to ignore or take these for granted – e.g., megahertz, flops. But within high-performance computing enterprises there are technical experts dedicated to developing and deploying new metrics and tools to keep track of usage – something that is more challenging when many computing cores are distributed around the globe working in concert.

I track the activities of one technical specialist, Brian Bockelman. Trained in computer science with a concentration in metrics, Bockelman has worked for many years to, as he puts it, "give estimates of the "size" of the Open Science Grid and demonstrate why such a number is hard to come by." (quotes in original) [2].

To measure the "size" of OSG, Bockelman et al. [3] first attempted the administration of a survey, but found responses were riddled with "human errors" as local administrators failed to supply the correct metrics. More importantly, the results of the survey were static even as new sites were quickly being added to OSG: "survey results would not scale as the grid grows." [2]

Instead, in the OSG they have relied on a piece of software called Gratia [3] that is used for job accounting. A job is a unit of work for an operating system. By installing Gratia at each OSG site they were able to track jobs: the OSG averaged between 5 and 11 million jobs per month between May 2008 and March 2009 [2]. Even this metric is crude, as it treats all jobs as though they have the same computational cost. They do not. And so Bockelman combined Gratia with a metric for aggregate computation: Wall hours; "if a job ran for one hour on one core consuming 50% the CPU, we say it has .5 CPU hours or 1 Wall hour." With this metric in hand, Bockelman was then able to extrapolate the growth of the OSG "using a linear fit based on the last 10 months, [Figure 2] shows the projection for the following 6 months" [2].

Based on his projection, Bockelman concluded "This burst of growth indicates the OSG is in a good position for delivering further growth when the LHC collisions start," but also added the caveat that growth is linear only over the academic year; during the summer, it stalls. He speculated: "It appears that the primary variable in grid usage is still sociological," [2].

Bockelman is neither a PI nor a project administrator. It is not only managerial actors who are concerned with scaling; we will encounter the deployment of scalar devices throughout sociotechnical systems and for many purposes. Even within the "depths of the machine" – and as with any scalar device – metrics and tools are developed to know and manage the growth the object. These indicators serve to inform actors about the future of OSG as they organize and plan to selectively allocate computing power where it is needed and to add more resources in advance of shortages.

DISCUSSION: What is to be done with large objects? Proliferate scalar devices

> One day the husband of the woman is called to the artist's studio. "What do you think?" asked Picasso, indicating the nearly finished picture. "Well…" said the husband, trying to be polite, "it isn't how she really looks." "Oh," said the artist, "and how does she really look?" The husband decided not to be intimidated. "Like this!" said he, producing a photograph from his wallet. Picasso studied the photograph. "Mmm…" he said, "small, isn't she?"
>
> – Gareth Morgan, Images of Organization [31]

[4] opensciencegrid.org In the past, I have investigated the delegation of coordinating work to software systems for cycle sharing in OSG [35].

Allow me to recapitulate the concept of *scalar agnosticism*. At the beginning of this paper I defined it as bracketing of any preconception of the largeness (or smallness) of the object of investigation. However, through the cases I have also attempted to elaborate another meaning: an agnosticism to what large *is*. In this paper we have encountered several variants on the size of infrastructure: the number of members of a project, the range and diversity of disciplines involved in development, a geographically distributed membership, a vast and unknown community of future users, and the projected growth of computing cycles.

Scaling has always also been temporal, whether this has been a meeting agenda that structures the activities of an upcoming get-together; knowing the prospective users of a community infrastructure; or predicting the cycles that will be needed in order to compute forthcoming particle collisions. Part of the goal in activities of scaling is to manage growth, and part of growth is what is yet to come. Scaling is a future oriented activity.

Each of these ambitions for growth present unique kinds of problems to know and manage the scale of an enterprise, and each has distinct techniques and technologies to manage that form of scale. In short, scaling (or scale) is not one thing. By taking an agnostic position, we have been freed to investigate what and how scale is encountered in such projects.

I write this partially because it seems to me that there is often a hubris associated with mastery of a particular scalar device, as though one technique had somehow solved the problem of scale. Once, such pride was the prerogative of the quantitative statistician; today the tables have shifted and I hear such claims mostly from social network analysts – but watch out, big data is well placed to attempt a coup.

What I have attempted to show is that no single scalar device can serve to represent or manage all forms of scale. A network diagram of author collaborations will tell you a great deal about the composition of a domain, or the relation between disciplines. But for all the "completeness" of these data, it will tell you nothing about how many servers will be needed to manage a website's traffic. And in turn, traffic indicators will not tell you why the communities of hydrologists and environmental engineers may chafe at having to work under the same umbrella; something a survey did moderately well.

Each of these approaches to scale provides a unique view and suggests different kinds of solutions to manage oncoming problems. But each device also generates exclusions and invisibilities.

In concluding my discussion of WATERS above, I mentioned Laura and Bob, real hydrologists with pseudonymous names. Laura trudges into wetland field-sites to collect and document her data on paper. She was irked that there was no place for her to recount this in a survey that assumed all data were digital. Bob uses surrogates, such as a declined average of eggs per nest, as a signal of pollutants in a river. There was no space for him to describe this rich method in the 'other' text-field available in the survey. A survey is a powerful device for capturing collective similarities and differences, but even the most well crafted survey apprehends only particular kinds of relations.

Laura and Bob know they are outliers – largely invisible to that scalar device – but they still wanted to have a voice in the design of the future infrastructure for their field. Their stories were captured instead by this ethnographer, recounted here in this paper, and in a handful of presentations back to WATERS PIs.

Ethnography too is a scalar device in such enterprises. This is why infrastructure developers invite investigators such as myself on-board. They hope that we will be able to help them understand things like the epistemic cultures of their user communities, to mitigate the difficulties of interdisciplinary collaboration, or to shape robust routines of communication.

Am I arguing that ethnography is somehow a better or less reductive scalar device? I am not. As with any other device, ethnography renders a particular representation of scale, myopic and revealing both.

In my experience, infrastructure developers implicitly agree. No single scalar device will suffice. They are forever seeking additional advice on their communities, better ways of organizing meetings, new forms of data visualization, and more agile methods for summarizing and communicating heterogeneous work. No approach is treated as a magic bullet, as if one universal representation of the scale of the enterprise will become available to topple all the others. There is no one scalar device to rule them all.

I have sat in rooms with principal investigators (or, information managers), as they poured over stacks of indicators in preparation for a decision. Multiple scalar devices are arranged idiosyncratically on tables and screens in order to stich together representations of their enterprise. From a formal standpoint, the methods that generated such indicators may be wholly incommensurable: notes from an All-Hands Meeting, user requirements scenarios, results of a survey, Gantt charts, and a handful of accumulated statistics. But in such rooms – what Janet Vertesi has identified as "seamful spaces" [42], in which local and practical solutions to the challenges of integration are enacted – no formal methodological justification is needed to mix and match these indicators. It is at the intersection of multiple scalar devices that decisions are made.

CONCLUSION: Ethnography of scaling... "Yes, but does it scale?"

This paper opened with the most common methodological question I receive as an ethnographer studying sociotechnical systems: "how can ethnography study large things?" I now conclude with the second most common question I get when I recount my ethnographic method, one that is more dismissive and exhibits less curiosity: "Yes ... but does it scale?"

I have always been baffled by this question.

When that question is asked, what come to mind are all the indicators produced about infrastructures that I have collected: troves of surveys and questionnaires, social network analyses, and benchmark metrics. I recall all the meetings where findings were presented, and the debates and conflicts that ensued; many of these events are documented only in my field notes. I also consider all the ways I have tracked these indicators as they were deployed to inform design decisions about a future sociotechnical system. Does ethnography scale? My answer is that I endeavour to scale exactly to the extent as do my informants.

At the root of this question, it seems to me, is a confusion about the object of ethnographic investigations. Scaling activities in all their forms are a crucial feature of infrastructure development, and sociotechnical systems more generally. One cannot observe activities of development without continuously encountering such indicators.

Perhaps because many scalar devices are quantitative or technical, there is an assumption that the (qualitative) ethnographer will skirt such activities. This is not the case. In the study of an enterprise where actors seek to represent and manage its size, *scalar devices are a part of the field of observation for the ethnographer*. Put more strongly, they *should be* objects of investigation.

As ethnographers our own methods should match our actors' nimbleness. In treating organizational action and technical design as practice, talk and material arrangement, scaling is rendered observable to the analyst. There is nothing in advance to limit ethnographic studies to those questions that are deemed of the "correct size" or "sufficiently social." I hope that the approach described here will open a terrain of research in studies of sociotechnical systems. We should travel across the scales mirroring the footsteps of our informants', and when we do so we will discover that scaling is the sometimes mundane, but often esoteric, work of actors. Rendered observable as a form of practice, any size-complex of the qualitative researcher dissolves.

One final note on scalar agnosticism. My first reaction when encountering indicators of scale is to treat them in the fashion described in this paper: as an activity of scaling oriented to knowing and managing the size of the object. However, once my investigation of these activities of scaling is completed, I remove the "bracket" that is my scalar agnosticism, and stuff these indicators into a black box, just as the actors do. Thereafter, as modalities are stripped from scalar devices [26], I treat visualizations and summaries in the way that developers do: largely as facts. In addition to the practices of scaling, there are many other activities that are relevant to understanding the development of infrastructure. And infrastructure is large. The statistics and visualizations they generate help me to know and manage my investigations of those infrastructures.

ACKNOWLEDGEMENTS

Earlier versions of this paper were presented at 'Scientific Practice as Ordinary Action' in Fribourg, SW; 'Mind and Society' at the University of Manchester, UK; 'The Ethnographer in the Network' at Princeton University, US, and an informal workshop at the Norwegian University of Science and Technology. I would like to thank the participants at those events for their feedback, to Marte Giskeødegård and Jennifer Feldman for their insightful comments on final revisions, and to Anat Leibler for comments on very early drafts. This research has been supported by NSF/VOSS award #0904145 'Delegating Organizational Work to Virtual Organization Technologies.'

REFERENCES

1. Beaulieu, A. From co-location to co-presence: Shifts in the use of ethnography for the study of knowledge. *Social Studies of Science*, 40, 3 (2010), 453-470.
2. Bockelman, B. *Usage of the Open Science Grid.* Managed Grids and Cloud Systems in the Asia-Pacific Research Community. Springer, 2010.
3. Bockelman, B., Canal, P., Mandrichenlo, I. and Pordes, R. *OSG Accounting Requirements*. 2008.
4. Boden, D. *The business of talk: Organizations in action.* Polity Press, Cambridge, UK, 1994.
5. Bowker, G. C. and Star, S. L. *Sorting things out : classification and its consequences*. MIT Press, Cambridge, Mass., 1999.
6. Callon, M. and Latour, B. *Unscrewing the Big Leviathan: how actors macrostructure reality and how sociologists help them to do so.* In Advances in Social Theory and Methodology: Toward an Integration of Micro- and Macro-Sociologies. Routledge, 1981.
7. Cambrosio, A., Keating, P. and Mogoutov, A. Mapping Collaborative Work and Innovation in Biomedicine: A Computer-Assisted Analysis of Antibody Reagent Workshops. *Social Studies of Science*, 34, 3 (2004), 325-364.
8. Edwards, P. *Infrastructure and Modernity: Force, Time, and Social Organization in the History of Sociotechnical Systems*. Modernity and Technology. MIT Press, 2003.
9. Emerson, R. M., Fretz, R. I. and Shaw, L. L. *Writing ethnographic fieldnotes*. University of Chicago Press, 2011.

10. Geertz, C. *The interpretation of cultures*. Basic Books, New York, 1973.
11. Geiger, R. S. and Ribes, D. The work of sustaining order in wikipedia: the banning of a vandal. CSCW 2010, 117-126.
12. Geiger, R. S. and Ribes, D. *Trace ethnography: Following coordination through documentary practices*. HICSS 2011.
13. Glaser, B. G. and Strauss, A. *The discovery of grounded theory: strategies for qualitative research*. Aldine Pub. Co., Chicago, 1973.
14. Hannerz, U. Being there... and there... and there! Reflections on multi-site ethnography. *Ethnography*, 4, 2 (2003), 201-216.
15. Heath, C. and Luff, P. Collaboration and control: Crisis management and multimedia technology in London Underground Line Control Rooms. *JCSCW*, 1, 1-2 (1992), 69-94.
16. Hilbert, R. A. Ethnomethodology and the Micro-Macro Order. *American Sociological Review*, 55, 6 (1990), 794-808.
17. Hinds, P. J. and Kiesler, S. *Distributed work*. MIT Press, 2002.
18. Howard, P. N. Network ethnography and the hypermedia organization: new media, new organizations, new methods. *New Media & Society*, 4, 4 (2002), 550-574.
19. Igo, S. E. *Subjects of Persuasion*. Social knowledge in the making. University of Chicago Press, 2012.
20. Jirotka, M. and Goguen, J. *Requirements Engineering: Social and Technical Issues*. Academic Press, New York, 1994.
21. Jirotka, M., Lee, C. P. and Olson, G. M. Supporting Scientific Collaboration: Methods, Tools and Concepts. *JCSCW* 2013, 1-49.
22. Keller, R. G. GEON (GEOScience Network) -- A first step in creating cyberinfrastructure for the geosciences. *Electronic Seismologist*, July/August (2003).
23. Knorr-Cetina, K. and Bruegger, U. Global Microstructures: The Virtual Societies of Financial Markets. *American Journal of Sociology*, 107, 4 (2002), 905-950.
24. Latour, B. Visualization and Cognition: Thinking with Eyes and Hands. *Knowledge and Society: Studies in the Sociology of Culture Past and Present*, 6 (1986), 1-40.
25. Latour, B. *The Flat-Earthers of social theory*. Accounting and Science. Cambridge University Press, 1996.
26. Latour, B. and Woolgar, S. *Laboratory life : the construction of scientific facts*. Sage Publications, Beverly Hills, 1979.
27. Lawrence, K. A., Finholt, T. A. and Kim, I. *Cyberinfrastructure for the WATERS Network: a Survey of AEESP and CUAHSI Members*. 2006.
28. Lee, C. P., Dourish, P. and Mark, G. *The human infrastructure of cyberinfrastructure*. CSCW, 2006.
29. Marcus, G. Ethnography in/of the world system: the emergence of multi-sited ethnography. *Annual review of anthropology*, 24, 1 (1995), 95-117.
30. Martin, A. and Lynch, M. Counting Things and People: The Practices and Politics of Counting. *Social Problems*, 56, 2 (2009), 243-266.
31. Morgan, G. *Images of Organization*. Sage Publications, Beverly Hills, 1986.
32. Ribes, D. *Universal Informatics: Building Cyberinfrastructure, Interoperating the Geosciences*. Unpublished Dissertation. University of California, San Diego, 2006.
33. Ribes, D. and Baker, K. S. *Modes of Social Science Engagement in Community Infrastructure Design*. Communities and Technology. Springer, 2007.
34. Ribes, D. and Finholt, T. A. Representing community: Knowing users in the face of changing constituencies. *CSCW*, 2008.
35. Ribes, D., Jackson, S. J., Geiger, R. S., Burton, M. and Finholt, T. Artifacts that organize: Delegation in the distributed organization. *Information and Organization*, 23, 1 (2012), 1-14.
36. Ribes, D. and Lee, C. P. Sociotechnical Studies of Cyberinfrastructure and e-Research: Current Themes and Future Trajectories. *JCSCW*, 19, 3-4 (2010), 231-244.
37. Rose, N. *Powers of Freedom: Reframing Political Thought*. Cambridge University Press, 1999.
38. Star, S. L. The Ethnography of Infrastructure. *American Behavioral Scientist*, 43 (1999), 377-391.
39. Star, S. L. and Ruhleder, K. *Steps Towards and Ecology of Infrastructure. CSCW* 1994.
40. Suchman, L. *Technologies of accountability: of lizards and aeroplanes*. Technology in Working Order. Routledge, 1993.
41. Vaughan, D. *The Challenger Launch Decision: Risky Technology, Culture, and Deviance at NASA*. University of Chicago Press, Chicago, 1996.
42. Vertesi, J. Seamful Spaces: Infrastructures in Interaction. *Science, Technology & Human Values* (forthcoming).
43. Weick, K. E. *Enactment processes in organizations*. New directions in organizational behavior. St. Clair, 1977.
44. Williams, R. and Pollock, N. Moving Beyond the Single Site Implementation Study: How (and Why) We Should Study the Biography of Packaged Enterprise Solutions. *Information Systems Research*, 23, (2012), 1-22.
45. Woolgar, S. Configuring the user: the case of usability trials. *A sociology of monsters: Essays on power, technology and domination*, 58 (1991), 66-75.
46. Yaneva, A. Scaling Up and Down: Extraction Trials in Architectural Design. *Social Studies of Science*, 35, 6 (2005), 867-894.

Enabling Relationship Building in Tabletop-supported Advisory Settings

Peter Heinrich, Mehmet Kilic, Felix-Robinson Aschoff, Gerhard Schwabe
University of Zurich, Department of Informatics
Binzmühlestrasse 14, 8050 Zurich, Switzerland
{peterhe,kilic,aschoff,schwabe}@ifi.uzh.ch

ABSTRACT
Recent research has shown that financial advisory encounters can successfully be supported with IT-artifacts. Tabletop scenarios, for example, can increase the transparency of the advisory process for customers. However, we have also had the experience that the relationship quality as experienced by customers can suffer severely when IT-artifacts are introduced. Based on these experiences, we developed guidelines for both, the artifact-design itself as well as for the environment in order to avoid this effect, and implemented them in one of our prototypes. The evaluation reveals that these measures proved to be effective. With the reported study, we seek to enhance our design knowledge of IT-supported advisory scenarios with a special focus on relationship building. In a larger context, we argue that the use of IT during sensitive face-to-face encounters will be of growing significance in the future but, as yet, is hardly understood. We make a contribution in this area with our generic requirements, design principles and evaluation.

Author Keywords
Tabletop, Relationship Building, Advisory Scenario

ACM Classification Keywords
H.5.3 [Group and Organization Interfaces]

1 INTRODUCTION

An advisory encounter is a crucial social process often taking place between the representative of an institution and a client. There are a number of different conceptualizations of the advisory process (see [25] for a discussion of different perspectives). In a general sense, one can describe an advisory process as the interaction between two persons, where one supports the other in solving certain problems for reaching certain decisions. Advisory encounters are interaction scenarios that have been known for a long time in the areas of medicine, law or sale.

CSCW'14, February 15 – 19, 2014, Baltimore, MD, USA.
Copyright 2014 ACM 978-1-4503-2540-0/14/02...$15.00.
http://dx.doi.org/10.1145/2531602.2531697

Recent research has demonstrated that these kinds of advisory scenarios can successfully be supported by IT-artifacts [19,25]. For example, Nussbaumer et al. [20] conducted a number of experimental tests in which the perceived transparency of a financial advisory process could eventually be increased. These experiments, however, showed that the quality of the information that is exchanged between the advisor and the client is not the only crucial factor; rather, the relationship between the client and the advisor can considerably suffer because of the introduced IT-artifact.

This is especially problematic because the quality of the relationship is a crucial factor for the advisory process. According to Jungermann [12], the social dimension of these interactions is at least as important as the information that is exchanged between the client and the advisor.

The crucial aspect of IT influence on relationship building in such sensitive face-to-face advisory scenarios has hardly been addressed by previous researchers. In addition, we lack empirically-founded design knowledge how these scenarios are to be conceptualized and implemented. This holds especially for the emerging technology of tabletops which are expected to change the advisory setting in many areas. Accordingly, we pursue the following research question: *How can we enable relationship building in a tabletop-supported advisory setting?*

By answering this question, we contribute to the design knowledge on sensitive face-to-face scenarios that are crucial in many areas such as financial transactions, legal advice and health issues. Based on the experiences of the evaluations in the financial advisory area, we develop a number of generic requirements and design principles to support relationship building between an advisor and a client. In this paper, we further demonstrate, how these design requirements and principles can be implemented in a tabletop supported advisory encounter. In an analysis of the time, spent for relationship building (mutual face gaze) we compare two tabletop systems: Prototype 1 that does not implement our design requirements and principles and Prototype 2 that does. The evaluation reveals that our guidelines prove to be effective.

2 BACKGROUND

Popular lore claims that there is no second chance to make a first impression. Indeed advisory scenarios are sensitive social interactions which can set the tone for the interactions to come. This is especially the case if the two parties meet only a few times or only once. The role of relationship has been intensely researched in the background of services selling [5] and e-Commerce [22]. Results from that research indicate that the relationship between seller and client is crucial for future sale interaction.

In our research, we focus especially on face-to-face advisory encounters in the financial area. These situations are characterized by the fact that the advisor and the client meet only a few times. Thus, the advisor does not have much time to win the respect and trust of the client. Misunderstandings, irritations or a negative personal atmosphere can hardly be corrected.

In this context, by relationship building we refer to the establishment of a trustful connection in which the client feels taken seriously, having his needs attended to and being treated respectfully. Overall the client should feel comfortable to reveal information that is important for the solution or decision making process.

In such a setting, establishing trust is key to a successful collaborative service encounter [12]. Advisors are trained to establish and maintain a personal relationship, and, for this reason, have thus long resisted using any technology during the actual service encounter, as they are afraid of interference [26].

2.1 The role of IT-artifacts in advisory encounters

Advisory services are normally performed in a structured way. In most cases, an investment advisory service will include the following steps: understanding the customer's situation and needs, analyzing her risk preferences and capability, proposing a strategic asset allocation to different asset classes (such as shares or bonds) and selecting specific products (c.f. [12] for an explicit phase model).

Although Stewart et al. [32] proposed collaborative interfaces for face-to-face sales-oriented collaboration, few studies have been undertaken, despite a rising interest in the marketing literature. There, the concept of value co-creation proposes a joint configuration as solution [23].

Apart from that, literature offers several good reasons to support these encounters with appropriate IT-artifacts:

- It has been shown that IT-artifacts can enable the customer to actively participate in the creation of a solution matching his problems [25].
- The IT-system can make the encounter more transparent by sharing information between client and advisor with the help of a shared artifact [20].
- (IT-)Artifacts can support both clients and advisors in the process of "common objectification" [35]. Weber et al. [35] describes common objectification as the act of sharing individual knowledge and expertise through materialized items created by the group members. An IT-system can provide such a shared information space to support this task.
- By providing a virtual form of reality, IT-artifacts can also foster efficient knowledge transfer by enabling situated learning in general [10] and also within the advisory encounter [9].
- IT-artifacts that are used by both advisor as well as client can be a valuable tool to document important information for later advisory sessions or services [WpHG][1].
- IT-artifacts like tabletop systems (in contrast to other display types) can help to seamlessly integrate traditional use of paper (e.g., proposed by [2,31]), which might still be required in such settings.

IT usage, however, also has its downsides. While necessary to achieve goals effectively, IT usage does consume precious time that could be spent otherwise in interpersonal communication. Thus, the more heavily these tools are used in the advisory situation, the less time there is available for relationship building.

2.2 Previous research in supporting face-to-face interactions with regard to relationship building

The connection between working with an artifact, as well as establishing and maintaining a personal relationship, has been an important design issue in CSCW research for more than two decades: "Successful technological augmentation of a task or process depends upon a delicate balance between good social processes and procedures with appropriately structured technology" [6]. Very early on, the importance of maintaining eye contact was a key challenge for collaborative rooms [15]. In those days embedded solutions connected single-user computers into a physical conferencing table. Working with these multi-user interfaces turned out to be challenging, as users had to align the actions of others into their own mental models. In consequence, systems were designed for aligning artifact related work with eye contact during distributed collaboration [16,18]. The importance of eye contact for interpersonal relations is also reflected by the literature from psychology: Research shows that eye contact can influence the interplay between two persons on various levels. For example, eye contact (see [13] for a comprehensive summary on this research) indicates

[1] WpHG: § 34 German Securities Trading Act

whether a person is paying attention to a certain situation, whether a person is perceived to be competent (more eye contacts are associated with more competence) and whether a person is perceived to be credible (more eye contacts are associated with more credibility). In addition, eye contact is generally perceived as an indicator of how much a person is attracted to another person.

Furthermore, eye contact serves as an important coordination function for turn taking in communication. For example, a speaker may hold a longer gaze at a person to indicate that he/she is done speaking and that it is the other person's turn to speak. This indicates that an IT-artifact can alter or disturb a communicational setting on a relatively subtle level. The participants might then develop a feeling of discomfort or confusion without really being able to describe the cause of this problem.

With the advent of large interactive displays, researchers started to focus on face-to-face interactions with "single display groupware" [32]. Using a single display reduced the cognitive effort of synchronous collaboration, as all participants could directly observe the actions of their collaborators. But not all display types seam to work equally well in service encounter settings: Regarding standard PC-systems, Novak et al. [19] have shown that a service encounter, supported by a standard PC-monitor, can even worsen the perceived information asymmetry. Regarding large displays, Rogers et al. [24] found, that horizontal oriented surfaces (like tabletop systems) foster cohesive group work far better, than vertical displays or standard PC-monitors. Tabletop environments, have further often been used in other group settings as a single shared artifact and been credited for their ease with interpersonal communication [8]. Researchers reported a significant increase in eye contact in contrast to using a desktop monitor as single display interface [11]. Further, a tabletop system closely resembles the known working environment to which clients and advisors are used to.

Tabletop computers can also ease aligning artifact manipulation and non-verbal communication [33]. The increasing sophistication of tabletop computers appears to be the solution for Scott et al.'s [27] design guideline: "Technology that provides little or no overhead to performing or switching between activities would allow users to transition easily between activities, focusing instead on communication." However, as we will show in this paper, the introduction of tabletop systems alone is not sufficient to realize successful relationship building. Further requirements need to be considered.

For tabletop activities in general, people favor to sit opposite to each other [27,30], and thus could establish eye contact by just lifting their heads and/or their eyes. Despite some advances of a face-to-face seating arrangement [17], the orientation of written information on tabletop computers remains an unsolved problem when users sit on opposing sides of the table. Thus, in recent publications [28,33], the settings comprise more people sitting in a 90 degree angle or beside one another when participants want to collaborate and use written information. This is also in line with the research of Wallace et al. [34], that describes that an adjacent (90 degree angle) seating arrangement is preferred over a face-to-face seating arrangement when working collaboratively. This seating arrangement appears to be a good compromise to support comprehension, coordination and ownership of objects [14]. This aspect is also related to the research on proxemic interaction and (IT-) artifact use as, for example, presented by Ballendat [1]. Proxemics describes how people interpret spatial distances to mediate relationships to other people and objects [7]. This line of research underlines the importance of environmental variables for the interaction between persons and between persons and artifacts. Up to now, this research, has been directed at larger changes in body movement, for example, when a person walks and her interpersonal distance to other persons or objects is changing (e.g. from the "public" distance to the "personal" distance). The aspects of body position we are focusing, on is on a smaller and more subtle scale. We will show how small modifications of body and head position in a face-to-face situation can influence the relationship between these two persons.

Based on this background, we do not limit our study to the user interface (UI) only. While being a central element of the interaction, the UI is only one component that influences the behavior of clients and advisors. One also needs to consider additional aspects, such as body positions or the questions what users do when they are not interacting with the artifact [1]. Thus, our analysis will target not only the UI but the advisory setting in general.

3 NAIVE DESIGN AND EVALUATION OF PROTOTYPE 1

In 2010, we started a joint research project with a major Swiss bank on improving their investment advisory service for their affluent customer segment (50'000 – 500'000 CHF). In the course of this collaboration, Prototype 1 was developed and tested. The main goal of this prototype was to improve the quality of the advisory process. One crucial aspect in this context was the transparency of the process and the exchanged information [20].

We used a tabletop system to provide a shared artifact workspace [25]. The prototype was designed to support financial advisory encounters within the property of the bank. Since it was not our primary goal to remove all forms of paper from the advisory process but to have it co-existing with an IT-artifact, a tabletop system provided a reasonable working environment that supported both styles at the same time. Note-taking especially was an example of key use of paper in this scenario. A tight and seamless integration (as mentioned in section 2.1) seamed not necessary for the purpose of note-taking.

The prototypes and test scenarios described in the following sections have also been published in Nussbaumer et al. [20,21] when researching the transparency of the process. In this paper, we focus on aspects of relationship building in these experimental scenarios that have not been published previously. To this end, we draw on additional data analysis and we explicate the design requirements and the design principles that were established with regard to the relationship dimension.

User Interface: The prototype was built on a Microsoft Surface table, intended to be used as a single shared artifact by both client and advisor. The user interface design of Prototype 1 guided the clients and advisors directly through a suggested advisory process. Each step of the advisory process (e.g., Personal Data, Risk Analysis, Financial Strategy, etc.) was supported by a dedicated screen. On top of the screen there was a navigable process map indicating the current step in the context of all the other steps. We call this the "slide-metaphor," as the visualization is similar to the way information is presented in PowerPoint. Figure 2 illustrates the visualization and interaction possibilities while defining an asset strategy. For a full view of the IT-supported advisory environment see Figure 6.

Body Position: During the advisory sessions, the client sat at the long end of the surface table, with the advisor sitting at the short end. The screen was oriented towards the client, i.e., the client could read texts without effort while the advisor had to mentally rotate the text 90 degrees (Figure 1).

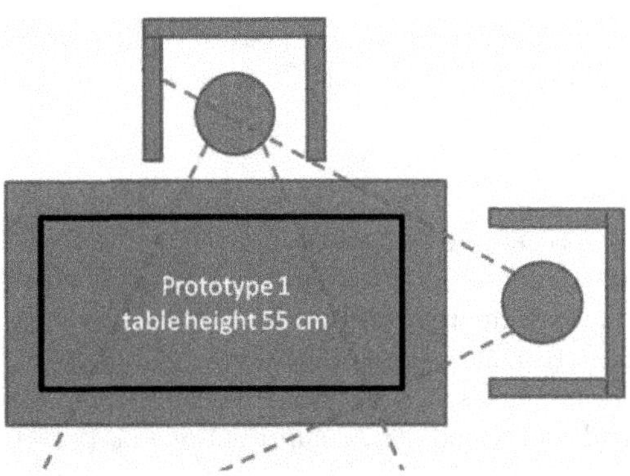

Figure 1: Seating arrangement of Prototype 1 (corner seating).

Evaluation: The prototype was evaluated in a realistic setting with four experienced financial advisors from a major Swiss bank and 12 test-clients. The tested scenario was that of a prospective customer. In the scenario they had to decide on an investment strategy to invest the fictional amount of about US$250,000. All test-clients received two treatments: one traditional pen and paper advisory and one IT-supported advisory encounter [21]. Half of the participants started with IT-supported advisory service, while the other half started with the traditional setting.

The IT-supported sessions were recorded on video. To compare the two experimental conditions, we conducted interviews in which we asked the participants about their experiences with the IT-supported and the traditional advisory scenarios. We analyzed the recordings of these interviews for all aspects of relationship building as well as for those factors that might affect this relationship building.

Results: The analysis of the interviews revealed that many participants referred to the relationship aspect of the situation. Out of 12 participants, ten participants mentioned this aspect in some form. They pointed out that they were too focused on the artifact, extremely distracted, and that the interpersonal contact without the artifact was more pleasant. One participant described this as: "I felt that I'm not in the focus, but the computer is"; another one pointed out, "It's like a triangle relationship, the advisor and table on one side and me on the other side."

Additional feedback included: "The traditional setting was more personal; in the IT-supported setting it felt like the table was in the focus not the advisory service." "During the IT setting, the personal aspect was lacking; everything went very quick, it would be better to somehow use it (the system) cooperatively." "The computer appears to be in between." "The most annoying was that he (the advisor) looked at the artifact, instead of looking at me."

In addition to this aspect, half of the participants also commented on aspects of distraction. Here, the participants described that there was so much information that they felt overwhelmed and were overly fascinated by the artifact. One participant reported: "You have to wait a while before you can say something." A second one felt overloaded with information coming from two sources: "A lot of information from the table, and the advisor and I have to handle this." Some also felt inhibited, stating: "One was so fascinated by the table that one did not ask questions." Finally, the surveys revealed that the participants preferred the traditional setting to the artifact-supported setting [21].

Figure 2: "Slide-metaphor" of the Prototype 1 (full extent of tabletop display, original interface was in German language).

4 PROBLEM IDENTIFICATION AND GENERIC REQUIREMENTS

The literature [8] describes numerous settings in which partners successfully collaborate while using shared artifacts on table-top computers. In our first evaluation, however, this did not seem to be the case. Based on the evaluation described in the previous section, we conclude that the scenario described for Prototype 1 does not lead to a functioning relationship between advisor and client in many cases. As seen in the evaluation, many participants accredited the presence of the IT-artifact for the disturbed interpersonal relationship. Therefore, our main solution objective is:

Solution Objective: Establish effortless relationship building in IT supported face-to-face advisory encounters.

With "effortless" we mean that it did not take the participants noticeable effort, i.e., more effort than s/he was used to from similar unsupported situations.

Similar to the work of Haller et al. ("Communication space" and "Task space") [8], we introduce the notion of spaces: "relationship building space" (RBS) and "artifact work space" (AWS) (Figure 3). Both RBS and AWS are physical spaces persons can use in their sole discretion. The AWS is defined as the space the persons look at if they want to work with the artifact. RBS on the other hand is defined as the space the persons look at when they want to engage in relationship building. The RBS therefore resembles the space where relationship building is possible from an external point of view.

However, humans are only able to focus on a single point in space at any given time. Thus, we end up with a mutually exclusive three state model of each participant being in one of: 1) in an artifact state (the person is focused on the artifact itself); 2) in a relationship state (the focus is on the other person, probably seeking eye contact), or 3), the person is looking somewhere else.

To visualize these states and transitions, we developed a state model (Figure 3) for single or two person situations.

This model describes the situation where one participant wants to change its state from being in AWS to RBS. As discussed in the literature section, people feel the need to engage in the RBS, for example, to signal a misunderstanding [13], to ground their communication [3] or to assess the personality of the other person. We assume relationship building to be efficient when both persons are in the RBS state at the same time.

In the discussion following, we focus on the transitions leaving the AWS states. We will argue under which circumstances people can enter RBS directly via transition "A" or why they fail and take transition "B" or "C" instead.

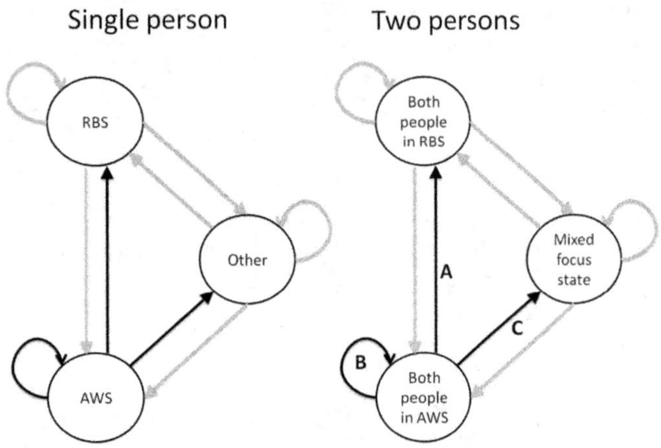

Figure 3: States of focus (left: single person; right: combined model for advisor and client).

The failed relationship building with Prototype 1 implies that the participants did not reach the RBS state often enough or did not stay there long enough.

For a successful transition into the RBS state, three things are necessary: First, both participants have to be aware of the existence of that state. Second, to be successful, the transition into the RBS-state has to be a coordinated transition, leading to both participants being in the RBS simultaneously (Transition A, Figure 3). Third, the affordance to transit into the RBS-state has to be low enough for the participants to switch deliberately into the RBS state.

The AWS state is inherently created with provision of the artifact to its users. However, the relationship building space does not seem to instantiate itself automatically. In order to ensure successful relationship building between client and advisor, that space has to be created and maintained throughout the session. Relationship building is not a one-time effort but rather an ongoing procedure running in parallel to the technical task of problem solving and decision making. This implies constant switching between the two spaces.

To motivate people to engage in the relationship building space, they have to be accommodated to it. In many non-IT-supported situations this happens intuitively when two persons interact with one another. However, it seems that this step is easily omitted when people are confronted with an attractive IT-artifact. Lacking such a relationship can hamper any further development of the relationship when using an IT-artifact right from the beginning. The first encounter in such a setting is probably crucial and sets the stage for the relationship that is established between the two. If the RBS is not introduced at the very beginning of the session, the advisor and client lack common ground [3].

***Generic Requirement 1**: Initially accustom the participants to the relationship building space and instantiate a basic relationship.*

While interacting with Prototype 1, participants complained about the process the IT-artifact imposed on the interaction between themselves and the advisor. One participant stated: "The process was predefined and it was difficult to ask questions." Another one said: "It should not be like an assembly line – it should not be that standardized." One participant suggested that there should be a period of talking to the advisor before the IT-artifact was introduced.

Even though it was not the intention at the time of development, we enabled the experience that participants as well as advisors followed the pre-given structure of the interface very strictly. As the visualized process had no relationship building related activities, they were simply omitted by the participants. One experience was that a process visualized by IT could have a much stronger effect on the socializing behavior of participants than was intended by the developers. While the process was meant rather to help participants not to forget anything important and to provide some orientation, the participants seemed to interpret the process as an instruction for behavior. Applied to our state model, instead of switching into the relationship building state, they stayed in the AWS state (transition "B", Figure 3). In contrast to transition A and C, transition B was explicitly expressed and visualized within the artifact design itself.

This led to the impression that personal or social aspects do not have any place in the advisory process. This aspect conflicts with the guidelines proposed by Ruth Cohn [4] for her Theme-centered Interaction Approach: Disruptions have priority, meaning that it does not make sense to continue with a process if there is conflict on a behavioral level. Thus, we formulate the following requirement:

***Generic Requirement 2**: Avoid UI designs that bind participants to the artifact space due to a prescribed process.*

In the first setting, the participants were sitting in a 90° orientation to each other. Due to the low table height, they had to bend a little over the artifact. To switch between the AWS and RBS, they had to at least rotate their heads towards each other. To get into a relaxed body position, they had to lean back and thus move their entire upper body.

We assume that these high switching costs hampered the transitions into the RBS. The participants referred to this issue, stating that the situation with the table was not very comfortable. One participant said: "It was disturbing because it [the table] was too low; I had to bend my head over it." Another one would even prefer to stand. To address this issue, we formulated the design requirement:

***Generic Requirement 3**: The physical effort to switch into the relationship building space (RBS) has to be low. Avoid the need for body movement at all.*

Another cause we assume to play a role is that a high cognitive effort can also reduce the ability to grasp the other person's state. We arrived at this conclusion after hearing the remarks of participants. A number of participants complained that they "had to concentrate too much on the tabletop," that "the advisor had to concentrate too much on the tabletop" or that "it was difficult to process the information and relate to the advisor at the same time."

As the interviews reveal, the participants were aware of their own cognitive effort required and the resulting lack of time to personally interact with the advisor. We assume that the constantly changing screen forced clients into building a new mental model for each screen – probably also trying to keep in mind the connection to the other hidden screens. This led to the effect that their focus was glued to the artifact space in a (subconscious) fear that they might miss something or that they would not be able to orient themselves again after returning from the relationship space. To address the cause, we formulated the design requirement:

***Generic Requirement 4**: The cognitive effort of leaving the artifact space has to be low.*

If one person is unaware of the other person's intention to switch into RBS, coordinated state switches are impossible or severely hampered at best. Humans only have a limited peripheral field of vision and a very limited area of focus. The advisor seeking eye contact with the client is probably one of the most important indicators that the advisor is seeking a connection with the client. The client, on the other hand, is irritated when he feels the need for attention when the advisor is engaged with the artifact.

The seating and body position in the first setting did not allow them to focus on the artifact while being able to track the other person's point of focus. The face of the advisor, for example, simply vanished out of the peripheral field of vision when the customer had to look at the center of the artifact. Thus, coordination might have been difficult, often resulting in uncoordinated space switches (transition "C", Figure 3). Therefore we propose:

***Generic Requirement 5**: Ensure effortless sensing of each other's space switches, utilizing the peripheral field of vision.*

5 DESIGN PRINCIPLES AND THEIR IMPLEMENTATION IN PROTOTYPE 2

Creating and maintaining the *relationship building space*:

To accommodate the person to the *RBS,* we suggest introducing a dedicated small talk phase prior to the artifact related work itself. In addition to accommodating the person to the space, the small talk phase is used to establish a first relationship between advisor and client. Thus, this intervention has actually two goals: Firstly, to make participants aware that a relationship building space exists and that it is accepted or even desired within the "interaction protocol" to switch into this state. Secondly, the two participants establish an initial relationship that makes it more likely for them to return to the relationship building state. This initial relationship should also lead to an interaction in which later disturbances (e.g. a short lack of eye contact) are not experienced as severe by the participants.

***Design-Principle 1** (to address generic requirement 1): Establish a basic relationship in IT-supported advisory sessions with a dedicated small talk phase at the beginning.*

Implementation: For the Prototype 2 evaluation, the advisors were instructed to be seated at the multi-touch-table but to disregard the artifact during the initial small talk phase; rather they should use a physical notepad and a pen to write down useful information during that phase, exactly what they were used to using in the traditional setting.

To overcome the interpretation of the rigid process visualization that no space was available to the relationship building activities, we suggest omitting any direct visual representation of the process.

***Design-Principle 2** (to address generic requirement 2): Omit any visualizations of a determined process and avoid any cue to the next activity in AWS.*

Implementation: To implement the described visual representation, we mapped each activity to a dedicated widget (software tool supporting the activity). All widgets were freely movable but initially arranged in a circular layout (c.f. Figure 5).

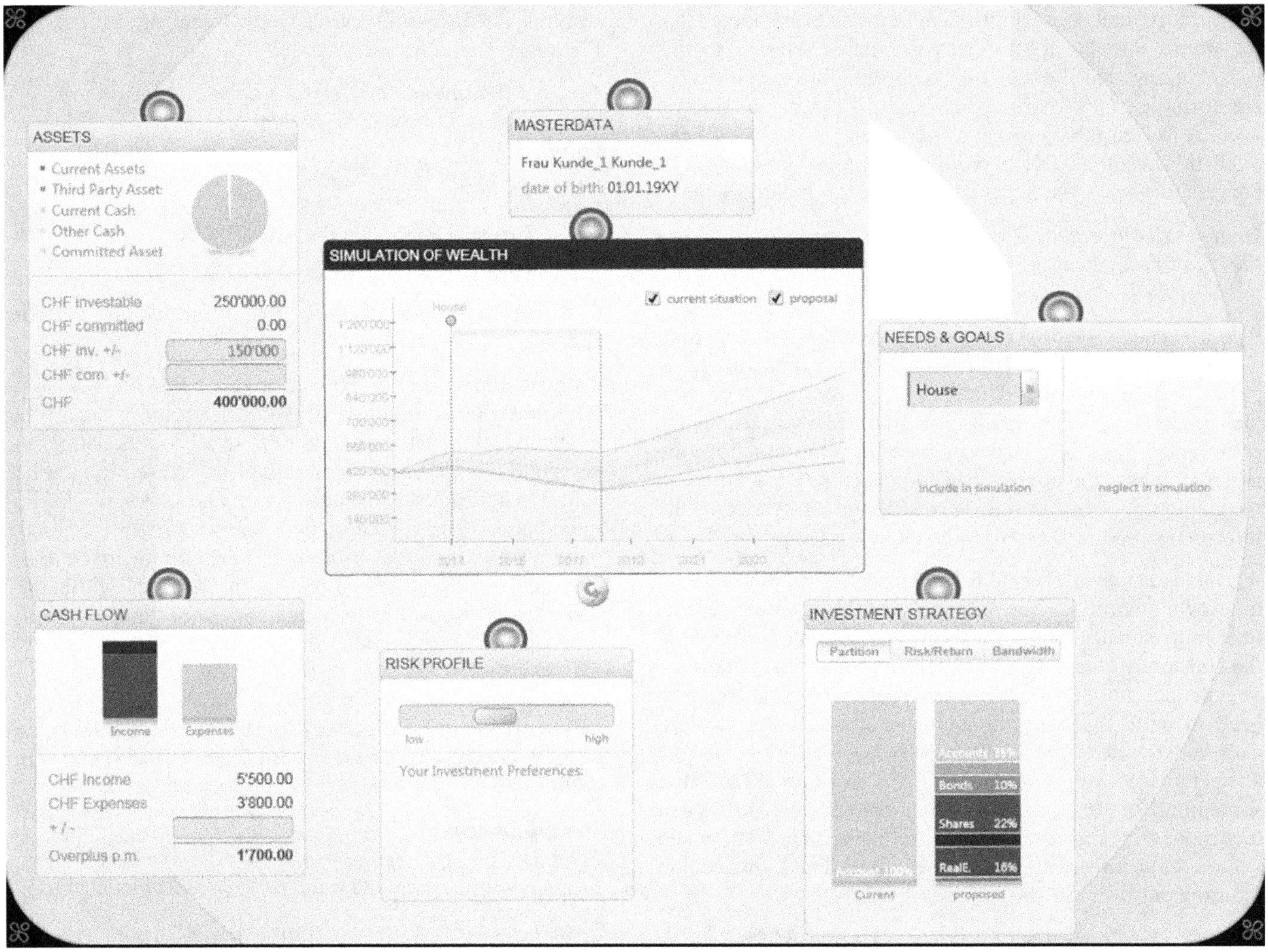

Figure 5: "Zoom and filter" metaphor of Prototype 2 (original interface was in German language).

Switching between *artifact work space* and *relationship building space*:

To enable easy switching between the spaces, we propose optimizing the seating position. This principle therefore addresses the environmental aspects rather than the artifact itself. The benefits of adjacent seating arrangements are described in section 2.3 in detail.

Design-Principle 3 *(to address generic requirements 3 and 5): Place the participants on adjacent sides around the table so that the RBS and AWS are reachable with minimal body and head movement.*

Implementation: For the second evaluation, we raised the table by 15 cm to a comfortable height of approximately 70 centimeters. This allowed the participants to sit in a slightly tilted, diagonal position and use the table as an arm rest. That seating position allowed participants to focus on the artifact while perceiving the other person's face in their peripheral vision (Figure 4). To switch the space in this arrangement, it is enough to move the eyes only, instead of the head or the whole body.

To make the interface more stable than the *slide metaphor* style of Prototype 1 we propose using abstraction layers where possible. Abstraction layers also help to reduce the visual complexity of the interface without restricting its functional complexity.

Design-Principle 4 *(to address generic requirement 2 and 4): Always display a complete picture of the situation at all times. Design for a stable UI and restrict visualization changes to portions of the screen only.*

Implementation: The UI of Prototype 2 was designed with a metaphor of "zoom and filter" [20,29], where only portions of the screen altered at any time. The interface consisted of single widgets, each addressing one activity. Each widget could extend the level of detail when needed (implemented as seen in Figure 5). With this design, only one widget could change its representation at any time, thus providing a mostly stable screen.

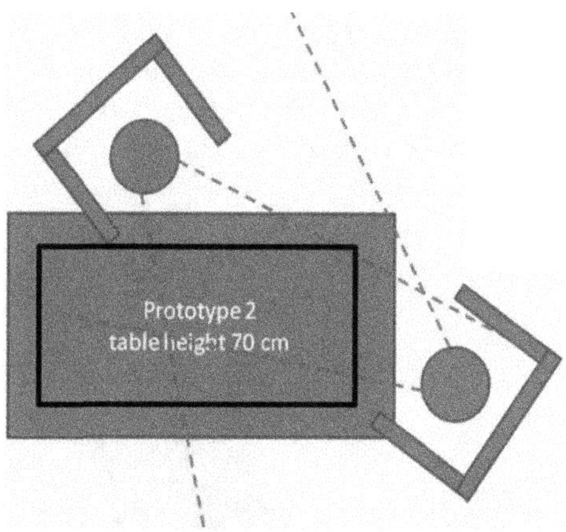

Figure 4: Seating position with Prototype 2 (diagonal seating)

6 EVALUATION OF PROTOTYPE 2

Prototype 2 was evaluated like the first one. The experimental evaluation involved 24 clients and 12 advisors in a within-subject design to compare the IT-supported encounter with its traditional counterpart (pen and paper) [20]. Half of the participants started with IT-supported advisory service, and the other half started with the traditional setting. Again, participants were interviewed regarding their experience with the two experimental conditions; the IT-supported sessions were videotaped and all sessions were observed by members of the research team.

The strong connection between eye contact and relationship development is reported in the literature [13], and so we use eye contact as an indicator for being in RBS. However, our video recordings did not allow us to determine eye contacts with certainty; accordingly, we refer to these episodes as "face-gazes." However, we assume that most of these face-gazes were actually eye contacts.

We conducted a systematic analysis of face-gazing behavior between clients and advisors. Thus, we opted to encode the viewing directions of both the advisors and clients.

All videos were manually encoded by two observers pressing buttons, each button representing one of the current viewing directions for each participant. This procedure was conducted for the IT-supported sessions of Prototype 2 as well as for the IT-supported sessions of Prototype 1. Each IT-supported test session was video-recorded during the evaluations with both faces and the artifact visible in the recording. We analyzed the 12 sessions of Prototype 1 and 12 sessions of the 24 recordings of Prototype 2 in order to have equal sample size.

The three distinct viewing-directions for each participant were "Focus on the other person" (person looking at the face of the other participant), "Focus on artifact" (person is looking at the artifact), and "Focus elsewhere" (person is looking in any other direction (c.f. Figure 6).

We sampled each recording for 20 second intervals out of every minute of video (second 0-20s, 60-80s, 120-140s, etc.). We expected the small-talk phase to have a lot of face-gazing by nature. We thus marked the point when the small talk phase was left and the participants started to work with the artifact.

7 RESULTS AND DISCUSSION

In this section, we first report the results of the interviews followed by the results of the face-gazing analysis. Subsequently, we describe the observed effects of our design guidelines.

Interviews: In contrast to the interviews that were conducted with the participants of Prototype 1, participants of the second evaluation hardly reported any problems with respect to the relationship between advisor and client. Only four out of 24 persons briefly mentioned this aspect (In Prototype 1 10 out of 12 clients mentioned this aspect).

Face-Gazing: Observing the session as a whole, the data show that sessions with Prototype 2 had nearly twice as many face-gazes or eye contacts as did sessions with Prototype 1. Figure 6 shows a state model of the two participants regarding their viewing directions. Face-gazing or eye contact was encoded when both participants looked at each other at the same point in time.

With Prototype 2, participants had an average mutual face-gazing ratio of 19.58% of the time, while they only had 10.75% with Prototype 1 (Figure 7). The difference is significant (two-sided t-test, $T(22) = 3.23$, $p = <.01$).

The difference in the face-gazing ratio could not simply be explained by the presence of the dedicated small talk phase. If excluding the small-talk phase from the sample, the length of the gazes was 17.08% for Prototype 2 and 9.33% for Prototype 1 (Figure 8), but still significantly different (two-sided t-test, $T(22)=2.93$, $p = <.01$).

In addition to this, we analyzed the absolute length of the mutual face-gazing episodes. This analysis revealed that there are more occurrences of longer length face-gazing contacts (10 seconds and more) for Prototype 2.

An interesting side aspect is that the data show that for both Prototype 1 and 2 the advisors in general focused on the clients more often than clients focusing on advisors. They spent over 30% of the session's time looking towards the clients.

Figure 6: States of view when working on the artifact.

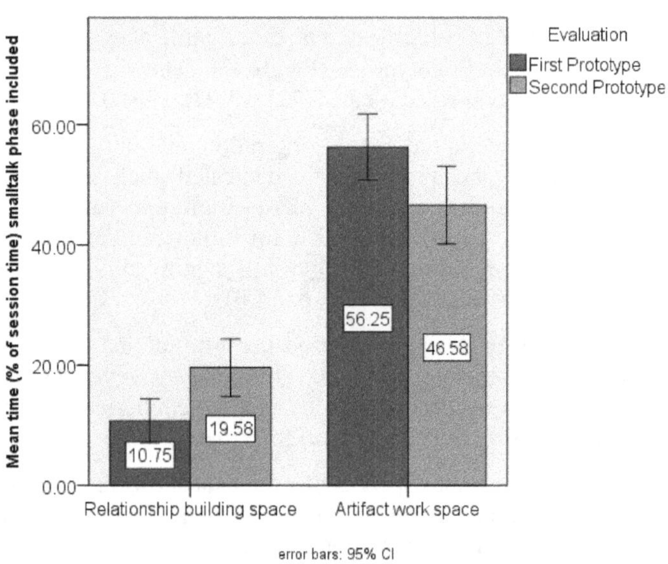

Figure 7: Mean time in the relationship building space with the small-talk phase included.

In greater detail, for Prototype 1 the advisors looked an average of 31.58% of the time towards the client and the client looked 16.83% of the time towards the advisors. For Prototype 2 the numbers were 38.08% for the advisor and 27.83% for the client. The difference for the client is significant (two-sided t-test, $T(22)=3.38$, $p<=0.01$). Without the small talk phase the average face-gazing time was 14.6% vs. 23.6% for the client (two-sided t-test, $T(22)=2.79$, $p<=0.05$) and 30.5% vs. 36.5% for the advisors.

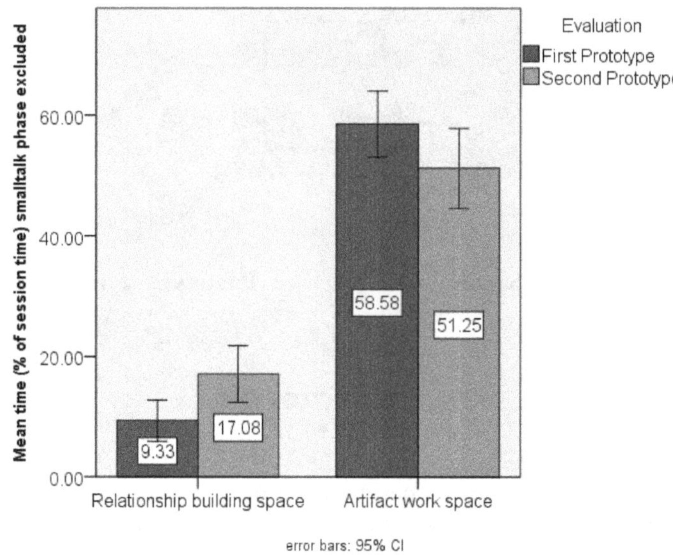

Figure 8: Mean time in the relationship building space without the small-talk phase.

Creating and maintaining the relationship building space:

The idea of having a dedicated small-talk phase at the beginning of the advisory endeavor was adopted well by the advisors. All sessions with Prototype 2 had an extensive small-talk phase (average of 10 minutes) between client and advisor prior to interacting with the artifact.

During that phase we could see a high degree of mutual face-gazing, supporting the assumption that mutual face-gazing moments are desired by both parties in such encounters. The additional dedicated small talk phase alone increased the overall amount of successful mutual face-gazing in comparison to that of the first evaluation. But even when subtracting these episodes from the face-gazing analysis, the situation for Prototype 2 still contained significantly more mutual face-gazing when compared to Prototype 1.

Switching between artifact work space and relationship building space:

The observation of the trials as well as the video recordings revealed the following aspects. The changes in table height had a strong effect on the predominant seating position. Due to the fact that the table was not square and people were seated relatively close to the artifact (in a 90 degree position), it was not possible for customers to focus on the artifact and simultaneously to have the advisor's face in their peripheral view. To gaze at the advisor's face, they had to leave the artifact focus and rotate their heads towards the advisor.

Now, with the rotated seating position of the second evaluation, customers had the face of the advisor and the artifact in nearly the same line of sight. Without the need to rotate their heads, they could sense when the advisor was looking at them and make direct eye contact when they felt it was appropriate.

This altered seating position, we believe, resulting from the change in table height, allowed customers to use the table as an armrest. Apparently, people prefer using a table as an armrest in such situations, as we also observed during the unsupported (pen and paper traditional style) advisory encounters.

These situations are sensitive to minute changes in the physical environment (like raising the table height by 15 cm), and the effects can be manifested in the overall impression of the participants.

We assume that the reduced cognitive effort on the part of the advisor as well as that of the client leads to increased chances that eye contact can be established. This is supported by our face-gazing data indicating that the advisor looks more often at the client in the Prototype 2 condition compared to in the Prototype 1 condition. This effect is even stronger for the clients. In the Prototype 2 condition the clients look considerably longer at the face of the advisor compared to in the Prototype 1 condition.

However, we mainly attribute the altered UI for the change in cognitive effort on the client side and the extended training period for the change of load on the advisor's side solely by argument. Since the experiment did not control for these variables separately, we cannot be certain.

8 LIMITATIONS

The analysis we conducted on our experimental scenarios did not allow us to control for all possible variables. Thus, we cannot be certain of the amount of influence of the different variables discussed or the directions of the influences. Our in-depth analysis, however, provides a rich understanding of the situation that would not have been possible in tightly controlled experimental settings.

The experiments were conducted in the Swiss financial sector, and their direct applicability is limited to this sector. We are confident it can be generalized in two directions: The results should be applicable to other Western countries, as underlying issues of principal agency conflicts and trust building are common there too. We believe they can also be generalized to other collaborative settings where establishing and maintaining personal relationships is crucial. Primary candidates are other sales oriented service encounters, e.g., in insurances or travel agencies. Conflict resolution meeting, consensus finding sessions or negotiations may also benefit from our results.

9 CONCLUSION

In this paper we described the severe effects of insufficient relationship building when working with IT-artifacts in advisory encounter situations. Based on observations and existing literature, we derived five generic requirements and four design principles that specifically address requirements for successful relationship building. These principles address the design of the artifact itself as well as the environment and process. In a subsequent evaluation with an enhanced prototype, following these guidelines, we found the effects of insufficient relationship building being reduced to the point of not being reported any longer by the majority of the test participants. Therefore, we conclude that systems following these guidelines should be able to maintain the level of relationship building compared to that of traditional settings.

In contrast to related work, this paper not only addresses the physical environment but also focuses on UI design issues related to relationship building. In the interviews we also found evidence that a suboptimal design of the IT-artifact can directly hamper relationship building.

Our contribution should help in the development of future collaboratively used IT-artifacts, thus directly contributing to the research stream of IT supported face-to-face collaboration [8].

By addressing the relationship building issue, we also enable practitioners in the finance industry to address a crucial aspect of their value proposition, i.e. a trusting relationship to their clients.

In this contribution, we focus on advisory scenarios, where the customer visits the advisor in her office because we believe that these settings have interesting characteristics from a scientific perspective as well as an increasing importance from a practitioner's perspective. From a research perspective, we helped understanding relationship building while working with IT artifacts in service encounters. For practitioners on the other hand, this contribution could be meaningful to design future systems without hampering the very fragile aspect of relationship building. Advisory scenarios are the central communication channels for several core disciplines in our current service economy, including medicine, law, finance and many sales processes. Advisory settings are always used when the information that is communicated is complex and/or very relevant to the perceiving person. This can mean that high amounts of money are involved as in financial situations or that the risks of certain procedures are very high such as in medicine or in legal advice.

It is therefore very important that the client is well informed to make an informed decision. This includes transferring the information as such, but it also includes the creation of a trustful relationship because the lack of such an relationship will also hamper the cooperation and the exchange of knowledge and advice (e.g., if persons do not ask relevant questions or conceal important information).

Thus, these kinds of processes are omnipresent in our current economic, medical and legal system with severe implications for the advised persons but possibly also for the advisor in case the advisor process fails. We believe that due to the awareness of the sensitivity of the process, the introduction of IT into these processes has hardly been undertaken.

The complexity of the transferred information, however, as well the challenging learning process that the participants of the advisory process have to go through, makes the introduction of IT very promising for the following reasons: The process of the advisory session can be supported in such a way that no central information aspects are omitted. Core aspects of the knowledge that has to be transmitted can be visualized and animated to improve the understanding of the complex subjects. Finally, the discussed topics can be documented and used to recall complex content after the end of the advisory session.

For these reasons, we expect an increased use of IT in such sensitive areas. These new opportunities, however, also impose new challenges for the design of advisory support systems. If we want to realize the benefits, we have to understand how these kinds of systems impact the relationship building between participants and be aware of the implications for the design. This article seeks to make a contribution in this direction.

10 ACKNOWLEDGEMENTS

The software was developed as part of the CTI project 'Banking Advisory 2.0' funded by the Swiss Federal Government. This was a group effort. We are grateful for the significant contribution of Philipp Nussbaumer, Inu Matter and Didier Bertschinger in designing the system and collecting evaluation data. We furthermore acknowledge the great support of Gerhard Buurmann (SDFB*), Anna Lang, Martin Scherrer and David Zysset in making this project a success.

* SDFB: swiss design institute for finance and banking

11 REFERENCES

1. Ballendat, T., Marquardt, N., and Greenberg, S. Proxemic interaction: designing for a proximity and orientation-aware environment. *ACM International Conference on Interactive Tabletops and Surfaces*, ACM (2010), 121–130.
2. Bonnard, Q., Jermann, P., Legge, A., Kaplan, F., and Dillenbourg, P. Tangible paper interfaces: interpreting pupils' manipulations. *Proceedings of the 2012 ACM international conference on Interactive tabletops and surfaces*, ACM (2012), 133–142.
3. Clark, H.H. and Brennan, S.E. Grounding in communication. *Perspectives on socially shared cognition 13*, APA (1991), 127–149.
4. Cohn, R.C. *Von der Psychoanalyse zur themenzentrierten Interaktion: Von der Behandlung einzelner zu einer Pädagogik für alle*. Klett-Cotta, (2000).
5. Crosby, L.A., Evans, K.R., and Cowles, D. Relationship Quality in Services Selling: An Interpersonal Influence Perspective. *Journal of Marketing 54*, (1990), 68–81.
6. Ellis, C.A., Gibbs, S.J., and Rein, G. Groupware: some issues and experiences. *Communications of the ACM 34*, (1991), 39–58.
7. Hall, E.T. *The hidden dimension*. Doubleday, 1966.
8. Haller, M., Billinghurst, M., Leithinger, J., Leitner, D., and Seifried, T. Coeno: enhancing face-to-face collaboration. *Proceedings of the 2005 international conference on Augmented tele-existence*, ACM (2005), 40–47.
9. Heinrich, P., Giesbrecht, T., Kilic, M., and Schwabe, G. Situated Learning in Bankberatungen. Bonner Köllen Verlag (2012), 261-266.
10. Herrington, J. and Oliver, R. Critical characteristics of situated learning: Implications for the instructional design of multimedia. *Learning with technology, proceedings of ASCILITE'95*, (1995), 235–262.
11. Inkpen, K.M., Hancock, M.S., Mandryk, R.L., and Scott, S.D. Collaboration around a tabletop display: Supporting interpersonal interactions. *tech report, Simon Fraser University*, (2002).
12. Jungermann, H. Advice giving and taking. *Proceedings of the 32nd Annual Hawaii International Conference on System Sciences, 1999. HICSS-32*, IEEE (1999).
13. Kleinke, C.L. Gaze and eye contact: a research review. *Psychological bulletin 100*, 1 (1986), 78-100.
14. Kruger, R., Carpendale, S., Scott, S.D., and Greenberg, S. How people use orientation on tables: comprehension, coordination and communication. *Proceedings of the 2003 international ACM SIGGROUP conference on Supporting group work*, (2003), 369–378.
15. Lewe, H. and Krcmar, H. The design process for a computer-supported cooperative work research laboratory: the Hohenheim CATeam room. *Journal of Management Information Systems*, (1991), 69–85.

16. Mantei, M. Capturing the capture concepts: a case study in the design of computer-supported meeting environments. *Proceedings of the 1988 ACM conference on Computer-supported cooperative work*, ACM (1988), 257–270.
17. Matsushita, M., Shirai, Y., Oguro, T., et al. A Face-to-face Collaboration Support System that Optimizes Direction of Projected Information to Each Stakeholder. *Transactions 46*, 7 (2005), 1603–1617.
18. Nguyen, D. and Canny, J. MultiView: spatially faithful group video conferencing. *Proceedings of the SIGCHI Conference on Human Factors in Computing Systems*, ACM (2005), 799–808.
19. Novak, J. Mine, yours... ours? Designing for principal-agent collaboration in interactive value creation. *Wirtschaftsinformatik 2009, Vienna*, (2009).
20. Nussbaumer, P., Matter, I., and Schwabe, G. "Enforced" vs. "Casual" Transparency – Findings from IT-Supported Financial Advisory Encounters. *ACM Transactions on Management Information Systems*, (2012), Article 11.
21. Nussbaumer, P. and Matter, I.S. What You See Is What You (Can) Get? Designing for Process Transparency in Financial Advisory Encounters. *Interact 2011*, (2011), 277-294.
22. Papadopoulou, P., Andreou, A., Kanellis, P., and Martakos, D. Trust and relationship building in electronic commerce. *Internet Research 11*, 4 (2001), 322–332.
23. Prahalad, C.K. and Ramaswamy, V. Co-creation experiences: The next practice in value creation. *Journal of interactive marketing 18*, 3 (2004), 5–14.
24. Rogers, Y. and Lindley, S. Collaborating around vertical and horizontal large interactive displays: which way is best? *Interacting with Computers 16*, 6 (2004), 1133–1152.
25. Schmidt-Rauch, S. and Nussbaumer, P. Putting Value Co-Creation into Practice: A Case for Advisory Support. *Proceedings of the 19th European Conference on Information Systems 2011*, (2011), Paper 138.
26. Schwabe, G. and Nussbaumer, P. Why IT is not being used for financial advisory. *Proceedings of the 17th European Conference on Information Systems 2009*, (2009), Paper 450.
27. Scott, S.D., Grant, K.D., and Mandryk, R.L. System guidelines for co-located, collaborative work on a tabletop display. *ECSCW 2003*, (2003), 159–178.
28. Shaer, O., Strait, M., Valdes, C., Feng, T., Lintz, M., and Wang, H. Enhancing genomic learning through tabletop interaction. *Proceedings of the 2011 annual conference on Human factors in computing systems*, ACM (2011), 2817–2826.
29. Shneiderman, B. The eyes have it: a task by data type taxonomy for information visualizations. *Visual Languages, 1996. Proceedings., IEEE Symposium on*, (1996), 336 –343.
30. Sommer, R. Personal Space. The Behavioral Basis of Design, Prentice-Hall, (1969).
31. Steimle, J., Khalilbeigi, M., Mühlhäuser, M., and Hollan, J.D. Physical and digital media usage patterns on interactive tabletop surfaces. *ACM International Conference on Interactive Tabletops and Surfaces*, ACM (2010), 167–176.
32. Stewart, J., Bederson, B.B., and Druin, A. Single display groupware: a model for co-present collaboration. *Proceedings of the SIGCHI conference on Human factors in computing systems: the CHI is the limit*, (1999), 286–293.
33. Tse, E., Greenberg, S., Shen, C., and Forlines, C. Multimodal multiplayer tabletop gaming. *Computers in Entertainment (CIE) 5*, (2007), Article No. 12.
34. Wallace, J.R. and Scott, S.D. Contextual design considerations for co-located, collaborative tables. *3rd IEEE International Workshop on Horizontal Interactive Human Computer Systems, 2008. TABLETOP 2008*, (2008), 57–64.
35. Weber, W.G. Organizational conditions fostering prosocial work orientations in teams. *Innovative Theories, Tools, and Practices in Work and Organizational Psychology. Seattle, WA: Hogrefe and Huber*, (2000), 75–96.

Can You Hear Me Now? Mitigating the Echo Chamber Effect by Source Position Indicators

Q. Vera Liao & Wai-Tat Fu
Department of Computer Science
University of Illinois at Urbana-Champaign
201 N. Goodwin Avenue, Urbana IL, 61801
liao28, wfu@illinois.edu

ABSTRACT

We examined how a source position indicator showing both valences (pro/con) and magnitudes (moderate/extreme) of positions on controversial topics influenced users' selection and reception of diverse opinions in online discussions. Results showed that the indicator had differential impact on participants who had varied levels of accuracy motives – i.e., motivation to accurately learn about the topic, by leading to greater exposure to attitude-challenging information for participants with higher accuracy motives. Further analysis revealed that it was mainly caused by the fact that the presence of position indicator increased the selection of moderately inconsistent sources for participants with high accuracy motives but decreased the selection of them for participants with low accuracy motives. The indicator also helped participants differentiate between sources with moderate and extreme positions, and increased their tendency to agree with attitude-challenging information from sources with moderately inconsistent positions. Participants with high accuracy motives were also found to learn significantly more about the arguments put forward by the opposite side with the help of the position indicator. We discussed the implications of the results for the nature of the echo chamber effect, as well as for designing information systems that encourage seeking of diverse information and common ground seeking.

Author Keywords

Selective Exposure; Motivation; Information Diversity.

ACM Classification Keywords

H.5.4 [Information Interfaces and Presentation]: Hypertext/Hypermedia-User issues.

General Terms: Human Factors; Design.

INTRODUCTION

Exposing people to challenging or alternative views is essential for promoting critical thinking and informed decision-making [19, 24], preventing or correcting inaccurate beliefs or even dangerous radicalization [32]. To encourage exposure to diverse opinions, researchers have stressed the necessity of providing "safe spaces" where people feel comfortable sharing their views and interacting with people of divergent perspectives [16, 32]. This "marketplace of ideas" is central to deliberative democracy [20], and also critical in many other information-seeking or decision-making contexts where people face controversies or choices [14].

Internet can be an ideal venue for such "marketplaces", given its provision of unprecedented access to information and people of widely varied backgrounds. Latest technology can further promote the access in a more centralized manner. For example, information aggregators allow users to view information from different sources at the same time. Social technologies, such as online discussion forum and social sharing service could assemble people of diverse opinions and open them up to opportunities for communication and education. On the other hand, critics have warned that, by facilitating easy control of one's own information diet, the Internet may exacerbate the "echo chamber effect" [1, 27] – i.e., that people may end up only interacting with others who share similar views. It is often attributed to a phenomenon called *selective exposure* to information, which can be defined as individuals' tendency to favor consonant information and avoid dissonant information. In other words, the increasing availability of diverse information on the Internet does not guarantee an equally diverse exposure to different perspectives if people lack the initiatives to attend to information that challenges their existing attitudes.

From this perspective, it is important for researchers to ask what can motivate Web users to attend to attitude-challenging information. Research in this area suggests that there are two critical aspects that impact selective exposure to information. First, researchers have studied how various design features [15, 17, 22, 28, 35] can promote exposure to diverse perspectives, such as better ways of organizing and presenting information of opposite stances. Second, recent research on Internet selective exposure suggests that there is a divergence on the motives of users to seek diverse information: while some users prefer avoiding dissonant information, some may not favor an exclusive diet of agreeable information [23]. In fact, psychological studies

CSCW'14, February 15–19, 2014, Baltimore, Maryland, USA.
Copyright © 2014 ACM 978-1-4503-2540-0/14/02...$15.00.
http://dx.doi.org/10.1145/2531602.2531711

have found two competing tendencies when people seek information [12] – a tendency to seek attitude-reinforcing information to avoid cognitive dissonance, and a tendency to achieve an accurate understanding of the reality by seeking relevant information regardless of its position (often called *accuracy motives*). Given that these tendencies often vary among individuals and topics, effects of certain interface designs on users' behavior may also vary.

In this paper, we studied how an interface feature indicating the position of the information source impacted users' selection and reception of attitude-challenging information through a laboratory experiment. More importantly, we studied its differential effects on users who had varied levels of accuracy motives. To the best of our knowledge, few studies have systematically examined the interaction between interface features and users' accuracy motives on the consumption of diverse information. However, given their key roles in influencing selective exposure tendency, the interaction may shed light on what designers can do to encourage attention and consumption of diverse information for users with different backgrounds and information needs.

The indicator feature we introduce here distinguishes itself from those in previous research in two aspects. First, we emphasize its reflection on the position of the information *source* rather than the *content* of a single piece of information. It is particularly pertinent to the design of social technologies. For example, it is common that on political discussion websites people indicate their political affiliation in their profile. Often we can also infer others' positions on particular issues based on more implicit information such as their previous posts, votes, groups they join or users they follow. This kind of data also makes it possible for, e.g., some forms of reputation or recommender system to infer the general position of the information source. We are interested in how explicit indication of such source position information could impact users' interaction with diverse information. Second, the indicator not only shows the valence, i.e., positive or negative, but also the magnitude, i.e., extreme or moderate, of the information source's position. We believe this is more ecologically valid as it is well known that people's attitudes are more likely distributed along a continuum rather than dichotomous. This would also allow us to study how the magnitude of discrepancy between the source position and user's pre-existing attitude impacts the consumption of information from diverse sources.

We expect the source indicator to have impact on different stages of users' information consumption, specifically, their selection, reception and learning outcomes of diverse opinions. For information selection, we are interested in whether the source indicator can motivate users to approach attitude-challenging information, i.e., reduce their selective exposure tendency. For information reception, we examine how the indicator can induce changes in users' perception of source positions and their agreement with different opinions. Last but not the least, we are interested in whether users can acquire new knowledge from diverse positions.

Biased views and inferior decisions are often caused by false perception of consensus or uniqueness (either side may possibly lead to bias [9, 28]), resistance to appreciating divergent opinions [16], and most importantly, ignorance of alternative views and facts that may challenge the existing views [8, 27, 31, 35]. Therefore, we believe the measurements of selection, position judgment, agreement and knowledge gain are important and especially pertinent to the goal of designing technological interventions that correct biased views and support informed decision-making.

In summary, we asked the following research questions:

RQ1: How does the indicator of positions of information sources impact users' selection of attitude consistent and inconsistent information (**RQ1a**)? Does it have differential impact on people who have high or low accuracy motives (**RQ1b**)?

RQ2: Do both the valence and magnitude of information source position reflected in the indicator affect users' selection of diverse information?

RQ3: Does the indicator have influence on users' perception of the information source's position *after* they process the information?

RQ4: Does the indicator influence users' agreement with the information from sources of different positions? As people with more extreme positions tend to hold stronger disagreement with opposing views, does the indicator moderate this tendency?

RQ5: Does the addition of the indicator feature lead to differences in users' knowledge gained on either side?

Before discussing the study, we will briefly review the selective exposure theory, previous research on designing interface for diversity seeking, and relevant psychological theories that motivated the design of the study.

RELATED WORK

In psychological research, selective exposure has been mainly explored based on the cognitive dissonance theory, which states that people are motivated to avoid the psychological discomfort incurred by having to reevaluate their prior decisions or existing attitudes [9]. A current focus of this research field is on identifying moderating variables that affect this tendency. In particular, research suggests that in some situations people are less likely to engage in selective exposure: i.e., when they are curious about the topic [9], when the dissonant information has high utility [31], when the decision is related to important outcomes [12, 30], or when the person is generally open-minded and value the norm of diversity [12]. Hart et al. [12] concluded that accuracy motive, defined as the desire to form accurate appraisal and valid representation of reality, is the underlying factor that promotes the tendency to process information in a more objective, open-minded fashion that fosters uncovering the truth.

Lately, selective exposure theory has attracted increasing attention from Web researchers [10]. The major concern is the fact that Internet users, who have increasing choices and autonomy to filter out disagreeable information, coupled with the wide adoption of personalization technologies that often provide only agreeable information, may isolate themselves into information "filter bubbles" [1, 27]. To cope with this problem, researchers have been developing systems that aim at exposing users to diverse perspectives in various domains such as politics [17, 22, 25], healthcare [15], news [28] and consumer reviews [36].

These designs mainly focused on ways of categorizing and presenting diverse perspectives. In many previous studies, dichotomous valence models (conservative/liberal, pro/con, etc.) were adopted to categorize information. This approach tends to ignore magnitudes of positions, even though attitudes often distribute along a continuum rather than dichotomy, and people with moderate positions may have distinctive perspectives from those with extreme positions [8, 29]. Moreover, there is substantial evidence that lower attitude discrepancy between the communicator and the recipient may decrease cognitive dissonance [0]. Therefore differentiating sources of moderate positions from the extreme ones may reduce users' resistance to dissonant opinions. A few previous studies provided evidence to support this idea. For example, OpinionSpace developed by Faridani et al. [5], a tool visualizing other voters' positions, uses spatial distance to represent the magnitude of opinion differences. However the study focused on examining the overall user experience without studying how magnitude information impacted users' information seeking process. ConsiderIt, developed by Kriplean et al. [17] aggregates public thoughts on controversial political issues, and provides users with top arguments on seven different stances distributed on a 1-support to 7-oppose scale. Qualitative results showed favorable user experience with this categorization method. However, there is still a lack of systematic examination of whether and how adding magnitude information in the categorization of positions will impact users' information selection and consumption.

Previous studies have explored interfaces that explicitly indicate stances by presenting information in either a two-column view or with inline labels. The former often listed opposite information side by side [17, 28], while the later used highlighting [23], tag [25] and image [11], etc., to indicate positions. The position indicator we introduced here belongs to the later category.

From a cognitive perspective, researchers argue that selective exposure can be attributed to people's tendency to preserve cognitive resource, as processing and counter-arguing challenging information demands more cognitive resources than consuming agreeable information [7]. Thus, reducing the demand of cognitive resource from other processes, e.g., interpreting and evaluating the message position [7, 33], could reduce the effect of selective exposure. Providing explicit labels of stances seems to be consistent with this notion of easing the processes involved in attending to and interpreting information. Research also suggests that explicitly indicating the stance of information could serve as a "reminder" that there exists different opinions, which may accentuate the benefit of, as well as the social norm, that one should balance his or her information seeking of diverse opinions [22, 25]. However, previous studies yielded mixed results of the effect of stance labeling on reducing selective exposure [23, 25].

Interestingly, in the Munson et al. [23] study, after distinguishing challenge-averse users (who prefer as much agreeable information as possible) from diverse-seeking users (who prefer at least some amount of challenging information), they examined the effect of highlighting agreeable items on challenge-averse users' satisfaction with using interfaces presenting information of varied levels of diversity. Surprisingly, overall they observed little effect of highlighting. In the condition in which the interface presented fewer agreeable items, it even slightly decreased challenge-averse users' satisfaction, possibly because the highlighting made it more explicit that there were fewer agreeable than disagreeable items. These mixed results raised the question of whether explicit indicators of positions could have differential effects on people with high or low accuracy motives. Specifically, we hypothesize that although the indicators can ease the cognitive demands and even "remind" users who have high accuracy motives to seek balanced information, the indicators may have little, or even negative effect on people with low accuracy motives by facilitating them to identify information to avoid. We will test this hypothesis in our study.

METHODOLOGY

In this experiment, we asked participants to browse comments from users who expressed their opinions in discussions of controversial issues in an online forum. We compared the condition where participants saw position bars indicating the users' positions on the particular issue to the control condition where the bars were hidden. We compared participants' selection of users and comments, perceived positions of the users, agreement with the comments, and knowledge gained between the two groups.

Participants

By posting recruiting ads in email newsletters, we recruited 32 participants from a Midwest college town in USA for the lab experiment. 20 of them are undergraduate or graduate students. The rest are a mix of faculties, university staffs, engineers, etc. They were randomly assigned to the group with position indicators (group 1) and control group (group 2). No significant difference in gender (group 1 43.8% male, group 2 37.5% male), age (group 1: M=32.0, SD=13.3, group 2: M=24.6, SD=8.5; $p=0.28$), education (25% in group 1 and 31.3% in group 2 are graduate students or have graduate degree, the rest are undergraduate or have bachelor degree) or political leaning (scale 1-conservative to 5-liberal, group 1: M=3.5, SD=0.9, group 2: M=3.5, SD=1.1; $p=0.85$) was observed between the two groups. Participants were compensated for $8 per hour and spent 1.5-2 hours on pre-tests and the experiment.

Task

In the experiment, we presented participants an interface of "user list" introduced as the result page of "user search" function of an online discussion forum (Figure 1). We will explain in detail how the users were created in the material section. Participants were instructed to imagine that they were visiting an online forum where people discussed controversial issues to learn about topics they were interested. They would eventually write their own posts. For each topic, the user list page suggested 32 users who were active in the discussion of the topic. Participants could click on any user to read his or her comment page (Figure 2), where one comment randomly chosen from the "top 3 comments" of this user would be presented, and participant could click "read more comments from this user" to read the other two, one at a time. Under each comment, there was a question asking participants to rate their agreement with the comment using a 1-disagree to 5-agree scale. They could return to the user list page to check other users at any moment. Once they clicked return (to leave the comment page of current user), they would be prompted to rate the user's position on the topic using a 1-pro to 5-con scale. They could click on any user and read as many comments as they wanted. When they were ready, they could proceed to the next page to write their own post. After submitting the post, they would proceed to the next task on a different topic. Each user on the experiment interface had a unique user name, which did not appear in more than one topic. The orders of topics, users, and the comments were randomized across participants.

Figure 1 presented the interface for the user list page. All 32 users were listed in this fashion, with a user name and an opinion summary generalizing the person's view. In the condition with position indicators, a bar showing the position of this user was added to the user profile, which indicated both the valence and the magnitude of this user's position, i.e., there were four kinds of position bars: 1) strong pro-a full green bar; 2) moderate pro- a ¾ green and ¼ red bar; 3) moderate con- a ¾ red and ¼ green bar; 4) strong con- a full red bar. As shown in Figure 1, images of thumb-up and thumb-down were added in the bar to indicate the meaning of the colors. Participants were told in the instruction that the website allowed other users to rate the position of users who participated in the discussions, and the position bar was calculated based on these ratings. In the control condition, this position bar was hidden in both the user list page and user comment page.

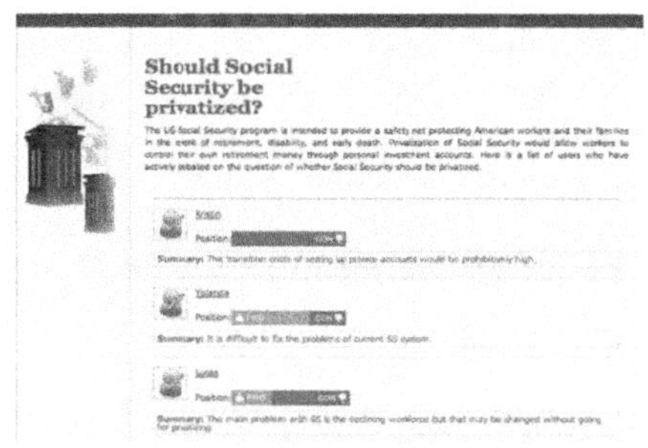

Figure 1. Interface for user list page

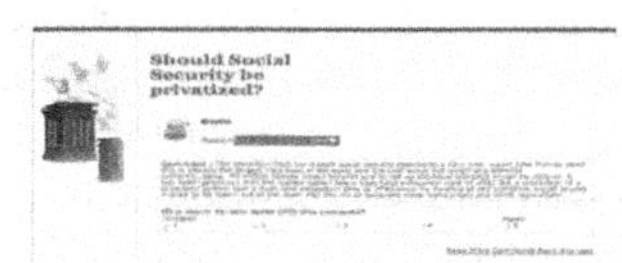

Figure 2. Interface for user comment page

Material

In a previous study [18], we identified a number of social, political and health related topics that have a balanced distribution of supportive and opposing attitudes in the similar population. We selected 6 topics from them (see Appendix A) for the experiment. Examples are "should

Category	Opinion Summary	Comment Examples
Strong pro	Drug advertisements inform patients about medical issues therefore should be encouraged.	An important benefit of direct to consumer advertising is that it fosters an informed conversation about health, disease and treatments between patients and their health care practitioners. Pharmacy members want patients and consumers to talk to their physicians about the medicines that may help them and to fully understand the known risks regarding these medicines.
Moderate pro	I do not have problem with advertisement about prescription drug as long as it provides unbiased information.	I do not have problem with advertisement about prescription drug as long as it provides unbiased information, meaning including both its benefits and side effects in a honest manner. A prescription drug is something that consumers should be making a rational decision about. And the more information consumers have, the better decisions they can make.
Moderate con	We should ban, or at least limit the advertisement of prescription drugs to avoid people making biased medical decisions.	I think that U.S. should limit the television commercials for prescription medications for this may influence the doctors and make a medication "more popular" without proper reason. Excessive promoting of medications using commercials may influence the "popularity" of a certain medication. It is a bad thing because people would more frequently ask for it.
Strong con	Drug advertisement is dangerous and should be banned as it may mislead patients.	Direct to consumer prescription drug ads, like most advertisements, are intended to sell the product being advertised. Such ads use marketing tactics that manipulate, create false impressions, and therefore mislead consumers instead of educating them about the drugs. It can be dangerous that patients start self-diagnosis by the information they get from advertisement.

Table 1. Example of Comments and Opinion Summary

social security be privatized?" and "should prescription drugs be allowed to directly advertise to consumers? ".

In the experiment, we created fictional users to control for the consistency of information and distribution of positions. To be ecologically valid, we obtained the material from real user posts on the Internet. We started by collecting 150-200 comments, with 60-100 words each, expressing varied opinions for each of the topics, from the online forums of debate.org, procon.org and Yahoo! Answers[1]. One graduate student and two undergraduate students worked on categorizing these comments into four categories: strong pro, moderate pro, moderate con and strong con (see Table 1 for examples). The inter-rater reliability (Fleiss Kappa) reached 0.85, which is often considered good agreement [6]. We categorized the comments with the following features to be moderate: 1) expressing indecisiveness by mentioning merits of both sides, but leaning towards one side; 2) supporting one side but with certain condition (e.g., "it is good if certain restriction applied"); 3) modest and/or uncertain tone (e.g., "I guess", "maybe"). In contrast, strong comments expressed one-sided and assured opinions and often with confident and strong tone (e.g., "I believe", "definitely").

For each topic, we created 32 users, with 8 under each of the four categories: strong pro, moderate pro, moderate con and strong con. For each user, we selected 3 comments from the corresponding comments pool to be his or her "top comments". As a priority, we grouped comments collected from the same real users together. Otherwise, we carefully selected and modified the comments minimally, if necessary, to make them reasonably consistent for a particular user. For each user, we created an "opinion summary" (see Table 1) by either choosing the first sentence of one of the comments or writing by ourselves.

Measurement

In this section, we will only introduce variables that were measured directly by questionnaires or the experiment platform. More indexes we defined for analyzing specific RQs will be introduced in the result section. A summary of all the variables used in the study can be found in Table 2.

Participants completed a demographic information questionnaire and a topic related questionnaire before the experiment. In the later, three attributes were measured for each topic: prior attitude, accuracy motive and knowledge.

Prior Attitude Index

Following [13], we used a 5-item semantic differential scale to measure participants' attitude on each topic. For example, when measuring participants' attitudes on vegetarianism, instead of directly asking whether they held positive or negative attitudes, we asked them to choose their opinions on vegetarianism based a 7-point Likert scale for five pairs of bipolar adjectives: unfavorable-favorable, unhealthy-healthy, bad-good, unnecessary-necessary, harmful-beneficial. We calculated the average ratings of the five items to be the participant's *prior attitude index* for the topic (Cronbach's α=0.96, good internal consistency [4]).

Accuracy Motive Index

Based on previous research [18], accuracy motive was measured by two items: 1) *how much are you interested in learning more about the topic*, and 2) *how much do you desire to know the truth of the topic regardless of your own position*. The answers were based on a 1-none to 7-a lot scale and we averaged the ratings to be the *accuracy motive index* (Cronbach's α = 0.88, good internal consistency).

Knowledge

For each topic, we asked participant to write down "what reasons or arguments immediately come to your mind for people who support or oppose the issue" using simple sentences such as "religious reason". They were asked to write pro-arguments and con-arguments in two separate bulleted lists. The same questions were asked again after the experiment. We counted the number of points that appeared in the post-experiment but not in the pre-experiment questionnaire as a proxy of participants' *knowledge gain* after browsing the website.

User and Comment Selection

One main focus of this study was participants' selection of users and comments of varied positions. The experiment platform, i.e., the website we used, was able to record which users and comments were clicked on.

RESULT

Participants in the condition with position bars selected a mean of 5.1(SD=2.7) users and read 1.8 comments (SD=0.8) from each user for each topic. Participants in the control condition selected a mean of 5.3(SD=2.7) users and read 1.7 (SD=0.8) comments from each user. No significant difference in the number of users ($p=0.69$) or comments per user ($p=0.60$) was observed between the two groups.

We were interested in the effect of the source position indicator on both the selection and processing of diverse information. To that end, we first investigated participants' selections of users of varied positions (**RQ1**), specifically how the valence and magnitude information showed by the indicator influenced the selection (**RQ2**). We then analyzed whether the position indicator had impact on participants' perception of the users' position *after* reading the comments (**RQ3**), and their agreement with the comments (**RQ4**). Lastly, we analyzed whether the selection of different users led to differences in participants' knowledge gained on either side (**RQ5**).

Prior Attitude Side and Relative User Position

[1] www.debate.org, www.procon.org, answers.yahoo.com

Index	Definition	Calculation
Prior Attitude Index	Reflects the participant's prior attitude on the topic based on 1-con to 7-pro scale.	Mean of ratings of the 5-item semantic differential scale on the particular topic measured in the pretest.
Accuracy Motive Index	Reflects the motivation the participant has for accurately learning about the topic.	Mean of the ratings of the 2-item accuracy motive scale on the particular topic measured in the pretest.
Prior Attitude Side	Reflects whether the participant has pro or con prior attitude on the topic.	Pro, if *Prior Attitude Index* >4 Con, if *Prior Attitude Index*<4
Attitude Extremity Index	Reflects extremity of prior attitude	| *Prior Attitude Index*-4|
Relative User Position	Reflects user's position as relative to participant's side.	If *Prior Attitude Side*=Pro, extremely/moderately pro (con) users coded *as extremely/moderately consistent*, (*inconsistent*) If *Prior Attitude Side*=Con, extremely/moderately pro (con) users coded *as* extremely/moderately *inconsistent* (*consistent*)
Selective Exposure Index	Measures user's preferential selection between attitude consistent and inconsistent users (or comments).	N (extremely consistent users) + N (moderately consistent users) –N (extremely inconsistent users) – N (moderately inconsistent users)
Position Judgment Index	Measures participant's position judgment of the particular type of users.	Mean of position ratings given to all users of the particular type
Relative Position Index	Measures participant's perception of the position of the type of users (extremely/moderately consistent or inconsistent) as relative to their own side	If *Prior Attitude Side*=Pro, *Relative Position Index* = *Position Index* If *Prior Attitude Side*=Con, *Relative Position Index* = 6-Position Index
Agreement Index	Measures participant's agreement with comments from the type of users	Mean of agreement ratings given to all comments from the type of users
Knowledge Gain Index	Reflects the new knowledge of arguments on either side gained by using the system	Number of points appeared in post-experiment recall test but not pre-experiment recall test listed on either side

Table 2. Summary of the measurements used in the current study.

First we coded each participant' prior attitude on each topic to be *pro* or *con* based on whether his or her *prior attitude index* is below or above 4, which is the neutral point of the scale and also the median among all participants. 20 out of the 192 cases where participants scored exactly 4 were removed from the analysis. Then we coded each user case to be *extremely consistent*, *moderately consistent*, *moderately inconsistent* or *extremely inconsistent* based on whether the user is on the same or opposite side of the participant's prior attitude, and their attitude magnitude (see Table 2 *Prior Attitude Side* and *Relative User Position*).

User Selection

Selective Exposure Index

To answer RQ1, how the position indicator impacted participants' selective exposure tendency, we created *selective exposure index*, calculated by the difference in the number of attitude consistent and attitude inconsistent users selected (see Table 2 *Selective Exposure Index*). A positive index indicated the exhibition of selective exposure, while negative indicated selection of more attitude inconsistent users, and its magnitude reflected the size of the difference.

Overall Selectivity of All Participants ***(RQ1a)***

We started by examining the indicator's overall impact on participants' selective exposure tendency. We ran a mixed-effect regression model on the *selective exposure index* by having the presence position bars (present=1, absent=0) as the fixed-effect independent variable (N=172). In all the mixed-effect regression models described in this paper, participants were included as random effects. We will only mention variables included as fixed effects in the remaining of the paper. We found a main effect of the presence of the position bars (β=-0.51, t (30)=-2.20, $p=0.04$, $f^2=0.03$), suggesting that, overall, position bar decreased participants' selective exposure.

Selectivity of Participants with High Versus Low Accuracy Motives ***(RQ1b)***

In RQ1b, we asked whether the position indicator would have differential impacts on users with varied levels of motivation to accurately learn about the topic (*accuracy motive*). To answer this question, we further examined the result by including the *accuracy motive index* and presence of position bars in the mixed-effect regression model on *selective exposure index* (detailed definition can be found in Table 2). Indeed, we found a significant interaction between *accuracy motive* and presence of position bars on the *selective exposure index* (β=-0.37, t(28)=-2.22, $p=0.03$, $f^2=0.09$). The significant interaction answered our research question in the affirmative, i.e., the effect of the position indicator on decreasing selective exposure depended on whether the participant had a high or low motivation to learn about the topic.

To more clearly visualize this two-way interaction, we chose to use median splits to show how the effect of the position bar depended on the level of accuracy motive. We should point out that the median splits were performed *only* for the visualization. The *accuracy motive index* was treated as a continuous variable in *all* regression models. In figure 3, we first preformed median splits to create the high or low accuracy motive groups, and we presented the mean *selective exposure ind*ex for each group. This visualization highlighted the two-way interaction between accuracy motive and presence of position bars: the presence of position bars decreased the selective exposure for topics in which participants had higher than average accuracy motive, as they selected more attitude inconsistent users. However, the bars had little impact on participants who had lower than average accuracy motive. The results suggested that the position bar was effective in mitigating the selective exposure tendency, but *only* for participants who had stronger motivation to learn about the topic.

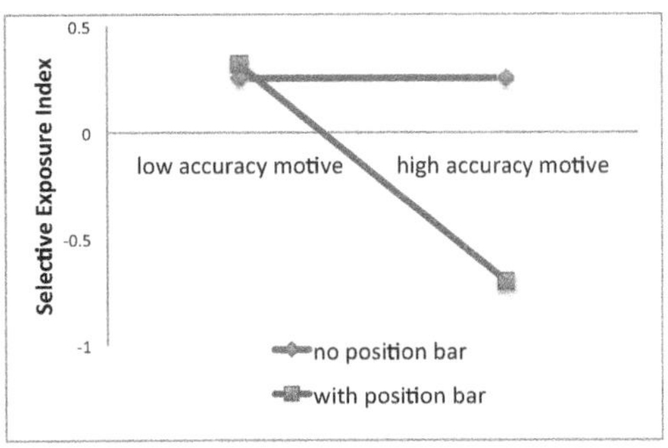

Figure 3. Average *selective exposure index*

To confirm this effect, we further investigated whether the same pattern of result was observed in the selection of the individual comments from the users. Since participants had the option to read from 1 to 3 comments from each user, we calculated the *selective exposure index* based on the number of comments they read as well. We observed the same trend that there was a significant interaction between *accuracy motive* and presence of position bars (ß=-0.68, t(28)=-2.20, $p=0.03$, $f^2=0.10$), indicating that with the presence of position bars participants were more likely to read comments of the opposite side for topics they had relatively high accuracy motives than those without the position bars.

To summarize the answer for RQ1, we found that the position bar had different impact on participants with varied levels of accuracy motives. Specifically, it increased their exposure to attitude-challenging information when participants *had high motivation to accurately learn about the topic*. However, for participants who had little interest in learning about the topic, the bar had little impact.

*Valence and Magnitude of Source Position on Participants' Selectivity (**RQ2**)*

Since the position bar not only provided the valence (pro/con) but also the magnitude (moderate/extreme) of users' stances, RQ2 asked whether participants differentially selected users indicated as one of the four *relative user positions*: *extremely consistent*, *moderately consistent*, *moderately inconsistent* and *extremely inconsistent*, coded as *Relative User Position* described in Table 2. We included *accuracy motive index*, presence of position bars (present=1, absent=0), the selected users' position valences (consistent=1, inconsistent=0) and magnitudes (moderate=0, extreme=1) in the mixed-effect linear regression model as independent variables to test how they impacted the percentage of the type of users selected (N=668, 4 categories for each of the 172 tasks). We found a significant three-way interaction among the presence of position bars, *accuracy motive*, and the selected users' valences of positions, (ß=-0.08, t (16)=-2.95 $p<0.01$, $f^2=0.04$), and a significant three-way interaction among the position bars, *accuracy motive*, and the selected users' magnitudes of positions (ß=-0.06, t (16)=-2.07, $p=0.04$, $f^2=0.07$). These significant interactions provided answers to RQ2 in the affirmative: both the valence and magnitude reflected in the position indicator affected participants' selection of users, and the selection differed between participants with varied levels of accuracy motives.

Given that we were interested in how the position bars would encourage exposure to attitude-challenging positions, we separated the selected users into two groups: attitude *consistent* users and *inconsistent* users. We then ran the regression analysis in each group to study how the interactive effects of the presence of position bars and *accuracy motive* would lead to different patterns of selection of users with extreme or moderate positions (i.e., position magnitudes).

For attitude inconsistent users, we ran a mixed-effect regression model on the selection percentages by including the presence of position bars, *accuracy motive index*, and the user's position magnitudes as independent variables. We found a significant three-way interaction among all the independent variables (ß=-0.06, t(24)=-2.18, $p=0.03$, $f^2=0.08$). It suggested that the position bar had differential effects on participants who had high and low accuracy motives on selecting inconsistent users with different attitude magnitudes. Figure 4 provided a clearer picture- *the position bars encouraged participants who had higher accuracy motives to select more moderately inconsistent users than those with lower accuracy motives*. No such difference was observed when the position bars were absent. To verify the conclusion, we ran a mixed-effect regression model on the selection percentages for *moderately inconsistent* users only by including *accuracy motive index* and presence of position bar as independent variables. Results showed a significant two-way interaction between the independent variables on the selection percentages (ß=0.05, t(28)=2.72, $p<0.01$, $f^2=0.10$). For extremely inconsistent users, we did not observe any statistically significant effect of the presence of position bars or *accuracy motives*. These results therefore provided further support for this conclusion.

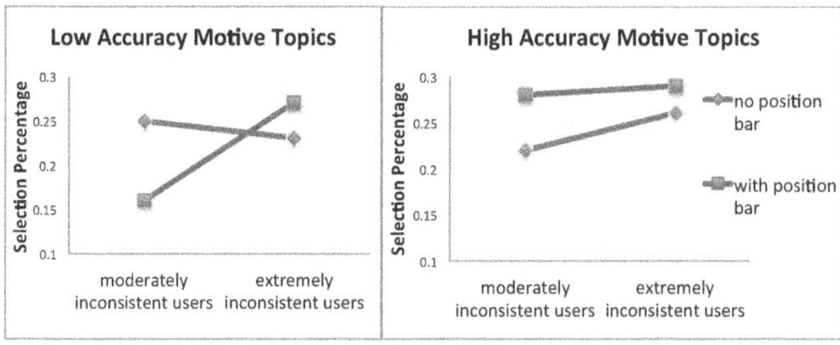

Figure 4. Selection percentage of attitude inconsistent users

For attitude consistent users, we ran the same mixed-effect regression model but did not find the three-way interaction to be significant. However, we found a significant two-way interaction between presence of position bars and *accuracy motives* (ß=-0.03, t (27)=-1.93, $p=0.05$, $f^2=0.03$), and a main effect of users' position magnitudes (ß=0.09, t (27)=4.52, $p<0.01$, $f^2=0.06$). The two-way interaction suggested that the position bars led to lower selection percentages only for participants with high accuracy motives, but not for those with low accuracy motives. This was consistent with the conclusion from the analysis of the *selective exposure index*: the position bar led participants with high accuracy motives, but not those with low accuracy motives, to select lower percentages of users with consistent positions. The main effect of position magnitude was caused by the fact that, regardless of the accuracy motive or presence of position bars, participants consistently selected more users with extremely consistent than moderately consistent positions. We speculated that it was caused by the fact that attitude consistent information would not lead to cognitive dissonance, thus neither the accuracy motives nor the presence of position bar impacted how likely participants selected users with moderately consistent or extremely consistent positions.

Interestingly, in the regression model for all users, the three-way interaction among users' attitude magnitudes, presence of position bars, and accuracy motives on the selection percentage implied that the position bar made participants who had low accuracy motives to be more selective towards users with extreme positions rather than moderate positions. By analyzing the total number of users selected, we found the accuracy motive had a marginally significant positive effect (ß=0.22, t (30)=1.69, $p=0.08$, $f^2=0.03$), showing that participants overall selected fewer users when they had relatively low accuracy motives. Given the low accuracy motives, it is likely that they were only willing to spend limited effort to understand the topic and may not be interested in knowing and weighing the detailed arguments, and therefore strategically chose to focus mostly on those standing at the extreme ends. In contrast, the greater motivation to form an accurate understanding of the topic might intrigue participants to seek for more detailed arguments from users of varied positions, including those with moderately inconsistent attitudes.

At the comment level, we performed the same analysis with the percentages of the selection of comments as the dependent variable in the regression model. We found a significant four-way interaction among presence of position bars, *accuracy motive*, users' valences and magnitudes of positions (ß=0.08, t (16)=1.93, $p=0.05$, , $f^2=0.08$). These results again suggested that the position bar had differential effects on participants with high and low accuracy motives on their tendency to read comments from different types of users. Closer examination revealed similar patterns as in the selection of users: with the position bars, participants with high accuracy motives read lower percentages of attitude consistent comments, but higher percentages of moderately inconsistent comments than participants with low accuracy motives, which resulted in overall lower selective exposure tendency of the former than the later.

In summary, our results provided affirmative answers to RQ2 by showing that both valence and magnitude information showed in the source position indicators had differential effects on users who had varied levels of accuracy motives. The most important result was that *with the position bars, participants with high accuracy motives selected more moderately inconsistent users than those with low accuracy motives.* As a result, the position indicators increased the exposure to attitude-challenging information for participants with high accuracy motives, but had no such impact for participants who had low accuracy motives.

Position Judgment

After examining the effect of the position bars on participants' selective exposure, the next question is to what extent the position bars could lead to changes in their *reception* of attitude inconsistent information. This leads to our RQ3: whether the source position indicator had influence on participants' perception of users' positions *after* they read their comments. To answer this question, we examined participants' position ratings (on a 1-pro to 5-con scale) given to each user after they read the comments. First, we looked at the correlation between participant's judgments and the "ground truth" (i.e., which we manipulated and checked in a pilot study, and coded as extremely pro user=1, moderately pro user=2, moderately con user=3, extremely con user=4). We found that the position bars significantly increased this correlation from 0.64 to 0.78 (Z=4.77, $p<0.01$). It indicated that after seeing the position bars, participants judgments of users' stances were closer to those indicated by the position bars, suggesting that the bar did influence their judgment of the positions of the users.

Relative Position Index

Another possible influence of the position indicator on participants' information reception is the extent to which a user was perceived to be different from one's pre-existing attitude. For example, if an attitude-inconsistent opinion had low reception, it might be judged to be more extreme than information the user had high reception with. To examine such judgment, we created an index called *relative position index* to measure participant's judgment on user's positions relative to the side of his or her pre-existing attitude. To do so, we first calculated *position judgment index* by the average ratings given to the four categories of users (extremely/moderately consistent or inconsistent). Since the position judgment used a 1-pro to 5-con scale, if the participant had positive prior attitude, the *relative position index* of each type of users would be equal the *position judgment index*. If the person had negative prior attitude, the *relative position index* would be calculated by 6 minus *position judgment index. Relative position index* reflected how far the participant perceived the type of users to be different from his or her prior attitude, with a higher number indicating that the users were perceived to be more different (see Table 2 *Position Judgment Index* and *Relative Position Judgment Index*).

*Participants' Judgments of Users' Positions (**RQ3**)*

We ran a mixed-effect regression model on the *relative position index* (N=535, 153 cases where the corresponding type of users were not selected were removed) by including the presence of position bars, user's position valences and magnitudes as independent variables. We found a significant three-way interaction among all the independent variables (ß = -0.78, t(24)=-2.46, $p=0.01$, $f^2=1.50$). All the other two-way and main effects, except for that between presence of position bars and users' position valences, were also significant. It suggested that the position bar had differential impact on participants' perceived relative positions of the users (see Figure 5). The Cohen's f^2 indicated that the interaction had a large effect size [3].

Given that we were interested in the difference in reception between attitude-consistent and inconsistent information, we unpacked the three-way interaction by running mixed-effect linear regression models on the *relative position index* among attitude consistent users and inconsistent users separately. We found a significant two-way interaction between users' opinion magnitudes and presence of position bars in the attitude inconsistent group ((ß = 0.59, t (28)=3.10, $p<0.01$, $f^2=0.25$), but not in the attitude consistent group (ß = -0.21, t (28)=-0.98, $p=0.33$). The results confirmed that the three-way interaction was caused by the difference in the reception of attitude-consistent and inconsistent information. In other words, *the position bars only led to significant differences in the position judgments of users with inconsistent positions*. Figure 5 illustrated this result: with the help of position bars, participants were better at differentiating between extremely and moderately inconsistent users. In fact, by examining moderately inconsistent users only, we found a significant main effect of the presence of position bars on the *relative position index* (ß = -0.33, t(28)=-2.00, $p=0.05$, $f^2=0.05$), suggesting that participants tended to perceive this group of users to be closer to themselves when the position bars were present than absent. This is consistent with the notion that people are inclined to perceive others of different opinions to be more extreme than they actually are. The position bar seemed to help to moderate their perception of moderately inconsistent sources to be less extreme.

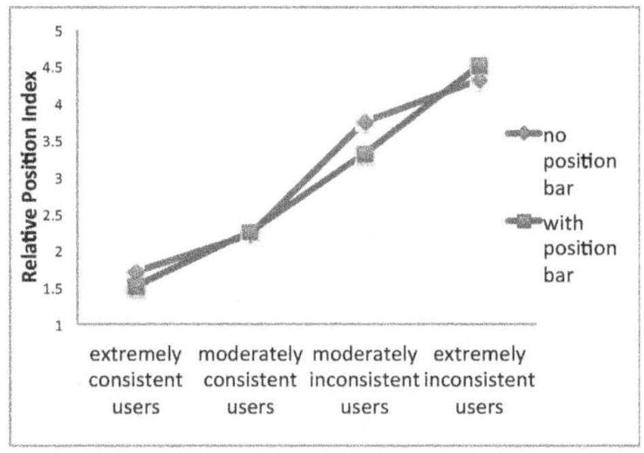

Figure 5. Average *relative position index*

Agreement

To further study how the position indicator influenced reception of diverse opinions, RQ4 asked whether the position bars also influenced participants' agreement with the comments from different types of users. To answer this question, we investigated participants' agreement ratings given to the comments (by a question under each user comment on the experiment interface). We expected that providing agreement rating would encourage more reflection of personal value than position judgment, for the later of which one could adopt a more third-person position. We therefore expected that agreement ratings would be impacted by the extremity of prior attitudes, as participants with more extreme prior attitudes would more likely have stronger disagreement with users who take opposite positions. Moreover, intuitively, if the participant was only moderately leaning towards one side, he or she might agree with users who were also in moderate positions more than those with extreme positions. Therefore, we examined participants' agreement by taking their prior attitude extremity into consideration.

Agreement Index and Prior Attitude Extremity Index

Agreement index was calculated by the average agreement ratings participants gave to all the comments they read and rated for the corresponding type of users for each topic (Table 2 *Agreement Index*).

Prior attitude extremity index was defined as the distance of one's *prior attitude index* from the neutral point, and was calculated by the absolute value of the *prior attitude index* minus neutral value 4. For example, if a participant scored 5 in the *prior attitude index*, he or she would be coded as *con* prior attitude with *prior attitude extremity index* of 1 (Table 2 *Prior Attitude Extremity Index*).

*Participants' Agreement with Comments from Users of Varied Positions (**RQ4**)*

We ran a mixed-effect regression model on the *agreement index* (N=535), with the presence of position bars, *prior attitude extremity,* users' position valences and magnitudes as independent variables. We found a significant three-way interaction among presence of position bars, *prior attitude extremity index*, and users' position valences (ß = -0.86, t(16)=-3.65, $p<0.01$, $f^2=0.36$), and a significant three-way interaction among presence of position bars, *prior attitude extremity*, and users' position magnitudes (ß = -0.47, t(16)=-2.12, $p=0.04$, $f^2=0.10$). The results suggested that the position bars differentially influenced users with moderate and extreme prior attitudes on their agreement with the comments from users of different positions.

To understand whether the position bars differentially impacted agreement with users of different positions, we separated the consistent and inconsistent users into two groups. For attitude inconsistent users, we ran a mixed-effect regression model on *agreement index* by including presence of position bars, *prior attitude extremity index* and users' position magnitudes as independent variables, and found a significant three-way interaction among them (ß=-0.41, t (24)=-1.91, $p=0.05$, $f^2=0.35$). The two-way interaction between *prior attitude extremity* and presence of position bars, and the main effect of *prior attitude extremity* were also significant.

Figure 6[2] explained the three-way interaction we found above: while the position bars did not have a significant impact on participants with moderate prior attitudes, they increased the agreement with moderately inconsistent users for participants with extreme prior attitudes, who tended to have lower agreement with attitude inconsistent comments than participants with moderate prior attitudes. To further verify this conclusion, we looked at the *agreement index* for moderately inconsistent users only. Indeed, we found the two-way interaction between *prior attitude extremity* and presence of position bars to be significant (ß=0.65, t (28)=3.73, $p<0.01$, $f^2=0.19$). It implied that, by helping participants to differentiate moderately inconsistent users from extremely inconsistent ones, participants who had extreme prior attitudes more likely agree with users with moderately inconsistent positions when the position bars were present than absent. For *agreement index* for extremely inconsistent users, we only observed significant main effect of *prior attitude extremity* (ß=-0.46, t (31)=-5.89, $p<0.01$, $f^2=0.25$), suggesting that the position bars did not have the same effect on agreement with users with extremely inconsistent positions. As expected, participants with extreme prior attitudes tended to disagree more with extremely inconsistent users than those with moderate prior attitudes regardless of the presence of position bars.

[2] As in previous figures, median splits on *prior attitude extremity* were used to illustrate the interaction in the figure, but not in the regression models.

For attitude consistent users, we ran the same mixed-effect regression model and did not observe the three-way interaction, but found a significant two-way interaction between participants' *prior attitude extremity* and users' position magnitudes (ß = 0.31, t (28)=2.89, p<0.01, $f^2=0.07$), indicating that regardless of the presence of position bars, participants with more extreme prior attitudes tended to agree more with users on the same side with extreme positions, while participants who had moderate prior attitudes tended to agree with users on the same side with moderate attitudes. This is consistent with the intuition that people tend to agree with others of similar positions.

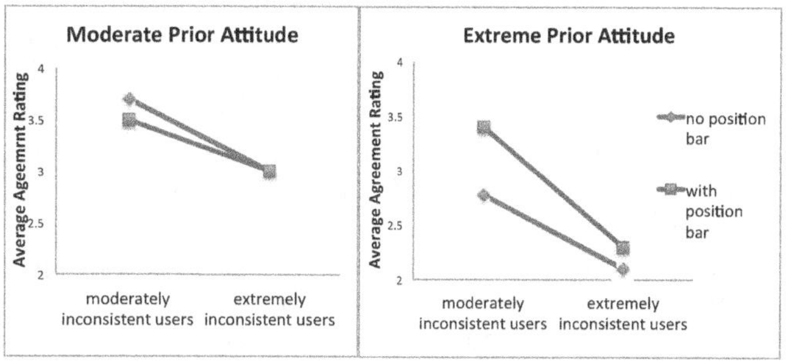

Figure 6. Average *agreement index* attitude inconsistent users

The analysis performed on position judgment and agreement revealed a consistent theme: the indicator showing both source position valence and magnitude was especially helpful for participants to differentiate between those who had moderately opposite stances from those with more extreme ones. Ultimately, the indicator seemed to help moderate participants' tendency to over-estimate the discrepancy of positions between themselves and the attitude-inconsistent information source, and induce more agreement with sources with moderately opposite positions. In general, the results showed that not only did the position bars reduced selective exposure, but also increased reception of attitude-challenging information.

Knowledge Gain (RQ5)

One important goal of exposing people to diverse opinions is to promote awareness of arguments on both sides in order to help them make informed decisions or form unbiased views. Last but not the least, we analyzed participants' knowledge gained on both sides as the outcome measurement. Specifically, we were interested in whether the differentiation in selection of information led to the difference in knowledge gained.

In the survey before experiment, we asked participants to list points that could "immediately come to mind" to support or oppose the topic. After the experiment, we asked them to do the same. We compared the two answers and counted how many points of attitude-consistent argument and inconsistent argument, respectively, appeared in the post-experiment questionnaire but not in the pre-experiment questionnaire. We used this number as a proxy measure of knowledge gain (see Table 2 *Knowledge Gain Index)* from using the system.

We ran a mixed-effect regression model on the *knowledge gain index* for the side opposite to participants' prior attitude (*attitude inconsistent knowledge gain*) by including presence of position bars and *accuracy motive index* as independent variables, and found a significant interaction between the two (ß=0.33, t(28)=3.10, $p<0.01$, $f^2=0.04$). Figure 7 illustrates the two-way interaction after we performed median splits of *accuracy motive index*: with the help of position bars, participants gained more knowledge of opposite side for topics they had high accuracy motives, but not for those who had low accuracy motives. For knowledge gained on arguments that people of similar attitudes make, we didn't observe any significant effect of position bars or accuracy motives. The result was consistent with the finding that participants, with the help of position bars, were exposed to attitude inconsistent users more for topics they had high accuracy motive. The results therefore further supported the conclusion that providing indicators of information source position is beneficial for users who are interested in accurately learning about the topic.

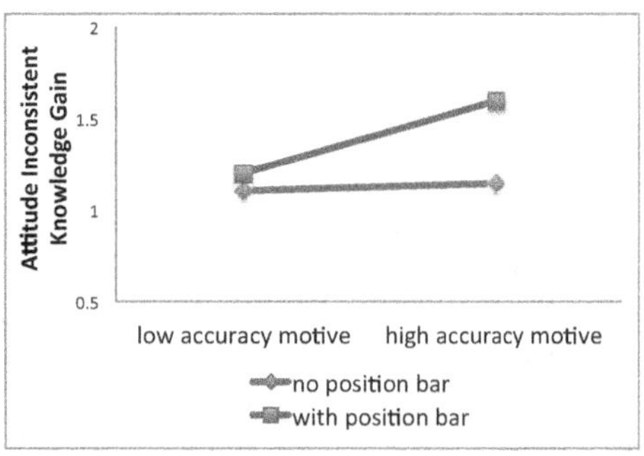

Figure 7. Average attitude inconsistent *knowledge gain*

DISCUSSION

Scholars have warned that the "echo chamber effect" on the Internet can exacerbate attitude polarization, as people may end up only interacting with others who share similar attitudes or opinions. In this experiment, in the hope of mitigating the problem, we introduced and tested the effects of an interface feature that indicated the information source's (in this study, the user) position, including both its valence and magnitude, on reducing the potential echo chamber effect. We found that it had differential effects on participants who had varied levels of motivation to accurately learn about the topic. Specifically, the indicator significantly decreased the selective exposure of participants who had high accuracy motives but had no such effect on participants who had low accuracy motives. The difference was caused by the fact that the multi-level position indicator encouraged participants who had high accuracy motives to select users with moderately inconsistent attitudes, but discouraged participants who had low accuracy motives from selecting information sources that were more neutral.

At the information reception stage, the indicator had influence on participants' perception of users and evaluation of information. Specifically, it helped participants to differentiate users who took moderately inconsistent stances from those who took extreme ones. As a result, participants eventually had a lower disagreement with comments from these moderately inconsistent users. Moreover, we found that, by encouraging exposure to attitude-challenging information, the indicator led to greater knowledge gained on the opposite side of their original positions for participants who had high accuracy motives.

The study has two main contributions. First, the results suggest that providing not only the valence but also the magnitude of information source position is useful for encouraging exposure to diverse information, which may facilitates the seeking of common grounds among people with different perspectives. Based on this result, we speculate that the group of people who are only moderately leaning towards the opposite side are critical for bringing in different perspectives without invoking strong resistance arising from cognitive dissonance. It is also possible that these people may provide distinctive insights that are useful for others to understand arguments from both sides. We believe that in many situations, identifying and explicitly indicating sources or arguments with moderate positions may allow them to function as "bridges" that increase the cohesion of groups with diverse opinions and contribute to more efficient "marketplaces" for idea exchanges.

Second, our results echoed suggestions from previous research [10, 23] that interfaces should be tailored for users with different levels of accuracy motives to achieve the goal of exposing users to challenging views, which highlighted the importance of personalization when designing for seeking diverse opinions. Our results showed that, when users are motivated to accurately learn about a topic thus interested in getting insights from people of varied positions, a non-dichotomous, more elaborate categorization of information combined with explicit indicators of such categories is useful.

Previous research suggests that high accuracy motive is often related to prioritizing the utility of information [34], and/or the social norm of valuing diversity [22]. By explicitly labeling the stances, it may better support the utility goal of seeking new, useful information. In addition, it may serve as a "reminder" that there exist diverse opinions, so as to further reinforce the normative goal of diversity seeking. However, when users have little interest in accurately learning about the topic, providing explicit labels of positions may sometimes exacerbate their biased selectivity between different stances.

From a design perspective, two issues emerged from this set of conclusions: the importance of inferring users' accuracy motivation levels and inferring the information sources' stances. Learning from research on personalization technologies, users' accuracy motives can be identified from either explicit inquiry or implicit inference based on their user profiles or previous behavior [21]. There are also conditions in which people are in general more motivated to accurately learn about a topic. For example, decision-making support tools will more likely target users who have high accuracy motives as the decisions are often related to important outcomes. Moreover, we argue that it is possible for designers to actively increase users' accuracy motive by, for example, providing simple interface cues that emphasize the social norm of valuing diversity [22] or highlight the utility of diverse or challenging information [34]. To infer information sources' stances, the literature has shown various ways of classifying, e.g., political positions or consumer opinions, based on either text based methods (e.g., machine learning, opinion mining, sentiment analysis [26]) or non-text features such as user voting or social network [37]. One future direction would be to develop methods that can accurately identify the "bridges" in an online opinion space, or information sources that can provide insights on both sides.

While much previous research alarmed the problem of selective exposure on the Internet, other questioned its existence as a universal phenomenon [23, 31]. Our study generated consistent results with the later, suggesting that there are important moderating variables that influence the exhibition of such behavior. In addition to exploring ways to mitigate selective exposure, future research should also focus on identifying and understanding these moderating variables, and examining their interactive effects with interface features.

In this study, given the limited time of use, we could not conclude whether participants became less polarized after using the system. Future work should focus on longer-term field studies, in which effects of information aggregator showing source positions on users' information seeking behavior as well as attitude change can be studied.

REFERENCES

1. Van Alstyne, M., & Brynjolfsson, E. (1996). Electronic communities: Global village or cyberbalkans?. In Proceedings of the 17th International Conference on Information Systems.
2. Aronson, E., Turner, J. A., & Carlsmith, J. M. (1963). Communicator credibility and communication discrepancy as determinants of opinion change. *The Journal of Abnormal and Social Psychology*, 67(1), 31.
3. Cohen, J. (1992). A power primer. *Psychological bulletin,* 112(1), 155.
4. Cronbach, L.J., Coefficient Alpha and The Internal Structure of Tests. *Psychometrika* 16, 3 (1951), 297-334.
5. Faridani, S., Bitton, E., Ryokai, K., & Goldberg, K. (2010). Opinion space: a scalable tool for browsing online comments. In Proc. CHI2010, 1175-1184).
6. Fleiss, L. (2011). Measuring nominal scale agreement among many raters. *Psychological Bulletin* ,76 (5), 378.
7. Fischer, P. (2011). Selective Exposure, Decision Uncertainty, and Cognitive Economy: A New Theoretical Perspective on Confirmatory Information Search. *Social and Personality Psychology Compass*, 5(10), 751-762.
8. Fischhoff, B., Slovic, P., & Lichtenstein, S. (1977). Knowing with certainty: The appropriateness of extreme confidence. *Journal of Experimental Psychology: Human Perception and Performance*, 3(4), 552.
9. Frey, D. Recent Research on Selective Exposure to Information. *Advances in Experimental Social Psychology* 19(1986), 41-80.
10. Garrett, R., Resnick, P. Resisting Political Fragmentation on the Internet. *Daedalus* 140, 4 (2011) 108-120.
11. Garrett, R. K., Stroud,N. (2012). Decoupling selective approach and selective avoidance. Paper to be presented at the National Communication Association, Political Communication Division, Orlando, FL.
12. Hart, W., Albarracín, D., Eagly, A. H., Brechan, I., Lindberg, M. J., & Merrill, L. (2009). Feeling validated versus being correct: a meta-analysis of selective exposure to information. *Psychological bulletin*, 135(4), 555.
13. Himmelfarb, S. The measurement of attitudes. In A.H. Eagly & S. Chaiken (Eds.), Psychology of Attitudes (1993), 23-88. Thomson/Wadsworth
14. Janis, I. L., & Mann, L. (1977). *Decision making: A psychological analysis of conflict, choice, and commitment* (p. 81). New York: Free Press.
15. Jiang, Y., Liao, Q., Cheng, Q., Berlin, R., Schatz, B. Designing and Evaluating a Clustering System for Organizing and Integrating Patient Drug Outcomes in Personal Health Messages. *In Proc. AMIA 2012*
16. Klayman, J. (1995). Varieties of confirmation bias. *Psychology of learning and motivation*, 32, 385-418.
17. Kriplean, T., Morgan, J., Freelon, D., Borning, A., Bennett, L. Supporting Reflective Public Thought with ConsiderIt. *In Proc. CSCW2012*, 265-274
18. Liao, Q. V., & Fu, W. T. (2013). Beyond the filter bubble: interactive effects of perceived threat and topic involvement on selective exposure to information. *In Proc. CHI2013*, 2359-2368.
19. Maass, A., & Clark, R. D. (1984). Hidden impact of minorities: Fifteen years of minority influence research. *Psychological Bulletin*, 95(3), 428-450.
20. Mendelberg, T. (2002). The deliberative citizen: Theory and evidence. *Political decision making, deliberation and participation*, 6(1), 151-193.
21. Mulvenna, M. D., Anand, S. S., & Büchner, A. G. (2000). Personalization on the Net using Web mining: introduction. *Communications of the ACM*, 43(8), 122-125.

22. Munson, S. A., Lee, S. Y., & Resnick, P. (2013). Encouraging Reading of Diverse Political Viewpoints with a Browser Widget. *In Proc. ICWSM 2013*

23. Munson, S. & Resnick P. Presenting Diverse Political Opinions: How and How Much. *In Proc. CHI2010*, 1457-1466.

24. Nemeth, C. J., & Kwan, J. L. (1987). Minority influence, divergent thinking and detection of correct solutions. *Journal of Applied Social Psychology*, 17(9), 788-799.

25. Oh, A., Lee, H., Kim, Y. User Evaluation of a System for Classifying and Displaying Political Viewpoints of Weblogs. In Proc. *ICWSM 2009*, 282-285

26. Pang, B., & Lee, L. (2008). Opinion mining and sentiment analysis.Foundations and trends in information retrieval, 2(1-2), 1-135.

27. Pariser, E. The Filter Bubble: What the Internet Is Hiding from You, Penguin Press, 2011

28. Park, S., Kang, S., Chung, S., Song, J. NewsCube: Delivering Multiple Aspects of News to Mitigate Media Bias. *In Proc. CHI2009*, 443-452

29. Petty, R. E., & Krosnick, J. A. (Eds.). (1995). *Attitude strength: Antecedents and consequences* (Vol. 4). Mahwah, NJ: Lawrence Erlbaum Associates

30. Sanders, GS; Mullen, B. 1982. Accuracy in perceptions of consensus: Differential tendencies of people with majority and minority positions. Eur J Soc Psychol 13(1): 57-70.

31. Sears, D. O., & Freedman, J. L. (1967). Selective exposure to information: A critical review. *Public Opinion Quarterly*, 31(2), 194-213.

32. Sunstein, C. R. (2009). *Going to Extremes: How Like Minds Unite and Divide: How Like Minds Unite and Divide*. Oxford University Press, USA.

33. Sweeny, K., Melnyk, D., Miller, W., & Shepperd, J. A. (2010). Information avoidance: Who, what, when, and why. Review of general psychology, 14(4), 340-353

34. Valentino, N. A., Banks, A. J., Hutchings, V. L., & Davis, A. K. (2009). Selective exposure in the Internet age: The interaction between anxiety and information utility. Political Psychology, 30(4), 591-613.

35. Vydiswaran, V., Zhai, C., Roth, D., Pirolli, P. Unbiased Learning of Controversial Topics. *In Proc. ASIST2012*

36. Yatani, K., Novati M., Trusty, A., Truong, K. Review Spotlight: A User Interface for Summarizing User Generated Reviews Using Adjective-Noun Word Pairs. *In Proc. CHI2011*, 1541-1550

37. Zhou, D. X., Resnick, P., & Mei, Q. (2011, May). Classifying the political leaning of news articles and users from user votes. *In Proc. ICWSM2011*, 417-424.

APPENDIX A: TOPICS USED IN THE EXPERIMENT

1. Should death penalty be allowed?
2. Should prescription drugs be advertised directly to consumers?
3. Should euthanasia be legal?
4. Do violent video games contribute to the increase of youth violence?
5. Should people become vegetarian?
6. Should social security be privatized?

Deep Twitter Diving: Exploring Topical Groups in Microblogs at Scale

Parantapa Bhattacharya
IIT Kharagpur, India
MPI-SWS, Germany

Saptarshi Ghosh
BESU Shibpur, India
MPI-SWS, Germany

Juhi Kulshrestha
MPI-SWS, Germany

Mainack Mondal
MPI-SWS, Germany

Muhammad Bilal Zafar
MPI-SWS, Germany

Niloy Ganguly
IIT Kharagpur, India

Krishna P. Gummadi
MPI-SWS, Germany

ABSTRACT

We present a semantic methodology to identify *topical groups* in Twitter on a large number of topics, each consisting of users who are experts on or interested in a specific topic. Early studies investigating the nature of Twitter suggest that it is a social media platform consisting of a relatively small section of elite users, producing information on a few popular topics such as media, politics, and music, and the general population consuming it. We show that this characterization ignores a rich set of highly specialized topics, ranging from geology, neurology, to astrophysics and karate – each being discussed by their own topical groups. We present a detailed characterization of these topical groups based on their network structures and tweeting behaviors. Analyzing these groups on the backdrop of the common identity and bond theory in social sciences shows that these groups exhibit characteristics of topical-identity based groups, rather than social-bond based ones.

Author Keywords

Topical groups; identity-based groups; Twitter; topical experts; seekers of topical information;

ACM Classification Keywords

H.3.5 On-line Information Services: Web-based services; J.4 Computer Applications: Social and behavioral sciences

INTRODUCTION

What is Twitter? Who says what to whom on Twitter? Recently these two questions about the fundamental nature of the Twitter microblogging site have attracted a lot of research attention. Early studies that attempted to answer these questions [16, 30] concluded that Twitter is more like a news media site than a social networking site, and that a small number of elite users consisting of celebrities, bloggers, media representatives, and organizations dominate and control the production and flow of information, which is then consumed by the masses of ordinary users in Twitter. These characterizations of the Twitter network have fostered the current popular perception of Twitter as a platform for getting information or public opinions on topics of general interest.

In this paper, we argue that it is time to revisit these two foundational questions about Twitter. Recently a lot of research has focused on mining user data to develop detailed characterizations of Twitter users. For instance, in our prior works [12, 25], we have proposed techniques to infer the biographical information and topical expertise of millions of Twitter users. These recent advances in accurately profiling large numbers of Twitter users enable us to dive deep into the Twitter network and explore several tens of thousands of *topical groups* that the earlier studies investigating these questions [16, 30] were oblivious to. Below, we summarize the three primary contributions of this paper.

1. Inferring topical groups at scale: A topical group is a collection of users that are interested in propagating or seeking information on a specific topic (e.g., music, politics, environment, neurology, forensics). In this paper, we propose a new *semantic approach* for detecting topical groups in Twitter. Our methodology first identifies *experts*, i.e., authoritative users, on a particular topic and then identifies *seekers*, i.e., followers of the experts on the topic. Unlike prior approaches, our method scales very well: using detailed data about 38.4 million Twitter users, we identify several thousand topical groups covering a wide variety of topics that Twitter users are interested in. The topical groups we identified cover 49.5% of all the users and 94.3% of all the links in the Twitter network for these 38.4 million users.

2. Characterizing the topical groups: We conducted a detailed characterization of the topical groups, focusing on their

CSCW'14, February 15–19, 2014, Baltimore, Maryland, USA.

ACM 978-1-4503-2540-0/14/02 ...$15.00.
http://dx.doi.org/10.1145/2531602.2531636

diversity, the users followed by them, and tweeting behaviors of these users.

(a) Diversity in topical groups: We discover a rich and diverse set of highly specialized and focused topical groups that lie embedded deep within the Twitter network. We find that these topical groups span a variety of niche topics, which range from 'geology' and 'neurology' to 'astrophysics' and 'karate'. These groups are often ignored by research studies today because (i) they are small in size, i.e., the number of group members is low, (ii) even the experts in these niche topical groups have relatively low overall popularity in the global network, and (iii) tweets relevant to the specific topics of interest of the groups are largely limited to the group members. Earlier studies that have attempted to characterize the Twitter network at-scale by looking at popular users or popular tweets have mostly overlooked the existence of these groups. Our work offers a different perspective on what the Twitter network is – a treasure-trove of diverse topical groups.

(b) Following and tweeting behaviors in topical groups: We also analyzed the *following* behavior of experts and seekers within a topical group, and the tweeting behavior of experts within a topical group. Our analysis provides several interesting insights: (i) within a topical group, the experts and seekers exhibit very different connectivities; the experts tend to be considerably more interconnected amongst themselves, while the seekers mostly connect to the experts and not amongst themselves, (ii) experts of niche topical groups, i.e., groups with a few tens to a few hundreds of experts, tend to be particularly tightly interconnected amongst themselves, (iii) the two-hop (and not one-hop) neighborhoods of experts include the majority of experts in the group for both niche and popular groups, (iv) experts, especially those in niche topical groups, tend to tweet on the topics of their expertise, and (v) tweets that are popular amongst experts in a topical group have a high likelihood of being related to the topical expertise of the group.

Overall, the observed behaviors of topical groups match closely with those expected of *identity-based groups* (rather than bond-based groups) in social sciences literature [22, 23].

3. Implications of the findings: Our findings about topical groups have important implications for researchers studying Twitter or designing various services on Twitter. We show that because of the relatively low interconnectivity between experts and seekers, it is difficult, if not impossible, to detect these topical groups by applying standard community-detection techniques on the Twitter network graph. We also demonstrate the significance of our findings by applying them in the context of two different applications: (i) Finding more experts in a topical group: we show how the tight interconnectivity between experts, especially in the case of niche topical groups can be leveraged to discover new (and otherwise missing) group members within the Twitter network, and (ii) Topical content recommendations: we show how the observation that experts in a group tend to tweet on topics relevant to the group can be used to build topical search and recommendation systems.

RELATED WORK

The present study focuses on identifying topical groups in Twitter and understanding their characteristics. There have been several prior studies on detecting and distinguishing between different types of user groups in social networks, in general, and Twitter, in particular. In this section, we discuss some of the major studies in each of these categories.

User groups in social sciences: The topic of user groups (or communities) in societies has been widely studied in behavioral sciences, and a variety of theories have been proposed to explain the formation of such groups [4, 8, 21, 29]. One of the most well-known theories on group formation, both in off-line and online societies, is the *common identity and common bond theory* [22, 23], according to which, the attachment of users to a particular group can be either identity-based or bond-based. Identity-based attachment holds when people join a group based on their interest in the group as a whole or in a well-defined common theme (topic) shared by the members. On the other hand, *bond-based* attachment is driven by personal social relations (bonds) among the members, and may be characterized by the absence of any central theme / topic of discussion within the group. According to this theory, the two types of groups differ in reciprocity of the interactions and the topicality of the discussions. Bond-based groups tend to have higher reciprocity among the members, whereas interactions in identity-based groups are generally not directly reciprocated. Also, the topics of discussion in bond-based groups tend to vary widely and cover multiple subjects, while in identity-based groups, they tend to be related to the common group theme.

There have been several attempts to distinguish between bond-based and identity-based groups, especially in the online world. For instance, [24] classified chats among users on a text-based communication platform into two categories – on-topic chats which centered around a common topic (examples of identity-based groups) and off-topic chats where people chatted on a variety of topics (examples of bond-based groups). More recently, [13] differentiated between the identity-based and bond-based groups (which they called topical groups and social groups respectively) in the Flickr social network.

In this study, we analyze the interconnections, interactions, and tweeting behaviors of *topical groups* in the Twitter social network. Our findings about the behaviors of users in the different topical groups conform to those one would expect to find in identity-based groups.

Detecting groups in social networks: Automatically identifying user groups in large social networks is a topic that has received a lot of recent research attention. A large number of algorithms have been proposed to identify user groups by detecting graph communities in social networks. These community-detection algorithms rely only on the network structure and identify groups of densely connected nodes in the network as communities; see [11] for a detailed review on such algorithms. The communities detected by such algorithms are known to mostly resemble bond-based groups [13]. In fact, the recent study [31] showed that communities identified from the network structure often do not conform to ground-truth groups that are explicitly defined by the nodes (members) in the network.

Detection of identity-based groups usually requires knowledge of groups defined explicitly by the nodes [13] or some semantic methodology based on the content generated in the OSNs (e.g., [24] analyzed the topicality of the conversations / chats among members). Unfortunately, not all social networks (for example, Twitter) allow users to form explicitly defined groups. In such systems, one would have to resort to semantic approaches for detecting identity-based groups.

In this study, we propose a semantic methodology to detect topical groups of Twitter users who are experts on or interested in a specific topic. We show that the semantically meaningful topical groups resemble identity-based groups, and are very different from the groups detected by standard community detection algorithms (which are likely to be bond-based).

Detecting groups in Twitter: There have been several efforts to identify groups of users having similar interests / characteristics in Twitter. They fall into two broad categories: (i) *graph-based approaches*: those that rely primarily on applying community detection algorithms on the Twitter follow-network [14, 28], and (ii) *semantic approaches*: those that rely on identifying groups of users with similar interests by analyzing either their profile meta-data (e.g., profile names, bios, URLs) or the content of their tweets [2, 3, 9, 30].

The graph-based approaches are scalable, but they would not be able to detect loosely connected groups of users (identity-based groups) driven by some common topical interest. The current semantic methods are better at identifying such groups, but they suffer from certain other drawbacks. First, studies using semantic methods are often limited to a few pre-selected (and popular) topics. Second, many users do not provide information about their topical interests in their profiles, and even if they did, it is unclear if they can be trusted. Similarly, users' tweets often contain conversation on day-to-day activities, making it difficult to identify meaningful topics from tweets [25, 27]. As a result, studies often focus on a few specific and popular topics. For instance, [2] focused on tweets posted by media sources on news, technology, sports, music, politics, business and fashion, while [9] characterized the users who tweet about certain events related to popular topics such as politics (Egyptian revolution, Wikileaks), music and entertainment (Academy Awards, Bonnaroo), environment (Earth Day), sports (Super Bowl) and technology (Release of ipad2).

In this paper, we propose a new semantic approach that scales well to identify several tens of thousands of identity-based groups on a diverse set of topics, covering several tens of millions of Twitter users. The only similar study we know of is [3], which studies the diffusion of popular as well as less popular topics identified using NLP techniques on tweets. However, the methodology used in the present study is very different, which can result in important differences in the topical groups identified. [3] identified topics from tweets and studied the networks among users who tweet on a common topic – so their topical groups include *ephemeral users*, who might have once tweeted about a topic, but do not have a long-standing interest in it. For example, many users might tweet about an election or a environmental disaster the day after the event, even if they have no specific interest in politics or environment. Such ephemeral users would be included in topical groups identified by [3], but not by our methodology.

User roles in spreading information in Twitter: There have been several studies on how information and news related to specific topics spread in Twitter [17, 19], which have classified the different roles played by users in this diffusion. For instance, [30] analyzed the flow of information from 'elite' users to their followers. [9] characterized three types of users – organizations, journalists / media bloggers and ordinary individuals – who post tweets about certain events. In this study, we distinguish between two types of users within a topical group – *experts* who are likely to be authoritative sources of information on specific topics, and *seekers* who are interested in gathering information on these topics.

INFERRING TOPICAL GROUPS

In this section, we discuss our methodology for inferring topical groups in Twitter. By topical groups, we refer to the set of Twitter users who are interested in propagating or receiving information on specific topics. Intuitively, our methodology for identifying topical groups consists of the following steps. First, we identify *experts*, i.e., authoritative users on a specific topic. Second, we find *seekers*, users interested in receiving information on that topic, by looking for users who follow multiple experts on the topic. Third, we group the experts and seekers of information on a specific topic into a topical group.

The primary challenge in our methodology lies in accurately discovering expert Twitter users on a wide variety of topics that might be of interest to Twitter users. For this, we utilize a semantic methodology for inferring topics related to individual users, which scales well with respect to both the variety of topics identified as well as the number of users for whom topics can be inferred. Our methodology relies on the Lists feature in Twitter.

List-based characterization of users

Lists are an organizational feature in Twitter, which users create to group experts on topics that interest them [20]. To create a List, a user specifies a name and an optional description for the List; the user can then add other users as members of the List. Table 1 shows a few examples of Lists, including their names, descriptions and some of their members. The key observation is that the List names and descriptions offer semantic cues to the expertise of the users included in them.

In our prior works [12, 25], we have shown that List names and descriptions can be leveraged to infer the topical characteristics of users. Specifically, we showed that List meta-data can be used to (i) accurately identify the topical characteristics for millions of Twitter users [25], and to (ii) find relevant experts on several tens of thousands of topics [12]. We leverage these prior works, and utilize Lists to identify experts on a wide variety of topics.

List Name	List Description	Members
News	News media accounts	nytimes, BBCNews, WSJ, cnnbrk, CBSNews
Music	Musicians	Eminem, britneyspears, ladygaga, rihanna, BonJovi
Tennis	Tennis players and Tennis news	andyroddick, usopen, Bryanbros, ATPWorldTour
Politics	Politicians & people who talk about them	BarackObama, whitehouse, nprpolitics, billmaher
Geology	Geology, Geophysics, Professionals and Students	Am Geophysical Union, Andy Fyon [Director, Ontario Geological Survey]
The Brain / Neurology	Information related to brain and neuro health	Neuroscience News, SarahJayneBlakemore [Cognitive Neuroscience Professor, UCL]
Forensics	Computer forensics, cyber forensics, phone forensics	Security Tube, Chad Tilbury [network security professional]
Chemistry	Resources on chemistry and its subfields	Clinical Chemistry, Anne Helmenstine [About.com writer on Chemistry]

Table 1: Examples of Lists: their names, descriptions, and some sample members. For less well-known experts, extracts from their Twitter account bio are also given within square braces.

The List-based methodology of identifying topical attributes of users has two key advantages. First, several recent studies [25, 27, 30] have shown that Lists help to infer topical expertise of users much more accurately, as compared to the contents of the tweets posted by the users. Second, since the List-based methodology relies on crowd-sourced social annotations (i.e., on Lists created by Twitter users themselves), it scales very well with respect to both the number of topics identified and the number of users for whom topics of expertise (and interest) can be identified. Note, that unlike most prior studies [2, 9, 30], we did not pre-select a small set of topics or events and identify users related to those topics. Instead, our List-based methodology automatically identifies experts on *any topic on which Twitter users have created Lists, i.e., any topic that interests Twitter users.* As we discuss in the next section, our methodology not only covers a large and diverse set of topics, but it also identifies hundreds of thousands of users who are experts on these topics.

Twitter data gathered

As stated above, we identify topical groups consisting of users who are experts or knowledge seekers on specific topics. Ideally, one would like to gather data about all users presently in Twitter and identify experts and seekers on any topic. However, given the restrictions on using the Twitter API for crawling, it is infeasible for us to gather data about the enormous number of users presently in Twitter (more than 550 million, as of May 2013 [1]). We started crawling users in Twitter network in the sequential order of their account creation date (using the Twitter API). We were able to gather detailed information of about 38.4 million users, including their profile information, their social links (followings), and the Lists in which they are members.

Using the data of the social links and the Lists, we constructed the Twitter *subscription network* in which there is a link from user (node) u to user v if u subscribes to the tweets posted by v. Note that in Twitter, user u can subscribe to v's tweets by either following v or by creating or subscribing to a List containing v as a member.

We also collected the tweets posted by all the users whom we identify as experts during the month of December 2012. Below, we describe how we identified topical experts and seekers in this dataset.

Identifying experts on a topic

To identify topics of expertise of an individual user u, we use the methodology proposed earlier by us in [12, 25] – collect the Lists which have u as a member, and extract the most common terms (topics) that appear in the names and descriptions of the Lists. Specifically, we identify a user u as an expert on some topic T if and only if u has been listed on T at least 10 times, i.e., topic T appears at least 10 times in the names or descriptions of the Lists containing the user. The threshold 10 is selected based on our observations in [12, 25]. Even after applying this threshold, we found that some popular Twitter users can be listed as experts on hundreds of topics. To limit the focus to the primary topics of expertise of an individual user u, we rank all of u's topics of expertise based on the number of times u is listed on each topic, and select the top 50 topics as u's primary topics of expertise. Similar to [12, 25], we considered as topics only unigrams (single words such as 'politics', 'music') and bigrams (two words which frequently occur together, e.g., 'social media', 'video game', 'bay area').

Using this List-based methodology, we identified *584,759 topical experts* on a large diverse set of topics, from among the 38.4 million users whose data we could gather. Table 2 shows some example topics and some of the Twitter users identified as experts on the topic, using this methodology. The table also gives the number of followers (indegree) of the experts in our Twitter subscription network. Note that the identified experts include not only globally popular users having millions of followers (e.g., Barack Obama, Lady Gaga), but also less popular ones having a few hundred to a few thousand followers. (For the less known experts, we also give extracts from their Twitter account bio in Table 2.)

Identifying seekers of topical information

Once we identify experts on a topic, identifying seekers of information on the topic (i.e., users interested in gathering information on the topic) is relatively straight-forward. Intuitively, if a user u subscribes to tweets from several experts on a certain topic, then u is likely to be interested in that topic. We considered u to be interested in topic T if and only if u subscribes to at least K experts on topic T. We experimented with varying values of K= 3, 5, and 10. While the number of seekers falls sharply as K increases, the high-level insights from the analysis using different values of K remain the same. So unless stated otherwise, the default value of K for the results presented in this paper is 3. Similar to the case of identifying topics of expertise, we found that many users in Twitter subscribe to experts on hundreds of topics. To focus on the primary topics of interest of an individual user u, we rank the topics of interest of u based on the number of experts she subscribes to on each topic, and then limit ourselves

Topic	Some experts identified by List-based method
Music	Lady Gaga (1.5M), coldplay (1.3M), Katy Perry (1.2M), Justin Timberlake (904K), Dallas Martin [VP, Warner Bros Records] (750), TenorRyan [Opera singing road warrior] (557)
Politics	Barack Obama (2.1M), Al Gore (1.1M), NPR Politics (976K), John McCain (887K), Bill Maher (285K), BristolRed [Chair of Bristol Labour Party] (631), Scott Fluhr [Harrison County GOP Chairman] (371)
Environment	TreeHugger.com (51K), GreenPeace USA (16K), Dennis Dimick [environment editor @natgeomag] (1328)
Neurology	Oliver Sacks (7K), Neurology Today (1K), MNT Neurology News (591), AAN Public (447), Neurology Journal (296)
Chemistry	ACS Pressroom [News from the American Chemical Society] (1173), Chemistry News (1108), chemheritage [Chemical Heritage Foundation Library] (856), Chemical Science (442)
Forensics	SANS Institute (4K), ForensicFocus (998), Michael Murr [Forensic Scientist] (618), Forensic Archaeology (265), Simon Whitfield [Digital Forensic Investigator] (144)
Geology	geosociety (1107), Kim Hannula [Structural geology professor] (382), Garry Hayes [Teacher of Geology] (232), Dave Mayer [Grad Student, Geoscientist] (158)

Table 2: Examples of topical experts identified by our List-based methodology [12, 25] for specific topics. Examples are shown for popular topics (music, politics, environment) as well as niche topics (neurology, chemistry, forensics, geology). For some of the less known experts, extracts from their Twitter account bio are also given within square braces. The numbers in parentheses give the approximate indegree of the expert in our Twitter subscription network (K: thousand, M:million).

to at most the top 50 topics (i.e., the 50 topics on which u subscribes to most experts).

Note that the set of experts and the set of seekers for a topic are not necessarily disjoint – a user can be both an expert and a seeker on the same topic. In fact, we find that a majority of experts on many topics are also seekers of information on their own topics of expertise.

We use the term 'topical group' to refer to the combined set of experts and seekers on a topic. Once we identify the topical group for a topic T, we can also construct the *topical-network* corresponding to T, by extracting the subgraph of the Twitter subscription network induced by the set of experts and seekers on topic T. In the subsequent sections, we analyze the properties of topical groups and topical networks corresponding to some specific topics.

Scalability of our approach

One of the primary advantages of the above approach is its scalability, with respect to the diversity in the topical groups identified and the number of users whose topical characteristics (expertise / interest) could be identified. The diversity in the topical groups will be studied in detail in the next section. Here, we demonstrate the scalability of the approach in characterizing a very large part of the Twitter network (especially the most popular / important part), by estimating the aggregate impact of all the topical groups that we detected.

We find that as many as 49.5% of all nodes and 94.3% of all links in the Twitter subscription network (for the 38.4 million users) are included in at least one of the topical groups that we extracted. While the experts across the different groups constitute only a small fraction of all users in the Twitter network (less than 1.5%), they include a large majority of the most popular users.

Figure 1 shows the fraction of all users having k or more followers in the Twitter, who are experts in some topical group. It is seen that more than 60% of all users having $k = 1000$ or more followers are included in the set of experts on some topic, and this fraction increases rapidly for higher values of k. Note, however, that *not* all experts have large numbers of followers; in particular, several of the experts in the niche topical groups are only moderately popular. Also, 65.2% of all links in the Twitter network are used to follow the experts.

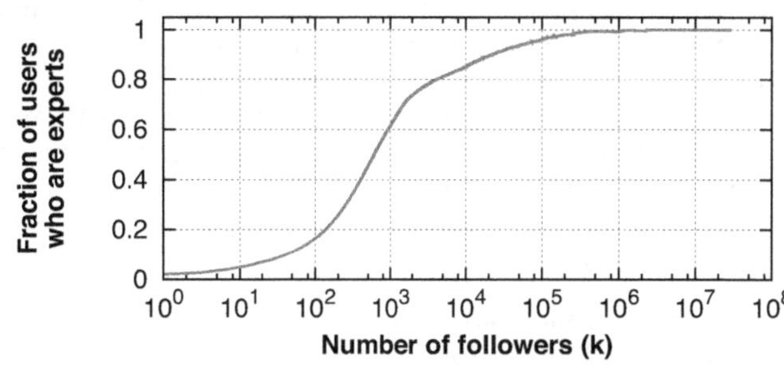

Figure 1: Fraction of all users having k or more followers who are experts – shown for all values of k.

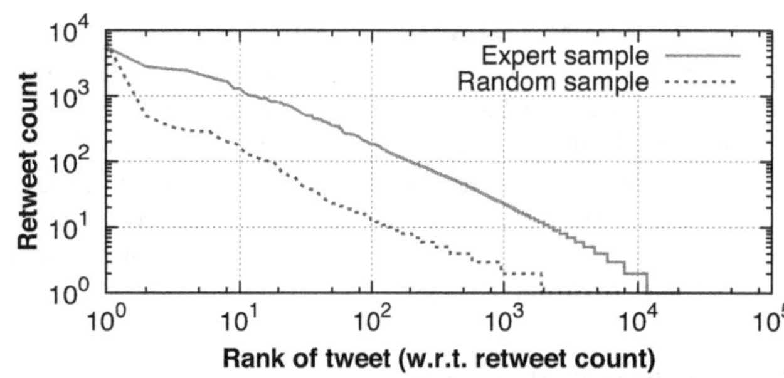

Figure 2: Distribution of the number of times a tweet is retweeted, for tweets posted by experts and tweets in the Twitter random sample. Tweets posted by experts are retweeted many more times than tweets in random 1% sample.

Hence, even though only a small fraction of all Twitter users are experts, a disproportionately large fraction of all follow links in Twitter point to them. Thus their aggregate followers (the seekers) include a substantial fraction of all users in the Twitter network.

Moreover, the content (tweets) posted by the experts constitute the most popular information in Twitter. The popularity of a given tweet in the Twitter network can be estimated by the number of times it has been retweeted in Twitter (also known as the retweet count of the tweet). We collected 100,000 tweets posted by the experts from diverse topical groups, and obtained the retweet counts for these tweets, using the Twitter API. As a baseline for comparison, we also considered 100,000 random tweets, randomly selected from a

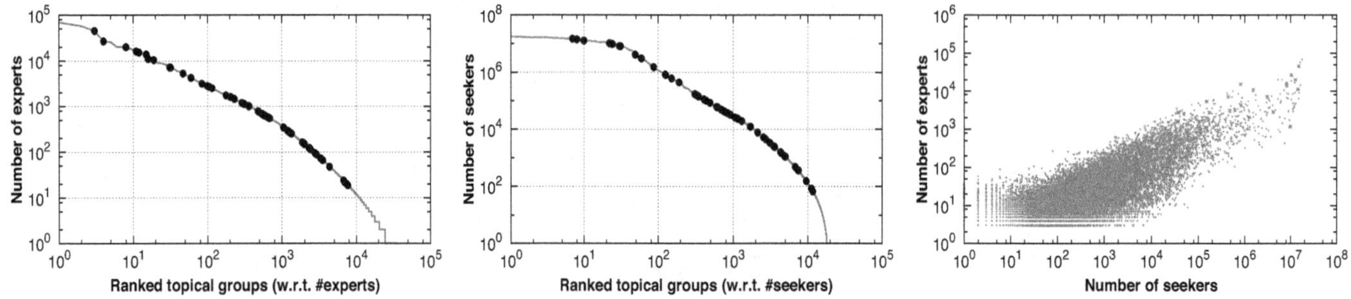

(a) Number of experts (b) Number of seekers (c) Scatter plot of experts and seekers

Figure 3: Distribution of the number of (a) experts and (b) seekers in various topical groups. Figure (c) shows a scatter-plot where the point (x, y) indicates a topical group having x seekers and y experts. Also indicated are the 50 topical groups that are studied in detail in subsequent sections (shown as black circles in (a) and (b), and red asterisks in (c).

1% random sample of all tweets made available by Twitter.[1] The popularity (retweet count) distributions of the random tweets and the experts' tweets is shown in Figure 2. The plot clearly shows that the tweets authored by the experts have an order of magnitude higher retweet counts than random tweets in Twitter. Thus the content posted by the experts is far more popular, and is retweeted numerous times by the seekers who follow the experts.

Taken together, the above discussion shows that the topical groups detected by the List-based approach constitute a significant portion of the Twitter network, thus highlighting the scalability of the approach.

CHARACTERIZING TOPICAL GROUPS

In this section, we present a detailed characterization of the topical groups in the Twitter network. We begin by exploring the diversity in the topical groups, both in terms of the topics they cover as well as their membership (i.e., the number of experts and seekers in the different groups). We then analyze the following and tweeting behaviors of the members of the groups, especially the experts.

Diversity in topical groups

As described earlier, the List-based methodology enables us to identify topical groups potentially on any topic on which a threshold number (10) of Twitter users created Lists. To investigate the diversity in the topics covered by the groups, we only considered those topics that correspond to words appearing in an English dictionary (and some very popular abbreviations of English words, such as 'celebs' and 'tech'). Note that by limiting our analysis to English language topics, we are potentially underestimating the diversity in topical groups.

Figures 3(a) and (b) respectively show the distribution of the number of experts and seekers in various topical groups, where the groups have been ranked in decreasing order of the number of experts and seekers respectively. The plots show that the number of experts and seekers in different topical groups vary by several orders of magnitude. We also checked the correlation between the number of experts and seekers in a group. Figure 3(c) shows a scatter plot of these two measures, where the point (x, y) indicates a topical group having x seekers and y experts. The plot shows that as the number of experts in a topic increases, the number of seekers on that topic also tends to increase. In fact, the number of experts and seekers are highly correlated, with a Pearson correlation coefficient of 0.7 across all topics. Thus, a small number of groups have tens of thousands of experts and hundreds of thousands of seekers interested in the corresponding topics, while there are a large number of groups that each have a few tens or hundreds of experts and a few hundred to a few thousand seekers.

As we shall see in the rest of this section, it helps to distinguish between the topical groups with a large numbers of experts and seekers and those with few experts and seekers. We consider a topic/group as *popular* if it has more than 1000 experts and more than 100,000 seekers. On the other hand, *niche* topics / groups are the ones containing fewer than 500 experts and 5000 seekers. Though these thresholds are somewhat arbitrary and can be altered, the high-level insights drawn in the study remain valid even if the thresholds are varied slightly. Note that our description of popular and niche groups is based on the number of experts and seekers identified from the Twitter data we gathered, and may not always agree with the corresponding notions in the off-line world. For instance, a certain topic may be generally discussed by many people in the off-line world, but if there are only a few hundred to thousand experts and seekers in Twitter on this topic, it would be considered as a niche topic in our study.

To explore the wide diversity of the topics of interest to the topical groups in Twitter, we partitioned the topical groups among several ranges of the number of experts and seekers, and show example topics / groups in each range in Table 3. The table illustrates the rich diversity of topics on which information is shared over the Twitter platform.

The cells in the bottom-right corner of Table 3 show the *popular topics* (in blue) having more than 1,000 experts and more than 100,000 seekers. These are the topics for which Twitter is generally known today, such as 'music', 'technology', 'politics', 'bloggers', 'celebrities', 'fashion', 'hollywood', and so on. As we move towards the top-left cornor of the table, both the number of experts and seekers decrease and topics become more specialized, like 'medicine', 'astronomy', 'yoga',

[1]Twitter provides a 1% random sample of all tweets in real-time, which we collected during December 2012.

No. of seekers	Number of experts					
	< 100	100 – 500	500 – 1K	1K – 5K	5K – 10K	> 10K
< 1K	(5416) *geology, karate, malaria, neurology, tsunami,* psychiatry, radiology, pediatrics, dermatology, dentistry	(132) volleyball, philosophers, tarot, perfume, florists, copywriters, taxi, esperanto				
1K – 5K	(915) *biology, chemistry, swimmers,* astrophysics, multimedia, semiconductor, renewable-energy, breast-cancer, judaism	(428) *painters, astrology, sociology, geography, forensics,* anthropology, genealogy, archaeology, gluten, diabetes, neuroscience	(17) architects, insurance, second-life, police, progressives, creativity			
5K – 10K	(166) *malware,* gnu, robot, chicago-sports, gospel-music, space-exploration, wall-street	(202) horror, agriculture, atheism, attorneys, furniture, art-galleries, ubuntu	(34) *psychology,* poetry, catholic, hospitals, autism, jazz	(2) coffee, dealers		
10K – 50K	(174) ipod, ipad, virus, Liverpool-FC, choreographers, heavy-metal, backstreet-boys, world-cup,	(312) *olympics, physics, theology, earthquake,* opera, makeup, Adobe, wrestlers, typography, american-idol	(146) *tennis, linux, astronomy,* yoga, animation, manga, doctors, realtors, wildlife, rugby, forex, php, java,	(67) *law, history, beer, golf,* librarians, theatre, military, poker, conservatives, vegan		
50K–100K	(7) bbc-radio, UK-celebs, christian-leaders, superstars	(61) *hackers, programmers,* bicycle, GOP, fantasy-football, NCAA, wwe, sci-fi	(35) *medicine, cyclists,* investors, recipes, NHL, xbox, triathlon, Google	(37) hotels, museums, hockey, architecture, charities, weather, space		
> 100K	(3) headlines, brits	(49) pop-culture, gospel, BBC, reality-tv, bollywood	(58) *religion,* actresses, gadgets, graphic-design, directors, lifestyle, gossip, commentators, youtube	(140) *books, government, comedy, environment, baseball, soccer, hollywood, iphone, economics,* money	(25) *fashion, education, wine,* photography, radio, restaurants, science, SEO	(17) *music, tech, business, politics, food, sports, celebs, health,* media, bloggers, travel, writers

Table 3: Examples of topical groups on different topics, along with the number of seekers and number of experts in each group. The total number of groups having a certain number of experts and seekers is indicated in each cell. The popular topics are the ones shown in blue color (bottom-right corner) and the niche topics are the ones shown in red (top-left corner). The topical groups chosen for detailed study in later sections are *italicized*.

'law', 'history', and 'psychology'; we refer to these as the 'intermediate topics'. The topics in this range also include *technological topics* such as 'hackers', 'linux', 'xbox', 'php', 'java' and 'Google', and *sport-related topics* such as 'golf', 'NHL', 'triathlon', 'hockey' and 'wrestlers'. Finally, the top-left corner of Table 3 contains the *niche topics* (shown in red) having fewer than 500 experts and fewer than 5000 seekers. Most of these topics relate to advanced scientific and technological disciplines like 'biology', 'chemistry', 'dermatology', 'astrophysics', 'geography', 'forensics', 'neuroscience', and 'diabetes'. The table shows that apart from the popular topics, Twitter also contains a collection of groups on a diverse set of highly specialized topics.

In addition to some illustrative topics, each cell in Table 3 also shows the number of topical groups with the number of experts and seekers in the corresponding ranges. We see that the number of niche topics is several orders of magnitude higher than the number of popular topics. For instance, there are more than 6000 niche topics having less than 500 experts and less than 5000 seekers, as compared to about 200 popular topics having more than 1,000 experts and 100,000 seekers. Most of the prior studies on Twitter have focused exclusively on the popular topics [30, 2, 14] and the presence of a large number of niche topical groups has largely been ignored in the literature.

Why niche topical groups are often overlooked

There are several potential reasons why niche topical groups are often overlooked by studies characterizing the Twitter social network. First, note that most niche topical groups have only a small number of experts and users interested in the topics. Second, many of the experts in the niche topical groups are not globally popular. For instance, experts in niche topics like 'neurology' or 'anthropology' rank quite low in global rankings of user influence (computed using metrics such as number of followers or PageRank over the follow network [26]). We computed the global PageRanks (over the Twitter follow network of 38.4M users) of the top experts in different topical groups and compared them. We found while the top experts in popular topical groups are ranked very highly (amongst the top 10 or top 100 users), the experts in niche topical groups are almost always ranked outside the top tens of thousands (or, in some cases, even outside the top hundreds of thousands) of users.

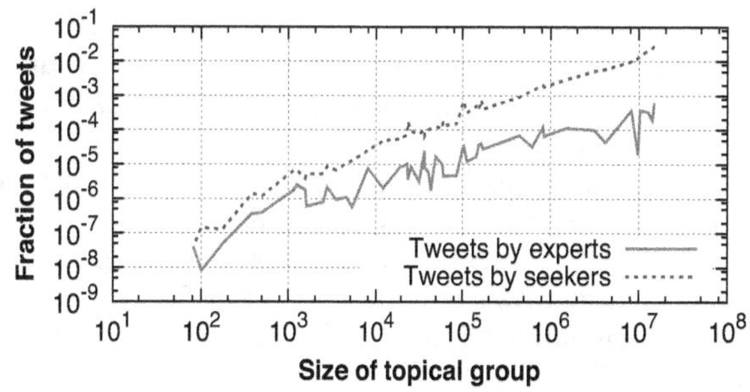

Figure 4: Fraction of tweets in the Twitter 1% random sample, which are posted by experts and seekers in the 50 selected topical groups.

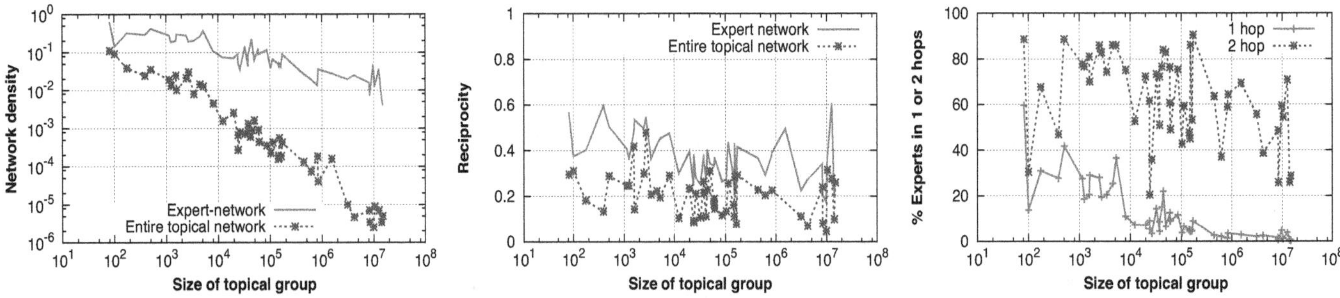

(a) Network density (b) Reciprocity (c) Experts within 1 or 2 hops

Figure 5: Network properties of the topical-networks (expert-seeker networks) and the expert-networks for the selected topics: (a) network density, (b) reciprocity, (c) mean percentage of all experts who are within 1 or 2 hops from a given expert.

Finally, much of the tweeting activity in Twitter is related to the popular topics. To show this, we considered the 1% random sample of all tweets provided by Twitter, during the month of December 2012, and measured the fraction of tweets that are posted by the experts and seekers in the 50 selected topics shown italicized in Table 3. Figure 4 plots this fraction against the size of the topical groups (measured as the total number of distinct users – experts or seekers – in the groups). The plots show that a considerably smaller fraction of the tweets are related to niche topics (smaller topical groups), as compared to those that are related to popular topics (large topical groups). So studies focusing on popular users or tweets would not capture the diverse set of niche topical groups. However, our analysis reveals that Twitter can also be a source of valuable information on specialized topics.

Following behavior and interactions in topical groups

We now conduct a detailed analysis of the *topical-networks*, i.e., the sub-graph of the Twitter subscription network induced by the set of experts and seekers in a particular topical group. We also separately study the network among the experts within the topical groups, which we refer to as *expert-networks*. Our analysis is done on a set of 50 topical groups that are shown italicized in Table 3 and also indicated in Figure 3.

Component and density analysis

We start by analyzing the number of strongly connected components (SCCs) in the topical-networks and the expert-networks.[2] Across all topics, the expert-network has a single giant SCC, which includes more than 90% of the experts on the topic. The experts who are not within the giant SCC are almost always singletons who are not directly connected to any other expert on the same topic. The entire topical-network also has a single giant SCC which contains almost all experts on the topic. However, a large majority of the seekers (who are not experts themselves) are not included in the giant SCC, which suggests that seekers are only loosely connected with the experts and other seekers. Intuitively, one would not expect seekers to be frequently followed by other seekers or experts.

[2]We also analyzed weakly connected components (WCCs), but the results are less interesting – across all topics, the entire topical-network forms a single WCC. In case of expert-networks as well, more than 99% of experts are in a single WCC for almost all topics.

Next, we computed the network density of the topical-networks and the expert-networks on each topic. We plot the density values in Figure 5(a) against the size of the topical group. Note that all the plots given henceforth have the size of topical groups on the x-axis – this is to highlight the fact that the niche topical groups corresponding to less popular topics (which appear towards the left in the plots) often exhibit very different characteristics than the large groups corresponding to the most popular topics (which appear towards the right in the plots).

Figure 5(a) shows that the topical-networks for the popular topics have very low densities. In fact, for the most popular topics, the densities of the topical-networks are comparable to that of the entire Twitter network (which is of the order of 10^{-7} [16]). However, the densities are relatively much higher for the niche topics.

Figure 5(a) also shows that across all topics, the expert-networks have much higher densities than the entire topical-networks. In particular, the expert-networks in niche topics have very high densities; for instance, for almost all topics having less than 1000 experts, the density of the expert-network is higher than 0.2. This shows that experts, specially in niche topics, are very well connected to other experts on the same topic. These results indicate the presence of strong *homophily* among the experts, in which the establishment of links occurs due to "immutable" similar characteristics [10], like expertise on a common topic. However, seekers do not exhibit strong homophily; they connect to other group members very sparsely, which explains the relatively low densities of the entire topical-networks.

Reciprocity

Next, we study the reciprocity of links in the topical-networks. For a given topic, we measure the fraction of links in the topical-network that are bi-directional, as a fraction of all node-pairs that are linked by at least one link (i.e., fraction of cases where both links $u \rightarrow v$ and $v \rightarrow u$ are present between users u and v). Figure 5(b) plots the reciprocity within the topical-networks and the expert-networks for the selected topics, against the size of the topical group. We observe that across all topics, reciprocity in the entire topical-network is low; for many of the topical-networks, reciprocity is lower than or around 0.22, which was observed to be the reciprocity of the global Twitter network [16]. This low reciprocity is expected, since experts are not likely to reciprocate links from ordinary seekers. However, reciprocity is relatively higher for the expert-networks, mostly varying between 0.3 and 0.6. Further, reciprocity is generally higher for the niche topics, and reduces for the more popular topics. However, there are a few popular topics that have high reciprocity, such as 'business' (0.6) and 'health' (0.49).

Proximity to experts

Network proximity to experts is important, since the closer a user is to an expert, the higher the chance that the user can receive information tweeted by the expert. Users get all information tweeted by their 1-hop neighbors and they can hear tweets from experts farther away through retweets. But, the chance of hearing information through retweets decreases dramatically with distance. So, next, we measure the fraction of all experts in an expert-network that lie within 1 or 2 network hops from an individual expert.

Figure 5(c) shows, for each of the 50 selected topical groups, the mean percentage of all experts in the group who are within 1 or 2 hops from a given individual expert (the mean is taken over all experts in the topical group). The plots show an interesting trend. While the fraction of all experts within 1-hop is *low*, particularly for the popular topics, the fraction of experts within the 2-hop neighborhood of an individual expert is generally high (60% – 80%) for most topics, including popular topics. Thus, a majority of experts on a topic lie within a 2-hop distance of any given expert on the topic. This is probably because the experts in a topical group are connected to each other relatively densely (see Figure 5(a)); hence, even if one connects to only a few experts in a topical group (1-hop), her 2-hop neighborhood would contain a significant fraction of all the experts in the group.

The above observation has a number of important implications for search and recommendation systems on Twitter. Most experts directly follow only a small fraction of all experts, so they are likely to receive only a fraction of the interesting content being posted by all experts on a topic. This motivates the need for topical search / recommendation systems that can suggest experts and information missing from the 1-hop neighborhood. The fact that a majority of experts could be found within one's 2-hop neighborhood suggests that search / recommendation systems could focus on mining information from the 2-hop neighborhood of a user.

Interactions among experts in topical groups

We now investigate whether the experts in a topical group personally interact with one another. In Twitter, a user u can personally interact with user v through a 'directed message' to v, by including a user-mention "@v" in a tweet. We say an expert u interacts personally with another expert v if u sends at least one directed message to v, i.e., if u mentions v at least once. We collected the tweets posted by all the topical experts during December 2012, and obtained the user-mentions in the tweets. For a given topical group, we construct a *mention-network* among the experts in the group, where there exists a directed edge $u \rightarrow v$ if u mentioned v at least once. Fig. 6 plots the density of the mention-networks for the experts in the 50 selected topical groups, against the group size.

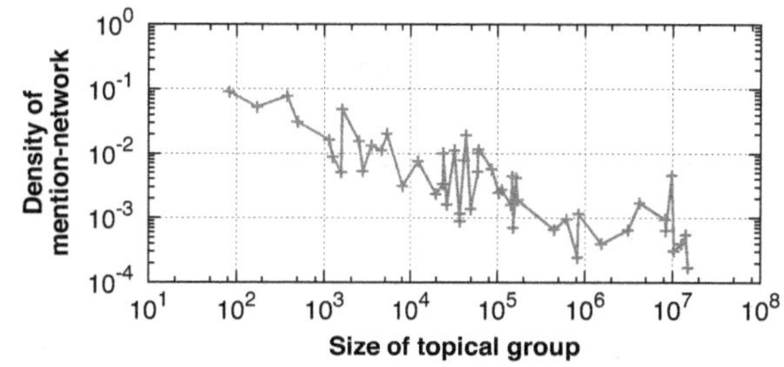

Figure 6: Density of the mention-network among experts for the selected topical groups.

We find that the densities of the mention-networks are much lower than the densities of the corresponding expert-networks (which consider subscription links, shown in Fig. 5(a)). This implies that the experts do *not* personally interact with most of the other experts in the same topical group that they are a part of.

Tweeting behavior in topical groups

In this section, we study the nature of the information being posted by experts in the topical groups. Specifically, we analyze whether experts tend to tweet more frequently on the topics of their expertise, and whether the content posted by multiple experts can be utilized to develop topical recommendation systems.

Methodology to ascertain topic of tweets

As stated earlier, we collected all tweets posted by all the topical experts on the 50 selected topics during the month of December 2012. We decided to focus on the tweets containing URLs (similar to [30]) as it is easier to infer topics related to the Web pages pointed to by the URL. We considered a tweet to be related to a topic if the URL contained in the tweet is related to the topic, which we ascertained using the following methodology.

We first obtained a set of keywords related to each topic. For a given topic T, we considered the experts in that topic and checked the 5 most frequent words extracted from the Lists of each expert (as described in the section *Inferring Topical Groups*). We selected the top 10 words which were associated with the most number of experts on topic T as the set of keywords related to T. For instance, for the topic 'religion', the set of keywords consists of words such as, 'christian', 'church', 'faith', 'catholic', 'atheists', 'pastors', and so on. These are essentially the words which co-occur most frequently with the word 'religion' in the Lists of the identified experts on religion.[3]

Next, to ascertain whether a URL is related to a specific topic, we used the AlchemyAPI service (`www.alchemyapi.com`), which uses natural language processing algorithms to extract semantic keywords from the contents of webpages. We considered a URL to be related to a topic if any of the keywords identified by AlchemyAPI for this URL occur within the set

[3]This is similar to the popular Information Retrieval technique of expanding search queries using words which frequently co-occur with the search terms [15].

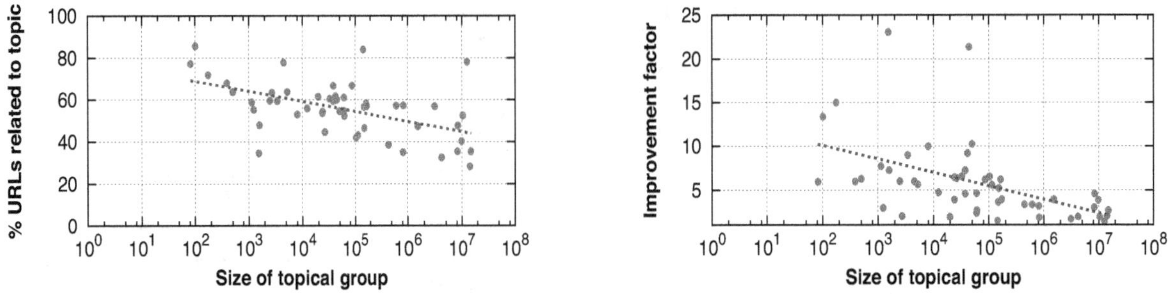

(a) Fraction of expert-URLs on topic (b) Expert-URLs vs random-URLs

Figure 7: (a) Percentage of expert-URLs on a topic (randomly sampled from among the URLs posted by experts in the corresponding topical group) which are related to the topic (b) Comparing the percentage of expert-URLs which are related to the topic, to the percentage of random-URLs (obtained from the 1% random sample provided by Twitter) related to a topic.

of keywords related to the topic, obtained by the aforementioned method.

Do experts tweet on their topic of expertise?
For each of the 50 selected topics, we randomly selected a set of 1000 distinct URLs from among the URLs posted by the experts on the topic. We refer to these sets as the *expert-URLs* on a topic.[4] As a baseline for comparison, we also randomly selected 1000 distinct URLs from Twitter's 1% random sample tweet stream. We refer to this set of randomly selected URLs as the *random-URLs*. We then used the AlchemyAPI service to extract topical keywords for each URL in the expert-URLs and the random-URLs sets.

Figure 7(a) plots the percentage of expert-URLs which were found to be related to the corresponding topic, against the size of the corresponding topical group. We find that for many of the groups, a large majority of the expert-URLs (posted by experts in that group) are related to the specific topic. The match is especially high for the niche topical groups, as shown by the decreasing nature of the logarithmic curve of best fit (obtained by the least-squares method) with increasing group size. Specifically, for as many as 36 groups, more than 50% of the expert-URLs were found to be related to the specific topic. These include mostly niche topical groups, but also a few popular groups such as 'books', 'government', 'fashion' and 'environment'.

Expert-URLs vs. random-URLs
We now examine whether expert-URLs (posted by experts in a topical group) tend to be more relevant to the topic of their expertise than random-URLs. We find that for many of the topics, especially the niche ones, the fractions of expert-URLs related to the specific topics are far higher than the fraction of random-URLs which are related to these topics. To quantify this, we measure the ratio between the percentage of expert-URLs and the percentage of random-URLs that were found relevant to a topic; we refer to this ratio as the *improvement factor* for the topic. Figure 7(b) plots the improvement factor for the 50 selected topics, against the size of the corresponding topical groups. It can be seen that the improvement factor is especially high (more than 10) for the niche topics such as 'psychology', 'karate', 'theology', 'neurology' and 'astrology', which are very rarely represented in the Twitter random sample.

Random URLs		Chemistry URLs		Malaria URLs	
Keyword	%URLs	Keyword	%URLs	Keyword	%URLs
likes	16.8	researchers	13.2	malaria	26.4
report	15.6	university	12.8	disease	11.6
gifts	10.8	science	8.0	cases	11.6
language	10.4	scientists	7.2	countries	11.2
gift	10.4	information	7.2	deaths	10.8
logos	10.0	team	6.8	mosquitoes	10.8
buttons	10.0	study	6.8	health	9.6
answers	10.0	results	6.4	africa	9.2
contact	9.2	research	6.0	number	8.8
sign	8.4	company	4.8	study	8.8
click	8.4	work	4.8	treatment	8.8
account	8.4	project	4.0	children	8.8
privacy	8.0	energy	4.0	dec	8.8
notes	8.0	percent	4.0	information	7.2
video	7.6	findings	3.6	areas	6.8

Table 4: Top 15 keywords identified by AlchemyAPI for (i) random-URLs derived from the 1% random sample of tweets provided by Twitter, (ii) expert-URLs in topic 'malaria', (iii) expert-URLs for topic 'chemistry'. Also shown are the percentage of URLs for which a given keyword was identified by AlchemyAPI.

Table 4 illustrates this further by showing the top 15 keywords identified by AlchemyAPI for most of the random-URLs in Twitter, and for the expert-URLs in the niche topics 'chemistry' and 'malaria'. For each keyword, the percentage of URLs (in the corresponding set) for which the given keyword was identified by AlchemyAPI is also given. It is clear that the experts in these topical groups primarily post content related to their specific topics of expertise, which are not captured in the Twitter random sample.

Note that some prior studies have attempted to use the random tweet sample provided by Twitter for topical search or recommendation [7]. Our analysis shows that the content posted by topical experts is a much richer source of topic-specific information than random tweet samples, especially for the niche topics. In the next section, we shall investigate whether the content posted by experts can be used for topic-specific recommendations.

[4]Throughout this section, we consider at most 1000 URLs per topic due to rate-limits on the use of the AlchemyAPI service.

IMPLICATIONS OF OUR FINDINGS

In this section, we discuss the implications of our detailed characterization of topical groups in Twitter. Specifically, we focus on implications for detecting topical groups in Twitter, and in developing improved topical recommendation systems in the future.

Topical groups are largely identity-based groups

As discussed in the Related Work section, several sociological theories have been proposed to explain the formation of groups / communities of users in social networks. According to the well-accepted common identity and common bond theory [22, 23], groups can be identity-based or bond-based, depending on the amount of reciprocity and personal interactions among the members, and the topicality of the discussions among the members [13]. We examined the topical groups for these characteristics, and observed low density and reciprocity and low levels of personal interactions (as estimated by the @user mentions). Also, a large fraction of the content posted by the experts in these groups are related to the specific topic of interest of the members of the groups. Based on these observations, it is clear that the topical groups closely resemble identity-based groups.

We also find that the experts in the topical groups post a significant amount of popular information (e.g., their tweets are highly retweeted by their followers) on the specific topics of interest of the group, hence users interested in a topic have a natural tendency to subscribe to these experts. Thus the formation of these topical groups can be explained by the common identity and common bond theory as being driven by the common interests / expertise of the members on the corresponding topic.

Detectability using community-detection algorithms

Another common approach to identify groups of related users is to use community detection algorithms [11] on the Twitter network graph. Since community detection algorithms rely only on the graph structure, they tend to scale better than semantic approaches that require gathering semantic annotations. However, prior studies [13] have shown that the communities identified by these algorithms are usually closer to bond-based groups and are less likely to detect identity-based groups (like our topical groups). Hence we now investigate whether our topical groups we detected could have been identified by such algorithms.

Using graph theoretic approach to identify communities

To investigate the pros and cons of the graph theoretic approach, we use the well-known BGLL community detection algorithm [5] on the Twitter subscription network described earlier.[5] BGLL detected a total of 686,296 communities. However 375,743 (54%) of these communities are of size 2, i.e., they are the isolated pairs of users only following each other. Figure 8 shows the sizes of the remaining 310,553 BGLL communities. They exhibit a wide variation in their size, with the median and average sizes of the communities being 3 and 108 members, respectively.

[5]Since BGLL runs on undirected networks, we considered all links of the Twitter network to be undirected.

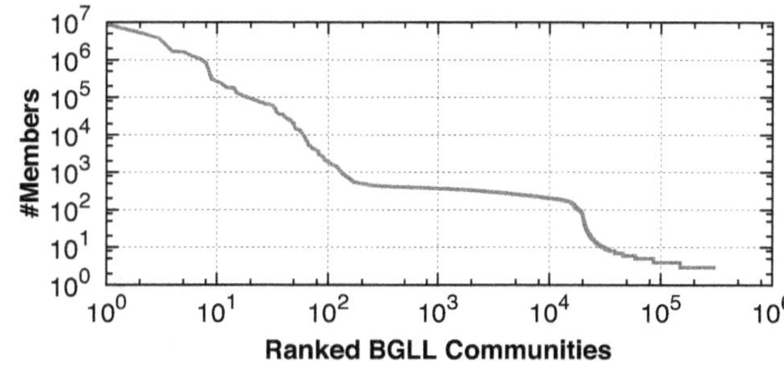

Figure 8: Number of members in the BGLL communities detected in the Twitter network, where communities are ranked in decreasing order of the number of members.

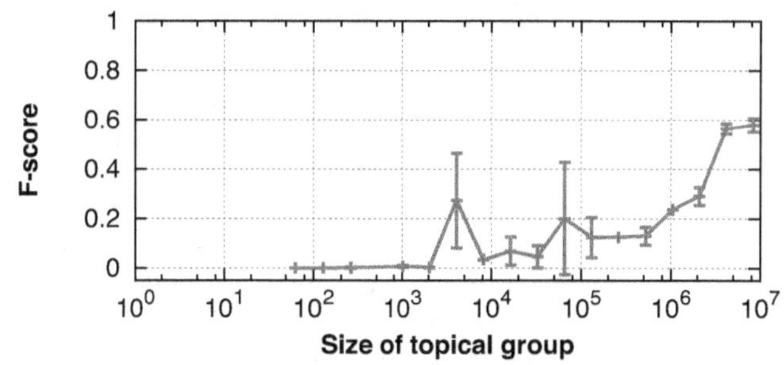

Figure 9: F-Score values between each topical group and the best matched BGLL community. The F-Scores for niche topical groups are low, indicating they are hard to detect by BGLL.

Comparing graph based approach and semantic approach

We begin by checking whether BGLL communities are able to capture at least some of the semantically meaningful topical groups. To this end, we considered the 50 topical groups (detected using the semantic approach) that were shown *italicized* in Table 3, and attempted to find the BGLL communities that most closely match each one.

We found the best matching BGLL community for each of the selected topical groups, according to the F-Score metric [31]. For a given pair of candidate BGLL community and topical group, the F-Score is the harmonic mean of the *precision* and *recall*, where the precision is the fraction of the members of the topical group who are also included in the candidate BGLL community, and the recall is the fraction of the members of the candidate BGLL community who are also included in the topical group. The F-Score takes values between 0 and 1, where 1 represents perfect match while 0 represents no match [31].

Figure 9 shows the F-Score for the selected topical groups, arranged in increasing order of the size of the group (i.e., the number of users in the topical group). It is seen that the smaller or niche topical groups (towards the left in the figure) have very low F-Score with even the best matched BGLL community. This shows that the graph theoretic approach (using BGLL community detection algorithm) is unable to detect the topical groups found using semantic approach, specially the smaller (niche) ones. In fact, we found that for a majority of the semantically meaningful topical groups, their members are spread over more than 100 different BGLL communities.

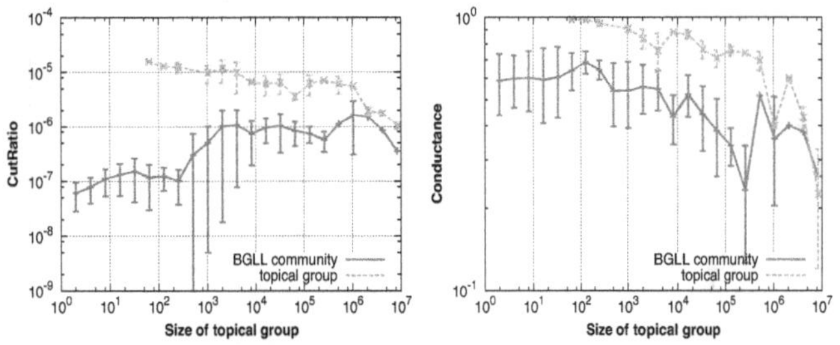

(a) Cut-ratio (b) Conductance

Figure 10: Comparison of community quality metrics between topical groups and BGLL communities. The cut-ratio and the conductance for topical groups are higher than for BGLL communities, thus making topical groups harder to detect using graph theoretic approaches.

Graph structure of topical groups

One reason why community detection algorithms might fail to detect semantically meaningful topical groups is that the semantic groups do not constitute good-quality communities *structurally*, i.e., the nodes do not form a distinctive community structure in the network graph. To test this hypothesis, we computed several metrics for community quality for the selected topical groups, and also for the BGLL communities. These metrics [18] indicate the quality of the community structure (within the global Twitter network) formed by the members of these topical groups and hint at the potential detectability of these topical groups using graph theoretic approaches. We consider the following two community quality metrics:

(1) *Cut-ratio*: The fraction of the number of external edges leaving a community to the total number of possible external edges. A lower cut-ratio implies better community structure.

(2) *Conductance:* The fraction of the number of internal edges inside the community to the total edges that point outside the community. A lower conductance shows better community structure.

Figure 10 shows the values of these metrics for the selected topical groups, as well as the BGLL communities. The BGLL communities exhibit good community structures (they do well on measures for community quality), while the topical groups show significantly worse community structure than the BGLL communities. These observations suggest that the topical groups do not conform to the standard graph theoretic measures of community quality, making it almost impossible to detect them through standard *graph-theoretic, semantic-agnostic* community-finding methods.

Developing topical recommender systems

We discuss how our improved understanding of topical groups can be leveraged towards (i) discovering more experts (missing members) in different topical groups, and (ii) discovering important topical information of interest to a topical group.

Recommending topical experts

Given a set of (known) experts in a topical group (i.e., on a topic), we investigate whether the expected tight interconnectivity between all experts in the group could be used to discover and recommend new (yet unknown) experts on the corresponding topic. Intuitively, the yet to be discovered experts would also be well connected to the known experts. So a simple technique to discover new topical experts would be to identify users in the Twitter network that are followed by the highest number of known experts and check their expertise. Such a technique might also be quite efficient as the number of Twitter users followed by multiple experts in a topical group tends to be quite small, especially for niche topics.

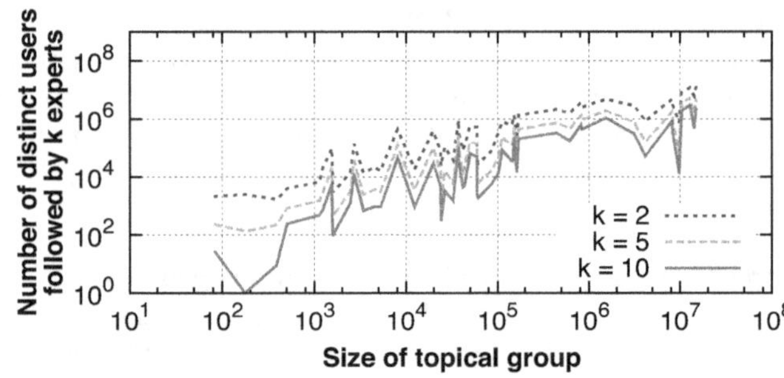

Figure 11: Number of distinct users who are followed by k known experts in a topical group, shown for k = 2, 5, 10.

Topical group	# known experts	# new experts discovered	
		on same topic	on any topic
Malaria	19	17	460
Karate	20	20	348
Chemistry	90	96	1342
Geography	124	103	2615
Sociology	157	231	4450
Physics	255	163	6673

Table 5: Number of new experts discovered among the users followed by known experts.

Figure 11 plots the number of distinct users who are followed by k experts in a topical group (for various values of k), against the group size. It shows that the number of distinct users followed by (k = 10) known experts is of the order of few hundreds for the niche topical groups to few million in the case of the most popular topical groups. We tested the likelihood that many of these users are yet undiscovered experts within their corresponding groups. We checked the expertise of these users using the same methodology as in [12, 25]. Table 5 shows the number of new experts that we discovered in the process for some niche topical groups. For several of the groups, the number of newly discovered experts doubles the size of known experts. These newly discovered experts are outside of the 38.4 million user accounts that we crawled as the seed data for our study.

These results show that an effective and efficient technique to search for new topical experts would be to look for users that are followed by a large number of known Twitter experts. Such a technique could not only be used to keep the list of experts up-to-date as new experts join Twitter in increasingly large numbers every day, but it could also be used to recommend other relevant topical experts to knowledge seekers who are already following a small set of known experts.

Recommending topical content

There have been several efforts to recommend interesting topical content to Twitter users who are interested in certain top-

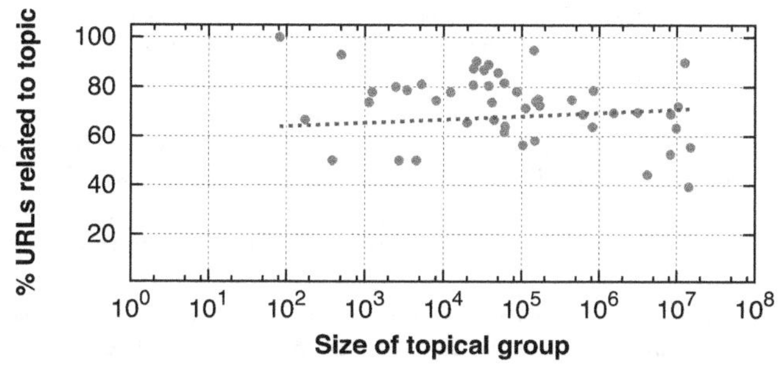

Figure 12: Fraction of the URLs posted by at least 3 distinct experts in a topical group, that are related to the topic. The results show that URLs that are tweeted by multiple experts in a topical group can be used for topical recommendations.

ics [6, 7]. A crucial challenge for such systems is to discover interesting content on specific topics. We now investigate whether the knowledge of a large set of topical experts can be utilized for recommendation of topical content. Intuitively, content that is posted by multiple experts in a topical group is more likely to be relevant and authoritative on the corresponding topic. Hence, for each topical group, we selected the URLs which were posted by at least 3 distinct experts in the topical groups, and used the AlchemyAPI service to check what fraction of these URLs were related to the topic.The results are plotted in Fig. 12, against the size of the topical groups. For 39 out of the 47 selected groups[6] , more than 60% of the expert-URLs that are posted by 3 or more experts were related to the specific topic. Interestingly, this is true not only for niche topical groups (e.g., 'malaria', 'iphone', 'geology', 'linux', 'medicine' and 'physics') but also for popular groups such as 'business', 'sports', 'health' and 'fashion'.

The above result shows that the content posted by multiple experts within a topical group is particularly useful for generating content recommendations to the users interested in that specific topic. Such recommendations are particularly useful for niche topics, where existing search / recommendation systems that rely on random samples from Twitter would struggle to provide good recommendations [7].

CONCLUSION

The primary contribution of this paper lies in identifying topical groups in Twitter at scale, and analyzing the characteristics of the topical groups. We utilized crowd-sourced social annotations to infer the topics of expertise and interests of individual Twitter users, and hence identified topical groups consisting of experts and seekers of information on specific topics. The identified topical groups span a wide diversity of topics, ranging from the most popular topics (e.g., 'politics', 'tech', 'music') to niche, specialized topics such as 'geology', 'forensics', and 'neurology'. We also show that these topical groups exhibit characteristics of identity-based groups, which makes it extremely difficult to detect these groups using graph theoretic community detection algorithms on the Twitter network graph.

[6]For three of the niche topical groups having only a few tens of experts, no URL had been posted by 3 distinct experts, hence this analysis was conducted for the remaining 47 groups.

This study firmly establishes that the popular Twitter microblogging site, beyond providing a platform for celebrities and news media to disseminate information about topics of general interest, is also facilitating the self-organization of a large set of niche topical groups consisting of local, topic-specific experts and dedicated followers. Finally, our analysis of network connectivity and tweeting behavior of users in such topical groups reveal several insights that have implications for designing search and recommendation services on Twitter. For instance, we show that the existing experts can act as a seed set to discover new experts, thus, facilitating dynamic update of the topical group. We also show that content posted by multiple experts in a topical group has a high probability of being topically relevant – this observation can be leveraged to generate topically relevant tweet recommendations. We believe that an interesting direction of future research would be to exploit the concept of topical groups for building such new services.

ACKNOWLEDGEMENTS

The authors thank the anonymous reviewers whose suggestions greatly helped to improve the paper. This research was supported in part by a grant from the Indo-German Max Planck Centre for Computer Science (IMPECS). P. Bhattacharya was supported by a fellowship grant from Tata Consultancy Services.

REFERENCES

1. Twitter Statistics, May 2013. **http://www.statisticbrain.com/twitter-statistics/** (Accessed October 15, 2013).
2. An, J., Cha, M., Gummadi, K., and Crowcroft, J. Media landscape in Twitter: A world of new conventions and political diversity. In *Proc. AAAI ICWSM* (2011).
3. Ardon, S., Bagchi, A., Mahanti, A., et al. Spatio-temporal analysis of topic popularity in Twitter. *arXiv:1111.2904v2 [cs.SI]* (2011).
4. Blanchard, A. L., and Markus, M. L. The experienced "sense" of a virtual community: characteristics and processes. *SIGMIS Database 35*, 1 (Feb. 2004), 64–79.
5. Blondel, V. D., Guillaume, J.-L., Lambiotte, R., and Lefebvre, E. Fast unfolding of communities in large networks. *Journal of Statistical Mechanics: Theory and Experiment*, 18 (October 2008).
6. Chen, J., Nairn, R., Nelson, L., Bernstein, M., and Chi, E. Short and tweet: experiments on recommending content from information streams. In *Proc. ACM CHI* (2010).
7. Choudhury, M. D., Counts, S., and Czerwinski, M. Find Me the Right Content! Diversity-Based Sampling of Social Media Spaces for Topic-Centric Search. In *Proc. AAAI ICWSM* (2011).
8. Cox, A. What are communities of practice? a comparative review of four seminal works. *Journal of Information Science 31*, 6 (2005), 527–540.
9. De Choudhury, M., Diakopoulos, N., and Naaman, M. Unfolding the event landscape on twitter: classification and exploration of user categories. In *Proc. ACM CSCW* (2012).
10. Easley, D., and Kleinberg, J. *Networks, Crowds, and Markets: Reasoning About a Highly Connected World.* Cambridge University Press, 2010.
11. Fortunato, S. Community detection in graphs. *Physics Reports 486*, 3-5 (2010), 75–174.
12. Ghosh, S., Sharma, N., Benevenuto, F., Ganguly, N., and Gummadi, K. Cognos: crowdsourcing search for topic experts in microblogs. In *Proc. ACM SIGIR* (2012).
13. Grabowicz, P. A., Aiello, L. M., Eguiluz, V. M., and Jaimes, A. Distinguishing topical and social groups based on common identity and bond theory. In *Proc. ACM WSDM* (2013).

14. Java, A., Song, X., Finin, T., and Tseng, B. Why We Twitter: Understanding Microblogging Usage and Communities. In *Proc. WEBKDD / SNA-KDD Workshop* (2007).

15. Jones, K. S. *Automatic keyword classification for information retrieval.* Butterworth, 1971.

16. Kwak, H., Lee, C., Park, H., and Moon, S. What is Twitter, a social network or a news media? In *Proc. ACM WWW* (2010).

17. Lerman, K., and Ghosh, R. Information contagion: An empirical study of the spread of news on Digg and Twitter social networks. In *Proc. AAAI ICWSM* (2010).

18. Leskovec, J., Lang, K. J., and Mahoney, M. Empirical comparison of algorithms for network community detection. In *Proc. ACM WWW* (2010).

19. Lin, C. X., Mei, Q., Han, J., Jiang, Y., and Danilevsky, M. The joint inference of topic diffusion and evolution in social communities. In *Proc. IEEE ICDM* (2011).

20. Twitter help center: How to use twitter lists. **http://tinyurl.com/lists-howtouse** (Accessed October 15, 2013).

21. McMillan, D., and Chavis, D. Sense of community: A definition and theory. *Journal of Community Psychology 14*, 1 (1986), 6–23.

22. Prentice, D. A., Miller, D. T., and Lightdale, J. R. Asymmetries in attachments to groups and to their members: Distinguishing between common-identity and common-bond groups. *Personality and Social Psychology Bulletin 20*, 5 (1994), 484–493.

23. Ren, Y., Kraut, R., and Kiesler, S. Applying Common Identity and Bond Theory to Design of Online Communities. *Organization Studies 28*, 3 (2007), 377–408.

24. Sassenberg, K. Common bond and common identity groups on the Internet: Attachment and normative behavior in on-topic and off-topic chats. *Group Dynamics Theory Research And Practice 6*, 1 (2002), 27–37.

25. Sharma, N., Ghosh, S., Benevenuto, F., Ganguly, N., and Gummadi, K. Inferring Who-is-Who in the Twitter Social Network. In *Proc. WOSN Workshop* (2012).

26. Talbot, D. How Google Ranks Tweets, Jan 2010. **http://www.technologyreview.in/web/24353/** (Accessed October 15, 2013).

27. Wagner, C., Liao, V., Pirolli, P., Nelson, L., and Strohmaier, M. It's not in their tweets: Modeling topical expertise of twitter users. In *Proc. ASE/IEEE SocialCom* (2012).

28. Wang, L., Lou, T., Tang, J., and Hopcroft, J. E. Detecting community kernels in large social networks. In *Proc. IEEE ICDM* (2011).

29. Wenger, E. *Communities of practice: Learning, meaning, and identity.* Cambridge University Press, New York, NY, USA, 1999.

30. Wu, S., Hofman, J. M., Mason, W. A., and Watts, D. J. Who says what to whom on Twitter. In *Proc. ACM WWW* (2011).

31. Yang, J., and Leskovec, J. Defining and evaluating network communities based on ground-truth. In *Proc. MDS Workshop* (2012).

Characterizing the Life Cycle of Online News Stories Using Social Media Reactions

Carlos Castillo
Qatar Computing Research Institute
Doha, Qatar
chato@acm.org

Mohammed El-Haddad
Al Jazeera
Doha, Qatar
mohammed.haddad@aljazeera.net

Jürgen Pfeffer
Carnegie Mellon University
Pittsburgh, USA
jpfeffer@cs.cmu.edu

Matt Stempeck
MIT Center for Civic Media
Cambridge, USA
stempeck@media.mit.edu

ABSTRACT
This paper presents a study of the life cycle of news articles posted online. We describe the interplay between website visitation patterns and social media reactions to news content. We show that we can use this hybrid observation method to characterize distinct classes of articles. We also find that social media reactions can help predict future visitation patterns early and accurately.

We validate our methods using qualitative analysis as well as quantitative analysis on data from a large international news network, for a set of articles generating more than 3,000,000 visits and 200,000 social media reactions. We show that it is possible to model accurately the overall traffic articles will ultimately receive by observing the first ten to twenty minutes of social media reactions. Achieving the same prediction accuracy with visits alone would require to wait for three hours of data. We also describe significant improvements on the accuracy of the early prediction of shelf-life for news stories.

ACM Classification Keywords
H.4.m Information Systems Applications: Miscellaneous;

Author Keywords
Web analytics; predictive web analytics; online news

1. INTRODUCTION
Traditional newspapers have been in decline in recent years in terms of readership and revenue; in comparison, digital online news have been steadily increasing according to both metrics.[1]

[1]http://stateofthemedia.org/2012/overview-4/key-findings/

CSCW'14, February 15–19, 2014, Baltimore, Maryland, USA.

ACM 978-1-4503-2540-0/14/02...$15.00.
http://dx.doi.org/10.1145/2531602.2531623

Recent surveys have shown that about half of the population of the US gets their news online, and about one third goes online every day for news.[2]

The study of patterns of consumption of online news has attracted considerable attention from the research community for over a decade. This research started with the analysis of access patterns to websites, and has expanded to include topics such as new engagement metrics, personalized news recommendations and summaries, etc. (see Section 2 for an overview).

One line of research looks at consumption and interaction patterns as a single time series and attempts several prediction tasks on it. For example, predicting total comments from early comments [18, 28], total visits from early visits [16], etc. More recent works incorporate attributes from each specific article (e.g. topic, source, etc.) into the prediction [4].

We adopt a novel approach, in which we integrate different types of interactions of users with an online news article including visits, social media reactions, and search/referrals. We evaluate our methods on data from Al Jazeera English, a large international news network, deeply characterizing different classes of articles, and predicting their total number of page views and their effective shelf-life (the effective shelf-life of an article is the time span during which it receives most of its visits).

The characterization and prediction of user behavior around news articles is valuable for a news organization, as it allows them (i) to gain a better understanding of how people consume different types of news online; (ii) to deliver more relevant and engaging content in a proactive manner; and (iii) to improve the allocation of resources to developing stories over their life cycle.

Our contributions. In this paper we present a qualitative and quantitative analysis of the life cycle of online news stories. Our main contributions are the following:

[2]http://www.people-press.org/2012/09/27/section-2-online-and-digital-news-2/

- We find that social media reactions can contribute substantially to the understanding of visitation patterns in online news.
- We characterize two fundamental classes of news stories: breaking news and in-depth articles, and describe the differences in users' behavior around them.
- We describe classes of short-term audience response profiles to news articles in terms of visits and social media reactions (decreasing, steady, increasing, and rebounding).
- We improve significantly the accuracy and timeliness of predictive models of total visits and shelf-life of articles, by incorporating social media reactions.

The remainder of this paper is organized as follows. Section 2 provides an overview of previous works related to ours. Section 3 introduces our data collection and defines the concepts and variables we use. The main results of our paper are presented as descriptive and predictive analysis in the two following sections: Section 4 describes user behavior with respect to different classes of articles, and Section 5 demonstrates the importance of incorporating social media information into the predictive modeling of visits. The last section concludes the paper.

2. RELATED WORK

One of the earliest published studies of user behavior in online news was conducted by Aikat [3], who studied the web sites of two large newspapers from November 1995 to May 1997. This work describes many of the patterns still seen in news sites today: visits occur mostly during weekdays and working hours; readers "skim" pages for information so dwell times tend to be short, and there are clear traffic "bursts" that can be attributed to specific news developments.

With the advent in recent years of what can be considered as new forms of journalism (blogs) and new propagation mechanisms for news (micro-blogs and online social networking sites), the volume of research publications in this area has increased considerably. In this section we overview a few previous works closely related to ours, but our coverage is by no means complete.

Behavioral-driven article classification. Previous works including [8, 19] that have studied online activities around online resources (e.g. visiting, voting, sharing, etc.), have consistently identified broad classes of temporal patterns. These classes can be generally characterized, first, by the presence or absence of a clear "peak" of activity; and second, by the amount of activity before and after the peak.

Crane and Sornette [8] describe classes of visitation patterns to online videos, and present models that are consistent with propagation phenomena in social networks. Lehmann et al. [19] extend these classes by observing that for Twitter "hashtags" (user-defined topics) the distributions of activity in different periods (before/during/after) induce distinct clusters of activity that can be interpreted considering the semantics of each hashtag. Romero et al. [25] describe how manually-assigned classes of hashtags are related to different shapes of the *exposure curve*: the probability that a user will propagate some information ("retweet" in the case of Twitter) after being exposed to the information by a certain number of her neighbors.

Yang and Leskovec [30] describe six classes of temporal shapes of attention. Attention is measured in terms of the number of appearances of a given phrase (of a variation of it) corresponding to an event. The patterns describe the distribution of attention over time, as well as the ordering in which different types of media (professional blogs, news agencies, etc.) "break" the story.

In general, previous works have established that the evolution of the popularity of different on-line items depends on their class. Figueiredo et al. [10] describe how YouTube videos that are posted to a "top" page on the website, and videos that are making use of professionally produced content, are different from randomly-chosen videos in terms of their visit patterns.

Recently, researchers at URL shortening service Bit.ly [6] described how an article's half-life (see definition in Section 3) is affected by topics, extending a previous observation than in general there are some topics that are more time-sensitive than others [12]. For instance, business-related articles have on average a longer half-life, while articles related to politics/celebrities/entertainment have an intermediate one. Sports-related articles have in comparison a shorter half-life. Previously, Bit.ly researchers [5] have shown that this half-life is also affected by the social media platform where the link is first posted (e.g. links on Facebook were longer-lived than links on Twitter).

We deepen and complement previous works on behavioral-driven characterization of online content, by describing the life-cycle of online news articles considering their visitation patterns as well as their social media reactions.

Prediction of users' activity. The prediction of the volume of user activities with respect to on-line content items has attracted a considerable amount of research. This is attested by a number of papers, some of which are outlined in Table 1. Another active topic that is closely related, but different, is that of predicting real-world variables such as sales or profits using social media signals (e.g. [13] and many others).

Over the years, the models used to predict user behavior in social media have increased in complexity. For instance, Bandari et al. [4] and Ruan et al. [26] incorporate into their models features extracted from the content of the articles, such as topics. Yin et al. [31] study voting behavior over on-line contents and describe a model that considers that users are divided into two popula-

Table 1. Selected references on predictive modeling of user behavior, sorted by publication year.

Reference	Collection	Input / Output
Tatar et al. [28]	20 Minutes	*input*: publication hour, number of comments after a short time, section; *output*: total number of comments
Brody, Harnad, and Carr [7]	arXiv pre-prints	*input*: short-term article downloads; *output*: long-term article citations
Lee, Moon, and Salamatian [18]	DPReviews / Myspace	*input*: time to first-comment, inter comment arrival stats; *output*: time to last comment
Lerman and Hogg [20]	Digg	*input*: visits; *output*: parameters of models that consider examination and promotion patterns
Kim, Kim, and Cho [16]	Blogs	*input*: clicks on first 30 minutes; *output*: clicks until end of lifetime
Yu, Chen, and Kwok [32]	Facebook pages	*input*: content and media type; *output*: number of FB likes/shares of each post
Lakkaraju and Ajmera [17]	Facebook pages	*input*: text- and other characteristics of the posting and the page; *output*: number of FB likes/shares of each post
Szabo and Huberman [27]	YouTube and Digg	*input*: views (Y), votes (D) in first 10d (Y), 2h (D); *output*: total number of views/votes
Bandari, Asur, and Huberman [4]	News aggregator	*input*: text analysis incl. topics, named entities, subjectivity, etc., source popularity; *output*: tweet count
Ruan et al. [26]	Tweets	*input*: topics, past tweets, content features, user features, etc.; *output*: tweet count for a given topic
Pinto, Almeida, and Gonçalves [24]	YouTube	*input*: time series of views in first 7 days; *output*: number of views after 30 days
Ahmed et al. [2]	YouTube, Digg, Vimeo	*input*: views (Y, V) and votes (D) over time; *output*: predict future popularity

tions: a group that follows the majority opinion, and a group that does not. Myers et al. [23] study models that describe user activity in terms of information propagations, including the presence of external influences, e.g. traditional media sources that can reach vast audiences, such as television networks. Huang et al. [15] consider an online model of social activities that evolves over time as more information becomes available.

In contrast with previous works, we focus on the dynamic relation between social media reactions and visits over time, and show that both are useful to understand the differences among classes of articles and to predict future visit patterns.

Analysis of news visits and social media responses. Dezso et al. [9] analyze the visits to a large news portal in Hungary. One aspect they study which is closely related to our work is the half-life of articles, which is shown to be distributed according to a power-law across a broad range, with a mean of 36 hours. Agarwal et al. [1] study the actions users perform after reading an article, which include printing, commenting, rating, and sharing through e-mail or social media. Their focus is on performing personalized recommendations, but they also uncover that article topics have an effect on the probability of each action, with a division between articles users read privately and articles they share publicly: "Users tend to share articles that earn them social prestige and credit but they do not mind clicking and reading some salacious news occasionally in private."

Social media reactions to traditional news media can vary not only in volume but also qualitatively. Hu et al. [14] record tweets during the broadcast of a speech of the US President. They observe that many tweets refer to the speech in general, except for certain topics which are discussed in more detail.

Finally, social media optimization company SocialFlow describes in a whitepaper [22] a comparative study of social media responses to several large media outlets: Al Jazeera, BBC News, CNN, The Economist, Fox News and The New York Times. Among other findings, they note that the probability that a user clicks on a tweet is higher for The Economist ($\approx 19\%$) than for Fox News ($\approx 16\%$), Al Jazeera ($\approx 11\%$) or The New York Times ($\approx 4\%$). However, followers of Al Jazeera are almost twice as likely to retweet article links than followers of the other channels.

In contrast with previous works, we consider jointly traffic to the website and social media reactions, as both constitute acts in which users engage with the news content. Additionally, we quantify the richness of Twitter messages over time measuring entropy and counting unique tweets, and show that these variables are key to more accurate predictions of future visits.

3. CONTEXT AND DATASET

In this section we provide some context to our research and describe the dataset that will be used on the remainder of the paper.

3.1 Traditional news and social media

Our dataset is provided by Al Jazeera English,[3] a well-established news organization that reaches hundreds of millions of viewers through its TV channel. Their website is divided into five major sections: News, In-Depth, Programmes, Sports, and Weather – plus a collection of blogs, which is outside the scope of this study. Approximately 40 editors/producers work on the areas of News, In-Depth, and Programmes.

The editors of Al Jazeera English maintain Facebook and Twitter[4] accounts (we call them "corporate accounts" in the rest of the paper) and use them actively to announce their content. This seems to be a standard practice adopted by all major media organizations in recent years. Each account (`facebook.com/aljazeera` and `@AJEnglish`) has over 1.5 million followers as of May 2013. Using these accounts, articles in the News section are shared immediately after being posted online. Articles on the In-Depth and Programmes sections are

[3] http://www.aljazeera.com/

[4] Currently Facebook and Twitter are the two most frequent sources of social media referrals to Al Jazeera. Reddit appears in a third place but only through few articles having extremely high visibility.

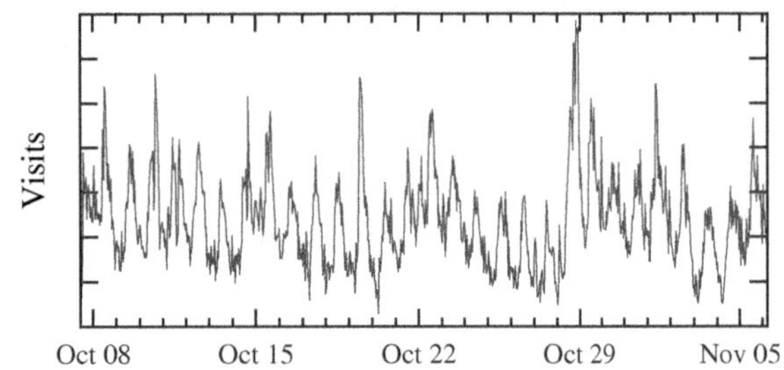

Figure 1. Overall visits to articles. Our study considers all articles posted from Oct. 8th to Oct 29th, 2012 (the graph extends until Nov. 6th).

shared throughout the day with the goal of maximizing audience reach across multiple time zones.

The corporate social media accounts re-share articles at different times of the day, sometimes up to 4 times, on a schedule determined by editors' judgment and designed to increase user engagement. Close attention is paid to the wording of the items posted in social media, including aspects such as their length and the use of hashtags in the case of Twitter. Editors use a variety of online tools to obtain low-latency analytics of traffic and social media, and to decide which hashtags and keywords to use in their postings.

More than half of the visitors to the Al Jazeera English website are from the USA, the United Kingdom, or Canada. According to an online survey taken by Al Jazeera English in 2011 ($n = 4,500$), 18% of respondents said they used Twitter, 42% Facebook, and 12% both.

Social media interactions and traffic to the website can complement or substitute each other. Most frequently, they complement each other: people click on the shared content and visit the website. Sometimes, the social media share can be a substitute for a visit to the article, such as when a video can be viewed directly on the social media site, or when the social media content itself delivers enough information to satisfy users without requiring them to click through to the full article.

For instance, the news "Pakistan's Malala now able to stand in UK" (19 Oct 2012) generated an unusually large number of shares on Facebook, but comparatively little traffic on the website. At the time, the student-activist was being treated from nearly-fatal wounds received ten days before, and it is likely that users who were following the story just wanted to express their relief or satisfaction at her recovery.

In summary, for Al Jazeera and for most large news organizations, social media is important both because it attracts more visitors to their website than any other external referrer, as well as because it provides more platforms in which to have an audience. Hence, many news organizations adopt an active role in social media in order to increase this positive effect.

Table 2. Summary statistics of our dataset.

	Total	Article avg.
Number of articles	606	-
Visits after 1 hour	260 K	430
Visits after 1 day	2.5 M	4,273
Visits after 7 days	3.6 M	5,971
Facebook shares	155 K	256
Tweets	80 K	133
Tweet entropy		5.6 bits
Fraction of unique tweets		19.9 %
Fraction of corporate retweets		36.8 %

3.2 Data collection

We focus on a period of three weeks between October 8th, 2012, and October 29th, 2012. The choice of this period is not random: it was a relatively stable period of traffic, only exhibiting a relatively minor peak on October 29th due to Hurricane Sandy. Figure 1 depicts the frequency of visits to all the articles in our dataset during the observation period.

The data collection is done via a "beacon" embedded in all article pages; this produces events that are processed using Apache S4,[5] a high-performance system for online processing, which is used to collect and aggregate the visits with a 1-minute granularity. For efficiency reasons, only articles obtaining at least 5 visits in a 10-hour window are monitored. The collected data is stored using a Cassandra[6] NoSQL database.

Our system also collects messages from Facebook (using the Facebook Query Language API) and Twitter (using their Search API). Both platforms have strict limitations on polling frequencies, which impose a trade-off between the number of articles we can monitor and the frequency with which we monitor them. To obtain more accurate results for popular articles, and after experimenting with different settings, we decided to poll social media reactions for articles that are within the list of the 30 most visited articles during each five-minute data collection window. We remark that this list varies considerably over time.

We selected a uniform random sample of articles whose first visit was recorded during the observation period, and kept only those accumulating at least 100 visits during their first week after publication. A total of 606 articles was included; this covers over 3.6 million visits and at least 235,000 social media reactions. Table 2 presents some summary statistics on this dataset.

3.3 Metrics

For each article we collected a number of metrics regarding user visits and social media reactions. First, we observed at a granularity of one minute the number of visits (page views) to each article, and the URL of the previous page seen by the users before reaching an article (referral). We bucketed the latter into four classes:

[5]http://incubator.apache.org/s4/
[6]http://cassandra.apache.org/

- internal links, mostly from the home page of the website: these are the majority of the traffic sources and comprise 70% of the visits;
- external links from other sources including social media sites, news aggregators, and others: 14%;
- direct links, which have an empty referral and correspond mostly[7] to people sharing news through instant messaging, e-mail, or other non-web application: 11%; and
- search referrals, basically links from organic search results: 5%.

We remark that this distribution of referrals corresponds to the articles in our sample, which do not include the homepage of the website, section index pages, or older articles. If we take those into account, the numbers are different, e.g. the search referrals account for 30% of the visits.

We also collected periodically the number of times an article has been shared on Facebook, and the content of any Twitter message containing the URL of the article, or a variant of the URL produced by a URL shortening service. We used this data to compute the following variables:

- Number of Facebook shares per minute (interpolated).
- Number of tweets per minute.
- Number of unique tweets per minute. A tweet is deemed *unique* if its edit distance with all previous tweets pointing to the same article (after discarding shortened URLs and "retweet" prefixes) is more than 10 characters.
- Tweet vocabulary entropy. To compute this, at any given point in time we create a document by concatenating all the tweets received up to that time. Then, we compute the entropy of the distribution of terms in that document.
- Number of corporate retweets per minute. A tweet is a "corporate retweet" if it includes "RT @AJEnglish" or "RT @AJELive" in its text. A tweet can be both corporate retweet and unique, as users are free to edit the retweet before posting it.
- Number of followers, friends (followees) and statuses of each of the users posting a tweet.

4. BEHAVIORAL-DRIVEN CLASSES

In this section we describe classes of articles according to patterns of user behavior.

4.1 News vs In-Depth

We observe that articles in the two larger sections of the Al Jazeera English website trigger distinct user behavior patterns: visits and social media reactions on articles in the News section (322 articles in our sample) are different from the ones on articles in the In-Depth section (139 articles).

[7]http://www.theatlantic.com/technology/archive/2012/10/dark-social-we-have-the-whole-history-of-the-web-wrong/263523/

Table 3. Top 10 most frequent words (stemmed and lowercased) in article titles in the "News" and "In-Depth" sections. Words that appear in both lists are italicized.

Top words (News, $n = 322$)			Top words (In-Depth, $n = 139$)		
Word	News	In-Depth	Word	News	In-Depth
us	34	17	*us*	34	17
kill	21	1	pictur	0	10
attack	19	0	obama	6	6
syria	15	4	interact	0	6
dead	15	1	america	0	6
protest	13	0	muslim	0	5
rebel	12	2	*syrian*	11	4
vote	11	3	*syria*	15	4
syrian	11	4	presid	4	4
pakistan	10	2	polici	2	4

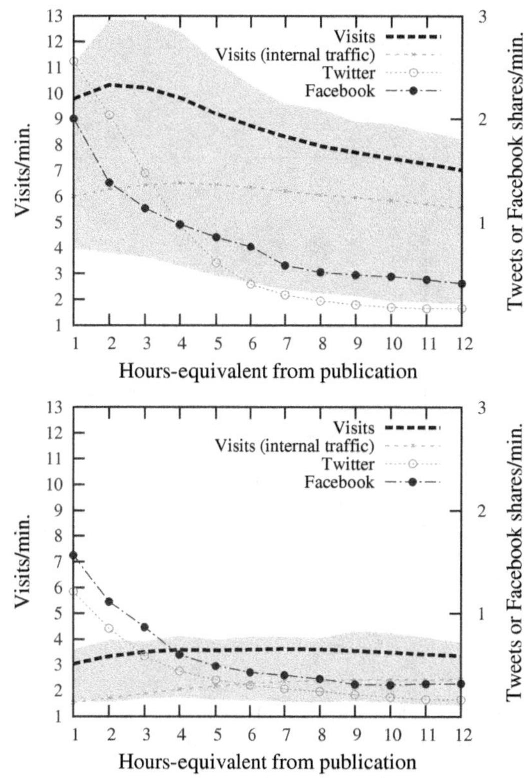

Figure 2. Visits per minute (left y-axis) as well as Tweets and Facebook shares per minute (right y-axis) for the first 12 hours. For visits, the shaded area covers 50% of the data (quantiles 0.25 to 0.75). Top: average for a News item. Bottom: average for an In-Depth item.

Titles. Table 3 includes the most frequent words in titles of articles in these two sections, after converting to lowercase and applying Porter's stemmer.[8] While in our sample the US and Syria appear prominently in both sections, articles in the News section include several violent acts, while articles in the In-Depth section are dominated by photos and political analysis. A chi-squared test comparing the entire distributions shows $p < 10^{-13}$, rejecting the hypothesis that they are equal.

[8]http://snowball.tartarus.org/algorithms/porter/stemmer.html

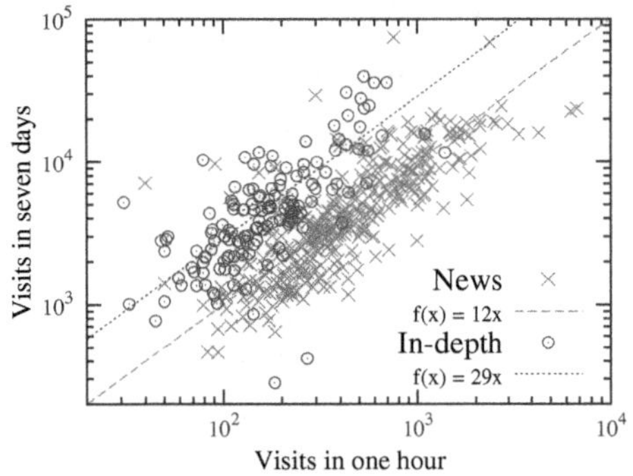

Figure 3. Visits in the first hour versus visits on the first week for articles in the two largest categories. A simple function that assumes that visits after seven days are a multiple of visits after one hour has been included, by performing a least-squares fit in the central portion of each distribution.

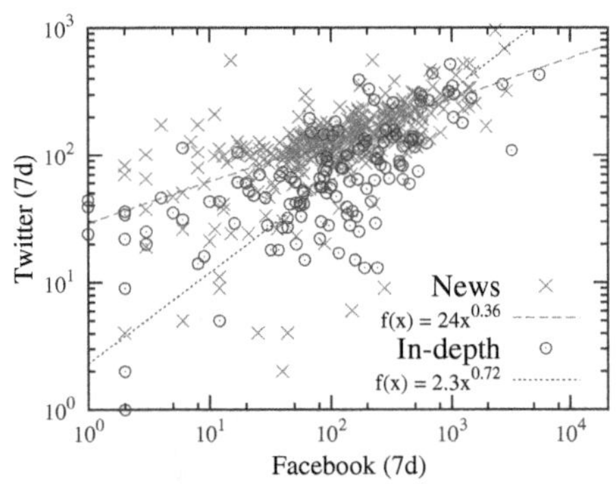

Figure 4. Differences in the distribution of Facebook vs Twitter shares. On average the ratio of Facebook shares to tweets is 1.9:1 (1.6:1 for News, 2.7:1 for In-Depth). The result of a least-squares fit in the central portion of each distribution is included.

Visits. Figure 2 (top) depicts the average time series of some variables for articles in the News section. Time is expressed in *hours-equivalent*, which are hours corrected by the seasonality (day-night, weekday-weekend) of traffic on the website, as in [27]. Initially there are a number of visits and activity on Twitter and Facebook, that decays rapidly after a short time. This is often the pattern in news media as observed e.g. by [9, 21] and others. After a few hours, a large amount of visits can be explained by "internal traffic", i.e. visitors arriving from the homepage of the site. For most articles, once the news article is displaced from the homepage by more recent items, its traffic slows down considerably.

The profile of visits to In-Depth articles can be more complex. Figure 2 (bottom) depicts the average series for these articles. We can observe that a sustained level of visits is observed during several hours, as the contents of these articles are not as time-sensitive as those of the News section. We remark that in both cases (News and In-Depth) there is considerable variability from one article to another.

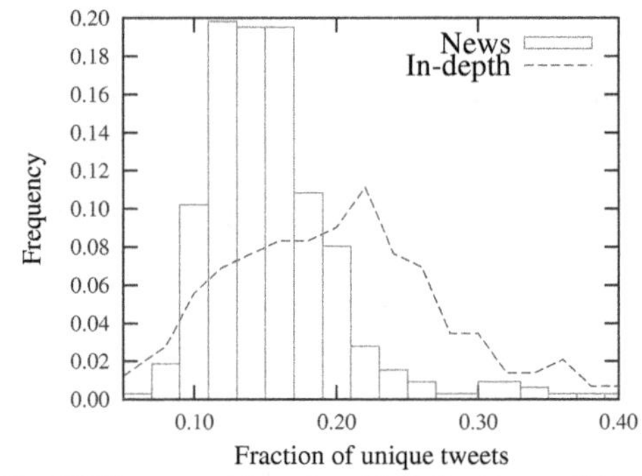

Figure 5. Differences in the distribution of the fraction of unique tweets. In both cases, Twitter activity is dominated by re-tweets or repetitions of the same tweets, but In-Depth articles attract more unique tweets.

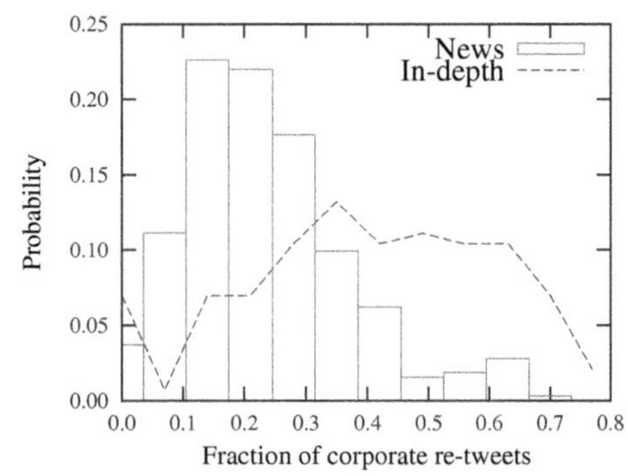

Figure 6. Differences in the distribution of fraction of corporate retweets. In-Depth articles have a larger share of re-tweets from the @AJEnglish and @AJELive accounts.

News items compared to In-Depth items have a more intense first hour, as can be seen in Figure 3. For News, visits in one hour are roughly 1/12th of the visits in the first week, while for In-Depth they are on average around 1/29th. The two groups are similar to "promoted" (homepage) and "not-promoted" stories in Digg as observed in [27].

This difference in behavior can to some extent be explained by the design of the website. News articles are displayed more prominently on the home page, with the most salient location being typically used by a news item; however, In-Depth articles are also visible across the website, including a prominent slot on the top right corner of every page. Additionally to the differences in social media sharing that we discuss next, we observe that long-lived News articles (in terms of effective shelf-life as defined in Section 5.2) tend to include analysis that would actually make them fit for the In-Depth section. Indeed, the top-3 longer lived News articles in our observation period are "Profile: Malala Yousafzai" (Oct 10th, 2012), "Syrian rebels in uneasy alliances" (Oct 25th, 2012), and "Malala is the daughter of Pakistan" (Oct 13th, 2012); their contents, while motivated by specific news events such as the Syrian conflict and the shooting of a school girl, do not describe the events but rather the context in which they are taking place.

Social media. On average the ratio of Facebook shares to tweets per article is 1.9:1, which is to some extent consistent with the survey described in Section 3.1 that indicated that there were twice as many website visitors using Facebook as there were Twitter users. Additionally, In-Depth articles are shared more on Facebook given the same level of activity on Twitter, as shown in Figure 4. On average News articles have 1.6 Facebook shares per tweet, while In-Depth articles have 2.7.

As shown in Figure 5 there is also a difference in the number of unique tweets. On average, 17% of the tweets about News articles are unique, versus 25% of the tweets about In-Depth articles. This means that a majority of users do not change the content of the tweets when clicking on the "tweet" button next to the articles, or when retweeting from another Twitter user.

There is also a difference in the number of corporate retweets, as shown in Figure 6. On average, 27% of tweets about News articles are corporate retweets, compared to 44% of tweets about In-Depth articles. This means that for In-Depth articles a larger share of Twitter activity can be attributed to users who are followers of @AJEnglish or @AJELive, and thus are probably more engaged with these Twitter accounts.

Anecdotally, we know that editors spend more time crafting tweets to promote In-Depth articles than News articles, given that the former are not as time sensitive as the latter. In the case of News, the headline is often posted without modifications to Twitter, which may produce a comparatively less appealing tweet.

4.2 Analysis of news articles

We observe that News articles have attention profiles that are quite predictable, while In-Depth and other article categories show significantly more variability. We focus on the first 12 hours-equivalent after publication of each article in the News section, and observe the time series of data from all sources including internal links, external links, search engines, and social media (similarly to the time series shown in Figure 2, but for each individual article instead of as an average). We then classify articles into several classes based on visit patterns that are apparent from these observations, starting with the largest class ("*decreasing*") and following with the other classes. The classification is done by the authors seeking consensus and discussing borderline cases.

At a high level, the classes of articles in our News sample can be roughly described by an "80:10:10 rule". The traffic to ~80% of the articles decreases monotonically during the first 12 hours, the traffic to ~10% does not decrease, and the traffic to the remaining ~10% decreases first, but then rebounds. Articles on each are listed in Appendix A.

Next we provide a brief description of each class and examples of stories appearing in each of them. We remark that in this work we do not attempt to provide a comprehensive content-based typology for news articles within each attention profile.

Decreasing (78%). The largest article class represents about 78% of the sample set. Articles in this class demonstrate an initial spike in visits following article publication, followed by a rather consistent drop in the number of visits, either immediately (244 articles), or after a short delay (7 articles).

Delayed onset traffic decreases have been observed before, such as in [21] with respect to the shooting in Aurora, Colorado, in 2012. This attention pattern can often be attributed to breaking news that resonates with readers located in a time zone that is off-peak when the article is first posted, such as when that portion of the audience is mostly asleep. A story about Hurricane Sandy's movement up the East Coast of the United States, for example, sees an initially sharp visit growth that begins to decline as the East Coast retires for the evening.

The predominance of this class of article indicates that while news itself occurs, and can even be covered, at a constant rate, in most cases readers will only be interested on a news article for a brief period of time after its publication.

Steady or Increasing (12%) Roughly 9% of the sample's articles retain relatively constant visitor rates during their first 12 hours. Compared to news categories with very short shelf-lives, such as sports news, these articles are remarkably consistent. In this subset of news articles, dramatic news and emotional stories appear to garner Facebook shares and, often as a result, extended shelf-lives.

In the U.S., multiple articles on Obama and Romney's sharp-tongued presidential debate drive consistent Facebook and Twitter responses for a relatively long period of time following the articles' publication. A poll on racism in the US has similar staying power and Facebook sharing. In Central Asia, the Taliban attack on Pakistani schoolgirl Malala appears in a number of these articles, where consistent Facebook sharing buoys the article traffic beyond average shelf-life. In Europe, furor over a seismology scandal is posted to Facebook, while in the Middle East, atrocities in the war in Syria and violence between Israel and Hamas also generate hours of steady traffic. Africa sees a new prime minister in Libya, the police shooting of 34 striking miners in South Africa, and a bomb attack on a church in Nigeria, all of which see sustained traffic thanks in part to significant Facebook and Twitter sharing many hours after their initial publication.

Stories in this group were mostly developing stories and many of them had regular updates. One such example is the story about Malala for which Al Jazeera sent a correspondent to the Swat Valley. Being a complex region to cover, a series of news articles and feature stories were written. In addition, Al Jazeera reached out to the

Reddit community for a Q&A session which topped the "Ask me anything (AmA)" section[9]. section.

A relatively small number of articles (3% of our sample) buck the usual trend and see increased page traffic as time passes after their publication, rather than a decline. To the extent that these articles can be generalized, they resemble the class of articles detailed above. Some of these articles were also updated with supporting content. For at least half of them, web producers added video packages after publication, which may explain to some extent the increase in visits.

Rebounding (10%). About 10% of the articles in our sample initially exhibit a decline in visits/minute, until a point where such decline is reversed. This "rebound" occurs either because of internal or external links.

In the case of internal traffic, the traffic patterns behind these rebounding articles sometimes reflect the common newsroom practice of linking to previous coverage in more recent articles. This practice provides additional background context to readers just arriving at the story, but also helps news organizations extract additional value from articles that are otherwise statistically becoming valueless. Stories that required a significant investment of resources to produce are also promoted more heavily than regular articles. We can see that in these cases, these internal links do indeed deliver readers to articles whose shelf-lives have nearly expired, when measured by homepage and social media traffic.

The articles that rebound as a result of external traffic are beneficiaries of attention directed from outside of the news organization (e.g. a social networking site, the website of another news network, etc.). Typically each observed burst in external web traffic can be tracked to a single source. Breaking stories can also gain visits as ongoing developments drive significant additional interest. This phenomenon is evidenced, for instance, by three rebounding articles tracking Hurricane Sandy's descent upon the United States.

In general, we see that when News articles cover topics that stray from "hard news", the article's attention profile reflects the increased variability seen in the In-Depth pieces. For example, some articles ostensibly cover specific actualities, but also bridge into long-standing issues: in the U.S., "Immigrant family in pursuit of the American Dream" and "Living the modern American Dream" stoke passions around immigration.

The sometimes blurry line between reporting on immediate actualities and longer-term trends like immigration is an area of tension in journalism, one identified by Galtung and Ruge when they asked "how do 'events' become 'news"'? [11].

[9]http://www.reddit.com/r/IAmA/comments/11p6q3/i_am_asad_hashim_journalist_for_the_al_jazeera/

Table 4. Modeling visiting volume after 7 days: Significance levels for regression models after 20 minutes.

Variable	In-depth		News	
Facebook shares	0.0349	*	0.0204	*
Twitter tweets	0.0026	**	<0.0001	***
Twitter entropy	<0.0001	***	0.0003	***
Twitter avg. followers	<0.0001	***		
Volume of unique tweets			<0.0001	***
Unique tweets %			<0.0001	***
Corporate retweets %	0.0092	**		

5. IMPROVING TRAFFIC PREDICTIONS USING SOCIAL MEDIA DATA

An increased amount of social media reactions is often correlated with more traffic to online articles. This is particularly marked in the case of non-decreasing and rebounding News articles, as well as In-Depth articles whose visitation patterns are more varied and less predictable than regular (decreasing) News articles. In this section, we combine social media reactions with early visitation measures to provide improved predictions of (i) the volume of visits to an article after 7 days from its publication and (ii) the effective shelf-life of articles, i.e. the time during which they will receive most of their visits. We begin by fitting models to our sample data, and then explore the practicality of this approach for new data.

5.1 Modeling visiting volume

Our first goal is to determine to what extent social media reactions can improve the prediction of the overall popularity (total number of visits) of an article. The dependent variable that we want to describe with our models is the total number of visits after 7 days ($v7d$). We use a straightforward approach to answer this question—linear regression models. We include the following variables (described in Section 3.3) as observed at the time at which the prediction is performed: number of visits (v), number of visits from link referrals (vr) and from "direct" traffic from e-mail/IM (vd), shares on Facebook (f), Twitter (t), mean number of followers of people sharing on Twitter ($foll$), entropy of tweets (ent), number and fraction of unique tweets (uni, $unip$) and fraction of corporate retweets (cp). We use a linear regression model that includes all first-order effects as well as second order interactions. We included second-order interactions because of the interdependency of the variables (e.g. an article with more visits is more likely to have more social media reactions):

$$lm(vis7d{\sim}v)$$

$$lm(vis7d{\sim}(v{+}vr{+}vd{+}f{+}t{+}foll{+}ent{+}uni{+}unip{+}cp)^2).$$

The distribution of visits to articles is log-normal distributed in our data, consistently with previous works [29, 4]. We log-transform $log(x+1)$ the visits as well as the volume of social media reactions. For t=5, 10, 15, ...we calculate the proportion of the explained variance of these two linear models. The result is shown in Figure 7.

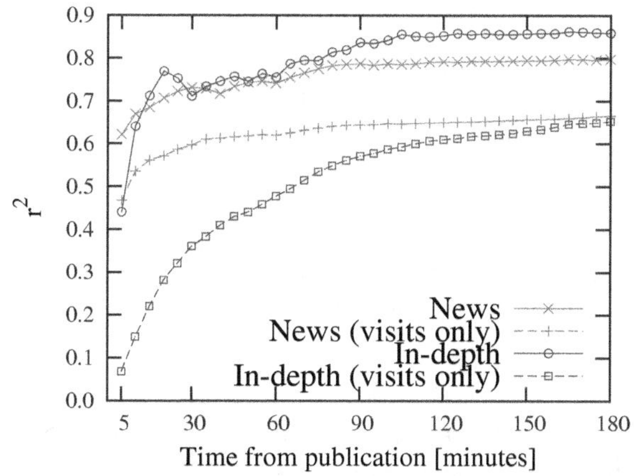

Figure 7. Proportion of explained variance (r^2) for the prediction of total volume of visits, for News and In-depth articles.

It takes about 3 hours to be able to explain > 0.6 of the variance for In-Depth articles, and the additional variables are profitable from the first minutes. After 10-20 minutes we observe the largest difference in our regression models (+0.5 in terms of r^2).

We take a closer look at the model variables after 20 minutes to identify the sources of this improvement. For this purpose we stepwise fit the model variables by AIC (Akaike information criterion) as implemented in `stats.step` in R. Table 4 shows the reliability of the Social media variables to serve as good predictor for the volume of visits after 7 days.

The fraction of traffic from different sources does not appear to be a reliable predictor when all variables are used for the model; when we reduce the model to exclusively these two variables, the traffic from e-mail/IM is a more reliable predictor than the traffic from external links.

Social media variables, particularly the number of tweets and the entropy of the vocabulary used in them, seem to be reliable predictors for both In-Depth and News articles. The number of followers of people posting an article on Twitter together with the fraction of corporate retweets seem to be particularly important for In-Depth articles. A possible interpretation is that the response to these articles has a larger component driven by influential accounts and the actions of Al Jazeera editors. In contrast, the number and fraction of unique tweets can be used for the prediction of traffic to News articles. Consequently, a rich online discussion around a breaking within its first minutes is a signal of potentially high and sustained user interest.

5.2 Modeling shelf-life

We define the *effective shelf-life* τ_ℓ of an article as the time passed between its first visit and the time at which it has received a fraction ℓ of the visits it will ever receive. In this work we set $\ell = 0.90$, but similar values (e.g. 0.85, or 0.95) yield similar results to the ones presented here. When $\ell = 0.50$ this is equivalent to half-life [5, 6].

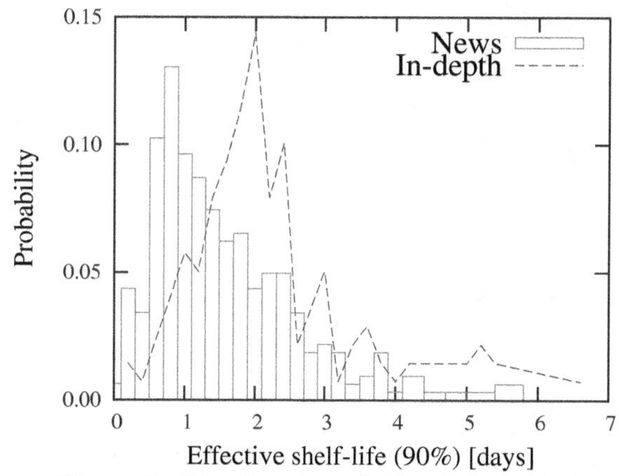

Figure 8. Distribution of effective shelf-life.

Table 5. Modeling effective shelf-life: Significance levels for regression models after 20 minutes.

Variable	In-depth		News	
Visits R^2	0.0005		0.0921	
Social media R^2	0.4457		0.2193	
Social media R^2 adjusted	0.2274		0.1505	
Twitter tweets	0.0138	*	0.0061	**
Twitter entropy	0.0027	**	0.0024	**
Twitter avg. followers			0.0001	***
Volume of unique tweets	0.0026	**		
Unique tweets %	0.0190	*	0.0445	*
Corporate retweets	0.0001	***		
Traffic from e-mail/IM	0.0482	*		

Given that our observation period is finite, we use a seven-day observation period as a proxy for the total number of visits the articles will ever receive, as for basically all the articles in our sample, there is little activity after 3 or 4 days. This is consistent with the experience of Al Jazeera editors and with observations in previous works (e.g. [30]). We remark however that there are rare cases where an article is "re-born" after weeks, for instance when it provides background information for a new development.

The distribution of the shelf-life for both classes is depicted in Figure 8. As observed in the qualitative analysis, the average shelf-life of In-Depth articles, 2 days and 9 hours, is longer than the one of News articles, 1 day and 16 hours. Their average half-lives are respectively 20 hours and 8 hours (both are shorter than the 36 hours observed by [9]).

We observe that the effective shelf-life of all articles is independent from their total number of visits after 7 days (Pearson's correlation $r = -0.03$). This will lead to low accuracy when predicting based solely on visits. For the predictive task the linear regression model setup is analogous to the one used to model visiting volume; this time the dependent variable is τ_{90}. Our focus is again on the variables after 20 minutes. Running the first regression model (only visits) for this time period reveals differences for News and In-Depth stories (Table 5). For News stories, at least 9.2% of effective shelf-life variance

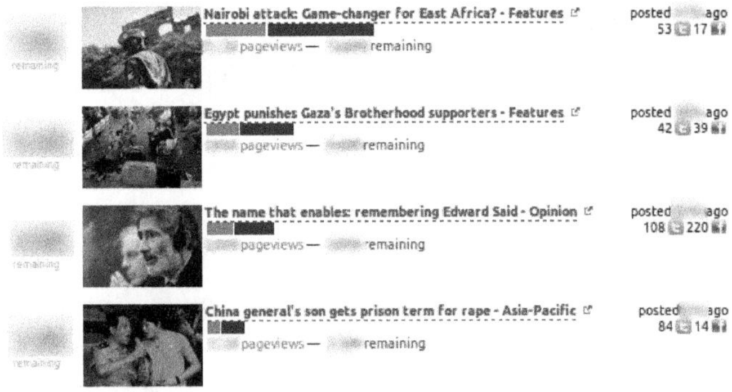

Figure 9. Screenshot of http://fast.qcri.org/ depicting predictions for four articles. Green bars indicate number of pageviews so far, gray bars indicate predictions. Exact numbers are business-sensitive so they are omitted.

can be described, while visits show no predictive information for In-Depth stories. Including social media variables changes this picture dramatically. Especially for In-Depth stories, a significant part of the variance can now be described. Stepwise fitting of the social media models shows that the number of Facebook shares and the traffic from external links are no reliable predictors for effective shelf-life. In contrast, all Tweet variables reach significant levels. For In-Depth articles corporate retweets and traffic from e-mail/IM also serve as reliable predictors.

In a nutshell, using social media variables to model effective shelf-life of stories can increase the accuracy of early prediction significantly. This is a very promising result for future research given that we describe the effective shelf-life pattern with data from one single time point without the use of time series or other elaborate models.

5.3 Online predictions

A live system implementing these ideas on data from the Al Jazeera English website is available online.[10] This allows us to further test the effectiveness of our methods in an online setting, in addition to the off-line tests we have described so far. Figure 9 shows a screenshot of this application.

The system collects data for all articles irrespective of their section, and produces predictions for all articles in the News section using one set of models, and for all the remaining articles (In-Depth, Videos, Programmes, etc.) using another set. In each model set there are models that are executed 1 hour, 6 hours, 12 hours and 24 hours after an article is published. The target variable in this live system is page-views after 3 days. Every 24 hours, it re-trains the models by adding the articles that have passed the 3-day deadline to the training set. After an initial warm up period of 3 weeks, we monitored all 350 article URLs published during a period of 1 week in July 2013 and kept all the predictions done by the system.

[10]http://fast.qcri.org/

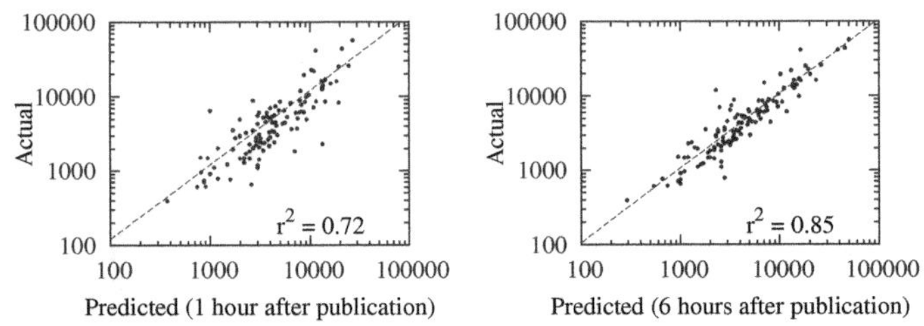

Figure 10. Predictions of visits after 3 days using the online system across all articles. Left: predictions 1 hour after publication. Right: predictions 6 hours after publication.

First, we evaluated the coverage of our system, which as explained in Section 3.2 is designed to focus on the top 30 most visited URLs in every 5-minute period. In practice, we produce predictions within 6 hours for 194 (55%) of the articles seen. Taking as comparison Google Analytics, which is also used by this website,[11] we observe that this covers 65% of the page-views to Al Jazeera English articles. We remark that this partial coverage is not an intrinsic aspect of the system, but a limitation of using public (instead of paid) access to Twitter's API.

Second, we evaluated the quality of the predictions. In order to do so, we store the predictions done by the different models. Conceptually, each of the 350 articles is in the testing set, and the training set is composed of all the articles published in the period of 1 to 4 weeks before its publication day. Figure 10 compares the actual number of page-views with predictions done 1 hour and 6 hours after an article is published. The quality of the predictions after one hour is similar to off-line tests ($r^2 = 0.72$) even when we are mixing articles from other sections; 134 articles (38%) not in News or In-Depth – but we also remark the predictive horizon of the live system is shorter (3 days vs 7 days). Predictions after 6 hours have $r^2 = 0.85$. The location of the best trade-off between timeliness and accuracy in the range of 1 to 6 hours is an important problem, which requires understanding how editors react to the predictions and use them in practice.

6. CONCLUSIONS

Main findings. By adopting an integrated view of users' behavior, we have observed that there are two classes of articles that generate qualitatively and quantitatively different responses from readers. News articles describing breaking news events tend to decay in attention shortly after they are published and thus have a shorter shelf-life. These articles also have more repetitive social media reactions, as most users simply repeat the news headlines without commenting on them. In-Depth items portraying or analyzing a topic tend to exhibit a longer shelf-life and a richer social media response, including more content-rich tweets in terms of vocabulary entropy and fraction of unique tweets, and more shares on Facebook for the same level of tweets.

[11]http://analytics.google.com/

By going deeper into the first few hours after publication of News articles, we found three distinctive response patterns in a roughly 80:10:10 proportion: decreasing traffic, steady or increasing traffic, and rebounding traffic. We found that there can be multiple causes for non-decreasing traffic, including the addition of new content to articles, social media reactions, and other types of referrals.

We have shown that social media signals can improve by a large margin the accuracy of predictions of future visits, as well as the accuracy of predictions of article shelf-life. In particular for In-Depth articles which exhibit more complex visit patterns over time, we have found that incorporating measures of the quantity and variety of social media reactions can lead to substantial gains in terms of prediction accuracy.

Practical significance. From the perspective of a news provider, while no automatic system can replace editorial judgment, understanding and predicting the life cycle of stories has three main benefits:

- In the case of News stories, knowing how the audience is interacting with an article is not just "nice to have", but increasingly a critical component in delivering timely and relevant content to an ever growing online audience.
- For In-Depth stories, which operate on a slower news cycle, knowing when to allocate additional time and resources can significantly improve the news planning process. This is particularly useful for an emerging class of news programmes that combine live online discussions with more traditional TV coverage.
- To a web producer, an article with a longer shelf-life means judicious time can be spent preparing backgrounder pieces which are valuable in providing context to a story. From a reach perspective, articles with steady or increasing levels of traffic translate into higher user engagement.

Our work depends on having access to a large repository of social media reactions. As more people get into social media (e.g. Twitter), this line of work will become more relevant and will be able to produce even higher quality predictions.

Limitations and future work. We combine findings from computer science, journalism, and media studies. The research presented here is more difficult to execute than the traditional single-discipline study, but we expect interdisciplinary work on this area to become increasingly common as our media and technology continue to converge.

Our data gathering system collects only aggregate information and does not attempt to link actions across sessions or users across platforms; this prevents us from separating post-read from pre-read sharing, an important distinction explored in [1]. Another limitation of our work is that we used data from a single website, and we are in the process of gathering data from other sources in order to strengthen our claims. We also used a manual process for categorization of the article classes (decreasing/steady/increasing/rebounding), and we did not attempt a comprehensive content-based classification of articles inside each class.

In this work, we used linear models and did not attempt anything more sophisticated. We do not claim that our models are the more accurate that can be built using this data, but used them to demonstrate in a clear way the importance of social media signals for the predictive tasks we undertake. Better models are definitively possible, and may yield even larger gains in accuracy when incorporating social media signals.

We also used a data-driven approach in which shelf-life is derived from observations. Alternatively, shelf-life can be derived by fitting a visitation curve produced by a parametrized model [29]. This may lead to an improvement in the prediction accuracy.

Reproducibility. The data sample used for this study, including feature vectors and the categorization of articles done during the qualitative analysis, is available for research purposes upon request. A live demo is available at http://fast.qcri.org/

Acknowledgments. The authors wish to thank Al Jazeera English for the data used for this study, Kiran Garimella from QCRI for his work in the live system, Janette Lehmann from Yahoo! Research for her valuable help and comments on an early version of this manuscript; Michael K. Martin and Ju-Sung Lee from Carnegie Mellon University for insightful discussions on regression models; and Edward Schiappa for his feedback on the methodology for the analysis of article classes.

Key references: [7, 27]

7. REFERENCES

1. Agarwal, D., Chen, B. C., and Wang, X. Multi-faceted ranking of news articles using post-read actions. In *Proc. of CIKM*, ACM (2012), 694–703.
2. Ahmed, M., Spagna, S., Huici, F., and Niccolini, S. A peek into the future: predicting the evolution of popularity in user generated content. In *Proceedings of the sixth ACM international conference on Web search and data mining* (New York, NY, USA, 2013), 607–616.
3. Aikat, D. News on the web. *Convergence: The International Journal of Research into New Media Technologies 4*, 4 (Dec. 1998), 94–110.
4. Bandari, R., Asur, S., and Huberman, B. A. The pulse of news in social media: Forecasting popularity. Feb. 2012.

5. Bitly Science Team. You just shared a link. how long will people pay attention? The Bit.ly blog, Sept. 2011.
6. Bitly Science Team. Halflife by topic. The Bit.ly blog, Nov. 2012.
7. Brody, T., Harnad, S., and Carr, L. Earlier web usage statistics as predictors of later citation impact: Research articles. *J. Am. Soc. Inf. Sci. Technol. 57*, 8 (June 2006), 1060–1072.
8. Crane, R., and Sornette, D. Robust dynamic classes revealed by measuring the response function of a social system. *PNAS 105*, 41 (October 2008), 15649–15653.
9. Dezsö, Z., Almaas, E., Lukács, A., Rácz, B., Szakadát, I., and Barabási, A. L. Dynamics of information access on the web. *Physical Review E (Statistical, Nonlinear, and Soft Matter Physics) 73*, 6 (2006), 066132+.
10. Figueiredo, F., Benevenuto, F., and Almeida, J. M. The tube over time: characterizing popularity growth of youtube videos. In *Proc. of WSDM*, ACM (2011), 745–754.
11. Galtung, J., and Ruge, M. H. The structure of foreign news. *Journal of Peace Research 2*, 1 (1965), 64–91.
12. Gharan, S. O., Ronaghi, F., and Wang, Y. What memes say about the news cycle? Tech. rep., Stanford University, 2010.
13. Gruhl, D., Guha, R., Kumar, R., Novak, J., and Tomkins, A. The predictive power of online chatter. In *Proc. of KDD*, ACM (2005), 78–87.
14. Hu, Y., John, A., and Seligmann, D. D. Event analytics via social media. In *Proc. of SBNMA*, ACM (2011), 39–44.
15. Huang, S., Chen, M., Luo, B., and Lee, D. Predicting aggregate social activities using Continuous-Time stochastic process. In *Proc. of CIKM 2012* (2012).
16. Kim, S.-D., Kim, S.-H., and Cho, H.-G. Predicting the virtual temperature of Web-Blog articles as a measurement tool for online popularity. In *Computer and Information Technology (CIT), 2011 IEEE 11th International Conference on*, IEEE (Aug. 2011), 449–454.
17. Lakkaraju, H., and Ajmera, J. Attention prediction on social media brand pages. In *Proc. of CIKM*, ACM (2011), 2157–2160.
18. Lee, J. G., Moon, S., and Salamatian, K. An approach to model and predict the popularity of online contents with explanatory factors. In *IEEE Conference on Web Intelligence* (2010).
19. Lehmann, J., Gonçalves, B., Ramasco, J. J., and Cattuto, C. Dynamical classes of collective attention in twitter. In *Proc. of WWW*, ACM (2012), 251–260.
20. Lerman, K., and Hogg, T. Using a model of social dynamics to predict popularity of news. In *Proc. of WWW*, ACM (2010), 621–630.
21. Lotan, G. Big data for breaking news: Lessons from #aurora, colorado. Tech. rep., SocialFlow, Aug. 2012.
22. Lotan, G., Gaffney, D., and Meyer, C. Audience analysis of major news accounts on twitter. Tech. rep., SocialFlow, Aug. 2011.
23. Myers, S. A., Zhu, C., and Leskovec, J. Information diffusion and external influence in networks. In *Proc. of KDD*, ACM (2012), 33–41.
24. Pinto, H., Almeida, J. M., and Gonçalves, M. A. Using early view patterns to predict the popularity of YouTube videos. In *Proc. of WSDM*, ACM (2013), 365–374.
25. Romero, D. M., Meeder, B., and Kleinberg, J. Differences in the mechanics of information diffusion across topics: Idioms, political hashtags, and ComplexContagion on twitter. In *Proc. of WWW* (2011).
26. Ruan, Y., Purohit, H., Fuhry, D., Parthasarathy, S., and Sheth, A. Prediction of topic volume on twitter. In *WebSci (short papers)* (2012).
27. Szabo, G., and Huberman, B. A. Predicting the popularity of online content. *Communications of the ACM 53*, 8 (Aug. 2010), 80–88.
28. Tatar, A., Leguay, J., Antoniadis, P., Limbourg, A., de Amorim, M. D., and Fdida, S. Predicting the popularity of online articles based on user comments. In *Proc. of WIMS*, ACM (2011).
29. Wu, F., and Huberman, B. A. Novelty and collective attention. *PNAS 104*, 45 (Nov. 2007), 17599–17601.
30. Yang, J., and Leskovec, J. Patterns of temporal variation in online media. In *Proc. of WSDM*, ACM (2011), 177–186.
31. Yin, P., Luo, P., Wang, M., and Lee, W. C. A straw shows which way the wind blows: ranking potentially popular items from early votes. In *Proc. of WSDM*, ACM (2012), 623–632.
32. Yu, B., Chen, M., and Kwok, L. Toward predicting popularity of social marketing messages. In *Social Computing, Behavioral-Cultural Modeling and Prediction*, J. Salerno, S. J. Yang, D. Nau, and S. K. Chai, Eds., vol. 6589 of *LNCS*, Springer (2011), 317–324.

APPENDIX

A. EXAMPLE ARTICLES

List of articles in the non-majority classes described in the qualitative assessment of Section 4.2. The data sample is available for research purposes upon request.

Delayed decreasing:

Hurricane Sandy moves up US Atlantic coast - Americas
Skydiver lands safely after record jump - Americas
Third-party candidates spar in US debate - Americas
Arrests by French police foiled 'bomb plot' - Europe
Scotland's independence referendum signed - Europe
Rival protesters clash in Egypt's capital - Middle East
Syria opposition 'captures' Assad soldiers - Middle East

Steady:

Bomb attack hits northern Nigerian church - Africa
Libya assembly elects new prime minister - Africa
Police admit 'overreacting' at Marikana - Africa
Marking the Cuban missile crisis - Americas
Obama and Romney face off in final debate - Americas
Obama and Romney meet in combative debate - Americas
Poll finds fresh increase in US racism - Americas
US exports to Iran soar despite sanctions - Americas
Asad Hashim: Ask Me Anything on Malala - Central & South Asia
Clerics declare Malala shooting 'un-Islamic' - Central & South Asia
India suspends Kingfisher licence - Central & South Asia
Pakistani schoolgirl Malala arrives to UK - Central & South Asia
Profile: Malala Yousafzai - Central & South Asia
Teenage rights activist shot in Pakistan - Central & South Asia
Italian seismologists could face jail term - Europe
Karadzic to begin Srebrenica defence at Hague - Europe
Russia says fighters killed in North Caucasus - Europe
Scientists found guilty in Italy quake trial - Europe
Bomb blast hits Damascus' Old City - Middle East
Fatah claims victory in West Bank poll - Middle East
Fighting dims hopes for Syria Eid truce - Middle East
Hariri calls on Lebanese to attend funeral - Middle East
Israel strikes Gaza after Hamas retaliation - Middle East
Marginalisation of disabled people in Egypt - Middle East
Palestinians vote in municipal elections - Middle East
Rights group says Syria used cluster bombs - Middle East
Syrian children killed in Idlib air raids - Middle East
US and EU urge political stability in Lebanon - Middle East

Increasing:

Colombia and FARC rebels launch negotiations - Americas
Immigrant family in pursuit of American Dream - Americas
Living the modern 'American Dream' - Americas
Man charged over attempted US bank bomb plot - Americas
Minors flee Central American violence - Americas
Anti-austerity protests erupt in Athens - Europe
Lithuanians vote out austerity government - Europe
Scientists await verdict in Italy quake trial - Europe
Assault on Yemen base blamed on al-Qaeda - Middle East
Qatari emir in historic Gaza visit - Middle East

Rebounding:

African and EU leaders to hold Mali summit - Africa
Evidence of mass murder after Gaddafi's death - Africa
Nigerian soldiers kill dozens of civilians - Africa
State-linked Libyan militias shell Bani Walid - Africa
Tunisia clash leaves opposition official dead - Africa
UN urges military action plan for Mali - Africa
Wounded Mauritania president flown to Paris - Africa
Argentine crew to vacate ship seized in Ghana - Americas
Armstrong 'unaffected' by doping report - Americas
Biden and Ryan set for crucial VP debate - Americas
Brazil forces set for raid on Rio slums - Americas
Candidates spar in US vice president debate - Americas
Cuba's Castro appears in public - Americas
First planet with four suns discovered - Americas
Forecasters predict 'serious' Hurricane Sandy - Americas
Hurricane Sandy approaches eastern US - Americas
Tsunami warning for Hawaii lifted - Americas
US deficit tops $1 trillion for fourth year - Americas
US East Coast prepares for Hurricane Sandy - Americas
Dozens dead in Afghanistan Eid suicide blast - Central & South Asia
Pakistan court probes bartering of girls - Central & South Asia
Pakistan teen activist in critical condition - Central & South Asia
Berlusconi vows to remain in political arena - Europe
Boxer a big hit as Ukraine readies for vote - Europe
EU leaders agree on banking supervisor - Europe
Germany's Merkel reassures Greece - Europe
Merkel arrives in Greece amid tight security - Europe
Russia demands Turkey explain intercepted jet - Europe
Russian opposition aide arrested - Europe
Baghdad area hit by more deadly Eid attacks - Middle East
Eid truce awaits Syrian government response - Middle East
Kuwait police fire tear gas at protesters - Middle East
Syrian forces continue to shell Aleppo - Middle East

Being A Turker

David Martin, Benjamin V. Hanrahan, Jacki O'Neill
Xerox Research Centre Europe
6 chemin de Maupertuis, Grenoble France
{david.martin, ben.hanrahan, jacki.oneill}@xrce.xerox.com

Neha Gupta
University of Nottingham
University Park NG7 2TD Nottingham
neha.gupta@xrce.xerox.com

ABSTRACT
We conducted an ethnomethodological analysis of publicly available content on Turker Nation, a general forum for Amazon Mechanical Turk (AMT) users. Using forum data we provide novel depth and detail on how the Turker Nation members operate as economic actors, working out which Requesters and jobs are worthwhile to them. We show some of the key ways Turker Nation functions as a community and also look further into Turker-Requester relationships from the Turker perspective – considering practical, emotional and moral aspects. Finally, following Star and Strauss [25] we analyse Turking as a form of invisible work. We do this to illustrate practical and ethical issues relating to working with Turkers and AMT, and to promote design directions to support Turkers and their relationships with Requesters.

Author Keywords
Ethnomethodology; content analysis; crowdsourcing; microtasking; Amazon Mechanical Turk; Turker Nation.

ACM Classification Keywords
H.5.3 Group and Organizational Interfaces – Computer, Supported Cooperative Work

General Terms
Human Factors

INTRODUCTION
The concept of crowdsourcing was originally defined by Jeff Howe of Wired Magazine as *"the act of a company or institution taking a function once performed by employees and outsourcing it to an undefined (and generally large) network of people in the form of an open call."* [8] This 'undefined network of people' is the key topic of this article. We present the findings of an ethnomethodological analysis of posts and threads on a crowdsourcing forum called Turker Nation[1]. We have sought to understand members of the crowd – their *reasoning practices, concerns,* and *relationships with requesters and each other* – as they are shown in their posts on the forum. We seek to present them as faithfully as possible, in their own words, in order to provide more definition to this network of people. We believe that this will be beneficial for researchers and businesses working within the crowdsourcing space.

Crowdsourcing encompasses multiple types of activity: invention, project work, creative activities, and microtasking. This latter is our focus here. The most well-known microtask platform is Amazon Mechanical Turk (AMT)[2], and the Turker Nation forum that we studied is dedicated to users of this platform. The basic philosophy of microtasking and AMT is to delegate tasks that are difficult for computers to do to a human workforce. This has been termed 'artificial artificial intelligence'. Tasks like image tagging, duplicate recognition, translation, transcription, object classification, and content generation are common. 'Requesters' (the AMT term for people who have work to be completed) post multiple, similar jobs as Human Intelligence Tasks (HITs), which can then be taken up by registered 'Turkers'. Turkers (termed 'Providers' by AMT) are the users completing the HITs, which typically take seconds or minutes paid at a few cents at a time.

For Amazon, the innovative idea was to have an efficient and cost effective way to curate and manage the quality of content on their vast databases (weeding out duplicates, vulgar content, etc.). While Amazon is still a big Requester, AMT has been deployed as a platform and connects a wide variety of Requesters with up to 500,000 Providers. However, Fort et al. [6] have performed an analysis on the available data and suggest that real number of active Turkers is between 15,059 and 42,912; and that 80% of the tasks are carried out by the 20% most active (3,011–8,582) Turkers. While these numbers are useful, the research community still has little deep qualitative knowledge about this workforce. Questions remain unanswered such as: how and what do they look for in jobs; what are their concerns; and how do they relate to requestors?

LITERATURE REVIEW
To date much of the research on AMT takes the employers' perspective, e.g. [14, 15, 17, 18], and this has in turn been highlighted [6, 16]. Silberman et al. [23] note that this mainstream research looks at how: *"[to] motivate better, cheaper and faster worker performance [...] to get good data from workers, quickly and without paying much."* When it comes to the Turkers themselves, research is more limited,

http://dx.doi.org/10.1145/2531602.2531663

[1] http://turkernation.com/forum.php

[2] http://www.mturk.com

mainly consisting of demographic [11, 20] and survey data. Ross et al. [20] found that the majority of Turkers (56%) are U.S. based, but there is a growing number of Indian Turkers (36%) and other nationalities. Nearly one-third of respondents had a median annual income of <$10,000. There has been an on-going debate about why Turkers turk – whether it is primarily for money (and thus is clearly work) or other reasons (e.g. enjoyment, pastime, etc.). This discussion largely stems from the low wages reported on AMT [20] meaning that it is hard for researchers to believe that people could be doing it for money. Interestingly, in most studies on this topic, money is reported as the primary motivator [2, 11, 13, 20]. However, for example, in [13] this is discounted as due to *"social desirability bias"*. The authors justified this decision by stating: *"bearing in mind the low payment level, this seems to be remarkable."* Other research has suggested a *"social desirability bias"* for US (compared to Indian) Turkers, but still considers that pay is a significant motivating factor [2]. Our paper contributes to this debate, showing that at least for posters on Turker Nation, the primary reason for Turking is to earn money, and that they orientate to AMT as a labour market. By examining how Turkers themselves talk about their wages and their reasons for Turking we give a more nuanced picture of what such low wages mean in practice (and why someone might 'choose' to earn so little).

There has been much less qualitative work into what it means to be a Turker, but notable exceptions to this are Silberman, Irani and colleagues [12, 22, 23]. For example, Irani had the intriguing idea of posting a HIT asking respondents to articulate a 'Turkers' Bill of Rights'[3]. A number of recurring topics were found in the 67 responses including unfair rejection of work, slow payment, low wage and lack of communication with requesters and AMT [24]. They posted questions on Turker Nation, interviewed Turkers via Skype and participated in various forums [23]. They identified the following set of problems for Turkers: employers who don't pay; identifying scams; the cost (to workers) of poorly designed tasks.

That research has been primarily concerned with the employers' perspective has had far reaching consequences. The design of AMT largely supports the needs of Requesters over those of Turkers. Two major examples of this are *information asymmetry* [3, 4, 23] and the *imbalance of power* [5]. Information asymmetry can most clearly be seen in the way reputations are handled. Whilst AMT provides means to rate Turkers' reputations, there is no equivalent means for rating Requesters [1, 23]. Furthermore AMT deliberately hides the relationship between Turkers and Requesters, often to the detriment of the Turker [3]. Requesters have better information on the Turkers than vice versa, as well as greater powers of redress. Felstiner [4] goes so far as to suggest that such *opacity* and lack of information ultimately can lead to *"deception"* and *"violation of privacy"* of workers. This has led Silberman et al. [23] to call for research which takes the workers' perspective in crowdsourcing as part of an effort to develop a fairer system of relationship-based crowdsourcing. As one step in this effort, Irani and Silberman [12] developed a plugin to AMT which enables Turkers to rate Requesters. This plugin provides a very useful resource for Turkers, enabling them to identify good and bad Requesters on the basis of their collective experience.

A parallel approach was taken by Kitter et al. [16] who used the question 'would we want our children to be crowdworkers' as a starting point for trying to create a common research agenda. They warn against the dehumanizing nature of crowdsourcing and specifically call out the need to *"improve task design through better communication"*.

Our study of Turker Nation adds to the research responding to the call to take the workers' perspective. Unlike most other research e.g. [13, 24] the data we collected is of conversations Turkers have amongst themselves, it is naturalistic and is not formulated in response to a research request or HIT. Silberman et al. [23] already showed the value of engaging in Turking forums to get access to the Turkers' perspective. The research reported here goes further with a more wide-ranging, systematic study of the posts of a subset of Turkers. The result is a deeper and more nuanced understanding of how Turkers operate as economic actors in the AMT labour market; how they reason, and how they make calculations and choices about who to work for, and on which jobs. We also look more deeply into their relationship with Requesters; how do they like relationships to work, and how do they respond emotionally and ethically? We also bring some understanding of Turk Nation as a community and draw attention to the extra hidden organizing work they engage in in order to manage their Turking work. We finish by discussing our findings in relation to Star and Strauss' [25] concepts of invisible and visible work and offering some design directions.

SETTING AND METHOD

The 'setting' for this ethnomethodological study is the forum of Turker Nation. We present an ethnomethdological analysis of forum posts on Turker Nation, focusing on a content analysis of posts publicly visible on the forum. For contextual understanding we also researched other places on the world wide web, particularly those discussed in the forum such as the sites for technologies like Turk Alert[4] (provides requester HIT alerts) and Turkopticon[5] (gives Turker ratings of requesters), script sites, blogs for both Turkers and Requesters, journalism sites, and crowdsourcing sites. We looked at Turker Nation as the core site but also followed debates and discussions 'off-site' (i.e. specifically when

[3] http://turkwork.differenceengines.com/blog/

[4] http://www.turkalert.com/

[5] http://turkopticon.differenceengines.com/

external material was discussed 'on site' or when forum members posted on external sites) to broaden and deepen our understanding.

The first author has been a member of Turker Nation for 7 months carrying out extensive (>200 hours) observation of the community, by reading public threads. Interaction was limited to an initial introductory post and several 'likes'. The materials collected were notes made while reading thoroughly and systematically through as many threads as possible. Hundreds of excerpts from posts and threads that were representative of often repeated topics, discussions, and reasoning were collected by taking screen shots. These have been transcribed for this paper with the original style maintained but with a few formatting changes (e.g. removing blank space) for presentational purposes.

Turker Nation is a general forum that concentrates on all topics to do with AMT. On joining the forum, members have limited access to various areas and threads. With increasing activity, members can increase access rights based on their usefulness to the community (engagement, sharing information and tips, scripts ideas, etc.). The majority of the public areas are devoted to issues directly related to being a Turker and doing AMT HITs. By far the largest area is the 'Requesters hall of fame/shame ratings' where Turkers can discuss their experiences with Requesters. Requesters may, and do, engage directly with Turkers in these threads. Other key areas relate to general discussions of AMT, problems, suggestions, computer tips, scripts, and tools. There is an area devoted to AMT and Turkers as represented in the media and academia. Also, there are various threads related to community communication and interests. In studying and reporting on Turker Nation we tried to cover as many public areas as possible, focusing on the key areas and threads (as indicated by post volume) and followed the threads as they unfolded and developed.

We think we should be clear about the data we discuss in this paper and who the Turkers are in relation to the wider population of AMT workers. AMT only provides payment in the form of money (as opposed to Amazon vouchers) to workers in the US and India and the main populations of workers are located in these countries. Turker Nation is but one forum and is primarily used by US workers, so, although we may use the shorthand of 'Turker' in this paper, we are only making claims about the Turker Nation community. The excerpts presented are instances of things we have many examples of, and whenever something unusual or debatable (attracting differing views) is presented we make this clear.

Our analytic approach is ethnomethodological [7]. Ethnomethodology has a long established history within CSCW dating from the early work of Suchman in the US [26] and the Lancaster group in the UK [9]. An ethnomethodological approach can be applied to a wide range of data; one form – conversation analysis (CA) [21] – focuses exclusively on transcribed conversations, while other studies have analysed text and reading practices [27], and still others have been applied to on-line interaction [19]. This approach is well equipped for understanding the activities undertaken on Turker Nation. Ethnomethodology involves detailed analysis of naturally occurring data. It eschews theorising and instead uses the data – in this case posts – to explicate how people organise their activities as a recognisable social accomplishment. A key focus here is on the actions Turkers are trying to achieve through their posts and everyday reasoning practices and understandings exhibited within them. In contrast to other qualitative approaches it does not use structured procedures for coding and organising data. This should not be mistaken for a lack of thoroughness as the collection of data is manual and extensive, and the phenomena reported on here are seen time and again in the data and are thus understood to be important and commonplace topics for the Turker Nation community. Our close analysis is augmented with understandings gained through our prolonged observation and reading of the forum posts. Topics were emergent in the data and we explicate the material in its own terms rather than fitting it to a theory or making judgments about the activity. We selected posts on commonplace topics we believe are interesting for the CSCW community.

FINDINGS

One way to describe AMT is as a labour market. Some, such as Tim Worstall (a blogger for Forbes) consider AMT as a relatively pure form of market; through mass individual actions of employers and workers the market falls into a fair equilibrium. Bad employers and workers are rooted out as their poor actions become visible. Wages or pricing settles to a 'natural' level such that *"apparently half a million people find work at pay rates they're entirely happy with but pay rates that are below minimum wage"* [28]. Given the research by Silberman et al. [12, 22] and Ipeirotis [10, 11] this argument seems shaky to us. In an attempt to get a clearer view on the matter, we present data on a set of emergent topics, posed as questions that probe AMT as a labour market from the point of view of the Turkers.

Why do turkers turk?

A key first question, however, is *do* Turkers orient to AMT as a *marketplace* where they sell their labour? Do they see themselves as working and are they primarily motivated by monetary gain? All the evidence from Turker Nation indicates that this is how they view themselves. Money, and the best way to earn it, underpins much of the discussion about AMT and we can establish it as the key reason why Turker Nation members do turking. We do not argue that other factors are never part of the experience, but that they are 'side benefits' alongside earning money. Interestingly, the Turkers themselves have discussed this very point in a Turker Nation thread about whether Turkers do HITs *"because you like them, regardless of what the pay is"*. A couple of representative responses are shown in example 1:

Example 1: Turkers Turking for Fun?

danturker[6]

This attitude would be requesters dream come true. The workers come here to have fun and play and the lousy pay for work is not an issue. This attitude helps create low pay for the AMT work force that does care about fair pay.

larak56

I agree with most everyone here. While I do find some of the HITS fun and actually learn an incredible amount by doing HITS, I do it for the cash.

While some Turkers did discuss the fact that they found some HITs to be fun, interesting, or educational (e.g. larak56) this was invariably related to comments about the HITs also paying well. Some Turkers did state they had made decisions to accept somewhat (but not much) lower pay if a task was more enjoyable. Other Turkers were more direct and dismissive. Danturker criticises the 'HITS for fun' attitude as bolstering up a wrong perception that Requesters do not need to pay good wages. The idea that Turkers' actions *en masse* send messages to Requesters and that Turkers are responsible for promoting fair pay is a dominant theme of Turker Nation discussions.

How much do Turkers make?

Given that Turkers are doing AMT work for money, is it *"remarkable"* given the *"low pay,"* or is it in fact just a relatively low paying job? We must bear in mind that the majority of contributors to Turker Nation are US based. There is an interesting thread where they discuss earnings for 2012 and we have picked out some representative posts:

Example 2: Turkers Establishing Pay Expectations

jimtexan79

I was hoping to make at least $3,650.00 (you know, 10 bucks a day) but, alas, I fell short. I blame all those summer months that I slacked off. :[

So, how much didja make? Was it what you hoped?

mwanza57

I made $1,179. Would love to double that for next year.

bubbles

$14,476.93 Hoping to do better this year.

defectturk

It is a full part time job for me. I can turk during slow periods at my day job and from 4-10 during the week I turk. Because of pay cuts at my day job I would have to be working a part time job outside the home if I did not turk. And yes, my boss is aware of my activities and when they cut our pay the last time, he openly told us that if we can find other work that he would be flexible in allowing it. Just trying to hold on until the housing market rebounds and keep the company in business. It is cool of him to allow it, but I would much rather have my salary back and drop turking.

The highest earnings we saw were ~ $15k for the year (see bubbles, but also defectturk). Such earnings are typically reported by people who appear to be experienced Turkers – through their posts and high status on Turker Nation. They state they only take well-paying, more professional AMT work. However, earnings otherwise are of all levels down to ~$50 a year. We can't make easy comparisons to an annual wage in more traditional labour markets, because we do not know the number of hours any one Turker has worked. We want to pick out a few more elements from the example that are also of interest:

Turkers are interested in comparison to gain information and knowledge: they start threads like this so they can understand where they are in relation to others and what earning potential they might reach and how quickly if they spend more time or progress to greater proficiency.

They set themselves targets: e.g. to make $10 per day (jimtexan79), or to double (or better) the last years' amount (mwanza57; bubbles).

The importance of their AMT income varies depending on earning ability and other life circumstances: as has been noted elsewhere, for some, AMT is their primary source of income, for others it is supplementary - sometimes to buy something special, sometimes to buy vital everyday things.

Why do they "choose this wage"?

Interestingly *"the current federal minimum wage is $7.25 per hour. If a minimum wage worker is employed full-time (forty hours per week for 52 weeks), that worker would earn $15,080 annually*[7]*"*. The best workers we are aware of from Turker Nation can make an equivalent yearly rate as working 40 hours a week at minimum wage. Again, we must note that we do not know how many hours these Turkers are working each week. Clearly, Turkers on Turker Nation are not getting rich, but are working in rather low paid work. We can imagine that the experiences of Indian Turkers may well be different, including, most obviously, that $15k a year in India would be considered a good wage.

Another feature of posts is that they reveal details of the way AMT work features in Turkers' lives and how they reason about their work. In bubbles' response to lypert she outlines her turking habits – 4-10 (pm) during the week but also during work time. She works in a full-time job relating to the housing market and her boss has allowed her to do AMT work during a period of market depression. For bubbles choosing turking is a product of current job market conditions rather than a preference; *"I would much rather have my salary back and drop turking"*.

From our extensive searches through the forum we see that even those doing AMT work just for extra money (e.g. a particular purchase) do so because they do not have enough money from other sources. What is also clear is that some are earning a good deal less than $15k *per annum* and using AMT as a means of helping to live 'hand-to-mouth':

[6] We have changed Turker aliases to add more anonymity.

[7] http://poverty.ucdavis.edu/faq/what-are-annual-earnings-full-time-minimum-wage-worker

Example 3: Turking Hand-to-Mouth

jane

I am having a hard time. Mentally, spiritually, physically, and especially financially. My roommate has been out of work for almost 2 months, and ran out of money a few weeks ago... I have to come up with $$ if he can't to keep this roof over my own head. And he does now have a job that he is in training for--tho he will not see any money from it for a few MORE weeks. In the meantime, rent is due today, and I don't have all of it. I am going to have to beg the office to take what I do have, and let me pay the rest next paycheck. I could stand that, if that were all there was, but the power and internet need to stay on, or NEITHER ONE OF US will have any income. I paid the power right before cut off last time--that means it can't be long before cut-off notice comes a-knockin again. I know the internet bill is like that too now... I have been beating my head in trying to do more turking, more anything online *[... rest of post omitted...]*

There is a forum area for 'prayers and good vibes,' where people share their problems, looking for support or advice. We see that some Turkers live in difficult circumstances, where AMT work is vital to generating enough income to make ends meet. For this 'digital underclass' who have difficulties accessing the regular labour market (e.g. being housebound, or living a disrupted life), AMT can form a *safety net*. In a modern version of living on the 'breadline' an internet connection has been promoted to the status of rent and vital utilities (like electricity and water), as something crucial to maintain. For jane, it is key for her continued access to the job market. Other discussions on the forum tell us that in the absence of other forms of assistance AMT has some benefits over traditional labour markets. Regular or set hours are not required, money does not have to be spent on transport costs, and judgments are restricted to the work you submit rather than your personal appearance and the way you present yourself.

How do turkers relate to requesters?

By far the largest area of Turker Nation is devoted to the 'Requesters hall of fame/shame'. What is clear is that for Turkers on Turker Nation, the primary concern is to find good Requesters and avoid bad ones. In straightforward cases, such as shown in example 4 and 5, forum participants simply describe their experience and subsequent assessment of particular Requesters. In example 4, you can see that the Turker explodeman provides the basic history (a week of work) and key components (all HITs approved, fair pay) for why they are a 'good requester'. In example 5, we see a contrasting assessment, this Requester is bad because of their 'mass rejection' and this is aggravated by their *"demeaning"* comments. To further substantiate the claim neilrsj notes they have also talked to other Turkers who have had similar experiences.

Example 4: A Good Requester

explodeman

All hits I have done for Project Tatooine[8] in the past week have approved and are fair pay. Good Requester.

[8] Requestor names have also been changed.

Example 5: A Bad Requester

neilrsj

Got a mass rejection from some hits I did for them! Talked to other turkers that I know in real life and the same thing happened to them. There rejection comments are also really demeaning. Definitely avoid!

Comments are peppered with references to pay, rejections, and responsiveness. Turkers' focus on pay and their ratings (key for future earnings) reinforce the view of turking seen as work. Interestingly, interactions with their 'employers' matter. This is shown most clearly in their use of emotional language. Emotional involvement happens even though the major part of the relationship is constituted simply in the process of choosing and submitting HITs, receiving approval (or not), and getting paid (or not). However, by doing HITs and communicating or miscommunicating, Turkers extrapolate opinions on Requesters based on sparse information. Good behavior (example 4) is lauded and shared, bad behavior is criticized and shared (example 5). When Requesters fail to acknowledge the relationship and the emotional and moral involvement Turkers have, there are consequences for both parties:

Example 6: Consequences of a Bad Requester

iambob

I have done a number of his hits. Then one day I get this email:

You received a bonus from Optimal Page Solutions for work related to. The value of your bonus is $0.01 USD yes ONE CENT

The requester included this note:

If you spent half the amount of time looking for a job as you spent scamming your way through Mechanical Turk HITs maybe you'd be able to find a real job...[9]

The next day I get a block message from him. WTF?! He asked for the work to be done and I did it. My hit total is under 2000 so I do not see how I am a scammer in his mind. I have done other similar real estate write ups with no issues.

Turkers are understandably offended when Requesters reject HIT submissions for reasons they do not understand. This not only deprives them of money they believe they have rightly earned, but it has a damaging effect on their approval rating. A high approval rating (90% or above) is a key metric for getting access to better paid and more professional, interesting work. Hasty judgments by Requesters result in unfair treatment of Turkers, and can rob them of pay for completed work and access to future work through potentially no fault of their own [22].

Insult is added to injury when comments are demeaning, as well as being seen as wrong. "*Blocking*" (see example 6) is when Requesters officially bar a Turker from working for them, which is a legitimate tool to have at their disposal if used fairly. However, if Amazon becomes aware of any Turkers getting too many blocks they may well suspend their account. We can easily see where the ire of iambob comes from, particularly when the avenues of redress are limited;

[9] The italicised text is a quote from the requesters email.

Turkers do not have a reciprocal system action to blocking (just avoidance and publicising) and it is complicated for them to prove their innocence. Actions can be taken against bad Requesters but the two sides are not treated in an even-handed manner.

Requester/Turker relationships

These posts so far demonstrate Turker-Requester relationships are more than the sum process of doing HITs and receiving pay. Many posts show that direct, open, polite, and respectful communication is highly valued:

Example 7: An Engaging Requester

modgirl

Great requester, honest, good communicator, cares about what is best for us as much as is best for him. Highly recommended.

You've proven to me that you are a good requester because you've asked here for help –you have my respect.

As with Modgirl, praise in posts for good communication is readily forthcoming and often effusive. This contrasts with the negative responses to adversarial or rude communication (examples 5,6). Modgirl, a Turker Nation moderator, later points the Requester to a thread that discusses good HIT design, and we have seen many examples where Turkers will fruitfully discuss HIT design directly with Requesters. As Kittur et al. [16] suggested it seems that good communication can improve HIT design. However it is not clear what proportion of requesters make use of this possibility or are even aware of it.

Threads on Requesters often contain assessments of their communication practices and their willingness to work with Turkers. They are not simply about unequivocally labeling Requesters good or bad. While some Requester threads are brief and clear – a few comments that endorse the original view – other threads have contrasting views put forward, and still others show how the relationship can evolve:

Example 8: Evolution of a Requester

Foldergirl

Does anyone know if he is a good requester to work for? He has 1 review on TO. I did a $.02 hit. Very quick and easy answer 10 multiple choice questions. Not been paid yet to report on the promptness. It is majority rules but answers are not opinions, I didn't know if that would make a difference or not.

Mezze

I did one hit yesterday, and its still pending. In my opinion the pay is too low for the time required, the pay is also too slow to look past its low payment all of which is assuming you get paid at all because it is majority rules graded. Big thumbs down for me.

jenny492

I just started working on his hits this week. I've probably done several hundred of his .15 hits. They all approved right away, and he got back to me quickly when I had a question. Thumbs up from me

Buffy

Evidently he learned from earlier experience. I have been doing work for him since last month. He is just super nice, normally online while the work is going on and answers any questions right away. The hits are now paying .15 each. My favorite requester.

In this example the Requester-Turker relationship seems to have matured positively, according to the Turkers. At first the posts indicated wariness, explicit in Foldergirl's post. This post also demonstrates the types of research and reasoning undertaken by Turkers in relation to Requesters. First, a poor "*review on Turkopticon*" is referenced. The HIT seemed "*quick and easy*" but there is concern over not being paid yet. There is further worry about the tasks being rewarded on 'majority rules' – which refers to HITs that are only accepted by the Requester if the Turker has responded with the same answer as 'the majority' of those doing the same HIT. "*Majority rules*" is a relatively common way to try to achieve good quality in tasks like tagging. Turkers consider these types of tasks risky, especially when they are subjective (e.g. an aesthetic judgment). However, in this case Foldergirl feels this should not be a problem, as the HITs are about *"answers"* (facts) not *"opinions."* The second post agrees with the first and is even more negative. The last two posts come from later in the thread but turn the initial posts around stating in various ways how things have changed; HITs are approved rapidly and the Requester is very available and responsive. This example demonstrates that Turkers may be more likely to come to negative conclusions when Requesters do not play by the 'rules' of good practice that Turkers orient to such as: designing tasks well; pricing them fairly; providing rapid approval and payment; responding to communication; and being polite. Lack of information seems to increase the *adversarial tension* between Turkers and their Requesters.

These longer threads always demonstrate the trajectory of a relationship between a set of Turkers and a Requester that may be rather complex, involving different topics and changing opinions both at an individual and at a group level. The posts often describe a summary of on-going individual experience and opinions, and there can be groupings around positive and negative views contained in a single thread. The Turkers are using the discussion to work out whether a Requester is good or bad. It is clear relationships with Requesters matter and that they are on-going and open to revision.

Turker workplace ethics

Turkers look for and expect good practice and ethics from Requesters, what about themselves? Often Turkers are thought of as having a significant amount of untrustworthy members amongst their ranks. While it is indeed true that there are some bad apples, the discourse seems to be weighted too negatively. In Turker Nation we see many examples where Turkers complain about being unfairly labeled as bots, spammers, and so forth (see example 6) and we have every reason to believe these people are genuine. The discourse within Turker Nation around cheating generally works as follows: cheating is generally frowned upon; if a Requester pays an insulting amount per HIT it is no shame if they fall prey to cheats or crooks; if a Requester designs their task badly and leaves it open to scams, that is their problem, but we can help them redesign their HITs if they care to consult us. All of this seems pretty fair, particularly as Turkers are also on the other end of nefarious activity – fraudster Requesters, badly designed HITs, unjust blocking and suspensions, and insulting pay and comments. In light of this, interestingly, the following post comes from a Requester blog:

Example 9: Accusation of Cheating[10]
mturkforum.com *(another popular forum)*[11] has become a huge problem for requesters. Every day there are discussions about the intricacies of HITs on this forum. How to work around qualifications, answers to qualifications, and answers to survey questions. I personally tried to inform the people on this forum and the forum admin that they are breaking requester rules along with Amazon Terms of Service, but it fell upon deaf ears. I was even banned for trying to help.

In highlighting this 'huge problem' the author directed the reader towards some examples such as the following:

There's a $1.20 survey by Tanika Sangakkara about culture and brands, the qualifying questions are about whether you are hispanic or not so if you qualify, easy money took me about 8 minutes.

Trying to take an objective look at this we can consider the reaction disproportionate. Upon examination of the post in question, there is no evidence that the poster is encouraging other Turkers to masquerade as Hispanic, it seems more like the commonly found posts which help one another to more efficiently direct their time. However, the Requester, who probably does not understand the requirements and challenges of Turker work (i.e. locating quality tasks is difficult) reads the post as 'cheating'.

Another way to look at Turker ethics would be to consider notions of blame and fault finding – do Turkers always look to blame and find fault with Requesters, or do they find fault with themselves? We have already seen that Turkers will praise and change their mind in relation to Requesters, what of the other side?

Example 10: Accepting Responsibility
lilacstripes
I do these HITs when I want something mindless or am short on time (read: two monster children hanging off me) Only had 1 rejection from them, which was fair (I wasn't paying close enough attention)

Example 10 shows a common phenomenon – if a rejection is fair from their understanding, or in the explanation they are given, Turkers on Turker Nation will generally admit fault. As should be becoming clear, everyday moral standards are not suspended by Turkers in the AMT marketplace. With the post from SeerKRap (example 11 below) we get an erudite example that encapsulates a number of elements we see time and again. First of all, rejections hurt, and it is acknowledged that Turkers will want to vent and flame. However, we see a lot of (often cooperative) activity where Turkers seek to make sense of why things have gone wrong and self-critical work is a part of this. They also look for causes that are technical or with HIT design, and Turkers are more tolerant of genuine mistakes, particularly when the Requester seeks to sort them out:

Example 11: Don't be too Quick to Damn
SeerKRap
... Plus I can see there are occasionally quirks within a Requester's system that cause problems, and in all fairness to the worker, that would piss me off too, if I felt I had put forth a noble effort, only to log into my stat sheet and find it splattered with double digit rejects. It is clearly evident that these "quirks" with the ProductHH system occurred a half a year back or more, and to my experienced knowledge, (and apparently others as well) have been satisfactorily corrected. In light of all of this, I have two comments about my ProductHH experience.
First of all, if someone has a "bad experience", then that problem is corrected, please come in here and let folks know about the positive side of a Requester. Some have, but then obviously, others have not. Also, I would caution on blackballing a Requester based on only one bad experience that involved one of those aforementioned "glitches" in the system.
Secondly, try please to avoid bashing a Requester during one of those heated moments, fresh after seeing the rejection box tallying up, and find out the truth before banging away on your keyboard in utter disgust, scaring the rest of us away from an otherwise potentially good Requester, only because you're miffed at your current situation. *... rest of post omitted ...*

Another interesting feature of this post is the *community orientation*. SeerKRap identifies personally and emotionally with flamers, but suggests that Turkers should try and be fair and objective. Objectivity is not only fair towards Requesters, but Turkers also cite the benefit to the community. If Requesters are unfairly 'blackballed' it is not only damaging to them, but may put off other Turkers from working for decent Requesters. As such, SeerKRap proposes it would be beneficial to inform the community that they have been hastily unfair. This type of perspective, expressed very clearly by SeerKRap, is borne out in multiple cases either through the actions of singular Turker Nation members or through the development of various discussions between Turkers. Notions of fair play and community ethics both within Turker Nation and in relation to AMT's healthy functioning as a marketplace are clearly important issues for them.

What pay do Turkers expect?

In the next 3 examples (12-14) we return to the notion of pay, but this time in terms of hourly rate per HIT. Various posts so far (e.g. in examples 6 and 8) talk directly about pay rate per HIT. In many of the discussions, particularly in relation to Requesters, we see extrapolations being made about how pay per HIT translates into pay per hour. Turkers also make judgments about whether these rates are worth it and in what

[10] http://turkrequesters.blogspot.fr/

[11] Turker Nation is strict compared to other forums. Their rules and large number of 'banned' members attests to this.

circumstances. The posts in example 12 are responses to a blog on a crowdsourcing site that claimed a pay rate of $4-6 was a reasonable rate:

Example 12: Establishing an Hourly Rate

Maryann

$6 an hour is actually better than the majority of requester's pay. I laughed a little when I read that though because that is how much I made at my first job when I was 15 years old working in an amusement park. [... *rest of post omitted* ...]

connorh

As for the suggestion to price $4-$6 an hour? Just perpetuates the 'digital sweatshop' instead of a global mutually beneficial workforce. Pathetic.

Interestingly $6/hour is not such a low rate for AMT in general. There are some HITs that pay a rate closer to $1 per hour. Regardless, in all of the discussions of pay, it is clear that the Turkers on Turker Nation orient to an idea of fair pay – and that that idea of fair pay is largely framed by the current minimum wage in the US ($7.25). Turkers index AMT pay to wages in more conventional realms of work: *"that is how much I made at my first job when I was 15 years old working in an amusement park"* and *"digital sweatshop"*. The comparison here by Turkers is to the rules or norms of the regular job markets of their country. More experienced Turkers who have been earning 'good' wages (~$10/hour and sometimes 'windfall' type jobs that could double or triple that) will not go near jobs that fall below ~$7/hour:

Example 13: An Attractive Wage

HoustonLady

I have been doing a lot of these transcription hits the last few days, and I have no complaints. They approve and pay quickly. The speakers are, for the most part, clear and easy to understand. I don't feel rushed and it takes me less than 2 for the 25-seconds-or-less ones, so the pay is definitely acceptable. $8 an hour is fine for me, sitting in my sweats at home.

HoustonLady makes her calculation of a worthwhile job clear. As shown clearly in the forum, when jobs become available Turkers often do an initial investigation; what does the HIT comprise, how long does it take, how quickly until I become proficient, and how much will I earn? These calculations help them to decide 'is it worth it for me?' Their community discussions with other Turkers also input into these calculations. A second feature is that even at $8/hour (quite high for AMT) they may still trade off the wage level against other factors, *"sitting in my sweats at home"*, that can make it a more attractive wage.

Of course calculations of 'worth it' or assessments of value are *relative to a person's situation* (in a general but also context specific sense) and what their 'goals' might be. In example 14 we see such a contrast. Defectturk's investigations have led her, on multiple counts (poor pay, HIT and interface design) to reject jobs by the requester. Majeski agrees with the assessment of pay but suggests that there are redeeming features that mean he sometimes does these HITs (to get his numbers up, they are easy to do taking little 'work,' and it saves spending time searching):

Example 14: Varying Expectations

defectturk

I would rather pull weeds, do laundry, wash the car, clean the toilet than work for this shit paying requester. Clunky interface, too many tags/ratings/whatever per hit, works out to about a buck an hour. They should be banned from mturk, or even better forced to work on their own shit paying hits.

majeski

I like to do their HITs when I want to get my numbers up. I usually plop on the couch, put TV on in the background and zone out with my laptop. The pay rate kinda sucks (except for the HITs where you found the twitter for a celebrity. I found that those pay pretty good) but I have never been rejected. It's not a bad option when there is nothing going on and you don't want to spend an hour of unpaid searching.

An important thing to realise is that broadly speaking the Turkers on Turker Nation fall into two categories, novice and experienced. Novices have to concentrate on getting their numbers up for both their approval rating (>90%) and their HIT count (1000 or even 5000). Approval rating is particularly important because it is more likely to be volatile when first turking, mostly because Turkers are learning both who the honest Requesters are and how to carry out tasks correctly. Also of note is that aspects of turking like simply searching for jobs can take a considerable amount time. The time spent learning and searching are clear examples of *invisible* work that Turkers must engage in, hence novices are often willing – like majeski – to accept poorer paying jobs as an interim means to the bigger goal of better paying (more interesting) work.

While experienced Turkers are not so concerned with HIT count, as it only increases, approval rating can rise and fall and is something that is of key importance to them. High approval rating is crucial in getting access to a wider selection of and better paying HITs.

This notion of a dual banded pay-rate marketplace is something Turkers are generally aware of and it draws a lot of discussion. Many Turkers (and especially the experienced Turkers on Turker Nation who work to levels of US minimum wage and above) are aware that this is a threat to the functioning of a fair pay market. Connorh is clear in his comment about *"digital sweatshops"* and defectturk suggests the $1/hour requester *"should be banned from mTurk"*.

Turker view of the market

Continuing on the subject of market we can transition into a final topic – Turker views on the AMT labour market as represented by their responses to the media (including academic papers). Based on their responses to various media reports on AMT and Turkers, it is clear that while it is considered important for Requesters and Turkers to adhere to Amazon's terms of service, they do not seem to want the US government to legislate and regulate AMT. This is not because they are happy with everything on AMT, but because the Turkers believe that their power to influence and manage the way the market works comes most fruitfully from their collective individual actions (e.g. in accepting and rejecting requesters on the basis of pay):

Example15: Reaction to AMT in the Media

modgirl

http://economix.blogs.nytimes.com/20...er=rss&emc=rss

Talk about unoriginal - I think one journalist from every news outlet drew a number out of a hat. The first person got to write the article on mTurk, and everyone thereafter put it through mTurk to have it rewritten sentence by sentence and then they got to publish it themselves.

Aren't any journalists focusing on something important? Why are they trying to take our work from us when jobs are so hard to find? If laws pass regulating hourly wages on mTurk, requesters will flee for the hills and we'll be FUCKED. Journalists, LEAVE US ALONE! We don't want your help.

PrettyPois

LOL the problem is that they (those who are writing) have jobs! They have decided to help us who don't. Armed with nothing beyond a surface level understanding of the turk-viornment and a savior complex more than likely brought on by the fact that they have jobs when no one else does, they just MUST fix what isn't broken. Hmm maybe it's jealousy that there are people who can make a living without having to punch a timeclock and drive to work. IDK. Makes me sick.

Turkers worry that 'interference' by journalists and academics – often done with noble intent – will actually just lead to closing AMT. When we consider AMT as an alternative to conventional labour markets and how it functions as a *safety net* for some, we can understand the worry. If AMT is closed down where else will they go to get this money? In addition to this fear their reactions are heightened by the sometimes condescending or demeaning tone of press and academic work. This work can fail to acknowledge that the Turkers are intelligent human beings making informed choices (even if in restricted circumstances) but instead sees them as people to be pitied and looked after. Modgirl and PrettyPois make these points very clearly. A key focus of these threads is often the misunderstanding and misrepresentation of Turkers and AMT work.

Example 16: Reaction to Academia

general65

I don't like it. Another idiot professor who thinks he knows what's best for the private market. This will only mean the government getting involved and regulating the requester's which in turn will end up in less pay for us. Someone please tell this idiot professor to stay in the classroom.

Turkers orient towards the idea that they can regulate the AMT marketplace through their actions. This is true to an extent, but may be problematic as organizing concerted action may be too difficult for these non-networked individuals [4] and it has been argued that Requesters benefit from the lack of cooperation amongst workers [5]. Their ability to influence the market depends upon how much solidarity workers show in their perspectives and actions (which is currently unknown), but could also be facilitated with tools developed to specifically to aid them. Some Turkers refer to Turker Nation as an informal *union* and they often praise collective agency.

Another side to this debate centres around distrust of conventional government. This is clear in example 16, where general65 forwards the view that government gets in the way of better functioning markets – legislation raises costs for employers which threatens market viability and/or workers take the 'hit' in their wage levels. While it is not clear that regulation would improve or ruin AMT for Turkers, a number of them certainly fear it would spell ruination. Differing political and market ideologies, and tensions between individual agency and collective action present complex challenges for designers and legislators, because catering for this diversity in opinion is not an easy task. Furthermore, we are very aware that in writing this paper we tread a fine line; maybe we *should* just be leaving Turkers alone, so we want to make two things clear: (1) we believe our approach means we accurately represent the Turkers of Turker Nation; and (2) our design approach will be to support the needs and practices of Turkers that we have identified.

DISCUSSION: VISIBLE AND INVISIBLE WORK

In an influential article, Star and Strauss discuss notions of 'visible' and 'invisible work' [25]. They provide a means for illuminating and connecting key findings in this article so we weave this analysis into our discussion through looking at turking as a form of invisible work. Star and Strauss analyse how some actors and their activities come to be labeled as *workers*, carrying out *work*. While other activities, ostensibly sharing key work-like features are not. They argue that work cannot be defined in any elemental sense (having a core set of features) but in a relational sense: it depends on who is viewing, defining and understanding the activity. E.g., traditionally the 'work' of home-keeping was not seen *officially* as work, it sat outside the regular labour market and was viewed more like a duty and the expression of love. Star and Strauss use the terms *invisible* and *visible* work to designate whether work gets seen and recognised. Of course, this again depends on perspective: who does the activity and who does the looking, and in some ways this relates to official or dominant 'truths' versus informal or marginal understandings. Finally, along with Star and Stauss we are not recommending *"more visibility in any simple sense."* Visibility implies recognition, official status and potentially better remuneration, but can also lead to surveillance, control and manipulation.

A Richer Understanding of Turkers

We have shown how some of the real people who turk orient to crowdsourcing. We are trying to redress the current balance in research which focuses more on the concerns of Requesters. We also seek to flesh out (and in some cases question) the typically quantitative analysis about users of

AMT. We have tried to make Turkers, their work and relationships with Requesters more visible *in their own terms* and to add to the rather small body of research that aims to make vivid the idea that *"Paid crowd workers are not just an API call"* [23].

In reporting our study of Turker Nation, we have elucidated the views of the posters on the work they do, the relationships with the people they work for, and the market they work in. Mainly, we focused on how they think, act and reason about turking as a job of work. In contrast to various opinions (e.g. 'they do it for fun' [13]) and despite the low wages, AMT, at least for the posters on Turker Nation, is clearly a labour market. This resonates well with Star and Strauss's analysis about labeling: if turking is seen as a leisurely pursuit, it does not have to be paid like 'real' work, which as we have seen is something *these Turkers* strongly reject. Labeling it as fun and leisure may be a misapprehension based on insufficient information. However in the some cases [13] it seems more problematic since they ignored the results from their survey that showed pay as the most important motivation. Are they willfully ignoring the obvious?

Information, Opportunity and Choice

Is then the view that crowdworkers are *"perfectly happy"* to work for extremely low pay (e.g. Tim Worstall's blog), the right one? No it is not. Equating a wage that people will accept with a wage that they are perfectly happy with is a fallacy unless they have sufficient *information, opportunity* and *choice*. However, as we have illustrated, information, opportunity, and choice are all rather limited. We have shown that Turkers search intensively for information not available on AMT as a means of being able to make more informed choices about AMT. Furthermore, whilst for some posters turking in itself really is a choice, for others it is less so. This is usually because opportunity and choice (and good wages) for them are restricted in other job markets, and for some, AMT operates as a *safety net.*

On AMT choice and opportunity are largely determined by experience, ratings, skills and qualifications, not to mention information. New Turkers will be more likely to accept low paid, easy work from credible requesters to increase their HIT count. Also, we see from the many 'war stories' on the forum that Turkers fall foul from taking chances on unknown (or even negatively rated) Requesters and HITs that turn out bad (in pay, honesty etc.). More experienced workers might even sacrifice pay to some extent if the work fits better with their requirements at that time (e.g. easy to do without requiring much concentration; a need to up reputation ratings). Pay value is also relative according to geography and HITs that are low value for US workers (e.g. $4/hour) will be more attractive to Indian Turkers.

Visibility within the Labour Market

Our study shows that that these Turkers orient to AMT as a labour market and illuminates in detail how they *operate as economic actors* – working things out, understanding and making decisions. As with traditional labour markets, the *relationship* between worker and 'work provider' is key. Once we start looking at the workers themselves, the idea that they are just cogs in a wheel is clearly false. Drawing again on Star and Strauss, we can see that turking fulfills a criterion of invisible work: work can be devalued or rendered invisible more easily when workers are seen as 'non-persons.' They go on to elucidate *"under some conditions, the act of working or the product of work is visible to both employer and employee, but the employee is invisible."* Their example looked at how domestic servants could become invisible at times while remaining in plain sight. In turking this invisibility is made easy by distance, anonymity, minimal communication, and electronic exchange. This in turn can lead Requesters and commentators to denigrate or misapprehend the work of Turkers, or at least not to see it as *work* as the Turkers do themselves. Conversely, some of these invisible features are appreciated by the workers – the anonymity, flexibility to work when you want, for whom you want, on what HITs you want are all major incentives for working on AMT. Thus Turkers also orient to *"positive invisibility"* – the freedom from surveillance, control, and intervention in their personal affairs.

Market Ethics

While one might think that anonymity would undermine ethics, genuine Turkers orient strongly to fairness. A desire to do things fairly is a characteristic of the forum; as we demonstrate there is a strong community orientation to judging Requesters fairly. It is important for Requesters to understand this aspect of their workforce and realize that nurturing and supporting relationships should be highly beneficial. Even though workers aim to reach the required standard for HITs using the minimum amount of time and effort, they are typically doing so in a genuine and fair way. The 'economy rule' applies for this relatively low paid piecework; Turkers *optimize* – they will not spend extra time getting things just right – the pay does not merit extras. Of course, Turkers fall foul of poorly designed HITs and HIT QA so it would not be a surprise if they sometimes take advantage of loopholes when weighted in their favour – it is at least an intentional exercise of minimal power – but the major orientation is to fairness.

Since it is the genuine Turkers that genuine Requesters want to attract, relationships matter. Requesters could usefully discuss problem HITs (e.g. when they are getting many apparently spam results) with the community on forums such as Turker Nation. A general principle of anonymity does not mean a desire for no communication and cooperation: Turkers on Turker Nation share information freely and work together to understand problems, Requesters, etc. and desire a degree of visibility and appreciation of their work, capabilities, and perspectives. All sides are likely to benefit when they orient to and invest in the relationships inherent in crowdsourcing, which are rendered less visible in AMT.

The Work to Make the Turking Work

An area of relative invisibility that our study has revealed is the work to make the turking work. This comprises the work Turkers do to find HITs, make good choices, learn and improve their skills and knowledge, and manage their AMT work. The more visible paid work is encapsulated in their HIT responses. This other, more deeply invisible work is unpaid and hidden, but it is necessary to get the best return on their turking. The forum and our examples show that quite a substantial amount of time is spent gathering information through turking and conversing to better optimize the time spent working on HITs. They share information on good and bad Requesters, pay rates per hour, how best to search, how best to monitor for good HITs being posted, what the best set up for your computer, keyboard, screen(s), browser is, how best to learn and progress at certain types of task, and how to manage turking and record keeping. These are all examples of the hidden work required to make turking work. Drawing again on Star and Strauss we can see that this work embodies classic features of invisible work – little of this effort has been rendered visible (except to the Turkers themselves) and as such, and because of the way the market works, it carries no direct monetary compensation. Instead, its value rests fully in the way it enables Turkers to operate more effectively.

Market Governance?

Once we face the fact that crowdsourcing is just a labour market like any other, questions of regulation come to the fore and indeed some legal cases are already underway that attempt to apply traditional labour laws to this market[12]. However, a number of Turkers on Turker Nation are unwelcoming about regulation from outside. Rather they believe that they can regulate the marketplace themselves through concerted cooperative action by choosing what jobs to do and what pay levels to accept. They do not want someone else to make decisions on their behalf. Again this resonates with the tension between invisibility and visibility and *"how the application affects relations of power and the nature of work"*. In this case AMT as a marketplace and technology is the 'application' and any subsequent technical and legal adjustments could clearly affect the 'nature of work' and 'power relations'.

Turkers are keen to retain their collective ability to make choices over becoming more visible and are concerned that visibility, monitoring and control would make things worse for them, or even close the market. However, it must be noted that concerted action, and making informed choices on jobs, is difficult due to the paucity of information and technical support for concerted action. For both work providers and workers to be able to make good decisions in the market, they would need very good information in order to understand the other people operating in the market such that they could price their requests or labour knowingly and truly comparatively. This is not the case, as the AMT platform is designed to provide little information on Requesters. This gives rise to suspicion, as well as the highly motivated search for better information, e.g. through forums, blogs etc. The key purpose of Turker Nation is the search for and sharing of information, most pointedly about Requesters but also about other Turkers.

[12] http://work3o.wordpress.com/2012/12/14/crowdflower/

Design Directions

What then does all this say for design? We believe this study has *ethical* and *practical* implications. Ethically we believe Turkers have sometimes been misunderstood and even denigrated. Practically, better understanding and engagement with Turkers can help design better HITs, and technologies to support Turkers and their relationships with requesters. The route taken by Irani and Silberman seems a good place to start; by helping Turkers to make better decisions within the market. Tools such as Turkopticon are first steps in this direction, but more can be done. A second complimentary approach is to design tools to support cooperation amongst Turkers so they can work together to exert more control on the functioning of the market.

Designers could also be thinking about how to create tools that make the functioning of the market more transparent, and that give better insight into communication patterns and relationships between Requesters and Turkers. Another important avenue of design is tools to help reduce and manage all the invisible background 'work to make Turking work' – since that is work for which Turkers are not paid but takes up a considerable amount of time.

CONCLUSION

We have rendered some of the invisible work of Turkers visible through an ethnomethdological study of Turker Nation forum showing how Turkers reason about and carry out their work activities. Some key findings are that they treat their activities as work where pay is the most important factor and that they understand and orient to AMT as a labour marketplace. Their biggest concerns are having enough information to make good decisions on selecting jobs, having good relationships with requesters, and how to act collectively. We find that the key function of Turker Nation is to help reduce the information deficit and promote better collective action. Based on this we suggest that technology directions that should support these needs. Finally, we draw on Star and Strauss's analysis and arguments about invisible and visible work to deepen our analysis and consider ethical issues relating to making Turkers and AMT work more visible, and what the implications of this might be.

ACKNOWLEDGMENTS

Our sincere appreciation goes out to all the Turkers whose thoughts and words are used in this article.

REFERENCES

1. Adda, G., Sagot, B., Fort, K., Mariani, J. Crowdsourcing for Language Resource Development. *5th Language and Technology Conference*. (2011).

2. Antin, J. and Shaw, A. Social desirability bias and self-reports of motivation: A study of amazon mechanical turk in the us and india. *In Proc. of CHI '12*, ACM press (2012), 2925–2934.
3. Bederson, B. B. and Quinn, A. J. Web workers unite! addressing challenges of online laborers. *In Proc. CHI EA '11*. ACM (2011), 97-106.
4. Felstiner, A. *Working the crowd: employment and labor law in the crowdsourcing industry*. http://papers.ssrn.com/sol3/papers.cfm?abstract_id=1593853 (2011).
5. Felstiner, A. *The weakness of crowds. Limn, Crowds and Clouds (2)*, 2013. http://limn.it/the-weakness-of-crowds/.
6. Fort, K., Adda, G. and Bretonnel Cohen, K. Amazon Mechanical Turk: Gold Mine or Coal Mine? *Computational Linguisitcs, 37, 2* (2011).
7. Garfinkel, H., *Studies in ethnomethodology*. Englewood Cliffs, N.J.: Prentice-Hall, (1967)
8. Howe, J. *Crowdsourcing: A definition*. (2006). http://crowdsourcing.typepad.com/cs/2006/06/crowdsourcing_a.html
9. Hughes, J., Randall, D., Shapiro, D. Faltering from Ethnography to Design. *In Proc of CSCW'92*. ACM (1992), 115-122
10. Ipeirotis, P. *Analyzing the Amazon Mechanical Turk marketplace*. CeDER Working Papers No. CeDER-10-04. (2010) http://hdl.handle.net/2451/29801
11. Ipeirotis, P. *Demographics of Mechanical Turk*. CeDER Working Papers No. CeDER-10-01. (2010) http://hdl.handle.net/2451/29585
12. Irani, L. and Silberman, M. S. Turkopticon: Interrupting Worker Invisibility in Amazon Mechanical Turk. *In Proc. CHI 2013*, ACM Press (2013).
13. Kaufmann, N., Schulze, T., and Veit, D. More than fun and money. Worker Motivation in Crowdsourcing – A Study on Mechanical Turk. *In Proc. Of AMCIS* (2011).
14. Kittur,A., Chi, E. H., and Suh, B. Crowdsourcing user studies with Mechanical Turk. *In Proc. of the CHI '08*. ACM, (2008), 453-456
15. Kittur, A., Smus, B. and Kraut, R. E. *CrowdForge: Crowdsourcing Complex Work*. Technical Report CMU-HCII-11-100, http://crowdresearch.org/blog/wp-content/.../CrowdForge_UIST_2011.pdf
16. Kittur, A., Nickerson, J. V., Bernstein, M., Gerber, E., Shaw, A., Zimmerman, J., Lease, M. and Horton, J. The future of crowd work. *In Proc. of CSCW '13*, ACM press, 1301–1318.
17. Kochhar, S., Mazzochi, S., Paritosh, P. The Anatomy of a Large-Scale Human Computation Engine. HCOMP'10. ACM press (2010). 10-17
18. Little, G., Chilton, L. B., Goldman, M. and Miller, R. C. Turkit: tools for iterative tasks on mechanical turk. *In KDD-HCOMP '09*, 2009.
19. O'Neill, J. & Martin, D. Text Chat In Action. *In Proc. Group '03,* ACM Press (2003), 40-49.
20. Ross, J., Irani, L., Silberman, M. S., Zaldivar, A., and Tomlinson, B. Who are the crowdworkers?: shifting demographics in mechanical turk. *In Proc. of CHI EA '10, ACM* (2010), 2863–2872.
21. Sacks, H. *Lectures on conversation*. (2 vols). Gail Jefferson (Ed.). Oxford: Basil Blackwell, (1992).
22. Silberman, M. S. What's fair? Rational action and its residuals in an electronic market. *Unpublished manuscript*, (2010). http://www.scribd.com/doc/86592724/Whats-Fair
23. Silberman, M. S., Irani, L., and Ross, J. Ethics and Tactics of Professional Crowdwork. *ACM XRDS, 17, 2* (2010)
24. Silberman, M., Ross, J., Irani, L. and Tomlinson, B. Sellers' problems in human computation markets. *In Proc. of HCOMP '10*. ACM Press (2010), 18-21.
25. Star, S.L. and Strauss, A.L. *Layers of silence, arenas of voice: The ecology of visible and invisible work'. CSCW Journal, 8*: 9-30. (1998)
26. Suchman, L. *Plans and situated action: the problem of human-machine communication*. Cambridge: Cambridge University Press (1987)
27. Watson, R., *Analysing Practical and Professional Texts; A Naturalistic Approach*. Farnham, Surrey: Ashgate, (2009).
28. Worstall, T. *On The New York Times Stupidity over Amazon's Mechanical Turk*. Forbes. http://www.forbes.com/sites/timworstall/2013/03/19/on-the-new-york-times-stupidity-over-amazons-mechanical-turk/

The Motivations and Experiences of the On-Demand Mobile Workforce

Rannie Teodoro, Pinar Ozturk*, Mor Naaman†, Winter Mason*, and Janne Lindqvist‡
Rutgers School of Communication & Information, 4 Huntington Street, New Brunswick, NJ 08901
*Stevens Institute of Technology, 1 Castle Point Terrace, Hoboken, NJ 07030
†JTCII, Cornell Tech, 111 8th Avenue, New York, NY 10011
‡Rutgers Department of ECE and WINLAB, 671 U.S. Route 1 South, North Brunswick, NJ 08902
rteodoro@rutgers.edu, pozturk@stevens.edu, mor.naaman@cornell.edu,
m@winteram.com, janne@winlab.rutgers.edu

ABSTRACT
On-demand mobile workforce applications match physical world tasks and willing workers. These systems offer to help conserve resources, streamline courses of action, and increase market efficiency for micro- and mid-level tasks, from verifying the existence of a pothole to walking a neighbor's dog. This study reports on the motivations and experiences of individuals who regularly complete physical world tasks posted in on-demand mobile workforce marketplaces. Data collection included semi-structured interviews with members (workers) of two different services. The analysis revealed the main drivers for participating in an on-demand mobile workforce, including desires for monetary compensation and control over schedules and task selection. We also reveal main reasons for task selection, which involve situational factors, convenient physical locations, and task requester profile information. Finally, we discuss the key characteristics of the most worthwhile tasks and offer implications for novel crowdsourcing systems for physical world tasks.

Author Keywords
Mobile workforce, physical world tasks, crowdsourcing services

ACM Classification Keywords
H.5.3 [Group and Organization Interfaces] Computer-supported cooperative work

General Terms
Human factors

INTRODUCTION
An emerging class of services connects workers to a variety of physical and virtual world tasks. These on-demand workforce services are often based on a simple model, where an individual or an organization ("requesters") creates tasks, which are offered to one or more participants in the system who can then accept the task based on its description and payoff. We refer to the workers who complete *physical* world tasks as the "on-demand mobile workforce," as they can choose when and where to work beyond the constraints of traditional office workspaces. We refer to workers who complete *virtual* tasks as the "on-demand virtual workforce," as their work occurs exclusively online.

On-demand mobile workforce services fall within the category of "crowdsourcing" [22], which connects large groups of workers with distributed micro-tasks that combine into a greater result. Crowdsourcing has received significant attention in the research community. Several methodological papers [35, 36] and reviews [32, 39] have covered crowdsourcing and human computation systems as a topic of research and as tools for research. In particular, Amazon's Mechanical Turk (AMT) [3] is potentially the most studied virtual crowdsourcing platform. While some services like Fancy Hands [12] allow more elaborate virtual tasks, at AMT most tasks do not require special skills and the market dynamics usually follow a model of very small payments for a large number of very simple tasks. Many studies describe how AMT can be used for automating online tasks such as object and image labeling and user studies [10, 20, 24, 27, 29, 33, 45]. The motivations of workers on AMT have also been studied extensively [23, 27, 37, 43], as we discuss later.

Increasingly, on-demand workforce services are leveraging the power of mobile workers operating in the *physical* world, often tied to specific locations. For example, services like TaskRabbit [49], Gigwalk [16], Field Agent [14], and Zaarly [54] facilitate the completion of physical world tasks that are location-dependent such as Ikea furniture assemblies, deliveries, basic house chores, price checks, and store audits.

Unlike their virtual counterparts, mobile workforce services depend on both virtual and location-dependent features. On-demand mobile workforce services must therefore carefully consider the productivity and sustained participation tradeoffs inherent in a distributed group of workers that operate online and offline. The complexity of the tasks

CSCW'14, February 15 – 19, 2014, Baltimore, MD, USA.

ACM 978-1-4503-2540-0/14/02...$15.00.
http://dx.doi.org/10.1145/2531602.2531680

offered through different mobile workforce services varies. Services like EasyShift [11] and Gigwalk mostly support low complexity tasks that require little time and cognitive effort to complete, comparable to AMT. Other services like TaskRabbit and Zaarly cater to more complex, multi-step tasks that require more cognitive effort.

Only recently, studies have begun to uncover the characteristics that make mobile workforce markets unique. For instance, Musthag and Ganesan [38] found that a small fraction of mobile workforce platform users—who they refer to as "super-agents"—perform more than 80% of the tasks and receive more than 80% of the total earnings. The authors show that these users were more willing to travel farther distances, incur larger travel costs and spend more time searching for jobs to complete. However, the authors do not provide insight into the motivations or considerations users make when initially joining a service, and electing to complete tasks. Understanding these user motivations and considerations is important for the development and improvement of on-demand mobile workforce services and tools [28].

In our study, we address this gap and provide an in-depth examination of the socio-technical factors contributing to worker participation in an on-demand mobile workforce service, including the motivations for signing up, and for accepting and completing physical world tasks. Improved understanding of these factors can encourage and sustain active participation in mobile workforce services.

The key research questions addressed in this study are thus:

1. What are the main motivations for *joining* on-demand mobile workforce services? (RQ1)
2. What are the main motivations for *selecting* certain tasks over other tasks? (RQ2)
3. What task characteristics did workers find more or less enjoyable and worthwhile? (RQ3)

To answer these research questions, we conducted semi-structured interviews with twelve on-demand mobile workforce workers from two distinct services: TaskRabbit and Gigwalk. Both services facilitate physical world tasks, but differ in many ways (as detailed below)—most prominently in terms of typical task complexity, worker application process, and worker profiles.

BACKGROUND AND RELATED WORK

In this section, we clarify the scope of the study and then review the previous work on on-demand workforce services, crowdsourcing physical world tasks, and the different motivations for completing tasks and following through with certain behaviors. We also describe the theoretical framework related to the study.

On-Demand Workforce Services

To outline the scope of this study, we offer an on-demand workforce services categorization based on the nature of tasks within the different services. We consider two dimensions: (1) the location of the tasks and (2) the complexity of the tasks.

The first dimension considers the extent to which tasks in the service occur within virtual or physical spaces. Virtual tasks occur within computer-based environments and often allow users to work from anywhere with an Internet or phone connection. Physical tasks occur outside of computer-mediated settings and in actual neighborhoods and offline locations. Still, the nature of whether requested tasks are completed in virtual or physical spaces varies depending on the service and requester expectations.

The second dimension reflects the complexity of tasks. Low complexity tasks require less time and cognitive effort to complete, whereas high complexity tasks require more time and higher levels of skill or expertise from users. For example, pet sitting or researching hotel costs require more time and steps than snapping a photo of a product while at the store. In this way, high complexity tasks often require individuals to use their own discretion when completing a task, compared to low complexity tasks that require little to no personal judgment for task completion.

Figure 1 graphically depicts the categorization and includes the dimensions of task location and task complexity on two intersecting continuums. Based on marketplace reviews, user testimonies, and our informal observations of the services, we placed four main on-demand workforce services to exemplify the quadrants of the categorization: Fancy Hands, Mechanical Turk, TaskRabbit, and Gigwalk. We note that services often offer a mix of tasks, where the general nature of tasks on a service is related to the service's affordances.

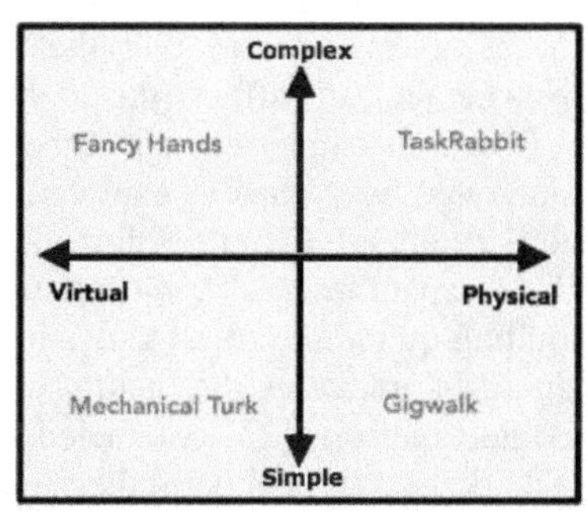

Figure 1. Categorization of on-demand workforce services.

Representing the top left quadrant, Fancy Hands is an on-demand workforce service of virtual assistants who fulfill requests from virtual locations and are capable of fulfilling recommendation-based complex tasks, which require discretionary practices, judgment calls, and needs assessment (more effort). Mechanical Turk, in the bottom left quadrant, also puts requesters in touch with virtual workers, but mostly serves as a micro-task market in which a large number of users complete minor tasks for small monetary or non-monetary compensation [27].

TaskRabbit and Gigwalk represent the top right and bottom right quadrants, respectively. These two quadrants represent the physical world tasks that require varying degrees of effort expenditure. Common requests posted in TaskRabbit include deliveries, furniture assemblies, and house chores. For Gigwalk, common tasks or "gigs" include store audits, price checks, customer interviews, and field photography. These gigs are often done while workers are already out and near the task locations. We again note that despite the general categorization, occasionally virtual tasks are offered in both these services, and tasks in both can vary in complexity. We focus on TaskRabbit and Gigwalk in this study.

Motivations and Crowdsourcing Systems

There is an abundant and long line of research on incentives and motivations, from psychological studies [4, 8, 53] to economic theory [13, 15, 17] to business and management research [18, 31]. At a high level, this body of research shows that people will work harder for the goals that they are rewarded for, but also provides clear evidence that a truly unified vision of the interactions between incentives and motivations in human behavior is unsettled.

Extrinsic motivations and intrinsic motivations have different implications for crowdsourcing systems. AMT, for instance, was originally designed for crowdsourcing human computation tasks, but has been since been appropriated for behavioral [37] and user studies [27]. Downs et al. [10] found that younger men (under 25) were more likely to try to game the system for monetary rewards while men over 30 and women of any age were more likely to take tasks seriously.

In AMT, Mason et al. [37] found that Turkers typically did more work when paid more but did not deliver better results. Mason et al. also found that the design of the compensation scheme can affect the quality of work considerably. Research suggests that when people are intrinsically motivated by desires to explore and learn, they will find the activity inherently interesting and pleasant, and will extend their capacities [8, 9, 44]. Kittur et al. [27] found that including quantitative and verifiable questions to experiments on AMT increases the quality of crowd work. Ross et al. [43] and Ipeirotis [23] conducted surveys of the motivations of Turkers, and in general they found that while money was cited as a reason for doing work—only 10-12% said money was irrelevant to their work—enjoyment of the task was necessary as well. This was captured by the fact that 69% of U.S. respondents in Ipeirotis' study indicated that "Mechanical Turk is a fruitful way to spend free time and get some cash." Choice, acknowledgement of feelings, and opportunities for self-direction work better to increase motivations.

Taken together, there is a need to examine what extrinsic and intrinsic factors contribute to the quality of work conducted especially with respect to physical world tasks.

The Theory of Planned Behavior

In this work, we mostly build on the theory of planned behavior (TPB) [1] to contextualize and analyze our findings. TPB considers the less active or visible factors that influence a person's intention to enact a certain behavior. Because members of the mobile workforce actively engage in the search for, implementation of, and completion of physical world tasks, TPB helps explicate a person's intention to engage in a specific behavior at a specific time and place.

Specifically, TPB considers the following constructs: (1) *attitude toward the behavior* (i.e., belief that the behavior leads to certain outcomes, evaluation of the outcome), (2) the *subjective norms surrounding the behavior* (i.e., belief referent or significant others think the behavior is preferred), and (3) *perceived behavioral control* (i.e., beliefs about control, likelihood of occurrence). These three factors ultimately predict and explain (4) *behavioral intention* and (5) *behavior*. Behavioral intention refers to the motivational factors or extent to which people try to perform a behavior while behavior refers to the actual actions an individual performs.

When applied to this study, TPB acknowledges that people's evaluations of the task and expected outcomes can and will drive behavior. As such, the heavy and sustained uses of mobile workforce services likely occur among individuals who have both the motivation (intention) and ability (behavioral control) to complete the requested tasks. The theory also suggests that users will likely complete tasks in line with normative beliefs or social acceptance regarding the task.

METHODS

This study seeks to understand mobile workforce members' motivations and considerations for completing physical world tasks. To uncover these motivations, we conducted twelve semi-structured interviews with experienced and active users of two mobile workforce services. In this section, we describe the sites for recruitment, the characteristics of participants interviewed, and the interview approach. We then discuss the themes that emerged from a qualitative analysis approach of interview transcripts.

Selecting the Recruitment Sites

With our categorization in mind, this study focuses on services that offer predominantly physical world tasks, and span the range between simple and complex task offerings. We selected TaskRabbit and Gigwalk as the main study sites based on popularity, diversity of physical world tasks, and geographic coverage. In the next sections, we briefly describe these on-demand mobile workforce services, their features and nuances, and the process of becoming a member.

TaskRabbit

TaskRabbit, located in the upper right corner in Figure 1, typically involves complex physical world tasks that require a substantial amount of effort, such as deliveries, pet sitting, and household chores. In TaskRabbit, individuals known as "TaskPosters" can simply signup and list errands or jobs they need completed. Then, prescreened helpers or "TaskRabbits" can bid on, negotiate, or accept the compensation for the task made by the TaskPoster. TaskRabbit describes their on-demand mobile workforce service as "neighbors helping neighbors" and a form of "service networking." As of May 2013, TaskRabbit claims to have over 4,000 Rabbits across nine different cities [48]. In order to become a TaskRabbit and before even bidding on tasks, applicants must go through a video interview, criminal background check, and pass a quiz about the TaskRabbit marketplace. Once accepted as a TaskRabbit, workers maintain profiles about themselves, which include their photos, bios, and any TaskPoster reviews about their previously completed tasks.

Gigwalk

Gigwalk, located in the bottom right corner of the categorization, usually involves micro (simple) tasks conducted in the physical world such as store audits, product reviews, and responses to client interviews. With a self-reported presence in 6,500 cities and four countries, Gigwalk boasts that people can turn their smartphone "into a second paycheck" and that businesses can leverage their very own "on-demand smartphone army" called "Gigwalkers." Gigwalkers' profiles include a small photo, first name, last name initial, and hometown. Gigwalkers must use a smartphone mobile phone app with GPS technology to find nearby "gigs" or posted tasks. The GPS location also helps clients verify where a gig was completed. Unlike TaskRabbit, any person can sign up and become a client or Gigwalker straight from his or her smartphone and post or complete gigs.

To summarize, TaskRabbit and Gigwalk facilitate physical world tasks but differ in terms of typical task complexity, task assignment and worker application process, and worker profiles. TaskRabbit tasks are usually personal requests from nearby individuals while Gigwalk gigs are usually generic requests from companies who need product or display checks among several distributed locations.

Recruitment Process

We recruited twelve participants organically, by posting a task or job in the respective systems for users to either bid on or accept. The task simply asked workers to participate in a phone interview with a researcher. Sample text from the task/recruitment notices read, "Are you at least 18 years of age? Do you use [mobile workforce service name]? Do you complete tasks of jobs that people post on mobile phone apps? If you answered YES to these questions, you may be eligible to participate in a phone interview." All participants, six from TaskRabbit (TR1-6) and six from Gigwalk (GW1-6), met a set of predetermined criteria. Participants are at least 18 years old, English-speaking, and familiar with and currently using an on-demand workforce mobile phone application or service. Table 1 depicts the characteristics of the participants interviewed.

	Sex	Age	App Name	Membership Length (Approx.)	Occupation
TR1	M	46	TaskRabbit	4 months	Electrician
TR2	F	25	TaskRabbit	9 months	Freelance graphic designer
TR3	F	21	TaskRabbit	1 year	Photographer, Personal assistant
TR4	F	27	TaskRabbit	1 year	Career advisor, graduate student
TR5	F	23	TaskRabbit	3 weeks	Micro-entrepreneur
TR6	F	27	TaskRabbit	1.5 years	Student
GW1	M	27	Gigwalk	1 year	Graduate student
GW2	F	26	Gigwalk	3 weeks	Unemployed, Special ed teacher
GW3	M	29	Gigwalk	9 months	Marketing professional
GW4	M	55	Gigwalk	5 months	Distribution manager
GW5	F	35+	Gigwalk	7 months	Management professional, Unemployed
GW6	F	36	Gigwalk	1 year	Homemaker

Table 1. Characteristics of interview participants.

Participants varied in terms of how they learned of the service. Seven of our participants found out about the service through friends or family (TR1, TR2, TR4, TR5, TR6, GW1, GW6). Meanwhile, others learned about the services through other companies (TR3), the app store (GW2, GW3), or online articles (GW4, GW5).

Overall, we interviewed eight women (75%) and four men (25%), ranging from 21 to 55 years old, who live in the United States. Their length of membership in the mobile workforce service ranged from novice (three weeks) to experienced (1.5 years). Subjects received $20 for participating in the interview, paid directly through the respective service.

Interviews

One of the authors conducted the semi-structured phone interviews with the mobile workforce service users. The interview questions inquired about workers' motivations for joining the on-demand mobile workforce services, job selection decision-making, and the factors contributing to the acceptance or denial of a task. All interviews were audio recorded and transcribed.

After completing the interviews, we reviewed the transcripts, annotated them for patterns, and extracted key themes. With this method, we closely examined, qualitatively assessed, and highlighted the critical features of the interview responses. This method is unconstrained and unbiased by pre-existing categories and uncovers the candid attitudes and behaviors of the mobile workforce members.

FINDINGS

Several themes emerged from the interview transcripts pertaining to participants' motivations and appealing task characteristics. We discuss first the main motivations for joining the on-demand mobile workforce, then the reasons behind task selection, and finally the characteristics that make jobs enjoyable and worthwhile.

Motivations for Joining On-Demand Mobile Workforce

The main motivations for joining mobile workforce services include, perhaps expectedly, monetary compensation, combined with personal control over one's schedule and actions.

Monetary Compensation: 'I do it for the money.'

Participants overwhelmingly listed monetary compensation as their main motivation for joining the on-demand mobile workforce services in the first place. Despite their different financial situations, many workers completed tasks for the purpose of supplemental income (Quotes 1, 2, 3).

"I am a stay-at-home mom so I would like to be able to make money but I cannot go out and get a job where I have to be some place at a specific time. I need to be flexible so I can take care of my family." - Quote 1 (GW6)

"I like having supplemental income... good experiences and having a little bit extra money." - Quote 2 (TR3)

"My main motivation is the compensation. I actually had surgery and wasn't released to go back to work... I ended up looking for something to keep me a little busy and also bring a little bit of money." - Quote 3 (TR4)

Some participants maintained full-time jobs (e.g., TR2, TR3, GW3, GW4) while others chose to complete tasks as they waited for full-time work (GW2, GW5), had free time outside of work and school (TR4, GW1), and/or looked for something to do (TR6, GW2, GW6). Others, more specifically in TaskRabbit, used the on-demand mobile workforce services as a way to build their clientele (TR1, TR5). The financial motivations for the on-demand mobile workforce parallel those of workers in the virtual crowdsourcing platforms like AMT [24], though it is clearly not the workers' only motivation.

Regarding the financial incentives, several suggestions for how to improve the compensation process emerged as subthemes from the interviews. While some workers appreciated not having to coordinate payments awkwardly in-person or worry about never getting paid (Quotes 4, 5), most workers expressed a desire for more payment regulation.

"I like not having to handle the money. So when I'm done with the task, it's not like they hand me [the money], 'Ok, here is the $20.' It's digital... I just mark it as complete and it goes through [TaskRabbit]." - Quote 4 (TR6)

"You have PayPal. If, let's say you completed a job, and somebody is not paying you I think it automatically pays you...it's regulated is what I mean." - Quote 5 (TR2)

According to interview responses, task requesters are very much "in the driver's seat" in terms of payment. They can view workers' task completion history, leave a positive or negative comment on a completed task, endorse or tarnish their worker reputation, and ultimately decide to compensate the workers or not. Requesters can delay (Quotes 6, 7) and even deny payments (Quote 8), offering very little support or payment protection for workers.

"One [disadvantage] comes to mind is the companies are in control of their payouts. Some companies will pay you right away, which is safe. Other companies don't." - Quote 6 (GW4)

"I would change the amount of time that a TaskPoster has to close a task. 72 hours is three days, I would make it into 48 hours." - Quote 7 (TR5)

"You go to places and you can't find what they're looking for. Then you don't get paid for that. It was all for naught." - Quote 8 (GW2)

Personal Control

All participants mentioned a desire for personal control as a main motivation for joining a mobile workforce service. Participants valued the ability to set their own schedules from any location, select what jobs they wanted to do, and negotiate rates based on the difficulty of the task and previous experiences (Quotes 9, 10). GW1, for instance, integrated gigs with her already planned shopping errands (Quote 11). GW2 and GW3 specifically cited not having a boss or a required time and place in which to report as a main motivation for completing these physical world tasks for compensation.

"If I'm out somewhere, if I have free time, I can look through the app and see what's available for tomorrow. I can do that anywhere." - Quote 9 (TR3)

"I can accept the job if I want to or I can just ignore it and not do it so I have a lot of control. So if the job is interesting, if it's local, if it looks like 'oh, I can do this,' then I can just accept it." - Quote 10 (GW6)

"I have told [my friends], sometimes you have a gig in Wal-Mart or in other stores that you go to all the time... spend few minutes shopping and you can get $7." - Quote 11 (GW1)

Additionally, the on-demand mobile workforce services allowed participants to personally control when and where they wanted to access the service. Overall, then, workers joined the mobile workforce to obtain income by completing jobs under one's personal control and convenience.

Motivations for Selecting Mobile Workforce Tasks

The desires for freedom and flexibility afforded by on-demand mobile workforce services allowed for the occurrence of some unique task selection practices. According to the interviews, the main motivations driving task selection over other tasks involved cost-benefit analysis regarding (1) situational factors, (2) physical location, and (3) the worker's evaluation of the task requester profile.

Situational Factors

Participants listed several situational or external reasons for selecting certain tasks over other tasks. Situational factors include the availability of time a person has (Quote 12), the timing of the task (i.e., completion due date, Quote 13), and even weather conditions (Quote 14). These situational factors are not directly related to the task itself, but influences whether or not a task is selected.

"Weekends, I'm off. I have more time. When I go on vacation and I travel a lot, I don't deal with it. I don't even like checking it." - Quote 12 (GW2)

"Saturdays are the only days I can spend with my husband. Those are the gigs that give you a lot of money, like between \$20-\$35 but those I do not take because those are times I spend time with my husband." - Quote 13 (GW1)

"I got drenched in the rain doing a task couple days ago. So I try to watch the weather to make sure I can go out and get something done. Otherwise I don't go out, and do a virtual task." - Quote 14 (TR5)

Convenient Physical Locations

Confirming existing literature [2], all participants cited the preference for completing nearby tasks or gigs. Participants consider the costs, benefits, and conditions associated with completing the physical world tasks, such as time spent traveling, gas, familiar/safe locations, and potential payout (Quotes 15, 16, 17).

"I look for the ones that are towards me, more accessible, either virtual job or job on a location. I want [the tasks] close by in my area. I like work that I can find work is not far away because I live in Los Angeles." - Quote 15 (TR3)

"I do not want to drive that far. If a gig is 10 miles away from my house, that's a lot of time and gas that I put into a \$5 to \$7 gig." - Quote 16 (GW1)

"If it's something that's close [I'll select the gig]. Not a lot of money for drive time and I don't have to worry about distance. It's my local area." - Quote 17 (GW4)

Evaluating the Task Requester

Generally, participants expressed preferences for tasks posted by requesters who have pictures and information verifying their identity on their profiles. TaskRabbit participants, who frequently complete tasks that require face-to-face contact with TaskPosters, stated that viewing a profile and immediately exchanging personal contact information helped alleviate their safety concerns about meeting TaskPosters in-person for the first time (Quote 18).

"I always favorably take [tasks] with the picture. Especially if I'm going to someone's house... Oh, I already know what you look like and you're waiting for me outside. I know who you are."- Quote 18 (TR3)

In line with online trust literature [47, 48], participants perceived requester profiles with pictures and other online memberships as more credible and trustworthy. TR5 compared TaskRabbit to Craigslist, a longstanding website for local classifieds and other forums. She described TaskRabbit as more "verifiable" versus the "kind of sketchy" proceedings in Craigslist (Quote 19).

"I like TaskRabbit because, most of the time, TaskPosters have their picture of their face so you can actually get an idea of who you are going to see...versus Craigslist, it's a long anonymous number that you're emailing." - Quote 19 (TR5).

If the requester's profile did not reveal identifying information, many of the participants admitted to completing small "investigations" of the TaskPosters or clients. TR4, for example, accepted a task to care for a woman's dog for five days while she was at a conference. Before arriving at the woman's home, TR4 searched for the TaskPoster on LinkedIn, a social networking site for professional networks, to verify her occupation and employment history (Quote 20). TR5 described similar practices: she frequently obtained TaskPosters' email addresses and used social media sites to find out some more information about the TaskPoster (Quote 21). GW5 also looked for additional information outside of the mobile workforce service based on information posted in the gig description. He eventually learned to question the vagueness of certain gigs and practice more discretion about selecting those gigs (Quote 22). Even GW6, who dedicated little research into verifying the identity of the gig client, said she certainly questioned the identity and legitimacy of the client and factored this into her ultimate decision to accept or deny a gig (Quote 23).

"I definitely looked her up on LinkedIn, because you know, she says, 'I'm going out of town for a conference' and I looked up her bio and she works for a company..." - Quote 20 (TR4)

"I'll email anonymous, I'll get their email back, search for anything I can find like Facebook." - Quote 21 (TR5)

"I learned to [investigate the clients]. Before I didn't care, particularly because [gig description] will just say 'the company'... but sometimes, who are these other guys?" - Quote 22 (GW5)

"There was a job that was posted anonymous and my husband said don't do that job because...I don't know if that's an actual business or an individual and we don't know if they're actually going to pay." - Quote 23 (GW6)

Workers discovered creative ways to learn about requesters. For example, TR4 evaluated task descriptions before placing bids on tasks (Quote 24). Specifically, she used the TaskPoster's attention to detail and assessment of a realistic deadline to gauge whether or not they could have a good professional relationship. TR2 and TR5 also factored task descriptions into their final decisions for task selection (Quotes 25, 26).

"The TaskPoster definitely plays a big role so I'll pretty much bid if only they have clearly written the description of

what they want and they seem to understand what is involved." - Quote 24 (TR4)

"There's this feeling of legitimacy versus something like Craigslist." - Quote 25 (TR2)

"Look at the way they write... For example, I need cleaning. It can be a cleaning of anything. I need organizing. It could be organizing 500 boxes. I'd like to have people that have details." - Quote 26 (TR5)

Workers wanted to learn about or implement a verification process for task requesters. More than half of the participants knew very little about requester verification (Quote 27) or did not know that requesters simply had to sign up with an email address, provide basic contact information, and a credit card in order to post a job. For the most part, participants trusted task requesters and assumed they went through some form of background check or verification process (Quote 28).

"I don't know what it takes to be a TaskPoster." - Quote 27 (TR1)

"I trust people a lot and not have a reason to not trust people on TaskRabbit yet. That (people not being who they say they are) hasn't crossed my mind." - Quote 28 (TR3)

Considerations for Task Characteristics

In addition to the motivations for task selection described above, task experiences might also affect workers' opinions on other tasks and influence their likelihood of choosing a similar task in the future. To investigate RQ3 (What task characteristics did workers find more or less enjoyable and worthwhile?), we asked participants to reflect on their most "memorable" task experiences and explain reasons for why that is. The wording of this question was intentionally neutral so that participants were free to compare task characteristics across positive, negative, and/or neutral tasks uninfluenced by the interviewer. Three themes emerged related to the appealing characteristics of jobs or tasks: (1) knowing the person behind the task, (2) knowing the reason or "story" behind why the task is needed, and (3) attaining experience.

Getting to Know the Person Behind the Task

Many participants expressed that getting to know more about the person posting the task made their experience more memorable and more enjoyable (Quotes 29, 30).

"I don't mind socializing at all... When I'm cleaning, I start a conversation. Like "Did you see that movie?" or " Where are you from" kind of thing."- Quote 29 (TR3)

"That one was a task to organize and clean a place in Brooklyn couple days ago... Next thing you know 'Hey, want to try fresh juice?' I'm like, 'Yeah, sure.' It was really awesome. It was fun."- Quote 30 (TR6)

Although participants generally understood and ultimately completed the objectives of the tasks (e.g., Ikea furniture assembly, package delivery, and grocery pickup), they appreciated getting to know the "person" behind the task (e.g., who is the requester, what is their background). Knowing this information was a common characteristic among memorable tasks as it lifted even if only slightly some amounts of uncertainty.

Knowing the Story Behind the Task

Participants sought to learn more about the "story" or agenda behind the posted task. This includes narratives surrounding why help was solicited in the first place.

The most fulfilling types of tasks involved learning about a TaskPoster's background and goals and obtaining positive reviews afterwards (Quote 31). For one task, a man hired TR6 to purchase flowers and deliver them while he and his girlfriend were on a bridge. During the delivery, TR6 said, "This is from someone who just adores you." TR6 highly regarded the thoughtfulness behind this task and subsequently selected several other surprise delivery tasks. TR1 recalled a task in which he rode his bike to a grave plot to ensure it was well maintained (Quote 32). According to TR1, tasks like this this had "meaning" and "made the world better."

"For the guy I delivered flowers for, how do you not like a guy like that? ...I learned a lot about [TaskPoster] and how long they have been dating, when they first started dating, and the long distance." - Quote 31 (TR6)

"I did drive my bicycle out to New Jersey to take a picture of somebody's parent's cemetery plot...I just thought it was just completely interesting that somebody would just take the trouble to do that." - Quote 32 (TR1)

In both TaskRabbit and Gigwalk, workers sometimes questioned the intentions and moral implications of the job postings, which contributed to them less likely to bid on or accept the job posted. GW5, for instance, became very selective and distrustful about the job postings after a client misled him into interviewing a competitor's customers. Other questionable tasks include payment for homework answers (TR2), pictures of private property for real estate companies (GW2, GW3, GW5), and a gig to mail lost cell phones to a company (GW4, GW5). Participants seemed to actively avoid what they perceived as more unethical types of jobs.

In analyzing our results, TaskRabbit and Gigwalk workers differed in their general impressions of the requesters and their intentions for learning more about the requesters. In TaskRabbit, participants were generally very positive about the TaskPosters and had few negative experiences to share. Several TaskRabbits described the experience of completing tasks similar to "helping a friend" or "helping a neighbor" (Quotes 33, 34).

"Everyone is super trusting in the site. Some people might see it as a bad thing. One of the things about TaskRabbit is that it's very much a community, people helping out other people. It's like doing odd jobs for your neighbor." - Quote 33 (TR3)

"I meet the TaskPosters, they're kind of more like a friend. It's what happens when I go out and meet TaskPosters. It's like helping out friends." - Quote 34 (TR5)

Gigwalk workers expressed more indifference towards virtual employers and referenced them as "companies" or "customers" (Quotes 35, 36), confirming the more corporate, for-profit nature of Gigwalk (Quote 37).

"You start to learn the companies and some are very particular... ultimately you don't have the last say. I'm pretty selective about who I work with." - Quote 35 (GW2)

"Whenever I complete a gig, you can actually send a message right to the customer. I always do that. That way, I can tell them about my experience, I can tell them I actually went into the store." - Quote 36 (GW1)

"I always have this assumption that they're white collar workers and they're just trying to find information like... it's cheaper for them to find out information if they have non-employees doing the work than to have paid employees." - Quote 37 (GW6)

Although workers' overall experiences in Gigwalk were positive, they proceeded more elusively (especially as mystery shoppers) and sometimes feigned interest in products or store displays to obtain information and mark tasks as complete. Unlike TaskRabbit, Gigwalkers assumed that requesters were companies checking in on their employees and products. In fact, those Gigwalkers that did express desires to learn about the persons and story behind the tasks did so because they questioned the legitimacy of the requesters and ethical nature of the tasks themselves (Quotes 38, 39).

"We all know what's really going on. People are stealing [these lost cell phones]." - Quote 38 (GW2)

"There are tasks that I won't do because it's unethical. People asking you to leave a positive review online, grading papers for teachers, writing student papers." - Quote 39 (TR2)

Defining Job Experience

There emerged a distinction between tasks providing *experience* or learned skills, versus tasks providing *an experience* or interesting memories. Only one participant (TR5) mentioned increased job experience as an end goal (Quote 40), but others described the appeal of learning and experiencing new and different things as an unintended consequence of completing their tasks.

"[TaskRabbit] is something I'm interested in doing because I'm starting a business of my own. I've been getting a lot of experience, more clientele." - Quote 40 (TR5)

For example, during a gig GW6 spent hours watching the Olympics with her family (Quote 41). TR6 purposefully bid on odd jobs so that she can experience something new and exciting and later tell others about them (Quote 42). Others recall the value of a job post hoc and cite positive experiences of meeting new people and animals (Quote 43), having novel ways to learn their city (Quotes 44, 45), and doing something different (Quote 46).

"Normally I don't watch the Olympics that much... it started out as a job and wound up being this really fun memory my kids will remember." - Quote 41 (GW6)

"Someday, I'll be a little old lady telling stories somewhere on a porch." - Quote 42 (TR6)

"One of the favorite things about the job is people who have pets. I love getting to meet animals." - Quote 43 (TR3)

"It's a good way for me to learn the city, different places, different stores, different neighborhoods all that kind of stuff. They really helped me that way."- Quote 44 (GW2)

"I just moved here to Houston. [Gigwalk] shows me a different side of the city that I wasn't familiar." - Quote 45 (GW1)

"Barbacking experience... I had a great time." - Quote 46 (TR2)

DISCUSSION

Interviews with our participants revealed several key themes about on-demand mobile workforce membership, task decision-making, and key job characteristics. To summarize the main findings with respect to our research questions:

- The main motivations for joining on-demand mobile workforce involve desires for monetary compensation and personal control over one's schedule and freedom to opt into or out of tasks. (RQ1)
- Situational factors such as the day of the week and weather conditions influence worker's task selection practices. Convenient physical locations and unambiguous profile information of task requesters also influence task selection practices as well. (RQ2)
- On-demand mobile workforce participants preferred knowing background information about task requesters and the original purposes for tasks. Workers also appreciated the non-financial incentives of new and different experiences that occurred as byproducts of task completion. (RQ3)

These results highlight similarities and differences among physical and virtual mobile workforce systems. Users of TaskRabbit, Gigwalk, and Amazon's Mechanical Turk mostly join the systems originally for monetary reasons, and as Silberman et al. [46] state, "are vulnerable to the whims of employers." If a task is not completed correctly as determined by the requester, the worker potentially receives poor reviews, a lower reputation, and ultimately less work and little to no money. As others [28, 46] have also observed, no matter the physical or virtual nature of the tasks, users want to secure the safety of their personal information and compensation.

One significant difference between the platforms is the risks associated with personal information and actual physical harm in the physical and virtual domains. In AMT, the personal risks of requesting and completing work are minimal; requesters and Turkers do not engage in an interpersonal exchange and are otherwise invisible to each other [25]. For TaskRabbit, however, users frequently need to reveal personal information. Rabbits can learn of work or home addresses, deliver sensitive packages, and care for living things such as pets and children. Thus, TaskRabbit requesters and workers have a much higher level of vulnerability than do requesters and workers from AMT and Gigwalk.

Also, unlike AMT or Gigwalk where both requesters and workers are anonymous, the TaskRabbit infrastructure minimizes risks for requesters by only completing background checks of workers and not requesters. Similar to the recommendations of Bederson and Quinn [5], the anonymity of requesters should be limited as this can create an imbalance of power in which requesters can post unethical tasks, refuse to pay, and create unfair reviews.

Theoretical Implications

This study offers implications for the theory of planned behavior, and the design of mobile workforce services, including future services that do not necessarily rely on monetary compensation (e.g. community volunteering marketplaces or time-banking).

In TPB, the constructs of attitude, subjective norms, and perceived behavioral control are predictive of behavioral intention and actual behaviors. In the context of this study, participants' attitudes towards the tasks and evaluations of their moral acceptability contribute to the likelihood of task selection and completion. Similar to the AMT findings of Kaufmann et al. [26], although we found support for extrinsic motivations as strong indicators for completing tasks, intrinsic motivations such as feeling enjoyment or solving challenges are important to task completion. This finding confirms the debatable role of monetary compensation as the main motivator, but highlights how attitudes towards tasks and requesters can outweigh the appeal of money, and affect behavioral intentions and outcomes.

Our study also provides support for a construct not included in TPB called "anticipated regret" [6, 34]. Anticipated regret involves the process of comparing the outcomes of the decision made with the outcomes of the decision not made. However, unlike previous studies [41], the anticipated regret in our study seemed to originate from worker evaluations of *sources* (i.e., task requesters, background stories) rather than evaluations of attitudes towards target behaviors (i.e., feelings towards the tasks), affective reactions (i.e., feelings towards performing the tasks), and anticipated affective reactions (i.e., feelings about having performed the tasks). Our findings also suggest that participants scrutinized the details of tasks and gauged the social acceptance of task completion. This tendency can tentatively suggest that volunteer- and exchange-based mobile workforce task can build on better familiarity with the person and their needs (e.g., in the style of micro-lending site Kiva [30]). This attitude may be a point of leverage for the execution of non-monetarily driven workforce services.

Implications for Design

We draw a few implications for designers and users of such platforms, based on the discussion above.

Requester Rating, Warranting

Our findings suggest that on-demand mobile workforce services should be more considerate of workers' attitudes and perceived norms and behavioral control surrounding the requested tasks. Extending the recommendations of previous AMT research [27, 46] and in line with TPB, on-demand mobile workforce services should notify both workers *and* task requesters that authentic profiles and requests will impact the quality of work given and received. Individuals prefer tasks with benefits that match their primary motives [21]. Because physical world tasks introduce a different set of risks compared to virtual world tasks (e.g., physical harm, deception), identifying information (social transparency) can ease workers' concerns with performing tasks and foster a community environment built on shared interests, a sense of belonging, and familiarity among members (i.e., develop positive attitudes and norms). In fact, platforms such as Turkopticon [25, 51], and TurkerNation [50] have emerged as ways to avoid exploitation and fraudulent tasks in AMT, but on-demand mobile workforce services could benefit from more robust, built-in evaluation systems that provide reviews for task requesters. In particular, internal rating systems of the task requesters, or any other form of vetting requesters supported by external social cues, might help workers manage expectations, prevent regret, and increase likelihood of task selection and completion.

Streamline Compensation Process

The findings on monetary compensation and personal control suggest a desire to maximize control over financial negotiations while relinquishing the responsibility for obtaining the compensation. On-demand mobile workforce service designers should consider automating requester-to-employee payments and procedures. TaskRabbit and Gigwalk currently require linking a credit card to the requester's account, but do not charge requesters until tasks are completed and evaluated. Timely payments can prevent payments from pending for long periods of time and ultimately sustain the membership of on-demand mobile workforce users.

Recommendations for Task Requesters

From the interviews with the workers there are some clear recommendations for requesters. Our analysis revealed the importance of communicating to the worker information about the task requester, and about the purpose for the task.

Reveal the Person

Not only does the practice of providing background information engender trust with the worker, it also provides additional motivation by creating a sense of purpose behind the task. The perceptions of the requesters were clearly very different between TaskRabbit and Gigwalk. On TaskRabbit, workers generally seemed less skeptical and more trusting of TaskPosters and the intentions of requests compared to Gigwalk. Gigwalk clients were perceived as more corporate and the workers clearly felt less regard for the clients and the jobs. This effect may have a number of implications, for example, to the cost or price offered for otherwise-equivalent jobs (e.g., what a worker is willing to do for a good cause), and is something to explore in future research. The desire to know the requester aligns our work with the theoretical framework of social transparency [48], which suggests that profile information increases credibility. This is in contrast to earlier studies by Riegelsberger and Sasse [40] on web sites listing staff photos, which were considered "manipulative."

Reveal the Context

As noted above, providing the workers with requester information and the context of the task can increase the workers' motivation to pick and complete the task. This implication supports findings on how task meaningfulness [7, 52] and fostered learning can improve labor supply in online crowdsourcing platforms [6, 28]. According to Hackman et al. [19], three "critical psychological states" describe factors that should enhance internal motivation to complete jobs: (1) experienced meaningfulness of the work, (2) experienced responsibility of the work, and (3) knowledge of results. First, the experienced meaningfulness of the work refers to when a person feels a task is worthwhile and important. If a person feels that his efforts are not important, he will likely feel unmotivated to complete the job. Work can be experienced as meaningful when there is (a) a clear cycle of perceived closure (beginning and ending of transformation process), (b) high visibility of the transformation, (c) high visibility of the transformation of the finished product, (d) transformation of considerable magnitude [52]. Second, the experienced responsibility of the work considers an autonomy dimension, where the work conducted by a person is one's own, and people feel their efforts are significant to accomplishing the task at hand. Lastly, having knowledge of results is a critical psychological state for motivation to complete a task. This means that a job must provide feedback about what is accomplished. Feedback can come from doing the task itself, or in the form of performance feedback from another worker or supervisor. Taken together, physical world tasks should capitalize on task features that promote these three critical psychological states.

We also saw that workers judged the potential trustworthiness and reliability of the requesters on the basis of their task descriptions, clearly favoring well-written tasks with unambiguous descriptions. Finally, providing workers with a bigger picture that contextualizes the task in a broader project can convey the sense that the worker is contributing to something greater and increase motivation to produce more and higher quality results [43]. All these factors can help requesters get jobs executed faster and perhaps completed quicker, and would be critical for volunteer-based mobile marketplace systems.

LIMITATIONS

This study has the following limitations. Our recruitment methods are of course biased due to availability and willingness of the workforce members to participate in a research task. Additionally, all of the participants demonstrate a high proficiency in terms of technological skills – all participants owned smartphones and PayPal accounts, for instance. While these demographics are probably common for current on-demand mobile workplace services in developed countries, the findings may not extend to other socio-economic groups and geographic regions. At the same time, our participants represented more than seven different states across the US and varied in terms of professional experience (mobile workforce or otherwise), age, and length of membership.

SUMMARY

We conducted interviews of mobile workforce service users to learn about their motivations, concerns, and practices. We found that individuals joined on-demand mobile workforce services for monetary reasons and sought personal control over their schedules, tasks, and compensation negotiations. Situational factors and convenience factored into a person's task selection process. Workers also preferred knowing information about the task requester and the purposes of the task. This study has broader implications for the ways in which people in local areas can leverage an effective, practical, novel and well-reasoned social and technical crowdsourcing application that organizes help and support in the physical world. Our findings could inform future development of mobile workforce services that are not strictly monetary, a challenge we intend to pursue next.

ACKNOWLEDGMENTS

This material is based upon work supported by the National Science Foundation under Grant Numbers 1211079 and 1211084. Any opinions, findings, and conclusions or recommendations expressed in this material are those of the author(s) and do not necessarily reflect the views of the National Science Foundation.

REFERENCES

1. Ajzen, I. The theory of planned behavior. *Organizational Behavior and Human Decision Processes 50*, 2 (1991).

2. Alt, F., Shirazi, A.S., Schmidt, A., Kramer, U., and Nawaz, Z. Location-based crowdsourcing: extending crowdsourcing to the real world. *In Proc. NordiCHI* (2010).
3. Amazon Mechanical Turk. http://www.mturk.com/
4. Ariely, D., Gneezy, U., Loewenstein, G., and Mazar. N. Large Stakes and Big Mistakes. *Review of Economic Studies 76*, 2 (2005).
5. Bederson, B. B., and Quinn, A. J. Web workers unite! addressing challenges of online laborers. *In Proc. CHI EA (2011).*
6. Bell, D.E. Regret in decision-making under uncertainty. *Operations Research 30* (1982).
7. Chandler, D. and Kapelner, A. Breaking monotony with meaning: Motivation in crowdsourcing markets. *Journal of Economic Behavior & Organization* (2013).
8. Deci. E.L. Effects of Externally Mediated Rewards on Intrinsic Motivation. *Journal of Personality and Social Psychology 18*, 1 (1971).
9. Deci, E.L. *Intrinsic motivation.* Plenum Press. (1975).
10. Downs, J.S., Holbrook, M.B. Sheng, S. and Cranor, L.F. Are your participants gaming the system?: Screening Mechanical Turk workers. *In Proc. CHI* (2010).
11. Easy Shift. http://www.easyshiftapp.com
12. FancyHands. http://www.fancyhands.com.
13. Fehr, E. and Falk, A. Psychological foundations of incentives. *European Economic Review 46*, 4 (2002).
14. Field Agent. http://fieldagent.net.
15. Gibbons, R. Piece-Rate Incentive Schemes. *Journal of Labor Economics 5*, 4,(1987).
16. Gigwalk. http://gigwalk.com.
17. Gneezy, U. and Rustichini, A. Pay Enough or Don't Pay at All. *Quarterly Journal of Economics 115,* 3 (2000).
18. Herzberg, F. One More Time: How Do You Motivate Employees? *Harvard Business Review* (1987).
19. Hackman, J. R. and Oldham, G. R. Motivation through the design of work: Test of a theory. *Organizational Behavior and Human Performance 16*, 2 (1976).
20. Heymann, P. and Garcia-Molina, H. Turkalytics: analytics for human computation. *In Proc. WWW* (2011).
21. Houle, B. J., Sagarin, B. J., and Kaplan, M. F. A functional approach to volunteerism: Do volunteer motives predict task preference?. *Basic and Applied Social Psychology 27*, 4 (2005).
22. Howe, J. The Rise of Crowdsourcing. *Wired Magazine,* (2006).
23. Ipeirotis, P. G. (2010). Demographics of Mechanical Turk (Tech. Rep. No. CeDER-10-01).
24. Ipeirotis, P.G., Provost, F., and Wang, J. Quality management on Amazon Mechanical Turk. *In Proc. HCOMP* (2010).
25. Irani, L.C. and Silberman, M. Turkopticon: Interrupting worker invisibility in amazon mechanical turk. *In Procs. CHI* (2013).
26. Kaufmann, N., Schulze, T., and Veit, D. More than fun and money. Worker motivation in crowdsourcing – A study on Mechanical Turk. *In Proc. AMCIS* (2011).
27. Kittur, A., Chi, E.H., and Suh, B. Crowdsourcing user studies with Mechanical Turk. *In Proc. CHI* (2008).
28. Kittur, A., Nickerson, J. V., Bernstein, M., Gerber, E., Shaw, A., Zimmerman, J., Lease, M. & Horton, J. The future of crowd work. *In Proc. CSCW* (2013).
29. Kittur, A., Smus, B., Khamkar, S. and Kraut, R.E. Crowdforge: Crowdsourcing complex work. *In Proc. UIST* (2011).
30. Kiva. http:// http://www.kiva.org.
31. Kohn, A. Why Incentive Plans Cannot Work. *Harvard Business Review* (1993).
32. Law, E. and von Ahn, L. *Human Computation.* San Francisco, CA: Morgan and Claypool (2011).
33. Little, G., Chilton, L.B., Goldman, M. and Miller, R.C. Turkit: Human computation algorithms on Mechanical Turk. *In Proc. UIST* (2010).
34. Loomes, G., and Sugden, R. Regret theory: An alternative theory of rational choice under uncertainty. *Economic Journal 92* (1982).
35. Malone, T., Laubacher, R. and Dellarocas, C. Harnessing Crowds: Mapping the genome of collective intelligence. MIT Sloan Working Paper (2009).
36. Mason, W.A. and Suri, S. Conducting Behavioral Research on Amazon's Mechanical Turk. *Behavior Research Methods* (2011).
37. Mason, W.A. and Watts, D.J. Financial incentives and the "performance of crowds." *In Proc. HCOMP* (2009).
38. Musthag, M. and Ganesan, D. Labor dynamics in a mobile micro-task market. *In Proc. CHI* (2013).
39. Quinn, A.J. and Bederson, B.B. Human computation: a survey and taxonomy of a growing field. *In Proc. CHI* (2011).
40. Reigelsberger, J. and Sasse, M.A.. Face it – Photos don't make a website trustworthy. *In Proc. CHI* (2002).
41. Richard, R., van der Pligt, J., and de Vries, N.K. Anticipated affect and behavioral choice. *Basic and Applied Social Psychology* (1996).
42. Rogstadius, J., Kostakos, V., Kittur, A., Smus, B., Laredo, J., and Vukovic, M. An Assessment of Intrinsic and Extrinsic Motivation on Task Performance in Crowdsourcing Markets. *In Proc. ICWSM* (2011).
43. Ross, J., Irani, L., Silberman, M. S., Zaldivar, A., & Tomlinson, B. (2010). Who are the crowdworkers?: Shifting demographics in Amazon Mechanical Turk. In Proceedings of the ACM conference on human factors in computing systems (pp. 2863–2872).
44. Ryan, R. M. and Deci, E. L. Self-determination theory and the facilitation of intrinsic motivation, social

development, and well-being. *American Psychologist 55*, 1 (2000).

45. Rzeszotarski, J.M. and Kittur, A. Instrumenting the crowd: Using implicit behavioral measures to predict task performance. *In Proc. UIST* (2011).
46. Silberman, M. S., Ross, J., Irani, L., and Tomlinson, B. Sellers' problems in human computation markets. *In Proc. HCOMP (2010).*
47. Steinbrueck, U., Schaumburg, H., Duda, S., and Krueger, T. A picture says more than a thousand words – Photograhps as trusts builders in e-commerce websites. *In Proc. CHI EA* (2002).
48. Stuart, H.C., Dabbish, L., Kiesler, S., Kinnaird, P., and Kang, R. Social transparency in networked information exchange: A theoretical framework. *In Proc. CSCW* (2012).
49. TaskRabbit. http://www.taskrabbit.com.
50. TurkerNation. http://www.turkernation.com.
51. Turkopticon. http://turkopticon.differenceengines.com.
52. Turner, A.N. and Lawrence, P.R. *Industrial jobs and the worker.* Boston: Harvard University Graduate School of Business Administration. (1965).
53. Tversky, A. and Kahneman, D. Rational Choice and the Framing of Decisions. *Journal of Business 59*, 4 (1986).
54. Zaarly. http://www.zaarly.com.

Information Extraction and Manipulation Threats in Crowd-Powered Systems

Walter S. Lasecki
Computer Science Department
University of Rochester
wlasecki@cs.rochester.edu

Jaime Teevan
CLUES Group
Microsoft Research
teevan@microsoft.com

Ece Kamar
ASI Group
Microsoft Research
eckamar@microsoft.com

ABSTRACT
Crowd-powered systems have become a popular way to augment the capabilities of automated systems in real-world settings. Many of these systems rely on human workers to process potentially sensitive data or make important decisions. This puts these systems at risk of unintentionally releasing sensitive data or having their outcomes maliciously manipulated. While almost all crowd-powered approaches account for errors made by individual workers, few factor in active attacks on the system. In this paper, we analyze different forms of threats from individuals and groups of workers extracting information from crowd-powered systems or manipulating these systems' outcomes. Via a set of studies performed on Amazon's Mechanical Turk platform and involving 1,140 unique workers, we demonstrate the viability of these threats. We show that the current system is vulnerable to coordinated attacks on a task based on the requests of another task and that a significant portion of Mechanical Turk workers are willing to contribute to an attack. We propose several possible approaches to mitigating these threats, including leveraging workers who are willing to go above and beyond to help, automatically flagging sensitive content, and using workflows that conceal information from each individual, while still allowing the group to complete a task. Our findings enable the crowd to continue to play an important part in automated systems, even as the data they use and the decisions they support become increasingly important.

Author Keywords
Crowdsourcing; privacy; security; extraction; manipulation

INTRODUCTION
Crowd-powered systems have recently become a popular way to surpass the capabilities of automated systems in many real-world domains. For instance, VizWiz [3] and Chorus:View [19] answer visual questions for the blind, Legion:Scribe [16] converts speech to text in real-time, Shortn [2] rephrases text into a more condensed form, Legion:AR [18] recognizes activities it has never seen before from video, Adrenaline [1] picks the "best" frame from a video, and Chorus [20] is an on-demand personal assistant capable of holding two-way conversations with a user. Each of these systems uses human intelligence to robustly solve a problem that artificial intelligence is not yet able to handle. However, doing so requires sharing potentially sensitive information with unknown people. For example, a photograph of a medication taken by a blind person for assistance reading the label (as in VizWiz) may include personally identifying information about the user. Figure 1 illustrates an example of a task where four workers are asked to extract text from an image of a credit card. Even if most workers are trustworthy, all it takes is one bad worker to steal the card number. Little is known about how systems can prevent unintentional extraction of data when using human intelligence as a computational resource [8].

CSCW'14, February 15 - 19 2014, Baltimore, MD, USA.
Copyright 2014 ACM 978-1-4503-2540-0/14/02 $15.00.
http://dx.doi.org/10.1145/2531602.2531733

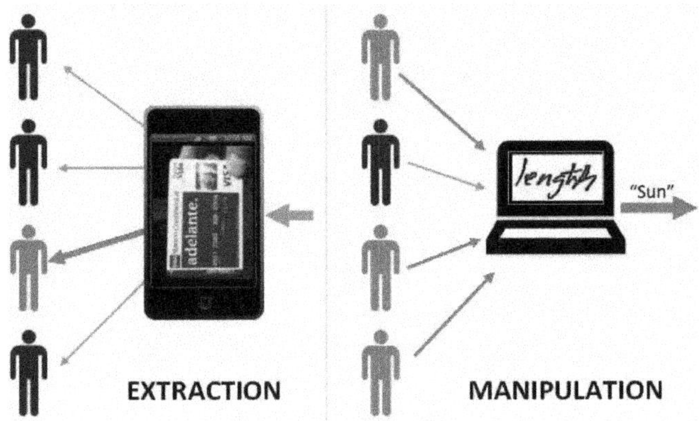

Figure 1. Crowd-powered systems are vulnerable to two types of attacks: unwanted information extraction (left), and malicious manipulative control (right).

The success of crowd-powered systems also means that the decisions made based on the input of crowd workers are becoming increasingly critical. For example, comScore is company that provides digital analytics to some of the world's largest enterprises, agencies, and publishers. Many significant business decisions are made based on comScore data, some of which are created using Mechanical Turk (www.mturk.com). As another example, Planet Hunters (www.planethunters.org) uses crowd input to determine where a new planet is most likely to be found, and then uses this information to dedicate scarce telescope resources. Responses collected from workers are used to power systems that do language translation [30], search results ranking [4], and even fine-grained image recognition [5]. With increased reliance on crowdsourcing to make real-world decisions, the potential for external manipulation could become a costly threat. Significant resources could be devoted to attacking crowd systems much in the way they are currently devoted to influencing search engine rankings. The search engine optimization market is estimated at $20 to $30 billion dollars in the United States alone [28], and poses a real challenge for search engines. As crowd systems become ubiquitous, they will likewise become targets for new types of malicious manipulative attacks, which perhaps even use the crowd itself. Figure 1 illustrates how a group of malicious crowd workers might convince a hand writing recognition crowd system to incorrectly interpret an image.

This paper lays the groundwork for addressing the threat of information extraction and manipulation in crowd systems by investigating the potential vulnerabilities of current crowdsourcing approaches. It contributes:

- An overview of the space of potential threats to existing crowd-powered systems and types of attacks,
- Tests that illustrate the viability of using Mechanical Turk to recruit workers for malicious attacks, and
- Ways to use the crowd to self-regulate against attacks for high-risk tasks, using various techniques.

We begin with a discussion of existing crowdsourcing practices. While previous efforts have explored how to combat worker errors and workers who want to be paid for doing as little work as possible, we highlight potential threats to crowd-powered systems, such as the extraction of valuable information from a task or the manipulation of a task's outcome. We study the feasibility of individual and group attacks, and analyze how group attacks can be organized by a group of malicious workers or by the hiring of workers by a malicious entity. We present the results of a study performed on Mechanical Turk with 1,140 unique workers that demonstrates the vulnerabilities of the current platform to malicious tasks that actively attack another task by directing workers. We analyze the behaviors of workers in contributing to these threats, and find that while such attacks can be successful; some workers are unwilling to participate. This suggests there is an opportunity for crowd systems to self-regulate to protect themselves, and we conclude with a discussion of how future crowd-powered systems might be designed to prevent information extraction and manipulation.

PRIOR WORK ON CROWDSOURCING

Crowdsourcing is a form of human computation that relies on a diverse group of nearly anonymous workers with unknown skills and reliability to contribute to a larger task by completing small pieces of the task called *micro tasks*. A *crowdsourcing platform* is the system that recruits crowd workers and connects these workers with micro tasks for them to perform. Within a crowdsourcing platform, a task *requester* is the individual or organization who creates a public call (in this case in the form of a description of the task) and hires crowd workers.

Systems that use crowdsourcing are at risk of attack because requesters know very little about the workers they hire and have limited means for quality control. Here we give an overview of what is known about crowd workers and how quality control is currently handled. We then highlight some of the vulnerabilities of crowd systems and discuss existing approaches to thwart malicious workers.

Understanding Crowd Workers

Crowd workers are remotely recruited by a crowd platform to micro tasks issued by a requester. Typically the crowd platform and requester are different entities, and the relationship between the requester and worker is mediated by the platform. As such, the relationship is very limited, with little information provided for context. The crowd employed by a system might consist of a few individuals or of a large population, and the requester might not even know what country the workers are each located in.

Members of a crowd have many different incentives for contributing, such as monetary payments in paid crowdsourcing or a desire to contribute to scientific research in citizen science projects. In this paper, we discuss how different motivations workers have may influence attacks in crowdsourcing. In our experiments, we focus on paid crowds recruited from Amazon's Mechanical Turk marketplace.

The most common approach (used by Mechanical Turk) for requesters to recruit workers on a crowd platform is for the requester to post a task, and then let workers choose which task they want to complete from a list of options. This is beneficial to requesters who can begin to use knowledge they retain between sessions [21] and beneficial to workers who can choose tasks they enjoy [27].

Quality Control in Crowdsourcing Systems

Because the relationship between a requester and worker is limited and workers are required to have little or no background knowledge, quality control is very important to the success of a crowd-powered system. As a result, maintaining quality is an active area of research [10,11].

Since individual workers' inputs are often error-prone, it is common for task requesters to implement agreement-based filtering (e.g., voting or averaging) or iterative workflows. Using contributions from a group of workers helps ensure the quality of the final output. It has been shown in previous work that collective responses result in better performance than any single worker could achieve [2,9].

Research in crowdsourcing has focused primarily on improving crowdsourcing quality based on responses collected from a group of error-prone workers. For tasks with one unknown correct answer, voting is one of the most

Figure 2. Prior systems such as Legion:AR have attempted to hide personal data from the crowd. Actors in the scene have been automatically identified and veiled in separate colors to preserve privacy and help workers identify which actor in the scene they should be focusing on. These veils can cover only the face (left two panels), or the entire silhouette of the user (right panel).

common techniques for aggregating multiple worker responses to predict the correct answer (e.g., Galaxy Zoo, Legion [16]). For estimation tasks, averaging responses is often an effective option (e.g., Legion:AR for image segmentation, Evanini and Zechner [6] for speech prosody). Other models of voting (e.g., ranked voting or tournament voting) have been used in idiom translation when majority voting alone is not successful [25]. Another common approach is to use iterative workflows for creating and revising content over a series of steps from multiple workers (e.g., TurKit [14] and Soylent [2]). Different than voting and averaging methods, which aggregate multiple workers' responses to the same micro task, iterative workflows involve individual or a small number of workers providing input at each step, which as we will see, may make these tasks more vulnerable to attacks from individuals or from groups of workers.

Existing Defenses Against Malicious Attacks

While quality control in crowdsourcing is an active area of research, little is known about coordinated malicious attacks on crowd systems. Efforts to avoid malicious workers have focused mostly on workers who want to strictly optimize their payment relative to the time or effort spent to complete a task [22]. These workers want to get paid the most for the least amount of effort, and they may take shortcuts (e.g., write scripts or give simplistic answers) to do so. However, in many important cases, workers are not just motivated by task payments, but also curiosity, beliefs, or interests. As crowd systems are used for increasingly valuable tasks, the payment involved may be minimal compared to the value of attacking the task. We identify two primary threats maliciously motivated workers pose to crowd systems beyond trying to optimize payments: 1) they can extract the private or sensitive information from tasks posted to a crowd platform, and 2) they can maliciously manipulate the outcomes of particular tasks.

Several existing approaches have been tried to prevent data leakage. The division of a task into micro tasks is typically used to allow multiple workers to contribute, facilitating agreement as well as simplification of the task. However, it can also be used to prevent any one crowd worker from seeing too much information, such as an entire medical record [25]. Legion:AR [18] used automatic methods to generate masks for specific pieces of information, such as a user's face (shown in Figure 2). Similarly, EmailValet [12] allows users to specify what data they share with the crowd.

Several existing approaches have also been explored to thwart task manipulation. Many of the crowd-based quality control measures designed to reduce noise and errors impede individual attempts to manipulate a task because they rely on agreement across different workers. However, coordinated efforts could create an artificial appearance of agreement. Gold standard tasks [13], where the requester knows the answer to a subset of questions, can be used to evaluate worker quality even when the majority is wrong, but must be generated a priori, which can be difficult or impossible in real-world settings.

Participants in a coordinated attack on a crowd-powered system can have varying motivations. For example, external influencers can recruit workers from existing markets by posting a task that asks workers to complete a different task. They may or may not get paid for the task they are asked to attack, depending on the request, but the net payment for completing the attack must be at least as high as that paid for the original task to incentivize opportunistic workers. Groups of individuals may also coordinate attack when it is in line with their beliefs or interests. For example, a group of users from 4Chan, Anonymous, or other similar community could attack a crowd-powered system as they have previously done to websites and service providers with denial of service attacks.

Web service attacks are frequently carried out using automated bots. While this represents a manipulation threat to systems relying on agreement, bots are relatively easy to detect in most crowd systems because the tasks require human understanding. When they do not, it is possible to add a ReCAPTCHA (www.google.com/recaptcha) task to check for worker authenticity.

Allowing workers to self-select tasks based on preference enables malicious workers or groups to target specific tasks and all give the same response. One way to avoid this is to directly route workers to particular tasks. Routing is supported by market places such as MobileWorks (www.mobileworks.com), and can be implemented on top of platforms that otherwise use self-selection [16, 17, 29]. Successful implementation of routing requires learning about individual workers' interests and capabilities for different tasks. To take advantage of this approach on an individual basis the requester must have enough active tasks to make the chance of returning to the same one very low.

These measures, however, only begin to address the threats posed to crowd systems as the data used by crowd systems and their outcomes become increasingly valuable. We now look more closely at the underlying vulnerability of crowd systems to information extraction and answer manipulation.

INFORMATION EXTRACTION

We call the threat of leaking private or sensitive information in tasks to others by posting tasks to crowd platforms the threat of *information extraction*. For instance, using a crowd captioning service such as Legion:Scribe [16] might result in letting workers hear a phone number, personal detail, or company secret. We discuss three types of potential types of threats related to workers extracting information from tasks: the thread of exposure, exploitation, and reconstruction.

Exposure

In some cases, a crowdsourcing task may contain information private or sensitive enough that were any worker to be *exposed* to the content, it would be harmful. For instance, a person using the crowd to help label and categorize their personal photos might consider an inappropriate or revealing picture to fall into this category. Exposure threats cannot be prevented by filtering workers since exposing the content even to honest workers is considered damaging. However, because the damage increases with each new worker exposed to the content, it can be limited by minimizing the number of workers that the information is shown to in situations where the content cannot be filtered prior to exposure to the crowd.

Exploitation

Often the concern with exposure of information is that the information could be exploited by the worker either for their own benefit or to harm the owner of the information. We call such threats as *exploitation* threats. For instance, a blind VizWiz user who turns to the crowd for image labeling might accidentally take a picture that includes their home address or credit card number. If a malicious worker were shown this image, that worker may steal this personal information. The difference between exposure and exploitation is that while exposure risks are always considered harmful, regardless of the worker, not all workers will actively exploit information.

Given no other knowledge of the workers, each worker hired for a task equally increases the risk of exploiting the information presented in the task. In such cases the risk of information explication grows linearly with the number of workers, as is the case with exposure. There may be opportunities for limiting exploitation threats if maliciousness of workers can be predicted.

Reconstruction

For some tasks, no individual piece of information incurs a large risk for the requester. For example, individual words in a private document usually do not hold enough context or meaning independent of the rest of the document to allow the worker to glean any valuable information. However, the more information that is revealed, the larger the potential risk that individually revealed pieces of information will come together to expose potentially harmful information about the requester. For instance, while information about a user's ZIP code, gender or date of birth alone reveals very little about them, knowing all three can be used to uniquely identify 87% of people in the United States [30]. We call such attacks as *reconstruction* attacks, since information extracted from individual tasks need to come together to cause damage for the requester.

Reconstruction attacks differ from exploitation and exposure attacks in that the harm to the requester (or benefit to the worker) grows non-linearly. Typically, the potential harm will grow either super linearly, or as a step function, meaning information either builds on prior knowledge to be more revealing (e.g., words in a document), or a certain subset of information must be recovered before anything important can be known (e.g., multiple partial images of a credit card number). This case differs from the previous cases because the harm from a set of revealed information is greater than the sum of the risks of each piece, meaning the risk grows *non-linearly*.

Prior examples of this type of attack in other domains have also shown that combining recovered records with other information can also result in an even larger privacy leak. For example, the information extracted from the Netflix challenge dataset, AOL search query logs, and Massachusetts medical records all appeared to preserve user anonymity on their own, but when joined with external databases, yielded personally identifying information.

Because the risk grows super-linearly due to the increase in context, the threat for requesters is significantly higher for group attacks. Reconstruction tasks with large numbers of individual pieces almost always require coordinated groups of workers (or bots) to successfully attack, since the number of tasks that must be viewed to cause harm can be high. By using a large enough group of workers, malicious entities can recover sizable portions of the information posted by a given task, even when the rate of workers outside of their group taking tasks is high.

Figure 3. Ambiguous text that could read in many ways, including as *gun, sun, lun, or fur*. The actual text is *fun*.

ANSWER MANIPULATION

Another type of threat to users of crowd-powered systems is that the answers they receive are intentionally incorrect due to workers manipulating the answers they provide. In this section, we discuss three areas of concern regarding workers manipulating tasks: classic manipulation, disruption, and corruption.

Classic Manipulation

Classic manipulation threats are ones where the worker or a group of workers changes the outcome of a task to reflect a particular outcome that is different from what the requester is looking for. We borrow the term *manipulation* from the breadth of research in election theory that strives to prevent this type of situation, in which one party attempts to attain undue influence [24]. Because most crowd systems use voting or other decision aggregation approaches to ensure quality, classic manipulation requires workers to comprise a large enough portion of the final contributing set to ensure the answer they want wins. Since this is not possible to do alone, workers must collaborate with others to successfully accomplish their goal.

Disruption

Another type of attack aims to simply disrupt the crowd-powered service. This means that the goal is to make the final result either any incorrect answer, or not allow the system to reach sufficient consensus to provide an answer at all. For tasks that use aggregation as a quality measure, disruption also requires a group of malicious workers, but it may not require them to coordinate on a fixed manipulation strategy. The difference between classic manipulation and disruption is the existence of an intended controlled outcome versus any outcome that stops the system from giving a valid response.

Corruption

Some crowdsourcing tasks ask sets of workers to contribute input, and then ask a different group to determine if that contribution was helpful or progressed the task. This process is repeated over and over with different workers until a final answer is reached (e.g., Wikipedia, TurKit [14]). Since these systems do not require that the entire crowd that contributed to a given piece be present throughout the lifetime of the decision process, the malicious input of a relatively very small group of workers can potentially destroy the progress made on the entire task.

Corruption can be manipulative or disruptive, and occurs in iterative workflows in which a small group can undo the progress of a much larger set if they can manipulate just one contribution and the corresponding verification step. To prevent corruption Wikipedia uses change logs that allow people to easily revert to prior versions. However, to the best of our knowledge most iterative workflows that run using Mechanical Turk do not protect themselves in this manner, meaning corruption of a task at any given point can prevent future good workers from repairing the damage.

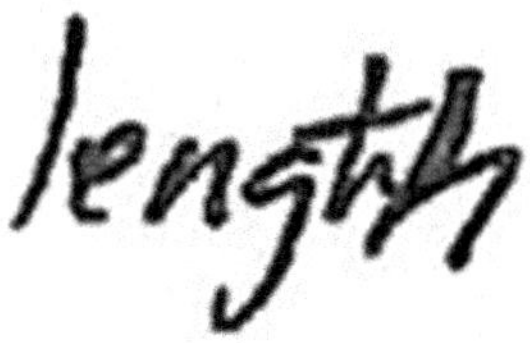

Figure 4. Easily read handwriting example which was used in our experiments. The text is *length*.

RAISING AN ARMY

While attacks on a crowd-powered system conducted by an individual require no coordination of effort or motivation, many of the most harmful potential attacks on crowd-powered systems involve coordinated effort by multiple workers. Group attacks can be carried out by a number of malicious workers organizing around a common objective. Such attacks can also be organized by a malicious entity directing a group of not necessarily malicious workers to execute an attack. This type of group attacks organized by a malicious entity may pose threats for the worker community since workers may be directed to carry out tasks with ethical or legal problems.

To understand how vulnerable crowd systems are to extraction and manipulation attacks, we conducted several experiments where we actively attacked a task of our own creation. We used crowds of people, recruited via the same crowdsourcing platform (in our case Mechanical Turk), to carry out the attacks. In doing so, our goal was to identify whether such attacks were feasible, and to build a picture of the different roles crowd workers take when asked to attack another task. We identify the following worker types as interesting to our analysis:

- **Passive workers** are not looking to find or capture any content. These workers might view unintended information (e.g., nude images), creating an exposure risk, but they will perform the task honestly and not misuse any information they are exposed to.
- **Opportunistic workers** do not actively seek sensitive information or chances to harm a task, but will seize such opportunities when presented. They may exploit the information they encounter, or perform a task incorrectly if paid to do so.
- **Malicious workers** actively seek information that they can exploit or try to manipulate tasks for personal gain. They may, for example, look for image recognition tasks that provide access to sensitive information.

Condition	Return Rate
Baseline	73.8%
Innocent	62.1%
Malicious	32.8%

Table 1. Extraction experiment return rates. Significantly fewer ($p < .0001$) workers were willing to copy task information to us when we asked a question that contained information that looked potentially sensitive.

Condition	Return Rate
Baseline	73.8%
Innocent	75.0%
Malicious	27.9%

Table 2. Manipulation experiment return rates. Significantly fewer ($p < .0001$) workers were willing to follow the manipulation instructions given in the attack task when the instructions clearly directed them to answer incorrectly.

- **Beneficent workers** are willing to go beyond completing the task correctly to further help the requester, instead of following economic incentives alone. This has been observed in terms of feedback on task design (including in this work), and reporting workers they see doing a task incorrectly [20].

As we vary the appearance of the attack we coordinate in our experiments in terms of maliciousness, we are able to identify passive workers (who will not complete tasks they see as potentially harmful), opportunistic or malicious workers (who are willing to complete potentially harmful tasks), and beneficent workers (who go above and beyond and contact us regarding the attack task).

EXPERIMENTS

Our goal was to test how viable it is to recruit a group of crowd workers to attack a different crowdsourcing task for us. We posted the two tasks under different requester names. In the first task (referred to as the *attack* task), workers were directed to follow a link to another task (the *target* task) that was visible on the crowdsourcing platform. This setup is illustrated in Figure 5. The target task always requested workers type the text they saw in an image. For example, users were asked to type the text shown in Figures 3 (perhaps “fun”, “lun”, “sun”, or “gun”) and 4 (“length”) or transcribe the text given on a credit card.

Since a worker’s hesitation to complete the attack task could possibly draw heavily on a moral component, we designed the attack task to either appear innocent or harmful (malicious). For the malicious condition of the extraction study, workers were asked to extract real-looking credit card information from the target task and return it to us. In the manipulation study, workers were asked to provide a clearly incorrect answer to the target task.

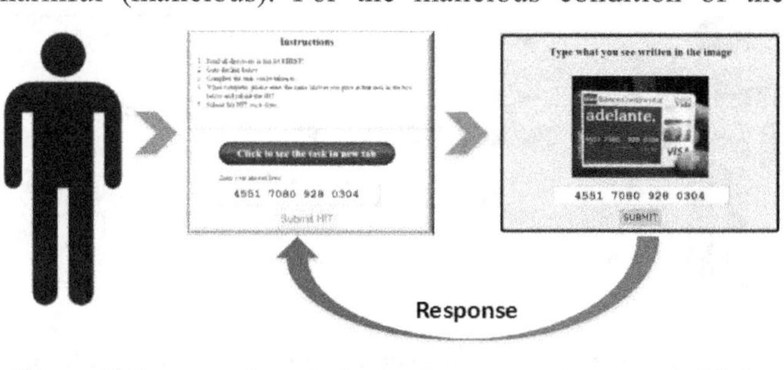

Figure 5. Layout of our information extraction tests. Initially the worker accepts our task, but then is redirected to another task where they are asked to return the answer they gave.

All workers were unique, and both tasks paid $0.05. In total, 1,140 workers completed our task, with at least 140 workers participating in each condition. In the baseline condition, the attack task directed workers to the target task and asked them to report back after completion by clicking a “done” button without extracting information or manipulating the target task. 73.8% of workers completed this baseline condition.

Extraction Study

Our first experiment tested whether or not crowd workers were willing to retrieve information and return it to us. We used the following conditions in the extraction experiments:

- **Baseline:** We used the same baseline described above.
- **Innocent:** Workers were shown a computer-generated picture of a credit card and asked to transcribe the text content. While this card had as much information on it as a real credit card (name, number, expiration date, etc.), the information was clearly fake (e.g. the card number was “01234[...]” and the name was “Card Holder”) and the picture was clearly not a real image.
- **Malicious:** To test the effect of perceived intentionality on the crowd, we ran the same extraction task with a photograph of a real-looking (but still fake) credit card. We expect this to appear to attentive workers as more of a threat than the artificial image.

We measured the rate of attack task response relative to the target task. In other words, we looked at how many workers who completed the task were willing to return the answer to us and get paid for the attack task. Our results are shown in Table 1. In all cases, a sizable portion of crowd workers were willing to extract information from other tasks. When the information being extracted appears innocuous, almost as many people (no significant difference) returned to provide the extracted information as they do when they are not asked to extract anything (62.1% v. 73.8%, $p > .1$). Even when asked to extract credit card information (the malicious case), workers were willing to do so 32.8% of the time, but this is a significant drop in return rate ($p < .0001$). We also saw a significant reduction in return rate (62.1% v. 78%) when completing the credit card task compared to the same baseline using the handwriting task ($p < .01$).

Manipulation Study

We also conducted a set of experiments to find out if workers were willing to actively manipulate a task based on our instructions. We again divided the conditions into two levels of potential harm and tested the following conditions:

- **Baseline:** We used the same baseline described above.
- **Innocent:** To see if the crowd would follow directions that overrode the instructions in a different task, we gave them a specific response to provide the target task in the instructions of the attack task. We used a handwriting example that was unclear what the true answer was (Figure 3), and provided a plausible solution (for this ambiguous task, workers were instructed to type "sun" when the correct answer was "fun"). We also ran another condition that asked workers to label the same image without instructions in order to get a baseline so we could detect a manipulative effect in the results.
- **Malicious:** To see if workers are also willing to knowingly provide false information (disobey the instructions of the target task at the request of the attack task), we created another task manipulation condition in which workers asked to respond the inner task in a way that is clearly incorrect. In this condition, the target task asked workers to transcribe an image (Figure 4) and the attack task instructed them to transcribe this image as "sun" (the answer is "length").

Our results, shown in Table 2, again demonstrate that people are willing to perform tasks that act on other tasks. As many people (no significant difference) were willing to complete the target task when instructed to manipulate it in an innocent fashion as were willing to complete the task when given no additional instructions (75.0% v. 73.8%, $p >$ .4. Interestingly, when the attack task instructed to give a clearly incorrect response to submit, a significant portion of the crowd refused to comply with the request to complete a task obviously incorrectly. We saw a significant ($p < .0001$) decrease the response rate for the malicious condition. We also want to know what those who did complete the task submitted, and what the final effect on the system was. For the malicious manipulation task, 28% who saw the word "length" (Figure 4), wrote "sun" as instructed. The rest correctly labeled the image despite initial instructions. Our results are shown in Table 3. This suggests that workers might be subject to intentional external biasing when they do not perceive the answer as obviously wrong.

Summary

Our results suggest that it is possible to mobilize the crowd to attack other tasks. When an attack task appears innocent to workers, they are as willing to complete the task as if they were not asked to extract or manipulate the target task. Even when the attack task appears likely to do harm (e.g., extracts credit card information or enter incorrect information), a significant portion of the crowd is willing to complete it, suggesting there are significant vulnerabilities for crowd systems to coordinated attacks.

Response	Baseline ("fun")	Innocent ("fun")	Malicious ("length")
"Sun"	12%	**75%**	28%
"Gun"	**36%**	16%	-
"Fun"	26%	7%	-
"Lun"	14%	1%	-
"Jun"	9%	1%	-
Other	3%	-	-
"Length"	-	-	**72%**

Table 3. Results from the manipulation experiment. While "gun" is the most commonly guessed word for this example when no instructions were given, the most popular answer in the innocent manipulation conditions is "sun", as instructed.

It is notable, however, that significantly fewer workers were willing to complete the attack task when it appeared malicious as when it appeared innocent, both in the extraction case and in the manipulation case. This suggests that some crowd workers can recognize the attack and object to it. Nonetheless, it appears possible to manipulate even these passive workers to act in ways that they would not intend if it the task appears innocuous, as many more workers gave different responses to the target task than they might naturally when given a plausible response.

DISCUSSION: SECURING AGAINST ATTACKS

Our findings demonstrate the vulnerability of existing crowdsourcing practices to extraction and manipulation attacks. Although there have been efforts for quality control in the presence of error-prone workers, little has been done on protecting these systems from the kind of threats studied in this paper. We believe that this same focus can and should be given to preventing systems from information extraction and from worker manipulation as well.

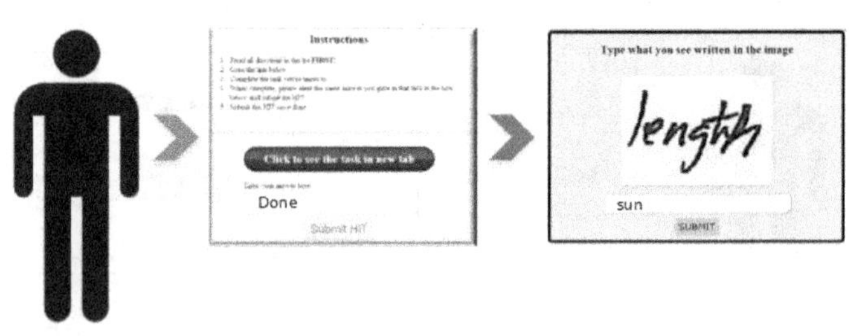

Figure 6. Layout of our information extraction tests. Initially the worker accepts our task, but then is redirected to another task where they are asked to provide a specified answer.

While our study showed a significant effect of changing the target task's content on workers' willingness to complete the attack task, our results do not show the exact reason why. In future work we would like to be able to isolate workers' reasons for participating and not participating in malicious extraction and manipulation tasks. Similarly, exploring trade-offs in worker motivation, such as the price paid for completing the target versus attack tasks, or the purpose of the task being completed, might impact workers' willingness to partake in potentially harmful actions. For example, if a worker was well paid to help a blind user in a system such as VizWiz, it might be the case that they are less likely to return user information to an attack task.

Our study was also carried out exclusively on Mechanical Turk, but provides a method of testing other crowdsourcing platforms that attain significant usage in the future.

Automation for Privacy Preservation

Previous work presented task-specific approaches for limiting information extraction from crowdsourcing tasks. As shown in Figure 3, face detection algorithms can be used to automatically detect and cover faces to protect privacy. Similar approaches can be used for text if the structure of private or sensitive information is known (e.g., SSN, credit card numbers and addresses). Another approach is dividing tasks into smaller pieces to limit information extraction. For example, the work by Little and Sun [15] proposed dividing images into pieces for protecting privacy. Similar approaches have been applied to OCR tasks such that no one worker gets the whole word, but multiple workers can each transcribe a set of letter that can then be recombined into the correct word for the requester. Such approaches help to prevent against extraction attacks from individuals. However, they are vulnerable against coordinated group attacks and may diminish performance of tasks that require contextual information about the entire task to be able to produce a solution. More attention is needed to generalize automated approaches for real-world tasks and offer solutions applicable to tasks that require context about the entire task.

Leveraging Reliable Workers

The results of our experiments showed that not all workers behave the same in extraction and manipulation attacks, especially when the nature of the attack is malicious. There are opportunities for designing workflows that can utilize reliable workers for early detection of information extraction and manipulation attacks. For instance, workers can be instructed to alert requesters about the existence of private or sensitive information. Iterative workflows can be designed to gradually release tasks – first to reliable workers and then to a larger worker pool based on feedback from the initial set of workers.

Reliable workers can also be of use to protect against manipulation attacks. As shown by our analyses, existing quality control approaches are effective to protect against individual manipulation attacks. Since workers in current crowdsourcing systems are mostly anonymous, large-scale manipulation attacks may need to reach workers with open calls as demonstrated in our experiments. Reliable workers that are aware of such attacks can alert requesters about manipulation attacks and aggregation mechanisms used for quality control can be adjusted accordingly. Workers can also be incentivized to report such attacks, helping to leverage opportunistic workers for the benefit of the task.

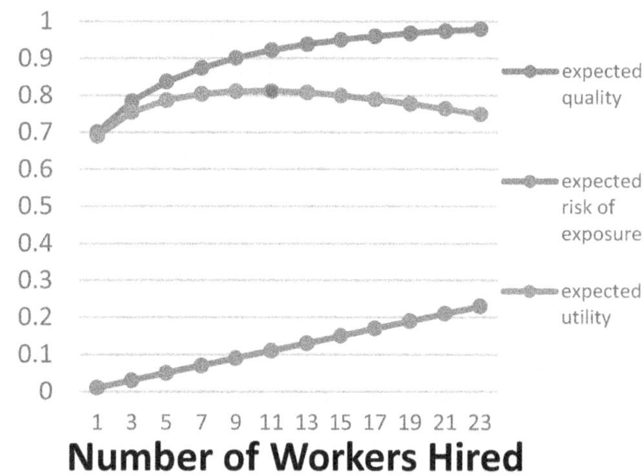

Figure 7. Tradeoff between expected quality of final decision, and the expected risk of exposing information to the crowd. The red dot at X=11 represents the number of workers that maximizes the expected utility for this example user.

Decision-Theoretic Analysis for Privacy Preservation

A common approach for quality control in crowdsourcing systems is hiring multiple workers for a task to eliminate the effect of errors from individual workers on the final result. As discussed above, hiring more workers increases the risk of information extraction. For instance, the risk of exposure may grow linearly in the number of workers hired for a task. This observation highlights a trade-off between higher quality output and higher risk of information extraction. Figure 7 shows an example of this trade-off. Given the probability of a task containing private or sensitive information, the risk of exposure (the expected number of workers exposed to the content) grows linearly with the number of workers hired for the task in this example. Based on majority voting applied for deciding the correct answer of the task, the expected quality (the probability of correctly identifying the answer) also grows with the number of workers hired. For a system that equally weights the utility for correctly identifying the answer and the cost for risking exposure, the expected overall utility of the system is also displayed in the figure. In this particular setting, hiring 11 workers (marked red in Figure 7) for a task maximizes the system utility. This case demonstrates a quality-risk trade-off, and highlights opportunities for designing dynamic decision-theoretic policies that reason about the risk of manipulation and extraction and use trusted workers in its workflow to minimize these threads.

CONCLUSION

In this paper, we studied the vulnerability of existing crowdsourcing practices to information extraction and manipulation threats from individual workers and groups. We demonstrated with experiments on the Mechanical Turk platform that a simple task design is sufficient to perform both an information distraction and manipulation attacks and workers have fewer tendencies to participate when tasks appear to be more malicious. We then outlined future directions for making crowdsourcing systems more resilient to these attacks.

As crowdsourcing becomes an integral component of many systems, threats such as the ones studied in this paper pose a significant danger. This paper is a first step towards understanding the viability of these threats as well as the behaviors of workers in their presence. We hope that gaining more understanding of these threats will influence further efforts in the future for more secure and resilient crowd-powered systems.

REFERENCES

1. Bernstein, M.S., Brandt, J.R., Miller, R.C. and Karger, D.R. Crowds in two seconds: Enabling realtime crowd-powered interfaces. In *Proceedings of UIST 2011.*
2. Bernstein, M.S., Little, G., Miller, R.C., Hartmann, B., Ackerman, M.S., Karger, D.R., Crowell, D. and Panovich, K. Soylent: A word processor with a crowd inside. In *Proceedings of UIST 2010.*
3. Bigham, J.P., Jayant, C., Ji, H., Little, G., Miller, A., Miller, R.C., Miller, R., Tatarowicz, A., White, B., White, S. and Yeh, T. VizWiz: nearly real-time answers to visual questions. In *Proceedings of UIST 2010.*
4. Chen, X., Bennett, P.N., Collins-Thompson, K. and Horvitz, E. Pairwise ranking aggregation in a crowdsourced setting. In *Proceedings of WSDM 2013.*
5. Deng, J., Krause, J., and Fei-Fei, L. Fine-Grained Crowdsourcing for Fine-Grained Recognition. In *Proceesings of CVPR 2013.*
6. Evanini, K. and Zechner, K. Using crowdsourcing to provide prosodic annotations for non-native speech. In *Proceedings of Interspeech 2011.*
7. Featured requester: Discover how comScore benefits from mechanical Turk. *The Mechanical Turk Blog*, March 2013. http://bit.ly/Ye64Sb
8. Harris, Christopher G. Dirty Deeds Done Dirt Cheap: A Darker Side to Crowdsourcing. In *SocialCom* 2011.
9. Kamar, E., Hacker, S., Lintott, C. and Horvitz, E. Combining human and machine learning intelligence in large-scale crowdsourcing: Principles, methods, and studies. *MSR-TR-2012-58*, 2012.
10. Kittur, A. and Kraut, R.E. Harnessing the wisdom of crowds in Wikipedia: Quality through coordination. In *Proceedings of CSCW 2008.*
11. Kittur, A., Nickerson, J.V., Bernstein, M., Gerber, E., Shaw, A., Zimmerman, J., Lease, M., and Horton, J. The future of crowd work. In *Proceedings of CSCW 2013.*
12. Kokkalis, N., Köhn, T., Pfeiffer, C., Chornyi, D., Bernstein, M.S. and Klemmer, S.R. EmailValet: Managing email overload through private, accountable crowdsourcing. In *Proceedings of CSCW 2013.*
13. Le, J., Edmonds, A., Hester,V., and Biewald, L. Ensuring quality in crowdsourced search relevance evaluation. In Proceedings of SIGIR 2010 Workshop on Crowdsourcing for Search Evaluation.
14. Little, G., Chilton, L.B., Goldman, M. and Miller, R.C. TurKit: Human computation algorithms on mechanical turk. In *Proceedings of UIST 2010.*
15. Little, G. and Sun, Y-A. Human OCR. *CHI 2011 Workshop on Crowdsourcing and Human Computation.*
16. Lasecki, W.S., Miller, C., Sadilek, A., Abumoussa, A., Borrello, D., Kushalnagar, R. and Bigham, J.P. Real-time captioning by groups of non-experts. In *Proceedings of UIST 2012.*
17. Lasecki, W.S., Murray, K.I., White, S., Miller, R.C. and Bigham, J.P. Real-time crowd control of existing interfaces. In *Proceedings of UIST 2011.*
18. Lasecki, W.S., Song, Y.C., Kautz, H. and Bigham, J.P. Real-time crowd labeling for deployable activity recognition. In *Proceedings CSCW 2013.*
19. Lasecki, W.S., Thiha, P., Zhong, Y., Brady, E. and Bigham, J.P. Answering Visual Questions with Conversational Crowd Assistants. In *Proceedings of ASSETS 2013.*
20. Lasecki, W.S., Wesley, R., Nichols, J., Kulkari, A., Allen, J.F. and Bigham, J.P. Chorus: A Crowd-Powered Personal Assistant. In *Proceedings of UIST 2013.*
21. Lasecki, W.S., White, S.C., Murray, K.I. and Bigham, J.P. Crowd Memory: Learning in the collective. In *Proceedings of Collective Intelligence 2012.*
22. Mason, W. and Watts, D.J. Financial incentives and the performance of crowds. In *Proceedings of HComp 2009.*
23. Massively multiplayer pong. http://collisiondetection.net, 2006.
24. Menton, C. and Singh, P. Manipulation can be hard in tractable voting systems even for constant-sized coalitions. *CoRR* abs/1108.4439.
25. Sun, Y-A. Roy, S. and Little, G. Beyond independent agreement: A tournament selection approach for quality assurance of human computation tasks. In *HComp 2011.*
26. Sweeney, L. Uniqueness of simple demographics in the U.S. population. In LIDAP-WP4, CMU. 2000.
27. Quinn, A.J. and Bederson, B.B. Human computation: A survey and taxonomy of a growing field. In *Proceedings of CHI 2011.*
28. Van Boskrik, S. US interactive marketing forecast, 2011 to 2016. *Forrester*. August 2011.
29. Von Ahn, L. Games with a purpose. *Comp.* 39(6), 2006.
30. Zaidan, O.F. and Callison-Burch, C. Crowdsourcing translation: professional quality from non-professionals. In *Proceedings of ACL-HLT* 2011.

How Physicians 'Achieve Overview': A Case-based Study in a Hospital Ward

Claus Bossen
Information Studies, Aarhus University
Helsingforsgade 14, 8200N Aarhus, Denmark
imvcb@hum.au.dk

Lotte Groth Jensen
Information Studies, Aarhus University
Helsingforsgade 14, 8200N Aarhus, Denmark
Lotte.Groth@stab.rm.dk

ABSTRACT
Clinicians' work in hospitals is safety- and time-critical, and often stressful due to the number and complexity of patient cases they must attend to. Therefore, how clinicians gather information, identify problems and make decisions concerning patients is a crucial concern, a process that can be labelled 'achieving overview'. In the process, clinicians use various artefacts amongst which medical records are central. Decades of experience is embedded in the structure and use of paper-based records. However, the development of electronic patient records (EPR) will change both structure and use of medical records, including 'achieving overview'. We conducted an ethnographic study in a hospital ward using paper-based medical records in order to understand how clinicians achieve overview. Inspired by the approach of exnovation, we elicit the use of paper-based records in order to inform the design of EPRs. We propose five axes which span out the process of achieving overview and describe implications for design of EPRs.

Author Keywords
Electronic patient records, ethnography, distributed cognition, healthcare, narratives, overview, sensemaking

ACM Classification Keywords
H.5.3 Group and Organization Interfaces

General Terms
Design; Human factors; Theory

INTRODUCTION
Health care work is often safety-critical and conducted under duress. Hence, gathering information about a situation or a patient's condition, constructing a coherent assessment and deciding what to do next are crucial tasks. The risk of making decisions that impair or are fatal to people puts immense pressure on health care professionals, who often have to act based on insufficient information. They are trained to do so and will rarely be reproached for it, unless they fail to notice or understand the significance of available information. However, gathering, presenting, and interpreting information and constructing a coherent assessment upon which to act are crucial in health care. This whole process can be labelled 'achieving overview'. As an initial working definition, achieving clinical overview is about *how health care professionals arrive at a sufficiently informed, accountable and coherent understanding of a situation, so that they are capable of acting consciously and with confidence.*

Because of the high-tension, safety-critical characteristic of health care work, health care staff are trained to work under stress, organisational routines have been established, and a variety of different artefacts have been developed to support health care professionals' information gathering, decision-making and coordination of work. As several studies within CSCW have shown, this is an inherently collaborative process, where health care staff communicate, collaborate, and move about [1; 19; 20]. Amongst the various artefacts used, the patient record is probably the most prominent [2], and it presents a well-known space within which health care professionals know how to act [32].

Patient records, paper-based or electronic, structure information in various ways: chronologically, problem-oriented, according to profession (physician and nursing patient records) and according to source (results from x-ray department, laboratory etc.). Ordering information is often based on standard terminologies for diagnoses, nursing interventions, drug identification and reimbursement (e.g. SNOMED CT, NANDA, ATC, DRG)[1]. Health care professionals are acquainted with these ordering standards, and the physical structuring of information in patient records thus resonates with mental orders that are known to health care professionals. However, in Europe and the USA hospitals are presently planning to, are in the process of, or have already implemented electronic patient records (EPR). Since the enabling capacities of paper and IT differ, the development of EPRs will entail changes in the ordering of patient records and its use in practice. Developing EPRs that present and order information in ways that facilitate

CSCW '14, February 15–19, 2014, Baltimore, Maryland, USA.

http://dx.doi.org/10.1145/2531602.2531620

[1]Systematized Nomenclature Of Medicine Clinical Terms; North American Nursing Diagnosis Association; Anatomical Therapeutic Chemical (Classification System); and Disease Related Groups.

clinicians' achievement of overview is hence a core challenge for present efforts to digitize health care work [27].

BACKGROUND

Our interest in and focus on 'overview' were spurred by a critical episode that took place when we did a longitudinal study into the implementation of an EPR in a regional hospital in Denmark. The EPR was cross-professional and meant to be used by various health care professions in the hospital, including physicians, nurses, physiotherapists, medical secretaries etc. It structured information in ways that partly overlapped with and partly deviated from the order and categories used in the paper-based patient record. A week into the implementation, the senior physicians demanded a meeting with the steering group responsible for implementing the EPR. Here the physicians passionately argued for significant changes to the EPR's display of information; too much information was presented to them in the EPR, some of it irrelevant, and the functionality to switch between views or scroll up and down was insufficient. They feared that they would miss available information, fail to find relevant information, and argued that the EPR did not help them generate a coherent understanding of a patient's situation. In their own words, they feared 'loosing overview'. The steering group immediately changed the display of information in the EPR to avoid a halt in the implementation process. The physicians' frustrations were somewhat lessened, and we as researchers were left with a strong impression of how an EPR might hinder rather than support achieving overview.

Digitisation of medical work is proceeding fast, and despite many setbacks and delays, there are no indications that it will stop. EPRs is one major IT infrastructure around which these efforts pivot with the hope of achieving better continuity and higher quality of patient care as well as more work and resource efficiency. The anticipated advantages of EPRs include updated data, immediately propagated across various settings and available to multiple clinicians at the same time. This is in contrast to working with paper-based patient records, where information is updated only when secretaries transcribe physicians' dictates, and information is only available to persons who can physically access the record, which is only available in one place at a time. Studies within CSCW have already shown that the shift from a paper- to IT-based media is not unproblematic. Paper is flexible and micro-mobile, which supports close collaboration in ways that IT-based documents do not [12; 13], and it allows easy and fluid annotations and juxtaposition of pages [26]. In contrast to office work, which experienced the first wave of digitisation, health care work is inherently mobile and collaborative in ways that are not supported by standard office computers [1; 9].

Ordering information in medical records in ways that support and augment clinicians' work is a central challenge. Orders based on, for example, source (e.g. x-ray department or laboratory) or transactions (e.g. admittance, ordering of medicine) provide little support for a cogent understanding of a patient's present state and problem. Problem-oriented records were proposed as early as 1969 as one answer to this, but have proven difficult to implement [4; 29]. According to a report by the National Library of Medicine, "The health care IT systems of today ... squeeze all cognitive support for the clinician through the lens of health care transactions and the related raw data, without an underlying representation of a conceptual model for the patient showing how data fit together and which data are important or unimportant. There is little or no cognitive support for clinicians to reason ..." [27: p40]. In this paper, we study clinicians' actual practices of achieving overview as a first step towards the goal of developing an understanding of how to order medical records. Such an investigation could start with practices based either on paper-based or on electronic patient records. The present case is inspired by the suggestion by Sellen and Harper (2002) that work practices that involve paper can be used as an analytical resource for design of IT. Electronic devices do not have to copy paper, and the affordances that paper supports should be understood in their practical and organisational context. However, more can be learned about the overall goals that paper serves, and this may inform design. Specific to health care, Berg and Toussaint (2003) call for analyses of paper-based patient records that bring forward their strengths and weaknesses in order to examine their integration with work practices and how this contributes to the performance of health care work [3]. In a broader perspective, such studies can be seen as examples of 'exnovation' [16]: a term proposed to describe how analysis of the mundane, routine practices can bring forward their invisible, taken for granted contribution to what actors try to achieve. 'Exnovation is the process of making existing strength of practices explicit by mapping the tacit resources of practitioners' [16].

In the following, we will pursue such a strategy of exnovation to bring forward how clinicians using paper-based patient records achieve overview. Paper-based work practices will provide an analytical resource for studying what 'achieving overview' means, and we will later conduct a follow-up study of clinicians working with a wholly digitised patient record. The focus will primarily be on physicians, because they are the central and ultimately responsible profession in hospitals. We are aware, as will also be evident from the empirical analysis, that medical work and achieving overview are collaborative endeavours that involve collaboration with other professions. We will continue the article in the following way. First, we present related work within CSCW on diagnosing and achieving 'overview'. Second, we describe the methods and setting of our case, and, third, continue to present the results of our analysis of the empirical data. Fourth, we discuss the implications of our case analysis for understanding overview and how this may inform the design of health care

IT in general and EPRs in particular. Fifth, we end the article by summarising the case and our conclusions.

WHAT IS 'OVERVIEW'? CONCEPTS AND THEORIES

Webster's Encyclopedic Unabridged Dictionary defines overview as 'a general outline of a subject or situation; survey or summary' (Webster's 1996: p1386), whereas the Oxford English Dictionary mentions 'Inspection; overseeing, supervision' and provides a more elaborate definition: 'A general survey; a comprehensive review of facts or ideas; a concise statement or outline of a subject. Also: a broad or overall view of a subject' (Oxford English Dictionary. Accessed online 30.1.2013). In the context of medical work, 'general outline', 'comprehensive review of facts' and 'concise statement of a subject' are all applicable and make sense. For example, clinicians construct a general outline of a patient case based on the temporal unfolding of their illness trajectories [28]; they make comprehensive reviews of facts when they go through a patient record and sum up cases, for example 'discharge summaries'; and they make concise statements of a subject when they make a diagnosis based on test results and the patient's account of his or her problem.

However, the process of *arriving at* the state of overview is less easily described as the definition of that state or noun. Within CSCW, a processual approach is represented by 'information seeking', which investigates the gathering and retrieval of information and stresses the temporal and collaborative characteristics of these activities [19] [21]. It tends though to focus on what triggers and facilitates information seeking rather than the establishment of a comprehensive understanding of and decision-making upon a situation or patient case. A collection of articles investigating 'diagnostic work' also adopts a processual approach. Diagnostic is "...the work of determining and categorizing ... trouble, and scoping for what to do about it (if anything) "[6: p110]. This includes not only medical work, but also that of web designers, ground control operators, engineers, and users of travel management systems. Diagnostic work is seen as cooperative, distributed, and technologically mediated and framed. The papers do not amount to a common theoretical framework, but argue for the need to conduct empirical research into the interactional processes of 'diagnostic work' [6]. Related to the issue of 'achieving overview' is the issue of 'awareness': actors' perception of their interactional space. 'Achieving overview' could be seen as a special instance of awareness: an actively pursued, reflective understanding of one or more patients' situation. Though central to CSCW and subdivided into situated, peripheral, temporal, etc., awareness, the term remains only loosely defined ([25]. For an overview, see [8]). .

While the above approaches are relevant, neither pinpoints 'achieving overview' precisely. However, in our search for broad, sensitising concepts and frameworks that may inform our investigation, we have come across three approaches that seem especially relevant: sensemaking, narrative theory and distributed cognition.

Sensemaking is the approach proposed by Weick [30], and focuses on how actors organise equivocal inputs in ways that make sense. Sensemaking can be described as a reciprocal, ongoing interaction between the search for information, meaning ascription and action. It is often instrumental, subtle, swift, social and easily taken for granted, but may become explicit when the environment conducts itself in unusual ways, or when actors cannot immediately engage with it. Sensemaking is a collaborative process to which communication is central. Analysing a hospital, Weick suggests that sensemaking is distributed across organisations and people:

> *... if knowledge about the correctness of treatment unfolds gradually, then knowledge of this unfolding sense is not located just inside the head of the nurses or physicians. Instead, the locus is system wide and is realised in stronger or weaker coordination and information distribution among interdependent healthcare workers.* [31: p412]

A central concept in sensemaking is 'functional deployment': imposing labels on interdependent events in ways that suggest plausible acts of management, coordination and distribution. For example, diagnosing a condition and thereby also suggesting future action.

Closely related, narrative theory focuses on how actors interpret and construct coherence when making sense of the world in which they act [14; 15]. For example, interpretations may take the form of stories based on a chronology of events or a narrative whose unifying structure is that of the plot. Such 'emplotment' is similar to functional deployment in sensemaking. It involves making a configuration in time, creating a whole or a story out of a succession of events. Actions, events and information take their meaning by belonging and contributing to the overall narrative. The narrative approach has been effectively used within health care as a way of understanding medical reasoning, such as physicians' ability to extract relevant elements from the history of illness and form a meaningful narrative which establishes causal relations. For example, Mønsted et al. [17] analyse physician-patient consultations and describe how physicians before meeting patients construct a proto-narrative based on the information available in patient records. Physicians then re-emplot this narrative when talking to and hearing patients' narratives. Mønsted et al. argue that the process in their case is not optimally supported technologically, because patient information is distributed over multiple systems and documents. Gaining an overview is hence a complex and cumbersome task [17].

Finally, the approach of 'distributed cognition' proposed by Hutchins and colleagues is relevant. Distributed cognition explicitly strives to get beyond a focus on the individual mind when analysing work settings. Instead, the distributed socio-technical system is the primary analytical unit, since most kinds of work are conducted by several people collaborating and using various artefacts. The approach sees itself as cognitive, because its focus is upon how people think, solve problems, predict and make decisions. It is distributive, because its concern is how information is represented and how representations are transformed and propagated during work activities, involving various people and artefacts [10; 11; 23].

> *Cognition is embodied. ... Minds are not passive representational engines, whose primary function is to create internal models of the external world. The relations between internal processes and external ones are far more complex, involving coordination at many different time scales between internal resources – memory, attention, executive function – and external resources – the objects, artefacts, and at-hand materials constantly surrounding.* [10: p177]

As information is propagated through minds, instruments, maps etc., it is transformed and the states of these entities are changed. The socio-technical system is 'computational' in transforming and changing information. As information is propagated across representational media – which can be internal as well as external to the mind – the various distributed entities are coordinated and work together. 'Overview', in this framework, can be seen as the result of computations by the use of various media. Distributed cognition shares with sensemaking and narrative theory the collaborative, communicative and distributed characteristic of acting and extends them by explicit incorporation of technologies and media. It has been applied in health care by, for example, Palen and Aaløkke (2006), who show that people at home make use of daily routines, inventory and materiality to remember to take their medication [18]. Likewise, Sarcevic et al. analyse interdisciplinary teamwork in trauma resuscitation based on distributed cognition [24].

In the following, we adopt the stance that the process of achieving overview is collaborative, communicative, distributed, and 'computational' by using various media. 'Functional deployment' and 'emplotment' are terms that propose initial understandings of the process of achieving overview. At the same time, we will argue that it is possible to go into more detail on how overview is achieved in practice. We will do this based on an ethnographic study, combining observation of and interviews with physicians in a university hospital. In the analysis we will propose that achieving overview can be described through five conceptual pairs spanning out five axes.

RESEARCH SETTING AND METHODS

The study was conducted by the second author in a ward for the treatment of liver and bowel diseases. The ward employs 135 clinical staff including 24 physicians, and has 22 beds and an outpatient clinic with approximately 14,000 appointments a year. The average length of patient stay is four days and covers a great diversity in length of stay. A considerable amount of the patients are admitted several times, because of different chronic conditions. The ward is part of a university hospital in Denmark, which has approximately 10,000 employees and 1,150 beds divided between 26 wards. On a yearly basis the hospital has approximately 82,000 discharges. An EPR had not yet been implemented in the ward. This ward was chosen for this study of overview, because of the complexity and long patient histories of the patients affiliated with the ward.

The ward routines included a morning conference attended by all present physicians, usually around 15. They subsequently split into two teams each covering one half of the ward and did pre-ward round conferences together with the nurses. On specific weekdays the physicians attended a diagnostic imagining or a pathology conference before the pre-ward round conference. After this, three or four physicians went to the outpatient clinic, one or two had on-call duties, and the remaining physicians did ward rounds, which lasted until late lunch. In the afternoon conference the physicians would follow up on new results and information generated during the day.

The physicians and the other professions in the ward used a mix of paper-based and digital artefacts. The most important and frequently used by the physicians were the following: the entirely *paper-based patient record* consisting of a paper sleeve containing loose sheets of paper organised by means of different tabs, which divided the record into various sections for very diverse information, ranking from insurance papers, x-ray descriptions and physicians' progress notes. The latter was the most used section by the physicians. The progress notes themselves were structured in different ways, using typography to mark selected parts. Progress notes were placed in the record by the nurses once they had been transcribed by a secretary. *Stationary computers* displaying *laboratory results* and *medication* in two different software programmes were found in both team offices. Laboratory results were displayed like a spreadsheet, enabling different views (e.g. numeric values or as a graph) and showing different time spans. Medication was displayed as an electronic list, one for each patient.

The medical ward divided its staff into two teams; each team was responsible for a group of patients and had its own team office used by physicians, nurses as well as health care assistants. A central artefact in these offices was a *whiteboard* displaying a chart containing information about the team's patients. The chart featured a row for each patient and was divided into columns for diagnosis, treatment plan, expected discharge, urgent problems etc. Information was updated several times a day by erasing text with a cloth and entering new information with a pen. The whiteboards functioned as a meeting point and as a central resource when the staff discussed patients.

Finally, two different *printed lists* used by physicians and nurses were important. One listed all the patients admitted to the ward and featured only a very limited amount of information. The other listed only a team's patients and featured a considerable amount of information in comparison with the other list. The physicians almost always carried these lists with them and frequently entered notes related to specific patients or to other things they needed to remember.

Data collection

Data were generated through ethnographic fieldwork. Around 60 hours of observation, distributed over 12 days and five months, was conducted by the same researcher, who followed the physicians around observing their work. All observations were conducted in the morning or in the afternoon. Initially, appointments were made in advance with a particular physician, but as the physicians became acquainted with the researcher, contact was made ad hoc with a diversity of physicians' tasks and experience in mind. Typically, observations started at the morning conference or the afternoon conference, which both were mandatory for the physicians.

No judgement about which situations to study was made in advance, but emerged in a grounded way; observations focused on physicians' actions and interactions with other staff and artefacts with a view to identifying situations in which overview was important, how overview was achieved, and which factors hindered or supported this process. When necessary and appropriate, clarifying questions were posed, and small informal interviews were conducted during observations. Field notes were taken, including both text and sketches, to capture actions, vocal and non-vocal. The notion of thick description guided the way data were recorded [5; 7]. Field notes were transcribed and extended as soon as possible after the observation.

Interviews with seven physicians were made to supplement observational data. The semi-structured interviews focused on physicians' accounts of what overview is and how they achieve it. The inclusion criteria for interviewees were diversity of physician experience. The interviewees consisted of six males and one female with experience in the ward ranging from six months to 20 years. All interviews lasted around one hour, were recorded and subsequently transcribed verbatim.

Analyses of the data were initially guided by the sensitising theoretical concepts and framework presented above, but with the intentional strategy to let other relevant issues and codes emerge from the data. During analyses transcribed field notes from observations and transcripts of interviews were looked through, with the purpose of finding thematic codes, capturing different aspects of 'achieving overview'. The preliminary set of codes was then discussed by the authors. After these discussions, additional codes were proposed, and a second round of coding was conducted. This resulted in codes like 'The physicians definition of overview', 'complete overview', 'sufficient overview', 'chronological overview', 'here&now status', 'different ways of conduction ward rounds' etc. As we went through the codes and their content we saw that some of them were clustered around the same underlying aspect, but representing opposite dimensions of the aspect. The different codes were then combined into five conceptual pairs structuring the presentation of findings. These codes are not based on quantified measurements, but were chosen because they were the ones most often found in the empirical material across multiple interviews and observations.

FINDINGS

A preliminary indication of what overview is about is provided by the physicians' own explanations and understandings during the interviews. This will provide some provisional clues about overview, but it will also show that its achievement can be difficult to conceptualise, because is it embedded in situated practices.

The physicians' understanding of overview

In the beginning of each interview the physicians were asked how they perceived overview and what overview looked like in their daily clinical practice. Generally they answered the question by explaining what kind of information they need in order to establish an overview. One physician explained it this way:

> *Well, it means to have everything available, that's what I would say. I think it means that I can be seated and read exactly what had happened yesterday. What did the blood samples say? What did the x-ray that I ordered this morning show? And what about the cultivation of blood? That I have everything right at my fingertips. Together with a nurse, who can tell me about the patient's conditions today. This clearly creates the optimal overview in my opinion.* (Female physician, one year of experience in the ward)

There are several significant clues in this statement. The ideal situation is to have all the information in one place ('be seated and read'), rather than, we surmise, to have to move around and search for information; to have exact information on different issues ('what happened yesterday'; what are the results of various test); to have unmediated access to information ('right at my fingertips'); and to collaborate with other actors ('together with a nurse').

However, most often the physicians found it somewhat difficult to talk about the process of establishing overview. When they talked about a process related to overview, it was in a generalised form like the following: Overview is to gather information, to know the patient history, to know the results of the test samples and to be aware of the treatment plan. Focus was on the process in patient history and not so much on the physicians' work process of establishing overview. They did not talk about how they gathered information or how they got to know the patient history. As one physician said:

> *It's important. As much information as possible. Both concerning what has been and how matters look like right now. Then you are able to make decisions on a better basis. Both concerning what to do right now and in general. ... The cool thing about being a physician is that you have some symptoms, and then you have some possible diseases, and then some tests to confirm or dismiss it. This is a connection you make all the time.* (Male physician, six months of experience in the ward)

Making a 'connection' between information and a problem, which can be seen as 'functional deployment' or construction of a narrative, is of course central to the process. However, the quote also points to central aspects of the process of achieving overview; 'as much as possible' expresses a wish for comprehensiveness, and 'has been' and 'right now' reveal a historical and a here&now aspect.

All the physicians had an opinion about what kind of information they needed in order to feel confident in the established overview, but it was difficult to establish in the interviews how they got this information or how they wanted to get this information. Hence, one of the purposes of the analysis below is to provide a conceptual frame through which it is possible to talk about what overview is about and how it is achieved.

Aspects of 'achieving overview'

Our empirical material and analysis reveal the existence of many 'different' aspects involved in the achievement of overview. In the following we present five conceptual pairs which outline different dimensions of overview. Examples from both interviews and observations will be inserted as the conceptual pairs are presented. The pairs are not to be seen as dichotomous concepts, but rather as poles which in practice may be intertwined and difficult to separate. Nor are they necessarily mutually exclusive. The achievement of overview is affected by different needs, contexts, situations etc. and often requires combination of poles.

Historical and here&now aspects

Historical overview refers to a chronological understanding of the patients' history going back as far as deemed relevant by the physician and the problem at hand. On the other hand, here&now overview is concerned with the present status of the patient – what is the situation right now?

The here&now aspect comes to the fore with stable patients, at first examinations of patients, or when a physician is under time pressure and needs to know whether a patient's condition is stable enough to justify the postponement of a thorough examination. Here&now is also relevant when a patient's condition is critical and action has to be taken immediately. The historical overview is relevant whenever a physician wants to understand symptoms, developments and the present state in a richer context of information. Often, the historical and the here&now aspects are entangled and achieved in parallel processes. Frequently, the information gathered in the process of establishing here&now overview is only meaningful if the physician has at least a minimal historical overview. A patient's weight, for example, is useless if you only have this one value, and the same is often truth for the value of a blood sample. On the other hand, information from the historical overview is often less meaningful and has little value as an indicator for action, if the physician is not aware of the current status of the patient.

This entanglement is seen in the following quote where a physician was asked: What does it mean for you to obtain overview in your daily clinical work? He answered:

> *Often it is like this – we go and see the patient and talk to them and talk about their problem. Often this one problem is, in quotes, a trivial problem. But almost all of them have something in the load. Things that are not insignificant for the current problem. In that case, if I meet unprepared, only focusing on the current problem, not aware of its background – then I will be set straight.* (Male physician, 10 years of experiences in the ward)

The following observation snippet also shows the entanglement of the historical and here&now aspects of achieving overview, and additionally displays the entangled use of different artefacts and actors in this establishment.

> *Observing one physician as he prepares for ward round. The physician looks at the computer to find test results from ordered samples. He expresses that he finds the results 'peculiar'. He then starts to discuss the results with another physician sitting next to him in the office. While they are discussing the results, they go further back in time on the computer to see test results from samples previously completed on the patient.* (Male physician, six months of experience in the ward)

The physician starts by looking on the computer in order to find the latest test results. He sits by himself and opens a spreadsheet displaying the results. He is puzzled and turns to another physician sitting next to him and they discuss the case. No evident explanation is found and they both turn to the computer and type a new interval into the spreadsheet, so test results are displayed further back in time, while they continue to discuss and try to find an explanation for the latest test results.

In order to pursue the here&now aspect, physicians use various artefacts and interaction processes. The most commonly used artefacts and interaction processes are the patient record with emphasis on physicians' notes, test results from, for example, blood samples, diagnostic imaging, urine samples etc.; conversations with patients, nurses and other physicians; physical examinations of the patients; and different kinds of conferences, like morning conferences in the ward, and cross-disciplinary conferences on e.g. pathology. Indeed, it is a very collaborative and interactional process. Pursuing the historical aspect, physicians often use the same artefacts as described above, but the most used artefact is the patient record, with special focus on physicians' notes and test results as described above. To a lesser extent, they use conferences, conversations with patients, nurses and other physicians and physical examinations to pursue the historical aspect.

Shared overview and individual overview

This conceptual pair illustrates an axis from the entire ward, trying to assess all of the patients, to the individual physician preparing for a patient during ward round or in the outpatient clinic.

Shared overview is established jointly among the clinicians and is concerned with a group of patients. The central situations through which shared overview is achieved, are the different kinds of joint conferences of physicians or of physicians and nurses. Individual overview is concerned with one patient at a time and requires more detailed information about this one patient. Individual overview is usually established concerning the patients that a physician is responsible for when he or she is on call. Individual overview is rarely an individual process, since other actors and artefacts contribute to this process. Overall, however, with respect to the individual overview, other actors do not have the same amount of information or the same overview as this one physician has of a particular patient. Indeed, shared overview informs the establishment of individual overview by providing information about patients in the ward for the physicians to build on. Also, individual overview helps clarify and enhance the shared overview.

During the day in the ward there is a tendency to go from establishing shared overview to establishing more individual overview, of course with exceptions and deviations. The day starts at half past eight with a morning conference. All the attending physicians meet at this conference. They are seated around two tables in the lunch room, often with the most experienced physicians gathered around one table and medical students and new physicians around the other table. Often present also is a nurse, whose task it is to contribute with updated information and function as a link between nurses and physicians. The physician who has been on night shift takes a book with a handwritten list of patients admitted during night shift. The physicians briefly audit all the patients admitted in the ward, with special focus on new patients. The central activity at the morning conference is information sharing and talk; furthermore, the physicians take notes on the printed lists. One physician described the benefit of the morning conference this way:

> *Well, it's sort of a broad briefing, these morning conferences. It's just a briefing on what we have in the house. What's new and what has happened, which we all ought to know about. Even if you do not participate in the actual work with the patient. If you encounter the patient during the day in one way or another. Or on call the following day, then you have some kind of overview, you know who the patient is.* (Male physician, five years of experience in the ward)

Some days the morning conference is followed by a more subject-specific conference, for example diagnostic imaging or pathology. The physicians have to move to another building to attend these conferences, and they often carry with them the printed lists and make annotations. On a large screen in the front of the room x-ray or MR images are presented and examined and discussed by the physicians, concerning their implications for the patients.

After these conferences, the physicians split into two teams, each responsible for a group of patients. The teams engage in separate pre-ward conferences, discussing their patients in more detail, now with the active participation of the nurses. Here, the most commonly used artefact is the whiteboard.

Afterwards, physicians prepare for ward round or other duties by establishing a more individual overview of the patients they are responsible for. Here the patient record and various test results are extensively drawn upon when establishing the individual overview.

At half past twelve all the attending physicians meet again and discuss almost all of the patients in the ward, now in the light of new knowledge generated during ward rounds or outpatient consultations. During this noon conference the physicians are seated around one table with a computer connected to a widescreen at the end of the table. On the widescreen they often display various test results concerning the patients they are discussing. In addition, almost all of the physicians bring the printed team lists and other artefacts like personal notes, and patient records are used in varying degrees. The physicians take turns and go through the patients they are responsible for. Either they ask the other physicians specific questions about a patient or they start a more general conversation about a patient – Are we on the right track with this patient? What do we do next? The physicians often use the printed team list when they go through their patients and add new notes to the list following the conversation. In this way they make plots and re-emplotments to the patient history, adding yet another layer of information, contributing to the on-going process of extending, change or modify the clinical overview.

An example of the achievement of individual overview is provided in the vignette below of a physician preparing for a ward round together with a nurse.

> *The physician starts a conversation with the nurse about the patient. During the conversation he makes notes on a printed list of the team's patients. Together they look up different test results on the computer. They are trying to find out if the patient receives the nutrition he needs. They look into different printed observation forms in the patient record on nutrition intake. Again the physician makes notes on the printed list of the team's patients.* (Male physician, six months of experience in the ward)

Whereas shared overview is primarily established by means of dialogue between physicians or between physicians and nurses and by using different kinds of common lists or displays with brief information about patients, individual overview is established through dialogue with other physicians, nurses or, notably, patients and by means of artefacts such as patient records, test results, observation forms, physical examinations etc.

Comprehensive overview and minimal overview

The golden standard with regard to overview is often perceived as complete overview; patients expect physicians to have complete overview of their individual illness history, and for physicians complete overview is an ideal, like when the physician in the first citation above wanted to have everything right at her fingertips.

In spite of this conception of complete overview, almost all the physicians talked about sufficient overview, which enables them to act. The physicians believed their main service was to make decisions about future actions for the patients. They did not seek to establish complete overview for its own sake. A physician expressed it this way when asked if he ever had complete overview:

> *No, of course, you never have. But a sufficient overview is what is needed. And that's what we try to achieve. It's in order to be able to make the correct decision. And the point is that you actually need quite a lot of things to achieve this.* (Male physician, 20 years of experience in the ward).

This quotation shows that even though physicians are aware that it is almost impossible to establish complete overview, they emphasise that sufficient overview often requires quite a lot of information to be regarded as sufficient.

Since the establishment of a complete overview is not attainable, it makes sense to conceptualise this dimension as spanned out between comprehensive and minimal aspects. Several factors influence the degree of comprehensiveness needed. First, a crucial task for the physicians is to determine if the patients in front of them are 'standard' patients. If not, they need a more comprehensive overview than when it comes to standard patients, where a minimal overview over the last test results will do. Likewise, if the patients are following a course of treatment and the patient condition is stable, the physicians only need a minimal overview of the patient history. On the other hand, to recapitulate or summarise a complicated treatment history requires a comprehensive overview.

A physician expressed the need for more or less comprehensive overview in the following way:

> *Like we talked about before. Well, you need to consider if this patient is a so-called standard patient. Which is a good thing to be. If he is not, well, then you need to dig a little deeper into it. Then I would read the physicians' notes a bit more carefully. Then I would look further back in time. What can we tell from the last scans? How widespread is this tumour?* (Male physician, 15 years of experience in the ward).

What counts as a comprehensive overview is very much context dependent. In some ways comprehensive overview is similar to the historical overview, but one difference is that a historical overview does not necessarily need to be comprehensive. A historical overview may only include a few central points, scattered across different time lines. Also, the historical-her&now aspects span out a temporal axis, while the comprehensive-minimal aspects concerns the amount of information needed. In their daily clinical practice, physicians strive for a sufficient overview that enables them to act. The amount of information needed to establish this sufficient overview may be comprehensive or minimal depending on various aspects.

Collaborative and single-handed decisions

During the observations in the ward it became evident that dialogue and conversation are central factor to the establishment of clinical overview. Physicians collect information about patients in various places, in various ways and by means of various artefacts. But it is often during conversations with colleagues that this information is transformed into a meaningful collection, which enables them to make decisions about future actions. During conversations physicians pick up the information gathered, put it together in new ways and make summaries for each other. Of course, a physician can go through the process single-handedly, but more often than not a certain amount of conversation is involved in the process of establishing overview. Often the physicians have qualified hypotheses about diagnoses and treatment plans and use conversations to challenge or confirm these. Observations also demonstrated the process of employment and re-emplotment or, in the words of Weick, functional deployment, as well as how the sociotechnical system performs various computations.

Conversations can take place between physicians, between physicians and nurses and between physicians and patients. Conversations are also central in establishing overview because of their ability to pass on information from one colleague to another. Several physicians argue that conversations significantly enhance their understanding of patient information. Reading the patient record is an essential first step, but discussing the information with someone else is even better. As one physician said:

> *But as I was saying, if it was the case that there was no nurse around, when we were talking about it, then I could go and read up on it by myself. But, well you know, the dialogue is often 10 times more valuable. Then you can also talk about what the real problem is.* (Female physician, one year of experience in the ward)

The quotation shows that something happens during conversations, something different from what takes place when physicians work on their own. Information is context dependent, and if the physicians engage in dialogue with colleagues, they can 'talk about what the real problem is'.

The process of establishing clinical overview and making decisions about future plans and actions for a patient is usually not a single-handed process. The complex and non-linear process of establishing clinical overview is a constant interplay between conversation and more single-handed processes. At the different conferences all the physicians and sometimes the nurses participate in multiple conversations and dialogues. Besides these more or less scheduled conversations, physicians participate in ad hoc conversations with other physicians, nurses and patients. In between all of this dialogue and conversation physicians work and gather information single-handedly and make decisions in the light of all the collected information. The following observation is an example of how conversation and dialogue may take place wherever there is room for it.

> *The physician is supposed to participate in a diagnostic imaging conference. We arrive in good time and stand outside the conference room, waiting for the surgeons to finish their conference. Three other physicians from the ward are also waiting outside and the four of them start to discuss some of the patients admitted in the ward. They discuss treatment plan, medication and single out what it is that makes these patients unique.* (Male physician, six months of experience in the ward)

Conversations are initiated when physicians walk from one building to another, meet in the corridor or the office, drink coffee in the lunch room etc. They range from brief exchanges to more detailed conversations about a patient.

Experienced and novice

Early in the data collection phase we sensed that experience is important for the ability to establish overview. Observing the role of experience in the process of establishing overview is rather difficult, since the differences between the physicians are within their minds. However, it is also evident from their behaviour, and observing them one can see that the more experienced physicians have slightly different working routines than the novice physicians.

One of the benefits of experience is the ability to act without spending time on profound considerations every time. The physicians ascribe this ability to the fact that with experience follows a degree of familiarity with numerous patient trajectories and courses of illness. Until something else manifests itself, they act upon this stock of experience, which makes the process of establishing overview smoother, less time-consuming and often less dependent on various artefacts. In addition, the more experienced physicians are often well-informed about theories and scientific evidence within their area of speciality. One physician expressed it this way:

> *... and the more experienced physician always has his working hypothesis in the back of his mind. Of course he tries to confirm or disconfirm it all the time, right. The more inexperienced collects information here and there and hopes for a hypothesis to manifest itself, right.* (Male physician, 20 years of experience in the ward).

This quotation once again demonstrates that the process of collecting information and ascribing meaning to this information, or as Weick would say, making sense of information, is perceived by the physicians as an important part of the establishment of overview. Virtually all the interviewed physicians had the perception that the described qualities enable the experienced physicians to sort and prioritise the extensive amount of information more easily and more quickly than the more inexperienced physicians. One physician said:

> *And I'm not able to make decisions if I'm unfamiliar with the patient history. And it is of course important to be able to single out what is important in all of these hundred pages you sometimes have. What is it, what are the important facts to be aware of? And I think experience is crucial in this process.* (Male physician, 20 years of experience in the ward)

What the physician says here is that the process of prioritising and sensemaking gets easier with experience and thereby also facilitates the establishment of overview.

Five conceptual axes

What emerges from the ethnographic fieldwork is the realisation that 'overview' is produced in various situations, settings and through the use of various artefacts.

Based on this we have tried to develop concepts which make it possible to talk about physicians' experience and practice of achieving overview. The proposed conceptual pairs and five axes are meant as analytical distinctions, which span different dimensions of what is implicated in 'overview' (Figure 1 below). In practice, physicians constantly combine and switch between the aspects in their work. However, the conceptual pairs may provide an initial analytical framework through which we can understand what overview is about and how physicians achieve it, even though they may not exhaust all dimensions of overview.

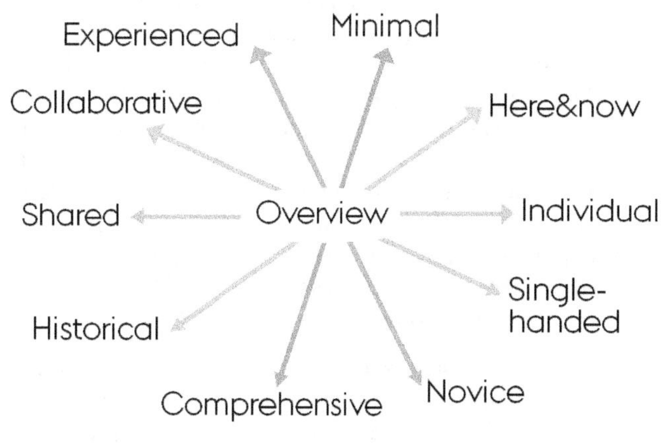

Figure 1. The five axes in which overview is spanned out.

DISCUSSION

We found the theoretical approaches of sensemaking, narratives and distributed cognition useful for framing the research into 'overview'.

Sensemaking as a process of reciprocal, ongoing interaction between the search for information, meaning ascription and action fits nicely with our empirical data. Also, it makes good sense to consider the distributed socio-technical system the primary analytical unit, as suggested by distributed cognition, and the achievement of overview a computational process across actors and artefacts. Achieving overview is not something that only takes place in the individual minds of physicians, as a process of absorbing and ordering information. The process is physical, social, technological and distributed, involving examinations of and dialogue with patients; conferences between physicians and with several professions; dialogue between physicians and with nurses; reading, looking into and carrying around artefacts such as team lists of patients, patient records, test results and laboratory tests on the computer. It becomes evident that the intertwined and complementary roles of these heterogeneous entities pass information around and transforms it. Cognition is embodied and interwoven with materiality [10].

Finally, the concepts of narrative and employment were also applicable. These are defined as pertaining not only to a level of discourse, the structure of a text or a talk, but also to action. Indeed, action is a kind of proto-emplotment where actors and materials are related to each other, so that emplotment may take place [14; 15]. In our case, we can see how physicians assemble and reassemble in different settings and groups, interact with other professions and patients, engage with different artefacts and thus construct proto-emplotments that later become actual emplotments.

However, while useful and adequate, these theoretical frameworks are not detailed enough for us to go into the specifics of the process. What emerged from our analysis of the data were the five conceptual pairs (Figure 1 above). They point out aspects that form and inform physicians' situated achievement of overview and can be said to span five dimensions: Historical and here&now concern how much of the *temporal* aspect of a patient's case should be drawn upon when producing overview; shared and individual concern the *numerical* aspect or how many patients the overview includes; collaborative and single-handed concern the *collaborative* aspect or whether an overview is produced individually or in a group; experience and novice concern *how knowledgeable* the person(s) constructing overview is(are); and comprehensive and minimal concern the *comprehensiveness of information* on a patient in the process of establishing overview.

These aspects are supported by a combination of artefacts and social techniques (dialogue, conference etc.), but not always in ideal ways; patient records are comprehensive with lots of detail, but inadequate for establishing shared overview of multiple patients, and, therefore, printed lists and whiteboards are used instead. These, on the other hand, lack the details that the records contain. Conferences are good for pooling expertise and developing shared overview, but at present they are only supported by the individually used printed lists and lack a shared artefact. Historical overview can be achieved through the details available in the patient record, but requires filtering all the information before a summary can be produced. Multiple summaries support historical overview of protracted patient cases, but are not found in one place in the record; they must be 'extracted' from the progress notes. Collaboration is supported by the micro-mobility of paper, but still requires moving around and looking from different angles and presupposes co-presence.

Related to the discussions upon awareness within CSCW, overview can be seen as a kind of 'situation awareness' and the five axes outlined resonate with the other kinds of awareness: The historical-here&now axis shares characteristics of 'temporal awareness', and the collaborative-single axis shares characteristics of 'team awareness'. As such the axes may comprise a condensation of various sub-kinds of awareness pursued in a given situation. However, within the broad range of awareness with CSCW (e.g. passive or active, sentience or understanding), the kind of overview in focus here is actively, purposefully acquired to form an understanding of a situation. The generalisability of the axes is probably limited. However, they could possibly contribute to the approach of information seeking that focuses on what triggers and facilitates search and retrieval of information, by suggesting more specifically the kinds of information sought for. Similarly, the axes possibly could span out the space within which 'diagnostic work' unfolds. For example, in a case of website breakdown, the trouble-shooting of web administrators could be said to have pursued a minimal, here&now rather than a comprehensive overview of the situation, because the organization prioritized speed over perfection. In these ways, the five axes may contribute to CSCW as a sensitizing framework of analysis.

Implication for design

From the perspective of digitisation, the paper-based socio-technical system of the patient record and related artefacts can be criticised for providing fragmented and incoherently updated information, only available at limited locations. EPRs can be seen as the answer to such criticism by providing updated, integrated information accessible to multiple persons at any number of locations at the same time. However, from the perspective of exnovation the paper-based socio-technical system emerges as an assembly of artefacts; each of these artefacts supports the process of achieving overview in limited ways, but together they flexibly facilitate the process. The first thing one must acknowledge is thus that achievement of overview is facilitated in different situations, through different kinds of artefacts and through different presentations of differentially filtered information. This also means that an EPR could not and probably should not be the only artefact to support the achievement of overview. Other artefacts, interactions with colleagues and patients, organisational setups etc. are equally important to consider.

This calls for artefacts that support different work situations, like working single-handedly, in groups, at patient bed, etc. Similar to the paper-based system's variety of lists, folders, records and whiteboards, the EPR should run on different platforms such as tablets, large displays, cell phones as well as on stationary computers. This also calls for supporting different ways of ordering and presenting information; summaries and views which present the most recent results and notes are necessary, but so are chronological views. Presentation and visualisation of information in EPRs is of crucial importance and have been done in many different ways so far (For a comprehensive overview, see [22]). On the basis of our analysis, one of the most important features must be the flexibility to easily move from a general overview to more detailed information and to easily shift the time span in the visualization.

One important point regarding these different artefacts and views is that they should enable the EPR to be part of the dialogues and conversations of physicians and other health professionals involved in the establishment of overview. Some essential parts of functional deployment, emplotment and computation that do not emerge when physicians work individually take place in these conversations. It is important to consider not only the artefacts, but also the processes in which the artefacts are involved.

More specific, initial requirements for EPRs arising from the above can be proposed starting with the position 'Shared overview' in figure 1 and going through the aspects clockwise. Shared overview is probably best facilitated by large displays with lists of patients and central patient information, making information about multiple patients available to groups. Individual overview, on the other hand, requires zooming in on the single patient with as much detail as appropriate. Collaborative overview requires a display that can be shared by two or more people in the many ad hoc conversations that take place, for example a display that can be carried and handed around like paper (like the printed lists), providing essential overview, but also making it possible to go into specifics. Furthermore, it should be easy to add information, so that the display can also function as an in-process working tool, not necessarily to be saved in the EPR. Experienced physicians will require a view that presents essential data to them as specialists, possibly even personalised data. While customised presentation of information might intuitively be the ideal solution for all physicians, this would in practice (apart from requiring huge customisation effort) only be suitable for highly specialised physicians, since such singular views would not support collaborative or shared overviews. Novice physicians, for example, need the EPR to present all information in well-known, ordered ways (e.g. chronologically, source-based, summaries in a separated folder), so that they can go through all relevant information in a structured way. A minimal overview would call for situated presentations of information; this could focus on patient trajectory (e.g. admission, transfer, and discharge), problem (ordered per diagnosis) or the most recent summary, prescriptions and examination results in one view. A comprehensive overview, on the other hand, requires that all information can be accessed and presented in ordered ways, similar to the information needs of novices. The here&now overview would require the most recent progress notes, prescriptions and examination results.

This discussion on implications for design, also addresses a difficult balance when setting up EPR systems between customised presentation of information, supporting individually shortcuts and work habits, and standardized supporting tools, which is easily recognisable. To meet this variation in preferences, the EPRs must be highly flexible.

A variety of visualization methods and flexibility of customization emerges as core requirement with regards to overview, because of its complexity and contingency. Overview of single, simple tasks is easy: knowing the present medication of a patient can be facilitated by a list, and her blood pressure levels over time can be visualized through a curve. However, assessing a patient's overall situation requires an integrated combination of various visualizations customized to the specific situation.

CONCLUSION

Based on ethnographic fieldwork at a hospital ward, we have described and analysed how clinicians achieve overview. We see this process as a result of a socio-technical system, where physicians and other professions through dialogue and by the use of multiple artefacts assemble information and construct narratives: Through storytelling and emplotment, narratives are constructed that ascribe meaning to disparate events and information, and form the basis of treatment and care. Based on analysis of our data, we suggest five axes that span out the space within which the process of achieving overview takes place. Physicians' situated decision-making takes place within the poles of shared-individual; collaborative-single handed; experienced-novice; minimal-comprehensive; and here& now-historical. These axes and their conceptual pairs can inform the design of EPR. Our own next step into the study and analysis of achieving overview is to conduct new empirical study in a ward with an EPR. This will test and refine the analysis presented here.

REFERENCES

1. Bardram, J. and C. Bossen Mobility Work: The Spatial Dimension of Collaboration at a Hospital. *Journ. of Computer Supported Cooperative Work.* **14**(2005), 131-160.

2. Berg, M. Accumulating and Coordinating: Occasions for Information Technologies in Medical Work. *Journ. of Computer Supported Cooperative Work.* **8**(4) (1999), 373-401.
3. Berg, M. and P. Toussaint The Mantra of Modeling and the Forgotten Powers of Paper: A Sociotechnical View on the Development of Process-Oriented ICT in Health Care. *International Journ. of Medical Informatics* 69(2-3) (2002), 223-34.
4. Bossen, C. Representations at Work: A National Standard for Electronic Health Records. *Proc. of CSCW 06,* 2006, ACM Press (2006), 69-78.
5. Bourgeault, I., R. Dingwall, R. de Vries, Eds. *Handbook of Qualitative Methods in Health Research*. Los Angeles, SAGE (2010).
6. Büscher, M., J. O'Neill, J. Rooksby. Designing for Diagnosing: Introduction to the Special Issue on Diagnostic Work. *Journ. of Computer Supported Cooperative Work*, 18(2-3) (2009), 109-128.
7. Crabtree, A. *Designing Collaborative Systems. A Practical Guide to Ethnography*. London, Springer (2003).
8. Gross, T. Supporting Effortless Coordination: 25 Years of Awareness Research. *Journ. of Computer Supported Cooperative Work,* Online June 2013, 1-50.
9. Hartswood, M., R. Procter, M. Rouncefield, R. Slack. Making a Case in Medical Work: Implications for the Electronic Medical Record. *Journ. of Computer Supported Cooperative Work,* 12(3) (2003), 241 - 266.
10. Hollan, J., E. Hutchins, D. Kirsch. Distributed Cognition: Toward a New Foundation for Human-Computer Interaction Research. *ACM Transactions on Computer-Human Interaction* 7(2) (2000), 174-196.
11. Hutchins, E. *Cognition in the Wild.* Cambridge, Mass & London, MIT Press (1995).
12. Luff, P. and C. Heath. Mobility in Collaboration. *Proc. of CSCW'98*, ACM (1998)**:** 305-14.
13. Luff, P., C. Heath, D. Greatbatch. Tasks-in-interaction: Paper and Screen based Documentation in Collaborative Activity. *Journ. of Computer Supported Cooperative Work*, ACM (1992).
14. Mattingly, C. The Narrative Nature of Clinical Reasoning. *The American Journ. of Occupational Therapy* 45(11) (1991), 998-1005.
15. Mattingly, C. The concept of therapeutic 'emplotment'. *Social Science & Medicine* 38(6) (1994), 811-822.
16. Mesman, J. *Uncertainty in Medical Innovation.* Houndsmill, Palgrave Macmillan (2008).
17. Mønsted, T., M. C. Reddy, J. P. Bansler. The Use of Narratives in Medical Work: A Field Study of Physician-Patient Consultations. *Proc of ECSCW'11*, Springer (2011).
18. Palen, L. and S. Aaløkke. Of pill boxes and piano benches: "home-made" methods for managing medication. *Proc. of CSCW'06,* New York, ACM (2006), 79-88.
19. Reddy, M. and P. Dourish. A Finger on the Pulse: Temporal Rythms and Information Seeking in Medical Work. *Proc. of the CSCW'02*. New Orleans, ACM Press (2002), 344-53.
20. Reddy, M., P. Dourish, W. Pratt. Coordinating Heterogeneous Work: Information and Representation in Medical Care. *Proc. of ECSCW'07*, Klüver (2001), 239-58.
21. Reddy, M. C. and P. R. Spence. Collaborative information seeking: A field study of a multidisciplinary patient care team. *Information Process& Management*. 44(1) (2008), 242-255.
22. Rind, A., T. D. Wang, W. Aigner, S. Miksh, K. Wongsuphasawat, C. Plaisant, B. Schneiderman. Interactive Information Visualization to Explore and Query Electronic Health Records. *Foundations and Trends in HCI* 5(3) (2011), 207–298.
23. Rogers, Y. and J. Ellis Distributed Cognition: an Alternative Framework for Analysing and Explaining Collaborative Working. *Journ. of Information Technology* 9(1994), 119-128.
24. Sarcevic, A., I. Marsic,R. S. Burd. Teamwork Errors in Trauma Resuscitation. *ACM Transaction on Computer-Human Interaction*. 19(2) (2012), 1-30.
25. Schmidt, K. The Problem with 'Awareness'. *Journ. of Computer Supported Cooperative Work* 11(3) (2002), 285-298.
26. Sellen, A. J. and R. Harper *The Myth of the Paperless Office*, MIT Press (2002).
27. Stead, W. W. and H. S. Lin *Computational Technology for Effective Health Care: Immediate Steps and Strategic Directions*. Washington, DC, USA, National Academies Press (2009).
28. Strauss, A., S. Fagerhaugh, B. Suczek, C. Wiener. *Social Organization of Medical Work.* Chicago & London, University of Chicago Press (1985).
29. Weed, L. L. *Medical Records, Medical Education, and Patient Care. The Problem-Oriented Record as a Basic Tool.* Chicago, Year Book Medical Publishers (1969).
30. Weick, K. E. *Sensemaking in organizations*. Thousand Oaks, Sage (1995).
31. Weick, K. E., K. M. Sutcliffe, D. Obstfeld. Organizing and the Process of Sensemaking. *Organization Science* 16(4) (2005), 409-421.
32. Østerlund, C. S. Documents in Place: Demarcating Places for Collaboration in Healthcare Settings. *Journ. of Computer Supported Cooperative Work* 17(2-3) (2006), 195-225.

Privacy Practices in Collaborative Environments: A Study of Emergency Department Staff

Alison R. Murphy
College of Information Sciences and Technology,
The Pennsylvania State University
arm193@ist.psu.edu

Madhu C. Reddy
College of Information Sciences and Technology,
The Pennsylvania State University
mreddy@ist.psu.edu

Heng Xu
College of Information Sciences and Technology,
The Pennsylvania State University
hxu@ist.psu.edu

ABSTRACT
Privacy research has long focused on the individual. Yet most organizations are highly collaborative where teamwork is the norm. To examine privacy practices in collaborative settings, we conducted an ethnographic study of a highly collaborative and information-intensive setting – an emergency department (ED). We found that ED staff's work practices did not always align with the organization's privacy policies and procedures. We then discuss the use of workarounds when privacy policies interfere with work practices, the challenge of assigning accountability for enforcing privacy in collaborative environments, and implications for technical and policy design. We conclude with some thoughts on the future of privacy research in collaborative settings.

Author Keywords
Privacy; collaboration; collaborative privacy practices; privacy policy; privacy design; computer supported cooperative work.

ACM Classification Keywords
H.5.3 [Group and Organization Interfaces]: Computer-supported cooperative work; K.4.1 [Public Policy Issues]: Privacy.

INTRODUCTION
Privacy research has long focused on the individual. Most technological safeguards and policies have been oriented towards *individual privacy practices (IPP)* [22]. IPP studies have focused on users protecting the privacy of their own information while using technology [27, 28], managing the privacy of their own information when collaborating with others [6, 24, 26], and making decisions on individual privacy [11, 21]. Consequently, privacy mechanisms and underlying conceptions of privacy are still primarily focused on individual users' perceptions and behaviors [3]. Yet, in many organizational settings, collaboration and teams are an integral aspect of the work. Therefore, we need to investigate how privacy policies and technologies impact collaboration in settings where teamwork is the norm.

For a variety of reasons, hospitals are one domain of particular interest for examining privacy. First, collaboration and multidisciplinary teams are essential aspects of work in this environment. Yet, in these settings, it is often unclear who is responsible for the information. Is it the patient care team member who retrieved the information? Is it the team member who the information was shared with? Is it the team member who used the information? The actions (i.e., policies and technologies) taken to protect information privacy in an individual work setting will affect only that particular individual. However, in collaborative environments such as intensive care units or emergency departments, privacy policies and technologies may impact not only an individual but also the collaboration amongst individuals. Second, hospitals face a number of additional legal requirements because of the personal health information (PHI) that they deal with on a daily basis. In the United States, hospitals must comply with two important laws that focus on patient information privacy and security – Health Insurance Portability and Accountability Act (HIPAA) [45] and Health Information Technology for Economic and Clinical Health (HITECH) [46]. HIPAA details a set of privacy rules related to personally identifiable health information and the penalties for violations of those rules. HITECH expanded the HIPAA privacy rules by stipulating requirements for electronic medical record systems to be held accountable to the security and privacy standards specified in the American Recovery and Reinvestment Act of 2009 [47]. These laws have driven the development of hospitals' information privacy policies and technologies. Finally, hospitals are facing an increasing number of privacy breaches and the consequences of these breaches can be severe [44]. For patients, it may have adverse effects on medical insurance and employment. For hospitals, privacy breaches may lead

CSCW'14, February 15–19, 2014, Baltimore, Maryland, USA.

ACM 978-1-4503-2540-0/14/02...$15.00.
http://dx.doi.org/10.1145/2531602.2531643

to problems, such as reputation and trust damage, monetary penalties, and civil and criminal liabilities.

CSCW researchers have been examining the role of collaborative artifacts (e.g., electronic medical record systems, whiteboards), as well as the daily work practices of the hospital staff for a number of years [17]. However, while researchers have examined privacy in different settings [31], there has been little work on privacy related issues in hospitals. Therefore, we investigated privacy issues through an ethnographic field study of the patient-care team members in the highly collaborative and information-intensive environment of an emergency department (ED) in a large academic hospital in the U.S. In particular, we are interested in examining the question of how organizational privacy policies are managed in this busy, collaborative ED environment. To address this question, we have focused on *collaborative privacy practices* (CPP). We conceptualize CPP as a set of activities that a group or team undertake to maintain the privacy of the information that they use in their work. This conceptualization shifts our focus of privacy management from the individual to the group, where multiple stakeholders are responsible for co-managing the privacy of information.

In the next section, we describe the current privacy research in CSCW. We then present our research methods and an overview of the ED environment. In the following section, we present the results of our field study and highlight the privacy practices that facilitate privacy management in the ED. Next, we discuss the tension between work practices and organizational privacy policies, the challenges of assigning accountability for privacy in collaborative environments, and some design implications. Finally, we conclude with thoughts on the direction of future CPP research.

LITERATURE REVIEW

Within CSCW, the tensions of group-level privacy practices have been identified by Palen and Dourish through their discussions on the *reflexive interpretability of action* (how users understand how their actions appear to others) and *mediation* (how interaction with others is conducted via a computer mediated environment) [31]. However, collaborative privacy practices by medical employees are more complex because the healthcare sector is an information-intensive industry, and a large percentage of its activities are dependent on the storage, sharing, processing, transfer, and analysis of sensitive patient data. Very limited studies in CSCW have discussed the need for studying collaborative privacy practices [6, 11, 29], which includes studying the privacy behaviors of groups who co-manage and share information within medical settings [11, 29]. In medical environments, information is not typically about the information handlers themselves (e.g., doctors handling patient information). However, these handlers are responsible for managing and protecting the privacy of this information in a collaborative fashion. For this reason, the handling of patient information results in a shared (vs. individual) responsibility for protecting patient privacy, which is of critical importance to health practices and to society as a whole.

Protecting information privacy within a collaborative environment is challenging. This is because organizations must develop effective technical mechanisms that protect privacy, while trying not to restrict the collaborative use of co-managed data [4, 5, 20, 32]. Additionally, these organizations must also implement organizational privacy policies that may restrict access and use of confidential information, while trying not to impede the staff's ability to do their work [13]. This literature review summarizes current studies related to the implementation of these privacy mechanisms and privacy policies within collaborative environments.

Technical Privacy Mechanisms

Privacy mechanisms are used within organizations to protect the confidentiality of information. This includes the use of access control mechanisms [4, 5, 20], audit trails [10, 15], and encryption [8, 30]. Many of these studies highlight the challenges of designing privacy mechanisms for collaborative organizations. Bartsch [4] described how authorization mechanisms tended to be too rigid and did not account for the staff's information needs changing over time. Bauer et al. [5] also found issues with collaborative organizations' access control mechanisms because of a gap between those who designed the mechanisms and those who used them. In some cases, the systems did not have the technical capabilities to implement the required tasks. There were also concerns about developing effective access control and security mechanisms for highly sensitive information (e.g., patients' mental health records) while balancing the need for reliable information availability for important users (e.g., doctors) [37].

Additionally, a few studies have pointed out the importance of understanding organizational work practices before implementing new privacy mechanisms [4, 5, 20]. Heckle et al. [20] described how neglecting to understand the staff's work practices before implementing a new access control mechanism led to implementation delays, additional costs, and negative attitudes towards the technology itself.

Organizational Policies and Procedures

Privacy policies are written guidelines that are used to train staff on regulatory, legal, and organizational requirements for protecting the confidentiality of information. This is especially important in healthcare organizations where regulations, such as HIPAA, can restrict the use and sharing of important information. Choi et al. [12] discussed how the implementation of privacy policies that assure regulatory compliance inevitably decrease the "ease and efficiency" of work practices. These privacy policies can even be in direct conflict with the work practices of the organization [38]. This can lead to serious issues, especially in healthcare organizations where restrictive policies can result in a negative impact to patient care [13]. A gap between policies and work practices can also result in the use of workarounds [1, 24]. These workarounds are temporary solutions that allow users to adapt technologies or processes in order to minimize interruptions [48]. However, the workarounds can deviate from the organizational policies, which could make the organization non-compliant with important regulations or laws.

There are also challenges in creating privacy policies for entire organizations. Turner & Dasgupta [43] described how the policies can become too generalized when including an entire organization within the same policy. These organization-wide policies can result in an inconsistent implementation of the policy within the separate groups.

These studies explore the impacts of both privacy mechanisms and organizational policies within collaborative environments. However, organizations cannot assure privacy based solely on the use of technical mechanisms and organizational policies [32]. The privacy practices of the staff must also protect privacy. There are studies that explore how employees' behaviors, or privacy practices, assure the confidentiality of information [35, 49]. Yet, these studies are limited and do not consider the impact that the privacy mechanisms and policies have on the work practices of the employees. Therefore, our study aims to better understand the collaborative privacy practices of the employees within a hospital's ED. This includes describing the impact that the organization's privacy mechanisms and policies may have on employees' privacy practices and work practices.

Summary

The need to balance the trade-off between privacy protection and work practices has been suggested by our literature review. However, within this body of literature, there lacks sufficient understanding of the underlying factors that determine the level of diligence of healthcare employees' handling patient information in their work practices. This is a significant exclusion because it is these medical employees who implement and comply with the technical and policy mechanisms to protect the privacy and confidentiality of patients' information. Therefore, we aim to gain an in-depth understanding about medical employees' privacy practices in terms of accessing, handling, and protecting patients' information in a collaborative environment.

In a recent interdisciplinary literature review, Smith et al. [39] have identified a lack of organizational privacy research in current literature, and the challenge is that organizational studies "are necessarily more complex and less conducive to 'quick' data collection techniques such as written and online surveys" (p. 1006). This gap in current privacy research has motivated us to conduct an ethnographic study to uncover the subtle organizational dynamics that drive privacy policies and practices.

METHODOLOGY

Research Site and Participants

We conducted this study in the ED of a large teaching hospital in northeastern United States. The ED has approximately 55,000 visits per year. The first author conducted 54 hours of observations and 4 hours of informal interviews with 7 clinical and non-clinical staff in the ED. We observed approximately 85 staff members, including: Physicians, residents, charge nurses, nurses, ED technicians, emergency medicine technicians (EMTs), pharmacists, transporters, care coordinators, social workers, registration assistants, chaplains, hospitality services, facilities, maintenance, and ED volunteers.

Phase	Description
(1) Familiarizing ourselves with the data	Transcribed interview notes and read transcriptions to ensure a general understanding of the data.
(2) Generating of initial codes	Labeled segments of data in a systematic way across all of the data.
(3) Searching for themes	Reviewed individual codes and identified preliminary themes.
(4) Reviewing themes	Reviewed preliminary themes to ensure they made sense across the entire data set.
(5) Defining and naming themes	Continuously refined each theme, identified a name for each theme, and defined the theme's boundaries.
(6) Producing the report	Presented themes with interesting examples that illustrate the individual themes.

Table 1: Braun & Clarke's six-phase thematic analysis approach

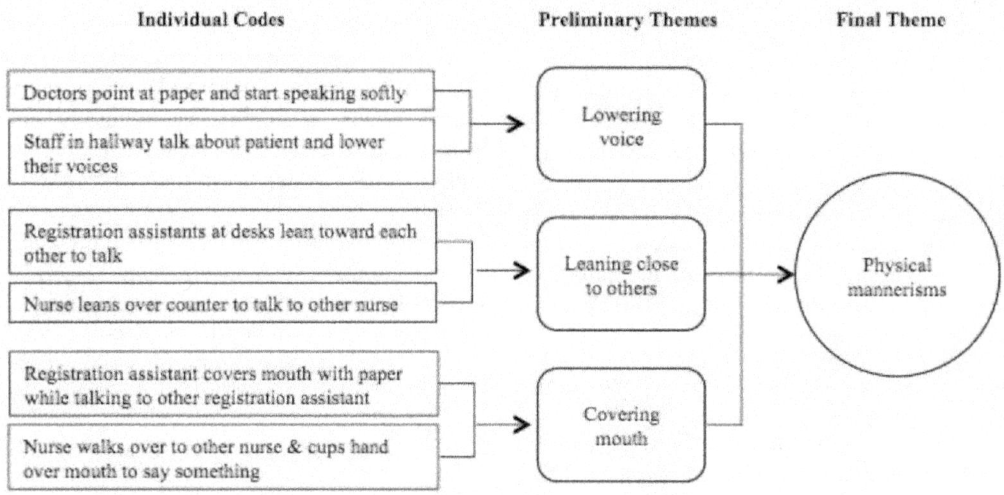

Figure 1: Example of theme generation using the thematic analysis approach

Data Collection

The 54 hours of observations were done in 2-5 hour increments over a 3-month period. Since the focus of the study was to understand the privacy practices of collaborative environments, we primarily focused our observations on two areas that had the largest amount of staff and information exchange: the registration area and the main nurses' station. We also observed the ED staff in hallways and at smaller nurses' stations. Detailed field notes were taken about the workflow, communication, collaboration, and technology use by both clinical and non-clinical staff. The field notes were then transcribed into an electronic document, resulting in 175 pages of data.

Data Analysis

The data was analyzed using Braun & Clarke's six-phase thematic analysis approach (Table 1) [9]. This general thematic analysis approach facilitates the process of becoming familiar with the data, systematically identifying codes and themes, and then defining and naming the common themes found across the entire data set. Through this analysis, we were able to identify types of privacy practices and mechanisms that helped facilitate privacy protection within the collaborative ED environment.

Figure 1 illustrates an example of how we generated individual codes, preliminary themes, and a final theme with this thematic analysis approach.

ED ENVIRONMENT

The ED is a fast-paced, collaborative environment where staff members have to work together to provide patient care. The staff includes clinical staff (e.g., physicians, residents, nurses, EMTs) and non-clinical staff (e.g., registration assistants, social workers, care coordinators, volunteers). The ED also sees a continuous influx of patients, visitors, and staff external to the ED (e.g., pharmacists, chaplains, specialized physicians).

Sources of Information

ED staff members received information from different sources. These sources included face-to-face communication, cell phones, pagers, desktop computers, laptop computers, computers-on-wheels (COWs), paper documents, white boards, and mounted electronic screens (e.g., tracking board).

The hospital policies state that the official patient medical records can be electronic, paper, or both; however, the ED used an EMR as its primary source of patient information. The hospital staff utilized computers throughout the ED to access the EMR. Desktop computers were found in patient rooms, nurses' stations, registration desks, and private offices. Some hospital staff (e.g., physicians, residents) carried laptops with them throughout the ED and used them to access the EMR at the nurses' stations and in private offices.

Some hospital staff frequently printed paper copies of patient records (called "face sheets") from the EMR. The staff carried these paper copies into patient rooms, took handwritten notes on them, and returned to their office computers to enter their notes into the EMR. When asked why they did this, they responded that it was more convenient and faster than having to log into the computer in the patients' rooms. They also stated that they preferred entering the patient information at their own computers to ensure that it was entered correctly into the system.

Organizational Privacy Policies

The ED staff had to attend mandatory training on organizational policies to make them aware of their responsibilities in protecting the confidentiality of patient information. The goal of these policies is to ensure that the hospital is in compliance with relevant federal and state laws and to protect the hospital from potential lawsuits. We reviewed 38 privacy policies that were part of the staff's training. The topics of the organizational privacy policies included:

- Access, use, and disposal of patient information (paper and electronic)
- Disclosure of information electronically (e.g., email, facsimile, telephone, photograph, electronic medical record systems)
- Disclosure of information to external reviewers (e.g., business associates, auditors, court order)
- Protecting the security of information (e.g., virus protection, remote access, password management, vendor system review, security controls, modifications and testing of computerized systems, eStorage)
- Printing of patient information
- Individuals' rights for requesting amendments, restrictions on disclosure, and confidential communication of patient information
- HIPAA accounting of disclosures
- Reporting of privacy practice complaints

In this section, we summarize the organizational privacy policies that are relevant to the observed activities within our study (verbal communication, physical mannerisms, technical mechanisms) in order to provide contextual background for this paper.

Access, Use, and Disclosure of Patient Information
The policies state that staff should use discretion when discussing patients and their medical information, especially in areas that are public or not soundproof. Also, the access, use, and disclosure of protected health information (PHI) in verbal, paper, or electronic form must be restricted to the minimal amount necessary to perform job requirements.

Appropriate Use of Information
The policies state that staff should limit the viewing and use of confidential information to only authorized individuals by protecting confidential documentation, positioning computer screens in a way that limits the view, and logging out of active sessions after use.

Access to Electronic Medical Records
The policies state that the staff are assigned individually identifiable usernames and passwords after obtaining the required management approval. The staff must not share their usernames and passwords with others. Additionally, the staff must use their own unique accounts when accessing and performing actions within the hospital's EMR system. This is because the use of the individual's username and password becomes a digital signature for any action performed by that account (e.g., adding, editing, deleting data).

Access within the Hospital
The policies state that the staff are assigned photo identification badges after obtaining the required management approval, which are programmed to allow access to the necessary restricted areas. The staff must not share their badges with others and only use their own badges when entering restricted areas.

ED Workflow
The ED workflow begins when patients enter the ED as either a *walk-in* or a *trauma*. The walk-ins enter through the registration check-in area where registration assistants enter the patient information into the EMR system. The registration assistants collect the patient's name, date of birth, social security number, zip code, and complaint (i.e., symptoms). This EMR data entry process generates a patient ID and alerts the charge nurse and attending physician of the new patient so that they can assign a patient-care team. Physicians are assigned to one of three areas in the ED and nurses are assigned to specific rooms. The triage nurses evaluate the patient, if needed, and then take them to an ED room. Depending on the room and location of the room, specific ED physicians and nurses, along with the ancillary staff, form the patient-care team for that patient.

If there is a trauma, the patient arrives through the ambulance entrance where a registration assistant assigns a patient ID in the EMR and collects as much information as possible depending on the patient's state. The trauma patients are then immediately brought to one of the designated trauma rooms. The registration assistant also alerts the ED of the trauma by sending out a page to certain staff. The trauma page alerts the charge nurse and attending physician, who assign a patient-care team for the trauma. The trauma page also alerts the registration assistants in the check-out registration area, who post the trauma information on the EMR's "tracking board" and compile a "trauma pack" depending on the type of trauma (e.g., dead-on-arrival, brain attack). An assigned nurse or ED technician pick-ups the trauma pack from registration and proceeds to the trauma room where the patient-care team is briefed on the patient's status.

Once the patient is in his/her ED room, the assigned physician and nurse(s) perform their patient care activities (e.g., evaluation, tests, medication administration, treatment). Registration assistants also visit the patient rooms to gather additional registration information, including demographic, insurance, and contact information. The registration assistants collect this information on a paper "face sheet" and then enter the information into the EMR back at their desk. A care coordinator is assigned to help the patient with financial assistance options, patient training, and external facility coordination (e.g., rehabilitation, assisted living). If the patient has any issues with drug, alcohol, or physical abuse, or psychiatric concerns then a social worker is assigned. Additionally, if the patient requests spiritual support, a chaplain is assigned as well. All members of the patient-care team log their activities in the EMR's "interdisciplinary narrative." This narrative is a real-time, chronological list of short updates about the patient's lab results, medication administration, and general assessments by the patient-care team. The physician and nurse also enter the patient's medical information into the EMR throughout their patient care activities. When patient-care team members need to discuss the patient, they frequently have the discussion at the main nurses' station that is centrally located in the ED.

If a patient receives visitors during their stay, the visitors arrive through the check-out registration area. The registration assistants provide the visitors with access to the ED. If the visitors are family members and the patient's registration information is not complete, then the registration assistants may ask the family members if they know the missing registration information (e.g., insurance, date of birth, address, phone number). The registration assistants then give the visitor the patient's room number and directions to the room. Visitors enter and exit through the access-controlled doors of the registration area.

When a patient is ready to be discharged, the patient-care team creates a discharge plan based on whether the patient will be admitted to the hospital, discharged to an external facility, or allowed to go home. Once the patient is discharged, the registration assistants check the patient out of the ED by logging his/her exit in the EMR and requesting any incomplete registration information.

FINDINGS

Sharing patient information is an integral part of patient care in the ED. However, because of the sensitive nature of patient information, there were various practices used to protect the privacy of this information. Through our analysis, we identified various privacy practices. We also identified several instances when organizational policies interfered with work practices. In these cases, the work practice was favored over the organizational privacy policy.

Types of Patient Information

The ED staff shared various kinds of patient information with one another.

- *Protected health information (PHI)* – Any specific medical information about a patient (e.g., the patient's symptoms, medications, test results, diagnosis);
- *Personally identifiable information (PII)* – Any information that could individually identify a patient (e.g., the patient's full name, date of birth, social security number, phone number, address);
- *Generalized information* – Any information that does not individually identify a patient or relate to his/her medical condition (e.g., the patient's food request, room number or location, physical description).

The staff members shared these three types of information in different ways. PHI was frequently discussed by all staff members because it was required by the patient-care team to determine a care plan for the patient. Yet, at the same time, staff members were typically more careful about openly discussing PHI with one another because of the confidential nature of the information.

PII was generally only discussed by the registration assistants because they were required to obtain demographic (e.g., ethnicity, age, gender, marital status) and identification information (e.g., social security number, phone number, address) from the patients. PII was openly discussed in the registration areas, but rarely shared anywhere else in the ED.

The generalized information was openly discussed by all ED staff. Since it was not personally identifiable information or sensitive medical information, there was little effort by the ED staff to protect the privacy of this information.

Privacy Practices

We observed various practices and mechanisms in the ED used to protect the privacy of patient information. These included physical mannerisms, secure spaces, physical proximity, ED access control, and information access control.

Physical Mannerisms

One of the primary methods of sharing information in the ED was verbal communication. The ED staff would frequently use certain physical mannerisms to prevent other individuals from overhearing their discussion. These practices included: lowering their voices, leaning closer to the person they were speaking to, and holding up their hand or a piece of paper to cover their mouth when speaking.

Two registration assistants are at their computers talking about three traumas that just arrived in the ED. The traumas were all children in the same family. One registration assistant describes to the other how the children's mother was outside the patient rooms crying and talking on her cell phone. She starts describing the medical state of the children. She then takes the piece of paper she's holding, puts it over her mouth, lowers her voice, leans into the other registration assistant, and continues to talk so that no one else in the area can hear them.

By putting the paper over her mouth, the registration assistant prevented visitors from hearing what she was saying. Her physical mannerism was also a signal to the other registration assistant that she was going to share some private information (i.e. PHI) about the case. This also made the second registration assistant more focused on the information that she was receiving.

Secure Spaces

ED staff also utilized what they considered secure spaces to share private information. For instance, although the registration desk and nurses' stations were open to the general hallways, there were a number of private offices available for use. One office was located through the nurses' station and was called the "physicians' area." Many times physicians would leave patient rooms and return to the physicians' area to have conversations with other patient-care team members. Registration assistants also used a back office in order to have private conversations:

During a shift change at the registration desk, a new registration assistant comes in and starts talking to the others about what has been happening in the ED that morning. Another registration assistant in the back office asked the new registration assistant to come into the office to "discuss a few things." They go into the office and close the door.

By using the private office and closing the door, the registration assistants were able to have a private conversation that could not be heard by the visitors in the waiting room and by other registration assistants at the desk.

Additionally, there were open spaces within the ED where the staff thought it was appropriate to talk about patient information. One of these designated areas was the main nurses' station. The nurses' station is a centralized location where various members of the patient-care team can meet, document and obtain information from the computers and phones, and create the patient-care plans. Around the nurses' station, patient-care teams would frequently talk about generalized information and PHI, since they had to discuss medical information; however, they took care not to discuss PII, which would identify the patient. Team members openly discussed patient conditions, tests, or diagnoses with other ED staff around the nurses' station counter.

A physician and four residents exit a patient's room. They gather around the main nurses' station counter and the physician summarizes the patient's condition based on the examination. He also mentions the patient's current medications. The residents take notes in their notebooks. The physician then asks them what tests they think should be run on the patient. The residents offer their opinions and the physician discusses the recommended tests with the residents.

Other ED staff just walked by the group or continued their own work at the nurses' station without paying attention to the discussion about the patient.

One area that was not considered a secure space was the open hallway. If the ED staff were in the hallways, they would frequently use physical mannerisms to protect PHI or go to a secure space to talk about patients. However, there were times when ED staff openly talked to patients about PHI in the hallways.

A patient with a neck brace is walking in the hallway and passes two registration assistants. One registration assistant asks how his neck is doing. The patient mentions that it's a bad neck sprain from the car accident and that he has to wear the brace for two weeks.

In this case, the registration assistants are expressing emotional support, which could be considered part of their job. However, showing support by talking about PHI in an open hallway does not align with privacy policies on protecting the confidentiality of the patient's health information in open spaces. In this case, the registration assistants prioritized their work practices over the organization's privacy policies in order to express their concern about the patient's condition.

Physical Proximity

ED staff members also protected the privacy of information sources. In any area where computers were visible from the general hallways, staff members either stayed close to the computer where they were logged in, or they logged out before leaving the area to ensure that private information was not left open.

The main nurses' station also had a charge nurse's area with an outward facing computer that did not timeout. This lack of timeout did not follow the organizational privacy policy, which states that computers will automatically logout after a certain period of inactivity. However, this was not the case with the charge nurse's computer. Although this information was left open, the charge nurse and other nurses were always very close to the open computer to prevent unauthorized individuals from accessing the system and viewing PHI.

The charge nurse has been standing by her computer all morning. When she has to speak to other nurses, she calls them over to her computer. When a trauma arrives in the ED, the charge nurse is called away for a meeting. The charge nurse asks another nurse to stay at the computer while she is away. The other nurse then takes over standing at the charge nurse's computer.

It seems that physical proximity was used as an important method of protecting the privacy of patient information.

ED Access Control

One of the primary ways of maintaining privacy was through controlling access to the ED. All six entrances into the ED, except for the main entrance where patients checked-in, were access-controlled. There were also four access-controlled doors internally that connected the registration areas to patient room hallways. ED staff used their badges to open the doors themselves or the registration assistants opened the door for patients, visitors, or external hospital employees. In addition, the lead registration assistant watched a video monitor of the doors that provided visibility of any attempts to enter the ED. Registration assistants also had to use a code to enter their own office, which contained confidential paper records and fax machines.

However, on occasion, the registration assistants opened the access-controlled doors for other employees (e.g., nurse who forgot her ID, nurse pushing a wheelchair, nurse with her hands full).

A nurse pushes a patient in a wheelchair through the registration area. A registration assistant at her desk looks up, sees them, and pushes a button to open the door that the nurse is walking towards. The door swings open for the nurse and patient. The nurse thanks the registration assistant for opening the door for them. The nurse and patient proceed through the door.

According to organizational privacy policies, the nurse was supposed to badge herself in so that the hospital has an accurate record of entry into restricted areas. However, clearly, she had difficulty doing this while pushing a patient, so the registration assistant did it for her. The opening of doors for other ED staff does not follow the organizational privacy policy for controlling access to the ED. Instead, the registration assistants chose to assist their colleagues by opening the doors. This is another case where privacy policies did not align with work practices, and the work practices took priority over the policy.

Both registration assistants and staff around the nurses' station also controlled access to the ED by frequently approaching people they did not know. They would ask unknown individuals whom they were visiting and if they needed help with anything. This included asking the researcher conducting the observations why she was there, as well as other visitors or staff in the hallways and waiting areas. For example, the charge nurse approached an unknown individual who was behind the nurses' station:

The charge nurse walks up to a person who just entered the nurses' station. The charge nurse introduced herself and asked who the person was. The person identified themselves as an inpatient staff member of the hospital. The charge nurse then said, "Oh okay, I had just never met you before."

Talking to unknown individuals helped to control access to the ED and protect the privacy of patients by ensuring only appropriate people were in the ED.

Information Access Control

The access control mechanisms built into the ED computers also helped to protect the privacy of information. These computer mechanisms include unique logins, inactivity timeouts, and disabling user access after too many incorrect attempts to login.

A registration assistant sits down at the registration desk and mentions that she cannot log into the system. She says she believes she is locked out because she keeps forgetting her password and entered it incorrectly too many times. Another registration assistant tells her to "call the helpdesk right away" so that she can get it fixed and get back into the system.

There were also computer mechanisms that protected information at the nurses' station. The main nurses' station was situated in the middle of the ED in an arc shape with a high counter on the exterior of the station for staff members to use for writing or working. There were six "Physician/Consult" computers on the nurses' station counter facing outward towards the ED hallways for physicians, nurses, and other ED staff to use during their daily work. These monitors included authorization mechanisms, which required a general password to login to the desktop. A nurse said that these general passwords "*change regularly*." These systems then required a unique username and password to login to the EMR system. We also observed that these monitors automatically logged out after approximately 10 minutes of inactivity. All other laptops and monitors in the ED were located behind the nurses' station and within patient rooms and offices, which could not be easily observed from the hallways.

There were times when the daily work practices would not align with the organizational policies. On occasion, nurses at the nurses' station would openly share the general password to log into the "Physician/Consult" monitors. This was not a password to the EMR system itself, but for accessing the computer at the nurses' counter. Although the organizational privacy policies state that users should not share passwords, nurses had to often share the password in order to continue doing their work. The nurses viewed the risk in this situation as low because the password could only open the monitor and they also recognized the person they were giving the password to as an authorized ED employee.

In another situation, a registration assistant entered information about a trauma patient into the EMR on another registration assistant's computer.

A registration assistant returns from getting information about a trauma patient. He begins entering the information into the system and asks the other registration assistants at their desks certain questions about how to enter the trauma data. He then says that he is late for a meeting. Another registration assistant offers to finish the data entry and says, "Want me to just do it on yours?" The registration assistant then sits down at the other registration assistant's computer and finishes entering the information.

In this case, the registration assistant entered information under another registration assistant's account. This is a clear violation of the organizational privacy policy that states that all staff must use their own unique accounts when performing actions in the system (e.g., adding, editing, deleting information). This illustrates another time when the work practice was prioritized over the organizational policy. In this case, the registration assistant had to input the patient information in a timely manner because the patient was a trauma case and the other patient-care team members needed that information as soon as possible.

DISCUSSION

The privacy of patient information is a priority to hospitals. Not only are U.S. hospitals legally required to protect patients' privacy because of HIPAA and HITECH compliance [25, 45, 46], but properly managing privacy also builds trust and improves communication between providers and patients [27]. Therefore, hospitals often develop organizational privacy policies based on legal requirements to define how the employees should protect the privacy of patients' medical information [38].

However, the existence of a law does not automatically translate into an explicit organizational privacy policy. Consequently, these policies can range from being very specific to very general. For example, our study hospital had a very specific policy about technical access control mechanisms at the system level. This policy had clear instructions for the assignment of unique usernames and specific requirements for creating secure passwords to use when logging into systems. This policy also had specific guidelines on the use of security mechanisms, such as automatic logout after a specific time of inactivity and system audit trails that capture who created, modified, or deleted information with the date and time of the action. However, other behavioral aspects of privacy policies were more vague. An example of this is a hospital policy about the verbal communication of patient information. This policy generally instructed the staff to use their own discretion when discussing patients and their medical information, especially in public areas, and to only discuss the minimum amount of information required to do their work. These vaguely written policies made the medical staff more aware of privacy requirements, but did not provide explicit guidelines.

Often, these policies are written for the entire hospital and not just one particular unit. Therefore, the policies do not necessarily account for the different activities and work practices in the different units. So, a busy unit, such as the ED, has to deal with same policies as a less busy unit, such as floor ward. Consequently, the staff of the particular unit has to develop approaches to manage these privacy policies in the context of their own work setting.

Our findings suggest a lack of clarity in translating some of those abstract policies into day-to-day work practices. One potential consequence of the ambiguity in the organizational privacy policies is the staff's use of workarounds to deal with specific privacy policies that affected their work practices. In this section, we will discuss several underlying factors for explaining the workarounds observed in our study. We will also discuss the accountability for privacy within highly collaborative environments and design implications based on our findings.

Privacy Policy Workarounds

Studies have highlighted the demanding and busy nature of the ED [1, 36]. In this environment, the ED staff often resorted to workarounds to deal with breakdowns or other problems in the unit [1]. This was also the case in our study when the organizational privacy policies or security mechanisms interfered with the staff's work practices. In particular, the staff used privacy workarounds in order to have constant access to information and to improve work efficiency.

Constant Information Access

From an organizational perspective, allowing employees to stay logged into an unattended computer can create a wide variety of problems ranging from allowing individuals unauthorized access to the information to disrupting the audit trail of who entered the information. Therefore, most systems have automatic logout mechanisms to prevent these problems. Yet, this may also create unintended problems, such as increasing the time it takes to access the information. In the ED, all the computers except one had an automatic logout feature. This computer with no auto-logout was at the nurses' station and was frequently used by the nurses. This seemed to clearly violate the organizational policies on automatic timeout. However, the ED staff had created a workaround, as described in the findings, to ensure the privacy of the information. The staff used *physical proximity* as a privacy mechanism for ensuring that only authorized individuals had access to the information. The charge nurse or other nurses always stood close to the open computer. The charge nurse even specifically asked another nurse to stand close to the computer when she had to step away. Therefore, in this workaround, the technical safeguard (automatic timeout) was replaced with a human safeguard (physical proximity). This allowed the information to be protected while at the same time assuring staff access to the information that they needed without disrupting their work practice by having to constantly log back into the computer.

In a dynamic and demanding environment like the ED, a patient's condition could change from moment to moment and the medical staff has to be able to quickly respond to this change. If the information needed by the medical staff to make urgent clinical decisions was unavailable due to strict access control, patients may miss the best treatment opportunities. Therefore, one of the major challenges in the ED is to ensure that information is available to the staff at a moment's notice. Yet, the need for constant information availability in the ED does not align with the hospital's privacy policies about automatic computer logouts. As Salomon et al. [37] pointed out, achieving a balance between constant information access and privacy compliance becomes particularly challenging in a medical context. Failure to address clinicians' information needs could lead to them using workarounds to bypass privacy protection mechanisms (e.g., automatic timeout features).

Improve Workflow Efficiencies

Another issue in the ED is the number of interruptions that affected the workflow in the unit. In the pursuit of privacy compliance, organizations enforce policies and technologies that may interrupt workflows or work practices. As a result, employees may not always comply with these organizational privacy policies and sometimes they try to minimize negative impacts of these policies on their work efficiencies through workarounds. For example, the hospital's privacy policy requires that ED staff badge themselves into any access-controlled areas so that the hospital can maintain an accurate record of who enters restricted areas in the hospital. However, there were times when registration assistants opened doors for other ED staff members who were supposed to use their own badges. The registration assistants performed this workaround if staff forgot their badges, were pushing a cleaning cart or wheelchair, or had their arms full. This workaround helped improve their work efficiency, but at the same time resulted in the inability to accurately track staff entry records.

Organizational privacy policies on data access/entry often conflict with the need for getting things done quickly in the ED. Similar to many organizations, the hospital's policy was that staff must enter information under their own username since that is the name associated with the entry in the audit trail. However, as described in the findings, we observed a situation where a registration assistant sat down at another registration assistant's computer to finish data entry for a patient. Getting the information into the system was a high priority because it was for a trauma patient and the trauma team needed access to any patient information as soon as possible. Yet, this was clearly in violation of the organizational policy on data access. However, the time saved by entering the information into the system under the other registration assistant's account instead of taking the time to save the information, log out the previous user, log back into the system, and find the patient record again outweighed the policy.

Similar to Smith [38], our study identified a "policy/practice gap," in which the staff's actual work practices are at variance with the official privacy policies. Negative effects of implementing privacy technologies and procedures on workflow and work efficiencies have been documented in the literature [12, 13]. Lovis et al. [26] identified one of the biggest challenges in privacy compliance in the medical context is to develop technologies and procedures that do not hinder the workflow and work practices of clinicians. In situations where privacy enhancing features and procedures disrupt their work efficiencies or workflows, staff try to minimize these negative impacts through workarounds to bypass privacy safeguards [1, 24]. Unattended workarounds can be potentially harmful to the overall organizational privacy compliance.

Accountability for Information Privacy in Collaborative Environments

Although there were situations where accountability for privacy violations was clear, there were a number of situations where it was not as obvious. For instance, in one case, the charge nurse asked another nurse to watch the no-logout computer while she left the area. In this case, the charge nurse clearly stated and assigned accountability to that nurse. However, in another situation, a registration assistant entered information under another registration assistant's account. In this case, it was not as clear about who was responsible for following the proper data entry policy. Was the first registration assistant responsible for logging out of the system before leaving the computer? Or was the second responsible for logging the previous user out of the system and logging back into the system with her own username and password? Or both?

The registration case illustrates how it is sometimes difficult to determine clear accountability in a collaborative environment where multiple people may be interacting with the same technologies. The first registration assistant may have assumed that the second would log out before continuing, while the second registration assistant may have assumed, based on previous practice, that she could use the account. Therefore, breakdowns in enforcing organizational policies can occur when there is ambiguity regarding who is accountable for privacy.

An additional issue to consider in collaborative settings is that the privacy practices may vary from person to person, which could create conflict or tension among the multiple information handlers. For example, certain areas of the ED were considered secure spaces to openly discuss private information. Physicians exited patient rooms and started openly discussing private patient information around the nurses' station. In this case, the physicians felt that they could freely discuss that private information because they were in a controlled-access ED around an area designated for other members of the patient-care team. However, it is possible that other ED staff members may not agree that physicians should be talking about private patient information in this area because visitors often walk by that area. They may believe that conversations about patients should occur in the private physicians' area located behind the nurses' station so that other patients and visitors do not hear the information being discussed.

In the ED, multiple staff members may access, use, and share a single patient's record. Therefore, staff members may have differing assumptions about whose responsibility it is to protect the privacy of that information. This is especially true when shifting privacy management from physical environments to computer-mediated environments [33]. There can also be overlapping accountability of specific privacy tasks, especially within fast-paced, highly collaborative environments such as EDs. All of these issues raise the question of who should be held accountable for managing the privacy of information.

Design Implications

In busy, information-intensive, and collaborative environments like the ED, it can be challenging to implement privacy policies that do not hinder the work practices of the staff. In this section, we discuss some technical mechanisms and policy mechanisms that could help address some of these challenges.

Technical Design

The ED staff used workarounds in order to improve their access to information. This included disabling the automatic timeout mechanisms to avoid repeatedly logging into the system, becoming locked out of the system because of forgetting one's password, and sharing passwords. Currently, the most common form of system access control in hospitals is the use of unique usernames and confidential passwords [3, 28, 50]. However, this method of access control can lead to concerns about users forgetting passwords or sharing passwords with others, and concerns about hackers using software to determine user passwords and gain unauthorized access to the system [28]. Therefore, other authentication methods have been suggested for the hospital setting.

One alternative access mechanism is smartcards, which are physical cards that users swipe or insert into the EMR system in order to confirm identity of the user [23]. Although these cards are portable and do not require password memorization, there can be problems with the cards potentially being lost, stolen, or damaged [21]. Another alternative access mechanism is the use of biometrics for user identification. Current biometric mechanisms include fingerprint, handprint, or retinal scans, as well as, face geometry technologies [21]. This alternative eliminates the need to memorize passwords or carry a smartcard. However, biometric authentication can be expensive to install and maintain for hospitals, and usability issues can result from environmental temperature, humidity, dirt, and the user's physical condition [18]. In addition, biometric authentication could lead to the users themselves having privacy concerns about the storage and use of their own biometric data [34].

Additionally, the ED staff also used workarounds to improve their workflow efficiencies. This included staff badging each other into restricted areas of the ED, instead of each staff member using his/her own badge. Currently, the most common form of physical access control in hospitals is the use of badges to open doors to restricted areas. This allows the hospital to accurately track the flow of people in restricted sections of the hospital. However, prior literature discusses an alternative to the use of badges for entry – radio frequency identification (RFID) tags.

RFID technology uses electronic chips to store and retrieve data. These chips, or "tags," are attached to objects or people, and the data is read by separate RFID "readers" [19]. The benefits of RFID are that the readers can scan tags while they are in motion and without direct line of sight to the tags [19]. This is beneficial for very busy environments, like hospitals. Within the medical context, RFID is typically used for medication, equipment, and patient tracking, but it has also been considered for staff tracking as well [16, 19].

Tracking hospital staff using RFID helped to improve the workflow of clinicians and quickly locate staff when they were needed for emergencies [16, 19, 53]. In our study, it was a common practice for staff to badge each other into restricted areas of the hospital. Embedding RFID tags into staff badges could be a potential solution for this issue by reducing workflow interruptions (e.g., stopping to find badge to hold to the door sensor) and preventing workarounds that lead to inaccurate records (e.g., badging in other staff). However, hospitals should also consider the negative impacts of using RFID to track staff.

RFID technologies can cause interference with other technologies, have high costs for installing and maintaining infrastructure, and lead to privacy and ethical issues [16, 19, 53]. In one study that explored the staff concerns of RFID tracking, nurses felt that they were "being watched by administration" and that there was increased work because maintaining the technology often fell upon them [16].

Therefore, these alternative technical mechanisms for accessing systems and entering restricted areas provide potential solutions to the policy workarounds described in this study. However, these alternatives raise additional issues regarding cost and privacy concerns. Hospitals will have to weigh the cost-benefit tradeoffs of choosing an alternative to the current technical mechanisms if they chose to explore alternative access control mechanisms.

Policy Design

Although technical design can address some of the tensions between organizational privacy policies and work activities, we also need to start re-thinking organizational privacy policy development and enforcement [14].

The "one-size-fits-all" privacy policy that most organizations have can lead to uneven application throughout the organization [43]. This approach does have the benefit of being much easier to develop, as well as ensure that there is a standard policy throughout the organization. However, these policies are also the ones that are most often violated because they do not account for the variance in work practices across departments. Therefore, organizations may write very general policies that give little guidance or more specific policies that will be often violated because they negatively impact the work practices in the department. Clearly, it is not a simple solution to write departmental-level privacy policies. There are issues with ensuring that departmental policies are in-sync with broader organizational policies, as well as the cost of developing and enforcing multiple different departmental policies. At the same time, this approach may be beneficial in terms of supporting, rather than hindering, departmental work practices.

Another important issue in implementing organizational privacy policies is ensuring that the users (i.e., clinical and non-clinical staff) have effective communication channels to share their feedback on privacy technologies and procedures with IT. One of the challenges that users often face is that privacy technologies and procedures are usually implemented on the basis of what is required by the privacy policies and do not account for the type of work practices in a department [4, 5, 12, 13, 20, 26]. This is a particular challenge in hospitals that have to comply with a number of legal requirements about ensuring the privacy of health information. Consequently, staff may see the privacy policies as a hindrance to their work. However, improving the communication channels between the two groups could help ensure that problems or issues are readily addressed.

CONCLUSION

An emergency department is a highly collaborative and busy environment where staff, patients, and visitors are all present. This means that there are a variety of challenges to managing information privacy in collaborative settings such as this. Therefore, the ED staff have developed various practices to try to help them manage these challenges.

More broadly, managing privacy is an important but challenging aspect of organizational work. Often times, work practices conflict with organizational policies and staff have to make daily decisions about whether to adjust their work or deviate from the policy. In collaborative environments, this can become even more problematic because of the larger number of people involved.

Through this research, we hope to improve our understanding of privacy practices in collaborative settings. We can then develop organizational policies that better match the on-going work, as well as begin to identify design requirements for the development of privacy-enhancing features that will also support the collaboration.

ACKNOWLEDGEMENTS

The authors are very grateful to the AC and anonymous reviewers for their constructive comments. We would also like to thank the ED staff and hospital CMIO for their willingness to participate in this study, as well as Saijing Zheng for her assistance in preliminary data analysis. This research is supported by the U.S. National Science Foundation under grant IIS-1017247. Any opinions, findings, and conclusions or recommendations expressed herein are those of the researchers and do not necessarily reflect the views of the National Science Foundation.

REFERENCES

1. Ash, J.S., Berg, M., and Coiera, E. Some unintended consequences of information technology in health care: The nature of patient care information system-related errors. *Journal of the American Medical Informatics Association, 11*, 2 (2004), 104-112.
2. Angst, C.M. and Agarwal, R. Adoption of electronic health records in the presence of privacy concerns: The elaboration likelihood model and individual persuasion. *MIS Quarterly, 33*, 2 (2009), 339-370.
3. Barrows, R.C. and Clayton, P.D. Privacy, confidentiality, and electronic medical records. *Journal of the American Medical Informatics Association, 3*, 2 (1996), 139-148.
4. Bartsch, S. Exploring twisted paths: Analyzing authorization processes in organizations. In *Proc. Network and System Security*, (2011), 216-223.
5. Bauer, L., Cranor, L.F., Reeder, R.W., Reiter, M.K., and Vaniea, K. Real life challenges in access-control management. In *Proc. CHI 2009*, ACM Press (2009), 899-908.
6. Belanger, F. and Crossler, R.E. Privacy in the digital age: A review of information privacy research in information systems. *MIS Quarterly, 35*, 4 (2011), 1017-1041.
7. Besmer, A. and Lipford, H.R. Moving beyond untagging: Photo privacy in a tagged world. In *Proc. CHI 2010*, ACM Press (2010), 1563-1572.
8. Bethencourt, J., Sahai, A., and Waters, B. Ciphertext-policy attribute-based encryption. In *Proc. IEEE Symposium on Security and Privacy*, (2007), 321–334.
9. Braun, V. and Clarke, V. Using thematic analysis in psychology. *Qualitative Research in Psychology, 3*, 2 (2006), 77-101.
10. Chen, Y., Nyemba, S., and Malin, B. Detecting anomalous insiders in collaborative information systems. *IEEE Transactions on Dependable and Secure Computing, 9*, 3 (2012), 332-344.
11. Chen, Y. and Xu, H. Privacy management in dynamic groups: Understanding information privacy in medical practices. In *Proc. CSCW 2013*, ACM Press (2013), 541-552.
12. Choi, Y.B., Capitan, K.E., Krause, J.S., and Streeper, M.M. Challenges associated with privacy in health care industry: Implementation of HIPAA and the security rules. *Journal of Medical Systems, 30*, 1 (2006), 57-64.
13. Coiera, E. and Clarke, R. e-Consent: The design and implementation of consumer consent mechanisms in an electronic environment. *Journal of the American Medical Informatics Association, 11*, 2 (2004), 129-140.
14. Culnan, M.J. and Williams, C.C. How ethics can enhance organizational privacy: Lessons from the choicepoint and TJX data breaches. *MIS Quarterly, 33*, 4 (2009), 673-687.
15. Fabbri, D. and LeFevre, K. Explaining accesses to electronic medical records using diagnosis information. *Journal of the American Medical Informatics Association, 20*, 1 (2013), 52-60.
16. Fisher, J.A. and Monahan, T. Tracking the social dimensions of RFID systems in hospitals. *International Journal of Medical Informatics, 77*, 3 (2008), 176-183.
17. Fitzpatrick, G. and Ellingsen, G. A review of 25 years of CSCW research in healthcare: Contributions, challenges, and future agendas. *Journal of CSCW*, (2012), 1-57.

18. Flores Zuniga, A.E., Win, K.T., and Susilo, W. Biometrics for electronic health records. *Journal of Medical Systems, 34*, 5 (2010), 975-983.

19. Fuhrer, P. and Guinard, D. Building a smart hospital using RFID technologies. In *Proc. European Conference on eHealth*, (2006), 131-142.

20. Heckle, R., Lutters, W. G., and Gurzick, D. Network authentication using single sign-on: the challenge of aligning mental models. In *Proc. Computer Human Interaction for Management of Information Technology*, (2008), 6-15.

21. Hewitt, B. Exploring how security features affect the use of electronic health records. *International Journal of Healthcare Technology and Management, 11*, 1 (2010), 31-49.

22. Hoadley, C.M., Xu, H., Lee, J.J., and Rosson, M.B. Privacy as information access and illusory control: The case of the Facebook news feed privacy outcry. *Electronic Commerce Research and Applications, 9*, 4 (2010), 649-664.

23. Hu, J., Chen, H.H., and Hou, T.W. A hybrid public key infrastructure solution (HPKI) for HIPAA privacy/security regulations. *Computer Standards and Interfaces, 32*, 5 (2010), 274–280.

24. Koppel, R., Wetterneck, T., Telles, J.L., and Karsh, B.T. Workarounds to barcode medication administration systems: Their occurrences, causes, and threats to patient safety. *Journal of the American Medical Informatics Association, 15*, 4 (2008), 408-423.

25. Liu, C. and Arnett, K.P. Raising a red flag on global WWW privacy policies. *Journal of Computer Information Systems, 43*, 1 (2002), 117-127.

26. Lovis, C., Spahni, S., Cassoni, N., and Geissbuhler, A. Comprehensive management of the access to the electronic patient record: Towards trans-institutional networks. *International Journal of Medical Informatics, 76*, 5 (2007), 466-470.

27. Mandl, K.D., Szolovits, P., and Kohane, I.S. Public standards and patients' control: How to keep electronic medical records accessible but private. *British Medical Journal, 322*, 7281 (2001), 283-287.

28. Medlin, B.D. and Romaniello, A. An investigative study: Health care workers as security threat suppliers. *Journal of Information Privacy and Security, 3*, 1 (2007), 30-46.

29. Murphy, A.R., Reddy, M.C., Xu, H., and Ringel, B. Exploring collaborative privacy practices. In *Proc. CHI 2011 Workshop "Privacy for a Networked World: Bridging Theory and Design,"* ACM Press (2011).

30. Narayan, S., Gagne, M., and Safavi-Naini, R. Privacy preserving EHR system using attribute-based infrastructure. In *Proc. ACM 2010 Workshop "Cloud Computing Security,"* ACM Press (2010), 47-52.

31. Palen, L. and Dourish, P. Unpacking "privacy" for a networked world. In *Proc. CHI 2003*, ACM Press (2003), 129–136.

32. Parks, R., Chu, C. H., and Xu, H. Healthcare information privacy research: Issues, gaps and what next? In *Proc. 2011 Americas Conference on Information Systems*, (2011).

33. Patil, S. and Kobsa, A. Privacy in collaboration: Managing impression. In *Proc. 2005 International Conference on Online Communities and Social Computing*, (2005).

34. Prabhakar, S., Pankanti, S., and Jain, A.K. Biometric recognition: Security and privacy concerns. *IEEE Journal of Security & Privacy, 1*, 2 (2003), 33-42.

35. Randell, R., Wilson, S., Woodward, P. and Galliers, J.R. The ConStratO model of handover: A tool to support technology design and evaluation. *Behaviour & Information Technology, 30*, 4 (2011), 489-498.

36. Reddy, M. and Dourish, P. A finger on the pulse: Temporal rhythms and information seeking in medical work. In *Proc. CSCW 2002*, ACM Press (2002), 344-353.

37. Salomon, R.M., Blackford, J.U., Rosenbloom, S.T., Seidel, S., Clayton, E.W., Dilts, D.M., and Finder, S.G. Openness of patients' reporting with use of electronic records: Psychiatric clinicians' views. *Journal of the American Medical Informatics Association, 17*, 1 (2010), 54-60.

38. Smith, H.J. Privacy policies and practices: Inside the organizational maze. *Communications of the ACM, 36*, 12 (1993), 105-122.

39. Smith, H. J., Dinev, T., and Xu, H. Information privacy research: An interdisciplinary review, *MIS Quarterly, 35*, 4 (2011), 989-1015.

40. Son, J.Y. and Kim, S.S. Internet users' information privacy-protective responses: A taxonomy and a nomological model. *MIS Quarterly, 32*, 3 (2008), 503-529.

41. Stutzman, F. and Kramer-Duffield, J. Friends only: Examining a privacy-enhancing behavior in Facebook. In *Proc. CHI 2010*, ACM Press (2010), 1553-1562.

42. Squicciarini, A.C., Xu, H., and Zhang, X. CoPE: Enabling collaborative privacy management in online social networks. *Journal of the American Society for Information Science and Technology, 62*, 3 (2010), 521-534.

43. Turner, E.C. and Dasgupta, S. Privacy on the web: An examination of user's concerns, technology, and implications for business organizations and individuals. *Information Systems Management, 20*, 1 (2003), 8-18.

44. U.S. Department of Health and Human Services. (2013). "Breaches Affecting 500 or More Individuals." Retrieved from:

http://www.hhs.gov/ocr/privacy/hipaa/administrative/breachnotificationrule/breachtool.html.

45. U.S. Department of Health and Human Services. (2013). "Health Information Privacy." Retrieved from: http://www.hhs.gov/ocr/privacy/.

46. U.S. Department of Health and Human Services. (2013). "HITECH Act Enforcement Interim Final Rule." Retrieved from: http://www.hhs.gov/ocr/privacy/hipaa/administrative/enforcementrule/hitechenforcementifr.html.

47. U.S. Government. (2013). "American Recovery and Reinvestment Act of 2009". Retrieved from: http://www.recovery.gov/About/Pages/The_Act.aspx.

48. Vogelsmeier, A.A., Halbesleben, J.R.B., and Scott-Cawiezell, J.R. Technology implementation and workarounds in the nursing home. *Journal of the American Medical Informatics Association, 15*, 1 (2008), 114-119.

49. Wears, R. L., Perry, S. J., Wilson, S., Galliers, J., and Fone, J. Emergency department status boards: User-evolved artefacts for inter-and intra-group coordination. *Cognition, Technology & Work, 9*, 3 (2007), 163-170.

50. Win, K.T. A review of security of electronic health records. *Health Information Management, 34*, 1 (2005), 13-18.

51. Xu, H., Dinev, T., Smith, H.J., and Hart, P. Examining the formation of individual's information privacy concerns: Toward an integrative view. In *Proc. International Conference on Information Systems*, (2008).

52. Xu, H., Teo, H.H., Tan, B.C.Y., and Agarwal, R. The role of push-pull technology in privacy calculus: The case of location-based services. *Journal of Management Information Systems, 26*, 3 (2009), 137-176.

53. Yao, W., Chu, C.H., and Li, Z. The use of RFID in healthcare: Benefits and barriers. In *Proc. 2010 IEEE International Conference on RFID Technology and Applications*, (2010), 128-134.

Institutional Logics of the EMR and the Problem of 'Perfect' but Inaccurate Accounts

Kathleen Pine[a] & Melissa Mazmanian[b]
[a]Intel Labs
[b]Department of Informatics, University of California, Irvine
{khpine, m.mazmania}@uci.edu

ABSTRACT

Electronic Medical Records promise to simultaneously enhance coordination and provide transparency and accountability in work process. As such, EMR are purported to benefit both hospitals and patients. In this paper we use grounded empirical data to explore how this promise plays out in the everyday tasks of healthcare providers. Building on the small body of CSCW literature that suggests that the accounting functions of EMR are impinging on the ability of medical personnel to coordinate work, we draw on the theoretical lens of new institutionalism to outline how certain institutional logics around safety and accountability are shaping the experience of EMR systems in situ. We suggest that the institutional logics that currently characterize U.S. healthcare are embedded in the EMR design itself, structuring how institutional values such as "safety" are achieved and evaluated. Using over one year of ethnographic research in an obstetrical unit, we find that the institutional logics of "safety" embedded in the EMR create negative organizational outcomes, effectively undermining coordination and necessitating inaccurate accounts of work. We provide design implications to address these issues in the current institutional environment and envision how systems might be designed to promote alternate logics of safety that are social, dynamic, and cast humans as expert agents in the system.

Author Keywords

Electronic Medical Records; Accountability; Coordination; Organizations; New Institutionalism; Safety; Medication; Ordering

ACM Classification Keywords

H5.3 Computer Supported Cooperative Work: Miscellaneous.

INTRODUCTION

Healthcare is currently facing myriad challenges. Rising costs have resulted in calls for increased efficiency in providing safe and effective healthcare.

CSCW'14, February 15–19, 2014, Baltimore, Maryland, USA.

http://dx.doi.org/10.1145/2531602.2531652

At the same time hospitals are experiencing mounting pressures to document every action and align daily work processes with pre-determined "care pathways" and evidence-based standards.

Technologically-based solutions, particularly Electronic Medical Records (EMR), are heralded by many as a pathway to address both of these challenges simultaneously. EMR are expected to increase coordination (thus enhancing effectiveness) and automatically document work process (thus allowing new forms of record keeping and evaluation). Using ICT to streamline workflow, import standards directly into practice, and enable digital retrieval of data used to evaluate practice [14], we can increase the quality, efficiency, and safety of healthcare [23]. In essence, EMR are imagined as systems that promote two related but distinct goals – coordination and accountability [15].

Looking for solutions to the complex challenges facing the healthcare system, policymakers have embraced the potential of EMR and are encouraging hospitals to implement these systems. The American Recovery and Reinvestment Act earmarked 20 billion in funding for initiatives related to EMR, and the Centers for Medicare & Medicaid Services are offering large incentives for implementing EMR. Beginning in 2015, organizations that have not begun using EMR in a meaningful way will be penalized through a downward adjustment in their Medicaid reimbursement. These policy changes are expected to dramatically accelerate adoption of the technology; rates are projected to exceed 70% by 2019 [35]. Development and implementation of EMR is a necessary priority for hospitals.

Yet, counter to expectations, a growing body of research is beginning to suggest that EMR provide only limited benefits and may actually hurt coordination and efficiency in primary clinical care. Beyond the challenges that occur during implementation that can lead to system failure [2], implementations of EMR support certain functions at the expense of others. For example, although EMR facilitates efficient data gathering for secondary purposes, efficiency of primary clinical care activities is simultaneously decreased [6,19].

The CSCW community has been at the forefront of responding to these challenges. Research in this arena has focused on enabling coordination by finding ways to better align EMR systems with everyday work practices in hospitals. Such scholarship suggests that effectiveness of EMR in primary care activities can be improved through leveraging appropriate social and organizational incentive structures, designing systems with a nuanced understanding of existing workflow, and designing work systems that facilitate collaborative work [34,29]. One notable line of work has examined "workarounds" in clinical practice (i.e. 13,42]. Workarounds are temporary practices used to handle exceptions to workflow. Both unexpected contingencies of work situations and inappropriately designed ICT systems give rise to workarounds [42]. However, this literature does not examine deeply a crucial factor that gives rise to workarounds on the first place: the accounting function of EMR, and the institutional logics that shape the work processes programmed into EMR.

Dourish noted over a decade ago that workflow technologies incorporate two related functions: coordination and accountability [15]. A handful of CSCW oriented studies on health ICT build on this insight. These scholars have begun to focus attention on the accountability function of EMR, suggesting that the accountability function might impinge on the coordinating function [7,8,9]. We contribute to this burgeoning stream of research and argue that the relationship between coordination and accountability needs to be further untangled through an examination of institutional logics.

Thus, we examine how EMR is designed with underlying logics of *safety*, a crucial goal of healthcare organizations at present. Using clinical ordering as a case, we empirically investigate how logics of coordination and accountability affect daily work processes and organizational effectiveness; trace the origins of existing logics; and envision how such systems might be designed differently to reflect alternative logics of "safety" in coordinating and accounting functions of ICT in hospital settings.

Specifically, we draw on over a year of ethnographic research in the obstetrical unit of a mid-size hospital to show how the dominant institutional logics of "safety" and "human error" figure in to the design of EMR. We conclude with a discussion of alternate design logics drawn from a discourse that is slowly gaining ground in the healthcare quality improvement literature that sees safety as sociotechnical and a situated accomplishment.

LITERATURE REVIEW

The Dual Role of EMR: Coordinating and Accounting

Medical records are complex sociotechnical artifacts that play a fundamental role in constituting what healthcare is and how such work gets conducted. The record is a coordinating device that allocates work and collects evidence of successful task completion, thus promoting processes of coordination and communication among heterogeneous teams of medical workers [5].

The shift to EMR is complex and, given the centrality of patient records in medical work, presents a myriad of design challenges. A rich body of CSCW related scholarship examines the situated practices of coordination in healthcare from a sociotechnical perspective. Key topics in coordination of medical work include: coordinating heterogeneous workflows [30]; the mobility of medical work [3]; informal, technology-mediated, and inter-organizational communication among providers [20,27,41, 42]; the role of informal documentation practices, transitional records, or "working records" in coordination [13,17]; and coordination surrounding handoffs [1,22,37].

Workflow systems such as EMR do not simply coordinate work, they also create accounts of work process. Thus, such technologies have a dual function in that they are both organizational coordinating devices and organizational *accounting* devices [15,21,36]. As mentioned above, Dourish [15] argues that workflow technologies provide a structure within which the activity of an organization is rendered visible and thus accountable to outsiders. Further, while the accounting function of workflow systems often goes unrecognized by scholars and designers, the accounts produced by such systems, and the promise of extended control through increased accountability, is a key driving force behind adoption and use of workflow technologies, including EMR [18].

The burgeoning stream of CSCW literature that discuss the accounting functions of EMR notes the potential downsides of the expanded use of EMR as an accounting tool. A handful of studies suggest that the accounting functions of EMR can interfere with situated coordination of work, thus leading to unintended negative consequences [7,8,9]. A recent meta-analysis goes so far as to assert that healthcare organizations are not actually re-shaping work practices around EMR systems in beneficial ways as had been previously hoped [19].

Claus Bossen, in particular, points to the emergence of a "flip over effect" where the work process embedded in EMR becomes a model *for* practice rather than a model *of* practice. This creates a situation where accountability does not emerge as a result of the work process representation inscribed in the EMR, but "at the cost of more work, redundancy of information, and the fragmentation of the overview of patient cases" [9, p. 490].

Such studies have begun to articulate the ways in which the dual functions of accountability and coordination designed into current EMR systems become problematic. However, scholars have yet to ask why these systems are being designed the way they are -- embedded with certain ideas about how work is coordinated, what kinds of accounts are legitimate, and how they should be created.

We argue that direct attention to such questions helps clarify why and how the accountability function of EMR matters for everyday practice and organizational effectiveness. Our logic is thus: healthcare organizations are embedded in the larger institutional environment of U.S. healthcare. As artifacts for coordinating and accounting, EMR are inscribed with particular ideas about what healthcare should look like; what is envisioned as "quality of care," where the sources of error lie, and how tasks should be ordered and delineated to reach certain metrics of care and effectiveness. These broader logics influence the design and implementation of EMR. They shape how work is coordinated by these systems. Equally important, they are the backdrops of accountability.

EMR and New Institutionalism

Specific healthcare organizations must demonstrate that they are responsive to, and oriented toward, the overarching goals, ideals, and logics of the broader healthcare system of which they are a part. In other words, hospitals are not accountable in a vacuum. They must provide accounts that make sense according to a specific institutional environment. New institutionalism, a theory that takes a sociological perspective of organizations and institutions, provides one way to gain traction on this dynamic.

New institutionalism takes the perspective that organizations are embedded in larger institutional environments and must survive within these environments. A key aspect of survival entails gaining *legitimacy* [12]. Organizations gain legitimacy by adhering to norms for conduct drawn from other organizations as well as larger arenas of policy, culture, and public opinion [26]. Scott [32] outlines three main pillars through which institutions create order: regulative, normative, and cultural-cognitive. For example, a healthcare organization is subject to regulatory standards and sanctions for failure to meet institutional standards, norms for how the organization should "behave" drawn from quality improvement repertoires, and cultural elements drawn from membership in professional groups. From this perspective, the production of accounts in healthcare organizations is directly related to survival.

Recent scholarship in this realm focuses on how institutional policies, norms, and beliefs are enacted at the micro-level. This work arises from the observation that changes, such as new rules or policies that come "from above" (the institutional level) often do not result in expected changes in organizations [24]. This line of work focuses on how institutional elements shape actions in the day-to-day life of organizational work, and how those working in organizations, in turn, reinforce, re-frame, or alter institutional conventions [24].

Taking the perspective that "institutional logics are instantiated in and carried by individuals through their actions, tools, and technologies" [28], we argue that institutional logics of U.S. healthcare are shaping the work processes embedded within EMRs [28], logic of EMR design itself, and the norms, myths, and beliefs about how key institutional values such as "safety" are achieved and evaluated. EMR carries institutional logics about healthcare work to the technical core of organizations and makes them central to individual work. Therefore we must examine these institutional logics if we are to gain new purchase on the debate about the accounting function of EMR and find useful footing to move forward.

RESEARCH CONTEXT

"We will make sure that every doctor's office and hospital in this country is using cutting edge technology and electronic medical records so that we can cut red tape, prevent medical mistakes, and help save billions of dollars each year."

-President Barack Obama, 12/6/2008

At present, practices of accountability in U.S. healthcare are shifting dramatically. Increasingly, hospitals and providers are being held accountable for the actual *content* of the work [38,40]. The organizational processes underlying basic activities such as ordering and dispensing medication are carefully examined by regulatory agencies and new quality surveillance organizations representing consumers. EMR and other ICT are seen as a key means through which this oversight can be achieved. Thus, we are currently designing and implementing the infrastructure through which a new generation of evidence-based medicine and best practices will be carried out.

A major focus of improvement efforts in the last decade has been around pinpointing errors and improving the safety of medical care. This focus was largely spurred by an influential report conducted by the Institute of Medicine in 1999 entitled "To Err is Human." This report points out that almost 100,000 people die in hospitals every year from medical errors [23].

Several stakeholders operating at the institutional level are shaping the norms, logics, and values being promoted in local healthcare organizations regarding safety. One example that is relevant to the current case is Leapfrog. The Leapfrog Group is a private organization that serves large consumers of healthcare (i.e. insurance companies) by administering a survey to hospitals that evaluates the hospitals' practices in terms of pre-determined metrics of quality and safety. Hospitals are ranked according to results and assigned a letter "grade." Results are made publicly available via a website (hospitalsafetyscore.org). These grades are increasingly important to hospitals; a poor grade can result in negative media coverage and significant financial loss. One of the safety items on the survey is a hospital's use of a computerized ordering system, and the specific work processes in which the computer system is employed for medication and other orders.

To maintain legitimacy in this institutional environment, hospitals must position themselves as healthcare organizations that engage in "safe" care. This vision of safety is then evidenced by adoption of tools and practices that adhere to prevailing logics about the sources of error and appropriate tactics of prevention. Further, they must demonstrate this position by creating visible accounts of work practice. In our fieldsite, a new EMR "went live" during the eighth month of observation (the midway point). At this time, medication ordering policies and protocols were changed in multiple ways. These changes happened in tandem with EMR implementation and directly responded to evolving institutional logics for safety, such as those assessed in the Leapfrog Survey.

In order to design EMR systems that support complex cooperative work practices in situ, we suggest that research needs to focus on how certain assumptions about accountability are being designed into EMR systems. In the rest of the paper, we explore how these shifts in understanding and assessing healthcare at the institutional level affect: how EMR systems shape practice at the micro-level; the ways in which the accounting function takes precedence over coordination in these systems; and why the cultivation of a "perfect" (if often inaccurate) account can undermine organizational effectiveness and the experience of care.

METHODS

Relying on ethnographic methods (observation and interviews), the bulk of data collection for this research occurred in a single site, the Labor & Delivery (L&D) unit of a mid-size teaching hospital (H1). The L&D unit of H1 has 14 beds and approximately 55 nurses who work 12 hour shifts from 7AM to 7PM. About 1,000 deliveries per year occur in H1. H1 is well equipped to handle both very high risk pregnancies and sick and premature infants, so the unit sees an exceptionally large number of high-risk cases. Additional data collection included both observations and interviews: we attended nursing and obstetrical conferences where safety and quality improvement were discussed; interviewed key informants working in obstetrics at other hospitals; and interviewed individuals working at a policy level on maternal care quality improvement and policy recommendations.

The first author conducted observations in the L&D unit of H1 for 16 months for periods of time ranging from four to fourteen hours during all times of the day as well as at night. Observations took place once or twice per week, intersected by three four-week periods away from the field in order to reflect and analyze data. We also conducted observations of unit and hospital-wide staff meetings, daily rounds, Practice Council, grand rounds, computer documentation training sessions, and various other education and training activities. Field notes were recorded using pen and paper and typed after leaving the field in the manner described by Emerson, Fretz, & Shaw [16].

Informants included bedside nurses, charge nurses, nurse managers, and several other interdisciplinary personnel. Nurses were the focus, in relation to the larger context of the obstetrical team. The first author also conducted a focus group interview with twelve L&D nurses and nine formal semi-structured interviews with bedside nurses in the L&D unit at H1, as well as interviews with nurse managers and various other stakeholders. In all, we conducted semi-structured interviews with 37 participants, a multitude of additional ethnographic interviews, and 400 hours of observation in H1.

FINDINGS

Micro-Institutional logics of medication safety

Observations in H1 made it clear that the larger institutional context is actively shaping the organizational context of the hospital. This was a huge factor in the everyday lives of clinicians. For example, the newly deployed EMR replaced an older-generation (implemented in 1990) computerized ordering system. The new EMR was embedded with up-to-date safety work processes and implemented in tandem with policy changes for medication and other medical orders. Changes included an organizational policy change stating that nurses were no longer able to manage and remove orders for medication as they had previously (only residents and attending physicians now had authority to do this). Simultaneously, the EMR was programmed with a permissions structure that placed large barriers in the way of nurses attempting to manage orders. Another change was an increase in system redundancies intended to prevent medication errors. All medication orders, regardless of risk, now had to be double-checked by a pharmacist and approved before administration could occur -- except in emergency circumstances, in which system over-rides or rapid protocols could be deployed. This requirement was programmed into the workflow logic of the EMR as well as the in-unit medication dispensary unit.

We found that local workers in the obstetrical unit were familiar with and fluent in the institutional logics for safety and error underlying these changes. For example, managers and bedside nurses alike often invoked the "swiss cheese" [1] model of patient safety. In explaining this statement informants described how the "swiss cheese" model envisions the hospital as a system comprised of multiple layers. Individual layers, be they organizational, technological, or human, are weak and full of holes, and can propagate errors. But, errors only reach the patient if holes in the different layers line up. Therefore, the system must contain redundancies, affordances, and obligatory passage points to prevent errors created in one part of the system from reaching the patient.

Personnel in H1 were not only cognizant of this broader institutional logic, they were acutely aware of the fact that these logics were driving technology and policy changes in

[1] This language is drawn from the work of Reason (1990) who first proposed the "Swiss-Cheese Model," now the dominant model for analyzing medical errors and patient safety mishaps (Perneger, 2005). We do not cite Reason directly since we are using informants' language and do not know how people developed an understanding of the "swiss cheese" model. Reason's name was not mentioned in conjunction with the error prevention model described by participants.

the hospital. The nurse manager, when queried about the changes in ordering process that were implemented when the EMR "went live," said: "That is all for safety, it comes from Leapfrog and their guidelines for safety." It is clear that the changes occurring in the hospital through EMR implementation, and affecting ordering practices, were both technological and political in origin, and operated at both the organizational (micro) and institutional (macro) levels.

Such changes to ordering instantiate certain norms, values, and logics of safety, agency, and medical work. In particular they represent two fundamental principles of "safety" as imagined in current medical discourses. First, such changes suggest that humans at all levels of complex organizational systems are the originators of errors. The system thus locates responsibility for the prevention of error outside of humans and in the purview of technical systems. An RN expressed this logic of locating safety with technical systems rather than people: "We are very safe here. We have a lot of systems in place to prevent errors, a lot of checks and balances."

Second, changes in ordering reflect an assumption that safety is not performed or enacted in daily practice. Rather, it is a semi-stable state that resides in organizational structures. Errors are thus seen as immutable events that are figured as existing almost independently from situated action. For example, nurses describe themselves as potential "goal keepers" protecting patients against errors. In order to perform these logics medical personnel must align personal actions with protocols and follow the directives of systems embedded with safety logics. This is easier said than done.

While medical personnel understand their work through a logic of safety that relies on preserving and following the system, personnel also carry situated logics of what constitutes good practice that can contradict (what we term) the "safety through systems" institutional logic.

For example, one morning a nurse felt frustrated because her patient was asleep but the worklist manager in the EMR listed that an order for a prenatal vitamin was past due. The nurse told the ethnographer that she did not want to wake her patient up for a vitamin even though she was going to have to provide a justification in the system for why the vitamin was given late. The nurse felt it was more important for the patient to sleep and she was angry that the system was prompting her to do something that went against her clinical judgment, telling the ethnographer: "Sometimes being a good nurse means breaking the rules."

In order to more fully articulate what "breaking the rules" looks like in daily practice, and the implications for coordinating, accounting, and organizational effectiveness, we present an ethnographic vignette drawn from fieldwork that is representative of our data on performances of orders work using the EMR. This vignette depicts a mundane yet emergent situation in which a nurse is compelled to take action in a manner not expected or prescribed by the EMR system and must deal with the fallout of this action. Three professionals are involved – a nurse, a pharmacist, and a resident. All become enrolled in the system's logic of how work *should* proceed. The story allows us to see how the institutional logics for safety conflict with situated logics of a nurse, resulting in some surprising and undesired effects.

Ethnographic Vignette: Changing an IV

Around 12:30pm, Sabrina (nurse) checks on her patient, who is being induced at 38 weeks for mild pre-eclampsia. The induction began around 6:00am that morning and Sabrina is worried her patient's contractions are not strong enough and that she will have a very long labor. The patient is tired and hungry, and Sabrina worries she might not make it through a long induction without extra energy. The patient has not eaten since dinner the previous night and Sabrina decides that in order to improve her situation the patient needs some sugar in her IV. Sabrina decides to switch her IV from lactated ringers (LR), or normal saline, to D5, a mixture of saline and sugar – this is a common practice, and can help give a patient the energy to withstand a long labor – for a tired and hungry patient will eventually become exhausted and ineffective at pushing. Once deciding on this course of action, Sabrina wants to get some sugar going ASAP for once a patient starts to go downhill it is hard to bring her energy back up. I follow her to the medication room to grab a bag of D5.

Back in the patient's room, Sabrina fills out a sticker to label the bag and replaces the old bag with the new D5 bag. All the while she is chatting with the patient and her husband about how she is giving her some "lunch" in liquid form that should help her to feel better. Sabrina types a note in the bedside flowsheet noting that she has hung D5.

Around 1:20pm, Sabrina is in the nurses' station. After hanging the bag, she now needs an official order for the D5 to be entered in Quest, the electronic medical record system used for ordering in the hospital. Quest requires Sabrina to create a record showing that the IV was ***first*** *ordered,* ***then*** *approved by the pharmacy, and* ***finally****, "completed" by the nurse.*

Since Sabrina has already hung the bag she attempts to enter an order for the D5 herself. The second year resident on duty is sitting next to Sabrina in the nurses' station. So, Sabrina tells the resident that she switched the IV and is entering a D5 order. The resident says, "OK, sounds good," so Sabrina spends a minute or so searching for the correct order in the system -- not a simple task as there are many potential orders for IV therapy.

I watch as Sabrina finds and selects the correct order. A box pops up requesting a password. Since Sabrina is a nurse and does not have jurisdictional authority over placing orders, she has to enter a special password to complete the ordering process. She tries several times, but her password doesn't work. 'Dammit" she mutters. Eventually, Sabrina turns to the resident sitting next to her and asks if the resident can enter the D5 order herself. The resident says "OK," gets up, and moves to a computer on wheels parked in the hallway. Sabrina turns and tells me, "Watch, she will be able to do it in seconds."

Seeing the resident is indeed entering the order Sabrina turns back to her computer and logs into a different computer program, QS, which is the bedside flowsheet program where nurses make notes about significant things that happen with the patient. She scrolls back through all of the notes she has recorded in the past hour, looking for the exact time she hung the D5. She then calls to the resident at the hallway computer that the D5 was hung at 12:30pm, so the resident can backdate the order for that time.

Sabrina tells me that now the pharmacy has to verify the D5 order and, once this has occurred, she will chart it as done in Quest. She logs into Quest and sees the D5 order, but she can't mark it as complete. If she does, she will receive an error message saying that the pharmacy has to verify the order before it can be completed. The pharmacy receives an alert each time a new medication order is entered and personnel from the pharmacy must review all medication orders in order to verify that each order is safe for that particular patient. Once the pharmacy verifies the order, the nurse can mark the order as complete. Around 2:00pm Sabrina checks to see if the pharmacy has verified the order yet. It has not, so Sabrina goes to lunch. She gets back around 3:00pm and is finally able to marked the order as complete in Quest.

Undermining coordination

When we examine how Sabrina goes about actually changing the IV, it is immediately apparent that the tasks she needs to perform to give what she considers good patient care do not align with the logics of the EMR. Further, the EMR adds time, burden, and coordination hurdles to what could be a relatively straightforward medical intervention.

There are multiple situational factors to take into account when understanding Sabrina's actions. The actions taken by a nurse take place in dialogue with a particular set of circumstances. The nurse has clinical expertise and knowledge of the patient's likely trajectory into the future. These factors prompt a clinical decision to act quickly to change the IV. All of the residents were off the floor (movement is common for residents) and this was not a "page-able" situation. While the sequence of actions technically deviates from protocol, Sabrina has the negotiated and informal authority to make this decision – she is confident that no resident would contradict this decision. In fact, the vignette reveals that both Sabrina and the resident she was working with both felt the decision was appropriate and justified. However, the vignette also suggests the significant burden placed on Sabrina in her attempts to create an account of the IV change in the EMR. One can imagine how her time and expertise might have been used differently in the service of patient care.

Sabrina is unable to violate the logics of the EMR when creating the account, because, as noted by Bossen [9], there is a "flip over effect" where the EMR is not a model *of* practice, but a model *for* practice. Thus, although the IV has been hung, Sabrina must follow the logics of the EMR. She is forced to have a resident enter the order, the order then must be verified by a pharmacist, and finally she is able to "complete" the order. Notably, this series of accounting steps extends for two hours after the IV has been hung, and takes no small amount of time, attention, and stress.

Another common example of the "flip over effect" we witnessed during fieldwork emerged when nurses needed to print transmittals for lab specimens. The programming of the EMR links printing a transmittal to collecting a specimen for an order that must be entered by a physician. The problem is exemplified by a situation where a nurse noticed that the physician had entered a wrong order (surprisingly typical since physicians must select orders from a litany of potential orders listed in a drop-down box) yet the nurse had already drawn the sample. The nurse needed to send the specimen to the lab to get blood work underway but was prevented from doing so. She could not print a transmittal that was not connected to a specific order, yet was unable to alter the order in the system herself and no physicians were available to alter the order (or to cancel the previous, faulty order). The nurse carried the blood vile in her scrubs pocket for over an hour waiting until someone was available to change the original order so a new transmittal could be acquired, delaying bloodwork and causing multiple inefficiencies.

Forcing a "perfect" account

The logics of the EMR are such that any post-hoc account of work process is subject to system requirements. In other words, the EMR produces a "perfect" account – even when that account is inaccurate. In the account of Sabrina's IV order, it will appear as if the doctor entered the order at 12:30pm, it will appear as if the pharmacy verified the order sometime between 12:30pm and 3:00pm, and that the nurse hung the IV sometime after the verification took place. In fact, Sabrina hung the IV at 12:30pm – when it was needed by the patient to assist in a difficult labor.

This official account will conflict with another account, the computerized bedside flowsheet, in which the nurse typed a note at 12:30 explaining the patient's symptoms, noting that she was hanging an IV, and that the residents were off the floor. It will also conflict with the time that the nurse wrote down on the sticker she placed on the IV bag when she hung it next to the patient's bed. It is important to note here that the nurse did not lie. Rather, she created accurate accounts in two places – although these accounts will reflect that protocol was not followed perfectly, since the situation required contingent work that deviated from protocol. However, the EMR is the primary source of "secondary" data used for billing, research, and regulatory accountability. The flowsheet is only used rarely. The primacy of the EMR is necessary in retrospective accounting for work practice. The "perfect" account is incompatible with the "accurate" account. If the flowchart is referenced in the future it will only cause confusion as to why the two records do not match.

The sequence of actions as it was recorded in the EMR makes it appear as if a resident entered an order for D5, the pharmacy verified the order, a nurse carried out the verified order and hung the D5, and the nurse then marked the order as complete in the EMR. What is interesting is that it looks this way because, basically, *it could not look otherwise.*

The account of work that the nurse must operate in terms of has been developed based on specific institutional logics emerging out of a specific view of safety. The current practice of accountability requires that the content of medical work increasingly contain a high degree of specificity and meet current standards for "best practice" [40]. Thus, the EMR's rendering of a routine includes the actions to be taken, the role and necessary qualifications of different types of participants, the sequence of actions, and so forth.

Thus, the EMR as a tool has an expanded capability to *audit action as it is actually happening*, meaning it is built to force certain actions to occur and to stop or slow down other actions. As we see in the vignette, this does not actually cause the nurse (in this instance) to suppress her own logic of practice, but it does make it difficult for the nurse to create an account of work *post hoc,* because she has to work through the account as if she is actually coordinating the work in the manner prescribed by the account itself.

This particular scenario, where an action precedes an order, occurred frequently with IV changes and other mundane-yet-urgent scenarios. Another "perfect but inaccurate accounts" scenario was one in which something was ordered by a physician, but not carried out by the nurse because the action was deemed inappropriate. This was sometimes due to errors in the orders programmed into the EMR itself. For example, we witnessed a scenario in which the nurse adjusted the fluid balance of multiple IVs because she knew that the protocol given in the EMR order was resulting in a fluid balance that was too high. So, the order in the system was not being followed exactly, but the actions were nonetheless "correct" and necessary for safe patient care.

Disrupting Organizations

Here we see that the EMR produces an account that is not only inaccurate, but can be detrimental to organizational effectiveness and patient care. This account leads to various organizational costs: time, attention, and energy expenditure on the part of the nurse, the pharmacist and the resident; post-hoc difficulties in establishing a "true" line of action; and possible damage to patient safety when the expertise of nurses is undermined by the logic of the system.

The IV change story provides insight into the complex and messy aspects of medical work that sit in inherent tension with the logics of the "perfect" account embedded in the EMR. This situation presents an instance of institutional logics about "safety through systems" emerging at the micro-level of the hospital unit.

The institutional logic of safety embedded in the EMR collides with necessities of the body and the situated, practices of providing medial care. There is simply no way for the nurse to change or mitigate the messiness of the situation presented to her. We chose to present an ethnographic vignette that highlights how the EMR can render basic and mundane tasks unfeasible. However, the choice of this example should not diminish the potential hazards associated with the supremacy of creating a perfect account. While we find the simple issue of inefficiency, previously highlighted by Greenhalgh et al. [19], organizational effects extend beyond inefficiency. Our findings thus suggest that the tension between logics of work and the logics of a perfect account are not simply impinging on the coordination of situated work and creating an inaccurate account, they suggest substantial implications for the organization.

We must also question the implications of bad, i.e. inaccurate data for healthcare more generally. If accounts of work are meant for secondary data purposes such as quality improvement and clinical research, it is worth exploring the impact of bad data more broadly. How useful is the data at the hospital's disposal? Where does this data 'go' and how does it reflect back on hospital practice? How do we understand what leads to medical errors or increased costs from accounts of work practices crafted by the EMR? In sum, what are the risks of measuring hospital effectiveness from inaccurate accounts, and what is the effect on research based on such data?

DISCUSSION

Our research reveals that institutional logics that understand "safety" as an organizational state that emerges when systems are in place to limit the situated contingencies of medical work underlie the design, implementation, and associated organizational processes for medication ordering in a hospital unit. This suggests that we need to understand ICT design, implementation, and use as political, as well as social and technical, phenomena. The EMR system effectively 'freezes' policy [10] and brings certain institutional norms, logics, and values for "safety" directly to the point of care. Further, our research reveals that the ways in which the accounting and coordinating functions of the EMR are designed lead to issues with organizational effectiveness. Specifically, the ways in which accounting is operationalized in the system we studied leads to inefficiencies in coordination and inaccurate accounts of work post hoc.

In line with prior research, we find that a tight coupling between the coordinating and accounting functions of the EMR is problematic. Further, similar to Bossen [9], we find that this coupling effectively inverts these functions, such that the work of making a perfect account directs and disrupts attempts to actually coordinate work. However, unlike past studies, our findings highlight the fact that although the account that is created in the course of changing the IV is "perfect," it is also inaccurate. What drives this sometimes problematic and potentially dangerous inversion between accuracy and perfection? We argue that the current institutional logics shape how EMR systems are imagined and implemented. Further, institutional level policies and measurement practices structure the nature of the accounts that EMR are designed to produce.

The theoretical lens of new institutionalism allows us to examine how the context and conversations around U.S. healthcare shapes the functionality of EMR systems at the micro-level in multiple ways. First, work process representations are imbued with a logic that clear delineation of work will increase safety by limiting human discretion over task and temporality. Thus, the work process representation is detailed and highly specified –including roles of actors, assigned actions, and specific sequences of steps that should be carried out. Second, because the EMR is designed with a logic of "safety through systems" it goes beyond simply delineating work in linear paths. It is designed to force certain actions, stop others, and pinpoint accountability when processes are not followed. Thus, the EMR system itself is designed with the notion that accounting and coordinating *should* be tightly coupled. Third, the system is designed with a logic that designing safety in systems is primarily a technical rather than a social concern. Errors are conceptualized as immutable entities that originate somewhere in a complex system and are prevented by various checks and "layers" designed into the work system through permissions and protocol. Finally, the dominant institutional logics of safety are reflected in the culture of the unit and the everyday discourse of workers.

Competing logics in healthcare

The current design of the EMR and accompanying policy changes are drawn directly from the dominant paradigm for healthcare safety. Informed by literatures of complex systems and safety science, the current safety paradigm of U.S. healthcare is reflected on the first page of the IOM's 1999 report:

Human beings, in all lines of work, make errors. Errors can be prevented by designing systems that make it hard for people to do the wrong things and easy for people to do the right things...In health care, building a safer system means designing processes of care to ensure that patients are safe from accidental injury (p. ix).

This perspective is formally termed Organizational Accident Theory (OAT) and at present forms the overarching framework for patient safety in the U.S. [25], and was formally adopted by the Institute of Medicine in 2000.

However, a small but expanding body of work on safety in healthcare organizations takes the view that safety is social, situated, and agentic. This literature conceptualizes safety as "...a dynamic social process of collective responsibility and adaptation" [25]. Further, this literature problematizes approaches to "human error" (and even the term itself) that attempt to design systems as if humans are cogs in a system who need stricter monitoring and regimentation [11,31]. Drawing on management literature on high reliability organizations, this school of thought argues that we must develop safe practices and cultures along with technical systems. Promoting safety through systems that limit human action with a heavy hand is not the best way to achieve such a safety culture; in fact, promoting in situ adaptation is key to achieving safety on an ongoing basis.

Implications of the "perfect" account

Here we come to another important question – what are the various goals embedded in accounts of work process? From the perspective of new institutionalism, creating a perfect account through the EMR allows hospitals to symbolically and legitimately operate in an institutional environment. However, accountability is also an important value in and of itself. This is particularly true for organizations that provide highly complex services with high social value [33]. Healthcare is a public good.

Our findings reveal that accounts produced by EMR are not necessarily accurate depictions of work process. This is not the fault of providers. The logics of the system simply do not allow the account to be otherwise. We are not suggesting that medical records were ever completely accurate. We know that this is not the case [21]. However, our findings do suggest that the mechanisms designed to create a "perfect" account may unintentionally necessitate inaccuracy.

Our findings also raise questions about post hoc data uses, such as clinical and quality improvement research [19]. As researchers prepare to make use of the deluge of data made available by the adoption of EMR systems, our findings suggest a note of caution is needed. In our ethnographic vignette, the bedside flowsheet program was a more accurate source of information about the events that occurred. It is possible that researchers may need to consider other sources of data, triangulate data culled from EMR systems with data from other accounts, or take the results of studies conducted using EMR-sourced data with caution.

Decoupling coordinating and accounting functions

In their classic work in new institutionalism, Meyer & Rowan [26] describe how organizations must "maintain face" in their larger institutional environments by adopting institutional standards, categories, and procedures, and that these often conflict with everyday uncertainties faced by organizations in the course of doing work. However, organizations may mitigate the impact of these conflicts through "decoupling" formal representations from everyday work practices – appearing to enact institutional standards in formal ways while continuing to work according to situational demands.

In the case of the EMR, institutional logics are built into the workflow technology itself, attempting to force actions in service of the formal account. Although EMR is designed to prevent decoupling by making it difficult or impossible to engage in work processes that do not match those programmed in the EMR, our data shows that workers effectively de-couple situated actions from EMR accounts of action. Further, we find that such de-coupling can promote situated and adaptive work processes that are beneficial. Although it may seem counter-intuitive, we propose that designing systems that allow for a degree of decoupling would prove beneficial for both the coordinating and accounting functions of EMR.

Implications for design

Design implications of this are twofold. First, in our current healthcare environment dominated by the "safety through systems" paradigm designers should consider what it would take to "decouple" the dual functions of workflow systems. In other words, what would it mean to decouple the formal need to create an account of work practice from the situated contingencies required by on-the-ground coordination?

Second, anticipating a possible shift in dominant logics stemming from the emerging conversation around healthcare as a dynamic social and technical process, we can begin to imagine designing an EMR system that reflects alternative logics of how to engender safe and effective healthcare.

Designing for decoupling

How might we design EMR for de-coupling? First, designers can recognize that hospitals need to produce charts that are detailed, accurate, and supportive of *in situ* coordination. This requires a delicate balance. At present, systems are designed with the assumption that real-time charting is ideal, and that clinicians will carry out work processes *through* the EMR, creating an account as by-product. However, it is essentially impossible to predict the intricate sequence of steps that clinicians will take in order to carry out a task. Thus, we propose that designing systems that facilitate what clinicians refer to as "backcharting," or charting after the fact, could result in more accurate accounts and less impact on coordination.

Supporting backcharting would require *decoupling* certain tasks in the EMR. Indeed, "forcing functions" are seen as a tool that promotes safety [4]. We argue that while tight coupling of tasks may be felicitous in certain instances, this technique can be quite problematic and should be deployed with care. For example, at present the tasks "collecting specimen" and "printing specimen transmittal" are coupled together. That is, the system assumes you cannot do one with the other and that they should proceed in a certain order. Yet, entering orders, collecting specimens, managing orders, preparing specimens, and engaging in double-checks can (and should) not always proceed in lock step. Designing systems that allow users to complete steps based on situated contingencies and then create accurate accounts of these steps would improve both efficiency of coordination and accuracy of accounts.

Another way to promote decoupling would be to increase use of unstructured data entry and narrative accounts of work. We found that accounts in the electronic bedside flowsheet were more accurate than those in the EMR. Because of the more open-ended interface clinicians were able to record narrative accounts of work more easily, and make "marks" on the flowsheet when significant events occurred but they did not have time to chart them. Automating some aspects of the process, such as providing markers for tasks completed or orders entered, while designing an interface that allows clinicians to chart either in the moment or go back and contextualize complex actions would increase efficiency and effectiveness during actual episodes of care.

We cannot discuss decoupling without acknowledging that a major potential benefit of EMR in terms of safety is decision support and systemic "hard stops" that prevent egregious errors. However, the present design of EMR does a poor job of distinguishing between situations in which an error has a large potential for harm versus those where the potential for harm is miniscule. The current mode of design has created a work system that feels like death from a thousand paper cuts – increasing complexity and heavy-handedness of the system have led to a proliferation of small inefficiencies and frustration.

Designing for a new safety paradigm

The emerging conversation in safety science and healthcare systems literature suggests an alternate path for re-imagining the design of EMR systems. What might it look like to create an EMR system designed with the notion that safety is "…a dynamic social process of collective responsibility and adaptation" [25]?

Such a system would be based on a logic of professional expertise and agency. In other words, hospital work is being carried out by skilled and mindful human agents. Thus, design interventions for safety such as redundancies and forcing functions would be deployed conservatively, with the understanding that such functions can undermine situated work. One possible solution would be to create a hierarchy of ordering functions in the EMR, such that only those actions that present high risk are subject to systemic design constraints.

Designing for "dynamic social processes of collective responsibility" would also inform such a system. One solution is to draw on recent work by Valentine and Edmondson [39] on the development of "team scaffolds." This approach recognizes the shifting and dynamic nature of teams in mission critical organizational environments (emergency rooms), and sees responsibilities as constantly in flux. An EMR design based on a team scaffold approach might imagine the "user" of an EMR system to be patient-centered "teams" lead by physicians or nurse practitioners. This approach would be based on the notion of appropriate fluidity of collective tasks and responsibilities. An EMR that supports teams of multiple users engaging in collective work would allow "captains" to cede discretion of certain tasks, such as manipulating orders, to other members of the team.

CONCLUSION

Our research suggests that it is imperative that CSCW researchers see design and implementation of EMR as occurring not just within sociotechnical systems, but also within systems that are political. Adoption of an EMR use of the system to produce real time accounts of work are necessary endeavors for hospitals hoping to maintain legitimacy in the current institutional environment of U.S based healthcare. We are currently building the infrastructure for new forms of evidence-based healthcare and oversight. However our findings show that EMR workflow tools designed to reflect a "safety through systems" logic are problematic for organizational effectiveness. The tight coupling of coordination and accountability built into current systems effectively inverts coordinating and accounting functions, hampering coordination and leading to the creation of a "perfect" but inaccurate account of work.

EMR systems are not simply tools for coordinating work or representing work practice. These systems are the manifestation of institutional logics about how healthcare should be practiced and attempt to dictate work along prescribed lines. In this view, it is not simply that increased accounting demands impinge on situated work practice, or that work process representations are out of synch with situated work practices. Rather, the very logic of work embedded in work process representations and the forcing functions of the EMR conflicts with situated practices and in-the-moment contingencies of doing work. By articulating the institutional logics embedded in current systems we are able to brainstorm how to re-design systems in the current institutional environment and envision how systems might be built to reflect evolving institutional logics of safe care.

ACKNOWLEDGMENTS

This work was supported by Agency for Healthcare Research and Quality grant R36 HS20753, as well as the Center for Organizational Research and UC Irvine's Graduate Council. We also wish to thank the following individuals: Professor Audrey Lyndon, UCSF, Professor Martha Feldman, UCI, and Dr. Christine Morton, CMQCC. Finally, we wish to thank the individuals and organizations who participated in our study.

REFERENCES

1. Abraham, J. and M. Reddy (2008). Moving patients around: a field study of coordination between clinical and non-clinical staff in hospitals. *Proc. CSCW 2008*, ACM Press, 225–228.
2. Anderson, J.G., Aydin, C.E., and Jay, S.J (1994). *Evaluating Health Care Information Systems: Methods and Applications*. Sage Publications, Thousand Oaks, CA.
3. Bardram, J. E., and Bossen, C. Mobility work: the spatial dimension of collaboration at a hospital. *Computer Supported Cooperative Work* (2005). 14(2), 131- 160.
4. Bates, D.W., and Gawande, A.A. (2003). Improving safety with information technology. *NEJM,* 348, 2536-2534.
5. Berg, M., and Bowker, G. The multiple bodies of the medical record: toward a sociology of an artifact. *The Sociological Quarterly*. (1997). 38(3), 513-537.
6. Berg, M. (2001). Implementing information systems in health care organizations: myths and challenges. *International Journal of Medical Informatics*, 64, 143-156.
7. Bjørn, P., and E. Balka. Health care categories have politics too: unpacking the managerial agendas of electronic triage systems. *Proc. ECSCW 2007*. Limerick: Springer (2007), 371–390.
8. Bossen, C. (2006). Representations at work: a national standard for electronic health records. *Proc. CSCW 2006.* ACM, 69–78.
9. Bossen, C. (2011). Accounting and co-constructing: the development of a standard for electronic health records. Computer Supported Cooperative Work, 20, 473–495.
10. Bowker, G.C. and Star, S. L. (1999). *Sorting Things Out: Classification and Its Consequences*, Cambridge, MA: MIT Press.
11. Dekker, S. W. A. (2006). *The Field Guide to Understanding Human Error*. Aldershot, UK: Ashgate Publishing Co.
12. DiMaggio, P.J., and W.W. Powell, (1991). Introduction. In *The New Institutionalism in Organization Analysis*. WW Powell and P.J. DiMaggio (eds.) Chicago: University of Chicago Press.
13. Chen, Y. (2010). Documenting transitional information in EHR. Proc. CHI 2010. ACM Press,1787–1796.
14. Dickerson, K., & Manheimer, E. The Cochrane Collaboration: evaluation of health care and services using systematic reviews of the results of randomized controlled trials. *Clin Obst & Gyn*, (1998). 41(2), 315-331.
15. Dourish, P. Process descriptions as organisational accounting devices: the dual use of workflow technologies. *Proc. GROUP 2001*, ACM Press (2001), 52–60.
16. Emerson, R.M., Fretz, R.I., and Shaw, L.L. *Writing Ethnographic Fieldnotes*. (1995). Chicago: The University of Chicago Press.
17. Fitzpatrick, G. Integrated care and the working record. *Health Informatics Journal*, (2004), 10(4), 291–302.
18. Fitzpatrick, G., and G. Ellingsen. A Review of 25 Years of CSCW Research in Healthcare: Contributions,

Challenges and Future Agendas. *Computer Supported Cooperative Work* (21 June 2012), 1-57.

19. Greenhalgh, T, H., W.W. Potts, G. Wong, P, Bark and D. Swinglehurst (2009). Tensions and Paradoxes in Electronic Patient Record Research: A Systematic Literature Review Using the Meta-narrative Method. *The Milbank Quarterly*, 87(4), 729–788.
20. Hartswood, M., R. Procter, M. Rouncefield and R. Slack (2003). Making a case in Medical Work: Implications for the Electronic Patient Record. *Computer Supported Cooperative Work*, 12, 241–266.
21. Heath, C. and P. Luff. (996). Documents and Professional practice: 'bad' organisational reasons for 'good' clinical records. *Proc. CSCW 1996*. ACM Press (1996), 354–363.
22. Hilligoss, B., and M. Cohen. (2011). Hospital handoffs as multifunctional situated routines: implications for researchers and administrators. *Advances in Health Care, 11,* 91-132.
23. Institute of Medicine. (1999). *To Err is Human: Building a Safer Healthcare System*. Kohn, L.T., Corrigan, J.M., & Donaldson, M.S. (Eds). Washington DC: National Academies Press.
24. Kellogg, K.C. (2009). Operating room: relational spaces and microinstitutional change in surgery. *The American Journal of Sociology,* 115(3), 657-711.
25. Lyndon, A., and Kennedy, H.P. (2010). Perinatal safety: from concept to nursing practice. *J Perinat Neonatal Nurs.*; 24(1): 22–31
26. Meyer, J.W., & Rowan, B. (1977). Institutional organizations: formal structure as myth and ceremony. *American Journal of Sociology*, 83, 340-63.
27. Østerlund, C. S. Documents in place: demarcating places for collaboration in healthcare settings. *Computer Supported Cooperative Work* (2007) 17, 195–225.
28. Powell, W.W., and J.A. Colyvas. (2008). Microfoundations of institutional theory. In *The SAGE Handbook of Organizational Institutionalism*, eds. Greenwood, R., Oliver, C., Sahlin, K., & Suddaby, R. Thousand Oaks, CA: Sage.
29. Pratt, W., Reddy, M.C., McDonald, D.W., Tarczy-Hornoch, P., Gennari, J.H. (2004). Incorporating ideas from Computer Supported Cooperative Work. *Journal of Biomedical Informatics*, 37, 28-37.
30. Reddy, M., P. Dourish and W. Pratt. (2001). Coordinating heterogeneous work: Information and representation in medical care. Proc. ECSCW 2001. 239–258.
31. Rochlin GI. (1999). Safe operation as a social construct. *Ergonomics,* 42(11):1549–1560.
32. Scott, W.R. (2001). *Institutions and Organizations*. Thousand Oaks, CA: Sage, 2nd ed.
33. Scott, W.R. (2003). *Organizations: Rational, Natural and Open Systems*. Prentice-Hall: Upper Saddle River, NJ. 5th ed.
34. Shekelle, P.G., and Goldzweig. C.L. (2009). *Costs and Benefits of Health Information Technology: An Updated Systematic Review*. London: Health Foundation for Southern California Evidence-Based Practice Center, RAND Corporation.
35. Steinbrook, R. (2009). Health care and the American Recovery and Reinvestment Act. *New England Journal of Medicine*, 360(11), 1057-1060.
36. Suchman, L. Making Work Visible. *Communications of the ACM*, (1995). 38 (9), 56–61.
37. Tang, C., and S. Carpendale (2007). An observational study on information flow during nurses' shift change. *Proc. ACM CHI 2007*, ACM Press, 219–228
38. Timmermans, S., and Berg, M. *The gold standard: the challenge of evidence-based medicine and standardization in health care*. (2003). Philadelphia: Temple University Press.
39. Valentine, M.A., and Edmondson, A.C. (2013). Team scaffolds: how minimal team structures enable role-based coordination. HBS Working Paper 12-062.
40. Wiener, C. L. *The Elusive Quest: Accountability in Hospitals*. (2000). New York: Walter de Gruyter.
41. Winthereik, B. R., and S. Vikkelsø (2005). ICT and integrated care: some dilemmas of standardising inter-organisational communication. *Computer Supported Cooperative Work*,14, 43–67.
42. Zhou, X., M. Ackerman and K. Zheng (2011). CPOE workarounds, boundary objects, and assemblages. In Proc. CHI 2011. *ACM Press*, 3353–3362

"It's in your Spinal Cord, It's in Your Fingertips": Practices of Craft in Building Software

Jessa Lingel
Microsoft Research
1 Memorial Dr. Cambridge, MA 02142 USA
jlingel@microsoft.com

Tim Regan
Microsoft Research
21 Station Rd. Cambridge, CB12FB, UK
timregan@microsoft.com

ABSTRACT
Drawing on interviews with 12 software engineers, we investigate the relationship between developers and the tools they use to build code through the lens of craft. We analyze different conceptualizations of craft in accounts of software development, including craft as a process of building, craft as materiality, and craft as a community of practice. By working through these different facets of craft, we investigate tensions of perceiving coding work as, on the one hand, highly rational, and on the other, deeply personal and embodied. In working through these tensions of code as abstract and concrete, cerebral and intuitive, we note implications for craft, both as a theory relevant to computer human interaction, and for paradigms of education in computer science.

Author Keywords
Craft, software engineering, tools, community of practice

ACM Classification Keywords
H.1.2. User/Machine Systems, Human Factors.

INTRODUCTION
This paper draws together a topic and a theoretical frame that are, at least at first glance, oppositional. Software engineering is typically characterized as rational, scientific, mathematical, logical and abstract [1, 3, 6, 11, 12, 19, 27]. Craft, in contrast, invokes notions of cultural tradition, intuition, the handmade and the tactile [2, 5, 13, 22, 26, 31]. Despite these ostensible disparities, human computing interaction (HCI) research has seen a burgeoning interest in studying craft and materiality as a highly useful way of understanding relationships between people and technologies, both in terms of theory and design [15, 17, 32]. In addition to the academic interest in these areas, there has been an attendant interest in the convergence of digital technologies and craft in both popular culture (as evidenced by the emergence and popularity of sites like Pinterest and Etsy) and software engineering as a profession (e.g. Etsy's Code as Craft blog[1]).

CSCW'14, February 15 – 19, 2014, Baltimore, MD, USA.
Copyright 2014 ACM 978-1-4503-2540-0/14/02...$15.00.
http://dx.doi.org/10.1145/2531602.2531614

The interest in craft from multiple audiences invites an investigation of how the production of code can itself be viewed as a craft. Moreover, analyzing connections between code and craft makes sense because it's a metaphor used by the people who develop code. For example, in the course of this study, participants both implicitly (without an interviewer asking) and explicitly (asking participants outright) identified their work as craft:

- Jack[2]: But every now and then, if you just keep working and working and working, you can just whittle [code] down to something very small and something very elegant, [so] that when people will read it, they understand it and they appreciate the kind of craft of it. That's what I like.
- Amit: You also have to sit there and think about a problem, that's the craft. You literally have to write it, you have to use your hands to write it, that's the craft.
- Mark: Yeah, [programming is] exactly the same [as craft]. All engineering's like that. We're making things, after all. There's a long tradition. That's exactly what it is. I can't really see the difference in that, it's a kind of craft. Potters were arguably the first engineers, really.

Although these three perspectives coalesce around craft as a term, starkly different associations emerge: craft as *process*, craft as *material*, and craft as *community*. Part of our objective in this paper involves addressing these varying ideas of craft as they relate to the work of building software. In doing so, we hope to provide 1). a multi-layered conceptualization of craft, lending clarity to a term that elicits complex and even contradictory meanings, and 2). a more nuanced discussion of how the concept of craft relates to software engineering, and to research on HCI research more generally.

A qualitative inquiry into software engineers and the connections they make between their work and craft contributes to software studies by providing a deeper understanding of coding processes that are typically deemed illegible or uncontrollable. In her feminist history of software

---

[1] See http://codeascraft.etsy.com/

[2] Throughout this paper, we use pseudonyms to provide confidentiality for participants.

development as a profession, Abbate [1] documents the shifting metaphors for characterizing coding work as rooted in mathematics, business and engineering, noting that across these paradigms, "managers found [the] creative, craftlike side [of coding] worrisome because it confronted them with a work process that they could neither understand nor control" (p. 93). Drawing on interviews with software developers, we analyze the creative, craftlike side of coding not as worrisome, but as conceptually productive for understanding the relationships between people, the products they build and the tools that they use.

PRIOR WORK: CONSTRUCTIONS OF CODE

Much of the existing qualitative HCI research on software engineers has focused on the workplace. Poltrock, Grudin and colleagues have conducted a number of studies investigating components of software development work, including the efficacy of collaborative software development via groupware [19] underlying causes of poor interface design in collaborative efforts to build software [18, 29]. In 1988, Curtis et al. [14] conducted a case study of software design in nine different software companies, where interviews identified key problems of process-related issues (silos of application knowledge, fluctuating design specifications and communication breakdowns), many of which persist two decades later. Although many of these investigations were motivated by a desire to provide insight into improving the efficiency and productivity of software development [39], studies of how software engineers conduct and conceptualize their work can also provide insight into wider questions of how power is distributed through networks of technological development For example, Takheytev [36] conducted an ethnography of software engineers in Rio de Janeiro, noting the ways that programmers evaluated their work in relationship to key centers of software production (i.e. Silicon Valley) even as they sometimes ignored the developments and successes of their local communities.

Beyond studies of coding as it takes place in the office, much of the qualitative research on coding, building and making has focused on relationships between people and technology. Kleif and Faulkner [23] conducted studies of robot hobbyists and software engineers to examine pleasures of technology, specifically in terms of gender. Usefully, their study separated relationships with technology and relationships with people about technology. In other words, Kleif and Faulkner were interested in the relationships that develop between people and the technology they build, as well as the relationships that develop between people as a result of working on technology together. Drawing on a range of empirical studies, McKenzie [27] addressed metaphors of "clarity and univocality" related to software, arguing that on closer examination of the social environments surrounding code, these metaphors become much more complex than mere descriptors of good or bad code. Reviewing comments posted by software engineers to the online forum Slashdot, Case and Piñeiro [7] argued that although programming is academically and professionally positioned as a highly rational, mathematical and scientifically-oriented process, programmers themselves often privilege the aesthetics and craft of coding. Like Case and Piñeiro, we share an interest in relationships between software engineers and the technologies they use and produce, as well as the tensions between producing code against a metric of efficiency versus aesthetics. To work through these issues (of relationships with technology and of discourses for talking about code) in an in-depth way, we investigate the production of software through a lens of craft.

Coleman [9] also studied software development outside the confines of the corporation, looking at open source hackers. In her dissertation, Coleman pointed out several useful tensions of coding work, including highly individualized labour amidst the need for collective approval, a theme that also surfaces among corporate software developers [36]. Although we focus on software development in a corporate context, our participants include developers in large corporations as well as start-ups, recentering our focus from a single institution to a wider community of practice, software developers writ large.

PRIOR WORK: CONSTRUCTIONS OF CRAFT

Interestingly, craft is often positioned relationally, as one half of a binary that brings its counterpart into conceptual relief. Craft is constructed as the less cerebral, quainter counterpart to high art [26], or as the individualized means of production in contrast to the impersonalized mechanisms of capitalist industry [5], or as part-time hobbying rather than full-time dedication to an artistic practice [2]. Craft is also positioned as production oriented, rather than the prototype orientation of a design mindset [31]. Our interest in craft as a concept seeks to work across these binaries, looking at the ways in which craft is used alternately and at once to talk about the production of software that is both functional and aesthetic, individually made but often constrained by institutional limitations, involving both concept development and production mentalities. In order to unpack these different conceptualizations, we address to relevant subsets of literature on craft: the relationship between craft and tools, and the way that community can surface through shared craft.

Craft and tools

Given the current interest in the extent to which the boundary between the digital (as abstract) and the material (as concrete) is easily blurred [17], we investigate the link between code, materiality and building things by focusing on the tools used to create software, as identified by developers interviewed in this study. Theoretical work on craft situates tools as both enabling and restricting imaginative processes of production. McCullough [26] situated tools in a socio-historical context:

> In the legacy of industrialism, we see an immediate source of the tool mentality in the psychological desire for containment, the wish for comprehensibility and control.

> A tool is for serving intent, whereas a medium might create intent, and a machine might work on its own. A tool does only what you tell it to do; it is never out of control (p. 78).

This resonates with Sennett's [33] definition of tools as facilitating innovation by organizing imaginative experience. For Risatti [31], "a tool is something used directly by the hand with an intention to make something by doing something to material" (p. 49). Tools are objects intended to construct other things, such that their value is defined in utilitarian terms, but for Risatti, tools "cannot be considered self-contained or self-relating things that exist in and of themselves; they are not ends in and of themselves" (p. 49). This argument is particularly complex in the context of software development in that coding work can involve bootstrapping, where (similar to carpentry) developers can use code to build software programs for the purpose of then building other products. For participants in this study, bootstrapping was referenced with a sense of cleverness and self-sufficiency, but did not change the fundamental relationship to tools as instruments of pragmatism and utility.

The above definitions of tools converge on positioning tools as rationalized structures operating in concert with but also providing direction for creativity. Although tools are effectively subverted to the intention (and skill) of the craftsperson, they also inhere boundaries and limitations. Our analysis situates tools of software development as assets that enable the production of code and helping to organize thought, as well as having limitations inherent to choosing one tool over another.

Craft and people

In thinking about the relationships between developers and the tools used to create software, we draw on Wenger's [41] work on communities of practice as well as Latour's [24] work on socio-technical networks of human and non-human actants. Regarding the former, we adopt Wenger's definition of a community of practice as encompassing both the "process of being active participants in the practices of social communities and constructing identities in relation to these communities" (p. 4). For Wenger, communities of practice centre not only on shared knowledge of the operations of producing something, but also the social and professional norms surrounding those activities. Software developers are a community of practice not only because they share knowledge of how to build products with code, but because they share standards of what constitutes good code [8, 9, 10, 36] and the social norms surrounding coding work.

Regarding relationships between people and tools, Latour [24] argued that technological work is distributed across a collection of elements that serve as nodes of possible subversion, (re)figuration and play. Latour critiqued sociotechnical studies that fail to take into account the extent to which technology possesses a kind of agency, calling this realm of actants and agents the "excluded middle." The excluded middle consists of those components that drop out of focus when we envision human interactions with technology. This in fact dovetails with a construction of tools as shaping craft where tools, craftspeople and labour are all intertwined in a mesh of affordances, limitations and objectives of production. For our investigation, we directed our attention to tools as the excluded middle of building software. Even as software engineers develop code in a process that can be highly individualized and creative, their efforts are shaped by the constraints and ethics embedded in the development tools that they use.

RESEARCH AGENDA

By investigating the extent to which software developers do or do not perceive their work as craft, we seek to address the complexity and conceptual fuzziness of craft as it relates to HCI by drawing on qualitative accounts from software engineers about their work. Because software is typically conceptualized as less physical than what one might think of as conventional craft materials (a potter's clay, a quilter's fabric) it makes for a particularly interesting case to study materiality, tools and craft. At the same time, we are also interested in coding as a process that has developed within a community of practice. With both functional and social dimensions to coding work in mind, key questions guiding this project include:

- To what extent do software engineers view their work as craft? What specific components and tools of coding work elicit these connections?
- What are the implications for paradigms of computer science education in thinking about software engineering as a craft (versus a science)?

Existing research on software engineers have already claimed the profession as a community of practice that share aesthetics of code [8, 28], relationships to the things they build [27] and, at least in the case of open source software [9, 10], a sense of personal ethics. In this project, we position software developers as a community of practice, with a specific focus on development tools, particularly in the Latourian sense of programmers and programming tools as a meshed network of creativity and production. These themes are tied to an interest in understanding how craft surfaces as a concept for understanding both the pleasures and frustrations of coding work. As well, craft offers a theoretical frame that allows for the re-evaluation of paradigms of education in computer science, where craft has historically been set up in opposition to analytical rationality and mathematics.

METHODOLOGY

Because we were interested in understanding the relationships between coding and craft in terms of everyday programming work, we took a qualitative approach for this project, combining interviews with a focus group. We began recruiting using convenience sampling at our research lab, interviewing five software engineers. Participants were chosen from a number of groups and departments (although none from our group) to provide diversity among the application areas of their coding work. The decision to use convenience sampling was intended as a jumping off point for conducting additional interviews outside our lab, allowing us to refine our interview protocol and develop additional questions. We then used our personal network as well as snowball sampling from the initial group of interviews to recruit and interview an additional seven participants. In order to gain access to knowledge about a wide range of development tools, we were interested primarily in people with significant industry experience. We also wanted to include women's experiences as developers, and deliberately sought out women coders to interview. In total, we conducted 12 semi-structured interviews with three women and nine men between the ages of 26 and 57 (average age, 38). Table 1 provides participant details.

	Name	Age	Sex	Length of time as developer
Internal	Amit	45	M	15
	Carlo	42	M	14
	James	50	M	27
	Mark	45	M	15
	Parth	38	M	20
External	Andrew	29	M	4
	Annie	26	F	4
	Jack	32	M	9
	Jess	31	F	9
	Mary	57	F	30
	Nick	36	M	15
	Sean	32	M	10

Table 1. Participant details. Pseudonyms are used to provide confidentiality. "Internal" refers to participants recruited from our place of work, external refers to participants who worked elsewhere.

Interviews were conducted during the summer of 2012. Nine took place face-to-face and three were conducted by Skype. Interviews lasted between 45 minutes and two hours. Our questions focused on the tools used to build software, working alone versus working collaboratively, and the actual process of coding. We also asked about changes in software development over time, focusing specifically on tools. Interviews were transcribed and coded using an open coding method [35, p. 143]. Both authors coded initial interviews separately, and then developed key themes and terms to continue coding remaining interviews. Themes revolved around craft, physicality of coding work, difficulties in explaining coding work to others and pleasures of programming.

Although interviews provided rich accounts of connections between coding and craft, we felt that an additional approach was needed to understand the extent to which programming tools do or do not shape code. To build on these themes, we conducted a focus group, in which we brought together three software engineers (recruited from our lab, but separate from the people interviewed previously). Drawing on ethnographic interview methods that utilize media objects as part of the interview process [34], we asked focus group participants to provide a piece of code from their past. As a group, participants examined the code (which ranged from 20 year old paper print outs to recent screen shots of coding in IntelliJ) and then talked about the tools used to develop it. Reviewing notes from the focus group as well as the audio recording, we further developed themes of tool use, technological change and ownership. We draw on both interviews and the focus group as sources for the following analysis.

FINDINGS

Our findings are structured around three connections between coding work and craft that emerged from interviews. First, we address references to craft as a process, looking specifically at relationships to tools in terms of selection, where participants discussed the benefits of being agnostic to tools like languages and editors, while also noting the ways that social status can be linked to a particular tool. Second, we consider craft as linked to embodiment, where (in something of a contradiction to voicing an agnostic attitude towards tools) participants described the deep attachment to tools, which was frequently associated with metaphors of embodiment and physicality. Third, we analyze references to craft and communities of practice, where participants voiced frustration with the extent to which their work was misunderstood or obscure to those outside the profession, intensifying the importance of communicating the intricacies of their code to others within their community of practice.

Craft and Process: The Right Tool for the Job

For many participants, references to craft were embedded in descriptions of software engineering as a process. Descriptions of tools in particular yielded detailed accounts of coding work as a series of decisions that had implications for one's overall relationship to software development. We use descriptions of tool selection as a grounded way of unpacking how participants talked about software development as a craft of unfolding decisions.

Editors and integrated development environments (IDEs) were unanimously listed as a tool by participants, and typically listed first. Amit's explanation of IDEs as a development tool describes both what IDEs are and why developers use them: "An IDE is a very concise way of describing a suite of tools that you need to write software. Well, you don't need it, you can just hack, pack and ship … But if you want to create quality software, bug free, performant, appropriately functional software, then you need to understand how to use all the tools." For Amit, building sophisticated, usable software requires the integrated functionality of IDEs, and he frames their use in terms of a responsibility to the finished product. Implicit in Amit's remarks is an awareness of the professional and design ramifications for selecting one tool over another in the context of a given project. Choosing to build a program in

Notepad versus IntelliJ, for example, carries with it certain professional associations, even if the programs built are identical to an end user. To understand the process of selecting tools as having import for developers as a community of practice, we consider some of the layered (and occasionally conflicting) accounts of choosing software development tools.

Decisions about choosing IDEs and languages were frequently couched in terms of picking "the right tool for the job," as demonstrated by Amit's assertion, "I don't have a favourite [editor], I'll just use whatever is best for the task at hand." Several participants described themselves as similarly agnostic to tools, which fits into a larger conceptualization of software development as firmly rooted in an ethic of problem solving. Parth described tool choice as a process of elimination, stating, "if you know what the project is … and you have experience of the strength and weaknesses of some tools, like some programming languages versus others, then the choice is narrowed down very quickly." The idea that a craftsperson's intentionality drives tool selection resonates with Risatti's positioning of tools entities of utility [30], instead of objects incidentally being put to a purpose. In this formulation, tools come into existence deliberately, to meet a need and facilitate a desired process. Related to this perception is a hands-off approach to telling others which tools to use. As Andrew explained, "Who am I to say 'do it this way' to you, because that's a personal choice. Like, do you really want to use a screwdriver to hammer something in? Go ahead. That's fine. I don't care, but I'm going to use my hammer." Viewing tools as instruments of problem solving shifts agency in tool selection to the craftsperson, where part of being skilled in a craft lies in the ability to choose tools.

Being skilled in a craft requires a thorough knowledge of tools, but an over-emphasis on process can position tools as less conceptual and almost trade-like, as described by James:

> Well there's always an applied thing. You don't have to understand the physics of fluid dynamics to be a plumber. [laughs] There is a point where some people are going to do more fundamental thinking. There's going to be some people that do some very applied work that says, just use this tool. That's your job in life. They don't have to know all of [the core principles]. Even if they knew a little bit … it would probably help them. But it's not strictly necessary. I think you could play more of an assistants' role. Vocational is the wrong word but more of an applied - you're good at using these things. You don't have to an expert on optics to be a great photographer to some degree.

James was hesitant to set up too simple of a binary between tools and concept development, yet it's nonetheless interesting that he draws on two distinct comparisons in this discussion – first a plumber, second a photographer. James is shifting between metaphors of describing tools as blue collar, repair-like work and instruments of artistry, but in both cases, the emphasis on tools de-intellectualizes coding work, drawing out negative connotations of craft as non-art and non-conceptual. It also speaks to a Latourian "excluded middle," where tools of actually writing code drop out of discourses of the intellectual and stimulating process of code. For Latour, an emphasis on tools as deferential to the problem at hand is a deprivileging of tools as having agency, affordances and limitations that actively shape processes of production [24]. This conforms to a craft-based conceptualization of tools as "serving intent" and furthermore underscores connections between tools, craft and vocation as fundamentally secondary to concept development and creativity. What emerges from these accounts is a conceptualization of tools as predominantly utilitarian, as a means of implementing cerebral abstractions of coding.

Craft and Embodiment: Coding, Code and Tactility

In contrast to either a purely rationalist approach or a rationale of conforming to community norms, participants also expressed a deep sense of commitment to a particular programming tool. For these developers, a sense of attachment arose from a kind of symmetry between a given tool and its associations in a wider community of practice. For example, Carlo, Jess, Nick and Sean all spoke of their preference of Emacs, which refers to a family of text editors characterized by their extensibility. This reputation for flexibility and configurability proved the biggest draw for people we interviewed. For Carlo, IDEs makes programmers lazy, where "tools like Visual Studios … limit" what programmers think of creating. This is in contrast to a perspective in which integration (of funcationalities ranging from debuggers to code repository management) is hailed as a major development in making programming work more efficient.

In contrast, Jack articulated the pro-integration viewpoint, saying, "all these IDEs, every single one that comes out is an improvement over the previous one. It's all about integration, making it easy to set up a new project that uses technology you've never used before." Proponents of Emacs, however, associated this packaging with a cut-and-paste mentality, as opposed to building something from the ground up. As Sean explained,

> You've got people who are interested in programming with very powerful tools. The IDE people are in the tools camp. That's a very interesting camp to be in. I'm in the language camp ... When I confront an IDE like Eclipse, or IntelliJ, or the Microsoft one, Visual Studio, I'm overwhelmed with options, and clutter, and it confuses the hell out of me. I don't know where to start … [Emacs is] one tool that would work for everything. It's like a really good common denominator tool that you can always fall back to.

Sean here sets up a divide between people who prefer IDEs as integrated and bundled ("the tools camp") versus editors as configurable and extensible ("the language camp"). Even as someone in the "language camp," however, Sean is clear that Emacs is also a tool, but importantly, a tool that inheres different possibilities for the kinds of coding work that can be undertaken. This association between tool choice and ideology moves past a traditional construction of tools as (solely) a force of structure and order [31], and speaks to the sociocultural norms that shape perceptions of tools and how they're used.

Other participants referenced a deep sense of attachment to particular coding tools, often expressed in terms of embodiment and physicality. In particular, these themes of attachment and intimacy surfaced when we asked about switching between editors. As Annie discussed: "In my fingers, I remember all the Emacs shortcuts for doing stuff, so when I'm in VisualStudio or in Notepad, I feel a little strange or a little lost because I can't do the things I want to do quickly." In part, this echoes McCullough's observation that the pleasure of using tools derives from extensive practice [26], where longstanding engagement with a tool effectively embeds the tool into the physical processes of use. This speaks to familiarity with a tool as part of one's embodied experience of a craft. This came out quite poignantly in Mary's assertion that, "once you're comfortable with a tool, it's in your spinal cord, it's in your fingertips ... Anytime you have to make a change, it interrupts the [coding] process until you retool or retrain." These descriptions are striking in the link between tool use and embodiment, as well as identification with tools being used in a craft. As Crawford argued, "from its earliest practice, craft knowledge has entailed knowledge of the 'ways' of one's materials - that is, knowledge of their nature, acquired through disciplined perception" [13, p. 21]. This knowledge of the affordances and limits of one's materials is part of the knowledge inherent in and constitutive of a community of practice.

Related to the embodiment of tools is the sense that the actual products that programmers make are tangible, which might strike some as odd given that the products are software. As Annie explained: "what I do is physical and tangible. I work on an app that people around me use. I'll look over and somebody will be on their phone [using the app] and to me that's incredibly tangible." Even the process of developing software felt tangible to some participants, as Andrew explained: "I like the concreteness of [coding] ... that you can see this program being built up. Even though I know it's a virtual thing, it's intangible, but it's real in some ways. You can make it do things. It can have an effect. You can push something into it and something will come back to you." These references to embodiment and tangibility return us to the link between craft, tools and materiality. There are two kinds of materiality being proposed here: fist, the sense of being physically involved in the production of code, where the body itself plays a role in the ability to create or improve code. Second, code retained notions of materiality because it produced material affects, such as the ability to gauge alterations in a program or product via iterations.

Craft and Communities of Practice

We discuss two focal points of software development as a community of practice: the first relates to how specific tools are associated with taste and professional identity among software engineers writ large. The second analyzes a frustration voiced by many participants that their work was poorly understood by non-developers, which as a consequence reinforced a guild-like mentality associated with crafts.

A Matter of Taste

For Risatti, "a tool is something used directly by the hand with an intention to make something by doing something to material. Because tools are used to make other things, they can be classified as objects having practical function, but they cannot be considered self-contained or self-relating things that exist in and of themselves; they are not ends in and of themselves" [31, p. 49]. Yet among participants, there are also certain external factors that influence the choice of one tool over another for programming work, where tools have purposes that are functional as well as symbolic [26]. One means of tracing symbolic associations of tools is to consider social norms for developers as a community of practice. Regarding these professional norms, Andrew described editors as "an issue of taste ... where certain program languages are considered a better expression than other languages." He went on to describe how this was also borne out in selecting an editor to use: "It's one of those superficial things, like you carry a certain book because you expect that someone will think something of your opinion. Programmers have taste. There are some things which are considered tasteful and some things which are not considered to be as tasteful." For example, using one IDE over another can mark a developer as "old school" or an "early adopter." As Annie explained: "There are some personalities at work at my company who, as soon as they see a new technology, want to try it out. They do that for a while, and that's not me. Once I find something that works for me, I stick with it." Annie's claim resists the idea that newer tools are always and necessarily better than existing ones, but continuing to work with an older editor by no means frees a developer from social connotations associated with too choice. For Wenger, communities of practice share knowledge not only of how to use a tools, but how to display that knowledge in ways that are tactful (or not) [38]. Choosing tools is rooted in how best to deal with the problem at hand, but complicating a purely rationalist account of tool selection are pressures of institutional and professional norms.

"This Strange, Arcane Profession"

Participants also noted that despite the fact that software itself has infiltrated innumerable levels of everyday life, programmers often feel that their work isn't well understood by those outside the field. Asked how he talks about his work to a general audience, James stated, "I would just say, "write software" and try and change the topic. In general, it's this strange arcane profession." Most participants agreed that their work was generally considered abstract at best and at worst, antisocial and dull. Jack offered an explanation of where this sense of obscurity originates:

> I think it's because it's a world of expertise that has no exposure outside of people who do it ... You watch *The Social Network*, which is the story about Facebook and Mark Zuckerberg. You don't see what coding is like even in that movie. You just see him typing and there's a glow of the screen on his face. It's just no use trying to explain something so abstract to someone in a social setting.

Several participants described a tactic of making their work more readily understood by focusing on the product of their work rather than the process. Nick described using this approach in talking about his company's work in the health care field:

> Usually people are more interested about what the software delivers in particular, as opposed to the actual software itself, unless they're software people ... Programming's a very esoteric activity, really, isn't it? Quite abstract, and if you don't do it, it's quite hard to grasp what someone does when they're programming.

Developers we interviewed perceive the end products that they're creating more recognizable than the process, such that the coded artifact is visible, legible even as the process underlying that work is obscure.

Tied directly to the link between code and invisibility, Sean voiced an interesting preference for the term programming over coding, because "coding for me speaks of obfuscation and hiding information. I try not to code, I try to program, if that makes any sense. I try to communicate from something to something." For Sean, the term coding implies hiding and obfuscation, which is in opposition to his personal ethics (such as advocating open source technologies) as well as his aforementioned perspective on code as communication.

Obscurity is not considered uniformly bad among programmers, as Parth explained: "I think it's quite great actually, that there's something that somebody has spent a lot of time, effort, and thought things through and ... nobody can see behind it. It's like a secret that you know, that I know, and other people know. Most people don't even know how it works." This echoes a guild or workshop mentality, where knowledge of how to do something is exclusive and even somewhat ritualized. As Sennett noted, "workshops present and past have glued people together through work rituals, whether these be a shared cup of tea or the urban parade; through mentoring, whether the formal surrogate parenting of medieval times or informal advising on the worksite; through face-to-face sharing of information" [33, p. 73]. In Sennett's view, workshops are sites of transfer, not only of professional knowledge but of professional norms (a focal point of communities of practice). Workshops are ritualized not only because of transferring knowledge but because they generate exclusivity based on the ability to make and evaluate a given set of artifacts. For Parth, there is an allure in a programmed artifact constructed via labor that is visible only to some. These two sentiments – the fatigue of not having one's work understood and the pleasure of exclusivity within a community of practice – are not so much mutually exclusive as sentiments that shift over time and from project to project.

DISCUSSION: CODE, COMMUNICATION AND CRAFT

We read a theme of communication as inherent to the craft of software development across concepts of tools, code and describing software engineering as a job. Interestingly, programmer Olivier Geoffroy has argued that software is uniquely capable of communicating craft: "normally you don't have a language for craft and it's very difficult to communicate" (cited in [6]). Part of the reason that craft conceptually evades language stems from the fact that the object itself is intended to communicate its purpose and (for the right audience) the processes of its formation: "[skill] in contemporary crafts can take a number of forms, but boils down to one basic premise: the ability to execute a difficult process, or processes, and communicate this directly through the object, or indirectly through knowledgeable and appreciative observers" [39, p. 145]. For Valentine and Follett, skill in craft is demonstrated through the crafted object, although (crucially) this communication may be experienced differently by those inside versus outside a community of practice. Unlike crafts that seem to operate outside language, writing software code in fact requires mastery of programming languages in order to function.

In looking at software development as a craft, code becomes a profound example of craft that takes place precisely through (programming) language(s). This is in keeping with thinking of tools as things that "send the message of clarity, of knowing which act should be done with which thing" [25, p. 94]. The difficulty of communicating the craft of coding centers on the illegibility of coding languages specifically and coding work more generally. Software developers that we interviewed were on the whole frustrated by the general lack of even basic knowledge of how coding works. Although one could argue that this is the case for any craft, there are two added tensions in the context of software development. First, the do it yourself (DIY) ethic that pervades both hacker [8], start up [24] and maker communities [8, lends itself to an ideology of self-teaching, even for those who have studied computer science in school. Second, given the enduring tension between offline (as concrete) and online (as abstract) we suspect that the inability of outsiders to understand coding work compounds the perception that it is abstract and immaterial.

Related to issues of legibility in terms of code are issues of collaboration and prestige - Coleman and Golub [10] point to the "uneasy fit between a world view that emphasizes the creative action of the individual and yet requires validation and recognition from a wider community." The wider community of software developers to which Coleman and Golub refer can be construed broadly (all software engineers, as brought together on Stack Overflow) or much more narrowly (one's development team). This need for validation is arguably heightened given how poorly understood development work tends to be outside the community of practice.

One consequence of coding being both procedurally and literally illegible to non-developers is the creation of an economy of intertwined understanding/affect and skill, alternately manifesting itself through inside jokes and economies of prestige. This is arguably the case for any profession that hinges on deep knowledge shared by a small group of people, but in the context of software, it's interesting to think of how this exclusivity manifests itself in the code itself, whether in idiosyncratic messages embedded in comments or hidden functions like Easter Eggs. But in addition to disparities in legibility between people who craft software and people who (solely) consume, it's notable (and perhaps paradoxical) that participants emphasized the importance of code being communicative – of explaining itself without unnecessary (or any) notation or commentary. Communication is thus both an evaluator metric of software development work work (borne out in the qualities that participants valued in code) and a metaphor relevant to key tensions within software development as a community of practice, where developers were frustrated by the perception that their work was "strange and arcane" to a general public, even as many took pleasure in the sense of exclusivity derived from thinking of code as communication work not only between a software program and a computer, but between craftspeople within a community of practice.

Implications for Theory

Earlier, we noted that craft often operates relationally, in that it is frequently defined as not art, not industrial and not design. In this section, we discuss how software development unfolds across these binaries, as suggested by our analysis of tools used in programming work.

Craft vs. Art

Where art is often constructed as aesthetic, thought-provoking and spiritual, an indication of socio-cultural esteem, craft is conceptualized as utilitarian and quotidian, referring to objects of the household rather than the museum. Underscoring this, participants often introduced a metric for evaluating code in terms of its functionality – during the focus group, as participants recounted early experiences coding other participants frequently questioned "Did it work?" as an initial means of response. Rather than evaluating code in terms of aesthetics or asking what one might have learned through making it, or even in terms of how something was made, code was frequently discussed in terms of functionality.

At the same time, developers frequently expressed a recognition and admiration of pretty code. As Annie commented, "When I see really pretty code, I really wish I could code like that. It's elegant. It's not verbose, but not so compact that you can't read it. It's easy to understand. It does what it looks like it's doing. It's neat. It's not brute force. It's not forced. It just flows." Similarly, Sean stated, "I get a lot of joy in making the code aesthetically pleasing to me, beautiful in terms of its layout, in terms of the naming of things, in terms of the flow of the codes. I quite like to look at the structure in terms of its 2D form on the page, how it moves in and out." Software is intended to do something, and is typically measured by the people who produce it in terms of how well it works. But without ignoring or understanding the importance of utility in conceptualizing craft, it's also important to note the aesthetic elements of craft. Coleman [9] argued that open source hackers

> often consider themselves to be artists, and see coding as a type of 'diligent craftsmanship' in which they imbue software with a unique element of their creative selves. Software developers construe their technical activity as inherently valuable avenues for highly creative forms of expression, even if they openly admit to various types of worldly and technical constraints (p. 262).

These tensions of producing aesthetically-pleasing code in the midst of technical constraints speak precisely to the experiences of developers we interviewed, but it's useful to note that these tensions were not experienced solely in terms of the code as a product, but also in the tools as part of the coding process.

Craft vs. Industry

Art and craft share a characterization of being handmade as opposed to artifacts that are made industrially, by machine. When participants position coding as craft, it was typically in reference to creating code as an embodied process, but also as a process of individual agency, as described by Parth:

> [Coding] is a craft because there's a lot of labor and sweat that goes into these artifacts. There is pride in making something. We don't have a way that I could say to a computer, 'Build me an X' and it would do it for me. You have to architect and think these things out. So I think craft is the right word.

Parth conjoins both the embodied and intentional elements of craft in this description where code is both something handmade (or at least, made through an effort of using one's hands) and something that cannot be manufactured without human deliberation. At the same time, code is produced through and intended to be used with machines. Moreover, institutional constraints (such as meeting client demands for a product compliant with a particular standard) were frequently cited by participants as a key source of tensions with elements of coding work that are more associated with craft, such as intuition for a particular problem-solving approach or taking the time to make code aesthetically pleasing. Part of the HCI interest in materiality stems from a push to consider material properties that shape interactions with numerous kinds of technologies [15, 17]. Given this attention on materiality as it affects understandings of socio-technical networks, our work provides instructive examples of just how deep issues of materiality run – all the way to software engineers' perceptions' of the development environments used to make software.

Craft vs. Design

Design inheres a notion of building prototypes, of the cerebral process of developing ideas for products or technologies. In contrast, craft is perceived as the fulfillment of design, the concrete production of abstract conceptions. In our interviews, some participants tracked this dynamic in terms of tools, where concept development was the interesting and primary work of programmers, and the actual use of tools to build code was deprivileged and secondary. This is arguably something of a sharpening of the "craft as vocation" assumption, in that it assigns key intellectual work to design and "hands on" technical work to implementation. This conceptualization is partly derailed by participants' repeated emphasis on problem solving and utility as deeply-entrenched metrics for evaluating code. Moreover, we would argue that throughout their descriptions of tools, participants frequently assigned both problem solving and concept development functions to the same tool – thus the binary of craft versus design effectively dissolves in the context of how tools are used in the craft of software development.

Implications for computer science education

Though mainly focused on a deeper understanding of the relationship between notions of craft and practices of software engineering, our analysis also points us to implications for computer science pedagogy. There has been a recent resurgence in a longstanding debate [11, 12, 21, 30] between teaching computing to children as a discipline, and teaching them how to use computers; between teaching computer science and teaching information and communication technology (ICT). Oscillations between claiming software development as alternately craft or science reveal changing assumptions not only in what programming is but also how it should be taught and how we think of the people who do coding work. Early on, developers sought to reclaim software engineering as firmly embedded within the sciences, marking it as a mature, scientific and rigorous practice, rather than the haphazard associations of craft [1]. In this line of thinking, software engineering began as craft and then (fortunately, in this view) developed into a legitimate science.

Though this debate started out in universities, it has been taken up by governments. Michael Gove, the UK's Secretary of State for Education since May 2010 said in 2012 that "long after the technologies [kids] used at school are obsolete - the principles learnt in Computer Science will still hold true" [30]. The goal is to reduce "demotivating and routine ICT activity" (i.e. where "material that the students already know is repeated) "in favor of the "recognition that Computer Science is a rigorous academic discipline" [12]. In this debate computing is seen as "a discipline, like mathematics or physics, that explores foundational principles and ideas" while ICT is "a skills-based course focusing, typically, on the use of applications" [11]. This is not an argument against tool use per-se, and in our study we found both sides represented among our participants. For example Mark stated "learning tools is not an issue really it's the underlying principles that are the important thing." In contrast, Mary noted of the Java IDE Eclipse "It would be fair to say Eclipse taught me Java," effectively assigning an instructive role to an IDE. Even as participants valued core principles of math and logic in their coding work, they also spoke of their attachment to tools and embodied components of labor, and as emblematic of their professional ethics and personal style. As such, craft becomes a means of conceptually situating software engineering in a way that accounts for the materiality of code, but it should also give pause in the context of educational policy that would emphasize rationality and logic at the expense of craft.

ACKNOWLEDGEMENTS

We would like to thank the Socio-Digital Systems group at Microsoft Research Cambridge for their feedback and support as this project was being conducted. We are also grateful to Tero Karppi, Ben Merriman and the anonymous reviewers for their feedback on this paper.

REFERENCES

1. Abbate, J. *Recoding gender: Women's changing participation in computing*, MIT Press (2012).
2. Adamson, G. *Thinking Through Craft*, Berg (2007).
3. Alt, C. Objects of our affection: How object orientation made computers a medium. In E. Huhtamo & J. Parikka (Eds.) *Media Archaeology*, UC Berkeley Press (2011).
4. Bowker, G. and Star, S. L. *Sorting Things Out,* MIT Press (1999).
5. Bratich, J. Z. The digital touch: Craft-work as immaterial labour and ontological accumulation. *Ephemera*, *10*, 3/4 (2010), 303-318.
6. Buxton, P. Hand, mind and hard drive. *Crafts*, May/June, (2003), 44-47.
7. Case, P. and Piñeiro, E. Aesthetics, performativity and resistance in the narratives of a computer programming community. *Human Relations 59*, 6 (2006), 168.
8. Chorianopoulous, K., Jaccheci, L., Salveson Nossum, A. Creative and open software engineering practices and tools in maker community projects. In *Proc. EICS '12*. ACM Press: New York, 333 - 334
9. Coleman, G. The Social Construction of Freedom in Free and Open Source Software: Hackers Ethics, and the Liberal Tradition. Doctoral dissertation, University of Chicago (2005).
10. Coleman, E. G., & Golub, A. Hacker practice: Moral genres and the cultural articulation of liberalism. *Anthropological Theory*, *8*, 3 (2008), 255-277.
11. Computing at School, The Challenge. http://www. computingatschool.org.uk/index.php?id=the-challenge

12. Computing in School. http://royalsociety.org/uploadedFiles/Royal_Society_Content/education/policy/computing-in-schools/2012-01-12-Computing-in-Schools.pdf

13. Crawford, M. *The Case for Working With Your Hands or Why Office Work is Bad for Us and Fixing Things Feels Good.* Penguin (2009).

14. Curtis, C., Krasner, H. & Iscoe, N. A field study of the software design process for large systems. *Communications of the ACM, 31* 1 (1988), 1268-1287.

15. Dourish and Melissa Mazmanian, "Media as Material: Information Representations as Material Foundations for Organizational Practice" (working paper presented at the Third International Symposium on Process Organization Studies, Corfu, Greece, June 2011).

16. Faulkner, W. 'Nuts and bolts and people': Gender-troubled engineer identities. *Social Studies of Science*, *37*, 3 (2007), 331-356.

17. Fernaeus, Y., Jonsson, M., and Tholander, J. Revisiting the Jaquard loom: Threads of history and current patterns in HCI. In *Proc. CHI 2012*, ACM Press (2012), 1593-1602.

18. Gentner, D. R. & Grudin, J. Why good engineers (sometimes) create bad interfaces. In *Proc. CHI '90*, ACM Press (1990), 277-282.

19. Grudin, J. Groupware and social dynamics: 8 challenges for developers. *Communications of the ACM 37* 1 93-105 (1994).

20. Hine, C. *Virtual Ethnography*, Sage (2000).

21. ICTs Programme Response. http://www.bcs.org/upload/pdf/ict-programmes-response-apr12.pdf

22. Kittler, F. A. *Gramophone, Film, Typewriter.* Stanford, Calif: Stanford Univ. Press (2006).

23. Kleif, T. and Faulkner, W. "I'm no athlete [but] I can make this thing dance!" - Men's pleasures in technology. *Science, Technology & Human Values, 28*,2 (2003), 296-325.

24. Latour, B. *Pandora's Hope: The Reality of Science Studies,* Harvard University Press (1999).

25. Marwick, A. Status update: Celebrity, publicity and branding in web 2.0. Doctoral Dissertation, New York University (2010).

26. McCullough, M. *Abstracting Craft: The Practiced Digital Hand,* MIT Press (1996).

27. McKenzie, A. *Cutting Code: Software and Sociality,* Peter Lang, (2006).

28. Piñeiro, E. The aesthetics of code. On excellence in instrumental action. Doctoral Dissertation, Royal Institute of Technology, Stockholm. (2003).

29. Poltrock, S. E. & Grudin, J. Organizational obstacles to interface design and development: Two participant observer studies. *ACM Transactions on Computer-Human Interaction 1* 1 52-80.

30. Removing ICT Programmes of Study, Attainment Targets and statutory assessment arrangements http://www.bcs.org/upload/pdf/ict-programmes-response-apr12.pdf.

31. Risatti, H. *A Theory of Craft: Function and Aesthetic Expression,* University of North Carolina Press (2007).

32. Rosner, D. K. Mediated crafts: digital practices around creative handwork. In *CHI '10 Extended Abstracts on Human Factors in Computing Systems* (CHI EA '10). ACM Press (2010), 2955-2958.

33. Sennett, R. (2008). *The craftsman*. New Haven: Yale University Press.

34. Spradley, J. *The Ethnographic Interview,* Holt, Rinehart and Winston (1979).

35. Strauss, A. L. and Corbin, J. M. *Basics of Qualitative Research: Grounded Theory Procedures and Techniques.* Thousand Oaks: Sage Publications (1990).

36. Takhteyev, Y. *Coding places: Software practice in a South American city.* Cambridge, Mass: MIT Press (2012).

37. Tannenbaum, J. G., Williams, A. M., Desjardins, A. Tanenbaum, K. Democratizing technology: Pleasure, utility and expressiveness in DIY and maker practice. In *Proc. CHI '13.* ACM Press, 2603-2612.

38. Taylor, T. L. Life in Virtual Worlds: Plural Existence, Multimodalities, and Other Online Research Challenges. *American Behavioral Scientist, 43, 3*, (1999), 436-449.

39. Valentine, L., and Follett, G., Eds. *Past, Present & Future Craft Practice*, NMS Press (2010).

40. Walz, D. B., Elam, J. J. & Curtis, B. Inside a software design team: Knowledge acquisition, sharing and integration. *Communications of the ACM 36* 10, (1993), 63-77.

41. Wenger, E. *Communities of Practice: Learning, Meaning, and Identity*, Cambridge University Press (1998).

Cultivating Practice & Shepherding Technology Use: Supporting Appropriation Among Unanticipated Users

Pablo-Alejandro Quiñones
University of Michigan
pabloq@umich.edu

ABSTRACT
Previous work has shown that the successful appropriation of technology into practice depends heavily on users' understandings and narratives around the technology's use. Who drives the successful appropriation process is still ill-defined within the literature. In this paper, we present a case study conducted in a research university, using interviews to understand staff practices and technology appropriation within their work contexts. We found that the successful appropriation of collaborative IT relies on the invisible work conducted by those people within groups who formally or informally aid their colleagues in the successful 'cultivation' of practices and sensemaking around technology—people we call shepherds. We draw parallels to other work that suggest the need for similar types of agents and close with a dialog concerning the challenge of establishing shepherding practices within large organizations.

Author Keywords
Appropriation; ecologies; practices; training; collaboration.

ACM Classification
H.5.3 [Information Interfaces and Presentation]: Group and Organization Interfaces – Computer-supported cooperative work.

General Terms
Human Factors; Design.

INTRODUCTION
The adoption and subsequent use of collaborative information and communication technologies (ICTs) have long been topics of interest to CSCW since its inception. A number of studies have explored barriers to the success of CSCW tools within organizations [17,18,19,33]. Such barriers include critical mass [17,19] and the disparities between those who will benefit from applications and those who must do additional work to supports its use [17,18]. CSCW has also examined how technology plays a role in a number of different contexts such as traditional workplace settings, online communities (e.g., Reddit), and social networks (e.g., Twitter, Facebook, etc.).

Of particular interest in this current research is the way in which technology is successfully incorporated into everyday practice (appropriation) within large organizations and identifying the key players who support this process. Specifically, this work explores the appropriation of two collaboration toolsets that support collaborative activities among administrators and office workers within a university setting. The first system, CTools, is a learning management system (LMS) that had been unexpectedly appropriated by the staff population. The other toolset was the Google suite of collaborative tools (primarily Docs/Drive and Sites), where staff were anticipated users. In uncovering why and how these systems were appropriated, a theme emerged—that certain individuals who would be influential in the process of adoption, cultivation of practices, and leading others in using (and learning to use) IT in the workplace would emerge.

Given the very different natures of the two systems' arrivals into the university at large and the vastly different circumstances for staff's appropriation of them, we use these two systems as parallel case studies for exploring the appropriation of technology and identifying the key agents in appropriating technology. We base our work in the appropriation literature—particularly that of Orlikowski [36, 37] and Draxler [10-12]—as well as through Nardi & O'Day's information ecologies framework [33], which frame our findings of limited appropriation practices due to the lack of system knowledge and training, revealing a lack of social agents to discover and promote alternate practices. Our findings reveal the need for leaders in the appropriation process (which we call *shepherds*). We discuss parallels between our own work and Orlikowski's work [38] over two decades prior to this paper, showing that shepherding and knowledge about IT continue to be issues in the appropriation of technology into practice for both target users and unanticipated users. We close by generalizing the issue of shepherding to other contexts and asking questions about who should be tasked with the creation of shepherds and how we might assist users of ICTs in becoming knowledgeable in re-appropriating their tools.

CSCW'14, February 15–19, 2014, Baltimore, Maryland, USA.

http://dx.doi.org/10.1145/2531602.2531698

RELATED WORK

Interpretive flexibility [37,40,41], which suggests that users are in control of creating narratives around the use of technology, results in the observation that all objects are open to interpretation. One example of interpretive flexibility comes from Madge et al. [31], who describe multiple possible interpretations of Facebook among educators, researchers, and students. Specifically, it can be interpreted as a potential environment to support teaching/learning. However, the authors found that college students interpreted it as a space for social interaction and not as a desirable learning space.

Compared to rigid technologies, flexible ones lend themselves to multiple interpretations and thus potential and existing users' interpretations of this technology may lead users to create narratives about its use—in turn, these narratives may lead to ICTs being implemented in ways that evolve over time [2,7,21,23,49] or in ways that may not even be those intended by designers [7,11,36,37]. *Appropriation* is a term that has been used to capture the ways in which these interpretations result in end use.

Draxler et al. [10] described appropriation as both as "an entangled, cooperative process of searching, becoming aware, installing, configuring and learning how to use new tools" (pg. 2835) and as "the social process of incorporating objects into one's life, including changes to the objects caused by modes of using it" (pg. 2835). Thus, appropriation focuses on the ongoing cycle whereby people adapt technology to their contexts while they themselves adapt to technological change—an act that is sometimes referred to as *mutual adaptation* or *co-evolution* [7,8,9,16,29,45]. As a result of the agency the people exert on technology use, appropriating technology is partly a matter of enacting practices and structures through technology use [39]. In this paper, we focus on appropriation as a process of emergently adapting the use of technology. This process keeps technology relevant to emergent contexts while also acknowledging the agency of the people using technology. This process also results appropriation by *unanticipated users* [43] and *bystanders* [13], users whose appropriations emerge despite not being the primary targeted user.

Though there are benefits to being able to adapt technology and practices, doing so requires effort on behalf of ITC users and stakeholders. Kling and Lamb assert that *articulation work* [25] is needed to make IT work and that users conduct this work, acting as social agents within their organizations [27]. Draxler and colleagues have similarly shown that the configuring and re-configuring these systems is a form of collaborative articulation work that occurs tangentially to the actual work being done and that these activities are an important part of appropriation [10-12].

What remains unclear from the points above are the necessary pre-conditions to successful appropriation and who plays the primary roles in ensuring appropriation work is occurring. The lack of clarity is due to two issues in the problematization of the appropriation process: first, there is the definition of successful/unsuccessful appropriation. The second issue are the numerous, conflicting, and sometimes overlapping characterizations of actors that various researchers in CSCW and IS have proposed as crucial to appropriation work.

The importance of sensemaking and knowledge in the appropriation of technology is highlighted both by sensemaking successes and failures that impact the ways in which ICTs are appropriated. MacLean [30] gives an example of an organizational success, where the existence of a 'tailoring culture' encouraged tailoring activities and the sharing of expertise, thereby allowing the system to be appropriated by users at many levels of expertise. Implicit in this finding is that users in the organization understood the system and thus were able to appropriate it. Okamura [35] proposed that users who act as *mediators* can successfully affect organizational use of ICT when they adapt a new collaborative technology to a context, modify the context, and support ongoing changes to the technology and context over time.

One example of an organization facing barriers to successful appropriation work is described in Orlikowski's study [37] of a group in an organization that adopted Lotus Notes. In this work, Orlikowski shows the importance of users' understanding of the system in their ability to appropriate it into their practices, describing both cognitive and structural barriers to its successful appropriation. She described cognitive barriers to appropriation—that the group she studied knew very little about Notes and why it was being implemented—a result of the lack of communication from the key decision-makers and implementers to the employees. As a result, these employees had formed weak understandings and thus appropriated Notes according to these weakly developed technological frames. She wrote, "If people have a poor or inappropriate understanding of the unique and different features of a technology they may rest using it, or may not integrate it appropriately into their work practices" (pg.364). The appropriation of the toolset was also negatively affected by the lack of appropriate types of training, which only reinforced disincentives to devising ways of appropriating technology that leveraged its capabilities.

The case study presented by Orlikowski demonstrates, among other things, the importance of people who are able to develop and cultivate practices around new technology. Other research has highlighted the importance of such local expert users in the context of tailoring activities [42]. Expert users are important for appropriation by target users and unanticipated users alike, though whether such experts exist among unanticipated user populations is questionable. Unanticipated appropriators could be experts at deciphering

IT, but it is just as likely that they are at a natural disadvantage to deciphering it. In the former case, users are able to interpret technology beyond the limits of design intent despite the lack of training; in the latter case, users may not know how to re-interpret IT due to a lack of official training. Because unanticipated users are unexpected, it is also questionable whether there are local agents in formal roles who are able to undertake the kind of training work to teach technology use and cultivate practices.

In establishing the role of users in establishing technology use and practice, Nardi & O'Day [33] identified a type of user that performs mediation work—*gardeners*. Gardeners are defined as informal actors who "translate concepts and mechanisms back and forth between the domain of work…and the technology itself" (pg.141), often informally training others in technology use, answering questions, setting standards, etc. Gardeners, through their tinkering spirit, might also spark change and lead others through the turbulence of transitions and sensemaking about technology. In their description, Nardi & O'Day relegate their work to the realm of the invisible, work that is an aside to the main missions of group work and that is unrewarded. Given these descriptions, gardeners would be aptly equipped to assist groups in the appropriation of collaborative technologies and social media by virtue of their expertise and local knowledge of the work that occurs within their groups. In previous work, Gantt & Nardi [14] distinguished between local developers (in formal positions) to gardeners (informal positions).

In a review of Information Ecologies, Ranney [43] highlighted what was perceived to be an oversight made by Nardi & O'Day, the importance of technical communication in technology and knowledge transfer. She discusses that the concept of gardeners overlaps with the field of technical communicators, practitioners who are involved researching and documenting various technical processes and products and sharing this knowledge to some audience. Technical communicators, in essence, have the power to design the kinds of human-human or human-information interactions that will help users in appropriating technology.

It is important, when considering users—either target users or unanticipated ones—to consider the process of appropriating technology as one that is collaborative and conducted by its users when they act as social actors within their organizations, exerting their agency while limited by structural components of the organization [27]. In their capacity as actors, users of collaborative systems appropriate these systems collaboratively, whether through single-user appropriations permeating throughout an organization, through designated group members, or anywhere in between [12]. This work explores both how users appropriated workplace technologies and those organizational actors who affected (or did not affect) the process of appropriation and end use of these ITCs.

RESEARCH SETTING

This research is concerned with unanticipated users and their appropriation of workplace technology. Of particular interest is technology use and practices among staff at a large research university, the University of Michigan. Within the University of Michigan, staff work in a 'social world' (borrowing the term from Strauss [48]) that co-exists with faculty and student worlds; each of these worlds has its own goals, practices, and structures in place. Staff's work situates them in a space that supports the research and academic missions at the university with the implication that they cross boundaries between the staff, student, and faculty worlds. Staff also work in positions dedicated to the administrative needs that allow the university to function.

Staff also work within communities of practice [28,51]—communities that are at times defined by their purposes (academic, research, or administrative support) and at other times defined by their academic or non-academic departments (locally called *units*). These layers of membership result in a complex set of boundaries that are continually crossed as part of daily responsibilities and practices. ICTs play a substantial role in staff's ability to work both within and across organizational boundaries.

CTools & Project Sites

The motivation of this research was centered on the observation that a large number of staff at our research site, University of Michigan, had adopted and appropriated a learning management system (LMS) known locally as CTools. CTools was designed to support teaching and learning in classroom settings between students, faculty, and teaching/learning content by creating a course-specific website for central course needs. The extent of staff's mass appropriation of the CTools platform came mostly as a surprise given the design intent underlying the course management system. Only a small subset of staff was considered to be potential users—those engaged in research or helping faculty to create their course sites—and even their use was expected to be relatively minimal. In that sense, staff were unanticipated and their use is similar to that of bystanders who became secondary users [13]. Since the discovery of staff's adoption, staff consistently outnumbered faculty in terms of the number of users and the amount of use, resulting in staff being the second largest group of users. Because of the extent of their use, staff are situated somewhere between primary and secondary users.

Within the CTools system, staff appropriated a toolset called Project Sites, a feature that allows any individual or group with university credentials to create a website that provides groups with access to the same tools found in Course Sites (shown in Figure 1, next page). Project Sites (and Course Sites) are flexible and customizable in that users are able to create a central site to meet a variety of

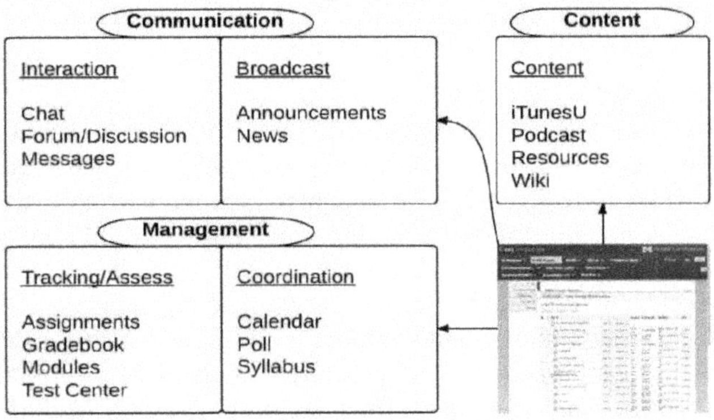

Figure 1. Project Sites tool diagram

needs, are able to select the tools they will use to achieve those ends, and because a number of the tools offer further options for customization.

These sites can be created for any reason and support user-content, user-process, and user-user interactions. Previous work [43] used log analyses and a values survey work and suggested that staff's appropriation of the Project Sites toolset had focused primarily on the use of the toolset for creating group repositories for their administrative kinds of activities. This research builds on this past work, further exploring both the role that the toolset played in staff practices and who was influential in the way it was appropriated—both formally and informally.

While Project Sites are flexible and tailorable to staff's given contexts, they are vastly different from the types of tailorable systems most commonly studied by researchers—systems that require end-user development or direct tailoring through plug-ins [10-12] and components [e.g., 52]. Instead, Project Sites lies somehwere in the middle of the tailorability spectrum, where customization of its features and applicability to various work contexts are possible, but changes to the tools themselves are not[1]. Configuration of Project Sites happens outside of the system, through interactions and decisions made in the social melieu, rather than being supported within the system.

Ecological Transition

During the initial phases of this research, the university made the decision to shift a number of its services to Google after a central deliberation process between the university administration and the Information Technology Services (ITS) to assess a number of options—a process that had been started by the central administration as part of a strategy for growing the university IT infrastructure and which resulted in an announcement of the transition on October 26,2012. The transition officially began on March 5, 2012 and concluded on August 31, 2012.

The 'migration', as it was called locally, meant that the university-supported email services would be supported by Google and the previous email interfaces would be replaced by Gmail though the university community would still be using the university-assigned credentials and email address, with the parallel effect that ITS would no longer support Outlook or Apple's Mail client, as all users would then gain access to the Google Calendar system and all other Google tools through their pre-existing university credentials. The number of tools that were made available to the campus community at large was extensive and included (but was not limited to) Google+, Google Docs/Drive, Google Chat, and Google Sites. Because Google's emergence into the university ecosystem was recognized as having a direct effect on the staff population, staff were in the group of anticipated users and there was a visible movement to provide training for staff.

Given the similarity between the systems' affordances and the differences in both the conceptualization of staff as intended users and how implementation occurred, Google proved to be an opportune comparison case to Project Sites. Much like for Project Sites, we aimed to discover those formal and informal influences on how Google's tools would be appropriated as well as uncovering the way in which these tools are interpreted.

RESEARCH PROBLEM & QUESTIONS

Project Sites and Google's collaboration tools are similar in that they support collaboration and were optional to adopt. The difference between the two toolsets, however, stems from their transitions into appropriation, where Project Sites was appropriated in a haphazard transition that was not uniform across the university compared to Google's tools, which emerged as options as part of a mandatory shift and a very visible campaign from ITS. The difference between the two cases suggests that staff have different degrees of knowledge prior to the appropriation process. Different people would also influence technology use and practices between contexts. These two cases highlighted the appropriation process among the same staff population from both the anticipated and unanticipated user perspectives, leading a number of research questions:

RQ1 How were Project Sites' and Google's toolsets interpreted and appropriated?

RQ2 How did knowledge about the two toolsets prior to the appropriation process explain how they were appropriated?

RQ3 Who were the influential people who drove technologies in the ecosystem?

RQ4 Who were the influential people who create knowledge regarding the toolsets and perform the

[1] In fact, the tools are themselves tailorable, but not from the users' end. Tools can be changed only through intervention from its university-level developers

appropriation work that makes sense of technology and drives its use?

METHODS

We conducted semi-structured interviews with staff at University of Michigan. Because of the size of the staff community (over 20,000 staff), we found it necessary to narrow down the scope of this study and chose to focus only on staff in office and administrative roles—staff who were critical to supporting the university's mission to support teaching/learning and the conduct of research. As a result, we excluded staff from health-related units (Medical School, Hospital, etc.). We had also excluded staff from the Libraries/Museums as well as staff in research and IT-related job roles because prior research had indicated very little use among these staff.

We collected interviews from twenty-four (24) participants across a number of units and roles. Participants were predominantly women (19 female, 5 male) and most participants were Caucasian (19 Caucasian, 4 African-American, 1 Asian-American). While we did not collect information pertaining to age, most participants were over the age of 40. The demographics we collected suggested that our sample was representative of university demographics, thus reducing the risk of potential biases.

We collected data from roughly equal numbers of staff from academic (N=13) and non-academic units (N=11). The staff we interviewed came from Office/Clerical (N=10) and Administrative positions (N=14). All of the participants had been at the university for at least 2 years.

Analytical Framework & Analysis

Interviews were recorded and transcribed. Transcripts were analyzed using a combination of coding techniques from a coding scheme that, among other things, was sensitive to activity theory and the ecological metaphor described by Nardi and O'Day, paying attention to the concept of *keystone species*—particularly the keystone species they call *gardeners*.

Because of the influence from Nardi & O'Day, Activity Theory (AT) was used to describe the entire system of work and activities beyond the individuals we interviewed. Activity theory, according to Bryant et al. [6], addresses activity in a sociotechnical system as 6 elements that can be summarized *subjects* in a *community* engaged in activities towards a set of *objectives* that are supported by *tools, rules,* and, *the division of labor.*

The final coding scheme used codes that were sensitive to the above frameworks by looking for tools, tool affordances, processes being supported, influential people (formal and informal), knowledge of tools (as well as inaccuracies in this knowledge), training, and obstacles in adopting or appropriating tools.

Thirteen interviewees had opted to participate in the think-aloud task. All interviewees' transcripts were coded for accuracy (correct understanding of tool functions) and for signs of guessing at tools' functions.

RESULTS

Overwhelmingly, staff described that their positions were highly collaborative and required substantial amounts of communication, knowledge creation, and knowledge sharing. With regard to information sharing, they were limited to centrally-supported core systems for university records and had many choices of platforms. Among the many tools that helped staff in these practices, the CTools Project Sites and Google toolsets filled roles that supported collaboration both within and across organizational boundaries by providing central spaces for work. The following sections describe how the tools were appropriated into practice and how knowledge served as a foundation, highlighting differences in the results of appropriation that were due in large part to knowledge about the systems and being target/unanticipated users.

Appropriation of Project Sites & Knowledge

Appropriation of CTools Project Sites

The interviews showed overwhelmingly that staff had appropriated the CTools Project Sites toolset as a repository, supporting their ability to store and share information and documents with collaborators. Staff most often described that Project Sites supported their storage and sharing activities within the context of working in committees, groups of staff in similar roles, groups defined by their unit affiliations, and (to a lesser degree) groups that included members who were outside of the university.

In working as a central location for sharing and storing information and important documents, Project Sites were reported to have removed the burden of finding ways to share information across intra-organizational boundaries mainly because access was (and continues to be) guaranteed as long as collaborators were also affiliated with the university. Staff often noted that a CTools feature ('Friend Accounts') supported the crossing of inter-organizational boundaries by allowing these users to invite non-university collaborators. Other sharing media—such as servers and intranets—failed to support sharing practices when staff needed central space for sharing and storage across their unit-defined boundaries. Thus Project Sites functioned as spaces that supported the flow of information without the limitation of boundaries.

Across the interviews, it was evident that staff had been using the toolset almost exclusively for the Resources tool, the main tool that supports uploading and downloading documents through a folder-based, hierarchical structure. The hierarchical and static nature of the file systems that the Resources tool created led to three of the participants comparing sites to a 'filing cabinet.'

Given that there were so many other available tools within the Project Sites toolset, the manner of its appropriation—which favored one tool and ignored the others—was striking. Some of the barriers to their adoption were organizational or professional—e.g., the use of the Chat tool being seen as unprofessional or the lack of critical mass to continue using a tool (such as the Schedule or Wiki tools). We similarly found that some non-tool features, like the ability to invite non-university collaborators to a site were not being used even though staff expressed their need for the features, suggesting inadequate system knowledge.

Staff were prompted to elaborate on the reasons why their appropriation of the toolset did not make use of other tools and features within the system. For the most part, staff felt that most of the other tools were not useful to them. This revealed two things: 1) this belief was held without understanding the tools and features, and 2) their belief that many of the tools were irrelevant to their needs—a belief based on a literal interpretation of those tools by their given, academically-oriented labels, not on potential uses.

Staff appropriation of Project Sites was also affected by their shortcuts in the site-creation process. Usually, staff reported that they purposefully ignored the list of tools while using and creating their groups' sites, choosing to only consider the Resources tool. In other instances, staff had learned to 'clone' an existing site, which had the effect of skipping the site set-up phase, a phase that opens opportunities for experimentation. In very rare occasions, staff reported looking briefly at help documents or tinkering with the tools, but this almost never resulted in other tools being adopted. Along a similar vein, staff did not conceive of appropriating tools because of a common perception among interviewees that many of the tools were specifically designed to serve faculty and students in a classroom setting (e.g., Assignments, Syllabus, etc.).

It was not the case that all staff interviewees were unable to experiment or find ways of appropriating the system to leverage its other features. There were rare cases where staff experimented with other tools. Those tools had usually either remained in disuse, were used inconsistently, or had been abandoned. One example was the use of the Schedule tool, which a few participants had experience with; two of these participants noted that they reduced the frequency with which they updated the calendar because they were unsure whether it was helping their coordination; another participant noted that she had stopped using the tool altogether for the vey same reason.

While there were general barriers to appropriating the system in ways that leveraged other tools, a minority of participants reported successes. One participant, P06 (a research administrator) noted successful use of the calendar and wiki to create an intranet for research proposals. In two other participants' groups, they were able to successfully appropriate the Wiki tool for intranets for collaborators spread across the university.

The appropriation of Project Sites as a repository also resulted from staff's perception that the intended use was in the classroom setting. In comparing that purpose to their own needs, staff distinguished their work and roles in the university as separate from those of faculty and students, while also confirming that they were not unanticipated users. This observation resulted in a narrative that prevented staff from appropriating Project Sites' features that they deemed incompatible because they had never been considered outside of the classroom. Regardless, staff had uncovered a common Project Sites configuration that used only the one tool that was unanimously believed to be compatible with the design intent and their needs. The appropriation of Project Sites as a repository worked well for staff because it successfully supported key file-sharing practices. However, in misunderstanding or not knowing about these other features, staff reported wishing for functions and tools that already existed. In this sense, the appropriation of Project Sites was not as effective as it could have been.

Developing Knowledge of Project Sites

The filing-cabinet interpretation and configuration persisted for a number of reasons, but the root of these reasons could be attributed to the knowledge that staff had about the system. Because the system was not designed for their use, staff's knowledge about Project Sites was mostly influenced by the people who exposed them to Project Sites in the first place. Throughout the interviews, staff described that they had learned about Project Sites through word-of-mouth interactions with each other and with faculty. These interactions emphasized that that staff could place documents on their group's site using the Resources tool, but underemphasized (or completely ignored) the other tools as well as other potential possibilities for use.

To further aggravate matters, staff denied receiving any other communication for new ways to appropriate Project Sites, which they suggested could improve their use of the toolset. While there was training available through ITS, staff did not realize this, thus they missed opportunities to learn to appropriate it in other ways. Staff's appropriation of Project Sites could have grown had they experimented with or learned about the tools. However, their knowledge was limited by a lack of information-seeking. Staff reported that they did not seek out information, particularly assistance in the form of technical communications that could teach them about the tools and diversify their use of the toolset because of time pressures and the perceived lack of incentives to conduct this appropriation work in their jobs.

This lack of knowledge about tools was also reflected in the talk-aloud/card-sort task. Aside from the Resources tool, staff's knowledge of the rest of the toolset was limited to those they had used (or attempted to use) previously—Chat, Announcements, Wiki, Calendar. The lack of knowledge and experience with tools resulted in staff having to guess the functions of the majority of the tools. Interestingly, once engaged in the think-aloud activity, staff were somewhat accurate with their hunches about tool use with only a few exceptions—the iTunesU, Podcast, News, Modules, and Test Center tools—all of which, coincidentally, are named in ways that favor literal interpretation into intended use by students and faculty. A few staff found ways of appropriating tools while sorting and thinking aloud. P07 and P19, for example, considered using the Assignments tool to create work assignments as a way of keeping track of progress within her group.

In summary, staff's lack of understanding of the Project Sites toolset can be attributed to the fact that they were unanticipated users who, once discovered as a dominant user group, were not adequately educated and trained in its use. Because there were no cultivators of new practices, staff remained uninformed. Even when information existed to address potential use, staff either failed to recognize that this information existed or they were too consumed in their actual work to engage in appropriation work. As a result of staff's lack of knowledge and lack of new practices, the appropriation of Project Sites, never evolved.

Appropriation of Google & Knowledge

Appropriation of Google Tools

At the time of the interviews, most staff were still recovering from the disruptions that rippled through their units and work groups as a result of the Google email migration. Regardless, most of the staff had strong inclinations about whether they would be adopting the optional Google tools (Docs/Drive and Sites) and a number of staff had already appropriated them into their everyday practices. All staff had at least some minor exposure to Google Docs (either creating a document or receiving an invitation to one in the past), whereas only two users had started using Google Sites.

Although staff reported knowing about the existence of Google tools prior to the transition, the potential to use them became much more tangible as a result of the email migration. As staff elaborated on the affordances and benefits of the tools, they mentioned that the Google tools provided staff with lightweight office applications with the additional benefits of supporting collaborative editing and sharing as well as easy access from their email.

Drive allowed for the creation of a cloud-based drive where users could share both Google Docs and other file types. The fact that Google Drive mimicked the affordances of the Resources tool was not lost on staff, yet its adoption was limited for a number of reasons, which included the lack of familiarity with the tools, that collaborative editing was not always desirable, and because sensitive/confidential information could not be kept in cloud-storage. When staff had adopted Drive, they had appropriated it into practice as a space for storing and collaboratively editing documents. None of the staff likened Drive to a filing cabinet, like they had with Project Sites, because Drive was perceived as a dynamic space as opposed to a static space—a distinction of instability versus stability. Because of this dynamic nature, it was only reportedly appropriate for work that was in progress.

Even towards the end of data collection (2 months after the migration), many of the interviewed staff still had lingering questions about Google Docs/Drive given that these tools still felt new. Of the relatively small number of active users in our sample (less than half), it remained unclear whether staff had yet to configure Drive for creating structured repositories. A number of staff reported that their focus remained on recovering from the email and calendaring changes and that this recovery period prevented them from learning about the applications and exploring ways to appropriate them.

We expected that the tool that most mimicked Project Sites, Google Sites, was going to replace or pose a challenge to Project Site use, resulting in the latter's disuse. Surprisingly, there were only five staff who recognized the tool and three who used this tool. The other two staff were familiar with the tool, but did not use it in their own work. The rest of the staff we interviewed either had no idea that the tool existed or they only had very vague or incorrect understandings of what Google Sites afforded. Those relatively few staff who adopted the tool, were still in the beginning stages of deciding on how to appropriate it.

Developing Knowledge of Google, Pre- & Post- Migration

Because the migration to Google was anticipated to affect the entire institution, ITS included staff as a target user group. By including staff as target users, ITS intended to consider the broader impacts on staff. In doing so, ITS developed assistance for staff for the email migration and, to some extent, training opportunities for the broader set of tools. Interestingly, this was lost on many staff, who expressed a lack of knowledge concerning how to appropriate the various collaboration tools, both pre- and post-migration. When prompted about their use of the Google tools, the two common methods were trial-and-error and hearing about potential uses from colleagues.

As part of the transition, staff were assisted in migrating their previous email to the Gmail client both by their local IT teams and by ITS. ITS went so far as to provide 'Google Assistants' to visit units for a day to help staff in the migration process. However staff noted almost unanimously, that they were only assisted through the email migration—a process that aided them in the technical aspect of changing tools, but which failed to both cultivate new email and calendar practices and ignored the adoption and appropriation of the rest of the tools (including the calendar tool). P07, a Research Administrator who had yet to participate in the email migration, described her upcoming support for the transition as consisting solely of the email migration with the possibility of some calendaring help.

P19 commented that the kind of training his unit received—again, email and calendar—did not address most of the issues work groups would actually face once the migration was complete, saying that

> *"... That one day, you were just getting organized and all your questions didn't come up until a week later when you're actually trying to start to use it; and by then, they were gone and I didn't know what to do."*

According to P19, ITS attempted to alleviate problems during the transition by assigning mediators in his unit who would be able to help them through their growing pains. P19 stated that these 'Google Reps' were staff who had received extra training in order to help their units in the transition, but who proved to know very little more than the staff they were supposed to assist. P19 describes his disillusionment with Google Reps:

> *"They had assigned one or two Google Reps, which were people here who had gotten a little extra training, but they're not IT people and they're not computer experts, so it was more like I would ask them and they'd be like, "Oh, let's see," and then they would start pushing buttons and I was like... Well, I can push buttons myself."*

The only real exceptions to the lack of Google knowledge and training came from a fraction of the interviewed staff—one who belonged to a unit that was already using Google tools prior to the university-wide transition, one who was exposed by her colleague, and the four staff who were from the School of Information. P06, a research Administrator in this unit, described that the local IT experts held training and Q&A sessions for staff, where she was able to learn enough about Google Sites to pursue them; she was able to learn the rest on her own.

Cultivators of Practice – Types of Gardening

As part of our research questions, we sought to uncover the people who were influential in the cultivation of practice within the staff world and differences in appropriation in the case of Project Sites and Google that could be due to membership un unanticipated and target user groups. Specifically, we expected to see staff themselves as the social actors to cultivate practices within Project Sites and a mix of both formal and informal actors in the context of Google.

As Nardi & O'Day suggested, there are people in sociotechnical ecologies that cultivate practices by virtue of their technical expertise—*gardeners*. Under the ecological framework, gardeners are technologically savvy technical experts who experiment with technology, introduce it to their colleagues, walk them through technology usage, and create new practices. Gardeners differ from the literature's various iterations of intermediaries between designers and users (e.g., mediators [35] and handymen [30]). Instead, they are portrayed as deeply embedded in what we've described as appropriation work. Of course, these experts may also perform mediation work as part of their activities.

From this perspective, gardeners can be any person who has any skill in technology and is involved in we've called appropriation work. Nardi & O'Day, like Draxler equate gardening activities as informal, invisible, thankless work to cultivate practices around technology and information.

Our results showed that gardening behavior among the interviewed staff and their groups was rare. Instead, staff were mostly focused on their activities and used technology to support them and in developing practices. Because appropriation work was perceived among this community as unrewarded and tangential to their jobs, only those staff who truly felt invested in cultivating new practices were involved in this type of work.

One reason why Project Sites had not been appropriated to leverage its capabilities was due to the narrative of use that had diffused through the staff world, but the reason why this narrative persisted is because there were no *gardeners* to cultivate new practices and to provide new examples of ways to reconfigure Project Sites. In the transition to Google, the lack of gardeners again led to staff's inability to engage in appropriation work. Without clear leadership, staff put off learning about new tools or used them in ways that were easily understandable to them.

Despite the widespread issues in appropriating collaboration technologies, there were a few examples of cultivators that could be gleaned from the interviews and we describe these below, also introducing new terminologies for describing formal vs. informal help and making further differentiations between those people who sparked change and those who do the invisible work of leading their colleagues through technological change. Specifically, we built on the idea of gardening as a type of appropriation work by refining it into distinct types of work—specifically, the introduction of tools (catalyzing) and guiding others in creating new practices around tools (shepherding). We also introduce formal farming as an extension of both developers and stakeholders at the organizational level.

Gardening as Catalyzing Change vs. Shepherding Use

Our data pointed that out that the lack of consistent guidance through the process of appropriating Project Sites and Google's collaboration tools resulted in poor knowledge about the tools which further inhibited the ability of staff to appropriate the toolsets. However, there were glimpses of people in local ecologies who were able to cultivate practices via gardening. Interestingly, these people emerged in the appropriation of the Google tools and no examples emerged concerning Project Sites.

P06, a research administrator, was clearly the leader in the adoption and appropriation of the Google Sites feature in her immediate work group and showed potential as a future gardener in other work groups given her familiarity with the Sites tool. P13, an Administrative Supervisor, collaborated with her work partner in collectively cultivating the potential uses of Google Sites, describing a hand-off process with her partner:

> *"She kind of starts things and then she hands them off to me and says, "**What do you think about this [tool]?" and I'm like, "Oh, yes. We can do this and we can do that.**" Then she's like, "Okay. I need you to finish it." Then, usually, **I get excited and I'll finish it.** That's how we're kind of a team in that way."*
> – P13, Admin Supervisor (emphasis added)

This particular example of appropriation work highlighted different facets that gardening work entails. First, there is experimentation and introducing a new tool (catalyzing), which is followed by making sense of the tool and determining how it can be used and adapted to the local context (gardening), and helping others in the process of leading others in use (shepherding).

Successful transitions and learning happened only where there were colleagues who were invested in the process of shepherding. The most striking example of successful shepherding was described by P23, the Director of a Women's Center, who recounted the story of her unit's transition to Google ahead of the rest of university. The Women's Center had appropriated of Google Docs/Drive because a set students who worked there as staff had suggested ways in which it could improve the unit's efficiency. These students were both familiar with Google's collaboration tools and with the local practices and structures of their unit, thus they were able to introduce the tools in a way that quickly diffused through the unit. P25, described them as catalysts, the term we adopted to describe these actors:

> *"They were trying to figure out, "Okay, who's going to do *this*, who's going to do *this*?" They said, "We'll put it on a spreadsheet on Google Docs," and **before you know it, the front office is using it. My assistant was sharing it with me. And everybody else was sort of spreading [it] throughout the Center**, how we can use these Google Docs."*
> – P23, Director (emphasis added)

P23 and her unit succeeded at appropriating Google Drive because of the combination of good ecological conditions for appropriation and the implied teaching that occurred that allowed the group to cultivate practices around its use.

Lastly, a number of participants indirectly mentioned the impact of a lack of shepherds or poor shepherding. P19's example of local Google assistants who knew little more than he did suggested these agents' ability to shepherd had been compromised. Other participants had noted that they attempted to incorporate some of Project Sites' tools besides Resources; but without informed, experienced leaders to help groups make sense of the tools and develop practices around them, the tools were abandoned.

Farmers - Formal Influencers on technology

Aside from end users involved in their own processes of appropriation, there were those people in ecologies whose jobs entailed deep involvement in the process of introducing and supporting IT use—specifically, IT staff and the university's central IT Office (ITS). In keeping to the Nardi & O'Day's metaphor of gardeners, we call these formalized influencers *farmers*. Farmers are related to technology champions in that they can introduce technology at the organizational level. Farmers are also closely related to technical communicators in that they have the power to impart technical knowledge either interpersonally or through documentation. Unlike programmers [14], farmers don't produce code, but rather produce decisions and support the ecology structurally and make it evolve. In describing farmers and farming work, we drew an important distinction: farmers are dedicated to technology and are involved in ecologies at a level that is separate from the work of end users. Their appropriation work, unlike gardening is not invisible because their primary role consists of supporting and evolving ecologies.

Because the university is large and decentralized, there were both farmers who were local to their units and those who were central to the entire university ecosystem. The difference in how staff described these players was a matter of proximity and ability to understand their work and processes. The difference, then, can be seen as one between farmers supporting local ecologies versus those supporting the entire organizational ecosystem.

Throughout the interviews, there was no mention of farmers (local or organizational) who were involved in cultivating practices around Project Sites among staff, though a few staff noted that they could reach the ITS Help Desk or their local IT personnel for technical problems. The previous observation that staff never realized training opportunities and never referred to help documentation points to the farming work that supported Project Sites use was ineffective at cultivating practices.

Staff identified the roles of the university's central administration and ITS as the main drivers of the shift in the ecology that led to the inclusion of Google tools, thereby equating them with Beath's concept of *technology champions*, visionaries who drive evolution of the ecosystem and who act as conduits for organizational change [4,5]. In terms of cultivating practices, however, staff perceived no intent at the organizational level to aid them in the adoption and appropriation of the Google tools.

Every participant noted support from their local IT staff with the migration to Google's email and calendaring tools, yet very few of these local farmers addressed use. From the participants we interviewed, only a few—all from the School of Information—received support that extended beyond the changes of email and calendaring and that delved into the other tools that staff would have access to. It was unclear whether the information sessions held by the IT groups actually resulted in shepherding, but the one participant who seemed the most affected by their guidance pointed to them as a catalyst for her further exploration of the Google Sites tool. Her description of how her interaction with this group of IT personnel helped motivate her in exploring technology overlapped with technical communicators. However, we found that in most cases staff had felt that technical communication was lacking. This particular group of local farmers point to the possibility that local formal IT experts can successfully take part in the appropriation work cultivate practices above an beyond any work they may do that catalyzes organizational change.

Paths to learning and appropriation

When people appropriate technologies, they can draw from their own tinkering experiences (i.e., explorative learning [11]) and through the collaborative sharing of successful configurations [12]. As previously mentioned, staff neither experimented with tools nor did they refer to help documents because of the additional and unrewarded nature of appropriation work in this setting. As a result, staff declared their networks to be most efficient paths:

> *"...this again is me not going out and searching for it, but if it's presented to me as a better way to do something, I would seriously consider it."*
> – P08, Business Admin

> *"I think the only way is if somebody tells me... I think it's going to be a word of mouth thing. That's how I found Google Drive..."* – P19, Sustainability Rep

These finding mirrored what Orlikowski called 'knowing in practice,' or rather, that knowledge forms via practice [36].

DISCUSSION

Learning to use technology and establishing practices around it is labor definitive of appropriation. Users, functioning as social actors [27] within their own ecologies, make sense of technology and their needs while adapting to changes in their sociotechnical ecologies and ecosystems. Following Orlikowski [36], by engaging in practices with technology, people learn to use technology and come to 'know in practice.' Project Sites, our primary interest, had been adopted unexpectedly by staff and thus we anticipated that, in appropriating it, staff would have engaged the toolset as social actors, developing a number of narratives around its use and perhaps evolve its use that was not limited by design intent. Because they were unanticipated, we expected little formal intervention in their development of practices, thus practices would be user-generated. As a comparison, we used Google's tools, which staff were expected to use and which we expected would have narratives around its use influenced by both staff and formal actors.

Staff suffered from a lack of knowledge in both cases regardless of their position as target or unanticipated users. Even though more than 20 years have elapsed between Orlikowski's study of Lotus Notes [38] and our study of our local LMS and Google tools, we were shocked to find that many of the problems that Orlikowski found regarding effective appropriation in 1992 are still endemic to today's organizations and the appropriation of technology. Orlikowski's findings suggested that the successful appropriation of Notes was due to two cognitive elements—1) the lack of communication about Notes and 2) insufficient or incorrect types of training—as well as three structural elements—1) the lack of reward systems, 2) failure to formulate new work procedures, and 3) culture/work norms that did not favor cooperation and sharing. Of these five issues, we found the first four to explain why Project Sites and Google's collaboration tools had been appropriated in a very limited way. Particularly, instead of finding that culture/norms prevented sharing of configurations of Project Sites, we found that sharing was inhibited by the fact that there were no local expert users [42] to cultivate new practices—a fact that emphasizes the extent to which appropriation by unanticipated user groups could differ from appropriation within target user groups. Specifically, it is not just that unanticipated users might have creative ways of interpreting and using technology, but that they may also appropriate technology without truly understanding it. The challenge is one of designing technology so that it can be appropriated by a wider audience of users aside from those that are anticipated—a challenge worthy of certain technologies and not others.

As Orlikowski noted, failures in training reinforced Notes' users' poor technological frames, thus their appropriation of the technology suffered. Among our staff, the perceived lack of training for Project Sites never challenged their frames of technology use, allowing staff to continue to follow the narrative of Project Sites as a repository, a narrative that persisted through word of mouth diffusion. Meanwhile, the Google training, which did not focus on the collaboration tools essentially led to the same outcome.

Much like the organization Orlikowski studied, staff at the university found that they lacked the reward for spending time on learning better techniques for appropriating the tools, primarily because of the added work. MacLean [30] had similarly noted that organizations have many people who are 'workers' who have little interest in technology and tailoring activities, focusing on accomplishing their tasks rather than the invisible and time-consuming gardening work [34] that establishes practices and impacts technology use. These assertions are akin to Grudin's assertion that a barrier to groupware success is the disparity between those who will benefit from an application and those who do additional work to support the application [17,18]. That is to say, that the articulation work needed to make IT needs to both feel as part of the job and also benefit those involved in the work. To that end, MacLean's suggestion of 'tailoring culture' [30] as a part of successful adaptation of tool is useful. Yet, it is less clear how to create this culture among unanticipated users when potential ways of appropriating technology may run contrary to perceptions of the design intent and appropriate uses.

Staff's appropriation of Project Sites was not poor *per se*, but it was not as effective as it could be because users did not understand the system they had appropriated as deeply as their faculty and student counterparts. This was particularly evident because so many participants wished that the system could provide affordances that were already built in. Their limited knowledge biased them away from other possible interpretations of the tools at their disposal and any potential benefits these tools could have were lost.

There were other potential barriers to multiple interpretations. For example, it is possible that these unanticipated users lacked the cognitive absorption [1], the psychological sense of ownership [15], or organizational reward structures [30] to pursue appropriation work. Yet, one might imagine different case with more expert users and engagement that could result in a wider variety of narratives and manners of appropriating technology. Thus, we continue to endorse the importance of expert individuals within organizations—much like Wulf [53] Pipek [42] and Draxler [10-12].

While this study did not uncover these types of expert users in the case of unanticipated users, comparing this case to one where the same population composed a target user group allowed these types of experts to surface *in absentia.* If we consider their broad definition of all the things a gardener might do, they include helping others with current technology, inciting change, and leading others in the creation of new practices in reaction to changes technology. We found that inciting change was not enough to change practices and appropriation by itself and that what was truly helpful towards appropriating technology was the type of technology leadership we called shepherding. Tyre & Orlikowski [50] note that there is a brief window of opportunity after implementation during which exploring and modifying technology happens. Shepherding, if done before narratives settle and become routine, can potentially improve the number of narratives that users can choose from and lead to more varied appropriations and higher adaptability.

Given that we—designers, researchers, and implementers of collaborative systems—know the importance of knowledge and leaders in the successful adoption and appropriation of technology, we are left with the challenges of creating knowledge and shepherds as part of the design and implementation process. We ask, who should bear the responsibility of establishing practice? Is it technical communicator? Or is it the responsibility of formally designated agents such as technical communicators or IT staff? We may consider people who informally distribute knowledge and initiate organizational change. We might place the responsibility with the people who are attempting to appropriate technology. Another remaining issue is creating informed, expert individuals and in them diffuse information in the context of unanticipated users.

In looking to our concept of farmers, it was evident that formal, dedicated technology experts in large organization may or may not be able to cultivate practice and perform appropriation work. Even formal, dedicated technology experts at the local level were unable to assist in appropriation work. This is especially true where the signal of top-down communication can easily be lost in the everyday noise of collaboration and work.

Lastly, appropriation work might be considered invisible work in that it is tangential to organizational goals. Though appropriation work is often invisible, it is not necessarily always the case. To the contrary, we found that appropriation work performed by gardeners was quite visible at the local ecological level when it was successful. On the occasions where gardening occurred and succeeded, those staff were recognized. The problem then becomes on of sharing the information outside to the greater organizational ecosystem.

Draxler et al. [10] posited support for appropriation work and making it visible to other users as design principles. We generally agree that facilitating appropriation and making the results of that work visible will aid in evolving technology use. Yet, it is also important to note that in following such design requirements, assumptions are made about the willingness and ability of end users to utilize search features, to know they should be wanting to reconfigure their work systems, and to potentially publicize their work—all issues that might be interpersonal or organizational in nature, rather than design-related.

Limitations & Future Work

In our analysis, we ignored the greater part of the tool ecology, having focused on Project Sites and Google's collaborative tools. As such, we omitted data that we collected about those appropriations as well as examples that highlighted the importance of catalyst, gardening, and shepherding work that form the greater umbrella of appropriation work. In other work, we are describing how the greater ecology works as a whole system of tools, appropriations, and social actors.

We also placed substantial weight on the importance of knowledge of the toolsets we studied and the lack of guidance (formal and informal) in the appropriation of ICTs. There were other barriers to developing different appropriation practices that were not discussed in this work—factors such as usability, convenience (or inconvenience), and critical mass. These issues would play a factor, for example, in the appropriation of new tools in Project Sites.

A number of staff at the university were excluded from the interview study because they were not related to the main missions of the university. Future work will address researchers, in particular, because they were conceived of as a small, but anticipated set of users. There may be interesting ways in which appropriation of Project Sites occurred for them as opposed to the other staff at the university.

Almost concurrent to the Google transition, the Hospital and Medical School made a transition in their medical records management system, which acts as a central patient-records information repository across all of the university's medical sites. The appropriation Project Sites within this community is likely to differ greatly from the rest of the university and the new medical records system is sure to add an interesting layer to the evolving practices of doctors, nurses, medical billers, and other professionals.

In this study, the underlying research interests led to interviews to question staff about their technology use and influences through an ecological lens. As a number of findings suggested, staff perceived the absence of training and support from the formal IT groups (which we called farmers), while the authors of this paper have been well aware of the various resources from these groups—ITS in particular. Future work will involve interviews with staff from ITS and unit-level IT staff to determine what appropriation support was provided and to trace the breakdowns that created barriers in information being transmitted from the central and local IT groups to staff.

To address the second point of generalizability to other contexts, it was clear that the comparative case study of two systems at this academic research institution was unique to this context—both in terms of the systems investigated and the organization itself. The story of these two toolsets presented the opportunity to study the influences on technology use influences with more than one toolset. The interviews revealed striking similarities between this work and previous work by other researchers. Despite the potential differences between various types of organizations and between tools, the appropriation of technology and cultivating good practices around technology is a universal problem. If a point is to be taken from this work, it is about the universal importance of helping users to do the work of establishing practices around technology, whether this is a collaborative system, social networks, etc.

Another limitation of this work is that interviews were conducted in the months immediately following the transition to Google, which included the email migration—a time when staff were still recovering from the technological shifts in the university ecosystem and when they were still in a sensemaking process around how to appropriate technology. While this was a good time to detect and explore shepherds in this phase, the inability to find them might have be due to the timing of the study. Future work will follow up with staff about sensemaking since our initial interviews and may perhaps uncover people who have influenced the appropriation of the tools much later in the process.

CONCLUSION

This work began with the premise that all technology is appropriated as users enact their practices and structures through ICTs, further suggesting that successful appropriation of ICT requires that users understand the technology they are trying to decipher—whether through experimentation, local experts, or training. This work highlighted the lack of clarity in who should be tasked with creating knowledge and establishing leaders in the appropriation of technology, noting both that this work is often invisible and tangential to the actual work of the group. Using a number of frameworks, the research examined the appropriation of two different systems and discovered parallels to other research that suggest the importance of knowledge and training in developing better appropriation practices. This work builds on previous research by further exploring who is involved in appropriation work, building on and refining the concept of *gardeners* [14,34] and putting the social actors in the context of unexpected users.

Wulf et al. [53] wrote that "the research challenge is to design innovative ICT applications so that their appropriation leads to (desirable) impacts on the applying social systems" (pg. 505). With a host of design methods and good intentions, technology may still fail to yield 'desirable outcomes' in the way it is appropriated simply because of organizational issues and the knowledge users have about the technologies they are about to appropriate. The challenge, then, is not just to design innovative ICTs with tailorable system design principles (e.g., [10]), but to consider the appropriation work that occurs at the user-level—supporting good understandings of technology and cultivating practices around it. Such work is akin to establishing what MacLean [30] called the 'culture of tailoring.' We suggest that these sociotechnical challenges become even more problematic in contexts where there are unanticipated users.

REFERENCES

1. Agarwal, R. & Karahanna, E. (2000). Time flies when you're having fun: cognitive absorption and beliefs about information technology usage 1. *MIS Quarterly*, 24(4), 665-694.
2. Andriessen, J.H.E., Hettinga, M., & Wulf, V. (2003). Introduction to Special Issue on evolving use of groupware. *Computer Supported Cooperative Work*, 12(4), 367-380.
3. Balka, E. & Wagner, I. (2006). Making things work: dimensions of configurability as appropriation work. In *Proceedings of the conference on Computer supported cooperative work* (CSCW '06), 229-238.

4. Beath, C. M. (1991). Supporting the information technology champion. *MIS quarterly*, 355-372.

5. Beath, C. M., & Ives, B. (1988). The information technology champion: aiding and abetting, care and feeding. In *Proceedings of the Hawaii International Conference on System Sciences (HICSS 1988)*, 115-123.

6. Bryant, S. L., Forte, A., & Bruckman, A. (2005). Becoming Wikipedian: Transformation of participation in a collaborative online encyclopedia. In *Proceedings of the conference on Supporting Group Work* (GROUP '05), 1-10.

7. Dourish, P. (2003). The Appropriation of Interactive Technologies. *Computer Supported Cooperative Work*, 12(4), 465-490.

8. Dourish, P. & Edwards, W.K. (2000). A Tale of Two Toolsets: Relating Infrastructure and Use in Flexible CSCW Toolsets. *Computer-Supported Cooperative Work*, 9, 33-51.

9. Dourish, P. (1998). Using Meta-Level Techniques in a Flexible Toolset for CSCW Applications. *ACM Transactions on Computer-Human Interaction*, 5 (2), 109-155.

10. Draxler, S., Stevens, G., Stein, M., Boden, A., & Randall, D. (2012). Supporting the social context of technology appropriation: on a synthesis of sharing tools and tool knowledge. In *Proceedings of the conference on Human Factors in Computing Systems (CHI 2012)*, 2835-2844.

11. Draxler, S. & Stevens, G. (2011) Supporting the Collaborative Appropriation of an Open Software Ecosystem. *Computer Supported Cooperative Work*, 20, 403-448.

12. Draxler, S., Jung, A., Boden, A., & Stevens, G. (2011). Workplace warriors: identifying team practices of appropriation in software ecosystems. In *Proceedings of the International Workshop on Cooperative and Human Aspects of Software Engineering* (57-60).

13. Ferneley, E. and B. Light (2008). "Unpacking user relations in an emerging ubiquitous computing environment: introducing the bystander." Journal of Information Technology 23(3): 163-175.

14. Gantt, M., & Nardi, B. A. (1992). Gardeners and gurus: patterns of cooperation among CAD users. In *Proceeding of CHI*. 107-117).

15. Gaskin, J., & Lyytinen, K. (2010). Psychological Ownership and the Individual Appropriation of Technology. In *Proceedings of the Hawaii International Conference on System Sciences (HICSS 2010)*, 1-8.

16. Girardin, F., & Blat, J. (2010). The co-evolution of taxi drivers and their in-car navigation systems. *Pervasive and Mobile Computing*, *6*(4), 424-434.

17. Grudin, J. (1994). Groupware and social dynamics: eight challenges for developers. *Communications of the ACM*, *37*(1), 92-105.

18. Grudin, J. (1988). Why CSCW applications fail: problems in the design and evaluationof organizational interfaces. In *Proceedings of the conference on Computer-supported cooperative work* (CSCW '88), 85-93.

19. Grudin, J. & Palen, L. (1995). Why groupware succeeds: Discretion or mandate? In *Proceedings of the European Conference on Computer-Supported Cooperative Work* (ECSCW '95), 263-278.

20. Grudin, J., & Pruitt, J. (2002). Personas, participatory design and product development: An infrastructure for engagement. In *Proceeding of the Participatory Design Conference* (PDC '02), 144-152.

21. Huysman, M., Steinfield, C., Jang, C., David, C., Huis in 't Veld, M., Poot, J., &Mulder, I. (2003). Virtual Teams and the Appropriation of Communication Technology: Exploring the Concept of Media Stickiness. *Computer Supported Cooperative Work*, 12(4), 411-436.

22. Johnson, R.R. (1998). *User Centered Technology: A Rhetorical Theory for Computers and other Mundane Artifacts*. NY: SUNY Press.

23. Karsten, H. (2003). Constructing interdependencies with collaborative information technology. *Computer Supported Cooperative Work*, 12(4), 437-464.

24. Kensing, F., & Blomberg, J. (1998). Participatory design: Issues and concerns. *Computer Supported Cooperative Work*, 7(3-4), 167-185.

25. Kling, R.,& Lamb, R. (1999). IT and organizational change in digital economies: a socio-technical approach. *ACM SIGCAS Computers and Society*, *29*(3), 17-25.

26. Koch, M., & Teege, G. (1999). Support for tailoring CSCW systems: adaptation by composition. In *Proceedings of Parallel and Distributed Processing*, (PDP '99), 146-152.

27. Lamb, R. & Kling, R. (2003). Reconceptualizing users as social actors in information systems research. *MIS Quarterly*, 197-236.

28. Lave, J & Wenger, E. (1991). *Situated Learning: Legitimate Peripheral Participation*. Cambridge: Cambridge University Press.

29. Leonard-Barton, D. (1988). Implementation as mutual adaptation of technology and organization. Res. Policy 17(5) 251–267.

30. MacLean, A., Carter, K., Lövstrand, L., & Moran, T. (1990, March). User-tailorable systems: pressing the issues with buttons. In *Proceedings of the SIGCHI conference on Human factors in computing systems: Empowering people* (pp. 175-182). ACM.

31. Madge, C., Meek, J., Wellens, J., & Hooley, T. (2009). Facebook, social integration and informal learning at university: 'It is more for socialising and talking to friends about work than for actually doing work'. *Learning, Media and Technology*, 34(2), 141-155.

32. Majchrzak, A., Rice, R. E., Malhotra, A., King, N., & Ba, S. (2000). Technology adaption: the case of a computer-supported inter-organizational virtual team. *MIS Quarterly*, 24(4), 569-600.

33. Markus, M.L. & Connolly, T. (1990). Why CSCW applications fail: Problems in the adoption of interdependent work tools. In *Proceedings of the conference on Computer-Supported Cooperative Work* (CSCW '90), 371-380.

34. Nardi & O'Day (1999). *Information ecologies: Using technology with heart.* Cambridge, MA: MIT Press.

35. Okamura, K., Orlikowski, W. J., Fujimoto, M., & Yates, J. (1994, October). Helping CSCW applications succeed: the role of mediators in the context of use. In *Proceedings of the conference on Computer Supported Cooperative Work* (CSCW '94), 55-65.

36. Orlikowski, W.J. (2000) Using Technology and Constituting Structures: A Practice Lens for Studying Technology in Organizations, *Organization Science*, 11(4), 404-428.

37. Orlikowski, W.J. (1992a). The duality of technology: rethinking the concept of technology in organizations. *Organization Science*, 3(3), 398-427.

38. Orlikowski, W.J. (1992b). Learning from Notes: organizational issues in groupware implementation. In *Proceedings of Computer-supported cooperative work* (CSCW '92), 362-369.

39. Orlikowski, W. J. (2000). "Using technology and constituting structures: A practice lens for studying technology in organizations." Organization Science 11(4): 404–428.

40. Pinch, T. J., & Bijker, W. E. (1984). The social construction of facts and artefacts: Or how the sociology of science and the sociology of technology might benefit each other. *Social Studies of Science*, 399-441.

41. Pinch, T. J., & Bijker, W. E. (1987). The Social Construction of Technological Systems: Or How the Sociology of Sciene & Technology Might Benefit Each Other. In W.E. Bijker, Hughes, T.P., & T.Pinch (Eds.),*The social construction of technological systems: New directions in the sociology and history of technology* (17-50). Cambridge, Ma: MIT Press.

42. Pipek, V., & Kahler, H. (2006). Supporting collaborative tailoring. In Lieberman, H., Paterno, F., & Wulf, V. (eds.): *End User Development*, 315-345. Springer: Netherlands.

43. Quinones, P.A. & Teasley (2013). Appropriation by Unintended Users: Looking Beyond Design Intent and Expected Use. In Proceedings *of CSCW,* 1515-1526.

44. Ranney, F. (2000). At the Heart of Information Ecologies: Invisibility and Technical Communication. *ACM Journal of Computer Documentation*, 24(2), 85-90.

45. Rogers, Y. (1994). Exploring Obstacles: Integrating CSCW in Evolving Organizations. In *Proceedings of the conference on Computer-Supported Cooperative Work* (CSCW '92), 67-77.

46. Schuler, D., & Namioka, A. (1993). *Participatory design: Principles and practices.* CRC PressI Llc.

47. Stevens, G., Pipek, V. and Wulf, V. (2009). Appropriation Infrastructure: Mediating appropriation and production work. *Journal of Organizational and End User Computing*, 22(2), 58-81.

48. Strauss, A. L. (1978). A social worlds perspective. *Studies in symbolic interaction, 1*, 119-128.

49. Torpel, B., Pipek, V., & Rittenbruch, M. (2003). Creating Hetergeneity – Evolving use of groupware in a network of freelancers. *Computer Supported Cooperative Work*, 12(4), 381-409.

50. Tyre, M. and W. Orlikowski (1994). "Windows of opportunity: Temporal patterns of technological adaptation in organizations." Organization Science 5(1): 98-118.

51. Wenger, Etienne (1998). *Communities of Practice: Learning, Meaning, and Identity*. Cambridge: Cambridge University Press.

52. Wulf, V., Pipek, V., & Won, M. (2008). Component-based tailorability: Enabling highly flexible software applications. *International Journal of Human-Computer Studies*, *66*(1), 1-22.

53. Wulf, V., Rohde, M., Pipek, V., & Stevens, G. (2011). Engaging with Practices : Design Case Studies as a Research Framework in CSCW. In *Proceeding of the conference on Computer Supported Cooperative Work (CSCW)* (pp. 505–512).

Designing for Repair? Infrastructures and Materialities of Breakdown

Daniela K. Rosner
Department of Human-Centered Design and Engineering, University of Washington
dkrosner@uw.edu

Morgan G. Ames
Center for Social Computing, Department of Informatics, UC Irvine
repair@morganya.org

ABSTRACT
This paper explores issues that come up in practices of breakage and repair through two projects: the "XO" laptops of One Laptop Per Child in Paraguay and public sites of facilitated repair in California, USA. Collectively drawing on 15 months of ethnographic fieldwork, 156 interviews, and archival research, we find that breakdown and repair are not processes that designers can effectively script ahead of time; instead, they emerge in everyday practice. These practices are shaped by material, infrastructural, gendered, political, and socioeconomic factors – such as manufacturing limitations, access to repair parts and expertise, and environmental convictions – which designers often did not, and may not have been able to, anticipate. We call the material realities and practices of repair *negotiated endurance*, which is illustrated by four themes from our findings: the negotiated identification of breakdown, collaborative definitions of worth, the fraught nature of collaborative expertise, and the gendered stakes of repair.

Author Keywords
Breakdown; design; infrastructure studies, maintenance; materiality; One Laptop Per Child; public sites of repair; repair; sociotechnical systems.

ACM Classification Keywords
K.4.0. Computers in Society: general.

INTRODUCTION
Over the last ten years, repair-oriented design, engineering, and policy-making have begun to take hold at local and global levels. Recent legislation reforms such as the Right to Repair Bill (http://righttorepair.org), for example, require automobile manufacturers to provide the same repair instructions and diagnostic data to consumers as they do to franchised dealerships. Going one step further, a few companies have proactively built repairability into their products. Patagonia has produced a jacket with a repairable zipper, asking consumers to take on fixing work themselves. Other projects enable repair through customization, such as the IKEA hacking movement wherein the modularity of mass-manufactured IKEA furniture turns unassembled pieces into LEGO-like reconfigurable units [34] or the GreaseMonkey browser plug-in that enables substantive end-user modification using the open standards of the Web [31]. Decades earlier, the Volkswagen Beetle of the 1960s was hugely popular around the world and often hailed as a force of democratization in part because of its ease of repair and modification [33].

On the other hand, within IT production one dimension of design is "planned obsolescence": the manner in which a product is built to last for only a few years rather than a lifetime, and meant to be replaced, not repaired. The phrase "planned obsolescence" was popularized in 1932 by Bernard London in his pamphlet entitled "Ending the Depression through Planned Obsolescence" [22]. The concept is canonized today in technological observations-made-rules such as Moore's Law, with its short turnaround for the doubling of computational power. In keeping with either Moore's Law or London's exhortation, a number of computers, electronics, and smaller consumer appliances have been designed to fail over time and be replaced. For example, battery-operated electronic products, notably recent releases of Apple iPhones and Macbook laptops, come with difficult-to-replace bonded batteries, and heating devices like toasters, hair dryers, and electric hot water kettles have flimsy resistive heating elements that are cheap to produce but not made to last.

In this paper, we explore the theoretical and material dimensions of breakdown and repair practices in the 'wild,' attending to the points at which obsolescence is thwarted and repairability is not realized, and the social implications of both. In the process, we introduce the notion of *negotiated endurance*. This refers to the process by which different actors – including consumers, community organizers, and others – drive the ongoing use, maintenance, and repair of a given technology through the sociocultural and socioeconomic infrastructures they inhabit and produce. In this framework, breakdown and repair are not simply planned or avoided through design, but instead actively produced and reconfigured through use.

We illustrate our argument with two case studies. The first chronicles the unexpected breakdowns and repair work on the "XO" laptops of One Laptop Per Child (OLPC) in Paraguay. The second explores the repair activities of the Fixit Clinic, a space where the public can bring broken appliances which volunteers help them repair. In both case studies, we explore how users approach breakdown and repair to provide new theoretical and practical insights into the design process. This

CSCW'14, February 15–19, 2014, Baltimore, Maryland, USA.

ACM 978-1-4503-2540-0/14/02...$15.00.
http://dx.doi.org/10.1145/2531602.2531692

involves questioning not only design for reparability in particular but also design practices in general – after all, products are all repairable to varying degrees, and breakdown and repair are often part of use even if not of design. Those who are engaged in repair practices both acknowledge and complicate the politics of design, especially design that is meant to encourage or discourage repair.

One contribution of this work is to theorize breakdown and repair as material states that are defined collaboratively in use. Moreover, both are closely tied to collective definitions of worth – as in, what is worth repairing. Why are people repairing or *not* repairing, and what does repair mean to them? How are objects designated as in need of repair in the first place? Our case studies show that breakage and repair both have multiple meanings and create different practices and roles, all of which offer different models of use and creativity.

Another contribution is to highlight the political and infrastructural aspects of breakdown and repair. This builds on the work of Steve Jackson and others in this area [16,17,18,19,28,37], testing the ability of these theoretical contributions to travel to new political, economic, and social contexts, including technology democratization projects in the Global South (OLPC) and countercultural urban repair initiatives (Fixit Clinic). In this framing, repair is a political act, a repurposing of designed objects in ways that may or may not have been planned. Tools or facilities for repair are similarly political in that they can rewrite conventional beliefs about what we can change and how we can change it, or be an admission that breakdown has occurred. Finally, our case studies highlight how repair can be a *privileged* practice, relying on certain kinds of materials (replacement parts, testing equipment) and forms of expertise to be carried out.

Related Literature on Repair

Before we turn to our case studies, we wish to acknowledge the small but vibrant ethnographic tradition that has emerged around the study of everyday maintenance in IT design. Decades prior to this work, Lucy Suchman, Julian Orr, and colleagues turned to the lives of photocopy machine repair workers to illuminate the limitations of codifying maintenance techniques [28,38]. Orr's influential accounts of particular diagnoses exposed skilled service work as "necessarily improvised, at least in diagnosis, and centered on the creation and maintenance of control and understanding" [28:161]. Orr showed how repair workers not only use manuals and codified organizational knowledge; workers also rely on the retelling of "war stories" – personal accounts from the field often shared over lunch or informal meetings. Each repair activity involves situated actions whose intent, in Suchman's terms, "must be contingent on the circumstantial and interactional particulars of actual situations" [38].

Others have studied practices and conceptions of consumer electronics disassembly in developing countries, as examples of thwarting planned obsolescence. Burrell [4], for example, describes how e-waste scavengers in Ghana, who are "invisible users" not planned for in the design process, retrieve parts from mobile phones, computers, and other electronics in landfills to reuse components and precious metals. Jackson et al. [18] further explore what they term "repair worlds" in Sub-Saharan Africa to show how information technology infrastructures are routinely maintained and extended.

Studying repair in the Global North, some work in HCI on sustainability has explored designing to enable maintenance and repair in order to support environmental concerns ([2] provides an example and [11] a summary), which we will see echoed in the motivations of the Fixit Clinic below. From "IKEA hacks" that rely on shared resources, online and off [34], to traditional crafts that can be learned through online how-to instructions [39], the Internet has created new opportunities kludging and hacking. Applying repair beyond hardware, Kelty [20] has studied the arcana of free software through the continuously rewritten fabric of the Internet. Beyond IT development, scholars have focused on a range of maintenance work, reconsidering aspects of building reconstruction [3], vehicle repair [8,9,15,22], electricity procurement [14], book restoration [35], routine work activities [16], and shared infrastructures [37].

Following from these scholars, this paper aims to examine practices of design and repair through the material conditions and cultural contingencies they surface. Drawing on two case studies that provide in-depth examinations of repair activity, we explore the myriad avenues in which repair work interfaces with design, especially the difficulties in designing to specifically enable or disable repair. This account illustrates some of the many complications that can arise in practice.

Methods

The methods used in this study are largely qualitative and ethnographic but also include quantitative and archival elements. For the first case study, the second author conducted six months of ethnographic fieldwork in Paraguay in 2010 as a volunteer for Paraguay Educa, as well as archival research on One Laptop Per Child (OLPC) between 2008 and 2013. Paraguay Educa is a small non-governmental organization (that is, a group not affiliated with the Paraguayan government, with funding sources independent of government support), founded and run by local Paraguayans, which purchased OLPC laptops for around $200 each (near the cheapest price the laptop, and its non-tablet successors, ever reached [42]) with funding from the SWIFT banking group, the Inter-American Development Bank, Itaipú Dam, and other donors, and brought them to Paraguay in 2009. In 2010 the project consisted of 4000 laptops in 10 schools, and as of this writing includes 9000 laptops in 36 schools. The second author observed the effects of broken laptops in classrooms and at home during the course of field observations, and interviewed 133 participants in Paraguay, including children who had laptops that were broken to varying degrees or had been repaired. She iteratively coded her fieldnotes and interview transcripts to identify the dominant themes across all sources, one of which was breakage and repair, the data presented in this paper.

The second author complemented this ethnography with quantitative data to corroborate her findings. Of particular importance to this analysis, she obtained from Paraguay Educa complete logs of laptop breakage reports and repairs filed by the Paraguay Educa support staff, which were all recorded in a system custom-built by a Paraguay Educa developer. This data included types of breakage for each laptop in the program, allowing layering of additional levels of analysis including the laptop owner's gender (categorized by their name, before anonymization of the dataset), grade (provided in the database), and whether they lived in the urban center or the rural outskirts of their city (determined by their school).

The first author conducted nine months of participant observation at seven public sites of repair (six Fixit Clinics and one Repair Cafe) in 2012 and 2013. She engaged in informal conversations at those events with roughly 60 participants. She also conducted extensive formal interviews with 23 participants, including leaders and participants in four public sites of repair (Fixit Clinic, Palo Alto Repair Cafe, Pasadena Repair Cafe, Fixer's Collective, and the Netherlands Repair Cafe), and leaders of related endeavors such as the Repair Clinic, Pasadena Repair Cafe, and the Flaming Lotus Girls. Lastly, she conducted in-depth research in the Fixit Clinic and Repair Cafe's online archives and in individual participants' collections. She transcribed her interviews and iteratively coded her fieldnotes and transcripts to find emergent themes.

CASE STUDY 1. THE CONTESTED REPAIRABILITY OF OLPC LAPTOPS IN PARAGUAY

One Laptop Per Child (OLPC) represents one of the largest experiments in laptop-driven learning underway. About two and a half million of OLPC's "XO" laptops are in use around the world, 85% of them in Latin America. It has also inspired derivative projects in both education and low-cost computing. Among the project's promises were that the XO laptop would be rugged enough to withstand the roughness of child use and so easy to repair that a child could do it. In this section, we explore the social implications of laptop breakages in the field, noting the ways that actual breakage departed from the idealized breakage that OLPC envisioned. The results make painfully concrete the possible material limitations of designing for repairability and the material requirements of repairwork. We also explore the implications that the approach OLPC encourages projects to take – every child owning their own laptop and being responsible for keeping it in good repair – has for social equity, one of the project's goals.

Figure 1. OLPC's "XO" laptops in Paraguay, one decorated with stickers by its owner.

OLPC's Idealized Repair Practices

OLPC's XO laptop is the first of its kind to combine an allegedly ruggedized design, an open-source educational software suite, and full (if intentionally underpowered) computer functionality. The XO has no internal moving parts such as fans or a hard drive to jam or break when dropped; minimal connectors to get broken or dirty (just USB and audio, both covered by the XO's antennae "ears" when the laptop is latched, plus a power connector and SD slot); a solid silicone membrane keyboard to make the laptop water-resistant; a thick plastic case to protect it from falls or other wear and tear; and only two sizes of screws – with extras included inside the handle – intended to make dismantling and repairing the laptop easier (see http://wiki.laptop.org/go/Disassembly and http://wiki.laptop. org/ go/ Screws). OLPC leaders, including the project's founder Nicholas Negroponte, demonstrated the ruggedness of the laptop during talks and events by flinging one across a stage, then picking it up and turning it on, leading to expectations among those interested in implementing their project that the laptop was very difficult to break [5,43].

OLPC hoped that in addition to making the laptop robust to the use of children, these design features would encourage children to tinker with the laptop's hardware (along with its open-source software) – in short, to be their own tech support, understanding the machine inside and out. OLPC's first Core Principle, Child Ownership, encouraged locally-run projects to give laptops to children directly so that they could take the laptops home and learn anywhere and anytime, not just at school [27]. They also maintained that child ownership would encourage children to take better care of their laptops, and even empower them to repair the laptops themselves [26,30], providing an excellent learning experience and making them comfortable with 'hacking' the laptop. Because the laptop was ruggedized, they theorized, the repairs that would need to be made would never be too serious [41].

Though expecting children to repair their own laptops has been called naïve or exploitative by some critics, OLPC leadership Nicholas Negroponte, Seymour Papert, and others have defended it as the perfect learning experience, taking advantage of children's supposedly natural proficiency with technology and allowing them to delve as deeply as possible into the workings of the machine. In a USInfo "Webchat" interview about OLPC in 2006, Papert directly claimed that having children repair the laptops is a matter of empowerment, not exploitation:

I believe in "Kid Power." Our education system underestimates kids. It infantilizes them by assuming they are incompetent. An eight-year-old is capable of doing ninety percent of tech support and a twelve-year-old one hundred percent. And this is not exploiting the children; it is giving them a powerful learning experience. [30]

To assist these repair activities, OLPC developers and volunteers populated OLPC's wiki with technical details about the laptop, often including descriptions and even debates about what the feature being discussed was meant to accomplish (see http://wiki.laptop.org/go/Battery_and_power for an example). While initially and ostensibly meant for laptop users at any level of expertise, over time this documentation became more and more aimed at people with a high level of technical proficiency. This tendency accelerated after the "Give 1, Get 1" XO laptops reached the hands of tens of thousands of OLPC enthusiasts across the United States and Canada around Christmas 2007 and 2008, before many OLPC projects around the world – including the one in Paraguay – had begun. As a result, most of these resources, which were nearly all in English, were aimed more at other tech-savvy enthusiasts than at novice users.

Breakage in Practice: OLPC's XO Laptops in Paraguay

Paraguay Educa, the locally-run non-governmental organization (NGO) in charge of the project of 9000 XO laptops in Paraguay (4000 first-generation XOs distributed in spring 2009, 5000 second-generation XOs distributed in spring 2011), initially embraced the Core Principles and central tenets that OLPC had laid out as important [1], including child ownership and the ruggedness of the XO. As a result of OLPC's framing of the project, the NGO Paraguay Educa, as well as other projects including the country-wide, government-run project in Uruguay, did not stress the importance of being careful with the laptop or work to procure and stockpile repair parts. However, as we will see and as has also been described elsewhere [46], limitations in the XOs' manufacturing process and the ways that children used laptops in practice – and the problems that resulted from both – differed from OLPC's initial expectations of ruggedness and ease of repair, which they had passed on to many of the early projects.

For one, the prevalence of cement corners and bumpy cobblestone streets in Paraguay meant that dropped laptops often did *not* emerge unscathed – and screens were the most frequent casualty. While the screen would generally survive impacts to the bumpered *edges* of the laptop, as would most likely happen in a demonstration onstage, some falls resulted in a direct impact to the screen surface itself, to which it was not nearly as robust. After an impact, a screen would often either go entirely black, rendering the laptop unusable (with no hookups for external screens nor a supply of external screens available), or would sport a cluster of permanently dead pixels, making it more difficult to use. Similarly, nearly every smartphone encountered in Paraguay had a cracked screen; one Paraguay Educa staff member cracked his the very day he bought it, much to his heartbreak. Though these smartphones could be repaired, the cost was prohibitive for even the relatively wealthy members of the NGO.

The location of the camera above the screen (like most laptops) also meant that children who were taking pictures with their laptops would often walk around with their laptops open and screens rotated to face out. While taking pictures was not that common an activity overall, one breakage of a screen rotated in this way was observed during fieldwork. Other observations involved close calls, as children sprinted across schoolyards or down cobblestone streets holding an XO on one arm, often open to play music. In interviews, children without working laptops or with laptop screens that had been replaced described using their XO on their bunk bed and accidentally dropping it a meter and a half to the floor, or putting it on a shelf or on top of a wardrobe only to have it jostled off. One child explained in an interview that she lent her laptop to her younger brother, and it was returned with a screen that no longer turned on, and no way for the family to afford the repair part. Overall, as of August 2010, one year and four months into the project, 403 (10%) of the 4000 laptops in use had unfixed broken screens.

Another part that often did not stand up to children's use was the AC adaptor. Though there was much early press regarding alternative power sources for XO laptops, nearly all in use around the world are charged conventionally by plugging them in to a power outlet. Through what was described by Paraguay Educa and OLPC technical staff in the field as a manufacturing flaw, the rubber used to make the cable for the first generation XO's adapter was stretchier than it should have been which, when combined with some students' tendency to swing their adapters or pull the adapters out of the wall by the cord, resulted in breakages. Still others suffered from a design defect that burned out the adapter unit itself. All in all, in August 2010, 21% of laptops had at one point logged a problem with charging, and 12% had unfixed adapters.

While these two parts broke an order of magnitude more often than most others, they were not the only breakages, and moreover, these logged breakages were not the only problems with using the machines. For example, the membrane keyboard of the first-generation XO was made slightly too thin to withstand heavy use, and over time the membrane cracked at the edges of the most-used keys, inviting fidgety students to pick at them further or eventually falling off on their own. In August 2010, 3% were logged as broken. The trackpad on the first-generation XO was notoriously buggy and difficult to use (see http://wiki.laptop.org/go/XO-1/Touchpad/Issues) – not technically "broken" (in the sense that it was not functioning as designed) but still an impediment to use. Also frustrating to students and teachers both was the laptop's slowness and its much-too-small one-gigabyte solid-state hard drive, which would fill up quickly with students' Internet-enabled media-centric usage patterns. These issues came to be collectively understood and discussed under the framework of breakage, though not all had a clear path for repair.

Even more troubling, breakages tended to recreate gendered and socioeconomic divisions. While *software* problems were roughly equal, an August 2010 data sample noted that more boys had *hardware* problems than girls (with a ratio of just over 4 boys for every 3 girls), especially the kinds of hardware problems that resulted from rough handling, following Paraguayan gender norms similar to those in the United States that generally allow boys to be more rambunctious than girls. Similarly, three laptops belonging to rural students had hardware problems for every two belonging to urban students per capita, though software problem reports were roughly equal between the two groups. This was perhaps a result of longer walks home and more unsupervised time as parents worked late. The potential for the project to be a social leveling force was thus undermined by laptop breakage.

A few of the employees from the NGO Paraguay Educa and OLPC noted that such problems were likely the result of the tradeoff between using more easily-serviceable parts and cost-cutting, with the decision often falling on the side of cutting costs to approach as closely as possible the $100 target price for the laptop (though it wasn't able to get much below $190). This meant that some parts were in fact epoxied to the motherboard and were nearly impossible to service. In this way, the idealism that OLPC initially had for the laptop being easily repairable was tempered by limitations imposed by the laptop's manufacturers, who were not as committed to the ideals of open hardware.

In sum, though OLPC's hardware designers anticipated some potential problems, their early claims that the laptop was unbreakable and that children could do the necessary repairs, as well as limitations in manufacturing, led to a number of problems among projects using first-generation XOs. The much larger project in Uruguay reported similar results [9,10,32]. In fact, estimates of the number of inoperably broken laptops in Uruguay ranged from 25% to 35% despite the government's extensive investment in repair facilities and subsidization of repair parts [36:11]. Several of these problems were fixed in the second-generation XO, but that does not help those who received first-generation laptops (and the second-generation XOs had their own manufacturing problems, such as a wireless card that failed more frequently). Though many technologists may think nothing of upgrading their devices frequently, hundreds of thousands of first-generation XOs are in use by students around the world, with little hope or budget for an upgrade, even after the laptop's five-year expected lifespan.

Material Requirements of XO Repairability

With the exception of power adapters, none of these breakages resulted in repairs that children could do without a supply of replacement parts. However, compounding the problems caused by laptop breakage, Paraguay Educa, being a small non-governmental organization running a relatively small project by OLPC's early expectations, had difficulty procuring these parts. According to Paraguay Educa's technical staff, OLPC told the NGO in 2009 or 2010 that they simply do not sell repair parts, since OLPC was too small to handle the maintenance of projects themselves. As a workaround, Uruguay's much larger government-run program went directly to the manufacturers to buy a large number of spare XO parts, and sold the NGO Paraguay Educa small batches of them out of goodwill – though much of this supply, especially the parts that broke most often, was quickly exhausted. As a result, during this fieldwork, just over one quarter of Paraguay Educa's laptops had documented but unfixed hardware problems. Of the 1095 unfixed hardware problems in Paraguay Educa's inventory system in August 2010, one year and four months since laptops were distributed, 474 involved a broken charger, 403 a broken screen, 139 a broken keyboard or trackpad, and 79 other hardware issues.

Some of these breakages could be repaired without replacement parts. One could borrow a charger or splice its cables for a temporary fix, tape bits of paper over the missing keys on the keyboard, or buy an external mouse if one's family was wealthy enough – some mice were observed in use, especially in the more wealthy private schools. However, a broken screen was particularly problematic. It was not only common, but it also rendered one's laptop unusable until a replacement screen was available and one's family saved 303,600 guaranies (about $65) to buy one. Only the charger broke more often, and only the motherboard cost more to replace.

Even when repair parts were available, many were prohibitively expensive for many Paraguayan families. While the official minimum wage in Paraguay in the second half of 2010 was 1,507,484 guaranies (about $320) a month [44], minimum-wage laws were under-enforced [40] and the majority of the population worked either in the exempt public sector or in Paraguay's still-extensive informal economy [13], making significantly less than minimum wage. In particular, rural families, many of them subsistence farmers with side businesses selling home-grown or homemade products on the side of the road, were unlikely to be able to afford repair parts, even though the repair *labor*, supplied by the NGO Paraguay Educa's technical support team that rotated through all of the schools in the program every week, was free. As a result, aside from chargers – which, with the possibility of splicing, had roughly equal rates of repair in urban and rural schools – most hardware problems were repaired roughly twice as often in urban schools as in rural schools. Thus, though the laptop program did help lessen the socioeconomic urban-rural divide in Paraguay, in some ways, the divide persisted in both breakage and repair rates.

One obvious solution to problems of breakage is one of more resources: extra laptops for school use, a consistent source of repair parts, and perhaps money to subsidize the cost of parts in cases of financial need, much like Uruguay's project had – though even with these resources, Uruguay's reported breakage rates were also quite high. Lacking these resources – as a small non-governmental organization dependent on donations and, like many small NGOs, often on the brink of running out of funding – Paraguay Educa had to look to other solutions. One initiative that they began during this fieldwork used parts from two broken laptops belonging to children in the same family (siblings or cousins) to make one working laptop that the children co-owned.

Other initiatives focused on changing the narrative from the one initially provided by OLPC – that laptops were rugged enough to even be thrown around – to one that emphasized their fragility and the responsibility of students or families in *preventing* breakage. During fieldwork in 2010, Paraguay Educa embarked on a campaign publicizing how to care for XO laptops, detailing under what conditions the laptops should be used (sitting down, the laptop resting on a solid surface, plugged in if possible), how to clean them, and how to do simple diagnostics. The NGO's trainers showed videos on the topic to students, and some teachers created and hung posters about how to care for XOs in their classrooms. The training sessions for teachers in the second phase of the project, who received second-generation XOs (with a 4GB hard drive and a better trackpad) in 2011, emphasized *not* OLPC's message about the ruggedness of the laptops but their fragility and the expense of repairs. While it was too early to assess the results of this campaign in 2010, of note here is that it departed from the story often told by OLPC and the press about the laptops to one based on what was happening to laptops on the ground. Along these lines, one of the more enthusiastic laptop users encountered during fieldwork was also one of the most fastidious and had independently concluded that the laptops needed to be cared for. She carefully swabbed her keypad and trackpad with an ethanol solution every day and exhorted her sixth-grade classmates to do the same.

Breakdown of laptops did lead to collaborative technology use – but not particularly the kind that OLPC, or students, really wanted. In the classroom, some teachers had students without working laptops pair up with those who did to do laptop work, but these students were often relegated to observation rather than active participation. Some children with broken laptops were able to borrow a laptop from a family member or (less commonly) a friend who rarely used theirs, though their use of the borrowed machine was generally more circumscribed than use of their own laptops would be, as the lender and borrower sought to balance memory usage, program installation or de-installation, and general care for the still-working machine. Moreover, since the lender had to reclaim their machine at least for classroom use and assignments, the borrower generally lacked the complete freedom with the borrowed machine that they would have with their own machine – or, in some cases, got the lender in trouble by deleting needed software or finished assignments. But more often, students with broken laptops just did not use a laptop anymore.

Practices of Repair in Paraguay

Though the leaders of OLPC hoped that children could do repairs themselves, almost all repairs were done by the NGO Paraguay Educa's teacher trainers or their technical support team, which consisted of two full-time staff members and a number of part-time volunteers from a local university. Some repairs, such as software re-installation, power cable splicing, and checking for loose connectors, could be done on-site at the schools, each of which the team visited once a week.

Some students and a few teachers took interest in these repairs, and the repair staff members were often surrounded by a cluster of students as they fixed laptops. A few teachers and students learned some basic diagnostics this way – one enterprising teacher offered a cable-splicing service for 5000 guaranies ($1), and one student made a point of getting the latest software from the repair staff and installing it himself on his friends' computers, though this often unfortunately overwrote all of their personal projects. Interestingly, most of the students who engaged with the repair staff were boys. Though several girls interviewed were just as interested in their laptops as the most interested boys, they had less interest in repair, labeling it as a "boy's activity," citing their shyness with the all-male repair staff, or saying they preferred to *prevent* breakage as reasons for not engaging. Even when female teacher trainers (or the author, also female) tried to engage them in repair, they were not interested.

Paraguay Educa's programming staff, which was quite skilled (even pushing software updates upstream to the official worldwide software distribution) and sometimes included international volunteers, also occasionally took on some repair and diagnostic work to discover software bugs to fix. They worked almost entirely at one particular school, taking about a day a week of one sixth-grade class to install new versions of the software and observe for bugs. The director of this school was the most outspoken in her support of the project, even incorporating it into her school's charter (and then trying to claim a greater share of scarce project resources in exchange). The international volunteer from OLPC who overlapped with several months of this fieldwork was even more proactive. He encouraged students, boys and girls alike (though girls were often shy with him), to learn to do basic hardware diagnostics – in effect running an informal repair clinic in the classroom, though in observations, such repair activities only happened hesitantly with his direct intervention and encouragement. He was moreover unique in this activity; other Paraguay Educa employees, while not avoiding students, also did not usually encourage them to become involved to that degree.

Almost all repairs that required a replacement part could not be done on-site, and required the repair staff to first wait for repair parts to be available (sometimes a long wait, as demand for some parts, especially screens and chargers, outstripped supply), and then to collect the cost of the part (sold at-cost to students) from the student's family – if they could afford it – before they could make the repair. After the cost was paid, they took the computer back to their office, did the repair, updated the software, and returned the computer to the child in a subsequent visit to their school. Sometimes long waits would lead to confusion and frustration on the part of students and teachers, who thought their laptops had been permanently confiscated when in reality they were just waiting for repair parts. And if families couldn't afford repair parts, as many rural families in particular could not, another site of socioeconomic division would emerge as laptops were relegated to the backs of closets or tops of shelves, reduced to "bricks."

CASE STUDY 2. FIXIT CLINIC AND PUBLIC SITES OF FACILITATED REPAIR

We have seen the complications that can arise from breakage and in repairing products designed to be easily repaired. What of products not necessarily designed for repair, but embedded in worlds with ample resources and expertise? To further explore contemporary landscapes of repair, we now delve into a world of nails, screwdrivers, and multimeters in urban repair clinics like the Fixit Clinic in the California East Bay. These community-supported events were created to help average consumers fix and learn to fix their broken products, such as an iPhone with a shattered screen, a toaster without heat, or a pair of old blue jeans ripped down the backside. Like the OLPC project in Paraguay, the organizers aimed to encourage learning through electronics tinkering which, as we will see, became difficult to support in practice.

The Material Infrastructure of the Fixit Clinic

In contrast to the limited material access in Paraguay, more expertise and infrastructure were available in the repair events in the Bay Area and more repair occurred as a result. The Fixit Clinic, our primary site of investigation, is a site of facilitated repair based in Albany, California, a city just east of San Francisco. Peter, an MIT engineering graduate, founded the project in late 2009 after years of trying to coordinate a free space with the requisite technical competencies to facilitate it. He had originally tried to partner with a local electronics dealer but found that the idea of teaching repair skills to the general public threatened the store's key demographic, the trade workers whose livelihoods depended on for-profit repair services. Eventually Peter found an available community space in Albany through local contacts and recruited his first repair volunteer through his conversations with the electronics store.

Since that time, Peter and his repair volunteers, or "coaches," have hosted more than fifty events in libraries, community centers, museums and hackerspaces (community-operated workspaces, often focused on electronics tinkering) across the Bay Area and beyond, including Minnesota, Colorado, Tennessee and Massachusetts. The events operated as "pop-up" affairs, with anywhere from ten to two hundred visitors and three to thirty repair-savvy volunteers descending on donated spaces with broken items in hand. Volunteers reported enjoying showing and telling visitors how to tinker with and interrogate mass-produced items, helping them take apart electronic devices, identify broken or missing parts, and understand the mechanisms underneath.

Over the past year, Peter's Fixit Clinic has become part of a growing network of parallel sites with such names as the Fixer's Collective (New York City), the Restart Project (London), and the Repair Cafe (Netherlands). While Peter named the Fixit Clinic for its emphasis on diagnosis, he admitted that his approach was largely aspirational. "We're going to try to fix it," Peter explained, "but it's not clear we're going to be able to." As his work reveals, the viability a fix is not dependent on the product alone, but on the many factors surrounding its use and repair, including the expertise of the volunteers, the amount of leisure time available, the ease with which the issue could be diagnosed, and the parts and tools coaches and visitors had available. These events present a case of extending the use of products not necessarily designed for repair to reveal tensions within: reuse versus recycling, serendipity over planning, and the promotion of technical expertise.

Locating Expertise and Participation

What it meant to restore or maintain an item not only depended on the owner's experience with the thing but also the nature and distribution of expertise at the Clinic. As in Paraguay, it was the facilitators of repair (the coaches), and not the participating owners of the devices, that were most often observed enacting repair through tinkering and disassembly.

At one Fixit Clinic in the Richmond area of San Francisco, three sisters in their early twenties brought in a broken sewing machine they had picked up on the side of the road. Once plugged in and turned on, the machine ran at a snail's pace and eventually stopped. Guided by E., a female coach and retired teacher, the sisters spent three hours taking the machine apart, oiling its parts, and trying to adjust a dial that seemed to have broken off. When E. decided the fix was beyond her, S., a male coach with a background in engineering, suggested replacing the purportedly missing part with a short peg. He inspected the machine and found three holes on the inside of the dial. To S., the holes looked as though they had once fit small pegs that enabled the dial to turn and adjust the motor. Taking S.'s advice, the sisters found a peg-like part that matched the diameter of the existing hole, picked up a screwdriver, and proceeded to twist the screw into the hole. Forty minutes later, after several passes between sisters, the screw was ground well inside the hole.

When the sisters returned the dial to its place on the sewing machine, the result was unexpected: the machine was unable to move at all. The machine, now less functional than when it entered the Clinic, was a mystery. *What did it look like before it broke?* Out of breath and depleted of ideas, the sisters decided to return home and bring back a second broken sewing machine they had acquired, which they hoped to use as a model for how the plastic dial should look and behave.

While the sisters were away, J., a male participant with a background in engineering joined the sisters' table and began inspecting the mechanism for turning the dial. He took apart the machine from the opposite end, unscrewed the compartment on the underside, and ultimately discovered a bobbin (a small spool of thread) rolling around in the bottom of the machine. With the bobbin removed, the machine suddenly began running smoothly.

This successful fix is worth considering for the kinds of expertise it brings to light. Despite their notable investments, neither the sisters nor the coaches were responsible for fixing the machine. The eventual fix was far simpler than anyone had suspected: removing a loose bobbin. Many fixes were like this, accomplished without owners' involvement or without their understanding of how or why a particular part failed. Disassembling and reassembling a device, and perhaps using an air spray to clear the inside of dust in between, would lead to mysterious functionality or new problems, some of which remained impossible to diagnose. Messing with a machine and exploring its possibilities for disassembly was the primary mode of repair, highlighting the value of tinkering and improvisation in the repair process.

Beyond the serendipitous character of the fix, the distribution of expertise that led to it was highly gendered. In the above vignette, it was the two male participants with engineering backgrounds, not the sisters or female coach, who decided the machine's fate, even when some of their suggestions were ultimately less critical to the fix. The fact that E. left the scene after designating her level of technical skill insufficient – though she could have discovered the bobbin herself if she had disassembled the machine, as J. had done – was representative of the majority of female participants observed passing work onto male volunteers or waiting for assistance before diving into disassembly, ultimately underestimating their mechanical competencies. Among the male participants, J. eventually fixed the machine, but S. provided advice that led to hours of trying to find and install a set of replacement pegs that never existed. The multiple interceptions of repair work by men at the Clinic were examples of broader patterns of gendered expertise and technical confidence in which some work is seen to appeal to, and align with, male over female volunteers and attendees. Peter noted,

If two or three women come to each Fixit Clinic – you know, women, because that's what they are [laughs] – and they repair fabric things there, and broken sewing machines come in, they take the lead in trying to repair those. And if not we know the other Fixit coaches will just come in.

In practice, the care of fabric, clothing, and jewelry fell to women, while male volunteers and attendees tended to take on electronics repair, reflecting the work of the tech-savvy international volunteer from OLPC and female students' relative disinterest in repair. Though organizers' aims were progressive, they still distinguished craftwork from mechanical repair and fell back on gendered divisions of labor.

Narratives of Empowerment & Sustainability

One key objective of the Fixit Clinic and other repair events was to enable learning through restoration: returning new screens to damaged iPhones, restoring heat to broken toasters, and patching a pair of tattered pants all while instilling an interest in technology development and innovation. At the Fixit Clinic, as for OLPC, repair work was seen to enable technological learning through tinkering with electronics. This motivation expanded to include ideas of technical empowerment – knowing more about technology and making more informed choices around technology as a result – and sustainability – advancing reuse over recycling and disposal.

In the case of empowerment, broken items became byproducts of diagnosis as well as materials to work with and absorb, offering new opportunities for reinvention. Peter explained:

Ultimately my surreptitious goal, which I conveyed to you the very first day, is that we're ultimately trying to get people to a place were they can help to make better policy choices. That we're demystifying technology so that when technology comes up as a societal issue people can participate in that dialogue more coherently than they're able to now.

The notion that repair work, and facilitated repair in particular, has the power to educate and transform how people see and understand technology was a common theme among coaches and organizers of the events, and was sometimes taken up by participants as well. At a Fixit Clinic in Minneapolis, a visitor brought broken antique radio that he and his girlfriend found at a thrift store. When they saw the radio, they immediately plugged it in and turned it on and the first sound they heard was an Otis Redding song that they both loved. After buying the radio and bringing it home, his girlfriend dropped it, rendering it dysfunctional. Bringing the radio to the Fixit Clinic, the visitor explained that his girlfriend's birthday was two weeks away and he wanted to repair it for her. "When he told that story," Peter later explained, "every coach was like: I want to work on that!" There were as many as five coaches vying to fix the broken radio, while Peter stood at the other side of the room already plotting to take a modern radio and somehow transplant it into the antique case as a last resort to get the radio functioning. After considerable tinkering, the Fixit Clinic coaches got the radio to play again. Several days after the Clinic, the visitor later emailed Peter to explain that before he gave the radio to his girlfriend he had checked it, and the radio was no longer working. The man opened up the radio, found that a speaker wire had gotten loose, and proceeded to fix the wire on his own. "So he was able to get it working without having to bring it to another Fixit Clinic," Peter exclaimed. According to Peter, attending the Clinic had given the man the confidence to take on his own repair. Yet, as in Paraguay, such independent repair work was uncommon (only three independent repair experiences were observed during nine months of fieldwork).

At repair events, rather than telling 'war stories' (such as the trials and tribulations that Orr's [28] copy machine repair technicians shared over lunch), coaches instead retold uplifting stories such as the radio gift as a way of rehearsing and reinforcing a desired narrative of *empowerment.* When the narrative did not match up, the story was not retold. One story rarely mentioned, for example, was of the many participants who came to fixing events for the free repair services rather than for the chance to learn about repair. For example, at a Repair Cafe in Palo Alto, an elderly man and his wife had brought in a slow-to-heat toaster he was given by his ex-wife. In use for over fifty years, the toaster was on its last legs; its mechanism for lowering the toast had weakened. Though his current wife was eager to see it die, the toaster symbolized memories the man was not ready to give up. The repair event was an opportunity to keep these memories alive, and all it took was waiting in line. During their time at the Cafe, the couple moved between a few sets of volunteers before someone discovered that the existing spring had loosened. The toaster's performance improved when a volunteer used the same spring at a quarter of its length, creating the necessary tension to lower and raise the toast. The couple had little to do with the fix but watched as the toaster became functional once again. As in Paraguay, empowering participants to do repairs themselves was an ideal state that rarely emerged in practice.

Linked to this idealization of repair were reflections on sustainability, consumerism, and mass manufacturing. Event attendees would comment on the environmental impact of fixing devices and organizers were eager to promote sustainable processes of repair and reuse over recycling. Before launching her events, for example, the founding organizer of the Netherlands based Repair Cafe had been a journalist focused on education and then, changing focus, environmental policy. But for her journalism was not enough:

I no longer wanted to be an outsider or just a neutral describer. But I wanted to do something myself. And I wanted to really add something. And this was what turned out to be the Repair Cafe.

The organizer described feeling a "sense of urgency" as she learned of the dangers of consumerism and energy use to environmental sustainability. This kind of urgency could be felt at multiple levels and in many capacities, as it related to local events and traumatic changes. The founder of the New York Fixer's Collective explained:

We wanted to take care of ourselves and not rely on experts for our needs. And when something big happens, like 9/11, people tend to want to come together. And just human contact is important. And, you know, you can't get that by Googling your answers online.

Even as devices were removed from participants' hands, the act of tinkering with technology and taking pleasure in its deconstruction was seen by the volunteers and event organizers to change how people approached not only their devices but also technology design more broadly. Repair work incited forms of innovation that were practical and collaborative – such as the three people helping to fix the Sunbeam toaster or the six people diagnosing the sewing machine. Despite this appearance of cooperative repair and reinvention, during observations, fixes were often born out of individual tinkering: one coach reusing a wobbly spring, or one volunteer discovering a loose bobbin. This tension between collaboration and individual work, as we have seen in the OLPC program, reveals how repair becomes a privileged act, supported by technical expertise, and, in doing so, becomes political, aimed at shifting how people learn and care for their environment. In this regard, repair work and its ideological aims become embedded in networks of practice that are local and specific.

DISCUSSION

Through stories of broken devices and tricky fixes – repairing things not meant to be repaired or not being able to repair things that were – our fieldwork has highlighted some of the complicated, contingent aspects of technology care and repair. We have seen that on the one hand, communities lacking repair infrastructure – even when they do have expertise – may be stymied by a device designed (or at least intended) to be repairable; while on the other hand, communities with access to a high degree of expertise and repair infrastructure can at times overcome even planned obsolescence.

In Paraguay, the material realities of the machine and the environment, perceptions of the usability and usefulness of the XO laptops, limited access to repair parts, and socioeconomic and gendered factors all shaped the laptops' repairability. Who required, paid for, and conducted repairs were all fraught categories, revealing persistent underlying inequalities and challenging the individualist narrative of the empowered child tinkerers able to repair their own laptops. While OLPC did attempt to specifically design to enable repair, the issues that still came up suggest that designing for repair is more complicated than it may initially appear.

In public repair events, by contrast, tinkering and customization could at times recover items that may have been designed to be discarded, not replaced. Though the work to achieve a fix was often far simpler than participants or coaches expected, it was still treated as privileged expertise, accomplished by the coaches rather than the participants. Despite this division of labor, the process of learning to fix consumer electronics was cast as political action, aiming to improve environmental awareness, inform policy-making at local and global scales, and ultimately promote greater empowerment of consumers and more environmentally responsible futures.

While there are differences between our two cases, there are also a number of material, social, and ideological parallels that help us understand repair in practice. In particular, both cases illustrate aspects of what we term *negotiated endurance*. By this we mean the ways that maintenance, care, and repair are negotiated – often collaboratively – in use and the meaning-making associated with use, rather than the meanings pre-specified by designers. In both case studies, we saw that the process of breakdown and repair was not something that device designers or event planners could effectively script ahead of time. Based on these observations, we argue that designers' intentions to plan or divert such outcomes can often be rendered ineffective without accounting for the specific material, economic and cultural infrastructures that are at play in use.

Although these results may point to a hopelessness in designing to enable (or disable) repair-work, as material realities disrupt design intentions, we feel that there is hope, and our findings should not be taken as a reason to abandon efforts to design to enable repair. Like those involved in repair – motivated in various ways by both ideology and necessity – we see breakdown and repair as integral parts of technology use. Moreover, despite the current trajectory toward even more disposable clothing and electronics, we believe that repair practices may well become more important as resources become more difficult to come by, as fewer can afford replacement, as landfills overflow, and as knowledge of what happens downstream when technology is abandoned becomes more widespread. While London hypothesized that planned obsolescence would drive the economy out of depression by stimulating spending, here we promote attending to repair activities as a source of new ideas and different opportunities for development in design and engineering.

As such, we turn to our case studies and the repair literature to highlight the importance of negotiated endurance. We highlight four themes that illustrate this concept as it relates to the CSCW community: the *negotiated identification of breakdown,* the *collaborative definitions of worth* in determining what to repair, the *fraught nature of collaborative expertise* that repair practices surfaced, and the *gendered stakes of repair* at play throughout. Each of these themes highlights material, social and ideological parallels between our case studies.

Negotiated Identification of Breakdown

One shared theme across our sites of repair is the different kinds of breakage that people not only recognized but also made use of while working with technology. For example, breakage was not viewed as a singular phenomenon; instead, definitions of breakdown lay on a continuum. Some breakage existed without rendering a device completely unusable, yet could still be significant to the user (such as the missing keys or difficult trackpad of the XO laptops, or the Sunbeam toaster that moved slowly as it retracted). Some aspects that were understood by participants as 'breakage,' indeed, had come with the device, such as the XO's small hard drive or the bonded batteries in some consumer devices. The emergence of particular ideas of breakage also may have a complicated relationship with expected lifespans of products. While the fieldwork in Paraguay was not after the XO laptops' expected five-year lifespan, the students using the laptops nonetheless did not have much hope for an upgrade after that time, meaning that these laptops will likely be asked to perform long beyond this timeframe. On the other hand, products that might still be under warrantee at the Fixit Clinic were sometimes turned away with advice to try the manufacturer first.

We also sometimes saw that breakage could be rehabilitated without repair in the conventional sense through processes of "upcycling" or reinvention, where creative reuse enabled participants to re-envision discarded things, such as the antique radio housing a modern one or one working XO laptop made from two broken ones. As a dimension of negotiated endurance, the emergence of conceptions of breakdown in practice rather than being predicted ahead of time illustrates some of the complications for repair-work in practice.

Collaborative Definitions of "Worth"

In both of our case studies, we found that what was deemed worth repairing was tied to the collective practices in which the devices were entrenched, including the repair's economic costs, socioeconomic constraints, demands on time and effort, and social rewards.

In Paraguay, many students' families' lack of disposable income made repairs unaffordable, even when repair parts were available. As a result, laptop repairs were generally less worthy than other pressing household expenses for which income was already reserved. Moreover, because most leisure activity on the laptops involved using them as a portal to music, videos, and videogames, many parents and teachers involved with the project initially saw the laptops as a "mere toy," not something worth taking care of or repairing. While it might be tempting to blame this framing on the fact that the laptops were given out to students and teachers for free, it was more the lack of initial messages of the expense of the laptop and its potential value in the classroom, combined with this collaborative sense-making, that led to this effect. Indeed, when Paraguay Educa noticed their non-use and breakage and started emphasizing their value in the classroom, opinions on the laptops' worth changed dramatically from a "mere toy" to a "learning device," even though usage patterns had not changed as much.

Participants in repair clinics had generally already decided that a device was worthy of repair – or at least investigation – by just showing up with it, though at times their presence was more due to curiosity than by the perceived value of what they brought. Still, stories of worth being collaboratively-defined abounded. While the antique radio provided an example of a formerly low-worth product taking on significance for a couple and then the Fixit coaches, there were also cases when coaches would advise against fixing objects, particularly when the object was cheap and the repair difficult (e.g. repairing the delicate wires of a phone charger) or if the device was expensive and "official" repair might be free (e.g. broken iPhones that could be taken to Apple's Genius Bar). In these cases, coaches steered participants toward particular conceptions of worth centered around repair. These collaborative definitions of worth arose as a second facet of negotiated endurance.

The Fraught Nature of Collaborative Expertise

In our two case studies, we found interesting negotiations around what constituted collaborative repair-work, which involved negotiating between repair ideals and practices on the ground. Overall, the notion of collaborative expertise did differ from commonly-held ideas of expertise as guarded and separated from everyday use – and, as Fixit founder Peter found, could even be threatened by it. For example, while the process of fixing a car is often considered "servicing" and the main points of collaboration are dropping off the car, agreeing to repairs, picking the car up, and paying, the Fixit coaches, as well as the one volunteer in Paraguay, wanted repair to be a deeply participatory endeavor and invited attendees to adjust and refigure electronic devices much like one might fiddle with a recipe – and work with each other to do so.

At the same time, we saw that in both case studies, those who actually diagnosed most problems and carried out most repairs were rarely the owners of the device (the students in

Paraguay or the participants in the Fixit Clinics). Though in both case studies the participants were meant to be more involved, they often gladly ceded control over the repair to the staff or coaches with the most experience. Thus, though these case studies were meant to challenge patterns of expertise and could raise interesting discussions about privileged work and paid labor as well as about the tendency to replace rather than repair, they ultimately reified notions of expertise.

Still, repair work in the Fixit Clinic and OLPC classrooms afforded opportunities for socialization and tinkering, even as they ultimately reified notions of expertise as the coaches or repair staff accomplished many of the repairs themselves (whether by proxy or directly). In this way, these forms of hands-on engagement both promoted and contested the collaborative character of expertise. The task of diagnosing and repairing was passed from coaches/staff to participants, and then back to the coaches/staff. Expertise began with an ideological stance (the importance of technological learning), but was then shaped by the social relations that emerge between device owners and the repair coaches/staff, tech-savvy individuals enabled by the material training they received. As such, repair expertise is a fraught collaborative endeavor, exposing a third dimension of negotiated endurance.

The Gendered Stakes of Repair

A final theme we observed concerned the broader sociological stakes of repair. At public sites of repair, such as the Fixit Clinic, as well as the classrooms, schoolyards, and homes of XO laptop use, we have seen how repair became a privileged practice, relying on infrastructures of diagnostic and repair parts, socioeconomic constraints in defining worth, and unevenly-available expertise, all of which may be easy to take for granted until they are absent. Repair did not always become "empowering" for users in these settings. Rather, it could become a bottleneck to a working laptop, an obstacle in the classroom, a divider between rich and poor. These sociological stakes are particularly important in projects like those described in our case studies, where one of the goals was to democratize technology use and repair. The complications that arose despite these best intentions highlight how complicated and stubborn these inequalities can be.

In particular, we want to take this opportunity to critically examine some of the gendered implications of repair work in our two case studies. Despite their progressive aims for inclusivity, both the Fixit Clinic and the non-governmental organization Paraguay Educa inadvertently prompted participants to enact traditional gender roles by selectively taking up and rejecting the work of repair in gendered ways, and not challenging the assumptions that participants brought to the table as well. In the Fixit Clinics, female coaches may be seen – and to see themselves – as lacking the competencies of their male counterparts and move toward "low-tech" processes of sewing and mending, which can often be seen as less skilled and less important [8]. In classrooms with OLPC laptops, female students were more careful with their laptops and shied away from repairs performed by the all-male repair staff and even female trainers (and the author). This reticence, and the fact that it was rarely challenged, reflected established Paraguayan gender dynamics that – much like gender norms in the United States – gave boys permission to perform both rambunctiousness (leading to breakage) and technical expertise (in repair).

At both sites, by articulating differences between material practices of craft and technology tinkering, participants distinguished male and female competencies and reaffirmed divisions between gendered metaphors for technology design, e.g., low-tech and high-tech, soft and hard, gentle and rough, shy and fearless, and so on. This echoes similar findings of other researchers regarding the gendered nature of tinkering, craft-work, and repair (e.g. [8,12]) and beyond (e.g. [25]), as well as gendered patterns of expertise in computing and engineering cultures more generally (e.g. [21,24,29,45]). Our account corroborates this literature and extends it to two new sites of repair-work that highlight the stubborn nature of these inequalities, particularly the ways that gender norms are collaboratively reinforced in practice.

CONCLUSION

Building on a lively tradition of infrastructure studies, this paper has presented a picture of repair that highlights its political stakes and social contexts. Our two cases have exposed instances of design for repair in and through practice, from programs aimed at increasing technological access and expertise overseas to local sites of technological learning concerned with enhancing public awareness of environmental impacts and technological possibility.

Our discussion describes four themes that emerged from both case studies: the cultural emergence of breakdown, collaborative definitions of worth, the fraught nature of collaborative expertise, and the gendered stakes of repair. All of these are part of what we call *negotiated endurance*, in which the lifecycles of the devices were not determined ahead of time but negotiated during use around these four themes. On the material level, manufacturing limitations, access to repair parts and infrastructure, warrantee status, and even the composition of roads factored into the maintenance and repair process, whether enabling or stymieing repair. On the social level, what was first considered "broken" and then determined to be "worth" repairing was something that depended on context, including access to disposable income, perceived value of the object, and perceived ease of repairs. Moreover, those who actually diagnosed most problems and carried out most repairs were the repair staff or volunteers rather than the owners of the device (the students in Paraguay or the participants in the Fixit Clinics). This last point also relates to ideological parallels between the cases: both OLPC and the Fixit Clinic hoped that participants would repair their own devices, finding empowerment along the way, and both 'designed' with this in mind (OLPC a laptop, Fixit Clinic an environment or experience). However, on-the-ground negotiations complicated these ideologies and brought out hidden constraints and biases that could thwart them, such as the gendered nature of repair in practice.

All together, these parallels undergird negotiated endurance, the work by which different actors – including consumers, community organizers, and others – drive the ongoing use, maintenance, and repair of a given technology around the different sociocultural and socioeconomic forces at play.

ACKNOWLEDGMENTS

This research was made possible by the gracious assistance of our participants. We also thank Fred Turner and Lilly Irani for their feedback on both of our projects, as well as the Hasso Plattner Design Thinking Research Program (HPDTRP) at Stanford for funding research at the Fixit Clinic.

REFERENCES

1. ABC Color staff. El proyecto "Una laptop por niño" comenzará a funcionar en Paraguay. *ABC Digital,* 2008.
2. Blevis, E. Sustainable Interaction Design: Invention & Disposal, Renewal & Reuse. *Proc. CHI '07,* ACM Press, (2007), 503.
3. Brand, S. *How Buildings Learn.* 1994.
4. Burrell, J. *Invisible Users: Youth in the Internet Cafes of Urban Ghana.* MIT Press, 2012.
5. Cellan-Jones, R. Negroponte - Throwing the Laptop. YouTube (video for *BBC News*), 2008. http://youtube.com/watch?v=-tqFEzDou6s.
6. Crawford, M.B. *Shop Class as Soulcraft: An Inquiry Into the Value of Work.* Penguin, 2010.
7. Dant, T. The Work of Repair: Gesture, Emotion and Sensual Knowledge. *Sociological Research Online* 15, 3 (2010), 7.
8. Dawkins, N. Do-It-Yourself: The Precarious Work and Postfeminist Politics of Handmaking (in) Detroit. *Utopian Studies* 22, 2 (2011), 261–284.
9. Derndorfer, C. Plan Ceibal Expands New Repair System to Address High XO Breakage Rates. *OLPC News,* 2011. http://olpcnews.com/countries/uruguay/plan_ceibal_expands_new_repair_system_to_address_high_breakage_rates.html.
10. Derndorfer, C. Plan Ceibal's 4-Year Cost Increases From $276 to $400. *OLPC News*, 2012. http://olpcnews.com/countries/uruguay/plan_ceibals_4_year_cost_increases_from_276_to_400.html.
11. DiSalvo, C., Sengers, P., Brynjarsdóttir, H. Mapping the landscape of sustainable HCI. *Proc. CHI '10,* ACM Press. 1975–1984.
12. Dunbar-Hester, C. Geeks, Meta-Geeks, and Gender Trouble: Activism, Identity, and Low-power FM Radio. *Social Studies of Science* 38, 2 (2008), 201–232.
13. Federal Research Division. Country Profile: Paraguay. 2005.
14. Graham, S., Thrift, N. Out of Order: Understanding Repair and Maintenance. *Theory, Culture & Society* 24, 3 (2007), 1–25.
15. Harper, D. *Working Knowledge: Skill and community in a small shop.* University Of Chicago Press, 1987.
16. Hencke, C.R. The Mechanics of Workplace Order: Toward a sociology of repair. *Berkeley Journal of Sociology* 44, (1999), 55–81.
17. Jackson, S.J., Pompe, A., Krieshok, G. Things Fall Apart: Maintenance, Repair, and Technology for Education Initiatives in Rural Namibia. (2010), 83–90.
18. Jackson, S.J., Pompe, A., Krieshok, G. Repair Worlds: Maintenance, Repair, and ICT for Development in Rural Namibia. (2012).
19. Jackson, S.J. *Rethinking Repair: Breakdown, Maintenance and Repair in Media and Technology Studies Today. In Media Meets Technology.* MIT Press, 2013.
20. Kelty, C. *Two Bits: The Cultural Significance of Free Software.* Duke University Press, 2008.
21. Kotamraju, N.P. Playing stupid, caring for users, and putting on a good show: Feminist acts in usability study work. *Interacting with Computers* 23, 5 (2011), 439–446.
22. London, B. *Ending the Depression through Planned Obsolescence.* 1932.
23. Maanen, J. V. Escape from Modernity: On the ethnography of repair and the repair of ethnography. *Human Studies* 13, 3 (1990), 275–284.
24. Nafus, D. 'Patches don't have gender': What is not open in open source software. *New Media & Society* 14, 4 (2011), 669–683.
25. Oldenziel, R. Boys and Their Toys: The Fisher Body Craftsman's Guild, 1930-1968, and the Making of a Male Technical Domain. *Technology and Culture* 38, 1 (2008), 60–96.
26. OLPC staff. About the Laptop: Hardware. OLPC Website, 2007. http://one.laptop.org/about/hardware.
27. OLPC staff. OLPC Principles and Basic Information. OLPC Wiki, 2012. http://wiki.laptop.org/go/OLPC_Principles_and_Basic_information .
28. Orr, J.E. *Talking about Machines: An ethnography of a modern job.* Cornell University Press, 1996.
29. Oudshoorn, N., Rommes, E., Stienstra, M. Configuring the User as Everybody: Gender and Design Cultures in Information and Communication Technologies. *Science, Technology & Human Values* 29, 1 (2004), 30–63.
30. Papert, S. Digital Development: How the $100 Laptop Could Change Education. *USINFO Webchat,* via *OLPC Talks,* 2006. http://olpctalks.com/seymour_papert/seymour_papert_usinfo.html.
31. Pilgrim, M. Greasemonkey Hacks: Tips & Tools for Remixing the Web with Firefox. O'Reilly Media, 2009.
32. Plan Ceibal. Síntesis del informe de monitoreo del estado del parque de XO a abril de 2010. 2010.
33. Rieger, B. From People's Car to New Beetle: The Transatlantic Journeys of the Volkswagen Beetle. *The Journal of American History* 97, 1 (2010), 91–115.

34. Rosner, D., Bean, J. Learning from IKEA Hacking: "I'm Not One to Decoupage a Tabletop and Call It a Day." *Proc. CHI '09*, ACM Press.

35. Rosner, D.K. The material practices of collaboration. *Proc. CSCW '12*, ACM Press, 1155.

36. Salamano, I., Pagés, P., Baraibar, A., Ferro, H., Pérez, L., Pérez, M. Monitoreo y evaluación educativa del Plan Ceibal. 2009.

37. Star, S.L., Strauss, A. Layers of silence, arenas of voice: The ecology of visible and invisible work. *Computer Supported Cooperative Work* (CSCW) 8, 1-2 (1999), 9–39.

38. Suchman, L.A. *Plans and situated actions: the problem of human-machine communication.* Cambridge University Press, Cambridge, 1987.

39. Torey, C., Churchill, E.F., Mcdonald, D. Learning How: The search for craft knowledge on the internet. *Proc. CHI '09,* ACM Press.

40. US State Department staff, Bureau of Democracy Human Rights & Labor. *2008 Human Rights Report: Paraguay.* 2009.

41. Vota, W. Joel Stanley's OLPC Job: Baking, Breaking Invincible XO-1. *OLPC News*, 2007. http://olpcnews.com/ hardware/screen/olpc_job_breaking_xo-1.html.

42. Vota, W. XO Laptop Price Increase & Maybe Decrease. *OLPC News*, 2009. http://olpcnews.com/sales_talk/price/xo_laptop_price_increase_204.html.

43. Vota, W. Negroponte Throws XO on Stage Floor "Do this with a Dell" - Everyone a Twitter. *OLPC News*, 2009. http://olpcnews.com/forum/index.php?topic=4597.0.

44. WageIndicator Team. Salario Mínimo: Paraguay. Tu Salario, 2011. http://tusalario.org/paraguay/Portada/salario/el-salario-minimo-mensual-es-de-1.341.775.

45. Wajcman, J. *Technofeminism.* Polity, 2004.

46. Warschauer, M. and Ames, M.G. Can One Laptop per Child Save the World's Poor? *Journal of International Affairs* 64, 1 (2010), 33–51.

Fast, Functional, and Fitting: Expert Response Dynamics and Response Quality in an Online Newcomer Help Forum

Hon Jie Teo
Virginia Tech
Blacksburg, VA, USA.
hjteo@vt.edu

Aditya Johri
George Mason University
Fairfax, VA, USA.
ajohri3@gmu.edu

ABSTRACT

In online communities a few experts are able to help a large number of help-seekers – whether in Q&A communities or other forms of online forums. How is this efficiency achieved? How useful is this help? We show that expert help-giving can be characterized as: (1) *Fast* – Most active help-givers gave response promptly and were most responsive during peak activity; (2) *Functional* – There was little duplication of help-giving effort; and, (3) *Fitting* – Initial responses were of high quality and reduced the need for further clarifications and corrections; high quality responses were provided earlier in the thread. Examination of differences across experts revealed that the most highly rated group of experts responded to 69% of the questions with a median response time of 16 minutes, twice as fast as other experts. Finally, we demonstrate the high quality of response through a taxonomy that characterizes expert responses as: *framing*, *guiding*, or *engaged* help.

Author Keywords

Online communities; Help-giving; Expertise dynamics.

ACM Classification Keywords

H.5.3 Information Interfaces and Presentation: Group and Organization Interfaces—*Computer-supported cooperative work*

General Terms

Human Factors; Design; Measurement.

INTRODUCTION

Research on online communities identified early on that a relatively small number of participants – usually experts – can provide help to a much larger number of newbies or newcomers [22]. Since then research on help-giving and expert behavior has proliferated as help-seeking behavior on the Internet has increased in popularity [1, 33]. This trend is reflected of late in the large number of question-answering (Q&A) sites that have mushroomed across the Web and studies of those sites [25, 38]. This expert-novice relationship, where a few experts are responsible for educating a large number of learners, is also mirrored in the recent rise of Massively Open Online Courses (MOOCs) [10, 14], illustrating another potential application area for this research.

CSCW'14, February 15 – 19, 2014, Baltimore, MD, USA.

ACM 978-1-4503-2540-0/14/02...$15.00.
http://dx.doi.org/10.1145/2531602.2531731

In this paper we present findings from a study that examined online help-giving behavior of experts to understand expert response dynamics and response quality across a range of measures within a single setting. Although earlier studies have looked at different aspects of help-giving, no study we are aware of has reported looking at a range of issues within a single setting. Our study of expert behavior is based on an online help forum for newcomers learning the Java programming language. The experts in this setting were proficient both with software programming in general and programming in Java more specifically. In addition, our research utilizes a concrete measure of expertise that distinguished between different levels of expertise to provide a more accurate understanding of expert dynamics. We now briefly review the literature on Q&A sites to situate our work and follow it up with our study design, findings, and a discussion.

HELP-GIVING IN ONLINE Q&A SITES

Although help-giving is common across a range of online communities, we situate our work within recent research on online Q&A sites which has looked directly at experts. Online Q&A sites are free-of-charge Web-based platforms in which users can freely post questions and interact with other users by providing potential answers to their questions, all of which is incentivized by a reputation system [32]. Studies suggest that Q&A sites are supportive environments where more than 88% of posed questions receive at least one answer [1, 25] and answers are typically of high quality [16]. Researchers also found some sites such as Yahoo! Answers attract a large and diverse user base [1] whereas other Q&A sites are more narrowly targeted. For instance, Stack Exchange is typically used by programmers due to the effectiveness of reviewing codes on the platform and access to a wide range of programming expertise [37]. Within studies of Q&A sites, the overarching topic of expertise has been an area of intense investigation as quality of expertise available and the way in which expertise dynamics works often determines the success of the site. Accurate and efficient means of Q&A expertise discovery improves system capability to swiftly identify, attract and retain expertise [30]. Yet, measuring or ascertaining expertise has been a difficult problem [18]. Often, answer quality is used to assess expertise. Answer quality is derived from user characteristics and discussion attributes [1, 24] or through counts of references to external resources [13] and the numbers of hyperlinks [16]. The focus is on indirect indicators of expertise such as graph-based algorithms and measures of users' answering ability. This emphasis on indirect indicators can be attributed to the presence of social voting systems in Q&A sites such as Yahoo! Answers and Stack Overflow. In these Q&A sites, users other than the questioner can also vote on the best answer. However the social voting feature is not prevalent in many other Q&A forums, including the research site in this study, where only the questioner has the discretion to vote on the best answer and award reputation points to the user with the best answer. Therefore, points awarded are based on the quality of the response as rated by the help-seeker providing a reliable metric to assess expertise. In sum, there is a range of proxy measures of expertise, but each measures only one of the several qualities of expertise. Moreover, these studies largely do not employ a direct marker of expertise

While measuring and ascertaining expertise remains a thorny issue, the ability of a small group of experts to support and help a large number of answer-seekers or newcomers is unquestioned [22]. A recent study reports that top 1% of top users contribute more than a quarter of answers in Stack Exchange [25]. These findings raise an important issue – how does the help-giving dynamic work? Yang and colleagues [39] examined an online help community (taskCn.com) and found that while there are no formal role specifications, experts tend to select tasks that are less popular to increase the chances of having their solution selected as the winning solution. Yang and Wei [40] studied another help community (Baidu.com) and uncovered a core group of members who actively engage in both asking and answering. They found that this core group of members tends to self-select easier questions to answer to enhance their community status. Posnett et al [31] examined user answering activities over time on Stack Exchange and found that the ability of users to answer and score points decreases over time and that the amount of time spent on site does not correlate with answering ability. In a nutshell, they suggest that experts' level of aptitude upon initial participation is predictive of future performance in the community and experts might not benefit from their tenure with the site. Hanrahan and colleagues [15] examined the same community and found little correlation between problem difficulty as indicated by the duration of specified question and the average expertise of involved answerers. Their findings suggest that experts do not necessarily participate in difficult questions but focus on easier to maximize their help-giving efforts and score as many points as possible. Pal and Konstan [29] similarly found TurboTax Live community experts demonstrate a question selection bias and prefer to answer questions where they may have a higher chance of making a contribution. Both studies suggest that expertise is influenced by the setup of the reputation system, and how being an expert answerer is less about being a "help-all" and more of picking the most favorable situation in which to offer help. Overall, help-givers and experts engage in a range of strategies to maintain their reputation while answering questions. This suggests that even though a formal organizing mechanism is absent in these online Q&A communities, some form of self-organizing occurs where experts selectively channel their efforts into areas where they see potential gains. *We found that in the literature, no one had looked at the organization of expert response behavior within the same study or context. So even though we have knowledge of a range of issues regarding expert behavior, this knowledge is piecemeal and not comprehensive.*

RESEARCH STUDY

Overall, as the previous review suggests, recent research on online Q&A sites has neglected to examine different groups of users based on explicit markers of reputation such as a badges or a status and no study has looked at a both patterns of expert behavior and the quality of their responses. In this paper our purpose was to utilize expertise markers to examine a range of issues regarding both response dynamics and quality. Furthermore, we wanted to look at a community that was domain-based and not social Q&A [12, 33] based as expertise plays a more important role in domain-based communities. We now discuss our research setting that allowed us to address these issues.

Research Site

Our data come from "New to Java" which is a community for those interested in learning more about the Java computing platform and programming language. We chose this site for two primary reasons. First, Java is a popular programming language used for application development in a wide variety of fields. There are currently more than nine million developers working with the language and more than one billion computer devices run Java[1]. Second, the complexity of Java (as an advanced programming language) attracts significant newcomers working on a diverse range of applications.

Data Collection

We collected forum data for over 10 years consisting of over 200,000 discussion messages (Figure 1). Over this period the community saw significant activity and the activity spiked in the late 2006-early 2007 period as Java was open sourced. Other than the increase in number of newcomers, we did not observe or find any other differences in terms of how community members responded to questions. The discussion forum data that we collected consisted of a total of 37,472 discussion topics which correspond to a question/answer ratio of 7.36, a figure which is close to that of Yahoo! Answers [1], and almost three times that of Stack Overflow [25] and Naver Knowledge iN [27]. Our data collection complied with both internal institutional IRB protocol and the 'terms of services' of the forum.

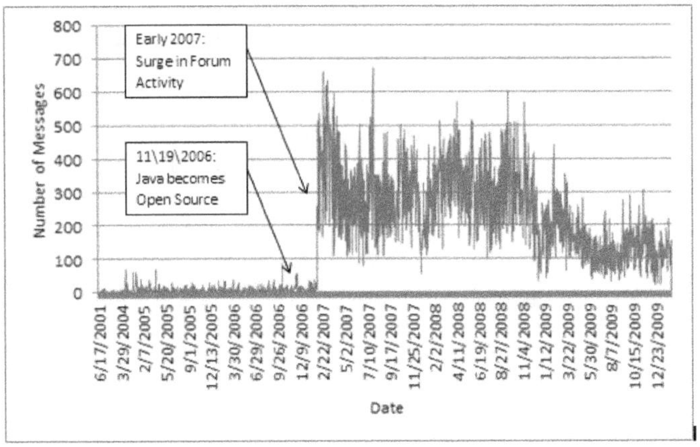

Figure 1: Community activity from 2001-2009

The data ranged from a time period between 2001 and 2009. User post counts (see Table 1) indicates that most users have less than 10 posts in this discussion forum with only 326 users having post counts more than 500. Therefore, similar to other help forums, the majority of users participate infrequently in contrast to a much smaller number of expert helpers who contribute much more frequently to the forums. There was very little to no off-topic discussion or postings on the forum. For findings presented in the first part of the study the entire data was analyzed. For the second part, we analyzed a subset of data as discussed later.

Post Count	Number of Users
0 to 10	14114
11 to 50	5076
51 to 500	1922
More than 500	326

Table 1: User Posts

DESCRIPTION OF THE 'NEW TO JAVA' FORUM

Given that the forum software in itself is a primary mechanism that structures online interaction, we first start by elaborating some structural features of the forum software present in the 'New to Java' online forum.

Forum Layout

Similar to other forums, this forum is made up of a collection of discussion topics created by help-seeking members (Figure 2). A discussion topic can be created by a member who submits a title defining his (or her?) request together with relevant message contents describing his request. The topic then forms the basis for subsequent interaction between the help-seeker and help-givers. The first post of each discussion thread is directed at a specific issue or topic and the following replies may not be focused on this issue or topic. As a form of incentive, the help-seeker has the discretion to give out "Duke" points[1] from 0-10 points to one specific member based on the quality and quantity of help given. This mechanism, also found in other help communities [1, 39], provides the original poser the option to rate other members that provide answers to questions. The given points are then stored on a cumulative basis against the help providers' username.

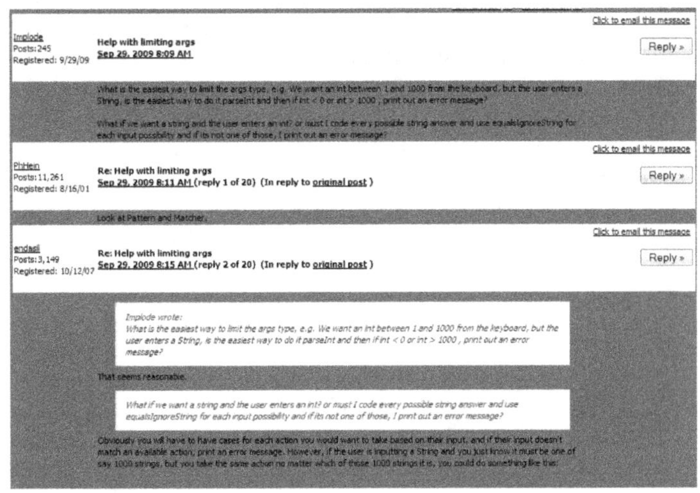

Figure 2: Example of a help request and follow-up discussion

User Profile by Status

Based on the distribution of points given by help-seekers to help-givers, the 'New to Java' forum classifies members by four distinct member profiles. The 'Duke status' of an individual member is determined on the basis of accumulated Duke points. The status of a newcomer to the community is set to Bronze by default and remains that way until the member receives 100 Duke points. Members with a 'Silver star' rating have between 100 to 500 Duke points. While Gold members have amassed Duke points in the 500 to 1000 range, Platinum members lie at the top of the rating scheme with more than a 1000 Duke points. The rating system is a cumulative assessment across all developer forums hosted by the company.

Table 2 describes the points required for each status and the number of members who have been accorded the status in the forums. It shows that a small number of members have accumulated a large number of Duke points across various forums – the total Duke star points accumulated by 43 active Platinum members exceed that of 21,395 members of

[1] 'Duke' is the mascot for Java.

all other statuses. Approximately 1.2% of registered users have either the Platinum, Gold or Silver statuses; a figure comparable with the widely recognized 1% rule [26].

Status	Required Duke Points	Members with Status	Total Duke Points	Average Duke Points
Bronze	0	21179	21,326	1.01
Silver	100	180	36,055	200.31
Gold	500	36	24,026	667.39
Platinum	1000	43	81,904	1904.74

Table 2. Community Status and User Count

Distribution of Help-Seeking and Help-Giving

Figure 3 describes the distribution of topic started by members across the four statuses. The numbers show Bronze members initiated 35,166 topics (93.8% of all topics in the forums) but helped with 2,171 topics not initiated by them. Platinum members on other hand started only 1,411 threads (3.7% of all topics in forums) and replied to 25,965 topics, which suggests that they are mostly engaged in help-giving. Gold and Silver members engage in help-giving, with each status helping with approximately 29% of all initiated topics while having only initiated less than 2% of all discussion topics.

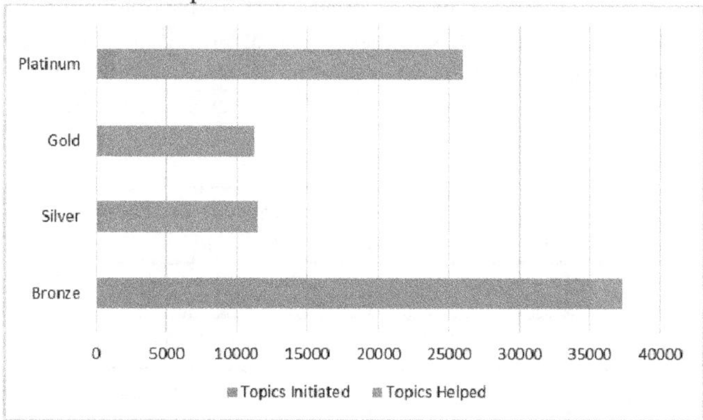

Figure 3: Topic and reply distribution across members based on their status

The descriptive statistics suggest a skewed phenomenon: (1) most help is sought by members (Bronze) who have not answered questions and, (2) most help is provided by members who at the time of data collection have accumulated a fair amount of Duke points (such as members from the Silver, Gold or Platinum statuses). These participation data are specific to just this forum as the users could have participated in other related forums hosted by Java/Oracle. *Overall, the forum worked in a similar fashion to Q&A sites as newcomers asked questions that were responded to by experts. Therefore we feel that a comparison with Q&A sites is justified.*

RESPONSE TIMELINESS

In the following section, we first establish that Platinum members are efficient help-givers through analysis of the timeliness of their first responses to help-seekers. Next, we describe how 'Platinum' members respond to questions across time and discussion topics to maximize their ability to respond to a large number of help requests. To empirically demonstrate these findings, we draw from temporal analysis of community activity to highlight the patterns in of help-giving across the 24 hour period. We then draw on descriptive statistics to demonstrate that there are on average less than two members of the same status on the same help discussion which allows helpers to distribute their expertise.

Timeliness of First Response across Statuses

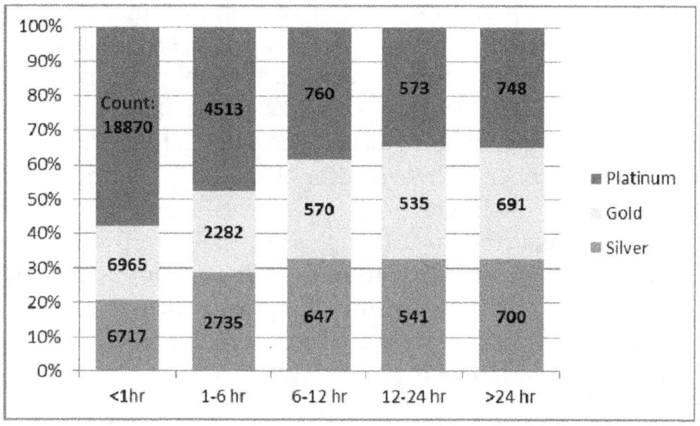

Figure 4: Distribution of response time based on member status

As a means to understand the timeliness of response to help-seekers' topic, we examined the average time taken to make a first response by the first member from each status group (see Figure 4). Based on an analysis of 37,474 topics, we found that more than half of the first response to each help request (68.0%) was provided within the first hour after the request was posted. We found that a relatively larger number of Platinum members replied within an hour (58.0% of all replying members) compared to members from Silver (20.6%) and Gold statuses (21.4%). This not only demonstrates that Platinum members help more, but that most of the help is given within a short time frame of 1 hour. These findings also suggest that helpers across the three statuses provided prompt help.

Status of User	Median Time
Platinum	16
Gold	29
Silver	36

Table 3: Median Response Time of First Response by Status

The median response time of 16 minutes for first response of Platinum users (see Table 3) is close to the reported median response time of 11 minutes on Stack Overflow, touted to be fastest Q&A site [25]. We however note the median response time of 16 minutes only correspond to the most reputable group of users – the Platinum users and not Gold or Silver users. The responsiveness of Platinum users is almost twice of that of Gold and Silver users.

Help-Giving Across Time

Our previous examination of the responsiveness of the help-giving users across the three statuses provide insights into the promptness of given help but reveal little about the distribution of help activities across distinct time periods where the number of requests for help may vary. To gain this perspective, we examined the distribution of help across the 24 hour time period for each member status (see Figure 5). We found that while Platinum members provide help throughout the 24 hour period, their levels of activities are close to that of Bronze members at certain time periods. For instance, help-seeking activities in the late nights (in EST) did not attract a proportional level of activity from the Platinum members. This however changes in daytime when the amount of help given by Platinum is much larger than the amount observed in late nights. As much help is sought during the day, this demonstrates to a certain extent how Platinum members are organized to provide help at the time when their expertise is most wanted – which is at daytime when bronze users are most active.

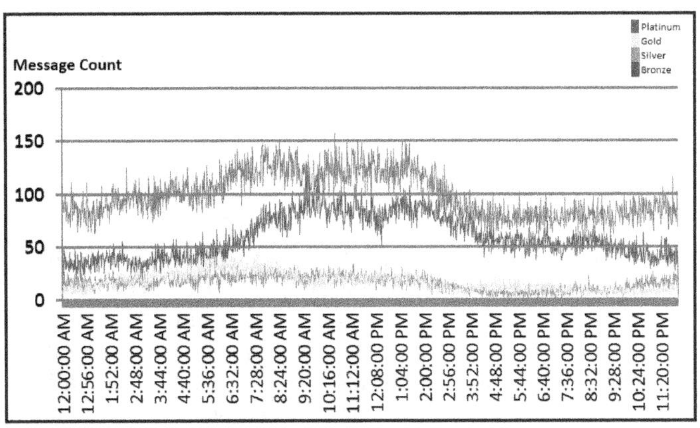

Figure 5: Community activity (time of the day normalized) across membership status

While Platinum members provided help at comparable levels to Gold or Silver members at late nights, the amount of help given by Platinum statuses was at least 3 times higher than both Silver/Bronze members at day time. The significance of the finding here is that there is a proportionally larger jump in Platinum users' help-giving activities from night time to day time where questions from other users arrive at the highest rate. This in turn suggests that Platinum users are more responsive to the rise of help request. In sum, we found evidence that the small number of Platinum members contribute to help-giving activities throughout the 24-hour period with extensive efforts going into the early morning to early afternoon period, when helps-seekers are most active. We found evidence that the Platinum members are efficient help-givers. Although their status could have been achieved solely by responding to a large number of questions and providing correct responses, consistent with prior work, we found them not only to be accurate but also highly efficient. We also observed that Gold and Silver help-givers provided help at a fairly consistent level which is reduced to minimal levels in the evening. This is despite more than four times as many Silver members as Platinum members and that the number of Gold members is close to that of Platinum members.

DISTRIBUTION OF EXPERTISE ACROSS THREADS

Help is primarily provided by members across the Silver, Gold and Platinum statuses to a relatively larger population. We analyzed 37,474 topics to understand how members from different status groups are distributed across the topics. Members of Bronze status were left out of this analysis since we previously established that they obtained few Duke points and rarely participated in help-giving or discussion beyond topics that they initiated. We found that 259 help-givers across the Silver, Gold and Platinum statuses replied to discussion topics. On average, not more than two members in the same status class featured in the same discussion topic (see Table 4). For every topic that they contributed to, we see on average 1.27 Silver and 1.20 Gold members helping with each topic. In particular for the Platinum status, this finding suggests that Platinum members demonstrate a tendency to seek efficiency by spreading their expertise to as many topics as possible.

Status	% of All Topic Helped	Mean unique membership status per topic / S.D.
Silver	30.1	1.27/0.64
Gold	30.0	1.20/0.505
Platinum	69.2	1.67/1.03

Table 4: Participation in discussions based on member status

It is noteworthy that while 43 Platinum members provided help to 69.2% of all topics in the forums, they managed to stay at less than two unique Platinum members for every discussion topic they engage in. This distribution of expertise and trust places in other members with similar status is a significant factor in helping core members become effective in help-giving. Although we do not have direct data on how they evaluated other members with similar status, the overall pattern of help-giving suggests that a lot of credence was placed in the point system. From our analysis of the content of the forum messages, it was clear that those with higher status commanded more attention. Furthermore, we observed that attaining Gold or Platinum status was extremely hard and required high amounts of involvement with the community. It was also observed that the status of members carried over to other

Java related online communities thereby investing the status system with more meaning and relevance. Indeed, in our site of study, it appears that the Silver and Gold users are selective in answering questions with both groups helping merely 30% of questions posted in the forums. Assuming that users spend similar amounts of time on the forums, the most reputable users (Platinum users) appear less selective with answering questions reaching 69.2% of questions. Our finding deviates from the work by Dearman and Troung [11] who reported that contributors to Yahoo! Answers offered answers to questions when they perceive that their answers will be well-received by the questioner and enjoy reasonable visibility. This possibly hints at differences in expert behavior across large Q&A only sites as opposed to more narrowly focused domain-based sites.

Having looked at the patterns of help-giving, we now examine the quality of help that was provided on the forum.

RESPONSE QUALITY

Prior research on online help communities uncovered various communication patterns in the help-giving process. For instance, [22] uncovered online help-givers spent a relatively smaller amount of time answering questions (2% of time spent) as compared to reading them (98% of time spent). In their study of the technical support forums of eight open source software projects, Singh and Twidale [35] found that the process of help-giving is seldom dyadic and often iterative, and the interactions between members are mostly many to many interactions (many help-seekers and many help-givers are involved). Singh et al. [34] examined help giving on seven online FLOSS technical support communities and found that help interactions were inefficient due to the wide variation in details provided by help-seekers which required extra sensemaking from the experts. As these studies indicate, much is left to learn about what forms of help is provided and how it is received by the help-seeker. The quality of help-giving – its accuracy, usefulness, and how it is conveyed– in particular is important to assess but has not received much attention in the literature.

In the following sub-sections, we present findings from our qualitative analysis of the textual contribution of members. Based on our analysis, we have classified help-giving under three dimensions: *framing help*, *guiding help*, and *engaged help*. To perform this analysis, we used a subset of our data. Discussion messages were collected from the most active discussion topics created in the month of September in year 2009 and which accounted for 9.4% of all topics started in the month. By only examining the most active discussion topics, we are able to focus on the discussion threads with sufficient content to analyze. In total, 1119 messages from 47 discussion threads amounting to a total of 108 pages of conservations were analyzed.

Framing Help

From our analysis, we found that help-givers gave framing help – to help them frame or reframe their questions – which might not be immediately useful to the help-seekers. We observed that help-givers at times declined to provide direct help specific to the question at hand. For instance, a help-giver offered this opinion in which he considered the help-seekers' question to be too broad:

I don't think anybody here has a problem with someone asking for help with homework. The problem--or one of them--is when they don't provide a clear, precise question. "Here's a bunch of code. It doesn't work," is not acceptable whether the question is homework or not. "Here's my code. It's supposed to generate the average, but the number is always off by a little bit," is a reasonable questions, regardless of whether it's homework or not.

Help-givers also suggested to the help-seeker to seek out further contextual information related to their questions when flaws are present in their questions. For example, a help-giver noticed an error in a help-seeker's question and suggested to the help-seeker to seek clarification from his/her instructor:

Maybe your instructor has made the (faulty) assumption that a file named Foo.class that the member will pick is guaranteed to have a public class simply named "Foo" (belonging to no package, so it is not "com.whatever.Foo")? You'd better ask him/her. Otherwise it appears that he/she is mistaken that you can simply derive the class name from the file name.

Guiding Help

Help-givers offered guidance which can assist help-seekers with their task at hand but not entirely resolve their challenges. Such help included commonly-found information and advice on how to seek out additional information. In our research, we found that help-givers often borrowed information from existing resources to assist the help-seekers. For instance, in a discussion on Java Programming Classes, a help-giver provided the following information directly quoting from the official manual:

6.4.3 The Members of a Class Type says: Members are either declared in the type, or inherited because they are accessible members of a superclass or superinterface which are neither private nor hidden nor overridden.

On occasions where external sites appeared to be relevant resources, help-givers provided URL links to external resources or code repositories. Resources recommended by the help-givers offered the help-giver-seekers immediate access to relevant information that could assist them with the task at hand. For example:

See if you can find record of this kind of GC [Garbage Collector]/finalizer bug at http://bugs.sun.com/.

Help-givers also prompted the help-seekers to look up specific information on the Internet. For example, help-givers recommended that help-seekers use search engines to obtain more information on "while loop" before returning to the task at hand:

You have to declare your input variable before you use it, just like any other variable. Google for java while loop example. I'm sure there'll be plenty.

Engaged Help

In discussion topics where expertise or context permitted, help-givers provided original codes, detailed explanation for a specific question and detailed procedures to assist with troubleshooting issues. Even though the production of source code may require a significant investment of time and effort, we observed that from time-to-time help-givers write original code and provide their code free-of-charge to the help-seekers. For example:

I hacked this up in about an hour as an example of how one should go about such stuff... it's not designed to fulfill your real requirements, of which I remain blissfully ignorant (and I would thank you to leave it so).This program displays: [Source Code Removed]

We observed that the contribution of detailed explanations proved to be a critical step towards resolving specific problems and questions. We found that help-givers typically provided well-described explanations when specific questions are asked. For example:

You are totally right Adams '==' operator compares the reference of 2 objects which cannot be the same at all cause different object instances refers to different addresses in memory. To compare object's contents taken from a certain class you need to override equals() method in (this class)which is inherited from Object class (Top class) and to do so you need to check that: 1- Objects are not null. 2- Objects are the same kind (taken from the same class) 3- The content of them are the same. It will be something like that: [Source Code Removed]

Some members at times sought help on issues that required specific actions to reach a resolution. For these members, help-givers provided detailed procedural instructions. For example, a help-giver offered detailed step-by-step procedures to assist with the establishment of the "classpath" parameter on a Windows System:

Here's the procedure for setting the classpath in Windows XP (I imagine Vista is somewhat similar):
Right click on the computer icon on the desktop
Select "properties"
Select "advanced" tab
Select "environment variables"
Create a new system variable called JAVA_HOME and give it a value of where your java.exe code is add this to your path variable %JAVA_HOME%\bin;%JAVA_ HOME%\lib

Distribution of Help Across Discussion Threads

Table 5 describes the distribution of help across the three dimensions. On average in all discussion topics, 40.4% of help were framing as compared to guiding forms of help (26.0%) and engaged help (33.6%). To deepen our analysis of the occurrence of the three dimensions of help, we also described the counts of help across the three dimensions in the first half and second half of all discussion topics. We conducted a Wilcoxon paired t-test and found significant differences for each of three dimension of help ($p<0.01$) over the two halves of discussion. Framing forms of help were more likely to occur in the second half of discussion whereas guiding and engaged help were more likely to occur in the first half of the discussion. As we earlier established most of the help were prompt (with 69% of first responses occurring in the first hour), this finding provided further support to our observation: help-givers were giving quality help in a prompt manner. Furthermore, from the two analysis we also know that Platinum members provided the help earliest and of highest quality.

Type of Help	**Avg. Count (Full Thread)**	**Avg. Count (1st Half)**	**Avg. Count (2nd Half)**
Framing	**6.79**	**2.02**	**4.89**
Provide Off-topic Opinion	5.40	1.43	4.04
Recommend Revisiting Original Source	1.38	0.43	0.85
Guiding	**4.37**	**2.64**	**1.98**
Quote Directly from Existing Material	1.45	0.81	0.64
Provide Link to External Resources	0.94	0.62	0.32
Advise to Use External Resource	1.98	0.83	1.15
Engaged	**5.64**	**3.64**	**2.00**
Write/Edit Code	1.51	0.96	0.55
Provide Detailed Explanations	1.96	1.15	0.81
Provide Step-by-Step Instructions	2.17	1.53	0.64

Table 5: Distribution of help across discussion threads -- classified according to quality and thread stage

DISCUSSION

Through this study we wanted to delve deeper into how help-giving is organized in online communities that support newcomers, a context similar to online Q&A sites. We found that newcomers were well supported in their quest for answers and that, as prior work has suggested, a small core of experts who are also the most active members of the community were able to provide timely and useful help to a really large number of newcomers. We synthesized several mechanisms used by experts to provide timely and useful help. Experts do not wait to provide help as they probably understand the need to get a quick response and also the traffic problems that might occur if posts are not responded to quickly. The promptness of the help given on the forum by the top 0.2% of all users is evident from several statistics – approximately 68.0% of first responses were generated within an hour of asking with a median time of 16 minutes, close to the median time of 11 minutes of the one of the fastest Q&A site StackOverflow [25].

Based on our findings that expert users provide high quality and fast help, we bring provide another perspective on expertise on Q&A sites. The maintenance of the most reputable users' presence on Q&A sites also requires them to provide swift response to questions to garner continual exposure and foster engagement with incoming help-seeking users. Therefore, our argument support previous findings that suggest that users do not get better with answering questions (or become experts) with more time spent in Q&A site and that the answering ability of user is evident from initial posts and persist throughout her tenure [31]. The presence of the Platinum users in the site of study can be understood as a group of users who already possess strong sets of skills and experiences organized to score as many points as possible and gain community exposure for professional reasons. We add to this line of work by highlighting the distinction between experts. The most reputable group of users, Platinum, which makes up 0.2% of all users or 17% of all expert help-givers, are not as selective in their engagement with questions as Silver and Gold users. They are also more prompt at providing answers. This is evident from their ability respond to approximately 69% of questions at a median response time of 16 minutes.

Our study also shows that expertise was well-distributed with less than two members of the same status participating on the same discussion. Experts monitored threads and if one expert – as indicated by the status – had already provided help they typically did not interfere and moved on to other threads. In other words, help giving was functional where the focus was on distributing but not duplicating efforts. Finally, they provided useful help to the questions. The appropriateness or fit of the responses is illustrated from findings from a content analysis of the forum messages. As prior work has suggested [4], newcomers' frame of questions shapes help-giving, but for the most part the experts take their role seriously and if possible provide appropriate help. These findings are important in light of the issues that we raised in our introduction.

The analysis of the quality of responses illustrates the high level of help provided suggesting that experts were able to scaffold the learning process of newcomers [28]. Even though in many instances the experts provided detailed and elaborated responses, it appeared from their responses, that they only did so when they were convinced that the help-seeker had put in enough effort to either find a workable solution or had enough prior knowledge to be receptive to their response (which they could gauge from the response from the help-seeker). In this sense, they illustrated an ability to work across the "zone of proximal development" of the learner [6] and even create conditions, through their framing and guiding responses, for the learner to raise their level of knowledge.

IMPLICATIONS

Design Implications

Scholars have studied online communities to understand motivation issues [23], issues of social cohesion and lack of social involvement [19], and have suggested ways to design online communities for sustained participation [20, 21]. One of the design implications from this study is the design of a reputation or "badge" mechanism for experts in online communities. Although it is hard to comment on how important a role was played by the status in the Java community, it is clear that the acted as an incentive [5]. Often after responding to questions experts would indirectly hint to the help-seeker that points are available for assigning. From a forum organization viewpoint, the mechanism seems to provide many advantages. For newcomers it provides a way to trust – or not – the responses they receive. It provides a mechanism for newcomer to move along a trajectory of increased participation and not only be aware of their progress, but have it be visible across the community. This "badge" mechanism, now becoming common across different kinds of communities, also makes it easier for those who running the community. It provides a mechanism for monitoring the progress and dynamics of the community – a critical issue in the age of digital big data. Of course, there can be a downside to the use of expertise symbols as well. There can be an unhealthy and unproductive competition. More but less useful help might be provided in order to garner points. The rating of the helper might unduly influence the help received – it might not be that useful or correct. But overall, our analysis, present in this paper but also otherwise, suggests that there were several checks and balances to ensure that the rating system function effectively. Most critically, since only the person who had started the thread, and asked for help, could assign 'Duke points' ensured quality control. The downside actually was that many help-seekers never assigned points even after receiving help, a shortcoming also observed in Yahoo! Answers [18], and there was no mechanism to correct this oversight.

Implications for Learning

Online communities, in addition to providing help, are also a critical avenue for technology-driven informal learning, especially around topics such as open source software, application development and programming languages [36]. They bring together practitioners, hobbyists, and students, and sometime experts [7, 9] to engage in information sharing and collaboration [8]. Although most of these communities do not form with the primary intent to educate others, many of them exist with the sole intent to provide help to learners and enthusiasts who are facing challenges with their task on hand. In this sense, these online help forums offer an accessible platform for discussion and collaborative learning for members of all levels of expertise [3, 7]. Finally, the recent rise and popularity of online education initiatives, particularly large setting such as MOOCs, also makes this work highly relevant. Many online education initiatives are working on the assumption that a small number of experts will be able to teach a large number of learners [10, 14]. The potential of such initiatives for educating a large number of people who do not have access to traditional learning opportunities – for various reasons – has been discussed at length – both positively and critically [2, 17]. The findings from our study are comforting to some extent as they show that managing a large number of learners – which is becoming a necessity – using a small group of experts is achievable. It remains to be seen what kind of a community structures will be needed to move beyond efficiency to create environments that can support deep learning.

Limitations

There are several limitations of this work. The forum supported newcomers learning a programming language that is hugely popular, and at one stage was open sourced and these characteristics might have shaped who participated and also the quality of their participation. Therefore, findings should be interpreted with caution when being applied to other online forums. The implications of our study are also limited as we do not directly ask users about their participation but have only analyzed their actions. Although we observed a pattern and have reported that, we can only hypothesize user intent but not report it directly. In our comparison of response time, we discuss our findings based on the assumption that users spend similar amounts of time on the forums. The forum participants, especially the experts, are mostly professionals highly engaged with using the software in their day to day work. In other online communities this kind of involvement might be limited. Finally, even though we use a longitudinal dataset, other communities have seen a shift in their expert-novice or mass-elite user dynamics over time [19] and similar changes can be expected in this community.

CONCLUSION

We present findings from a study of how expertise dynamics works on an online Java programming help forum. Our work confirms the findings from earlier studies which have demonstrated that in online help forums a few experts are able to support a large number of newcomers. In addition, our findings provide evidence supporting an observation made from a review in other similar studies on user behavior in online communities – that expert behavior is self-organized in the absence of external guiding forces. The most reputable experts provide quick and high quality help and are able to cover a large number of questions by answering close to 70% of all questions quickly at a median response time of 16 minutes. Self-organizing is further demonstrated from limited duplication of expert help. Overall, this study suggests that even though help-giving on online forums is voluntary, it self-organizes to provide fast, functional, and fitting help.

ACKNOWLEDGMENTS

We thank Rakim Mitra for assistance with data collection. This material is based upon work supported, in part, by the U.S. National Science Foundation under Grants EEC-0954034 & EEC-0935143.

REFERENCES

1. Adamic, L.A., Zhang, J., Bakshy, E., and Ackerman, M.S. Knowledge sharing and yahoo answers: everyone knows something. In *Proc. WWW 2008* , ACM Press (2008), 665-674
2. Anderson, N. Elite education for the masses. *Washington Post*, November, 3, 2012.
3. Barab, S., & Kling, R. (2004). *Designing for virtual communities in the service of learning*. Cambridge University Press.
4. Burke, M., & Kraut, R. Mind your Ps and Qs: the impact of politeness and rudeness in online communities. In *Proceedings of the 2008 ACM conference on Computer supported cooperative work* (pp. 281-284). ACM.
5. Cheshire, C. Selective incentives and generalized information exchange. *Social Psychology Quarterly*, 70:82–100, 2007.
6. Cole, M. (1985). The Zone of Proximal Development-Where Culture and Cognition Create Each Other. In, Wertsch, J.V. (Ed.). *Culture, Communication and Cognition: Vygotskian Perspectives*. Cambridge University Press. pp. 146-161.
7. Cranshaw, J. and Kittur, A. The Polymath Project: Lessons from a successful online collaboration in mathematics. In *Proc. CHI 2011*, 1865–1874. ACM Press.
8. Crowston, K. and Howison, J. The Social Structure of Free and Open Source Software Development. *First Monday*, 10, 2, (2005).
9. Crowston, K., Li, Q., Wei, K., Eseryel, U. Y., and Howison, J. Self-organization of teams for free/libre open source software development. *Information & Software Technology*, 49, 6, (2007), 564-575.
10. Daniel, J. Making sense of MOOCs: Musings in a maze of myth, paradox and possibility. *Journal of Interactive Media in Education*, (2012) 3.

11. Dearman, D., & Truong, K. N. (2010). Why users of Yahoo!: answers do not answer questions. In *Proceedings of CHI* (pp. 329-332). ACM.
12. Gazan, R. (2011). Social Q&A. *JASIST*, 62(12), 2301-2312.
13. Gazan, R. (2006). Specialists and synthesists in a question answering community. *Proceedings of ASIST*, 43(1), 1-10.
14. Glance, D., Forsey, M. and Riley, M. The pedagogical foundations of massive open online courses. *First Monday*, Volume 18, Number 5 - 6 May 2013 |http://firstmonday.org/ojs/index.php/fm/article/view/4350/3673
15. Hanrahan, B. V., Convertino, G., & Nelson, L. (2012, February). Modeling problem difficulty and expertise in stackoverflow. In *Proceedings of CSCW* (pp. 91-94). ACM.
16. Harper, F. M., Raban, D., Rafaeli, S., & Konstan, J. A. (2008). Predictors of answer quality in online Q&A sites. In *Proceedings of CHI* (pp. 865-874). ACM.
17. Johri, A. & Teo, H. J. (2012). Assessing the Effectiveness of Open Innovation as a Model for Re-designing Design Learning. *International Journal of Engineering Education*, 28(2): 374-380.
18. Jurczyk, P., & Agichtein, E. (2007). Discovering authorities in question answer communities by using link analysis. In *Proceedings of CIKM* (pp. 919-922). ACM.
19. Kittur, A.,Chi, E. H., Pendleton, B. A., Suh, B. and Mytkowicz, T. Power of the few vs. wisdom of the crowd: Wikipedia and the rise of the bourgeoisie. *In Proc. CHI 2007*, ACM Press (2007).
20. Koh, J. Kim, Y.-G., Butler, B. and Bock, G.-w. Encouraging participation in virtual communities. *Communications of the ACM*, 50:69–73, 2007.
21. Kraut, R. E. & Resnick, P. (2012). *Building successful online communities: Evidence-based social design*. Cambridge, MA: MIT Press.
22. Lakhani, L. and von Hippel, E. How Open Source Software Works: "Free" User-to-User Assistance, *Research Policy* 32, 6, (2003), 923-943.
23. Lampe, C., Wash, R., Velasquez, A. and Ozkaya, E. Motivations to participate in online communities. In *Proc. CHI 2010*, 1927–1936. ACM Press.
24. Liu, Y., Bian, J., & Agichtein, E. (2008). Predicting information seeker satisfaction in community question answering. In *Proceedings of SIGIR* (pp. 483-490). ACM.
25. Mamykina, L., Manoim, B., Mittal, M., Hripcsak, G. and Hartmann, B. Design lessons from the fastest Q&A site in the West. In *Proc. CHI 2011*, 2857–2866. ACM Press.
26. McConnell, B., and J. Huba. 2006. *Citizen marketers: When people are the message*. Chicago: Kaplan.
27. Nam, K. K., Ackerman, M. S., & Adamic, L. A. (2009). Questions in, knowledge in?: a study of naver's question answering community. In *Proceedings of CHI* (pp. 779-788). ACM.
28. Pea, R. D. (2004). The social and technological dimensions of scaffolding and related theoretical concepts for learning, education, and human activity. *The journal of the learning sciences*, 13(3), 423-451.
29. Pal, A., & Konstan, J. A. (2010). Expert identification in community question answering: exploring question selection bias. In *Proceedings of CIKM* (pp. 1505-1508). ACM.
30. Pal, A., Farzan, R., Konstan, J. A., & Kraut, R. E. (2011). Early detection of potential experts in question answering communities. In *User Modeling, Adaption and Personalization* (pp. 231-242). Springer Berlin.
31. Posnett, D., Warburg, E., Devanbu, P., & Filkov, V. (2012). Mining Stack Exchange: Expertise is Evident From Initial Contributions. In *2012 ASE International Conference on Social Informatics*.
32. Roush, W. (2006). What's the best Q&A site? Technology review. Retrieved January 6, 2009, from http://www.technologyreview.com/communications/17932/?a=f
33. Shah, C., Oh, S., & Oh, J. S. (2009). Research agenda for social Q&A. *Library & Information Science Research*, 31(4), 205-209.
34. Singh, V., Twidale, M. and Rathi, D. Open Source Technical Support – A look at Peer Help Giving. In *Proc. HICSS 2006*, IEEE Press (2006).
35. Singh, V and Twidale, M.B. The Confusion of Crowds: non-dyadic help interactions. In Proc. *CSCW 2008, ACM Press (2008)*. 699-703.
36. Sowe, S.K., Stamelos, I. and Angelis, L. Understanding knowledge sharing activities in free/open source software projects: An empirical study. *Journal of Systems and Software*, (2007).
37. Treude, C., Barzilay, O., & Storey, M. A. (2011, May). How do programmers ask and answer questions on the web? In *Proceedings of ICSE* (pp. 804-807). IEEE.
38. Uduwage, A. & Konstan, J. (2012). The Answer Is Out There: Online Q&A Sites. *IEEE Computer*, July 2012, pp. 90-92.
39. Yang, J., Adamic, L. A., and Ackerman, M. S. Competing to share expertise: The taskCn knowledge sharing community. In *Proc. ICWSM 2008*, The AAAI Press (2008).
40. Yang, J. and Wei, X. Seeking and offering expertise across categories: A sustainable mechanism works for baidu knows. In *Proc. ICWSM 2009*, AAAI Press (2009).

How Social Q&A Sites are Changing Knowledge Sharing in Open Source Software Communities

Bogdan Vasilescu[1,2], **Alexander Serebrenik**[1], **Premkumar Devanbu**[2], **Vladimir Filkov**[2]

[1]Eindhoven University of Technology, The Netherlands, {b.n.vasilescu, a.serebrenik}@tue.nl

[2]University of California, Davis, USA, {devanbu, filkov}@cs.ucdavis.edu

ABSTRACT

Historically, mailing lists have been the preferred means for coordinating development and user support activities. With the emergence and popularity growth of social Q&A sites such as the StackExchange network (*e.g.*, StackOverflow), this is beginning to change. Such sites offer different socio-technical incentives to their participants than mailing lists do, *e.g.*, rich web environments to store and manage content collaboratively, or a place to showcase their knowledge and expertise more vividly to peers or potential recruiters. A key difference between StackExchange and mailing lists is gamification, *i.e.*, StackExchange participants compete to obtain reputation points and badges. In this paper, we use a case study of R (a widely-used tool for data analysis) to investigate how mailing list participation has evolved since the launch of StackExchange. Our main contribution is the assembly of a joint data set from the two sources, in which participants in both the `r-help` mailing list and StackExchange are identifiable. This permits their activities to be linked across the two resources and also over time. With this data set we found that user support activities show a strong shift away from `r-help`. In particular, mailing list experts are migrating to StackExchange, where their behaviour is different. First, participants active both on `r-help` and on StackExchange are more active than those who focus exclusively on only one of the two. Second, they provide faster answers on StackExchange than on `r-help`, suggesting they are motivated by the *gamified* environment. To our knowledge, our study is the first to directly chart the changes in behaviour of specific contributors as they migrate into gamified environments, and has important implications for knowledge management in software engineering.

Author Keywords

Crowdsourced knowledge; social Q&A; mailing lists; open source; gamification.

ACM Classification Keywords

H.5.3. [Information Interfaces and Presentation (e.g. HCI)]: Computer-supported cooperative work

CSCW'14, February 15–19, 2014, Baltimore, Maryland, USA.

ACM 978-1-4503-2540-0/14/02...$15.00.
http://dx.doi.org/10.1145/2531602.2531659

INTRODUCTION

Historically, mailing lists have been the preferred medium for coordinating development and user support activities [16, 31,32]. In particular, mailing lists have been viewed as the *de facto* communication medium between *knowledge seekers* (*e.g.*, users of the software asking for support) and *knowledge providers* (*e.g.*, other users, more knowledgeable about the topic, or the developers themselves) in models of knowledge sharing in open source [32]. The two categories of knowledge actors have been reported to co-exist in a symbiotic relationship, wherein "the community learns from its participants, and each individual learns from the community" [32]. However, their motivations for participation may differ. For instance, knowledge seekers may directly benefit from having their problems solved, while knowledge providers may be motivated intrinsically (*e.g.*, by altruism), or by learning about the problems experienced by other users [20, 32].

Recent years have witnessed the emergence and growing popularity of software-development-related social media sites, such as GitHub[1] (coding), Jira[2] (issue tracking), or the StackExchange network (question and answer websites, *e.g.*, StackOverflow for "professional and enthusiast programmers,"[3] or CrossValidated for "statisticians, data analysts, data miners and data visualization experts"[4]). Such sites are rapidly changing the ways in which developers collaborate, learn, and communicate among themselves and with their users [4, 8, 9, 30, 34]. Moreover, they are offering different socio-technical incentives to their participants, *e.g.*, rich Web 2.0 platforms to store and manage content collaboratively, or a place to showcase their knowledge and expertise more vividly to peers and potential recruiters [8]. In addition, StackExchange sites employ *gamification* [11] to engage users more: questions and answers are voted upon by the community; the number of votes is reflected in the poster's *reputation* and *badges*; exceeding various reputation thresholds grants access to additional features (*e.g.*, moderation rights on topics and posts); reputation and badges can also be seen as a measure of one's expertise by potential recruiters [8], and are known to motivate users to contribute more [1, 2, 10, 42]. Activity on StackExchange sites can also elevate one to celebrity status within the developer community (see, *e.g.*, the discussion around Jon Skeet[5], the most prolific contributor to StackOverflow).

[1]`https://github.com`

[2]`http://www.atlassian.com/software/jira`

[3]`http://stackoverflow.com`

[4]`http://stats.stackexchange.com/`

[5]`http://meta.stackoverflow.com/q/9134`

Naturally, the richer user interfaces, wider audiences, or different incentives and motivations for participation inherent in social Q&A sites are challenging the supremacy of mailing lists as the *de facto* communication medium between knowledge seekers and knowledge providers. For example, StackOverflow is known to provide good technical solutions [25] and to provide them fast [23]. At the same time, mailing list participants are signalling the need for more modern support,[6] and are even promoting a transition to StackExchange.[7] Our goal here is to study in detail the effects of such a transition on contributors and their work. Are mailing list participants transitioning to StackExchange? If so, do they behave differently on StackExchange than on the mailing list?

To study the phenomena associated with such a transition, we need a *longitudinal data set* combining mailing list and StackExchange activity, wherein participants overlap. In this paper we create such a data set for R [28], a popular data analysis software, by integrating mailing list activity and StackExchange activity (the latter under the `[r]` tag). Using this data set, we find that:

- activity on `r-help` (the main user support mailing list for R) has been consistently decreasing since around 2010 (*i.e.*, participants are asking fewer and fewer questions), while at the same time the number of R-related questions asked on the two main StackExchange sites for R (CrossValidated and StackOverflow) has been accelerating.
- participants in the two communities overlap, but different categories of `r-help` contributors are "attracted" differentially by StackExchange. For example, the proportion of mailing list users active on StackExchange is much higher among R developers than non-developers.
- the levels of activity for `r-help` participants who are also active on StackExchange differ relative to those who restrict themselves to either the mailing list or to StackExchange: those participating in *both* `r-help` and StackExchange are more active.
- knowledge providers active in both communities answer questions significantly faster on StackExchange than on `r-help`, and their total output increases after the transition to StackExchange.

Apart from uncovering interesting phenomena, these findings reveal that knowledge management in open source is changing, and that the different socio-technical incentives offered by Q&A sites such as StackOverflow enhance participation in these communities, facilitate user contributions and foster productivity. Therefore, our findings could inspire start-up open source or commercial projects looking to establish user support platforms, or stakeholders interested in knowledge management in general.

The rest of the paper is organised as follows. We first focus on the background underlying knowledge-sharing in open source and present our research questions. Then, we describe the data set and data gathering process, followed by our methods, results, and concluding sections.

[6] http://goo.gl/0i4j1n, http://goo.gl/6h8bMa

[7] http://goo.gl/aeoBJA http://goo.gl/OtzZT5

Background

The importance of user support for the adoption, growth, and success of open source projects is well-recognized [3,20,35]. Traditionally, user support was organised through mailing lists, forums, user groups, etc. However, as new venues of information and tools for information access emerge (*e.g.*, weblogs, wikis, social Q&A sites), people's online information seeking behaviour is also evolving [12,29]. When it comes to user support activities around open source software, though, what is common among both traditional and new venues of information is that this "mundane but necessary task" [20] is typically carried out by unpaid volunteers. Often, the developers themselves take part in these activities, but thriving open source projects also succeed in enlisting some of their users to offer assistance to peers. But what motivates knowledge providers to answer other people's questions? Together with online information seeking behaviours, these motives are also evolving.

In traditional information-sharing venues, *knowledge-providers* participate for reasons related to, albeit different, than those of *developers* contributing to open source. Developers contribute for reasons such as: a direct need for the software; enjoyment of the work itself; or the enhanced reputation arising from high-quality contributions [20]. Knowledge-providers, on the other hand, are reportedly motivated by: learning about problems other users are experiencing; an enhanced feeling of being part of a community; personal benefits of learning through teaching; an enhanced likelihood of receiving help in the future; or a sense of obligation from having received help from others in the past [20,24].

As social Q&A sites, *e.g.*, the StackExchange network, are becoming more popular, instances of what the economic literature calls "signalling incentives" start to better explain what motivates knowledge providers to help others [21], in addition to the previous reasons. Career concerns (*e.g.*, online activities in social Q&A sites are more visible to employers and recruiters, who may use them to find qualified people [8]), or a desire for peer recognition (*e.g.*, reputation building) are among the listed motives [20,21,24]. However, such signalling incentives may not be equally applicable to all knowledge providers. For example, we can expect that more knowledgeable providers would draw greater benefit from signalling, and thus signal more. Therefore, to obtain a more fine-grained understanding of the transition from traditional information venues to social Q&A, it is important to distinguish between different groups of participants (*e.g.*, developers, with likely more knowledge about the software, versus non-developers).

Another dimension of social Q&A participation incentives arises from *gamification*, *i.e.*, using elements of game design in non-game contexts [10, 11]. Gamification has been widely used in online platforms in recent years, where it was shown to motivate users to contribute more [1,2,10,42], and there are many psychological theories that can explain why [40]. The blueprint[8] that all current implementations of gamification (including all StackExchange sites) follow as-

[8] http://codingconduct.cc/Meaningful-Play

sumes stimulating users to perform a desirable activity by awarding them points. Specifically, users (i) are rewarded with points to encourage the desired behaviour (and may be subtracted points to sanction undesired behaviour); (ii) are awarded badges after collecting sufficiently many points or when performing certain activities; and (iii) have their progress tracked and their achievements displayed publicly in a leaderboard, to create competition between them. On StackExchange sites, the goal of "the game" is to have participants teaching and learning from each other[9] by asking relevant questions and providing helpful, well-documented and clear answers. Users receive reputation points when fellow users vote up their questions and answers. In turn, reputation points or directly generating *good* content translate to badges (*e.g.*, "Famous Question", if a question received 10,000 views, or "Legendary", if the user earned 200 reputation points daily 150 times). Top performing users in terms of their reputation count (either at week, month, quarter, year, or overall level) are displayed in public leaderboards. Exceeding various reputation thresholds grants users additional privileges on StackExchange sites, including at the higher end, the privilege to help moderate the site.

Therefore, coming back to our study of mailing lists, it seems that the different incentives, inherent to social Q&A sites, have the potential to "disrupt" mailing list activity and catalyze a transition to social Q&A, for knowledge seekers and knowledge providers alike. Seekers may turn to StackExchange expecting faster answers and a wider expert audience. Providers may transition to it to satisfy a rising demand for information, or pursuing signaling incentives and recognition. The latter is, for instance, supported by "alpha-male" behaviours self-reported by Apache help forum knowledge providers interviewed by Lakhani and von Hippel [20]: those wanting to be known as "the" expert in a particular aspect of Apache "would strive to answer all questions associated with their area" and seek to "drive out all other information providers from [that] chosen field of expertise". In the presence of gamification, such as on StackExchange sites, such behaviours may be even further accentuated. For example, StackOverflow is said to suffer from the *fastest gun in the West problem*:[10] to maximise their chances of collecting up-votes from their peers, participants would race to answer questions as quickly as possible, rather than as correctly or as exhaustively as possible. The said problem is based on the anecdotal belief that given two answers of comparable quality, it is the earliest that would typically receive the most votes, or that one might refrain from answering altogether if someone else already offered a similar solution.

Research Questions

In this paper, our goal is to analyze a mature and vibrant community where knowledge-transfer is transitioning from an older, mailing list modality to a new, social Q&A modality, and understand some of the effects of that transition. We chose the R software community.

[9] http://goo.gl/4kPzBP

[10] http://meta.stackoverflow.com/q/9731/182512

> **Research Question 1:** Can we find evidence in the R community for a decreasing popularity of the mailing list and an increasing popularity of StackExchange?

RQ1 Discussion. R [28], a popular data analysis software, makes for an interesting case study since there have been initiatives by members of its community to promote a transition to StackExchange.[11]However, to quantitatively assess this phenomenon, we first need to construct a historical data set combining mailing list and StackExchange activity for R, , and identify participant overlap (if any). Given such a data set, we can then evaluate activity in the two communities, and look for transition phenomena. To the best of our knowledge, we are the only ones creating and analysing such overlapping data sets between StackExchange and open source communities [38].

In addition to the potentially different motivations driving participants, other factors may influence these phenomena. The R mailing lists have been around since 1997, while StackOverflow, the first of the StackExchange sites, was only launched in 2008. The relative maturity of the former compared to the latter, as well as the direct contact with R developers, may mean that mailing lists are seen as well-established "educational institutions" by R users, *i.e.*, the default go-to place for requesting R support. Moreover, not all mailing list discussions are equally as well suited for StackExchange, hence not all are at risk of being subsumed. For example, StackExchange discourages questions that are too broad or primarily opinion-based.[12] Such questions may therefore only be suitable for the mailing lists. In other words, despite addressing some mailing lists limitations (*e.g.*, pertaining to user interface), StackExchange may not be a complete substitute.

On the other hand, R users asking questions on StackOverflow may be given answers referring to earlier posts from `r-help`.[13] This suggests that mailing lists may not be as well indexed by search engines (hence solutions posted there may not appear as high up in the results list), or that the mindset of users (asking directly on a StackExchange site) is altogether changing in disfavour of the mailing lists. In addition to the factors above, the two communities also show signs of symbiosis. For example, StackOverflow discussions are being followed by R developers and bug reporters, who use the feedback received from this community to stir up development discussions on `r-devel`,[14] the other main mailing list for R, dedicated to developers. The varying and synergistic activities of developers and knowledge-providers on mailing lists and Q&A sites suggest that some developers and knowledge-providers in R are splitting their time between the two, while others, perhaps, are not. Thus, R, a project with a knowledge-exchange in transition, includes some participants who stay with the old, some who are in transition, and some who go entirely with the new. It would

[11] http://goo.gl/aeoBJA http://goo.gl/OtzZT5

[12] http://meta.stackoverflow.com/a/10582

[13] http://stackoverflow.com/a/1996404 http://stackoverflow.com/a/4947528

[14] http://goo.gl/6UAUgr http://stackoverflow.com/a/1321491

be important to understand if this transition is in fact taking place, and to what degree. Community processes for answering user questions on-line are a vital component of the industry, and it is important to understand and promote this important process.

> **Research Question 2:** How do the contributors active both on the mailing list and on StackExchange differ from those focused on a single community (either of the two) in terms of their activity levels?

RQ2 Discussion. The different socio-technical incentives inherent in social Q&A (*e.g.*, related to user interface, potentially wider audiences, and gamification) may result in StackExchange becoming more attractive, *i.e.*, taking over (part of) the mailing list activity, and engaging (part of) the mailing list community. Previous studies (*e.g.*, [8]) argue that one's activity in social media can be used as a signal of qualifications and, similarly, one's reputation in social media as a signal of references from peers. Are there mailing list participants active also on StackExchange sites? Who are they and how do they differ (in terms of their activity levels) from other mailing list or StackExchange participants, who choose to focus solely on the mailing list or solely on StackExchange? Are developers more likely to be active both on `r-help` and on StackExchange (*i.e.*, to "signal" more) than non-developers?

> **Research Question 3:** For the contributors active both on the mailing list and on StackExchange, can we find differences in their behaviour in one community versus the other?

RQ3 Discussion. If StackExchange sites are attracting mailing list participants (*e.g.*, knowledge seekers looking for faster answers or a wider expert audience, or knowledge providers looking to satisfy a demand for knowledge, "signal" their "fitness" as experts, or engage in the game for reputation and badges), we should observe a decreasing trend in the mailing list activity concomitant with an increasing trend in StackExchange activity for those participants (especially knowledge providers) active on both. Moreover, gamification, one of the key differences between `r-help` and StackExchange sites, might influence `r-help` participants active on StackExchange to adopt a different behaviour on StackExchange [1, 2, 10, 42]. For example, in order to "survive" in the game for reputation and badges, they might have to provide faster answers than they do on the mailing list. Can we observe such a trend? Do participants active both on `r-help` and on StackExchange behave differently when on the mailing list than when on StackExchange sites? If answers are indeed quicker, and the speed is somewhat attributable to "game-playing", this might confirm that gamification is a useful adjunct in the design of Q&A fora.

RELATED WORK

Our work touches upon different fields of research. First, mail archives have been studied since as early as 2006 (see recent review by Squire [33]), *e.g.*, to understand knowledge sharing [32] and how users of the software get help [31]. Bettenburg *et al.* [5] identified challenges that arise when using off-the-shelf techniques for processing mailing list data. Singh *et al.* [31] and Guzzi *et al.* [16] qualitatively studied the types of discussions that occur in mailing lists, the types of questions asked and the types of responses that are given. For example, Singh *et al.* [31] reported that about 90% of the questions being asked in the online support forums of a number of open source projects are related to problem solving and information seeking, while the remaining can be classified as social discussions or feature requests.

Second, StackExchange (in particular StackOverflow) is receiving increasing attention from researchers, as witnessed by the growing number of papers using StackExchange data published each year,[15] as well as the yearly mining challenge of the International Working Conference on Mining Software Repositories (MSR) choosing StackOverflow as its topic in 2013. For example, Anderson *et al.* [1] investigated the dynamics of the StackOverflow community and found, *e.g.*, significant assortativity in the reputations of co-answerers, or relationships between reputation and answer speed. Vasilescu *et al.* [36, 37] studied the representativeness and activity of genders on StackOverflow compared to traditional mailing lists, and found StackOverflow to be a relatively "unhealthy" community, in which women disengage sooner although their activity levels are comparable to men's. Also related to the current topic is our previous study [38] of the interplay between StackOverflow Q&A activities and the development process, reflected by code changes committed to GitHub by developers also active on StackOverflow. There we found that the more prolific StackOverflow experts (*i.e.*, those providing the most answers) are also very active GitHub committers, and that in general participating in StackOverflow catalyses committing to GitHub.

Third, numerous studies focused on the motivations of participants in knowledge-sharing (online) communities. For example, Lin [22] analysed the effects of extrinsic and intrinsic factors in explaining the knowledge sharing intentions of a number of employees from fifty large organisations in Taiwan. Hendriks [17] proposed a theoretical model linking the variables and motivators involved with sharing knowledge using ICT. Sowe *et al.* [32] discussed the altruistic sharing of knowledge between participants in the Debian mailing lists. Deterding *et al.* [10] presented a number of views on how gamification impacts participation of users in online communities. Zhuolun *et al.* [42] studied the value of using badges in StackOverflow, and found that this reward system helps cultivate users' loyalty to the community.

Finally, R has been the object of two recent studies [13, 41]. German *et al.* [13] found differences in the growth rate as well as the way in which active contributors are attracted between user-contributed packages and core packages. Voulgaropoulou *et al.* [41] analysed the quality of 508 R packages and found, *e.g.*, that changes in social attributes such as the number of developers do not influence the code quality.

Source	Period	#messages #threads	#participants #unique	Multiple aliases
r-help	4/1997–	344,854	33,338	≃15%
	3/2013	97,125	28,096	
StackOverflow [r]	9/2008–	67,248	10,534	≃2%
	3/2013	24,957	10,284	
CrossValidated [r]	7/2010–	7,351	2,312	≃1%
	3/2013	3,208	2,285	

Table 1. Basic statistics for the two data sources.

METHODOLOGY

As case for our case study we selected R [28], a popular data analysis software, for several reasons: First, R is a typical example of an open-source software ecosystem, comprising a (relatively) closed *core of developers providing the basic functionality* and coordinating new releases, various developers *contributing patches and bug fixes*, numerous developers *contributing packages* (plugins) that extend the functionality beyond that provided with each release, and a *plethora of users*. Other examples of such ecosystems include the Eclipse IDE and its third-party plugins, or the Python/Ruby/LaTeX programming languages and their various contributed packages/gems. Second, R has been evolving for almost 20 years, and its entire history of mailing list communication is archived and publicly available. Third, R has been the recent subject of an extensive study of its evolution [13]. Fourth, R promises to provide broader relevance outside the software developers' community, as many users and contributors are data analysts from different domains such as economics or biology, with none or limited software engineering experience.

Data extraction. We integrated data from two different sources: the community behind the main R user support mailing list (`r-help`), and the StackExchange R subcommunities behind StackOverflow and CrossValidated, the StackExchange websites containing the most R-related (`[r]`-tagged) questions and answers.

`r-help` is the principal mailing list for user support in R. It hosts discussions about problems and solutions using R, as well as announcements about the availability of new functionality and documentation. Moreover, it mirrors announcements from `r-packages` on new or enhanced contributed packages, or major developments from `r-announce`. The other major mailing list for R is `r-devel`, targeting developers, testers and bug reporters, with topics that are considered "too technical" for `r-help`'s audience. The `r-help` archives can be downloaded in standard mbox format.[16] We wrote Python scripts to automatically download, extract, and parse the archives, which date as far back as April 1997.

For each `r-help` participant we recorded their role: (i) *core developer, i.e.*, the 22 developers with "write access to the R source" since its inception;[17] (ii) *peripheral developer, i.e.*, the 43 developers who "contributed by donating code, bug fixes and documentation";[17] (iii) *package author/maintainer, i.e.*, the 2617 developers maintaining or having authored packages on CRAN, the largest R package repository;[18] (iv) *user, i.e.*, those not fitting in any of the previous categories.

StackExchange is a network of Q&A sites started in 2008, now comprising more than 100 sites on different topics, such as English language, video gaming, photography, or parenting. All have similar look and feel, and function by the same principles: participants can ask and answer questions; questions are organised by tags (*e.g.*, `[r]` for R-related questions) and voted upon by members of the community, with votes translating to reputation points and badges; questions and answers can be edited and improved by other members with sufficiently high reputation; each participant has a dedicated profile page, combining the representation of oneself (self-determined, *e.g.*, name, location, or personal website) with activity-related information (automatically provided, *e.g.*, a list of the answers provided, the total reputation count, or a list of badges); users can subscribe to tags and receive email notifications when new questions are being asked (less practical for high-volume tags such as `[c#]`, `[java]`, or even `[r]`, the latter receiving around 500 questions per week at the time of writing), or simply browse the website.

StackExchange releases quarterly data dumps in XML format from all the websites under its umbrella. We explored the one dated March 2013,[19] using Python scripts to parse the XML archives. We restricted our analysis to StackOverflow (a generic programming Q&A site, and the first and largest StackExchange member) and CrossValidated (dedicated to statistics). This left out a number of other StackExchange websites where questions tagged `[r]` occasionally (*i.e.*, very infrequently) pop up, such as TeX or GIS, as well as all the activity on StackOverflow and CrossValidated which did not occur within the `[r]` tag. The oldest StackOverflow questions tagged `[r]` are dated September 2008. CrossValidated hosts `[r]`-tagged questions dating as far back as July 2010. The `[r]` activity on both websites mainly targets R users as opposed to R developers (hence the comparison to `r-help` is sound), although R developers may also follow it, as discussed in the introduction.

The organization of StackOverflow and CrossValidated in terms of questions, answers, tags, badges and reputation points is the same, with the only difference being the target audience, programmers in the former vs. data analysts in the latter. Therefore, we expect that differences between StackOverflow and CrossValidated should not affect data collection, analysis and interpretation. Table 1 lists some basic statistics about the data sources.

Identity merging. One of the biggest challenges when mining software repositories is *identity merging* [6, 14, 19, 39]. Both within a single repository (*e.g.*, mailing lists), as well as across repositories (*e.g.*, mailing lists and StackExchange), the same person may use different aliases, *i.e.*, different (*name, email*) tuples. For instance, *John Smith* may go by (*John Smith, johnsmith@gmail.com*), (*John, john@smith.com*), etc. The extent of the problem is unpredictable, *e.g.*, one of the Gnome developers reportedly used 168 different aliases in the source code repository [39].

[15] `http://meta.stackoverflow.com/q/134495`

[16] `http://www.r-project.org/mail.html`

[17] `http://www.r-project.org/contributors.html`

[18] Comprehensive R Archive Network `http://goo.gl/hHJROZ`

[19] `http://www.clearbits.net/torrents/2121-mar-2013`

A solution is to merge identities, and existing approaches are very diverse. For example, Bird *et al.* [6] try to match full names or email addresses shared by different aliases, and use heuristics to "guess" email prefixes based on combinations of name parts (*e.g.*, *jsmith* is likely to belong to *John Smith*). Kouters *et al.* [19] use Latent Semantic Analysis (LSA), a popular information retrieval technique, and report better results in presence of very noisy data. However, all existing approaches are known to produce false positives and false negatives [14]. We followed different approaches for `r-help` and for StackExchange.

StackExchange. The email addresses of the StackExchange participants are not publicly available for privacy reasons, but their MD5 hashed versions are offered instead. Since it is highly unlikely for two different email addresses to share an MD5 hash, we performed identity merging on the StackExchange data if two MD5 hashes coincided. This process resulted in a reduction in the number of participants of approximately 2% on StackOverflow and 1% on CrossValidated.

We decided to limit the identity merging *solely* to the case above due to the following reasons. First of all, on StackExchange as opposed to the mailing lists users have *accounts* and can log in using a password. This suggests that the incidence of multiple aliases (*i.e.*, accounts) by the same person should be much lower than on the mailing lists, where one is more likely to send an email, *e.g.*, from the account which is most at hand at any given time. While it is common for people to own multiple email accounts (*e.g.*, employer-related, open-source-related, private, etc.), we believe it to be less common for the same person to own multiple accounts on the same StackExchange site (at least because one cannot integrate the activity and reputation points earned using each). Moreover, since the email addresses are not publicly available, identity merging would rely solely on names, increasing the likelihood of false positives.

Mailing list. For `r-help` we performed a fixed-point computation: for each email address, we (i) collected all other email addresses having the same prefix (*e.g.*, for *john.smith@gmail.com* we collected *john.smith@hotmail.com*), as long as the prefix did not consist of a single word (*i.e.*, contained either a dot or an underscore character); and (ii) collected all the different names associated with it (*e.g.*, *John Smith* and *John* if both used the email address *john.smith@gmail.com*). Then, for each of these names we collected the different email addresses with which they were associated (*e.g.*, *John Smith* might be associated with both *john.smith@gmail.com* and *johnny@gmail.com*), and repeated the process until a fixed-point was reached. Checks for a minimal length of the email prefixes and names were used to limit the number of false positives. Applying this technique resulted in a reduction in the number of participants of approximately 15%. Among the users with the most aliases were, *e.g.*, an active participant with ten different emails under the same name, or one of the peripheral R developers with two email addresses and nine different variations of his name.

Intersecting the two data sets. A prerequisite for studying migration phenomena from the mailing lists to StackExchange was computing the overlap between the two communities. First, we made use of the fact that email addresses are available for the mailing list participants, as opposed to only MD5 hashes for the StackExchange users. As a result, we merged a mailing list user with one on StackExchange if the MD5 hash computed for any of the former's email addresses (there might have been multiple after identity merging on the mailing list) was identical to the MD5 email hash of the latter. Then, to expand the merges beyond only matching email addresses, we followed a fixed-point approach similar to the one described above, using names and email address prefixes (*e.g.*, *John Smith* from StackExchange with *John Smith* from `r-help`, despite the latter not having an email address that matches the former's MD5 hash). As a side effect, at this step two StackExchange users could have been merged to the same `r-help` individual, hence also among themselves (in addition to the merges using MD5 hashes discussed in the previous paragraph), if their MD5 hashes matched email addresses known to belong to this `r-help` individual.

Using this approach we found that approximately 15% (or 3,894) of the `r-help` unique participants (*i.e.*, after identity merging) have StackOverflow accounts, and 5% (or 1,159) have CrossValidated accounts.[20] These numbers are influenced by the difference in age between the two communities, since `r-help` started in 1997, while StackOverflow only in 2008 and CrossValidated in 2010: part of the overall mailing list population is not active anymore, as observed also for other open source projects [7]. The size of the overlap increases (*e.g.*, to slightly over 20% for StackOverflow) when considering only the `r-help` participants active starting with September 2008. Variations may also occur between different user groups (*e.g.*, knowledge seekers and knowledge providers). For example, the activity of open source contributors typically follows very skewed distributions [39], *i.e.*, most have very few contributions. Hence, it seems more likely that active knowledge providers would participate in StackExchange than one-time knowledge seekers.

Comparing apples and oranges. Our goals include understanding how the amount of activity differs between mailing lists and StackExchange, and whether mailing list participants are migrating to StackExchange. However, *activity* is organised in different ways in the two communities. On StackExchange users ask questions and typically receive several answers from other members of the community. Answerers "compete" with each other at offering good answers, as reflected by the up votes received from other members of the community. If a question was ill-formulated, *e.g.*, as signalled by other users through comments, the original poster has the option of editing and improving it any number of times. Similarly, if the answers were incomplete, the answerers or any other members of the community have the option of updating them. Questions may remain unanswered. Acknowledgements for answers that solve the original problem can be made by the original poster by *accepting* one answer using a dedicated button, and/or *posting comments* to the others (we do not consider comments). The standard structure

[20]Having a StackExchange account does not guarantee having engaged in Q&A there, hence a smaller fraction will have actually been *active* on StackExchange.

of a Q&A post is therefore *one question followed by zero or more answers, typically offered by different people.*

The equivalent communication structure on mailing lists is represented by *discussion threads*. The first new message with a particular topic (subject) is the one starting the thread (*i.e.*, the question). Similarly to StackExchange, it can remain unanswered, or it can receive responses identifiable as messages sent In-Reply-To the original message, or to other messages within the same discussion thread. However, as opposed to StackExchange, the original poster and the answerers can all appear multiple times within a thread.

Therefore, to avoid comparing apples to oranges when comparing activity on the two communication media, we (i) grouped related email messages into discussion threads, operation known as *threading*; and (ii) discounted multiple answers by the same person, and discounted the original poster as answerer within the same thread. Due to numerous caveats, threading is a non-trivial operation, typically taken lightly in the literature. We used a slightly modified version of Zawinski's algorithm[21] (based on Kuchling's Python implementation),[22] to the best of our knowledge the leading publicly-available threading algorithm. The number of distinct threads obtained for `r-help` is displayed in Table 1. For the StackExchange websites, the number of threads is the same as the number of questions, by definition.

User survey. To better understand the context of our research, related to changes in information seeking and information providing behaviours in the R community, we augmented the quantitative study with a user survey,[23] used to triangulate the quantitative findings. We asked the participants for: background information about their occupation, experience with R and involvement in the development of R (*e.g.*, as core developers, package maintainers, users); their information seeking behaviour (*e.g.*, how frequently they need information, where and how they search for it, how satisfactory what they find is, what their preferred information seeking medium is, and whether anything has changed in their seeking behaviour over the years); and their information providing behaviour (how often and by what means they share information with others, and what motivates them to do so). Survey participants were recruited by posting an ad about the questionnaire on various channels, such as `r-help`, the StackOverflow Meta (the site for meta-discussion of the StackExchange family of Q&A websites, where the maintainers of StackExchange also hang out), the StackOverflow R chat room, Google groups, other French, Russian or German fora, our own LinkedIn, Twitter, Google+ or Facebook profiles, or by contacting R developers directly.

RESULTS

Overall knowledge seeking activity. We start by analysing the activity on `r-help` (Figure 1). After an initial increase in the number of threads started (questions asked) each month, we observe drops in recent activity (since 2010). It is interesting to note that the 2010 inflection point is synchronised with initiatives to promote StackExchange among R users,[24] as illustrated by this excerpt from a blog entry:[25] "*Young experts don't want to have to monitor email all day to be part of the discussion. Their answers belong on a website with a normal content management system, with good search functions and user interactions. Go* [to StackExchange and] *sign up.*" On the other hand, `[r]` activity on StackExchange and in particular StackOverflow (Figure 1) grows at an increasing rate. The fraction of `[r]` questions relative to all questions grows linearly[26](*i.e.*, `[r]` gains popularity).

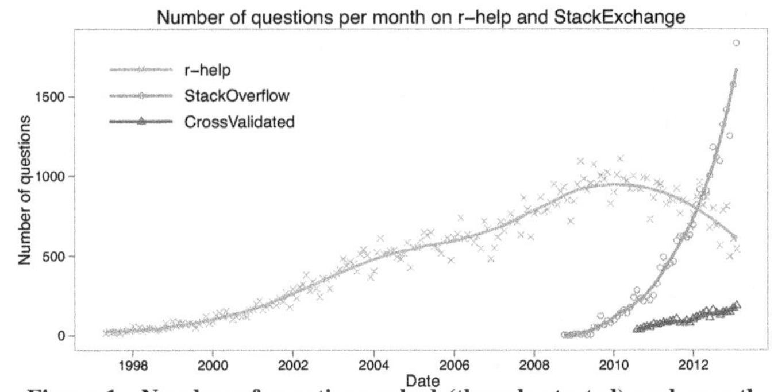

Figure 1. Number of questions asked (threads started) each month on `r-help` and StackExchange (StackOverflow and CrossValidated) in the `[r]`-tag. The trend curves are Loess curves with 0.5 span.

> **RQ1.** Knowledge seeking on `r-help` decreases sharply since around 2010. At the same time, the number of R-related questions asked on StackOverflow and CrossValidated grows at an increasing rate.

Structure of the community. Recall that we have distinguished between different roles within the `r-help` population. Here we wish to understand the knowledge seeking and knowledge providing activities of the different roles. Developers (mostly package authors/maintainers) are responsible for starting only a small fraction of the discussion threads (approximately one tenth in recent years), as depicted in Figure 2, top. Non-developers, the vast majority of question askers, are most responsible for the decreasing activity on `r-help` since 2010. The situation is reversed for thread answerers (Figure 2 bottom). The R core developers and the package authors/maintainers are responsible for most replies to threads started on `r-help`. However, since the decrease in new `r-help` threads started in 2010, the answering activity of developers (package authors/maintainers in particular) has also decreased the most. Both users and developers may be tempted by StackExchange, *e.g.*, one in search of better or faster answers, the other—of recognition.

Activity of contributors engaged in both communities. In this section we focus on those mailing list participants who were also *active* on StackExchange. To control for the difference in age between `r-help` (started in April 1997) and StackExchange (started by StackOverflow in September 2008), we only consider the mailing list participants starting

[21] `http://www.jwz.org/doc/threading.html`

[22] `https://github.com/akuchling/jwzthreading`

[23] `http://goo.gl/mZtz9X`

[24] `http://goo.gl/0i4j1n`, `http://goo.gl/jSZQFZ`

[25] `http://goo.gl/12nJxe`

[26] `http://goo.gl/gWKxbQ`

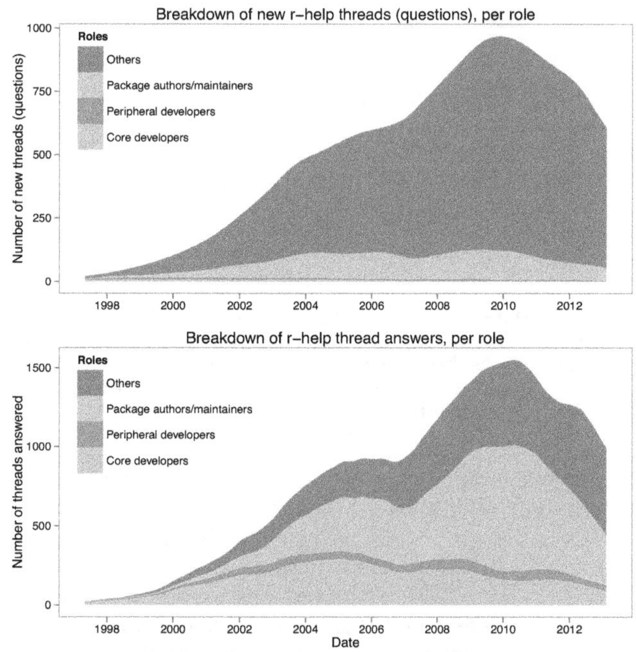

Figure 2. Breakdown of new threads (top) and thread answers (bottom) on `r-help` by initiator role. Only the *trend* component of each time series is displayed, after using a seasonal-trend decomposition procedure based on Loess. The top plot corresponds to Figure 1.

with September 2008. While we were able to link approximately 20% (from September 2008, or 15% overall) of the `r-help` participants with StackExchange accounts (either StackOverflow, CrossValidated, or both), we also observed that not all of them have actually engaged in `[r]`-tagged Q&A on the two StackExchange sites. Indeed, only 7.8% (or 1,293 out of 16,569) have asked or answered at least one `[r]`-tagged question on StackOverflow or CrossValidated.

Different population subgroups again exhibit different behaviour (Figure 3): the fraction of participants with StackExchange accounts is much higher among developers (core, peripheral, or package authors/maintainers) than non-developers (left); within those with StackExchange accounts, developers are also more likely to have been active (*i.e.*, to have engaged in Q&A) than non-developers (right). The groups of core and peripheral developers are too small to enable statistically significant comparisons (*e.g.*, we linked only 8 out the 18 core developers active on `r-help` since September 2008 with StackExchange accounts; out of these, only 5 asked or answered at least one question on StackExchange). However, when considering the core, peripheral, and package developers together, the differences in joining and contributing to StackExchange between developers and the users become statistically significant and the effect sizes practically significant (Table 2). For example, developers (183 active out of 331 with StackExchange accounts) have between a 1.34 and 1.66 times higher chance of being active on StackExchange than users (second row).

The more things you do, the more you can do. Actively contributing to both communities requires dividing one's time between them. Do mailing list participants contribute more or less to `r-help` if they are also active on Stack-

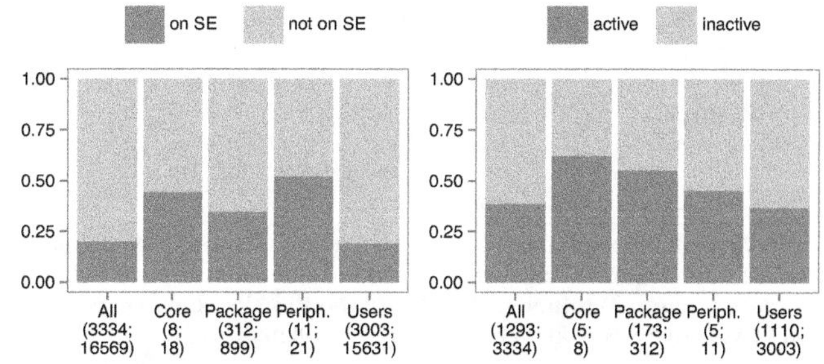

Figure 3. *Left:* Fraction of `r-help` participants (starting with September 2008) with StackExchange accounts, by role. *Right:* Among those with StackExchange accounts, the fraction that asked or answered at least one question. The absolute values are displayed under each label.

Outcome	Devs (D)	Users (U)	χ^2 (p-val)	D-U (CI)	RR (CI)
Have SE accounts	331/938 (35.28%)	3,003/15,631 (19.21%)	141.28 (<2.2E-16)	.16 (.13, .19)	1.83 (1.67, 2.01)
Active on SE	183/331 (55.3%)	1,110/3,003 (36.9%)	41.39 (1.2E-10)	.18 (.12, .24)	1.49 (1.34, 1.66)

Table 2. Results of statistical testing for the Figure 3 cases. D-U (CI): Estimate and 95% confidence intervals for the difference of proportions. RR (CI): Risk ratio by unconditional maximum likelihood estimation and 95% confidence intervals using normal approximation.

Exchange? To answer this question, we recorded for each `r-help` participant a flag indicating whether or not he or she was active on StackExchange in the `[r]` tag, the number of threads started and the number of threads answered on the mailing list. To control for differences in age, we again restricted the counts to posts after September 2008. Depending on their `r-help` activity types, three groups of participants emerged (Table 3): (i) those who only started threads; (ii) those who only replied to threads; and (iii) those who both started and replied to threads. For each group we compared the amount of activity (number of threads started for (i) and (iii), and number of threads answered for (ii) and (iii)) between those active and those inactive on StackExchange using the Wilcoxon-Mann-Whitney test (since activity is not normally distributed). In all cases, the results reveal that the mailing list participants who also contributed to StackExchange are more active than those who did not. For example, the median number of threads answered is 4 among those who ask and answer on `r-help` *and* engage on StackExchange, compared to 1 for the others.

Next we compared the StackExchange activity for `r-help` participants also active there to that of the rest of the StackExchange `[r]` community: which were more prolific? Similarly, we distinguished between exclusive askers, exclusive answerers, and users who both asked and answered questions (Table 4). Similar comparisons using Wilcoxon-Mann-Whitney tests show that among the StackExchange `[r]` population, those who also participate in `r-help` are more active. For example, the median number of `[r]` answers for those who ask and answer on StackExchange *and* contribute to the mailing list is 3, as opposed to just 1 for the others.

These results show that the most prominent mailing list participants "signal" the most both on the mailing list and on StackExchange. The group of users who participate in the R mailing lists *and* engage in `[r]` Q&A on StackExchange are the most active contributors relative to the other mail-

Activity on `r-help`\SE	No account or inactive (N)	WMW comparison (p-val)	Active (A)
Only ask	11,724	Asking: A>N (4.7E-14)	790
Only answer	1,413	Answering: A>N (4.2E-3)	123
Ask, answer	2,139	Asking: A>N (2.83E-8) Answering: A>N (<2.2E-16)	380
Total	15,276		1,293

Table 3. Activity comparisons for three groups of `r-help` participants also active on StackExchange relative to the other `r-help` participants (Wilcoxon-Mann-Whitney tests with Benjamini-Hochberg correction). StackExchange = StackOverflow + CrossValidated.

Activity on SE \ `r-help`	Inactive (N)	WMW comparison (p-val)	Active (A)
Only ask	5,464	Asking: A>N (5.25E-5)	794
Only answer	2,824	Answering: A>N (<2.2E-16)	338
Ask, answer	1,470	Asking: A>N (3.24E-12) Answering: A>N (<2.2E-16)	564
Total	9,758		1,696

Table 4. Activity comparisons for three groups of StackExchange contributors also active on `r-help` relative to the other StackExchange participants (Wilcoxon-Mann-Whitney tests with Benjamini-Hochberg correction). StackExchange = StackOverflow + CrossValidated.

ing list participants and, similarly, the most active contributors relative to the other StackExchange participants. This result is in line with a recent observation made by Posnett *et al.* [27] in their study of expertise on StackExchange: "*expertise is present from the beginning* [of one's participation], *and doesn't increase with time spent with the community. [...] In other words, experts join the community as experts, and provide good answers immediately.*" Assuming the number of answers one provides to be a proxy for their expertise, we showed, *e.g.*, that StackExchange experts (*i.e.*, heavy answerers) stem from mailing list experts. Recently we made a similar observation about GitHub developers active on StackOverflow [38]: those who provide the most answers are also those who perform the most commits.

> **RQ2.** The more things you do, the more you can do: Contributors to both communities (more likely developers than non-developers) are more active than those who focus on just one.

Behavioural differences. We compared the question answering activity on `r-help` for two groups of knowledge providers: those with (denoted "`r-help` and StackExchange") and those without (denoted "only `r-help`") StackExchange accounts (Figure 4). For each group we plotted the total number of answers given to `r-help` threads each month (denoted "On `r-help`"); for the "`r-help` and StackExchange" group, we also plotted the number of answers given to StackExchange questions each month (denoted "On StackExchange").

We draw the following observations. The inflection point (mid 2010) in the number of answers given to `r-help` threads by the "`r-help` and StackExchange" group coincides with the inflection point in general activity trend on `r-help`, depicted in Figure 1 top. This should not come as a surprise. In the previous sections we have seen that it is those mailing list participants that are also active on StackEx-

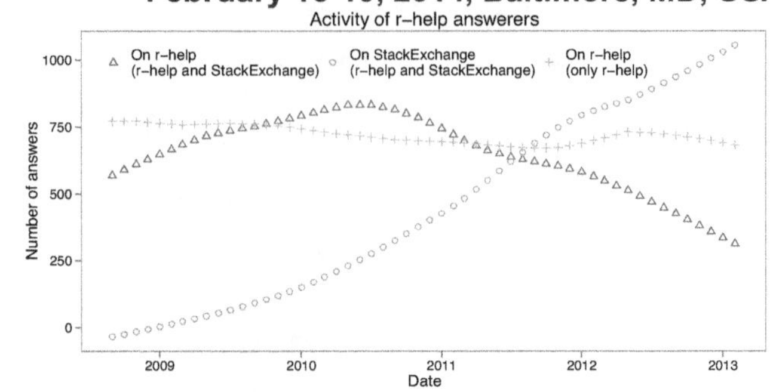

Figure 4. Number of questions answered on `r-help` (after September 2008) and StackExchange each month: participants exclusive to the mailing list versus those also active on StackExchange. Only the *trend* component of each time series is displayed, after using a seasonal-trend decomposition procedure based on Loess.

change that are most active, *i.e.*, the activity drivers or trend setters (both relative to the other mailing list participants as well as to the other StackExchange participants). Therefore, it is natural that they also exhibit a decreasing trend in activity since mid 2010. However, it is interesting to observe that the activity trend of the `r-help` knowledge providers without StackExchange accounts remains relatively constant (or decreases much slower). Corroborated with the increasing trend in answering activity on StackExchange by mailing list participants active on StackExchange, this suggests that R mailing list experts are migrating to StackExchange.

However, not all members of the "`r-help` and StackExchange" group exhibit similar patterns (Figure 5). For example, participant 3513 (topmost subfigure) *is* the norm: single-handedly responsible for approximately one fifth of the total number of answers, he exhibits a similar decreasing trend in activity as the entire group. In contrast, participant 9440 (second topmost subfigure) has migrated entirely to StackExchange in the second half of 2010. Participant 209 (second bottommost subfigure) has been active on both `r-help` and StackExchange ever since the beginning, albeit not as intensively on StackExchange; over the years he has become increasingly disinterested in `r-help`, without becoming more interested in StackExchange. Finally, participant 9859 (bottommost subfigure) is barely active on StackExchage, but is becoming increasingly more active on `r-help`.

Next we investigated whether there are significant differences between the speed with which `r-help` participants also active on StackExchange answer questions on `r-help` versus on StackExchange. If the incentives on StackExchange (*e.g.*, gamification, more attractive user interface) do not influence behaviour, then we should not observe any meaningful differences. If instead users are engaging in the race for reputation and badges, then they might try to answer more questions (we have already seen this in the previous section) as well as answer questions faster on StackExchange than on the mailing list, where they are not "rewarded" for their haste. To test this hypothesis, we compute for each member of the "`r-help` and StackExchange" group the time intervals between their first answer within a thread and the thread start (for all threads for which they provide answers), on the one hand, and between their first answer to a StackExchange question and the question date (for all questions they answer), on the other hand. Then, us-

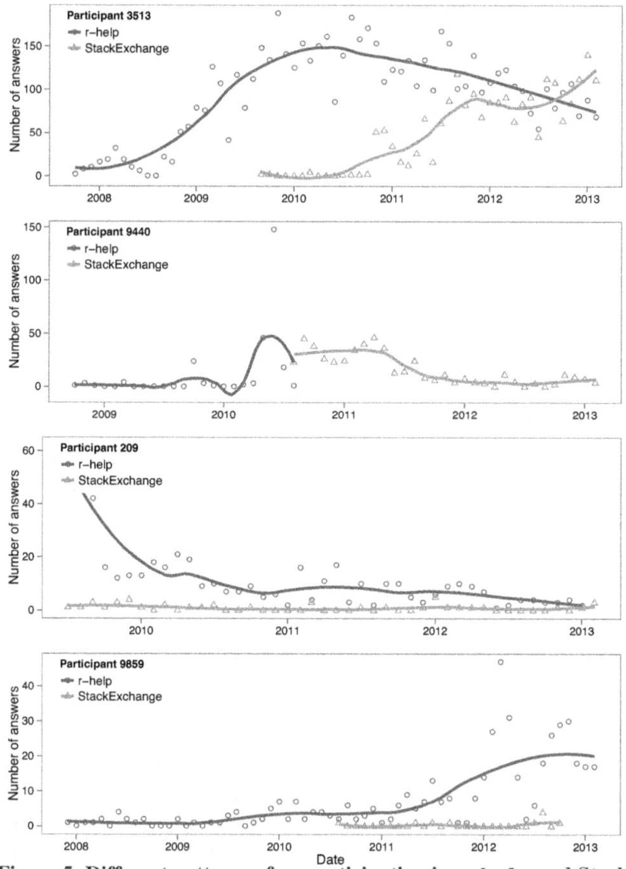

Figure 5. Different patterns of co-participation in `r-help` and StackExchange for knowledge providers (Loess curves with 0.5 span).

ing a Wilcoxon-Mann-Whitney test we compare two large groups of `r-help` and StackExchange time deltas obtained by concatenating the intervals for all "`r-help` and StackExchange" members (Figure 6).

Our results show that the StackExchange answers are significantly faster ($p < 2.2\text{E-}16$), with a median of 47 minutes versus 3 hours on `r-help`. This confirms that `r-help` participants behave differently when on StackExchange, where they are rewarded for their efforts more. To further put these results into context, note that on mailing lists a knowledge provider is *passively* (automatically) provided with opportunities to answer questions (by receiving emails with new questions directly, or in the form of a digest); on StackExchange, although subscribing to tags (to receive notifications of new questions) is possible, knowledge providers will frequently *actively* pursue new questions being asked by browsing the site,[27] and will rush to answer them.

> **RQ3.** Knowledge providers active both on `r-help` and on StackExchange (*i.e.*, the mailing list experts) are migrating to StackExchange, where they answer questions significantly faster than on the mailing list.

Triangulation

In this subsection we compare the quantitative findings with the user survey results. We received 115 responses. One respondent participated twice, and two respondents did not consent to participate in the survey, leaving 112 valid responses, mostly from academics (32% of the respondents), statisticians (35%), students (14%), and software engineers (6%). Most respondents described themselves as R users (51%), or authors or maintainers of R packages (35%). We also received two responses from the core developers. We stress that the survey was not intended for quantitative analysis; rather, it served to triangulate the earlier findings.

[27] `http://meta.stackoverflow.com/q/40927/182512`

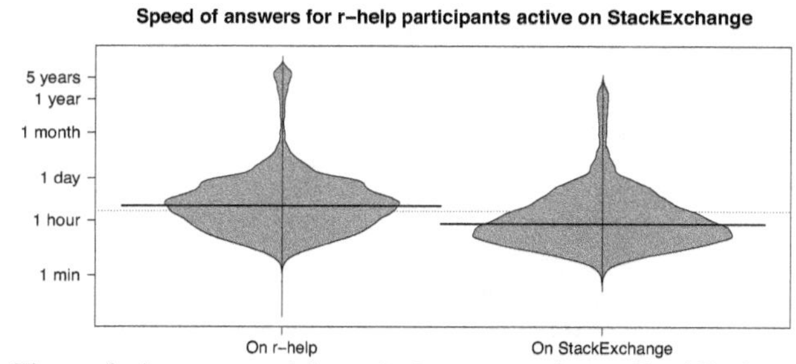

Figure 6. Answer speed for `r-help` users active on StackExchange. Beans: corresponding density shapes. Longer horizontal lines: medians per group. Dashed line: median over all groups.

Our first empirical finding was the evidence of a transition in seeking support from the mailing list to StackExchange: while activity on `r-help` decreases sharply since around 2010, the number of R-related questions asked on StackExchange grows at an increasing rate. In order not to impose our perception of transition on the survey participants, we opted for an open question, and asked whether the participants have experienced changes in their information seeking behaviour over the years. On the one hand, we observed that all survey participants reporting changes related to the mailing lists indicated disengagement, *e.g.*, "*Google is getting better at finding answers related to R so I use it more. I rely less on going directly to mailing lists now*" (user and documentation contributor, statistician/data analyst, 6 years of experience), or "`r-help` *used to be very helpful. But as the number of posts has gone up, I find that reading it is not as useful as it had been*" (package maintainer, academic, 8 years of experience). On the other hand, when the survey participants reported changes related to StackExchange sites, they are much more positive, *e.g.*, "*StackExchange has become more prevalent and more useful in the last two years*" (user, academic, 5 years of experience), or "*I started using RSeek.org, but currently I prefer stackoverflow.com, whose question database is increasing*" (user, statistician/data analyst, 6 years of experience). Still, these observations should be placed in the right context: more than half of the respondents are satisfied with the quality of the answers found in the mailing list archives, and more than a third will occasionally share their knowledge through mailing list discussions.

Our next empirical finding was that developers are more likely to be active on StackExchange than non-developers. To confirm it, we asked the survey participants what motivates them to contribute their knowledge. While numerous reasons such as reciprocity have been named both by the users and by the developers, developers are the only ones that mentioned StackExchange and gamification explicitly: "*In case of StackExchange, the reputation ratings are a nice little*

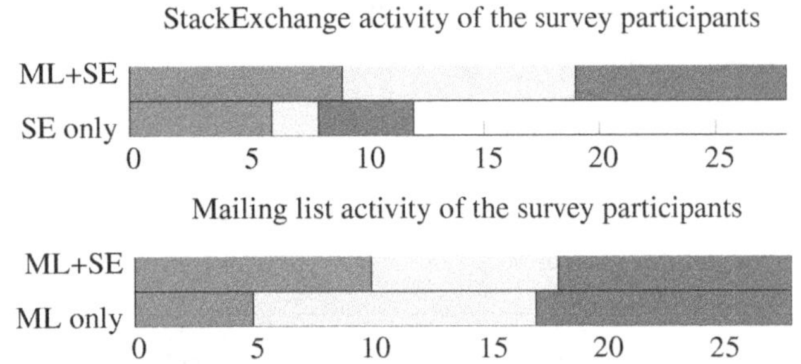

Figure 7. Number of survey participants frequently (green), occasionally (yellow) and rarely (red) sharing knowledge about R on StackExchange (SE) and mailing lists (ML).

incentive," (academic, package maintainer, 6 years of experience), or "[I am motivated by] *peer recognition/gamification within StackOverflow*" (academic, contributes to documentation, submits bugs, 5 years of experience). Moreover, developers put more stress on being motivated by the desire to enhance one's own reputation ("*wanting to be seen as a relative expert in some sub-domain*"; academic, contributes to documentation, submits bugs, 5 years of experience) and on evangelisation ("*I like to promote R because I think it's a great tool to learn about the principles of statistics and programming*"; academic, submits bugs, 4 years of experience). We believe that StackExchange is a better platform for these goals than mailing lists, since StackExchange quantifies one's reputation and makes it visible to everyone (see previous discussion of the gamification blueprint), as opposed to the mailing lists lacking commonly agreed upon and readily accessible representations of reputation. Moreover, StackExchange is a multi-topic community, hence better suited to evangelisation than "preaching to the choir" on a mailing list.

The empirical study also showed that contributors active both on the mailing list and on StackExchange are more active than those focused on only one of the two. To triangulate this finding, we asked the survey participants how often they share information about R by replying to threads on R mailing lists, and by answering questions on StackExchange. Figure 7 shows that survey participants active in both communities are more actively participating in the mailing list discussions than those active only on the mailing lists, *i.e.*, it supports the findings of the empirical study. A similar observation can be made for the StackExchange activity, although disparity between the numbers of survey respondents active only on StackExchange (12) and active in both communities (28) hinders interpretation in this case.

Finally, in the empirical study we observed that knowledge providers active both on `r-help` and on StackExchange (*i.e.*, the mailing list experts) are migrating to StackExchange and are answering questions faster there than on the mailing list. To confirm, we revisited the survey questions about changes in information seeking behaviour and motivations for sharing knowledge. Half of the survey participants reporting changes related to the mailing lists explicitly indicated their transition to StackExchange websites, *e.g.*, due to an easier user interface, a friendlier community, or the sites being better indexed by the search engines. In addition, although not explicitly commenting on the speed with which they provide answers, respondents who contribute their knowledge to StackExchange acknowledged gamification (*i.e.*, reputation building) as important, *e.g.*, "[I am motivated to answer questions on StackExchange because] *it's a game, which also serves a good purpose*" (academic, package maintainer, contributes to documentation, submits bugs, 6 years of experience). Not everyone is attracted by the StackExchange incentives, though. R users might still prefer to offer support via the mailing lists, *e.g.*, "*mailing lists are very nice to read and to reply to, due to their text-only policy*" (academic, package maintainer, 11 years of experience).

IMPLICATIONS

In this section we review the implications of our study for Q&A sites design, knowledge communities and future research.

Implications of our work for *Q&A site designers* are twofold. First of all, we have observed that the movement to social, gamified Q&A is correlated with an increase in the engagement of knowledge providers, and the rapidity of response. This finding suggests that *Q&A site designers* should consider gamification elements to increase engagement of the participants, and, indirectly, popularity of their sites. Second, we have seen that users and developers exhibit different behaviour (*e.g.*, developers are more likely to be active on StackExchange). This means that the Q&A site designers should cater for different groups of community members (*e.g.*, developers and users) having different needs and expectations, by providing different knowledge sharing channels involving different participation and reward mechanisms. This is also why we do not believe that `r-help` will eventually die off, as StackOverflow and `r-help` users have explained: "*If you have a problem and you are* completely stuck, *ask a question on the mailing list*"[28] and "*Although many people there [StackOverflow] gave very detailed answers, I have the feeling that there is much more wisdom on the subject that is still only available in this mailing list*".[29]

For *knowledge communities* our findings suggest that a move to gamified social Q&A can be a beneficial strategy when searching for a better visibility and contributors' activity. We believe that gamification may be of particular interest in closed environments, such as commercial corporations, where knowledge is proprietary, and the set of potentially knowledge providers is closed. Furthermore, the aforementioned distinction between different groups of community members, and different knowledge sharing channels required, suggests that knowledge communities might prefer to combine different knowledge channels.

Finally, our findings provide new insights for *researchers* of collaborative software engineering. While there is a significant body of work on why gamification features should positively influence participation in knowledge communities, facilitate user contributions and foster productivity, our study adds concrete evidence that gamification features or community design affect productivity of the contributors.

[28] `http://stackoverflow.com/a/3382477`

[29] `http://goo.gl/CoJIyp`

THREATS TO VALIDITY

Despite our detailed efforts in experimental design, data gathering and data analysis, we do note several threats to the validity of our methodology and conclusions. The core step in the data gathering, extracting information from the StackExchange data dump and the mail archives, is subject to threats to validity akin to those identified for digital trace data [15, 18]. Following the classification of Howison [18], *system and practice issues* in our work may be related to communication through other mailing lists than `r-help` and other StackExchange sites than StackOverflow and CrossValidated. Indeed, advanced R packages such as `lme4` have separate mailing lists,[30] and experts working with these packages might prefer not to migrate to StackExchange. However, `r-help`, StackOverflow and CrossValidated are the biggest platforms of their kind. We also knowingly omitted other venues where knowledge exchange happens, *e.g.*, Google+ groups or individual blogs. Our results are very strong, and give us confidence that StackExchange is a good representative of the missing Q&A communities.

Moreover, the data extracted is subject to potential *reliability* threats arising from missing messages from mail archives, and questions and answers being deleted from StackExchange. Indeed, as indicated by one of the survey participants, StackExchange sites encourage the participants "*to ask well-formed questions, leading to well-formed answers*", while ill-formed questions are being removed. Question or answer removal might lead to underestimating the activity of the StackExchange contributors, as well as the overlap between StackExchange and `r-help`. Similarly, removal of StackExchange accounts might lead to underestimation of the overlap. Another reliability threat is related to multiple system representations of a single individual, which again might incur an underestimate of the overlap between StackExchange and `r-help`. We have explicitly addressed this threat when discussing identity merging in the methodology section: while no data gathering is perfect, our efforts are particularly detailed, and have been shown elsewhere to work satisfactorily. Finally, reliability might be threatened by noise in the data, such as spam messages stored in the mail archives.

The next group of threats to validity refers to *representation of the data extracted in the model* of one question followed by multiple answers. While the distinction and relation between questions and answers on StackExchange is explicit in the data organisation, the natural counterpart in the mailing lists is the discussion thread (see "Comparing apples and oranges" in the methodology section). Recognition of the discussion thread starter as the asker, and other thread participants as answerers can, however, be threatened by the thread starter posting an announcement rather than a question, as well as by thread participants trying to clarify the intention of the thread starter rather than answering her questions. We have performed an informal evaluation of the discussion threads in `r-help` and observed that the lion's share of threads adhere to the "question and answers" model similar to StackExchange.

[30] `http://goo.gl/ofUT3L`

Temporal aggregation threats arise when aggregating events that occur at different points in time (cf. Figures 1 and 4). Indeed, inappropriate choice of the time granularity might have made our work subject to ecological fallacy [26]. However, our choice for month as the basic time unit stems from the way traditional mail archives are presented (per month) as well as the literature.

CONCLUSIONS

Using an *aligned, longitudinal* data set which connects the same people over time in different knowledge-transfer venues, we have been able to examine the phenomena associated with the transition to StackExchange from the mailing lists.

Future research directions would involve designing and setting up follow-up interviews with R developers and users to address the causality of user migration between different mailing lists and StackExchange: which incentives such as more modern user interface, potentially wider audiences, and gamification are perceived as most important for different subgroups within the R community? Understanding causality could result in quantitative predictive models of user behaviour in the presence of various incentives.

ACKNOWLEDGEMENTS

We thank the anonymous reviewers for their numerous remarks that helped us improve the paper significantly. Vasilescu gratefully acknowledges support from the Dutch Science Foundation (NWO) through the project NWO 600.065.120.10N235. Filkov gratefully acknowledges support from the US Air Force Office of Scientific Research through the project FA955-11-1-0246. Devanbu gratefully acknowledges support from the NSF, grants CISE SHF MEDIUM #0964703 and CISE SHF EAGER #1247088. Part of this research has been carried out during Vasilescu's visit at the University of California, Davis, USA.

REFERENCES

1. Anderson, A., Huttenlocher, D. P., Kleinberg, J. M., and Leskovec, J. Discovering value from community activity on focused question answering sites: a case study of Stack Overflow. In *Proc. KDD*, ACM (2012), 850–858.
2. Antin, J., and Churchill, E. F. Badges in Social Media: A Social Psychological Perspective. In *Proc. CHI*, ACM (2011).
3. Bagozzi, R. P., and Dholakia, U. M. Open source software user communities: A study of participation in Linux user groups. *Management Science 52*, 7 (2006), 1099–1115.
4. Begel, A., Bosch, J., and Storey, M.-A. Social networking meets software development: Perspectives from GitHub, MSDN, Stack Exchange, and TopCoder. *IEEE Software 30*, 1 (2013), 52–66.
5. Bettenburg, N., Shihab, E., and Hassan, A. E. An empirical study on the risks of using off-the-shelf techniques for processing mailing list data. In *Proc. ICSM*, IEEE (2009), 539–542.
6. Bird, C., Gourley, A., Devanbu, P. T., Gertz, M., and Swaminathan, A. Mining email social networks. In *Proc. MSR*, ACM (2006), 137–143.
7. Bird, C., Gourley, A., Devanbu, P. T., Swaminathan, A., and Hsu, G. Open borders? Immigration in open source projects. In *Proc. MSR*, IEEE (2007), 6.
8. Capiluppi, A., Serebrenik, A., and Singer, L. Assessing technical candidates on the social web. *IEEE Software 30*, 1 (2013), 45–51.
9. Dabbish, L. A., Stuart, H. C., Tsay, J., and Herbsleb, J. D. Social coding in GitHub: transparency and collaboration in an open software repository. In *Proc. CSCW*, ACM (2012), 1277–1286.

10. Deterding, S. Gamification: designing for motivation. *Interactions 19*, 4 (2012), 14–17.
11. Deterding, S., Sicart, M., Nacke, L., O'Hara, K., and Dixon, D. Gamification: Using game-design elements in non-gaming contexts. In *Proc. CHI*, ACM (2011), 2425–2428.
12. Gentle, A. *Conversation and Community: The Social Web for Documentation*. XML Press, 2009.
13. German, D. M., Adams, B., and Hassan, A. E. The evolution of the R software ecosystem. In *Proc. CSMR*, IEEE (2013).
14. Goeminne, M., and Mens, T. A comparison of identity merge algorithms for software repositories. *Science of Computer Programming* (2011).
15. Goggins, S., Mascaro, C., and Valetto, G. Group informatics: A methodological approach and ontology for understanding socio-technical groups. *JASIST 64*, 3 (2013), 516–539.
16. Guzzi, A., Bacchelli, A., Lanza, M., Pinzger, M., and van Deursen, A. Communication in open source software development mailing lists. In *Proc. MSR*, IEEE (2013), 277–286.
17. Hendriks, P. Why share knowledge? The influence of ICT on the motivation for knowledge sharing. *Knowledge and Process Management 6*, 2 (1999), 91–100.
18. Howison, J., Crowston, K., and Wiggins, A. Validity issues in the use of social network analysis with digital trace data. *Journal of the Association for Information Systems 12* (2011).
19. Kouters, E., Vasilescu, B., Serebrenik, A., and van den Brand, M. G. J. Who's who in Gnome: Using LSA to merge software repository identities. In *Proc. ICSM*, IEEE (2012), 592–595.
20. Lakhani, K. R., and von Hippel, E. How open source software works: "free" user-to-user assistance. *Research Policy 32*, 6 (2003), 923–943.
21. Lee, S., Moisa, N., and Weiss, M. Open source as a signalling device - an economic analysis. Working Paper Series: Finance and Accounting 102, Department of Finance, Goethe University Frankfurt am Main, 2003.
22. Lin, H.-F. Effects of extrinsic and intrinsic motivation on employee knowledge sharing intentions. *J. Information Science 33*, 2 (2007), 135–149.
23. Mamykina, L., Manoim, B., Mittal, M., Hripcsak, G., and Hartmann, B. Design lessons from the fastest Q&A site in the west. In *Proc. CHI*, ACM (2011), 2857–2866.
24. Oram, A. Why do people write free documentation? Results of a survey. `http://www.onlamp.com/lpt/a/7062`, 2007.
25. Parnin, C., Treude, C., Grammel, L., and Storey, M.-A. Crowd documentation: Exploring the coverage and the dynamics of API discussions on Stack Overflow. Tech. rep., Georgia Institute of Technology, 2012.
26. Posnett, D., Filkov, V., and Devanbu, P. T. Ecological inference in empirical software engineering. In *ASE* (2011), 362–371.
27. Posnett, D., Warburg, E., Devanbu, P., and Filkov, V. Mining Stack Exchange: Expertise is evident from earliest interactions. In *Proc. ASE SocialInformatics*, IEEE (2012), 199–204.
28. R Development Core Team. *R: A Language and Environment for Statistical Computing*. R Foundation for Statistical Computing, Vienna, Austria, 2010.
29. Shah, C., Oh, S., and Oh, J. S. Research agenda for social Q&A. *Library & Information Science Research 31*, 4 (2009), 205–209.
30. Singer, L., Filho, F., Cleary, B., Treude, C., Storey, M., and Schneider, K. Mutual assessment in the social programmer ecosystem: An empirical investigation of developer profile aggregators. In *Proc. CSCW*, ACM (2013).
31. Singh, V., Twidale, M. B., and Nichols, D. M. Users of open source software - How do they get help? In *Proc. HICSS*, IEEE (2009), 1–10.
32. Sowe, S. K., Stamelos, I., and Angelis, L. Understanding knowledge sharing activities in free/open source software projects: An empirical study. *JSS 81*, 3 (2008), 431–446.
33. Squire, M. How the floss research community uses email archives. *IJOSSP 4*, 1 (2012), 37–59.
34. Storey, M.-A. D., Treude, C., van Deursen, A., and Cheng, L.-T. The impact of social media on software engineering practices and tools. In *Proc. FoSER*, ACM (2010), 359–364.
35. Swisher, J. Open source user assistance: Ensuring that everybody wins. *Open Source Business Resource* (2010).
36. Vasilescu, B., Capiluppi, A., and Serebrenik, A. Gender, representation and online participation: A quantitative study of StackOverflow. In *Proc. ASE SocialInformatics*, IEEE (2012), 332–338.
37. Vasilescu, B., Capiluppi, A., and Serebrenik, A. Gender, representation and online participation: A quantitative study. *Interacting with Computers* (2013), 1–24.
38. Vasilescu, B., Filkov, V., and Serebrenik, A. StackOverflow and GitHub: Associations between software development and crowdsourced knowledge. In *Proc. ASE SocialCom*, IEEE (2013), 188–195.
39. Vasilescu, B., Serebrenik, A., Goeminne, M., and Mens, T. On the variation and specialisation of workload–A case study of the Gnome ecosystem community. *Empirical Software Engineering* (2013), 1–54.
40. Vassileva, J. Motivating participation in social computing applications: a user modeling perspective. *User Modeling and User-Adapted Interaction 22*, 1-2 (2012), 177–201.
41. Voulgaropoulou, S., Spanos, G., and Angelis, L. Analyzing measurements of the R statistical open source software. In *Proc. SEW*, IEEE (2012), 1–10.
42. Zhuolun, L., Huang, K.-W., and Cavusoglu, H. Can we gamify voluntary contributions to online Q&A communities? Quantifying the impact of badges on user engagement. In *Proc. WISE* (2012).

Collaborative Problem Solving: A Study of MathOverflow

Yla R. Tausczik
Human-Computer Interaction Institute
Carnegie Mellon University
ylataus@cs.cmu.edu

Aniket Kittur
Human-Computer Interaction Institute
Carnegie Mellon University
nkittur@cs.cmu.edu

Robert E. Kraut
Human-Computer Interaction Institute
Carnegie Mellon University
robert.kraut@cmu.edu

ABSTRACT
The Internet has the potential to accelerate scientific problem solving by engaging a global pool of contributors. Existing approaches focus on broadcasting problems to many independent solvers. We investigate whether other approaches may be advantageous by examining a community for mathematical problem solving – MathOverflow -- in which contributors communicate and collaborate to solve new mathematical "micro-problems" online. We contribute a simple taxonomy of collaborative acts derived from a process-level examination of collaborations and a quantitative analysis relating collaborative acts to solution quality. Our results indicate a diversity of ways in which mathematicians are reaching a solution, including by iteratively advancing a solution. A better understanding of such collaborative strategies can inform the design of tools to support distributed collaboration on complex problems.

Author Keywords
Problem solving; scientific collaboration; crowdsourcing; Q&A sites

ACM Classification Keywords
H.5.3. Information Interfaces and Presentation: Group and Organizational Interfaces.

INTRODUCTION
The Internet has enabled scientific problem solving on a global scale, where individuals can contribute their expertise to solve challenging problems in domains ranging from finding a red balloon [38] to software engineering [25] to R&D [16]. Increasing our collective ability to tackle such problems could significantly impact progress in science, technology, and innovation. Many approaches, such as Innocentive, the Climate Collaboratorium, or TopCoder, focus on broadcasting a scientific problem to many contributors under the assumption that at least one may have a valuable solution. In such systems the "solvers" are generally individuals or small teams who work independently [16,25].

However, despite the large number of "open call" approaches to scientific problem solving online, examples of deeply interactive and collaborative problem solving on the internet remain few and far between. Notable exceptions in which contributors communicate with and build on each others' work include the Polymath Projects and MathOverflow, in which anyone with an internet connection can be involved in the collaborative solution to an unsolved mathematics problem. Such collaborative problem solving approaches raise challenges when involving many contributors, including reaching a shared understanding of the problem, which itself may be ill-defined, decomposing an interdependent problem into subproblems, and coordinating the efforts of many contributors, each with varied expertise and commitment levels. Previous work has begun to characterize such collaborative problem solving communities, describing the leadership structure and showing that even peripheral contributors make meaningful contributions [6]. In this paper we contribute a detailed process-level understanding of the collaborative activities that happen in one such community, MathOverflow, and quantify the effects of different collaborative activities on solution quality. Our results have implications for systems aimed at supporting large-scale, collaborative scientific problem solving.

RELATED WORK
Collaboration in science is becoming even more important, and our ability to tackle scientific questions may be aided by online systems to improve and open up scientific problem solving. We know from the literature on small group problem solving and peer-production that carefully designing and structuring interactions is important to elicit good work. Yet, it is not clear how to structure interactions for the specific domain of scientific problems. Below we describe this related work and why it motivates our process-level examination of MathOverflow.

Scientific Collaboration
Studies of global patterns of scientific collaboration have shown that science is increasingly being driven by collaboration [7, 43], with more multi-authored grants and papers being published more [14] with more successful outcomes than single-authored papers: they are cited more often and are published in more prestigious journals [31, 41]. However, these studies have focused on global patterns of

CSCW '14, February 15–19, 2014, Baltimore, Maryland, USA.

ACM 978-1-4503-2540-0/14/02$15.00.
http://dx.doi.org/10.1145/2531602.2531690

collaboration in science, such as who collaborates with whom, and have not investigated the mechanics of the collaboration process -- e.g., how scientists jointly pose questions, develop ideas, and refine solutions.

Another branch of social studies of sciences have examined the cognitive processes that take place among scientists working together. For example, Dunbar and colleagues identified the use of analogy as an important cognitive process in developing hypotheses in a new experimental domain [11]. However, these studies typically focus on the practices in a single lab or a few labs and are limited to explicit discussions between scientists rather than following the entire trajectory of an idea (e.g., [26]).

Finally a third branch of studies has questioned the degree of true collaboration in science. They find that scientific collaboration often involves large multi-institutional collaborations, in which there is little communication and coordination [9]. Institutional barriers and reward structures impede the ability for true large-scale collaboration even when co-authoring papers, or sharing data or equipment [9]. Entrenched status hierarchies and competition among individuals for recognition create non-collaborative environments in which being helpful and making small contributions without acknowledgement as an author is costly [2]. Even physical distance can present a barrier to traditional forms of collaboration [29]. Current scientific collaboration may only make use of limited forms of collaboration that in particular don't scale.

Small-Group Problem Solving

The costs and inefficiencies of communicating in small groups highlight the importance of structuring collaboration and assistive technology. Early work on small group decision-making found discussions to be fraught with unexpected inefficiencies and biases [19]. Despite expected gains from multiple-perspectives and unique expertise, experiments in which information was distributed among group members showed that groups spent the majority of time discussing common knowledge rather than unique knowledge [36]. Structuring the group's interaction, for example by making individual's area of knowledge known, has been shown to reduce some of the inefficiency [37]. The medium through which a group communicates can also reduce inefficiencies; using computer-mediated communication has been shown to keep students' problem-solving discussions more task-focused [18].

Collaborative Sensemaking, Peer-production, and Crowdsourcing

Peer production and crowdsourcing have emerged as powerful mechanisms for sharing information (e.g. Usenet [42], StackOverflow [27]), building rich artifacts (e.g. open-source software [10], Wikipedia [20]), and accomplishing complex tasks (e.g. CrowdForge [22]) by facilitating collaboration among many individuals [5]. These systems highlight the importance of structuring collaboration to reduce the costs of coordination [20], focus discussion [23], and represent knowledge in ways that facilitate making inferences [34]. Below we focus on two strategies that are most relevant to collaborative problem-solving on MathOverflow: broadcasting difficult problems to a large audience of potential experts and dividing work into sub-problems to involve a large number of people while keeping coordination costs low.

Platforms such as Innocentive, TopCoder provide good models of broadcasting difficult problems to a large crowd [16, 25, 24]. These systems work by running competitions among individuals or small teams to solve complex, difficult problems. They have been very successful at solving difficult problems quickly by reaching individuals who have the insight or unrealized expertise to solve the problem. However, these systems primarily focus on a broadcast model with little communication or coordination between individuals or small teams of individuals.

Another strategy focuses on decomposing a problem into subtasks that can be assigned to different workers. Crowdsourcing systems such as CrowdForge, Soylent, and Turkomatic, make use of a crowd of novices to do complex tasks by breaking them into sub-tasks and using workflows to handle dependencies between tasks [22, 3, 24]. These implementations have successfully enabled novices to do complex tasks that require interdependence, like writing an article, but are challenging for more complex unsolved problems in which the problem may be underspecified, there is no clear way to go about solving the problem, and partial answers may be incorrect, incomplete, and not on a path to a final solution.

Polymath and MathOverflow

Mathematicians have started to make use of user-generated content platforms to build large-scale collaborations to solve research-level mathematics problems. The Polymath Projects began as an attempt by Timothy Gowers, a senior mathematician at Cambridge University, to create massively collaborative mathematics [6]. During the Polymath 1 Project a new proof to an important theorem, was solved in 155 involved blog posts made by a total of 39 unique users [6]. On MathOverflow (mathoverflow.net), an online community of mathematicians, members solve small novel mathematical problems or "micro-problems". By micro-problems we mean relatively small problems which may not themselves qualify as publishable results, but are nonetheless novel to the mathematicians involved, enriching the participants' own knowledge and work practices and occasionally contributing to published research.

While past research has described these projects and attempted to evaluate whether everyone really makes meaningful contributions [6,39,40] no one has yet examined contributions to these collaborations at a process-level. In this paper we develop a deeper, process-level understanding of collaboration by examining individual contributions to

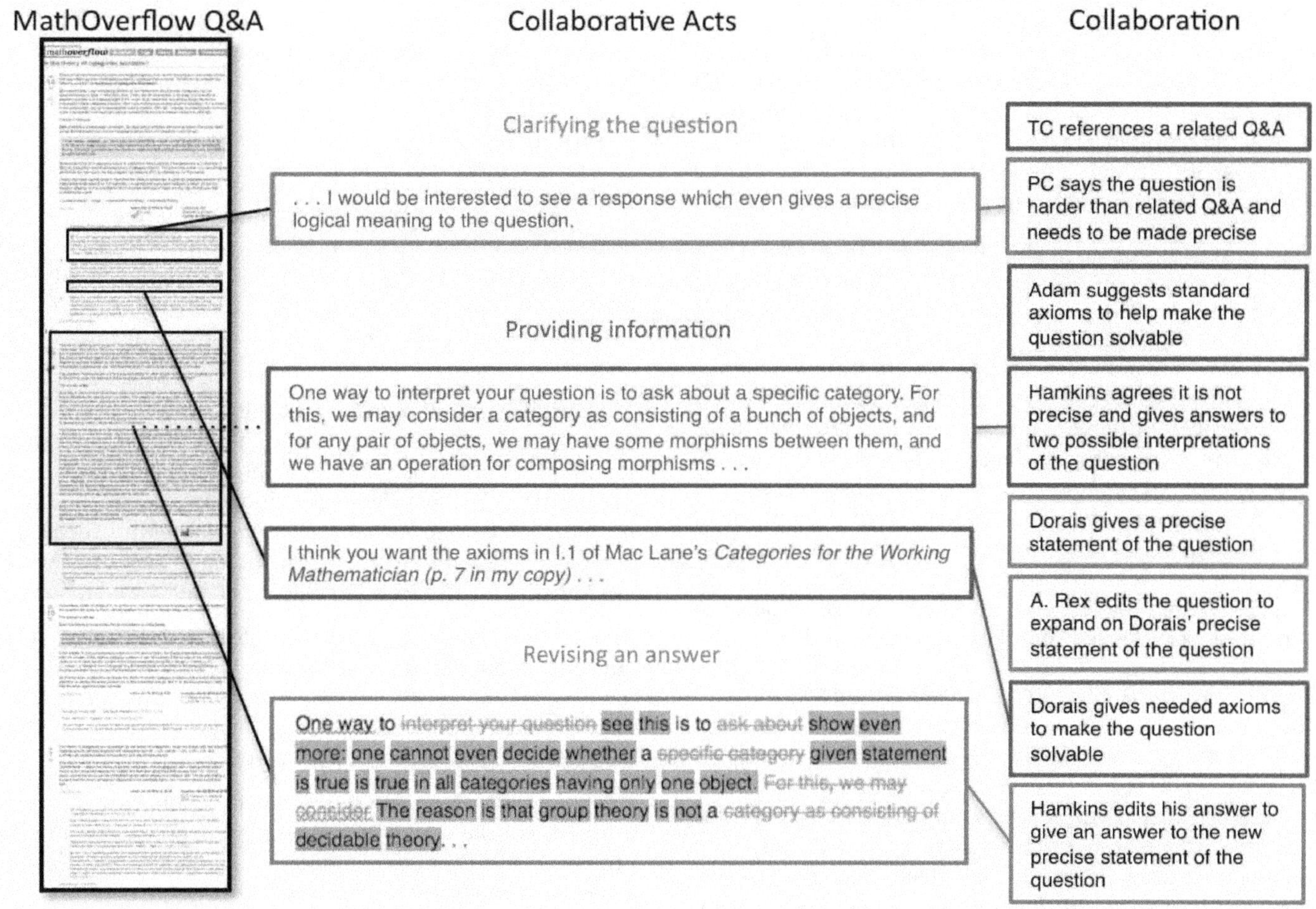

Figure 1: MO question "Is the theory of categories decidable?" The left column shows the entire MO Q&A (comments are threaded within the question and answers). The middle column shows a few examples of collaborative acts (excerpts). The right column shows a description of early contributions in chronological order and shows how a collaboration unfolds.

solving a problem on MathOverflow. MathOverflow provides rich archival data to survey many examples of distributed collaborative problem solving in practice.

STUDY OVERVIEW

As discussed above, while large-scale collaborative scientific problem solving has significant potential, little research has to date examined the low-level mechanisms by which collaboration takes place and their impact on the resulting quality of the solution. In the studies below we begin to build up our understanding of online collaborative problem solving at a process level, and investigate the impact of those processes on solution quality. In Study 1 we use a grounded theory approach on a sample of MathOverflow questions to build up a taxonomy of "collaborative acts" which describe the collaboration processes involved. We leverage structured interviews with active participants in the collaborations to provide insights on how the collaborative acts fit together and lead to the development of a final solution. In Study 2 we use this taxonomy and insight from interviews to quantify the impact of collaboration processes on resulting solution quality. Finally, we discuss implications of our results for the design of large-scale collaborative problem solving systems.

RESEARCH SITE

MathOverflow (MO) is a mathematical question and answer site started in September of 2009. Contributors ask and answer research level mathematics questions through an implementation of the StackExchange platform (stackexchange.com). MO is primarily an academic community [40] and is viewed as a professional outlet for mathematics research.

MO provides a number of advantages that make it an ideal platform for examining collaborative problem solving. (1) The problems require higher order cognition to solve. Many prior studies of collaborative problem solving are artificial in the sense they examine the process by which groups go about solving well-defined problems with pre-defined solutions, such as insight problems or constraint satisfaction problems [18]. However, many real-world problems that are done collaboratively such as scientific discovery, design, or innovation are difficult and ill-defined. (2) Because all the communication in MO is text-based and archived, it preserves the record of the collaboration practices used by ad hoc groups, practices which are often invisible in studying other types of collaborations. MO shares this quality with other recent online collaborations such as the Polymath Projects [6]. However, MO has further benefit lacking in these other collaborations (3) MO of hosting scores of groups and providing many data points.

As of September, 2011 there were 22,531 questions posed on MO. The questions on MO are very different from other Q&A sites. The intention of the site is for researchers to ask and answer small, novel problems that arise in doing mathematics research. Thus, questions are difficult enough that they require original work, but not so difficult that they are unsolvable. Successful questions on MO are small steps in the process of building a larger mathematical contribution. For example, a MO Q&A might represent one section of a mathematical publication. Despite being small problems, most of the problems are difficult and only experts in the field can solve them. At the time of the writing of this paper 66 published journal article or preprints acknowledged contributions made on MO.

STUDY 1: IDENTIFYING COLLABORATIVE ACTS

How does collaborative problem solving occur on MathOverflow? And what strategies are most successful? There are a number of possibilities, ranging on a spectrum of interdependence to independent. At one end of the spectrum there is a somewhat romantic view of collaborative problem solving in which there is a special connection between collaborators and ideas emerge from deep conversations. This view would suggest a highly interactive and interdependent process of collaboration on MathOverflow.

On the other end of the spectrum, MathOverflow might succeed because it is a good platform for broadcasting a problem to a large enough crowd of people where at least one person with appropriate expertise can solve the problem by him or herself. Indeed, its structure as a Q&A site (based on the StackOverflow Q&A system) might suggest exactly this: users submit independent answers to questions, with more popular answers receiving upvotes.

To understand global patterns of collaboration on a problem, in Study 1, we first examine each contribution to a problem individually. We categorize contributions into what we call types of collaborative acts, or a single contribution contributing to a larger collaboration. For example, a collaborative act might be providing a critique of an answer, in which the larger collaboration is made up of many answers, critiques, and revisions. We find that features supporting meta-commenting (i.e., commenting on others' answers, or even on the question itself) provide an avenue for more interactive collaboration. Indeed, as we will discuss below, such features support a rich and varied methods of collaborating. By leveraging interviews with the most active members of the site we provide context to understand the collaborative acts we identified as well as uncovering ways that the acts may lead to better answers.

Background

Collaboration on MO begins with a question. For example, in Figure 1, A. Rex asked the question "Is the theory of categories decidable?" which he explained in a few paragraphs (MO question 12732). His question was a broad big-picture question. In order to be addressed it required an exploration and elaboration of the relevant mathematical concepts.

The original question was ambiguous and too broad in scope. Early respondents, in trying to provide information to solve the problem, pointed to problems with phrasing. For example, PC, a professor, mentions in a comment: *"it is not obvious how to formalize this decidability statement"* and says *"I would be interested to see a response which even gives a precise logical meaning to the question."*

Joel David Hamkins, another professor, reiterated PC's concerns in the first proposed solution. *"I believe that there are several reasonable interpretations, totally different in nature"*. He then outlines two interpretations of the question and provides solutions to both interpretations.

Next, the problem began to take shape. Following attempts at clarifying the question, François G. Dorais a professor, provided what was being requested. He wrote *"Maybe I'm misreading the question, but it made perfect sense to me."* He then gave a precise logical statement of the question. The original question asker A. Rex in a major edit to the question expanded on this new understanding of the problem. At this point, although the problem was finally taking shape, it was still not clear that this was the right way to think about the problem.

Hamkins and Dorais then grappled with whether this was the best understanding of the problem as they worked to solve it. Hamkins wrote *"@Dorais: Yes, I think this must be the best way to think about it"* and then connected the new understanding of the problem to part of his original solution. Dorais then countered *"@[Hamkins]: I don't think it's that easy"*. The back-and-forth continued and eventually Hamkins and Dorais simultaneously posted solutions that were conceptually equivalent.

Although, Hamkins and Dorais posted solutions that answered the general case of the problem, they were unable to answer the more specific case asked by A. Rex. The specific case required different mathematical machinery in an area in which neither was an expert. A day later this specific case was filled in by Bjorn Poonen, a professor with more expertise in that area. At the beginning of his answer he wrote *"This answer builds on those of F. G. Dorais and Joel David Hamkins to answer your 'specific question', the question left open by them"*. Finally, the problem was fully solved.

By the end, 9 users made contributions, with substantial solutions from 3 users, Hamkins, Dorais and Poonen. We will return to this example later. We analyzed a random sample of 150 MO collaborations similar to this one to conduct our study.

Methods

Open Coding

Because there is little systematic and comprehensive research on the mechanisms by which collaborative problem solving takes place, a bottom-up approach was taken to fully explore the possible ways that individuals collaborate. To begin we focused on the most basic element of collaboration, a single contribution, which we call ***a collaborative act***. Collaborative acts were identified using an open coding by multiple coders. A deeper understanding of the collaborative acts was developed by conducting semi-structured interviews.

A grounded theory approach was used to identify collaborative acts inductively [13]. 150 collaborations on MO, which encompassed 737 contributions, were studied in detail by four independent judges.

Question-answer posts were randomly selected from the publicly accessible database dump generated September 2011. These posts were screened to ensure they met the inclusion criteria. Those questions that were critiqued by community members as too easy (e.g. closed, redirected to a lower level site), related to the discipline of mathematics but not a mathematics problem (e.g. career advice, questions about teaching math), or requests for known information (e.g. reference request, or a request for what is known in an area) were excluded. This left research level questions that were about a specific problem. The first 150 that met the criteria were selected for the final coding.

Four coders (including the first author) coded the contributions. Each coder had undergraduate level mathematics expertise. Two of the raters had or were working on a B.A. in mathematics and had taken upper division undergraduate coursework in mathematics. Two of the raters were M.A. level engineering students and had taken lower division undergraduate coursework in mathematics. Each contribution was coded by at least 3 raters. Every comment, answer, or edit was considered as a potential contribution to a collaboration. In total there were 737 contributions. Coders viewed each contribution individually and in the order they had been published on MO using a specially designed website.

During open-coding many sub-categories were identified, such as providing a complete answer (e.g. proof), supporting the previous contribution, and changing the focus of the question. In later phases of coding these subcategories were grouped into larger categories and a questionnaire was developed to help code contributions. Classification into concrete sub-categories was used as a technique to guide the creation of more abstract categories to describe collaborative acts, and to reinforce category definitions to ensure inter-rater reliability was high. Using this questionnaire the coders rated whether the contribution:

1. *provided information* ("Does this contribution provide new information that contributes or could contribute to a solution, whether or not correct*?")*

2. *clarified the question* ("Does this contribution modify the original question or ask that it is clarified?")

3. *critiqued an answer*("Does this contribution evaluate, ask for clarification?")

4. *revised an answer* ("Does this contribution improve on, or answer a related question about all or part a previous contribution?")

5. *extended an answer* ("Does this contribution contribute a new answer that incorporates previous ideas?")

For each question about the contribution the coders rated the question on a 5 point Likert scale from 0 to 4 labeled as 'Not at all' to 'Extensively', as well as indicating the category subtype if applicable (e.g. "It provides a complete answer (e.g. proof)". Collaborative acts were rated on a 5-point scale to assess the magnitude of the contribution for use later in quantitative analyses. There was significant variation in the magnitude of contributions; for example, one contribution might provide a useful definition while another might provide a complete proof, these were rated as 1 and 4 respectively on a 5-point scale. In the questionnaire, critiquing and revising an answer were grouped together; in the final analyses they were separated using subcategory ratings as it became apparent that the two represented distinct types of contributions.

Semi-structured Interviews

The first author also conducted semi-structured interviews with active MO contributors to better understand the collaborative acts, the role they played in the collaborations, and how they contributed to the development of a final solutions. Thirty-five of the most active users from MO who had listed an email address or a website with an email address on their MO profile page were contacted by email. All of these community members had made at least 350 contributions. Of those contacted 22 agreed to be interviewed, and 16 were eventually interviewed. The most active contributors were contacted because they have the most familiarity with the site and have been exposed to a variety of different collaborations.

The interviewees were all male; they were current Ph.D. students or graduates (n = 6 interviewees), postdoctoral fellows (n = 1), or professors (n = 9) in mathematics. Interviewees were asked a series of questions, including to briefly explain why they contributed to MO, to discuss the kinds of collaboration that they had observed on MO, and about specific contributions from their personal collaborations on MO. The interviews were conducted by phone or skype call with at minimum audio (n = 9); instant messenger (n = 2); or email (n = 5). The interviews by phone and skype were recorded and transcribed (M = 42 min); the interviews by instant messenger (M = 1,803 words) and email (M = 980 words) were saved.

The interviewer presented interviewees with examples of contributions from Q&A collaborations that the interviewees had participated in. Interviewees were sometimes the author of the selected contribution and sometimes peripherally involved. Interviewees were asked to explain in detail the process by which the question was solved and how the specific contribution fit into the final solution. Transcripts of the interviews were divided into sections based on the type of collaborative act represented by the specific contribution and quotes were pulled from the transcripts to illustrate different ways interviewees described the collaborative act and how it fit into the larger search for a solution.

Results

Collaborations on MO questions were small to moderate in size (1 to 14 distinct contributors per question, M = 4.23, Mdn = 4). However, many more users viewed a question than contributed (42 to 2,993 views, M = 384, Mdn = 298.5). Almost all questions received some contributions (0 to 39 comments, answers, and edits, M = 9.51, Mdn = 7). This work usually resulted in at least one answer (0 to 8 answers, M = 1.68 answers, Mdn = 1). Only 5 out of 150 questions in the corpus received no answers.

Five categories of contributions emerged; evidence from coding confirmed that the identified collaborative acts form a good taxonomy. Independent raters were able to reliably identify the collaboration acts. Intraclass correlations were calculated as a measure of inter-rater agreement among the 3 raters; agreement was moderate to high (see Table 1). This suggests that the collaboration acts represent real and detectable ways in which individuals are working together.

The collaborative acts were common enough to describe the important ways in which individuals contribute. Each type of collaborative act identified was present in at least 20% of question-answers examined and at most 91% of question-answers (see Table 1). While the collaborative acts are conceptually distinct, representing unique categories developed during open-coding, in practice they often co-occurred in solving the same problem. All of the collaborative acts were highly correlated with providing information ($r(148) = 0.44 - 0.69$, $p < 0.001$). Controlling for the relationship between information and collaboration, critiquing an answer was correlated with revising an answer and clarifying the question (*partial* $r(147) = 0.39$, $p < 0.001$; *partial* $r(147) = 0.20$, $p = 0.01$); and extending an answer was correlated with revising an answer and clarifying the question (*partial* $r(147) = 0.20$, $p = 0.02$; *partial* $r(147) = -0.30$, $p = 0.001$).

Collaborative Acts	Inter-rater agreement (ICC)	Frequency
Providing information	0.887	91.3%
Clarifying the question	0.817	38.0%
Critiquing an answer	0.829	45.3%
Revising an answer	0.733	42.7%
Extending an answer	0.651	22.0%

Table 1: Collaborative acts, building blocks of collaborations, and the percent of the 150 Q&A collaborations in which they are present.

Semi-structured interviews with frequent contributors provided confirmation that the collaborative acts identified by non-participants were sensible to active participants as well as a deeper understanding of when and how the collaborative acts contributed to a final solution. Below we describe the identified collaborative acts with descriptions from interviews and examples from the dataset to provide context.

Providing Information: was the most common type of contribution; 91.3% of questions received a contribution that provided information. Providing information can mean providing a complete solution to the problem. Interviewee 14 wrote *"Usually, I participate in MO as an individual, reading and then answering a question completely by myself."* However, often provided information was not a solution in itself but background information that was useful for understanding the problem and needed for the solution. For example, in response to the question "Is the theory of categories decidable?" discussed above, many users provided information about the definitions needed to understand the problem. Adam described a common way of defining the axioms that were needed to clarify and solve the problem. His comment received 2 votes indicating others thought is was important. Dorais later cited a reference giving specific axioms that could be used, he wrote *"I think you want the axioms in I.1 of Mac Lane's Categories for the Working Mathematician (p. 7 in my copy)."*

Clarifying the Question: There were a few different reasons the users clarified the question. Understanding the problem was often a necessary step before the problem could be solved. Many interviewers stressed the importance of having a precise statement of the problem. Some questions on MO have mistakes, do not provide enough information, or are vague. Interviewee 2, a graduate student, mentioned that *"a fairly common thing is that people will ask a question but will word it in such a way that it is completely not clear what they want. And then at the best the comments and requests for clarification really are kind of 'I'd like to answer your question I don't know what your question is. Here is one possible question. Is this it?'"*

At other times, a question may have been clear but it not the question that the question asker meant to ask or should have asked. Interviewee 3, a professor, mentioned that *"often times when people ask questions they are not even really sure of what question they want to ask"*. The asker may have needed help clarifying the question because he or she did not have enough expertise to frame the question in the right way. The interviewee described a case where *"the literal answer to the question [the question-asker] asked [was] not nearly as interesting as a nearby question, so [the interviewee and others] sort of pushed him toward that question and [the interviewee and others] tried to explain why that other question was really the one he had lurking in his mind even though it [was] not what he actually asked."* There were often multiple ways to phrase or describe a problem. Coming up with the right way of thinking about it early on helped make it solvable. Clarifying the question draws on community members expertise to fill in gaps left by the question asker. The asker may have needed additional information in order to ask the "right" question. Even after a question was clarified, there may have been a period of uncertainty and refinement, until a new understanding of the problem led to a solution.

Critiquing an Answer: Solutions were evaluated by the larger community on MO. Corrections, critiques and comments about an answer filtered out bad solutions. Critiques also helped guide the original answerer to improve his or her solution. Answers were critiqued when others believed the solution or partial solution was incorrect or could have been improved. In many cases this led to a much better solution when the problems were addressed. Interviewee 6, a professor, described a situation in which he had edited his answer. He said *"I was getting into this question partially to learn the material ... I looked up some references and learned some more. Based on the comments I hadn't really learned the specific material that well, so my first answer was not that great so I revised it to make it better. Draft 1 was a B minus paper I got some comments and the second draft was an A minus paper so that was better. ... my first answer was sloppy and it needed to be rewritten."* In this case, he acknowledged that his first solution was not very good. However, without being critiqued, he would not have known that his solution needed more work.

In other cases, the corrections may not have corrected the substantive nature of the solution. For example, Interviewee 2, a graduate student, submitted an answer that included some mistaken assumptions about a theorem, someone pointed out the mistake and he fixed his answer by being less specific. About the changes Interviewee 2 wrote *"rather than trying to fix the details of my answer I basically decided to give what amounts to the same answer at the conceptual level"*. In this case, the errors in his answer were not central to the argument he was making. Even though minor critiques like this one did not challenge the main substance of the solution, they were important in preventing incorrect statements. In the classification scheme critiques to an answer were distinguished from revisions of an answer and extensions of an answer, by limiting it to contributions that pointed out errors or suggested ways to improve an answer without making these improvements or modifications themselves (e.g. suggesting a way to close a hole in a proof without actually carrying out the steps to fix the proof).

Revising an answer: Critiques of an answer often led to substantive revisions of an answer. As we mentioned above, Interviewee 6 described how his answer progressed from a B minus paper to an A minus paper because of substantial revisions, which were inspired by critiques of his original answer. Multiple revisions were common on MO. Interview 3 described an answer to one of his questions. He said *"I remember that [MO user's answer] maybe changed the most. I think [MO user] had maybe some incorrect answers at the beginning . . . I think that the first version was problematic. Or something like that. Later versions were useful."* Through revisions a more valuable solution emerged. In the classification scheme revising an answer was distinguished from extending an answer by limiting it to answers that corrected an existing answer rather than took an answer in a new direction (e.g. revising an answer to close a hole in a proof as opposed to taking a related but different approach to reach a new proof).

Extending an Answer: Sometimes a final solution emerged from the ideas of multiple users, each with his own insights. Interviewee 13, a professor, describes this type of collaboration as an idealized prototype in which *"one person might suggest a refinement of a definition, or suggest a vague idea which is subsequently given legs by another researcher,"* and later described an instance of this collaboration. He and another user had submitted similar answers, then a third person extended their answer *"[third person]'s answer came later, as I recall, and extends the same idea to give a more striking instance of the phenomenon. I think that his answer builds on the idea we used, but required his insight to see it through."* In this example, the question could not have been solved without the insights of multiple users. This is similar to Poonen's role in the collaboration surrounding the question "Is the theory of categories decidable?" Using his expertise, he was able to solve the original question posed by A. Rex, after Hamkins and Dorais had worked out a slightly different (and less specialized) case. The final solution was a combination of work by all three.

Extending an answer also occurred when users added to an answer by providing insight from another perspective. This insight was not needed to solve the problem, but it made the solution better by elaborating on the idea. Interviewee 12, a professor, described why he sometimes adds to a solution, *"one thing that happens a reasonable amount is me reading an answer, saying 'Hmm, that's not wrong, but not how I would have put it either.' and writing an answer which tries to put what I think is a better spin on things."* Compared to revising an answer extending an answer added substantive content the Q&A collaboration that was considered to be a significant portion or a complete answer in itself.

Summary

Collaboration was diverse and fell on the spectrum between independent and interdependent generation of answers. Providing information was the most common collaborative act. However users also made a variety of other kinds of contributions that built on existing work including clarifying the question, critiquing answers, revising answers and extending answers.

Contributions often built on existing work by revising or extending answers; we will refer to these contributions as *secondary, additive work* because they append complete or partial answers to existing work. The design of the Q&A platform used for problem solving on MO suggested that collaboration might take place primarily through independent contributions that provide information; we will refer to these contributions as primary additions. Despite the limitations of the Q&A platform we found multiple ways in which users made use of the limited features to revise or extend existing work. Interviewees suggested that these secondary additions were often as important as primary additions in developing a solution. For example, in solving the question "Is the theory of categories decidable?" the answer that Poonen gave, which extended the answers of Hamkins and Dorais, was as important as the answers given by Hamkins and Dorais in solving the problem. Remember Hamkins and Dorais were able to answer the question posed by A. Rex in the more general case, but only Poonen was able to answer the specific case asked by A. Rex.

Contributions also built on existing work by evaluating and critiquing that work; we will refer to these contributions as *indirect, evaluative work*. A substantial amount of work was in the form of critiquing the question or answers, identified as clarifying the question and critiquing an answer respectively. These contributions did not directly provide answers or parts of answers, but instead indirectly contributed to answers by asking questions, providing clarification, pointing out errors, and making suggestions. Interviewees suggested that these contributions were important in encouraging better answers. For example, in solving the question "Is the theory of categories decidable?" there was a lengthy discussion among several contributors about how the question should be reformulated to be logically precise. Without the clarification of the question, Hamkins, Dorais, and Poonen's final answers would not have been given. Despite the importance of this indirect, evaluative work, it also created some confusion. In the case discussed above, there was a period of a few hours where the correct version of the question was unclear, leading to uncertainty as to whether the original version of Hamkins' answer was sufficient.

In Study 2 we directly test whether these contributions add value to collaborations.

STUDY 2: THE IMPACT OF COLLABORATIVE ACTS ON SOLUTION QUALITY

Collaboration is often assumed to be valuable and there is evidence showing that collaborative work in aggregate when compared to independent work is often superior. Pairs outperform individuals in lab tasks simulating scientific discoveries [28]. Co-authored scientific papers are cited more often and appear in more prestigious journals than single-authored papers [14,31,41]. Teams developing inventions create more influential patents and fewer very poor patents [35]. However, less is known about the value that different types of contributions make to a collaborative outcome. In this study we evaluate what value, if any, each type of collaborative act identified in Study 1 added to the solution quality.

In Study 1 we found that solutions often grow organically and become better through additions of answers or parts of answers. *Primary additions*, which are defined as providing information independent of existing work on a problem, are expected on average to increase a Q&A's solution quality by providing the first solution or a better solution. *Secondary additions*, such as revisions and extensions of answers, are expected, based on Study 1, to be as important as primary additions and to increase a Q&A's solution quality by improving, completing, or surpassing existing solutions. Thus we predict that all additions, primary and secondary, will increase a Q&A's solution quality.

In Study 1 we found that *indirect, evaluative contributions*, such as clarifying the question and critiquing an answer, were common and important in encouraging better answers. These contributions are expected to increase a Q&A's solution quality by making the question easier to answer or by pointing out ways to fix an answer. They are expected to encourage and enable the creation of better solutions.

While both additive and indirect, evaluative contributions might improve solution quality, they might do so in different ways and under different conditions. For example, while additive contributions might immediately affect solution quality by providing a better solution, indirect contributions rely on subsequent contributions to have an impact, and so they might not cause an immediate improvement in the solution. In fact, it is possible that indirect contributions could even *decrease* perceived solution quality in the short term, because clarifying a question or critiquing an answer might reduce the relevance or highlight flaws in existing solutions. In Study 1 we found that these evaluative contributions can sometimes create a period of confusion by calling into question and devaluing accepted information.

Below we operationalize quality in MathOverflow and examine the association of collaborative acts on quality over time.

Method

By tracking changes in solution quality over time we were able to evaluate the impact of each type of collaborative act on the change in solution quality.

Outcome Variable

Users vote on the quality of answers by voting an answer score up or down. **Solution quality at time t** was operationalized as the maximum score an answer to a question received during hour t. For example, if a question had no answers at hour t it was given a score of 0, if a question had two answers scoring 2 and 5 during hour t, it was given a score of 5. This operationalization involves a few assumptions. First, users' ratings of answer quality approximate objective answer quality. Solution quality is difficult to measure objectively, particularly for research level mathematics because there are few qualified judges. The answer score represents a good approximation because MO users are some of the few judges who can judge the quality of an answer [39]. Second, the solution to a problem is best judged by the quality of its best answer. There are a few alternative metrics including sum of the quality of all answers and the average quality of all answers to a question. The score of the best answer seemed the most logical because it does not penalize for extraneous wrong content, while also not rewarding extraneous beneficial content. In this case it was the most stringent test that the additional collaborative activity was actually adding value to the final best answer. Third, studying changes in the score of an answer in units of hours is meaningful. While one hour is a short interval votes accrue quickly and predictably on MO. An answer in its first hour typically receives 15% of the votes it will receive overall and more importantly the score in the first hour is significantly correlated with its final score ($r(250) = 0.44$, $p < 0.001$). Due to the constraints of the data on MO, scores are not available in units shorter than one hour. Thus an hour is the shortest unit of analysis to measure changes in solution quality. For simplicity the analysis was limited to the first two days after a question was posted, because this was the period in which the majority of activity occurs (81.5%).

Predictor Variables

Providing information at time t was measured as the sum of the score given to each contribution categorized as providing information during hour t (contributions were rated by coders on a scale 0 to 4, scores were scaled to be from 0 to 1 and the average was used, see Study 1). For example if there were two contributions in the hour classified as providing information and given scores of 0.5 and 0.75, then the total score for the hour for providing information was 1.25.

Clarifying the question at time t was measured as the sum of the score given to each contribution categorized as clarifying the question during hour t. Each contribution was rated and the scores were scaled to be from 0 to 1 to indicate how much it clarified the question (see Study 1).

Collaborative Acts	Mean # (SD)	Avg. Score
Providing information	2.57 (2.18)	0.44
Clarifying the question	1.32 (1.89)	0.38
Critiquing an answer	1.26 (1.97)	0.46
Revising an answer	0.73 (1.35)	0.28
Extending an answer	0.25 (0.50)	0.45

Table 2: Mean (standard deviation) number of collaborative acts in a Q&A and average score per collaborative act from 0-1.

Critiquing an answer at time t was measured as the sum of the score given to each contribution categorized as critiquing an answer during hour t. Each contribution was rated and the scores were scaled to be from 0 to 1 to indicate how much it critiqued an answer.

Revising an answer at time t was measured as the sum of the score given to each contribution categorized as revising an answer during hour t. Each contribution was rated and the scores were scaled to be from 0 to 1 to indicate how much information it provided.

Extending an answer at time t was measured as the sum of the score given to each contribution categorized as extending an answer during hour t. Each contribution was rated and the scores were scaled to be from 0 to 1 to indicate how much information it provided.

Covariates

Several control variables were included in the models as covariates.

Solution quality at time t-1. The outcome of interest was the change in solution quality in a given hour. Solution quality in the previous hour was included to control for solution quality up until the hour of interest [8].

Question. A dummy variable for each question was included to control for unmeasured differences at the question level that did not vary with time, such as poor quality question or a question attracting more contributors. In other words the question was included as a fixed effect to control for differences between questions. Models including the question as a random effect instead resulted in results that are substantively the same as those we report below; we report the results with question as a fixed effect because it is a stricter control.

Time. The hour since the question was posted was included to control for systematic changes in a collaboration that depended on how long it had been active on the site. For example, questions receive more attention shortly after they are posted rather than later.

Linear regression models were constructed with predictors, covariates, and the outcome variable. We had hypothesized that clarifying the question and critiquing an answer would have delayed impact on solution quality. Therefore, we tested two regression models, one that did not consider downstream impact of contributions and one that did. Model 1 considered only immediate increases in solution quality that occurred in the same hour as the contribution. To examine possible delayed impact clarifying the question and critiquing an answer Model 2 examined increases in solution quality up to three hours later. Partial R^2 were calculated for the addition of the collaborative acts into the models and Akaike Information Criterion (AIC) were calculated to compare Model 1 and 2.

Results

Primary and secondary additions had a direct and immediate impact on solution quality. Both Model 1 and Model 2 showed that providing information, revising an answer, and extending an answer all significantly predicted an immediate increase in solution quality (See Table 3). Over the course of an hour, one additive contribution typically increased the score of the best solution by 0.35-0.51 points. Sometimes this meant a new best solution replacing the old best solution. On average the best solution's quality score increased by 0.06 points per hour (SD = 0.30 points), so the value of an addition is relatively large.

Indirect, evaluative contributions had a delayed impact on solution quality. A comparison of Model 1, which only included immediate effects of contributions on solution quality and Model 2, which included up to 3 hour delayed effects of contributions for clarifying the question and critiquing an answer showed that Model 2 was superior. Model 2 explained slightly more variance and had a better AIC value (see Table 3). A model comparison test revealed that Model 2 was significantly better. Model 2 showed that clarifying the question had a negative effect on solution quality in the first two hours—a clarification of the question lowered the best solution quality by 0.08 points in these two hours—while critiquing the answer had no effect (see Table 3). Model 2 also showed that clarifying the question and critiquing the answer had a positive effect on the best solution quality after three hours. The inclusion of a clarification of the question or critique of an answer after three hours increased the best solution's quality by 0.16 and 0.08 points respectively.

Overall the collaborative acts only explained a small amount of variance in change in solution quality, 3.3%. This may be largely due to the large amount of random chance and unexplained factors in the ratings of answers on MO and is a limitation of this method. The amount of variance explained is comparable to other studies of answer quality on MO [39].

Summary

Past literature has shown that, in aggregate, collaboration improves solutions compared to independent work. Study 2 tested at a process level the specific types of collaborative acts that lead to increased solution quality. We had predicted and found that adding a new answer or parts of an answer, whether independent of existing work in the case of providing information or building on existing work, in the case of revising an answer or extending an answer increased solution quality. Further, we found that revising and extending an answer had an equal effect on solution quality as providing information. This finding demonstrates that building on existing work is as valuable as adding an original contribution.

All the collaborative acts increased solution quality, but through different ways. While additions had a direct effect on solution quality, evaluative contributions, such as clarifying the question and critiquing an answer, had a delayed impact on solution quality. One explanation is that clarifying the question and critiquing the answer improve quality by inspiring other improvements, such as revisions or new answers within a few hours. But in the short-term clarifying a question had little effect and clarifying the question had a negative effect on solution quality, because they bring into question the adequacy of current solutions. Although critiques and clarifications eventually had a positive impact on solution quality the effect was smaller than the effect of direct contributions.

	Model 1: Change in Solution Quality	**Model 2: Change in Solution Quality**
Provided information	0.35***	0.35***
Clarified the question	-0.12**	-0.08*
an hour ago		-0.08*
two hours ago		0.16***
Critiqued an answer	0.04	-0.04
an hour ago		0.04
two hours ago		0.08*
Revised an answer	0.51***	0.51***
Extended an answer	0.43***	0.43***
Partial R^2	3.1%	3.3%
AIC	674.7	659.2
Model Comparison	$F(4) = 5.88, p < 0.001$	

Table 3: Regression models showing the impact of collaborative acts on solution quality, with and without delayed effects. * p < 0.05, ** p < 0.01, *** p < 0.001

DISCUSSION

We examined collaborative scientific problem solving in the context of MathOverflow, a site in which anyone connected to the Internet can pose, answer, critique, or improve a problem. By characterizing a sample of posts to the site we proposed a simple taxonomy of collaborative acts in which users engage, including both direct contributions (e.g., providing answers) as well as indirect contributions (e.g., clarifying the question, critiquing answers). A quantitative analysis relating collaborative acts to solution quality showed that quality improved for both direct and indirect contributions, but that indirect contributions had a delayed effect on quality. Below we discuss the implications of these results for existing Q&A systems which are being repurposed for scientific problem solving, as well as the design of novel systems that could better support such activities.

Repurposing Q&A Platforms for Problem Solving

Increasingly Q&A platforms are being repurposed for other uses, including as a repository of knowledge, in the case of Stack Overflow [1], and as a problem-solving platform, in the case of MathOverflow. Q&A systems are designed to support one form of collaboration very well. They support the selection of the best answer among many, by broadcasting a question to a large group, allowing multiple independent answers, and rating of answers through voting by a large audience. Our analyses of the ways mathematicians have been collaborating suggest some concrete changes to Q&A platforms that could enhance other forms of collaboration.

First, Q&A platforms could include more suitable tools to facilitate building on existing work. A major finding of this paper is that MO users often advance a solution by building on others' work. Better tools might make it easier to building on others' work making it even more common. For example, better versioning tools that could connect related ideas or answers together and allow joint ownership of answers might encourage building on existing work. At the moment answers can be revised, but there is no tool to link an answer that develops as an extension of another answer to its precursor. Also, in practice other users are hesitant to directly edit someone's answer because of the perceived ownership over an answer. Tools to gather ideas into an answer and share ownership might make people less hesitant about adding to other people's work. Another possible change would be to create a section for partial work to elicit more contributions that could be built upon. At the moment users sometimes include definitions, related work, partial ideas in the comments sections by convention; if there were an explicit section more content might be added in a more systematic way. Better tools to support building on existing work might encourage even more additions and increase the prominence of these later contributions.

Second, Q&A platforms could include better incentives to encourage indirect contributions. Our results provide quantitative evidence that good answers come about not just from more people providing answers, but also by fixing errors, filling in gaps, being inspired by existing work, and adding additional perspectives. These secondary additions are as valuable in reaching a final solution as primary additions. Thus, figuring out ways to support and inspire iterating on solutions is important. However, Q&A platforms generally award reputation points to answers and not to indirect contributions. One way of supporting this indirect work may be to provide rewards for downstream effects that are not immediately recognizable as useful. For example, a flat number of reputation points could be awarded to evaluations of either the question or answers or an evaluation could receive the same number of reputation points as a contribution it inspires but from a separate "indirect" reputation pool.

Third, Q&A platforms could include mechanisms to keep people involved in a Q&A for longer. The importance of building on existing work and indirect, evaluative contributions suggest that continued interaction and revisiting a Q&A may lead to improvements in solution quality. Q&A platforms could use alerts and content prioritization to bring authors of the question, authors of answers, and potential experts back to a Q&A multiple times as work progresses. It also suggests that there may be value recommending specific tasks to specific users, such as bring in a user to review a particular answer that is in their area of expertise.

Large-scale Collaborative Problem Solving Systems

Given better tools to collaborate we might see a proliferation of larger scale collaborations. Even with the limitations of the Q&A platform we see people eking out ways to collaborate in complex ways. Q&A platforms support basic ways to enable large scale collaboration, such as the ability to find experts within a crowd and to select the best solutions among many. More support is needed to enable users to build on each others' work such as ways to iterate on solutions, ways to inspire new solutions from partial ideas, and ways to elicit and represent multiple perspectives. Trying to shoehorn such functionality into existing Q&A platforms (such as MathOverflow) or blogs/discussion boards (such as The Polymath Projects) may not be the most effective approach. New systems for collaborative problem solving could be built from the ground up to address not only the issues identified above but also fundamental crowd coordination issues such as expertise identification, support for subteams, decomposition of tasks while maintaining interdependencies, task routing, and quality control [21]. Matching the motivations for participating in such systems with the already-existing reward structure for professional advancement in science will be a key challenge to overcome as well.

Limitations

In this paper we developed identified a set of collaborative acts that describe the types of contributions to collaborations at a process-level. However, the observations were built from the examination a single site, MathOverflow, with problems all from the single domain of mathematics. To ensure that the set of collaborative acts and their assessed value generalizes and is not site or domain specific future research will need to examine the set of collaborative acts in other domains of problem solving in which collaboration occurs through other media. Nor are the collaborative acts that we describe comprehensive, and we anticipate that future research will expand on this work to better test which are most effective and how they fit together.

CONCLUSION

In this paper we identified a set of collaborative acts that describe at a process-level how collaboration transpires in solving complex, difficult problems. A quantitative analysis relating collaborative acts to solution quality suggested that some types have an immediate effect while others have a delayed and indirect effect on improving solution quality. Together these findings inform the design of tools to aid large-scale collaborative problem solving.

ACKNOWLEDGMENTS

Preparation of this manuscript was aided by funding from the National Science Foundation (IIS-1149797, IIS-1217559, OCI-0943148, IIS-0968484, ISS-1111124), Bosch, Google, Microsoft and Center for the Future of Work. We would also like to thank Justin Cranshaw for his help.

REFERENCES

1. Anderson, A., Huttenlocher, D., Kleinberg, J., & Leskovec, J. Discovering value from community activity on focused question answering sties: A case study of Stack Overflow. In *Proc KDD'12,* ACM Press (2012), 850-858.
2. Birnholtz, J. P. What does it mean to be an author? The intersection of credit, contribution, and collaboration in science. *Journal of the American Society for Information Science and Technology 57,* (2006), 1758-1770.
3. Bernstein, M. S., Little, G., Miller, R. C., Hartman, B., Ackerman, M. S., Karger, D. R., Crowell, D., & Panovich, K. Soylent: A word processor with a crowd inside. In *Proc UIST 2011*, ACM Press (2011), 313-322.
4. Blumenstock, J. E. Size matters: Word count as a measure of quality on Wikipedia. In *Proc. WWW 2008*, ACM Press (2008), 1095-1096.
5. Chi, E. H., Pirolli, P., Suh, B., Kittur, A., Pendleton, B., and Mytkowicz, T. Augmented social cognition. In *AAAI Spring Symposium: Social information processing,* (2008), 11-17.
6. Cranshaw, J. and Kittur, A. The Polymath Project: Lessons from a successful online collaboration in mathematics. In *Proc. CHI 2011,* ACM Press (2011), 1865-1874.
7. Cronin, B. *The Hand of Science: Academic Writing and its Rewards.* Scarecrow Press, Lanham, MD, 2005.
8. Cohen, J., Cohen, P., Wes, S. G., & Aiken, L. S. *Applied Multiple Regression/Correlation Analysis for the Behavioral Science.* Hillsdale, NJ: Lawrence Erlbaum Associates (2003).
9. Cummings, J. N., & Kiesler, S. Collaborative research across disciplinary and organizational boundaries. *Social Studies of Science 35* (2005), 703-722.
10. Dabbish, L., Stuart, C., Tsay, J., and Herbsleb, J. Social coding in GitHub: Transparency and collaboration in an open software repository. In *Proc. CSCW 2012,* ACM Press (2012), 1277-1286.
11. Dunbar, K. How scientists think. On-line creativity and conceptual change in science. Eds. Ward, T. B., Smith, S. M., Vaid, J. In *Creative thought: An investigation of conceptual structures and processes.,* (pp. 461-493), American Psychological Association, Washington DC, 1997.
12. Fiske, D. W., and Fogg, L. But the reviewers are making different criticisms of my paper! Diversity and uniqueness in reviewer comments. *American Psychologist 45* (1990), 591-598.
13. Glaser, B. G., and Strauss, A. L. *The Discovery of Grounded Theory: Strategies for Qualitative Research,* Aldine, New York, 1967.
14. Gordon, M. D. A critical reassessment of inferred relations between multiple authorship, scientific collaboration, the production of papers and their acceptance for publication. *Scientometrics 2* (1980), 193-201.
15. Hesse, M. B. *The Structure of Scientific Inference.* Macmillan, London, (1974).
16. Jeppesen, L. B., and Lakhani, K. R. Marginality and problem solving effectiveness in broadcast search. *Organization Science 21* (2010), 1016-1033.
17. Jonassen, D. H. Instructional design models for well-structured and ill-structured problem solving learning outcomes. *Educational Technology Research and Development 45,* (1997), 65-94.
18. Jonassen, D. H., and Kwon, H. Communication patterns in computer mediated versus face-to-face group problem solving. *Educational Technology Research and Development 49,* (2001), 35-51.
19. Kerr, N. L., and Tindale, R. S. Group performance and decision making. *Annual Review of Psychology 55,* (2004), 623-655.

20. Kittur, A., and Kraut, R. E. Harnessing the wisdom of crowds in Wikipedia: Quality through coordination. In *Proc. CSCW 2008,* ACM Press (2008), 37-46.

21. Kittur, A., Nickerson, J. V., Bernstein, M. S., Gerber, E. M., Shaw, A., Zimmerman, J., Lease, M., and Horton, J. J. The future of crowd work. In *Proc. CSCW 2013,* ACM Press (2013), 1301-1318.

22. Kittur, A., Smus, B., Khamkar, S., & Kraut, R. E. CrowdForge: Crowdsourcing complex work. In *Proc. UIST 2011,* ACM Press (2011), 43-52.

23. Klein, M. How to harvest collective wisdom on complex problems: An introduction to the MIT deliberatorium. (2011) *Working paper.*

24. Kulkarni, A. P., Can, M., & Hartmann, B. Collaboratively crowdsourcing workflows with turkomatic. In *Proc. CSCW 2012,* ACM Press (2012), 1003-1012.

25. Lakhani, K. R., Garvin, D. A., & Lonstein, E. Top Coder (A): Developing software through crowdsourcing. *Harvard Business School Case* (2012), 610-632.

26. Latour, B., and Woolgar, S. *Laboratory Life: The Construction of Scientific Facts.* Princeton University Press, Princeton NJ, 1979.

27. Mamykina, L., Manoim, B., Mittal, M., Hripcsak, G., Hartmann, B. Design lessons from the fastest Q&A site in the west. In *Proc. CHI 2011,* ACM Press (2011), 2957-2967

28. Okada, T., and Simon, H. A. Collaborative discovery in a scientific domain. *Cognitive Science 21* (1997), 109-146.

29. Olson, G. M, & Olson, J. S. Distance Matters. *Human-Computer Interaction 15,* (2000), 139-178.

30. Pennington, N., Lee, A. Y., and Rehder B. Cognitive activities and levels of abstraction in procedural and object-oriented design. *Human-Computer Interaction 10* (1995), 171-226

31. Persson, O., Ganzel, W., and Danell, R. Inflationary bibliometric values: The role of scientific collaboration and the need for relative indicators in evaluation studies. *Scientometrics 60* (2004), 421-432.

32. Schoenfeld, A. H., and Herrmann, D. J. Problem perception and knowledge structure in expert and novice mathematical problem solvers. *Journal of Experimental Psychology 8* (1982), 484-494.

33. Shin, N., Jonassen, D. H., and McGee, S. Predictors of well-structured and ill-structured problem solving in an astronomy simulation. *Journal of Research in Science and Teaching 40* (2003), 6-33.

34. Shrager, J., Billman, D., Convertino, G., Massar, J. P., & Pirolli, P. Soccer science and the Bayes community: Exploring cognitive implications of modern scientific communication. *Topics in Cognitive Science 2,* (2010), 53-72.

35. Singh, J., and Fleming, L. Lone inventors as sources of breakthroughs: Myth or reality? *Management Science 56* (2009), 41-56.

36. Stasser, G., and Titus, W. Pooling of unshared information in group decision making: biased information sampling during discussion. *Journal of Personality and Social Psychology 48,* (1985), 1467-1478.

37. Stasser, G., and Titus, W. Hidden profiles: A brief history. *Psychology Inquiry 14,* (2003), 304-313.

38. Tang, J. C., Cebrian, M., Giacobe, N. A., Kim, H., Kim, T., & Wickert, D. Reflecting on the DARPA Red Balloon Challenge. *Communications of the ACM 54,* (2011), 77-85.

39. Tausczik, Y. R., and Pennebaker, J. W. Predicting the perceived quality of online mathematics contributions from users' reputations. In *Proc. CHI 2011,* ACM Press (2011), 1885-1888.

40. Tausczik, Y. R., and Pennebaker, J. W. Participation in an online mathematics community: Differentiating motivations to add. In *Proc. CSCW 2012,* ACM Press (2012), 207-216.

41. Thagard, P. Collaborative knowledge. *Nous 31* (1997), 242-261.

42. Turner, T. C., Smith, M. A., Fisher, D., and Wlser, H. T. Picturing Usenet: Mapping computer-mediated collective action. *Journal of Computer-Mediatied Communication 10* (2005).

43. Wuchty, S., Jones, B. F., and Uzzi, B. The increasing dominance of teams in production of knowledge. *Science 316* (2007), 1036-1039.

Creepy but Inevitable? The Evolution of Social Networking

Hui Zhang
University of Washington
Seattle, Washington
huizhang@uw.edu

Munmun De Choudhury
Microsoft Research
Redmond, Washington
munmund@microsoft.com

Jonathan Grudin
Microsoft Research
Redmond, Washington
jgrudin@microsoft.com

ABSTRACT
This paper focuses on the fifth year of a cross-sectional trend study of enterprise social networking. Several stable patterns are evident—some activities have plateaued, others steadily increase in frequency. The fifth year did see a new development: As social networking companies visibly embraced behavior tracking and targeted advertising, concerns shifted from boundary regulation within personal networks to unsettling evidence of activity monitoring. However, benefits of use continue to outweigh drawbacks.

Author Keywords
Social networking; Facebook; LinkedIn; Twitter; Boundary

ACM Classification Keywords
H.5.3 Group and Organization Interfaces

INTRODUCTION
At the end of our first interview, we asked a 30-year-old senior program manager, "What haven't we asked (about her use of social networking) that might be noteworthy."

She replied, "I don't know how Facebook is using my information. Somehow, whenever I type in something, the marketing ads on Facebook seem to match what I typed in, so that's creepy..."

One of us said, "When I go to the supermarket I have a card and they scan things in and I get these offers that are clearly tuned to me because they're things I bought before, (sometimes) I get one free, so that doesn't seem creepy..." She was nodding. "So what's your feeling as to why it feels creepier with Facebook?"

She replied, "When I'm in the grocery store and that happens, I've physically purchased something at that specific place. But if I'm in conversation with somebody and said 'Oh yeah, I'm looking for a house,' and then some random person back there comes up and says 'I have five houses in that area,' it's super creepy."

CSCW '14, February 15–19, 2014, Baltimore, Maryland, USA.

Copyright 2014 ACM 978-1-4503-2540-0/14/02...$15.00.
http://dx.doi.org/10.1145/2531602.2531643

A senior software design engineer explained why she has resisted her partner's constant encouragement to join Facebook. "I do not like how much information they collect about people (and) I don't need that kind of potential time sink." But without rancor, she said "Facebook I see as an inevitable thing. One day I will have to have a Facebook account. I am holding out as long as I can."

In ten years, social media went from relative obscurity to over a billion active users [14]. LinkedIn, Facebook, and the once-popular MySpace and Orkut were launched in 2003 and 2004; predecessors Friendster and Plaxo in 2002. New users and sites appear and established sites evolve, but as experience accumulates, habits and social conventions form. Where designers cannot or do not address challenges, people find workarounds.

The initial public offerings of LinkedIn and Facebook in 2011 and 2012 indicated that investors believe that the rapid rise and fall of major sites is over. Obligations to shareholders and regulators require a new level of corporate responsibility and oversight. These sites responded to the heightened attention to revenue and profitability by expanding on-site advertising. Their valuations have risen.

For five years, we have studied the use of social networking sites for personal and professional purposes by Microsoft employees. Not a typical company, Microsoft has many early adopters of digital technologies, although fewer than half of the employees are engaged in product development.

Trends within the organization over the first four years were previously published [1]. This paper focuses on two unexpected deviations in 2012. (1) Daily LinkedIn by employees has risen significantly. Daily Twitter use plateaued at a much lower rate, yet occasional Twitter use is rising. To understand these phenomena, we interviewed 46 employees. (2) The interviews revealed that although people expressed the same moderate level of overall concern about social networking sites, the nature of those concerns in our population has shifted dramatically.

In 2008, most Microsoft employees were active on at most one social networking site. Their principal concern was that as their network expanded to include friends, family, and professional contacts, communication was inhibited [34]. Challenges in boundary management may still afflict some populations. Ours, typically thirty-somethings with several years' social networking experience, described ways that they had reestablished boundaries.

Despite media accounts of risks in social network use, the proportion of people reporting major security concerns leveled off or declined over the years as they gained a sense of control. However, a new concern appeared: Through targeted advertising, people are more aware of how personal conversations and information are monitored and used. The words "creepy," "weird," and "unnerving" arose without prompting in many interviews.

Nevertheless, abandonment rates are low. Almost all employees have integrated social networking into their lives and show no sign of giving it up, although some take steps to counter developments that make them uneasy.

This paper has two threads. (1) The five-year cross-sectional trend study, a unique look at organizational aspects of sites that are also used for personal purposes. (2) The shift in concerns, which has broad implications that are primarily in the personal sphere.

RELATED LITERATURE

The pace of change complicates efforts to interpret the literature. To understand a study conducted in mid-2006 requires keeping in mind that Facebook was then open only to students and that MySpace was dominant, getting more visits than Google. Some studies do not report when data were collected, which impedes efforts to identify shifting patterns of use.

Treem and Leonardi [40] acknowledge the challenge that rapid change creates in pulling together studies from different times and places. Their survey identifies conceptual aspects of social media use in organizations that appear consistently, such as the visibility and persistence of activity and the associations of groups of users.

Studies vary as to whether sites are used at work, by the general population, or by students, and vary as to the aspects of use that are considered. Our study examines workplace use but includes personal uses as well. Many in our population began using social networking sites as students, so our brief review covers all three focuses. We separately review studies of boundary regulation, a topic that is particularly salient to our analysis.

Workplace studies

Internal sites. Most workplace studies are of volunteers using proprietary systems accessible only to employees. Most volunteers are relatively active and positive. IBM prototypes such as Beehive and BlueTwit dominate early research on enterprise behavior. The studies identified the potential of social networking to strengthen ties and develop social capital [8, 10, 14, 16, 18, 19, 36, 39, 48]. The studies guided systems research, development, and deployment, as did similar non-IBM studies [e.g., 4, 49]. The latter examined the use, by 1.5% of an organization, of Yammer, a Twitter-like tool with posts of unlimited length. It was used to broadcast work-related status, questions or directed messages, and links to external information.

External sites. Publicly available sites such as Facebook and Twitter are used formally for recruiting and marketing [e.g., 43]. Some enterprises prohibit informal access to external sites from workplace computers, but many including Microsoft do not. With smartphones enabling access, blocking employee use during the day is difficult.

Zhao and Rosson [50] studied 11 heavy users of Twitter. Heavy users are by definition atypical, but they can identify useful features. Their uses were similar to those noted above for Yammer. Ehrlich and Shami [12] compared use of Twitter and BlueTwit by 34 employees who used both. With BlueTwit there was less status posting and more information and comments directed to specific individuals. Thom and Millen [38] described a Twitter-based event organized to capture organizational culture. The effort was deemed a success although less than one-fifth of 1% of employees posted.

Surveys of communication practices at a small company in May 2008 and May 2009 found Facebook, LinkedIn and Twitter use increasing, with weekly use the norm for Facebook and Twitter [42]. The authors forecast that Twitter would thrive. We found a similar pattern in 2008-2009, but daily Twitter use plateaued in 2011 at around 10%.

Rooksby & Sommerville [33] identified problems with the use of internal and public sites to support productivity in a large government agency. Lampe et al. [26] surveyed Facebook use by university staff. Although diverse networks are reportedly effective for getting questions answered, they found little use of social networks for Q&A.

General population

Much of the research literature and media attention is focused on Facebook and Twitter use by the general population. Wilson et al. [46] surveyed 412 articles on Facebook research, grouping them into user characterizations, user motivation, presentation of self, privacy and disclosure, and Facebook's role in interactions.

Most Facebook research is through surveys and interviews, although researchers at Facebook publish server log studies [e.g., 5, 6]. The Twitter API provides streams from users who do not opt out, enabling collection and analysis of large-scale samples [e.g., 27, 30].

The general population differs in makeup from most workplaces. A higher proportion of Twitter users are black and Hispanic than the general population [35]. Teens are heavily represented and may have less complex social networks than older users—acquiring professional colleagues can change social network composition [34].

Nevertheless, such studies can provide indicators. Naaman et al. [30] found that Twitter users clustered into those who post about themselves and those who relay information. Wang et al. [45] describe regrets over Facebook posts. This is a possible step toward more mature use, just as early concerns with email flaming receded over time.

Student use

Students are a significant segment of the general user population. Students differ in important respects from our career- and family-engaged population, few of whom are younger than 25. Nevertheless, all employees were once students and many began using social networking sites as students, arriving at Microsoft with habits and expectations.

Studies published before 2009 [2, 21] noted that students generally opted either for MySpace or for Facebook based on their career aspirations. We also found a tendency to use a single site in 2008, but this changed over time.

In a 2007 survey of undergraduates [17], women expressed more concerns about privacy. We did not find this in our samples surveyed later. In surveys conducted from 2005 to 2008, many undergraduates' Facebook networks resembled IM or SMS buddy lists [24, 25]; they then slowly added family members and past classmates. We found that networks often expanded significantly after employment.

Surveying college students from 2006 to 2010, Tufekci [41] charted a decline in allowing open access to Facebook profiles. Attitudes toward privacy depended on whether the goal was primarily to communicate with existing friends or to find people with common interests. Twenty percent of those surveyed had dropped Facebook once, but most resumed using it. Non-use was considered "resistance" or a "faux pas." Limiting access was considered a better approach. Women reported more use of access controls.

Boundary regulation

> "By proper scheduling of one's performances, it is possible not only to keep one's audiences separated from each other (by appearing before them in different front regions or sequentially in the same region) but also to allow a few moments in between performances so as to extricate oneself psychologically and physically from one personal front, while taking on another." – Erving Goffman, quoted in Hogan [22]

Goffman's observation pinpoints a dilemma posed by social media. Conversations are persistent, so we cannot use temporal sequencing to address the different audiences that he identified as integral to social life. When we access our audience through the same device or devices, separation does not occur, or occurs in distinct digital spaces.

A good review of issues in boundary regulation appears in Stutzman and Herzog [37]. It is sometimes called context collapse, although the process is typically gradual. An employee with a network of friends adds co-workers who are also friends, then gets requests from other colleagues, customers, and so on. Posting becomes more awkward, but a moment calling for radical reorganization may not present itself.

Studies of boundary regulation issues arising in social media use date back to at least early 2007 [11]. In 2008, it was the primary concern found in the first year of this cross-sectional trend study: Skeels and Grudin [34] focused on the many problems created as Facebook users added, sometimes under pressure, 'friends' who were family members, managers, customers, and others.

Issues found in enterprises can surface in other populations. Two studies used advertising to recruit Facebook [15] and Google+ users [23]. The former reported that individual sites do not support people's faceted lives; the latter explored how friend circles can address these tensions. Ellison et al. [13] conclude that suboptimal use of access control features could prevent Facebook users from maximizing social capital. Woelfer & Hendry [47] describe homeless users who resolve tremendous disparities across their contacts through multiple online identities on one site. Stutzman and Hartzog [37] recruited 20 adults aged 25 to 60 who also created multiple identities on a single site. Our sample did not create multiple identities on one site, but their observations of why and how their participants differentiated groups is consistent with our observations below of why and how our participants use multiple sites.

SURVEY AND INTERVIEW METHODS

The two direct ways to identify change over time are with longitudinal studies of a fixed population or with a cross-sectional trend study, in which different members of the same group are studied at regular intervals. We chose the latter approach out of concern that taking a survey or being interviewed would alter behavior, especially in the early years when many people had not heard of these sites. In addition, employee turnover or annoyance with repeated solicitation could diminish the sample size.

Starting in mid-2008 we sent a survey invitation annually to 1000 employees randomly selected from the Microsoft address book. The survey covered attitudes and behaviors around the use of social networking for work and personal purposes. Demographic information was collected, including age, gender, geographic location, level, role, and years of use. Previous respondents were excluded to avoid influence from exposure to the survey. As an incentive, participants were entered in drawings for digital appliances.

Key survey questions are whether social networking is considered useful for fun, personal networking, external professional networking, and networking within the company. We ask the frequency of visiting different sites and engaging in diverse activities. We inquire into the use of access control mechanisms and their level of concern, with optional open-ended opportunities to elaborate.

The 2012 survey analysis revealed departures from past surveys. To understand these, we conducted 46 semi-structured interviews of respondents who indicated that they were open to follow-up. Interview selection criteria are discussed below. Most interviews were 45 to 60 minutes. Thirty were conducted in or near the informant's office, 16 by teleconference. Each was attended by at least two researchers who took notes and recorded with permission.

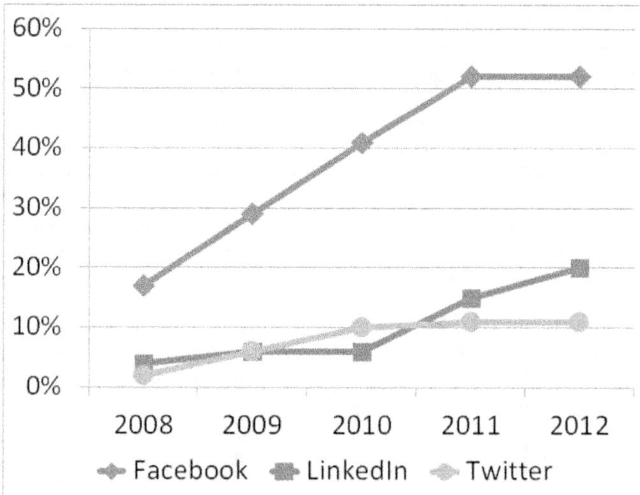

Figure 1. Daily use of sites as percentage of all employees.

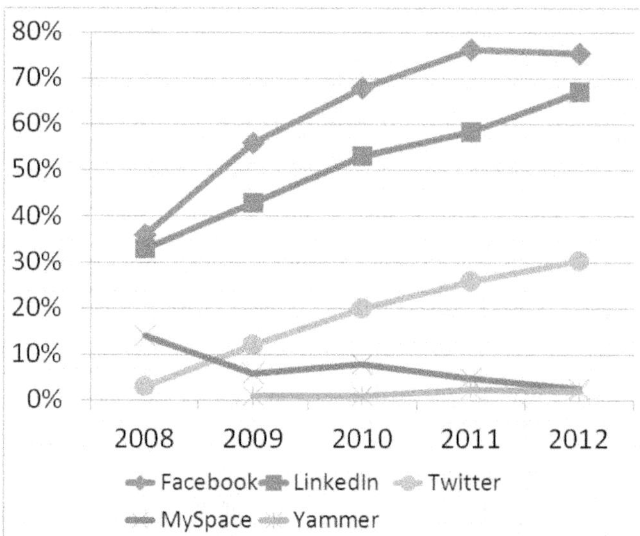

Figure 2. Occasional or more frequent use. Not shown: In 2012, Foursquare 10%, Pinterest and Google+ 7.5%, Instagram 2%.

Our approach to interviews was grounded—we had no hypotheses, we were there to listen. However, as a result of the survey results discussed below, we included employees who use Facebook or LinkedIn several times a day, occasional Twitter users, and a few employees who do not use social networking at all. We selected employees in Asia, Europe, Latin America, and various parts of North America to look for indications of differences based on culture or distance from headquarters. We included people sceptical of the usefulness of social sites for internal networking and some who had indicated that they had major concerns. Included were a few executives, some managers, and many individual contributors (non-managers), covering a range of ages and lengths of time with the company.

After each interview, a researcher used the notes and a full re-audit of the recording to compose a detailed summary. Quotations were transcribed and checked by two authors.

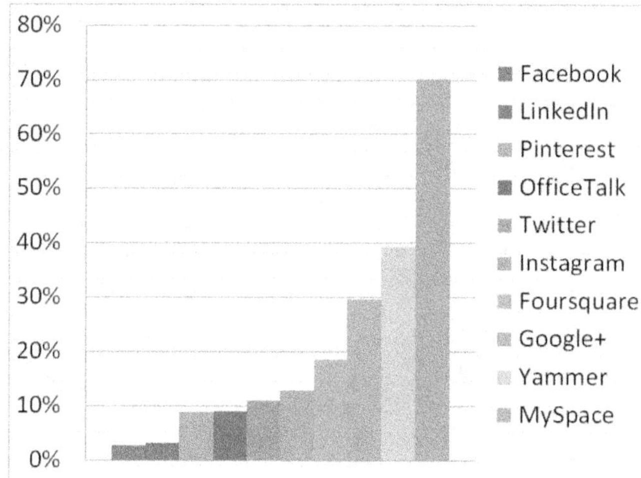

Figure 3. Churn (abandonment) rate.

An open-ended question, "If you have concerns (or know others who do) please describe them," drew 1232 comments over five years. We used a variant of the Miles and Huberman [29] coding method to tag each with a label identical or close to what was written, then grouped the resulting subcategories into higher-level categories. Any that did not cover 2% of the respondents in a year were dropped from the analysis, yielding 18 categories.

As discussed in the results section, the overall level of employee concern about social networking has never been high. Responses to the open-ended comment on concerns vary in detail. Some type "privacy," with no subcategory; others are more specific. This is discussed further when we cover the shift in concerns expressed over the years.

RESULTS

Survey response rates were over 40% every year, high for a long survey. Respondent demographics (ages, gender, and roles) were within 1% to 2% of those published for the company. In general, 95% confidence intervals for the results reported in this paper range from ±2% to ±4%.

Over half of all employees now report daily use of Facebook (Figure 1), although it appears to have leveled off (as has 'several times a day,' at 22%). Daily Twitter use plateaued at 11%. A surprise was that *daily* use of LinkedIn is twice as high as Twitter: one-fifth of employees in a company that is not experiencing high turnover.

Figure 2 shows that 'occasional' use of Twitter continues to climb and occasional LinkedIn use is very high. New social networking entries attracted attention (see caption). Figures 1 and 2 apply to the overall employee population: 50,000 are daily Facebook users, around 65,000 are at least occasional LinkedIn users, and so on.

Figure 3 shows the percentage of people who report once having had a profile but no longer using a site. In light of mass media articles describing Facebook burn-out, it is striking that fewer than 3% of its many users reported abandoning it. Twitter churn is almost four times as high. Pinterest is the 'stickiest' newcomer. The internal social networking platform Yammer has low adoption and high abandonment, but it competed the last two years with an internally-developed prototype system. (Yammer was bought by Microsoft soon after this survey.)

These analyses raised questions: What are heavy LinkedIn users doing? What are occasional Twitter users using it for? Why aren't they progressing to daily use as Facebook and LinkedIn users did? Why is Facebook so sticky? What could explain Foursquare's relatively high adoption—and abandonment—rates? Qualitative findings from interviews and open-ended survey questions that address these questions are covered in the next two sections.

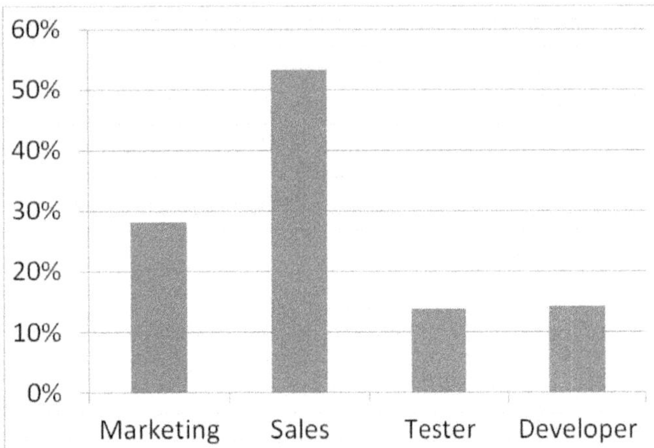

Figure 4. Daily LinkedIn use over major job roles.

Daily LinkedIn use

Many people assume that a steep rise in LinkedIn use signals that employees are considering new jobs. However, low employee turnover and our data tell a different story.

Although Microsoft develops technology, 45% of the employees are in product development groups, 45% are in sales and marketing divisions, and 10% support operations. Four major roles are Developer, Tester, Marketing, and Sales. Most sales and marketing staff are located in the field. LinkedIn use varies with role (Figure 4).

In sales and marketing, LinkedIn is used for customer contact, to recruit, to participate in professional LinkedIn groups, to stay in touch with past colleagues and alumni, and to follow technical news. For some, LinkedIn is a primary communication medium as well as the first place to check out a new contact.

What of testers, developers, and others who have little customer contact? Peak use for some coincided with past job searches, but many continue to use it regularly, exploiting advantages that LinkedIn has over business card exchange [1, 34]. They also use LinkedIn alumni groups and other groups. Developers and testers scan job openings that arrive via LinkedIn because it is nice to feel sought and useful to see the job skills that are listed. One tester takes training courses to acquire skills that are sought in LinkedIn job descriptions, figuring it could prove useful some day.

Occasional Twitter use

On a typical day, 8% of adult Americans use Twitter [35]; therefore, even fewer are daily users. Twitter use is not representative [27] and may skew toward demographic groups that are underrepresented in technology companies, so why do we find 'occasional' Twitter use increasing? Several interviewees reported rarely or never posting to Twitter, yet valuing it as a news source. They occasionally follow celebrities, Olympics, CNN headlines, and so on. An Egyptian tester considered its coverage of demonstrations in Cairo faster and more trustworthy than official media. Some people follow or post about local events or product launches. A developer who said he has only posted about 25 times in 3 years said:

> "(Twitter) is very useful for finding out local news... Near our house some guy barricaded himself in his house and said he had a bomb or something and we were like 'what's going on?' There were cops all around the place. (We) started looking on Twitter and searching for Wallingford and were able to figure out fairly quickly what was going on. I was even able to contribute! I saw a little bomb robot going down the road! So I posted that.
>
> "I've done that a number of times. There was a fire down in Renton one time and we saw smoke and tried 'smoke, Renton.' We were able to figure out what's going on before the news stations were even getting that information."

A marketing executive, finding the Disneyland parking lot closed, used Twitter to quickly learn that the theme park was open and to locate nearby free parking.

For our population, tweeting about self is rarer than using Twitter for information consumption or information seeking [30]. Whether as a source of news or to publicize one's work, most use is occasional.

Internal uses of social networking

The question of most interest to enterprises is whether internal use of sites that also include non-employees will benefit an organization by improving social capital and work productivity. We explored this issue in depth for 2008-2011 in [1]. In 2012 there was little change: 20% of the employees are negative and close to 30% are undecided about internal utility.

Men are more often negative sbout internal use than women. Workers around the company headquarters are more negative than those in the field, many of whom use LinkedIn. Only 15% of employees in sales are negative about internal utility, versus 25% of developers. In 2008, managers were more negative than individual contributors. Although both groups are now less sceptical, more managers shifted; on average they are now more positive. Individual contributors who communicate in person with collocated peers may find internal networking less useful.

Partially collocated group members are the most positive. Not surprisingly, employees with major concerns about social networking are less optimistic about internal use.

New social networking sites

The rise of new social sites shows that existing sites do not meet all needs. However, the challenge facing a new site was summed up by a designer who said, "(Facebook) seems like a monopoly. I can't post to five different things." Some people liked the design of a new site but said it never attracted enough of their friends to be useful. Internal sites suffered from a perception of low signal-to-noise ratio or insufficient ease of access: People want to browse all their sites quickly; for example, when they have a few free minutes and a smartphone in hand.

Foursquare's game element may contribute to its substantial adoption—and its high churn. After working hard to become 'mayor' of a sushi restaurant, one informant could either work to defend his title, watch himself lose it, or drop Foursquare, which is what he did. Pinterest had less adoption but very low churn: People whose use had declined spoke of it fondly and some expected to resume.

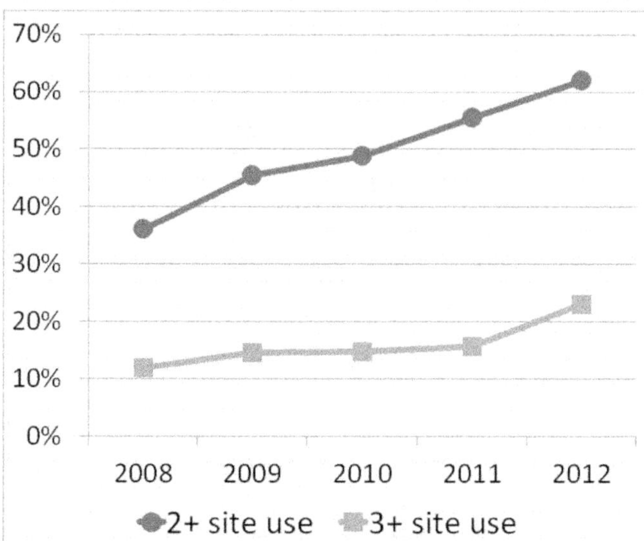

Figure 5. Occasional or more frequent use over time.

The use of multiple sites

Figure 5 shows increasing use of multiple sites. Facebook for personal networking and LinkedIn for professional networking is common, but people described a variety of ways to segment audiences. People differ as to which sites they are more selective about. Figure 5 misses the use of LinkedIn or Facebook groups and pages to segment audiences. Interfaces that support quick scanning of sites are popular; sites that are not covered can be overlooked.

These approaches to boundary regulation, to restoring Goffman's sequential 'performances,' came as experience with social networking increased. In 2008, 1-2 years was the median and mode; only 9% reported 5+ years. In 2012, 44% reported 5+ years of use and only 9% fewer than three years. People found conventions and solutions that worked for them—usually using multiple sites, sometimes using grouping features that sites provide. A technology that is deeply integrated into the lives of many people is reaching maturity on some dimensions even as it evolves and provokes new responses. Implications of this, and new challenges, are considered in the Discussion.

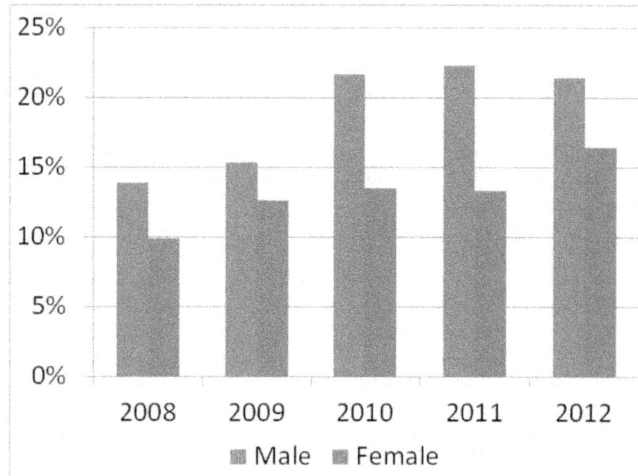

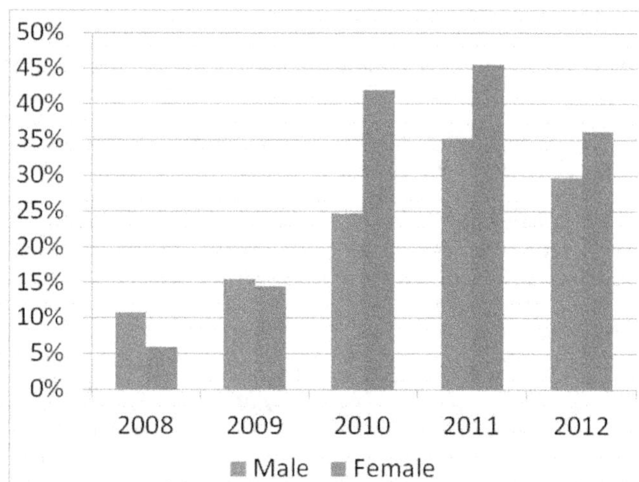

Figure 6. Major concerns (top). Heavy access control (bottom).

Concerns

The survey asked whether people had major concerns about social networking sites, minor concerns, or no concerns. Most reported minor concerns, but as seen in Figure 6, reports of major concerns rose until 2010, then leveled off. Reported use of access controls also jumped in 2010, continued to rise in 2011, and declined in 2012. Gender differences were initially minor, but by 2010 more women used access controls heavily and fewer expressed major concerns.

For those expressing concerns, the nature of the concerns shifted sharply. The open-ended survey comments revealed transitions in 2010 and 2012. Boundary maintenance problems were the greatest concern in 2008. In 2010, perhaps influenced by media stories, general privacy and security concerns leaped from 40% to 59% of all concerns, and the first concerns were reported about content ownership, the permanence of information on sites, and reduced off-line interaction with friends. 2012 brought the first explicit mention of targeted advertising, which together with the related topics of 3rd party access to personal information, misuse of data, and profiling outnumbered concerns about improper content, access by children, usage, safety, and wasted time.

Concerns about mixing personal and professional information declined over the past two years. Early concerns over unwanted contacts, spam, and insufficient access control have disappeared. People explicitly noted that they had found ways to cope. One summarized his response to spam: "Hide all Farmville."

Creepiness

People did not object to targeted advertisements in principle. They are familiar with ads placed in search results. Their comments focused on visible reminders that private conversations are being mined. The person quoted at the beginning of the paper is one of several using the words 'creepy,' 'weird,' or 'unnerving.' A few more examples that revealed uneasiness:

> "Why is that pair of shoes following me around the web? That's creepy."

> "I don't mind being advertised to, but there's ways that are uncomfortable... I want to say that I 'like' stuff, like Batman... So I 'like' Breaking Bad, but I didn't realize that I was instantly going to start getting a feed from the show... I might like going to Target every once in a while, but if I 'like' Target on Facebook all of a sudden I'm clogging my feed... There are some smaller businesses and smaller websites that I don't mind 'liking' because I want to help their business."

> "You get this very clear evidence that they are mining the things you're posting, mining your data... Ads targeted at my age... like, get ripped now, exercise at..., or if I post something on biking then I started getting all kinds of bike ads... Some targeted ads are better but then they start pigeon-holing you. So 'You're clearly a 40-year old white guy, you probably need to lose weight...' Stuff for knee surgery and spinal surgery... I guess my age group and my cohort talking about their injuries... And a lot of dating stuff, meet local women... (I just changed my marital status.) You'd get these kind of weird things, not really offensive or anything, just unnerving."

> "Creepy, but kind of cool."

After interacting with French colleagues, one informant encountered ads in French, a language he doesn't speak.

People were uncomfortable, but not angry. No one reported dropping a site because of evidence that they were targeted. However, several said that they dropped apps and games altogether, or that they refuse to download anything that asks to access information such as location, photos, or contacts when they do not see why such information is needed for the app or game to work.

Other concerns

Another form of behavior tracking is users tracking one another. The complexity of this issue is seen in the comments of a recent hire. He spoke of the "immorality" of letting people see who had viewed one's site. He joked about funny possible misunderstandings. He knew that Facebook does not allow you to see who has viewed your profile, but that LinkedIn does:

> "The thing I don't like about LinkedIn is that I'm always afraid to look at people's pages, because then they can see that I looked at it, and I might just be looking for some inane reason... One of my friends said 'you're stalking me!' because I went and looked at his page."

Then, without noting a contradiction or qualifying his long diatribe on this topic, he said, "When I was looking for a job it was helpful. I could see who was looking at my page. I could see if a recruiter was. I could contact people."

Potential risk in revealing your location to online friends (or 'friends of friends') through posts or check-ins is a non-issue for some people and a huge issue for others. Some parents express concerns about the safety of their children. More often the concern was for property. For example,

> "I don't want 'Hey, I'm going on vacation' messages or 'I'm in Virginia at this place,' going out to the world... I don't want someone coming to my house and stealing my stuff... I trust my friends, I don't trust everybody. I know that people will see your driveway has newspapers in it and they'll target your house... I don't want Facebook to be another way for someone to see that, because we have someone pick up our newspaper."

Inevitability

The overall rise in frequency of use and low rates of abandonment speaks to the stickiness of social networking. For now, it is woven into people's lives. Markedly fewer younger employees express major concerns (Figure 7).

> "These ecosystems, they kind of suck you in, like gmail... Then you think about leaving, and you're just stuck. Facebook's kind of the same way. It's hard to break out of it, which is great for them but it makes me feel a little fenced in."

> "Any time that I try to organize a dinner party with more than say five guests, logistically it starts getting complicated (without Facebook). I know there are things like Evite, but most of my friends would use Facebook..."

DISCUSSION

> "There is no big brother, we're all big brother, we're all spying on each other... We're entering an age where privacy is going away in a lot of ways anyway, so I might as well embrace some of this. There will be so much noise out there, how will they be able to pinpoint me? If everybody's not private, then everybody's private. No privacy leads to all privacy. How are they going to be able to pinpoint?" – Software engineer

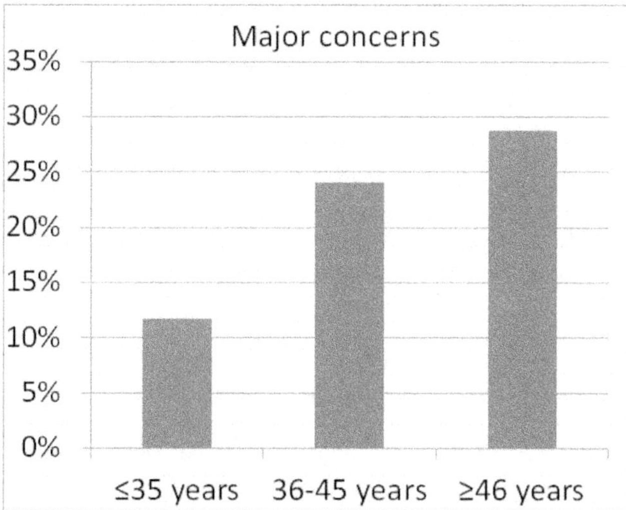

Figure 7. Major concerns by age.

Facebook was largely unknown prior to its public release in late 2006. In 2012 it reported having a billion active users. Features changed steadily—Facebook added access control mechanisms, became an application platform, introduced advertisements, and so on. People using social networking sites develop personal and social conventions. Given this unparalleled dynamism, consideration of dates and user populations is critical to understanding studies.

Insights can be gleaned by carefully merging the results of independent studies. A cross-sectional trend study such as ours can identify phenomena with greater confidence, bearing in mind that it may not generalize to other populations. By identifying significant shifts over five years, we know that past findings may not hold today. In some respects there is a pattern of maturing use, yet we also see experimentation and new behaviors. With millions of new young users each year, innovation is inevitable.

Given that there is a finite number of people on the planet and only 24 hours in the day, activity will level off. With years of experience, people discover what they find useful and comfortable. New features and sites appear, but there is more behavioral inertia.

In 2008, we set out to understand the impact of social networking sites on one workplace. The first survey revealed a range of attitudes and identified how some employees used public sites in ways that they felt helped them work better [34]. Their major concern was the difficulty of boundary regulation on sites that increasingly included work colleagues, personal friends, and family members. In 2012 we published a paper that details workplace trends over four years, 2008 to 2011 [1]. Most did not change appreciably in 2012, so readers interested in more depth on these issues can refer to it.

The following discussion focuses on concerns expressed by a significant minority. Concern with boundary regulation receded in our population as people became active on multiple sites and in different groups on some sites. Concerns over monitoring revealed by targeted advertising are significant although not an enterprise issue. We conclude with discussion of location tracking, one form of monitoring, and gender differences.

Boundary regulation

A decade ago, most users had few online friends and experienced few conflicts. Boundary regulation was less an issue for Friendster, MySpace and other early sites. Facebook was initially used by students who saw it as an enhanced space to interact with IM buddies [24]. By 2008, students were often adding family members [25], but Facebook had few access controls. Subsequently, as adults (faculty, corporate users, etc.) joined in growing numbers, boundary issues became significant. What should a student do when a teacher asked to be a friend, and vice versa? Could I refuse my manager, vice president, or customer? Probably not, but it affected what I posted about.

At Microsoft in 2008, this was the problem most often cited by the minority of employees then active on social networking sites. Virtually all had past schoolmates, family members, and friends in their networks, and were now adding colleagues. Few were active on more than one site. Several people interviewed in 2008-2009 remarked that they *should* use Facebook's new access control features to create multiple groups, but only one had done so.

Site designers did little to solve the problem. Interest groups are used, but there is little segmentation of 'friends.' Some people tried but now report only posting to 'All.'

Our workforce primarily coped by adopting different sites for different social groups. There was no single pattern in how Facebook, LinkedIn, Twitter, restricted Facebook pages, LinkedIn groups, and specialized sites are used. No one used multiple identities on one site as did Stutzman and Harzog's [37] carefully recruited sample, but motives for using multiple sites were similar, albeit with little use of pseudonyms to shield identity. The focus was on directing different kinds of messages to appropriate audiences.

Many of our participants explicitly said that they have things under control. Some noted that other people, people who do not make adequate arrangements, could get in trouble. Incidents arise—one person discovered to his horror that LinkedIn was displaying his Twitter feed. But he quickly fixed it. Another said of unwanted intrusions, "It's easier to turn off now, so I feel more protected."

Given the drumbeat of negative media stories about social media, our 2012 decrease in 'many concerns' might be a surprise. Tufekci [41] reported reduced concerns among long-time site users. Every day more of us are long-time users. We find solutions that work for us.

Even if these concerns fade over time, designers have reasons to improve our options. They may prefer that users spend more time on their site, rather than skip off to other sites. Also, every year, millions of people use their first social networking site or take their first job. Teenagers, who were absent from our sample, will likely encounter the boundary challenges that our population did five years ago.

Targeted advertising: A new concern

People may have known that tracking was possible, but it was not among the concerns expressed in our early surveys or in other studies. In 2009, Raynes-Goldie [32] examined privacy concerns among "twenty-somethings," focusing on control of who saw what—boundary regulation—and explicitly reported *not* finding concerns about the use of personal information. Interviews conducted in 2009 into location-tracking Google Latitudes found concern with maintaining social boundaries, but even when the experimenters asked directly they found that use of personal information was not a concern [31].

What changed for some people is that the hypothetical became the reality. It is in your face. "Why are these shoes following me around the web?" As public companies, LinkedIn and Facebook are under pressure to show profitability and expand uses of targeted advertising. Public awareness is amplified by Google, as it partners with other site owners to place targeted ads. Facebook is also placing targeted ads on third-party mobile applications [7].

Why are people who are familiar with targeted ads in search engine results uncomfortable? A person approaches a search engine with a question. An ad that is related to the current query is like a friend who makes a relevant suggestion in the course of a conversation. On a social networking site, one discovers that a discussion with friends is being listened to, resulting in an advertisement that is often only loosely tied to the conversation. It is different.

How people and sites will adjust to this in the long term remains to be seen. For now, in our sample, those who are uncomfortable are not outraged. "Not offensive, just unnerving," one said. Frequency of daily Facebook and Twitter use has plateaued, and we read reports of similar retrenchment more broadly, but the rate of abandonment is remarkably low.

However, several respondents now draw a line at apps and games that demand access to personal information that does not seem necessary. Some said emphatically that they removed or refused to download them, a trend echoed in a September 2012 Pew report on smartphone use [3].

On the other hand, a game designer observed that he did not understand why some games asked for so much information, but added, "I think people are becoming really desensitized to it… I wouldn't be surprised if people became really desensitized to it really quickly."

He may be right, but some people are sensitive now. A 2005 study that quaintly called this now-ubiquitous information collection "spyware" reported that people do not read application EULAs (end user license agreements) that reveal such data collection [20]. Another study showed that people are surprised when they are told what is collected [28]. Targeting advertisements reveal what is collected and push some people to pay closer attention to EULAs.

Will more people look closely? Will those who do so relay their findings, perhaps on social networking sites, to inform a larger community? We don't know, but app developers might be advised to ask only for what they need and let prospective users know why the app needs it.[1]

Location tracking

The safety of location information is an area of heightened concern. Although this is a topic dear to privacy experts and the mass media, early studies reported that users are wholly unconcerned about it [31, 32]. Many people tweet their location or check in on Facebook or Foursquare, and some of our informants reported positive experiences. Others abandoned location tracking only because it led to no encounters for them. However, others described robbery and stalking concerns. Fear of "a friend of a friend" can motivate people to set access controls: Restricting messages to a closer circle to increase the sense of security.

Gender

A finding that surprised some is that men expressed greater concern about social networking than women. Female students expressed significantly more concerns in mid-2007 [17]. But later surveys found women using access controls more heavily [41], a trend seen also in our study. This was correlated with women having fewer concerns. Women may organize their online worlds in ways that make them comfortable. It is also possible that women working for a 75% male technology company are not easily intimidated.

CONCLUSION

"Before Facebook, how did we know what people were listening to on Spotify?" – A joke recounted in an interview.

With change so rapid, it is difficult to remember how life used to be and anticipate with confidence what is coming. Site designers and frequent site visitors accumulate experience, learn to avoid pitfalls, and bend a new medium to their purposes.

Facebook, LinkedIn, Twitter, Pinterest, Instagram and so on are not just places we visit, they house spaces we shape and spend time in. In 2008, most site users had one large room that was growing crowded. Many resolved this by finding or creating different spaces in which to hold different conversations. Now some are unsettled to discover that

[1] At an abstract level, the monitoring of conversations by site owners or intelligence agencies are forms of boundary regulation, differing in that these 'friends' are uninvited. Coping strategies seem limited. Sites could let people pay to opt out. People could shift to highly encrypted channels.

their conversations are being listened to by the architects, who strive to balance helpfulness and intrusiveness as they put up billboards or interject comments. To find a comfort level that supports these free services requires ongoing, delicate negotiations.

We surveyed and interviewed a diverse but not fully representative set of people. There were no teenagers. Most are over thirty, economically secure, and relatively well-informed about technology. They have a wide range of jobs and are drawn from around the world. In general, they seemed uninhibited in their responses.

Even savvy people are feeling their way forward in this new world. Recall the developer who said, "How will they be able to pinpoint me? If everybody's not private, then everybody's private. No privacy leads to all privacy. How are they going to be able to pinpoint?" There is an answer: "With computers." Research can guide the developers and the users of these helpful and intrusive technologies.

ACKNOWLEDGMENTS

Anne Archambault worked on this for three years, Meredith Skeels worked on the first year, and Gina Venolia assisted throughout. We thank Cliff Lampe for comments and the CSCW 2014 coordinator/shepherd who saw value that mostly eluded the previous 15 conference reviewers.

REFERENCES

1. Archambault, A. & Grudin, J. 2012. A longitudinal study of Facebook, LinkedIn, & Twitter use. *Proc. CHI 2012*, 2741-2750. ACM.
2. boyd, d. 2008. Taken out of context: American teen sociality in networked publics. PhD Dissertation, University of California-Berkeley.
3. Boyles, J.L., Smith, A. & Madden, M. 2012. Privacy and data management on mobile devices. Pew Internet. http://www.pewinternet.org/Reports/2012/Mobile-Privacy.aspx
4. Brzozowski, M.J., Sandholm, T. & Hogg, T. 2009. Effects of feedback and peer pressure on contributions to enterprise social media. *Proc. GROUP 2009,* 61-70.
5. Burke, M. & Kraut, R. 2013. Using facebook after losing a job: Differential benefits of strong and weak ties. *Proc. CSCW 2013,* 1419-1430. ACM.
6. Burke, M., Kraut, R. & Marlow, C. 2011. Social capital on Facebook: Differentiating uses and users. *Proc. CHI 2011,* 571-580. ACM.
7. Constine, J. 2012. Facebook beta launches new mobile ad network using your data to target you with banner ads in other apps. TechCrunch, September 18th. http://techcrunch.com/2012/09/18/facebook-mobile-ad-network/
8. DiMicco, J., Geyer, W., Millen, D.R., Dugan, C. & Brownholtz, B. 2009. People sensemaking and relationship building on an enterprise social networking site. *Proc. HICSS 2009.* IEEE.
9. DiMicco, J.M. & Millen, D.R. 2007. Identity management: Multiple presentations of self in Facebook. *Proc. Group 2007*, 383-386. ACM.
10. DiMicco, J., Millen, D.R., Geyer, W., Dugan, C., Brownholtz, B. & Muller, M. 2008. Motivations for social networking at work. *Proc. CSCW 2008*. 711-720.\
11. Efimova, L. & Grudin, J. 2007. Crossing boundaries: A case study of employee blogging. *Proc. HICSS'07.*
12. Ehrlich, K. & Shami, N. S. 2010. Microblogging inside and outside the workplace. *Proc. ICWSM 2010.* AAAI.
13. Ellison, N., Vitak, J., Steinfield, C., Gray, R., & Lampe, C. 2011. Negotiating privacy concerns and social capital needs in a social media environment. In S. Trepte and L. Reinecke (Eds.), *Privacy online,* 19-32. Springer.
14. Facebook Inc. 2013. First Quarter 2013 Results. http://investor.fb.com/releasedetail.cfm?ReleaseID=761090
15. Farnham, S. & Churchill, E. 2011. Faceted identity, faceted lives: Social and technical issues with being yourself online. *Proc. CSCW 2012,* 359-368. ACM.
16. Farzan, R., DiMicco, J.M., Millen, D.R., Brownholtz, B., Geyer, W. & Dugan, C. 2008. Results from deploying a participation incentive mechanism within the enterprise. *Proc. CHI 2008*, 563-572. ACM.
17. Fogel, J. & Nemad, E. 2009. Internet social network communities: Risk taking, trust, and privacy concerns. *Computers in Human Behavior, 25,* 1, 153-160.
18. Geyer, W., Dugan, C., Brownholtz, B., Masli, M., Daly, E. & Millen, D.R. 2011. An open, social microcalendar for the enterprise: Timely*? Proc. CHI 2011,* 247-256.
19. Geyer, W., Dugan, C., DiMicco, J., Millen, D.R., Brownholtz, B. & Muller, M. 2008. Use and reuse of shared lists as a social content type. *Proc. CHI 2008*, 1545-1554. ACM.
20. Good, N., Dhamija, R., Grossklags, J., Thaw, D., Aronowitz, S., Mulligan, D. & Konstan, J. 2005. Stopping spyware at the gate: A user study of privacy, notice, and spyware. *Proc. SOUPS 2005*, 43-53. ACM.
21. Hargittai, E. 2007. Whose space? Differences among users and non-users of social network sites. *Journal of Computer-Mediated Communication, 13, 1, article 14.*
22. Hogan, B. 2010. The presentation of self in the age of social media: Distinguishing performances and exhibitions online. *Sci Technol Soc, 30,* 377–386.
23. Kairam, S., Brzozowski, M., Huffaker, D. & Chi. E. 2012. Talking in circles: Selective sharing in Google+. *Proc. CHI 2012,* 1065-1074. ACM.
24. Lampe, C., Ellison, N. & Steinfield. 2006. A Face(book) in the crowd: Social searching vs. social browsing. *Proc. CSCW 2006,* 167-170. ACM.
25. Lampe, C., Ellison, N. & Steinfield. 2008. Changes in use and perception of Facebook. *Proc. CSCW 2008,* 721-730. ACM.

26. Lampe, C., Vitak, J., Gray, R. & Ellison, N. 2012. Perceptions of facebook's value as an information source. *Proc. CHI 2012,* 3195-3204. ACM.

27. Laporte, N. 2013. Why TV execs are still skeptical of Twitter's power to attract eyeballs. *Fast Company.* http://www.fastcompany.com/3019669/

28. Lin, J., Amini, S., Hong, J.I., Sadeh, N., Lindqvist, J. & Zhang, J. 2012. Expectation and purpose: understanding users' mental models of mobile app privacy through crowdsourcing. *Proc. Ubicomp 2012,* 501-510. ACM.

29. Miles, M. B. & Huberman. A. M. 1999. *Qualitative data analysis.* New York: Sage.

30. Naaman, M., Boase, J. & Lai, C.H. 2010. Is it really all about me? Message content in social awareness streams. *Proc. CSCW 2010,* 189-192. ACM.

31. Page, X., Kobsa, A. & Knijnenburg, B.P. 2012. Don't disturb my circles! Boundary preservation is at the center of location-sharing concerns. *Proc. ICWSM 2012,* 266-273. AAAI.

32. Raynes-Goldie, K. 2010. Aliases, creeping, and wall cleaning: Understanding privacy in the age of Facebook. *First Monday, 15,* 1.

33. Rooksby, J. & Sommerville, I. 2012. The management and use of social network sites in a government department. *Computer Supported Cooperative Work, 21,* 4-5, 397-415.

34. Skeels, M. & Grudin, J. 2009. When social networks cross boundaries: A case study of workplace use of Facebook and LinkedIn. *Proc. Group 2009,* 95-104.

35. Smith, A. & Brenner, J. 2012. Twitter use 2012. Pew Internet. http://www.pewinternet.org/Reports/2012/Twitter-Use-2012/Findings.aspx

36. Steinfield, C., DiMicco, J.M., Ellison, N.B. & Lampe, C. 2009. Bowling online: Social networking and social capital within the organization. *Proc. Communities and Technology 2009.*

37. Stutzman, F. & Hartzog, W. 2012. Boundary regulation in social media. *Proc. CSCW 2012,* 769-778. ACM.

38. Thom, J. & Millen. D.R. 2012. Stuff IBMers say: Microblogs as an expression of organizational culture. *Proc. ICWSM 2012.* AAAI.

39. Thom-Santelli, J. & Millen, D. 2009. Learning by seeing: Photo-viewing in the workplace. *Proc. CHI 2009,* 2081-2090. ACM.

40. Treem, J. & Leonardi, P. 2012. Social media use in organizations: Exploring the affordances of visibility, editability, persistence, and association. *Communication yearbook, 36,* 143-189.

41. Tufekci, Z. 2012. Youth and privacy in public networks. *Proc. ICWSM 2012,* 338-345. AAAI.

42. Turner, T., Qvarfordt, P., Biehl, J.Y., Golovchinsky, G., & Back, M. 2010. Exploring the workplace communication ecology. *Proc. CHI 2010,* 841-850.

43. Voida, A., Harmon, E. & Al-Ani, B. 2012. Bridging between organizations and the public: Volunteer coordinators' uneasy relationship with social computing. *Proc. CHI 2012,* 1967-1976. ACM.

44. Wang, Y. & Kobsa, A. 2009. Privacy in online social networking at the workplace. *Proc. CSE 2009*, 975-978.

45. Wang, Y., Norcie, G., Komandura, S., Acquisti, A. Leon, P.G. & Cranor, L. 2011. "I regretted the minute I pressed share": A qualitative study of regrets on Facebook. *Proc. SOUPS 2011.*

46. Wilson, R. E., Gosling, S. D. & Graham, L. T. 2012. A review of Facebook research in the social sciences. *Perspectives on Psychological Science, 7,* 3, 203-220.

47. Woelfer, J. & Hendry, D. 2012. Homeless young people on social network sites. *Proc. CHI 2012.* 2825-2834.

48. Wu, A., DiMicco, J. & Millen, D.R. 2010. Detecting professional versus personal closeness using an enterprise social network site. *Proc. CHI 2010,* 1955-1964.

49. Zhang, J., Qu, Y., Cody, J. & Wu, Y. 2010. A case study of micro-blogging in the enterprise: Use, value, and related issues. *Proc. CHI 2010*, 123-132. ACM.

50. Zhao, D. & Rosson, M.B. 2009. How and why people Twitter: The role that micro-blogging plays in informal communication at work. *Proc. GROUP 2009*, 243-252.

Understanding Employee Social Media Chatter with Enterprise Social Pulse

N. Sadat Shami[1], Jiang Yang[1], Laura Panc[1], Casey Dugan[2], Tristan Ratchford[2], Jamie Rasmussen[2], Yannick Assogba[2], Tal Steier[3], Todd Soule[2], Stela Lupushor[1], Werner Geyer[2], Ido Guy[3], Jonathan Ferrar[1]

[1]IBM, 1 New Orchard Road, Armonk, NY 10504, USA
{ sadat, yangjiang, lpanc, stela.lupushor, jaferrar } @ us.ibm.com
[2]IBM Research, 1 Rogers St., Cambridge, MA 02142, USA
{ cadugan, tratch, jrasmus, yannick, tssoule, werner.geyer } @ us.ibm.com
[3]IBM Research, Mt. Carmel, Haifa 31905, Israel { ido, talst } @ il.ibm.com

ABSTRACT
The rise of social media in the enterprise has enabled new ways for employees to speak up and communicate openly with colleagues. This rich textual data can potentially be mined to better understand the opinions and sentiment of employees for the benefit of the organization. In this paper, we introduce Enterprise Social Pulse (ESP) – a tool designed to support analysts whose job involves understanding employee chatter. ESP aggregates and analyzes data from internal and external social media sources while respecting employee privacy. It surfaces the data through a user interface that supports organic results and keyword search, data segmentation and filtering, and several analytics and visualization features. An evaluation of ESP was conducted with 19 Human Resources professionals. Results from a survey and interviews with participants revealed the value and willingness to use ESP, but also surfaced challenges around deploying an employee social media listening solution in an organization.

Author Keywords
Social media; workplace; social analytics; social listening.

ACM Classification Keywords
H.5.3 [Information Interfaces and Presentation]: Group and Organization Interfaces.

INTRODUCTION
The importance of employee feedback to an organization's well-being is well known and extensively studied [19]. In today's complex business environment constant change is the norm. Traditional top-down decision-making is becoming increasingly difficult because of the complexity and amount of information needed. Involving employees by enabling constructive, change-oriented communication behaviors, often called 'employee voice' [19], has been shown to improve organizational performance [10, 22]. The notion of employee voice has been studied in many contexts (e.g. [10, 22, 27]). There are various ways in which employees can speak up and provide their input, e.g. direct feedback and discussions with leadership, suggestion boxes, surveys etc.

CSCW'14, February 15 - 19 2014, Baltimore, MD, USA
Copyright 2014 ACM 978-1-4503-2540-0/14/02...$15.00.
http://dx.doi.org/10.1145/2531602.2531650

Different methods of soliciting employee feedback have both advantages and disadvantages. Management willingness to hear employees can create a culture of openness and two-way communication [10]. However, direct feedback to leaders can be hampered by power differences and might only revolve around localized issues. Surveys, on the other hand, are typically anonymous and allow employees to speak more openly without the fear of retribution. When properly administered, surveys can be a powerful tool for understanding employee voice [25]. They allow an organization to obtain responses on targeted questions of interest from a potentially large number of employees. Like any research tool, surveys have their limitations as well. Once a year surveys may not surface emergent issues experienced by an employee population. More frequent (e.g. quarterly) surveys may cause employees to feel survey fatigue and are costly to administer. A proper survey takes time to design, deploy, and analyze. This time requirement may prevent an organization from being aware of or responding to an issue affecting the employee experience right away. Furthermore, if the response rate of a survey is low, it may not be representative of the entire workforce.

The advent of social media in the enterprise provides a new opportunity for organizations to take advantage of the unstructured content being generated by employees. By definition, social media is more informal, and is a medium where employees spontaneously share information and express opinions, often without prompting. Compared to surveys, social media content can potentially be leveraged to provide a more 'real-time' understanding of the employee experience.

Social media listening has most commonly been used in domains such as marketing to monitor brand sentiment and engage with customers [9, 20]. It has also proven useful as an early warning system for crises [24] and responding to them [45]. We see great potential in social media listening to provide useful insights about workforce opinions and sentiment. While analyzing social media content is not 'employee voice' in the traditional sense, it does provide an additional source of information for an enterprise to glean business-relevant input from employees. This potential benefit does come with challenges. These include respecting employee privacy, filtering out noise from social media, representativeness, and validity of the data.

Listening to employee social media chatter differs in important ways from other forms of social media listening such as listening to customers. Social media listening by an employer could be viewed by some as employee monitoring with the intent to discipline offending employees. The realization that one's employer may be analyzing public social media chatter can cause an employee to self-censor and temper expressions of negativity. Taken to the extreme, it may reduce levels of participation in public social media.

Fear of speaking up or organizational silence is not a new phenomenon. Studies conducted *before* the advent of social media found that many employees choose the safe option of silence, even when sharing their thoughts would help the organization [33]. Social media is becoming a channel through which many are getting increasingly comfortable to share their thoughts and opinions about various issues. In order to encourage speech, researchers recommend management to explicitly invite and acknowledge employees' ideas through cultivating a culture that makes employees safe enough to contribute fully [11]. By allaying fears of negative repercussions, management can position social media as a real-time channel for employees to express themselves. Unquestionably, this depends on how successful an organization is in engendering the trust of its employees.

In this paper, we introduce Enterprise Social Pulse (ESP) – a social listening tool that allows analysts in the Human Resources (HR) or a related business function of an organization to gain real-time insights from workforce social media content in addition to other channels such as surveys. ESP aggregates employee social media chatter from internal and external sources, combines it with enterprise data, and supports search, data segmentation, filtering, analytics and visualization. The paper is organized as follows. We first review related work on soliciting employee feedback, the use of social media by employees, and tools for understanding employee sentiment from social media. We then discuss the design principles and design requirements that motivated and shaped ESP, and describe its various features. A description of a user study evaluating ESP, and three mini case studies of real-world usage follow. We conclude with a discussion of the issues encountered in the deployment of ESP, and offer practical suggestions to those interested in deploying such a tool to understand employee chatter.

BACKGROUND LITERATURE

The importance of employee comments and suggestions intended to improve critical work processes are essential to organizational performance [10]. Many scholars have highlighted the virtues of this for organizational health [16, 40] and effective decision making [35]. In a complex world, leaders need input from across the organization to understand the impact of internal practices on the employee experience [43]. Additionally, channels that allow for employee voice are viewed positively, because they signal that employees are valued members of the organization [29]. If employees feel their organization values them, they will be more likely to identify with and trust the organization [12]. Studies have shown that employees evaluate management decisions more favorably when those decisions allow for employee input, even when the input does not have much impact on decision outcomes [46].

Surveys are the most common form through which organizations solicit employees' opinions. Almost three out of every four large organizations in the United States surveys its employees [23]. Employee surveys allow an organization to diagnose itself, evaluate programs and policies, transmit corporate values, and provide an avenue for feedback on decision making [44]. Employee surveys can help management understand the degree to which an organizational strategy is being implemented and the alignment of the organization's policies to achieving strategic goals [41]. Ever since employee surveys were developed in the 1930s, they continue to be a popular instrument for information gathering, communication, and decision making [31]. The data generated through surveys can be quantified and compared against prior time periods or industry averages.

Research has found that a quick response to issues arising from an employee survey is crucial for building employee commitment [28]. Employees become frustrated when the turnaround time for surveys is slow. Employees can perceive this as inaction. Consequently, traditional surveys, with report back 4-6 months after administration, can be viewed as failing at their objective to open the lines of communication between employer and employee [28].

Real-time analysis of social media content of employees may ameliorate this problem of turnaround time. The use of various forms of internal and external social media such as social network sites, blogs, microblogs, forums, and online communities is proliferating in organizations. According to a survey conducted by global consulting firm McKinsey, 65% of companies reported the use of social technologies in their organizations [5]. Surveys of Microsoft employees conducted annually from 2008 to 2011 found gradual increase of the use of Facebook, LinkedIn and Twitter [1].

Increased adoption of social media by employees presents an opportunity for an organization to better understand employees' thoughts and opinions through social listening.

The analysis of unstructured social media text has been used in a variety of contexts from government services [37], to marketing [21] and finance [15]. The domain of 'crisis informatics' provides a good example of how the noise in social media can be reduced to provide positive outcomes in near real-time For example, Palen et al. [36] provide a framework by which people can judge the helpfulness of information by establishing source-level and individual-level credibility. In the deluge of social media, accuracy is ideal, but not the measure by which people can utilize information. In their framework, *helpfulness* is the critical criteria rather than producing the 'right' answer. Social media use in organizations where identity is clearly delineated may suffer less from concerns of credibility. Nonetheless shifting away from precision as a gold standard in evaluating social media content is useful, and one that we will draw on in understanding employee chatter.

Researchers have built visualizations that allow near real-time analysis of unstructured social media content. Such visualizations help make sense of the large amount of text generated in social media. For example, Eddi provides an interface for browsing Twitter streams that clusters tweets by topics [4]. TwitInfo is a Twitter based event tracking interface that can collect, aggregate, and visualize tweets about user-specified events as they unfold [30]. In an enterprise context, Streamz uses a faceted search approach to provide advanced capabilities of search, navigation, and visualization over an enterprise activity stream [18].

There has been less focus on tools to understand employee social chatter within the context of an enterprise. Previous work has analyzed textual patterns in email to understand phenomena such as organizational hierarchy [14] and newcomer socialization [48]. De Choudhury and Counts analyzed 204,284 posts from 22,968 Microsoft employees that used an internal microblogging tool called OfficeTalk [7]. Using a psycholinguistic lexicon known as LIWC (http://www.liwc.net) to analyze the content, they found that employees generally express positive affect throughout the workday, but exhibit a sharp drop in positive affect when working afterhours.

There are several ways we believe our work provides a novel contribution. We are not aware of any tool that allows an organization to intelligently mine the content of chatter generated by employees on internal and external social media. The design principles embedded in our approach respect employee privacy while allowing the organization to make sense and act on employee chatter. Additionally, we provide practical steps for deploying an employee social media listening tool in an organization.

ENTERPRISE SOCIAL PULSE (ESP)

At its most fundamental level, ESP aims to answer the questions: 'What are my employees talking about? And what is the sentiment of the chatter?' It is a tool meant for analysts in Human Resources or other business function of a company, such as workforce communications, with the responsibility to understand employee chatter and identify input valuable to the organization.

ESP requirements and design principles were generated through persona development in interactive workshops among designers, engineers, and HR professionals. For example, HR needed to compare specific employee segments across business units and countries. This led to a requirement to have filters based on employee demographics. The need to understand employee opinions on particular policies or events required the ability to search. The need to understand emerging chatter led to a requirement of topic extraction and top lists.

Design Principles

Augment, not replace

We do not view social media as a substitute for other ways of collecting input from employees (e.g. surveys). Previous research suggests that social media content can supplement but not replace surveys in areas where precise estimates and correlations are required [34]. Rather, the goal of ESP is to 'fill in the gap' in between periodic surveys without putting a burden on the respondents. In addition to the topics traditionally investigated through surveys and other means such as 'Employee Satisfaction' and 'Business Improvement', ESP is intended to provide a real-time expression of employee thoughts, opinions, and sentiment on any emerging or continuing issue. For example, ESP may identify chatter about a social campaign on 'Women in Tech', and the scale of the chatter can be ever evolving and new relevant topics can keep emerging over time.

Establish authentic employee content

A challenge in understanding employee chatter through social media is identifying employees on social media, especially in external social media. We are only interested in understanding the chatter of current employees. While former employees, former interns and other entities may be discussing topics related to the company, analyzing such discussion is outside the scope of ESP. As we explain in the next section, we used a crowdsourced approach to identify current employees and allow them to opt-into having their external social media content mined. Anonymized social media content is matched with demographic characteristics to allow an analyst to segment the data along different dimensions and obtain fine-grained understanding of employee chatter.

Only mine public data

Social media can be both private and public. ESP only mines content that is made public by the author. In other words, ESP aggregates content that anyone can read and potentially analyze. ESP does not mine email or instant messaging communication. ESP excludes content from countries where there are restrictions of mining public social media content (e.g. Germany, Austria, Netherlands).

Respect employee privacy

ESP operates under the principle that the company is not interested in what specific individuals are saying. Rather it is interested in what they are saying at an aggregated level. If enough employees are saying the same thing, that likely deserves the attention of the company. ESP goes to great lengths to respect employee privacy. First, all social media content is anonymized at the point of collection (details are provided in the next section). Secondly, ESP has different levels of access control. We restrict view access to individual social media posts (called 'snippets' in ESP) because search engines often store social media content, and searching for such content can reveal its author's identity. Snippet-level access is required when there is a need to make sense of the context in which topics are being discussed to provide richer insights to business leaders. Only a handful of 'admin' level users (less than 15) can view social media snippets. These 'admin' level users are those analysts who already have access to sensitive employee data because of their job responsibilities. Others with 'business user' level access can only view analytics in aggregate form.

Within ESP, social media content is associated with demographic characteristics of the authors. In order to prevent inferring identity when searching within ESP, snippets are shown only when the search returns more than 20 snippets. When a search result returns less than 20 snippets, a message notifies the user that results cannot be displayed to protect privacy. Additionally there are only two demographical filters that can be applied at a time, which limits the ability to drill into a very narrow employee segment. Since identity information cannot be linked to individual snippets, the company cannot contact an employee based on what he or she said.

Respect Terms of Use of sites mined

ESP adheres to the Terms of Use of the sites that it mines content from.

System Description

Data flow to ensure privacy

ESP currently collects data from one internal source and one external source but can be configured for additional data sources. Internal data is provided by a social platform used in the company. This platform supports microblog status updates, blogs, bookmarks, and community forums. By default, all employees have a profile on this social platform. All content authored by an employee is associated with their identity – nothing is anonymous.

The external data that ESP analyzes comes from Twitter. We are only interested in Twitter content from our employees. Identifying employees of a particular company on Twitter is a non-trivial task. We use the Twitter user search API to do this. Querying the API with the name of the company returns a set of matching users. We also aggregate users on Twitter lists that contain the company name. From this seed list of users, we ask employees to identify those that they know through an internal crowdsourcing service. Employees were interested in finding their colleagues on Twitter and were generally supportive of performing the identification task (more details on the service can be found in [26]). Once an employee is identified, she receives an email asking if she would like to opt into the service. If she declines, her tweets are not collected. So far, out of 4,462 invited users of the crowdsourcing service, 1,827 (41%) employees have opted-in and 177 (4%) explicitly denied being listed. The remaining users are pending as invitations to this service are distributed through email and can often get ignored. Content from employees that have not taken any action on the email is not analyzed in ESP. Employees who opted in come from all business units across 55 countries, which is a fairly representative sample of the organization. Analysis of the demographic characteristics of those that opted out revealed no significant differences from those that opted in.

Once social media content from the internal and external sources are collected, identity is anonymized using an MD5 cryptographic hash function. A given string (e.g. an email address) will always resolve to the same 32 character MD5 hash. Once hashed, there is no technical way to reverse the hash and recover the original string. Any references to an identity within the social media snippet (e.g. @username) are not hashed. However, as mentioned, the actual social media snippet is viewable to a small set of authorized users.

In order to provide useful segmentation of the data, identity information from the corporate directory and the HR data warehouse are also hashed using the same MD5 cryptographic hash function. This enables ESP to match social media content with employee demographic characteristics, while keeping the identity anonymous.

Text Analytics on Social Media

ESP currently provides two types of analysis: Topic extraction and sentiment analysis. These two types of analysis are available during search and for the demographic segmentations supported by our system.

Topic extraction first extracts candidate noun phrases [39] from the snippets using the OpenNLP open source project [2]. These candidates are then assigned with scores using the KL+TB method, which has been previously shown to be effective for term extraction in social streams [6]. This method first assigns a score with a noun phrase based on its Kullback-Leibler (*KL*) measure [3], which is a non-symmetric distance measure between two given distributions. KL favors noun phrases that maximize the KL divergence between the language model of the current subset of snippets and the language model of the entire ESP dataset. On top of the KL statistical score, a tag-boost (*TB*) is applied, which promotes keywords that are likely to appear as tags, based on a given well-tagged folksonomy. The folksonomy generated from a social tagging application deployed in the company was used to this end.

Sentiment analysis is the task of finding the opinions of authors about specific entities [13]. ESP uses a commercial sentiment analysis engine to parse social media data and assign a sentiment value (e.g. positive, negative, neutral) to each snippet. Sentiment analysis is still an evolving science since human language is filled with irony, sarcasm, humor etc. This is exacerbated in social media. In order to measure the accuracy of the sentiment, a reliability analysis was performed. A random sample of 500 snippets was collected with their associated sentiment as detected by the sentiment analysis engine. A researcher then went through these same 500 snippets and classified their sentiment. An inter-rater reliability was performed comparing the machine and human rater. The level of agreement for positive, negative, and neutral sentiment was 0.76 ($p < 0.001$) using Cohen's Kappa [8]. Realizing that sentiment classification by the machine needs to be improved for the company to make decisions based on ESP data, the team implemented a feature that allows a human analyst to correct or verify the sentiment of a given snippet.

Once social media content is anonymized, matched with anonymized employee records from the corporate directory and HR data warehouse, it is run through the sentiment analysis engine, and stored in the ESP database. Data is then surfaced through the ESP user interface. Data is stored and available for querying within less than 5 minutes of being generated, providing near real-time access to employee social media content.

ENTERPRISE SOCIAL PULSE FEATURES

Below is a summary of the various features in ESP. All features are available to all users unless otherwise stated.

Organic results and keyword search

When an analyst wants to get a general understanding of employee chatter within a given timeframe, she can view the 9 portlets in the 'Overview' tab of ESP (Figure 1). This provides 'organic' results without having to enter any search term(s). An analyst can also perform a keyword search when she is interested in understanding the chatter around a particular topic. The content of the 9 portlets will change based on the search term entered. Often times multiple keywords are needed to express a topic. ESP allows the aggregation of multiple keywords into a single user defined 'concept'. ESP supports both keyword searches and searches on 'concepts'. Below we briefly describe the contents of the most important portlets.

Overview

This portlet provides summary information about the volume of social media content and associated sentiment. The sentiment analysis engine breaks the social media content into snippets and uses an NLP approach to

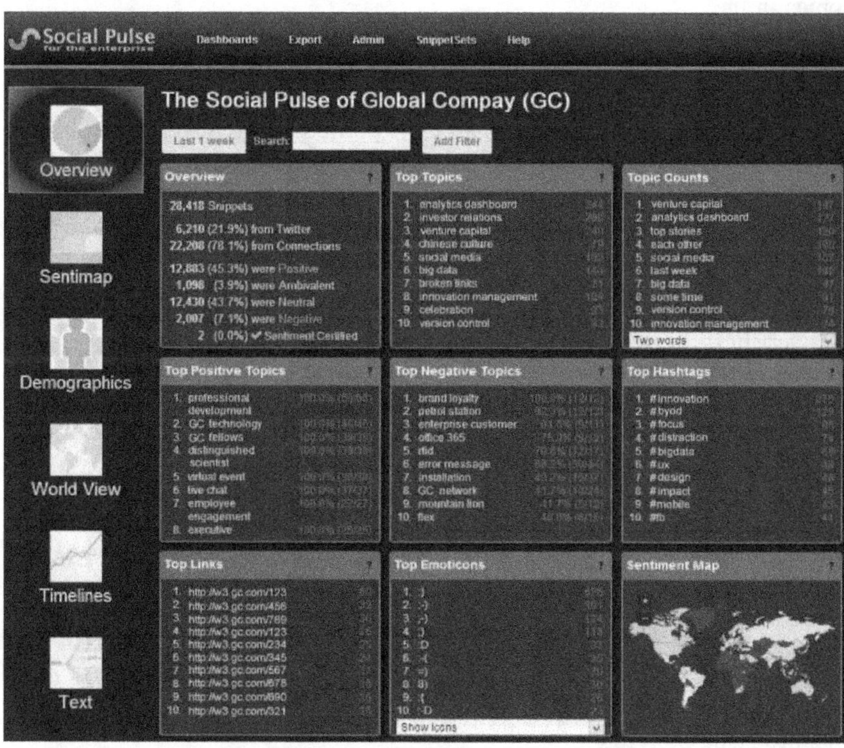

Figure 1. Overview tab in ESP showing 9 portlets. Portlet content was modified to protect confidentiality.

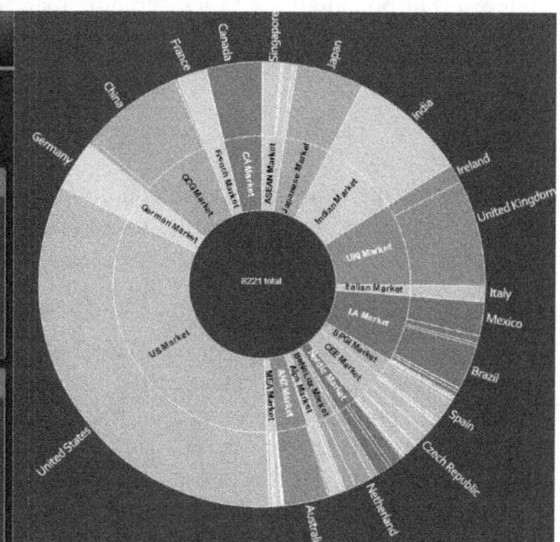

Figure 2. Sunburst visualization of the number of employees posting social media content by country in a week.

determine the sentiment score of the snippet. If there are one or more positive phrases detected – the sentiment of the snippet is determined as positive. Similarly, negative sentiment is assigned to a snippet when one or more negative phrases are found. Ambivalent sentiment indicates that an equal amount of positive and negative phrases have been found. Neutral means the snippet does not contain any positive nor negative phrases.

Top Topics
This portlet helps users identify prominent and trending topics in the set of snippets being analyzed, based on the KL+TB measure explained previously. The KL+TB score can sometimes be higher for topics with lower counts (listed next to the topics).

Topic counts
This portlet lists top topics based on strict frequency counts. It allows showing one-word topics, two-word topics, or three-word topics. It offers a different way to identify important topics in parallel with Top Topics.

Top positive topics and Top negative topics
These two portlets list top topics with extreme sentiment scores. The system first calculates top-k topics using the KL+TB measure (currently k is set to 1,000) that pass a count threshold (currently set to 10) and considers those that have the highest portion (shown next to the topics) of positive or negative snippets as Top Positive or Top Negative, respectively. This feature is particularly helpful in identifying topics with strong sentiment and thus of great interest, but potentially with less volume than topics in the general Top Topics list.

Sentiment map
This portlet visualizes the geographical distribution of sentiment such that users can quickly compare across countries. In the world map, each country's color reflects its ratio of positive (more green) to negative (more red) snippets.

Data segmentation and filtering
ESP supports segmentation of data based on characteristics such as business unit, geography, job category, work location, years of service, manager/non-manager, performance rating etc. In fact, there are 40 filters to segment the data. However only two can be applied at a time given the privacy considerations discussed earlier. Any search on ESP can be filtered based on these dimensions. Search and segmentation based on filters are available in all the tabs in ESP. For example, the 'Demographics' tab in ESP provides a breakdown of the set of snippets being analyzed by characteristics such as work location, manager / non-manager, performance rating, business unit, country etc. Figure 2 shows a sample visualization of the 'employees by country' portlet in the 'Demographics' tab

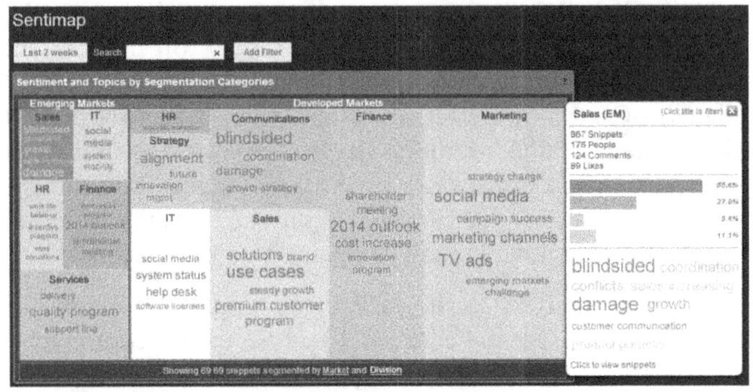

Figure 3. 'Sentimap' Tree Map visualization.

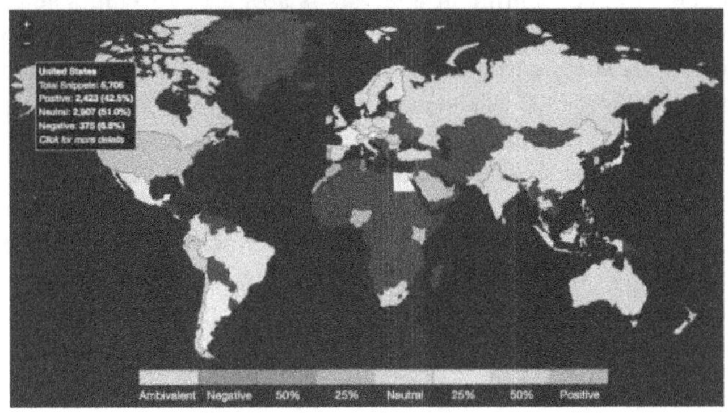

Figure 4. 'World View' for a given week. Sentiment color is overlayed on top of countries, and hovering over a country reveals more details.

for a given set of snippets. Additionally, users can specify or search within a custom date range.

Custom dashboard
An analyst may want to follow a particular business unit, geography or other demographic segment. ESP has the ability to set up all the 9 portlets in the 'Overview' tab pre-filtered based on an analyst's needs and saved such that an analyst can monitor the social stream of interest without having to specify filter(s) every time.

Analytics and visualization
ESP supports a variety of interactive visualization features. We briefly describe them below.

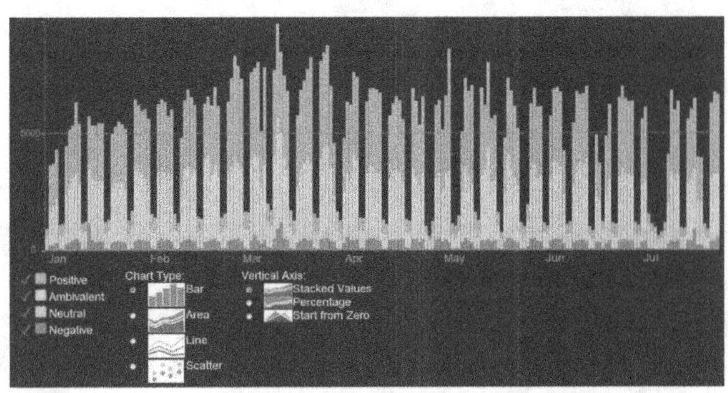

Figure 5. 'Timelines' tab showing sentiment over time.

Sentimap

The 'Sentimap' tab displays a visualization known as a 'Tree Map' [42] which compares volume, sentiment, and topics all at once across groups. Each cell represents a category of content (e.g. data source, sentiment) or authors (e.g. business unit, country). The size of the cell represents the number of snippets from that category, and the color of the cell represents the aggregate sentiment for those snippets. Top topics of the snippets from each category are also shown and sized according to frequencies. Figure 3 shows an example sentimap where the user is hovering over the 'Sales' cell to reveal more information about it. The terms 'blindsided' and 'damage' show high volume of primarily negative sentiment.

World view

The 'World View' tab displays a bigger version of the 'sentiment map' found in the 'Overview' tab. The map is interactive and provides more screen real-estate for the analyst to get a sense of the data through contextual hovers that display information by country (Figure 4).

Timelines

The 'Timelines' feature shows the variation of volume and sentiment of snippets over a selected time range. As shown in Figure 5, bars are colored by sentiment type and sized by daily volume. Multiple interactive features are offered to help visualize the data, such as legends that can be reordered/removed, and chart type/axis options.

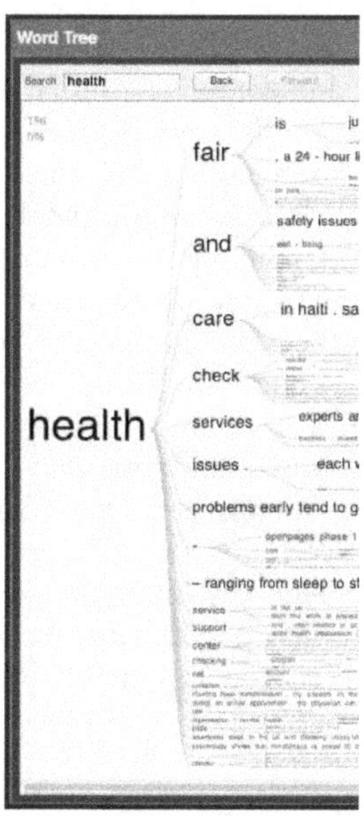

Figure 6. Word Tree visualization showing words that appear after 'health'.

Figure 7. 'Table of snippets' showing sample snippets.

Events

Many times certain events trigger social chatter. The 'Events' tab (not shown) allows an analyst to analyze this chatter by specifying a specific date and looking at the list of topics a) before that date, b) after that date, and c) shared across that date. It also determines if the event generated enough "buzz" to break through as a topic after it occurred.

Word tree

The word tree visualization [47] resides within the 'Text' tab and plots the word/phrase associations around a

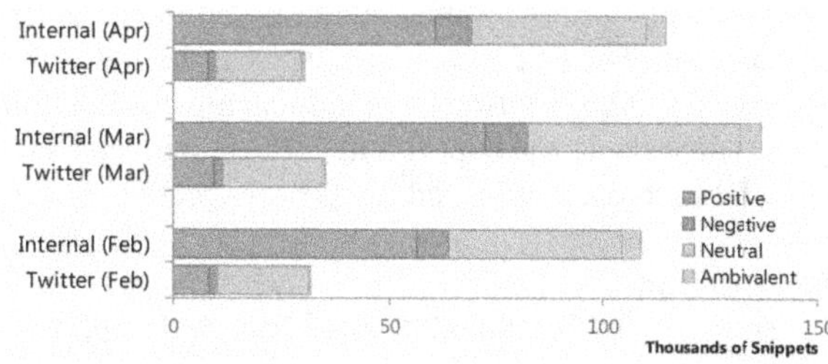

Figure 8: Volume of chatter by source (Feb – April, 2013).

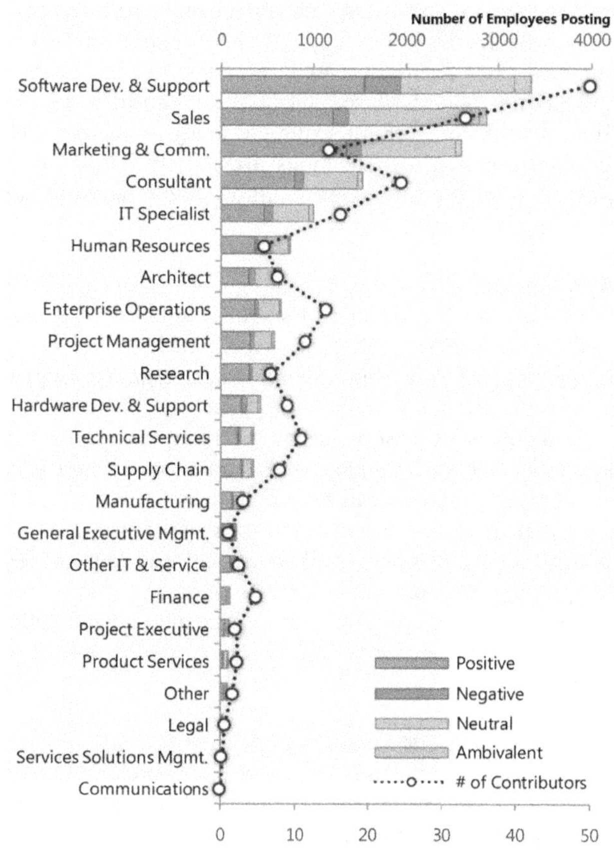

Figure 9: Volume of chatter by job role (Feb-April, 2013).

keyword being searched (Figure 6). Only users with 'admin' level access are allowed to view this tab. This visualization lets an analyst search for a word and see common phrases that appear before or after it, weighted by occurrence in the set of snippets being analyzed.

Data export

An analyst may want to perform advanced statistics or visualize the data in a manner different from ESP. In order to support this, ESP allows up to 10,000 rows of the social media snippets augmented by selected demographic data to be exported as a comma or tab delimited file. This feature is only available to users with 'admin' level access.

Table of snippets

Snippets can be sorted by date, source, sentiment, number of likes and number of comments. They can be individually selected to fix their sentiment or added to a collection of snippets (snippetset) for export and further analysis. This is only available to users with 'admin' level access (Figure 7).

Implementation

The system is implemented as a J2EE web application across two server nodes. One server manages the real-time data collection and serves as database server, the other server manages the web application and indexing of the data. We used Lucene (http://lucene.apache.org/) as a basic indexing technology but applied the organization's own adaptation of faceted search to support the various segmentation options described above. Sentiment analysis is done with a commercial sentiment analysis package. The user interface and visualizations are mostly based on the d3-dojo (https://github.com/sdqali/d3-dojo) and jQuery (http://jquery.com/) libraries.

DATA VOLUME

Figure 8 shows the volume of social chatter for the entire months of February through April 2013. We see a consistent pattern of more positive than negative snippets across time. Figure 9 shows how different job roles have different levels of posting behavior during the same time period. Software developers, and employees in Sales and Marketing & Communications are the most active. The data shows that there is representation of all business units and job roles in the company, albeit in varying degrees. The demographic distribution of posts largely matches the employee distribution, with software developers and sellers being a large proportion of the employee population of the organization.

USER EVALUATION

We conducted a user study to evaluate how well ESP meets the needs of HR professionals interested in understanding employee social media chatter. We utilized both quantitative and qualitative methods for this purpose.

Participants

We recruited 19 HR professionals of a large Information Technology company through email invitation. The majority of participants had been at the company for over five years. Participants originated from 4 countries (USA, Canada, China, Australia) and 10 of them were female. They held job responsibilities such as workforce analytics, employee engagement, employee & labor relations, talent partner, workforce enablement, HR location leader, and HR director. They had non-technical backgrounds.

Training

Participants were first required to complete an online course on data privacy. The course lasted about half an hour. The goal of the course was to educate participants on handling sensitive employee data. Following the course, participants were required to attend an hour-long training session on how to use ESP. In addition to receiving a tutorial on how to use the different features of ESP, this training session allowed participants to ask any questions they had. The training was recorded and the video was made available to access afterwards as needed. Additionally, we were available for one-on-one follow-up sessions with participants in case they needed further instructions or clarifications on using ESP. For the purposes of the study all participants were temporarily given admin access.

Task

Participants were given two weeks to familiarize themselves with ESP and complete a research task. The task consisted of thinking of any business question that participants wanted to answer, and then using ESP to explore that question. Results of the analysis were to be documented in a report. The report, similar to the task, was open-ended and participants could choose any format, framework, or length for their reports. The goal of this task-oriented method was not to study or compare task completion effectiveness but rather encourage authentic use of ESP in order to collect qualitative data about the value and usage of ESP for HR professionals. Some examples of business questions our participants explored include understanding employee sentiment on professional development and training, performance reviews, work life balance, LGBT and marriage equality, the onboarding experience, seller experience etc.

Survey and Interview

Upon submission of their reports, participants were asked about their experience using ESP through a survey. The survey consisted of 40 questions and took approximately 15 minutes to complete. The majority were Likert-scale questions to evaluate individual or overall features, with some open-ended ones asking for insights and comments. 18 of 19 participants completed the survey. At the conclusion of the survey, participants had the option of signing up for an interview. 12 of 19 participants signed up to be interviewed.

We conducted semi-structured interviews to elicit richer understanding of users' experience and expectations. We followed a semi-structured interview protocol, referred to interviewees' survey responses and reports, and probed when necessary. Two people conducted most interviews, with one person guiding the interview while the other took notes. Interviewers were not involved in the engineering and design of ESP. This was mentioned to interviewees to encourage them to be frank and honest in their responses. All interviews were recorded with the participants' permission and lasted on average about 45 minutes. Repeatedly listening to recordings and working over transcripts allowed us to identify emergent themes from interviews. Overall, the study lasted two weeks, with an additional day for those that signed up to be interviewed.

RESULTS

Survey: Evaluating ESP features

An overwhelming majority (17 of 18) of our participants see themselves using ESP going forward. About a third would use ESP monthly, while another third would use it weekly and a quarter of participants would use after an event of interest. 4 of 18 respondents are currently conducting searches/analysis on employee social media chatter (without using ESP). Most of those conducting social media searches believe that ESP can considerably improve their understanding of employee chatter. We were pleased to hear this from that sub-population as they are familiar with the challenges of social media listening. The responses to our Likert-scale questions (Figure 10) reveal that the majority of respondents view ESP as a valuable tool to gather workforce insights. However, concerns remain about the representativeness of the data, which is consistent with prior research [34].

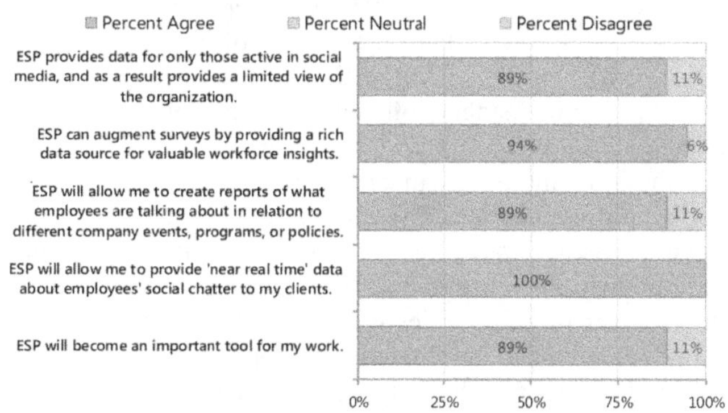

Figure 10. Survey results. $N = 18$.

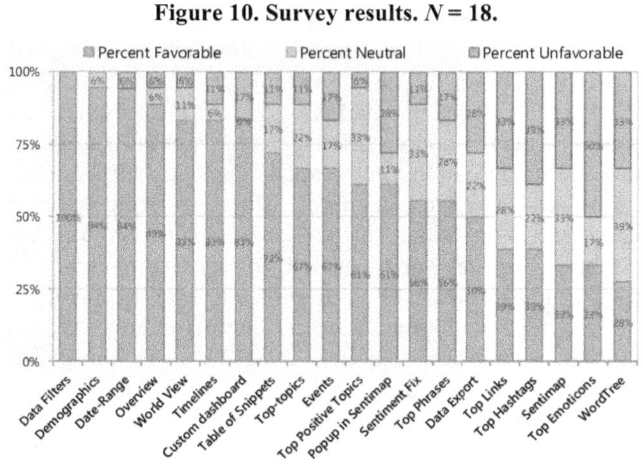

Figure 11. Usefulness of various ESP features. $N = 18$.

Figure 11 shows responses to a question asking about the usefulness of different ESP features ("How useful do you consider this feature to your analytic/research work?"). The scale ranged from 1=Not useful at all, to 5=Very useful. Values of 4 and 5 are pooled into the 'favorable' category while values of 1 and 2 are 'unfavorable', with a value of 3 considered 'neutral'. Data filters were found unanimously to be the most useful (100%). Also scoring high are the 'Demographics' tab, the ability to search/filter within a date range, and the 'Overview' tab. The 'Word Tree' was considered the least favorable. This visualization uses Java. Many participants reported experiencing issues with Java on their browsers.

Interviews: Deeper investigation

Our interview sessions provided further fine-grained detail and richer insights about the experience of using ESP and the challenges encountered.

General positive reaction

The interviews confirmed the positive findings of the survey.

"Until you have a tool like Social Pulse where you can actually read the comments yourself and interpret what that reaction is - now you have some strong intellectual capital to use to either explain to our executives that everything is okay, or explain to them what some of the root cause issues are being identified."

Participants felt ESP provided a unique service not available through other tools.

"Without this tool, how would I be able to access all the forums, communities, blogs to see the information? It's not possible."

The majority of participants appreciated the flexibility of the tool and its drill-down capabilities.

"There is a really good blend of high level synopsis stuff as well as down in the weeds detail oriented stuff. And you can go to whatever level of detail you choose to."

Value of data segmentation

Several participants mentioned the value of demographic segmentation to understand employee chatter.

"It is useful to get those kind of demographics – what part of the business is something coming from? Is it a global issue, or is it a predominantly North American issue? ...

The issues that you are going to experience in India and China could be significantly different in that the maturity of the business is so young, you know, the issues that you are facing in a major market may be totally different. The things you want to do or focus on will be different depending on your demographics."

"Demographics will tell you a lot about the data. Does a manager have a different view than an individual contributor? Does a high performer have a different view than a low performer? Or, does everyone have the same opinion, and what does that tell you? Being able to classify into meaningful groups helps give you more context to draw conclusions about what the data is actually telling you."

Value of real-time

The majority of participants felt the main value in ESP was in its capability to provide real-time insights.

"I left Social Pulse running in the background, and in the course of an hour, I could see the comments increasing. It was very real-time, which was impressive to me."

Different uses of the tool

In addition to the business questions participants showcased in their reports, they were often inspired to talk about more possibilities of using ESP, for example:

"In a micro way, following an incident of some type I think it will be very insightful. Where is social media lighting up regarding that incident or topic?"

"I can see particularly in the acquisition/integration side of my job incorporating some of the Social Pulse analysis and sentiment tracking. Morale and change-management in acquisitions is a very big topic. It's commonly reported that people issues and culture change are the reasons for failure in acquisitions."

Lack of data

Some participants found that there wasn't enough social chatter on their topics of interest to provide business value.

"The more detailed I got in my search, I would pretty much go from 20 snippets to 0."

Participants noticed that there were usually more positive comments than negative comments, and that employees may be self-censoring.

"The one thing that I worry about is that there aren't many negative comments. Obviously we'd like to work in a positive environment. But I believe, my own theory is that there is more negativity on some of these subjects than what is appearing [in ESP]. That causes me concern that we would be drawing conclusions when people are self-filtering."

Lack of confidence in sentiment analysis

Participants understood the limitations of the sentiment analysis algorithms. However, this did not keep them from raising concerns.

"If I'm taking this very seriously, then it is imperative that I take these snippets as seriously as well. And for that the sentiments have to be correct, you know... It's important that it's correct."

BRIEF CASE STUDIES OF POST EVALUATION USAGE

Based on the results of the evaluation, the organization has decided to rollout ESP to a wider population of HR professionals and other employees whose job responsibilities involve understanding the employee experience and/or analyzing social media chatter. Below we describe three mini case studies that showcase the usage of ESP to deliver business value.

Understanding overall health of the company

A monthly report based on exported data from ESP summarizing social media trends at the company such as changes in volume, sentiment, and top topics segmented by geography and business unit is sent to senior leaders, including the CEO. After the first of such reports was sent, the senior leadership has continued to request monthly updates and analysis of changes over time. The adoption of ESP reports as part of a wider set of reports sent to senior leaders to help understand the impact of change initiatives within the company is suggestive of the insights ESP can provide. Senior leaders roll out different communications, change initiatives, programs and policies in the company, and they are interested in understanding if these generate any employee chatter. The ability to search social media content using specific keywords related to these communications, programs and policies, and analyze chatter over time, provides useful input to decision makers in understanding if employees are adopting the change, and sharing information about it through social media.

Understanding reputation as an employer

A specific business unit of the organization was interested in the perception of their employees about the work experience in growth markets. A team examined the internal Human Resources Management System (HRMS) to analyze data on employees voluntarily leaving the business unit in growth market countries. They supplemented this data with anonymous snippet commentary from ESP. Searching for keywords related to career, recognition, strategy, and job/work allowed the team to surface content that provided additional context and richness to the quantitative data extracted from the HRMS. This provided insights into specific attrition levers that the business unit could use to implement pre-emptive strategies to address voluntary attrition of high performers. Additionally, we found that certain keywords (e.g. re-org) are not used much, likely because they touch on sensitive issues. A further challenge with a keyword-based approach is that employees might be discussing the topic of the keyword without using the specific keyword itself. To address this limitation, we encouraged employees to use hashtags. This allows them to view related content by clicking on a hashtag in the social platform used by the company, and also enables ESP to aggregate related snippets.

Fine-tuning and aligning internal and external messaging

The business unit of the company that specializes in outsourcing wanted to know if the language used in relation to the term was consistent across the company. This can improve the brand messaging of the business unit around outsourcing. A team uses ESP to measure this on a monthly basis. Additionally, they examine if the volume of conversation around outsourcing is growing, and identify demographics of employees engaging in these conversations. Using ESP to analyze data over several months, the team found that the terms 'outsourcing', 'company' and 'BPO' were most used externally, while 'outsourcing' and 'sourcing' were mentioned most internally. Through this analysis, the team recommended the use of the term 'sourcing' in all internal and external messaging in order to have consistent communication. Moreover, they were able to identify peaks in conversation and the reasons behind the peaks. For example, ESP data revealed that a service agreement contract led to a significant peak in volume toward the end of July 2013. Most of the posts on outsourcing were from sellers and employees in the software business unit, accounting for 42% of the conversation in total.

DISCUSSION

With the advent of social technologies, communication is increasingly going from one-way and two-way to multi-directional. Employees are already active on social media. As more people that have grown up with social technologies enter the workforce, social media in general and internal social media in particular will become a strong platform for employee expression. Organizations are beginning to realize the value of instant, real-time data on what their employees are thinking. Consequently, tools are needed to mine social content in order to deliver insights to the organization about the employee experience. Our design of ESP was a means to that end of delivering immediacy of insight. ESP promotes understanding employee social chatter while preserving the privacy of employees.

Our interviews revealed that HR professionals did not really have any tool to systematically gather and analyze employee social media content prior to ESP. The employees that performed searches would frequent employer review sites, or do manual searches on Google or Twitter. However there was no way to verify that the people posting were actually employees of the company. Perhaps this explains why our study participants were so enthusiastic about continuing to use ESP in the future. The in-situ evaluation of ESP using employees to perform a real business task lends ecological validity to the findings. The continued use of ESP, such as those mentioned in the mini case studies, shows the promise of ongoing business insights.

The wider use of ESP in the organization paves important avenues for future research. Tools such as ESP are only as good as the data employees are willing to provide through their participation in social channels. Without strong support from management and a culture that encourages employees to voice their thoughts, tools such as ESP cannot be effective. We plan to conduct a longitudinal study to draw out the nuances in which ESP may play a role in understanding the employee experience. At the very least, the existence of ESP provides a signal to employees that the organization is interested in listening to their thoughts to drive positive change. In order to strengthen that signal, we are planning to make some of the ESP visualizations publicly available inside the organization.

A challenge with social media is the representativeness of the data. Surveys also face this challenge when low response rates are encountered. Our participants clearly felt that ESP provides over representation of employee segments active in social media, and under representation of others. With ESP, the results are shown along with the underlying employee demographics of the data. This helps analysts interpret the data better, and aids decision-making. Contextualizing the data in such a manner allows a business leader to determine how much credibility she will lend to the social data during decision-making.

In deploying ESP, the greatest challenge we faced was with ensuring we respect employee privacy. We have discussed the technical solution in previous sections. Just as important is handling the organizational processes. We went through a couple of steps to ensure global deployment of ESP. First, we had a series of meetings with the Chief Privacy Officer and her legal team to make sure ESP conforms to the company's Social Media Policy and respects all labor laws. We worked with work councils in the European Union to determine which data fields could be collected. We adhered to all country specific work council restrictions. We developed a Terms of Use (ToU) of ESP in consultation with the company's legal team. The ToU clearly specifies the purpose of ESP and how data will be used. The salient aspects of the ToU include the prohibition of sharing ESP confidential data with others that do not have a business need, and that violation of agreed usage terms can result in disciplinary action.

An important component of the deployment plan was to communicate to employees through an article published on the Intranet and shared through social channels. The article includes a description of ESP, who has access to it, and what it is being used for. It is important to be transparent with employees and obtain consent when required. We have plans for deploying a public widget on the Intranet incorporating data from some of the portlets in the 'Overview' tab, allowing all employees to see the type of analytics and visualization an analyst sees. However, this was not part of the initial deployment.

One of the findings of our user study was that many employees appeared to be reluctant to express overtly negative sentiment. Out of the 2.6M snippets in ESP to date, 51.8% are neutral, 37.8% are positive, 7.2% are negative, and 3.1% are ambivalent. This is consistent with prior studies showing that even the most proactive or satisfied employees are likely to "read the wind" as to whether it is safe and/or worthwhile to speak up in their organization [32]. At the same time, research has found that individuals have a strong need for control over decisions that affect them [17, 38]. An important way in which employees gain a sense of control over their environment is by expressing their opinions [29]. Through such expression they can make their opinions heard and influence decisions that affect them. Our motivation behind creating ESP was to allow organizations to make the opinions and sentiment of their employees more accessible. Although ultimately it comes down to a matter of trust, we believe the privacy features enabled in ESP can encourage more employees to express themselves without fear of negative consequences. Furthermore, an organization would rather have employees express negative sentiment behind the firewall rather than repress it or express it externally.

Another issue that surfaced in our user study was the lack of relevant content related to a specific business question. There are two issues here: one involving noise, and another regarding the sparseness or complete lack of data.

With respect to noise, we refer to Palen et al.'s notion of 'helpfulness' and moving away from precision as a gold standard in retrieved social media results [36]. In this context, helpfulness is *relative to what is needed.* In relation to employee chatter, often times what is needed is some clue that can allow an analyst to dig deeper and determine if something is of concern or not.

With respect to the sparseness or lack of data, we anticipate that as more employees embrace social media, there will be more content to mine. We plan on adding more data sources as ESP has the ability to manage multiple data sources. Passive listening may not surface data from all employee segments. To compensate for under representation of certain employee segments in the data, a more 'active' and directed approach could be taken. For example, a quick poll targeted at an employee segment that is under-represented in ESP data can help provide more complete data in answering a business question. In our future work, we plan to integrate quick polls into ESP to further enrich the capabilities of surfacing employee sentiment.

CONCLUSION

In this paper we have described a new tool for mining internal and external social media to understand employee chatter while respecting employee privacy. ESP was found to be very useful in providing near real-time data about employee social chatter, which can allow analysts to create better reports describing the employee experience. We believe that ESP will be beneficial for companies with an active social media footprint and the business need to understand employee chatter. Technological challenges such as the limitations of sentiment analysis, and cultural barriers such as self-censorship and the lack of relevant social media content remain. As technology advances, one can see the technological challenges dissipate. The cultural barriers may need more time to overcome.

REFERENCES

1. Archambault, A. and Grudin, J. A longitudinal study of facebook, linkedin, and twitter use. In *Proc. CHI 2012*, ACM Press (2012).
2. Baldridge, J. *The opennlp project*, 2005.
3. Berger, A. and Lafferty, J. Information retrieval as statistical translation. In *Proc. SIGIR 1999*, ACM Press (1999).
4. Bernstein, M. S., Suh, B., Hong, L., Chen, J., Kairam, S. and Chi, E. H. Eddi: interactive topic-based browsing of social status streams. In *Proc. UIST 2010*, ACM Press (2010).
5. Bughin, J. and Chui, M. The rise of the networked enterprise: Web 2.0 finds its payday. (2010), Retrieved May 27, 2013, from http://www.mckinsey.com/insights/high_tech_telecoms_internet/the_rise_of_the_networked_enterprise_web_20_finds_its_payday.
6. Carmel, D., Uziel, E., Guy, I., Mass, Y. and Roitman, H. Folksonomy-based term extraction for word cloud generation. *ACM Transactions on Intelligent Systems and Technology (TIST)*, 3, 4 (2012).
7. Choudhury, M. D. and Counts, S. Understanding affect in the workplace via social media. In *Proc. CSCW 2013*, ACM Press (2013).
8. Cohen, J. A coefficient of agreement for nominal scales. *Educational and Psychological Measurement*, 20 (1960), 37-46.
9. Crawford, K. Following you: Disciplines of listening in social media. *Continuum: Journal of Media & Cultural Studies*, 23, 4 (2009), 525-535.
10. Detert, J. R. and Burris, E. R. Leadership behavior and employee voice: Is the door really open? *Academy of Management Journal*, 50, 4 (2007), 869-884.
11. Detert, J. R. and Edmondson, A. C. Why Employees Are Afraid to Speak. *Harv.Bus.Rev.*, 85, 5 (2007), 23-25.
12. Eisenberg, R., Fasano, P. and Davis-LaMastro, V. Perceived organizational support and employee

diligence, commitment, and innovation. *Journal of Applied Psychology*, 75 (1990), 51-59.

13. Feldman, R. Techniques and applications for sentiment analysis. *Commun. ACM*, 56, 4 (2013), 82-89.

14. Gilbert, E. Phrases that signal workplace hierarchy. In *Proc. CSCW 2012*, ACM Press (2012), 1037-1046.

15. Gilbert, E. and Karahalios, K. Widespread worry and the stock market. In *Proc. ICWSM 2010*, (2010).

16. Glauser, M. J. Upward information flow in organizations: Review and conceptual analysis. *Human Relations*, 37 (1984), 613-643.

17. Greenberger, D. B. and Strasser, S. The development and application of a model of personal control in organizations. *Academy of Management Review*, 11 (1986), 167-177.

18. Guy, I., Steier, T., Barnea, M., Ronen, I. and Daniel, T. Swimming against the streamz: search and analytics over the enterprise activity stream. In *Proc. CIKM 2012*, ACM Press (2012).

19. Hirschman, A. O. *Exit, voice, and loyalty: Responses to decline in firms, organizations and states*. Harvard University Press, Cambridge, MA, 1970.

20. Hoffman, D. L. and Fodor, M. Can you measure the ROI of your social media marketing. *MIT Sloan Management Review*, 52, 1 (2010), 41-49.

21. Kaschesky, M., Sobkowicz, P., Lobato, J. M. H., Bouchard, G., Archambeau, C., Scharioth, N., Manchin, R., Gschwend, A. and Riedl, R. Bringing Representativeness into Social Media Monitoring and Analysis. In *Proc. HICSS 2013*, IEEE Computer Society (2013), 2003-2012.

22. Kiker, D. S., Kiker, M. B. and Perry, M. Constructive challenge: employee voice, helpfulness and task performance on organizational rewards. *Journal of Management and Marketing Research*, 13 (2013).

23. Kraut, A. Moving the needle: Getting action after a survey. In A. Kraut (Ed.), Getting action from organizational surveys: New concepts, technologies and applications. San Francisco: Jossey-Bass, 2006.

24. Lampos, V. and Cristianini, N. Tracking the flu pandemic by monitoring the social web. In *International Workshop on Cognitive Information Processing (CIP) 2010*, (2010), 411-416.

25. Lawler, E. *High-Involvement Management. Participative Strategies for Improving Organizational Performance.* Jossey-Bass Inc. Publishers, 1986.

26. Lee, T. Y., Dugan, C., Geyer, W., Ratchford, T., Rasmussen, J., Shami, N. S. and Lupushor, S. Experiments on Motivational Feedback for Crowdsourced Workers. In *Proc. ICWSM 2013*, (2013).

27. LePine, J. A. and Van Dyne, L. Voice and cooperative behavior as contrasting forms of contextual performance: Evidence of differential relationships with Big Five personality characteristics and cognitive ability. *Journal of Applied Psychology*, 86, 2 (2001).

28. Lilienthal, P. If you give your employees a voice, do you listen? *The Journal for Quality and Participation*, 25, 3 (2002), 38-40.

29. Lind, E. A. and Tyler, T. R. *The social psychology of procedural justice.* Plenum, New York, 1988.

30. Marcus, A., Bernstein, M. S., Badar, O., Karger, D. R., Madden, S. and Miller, R. C. Twitinfo: aggregating and visualizing microblogs for event exploration. In *Proc. CHI 2011*, ACM Press (2011).

31. McConnell, J. *How to Design, Implement, and Interpret an Employee Survey.* Amacom, New York, 2003.

32. Miliken, F. J., Morrison, E. W. and Hewlin, P. F. An exploratory study of employee silence: Issues that employees don't communicate upward and why. *Journal of Management Studies*, 40 (2003), 1453-1476.

33. Morrison, E. W. and Milliken, F. J. Organizational silence: A barrier to change and development in a pluralistic world. *Academy of Management Review*, 25, 4 (2000), 706-725.

34. Murphy, J., Kim, A., Hagood, H., Richards, A., Augustine, C., Kroutil, L. and Sage, A. Twitter Feeds and Google Search Query Surveillance: Can They Supplement Survey Data Collection? In *Association for Survey Computing 6th International Conference*, (2011).

35. Nemeth, C. J. Managing innovation: When less is more. *California Management Review*, 40, 1 (1983), 59-74.

36. Palen, L., Vieweg, S. and Anderson, K. M. Supporting "Everyday Analysts" in Safety-and Time-Critical Situations. *The Information Society*, 27, 1 (2011), 52-62.

37. Paris, C. and Wan, S. Listening to the community: social media monitoring tasks for improving government services. In *Ext. Abstracts CHI 2011*, ACM Press (2011), 2095-2100.

38. Parker, L. E. When to fix it and when to leave: The relationship among perceived control, self-efficacy, dissent and exit. *Journal of Applied Psychology*, 78 (1993), 949-959.

39. Rijkhoff, J. *The noun phrase*. Oxford University Press, 2004.

40. Saunders, D. M., Sheppard, B. H., Knight, V. and Roth, J. Employee voice to supervisors. *Employee Responsibilities and Rights Journal*, 5 (1992), 241-259.

41. Schneider, B., Ashworth, S., Higgs, C. and Carr, L. Design, validity and use of strategically focused employee attitude surveys. *Personnel Psychology*, 49, 3 (1996), 695-705.

42. Shneiderman, B. Tree visualization with tree-maps: 2D space-filling approach. *ACM Transactions on Graphics (TOG)*, 11, 1 (1992), 92-99.

43. Senge, P. M. *The fifth dscipline: The art and practice of the learning organization.* Doubleday, New York, 1990.

44. Smith, F. *Organizational Surveys: The Diagnosis and Betterment of Organizations Through Their Members.* Lawrence Erlbaum 2003.

45. Starbird, K. and Palen, L. Working and sustaining the virtual "Disaster Desk". In *Proc. CSCW 2013*, ACM Press (2013).

46. Tyler, T. R., Rasinski, K. and Spodick, N. The influence of voice on satisfaction with leaders: Exploring the meaning of process control. *Journal of Applied Social Psychology*, 15 (1985), 700-724.

47. Wattenberg, M. and Viegas, F. B. The Word Tree, an Interactive Visual Concordance. *IEEE Transactions on Visualization and Computer Graphics*, 14, 6 (2008), 1221-1228.

48. Yang, J., Adamic, L., Ackerman, M., Wen, Z. and Lin, C.-Y. The way I talk to you: Sentiment expression in an organizational context. In *Proc. CHI 2012*, ACM Press (2012).

Most Liked, Fewest Friends: Patterns of Enterprise Social Media Use

Gloria Mark[1], Ido Guy[2], Shiri Kremer-Davidson[2], Michal Jacovi[2]

[1]Department of Informatics
University of California, Irvine
Irvine, CA 92697-3440 USA
gmark@uci.edu

[2]IBM Haifa Research Lab
Mt. Carmel
Haifa 31905, Israel
{ido, shiri, jacovi}@il.ibm.com

ABSTRACT

Enterprise social media can provide visibility of users' actions and thus has the potential to reveal insights about users in the organization. We mined large-scale social media use in an enterprise to examine: a) user roles with such broad platforms and b) whether people with large social networks are highly regarded. First, a factor analysis revealed that most variance of social media usage is explained by commenting and 'liking' behaviors while other usage can be characterized as patterns of distinct tool usage. These results informed the development of a model showing that online network size interacts with other media usage to predict who is highly assessed in the organization. We discovered that the *smaller* one's online social network size in the organization, the more highly assessed they were by colleagues. We explain this inverse relationship as due to friending behavior being highly visible but not yet valued in the organization.

Author Keywords

Social media; network size; enterprise; collaboration; factor analysis; social media platform

ACM Classification Keywords

H.5.3 [Information Interfaces and Presentation (e.g., HCI)]: Group and Organization Interfaces; K.4.m [Computers and Society]: Miscellaneous.

INTRODUCTION

Social media continues to gain ground in the enterprise for a wide range of business purposes. A recent report by Gartner [11] predicted that social media will transform communication and data-sharing in the enterprise. In fact, they predict that by 2016, for a third of businesses who adopt social media, it will achieve as much importance for the organization as email and telephone today have in connecting people, exchanging informal knowledge, and in social filtering of information.

Social network sites (SNS) are a particular type of social media that have been attracting a great deal of interest by practitioners for their potential to leverage social connections within and outside of the enterprise. Researchers have focused on advantages that SNSs have for the organization such as enabling career trajectories and maintaining awareness of organizational dynamics [28].

However, despite the argued potential for SNSs and integrated social media platforms to be an impetus for change in the enterprise, little attention has been given to the ways they might create an impact. Historically enterprises have focused on the technical aspects of IT deployment, e.g. through providing helpdesk and training classes. However, given the growing adoption of social media in and out of the enterprise, it is timely to take a closer look at the social usage of integrated social media platforms.

Numerous studies have examined individual social media applications in the enterprise [e.g. 6, 8, 10, 21, 30, 35, and for a review, see 32]. However, enterprises are now introducing comprehensive social media platforms which include social networks, blogs, wikis, forums, people tagging, file sharing, and more. Fewer studies have examined how data from social media platforms could be used to understand organizational behavior [8, 16, 17].

In this paper we focus on social media usage in an enterprise from two perspectives to gain insights into the organization. First, we examine large-scale patterns of use to identify the types of roles users adopt when using enterprise social media platforms. For example, users might tend to be content creators, commenters, or followers. Second, we examine how one's network size can inform the organization about the user. We had the opportunity to collect comprehensive use of a broad social media platform in a global enterprise to investigate these questions. This paper is part of a larger project examining insights from large-scale enterprise social media use. In another study, a novel methodology is applied as a descriptive model to social media to examine how the traces from the media can infer reputation in the organization [18].

CSCW'14, February 15 - 19 2014, Baltimore, MD, USA

http://dx.doi.org/10.1145/2531602.2531662

RELATED RESEARCH

Broadly, we are interested in how social media usage can reveal insights about contributors. Researchers such as boyd [2] and Grudin [12] have argued that social media differs from other types of organizational communication media in that it enables people's actions to become visible in the organization. Unlike users' actions with personal information systems such as file management, phone, and email, what users do on an enterprise social media platform is typically visible to all who use the system. Treem and Leonardi [32] claim that the specific affordances of social media are that it makes users' behaviors, knowledge, preferences, and online social networks visible to others in the organization. It is feasible then that enterprise social media use could provide a means to examine users' behavior and knowledge, through making online information and actions visible. Such data was formerly difficult to obtain through other methods such as ethnography or collecting email records. Further, social media data provides information on a macro scale which can allow the examination of patterns of behavior in the organization.

Social media as behavioral communication

Enterprise social media use may also reveal insights about colleagues' relations to each other, in addition to the social information that face-to-face interaction yields. People have reported that they use social media to learn about others' behaviors in the organization, which DiMicco et al. [8] termed 'people sensemaking'. Enterprise social media usage might communicate both explicit and tacit knowledge about users. Tacit knowledge refers to knowledge that is not explicitly represented but rather is gleaned through informal, non-codified means [26]. By interacting with others in a social media platform, people may gain impressions or understandings about their colleagues, based on their actions. Being socially tagged by others contains implicit meanings, as does having someone share your files or 'like' your blog. For example, these actions might lead one to judge someone's importance or potential influence in the organization. Thus, people may communicate information about themselves through their online behaviors though the information may not be explicitly articulated. Social media usage can also communicate explicit knowledge about people. The content that people post in wikis, blogs or forums could demonstrate their expertise in areas [14]. Their posts could also communicate that they are knowledgeable about the organization, and therefore could be influential. For example, the use of social tagging was found to explicitly (and intentionally) communicate social connections [30].

Thus, social media might not only be a useful source of information to researchers, but it may also contribute signals to colleagues about other users. If social media can indeed provide visibility of users' online actions as many suggest, then we envision two approaches for how we, as researchers, might use this data to understand organizational dynamics. Our first question then, is if an organization has adopted a broad social media platform, can we identify user preferences for different social media applications within such a platform? Can we find different patterns of user groups in the organization such as contributors, followers, or commenters? In contrast to focusing on a person's usage of a single social media tool, how might people in an organization behave with a broad social media platform that offers a SNS, wikis, blogs, tagging, forums, and file sharing? One person may specialize in blogging while another in wiki creation and editing. Then again, others may adopt roles of commenting across different applications. We feel that identifying distinct patterns of social media use can provide benefits for the organization in understanding dynamics such as communication patterns, and how knowledge sharing and production occurs.

Second, within the context of an integrated social media platform, we can focus specifically on SNSs since they have received attention for their growing importance in the organization [cf 11]. Following the notion that social media makes a person's online actions visible, what could a person's online SNS usage reveal about their behavior in the organization? Could a person's SNS behavior in the organization reveal who might be considered cooperative, or who might be viewed to be a good colleague to work with, e.g. as collaborative tagging has been used to identify experts in the organization [19]? A very visible behavior with SNS is "friending" behavior [2]. Do colleagues value someone who is very active with "friending" in the enterprise?

However, we hypothesize that, in an environment with a range of social media options available to users, SNS usage would not be the sole influencing factor on colleagues' perceptions of one another. We therefore are interested to examine how SNS usage interacts with other social media use. If indeed SNS usage is consistent with colleagues' high regard of the user in the organization, then what other social media usage might interact with SNS usage to also predict high regard?

Other studies of enterprise SNS use have explored motivations and types of connections [7] as well as outcomes of SNS usage such as social capital [29]. Wu et al. [35] asked employees in an organization to rate their closeness with each other and found significant correspondence with SNS usage. To our knowledge, enterprise SNS usage, along with other social media usage, has not been examined in terms of what it communicates about colleagues in an organization.

ONLINE NETWORK SIZE AND ASSESSMENT

We have argued that SNSs can make a person's online network visible, which can offer cues about that person. One very visible cue is the size of one's network which might communicate how well-liked or socially attractive that person is. Tong et al. [31] found a curvilinear relationship between Facebook friends and social attractiveness: those with a moderate number of friends were judged to be the most socially attractive and those with the lowest and highest number of friends were judged to be the least socially attractive. Utz [33] found that personality played a role in judging online network size: those with introverted and fewer friends were judged as more socially attractive.

However, network size on SNSs like Facebook may be regarded differently than the social network size of offline friends. Offline social networks in organizations have been shown to have optimal network configurations associated with group effectiveness [25]. Research has shown that the more friends one has in their offline social network, the more positive traits one is judged to have [24]. Those people more sociable and with higher self-esteem are more popular in both their offline and online friend networks [36]. Yet the notion of online SNS connections as "friends" has been brought into question. Due to the technological ease of "friending" (i.e. with a click), SNS friends may not be considered close friends in the same way they are considered in offline relationships [2]. Utz [33] in fact found that popularity in online SNSs do not necessarily correspond with popularity of offline friends.

Online networks in an enterprise can reveal work-related information about a person. Gao et al. [9] found that those in a U.S. enterprise were more interested to collaborate with someone when their network contained experts, which in turn was related to influence in the organization. These researchers also found that a person's reputation was connected to the desire to collaborate with that person. However, network size was not found to be related to the desire to collaborate.

Thus, it is possible that one's network size in an enterprise could reveal traits of that person, and by taking a macro view, a person's network size could reveal how others in the organization regard them. It is an open question how online network size corresponds to colleagues' assessment of others in an enterprise.

Mechanisms of SNS influence

There might be direct and indirect reasons for why we might expect a relationship between a person's SNS usage in the enterprise and colleagues' perceptions of them. One direct mechanism that could explain this relationship is through social capital. Social capital refers to the resources that people gain through their interactions with other people [5]. Social network sites, and social media usage in general, can be an indirect way that people gain benefits from others. Strong relationships have been found between the use of Facebook, in terms of network size and the accumulation of social capital [10, 34]. The use of an enterprise social network site was also found to be positively associated with gaining social capital, e.g. in employees' willingness to give back to the company [29]. Social capital can serve as a basis for developing trust and can be associated with reputation [23]. Networks can also provide expertise as a resource [9].

We may expect then, that people accumulate social capital through SNS use, and that social network size in the enterprise could be associated with colleagues' positive perceptions of them.

However, SNS friends include weak as well as strong ties. A person may be barely acquainted with some in their social network [2]. In the enterprise it is unclear how the proportion of weak and strong ties compare with those in SNS site networks more broadly.

SNS usage however, may interact with other types of social media use in a broad platform. With enterprise social media in general, people could be perceived as doing favors for others either directly or indirectly, e.g. by commenting on their blogs, contributing to their wikis, tagging others, or friending others. More broadly, people can be perceived positively when they contribute to the enterprise through social media, e.g. by creating forums, wikis, or contributing information to corporate blogs. This could be perceived by colleagues as having impact by contributing to the greater good of the organization [30]. Therefore, it would not be surprising that people who contribute to social media in an enterprise might be perceived favorably by their colleagues.

Another direct mechanism to explain why SNS use, and social media usage in general, might be related to colleagues' perceptions of others is that people who contribute content to an enterprise social media system might be considered cooperative. Collaborative behavior is associated with desirable traits such as reputation [9] and trust [20]. Some evidence exists to support this notion. Kosonen and Kianto [21] found that wiki use encouraged collaborative behaviors in the organization.

However, a relationship between online SNS and social media usage, and colleagues' perceptions of that person, may be due to indirect factors. Correlation does not imply causality. There may be other underlying traits than the actual social media usage that influence a colleagues' judgment about that person. For example, people who are heavy social network users might also be very personable offline. Some indirect evidence supports this notion as there is some correspondence with personality traits and SNS usage [27]. Users of other social media such as wikis or blogs might also be people who are experts in their fields, are opinion leaders, and have other traits regarded positively in the organization. So actions with social media per se may not directly communicate signals about a person's behavior to others, but rather it may co-occur with *other* traits that the user has.

Therefore, we argue that online enterprise social media platforms can make users' online actions visible, and that this information could contribute to the opinions that colleagues form of social media users [cf 8]. People's online actions with the system may create positive impressions through the accumulation of social capital or through their online contributions which might be perceived as cooperative. Our position is that mining such data in the aggregate can be used as a way to investigate organizational behavior. We therefore ask the following research questions concerning enterprise social media use:

RQ1: Can we identify different patterns of enterprise social media use when people have access to a broad platform? Do people tend to exhibit particular patterns of social media usage, or is it rather ad hoc? For example, there might be people who are creators, i.e. they tend to create blogs, forums and wikis. Or there might be people who are commenters, who tend to comment on blogs, forums and wikis but not initiate new blogs, forums or wikis. There may be people who are active on social network tools but tend to not use other types of media. There could be people who specialize in maintaining blogs but not other media. Understanding platform-wide patterns of use can reveal insight both into individual behavior, and also on a macro level, how social media is used in an enterprise. These results can then be used to inform a model of SNS usage, addressed in our next research question.

RQ2: Does a person's online social network site behavior in the organization correspond to how they are perceived in the real work environment? In particular, can online social network behavior of enterprise employees predict who would be desirable to work with in the organization? Given that SNS use is becoming more widespread in enterprises, can we utilize it to locate someone who might make a good collaboration partner? For example, consider a manager who is looking to choose someone for an important task force. Can use of online social networking, in conjunction with patterns of social media use (see RQ1), be used as a determinant of who might be a good choice? On the one hand, managers can ask about various people through word-of-mouth. But perhaps social media use in the aggregate could also provide valuable information about which person might make a good choice. Following [8], we might expect that there is a correspondence between SNS usage and users' positive assessments of others. Though cues such as profile information have been examined with SNS use [cf 33], we focus on the variable of network size, which is quantifiable in the context of large-scale data analysis.

RESEARCH SETTING AND STUDY

As a first step to understanding how social media use can reveal perceptions and patterns of behavior in an enterprise, we collected large-scale data use of an enterprise social media platform--a broad spectrum of variables related to social media.

Research setting

Our study was conducted in a large global enterprise with over 400,000 employees. The organization employs a social media application platform behind its firewall. The platform consists of a blogging system that allows employees to author blog posts, comment on them, and 'like' them; a file sharing system that allows employees to upload files, share files with others (including ones they did not originally upload), to comment on files, and like them; a forum system that enables the initiation of forum threads and to reply on existing threads; an enterprise SNS that allows employees to reciprocally connect with each other, follow each other, post messages or comments on each other's boards, and tag one another; and a wiki system that allows employees to co-edit wiki pages, comment on them, and like them.

All of these applications have been in wide use (by over 20,000 users) over the past three years in the organization. We scraped the data using the platform's public API and collected a total of 57 variables over the prior two years, reflecting different aspects of the social media use, described above. The variables include actions that the user initiates, such as uploading a file or commenting on a wiki page, and actions that other users do on that user's content, such as tagging or following her, or her content, e.g. the number of downloads of her files or the number of edits to her wiki pages. Table 1 gives examples from different categories of the 57 social media variables collected. Figure 1 shows a distribution of the usage of five different applications which our paper focuses on, for 20,772 users.

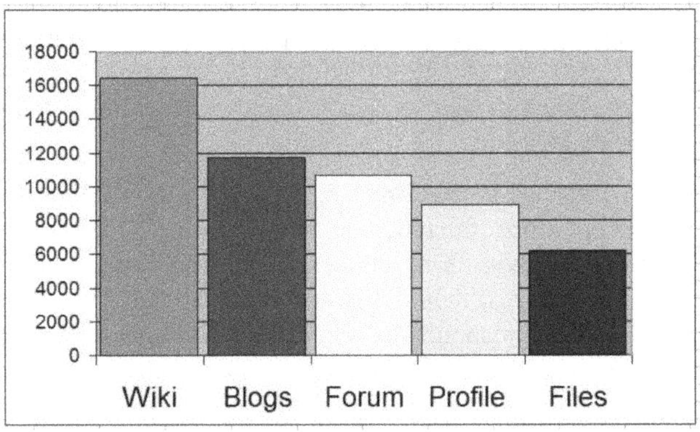

Figure 1. Usage of five social media applications (focused on in this paper) in a two-year period by the 20,772 most active users.

Survey

To examine how SNS usage relates to colleagues' perceptions of a user (RQ2), we asked colleagues to rate each other in a survey. Considering the notion, as we discussed, that social media contributors might be viewed as having positive traits through their online behavior, and informed by the work of [9, 20, 23], we hypothesized that desirable traits would include someone who might be considered reputable, trustworthy, an opinion leader, someone who could impact the company, and someone considered an expert in their field.

Category	Examples of social media variables	
	User's actions	Actions by others on the user or her content
Blogs	# blogs created # blog posts created	# comments on one's blog
Files	# files downloaded # files liked # comments placed on files	# of user's files downloaded by others # of comments others placed on user's files
Forums	# forums created	# posts from others in one's forum
Social networking	network size # of others the user follows	# of others who follow the user
Wiki use	# wiki pages edited # wikis one created	# of comments on one's wiki pages

Table 1. Examples of social media variables collected from the enterprise social media platform.

Using the SONAR aggregation system [15] we extracted social network information from public social media in the enterprise. SONAR yields for each person a list of people with whom they are acquainted. Each person on the list has a score reflecting the degree of acquaintance with the target person. To minimize false alarms, i.e. cases where people were on the list but not well acquainted with the target, we filtered the list using a score threshold. Then we further filtered out people who were active in less then three categories of social media usage (e.g. see Table 1). We then took the top 30 people and presented it in lists of 10 individuals each. Thus, if the SONAR results produced a list of 33 individuals, the top 30 (according to their score) would be randomized into three lists of ten people each and presented to participants. Participants could mark individuals who they did not know, and these individuals were not considered in our analysis (13.5% of people on the lists were marked as unfamiliar).

The survey was sent to 2,474 employees who were identified to be acquainted with at least 10 individuals who had substantial data in the enterprise social media platform (active in at least 3 categories of Table 1). We had 554 respondents (response rate of 22%), who rated a total of 1,073 sets of 10 individuals.

Target users were then given a set of five questions, shown in Appendix A. Users then reviewed the lists of individuals and were asked to choose from each list between 1 to 3 people who best fit each question.

RESULTS

Overview of social media use

First we present an overview of social media use in the organization. Table 2 shows mean usage for selected variables that are representative of the main categories. Data is used only from those individuals who were rated by colleagues, N=3,320. These individuals represent heavy users of the social media platform. As we would expect, the distribution of the total number of activities is a long tail. Most users use 2-3 different social network systems.

Variable	Mean (s.d.)	Range
# blog posts created	6.6 (29.6)	0-738
# files liked	0.6 (3.9)	0-96
# forums created	0.4 (1.3)	0-20
# people tagged	5.3 (61.6)	0-3015
# of wiki pages edited	19.2 (65.0)	0-2051
Network size	45.5 (70.4)	0-1653
Number of followers	2.9 (7.6)	0-235

Table 2. Sample usage (mean, s.d., range) for representative variables of the main categories. N=3320.

Patterns of social media use

Our first research question asked what kinds of patterns of social media use we might identify in an enterprise. For example can we find that people tend to be creators while others might tend to be commenters? Do people tend to "specialize" in different usage of social media?

We chose to examine 20,772 of the most active social media users in the enterprise. These users were selected based on having data in at least 5 of the 57 social media variables.

We conducted a factor analysis on the collected social media variables. Factor analysis is a statistical technique that enables a researcher to uncover a "structure" among a large number of correlated variables, by explaining the variability through latent variables or factors [22]. Our goal was to use factor analysis to uncover "unobserved variables" among our observed variables so as to identify patterns of behavior with social media use. Factor analysis results in each variable being primarily associated with a distinct factor.

Of the initial 57 variables, many of the variables were very highly correlated as they were measuring very similar activities. In terms of a factor analysis, we wanted to include variables in the analysis that were measuring distinct (though possibly related) activities. We thus averaged together those social media usage variables that were highly correlated, and that logically seemed to be measuring the same thing, to create an averaged measure. Here are some examples of the social media indicators that were highly correlated, and with which we created a composite average measure:

-*Board commenting*: Number of people whose boards one commented on, Number of comments placed on boards

-*Post replies*: Number of people whose posts one liked, Number of posts one liked

-*File commenting*: Number of files one commented on, Number of comments placed on files

Factor	Social media variables
1. Liking and commenting activity	Number of file liking; board commenting; blog post commenting
2. Wiki activities	Number of people whose wiki pages user edited; number who edited user's wiki pages; overall edits to user's wiki pages; user's wiki creation and editing actions
3. Actions on user's files	Number of user's files shared by others; number of people who shared user's files w/others; number who downloaded user's files
4. Blog activities	Number of blog posts user created; number who commented on user's posts; overall liking activities of user's posts
5. Social networking activities	Number of friends; number of followers; number of people the user is following, tagging activities by others on user; peoples' activities on user's board (writing and commenting)
6. Social use of one's file information	Number of people who placed user's files in their folders; overall commenting and liking activities on user's files
7. Forum activities	Number of topics, forum entries, communities created; overall replies to user's entries

Table 3. Factor analysis results: variables that loaded onto separate factors along with interpretations.

-*Files in folders*: Number of files placed in folders, Number of times one placed files in folders

-*Topic replies*: Number of people whose topics one replied to, Number of topics one replied to, Number of replies on topics

This reduced our dataset to 32 social media variables, which were based on the original variables and composite variables based on highly correlated variables that were averaged together. A factor analysis was done on these 32 social media variables to examine what factors could be identified. We used a Varimax rotation with a Kaiser normalization. A scree plot[1] revealed that seven factors should be used, accounting for 49.0% of the variance. Table 3 shows the social media activity variables that loaded onto the separate factors. In the right hand column are the specific variables that loaded onto the factors. Again, note that each variable primarily loads onto a separate factor. In the left column are our interpretations of these factors.

Our interpretations of these factors are as follows. Most factors (6 out of 7) fall along the separate types of social media categories described in Table 1. The exception is factor 1, which concerns more general activity of liking and commenting across different applications. This factor explains, for example, that people who like files also tend to comment on boards and these same people who comment on boards also tend to comment on blog posts.

Factor 2 clearly points to wiki use. It is interesting to note that some of the variables refer to one's actions in creating or editing wiki pages; other variables refer to others' edits on the wiki pages that one created. The reason is that wiki page creation and also editing by others is very much intertwined. The more wiki pages one has, the more likely it is to receive edits. But nevertheless, it is possible that number of edits by others could be an indication of the quality or maturity of one's wiki writing.

Factor 3 indicates actions by others on the user's files. This includes file sharing and downloading.

Factor 4 explains blog use, again, in terms of both the blog posts created as well as others' actions (commenting, liking) on one's blogs. This could indicate the interest level that others have in one's blogs, which could be a proxy for how interesting the blog is perceived to be by others.

Factor 5 represents social networking activity, in terms of friending, having followers or being followed, being tagged by others, and others' activity on one's board.

We call Factor 6 social use of file information, as it involves other's social input to a user's files: commenting and liking them.

Factor 7 identifies forum activity. This factor identifies a user's creation of topics, forum entries, and communities and also others' replies to the topics that the user created. Again, the more topics that one creates, the more opportunity there is for others to reply to one's topics. Thus, topic creation, and the activity of others replying to the user's topics, are deeply intertwined.

Thus, the factor analysis revealed two types of broad patterns of social media platform use. First, factor 1 (liking and commenting) explained most of the variance and is a social media activity that cuts across different tool use. Second, there are patterns that fall along the lines of distinct social media tool use, as we found with factor 2 (wiki use), factor 3 (file use), factor 4 (blog use), factor 5 (social networking), and factor 7 (forum activities). It is interesting to note that factor 3 and factor 6 show distinct uses of dealing with files. Factor 3 is more of an "operational" usage of files whereas factor 6 shows more of a social usage of files, involving annotating and liking files. Thus, there are clusters of user

[1] A scree plot is used to determine the number of factors to select based on a visual analysis of when the curve flattens.

roles that can be identified, based on distinct tool use, and also commenting/liking. These results can then be used to inform our model for the next research question.

RQ2: Social network size as a predictor

Our second research question asked whether SNS usage in the enterprise can serve as a predictor to find people who are positively evaluated.

For each survey question (see Survey section) we divided the number of times each individual was selected by colleagues by the number of times each individual was presented to people in the list as described earlier. This was a way to normalize the responses: i.e. a person may have been presented 5 times and selected 5 times, or presented 20 times and selected 5 times. We only consider people who were selected and presented two or more times; our reasoning is that a presentation or selection of just once could be an outlier and no selections at all indicate that no one regards that person highly. We only considered people who were selected on all five survey questions at least once. A person, for example, who was selected as reputable (Q1) and able to keep information secure (Q2) but not selected as an opinion leader (Q3) or having impact (Q4) or expertise (Q5) might not represent someone who has achieved high regard in the organization. Choosing people in the organization who were selected on all five survey questions enables us to focus on a clear set of people who are consistently "highly assessed" by two or more people. This enables us to be reasonably confident that we are working with a set of people who are rated consistently positive along what we consider to be desirable traits to have in the organization. This yielded a set of 79 individuals.

The responses to the five questions were strongly correlated and highly significant, with correlations ranging from .68 to .85, $p<.0001$. This suggests that these five questions may represent the same underlying social construct. A factor analysis using a Varimax rotation revealed that all of the responses fall along a single factor, with nearly equal factor scores (ranging from .83-.89), explaining 74.5% of the variance. Therefore, an additive model is appropriate. The measures from each individual question (in Appendix A) were thus added together to produce a single measure of "High Assessment". In summary, our target dataset has people who received consistent positive ratings from colleagues, along with 57 measures of their social media usage[2].

Our target variable of interest was Network Size, a measure of the number of friends that one has in their enterprise social network (similar to Facebook friends). To reduce our set of variables, we first ran a stepwise regression on the 57 social media indicators using High Assessment as the dependent variable, to see what variables were significant predictors. We found that the best fitting model included Network Size and Total Followers as significant predictors of High Assessment: $F(2,77)=15.77$, $p<.0001$. $R^2=29.6$. Total Followers is a measure of the number of followers one has. The variance inflation factor (VIF) was 1.5, which indicates that multicollinearity is not a problem.

As our theoretical interest was in Network Size, we then focused on developing a model using Network Size as a predictor of High Assessment. We hypothesized that Network Size may actually be a *mediator* of the effect of other social media usage on High Assessment. In other words, Network Size may be influenced by other social media variables, which in turn may influence colleagues' assessment. Informed by our factor analysis results in RQ1, we chose other variables to include in the model. Our theoretical reasoning was that these variables represented the most active (and perhaps visible) types of social media use.

We chose the following variables to control for, to include in our model: number of (professionally-related) files liked (in Factor 1), number of corporate wiki pages edited (in Factor 2), number of corporate blog posts created (in Factor 4), number of people tagged in the enterprise and total followers one has (in Factor 5), and number of corporate-related forums created (in Factor 7). We did not include a variable based on Factors 3 and 6, since they also concerned file activity and we have this represented by the variable of number of files liked in Factor 1.

We tested the model using hierarchical regression analysis with Network Size as an independent variable, controlled by Files Liked, Wiki Edits, Blog Posts, People Tagged, Number of Followers and Forums Created. Figure 2 shows a diagram of the model based on the results. The model as shown in Figure 2 is a significant predictor of High Assessment ($F(7, 77) = 6.55$, $p<.0001$, and the overall R^2 of the model explains 39.6%[3] of the variance of High Assessment. Adding Network Size alone to the model, given that all other variables are included, adds 32.1% of the explained variance (R^2) of High Assessment: F change $(2, 70) = 18.86$, $p<.0001$.

[2] For this analysis, we used the full set of 57 measures. For the factor analysis, we combined highly correlated variables.

[3] We would like to emphasize that this is a very high percent variance explained, mostly due to Network Size (32.1%).

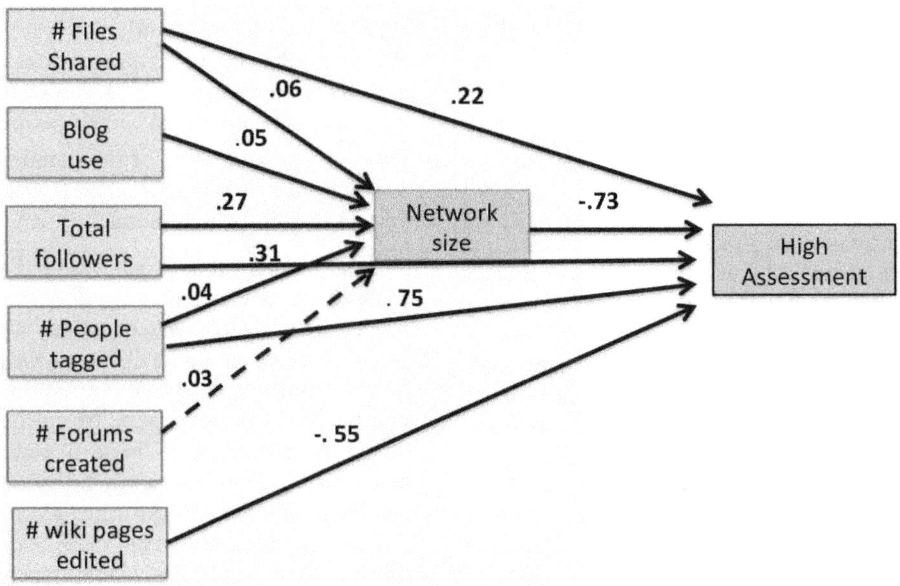

Figure 2: Model of network size as a mediator of social media use on colleague's positive assessment. All arrows show relations with significance levels of p<.01. Dotted line refers to a relation of p<.08. Standardized beta coefficients are shown on arrows.

Table 4 shows the beta coefficients in the model. Note that in Figure 2, though the standardized beta coefficients might be small, because the sample size is relatively small, these indicate significant weights.

	B	t	p
Network Size	-1.67	-6.03	.0001
Files Shared	.03	2.18	.03
Blog Use	-.002	-.57	.57
Total Followers	.02	2.65	.01
People Tagged	.002	2.60	.01
Forums Created	-.05	-.97	.34
Wiki Pages Edited	-.03	-2.07	.04

Table 4. Beta coefficients for factors in the model of Figure 2. N=77.

The results in Figure 2 show that counter-intuitively, there is an *inverse* relationship between Network Size and High Assessment. The results show that the smaller one's network (the fewer friends one has in their online enterprise social network), then the *higher* one is assessed by colleagues.

The numbers by the arrows in Figure 2 indicate the standardized beta coefficients which allow us to compare the relative effects of the variables. The model illustrates several relations. Network Size has a very strong negative effect on Assessment, based on its standardized beta coefficient of -.73, relative to the other coefficients in the model. File Sharing has a moderate effect (.22) and Tagging has a very strong effect, with a coefficient of .75. Number of Wiki Page Edits also has a strong but negative effect on Assessment with a coefficient of -.55. Total Followers has a moderate positive effect on Assessment.

Though Network Size significantly and strongly (inversely) predicts High Assessment, it is actually mediated by other variables. Blog Use, Files Shared, Forums Created, Total Followers and People Tagged indirectly affect High Assessment through their significant effect on Network Size. This shows that Network Size is a partial mediator of the relation of social media use to High Assessment. Again, as Network Size increases, people are *less likely* to rate that person with a positive assessment. In other words, the larger one's social network in the enterprise, the lower they are rated by colleagues. This is a puzzling result and we chose to examine it further in the next section.

Opportunity cost

One explanation for the inverse relationship of Network Size and colleagues' ratings is *opportunity cost.* An opportunity cost, originating in microeconomic theory, refers to the idea that if one alternative is chosen, one loses a potential gain from the alternatives that one did not choose [4]. Thus, given that in the enterprise one has limited time constraints, by choosing to use one form of social media, one loses the potential gain by not using another form of social media. When one invests time in building and maintaining friends through an enterprise social network site, there is less time to engage in other social media usage in the broad platform. It is possible that people with fewer friends in the enterprise might actually spend more time using social media on more "professional" or "serious" activities, such as those identified in our factor analysis: file sharing (factor 3) or writing in a company wiki (factor 2) or blog (factor 4). It might be that 'friending' in an enterprise would be perceived to be wasting time. This could explain why people with the smallest network size were the most highly regarded—perhaps they are the ones who do "serious" work.

To test this notion, we first examined our target dataset used in Figure 2, of those people with the most positive assessments in the organization. We divided people's network size into three levels based on a histogram with roughly equal cases per level: low (mean friends = 29.6), medium (mean friends = 95.8), and large (mean friends = 246.4). We consider the following variables used in our model in Figure 2 to be "serious" social media use, i.e. what might be considered more central to enterprise work: blog use (number of posts to corporate blogs), file activity (number of professionally-related files liked), wiki use (number of corporate wiki pages edited), forum use (number of forums created on the enterprise network), and tagging others (number of tags given to others in the organization).

An ANOVA revealed that only blog use showed a significant difference between friend levels ($F(2,77)=3.37$, $p<.04$, with low friends having the lowest blog use (mean blog use = 7.4), then medium friends (mean blog use = 13.3), and then high friends (mean blog use = 44.7). We found no significant differences among any of the other four "serious" social media variables on the low, medium, or high friend levels. In sum, the results indicate no support for opportunity cost.

However, it is possible that this set of highly rated people are special cases. Perhaps we would find evidence for an opportunity cost with a broader set of social media users than just the highest rated by colleagues. We used the data of people who received at least one rating on one survey variable (N=3,320). We divided people's network size into three friend levels based on a histogram with roughly equal cases per level: low (mean=8.5), medium (mean=26.2), and large (mean=99.9). An ANOVA showed that for all the "serious" social media use variables, there were significant differences between the friend size groups: low, medium, high (Table 5). Contrary to our expectations, with the exception of forum creation, the data shows that as one's network size increased, the social media activity also increased for our selected variables. Therefore, opportunity cost does not seem to explain the inverse relationship of Network Size on High Assessment.

DISCUSSION

Together, our findings suggest that the usage of social media in an enterprise can help reveal insights about how employees use it. Our first research question examined whether we could identify patterns of social media use within an enterprise social media platform.

	Number of Friends					
	Low (L)	Medium (M)	High (H)	F	p	Bon-ferroni Tests*
Blogs	3.57 (13.7)*	3.80 (14.1)	12.35 (46.8)*	32.17	.0001	L-H; M-H
Files	.09 (.95)	.30 (2.2)	1.39 (6.2)	35.48	.0001	L-H; M-H
Forums	.33 (1.31)	.28 (.96)	.59 (1.7)	17.71	.0001	L-H; M-H
Tags	.22 (1.35)	1.58 (13.8)	13.88 (105.2)	16.47	.0001	L-H; M-H
Wikis	14.44 (39.7)	17.41 (40.1)	25.28 (97.0)	8.00	.0001	L-H; M-H

Table 5. Mean (s.d.) of different social media usage, for low, medium, and high levels of friends in one's social network. All Bonferroni tests shown are significant at p<.01. N=3320.

We discovered that social media use falls mostly into factors associated with distinct tool use. Informed by these factors, for our second research question we developed a model showing that in conjunction with other social media usage, Network Size is a strong predictor of whether a person in the enterprise is highly reputable. However, Network Size revealed a surprising result: an *inverse* relationship with High Assessment, which we will address shortly.

Social media use in an enterprise platform

An integrated social media platform offers users in the enterprise a choice of media. The factor analysis results showed that there are indeed distinct identifiable patterns of use that mostly correspond to individual social media tools. However, the first factor, commenting and liking, indicates that most of the variance of broad social media use can be explained by these behaviors. These results together suggest that users might "specialize" in different types of media use: as commenters/likers, or as bloggers, wiki users, file sharers or forum contributors. These findings relate to the notion of compensatory fit of Gulatti and Puranam [13]: activities in the informal organization can enhance the effectiveness of the formal organization. Our results provide a first step in investigating more clearly how social media platform use contributes to those informal activities by identifying user roles with social media. Focusing on particular types of media could develop user skills in this media, such as becoming expert bloggers or wiki contributors. The development of such skills could provide benefits to the organization as opposed to using social media platforms in a more *ad hoc* manner.

The factor analysis results revealed that contributing content, and having others react to that content, is very much intertwined, as evidenced by these actions loading onto the same factors. We found that factor 1 revealed that behaviors of commenting and liking, but also having one's contributions commented upon and liked, loaded on to the same factor. Similarly, factors that showed wiki and blog use indicated the same types of interdependent actions, both creating content and having others comment on that content. One explanation for these patterns of interdependent use might be found from the study of Brzozowski et al. [3] who found that comments on blogs encouraged further blog posting by the author. In a cyclical manner, the relationship of contributing and being commented upon with other forms of social media can be mutually reinforcing.

Understanding broad patterns of enterprise social media use can inform the design of social media platforms. For example, a platform might adapt to a user's pattern of preference for tools. A related idea is that notifications can be geared to a user's social media preference so that they are not overloaded with too many different updates.

Network Size and visibility

We found that Network Size was the strongest (negative) predictor of people's ratings of their colleagues. This result occurred with the most highly rated individuals. Network Size, however, was a partial mediator of other social media usage. Its negative weight in the model indicates that it actually could be a *suppressor* of the effects of other social media usage on High Assessment, i.e. it could suppress the effects of Files Shared and Total Followers.

Our finding of Network Size contrasts with that of Tong et al. [31] who found a nonlinear relationship of number of Facebook friends and social attractiveness. Several aspects of the studies are notable in their differences. First, an assessment of social attractiveness of undergraduates in the Tong et al. study is very different than an assessment of traits for an organization's employees as in our study. Second, the mean number of friends in our study was 45.5 whereas the students in the Tong et al. study had a mean of 395 friends. Our result is closer to that of Utz [33] who found that people with introverted and fewer friends are judged more socially attractive. Extending this to an enterprise context, it may be possible that in assessing others, the *type* of friend is important in connections and not necessarily the size of the network.

We hypothesized that opportunity cost could explain the negative relation of Network Size to High Assessment but we did not find evidence to support this notion. We provide an alternative interpretation of the negative relation of Network size on High Assessment as follows. Researchers of social media effects in the enterprise have argued that social media makes people's behavior visible [2, 12, 32]. It is possible that social network use, i.e. 'friending', is more visible in the enterprise than other types of social media usage. When one requests someone to be a friend on a social network site, it is a direct communication with another person and thus is very visible. In contrast, other types of social media activity such as blog use or forum creation may be less visible. One needs to seek out a wiki or blog, or subscribe to notifications of new content. If it is indeed the case that friending behavior is very visible and that 'friending' in an enterprise might be considered frivolous or non work-related, then this could explain the negative relation with High Assessment. One interpretation is that friending is not valued yet in the enterprise. However, another possible interpretation is that friending may be less relevant in an enterprise when there are so many other options for communicating with someone, especially through a broad social media platform.

How can we explain the negative relation of Wiki use (i.e. wiki pages edited) with High Assessment? Our interpretation is that Wiki use and High Assessment have actually an underlying covariate in common. Wiki edits involve technical, fact-oriented content contribution. The people selected as having "High Assessment" might be people who are instead content creators, or more active social media "leaders". Evidence for this is found in our model with the significant predictor of Files Shared. People who share files to others may be more active in the organization and thus, perhaps assessed higher as a result. Perhaps those who do technical Wiki edits are not those who are also content creators. Indeed, our factor analysis results showed that wiki use loads onto a separate factor than other social media behaviors. It is thus possible that wiki users have traits that are different than those who are most highly regarded in the organization.

Limitations

The underlying variable that we created based on the five survey questions may have actually measured some other construct than what we call "High Assessment". People could have instead rated others based on people they like or admire. If this were the case, then our interpretation for the model in Figure 2 would be that file sharing, tagging, followers, and wiki use, mediated (negatively) by network size, predict colleagues' liking or admiration for other people. This would then suggest that people's SNS usage and use of social media is correlated with a dimension such as respect. This is entirely possible. With this interpretation, perhaps those who spend their time "friending" in the organization are not the people who are highly respected or admired.

Our dataset was deliberately limited to people who were highly perceived by their colleagues (they were presented to, and selected by, at least two target users.), Therefore, our results would hold for highly regarded people and would not necessarily be generalizable to a broader set of people in the enterprise. This research was a first step in assessing the relationship of Network Size to colleague's ratings. We hope that our study can spark further research to examine this phenomenon for a more varied set of users.

Another limitation is that our study focused only on behavioral factors related to social media platform use. We did not include institutional factors, which would be a fruitful area of research for future study.

We wish to note that the 'friending' feature exists longer (about five years) in the organization than the 'following' feature (about 2.5 years) and thus its resulting network is denser. Thus, it is possible that the differences in density could have influenced our model.

CONCLUSIONS

Broad social media platforms as well as social network use in the enterprise is still a relatively new phenomenon, compared to the use of more traditional media such as email. Employees in the enterprise do exhibit distinct patterns of use (as opposed to ad hoc usage) when they have broad social media platforms available. Our finding of a negative relation of Network Size on colleagues' positive assessment raises questions about the claim that electronic social networks will become the most valued communication medium in the enterprise [11]. That may be the case, but currently our results indicate that friending is not a trait associated with the most highly assessed colleagues. In all, our results suggest that the role of social media in the enterprise is complex and they raise new questions on how its usage can impact organizational behavior.

ACKNOWLEDGMENTS

We thank Judy Olson, Cory Knobel, Bart Knijnenburg and Xinru Page for their valuable comments.

REFERENCES

1. Baron, R. M., & Kenny, D. A. The moderator-mediator variable distinction in social psychological research: Conceptual, strategic and statistical considerations. *Journal of Personality and Social Psychology*, 51, (1986), 1173-1182.
2. boyd, d. Social network sites as networked publics: Affordances, dynamics and implications. In Z. Papacharissi (Ed.), *A Networked Self: Identity, Community, and Culture on Social Network Sites*. New York: Routledge, (2010), 39–58.
3. Brzozowski, M., Sandholm, T., & Hogg, T. Effects of feedback and peer pressure on contributions to enterprise social media. *Proceedings of the 2009 International Conference on Supporting Group Work*. NY: ACM Press, (2009), 61–70.
4. Buchanan, J. M. Opportunity cost. *The New Palgrave Dictionary of Economics*. 2nd Ed. S. N. Durlauf & L E. Blume (Eds.). Palgrave Macmillan, (2008).
5. Coleman, J. S. Social capital in the creation of human capital. *American Journal of Sociology*, 94(Supplement), (1988), S95–S120.
6. De Choudhury, M. and Counts, S. Understanding affect in the workplace via social media. *Proceedings of CSCW'13*, (2013), 303-316.
7. DiMicco, J, Millen, D., Geyer, W., Dugan, C., Brownholtz, B. and Muller, M. Motivations for social networking at work. *Proceedings of the 2008 ACM conference on Computer supported cooperative work*, (2008), 711-720.
8. DiMicco, J., Geyer, W., Millen, D. R., Dugan, C., & Brownholtz, B. People sensemaking and relationship building on an enterprise social networking site. *Proceedings of the 42nd Annual Hawaii International Conference on System Sciences*, (2009).
9. Gao, G., Hinds, P. and Zhao, C. Closure vs. structural holes: How social network information and culture affect choice of collaborators. *Proceedings of CSCW'13*, (2013), 5-18.
10. Ellison, N., Steinfeld, C. and Lampe, C. The Benefits of Facebook "Friends:" Social Capital and College Students' Use of Online Social Network Sites. *Journal of Computer-Mediated Communication,* 12, (2007), 1143–1168.
11. Gartner. Gartner Says 80 Percent of Social Business Efforts Will Not Achieve Intended Benefits Through 2015, 2013, http://www.gartner.com/newsroom/id/2319215.
12. Grudin, J. Enterprise knowledge management and emerging technologies. *Proceedings of the 39th Annual Hawaii Int'l Conference on System Sciences*, (2006).
13. Gulatti, R. and Puranam, P. Renewal through reorganization: The value of inconsistencies between formal and informal organization. *Organization Science,* 20(2), (2009), 422-440.
14. Guy, I. Avraham, U., Carmel, D., Ur, S., Jacovi, M., & Ronen, I. Mining expertise and interests from social media. *Proc. WWW '13,* (2013), 515-526.
15. Guy, I., Jacovi, M., Shahar, E., Meshulam, N., Soroka, V., & Farrell, S. Harvesting with SONAR: the value aggregating social network information. *Proc. CHI'08*, 2008, 1017-1026.
16. Guy, I., Ur, S., Ronen, I., Perer, A., and Jacovi, M. Do you want to know? Recommending strangers in the enterprise. *Proceedings of CSCW'11*, (2011), 285-294.
17. Jacovi, M., Guy, I., Ronen, I., Perer, A., Uziel, E., Maslenko, M. Digital traces of interest: Deriving interest relationships from social media interactions. *Proceedings of the 12th European Conference on Computer Supported Cooperative Work* (ECSCW'11), 24-28 September 2011, Aarhus Denmark, (2011), 21-40.
18. Jacovi, M., Guy, I., Kremer-Davidson, S., Porat, S., & Aizenbud-Reshef, N. The perception of others: inferring reputation from social media in the enterprise. *Proc. CSCW'14*, ACM Press, (2014).

19. John, A., & Seligmann, D. Collaborative tagging and expertise in the enterprise. *Proceedings of WWW'06,* NY: ACM Press, (2006).

20. Jones, G. and George, J. The Experience and evolution of trust: Implications for cooperation and teamwork. *The Academy of Management Review*, 23 (3), (1998), 531-546.

21. Kosonen, M. and Kianto, A. Applying wikis to managing knowledge—A socio-technical approach. *Knowledge and Process Mgt*, 16(1), 2009, 23–29.

22. Lawley, D. N. and Maxwell, A. E. *Factor analysis as a statistical method.* New York: American Elsevier Pub. Co. (1971).

23. Nahapiet, J. and Ghoshal, S. Social capital, intellectual capital, and the organizational advantage. *The Academy of Management Review*, 23 (2), (1998). 242-266

24. Parkhurst, J. and Hopmeyer, A. Sociometric popularity and peer-perceived popularity : Two distinct dimensions of peer status. *The Journal of Early Adolescence*, 18(125), (1998).

25. Oh, H., Chung, M., and Labianca, G. *The Academy of Management Journal*, 47(6,) (2004), 860–875.

26. Polanyi, Michael, *The Tacit Dimension*, Chicago: University of Chicago Press, (1966).

27. Ross, C., Orr, E., Sisic, M., Arseneault, J., Simmering, M., and Orr, R. Personality and motivations associated with Facebook use. *Computers in Human Behavior* 25, (2009), 578–586.

28. Skeels, M. and Grudin, J. When social networks cross boundaries: A case study of workplace use of facebook and linkedin. *Proceedings of ACM Group'09*. (2009).

29. Steinfeld, C., DiMicco, J., Ellison, N., and Lampe, C. Bowling online: Social networking and social capital within the organization. *Proceedings of C&T'09*, (2009).

30. Thom-Santelli, J. and Muller, M. and Millen, D. Social tagging roles: Publishers, evangelists, leaders. *Proc of CHI'08*. NY: ACM Press, (2008), 1041-44.

31. Tong, S., van der Heide, B., Langwell, L., and Walther, J. Too much of a good thing? The relationship between number of friends and interpersonal relationships on Facebook. *Journal of Computer-Mediated Communication*, 11, (2008), 531-549.

32. Treem, J. R. and Leonardi, P. Social Media Use in Organizations Exploring the Affordances of Visibility, Editability, Persistence, and Association. *Communication Yearbook*, 36, (2012), 143-189.

33. Utz, S. Show me your friends and I will tell you what type of person you are: How one's profile, number of friends, and type of friends influence impression formation on social network sites, *Journal of Computer-Mediated Communication*, 15, (2010), 314-335.

34. Valenzuela, S., Park, N., Kee, K. Is There Social Capital in a Social Network Site? Facebook Use and College Students' Life Satisfaction, Trust, and Participation. *Journal of Computer-Mediated Communication*, 14(4), (2009), 875–901.

35. Wu, A., DiMicco, J. M., & Millen, D. R. Detecting professional versus personal closeness using an enterprise social network site. *Proceedings of CHI'10*, NY: ACM Press, (2010), 1955–1964.

36. Zwica, J. and Danowski, J. The faces of Facebookers: Investigating social enhancement and social compensation hypotheses: predicting Facebook and offline popularity from sociability and self-esteem, and mapping the meanings of popularity with semantic networks. *Journal of Computer-Mediated Communication*, 14(1), (2008), 1-34.

APPENDIX A

Q1. CNN is making a new documentary series about reputable people. Gamma[4] was asked to identify a group of the most reputable Gamma employees in various fields, to be included in a chapter about IT companies. Imagine you are sitting on the selection committee, and that the list below contains the 10 finalists. Who would you nominate?

Q2. You just got some really exciting news, but were asked to keep it under wraps until the formal announcement. You were given permission to share this news with up to three people. Suppose these people you were going to tell are ones from the list below. Who would you tell?

Q3. A group at Gamma Research has developed a new tool for internal use. The group is looking for early adopters who would be willing to use the tool and later spread it across Gamma. Imagine you are sitting on the committee responsible for picking these early adopters. The list below contains the 10 finalists. Who would you pick?

Q4. To celebrate its second centennial, Gamma is announcing an award for people whose work had the most impact on the company. Imagine you are sitting on the committee responsible for picking these people. The list below contains the 10 finalists. Who would you nominate for the award?

Q5. Gamma has created a new forum of experts, and is looking for people who are experts in their field to act as the core team of the forum. Imagine you are sitting on the committee responsible for picking this core team. The list below contains 10 finalists. Who would you pick?

---

[4] A pseudonym is used for the organization name.

Understanding Individuals' Personal Values from Social Media Word Use

Jilin Chen*, Gary Hsieh†, Jalal Mahmud*, Jeffrey Nichols*

*IBM Almaden Research Center
650 Harry Road, San Jose, CA 95120, USA
{jilinc, jumahmud, jwnichols}@us.ibm.com

†Human Centered Design & Engineering
University of Washington
Seattle, WA 98195, USA
garyhs@uw.edu

ABSTRACT

The theory of values posits that each person has a set of values, or desirable and trans-situational goals, that motivate their actions. The Basic Human Values, a motivational construct that captures people's values, have been shown to influence a wide range of human behaviors. In this work, we analyze people's values and their word use on Reddit, an online social news sharing community. Through conducting surveys and analyzing text contributions of 799 Reddit users, we identify and interpret categories of words that are indicative of user's value orientations. Using the same data, we further report a preliminary exploration on word-based prediction of Basic Human Values.

Author Keywords

Basic Human Value; word use; social media

ACM Classification Keywords

H5.3. Information Interfaces and Presentation

INTRODUCTION

Social media users are not homogenously motivated. Just because two people both "participate" on the same social media platform, it does not mean that they use it for the same reasons or interact with the platform in the same way. In fact, what they hold to be important can differ drastically and as a result they most likely will behave differently. For example, while some may be more focused on job-related uses because they are interested in advancing themselves and demonstrating their competency, others may be more likely to provide social support and be more interested in helping others who have questions or problems.

Schwartz's theory of Basic Human Values [36] provides us a rigorous framework in reasoning about these different motivations. As a theory of values [32, 34], the theory of Basic Human Values defines a motivational construct, capturing desirable, trans-situational goals of people's lives into several distinct dimensions. These value dimensions have been shown to affect a wide range of offline behaviors, including choice of degree major in college, consumer decisions [30], religiosity [6, 38], pro-environmental behavior [16], etc.

Despite these results, to date we have little knowledge on whether and how these value dimensions manifest in online social media. Do our values draw us towards certain discussions, or lead us to more frequently employ certain words? And if they do influence our word use, what words are indicative of which value dimensions? Answering these questions can lead to more effective tailored persuasive messages or incentives to tackle the under-contribution problem plaguing many social media services [22].

In this work, we present the first analysis of associations between people's Basic Human Values and their word use in online social media. We recruited users from Reddit, a popular social news sharing community, and measured their personal values through the established Portrait Values Questionnaire [35]. We also collected their posts on Reddit, and measured their word use in a number of word categories as defined by the Linguistic Inquiry and Word Count (LIWC) dictionary [27]. Following methodologies established in prior analyses (e.g. Yarkoni [44]), we correlated users' values with word use, and identified LIWC word categories that are associated with different value dimensions. We further explored the prediction of Basic Human Values based on word use.

This work contributes to both theory and practice. On the theoretical side, as the first study that relates Basic Human Values to social media word use, this work furthers our understanding of how people's values manifest in their everyday online discussions. On the practical side, this work investigates to what extent people's values can be predicted from their writing on social media. Such predictions can be potentially useful in a wide variety of practical scenarios, such as recruiting pro-social individuals for volunteer efforts or offering extrinsic recognitions to achievement-motivated contributors.

BACKGROUND AND RESEARCH QUESTIONS

In this section we describe the Basic Human Values proposed by Shalom Schwartz [34]. We then briefly review prior research that relates word use to values, personalities, and other attributes. Lastly, we introduce the two research questions that guide the rest of this paper.

CSCW'14, February 15–19, 2014, Baltimore, Maryland, USA.
Copyright © 2014 ACM 978-1-4503-2540-0/14/02...$15.00.
http://dx.doi.org/10.1145/2531602.2531608

Basic Human Values

According to the theory of values, values convey what is important to an individual. Values are "desirable, trans-situational goals, varying in importance that serve as guiding principles in people's lives" [36]. Schwartz summarizes five features that are common to all values: (1) values are beliefs; (2) values are a motivational construct; (3) values transcend specific actions and situations; (4) values guide the selection or evaluation of actions, policies, people and events, and (5) values are ordered by relative importance [34].

Values have been found to correlate to a wide variety of behaviors [35]. Research suggests that people behave according to their values for two reasons. First, they seek consistency between their beliefs and actions (e.g., Rokeach [32]). Second, actions consistent with values are rewarding, since they allow people to obtain what they believe in. Studies have showed that people do want to act accordingly to their values in hypothetical situations [9, 33].

A few different values dimensions have been proposed [17, 20, 32, 34]. In this work, we focus on the Basic Human Values derived by Schwartz [34] for a number of reasons. First, Schwartz' values discriminate among individual people instead of national cultures. Second, Schwartz' values are not limited to work but also include values from different life domains. Third, they were developed through surveys of people across 67 countries, are well studied and tested, and they have been included in the European Social Survey [35].

Schwartz and colleagues propose 10 Basic Human Values, which map onto 5 higher-level value dimensions [34]. As represented in Figure 1, the circumplex structure in Schwartz' Value Theory indicates relations of conflict and congruity across values. The closer any two values are to one another, the more similar their underlying motivations, and vice versa. Below, we introduce the five value dimensions:

Self-transcendence encompasses two basic human values involving concern for the welfare and interests of others: (1) *universalism*, to pursue understanding, appreciation, tolerance and protection for the welfare of all people and for nature; and (2) *benevolence*, to pursue the preservation and enhancement of the welfare of people with whom one is in frequent personal contact.

Self-enhancement encompasses two basic human values related to the pursuit of self-interests: (1) *power*, to pursue social status and prestige, control or dominance over people and resources; and (2) *achievement*, to pursue personal success through demonstrating competence according to social standards.

Conservation encompasses three basic human values related to self-restriction, order, and resistance to change: (1) *conformity*, to pursue restraint of actions, inclinations, and impulses likely to upset or harm others and violate social expectations or norms; (2) *tradition*, to pursue

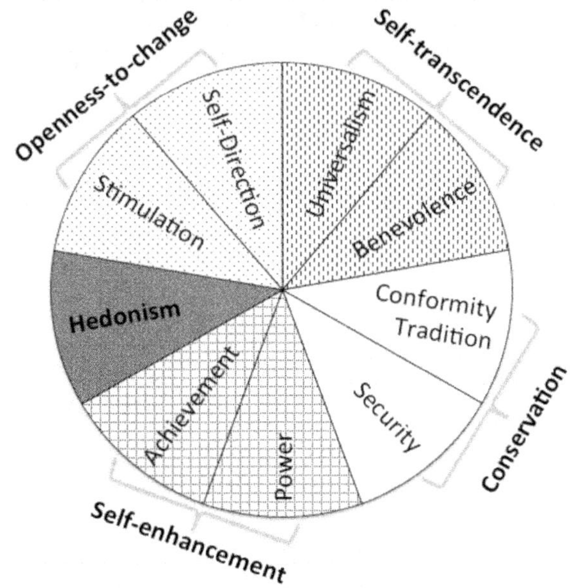

Figure 1. Schwartz' Values

respect, commitment, and acceptance of the customs and ideas that traditional culture or religion provide the self; and (3) *security*, to pursue safety, harmony, and stability of society, of relationships, and of self.

Openness-to-change encompasses two basic human values related to the desire for independence and new experiences: (1) *stimulation*, to pursue excitement, novelty and challenges in life; and (2) *self-direction*, to attain independence in thought and action—to choose, create, and explore.

Hedonism refers to the pursuit of pleasure and sensuous gratification for oneself. It is about seeking pleasure, enjoying life and self-indulgence. According to Schwartz [35], hedonism can be categorized under openness-to-change 75% of the time, but may also be related to self-enhancement. To keep the effects distinct, in our analyses, we keep hedonism as a separate value.

To measure people's value orientations, we use the Portrait Value Questionnaire (PVQ) developed by Schwartz (see Schwartz [35] for review). The 21-question version takes about 5-6 minutes to answer, and has been completed by respondents from 18 nations. We describe measurements of values in more details in the methodology section.

Word Use, Value and Personality

In this work we analyze the associations between people's values and their word use in social media, guided by the hypothesis that word use is influenced by values.

The link between values and text has been proposed, but not conclusively established. Some recent research [10, 21, 41] has explored machine annotation of values expressed in text documents, as perceived by the readers. This recent research suggests that certain words are interpreted to convey certain values. In contrast to these efforts that focused on if and how readers perceive the values within text documents, our focus is on how people's own writing reveals their personal values. In other words, whether personal values influence word use in writing.

Our research methodology is borrowed from prior research that related people's word use to personality. Early works (e.g. Fast et al. [7], Mairesse et al. [25]) collected writing samples in experimental settings, and correlated the word use to writers' personality. Gill et al. [12] and Yarkoni [44] analyzed web blogs and correlated their word use with personality dimensions. Several recent papers [13, 14, 39] used text snippets on Facebook and Twitter to predict personality. A majority of these prior works followed a common research methodology: They first identified psychologically-meaningful word categories within the Linguistic Inquiry and Word Count (LIWC) dictionary [27, 28], and transformed people's writings into word counts for these word categories. The word counts were then correlated to people's personality, measured through established personality questionnaires.

We follow this methodology in analyzing the association between word use and Basic Human Values, for three reasons: 1) both personality models and value models are psychological constructs that characterize people's emotional, attitudinal and behavioral patterns on several meaningful dimensions; 2) like the case of personality, we aim to find meaningful and systematic associations between word use and psychological constructs, making LIWC an appropriate instrument; 3) like the case of personality, we can take advantage of reliable ground truth from established psychometric questionnaires.

Word-Based Prediction of Other Attributes

More broadly, prior data mining research has explored algorithms that use word-based features to predict other attributes, such as sentiment (see Pang et al. [26] and Liu [23] for reviews) and political polarization (e.g. Cohen [3]). This work complements such prior research by exploring Basic Human Values, a set of attributes that have not been studied before.

Meanwhile, our work also differs from prior data mining research on our research goals and methodology. A vast majority of data mining research on sentiment and political polarization aims to optimize prediction accuracy, and is generally uninterested in the underlying interpretation of word use; indeed, word-based features are often treated as yet another feature set and nothing else. In contrast, our investigation primarily aims to understand how and why Basic Human Values manifests in people's word use, and considers the exploration of prediction accuracy only as a secondary goal. Our work is thus more similar to what Dehghani et al. [5] and Graham et al. [15] have done on characterizing political polarization.

Research Questions

We now introduce our two research questions:

RQ1: Are there any systematic associations between people's Basic Human Values and their word use in online social media? If so, what these associations are, and why?

RQ2: To what extent can we predict people's values solely from their social media word use?

Answers to these questions are particularly valuable due to the roles of Basic Human Values in people's motivation. Researchers have long posited the matching hypothesis [4, 19, 29], i.e. effective persuasive messages and rewards need to target individual's underlying reasons for participation. As a result, through relating people's word use to their values, this work can reveal deeper insights into people's motivation, inform more engaging designs, and lead to impacts that are lacking from existing research on other attributes such as personality and sentiment.

REDDIT AS A SOCIAL MEDIA PLATFORM

We based our word use analysis on participants recruited from Reddit. Founded in 2005, Reddit is one of the most visited social news sites. At the time of our study, Alexa ranked Reddit 8th in the News category, and 136th overall in the world.

Reddit is organized as an aggregation of over 67,000 subReddits, i.e. subcommunities built upon a specific topic, interest, or functionality. Registered users can submit content to any of these subReddits in the form of a link or user-generated text (formally known as self post). Other users can comment on each other's posts and comments, thus giving a tree structure to the content on Reddit, with a post as the root and comments as lower level nodes.

When visiting Reddit, users are first directed to their frontpage, which shows the "hottest" submitted content. Users may also customize their frontpage by subscribing to various subReddits. They can also navigate to each subReddit, which shows only the contents posted specifically to that subReddit. Registered users can up or down-vote the submitted post or comment. The accumulated votes from all users can then affect the visibility of a post or a comment under a post.

There are two key reasons why Reddit was chosen as the focus of this work. First, the functions of Reddit are simple but representative of a wide range of different social media. Like most other sites, it enables users to submit content, comments, maintain a profile, and curate content. Thus, the findings from the study of Reddit may help us understand general social media word usage.

Second, unlike many other social media sites that oftentimes focus on specific interests or functions, Reddit welcomes users with a wide-range of interests through their subReddit design. This may provide us with a better variety of participants and texts than other interest- or function-focused social media. For example, the *r/askReddit* subReddit works like a Q&A site where people post questions and others answer the question by commenting, while the *r/worldnews* subReddit is essentially a world news aggregator where users post links from major news sites from all over the world.

METHODOLOGY

We recruited participants on Reddit through posting a public invitation. We measured the Basic Human Values of the participants through a survey, and collected their most recent posts/comments on Reddit, from which we measure their word use and general Reddit usage. We then performed a correlation analysis, a regression analysis, and a classification study to answer the two research questions.

Data Collection

We submitted a post to the *r/self* subReddit, inviting Reddit users to participate in our survey. The *r/self* subReddit is a general purpose subReddit that is "a place to put self-posts for discussion, questions, or anything else you like". Besides posting to *r/self*, we also cross-posted our survey to multiple other subReddits in order to gain more attention. Reddit users were told that they would be entered into a drawing for one of multiple $100 Amazon Gift Cards or a donation of the same amount to a charity of their choice.

The survey first invited the Reddit users to provide their Reddit username or an email address, and then asked users to fill out the Portrait Value Questionnaire (PVQ) developed by Schwartz and colleagues to measure individual's value orientations [35]. The survey also contained several questions about the demographics of the survey participants. Duplicate questions were included in our survey to help filter low quality responses.

The PVQ includes 21 items that require responses on a 6-point Likert scale. There are 2 items for each of the 10 value types discussed above, except for Universalism, which contains 3 questions. Each item describes a third person (she or he), and survey takers were asked to rate how much this person in the question is like them. As per their instructions, we used the normalized version of the rating for each respondent in our analysis as these ratings indicate the relative, and not absolute importance of various goals in individuals' lives [37].

Our calculated Cronbach's alphas (a measure of internal consistency for psychometric questionnaire results) for each of the 10 Basic Human Values range from 0.27 to 0.78. In the design of the PVQ, Schwartz has explained that these low alpha ratings are acceptable, because some of the questionnaire items are designed to measure different underlying goals [35]. Nonetheless, to further ensure the reliability of value measures, we decided to focus on the 5 higher-level value dimensions in this work, thus increasing the number of questionnaire items per dimension from 2 to 4. The resulting alphas were all above 0.50 for our final analysis dataset.

Along with the survey, we also collected the 1,000 most recent posts/comments (fewer for those with less than 1,000 total posts) for each user who provided us with a valid username in the survey (using Reddit API). The collected information is used to measure word use.

Measures

We measured word use with the Linguistic Inquiry and Word Count (LIWC) 2007 version [27]. LIWC is the most commonly used language analysis tool for investigating the relation between word use and psychological variables [40]. The LIWC 2007 dictionary defines over 60 word categories, each containing dozens or hundreds of words.

For each Reddit user we computed one LIWC measure for each LIWC category based on the user's posts/comments. First, we counted the number of times each word in that category was used by the user, and then we divided that count by the total number of the user's words for normalization. Each LIWC measure thus represents the frequency of word use in one LIWC category.

A few LIWC categories form hierarchical relationships to each other. For example, the category *pronouns* can be broken into *personal pronouns* and *indefinite pronouns*, and *personal pronouns* can be further broken into several specific categories such as *first-person plural*. Because in this case the LIWC measure of a high level category is simply the sum of the measures for all its subcategories, in our analysis we omitted 14 high-level LIWC measures to avoid duplication (e.g. *pronouns* and *personal pronouns*).

For exploring value prediction we also computed a few other generic measures per user, including the number of posts/comments, the average number of sentences per post/comment, the average number of words per sentence, and the number of up and down-votes received in total. We omit these measures in this paper as none of them showed predictive power beyond the LIWC measures.

Analytical Approach

RQ1: Values and Word Use

We identify the associations between Basic Human Values and word use through a correlation analysis and an analysis of regression coefficients.

In the correlation analysis, we correlate the LIWC measures with the five value dimensions, and use the correlation significance to measure reliability. This analytical approach has been the established way for identifying associations between word use and personality in a large body of prior work [7, 13, 14, 31, 44].

To control for the large number of concurrent statistical significance tests, we corrected significance levels using a False Discovery Rate (FDR) criterion [2], which adaptively controls the false positive rate for all correlations deemed significant. The FDR was set to 0.05; in other words, any correlation that we report as significant has only a 5% probability on average of being a false positive. The equivalent p-value on our dataset was 0.014.

We also analyze the associations through linear regressions that predict value dimensions using LIWC measures. A challenge here is the collinearity between LIWC measures. For instance, while the LIWC measure *articles* has no significant correlation with self-transcendence and is not a significant predictor in a univariate regression of self-

	Mean	Std Dev	Correlations			
			2	3	4	5
1.Self-Transcendence	.85	.63	**-.58**	**-.20**	**-.07**	**-.23**
2.Self-Enhancement	-.50	.73	-	**-.25**	**-.19**	-.02
3. Conservation	-.86	.66		-	**-.66**	**-.34**
4. Openness-to-Change	.44	.60			-	**.61**
5. Hedonism	.26	.95				-

Table 1. Basic Human Values of Participating Reddit Users. Significant correlations shown in bold.

transcendence, it would become significant in a full linear regression due to its collinearity with other LIWC measures. Reporting *articles* as a significant predictor from this full regression would have been highly misleading.

As a result, we have conducted a Lasso penalized linear regression [11], using the R glmnet implementation. This approach alleviates the collinearity among LIWC measures by shrinking the coefficients of weak and/or correlated measures to zero. As suggested by Wu et al. [43], while there is no well-established way to assign p-value to regression coefficients in this case, a plausible approach is to calculate the univariate p-value for each non-zero coefficient separately and then apply FDR correction. This p-value calculation is equivalent to the significance calculation we used in our correlation analysis.

To help explain the LIWC word category and illustrate actual word usage behind each LIWC measure, for each LIWC measure we counted how many times words in the LIWC category were used in our Reddit dataset, and selected a few example words from the most frequently used words.

RQ2: Prediction Potential

To understand the prediction potential of the LIWC measures, we conducted a regression analysis and a machine learning classification study. In the regression analysis, we formulated linear regressions to predict each of the five value dimensions using LIWC measures. We evaluate prediction strength through R^2 and the correlation between the regressed value and true value. These two metrics reflect overall how well the regression can approximate the value dimensions.

A few prior papers have evaluated regression results using error measures such as MAE and RMSE [13, 14, 31]. Sumner et al. [39] have however argued that such evaluation is inadequate, as these error measures can often mask large errors on a unimodal population distribution if the algorithms predict a majority of individuals around the population mean. As all of our five value dimensions had unimodel distributions, we followed the advice of Sumner et al. and supplemented the regression analysis with a machine learning classification study.

In the classification study, we used supervised binary machine learning algorithms to classify individuals with above-median levels of each value dimension. We experimented with a number of classifiers from the WEKA machine learning toolkit [42], including logistic regression, naive Bayesian classifier, a variety of support vector machines and a variety of decision tree-based classifiers. Classifiers were evaluated using Area Under the ROC Curve (AUC) values under 10-fold cross validation. The AUC value is equivalent to the likelihood that a classifier ranks a randomly chosen positive instance higher than a randomly chosen negative one, and has been widely used to indicate the practical performance of binary classifiers [8].

RESULTS

For the survey, after removing incomplete responses, those that were completed too quickly (<5 minutes), and those that failed our consistency checks (low variance across all items and high discrepancies between duplicate items), we ended up with 1305 Reddit users with valid responses. To ensure the quality of LIWC measures, we included in our final dataset only users for which we could collect at least 100 posts/comments through the Reddit API. Our final analysis dataset contained 799 Reddit users.

Participating Users

The majority of our users identified themselves as male (65%), between the ages of 21 and 29 (51%), and had at least some college education (>80%).

On average, these users had been members of Reddit for 20 months and were fairly heavy users, spending between 1 to 4 hours on the site per day (70%).

On average each user had 599 posts/comments with over 20,000 words. The median was 566 posts/comments and about 15,500 words.

Our users' posts and comments spread over more than 4,000 subReddits, covering a diverse set of topics (e.g. *r/gaming*, *r/politics*, *r/fitness*, *r/canada*, *r/android*) and functions (e.g. *r/askReddit* for Q&A, *r/worldnews* for news aggregation).

Table 1 shows the mean, standard deviation, and correlation of the participating users' value dimensions. The moderate standard deviations indicate a healthy spread of values across our Reddit users. The correlations support the circumplex structure between values (Figure 1), i.e. the opposing relationship between self-transcendence and self-enhancement (corr = -.58), the opposing relationship between conservation and openness-to-change (corr = -.66), and the proximity between openness-to-change and hedonism (corr = .61).

RQ1: Values and Word Use

Table 2 shows Pearson correlations and the standardized regression coefficients between the LIWC measures and the value dimensions. The table groups the LIWC measures by high-level LIWC categories, and each LIWC measure is accompanied with a few example words used by our Reddit users. To save space, we omitted from Table 2 LIWC measures with no significant correlations and no significant non-zero coefficients.

The correlation analysis and the regression analysis mostly agree, with a few exceptions due to collinearity among the LIWC measures. For instance, while the LIWC measures *swear words* and *anger* both significantly correlate with self-transcendence, the regression coefficient of *anger* is absorbed by *swear words* due to the collinearity between the two measures. In general, as the regression analysis handles collinearity better, below we focus our description on the regression coefficients.

We explain the significant regression coefficients in Table 2 by the five value dimensions, using the example words and the interpretations of LIWC from Tausczik et al. [40]. These significant coefficients (shown in bold in Table 2) indicate reliable associations between value dimensions and the LIWC measures: A positive coefficient between a

LIWC Measures	Example Words from Reddit Users	Self-Transcendence		Self-Enhancement		Conservation		Openness-to-Change		Hedonism	
		Corr.	Coef.	Corr.	Coef.	Corr.	Coef.	Corr.	Coef.	Corr.	Coef.
Linguistic Processes											
First-person plural	we, us, our, ours	**.150**	**.069**	**-.099**	**-.025**	-.065	-.021	.041	.014	-.071	-.011
Third-person singular	she, her, him, his	**.084**	-	-.035	-	.005	-	-.060	-	-.037	-
Common verbs	is, have, was, would, get, think	**.111**	**.020**	-.013	-	-.036	-	-.025	-	.024	-
Auxiliary verbs	is, have, would, will, could, can	**.101**	-	.019	-	-.062	-	-.024	-	.017	-
Past tense	was, had, got, thought, used, went	.022	-	-.027	.022	**.075**	-	**-.086**	**-.017**	-.002	-
Present tense	is, have, get, think, know, make	**.097**	**.025**	.001	-	-.088	-.010	.039	-	.055	-
Prepositions	to, of, in, for, on, with	**.131**	**.071**	**-.102**	**-.010**	-.050	-	.016	-	**-.154**	**-.067**
Conjunctions	and, but, if, as, or, so	**.150**	**.026**	**-.088**	-	-.015	-	-.030	-	-.052	-
Swear words	shit, fuck, hell, damn	.007	.034	-.016	-.015	**-.107**	**-.045**	**.141**	**.065**	**.158**	**.051**
Social Processes											
Family	parent, family, dad, husband	**.122**	**.007**	**-.108**	-	**.133**	**.093**	**-.160**	**-.121**	**-.140**	**-.157**
Friends	friend, girlfriend, neighbor, roommate	**.093**	-	-.064	-	-.034	-.029	.020	.028	.028	.042
Humans	people, guy, man, girl	**.128**	**.008**	-.067	-	-.077	-.015	.020	-	-.006	-
Affective Processes											
Anxiety	worry, crazy, awkward, afraid	**.177**	**.026**	**-.145**	**-.056**	.000	-	-.037	-.012	**-.110**	**-.080**
Anger	shit, fuck, kill, hate	.007	-	.010	-	**-.113**	-	**.111**	-	**.109**	-
Sadness	hurt, sad, depressing, disappointing	**.089**	**.010**	-.020	-	-.006	-	-.042	-.008	-.052	-.022
Cognitive Processes											
Insight	think, know, reason, question	**.107**	**.012**	-.015	-	-.064	-	-.008	-	-.068	-
Causation	because, why, reason, since	.016	-	.036	-	**-.083**	-	.040	-	-.012	-
Discrepancy	if, would, should, could	**.085**	-	.030	.004	-.012	-	-.074	-.014	-.082	-.049
Tentative	if, something, probably, might	**.081**	-	-.022	-	-.033	-	-.020	-	-.070	-
Certainty	all, always, never, everything	.032	-	-.025	-	**-.123**	**-.048**	**.136**	**.077**	.066	.028
Inhibition	keep, stop, wait, hold	**.103**	**.043**	-.061	-.038	-.017	-	-.009	-	-.051	-
Inclusive	and, with, we, include	**.184**	**.006**	**-.172**	**-.047**	-.039	-.034	.034	.042	**-.085**	-
Exclusive	but, without, rather, unless	**.085**	-	-.002	-	-.057	-	.008	-	.022	-
Perceptual processes											
See	see, watch, color, red	**-.135**	**-.043**	.001	-.010	**.107**	**.039**	.013	-	**.120**	**.021**
Hear	say, hear, music, song	-.005	-	-.012	-	-.008	-	.033	-	**.110**	**.044**
Feel	feel, feeling, soft, hard	**.086**	-	**-.098**	-	-.020	-	.039	-	-.017	-
Biological processes											
Health	health, doctor, medicine, drug	**.182**	**.043**	**-.091**	-	-.034	-	-.040	-	-.084	-
Sexual	love, sex, penis, porn	.032	-.008	.008	.016	-.058	-	.032	-	**.102**	**.022**
Personal concerns											
Work	work, school, job, team	**-.090**	**-.047**	**.105**	**.061**	.043	-	-.084	-.028	**-.160**	**-.132**
Leisure	game, movie, music, beer	**-.136**	**-.020**	.043	-	.049	-	.029	-	**.128**	**.042**
Home	home, family, apartment, shower	**.096**	**.031**	**-.152**	**-.075**	**.104**	**.007**	-.061	-	**-.095**	-

Table 2. Pearson Correlations and Standardized Regression Coefficients Between Value Dimensions and LIWC Measures

1) Regression coefficients are computed through Lasso penalized linear regression, which handles collinearity among LIWC measures by shrinking the coefficients of weak and/or correlated measures to zero (marked as "-" in the table).
2) **Significant** correlations and regression coefficients are shown in **bold**, for which the false discovery rate (**FDR**) was set to be **0.05**;
3) Measures with **no significant correlations** and **no significant non-zero coefficients** are **omitted** from the table;
4) **Example words** in the table are chosen from words frequently used by our Reddit users to **represent the actual word usage** that contributed toward the LIWC measures.

Value Dimensions	R^2 of Linear Regression	Correlation between the Regressed Value and the True Value
Self-Transcendence	17.0%	0.39
Self-Enhancement	13.8%	0.35
Conservation	15.4%	0.37
Openness-to-Change	18.1%	0.41
Hedonism	18.2%	0.41

Table 3. Strength of Linear Regressions.

LIWC measure and a value dimension means that people who are high on the value dimension use words in the LIWC category more frequently than the average population.

Self-Transcendence

Self-transcendence significantly associates with a number of measures. First, it is positively associated with a few word categories that indicate an attention focus on others and the larger group (*first-person plural*, *humans*, *inclusive*). Second, it is positively associated with words expressing anxiety and sadness (e.g. "worry", "sad"), and words expressing inhibition (e.g. "stop", "wait"). Third, it is positively correlated with measures that indicate more complex language and more in-depth thinking, including the use of prepositions, conjunctions, and words from the LIWC *cognitive processes* categories.

A possible explanation for these correlations is that Reddit users with high self-transcendence give more advice to others in their comments: these advice comments likely mention the group and other people more frequently, show worries, concerns and inhibition, involve more in-depth thinking, and are generally more complex. These findings complement a previous analysis of Reddit showing that people who value self-transcendence are more likely to voluntarily help newcomers on Reddit [18].

Additional associations in social processes and personal concerns categories indicate that people with high self-transcendence write more about family, health, and home-living issues, and less about work-related issues and leisure activities.

Self-Enhancement

Self-enhancement shows the opposite associations with self-transcendence on many measures. These associations indicate that Reddit users with high self-enhancement write less about the larger group, express less anxiety, and use fewer prepositions. Like the case of self-transcendence, this result may suggest that people with high self-enhancement give less advice to others in their comments compared to the average population.

Additional associations in social processes and personal concerns categories suggest that people with high self-enhancement write more about work and less about home-living issues. These results highlight both the achievement and power values in self-enhancement.

Value Dimensions	Classifier Achieving the Highest AUC	AUC	TPR	TNR
Self-Transcendence	Random Forest	.60	.67	.50
Self-Enhancement	REPTree	.56	.54	.57
Conservation	Logistic Regression	.59	.56	.57
Openness-to-Change	Logistic Regression	.61	.59	.57
Hedonism	Logistic Regression	.61	.53	.63

Table 4. Predicting the Top 50% Users on Value Dimensions.

Reporting the best performing WEKA classifier among logistic regression, naive Bayesian classifier, a variety of support vector machines and a variety of decision tree-based classifiers.

Conservation

Conservation is negatively associated with the use of swear words and the use of words suggesting absolute certainty (e.g. "always", "everything"). These associations seem to suggest that people with high conservation exhibit more self-constraint in their writing, using fewer swear words and making fewer strong absolute statements so as to avoid upsetting other people. Not upsetting other people is a defining goal of conformity, a facet under conservation.

Additional associations in social processes and personal concerns categories suggest that people with high conservation write more about family and home-living issues, indicating their elevated interest in these topics.

We also observed a significant positive association between conservation and the *see* category (e.g. "see", "red"), for which we lack a clear explanation.

Openness-to-Change

Openness-to-change shows the opposite associations with conservation. These associations suggest that people with high openness-to-change write less about the past and family, use more swear words, and use more words that suggest absolute certainty. This result seems to suggest that people who seek excitement and independence (the two facets under openness-to-change) tend to be less constrained by society's rules, and are less constrained and more confident in their writing.

Hedonism

Hedonism shares a number of common associations with self-enhancement and openness-to-change. Like the case of self-enhancement, people with high hedonism express less anxiety and use fewer prepositions. Like the case of openness-to-change, people with high hedonism also use more swear words and use fewer words about family.

In addition, we have found that people with high hedonism write more about color, music, sex and leisure activities, and less about work related issues. These findings match the common image of hedonism.

RQ2: Prediction Potential

We report the strength of regression in Table 3. The R^2 of the linear regressions were small but substantial across all five value dimensions, ranging from 13.8% to 18.2%. The correlation between the regressed value and the true value was moderate, ranging from 0.35 to 0.41.

Table 4 shows the classification results under 10-fold cross validation. Following Sumner et al. [39], for each value dimension we report the best WEKA classifier in terms of AUC, as well as the AUC value, the true positive rate (TPR) and the true negative rate (TNR) of the best classifier under 10-fold cross validation. As flipping a coin would have achieved exactly .50 for AUC, TPR and TNR, we can conclude that in this classification task, the classifiers offered a real but small improvement over random chance.

Overall, we have demonstrated that word use on Reddit indeed contains predictive information of people's values, and can potentially be used to rank people based on their values. We also found that the prediction is not strong enough to allow accurate prediction of an individual's value in the binary classification setting proposed by Sumner et al. [39].

DISCUSSION

RQ1: Values and Word Use

One of the main contributions of this work is to show that personal values can influence word use. Indeed, the results in Table 2 indicate the existence of numerous reliable associations between personal values and word use.

More importantly, these associations suggest a number of potential mechanisms through which personal values affect word use. Below we summarize two major mechanisms that seem to function across value dimensions.

One such mechanism is thinking styles. The use of words from the LIWC *cognitive processes* categories are known to reflect people's thinking process [40]. In our case, we have found that people with high self-transcendence, perhaps due to their elevated desire to help others [18], try harder to interpret other people's situations, and therefore use more *cognitive processes* words. Similarly, we have found that people with high openness-to-change, perhaps due to their elevated desire to drive their own lives, are often more confident in their reasoning, and therefore use more words indicating certainty.

Another mechanism is attention focus. The use of certain pronouns and verbs is known to indicate people's specific focus of attention [40]. In our case, we have found that people with high self-transcendence, perhaps due to their elevated interest in the wellbeing of others, pay more attentions to others, and thus use the word "we" and other group-oriented words more often. Similarly, we have found that people with high conservation, perhaps due to their elevated attachment to established status quo, pay more attention to the past, and thus use past tense more often.

Attention focus also manifests in the use of content words [40]. As Reddit users participate in discussions at will, it is likely that their increased use of certain content words is due to their elevated interest in related discussions. For instance, people with high self-enhancement, perhaps due to their elevated desire for power and achievement, care more about work-related topics, and thus participate more in work-related discussions and use more work-related words. Similarly, people with high hedonism, perhaps due to their elevated interest in leisure and entertainment, participate more in such discussions, and thus use more words related to color, music, and leisure activities.

As our analysis is based on one social media site, one may wonder how the word use patterns and mechanisms we identified may generalize to other forms of social media. First, it should be noted that people's value orientations have been shown to be trans-situational [36] and do not vary greatly between different contexts. Second, due to the wide variety of topics covered in Reddit and the wide range of subReddits our users were involved in, we believe our results will likely generalize to other forum-like social media, such as social news sites, forums, and Q&A sites. However, characteristics and affordances of various media can and do influence communication behaviors. For example, while people with high self-transcendence may write many long advice comments with in-depth thinking, they simply would not be able to write these long comments on Twitter due to the 140 character limit.

RQ2: Prediction Potential

Our regression analysis (Table 3) confirms that word use on Reddit indeed contains predictive information of people's values. This finding demonstrates the potential of ranking social media users based on their motivational values expressed in their word use. Although in this study we did not explore ranking algorithms in detail, learning-to-rank algorithms [24], a class of advanced ranking algorithms developed in recent years, may be a promising candidate for further harnessing the predictive information from word use.

Meanwhile, our classification study indicates that word use by itself cannot accurately predict an individual's value in a binary classification setting. On all value dimensions the classification was better than random, and yet no algorithms performed particularly well (Table 4). This overall result is comparable to the state-of-art results on personality classification. For example, Sumner et al. [39] explored a large number of text-based classifiers, and reported that the best classifiers they explored were only slightly better than random chance in classifying people on personality dimensions. As a result, it is perhaps more promising to explore sophisticated topic modeling (e.g. LDA with topic-in-set knowledge [1]) and/or other information sources (e.g. the social network of the users) to further improve classification accuracy.

The ranking and classification of motivational values can be useful in many practical scenarios. For instance, our linear regression of self-transcendence is strong enough that if we rank all of our Reddit users according to our prediction, the majority of the top users in the ranked list would have above-mean self-transcendent orientation. This ranking can therefore be used to find high self-transcendent people for performing volunteer work, as these people will be more intrinsically motivated to help others.

The prediction of personal values can also help other meaningful prediction tasks due to values' trans-situational nature [36]. For instance, as recently reported by Cohen et al. [3], most existing political polarization classifiers transferred poorly from political elites to ordinary people, because ordinary people do not use strong partisan-specific language and vocabularies as often as political elites. Incorporating language signals indicating personal values might improve the situation, because such signals may be more revealing of the fundamental beliefs of individuals.

CONCLUSION AND FUTURE WORK

In this work, we have analyzed people's value and word use in social media. We identified a number of word categories that are associated with each value dimension, and found reasonable explanations for a vast majority of them. We also explored and confirmed word use in social media as a potential predictor of people's values.

There are a number of promising future directions. On the theoretical side, future research can expand from the 5 high-level value dimensions in this work to the 10 low-level value dimensions (Figure 1). It would also be valuable to better understand the mechanisms through which values influence word use. In this work we have discussed such mechanisms based on prior literature; future work is needed to directly validate these proposed mechanisms. Lastly, future work could extend our investigation of word use into other important online behaviors, such as the formation of social interactions.

On the practical side, future research can employ more sophisticated topic modeling approaches such as LDA, investigate value prediction on alternative social media platforms (e.g. Twitter), and explore stronger prediction algorithms by incorporating other signals, such as social network structures and temporal activity patterns.

ACKNOWLEDGEMENTS

We thank Yiran Chen for his help with data collection.

This research was sponsored by the U.S. Defense Advanced Research Projects Agency (DARPA) under the Social Media in Strategic Communication (SMISC) program, Agreement Number W911NF-12-C-0028. The views and conclusions contained in this document are those of the author(s) and should not be interpreted as representing the official policies, either expressed or implied, of the U.S. Defense Advanced Research Projects Agency or the U.S. Government. The U.S. Government is authorized to reproduce and distribute reprints for Government purposes notwithstanding any copyright notation hereon.

Funding for the second author, Gary Heish, was provided by National Science Foundation grant #1348542.

REFERENCES

1. Andrzejewski, D., & Zhu, X. 2009. Latent Dirichlet Allocation with topic-in-set knowledge. In NAACL HLT 2009 Workshop on Semi-Supervised Learning for Natural Language Processing (pp. 43-48).
2. Benjamini, Y.; Hochberg, Y. 1995. Controlling the false discovery rate: a practical and powerful approach to multiple testing. Journal of the Royal Statistical Society, Series B (Methodological 57 (1): 289–300.
3. Cohen, R., and Ruths, D. 2013. Classifying Political Orientation on Twitter: It's Not Easy!. In ICWSM'13.
4. DeBono, K. G., & Telesca, C. 1990. The Influence of Source Physical Attractiveness on Advertising Effectiveness: A Functional Perspective1. Journal of Applied Social Psychology, 20(17), 1383-1395.
5. Dehghani, M., Gratch, J., Sachdeva, S. & Sagae K. 2011. Analyzing Conservative and Liberal Blogs Related to the Construction of the 'Ground Zero Mosque'. In CogSci'2011.
6. Devos, T., Spini, D., & Schwartz, S. H. 2002. Conflicts among human values and trust in institutions. British Journal of Social Psychology.
7. Fast, Lisa A.; Funder, David C. 2008., Personality as manifest in word use: Correlations with self-report, acquaintance report, and behavior. Journal of Personality and Social Psychology, Vol 94(2), 2008.
8. Fawcett, T. 2006. An introduction to ROC analysis. Pattern Recognition Letters, 27, 861–874
9. Feather, N. T. 1995 Values, valences, and choice: The influences of values on the perceived attractiveness and choice of alternatives. Journal of Personality and Social Psychology, 68(6), 1135-1151
10. Fleischmann, K. R., Oard, D. W., Cheng, A. S., Wang, P., & Ishita, E. 2009. Automatic classification of human values: Applying computational thinking to information ethics. In ASIST, 46(1), 1-4.
11. Friedman, J., Hastie, T., and Tibshirani, R. 2010. Regularization paths for generalized linear models via coordinate descent. Journal of Statistical Software, 33(1), 1-22.
12. Gill, A.J., Nowson, S., Oberlander, J. 2009. What Are They Blogging About? Personality, Topic and Motivation in Blogs. In ICWSM'09.
13. Golbeck, J. Robles, C., Edmondson, M., Turner, K. 2011. Predicting Personality from Twitter. In Proc. IEEE SocialCom.
14. Golbeck, J. Robles, C.,Turner, K, Turner, K. 2011. Predicting Personality with Social Media. In.CHI'11 Extended Abstracts.
15. Graham, J., Haidt, J., & Nosek, B. A. 2009. Liberals and conservatives rely on different sets of moral foundations. Journal of personality and social psychology, 96(5), 1029.
16. Grunert, S. C., & Juhl, H. J. 1995. Values, environmental attitudes, and buying of organic foods. Journal of Economic Psychology, 16(1), 39–62

17. Hofstede, G. 1980. Culture's consequences: International differences in work-related values. Beverly Hills, CA: Sage.

18. Hsieh, G., Hou, Y., Chen, I., Truong, K. "Welcome!": Social and Psychological Predictors of Volunteer Socializers in Online Communities. In CSCW'13.

19. Hullett, C., & Boster, F. 2001. Matching messages to the values underlying value-expressive and social-adjustive attitudes: Reconciling an old theory with a contemporary measurement approach. Communication Monographs, 68(2), 133-153.

20. Inglehart, R. 1971. The Silent Revolution in Europe: Intergenerational Change in Post-Industrial Societies', American Political Science Review, 65:4, 991–1017.

21. Ishita, E., Oard, D. W., Fleischmann, K. R., Cheng, A. S., & Templeton, T. C. 2010. Investigating multi-label classification for human values. In ASIST, 47(1), 1-4.

22. Kraut, R. E. & Resnick, P. 2012. Building successful online communities: Evidence-based social design. Cambridge, MA: MIT Press.

23. Liu, B. 2012. Sentiment analysis and opinion mining. Synthesis Lectures on Human Language Technologies, 5(1), 1-167.

24. Liu, T. Y. 2009. Learning to rank for information retrieval. Foundations and Trends in Information Retrieval, 3(3), 225-331.

25. Mairesse, F., Walker, M. 2006. Words Mark the Nerds: Computational Models of Personality Recognition through language, In Proc. of CogSci 2006.

26. Pang, B. and Lee, L. 2008. Opinion mining and sentiment analysis. Foundations and Trends in Information Retrieval (2).

27. Pennebaker, J. W., Chung, C. K., Ireland, M., Gonzales, A., & Booth, R. J. 2007. The development and psychometric properties of LIWC2007 [LIWC manual]. Austin, TX: LIWC.net.

28. Pennebaker, J.W., Francis, M.E., Booth, R.J., 2001, Linguistic Inquiry and Word Count. Erlbaum Publishers, Mahwah, NJ.

29. Petty, R. E., & Wegener, D. T. 1998. Matching versus mismatching attitude functions: Implications for scrutiny of persuasive messages. Personality and Social Psychology Bulletin, 24(3), 227-240.

30. Puohiniemi, M. 1995. Values, Consumer Attitudes and Behavior: An Application of Schwartz's Value Theory to the Analysis of Consumer Behavior and Attitudes in Two National Samples. University of Helsinki, Helsinki, 1995

31. Quercia, D., Kosinki, M., Stillwell, D., and Crowcroft, J. 2011. Our Twitter profiles, our selves: predicting personality with Twitter. In SocialCom'11.

32. Rokeach, M. 1973. The Nature of Human Values. Free Press, New York, USA

33. Sagiv, L., & Schwartz, S. H. 1995. Value priorities and readiness for out-group social contact. Journal of Personality and Social Psychology, 69(3), 437-448.

34. Schwartz, S. H. 1994. Are There Universal Aspects in the Structure and Contents of Human Values? Journal of Social Issues, 50(4), 19-45

35. Schwartz, S. H. 2002. A Proposal for Measuring Value Orientations across Nations. Chapter 7 in the Questionnaire Development Package of the European Social Survey.

36. Schwartz, S. H. 2006. Basic human values: theory, measurement, and applications. Revue Française de Sociologie, 47(4).

37. Schwartz, S. H. 2009. Draft Users Manual: Proper Use of the Schwarz Value Survey, version 14 January 2009. Compiled by Romie F. Littrell. Auckland, New Zealand: Centre for Cross Cultural Comparisons, http://www.crossculturalcentre.homestead.com.

38. Schwartz, S. H., & Huismans, S. 1995. Value priorities and religiosity in four Western religions. Social Psychology quarterly, 58, 88-107.

39. Sumner, C., Byers, A., Boochever, R., and Park, G, J. 2012. Predicting Dark Triad Personality Traits from Twitter usage and a linguistic analysis of Tweets, 11th IEEE International Conference on Machine Learning and Applications, 2012, pp. 386-39.

40. Tausczik, Y. R. and Pennebaker, James W. 2010. The Psychological Meaning of Words: LIWC and Computerized Text Analysis Methods, In. Journal of Language and Social Psychology 29 (1), 24-54.

41. Templeton, T. C., Fleischmann, K. R., & Boyd-Graber, J. 2011. Simulating audiences: Automating analysis of values, attitudes, and sentiment. In PASSAT/SocialCom, pp. 734-737.

42. Witten, I.H., Frank, E., and Hall, M.A. 2011. Data mining: Practical machine learning tools and techniques, 3rd Edition. Morgan Kaufmann.

43. Wu, T. T., Chen, Y. F., Hastie, T., Sobel, E., and Lange, K. 2009. Genome-wide association analysis by lasso penalized logistic regression. Bioinformatics, 25(6), 714-721.

44. Yarkoni, T. 2010. Personality in 100,000 words: A large-scale analysis of personality and word usage among bloggers. Journal of Research in Personality.

Cursing in English on Twitter

Wenbo Wang, Lu Chen, Krishnaprasad Thirunarayan, Amit P. Sheth
Kno.e.sis Center, Wright State University
Dayton, OH 45435 USA
{wenbo, chen, tkprasad, amit}@knoesis.org

ABSTRACT
Cursing is not uncommon during conversations in the physical world: 0.5% to 0.7% of all the words we speak are curse words, given that 1% of all the words are first-person plural pronouns (e.g., we, us, our). On social media, people can instantly chat with friends without face-to-face interaction, usually in a more public fashion and broadly disseminated through highly connected social network. Will these distinctive features of social media lead to a change in people's cursing behavior? In this paper, we examine the characteristics of cursing activity on a popular social media platform – Twitter, involving the analysis of about 51 million tweets and about 14 million users. In particular, we explore a set of questions that have been recognized as crucial for understanding cursing in offline communications by prior studies, including the ubiquity, utility, and contextual dependencies of cursing.

Author Keywords
Profanity; Social Media; Twitter; Emotion; Gender Difference; Cursing.

ACM Classification Keywords
J.4 SOCIAL AND BEHAVIORAL SCIENCES: Psychology

General Terms
Human Factors; Experimentation; Verification.

INTRODUCTION
Do you curse? Do you curse on social media? How often do you see people cursing on social media (e.g., Twitter)? Cursing, also called swearing, profanity, or bad language, is the use of certain words and phrases that are considered by some to be rude, impolite, offensive, obscene, or insulting [26]. In this paper, we use cursing, profanity and swearing interchangeably. As Jay [6] pointed out, cursing is a "rich emotional, psychological and sociocultural phenomenon", which has attracted many researchers from related fields such as psychology, sociology, and linguistics [7, 8].

CSCW'14, February 15 - 19 2014, Baltimore, MD, USA

ACM 978-1-4503-2540-0/14/02$15.00.
http://dx.doi.org/10.1145/2531602.2531734

Over the last decade, social media has become an integral part of our daily lives. According to the 2012 Pew Internet & American Life Project report [25], 69% of online adults use social media sites and the number is steadily increasing. Another Pew study in 2011 [24] shows that 95% of all teens with ages 12-17 are now online and 80% of those online teens are users of social media sites. People post on these sites to share their daily activities, happenings, thoughts and feelings with their contacts, and keep up with close social ties, which makes social media both a valuable data source and a great target for various areas of research and practice, including the study of cursing. While the CSCW community has made great efforts to study various aspects (e.g., credibility [13], privacy [1]) of social networking and social media, our understanding of cursing on social media still remains very limited.

The communication on social media has its own characteristics which differentiates it from offline interaction in the physical world. Let us take Twitter for example. The messages posted on Twitter (i.e., tweets) are usually public and can spread rapidly and widely through the highly connected user network, while the offline conversations usually remain private among the persons involved. In addition, we may find that more of our actual exchange of words in the physical world happens through face-to-face oral communication, while on Twitter we mostly communicate by writing/typing without seeing each other. Will such differences lead to a change in people's cursing behavior? Will the existing theories on swearing during the offline communication in physical world still be supported if tested on social media?

To address such differences, this paper examines the use of English curse words on the micro-blogging platform Twitter. We collected a random sampling of all public tweets and the data of relevant user accounts every day for four weeks. We first identified English cursing tweets in the collection, and extracted numerous attributes that characterize users and users' tweeting behaviors. We then evaluated the effect of these attributes with respect to the cursing behaviors on Twitter. This exploratory study aims to improve our understanding of cursing on social media by exploring a set of questions that have been identified as crucial in previous cursing research on offline communication. The answers to these questions may also have valuable implications for the studies of language acquisition, emotion, mental health, verbal abuse, harassment, and gender difference [6].

Specifically, we examine four research questions:

- Q1 (*Ubiquity*): How often do people use curse words on Twitter? What are the most frequently used curse words?
- Q2 (*Utility*): Why do people use curse words on Twitter? Previous studies [6] found that the main purpose of cursing is to express emotions. Do people curse to express emotions on Twitter? What are the emotions that people express using curse words?
- Q3 (*Contextual Variables*): Does the use of curse words depend on various contextual variables such as time (when to curse), location (where to curse), or communication type (how to curse)?
- Q4: Who says curse words to whom on Twitter? Previous research [5, 11] suggested that gender and social rank of people play important roles in cursing; do they also affect people using or hearing curse words on Twitter?

The remainder of the paper proceeds as follows. We first review the related work in the next section. We then describe the data and methods, including an overview of the data and how we obtained it, the methods to identify cursing tweets and to extract various attributes, the exploration of the above mentioned questions, and the implications of the results. Finally, we close with a summary of this study.

RELATED WORK

We first consider the previous research on cursing in offline communications, and organize them into four groups corresponding to the four questions we address in this study. Then we discuss the efforts that have been made to understand the cursing phenomenon on social media.

The Ubiquity of Cursing

Cursing is more common than people might think. Jay [4, 6] found 70 curse words in an 11,609-word tape-recorded conversation of elementary school students and college students. In another study [12], Mehl and Pennebaker reported that curse words occurred at a rate of 0.5% over two 2-day periods among undergraduate students, which may not seem significant except that the first person plural pronouns – words like *we*, *us*, and *our* – occurred at a 1.0% rate. They also found substantial differences among individuals regarding curse words usage: the word rates varied from a minimum of 0% to a maximum of 3.4%. Some recent studies suggest that people have been hearing and using profanity more often than ever before [27], and more (a 69% increase) and harsher curse words have been used in TV programs in 2010 compared to 2005 [22]. Researchers also found that a few most frequently used words (e.g., *fuck*, *damn*, *hell*, and *shit*) account for most of the cursing expressions in conversations (a long tail phenomenon)[4].

The Utility of Cursing

Cursing is not as negative or harmful as it may seem at first glance. Prior studies [4, 5, 11, 14] suggest that the main reason that people use swearing words is to express some strong emotions, especially anger and frustration, for emphasis. As a common conversational practice, cursing rarely results in obvious harm. Only when cursing occurs in the form of insults toward others, such as name calling, harassment, hate speech, and obscene telephone calls, it becomes harmful [7]. Researchers also found other positive effects could be achieved by swearing. For example, Stephens et al. [17] reported that swearing increased pain tolerance and decreased perceived pain compared with not swearing. In addition, people may find relief and positive effects of laughing at jokes, humour and sarcasm in which curse words are used [5, 7].

Contextual Variables

Prior studies suggest that cursing is very sensitive to contextual influences [5]. More specifically, people's propensity to curse, the particular curse words people use, and how others perceive the cursing behavior, are dependent on various contextual variables. Generally, the context of cursing activity is defined by those variables about *when*, *where*, *how*, *who* and *with whom* the cursing occurs. Among those variables, while *who* and *with whom* variables have attracted the most attention from researchers, physical location has also been recognized as important [4, 5, 8]. Researchers [8] found that "people are more likely to swear in relaxed environments than in formal environments" (e.g., pub vs. office). Since such observations were made in the setting of oral communication in physical world, it is not clear whether physical location still matters for cursing on social media which occurs as written messages in digital world. In addition, little is known about how *when* and *how* factors would affect cursing. In this study, we examine the effect of location variable as well as the variables of time during a day, day in a week and message types, on cursing on social media.

Who Says Curse Words to Whom

There have been a considerable number of studies on understanding the characteristics of people who use and hear curse words. A set of important variables have been identified and investigated [4, 5, 11], including gender, age, race, religion and power. Unfortunately, many of these variables such as age, race and religion remain difficult to measure on Twitter, thus, we limit our focus on gender and power. Some well-recognized patterns about gender in swearing research include: (1) Gender affects cursing frequency. Many studies [9, 12, 19, 15] suggest that men curse more frequently than women. (2) Gender affects the choice of curse words. For example, according to a study in 2006 [11], women used the words *god*, *hell*, *bitch*, and *piss* more often than men, and men used the words *fuck* and *cunt* more often than women. (3) People are more likely to curse in same-gender contexts than in mixed-gender contexts [8, 15]. People's power or social rank also plays a role in cursing. McEnery [11] found that frequency of cursing is inversely proportional to the social rank.

Cursing on social Media

Only a few efforts have been made to explore cursing on social media. Thelwall [19] studied the use of curse words in MySpace profiles and the effects of gender and age factors. Sood et al. [16] investigated profanity usage in Yahoo! Buzz communities and found that different communities (e.g., politics or sports) use profanity with varied frequencies and in different ways. Turning to Twitter, Bak et al. [2] studied self-disclosure behavior in Twitter conversations. As one aspect of self-disclosure, profanity was used more frequently between users with higher relationship strength. While other researchers have mainly focused on investigating algorithms to automatically detect offensive tweets [30, 31], our understanding of the basic questions regarding the use of offensive words on Twitter still remains unexplored, such as why people use curse words, who uses it, and whether these words are always harmful and should be removed. The insights gained in this study can shed light on these questions.

METHOD AND ANALYSIS

Data Collection

Twitter provides a small random sample of all public tweets via its *sample API* in real time [1]. Using this API, we continuously collected tweets for four weeks from March 11th 2013 to April 7th 2013. We kept only the users who specified 'en' as their language in profiles. Further, we utilized Google Chrome Browser's embedded language detection library to remove non-English tweets [2]. In total, we gathered about 51M tweets from 14M distinct user accounts.

Spam on Twitter may impede the delivery of quality results from data analysis. To examine the spammers in our dataset, a random set of 200 user accounts were selected and manually verified based on the content of tweets and their profile (using the number of friends, followers, etc.) attached with each account. Of the 200 accounts, 5 (2.5%) were identified as spammers, and there were 88 tweets in our dataset from these 5 spammers, accounting for 1.32% of all 6678 tweets posted by these 200 users. On the other hand, we observed that there were some accounts that posted suspiciously frequently, and it could harm our analysis if they were spammers. Thus, we manually verified the top 1000 accounts which posted most frequently in our dataset, and removed the identified spam accounts and their tweets. Not surprisingly, among the 1000 accounts, there were 19 spammers in the top 100 accounts, 15 spammers in the following 100 accounts, and then this fraction kept diminishing, with only 3 spammers identified in each of the last two sets of 100 accounts. Totally, we removed 68 spammers and 89,556 tweets from our dataset.

Cursing Lexicon Coding

To create a lexicon of curse words for this study, we first collected existing curse word lists from Internet used by native English speakers for cursing on social media. Besides the curse word list [23] that have been used by existing studies [16, 30], we collected additional curse word lists from [28, 21, 20] to increase the coverage. After merging the above word lists, we found that a few non-curse words were also included, e.g., *sexy*. Also, there are some non-English words, e.g., *buceta*, which means *pussy* in Portuguese. Moreover, some words can be used in both cursing and non-cursing contexts: *gay* in *"you are so gay"* conveys cursing, but gay

[1] `https://dev.twitter.com/docs/api/1.1/get/statuses/sample`

[2] `https://pypi.python.org/pypi/chromium_compact_language_detector/0.2`

Statistics	Min	Max	Mean	Median	Std. Dev.
Overall Tweets	1.0	4124.0	3.56	2.0	8.00
Cursing Tweets	1.0	549.0	1.78	1.0	2.39

Table 1. Statistics of overall tweets and cursing tweets per user

in *"Bill Clinton urges Illinois to approve gay marriage bill"* does not convey cursing . To achieve high precision in identifying cursing expressions, we keep only the words that are mostly associated with cursing connotation.

Specifically, to retain these curse words, we asked two college students who are native English speakers to independently annotate the collected words in the context of social media with the following labels: 1 - the word is mostly used for cursing, 2 - the word can be used for both cursing and non-cursing purposes, 3 - usually the word is not used for cursing, or 4 - I do not know its meaning. Cohen's Kappa between the labels chosen by the two students was 0.5582. In the end, we kept only 788 words that received label '1' from both students to emphasize high precision. Besides correctly spelled words, (e.g., *fuck*, *ass*), the lexicon also included different variations of curse words, e.g., *a55*, *@$$*, *$h1t*, *b!tch*, *bi+ch*, *c0ck*, *f*ck*, *l3itch*, *p*ssy*, and *dik*.

We call a tweet *cursing tweet* if it contains at least one curse word. Twitter users may use different variations of the same word, so we first simply compare words in a tweet against all the curse words in the lexicon. If there is no match, we remove repeating letters in the words (e.g., fuckk → fuck) of a tweet and repeat the matching process. We also convert digits or symbols in a word to their original letters: e.g., 0 → o, 9 → g, ! → i. Moreover, based on our observations, the following symbols, '_', '%', '-', '.', '#', '\', '"', are frequently used to mask curse words: *f_ck*, *f%ck*, *f.ck*, *f#ck*, *f'ck* → *fuck*. We apply the edit distance approach similar to [16] to spot curse words with mask symbols. Namely, if the edit distance between a candidate word (*f_ck*) and a curse word (*fuck*) equals the number of mask symbols (1 in this case) in the candidate word, then it is a match. Table 1 provides an overview of the per-user count of the number of overall tweets and cursing tweets in our data collection.

To evaluate the accuracy of this lexicon-based method to spot cursing tweets, we drew a random sample of 1000 tweets, and asked two annotators to manually label them as cursing or non-cursing independently. Finally, there were 118 tweets labeled as cursing tweets for which both annotators agreed on their labels, and the other 882 tweets were labeled as non-cursing ones. We then tested the lexicon-based spotting approach on this labeled dataset, and the results showed that this lexicon-based method achieved a precision of 98.84%, a recall of 72.03% and F1 score of 83.33%. As expected, this lexicon-based approach for profanity detection provides high precision but lower recall, which is mainly due to the variations in curse words (e.g., due to misspellings and abbreviations) and context sensitivity of cursing. Though we believe that, for this work, high-precision is preferred and recall of 72.03% is considered reasonable, more sophisticated classification methods that can further improve the recall remain an interesting topic for future work.

Cursing Frequency and Choice of Curse Words

Prior studies have found that 0.5% to 0.7% of all the words we speak in our daily lives are curse words [4, 12]. Turning to Internet chatrooms, Subrahmanyam et. al. [18] reported that 3% of utterances contain curse words. Our comparison of cursing frequencies from different studies is shown in Table 2. Compared with existing studies, our estimate of cursing frequency was conducted for a significantly larger population: 14 million Twitter users and 51 million tweets. After removing punctuation marks and emoticons, we find that curse words occurred at the rate of 1.15% on Twitter, which is more than twice the rate (0.5%) in [12]. About 7.73% of all the tweets in our collection contain curse words, namely, one out of 13 tweets contains curse words. If we consider one tweet as roughly one utterance, this rate is also more than twice the rate (3%) in [18].

Besides the cursing frequency, we are also interested in the question: Which curse words are most popular? We manually grouped different variations of curse words into their root forms, e.g., *@$$*, *a$$*, → *ass*. If a curse word is the combination of two or more words, and one of its component words is also a curse word, then it will be grouped into its cursing component word, e.g., *dumbass*, *dumbasses*, *@sshole*, *a$$h0!e*, *a55hole* → *ass*. All the 788 curse words are grouped into 89 distinct groups based on the root curse words and the frequencies of the top 20 words are shown in Figure 1. The most popular curse word is *fuck*, which covers 34.73% of all the curse word occurrences, followed by *shit* (15.04%), *ass* (14.48%), *bitch* (10.34%), *nigga* (9.68%), *hell* (4.46%), *whore* (1.82%), *dick* (1.67%), *piss* (1.53%), and *pussy* (1.16%).

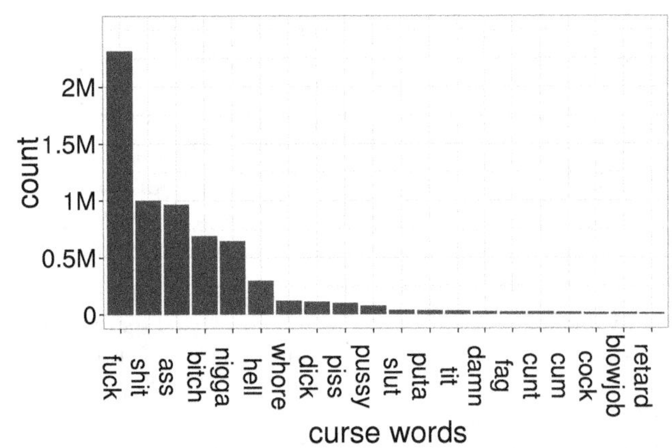

Figure 1. Frequencies of curse words: Only top 20 curse words are shown due to space limitation.

Realizing that only a small subset of curse words occurs very frequently, we also draw the cumulative distribution of top 20 curse words. We find that the top seven curse words – *fuck*, *shit*, *ass*, *bitch*, *nigga*, *hell* and *whore* cover 90.55% of all the curse word occurrences.

Cursing vs. Emotion

Psychology studies [8] suggest that "the main purpose of cursing is to express emotions, especially anger and frustration." Thus, we aim to explore emotions expressed in cursing

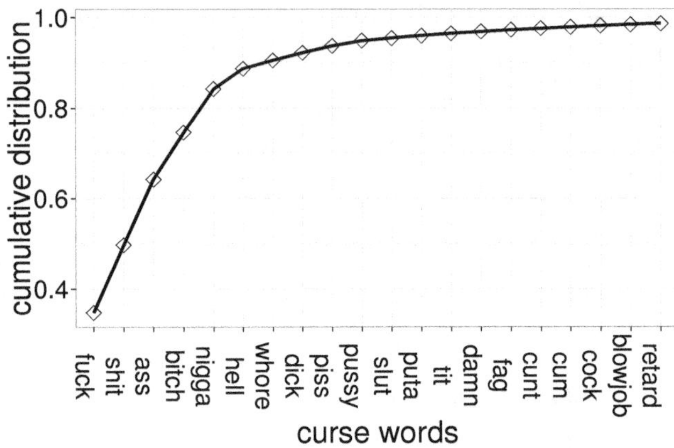

Figure 2. Cumulative distribution of curse Words: The top 7 curse words cover more than 90% of all the curse word occurrences.

tweets and compare them with those in non-cursing tweets. We adapted the emotion identification approach from our prior work [29] to automatically detect emotions expressed in tweets. The basic idea is to leverage ending emotion hashtags to automatically create labeled training data. For example, the tweet *"And all I need is one fuckin sheet stamped! #rage"* will be labeled with emotion *anger* and added into training data after removing the ending emotion hashtag "#rage". In this way, we collected a large number of self-labeled tweets covering seven emotions: *joy*, *sadness*, *anger*, *love*, *fear*, *thankfulness* and *surprise*. We collected about 2 million tweets for training, 250 thousand tweets for testing and nearly 250 thousand tweets for algorithm development, all of which were used in our experiment. We did not apply all the features used in [29], instead, we applied a combination of unigram, bigram and LIWC [3] features. LIWC features refer to the percentages of positive and negative emotion words according to LIWC dictionary. This combination achieved a reasonably good accuracy, very close to the best performance achieved by incorporating more features, according to the feature engineering experiments (Refer to Table III in [29]).

We train seven binary classifiers for seven emotions, such that for each emotion e_i, the corresponding classifier C_{e_i} predicts the probability p_j of a tweet t_j expressing the emotion e_i: $p_j = C_{e_i}(t_j)$. Specifically, we train a binary classifier C_{e_i} by selecting all the tweets of a specific emotion (e.g., *anger*) and randomly selecting the same number of tweets that do not express this emotion (the tweets may express other emotions such as *sadness*, *love*, etc.) For a given tweet t_j, we apply all the seven classifiers. If a classifier C_{e_i} provides the highest probability that t_j expresses the emotion e_i among all the classifiers, and this probability is greater than or equal to the predefined threshold τ, we conclude that the emotion e_i is expressed in t_j; otherwise, t_j is labeled as *other*.

$$\begin{cases} Emotion\ e_i & i = \arg\max_k \{C_{e_k}(t_j)\}\ and\ C_{e_i}(t_j) >= \tau \\ Other & Otherwise \end{cases} \quad (1)$$

[3] http://www.liwc.net

	Mehl 2003 et. al. [12]	Subrahmanyam 2006 et. al. [18]	**Twitter**
Subject	52 undergraduates	1,150 chatroom users	14 million Twitter users
Sample	4 days' tape recording	12,258 utterance	51 million tweets
Cursing Frequency	0.5% of all words	3% of all utterances	1.15% of all words 7.73% of all tweets

Table 2. Cursing frequency over different datasets: Cursing on Twitter is much more frequent than that in the other two datasets – 1.15% of all words vs. 0.5% of all words, and 7.73% of all tweets vs. 3% of all utterances

Intuitively, higher the value of τ, higher is the precision of identifying the seven emotions, at the expense of recall. To find a τ that provides high precision and reasonable recall, we tried a series of τ values on the development dataset: starting from 0, with an increment of 0.02, and ending at 1.0. We plot the precision and recall of individual emotion classifiers as well as the combined classifier in Figure 3. As we can see from the figure, with the increasing value of τ, the precision increases, while the recall decreases. Emotion classifiers that are on the upper right perform better than those on the lower left. Since we are interested in only the emotions that we can predict with high precision, we skip detecting emotion *surprise* and *fear*, for which the highest precision is less than 65%. We select $\tau = 0.88$ for later emotion identification, with which the combined classifier achieves good a precision while retaining a reasonable recall among all the values of τ we have tested using the development dataset.

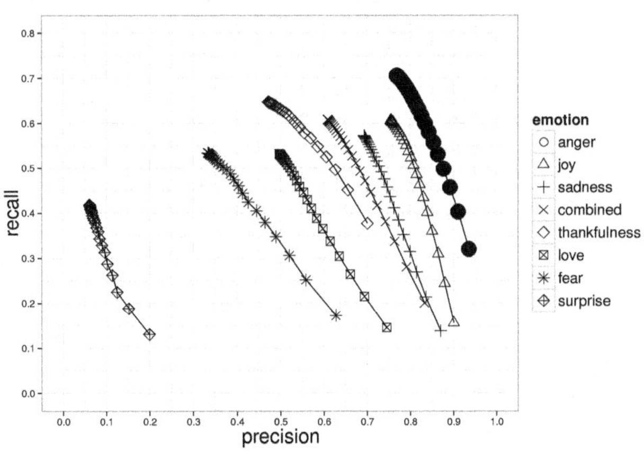

Figure 3. Performance of emotion identification on the development dataset

We then train the classifiers on the training dataset and apply the combined classifiers to the testing dataset. The results are shown in Table 3. Among all the five emotion categories, precision ranges between 56.04% (*thankfulness*) and 84.66% (*anger*), recall ranges between 37.22% (*love*) and 57.01% (*thankfulness*), and F1-score ranges between 45.86% and 68.11%. The combined classification achieves a micro-averaged precision of 76.17%, a micro-averaged recall of 46.07%, and a micro-averaged F1-score of 57.41%. This performance is quite reasonable considering that it is a multi-class classification problem.

Finally, we apply the combined classifier to the 51 million cursing tweets, and obtain the emotion distributions on both cursing and non-cursing tweets, which is shown in Figure

Emotions	Precision (%)	Recall (%)	F1-score (%)
anger	84.66	56.97	68.11
joy	82.77	44.81	58.14
sadness	76.05	39.34	51.86
love	59.72	37.22	45.86
thankfulness	56.04	57.01	56.53
combined	76.17*	46.07*	57.41*

Table 3. Performance of emotion identification on the testing dataset. * micro-averaged metrics. (*Surprise* and *Fear* were dropped because we couldn't detect it with a reasonably high precision on the development dataset)

4. Not surprisingly, cursing is associated with negative emotions: 21.83% and 16.79% of the cursing tweets express sadness and anger emotions, respectively. In contrast, 11.31% and 4.50% of the non-cursing tweets express sadness and anger emotions, respectively. This can be explained by the fact that curse words are usually used for venting out negative emotions, especially anger and sadness. However, we also find that 6.59% of cursing tweets express love. One reason is that curse words can be used to emphasize emotions, including positive ones such as love: e.g., ***"fucking** love you."* Another reason is that certain curse words are used between close friends as a playful interaction, e.g., close female friends call each other *whore*. To better understand how curse words are used to express emotions in tweets, we list some example cursing tweets in Table 4.

In addition, we also examined the frequency of cursing in each type of emotional tweets. As we expected, 23.82% angry tweets and 13.93% sad tweets contain curse words, which are much higher than the rate of curse words in other emotional tweets, such as love (4.16%), thankfulness (3.26%) and joy (2.5%), or the remaining tweets that are not labeled with any of these five emotions (6.39%). This again shows that curse words are often used to express negative emotions.

Cursing vs. Time

Previous study [10] has shown marked difference in emotions (e.g., stress, happiness) expressed between weekdays and weekend, or between morning and night. Similarly, we investigate the relationship between cursing and two types of time periods: times during a day and days of a week. For each tweet, Twitter provides a timestamp based on UTC timezone, indicating when the tweet was posted. However, it makes more sense to use local time when the tweet was posted, so we calculate the corresponding local timestamp for every tweet whose sender has specified timezone in his/her profile. In Figure 5, the lines with triangles and crosses stand for the volumes of overall tweets and cursing tweets, and the line with circles stands for the ratio of cursing tweets to overall

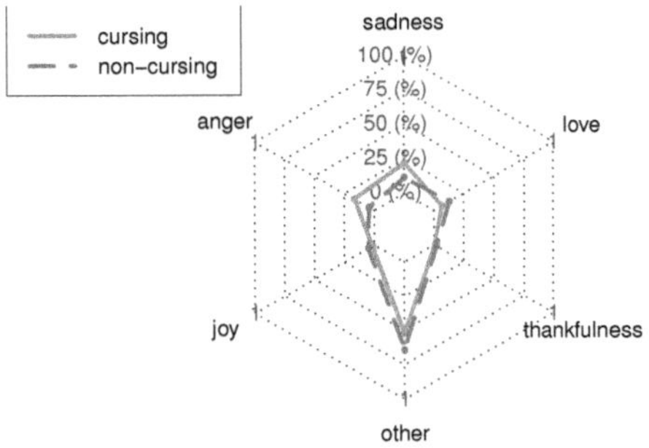

Figure 4. Emotion distributions in both cursing and non-cursing tweets. It shows that curse words are usually used for venting out negative emotions: 21.83% and 16.79% of the cursing tweets express sadness and anger emotions, respectively; in contrast, 11.31% and 4.50% of the non-cursing tweets express sadness and anger emotions, respectively

sadness	"Where da **fuq** is the sun at, this weather is so #depressing" "My life fell apart a long **ass** time ago.. So everythings normal i guess."
anger	"Soo **pissed** off" "People laugh when I say I work at McDonald's. And I say, **bitch** at least I have a job! At least I don't bother my parents asking them for $$$"
love	"Across the ocean, across the sea starting to hate the **fucking** distance between Justin Bieber and me." "@user you little **whore** TAKE ME WITH YOU" "Dear Marilyn Manson, I **fucking** love you and your music. The end."

Table 4. Example tweets in which curse words are used to express different emotions.

tweets. A flat segment of the line with circles suggests the cursing ratio is stable – the increment of cursing tweets keeps pace with that of overall tweets. A rising line segment with circles suggests that the increment of cursing tweets outpaces that of overall tweets. A falling line segment with circles suggests that the increment of cursing tweets is outpaced by that of overall tweets.

We have the following interesting observations from Figure 5. First, the pattern of overall tweet volume fits humans' diurnal activity schedule: it starts rising at 5 am when people get up at the beginning of a day. From then, it keeps rising, and reaches a small peak around lunch time. It keeps rising until it reaches the peak of the day around 9 pm, after which people start preparing to go to sleep. Second, cursing is ever-lasting: the black cursing ratio line with circles always stays above 0, suggesting that people curse all the time throughout the day. Third, the increment of cursing outpaces the increment of overall tweet volume during most of the day time: people curse more and more as they go through the day! In particular, there are two sharp rising slopes: 6 am - 11 am and 3 pm - 1:30 am. We speculate that Twitter users being in good mood during lunch contributes to the flat ratio line segment between 11 am - 2 pm (lunch time). It seems that midnight to 1:30 am is the *high time* for cursing. After that, the volume of cursing tweets decreases faster than the overall tweets.

We now explore the popularity changes of top seven curse words (refer to Figure 1) at different times of a day to gain more insights. We define *relative frequency* for a curse word as its total number of occurrences in any tweet divided by the total number of tweets in a predefined time window. Three representative time windows are selected: 12 am - 2 am, 5 am - 7 am and 12 pm - 2 pm. We observe that the relative frequencies for all top seven curse words keep increasing from 5 am - 7 am to 12 pm - 2 pm and from 12 pm - 2 pm to 12 am - 2 am. On average, from 5 am - 7 am to 12 am - 2 am, the relative frequencies of top seven curse words have increased by 144.05%. In descending order of their relative increase of relative frequencies, top seven curse words rank as follows: *nigga* (262.55%), *ass* (200.70%), *bitch* (199.61%), *shit* (118.86%), *whore* (91.74%), *fuck* (81.93%) and *hell* (52.98%).

To explore how people curse during different days of a week, we plot the ratio of cursing tweets to total tweets each day for four weeks, separately, in Figure 6. The general trend is that users start with relatively high cursing ratios on Mondays, Tuesdays and Wednesdays, then the ratios keep decreasing on the following three days, and reaches the lowest point on Saturdays. Then they start rising up on Sundays. To see the general trend clearly, readers are referred to see the four-week average ratio in the plot. Although we observe this general pattern across four weeks, we are still unclear about the reason. We are interested in the popularity changes of top seven words during different days of a week, similar to those at different times of a day. We select the following two time windows: Monday-Tuesday and Friday-Saturday. On average, from Friday-Saturday to Monday-Tuesday, the relative frequencies of top seven curse words have increased by 10.28%. In descending order of their relative increase of relative frequencies, top seven words rank as follows: *bitch* (14.75%), *shit* (13.10%), *nigga* (11.54%), *whore* (9.64%), *ass* (9.40%), *hell* (7.08%) and *fuck* (6.45%).

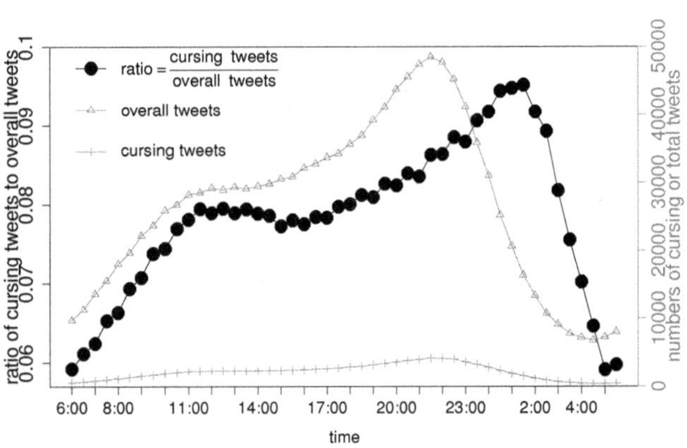

Figure 5. Cursing Volume at Different Times of Day

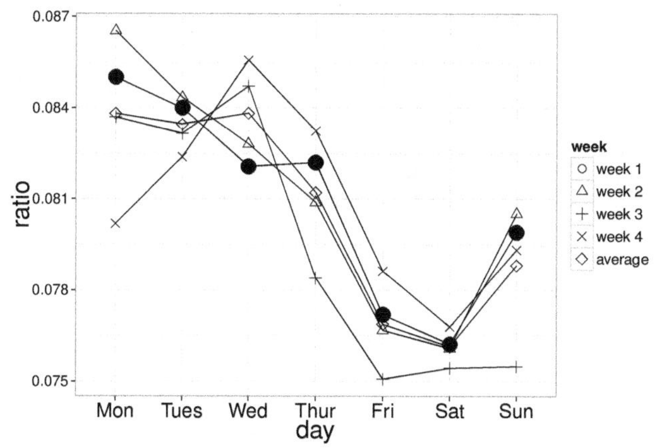

Figure 6. Cursing Volume in Different Days of Week

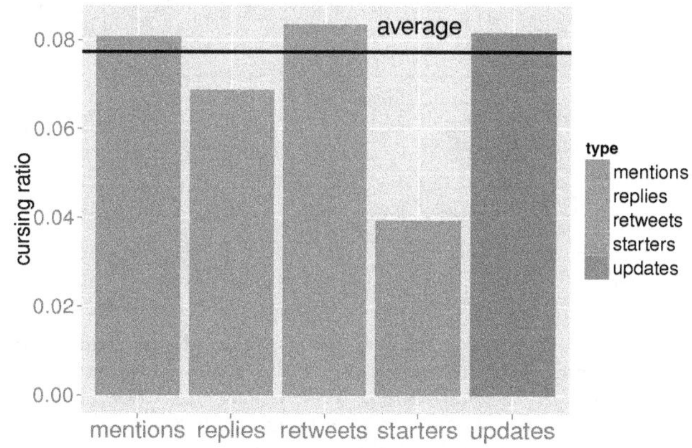

Figure 7. Cursing Ratios in Different Types of Messages

Cursing vs. Message Type

Tweets can be grouped into different message types and we are curious whether users curse differently in different types of tweets. Specifically, *retweet* refers to the tweet that is simply a re-posting of a tweet from another user. If a user receives a tweet from another user, and this user clicks on *reply* button to write a new tweet to reply to this tweet, then this newly posted tweet is called a *reply*. If a user starts sending a tweet to another user, and this tweet is not a reply to any other tweet, we name it a *starter*. If a tweet mentions another user, and it is neither a *reply* nor a *starter*, we call it a *mention*. If a tweet does not belong to any of the above categories, it is an *update*.

We plot the ratio of cursing tweets in each message category in Figure 7, where the black horizontal line stands for the average ratio of cursing tweets to all the tweets. It is interesting to note that although we see quite a bit of cursing messages on Twitter in general, when the messages are sent to other users, the cursing ratios are below average. The ratio of cursing tweets in *starters* is 3.93%, which is only 51.01% of the average cursing ratio. This suggests that users perform self-censorship to some extent when they directly talk to other users. When they post updates about themselves or simply mention other users' names, they do not pay as much attention to the use of curse words. Another interesting observation is that the highest cursing ratio occurs in *retweets*. Sood et. al. [16] found that "*profane comments are more popular or more widely read than non-profane comments*" by receiving thumb ups and downs in Yahoo! Buzz. We are interested in assessing whether use of curse words can help draw other users' attention so as to be retweeted. However, Pearson's product-moment correlation analysis between whether a tweet has curse words and the number of times it is retweeted suggests a negligible correlation: $r = -0.00154, p < 2.2e - 16$. We perform the same analysis on whether a tweet has curse words and whether it is retweeted, and find a stronger but still very weak positive correlation: $r = 0.03366, p < 2.2e - 16$. Similarly, a negligible correlation is also observed between whether a tweet has curse words and whether it has been favorited: $r = 0.005436, p < 2.2e - 16$.

Cursing vs. Location

Location also affects the way people curse in physical world. Cameron [3] found that people curse more at parties than they do at work places. Jay [4] has a similar discovery obtained by investigating cursing frequency at different campus locations: people tend to curse more in relaxed environments (e.g., college dorms vs. Dean's office). Compared with physical world conversations, tweets are posted in digital world: a user can use curse words without being noticed by surrounding people. Does physical locations still affect Twitter users' cursing frequency? Luckily, a Twitter user's location can be inferred via geo-enabled tweet feature. This feature provides the latitude and longitude of the user's location, along with the usual tweet content.

Given a pair of latitude and longitude, Foursquare's venue search API [4] returns a list of nearby venues, as well as the distances. If the distance from the user's location to the nearest venue is less than 50 meters, we assume the user posted the tweet from that venue. For every venue, we retrieve its immediate category and upper category from Foursquare, e.g., a venue is under Asian Restaurant (immediate category), and Asian Restaurant is under Food (upper category). We made very few changes to the Foursquare category hierarchy to reduce ambiguous information, e.g., we deleted *other places* from the hierarchy, because we have no idea what the name suggests. We also removed categories if they have very sparse tweets. Table 5 shows the different categories of venues, the raw number of cursing tweets and the ratio of cursing tweets to all the tweets sent from venues of the same category.

We have the following observations: a) The pattern of more swearing in more relaxed environment still holds, e.g., cursing ratios in a descending order are: Residence (7.08%) > Shop & Service (6.41%) > Nightlife Spot (6.37%) > Entertainment & Recreation (5.71%) > Professional Places (5.64%) > Travel & Transport (5.34%). However, the gaps are much less than those in physical world, partly due to the fact that communications happen in digit world. b) Two exceptions, College Academic Place and High School, have

[4] `https://developer.foursquare.com/docs/venues/search`

Venues	Cursing Tweets (#)	Cursing Tweets (%)
Field (Nature)	380	**4.97**
Travel & Transport	621	5.34
Food	2814	5.35
Professional Places	2020	5.64
Entertainment & Recreation	1305	5.71
Arts	195	5.77
Nightlife Spot	1063	6.37
Shop & Service	3036	6.41
College Academic Place	1155	6.45
Residence	2198	7.08
High School	339	**9.36**

Table 5. Cursing ratios from different places. Field: lakes, Beach, Mountain, etc.; Travel & Transport: Train, Plane, Ferry, etc.; Professional Places: Police Station, City Hall, Office, etc.; College Academic Place: Law School, Engineering Building, Math Building, etc.; Residence: Home, Residential Building, Hotel, etc.

very high cursing rates. This suggests that young high school and college students tend to use more curse words, even in educational places. c) We speculate that users are usually in a good mood while out in the nature, and that is why its cursing ratio is the lowest (4.97%) among all the venues.

Cursing vs. Gender

Another interesting question about cursing is "*who says curse words to whom*". We first explore the gender factor in this section, and then discuss the effect of social rank in the next section. Prior studies have found that gender affects the cursing frequency and the choice of curse words, in addition, people curse more in same-gender contexts than in mixed-gender contexts [12, 11, 8, 15]. We explore whether these hypotheses still hold when people send messages to each other on Twitter. In order to study the gender difference, we first apply an algorithm to recognize the gender of users in our data collection. A person's gender can be revealed by his/her first name: Linda, Lisa, Betty, etc. are usually females' names; John, Paul, William, etc. are male names. US Census Bureau [5] provides 1,219 most popular male names and 4,275 most popular female names. We calculate the "maleness" or "femaleness" by dividing the number of male/female people using this name by the overall size of the population. If a name has a high female percentage and a low male percentage, e.g., Mary: Male 0.009%, Female: 2.629%, then the corresponding person is mostly female. If the female and male percentages of a name are close, e.g., Morgan: Male 1.8%, Female: 2.2%, it suggests that this name is usually used for both genders. If a name is missing from male (female) name list, we take it as female (male). Our algorithm will label a user as female when the female percentage divided by the male percentage is greater than or equal to four; if the male percentage divided by the female percentage is greater than or equal to four, the user will be labeled as male; otherwise, the user will be labeled as unknown.

Overall, this algorithm identified 4,639,204 females and 3,826,701 males in our Twitter user collection. Recall that previously we grouped tweets into five categories: *mention*, *reply*, *retweet*, *starter* and *update*. Here we consider only

[5] `https://www.census.gov/genealogy/www/data/1990surnames/names_files.html`

Sender	Recipient	Cursing Tweets (#)	Cursing Ratio (%)
F	M	3,808	**3.81**
F	F	3,977	3.98
M	F	4,192	4.19
M	M	5,483	**5.48**

Table 6. Cross Gender Cursing Statistics. Statistics of each row are drawn on randomly sampled 100K tweets. Reported *cursing ratio* in each row is the percentage of cursing tweets out of all the tweets within each corresponding group.

Word	F→F	F→M	M→F	M→M	χ^2
fuck	1236	1284	1359	**2069**	308.89***
shit	670	661	831	**1159**	195.61***
nigga	119	171	201	**338**	126.59***
bitch	**475**	273	281	298	83.46***
hell	334	315	349	**532**	79.43***
dick	54	67	80	**137**	47.49***
cunt	22	24	26	**60**	29.70***
fag	20	29	26	**58**	25.83***
pussy	25	25	33	**60**	23.13***
slut	**50**	30	24	17	19.99***
ass	**1091**	1030	970	922	16.07**
bastard	9	14	18	**32**	16.04**
piss	95	91	107	**143**	15.41**
cock	14	15	25	**37**	15.15**
whore	**92**	68	68	50	12.82**

Table 7. The frequency of curse words out of 100K tweets posted or received by males and females. *** $p \leq 0.001$, ** $p \leq 0.01$

reply and *starter*, since they represent targeted messages between Twitter users with explicit message sender (*who*) and recipient (*to whom*) specified. These messages are further divided into four groups based on gender – *female to female*, *male to female*, *female to male* and *male to male*. To make results comparable, we randomly sampled 100K tweets from each of these four groups and statistics are shown in Table 6.

Comparing the same-gender contexts (*F to F* and *M to M*) with the mix-gender contexts (*F to M* and *M to F*) in Table 6, we observe that people are more likely to use curse words within the same-gender context, and this tendency is more obvious when the message senders are males (5.48% vs. 4.19%). This is consistent with the findings in prior studies [8, 15] on offline communications. Moreover, Male-to-Male communication has the highest cursing ratio: 5.48%, while Female-to-Male has the lowest cursing ratio: 3.81%.

Regarding the preference of curse words, out of randomly sampled 100K tweets for each of the four groups (see Table 7), we also find clear difference between females and males. There are a set of words that are used significantly more often by males than by females, for example, *fuck*, *shit*, and *nigga*. Some other words are significantly overused by females, such as *bitch* and *slut*. It is also interesting to observe that such differences are more apparent between two same-gender contexts – *F to F* vs. *M to M*. This suggests that the genders of both "*who*" and "*whom*" matter in the choice of curse words.

Cursing vs. Social Rank

We now look into the relationship between social rank and cursing behavior. Within a society, it is expected that higher the social rank of a person, the less cursing the person performs [8]. We use the number of followers on Twitter as

User Group	Sender				Recipient			
	Cursing Tweet (#)	Cursing Ratio(%)	$\mu_{followers}$	$\sigma_{followers}$	Cursing Tweet (#)	Cursing Ratio(%)	$\mu_{followers}$	$\sigma_{followers}$
top 1%	146,035	5.98	67,810	408,228.8	49,069	3.91	155,000	650,825.3
1% - 10%	847,467	**8.78**	1,923.00	1,481.60	101,983	6.11	3,764.00	3,744.18
10% - 40%	1,744,258	**8.75**	400.10	148.20	289,035	**7.96**	565.70	219.82
40% - 90%	1,116,645	6.62	101.60	60.58	258,984	6.26	172.20	71.85
90% - 100%	77,523	4.00	2.30	2.91	28,348	4.56	29.91	15.77

Table 8. Cursing Ratio vs. Social Ranking (followers) for both Senders and Recipients. μ population mean, σ standard deviation. For senders and recipients, we show statistics regarding their posted and received tweets, respectively

Word	top 1%	1-10%	10-40%	40-90%	90-100%	χ^2 * **
fuck	2621	3306	**3399**	2814	1265	1093.81
ass	744	**1624**	1607	1027	675	738.11
nigga	563	**1354**	1131	564	696	603.74
shit	986	1588	**1614**	1221	668	534.82
bitch	779	**1224**	1095	763	596	301.16
cock	30	24	19	22	**129**	199.26
blowjob	24	16	15	16	**89**	128.56
dick	178	**203**	169	130	64	78.92
piss	98	119	**159**	148	54	60.98
whore	167	**205**	183	136	95	46.85
pussy	151	**160**	117	76	101	40.18
hell	286	358	**375**	357	253	34.73
slut	**71**	41	50	54	25	23.79

Table 9. The frequency of curse words out of 100K tweets based on the social rank (follower counts) of senders. χ^2 results are based on the comparison of frequencies of each word across different sender groups. *** p≤0.001 for all the values in this column

Word	top 1%	1-10%	10-40%	40-90%	90-100%	χ^2
ass	618	1521	**2284**	1590	1034	1119.08***
nigga	243	674	**892**	471	266	599.30***
shit	628	1089	**1428**	1090	774	387.95***
fuck	1556	1875	**2330**	2023	1507	250.08***
bitch	350	533	**643**	458	346	136.78***
hell	244	431	**522**	434	370	105.54***
pussy	62	**88**	71	52	39	22.20***
whore	92	128	**145**	102	92	20.08***
slut	**56**	27	32	35	24	18.24**
dick	124	133	**134**	110	84	14.80**
piss	65	80	96	**107**	93	11.82*

Table 10. The frequency of curse words out of 100K tweets based on the social rank (follower counts) of recipients. χ^2 results are based on the comparison of frequencies of each word across different recipient groups. *** p≤0.001, ** p≤0.01 * p≤0.05

an approximation to the social rank in digital world. We sort both senders and recipients based on the descending order of their number of followers, and then divide them into five groups: top 1% (who have the highest numbers of followers), then followed by 1% - 10%, 10% - 40%, 40% - 90%, 90% - 100%. In Table 8, we show the raw numbers of posted/received cursing tweets, the ratio of posted/received cursing tweets out of overall tweets, the mean and standard deviation of followers that the group users have, within each sender/recipient group.

The top 1% senders do curse, but it is less than what we expected. We also observe bell-shaped distributions in cursing ratios for both senders and recipients: the middle sender groups (1%-10% and 10%-40%) curse the most, while the middle recipient group (10%-40%) receive tweets with the highest cursing ratio. Senders from the bottom group, who may have recently joined Twitter, and have very few followers (mean: 2.3), curse the least among all sender groups. Turning to recipients, the cursing ratio among tweets received by the top 1% group, is the lowest across all recipient groups: these popular users receive a lot of friendly messages from their fans, e.g., "*@Harry_Styles follow me babe<3*", "*@NiallOfficial I can't sleep :(*"

Besides the cursing ratios in tweets that are posted/received by different user groups, we are also interested in the curse word choices across all groups. To make the results comparable, we randomly sampled 100K posted tweets from each sender group and counted the corresponding frequencies of curse words in Table 9. We did the same to all the tweets received by different recipient groups in Table 10. We observed that the same word can be used at different rates across groups: 10-40% sender group used *fuck* 3,399 times out of 100K posted tweets, while 90-100% sender group used it only 1,265 times; 10-40% recipient group received *ass* 2,284 times out of 100K received tweets, while top 1% recipient group only received it 618 times. We find that, for the same word, its post/received volumes usually achieve highest frequencies in 1-10% and 10-40% for sender groups, and 10-40% for recipient groups with a few exceptions. The reason why top 1% sender group used *slut* word the most is because there are a few popular Twitter accounts that posted funny tweets about the word *slut*. We also found some porn accounts in 90-100% sender group that aggressively posted porn links, which explains the peaks for the words *cock* and *blowjob* in this group. The reason why top 1% recipient group received more tweets containing *slut* is because some fans like to call celebrities *slut* regardless of their gender for fun, e.g., "*@taylorswift13 slut*", "*@Harry_Styles slut drop on my follow button :))))))))*"

LIMITATIONS

This study is limited in several ways. Firstly, our exploration is based on a random sampling of tweets posted by Twitter users, and our results may be biased towards these users, who may not statistically represent users in other social media websites or mirror overall population in the real world. Thus our findings may turn out to be different on other datasets or social media platforms. Though the findings may not be generalized beyond Twitter, the analysis framework can be applied to cross-platform studies which we would like to pursue in our future work. Secondly, with such a large amount of data, it is impossible to manually label all the tweets/users. Because of this, we employed automatic approaches to labeling, profanity, emotion, gender, etc. Though these techniques have been used in many studies, they are not perfect. It is important to note that we always choose precision over recall when designing these techniques. Further improving any of these approaches would be an interesting topic for future research. Moreover, in a few tasks, we relied on self-reported data, such as users' names and geo-locations. Using self-reported data may lead to bias toward users who opt to share such information. Further, we do not segment Twitter user accounts into different types, e.g., celebrity, media, organization or regular personal accounts. Users from these different categories may curse in varied manner, and it would be interesting to examine the differences. Other topics as for extension of this study are the comparative study of native speakers and non-native speakers in using curse words, and the explorations of cursing behavior in languages other than English. Finally, this work is mostly descriptive, which provides insights on the *what* aspect of the cursing phenomenon on Twitter. In order to achieve deeper understanding on *why*, e.g., why people choose particular curse words they use, why people's cursing behaviors depend on certain contextual variables, etc., user surveys and qualitative analysis will be needed.

CONCLUSION

In this paper, we investigated the use of curse words in the context of Twitter based on the analysis of randomly collected 51 million tweets and about 14 million users. In particular, we explored four questions that have been identified as important by the prior swearing studies in the areas of psychology, sociology, and linguistics.

Regarding the question of *ubiquity* of cursing on Twitter, we examined the frequency of cursing and people's preference in the use of specific curse words. We found that the curse words occurred at the rate of 1.15% on Twitter, and 7.73% of all the tweets in our dataset contained curse words. We also found that seven most frequently used curse words accounted for more than 90% of all the cursing occurrences. The second question we studied is the *utility* of cursing, especially the use of cursing to express emotions. We built a classifier which identified five different emotions from tweets – *anger*, *joy*, *sadness*, *love*, and *thankfulness*. Based on the classification results, we found that cursing on Twitter was most closely associated with two negative emotions: *sadness* and *anger*. However, curse words could also be used to emphasize positive emotions such as *joy* or *love*.

Prior studies suggest that cursing is sensitive to various contextual variables. We focused on examining three contextual variables regarding *when*, *where* and *how* the cursing occurs. We found that the pattern of overall tweet volume matches peoples diurnal activity schedule, and people curse more and more after they getup in the morning till sleep hours of the night. Our study of the relation between cursing and message types suggests that users perform self-censorship when they talk directly to other users. We find that users do curse more in relaxed environments, but the differences across different environments are very small, partly due to the fact that Twitter messages are posted in virtual digital world.

The last question we tried to investigate is about *who says curse words to whom*. We examined the gender and social rank factors and how they might affect people's cursing behaviors on Twitter. Our results support the findings from prior studies that gender and social rank relate to people's propensity to curse and the choice of curse words. Specifically, men curse more than women, men overuse some curse words different from what women use and vice versa, and both men and women are more likely to curse in the same-gender contexts. Turning to social rank, high rank users do curse less than most low rank users; the ratios of using/receiving curse words achieve highest numbers in 1%-10%, 10%-40% sender groups, and 10%-40% recipient group.

ACKNOWLEDGMENTS

This research was supported by US National Science Foundation grant IIS-1111182: SoCS: Social Media Enhanced Organizational Sensemaking in Emergency Response. Any opinions, findings, and conclusions or recommendations expressed in this material are those of the authors and do not necessarily reflect the views of the National Science Foundation.

REFERENCES

1. Almuhimedi, H., Wilson, S., Liu, B., Sadeh, N., and Acquisti, A. Tweets are forever: a large-scale quantitative analysis of deleted tweets. In *Proceedings of the 2013 conference on Computer supported cooperative work*, ACM (2013), 897–908.
2. Bak, J. Y., Kim, S., and Oh, A. Self-disclosure and relationship strength in twitter conversations. In *Proceedings of the 50th Annual Meeting of the Association for Computational Linguistics: Short Papers-Volume 2*, Association for Computational Linguistics (2012), 60–64.
3. Cameron, P. Frequency and kinds of words in various social settings, or what the hell's going on? *The Pacific Sociological Review 12*, 2 (1969), 101–104.
4. Jay, T. *Cursing in America: A Psycholinguistic Study of Dirty Language in the Courts, in the Movies, in the Schoolyards, and on the Streets.* John Benjamins Publishing Co, 1992.
5. Jay, T. *Why we curse: A neuro-psycho-social theory of speech.* John Benjamins Publishing, 2000.
6. Jay, T. The utility and ubiquity of taboo words. *Perspectives on Psychological Science 4*, 2 (2009), 153–161.
7. Jay, T., et al. Do offensive words harm people? *Psych. Pub. Pol. and L. 15* (2009), 81–315.
8. Jay, T., and Janschewitz, K. The pragmatics of swearing. *Journal of Politeness Research. Language, Behaviour, Culture 4*, 2 (2008), 267–288.
9. Jay, T. B. Sex roles and dirty word usage: a review of the literature and a reply to haas. *Psychological Bulletin 88*, 3 (1980), 614–621.
10. Kamvar, S. D., and Harris, J. We feel fine and searching the emotional web. In *Proceedings of the fourth ACM*

international conference on Web search and data mining, ACM (2011), 117–126.

11. McEnery, T. *Swearing in English: Bad language, purity and power from 1586 to the present*, vol. 1. Psychology Press, 2006.
12. Mehl, M. R., Pennebaker, J. W., et al. The sounds of social life: A psychometric analysis of students' daily social environments and natural conversations. *Journal of personality and social psychology 84*, 4 (2003), 857–870.
13. Morris, M. R., Counts, S., Roseway, A., Hoff, A., and Schwarz, J. Tweeting is believing?: understanding microblog credibility perceptions. In *Proceedings of the ACM 2012 conference on Computer Supported Cooperative Work*, ACM (2012), 441–450.
14. Nasution, R. F., and Rosa, R. N. Swearwords found in chat room yahoo messenger (page: 84-93). *E-Journal English Language and Literature 1*, 1 (2012).
15. Pilotti, M., Almand, J., Mahamane, S., and Martinez, M. Taboo words in expressive language: Do sex and primary language matter? *American International Journal of Contemporary Research 2*, 2 (2012), 17–26.
16. Sood, S., Antin, J., and Churchill, E. Profanity use in online communities. In *Proceedings of the 2012 ACM annual conference on Human Factors in Computing Systems*, ACM (2012), 1481–1490.
17. Stephens, R., Atkins, J., and Kingston, A. Swearing as a response to pain. *Neuroreport 20*, 12 (2009), 1056–1060.
18. Subrahmanyam, K., Smahel, D., Greenfield, P., et al. Connecting developmental constructions to the internet: Identity presentation and sexual exploration in online teen chat rooms. *Developmental psychology 42*, 3 (2006), 395.
19. Thelwall, M. Fk yea i swear: Cursing and gender in a corpus of myspace pages. *Corpora 3*, 1 (2008), 83–107.
20. Banbuilder - PHP curse word function and word list for application developers, moderators, etc., March 2013. `http://banbuilder.com/`.
21. BannedWordList.com - a resource for web administrators, March 2013. `http://www.bannedwordlist.com/`.
22. Habitat for Profanity, July 2010. `http://www.parentstv.org/PTC/publications/reports/2010ProfanityStudy/study.pdf`.
23. List of Bad Words, March 2013. `http://www.noswearing.com/dictionary/`.
24. How American teens navigate the new world of "digital citizenship", November 2011. `http://pewinternet.org/Reports/2011/Teens-and-social-media/Summary/Findings.aspx`.
25. Pew Internet: Social Networking (full detail), Febrary 2013. `http://pewinternet.org/Commentary/2012/March/Pew-Internet-Social-Networking-full-detail.aspx`.
26. Profanity - Wikipedia, the free encyclopedia, March 2013. `http://en.wikipedia.org/wiki/Profanity`.
27. Watch your mouth! Americans see profanity getting worse, poll finds, March 2006. `http://www.nbcnews.com/id/12063093/from/RS.4/?GT1=7938#.UaKaG2cSpZo`.
28. Bad words list, March 2013. `http://urbanoalvarez.es/blog/2008/04/04/bad-words-list/`.
29. Wang, W., Chen, L., Thirunarayan, K., and Sheth, A. P. Harnessing twitter" big data" for automatic emotion identification. In *Privacy, Security, Risk and Trust (PASSAT), 2012 International Conference on and 2012 International Confernece on Social Computing (SocialCom)*, IEEE (2012), 587–592.
30. Xiang, G., Fan, B., Wang, L., Hong, J., and Rose, C. Detecting offensive tweets via topical feature discovery over a large scale twitter corpus. In *Proceedings of the 21st ACM international conference on Information and knowledge management*, ACM (2012), 1980–1984.
31. Xu, J.-M., Zhu, X., and Bellmore, A. Fast learning for sentiment analysis on bullying. In *Proceedings of the First International Workshop on Issues of Sentiment Discovery and Opinion Mining*, ACM (2012), 10.

How to See Values in Social Computing: Methods for Studying Values Dimensions

Katie Shilton
College of Information Studies
University of Maryland, College Park
kshilton@umd.edu

Jes A. Koepfler
College of Information Studies
University of Maryland, College Park
koepfler@umd.edu

Kenneth R. Fleischmann
School of Information
University of Texas at Austin
kfleisch@ischool.utexas.edu

ABSTRACT
Human values play an important role in shaping the design and use of information technologies. Research on values in social computing is challenged by disagreement about indicators and objects of study as researchers distribute their focus across contexts of technology design, adoption, and use. This paper draws upon a framework that clarifies how to see values in social computing research by describing *values dimensions*, comprised of *sources* and *attributes* of values in sociotechnical systems. This paper uses the framework to compare how diverse research methods employed in social computing surface values and make them visible to researchers. The framework provides a tool to analyze the strengths and weaknesses of each method for observing values dimensions. By detailing how and where researchers might observe interactions between values and technology design and use, we hope to enable researchers to systematically identify and investigate values in social computing.

Author Keywords
Value sensitive design; values in design; research methods

ACM Classification Keywords
K.4.2 Social Issues

INTRODUCTION
Social computing research studies sociotechnical factors in the design, deployment, and use of computing systems [49,61]. This work considers *values* as important to a technology's fit into, and impact on, the world [10,22,40]. Social computing research has developed a rich body of work exploring the role of values in, for, and from information technology design [10,12,17,22,40]. However, there is a lack of precision in how the construct of values is defined, applied, and investigated. Values are understood to contribute to technology design, to shape affordances that mediate technology use, and to pervade the social contexts mediated by technology [28,60]. Values are also personal, shaping how people evaluate their behaviors, respond to others, and make judgments [47,50].

CSCW'14, February 15 – 19, 2014, Baltimore, MD, USA.

ACM 978-1-4503-2540-0/14/02…$15.00.
http://dx.doi.org/10.1145/2531602.2531625

While values are increasingly considered in relation to design [30], these various definitions suggest diverse understandings and uses of values in the social computing literature. Social computing's focus on the intersection of social behavior and computational systems creates significant challenges for values research. Should we look for values in communities, or in interactions between people and technologies? Should we look for values in technologies themselves, or in the design groups responsible for those technologies? Design research traditions do not currently provide a theoretically-grounded discussion of where values occur in sociotechnical systems, and subsequently what methods can best study those values. Values in social computing are sometimes core beliefs held by people; sometimes attributes of systems and policies; and sometimes features of contexts, users, or technologically-mediated interactions. For example, values of import to researchers may be the personal values of the end users (i.e. dignity) or embedded within the heuristic principles of a technology (i.e. freedom from bias). A social computing study on privacy, for example, may struggle to specify whether privacy is a value of a person or group, a value intentionally embedded within a technology by designers, or a value materialized by a technology's affordances through human interaction. There have been few efforts to connect these understandings and uses of values through empirical research and theory-building.

To answer these questions and improve the precision of our methods, we separate the <u>source</u> of values from <u>attributes</u> of values themselves. We have developed a framework defining sources and attributes of values along six dimensions, as a heuristic to support research in social computing [53]. This paper reviews existing methods in values and social computing research, and uses the framework to highlight indicators for values to which each method is particularly suited: how each method sees values. This analysis illuminates the impact that methodological choices have on the values we investigate, and illustrates a range of qualitative and quantitative methods for observing values across different dimensions in social computing. The analysis also exposes gaps in the literature and opportunities for future interrogation of how researchers choose values to study. We hope to engage researchers by providing a heuristic to better describe the sources and attributes of values, and by cataloging methods to examine how values impact both the design process and the technologies that result from that process.

VALUES IN SOCIAL COMPUTING

Research emphasizing the values incorporated into, and embodied in, technologies is often grouped under two theoretical umbrellas: Values in Design (VID) (http://www.nyu.edu/projects/nissenbaum/vid/) and Value Sensitive Design (VSD) (http://www.vsdesign.org/). There is also a related body of research in worth-centered design, which examines design contexts in terms of "worth" and "value propositions" [10]. This paper focuses primarily on the VID and VSD traditions. The similar traditions of VID and VSD, developed in the human-computer interaction (HCI), information studies, and media studies literatures, explore the ways in which moral or social values become part of technological artifacts. Values research in these traditions is characterized by a proactive perspective, seeking to influence technology during the design process [20]. This literature highlights the discursive nature of values embedded in technologies, which are shaped endogenously by their designers and technical affordances, as well as exogenously by users and use contexts [22].

These influential traditions have also received calls for refinement [1,2,34,48]. For example, Le Dantec et al. write: "What is needed is more prescription in methods that inform value-centered investigations, and less prescription in the kinds of values considered" [34]. In response, this paper uses the values dimensions framework as a lens to examine methods for values research in social computing. As three researchers with different backgrounds and approaches to values and social computing, we struggled to communicate what values were in our work, and where they intersected with social computing. As we began to compare our empirical projects, which have employed methods such as ethnography of computing design, content analysis of values in online communication, and interviews focused on values in computing, we realized that we needed to separate the source of the values under investigation from the attributes of the values themselves. We iterated on dimensions to describe the source and attributes of values over dozens of drafts, challenging and refining the emerging framework using case studies from the HCI, values and design, and social computing literatures. Because construction of such a framework is in itself a values-laden task, we do not claim that ours is comprehensive or singular. Instead, drawing on the needs of social computing research projects, we claim that it is useful for providing a more precise vocabulary for describing values research, as well as suggesting a set of methods demonstrated to be appropriate for studying values dimensions of interest to social computing researchers.

VALUES DIMENSIONS

We draw distinctions between dimensions that describe the source of the value – the setting, environment, or context from which values are elicited – and dimensions that describe attributes of the values themselves [53]. The term "dimensions" connotes continual spectra between extremes, rather than dichotomous pairs of attributes. The first three dimensions of the framework relate to the source of values; the remaining three are attributes of values themselves [53].

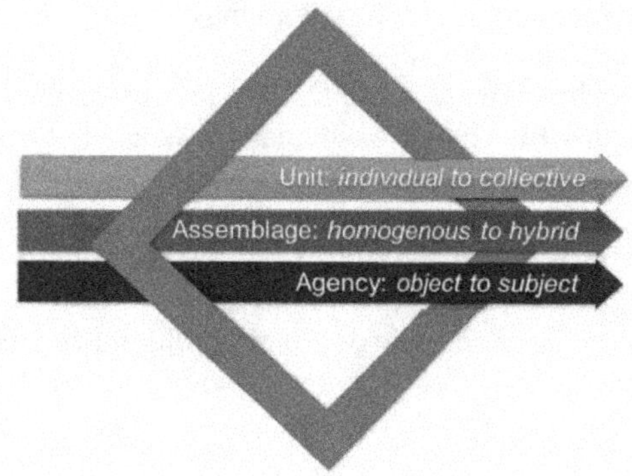

Figure 1: Dimensions Describing the Source of Values

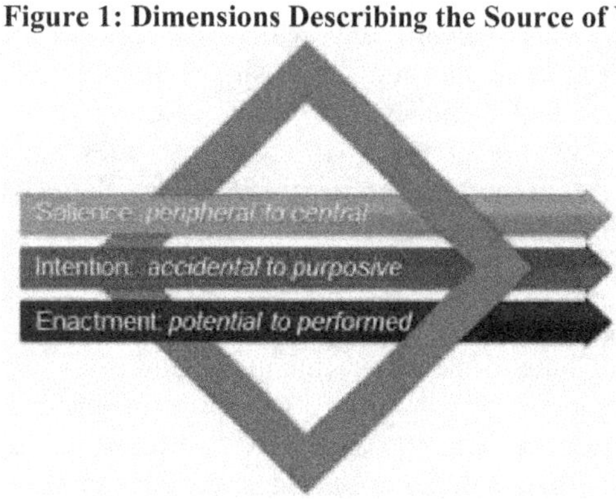

Figure 2: Dimensions Describing Attributes of Values [53]

The first source dimension describes the Unit from which values are elicited, moving from values of an *individual* to a *collective* [53]. Points along this continuum might include individuals, families or work groups, institutions, sub-cultures, and cultures. Values of an *individual* source are held by a person and are a core component of his or her identity [51]. Values of *collective* sources are the goals embedded in a given sociotechnical context [39].

The second source dimension describes the Assemblage of the source, moving from values of *homogenous* to *hybrid* human and technological actors [53]. Values in a design project might emerge from a relatively homogenous set of actors – a group of people belonging to a single demographic, for example, or technologies of similar types. Or the source of values may be a *hybrid* assembly that combines people entangled with technologies – groups of human actors embedded in an augmented reality video game simulation, for example. Points on this dimension include sources ranging from an all-machine group or a homogenous group of humans to diverse humans of various types to groups of human actors interacting with multiple sociotechnical systems.

The third source dimension describes the Agency of a source, moving from *object* to *subject* [53]. Agency takes into account the degree of autonomy and self-determination sources have in possessing and expressing values. *Objects* have values ascribed to them while *subjects* have the ability to determine and express their own values. For example, humans are often treated as *subjects* who may express their own values, and machines are often *objects* to which humans ascribe values. But because this is a spectrum, there are many examples in which non-humans take agency or humans lose agency. For example, humans are sometimes considered objects in specific situations or stages of life [26]. Cyborg hybrids [25] blend *object* and *subject*: cyborgs are likely to both express agent values as well as have values ascribed to them. Similarly, autonomous machines [35] can be studied as *subjects* with their own agent values, as well as *objects* with ascribed values.

The first attribute dimension, Salience, is a continuum from *peripheral* to *central* values [53]. A primary challenge for values researchers is identifying which values are of particular importance in a technology design or use context. The qualifier "salient" implies that some values will be more important in one context, while other values have more importance in another context [56]. The Salience dimension depends on the source of the values (i.e. the first three dimensions) such as individuals, groups, or social context.

The second attribute dimension, Intention, describes the degree to which a designer or system intends to materialize a value on a continuum from *accidental* to *purposive* values [53]. Values are surfaced, exposed and negotiated through design. This negotiation affects the shape and characteristics of the resulting technology, and eventually the social impact of design products [34]. *Purposive* values are those intentionally built into a technology's affordances and policies by its designers. Examples might include Winner's "technical arrangements as forms of order," in which artifacts are "deliberately designed to achieve a particular social effect" [62:123], as well as Suchman's observation that some early CSCW technologies "cast [computer scientists] into the role of designer not only of technical systems but of organizations themselves" [57:186–187]. Towards the other end of the dimension, *accidental* values are unintentional features or biases embedded in a technological system [21].

The third attribute dimension, Enactment, is the degree to which values are enacted within a sociotechnical system [53]. The Enactment dimension highlights a continuum between *potential* and *performed* values. "Potential" is used in the same sense as potential energy: *potential* values are present but inert. *Performed* values are those that an actor or system materializes in the world. "Performed" is used as it is increasingly employed in science and technology studies, to describe a factor that makes a difference or brings about the world it envisions [37,42].

This paper applies the framework to empirical studies in social computing to illustrate the precision it adds to our understanding of the intersection of values and design. To classify studies, we asked the following questions:

- Does a study illuminate the values of individuals, groups, or societies? (Unit)
- Does a study illuminate the values of people, technologies, or blended sociotechnical systems or cyborgs? (Assemblage)
- Does a study illuminate the degree to which people, systems, or materials determine their values? (Agency)
- Does a study illuminate the degree of importance of various values to stakeholders or systems? (Salience)
- Does a study illuminate the degree to which participants mean to materialize a value? (Intention)
- Does a study illuminate the degree to which values are materialized in a system or setting? (Enactment)

Like any classification project, application of this framework to existing studies is challenging and leaves room for debate. We make these classificatory choices to illustrate how using the six dimensions can unpack values investigations in social computing. Researchers can look for the values at their sources, examine attributes of values themselves, or both. Returning to our earlier example, a social computing study on privacy could use these dimensions to specify whether privacy is an intended goal of a technology, a core value of an individual or group, or some combination of the two.

METHODS TO STUDY VALUES IN SOCIAL COMPUTING

Each dimension can be studied with a variety of empirical methods; however, each method elicits some dimensions more effectively than others. The following sections describe methods used to study sources and attributes of values in social computing research. Considering how methods surface different dimensions moves the field closer to providing greater prescription in methods for values research in social computing [13].

Ethnographies of Computing Design and Use

Social computing research frequently uses observation methods to discern how values are selected and incorporated into system features and policy, or applied within varying use contexts. Ethnographic methods are common in the values and design literature, and provide techniques to observe a broad range of values dimensions during design and use of social computing systems.

Ethnographies of technology design often embed an observer or participant-observer in a laboratory, workplace, or other design environment to study the dynamics and decisions of computing design [41]. Ethnographies of computing design are particularly suited to studying attribute dimensions of Salience, Intention, and Enactment (for example, *central* values of a design team that are *purposively* built into technical features) among *collective*, *hybrid,* and *subject* sources (for example, a group of people making values decisions while interacting with material constraints of technological systems). In the VSD and VID traditions, ethnographies of design have included observations of artificial intelligence laboratories [18], open source software development [29], and Web 2.0 technology development [44].

For example, Shilton used participant-observation to study values in a lab developing mobile phone systems to gather data about people and their environments [56]. We classify her study as focused on both ends of the Salience, Intention, and Agency dimensions, because she examined what values were important to the team, and examined how the team tried to build those values into technical features. Shilton observed that engineers' ability to transform *peripheral* to *central* values into *performed* features was impacted by work practices. Self-testing practices within the laboratory surfaced previously *peripheral* values such as equity, as designers confronted with their personal data debated who they would be willing to share that data with, and what power dynamics that data revealed. *Peripheral* values such as consent were also enforced by institutional policies such as IRB requirements, and were therefore *performed* within user interfaces. Enforcing access control and data retention policies to protect the *central* value of privacy required careful data practices, making this value difficult to incorporate into technical features. These tensions illustrated challenges to the Agency dimension: though designers felt privacy was important, it was challenging to *perform* that value in technical products.

Ethnographic observation of technology use can also reveal values dimensions in social computing. Observation of users can reveal how the *central* values of *hybrid collectives* impact the *performed* values of technology in use. For example, Ames et al. observed how parents' attitudes about their children's use of technology were modulated by values attributed to social class [3]. We classify the source of parents' values in this framing as the *collective* of their class membership. Their *collective* values in turn impacted their technological practices. For example, middle-class parents in the study disallowed television but encouraged phone calls to long-distance family, attempting to *perform* values of connection by restricting or encouraging use of particular technologies. Similarly, Alsheikh et al. demonstrated how participants used technologies to *perform collective* Islamic values in long-distance romantic relationships. Because video chat used by unmarried couples could undermine *ikhtilat*, or cultural conventions that regulate mixing between the sexes (which we frame as *accidental* and *potential* values of video chat software), respondents reported using voice chat instead of video to *perform* their values [2]. Roberson and Nardi used ethnography to explore how homeless users employed mobile technologies (what we classify as a *hybrid collective* of people and systems) to *perform* values of survival (such as finding food and shelter) and social inclusion (such as establishing ties with the housed) [46].

Ethnography can study both values attributes and sources of values such as *hybrid*, *collective* configurations of designers, users, and technologies, but has limited scalability and generalizability. Future work mapping social computing studies along the dimensions framework might aid in comparison of similar attributes and sources of values across studies.

Sources of Values	Attributes of Values
individual ⇔ **collective**	**peripheral ⇔ central**
homogenous ⇔ **hybrid**	**accidental ⇔ purposive**
subject ⇔ object	**potential ⇔ performed**

Table 1. Dimensions highlighted by ethnographies

Values Advocacy

An alternative approach to studying and simultaneously influencing the Intention and Enactment of values in design contexts is inserting an advocate for particular values onto design teams. This approach is formally codified in some research areas due to grant guidelines that include "Ethical, Legal and Other Societal Issues" (ELSI) requirements. Van der Berg [59] and Rabinow and Bennett [45] relate mixed success intervening in biotechnology design labs. A project led by Fisher [11] embedded humanities graduate students in science laboratories to influence ethical decision points. Guston and Sarewitz propose a method for social scientists to intervene in design with "Real-time Technology Assessment" [23:93]. Manders-Huits and Zimmer [38] also conducted work as values advocates in commercial design settings.

A values advocate focuses on ethical and values-based concerns during design [20,38]. As Friedman et al. [20] describe the role, advocates lead conceptual investigations, enumerating stakeholders (what we would categorize as one or more *collective* sources of values) and how system features impact those *collectives* by identifying both *accidental* and *purposive* values within systems. Advocates also facilitate technical investigations into how system properties materialize values. Advocates therefore investigate the intersection between Intention (what the system designers built into properties) and Enactment (the degree to which those properties make a difference) [20]. Finally, advocates undertake empirical evaluations of user experience, testing whether *purposive* values were *performed.*

Values advocates may also discuss the Salience of values. As a values advocate during the ethnography described above, Shilton [56] facilitated discussions of the *hybrid* context of people using mobile sensing systems to build consensus around *peripheral* and *central* values (e.g. privacy, consent, equity, and forgetting) of the lab *collective*. Her intervention also helped operationalize those values in features (such as user interface considerations, data retention procedures, and secure data storage [54]), materializing *purposive* values into *performed* values.

Because values advocacy introduces values discussions into a design setting, it can be difficult to determine the *peripheral* and *central* values in the context before the advocate arrived. It is also a time- and resource-intensive method for values investigation. And at times, full membership in the design team can compromise a values advocate. There is a large literature in sociology discussing insider versus outsider status, and the line between participant-observation and participation [36].

There is also controversy surrounding what or whose values advocates should promote [5,34]. Advocates may introduce discussion of values writ large, or may focus on instilling a particular set of values. Both interventions qualify as values advocacy. Values discussions might focus on helping a *collective* define their *central* or *peripheral* values, or advocates may focus on encouraging particular *purposive* and *performed* values.

Sources of Values	Attributes of Values
individual ⇔ **collective**	**peripheral ⇔ central**
homogenous ⇔ **hybrid**	**accidental ⇔ purposive**
subject ⇔ object	**potential ⇔ performed**

Table 2. Dimensions highlighted by values advocacy

Design Activities

A targeted intervention method is the use of design activities – focused games, toolkits, or structured conversations with designers – to elicit discussion and considerations of values. One example is the deployment of values levers: practices or interventions within design meant to build consensus around values as important design concerns [55]. An example of a values lever is having designers pilot their own software, which can highlight instances where a system's *performed* values conflict with the lab's or an individual's *peripheral* to *central* values.

Researchers have also developed card-based design activities to elicit *peripheral* to *central* values of designers and stakeholders (i.e. *individuals*), or *hybrid* design settings. These activities stem from a longer tradition of design games in participatory design [6]. One example is the Envisioning Cards [19]. These cards are intended to provoke conversations about values issues before, during, or after design. The cards have four categories, each of which evokes questions about sources and attributes of values. Stakeholder cards evoke Units (*individual* to *collective*) and Assemblages (*homogenous* to *hybrid*). Time cards evoke future impacts, with a focus on appropriation and integration of a system in social contexts. We classify this as a focus on the future Enactment of values, including those both *potential* and *performed.* Values cards explicitly draw attention to what individuals or groups think is important, highlighting the Salience of values from *peripheral* to *central.* Pervasiveness cards, designed to emphasize "systemic interactions" [19:1146] may raise discussions of Agency (such as whether a pervasive system takes on a *subject* role with its own values impacts) as well as Enactment (such as whether a *purposive* value remains *potential* when a system is embedded in a larger system.).

Similarly, the Grow-A-Game cards [4] are a tool to help groups brainstorm and design games based around a set of prescribed values. By assigning a familiar game (such as Checkers or Pac Man), and then assigning a particular value (such as generosity, peace, or autonomy), this method encourages a team to rethink game mechanics and play based upon an assigned value. The Grow-A-Game cards create a *hybrid* environment where people interact with, and are constrained by, game mechanics. Both the players and the game have *subject* properties: the players as *subjects* who decide upon new rules, and the game's mechanics that limit the range of possibilities. Finally, by prescribing values, Grow-A-Game encourages discussion of *purposive*, *performed* values as players build infrastructures that materialize their assigned values.

Related to cards are design activities intended to elicit discussion of values. Cultural probes have been used to foster discussion of values in computer-supported collaborative work across disciplines [24], which we classify as drawing attention to values in *hybrid collectives*. Reflective design [52] focuses on bringing unconscious choices in design (which we classify as *accidental* values) to the surface to critique and evaluate their impact.

Sources of Values	Attributes of Values
individual ⇔ collective	**peripheral ⇔ central**
homogenous ⇔ **hybrid**	**accidental ⇔ purposive**
subject ⇔ object	**potential ⇔ performed**

Table 3. Dimensions highlighted by design activities

Interviews

Interviews with developers can be used to study all source dimensions, as well as attribute dimensions such as Salience and Intention. Fleischmann and Wallace [16] used interviews to study values in the design of computational models in corporate, academic, and government research labs. They interviewed modelers by asking questions about what role values played in the design of their models and if they observed value conflicts between their organization and other stakeholders such as clients and users [15,16]. Because they asked directly about the importance of values, they observed values that were *central* and *purposive* at specific labs, such as transparency in the corporate lab [15]. Questions about values conflicts [14,16] also elicited Agency dimensions. The interviews revealed the relationship between the values of the designers on the *subject* side of the Agency dimension, and the values embedded in models on the *object* side of that dimension.

Interviews with users can also elicit important findings for values in social computing research. Le Dantec and Edwards used interviews to ground a values-sensitive design project for a homeless population [33]. They used photo-elicitation interviews (a diary study in which participants use cameras to prompt discussion during interviews) to ask *individuals* about their interactions with technologies, which we classify as *hybrid* sources. Homeless participants photographed objects they used in their daily lives, and researchers asked questions about the photographs to explore values along the Salience dimension (such as the *central* value of connectedness) and Agency dimension (such as the features of mobile phones that enabled connectedness). Poole et al. also used an adapted interview technique combining interviews and photo elicitation to study *individuals'* values in a *hybrid* setting: the ubiquitous computing environment of RFID technologies [43]. These interviews revealed the Salience of diverse values, including system trust, data protection, consumer choice, and precise divisions of social appropriateness for RFID tracking of humans.

Interviews face potential self-selection bias and social desirability bias. In particular, researchers risk proscribing values of the source by priming respondents. But if interviewers avoid naming explicit values, interviews may suffer in clarity of focus. Interviews benefit from combination with other methods to elicit *central, purposive* values such as surveys or ethnographies.

Sources of Values	Attributes of Values
individual ⇔ collective	**peripheral** ⇔ **central**
homogenous ⇔ **hybrid**	accidental ⇔ **purposive**
subject ⇔ **object**	potential ⇔ performed

Table 4. Dimensions highlighted by interviews

Content Analysis

Content analysis can overcome limitations such as social desirability and self-selection biases by evaluating existing documents such as public hearings [8] or social media [31]. Fleischmann et al. used this approach to study values in found data [13,31], and explored scaling content analysis using automation [27] and crowdsourcing [58]. Values detected via content analysis are those invoked most frequently in texts, so tend to be what we classify as *central* (important to individuals who invoke them); *purposive* (intentionally embedded in texts); and *performed* (brought into being through their invocation in text). Content analysis mainly focuses on actors towards the *subject* end of the Agency dimension, but facilitates studies of diverse Units (ranging from *individual* writers to *collective* group conversations) and Assemblages (ranging from analysis of content in non-mediated to computer-mediated settings).

A challenge for content analysis is achieving sufficient inter-coder agreement to ensure reliability of coding procedures. In addition, developing and testing a coding rubric is time- and labor-intensive. However, content analysis of found data is more scalable than field research methods and may be applied to large datasets [13].

Sources of Values	Attributes of Values
individual ⇔ **collective**	peripheral ⇔ **central**
homogenous ⇔ **hybrid**	accidental ⇔ **purposive**
subject ⇔ object	potential ⇔ **performed**

Table 5. Dimensions highlighted by content analysis

Technical Investigations

Friedman et al.'s work suggests that "technological properties and underlying mechanisms support or hinder human values" [20:4], and argue that values can be elicited through technical investigations: systematic examination of the components and operation of a technology. We classify these investigations as focused upon the Intention and Enactment dimensions of *hybrid*, *subject* systems, because they look at designed features and the values impact of those features upon larger systems. Similarly, Brey [7] proposes disclosive computer ethics, which describes similar technical investigations focused on whether a chosen value (such as privacy or democracy) is supported by technical features. Because of the focus on system support for a value, we classify these as *potential* to *performed* values. Nissenbaum [39] provides a heuristic to determine whether systems uphold the values of a *collective* (a social group), *hybrid* (involving both technological and human agents) context or system. The heuristic includes examining whether the information transmission principles of a system match the roles, activities, and norms of the context in which a system is deployed.

Technical investigations provide systematic ways to evaluate values along the Enactment dimension within technologies that are already built and in use, when values are *potential* or *performed*, but therefore concretized and difficult to alter. Post-hoc technical investigations are excellent for descriptive work, but less useful for investigating the values reasoning behind system decisions.

Sources of Values	Attributes of Values
individual ⇔ **collective**	peripheral ⇔ central
homogenous ⇔ **hybrid**	**accidental ⇔ purposive**
subject ⇔ object	**potential ⇔ performed**

Table 6. Dimensions highlighted by technical investigations

Sources of Values	Attributes of Values
individual ⇔ **collective**	peripheral ⇔ **central**
homogenous ⇔ **hybrid**	accidental ⇔ **purposive**
subject ⇔ object	potential ⇔ performed

Table 7. Dimensions highlighted by surveys

Surveys

A common approach to studying the Salience of values within Units (often starting with *individual* values and then aggregating results to study values of the *collective* values of a group or culture) has been to use values inventories: surveys in which individuals rate the relative importance of a list of values or value statements [9]. This approach assumes a source of values towards the *subject* end of the spectrum (able to have and express values). Perhaps best-known is the Schwartz value inventory, comprised of 56 human values organized into ten value types [51]. This framework underlies the Portrait Values Questionnaire (PVQ), developed to study the relative importance of each value type across *individuals* to *collectives*. The PVQ has been found to provide comprehensive coverage of *central* values recognized across *collective* cultures [51].

Constructing surveys to find values in *hybrid* sociotechnical contexts, rather than values of *individuals*, is a challenge for social computing researchers. To address this challenge, value surveys can be altered to fit social computing contexts. For example, Koepfler conducted a survey that examined *central* values (by asking the relative importance of values to survey participants) of collectives (multiple stakeholders related to the social issue of homelessness) within the technologically-mediated and therefore *hybrid* context of Twitter [32]. Broadmindedness emerged as a shared *central* value in the context of Twitter for all of the stakeholders pointing to a potentially shared *central* value among all stakeholder groups. Wealth and equality were *central* to those who had experienced homelessness, but no other groups, pointing to potentially conflicting *central* values among different stakeholder groups. These sociotechnical value portraits offered a starting point for engaging with the study of values along the Salience dimension in the design of *hybrid* social computing environments such as online communities. When administered at the beginning of a design process, surveys might also elicit values along the Intention dimension by asking designers about *purposive* values in their systems.

Survey methods are not ideal for addressing all values dimensions, however. Because surveys do not assess technology directly (e.g. we cannot yet ask a technology about its central values), they cannot assess values *performed* after the completion of design or deployment, and are unlikely to find *accidental* values. And because surveys are designed to elicit a respondent's *central* values, they may not capture *peripheral* values.

DISCUSSION

Applying the values dimensions to social computing research highlights the ways in which a variety of methods afford the study of specific dimensions, and also highlights dimensions that are less explored in current research. Though not exhaustive, this analysis illustrates that methods reviewed here all consider <u>source</u> dimensions (Unit, Assemblage, and Agency). This is not surprising; the source of values is an important consideration for researchers as they define the boundaries of their study and their objects of interest (e.g. groups or individuals, people or machines). The analysis also illustrates that methods address the <u>attributes</u> dimensions quite differently. Methods that interrogate groups of people, or their expressions and communications (such as ethnographies, interviews, content analysis and surveys) often highlight values along the Salience dimension. Methods that interrogate design processes (such as ethnographies, values advocacy, design activities, and interviews) often highlight values along the Intention dimension. And methods that interrogate technologies in use (such as ethnographies, technical investigations, and content analysis) often highlight values along the Enactment dimension.

These distinctions provide a heuristic for planning future values research in social computing. Researchers focused on values and agency, for example, might find ethnography, design activities, or interviews better suited to determining when values are ascribed to humans or systems. Researchers focused on values underlying design decisions, or looking for values conflicts between designers and users, might first consider surveys or content analysis methods to elicit *central* values. For example, Walmart is piloting a new smartphone checkout option in stores [63]. Introducing mobile applications into physical shopping experiences may raise concerns for values such as privacy, consent, or equity. A social computing researcher might consider *central* values of *individual subject* Walmart shoppers within this *hybrid* human-mobile device context. A mixed-methods approach of interviews and technical investigations would be well suited to investigating these dimensions. Or a researcher might consider *performed* values of the *object*, *hybrid* mobile system. Technical investigations and participant-observation through use of the system would illuminate these dimensions. Evaluating the effectiveness of the dimensions framework for planning and conducting values in social computing research will be a critical next step for this work.

The dimensions framework also exposes the fact that methods widely used in values and design research are frequently better suited for addressing values towards one end of a dimensions spectrum. For example, surveys are useful for studying values of *subject* actors on the Agency dimension (i.e. it is difficult to survey *object* machines in a sociotechnical system). And both interviews and surveys can solicit *central* and *purposive* values (what people say they care about and do), but may not pick up *peripheral* or *accidental* values as effectively. Indeed, many of the methods discussed are excellent for eliciting *central*, *purposive*, and *performed* values on the attributes dimensions. An opportunity for social computing research is to develop methods and cases that can observe *peripheral*, *accidental*, and *potential* values more effectively. These less visible attributes of values are currently underrepresented in values and design research, but could provide new concepts and domains for analysis. Future work should adapt existing methods or explore new methods to collect data at underrepresented ends of dimensions. For example, developing interview methods to elicit peripheral values, or methods beyond technical analysis to examine accidental values, would advance values research in social computing.

Though the dimensions framework enables description of sources and attributes of values in social computing, a final challenge remains: identifying which values are important in a research context [5,34]. Should researchers explore intrinsic values such as justice and virtue? Or instrumental values such as privacy, openness, or trust? Is there a list of prescribed values for which researchers should look, or should researchers examine emergent values? We believe that values may be found using preexisting inventories, or *in situ* through observation. Researchers should identify their approach and be aware of its limitations. *A priori* approaches using values inventories risk missing values important to research subjects. *In situ* approaches, also known as descriptive ethics [12], risk comprehensiveness by focusing on a subjective set of values.

CONCLUSION

Our application of the values dimensions framework to social computing highlights the fact that values are not fixed in people, or systems, or use contexts [22]. Instead, values can be observed among a complex collection of designers, artifacts, infrastructures, social contexts, and use practices. Values researchers must therefore distribute their focus across contexts of design, adoption, and use.

To support a more unified conversation, we suggest that researchers use a shared vocabulary for describing where in the social computing ecology values are being investigated, without prescribing what values should be considered. We believe that researchers can more precisely describe, operationalize, and study values in social computing by considering dimensions that describe where and how values occur in technology contexts. Values dimensions include the source of the value – the setting from which values are elicited – as well as attributes of the values themselves. Mixed methods and a consistent vocabulary for describing where in the design ecology values are being investigated will be critical to this emerging research agenda.

ACKNOWLEDGMENTS

This material is based in part upon work supported by the National Science Foundation under Grants No. SES-0521117, SES-0646392, IIS-0729459, IIS-0832873, and CNS-1040868.

REFERENCES

1. Albrechtslund, A. Ethics and technology design. *Ethics and Information Technology 9*, 1 (2007), 63–72.
2. Alsheikh, T., Rode, J.A., and Lindley, S.E. (Whose) value-sensitive design: A study of long- distance relationships in an Arabic cultural context. *Proc. CSCW 2011*, ACM (2011), 75–84.
3. Ames, M.G., Go, J., Kaye, J., and Spasojevic, M. Understanding technology choices and values through social class. *Proc. CSCW 2011* ACM (2011), 55–64.
4. Belman, J., Flanagan, M., Nissenbaum, H., and Diamond, J. Grow-A-Game: A tool for values conscious design and analysis of digital games. *Proc. DiGRA 2011,* (2011), 14–17.
5. Borning, A. and Muller, M. Next steps for value sensitive design. *Proc. CHI 2012*, ACM (2012), 1125–1134.
6. Brandt, E. and Messeter, J. Facilitating collaboration through design games. *Proc. PDC 2004, Volume 1*, ACM (2004), 121–131.
7. Brey, P. Method in computer ethics: Towards a multi-level interdisciplinary approach. *Ethics and Information Technology 2*, 2 (2000), 125–129.
8. Cheng, A.-S., Fleischmann, K.R., Wang, P., Ishita, E., and Oard, D.W. The role of innovation and wealth in the net neutrality debate: A content analysis of human values in congressional and FCC hearings. *Journal of the American Society for Information Science and Technology 63*, 7 (2012), 1360–1373.
9. Cheng, A.-S. and Fleischmann, K.R. Developing a meta-inventory of human values. *Proc. ASIST 2010 47*, 1 (2010), 1–10.
10. Cockton, G. From quality in use to value in the world. *Proc. CHI 2004*, (2004), 1287–1290.
11. Fisher, E. Ethnographic invention: Probing the capacity of laboratory decisions. *NanoEthics 1*, 2 (2007), 155–165.
12. Flanagan, M., Nissenbaum, H., and Howe, D.C. Embodying values in technology: Theory and practice. In J. van den Hoven and J. Weckert, eds., *Information Technology and Moral Philosophy*. Cambridge University Press, Cambridge, 2008, 322–353.

13. Fleischmann, K.R., Cheng, A.-S., Templeton, T.C., et al. Content analysis for values elicitation. *Proc. CHI 2012, Workshop on Methods for Accounting for Values in Human-Centered Computing*, ACM (2012).
14. Fleischmann, K.R., Wallace, W.A., and Grimes, J.M. How values can reduce conflicts in the design process: Results from a multi-site mixed-method field study. *Proc. ASIST 2011, 48*, 1 (2011), 1–10.
15. Fleischmann, K.R. and Wallace, W.A. Ensuring transparency in computational modeling. *Commun. ACM 52*, 3 (2009), 131–134.
16. Fleischmann, K.R. and Wallace, W.A. Value conflicts in computational modeling. *Computer 43*, 7 (2010), 57–63.
17. Fleischmann, K.R. Digital libraries and human values: Human-computer interaction meets social informatics. *Proc. ASIST 2008, 44*, 1 (2008), 1–17.
18. Forsythe, D.E. *Studying those who study us: An anthropologist in the world of artificial intelligence*. Stanford University Press, Palo Alto, CA, 2002.
19. Friedman, B. and Hendry, D.G. The envisioning cards: A toolkit for catalyzing humanistic and technical imaginations. *Proc. CHI 2012*, ACM (2012), 1145–1148.
20. Friedman, B., Kahn, P.H., and Borning, A. Value sensitive design and information systems. In D. Galletta and P. Zhang, eds., *Human-Computer Interaction and Management Information Systems: Applications*. M.E. Sharpe, New York, 2006.
21. Friedman, B. and Nissenbaum, H. Bias in computer systems. In B. Friedman, ed., *Human values and the design of computer technology*. Cambridge University Press, Cambridge and New York, 1997, 21–40.
22. Friedman, B., ed. *Human values and the design of computer technology*. Cambridge University Press, Cambridge and New York, 1997.
23. Guston, D.H. and Sarewitz, D. Real-time technology assessment. *Technology in Society 24*, 1-2 (2002), 93–109.
24. Halpern, M.K., Erickson, I., Forlano, L., and Gay, G.K. Designing collaboration: comparing cases exploring cultural probes as boundary-negotiating objects. *Proc. CSCW 2013,* ACM (2013), 1093–1102.
25. Haraway, D. The cyborg manifesto and fractured identities. In *Social Theory: The Multicultural & Classic Readings*. Westview Press, Boulder, CO, 1985, 597–604.
26. Himma, K.E. A dualist analysis of abortion: Personhood and the concept of self qua experiential subject. *Journal of Medical Ethics 31*, 1 (2005), 48–55.
27. Ishita, E., Oard, D.W., Fleischmann, K.R., Cheng, A.-S., and Templeton, T.C. Investigating multi-label classification for human values. *Proc. ASIST 2010,47*, 1 (2010), 1–4.
28. Kaptelinin, V. and Nardi, B. Affordances in HCI: toward a mediated action perspective. *Proc. CHI 2012,* ACM (2012), 967–976.
29. Kelty, C.M. *Two bits: The cultural significance of free software*. Duke University Press, Durham, NC, 2008.
30. Knobel, C.P. and Bowker, G.C. Values in design. *Communications of the ACM 54*, 2011, 26–28.
31. Koepfler, J.A. and Fleischmann, K.R. Studying the values of hard-to-reach populations: content analysis of tweets by the 21st century homeless. *Proc. iConference 2012*, ACM (2012), 48–55.
32. Koepfler, J.A., Shilton, K., and Fleischmann, K.R. A stake in the issue of homelessness: Identifying values of interest for design in online communities. *Proc. C&T 2013*, ACM (2013).
33. Le Dantec, C.A. and Edwards, W.K. Designs on dignity: perceptions of technology among the homeless. *Proc. CHI 2008*, ACM (2008), 627–636.
34. Le Dantec, C.A.L., Poole, E.S., and Wyche, S.P. Values as lived experience: evolving value sensitive design in support of value discovery. *Proc. CHI 2009*, ACM (2009), 1141–1150.
35. Lin, P., Abney, K., and Bekey, G. Robot ethics: Mapping the issues for a mechanized world. *Artificial Intelligence 175*, 5–6 (2011), 942–949.
36. Lofland, J., Snow, D., Anderson, L., and Lofland, L.H. *Analyzing social settings: a guide to qualitative observation and analysis*. Wadsworth/Thomson Learning, Belmont, CA, 2006.
37. MacKenzie, D. *An engine, not a camera: how financial models shape markets*. The MIT Press, Cambridge, MA and London, 2008.
38. Manders-Huits, N. and Zimmer, M. Values and pragmatic action: The challenges of introducing ethical intelligence in technical and design communities. *International Review of Information Ethics 10*, (2009), 37–44.
39. Nissenbaum, H. *Privacy in context: Technology, policy, and the integrity of social life*. Stanford Law Books, Stanford, CA, 2009.
40. Nissenbaum, H. From preemption to circumvention: if technology regulates, why do we need regulation (and vice versa)? *Berkeley Technology Law Journal 26*, 3 (2011), 1367–1386.
41. Plowman, T. Ethnography and critical design practice. In B. Laurel, ed., *Design research: methods and perspectives*. MIT Press, Cambridge, MA, 2003.
42. Pollock, N. and Williams, R. The business of expectations: How promissory organizations shape technology and innovation. *Social Studies of Science 40*, 4 (2010), 525–548.
43. Poole, E.S., Le Dantec, C.A., Eagan, J.R., and Edwards, W.K. Reflecting on the invisible: understanding end-

user perceptions of ubiquitous computing. *Proc. UBICOMP 2008*, ACM (2008), 192–201.

44. Postigo, H. Questioning the Web 2.0 discourse: Social roles, production, values, and the case of the human rights portal. *The Information Society 27*, 3 (2011), 181–193.
45. Rabinow, P. and Bennett, G. *Ars synthetica: Designs for human practice*. Rice University Connexions Web site, Houston, TX, 2008.
46. Roberson, J. and Nardi, B. Survival needs and social inclusion: technology use among the homeless. *Proc. CSCW 2010*, ACM (2010), 445–448.
47. Rokeach, M. *The nature of human values*. Free Press, New York, 1973.
48. Saab, D.J. An ethnorelative framework for information system design. *Proc. AMCIS 2008*, Association for Information Systems (2008), 1–14.
49. Schuler, D. Social computing. *Communications of the ACM 37*, 1 (1994), 28–29.
50. Schwartz, S.H. Universals in the content and structure of values: Theory and empirical tests in 20 countries. In M. Zanna, ed., *Advances in experimental social psychology*. Academic Press, New York, 1992, 1–65.
51. Schwartz, S.H. Value orientations: Measurement, antecedents and consequences across nations. In R. Jowell, C. Roberts, C. Fitzgerald and G. Eva, eds., *Measuring attitudes cross-nationally: Lessons from the European Social Survey*. Sage Publications, London, 2007, 169–203.
52. Sengers, P., Boehner, K., David, S., and Kaye, J. Reflective design. *Proc. Critical computing 2005: between sense and sensibility*, ACM (2005), 49–58.
53. Shilton, K., Koepfler, J.A., and Fleischmann, K.R. Charting sociotechnical dimensions of values for design research. *The Information Society 29*, 5 (2013).
54. Shilton, K. This is an intervention: Foregrounding and operationalizing ethics during technology design. In *Emerging Pervasive Information and Communication Technologies (PICT). Ethical Challenges, Opportunities and Safeguards*. Springer, New York, In Press.
55. Shilton, K. Values levers: Building ethics into design. *Science, Technology & Human Values 38*, 3 (2013), 374 – 397.
56. Siegrist, M., Cvetkovich, G., and Roth, C. Salient value similarity, social trust, and risk/benefit perception. *Risk Analysis 20*, 3 (2000), 353–362.
57. Suchman, L. Do categories have politics? The language/action perspective reconsidered. In B. Friedman, ed., *Human values and the design of computer technology*. Cambridge University Press, Cambridge and New York, 1997, 91–105.
58. Templeton, T.C. and Fleischmann, K.R. The relationship between human values and attitudes toward the Park51 and nuclear power controversies. *Proceedings of the American Society for Information Science and Technology 48*, 1 (2011), 1–10.
59. van der Burg, S. Imagining the future of photoacoustic mammography. *Science and Engineering Ethics 15*, 1 (2009), 97–110.
60. Verbeek, P.-P. Materializing morality. *Science, Technology & Human Values 31*, 3 (2006), 361 –380.
61. Wang, F.-Y., Carley, K.M., Zeng, D., and Mao, W. Social computing: from social informatics to social intelligence. *IEEE Intelligent Systems 22*, 2 (2007), 79–83.
62. Winner, L. Do artifacts have politics? *Daedalus 109*, 1 (1980), 121–136.
63. Wohlsen, M. To beat Amazon, Walmart is treating its stores like apps. *Wired.com*, 2013. http://www.wired.com/business/2013/03/walmart-treats-stores-like-apps/.

De-Virtualizing Social Events: Understanding the Gap between Online and Offline Participation for Event Invitations

Ai-Ju Huang[1], Hao-Chuan Wang[2], Chien Wen Yuan[3]

[1,2]Institute of Information Systems and Applications
& [2]Department of Computer Science
National Tsing Hua University, Taiwan
[1]s100065506@m100.nthu.edu.tw,
[2]haochuan@cs.nthu.edu.tw

[3]Department of Communication
Cornell University
Ithaca NY 14850 USA
cy294@cornell.edu

ABSTRACT

One growing use of computer-based communication media is for gathering people to initiate or sustain social events. Although the use of computer-mediated communication and social network sites such as Facebook for event promotion is becoming popular, online participation in an event does not always translate to offline attendance. In this paper, we report on an interview study of 31 participants that examines how people handle online event invitations and what influences their online and offline participation. The results show that people's event participation is shaped by their social perceptions of the event's nature (e.g., public or private), their relationships to others (e.g., the strength of their connections to other invitees), and the medium used to communicate event information (e.g., targeted invitation via email or spam communication via Facebook event page). By exploring how people decide whether to participate online or offline, the results illuminate the sophisticated nature of the mechanisms that affect participation and have design implications that can bridge virtual and real attendance.

Author Keywords

Participation; social network sites; computer-mediated communication; online events.

ACM Classification Keywords

H.5.3 **[Group and Organization Interfaces]:** Computer-supported cooperative work. H.5.m **[Information interfaces and presentation (e.g., HCI)]**: Miscellaneous.

INTRODUCTION

Social network sites (SNSs) are increasingly used to support event planning, such as recruiting and mobilizing people around the world [17, 26]. The use of SNSs has many benefits, including reaching out to potential event participants and collecting pre-commitment to attending an event through online social networks [17]. This approach facilitates resource allocation in terms of event planning and personnel deployment.

However, although the cost of initiating and managing events online tends to be low, event participation outcomes may not be as promising. One of the downsides to use SNSs or other computer-mediated communication (CMC) tools to disseminate and manage event invitations is that one's online response to an event page or a web forum does not always translate to actual attendance offline [12, 15, 25]. Anecdotal evidence often shows that anxious hosts continually seek ways to solve the problem of people hitting "Join" or "RSVP" via SNSs (e.g., Facebook) or other e-invitation sites but ending up with no show.

We broadly define event participation as any form of response to online (i.e., over technological mediation) or offline (i.e., face-to-face) event invitations. A gap may exist between online and offline participation. Using an online event call to motivate offline participation may be difficult because the cost of offline participation may be high [35], and the properties of certain existing technological designs may not be effective in motivating offline participation.

Research around the issue has focused on participation in the context of political and social movements (e.g., demonstration, election etc.). Previous studies have investigated how political events can be successfully mobilized via Facebook [16], how different media (e.g., technologically-mediated versus face-to-face) affect participation in online and offline activities [26, 35], and how messages exchanged through online social networks affect the behavioral outcomes [3]. However, few studies attempt to take a broader perspective to include non-political, everyday, and personal events such as birthday parties or cultural activities into consideration. Little is known about how people make decisions about online invitations in general.

From the design perspective, this possible mismatch between response choices on SNSs or other CMC tools and people's offline behaviors can be a signal of design failure. Online response choices are not necessarily good indicators

CSCW '14, February 15–19, 2014, Baltimore, Maryland, USA.

http://dx.doi.org/10.1145/2531602.2531606

of offline behaviors, which raises concerns about whether the original designs, such as features for event planning on SNSs, meet the intended design goals.

As event planning of all types is increasingly virtualized through the use of communication technologies, it is important to examine how event invitations move from the offline, socio-physical world to the online space and are disseminated through computer networking. Moreover, it is valuable to tackle this issue through users' perspective by exploring how they perceive and react to this change. To guide our investigation, we conceptualize the challenge of motivating offline behavior through online communication as a bottleneck in the *de-virtualization of events*. Not all events require offline participation, and a lack of offline participation may not be a problem for some events. However, in circumstances in which offline participation is required, understanding the gap between online and offline participation and the best way to de-virtualize these events is crucial. Without successful de-virtualization, it may be difficult to ground event planning and resource allocation in practice. Moreover, repercussions may follow, such as deteriorated social relationships between hosts and invitees as well as users' perceptions of the functions of the interfaces, without successful de-virtualization.

This paper contributes to an understanding of how people handle event invitations, ranging from personal events to social movements, that require offline participation when the initiation, development, communication, and some forms of participation in the events are virtualized and occur in the online space. We present the results of interviews in which we examined people's management of event invitations as well as their concerns and reasoning. We asked interviewees to recall their previous experiences in handling event invitations. We investigated whether gaps existed between online and offline forms of participation. Finally, if gaps existed, we examined the social mechanisms behind these gaps and the implications for future design.

BACKGROUND

(De-)Virtualization of Social Events

We observe a trend of social activity virtualization from the socio-physical, offline world to computer-mediated, online spaces. This trend is not surprising given that the costs of offline participation, such as the physical planning and attendance of an event, can be much higher than the online equivalents, such as chatting through instant messages or posting on a forum. Offline participation tends to be financially more expensive and more time consuming than many forms of online participation. In the work domain, it has become common to replace some face-to-face meetings with online discussion to reduce costs [19, 40]. Some collaboration may even occur only "virtually" through the mediation of technology, such as Wikipedia or human computation games that require a large crowd of people around the world to interact and contribute [36].

SNSs provide features that support the initiation and management of social events [16, 17]. Facebook's event pages, for example, allow users to create social events, send event invitations to others, and gather people's support and attendance decisions. For hosts, this is a convenient way to spread information about an event and reach a group of guests, and this approach requires less preparation time than other methods. It is easy for a guest to RSVP to an event to which s/he is invited through Facebook event pages. Event-supporting technologies of this sort are designed to support social event planning [21], although the actual effects of existing designs remain unclear.

Note that not all social events can be virtualized. There are cases in which physical presence and attendance are instrumental to the success of the event, which can be as personal as a birthday party or as public as a political demonstration. For example, researchers have begun to observe a phenomenon called slacktivism (combining "slacker" and "activism"). Slacktivism is used to describe the scenario in which people engage in low-cost and low-risk action online without participating in related in-person activities [30]. To event organizers, online participation, in the form of such actions as electronic petitions or information sharing, is typically considered a mediating step preceding offline participation; presence at actual social events is still expected [23, 25]. However, some participants may behave differently, treating online participation as the end rather than the means to an activity. Most research now focuses on the gap between online and offline participation for political or public events, and work on participation in everyday, personal events remains limited.

People's restriction of their event participation to the online space calls into question the impact of such online participation. The lack of a real-world presence does not necessarily indicate a lack of impact. A recent study shows that people who have signed an online petition are more likely to donate to charity than those who have not [23]. However, when offline participation is vital to the success of an event, whether personal or public, an understanding of what factors influence offline presence can better reveal the properties of event virtualization.

Social Connection, Interaction, and Participation

Recent work shows that social ties and social interaction contribute positively to event participation. For example, people are more willing to accept invitations sent by people they already know [28]. Zhang et al. study the integration of online and offline social interaction, noting that people's role identity in sport clubs on Facebook shapes their degree of participation [41]. This work highlights the individual's identity as a key factor in calls for offline action. Bond et al. explore how messages exchanged online and the strength of social ties affect political mobilization. Their results reveal that information distributed through multiplex networks in which people are connected both online and offline trigger event participation [3].

Along these lines, there is reason to believe that SNSs and online communication may encourage offline participation through the moderation of social relationships. Prior studies have made similar observations, showing that some social activities appear to benefit from the use of CMC and SNSs [16, 31]. The interactive features of SNSs (e.g., Facebook event pages) are designed to support information exchange and socialization online. Thus, it is possible for people to strengthen social connections when they socialize with their online contacts increasingly more over time [2, 10, 37]. In addition, online social interaction may facilitate the building of common ground [7], which is instrumental for collaboration among people. Therefore, technology-mediated interaction may positively contribute to offline participation decisions through increased interactivity and social connectivity.

In summary, although real-world social ties and interaction have been established as crucial to offline participation, the interactive features of SNSs may compensate for the limitations of virtualized, online communication, leading to a large amount of offline participation.

Medium Difference and Specificity

Different communication media have different properties or features and influence people's communication behaviors accordingly (cf. [38]). For example, in sense-making communication, rich, visible media (e.g., face-to-face or video) can often lead to more efficient communication because the establishment of mutual knowledge or common ground is facilitated when visibility is afforded [34].

Because of different media affordances, issues concerning cross-media event planning, such as the processes of the virtualization (from offline to online) and de-virtualization (from online to offline) of social events, may benefit from focused discussion on the role of media characteristics in event planning. SNSs such as Facebook allow people to express intentions to participate online by clicking "Like" or "Join" on an event page, for example. However, it is unclear whether symbolic support of this sort is representative of offline behaviors. One possibility is that people may perceive it to be more suitable to take certain types of action online and other types offline. Initial studies show that certain types of online communication (e.g., emails) tend to trigger only online behaviors, whereas face-to-face communication tends to better motivate offline behaviors [35]. In a similar fashion, SNSs may be more useful in calling for virtual support (e.g., "join an online group"), although perhaps not in-person attendance.

Another characteristic of SNSs is that they may become public or semi-public spaces (e.g., Facebook walls) where social interactions between people are displayed to irrelevant third parties [4]. Information provided on many types on SNSs, including personal or interactional information, allows users to manage their representations of themselves [5]. Following Goffman's theory of impression management [14], we can view SNSs as a front stage on which individuals present their ideal selves [4, 18]. When displayed publicly to SNS friends, reactions to event invitations can be part of one's online (i.e., onstage) self-presentation and are distinguishable from offline images and behaviors. It is possible for people to join groups on Facebook without any interest in offline participation. Participation in online groups or an agreement to attend an event may simply be a way to maintain one's personal profile [9] or present one's views or interests [15].

THE CURRENT STUDY

Previous work has revealed a complex set of conjectures and observations regarding the relation between online communication and participation through the use of any form of CMC and SNS and offline participation in events. To resolve this issue, it is important to study individuals' perceptions and strategies for handling technology-mediated event invitations.

We conducted an in-depth interview study that explored how people handle event invitations distributed via communication technologies and what factors influence people's online and offline participation behaviors.

METHOD

Participants

We recruited our interviewees from the largest Bulletin Board System (BBS) in Taiwan, *ptt.cc*. According to official ptt.cc information, the site has a total of approximately 1.5 million users [29]. To obtain a sample of the general public, we posted the recruiting message on a local discussion board (Hsinchu) and a board specific to the recruitment of questionnaire respondents and study participants (Q_ary). The recruiting message contained the research description and a link to a Google Document form to sign up for the study.

A total of 31 Taiwanese interviewees participated in the study (17 male, 14 female). Of the participants, 18 were college students, and 13 were non-students with various occupations (e.g., software engineers, salespersons, preschool teachers). In terms of age distribution, all were under 45. Fifteen interviewees were between 18 and 25 years old, 12 were between 26 and 35, and the remaining four were between 36 and 45. To address our research question, our interviewees were required to be CMC or SNS users and to have experience in receiving and handling event invitations mediated by some type of communication technology.

Materials and Procedure

This study identified people's experiences in handling technology-mediated event invitations. Before the interviews, we created an online survey using Google

Documents that asked interviewees to recall and provide information about events they had attended or agreed to attend but ultimately did not attend. To allow the interviewees to provide information on the events documented during the interview, the survey asked for the title, the hyperlink (if available), and the medium used to mediate the event invitation (e.g., email, instant messaging, Twitter, Facebook, Google+, BBS). At the end of the survey, we also collected demographic information on the respondents.

One week later, we conducted one-on-one interviews and asked our interviewees to reflect on their experiences handling event invitations with the aid of information collected using the pre-interview survey. The semi-structured in-depth interview process allowed the interviewees to articulate how they grappled with the issues addressed in our research. We asked them what events they reported in the survey, how they handled the event invitations, and whether they actually attended the events. To support and better customize each interview, we checked the event hyperlinks our interviewees provided prior to the interview whenever necessary.

Each interview lasted approximately 40 minutes, and all of the interviews were audio-recorded. Most of the interviews were conducted face-to-face at the university, with the exception of two that were conducted over Skype because the interviewees could not meet in person. The audio records were transcribed verbatim, including interviewees' emotional reactions (e.g., laughing) and moments of hesitation. All of the interviews were conducted, transcribed, and analyzed in Mandarin Chinese.

Data Analysis

To determine whether a gap exists between people's online and offline participation, the size of the gap, and why such a gap may exist, we first identified the event types recalled by our interviewees. Then, we examined how the interviewees' responses to event invitations depended on the communication media, the interface design, and their relationships and social interactions with the event host and other invitees. Important themes were identified and are presented in the following section. The transcripts were analyzed in an iterative manner until salient themes emerged. All quotes presented in the next section were translated into English for the sake of clarity in the paper.

Event Classification

In the transcripts, only specific referenced events were counted and analyzed. For example, if an interviewee expressed a specific experience by making a statement such as, "Once, there was a high school reunion...," referring to a particular time or place, we identified such an incident as one event. Conversely, if a description such as "I always ignore invitations to demonstrations" was given, we did not identify the statement as referring to any type of event because it refers to a general experience rather than a specific case.

Types of Responses

There are four possible ways to handle online event invitations. The first is to accept the invitation by, for example, leaving a message expressing an intention to attend by clicking on the "Join" button on the Facebook event page. The second is to decline the invitation by conveying one's unavailability, such as by clicking on the "No" button on Google+. The third is to provide an uncertain response, such as clicking on the "Maybe" button on a Facebook event page. The last is to ignore the invitation by not responding. In the transcript, we identified the respondents' offline behavior for each event: whether the person attended the event (i.e., attendance) or did not attend (i.e., absence).

Emerging Themes

During the coding process, we highlighted recurring ideas that represented people's perceptions, thoughts, and behaviors with regard to the online event invitations across interviews. Important themes are identified and presented in this paper.

RESULTS

In this section, we first present the results of the event classification. We determined the frequency of different types of online and offline event participation to establish whether a gap exists between online and offline participation. We then examined the themes that emerged from the coded transcripts in an attempt to explore the reasons behind people's decisions and behaviors.

First, we confirmed that a gap exists between online and offline participation. We discovered that the communication platform and the platform's technical features matter when people evaluate events and make decisions accordingly. We then identified themes that address how people perform evaluations and make decisions. The themes revolve around the nature of the events, including public and private events, and people's relationships with the event hosts.

Gap between Online and Offline Participation

Based on events identified and extracted from the transcripts, we determined whether online responses were consistent with offline behavior. In total, 79 events were reported during the pre-interview survey and the interviews. The majority of the event invitations (62 events, or 78% of the events) were sent through Facebook. Seven events were sent from particular event websites, and the rest were sent through other channels, such as instant massaging, BBS, or email.

Table 1 shows the interviewees' responses to event invitations they received. After excluding 12 cases in which the interviewee did not remember how s/he replied, of the remaining 67 events, 43 accepted, 19 ignored the invitation, one responded ambiguously (i.e., with uncertainty), and four declined. The 43 invitations that were accepted were reported by and distributed among 15 interviewees. Interestingly, of the 43 accepted event invitations, 17 (39.5% of accepted events) did not result in actual attendance.

The descriptive statistics show that the most popular form in which the interviewees received invitations was Facebook. We also confirmed the presence of a gap between online and offline participation. A high proportion of accepted events did not result in attendance, raising the question of why people committed to attending events online but skipped them offline.

Roles of Interface Features

Several salient themes emerged from the data. The first theme that emerged from the interviews is the role of interface features, which shaped the way people responded to the invitations. SNSs such Facebook and Google+ allow for explicit event creation and management, so people can initiate events, edit event details, and send invitations to invitees. SNSs also allow invitees to reply to invitations by clicking on buttons such as "Join," "Maybe," and "Decline" on Facebook or "Yes," "Maybe," and "No" on Google+.

The majority of the invitations that our interviewees reported were sent from Facebook, so our discussion concentrates on these. We describe how our interviewees perceived the interface features (e.g., buttons) of the invitations and the impacts of these features on their responses to the invitations. The interviewees were anonymized and are presented in the following format: "number-F/M-S/N" ("F": female, "M": male, "S": student, "N": non-student).

Social Meanings of Reply Buttons

Although Facebook provides a set of buttons to allow people to easily express their intention to participate, different people may interpret the meaning of these buttons differently. Twelve of our interviewees claimed that clicking the "Join" button on an event page is *not* a promise that one will actually attend the event.

"This is not a contract that can force you to execute. I click 'Join' only to indicate the inclination. It implies that 'I most likely will attend' or 'I most likely won't go.'" (1-M-S)

Offline Behavior	Online Response				
	Accept	Uncertain	Decline	Ignore	Total
Attendance	26 (60.5%)	0 (0%)	0 (0%)	2 (10.5%)	18
Absence	17 (39.5%)	1 (100%)	4 (100%)	17 (89.5%)	39
Total	43	1	4	19	67

Table 1. The number of specific events identified in the interviews by type of online response and offline behavior.

One useful function that Facebook provides is the ability to remind users of events that they have agreed to attend and notify them of updates to and the times of these events. Three interviewees appropriated this function for personal information management. They clicked on response buttons on Facebook event pages so that Facebook could help them remember the events rather than to indicate an intention to attend.

"I clicked 'Join' because the event looked good. Basically, it was similar to writing a memo saying, 'I want to go to this event'...so if I can't attend at the time, I won't change my response on the page to 'Maybe' or 'Not going.'" (30-F-S)

Similar to interviewee 1, interviewee 25 noted that the literal meaning of "Join" was overestimated and treated lightly, suggesting that people clicked on this button without a great deal of consideration. Decision making regarding event participation is taken less seriously on SNSs.

"No one responds seriously. They take a look and think maybe they are available to go, and then click 'Join,' but forget about it within the next second." (25-F-S)

In contrast to agreement, a refusal to participate is accompanied by considerable thought. Eleven interviewees thought seriously about the meaning of clicking the "Decline" button because they were concerned about the negative impact that it would have on the event or the host.

"If the number of people who have declined is higher than the number of people who have joined, one thing I will consider is the host's feelings. The other thing is that it may cause others who see the page to wonder why they are going to an event no one wants to go to." (10-M-N)

Furthermore, according to three interviewees' reports, "Decline" indicates not only an unwillingness to attend but also an opposition to the event. If they cannot make an event, they prefer to ignore the invitation rather than provide a definite negative response. Erroneous attribution regarding their stance on the event can thus be avoided.

"If the event concerns some issues that I disapprove of, of course I will click 'Decline.' However, if I support its standpoints, I won't click 'Decline' whether I will attend or not." (31-F-S)

"If I click 'Decline,' it feels like it's because I think the one who invited me made some mistakes." (07-F-S)

The meaning of the choice to "Join," "Decline," or not reply extends beyond what was suggested when our interviewees made the decision upon receiving an invitation. Although people differed in their evaluations and perceptions of the events they agreed to attend, they weighed a negative decision more heavily because rejection can have unintended social consequences. In the following, we discuss the interviewees' evaluations and perceptions used to reach their attendance decisions.

Targeted versus Spam Communication

Some interviewees had experiences of being both invitees and event hosts, so they were familiar with the procedure used to create events and the associated costs of initiating events on Facebook. Their perceptions of the cost of event management on different sites or through different media became a criterion for their evaluation of the importance of the events.

"Facebook provides a template for you to create events, and you just have to fill in the blanks. However, with websites, you have to establish it from scratch...If someone builds a website for the event, I think it must be serious, or the host won't be willing to build the website." (09-F-S)

"Currently, many people create events on Facebook, and if you want to go, click 'Join'; if not, then ignore it. I sense that many people do that, and the event can fall apart. However, if the event host invites me by phone, it indicates that s/he really takes the event and my attendance seriously; otherwise, s/he won't call everyone one by one." (20-F-N)

Eleven interviewees noted that the low cost and the ease of inviting people on Facebook suggested that the host had not taken the invitation seriously, especially if the list of invitees is large and all-inclusive. In such cases, the response was weighed as much as the effort the event hosts spent on the events; the invitees tended to treat such events lightly and ignored the invitations.

"When you use Facebook, you can invite all your friends on your list with one click. It can be done as easily as spam. However, with e-mail, you have to screen who may be more interested in the event and even write down some words for the invitation." (31-F-S)

"If it's instant messaging, that's a personal invitation. That is more sincere and is not a random attempt." (19-M-N)

If the invitations are not sufficiently targeted, people's intentions to reply or attend may be low. Interviewees compared invitations sent through different media. The data show that if a public medium is used and if it is easy to invite participants, the invitation appears less formal and less personal.

"I think email can be replied to personally, and it's private. Facebook seems still semi-public even when we use group chat. I think a Facebook invitation is more casual in that the event hosts invite participants by clicking on them without concern. However, email may require event hosts to search for the list. Even if they just select all the people on the list, they should have contacted you before, and that makes me feel...it's more close to me." (28-F-S)

If an invitation was more personal, the interviewees took it more seriously and tended to provide an unambiguous answer instead of ignoring the invitation. In other words, the personalization of the invitation has a positive relationship with perceived accountability [32]. In our data, the level of personalization was evaluated based on the media used to send the invitation. Our interviewees applied different strategies when replying to invitations sent through different media.

"I always indicate clearly whether I will go or not in response to invitations sent through instant messaging, as it feels closer to being invited on a one-on-one basis." (30-F-S)

To our interviewees, the perception of the directness of the invitation/communication was vital to the decision regarding attendance and commitment to the decision. The undirected approach of invitation dissemination, although efficient on the hosts' end, was taken less seriously by the invitees.

Public Events with a Mass Audience

In addition to the perception of whether an invitation is communicated in an undirected or directed way, the nature of the event, such as whether it is a public or a private activity, elicits different reply strategies from users. Public events on Facebook allow access to everyone (based on privacy settings) and may feature an invitee list or participant list with hundreds of people. We found that the public nature of the event and the visibility of the participant and invitee lists may affect people's intentions to respond to such an invitation and their offline participation.

Public Image Maintenance and Conflict Avoidance

On Facebook, if individuals "Join" an event set as "Public," information regarding their attendance is shown on their personal walls by default. When managing invitations, our interviewees' changed their behaviors in response to such a public display to maintain their public images. Sometimes they even use such an invitation as an opportunity to reveal their tastes or interests to others. This online representation is expected to facilitate conversation with an interested audience. The online display of event participation is also considered a less socially intrusive method of self-promotion.

"If there is an Audi or Mercedes-Benz exhibition, I will click 'Join' to let others know, 'Wow, it is so cool that you go to this event,' and it opens conversation...but if you have no interest in this, and I keep telling you directly that I went to a Mercedes-Benz exhibition today, or posting it on others' walls, people will think I am nuts." (10-M-N)

However, if the event was related to controversial issues (e.g., anti-nuclear power, anti-media monopoly in Taiwan) or was in conflict with their online personal identity, the interviewees tended to be reserved in terms of expressing their intention to join.

"Everyone has his/her own standpoint, and I don't want to be labeled. To some degree, I am afraid that my friends will think I am a certain kind of person because I join some events. Therefore, I will avoid clicking 'Join' for an event that states certain positions." (02-M-S)

Event attendance becomes part of one's online representation. To display an ideal image, nine interviewees reported that they attempted to show the best part of themselves and avoided possible conflicts. One way to ease the tension resulting from this conflict is to remain within the mainstream. Due to the bandwagon effect [24], the majority opinion prompts people to side with the majority view. This effect relieves people of the pressure of taking an explicit stance or incurring conflict.

"From the side of public opinion, if everyone supports this event, of course you will click 'Join.' It means that I have the same opinion as the mainstream." (01-M-S)

The discrepancy between online and offline representation sometimes produces an inconsistency between online and offline participation. To protect their privacy, individuals may not click on "Join" online but may still attend the event offline. One of the interviewees described his experience regarding an invitation to a rock festival. He went to the event with his friends without accepting the invitation online because he did not want others to know what he was doing (24-M-S).

The negotiation between online and offline images is especially apparent in situations in which people use Facebook to maintain offline relationships [11, 22]. People feel tension when dealing offline with the consequences of their online behaviors.

"Because my Facebook friend list consists of my teachers, relatives, and elders, they are going to tell me that they see that I clicked on the anti-nuke demonstration or something, and ask questions like, 'How can you students be so available as to join such events?' " (09-F-S)

In alignment with the notion of context collapse [39], people cannot easily adapt their self-presentation to different audiences and contexts with a single, shared information space (e.g., a Facebook wall). The multiplex networks on SNSs make it difficult for the interviewees to manage a consistent online/offline presentation. As a result, our interviewees employed other strategies, such as following the majority view or hiding their real thoughts, to respond to public event invitations to maintain their ideal self-representation on the front stage.

Social Loafing

Studies on social loafing posit that individuals reduce their group work efforts when the number of people in the group grows [13]. On a Facebook event page, the names and number of participants and invitees are disclosed. Ten interviewees mentioned that they were aware of the number of other invitees and attendees. Hence, they were less concerned about their response because they believed that no one would notice their absence and thus did not feel pressured to attend the event. The display of this information appears to result in social loafing.

"When there are only a few people, maybe just five, being invited, every decision of each individual is obvious. However, it doesn't really matter if someone clicks 'Join' or not in the event with 1,000 people invited." (01-M-S)

A large number of attendees may lead to social loafing in a form similar to slacktivism when the event concerns political movements. Social loafing may explain the difficulty of de-virtualizing such online events. People depend on others' actions without taking theirs seriously or think that their actions do not count as much when the denominator is large.

"For the recent anti-nuke demonstration, I clicked 'Join' on the event page, but just for moral support. That event did not really need my actual attendance." (22-M-S)

In other words, a perception of a large number of both *invitees* and *attendees* may trigger social loafing during the decision and action stages.

Within-Group Private Events

Based on the descriptions given by our interviewees, private events restrict information access to those who are invited. Usually, private events are held within private social groups (e.g., high school classmates, family) containing individuals who know one another and have had prior offline social interactions. A sense of social obligation among individuals may create pressure to honor their commitment to attendance. In addition, a prior relationship implies that the host has multiple ways of contacting the participants, such as phone calls, emails, or IM. Multiple ways of staying in touch may also contribute to increased levels of offline participation.

Social Obligation

For private events, both the host and the participants are usually people who meet each other offline and have an expectation of persistent future interactions, which results in a sense of social obligation and prompts more definite responses. Twelve interviewees reported that, unlike public events for which they tended to ignore invitations, they gave precise responses for private events.

"For a private event, I will indicate clearly whether I will join or not. However, for those public events, I do nothing if I won't engage." (02-M-S)

In addition to the decision stage, social obligation plays an important role at the action stage for private events. Most of our interviewees reported that they would not be absent from such events because they were worried about being blamed by the members of the social group. In other words, the expected interaction and identifiability in the group caused our interviewees to self-censor when making a decision to avoid possible social sanctions.

"In such a private event, honestly, everyone knows each other. You can't act like you did for the public events—clicking 'Join' but being a no-show. That will get you in trouble." (23-M-S)

"Like a class reunion, the participants are all my friends, and I think the host relies on the Facebook event page to do the head counts. No-shows will cause them trouble. " (30-F-S)

In comparison with public events, private events cause people to care about their decision, commitment, and action, either for their sake or for the hosts' sake.

Confirmation through Different Media

Prior relationships usually indicate that people have multiple ways of connecting to each other. Ten interviewees talked about the experience of making use of such connections to ensure participation. For example, the host can make a phone call to everyone on the "Going" list for double confirmation (if one clicks on "Join" on the event page, his/her name and photo show up on the "Going" list).

"My friends, especially very close ones, they create the Facebook events just for fun. A phone call is coming up anyway, for they think I may miss the information." (16-M-S)

In addition to Facebook events, other online communication tools are used to raise awareness of the event or to confirm attendance.

"Facebook event invitations are not completely reliable. I most likely send an instant message through both Facebook and Windows Live Messenger, even send a Line message by cellphone." (18-M-N)

"Before the event, we will open a chat room in Facebook message, and it will present who has seen the reminder message. We use it confirm that everyone has gotten the information." (07-F-S)

The event planning process does not always move from online to offline. Some interviewees noted that the reverse route produced even stronger confirmation of attendance. People proposed an event and counted who would join in advance when they met offline. As the meet-up time approached, they created a Facebook event with more details regarding time and location and other information to raise awareness and receive final confirmation.

"Facebook is like an assisting tool... I will make sure my event guarantees a certain level of attendance before I create it." (06-M-S)

"For all the private events with usually a small number of people, first, we ascertain we are going out together; then, we create Facebook events for a real confirmation of attendance." (07-F-S)

Our data show that using different communication tools to convey a message or combining online and offline communication are ways of raising people's awareness of and commitment to an event and increasing the likelihood of response and attendance.

Social Ties with Others

Regardless of whether an event is public or private, people's decisions regarding the event invitation appear to differ depending on whether it is received from a friend or an acquaintance.

"It depends on who invited you. If he/she is not so important, I will most likely click 'Maybe' or just ignore the invitation. If he/she is important or is my close friend, I am certain to reply. Moreover, for events for which I'm not sure whether I can go, I will click 'Join' and leave a comment like, 'I'm not sure if I am available that day, but I will try my best to attend' on the event page." (21-F-N)

Strong social ties entail mutual trust, which influences invitees' evaluations of the information (e.g., the number of participants) on the event page. However, even if the event is public, being invited through strong ties increases the possibility of eventual attendance.

"Today, I create an event and tag others' names, hoping they reply to the invitation. For people tagged, they can't miss my message. I just treat those who do not respond as if they are not going to join us to do the head counts. The thing is, it only works when you know all your invitees. If there is a stranger, he is the weakest link." (23-M-S)

The interviews also indicate that strong ties with the attendees are important to the host as well because these relationships help to guarantee attention to and attendance at events.

Motivating Offline Participation

Public events can lead to social loafing. However, strong social ties can be a solution to this problem. Six interviewees described how seeing other friends on the "Going" list could improve people's intentions to join a public event and their subsequent joining behaviors.

"If my close friends are on the list, I will send instant messages to ask them. If they are certain to go, okay, then I will go, too." (09-F-S)

"When I first see the (public) event, I see if my friends are going...I will ask them how the event is. If it is fun, then I will join." (23-M-S)

Because of the information that is publicly displayed on Facebook, people who know each other can form a small group and attend a public event. Offline social relationships facilitate the de-virtualization of online participation into offline participation.

"When there are thousands of people clicking 'Join', to be honest, your attendance does not matter, unless there is someone who draws you in. For example, you see your friend is on the list, and that friend you haven't met for a long time...Therefore, it's often the case that a couple of friends attend the social movement together. This helps maintain the offline attendance level." (11-M-N)

Difficulty of Declining

Social obligation derived from relationships characterized by strong ties not only encourage people to participate offline but also make it difficult for interviewees to decline an invitation because "Decline" may imply disapproval of the host or the event, as previously mentioned.

"I found that if I click 'Decline', the event holders will be disappointed because they assume that I do not want to go rather than that I have no time. Therefore, I click neither 'Join' nor 'Decline' in the end." (4-F-S)

In a way, social relationships between the host and the invitees sanction the invitees' decision. When responding, people prioritize the relationship over their interest in the event or their availability.

"For acquaintances, I click 'Decline'. For close friends, I click 'Maybe' or 'Join', but if I won't go, I make a phone call to explain why I can't go." (16-M-S)

Seven interviewees viewed the choice of "Decline" as an impolite and thoughtless behavior, especially when the event was initiated by people with whom they had strong connections. Therefore, they clicked "Join" out of courtesy, not as an indication of commitment or attendance.

"Our department created an event last afternoon, and I clicked 'Join' merely out of courtesy." (02-M-S)

An invitation through strong ties is a double-edged sword; it helps to ensure attendance but introduces uncertainty to offline attendance. Seven interviewees indicated a sense of social obligation to accept invitations although they were sure that they would not attend, allowing them to save face for the host and avoid social sanctions.

"Information on Facebook is visible to everyone, and I think it could be a problem for that...I saw my friends all clicked 'Join', and I found it embarrassing if I didn't. Then, I clicked it, but I wouldn't go." (12-M-S)

"...if he asked me to come, of course I said, 'Yes, yes, I will'. You have to support him, right? So I click 'Join', but I ultimately didn't attend." (06-M-S)

DISCUSSION

Based on the events identified in the interview transcripts, different types of online responses and actual attendance show that a gap exists between online and offline participation ("the gap," hereafter). Other recent works have identified similar results [12, 25, 35, 41]. In socio-psychological research, the association between attitude and behavior is unclear [1]. Attitudes displayed are not necessarily consistent with behaviors. Although technologies such as SNSs and CMC provide convenient tools with which people can express their support and commitment, what people say (online participation) is not necessarily equal to what they do (offline participation).

The current work explored why this gap occurs and clarifies how and why the de-virtualization of social events at the individual level may be difficult. We found that perceptions regarding interface features and communication platforms (e.g., the meanings of reply buttons on Facebook), the social nature of the event (e.g., public versus private events), and social ties (e.g., relationships to the event host and other invitees/attendees) are important factors.

The first factor in the gap is related to how people perceive the meanings of the interface features of the communication platforms used to communicate events. Surprisingly, people can attach non-literal, social meaning to response buttons (accept, decline, maybe). For example, clicking "Accept" on Facebook becomes a way to express attendance uncertainty to save face for both the host and the invitee. The selection of "Decline" expresses one's opposition to the event. Such appropriation can lead to the miscommunication of intention, especially when the invitee and the host do not share the same interpretation frameworks. It appears that people may form implicit norms regarding the social meanings of these buttons. However, because this sort of social interpretation is implicit, inconsistency in interpretations may create false expectations and inaccurate estimations of the number of actual attendees at offline social events. Current interfaces do not support the nuanced appropriation and interpretation of the choice buttons. A lack of design subtlety gives users less flexibility to express their genuine intentions online that accompany their offline behavior.

It is also interesting that the interviewees were aware of the costs associated with online event communication. The literature focuses primarily on the costs associated with offline participation and considers online participation a low-cost and low-risk activity [30]. The cost-efficiency of online participation may reduce people's interest in participating in offline activities [25]. However, event communication and arrangement involve effort from the host in addition to the invitees. With CMC and SNSs, both the cost of participation and the cost of event planning decrease. The host's lack of effort in initiating event invitations on SNSs appears to lessen invitees' evaluations of the event.

For event invitations targeted at a large audience, the invitation is easily distributed with the aid of features provided by SNSs. For example, on Facebook, little effort is required to recruit participants using features provided on the event page. When the cost of recruitment is low, invitees are unlikely to reciprocate through offline attendance; they may return a mouse click, at most.

Second, we found that people use different response strategies for public and private events. The social nature of an event has an impact on people's participation because it triggers perceptions of being part of a large crowd or a small group and indicates how identifiable the individual is in the context of the social event.

With online event invitations, information that is displayed regarding how many people plan to attend the event and these people's identities is an important cue that influences invitees' behaviors. Our interviewees reported a weaker motivation to join a public event when they knew that many people were attending. Because the cost of online participation on SNSs is low, a new form of social loafing behavior emerges in the form of an online expression of support (i.e., clicking "Join" on the Facebook event page but failing to actually attend offline). Slacktivism with regard to political events may occur for this reason. Conversely, an underestimation of the number of participants may trigger participation [27]. The perceived size of participation, either overestimation or underestimation, appears to influence individual action.

Private event invitations tend to de-virtualize social events relatively better, channeling people's online commitment to offline attendance. Consistent with work on the mobilization of online communicators [3, 32], tie strength appears to correlate with whether people will join an event. People may be more willing to attend an event when they discern that their close friends also plan to do so, suggesting that existing connections and community bonds play a role. At the same time, because people also use Facebook to sustain their relationships with people they have met offline [22], an influence of strong ties is present online. One possibility is that information disseminated via these strong ties may easily dominate one's online information processing, resulting in limited attention to weak tie-mediated event information. The mobilizing effect of event invitations mediated by weak ties may thus be further attenuated. Although we believed that interaction on SNSs may facilitate socialization and may compensate for the weakness of weak ties in the de-virtualization of social events, we did not observe cases supporting this assumption. Further design efforts may be required to support this scenario.

Relationship concerns can be a double-edged sword. Our data reveal that strong ties may promote offline participation through perceived social obligation, but it may also become difficult for people to decline events that they would not or should not attend. Although extensive research has examined the relationship between social ties and participation [3, 8, 15, 16, 33, 41], the negative side effects have received limited attention.

Impression management is another concern on SNSs because participation information is displayed to other invitees or on one's personal network. Previous studies have shown that individuals leverage SNS profiles and online group affiliation as resources to shape their online self-presentations [9, 12, 15]. Our study sheds light on how concerns about impression management interact with the content and context of events to affect people's event participation. For example, people choose to participate in or avoid certain events online or offline to maintain their image.

People can develop sophisticated strategies for event participation to meet their need for impression management, such as offline attendance at an event without an online expression of support to avoid an explicit affiliation with any stance. People also have a need to differentiate their online image for different groups of SNS contacts (e.g., family, colleagues, close friends), such as by displaying event participation information to some parties but not others.

Comparison between Invitations via Different Media

In our results, the media used and the perceived sincerity of event hosts constituted one reason for the gap between online and offline participation. Interviewees identified the differences among invitations sent via different media, such as Facebook events, instant messaging, phone, email, and face-to-face communication. Based on the evaluation of the media used, they determined whether the invitations were important enough to merit a reply. In addition, they made attendance decisions according to the perceived costs of event arrangement. Our data show that when people receive invitations through relatively personal and private media, such as face-to-face interactions, phone, or even instant messaging, they feel that the event hosts care significantly more about their attendance than they would if they used a more social and public medium, such as a Facebook invitation. They know that the event hosts have made a special effort to invite them instead of randomly selecting individuals from long lists. At the same time, social loafing is less likely to occur with offline acceptance or online instant messages because people cannot determine the number of participants, which is disclosed on SNSs, or the hosts are individuals with whom they have consistent interactions. Therefore, they make their decision more carefully and are more likely to keep their promise of offline participation. The attitude toward the event indicated by their online participation corresponds more closely to the targeted offline participation behavior [1].

Face management in SNSs corresponds closely to Brown and Levinson's study, in which people developed politeness strategies to avoid making others feel uncomfortable and to maintain others' self-esteem [6]. We found that rather than directly declining invitations in SNSs, people often employ off-the-record strategies of refusal by expressing their intentions indirectly offline or via other media (e.g., instant messaging). As one interviewee explained, she turned down a wedding invitation over the phone. She made an excuse such as, "*I am not sure if I will be available that day. Let me check my schedule*" and then called back later to apologize because she could not attend the wedding (26-F-N). This sort of complicated decision-making and communication process is reduced to the click of a button on SNSs. The interface design may make people feel that it is difficult to decline event calls; thus, they click "Join" to maintain politeness. Current SNS designs may not be able to support the intricate social protocols behind declining invitations that people practice offline.

DESIGN PROPOSALS

Based on the results, we propose a number of initial ideas for supporting people in extending their online participation to offline attendance and for better de-virtualization of social events. We believe that the design space constructed on the obtained understanding is significant and sophisticated. Therefore, our proposals are intended to demonstrate rather than to limit ways to design and redesign tools for event management and communication.

First, to increase the effectiveness of online event invitations and to encourage offline participation, it may be necessary to explicitly present the host's effort and the value of participation in the event to the invitees. For example, the SNS's interface for event creation may request that event creators provide more detailed and personal invitation messages, and the human effort of personalization must be visible to the invitees.

Another proposal involves making people feel more comfortable declining an event invitation so that invitees' online responses are less ambiguous and more reliable for event management. One respondent indicated a possible strategy: *"I click 'Join' first and then post a message to apologize that I won't attend"* (2-M-S). Instead of relying on a single button (Accept, Decline, etc.) to express a decision, clearly distinguished buttons can indicate support of the event (such as a thumbs-up) and the intention to attend. Alternatively, both the invitees and the event host could be allowed to express their intentions flexibly with open-ended, short messages. This design could also use text processing and machine learning techniques to automatically estimate the likelihood of actual attendance. In this case, machine processing could be used to aid people in maintaining the desired ambiguity.

Because people tend to loaf more in larger groups [20] and are more willing to attend private events than public ones, it may be effective to manipulate perceived group size and privacy through design. One possible design involves the transformation of public events into more private ones, such as by partitioning a loosely connected event group into multiple subgroups in which social connections among group members become relatively stronger and more private. In this way, group size decreases and the perception of privacy increases.

Because information on event participation on SNSs can influence how one is viewed and valued by other people, it may be helpful to consider the benefits and costs of displaying information on online participation (e.g., attending an event) and offline participation (e.g., a status or photo indicating physical presence) as well as the (in)consistency between the two.

LIMITATIONS

This study has two main limitations. First, because this study is an interview study, data collection is inherently connected to the properties and constraints of self-reporting. The recollection of information related to event participation through memory recall may not be completely reliable, and interesting phenomena may be missing from our interviews. However, the themes that emerged from the current transcripts appear to make a great deal of sense and have triggered useful insights. Future investigation will benefit from the use of other methods in the triangulation of our results.

Second, because our interviewees are Taiwanese living in Taiwan, the results reported may be culture-specific. Although limited clues allow for the determination of whether the perceptions, thoughts, and behaviors related to event participation identified in this work are specific to the domestic culture or are universal, it is reasonable to suggest that culture may play a role in group-related processes such as social loafing and obligation. The cross-cultural aspect is especially worth further investigation.

CONCLUSION

This paper presents an interview study intended to increase understanding of people's experience and practice handling of distributed event invitations. From these interviews, we gained a richer and deeper understanding of how people handle online event invitations, the shape of online and offline participation behaviors, and the gap between the two. We developed the notion of de-virtualization to describe social events that are developed online but that aim to provoke participation offline, and we examined why this may be a challenging task and how we can address this challenge through design.

The results reveal reasons for participation and non-participation both online and offline. The wide dissemination of e-invitations does not necessarily guarantee high participation. This study contributes to the literature by showing that social perceptions of the nature of an event (e.g., public or private), relationships to others (e.g., the strength of connections to other invitees), and the medium used to communicate event information (e.g., targeted invitation via email or spam communication via a Facebook event page) are possible key factors. Future designs may leverage these understandings to better bridge people's online and offline participation in events that require physical presence and real-world attendance.

REFERENCES

1. Ajzen, I. and Fishbein. M. Attitude-behavior relations: A theoretical analysis and review of empirical research. *Psychological bulletin 84,* 5 (1977), 888-918.
2. Brandtzæg, P. B. and Heim, J. Why people use social networking sites. *Lecture Notes in Computer Science 5621,* (2009), 143-152.
3. Bond, R. M., Fariss, C. J., Jones, J. J., Kramer, A. D. I., Marlow, C., Settle, J. E. and Fowler, J. H. A 61-million-person experiment in social influence and political mobilization. *Nature 489,* (2012), 295-298.
4. Boyd, D. and Ellison, N. Social network sites: Definition, history and scholarship. *Journal of Computer-Mediated Communication 13*, 1 (2007), 210-230.
5. Boyd, D. "Why youth (heart) social network sites: The role of networked publics in teenage social life." Youth, identity, and digital media. *Digital Media and Learning,* (2008), MA: MIT Press, 119–142.
6. Brown, P. and Levinson, S. C. Politeness: Some Universals in Language Usages. (1987), Cambridge: Cambridge University Press.
7. Clark, H. H. and Brennan S. E. Grounding in communications. *Perspectives on Socially Shared Cognition,* (1991), Washington DC: APA, 127-149.
8. Diani, M. Social Movement Networks Virtual and Real. Information. *Communication & Society 3*, 3 (2000), 386- 401.
9. Ellison, N. B., Hancock, J. T. and Toma, C. L. Profile as promise: A framework for conceptualizing veracity in online dating self-presentations. *New Media & Society 14*, 1 (2012), 45-62.
10. Ellison, N. B., Lampe, C. and Steinfield, C. Social network sites and society: Current trends and future possibilities. *Interactions 16*, 1 (2009), 6-9.
11. Ellison, N. B., Steinfield, C. and Lampe, C. The Benefits of Facebook ''Friends'': Exploring the relationship between college students' use of online social networks and social capital. *Journal of Computer-Mediated Communication 12*, 4 (2007), 1143-1168.
12. Evans-Cowley, J. S. Planning in the age of Facebook: the role of social networking in planning processes. *GeoJournal 75,* 5 (2010), 407–420.
13. Geen, R.G. Social Motivation. *Annual Review of Psychology 42,* (1991), 377-399.
14. Goffman, E. The presentation of self in everyday life. (1959), NY: Anchor Books.
15. Gustafsson, N. and Wahlström, M. Virtual mobilisation? Linking on-line and off-line political participation among Swedish Facebook users: Courtesy and irritation. *The XV NOPSA conference 2008, workshop 'Globalization as Individualization and Destabilization'.*
16. Harlow, S. Social media and social movements: Facebook and an online Guatemalan justice movement that moved offline. *New Media & Society 14,* 2 (2012), 225-243.
17. Harlow, S. and Harp, D. A cross-cultural study of social networking sites and online and offline activism in the United States and Latin America. *Information, Communication & Society 15*, 2 (2012), 196-216.
18. Hogan, B. The presentation of self in the age of social media: Distinguishing performances and exhibitions online. *Bulletin of Science Technology & Society 30*, 6 (2010), 377-386.
19. Jonassen, D. H. and Kwan II, H. Communication patterns in computer mediated versus face-to-face group problem solving. *Educational Technology Research and Development 49*, 1 (2001), 35-51.
20. Karau, S. J. and Williams, K. D. Social loafing: A meta-analytic review and theoretical integration. *Journal of Personality and Social Psychology 65,* 4 (1993), 681-706.
21. Khan, Z. and Jarvenpaa, S. L. Exploring temporal coordination of events with Facebook.com. *Journal of Information Technology 25,* (2010), 137–151.
22. Lampe, C., Ellison, N. B. and Steinfield, C. A Face(book) in the crowd: Social searching vs. social browsing. In *Proc. CSCW 2006*, ACM Press (2006), 167-170.
23. Lee, Y. -H. and Hsieh, G. Does slacktivism hurt activism?: The effects of moral balancing and consistency in online activism. In *Proc. CHI 2013*, ACM Press (2013), 1-10.
24. Marsh, C. Back on the bandwagon: The effects of opinion polls on public opinion. *British Journal of Political Science 15*, 1 (1985), 51-74.
25. McCafferty, D. Activism vs. slacktivism. *Communication of the ACM 54*, 12 (2011), 17-19.
26. Nielsen, R. K. Mundane Internet tools, mobilizing practices, and the coproduction of citizenship in political campaigns. *New Media & Society 13,* 5 (2011), 755-771.
27. Oliver, P. "If you don't do it, nobody else will": Active and token contributors to local collective action. *American Sociological Review 49,* 5 (1984), 601-610.
28. Paris, C. M., Lee, W. and Seery, P. The role of social media in promoting special events: Acceptance of Facebook 'events'. *In Proc. Information and Communication Technologies in Tourism 2010*, Springer Vienna (2010), 531-541.
29. PTT official Facebook page. https://www.facebook.com/PttTW/info
30. Rotman, D., Vieweg, S., Yardi, S., Chi, E., Preece, J., Shneiderman, B., Pirolli, P. and Glaisyer, T. From

slacktivism to activism: participatory culture in the age of social media. *Ext. Abstracts CHI 2011,* ACM Press (2011), 819-822.

31. Starbird, K. and Palen, L. (How) will the revolution be retweeted?: Information diffusion and the 2011 Egyptian uprising. In *Proc. CSCW 2012*, ACM Press (2012), 7-16.

32. Stefanone, M. A., Kwon, K. and Lackaff. D. The value of online friends: Networked resources via social network sites. *First Monday 16*, 2 (2011).

33. Teorell, J. Linking social capital to political participation: Voluntary associations and networks of recruitment in Sweden. *Scandinavian Political Studies 26*, 1 (2003), 49-66.

34. Veinott, E. S., Olson, J. S., Olson, G. M. and Fu, X. Video helps remote work: Speakers who need to negotiate common ground benefit from seeing each other. In *Proc. CHI 1999*, ACM Press (1999), 302-309.

35. Vissers, S., Hooghe, M., Stolle, D. and Mahéo, V. The impact of mobilization media on offline and online participation: Are mobilization effects medium-specific. *Social Science Computer Review 30*, 2 (2012), 152-169.

36. von Ahn, L. and Dabbish, L. Labeling images with a computer game. In *Proc. CHI 2004*, ACM Press (2004), 319-326.

37. Walther, J. B. Interpersonal effects in computer-mediated interaction: A relational perspective. *Communication research 19*, 1 (1992), 52-90.

38. Wang, H.-C., Fussell, S. R. and Setlock, L. D. Cultural difference and adaptation of communication styles in computer-mediated group brainstorming. In *Proc. CHI 2009*, ACM Press (2009), 669-678.

39. Wesch, M. YouTube and you: Experiences of self-awareness in the context collapse of the recording webcam. *Explorations in Media Ecology 8*, 2 (2010), 19-34.

40. Young, D. P. The relationship between electronic and face-to-face communication and its implication for alternative workplace strategies. *Facilities 13*, 6 (1995), 20-27.

41. Zhang, S., Jiang, H., and Carroll, J.M. Integrating online and offline community through Facebook. In *Proc. CTS 2011*, IEEE (2011), 569-578.

Awkward Encounters of an "Other" Kind: Collective Self-Presentation and Face Threat on Facebook

Eden Litt[1], Erin Spottswood[2], Jeremy Birnholtz[1], Jeff Hancock[2], Madeline E. Smith[1], Lindsay Reynolds[2]

[1] Department of Communication Studies
Northwestern University
Evanston, IL 60208

[2] Department of Communication
Cornell University
Ithaca, NY 14850

eden.litt@u.northwestern.edu, els263@cornell.edu, jeremyb@northwestern.edu, jth34@cornell.edu, madsesmith@u.northwestern.edu, llr48@cornell.edu

ABSTRACT

While we tend to think of self-presentation as a process executed by the self, reputation management on social network sites, like Facebook, is increasingly viewed as a collective endeavor. The information users share about one another can have significant impacts on impression formation, and at times this other-generated content may be face threatening, or challenging to one's desired self-presentation. However, we know little about the nature of these other-generated face threats and the ways that people perceive them. Using an online survey of 150 Facebook users, we report on what these users consider to be other-generated face threats and how they feel after experiencing them. Results suggest that many face threats result from other Facebook users neglecting or misunderstanding a target's audience and/or self-presentation goals, as well as a target's fear of creating an unwanted association with another Facebook user. Experience of these threats is affected by both individual and situational factors. We also report on a new unique measure capturing Facebook skills.

Author Keywords

Facebook; social media; audience; face; self-monitoring; face threats; privacy; skill; Facebook skills scale

ACM Classification Keywords

H.5.2 [Information Interfaces and Presentation]: User Interfaces - Interaction styles.

INTRODUCTION

As people increasingly share their life updates online, social network sites like Facebook have become online repositories of digital self-presentations. This requires vigilance about controlling access to information and active management of online presence through social strategies, like selectively posting content, in addition to technological strategies, like using privacy settings to restrict the visibility of content to certain audiences [28].

CSCW'14, February 15 – 19, 2014, Baltimore, MD, USA.

http://dx.doi.org/10.1145/2531602.2531646

While these strategies can be effective for controlling access to content users post themselves, people often have trouble understanding their audience and privacy settings on social network sites [1, 3, 25, 27]. Recent work by Bernstein and colleagues [3], for example, shows that people significantly underestimate their audience for content they post on Facebook. If this is the case for people's own posts – where they are more likely to have some awareness of their potential audience and privacy settings – the effect could be even stronger for posts about or targeted at another individual (e.g., posts on another's Facebook profile or tagged photos).

Consider the example of Alex tagging a Facebook photo of Bill at a party. Facebook's interface provides Alex with little information about Bill's privacy settings including the visibility of tagged photos, or how many and which of Bill's Facebook friends might see the photo.

Despite the prevailing focus in the social network site literature on self-presentation as an individual act, people's identities are collectively constructed [18, 33, 41]. Audiences form impressions based on a combination of content and behavior produced by both the self and others [17, 18, 41, 42]. In some cases, content generated by others can carry more weight than self-generated content in the impression formation process [41].

While people generally aim to preserve each other's positive social identity and/or autonomy during social interactions [7], sometimes others intentionally or inadvertently produce a "face threat." That is, they say or do something disharmonious with one's self-presentation [13, 17]. On Facebook and other social network sites, face threats generated by others may play an outsized role in self-presentation because others posting content about an individual (the "target") may not care about or understand the target's audience or self-presentation goals.

Research in face-to-face (FtF) contexts has explored the face-threatening situations people encounter, and the individual and situational factors that affect people's ability to manage and recover from these situations [12, 31]. While scholars have explored face threats on social network sites, they have mainly focused on information that users regret sharing about themselves [37, 43]. Comparatively, little work has focused on face threats from content generated by others, even though this content also plays a role in online identity construction.

In this study, we draw on data from an online survey of Facebook users to explore other-generated face threats. We describe the types of situations that lead to perceptions of face threats, while highlighting factors that influence the perceived severity of these threats. Our results suggest that the majority of other-generated face-threatening situations occurred because other Facebook users did not take into account the target's collapsed audiences and revealed something that a particular audience member(s) should not have seen. We also find systematic differences in how people feel after experiencing an other-generated face-threatening encounter, with factors like users' perceived Facebook skills and audience composition influencing the severity of the perceived face threat.

BACKGROUND

To better understand the nature of face threats presented by others on Facebook and how they are experienced, we explore and classify the types and origins of face-threatening scenarios, and then measure how specific individual- and situation-level factors influence people's perceptions. In this paper, we use the term "post" to refer to any content generation behavior, including commenting on or liking existing content, linking to outside content (e.g., news story, video clip, etc.), and uploading and/or tagging a photo that is viewable or accessible to people other than the poster. We use "other-generated posts" to refer to posts that affect, but are not generated by, a particular user, whom we refer to as the "target" of the post.

Types of Face Threats on Social Network Sites

Self-presentation, or impression management, "refers to the process by which individuals attempt to control the impressions others form of them" [23: 34]. Individuals selectively disclose information and alter their behaviors depending on who is in the audience, often looking to others for confirmation [18].

Though we often think of self-presentation as being carried out by the self, managing personal information and identity is a collective process [33]. On social network sites like Facebook, others contribute to self-presentations through photos, comments, likes, and tags. Posts by other users can affect one's self-presentation, sometimes even more than one's own posts [41].

Generally people attempt to preserve the face of others by behaving in ways motivated by self- and mutual-respect [17]. Examples include respecting one another's privacy and abstaining from criticizing one another publicly [2]. Despite these prevailing norms, situations sometimes occur in which people's desired self-presentation is challenged. A face threat is a verbal or non-verbal communication act that challenges a person's desired self-presentation [13, 17]. Face threats can vary in their severity and consequences [33] and can be brought on by the self (e.g., spilling a drink at a party in front of others), or by others (e.g., one person mocking another) [13].

Past research on social network sites highlights how such environments may increase the frequency of face-threatening encounters [22, 28, 30, 37, 43], and how users engage in a variety of strategies to prevent and react to face-threatening acts, including use of their privacy settings to restrict content visibility, blocking people completely, and removing content they regret sharing [28, 35, 43]. We know less, however, about how other-generated Facebook posts influence the extent to which a user experiences and manages face threats on the site.

There are two primary reasons to believe that these threats may be perceived differently than those generated by the self. First, others tend to have less information about the potential audience for a post, so they may be more likely to misjudge who will see a post or what constitutes normatively acceptable behavior for a particular audience. Relatedly, others may have a less direct interest or may be less motivated to understand another's audience or present a consistently positive image of the target.

Second, studies have suggested that people's associations with certain others (e.g., those who are more attractive, etc.) can affect impression formation [42]. Thus, the actions of others might affect the target's self-presentation simply by creating an association between the target and other or between the target and the other's behavior. We therefore asked:

RQ1: *What are the types of other-generated face-threatening situations people encounter on Facebook? How do others influence the target's self-presentation, and what is the nature of this influence?*

Face Threat Severity

After encountering face threats, people experience a range of emotions including "self-conscious, awkward, discomforted, and exposed" feelings [31: 192]. Research on face threats in FtF settings, however, suggests that people's experience and reactions to face threats vary based on both individual differences as well as situation-level factors [13, 17]. To date we know little about how these translate on social network sites.

Individual Influences on Face Threat Severity

Based on past research in FtF settings, one factor likely to affect how people experience and cope with face-threatening situations is self-monitoring. Self-monitoring describes people's level of concern for abiding by social norms and their ability to modify their self-presentation accordingly [38]. High self-monitors are individuals who strive to act in socially appropriate ways according to their perception of what their audience expects [38, 39]. Low self-monitors are more motivated by their internal thoughts and values and are less concerned with situational cues and expectations [38].

Given that high self-monitors are more attuned to their self-presentations, fitting in, and potential negative consequences of face threats, we predict they are likely to be less comfortable than low self-monitors in allowing elements of their self-presentation to be collectively constructed. We therefore predicted that:

***H1:** There will be a positive relationship between self-monitoring and perceived face threat severity; higher self-monitors will perceive other-generated posts as more face threatening.*

While self-monitoring may be an important attribute, because of the audience and privacy challenges social network sites present to users [25, 29, 40], successful self-presentation in these spaces requires technological skills in addition to social skills [19, 25]. In FtF settings a person may be able to get through a face-threatening situation by social adroitness alone [36, 38], but the same embarrassing situation on a social network site may escalate unless the person has additional skills to manage the situation [5, 21]. While Internet skills have traditionally been linked with people's positive and negative experiences online [14], as people increasingly engage in a more diverse array of activities online, users need additional skills reflective of these more nuanced activities. For example, successful self-presentation on Facebook requires knowledge and understanding of tools that allow one to post, edit, and remove content as well as alter privacy settings and control one's audience.

Both general Internet-related and Facebook-specific skills may play important roles in how people experience face-threatening encounters online. However, the relationship between these factors is hard to predict. On the one hand, higher Internet and Facebook skills may both lead to people feeling more face threat severity. People with higher Internet skills may react more strongly because they tend to have a better understanding of the way privacy functions online more generally, and they may have a better understanding of online self-presentations and the role that other-generated content can have during impression formation. Those with higher Facebook skills may also feel more face threat severity because they are more cognizant of their audience on Facebook, have more awareness of the way the site's algorithm functions, and have a better understanding of how many people might have witnessed the encounter.

On the other hand, people with higher Internet and Facebook skills may actually feel lower levels of face threat. Higher Internet skills may give users more working knowledge to remediate the situation regardless of their Facebook skills. For example, even if they don't know how to remove face-threatening content or alter their privacy settings, they may be more likely to know that these remedial solutions are even possible, or know how to search and find solutions. Likewise, higher Facebook skills, particularly those related to self-presentation, may mitigate the effects of a face-threatening situation because they offer users tangible Facebook-specific solutions.

However, it may actually be that the two skillsets function differently. For example, those with higher Internet skills may have a better conceptual understanding of face-threatening repercussions leading to more anxiety after a face-threatening post; while those with more nuanced Facebook skills may find the situation less severe because they can engage the remedial tools to manage the situation.

***RQ2:** How do perceived Internet skills impact how severely people perceive an other-generated face-threatening situation?*

***RQ3:** How do perceived Facebook skills impact how severely people perceive an other-generated face-threatening situation?*

Situational Influences on Face Threat Severity

Given the collective construction of self-presentation and identity, it is insufficient to examine only individual differences. We must also examine attributes of the situation, including the nature of the threat, the person generating the threat, and the potential audience.

One key attribute of the situation is whether the threat is perceived as deliberate or not. Goffman [17] identified a range of perceived intentions from *innocent mistakes,* where the person did not mean to embarrass the target, to *intentional offenses*, where the person deliberately aimed to embarrass the target.

As people perceive face threats by others as more intentional, we argue they will perceive them as more severe. This is because, while one might forgive or try to look past an inadvertent error, believing somebody was deliberately causing damage or embarrassment could cause pain or emotional harm [13]. We predicted:

***H2:** There will be a positive relationship between perceived intentionality and perceived severity of face threat; participants who think the other's actions were intentional will perceive the other-generated post as more face threatening.*

Another factor linked with one's experience after a face-threatening act is closeness with the other [30, 34]. FtF studies have found that the frequency of face threats tends to be lower in closer relationships because close contacts know what makes one another tick [32], and they tend to be more aware of each others' self-presentation goals. As a result, people expect their close contacts to be more sensitive to their self-presentation goals, particularly in public settings [2], including Facebook [8]. Furthermore, closer contacts' actions may carry more weight during impression formation because outsiders assume they know more about the individual. While face-threatening encounters may be less likely in close relationships with others, because of the high expectations embedded within close relationships and the potential weight their content may carry, when others produce face threats we hypothesize that:

H3: There will be a positive relationship between closeness to the other and perceived severity of face threat; participants who report being relationally closer to the other will perceive the other-generated post as more face threatening.

Audience influences on face threats

While prior literature on face threats has not explicitly discussed audience attributes, mediated environments like Facebook have brought these contextual factors to the fore. Research already finds that public face threats carry more weight and dissatisfaction than private ones [12], and face threats on social network sites are "public-by-default, private-through-effort" [6: 11].

Given that social media sites can make it difficult to segment one's audience [40], the size and diversity of one's audience may exacerbate how severe one perceives face threats to be when a faux pas occurs on these sites. For example, larger audiences may lead to more feelings of embarrassment because there are more eyes to witness the social faux pas. Similarly, an individual who experiences something embarrassing in front of a more diverse audience composed of co-workers, friends, and family members may experience the situation more severely than one who makes a faux pas visible only to friends.

H4: There will be a positive relationship between audience size and perceived severity of face threat; participants with larger contact lists will perceive the other-generated post as more face threatening.

H5: There will be a positive relationship between audience diversity and perceived severity of face threat; participants with more diversely configured contact lists will perceive the other-generated post as more face threatening.

METHOD

Participants and Procedure

Participants were recruited through flyers posted in a large Midwestern city near the lead author's university, from an online recruitment website at the second author's university, and from advertisements on Craigslist. Participants completed an anonymous online questionnaire (see Appendix for example items). As compensation, participants received a $5 gift card to their choice of Starbucks or Amazon. A total of 165 people completed the survey, but 15 of these cases were eliminated because they did not include a face threat, or did not provide usable data, resulting in N=150. Participants ranged in age from 18 to 85 (M=25, SD=9.2). They were racially diverse with just under half identifying as non-white. About three quarters (74%) were female; 61% were undergraduates and others included those working full or part time, graduate students, and those unemployed or unable to work.

Measures

General information is provided here about the study's measures. Scale items are included in the Appendix.

Face Threats and Impact

Participants were first asked via an open-response question to share a recent story about a face-threatening experience on Facebook. To measure severity of face threat, the dependent variable, participants then responded to seven 5-point Likert scale items (1= "strongly disagree" to 5= "strongly agree") developed for this study. Items included, for example, "I felt awkward" and "I felt it made me look bad." Items were averaged (Cronbach's α=0.8) to yield a severity score (M=3.9, SD=0.7).

Individual-Level Factors

Self-monitoring was measured using a scale by Lennox and Wolfe [24], which has been used in prior studies on social media [e.g., 10]. Using 13 5-point Likert scale items (same anchors as above), participants indicated agreement with items including, "I have the ability to control the way I come across to people depending on the impression I wish to give them." Items were averaged (Cronbach's α=0.8, M=3.7, SD=0.5).

To measure perceived Internet skills, we used Hargittai's [20] scale on which participants rate their familiarity with six computer- and Internet-related items, such as "PDF" and "Wiki," using a 5-point scale (1= "no understanding" to 5= "full understanding"). Items were averaged to give a composite perceived Internet skills score (Cronbach's α=0.9, M=3.4, SD=0.9).

To measure perceived Facebook skills, we created a similar but novel index in which participants rated their understanding of eight Facebook activities (e.g., untagging oneself from photos and limiting access to one's profile) with 5-point scales (same anchors). Inter-item reliability was high (Cronbach's α=0.9, M=4.4, SD=0.8) and an exploratory factor analysis revealed that all scale items loaded onto one factor, suggesting that the items (e.g., posting, editing, and removing content, as well as adjusting privacy settings) were all tapping a single dimension of Facebook skills (see Appendix).

Situation-Level Factors

To measure closeness with the "other," participants indicated how close they were on a 5-point scale anchored by "no relationship at all" to "very close" (*M*=3.4, *SD*=1.2). For the other's perceived intentionality, participants indicated agreement (on a 5-point scale) with five statements, including "his/her actions were not meant to be harmful" (reverse coded) and "his/her actions were on purpose" (Cronbach's α= 0.8, *M*=2.6, *SD*=1.0).

We measured audience size and diversity using modified versions from [40] in which we asked participants about the size of their Facebook network (e.g., "About how many total Facebook friends do you have?" and "Do your Facebook friends include any of the following groups? Check ALL that apply," with choices indicating work, social, school, family, etc.).

Participants' reported Facebook network sizes ranged from five to 3,500, averaging 655.8 friends (*SD*=569.8). This included, on average, six different categories (e.g., friends, teachers/professors, people they didn't know; see Appendix for complete list). While we recognize these may not align with who is actually in the audience, we argue that it is the perception of their audience that matters for face-threatening experiences [25]

Analysis

To analyze the face threats participants provided, two judges independently coded participants' responses using an iteratively refined version of Miller's [31] coding scheme. After the final coding scheme was established, all data were recoded. Inter-rater reliability for types of face threats was acceptable (Cohen's kappa=.73) [16]. After discussing the discrepancies among the coders and authors, an independent judge knowledgeable with face-related literature settled the remaining discrepancies.

To evaluate our hypotheses, we ran an ordinary least squares (OLS) regression with severity of face threat as the dependent variable. We included three blocks of predictor variables in the model: (1) demographics, (2) individual-level, and (3) situation-level. All independent variables were tested for multicollinearity; tolerance values ranged from .71 to .98 and VIF values ranged from 1.02 to 1.50, indicating that multicollinearity is not a concern [11] (see Table 2).

RESULTS

Overall, people shared a range of stories from minor situations, such as friends posting photos in which the target looked unattractive, to crises with social and emotional consequences like trouble at school or work.

Types of Other-Generated Facebook Face Threats

To highlight the collective self-presentation process and others' influence on self-presentation (RQ1), we explore the face threat examples participants provided. Our results suggest four primary types of other-generated face threats: norm violations, ideal self-presentation violations, association effects, and aggregate effects (see Table 1 for more details on the categories and their frequencies).

Norm Violations

As Goffman [17] noted, behavioral norms are dependent on context and audience, and people use a range of cues to determine acceptable behavior. In the privacy of their own homes or in the company of close friends, for example, people may engage in behavior that would be considered inappropriate or counter-normative in public or with varying audiences.

While participants shared stories in which others had revealed their counter-normative public behavior (such as exposing the target hurting someone else or picking food out of their teeth), this only happened in a small percentage of stories submitted (6%), such as in the example below from a 22-year-old female:

I have a picture that was recently tagged to me on Facbeook [sic]. Unfortunately it is an unattractive picture where I am picking food out of my teeth. This is an embarrassing and unflattering picture that I would not like to be on spread across the internet.

The relative lack of stories regarding publicly inappropriate behavior is likely because politeness and pro-social behavior typically discourage exposing one another's private behavior. Instead, the overwhelming majority of norm violation stories submitted (39.3%) showcased others exposing the target engaged in behavior that was normatively acceptable to one sub-audience on Facebook, but counter-normative to another.

One attribute of Facebook that makes it particularly easy to present an inadvertent face threat is that the system provides few cues about the potential audience for a post, particularly those involving somebody else. While the targets may be aware of their privacy settings and the diversity of their friend networks, others are often not aware of these parameters when they post content involving the targets. This is particularly challenging for users who have diverse audiences spanning groups with varying norms or standards.

While the targets may have wanted to engage in selective self-presentation with these various audiences, or not even share the information on Facebook at all because of their audience diversity, others did not always take such collapsed audiences into account. This could be because they were unmotivated or unaware of these preferences and/or audiences. The content of these posts ranged from inadvertently sharing unflattering photos with the target's crush to exposing an individual's lie. As a 20-year-old female described:

I went to a concert with a friend. I had to miss a mandatory meeting to be there, so I blocked all the friends who were going to the meeting from my excited status abou [sic] the concert. The friend I was going with didn't know I wasn't supposed to be going so tagged me in a status saying I was at the venue. My meeting friends found out and were super angry. If he didn't post his status, I wouldn't have gotten in trouble.

In another example, a 21-year-old female discussed a post by her boyfriend that she didn't want certain people to see:

I felt uncomfortable when my boyfriend posted an article about condoms on my facebook wall... my mom reads my Facebook, and I didn't want her to see that (even though she knows we are sexually active).

Many of these norm-violating stories involved alcohol. As one 20-year-old male shared:

Someone posted a picture of me at a party where I was obviously intoxicated. My friends and family are friends with me on facebook and probably wouldn't condone such behavior. Also, I don't want any future employers to see that image an [sic] get the wrong idea of who I am and what I do.

While being drunk at a party was normative for this young adult, the person worried about how his overall audience, which also included other friends, family, and potential future employers, might form negative impressions based on these behaviors.

These stories highlight how the risks around counter-normative social behavior are distributed differently on Facebook. Where poor judgment (and poor behavior) in FtF situations typically has negative consequences primarily for the person engaging in the behavior, poor judgment in posting content by others can have serious consequences for the target. That is, there is an asymmetry in consequences between poster and target. This is true in cases where the target is acting acceptably in context (such as merely attending a concert, as in the example above, where others might reasonably not know that the behavior is intended to be protected from certain audience members) and for those where the target might more clearly expect others present to protect his/her privacy (as in the teeth-picking example, where revealing the behavior is likely embarrassing in most audiences).

Ideal Self-Presentation Violations

While self-presentation on Facebook is a collective process as described above, it is also the case that others may not be as sensitive as the targets to concerns about their desired self-presentation. Others may be more interested, for example, in their own self-presentation or with sharing images of the target in a particular place or setting, with less regard for whether the posted content is consistent with the target's ideal self-presentation.

The second most common type of other-generated face-threatening situation (28.7%) occurred when others shared something about the targets that detracted from their ideal self-presentation. These were situations that would have happened regardless of who was in the audience; the targets likely did not want *anyone* to form impressions based on the shared content.

While the targets were not engaging in what others would consider counter-normative behavior in the posted content, they were not meeting their own personal self-presentation ideals. The majority of these were simply unflattering photos. As a 33-year-old female explained:

...I was a bridesmaid in a wedding, so I was the subject of many photos. One photograph of me was particularly unflattering. My head was turned a certain way, so I looked like I had an enormous double-chin [sic]. I was

	Definition	%	Example
Norm Violations	The target worries about self-presentation because the other posts content showcasing the target engaged in norm-violating behavior (whether toward a public and/or sub-audience).	45.3	*My friend posted a picture of me doing hookah once. even though it is legal, i did not want my family on facebook to see me smoking, so i asked my friend to un-tag me from the picture, which she did.*
Ideal Self-Presentation Violations	The target is concerned about self-presentation because the other's content is disharmonious with his/her ideal self-presentation (even though the content refers to normative behaviors).	28.7	*My friend posted a really unattractive picture of me that I did not want other people to see.*
Association Effects	The target worries about self-presentation because of another's self-presentation. The posting does not directly involve the target, but he/she worries that others will negatively judge him/her because of the other's behaviors.	21.3	*One time a friend posted a link to an image that she thought was funny on my wall...I was slightly embarrassed because I did not find the image funny and I was worried about how my other Facebook friends would think of me for having the link on my wall. I did not want my other Facebook friends to think that I was the type of person to find the image funny. In the end, I hid the link.*
Aggregate Effects	The target becomes self-conscious about self-presentation because another's posting draws attention to it.	4.7	*A friend of mine commented on a picture I forgot I had posted of me with my ex boyfriend and it showed in the newsfeed.*

Table 1. Types of other-generated face threats.

already insecure about my weight gain, but this photo made me look even larger than I actually am.

As this example shows, the target was sensitive about her appearance in ways that the poster may not have been aware of or did not realize. What is unique about this scenario, in contrast to the norm violations described above, is that the audience may not have even noticed the unflattering photo or information. It is only the presence of the information, discovered or not, that is needed for the face threat to be perceived.

Association Effects

It is well known that the company people keep can affect others' impressions of them [42]. The third most common face-threatening scenario (21.3%) reported was when others had engaged in behavior or shared content that did not directly involve the target, but was face threatening because the target did not want his or her audience to form impressions based on the other's posting. For instance, a 25-year-old female shared the following:

*Someone posted a link to a video about wealth inequality on my facebook wall (and about occupy), thinking I would be interested and have a similar critique of politics in the US. It was awkward because I didn't want people to think I was still involved in occupy and the whole *get money out of politics* thing. My political critique is definitely anarchist, not liberal, and I felt awkward being pegged as something different than what I am.*

This example illustrates political views, but the same could happen with any behavior where there is variation in norms across social settings. People fear that others' judgment around norms can have consequences for them, even in cases where the target has engaged in no questionable behaviors. In another instance, a 51-year-old female shared how another's post might influence the way people perceive her:

I am a person in recovery and have been for decades, I only post positive inspirational stuff that is uplifing [sic] and will never post anything political and stay away from religous [sic] posts...Forinstance [sic], I had someone post a Marajuana [sic] leaf and other subjects about illegal substances. I deleted it, unfriended them and even apologized to anyone that may have seen it as I don't want anyone to get the wrong impression and assume I may have backslid.

While the target did not engage in any counter-normative behavior, she still feared that this content might impact her self-presentation.

Aggregate Effects

As a service that broadcasts user behavior and allows people to comment on and share their own and others' content, others' behavior on Facebook can significantly alter the visibility of one's self-presentation. A photo of the target, for example, that is repeatedly "liked" or commented on might show up in many people's News Feeds and receive additional attention [9]. This highlights another challenge to self-presentation on Facebook. Others' behavior can draw unwanted attention to otherwise mundane or dated content in ways that people fear can affect impression formation.

This last type of other-generated face threat, reported in 4.7% of cases, described when participants felt embarrassed because of extra attention paid to them. The shared information did not display the person engaged in counter-normative or unflattering behavior, but additional viewing of the content or knowledge that it was being broadcasted in the News Feed led to feelings of face threat. A 20-year-old female summed this up:

I recently wrote an endorsement for a student group candidate, and attached a photo of myself to it on a website. Pretty soon, to my embarrassment people were commenting on my photo on my Facebook wall, noting how nice it looked, but to a point where the attention made me uncomfortable.

This example highlights that even simple behavior by multiple others acting independently – such as commenting or liking – can have significant effects in the aggregate. The others in this case likely felt that they were being polite and flattering in responding positively to the photo, and had no idea that their behaviors were contributing to an aggregation that became embarrassing.

All of these categories and examples highlight how self-presentation on Facebook is collectively constructed, and others' behavior can affect self-presentation. These sometimes result from errors in audience judgment, neglect of others' self-presentation goals, but they can also result from simple aggregations or broadcasts of otherwise polite and innocuous behaviors. In the next section we turn to understanding how people interpret and experience these situations.

Effects on Face Threat Severity

Our next research questions and hypotheses asked about factors that affect how people experience face threats on Facebook. Table 3 contains the OLS model described above, with face threat severity as the dependent variable. In Model 1 we tested for effects of demographic factors including gender and age, but neither value nor the overall initial model was significant, $F(2,142) = .30, p = 0.74$.

Individual-Level Factors

In Model 2, we included the individual-level factors leading to a significant increase in R^2, to 0.20, $F(5,139) = 6.74, p < 0.001$.

We first examined self-monitoring, which H1 predicted would have a positive relationship with face threat severity. As Table 3 shows, the data support this hypothesis ($\beta = .38, p < .001$). This suggests that those with higher self-monitoring levels will feel more emotion

	Gender	Age	Self-Monitoring	Perceived Internet Skill	Perceived Facebook Skill	Closeness with Other	Other Perceived Intentionality	Audience Diversity	Audience Size
Age	-0.13	——							
Self-monitoring	0.16*	-0.09	——						
Perceived Internet Skill	-0.21**	0.04	0.16*	——					
Perceived Facebook Skill	0.13	-0.37**	0.32**	0.28**	——				
Closeness with Other	0.11	-0.09	0.13	-0.06	0.06	——			
Other Perceived Intentionality	-0.23**	0.10	-0.03	0.07	0.00	-0.15	——		
Audience Diversity	0.00	-0.15	0.17*	0.15	0.09	0.04	0.05	——	
Audience Size	-0.05	-0.27**	0.03	0.00	0.23**	-0.05	0.12	0.20*	——
Time Since Situation	0.18*	-0.15	-0.01	-0.15	-0.08	0.21**	-0.16	0.15	0.06

Notes: * p < .05, ** p < .01. Two-Tailed.

Table 2. Correlation matrix of predictor variables.

when they encounter an other-generated Facebook threat. This may be because the very identity that they work so hard to craft and monitor is at stake. Because high self-monitors tend to modify their self-presentation based on their audience, they may find spaces like social network sites particularly stressful because they must present in spaces that collapse the very social contexts on which they rely.

In response to RQ2 about perceived general Internet skills, Table 3 shows there was a positive relationship with perceived severity. Those with more perceived general Internet skills may feel more at risk because they may be more cognizant of the collective self-presentation process and understand that other-generated information may pose a threat to their offline reputation. For example, many scenarios participants provided highlighted users being concerned that future employers might form impressions based on the face-threatening post.

Interestingly, perceived Facebook skills had a different effect. In response to RQ3, there was a negative relationship between perceived Facebook skills and face threat severity. This finding suggests that feeling that one knows more about Facebook's features may reduce the severity of face threat. Perceived Facebook skills may ameliorate the feeling of face threat because skilled users know how to resolve the situation (e.g., make the face-threatening content disappear), and/or prevent it from worsening.

Situation-Level Factors

In Model 3, we include the situation-level factors leading to another statistically significant increase in R^2, to 0.34 $F(10, 134) = 6.93$, $p < 0.001$. Even while controlling for these additional factors, all three individual-level factors remain significant with similar relationships to Model 2.

H2 predicted a positive relationship between severity and participants' perceptions of the others' intentionality. Consistent with this hypothesis, participants perceived the situation more severely if they felt the other more intentionally embarrassed them, even when controlling for the other factors in the model.

Next, H3 predicted a positive relationship between relational closeness to the other and perceived severity. However, we do not find support for H3. There was no evidence that the closeness between two individuals relates to face threat severity. These results may in part be because the variable was slightly negatively skewed.

H4 predicted a positive relationship between audience size and perceived face threat severity. The data did not

Model	1	2	3
Demographic			
Gender	0.03	0.05	0.14
Age	-0.05	-0.11	-0.13
Individual-level			
Self-monitoring		0.38***	0.35***
Perceived Internet skill		0.23**	0.19*
Perceived Facebook skill		-0.23*	-0.28**
Situation-level			
Perceived Closeness			0.00
Perceived intentionality			0.26**
Audience diversity			0.17*
Audience size			0.09
Time since situation			-0.18*
R^2	0.00	0.20***	0.34***

Notes: * p < .05, ** p < .01, *** p < .001. All values are standardized β coefficients.

Table 3. OLS regression models showing effects on perceived severity of face threat.

support H4. Participants' reported audience size did not influence perceived severity. In interpreting this result, it bears mentioning that most participants reported a relatively large number of Facebook friends such that even a "small" audience among our participants may be just as face threatening as a larger one.

H5 predicted a positive relationship between audience diversity and severity. There is support for H5. Diversity of participants' Facebook audience influenced their perception of face threat severity, with those having more diverse audiences (i.e., the more types of people users have in their audience) reporting higher levels of severity. Given the findings regarding audience size, the number of people witnessing the situation seems to be less consequential than to which groups a particular face threat might be visible.

This is consistent with our qualitative evidence presented earlier in which participants experienced face threats due to information shared with an inappropriate sub-audience, and builds on this finding by suggesting that increasing diversity in the audience means increased face threat severity.

DISCUSSION

Theoretical Implications

While we tend to emphasize the 'self' when thinking about and researching self-presentation, our study highlights that *others* can influence and pose challenges to our self-presentation goals on social network sites like Facebook. While others influence self-presentation and threaten face in a range of situations, our results showcase unique attributes of social network sites that can make this particularly challenging.

Audience Matters

A clear theme in our results was the role of audience. Many threats to individuals' online presence stemmed from people's (in)ability or lack of care in judging the potential audience for a post and its effects. While this may be true of individuals posting content to their own audiences [1, 3], this seems particularly true when someone else posts something—likely because others have even fewer audience cues, and may be attending to their own self-presentation goals and audiences. The majority of other-generated face threats described by our participants occurred primarily because others had difficulty navigating and/or lacked motivation in understanding the targets' diverse audiences. They often shared information about the target that may have been normative in one context or with one audience, but violated another audience's expectations (both of whom were in the same overall Facebook audience). Not knowing who is in the potential audience for a post or the norms for different groups in an audience makes it particularly difficult to know whether or not shared content is likely to present a face-threatening scenario. This resulted in many frustrating or difficult experiences for our participants, who then had to deal with the face threat consequences.

The quantitative results also reflected aspects of audience concerns. While audience size did not affect face threat severity, the diversity of the audience did have a positive relationship with severity. People with more groups represented in their Facebook networks experienced face threats as more severe, thus suggesting that information crossing group boundaries is potentially an ongoing and stressful issue.

Collective Self-Presentation is Complex

Another clear theme in our results was that even sharing socially appropriate information could be perceived as face threatening, such as when others' shared content goes against a person's ideal self-presentation. However, perhaps the most interesting cases of this occurred when others interacted with otherwise innocuous content (such as "liking" or adding harmless comments) that eventually garnered extra attention in people's News Feeds leading to an inadvertent face threat because of the increased visibility [9]. Individuals felt a similar sense of embarrassment when a post drew attention because another's presence created an unwanted association. Targets were concerned that people would form impressions based on others' self-presentations. This echoes the warranting principle [41], and leaves open the question of whether these concerns are borne out in actual negative impressions.

These cases highlight how collective self-presentation on Facebook can extend well beyond notions of context collapse explored in prior work [4, 29]. In these examples, the visibility of certain behaviors begets further visibility of both individuals and content; and this can have unpredictable consequences for impression formation. This suggests a need to reconsider notions of collective self-presentation in light of this complexity.

Skills Matter

While all participants reported face threats they had experienced recently, our results suggest that some individuals are more concerned about collective self-presentation and other-generated face threats than others. As might be expected, higher self-monitors reported more severe face threats. Since many of participants' reported situations revolved around norm violations and audience awareness, it is understandable that people who are more concerned with social appropriateness would interpret these situations with more affect [10, 38, 39].

Perhaps more importantly, people's perceived general Internet and more specific Facebook skills impacted their experience of face threats even when controlling for this social skill. However, these technological skillsets seemed to function in different ways. General Internet skills seemed to tap into participants' understanding of the importance of their online presence; those with more Internet skills perceived face threats more emotionally, likely because they understood the potential reputational harm that could come from the threat [5, 21, 26].

Facebook skills, however, seemed to play a remediating role for participants. Those who perceived a better understanding of Facebook's features, including those needed for self-presentation management, likely felt less face threat after an encounter because they knew how to use the technology to ameliorate the situation. These results highlight the importance of both general and more nuanced skills, and the need for more studies capturing users' technological skills. We have developed and tested the novel perceived Facebook skills measure used in this study in hopes that other scholars will use it in future Facebook-related research.

Design Implications

In contrast to the prevailing focus on self-presentation and privacy management as individual activities, we urge designers to consider these acts as collective processes.

Following from our consideration of audience and others' frequent audience inconsideration, one possibility would be a feature that provides potential audience cues for a particular post. For example, an audience cue feature might allow a poster to see a post's potential visibility (in terms of the target's selected groups and privacy settings). Another feature might allow others to restrict posts involving the target to certain individuals or groups already configured by the target. Designers may also want to consider tools that allow users to anonymously suggest content be removed to other users, taking some of the pressure off the face-threatened individual.

Given that perceived Facebook-specific skill relates to a person's face-threatening experience, part of the issue may be that users are not aware of existing tools or do not know how to use them. Half of the participants reported the face-threatening content is still visible to at least some of their network contacts—future work should investigate why. Other researchers have suggested incorporating "privacy nudges" that could alert users when they are about to post something that may be face threatening to themselves or others (e.g., images with alcohol) [37, 43].

Building on the idea of privacy nudges, we also have suggestions for the complex situations of aggregation and association effects. Sites have detailed logs of content that are regularly used to increase the visibility of certain content or people. In the interest of helping users avoid the face threats described here, designers could use this information to decrease visibility. A post from a long-lost relative, for example, might trigger a "Somebody new is posting on your Timeline. Make this visible to everybody?" message. Similarly, a photo getting a lot of attention could prompt a message such as "Your friends like this photo. Is it ok to show it to more of them?"

Limitations and Future Directions

There are a few limitations to consider in interpreting these results. While our sample was diverse in some respects, it had a disproportionate number of females and undergraduate students. It is worth noting however, that young adults tend be some of the most common and active users on the site [15]. Given that we collapsed different types of posts (e.g., comments, likes, photos etc.), these results may not capture important differences linked with the posting format that future research will need to explore. Furthermore, our data are correlational and self-reported indicating they may contain biases due to social desirability effects and memory recall issues. Additionally, it is worth reiterating that many of the variables used in this study focused on participants' perceptions (e.g., Internet skills and/or others' intentionality), which may not reflect users' actual experiences and may have been influenced by the participants' current mental state. Future experimental work can strengthen these results.

Future research may also wish to explore how people take specific actions to resolve face-threatening acts and the extent to which these mitigation processes are collective versus individual. For example, when do users untag and/or remove the content? When does a person confront the other? While these findings provide foundational work on collective self-presentation and face-threatening experiences in networked environments, there are many more questions to be answered.

ACKNOWLEDGMENTS

This work is supported in part by the National Science Foundation (IIS-0915081 and DGE-0824162). We acknowledge research assistance from Anne Oeldorf-Hirsch, Grace Rojek, Anita Gallant, and Jessie Taft, as well as invaluable insights from two anonymous reviewers and the Associate Chair.

REFERENCES

1. Acquisti, A. and Gross, R. Imagined communities: Awareness, information sharing, and privacy on the Facebook. In *Proc. Privacy Enhancing Technologies Workshop* (2006), 36-58.
2. Argyle, M. and Henderson, M. The rules of friendship. *Journal of Social and Personal Relationships*, 1, 2 (1984), 211-237.
3. Bernstein, M. S., Bakshy, E., Burke, M. and Karrer, B. Quantifying the invisible audience in social networks. In *Proc. CHI* (2013), 21-30.
4. boyd, d. Social network sites as networked publics: Affordances, dynamics, and implications. In Z. Papacharissi, ed. *Networked self: Identity, community, and culture on social network sites.* Routledge, New York, 2010.
5. boyd, d. and Hargittai, E. Facebook privacy settings: Who cares? *First Monday*, 15, 8 (2010).

6. boyd, d. and Marwick, A. Social privacy in networked publics: Teens' attitudes, practices, and strategies. In *Proc. A Decade in Internet Time: Symposium on the Dynamics of the Internet and Society,* 2011.

7. Brown, P. and Levinson, S. C. *Politeness: Some universals in language usage*. Cambridge University Press, Cambridge, 1987.

8. Bryant, E. M. and Marmo, J. The rules of Facebook friendship: A two-stage examination of interaction rules in close, casual, and acquaintance friendships. *Journal of Social and Personal Relationships*, 29, 8 (2012), 1013-1035.

9. Bucher, T. Want to be on the top? Algorithmic power and the threat of invisibility on Facebook. *New Media & Society*, 14, 7 (2012), 1164-1180.

10. Child, J. T. and Agyeman-Budu, E. A. Blogging privacy management rule development: The impact of self-monitoring skills, concern for appropriateness, and blogging frequency. *Computers in Human Behavior*, 26, 5 (2010), 957-963.

11. Cohen, J., Cohen, P., West, S. G. and Aiken, L. S. *Applied multiple regression/correlation analysis for the behavioral sciences*. Lawrence Erlbaum Associates, London, 2003.

12. Cupach, W. R. and Carson, C. L. Characteristics and consequences of interpersonal complaints associated with perceived face threat. *Journal of Social and Personal Relationships*, 19, 4 (2002), 443-462.

13. Cupach, W. R. and Metts, S. *Facework*. Sage Publications, Thousand Oaks, CA, 1994.

14. DiMaggio, P., Hargittai, E., Celeste, C. and Shafer, S. Digital inequality: From unequal access to differentiated use. In K. Neckerman, ed. *Social Inequality*. Russell Sage Foundation, New York, NY, 2004.

15. Duggan, M. and Brenner, J. *The demographics of social media users — 2012*. Pew Internet & American Life Project, 2013.

16. Fleiss, J. L. Measuring nominal scale agreement among many raters. *Psychological Bulletin*, 76, 5 (1971), 378–382.

17. Goffman, E. *Interaction ritual: Essays in face-to-face behavior*. Transaction Publishers, New Brunswick, NJ, 1967.

18. Goffman, E. *The Presentation of Self in Everyday Life*. Doubleday, New York, 1959.

19. Hargittai, E. Digital na(t)ives? Variation in Internet skills and uses among members of the "Net Generation". *Sociological Inquiry*, 80, 1 (2010), 92-113.

20. Hargittai, E. and Hsieh, Y. P. Succinct survey measures of Web-use skills. *Social Science Computer Review*, 30, 1 (2012), 95-107.

21. Hargittai, E. and Litt, E. New strategies for employment? Internet skills and online privacy practices during people's job search. *IEEE Security & Privacy*, 11, 3 (2013), 38-45.

22. Lampe, C., Ellison, N. B. and Steinfield, C. Changes in use and perception of Facebook. In *Proc. CSCW* (2008), 721-730.

23. Leary, M. R. and Kowalski, R. M. Impression management: A literature review and two-component model. *Psychological Bulletin*, 107, 1 (1990), 34-47.

24. Lennox, R. D. and Wolfe, R. N. Revision of the Self-Monitoring Scale. *Journal of Personality and Social Psychology*, 46, 6 (1984), 1349-1364.

25. Litt, E. Knock, knock. Who's there? The imagined audience. *Journal of Broadcasting & Electronic Media*, 56, 3 (2012), 330-345.

26. Litt, E. Understanding social network site users' privacy tool use. *Computers in Human Behavior*, 29, 4 (2013), 1649–1656.

27. Liu, Y., Gummadi, K. P., Krishnamurthy, B. and Mislove, A. Analyzing Facebook privacy settings: User expectations vs. reality. In *Proc. Internet Measurement Conference* (2011), 61-70.

28. Madden, M. and Smith, A. *Reputation management and social media: How people monitor their identity and search for others online*. Pew Internet & American Life Project, Washington, D.C., 2010.

29. Marwick, A. and boyd, d. I tweet honestly, I tweet passionately: Twitter users, context collapse, and the imagined audience. *New Media & Society,* 13, 1 (2011), 114–133.

30. McLaughlin, C. and Vitak, J. Norm evolution and violation on Facebook. *New Media & Society*, 14, 2 (2012), 299-315.

31. Miller, R. S. The nature and severity of self-reported embarrassing circumstances. *Personality and Social Psychology Bulletin*, 18, 2 (1992), 190-198.

32. Mills, J. and Clark, M. S. Exchange and communal relationships. *Review of Personality and Social Psychology*, 3 (1982), 121-144.

33. Petronio, S. *Boundaries of privacy: Dialectics of disclosure*. State University of New York Press, Albany, NY, 2002.

34. Petronio, S., Olson, C. and Dollar, N. Privacy issues in relational embarrassment: Impact on relational quality and communication satisfaction. *Communication Research Reports*, 6, 1 (1989), 21-27.

35. Raynes-Goldie, K. Aliases, creeping, and wall cleaning: Understanding privacy in the age of Facebook. *First Monday*, 15, 1 (2010).

36. Schlenker, B. R. *Impression management: The self-concept, social identity, and interpersonal relations.*

Brooks/Cole Publishing Company, Monterey, CA, 1980.

37. Sleeper, M., Cranshaw, J., Kelley, P., Ur, B., Acquisti, A., Cranor, L. and Sadeh, N. "I read my Twitter the next morning and was astonished": A conversational perspective on Twitter regrets. In *Proc. CHI* (2013), 3277-3286.

38. Snyder, M. Self-monitoring of expressive behavior. *Journal of Personality and Social Psychology*, 30, 4 (1974), 526-537.

39. Turnley, W. H. and Bolino, M. C. Achieving desired images while avoiding undesired images: Exploring the role of self-monitoring in impression management. *Journal of Applied Psychology*, 86, 2 (2001), 351.

40. Vitak, J. The impact of context collapse and privacy on social network site disclosures. *Journal of Broadcasting & Electronic Media*, 56, 4 (2012), 451-470.

41. Walther, J. B., Heide, B. V. D., Hamel, L. M. and Shulman, H. C. Self-generated versus other-generated statements and impressions using computer-mediated communication: A test of warranting theory using Facebook. *Communication Research*, 36, 2 (2009), 229-253.

42. Walther, J. B., Van Der Heide, B., Kim, S., Westerman, D. and Tom Tong, S. The role of friends' appearance and behavior on evaluations of individuals on Facebook: Are we known by the company we keep? *Human Communication Research*, 34 (2008), 18-49.

43. Wang, Y., Norcie, G., Komanduri, S., Acquisti, A., Leon, P. G. and Cranor, L. F. I regretted the minute I pressed share: A qualitative study of regrets on Facebook. In *Proc. SOUPS* (2011), Article 10, 16 pages.

APPENDIX

Severity of face threat scale

How did the post make you feel? Please indicate how much you agree or disagree with the following statements.

1. I felt awkward.
2. I felt embarrassed.
3. I felt uncomfortable.
4. I felt flustered.
5. I felt uneasy.
6. I felt exposed.
7. I felt it made me look bad.

Response options: Strongly Disagree, Disagree, Neither Agree nor Disagree, Agree, Strongly Agree

Facebook skill

Generally speaking, how well do you know how to do the following activities on Facebook? Please indicate your understanding of the following Facebook activities.

1. Posting a status update
2. Tagging a photo
3. Editing a posted comment
4. Untagging yourself from a photo
5. Deleting a post from your profile
6. Deleting a posted photo
7. Hiding a post on your profile
8. Limiting access to view your profile

Response options: No understanding, Little, Some, Good, Full understanding

Perceived closeness

How close were you to this person prior to this embarrassing incident?

Response options: No relationship at all, Not close, Somewhat close, Close, Very close

Perceived intentionality

The following questions are about the person who posted the embarrassing content on Facebook. Please indicate the extent to which you agree or disagree with each of the following statements.

Thinking about the person who embarrassed you, would you say that…

1. …his/her actions were not meant to be harmful.
2. …his/her actions were rude.
3. …his/her actions were insensitive.
4. …his/her actions showed disrespect towards me.
5. …his/her actions were on purpose.

Response options: Strongly Disagree, Disagree, Neither Agree nor Disagree, Agree, Strongly Agree

Facebook audience size

About how many total Facebook Friends do you have? If you're not sure, take your best guess. [Open-ended]

Facebook audience diversity

Do your Facebook friends include any of the following groups? Check ALL that apply.

1. Boyfriend/Girlfriend/Spouse
2. Friends
3. Acquaintances
4. Family members
5. Classmates (Current or former)
6. Teachers/Professors (Current or former)
7. Co-workers/Colleagues/Clients (Current or former)
8. Boss/Manager (Current or former)
9. Potential employers/Recruiters
10. People I don't know
11. Other

"You Can't Block People Offline": Examining How Facebook's Affordances Shape the Disclosure Process

Jessica Vitak
College of Information Studies
University of Maryland
4105 Hornbake Bldg, South Wing
College Park, MD 20742
jvitak@umd.edu

Jinyoung Kim
College of Information Studies
University of Maryland
4105 Hornbake Bldg, South Wing
College Park, MD 20742
jkim0204@umd.edu

ABSTRACT
Guided by the underlying question of how—if at all—the self-disclosure process varies online, the present study explores the self-disclosure practices of 26 American graduate students on Facebook through in-depth interviews. Building on work by Derlega and Grzelak [12] on self-disclosure goals and focusing on the affordances of the site, findings reveal both commonalities with and extensions to existing communication research on self-disclosure, as users saw both benefits and drawbacks to the high visibility and persistence of content shared through the site. Furthermore, users employed a wide spectrum of strategies to help them achieve their disclosure goals while decreasing perceived risks associated with making disclosures in a public forum. Importantly, these strategies generally sought to recreate the offline boundaries blurred or removed by the technical structure of the site and allow users to engage in a more strategic disclosure process with their network.

Author Keywords
Privacy; self-disclosure; impression management; social network sites; Facebook; context collapse

ACM Classification Keywords
H.5.3. Group and Organization Interfaces – Web-based Interaction

INTRODUCTION
Social network sites (SNSs) continue to become an increasingly embedded part of daily life for the average Internet user, with recent Pew Internet data showing that 72% of all online American adults maintain a profile on a site like Facebook [7]. These sites are distinguished from other communication technologies in that users can (1) create profiles containing user-, other-, and system-provided data; (2) articulate a list of connections (e.g., Facebook "Friends"); and (3) consume, produce, and interact with user-generated content [13]. Furthermore, SNSs are distinguished from other forms of media by containing a number of unique affordances, including the visibility and persistence of content, the association of connections, and the editability of content [33], which researchers have argued lower the costs to interacting with and maintaining a large network of connections.

Self-disclosure—the process through which we share information about ourselves with others—is central to many people's use of SNSs. For example, among American adult Facebook users, 44% update their status at least weekly (15% daily), while 53% of users comment on a Friend's status (21% daily), and 48% comment on a Friend's photo at least weekly (20% daily) [17]. As with their disclosures and interactions in other settings, SNS users must balance disclosure-based goals (e.g., increasing intimacy, relieving distress) with a variety of potential risks (e.g., hurt feelings, reduced integrity). On Facebook, the most popular SNS, users' disclosures are typically visible to most—if not all—of their Friend network. To mitigate the tensions between disclosure goals and risks, users may employ a variety of system-based and behavioral strategies that both take into consideration SNSs' affordances and take advantage of the various features available on the site.

The following paper presents results from a qualitative study of Facebook users to gain a deeper understanding of technology's impact on the disclosure process by focusing on users' self-identified goals and risks, a traditional approach to studying disclosures [12, 23]. However, the present study extends this research to SNSs to consider the role that the sites' affordances may play in shaping the disclosure process and creating a different interaction experience as communication moves from a dyadic to group or *masspersonal* setting. In addition, the study presents a set of strategies participants reported engaging in as part of their disclosure process on Facebook, many of which emerged as a direct result of the site's affordances and most of which were employed to enable them to achieve specific self-disclosure goals while minimizing the risks associated with those disclosures. Overall, the participants' narratives highlight an often-complex thought process behind disclosing personal information on SNSs, involving many of the same goals and risks that people associate with traditional communication practices, but with both more and less control of distribution of information.

CSCW'14, February 15–19, 2014, Baltimore, Maryland, USA.
Copyright © 2014 ACM 978-1-4503-2540-0/14/02...$15.00.
http://dx.doi.org/10.1145/2531602.2531672

These findings offer important insights into communication theory as it continues to expand into the realm of computer-mediated communication.

SELF-DISCLOSURES, ON- AND OFFLINE

Historically, self-disclosure has been defined as a process of dyadic communication in which an individual shares personal information with another [11, 38]. This process is essential to the relationship formation and maintenance process, as increased disclosures between relational partners leads to increased relational closeness [2]. Self-disclosure via verbal communication has been examined by numerous researchers over the last half century (e.g., [2, 23, 38], focusing on both the characteristics of disclosures as well as the process through which individuals make decisions regarding what and with whom they should share.

With the rise and increasing popularity of social media, disclosure practices have shifted in several important ways, most notably that users of these sites, by default, make disclosures to a wide audience rather than in a dyadic or small group setting. Furthermore, these sites contain a number of affordances—including visibility, editability, and persistence of content and association of connections [33]—that shape interactions and disclosure behaviors. These factors have significant implications for communication theories related to self-disclosure and relationship maintenance.

A critical piece in the self-disclosure research is the role of privacy. Some notable researchers have described privacy as a boundary regulation process by which a person manages others' access to personal information [1, 11]. An individual controls the boundary of information by manipulating the depth, breadth, and frequency of disclosures. That said, individuals might freely forgo privacy when they have a specific goal associated with their self-disclosure, such as increasing the level of intimacy with their partner or creating a desired impression [11, 16].

In the following sections, we review literature related to self-disclosure, specifically focusing on the area of goals and risks identified in more traditional, dyadic, offline settings. We also provide an overview of research on SNS disclosures, focusing on the role of affordances. Finally, we look at the role privacy plays in self-disclosure. These sections provide a background for our two research questions, which examine how Facebook users' self-disclosure practices compare with those employed in more private, dyadic communication (RQ1), as well as seek to identify the strategies users employ to help mitigate any risks they identify as barriers to making disclosures through the site (RQ2).

Disclosure Goals and Risks

Building on Derlega and Grzelak's [12] functional theory of disclosures, the disclosure decision model [23] identifies the cognitive process behind individuals' self-disclosure decisions and argues that self-disclosures fulfill specific roles within interpersonal relationships. Like its predecessor, the model identifies five primary disclosure goals, the first three of which are interpersonal in nature, while the latter two are associated with intrinsic rewards. Social approval involves garnering support and affection from others [3]. Intimacy relates to building a closer relationship with the recipient. Social control is a form of selective self-presentation [15] where individuals convey "packaged information" [12] to manage the impressions of others—often those in positions of power. Identity clarification helps individuals formulate their own ideas more clearly and sometimes elicit reactions from others, but does not necessarily involve others as recipients in the process [8]. Finally, self-disclosure may relieve distress through the process of catharsis, whereby individuals are able to release emotions by sharing bad experiences [29].

In addition to disclosure-based goals, researchers have identified four relational risks associated with disclosing information: social rejection, hurt feelings, reduction of integrity, and loss of control [4, 25]. The first two risks may impact one's interpersonal relationship with message recipients, while the latter two risks threaten one's self-concept and impression management. First, when a disclosure contains negative information, it may lead to social rejection by the recipient; this could take the form of formal or informal exclusion from events or social circles. Likewise, the discloser may hurt the recipient's feelings by revealing negatively valenced information, or if the discloser lacks prudence in making the disclosure [4, 27]. Next, disclosing information may alter existing impressions of the discloser when that information is inconsistent with previously disclosed information or projects an image other than what the recipient desires, leading to a reduction in integrity [27]. Finally, self-disclosure may jeopardize the discloser's power to regulate situations and outcomes [27]. For example, a teacher's professional image can be harmed when non-professional information becomes visible to her students, which could in turn affect power dynamics and decrease her ability to control students in the classroom.

Affordances and Disclosures on Social Network Sites

Self-disclosure is at the core of SNS use, and users disclose a variety of information through both static profile fields (e.g., birth date, location, employment) and through more interactive features such as status updates, Wall posts, and comments. Gross and Acquisti [16] argued SNS' affordances—i.e., the unique set of characteristics that enable action on the sites—create a new context for self-disclosure and influence users' behaviors related to revealing and concealing personal information.

In general, SNSs affordances enable users to engage in content distribution, sharing, and consumption at a lower cost and in less time than would be otherwise possible without the technology. For example, Treem and Leonardi [33] have identified four primary affordances of SNSs: visibility, persistence, editability, and association. SNSs both increase the visibility of disclosures and lower the search costs to locating disclosures (e.g., via the organization of information in the profile page); disclosures are archived and remain searchable long after they are first posted; users can carefully craft disclosures by drafting and editing messages both before and after posting them to the site; and disclosed information is associated with both the discloser and, if directed at another person, the recipient of that content (as in the case of a Wall post, tagged post, or comment).

These affordances create a significantly different interaction environment than that described in traditional models of disclosure processes [12, 23]. On sites like Facebook, users are encouraged to engage in public, one-to-many forms of self-disclosure rather than more private, dyadic communication. An important question to consider, then, is how these affordances impact users' self-disclosures on the site, especially in light of research linking SNS use to various positive relational outcomes (e.g., [34, 35]). Therefore, our first research question looks at Facebook users' self-reported disclosure goals, as well as the risks they identify as potential barriers to making disclosures through the site.

RQ1: What self-disclosure (a) goals and (b) risks do Facebook users identify when using the site?

Managing Privacy and Self-Disclosure on SNSs

Broadly speaking, discussions of privacy on SNSs have described users' attitudes toward privacy (e.g., risks/concerns), their privacy behaviors (i.e., settings), or the relationship between these variables and users' disclosure habits [16, 31, 35]. Research has also pointed to the blurred boundary between public and private information on SNSs, where privacy settings and audience visibility may vary for individual pieces of content, and users may fail to recognize the full audience for a given disclosure [5]. Users identify a variety of privacy concerns that may serve as barriers to their engagement in self-disclosure on the site, many of which align with the previously identified disclosure risks [35], as well as more general privacy concerns such as identity theft or cyberstalking [31].

That said, the average SNS user discloses a significant amount of information through the site; therefore, many users likely develop one of more strategies to manage the blurry boundaries and overcome any privacy concerns they may harbor. Understanding the strategies individuals employ to manage and curate their online identity is becoming an especially important area of research as more people join these sites and share personal information [7, 17], and this area of research is still in its nascent stages.

Facebook offers a number of ways to manipulate privacy settings to help users engage in boundary regulation regarding their disclosures. For example, users can limit access to each piece of content they share on the site by setting it to be visible to a set of Friends or, conversely, to be hidden from a subset of their Friend network. Use of these features may allow for more nuanced self-disclosures; for example, Vitak [35] found that those who used Friend Lists to allow for more targeted message dissemination reported disclosures to those Lists were more honest, sincere, intimate, and detailed than posts made to their full network. Lampinen and colleagues [19] labeled this type of behavior as a *preventive* strategy and found that users employ them to recreate offline boundaries.

An additional preventive strategy users engage in that is indirectly discussed by Lampinen and colleagues [19] is self-censorship; this strategy involves controlling the content of disclosed information in various ways. For example, users' disclosure decisions (i.e., whether they post a piece of content, as well as the content of the message) may be guided by the "lowest common denominator" in their network, i.e., the Friend(s) for whom a given disclosure might be problematic, such as a family member or authority figure [18]. Operationalizing self-censorship as starting to make a disclosure (i.e., entering text into a status update or comment box) but not publishing it, researchers at Facebook recently found that 71% of Facebook users engage in "last minute" self-censorship, which the authors argue is driven by audience considerations [10]. Finally, moving beyond individual people or groups, specific topics (e.g., politics, personal opinions, logistics) are generally the subject of self-censorship on Facebook, as users seek to avoid interpersonal conflict [28].

Self-censorship also involves behaviors related to the editability affordance of SNSs, whereby individuals review and manage content that has already been disclosed. A recent report by the Pew Internet Project and the Berkman Center reveals that teens engage in a wide variety of privacy management strategies [21]. The report found that 59% of SNS-using teens have edited or deleted something they posted in the past, while 53% have deleted comments others posted to their account, and 74% have deleted a Friend from their network.

Another strategy for managing content involves cloaking or otherwise hiding the true meaning of a message of content behind content that only a portion of one's network understands. Danah boyd [6] refers to this practice as "social steganography" and has found it to be a common practice in her ethnographic work with teenagers. This is reinforced through recent empirical work by Pew Internet, which found that 58% of teens report using inside jokes or coded messages on SNSs to ensure that only some friends understand a given message [21].

Even more extreme management strategies involve controlling access at the account level, either by deactivating/reactivating one's account or creating multiple accounts. This is not likely to be a common practice due to the high management costs, but research has identified some evidence of both behaviors. For example, in a broad-based survey question, Pew Internet found that 31% of teens reported deactivating or deleting a social media profile [21]. Other studies using non-teen samples have identified users creating multiple profiles on social network sites, for reasons ranging from privacy purposes to identity management (e.g., [32, 37]).

We expect that Facebook users will identify a variety of potential risks to sharing personal information through the site, especially related to privacy. Therefore, our second research question seeks to understand the various strategies users employ to help mitigate these risks or, alternatively, if there are situations in which users perceive the risks to be too high to make disclosures through the site.

RQ2: What strategies do Facebook users employ to mitigate self-disclosure risks and privacy concerns?

METHODS

During April 2011, a random sample of 2000 American graduate students at a large Midwestern university was invited, via email, to participate in a study regarding their use of online communication tools. Participants completed a survey that assessed their use of social media and, at the conclusion of the survey, those who used Facebook were invited to enter their email address if they were interested in participating in a 45-minute follow-up interview. Participants were also invited to enter their email into a drawing for one of ten $25 Amazon gift cards. This paper only presents results from the interview data; to view results from the survey data, see Vitak [35].

The survey remained open for two weeks and drew a response rate of approximately 25% (N=486); of these, 386 participants reported having an active Facebook account and 169 provided an email address as a possible interview participant. For this research project, the primary goal of conducting interviews was to gain deeper insight into users' privacy management and self-presentation practices on SNSs; therefore, a form of purposive sampling known as criterion sampling [24] was employed. Criterion sampling involves selecting cases that meet a pre-determined set of criteria to identify "information rich" cases (p. 238) and help identify weaknesses in a system that may help lead to overall system improvements. In the case of Facebook, studying users who are highly engaged in self-monitoring and self-presentational practices may help us understand gaps in privacy or other behavioral practices that a survey of general users would not reveal.

Therefore, for this sample, the primary criteria employed for interview selection were use of the "Friend Lists" feature or advanced privacy settings on Facebook (which indicated engagement in privacy and audience management beyond use of basic privacy settings) and, in the case of Twitter users, maintaining more than one profile on the site (which indicated an effort to segment audiences or engage in selective self-presentation).[1] From these criteria, 38 participants were emailed requesting an in-person interview; 26 attended one over the following three weeks (see Table 1 for detailed descriptives for each interview participant). All participants received a $15 Amazon gift card. Among interview participants, 16 (62%) were female, with an average age of 29 (range: 22-53, *SD*=6). The sample included 22 White, two African American, one Latino, and one multiracial participant. Participants had an average of 500 Facebook Friends (median=433, SD=360) and spent 55 minutes a day on the site (*SD*=37.82).

The first author conducted each of the interviews in an on-campus lab during April and May 2011. Interviews were semi-structured and lasted between 30 and 95 minutes. During the interviews, participants were asked a variety of questions about their use of the site, their disclosure and interaction behaviors with their networks, their privacy attitudes and behaviors, and their impression management strategies.[2] Following completion of the interviews, they were transcribed by two undergraduate research assistants and checked by the first author to ensure accuracy. Prior to analysis, both authors read the interviews and created a codebook based on the guiding theories (i.e., disclosure goals and risks, affordances, privacy) as well as various characteristics of disclosures (e.g., inappropriate, self-presentation), and expected risk management strategies based on existing literature (e.g., targeted disclosures, lowest common denominator).

Analysis was conducted by the authors in Dedoose, an online qualitative software program, whereby individual participants' data were used to refine themes related to the research questions as they emerged [20]. Line-by-line coding of each transcript was employed using complete thoughts as the unit of analysis to establish themes across the corpus [30]. The second author coded each interview in this manner and then met with the first author to review codes, discuss instances of where application of a code was unclear, and to review the codebook to ensure the necessary excerpts were being captured. Following this discussion, the first author completed a second round of coding on the entire corpus. At the completion of the second round of coding, the excerpts were exported into Excel spreadsheets, and the second author created a meta-matrix [22] to help identify patterns across participants, establish representativeness of findings, and detect negative cases.

---

[1] While 16 interview participants maintained one or more Twitter accounts, in the present analyses we focus only on their discussion of their Facebook use.

[2] Questions about disclosure goals and risks were not directly probed; rather, the themes discussed in the findings emerged from more general discussions of users' disclosure practices on the site and their concerns about communicating information over a semi-public channel.

Name	Sex	Age	Race	Total FB Friends	Facebook Friend Diversity[1]	Privacy Concerns[2]	Advanced Privacy Settings?[3]	Use Friend Lists?[4]	Use Twitter? (Multiple Accounts?)
Brandon	M	27	White	525	8	2.33	Yes	Yes	No (n/a)
Christina	F	33	White	280	12	3.33	Yes	Yes	Yes (Yes)
Dana	F	25	Black	750	11	2	Yes	Yes	Yes (No)
Evelyn	F	28	White	477	7	3	Yes	Yes	Yes (No)
Fiona	F	28	White	700	10	3	Yes	Yes	Yes (Yes)
Gabriel	M	33	White	400	12	3.33	Yes	Yes	No (n/a)
Hilary	F	22	White	1400	8	2.67	Yes	Yes	Yes (No)
Irene	F	31	White	165	7	4	Yes	Yes	Yes (No)
Jennifer	F	22	Latino	1600	5	3.67	Yes	Yes	Yes (Yes)
Katie	F	28	White	315	11	2	Yes	Yes	Yes (Yes)
Laura	F	23	White	500	8	4	Yes	Yes	No (n/a)
Marshall	M	27	White	251	10	2.67	No	No	Yes (Yes)
Nick	M	29	White	700	13	2.67	No	No	Yes (Yes)
Owen	M	35	White	830	6	4	No	Yes	Yes (Yes)
Peter	M	35	White	337	10	1.33	Yes	Yes	Yes (Yes)
Kim	F	26	White	368	7	3.67	Yes	Yes	No (n/a)
Rachelle	F	25	White	548	8	4	Yes	Yes	No (n/a)
Stephanie	F	25	White	302	8	3	Yes	Yes	No (n/a)
Cindy	F	28	White	82	11	4.67	Unsure	Yes	No (n/a)
Tania	F	28	White	120	8	4.67	Yes	Yes	No (n/a)
Zara	F	27	Black	370	8	2	No	Yes	No (n/a)
Will	M	28	White	465	10	3.33	Yes	Yes	No (n/a)
Thomas	M	29	Multi	120	5	1.67	Yes	Yes	No (n/a)
Ryan	M	28	White	500	10	3	Yes	Yes	No (n/a)
Victoria	F	53	White	200	7	2	No	No	Yes (Yes)
Aaron	M	31	White	701	11	2.67	Yes	No	No (No)
Sum/Avg	62%F	29	85%W	500	8.88	3.03	92%Y	85%Y	54%Y (35%Y)

[1] Participants were asked to indicate whether they had Facebook Friends in 12 relational categories, plus an "other" option. The score was then computed by adding up each category they indicated being present in their network (range: 5-13).

[2] Three-item scale measuring individuals' concerns related to sharing information through the site, measured on a Likert-type scale ranging from 1=Strongly disagree to 5=Strongly agree.

[3] Question: "Have you ever used the advanced privacy settings so that only some of your friends can see an update or photo?"

[4] Question: "Have you created 'Friend Lists' so you can post updates just to a subset of your Facebook Friends?"

Table 1: Interview participant demographics

FINDINGS

Below we present findings related to our two research questions, first highlighting trends in the data related to participants' self-identified disclosure goals and risks associated with making disclosures on Facebook (RQ1), and second by evaluating the various strategies participants identified using to help mitigate those risks (RQ2).

Self-disclosure Goals on Facebook

The first part of RQ1 focused on identifying the self-disclosure goals SNS users may have while sharing information through the site. Though participants were not directly prompted about each of the five goals identified in Derlega and Grzelak's [12] research, we found evidence of each goal in participants' comments about their motivations for using the site. Furthermore, we saw evidence of a sixth self-disclosure goal among participants, which we have labeled "personal record"; this goal reflects how SNS users are able to merge dyadic communication goals with the site's affordances (e.g., persistence) to create a new form of self-expression that mixes a traditionally private activity (journaling) with the increased visibility of status updates. Below, we discuss how these goals manifested in further detail.

Social approval goal

Many participants reflected on having a goal of social acceptance when they made self-disclosures, describing instances in which they would share information specifically because they thought their friends would be interested in it. For example, Christina said, "I'll share news stories or things I find interesting because I know largely it's teachers who are my friends, so I know who my audience is and I think about what they would want to see." Fiona, Nick, and Peter shared similar comments about posting status updates that because they believe they'd appeal to their Friends. At other times, participants made self-disclosures through the site because they expected their Facebook Friends to find enjoyment or humor in the content, which would also meet the social approval goal. For example, Laura said, "I'm friends with a lot of my co-workers on Facebook, so if something funny or stupid happens at work, I'll post it because I know people will appreciate it."

Social control goal

As this sample was comprised of graduate students—many of whom had friended faculty members (54%) or previous (46%) or current (27%) students, while others were on the job market or working professionals—participants were highly cognizant of their self-presentation online and nearly all made references to engaging in some degree of social control in their self-disclosures. A recurring theme among the participants was the struggle between wanting to engage and share content with some portions of their network while maintaining a certain restraint with other portions, or trying to keep up a "clean" image for specific audiences. Ryan, who was getting ready to go on the job market, captured this struggle:

> "...you have to kind of negotiate a lot of interactions at times. Because like, for instance, I'm on the job market next year. I'll be finishing up my degree, putting myself up on the academic job market and the colleagues on there I have are people that could potentially be on hiring committees next year. So I'm trying to navigate that space of the personal where you're trying to have fun, have status updates, write back to people on your Wall, but also do it in a way that's rhetorically effective... but it is kind of a fine line because you want also the people on these hiring committees and potential colleagues and such to see you as human too."

Ryan's comment represents a prudent self-disclosure process of participants navigating their self-presentation to find the proper balance to appeal to all relevant audiences—in this case social and professional—in order to reap multiple benefits (interpersonal relationships with friends and potential employment opportunities). It also highlights how the affordances of the site may impact various user goals. In Ryan's case, the goal of social control is influenced largely by his network composition, or the association affordance, which makes connections visible to one another and links content to connections. Furthermore, the visibility of content, especially through the News Feed but also through the user's profile, may make users think twice before sharing certain types of information, especially if they have a goal related to curating a specific image, such as that of the ideal new faculty hire. For example, Stephanie said, "I just wanted to be on the safe side and I also have classmates who I just feel like I should keep some professionalism with, so I just try to, still show my personality, but not everything."

Intimacy goal

Self-disclosures may serve a goal of increasing or maintaining relational closeness with members of one's network, especially if specific friends are geographically dispersed. Most participants referenced sharing various types of content (e.g., greetings, wishes), writing supportive comments, and "liking" Friends' posts. In some instances, these forms of interaction may have served a maintenance purpose; for others, they helped bring Friends closer together. For example, Brandon said he had a group of about 20 close friends on Facebook who "constantly keep in touch" through the site. Likewise, Laura said she maintains a private message thread with 10 close friends from college where they keep each other updated on what's going on in their lives. Notably, some participants said that for more intimate interactions, they chose to use channels other than Facebook. For example, Evelyn said: "If you're a really close friend, I probably won't post on your Wall either because I'm going to call you. I'm not going to post on you Wall. That seems tacky."

Identity clarification goal

Self-disclosure on Facebook also functions to clarify users' opinions or beliefs on various issues by providing a platform for them through which they can engage in self-reflection (via self-disclosure) or interaction with others. A common practice many participants referenced was sharing links to news stories on issues that mattered to them—whether it was abortion (Fiona), politics (Aaron), or their field of research (Brandon)—and participants presented these updates when they thought the issue should be addressed, even though the content of the messages sometimes threatened other goals such as social approval. Another aspect of identity clarification is that individuals can use Facebook to focus on a specific aspect of their identity; for example, Dana, a mom and wife, purposefully does not share those aspects of herself on the site:

> "I have an 8-year-old so my life is SpongeBob most of time, and that is **not** reflected [in my profile]...I'm not a wife, I'm not a mom, I'm just Dana on Facebook and these are Dana's interests and this is Dana's space. And if you meet me, it's going to be different. I'm going to have mayonnaise on my shirt from fixing that sandwich or something like that. So I think that's the primary difference. It's not a different me, but it's just me undiluted if that makes sense."

For Dana, Facebook serves an important role by allowing her to express herself and interact in ways she feels otherwise constrained in her day-to-day life as a wife and mother.

Relief of distress goal
The final of the five goals identified in Omarzu's [23] research was reflected in just a few participants' comments. Marshall described a cathartic role of self-disclosure, saying if he was "frustrated or angry," the site provided an outlet for channeling those emotions. However, most participants who referenced these types of posts only mentioned them when talking about Friends' posting habits and generally expressed annoyance with using Facebook for this kind of disclosure, at least those who did so publicly. Overall, participants viewed Facebook as a place for sharing positive news and information more so than a place to disclose negative emotions or experiences. If people did use Facebook to achieve this goal, it was seen as more acceptable when they used a private over a public channel, as Gabriel described doing.

Personal record goal
In addition to identifying goals consistent with previous research, we also identified an additional self-disclosure goal. Like identity clarification and social control, the personal record goal is associated with intrinsic rewards and is related to the desire to keep an online diary of events in one's life. This goal is facilitated by the affordances of the site, especially the persistence of content, which allows users to maintain a virtual archive of content for as long as they maintain an account, as well as editability, which gives users control over both the content of posts as well as their visibility (i.e., which Friends can view individual posts). Katie described one way in which this goal is achieved:

> "I status update a lot, mainly because we [academics] have a job where you don't get to see a lot of your products, so as soon as I'm done with something, I'm like, 'Ooh, I just finished X.' So I feel like something has happened."

By announcing the event on Facebook, Katie felt a certain sense of fulfillment. Other participants mentioned posting about life events and achievements such as marriage, pregnancy, or graduation. For example, Laura mostly used Facebook to share her big events such as her acceptance to medical school, and Dana posted whenever a major life transition happened (e.g., marriage, pregnancy). It is important to note that these types of postings are often driven by other goals (e.g., social approval, intimacy), but at the same time, users can avail themselves of the Wall on Facebook to log lifetime stories, and they are not only able to keep track of what they disclose, but the interactions associated with that disclosure, such as how many "likes" Dana got when she announced her marriage. For some people, these notes, like a collection of letters and diary entries in a box, appears to carry significant emotional meaning; during her interview, Victoria vividly remembered her last birthday, saying, "I had 150 happy birthday messages on Facebook. I was like, that was pretty cool, I wouldn't have ever gotten 150 people saying happy birthday to me ever before in my life."

Finally, as with other social media, Facebook allows users to upload and share content originally created through another application. In this way, Facebook may become a central repository that houses all-important "digital disclosures" people make online. While not explicitly referenced by many participants, we expect that this behavior was more common than we found in the interviews because it was not directly addressed through any questions. For example, Cindy noted that she used Facebook to keep track of the books she reads through the Goodreads application, which automatically pushed the content to Facebook. In addition to fulfilling a personal record goal, these behaviors may also support goals of identity clarification and social control.

Self-disclosure Risks on Facebook
As with the disclosure goals, we found that Facebook users' self-identified disclosure risks generally corresponded to those identified in previous research. In general, the two interpersonal risks—social rejection and hurt feelings—tended to be discussed together, as did the two impression management-based risks, reduction of integrity and loss of control. In addition to these risks, our participants also described a variety of risks they faced when using Facebook that reflected the role that the site's affordances play in creating and/or increasing users' concerns about sharing information.

Interpersonal-based risks
A primary concern for Facebook users in this sample was that their behaviors on the site could result in stigma and/or avoidance on or off the site. This concern was most often manifested in comments related to the social rejection risk, which a majority of our participants mentioned when describing their disclosure habits on the site. Over-sharing, complaints, and "boring" content were mentioned as potential causes of social rejection. For example, Laura worried that her Friends might not be interested in what she shared, Will felt that talking about divisive issues might alienate some people he wanted to stay in touch with, and Gabriel consciously tried to not be one of the complainers he disliked. These examples highlight how social rejection could interfere with the self-disclosure goals, especially those related to interpersonal relationships (i.e., social approval, intimacy, and social control). Avoidance of certain topics seen as taboo or "inappropriate" also reflected these perceptions.

In addition to fears of social rejection, participants described concerns related to hurting Friends' feelings through their self-disclosures. This risk was especially complicated by the fact that Facebook does little to distinguish between offline boundaries and relational contexts, making selective self-presentation more difficult than in offline environments. Christina described a situation where she perceived making a positive disclosure could hurt some Friends' feelings:

> "When I got accepted here into the PhD program, I knew some of my Facebook Friends had applied and been rejected and so I kind of kept it to myself. ...I guess kind of always worried about sounding braggadocio, you know, I just don't want to put myself out there in that way. I think I try to think about how people's feelings are impacted because it is a social space."

Even though being accepted to a PhD program was a major achievement for Christina—and one that most people would be excited to share with their networks—she was more concerned about those network members who had not been accepted and did not want to hurt their feelings by sharing her good news. In this case, the conflict between her disclosure goal and perceived risks negatively affected her decision to disclose the information.

Participants described a variety of anecdotes highlighting the role that Facebook's affordances played in increasing interpersonal risks associated with making disclosures on Facebook. Katie talked about an incident when a Friend posted a video on her Wall; while she thought it was funny, she said she quickly realized it might be offensive to other people in her network. Likewise, Zara talked about problems derived from multiple and cross-cutting associations; she described an incident where she really wanted to comment about something happening in a class, but decided not to because she was Friends with one of the people in the class, and the comment may have hurt his feelings. In this way, our participants generally tried to avoid negatively affecting others' feelings, especially when they were likely to have future interactions with that person.

Impression management-based risks

The majority of participants expressed concerns with presenting information consistent with their self-perception, and they expressed concerns over the reduction of integrity and loss of control that errant disclosures could cause. Inappropriately tagged photos, a wayward comment from a Friend, or poor judgment in their own disclosure decisions could damage their public image, which was especially of concern to participants in this sample, as many were actively on the job market. Several described being very careful not to disclose unnecessary information that contradicted their public images; for example, Brandon and Laura referenced concerns about potential employers accessing old pictures from when they were younger. Jennifer echoed this, saying, "I have an image to upkeep, and I don't want people to think less of me because of some particular incident."

The social roles of our participants (e.g., student, teacher, employee) made them reconsider their postings due to the inherent power structure of relationships within their networks. Comments often reflected both impression management-based risks (i.e., loss of control and reduction of integrity) concurrently; for example, some participants noted that content that could be perceived as negative—such as photos from an event at a bar—could lower perceived integrity in the eyes of a potential employer and could impact their ability to maintain control over students in the classroom. In both of these situations, participants were describing situations in which they were in a position of power (in the case of students) or were subject to the decisions of others (in the case of prospective employers). Other instances of these risks included when a disclosure initiated unwanted interactions and the participant lost control of content posted on their Facebook Wall.

Affordance-based risks

An overarching theme that emerged from participants' comments about risks associated with making disclosures through Facebook related to how the site's affordances shaped how and by whom disclosures could be viewed. For example, the high visibility and persistence of content on Facebook makes it easier for users to locate posts through both the News Feed and users' profiles; compared with the more ephemeral—and less public—alternative forms of communication, these affordances led many participants to "think twice" before sharing content. For example, Aaron compared Facebook to a public square: "I consider Facebook the most public space. I consider if I went out into the middle of a crowded space and yelled something; it's the equivalent." Irene said she tends to be much more careful making disclosures on Facebook than she does in face-to-face conversations because Facebook disclosures remain long after the conversation: "My interactions with people, especially the public interactions on Facebook, are pretty...reserved...it's always with this idea in the back of my head that this is going out in public and it will be there forever."

Self-disclosures on Facebook are associated with network members in multiple ways (e.g., tagging, mentions, comments), and these connections sometimes led to increased concerns related to self-presentation and privacy. For these reasons, self-disclosures are carefully thought out. Zara's remark reflects the mental processes in making self-disclosures.

> "If you post this, are you okay with people, everyone seeing this? Is that okay with you? I think twice about it. And if I think it's not a big deal, then I'll go ahead and do it. But if I'm thinking about the repercussions of it; if I can think of a few, then I won't do it."

Some of the "repercussions" of self-disclosure are related to the inherent tensions created by the technical structure of networks on Facebook, a concept known as context collapse. In offline environments, individuals have a much greater degree of control over their self-presentation because their audience is generally predictable; on sites like Facebook, however, contacts from various contexts are flattened into a single, homogenous group, which makes it more difficult to engage in varied self-presentation. Users must instead disclose information to various audiences simultaneously, and this increases the likelihood of other types of risks occurring. For example, Dana said:

> "If I post 'I'm bored right now' at 4:30 and a colleague sees it, they know I was in class at 4:30. And you don't know whose advisor is who, and they're like, 'oh yeah, she posted she was bored while she was in your class.' And that would be bad, so I worry about things like that getting around."

This example reflects the complexities of making disclosures to a diverse and sometimes unknown audience and hints at potential risks—in this case, risks associated with Dana managing a certain impression as a grad student.

Finally, several users expressed doubts about the privacy of content on the site, even when using private channels or employing Facebook's many privacy features. For example, Kim and others noted that Facebook is a public site and privacy settings do not guarantee that information will remain private. Likewise, Ryan's comments pointed to Facebook's frequent changes to privacy settings, which may even increase concerns of the savviest users:

> "Even if it was one of those things where I added those seven or eight people that are like my closest friends and family, and it was just a Facebook group, I'd still be kind of wary about putting certain things online I think. Just because you just never know if one day your settings...Facebook makes some updates and your settings change and suddenly something is open that wasn't open."

Risk Management Strategies Employed by Users

Facebook contains several features users can manipulate for boundary regulation. Once the technical connection is established vis-à-vis "Facebook Friends," users can control access to content at a high level—through blocking and unfriending—as well as at a more granular level through advanced privacy settings such as Friend Lists and Private Groups. While our participants noted various risks to making self-disclosures on Facebook, they also engaged in various strategies to help mitigate those risks. These strategies fell into four broad categories, which we have labeled network regulation, targeted disclosure, self-censorship, and content regulation.

Network regulation strategy

Network regulation is a type of preventive strategy that limits the *official* recipient of disclosures. Our participants sometimes rejected or left a friend request unanswered in order to regulate information boundaries. A common example mentioned by participants who were also teachers was Friend requests from their students. Gabriel explained why he decided not to accept friend requests from students.

> "I worked with undergraduate students for seven years and five of those were Facebook years... So they'd friend me...and it was a power dynamic, like I was in charge of where they lived, so I didn't want to create unnecessary power dynamics that were inappropriate."

Gabriel described the additional regulation work that would have been required of him if he were to allow students into his network, coming to the conclusion that it was not a good idea. Sometimes, decisions are made to avoid efforts to maintain the boundary that is often perceived much more complex than preventive strategies. Offline relationships that involve power dynamics can disrupt their self-disclosure practices and because, in this case, having students as Facebook Friends creates risks such as reducing integrity as a teacher and losing control over in the classroom. Thus, Gabriel could simply avoid these risks with network regulation (i.e., rejecting the Friend requests). However, in some situations, users described feeling social pressure to accept Friend requests, even if they'd rather not have that person in their network. Evelyn, who had a public relations job in a small town, felt pressured to accept a Friend request from the town's mayor because ignoring it could create tension in their offline relationship. Dana echoed this sentiment when referencing Friend requests from coworkers, saying, "You can't reject colleagues. So if you're in class with them, you can't say no." Other participants also mentioned similar cases where they could not manage the boundary to their liking due to offline pressures.

Social pressures affected use of other network regulation strategies as well, including the Chat visibility features, "hiding" Friends from their News Feed, and defriending. Becoming "invisible" on Facebook's Chat client was mentioned by most participants who used Chat—which was a minority of participants—as one way they avoided unwanted interaction with specific individuals or groups of Friends. Several participants also said they preferred hiding an "annoying" Friend or someone with whom they shared different ideological beliefs rather than defriend them; this was often because of the underlying relationship with the person. When asked why they chose to "hide" a Facebook Friend rather than defriend the person, many people expressed hesitancy to sever that tie, even virtually. For example, following a high school reunion, Irene opted to hide several high school friends: "We were good friends 10 or 15 years ago, but we're not really that close now. So I feel bad to defriend them, but I don't really want to get frequent updates on what's going on in their lives." It is important to note that hiding does nothing to mitigate risks, as it only makes Friends invisible to the user and does nothing to prevent that person from viewing content.

Targeted disclosure strategy

While the above strategy provides a more broad-based level of coverage, Friend Lists manage disclosure boundaries at a much more granular level. It is no surprise that the vast majority of participants (85%) in this sample used Friend Lists to recreate some of their offline contexts and segment content distribution to specific subsets of their network[3]; however, exploring this as a strategy is still useful because the participants describe a wide range of Friend List uses, thus providing the "rich information" sought through this sampling technique.

As mentioned above, participants used targeted disclosures in a variety of ways; sometimes the purpose was to single out the people in their network for whom their messages were most relevant. For example, Irene disclosed her school union-related updates selectively to just those Friends for whom she felt the content was relevant:

> "It's kind of a courtesy not to bother people with things they don't need to know about. But also, just focusing like, you guys need to know about so I'm going to focus it just to you guys."

By using targeted disclosures, she could effectively communicate with people who might want to know the information, while avoiding risks such as social rejection. More often, targeted disclosures were used to hide content from a group of people. Stephanie described a group of Friends (i.e., some family and faculty) for whom she limited access to her sexual orientation because she had not yet disclosed that information. This strategy was also widely used to exclude a small subset of Friends from viewing status updates and photos. For example, Tania placed a group of acquaintances on a List to limit their access to her Facebook updates, which she called her "don't see" group. Her default settings for status updates were set to all friends other than this group. Fiona accepted Friend requests from current students or faculty members without hesitation, but placed them in a "Limited List" that did not have access to the majority of the content she shared. Private messages were also used to target specific recipients; both Brandon and Laura referenced using private messages to keep in touch with groups of close friends; this may have been done as much for an organizational purpose as for keeping the information private, but by using private messages, the groups may feel more open in what they share with each other.

However, targeted disclosures are sometimes laborious and require self-efficacy on the part of users. Stephanie explained some reasons why she did not use advanced privacy settings other than for Chat and her relationship status.

> "I guess it's kind of hard to do on there. You have to really know what you're doing with the privacy settings, and I don't want to bother with it. It's not that important to me to post [things I wouldn't want my mom to see] anyways, so I just let it be."

[3] The percentage was so high because it was one of the selection criteria for interviews. Among the survey of Facebook users (N=486), 17% reported using Friend Lists.

Self-censorship strategy

Participants also managed their disclosures by engaging in various forms of self-censorship, ranging from strategies resembling Hogan's [18] lowest common denominator (LCD) to consciously deciding to not engage in self-disclosure. Applying a LCD strategy, one might choose to engage in some form of self-censorship—either by not posting content or altering the message itself—if it is determined that that original message will offend the lowest common denominator. This strategy was reflected in several participants' comments about engaging in a sometimes-prolonged thought process before sharing content on the site to evaluate the potential risks of making that disclosure. For example, Jennifer said: "I definitely consider who is going to see it, if I want them to see it. Obviously if I don't want one person to see it, I'm not going to put it up there. Period." In addition to technical features such as Friend Lists and advanced privacy settings, Jennifer thought about whether posting is acceptable to anyone in her network. Likewise, Victoria pointed to the diversity of her Friend network and the role that played in how she made decisions about what to post on the site:

> "I'm communicating to people from all walks of my life, and I want to make sure that what I'm putting out there is appropriate for everybody that's going to see it. And so I do have that moment of censoring everything before I put it to make sure, 'Oh yeah, there's these people seeing it.'"

Participants sacrificed self-disclosure goals if they thought potential risks overrode the goal. Rachelle tried to keep her profile generic due to the presence of her professional connections in her Friend Lists. Sometimes, participants imposed self-censorship to maintain self-presentation on Facebook. For example, Gabriel kept certain postings to himself because he did not "want to put that kind of persona out."

Content regulation strategy

A final strategy for mitigating risks of disclosing personal information through Facebook, content regulation, involves moving communication to other channels or communicating through the site, but in code. Brandon used email to share interesting information because of potential social rejection risks of posting it publicly on Facebook. Alternatively, participants controlled the depth of information shared by intentionally cloaking the details in a form of social steganography. While not mentioned by many participants, in Katie's case, this strategy was related to the goal of relieving distress.

> "So there was some...assignment, somebody had named a fictional character Dr. [X]. And we just thought that name was really funny. And so eventually, it had nothing to do with that original project, but anytime we

> were complaining about a class we were in, we were like, 'Oh my gosh, Dr. X is going on and on and on.' 'I can't believe these X assignments.'"

Katie used a pseudonym to conceal the real identity of the professor she and her friends were talking about, as their conversations were happening in pseudo public spaces (i.e., Facebook and Twitter), but only the circle of friends understood the true identity of the person. In this case, through use of coded information, the group of students was able to use Facebook to relieve stress during what was otherwise a very stressful semester. Conversely, ambiguous content can also hurt the person who is the focus of the post, if s/he is able to interpret the message. Will gave an example, saying, "maybe your ex posts something that you know is about you, but nobody else does, and so it pisses you off."

DISCUSSION

This study examines Facebook users' self-disclosure practices through an evaluation of their self-identified disclosure goals and risks, as well as a discussion of the various strategies users employ to mitigate those risks and remain engaged users of the site. Facebook is driven by social interaction, and research shows that in order for users to reap the full benefits of the site, they need to be engaged through both self-disclosure [35] and interaction with other users [9, 14]. Furthermore, Facebook's affordances, including the visibility, persistence, and editability of content as well as the association of connections [33], impact users' goals, perceived risks, and impression management strategies when making disclosures through the site.

Implications for research and theory

The disclosure process is at the core of many communication theories, yet little work has been done to connect more traditional models of communication, such as Derlega and Grzelak's [12] and Omarzu's [23] work to new forms of mediated communication, which, as boyd [5] has noted, create invisible audiences, blur lines between public and private, and collapse contexts. In combination with the affordances described by Treem and Leonardi [33] that are unique to these sites, users' behaviors on SNSs should be evaluated to determine how they deviate from what we have already established in existing theories of communication and relationship maintenance.

The present study offers a preliminary step at evaluating how two important disclosure attitudes—goals and risks—are reflected in a very non-traditional disclosure space. Unlike the dyadic disclosure environment described in theory, Facebook disclosures and interactions are generally broadcast to one's entire network via status update (or a subset thereof). Perhaps unsurprisingly, while each of Derlega and Grzelak's [12] original five disclosure goals was referenced across the corpus, the high visibility of many forms of disclosure in Facebook and diffuse association between contacts (both within their immediate and extended network) affected some users' goals, especially social control, which is often employed in situations when the discloser is in a subservient position to the recipient of the disclosure [12]. Among our sample, participants repeatedly referenced instances in which their disclosure goal was to portray a specific image—typically a professional one—because they were concerned about an existing or potential audience viewing the content and wanted to ensure the generated impressions were consistent with those desires.

Remarks related to the social control goal, as well as to related risks (e.g., loss of control, reduction of integrity) can be examined in terms of Goffman's front stage and backstage performances [15]. Offline, the boundaries between the front stage, where individuals engage in more formal performances for an audience (e.g., at a job interview) and the backstage, where individuals can "step out of character" (e.g., at home with friends) are relatively clearly delineated. On Facebook, however, these boundaries become blurred due to the flattening of different groups into a single group (i.e., Facebook Friends) in a process known as context collapse [5, 35]. While not unique to SNSs, context collapse is exacerbated by these sites' affordances, and participants often struggled to balance front stage performances—in this case, that of a reputable graduate student, instructor, and/or employee—and backstage performances, which typically took the form of more intimate, off-the-cuff interactions with friends that were facilitated by the site's many quick and convenient communication features.

Context collapse reduces costs associated with communicating to a large and diverse audience; however, for many participants, it also increased risks to making disclosures due to concerns about various parts of their audience. Therefore, it was unsurprising that participants engaged in a wide variety of strategies to help mitigate the risks associated with making disclosures on a site where the average participant had 500 Friends. Some of these strategies were relatively cost-intensive; for example, the Friend List strategy required users to go through their entire network and manually enter every Friend they wanted on a particular List.[4] Creating these Lists requires a certain amount of skill, which not all users possess, especially older and less engaged users not captured in this sample (e.g., [36]), but who make up an increasingly larger proportion of the total Facebook population [7]. Furthermore, managing Lists is complicated by the addition of new Friends to one's network and new privacy features from Facebook, and some participants expressed frustration

[4] When these data were collected, Facebook had not yet rolled out its "Smart Lists" feature (see: https://www.facebook.com/notes/facebook/improved-friend-lists/10150278932602131).

with the technology or said they had created some Lists but did not use them.

The relationship between privacy and disclosure has been studied in offline settings for decades, most famously by Irwin Altman [1], who argued that individuals achieve privacy by regulating their social interactions. In offline settings, boundary regulation may be achieved by closing a door or choosing a location to meet. Building on Altman's work, Petronio's [26] Communication Privacy Management Theory offers individuals with a framework through which to use when deciding whether or not to reveal (i.e., disclose) or conceal (i.e., keep private) a piece of information, arguing that once information is disclosed, it is no longer private.

On SNSs, interactions vary in a number of important ways. Boundary regulation is not nearly as simple as closing a door; as seen in the interviews presented in this study, Facebook users come up with a variety of methods to enable them to interact with their network while still maintaining some degree of privacy; yet at times, they still decide that the best decision is to self-censor their posts, which is in line with other research in this area [19]. Furthermore, the invisible audience paired with highly visible content likely plays a significant role in self-presentation, especially when users have goals related to strategic self-presentation, as was the case for many participants in this sample. Even when users are not trying to present a specific image in their disclosures, it may only take one negative experience—whether personal or witnessed—to change a user's privacy and disclosure habits.

Finally, an important component to theory-driven research is to extend theory, and this study offers contributions in this regard as well. In examining users' disclosure goals, some participants specifically referenced the site's utility in keeping track of their day-to-day activities, as well as important life events. In this way, the site served as a form of digital diary, with the persistence of searchability of content making it easily accessible and reviewable over time, both by the individual and by others, and the visibility and editability enabled other users to add to the content, such as when someone posted an engagement notice and Friends wrote congratulatory notes. Facebook's affordances may help move this personal record far beyond any diary by making it interactive and editable. The search function, especially now with newer features like Timeline, Graph Search, and the ability to download one's profile information, enable users to keep track of everything going on in a specific moment of time through notes, pictures, and interactions and then revisit them at a later date. This could be especially useful to people tracking a specific goal, like someone training for a marathon who posted their daily workouts to the site, to be able to go back and see their progress over time.

Perhaps more than any of the other goals, engagement in the personal record goal on Facebook leaves the user most exposed to potential disclosure-based risks, as these disclosures suggest revealing both a high quantity and quality of information. That said, as SNSs become one of the most important platforms that integrate information that was generated outside of Facebook, the personal record goal would become an important function among SNS users in the future.

Implications for site design

The frustrations voiced by some of our participants—and subsequent decisions to either not use the technical solutions provided by Facebook or to not interact through the site because of perceived risks—calls for design solutions that account for the affordances of the site and their impact on self-disclosure and boundary regulation processes. Whereas offline self-disclosure is built on the dyadic boundary that generally avoids information leakage to third parties [11], SNS users have much less control over the boundary regulation process because it is often difficult—if not impossible—to know one's full audience on the site [5]. Even when a discloser has a good sense of her audience, the message recipients may not, which could lead to awkward situations if information is shared with unintended parties. Facebook could look to sites like Google+, which makes disclosure boundary information (i.e., a full list of people with whom a user shares an update) visible to everyone who can see the update. This strategy of transparency lowers the risks associated with making disclosures in these spaces.

A second design feature to consider when discussing self-disclosure goals and risks is Timeline. Facebook's most recent profile overhaul places the persistence and visibility affordances of the site at the forefront by simplifying the process of searching and moving through a user's profile, as well as giving users the ability to highlight or minimize individual pieces of content. For a user with disclosure goals related to identity clarification or creating a personal record, these developments are likely welcome, but they also introduce a number of risks, especially when one considers how users' Friend networks—and disclosure habits—have likely evolved over the course of their membership. Facebook has taken some steps to help users minimize unwanted or embarrassing encounters due to years-old content suddenly becoming much more visible, but as several participants in our interviews noted, Facebook's privacy settings may be viewed as overly complex to some. Creating simpler ways to manage the visibility of older self-disclosures—and clearly articulating these methods to users—should be a goal of the site.

Limitations

This study employed qualitative interviews to gain deeper insights into SNS users' disclosure behaviors and risk management strategies. As it employed purposive, rather than random sampling, caution should be taken in interpreting findings, as the small, homogenous sample of highly engaged, largely white, American graduate students limits the generalizability of findings. The choice of graduate students over other populations was motivated by the likelihood that they would have more (diverse networks than other populations (e.g., undergraduate students), and that they would potentially experience a variety of situations on Facebook involving power disparities, such as student or faculty connections, and significant impression management concerns, such as those related to seeking a job. To some degree, all Facebook users experience these types of issues, but they were expected to be magnified within this population; therefore, the findings presented here, especially regarding engagement in risk management strategies, may not reflect that of a more heterogeneous population. Additional research should be conducted to confirm the findings using more diverse sampling techniques.

CONCLUSION

Through this qualitative study, we have gained a deeper understanding into how individuals navigate the communication process on social network sites. Once viewed through a more simplistic lens of dyadic communication in which interaction partners exchanged increasingly intimate personal disclosures as a method of relational development, self-disclosure in the more dynamic world of social media involves both dyadic and group communication across public and private channels with known and unknown audiences of various sizes. While many of the goals and risks are similar, they are influenced by the affordances of the sites, which also affects the strategies users employ when making decisions about what—and with whom—to disclose.

We believe this study provides an important contribution to a growing body of research on how new communication technologies affect relationship maintenance practices, as well as how the affordances of social network sites are changing how we interact with a variety of others, especially as individuals face new challenges such as collapsed contexts when disclosing information online.

ACKNOWLEDGMENTS

This study was funded by a research grant from the College of Communication Arts and Sciences at Michigan State University. The authors would like to thank Drs. Jennifer Golbeck, Beth St. Jean, and Dana Rotman for their feedback on an earlier draft of this paper, as well as the thoughtful comments from the anonymous reviewers, which helped strengthen the paper.

REFERENCES

1. Altman, I. *The Environment and Social Behavior: Privacy, Personal Space, Territory and Crowding*. Brooks/Cole. Monterey, CA, 1975.
2. Altman, I. and Taylor, D. *Social Penetration: The Development of Interpersonal Relationships*. Holt, New York, 1973.
3. Baumeister, R.F. A self-presentational view of social phenomena. *Psychological Bulletin 91*, 1 (1982), 3–26.
4. Baxter, L.A. and Montgomery, B.M. *Relating: Dialogues and Dialectics*. Guilford Press, New York, 1996.
5. boyd, d. Social network sites as networked publics: Affordances, dynamics, and implications. In Z. Papacharissi, ed., *Networked Self: Identity, Community, and Culture on Social Network Sites*. 2010, 39–58.
6. boyd, d. Networked privacy. *Surveillance & Society 10*, 3 (2012), 348–350.
7. Brenner, J. and Smith, A. 72% of Online Adults are Social Networking Site Users. *Pew Internet Project*, 2013.
8. Buhrmester, D. and Prager, K. Patterns and functions of self-disclosure during childhood and adolescence. In K. Rotenberg, ed., *Disclosure Processes in Children and Adolescents*. Cambridge University Press, Cambridge, UK, 1995, 10–56.
9. Burke, M. Kraut, R. and Marlow, C. Social capital on Facebook: Differentiating uses and users. In *Proc. CHI*, ACM Press (2011), 571-580.
10. Das, S. and Kramer, A. Self-censorship on Facebook. *International Conference on Weblogs and Social Media*, In *Proc. ICWSM*, AAAI Press (2013).
11. Derlega, V.J. and Chaikin, A.L. Privacy and self-disclosure in social relationships. *Journal of Social Issues 33*, 3 (1977), 102–115.
12. Derlega, V.J. and Grzelak, J. Appropriateness of self-disclosure. In G.J. Chelune, ed., *Self-Disclosure: Origins, Patterns, and Implications of Openness in Interpersonal Relationships*. Jossey-Bass, San Francisco, 1979, 151–176.
13. Ellison, N. and boyd, d. Sociality through social network sites. In W.H. Dutton, ed., *Oxford Handbook of Internet Studies*. Oxford University Press, Oxford, 2013, 151-172.
14. Ellison, N., Vitak, J., Gray, R., and Lampe, C. Cultivating social resources: The relationship between bridging social capital and Facebook use among adults. *Journal of Computer-Mediated Communication*, (in press).
15. Goffman, E. *The Presentation of Self in Everyday Life*. Doubleday Anchor, New York, 1959.
16. Gross, R. and Acquisti, A. Information revelation and privacy in online social networks. In *Proc. ACM workshop on Privacy in the electronic society 2005*, ACM Press (2005), 71–80.
17. Hampton, K.N., Goulet, L.S., Rainie, L., and Purcell, K. Social networking sites and our lives. *Pew Internet Project*, 2011.
18. Hogan, B. The Presentation of self in the age of social media: Distinguishing performances and exhibitions

Online. *Bulletin of Science, Technology & Society 30*, 6 (2010), 377–386.

19. Lampinen, A., Lehtinen, V., Lehmuskallio, A., and Tamminen, S. We're in it together: Interpersonal management of disclosure in social network services. In *Proc. CHI*, ACM Press (2011), 3217–3226.
20. Lincoln, Y.S. and Guba, E.G. *Naturalistic Inquiry*. Sage Publications, Beverly Hills, CA, 1985.
21. Madden, M., Lenhart, A., Cortesi, S., Gasser, U., Duggan. M., Smith, A., and Beaton, M. Teens, social media, and privacy. *Pew Internet Project*, 2013.
22. Miles, M.B. and Huberman, A.M. *Qualitative Data Analysis*. Sage Publications, Newbury Park, CA, 1994.
23. Omarzu, J. A disclosure decision model: Determining how and when individuals will self-disclose. *Personality and Social Psychology Review 4*, 2 (2000), 174–185.
24. Patton, M.Q. *Qualitative Research & Evaluation Methods*. Sage Publications, Thousand Oaks, CA, 2002.
25. Parks, M.R. Ideology in interpersonal communication: Off the couch and into the world. *Communication Yearbook 5*, (1982), 79–107.
26. Petronio, S. *Boundaries of Privacy*. State University of New York Press, Albany, NY, 2002.
27. Rosenfeld, L.B. Self-disclosure avoidance: Why I am afraid to tell you who I am. *Communication Monographs 46*, 1 (1979), 63–74.
28. Sleeper, M., Balebako, R., Das, S., McConahy, A.L., Wiese, J., and Cranor, L.F. The post that wasn't: Exploring self-censorship on Facebook. *In Proc. CSCW,* ACM Press (2013), 793–802.
29. Stiles, W.B., Shuster, P.L., and Harrigan, J.A. Disclosure and anxiety: A test of the Fever Model. *Journal of Personality and Social Psychology 63* (1992), 980–988.
30. Strauss, A. and Corbin, J. *Basics of Qualitative Research: Techniques and Procedures for Developing Grounded Theory*. Sage Publications, Thousand Oaks, CA, 1998.
31. Stutzman, F., Capra, R., and Thompson, J. Factors mediating disclosure in social network sites. *Computers in Human Behavior 27*, 1 (2011), 590-598.
32. Stutzman, F. and Hartzog, W. Boundary regulation in social media. In *Proc. CSCW*, ACM Press (2012), 769-778.
33. Treem, J.W. and Leonardi, P.M. Social media use in organizations: Exploring the affordance of visibility, editability, persistence, and association. *Communication Yearbook 36* (2012), 143-189.
34. Vitak, J. *Keeping connected in the Facebook age: The relationship between Facebook use, relationship maintenance strategies, and relational outcomes*. PhD dissertation, Michigan State University. East Lansing, MI.
35. Vitak, J. The impact of context collapse and privacy on social network site disclosures. *Journal of Broadcasting and Electronic Media, 56,* 4 (2012), 451-470.
36. Vitak, J. and Ellison, N.B. 'There's a network out there you might as well tap': Exploring the benefits of and barriers to exchanging informational and support-based resources on Facebook. *New Media & Society 15*, (2013), 243–259.
37. Vitak, J., Lampe, C., Ellison, N., and Gray, R. "Why won't you be my Facebook Friend?": Strategies for dealing with context collapse in the workplace. In *Proc. 7th Annual iConference*, ACM Press (2012), 555-557.
38. Wheeless, L.R. and Grotz, J. Conceptualization and measurement of reported self-disclosure. *Human Communication Research 2*, 4 (1976), 338–346.

Family Matters: Control and Conflict in Online Family History Production

Heather Willever-Farr
The iSchool at Drexel
Philadelphia, PA 19104
hlw29@drexel.edu

Andrea Forte
The iSchool at Drexel
Philadelphia, PA 19104
aforte@drexel.edu

ABSTRACT

Findagrave.com and Ancestry.com are sites that support the cooperative creation of public historical resources. These sites of cooperative production have attracted tens of thousands and millions of contributors respectively, yet they embrace content standards, social norms, and models of editorial control that differ radically from the well-studied exemplar of Wikipedia. In this study, we investigated how Ancestry.com and Findagrave.com support production of historical resources through analysis of message boards and interviews with participants. We found that these sites are not only places for building a historical resource, but simultaneously serve as opportunities for public memorialization and familial identity construction. Notably, we found that contributors to these websites embrace the idea of familial oversight of biographical information in order to maintain high standards of quality, and they harbor a corresponding skepticism of the open editing practices that have become a hallmark of many open collaboration projects.

Author Keywords

Peer production; crowd sourcing; socio-technical systems; family history; genealogy.

ACM Classification

H.1.2 [Models and Principals]: User/Machine Systems – Human Factors.

INTRODUCTION

A middle-aged woman lost her beloved husband 6 years ago and spent considerable time writing a biographical sketch of her husband and photographing his grave. She then uploaded these memoirs, along with some personal photos of him, to the user-contributed website Findagrave.com. Soon after, she was shocked and angered to find that an Ancestry.com subscriber had copied and pasted the content and images to a family tree for a family that was not related to her husband. The subscriber conducted careless research and had misidentified her husband as a family member.

CSCW'14, February 15–19, 2014, Baltimore, Maryland, USA.
Copyright © 2014 ACM 978-1-4503-2540-0/14/02...$15.00
http://dx.doi.org/10.1145/2531602.253173

This true story (provided by a participant of this study) points to problems arising in the burgeoning and diverse family history research (FHR) community that is engaging in the production of family histories on the web. Millions of family history researchers (FHRs) are cooperatively building web-accessible archives filled with information and images pertaining to deceased individuals for personal use and for public consumption. Yet, we know little about how their production activities are coordinated and constrained by the different systems that support family history work.

In this paper, we explore these phenomena through the lens of two different family history production websites: Findagrave.com and Ancestry.com's family tree archive. Both the family tree archive and Findagrave.com represent the convergence of personal family history building and the creation of a public historical resource. This juxtaposition highlights the fact that online production activities can have multiple meanings. Unlike Wikipedia, where identity building and memorialization are not formally considered to be part of the encyclopedic enterprise, family history production sites exist to meet family members' wants and needs as they construct histories about their kin.

LITERATURE REVIEW

Understanding the online production of family histories involves not only understanding the practices and information behaviors of FHRs, a topic that has been addressed by researchers in library science and archival studies, but also the phenomena of virtual memorialization and the organization of peer production communities, both of which have drawn the attention of CSCW and social computing researchers. We draw on literature from these diverse disciplines to motivate our research questions and situate the phenomena we investigated.

Online Practices of Family History Researchers (FHRs)

Little is known about the socio-technical aspects of family history production in open collaboration environments. We are aware of only one study of FHRs' collaborative online production activities, which explores peer indexing projects. Peer indexing involves volunteers extracting data from digitized government documents, such as census records, and uploading transcribed data to family history websites. Hansen et al. compared two different types of quality control methods—arbitration and peer review—to determine which might prove to be more efficient and provide more accurate peer indexing on FamilySearch.org [16]. They found that the peer review method took considerably less time to resolve transcriptions errors than arbitration but with slightly less accuracy.

Most research on FHRs has focused on how they share information, advice, and instructional guidance either virtually or face-to-face [7, 29, 34, 36]. These activities have been found to be the foundation of a reciprocal information sharing culture that FHRs draw upon to meet individual information needs [14, 29]. Yakel and Torres found that in face-to-face genealogy society meetings informal information sharing took the form of instructional guidance, which served as a means to bring less experienced FHRs into the family history community of practice [36]. Yakel, Fulton, and Tucker found that web-based chat rooms and forums were also important communication channels for informal information sharing among FHRs [14, 29, 34]. Using a quantitative approach, Veale studied a FHR newsgroup and found that participants got to know one another and interacted in long threads that suggest rich conversations [30]. One might imagine that such online forums provide an opportunity for the kind of community building and enculturation found to be important in face-to-face interactions. However, Willever-Farr, Zach, and Forte studied the exchanges of FHRs on a popular message board on Ancestry.com and found that the abundance of online genealogical data and the structure of technological tools available to FHRs appeared to inhibit them from providing one another with guidance on *how* to find family history data and instead encouraged them to provide family data outright with no instruction in their exchanges on the message board [33]. Instruction on how to conduct research may be critical for newbies as family history is a learned practice involving original research that requires participants to: 1) locate relevant data on deceased individuals from a sea of information scattered across virtual and brick and mortar repositories; 2) verify the relevancy of found data based on contextual or other confirmatory evidence; and 3) use that data to construct family trees and/or family history narratives [7].

Memorialization and Grieving

The literature on FHRs' information behaviors has examined online information sharing behaviors, but does not discuss online memorialization and the virtual representation of family history. There is, however, a growing corpus of literature that has explored the ways in which online spaces are used for memorialization and as a part of the grieving and mourning process.

In contrast to physical memorials, virtual memorials can be modified over time by loved ones and others [17, 24] and free bereavement from one ritual place and time (such as face-to-face funerals or physical graves) [17]. Online memorials provide the bereaved with a virtual space in which they can grieve whenever and however they wish. Virtual memorials also shift death and bereavement from the private sphere of family and local community into the public sphere of the Internet [15, 32]. These public virtual spaces allow for "a unique form of communal discourse" [4] among grievers within and outside of the deceased's immediate social networks and provide a sense of community centered on mourning [2, 17, 24]. Other researchers have found that virtual memorials blur boundaries between the living and the dead and enable relationships with the deceased after death [24], which can extend bereavement and the social lives of the dead indefinitely [22].

Virtual memorials may enable details about the deceased to persist on the Internet indefinitely, creating an "immortal" identity for the deceased that is managed by others [4]. Virtual memorials, therefore, raise questions about who manages the content and potential conflicts over content decisions. On one website, MyDeathSpace.com, anyone can upload a MySpace profile of a deceased individual without the consent of family and/or friends of the deceased [25]. Ryan and Sofka found that some individuals were shocked and disturbed to find deceased family member's profiles online [25, 26]. The content of some memorial postings may be of upsetting to family, friends, and other members of the mourning community; in many instances anyone can post to virtual memorials creating more opportunities for diverse responses to death and potential conflict [32]. For example, postings that express death in religious terms may be offensive to nonbelievers [24]. Internet trolls and spam robots can also lead to unwanted and offensive content being placed on virtual memorials [23].

Managing Online Biographical Content

The difficulties of managing online biographical content have been explored by researchers of open collaboration on Wikipedia. Wikipedia is an online encyclopedia that relies on an open editing model in which anyone can contribute and edit articles on a myriad of topics, including biographies of deceased and living people. Like any Wikipedia article, biographies are expected to follow Wikipedia's established content policies, including Neutral Point of View (NPOV), Verifiability (V), and No Original Research (NOR). Biographical articles, particularly those about living people, have captured researchers' attention in part because they have necessitated a lot of policy intervention [12, 18]. In particular, "the impact on biographies of living persons (BLPs) in Wikipedia is that what used to be a tightly controlled artifact, created for a very small number of subjects, can now be created for and about anyone" [18]. Unsurprisingly, BLPs and attendant policies have created conflict among contributors. Joyce, Butler, and Pike assert that conflict arises largely through differences in goals between and within groups on Wikipedia and that these differences are embodied in artifacts they refer to as "contentious objects" [18]. Contentious objects are elements in a social organization that serve as a common object of activity, but these activities contain elements of unrealized conflict. For the Wikipedia community, BLPs are particularly contentious objects.

Conflict over BLPs or other types of content on Wikipedia is typically resolved through various avenues that ideally involve rational discourse and consensus building. For example, "talk" pages that are separate from the encyclopedia content are spaces for contributors to discuss content changes and resolve disputes related to a specific article [31]. Additionally, a revision comment field, which is a free-form text field supplied by each contributor when submitting an edit, is available for the contributor to describe what kind of changes he/she made and why [27]. As a last resort, the Arbitration Committee can be called upon to resolve a dispute among contributors [12].

Avenues for resolving disputes are a critical feature of Wikipedia, as conflict resolution is becoming a mainstay in the development of many Wikipedia articles, whether the content encompasses BLPs or other types of content. Kittur, Suh, Pendleton, and Chi found conflict impacts activity at the article level: the number of article edits is decreasing, while the overhead (the number of edits intended for communication and policy making) is increasing for individual articles [19]. Later, Suh, Chi, Pendleton, and Kittur developed a user conflict model for Wikipedia ("Revert Graph") based on revert activity (revisions that void previous edits) and found four social patterns of conflict. The authors observed that conflict was not always tied to a specific piece of content—disagreements among user factions often propagated from one article into others [27]. Territorialism, the expression of ownership towards an object, is another source of contention among Wikipedia contributors. Territorial behaviors, if left unchecked, may result in conflicts over ownership and hinder cooperation. In Wikipedia such territorialism is discouraged, although Thom-Santelli, Cosley and Gay found in an interview-based study that some Wikipedia editors develop the means to take "ownership" of articles by being the primary contributor to the article, being the initial content creator, being the main reviser of the content, and/or using an editing style that bolsters his/her primary contributor role [28]. Reasons for this behavior included commitment to producing quality articles that would stand up to heavy critique, rectifying vandalism, and removing erroneous information or unsupported assertions.

Research Questions

The high-level question that motivates this work is, "What are the social and technical features of open collaboration systems that support family history researchers?" Given the peculiar juxtaposition of personal and public concerns that characterize online family history construction and the breadth of literature that highlights the contentious nature of online biographical materials, we specifically wondered:

- What tensions and conflicts arise as FHRs simultaneously engage in the personal work of constructing the story of their own families and the public construction of a historical resource?
- How do FHRs negotiate these tensions and resolve conflicts?
- How do the systems that support online production of family histories constrain and support negotiation of these tensions?

METHODS

To answer these questions, we undertook a qualitative study using multiple data sources. The primary empirical support for our analysis comes from message board/forum data and interviews with FHRs.

To begin, we selected two family history production websites to examine: Findagrave.com (Find A Grave) and Ancestry.com (Ancestry). These popular websites were chosen because of their prominence, the number of contributors involved, the historical value of the materials being archived, and the potential differences that may exist between family history production on a commercial website vs. a community-run website. To better understand how the sites support production and what kinds of technological constraints they impose on production activities, we spent months observing activity and trying out both Ancestry and Find A Grave. We also examined the sites' terms of service and guidelines to understand the production rules. These observations raised many questions about how people perceive their activities. Did people view their work on these sites as building a public resource or as a personal project? For what audience was this often painstaking work intended? What kind of research experience do contributors bring to the sites? As these questions accumulated, we developed an interview guide to explore Ancestry and Find A Grave contributors' experiences and perceptions of the sites.

We sought to interview individuals who had provided content on both websites, and used message boards and word-of-mouth on both Ancestry.com and Findagrave.com to recruit participants. Eight individuals agreed to be interviewed: six women and two men. Participant ages ranged widely: one in his 20s, three in their 40s, two in their 50s, and two in their 60s. All eight interviewees had contributed content to both websites and had participated on both of the sites' message boards/forums. Interviews lasted from 40 minutes to 2.5 hours; most interviews were over an hour in length. Interviews were recorded and transcribed. The first author performed three iterations of coding to identify thematic patterns in the transcribed data using Atlas.ti (open coding) [6]. Both authors discussed and worked with the resulting codebook to refine and further articulate the relationships among codes (axial coding) [6].

Interviews revealed that production problems were sometimes hashed out on Ancestry's message boards, Find A Grave forums, or via private messaging. Although private message exchanges are not observable, message board/forum posts are publicly available, and we collected a strategic sample of public discussion threads to further understand the dynamics of online family history production. Similar to the method used by Forte, Humphreys, and Park [11], we used the codebooks developed from interview data to inform our analysis of public message board/forum posts.

Ancestry and Find A Grave message boards are different and required different sampling strategies to assemble a corpus for analysis. Although interviewees had identified the Ancestry message boards as an important communication channel for discussing community issues and airing grievances, we knew from existing research [33] that much of the content on these boards involved help requests that are not clearly related to the production of artifacts on the site. Some interviewees, fortunately, mentioned that discussions regarding family tree production were often conducted on the "Ancestry" threads. This pointed researchers to a section of the message boards which enabled the researchers to identify specific boards that might provide additional information on production activities on the site. This yielded 5 message boards with 1,512 total posts between January 1, 2011 and March 1, 2013. Compared with Ancestry, Find A Grave forums are smaller in number, and we knew less about their composition. As a result, we initially read all 2,291 posts for the period January 1, 2013 to March 1, 2013 to get a sense of the content of the different forums. Forums that were overtly off-topic, such as discussions about politics or vintage cars were discarded, leaving 5 forums to explore. For the time period January 1, 2011 to March 1, 2013, there were 763 posts on the 5 production-oriented Find A Grave forums. We analyzed a total message board corpus of 2,275 posts.

Finally, we used the interview codebook to categorize content from all the posts, which worked well and yielded a rich set of complementary data from both intervention-based interviews and naturally-occurring online discussions. Production-oriented posts involved discussions about three topics: technical problems with the website, problems associated with use of copyrighted materials in user-contributed content, and problems with inaccurate user-contributed family histories. The posts strongly iterated the interview findings, which further strengthened our confidence in the validity of our interpretations. Content inaccuracies, technical glitches resident in studied website infrastructures (e.g. photo upload problems), and copyright issues were mentioned by both posters and interviewees. This paper explores one of those issues—inaccuracies in user-contributed family histories—which appeared to be creating wide-spread conflict among contributors. Our future research plans include exploring the copyright issues associated with family history production.

RESEACH SETTINGS

Find A Grave and Ancestry support FHRs in different ways. Each of these sociotechnical systems are influenced by the website owners and administrators, as well as the contributors. This section will give an overview of the production systems, artifacts, and guidelines that set the stage for family history work on each site.

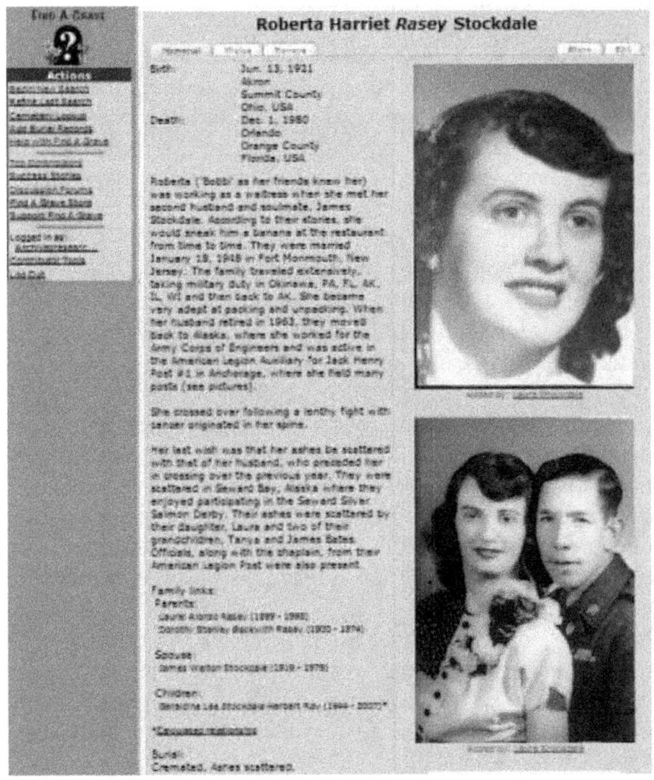

Figure 1: Find A Grave memorial.

Findagrave.com

On Find A Grave, tens of thousands of contributors have uploaded artifacts related to deceased individuals. Each entry for a deceased person is called a memorial and typically includes a biographical sketch of the deceased, images of the grave marker, and sometimes images of the deceased. In addition, any registered user can upload virtual memorial tokens (e.g. virtual flowers) to the memorial. Submitters retain editorial control of memorials they create.

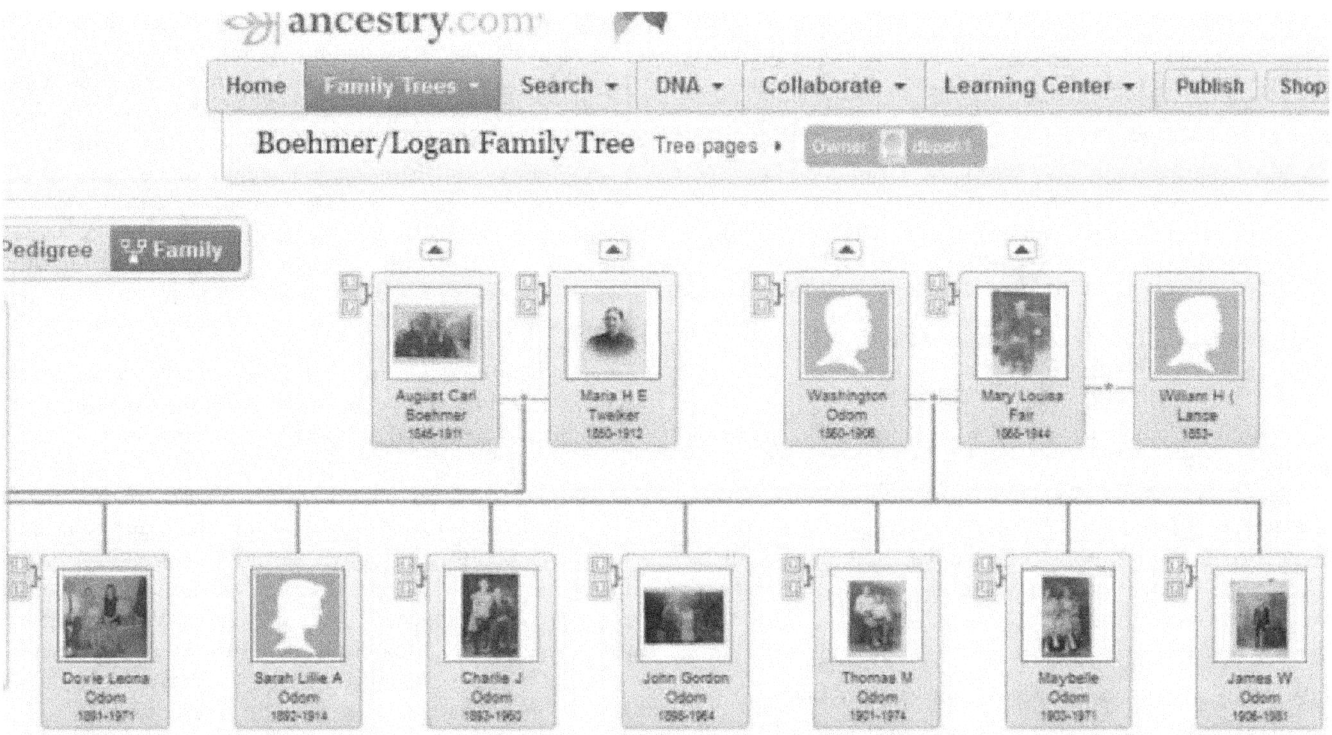

Figure 2: Ancestry.com family tree

In the case of famous persons and Medal of Honor recipients, the site itself retains editorial control. Find A Grave is free to use and all of its content is freely accessible. There is no licensing requirement for submitted content beyond the requirement that it not infringe on intellectual property laws of any country.

The Find A Grave website is maintained by its founder, Jim Tipton, who first developed the website as a place for contributors to provide content about famous persons' graves [9]. Over time, interviewees stated that the site has become more family-history oriented, as more and more FHRs have added content to the site. Features such as the ability to hyperlink memorials to the memorials of related individuals have been added to meet the needs of FHRs. The Find A Grave website is currently administered by Tipton and six additional volunteers who, together, manage conflicts among contributors and resolve other problems and technical issues. The site also features discussion forums for socializing and help seeking.

Ancestry.com

Ancestry is a comparatively large site owned by a private equity firm and for a subscription fee provides online access to records and family tree production tools. In 2012, Ancestry reported over 2 million paid subscribers [1]. Through arrangements with archival repositories in both the US and Europe, Ancestry has digitized, indexed, and transcribed records and made them available to subscribers through online databases. In addition to providing access to records and transcribed data, Ancestry's family tree production tools enable subscribers to enter basic information about deceased individuals and record their relationships to others. Documents, images, and videos can be uploaded and linked to individuals represented in the tree. To build family trees on the website, subscribers can search Ancestry's databases for deceased individuals by name, date, and other variables and then populate their family trees with the found information and images. Ancestry also provides a hint feature: once a contributor creates a portion of a family tree, the website will generate "hints" that appear as shaking leaves. These hints are automatically generated and may lead to relevant transcribed data or digitized records, such as census records, military records, and other user-contributed family trees. Ancestry encourages contributors to make their trees publicly viewable (to Ancestry subscribers) and to connect individuals represented in their family trees to related individuals in others' trees. These links have the potential to transform isolated family tree building projects into contributions to an extensive public resource—a world-wide kinship graph.

Contributors, however, have control over whether to make their tree public or private and whether to allow their trees to be connected to others. Other features of Ancestry include free, public message boards, and a private messaging function for users with accounts. Message boards are moderated by volunteer administrators.

FINDINGS

Through interviews and analysis of contributor posts three themes were uncovered: representation of family; conflict between experienced, meticulous researchers and careless researchers; and awareness of family history production as a public resource and the need for accuracy.

Family Matters: The Representation of Kin

All of the interviewees, as well as many Find A Grave and Ancestry forum/message board participants, spoke or wrote of the importance of controlling the content of their own family information on FHR websites. They referred to two concerns:

- the public portrayal of family members, and
- the accuracy of content about relatives.

How relatives are remembered was a primary concern of family history contributors. Family trees and Find A Grave entries were viewed as means of memorializing and presenting information about the deceased for future generations. Thus, deceased relatives' identities were at stake in the creation of virtual memorials or family trees, as one interviewee explained:

> "So my family, we have two Frank Greeleys and I posted a picture of one online. On Find A Grave. Well, I see it on Ancestry that that picture is attributed to both of the Frank Greeleys. And it's anymore, people just grab the wrong picture and upload the wrong person and then they never go back and check and so I think that's another thing that we're running into. That people just aren't checking and not realizing that just because you have a picture of someone with this name, it doesn't mean that it's definitely this person. You have to look and be like, well, there's two of them. So obviously you have to look at both. So which one could it be?...Future generations are going to be like, I found five different family trees and they're all different and which one is correct?"

Contributors' heighted sense of the role virtual family histories will play in the collective memory of their family's past influenced their thinking about editorial control. They want to create and control their family stories for their own families, but many also want to add content to the websites about non family members for use by non-related researchers. This raises the question of how does one build policies, norms, and permissions on a collaborative platform that respects the existential need of families to control the representation of kin, as well as supporting the production of a historical resources for broader publics?

We found that Ancestry and Find A Grave take similar approaches but with one significant difference. Both are premised, in part, on the idea that people will generate content about their own families. Ancestry.com does not provide community guidelines that address an individual's right to control content about his/her own family; however, guidelines and even site infrastructure generally assume that contributors are creating family trees for their own families and should have the right to retain editorial control of the family trees they created. Contributors can invite specific individuals (presumably family members) to collaborate on a family free, but cannot make a tree editable by the public. The only other opportunities for cooperative production are linking trees with other contributors' trees (if the other contributors approve) or offering suggestions (such as corrections) or other information to other contributors by way of messaging.

Find A Grave takes a slightly different approach. The website provides opportunities for joint construction of content by family and non-family contributors. On the site, any registered user can create a memorial for a deceased person, as long as one does not already exist for that individual. The original creator of the memorial retains editorial control of biographical information in the memorial, but any registered contributor can upload photographs to the memorial, as well as virtual memorial tokens (such as virtual flowers). This hybrid approach to editorial control (keeping images of graves or memorial tokens and textual authorship separate) facilitates cooperation among family and non-family contributors, and supports the development of Find A Grave as a public resource. The editorial structure of the site, for example, allows non-family members to provide grave images for other contributors' memorials thereby creating richer and more complete memorials. One forum poster attested to the importance of this hybrid approach:

> "...I also have to say that I love the way that Find a Grave works. If I make a memorial for a relative who is buried hundreds of miles away and if I make a request for a photo of the headstone, some wonderful volunteer will go out and take a picture for me and post it to the memorial, FOR FREE. Very little else in my world today comes close to this concept."

When it comes to biographical content of memorials, however, Find A Grave production guidelines explicitly favor family control. According to the Find A Grave's "Family First" policy, a direct relative within four generations (siblings, parents, grandparents, and great-grandparents) has the editorial rights to a related family member's biographical content ("the memorial") if the original contributor is not a direct family member. If the original contributor refuses to transfer the memorial, direct relatives can take up their case with volunteer administrators, who serve as community mediators. Similarly, a Find A Grave guideline states that if a family member does not want their relative memorialized on the site (in the instance that a nonrelated person created the memorial), original contributors are expected to take the memorials down; when a memorial "owner" dies the website states that the "management of your memorials may be passed on to the family members of the memorials that you have created" [10].

Echoing the Ancestry and Find A Grave production rules and guidelines, interviewees and posters voiced support for familial ownership or restricted editorial control of memorials and family trees. One might expect that the desire to control potentially negative content about family members was a key motivating factor in FHR's desire for restricted editorial controls. In fact, interviewees never mentioned this and few message board posts addressed this issue. The more prominent concern was accuracy of biographical information, not whether the content was flattering. Contributors feared that if anyone could modify content about their family members, lots of inaccurate information might be added. Inaccurate information was tantamount to besmirching their relatives' reputation, as one Ancestry message board poster declared:

> "People that play fast and loose with facts when they simply collect names on their trees are creating problems for those people that care about truth in their family histories. It's also disrespectful to the ancestors and the lives they led to deliberately disregard facts. Even if the lives they led were less than 'admirable'."

"Getting the facts right" about one ancestors for current and future generations appeared to be a key motivating factor for contributing and controlling content.

A Battle Over Accuracy: The Clash Between Careful Researchers and "Clickologists"

Fears of inexperienced FHRs polluting others' family trees or memorials with inaccurate information contributed to the study participants' strong desire to control content on their family trees and memorials. Most interviewees saw themselves as serious, experienced FHRs. Many posters on the message boards and forums we examined touted their experience level and their careful and thorough research practices in discussions. These vocal, central members of the FHR community stress the importance of careful research and the collection of evidence to back up historical claims about family members. Since the majority of records or documents about deceased individuals are not digitized, collecting evidence often entails traveling to brick and mortar archives and graveyards. Many experienced FHRs have developed artifactual literacy (the ability to analyze and interpret primary documents), subject knowledge (such as knowledge of the history of a geographical region), as well as "archival intelligence" or knowledge of archival principles and practices [7, 35]. These literacies enable FHRs to triangulate data from various sources to ensure that found information is relevant to their ancestors.

The FHRs we studied prided themselves on these skills; however, they also frequently lamented FHRs who were careless in their research practices and who cared more about increasing the size of their family trees or the number of memorials they contributed than about accuracy. In fact, Ancestry was seen as a provocateur of poor quality family histories on the web. Many asserted that Ancestry had so lowered the bar for entry into family history construction that people were creating content without really knowing how to properly conduct family history research. Contributors referred to such FHRs as "clickologists" and "half researchers" as they populated their trees and memorials without attempting to verify that the information was actually about their relatives. Many asserted that Ancestry had encouraged "clickologist" behavior by suggesting that a subscription would allow people to create an accurate family tree in a weekend with the tools and data on the site.

Automation also played an insidious role. Some complained that inexperienced researchers mindlessly accept Ancestry hints—the little shaking leaves ("poison ivy" or "poison leaves" as two interviewees described them) offered by the sites' automatic search feature—without verifying the data, leading to family trees full of erroneous information or "genealojunk." According to many FHRs, Ancestry's algorithms that identify potential kinship links do a poor job at triangulating data from different documents and data points, leading to many false positives. Yet, inexperienced FHRs still click on them and populate their trees with the incorrect data. This has created a domino effect as erroneous information propagates from tree to tree. An Ancestry message board poster commented on the problem:

> "Most of the trees on Ancestry are rubbish anyway - at least the hundreds of trees claiming to have relatives of mine on them. Proper family history research requires that you locate and examine the sources of every entry yourself. Just grabbing junk lists of names from Ancestry is another game altogether. To be certain that you have the correct ancestors you MUST see the BMD certs and the Parish Records (or DEFINITE images of them) YOURSELF."

An interviewee similarly opined:

> "Well sometimes those little leaves are poison ivy. And people will ask us to trees that are no true facts. Like my husband, after I tried to get some people to make some corrections I just went ahead and made my tree private...My husband is a direct descendant from a woman who had a child and he was born in the 1830's and she never married. She never had any more children...but people keep wanting to marry her off and have her with two or three other children and I email them and I say look, Nancy never had any other children. She never married. Your information isn't correct. But it's still perpetrating a falsehood. So that's the only reason I went private but most anybody who asks

> me, I give them access or I give them what they want to know."

On Find A Grave, contributors also indicated concern about "half researchers" and "half-fast researchers" adding or editing content on their family's memorials. Negative experiences with careless researchers appeared to be a strong motivating factor for the studied contributors to maintain control of their own family trees or memorials. These experiences beget skepticism of radically open editing policies and colored our interviewees views of sharing content and working collaboratively with others to build family history content for the wider public.

Family History as Public Resource: Conflicted Views of Sharing and Editorial Control

All interviewees described a similar trajectory from researching their own families and sharing family history content on FHR-oriented websites to conducting research about non-family members. Contributors moved from meeting an immediate personal information need to attempting to meet the potential needs of future researchers. Among interviewees who described contributions to Find A Grave, it was evident that they viewed the site as a historical resource for the public and not only a resting place for their own family history. For example, interviewees described visiting graveyards that were geographically close to them in order to collect and share information about non-related individuals buried there. Others described collecting information on deceased individuals at local archives and adding this information to Find A Grave because others may need that information. One interviewee who had been contributing content pertaining to non-related individuals to Find A Grave for over four years described her motivations for contributing:

> "What's important to me is I get a kick out of somebody's page (memorial) and seeing who their parents were and who their children were. And it hurts me that I can't make it totally complete…So if I can look for it, and I can find it, I'm going to put it up there. And if I don't know, I've even had times when I've been looking for newspapers in the obituaries and stuff. And if I see something that's really interesting, I'll just grab that one and put it up too…"

To build Find A Grave as a public resource coordination among volunteers was frequently needed. Often coordination occurred at the local level, as one interviewee recalled:

> "There are a couple people here in town, I know if a request comes through for Central Cemetery I just delete it because there's two people who have that market cornered… it's a waste of my time to go over there because I know these people know where all these sections are and they know exactly where to go so I can save my efforts for something like St. Mary's Chapel."

Coordination also took place virtually among contributors who were not co-located. Many interviewees spoke of meeting other contributors on one of the Find A Grave forums, and deciding to partner with them to create memorials. For example, one interview described her relationship with an older woman who enjoyed finding facts about deceased individuals but could not take grave photos. She decided to partner with her: she would take grave photos and her volunteer partner would develop the biographical information. Other contributor efforts were responsive to specific needs of other contributors. All the interviewees had responded to requests for grave photographs on Find A Grave's request thread, and uploaded the requested grave images to memorials.

Contributors were not only concerned about the accuracy of their own family histories, many also expressed concern about Find A Grave's overall accuracy and completeness as a public resource. Despite the general agreement with familial oversight of content, concern for the site as a public resource evoked frustration with restricted editorial controls. Interviewees and forum posters were frustrated that poorly researched memorials could not be corrected unless the owner decided to edit the memorial based on their suggested corrections. If the owner of the memorial did not respond to suggested corrections, their only recourse was to bring the problem to one of the site's six administrators or the site owner in hopes they could mediate a solution. The following Find A Grave forum poster described this frustration:

> "Unresponsive contributors…I am in the same spot with a contributor who has never responded to my suggestions. Everyone has a story about this. I could wait forever for a response but it will not be forthcoming. That alone causes more work for both us and admin."

Interviewees and forum posters alike suggested that the Find A Grave administrators were overwhelmed with the number of complaints they receive and the number of requests for revisions and memorial ownership transfers. We repeatedly observed frustration with the long lag times between posting a concern or problem on one of the website forums and administrators resolving the problem.

Administrators are not only responsible for addressing errant inaccuracies here or there brought to their attention by other contributors, but also are responsible for resolving problems with slews of "bogus" memorials generated either by contributors who wanted their relatives represented on Find a Grave but did not locate correct burial information, or by contributors who wanted a high number of contributions without doing the necessary work. One interviewee described such an occurrence when two contributors decided to boost the number of memorials on the site:

> "There are certainly some problems with it being as big as Find A Grave is. They just hit their, oh, a big number, a big nice round one with lots of zeros behind it. Apparently, two people were actually fighting over who would get there, and they were entering bogus memorials to get there. And I don't know what the number is, but that magic number with all the zeros is now gone, because somebody pointed out in the forums that they were doing this, entering bogus memorials, and they removed it."

The same interviewee similarly described the fabrication of an entire graveyard full of deceased relatives:

> "There's people who play with the numbers, and they play with getting their genealogy up there whether they know where people were buried or not. There was a lady who put in all the relatives, whether she knew where they were buried or not, which is a big no-no. And it's just like, she put in people so that there is a whole cemetery out there... something like Smith's cemetery...But there is 500 burials in there, it's like, really? I started looking at it and 99% of them all died in 1880, 1870, 1900 – on the census years. She was creating people from the census records and burying them in that cemetery."

The interviewee described her dismay that these bogus memorials were never taken down, because while they appeared incorrect, the administrators could not prove they were incorrect without visiting the cemetery, which was not feasible.

Frustrations with inaccuracies generated by other contributors and unresponsive contributors did not stop most of the interviewees from continuing to contribute content, but it did cause them to avoid contributors with whom they had problematic experiences. A few participants reported that frustration with problem contributors led them to stop offering any corrections. As one interviewee stated, "Now, you go do your thing and I'll do my thing, because I have run into so much that it's like you know you can't convince some people that they are wrong." Another interviewee described how she maintains content on Find A Grave for another contributor who was tired of dealing with contentious exchanges between contributors:

> "She would gather all the information together, send me a spreadsheet. I would put the spreadsheet online, and that way she doesn't have to deal with all of the communication from various people. So my name is on it, but I really haven't done any work. She just didn't want to have to deal with some of the other people...So there's a lot of fighting. And along with it have come people who have decided that rules don't apply. And it's their family. I call them the but, but people. But, but, but it's my family. I can do what I want with them. So I know there are a lot of people who have stepped away. Old-timers."

Problems with inaccuracies and conflict between contributors may be even more of a stumbling block for cooperative production on Ancestry. Problems with inaccuracies led all but one of the interviewees and many of the studied posters on Ancestry's message boards to make their family trees "private" or not allow others to connect to their trees. By not making their trees public and not allowing connections, they made a choice to not share their family histories with other Ancestry subscribers and to limit their cooperative production activities. This choice was the result of their concern that information and images from their carefully researched family trees was being lifted without their permission and placed on family trees that were for families that were not related, because the tree builder did not conduct careful research. As one forum poster on Find A Grave concluded:

> "Half-fast researchers are what poison Ancestry.com trees...I warn new researchers to RUN from those, and do their own primary research. Those sources are a thousand times more accessible than they were when I started, but sometimes you have to get off the couch and do the legwork yourself. The point-and-click researchers who think info needs to come to them are the same ones who think others are 'meanies' when actual re-search-ers do re-search and then don't share everything freely. Screw your time, effort, gas, injuries, bug bites, sun burns."

An Ancestry poster described his decision to no longer allow others to view or connect to his family trees:

> "Two so called members of Ancestry have latched themselves on to my great great grandparents James Cassidy and Ann Mooney but they have latched on to the wrong James and Ann. No proper research or cross referencing done whatsoever. NO REDRESS WHATSOEVER HOW CAN ANCESTRY HAVE ANY CREDIBILITY IF THEY ALLOW THIS TO CARRY ON? It's a money making machine with no desire to make this a serious family history research site and that is very sad. So be warned. For research purposes they are absolutely wonderful. For showcasing your work or sharing your data a total unmitigated disaster, especially ANCESTRY. If you do upload your family tree KEEP IT PRIVATE! Invitation only!"

Poor research practices and inaccuracies appear to be hindering cooperative work on both Ancestry and Find A Grave.

DISCUSSION

Websites for family history production attract millions of contributors. It is unclear, however, whether a large number of participants is sufficient to sustain the long-term cooperative production of an accurate family history resource for current and future generations. The need to not only attract participants, but enculturate them into the practices of a community has been recognized as a primary challenge for open collaboration systems [13]. This often entails interactions among more and less experienced contributors; however, we observed that at times conflict over accuracy has pitted experienced, careful researchers against less experienced researchers who are viewed as careless. Thus, the very individuals who could be mentoring and teaching newcomers about good research practices are angry and lose patience with the restrictions and editorial controls on both Ancestry and Find A Grave. Many committed contributors want the content to be accurate but must rely on others to address inaccuracies and have few avenues to teach newly minted contributors good research practices.

We have noted that the culture of the FHR community stresses the importance of helping others with their family history research [14, 33], and in face-to-face environments this often takes the form of informal instruction [36]. In a virtual environment with information about deceased persons at the researchers' finger tips, "help" often takes the form of sharing data instead of providing instruction [33]. Our findings suggest that less experienced contributors may need instruction on good research practices in order for them to be able to create quality content online. This raises a broader question -- what is the most appropriate model for online FHR communities to bring newcomers into the community of practice?

There is a wealth of work on the socio-technical features of Wikipedia that support new participants. These range from technical features of the wiki permissions system that allow newcomers to start contributing in small ways, enabling them to "learn the ropes" through *legitimate peripheral participation* [3], to social interventions like welcome messages, and offers of assistance [5] to extensive education efforts like the Teahouse [21], which provides a nurturing social space for newcomers and efforts to train college students to contribute [8].

These approaches, however, rely on open editing systems. In contrast, we found that *familial oversight* is an important feature of sites that support family history production. Yet these restrictions raise the bar for participation and reduce the opportunities for low-risk peripheral participation that could ease new contributors into the creation of biographical content. For example, on Ancestry.com, one must create a family tree in order to make an original contribution and populate it with all the requisite information. One obvious solution is to allow families to choose whether they want to open their family tree or memorial for editing, thus creating some opportunities for newbies to make small edits. We found, however, that experienced FHRs are resistant to open editing, and may not welcome this possible solution.

Ancestry has attempted to solve the newbie problem by automating some of the family tree-building process, thus lowering the bar for newcomers. Yet, we learned that this approach has not proved effective for enculturating newcomers, who tend to rely on a recommendation engine to identify family links without understanding how to verify the quality of recommendations. Instead of encouraging newcomers to learn how to construct family histories and conduct research, this approach has led to family trees and memorials littered with incorrect information and a general distrust of automated tools among experienced FHRs.

Other possible solutions may alleviate or lessen problems with content inaccuracies on Ancestry and Find A Grave. First, we suggest that both websites include a tagging feature that enables contributors to indicate that specific information included on their memorials or family trees is not yet verified. Interviewees mentioned that they often collected data and placed it on memorials or family trees before fully verifying the data. Only later did they find corroborating information sources or deleted the data when further research suggested the data was incorrect. To help newcomers or any contributor struggling with confirming the accuracy of found data, an additional tagging feature would enable contributors to indicate to others that they needed help finding confirmatory evidence for specific found data. Such a tagging feature may encourage cooperation among content contributors and increase awareness of the importance of finding confirmatory evidence to support the relevancy of found data. However this tagging function does not fully address the problem of newcomers learning the craft of genealogical research.

As was found in a previous study of Ancestry message boards, unstructured discussion spaces do not necessarily facilitate the exchange of instructional guidance. Yet, research on FHRs in face-to-face contexts suggests that many experienced practitioners are committed to helping newcomers learn the craft. We also found that the interviewees wanted to help others but were frustrated with online spaces that did not provide good opportunities for learning to take place before contributors were producing content. Given the willingness of many FHRs to help others learn the craft, it makes sense to provide virtual spaces to better facilitate learning that are more robust than typical message boards. The FHR environment—full of people who want to learn how to find good information as well as experts who want to help—make it a rich context for experimentation with online learning.

We suggest that family history "learning spaces" should support both synchronous and asynchronous interactions between experienced FHRs and newcomers. These learning spaces could include resources, such as learning modules and video tutorials, to which experienced FHRs could direct newcomers, as well as "practice" spaces in which newcomers could work with experienced FHRs to build memorials or family trees. Such learning spaces may be a means of bringing newcomers into the family history community of practice and ultimately may help improve problems with content inaccuracies on the sites. Our future research plans include exploring the potential of community learning spaces for improving the quality of user-contributed family history content.

LIMITATIONS

The opinions and perceptions of interviewees and studied forum/message board posters may not be representative of the many potentially diverse opinions of Find A Grave and Ancestry contributors, such as those of novices. It is also impossible to tease out whether system design on the two sites, particularly the inclusion of restricted editing controls, has influenced contributors' bias against open editing systems for family history production.

CONCLUSION

High quality family history content requires that contributors are well versed in locating information from a number of sources and triangulating that information to ensure that found information is correct. Without such expertise, content can be inaccurate and result in the misrepresentation of the deceased. In other virtual production communities, good research practices are also needed to create accurate content. As a result, it is important that we develop socio-technical systems that will help new contributors learn good research practices. This paper proposes some possible solutions, but more research is needed to fully address this challenge.

ACKNOWLEDGEMENTS

We would like to thank Katherine McCain for bringing Find A Grave to our attention and for her insights about family history production. This work is supported by the National Science Foundation, CISE IIS-1253302.

REFERENCES

1. Ancestry.com Inc. Reports Q3 2012 Financial Result. *http://ir.ancestry.com/releasedetail.cfm?ReleaseID=716064/*
2. Brubaker, J. R. and Hayes, G. R. We will never forget you [online]: An empirical investigation of post-mortem Myspace comments. In *Proc. CSCW 2011*, ACM Press (2011), 123-132.
3. Bryant, S. L., Forte, A., and Bruckman, A. Becoming Wikipedian: Transformation of participation in a collaborative online encyclopedia. *Proc. Supporting Group Work*, ACM Press (2005), 1-10.
4. Carroll, B. and Landry, K. Logging on and letting out: Using online social networks to grieve and to mourn. *Bulletin of Science, Technology & Society 30*, 5 (2010), 341-349.
5. Choi, B., Alexander, K., Kraut, R. E. and Levine, J. M. Socialization tactics in Wikipedia and their effects. *Proc CSCW 2010*, ACM Press (2010), 107-116.
6. Corbin, J. and Strauss, A. *Basics of qualitative research: Techniques and procedures for developing grounded theory*. Thousand Oaks, Ca.: Sage Publications, Inc., 2008.
7. Duff, W. M. and Johnson, C. A. Where is the list with all the names? Information-seeking behavior of genealogists. *American Archivist 66*, 1 (2003), 79-95.
8. Farzan, R. and Kraut, R.E. Wikipedia classroom experiment: Bidirectional benefits of students' engagement in online production communities. *Proc. CHI 2013,* ACM Press (2013), 783-792
9. Findagrave.com. http://www.findagrave.com/cgi-bin/fg.cgi?page=whois/
10. Findagrave.com. http://www.Find A Grave.com/cgi-bin/fg.cgi?page=listFaqs/
11. Forte, A., Humphreys, M. and Park, T. Grassroots professional development: How teachers use Twitter. *Proc. International Conference on Weblogs and Social Media (ICWSM)*, Association for Advancement of Artificial Intelligence (2012), 106-113.
12. Forte, A., Larco, V. and Bruckman, A. Decentralization in Wikipedia governance. *Journal of Management of Information Systems 26*, 1 (Summer 2009), 49-72.
13. Forte, A. and Lampe, C. Defining, understanding and supporting open collaboration: Lessons from the literature. *American Behavioral Scientist* 57, 5 (2013), 535-547.
14. Fulton, C. Quid pro quo: Information sharing in leisure activities. *Library Trends 57*, 4 (2009), 752-768.
15. Gibson, M. Death and mourning in technologically mediated culture. *Health Sociology Review* 16, 5 (2007), 415-424.
16. Hansen, D. L., Schone, P. J., Corey, D., Reid, M., and Gehring, J. Quality control mechanisms for crowdsourcing: peer review, arbitration, & expertise at Familysearch indexing. *Proc. CSCW 2013*, ACM Press (2013), 649-660.
17. Hess, A. In digital remembrance: vernacular memory and the rhetorical construction of web memorials. *Media, Culture & Society* 29, 5 (2007), 812-830.
18. Joyce, E., Butler, B. and Pike, J. Handling flammable materials: Wikipedia biographies of living persons as

contentious objects. *Proc. iConference 2011*, ACM Press (2011), 25-32.

19. Kittur, A., Suh, B., Pendleton, B. A., and Chi, E. H. He says, she says: Conflict and coordination in Wikipedia. *Proc. CSCW 2007*, ACM Press (2007), 453 – 462.

20. Luther, K. and Bruckman, A. Leadership in Online Creative Collaboration. *Proc. CSCW 2008*, ACM Press (2008), 343-352.

21. Morgan, J. T., Bouterse, S., Walls, H,. and Stierch, S. Tea and sympathy: Crafting positive new user experiences on Wikipedia. *Proc..CSCW 2013*, ACM Press (2013), 839-848.

22. Mitchell, L. M., Stephenson, P. H., Cadell, S., and Macdonald, M. E. Death and grief on-line: Virtual memorialization and changing concepts of childhood death and parental bereavement on the Internet. *Health Sociology Review 21*, 4 (2012), 413-431.

23. Phillips, W. LOLing at tragedy: Facebook trolls, memorial pages and resistance to grief online. *First Monday 16*, 12-5 (2011).

24. Roberts, P. Here today and cyberspace tomorrow: Memorials and bereavement support on the web. *Generations 28*, 2 (2004), 41-46.

25. Ryan, J. (2008). The virtual campfire: An ethnography of online social networking. Master's thesis, Wesleyan University. http://www.thevirtualcampfire.org/virtualcampfire.htm

26. Sofka, C. J. Adolescents, technology, and the Internet: Coping with loss in the digital world. *Adolescent Encounters with Death, Bereavement, and Coping*. New York: Springer, 2009, 155-173.

27. Suh, B., Chi, E. H., Pendleton, B. A., and Kittur, A. Us vs. them: Understanding social dynamics in Wikipedia with revert graph visualizations. *Visual Analytics Science and Technology,* 2007, 163-170.

28. Thom-Santelli, J., Cosley, D. R., and Gay, G. What's mine is mine: territoriality in collaborative authoring. *Proc. CHI 2009*, ACM Press (2009), 1481-1484.

29. Tucker, S. N. *The most public of all histories: Family history and heritage albums in the transmission of records*. Ph.D. Dissertation, University of Amsterdam, Amsterdam, Netherlands (2009).

30. Veale, K. Discussing our family trees: Finding community-based communication in genealogical newsgroups. *The Journal of Education, Community and Values: Interface on the Internet 4*, 4 (2004).

31. Viégas, F. B., Wattenberg, M., and Dave, K. Studying cooperation and conflict between authors with history flow visualizations. *Proc. CHI 2004*, ACM Press (2004), 575-58.

32. Walter, T., Hourizi, R., Moncur, W., and Pitsillides, S. Does the internet change how we die and mourn? Overview and analysis. *OMEGA--Journal of Death and Dying* 64, 4 (2011), 275-302.

33. Willever-Farr, H., Zach, L., and Forte, A. Tell me about my family: A study of cooperative research on Ancestry.com. *Proc. iConference* 2012, ACM Press (2012), 303-310.

34. Yakel, E. Seeking information, seeking connections, seeking meaning: Genealogists and family historians. *Information Research 10*, 1 (2004), paper 205.

35. Yakel, E. and Torres, D. A. AI: archival intelligence and user expertise. *American Archivist 66,* 1 (2003), 51-78.

36. Yakel, E. and Torres, D. A. Genealogists as a 'community of records.' *American Archivist 70*, 1 (2007), 93-113.

"Our Life is the Farm and Farming is Our Life": Home–Work Coordination in Organic Farm Families

Gilly Leshed
Cornell University
Ithaca, NY, USA
gl87@cornell.edu

Maria Håkansson
Chalmers University of Technology
Gothenburg, Sweden
maria.hakansson@chalmers.se

Joseph 'Jofish' Kaye
Yahoo Labs
Sunnyvale, CA, USA
jofish@yahoo-inc.com

ABSTRACT
We present a qualitative study of 13 farm families who intentionally *merge* their home and work lives. This is in contrast to most families studied in CSCW, who are urban/ suburban, white-collar and often dual-income, where the goal is to *balance* separate home and work spheres. We analyze the farm families' coordination practices along three dimensions – space, time, and roles – and contrast their experiences to what is known in CSCW about family coordination practices. Through this, we reveal blind spots in CSCW's study of and support for family coordination toward building better tools to support such activities. We emphasize considering co-location rather than assuming geographic distribution across life spheres, the value of natural rhythms in understanding and supporting family life, and how taking on simultaneous roles can be viewed as a life goal rather than a source of conflict.

Author Keywords
Home–work split; families; coordination; farms; rural; family business; qualitative studies.

ACM Classification Keywords
H.5.3 Group and Organization Interfaces: CSCW.

General Terms
Human Factors; Design.

INTRODUCTION
Family life has been of great interest to the CSCW and HCI communities in the past years, with a special interest in understanding family coordination practices and directing design efforts to support and improve these practices. Existing work, however, has favored white-collar, middle-class, dual-income, and urban/suburban families, and the activities and values related to living such lives [e.g., 6,9,12,25, 28,29,32,33,36,37]. According to the sociology literature [26], these families experience a *home–work split*, where in general, home is separate from work and other activities such as school, and significant effort goes into coordinating between these different spheres. As a result, we have gained valuable insights into the busy lives of families who are trying to "juggle" everything in everyday, modern life. Furthermore, we have seen how information and communication technologies (ICTs) on the one hand enable the coordination [e.g., 8,24,29], but on the other hand increasingly challenge this split by blurring its boundaries [22,23].

Aside from a few recent exceptions (e.g., divorced families [27,43], low-income families [42], and migrant families [40]), we have fewer insights into the coordination practices of families who organize their lives differently. In this paper, we focus on families who are *intentionally interweaving home and work* and thus do not experience the same home–work split, asking *what does family coordination look like in such families?* By studying coordination practices in families that experience a different way of organizing home and work in family life, we identify blind spots in the research and design space in CSCW for families in general and family coordination in particular.

To this end, we chose to study farm families because of their practice of combining home and work on the farm. We report on a qualitative study of 13 small-scale organic farm families in the US. In our visits to their farms, we encountered love of the outdoors, respect for natural and seasonal rhythms, and responsible children helping their parents, as well as homes that were messy, heavy and stress-inducing workloads, and family conflicts. We organize and discuss our findings in three dimensions of family coordination: *space*, *time*, and *roles*. Finally, we contribute new insights including the importance of considering co-location rather than assuming geographical distribution across life spheres; the value of natural rhythms in understanding and supporting family life; and how taking on simultaneous roles can be viewed as a life goal rather than a source of conflict.

RELATED WORK
Before turning to our study, we review related work. We begin by reviewing studies and designs that focus on family coordination practices and tools. We then discuss theories and studies that articulate home and work as two separate spheres with the difficulties of balancing between the two.

Family Coordination
Family life involves ensuring that all family members participate in school, work, extracurricular activities, special events and appointments, that children and adults are nurtured, and that the house is maintained. This multitude of activities re-

CSCW'14, February 15 – 19, 2014, Baltimore, MD, USA.

ACM 978-1-4503-2540-0/14/02...$15.00.
http://dx.doi.org/10.1145/2531602.2531708

quires continual organization and coordination, of multiple family members with conflicting schedules, and changing task dependencies [7,21]. HCI and CSCW research has focused on understanding the *practices* of family coordination, as well as the *tools* used by and designed for families to enhance their coordination practices.

Coordination Practices

Family coordination has been examined from two primary perspectives, *functional* and *socio-emotional*. The *functional* aspect of coordination ensures that family members complete tasks, carry out activities and attend events. Awareness of family members' schedules, locations, and activities, has been found to be key for effective family coordination [9,25,28,29]. For instance, awareness of family members' schedules is important for coordinating childcare and visits, especially across households (e.g., grandparents) [29]. However, family members often have an incomplete awareness of each other's schedules, which may contribute to scheduling conflicts [9]. Working parents use mobile phones heavily to overcome gaps in this awareness, especially during transition times between activities and locations [28]. According to [25], families vary in the level of internal knowledge of each other's schedules, and as such their involvement in coordination practices varies.

Beyond getting family-oriented tasks done, family coordination has also been examined from the perspective of the *socio-emotional* role it serves in the family. According to [37], family members help define and maintain social order through practices of organizing everyday family life. Thayer et al. [38] describe the use of shared digital calendars in managing friendships and intimate relationships. Sellen et al. [33] found that a home messaging system designed for sending reminders also supported expressing affection and marking identity by family members. Brown et al. [2] found that being aware of each other's activities and locations enhanced emotional connection within the family more than it enabled coordination.

Tools for Coordination

A central point of interest in CSCW and HCI is the tools that families use to coordinate their activities, as well as designing tools for family coordination. Home-based tools, physical or digital, often include calendars [9,24,25,29], lists and reminder systems [36], messaging systems [33], and systems that mix few functions together [6,37]. These tools have been described as "artful" [37], in that they are often reflectively designed, appropriated, and negotiated by family members to fit their changing needs over time. And while such tools are designed to streamline coordination practices, substantial work goes into creating, updating, synchronizing, and maintaining them [25,29].

Just as coordination practices extend beyond the household walls, so do coordination tools. Grimes & Brush [12] found that working parents often schedule and coordinate family activities and events while at work, and other studies described the challenge of coordinating family activities when outside the home and away from their home-based coordination tools [25,29]. Mobile phones take this a step further, allowing families to coordinate their activities on the go. This allows for micro-coordination during transition times between activities [28], which can be supported by mobile applications that locate members at any given moment [8].

Home–Work Split

We see the articulation of coordination practices and the study and development of tools to support such practices as being the core of CSCW. However, the populations studied and designed for in the CSCW literature are often white-collar, middle-class, dual-income, and urban/suburban families, who have been depicted as "juggling" generally separate home and work activities. However, in the families that we study in this paper, the division between home and work manifests in a distinctly different manner.

Home and work are two fundamental areas in human activity and emotional investment. They are not just places, but categories combining conceptual, social-structural and spatio-temporal aspects, together contributing to two "experiential realms" [26]. Theories have been developed around how these two spheres are segmented or integrate, how boundaries are negotiated and crossed back and forth, and where and how conflicts occur when expectations, roles, activities, and time demands contradict between home and work [1,4,26]. There are also positive models for positive spillovers and enrichment between home and work [10,13].

The assumption behind all these theories is that work and home are separate worlds, and that a boundary, more or less blurred depending on the context, can be drawn between the two. But historically, in pre-industrialized societies, there were no boundaries between work and home: all household members had to participate in subsistence activities in order to have food on the table, roof over their head, and clothes on their back [15]. While gendered roles were distinct – women cooking, sowing, and childrearing, and men doing field work, hunting, and wood cutting – all family and household members, including children, participated in unpaid and paid labor to survive [5,30,35]. The industrial revolution introduced a distinction between the spheres of home and work, pushing men toward participation in paid labor outside the home, women to home economics, and children to school activities [5,15].

In the recent decades, these spheres are increasingly becoming blurred, although we argue that the kind of blurring between home and work is not taking us back to pre-industrialized times when households were self-sufficient, but creating new experiences with new opportunities and challenges. Several factors are involved, including increased participation of women in the workforce [31] and information and communication technologies (ICT) [3]. The latter is of particular interest to the CSCW community. First, ICTs introduce opportunities and challenges related to telecommuting [14,20,32]. Using technology to connect to the office and work from home has been linked to greater productivity and flexibility experiences but also to a more problematic work–life balance [11,16]. Second, ICTs, and especially mobile technology and Internet applications, offer new ways of participating in home and work activities beyond spatial constraints of workplace vs. home and temporal constraints of work vs. non-work hours. Individuals can do work such as checking email while outside of the workplace and work hours [23], and they can accomplish home tasks such as scheduling family activities while in the office [12]. While this may lead to feelings of greater autonomy to control when and where work and family activities are getting done, it may also be linked to tensions within the workplace and the family around increased commitment, attention, and privacy [12,23].

The new ways in which home and work are being experienced also require families to practice new ways of coordinating their life at the boundaries between the two. From a spatio-temporal perspective, external schedules from work, school, and extracurricular activities impose on the family distinct times, locations, and participants for each activity, leaving the family to figure out how to "juggle" everything effectively. The CSCW literature on coordination practices and tools reviewed above exemplifies the efforts toward the effective coordination between all these spheres of activities. In addition, home–work split also helps shape coordination through the perspective of roles, by defining what individuals are expected to do in each sphere. When the lines are blurred, however, individuals might find it difficult to comply with multiple roles they assume (e.g., parent and employee) [1]. For example, attending to work emails at home might conflict with pressures from the family to attend to family affairs, and makes it difficult for the family to coordinate their activities by expecting the individual to act as a parent and not as an employee.

By contrast, in our field study, we wanted to understand what family coordination looks like when one of the life goals of the family is to merge home and work rather than keep some boundaries (more or less blurred) between the two. As we will show, the families we studied also work hard, "juggle", and experience conflicts, but their approach to coordinate their life and overcome the conflicts comes from a perspective of attempting to merge home and work, rather than delineate the lines between the two. We believe that by understanding this approach and the practices associated with it, we can uncover new ways of thinking about and designing for family coordination in the CSCW field.

FARM FAMILY STUDY

In the spring of 2012, we visited 13 small-scale organic farms in upstate New York to understand the coordination practices that the families living on these farms carry out and experience in their everyday lives. We conducted interviews with as many family members as possible during our visits, went on farm tours, and afterwards visited their websites, blogs, and Facebook page for those families who had online presence associated with the farm.

Sociologists have a long tradition of studying rural life [for a recent overview, see 41], as well as modernization and technological development in rural life [e.g., 19], which go beyond the scope of this paper. However, because rural life is highly diverse [41], we want to stress that this study looks at small-scale organic farming as *one* particular way of experiencing rural family life. Small-scale farm families are characterized by family farm ownership, operation, management, and labor, by integration of work and home, by a seasonal rhythm of production, and above all, by a commitment to certain values [34].

Farm families can be seen as similar to home business owners and teleworkers in that home and work often occupy the same physical space. For teleworkers, this is associated with challenges and practices around keeping the boundaries between home and work in their roles, activities, and time commitments [e.g., 14,20,32]. In contrast, farm families combine home and work on several dimensions, for example, through homesteading activities as part of their home and farm business practices. As Strange says *"family farming may be a business, but it is not just a business. It is a way of life as well."* [34, p.35].

Participants

We recruited our participants through handouts and advertisements in local farmers' markets and through snowball sampling. The authors are familiar with the local market settings from being regular customers, but we did not know any of the farm families before this study began.

The families vary in the size of the family and ages of children (Table 1; all names of people and farms are pseudonyms). Altogether, 11 pre-school children are looked after at home, 8 school-aged children are homeschooled, and 11 children go to public schools or pre-schools in nearby towns. In Hickory Hill, Foxtail, and Halfmoon some children are homeschooled and others attend public schools depending on their preference. Most of the adult participants did not grow up on farms: these are not life-long farmers but people who have made a deliberate decision as adults to go into farming. In 10 families, one adult works part-time or full-time outside of the farm to help with financial security, leaving the farm to go to their outside job, sometimes daily and sometimes as rarely as once a month.

The farms also vary in the kind of business and foods they grow and sell, including vegetables, fruit, meat animals, honey, flowers, and farm products: cheese, cider, fiber, jam, cooked foods. Their sizes range between 1-150 acres, which is considered small-scale (the US average farm size is 420 acres, and 194 acres in New York State [39]). Their farming practices are strongly influenced by the weather and seasons. In this area, there is generally ample rainfall, but harsh winters with heavy snowfall and freezing temperatures. Although not all the farms are certified organic because of the financial cost and bureaucracy involved, all except Forest Creamery and Harmony consider themselves organic in terms of methods and philosophy. Seven farms have 1-5 employees or interns working on the farm in an ad-hoc manner, seasonally, or year-round.

The farms' primary source of income is selling directly to customers: at one of the area's local weekly farmers' markets, through a *Community Supported Agriculture* (CSA) program, or by selling to local supermarkets and restaurants. Again, in terms of farm business, we want to stress that these represent a particular kind of farmers, and their practices and values may differ from those on large-scale industrial farms, and farms that produce other products, such as grain and dairy.

Interviews

We carried out in-depth qualitative family interviews and farm tours, which together lasted 2-4 hours for each family. Overall, 53 individuals in these families were present in our interviews, of whom 12 were children under the age of 5 who did not actively answer questions. Families were compensated with a $100 gift card to a local store of their choice, and we brought a light meal to each interview as a way of making it easier for the families to participate despite facing a busy season. The meal was also an icebreaker, and often the families chose to eat as we interviewed them, and some invited us to join the meal.

The interviews were semi-structured and open-ended, and we often followed needs dictated by the family and the farm: in bad weather, we limited the farm tour; when the farm or a toddler needed attention, we stayed with the remaining part of the family to complete the interview. Despite these limitations, we covered questions about the farm business, everyday activities in the farm and the family, how all these activities are coordinated among family members, and how participants feel about and value being a farm family. We also asked participants to show and tell us about ICTs they use, and the tools and artifacts (digital and non-digital) they use for organizing, coordinating, and managing their activities, tasks, and time, and how these tools are used in the course of their everyday life. These coordination tools and ICTs included family calendars, to-do lists written on scrap paper and chalkboards on barn walls, computer spreadsheets, and seeding maps and diaries. Interviews and tours were audio-recorded, and we took photographs of objects they showed us in their homes and farms for further analysis. Audio-recordings were fully transcribed and we applied open-coding to search for common concepts and identify themes that reoccur in the data.

COORDINATING HOME AND WORK ON THE FARM

These families deliberately interweave home and work, which has implications not necessarily for the quantity of coordination – these families routinely juggle activities, handle interdependencies, and multitask – but for the quality of how and what their coordination practices look like. As a way of understanding what it means to interweave and coordinate home and work on these farms, we have chosen to look at the empirical data in terms of three dimensions of coordination: *space*, *time*, and *roles*. Although additional dimensions may exist, we are particularly interested in these three, because for each activity family members need to coordinate where it will happen (space), when (time), and who will carry it out (role). These are not exclusive categories; they overlap and merge, but provide a useful set of lenses for understanding and characterizing our participants' experiences and practices.

Space

For our families, there is generally one physical space where most farm work and family activities happen, and they some-

Farm Pseudonym	Primary farm business	Year started on this land	Parents	Adult children	School-age children	Pre-school children	Other participants
Spirit Hill	Vegetables & beef	1992	Mary & Don*	3 daughters 1 hour away*			
Kane Acres	Meat animals	1996	Katie & Mitch		Rachel 14		
Foxtail	Sheep fiber, B&B	1999	Julie & Dave		Beth 18, Bonnie 16, Anika 14, Sean 13, Amy 11, Isaac 8, Mindy 7	Cindy 4, Paige 10m	
Hickory Hill	Vegetables & fruit	2000	Carol & Rob		Vicky* 14, Sophie* 10, Ruth* 7	Micah 5, Riley & Sydney 18m	
Harmony	Honey & jams	2002	Sue & Bob	Bob Jr.*, Aaron*(grandson)			Carly (employee)
Skylark	Vegetables	2003	Lori & Marty		Grace 5	Eric 2, Ross 4m	
Greenwood	Vegetables	2005	Diane & Mark	Natalie, Dan, Marie			
Singalong	Vegetables	2006	Emma & Peter		Yana 5	Sam 3	
Forest Creamery	Cheese	2006	Nina & James*		Leah* 15, Logan* 11		
Oak Ridge	Vegetables	2008	Naomi & Toni			Cara 3, Anna 7m	
Halfmoon	Pasture poultry	2009	Linda & John*	Wendy, Ashley*	Tyler 17, Zion 15, Megan 12		
White Birch	Flowers & vegetables	2009	Wanda & Jim	Stacy*			
Eden	Hard apple cider	2010	Amy & Eli			Lucy 5, Zach 2	

Table 1. Farm families in the study, farm business and children's ages (*individual not present at interview)

times use the terms "farm" and "home" interchangeably to refer to the physical space that occupies both. For our participants, occupying the same physical space is about sharing and experiencing life together. Several of the participants strongly appreciate being able to see their families throughout most days:

"[We] actually have a pretty good life. I mean, compared to say two people who work outside of their homes and have kids. You know, we don't really calculate it into the factor, but I came home for lunch yesterday. I always come home and have lunch. I breastfeed Zach, or you know, we're together, we see each other. The kids are able to be involved in our work to some extent, and I think that's a benefit for them." – Amy, Eden

"The best part is that we're all working around each other. The time we see each other isn't just two hours in the evening. Everything we do is happening on the farm: swimming, horseback riding, working, it's all here. Our life is the farm and farming is our life." – Mitch, Kane Acres

This integration has implications for how activities are coordinated and when they are carried out all in one place, how spaces divided into subspaces and modified to fit the needs of several different activities, and how farm and family are coordinated when leaving to go off the farm.

All in One Place

The occupation of the same physical spaces for home, family, farm, and business activities often alleviates issues in coordinating activities over distance, since family members are generally nearby each other during the day. These families have on-going conversations throughout the day about prioritizing and coordinating what needs to be done depending on the circumstances, and about life in general. The conversation happens primarily *face-to-face*, during breaks or when working together:

"We also have a brief farm meeting every morning. Mitch and Ethan [intern] do chores and talk together every morning. Mitch comes back at 9. I'll have a little chat with him as well: we'll probably go over the what needs to be done that day, what we're probably going to do together, what I need him to take care of, things like that. 'Cause it changes so much on a daily basis, we need to keep talking. We're always all working together 'cause it's a small farm. We're able to communicate." – Katie, Kane Acres

When there seem to be no spatial boundaries where family life and farm work start and end respectively, families make decisions about how to use the spaces they occupy to fit multiple activities. For example, the farm kitchens are used for a wide range of activities including family meals, meetings with workers (sometimes with meals), schoolwork, planning, and preparing produce and foods to sell at the market. Many gardens contain plants intended both for the market and for homesteading. At Singalong, a swing set is deliberately placed near the greenhouses to be able to watch the kids while doing farm work. At Oak Ridge, one of the rooms in

Figure 1. Computer and tomato seedlings inside the home at Oak Ridge

Figure 2. The teenage children at Halfmoon are in charge of daily moving the chicken pen to fresh pasture

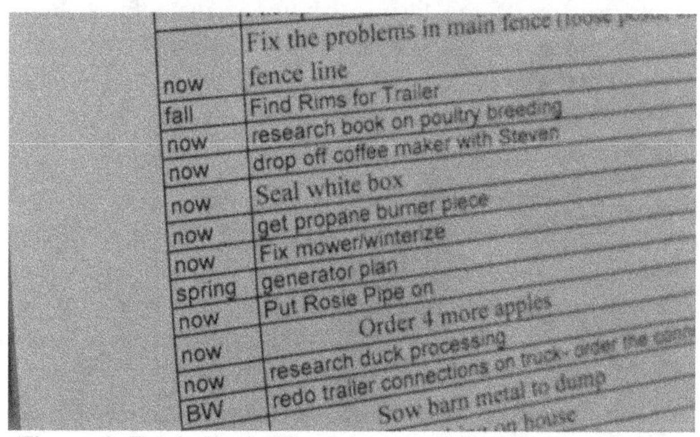

Figure 3. To-do list in Kane Acres, mixing home and farm tasks and prioritizing seasonally

the house has been turned into the office and now holds their "*information center*" with a computer, phone, printer, and filing cabinet (Figure 1). However, because they currently lack a heated greenhouse, the same room also holds trays of tomato seedlings that will be later transplanted outside and that need frequent watering. It happened to be the only room with available space that is located off the kitchen and living room, so that Naomi can both watch the children and do some watering or computer work.

Keeping everything on the farm further means that some families have customers, workers and interns coming regularly to the farm. The farm spaces then need to be organized in a way that allows these external members to participate in some activities, but without disrupting other activities. Kane Acres, Singalong, Eden, and Skylark farm each have workers/interns who live in separate accommodations on the farm, and some of them have meals with the families. At Kane Acres, they have designed a shed for customers to pick up ordered meat independent of supervision in order to avoid being disturbed during the days when they farm or are inside the house: "*The only way that it really works is that we don't spend a lot of time at it. I mean if we went over there every time somebody showed up, it would be a full-time job some days*." (Katie) They have also deliberately designed their farm website to provide up-to-date, relevant information (e.g., pricelists and availability) for current and future customers, and this online space serves as a "buffer" against disruptions from phone calls and face-to-face questions from customers.

There are also conflicts when interweaving home and work in one place. Interviewees complained about the difficulty to keep order when family, farm work, and business work are so permeated into each other. For instance, Nina at Forest Creamery asked to hold the interview out in the yard, saying she was too embarrassed to let us into her messy house. Kane Acres and White Birch talked about how they have divided the responsibility of different spaces on the farm, simply because they cannot agree on how to do it, and preferring different approaches and styles. Customers who come to the farm are sometimes unaware that as they participate in a business transaction with the farmers they are possibly invading the privacy of the farmers' home. Nina told us how a group of customers once came on a Sunday evening when the creamery was closed and she was watching TV with her son. They saw her through the window and refused to leave until she came out and served them.

Indoor and Outdoor

Instead of a spatial separation between home and work spaces, we found that families distinguish between *indoor* and *outdoor* spaces, which both involve different aspects of family and work. "Indoor" is usually the house or space where the family lives (at Skylark this is a renovated attic built on top of a farm building), but it can also be other enclosed spaces protected from the weather, such as a shed for processing farm produce. "Outdoor" refers to everything else including fields, greenhouses, gardens, and various buildings for machines and animals. The families describe how usually labor-intensive physical farm work activities happen outdoors, whereas less physical activities including business (e.g., accounting), production and preparation work (e.g., washing vegetables, making jam), and children's school work happen indoors. Socializing with family, friends, and even business-related contacts, as well as childcare, happen both outdoors and indoors depending on what is going on at the moment.

Factors such as weather, the growing season, and childcare often influence whether activities will be carried out indoor or outdoor. For instance, families with small children constantly coordinate outdoor farm work and (indoor/outdoor) childcare: one parent usually stays indoors to watch the children and simultaneously do tasks like computer work (communication, marketing, ordering, accounting, etc.) or housework, or does light outdoor work like transplanting while keeping an eye on the children. Carol gets her outdoor activities done by having one of the older children stay inside and watch the twins after she put them to sleep.

Many participants expressed a love for the outdoors, and clearly prefer outdoor farm work to indoor activities. The latter are often put off and "saved" for days with bad weather (or even for the winter when there is less to do outside): Nina saves "*cheese turning*" in the cool storage room for when it is hot outside, Peter postpones paper work until rainy days, and at Kane Acres indoor leisure activities like movie watching, reading, and longer meals are saved for the winter season.

Off the Farm

Although a lot of what is going on in these families takes place *on* the farm, a number of important activities including the farmers' market, public school, outings, errands, and part-time jobs happen *off* the farm. Some families appreciate going off the farm, to have time for themselves or to socialize. For example, Eli at Eden enjoys working twice a month as a lawyer in a nearby town: *"It's an easy vacation day. That job is so easy. [...] [And] I go out to lunch."* On the other hand, leaving the farm sometimes becomes a disruption, because those staying on the farm need to pick up all the tasks: farm work, house work, child care, etc.

As a result, some individuals try to minimize their outings as a way to keep as many of their activities as possible on the farm. For example, Wanda at White Birch is doing all her cooking and pickling for the market at the local community center because it has a licensed commercial kitchen, which she has not. She finds it frustrating to have to leave the farm, and is currently dealing with the situation by going to the center on certain days, and premeasuring and packing ingredients beforehand to make sure that she can use the kitchen efficiently once she is there. However, Wanda and Jim are currently going through the legal requirements of turning their porch into a commercial kitchen, which will allow her to cook at home in the future without having to coordinate *on* and *off* the farm. For them, it is clear that they prefer to keep these activities on the farm.

Another strategy includes efficiently getting as many activities as possible in any one outing. Because these families live in a rural area and have to drive to get to a town, many errands and outings are planned in advance and also scheduled for one trip. Participants often bring cell phones so that they can reach each other. For example, Dave at Foxtail, working outside the farm, coordinates in the morning with Julie and the older children of any errands that they will want him to run while he is out, drop-offs and pick-ups needed for any children at the end of the day, and he also expects a phone call at the end of his workday of what groceries are missing for dinner and need to be shopped for.

Time

For our participants, merging family and work on the farm often means that things happen not only at the same place, but also at the same time: children, plants, animals, product processes, and the business side of the farm all constantly need attention. When the families were describing their days, family care, chores, homesteading, farm work, and business activities all happen simultaneously.

Emerging from the interviews, we identified two main temporal rhythms that influence and guide these families' lives, as well as create tensions: *natural* and *structural rhythms*. These rhythms in particular characterize farm families, as their sources of income and lifestyle depend particularly on both natural rhythms of seasons and growth and structural rhythms of market days, work schedules, and school years. The families therefore need to balance, coordinate, and align their activities across these rhythms, described below.

Natural Rhythms

Although we visited each family once, and thus cannot make any claims based on long-term observations, the families themselves shared many accounts about temporal patterns in their lives. We see natural rhythms as patterns and sequences such as seasonal cycles that affect vegetable and animal growth, human bodily needs and growth, and homesteading processes that require following sequential activities (e.g., making sourdough bread). For example, several of our participants grow vegetables. They order the seeds and plan the plots in the winter; plant the seeds in the early spring inside the house/greenhouse; transplant the seedlings in the field after the last threat of frost; continue to weed, water, watch for pests, and take care of the plants; and finally harvest and prepare the produce for selling in the summer. Similarly, chickens arrive at Halfmoon as one-day-old chicks; are moved after a few days from the brooder to the pen; the pen then needs to be physically moved over the pasture twice daily to give the chickens fresh grass, and they need to be watered daily (Figure 2); after 8 weeks the chickens are butchered in the barn on *"processing day"*; and are frozen and finally sold. Both growing vegetables and raising chicken involve natural rhythms – both in the short-term daily work on the farm and in the long-term perspective of the season – and they have to be coordinated with other natural rhythms and with structural rhythms like the weekly market, which we will return to below.

Understanding and paying attention to natural rhythms like the ones above is key for the families and their farm work. This is particularly important as the growing season ramps up, as Katie says: *"During the growing season, you really have to prioritize. What absolutely has to be done today?"* (Figure 3) Knowing how to prioritize based on weather, growth, demand, and resources at hand (e.g., workers and childcare) requires a lot of experience and skills, along with a great deal of *flexibility* in both work and family life in general. For instance, breaks and family meals can happen at varying times or on the fly depending on what needs to be done outside in the field that day. The families also talked about how the flexibility of farm life allows people to follow their own personal natural rhythms. When coordinating farm work and family care, Katie takes into account that she is a *"slow hatch"* in the morning while Mitch is not; Naomi lets Cara sleep in; Mary and Don eat dinner in the morning instead of evening because they rise early; and Carol serves breakfast at three different times to accommodate Rob and all six children of varying ages and needs. However, the flexibility can also be experienced as problematic, as Naomi and Carol point out. Both told us they sometimes both wish there was *more* structure in the farm work, which they think would allow them to plan *their* activities better instead of being "on-call" with e.g., food.

Natural conditions can change quickly, making farm work and family life highly dynamic: equipment breaks, a cow calves early, a storm arrives, vegetables ripen early, or a child gets sick. The families deal with these changing conditions by flexibly shifting priorities and relying on ad-hoc support from extended family and a network of friends, neighbors, and workers. Peter provides an illustrative example of how changing weather conditions provided an opportunity to get a major job completed:

"I went to do some maintenance on a few pieces of our equipment, then I realized it was no longer windy, so I got everyone [workers and Emma] together at 10 and then we spent 10-noon putting on another piece of plastic and getting the other greenhouse ready and then we had a half hour lunch and went back out and got everything prepped for the afternoon working on the other greenhouse."

Structural Rhythms

Besides doing farm and family work that follow natural rhythms, our participants also take part in social institutions with their own structural rhythms: farmers' markets, school, work, religious practices, organized leisure activities, etc. Our participants described their daily, weekly, monthly, and yearly patterns related to those structural rhythms: school year calendars and daily schedules, weekly schedules of part time work and daycare, weekly activities like music lessons, Sunday church visits, monthly volunteer days, and so on. Like other studies of family coordination [9,25], our families are continually involved in coordinating these activities within the family and with outside entities (e.g., carpooling and external childcare). This happens through family calendars, daily to-do lists, and through conversations during breaks and meals and throughout the day.

Our participants also describe how they need to coordinate *between structural and natural rhythms*, because natural rhythms on the farm cannot be ignored, *"or something will die or give birth outside or be a disaster"* (Katie, Kane Acres). Participants therefore often support each other and rely on external help so they can participate in structural activities. For example, Emma at Singalong explains that it is only after they hired workers that she can regularly take 5-year-old Yana to ballet classes and have play dates. Another solution is to do the necessary farm chores before and after the structured activities like part-time jobs, which Mitch, Rob, and Eli do when they have to leave the farm. Yet another more fundamental strategy is to align the structured activities to fit the natural rhythms, and vice versa. In the homeschooling households, for example, the school year is shifted so that the children can help out more on the farm during the busy growing season. At Foxtail, the school year is aligned so that it ends when the lambs are born:

"From when lambs are born it just gets pretty intensive. [...] And also our home school starts the first Monday in August, and so we generally are wrapping up around the time that the chores start to pick up again." – Julie, Foxtail

The opposite is how they try to fit the natural rhythms with the structural rhythms of the farmers' market, such as by balancing and sometimes compromising between harvesting at the peak when the vegetables are the best and waiting for a market day. Several farmers also talked about how they are exploring hardier crops in combination with green houses/hoop houses to try to extend the season in order to be able to join a recently emerging winter market.

A special consideration for all our participants is the farmers' market, which requires significant coordination between activities related to structural and natural rhythms. Farmers' markets are seasonal and happen on certain day(s) of the week. In the long term, the farmers need to skillfully plan their business so that they have enough fresh produce throughout the market season. In the short term, the farmers need to harvest, prepare and pack their produce for the market day, organize, and man a stall at the market, and finish by cleaning and packing away the containers and doing the book work. This often means that during market season, the week is structured around market day for the entire family. At White Birch, they prepare for the Saturday market day on Thursday and Friday, rest on Sunday, and then spend Monday through Wednesday *"trying to catch up on all the things that we haven't managed to do yet."* (Wanda). The entire family is involved either directly or indirectly, and childcare sometimes needs to be organized or have one spouse/sibling stay with the young children. Many of the older children help pack and unpack the truck and sell at the market. However, as Carol says below, young children are more challenging, because the parents need to dedicate full attention to customers at the market:

"*My seven□year□old's always like, can you read this to me? [...] But you can't look disengaged. You have to always be ready for, 'Oh no, I'm right here for your customer base.' Because if people feel like they're interrupting you, they're less likely to do so. And they want to just walk by and smile and then go on to the next person. And so you have to be available.*" – Carol, Hickory Hill

Roles

Finally, we look at how roles are coordinated in these families when home and work are interwoven on the farm. Our participants' accounts point to how they simultaneously serve in multiple roles, and how roles are uniquely divided within the family to "make it all happen."

Managing Multiple Simultaneous Roles

Our participants take on many roles in their daily life on the farm: parent, spouse, farmer, colleague, businessperson, friend, educator, social advocate for organic food, and in some cases manager. Oftentimes they are seamlessly shifting between activities related to the various roles that they have, as Mitch at Kane Acres describes: "*The fluidness of our day, it's not uncommon [...] that I'm doing farm work, [Workplace] work, housework and maybe even mixing those all up.*" For the homeschooling families in particular, the family members might serve in multiple roles in the same activity. For example, when working with 11-year-old Amy in the garden, Julie is a parent spending time with her daughter, an educator teaching her daughter important gardening skills, and a homesteader growing her own food.

For our participants, the social and business life are often intertwined as well, which they see as an important part of being organic farmers in the local community. For instance, as a result of spending many hours selling vegetables in the on-farm CSA shed at Singalong, Emma and Peter have become friends with many of their customers, which means that spending time in the shed is not only about selling but also about socializing. Many see the farmers' market as a valuable opportunity to get to know their customers better and advocate for organic food, as well as learn from other farmers at the market. Several of the families socialize on a regular basis with other farmers as well as with their workers, like Amy describes below:

"We're having a potluck at [the park] on Sunday, and it's going to be fun. [...] there's a playground at the park, it'll be fun for the kids but we're meeting to discuss plans with this group of people to do a cider promotional week [...] Like the business infiltrates our lives. [...] A lot of our friends are related to the business though. I mean we actually have very few friends that aren't involved in either farming or cider making." – Amy, Eden

Sometimes simultaneity of roles, especially farmer, businessperson, and parent, involves conflicts that need to be resolved, because it requires being in several mindsets at the same time. For example, as described earlier, taking young children to the market can be stressful because all attention needs to be dedicated to customers, and it is difficult to take the role of a parent at the same time. As a result, the parents talked about how they often choose activities that the children can take part in. For example, tractor work is a good activity to do with children – the young ones can ride along (e.g., Eden), and the teenage children get excited about driving it (Hickory Hill). Being a farmer, a businessperson, a parent, and an educator, also means that children can get involved in farm and business activities as part of their schoolwork. For example, Megan at Halfmoon is in charge of the egg-laying chickens and is working on a chart to track income and expenses as part of a math project.

Division of Labor

Finally, taking on certain roles also has implications for how farm work and family life get divided and coordinated between family members. First, our participants described how their preferences, or skills that they brought to the farm or developed over time dictates who does what. For example, Toni at Oak Ridge has a degree in agriculture, while Naomi has retail experience, which makes it natural for them to divide the work so that he does more fieldwork and she is in charge of the business side of the farm. At Greenwood, Diane says that the customers like hearing Mark tell them about how to cook and preserve vegetables, so *"I'll let him schmooze all of them while I'm doing all the other [display and finances]."* Wanda at White Birch explains:

"[Jim] has got way more experience gardening and farming than I do. I love the animals, so that's a natural division. [Jim] made the chicken coops because I can't. I'm lucky to hit a nail in properly. I'm not like that. I think that's contributed to a lot of the division."

Second, our participants brought up gender as an important factor in dividing work and family life, which came up in discussions around pregnancies, having babies, and breastfeeding. They explained how being pregnant and nursing infants change what a mother can do on the farm, which means she takes on more physically lightweight farm work, indoor work, or work that can be easily interrupted. They see this division of labor as helpful in coordinating activities between the parents, but are sometimes frustrated about the fact that the division stays beyond the infant years and is hard to change. Emma at Singalong explains how their skills and roles were developed over the childrearing years:

"I used to do a lot of mechanical stuff. I just don't do it anymore 'cause your hands get so gross, like all that oil and everything, and it's just not good to have that around small kids... When I used to have my own farm, I did all the roles. It is true when you have a little baby it's way easier to do the greenhouse seeding and so I haven't gotten to field seeding for like 4 years. And now Peter has 4 years of doing field seeding experience on me and I have tons of years' greenhouse seeding on him."

DISCUSSION

In our study, we have looked at a group of families who deliberately merge home and work, and analyzed family coordination in the dimensions of space, time, and role, to understand what it means to interweave everything on the farm. As we have seen, coordination efforts exist also in these families, and, like other families, they struggle to accomplish their desired activities within the boundaries of time, cost and energy. It is not the *quantity* of their coordination practices that is different from those of families that have been previously studied in CSCW, but the *quality* of the coordination looks different, and happens for different reasons and values. We argue that *merging home and work* in the families we studied is different from *boundary blurring* that we have seen in the literature on family coordination. This is because farm families intentionally embrace the merging of home and work, rather than view the blurring as a consequence that needs to be dealt with as a result of a chosen lifestyle. We do not make a judgment over what life choices, values, and coordination practices are better or worse, but we do provide new perspectives on family coordination that we believe CSCW can learn from this study.

We now step back and discuss how these insights can help us rethink family coordination research and design. We do so through the perspectives of the three dimensions of coordination we identified in our analysis – space, time, and roles – revisiting how the existing literature on family coordination sees them, and looking at the new insights that we have learned from the farm families. In doing so, we will also point at implications for design and future work on family coordination in CSCW.

Space

An interest in the role that location plays in family coordination follows CSCW's long history of understanding co-located and distributed coordination, driven by a fundamental promise that technology will help overcome problems that occur over distance. The assumption in existing research in CSCW is that a geographical split between home and work exists, leading to a need to understand and improve coordination practices and tools used across the different locations that family members inhabit – home, work, school, on the go, etc. Knowing where family members are and planning where they should be at any given time are key in the research and design efforts on family coordination [e.g., 2,8,9,28]. And while much research has shown the centrality of the home as a place for the family to gather, organize and coordinate their activities, and as such shape social structures within the family [6,25,33,37], family coordination research and design extend beyond the home to other locations, such as at work and when on the move [2,9,12,17,28].

However, when home and work are not physically separate, as we have seen in our study, coordination around space involves different practices and strategies. We have seen a strong emphasis on the value of wanting to be together at home and on the farm, and organizing these spaces in ways that allow this to happen as much as possible: e.g., through homesteading activities, homeschooling, and assigning spaces for different purposes. This means that these families assume co-location rather than geographical distribution and that they can talk about coordinating their activities throughout the day. For these families, digital support for mediating geographically-distributed coordination might not be the right solution because they value and practice more unmediated face-to-face interactions. Further, many families we interviewed value being outside rather than inside, and many activities they engage in outside do not lend themselves to weather-sensitive digital solutions. Understanding families' values around co-location and distribution and about technologically-mediated family coordination might be an interesting direction for the CSCW research and design community, to avoid the immediate assumption that a technological solution for geographical distribution of a family is what families want and need (e.g., the digital calendar in [24] as a response to a study of family coordination practices [25]).

Another implication related to the spatial merging of home and work on the farms we studied comes from our observation that there is a broader set of people that inhabit the home and farm than just the family members: workers living and sometimes eating with the family on the farm, customers coming to the farm, and neighbors regularly stopping by to chat and help. Besides creating a strong sense of a local community, this points to the question of who we usually think of and represent in family coordination technologies. Often it is family and sometimes extended family members, but less often we think of neighbors and other people who are close. Tools are often visible and accessible by people outside the immediate nuclear family: family calendars are located in kitchens visited by workers and friends, family computers with personal photos are used by farm workers to access work files, and Facebook pages mix family photos and farm promotion. We suggest that there is room to reconsider the assumption that the home is a private retreat from the public life that happens outside of the home (e.g., family events on a workplace calendar are problematic from a privacy perspective [12]). We already see how social media and mobile devices are blurring the lines between public and private – what would family coordination look like if we relax this assumption in our designs of family coordination tools?

Time

Based on studies of practices of research scientists, Jackson et al. discuss *organizational rhythms:* the socially constructed pattern of deadlines, conferences and meetings, which structure professional scientific life [18]. Previous work on families has emphasized family coordination around temporal patterns that we label *structural rhythms,* associated with social structures: school, work, religion, government authorities, etc. [9,12,24,25,29]. By structural rhythms we emphasize both the larger sense of societal and governmental structures, and local organizations, extended family, and informal groups of friends. Abiding by structural rhythms using calendars and schedules brings order to society: social structures can function systematically and orderly around daily and weekly schedules, national and religious holidays, summer vacations, etc. [44].

Our findings resonate with the CSCW literature around structural rhythms, but we want to build on this work by drawing attention to the role of *natural rhythms*. By this, we mean the temporal patterns associated with natural and biological states that are not dictated by social structures or organizations: sleep/wake and appetite/fullness cycles, growth, maturity, and aging of the body and mind, seasonal weather changes, etc. There is an analogy to Jackson el al.'s *biographical* and *phenomenal* rhythms in scientific practices, but we want to emphasize the role of human bodily rhythms, ranging from daily patterns of sleep/wake, appetite/fullness, to seasonal factors and lifetime-long cycles of birth, aging and death as family members are born, grow up and become productive members of the farm family, leave the farm and die.

In the case of farm families, natural rhythms fundamentally affect their life, creating a sort of "organic" existence where tasks and activities are changed on the fly depending on sometimes highly volatile conditions. However, natural rhythms affect us all, not only farmers who work in the field: parents with young children know that coordinating family activities can be anything but straightforward. Yet natural rhythms such as sleep/wake and appetite/fullness, infancy, puberty, aging, as well as outside forces such as weather, and their interplay with structural rhythms, have to date largely escaped the CSCW literature on family coordination.

Paying attention to *both* structural and natural rhythms, not exclusive to the life of farm families, suggests a very different understanding of the role of time in family coordination and organization. At the home–work boundaries, workplaces' bureaucratic structures consider biological natural rhythms through standardized work hours and lunch breaks, rest days, and retirement regulations. Families develop and negotiate routines, such as daily dinner and bedtime routines, to synchronize structural and natural rhythms. We also call CSCW researchers and designers to pay attention to the need to coordinate and synchronize structural and natural rhythms, and to the difficulties that ensue when those various temporal rhythms are not well synchronized.

Roles

As others have observed [12,32], family members often simultaneously perform multiple roles, such as parent and farmer, rather than switching back and forth between them [1]. Our findings highlight the efforts that our participants make to have different roles *cooperate* with each other, rather than *conflict*. Tensions between roles still exist: Carol finds it difficult to be both a mother and a businessperson at the same time at the market. For our participants, the goal is not to balance or find the right boundaries between roles, but to integrate them, and thus tensions arise in situations when the families find it problematic to take on simultaneous roles.

When work life intrudes home life and vice versa, it has so far been explored from the perspective of balancing or boundary blurring between the two. However, this perspective perpetuates an assumption of separation between the two spheres of home and work. Steeped in a worldview where work and home are separate spheres that need to be "balanced", especially when the boundaries between the two are blurred given telework opportunities or mobile technologies, we may be missing other interesting perspectives for further exploration. Our findings point to a different perspective:

tensions are understood from the mindset that home and work *could* be one, and tensions arise when separation between the two happens. Embracing this new mindset—that home and work together (not balanced, not blurred, but one) contribute to the wholeness of individuals, families, and organizations—could expand the opportunities and possibilities for CSCW research and design.

Limitations

We recognize a limitation in our study in that we did not look more in-depth at the role of ICT when having this particular mindset, and we therefore believe that it would be a valuable direction for future work to specifically study ICT in families that merge home and work. We suggest that the role of coordination tools, including ICTs, in experiencing home and work could be seen in the perspective of the life choices that individuals, and families, make. Cultural background, upbringing, socio-economic class, career choices, and life circumstances help shape individuals' expectations about when and how to segregate, blur, or merge home and work. Different families might have different degrees of control [e.g., 23]; an employer may impose on its individuals to work extra time, or may limit taking personal time off to handle family matters. The use of ICT then becomes one factor in a broader setting of life choices and everyday practices, for example, when one carries smartphones that connect them simultaneously to the workplace and to the family in one device. What our study suggests is that assumptions that the goal is "balancing" home and work may not be generally appropriate, and that our participants concerns about "integrating" home and work articulates a powerfully different set of values.

CONCLUSION

We have presented a study of farm families who *intentionally interweave home and work*, in order to understand what family coordination looks like in families who do not experience a home–work split. We analyzed how they coordinate their lives at three dimensions: *space*, *time*, and *roles*. We found that they coordinate through locally meaningful definitions of space (indoor/outdoor/off the farm), through two rhythmic temporalities (natural/structural), and by taking on simultaneous roles and attempting to align them with each other. These findings point at a couple of valuable insights for CSCW in studying and designing for family coordination and family life in general, including: considering co-location rather than geographical distribution across life spheres; the value of natural rhythms in understanding and supporting family life; and how taking on simultaneous roles can be viewed as a life goal rather than a source of conflict. We argue that these insights are important for better understanding what we mean in CSCW when we talk about work-life balance, and the blurring of boundaries between home and work. They also suggest the value in exploring other mindsets/life choices where families attempt to unify rather than to balance different spheres.

In addition, at a meta-level, our study contributes to expanding the range of cooperative groups studied in CSCW: this is a variety of family that has not been looked at before. It emphasizes, yet again, the importance of understanding people's values as articulated through their practices. More specifically, our study contributes new insights about how family coordination looks like when merging home and work, and how this is different from how CSCW so far has understood family coordination and designed for family coordination.

ACKNOWLEDGEMENTS

We warmly thank the families for their time and for opening their homes to us. Thanks to Monika Roth at the Cornell Cooperative Extension for helping with recruitment, and to Susie Forbath for helping run the study. This work has benefitted from advice from Phoebe Sengers, Steven Jackson, Carl DiSalvo, Alex Taylor, Eric Baumer, Alex Thayer, members of the ISTC-Social, and the anonymous reviewers. This work was funded by a Nokia Global University Funding grant, and by the Intel Science and Technology Center (ISTC) for Social Computing.

REFERENCES

1. Ashforth, B.E., Kreiner, G.E., & Gugate, M. 2000. All in a day's work: Boundaries and micro role transitions. *Academy of Management Review*, 25(3), 472-491.
2. Brown, B., Taylor, A.S., Izadi, S., Sellen, A., Kaye, J.'J.', & Eardley, R. 2007. Locating family values: a field trial of the whereabouts clock. *Proc. UbiComp '07*. 354-371.
3. Chesley, N. 2005. Blurring boundaries? Linking technology use, spillover, individual distress, and family satisfaction. *J. Marriage & Family*, 67(5), 1237-1248.
4. Clark, S.C. 2000. Work/family border theory: A new theory of work/family balance. *Human Relations*, 53, 747-770.
5. Cowan, R. 1983. *More work for mother*. Basic Books.
6. Crabtree, A., & Rodden, T. 2004. Domestic routines and design for the home. *CSCW, 13*, 191–220.
7. Darrah, C.N., Freeman, J.M., & English-Lueck, J.A. 2007. *Busier than ever! Why American families can't slow down*. Stanford, CA: Stanford University Press.
8. Davidoff, S., Ziebart, B.D., Zimmerman, J., & Dey, A.K. 2011. Learning patterns of pick-ups and drop-offs to support busy family coordination. *Proc. CHI '11*. 1175-1184.
9. Davidoff, S., Zimmerman, J., & Dey, A.K. 2010. How routine learners can support family coordination. *Proc. CHI '10*. 2461-2470.
10. Greenhaus, J.H., & Powell, G.N. 2006. When work and family are allies: A theory of work-family enrichment. *Academy of Management Review*, 31(1), 72-92.
11. Gregg, M. 2011. *Work's Intimacy*. Polity Press.
12. Grimes, A., & Brush, A.J. 2008. Life scheduling to support multiple social roles. *Proc. CHI '08*. 821-824.

13. Grzywacz, J.G., & Marks, N.F. 2000. Reconceptualizing the work–family interface: An ecological perspective on the correlates of positive and negative spillover between work and family. *Journal Of Occupational Health Psychology*, 5(1), 111-126.
14. Habib, L., & Cornford, T. 1996. The virtual office and family life. *Proc. SIGCPR '96*, 296-304.
15. Hareven, T.K. 1991. The home and the family in historical perspective. *Social Research*, 58(1), 253-285.
16. Hill, E., Miller, B.C., Weiner, S.P., & Colihan, J. 1998. Influences of the virtual office on aspects of work and work/life balance. *Personnel Psych.*, 51(3), 667-683.
17. Hoefnagels, S., Geelhoed, E., Stappers, P.J., Hoeben, A., & van der Lugt, R. 2004. Friction in scheduling and coordinating lives of families: Designing from an interaction metaphor. *Proc. DIS '04*, USA, 321-324.
18. Jackson, S.J., Ribes, D., Buyuktur, A., & Bowker, G.C. 2011. Collaborative rhythm: Temporal dissonance and alignment in collaborative scientific work. *Proc. CSCW '11*, 245-254.
19. Kline, R.R. 2000. *Consumers in the country: Technology and social change in rural America*. Baltimore, MD: Johns Hopkins University Press.
20. Koehne, B., Shih, P.C, & Olson, J.S. 2012. Remote and alone: Coping with being the remote member on the team. *Proc. CSCW '12*, 1257-1266.
21. Malone, T.W., & Crowston, K. 1994. The interdisciplinary study of coordination. *ACM Computing Surveys,* 26(1), 87-119.
22. Mazmanian, M.A., Orlikowski, W.J., & Yates, J. 2005. CrackBerries: The social implications of ubiquitous wireless e-mail devices. *IFIP 185/2005*, 337-343.
23. Mazmanian, M., Orlikowski, W. J., & Yates, J. 2013. The autonomy paradox: The implications of mobile email devices for knowledge professionals. *Organizational Science*, February 2013, 1-21.
24. Neustaedter, C. & Bernheim Brush, A.J. 2006. "LINCing" the family: the participatory design of an inkable family calendar. *Proc. CHI '06*, 141-150.
25. Neustaedter, C., Brush, A.J., & Greenberg, S. 2009. The calendar is crucial: coordination and awareness through the family calendar. *ToCHI*, 16(1), 1-48.
26. Nippert-Eng, C.E. 1996. *Home and work: Negotiating boundaries through everyday life*. U. of Chicago Press.
27. Odom, W., Zimmerman, J., & Forlizzi, J. 2010. Designing for dynamic family structures: divorced families and interactive systems. *Proc. DIS '10*, 151-160.
28. Palen, L., & Hughes, A. 2007. When home base is not a place: parents' use of mobile telephones. *Personal Ubiquitous Computing,* 11(5), 339-348.
29. Plaisant, C., Clamage, A., Hutchinson, H., Bederson, B.B., & Druin, A. 2006. Shared family calendars: promoting symmetry and accessibility. *ToCHI*, 13(3), 313-346.
30. Pleck, E.H. 1976. Two worlds in one: Work and family. *Journal Of Social History*, 10(2).
31. Pleck, J.H. 1977. The work-family role system. *Social Problems*, 24(4), 417-427.
32. Salazar, C. 2001. Building boundaries and negotiating work at home. *Proc. GROUP '01*, 162-170.
33. Sellen, A., Harper, R., Eardley, R., Izadi, S., Regan, T., Taylor, A.S., & Wood, K.R. 2006. HomeNote: supporting situated messaging in the home. *Proc. CSCW '06*. 383-392.
34. Strange, M. 2008. *Family farming: A new economic vision*. The Institute for Food and Development Policy.
35. Strasser, S. 1982. *Never done: A history of American housework*. NY: Pantheon Books.
36. Taylor, A.S., & Swan, L. 2004. List making in the home. *Proc. CSCW '04*. 542-545.
37. Taylor, A.S. & Swan, L. 2005. Artful systems in the home. *Proc. CHI '05*. 641-650.
38. Thayer, A., Bietz, M.J., Derthick, K., & Lee, C.P. 2012. I love you, let's share calendars: calendar sharing as relationship work. *Proc. CSCW '12*. 749-758.
39. US Department of Agriculture. 2012. *Farms, land in farms, and livestock operations, 2011 summary*. Retrieved from http://www.nass.usda.gov.
40. Wyche, S.P., & Grinter, R.E. 2012. This is how we do it in my country: A study of computer-mediated family communication among Kenyan migrants in the United States. *Proc. CSCW '12*, 87-96.
41. Woods, M. 2011. *Rural*. New York, NY: Routledge.
42. Yardi, S. & Bruckman, A. 2012. Income, race, and class: exploring socioeconomic differences in family technology use. *Proc. CHI '12*. 3041-3050.
43. Yarosh, S., Chew, Y.C., & Abowd, G.D. 2009. Supporting Parent–Child Communication in Divorced Families. *IJHCI* 67(2), 192-203.
44. Zerubavel, E. 1981. *Hidden rhythms: schedules and calendars in social life*. University ofhicago Press.

Account Sharing in the Context of Networked Hospitality Exchange

Airi Lampinen[1,2,3]

[1] Microsoft Research
1 Memorial Drive,
Cambridge, MA 02142, USA
airi.lampinen@helsinki.fi

[2] Helsinki Institute for Information Technology HIIT/Aalto University
P.O. Box 15600,
00076 Aalto, FINLAND

[3] University of Helsinki
Department of Social Research
P.O. Box 54, 00014 University of Helsinki, FINLAND

ABSTRACT

This paper examines account sharing in the context of networked hospitality exchange. I discuss the dynamics of account sharing based on a qualitative interview study with multi-person households who offer to host visitors via Couchsurfing.org. Findings reveal that multi-person households that engage in account sharing face several challenges, including presenting multiple people in one profile, coordinating negotiations over access to domestic space, and representing in a fair way the reputation hosts have accumulated together over time. Amidst the rising rhetoric of a 'reputation economy', this paper calls for engaging the inclusions, exclusions, and inequalities that reputation metrics may renew or create, especially if they fail to acknowledge people's account sharing practices. Furthermore, this paper encourages adopting a design focus beyond individuals in order to support maintaining shared accounts and interacting with others through them. The findings have implications for a variety of hospitality exchange services and other online systems.

Author Keywords

Sharing; account sharing, online profile; social network service; Couchsurfing; reputation

ACM Classification Keywords

H.5.m. Information interfaces and presentation (e.g., HCI): Miscellaneous.

INTRODUCTION

Studies on password sharing in diverse contexts [5,7,10,11] have pointed out challenges resulting from a disregard of people's practices and called for holistic approaches to designing systems and security policies. For instance, focusing merely on password strength and change frequency may not be useful if organizational security ignores people's everyday practices of password sharing [7]. Characterizing password sharing as a nuanced practice in which people engage with thought and care, Kaye [5] counters the more traditional conceptualization that frames it as a deviant practice that should be stamped out.

This paper examines the broader issue of *account sharing* in the context networked hospitality exchange. 'Network hospitality' [4] refers to how those engaging with hospitality exchange services, such as Couchsurfing.org[1], connect to one another using online social networking systems, as well as to the kinds of relationships they perform when they meet face-to-face. On Couchsurfing.org, members can engage in hospitality exchange by hosting visitors ('couchsurfers') or by staying with others as guests.

In order to unravel practices of account sharing in the context of networked hospitality exchange, I present a qualitative study on multi-person households who offer to host strangers in their homes through Couchsurfing.org. Findings illustrate that beyond sharing credentials, account sharing involves complex negotiations over how to present multiple people in a single profile, how to coordinate the households' outfacing communication and decisions over whether to grant potential visitors access to the home, as well as how to share fairly the benefits of a good reputation.

While the analysis in this paper focuses on a single system that fosters non-monetary network hospitality, the issues it raises have implications for a variety of online systems. First, there is a growing number of similar hospitality exchange services, such as Bewelcome[2] and Hospitality Club[3]. Furthermore, when it comes to account sharing, sites that make a business out of helping people monetize their willingness to make domestic spaces or other tangible resources available to others are likely to encounter similar issues. The paper concludes with a discussion of designing for shared use and an invitation to consider how a design focus beyond individuals could help support users' efforts

CSCW'14, February 15 - 19, 2014, Baltimore, MD, USA.

ACM 978-1-4503-2540-0/14/02$15.00.
http://dx.doi.org/10.1145/2531602.2531665

[1] http://www.couchsurfing.org/

[2] http://www.bewelcome.org/

[3] http://www.hospitalityclub.org/

to maintain shared accounts as well as to interact and exchange with others through them.

HOSPITALITY EXCHANGE VIA COUCHSURFING.ORG

The empirical site of this study, Couchsurfing.org, is a social network site (SNS) focused on hospitality exchange. Members can offer to host couchsurfers at their home or request to stay as guests. While it is possible to solely host or surf, over time members tend to engage in both ways [6]. As a rule, couchsurfing involves no monetary exchange as stays take place with the broad goal of promoting intercultural experiences and understanding between people of different backgrounds [6].

Prior research on Couchsurfing.org has examined practices of writing references, the small testimonials that guests and hosts post to one another after visits [13] and disclosing information in online profiles [8]. Accumulating references to the profile is an important way for profile owners to establish a trustworthy reputation within the network. Notions of reciprocity and trust [6,9] have attracted scholarly attention, as trust has been deemed crucial for letting a stranger sleep in one's home or for staying on someone else's couch. Recent studies [1,3,14] have considered how people negotiate access to personalized spaces and adopt roles that help achieve comfortable interactions.

The main emphasis in prior work has been on dynamics of host-guest relationships, accompanied with the occasional remark that encounters do not necessarily take place in host-guest dyads: people often share their homes with others who may get involved in hosting more or less voluntarily. This paper examines the dynamics of hosting together with other household members from the perspective of account sharing. Couchsurfing.org embraces account sharing in that whenever new members set up a profile on the site, they are given an opportunity to indicate that the profile represents 'several people'. The opportunity to create a profile that explicitly represents more than one person makes the site an opportune location for examining how small groups (here, households of more than one person) negotiate presenting themselves and their home through a shared account and through offline interactions resulting from engaging others via the service.

Next to maintaining a profile, accounts allow members to send and receive requests for a stay ('CouchRequests'), send private messages to others, and to write and receive references – small testimonials that hosts and guests write to evaluate one another. It is customary for both guests and hosts to post these references to one another's profiles after visits. Accumulating references to the profile is an important way for profile owners to establish a trustworthy reputation within the network. In terms of interactivity, it is also possible to engage in broader conversations in a discussion forum embedded on the site.

Couchsurfing.org profiles serve to present two interwoven but distinguishable aspects of households: the domestic space and the people who live in it. The main part of the profile is taken up by personal information, including (1) brief items, such as age, gender, occupation, location, where one grew up, and since when one has been a member of the community; (2) free-length verbal descriptions of one's preferred ways of participating in the Couchsurfing community, one's couchsurfing experiences, as well as interests, and (3) photos. The profile contains an SNS-style list of Couchsurfing.org friends, and finally but crucially, the references one has received, categorized in a table both according to whether the feedback is positive, neutral, or negative, and in terms of whether it has been given by visitors, hosts, or people met while traveling. Although it is technically possible to make a profile for representing 'several people', the structure of the profile is best suited for individual users.

As for hosting, profiles require members to indicate whether they have 'a couch' available, whether they can host at the moment, and, if so, provide more information on the type of accommodation they have to offer. A free text field titled 'Couch Information' is used not just to describe the space but also to communicate expectations and restrictions, such as the appropriate length of stay or the maximum number of surfers welcome at a time.

MATERIAL AND METHOD

This paper presents results from a qualitative case study consisting of in-depth, semi-structured interviews with altogether sixteen people (eight women and eight men) from eight households of more than one people (heterosexual couples, housemates, and a heterosexual family with a child) who offer to host couchsurfers. Participants' ages ranged from 10 to 56 years, with most participants in their mid to late twenties. One of the couples was initially interviewed with the purpose of piloting the interview procedure. Since no major changes were made to the procedure after the pilots, it was deemed appropriate to include transcripts of these interviews in the analysis.

Apart from pilot interviewees (contacted through the author's colleagues), all interviewees were recruited through direct messages to Couchsurfing profile owners whose profiles were listed as 'several people'. The interviews took place in two metropolitan areas in the USA in July and August 2012. They were conducted in the participants' homes (apart from the over-the-phone pilot interviews). The interviews ranged from 30 to 70 minutes in length. Each interviewee received $20 as compensation for participation. All interviews were conducted and transcribed in English.

The interview transcripts were analyzed by first searching for all mentions of participants' Couchsurfing accounts and practices relating to them. This subset of the research material was, then, categorized further, narrowing in on notions of (1) setting up and maintaining profiles, (2) handling CouchRequests, and (3) writing and receiving references after hosting couchsurfers. Finally, the interview sections classified to each of these categories were open-coded to understand how households deal with different aspects of hosting couchsurfers. The coding was focused on how members of households divided responsibilities, how they cooperated with one another, and what kinds of reasoning and criteria they expressed for the choices they made in the course of hosting. The names used in conjunction with interview excerpts are pseudonyms, used to protect the participants' anonymity.

The material provides rich detail about participating households but there are two key limitations that should be kept in mind in considering the findings. First, the study builds on a convenience sample that is limited to people living in urban metropolitan areas in the USA. Thus, the findings are not generalizable as a broader depiction of how hosts or guests use Couchsurfing.org. Second, although the material includes different types of households, ranging from self-defined domestic partnerships to a set of housemates, it is not in the scope of this study to systematically address how different types of households may differ in how their members think about and act on issues related to account sharing. Third, the study focuses on *hosting*. As such, it does not speak to account sharing challenges specific to staying as a guest, although members from six households had couchsurfing experience, too.

FINDINGS

Presenting Multiple People in a Single Profile

On Couchsurfing.org, profiles serve to present households both in terms of the domestic space and the people who live in it. While the site allows for stating explicitly that a profile represents more than one person, participants deemed it difficult to construct their profiles in a way that would speak coherently for everyone in the household. Christina, who lives with her partner and daughter, explained how Couchsurfing.org falls short in supporting account sharing:

"*Right now, it's just male, female, or multiple people. And then you can put multiple pictures or you can describe, but there's no way to actually say we are this person, this person and this person. And not all of us have a way to log in and see the site unless we just share my login.*"

Christina's account illustrates how treating 'several people' as a straightforward unit can be problematic and discourage equal participation.

Next to presenting the hosts to potential guests, profiles are used to communicate expectations and restrictions. Profiles are critical for structuring a household's Couchsurfing experiences since they have an impact on the requests the household receives. Given this power, it is important to understand how households create and maintain their profiles, and how design shapes these choices.

Three couples had created their profiles together from scratch. In two other instances, an individual in each household reported having been in charge of setting up the profile, assuming the responsibility to craft the presentation of the entire household. Showcasing how account sharing is welcomed but not fully supported on the site, a further three households reported challenges related to repurposing an initially individual account for shared use. Prateek had created his Couchsurfing profile before moving in with his partner, Jane. The couple found it difficult to turn an individual profile into a shared one. Prateek described how the profile was now an attempt to present both of them:

"*I don't think I have a photograph of her. [..] The profile still says -- it's still of me and it refers to her everywhere else. It'll talk about me and my partner, Jane.*"

However, now that Jane was increasingly involved in couchsurfing, she explained why she and Prateek decided to repurpose the profile to represent her, too:

"*I realize that I might also be traveling [..] I realized it might help for me also to have my name on the profile, just so that I can link to it.*"

The household consisting of unrelated individual housemates offered a contrast to the cooperativeness of couples. The housemates conceived of profile maintenance as a more individual activity and, unlike most participants, did not share account credentials. Next to Kevin whose profile was used for hosting, Matt had a personal profile that he used when travelling. It is important to bear in mind that multi-person households vary in their preferences and practices when it comes to account sharing.

To sum up, most participating households had an individual in charge of interacting with the website on behalf of everyone. In some cases, other household members had not seen the site or knew little of its features. This need not mean that they do not act actively as hosts by interacting with guests or shouldering other hosting tasks, only that they had little to do with managing the account online.

Negotiating over Access to Domestic Spaces

In setting up a profile, even one that is explicitly about 'several people', Couchsurfing allows for inserting only one e-mail address to which the system forwards messages, such as CouchRequests, that other members send to profile owner(s). Messages can be read directly on the website, too. Many households shared credentials in order to provide multiple people with access to the profile and messages. In practice, though, receiving messages to an e-mail inbox was a functionality participants relied on, as it spared them the effort of checking yet another account separately.

Being able to redirect incoming messages only to one e-mail address enforced the tendency for one individual to become a gatekeeper to the household's account. To overcome the issue, Kate and Jeff, a recently married couple, had created a separate e-mail account with the sole task of forwarding redirected messages to their primary e-mail addresses. This allowed both partners equal access to messaging. As Jeff explained, this was a priority for the couple since, for them, hosting was pronouncedly a shared activity:

"We definitely always look at the request and talk about it together [..] I don't think one of us would say yes or no to someone before we had talked about it."

It was, however, more common that the person receiving the messages forwarded them to others or brought them up with them in face-to-face conversations. Jane described how she and Prateek tend to handle requests:

"*Yeah usually the way we do it is he checks the account, but he sends me the details and then we discuss whether those days work and then I respond to him and he writes back and then he starts cc'ing me on any email exchanges he has.*"

While some reported forwarding all messages diligently, in other cases the person in charge filtered CouchRequests and brought only part of the requests into shared consideration. Christina explained that she curates carefully which CouchRequests to bring into discussion with her partner, a somewhat reluctant host. She engaged in this filtering as a strategy to make hosting more meaningful for her partner and, thus, to keep receiving couchsurfers in their home – an activity she found very enjoyable. Furthermore, Christina made an interesting distinction between asking for permission from her partner and offering notice to her daughter. According to Christina, the latter enjoyed having visitors around and, as a result, there was not really a need to consult with her as for who could be invited to stay.

It was typical for the participating households to drop hosting if there was a disagreement over whether to host. In making decisions over whether to accept a request, hosts considered primarily whether the timing of a proposed visit worked for them and whether the requester seemed like a person they would like to meet. Participants evaluated potential guests based on how the request was phrased, what the requester's profile looked like, and, especially, what kind of references s/he had received and given. These priorities highlight the importance of references.

Establishing a Trustworthy Reputation

As references provided and received after visits accumulate members' reputation within the Couchsurfing network, they affect members' chances to couchsurf as well as to host. Jeff and Kate had agreed to share the important task of writing references. They said that they might just discuss what kind of a reference to give for a recent visitor, and then one of them would go and write it. Jeff explained that it was more likely, though, that they would end up writing it together:

"*Yeah, I would guess that we'd probably write it, because I bet, like, if we had a really fun time, then we would probably want to, like, sit together, and say, oh, this was fun, that was fun, and write about it. And if we were like, a little peeved, then I think we would want to, like, talk together about how to be polite but also be honest".*

In most cases, though, the person in charge of the account assumed responsibility of writing references, as well. In some households, others knew little about references. During the interviews, Christina asked both her partner and her daughter whether they "*even know that I write references*". Both responded that they had seen references in the profiles of potential visitors. They had, however, not really considered providing references as something they or their household members would do, too. Similarly, Mike's partner Daniela stated that the interview was "*the first time I'm hearing about feedback*". Not knowing what kind of a reputation one's household has online may be problematic, for instance, by lessening opportunities to benefit from a good reputation accumulated through joint hosting efforts.

DESIGNING FOR SHARED USE

While Couchsurfing.org allows users to set up 'several people' profiles, the site is limited in its support of account sharing. The structure of profiles is not convenient for presenting multiple people, nor is the messaging system set up to encourage multiple profile owners to cooperate in handling requests on the site. Examination of what it means to use a single account as a multi-person household revealed that core challenges users face include presentation of multiple people in one profile, coordination of negotiations over access to domestic space, and representing in a fair way the reputation hosts have accumulated together over time so that all household members have an opportunity to benefit of joint hosting efforts. While it may not be possible, or even desirable, to 'design away' all of the messiness of engaging in network hospitality as a multi-person household, it is worthwhile to consider both designing for shared use and the tradeoffs related to such alternative design choices.

Shared Profiles and Reputation

While participation on Couchsurfing.org does not strictly require reciprocity, positive references on a profile serve to establish a reputation for the profile owners, casting them as good community members who are safe to interact with and worthy of being hosted based on the hospitality they have offered to others. Thus, a profile that showcases positive references is likely to increase its owners' success in requesting a place to stay (or in receiving visitors to host). The study found participants struggling with how to present multiple people in a single profile and, especially, how to repurpose originally individual profiles for shared use. Household members who are not visibly represented in a shared profile may end up with fewer opportunities to benefit from the household's jointly accumulated reputation, for instance when traveling independently.

Furthermore, current design provides little assistance for transferring reputation to a new context. The research material does not include examples of how households manage accounts when they grow apart, probably due to sampling only 'several people' profiles and due to interviewing participants only at one point in time. Yet, such changes, too, are an inevitable part of social life: housemates move in and out, couples may break up, and as children grow up, they tend to leave their childhood homes. This introduces challenges on Couchsurfing.org, for instance in terms of continuing participation as a reputed member after a life change, but the consequences could be much more troubling in other systems that use the social and economic value of reputation more systematically as a condition for participation and related benefits.

One way to rethink multi-person profiles would be to design them as collections of components that can be combined and decomposed as needed – much like pieces of a small puzzle. Next to a joint part, dedicated to representing the domestic space and other shared information specific to the household, each household member could have a personal component of their own. This would allow for distinguishing between the particular offer of hosting guests in a specific setup and the more permanent identities of the participating individuals.

Portable personal profile components would equip users with means to go through life changes without needing to recreate their profiles from scratch. This affordance would be valuable in systems where reputation metrics are important and affect opportunities for participation, such as Couchsurfing.org. Such a design could mitigate some of the issues around representing everyone involved. Also, it could help make profile components more durable over time, leading to more lasting self-presentations and reputation metrics. However, there are some important trade-offs to consider. The proposed structure could make the system more complicated to use, and it might even discourage participation if household members with lesser interest in the activity were forced to engage with online aspects of hosting. Finally, people may have good reasons for wanting a fresh start. If re-using personal parts of profiles became a norm, this option might be less readily available. As such, it would seem advisable to make the re-use of profile components an option, not a requirement.

Shared Access and Awareness

Some participants were not contented with the affordances Couchsurfing.org provides for cooperative coordination. For instance, allowing users to redirect their messages to only one e-mail address had pushed participants to create varied practices to ensure sufficient shared awareness of the household's communication with other members of the Couchsurfing community. When it comes to facilitating cooperation among multiple household members who are sharing an account, however, seemingly easy fixes, such as allowing multiple redirect addresses, may introduce inadvertent challenges. Group-level coordination is not an issue that could be 'solved by design'. Here, it would seem recommendable to simply provide users with the option of redirecting messages to multiple e-mail addresses.

Users' preferences and practices are contextual and vary from group to group. When it comes to practices of account sharing, no single design will fit the needs of all households. It is preferable to provide account owners with meaningful choice, helping them make decisions that suit their particular needs: On Couchsurfing.org, some households are comfortable with delegating authority over the account to an individual gatekeeper. Others would appreciate mechanisms that provide all household members with equal access to the account.

Beyond the particular functionalities of Couchsurfing.org, asking people to consider clearly articulated choices when they are setting up a shared account in an online system could help them reflect on and discuss together how to handle their account. For example, Couchsurfing.org could help mitigate the challenges of coordinating hosting activities via a shared account by explicating more clearly the choices households need to make in engaging with the community as a small group. Next to options from which to select in setting up a profile, the setup process could be accompanied with a short list of issues household members should agree upon and examples of how others have resolved them. The list could include topics such as who maintains the profile, how decisions over whom to host are made, and who answers messages and writes references.

CONCLUSION

Challenges of account sharing in the context of hospitality exchange include (1) presenting multiple people with a single profile, (2) coordinating and negotiating how the household responds to requests it receives, and (3) sharing the benefits of a good reputation in a fair way.

While Couchsurfing was selected as a study site as an especially illustrative example of what is at stake in account sharing, the issues raised in this paper are not confined to the system or even to other similar non-monetary networked hospitality exchange services, such as Bewelcome and Hospitality Club. Further parallels can be found, for instance, from sites like Airbnb[4] and Bizpora[5] that help people monetize their willingness to make domestic spaces available to others. Here, too, the need to negotiate with other household members over access to domestic spaces may arise, with the added question of how the exchange of money between hosts and visitors affects the dynamics of the situation. Beyond the scope of physical space, similar issues are important for other 'collaborative consumption' systems that facilitate, for instance, local

[4] https://www.airbnb.com/

[5] https://www.bizpora.com/

online exchange or ridesharing. Here, sharing and exchanging can concern goods that are co-owned by multiple people. Questions of accumulating a reputation and achieving satisfactory coordination of exchange activities are of crucial importance also in this context.

On Couchsurfing.org, members may face challenges due to the scarce support for account sharing, for example in how to continue participation as a reputed member after a life change. However, consequences could be much more troubling in other systems that use the social and economic value of reputation more systematically as a condition for access to participation and other valued resources. Further analysis is needed, among others, of how account sharing practices in the context of non-monetary network hospitality differ from those related to hospitality exchanges that involve monetary transactions, such as the activities facilitated by Airbnb and Bizpora.

Another topic for future study is analyzing systematically whether and how different types of households differ in terms of their preferences and practices for account sharing. It would also be worthwhile to scrutinize account sharing practices in systems other than Couchsurfing.org to better understand how challenges related to account sharing differ in different communities and how they are shaped by differing user interfaces. Also, it remains an open question how well these findings that are related to the sharing of physical space can be applied to the sharing of other types of resources, such as cars, bikes, or other tangible items.

Amidst the rising rhetoric of a 'reputation economy' [see, e.g. 2], we need to engage in a conversation over the inclusions, exclusions, and inequalities that reputation metrics may renew or create, especially if they fail to acknowledge people's account sharing practices. This paper calls for adopting a design focus beyond individuals in order to unlock the potential for catering to users' goals and needs in maintaining shared accounts and in interacting with others through them. This is an increasingly critical issue as systems that facilitate network hospitality and other forms of collaborative consumption permeate the everyday lives of a growing number of people.

ACKNOWLEDGMENTS

I conducted the research for this paper during my internship at Microsoft Research New England. I am indebted to Mary L. Gray, Nancy Baym, and other members of the Social Media Collective for their advice and support. The work was finalized with the support of funding from the TEKES project FuNeSoMo. I wish to acknowledge the participants without whom this project would not have been possible. Finally, I am thankful for my HIIT colleagues as well as for the anonymous reviewers whose feedback helped me improve the paper significantly.

REFERENCES

1. Bialski, P. (2011). Technologies of hospitality: How planned encounters develop between strangers. *Hospitality & Society 1*(3), 245–260.
2. Botsman, R. (2012) 'Welcome to the New Reputation Economy' in Wired, September 2012: http://www.wired.co.uk/magazine/archive/2012/09/features/welcome-to-the-new-reputation-economy?page=all (accessed on May 31, 2013)
3. Buchberger, S. (2011). Hospitality, secrecy and gossip in Morocco: Hosting CouchSurfers against great odds. *Hospitality & Society 1*(3), 299–315.
4. Germann Molz, J. (2011). CouchSurfing and network hospitality: "It's not just about the furniture''. *Hospitality & Society 1*(3), 215–225.
5. Kaye, J. 'J.' Understanding Self-reported Password Sharing Strategies. *In Proc. CHI'11,* ACM Press (2011).
6. Lauterbach, D., Truong, H., Shah, T. and Adamic, L. Surfing a Web of Trust: Reputation and Reciprocity on CouchSurfing.com. *In Proc. IEEE Social Computing 2009,* IEEE Press (2009).
7. Inglesant, P.G. and Sasse, M.A. The true cost of unusable password policies: password use in the wild. *In Proc. CHI'10,* ACM Press (2010).
8. Peterson, K. & Siek, K. (2009). Analysis of information disclosure on a social networking site. In: AA Ozok & P Zaphiris (Eds) *Online Communities*, 256–264. Springer-Verlag, Berlin, Germany.
9. Rosen, D., Lafontaine, P.R., & Hendrickson, B. (2011). CouchSurfing: Belonging and Trust in a Globally Cooperative Online Social Network. *New Media and Society, 13*(6): 981–98.
10. Singh, S. Secure shared passwords: the social and cultural centered design of banking. *Journal of Financial Transformation, 23*, (2008), 110–114.
11. Singh, S., Cabraal, A., Demosthenous, C., Astbrink, G. and Furlong, M. Password Sharing: Implications for Security Design Based on Social Practice'. *In Proc. CHI'07, ACM Press (2007).*
12. Tan, J-E. (2010). The Leap of Faith from Online to Offline: An Exploratory Study of Couchsurfing.org. In: A Acquisti, S W Smith, & A-R Sadeghi (Eds.) *TRUST 2010*, LNCS 6101, 367–380.
13. Teng, C-Y., Lauterbach, D., & Adamic, L. (2010). I rate you. You rate me. Should we do so publicly? In *Proceedings of the 3rd Workshop on Online Social Networks.*
14. Zuev, D. (2011). CouchSurfing as a spatial practice: Accessing and producing xenotopos. *Hospitality & Society 1*(3): 227–244.

Achieving Convergence in Operational Transformation: Conditions, Mechanisms and Systems

Yi Xu, Chengzheng Sun, Mo Li
School of Computer Engineering, Nanyang Technological University, Singapore

ABSTRACT
In this paper, we present a comprehensive and in-depth study on convergence preservation and avoidance in Operational Transformation (OT) systems. In this study, we discovered basic conditions, transformation patterns, and mechanisms for avoiding Convergence Property 2 (CP2), and established CP2-avoidance correctness of seven major OT systems. Furthermore, we proposed improvements to existing systems and designed a new OT system capable of avoiding CP2 with a unique combination of novel features. These results contribute significantly to the advancement of OT and collaboration-enabling technology.

Author Keywords
Operational Transformation; consistency maintenance; convergence; real-time collaborative applications.

ACM Classification Keywords
H.5.3 [**Information Systems**]: Group and Organization Interfaces – Synchronous Interaction, Theory and Model.

INTRODUCTION
Consistency maintenance is a main challenge in building real-time collaborative applications over high latency communication environments like the Internet [4, 17]. Due to its non-blocking, fine-grained concurrency, and unconstrained interaction properties, Operational Transformation (OT) is particularly suitable for consistency maintenance in such environments, and has been increasingly adopted in industrial applications, e.g. Google Wave/Docs[1], IBM OpenCoWeb[2], and Codoxword[3].

In OT-supported real-time collaborative editing applications, multiple users may freely and simultaneously generate editing operations, which may be transformed and executed in different orders at different collaborating sites [1, 2, 3, 18, 24]. Document *convergence* is a key consistency requirement: the final documents at all sites must be *identical* after executing the same group of operations [18]. Past research has discovered important transformation properties for achieving convergence. In the first OT system [3], a transformation property, *Convergence Property 1* (*CP1*)[4], was identified, which ensures the same document is produced by executing two concurrent operations in different orders. Follow-up research found CP1 was insufficient to ensure convergence under certain circumstances, and added another transformation property, *Convergence Property 2* (*CP2*)[5], which ensures the same operation is produced in transforming one operation against two concurrent operations in different orders (see the next section for precise definitions of CP1 and CP2).

There exist two general approaches to achieving convergence in OT: one is to design application-specific transformation functions capable of preserving CP1/CP2; the other is to design generic control algorithms capable of avoiding CP1/CP2. Past research has found that it is relatively easy to preserve CP1 by transformation functions and to avoid CP2 by control algorithms. Multiple CP1-preserving transformation functions for a variety of data and operation models have been designed [1, 11, 14, 20, 24]; and numerous control algorithms capable of avoiding CP2 have been invented [8, 10, 15, 16, 18, 21, 23]. An OT control algorithm is said to be able to avoid CP2 if it works with transformation functions capable of only preserving CP1 for achieving convergence. There were some attempts to design transformation functions for preserving CP2 in character-wise text editing systems [6, 7, 12], but avoiding CP2 by control algorithms has been favored due to its advantage of being generic and applicable to different data and operation models for supporting a range of applications. Recent OT systems for advanced collaborative applications, e.g. 2D spreadsheets [22] and 3D digital media design systems [1], have been designed with a combination of transformation functions[6] for preserving CP1 and control algorithms for avoiding CP2 [21].

Despite the wide adoption of the CP2-avoidance strategy in OT systems, the basic conditions and mechanisms for CP2-avoidance have not been well-understood. Most OT systems that claimed CP2-avoidance had justified their claims by showing the absence of transforming an operation against the same pair of operations in different orders, which is intuitive-

[1] http://docs.google.com
[2] https://github.com/opencoweb/coweb#readme
[3] http://www.codoxware.com

[4] CP1 was named as *Transformation Property* (*TP*) in [3], and *Transformation Property 1* (*TP1*) in [14].
[5] CP2 was named as *Transformation Property 2* (*TP2*) in [14], which is the same as *Transpose Property 5* proposed in [11].
[6] Transformation functions must preserve, in addition to generic CP1, application-specific *combined effects* for concurrent operations [1, 20, 22] or *operation intentions* [18].

CSCW'14, February 15 – 19, 2014, Baltimore, MD, USA.

http://dx.doi.org/10.1145/2531602.2531629

ly derived from CP2 (see details in the next section) [8, 15, 23]. However, more recent research has found the mere absence of transforming the same pair of operations in different orders is *insufficient* to avoid CP2 (see the next section for a counter-example), and a correct condition of avoiding CP2 is: *to avoid transforming two operations in different contexts* [21]. The discovery of this condition has advanced OT knowledge, but also cast doubt on the CP2-avoidance claims of prior OT systems: are they really able to avoid CP2? After all, they were either not verified or verified by an insufficient condition. Resolving this doubt is important as it is related to the correctness of a large number of major OT systems [8, 10, 15, 16, 18, 21, 23, 24], some of which are being used in industrial applications with millions of users, e.g. the Jupiter OT [10] is the basis for Google OT [24, 16], which is used for Google Docs; and COT [21] is used in Codoxword and IBM OpenCoWeb. As OT is increasingly applied to a wider range of real-world applications and used by more and more people, ensuring and verifying correctness of its core algorithms become more and more important.

To address these open issues, we set out to study seven major OT systems that claimed or was recognized for being capable of avoiding CP2, including Jupiter[7][10], NICE[15], Google OT [24,16], SOCT3 and SOCT4 [23], TIBOT [8], and COT [21], with the following objectives: (1) to validate whether they indeed meet the correct CP2-avoidance condition; and (2) to find out how and why they did it (if they can). From this study, we have not only achieved the original objectives, but also made important discoveries in CP2-avoidance conditions, and basic transformation patterns and mechanisms that can be used to avoid CP2 in different OT systems. Furthermore, we proposed improvements to examined systems and designed a new OT system capable of avoiding CP2 with a unique combination of novel features. We report these research findings in this paper.

The rest of this paper is organized as follows. First, we introduce background knowledge related to this work. Then, we discuss CP2-avoidance conditions. Next, we present basic CP2-avoidance transformation patterns and mechanisms. Based on these patterns and mechanisms, we present our CP2-avoidance validation of seven systems. Furthermore, we propose improvements to Jupiter and Google OT, present the design of a new OT system, and discuss ideas of future work inspired by this study. Finally, we summarize the main contributions of this work.

BACKGROUND KNOWLEDGE

Causal and Total Ordering Relations

Following Lamport [5], the causal ordering relation of operations is defined as follows [3].

Definition 1. Causal Relation "→". *Given two operations O_a and O_b, generated at site i and j, respectively, O_a is causally before O_b, denoted by $O_a \rightarrow O_b$, if and only if: (1) i=j and the generation of O_a happened before the generation of O_b; (2) i≠j and the execution of O_a at site j happened before the generation of O_b; or (3) there exists an operation O_x such that $O_a \rightarrow O_x$ and $O_x \rightarrow O_b$.*

Definition 2. Concurrent Relation "||". *Given two operations O_a and O_b, O_a and O_b are concurrent, denoted by $O_a \| O_b$, if and only if neither $O_a \rightarrow O_b$ nor $O_b \rightarrow O_a$.*

In real-time collaborative editing systems, operations with causal relationships are executed in their causal orders; but concurrent operations may be executed in any orders [3, 17]. In OT systems, concurrent operations are transformed to achieve consistency, but transformation orders are also governed by causal relations among operations.

Definition 3. Total Ordering Relation "⇒". *A relation "⇒" is a total ordering relation among operations in a session if the following statements hold for any operations O_a, O_b, and O_c, where $O_a \neq O_b \neq O_c$: (1) if $O_a \Rightarrow O_b$ and $O_b \Rightarrow O_c$, then $O_a \Rightarrow O_c$ (transitivity); and (2) $O_a \Rightarrow O_b$ or $O_b \Rightarrow O_a$ (totality).*

In contrast to the causal relation, which defines a partial ordering relation among operations, a total ordering relation is a complete ordering relation among operations. The "totality" condition in the total ordering relation means that all operations are ordered under "⇒". In this work, we are particularly interested in a special class of total ordering relations that are consistent with the causal ordering relation among the same group of operations, i.e. for any O_a and O_b, if $O_a \rightarrow O_b$, then $O_a \Rightarrow O_b$. In the rest of this paper, we assume "⇒" is always consistent with "→". As will become clear later, such total ordering relations play a key role in defining CP2-avoidance conditions.

Operation Context and Context-based Conditions

In OT systems, every operation O is associated with a *context*, which represents the document state on which O is defined [17, 18, 21]. For the purpose of OT design, the context of O needs not be represented by a real document state, but can be represented by a *set* of operations (in their original forms) that have been executed to create the state on which O is defined [21].

Definition 4. Document State Representation. *A document state, denoted as S, can be represented as follows:(1) the initial document state is represented as an empty set $S = \{\ \}$; (2) after executing an operation O on the document, the new state is represented by: $S = S \cup \{org(O)\}$, where org(O) represents the original form of O; if O is an original operation (generated by a user), $org(O) = O$.*

Definition 5. Operation Context Representation. *The context of an operation O, denoted as C(O), is represented as follows: (1) for an original operation O, $C(O) = S$, where S is the document state from which O is generated; (2) for a transformed operation O', $C(O') = C(O) \cup \{org(Ox)\}$, where $O' = T(O, Ox)$, and T is a function that transforms O into O' according to the impact of Ox.*

The significance of operation context is that it provides the ground for interpreting the effect of an operation and for

[7]When Jupiter OT was published in 1994 [10], CP2 had not yet be identified as an OT convergence requirement. So Jupiter OT was not designed to purposely avoid CP2, but to rely solely on CP1 to achieve convergence.

reasoning about the relations among operations, which are essential for ensuring correct operation execution and transformation [17, 18, 21]. Among others, two context-based conditions are directly relevant to this work:

1. *Context-equivalence condition for execution*: given an operation O and a document state S, O can be correctly executed on S only if $C(O) = S$.
2. *Context-equivalence condition for transformation*: given two operations O_1 and O_2, they can be correctly transformed with each other, by invoking $T(O_1, O_2)$ or $T(O_2, O_1)$, only if $C(O_1) = C(O_2)$.

In theory, any operation (either original or transformed) has a context, but operations included in a context are all in original forms. Causal and total ordering relations are defined only among original operations [21]. For notation conciseness, however, we assume an automatic operation form conversion, from "O" to "$org(O)$", whenever "$\rightarrow$", "$\|$", "$\Rightarrow$" and other context set operators (e.g. "$\cup$") are used, e.g. "$O_a \Rightarrow O_b$" means "$org(O_a) \Rightarrow org(O_b)$". When we say an operation O is in an operation context, we mean $org(O)$ is in a context. We use the notation $O_a\{b\}$ to denote that O_b is in the context of O_a, which can be used to represent the result of transforming O_a against O_b, i.e. $O_a\{b\} = T(O_a, O_b)$. If O is generated from an initial document state, no operation is included in its context, so it can be expressed as $O\{\}$ or simply O.

Convergence Properties

Convergence Property 1 (CP1): Given O_a and O_b defined on the state S, if $O_a\{b\} = T(O_a, O_b)$, and $O_b\{a\} = T(O_b, O_a)$, the following holds:

$$S \circ O_a \circ O_b\{a\} = S \circ O_b \circ O_a\{b\},$$

which means the same document is produced by applying O_a and $O_b\{a\}$ in sequence on S, and applying O_b and $O_a\{b\}$ in sequence on S, respectively.

Convergence Property 2 (CP2): Given O_a, O_b and O_c defined on the same state, if $O_c\{b\} = T(O_c, O_b)$ and $O_b\{c\} = T(O_b, O_c)$, the following holds:

$$T(T(O_a, O_b), O_c\{b\}) = T(T(O_a, O_c), O_b\{c\}),$$

which means the same operation is produced by transforming O_a against O_b and then $O_c\{b\}$, and transforming O_a against O_c and then $O_b\{c\}$, respectively.

CP2-AVOIDANCE CONDITIONS

An Insufficient CP2-Avoidance Condition

CP2 requires the same operation is produced in transforming one operation against the same pair of operations in different orders, so it is intuitive to derive: *CP2 can be avoided if an OT system can avoid transforming an operation against the same pair of operations in different orders.* This condition has been explicitly or implicitly used to validate CP2-avoidance in several OT systems [8, 15, 23], but it is insufficient to achieve convergence.

A counter-example to this condition is given in Figure 1. In this scenario, there are three operations: $O_1 = I(2, x)$ (to insert "x" at position 2), $O_2 = D(1, b)$ (to delete "b" at position 1), and $O_3 = I(1, y)$ (to insert "y" at position 1), concurrently generated from the same initial document state "abc". All possible execution and transformation paths of these operations are illustrated in a Context-based Operation Transformation Space (COTS)[8] in Figure 1.

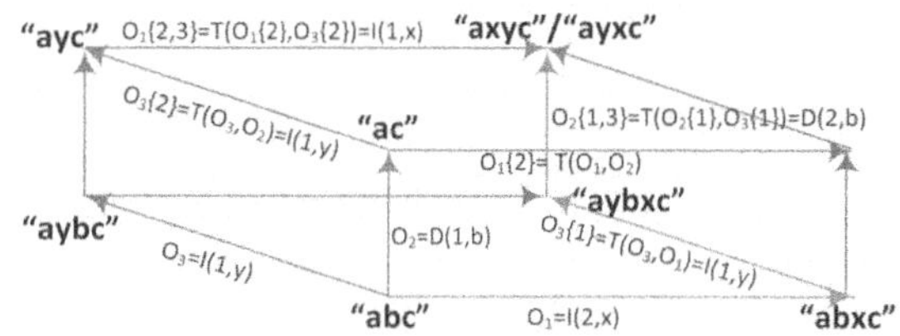

Figure 1: A counter-example to the insufficient CP2-avoidance condition (assuming *priority*(O_1) > *priority*(O_3)).

Suppose an OT system forces operation execution and transformation along only two paths in Figure 1:

1. In one path, O_2, $O_3\{2\}$ and $O_1\{2, 3\}$ are executed in sequence, where:
   (1) $O_3\{2\} = T(O_3, O_2) = I(1, y)$;
   (2) $O_1\{2, 3\} = T(O_1\{2\}, O_3\{2\}) = I(1, x)$;
   which results in a final state "axyc";
2. In another path, O_1, $O_3\{1\}$ and $O_2\{1,3\}$ are executed in sequence, where:
   (1) $O_3\{1\} = T(O_3, O_1) = I(1, y)$;
   (2) $O_2\{1, 3\} = T(O_2\{1\}, O_3\{1\}) = D(2, b)$;
   which results in a final state "ayxc".

Clearly, no operation has ever been transformed against two other operations in different orders along these two paths, but the final states produced by the two paths are not identical – convergence is not ensured, which means the condition is insufficient to achieve convergence.

A General CP2-Avoidance Condition

A correct and general CP2-avoidance condition was discovered in [21], which can be stated as: *CP2 can be avoided if an OT system can avoid transforming the same pair of operations in different contexts.*

It can be seen that transformations along the two divergent paths in Figure 1 violate this condition:

1. O_2 and O_3 are transformed under different contexts: $T(O_3, O_2)$ in 1-(1) vs $T(O_2\{1\}, O_3\{1\})$ in 2-(2).
2. O_1 and O_3 are also transformed under different contexts: $T(O_1\{2\}, O_3\{2\})$ in 1-(2) vs $T(O_3, O_1)$ in 2-(1).

The condition in [21] requires the contexts of any two operations are always the *same* whenever they are transformed with each other, but it does not specify what concrete conditions the contexts of two operations should meet when they are transformed. This CP2-avoidance condition is general but unsuitable for direct use in validating specific OT systems. In this work, we discovered a special CP2-avoidance condition that satisfies the general condition and also defines concrete

[8] In a COTS, a vertex represents a document state, and an arrow represents an operation: the starting vertex of the arrow represents the definition state of the operation, and the ending vertex represents the resulting state of the operation. A correct COTS is one that ensures there is only one label for each vertex or arrow.

context conditions between two operations for avoiding CP2; and we use this new condition to validate seven OT systems.

A Special CP2-Avoidance Condition

Definition 6. Totally Ordered and Equivalent Context Relation "$\stackrel{\Rightarrow}{=}$". *Given a "$\Rightarrow$" among all operations in a session, two operations O_a and O_b have a Totally Ordered and Equivalent Context Relation, denoted by $C(O_a) \stackrel{\Rightarrow}{=} C(O_b)$, when the following conditions are met: (1) $O_a \Rightarrow O_b$; (2) $C(O_a) = C(O_b)$; and (3) O_x is included in $C(O_a)$ and $C(O_b)$ if and only if:*

1. $O_x \Rightarrow O_a \Rightarrow O_b$; *or*
2. $O_a \Rightarrow O_x \Rightarrow O_b$ *and* $O_x \rightarrow O_b$.

The "$\stackrel{\Rightarrow}{=}$" relation requires the contexts of O_a and O_b include all and only those operations that are totally before both O_a and O_b, and those that are totally between O_a and O_b and causally before O_b. The following theorem establishes the uniqueness of the context under this relation.

Theorem 1. *For any two operations O_a and O_b in a session, operations included in their contexts are uniquely defined if $C(O_a) \stackrel{\Rightarrow}{=} C(O_b)$.*

Proof: In a given session, the causal ordering relation "$\rightarrow$" between any pair of operations must be fixed; and, under a given total ordering relation "$\Rightarrow$", the total ordering among all operations must be unique by Definition 3. The theorem follows directly from the uniqueness of the "$\Rightarrow$" and "$\rightarrow$" relations among operations in the same session and the definition of "$\stackrel{\Rightarrow}{=}$".

The general CP2-avoidance condition can be restated as follows: *CP2 can be avoided if an OT system can ensure the same pair of operations are transformed always on the same context.* This restatement highlights the *context uniqueness* essence of CP2-avoidance. The following theorem establishes a special CP2-avoidance condition.

Theorem 2. *CP2 can be avoided if an OT system can ensure a pair of operations O_a and O_b are transformed only if $C(O_a) \stackrel{\Rightarrow}{=} C(O_b)$.*

Proof: It is derived directly from the general CP2-avoidance condition and the uniqueness of the context of O_a and O_b under $C(O_a) \stackrel{\Rightarrow}{=} C(O_b)$ (Theorem 1).

We will show this special condition is general enough to cover all existing OT systems capable of avoiding CP2.

CP2 AVOIDANCE MECHANISMS AND PATTERNS

In this section, we discuss the basic mechanisms and transformation patterns that are required to meet the special CP2-avoidance condition.

Total Ordering Schemes

A total ordering relation "$\Rightarrow$" among operations in a session is at the core of the special CP2-avoidance condition, so a total ordering scheme is a basic mechanism for achieving CP2-avoidance in OT systems.

For a group of n operations in a session, there may be a maximum of $n!$ ways of totally ordering them. The special CP2-avoidance condition only requires the same "$\Rightarrow$" is used to order all operations in the same session, without imposing constraints on specific total ordering relations or ways of creating such total ordering relations. We describe three types of total ordering schemes below.

An OT system may use an *implicit* total ordering scheme based on a central server for broadcasting operations among collaborating sites: each site connects and sends local operations to the server via a FIFO (First In First Out) communication channel (e.g. a TCP connection); and the central server serializes operations and broadcasts them among all sites. The operation *serialization* order at the server *implicitly* forms a total order among all operations. This kind of total ordering scheme can be found in Jupiter [10], Google OT for Wave/Docs [16, 24], NICE [15], and Codoxword [21].

An OT system may also use an *explicit* total ordering scheme based on a special sequencer, which does not broadcast operations but only generates continuous sequence numbers for ordering operations. After generating a local operation, a collaborating site requests the central sequencer for a sequence number to timestamp this operation. In this way, all operations are totally ordered by sequence numbers. This total ordering scheme is used in SOCT3 and SOCT4 [23].

A total ordering scheme can be based on a distributed timestamping scheme without involving any central server/sequencer: collaborating sites use special rules to broadcast and timestamp operations so that a total ordering relation among all operations can be unambiguously derived. One example of such distributed schemes is the Time-Interval-Based OT system TIBOT [8].

One way or another, all existing OT systems that claimed or were recognized for CP2-avoidance have a total ordering scheme. However, the formation and use of such total ordering schemes may be implicit in these systems.

Operation Sequence and Transformation Patterns

We have identified several basic operation sequences and transformation patterns that can be used to ensure $C(O_a) \stackrel{\Rightarrow}{=} C(O_b)$ in transformations, which are described below.

Definition 7. Totally-Ordered and Contextualized Operation Sequence (TOCOS). *Given a list of operations $L = [O_1, O_2, ..., O_n]$ and a "$\Rightarrow$" among all operations in a session, L is a TOCOS if it is an empty list or a list with one operation, or the following holds (when $n \geq 2$): (1) $O_i \Rightarrow O_j$, for $1 \leq i < j \leq n$; and (2) $C(O_{i+1}) = C(O_i) \cup \{O_i\}$, for $1 \leq i < n$.*

All operations (if any) in a TOCOS are required to be totally ordered and contextualized, i.e. the context of an operation O_{i+1} must include O_i and all operations in the context of O_i. Contextualization can be achieved at the time of operation generation if $O_i \rightarrow O_{i+1}$, or by transformation if they are concurrent, i.e. $O_i || O_{i+1}$.

Based on TOCOS, we define two basic operation sequence patterns related to avoiding CP2.

Definition 8. ***Operation Sequence Pattern 1 (OSP1).*** *Given a TOCOS $L=[O_1, O_2, \ldots, O_n]$ and an operation O_x that is not in L, L is an OSP1 with respect to O_x if L is an empty list or the following conditions hold: (1) $C(O_1) \stackrel{\Rightarrow}{=} C(O_x)$; (2) $O_n \Rightarrow O_x$; and (3) L includes every operation O_y in a session, such that $O_y \parallel O_x$ and $O_1 \Rightarrow O_y \Rightarrow O_n$ (when $n \geq 2$).*

The first operation (if any) in L must have the "$\stackrel{\Rightarrow}{=}$" relation with O_x; all operations in L must be totally ordered before O_x; all operations that are concurrent with O_x and totally ordered between O_1 and O_n must be included in L.

Definition 9. ***Operation Sequence Pattern 2 (OSP2).*** *Given a TOCOS $L = [O_1, O_2, \ldots, O_n]$ and an operation O_x that is not in L, L is an OSP2 with respect to O_x if L is an empty list or the following conditions hold:(1) $C(O_x) \stackrel{\Rightarrow}{=} C(O_1)$; (2) $O_i \rightarrow O_j$, for $1 \leq i < j \leq n$ (when $n \geq 2$); and (3) L includes every operation O_y in the session, such that $O_1 \rightarrow O_y \rightarrow O_n$.*

O_x must have the "$\stackrel{\Rightarrow}{=}$" relation with the first operation (if any) in L, which implies O_x is totally ordered before all operations in L; all operations in L must be causally related; and all operations that are causally ordered between O_1 and O_n must be included in L.

The following LT function transforms an operation O against a sequence of operations in L to produce $O\{L\}$.

List Transformation: $LT(O, L) = O\{L\}$

1. $O\{L\} := O$;
2. **for** $(i = 1; i \leq |L|; i{+}{+})$ {
   $O\{L\} := T(O\{L\}, L[i])$;}

The SLT function symmetrically transforms an operation O with operations in L to produces $O\{L\}$ and $L\{O\}$.

Symmetric List Transformation: $SLT(O, L)=(O\{L\}, L\{O\})$

1. $O\{L\} := O$;
2. **for** $(i = 1; i \leq |L|; i{+}{+})$ {
   $L\{O\}[i] := T(L[i], O\{L\})$;
   $O\{L\} := T(O\{L\}, L[i])$; }

$LT(O_x, L)$ and $SLT(O_x, L)$ define two basic CP2-avoidance transformation patterns under the condition that L is an *OSP1* or *OSP2* with respect to O_x, which is established by the following theorem.

Theorem 3. *If L is an OSP1 or OSP2 with respect to O_x, CP2 is avoided in all transformations in $LT(O_x, L)$ and $SLT(O_x, L)$.*

Proof: Consider the transformation pattern: $LT(O_x, L)$ where L is an *OSP1* with respect to O_x. From Definition 8, we know $C(L[1]) \stackrel{\Rightarrow}{=} C(O_x)$. Therefore, CP2 can be avoided in $T(O_x, L[1])$ by Theorem 2. After this transformation, O_x becomes $O_x\{L[1]\}$, which implies $C(L[2]) \stackrel{\Rightarrow}{=} C(O_x\{L[1]\})$ by Definition 6 and Definition 8, hence CP2 can be avoided in $T(O_x\{L[1]\}, L[2])$. By a deductive argument, CP2 can be avoided in every transformation in $LT(O_x, L)$. Following the same reasoning, CP2 can be avoided in all transformation patterns stated in the theorem.

VALIDATING OT SYSTEMS FOR CP2 AVOIDANCE

One major challenge in this work is the diversity of the systems to be examined: they were designed for different purposes and had major differences in: (1) system structures, e.g. some use a central server and some do not; (2) operation propagation protocols, e.g. some delay propagating operations until certain conditions are met, and some do not; and (3) mechanisms and algorithms, e.g. some use state/context-vectors, and some do not; some are based on two-dimensional (2D) state-spaces, and some use one-dimensional (1D) buffers. These systems were designed by different research groups and described in different styles and terminologies, which present challenges to figure out their real similarities and differences.

Our approach to addressing these challenges is to devise a general framework encapsulating the basic mechanisms and transformation patterns that may occur at three critical locations: (1) local sites, where operations are generated; (2) the server site (optional), where operations are broadcast to other sites; and (3) remote sites, where operations generated by other sites are replayed. Then, we dissect the seven OT systems one-by-one to extract relevant schemes and algorithms, and describe them uniformly in terms of the basic mechanisms and patterns under the framework. Finally, we validate CP2-avoidance by matching their transformation patterns with CP2-avoiding transformation patterns established in the prior section.

In addition, we use a running example to illustrate how the seven systems work in concrete scenarios, in which there are three collaborating sites (plus an optional server) and four operations with causal relations: $(O_1 \rightarrow O_4) \parallel (O_2 \rightarrow O_3)$, and total ordering relations: $O_1 \Rightarrow O_2 \Rightarrow O_3 \Rightarrow O_4$.

Jupiter

In the Jupiter system [10], collaborating clients are connected to a central server via TCP connections in a star-like topology. A client can communicate directly with the server only; the server sequentially processes and broadcasts operations among all clients.

Local processing

When O_x is generated by a client, it is executed immediately at the local site and propagated to the server as-is. Local operations are propagated sequentially and saved along the local dimension of a 2D state-space.

Server processing

The server maintains multiple 2D state-spaces[9], one for every client. A state-space consists of a *local* dimension for operations from the corresponding client, and a *global* dimension for operations from all other sites. The server handles O_x as follows:

1. locates the space for the client from which O_x comes;
2. searches this space to find the state that matches the context of O_x, and saves O_x at this matching state along the local dimension;

[9]The multiple 2D state-spaces maintenance was not reported in the Jupiter paper [10]. The description here is based on our understanding and derivation from other sources [9, 16, 24].

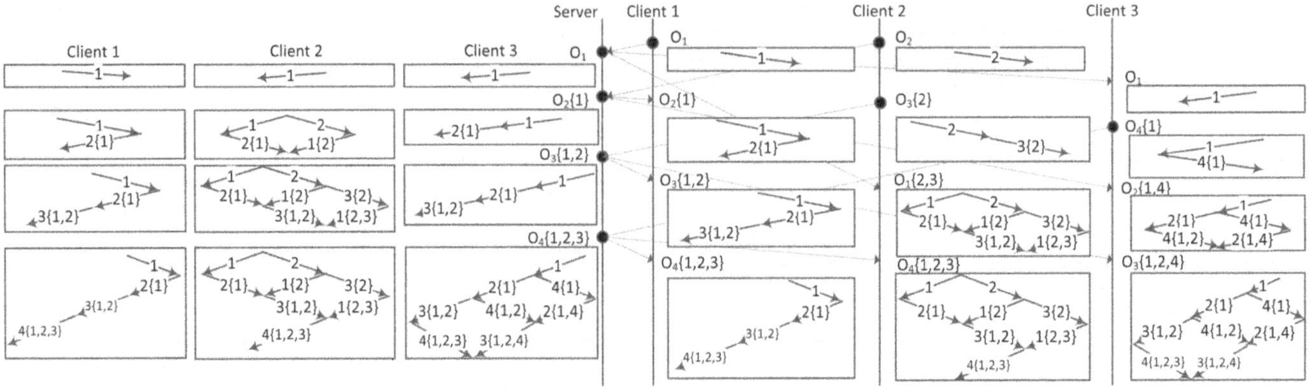

Figure 2: Jupiter: the server maintains three 2D state-spaces; each client maintains a single state-space; in a 2D state-space, an operation $O_n\{m\}$ is represented by arrow labeled by $n\{m\}$ (for conciseness), the local dimension is represented by south-east arrows, and the global dimension represented by south-west arrows.

3. transforms O_x symmetrically with a sequence of operations, denoted as L_1, consisting of operations along the global dimension from the matching state to the final state of the space; this transformation can be expressed as: $SLT(O_x, L_1) = (O_x\{L_1\}, L_1\{O_x\})$[10];
4. propagates $O_x\{L_1\}$ to other clients;
5. saves $O_x\{L_1\}$ at the end of the global dimension of every other state-space maintained by the server.

Remote processing

Each client maintains a state-space similar to that at the server. Jupiter handles $O_x\{L_1\}$ at a remote site as follows:

1. searches the space to find a matching state for $O_x\{L_1\}$, and saves $O_x\{L_1\}$ at this matching state along the global dimension;
2. transforms $O_x\{L_1\}$ symmetrically with a sequence of operations, denoted as L_2, consisting of operations along the local dimension from the matching state to the final state of the space; this transformation can be expressed as $SLT(O_x\{L_1\}, L_2)=(O_x\{L_1, L_2\}, L_2\{O_x\})$;
3. executes $O_x\{L_1, L_2\}$.

CP2-avoidance validation

It can be shown that L_1 is an OSP1 with respect to O_x for $SLT(O_x, L_1)$, and L_2 is an OSP2 with respect to $O_x\{L_1\}$ for $SLT(O_x\{L_1\}, L_2)$ because:

1. all operations in L_1 and L_2 are:
   (1) totally ordered by the server serialization;
   (2) contextualized by transformations in *SLT;*
   (3) concurrent with O_x as they are generated by other clients before O_x reaches these clients, and O_x is generated before they reach O_x's local site;
2. L_1 contains all operations that are totally before O_x, and $L_1[1] \underline{\Rightarrow} O_x$;
3. L_2 contains operations that are totally after O_x and causally related with each other, and $O_x\{L_1\} \underline{\Rightarrow} L_2[1]$.

By Theorem 3, Jupiter CP2-avoidance is confirmed.

[10] For conciseness, details of using intermediate transformation results created during *SLT/LT* to update 2D state-spaces and other buffers for all systems are omitted.

An example

Consider operation $O_3\{2\}$ at Client *2* in Figure 2. Upon generation, it is executed immediately, appended at the end of the local dimension of a 2D state-space, and propagated to the server. At the server, the state-space for Client *2* is firstly located and searched to find the matching state at the end of O_2. Then, $O_3\{2\}$ is saved after O_2 along the local dimension, and symmetrically transformed with $O_1\{2\}$ along the global dimension, which produces two transformed operations: $O_3\{1,2\}$ and $O_1\{2,3\}$, which are placed in corresponding dimensions of the state-space. $O_3\{1,2\}$ is propagated to Clients *1* and *3*, and appended to the ends of global dimensions of their state-spaces as well. When $O_3\{1,2\}$ arrives at Client *3*, it is saved at the matching state at the end of $O_2\{1\}$ along the global dimension, then symmetrically transformed with $O_4\{1,2\}$ along the local dimension, which produces two transformed operations: $O_3\{1,2,4\}$ and $O_4\{1,2,3\}$ in corresponding dimensions of the state-space. Finally, $O_3\{1,2,4\}$ is executed at Client *3*.

NICE

The NICE system [15] is also based on a central server for serializing and broadcasting operations. NICE supports OT-based flexible notification for both real-time and non-real-time collaboration. We extract and describe only the relevant consistency maintenance aspects below.

Local processing

NICE handles local operations in the same way as Jupiter, except using a 1D buffer to save local operations.

Server processing

The server maintains multiple 1D buffers, one for every client to maintain operations that are from other clients and have been broadcast. The server handles O_x as follows:

1. locates the buffer for the client from which O_x comes;
2. searches the buffer to find the matching state for O_x;
3. transforms O_x symmetrically with a sequence of operations, denoted as L_1, starting from matching state to the end of the buffer; this transformation can be expressed as: $SLT(O_x, L_1) = (O_x\{L_1\}, L_1\{O_x\})$;
4. propagates $O_x\{L_1\}$ to other clients;
5. saves $O_x\{L_1\}$ at the end of every other 1D buffer.

Remote processing

NICE handles $O_x\{L_1\}$ at a remote site as follows:

1. searches the buffer for the state that matches the context of $O_x\{L_1\}$ (this state may not exist);
2. transforms $O_x\{L_1\}$ symmetrically with a sequence of operations, denoted as L_2, consisting of operations from the matching state (if exists) to the end of the buffer; this transformation can be expressed as $SLT(O_x\{L_1\}, L_2) = (O_x\{L_1, L_2\}, L_2\{O_x\})$;
3. executes $O_x\{L_1, L_2\}$ (no need to save it in the buffer).

CP2-avoidance validation

It can be shown that L_1 is an OSP1 with respect to O_x in $SLT(O_x, L_1)$; and L_2 is an OSP2 with respect to $O_x\{L_1\}$ in $SLT(O_x\{L_1\}, L_2)$ by the same reasoning as that for Jupiter. By Theorem 3, NICE CP2-avoidance is confirmed.

An example

Consider operation $O_3\{2\}$ at Client *2* in Figure 3. Upon generation, it is executed immediately at Client *2*, appended at the end of the local buffer, and propagated to the server. At the server, the buffer for Client *2* is located and searched to find the matching state at beginning of the buffer. Then, $O_3\{2\}$ is symmetrically transformed with $O_1\{2\}$, which produces two transformed operations: (1) $O_3\{1,2\}$ is propagated to Clients *1* and *3*, and appended to the ends of their buffers as well; (2) $O_1\{2,3\}$ is used to replace $O_1\{2\}$ in the buffer for Client *2*. When $O_3\{1,2\}$ arrives at Client *3*, it is symmetrically transformed with $O_4\{1,2\}$ since they share the same state, which produces two transformed operations: $O_3\{1,2,4\}$ is executed; and $O_4\{1,2,3\}$ is used to replace $O_4\{1,2\}$ in the buffer.

Google OT for Google Wave and Docs

Google OT for Google Wave and Docs [9, 16, 24] is adapted from Jupiter, with the same star-like architecture and a central server for serializing and broadcasting operations. Google OT adds a *stop-and-wait* propagation protocol between each client and the server. As a result, a single 1D buffer at the server is adequate to maintain all possible states for transformation, which eliminates multiple 2D state-spaces in Jupiter.

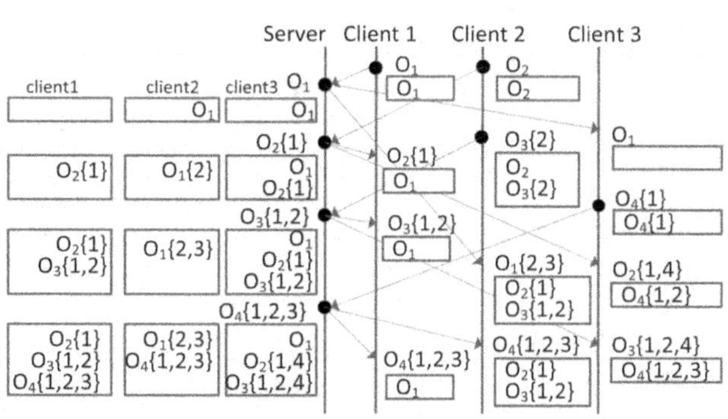

Figure 3: NICE: the server maintains three 1D buffers; each client maintains one buffer.

Local processing

When O_x is generated by a client, it is executed immediately and saved in the local dimension of a 2D state-space. However, O_x is not propagated to the server until the prior local operation O_{x-1} (if any) has been acknowledged by the server. Consequently, when O_x is propagated, it must have been symmetrically transformed with a sequence of remote operations (if any), denoted as L_1, that are propagated from the server (see the follow-up description for remote processing) and totally before O_{x-1} (hence before O_x as well). This transformation can be expressed as: $SLT(O_x, L_1) = (O_x\{L_1\}, L_1\{O_x\})$; the transformed operation $O_x\{L_1\}$ is propagated to the server.

Server processing

The server maintains a single 1D buffer for keeping track operations from all clients in a totally ordered and contextualized fashion. The server handles $O_x\{L_1\}$ as follows:

1. searches the 1D buffer to find the state that matches the context of $O_x\{L_1\}$;
2. transforms $O_x\{L_1\}$ against a sequence of operations, denoted as L_2, from the matching state to the end of the buffer; this transformation can be expressed as $LT(O_x\{L_1\}, L_2) = O_x\{L_1, L_2\}$;
3. appends $O_x\{L_1, L_2\}$ at the end of the buffer (other operations in the buffer remain unchanged); and
4. propagates $O_x\{L_1, L_2\}$ to all sites, including the originating site of $O_x\{L_1\}$ as an acknowledgement.

Remote processing

At each client site, there is a 2D state-space similar to Jupiter. The handling of $O_x\{L_1,L_2\}$ at a remote site is also similar to handling $O_x\{L_1\}$ in Jupiter: $O_x\{L_1,L_2\}$ will be symmetrically transformed with a sequence of operations, denoted as L_3, consisting of operations along the local dimension from the state that matches the context of $O_x\{L_1,L_2\}$ to the final state of the state-space. This transformation can be expressed as $SLT(O_x\{L_1,L_2\},L_3)= (O_x\{L_1, L_2,L_3\}, L_3\{O_x\})$. Finally, $O_x\{L_1,L_2,L_3\}$ is executed.

CP2-avoidance validation

It can be shown that L_1 is an OSP1 with respect to O_x in $SLT(O_x, L_1)$, L_2 is an OSP1 with respect to $O_x\{L_1\}$ in $LT(O_x\{L_1\}, L_2)$, and L_3 is an OSP2 with respect to $O_x\{L_1, L_2\}$ in $SLT(O_x\{L_1,L_2\}, L_3)$ by following the same reasoning as for Jupiter. By Theorem 3, Google OT CP2-avoidance is confirmed.

An example

Consider operation $O_3\{2\}$ at Client *2* in Figure 4. Upon generation, it is executed immediately and appended at the end of the local dimension of a 2D state-space. It is not propagated to the server until it has been transformed with O_1 and Client *2* has received the acknowledgement of $O_2\{1\}$, which is the prior operation causally before $O_3\{2\}$. The transformed operation $O_3\{1,2\}$ is propagated to the server. At the server, the matching state is located at the end of $O_2\{1\}$ in the buffer and there is no other operation shares this state, so $O_3\{1,2\}$ is appended to the end of the buffer and then propagated to all clients. When $O_3\{1,2\}$ arrives at Client *3*, it is handled in exactly the same way as in Jupiter.

Consider another operation $O_4\{1\}$ at Client *3* in Figure 4. Upon generation, it is executed immediately and saved. It is immediately propagated to the server since it is the first local operation at Client *3*. At the server, the matching state is at the end of O_1 in the buffer, so $O_4\{1\}$ is transformed with $O_2\{1\}$ and $O_3\{1,2\}$ in sequence to produce $O_4\{1,2,3\}$, which is appended at the end of the buffer and propagated to all clients. When $O_4\{1,2,3\}$ arrives at Client *1*, it is executed without transformation and appended at the end of the state-space along the global dimension.

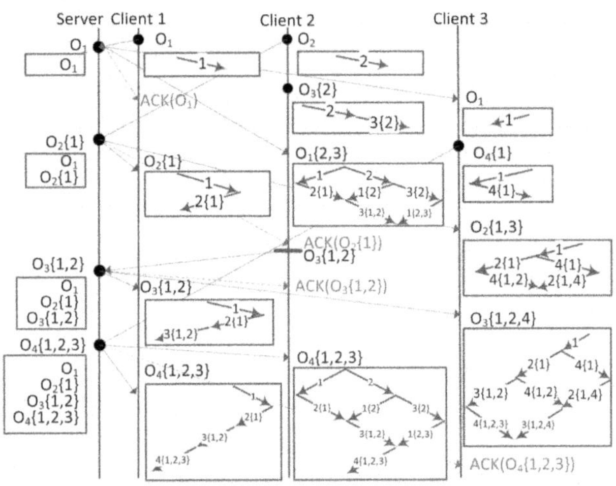

Figure 4: Google OT: the server maintains a single linear buffer; each client maintains one 2D state-space; local operations are acknowledged by the server.

SOCT3

Different from all prior systems, SOCT3 uses a central sequencer, which issues continuous sequence numbers to totally order operations, but is not involved in transforming or broadcasting operations. In addition, SOCT3 also uses state-vectors (SV) to capture concurrency relations among operations.

Local processing

When O_x is generated at a site, it is executed immediately, and timestamped by a sequence number acquired from the sequencer and a state-vector. Local operations are propagated as-is in sequence and saved in a history buffer (*HB*).

Remote processing

SOCT3 handles O_x at a remote site as follows:

1. waits until all operations with smaller sequence numbers have been executed at this site;
2. copies *HB* into *HB'*, and splits *HB'* into two totally ordered and contextualized sub-lists: HB'_1 with operations that are causally before O_x, and HB'_2 with operations that are concurrent with O_x, which can be achieved by using SV timestamps and a *transpose* procedure to reorder operations;
3. transforms O_x against operations in HB'_2, which can be expressed as $LT(O_x, HB'_2) = O_x\{HB'_2\}$;
4. executes $O_x\{HB'_2\}$; and
5. saves $O_x\{HB'_2\}$ at the end of *HB* and transposes it to the position determined by its total ordering in *HB*.

It is worth highlighting that *HB'* is created only for transforming O_x for execution, while *HB* always maintains operations that are totally ordered and contextualized.

CP2-avoidance validation

We can use the total ordering position of O_x to split HB'_2 into two sublists: $HB'_2 = HB'_{2\text{-}1} + HB'_{2\text{-}2}$, where $HB'_{2\text{-}1}$ contains operations totally before O_x and $HB'_{2\text{-}2}$ contains operations totally after O_x. Then it can be shown that $HB'_{2\text{-}1}$ is an OSP1 with respect to O_x; $HB'_{2\text{-}2}$ is an OSP2 with respect to $O_x\{HB'_{2\text{-}1}\} = LT(O_x, HB'_{2\text{-}1})$ by following similar reasoning as for the Jupiter case, except that the total ordering of operations is defined by sequence numbers and concurrent operations are detected by SVs.

One special complication in SOCT3 is the use of a transpose procedure to reorder operations in *HB*. This transpose procedure involves a pair of *reversible* inclusion/forward and exclusion/backward transformation functions [23], which is non-trivial to achieve [18, 21].

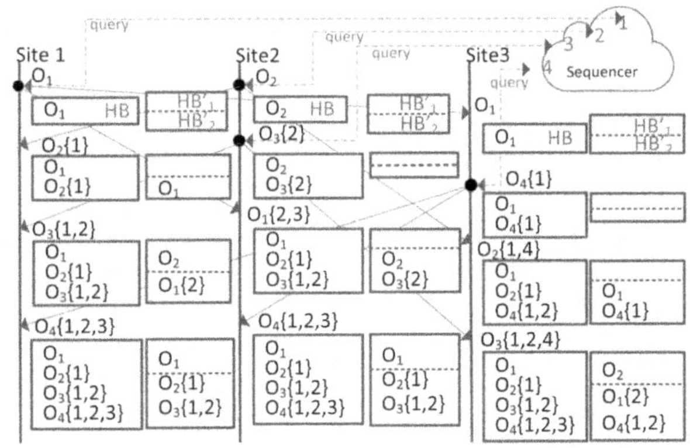

Figure 5: SOCT3: there is a central sequencer for issuing continuous numbers to totally order operations.

An example

Consider operation $O_3\{2\}$ at Site *2* in Figure 5. Upon generation, it is executed immediately, timestamped by a sequence number "3" and a SV, appended at the end of the local *HB*, and propagated to Site *1* and Site *3*. When $O_3\{2\}$ arrives at Site *3*, it waits until operations with sequence numbers smaller than "*3*" have been executed. Then, the original $HB = [O_1, O_2\{1\}, O_4\{1,2\}]$ is copied into *HB'* and split into two sub-list: $HB'_1 = [O_2]$, and $HB'_2 = [O_1\{2\}, O_4\{1,2\}]$ by using *SV* timestamps and the transpose procedure. $O_3\{2\}$ is transformed with concurrent operations in HB'_2 to get $O_3\{1,2,4\}$. The transformed operation $O_3\{1,2,4\}$ is executed, appended at the end of the original *HB*, and transposed to the position determined by the sequence number "3" to produce $HB = [O_1, O_2\{1\}, O_3\{1,2\}, O_4\{1,2,3\}]$.

SOCT4

SOCT4 follows SOCT3 in using a central sequencer to totally order operations, but eliminates the use of state-vectors for capturing concurrency relations and the transpose procedure for reordering operations in *HB* by globally serializing operation propagation.

Local processing

When O_x is generated, SOCT4 handles it as follows:

1. executes O_x immediately and acquires a sequence number from the central sequencer to timestamp O_x;
2. saves O_x in *HB*, and waits until O_x has been symmetrically transformed with a sequence of (remote) concurrent operations, denoted as L_1, that are totally before O_x; this transformation can be expressed as: $SLT(O_x, L_1) = (O_x\{L_1\}, L_1\{O_x\})$;
3. propagates $O_x\{L_1\}$ (serialized operation propagation).

Remote processing

SOCT4 handles $O_x\{L_1\}$ at a remote site as follows:

1. waits until all operations that are totally before $O_x\{L_1\}$ have been executed at this site;
2. transforms $O_x\{L_1\}$ symmetrically with a sequence of local operations that are totally after it in *HB*, denoted as L_2; this transformation can be expressed as: $SLT(O_x\{L_1\}, L_2) = (O_x\{L_1, L_2\}, L_2\{O_x\})$;
3. executes $O_x\{L_1,L_2\}$ (no need to save it in the buffer).

CP2-avoidance validation

It can be shown that L_1 is an OSP1 with respect to O_x in $SLT(O_x, L_1)$, and L_2 is an OSP2 with respect to $O_x\{L_1\}$ in $SLT(O_x\{L_1\}, L_2)$ by the same reasoning as for Jupiter. By Theorem 3, SOCT4 CP2-avoidance is confirmed.

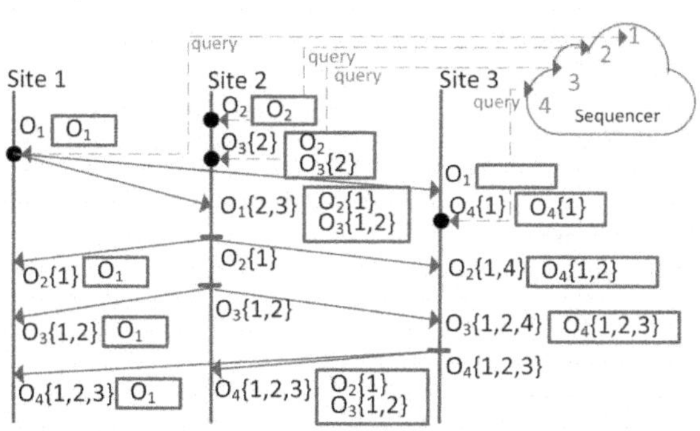

Figure 6: SOCT4: there is a central sequencer; each site maintains a buffer for locally generated operations only.

An example

Consider operation O_2 at Site *2* in Figure 6. Upon its generation, it is executed immediately at Site *2*, timestamped by a sequence number "*2*", and appended at the end of the local buffer. It is not propagated until it has been symmetrically transformed with O_1, which is the only operation totally before it. The transformed operation $O_2\{1\}$ is propagated to Site *1* and Site *3*. When $O_2\{1\}$ arrives at Site *3*, it is symmetrically transformed with $O_4\{1\}$ that is totally after it to produce two transformed operations: one is $O_4\{1,2\}$, which replaces $O_4\{1\}$ in the buffer; the other is $O_2\{1,4\}$, which is executed at Site *3*.

TIBOT

TIBOT (Time-Interval Based OT) is unique in using a distributed scheme to totally order operations, without using any central server. Collaborating sites may communicate with each other in any way that ensures reliability and the FIFO property.

Each site maintains a local timer (a numeric counter) with continuously increasing *Time-Interval* (*TI*) values: *0*, *1*, *2*, ..., etc. Timers at different sites must take the same sequence of values, but may tick at different speeds and need not be synchronized.

TI-based Timestamping Scheme: when an operation is generated at a site, it is timestamped by a tuple <*TI*, *SI*, *SN*>, where *TI* is the local timer value, *SI* is the local site identifier, *SN* is the local operation sequence number.

TI-based Total Ordering Scheme: for any two operations O_a and O_b, with timestamps T_a and T_b, respectively, $O_a \Rightarrow O_b$ *if and only if*: (1) $T_a.TI < T_b.TI$; or (2) $T_a.TI = T_b.TI$ and $T_a.SI < T_b.SI$; or (3) $T_a.TI = T_b.TI$ and $T_a.SI = T_b.SI$ and $T_a.SN < T_b.SN$.

Local processing

When O_x is generated, TIBOT handles it as follows:

1. executes O_x immediately and timestamps it with T_x;
2. saves O_x in a history buffer (*HB*) and waits until: (1) the local timer has been advanced to a value larger than $T_x.TI$; and (2) O_x has been transformed with a sequence of remote operations, denoted as L_1, which includes all operations whose *TI*s are smaller than $T_x.TI$; this can be expressed as $LT(O_x, L_1) = O_x\{L_1\}$;
3. propagates $O_x\{L_1\}$ with the same timestamp T_x.

Two important operation propagation schemes:

1. All local operations generated during the same time interval are packaged and propagated to remote sites together, which not only reduces communication overhead, but also simplifies derivation of total order relations at remote sites.
2. If there is no operation generated at a site during a time interval, this site is required to broadcast a special message, with a timestamp <*TI*, *SI*, *nil*>, at the end of each time interval. Such special messages are needed to enable the derivation of TI-based conditions and total ordering relations among operations, which are essential in TIBOT.

Remote processing

TIBOT handles $O_x\{L_1\}$ at a remote site as follows:

1. waits until: (1) the local timer has advanced to a value greater than $T_x.TI$; (2) local operations with *TI*s equal to the $T_x.TI$ have been propagated; and (3) all operations totally before $O_x\{L_1\}$ have been executed at this site;
2. undoes a sequence of (local) operations in *HB*, denoted as L_{undo}, which are totally after $O_x\{L_1\}$;
3. transforms $O_x\{L_1\}$ against a sequence of operations in *HB*, denoted as L_2, whose *TI*s are the same as $T_x.TI$; this can be expressed as $LT(O_x\{L_1\}, L_2) = O_x\{L_1, L_2\}$;
4. executes $O_x\{L_1, L_2\}$ and saves it in *HB*;

5. transforms operations in L_{undo} symmetrically with $O_x\{L_1, L_2\}$; this transformation can be expressed as $SLT(O_x\{L_1, L_2\}, L_{undo}) = (O_x\{L_1, L_2, L_{undo}\}, L_{undo}\{O_x\})$;
6. re-executes transformed operations in $L_{undo}\{O_x\{L_1, L_2\}\}$ and saves them sequentially in *HB*.

CP2-avoidance validation

It can be shown that L_1 is an OSP1 with respect to O_x in $LT(O_x, L_1) = O_x\{L_1\}$, L_2 is an OSP1 with respect to $O_x\{L_1\}$ in $LT(O_x\{L_1\}, L_2)$; and L_{undo} is an OSP2 with respect to $O_x\{L_1, L_2\}$ in $SLT(O_x\{L_1, L_2\}, L_{undo})$ by following the same reasoning as for Jupiter, except that the total ordering and concurrency relations among operations are detected by TI-based distributed timestamps. By Theorem 3, TIBOT CP2-avoidance is confirmed.

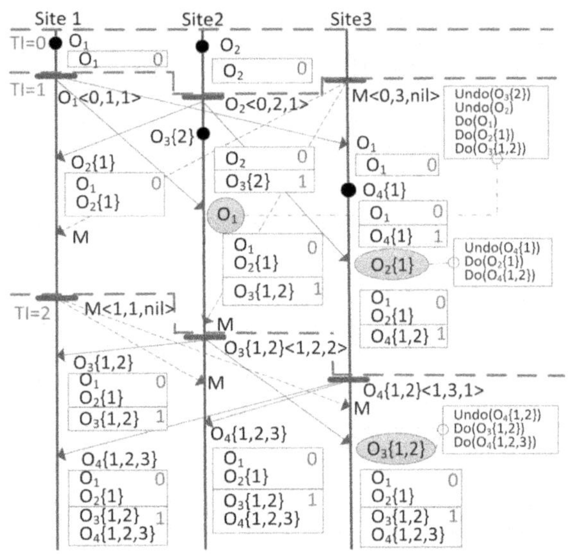

Figure 7: TIBOT: each site maintains an independent timer and a linear HB; operations may be undone and redone; special message M is sent if no local operation to propagate.

An example

Consider operation O_2 generated during $TI = 0$ at Site *2* in Figure 7. Upon generation, it is executed immediately, timestamped with <*0, 2, 1*>, and saved at the end of the *HB*. O_2 is not propagated until its timer has advanced to $TI = 1$. TIBOT handles O_2 at remote sites as follows:

1. At Site 1: Step 1, the following conditions are met: (1) local timer has advanced to $TI=1$; (2) local operation O_1, with the same $TI=0$ as O_2, has been propagated; and (3) O_1 is the only operation totally-before O_2 and has been executed. Step 2, there is no local operation totally-after O_1, so nothing to undo. Step 3, O_2 is transformed with O_1 to produce $O_2\{1\}$. Step 4, $O_2\{1\}$ is executed and saved in *HB*. There is nothing to re-transform and redo in Steps 5 and 6.
2. At Site 3: Step 1, the following conditions are met: (1) local timer has advanced to $TI=1$; (2) there is no local operation during $TI=0$ and a special timestamp message M<*0, 3, nil*> has been propagated; and (3) O_1 is the only operation totally-before O_2 and has been executed. Step 2, local operation $O_4\{1\}$ is undone as it is totally after O_2. Step 3, O_2 is transformed with O_1 to produce $O_2\{1\}$. Step 4, $O_2\{1\}$ is executed and saved in *HB*. Step 5, $O_4\{1\}$ is transformed with $O_2\{1\}$ to produce $O_4\{1,2\}$. Step 6, $O_4\{1,2\}$ is re-executed and saved in *HB*. $O_4\{1,2\}$ is propagated when *TI* is advanced to *2*.

COT

Among seven OT systems, COT (Context-based OT) [21] is unique in supporting both consistency maintenance and *group undo* (initiated by users, not as internal concurrency control mechanisms) [11, 13, 21]. In this study, we focus on COT's consistency maintenance (convergence) aspects only. To avoid CP2, COT specifies a total ordering relation among operations and uses this relation to control operation execution and transformation orders, but leaves the schemes to achieve such ordering unspecified. In other words, COT may adopt a server-based or a distributed scheme that is able to meet the specified total ordering requirements. In the following, we sketch COT under the assumption that every collaborating site is connected to a central server via a TCP communication channel; the server broadcasts and serializes operations, but does not transform operations.

COT is also special in decoupling its operation buffering scheme from the core algorithm. The basic COT buffering scheme requires saving operations in original forms only. However, more sophisticated COT buffering schemes may selectively save operations in transformed forms to eliminate re-transformations [21]. For simplicity, we assume the basic buffering scheme in COT description.

Local processing

When an operation O_x is generated at a site, it is executed immediately and timestamped by a Context-Vector (CV) for capturing causal/context relations among operations, and propagated as-is to remote sites (via the server). All local operations are saved in original forms in a local buffer, called *Document State* (*DS*), which may be implemented as a set or other suitable data structures.

Server processing

The server broadcasts O_x to all sites, including the site which O_x comes from, which serves as a notification of its total ordering based on the server serialization.

Remote processing

COT handles O_x at a remote site as follows:

1. waits until all operations that are totally before O_x have been executed at this site;
2. finds all operations in the local *DS* that are concurrent with O_x by using their context-vectors;
3. contextualizes those operations into a sequence of operations, denoted as *L*, which are totally ordered according to the server serialization;
4. transforms O_x against operations in *L*, which can be expressed as: $LT(O_x, L)=O_x\{L\}$;
5. executes $O_x\{L\}$;
6. saves the original O_x in the local *DS*.

CP2-avoidance validation

We can use the total ordering position of O_x to split L into two sublists: $L = L_1 + L_2$, where L_1 contains operations totally before O_x and L_2 contains operations totally after O_x. Then, it can be shown that L_1 is an OSP1 with respect to O_x in $LT(O_x, L_1)$, and L_2 is an OSP2 with respect to $O_x\{L_1\}$ in $LT(O_x\{L_1\}, L_2)$ by following the same reasoning as for prior systems, except concurrency relations among operations are detected by context-vectors. By Theorem 3, COT CP2-avoidance is confirmed, which is consistent with prior verification based on the general CP2-avoidance condition [21].

An example

Consider operation $O_3\{2\}$ at Client *2* in Figure 8. Upon generation, it is executed immediately, saved in the local *DS*, and propagated to the server. The server broadcasts $O_3\{2\}$ to all clients. When $O_3\{2\}$ arrives at Client *3*, the local $DS=\{O_1, O_4\{1\}, O_2\}$. From *DS*, COT finds a subset of two operations $\{O_1, O_4\{1\}\}$ which are concurrent with $O_3\{2\}$, and converts the subset into a totally ordered and contextualized list $L= [O_1\{2\},O_4\{1,2\}]$. Then, $O_3\{2\}$ is transformed against L to get $O_3\{1,2,4\}$. Finally, $O_3\{1,2,4\}$ is executed on the local document, and original operation $O_3\{2\}$ is saved in the local $DS = \{O_1, O_4\{1\}, O_2, O_3\{2\}\}$.

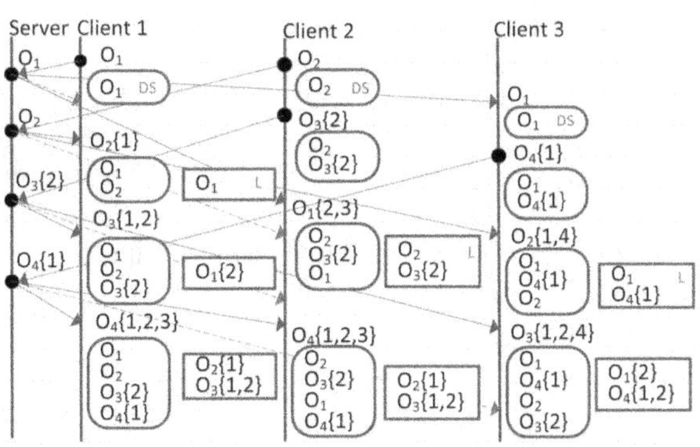

Figure 8: COT: every client maintains a document state *DS* containing executed operations in their original forms; concurrent operations are extracted from *DS* and contextualized in *L* in a totally ordered fashion for transformation.

Summary of CP2-avoidance Validation

CP2-avoidance validation results for seven OT systems are summarized in Table 1. As all transformations performed by these systems can be expressed by the basic CP2-avoiding operation sequences and transformation patterns established in this work, we have confirmed CP2-avoidance correctness for all systems:

1. COT was verified for its CP2-avoidance by using the general CP2-avoidance condition [21]; this work is a reconfirmation of its correctness based on the special CP2-avoidance condition.
2. Jupiter and Google OT were designed to solely use CP1-preserving transformation functions for convergence, which is essentially the same as what is meant by CP2-avoidance; this work establishes their correctness in achieving convergence without requiring transformation functions to preserve CP2.
3. NICE, TIBOT, and SOCT3/4 were designed to avoid CP2 but verified by using the insufficient condition. It is not surprising that these systems were able to meet the insufficient condition because they can satisfy the special CP2-avoidance condition (in this work), which satisfies the general CP2-avoidance condition (according to Theorem 2), which implies the insufficient CP2-avoidance condition, as proven in [21]. The value of this work is to establish their CP2-avoidance correctness on a sound ground.

Conversely, these validation results have also confirmed the generality and effectiveness of the basic CP2-avoidance conditions, mechanisms and transformation patterns, and validation framework, for studying and verifying a variety of OT systems.

OT Systems	Operation Sequences and Transformation Patterns at Three Locations		
	Local	Server	Remote
Jupiter OT	O_x	$SLT(O_x,L_1)$, L_1 is an OSP1 with O_x	$SLT(O_x\{L_1\},L_2)$ L_2 is an OSP2with $O_x\{L_1\}$
NICE	O_x	$SLT(O_x,L_1)$, L_1 is an OSP1 with O_x	$SLT(O_x\{L_1\},L_2)$, L_2 is an OSP2 with $O_x\{L_1\}$
Google OT	$SLT(O_x, L_1)$, L_1 is an OSP1 with O_x	$LT(O_x\{L_1\},L_2)$ L_2 is an OSP1 with $O_x\{L_1\}$	$SLT(O_x\{L_1,L_2\}, L_3)$, L_3 is an OSP2 with $O_x\{L_1,L_2\}$
SOCT3	O_x	*Sequencer*	$SLT(O_x, HB'_2)$, $HB'_2=HB'_{21}+HB'_{22}$, HB'_{21} is an OSP1with O_x HB'_{22} is an OSP2 with $O_x\{HB'_{21}\}$
SOCT4	$SLT(O_x, L_1)$, L_1 is an OSP1 with O_x	*Sequencer*	$SLT(O_x\{L_1\},L_2)$, L_2 is an OSP2 with $O_x\{L_1\}$
TIBOT	$LT(O_x, L_1)$, L_1 is an OSP1 with O_x	*N.A.*	$LT(O_x\{L_1\}, L_2)$, L_2 is an OSP1 with $O_x\{L_1\}$; $SLT(O_x\{L_1, L_2\}, L_{undo})$, L_{undo} is an OSP2 with $O_x\{L_1,L_2\}$
COT	O_x	*Serialization and broadcast*	$LT(O_x, L)$, $L=L_1+L_2$, L_1 is an OSP1 with O_x, L_2 is an OSP2 with $O_x\{L_1\}$

Table 1: CP2-avoidance validation summary

NEW SYSTEMS/IDEAS INSPIRED BY THIS STUDY

This study has not only enabled us to discover the basic conditions and transformation patterns for CP2-avoidance and to validate existing OT systems, but also inspired us to identify improvements to these OT systems, devise new OT systems capable of avoiding CP2 with unique combinations of novel features, and ideas for future exploration.

Improvements to Jupiter and Google OT

From NICE, we learned 1D buffers are adequate to achieve CP2-avoidance with simple control algorithms. By comparing Jupiter with NICE, we observed their CP2-avoiding operation sequences and transformation patterns and locations are the same (as shown in Table 1), and their main differences lie in the use of 2D state-spaces (in Jupiter) vs. 1D buffers (in NICE). From this observation, we derive

Jupiter can be simplified by replacing all 2D state-spaces with 1D buffers similar to NICE, without losing any capability or complicating any aspect of Jupiter.

Google OT has replaced the multiple 2D state-spaces in Jupiter server with a single 1D buffer, at the price of a *stop-and-wait* synchronization between each client and the server, but still maintains 2D state-spaces at client sites. Based on the same NICE insight, Google OT can also be simplified by replacing 2D spaces with 1D buffers.

A New OT System: TIBOT 2.0

Compared to other six OT systems, TIBOT is unique not only in its distributed total ordering scheme, but also in its capability of avoiding both CP1 and CP2, which is only achieved by the prior GOT system [18]. But TIBOT avoids both CP1 and CP2 without using state-vectors or exclusive transformation, which is an advantage over GOT. Similar to GOT [18], TIBOT has used an *undo/transform-do/transform-redo* scheme to enforce a totally ordered transformation among all operations and never transform a pair of operations in different orders. However, past research has found undo/redo-based concurrency control schemes are inefficient and may cause interface abnormality to end-users, so most OT systems have been designed to avoid internal undo/redo.

Inspired by the insights drawn from this study, we propose a new OT system, named as TIBOT 2.0, which inherits from TIBOT the basic time-interval-based distributed total ordering and shares the same local processing and propagation control schemes as TIBOT, but has a significantly re-signed remote processing to eliminate undo/redo. We describe TIBOT 2.0 remote processing below.

Remote processing in TIBOT 2.0

TIBOT 2.0 handles $O_x\{L_1\}$ at a remote site as follows:

1. waits until: the same conditions as specified in Step 1 in the original TIBOT;
2. transforms $O_x\{L_1\}$ against a sequence of operations in *HB*, denoted as L_2, which includes all operations with *TI*s equal to $T_x.TI$ and totally before $O_x\{L_1\}$; this transformation can be expressed as $LT(O_x\{L_1\}, L_2) = O_x\{L_1, L_2\}$;
3. saves $O_x\{L_1, L_2\}$ at the end of L_2 in *HB*;
4. transforms $O_x\{L_1, L_2\}$ symmetrically with a sequence of operations in *HB*, denoted as L_3, which are totally after $O_x\{L_1, L_2\}$; this transformation can be expressed as $SLT(O_x\{L_1, L_2\}, L_3) = (O_x\{L_1, L_2, L_3\}, L_3\{O_x\})$;
5. executes $O_x\{L_1, L_2, L_3\}$; replaces L_3 with $L_3\{O_x\}$ in *HB*.

The key insight in TIBOT 2.0 is (in Step 4) to transform $O_x\{L_1, L_2\}$ symmetrically with a sequence of operations in L_3, which are totally after $O_x\{L_1, L_2\}$. This symmetric transformation replaces undoing and redoing the same sequence of operations in L_{undo} (= L_3) in Steps 2 and 5 of the original TIBOT. This is the key to avoiding CP2 without undo/redo (but giving up CP1-avoidance as CP1 can be easily achieved by transformation functions).

In addition, TIBOT 2.0 made other subtle but important technical changes (due to the elimination of undo/redo):

- Step 2: the condition for transformation of $O_x\{L_1\}$ has been enhanced to require operations in L_2 to be totally before $O_x\{L_1\}$ as well as having *TI*s equal to T_x, which is in contrast to requiring *TI*s equal to T_x only in Step 3 in the original TIBOT.
- Step 5: $O_x\{L_1, L_2, L_3\}$ is executed to achieve the original effect of O_x, which is in contrast to executing $O_x\{L_1, L_2\}$ in Step 4 and re-executing undone operations in Step 6 in the original TIBOT.

TIBOT 2.0 is unique in avoiding CP2 by distributed total ordering (no central server) without undo/redo. It can be shown that L_2 is OSP1 with respect to $O_x\{L_1\}$ in $LT(O_x\{L_1\}, L_2)$, and L_3 is OSP2 with respect to $O_x\{L_1, L_2\}$ in $SLT(O_x\{L_1, L_2\}, L_3)$ by following the same reasoning as in validating other systems.

In Figure 9, we illustrate the working of TIBOT 2.0 under the same working example. Consider O_2 at Site *2*, local processing of O_2 is the same as in the original TIBOT. TIBOT 2.0 handles O_2 at Site *3*, where $HB = [O_1, O_4\{1\}]$, as follows. Step 1, the same conditions are met. In Step 2, O_2 is transformed with $L_2 = [O_1]$, which is totally before O_2, to produce $O_2\{1\}$. Step 3, $O_2\{1\}$ is saved in *HB* after O_1. Step 4, $O_2\{1\}$ is symmetrically transformed with L_3=$[O_4\{1\}]$, which is totally after $O_2\{1\}$, to produce $O_2\{1,4\}$ and $O_4\{1,2\}$. Step 5, $O_2\{1,4\}$ is executed at Site *3*, and $O_4\{1,2\}$ is saved to replace $O_4\{1\}$ in *HB*. By comparing Figure 9 with Figure 7, we can see the undo/redo processes for O_1, $O_2\{1\}$ and $O_3\{1,2\}$ have been eliminated, and their execution forms have also been changed due to changes in Step 5 of TIBOT 2.0.

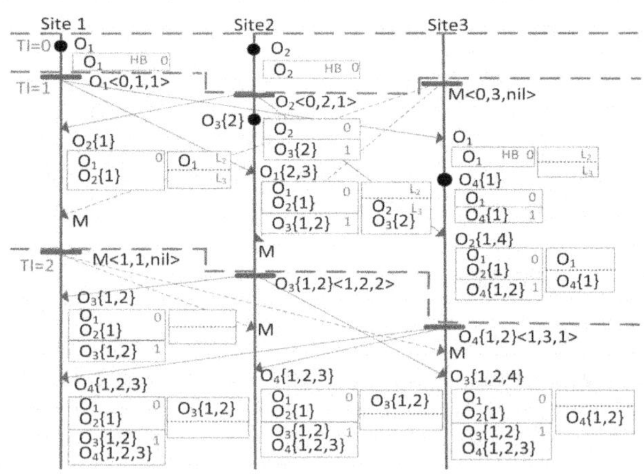

Figure 9: TIBOT 2.0: achieving CP2-avoidance without undo/transform-do/transform-redo or a central server.

Seeking Alternative CP2-avoidance Conditions

From this study, we have found all existing systems capable of avoiding CP2 meet the same special CP2-avoidance condition as specified in Definition 6. However, this is only one possible specialization of the general condition, which requires operations in the context of two operations to be the same whenever they are transformed with each other.

One interesting question arises: are there other possible specializations of this general CP2-avoidance condition? The answer is *yes*.

One alternative specialization is to restrict operations in the context of O_a and O_b to be totally before both O_a and O_b only, i.e. $O_x \Rightarrow O_a \Rightarrow O_b$, (keeping Condition 2-1 in Definition 6), but disallow operations that are totally ordered between O_a and O_b (removing Condition 2-2 in Definition 6). This specialization is valid as it still ensures the context uniqueness of two operations whenever they are transformed and meets other established context-based conditions [21]. However, careful examination reveals this specialization would prohibit users from generating operations continuously, which is undesirable.

Seeking for other valid and desirable special CP2-avoidance conditions (e.g. to get rid of totally ordering operations) is an interesting direction for further research as it may inspire invention of novel OT systems for meeting special algorithmic or application needs in the future.

CONCLUSION

In this work, we have conducted a comprehensive and in-depth study on convergence property preservation and avoidance in OT systems in general, and in validating CP2-avoidance for seven major OT systems: Jupiter, NICE, Google OT, SOCT3, SOCT4, TIBOT, and COT. From this study, we have made three major contributions: (1) establishment of CP2-avoidance correctness of seven major OT systems; (2) discovery of CP2-avoidance conditions, operation sequence and transformation patterns, basic mechanisms and a general framework for studying a diverse range of OT systems; and (3) improvements to existing systems (Jupiter and Google OT for Wave and Docs), and design of a new system TIBOT 2.0 – the first OT system based on a distributed total ordering scheme and capable of avoiding CP2 without using undo/redo. These results have significantly contributed to the advancement of OT knowledge and technique, and collaboration-enabling technology in general.

Inspired by the insights from this study, we are designing new OT systems to support both consistency maintenance and group undo, without using vector-based schemes, in large scale collaborations with an arbitrary number of dynamic collaborating users. Other major efforts in our group are devoted to applying OT technologies to advanced real-world collaborative applications.

ACKNOWLEDGEMENT

This research is partially supported by an Academic Research Fund Tier 1 Grant from Ministry of Education Singapore, and by NTU NAP Grant M4080738.020. The authors wish to thank anonymous reviewers for their insightful and constructive comments and suggestions.

REFERENCES

1. Agustina and Sun, C. Dependency-conflict detection in real-time collaborative 3D design systems. *ACM CSCW* (2013), 715 – 728.
2. Begole, J., Rosson, M.B. and Shaffer, C.A. Flexible collaboration transparency: supporting worker independence in replicated application-sharing systems. *ACM TOCHI* 6, 2 (1999), 95 – 132.
3. Ellis, C. A. and Gibbs, S. J. Concurrency control in groupware systems. *ACM SIGMOD* (1989), 399–407.
4. Greenberg, S. and Marwood, D. Real time groupware as distributed system: concurrency control and its effect on the interface. *ACM CSCW* (1994), 207 – 217.
5. Lamport, L. Time, clocks, and the ordering of events in a distributed system. *CACM 21*, 7 (1978), 558-565.
6. Li, R. and Li, D. A landmark-based transformation approach to concurrency control in group editors. *ACM GROUP* (2005), 284 – 293.
7. Li, D. and Li, R. An admissibility-based operational transformation framework for collaborative editing systems. *JCSCW 19, 1* (2010): 1 – 43.
8. Li, R., Li, D. and Sun, C. A time interval based consistency control algorithm for interactive groupware applications. *IEEE ICPADS* (2004), 429 – 436.
9. MacFadden, M. The client stop and wait operational transformation control algorithm. *Solute Consulting*, San Diego, CA, 2013.
10. Nichols, D., Curtis, P., Dixon, M. and Lamping, J. High-latency, low-bandwidth windowing in the Jupiter collaboration system. *ACM UIST* (1995), 111-120.
11. Prakash, A. and Knister, M. A framework for undoing actions in collaborative systems. *ACM TOCHI 1, 4* (1994), 295 – 330.
12. Oster, G., Molli, P., Urso, P. and Imine, A. Tombstone transformation functions for ensuring consistency in collaborative editing systems. *IEEE CollaborateCom* (2006).
13. Ressel, M. and Gunzenhauser, R. Reducing the problems of group undo. *ACM GROUP* (1999), 131–139.
14. Ressel, M., Ruhland, N. and Gunzenhauser, R. An integrating, transformation-oriented approach to concurrency control and undo in group editors.*ACM CSCW* (1996),288 – 297.
15. Shen, H.F. and Sun, C. Flexible notification for collaborative systems. *ACM CSCW* (2002), 77 – 86.
16. Spiewak, D. Understanding and applying operational transformation. http://www.codecommit.com/blog/ java/understanding-and-applying-operational-transformation.
17. Sun, C. and Ellis, C. Operational transformation in real-time group editors: issues, algorithms, and achievements. *ACM CSCW* (1998), 59 – 68.
18. Sun, C., Jia, X., Zhang, Y., Yang, Y., and Chen, D. Achieving convergence, causality-preservation, and intention-preservation in real-time cooperative editing systems. *ACM TOCHI 5,1* (1998), 63 – 108.
19. Sun, C., Xia, S., Sun, D., Chen, D., Shen, H. and Cai, W. Transparent adaptation of single-user applications for multi-user real-time collaboration. *ACM TOCHI 13, 4* (2006), 531 – 582.

20. Sun, C. OTFAQ: operational transformation frequent asked questions. http://cooffice.ntu.edu.sg/otfaq.
21. Sun, D. and Sun, C. Context-based operational transformation in distributed collaborative editing systems. *IEEE TPDS* (2009), 1454 – 1470.
22. Sun, C. Wen, H. and Fan, H. Operational transformation for orthogonal conflict resolution in collaborative two-dimensional document editing systems. *ACM CSCW* (2012), 1391 – 1400.
23. Vidot, N., Cart, M., Ferrie, J. and Suleiman, M. Copies convergence in a distributed real-time collaborative environment. *ACM CSCW* (2000), 171 – 180.
24. Wang, D., Mah, A. and Lassen, S. Google wave operational transformation. *http://www.waveprotocol.org/whitepapers/operational-transform.*
25. Xu, Y., Agustina, and Sun, C. Exhaustive search of puzzles in operational transformation. *ACM CSCW* (2014).

Exhaustive Search of Puzzles in Operational Transformation

Chengzheng Sun, Yi Xu, and Agustina
School of Computer Engineering, Nanyang Technological University, Singapore

ABSTRACT
Operational Transformation (OT) is a collaboration-enabling technology and increasingly adopted in a wide range of real-world applications. One long-lasting issue in OT research is detecting and resolving puzzles – subtle and characteristic collaborative editing scenarios in which an OT system may fail. After many years of extensive search and research, a variety of intricate puzzles have been detected and resolved. However, it remains open whether all puzzles, under certain well-defined conditions, have been discovered. To address this issue, we set out to devise a system of verification frameworks and a software tool, that are independent of specific OT algorithms and able to exhaustively cover all possible transformation cases in which puzzles (if any) will manifest themselves. With the support of these tools, we verified OT correctness and concluded: *all puzzles, under basic data and operation models and established transformation properties, have been discovered and resolved.* Our discoveries help resolve a number of long-standing mysteries surrounding OT correctness and contribute to the advancement of OT fundamental knowledge and technology.

Author Keywords
Operational Transformation; transformation property; puzzle detection and resolution; real-time collaborative editing.

ACM Classification Keywords
H.5.3 [**Information Systems**]: Group and Organization Interfaces – Synchronous Interaction, Theory and Model.

INTRODUCTION
Operational Transformation (OT) is a collaboration-enabling technology invented by CSCW researchers and has been a technical research subject in CSCW in the past two decades [1-9,11-29]. Due to its unique combination of non-blocking, fine-grained concurrency, and unconstrained interaction properties, OT is particularly suitable for supporting real-time collaboration over the Internet, and has been increasingly adopted in industrial applications, e.g. Google Wave/Doc[1], IBM OpenCoWeb[2], and Codoxware[3].

[1] http://docs.google.com
[2] https://github.com/opencoweb/coweb#readme
[3] http://www.codoxware.com

CSCW'14, February 15–19, 2014, Baltimore, MD, USA.

http://dx.doi.org/10.1145/2531602.2531630

One long-lasting issue in OT research is detecting and resolving puzzles – subtle and characteristic collaboration scenarios in which an OT system may fail to produce correct results. After many years of extensive search and research, a variety of intricate puzzles and their variations have been discovered and resolved [12,14-16,20-22,24,28]. For over one decade, there has been no new type of puzzle detected despite of continuous efforts by some dedicated researchers.

However, the mere absence of new puzzle discovery is not a proof that no more OT puzzle exists. It remains open whether all puzzles have indeed been detected. Resolving this open issue is important. For researchers, who design and verify OT algorithms, it is important for them to know what correctness issues have been solved or open, so that they can avoid wasting time on issues that had long been solved and devote efforts to open challenges. For practitioners, who adopt and implement OT algorithms to support real-world applications, it is important for them to know which OT algorithms are correct under what conditions, so that they can avoid wasting time in reinventing the wheel or choosing OT techniques that mismatch their target applications. Correctness is particularly important for mission-critical applications that require verification of core algorithms [17].

To solve this open issue, we set out to devise a system of verification frameworks that are independent of specific OT algorithms and able to efficiently and exhaustively cover all possible transformation cases in which puzzles (if any) will manifest themselves. We also developed a software tool to automate the verification process. In this paper, we present our verification frameworks and main research discoveries.

The rest of the paper is organized as follows. First, we briefly introduce prerequisite OT knowledge related to this work. Next, we review prior work on experimental puzzle detection and theoretic verification. Then, we formalize the basic data and operation models, specify combined-effects for concurrent operations, and define a general transformation matrix for verification. Based on these formalizations, we describe verification frameworks and discuss verification discoveries. Finally, we summarize major contributions and suggest future directions.

PREREQUISITE KNOWLEDGE
OT for Real-time Collaborative Editing Systems
Real-time collaborative editing systems allow geographically dispersed people to edit shared documents and see each other's updates instantly over the Internet. Most real-time collaborative editors have adopted the strategy of replicating the shared documents and the co-editing application among multiple collaborating sites. Replication has advantages of masking network latency and helping achieve fast local response, but also has a major problem: consistency maintenance of multiple replicas in the face of concurrent editing, which OT was originally invented to solve [6].

In over two decades, OT has evolved from supporting collaborative editing of plain text documents [6, 16, 20, 21], to rich-text documents [23], two-dimensional (2D) spreadsheets [26], and three-dimensional (3D) digital media [1, 2]. A pair of *basic* data and operation models, originated and generalized from text editing, have served as the foundation of most existing OT systems: (1) the basic data model is a sequence of data objects (of any type and size), which can be accessed using positional references; and (2) the basic operation model includes two operations: *insert* and *delete* of a single object, which can be directly manipulated by transformation functions. Past research has invented a core body of OT techniques for the basic data and operation models; and most OT verification work, including this paper, has focused on them due to their foundation role in supporting real-world applications. Core OT techniques, however, provide the foundation but not the complete solution for real-world applications: they can be directly used for applications that are restricted to insert and delete operations on a sequence of objects, but require significant extensions for supporting office productivity tools and 2D and 3D computer-aided design systems, which are frontiers of current OT research and application. Prior research has invented promising techniques, such as *Transparent Adaptation* techniques used in CoWord [23] and CoMaya [1, 2], to bridge the gap between core OT techniques and complex models in real-world applications [1, 2, 23, 26, 27].

Basic Ideas for Consistency Maintenance and Undo

The basic OT idea for consistency maintenance can be illustrated in a *Space-Time-Diagram* (STD) in Figure 1(a). The initial document contains a string *"abc"*, replicated at two collaborating sites; two operations: $O_1 = D(1,b)$ (to delete *"b"* at position *1*), and $O_2 = I(3,e)$ (to insert *"e"* at position *3*) are *concurrently* generated. At site *1*, O_1 is first executed to get the document *"ac"*. Then, O_2 arrives and is transformed against O_1, i.e. $T(O_2,O_1) = I(2,e)$, whose position is decremented to compensate the left-shifting effect by O_1. Executing $I(2,e)$ on *"ac"* inserts *"e"* at the end of document to get a new state *"ace"* (note: if O_2 were executed in its original form, it would cause an error as its insert position is beyond the current document length). At site *2*, O_2 is first executed to get the document *"abce"*. Then O_1 arrives and is transformed against O_2, i.e. $T(O_1,O_2) = D(1,b)$, which makes no change because O_2 has no impact on O_1. Executing $D(1,b)$ on *"abce"* deletes *"b"* at position *1* and get the document state *"ace"*, which is identical to the state at site *1* and also achieves the original effects of both O_1 and O_2. In summary, the basic idea is to transform an operation according to the effect of concurrent operations so that the transformed operation can achieve the correct effect and maintain document consistency.

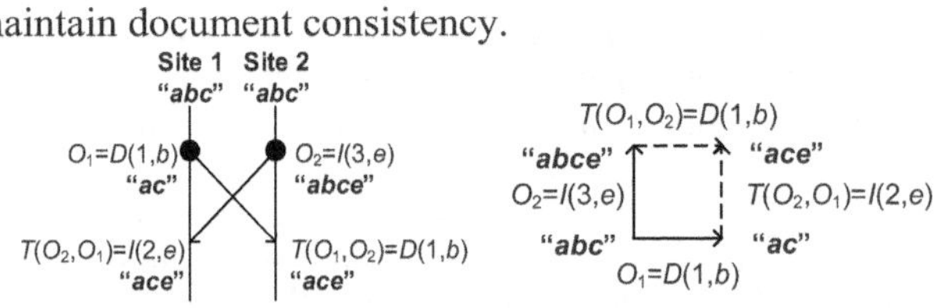

(a) Space-Time Diagram (b) Context-based OT Space

Figure 1. Basic idea of OT for consistency maintenance.

The same scenario can also be illustrated using a different diagram, called *Context-based Operational Transformation Space* (COTS), in Figure 1(b), where a vertex represents (and is labeled by) a document state, and an arrow represents an operation; the starting vertex of an arrow represents the definition state of the operation, and the ending vertex represents the resulting state of the operation. A correct COTS possesses the following property[4]: there is only one label for each vertex or arrow.

Another major OT functionality is supporting user-initiated *undo* – a mechanism for error recovery and alternative exploration, which is commonly available in single-user interactive applications but challenging to support in collaborative systems [14-16, 22, 24]. A user may issue *Undo*(O) to reverse the effects of an executed operation O. In OT undo solutions, undoing O is achieved by executing an *inverse* operation $!O$ with the following effect: $S \circ O \circ !O = S$, i.e. applying O and $!O$ on the document state S in sequence would restore S. $!O$ can be executed as-is if it is executed immediately after executing O on S; otherwise, $!O$ must be transformed and treated in the same way as concurrent operations. In this paper, we verify transformation properties related to both consistency maintenance and undo.

Control Algorithms and Transformation Functions

An OT system contains two key components: control algorithms and transformation functions [6,12,15,20,21,23,24, 26,27], as shown in Figure 2. Control algorithms are responsible for determining which operations should be transformed with which others and in what orders, and they are *generic* in the sense they work on generic relations (context [24] and/or causality [10]) among operations. On the other hand, transformation functions perform actual transformations between two operations, according to their types, target object relations and other parameters, which may be *application-specific*. The number and types of transformation functions are related to the data and operation models that an OT system is to support. Residing between control algorithms and transformation functions is a collection of transformation properties and conditions that define correctness requirements of an OT system and also divide correctness responsibilities between these two components.

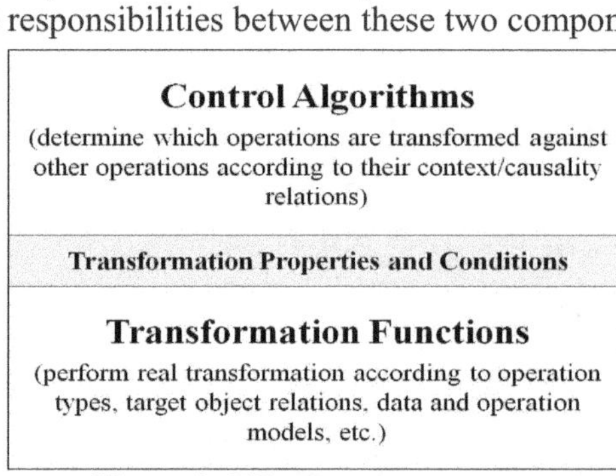

Figure 2. OT system components.

[4] The COTS is an extension of the Interaction Graph in [16] to represent all operations in an OT system supporting both do and undo in an integrated context space [24].

The correctness of an OT system depends on individual correctness of control algorithms and transformation functions and their correct integration. This work focuses on verification of transformation functions. For verification of control algorithms, the reader is referred to [15,21,22,24,29].

Transformation Properties

Past OT research has established a comprehensive set of transformation properties as OT algorithmic correctness criteria [6,14,16,21,22,24,27]. Transformation properties and OT puzzles are intimately related: violation of any transformation property would result in incorrect transformation results, which may lead to inconsistent documents and manifest themselves as puzzles. In other words, transformation property violation is the root of puzzles, whereas puzzles are the phenomena of transformation property violation. In this work, our approach to searching OT puzzles is by verifying transformation properties. We focus on the following properties:

1. **Convergence Property 1 (CP1):** Given O_1 and O_2 defined on the state S, if $O_1^{O2} = T(O_1,O_2)$, and $O_2^{O1} = T(O_2,O_1)$, the following **CP1-equation** must be held:
   $$S \circ O_1 \circ O_2^{O1} = S \circ O_2 \circ O_1^{O2.}$$
   which means that applying O_1 and O_2^{O1} in sequence on S has the same effect as applying O_2 and O_1^{O2} on S.
2. **Convergence Property 2 (CP2):** Given O_1, O_2 and O_3 defined on the same state, if $O_3^{O2}=T(O_3,O_2)$ and $O_2^{O3}= T(O_2,O_3)$, the following **CP2-equation** must be held:
   $$T(T(O_1,O_2),O_3^{O2}) = T(T(O_1,O_3),O_2^{O3})$$
   which means transforming O_1 against O_2 and O_3^{O2} equals to transforming O_1 against O_3 and O_2^{O3}. Alternatively, the CP2-equation can be expressed as:
   $$T(O_1^{O2},O_3^{O2}) = T(O_1^{O3},O_2^{O3})$$
   where $O_1^{O2} = T(O_1, O_2)$, and $O_1^{O3} = T(O_1,O_3)$.
3. **Inverse Property 1 (IP1):** Let $!O$ be the inverse of operation O and S be a document state, then the following **IP1-equation** must be held:
   $$S \circ O \circ !O = S$$
   which means applying O and $!O$ on S has no effect.
4. **Inverse Property 2 (IP2):** Given O_1 and O_2 defined on the same state, and $!O_2$ as the inverse of O_2, then the following **IP2-equation** must be held:
   $$T(T(O_1,O_2),!O_2) = O_1$$
   which means that transforming O_1 against O_2 and $!O_2$ in sequence has no effect on O_1.
5. **Inverse Property 3 (IP3):** Given O_1 and O_2 defined on the same state, if $O_1^{O2}=T(O_1,O_2)$, $O_2^{O1}=T(O_2,O_1)$ and $(!O_2)^{O1} = T(!O_2,O_1^{O2})$, then the following **IP3-equation** must be held:
   $$(!O2)^{O1} = !(O2^{O1})$$
   which means that $(!O2)^{O1}$, the outcome of transforming the inverse $!O_2$ against O_1^{O2}, equals to $!(O2^{O1})$, the inverse of the outcome of transforming O_2 against O_1.

The reason for focusing on these five properties is that CP1 and CP2 are the transformation properties governing convergence, and IP1, IP2, and IP3 are governing transformations related to undo. Formally, an OT puzzle can be defined as a case of violating a transformation property. By exhaustively searching verification cases with respect to these properties, we will be able to detect all possible puzzles related to them and answer the question whether all consistency and undo puzzles have been found. Past research had detected various convergence and undo puzzles under different OT systems [4,9,11,14,15,16,18,20,21,22, 24]. We predict all those known and unknown (if any) puzzles would manifest themselves in our verification frameworks, provided our theory that a puzzle is violation of a property is correct and our verification cases are exhaustive.

CP1 and CP2 were found to be necessary and sufficient conditions to achieve convergence in OT systems that allow operations to be transformed in any orders, such as the adOPTed system [15]. However, they are not unconditionally required. For example, CP1 is not necessary in an OT system, such as GOT [21], that never transforms two operations in different orders; CP2 is not necessary for OT systems that impose special transformation orders among operations [29], including Jupiter [12], Google Docs, NICE [19], SOCT4 [28], and COT [24]. CP1 and CP2 are not sufficient either: transformation functions must meet, in addition to convergence, the *intention-preservation* requirement [20,21]. In this paper, we will formally specify and verify this requirement as *combined-effects* of concurrent operations under the basic data and operation models.

We should point out that T in all transformation properties represents *Inclusion Transformation* (*IT*) functions, which are used in all existing OT systems [1,2,12,13,15,16,19,21, 22,24,26,28]. However, some OT systems also use *Exclusion Transformation* (*ET*) functions [21,22,28], which are reverse functions to *IT*. If both *IT* and *ET* are used in an OT system, they are required to preserve the *Reversibility Property* (RP) [21]: if $O_1^{O2} = IT(O_1,O_2)$, then $ET(O_1^{O2},O_2) = O_1$. Alternatively, RP can be expressed as:

$$ET(IT(O_1,O_2),O_2) = O_1.$$

By substituting T with IT, IP2 can be expressed as:

$$IT(IT(O_1,O_2),!O_2) = O_1.$$

By comparing RP and the above IP2, we found RP can be converted into IP2 by replacing *ET* with *IT* and O_2 with $!O_2$. This insight suggests an IP2-preserving *IT* function can be used as an RP-preserving *ET* function by replacing O_2 with $!O_2$. Furthermore, past research has also found an OT system (for both consistency maintenance and undo) can be based on *IT* functions only, without using any *ET* function [15,16,24]. For these reasons, we do not consider *ET* and RP, but focus on verification of *IT* with respect to IP2 (and other transformation properties) in this paper.

Finally, we highlight that all transformation properties share one common condition: *if two operations are transformed by function T, they must be defined on the same state.* This condition is guaranteed by suitable OT control algorithms [12,16,19,20,21,22,24,28]. An OT-based collaborative editing system can support multiple users to generate any number of operations with arbitrary causal relations. Possible scenarios and relations among operations are arbitrary and infinitive. Under correct control algorithms, however, every pair of operations being transformed by T are guaranteed to be defined on the same state. Therefore, there is no need to model causal relationships among operations for verifying transformation properties and functions, and this insight leads to significant simplifications in our verification frameworks, compared to prior verification work [4].

PRIOR WORK

Ad Hoc Puzzle Detection

An experimental approach, called *puzzle-detection-resolution,* has been commonly adopted in prior research for searching OT puzzles [14-16,21,22,24,27]. This approach suits well with the complex nature of puzzle issues, and has proven its effectiveness in detecting and solving all known puzzles, including the *dOPT* puzzle related to OT control algorithms [6,12,16,20,21], the *False-Tie* (*FT*) puzzle related to violating document convergence [20], and undo puzzles that violate *undo effects* and may cause inconsistency [14,15,22,24]. Despite its effectiveness and success, the ad hoc and informal nature of this approach makes it unsuitable for systematic and formal verification: ad hoc search can detect the existence of puzzles, but cannot prove the absence of puzzles. Another problem is that it requires researchers to have intimate knowledge of specific OT algorithms to be able to detect and resolve puzzles in those algorithms.

In this work, we generalize this ad hoc puzzle detection approach into a *systematic and exhaustive puzzle search* approach, which is grounded on established transformation properties, without using the knowledge of specific OT algorithms. This generalized approach has enabled us to not only detect all puzzles already discovered by the traditional approach, but also prove the absence of any new puzzle.

Theoretic Verification Work

Theoretic verification plays an important role in OT correctness study and may be conducted manually or by using computer-aided tools. Prior work had used automatic *theorem-provers* [9] and *model checkers* [4] to assist the verification of convergence properties CP1 and CP2 [4, 9]. Using generic verification tools necessitates the mapping between OT verification problems and theorem-proving or model-checking problems in mathematical logic formalisms. People who are acquainted with such formalisms may not have adequate knowledge of OT, and vice versa. This knowledge gap may cause modeling and specification errors, which may lead to false verification results, as reported in [4, 9, 11]. Another challenge is result interpretation, e.g. whether an unproven logic formula reveals an OT puzzle or the incompleteness of the proving system, and how to establish connections between formal verification results and OT puzzles (if any), which is crucial for any verification approach to be useful for studying OT correctness.

One often-cited reason for using computer-assisted verification tools is that transformation property verification is an *exponential explosion* problem that is too complex and "even impossible" for manual checking [4,9]. A state explosion problem was reported in a model checker, based on the following modeling [4]:

1. A collaborating editing session is modeled as an arbitrary number of users; each user may generate an arbitrary number of operations at any time; operations may have arbitrary concurrency/causality relationships.
2. A document is modeled as a string of characters with a length $L = 2 \times n$, where n is the total number of operations in a simulated co-editing session; and each character in the string may take one of 2 values: 0 or 1.
3. An operation may take one of 2 types: *insert* or *delete* (character-wise); each operation may take one of L positions; and an *insert* has an additional character parameter, which may take one of 2 values: 0 or 1.

The following formula gives the total number of states the model checker has to check to assess whether convergence is preserved in a simulated session with n operations [4]:

$$((2 + 1) \times L)^n = (6 \times n)^n .$$

The model checker has to check $5832 = (6 \times 3)^3$ states for a session with 3 operations, and $331776 = (6 \times 4)^4$ states for 4 operations, which had exceeded the capability of the used model-checking system [4]. As the number of operations n can be arbitrarily large in this modeling, it is impossible to exhaustively check all possible states. On the other hand, limiting $L = 2 \times n$ and character values to be 0 or 1 makes this modeling highly restrictive as well.

The ability to cover all verification cases is essential to answer the question whether all puzzles have been found. As will become clear in this paper, our verification frameworks can efficiently model the verification problem with less than 100 verification cases; and exhaustively cover all verification cases without suffering from exponential case explosion. Moreover, our exhaustive coverage is achieved without imposing restrictions on the data and operation modeling: a document string may have an *arbitrary* length (unrelated to the number of operations); each character may take an *arbitrary* value from any valid set of characters (unlimited to two values: 0 or 1); and an operation may also take an *arbitrary* position in a document. Furthermore, our verification frameworks are based on original OT data and operation formalisms and transformation properties (e.g. transformation property equations are *directly* used in our verification frameworks), which help achieve correct specification and result interpretation. Last but not least, our verification covers not only CP1 and CP2, but also combined-effects (to be defined later) and undo-related properties (IP1/IP2/IP3), which were never addressed in prior work.

FORMALIZATION OF DATA AND OPERATION MODELS

We have chosen character strings and character-wise operations as the data and operation formalisms as they are precise enough for the purpose of verification and directly correspond to the basic OT data and operation models. Conclusions drawn from this formalization are generally applicable to any object sequences.

Data Model Specification

A document state S is represented as a string of characters:

$$S = "c_0\, c_1\, c_2 \ldots c_{p-1}\, c_p\, c_{p+1} \ldots c_{n-1}"$$

where c_p, $0 \leq p \leq n-1$, represents a character. The following notations are used for convenience of expression:

1. $|S|$ is the length of the string S.

2. $S[p]=c_p$, $0 \le p \le |S|-1$, is the character at position p in S.
3. $S[i,j]="c_i c_{i+1} \ldots c_{j-1} c_j"$, $0 \le i \le j \le |S|-1$, represents a sub-string of characters with positions from i to j, inclusively, in S. For notation convenience in state expressions, $S[i,j]$ represents an empty string in case that $i>j$.
4. $S[i,j] + S[m,n]="c_i c_{i+1} \ldots c_{j-1} c_j c_m c_{m+1} \ldots c_{n-1} c_n"$, represents the concatenation of two sub-strings.

Operation Model Specification

The operation model consists of two operations:

1. $I(p, c)$: to insert a single character c at position p;
2. $D(p, c)$: to delete a single character at position p. The parameter c is used to record the deleted character for the purpose of supporting undo.

Insert and delete operations are inverses of each other, i.e.

1. $!I(p, c) = D(p, c)$;
2. $!D(p, c) = I(p, c)$.

From the basic operations and their inverses, we have:

1. $S \circ I(p, c) \circ !I(p, c) = S \circ I(p, c) \circ D(p, c) = S$;
2. $S \circ D(p, c) \circ !D(p, c) = S \circ D(p, c) \circ I(p, c) = S$.

which means that *IP1*-equation: $S \circ O \circ !O = S$, is preserved by definition for any O in the basic operation model.

Specification 1: Effect of a Single Insert Operation

Given an insert operation $I(p, c)$ defined on a state S, where $0 \le p \le |S|$. The effect of $I(p, c)$ on S is to convert S into the following new state S':

$$S' = S \circ I(p, c) = S[0, p-1] + "c" + S[p, |S|-1],$$

with the following $S' \leftrightarrow S$ mapping relationship:

1. $S'[0, p-1] = S[0, p-1]$, when $p \neq 0$;
2. $S'[p] = c$;
3. $S'[p+1, |S'|-1] = S[p, |S|-1]$, when $p \neq |S|$.

Informally, the effect of an insert operation $I(p, c)$ is to insert a new character c at position p in S, which will *right-shift* characters *at* and *on the right* of $S[p]$ by one position, but keep characters *on the left* of $S[p]$ unchanged.

Specification 2: Effect of a Single Delete Operation

Given a delete operation $D(p, c)$ defined on the state S, where $0 \le p \le |S|-1$. The effect of $D(p, c)$ on S is to convert S into the following new state S':

$$S' = S \circ D(p, c) = S[0, p-1] + S[p+1, |S|-1],$$

with the following $S' \leftrightarrow S$ mapping relationship:

1. $S'[0, p-1] = S[0, p-1]$, when $p \neq 0$;
2. $S'[p, |S'|-1] = S[p+1, |S|-1]$, when $p \neq |S|-1$.

Informally, the effect of a delete operation $D(p, c)$ is to delete a character at position p in S, which will *left-shift* characters *on the right* of $S[p]$ by one position, but keep characters *on the left* of $S[p]$ unchanged.

Exhaustive Coverage of Arbitrary Positions and States

Under the basic data and operation models, a document state S may have an arbitrary (and theoretically unlimited) length $|S|$, and each position in S may contain an arbitrary character from the ASCII character set; and an operation O may have an arbitrary position p in the range $0 \le p \le |S|$, and may affect the positions of an arbitrary number of characters in S, as defined in Specifications 1 and 2. These arbitrary parameters and their combinations present major challenges to achieving exhaustive coverage of all possibilities in OT verification, which caused exponential explosion problems as discussed in the "Prior Work" section.

The solution to this challenge lies in the following key insights in our data and operation modeling. First, $S' \leftrightarrow S$ mappings establish one-to-one positional correspondences between S' and S, and serves as a formalism of representing arbitrary lengths and characters in S' in terms of S (and vice versa), without knowing specific lengths and values of those characters in S. This formalism provides the foundation for checking the equivalence of two states, without knowing specific contents of these states.

Second, the effect of O on S can be partitioned into three *uniform effect ranges*:

1. $S[0,p-1]$, the *left* effect range of p;
2. $S[p]$, the effect range at p; and
3. $S[p+1,|S|-1]$, the *right* effect range of p.

The effect of O in each range is *uniform* in the sense that all positions in the same range are affected by O in the same way, though the effect in different ranges may be different. This effect uniformity provides the foundation for reducing arbitrary possibilities to a fixed number of possibilities.

The significance of these insights will become clear when we define combined-effects of concurrent operations and derive exhaustive verification cases.

UNION-EFFECTS AND TRANSFORMATION MATRIX

Combined-Effects of Concurrent Operations

In the absence of concurrency, the single-operation effect specification is adequate for a user to understand the behavior of an editor (e.g. a single-user editor). In the presence of concurrency in collaborative editing, however, we need to define *combined-effects* for concurrent operations, independent of their execution orders.

To specify combined-effects, we need first determine all possible cases. Given two operations defined on the same state, they may have three possible position relationships: $p_1 < p_2$, $p_1 = p_2$, $p_1 > p_2$, which directly correspond to three uniform effect ranges of each operation. Under each specific position relationship, two operations may affect each other in a uniform way, and their combined-effect can be uniformly specified in a single effect expression. Based on this observation, an exhaustive set of combined-effect cases for two operations are derived as follows. First, there are three different operation type combinations: I-I, D-D, and I-D (D-I is the same type combination). Second, for each type combination, there are three position relationships based on the uniform effect ranges of each operation. In total, there are $3 \times 3 = 9$ combined-effect cases for two operations.

The second issue is to specify concrete combined-effects for all possible cases. Different collaborative applications may choose different combined-effects for meeting specific needs. Most OT systems have (implicitly) adopted a special combined-effect, named *Union Effect* (*UE*) in this paper.

We specify union effects under all *9* possible cases in the column $UE(O_1,O_2)$ in Table 1. The $UE(O_1,O_2)$ is a formal specification of the general *intention-preservation* requirement under the basic data and operation models [21,20]. The $UE(O_1,O_2)$ has the merits of retaining the *original-effect* of individual operations, and preserving *all-operation-effects* under all circumstances. Such union effects have been commonly supported by OT systems, but this work is the first to give it a formal specification.

Two cases in $UE(O_1,O_2)$ deserve special attention. One is Case 2 (*insert-insert-tie*): $I(p_1,c_1)$ and $I(p_2,c_2)$ with $p_1 = p_2$. In this case, two possible combined-effects: "c_1c_2" and "c_2c_1" are specified as valid union effects. An OT system is free to support any of them, so this combined-effect introduces *non-determinism* to $UE(O_1,O_2)$. Such a union effect is not the only possibility for the *insert-insert-tie* case. Other possibilities are: only one result is accepted as valid; none of them is accepted; or two characters are merged into one if they are the same [6]. Nearly all OT systems have chosen the same effect as in $UE(O_1,O_2)$ due to its ability of preserving all operation effects and intuitiveness to end-users.

O_1 O_2	PR	$UE(O_1,O_2)$	#
$I(p_1,c_1)$ $I(p_2,c_2)$	$p_1<p_2$	S[0,p₁-1]+"c₁"+S[p₁,p₂-1] +"c₂"+S[p₂,|S|-1]	1
	$p_1=p_2$	S[0,p₁-1]+"c₁c₂"+S[p₁,|S|-1] S[0,p₁-1]+"c₂c₁"+S[p₁,|S|-1]	2
	$p_1>p_2$	S[0,p₂-1]+"c₂"+S[p₂,p₁-1]+"c₁"+ S[p₁,|S|-1]	3
$I(p_1,c_1)$ $D(p_2,c_2)$	$p_1<p_2$	S[0,p₁-1]+"c₁"+S[p₁,p₂-1]+S[p₂+1,|S|-1]	4
	$p_1=p_2$	S[0,p₁-1]+"c₁"+S[p₁+1,|S|-1]	5
	$p_1>p_2$	S[0,p₂-1]+S[p₂+1,p₁-1]+"c₁"+S[p₁,|S|-1]	6
$D(p_1,c_1)$ $D(p_2,c_2)$	$p_1<p_2$	S[0,p₁-1]+S[p₁+1,p₂-1]+S[p₂+1,|S|-1]	7
	$p_1=p_2$	S[0,p₁-1]+S[p₁+1,|S|-1]	8
	$p_1>p_2$	S[0,p₂-1]+S[p₂+1,p₁-1]+S[p₁+1,|S|-1]	9

Table 1. Union effect specification. PR: Position Relationship.

The other special union effect is Case 8 (*delete-delete-tie*): $D(p_1,c_1)$ and $D(p_2,c_2)$ with $p_1 = p_2$ and $c_1 = c_2$. In this case, only one character c_1 is deleted, which is the same as a single delete operation effect. It is also possible to define other combined-effects for this case, e.g. none of the deletes has an effect (so the character remains). However, all OT systems have adopted the same union effect for the delete-delete-tie case, based on similar reasons as the insert-insert-tie case. This introduces *non-serialisability* to $UE(O_1,O_2)$ as no serialization scheme is able to achieve such a combined-effect. As will become clear later in this paper, *non-determinism* and *non-serialisablilty* properties in $UE(O_1,O_2)$ have intricate relationships with all puzzles related to transformation properties.

Integrating UE and CP1 Requirements

Given two operations O_1 and O_2 defined on the same state S, transforming O_1 against O_2 is to produce $O_1^{O2} = T(O_1,O_2)$ as follows: (1) assume O_2 has been executed; (2) assess the execution effect of O_2 on the state S; and (3) derive O_1^{O2} so that executing O_1^{O2} after O_2 on S would produce the union effect specified in $UE(O_1,O_2)$, i.e.

$$UE(O_1,O_2) = S \circ O_2 \circ O_1^{O2}.$$

In addition, transformation must satisfy the CP1-equation:

$$S \circ O_1 \circ O_2^{O1} = S \circ O_2 \circ O_1^{O2}.$$

For transformation to be meaningful (in terms of $UE(O_1,O_2)$) and consistent (by CP1), the following new property equation, denoted as *UE-CP1*, must be satisfied:

$$UE(O_1,O_2) = S \circ O_1 \circ O_2^{O1} = S \circ O_2 \circ O_1^{O2}.$$

Transformation Matrix as Verification Target

We use the Transformation Matrix (TM) in Table 2 to represent all results of transforming O_1 against O_2. The TM consists of four rows corresponding to four operation type permutations[5]: I-I, I-D, D-I and D-D. Each type permutation is divided into three sub-rows according to three position relationships. Entries in column $TM(O_1,O_2)$ represent results of transforming O_1 against O_2 for individual cases.

O_1 O_2	PR	$TM(O_1,O_2)$	#
$I(p_1,c_1)$ $I(p_2,c_2)$	$p_1<p_2$	$I(p_1,c_1)$	1
	$p_1=p_2$	$I(p_1,c_1)$ if priority(O_1)> priority(O_2) $I(p_1+1,c_1)$ if priority(O_1)<priority(O_2)	2
	$p_1>p_2$	$I(p_1+1,c_1)$	3
$I(p_1,c_1)$ $D(p_2,c_2)$	$p_1<p_2$	$I(p_1,c_1)$	4
	$p_1=p_2$	$I(p_1,c_1)$	5
	$p_1>p_2$	$I(p_1-1,c_1)$	6
$D(p_1,c_1)$ $I(p_2,c_2)$	$p_1<p_2$	$D(p_1,c_1)$	7
	$p_1=p_2$	$D(p_1+1,c_1)$	8
	$p_1>p_2$	$D(p_1+1,c_1)$	9
$D(p_1,c_1)$ $D(p_2,c_2)$	$p_1<p_2$	$D(p_1,c_1)$	10
	$p_1=p_2$	NULL	11
	$p_1>p_2$	$D(p_1-1,c_1)$	12

Table 2. Transformation Matrix TM(O₁, O₂).

We have filled entries in $TM(O_1,O_2)$ with transformation results derived from $UE(O_1,O_2)$ and UE-CP1. In most cases, convergence is guaranteed as long as the union effect is achieved. In two cases, however, special measures have been taken to achieve UE-CP1. In the insert-insert-tie case, a priority-based tie-breaking rule, which ensures a total ordering among all operations, is used. In the delete-delete-tie case, the result is the special operation NULL[6].

From $TM(O_1,O_2)$, it is straightforward to design concrete transformation functions. One possible set of transformation functions capable of producing the same transformation results as $TM(O_1,O_2)$ is given in APPENDIX. Conversely, we can also derive $TM(O_1,O_2)$ from existing transformation functions. In our verification frameworks, $TM(O_1,O_2)$, rather than specific transformation functions, is used for verification, which allows us to verify both existing and new transformation functions whose transformation results are captured in $TM(O_1,O_2)$. This approach is in contrast to prior verification work, which all used specific existing transformation functions for verification [4,9].

VERIFICATION FRAMEWORKS

Based on the formalization of data and operations models, $UE(O_1,O_2)$, and $TM(O_1,O_2)$, we devised a system of frameworks to verify UE-CP1, CP2, IP2 and IP3 (IP1 is preserved by the operation model definition), respectively.

[5] Type permutations (in which orders matter) are different from type combinations (in which operation orders do not matter), e.g. D-I and I-D are different type permutations, but the same type combination.

[6] *NULL* has the following properties: $S \circ NULL = S$; $T(NULL, O) = NULL$; $T(O, NULL) = O$.

Each framework contains two key components: (1) an exhaustive set of verification cases; and (2) a verification process based on the corresponding property equation.

UE-CP1 Verification Framework

Exhaustive UE-CP1 verification case derivation. UE-CP1 involves two independent operations O_1 and O_2. The two operations may have three different operation type combinations: I-I, D-D, and I-D (D-I is the same type combination). For each combination, two operations have three possible position relationships. In total, there are $3\times 3= 9$ cases.

Specification 3: UE-CP1 Verification Process

Given all *UE-CP1* verification cases, the verification process works on each case one-by-one as follows:

1. Derive $S_{12} = S \circ O_1 \circ O_2^{O1}$:
   (1) Derive $S_1 = S \circ O_1$ and $S_1 \leftrightarrow S$ mappings, according to Specifications 1&2.
   (2) Derive $O_2^{O1} = T(O_2,O_1)$, according to types and position relationships of O_1 and O_2 by consulting the $TM(O_1,O_2)$.
   (3) Derive $S_{12} = S_1 \circ O_2^{O1}$, according to Specification 1&2.
   (4) Derive $S_{12} = S \circ O_1 \circ O_2^{O1}$, by $S_1 \leftrightarrow S$ mappings associated with O_1.
2. Derive $S_{21} = S \circ O_2 \circ O_1^{O2}$ by following similar steps.
3. Check the UE-CP1-equation: $S_{12} = S_{21} = UE(O_1,O_2)$. If the equation is satisfied, this is a UE-CP1-confirmation case; otherwise, it is a UE-CP1-violation case.

Steps in the UE-CP1 verification process are well defined by the UE-CP1-equation, Specification 1 and 2, $TM(O_1,O_2)$, and $UE(O_1,O_2)$. Step 1-(4)/2-(4) is a special step to convert S_1/S_2-based representations of S_{12}/S_{21} into S-based representations so that they can be literally compared for equivalence. The correctness of this conversion is ensured by the correctness and completeness of $S_1 \leftrightarrow S/S_2 \leftrightarrow S$ mappings. We illustrate one UE-CP1 case verification in Table 3, and provide all verification cases and results in APPENDIX.

UE-CP1 Verification Case: $O_1 = I(p_1, c_1)$, $O_2 = D(p_2, c_2)$, $p_1<p_2$	
1	**Derive $S_{12}=S\circ O_1\circ O_2^{O1}$**
(1)	$S_1=S\circ O_1=S[0,p_1-1]+$"$c_1$"$+S[p_1,\vert S\vert-1]$ // by Specification 1 $=S_1[0,p_1-1]+S_1[p_1]+S_1[p_1+1,\vert S_1\vert-1]$ // $S_1\leftrightarrow S$
(2)	$O_2^{O1}=T(O_2,O_1)=D(p_2+1,c_2)$ // derived from row #9 in **TM(O₁,O₂)**
(3)	$S_{12}=S_1\circ O_2^{O1}=S_1[0,p_2] + S_1[p_2+2,\vert S_1\vert-1]$ // by Specification 2
(4)	$S_{12}=S\circ O_1\circ O_2^{O1}=S_1[0,p_2]+S_1[p_2+2,\vert S_1\vert-1]$ $=S_1[0,p_1-1]+S_1[p_1]+S_1[p_1+1,p_2]+S_1[p_2+2,\vert S_1\vert-1]$ // a middle step $=S[0,p_1-1]+$"c_1"$+S[p_1,p_2-1]+S[p_2+1,\vert S\vert-1]$ // by $S_1\leftrightarrow S$
2	**Derive $S_{21}=S\circ O_2\circ O_1^{O2}$**
(1)	$S_2=S\circ O_2=S[0,p_2-1]+S[p_2+1,\vert S\vert-1]$ // by Specification 2 $=S_2[0,p_2-1]+ S_2[p_2,\vert S_2\vert-1]$ // $S_2\leftrightarrow S$
(2)	$O_1^{O2}=T(O_1,O_2)=I(p_1,c_1)$ // derived from row #4 in **$TM(O_1,O_2)$**
(3)	$S_{21}=S_2\circ O_1^{O2}=S_2[0,p1-1]+$"$c_1$"$+S_2[p_1,\vert S_2\vert-1]$ // by Specification 1
(4)	$S_{21}=S\circ O_2\circ O_1^{O2}=S_2[0,p1-1]+$"$c_1$"$+S_2[p_1,\vert S_2\vert-1]$ // $=S_2[0,p_1-1]+$"c_1"$+S_2[p_1,p_2-1]+S_2[p_2,\vert S_2\vert-1]$ //a middle step $=S[0,p_1-1]+$"c_1"$+S[p_1,p_2-1]+S[p_2+1,\vert S\vert-1]$ // by $S_2\leftrightarrow S$
3	**Check UE-CP1-Equation: $S_{12}=S_{21}=UE(O_1,O_2)$** by comparing the results in 1-(4) and 2-(4) and row #4 in **$UE(O_1,O_2)$**. The equation is satisfied, so this is a UE-CP1 confirmation case.

Table 3. An example case in UE-CP1 verification.

CP2 Verification Framework

Exhaustive CP2 verification case derivation. CP2 involves three independent operations O_1, O_2 and O_3. As each operation may independently take one of two different types – *insert* or *delete*, there exist $2^3 = 8$ different type permutations. Furthermore, three independent operations may have thirteen position relationships, according to a set of three operators: {<, =, >}:

1. Six cases where all three positions are different: (1) $p_1<p_2<p_3$, (2) $p_2<p_1<p_3$, (3) $p_2<p_3<p_1$, (4) $p_1<p_3<p_2$, (5) $p_3<p_1<p_2$, (6) $p_3<p_2<p_1$;
2. Six cases where two positions are the same but one position is different: (1) $p_1=p_2<p_3$, (2) $p_3<p_1=p_2$, (3) $p_1=p_3<p_2$, (4) $p_2<p_1=p_3$, (5) $p_2=p_3<p_1$, (6) $p_1<p_2=p_3$;
3. One case where all positions are the same: $p_1=p_2=p_3$.

In total, there exist $8 \times 13 = 104$ different combinations of operation type permutations and position relationships. Each of them could make a CP2 verification case by transforming O_1 against O_2 and O_3 in different orders. However, careful examination reveals that nearly half of those CP2-equations are actually redundant. After eliminating redundant cases, there are a total of *58* distinctive CP2 verification cases to be checked.

Specification 4: CP2 Verification Process

Given all CP2 verification cases, the verification process works on each of these cases as follows:

1. Derive $O_1^{O2,O3} = T(O_1^{O2},O_3^{O2})$:
   (1) Derive $O_1^{O2} = T(O_1,O_2)$ and $O_3^{O2} = T(O_3,O_2)$, according to types and position relationships among O_1, O_2 and O_3, by consulting the TM.
   (2) Derive position relations between the transformed operations O_1^{O2} and O_3^{O2}, according to the original position relations, and transformed positions.
   (3) Derive $O_1^{O2,O3} = T(O_1^{O2},O_3^{O2})$, according to the operation types of O_1 and O_3 and the derived position relationship in Step(2), by consulting the TM.
2. Derive $O_1^{O3,O2}=T(O_1^{O3},O_2^{O3})$ by similar steps.
3. Check the CP2-equation: $O_1^{O2,O3}= O_1^{O3,O2}$. If the equation is satisfied, this is CP2-confirmation case; otherwise, it is a CP2-violation case.

Steps in the CP2 verification process are well defined by the CP2-equation and the TM. Step 1-(2)/2-(2) is special for CP2-verification as it involves deriving new position relationship between transformed operations. Such position relationship is required in using the TM to derive $O_1^{O2,O3} = T(O_1^{O2},O_3^{O2})$ in Step 1-(3)/2-(3). This position relation derivation is supported by a Position Relationship Derivation Matrix (PRDM) in APPENDIX.

IP2 and IP3 Verification Frameworks

Exhaustive IP2 and IP3 verification case derivation. IP2 and IP3 verification frameworks are closely related and discussed together. IP2/IP3 involves two independent operations O_1 and O_2, plus an inverse $!O_2$, which is not an independent operation but derived from O_2. Each independent operation may take one of two types – insert or delete, so there exist $2^2 = 4$ operation type permutations. Furthermore, each pair of operations may have three different positional relationships. Therefore, there are a total of $4\times 3=12$ distinctive IP2/IP3 verification cases.

Specification 5: IP2 Verification Process
Given the set of IP2 verification cases and $TM(O_1,O_2)$, the IP2 verification process works on each case as follows:

1. Derive $O_1^{O2,!O2}$:
   (1) Derive $O_1^{O2} = T(O_1,O_2)$, according to types and position relationships between O_1 and O_2 by consulting the TM.
   (2) Derive position relationship between transformed operation O_1^{O2} and $!O_2$.
   (3) Derive $O_1^{O2,!O2} = T(O_1^{O2},!O_2)$ according to types of O_1 and $!O_2$ and derived position relation in 1-(2), by the TM.
2. Check the IP2-equation: $O_1 = O_1^{O2,!O2}$. If the equation is satisfied, this is an IP2-confirmation case; otherwise, it is an IP2-violation case.

Specification 6: IP3 Verification Process
Given the set of IP3 verification cases and $TM(O_1,O_2)$, the IP3 verification process works on each case as follows:

1. Derive $!O_2^{O1}$:
   (1) Derive $O_1^{O2} = T(O_1,O_2)$, using types and position relationships between O_1 and O_2 to consult the TM.
   (2) Derive position relationship between transformed operation O_1^{O2} and $!O_2$.
   (3) Derive $!O_2^{O1} = T(!O_2,O_1^{O2})$ by using types of O_1 and $!O_2$ and derived position relation in Step (2) to consult the TM.
2. Derive $!(O_2^{O1})$:
   (1) Derive $O_2^{O1} = T(O_2,O_1)$, by using operations types and position relationships in the case to consult the TM.
   (2) Create an inverse operation $!(O_2^{O1})$ from O_2^{O1}.
3. Check the IP3-equation: $!O_2^{O1} = !(O_2^{O1})$. If the equation is satisfied, this is an IP3-confirmation case; otherwise, this is an IP3-violation case.

Steps in the IP2/IP3 verification process are well defined by the IP2/IP3-equation and the TM. Step 1-(2) involves deriving position relationships between a transformed operation and an inverse operation, supported by the same PRDM.

VERIFICATION TOOL

Based on the derived verification cases and the verification process specifications, we have developed a software tool, named *OTX* (*OT eXplorer*), to automate the verification process. OTX was originally developed to support development of STD-/COTS-based benchmarking suites for testing and validating real OT implementations [25], and has been extended to support automatic verification of transformation properties. The main benefit of using OTX is not so much about saving time (as the number of verification cases is not unmanageable and each verification case is simple), but more about using OTX to support experimentation with alternative transformation designs, based on different operation models, combined-effects, and transformation matrixes. We have executed all verification processes both manually and by using OTX. We present main verification discoveries in this paper, and provide full verification results in APPENDIX.

VERIFICATION DISCOVERIES

UE-CP1 Verification Discoveries

Based on UE-CP1 verification results, we declare *TM*(O$_1$, O$_2$) *can preserve UE-CP1 under all cases.* This work is the first to formally define and verify both UE and CP1 for transformations defined on the basic data and operation models and to draw the conclusion on UE-CP1 correctness. In fact, convergence can be trivially achieved if UE (or other suitably defined combined-effects) were not considered [16,20,21]. It is essential for OT systems to achieve UE and convergence properties at the same time, and to verify both of them in an integral way.

CP2 Verification Discoveries

Based on CP2 verification for all *58* cases, we discovered $TM(O_1, O_2)$ can preserve CP2 under *57* cases, but violate CP2 in one case: $O_1 = I(p_1, c_1)$, $O_2 = D(p_2, c_2)$, and $O_3 = I(p_3, c_3)$, where $(p_1-1) = p_2 = p_3$.

CP2-violation vs. the FT Puzzle

The CP2-violation case is a general description of the well-known *False-Tie (FT)* puzzle [21]. This puzzle involves an *insert-insert-tie,* which is considered as a *false-tie* because the tie was not originally generated by users but created by transformation; this FT may result in inconsistent states if a normal tie-breaking rule is applied.

A concrete FT puzzle can be created by instantiating the general CP2-violation case with specific operations $O_1 = I(2, x)$, $O_2 = D(1, b)$, and $O_3 = I(1, y)$, where $((p_1=2) - 1) = (p_2=1) = (p_3=1)$, generated from the same state *"abc"*, as shown in the COTS in **Figure 3**.

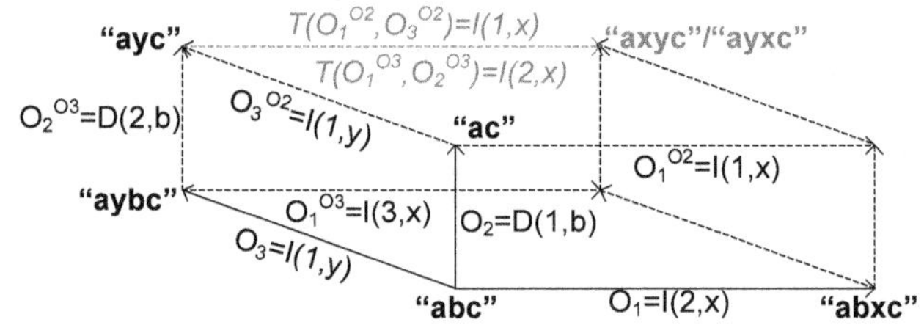

Figure 3. Illustrating the False-Tie puzzle and CP2 violation.

This COTS contains one arrow labeled by two different operations and one vertex labeled by two different states, which are resulted from transforming O_1 against O_2 and O_3 along two different paths:

1. One is transforming O_1 against O_2 and O_3^{O2} in sequence: $T(O_1^{O2}, O_3^{O2}) = I(1, x)$, which involves an FT as the two inserts $O_1^{O2} = I(1, x)$ and $O_3^{O2} = I(1, y)$ are created by transformations, and this FT is resolved by a tie-breaking scheme based on the *priority*(O_1) > *priority*(O_3) (so $I(1, x)$ remains unchanged).
2. The other is transforming O_1 against O_3 and O_2^{O3} in sequence: $T(O_1^{O3}, O_2^{O3}) = I(2, x)$, where $O_1^{O3} = I(3, x)$ and $O_2^{O3} = D(2, b)$.

CP2 is violated as $I(1, x) \neq I(2, x)$, which results in divergent final states: *"axyc"* ≠ *"ayxc"*.

Since the discovery of the basic FT puzzle in [21], various CP2-violation scenarios have been reported in different OT systems [4,9,11,18] and CP2-violation phenomena became a main mystery surrounding OT correctness. However, examination of all reported CP2-violation cases revealed that they were just variations of the FT puzzle, i.e. CP2-violation occurs only if an FT is involved. Based on the exhaustiveness of our CP2 verification, we confirm: *the FT puzzle is the only possible case for CP2-violatio*n, which means all puzzles in relation to CP2 have been discovered.

CP2-Preservation vs. FT-Solution

Based on CP2 verification discoveries, we assert that CP2-preservation can be achieved by solving the FT puzzle at the transformation function level. The general CP2-violation description also provides hints on how to resolve the FT puzzle: as the FT occurs only under circumstances that involve *delete* and *insert* operations with special position relationships, it is advisable to *localize* an FT solution in transformation functions related to *delete* and *insert* operations only, without disturbing the rest of the system, e.g. transformation functions unrelated to *insert*/*delete,* data and operation models, or control algorithms.

Past research has found that CP2 is not unconditionally required. CP2-violation can be and has been solved, without an FT-solution in transformation functions, by CP2-avoidance schemes in OT control algorithms [12,19,21,24, 28,29].

IP2 and IP3 Verification Discoveries

Based on IP2 and IP3 verification results for all *12* cases, we discovered $TM(O_1, O_2)$ can preserve IP2 and IP3 under ten cases, but violate IP2 and IP3 in following two cases:

1. $O_1=I(p_1,c_1), O_2=D(p_2,c_2)$, and $!O_2=I(p_2,c_2)$, $(p_1-1)=p_2$.
2. $O_1=D(p_1,c_1)$, $O_2=D(p_2,c_2)$, and $!O_2=I(p_2,c_2)$, $p_1=p_2$.

IP2/IP3-violation vs Undo Puzzles

The two IP2 and IP3-violation cases are general descriptions of all known undo puzzles, previously discovered in different OT systems [14,15,16,22]. *DistEdit* was the first OT undo solution [14], which undoes an operation in a history buffer by transposing (by using transformation) this operation to the end of the buffer, then creating an inverse of the transposed operation to achieve the desired undo effect. *DistEdit* is unable to undo an operation if this operation *conflicts* with any operation on the way to the end of the buffer. Two editing operations (*insert* and *delete*) may conflict if they affect *adjacent* or *overlapping* characters in the document [14]. These conflict scenarios were the earliest reported undo puzzles, which were late rediscovered in follow-up OT undo solutions *adOPTed* [15,16] and *ANYUNDO* [22], but under different names. All undo puzzles are just special instances of general IP2/IP3-violation cases discovered in this work. Based on the exhaustiveness of IP2/IP3 verification cases, we confirm: *all undo puzzles in relation to IP2/IP3 have been found.*

Classification of Undo Puzzles

Based on the two general IP2/IP3-violation cases, we can classify all undo puzzles into two groups. One group can be described by IP2/IP3-violation Case 1. In Figure 4(a), we illustrate an instance of this group, where the initial state is state *"axb"*, $O_1=I(2, y)$, $O_2=D(1, x)$, and $!O_2=I(1, x)$, with a position relationship $(p_1 - 1) = p_2$. Using $TM(O_1, O_2)$, we can derive $O_1^{O2}=T(O_1, O_2)=I(1,y)$, and $O_2^{O1}=T(O_2, O_1)=D(1,x)$. After applying O_1 and O_2 (and one of them is transformed) in different orders on *"axb"*, the same state *"ayb"* will be reached (guaranteed by the *UE-CP1* preservation of $TM(O_1, O_2)$). Then, if O_2 is undone, the state should become *"axyb"*, in which the effect of O_2 is eliminated but the effect of O_1 is retained, according to the established *undo effect* requirement in [14,15,22]. However, an incorrect state *"ayxb"* could be produced by:

1. executing $I(1, y)$ on state *"axb"*, where $I(1, y)$ is obtained by $T(I(1, y), I(1, x)) = I(1, y)$), which violates IP2 as $I(1, y)=T(T(O_1, O_2),!O_2) \neq O_1$; *or*
2. executing $I(2, x)$ on state *"ayb"*, where $I(2, x)$ is obtained from creating an *inverse* $!O_2=I(1, x)$ and performing $T(I(1, x), I(1, y)) = I(2, x)$), which violates IP3 as $I(2, x) \neq !T(O_2, O_1) = I(1, x)$.

The above IP2-violation case involves an *insert-insert-tie* ($I(1,x)$ vs $I(1,y)$) and this tie is resolved by using $priority(O_1) > priority(O_2)$ (assuming the priority of $!O_2$ is the same as O_2). Reversing the priority could solve the puzzle in this scenario, but will fail in another similar scenario where $O_1 = I(1, y)$, which is why this puzzle was named *insert-insert-tie* dilemma in [22]. As the order of *"x"* and *"y"* is reversed in the final state *"ayxb"* (compared to the correct undo effect "*axyb*"), this puzzle is the root of the *order-puzzle* in [15,16]; O_1 and O_2 also have an *adjacent-conflict* relationship as defined in [14].

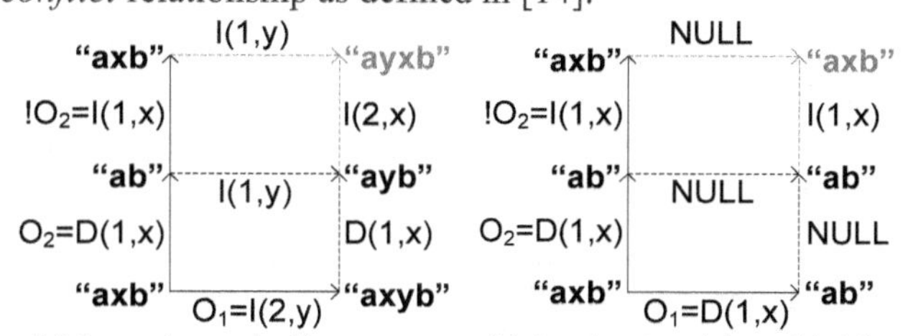

(a) *Insert-insert-tie dilemma, order-puzzle, adjacent-conflict.* (b) *Overlapping-delete, del-del-puzzle, overlapping-conflict.*

Figure 4. Illustrating undo puzzles and IP2/IP3-violation.

The other group can be described by IP2/IP3-violation Case 2. In Figure 4(b), we illustrate an instance of this group, where the initial state is state *"axb"*, $O_1=D(1, x)$, $O_2=D(1, x)$, and $!O_2=I(1, x)$, with a special position relationship: $p_1=p_2$. After applying O_1 and O_2 (and one of them is transformed) in different orders on "*axb*", the same state *"ab"* will be reached. Then, if O_2 is undone, the state should remain *"ab"* because undoing one overlapping delete O_2 should not recover *"x"* as the effect of O_1 should be retained according to the *undo effect* requirement in [14,15, 22]. However, an OT system may prematurely recover *"x"* to produce *"axb"*, which could be produced by:

1. executing *NULL* on *"axb"*, where *NULL* is obtained by $T(NULL, !O_2)$, which violates IP2 as $NULL=T(T(O_1, O_2),!O_2) \neq O_1$; or
2. executing $I(1, x)$ on *"ab"*, where $I(1, x)$ is obtained by creating $!O_2=I(1, x)$ and performing $T(I(1, x), NULL)$, which violates IP3 as $I(1, x) \neq !T(O_2, O_1)=NULL$.

If this scenario is extended to undo O_1 as well, the final state would become *"axxb"*, which is not the initial state *"axb"* (after undoing both O_1 and O_2) and thus violates the *undo property* as well [22]. In this undo puzzle scenario, both O_1 and O_2 are *delete* operations and have an *overlapping-conflict* relationship according to [14]; this puzzle was named *del-del-puzzle* [15], and *overlapping-delete puzzle* [22], respectively, for obvious reasons.

Connections between IP2/IP3-violation and CP2-violation
By comparing verification results between IP2/IP3 and CP2, we discovered an interesting connection between undo puzzles (related to IP2/IP3-violation Case 1, as illustrated in Figure 4(a)) and the FT puzzle: one side of the IP2/IP3-equation is a deterministic result, but the other side contains an *insert-insert-tie* that has to be resolved by a tie-breaking rule. This *insert-insert-tie* is an FT because the tie is not original but created by transformation, and it plays exactly the same role as the FT does in the CP2-violation case. From this observation, we deduce: the FT phenomenon is a common cause in CP2-violation and IP2/IP3-violation Case 1, which provides hints for an *integrated* FT solution for preserving CP2, IP2 and IP3.

IP2/IP3-Preservation vs. Undo-Puzzle-Solution
Based on IP2/IP3 verification discoveries, we can assert that IP2/IP3-preservation can be achieved by solving known undo puzzles at the transformation function level. The general IP2/IP3-violation description of undo puzzles and their connections to CP2-violation also provide hints on how to resolve them: an FT solution at the transformation function level may resolve both CP2-violation and IP2/IP3-violation Case 1. Solutions for the IP2/IP3-violation Case 2 should focus on transformation functions related to two *delete* operations only.

Past research has also found that IP2 and IP3 are not unconditionally required; IP2 and IP3 can be and have been solved by breaking their preconditions at the OT control algorithm level [15,22,24], without requiring undo puzzle solutions in transformation functions.

OT Puzzles vs. Non-determinism and Non-serializability
Last but not least, we found that all OT puzzles, related to transformation properties, are rooted in the two common properties of OT systems:

1. *Non-deterministic* combined-effects for *insert-insert-ties* (some of them are FTs), which is achieved by using a tie-breaking rule. This combined-effect and achieving technique are responsible for CP2-violation and IP2/IP3-violation Case 1.
2. *Non-serialisable* combined-effects for *delete-delete-ties*, which is achieved by using a special operation NULL. This combined-effect and achieving technique are responsible for IP2/IP3-violation Case 2.

The above combined-effects and achieving techniques have been adopted by nearly all OT systems based on basic data and operation models, which explains why the same puzzles occur in different OT systems, independent of their algorithmic designs and functionalities.

CONCLUSIONS

This is the first work to verify OT correctness in both consistency maintenance and undo, with respect to established transformation properties, including UE-CP1, CP2, IP1, IP2, and IP3. In this work, we have contributed a novel system of verification frameworks, a software verification tool, and important verification discoveries.

OT puzzles were notoriously difficult to detect as they were often hidden in intricate scenarios and took varying forms in different OT systems. It is amazing to see all those puzzles manifesting themselves under verification frameworks that are solely based on data and operation models and transformation properties, independent of specific OT algorithms. Furthermore, our verification frameworks are able to exhaustively cover all verification cases, without exponential case explosion, which is essential to achieving exhaustive search of all OT puzzles. Main innovations in our verification frameworks include: formalization of basic data and operation models, formal specification of union effects as a specialization of the intention-preservation requirement, integration of union effects with convergence properties, general transformation matrix for verifying existing and new transformation functions, exhaustive verification case derivation methods based on uniformed effect ranges, and verification processes based on property equations.

The main discovery from this study is: *all OT puzzles, in relation to established transformation properties under the basic data and operation models, have been discovered.* Moreover, we discovered general descriptions and classifications of all puzzles, and connections among seemly unrelated transformation properties and puzzles. These discoveries help resolve a number of long-standing mysteries surrounding OT correctness and contributed to advancement of OT fundamental knowledge and technology. Past research has solved all discovered puzzles and many solutions are based on generic control algorithms [29], which are applicable to a wide range of applications.

We have extended our verification frameworks to cover string-wise operations and implemented this extension in OTX. The extension from char-wise to string-wise operations has increased the number of verification cases (e.g. from less than one hundred to several hundreds for CP2 verification) and operation overlapping cases (e.g. from a single delete-delete-tie case to multiple partial delete-delete overlapping cases and new delete-insert overlapping cases). This extended work has reconfirmed the effectiveness of the general verification framework and main discoveries reported in this paper, and also made interesting new discoveries, which will be reported in the future.

While core OT techniques under basic data and operation models have been thoroughly studied, new and significant challenges lie in applying core OT techniques to advanced real-world applications [1, 2, 23, 26, 27], that are based on complex data and operation models with domain-specific constraints on conflict resolution and consistency requirements. Existing and emerging real-world applications continue to provide exciting opportunities and fresh stimuli to ongoing and future OT research and innovation.

ACKNOWLEDGEMENTS

This research is partially supported by an Academic Research Fund Tier 1 Grant from Ministry of Education Singapore. The authors wish to thank anonymous reviewers for their insightful and constructive comments and suggestions.

REFERENCES

1. Agustina, Liu, F., Xia, S., Shen, H.F. and Sun, C. CoMaya: Incorporating advanced collaboration capabilities into 3D digital media design tools. *ACM CSCW* (2008), 5 – 8.
2. Agustina and Sun, C. Dependency-conflict detection in real-time collaborative 3D design systems. *ACM CSCW* (2013), 715 – 728.
3. Begole, J., Rosson, M.B. and Shaffer, C.A. Flexible collaboration transparency: supporting worker independence in replicated application-sharing systems. *ACM TOCHI* 6, 2 (1999), 95 – 132.
4. Boucheneb, H. and Imine, A. On Model-checking optimistic replication algorithms. *FORTE on Formal Techniques for Distributed Systems* (2009),73 – 89.
5. Davis, A., Sun, C. and Lu, J. Generalizing operational transformation to the standard general markup language. *ACM CSCW* (2002), 58 – 67.
6. Ellis, C. A. and Gibbs, S. J. Concurrency control in groupware systems. *ACM SIGMOD* (1989), 399 – 407.
7. Gu, N., Yang, J. and Zhang, Q. Consistency maintenance based on the mark & retrace technique in groupware systems. *ACM GROUP* (2005), 264 – 273.
8. Ignat, C. and Norrie, M.C. Customizable collaborative editor relying on treeOPT algorithm. *ECSCW* (2003), 315 – 334.
9. Imine, A., Molli, P., Oster, G. and Rusinowitch, M. Proving correctness of transformation functions in real-time groupware. *ECSCW* (2003), 277 – 293.
10. Lamport, L. Time, clocks, and the ordering of events in a distributed system. *CACM 21*, 7 (1978), 558 – 565.
11. Li, D. and Li, R. Preserving operation effects relation in group editors. *ACM CSCW* (2004), 427 – 466.
12. Nichols, D., Curtis, P., Dixon, M. and Lamping, J. High-latency, low-bandwidth windowing in the Jupiter collaboration system. *ACM UIST* (1995), 111 – 120.
13. Palmer, C.R. and Cormack, G.V. Operation transforms for a distributed shared spreadsheet. *ACM CSCW* (1998), 69 – 78.
14. Prakash, A. and Knister, M. A framework for undoing actions in collaborative systems. *ACM TOCHI 1, 4* (1994), 295 – 330.
15. Ressel, M. and Gunzenhauser, R. Reducing the problems of group undo. *ACM GROUP* (1999), 131 – 139.
16. Ressel, M., Ruhland, N. and Gunzenhauser, R. An integrating, transformation-oriented approach to concurrency control and undo in group editors. *ACM CSCW* (1996), 288 – 297.
17. Robert, C. S. Collaborative editing for mission control. *Third Int. Workshop on Collaborative Editing Systems*, in conjunction with *ACM GROUP* (2001).
18. Shao, B., Li, D. and Gu, N. A sequence transformation algorithm for supporting cooperative work on mobile devices. *ACM CSCW* (2010), 159 – 168.
19. Shen, H.F. and Sun, C. Flexible notification for collaborative systems. *ACM CSCW* (2002), 77 – 86.
20. Sun, C. and Ellis, C.A. Operational transformation in real-time group editors: issues, algorithms, and achievements. *ACM CSCW* (1998), 59 – 68.
21. Sun, C., Jia, X., Zhang, Y., Yang, Y, and Chen, D. Achieving convergence, causality-preservation, and intention-preservation in real-time cooperative editing systems. *ACM TOCHI 5, 1* (1998), 63 – 108.
22. Sun, C. Undo as concurrent inverse in group editors. *ACM TOCHI 9, 4* (2002), 309 – 361.
23. Sun, C., Xia, S., Sun, D., Chen, D., Shen, H. and Cai, W. Transparent adaptation of single-user applications for multi-user real-time collaboration. *ACM TOCHI 13, 4* (2006), 531 – 582.
24. Sun, D. and Sun, C. Context-based operational transformation in distributed collaborative editing systems. *IEEE TPDS 20, 10* (2009), 1454 – 1470.
25. Sun, C., Agustina, and Xu, Y. Exploring operational transformation: from core algorithms to real-world applications. *ACM CSCW* (2011) *demo.*
26. C. Sun, Wen, H. and Fan, H. Operational transformation for orthogonal conflict resolution in collaborative 2-dimensional document editors. *ACM CSCW (2012),*1391 – 1400.
27. Sun, C. OTFAQ: Operational Transformation Frequently Asked Questions and Answers. http://www.ntu.edu.sg/home/czsun/projects/otfaq
28. Vidot, N., Cart, M., Ferrie, J. and Suleiman, M. Copies convergence in a distributed real-time collaborative environment. *ACM CSCW* (2000), 171 – 180.
29. Xu, Y., Sun, C. and Li, M. Achieving convergence in operational transformation: conditions, mechanisms and systems. *ACM CSCW* (2014).

APPENDIX of this paper can be found at http:// www.ntu.edu.sg/home/czsun/cscw2014_239_Appendix.pdf.

A Partial Replication Approach for Anywhere Anytime Mobile Commenting

Huanhuan Xia[1], **Tun Lu**[1], **Bin Shao**[2], **Guo Li**[1], **Xianghua Ding**[1], **Ning Gu**[1]

[1]School of Computer Science, Fudan University, Shanghai, China

[2]Microsoft Research, Beijing, China

{huanhuanxia,lutun}@fudan.edu.cn, binshao@microsoft.com, {guoli,dingx,ninggu}@fudan.edu.cn

ABSTRACT

Commenting systems play increasingly important roles in the interactive web applications. Meanwhile, more and more web applications are visited on mobile devices. However, the intermittent connection of mobile networks and resource limitation of mobile devices pose great challenges, mainly in terms of interactive responsiveness and data consistency. In this paper, we present the first work of partial replication solution based on collaborative editing techniques, which can address the issues of local responsiveness and resource limitation on mobile commenting systems. We report how we address the consistency maintenance challenges that come with the partial replication approach. With this approach, users are allowed to smoothly comment anywhere anytime. The comment thread can be incrementally updated and automatically synchronized with strong data consistency guarantees. We implemented a system prototype called Hydra and evaluated it on a real data set.

Author Keywords

Commenting System; Partial Replication; Consistency Maintenance; Synchronization.

ACM Classification Keywords

H.5.3 Information Systems: Group and Organization Interfaces; C.2.4 Computer Systems Organization: Distributed Systems—*Client/Server*.

General Terms

Algorithms, Experimentation, Performance

1. INTRODUCTION

The last few years have witnessed that the Web has been evolving into an interactive and collaborative platform for a great variety of web media, such as news, blogs, goods, music, videos, tweets. Commenting systems can greatly improve user interaction and collaboration on the web media, by which users express their individual opinions or sentiments, and even contribute their insights, knowledge and creativity. There are many popular commercial commenting systems such as Disqus[1], IntenseDebate[2] and Livefyer[3], which are widely adopted by web sites to encourage user interaction and participation. Taking Disqus for example, it has over 70 million users; over 1.4 million sites are using its commenting service; and about hundreds of thousands of comments are generated everyday.

With the rapid development and penetration of mobile technologies, commenting activities become more pervasive. Marketing-Charts' mobile research found that 34% Facebook users and 43% Twitter users access their accounts via mobile phones [2]. For Sina Weibo, the biggest microblogging system in China, 60% active users are mobile [1]. And the growth still continues. The mobile users of Twitter increased 182% in 2011 [3].

However, we are still in the era when the internet mainstay is not optimized for mobile devices. Specifically, most existing commenting systems do not pay enough attention to mobile users. Even some commenting systems have already taken the screen size into consideration, many of them overlooked another important difference between desktop PCs and mobile devices, namely, network connection. Most mobile users can surf the web, but not in a comfortable way due to intermittent connection and high latency issues of mobile networks.

The network connection issues make smooth commenting without disruption a big challenge in the mobile environment. Users need to wait for the server response after clicking the submit button. It usually gives users a long pause in the high-latency mobile network. Even worse, sometimes nothing but a failure notification is returned after the long pause when the network connection is temporarily unavailable . And this really leads to bad user experience.

A widely used approach to addressing this problem in disconnected environments is *optimistic replication* [18]. With local data replica, operations can be performed on the local replica immediately in a non-blocking way. It is especially promising to solve the responsiveness problems in mobile environment by allowing offline operations when network is disconnected. However, replication can lead to data inconsistency. How to make an optimal trade-off between high responsiveness and

[1]http://disqus.com

[2]http://intensedebate.com/

[3]http://www.livefyre.com/

CSCW'14, February 15–19, 2014, Baltimore, Maryland, USA.
Copyright © 2014 ACM 978-1-4503-2540-0/14/02...$15.00.
http://dx.doi.org/10.1145/2531602.2531609

data consistency is a key technical challenge of interactive applications, such as online gaming [26], co-authoring [6, 23] and collaborative software development [10].

Collaborative editing techniques, such as Operational Transformation (OT) [6, 23] and Address Space Transformation (AST) [7], are representative optimistic concurrency control methods to address this challenge. To achieve high responsiveness, they adopt the *full replication architecture*. Local operations can be applied immediately on the local replica to obtain unconstrained local user experience. To maintain the data consistency, before applying the remote operations on local data replica, the remote operations (as in OT) or local data replica (as in AST) are transformed to correctly incorporate the effects of remote operations.

However, it suffers from resource constraints, and is usually not necessary, to make full replicas for a commenting system on mobile devices. Due to the spotty nature of comments and the diversity of user interests, a user may slide many screens before encountering worth-reading items, which makes full replication useless in most cases. *Partial replication* of the online content can not only save the network bandwidth and battery life of the device, but also potentially make better user experience of web surfing. Besides consistency maintenance issue, partial data replication brings new challenges to OT and AST.

In this paper, we contribute a novel partial replication approach to anywhere anytime mobile commenting experience. It can be used by existing commenting systems to fetch and construct a comment thread incrementally for mobile users, achieve high local responsiveness in intermittent mobile networks, and synchronize the states of comment threads automatically with strong data consistency guarantees. It is important to note that local responsiveness is different from real time synchronization: the former can be achieved through data replication, whereas the latter relies on network conditions.

The contribution of this work are threefold. First, to the best of our knowledge, it is the first work of applying collaborative editing techniques in partially replicated architecture for mobile commenting. Second, we addressed data consistency maintenance issues that come with partial replication approach by devising a partial replication scheme and a synchronization protocol to synchronize the states of comment threads. Third, a scalar timestamp based synchronization protocol is designed for achieving efficient and scalable commenting systems.

The rest of the paper is organized as follows. Section 2 lays out the approach overview and points out the technical challenges that have not been fully addressed by prior work. The partial replication of comment threads and the corresponding replication synchronization protocol are elaborated in Section 3 and 4, respectively. Section 5 introduces the underlying consistency maintenance technique in our approach. Our approach is evaluated in Section 6. Related work is discussed in Section 7. Section 8 concludes the paper by summarizing our contributions and discussing possible future research direction.

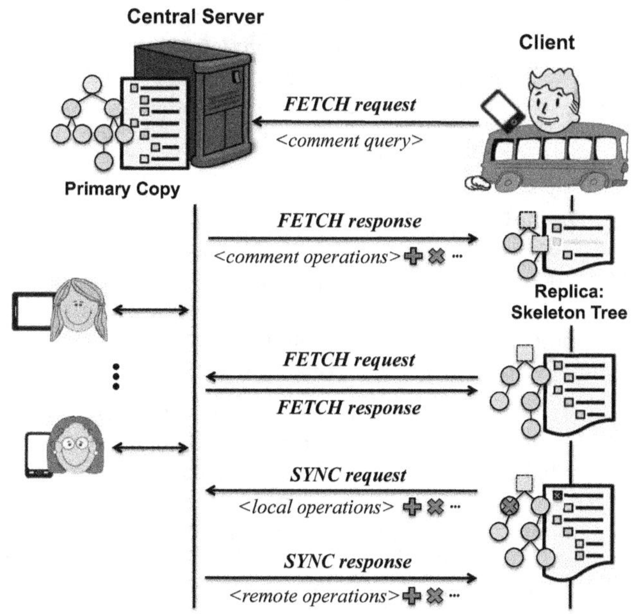

Figure 1. Approach sketch.

2. OVERVIEW

2.1 Approach Sketch

A commenting system consists of a dedicated server and a number of clients as shown in Figure 1. For each comment thread, the primary copy is maintained by the central server. Users can fetch and replicate any comments they want in the thread, and local replicas are built incrementally on their client devices.

When a user starts to participate in an online discussion, a *FETCH* request will be sent to the server specifying what comments are requested by the user, for example, the latest comments. The requested comments will be returned to the client in the form of commenting operations, and are maintained in a special data structure of the replica, which is called the *skeleton tree* in our approach. The skeleton tree is responsible for organizing the replicated comments and maintaining their relationships, i.e. the parent-child relationship and sibling relationship. To avoid transferring unnecessary data and thus save the bandwidth of mobile users, the central server tracks the states of each replica and responds to client's subsequent *FETCH* requests incrementally.

Users are allowed to freely perform commenting operations on their local replicas in a non-blocking way, even in disconnected situations, e.g. posing, editing or deleting comments, voting for other users' comments etc.. Local operations are executed immediately by the clients. Offline local operations will be submitted to the server in a *SYNC* request to synchronize the local replica with the primary copy when the network is available. The primary copy on the central server will get updated by integrating client's local operations, and the operations from other users will be identified and returned to the client for updating the local replica.

In replica synchronization, concurrent operations may cause conflicts and lead to inconsistent comment thread state. In our approach, AST [7] (Address Space Transformation), which is originally proposed for group editing, is used to maintain the data consistency. Before executing a remote commenting operation, the concurrent operations are identified to transform the local replica or the primary copy to the state in which the operation was generated.

2.2 Technical Challenges

Existing collaborative editing techniques require that the shared document are fully replicated on all collaborative sites. To use them for consistency maintenance in partial replication and synchronization of comment threads, the following technical challenges must be addressed:

- First, *how to partially replicate a comment thread and incrementally construct the replica.* In collaborative editing, the shared document is fully replicated on all collaborative sites. However, in commenting systems, users may want any part of a comment thread. Moreover, during a comment conversation, users may fetch their required comments via several *FETCH* requests. Therefore, a replication scheme must be designed for incrementally constructing the replica to save the bandwidth of mobile users.
- Second, *how to identify concurrent operations and correctly transform the comment thread state.* In collaborative editing, fully shared document and the complete operation history can be used to easily identify concurrent operations. In AST, the document transformation is realized by traversing the whole document. So when the comment thread is partially replicated, the AST must be adapted and the replication scheme should ensure adequate information can be provided for AST to correctly perform the transformation.
- Third, *how to meet the scalability requirement of commenting systems and support user's dynamic participation.* Unlike collaborative editing, a hot topic may attract thousands of users in a short time, and users often join and leave a conversation highly dynamically. Most existing collaborative editing algorithms use vector timestamps to determine the concurrent relation between operations. The size of the vector timestamp is proportional to the number of the participants and will consume considerable mobile bandwidth under high degree of concurrency. Therefore, in our approach, an efficient concurrent operation detection method and a scalable synchronization protocol based on the scalar timestamp are devised for large-scale commenting systems.

3. PARTIAL REPLICATION OF COMMENT THREADS

Almost all existing commenting systems fetch a comment thread incrementally, for example, loading a comment thread page by page, expanding the nested comments only if a user wants to read more. In addition to these common schemes, a commenting system can even track and learn user commenting behaviors, and provide personalized commenting experience. Our approach allow clients to incrementally fetch comments with different schemes (e.g. "next 20 comments", "all comments posted by Alice" etc.). However, how to define a comment query and perform a query are application specific, and it is not the focus of this paper.

In this section, we first introduce a tree structure for modeling comments threads. Then we explain how a tree-structure comment thread is partially replicated on clients as well as the process of incrementally constructing a partial replica.

3.1 Comment Tree Structure and Primitive Operations

User interactions in a comment thread naturally form a tree structure. Although it is not necessary for all commenting systems to store comment threads as tree structures, it would be very convenient to hide the differences of various physical storage models (e.g. database, xml, disk file etc.) using a generic data structure. In our approach, a comment thread is modeled as a generic tree structure of a set of comments. A comment is uniquely identified by a global identifier and has a set of attributes, e.g. *author*, *content*, *likes* (i.e. the number of users who like the comment) etc.. Replies to the same parent comment node constitute an ordered list of child comment nodes. Therefore, a tree structure for modeling a comment thread is defined as a comment node set $\{N|N = \langle id, parent, children, attributes\rangle\}$, where:

- $N.id$ denotes the global unique identifier of N;
- $N.parent$ denotes the parent comment node of N;
- $N.children$ denotes the child comment node list of N;
- $N.attributes$ denotes the attributes of N, which is a set of name-value pairs.

Various comment operations are supported by different commenting systems, and typical comment operations include *Post* (post or reply a comment), *Edit* (edit the comment content), *Delete* (delete an existing comment), *Like* (like a comment by another user) etc.. For general purpose, four primitive operations on the tree structure are defined as follows:

- *Append (parentId, id, attributes)*: Create a new comment node with id and $attributes$, and add it to the end of the child node list of the parent node indicated by $parentId$.
- *InsertBefore (parentId, refId, id, attributes)*: Create a new comment node with id and $attributes$, and insert it before the existing child node indicated by *refId* in the child node list of the parent node indicated by $parentId$.
- *Delete (id)*: Delete the comment node indicated by id.
- *Update (id, name, value)*: Update the attribute indicated by $name$ of the comment indicated by id with the $value$.

The structural operations *Append*, *InsertBefore* and *Delete* can support adding or deleting a node at any position in a tree structure. The *Update* operation can be used to change the content of a comment. Note that the comment content represented as a set of *attributes* is application-specific. In a commenting system, in general, a comment has two types of attributes: *string-valued attribute* (e.g. author name, content) and *numerical attribute* (e.g. the number of likes). The string-valued attributes are commonly not allowed to be modified (e.g. the author's name) or only allowed to be modified by the comment's author (e.g. the comment's content). The numerical attributes are allowed to be updated by any user in an incremental manner, e.g. the value of *'likes'* of the comment *'A'* will be increased by 1 after the operation *Update(A, 'likes', 1)* is executed. Each comment node is associated with

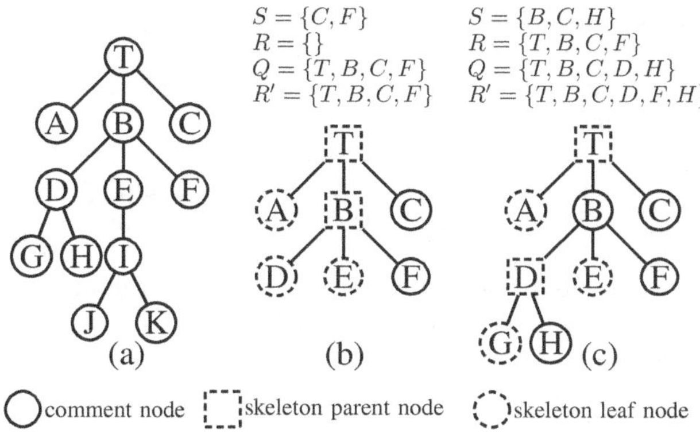

Figure 2. An example comment tree structure and the incremental update of the partial replica. (a) The example comment tree structure. (b) The replica after comments *C* and *F* are fetched for the user. (c) The updated replica after comments *B*, *C* and *H* are fetched.

a history buffer which logs the operations that have been executed on this node.

3.2 Primary Copy and Partial Replicas

Figure 2 (a) shows the tree structure of an example comment thread. It is stored as a *primary copy* at the server side. Users may want only a specific set of comments when they participate in the online discussion, and the required comments, for example the comments *C* and *F*, may be distributed within the tree structure arbitrarily. It does not make sense for a comment thread to only replicate and store the required nodes on the client independently. The relationships between the replicated nodes must be preserved and consistent with those in the primary copy, including the *parent-child* and *sibling* relationships.

To preserve the relationships between the replicated nodes, the rule "*If a comment node is replicated, its parent node (if any) must also be replicated*" is applied when replicating a subset of a comment tree structure. In this way, it is easy to show that all replicated nodes can be organized in a single rooted tree structure on the client, and the parent-child relationships are naturally preserved. As shown in Figure 2 (b), when comment nodes *C* and *F* are required to be replicated, their parent nodes *B* and *T* (which is also *B*'s parent node) are replicated on the client as well. The tree structure of the partial replica is called *skeleton tree* in our approach, and the parent nodes replicated to form the skeleton tree, e.g. *B* and *T*, are called *skeleton parent nodes*.

When a node is replicated, the history operations logged in its history buffer will be transferred to the client and executed. As shown in Figure 2 (b), the *skeleton leaf nodes A*, *D* and *E* are also generated in the skeleton tree after executing history operations logged in *T* and *B*, respectively. The skeleton leaf nodes are not explicitly required to be replicated on the client, however, they are important for maintaining consistent sibling relationships across replicas. The underlying consistency maintenance technique will be elaborated in Section 5. It should be pointed out that, to save the bandwidth of mobile users, all skeleton nodes, including the skeleton parent and skeleton leaf nodes, are maintained in the skeleton tree without content data (i.e. the nodes' attributes).

3.3 Incremental Construction of Partial Replicas

When a user starts to participate in an online discussion, the first *FETCH* request will be sent to the server to fetch the specific comments wanted by the user. The initial skeleton tree can be constructed from top to bottom by executing the operations returned to the client. When subsequent *FETCH* requests are sent to refresh the current replica or fetch additional comments for the user, some of the required nodes may exist in the client replica. To save the bandwidth of mobile users, the client replica should be updated incrementally. In other words, only incremental operations should be returned by the server to update the skeleton tree of the partial replica.

To determine which nodes should be replicated and how to respond to a *FETCH* request in an incremental manner, the server maintains a *replica metadata* for each replica to track the replica's state. It records which nodes have been replicated and their *replication types* in the skeleton tree. *CN* and *SN* denote the replicated comment node and skeleton parent node, respectively.

Algorithm 1 $Fetch(R, Request) : Response$

1: $Response \leftarrow Sync(R, Request)$
2: $S \leftarrow$ *comments specified by* $Request.query$
3: $Q \leftarrow$ *required nodes for replicating nodes in* S
4: **for** each $N \in Q$ **do**
5: *Determine what data should be returned to the client for* N *according to* N*'s replication type, and update* R *and* $Response$.
6: **end for**
7: **return** $Response$

Given the replica metadata *R*, Algorithm 1 specifies the procedure of responding to a *FETCH* request which consists of a comment query and unsubmitted client operations before the request. The server first calls Algorithm *Sync*, which is elaborated in next section, to execute the client's local operations within the request (line 1), and then performs the query on the latest primary copy to get the comment set *S* wanted by the client (line 2). For example, $S = \{B, C, H\}$ in Figure 2 (c) indicates that the comments *B*, *C*, and *H* are required by the client. According to the replication rule described above, the nodes that should be replicated are identified and stored in $Q = \{T, B, C, D, H\}$ (line 3). The set Q can be calculated by including all nodes on the paths from the root to the nodes in *S* (e.g. $Q = \{T, B\} \cup \{T, C\} \cup \{T, B, D, H\}$).

Because some of nodes in *Q* may have existed in the client's replica, the server determines what data should be returned for each node $N \in Q$ according to their replication types as follows (line 4-6):

- Case 1: $N \notin R \wedge N \notin S$. N will be replicated as a new skeleton parent node, e.g. *D* in Figure 2 (c), so only the history operations on N will be returned to construct its child node list. *Update* operations and *attributes* fields of *Append* and *InsertBefore* operations will be excluded. N's replication type is set as *SN*.

- Case 2: $N \notin R \wedge N \in S$. N will be replicated as a new comment node, e.g. *H*. Similarly with Case 1, history operations on N will be returned. In addition, N's attributes will returned as well. N's replication type is set as *CN*.
- Case 3: $N \in R \wedge N \notin S$. N has existed in the replica and is not wanted by the user, e.g. *T*, so nothing needs to be done.
- Case 4: $N \in R \wedge N \in S$. If N is currently replicated as skeleton parent node, e.g. *B*, N's attributes will be returned to the client and its replication type will be changed from *SN* to *CN*, otherwise nothing needs to be done for N, e.g. *C*.

Note that Algorithm *Sync* is called at line 1 to update the primary copy and identify incremental remote operations for the replicated nodes. So actually, for $N \in R$ in Case 3 and 4, incremental operations on N (if any) will also be returned to the client. This can be considered as the synchronization of the two corresponding nodes between the client and the server, and it will be elaborated in next section.

When the client receives the response returned from the server, it first executes the incremental operations within the response to update the structure of the skeleton tree, and then sets the *attributes* fields of the nodes whose contents are also returned along with the operations.

4. PARTIAL REPLICA SYNCHRONIZATION

In this section, we introduce how replicated nodes are synchronized with their corresponding nodes on the server. A batch of local operations, which are executed since the last synchronization with the server, are incrementally submitted using a single *SYNC* message. Then the server applies all received operations on the primary copy. After that, remote operations which are concurrent with the submitted operations are identified and returned to update current client's local replica.

4.1 Concurrent Operation Detection

In a typical commenting system, a server may serve thousands of online users at the same time, and users may join and leave a discussion dynamically. Therefore, the concurrent operation detection method must be efficient enough. In this section, a concurrent operation detection method with $\log(n)$ time complexity is presented, where n is the length of a node's operation history buffer.

On the server side, the received operation sequences will be stored in the sequence history buffers (*SHB*) of corresponding nodes in the order of execution time. On the client side, an operation sequence that has been synchronized with the server is stored in the *SHB* of the corresponding node, and operations that have not been submitted to server are stored in the local history buffer (*LHB*). Each sequence S_i in the history buffer is a tuple $\langle R, T, T', L\rangle$, where:

- $S_i.R$ denotes the replica on which S_i was generated;
- $S_i.L$ denotes the list of operations constituting S_i;
- $S_i.T$ denotes the finish time of executing S_i on server;
- $S_i.T'$ denotes the finish time of $S_i.R$'s last synchronization with the server.

Here $S_i.T$ and $S_i.T'$ are global scalar timestamps, which can be realized by real time or logic time on the server. Some existing centralized collaborative systems adopt two-dimensional timestamp, one dimension is for the client, the other is for the server. For example, Jupiter [13] uses two-dimensional timestamps to transform concurrent operations in the transformation state space. However, Jupiter assumes the shared object is fully replicated. If the shared object is partially replicated on individual clients, two-dimensional timestamps generated in local partial states are not comparable globally.

For any sequence S in the *SHB* of a comment node N, S is generated after $S.T'$. When S is generated on the replica $S.R$, all sequences before $S.T'$ must have been executed on $S.R$, and no sequence after $S.T'$ is returned and executed on $S.R$. Sequences generated on the same local replica are submitted and executed on the primary copy in their generating orders. Therefore, given two sequences S_i and S_j in the *SHB* of a node N, where $0 \le i \le j < |N.SHB|$, one of the following relations is hold between S_i and S_j:

- *casually-before*: $S_i \to S_j$. S_i happens before S_j if $S_i.T < S_j.T'$ or $S_i.R = S_j.R$;
- *concurrent*: $S_i \parallel S_j$. S_i is concurrent with S_j if $S_i.T > S_j.T'$ and $S_i.R \neq S_j.R$.

Since operations in a sequence are ordered by their generating times, the relations between two operations can also be specified as following: Given two operations O_1 and O_2, where $O_1 \in S_i.L$ and $O_2 \in S_j.L$,

- $O_1 \to O_2$: O_1 happens before O_2 if $S_i \to S_j$ or $S_i = S_j$ and O_1 is before O_2 in $S_i.L$.
- $O_1 \parallel O_2$: O_1 is concurrent with O_2 if $S_i \parallel S_j$.

Given an operation sequence, concurrent operation sequences are those whose execution times T are greater than $S.T'$ except for those from $S.R$, where T' is the time of the last synchronization time of an operation sequence S. Because operation sequences are ordered by their execution times T in the *SHB* of a node, a binary search can be performed on the *SHB* to identify all concurrent sequences that have not been executed on the replica.

4.2 Partial Replica Synchronization

A synchronization process can be started manually, triggered periodically, or triggered automatically when the mobile device is reconnected. Figure 3 illustrates two synchronization processes between a client and the server.

When the local operation sequence S_j is ready to be submitted to the server at the state (1), i sequences (i.e. $S_{0..i-1}$ in *N.SHB*) have been synchronized with the server. The sequence S_j was generated after the client's last synchronization with the server, and the finish time T_1 of the last synchronization will also be submitted to the server with S_j to identify concurrent remote operation sequences.

After the *SYNC* request is received from the client at the state (2), j sequences (i.e. $S_{0..j-1}$ in *N.SHB* shown in Figure 3) have been received and executed on the primary copy. The server first identifies the concurrent sequences after $S_j.T' =$

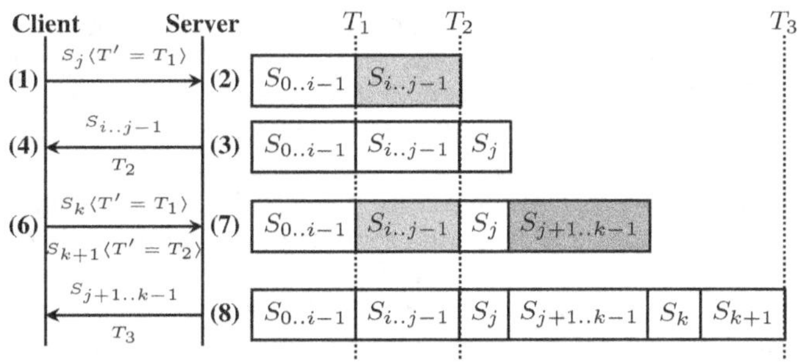

Figure 3. Illustration of two synchronization processes between a client and the server.

State	SHB	LHB
(1)	$S_{0..i-1}$	$S_j\langle T' = T_1\rangle$
(4)	$S_{0..i-1}$	$S_j\langle T' = T_1\rangle$, $S_k\langle T' = ?\rangle$
(5)	$S_{0..j}$	$S_k\langle T' = T_1\rangle$
(6)	$S_{0..j}$	$S_k\langle T' = T_1\rangle$, $S_{k+1}\langle T' = T_2\rangle$

Table 1. The *SHB* and *LHB* on the client shown in Figure 3.

T_1 for S_j, i.e. sequences $S_{i..j-1}$. After executing operations in S_j and adding it into *N.SHB* at time T_2 (shown as state(3)), the server returns the concurrent sequences $S_{i..j-1}$ and T_2 to the client.

During the synchronization, i.e. before responded by the server, local operations on the client replica are still allowed to be executed for high local responsiveness. For example at the state (4), besides the sequence S_j that is submitted to the server, the local operations generated during the synchronization are stored in the sequence S_k in *N.LHB*. After receiving the *SYNC* response, the client first executes remote operation sequences on N; then moves S_j into *N.SHB* and sets $S_k.T'$ for the next synchronization (shown as state (5)). It is worth to note that, $S_k.T'$ is set to $S_j.T' = T_1$ rather than the finish time T_2 of the current synchronization. This is because the operations in S_k are executed on the replica which have not integrated the operations in $S_{i..j-1}$, therefore, when S_k is submitted to the server in the next synchronization, $S_{i..j-1}$ must be identified as concurrent remote sequences for correctly executing S_k on the primary copy.

For the operations executed locally after the synchronization, i.e. S_{k+1} in *N.LHB* at state (6), they are generated after $S_{i..j-1}$ and S_j have been executed on the replica, so when it is submitted to the server, T_2 will be used to identify its concurrent remote sequences $S_{j+1..K-1}$ at the state (7) on the server. It is easy to show that, in a *SYNC* request, there are at most two local sequences for a node to be submitted to the server. After executed on the server, S_k and S_{k+1} submitted by the client are sequentially added into *N.SHB* (as shown in state (8)). The finish time T_3 of the synchronization and the concurrent sequences $S_{j+1..K-1}$ after T_2 are returned to the client.

Given the replica metadata R of the client from which the *SYNC* request is received, Algorithm 2 specifies the procedure of responding to a synchronization request. The server first executes the submitted operations for each node N in the request (lines 1-9) to update the primary copy. For each operation sequence S of N, the concurrent operations in *N.SHB* are identified (line 3), and then Algorithm *Execute* is called to execute the operations in S (line 5). An underlying consistency maintenance technique, which will be presented in next section, is used in *Execute* to maintain the consistent sibling relationships across replicas and resolve operation conflicts automatically. S is appended into the node's history buffer after the operations in it are executed (line 6). Note Algorithm *Execute* returns a list of comment nodes which are created on the client. These nodes should be added into the replica metadata R as the replication type *CN* (line 7). After all submitted operations are executed on the primary copy, concurrent operation sequences are identified for each nodes in the replica and added into the response (lines 11-14). However, for nodes that are replicated on the client as skeleton parent node, *Update* operations on them are excluded. Finally, the finish time of this synchronization process is set for the replica metadata and the response (line 15).

Algorithm 2 $Sync(R, Request) : Response$

```
1:  for each N ∈ Request do
2:      for each operations sequence S of N do
3:          CSL ← {S'|S'∈N.SHB ∧ S'∥S}
4:          S.T ← now
5:          NL ← Execute(N, S, CSL)
6:          Append S into N.SHB.
7:          Add nodes in NL into R as CN.
8:      end for
9:  end for
10: Response ← [ ]
11: for each N ∈ R do
12:     CSL ← {S'|S'∈N.SHB ∧ S'.T>R.T' ∧ S.R≠R}
13:     Add CSL into Response for N. Update operations are
        excluded if N is replicated as a skeleton parent node.
14: end for
15: Response.T' ← R.T' ← now
16: return Response
```

When the client receives the response returned from the server, it first executes the remote operations within the response to update the replica. Similarly with the operation execution on the server side, Algorithm *Execute* will be called for consistency maintenance and conflict resolution. However, it should be noted that, besides concurrent operations in a node's *SHB*, all operations in the node's *LHB* (if any) are also concurrent with the returned remote operations targeting the same node. After the remote operation are executed, the last synchronization time will be set for operation sequences in *LHB* , and the submitted sequences will be moved from *LHB* to *SHB*.

5. CONSISTENCY MAINTENANCE

For high local responsiveness, the shared comment thread is replicated on clients and operations are allowed to be concurrently performed on any part of the local replicas. When a local operation is submitted to the server or a remote operation is returned to the client, the state of the tree structure may be different from the state in which the operation was

Algorithm 3 Execute(N, S, CSL):L

1: **for** each $o \in CSL$ **do**
2: *Exclude o's effect on its affected node.*
3: **end for**
4: $L \leftarrow [\,]$
5: **for** each $o \in S$ **do**
6: *Execute o on the node N.*
7: *Put o's affected node into L if o is an Append or an InsertBefore operation.*
8: **end for**
9: **for** each $o \in CSL$ **do**
10: *Restore o's effect on its affected node.*
11: **end for**
12: **return** L

generated. Naively applying concurrent operations will lead to inconsistent data replica even corrupt data replicas.

In this section, an AST (Address Space Transformation) based consistency maintenance technique designed for partial replication architecture is elaborated. Note that we only focus on maintaining the syntactic not semantic consistency (e.g. a user posts a same comment twice in a short time or deliberately posts the answer before the question). The semantic inconsistency issues usually cannot be resolved solely by technical approaches without human interventions.

5.1 AST Basis

AST is originally proposed in [7] for collaborative editing of linear character documents. It ensures that the order of linear character nodes is consistent across all replicas after the same group of operations are executed at all collaborative sites. One of the most important advantages of AST is that a remote operation can be directly executed in its original form, as long as the address space on which this operation was generated exists and all concurrent operations' effects are excluded.

To ensure a remote operation can be correctly executed, AST transforms the address space (i.e. the comment tree structure) to the state at which the operation was generated. This is realized by excluding the execution effects of all concurrent operations. The effects of concurrent operations will be restored after the remote operation is executed. In order to achieve the address space transformation, AST logs all history operations and marks deleted nodes as *ineffective* rather than really removing them from the address space.

In AST [7, 25], history operations are associated with their target nodes. The address space transformation is achieved by the *Retracing* procedure [7], which visits all the nodes and determines their *effective/ineffective* marks to exclude or restore the effects of concurrent operations. However, it is not applicable for partial replication of the tree structure, since a node may not exist in a partial replica.

5.2 Adapting AST for Partial Replication

We have two observations on address space transformation. One is that a concurrent operation does not need to be considered in an address space transformation, if it has no effect on the execution of a remote operation, i.e. there is no conflict between the two operations. Another one is that the essence of address space transformation is to exclude or restore the execution effects of conflict concurrent operations, and it is unnecessary to traverse all the nodes as long as all conflict concurrent operations can be identified. By reviewing the tree structure and its primitive operations, we note that the conflicts of concurrent operations are confined to a node and its children, since the nodes are addressed by global identifiers. Specifically, for concurrent *Append*, *InsertBefore* and *Delete* operations, conflicts can be caused only when their target nodes share the same parent node. The *Update* operations only affect the content of comment nodes and have no effects on the structure of the comment thread, so they do not conflict with the other types of operations.

Therefore, to adapt AST for partial replication of the tree structure, history operations logged in their affected nodes are moved to the history buffer of the parent nodes. Each node maintains an *effectiveness counter*. When a node is created by an *Append* or *InsertBefore* operation, its effectiveness counter is initialized to 1. If a *Delete* operation is executed on the node, its effectiveness counter is decreased by 1. A node is *effective* if and only if its effectiveness counter equals 1. To execute a remote operation, after the concurrent operations are identified, the address space is transformed by directly manipulating the effectiveness counters of the concurrent operations' affected nodes. The partial replication mechanism (in Section 3) and the synchronization protocol (in Section 4) ensure all conflict concurrent operations that may lead to conflicts can be efficiently identified for executing a remote operation.

Given the sequence list of concurrent operations *CSL*, Algorithm 3 specifies the procedure of executing a remote operation sequence S on the node N. Since the operations in S are sequentially generated on their corresponding local replicas, they can be correctly executed in order (lines 5-8) after the effects of concurrent operations are excluded (lines 1-3). Concurrent operations' effects are restored (lines 9-11) after the remote operations are executed. The algorithm *Execute* returns a list of nodes which are created by *Append* and *InsertBefore* operations.

The *Delete* operation can be executed directly by decreasing the *effectiveness counter* of its affected node by 1. The *Append* and the *InsertBefore* operations can be executed by inserting a new node between two reference nodes. Due to concurrent insert operations and preceding delete operations, there may exist ineffective nodes between the two reference nodes. The procedure *RangeScan* [7] will be called to insert the new node at the correct position in the range of ineffective nodes and ensure a consistent sibling node order across all replicas.

Figure 4 illustrates the operation execution and conflict resolution. The node N as well as its children A and B are replicated on both client 1 and 2. N's initial states (Figure 4(b)) on the server, client 1 and client 2 are identical to each other. The server receives O_1 and O_2 from client 1, followed by O_3 from client 2 (Figure 4(a)). O_1 inserts X before B, and then

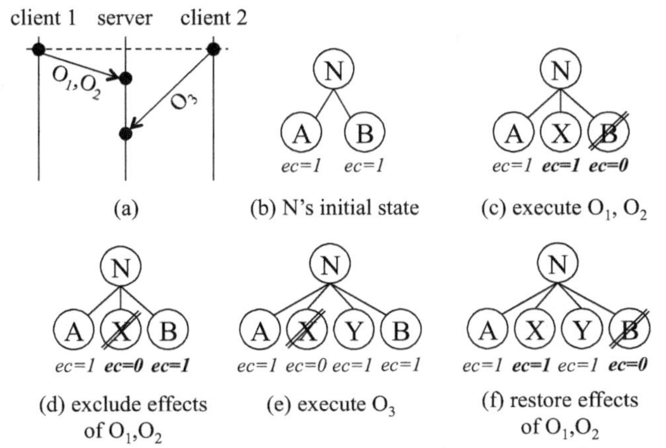

Figure 4. Examples of operation execution and conflict resolution. O_1=***InsertBefore(N,B,X)***, O_2=***Delete(B)*** **and** O_3=***InsertBefore(N,B,Y)***. ***ec*** **is short for** ***effectiveness counter.***

O_2 deletes B by decreasing B's effectiveness counter by 1 (Figure 4(c)).

O_3's execution is slightly different, because it is concurrent and conflict[4] with O_1 and O_2. Before executing O_3, effects of O_1 and O_2 must be excluded by decreasing X's effectiveness counter by 1 and increasing B's effectiveness counter by 1, respectively (Figure 4(d)). Y, which is intended to be inserted before B (i.e. between A and B), is inserted after the ineffective node X (Figure 4(e)) by calling the procedure *RangeScan*. O_1 and O_2's effects are restored after O_3's execution (Figure 4(f)). After concurrent operations O_1 and O_2 are returned to and executed on the client 2, N's state on the client 2 will be consistent with the one shown in Figure 4(f).

For two *Update* operations targeting the same *attribute* of a node, if the attribute is numerical, they do not conflict with each other since the target attribute is incrementally updated; otherwise, due to the attribute is only allowed to be updated by the comment's author, the conflict can be automatically resolved in a *"Last-Write-Win"* manner. Specifically, the execution of an *Update* operation is different between the server and the client. On the server side, an *Update* operation can be directly executed; while on the client side, a remote *Update* operation will be discarded if it targets a string-valued attribute which has been updated by an unsubmitted local operation.

Operations can be executed in linear time. Since an operation's effect can be excluded or restored by manipulating the affected node's *effectiveness counter* in constant time, the address space transformation can be done in $O(k)$ time, where k is the number of concurrent operations in *CSL*. Primitive operations can also be executed in constant time. So, *Execute*'s time complexity is $O(k + |S|)$.

6. EVALUATION

We have implemented a system prototype called Hydra and have evaluated it using the real comment data crawled from Disqus, which is a popular 3rd party commenting system used by CNN, FoxNews, Time, and Engadget etc. First, we analyze the characteristics of the Disqus comment data. Then, we present the experimental evaluation results.

6.1 Analysis of Disqus Comment Threads

We collected 32,289 comment threads with 8,612,658 comments from Disqus. Disqus lists the latest articles from the web content providers in its Explore Page [5]. We use those article URLs to crawl the articles and their comment threads. These comment threads can be constructed as tree structures in 3.3 seconds, 0.1 milliseconds per thread on average. Figure 5 shows the distribution of the comment thread size. About 25% of the threads consists of less than 10 comments, and 10% of the threads consists of more than 500 comments. On average, a comment thread consists of 267 comments contributed by 115 users. The largest thread consists of 30,232 comments, and the most popular comment conversation attracts 28,652 users. This suggests Hydra has to scale to a large comment thread size and a large number of participants.

In the crawled dataset, each user posted 2.32 comments on average. And the most active user posted 850 comments in a single comment thread. We examined the user interactions in the collected comment threads, and considered a reply to another user as an interaction between the two users. About 49% of users read and replied to other users' comments. Only 40% of comments were directly posted to the original web content, while 60% were replied to others' comments. These observations suggest user interactions accounted for a large proportion of comment threads.

6.2 Evaluation of Hydra

We implemented a system prototype called Hydra and a baseline commenting system to evaluate our approach.

- Client side response time was measured to evaluate the local responsiveness in real mobile environments.
- Network bandwidth usage was measured to evaluate the efficiency of partial replication approach.
- The server side response time and throughput were measured to evaluate the system scalability.

Experiment setup

Both the baseline system and Hydra were implemented as web-based commenting systems. For Java servlets were implemented in the baseline server to process comment fetching, posting, editing and deleting requests from clients. The partial replication algorithms were implemented in Hydra serve to process *FETCH* and *SYNC* requests from clients. They were deployed in the same Apache Tomcat server running on a virtual machine with four 2.8 GHz X5600 CPUs, 16G main memory. The operating system is Windows Server 2008 R2.

The evaluation experiments were conducted on the real data set crawled from Disqus. Users commenting behaviors in the

[4] B has been concurrently deleted by O_1, and a new node X has been concurrently inserted between A and B by O_2.

[5] http://disqus.com/explore/

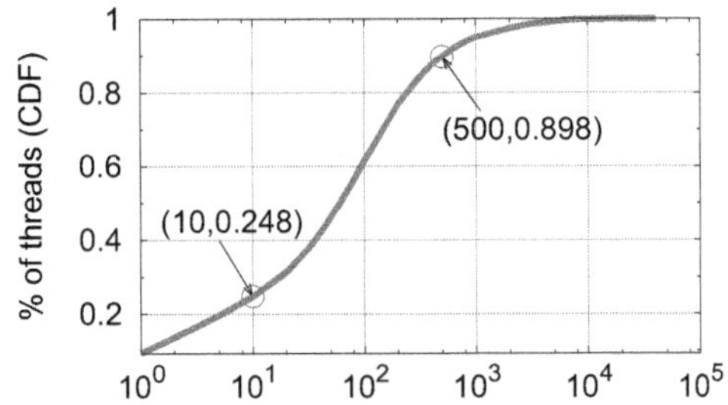

Figure 5. Comment thread size distribution.

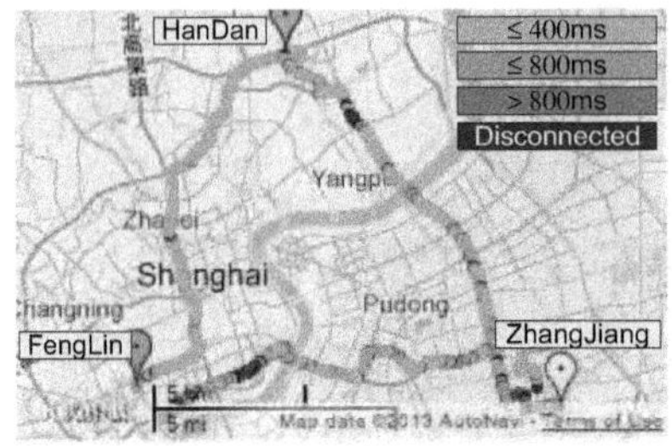

Figure 6. Mobile network RTTs between 7:00 a.m. to 9:00 a.m. in Shanghai.

Figure 7. Mobile network RTTs between 12:30 p.m. to 2:30 p.m. in Shanghai.

data were simulated in the chronological order of the comments to generate the client commenting requests. A centralized monitor program was implemented to schedule the commenting clients. Before posting, deleting or editing a comment, the comments depended on by current operation must be fetched first if they did not exist on the client. Since comment deletion and update information cannot be obtained and inferred lexically from the crawled data set, these operations were generated and randomly distributed among comment insertion operations to validate the correctness of operation executions. Users' commenting operations in Hydra were executed immediately on the local replica, while users' operations in the baseline system can only be executed after they were responded by the remote server. The simulation experiment was repeated four times to measure the local responsiveness, network bandwidth usage of mobile clients, and the server side performance.

Local responsiveness

Local responsiveness was measured in real mobile environments. We repeated the experiment twice at different time in a day. They were conducted on school buses between three campuses of Fudan university (i.e. HanDan campus, FengLin campus and ZhangJiang campus shown in Figure 6 and 7). The baseline client and Hydra client were run on a laptop which was connected to China Unicom's 3G mobile network via a laptop connect card. Meanwhile, we also implemented an Android application to record the locations and the round trip time (RTT) of the mobile network.

As expected, the mobile network was intermittent in the experiments. And we observed that the mobile network signal strength had no significant differences at different locations in Shanghai, but changed significantly with the change of time. The network RTTs were marked at different locations on the maps shown in Figure 6 and 7. Figure 8 shows the average local response time under different network conditions for Hydra client and the baseline client. Local response time of Hydra client is consistently close to zero. It means Hydra can provide high local responsiveness for users anywhere anytime. However, local response time of the baseline client increases with larger network RTT, and it can reach tens of seconds in the experiment.

Bandwidth saving

To save the bandwidth of mobile users, the structure of a comment thread is partially replicated on the client; the comment content is replicated if and only if it is explicitly required by a user. The bandwidth usage of each Hydra client can be calculated using the following formula:

$$B_H = b_c \cdot C + b_o \cdot R \tag{1}$$

where C is the number of comments required by a user; R is the number of nodes in the skeleton tree of a replica; b_c is the average comment size in bytes; and b_o is the average commenting operation size in bytes.

Existing collaborative editing techniques (such as OT and AST) can also be used to achieve high local responsiveness if the shared comment thread is fully replicated, we compared Hydra client's bandwidth usage with the following two full replication schemes:

- *Full-Structure-Partial-Content* (F_1): the structure of a comment thread is fully replicated, but the comment content is replicated if and only if it is explicitly required by the user.
- *Full-Structure-All-Content* (F_2): the full structure of a comment thread and its content are both replicated on the client.

Similarly, the bandwidth usage of the clients adopting the full replication schemes F_1 and F_2 can be calculated using the following two formulas respectively:

$$B_{F_1} = b_c \cdot C + b_o \cdot P \tag{2}$$
$$B_{F_2} = b_c \cdot P + b_o \cdot P \tag{3}$$

where P is the number of comments in a comment thread. Therefore, compared with the two full replication schemes, the percentage of bandwidth saved by Hydra are:

$$\delta_{F_1} = \frac{B_{F_1} - B_H}{B_{F_1}} = \frac{P - R}{P + \alpha \cdot C} = \frac{1 - \frac{R}{P}}{1 + \alpha \cdot \frac{C}{P}} \tag{4}$$

$$\delta_{F_2} = \frac{B_{F_2} - B_H}{B_{F_2}} = 1 - \frac{R + \alpha \cdot C}{P + \alpha \cdot P} = 1 - \frac{\frac{R}{P} + \alpha \cdot \frac{C}{P}}{1 + \alpha} \tag{5}$$

where $\alpha = \frac{b_c}{b_o}$ and it equals 4.9 in the prototype implementation. We can see that the percentage of bandwidth saved by Hydra is the function of two ratios: $\frac{C}{P}$ and $\frac{R}{P}$. The ratio $\frac{C}{P}$ denotes the percentage of the comments required by a user, and the ratio $\frac{R}{P}$ denotes to what extend the comment thread is partially replicated.

In the experiment, for comment threads that consist of more than 50 comments, the average percentages of bandwidth

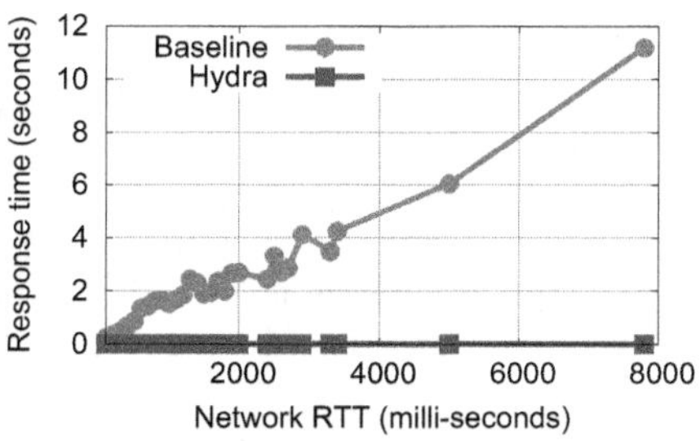

Figure 8. Response times of Hydra and Baseline clients with different network RTTs.

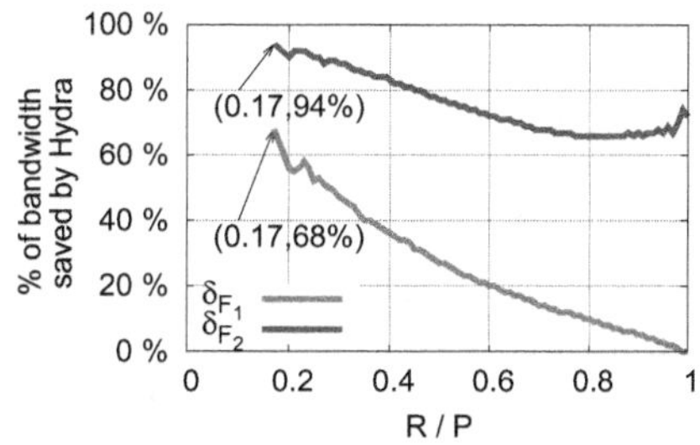

Figure 9. Average percentage of bandwidth saved by Hydra for different replication ratios.

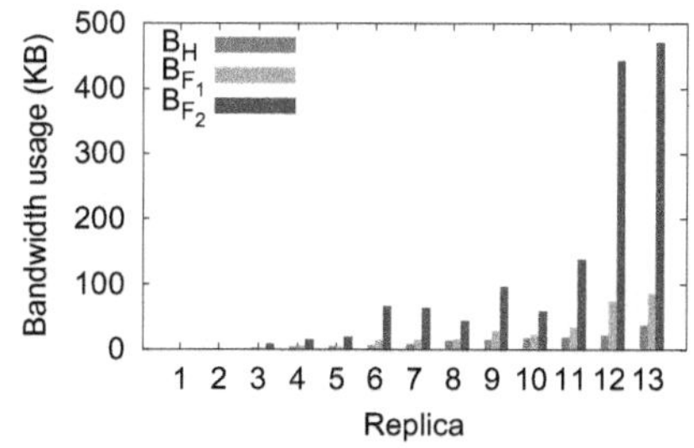

Figure 10. Bandwidth usage comparison of Hydra, F_1 and F_2 clients in an example comment thread.

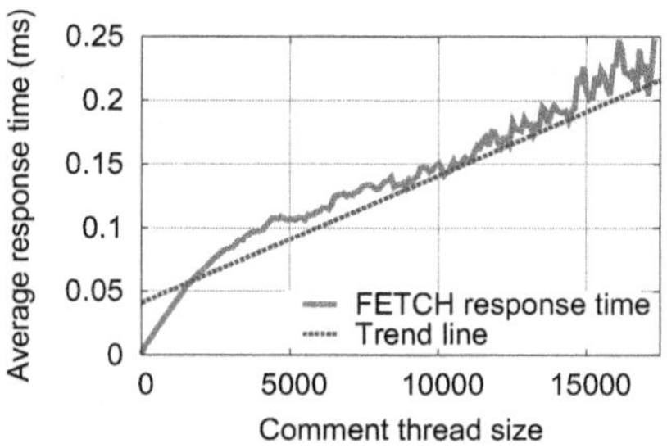

Figure 11. *FETCH* response time to the primary copy size.

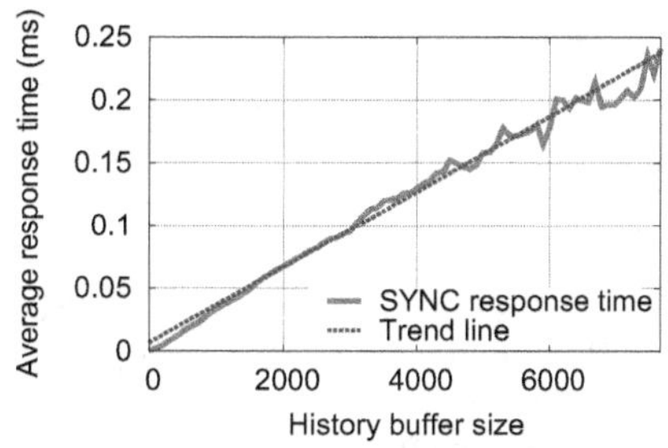

Figure 12. *SYNC* response time to the number of history operations in *SHB* on server.

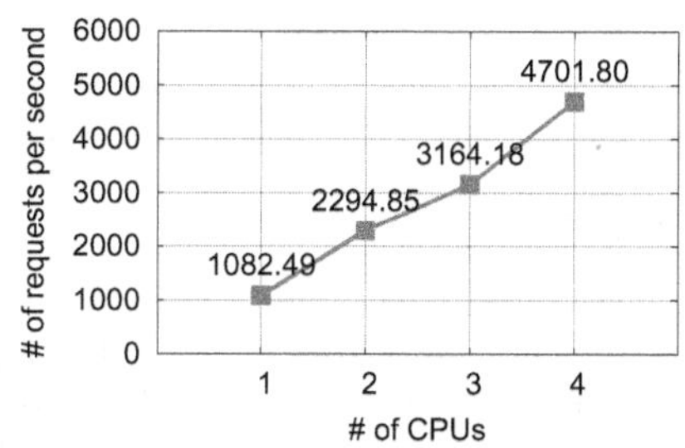

Figure 13. Hydra server throughput when configured different number of single-core CPUs.

saved by Hydra $\bar{\delta}_{F_1}$ and $\bar{\delta}_{F_2}$ were 15.6% and 69.8%, respectively. Figure 9 shows $\bar{\delta}_{F_1}$ and $\bar{\delta}_{F_2}$ for different replication ratios $\frac{R}{P}$. Compared with F_1, the smaller the replication ratio is, the more bandwidth Hydra saves. Compared with F_2, the bandwidth percentage saved by Hydra first decreases and then increases with the increase of the replication ratio. This is because, for large and flat comment threads, the replica size is close to the size of the whole thread even if only a small portion of comments are required by a user. Therefore, in the case where $\frac{R}{P}$ is close 1 and $\frac{C}{P}$ is very small, Hydra can save considerable bandwidth for users compared with F_2.

The minimum of the replication ratios equals 0.17 in the experiment. The corresponding comment thread contained 573 comments and 13 users' replicas. Figure 10 compares the bandwidth usage of Hydra, F_1 and F_2 clients for each user's replica in this comment thread. We can see that the bandwidth usage on the Hydra client is much less than that on F_1 and F_2 clients. For example, the F_1 and F_2 clients consumed 86KB and 471KB of user#13's bandwidth respectively, while the Hydra client only consumed 38KB.

Server side performance

The server side response time and throughput were measured to evaluate the system scalability. Figure 11 and 12 show the execution times of processing *FETCH* and *SYNC* requests, respectively. They are less than 0.25 milliseconds in the experiment, which are negligible compared with the network latency. In addition, the execution times of processing *FETCH* and *SYNC* requests increase linearly with the growth of the comment thread size and the history buffer size, respectively.

Four pressure tests were performed to measure the throughput of Hydra server. The Hydra server was configured with 1, 2, 3, 4 single-core CPUs, respectively. And it was running at 100% CPU usage using excessive commenting requests. Figure 13 shows the throughput under different CPU configurations. The Hydra server throughput is around 1000 requests per second per core on average, and it scales linearly with the number of CPU cores.

7. RELATED WORK AND DISCUSSION

Replication is widely adopted to offer high availability in distributed systems, such as [14, 17, 19]. As an important category of interactive systems, group editors [6, 23] fully replicate the shared document at all clients for high local responsiveness using optimistic concurrency control approaches such as OT (Operation Transformation) [6, 23] and AST (Address Space Transformation) [7]. Over the past two decades, a lot of work has been done for collaborative editing in fully replicated architecture to maintain consistency of replicas and automatically resolve conflicts in P2P architecture [6, 23, 11, 7, 15], client-server architecture [13, 21], mobile environment [20, 22], tree structure of document [5, 8, 25], etc..

However, as analyzed previously, full replication is usually not adopted under a bandwidth-minded environment, such as on mobile devices. To mitigate the problems caused by intermittent connection, online contents are usually prefetched and cached [4, 9] for local responsiveness of content retrieval. The cached content is actually a portion of the whole content, however, they are usually static where no concurrently editing is allowed. Prefetching and cache technologies can be leveraged to decide when and what content to fetch for comment retrieval and our approach can be adopted to maintain the replicated data and ensure high responsiveness of local operations.

Both OT and AST are potentially promising approaches that can be adapted for partial replication. But to the best of our knowledge, this is the first work proposing a complete solution to applying collaborative editing techniques for partial replication of comment threads. Although AST is used as the underlying consistency maintenance technique in our approach, actually, the partial replication scheme and the synchronization protocol can also be integrated with OT. More specifically, they can ensure right and enough information exchanged between client and server, so that a transformation can be conducted for a remote operation to be executed in a "right" address space (for AST) or in a "right" form (for OT). However, the primitive operations with global identifiers for AST, which enables efficient target nodes addressing, need to be redefined using positional parameters for OT-based partial replication.

Sync [12] is a Java framework for developing mobile collaborative applications, which allows developers to implement the merge matrix to resolve the conflicts in different applications. The main contribution of this paper is a partial replication approach, which has not been addressed in the Sync framework.

Docx2Go [16] is a framework for collaborative editing of XML-based documents on mobile devices, which is the most related work to ours from some technical perspectives. In terms of working on mobile devices anywhere anytime, our system design goal resembles that of Docx2Go. Both Docx2Go and our approach adopt partial replication to accommodate mobile devices. The major differences between our approach and Docx2Go are synchronization mechanisms, conflict resolution and consistency maintenance methods. In Docx2Go, replicas are synchronized by exchanging data of element while operations are exchanged in our system. Due to the difference in manipulated elements and structure, the conflicts in Docx2Go are manually or automatically resolved by merging two conflict versions of an element, but conflicts of tree structure manipulation will be resolved automatically in our system. For consistency maintenance, Docx2Go uses *position indicator* [24, 15] to determine a consistent order of sibling nodes, but its unbounded position indicator and version vector are not suitable for Internet-scale commenting and mobile device with limited resources. Our scalar timestamp based concurrent operation detection and efficient operation integration on server side can ensure higher scalability.

8. CONCLUSION

To address the technical challenges brought by mobile networks, we contribute a novel partial replication approach to address the responsiveness and consistency maintenance issues for anywhere anytime mobile commenting. The main technical contributions are threefold: 1) To the best of our knowledge, it is the first work of applying collaborative editing techniques to achieve high local responsiveness in mobile commenting; 2) A holistic approach for partial replication and synchronization of tree-structure comment threads are proposed; 3) A scalar timestamp based synchronization protocol is designed to meet the scalability requirements of commenting systems and users' dynamic participation.

A prototype system called Hydra was implemented to evaluate our approach. The evaluation results show that our approach is capable of providing high local responsiveness for users in high-latency networks, save bandwidth of mobile users compared with full replication approaches. And it has high efficiency and good scalability for achieving large scale commenting systems.

Existing commenting systems can leverage our approach to achieve high local responsiveness in intermittent mobile networks and do not need to worry about the issues of replication, synchronization and data consistency of comment threads. In the future, we will integrate our approach with existing commenting systems, and conduct user experience studies to better evaluate our approach from the perspective of usability.

ACKNOWLEDGMENTS

We thank Silvia Lindtner for her great help with the paper revision. The work was supported by the National Natural Science Foundation of China (NSFC) under Grants No.61272533, No.61332008, No.61300201, and Shanghai Science & Technology Committee Project under Grant No.11JC1400800 and No.13ZR1401900.

REFERENCES

1. `http://socialmediainasia.blogspot.com/2012/05/more-than-60-of-sina-weibo-active-users.html`.

2. More than talk: Action in mobile marketing. `http://www.hubspot.com/more-than-talk-action-in-mobile-marketing/`.

3. Twitter statistics - updated stats for 2011. `http://www.marketinggum.com/twitter-statistics-2011-updated-stats/`.

4. Billsus, D., Pazzani, M. J., and Chen, J. A learning agent for wireless news access. In *Proceedings of the 5th international conference on Intelligent user interfaces*, IUI '00, ACM (New York, NY, USA, 2000), 33–36.

5. Davis, A. H., Sun, C., and Lu, J. Generalizing operational transformation to the standard general markup language. In *Proceedings of the 2002 ACM conference on Computer supported cooperative work*, CSCW '02, ACM (New York, NY, USA, 2002), 58–67.

6. Ellis, C. A., and Gibbs, S. J. Concurrency control in groupware systems. In *SIGMOD '89: Proceedings of the 1989 ACM SIGMOD international conference on Management of data*, ACM (New York, NY, USA, 1989), 399–407.

7. Gu, N., Yang, J., and Zhang, Q. Consistency maintenance based on the mark & retrace technique in groupware systems. In *Proceedings of ACM GROUP'05 Conference on Supporting Group Work* (Nov. 2005), 264–273.

8. Ignat, C.-L., and Norrie, M. C. Customizable collaborative editor relying on treeopt algorithm. In *Proceedings of the eighth conference on European Conference on Computer Supported Cooperative Work*, ECSCW'03, Kluwer Academic Publishers (Norwell, MA, USA, 2003), 315–334.

9. Jiang, Z., and Kleinrock, L. Web prefetching in a mobile environment. *IEEE Personal Communications 5* (1998), 25–34.

10. Lautamäki, J., Nieminen, A., Koskinen, J., Aho, T., Mikkonen, T., and Englund, M. Cored: browser-based collaborative real-time editor for java web applications. In *Proceedings of the ACM 2012 conference on Computer Supported Cooperative Work*, CSCW '12, ACM (New York, NY, USA, 2012), 1307–1316.

11. Li, D., and Li, R. An admissibility-based operational transformation framework for collaborative editing systems. *Computer Supported Cooperative Work 19*, 1 (2010), 1–43.

12. Munson, J. P., and Dewan, P. Sync: a java framework for mobile collaborative applications. *Computer 30*, 6 (1997), 59–66.

13. Nichols, D. A., Curtis, P., Dixon, M., and Lamping, J. High-latency, low-bandwidth windowing in the jupiter collaboration system. In *UIST '95: Proceedings of the 8th annual ACM symposium on User interface and software technology* (Pittsburgh, Pennsylvania, USA, 1995), 111–120.

14. Petersen, K., Spreitzer, M. J., Terry, D. B., Theimer, M. M., and Demers, A. J. Flexible update propagation for weakly consistent replication. In *SOSP '97: Proceedings of the sixteenth ACM symposium on Operating systems principles* (New York, NY, USA, 1997), 288–301.

15. Preguiça, N., Marquès, J. M., Shapiro, M., and Leia, M. A commutative replicated data type for cooperative editing. In *29th IEEE International Conference on Distributed Computing Systems (ICDCS 2009)*, IEEE Computer Society (Montreal, Québec, Canada, 2009), 395–403.

16. Puttaswamy, K. P., Marshall, C. C., Ramasubramanian, V., Stuedi, P., Terry, D. B., and Wobber, T. Docx2go: collaborative editing of fidelity reduced documents on mobile devices. In *Proceedings of the 8th international conference on Mobile systems, applications, and services*, MobiSys '10, ACM (New York, NY, USA, 2010), 345–356.

17. Ramasubramanian, V., Rodeheffer, T. L., Terry, D. B., Walraed-Sullivan, M., Wobber, T., Marshall, C. C., and Vahdat, A. Cimbiosys: a platform for content-based partial replication. In *Proceedings of the 6th USENIX symposium on Networked systems design and implementation*, NSDI'09, USENIX Association (Berkeley, CA, USA, 2009), 261–276.

18. Saito, Y., and Shapiro, M. Optimistic replication. *ACM Computing Survey 37*, 1 (2005), 42–81.

19. Salmon, B., Schlosser, S. W., Cranor, L. F., and Ganger, G. R. Perspective: semantic data management for the home. In *Proccedings of the 7th conference on File and storage technologies*, FAST '09, USENIX Association (Berkeley, CA, USA, 2009), 167–182.

20. Shao, B., Li, D., and Gu, N. A sequence transformation algorithm for supporting cooperative work on mobile devices. In *CSCW '10: Proceedings of the 2010 ACM conference on Computer supported cooperative work* (Savannah, GA, USA, 2010).

21. Shao, B., Li, D., Lu, T., and Gu, N. An operational transformation based synchronization protocol for web 2.0 applications. In *Proceedings of the ACM 2011 conference on Computer supported cooperative work*, CSCW '11, ACM (New York, NY, USA, 2011), 563–572.

22. Shen, H., and Reilly, M. Personalized multi-user view and content synchronization and retrieval in real-time mobile social software applications. *J. Comput. Syst. Sci. 78*, 4 (2012), 1185–1203.

23. Sun, C., and Ellis, C. Operational transformation in real-time group editors: issues, algorithms, and achievements. In *Proceedings of the ACM Conference on Computer-Supported Cooperative Work* (Dec. 1998), 59–68.

24. Weiss, S., Urso, P., and Molli, P. Logoot: A scalable optimistic replication algorithm for collaborative editing on p2p networks. In *ICDCS*, IEEE Computer Society (2009), 404–412.

25. Yang, J., Wang, H., Gu, N., Liu, Y., Wang, C., and Zhang, Q. Lock-free consistency control for web 2.0 applications. In *WWW* (2008), 725–734.

26. Zhao, S., Li, D., Lu, T., and Gu, N. Back to the future: a hybrid approach to transparent sharing of video games over the internet in real time. In *Proceedings of the ACM 2011 conference on Computer supported cooperative work*, CSCW '11, ACM (New York, NY, USA, 2011), 187–196.

Monitoring Email to Indicate Project Team Performance and Mutual Attraction

Sean A. Munson
Human Centered Design & Engineering
DUB group, University of Washington
smunson@uw.edu

Karina Kervin, Lionel P. Robert Jr.
School of Information
University of Michigan
{kkervin,lprobert}@umich.edu

ABSTRACT
Many managers and mentors for project teams desire more efficient and more effective ways of monitoring and predicting the quality of social relationships and the performance of teams under their purview. A previous study [13] found that one form of linguistic mimicry, linguistic style matching, and some lexical features indicated team performance and mutual attraction in short-term, laboratory tasks. In this paper, we evaluate whether these measures also work as indicators for performance, shared understanding, and team trust in longer-duration project teams, using only limited, unobtrusively obtained communication traces. In our four-month evaluation using student project team emails, we found no support for LSM or most of the previously identified measures as practical indicators in our field setting. We did find some support for using future-oriented words to indicate team performance over time.

Author Keywords
Email, groups, workgroups, performance, LIWC, team, process, language, mimicry, trust, mutual attraction, computer-mediated communication

ACM Classification Keywords
H.5.e. Group and Organization Interfaces: Computer-supported cooperative work

INTRODUCTION
Managers and project team leaders regularly seek more accurate or more efficient ways to keep track of the health and performance of the teams they manage [19, 20]. Team members also may benefit from better awareness of their team's performance [16]. Despite the importance of team performance and functioning in many workplaces, relatively little is known about effective and unobtrusive indicators of team performance and processes [4].

CSCW'14, February 15 - 19 2014, Baltimore, MD, USA

ACM 978-1-4503-2540-0/14/02...$15.00.
http://dx.doi.org/10.1145/2531602.2531628

In efforts to find unobtrusive indicators – with respect to additional work for team members and leaders, if not with respect to privacy – several researchers have mined face-to-face or electronic communication among different types of teams or workgroups. Measures extracted from this communication, such as affect, linguistic style, coordination routines, and communication volume (number of messages or word count), have been found to be valuable indicators in such diverse teams as the electronic communication of Wikipedians [9], face-to-face interactions among teams in simulated search and rescue missions [11], and student teams [7, 6]. While some of these indicators are easily automated, others have required extensive human coding of communication logs.

Linguistic mimicry between dyads or among small teams is one particularly promising indicator that can be easily automatically extracted from communication records. Linguistic mimicry is the extent to which people align in the cognitive complexity, formality, emotionality, and/or terms in their communication [5, 22]. In a laboratory setting, Gonzales et al. used one measure of linguistic mimicry, linguistic style matching (LSM) [21], as an indicator for group cohesion and, in computer-mediated settings, team performance [13].

In this paper, we present a study that replicates Gonzales et al.'s approach [13] in the field. We evaluate LSM as an indicator of mutual attraction, operationalized as trust and shared understanding, and performance in real-world project teams whose members communicate in-person, by email, and through other channels. We chose to use team emails as the source data, restricting ourselves to data that might be reasonably obtained in a corporate or educational environment, by mining the digital traces of communication among team members as they go about their work. We selected emails because groupware that integrates with activities and tools that people already use may have lower barriers to adoption and continued use [14]. Other than an initial setup, tracking team emails requires no further work from team members. Supporting this choice, [21] notes that emails are one form of communication to which the LSM metric should be applicable. As a secondary goal, we evaluated other linguistic indicators that Gonzales et al. [13] found indicated performance or mutual attraction. This included the use of first-person plural pronouns and word count to indicate group cohesion and future- and achievement-oriented language for performance.

This study, then, is an important step toward assessing the feasibility of using LSM and other linguistic measures as indcators of performance and mutual attraction among real-world project teams. In our setting and with our collected data, we did not find that linguistic mimicry was an indicator of team trust, shared understanding, or team performance. Of the other indicators evaluated, we found only the proportion of future-oriented words to be indicative of performance and none to be indicators of team trust or shared understanding.

In the remainder of this paper, we present additional background on linguistic mimicry and the particular measure, Linguistic Style Matching (LSM), that [13] and we used, the details of our study design, our analysis, and details of our results. We then discuss the implications of these findings and conclude with ideas for future work.

RELATED WORK AND MOTIVATION

Previously, linguistic mimicry has been used as an indicator for team performance [13, 32], group cohesion [13], and trust [29]. Niederhoffer and Pennebaker propose one measure of similarity in text, Linguistic Style Matching (LSM), based on conversation participants' use of function ("content-free") words, such as adverbs, articles, auxiliary verbs, conjunctions, negations, prepositions, pronouns, and quantifiers [21]. Function words occur frequently and are context-independent, so similarity in the use of these words may be a better indicator of convergence in conversation style than similarity in use of words that are task-specific. For example, if project teams are working in different domains, their use of task-specific words may vary from project to project, but function words will be present across all communication. Similarly, function words will be present regardless of whether teams are communicating to socialize or to accomplish work [13], and so this measure can be used across messages in which participants are catching up about the weekend, planning a bonding happy hour, planning tasks for an upcoming deliverable, or sharing thoughts about the content of that deliverable.

In a short-duration lab experiment, Gonzales et al. found that groups' LSM scores were correlated with self-reported measures of group cohesion in both face-to-face (FTF) and computer mediated (CMC) contexts and are correlated with performance in the FTF, but not the CMC, context [13]. In the same study, Gonzales et al. also found a positive correlation between future-oriented words and performance, a negative correlation between achievement oriented words and performance, a positive correlation between word count and team cohesiveness, and a negative relationship between use of first-person plural pronouns and team cohesiveness. While this work is promising, we were curious if we could reproduce these results in a setting that is more authentic for many types of collaboration: longer-duration, real-world tasks in which participants communicate across diverse media, only some of which is unobtrusively observable.

We are not the first to study the application of the LSM measure to real-world settings or tasks. LSM, alongside other measurements, has been used to provide real-time feedback that has improved the performance of poorly functioning classroom teams [31]. In another context, higher LSM between hostage takers and hostage negotiators has been found to be correlated with successful outcomes [32].

In this study, we evaluated the potential of LSM as an indicator of team performance, team trust, and shared understanding in project teams whose members communicate in-person, by email, and through other channels. We further restricted ourselves to data that might be reasonably obtained in a corporate or educational environment, simply by mining the digital traces of communication among team members as they go about their work. Prior work has shown that mining online discussion patterns can indicate students' performance and retention [6]. Unlike [6], however, we study communication only among project group members and analyze the content of that communication, rather than the network of communication among an entire class of students. Our outcomes are also at the group, rather than individual, level.

We sought to replicate Gonzales et al.'s study of LSM [13] among teams working on longer-term projects with greater authenticity to the workplace. We also wanted to be able to distinguish between two forms of cohesiveness, or mutual attraction, among teams: shared understanding and team trust. Thus, we designed a study to test the following hypotheses about LSM's value as an indicator:

- **H1a.** Higher LSM will correlate to greater team trust.
- **H1b.** Higher LSM will correlate to greater team shared understanding.
- **H2.** Higher LSM will correlate to greater team performance on class assignments.

We also developed hypotheses based on the other linguistic indicators identified by Gonzales et al. [13], again dividing team cohesiveness into team trust and shared understanding:

- **H3a.** A lower proportion of first-person plural pronouns will correlate with greater team trust.
- **H3b.** A lower proportion of first-person plural pronouns will correlate with greater shared understanding.
- **H4a.** Greater word count overall will correlate with greater team trust.
- **H4b.** Greater word count overall will correlate with greater shared understanding.
- **H5.** A higher proportion of future-oriented words will correlate with higher performance.
- **H6.** A higher proportion of achievement-oriented words will correlate with lower performance.

If these hypotheses were to be supported – indicating that [13]'s measures work for longer-term communication routines in complex teams – these indicators could be useful for efforts to build dashboards that give managers, mentors, teams, and team members visibility of and feedback on their performance, processes, and communication styles (e.g., [15, 3]). Such dashboards have historically been more limited to providing feedback on specific, shorter-duration interactions, even when used among longer term project teams (e.g., [10, 18, 31]).

STUDY DESIGN

We chose to evaluate LSM's ability to indicate team performance, trust, and shared understanding among groups in an introductory masters-level course at the University of Michigan School of Information. In this course, students are assigned to groups of four to six students (in one team, three) to work on a semester-long project. Each project team is assigned to an external client who has an information-centric process. Each team is tasked with interviewing client stakeholders, identifying themes in the interview data, modeling the client's process, and providing recommendations to improve the client's process.

The selection of this site and context was advantageous for several reasons. First, each team worked on an authentic project, yet each project was bounded in time to one semester. Each project team earned several grades over the course of the semester, including a final report grade, which could be used as performance measures.

At the beginning of the Fall 2012 semester, we introduced the study to teams during a class session. Afterwards, they had the opportunity to review the informed consent materials and decide whether to participate. Each participating project team created a group mailing list and was instructed to add a unique email address, supplied by the research team, as a subscriber to this list. Email sent to that address would be accessed by our data analysis scripts. Students were asked to carbon-copy that address on any email communication they sent off-list, including communication between individuals on the team. Researchers and instructors informed the students that the instructors would never have access to the email sent to this address, and that copying this list on email between team members would earn students one point of extra credit in the course.

There were 44 project teams in this course. 30 project teams, including a total of 137 subjects, participated in this study. One of these teams did not continue automated email address in their communication after the second week, and so they are excluded from the data analysis and result. Additionally, in two further teams, only one or two team members appeared to reliably use the automated email address in their communication (with less than four emails from some team members), so we excluded those teams as well. This left 27 project teams and a total of 124 students (50 men and 74 women). Most teams were gender-balanced or approximately gender-balanced, but two teams were all-female, two teams were 75% female, and two teams were 25% female. From these 27 teams, we collected and analyzed 6993 emails (after excluding automated messages, messages from the team's clients, and messages from instructors), an average of 259 emails per team. We were unable to collect emails that team members sent to each other individually rather than by using the distribution list. Typically, email collection began late in the second week or early in the third week of the semester.

We were also concerned that there may be a self-selection confound in this study: perhaps deciding to participate in the study in a timely manner was indicative of a well-functioning team, which would mean that our data did not include LSM scores from low-performing teams. To check for this confound, we compared the course grades from participating teams to the grades for teams not participating and found no differences in either the mean or distribution of scores.

Measures

Our analysis was conducted at the team level, using demographics of the teams, the emails to the distribution list, a survey that included measures of trust and shared understanding, and their assignment grades. Participants completed surveys individually. We distributed the survey electronically after the end of the semester; students had received their final grades by the time they took the survey.

Linguistic Mimicry

In addition to our focus on real–world, 14-week semester–long projects, a notable difference from Gonzales et al.'s study is that they used transcripts of synchronous communication as an input in both the CMC and FTF conditions, while we use asynchronous communication (email) as the input. The emails were analyzed according to the LSM approach described in [13]. To summarize, Gonzales et al. input transcripts of interactions (in our case, emails) into the Linguistic Inquiry and Word Count (LIWC) language analysis tool [23], which is capable of outputting word counts for specific categories of words, including function words. LIWC is used to measure the frequency with which each group member uses nine types of function words: auxiliary verbs (e.g., can, has, am), articles (e.g., a, an, the), personal pronouns (e.g., her, I, we, they, you), indefinite pronouns (e.g., anyone, someone, others), prepositions (e.g., about, at, unless, till), negations (e.g., not, never, nor, nowhere, without), conjunctions (e.g. also, though, but, while), and quantifiers (e.g., all, besides, best, worst, some). For each of the nine categories c, the percentage of an individual n's total words ($p_{c,n}$) was calculated, as well as the percentage of the group's total words (p_{Gc}). This allows the calculation of an individual's similarity against the group, per word category, as

$$LSM_{c,n} = 1 - \frac{|p_{c,n} - p_{Gc}|}{p_{c,n} + p_{Gc}}$$

The group G's average for category c is the average of the individual scores:

$$LSM_{Gc} = \frac{\sum_{n \in G} LSM_{c,n}}{|G|}$$

And the LSM across the nine categories is simply:

$$LSM_G = \frac{\sum_{c=1}^{9} LSM_{Gc}}{9}$$

Moving from face-to-face or computer mediated chats to emails required deciding which text to input into this analysis process. We excluded automated emails sent from collaboration tools (e.g., Google Docs or the University's course management system), emails sent from the client organization, and emails sent from the instruction team. Within each email, we excluded quoted reply text and signature lines. Emails sent after the last assignment was due were excluded.

Mutual Attraction

To measure team cohesion, prior researchers [13, 31] have used the Interaction Rating Questionnaire (IRQ). The IRQ was developed for experiments studying linguistic style matching [21] in specific, temporally-bounded interactions (e.g., a chat). Because we were assessing interactions over the course of a semester, we did not feel the IRQ was the most appropriate measure for our study.

We instead looked to other measures of team cohesion or mutual attraction. We also wanted to be able to distinguish which components of mutual attraction LSM indicates. LSM is thought to be a useful indicator in part because mimicry represents improved shared understanding [12, 13]. Researchers have also commonly used team trust as a measure of mutual attraction [26, 27], and it has been found to be a primary factor in team cohesion [8]. Thus, we chose to include short measures for team trust and shared understanding in the survey. We selected:

- **Team Trust**: four items from Simons and Peterson [30].
- **Shared Understanding**: five items from Ko, Kirsch, and King [17].

We had also intended for the survey to include a three item measure of team cohesion, not differentiated as team trust and shared understanding. A survey configuration error prevented these questions from being displayed.

We also added disposition to trust as a control variable for use in models indicating trust. This was based on a six-item measure from Schoorman, Mayer, and Davis [28].

Task Performance

To measure task performance, we collected the team's grades on each of the four group assignments on which there was variance in grading (i.e., not the assignments that were simply credit/no credit). These assignments included a model of the process the team was studying, an affinity diagram and walkthrough, a final presentation, and a final report. All analyses were conducted without including the extra credit received for participation in this study.

RESULTS

In all of the following analyses, we controlled for group size and sex (measured as percentage of the team who was male), which were also control variables in [13]. Because grades and instruction were determined in part by the teaching assistant who taught the team's course section, we evaluated whether we should control for each team's assigned teaching assistant. After finding no differences in the distributions of grades between teaching assistants, we elected to drop this control variable out of concern that its inclusion (there were six teaching assistants and thus five dummy variables) would lead to overfitting of the models.

Linguistic Style Matching

We evaluated LSM as an indicator for both mutual attraction and team performance. Teams' LSMs varied from 0.822 to 0.94 ($\mu = 0.90$, median $= 0.90$).

H1. Mutual attraction

Based on Gonzales et al.'s findings, we expected to find that LSM was indicative of the two measures for mutual attraction we collected: shared understanding and team trust. We constructed OLS regression models with shared understanding and trust as dependent variables and our control variables and LSM as the independent variables. As one would expect, a greater disposition to trust indicated higher reported trust among teams ($\beta = 0.79$ ($p < 0.001$); $F = 3.854$ ($p < 0.05$) adjusted $R^2 = 0.26$), and so we also included disposition to trust as a control variable in our model for LSM based on team trust.

LSM was not a statistically significant indicator for either shared understanding or team trust, and observed effects were in the opposite direction of what was hypothesized. Thus, we did not find support for H1a or H1b.

H2. Performance

We next assessed whether a group's LSM score is indicative of their overall performance. We operationalized each group's performance as the overall score of all of the group's assignments ($p_{overall}$), weighted according to how course grades were determined. Participating teams' overall scores varied between 48.2 and 53.1 ($\mu = 50.8$, stdev$= 1.3$); the maximum possible was 55). We constructed OLS linear regression models for performance as a function of the LSM score, controlling for team size and sex. LSM was not a significant indicator of performance in either of these models. Furthermore, the observed effect of a 0.01 increase in LSM was -0.04 (95% confidence interval: -0.27 to 0.18).

Other Linguistic Indicators

We then tested the other linguistic indicators that Gonzales et al. [13] identified for cohesion and performance.

We first tested the indicators [13] identified for cohesion. We generated separate OLS models that indicated shared understanding and team trust based on word count, word count per person (since our teams varied in size), and proportion of first person plural pronouns. There did not appear to be effects of any meaningful size and none were statistically significant, and so we find no support for hypotheses H3a, H3b, H4a, or H4b.

We then tested the indicators that Gonzales et al. [13] identified for team performance. In their study, a higher proportion of achievement words negatively indicated performance and that a higher proportion of future-oriented words positively indicated performance.

Among the teams in our study, the proportion of future-oriented words was a positive indicator for the overall score (Table 1). A 1% increase in use of future-oriented words would correspond to a 1.6 point increase in overall score (95% confidence interval: 0.5 - 2.25 points). We also checked this effect on each of the assignments that comprise the overall score. It was a positive indicator for the modeling assignment (A1) and affinity diagram and walkthrough grades (A2). It was not an indicator for scores on the final report (A3)

Table 1. OLS models for team grades on different assignments as indicated by proportion of future-oriented words used.

	$S_{overall}$			S_{A1}			S_{A2}			S_{A3}			S_{A4}		
	B	SE	p	B	SE	p	B	SE	p	B	SE	p			
Intercept	51.30	2.44		95.10	7.22		90.60	5.17		92.18	6.27		90.86	7.11	
Team size	-0.43	0.39	n.s.	-1.89	1.77	n.s.	-0.81	0.78	n.s.	0.19	1.02	n.s.	0.17	1.16	n.s.
Prop. Male	-3.38	1.26	n.s.	-8.25	3.72	0.037	-4.63	2.49	0.080	-6.23	3.23	0.07	-7.25	3.67	0.06
Prop. Future-oriented words	163.90	57.56	0.01	381.74	164.22	0.029	351.44	112.47	0.005	60.48	142.80	n.s.	186.09	161.88	n.s.
Adjusted R^2	0.36			0.27			0.54			0.03			0.05		
F-statistic on 3 & 23 dof	2.90		0.06	4.28		0.015	4.92		0.008	1.25		n.s.	1.46		n.s.

and presentation (A4). Additionally, a more conservative approach of applying a family-wise correction (and inflating the standard errors) would cause all confidence intervals to include zero, eliminating this effect. Thus, we find limited support for H5, that use of a higher proportion of future-oriented words indicates higher team performance, but use of this metric in this context merits further investigation.

In our data, the proportion of achievement words was not a indicator of performance, and thus we find no support for H6.

LIMITATIONS

Our context deviated in many ways from that tested by Gonzales et al. [13]. Their study used synchronous communication in a short-term (20 minute) task with answers that were verifiably correct or incorrect. All groups were same sex. Teams were 4-6 people. While our teams were similarly sized, they were mixed-sex. The project was a semester (14 weeks) in duration. The instruction team evaluated performance (according to rubrics and example assignments), and performance was subject to outside factors such as the specific problem and each team's clients' support and cooperation. We also were only able to capture a small portion (the email) of each team's communication. We chose this context as it was highly authentic and similar – apart from the performance evaluation – to how teams in many organizations function: similarly sized, working on similar but non-identical tasks, for different clients or stakeholders.

Because we deviated in many ways from the original experiment, it is not possible to determine which of these dimensions cause LSM to be a less effective indicator in this context. Future work may wish to systematically explore different dimensions – variance in specific project, task duration, whether the task is verifiably true or false or allows for more creativity, team size, team composition, communication synchronicity, and completeness of captured communication – and when LSM is or is not a indicator for team process and performance, either in the lab or in the wild. Finally, by having only measures for two aspects of mutual understanding or team cohesion – team trust and shared understanding – and not an overall measure for team cohension, it is possible that our study failed to measure some element of team cohesion for which LSM would have been an indicator.

We also chose student teams as a proxy for workplace teams. This allowed us to use grades as a standardized performance measure and offered considerable control for factors such as project duration and specific deliverables (since all had the same assignments and schedule). While our student teams had many similarities to many workplace teams – they worked with different, client organizations to make recommendations addressing clients' real problems – they are not the same as workplace teams. Our teams, for example, had their deliverables determined by an outside, third party (the instructors), and their primary goal was learning, with solving clients' problems as a secondary goal. This is a limitation of this study, but one that makes us still more skeptical that LSM and the other measures in [13] are appropriate for longer-term, real-world teams. If these measures are not good indicators even among such controlled teams and tasks, what potential do they have for more diverse projects?

DISCUSSION

Our work does not suggest that the combination of LSM and automatic email harvesting from project teams is an effective tool for monitoring teams' cohesion (H1a, H1b) and indicating performance (H2). We do find some support for using the proportion of future oriented words to indicate team performance. Further work may still be warranted to see whether our results hold in other settings, such as project teams in actual workplaces. Additionally, we believe that this approach should be explored for indicating the performance of open source software teams, for whom the majority of communication occurs electronically, and would be less subject to our inability to collect face-to-face or phone communication.

LSM

We found no support for using LSM to indicate mutual attraction or performance among student teams engaged in real-world projects over the duration of a semester. This suggests at least one important limit to the practical applications of LSM.

While our study had limited power and we cannot reject the idea that LSM measured in asynchronous communication correlates with team performance or mutual attraction in longer-term teams, we are skeptical that LSM is a practical measure for the type of data and teams that we examined. A study with more teams would give more statistical power, but even if it were to identify a correlation between LSM and performance, it is likely that this correlation is too small to be practically useful. Furthermore, in even less-controlled settings, it seems like any effect would be lost among other variables for which we cannot adequately control. While past work suggests that LSM is a valuable indicator in many types of interactions, the teams' work on projects in our study does not appear to be one of them. Future research may inform whether this limitation is because this context has too many uncontrolled factors (e.g., differences in clients being studied), email logs are too limited of a signal when teams are also communicating through other channels, a semester is too long of a period for LSM to be applicable, or some other reason.

Exploration: LSM over time

Seeking explanations for our negative result, we were curious whether a semester was too long of a period for LSM to be valuable. Perhaps all teams eventually converge, and what matters is their rate of convergence, or how much the team's language converges. Thus, we explored whether mimicry increased over time, operationalized as whether teams' LSM scores were higher at the end of the semester than at the start. In a paired t-test, LSM scores were no higher in the second half of the semester than the first half, or in the last quarter of the semester than the first quarter. Observed differences were very small (0.005 and 0.008, respectively, and with little variance), so even if our test was under-powered, any actual change over time is likely negligible. This would be consistent with findings that style matching occurs very quickly (in a matter of seconds in face-to-face interactions) [22].

Had we observed changes in LSM over the semester, we would have been curious if the changes (rather than raw score) indicated our measures of mutual attraction or performance. As a further check, we analyzed the emails from the two weeks before each group assignment's due date to see if the LSM score from this more limited set of messages was an indicator of short-term performance: the grade on that particular assignment. These models were also not indicative of performance.

Future-oriented words

A higher proportion of future-oriented words used in team messages was indicative of higher team performance, as it was in [13]. This is consistent with other findings that future-oriented attitudes or scenarios can indicate performance (e.g. [25, 33]), but the ability to detect this in limited, text-based behavior traces is exciting. Though we do not fully understand its limits, the robustness of this result across two different studies and contexts is notable. With further refinement, this measure may be suitable for use in team dashboards or to provide visibility of potential performance issues to management.

There are, however, many questions that remain to be answered. How robust is this result? Why was it a indicator for early assignments but not later assignments? Our study does not offer an explanation, but earlier work encourages some speculation. The theory of achievement motivation [24, 25] predicts that the effects of future-oriented scenarios are greater when success at the current task is perceived to be an immediate prerequisite for future success. Our teams may have perceived success on the earlier assignments to be a prerequisite for success on the latter assignments - i.e., they would not be able to produce good quality final reports if they were not able to produce good process models (A1) or affinity diagrams (A2) - but not have perceived success on the final assignments as a prerequisite for any future success. This does not explain the indicative ability of future oriented words in [13], though, as their tasks had no dependencies. We hope that future research will address these questions.

Obtrusiveness

We selected email because it was practical to collect and fairly unobtrusive on teams' work practices. Beyond adding the collection email address to their distribution list and remembering to use that distribution list, this approach required no additional work from team members. Of the 30 teams that opted-in to the study, 27 appear to have remembered to use the distribution list in at least a substantial portion of their email communication, suggesting that our assumptions were reasonable.

Our study does not, however, address how intrusive such a monitoring system is from a privacy or autonomy perspective. While a production-system could further protect users' privacy by consuming emails as they are received – storing only word counts – rather than storing messages to be analyzed post-hoc, as they were in our study, team members may still resist such a system. There is a long history of workers perceiving performance monitoring as intrusive or diminishing their autonomy [2]. If dashboards are to be built to indicate team performance or process based on email or other communication traces, there remains a question of whether the project team members will be willing to allow their email to be monitored in this way, or whether such an application is "snoopware" [1] that people would choose to avoid. Future research should address this question before such systems are built and deployed.

CONCLUSION

This study contributes to the literature by evaluating indicators previously found to be valuable for indicating team performance and cohesion in the lab in a field setting, among real-world teams and over a three-month project. We were optimistic that LSM and the other indicators identified in [13] would prove to be useful indicators of team performance, shared understanding, or trust in the field. Had this turned out to be the case, it would have opened the door for management dashboards or other tools to monitor team performance and functioning based on these measures.

Instead, we find no support for using the majority of indicators identified by Gonzales et al. [13]. There are many possible reasons for this, some of which we discuss above. While this is disappointing from a practical standpoint, it helps to better understand in which situations and for what LSM and other metrics may or may not be useful indicators.

We also found that one measure – proportion of future-oriented words used – which indicated team performance in a short-term, lab setting may also indicate team performance in a semester-long educational setting, but not for all assignments. Due to the limitations of this study, these results should receive further scrutiny in future research. Future work should also explore conditions in between those we tested and those tested by Gonzales et al. to better understand the limits of these measures and why they do or do not work in different contexts.

ACKNOWLEDGEMENTS

We thank to the students and instructors who helped make this experiment possible. This study also benefited from feedback from participants in the Social Computing seminar in Fall 2009, especially Paul Resnick and Eytan Bakshy. Anonymous reviewers' comments and suggestions substantially improved this manuscript.

REFERENCES

1. Allen, J. Groupware and social reality. *Computers Society 22*, 1-4 (1992), 24–28.
2. Ball, K., and Wilson, D. C. Power, control and computer-based performance monitoring: Repertoires, resistance and subjectivities. *Organization Studies 21*, 3 (2000), 539–565.
3. Biehl, J. T., Czerwinski, M., Smith, G., and Robertson, G. G. Fastdash: a visual dashboard for fostering awareness in software teams. In *Proceedings of the SIGCHI Conference on Human Factors in Computing Systems*, CHI '07, ACM (New York, NY, USA, 2007), 1313–1322.
4. Brannick, M. T., and Prince, C. W. An overview of team performance measurement. In *Team Performance Assessment and Measurement: Theory, Methods, and Applications*, M. T. Brannick, E. Salas, and C. W. Prince, Eds. Lawrence Erlbaum, Mahwah, New Jersey, 1997.
5. Brennan, S. E., and Clark, H. H. Conceptual pacts and lexical choice in conversation. *Journal of Experimental Psychology: Learning, Memory, and Cognition 22*, 6 (1996), 1482.
6. Chen, G., Wang, C., and Ou, K. Using group communication to monitor web-based group learning. *Journal of Computer Assisted Learning 19*, 4 (2003), 401–415.
7. Chioccio, F. Project team performance: A study of electronic task and coordination communication. *Project Management Journal 38*, 1 (2007), 97–109.
8. Cohen, S. G., and Bailey, D. E. What makes teams work: Group effectiveness research from the shop floor to the executive suite. *Journal of Management 23*, 3 (1997), 239–290.
9. Danescu-Niculescu-Mizil, C., Lee, L., Pang, B., and Kleinberg, J. Echoes of power: language effects and power differences in social interaction. In *Proceedings of the 21st international conference on World Wide Web*, WWW '12, ACM (New York, NY, USA, 2012), 699–708.
10. DiMicco, J., and Bender, W. Group reactions to visual feedback tools. In *Persuasive Technology*, Y. Kort, W. IJsselsteijn, C. Midden, B. Eggen, and B. Fogg, Eds., vol. 4744 of *Lecture Notes in Computer Science*. Springer Berlin Heidelberg, 2007, 132–143.
11. Fischer, U., McDonnell, L., and Orasanu, J. Linguistic correlates of team performance: Toward a tool for monitoring team functioning during space missions. *Aviation, Space, and Environmental Medicine 78*, 1 (2007), 86–B95.
12. Giles, H., and Coupland, N. *Language: Contexts and consequences*. Thomson Brooks/Cole Publishing Co, 1991.
13. Gonzales, A. L., Hancock, J. T., and Pennebaker, J. W. Language style matching as a predictor of social dynamics in small groups. *Communication Research 37*, 1 (2009), 3–19.
14. Grudin, J. Groupware and social dynamics: Eight challenges for developers. *Communications of the ACM 37*, 1 (1994), 92–105.
15. Grudin, J., and Poole, E. S. Wikis at work: success factors and challenges for sustainability of enterprise wikis. In *Proceedings of the 6th International Symposium on Wikis and Open Collaboration*, WikiSym '10, ACM (New York, NY, USA, 2010), 5:1–5:8.
16. Hacker, M. E., and Lang, J. D. Designing a performance measurement system for a high technology virtual engineering team a case study. *Integrated Manufacturing Systems 2*, 3 (1999), 225–232.
17. Ko, D.-G., Kirsch, L. J., and King, W. R. Antecedents of knowledge transfer from consultants to clients in enterprise system implementations. *MIS Quarterly 29*, 1 (2005), pp. 59–85.
18. Leshed, G., Perez, D., Hancock, J. T., Cosley, D., Birnholtz, J., Lee, S., McLeod, P. L., and Gay, G. Visualizing real-time language-based feedback on teamwork behavior in computer-mediated groups. In *Proceedings of the SIGCHI Conference on Human Factors in Computing Systems*, CHI '09, ACM (New York, NY, USA, 2009), 537–546.
19. MacBryde, J., and Mendibil, K. Designing performance measurement systems for teams: theory and practice. *Management Decision 41*, 8 (2003), 722–733.
20. Meyer, C. How the right measures help teams excel. *Harvard Business Review*, 5 (1994), 95–103.
21. Niederhoffer, K. G., and Pennebaker, J. W. Linguistic style matching in social interaction. *Journal of Language and Social Psychology 21* (2002), 337–360.
22. Pennebaker, J. W. *The Secret Life of Pronouns: What Our Words Say About Us*. Bloomsbury Press, 2013.
23. Pennebaker, J. W., Booth, R. J., and Francis, M. E. Linguistic inquiry and word count (LIWC): A computerized text analysis program, 2007.
24. Raynor, J. O. Future orientation and motivation of immediate activity: An elaboration of the theory of achievment motivation. *Psychological Review 76*, 6 (1969), 606–610.
25. Raynor, J. O., and Rubin, I. S. Effects of achievement motivation and future orientation on level of performance. *Journal of Personality and Social Psychology 17*, 1 (1971), 36–41.

26. Robert, L. P., Dennis, A. R., and Ahuja, M. Social capital and knowledge integration in digitally enabled teams. *Information Systems Research 19*, 3, 314–334.

27. Robert, L. P., Dennis, A. R., and Hung, C. Individual swift trust and knowledge-based trust in face to face and virtual team members. *Journal of Management Information Systems 26*, 2 (2009), 241–279.

28. Schoorman, F. D., Mayer, R. C., and Davis, J. H. Organizational trust: Philosophical perspectives and conceptual definitions. *The Academy of Management Review 21*, 2 (1996), 337–340.

29. Scissors, L. E., Gill, A. J., and Gergle, D. Linguistic mimicry and trust in text-based cmc. In *Proceedings of the 2008 ACM conference on Computer supported cooperative work*, CSCW '08, ACM (New York, NY, USA, 2008), 277–280.

30. Simons, T. L., and Peterson, R. S. Task conflict and relationship conflict in top management teams: The pivotal role of intragroup trust. *Journal of Applied Psychology 85*, 1 (Feb. 2000), 102–111.

31. Tausczik, Y. R., and Pennebaker, J. W. Improving teamwork using real-time language feedback. *CHI 2013* (2013), 459–468.

32. Taylor, P. J., and Thomas, S. Linguistic style matching and negotiation outcome. *Negotiation and Conflict Management Research 1*, 3 (2008), 263–281.

33. Weitzenkorn, S. D. An adjusted measure of achievement motivation for males and females and effects of future orientation on level of performance. *Journal of Research in Personality 8*, 4 (1974), 361–377.

Editing Beyond Articles: Diversity & Dynamics of Teamwork in Open Collaborations

Jonathan T. Morgan
Wikimedia Foundation
San Francisco, CA USA
jmorgan@wikimedia.org

Michael Gilbert[1], David W. McDonald[2], Mark Zachry[1]
[1]Human Centered Design & Engineering
[2]The Information School
University of Washington Seattle, WA USA
{mdg, dwmc, zachry} @uw.edu

ABSTRACT
We report a study of Wikipedia in which we use a mixed-methods approach to understand how participation in specialized workgroups called WikiProjects has changed over the life of the encyclopedia. While previous work has analyzed the work of WikiProjects in supporting the development of articles within particular subject domains, the collaborative role of WikiProjects that do not fit this conventional mold has not been empirically examined. We combine content analysis, interviews and analysis of edit logs to identify and characterize these alternative WikiProjects and the work they do. Our findings suggest that WikiProject participation reflects community concerns and shifts in the community's conception of valued work over the past six years. We discuss implications for other open collaborations that need flexible, adaptable coordination mechanisms to support a range of content creation, curation and community maintenance tasks.

Author Keywords
Wikipedia; group work; group dynamics; open collaboration

ACM Classification Keywords
H.5.3 [Information Interfaces and Presentation]: Group and Organization Interfaces – Computer-supported cooperative work

General Terms
Human Factors, Theory, Measurement

INTRODUCTION
The Internet has fostered many new ways for volunteers to organize around a common cause, but few of these initiatives have had the longevity or impact of Wikipedia. Wikipedia is one of the most visibly successful examples of large-scale, open collaboration. The English language edition has been a hive of activity for the past 10 years, with tens of thousands of regular contributors logging in each month to build and maintain the encyclopedia. The community around Wikipedia has certainly changed over that time. While Wikipedia's readership and article base has grown steadily, its active contributor base, which grew exponentially until late 2007, has ebbed in recent years [30][14]. Yet even with that ebb, tens of thousands of dedicated editors still contribute to Wikipedia, working together to coordinate their activities.

CSCW'14, February 15–19, 2014, Baltimore, Maryland, USA.

ACM 978-1-4503-2540-0/14/02...$15.00.
http://dx.doi.org/10.1145/2531602.2531654

One key type of coordination is the WikiProject. A WikiProject is a collaborative effort organized around topic areas of interest or specific work activities. Previous research has shown that WikiProjects can play an important role in coordinating different tasks around editing Wikipedia articles. WikiProjects can also serve important social functions for those involved, who often become both more productive and more engaged in the editing community [16][11]. In this respect WikiProjects fill similar roles to work groups, teams and task forces in other settings, from World of Warcraft guilds [27] and Open Source software development projects [8] to offline groups [1].

Previous studies of WikiProjects present a compelling but incomplete picture. They have tended to focus on projects that coordinate work around particular encyclopedia topics (like military history, medicine, or feminism), on the largest and most active projects, and on project activities during Wikipedia's growth years. However, research on other online collaborations [15][20][25] suggest that teams within the same system vary greatly in the work they do and the ways they organize their work. Furthermore, both the teams themselves and the nature of the work they perform can change over time. The evolution of other coordinating structures on Wikipedia such as community policies [2][14] suggest that WikiProjects likewise have the potential to adapt to environmental shifts. How the universe of WikiProjects has changed in response to the changing environment in Wikipedia has not been examined.

Investigating how WikiProjects have adapted to environmental change can inform our understanding of the specialized work activities necessary to maintain a mature peer production community. It may also reveal patterns of participation that illustrate shifts in the community's priorities and work activities, and provide new insights into how open collaborations adapt and persist during periods of change. This could inform the design of tools to encourage participation in other open collaborations, and help designers and community managers address shifts in member activity and motivation [28].

In this paper, we analyze 978 WikiProjects that have achieved sustained activity at some point in Wikipedia's history. Our investigation combines interviews with Wikipedia editors, content analysis of WikiProject pages, and quantitative analysis of edit logs between 2002 and 2012. To characterize the diversity of work activities coordinated through WikiProjects, we draw a distinction between *conventional* WikiProjects that are generally scoped around an encyclopedic topic and focus on coordinating article editing tasks, and *alternative* WikiProjects in which the project scope and/or primary tasks differ significantly from the conventional model. Our analysis unpacks key relationships between the creation of and participation in alternative WikiProjects, environmental changes within Wikipedia, and the editing community's perceptions of valued work. We close with a discussion of the current role of alternative WikiProjects in Wikipedia and present implications for supporting a wide range of specialized workgroups in other open collaborations.

BACKGROUND AND RELATED WORK

Two key challenges for open collaborations are helping potential contributors find productive and engaging ways to get involved and ensuring sustained productivity and project maintenance despite low levels of member commitment and rapid member turnover [10]. Open collaboration systems address these challenges by *keeping barriers to participation low* and by *supporting the development of persistent social structures*. Low barriers to participation help assure that community members who leave are replaced by a steady stream of new contributors, and persistent social structures help organize and integrate contributions and maintain a sense of community and continuity.

One of the ways that Wikipedia keeps its barriers low is by allowing editors to decide for themselves where, when, how, and how much they will edit. In order to ensure that these contributors and their contributions are successfully integrated, the Wikipedia community has developed a variety of social structures—such as community rules and awards—and embedded them into the website itself. Over time, these social structures have proliferated and developed complex internal structures and inter-relationships as community members adapt and refine them to better suit community needs or address new community concerns.

WikiProjects are a prime example of a persistent, community-created social structure that addresses the challenges of open collaboration. Since the first WikiProjects were created in 2002, thousands of projects have been founded and tens of thousands of Wikipedia

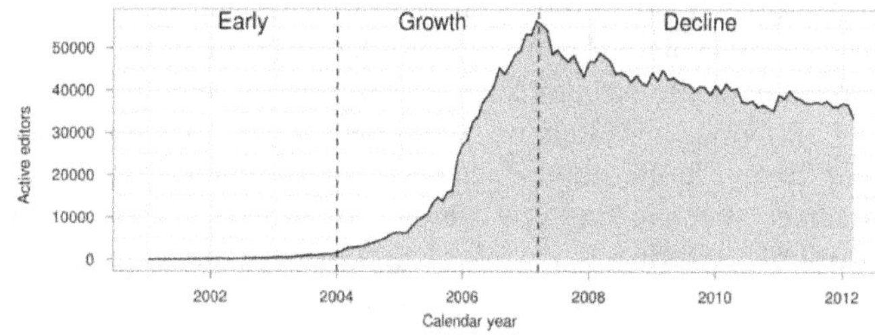

Figure 1. Rise and decline of active Wikipedia editors. Source: Wikimedia Commons *The_English_Wikipedia_Decline.png*

editors have participated. WikiProjects come in all sizes: some projects may host dozens or even hundreds of participants within a single month, while others only have a handful of members. Despite an overall decline in active editors on the English Wikipedia since 2007, hundreds of WikiProjects are still active in 2013 [39].

One reason WikiProjects have flourished may be that they resemble Wikipedia as a whole in their openness and flexibility. Each project is a relatively autonomous and informal entity with no official control over the domain of wikiwork it focuses on [11]. Anyone can create a new WikiProject around any work activity they think is important, and others can participate in that project in whatever way they choose [23]. Within these broad parameters, different WikiProjects are free to develop their own individualized strategies for motivating members and coordinating work.

A lot of the useful work on Wikipedia does not involve writing encyclopedia articles. Kriplean et al. [18] found that editors give one another specialized awards called Barnstars to recognize a variety of valuable contributions beyond editing articles: from meta-work such as developing specialized tools, to work that sustains the community such as conflict mediation. Barnstars are also awarded to recognize positive personal qualities like leadership or civility reflected in the performance of work. Given the broad leeway that WikiProjects have in the work they focus on and the way they organize, it is reasonable to expect that different projects also exhibit a degree of specialization and address valuable work beyond editing articles.

The work that is most valuable to Wikipedia may have changed over the course of its 12-year history. In particular, the decreasing rate of new article creation and article development over the past six years has potential ramifications for WikiProjects that focus on major topics, which may now direct more of their energy towards curating existing content than creating new content. Furthermore, the Wikipedia community's growing awareness of other emerging concerns seems to be reflected in the names of newer projects such as *WikiProject Editor Retention* and *WikiProject Cooperation*.

In order to understand the ways Wikiprojects may have adapted it is necessary to examine the diversity of projects and project work. Studies of FLOSS projects have shown that both the size of a project and the nature of its work are reflected in the structure and activities of the project [15, 37]. Previous research on WikiProjects has demonstrated that many large, topic-focused projects have developed diverse mechanisms to fulfill members' needs and coordinate editing work. We believe that smaller projects and projects that focus on alternative forms of work may exhibit even greater diversity.

Several previous studies have examined the work productivity of WikiProjects—operationalized as the number of edits made by project members to articles within the project's topical scope. Kittur et al. [16] examined the impact of project membership on users' editing behavior in a set of 73 topic-focused WikiProjects and found that editors who joined a project became more productive Wikipedians, communicated more with other editors, and engaged in 'good citizenship' activities like reverting vandalism to articles at a higher rate. A series of studies led by Chen [4] and Wang [34] that investigated the relationship between the group structure and work productivity in more than 300 topic-focused WikiProjects found that projects with a mix of veteran editors and relative newcomers made more edits to articles. However, the work productivity of veteran editors in these projects declined significantly more quickly than that of younger editors. The authors suggest that the decline in veteran productivity may be due to these editors taking on community maintenance and coordination roles within the project that were not counted as work in their analysis.

Several other studies have shown that such coordination work is important to a project's productivity. In a study of 310 topic-focused WikiProjects on the French Wikipedia, Ung & Dalle [32] demonstrated a correlation between coordination activity on the project talk page and 'bursts' of editing activity on project-related articles. Supporting Wang et al.'s post-hoc hypothesis on the importance of coordination work, they found that in the majority of cases there was little intersection between a project's most active content producers and its most active coordinators. A study by Zhu et al. [38] found that Collaborations of the Week (COTWs), structured editing events organized by some WikiProjects, were effective at mobilizing project participants to edit articles together, and that participating in a COTW also boosted editors' subsequent productivity.

Other studies describe WikiProjects as a site of both coordination work and social interaction. Two studies led by Forte [9,11] based on interviews with 15 members of *WikiProject Military History* detail a variety of sophisticated coordination mechanisms that that project had developed such as a project newsletter, specialized task lists and task forces, and topic-specific article formatting guidelines and article assessment criteria. They also found that members appreciated *Military History* for its social functions: participating provided opportunities to find new collaborators, get expert help, protect and advertise their work, and network socially.

While these studies demonstrate that the role of WikiProjects extends beyond production work, it is not known whether the projects previously studied reflect the range of coordination mechanisms and group dynamics among the hundreds of other projects on Wikipedia. For example, WikiProject participants interviewed in Krieger et al. [17] stated that they seldom referred to project task lists when deciding what to work on, and suggested that COTWs were often unsuccessful at mobilizing collaboration even when they were prominently advertised. An analysis of coordination practices across a sample of 138 WikiProjects by Morgan et al. [23] found evidence that project members generally worked independently of one another and primarily used the project talk page to ask for advice or pass on generally relevant information [23], a lightweight approach to coordination more common in FLOSS projects than in offline groups or other virtual teams [15, 37]. This study also found only limited evidence that WikiProject members exhibit behaviors related to group identification, such as in-group favoritism, in their interactions on the project talk page.

Current study

Given the intriguing but inconsistent picture of WikiProject collaboration presented by these previous studies, we believe that these complex coordination structures warrant further investigation. Our analysis complements and contextualizes the existing body of research on WikiProjects by examining WikiProject participation over time across a large and heterogeneous set of active projects. We expand the scope of analysis in three ways in order to account for a greater diversity of projects and practices.

Examine a greater range of production work. Many WikiProjects have a topic focus, and several previous studies have operationalized the production work of WikiProjects by measuring edits by a project's members to articles within that project's scope [16][5][32][34][4][9]. However, this may not be an effective metric for quantifying the work of WikiProjects organized around editing tasks that span topical boundaries such as *WikiProject Stub Sorting*, or projects that may primarily coordinate non-editing-related activities such as *WikiProject Dispute Resolution*.

We conceptualize these as *alternative* WikiProjects and examine the work they do within and outside article space.

Investigate a larger, more diverse set of projects. Exceptionally large and active WikiProjects, like those studied in Forte et al. [9,11], Zhu et al. [38], and Kittur et al. [16] are unlikely to be structurally or functionally similar to hundreds of smaller and less active WikiProjects. Zhu et al. [38] acknowledge that COTWs were only used consistently in 13 of the largest WikiProjects, and suggested that other projects may have stopped running

COTWs or decided not to adopt this approach because of its high coordination cost. *WikiProject Military History,* studied by Forte [9,11], is one of the largest, oldest and most organized projects on Wikipedia with 1170 active members and 1000 monthly edits in 2007. Smaller WikiProjects may lack the critical mass of highly invested participants necessary to sustain sophisticated collaboration mechanisms like monthly newsletters and COTWs, and their members may not experience the same sense of group identity or engage in the same degree of social interaction or direct collaboration.

We seek to describe a wider variety of coordination practices by collecting data from 978 active projects and interviewing members of multiple alternative WikiProjects.

Analyze project activity over time. Finally, with few exceptions [13, 23], previous studies of WikiProjects on the English Wikipedia have examined data from Wikipedia's peak years (2006 – 2008). Wikipedia has changed dramatically since then: for example, there are an increasingly smaller number of articles on major topics that need writing or significant expansion, and an increasing number of quality control tasks being performed by bots [30]. Furthermore, as contribution volume dropped off and the community itself began to shrink after 2007, the social system of Wikipedia began to change in significant ways. The community has grown more mistrustful of the motives of outsiders in recent years, and it has become more difficult for newcomers to contribute [14]. Both of these factors are thought to have contributed to the current editor decline [14, 30].

These findings suggest both a change in the social climate of Wikipedia, as well as a shift away from direct editing work as the primary mode of contribution towards more of the meta-work activities—such as border patrol, community support, administrative work and meta-content work—described in Kriplean et al.'s [18] barnstar analysis. Some factors that contributed to Wikipedia's rise—its openness to new contributors, its adaptable community rules—have grown more rigid, possibly precipitating or contributing to its decline [14]. Other important coordination mechanisms, such as WikiProjects, have not been examined in this new environment: how have WikiProjects weathered Wikipedia's climate change?

METHOD

We gathered our edit log data from toolserver.org[1], a public data repository hosted by the Wikimedia Foundation that maintains a nearly live mirror database of the English Wikipedia. We conducted queries against the Toolserver database, parsing results to create our own metadata about WikiProjects and cached results to offload subsequent processing.

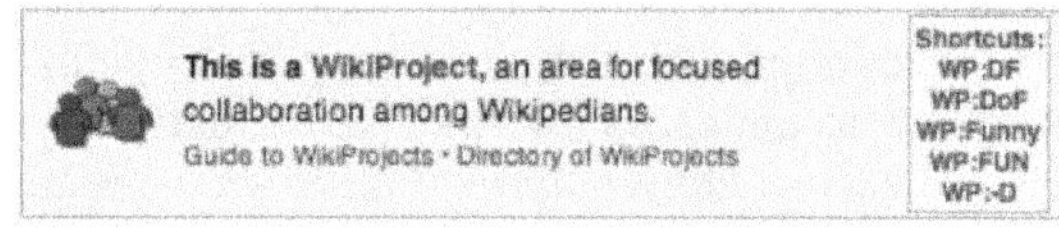

Figure 2. WikiProject banner from the *Department of Fun* project

While WikiProjects share many common features, each project is individual and is not required to adhere to any specific naming or formatting conventions. In order to identify WikiProjects, we considered all of the pages in the project namespace that either displayed the WikiProject banner (see **Figure 2**) or had "WikiProject" in the page title. We excluded pages that met these criteria, but which were a subpage of some other page. As well, we considered any redirects and included the page to which a redirect pointed if the page met our inclusion criteria. This resulted in a set of 1868 total WikiProjects as of May 2013.

Identifying Active WikiProjects

Some WikiProjects sustain regular participation from a large number of editors for many months or years. However, many WikiProjects that are created never garner significant participation over a sustained period of time. Measuring project activity in terms of edits by declared project members to articles is unsuitable as a universal measure of WikiProject activity simply because not all WikiProjects focus on editing a restricted set of articles and because project member lists do not accurately reflect project participation [23].

However, edits to project pages, whether made by declared members or non-members, are likely to reflect the overall level of community investment in a project's work. We define an active WikiProject as one that averaged 10 edits per month to the project page and any sub-pages including talk pages (i.e., the approximate lower bound for active project from Forte et al. [9]) for at least one calendar year. We exclude edits by unregistered editors and automated bots. 978 of the WikiProjects we identified (52%) were defined as current or formerly active projects using these criteria.

Identifying Alternative WikiProjects

Many WikiProjects focus on editing articles on particular topics and this norm has been formalized in a template for creating a new WikiProject provided by the *WikiProject Council* (which is itself a WikiProject). The template states *"Several Wikipedians have formed this collaboration resource and group dedicated to improving Wikipedia's coverage of [some topic] and the organization of information and articles on this topic"*[2]. This template provides top-level page section headings for the project to define its goals (the intended impact of the project), scope

[1] http://toolserver.org/

[2] http://enwp.org/Template:WikiProject

(the boundaries of the project's work), and tasks. WikiProjects that follow this template are often organized around encyclopedic topics, as provided in the outline. We define these projects as *conventional* WikiProjects because they follow the common conventions of WikiProject organization, goals, scope, and tasks.

A number of WikiProjects deviate from this conventional description. These projects may still use the template provided by the WikiProject Council, but the scope, goals, and tasks defined by the project point clearly to other types of work, with goals and scope that are not focused on encyclopedic content, or else they focus on work that spans multiple topical categories. We define these projects as *alternative* WikiProjects because their activities do not follow the conventional pattern of coordinating a *loosely defined* range of article creation and curation-related activities within a *well defined* topic area. Thus we define alternative WikiProject only *negatively*—the criterion for identification is deviation from the norm in stated goals, scope or primary tasks—in order to avoid forcing artificial distinctions onto our data and to allow patterns to surface in the analysis.

To identify alternative projects, we examined the current project page of each active project in our sample, identifying each of the 978 active WikiProjects as either conventional or alternative based on that project's conformity with the WikiProject template. This first pass of coding was binary: is this a conventional project or does it deviate from the norm in its goals, scope, or tasks? Initial coding and subsequent peer-review resulted in a final set of 131 out of 978 active projects (12%) labeled as alternative.

Classifying Alternative WikiProjects

Kriplean et al.'s barnstar categories, which were developed through a grounded coding approach on a similar dataset, serve as a set of sensitizing concepts [3] and a minimal structure that provide a useful descriptive framing for the work of alternative WikiProjects. That study analyzed the work activities described and acknowledged in barnstars, some of which were even developed by WikiProjects. The coding scheme naturally includes the type of editing work found in conventional, topically oriented WikiProjects, but also includes dimensions of wikiwork outside the scope of content production such as dispute resolution, question answering, vandalism detection and removal, template creation, participation in formal review processes, administrative activities, and other forms of meta-work.

Two independent coders classified the focal type of work claimed by each alternative project as described on the WikiProject's main page, focusing on the goals, scope, and tasks. Projects were classified according to the five top-level categories from the Barnstar Wikiwork coding scheme. The second-tier codes from that coding scheme were used to inform our decisions of which top-level code

Table 1. Work activities of alternative WikiProjects, classified according to valued work codes from Kriplean et al. 2008.

Editing work	creating content; starting articles; adding images; citing sources	57	**39%**
Meta-content work	template design; process design; classification	43	**29%**
Social & community support actions	mentorship; recognizing achievement of others; question-answering	22	**15%**
Collaborative action and disposition	policy interpretation; integrity; conflict mediation; explanation	10	**7%**
Administrative	determining article status; privilege granting; formal mediation	7	**5%**
Border patrol	spam removal; vandal fighting; copyright violations	7	**5%**
Undifferentiated work	*(not addressed in this study)*	1	**1%**
Total		147	100%

to use. Both tiers of barnstar codes are presented alongside our results in **Table 1.**

Each coder was to identify and code the most predominant claim of work. In rare cases where it was difficult to identify a predominant form of work, two codes were applied. 16 of 131 alternative projects (12%) were coded with two different codes. Discrepant codes were discussed and resolved through adjudication. The full list of categorized alternative WikiProjects is available[3].

Characterizing participation in Alternative WikiProjects

The project pages provide a structural framework for project work, but it is editors who perform that work. In order to deepen our understanding of why editors do the work they do and the way they experience participation, the first author performed 18 semi-structured interviews with WikiProject members.

The interviews were conducted as part of a larger research study focused on understanding editors' motivation and involvement in WikiProjects (both conventional and alternative) and on identifying important technical and social factors that had impact on the success of projects. The first nine interviews were conducted by the first author with members of *WikiProject Military History* in 2011 in conjunction with an informal self-assessment undertaken by members of that project. Eight of these interviews were conducted with project members, and a ninth with the assessment facilitator, who was also a member and founder of several WikiProjects. The second set of nine interviews were conducted in parallel with the current study, using a refined and expanded version of the initial protocol. Several

3 http://meta.wikimedia.org/wiki/Research:WikiProjects_as_Virtual_Teams/Nontraditional_wikiprojects.

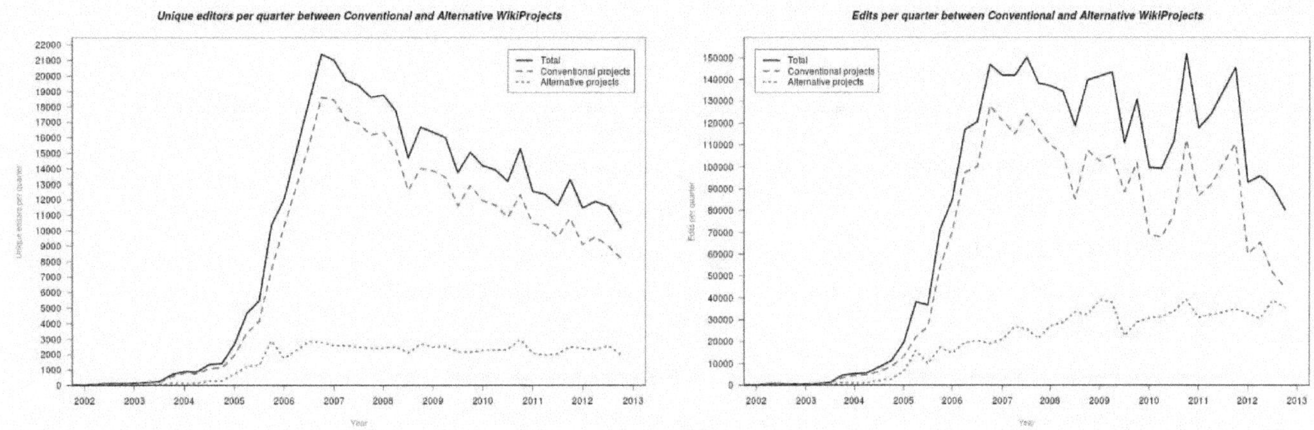

Figure 3. Number of edits to WikiProject pages (left) and registered editors participating in WikiProjects over 10 years. Alternative WikiProject activity (dotted red) is lower but more stable than in conventional WikiProjects (dashed green).

initial interview candidates were approached initially because they mentioned WikiProject participation on their userpages or on personal profiles they created on the Wikipedia Teahouse [22]. Other interview candidates were approached in person at a local Wikipedia Edit-a-thon. Additional interviewees were identified through snowball recruitment. 14 interviews were conducted face to face, over Internet Relay Chat, or by Google Hangout. Four of the initial nine interviews were conducted over email.

Members of the research team analyzed written interview transcripts and identified passages related to projects that had been identified as alternative in the first coding pass. Passages were then sorted by project, and by whether they reflected a) *the editor's motivation for founding or participating in the project* and b) *goals of the project or the activities the project focuses on* (interviewee must identify as a participant). These motivations and activities informed our categorization of the other alternative projects. Data from the interviews and examination of the project pages were used to develop case studies of projects in each of five top-level barnstar wikiwork categories, which are presented below.

FINDINGS

Our analysis indicates that overall WikiProject participation **(Figure 3)** has declined in step with the overall active editor base of Wikipedia **(Figure 1).** WikiProjects are still a major site of editor activity—during the first three quarters of 2012, an average of 11,229 editors made 88,943 edits to WikiProject pages per quarter. However, these figures represent a 46% and 38% decrease in activity from the first three quarters of 2007, when both general editing activity and WikiProject participation were at their greatest level.

Between 2007 and 2012, the number of editors participating in conventional WikiProjects decreased by 51%, and the number of edits to these projects decreased by 56%. However participation in alternative WikiProjects shows a different trajectory: the number of participating editors has declined much less dramatically (13%) and the number of edits to alternative WikiProject workspaces has increased steadily to an average of 35,035 edits per quarter in 2012, compared to 22,300 edits per quarter in 2007—an increase of 57%.

The contrast between the relative stability—and even growth—in alternative WikiProjects and the decline of conventional project activity suggests that alternative WikiProjects are an increasingly prominent part of the WikiProject ecology. This may be due to their ability to provide editors with opportunities to perform valuable and engaging work in the mature peer production system of Wikipedia.

However while the proportion of WikiProject activity within alternative projects has increased from 16% in 2007 to 39% in 2012, conventional WikiProjects still make up the majority of active projects. The lists of the Top 20 WikiProjects in **Table 2** demonstrate that the decline in WikiProject participation has not made conventional projects obsolete. Many historically active topic-focused projects like Military History are still among the most active projects in 2012. However, participation patterns have changed: fewer than half of the top projects in 2007 are still in the top 20. Furthermore, there seems to be a greater churn among alternative WikiProjects: 75% (6/8) alternative projects in 2012 were not among the most active projects in 2007, compared with 50% (6/12) of conventional projects. Historically active alternative projects with names that suggest a focus on content creation, such as *WikiProject Missing Encyclopedia Articles,* have been replaced by different alternative projects whose focus is not known. Below, we investigate the work performed by several of these new alternative WikiProjects.

Table 2. Top 20 WikiProjects by annual edits to project pages in 2007 and 2012. Alternative Project names are highlighted and italicized. An asterisk indicates a project that was not among the top 20 in 2007.

Edit rank	2007	2012
1	WikiProject Military history	*WikiProject Deletion sorting*
2	*WikiProject Deletion sorting*	WikiProject Military history
3	WikiProject Video games	WikiProject Football
4	WikiProject Biography	*WikiProject Articles for creation**
5	WikiProject Professional wrestling	*WikiProject Guild of Copy Editors**
6	WikiProject Football	WikiProject Television Stations*
7	*WikiProject Red Link Recovery*	WikiProject Video games
8	WikiProject U.S. Roads	WikiProject Medicine*
9	*Department of Fun*	WikiProject Film
10	*WikiProject Spam*	WikiProject U.S. Roads
11	WikiProject Anime and manga	*WikiProject Wikify**
12	*WikiProject Missing encyclopedic articles*	WikiProject Chemicals*
13	*WikiProject Council*	*Department of Fun*
14	WikiProject Film	*WikiProject Resource Exchange**
15	*WikiProject Stub sorting*	WikiProject Birds*
16	WikiProject Comics	*Counter-Vandalism Unit**
17	WikiProject Cricket	WikiProject India*
18	WikiProject Novels	*WikiProject Good articles**
19	WikiProject LGBT studies	WikiProject Mathematics
20	WikiProject Mathematics	WikiProject National Register of Historic Places*

Range of work activities in alternative WikiProjects

Just as barnstars acknowledge the variety of work beyond editing articles, alternative WikiProjects are used to coordinate many of these same work activities. **Table 1** illustrates the distribution of assigned wikiwork codes to the alternative WikiProjects in our study. In this section, we draw on findings from our interviews with Wikipedians to show how WikiProjects both reflect the Wikipedia community's conception of valued work and provide a mechanism for performing that work across topical, temporal, and even ideological boundaries.

Editing Work (39%). Kriplean et al. found that editing work was the largest single work category for which editors awarded barnstars [18]. We show similar results among alternative WikiProjects. Like conventional WikiProjects, many alternative projects address the fundamental work activity on Wikipedia: making edits to articles. However, while conventional WikiProjects focus on a specific topic area and coordinate a range of activities to improve coverage of that topic, alternative projects like *WikiProject Unreferenced BLP Rescue* (founded 2010), coordinate a single, specific task. The goal of Unreferenced BLP Rescue was to systematically eliminate a backlog of biographical articles about living people (BLPs) that had been tagged by other editors as lacking sources. Providing sources for BLPs is particularly important work because of notorious, high profile controversies that uncovered untrue and unsourced statements in articles about public persons such as American journalist John Siegenthaler. In 2009, the Wikimedia Foundation passed a resolution on the importance of *"neutrally-written, accurate and well sourced articles on living people"* [12]. This project's approach—setting monthly targets and efficiently coordinating work around those specific target articles—was successful in mobilizing participation by a large number of editors to eliminate the existing backlog over the course of 15 months. The project also streamlined Wikipedia's article deletion process to combat future backlogs:

> *"The project that handled referencing BLPs they managed to really kind of promote systemic change in the way BLPs are handled... they created a new deletion process, the 'Sticky prod'[4], with BLPs that don't have*

[4] http://enwp.org/WP:Proposed_deletion#Sticky_prod

> *references are automatically deleted after a certain time. This was a huge change in the approach." [participant 11]*

All of the articles within the scope of Unreferenced BLP Rescue are also within the scope of *WikiProject Biography*, one of the largest and oldest conventional WikiProjects (f. 2002). Specialized subgroups like Unreferenced BLP Rescue are frequently set up as task forces within parent projects [11]. Although task forces are generally fairly autonomous of their parent project, one interviewee suggested that Unreferenced BLP Rescue may have benefitted from being a distinct project because it increased the project's visibility within the community, allowing it to draw in editors who were not interested in writing biographical articles, but enjoyed hunting for sources.

Another alternative project that coordinates direct article editing is *WikiProject Wikify* (f. 2006). This project also chose a limited and well-defined set of editing activities, namely *wikification*—the practice of fixing wikitext markup, adding internal links between related articles, and standardizing the basic page layout of articles. This project differs from conventional projects in that it takes the whole encyclopedia as its scope. One Wikify member, who has often served in an unofficial coordinator role for the project, was drawn to the project as a new editor because he viewed wikification as a simple way to improve the overall credibility of Wikipedia:

> *"...for me it was like here's this thing it's got these goals and it wasn't a difficult thing to do, especially once you learn how to wikify an article... I consider that process really important because there was an article that I didn't really change the content to but one of the greatest improvements I've made to an article was just through wikifying it because it makes it look like it's encyclopedic." [p8]*

Like Unreferenced BLP Rescue, Wikify conducts structured collaboration drives, in which editors informally compete to wikify the most articles within a given month. While some conventional WikiProjects also conduct collaborations of the week [38], these events focus on improving a single article, usually with the intent of gaining official acknowledgement that the article is of Good or Featured status, a community-wide designation that is determined through an official peer-review process. Contributions like wikification that do not involve adding substantial content may not be as well acknowledged in topical WikiProjects. Furthermore, creating and applying consistent wikification standards may be difficult to do within conventional projects, since these projects often create their own local style guides and formatting conventions [9].

Meta-Content Work (29%). Our second most frequent work category, meta-content work, was the primary focus in 29% of alternative WikiProjects. As the name suggests, meta-content work covers a wide range of activities that do not involve editing articles directly. Some of the projects in this category, such as *WikiProject Infoboxes* (f. 2007) and *WikiProject Disambiguation* (f. 2005), build and maintain Wikipedia's template and category infrastructure. WikiProject Disambiguation creates disambiguation pages for commonly confused titles. These pages are located in the article namespace, but rather than presenting original content they function as a reader-facing index to the content of the encyclopedia. Another alternative WikiProject, *Stub Sorting* (f. 2004) builds and maintains a complementary editor-facing index: it builds lists of categories and subcategories of stubs (very short articles) arranged by topic. Other editors and WikiProjects can use these lists to identify articles with their area of interest that need substantial improvement.

Other projects in the meta-content work category focus on editing activities at an even greater remove from articles themselves. *WikiProject Deletion Sorting* (f. 2005) performs similar work to *Stub Sorting*, but instead of categorizing articles it categorizes previous discussions at the Articles for Deletion noticeboard (AFD) according to the topic of the article under consideration to be deleted. According to one long-time member of Deletion Sorting, the goal of this work is to improve the decision-making process around article deletion:

> *"Deletion Sorting I kind of went into that with the aim, the idea that this was a problem that needed to be solved... AFD was becoming very high-volume at that point and a lot of discussions were going by with not much input. And sometimes they could have benefitted from input from for example people in the UK, or Chemists, or whatever. So the idea was that we would have a list of chemistry-related deletion discussions and a list of England-related deletion-discussions so that people who were interested, it was a resource for them to use if they wanted." [p9]*

The *Help Project* curates pages in the Help namespace, a set of editor-facing pages devoted to tutorials and how-to guides related to technical topics such as how to redirect a page or create a table in wiki-markup. There are thousands of help pages on Wikipedia, but they are often incomplete, out-of-date, hard to find, and dense with technical jargon. The Help Project (f. 2006) is dedicated to making these help pages more helpful, and making the best ones easier for editors in need to find. One current member describes how the Help Project provides an alternate way to contribute content to Wikipedia for editors whose interests may lie outside of encyclopedia articles, but who want to create resources that may be read and used by thousands of other editors.

> *"I'd been interested in a lot of this meta stuff and I'd kind of touched on Help pages before and made a few edits and done categorization and stuff... I saw someone*

had proposed this project to improve the help pages and I thought "God, yes they really do need improving" [p9]

Another alternative project that curates meta-content resources that are primarily editor-facing is the *WikiProject Council* (f. 2006). The Council is in some ways the most meta project of all: a WikiProject founded to help coordinate WikiProjects. Its pages provide a central hub for WikiProject-related guidance and discussions. It maintains a WikiProject Directory with lists of projects sorted by their type and how active they are believed to be, making it easier for editors to find WikiProjects that they may be interested in joining. The council also provides templates, style guides and how-to's for creating a WikiProject. As the Council's founder explains:

"My initial idea in creating it was actually to bring together the coordinators of the various active projects so that we could discuss common strategies and share best practices." [p6]

Stub Sorting, Deletion Sorting, the Help Project and the WikiProject Council all create and maintain important resources that support content creation, but indirectly: making it easier for editors to find interesting work to do, aiding in group decision-making, clarifying complex technical problems, and helping people create and maintain their own autonomous work groups.

Social and Community Support Actions (15%). The WikiProject Council is a good example of a project that plays multiple roles: in addition to performing the valuable meta-content work, it also provides a forum for social and community support activities. The Council provides a proposal board where editors interested in creating a new WikiProject can draft a project plan and receive feedback. Other editors can indicate their interest in participating by signing up for the proposed project. While the Council has no authority over whether or not a project is created, the structured proposal process provides mentorship and guidance and also regulates the creation of projects that may be unlikely to succeed:

"It's made the process of creating new WikiProjects marginally more complex which weeds out some of the most unsuitable candidates. One of the main reasons WikiProjects fail is because they choose an unsuitable scope. The proposal process provides an opportunity for someone to point that out, and ideally redirect the proposer's energy towards something more productive." [p6]

The WikiProject Council was founded near the peak of both editing activity and WikiProject activity (426 new projects were founded in that year alone). Channeling thousands of new editors' efforts towards areas where they would have the greatest positive impact may have been seen as a productive approach, even in a community that is generally leery of bureaucracy.[5]

Several recently-founded social and community support projects address issues related to the editor decline. These projects employ different strategies to recruit new editors and retain existing ones. *Today's Article for Improvement* (TAFI) (f. 2012) organizes Collaboration of the Day, which functions like a Wikipedia-wide Collaboration of the Week [38]. Project contributors select an article to collaboratively boost to Featured Article status from a list of proposed collaborations. While improving article quality is one of the primary functions of conventional WikiProjects, TAFI differs from the norm not just in its broader scope, but in its goals:

"The main motive was to create a good enough framework for all editors and collaborators to come in... It was as much of a "Rope in the newcomers" thing as "Improve the important articles" [p1]

Inviting newcomers to work collaboratively on improving an article alongside more experienced editors who are there to provide friendly guidance and constructive criticism provides an opportunity for direct mentorship, which has been shown to be successful but rare on Wikipedia [26]. As of mid-2013 TAFI members are working to feature the current Collaboration of the Day on the front page of Wikipedia in an effort to convert Wikipedia readers to editors.

Another recently-founded (2012) alternative WikiProject, *Editor Retention* (f. 2012), has a complementary focus: it provides a forum for discussing strategies for retaining established editors, who often leave Wikipedia because of negative social experiences or a feeling that their work is not acknowledged [35]. In service of this goal, Editor Retention runs an Editor of the Week board, a "place to nominate someone for Editor of the Week recognition: an unsung hero who has been doing great work for months but is not well-known."

Many members of the Wikipedia community have suspected for years that their shrinking community is partially due to new editors having difficulty learning the ropes and having few opportunities to interact with the Wikipedia community in positive ways, a theory supported by recent research [14][22]. The creation of projects like Today's Article for Improvement and Editor Retention demonstrates how the WikiProject model for group collaboration can be adapted to address these emerging community concerns.

Collaborative Actions and Disposition (7%). Following Kriplean et al. [18], we distinguish the Collaborative Actions and Disposition category from Social and Community Support Actions by direct implication of

[5] see http://enwp.org/WP:NOTBUREAU

collaborative activities such as dispute resolution or helping individuals adhere to formally-stated Wikipedia policies such as Neutral Point of View, Notability and Civility. Several alternative WikiProjects have been founded to support conflict resolution within topic areas that reflect geo-political controversies. *WikiProject Israel Palestine Collaboration* (f. 2008) was founded to:

> *"create a more hospitable editing environment for Category:Israeli–Palestinian_conflict related topics, including through a) actively seeking the cooperation of people who are uninvolved or hold strong and differing points of views[sic] and b) preventing and resolving disputes about the application of Wikipedia policies to these articles."* [40]

Similar projects include *Ireland Collaboration* (f. 2008) and *Sri Lanka Reconciliation* (f. 2007). These projects provide a space for coordination, discussion and conflict resolution among individual editors interested in these topics, as well as between WikiProjects. The member list of Israel Palestine Collaboration includes members of the conventional WikiProjects *Israel* and *Palestine*, as well as unaffiliated editors. By providing a neutral space for cross-project dialogue, as well as oversight and informal mediation, these alternative projects play an important meta-role within topical domains where civility, neutral point of view, and verifiability are crucial but may be difficult to adhere to, even by other WikiProjects.

Another project geared towards both supporting cooperation and assuring adherence to Wikipedia policy is *WikiProject Cooperation* (f. 2012), which aims to help editors who have a potential conflict of interest related to an article that they would like to edit, such as a financial stake in the organization the article describes.

> *"[WikiProject Cooperation] is trying to advance a model of cooperation with paid editors... They have a paid editor help board on which paid editors can come and have their drafts reviewed. Interestingly there's a counter-organization called WikiProject Integrity which is very skeptical of this model..." [p10]*

Paid editing has been a known issue on Wikipedia since at least 2007, when Virgil Griffith's WikiScanner tool [41] first revealed that thousands of anonymous edits to Wikipedia articles were being made from corporate IP addresses. Paid editing has increased on Wikipedia as the website's popularity search ranking has risen, but Wikipedia lacks both official policies on paid editing and mechanisms for enforcing compliance. Like WikiProject Israel Palestine Collaboration, WikiProject Cooperation exists to help paid editors who are acting in good faith and would like to adhere to the rules of the site. Submitting their drafts for review may provide those editors with some assurance of protection for their work, a function that some conventional WikiProjects perform for their members [9].

Border Patrol (5%). Not all projects or editors on Wikipedia act with a deliberately cooperative spirit: a more common approach to unwanted content and users on Wikipedia is to revert first, and ask questions later. *WikiProject Spam* (f. 2005), one of the most active alternative WikiProjects, functions primarily as a noticeboard for reporting instances where obviously biased or trivial content has been added to articles. Another more recent border patrol project is *WikiProject Integrity* which exists *"to discuss, raise awareness of, and hopefully address issues regarding paid editing on Wikipedia"* [42]. Integrity was originally founded in early 2012 as WikiProject Paid Advocacy Watch, nearly simultaneously with WikiProject Cooperation, and re-named in 2013 as part of what one interview participant referred to as a "re-branding" effort. Integrity addresses the same issue as Cooperation but takes the approach of WikiProject Spam: it maintains a noticeboard for reporting possible instances of paid editing. The project is also attempting to promote adoption of an official Wikipedia policy for addressing issues of paid editing in articles.

While Paid Advocacy Watch and Cooperation take different approaches, they share members and have collaboratively created a detailed how-to guide—the *Plain and Simple Conflict of Interest Guide* [43]—which is intended to help new editors understand the concept of Conflict of Interest (COI) and contribute more productively when they have a potential COI. Because WikiProjects are open, autonomous, and have no formal authority, these two projects are able to work together even though some members have incompatible ideological stances. Like the talk page of WikiProject Israel Palestine Collaboration, the Plain and Simple Conflict of Interest Guide provides a common space for editors in both projects to work together to address a pressing community concern.

Complex tasks like conflict mediation and outreach requires active coordination among many different stakeholders. The cases of Integrity and Cooperation, and of Israel Palestine Collaboration demonstrate that sustained cooperation is possible even between groups with different ideologies. If Wikipedia's editor base continues to shrink, it may be more difficult to sustain cooperation among these alternative projects, even as the need for them grows. Border patrol projects may be more successful in the long run because they require less coordinated effort to maintain, which may exacerbate Wikipedia's current tendency to revert first and ask questions later.

Administrative Actions (5%). Work categorized in the administrative action category pertains to actions taken by administrators and to acknowledge participation in formal processes like Articles for Deletion (AfD) or Featured Article Review [18]. Only seven alternative WikiProjects deal directly with administratorship or other formal processes. In part this may be because WikiProjects themselves have no formal authority to dictate policy or enforce decisions [9]. Other groups on Wikipedia like Arbitration Committee (ArbCom) or the Featured Article Committee (FAC) are vested with the formal authority and technical permissions necessary to make binding decisions—respectively, to block or ban a user account, and to decide what articles are featured on the front page of Wikipedia. These groups are not referred to as 'WikiProjects' and use neither the name or the template. They also differ from the WikiProjects we examined in other important ways. For example, both ArbCom and FAC lack open and egalitarian membership—members are appointed or elected to official roles. Other group workspaces on Wikipedia, such as the Good Articles nomination page, are designed to support case-by-case decisions about the quality designation of articles, and do not list members at all.

However, we find that in several cases alternative WikiProjects exist to support these formal processes. The *Featured Article Team* (FAT) (f. 2007) provides newer editors with informal peer feedback in preparation for nominating an article for formal peer review. Another alternative project, *WikiProject Arbitration Enforcement* (f. 2010), supports the other end of an official process: coordinating the enforcement of binding arbitration decisions issued by ArbCom by "listing the administrators who make themselves available for taking enforcement action in these areas, providing spaces to track recurring and longtime problems [and] making AE precedents and best practices more accessible"[44]. This may reflect a further attempt at decentralizing Wikipedia's governance by reducing the burden of monitoring compliance on ArbCom in an increasingly conflict-driven community.

Projects that deal with administrative actions provide support for the (relatively few) official, centralized governance mechanisms of Wikipedia and also provide support for the editors who interact with those processes. They also provide a way for more editors to participate more directly in governance and formal review processes, and even lobby for regime change. As Wikipedia's official policies have grown more calcified and difficult to change [14], participating in these informal projects may be an effective way for everyday editors to have an impact on community rules, norms and processes.

DISCUSSION

> *"WikiProjects divide so much into the different kind of work they do. Projects that are gathered around specific article subjects might lose steam once coverage of that subject becomes more complete." [p11]*

As the work of improving Wikipedia shifts increasingly aware from content creation and towards content curation, alternative WikiProjects may become even more important for maintaining the quality of the encyclopedia. Many valuable editing tasks, such as wikifying articles, span topic boundaries. Other tasks that focus effort within existing topical boundaries, such as eliminating backlogs, may benefit from the specialized coordination mechanisms, autonomy, and visibility that comes with setting up a stand-alone project. Meta-content work coordinated through alternative WikiProjects also helps the community maintain its organizational memory of past decisions (Deletion Sorting) and help contributors can find articles that match their interests and need substantial improvement (Stub Sorting).

As Wikipedia's social climate has evolved, new barriers to participation have arisen. Many alternative WikiProjects such as TAFI and Editor Retention, focus on newly-recognized community concerns such as the decline in retention of new editors and the shortening productive lifespan of established editors. The relevance of these newer alternative projects to the community's current needs may be part of the reason why the level of activity within the set of alternative WikiProjects has increased over the past six years while activity within conventional WikiProjects, and within Wikipedia as a whole, have decreased.

In addition to highlighting the importance of alternative WikiProjects to the health of the modern Wikipedia ecosystem, our findings illuminate other important ways in which WikiProjects differ from one another. While projects like Military History maintain a high degree of engagement by fostering a collaborative atmosphere, one interviewee's description of the task of Deletion Sorting suggests that it is a relatively solo effort:

> *"So basically we had a script which would pop up when you're on [the Articles for Deletion noticeboard] and for each debate you could click and then select which category it should be in. And it would then put it in that category it would put it on that list so that people would know, and then leave a small notice saying "This discussion has been listed in the list of chemistry related deletion discussions." [p9]*

Several other interviewees also described their work within WikiProjects as largely autonomous. One interviewee struggled to name a single other regular participant in their primary WikiProject! Taken together with findings from previous research on coordination in WikiProject talk pages [23], these descriptions of project life suggest that many Wikipedians do not experience WikiProjects as groups, but rather as interest-based coordination spaces that can support both independent and collaborative participation. These findings have ramification for the theoretical and methodological approaches researchers use to study WikiProjects and also for the tools that designers and community managers develop to support the work of WikiProjects and other open teams.

WikiProjects exist on several other Wikimedia wikis that are not encyclopedias[6], and groups called WikiProjects exist within other wiki-based online communities, such as Open Street Map[7] and Wikia[8]. The degree to which these groups resemble Wikipedia WikiProjects in their diversity of roles, goals, and practices has not been studied but could illuminate whether WikiProjects' pivotal role in coordinating work around critical tasks on English Wikipedia represents a special case or a general trend within open collaborations.

One domain of open collaboration that may benefit from fostering WikiProject-like groups is citizen science. Rotman [29][28] has suggested that better support for federated, task-based subgroups in the Encyclopedia of Life project could help encourage collaboration, foster a stronger sense of community, and aid in the development of a common taxonomical classification standard. In designing affordances to support such subgroups in the system, it may be helpful to follow a WikiProject model—allowing contributors to create new groups and group workspaces freely and dynamically, in response to their own shifting interests and the overall project's evolution.

Other citizen science projects such as Zooniverse already contain a federated system of different collaborations that participants can move between [19]. However, research funding is required to start a new Zooniverse subproject. Despite this constraint, in 2011 a group of volunteer participants in the climatology Zooniverse project *OldWeather* undertook their own independent research project, tracking the spread of the 1919 Spanish Flu pandemic through 'sick lists' in archived ship log data [31]. Explicitly supporting self-organized citizen research initiatives like this one could encourage more people to contribute to Zooniverse and also yield valuable scientific discoveries.

Implications for Design

Directing people towards engaging and important activities and allowing them to coordinate those activities in their own way is key to sustaining an open collaboration. Based on our examination of the range of work activities that all WikiProjects perform—not just conventional ones—and the different ways editors work within those projects, we offer the following set of design suggestions for supporting WikiProjects and open teams in related systems.

General requirements. While many excellent information visualization (i.e. [33]), task recommendation, and vandal-fighting tools have been developed on Wikipedia, most of these tools are intended for use by individuals rather than groups, and are designed to support article production activities. Tools designed to support WikiProjects and similar open groups should allow these groups to maintain the openness and flexibility that enables them to support a wide variety of tasks and diverse ways of working, while minimizing the effort required to maintain project resources. Building effective tools in this design space require a nuanced understanding of which features can be baked in to the platform, or made available as opt-in modules, and which ones need to remain open to creative reconfiguration and remixing by user-designers. Below we provide some specific suggestions.

Socially intelligent task routing. Many WikiProject participants report that they do not use WikiProject task lists, preferring to work more independently [17]. One successful tool that supports this task management style, SuggestBot [6], uses Wikipedia's template and category structure to generate a list of task recommendations for a user based on articles they previously edited. Intelligent task routing tools like SuggestBot could be designed to recommend tasks beyond editing, such as sorting deletion discussions or improving help pages. *Socially intelligent* routing tools could also recommend WikiProjects that an editor may want to join based on their edit history or stated interests. A research prototype system called WikiTasks [17] allowed WikiProject members to provide contextual information about the tasks they request and let other users publically claim requested tasks. These detailed annotations could be useful for helping editors understand the scope and nature of a task, and also have the potential to serve as *practice proxies* [24] that teach new editors norms of participation.

Social translucence visualizations. Wiki pages do not surface activity well. It is difficult to tell who is active on a page without digging into the edit histories, or to distinguish a living project from a moribund one. Social translucence tools such as the Re:Flex toolbar [21] show who the most active editors are on a particular wiki page, and also let users to see what other pages these editors are editing and who they communicate with. Re:Flex and similar tools that visualize dynamic relationships and activity networks could help WikiProject members find both potential collaborators and relevant tasks.

Leaderboards. Metadata about project participants' recent editing activities could also be leveraged to visualize activity at the project level. Configurable leaderboards like CommunityCompare [36] could be enabled on WikiProjects to visualize the project's recent and historical activity across multiple dimensions of work. For example, featuring the most active contributors to the project workspace provides public acknowledgment for the (often invisible) work of project coordinators, which may encourage them to continue participating longer. Leaderboards can also be used to track progress towards group goals—our interviewees described handmade leaderboards in use among several projects for this purpose. Automating this feature reduces the administrative cost of conducting

[6] e.g. http://www.mediawiki.org/wiki/Project:WikiProject_Extensions
[7] http://wiki.openstreetmap.org/wiki/WikiProject_Haiti
[8] http://entourage.wikia.com/wiki/Entourage_Wiki:WikiProject

focused editing drives and COTWs, potentially encouraging more direct collaboration among project members and deepening their commitment to the project and the community.

CONCLUSION

To understand and support group work in open collaborations, we need empirical investigations into actual work practices across a diverse set of groups. In this study we have made an attempt to more fully characterize the range of work performed by one type of group, WikiProjects, within one of the largest and longest-lived open collaborations, English Wikipedia. We have made four primary contributions to research:

- Characterized alternative WikiProjects, an important sub-set of WikiProjects that do not focus on general improvements to articles within a particular encyclopedia topic area.
- Presented empirical data on the range of work activities performed by these projects.
- Described how these projects facilitate collaboration around emergent problems and current community concerns.
- Demonstrated that participation in alternative WikiProjects has remained relatively stable, and even increased by some measures, as participation within conventional WikiProjects and Wikipedia as a whole has declined since 2007.

Participating in Wikipedia involves editing beyond articles. Wikiwork increasingly involves filling in around the edges, increasing the overall quality of the encyclopedia (not just a particular topic), and actively recruiting and retaining productive contributors. If Wikipedia remains open and active, these alternative ways of contributing will only grow more important. The fact that Wikipedians have successfully adapted WikiProjects, a mechanism originally designed for coordinated content creation, to effectively manage these emerging work activities demonstrates the resilience of open collaboration systems and also suggests a potential strategy for replicating the success of Wikipedia in new domains of open collaboration.

ACKNOWLEDGEMENTS

This work is supported in part by the National Science Foundation under Grants IIS-0811210 and IIS-1162114, and by the Wikimedia Foundation through its 2011 Summer of Research program.

REFERENCES

1. Arrow, H., McGrath, J.E., and Berdahl, J.L. *Small groups as complex systems : formation, coordination, development and adaptation.* Sage Publications, Thousand Oaks, Calif., 2000
2. Beschastnikh, I., Kriplean, T., and McDonald, D.W. Wikipedian self-governance in action: Motivating the policy lens. *ICWMSM 2008*
3. Blumer, H. What is wrong with social theory? *American sociological review 19*, 1 (1954), 3–10
4. Chen, J., Ren, Y., and Riedl, J. The effects of diversity on group productivity and member withdrawal in online volunteer groups. *CHI 2010*
5. Choi, B., Alexander, K., Kraut, R.E., and Levine, J.M. Socialization tactics in wikipedia and their effects. *GROUP 2010*
6. Cosley, D., Frankowski, D., Terveen, L., and Riedl, J. Using intelligent task routing and contribution review to help communities build artifacts of lasting value. *CHI 2006*
7. Cosley, D., Frankowski, D., Terveen, L., and Riedl, J. SuggestBot: using intelligent task routing to help people find work in wikipedia. *IUI 2007*
8. Ducheneaut, N. Socialization in an Open Source Software Community: A Socio-Technical Analysis. *Computer Supported Cooperative Work (CSCW) 14*, 4 (2005), 323–368.
9. Forte, A., Kittur, N., Larco, V., Zhu, H., Bruckman, A., and Kraut, R.E. Coordination and beyond: social functions of groups in open content production. *CSCW 2012.*
10. Forte, A. and Lampe, C. Defining, Understanding, and Supporting Open Collaboration: Lessons From the Literature. *American Behavioral Scientist*, (2013).
11. Forte, A., Larco, V., and Bruckman, A. Decentralization in Wikipedia governance. *Journal of Management Information Systems 26*, 1 (2009), 49–72
12. Foundation, W. Biographies of living people. *Wikimedia Foundation Resolutions*, 2009. http://wikimediafoundation.org/wiki/Resolution:Biographies_of_living_people
13. Gilbert, M., Morgan, J.T., McDonald, D.W., and Zachry, M. Managing Complexity: Strategies for group awareness and coordinated action in Wikipedia. *OpenSym 2013*
14. Halfaker, A., Geiger, R.S., Morgan, J., and Riedl, J. The Rise and Decline of an Open Collaboration System: How Wikipedia's reaction to sudden popularity is causing its decline. *American Behavioral Scientist* (2013).
15. Heckman, R., Crowston, K., Eseryel, U.Y., Howison, J., Allen, E., and Li, Q. Emergent decision-making practices in free/libre open source software (FLOSS) development teams. *International Federation for Information Processing Publications, IFIP 234* (2007), 71
16. Kittur, A., Pendleton, B., and Kraut, R.E. Herding the cats: the influence of groups in coordinating peer production. *WikiSym 2009*
17. Krieger, M., Stark, E.M., and Klemmer, S.R.S.R. Coordinating tasks on the commons: designing for personal goals, expertise and serendipity. *CHI 2009*

18. Kriplean, T., Beschastnikh, I., and McDonald, D.W. Articulations of wikiwork: uncovering valued work in wikipedia through barnstars. *CSCW 2008*
19. Lehan, C. and Gay, P. User Movement Across the Zooniverse. *American Astronomical Society Meeting Abstracts #217*, (2011), #344.01.
20. Luther, K., Fiesler, C., and Bruckman, A. Redistributing leadership in online creative collaboration. *CSCW 2013*
21. McDonald, D.W., Gokhman, S., and Zachry, M. Building for social translucence: a domain analysis and prototype system. *CSCW 2012*
22. Morgan, J.T., Bouterse, S., Stierch, S., and Walls, H. Tea & Sympathy: Crafting Positive New Editor Experiences on Wikipedia. *CSCW 2013*
23. Morgan, J.T., Gilbert, M., McDonald, D.W., and Zachry, M. Project talk: Coordination work and group membership in WikiProjects. *OpenSym 2013*
24. Mugar, G., Østerlund, C., Hassman, K.D., Crowston, K., and Jackson, C.B. Planet Hunters and Seafloor Explorers: Legitimate Peripheral Participation Through Practice Proxies in Online Citizen Science. *CSCW 2014*
25. Muller, M., Ehrlich, K., Matthews, T., Perer, A., Ronen, I., and Guy, I. Diversity among enterprise online communities: collaborating, teaming, and innovating through social media. *CHI 2012*
26. Musicant, D.D.R., Ren, Y., Johnson, J.A., and Riedl, J. Mentoring in Wikipedia: a clash of cultures. *WikiSym 2011*
27. Nardi, B. and Harris, J. Strangers and friends: Collaborative play in World of Warcraft. *CSCW 2006.*
28. Rotman, D., Preece, J., Hammock, J., et al. Dynamic changes in motivation in collaborative citizen-science projects. *CSCW 2012*
29. Rotman, D., Procita, K., Hansen, D., Sims Parr, C., and Preece, J. Supporting content curation communities: The case of the Encyclopedia of Life. *Journal of the American Society for Information Science and Technology 63*, 6 (2012), 1092–1107.
30. Suh, B., Convertino, G., Chi, E.H., and Pirolli, P. The singularity is not near: slowing growth of Wikipedia. *WikiSym 2009*
31. The Zooniverse. HMS Africa in action against Orthomyxoviridae. *Old Weather Blog*, 2011. http://blog.oldweather.org/2011/01/12/hms-africa-in-action-against-orthomyxoviridae/
32. Ung, H. and Dalle, J.-M. Project management in the Wikipedia community. *WikiSym 2010*
33. Viégas, F.B., Wattenberg, M., and Dave, K. Studying cooperation and conflict between authors with history flow visualizations. *CHI 2004*
34. Wang, L.S., Chen, J., Ren, Y., and Riedl, J. Searching for the goldilocks zone: trade-offs in managing online volunteer groups. *CSCW 2012*
35. Wikimedia Foundation. Former Contributors Survey Results. *Wikipedia Strategic Planning Initiative.* http://strategy.wikimedia.org/wiki/Former_Contributors_Survey_Results.
36. Xu, A., Chen, J., Matthews, T., Muller, M., and Badenes, H. CommunityCompare: Visually comparing communities for online community leaders in the enterprise. *CHI 2013*
37. Yamauchi, Y., Yokozawa, M., Shinohara, T., and Ishida, T. Collaboration with Lean Media: how open-source software succeeds. *CSCW 2000*
38. Zhu, H., Kraut, R., and Kittur, A. Organizing without formal organization: group identification, goal setting and social modeling in directing online production. *CSCW 2012*
39. WikiProjects by changes. *Wikipedia Database Reports.* http://enwp.org/WP:Database_reports/WikiProjects_by_changes.
40. WikiProject Israel Palestine Collaboration. *Wikipedia.* http://enwp.org/WP:WikiProject_Israel_Palestine_Collaboration#Purpose.
41. WikiScanner. *Wikipedia.* http://enwp.org/WikiScanner.
42. WikiProject Integrity. *Wikipedia.* http://en.wikipedia.org/wiki/Wikipedia:WikiProject_Integrity#Overview.
43. Plain and Simple Conflict of Interest Guide. *Wikipedia.* http://enwp.org/WP:Plain_and_simple_conflict_of_interest_guide.
44. WikiProject Arbitration Enforcement. *Wikipedia.* http://enwp.org/WP:WikiProject_Arbitration_Enforcement#top.

Playing Well with Virtual Classmates: Relating Avatar Design to Group Satisfaction

Rabindra Ratan
Dept. of Telecommunication, Information Studies, and Media
Michigan State University
rar@msu.edu

Béatrice S. Hasler
IDC Herzliya, Sammy Ofer School of Communications
Kanfei Nesharim, Herzliya, Israel
hbeatrice@idc.ac.il

ABSTRACT

Virtual environments facilitate group collaboration through avatars. While many studies have examined the effects of avatar attributes on users' behaviors and attitudes, few have explicitly tested how elements of avatar design relate to group satisfaction. The present study fills this gap using data from a field study with student groups in a collaborative virtual environment. Customizing an avatar to express identity was found to relate to more satisfaction with group collaboration, while similarity between the avatar and user's gender traits was related to less group satisfaction. Further, groups with fewer active members reported higher group satisfaction. Unexpectedly, number of customizations and using a face-similar were not related to group satisfaction, potentially due to limitations in the present design for which future research can account. These findings suggest that avatar design elements play an important role in collaborative virtual environments.

Author Keywords
Avatars; avatar body-connectedness; avatar identity-expressiveness; avatar gender-likeness; group collaboration; group satisfaction; collaborative virtual environments

ACM Classification Keywords
K.3.1 Computer Uses in Education; K.4.3 Computer-supported collaborative work; H.5.1 Multimedia Information Systems

General Terms
Human Factors

INTRODUCTION

Virtual environments are being increasingly used as group collaboration tools. Such environments present excellent platforms for collaborative group processes because they can bring people together from geographically and culturally diverse locations and facilitate the sharing and construction of knowledge within these groups [14, 10]. Such virtual group interactions are often mediated by customizable virtual self-representations (i.e., avatars), and the attributes of these avatars are likely to relate to such interactions, given that various elements of avatar use have been found to influence users' behaviors and attitudes in single-user contexts. For example, the extent to which an avatar resembles its user has been found to influence the users' eating [11] and exercise [12] behaviors, while avatar height and attractiveness have been found to influence negotiation acumen and social confidence, respectively [35].

The present paper extends this research into group contexts and focuses on the role of users' avatar design decisions and psychological connections to an avatar. Users design their avatars in a variety of ways according to the specific virtual environments in which the avatars exist [7]. Some virtual environments offer only a few choices of preset avatars, while others facilitate highly realistic avatars about which the user can make many design decisions. Some of the latter even allow users to paste digital pictures of their own faces onto the avatars' heads. However, individuals vary in the psychological connections they have to their avatars [26, 32], and so a given avatar design type will be experienced differently across individuals. The present paper extends the research on avatar design type and psychological connection to an avatar to the group collaboration context. Specifically, this study examines the relationship of these avatar-related attributes with one element of this group context: satisfaction with the collaboration process, which is an important factor in computer-supported group collaboration [2, 34, 23].

AVATARS, GROUPS, AND CUSTOMIZATION

Just as avatar attributes influence user behaviors and attitudes in solitary or interpersonal contexts, they also influence group collaboration. For example, participants who were assigned to use an avatar with a black cloak reported lower group cohesion than those who were assigned to a white cloak avatar, presumably because the color black carries negative associations and thus primed participants with negative emotions [24]. Another series of

CSCW'14, February 15 – 19, 2014, Baltimore, MD, USA.

ACM 978-1-4503-2540-0/14/02...$15.00.
http://dx.doi.org/10.1145/2531602.2531732

studies has found that people who were assigned to use uniform avatars in a group context reported more group cohesion because they felt deindividuated and thus more similar to the other group members [17-19]. However, this line of research also suggests that the lack of uniqueness invoked by the uniform avatars leads group members to strive for individuality by disagreeing with group members about the task at hand. These studies suggest that avatar attributes assigned in an experimental context affect the ways that users interact in the group, but they do not provide insight into such effects in practice, where users often make choices about their avatar's attributes.

Such choices over avatar characteristics, even as simple as choosing one avatar from a small set, has been found to influence the avatar use experience [21]. One important distinction in the way that users make choices about, or customize, their avatars is the extent to which the avatar reflects an ideal self versus an actual self [15]. For example, Bessiere [3] found that online gamers with high depression or low self-esteem designed avatars that emphasized the ideal self, while online gamers with low depression or high self-esteem designed avatars that emphasized the actual self. Similarly, Dunn and Guadagno [8] found that people designed avatars that are consistent with male and female body ideals and that certain personality characteristics predicted numerous aspects of avatar design, such as attractiveness and skin tone variability. Further, Ducheneaut et al. [5] found that across multiple virtual contexts, hairstyle is one of the most important facets of avatar customization, though different styles of avatar presentation are associated with different demographics of avatar users. These studies suggest that avatar customization is an important factor of avatar use, but do not provide insight into how such customization may relate to the actual experience of using the avatar.

In an attempt target the intersection of these two lines of research – on group interactions related to avatar attributes and on avatar customization – the present research examines the relationship between avatar customization and group collaboration. Given that avatar attributes are related to group behaviors, and that avatar customization focuses on changing an avatar's attributes, then it follows that avatar customization may be related to avatar-based group collaboration. In order to examine whether this is the case, we pose the following question.

RQ1: Is the amount that an individual customizes an avatar for use in a virtual group associated with group satisfaction?

There is one specific type of customization that is becoming increasingly popular, due to the proliferation of digital cameras in computing devices, that has not received much attention in previous literature: putting one's own face onto the avatar. This type of customization leads to a high level of similarity between the avatar and the user's facial appearance, thereby allowing the users to project their "real" identity [29]. Previous research has found that avatar anthropomorphism, realism, and gender similarity contribute positively to avatar homophily (the extent to which an avatar is rated as similar to or representative of the self), which in turn contributes positively to the desirability of using the given avatar in a virtual environment [13, 22]. Further, Shami et al. [28] found that participants preferred, as reflected by duration of use, avatars that were paired with a face picture (in comparison to no-picture avatars, no-avatar pictures, or neither avatar nor pictures), likely because the combination of an avatar with a face picture provided the most cues to identity and intentions. This suggests that such face-similar avatars would contribute positively to the avatar use experience. Further, using a face-similar avatar may be positively related to collaborations with group members because it may increase the feeling of having a persistent identity, which is a contributor to trust between group members in virtual environments [27]. However, in contrast to this argument, a face-similar avatar does not allow the user to selectively self-present, and thus the user may not feel as comfortable using this avatar in a social context [33], which could detract from satisfaction with group collaboration. The present research examines this question.

RQ2: Is the use of a face-similar avatar related to group satisfaction?

PSYCHOLOGICAL CONNECTION TO AVATAR

Given the large range of customization options often provided in the avatar-design process, people psychologically connect to their avatars in different ways and to different extents [26, 31]. For example, people who have "chronic", close psychological connections to their avatars were found to incorporate their avatars' attributes in their self judgments (of body size) more than people with distant psychological connections to their avatars [4]. Thus, psychological connections to avatars may also be related to satisfaction with avatar-based group collaboration. The present study examines three types of psychological connections to avatars: avatar body-connectedness, avatar identity-expressiveness, and avatar gender-likeness.

Body and Identity Avatar Connections

The notions of avatar body-connectedness and avatar identity-expressiveness presented here are derived from a one particular approach to understanding the concept of self-presence, which is broadly defined as the extent to which the self is "present" in an avatar [26]. Given that there have been numerous disparate explanations and operationalizations of self-presence, this study utilizes two of the three subfactors of self-presence offered by the aforementioned approach and then describes them using terminology that we believe more accurately reflects their essence. Specifically, avatar body-connectedness is based on the concept of body-level ("proto") self-presence, which is defined as the extent to which an avatar is integrated into body schema. In other words, an avatar user experiences some amount of an avatar body-connectedness when she feels as though the avatar is integrated with her body in a way that allows her to naturally interact with the virtual environment through the avatar, to some extent. Avatar identity-expressiveness is based on the concept of identity-level ("extended") self-presence, which is defined as the extent to which the avatar reflects the user's personal identity outside of the virtual environment. In other words, the more an avatar user expresses elements of his personal identity (e.g., name, race, age) through the avatar, the more he should feel a sense of avatar identity-expressiveness. It is important to note that this is distinct from the concept of identification [5], which describes how people understand and empathize with media characters that have existing identities.

There has been some work comparing avatar customization to these two types of avatar connections. For example, participants who designed an avatar to resemble themselves reported more avatar identity-expressiveness than participants who were assigned to use a generic avatar, and those who designed an avatar of the same gender reported stronger avatar body-connectedness than participants who designed an opposite-gender avatar [25]. The former finding is straightforward: as participants customize an avatar to look like themselves, they imbue their own identity characteristics into the avatar and thus the avatar expresses the user's identity more. The latter finding is potentially explained by the physical similarity between the avatar and the user, i.e., the more the avatar looks like the user, the more she feels a connection between the avatar and her body schema. This explanation is consistent with neuroscientific research findings that non-body parts are integrated into the user's body schema more easily when those non-body parts resemble the actual body part in appearance or are oriented realistically [1, 9, 31]. In other words, people are generally more capable of embodying an avatar of a matched gender than an oppositely gendered avatar because of the physical similarities in body schema.

Gender-based Avatar Connections

The other type of psychological connection to avatars examined here relates to the similarity between the avatar and the user's gender. In addition to being treated as a binary identity attribute (i.e., male versus female), gender is also considered to be an element of personality that exists on sliding scale (i.e., from masculine to feminine) [6]. This understanding of gender as a continuous construct can apply to avatars as well as their users. Thus, avatar gender-likeness is defined as the extent to which the avatar's gender is perceived as similar to the user's own gender.

Previous studies have examined the similarity between users and avatars for other elements of personality (e.g., extroversion). Specifically, participants responded to versions of the Big Five personality inventory with respect to their own and their avatar's personality [3, 7]. The researchers then took the difference between the personality measures for the individual and the avatar. Smaller differences indicated greater avatar personality similarity between the user and the avatar. In both studies, participants idealized their avatars' personalities more than their own. Further, Duchenaut et al. [7] found that people with greater avatar personality similarity were more satisfied with and attached to their avatar and also spent more time playing as their avatar.

The present study utilizes a similar approach to building a construct based on the similarity between two continuous trait-level characteristics, one regarding the avatar and the other regarding the user. However, this study focuses on gender instead of other personality constructs. Unlike these other constructs, gender is more clearly associated with customizable avatar characteristics (e.g., hairstyle, clothing color) and thus is easier to attribute to an avatar than psychological traits that are more vaguely apparent in the avatar's customizable characteristics.

Psychological Connections and Group Satisfaction

Just as amount or type of avatar customization may relate to group satisfaction, as explored through RQs 1 and 2, the types of psychological connection to avatars explored here may also relate to group satisfaction. On the one hand, having a closer psychological connection to an avatar may increase the comfort that the user has while using this avatar, which would put the user more at ease in group collaboration and thus may increase group satisfaction. Or alternatively, having a close psychological connection to the avatar may increase the extent to which the user feels as though she has a unique or persistent identity in the group, which, as described with respect to RQ2, may contribute to trust and thus satisfaction between group members. On the other hand, the closer psychological connection to the avatar may hinder the user's ability to selectively self-present through the avatar and thus may detract from group communication. This potential relationship is explored through a research question.

RQ3: Is group satisfaction associated with any of the types of psychological connections to avatars (i.e., body-connectedness, identity-expressiveness, or gender-likeness)?

METHOD

We conducted an uncontrolled field study within the context of a semester-long online course that included interactions between students through avatars in a virtual environment. While this method offered limited control over the participants' experiences and the variables of interest, thereby limiting our ability to establish causal links, this type of natural setting provides a high level of ecological validity (e.g., students had real learning motivations), which is valuable given the increasing popularity of online teaching environments. Further, given the 10-week duration of the study, participants were able to develop a strength of interpersonal relationships with each other that is impossible in a single-session, controlled social interaction. Also, by using a diverse, intercultural selection of participants (details below), the study generalizes to a wider population. In summary, by sacrificing control over the variables, the present study provides higher levels of ecological and external validity.

Participants and Procedure

Participants included 154 students (119 male, 35 female) between the ages of 19 and 42 (M = 23.53, SD = 2.69, inner quartile range 22-24) who collaborated in 62 virtual teams of four to six members each throughout the 10-week Fall 2010 semester. The study was conducted in the context of a global lecture series called "The ShanghAI Lectures" (http://shanghailectures.org; see [20] for more details) on embodied – natural and artificial – intelligence. The lecture series by the Artificial Intelligence Lab of the University of Zurich (presented for the first time in Fall term 2009 from Shanghai Jiao Tong University) connects about 15 universities worldwide every year via videoconference. The students represented over 25 nationalities, with the top three being Chinese (N = 56), Swiss (N = 26), and German (N = 17). Student teams were comprised of members from the same continent (i.e., either Asia or Europe), but most team members were unacquainted with each other prior to the course.

In addition to the traditional elements of the online class (e.g., viewing video-recorded lectures), students were required to participate in virtual discussion sessions every other week and, in between these meetings, to engage in group exercises in the virtual environment as well. The present study focuses on the group exercises, which included activities such as building a "cozy and unique" virtual team room in which the group could meet, assessing the artificial intelligence of a virtual robot, and examining sets of virtual self-assembling objects.

The virtual collaboration platform used in this course, "UNIworld" (screenshot in Figure 1), which was developed based on the open-source toolkit "Open Wonderland" (version 0.5) (http://openwonderland.org). Open Wonderland offers public and private chat and "spatial audio" (i.e., automatic volume adjustment according to the distance between avatars). Further, students could perform a set of 14 basic postures and gestures through their avatars using keyboard commands or by clicking corresponding buttons. Collaborative work was supported by in-world application sharing tools, such as web browsers, video-players, PDF viewers, text editors, and whiteboards. It should be noted that teams could use additional media to schedule meetings and coordinate tasks.

Students were given the option to use a default avatar or a customized avatar using in-world tools. Further, they could put a picture of their own face on the avatar's head (screenshot examples in Figure 2). Participants began with a cartoon-style default avatar and could customize gender, clothing accessories, and color of skin, hair, pants, shirt, and shoes. In comparison to other virtual world applications (e.g., Second Life), freedom to customize avatar appearance was limited in UNIworld. These customizations were categorical and did not allow for gradual changes. Face-pic avatars were created with a special website that facilitates the creation of photorealistic avatars (http://evolver.com). Students could upload a photograph of themselves, export the avatar file from evolver.com, and then import it into UNIworld and use it as any other Wonderland avatar (i.e., navigate, speak, and write).

Figure 1: Screenshot of the collaborative virtual environment.

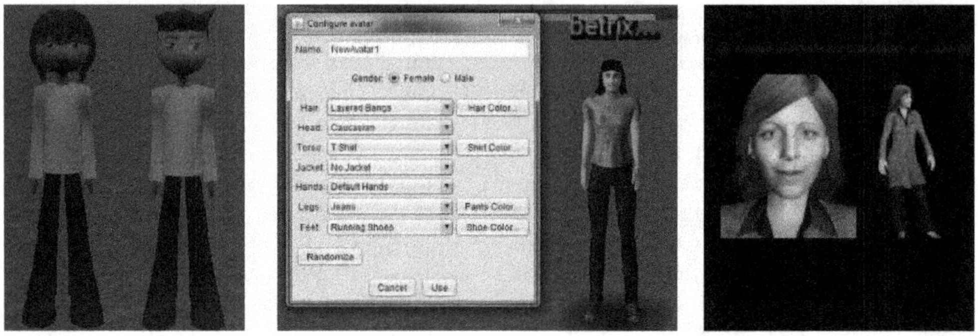

Figure 2: Avatar options: default (left); customized example (center); personalized example (right).

Upon registration for the lectures, the students were requested to choose an avatar name and to fill in a profile page on the course website. The online registration form contained a description of the purpose of the research project, the kind of data to be collected, and privacy protection procedures. The students were also required to read and respond to an informed consent form. Participation in the research project was an optional part of the lectures, which had no bearing on their academic evaluation.

Participants responded to two surveys throughout the course of the project. The first, which was administered after the first group exercise, included questions about technology use habits and psychological personality traits of the participant. The second survey was administered after the final group exercise, about six weeks after the first survey. This included questions about self-presence and psychological personality traits of each participant's avatar. There were also numerous questions in both surveys not discussed presently. Students received extra credit points for completing the surveys, which led to a high response rate (83%).

Measures

Avatar customization count, derived from logs of the participants' behavior in the virtual world, was simply the raw count of the number of times a change was made to any of the avatar's attributes.

Because the behavior logs did not record whether a participant used a face-similar avatar, the measure of such use was determined from the responses to the question "How often did you use a personalized avatar that you created on evolver.com based on your photograph?" Participants who responded with "occasionally" (N = 36), "often" (N = 2), or "always" (N = 3) were classified as face-similar avatar users, where those who replied "never" (N = 113) were not.

The measures of avatar body-connectedness and avatar identity-expressiveness were drawn from a previously validated questionnaire designed to measure the subfactors of self-presence [26]. Participants used a 5-point Likert scale, ranging from "not at all" to "absolutely" to respond to the questions about their connections to their avatars. The items for each construct (see Figure 3) were averaged to form composite measures, with Cronbach's alphas of .91 for avatar body-connectedness and .83 for avatar identity-expressiveness.

Avatar gender-likeness similarity was measured in a similar method as in the aforementioned studies [7, 3]. Participants responded, on 5-point Likert scales ranging from "not at all" to "extremely", to 22 adjectives about gender traits ([6], see Figure 4) as they applied to themselves (first survey) as well as their avatars (second survey). The absolute value of the difference between these scores indicates the extent to which the avatar ratings differed from the self ratings. We performed this calculation for the masculine and feminine gender items separately, resulting in two separate measures. These scores were reverse coded so that larger values indicated greater similarity between the two related ratings.

Avatar Body-Connectedness

1. When using the virtual environment, how much do you feel your avatar is a part of your body?
2. When using your avatar, to what extent do you feel like your arm is elongated into the virtual environment through your avatar?
3. When using your avatar, to what extent do you feel like you can reach into the virtual environment through your avatar?
4. When using the virtual environment, how much do you feel like your avatar is an extension of your body within the game/virtual environment?
5. When using the virtual environment, to what extent do you feel like your hand is inside of the game/virtual environment?

Avatar Identity-Expressiveness

1. To what extent is your avatar's gender related to some aspect of your personal identity?
2. To what extent is your avatar's race related to some aspect of your personal identity?
3. To what extent is your avatar's clothing related to some aspect of your personal identity?
4. To what extent does your avatar's profile info represent some aspect of your personal identity?
5. To what extent does your avatar's name represent some aspect of your personal identity?
6. To what extent is your avatar's appearance related to some aspect of your personal identity?

Figure 3. Self-presence questionnaire items [26].

Group satisfaction was operationalized through a measure of satisfaction with the process of in-world collaboration tasks using Suh's [30] Performance Perception Questionnaire. Participants rated five semantic differentials with respect to the group collaboration process in response to the question "How would you describe the problem solving (or negotiation) process you and your team members used?" on a 7-point scale: efficient – inefficient, uncoordinated – coordinated, fair – unfair, understandable – confusing, dissatisfying – satisfying. Cronbach's alpha for this measure was .87.

Two measures of technology use habits, computer use time and video game frequency, were included as controls because of the potential effect that they may have on choice of avatar type and psychological connections to avatars. Specifically, people who are more comfortable with technology may be more willing to customize or personalize their avatar and may also feel a different type of connection to their avatars than people who are less comfortable with technology. Participants estimated the number of hours per week they spend on a computer and the frequency with which they play computer or video games on a 5-point scale ranging from "I do not play computer/video games" to "every day".

The extent to which students were actively engaged in the class varied, especially because some students were not taking the class for credit. Such variance in individual engagement (e.g., showing up for virtual group meetings) was likely to influence the experience for the students. For example, being on a team with only two active members would be more intimate than being on a team of four active members. In order to account for this variance at the group level, and given that only active team members were likely to complete the final survey, we included a count of such completions ("active member count") in our analysis.

Personality
(M) Competitive, daring, adventurous, aggressive
(F) Affectionate, sympathetic, gentle, sensitive
Cognitive
(M) Good with numbers, analytical, good at problem solving, quantitatively skilled
(F) Imaginative, intuitive, artistic, creative
Physical
(M) Rugged, muscular, physically strong, burly
(F) Cute, gorgeous, beautiful, pretty

Figure 4. Subconstructs and adjectives for gender measure [6]

	N	M	SD	Min	Max
Group Process Satisfaction	154	4.85	1.21	1	7
Customization Count	140	9.42	9.55	0	57
Avatar Body-Connectedness	152	2.38	0.96	0	4
Avatar Identity-Expressiveness	152	2.75	0.97	0	5
Avatar Gender-Likeness_Masculine	144	8.69	3.07	0	12
Avatar Gender-Likeness_Feminine	144	8.70	3.18	0	12
Computer Hours per Week	146	37.78	20.42	1	120
Frequency Video Games	146	3.10	1.29	1	5
Response Rate	154	3.08	1.18	1	6

Table 1. Descriptive Statistics

The descriptive statistics for all measures can be found in Table 1. For the analysis, in order to account for variance in the distribution of this data, we mean centered all of the independent variables, except for the face-similar avatar use, which was calculated as a binary metric, as described above.

RESULTS

Multilevel modeling was used to examine the effects on group satisfaction. This approach accounts for interdependence among the observations. Specifically, it controlled for team effects, given the potential for dependency among team members, when examining the relationship between an individual's customization or avatar connections with group satisfaction.

In order to determine the degree of within-group interdependence, we calculated the intraclass correlation coefficient (ICC). The intercept estimate was .54, and the residual was 1.03, and so the ICC was calculated to be .34. This suggests that 34% of the variance in group satisfaction is explained by the team structure, which confirms the importance of multilevel modeling.

The fixed factors of interest in this model included customization count, use of a face-similar avatar, avatar body-connectedness, avatar identity-expressiveness, and the two measures of avatar gender-likeness (masculine gender-likeness and feminine gender-likeness). Further, as fixed factor control variables, we included computer hours per week and frequency playing of video games. Active member count for each group was included as a random factor because of the potential influence on group satisfaction.

The results of this analysis (Table 2, Fixed Effects) indicate no difference in group satisfaction related to customization (RQ1) or using a face-similar avatar (RQ2). However, group satisfaction was positively related to avatar identity-expressiveness and negatively related to the masculine avatar gender-likeness measure (RQ3).

Fixed Effects

	Estimate	Std. Error	df	t	p	
Intercept	4.87	0.12	39.63	42.10	0.00	
Customization Count	0.01	0.01	115.33	1.38	0.17	
Face Similar Avatar	-0.14	0.25	130.96	-0.56	0.58	
Avatar Body-Connectedness	-0.10	0.13	120.65	-0.76	0.45	
Avatar Identity-Expressiveness	0.25	0.12	119.59	2.14	0.03	*
Avatar Gender-Likeness_Masculine	-0.16	0.07	121.19	-2.26	0.03	*
Avatar Gender-Likeness_Feminine	0.06	0.06	122.57	0.93	0.36	
Computer Hours per Week	0.00	0.00	124.86	-0.82	0.41	
Frequency Video Games	0.00	0.07	126.86	0.04	0.97	

Random Effects

	Estimate	Std. Error	Wald Z	p	
Residual	0.83	0.13	6.55	0.00	
Intercept	0.08	0.17	0.49	0.63	
Active member count (AMC)	0.377162	0.207808	1.81495	0.0695	†
Intercept-AMC correlation	-0.18	0.09	-1.93	0.05	†

Note: †p < .10, *p < .05, **p < .01

Table 2. Multilevel model on group satisfaction

We also found an unexpected negative relationship between active member count and group satisfaction, as indicated by the negative correlation between the random effects intercept and the active member count (p = .05). This suggests higher group satisfaction for smaller groups.

DISCUSSION

Building on research about the effects of avatar use on behaviors and attitudes, the present study examines how avatar design and psychological connections to avatars relate to group satisfaction (i.e., satisfaction with the group collaboration process). Data collected from a virtual world-based lecture series in which students collaborated on small group projects suggest that psychological connection to the avatar as measured by avatar identity-expressiveness was associated with more group satisfaction, while psychological connection to the avatar as measured by masculine avatar gender-likeness was associated with less group satisfaction. The opposing direction of these relationships is interesting and suggests that psychological connections to an avatar do not relate to avatar-based group collaboration in uniform ways. The unexpected finding that groups with smaller active member counts were associated with more group satisfaction suggests that collaborative virtual environments may be inefficient for larger groups, perhaps due to limitations in the channels used for communication. Our expectations of a relationship of group satisfaction with avatar customization and with using a face-similar avatar were not supported, but we believe this was due to specific aspects of the present study and thus that differently designed research may discover such relationships in the future. Below, we examine the implications of the specific findings and non-findings as well as considerations for design of collaborative virtual environments platforms.

The positive relationship between avatar identity-expressiveness and group satisfaction may suggest that customizing an avatar to express identity may increase the comfort with using with that avatar within the group setting. Or alternatively, using an avatar that closely reflects an individual's offline identity may increase the user's feeling of accountability to others, which is consistent with other research on trust between group members in virtual environments [27]. However, such causal interpretations should be treated cautiously because it is also possible that elements of the group interactions influenced the extent to which the user customized the avatar as expressive of identity, or that a third variable affected both. In either direction, as cause or effect, this finding still highlights the importance of being able to express personal identity through an avatar within the group collaboration process. But if the causal link from avatar identity-expressiveness to group satisfaction were accepted, this would suggest that collaborative virtual environments could improve group satisfaction by allowing (or encouraging) users to imbue aspects of their offline identity into their avatars.

The negative relationship between masculine avatar gender-likeness and group satisfaction does not lend itself to a clear interpretation. It is possible that having a close psychological connection to the avatar's gender hinders the user's ability to selectively self-present through the avatar and thus constrains group communication. However, this does not seem likely, given that a similar relationship was not found for the feminine avatar gender-likeness measure. Another explanation, which is more consistent with research on gender differences in gaming [15], is that masculine avatars tend to be used for more competitive and less social activities. Given that people sometimes conform to their behavioral expectations regarding their avatar's identity [35], it may be that masculine participants who customized masculine avatars conformed to the expectation that masculine avatars are unfriendly. However, as with the previous finding, such a causal explanation should be treated with caution. It is also possible that negative elements of the group interactions encouraged participants to customize their avatars to be consistent with their own masculine gender, or that a third variable influenced both masculine customization and group satisfaction in the same direction. Another important consideration is the gender skew of the sample (77% male). If there had been more female participants, perhaps the relationship feminine avatar gender-likeness and group satisfaction would have been significant, possibly in the opposite direction, or would have cancelled out the relationship between masculine avatar gender-likeness and group satisfaction. In any case, the present finding still suggests that avatar gender plays a meaningful role in the experience of avatar use and may be related to the outcomes of such use. If the causal link from masculine avatar gender-likeness to group satisfaction were accepted, this would suggest that collaborative virtual environments could improve group satisfaction by not providing avatar customization options that are strongly masculine or otherwise anti-social.

The finding that group satisfaction was higher for groups with smaller active member counts, though unexpected, provides interesting implications. Namely, it suggests that the quality of communication in collaborative virtual environments decreases as the number of communicators increases. This is consistent with a media richness theory argument – that as the number of channels decreases, the quality of communication decreases – though this theory has not received consistent support [30]. The communication channels provided by the collaborative virtual environment (e.g., text chat) may privilege communication between smaller groups, for example, by not providing clear cues to help users distinguish who is communicating to whom. An alternative explanation in the opposite causal direction is that strongly positive communication between a small number of group members alienated the other group members, resulting in those members withdrawing from the group or continuing on but being displeased with the group. This would have led the average group satisfaction to be high for those groups in which the alienated members departed, and low for those groups in which the displeased members stayed on. While such dynamics were not the focus of the present study, they are interesting to note and future research may be better equipped to examine them directly. And regardless of the directionality, one potential implication for the design of collaborative virtual environments is that the communication channels should be examined for groups of varying sizes.

The lack of a significant relationship between group satisfaction and avatar customization and may suggest that the amount of customization alone does not play a role in the way the avatar is used in a group setting. Similarly, using a face-similar avatar compared to a typical avatar may not relate to differences in the uses of the avatar. However, such claims cannot be supported by the present null findings. Further, the present design was an uncontrolled field study and so there were many potential aspects of the participants' experience that may have detracted from this relationship. Most notably, the groups were not required to communicate only in the virtual environment. Some groups used external communication tools (e.g., Skype, email) to coordinate their group activities. It is possible that such communication influenced group satisfaction and thus added noise to the data. Alternatively, the customization options provided in the environment may have seemed unnatural, while face-similar avatar use may have seemed too intrusive or time consuming for some users. Future research could tease out these limitations by utilizing a controlled experimental design. Specifically, by assigning participants to customize their avatars at differing amounts of input and face-similarity, such research may discover a relationship between these conditions and elements of group collaboration that results from using these avatars.

This relates to another limitation of this study that would have been notable if avatar customization had been found significantly related to group satisfaction. Namely, although the avatar customization measure came from a log-based count taken throughout the course of the study, well before these self-report variables were measured, it would still have been possible for variables unaccounted for in this analysis to have influenced both the amount of customization as well as the self-report variables. For example, an individual's choice to engage in more avatar customization may be caused by a specific personality trait, such as extroversion, and this trait may also contribute to more positive group collaboration. Similarly, students who were more excited about the class may have put more energy into customizing their avatars as well as engaged more in the group collaboration, thereby increasing their satisfaction. Thus, a relationship between avatar customization and group satisfaction would have been potentially spurious and instead the result of a third variable that was unaccounted for in the dataset. Future research could address this through a controlled experimental design. One approach would be to compare three conditions of avatar design: undirected customization, forced high customization, and forced low customization.

In general, this uncontrolled field study was unable to make strong claims of causation in the observed relationships because of the limitations of using cross-sectional data (e.g., questionnaire response habits). Another limitation relates to context in which the participants interacted. Specifically, given that it was an AI course, it attracted technologically-oriented students who had a fair amount of gaming experience. On the positive side, this context is generalizable to other online courses that focus on technology-related content. On the negative side, this means that generalizability is limited for virtual collaborative work that occurs outside of a learning environment, for online courses that focus on non-technology topics, and for virtual collaborations between people who are less adept at or interested in using technology.

While recognizing these limitations, the present approach allowed for the examination of avatar design in a natural setting, thereby providing a higher level of ecological and external validity than usually offered by most controlled experiments. The findings suggest that avatar design matters in the implementation of real collaborative virtual environments and that the users' psychological experience with their avatars play an important role in the outcomes of such use.

CONCLUSION

Overall, this research offers a novel examination of how avatar customization and psychological connection to avatars relate to group satisfaction in virtual environments. As part of the growing body of research on how avatar attributes influence their users, this study contributes to the understanding of the phenomena of avatar use as well as to some simple principles for the implementation of avatar design systems in collaborative virtual environments.

ACKNOWLEDGMENTS

We greatly appreciate the reviewers of this manuscript who not only provided thorough feedback but also shepherded us through greater process of improving our thinking and writing. This was especially true for the review coordinator, who provided helpful and constructive syntheses of all of the feedback. And lastly, we thank David Reyes for his statistics consulting on how to (properly) conduct multilevel modeling.

REFERENCES

1. Armel, K. and Ramachandran, V. Projecting sensations to external objects: Evidence from skin conductance response. *Proc. of the Royal Society B: Biological Sciences, 270* (2003), 1499-1506.
2. Baltes, B. B., Dickson, M. W., Sherman, M. P., Bauer, C. C. and LaGanke, J. S. Computer-mediated communication and group decision making: A meta-analysis. *Organizational Behavior and Human Decision Processes 87*, 1 (2002), 156-179.
3. Bessiere, K., Seay, A. and Kiesler, S. The ideal elf: Identity exploration in World of Warcraft. *CyberPsychology & Behavior 10*, 2 (2007), 530-535.
4. Chandler, J., Konrath, S. and Schwarz, N. Online and on my mind: Temporary and chronic accessibility moderate the influence of media figures. *Media Psychology 12,* 2 (2009), 210-226.
5. Cohen, J. Defining identification: A theoretical look at the identification of audiences with media characters. *Mass Communication and Society 4*, 3 (2001), 245-264.
6. Diekman, A. B. and Eagly, A. H. Stereotypes as dynamic constructs: Women and men of the past, present, and future. *Personality and Social Psychology Bulletin, 26* (2000), 1171-1188.
7. Ducheneaut, N., Wen, M. H., Yee, N. and Wadley, G. Body and mind: a study of avatar personalization in three virtual worlds. *Proc. of the 27th International Conf. on Human Factors in Computing Systems.* 1151-1160 (2009). ACM.
8. Dunn, R. A. and Guadagno, R. E. My avatar and me - Gender and personality predictors of avatar-self discrepancy. *Computers in Human Behavior 28,* 1 (2012), 97-106. doi: 10.1016/j.chb.2011.08.015
9. Ehrsson, H., Spence, C. and Passingham, R. That's my hand! Activity in premotor cortex reflects feeling of ownership of a limb. *Science 305,* 5685 (2004), 875-877.
10. Erickson, T., Shami, N. S., Kellogg, W. A. and Levine, D. Synchronous Interaction Among Hundreds: An Evaluation of a Conference in an Avatar-based Virtual Environment. *Proc. CHI* 2011, ACM Press (2011), 503-512.
11. Fox, J., Bailenson, J. and Binney, J. Virtual experiences, physical behaviors: The effect of presence on imitation of an eating avatar. *Presence: Teleoperators and Virtual Environments 18,* 4 (2009), 294-303.
12. Fox, J. and Bailenson, J. Virtual self-modeling: The effects of vicarious reinforcement and identification on exercise behaviors. *Media Psychology 12,* 1 (2009), 1-25.
13. Hamilton, M. A. and Nowak, K. L. Advancing a Model of Avatar Evaluation and Selection. *PsychNology Journal 8,* 1 (2010), 33-65.
14. Hasler, B. S. Intercultural collaborative learning in virtual worlds. In R. Hinrichs & C. Wankel (Eds.), *Transforming virtual world learning. Cutting-edge technologies in higher education* (Vol. 4, pp. 271-310) (2011). Bingley, UK: Emerald Publishing.
15. Huh, S. and Williams, D. Dude looks like a lady: Gender swapping in an online game. *Online worlds: Convergence of the real and the virtual.* Springer London (2010), 161-174.
16. Jin, S. A. Avatars mirroring the actual self versus projecting the ideal self: The effects of self-priming on interactivity and immersion in an exergame, Wii Fit. *CyberPsychology & Behavior 12,* 6 (2009), 761-765.
17. Kim, J. Balancing uniqueness and assimilation in computer-mediated groups. *Computers in Human Behavior 26*, 4 (2010), 778-784.
18. Kim, J. and Park, H. S. The effect of uniform virtual appearance on conformity intention: Social identity model of deindividuation effects and optimal distinctiveness theory. *Computers in Human Behavior 27*, 3 (2011), 1223-1230.
19. Kim, J. Two routes leading to conformity intention in computer-mediated groups: Matching versus mismatching virtual representations. *Journal of Computer-Mediated Communication 16*, 2 (2011), 271-287.
20. Labhart, N., Hasler, B. S., Zbinden, A. and Schmeil, A. The ShanghAI Lectures: A global education project on artificial intelligence. *Journal of Universal Computer Science, 18* (2013), 2542-2555.
21. Lim, S. and Reeves, B. Being in the game: Effects of avatar choice and point of view on psychophysiological responses during play. *Media Psychology 12,* 4 (2009), 348-370.
22. Nowak, K., Hamilton, M. and Hammond, C. The effect of image features on judgments of homophily, credibility, and intention to use as avatars in future interactions. *Media Psychology 12,* 1 (2009), 50-76.
23. Olaniran, B. A. A model of group satisfaction in computer-mediated communication and face-to-face meetings. *Behaviour & Information Technology 15,* 1 (1996), 24-36.

24. Pena, J., Hancock, J. and Merola, N. The priming effects of avatars in virtual settings. *Communication Research 36,* 6 (2009), 1-19.
25. Ratan, R. A. *Self-Presence: Body, emotion, and identity extension into the virtual self. Unpublished doctoral dissertation* (2011). University of Southern California.
26. Ratan, R. A. Self-presence, explicated: Body, emotion, and identity extension into the virtual self. In R. Luppicini (Ed.), *Handbook of Research on Technoself* (2012). New York, NY: IGI Global.
27. Ratan, R., Chung, J., Shen, C., Williams, D. and Poole, M. Schmoozing and Smiting: Trust, social institutions and communication patterns in an MMOG. *Journal of Computer-Mediated Communication, 16*(1), (2010), 93-114.
28. Shami, N. S., Cheng, L.-T., Rohall, S., Sempere, A. and Patterson, J. Avatars Meet Meetings: Design Issues in Integrating Avatars in Distributed Corporate Meetings. *Proc. GROUP 2010*, ACM Press (2010), 35-44.
29. Shami, N. S., Erickson, T. and Kellogg, W. Common Ground and small group interaction in large virtual world gatherings. *Proc. ECSCW 2011*. Springer London (2011), 393-404.
30. Suh, K. S. Impact of communication medium on task performance and satisfaction: an examination of media-richness theory. *Information & Management 35,* 5 (1999), 295-312.
31. Tsakiris, M. and Haggard, P. The rubber hand illusion revisited: Visuotactile integration and self-attribution. *Journal of Experimental Psychology-Human Perception and Performance 31,* 1 (2005), 80-91.
32. Van Looy, J., Courtois, C., De Vocht, M. and De Marez, L. Player identification in online games: validation of a scale for measuring identification in MMOGs. *Media Psychology 15,* 2 (2012), 197-221.
33. Walther, J. B. Selective self-presentation in computer-mediated communication: Hyperpersonal dimensions of technology, language, and cognition. *Computers in Human Behavior 23,* 5 (2007), 2538-2557.
34. Walther, J. B. and Bazarova N.N. Validation and application of electronic propinquity theory to computer-mediated communication in groups. *Communication Research 35*, 5 (2008): 622-645.
35. Yee, N., Bailenson, J. N. and Ducheneaut, N. The Proteus effect: Implications of transformed digital self-representation on online and offline behavior. *Communication Research* 36, 2 (2009), 285-312.

The Kernel of a Research Infrastructure

David Ribes
Communication, Culture & Technology (CCT)
Georgetown University
3520 Prospect St. NW, Suite 311
Washington, DC, 20057
dr273@georgetown.edu

ABSTRACT

Infrastructure makes it easier, faster or possible for investigators to study objects of research. It does so by making available consistent and stable resources and services such as data, collaboration tools, sites of sample collection, or calibrated instruments. This paper offers the concept of the *kernel of a research infrastructure* as a new unit of analysis for investigating the enabling capacities of infrastructure. The kernel is the core resources and services an infrastructure makes available (called the cache), as well as the work, techniques and technologies that go into sustaining that availability (called addressing). By inspecting and comparing the kernel of two long-term scientific enterprises, this paper demonstrates how focusing on the kernel can help explain key qualities of research infrastructure such as flexibility and persistence in the face of dramatic changes to the objects, methods and practice of science.

Author Keywords

Infrastructure; long-term; sustainability; change; technoscientific flexibility; science; ethnography and archival research; grounded theory; kernel

Categories and Subject Descriptors

J.4 [**Social and Behavioral Sciences**] Sociology
K.4.3 [**Organizational Impacts**] Computer-supported cooperative work

General Terms

Management, Design, Human Factors, Theory

INTRODUCTION

Research infrastructures offer resources and services in the support of scientific and scholarly inquiries. They make it easier, or possible, for investigators to explore their objects of research. What particular resources and services are made available varies greatly by infrastructure. In studies *of* infrastructure, the most well investigated service has been facilitating communication and coordination [31], such as supporting geographically distributed collaboration or helping heterogeneous researchers work across disciplinary boundaries [26]. Also well investigated have been the archival functions of infrastructure, such as making it easier to curate scientific data [3], share them with colleagues [4] or enable reuse [12]. But infrastructures may offer other resources and services, less explored but equally important to the accomplishment of science, for example, analytic functions such as offering software tools [16] to support data visualization or making computing 'cycles' available [38]. Infrastructures may offer standardized instruments that enable the comparison of data across time and space [34]. They may play more cultural roles, such as offering researchers identity and affiliation, a venue for community formation, or a sense of vocation [17].

This paper offers the concept of *the kernel* as a new unit of analysis for the investigation of research infrastructure. The kernel is the core resources and services that an infrastructure makes available *and* the work, techniques and technologies that seek to sustain the availability of those resources over time. These two aspects of the kernel must always be taken together. A kernel approach examines resources and services as *entangled* with the work, techniques and technologies used to ensure their availability *as* resources and services.

For example, data is one such resource: some research infrastructures seek to make data sharing easier, for instance, in order to encourage reuse. Within such infrastructures there are actors (e.g., information managers) tasked with ensuring that those data remain available, well described, and in accessible repositories – in a kernel approach, this work is called *addressing*. The activities of sustaining availability of those data are entangled with the data themselves, for example, through the calibration of instruments [19], through data's redescription in metadata specifications [28], or by the ongoing maintenance work to keep data available online by web-service.

However, data are only one resource that infrastructure may seek to make available. This paper will focus on the set of core resources and services offered by particular infrastructures – in a kernel approach this is called *the cache*.

Focusing on the kernel, the cache and addressing will help explain many of the central capacities of infrastructure to enable and facilitate scientific research. By definition, a research infrastructure may have many purposes [41],

CSCW'14, February 15 - 19 2014, Baltimore, MD, USA
Copyright 2014 ACM 978-1-4503-2540-0/14/02©$15.00.
http://dx.doi.org/10.1145/2531602.2531700

however, one of the most explicit goals is the ability of infrastructure to support the investigation of new objects of research. *How do actors work to make the resources of infrastructure available for the investigation of new objects of interest?*

Focusing on the kernel will also help us understand the longevity of certain research infrastructures in the face of great transformations to the landscape of science. This is called *technoscientific flexibility*. Today, we consider flexibility to be a sought after virtue in the design of information systems. Flexibility may refer to, for example, the ability of a system to respond to changing user needs or to smoothly embrace emerging technologies [8]. But the ability to adapt to new scientific objects is a particular kind of capacity; for research infrastructure it is seminal, but one that has received very little scholarly attention. Focusing on the kernel will contribute to understanding technoscientific flexibility: *techniques, technologies and organizational innovations to adapt to changes in scientific objects, instruments and methods of investigation.*

To elaborate a kernel approach, this paper draws on an ongoing comparative study of two long-term research infrastructures: the MACS is the Multi-Center AIDS Cohort Study, and LTER is Long-Term Ecological Research. The empirical portions of this paper are dedicated to exploring the MACS and LTER kernels – which share surprising similarities given their distinct research concerns, while differing in revealing ways. The MACS is a *trim-poodle infrastructure* because it has a *single-core* kernel: its members work to standardize all their data and specimens and house them in common repositories. LTER is a *shaggy dog infrastructure* because it has a *multi-core* kernel: the diversity of their scientific materials and objects of study has posed great difficulties for standardization; today they have multiple repositories and standards for their data and materials.

The paper concludes with a discussion of how a kernel approach can serve to evaluate research infrastructure's ability to support the investigation of new objects of research.

What do we gain from a kernel approach? Understanding persistence, materiality and flexibility

The study of infrastructure has a strong intellectual lineage in CSCW [41]. A common focus has been on infrastructure that supports the doing of science, social science or humanities scholarship [31], often under the titles of collaboratory [13], cyberinfrastructure or eScience [39], but which in this paper will simply be called research infrastructure.

A great deal of research *on* infrastructure has focused on supporting collaboration of scientists [31]. A second focus has been to investigate how infrastructure supports data sharing and reuse [6, 42]. The two cases explored in this paper share these goals: the MACS and LTER are cross-disciplinary and seek to make their data available for new investigations. However, they also offer additional resources and services.

A kernel approach focuses on how infrastructures support the investigation of new objects of research, and to do so will broaden the analysis to include additional kinds of key resources and services – for example, the *materials* of science such as specimens and samples, along with where those materials come from. This approach places at center-stage renewal of the availability of resources and services: *supporting the ongoing investigation of new and old objects of research is the central goal of research infrastructure, and regenerating access to key resources and services is the central activity that enables infrastructure to do so.*

The Kernel

The driving metaphor in this paper is not about corn – a seed that grows or pops – it is a secondary metaphor inspired by software engineering. A kernel is the most important part of an operating system (OS), providing an abstraction layer that makes system resources available for applications.

Imagine the classic representation of the computing stack: interface and applications on the top, hardware on the bottom, and the operating system mediating these from between. From the perspective of the user, the kernel is essentially opaque, a black box that handles the operations "below." A user need not understand the machine language of device drivers, such as printers or scanners, or how to allocate activity in the central processing unit. An OS kernel is the infrastructure of practical computing, making the coordination of heterogeneous components appear seamless.

However, if we were to open this black box, as programmers that work on a kernel do, we would find millions of lines of code, built up and torn down over years or decades, sedimented by each additional contribution that sought to sustain the operations of a legacy device or enshrine a new computational capacity. It is from this perspective that this paper approaches the kernel – "from below," as an infrastructural inversion [5].

The kernel of a research infrastructure seeks to make certain resources that are needed in a scientific investigation available for use. It comprises two entangled aspects: the cache and addressing (see Figure 1).

The cache refers to the resources and services that an infrastructure makes available to support scientific investigations. In the cases explored in this paper, MACS and LTER, their caches have four features:

i. sites of ongoing data and specimen collection;
ii. an archive of data and specimens;
iii. standardized instruments, and;
iv. affiliated heterogeneous experts.

Other infrastructures offer altogether different configurations of resources and services. For example, GEON and LEAD [36], cyberinfrastructure for the earth and atmospheric sciences respectively, had no sites of collection, instruments, or data of their own. Instead their cache comprised data integration and visualization tools, i.e., they offered resources and services to interoperate data from heterogeneous databases and helped to make those data comprehensible by providing tools to render them in domain-specific visualizations. The Open Science Grid (OSG) offers only access to vast amounts of distributed processing power and storage [38]. We will return to these examples in the discussion.

The question: "What resources and services?" has as many answers as there are infrastructures – it is an empirical question that can only be answered in the particular. The composition of the cache is specific to the history of an infrastructure.

Over time, new kinds of resources and services that an infrastructure may offer are innovated – such as data integration or cycle sharing – but the "classic resources" remain just as important to doing science. The emphasis in recent studies of infrastructure development efforts has been on digital resources, such as data. However, within science, materials, such as specimens and samples, are crucial for inquiry. For example, one of the most valuable resources that the MACS offers its members is a specimen archive of blood that goes back nearly thirty years. The LTER site in Baltimore offers something similar yet distinct: an archive of stream water samples that stretches back thirteen years. To illustrate the kernel, we will return to the examples of blood and water throughout the paper.

The key point in examining a cache is to expand the unit of analysis to include all the core resources and services an infrastructure makes available, eschewing any fixation on 'high tech' resources in favor of understanding how features of the cache – new and old, material and computational, digital and paper based – are rendered available for the investigation of a research object.

The second aspect of the kernel is called addressing, which refers to the work, techniques and technologies that seek to ensure that resources and services are available for use, in a stable manner, and over time. As with the cache, addressing is highly heterogeneous and specific. Returning to blood and water, we will find that such scientific materials are not distinct from the information systems of infrastructure: an aliquot of blood is only meaningful if it continues to be tied to the individual who donated it, their blood pressure, their weight, and all the other blood samples they have donated over the years. Water must be tied to the stream that it came from and the date of its collection. All of these data are recorded in tandem with collection of blood and water: an information management issue. Within the MACS and LTER there are actors who work to ensure that those samples are collected in comparable ways across the years;

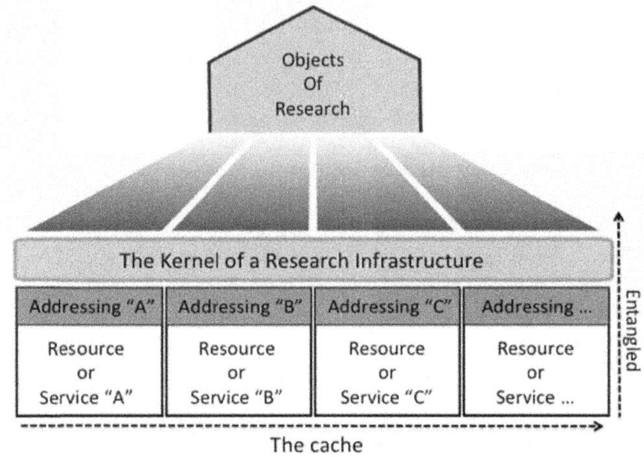

Figure 1: The kernel of a research infrastructure. Resources and services are made available for the investigation of objects of research through ongoing activities of addressing. ***Image credit: Jake Fagan***

that they are labeled and stored in ways that will preserve their useful material qualities; and that they can be retrieved for later use with relative ease. All of these, and many more, are the activities of addressing.

The term "entangled" is essential to understanding the relationship between the cache and addressing. To clarify what is meant by entanglement, an example from traditional infrastructure is revealing: we may initially think that drinking water and the pipes that deliver it to our home should be thought of as discrete, however this is misleading. Part of the infrastructure of drinking water includes filtering silt, extracting pollutants, inspecting for bacterial cultures, and adding chlorine. *Infrastructure transforms that which it makes available.* If anything other than water in this form were to pour from our taps, we would consider the infrastructure to be broken, dangerous, a matter of public safety and welfare. Similarly, a research infrastructure operates upon its resources: data must be cleaned, standardized and annotated; instruments calibrated across geographic sites and over time; specimens preserved in the same manner, properly stored and labeled [37]. The term entangled will serve as a shorthand to remind us that in the approach outlined in this paper we should not distinguish the resources and services of a research infrastructure from the work of regenerating their availability[1].

The final aspect of the kernel is that it facilitates change to itself. That is, many actors within infrastructure are reflexively engaged in a process of monitoring the kernel and the research activities it is intended to support. As

[1] The concept of entanglement is a departure from the kernel OS metaphor. In its software sense, a kernel is distinct from the resources that it makes available, i.e., the operating system is not the printer, memory or CPU. However this makes little sense for a kernel approach to infrastructure. Notably, the term 'entangled' is not native to the vocabulary of OS kernels, it is an intentionally mixed metaphor so as to better remind of this break.

research goals shift over time, the kernel itself must change to support the investigation of new objects. For example, over time new disciplinary specialists have joined LTER: as ecology has become more and more concerned with human ecologies (e.g., a city), LTER has added specialists concerned with human activity: social scientists. Social scientists have different instruments and different kinds of data (e.g., surveys) and consequently the LTER kernel has been adapted to help facilitate these kinds of inquiries and preservation of these kinds of data.

The kernel is built with a prospective expectation of change and there are procedures and technologies within the operations of infrastructure that facilitate such changes to the kernel – these are examined below as *elaboration* and *extension*.

Paul Edwards, in his studies of another large-scale and long-term research infrastructure – the vast machine of climate science – has noted that "infrastructure" is a particularly useful concept for understanding flexibility in science:

> The concept of knowledge infrastructure [see 10] resembles the venerable notion of scientific paradigms, but it reaches well beyond that, capturing the continuity of modern science, which keeps on functioning as a production system even while particular theories, instruments, and models rise and fall within it. [.] I prefer the language of infrastructure, because it brings home fundamental qualities of endurance, reliability, and the taken-for-grantedness of a technical and institutional base supporting everyday work and action. [9]

The concept of the kernel, repurposing of its features such as data and experts, and change to the cache through elaboration and extension, are contributions to understanding *technoscientific flexibility*: how infrastructure prepares, manages and responds to change in science even as its objects of research, methods of investigation, and the experts who enact that research are transformed.

CASES AND METHOD

The design of this study is historical-comparative and ethnographic-comparative. Comparisons are of two case studies of infrastructure supporting scientific research, founded approximately thirty years ago, and continuing in the present.

The MACS – The Multicenter AIDS Cohort Study

The MACS was founded in 1983 to investigate the causes and modes of transmission of a very poorly understood disease: Acquired Immunodeficiency Syndrome (AIDS). To do so, the MACS was established as a multicenter study, a distributed biomedical organization in four American cities: Los Angeles, Pittsburgh, Baltimore and Chicago. In these cities they recruited thousands of gay or bisexual men (the most visible 'at risk' population), and tracked them over time – as a prospective cohort – by administering biannual questionnaires (ranging in topic from social activities and locations, to toxic exposures and sexual behaviors) and medical interventions (measurements, such as blood pressure; or, specimen collection, such as blood, urine, semen, etc.).

LTER – Long-Term Ecological Research

LTER was founded in 1980 to "understand general ecological phenomena which occur over longer temporal and spatial scales" [27]. The sense within the scientific community was that to study ecological change, which occurs over decades or centuries, the investigation itself should be temporally scaled to match. To do so, LTER established six sites for long-term data and sample collection. Over time LTER has added many new sites and has shut down others; in 2013 it has twenty-six sites of investigation. These sites span a great array of terrestrial and aquatic ecosystems such as deserts, prairies, lakes, and estuaries. For example, the Hubbard Brook site is focused on forests and small streams. There, they have tracked the temperature of streams for over thirty years; they also sample those streams by bottling water and silt.

Method

This paper is focused on theory exposition in the Grounded Theory tradition [7]. The paper targets (or *theoretically samples* [14]) the empirical features of the MACS and LTER most relevant to understanding the cache, addressing and change to the kernel.

In order to track change to science in these research infrastructures, my research team inspected the corpus of associated publications within each infrastructure, year-by-year over each thirty-year history e.g., scientific publications, funding proposals, reports, requests for proposals (RFP), and other documentary sources including archived websites.

Members of my research team participated ethnographically in current activities, such as data collection outings, All-Hands meetings, executive and advisory meetings. I have worked closely with six sites of LTER over nine years, have been an observer of the MACS for two years as well as participating in the design of a study for its Baltimore site; one of my research assistants worked for the MACS for one year.

To better understand information management practices, I theoretically sampled portions of data archives in the MACS and LTER. Finally, I have interviewed members of these organizations, including scientists, technicians and staff; in the MACS this has included interviews and focus groups with participants (subjects) in the study from the Baltimore/Washington site.

THE MACS AND LTER KERNELS

For two enterprises dedicated to studying very different objects, the MACS and LTER have surprisingly similar kernels. Both organizations have sought to persistently make available four sets of resources and services. This section outlines each feature of the cache in turn: sites, archives, instruments and experts. The next section will explore how each feature has enabled the MACS and LTER to continue supporting science in the face of fundamental transformations to their objects of research.

The cache: Resources and services of MACS and LTER

i. Ongoing sites of data and sample collection

When we think of doing science we often think of data, but in long-term collection enterprises such as the MACS and LTER, *the source* of those materials is nearly as important as the data and specimens themselves. The term 'site' refers to the source of collection for scientific materials. The heart of a prospective longitudinal study is the ability to ongoingly produce novel data and samples, i.e., when one cannot answer a research question using extant data and samples, ongoing sites enable the collection of new materials to do so.

In the MACS, the sites of collection are the cohorts of gay and bisexual men who have, for the last thirty years, every six months, travelled to clinics in their respective cities to once again fill out questionnaires and donate the blood and tissues that then become specimens. All data and specimens come from these men and two further cohorts that have been recruited since: nearly 5000 from the first cohort recruited in 1984-5, with a total of nearly 7000 across all cohorts. The MACS continues to track the men who remain in the study to this day.

In LTER the sites of collection – and what is collected – are far more diverse. In 1980, LTER was founded with only six sites, today there are twenty-six. Each site is distinct and the focus of different kinds of research; members collect many different kinds of data and samples. An example that will serve as a touchstone throughout the paper is drawn from the Baltimore Ecosystem Study (BES) site of LTER where every week a team of technicians and graduate students head out in a van to circle the Baltimore area, stopping at twelve spots to measure stream temperatures, to check local rainfall levels and to collect four bottles of stream water.

ii. Archives of data and specimens

The MACS and LTER have a mandate to keep data and specimens available for the investigation of new and old objects of research. Longitudinal datasets and collections are key contributions of both enterprises, allowing their scientists to explore their most ambitious and central objects: the natural history of HIV/AIDS (i.e., how the disease progresses and varies in individuals over time), and ecological change that occurs over decades.

When the participating men in the MACS come to clinics they enact a routine called "the visit" in which they fill out questionnaires on their well-being, sexual behaviors, drug use, medications, and many others. For the core questionnaires that have been administered since 1984, to this day, the men continue to fill out bubbles on "scantron forms" using a #2 pencil. During a visit, blood is always taken; other materials have come and gone. Depending on when in the thirty-year history of the MACS we were to join the visit, we could observe the collection of other materials such as urine, fecal swabs, or throat gargles. In 2012, the MACS reported the storage of 1,638,409 aliquots of urine, cells, plasma and serum.

Samples are not simply a step in the translation of a site into data [22]; they have value unto themselves. Just as with data, they are preserved and curated. In LTER/BES two of every four bottles of water that leave each streambed in Baltimore are ported to Millbrook, New York. There they are placed in cold storage with thousands of other bottles, neatly identified with glued-on labels that mark their site and time of collection. Samples are not discrete from data, they too are entangled, i.e., a sample of water is only scientifically meaningful if it is tied (with data), to a specific place of collection, a specific time, and all the rest of the water and other data collected from that streambed over the years.

These scientific data and materials circulate in many ways across their respective scientific communities. Today, the most well documented data are available online for immediate download; other datasets are available upon request; and still others exist only as paper documents in filed archives. Available in principle, such data may be tedious or impossible to access in practice. Similarly, scientists can gain access to material samples. Ecologists travel directly to the sites of cold storage to analyze stream samples, or, a styrofoam-packed and frozen aliquot of blood can be delivered to biomedical researchers by courier.

iii. Standardized instruments

Instruments (and their associated practices) are the devices that transform sites, materials and subjects into data – they are key information technologies in the doing of science. Both the MACS and LTER are geographically distributed organizations with the goal of longitudinal synthesis and comparison. Comparing data and samples across time and space (usually) means collecting them and analyzing them in comparable ways, and this requires the ongoing standardization of instruments.

For example, a key instrument for the MACS has been the flow cytometer. This largely automated machine runs a laser over flowing tissues, such as blood, in order to classify and count entities like CD4 white-blood cells [19]. Previous to the availability of the HIV test in 1985, measuring CD4 counts (then called T-helper cells) was one of the only methods for detecting AIDS before the onset of symptoms.

At the founding of the MACS, the principal investigators decided to buy the same kind of flow cytometers from the same vendors, using the same reagents to mark cells, and to use the same brand of calibration beads to standardize them. Even this is not enough: on a regular basis, the very same specimen of blood is circulated across the four sites of the MACS to compare measurements for each instrument. Without this work of ongoing standardization, comparing across sites would be methodologically challenging or impossible.

In LTER/BES, they have considered automating the collection of stream samples. They sought to delegate the weekly work of bottling water to machines by installing a device at each site that 'sips' the stream at regular intervals. However, such a transformation in the sampling method threatened the comparability of the archive: water collected in a new manner could shift key measures in ways that biased the data. To this day in Baltimore they run the automated machines *and* continue to slog into the middle of the stream to collect bottled samples by hand. Now two sets of data, one goes back a decade longer than the other, preserving comparability at the expense of more labor.

iv. Heterogeneous experts

HIV disease and ecology are complex; they do not sit tidily within the confines of disciplines. To support ongoing investigation, the MACS and LTER maintain a network of heterogeneous experts. The MACS' founding members were epidemiologists, virologists, and research doctors. But illness is as a much a sociological object of research as a biological and medical one. In its thirty years the MACS has increasingly extended its base of expertise to sociologists, psychologists and many others.

Experts are not only scientists. LTER has an information manager at each of its twenty-six sites. These specialists are specifically tasked with curating an ongoing archive, facilitating data sharing, and prospectively planning for a technologically evolving datascape, i.e., from flat-files and floppy disks in 1980, to relational databases, web-services and metadata specifications in 2013.

Facilitating communication between its geographically distributed members is also a service the MACS and LTER offer, often through relatively "low-tech" approaches such as member directories, but more recently through specialized discovery tools. Both organizations host face-to-face gatherings, e.g., "All-Hands" meetings that assemble the majority of their members, or more targeted get-togethers by topic or goal. Such meetings are opportunities to share findings, methods and common challenges, but also, to get to know each other *as* MACS and LTER members, rather than as specialists at disciplinary conferences.

CHANGING OBJECTS OF RESEARCH

Change to the very root of the scientific enterprise can be vividly illustrated through both the MACS and LTER. This section outlines changes in broad strokes. The next section inspects these changes more granularly to explore how the MACS and LTER caches helped them adapt to these changes.

When the MACS was founded in 1983, no causal agent for AIDS was known. A central goal of the MACS was to participate in the search for AIDS' etiology. It was a year later, in 1984, that French and American researchers identified the Human Immunodeficiency Virus as that agent, and it was not until 1985 that a commercial assay became available to test the thousands of men in the study for that retrovirus.

I will not further recount this story, which is described in greater detail elsewhere [40], but instead emphasize the technoscientific change: What the MACS was tasked to study in 1983, its object of research, was a newly recognized but unknown and ultimately deadly disease, AIDS. At that time many causes were posited – an infectious agent, yes, but environmental and behavioral causes were also being explored. The initial purpose of the MACS was to help pin down a cause. That mission vanished with the discovery of HIV. This is quite literally an ontological transformation: in 1983 we had no recognized such entity in the world, and in 1985 we had both HIV and people who were seropositive. Thereafter the MACS became a study of the natural history of HIV.

In LTER scientific change has been less immediate and life-and-death, but ultimately, one that is proving to be part of a more radical cosmological shift. LTER was founded as a study of six sites, each a distinct biome: a large, naturally occurring collection of flora and fauna. In 1980, the framing was largely that these biomes would be studied discretely and comparatively, as unique biomes. Since then the science in LTER has gone through two major refigurings. Firstly, it is now a much more globalized enterprise; biomes are still units of comparison, but they are also modeled as part of an interconnected global system. LTER collaborates and coordinates with "other LTERs" all over the world through its international coordinating body: ILTER. Secondly, humans are increasingly framed as part of ecology rather than an experimental variable to be controlled ("disturbances" as they were called in 1980 [29]). The first six biomes were chosen largely for their purity: "areas of relatively pristine, preserved ecosystems" [27]; they were "nature on its own," devoid of human intervention. Today, in tandem with changes in climate science, humans are treated as important actors in reshaping *and* sustaining ecological biomes. In short, the vision of LTER today is more globalized, and the role of humans to ecology is more central.

Change to the kernel: Repurposing, elaborating & extending

The narratives above are a view of scientific change from "1000 kilometers up." Each of these broader changes was actualized as innumerable more granular reorientations in objects of research. This section will focus on how each kernel was *repurposed* for the investigation of these new objects, and then examine two forms of punctuated change to the kernel: *extension* and *elaboration*.

The public announcement of HIV as the cause of AIDS came twenty-three days after the MACS had begun to recruit a cohort. And yet, even as their new study lost its founding purpose, the MACS principal investigators do not recount any sense of crisis. The MACS, in 1984, was in a scientifically enviable position to investigate this new retroviral entity. This is because the MACS kernel had been assembled with the breadth of materials, instruments and experts needed to render HIV a researchable object.

Inspecting each feature of the kernel in turn: the relevant specialists – virologists – were already part of the MACS team; they were readily equipped with the instruments and techniques of their craft; they were already collecting the behavioral data that would become most relevant in understanding transmission in gay men: anal intercourse and intravenous drug use; they were already collecting the material that would most closely come to be associated with transmission: blood.

This is called *repurposing the kernel*: resources and services collected for one purpose are thereafter used for the investigation of new objects of research. For example, blood, collected for the investigation of many possible causes (e.g., it can be screened for pathogens, but can also be used to track drug use or environmental exposures), was repurposed as a key material in the investigation of HIV disease.

The latter is an important point in understanding the capacity of the MACS to adapt to these changes. In the study of cyberinfrastructure, and CSCW studies of scientific work, we have greatly emphasized the importance of data reuse, particularly data in a digital form. In a recent review article, Jirotka, Lee and Olson [18] have called data the "lifeblood of science," a phrase which recurs throughout the literature [32, 40].

Data *are* central to science; the argument in this paper is that the focus on data has thus far come at the expense of a concern with the materiality of scientific resources.

In the study of AIDS, the lifeblood of HIV research has been … blood. In 1985, when the test became available, MACS researchers did not re-inspect their data (nothing to see!), rather they turned to their archives of blood. By retesting these specimens they were able to reclassify the participating men from 'at risk' of contracting AIDS to either HIV-positive or negative – a new category in the columns of their databases. Over time MACS researchers tested the entire specimen archive, producing for each HIV-positive man a new retrospective history of their seroconversion. The blood archive permitted the MACS to push this newly generated diagnostic status back in time [23]: thereafter, for some men, they had always already been infected before the discovery of HIV or the availability of a test.

This is called *elaboration of the kernel:* a change to the cache resulting from the addition of new instruments and categorizations. The sites of collection remained "the same men," but through the HIV test and, essentially, the incorporation of a new variable for each man – serostatus – the study design was transformed in ways that would allow the MACS to continue its investigations following the discovery of HIV. For example, in certain studies the HIV-negative men are used as "controls" to compare with HIV-positive men; they are comparable in that they are demographically similar (e.g., gay, actively sexual, living in the same cities) but with a key difference, serostatus. This comparison enables the isolation of a "natural history of HIV" from the general trajectory of being a gay sexually active American male.

The test is now a routine part of the MACS kernel: it is administered at each six-month visit; the results are carefully catalogued in the data archives. The instrument has been added to the cache, now standardized across the 4 sites.

This point is also crucial in understanding elaboration of the kernel. New instruments cannot simply be "dropped in" to the cache. The HIV test had to be addressed for use in the MACS. In the months and years following the availability of the HIV test, MACS scientists tested the test itself. On the one hand, the validity of the test is important (and scientists report that the early tests produced many false negatives and positives), but for a longitudinal study, the reliability of the test was also critical: ensuring comparability of results (data) over time, and across the 4 sites, is a central service of the MACS. In the end, as with the flow cytometers described above, the MACS chose one HIV test vendor and developed cross-site protocols that sought to routinize the practical execution of the test across sites.

Let us now turn to LTER's refiguration as it began to more centrally include human impact and interrelations with ecology. This is an *extension of the kernel*: the addition of new features to the cache in order to investigate objects of research not originally within the purview of the research infrastructure. A clear example of extension is the addition of urban-ecological sites to LTER.

In 1997, LTER added two new sites of data and specimen collection: the Baltimore Ecosystem Study (BES) and Central Arizona-Phoenix (CAP). With these urban sites came a more systematic integration to LTER of experts focused on, for example, social, psychological and economic objects: social scientists. These new scientists initiated the collection of new data and specimens using new instruments that made urban-ecology researchable, for example: quantifying the coverage of impervious surfaces such as paved roadways; measuring fertilization of lawns with nitrogen-based compounds; or surveying attitudes towards urban parks.

These new sites of collection were different than those of LTER in the past: they were no longer "nature on its own," but instead, as LTER scientists put it, socio-ecological systems. The extensibility of the LTER kernel facilitated the investigation of entirely new objects of research. As LTER scientists have become more interested in the role of humans in ecology, this adaptability of the cache has made new science possible within an old infrastructure. This is technoscientific flexibility.

ADDRESSING: Sustaining and managing change to the kernel

The cache, though, is not "just available," for use. It is worked over continuously to sustain its readiness for future use. As Star reminds us, *infrastructure is relative* [41]: one person's taken for granted resources and services are another person's everyday work of renewing their availability. These are the activities of addressing.

In many senses, the purpose of research infrastructure is to help facilitate technoscientific change, or, as a recent visionary text put it: "revolutionizing science through cyberinfrastructure"[1]. In this paper I have recounted exemplars of such change and how infrastructure supported these new investigations. And yet, these changes are also highly disruptive to scientists and to research infrastructure itself: new theories challenge old; novel instruments are interrogated as producing false findings; and, new methods may leave some scientists feeling like old researchers.

However, in addition to finding tensions within infrastructure there is also long-term cooperation, and this is the key to adapting to new circumstances.

Counter-intuitively, one of the most important strategies for remaining flexible is to keep doing the same thing. More precisely, a central quality of infrastructure is to sustain a consistent level of services and resources. Following the kernel metaphor, these are the activities of *addressing,* in the sense of generating a location within an address space. In the terminology of the kernel, addressing is work to sustain the entanglement of the cache with the kernel.

More concretely, addressing refers to the heterogeneous work, techniques and technologies of those actors that seek to regenerate access to the resources and services of infrastructure. For example, data, particularly data collected somewhere else for some other purpose, are always in danger of losing their meaning and thus their value for reuse in a future investigation. Methods of addressing data may include, for example, careful annotation of who, how and when they were collected [11], or more ambitiously, developing common metadata specifications or semantic representations such as computational ontologies [35].

However, data are only one example: the work of addressing is as diverse and detailed as the range of resources and services that a research infrastructure may avail. Addressing *is* maintenance, repair and upgrade, but these terms are too narrow to cover the full range of activities we find that seek to renew readiness of the cache. We have already seen several other examples of addressing in this paper, e.g., the MACS and LTER regularly organize face-to-face meetings and create online venues, such as forums and webpages, to renew the social ties of their members. We have also seen that instruments (flow cytometers, HIV tests, and water collectors) must be continuously calibrated to ensure comparability. Standardizing is never complete: instruments are forever threatening to "disentangle" and lose their potential to support future research.

The recurrent night terror of disentanglement

In the first ethnography of a scientific laboratory, the observer, now Latour-as-demon, imagined himself trolling through a lab and disentangling samples from the notebooks that gave them meaning:

> Entering the deserted laboratory at night, he opens one of the large refrigerators [.] Each sample on the racks [.] is labeled with a long code number which refers back to the protocol books. Taking each sample in turn, the observer peels off the labels, throws them away and returns the naked samples to the refrigerator. Next morning, he would doubtless witness scenes of extreme confusion. No one would be able to tell which sample was which. It would take up to five, ten, and even fifteen years (the time it took to label the samples) to replace the labels.[24]

Fanciful as this tale may seem, it is a recurrent topic in discussions with the technicians and scientists dedicated to the assembly and care of their archives. In an interview discussing the cold storage of stream water samples, one LTER/BES scientist recounted his own terror:

> That's one long-term study we haven't done: the life of the label glue over time. I dread to think that one day we'll walk into the cold storage room and hundreds of labels will be lying scattered beside the bottles. But I think the extra label tape we put on the lids will hold up.

Labels are the physical point of contact between specimens and the digital databases that track all the details that give those samples meaning. Without a sustained connection to data, the bottles contain mere water, not scientific samples.

Kernel Inversions

Fears of disentanglement do not remain abstractions, they become the topic of what Geoffrey Bowker has called *infrastructural inversions* [5]: a figure /ground reversal in which members turn their attention from their objects of research to the infrastructure that makes that work possible. For instance, in an attempt to strengthen the connection between sample and data, a World Health Organization technical report in 1968 encouraged researchers to use a diamond to directly inscribe identifying codes onto glass vials containing scientific materials rather than relying on glued labels [33].

The link to a label (and thus to data) is only one way that a sample may loose its value. For example, in the MACS, specimens of the blood archive are thawed to check the continued viability of peripheral blood mononuclear cells

(PBMCs – blood cells with a round nucleus, key to immune system function). During a six year-long testing period:

> recently cryopreserved PBMC from HIV-1-infected and HIV-1-uninfected participants at each MACS site were thawed and evaluated. The median recoveries of viable PBMC for HIV-1-infected and -uninfected participants were 80% and 83%, respectively. [2]

Within this study, they found that one of the four MACS sites had a markedly lower recovery rate, and identified the use of "an automated particle counter that was out of calibration and required servicing by the manufacturer." [2]. Such ongoing quality assessment procedures help laboratories improve protocols and performance "to ensure optimal cryopreservation [.] for future studies." [2].

Addressing is an umbrella term for many activities already named within studies of infrastructure, such as maintenance, repair, upgrade, calibration or quality control; but there also many other activities that sustain availability of the cache that, as of yet, have received little scholarly attention.

Protecting and renewing the sites of specimen and data collection is another revealing addressing activity, almost completely unexplored in the literature [though see 21]. From its founding documents, three of the six criteria for funding an LTER site referred to securing the sites of collection: "The principal investigators [.] should consider site integrity, conflict in use of a site, and long-term agreements with site owners." [29]. LTER's sites are (also) real estate that may occasionally change owners and is sometimes transformed into developed land, making impossible further collection of materials.

Even at the urban sites, where human activity is expected, delicate instrumentation can be disturbed. At the streambeds of urban Baltimore, investigators have reported that "kids just love to pee in things!" (interview) such as the metricized plastic tubes they use to measure rainfall. In response, to protect the integrity of the measurement, they have sought to hide these water collectors from the casual passerby.

The MACS reveals a more peculiar form of addressing of its sites of collection, which in biomedical studies is called retention. The participating men can withdraw at any point: they are tied to the MACS only by their willingness to donate their time and bodies to this ongoing enterprise; some men have done so twice a year for nearly thirty years! Keenly aware of the danger of attrition (which could transform the study from a prospective to a retrospective investigation), MACS members work diligently to make it easier for men to participate: i.e., holding the visits in multiple locations in a city to ease the burden of travel; curbing the time and effort men must expend at clinics by truncating questionnaires and minimizing invasive specimen collections; and, by demonstrating their appreciation for the men's volunteered participation by throwing "thank-you" parties at key anniversaries such as the 25th in 2009.

The techniques and technologies described here only begin to scratch the surface of the varieties of addressing work found in these research infrastructures. All of these activities are oriented to preserving availability of resources and services for future investigations. Without them, instruments data, samples, sites, experts and instruments would disentangle; rather than infrastructure they would become suspect measurements, common blood and water, and scattered scientists working on their own.

Can a feature of the cache be meaningfully disentangled from the kernel? Or, more concretely, can data and specimens circulate "outside their infrastructure" without losing their value? This is a complex question, well beyond the scope of this paper, but the short answer is: Yes, but only if they become entangled with another infrastructure. Some data already rely on other infrastructures. Consider the temperature of a stream: such a measurement, taken in degrees centigrade at BES/LTER, can be shared relatively easily across the globe, but this is only because it relies on a an extant global metrological network [30]. Metadata standards [28] can be developed to help data travel, but of course, those data can only do so once they have been redescribed in the metadata specification – a new entanglement with another infrastructure. Further development of this topic will have to await another paper.

SHAGGY DOG AND TRIM POODLE INFRASTRUCTURES

This section compares and contrasts the MACS and LTER kernels, which are revealing of vastly varying possible kernel architectures. The discerning reader may have noticed that this paper has thus far treated the MACS as a whole, while many of the LTER narratives have been drawn from a single site in Baltimore. This is because LTER is a shaggy dog infrastructure and the MACS is a trim poodle.

A *"shaggy dog story"* is one that continues endlessly without coming to a clear point or conclusion[2]. It does not have a punch line. Such stories have an iterative "and then this happened, and then that" quality. Analogously, a shaggy dog infrastructure has fuzzy boundaries, loosely defined membership, and multiple ongoing research approaches across heterogeneous disciplinary fields. A trim poodle infrastructure has much cleaner boundaries: who is or is not a member is clear, what resources are available are commonly defined and its investigations target a circumscribed set of objects.

As Robert Kohler recalls from when he began to study the history of field ecology: "It was interesting but boundless, with few familiar landmarks, and easy to get lost in.

[2] I attribute this colorful language to Geoffrey Bowker, who has long quipped that all infrastructures are shaggy dog stories.

Finding a coherent narrative structure also proved irksome," [21]. This is the case with LTER, which I have studied for many more years than the MACS, but which has proven recalcitrant to a concise narrative. In contrast, the MACS, while still complex and gnarled, immediately lent itself to more succinct storytelling. The histories of these infrastructures recounted above are both vastly figurative, but far more so of LTER than of the MACS.

Shaggy dog and trim poodle are Weberian *ideal types*, they do not accurately describe the real-world complexity of infrastructure. However, ideal types are useful in constructing comparative analysis. We can explain part of these infrastructures' "trim" and "shaggy" qualities by comparing their kernels.

Single-Core and Multi-Core Kernels

LTER has a multi-core kernel, while the MACS has a single-core. A core occurs when efforts are made to centralize, collect or standardize features of the kernel in a common way across time or sites. The concept of a core can help us understand why LTER is a shaggy dog, and the MACS a trim poodle.

Ecology is complex. LTER scientists have innumerable objects of research from soil types to stream chemistry, forest growth and animal populations, from microorganism cultures to watersheds. In contrast, while the MACS certainly investigates many things, generally speaking it has a much narrower set of research objects, and, more importantly, all data and specimens are drawn from the common subject pool of gay and bisexual men in four American cities.

A "core" should not be confused with a site. LTER has twenty-six geographic sites, while the MACS has four. The MACS has a single core because members work to address all their materials, sites of collection and instruments in such as way as to make them comparable. There is an effort to collect the same data, in the same way, at all sites, and to send all of these to a single data management center in Baltimore at Johns Hopkins University. Specimens are transported to a single repository. In turn, all access to data or new requests for specimens go through a single obligatory passage point: the data management center at Johns Hopkins.

Shagginess or trimness is not only a matter of social organization; the objects of investigation will also play a role. Consider, once again, the role of blood in the MACS: it is the material for measuring immune function, for testing the presence of HIV virus itself, for the key markers that (today) transition a person to having AIDS (CD4 counts), and of what has often been called the "golden key" metric of viral load. No such "key" exists for ecology. Shagginess of infrastructure is partially linked to the shagginess of the objects of investigation.

Obviously, efforts to create a single core are never complete. We have seen above how a single instrument out of alignment at one MACS site led to miscounting viable blood cells. There are many other ways that the four sites differ from each other. For example, following the discovery of HIV and an emerging scientific consensus about the centrality of blood for its investigation, the MACS as a whole stopped collecting many specimens, such as stools[3]. However, the Pittsburgh site continued to collect stools for many years afterwards, based on the principal investigator's continuing interest in stomach flora. Generally speaking, in the MACS there is an ongoing effort to generate a single common core to the study; in practice, its realization is a matter of degree. It is this sense that "trim poodle" or "single core" are ideal types.

In contrast, LTER has many cores. The water samples from Baltimore described in this paper, end up in Millbrook, New York. There they are stored with stream samples from that site and with those of the Hubbard Brook site. The methods at Hubbard Brook and Baltimore are ongoingly standardized: by sharing common data and sample protocols, water is collected, analyzed and stored in the same ways for these two sites. In this sense these two sites form a single core for stream water materials. But LTER has many other such cores, e.g., at the Kellogg Biological Station in Michigan they preserve many kinds of plant specimens [6], while at a discontinued LTER site called North Inlet in South Carolina, ecologists still maintain a collection of preserved fish in jars. It is difficult to say with any certainty how many cores LTER may have; a fuzzy kernel is a quality of a shaggy dog infrastructure.

The fuzzy boundaries of the kernel

I once owned a shaggy black dog called Sisco. I enjoyed watching as he would sit on my black shag rug and use his tongue to clean his paws. He often licked a full inch of dark carpet beyond his paw, unaware or indifferent to the limits of Sisco. Shaggy dog infrastructures are this way too.

In an early study of cyberinfrastructure, Charlotte Lee et al. identified the common occurrence of fuzzy membership [25]: a respondent would point her in the direction of another member to interview, but when she arrived, the indicated person would admit no sense of affiliation to the infrastructure. More generally, this is true of all features of the kernel: what is, or is not, part of the cache is easily identified in a trim poodle infrastructure and the source of contestation or confusion in a shaggy dog infrastructure.

---

[3] Cuts or eliminations to the kernel are called *shedding*, which is as important as the additive activities of elaboration or extension inspected in this article. The kernel does not only grow over time, it is also necessarily – and often controversially – reduced. A further discussion of shedding will appear in forthcoming research.

In terms of membership, it is common for many affiliated researchers, such as graduate students working on LTER projects, to be unaware of any association. In contrast, researchers in the MACS are almost always aware of the use of those subject cohorts and datasets. The case is similar for other features of the cache, e.g., in those LTER sites with very little social scientific investigation (for example, Palmer station in the Antarctic) researchers are less likely to be aware of the methods, instruments and objects of analysis used by social scientists.

Over the years LTER members have sought to address their kernel in order to *trim the shaggy dog*; some of these efforts have been successful, others have vanished without a trace. A most notable success in LTER has been the establishment a network-coordinating center in 1983 to facilitate communication and collaboration across its sites. However, other addressing efforts have come and gone; for example, beginning in 1988 a single Minimum Site Installation (MSI) was implemented in LTER, defining the information technologies that each site should have. This MSI has rarely reappeared in LTER documentation since. A mixed success (thus far) is the effort to develop a common Ecological Metadata Language (EML), which received uneven uptake across the twenty-six sites [28]: today some data are well described in EML, others not at all.

Are the terms shaggy and trim necessarily valuations of these infrastructures? Is trim good and shaggy bad? Certainly, managerial actors tend to prefer a trim structure: standardized data, well catalogued specimens and a clearly defined membership. But shaggy dog infrastructures do 'work.' As Lee et al. note of fuzzy membership: "Participants can successfully accomplish work with a partial view of the organizational membership and structure." There may even be advantages to a shaggy kernel, as with long discussed tension between standardization and flexibility [15]: the loose cross-site coupling found within shaggy dog infrastructures may enable a more nimble adaptation to new research objects or changes to the kernel.

Understanding shaggy and trim qualities, and their implications, requires a much more extensive analysis than is possible in this paper – it is simultaneously a sociotechnical, scientific and institutional matter[4] – but comparing the MACS and LTER kernels has allowed us to begin appreciating their trim and shaggy silhouettes.

DISCUSSION: A kernel approach

The most significant methodological reorientation in a kernel approach is to place supporting the investigation of objects of research at the center of the analysis. The study of infrastructures must be closely tied to the specific research practices they enable, the materials to do so, and the shifting orientation of investigators to novel phenomena. The intellectual contributions of a kernel analysis follow from this reorientation.

In many publications that take cyberinfrastructure as their topic, it is common to find the objects of investigation identified only briefly in the description of the case. Occasionally, objects are altogether absent in such papers and only the disciplines supported are described – as though disciplines can stand in for their objects. Such papers thereafter move on to topics greatly abstracted from the doing of a particular science, e.g., user needs, data sharing, supporting collaboration, disciplinary culture.

A kernel approach insists that the analysis return to actors' research orientation: sharing data about what? collaborating for what purpose? And most importantly, how do these resources and services support investigation (or not)? This paper has made many general points about research infrastructure, but the analysis has always returned to participants' activities of investigating AIDS and ecology.

By returning to the objects of investigation, and tracking their ongoing transformations over time, it has become possible to characterize a particular form of resilience and plasticity thus far largely ignored in studies of research infrastructure: technoscientific flexibility. Infrastructure may be characterized by other forms of flexibility – such as an adaptability to change in its information technologies or its funding arrangements – but a unique feature of both the MACS and LTER is that they have persisted in the face of radical reconfigurations to their scientific methods and objects. More than this: they have continued to conduct investigations within their fields. Without this capacity they would cease to be research infrastructure.

Even while insisting on being specific about objects, the kernel has also served as a new unit of analysis that facilitates a rigorous comparison of infrastructures. We need not ignore the specificity of research objects and practices in order to generalize or to compare. In this paper the leverage of the analysis has come, first, by analyzing infrastructures that offer similar resources and services, and then, through outlining their shaggy and trim qualities, by contrasting the integration of their cores.

This is one possible comparative design. Juxtaposing distinctly different kernel architectures can also be revealing. For example, GEON and LEAD, which I have investigated in the past [36], did not offer their own data and specimens or sites of collection as resources. Instead they gathered the heterogeneous datasets of other enterprises and sought to integrate those data. The service they offered was data interoperation; addressing in such endeavors was rooted in sustaining the links across datasets that scientists used for their inspection of new objects. This is a common architecture within some contemporary

[4] For instance, the MACS has been the beneficiary of many national and international efforts by the institutions of biomedicine to standardize materials and instruments [20].

cyberinfrastructure projects, which emphasize data integration over collection.

Comparing GEON and LEAD's kernel architectures with the MACS and LTER's could be revealing, e.g., on the one hand GEON and LEAD did not need to expend efforts curating data and specimens, nor stewarding the sites of collection, but, on the other hand, data and specimens are a form of scientific capital: without them, such projects may lack the resiliency that comes from holding these repurposable scientific materials.

Thus, a second reorientation in a kernel approach is to be specific about the resources and services that are made available. The kernel is a broad concept; it includes many things traditionally within the purview of infrastructure studies – such as data or maintenance – but it also encourages the analyst to inspect the full range of a cache and its unique forms of addressing. Such an investigation will reveal many surprising resources and ways of sustaining them. Keeping a research infrastructure running is, as we know, annotating data and upgrading a computer, but it is also throwing parties for dedicated volunteers, or hiding instruments from children who want to pee in them.

Other resources that have come to be considered almost synonymous with research infrastructure may altogether fall away in the study of a particular kernel. Consider, for example, the most commonly investigated service of infrastructure (in CSCW): supporting collaboration.

Research infrastructures are often evaluated for their ability to encourage interdisciplinarity or sustain a distributed organization. However, research infrastructures seek to support collaboration only to the extent that its developers consider collaboration to be important in the investigation of new objects. This is not always the case.

For instance, the Open Science Grid (OSG) specifically seeks to minimize the need for human communication. It seeks to support research by making computing power available 'on tap.' Having to go through a human gatekeeper or fill out tedious paperwork in order to gain access to cycles is seen as a hindrance to the doing of science, a waste of time for all members. Instead, the OSG (and grid and cloud computing more generally) is developed with the goal of minimizing the need for scientists to communicate or collaborate: negotiations for access to cycles and storage are largely delegated to the computational system [38]. The hope is that this will free scientists from such tedious activities so they may focus on their research. While coordination is certainly occurring in OSG, we should no more think of this as "collaboration" than you would call pouring water from a tap collaboration with your local waterworks utility.

Finally, the third reorientation in a kernel approach is to recognize that an infrastructure does not simply 'have' resources and services, there are always actors tasked with sustaining, renewing, adding or shedding features of the kernel. Addressing is the work, techniques and technologies that render features *as* resources and services, available for the investigation of new and extant objects.

Notably, while analyzing two thirty-year enterprises, I have not characterized the MACS or LTER as having a 'foundation' that has remained stable across their decades of operation. Neither the cache, nor the objects of investigation have remained consistent across the years. The kernel is more process than thing. I have named only a few of the processes that have changed the kernel in a punctuated manner: elaboration, extension and shedding. There is a great deal more to be written about these changes and certainly many more kinds of such transformations. But the central activity of the kernel is addressing, an ongoing working over of the things of infrastructure (data, specimens, instruments) and people (experts & subjects) to make them the same, comparable, accessible, preserved, or continuing to contribute.

What is not part of the kernel?

At the edges of the kernel and beyond, we will find countless activities, still within the bounds of "an infrastructure," but that have not been part of this analysis. Most notably, one activity that is not "part" of the kernel is an investigation conducted using the resources and services of that infrastructure.

This paper has approached the kernel "from below," focusing on the activities that develop and renew the resources of a research infrastructure. Returning to our guiding metaphor of the kernel of an operating system, what remains to be investigated is approaching the kernel "from above," as a user or "application." To say that the cache is addressed in an effort to regenerate access is not the equivalent of actually gaining access to these resources. How do scientists conducting a study draw on the resources of the kernel, and what challenges do they encounter in practice? For example, in the MACS and LTER, use of the finite materials from the blood and water archive are carefully deliberated. Some resources are available in principle, but in practice are challenging or impossible to access: poorly documented data, or very new data with value for current research that is reserved for core members. Studying how resources are accessed and deployed for particular investigations in practice is one next step in understanding the operations of the kernel.

Conclusion: Evaluating research infrastructure

This paper has presented a framework for understanding how old organizations have sought to renew themselves to sustain value for new science. This comparative investigation of the past and the present of two research infrastructures has sought to understand what kinds of changes they have encountered over time, and what strategies they have employed in the face of transformations to the landscape of their science. MACS and LTER are active today, continuing to investigate HIV disease and global ecologies; they also continue to plan and organize for a future that promises many ongoing alterations to their research landscapes.

We can expect but not precisely predict continuing transformations to the scientific ecologies of today's research infrastructure. New research infrastructure projects, i.e., cyberinfrastructure, will face a different and unique set of challenges than those of the past thirty years. From our vantage point, we can only sketch these oncoming scientific changes, but by investigating the past and present of infrastructures that have weathered transformations, this research has sought to inform future infrastructure development efforts by articulating strategies of the long-term: organizational forms and methods of design with a track-record of facilitating responsiveness to change.

Considered in this manner – framing research infrastructure as the repurposing, elaborating and extending the kernel, could serve to develop methods for evaluating the ability of research infrastructure to support future research. Defining 'progress in science' is a notoriously fraught philosophical endeavor, but evaluating a research infrastructure according to its ability to support the investigation of new objects could serve as a new metric: What does it take to gain access to data and specimens for repurposing in new investigations? How much work does it take to add a new instrument? Are seasoned scientists and diverse specialists easily available to help navigate the use of resources and services?

Posing the evaluation of research infrastructure in this manner leads to a deeper, more troubling question: are there objects of research that a kernel architecture makes wholly impossible to investigate? Consider: the MACS is rooted in the study of American bodies. While there are certainly many similarities between HIV disease in the U.S. and the natural and treated histories of HIV around the globe, today we also know that AIDS manifests in distinctly different ways in the developing world. The MACS has contributed enormously to our knowledge of HIV disease, and to our ability to manage that illness; but our understanding of specific variation in the developing world has come from other investigations. By virtue of their architecture, there are limits to the flexibility of any kernel that may render entire domains of inquiry opaque.

ACKNOWLEDGEMENTS

Jessica Beth Polk was an invaluable collaborator and field worker during investigations of the MACS, and in the development of the kernel concept. This paper was presented at a workshop in the Department of Informatics at the University of Oslo; I would like to thank the participants at that event for their feedback and to Jennifer Feldman for her insightful comments on final revisions. This research has been supported by NSF/VOSS award #0904145 'Delegating Organizational Work to Virtual Organization Technologies.'

REFERENCES

1. Atkins, D. E. C. *Revolutionizing Science and Engineering Through Cyberinfrastructure*. National Science Foundation, Washington, DC, (2003).
2. Aziz, N., Margolick, J. B., Detels, R., Rinaldo, C. R., Phair, J., Jamieson, B. D. and Butch, A. W. Value of a quality assessment program in optimizing cryopreservation of peripheral blood mononuclear cells in a multicenter study. *Clinical and Vaccine Immunology,* 20, 4 (2013), 590-5.
3. Baker, K. S. and Yarmey, L. Data stewardship: Environmental data curation and web-of-repositories. *International Journal of Digital Curation*, 4, 2 (2009), 1-12.
4. Birnholtz, J. P. and Bietz, M. J. Data at work: supporting sharing in science and engineering. *GROUP (2003), 339-348.*
5. Bowker, G. C. *Science on the Run: Information Management and Industrial Geophysics at Schlumberger, 1920-1940.* MIT 1994.
6. Burton, M. and Jackson, S. J. *Constancy and Change in Scientific Collaboration: Coherence and Integrity in Long-Term Ecological Data Production.* HICSS, (2012), 353-362.
7. Charmaz, K. *Constructing grounded theory*. Sage (2006).
8. Dourish, P. and Edwards, W. K. A Tale of Two Toolkits: Relating Infrastructure and Use in Flexible CSCW Toolkits. *JCSCW* 9, 1 (2000), 33-51.
9. Edwards, P. N. *A vast machine: computer models, climate data, and the politics of global warming*. MIT, 2010.
10. Edwards, P. N., Jackson, S. J., Chalmers, M. K., Bowker, G. C., Borgman, C. L., Ribes, D., Burton, M. and Calvert, S. *Knowledge Infrastructures: Intellectual Frameworks and Research Challenges*. Deep Blue, Ann Arbor, 2013.
11. Edwards, P. N., Mayernik, M. S., Batcheller, A. L., Bowker, G. C. and Borgman, C. L. Science friction: Data, metadata, and collaboration. *Social Studies of Science*, 41, 5 (2011), 667-690.
12. Faniel, I. M. and Jacobsen, T. E. Reusing Scientific Data: How Earthquake Engineering Researcher Assses the Reusabilty of Colleagues' Data. *JCSCW*, 19, 3-4 (2010), 355-375.
13. Finholt, T. A. Collaboratories. *Annual Review of Information Science and Technology*, 36, (2004), 73-107.
14. Glaser, B. G. and Strauss, A. *The discovery of grounded theory: strategies for qualitative research.* Aldine, 1973.
15. Hanseth, O., Monteiro, E. and Hatling, M. Developing Information Infrastructure: The Tension between

Standardization and Flexibility. *Science, Technology & Human Values*, 21, 4 (1996), 407-426.

16. Howison, J. and Herbsleb, J. D. *Incentives and integration in scientific software production.* CSCW (2013), 459-470.
17. Jackson, S. J. and Barbrow, S. Infrastructure and vocation: field, calling and computation in ecology. *CHI* (2013), 2873-2882.
18. Jirotka, M., Lee, C. P. and Olson, G. M. Supporting Scientific Collaboration: Methods, Tools and Concepts. *JCSCW* (2013 online first), 1-49.
19. Keating, P. and Cambrosio, A. *Interlaboratory life: regulating flow cytometry.* The Invisible Industrialist: Manufacturers and the Construction of Scientific Knowledge. MacMillan (1998) 250-95.
20. Keating, P. and Cambrosio, A. *Biomedical platforms.* MIT Press, (2003).
21. Kohler, R. E. *Landscapes and labscapes: Exploring the lab-field border in biology.* University of Chicago Press, (2002).
22. Latour, B. *Circulating reference: Sampling the soil in the Amazon forest.* Pandora's Hope. Harvard Press, Cambridge, (1999), 24-79.
23. Latour, B. On the partial existence of existing and nonexisting objects. *Biographies of scientific objects,* University of Chicago Press (2000), 247-269.
24. Latour, B. and Woolgar, S. *Laboratory life: the construction of scientific facts.* Sage Publications, Beverly Hills, 1979.
25. Lee, C. P., Dourish, P. and Mark, G. *The human infrastructure of cyberinfrastructure.* CSCW (2006) 483-92.
26. Lee, E. S., McDonald, D. W., Anderson, N. and Tarczy-Hornoch, P. Incorporating collaboratory concepts into informatics in support of translational interdisciplinary biomedical research. *International journal of medical informatics*, 78, 1 (2009), 10-21.
27. LTER *A long-range Strategic Plan for the Long Term Ecological Research Network.* LTER Network Office, 1989.
28. Millerand, F., Ribes, D., Baker, K. S. and Bowker, G. C. Making an Issue out of a Standard: Storytelling Practices in a Scientific Community *Science, Technology & Human Values*, 38, 1 (2013), 7-43.
29. NSF. *LTER Request for Proposals.* 1980.
30. O'Connel, J. Metrology: 'The Creation of Universality by the Circulation of Particulars'. *Social Studies of Science*, 23 (1993), 129-173.
31. Olson, G. M., Zimmerman, A. and Bos, N. *Scientific collaboration on the internet.* MIT Press, 2008.
32. Onsrud, H. J. and Campbell, J. Big opportunities in access to "Small Science" data. *Data Science Journal*, 6 (2007), 58-66.
33. Radin, J. Latent Life: Concepts and Practices of Human Tissue Preservation in the International Biological Program. *Social Studies of Science* (Online First).
34. Ranon, R., Marco, L. D., Senerchia, A., Gabrielli, S., Chittaro, L., Pugliese, R., Cano, L. D., Asnicar, F. and Prica, M. *A Web-based Tool for Collaborative Access to Scientific Instruments in Cyberinfrastructures.* Grid Enabled Remote Instrumentation. Springer US, (2009).
35. Ribes, D. and Bowker, G. C. Between meaning and machine: learning to represent the knowledge of communities. *Information and Organization*, 19, 4 (2009), 199-217.
36. Ribes, D. and Finholt, T. A. The long now of technology infrastructure: Articulating tensions in development. *Journal for the Association of Information Systems (JAIS): Special issue on eInfrastructures*, 10, 5 (2009), 375-398.
37. Ribes, D. and Jackson, S. J. *Data Bite Man: The Work of Sustaining a Long-Term Study.* "Raw Data" is an Oxymoron. MIT Press (2013) 147-166.
38. Ribes, D., Jackson, S. J., Geiger, R. S., Burton, M. and Finholt, T. Artifacts that organize: Delegation in the distributed organization. *Information and Organization*, 23, 1 (2012), 1-14.
39. Ribes, D. and Lee, C. P. Sociotechnical Studies of Cyberinfrastructure and e-Research: Current Themes and Future Trajectories. *JCSCW* 19, 3-4 (2010), 231-244.
40. Ribes, D. and Polk, J. B. Historical Ontology and Infrastructure. *iConference* (2012), 252-264.
41. Star, S. L. and Ruhleder, K. Steps Toward an Ecology of Infrastructure: Design and Access for Large Information Systems. *Information Systems Research*, 7, 1 (1996), 111-134.
42. Vertesi, J. and Dourish, P. *The value of data: considering the context of production in data economies.* CSCW, 2011, 533-542.

The Policy Knot: Re-integrating Policy, Practice and Design in CSCW Studies of Social Computing

Steven J. Jackson
Dept. of Information Science
Cornell University
sjj54@cornell.edu

Tarleton Gillespie
Dept. of Communication
Cornell University
tlg28@cornell.edu

Sandy Payette
Dept. of Communication
Cornell University
sdp6@cornell.edu

ABSTRACT
In CSCW and information science research today, the worlds of design, practice, and policy are often held separate, speaking to different audiences, venues, and fields of expertise. But many growing areas of CSCW work, including mobile, cloud, and social computing, run into problems precisely at this intersection. This paper presents a model for understanding processes of change and emergence in social computing in which policy, practice, and design show up in the form of complex interdependencies, or knots, that collectively determine the shape, meaning, and trajectory of shifting computational forms. We then apply this model to two recent social computing controversies: the 2011 privacy scandal surrounding the location-aware mobile app Girls Around Me; and controversies surrounding the 2010 launch of the Google Buzz social network. We argue that better attention to the mutually constitutive relations between design, practice and policy can expand the reach, depth, and impact of CSCW scholarship.

Author Keywords: policy, privacy, design, practice, mobile applications, social computing.

ACM Classification Keywords: H.5 Information Interfaces and Presentations; K.4.1 Public Policy Issues K.4.3 Organizational Impacts; K.5.2 Government Issues

INTRODUCTION
Emergent forms of social computing very often push the boundaries of design and practice simultaneously, producing challenges and problems for each. New social computing tools and systems may provoke CSCW researchers to think differently about the range of human interactions that can be built and imagined around them. At the same time, changes in social computing practice can push back on design, as users and communities enact and repurpose technologies in ways unimagined by their designers. This meeting point (or sometimes gap [1]) between technical design and social practice constitutes a traditional heartland of CSCW concern, and plays a central role in defining the shape, meaning and generativity of social computing today.

CSCW'14, February 15 – 19, 2014, Baltimore, MD, USA.

ACM 978-1-4503-2540-0/14/02...$15.00.
http://dx.doi.org/10.1145/2531602.2531674

But this two-dimensional story captures only part of the dynamic by which new technological forms emerge and gain force in the world. This paper seeks to extend the analytic range of CSCW by arguing that emergent social computing practices and design often impact and are impacted by structures and processes in the realm of policy, with effects formative for each. Emergent technologies may suggest problems and possibilities for both social practices and the formal rules and institutions that govern them. New practices may challenge both designers and policymakers to rethink core assumptions of their work. And emergent policy arrangements may shift the institutional terrain that designers and users operate on, foreclosing some possibilities for action while opening up others.

This claim reverses how policy is sometimes thought about and practiced in CSCW scholarship. Too often (when policy is thought about at all) it is imagined to come *after* design and practice, in both time and importance. Under this basically linear presumption, emergent technologies are first designed; users then adopt and adapt them in contexts of situated practice; and on occasion, when a dispute emerges, aggrieved stakeholders turn to public agencies or the courts to clean up the mess. We argue that this presumptive sequence is both wrong and deeply limiting to work in the field, for at least two reasons: first, because it removes important questions of oversight, governance and control from the heart of CSCW scholarship; and second, because it fails to recognize how policy – large and small, enacted by public bodies or private organizations – may precede and prefigure design and practice. Reframing the relationship between these three core elements (and reviving CSCW attention to policy more generally) can therefore help to expand the analytic scope and range of CSCW scholarship – perhaps especially around emerging technological forms like social, cloud, and mobile computing.

Under the alternative model advocated here, the nominally separate moments of design, practice and policy show up as deeply intertwined, with no presumptive ordering in time or priority between them. They are mutually constitutive (or 'co-productive' [42]), informing one another in forceful and sometimes subtle ways that feed back into the independent constitution of each (while sometimes erasing the traces of their connection, making it possible for observers to tell design-, practice- or policy-only stories). This three-way back and forth plays out across the complex unfolding of time, in processes of emergence that *themselves* give form to many of the languages and effects – determinism, dependency, trajectories, diffusion, etc. – through which we try to account for and make sense of the dynamics of computational innovation and change.

Our preferred metaphor for this set of relations is the *knot*: the multiple gatherings and entanglements through which worlds of design, practice and policy are brought into messy but binding alignment. Knots highlight both contingency and the work of assemblage: they help map the precise points of connection by which processes of design, practice, and policy are brought together (or held apart), often while establishing while twisting together the 'autonomous' constitution of each. Knots help account for the existence of durability and order through time, in that once knotted they tend to hold fast, ensuring "sticky" and stepwise progressions from old to new: a key challenge in rapidly changing fields. Knots highlight the irresolvable complexity of sociotechnical worlds and the analytic stories we must tell around them, ensuring work for CSCW and allied fields for generations to come. And knots provide an analytically compelling account of change and innovation: it is through processes of unwinding and retying, loosening and tightening, straightening and reweaving that the worlds of social computing, past, present and future, are formed.

This paper develops these points through analysis of two recent controversies: the 2011 privacy scandal surrounding the location-aware mobile app Girls Around Me, and controversies surrounding the 2010 launch of the Google Buzz social network. We conclude by arguing for the contributions that "knot-like" thinking can make to CSCW research around social computing, innovation, and problems of socio-technical change.

WEBS, GAPS, AND KNOTS: CSCW AND POLICY RESEARCH IN HISTORICAL PERSPECTIVE

CSCW and information science scholarship has long had an ambiguous relationship to work in technology policy. On one hand, policy concerns were central to some of the key movements and influences that informed the founding of the field. And since then, specific policy issues (most notably privacy) have periodically emerged as concerns within many of the immediate contexts examined by CSCW researchers (though called out with varying degrees of attention). On the other hand, organized approaches to policy as a site and modality of CSCW work have been rare, and the field's own recent efforts to connect or contribute to wider policy debates, with few exceptions, have been limited.

This has not always been the case. Early work in CSCW and allied fields showed a deliberatively ambitious breadth, seeking to situate micro and design-oriented accounts of collaborative work within larger systems of practice and order. CSCW work informed by the social informatics tradition of scholars like Kling, King, Scacchi, and other members of the Irvine School adopted a notably holistic orientation, embedding questions of design, use, and collaboration in an expansive context that included organizations, institutions, and systems of public policy. In this understanding, specific artifacts, collaborative practices, and design interventions operated against the backdrop of a broader canvas that could be shaped (and misshaped) by forces and institutions operating at the level of policy. The assemblage as a whole constituted what Kling termed the "web of computing": roughly, the broader set of actors, systems, organizations, rules, and institutions within which discrete computing interventions and computerization "movements" unfold [44,45,46,47].

The same expansive orientation characterized early CSCW work sourced from other theoretical traditions, including cybernetics, activity theory, and symbolic interactionism. Important work by scholars like Grudin [34], Engestrom [24], Nardi [57], and Star and Ruhleder [51] described a world in which application failures, activity systems, and infrastructures lived within larger systems of interaction that ran all the way up and down: from fine-grained details of design and practice to the exigencies of law, institutions, and other mechanisms for the large-scale organization of collective choice and power. The net result was analytical scale and suppleness, as well as an in-principle commitment to tracing the shaping and consequences of emergent computing practices beyond and outside their moments of design and early adoption.

However, this explicit attention to scale, perhaps especially at higher levels of aggregation, attenuated as the field moved on to new concerns in the later 1990s and 2000s. The field turned to the new possibilities of practice and design that were emerging, as successive waves of computing pushed CSCW beyond its traditional workplace groundings and in an increasingly 'social' direction.

Core CSCW work from this period did vital work to sort out the relationship, theoretical and empirical, between the shape and affordances of designed technology and the complex worlds of practice that such design-level interventions were meant to address. This included strategic attention to more thoughtful transits between social practice and technical design, which had gradually solidified as the two dominant pillars of CSCW scholarship. But it also directed attention to the potential *irreducibility* of these worlds, arguing for the ways in which technological design, like other efforts at formalization, must always operate at some distance from the complexities and subtleties of practice. Work by Ackerman on the "social-technical gap" points to the necessary "divide between what we *know* we must support socially and what we *can* support technically" [1]. From this perspective (and citing a rich tradition of CSCW work grounded in pragmatist, ethnomethodological, activity theory, and structuration approaches) the world of practice is fluid, nuanced, emergent, contextually shaped, and above all navigated by artful social actors with extraordinary (if often invisible) skill, flexibility, and care. By contrast, technical systems meant to support collaborative action may be excessively fixed and rule-bound ("brittle"), lack nuance, struggle with ambiguity, and fail to accommodate the kind of flexibility and discretion regularly deployed by competent social actors in the everyday run of their work.

More recent CSCW work has sometimes addressed policy-relevant themes, but rarely as a first-order priority of work. A variety of workshops, panels, and tutorials have sought to bring questions of law and policy to the attention of CSCW scholars, on topics ranging from privacy and data sharing to medical information and scientific infrastructure [52,64]. CSCW research papers, most notably in the area of privacy, have documented user attitudes and responses to organizational and public policies embedded in specific social computing applications (e.g., Facebook, third party apps, etc.) [4,31,50,72]. Others have explored privacy dynamics in the context of medical care, with special attention to design, user attitudes, and practices [17,61]. Still other researchers have investigated the connections between CSCW tools and research programs around collaborative scientific work, and more broadly the organizational, institutional, and national-scale policies related to scientific funding and data-sharing that may alternatively advance or frustrate such efforts [6,22,39,43,70,71].

But this work constitutes a vanishingly small proportion of CSCW work in general and rarely acknowledges the generative three-way relation of design, practice, and policy argued for here. Nor does it typically address policy itself as a legitimate site and target of CSCW work (as opposed to positioning policy as the external backdrop against which such work unfolds). For example, witness the relative paucity of discussions around 'implications for policy' in comparison to 'implications for design' in the discussion sections of CSCW papers and presentations [18,40].

There are several possible reasons for this absence. With important but limited exceptions, the disciplinary education of CSCW scholars in computer and information science and allied fields has tended *not* to include the kinds of legal and institutional training central to work in technology law and policy. Similarly, scholars in technology policy have paid scant attention to CSCW and other fields where technical design figures centrally. Because of this disconnect, there may be widespread misconception within the CSCW community that policy is necessarily static, irrelevant, or purely reactive to questions of design and practice - perhaps especially under the conditions of emergence and rapid change that characterize the worlds of mobile, social, and ubiquitous computing today. This connects in turn to a larger error in the way that technology law and policy has been sometimes thought about and practiced: as an arcane and largely foreign set of rules that stands outside the real worlds of practice they are meant to govern.

This error of omission becomes immediately apparent when we switch from the abstraction of concepts to the concreteness of real-world social computing problems. In such contexts, researchers without legal training are often surprised (and frustrated) by the apparent relativity and context-dependency of the law. Privacy law, for example, remains deeply embedded in norms and subjective orientations that both live at the level of practice and are deeply inflected, sometimes serendipitously, by the designed form of existing technologies. Policy debates often assume these design-contingent features of social practice as they anticipate regulation of new technical forms – which may in fact operate on a substantially different basis of design and practice. Under the dominant "reasonable expectation" test established by Katz v. U.S. (1969), for example, courts are asked to weigh potential privacy violations against two notably fuzzy standards: whether the individual in question has demonstrated a "subjective expectation" of privacy (for example, by closing a phone booth door!); and whether the court (and society as a whole) is prepared to recognize that expectation as "reasonable". Courts weighing privacy violations also draw a postal-based distinction between 'envelope' and 'content' information, granting the former less constitutional protection than the latter on the grounds that information like addressing or numbers dialed has always been more exposed and therefore 'public' than the materials contained on the 'inside' of private letters and conversations. U.S. constitutional protections against "illegal search and seizure" – a category now expanded to include government intrusions on private information of all kinds, from phone taps and library records to the domestic surveillance activities of the U.S. National Security Agency recently uncovered by the Wikileaks and Edward Snowden whistleblower cases - remain almost entirely dependent on these kinds of highly subjective and context-dependent assessments of privacy.

The same complex relation to design and practice shows up in the nuanced application of the fair use balancing tests used to carve out exceptions to U.S. copyright law. Designed as a heuristic rather than as a set of hard-and-fast rules (as discretionary legal standards are sometimes misinterpreted), the four factors of fair use, manifestly *cannot* be reduced to a simple set of rules and prescriptions (despite periodic attempts to do so) [2]. This makes them famously hard to design for in technology systems that would permit some kinds of copying as fair and restrict others as infringing [29].

This double embedding of policy – in discretionary and subjective assessment, and in past forms of design and practice – is more than a simple error or limit, or reflection of the fact that law and policy have somehow failed to 'keep up' with the pace of social and technological change. Indeed, echoing a longer line of legal and policy scholars, we'd argue that the kinds of flexibility built into things like reasonable expectation or fair use balancing tests are precisely what allows law and policy to grow and remain relevant over time, and our systems of order and governance to remain supple and 'live,' rather than fossilized remains of a different sociotechnical moment. Such properties become particularly important at moments of rapid change and emergence, such as those characterizing social computing today (and indeed many other areas of CSCW scholarship).

But it is also a source of complexity and complication. It is *not* the case that emergent forms of design and practice can look to policy as a fixed and stable point of reference around and against which to evolve. Nor will law and policy always provide clear answers to the challenges posed by emergent design and practice, since one of the things that such developments may challenge is the terrain of policy itself. Instead, we live in a world where all three are changing together, in complex, interlinked, and mutually constitutive ways. CSCW efforts to understand and contribute to such changes need to take on this complexity..

POLICY AND EMERGENCE IN SOCIAL COMPUTING: UNDERSTANDING THE KNOT

For purposes of clarity (and because the term is subject to a wide variety of uses and interpretations) it may be useful to say an additional word about what we mean to include under the category of policy. As developed here, "policy" means something wider, though not limitless, than is often meant in common parlance. Certainly, policy includes the forms of public law that regulate technology design and use. This includes both the public bodies and processes charged with establishing laws and regulations (e.g. the U.S. Congress and its relevant sub-committees, the United nations and their more technology-focused working groups) and the public agencies charged with implementing them: the courts, state regulators, and a wide variety of administrative agencies (e.g. the U.S. Federal Communications Commission, Federal Trade Commission, the European Commission, etc.). But it also includes a wide range of rules and procedures set by private firms – software licenses, end user license agreements, policies for app developers, and at the limit corporate philosophies (where actually backed and followed through in organizational practice) – that may intersect with formal law and policy in complex ways.

While policy is often formally expressed through legal and contractual language designed to bind with precision the range of allowable practice, it also depends on a wider set of ideas and tropes to which formal law and policy very often return (in more and less explicit ways). As alluded to above, technology law and policy is full of reference to figures like 'reasonable actors' and 'persons having ordinary skill in the art' which are meant to infer cultural baselines of expectation and normalcy. Where formally expressed rules and cultural norms are out of step, as Jessica Litman has argued for the case of copyright, or where norms and values may be shifting (as some have argued for privacy), deep instabilities in law and policy can ensue.

Under present institutional configurations, the world of policy is also organized into distinct issue spaces (e.g. privacy, telecommunications, antitrust, security, intellectual property, etc.) governed by usually separate regulatory bodies, logics, and processes. Any given instance of technology design and practice may cross and implicate more than one of these, producing additional jurisdictional and practical complexity. Gathering this range and complexity into a single definition (and borrowing from international relations scholar Stephen Krasner's description of transnational regimes [49]), we define policy here simply as the "set of explicit or implicit principles, norms, rules, and decision making procedures around which actor expectations converge."

When brought back together with design and practice as advocated above, the relationship between design, practice, and policy might be modeled after something like a mutually causative triangle, in which each pole interacts with the other two in mutually transformative ways:

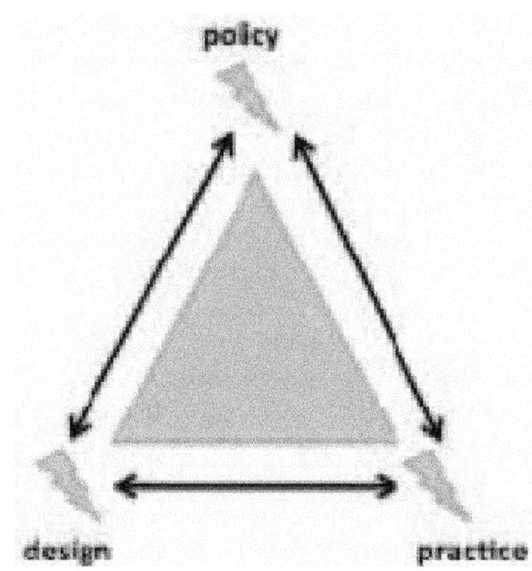

Figure 1. Design, practice, and policy as co-constitutive

Understood in any particular case, however, the story rapidly becomes more complicated than the clean and linear geometry of the triangle will allow. To get at this process, we must unpack the simple lines of the triangle and replace straight-line connections with more supple threads or strands that intersect and combine in specific and sometimes unpredictable ways. The entanglement of design, practice, policy can be better understood as strands woven together, yielding one or more integrated or interlinked entities. In moments of formation, we may see these strands coming together (as in the right side of Figure 2 below); once accomplished, these separate strands may blend into the appearance (and reality!) of a single unified force, all the stronger for their combination and mutual reinforcement: practices valorized through law, law passed into code, etc. But knots can also come apart, fraying through time and change and through the forms of tension and friction that remain endemic to such combinations. The net result of these activities constitutes the landscape or 'web' [46] of social computing, as it grows, shifts and evolves over time.

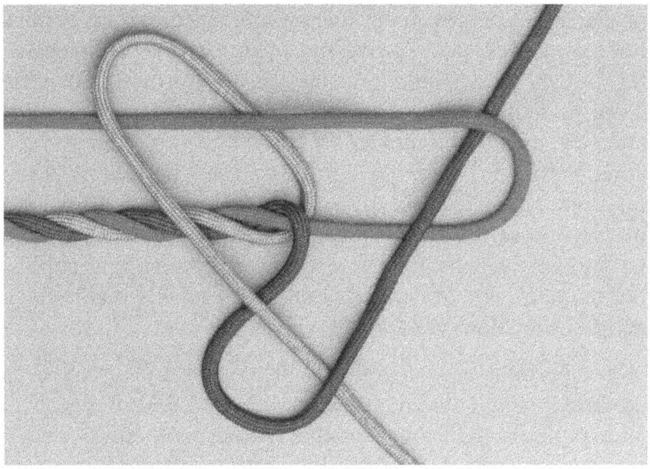

Figure 2. The Design, practice, and policy knot

These three-way intersections between design, practice, and policy show up with particular complexity and importance during periods of formation and emergence, such as those characterizing the world of social computing today. As work in the history and sociology of technology has demonstrated, new technologies in their formative states typically experience complex and uncertain trajectories during which multiple dynamics are being sorted out at once: the design of individual objects or tools, the imagination of their uses and users, and the broader social context in which emerging technologies and practices will fit [5,8,42,48,54,63]. Historians of technology have called attention to the conflictual processes of 'stabilization' or 'closure' through which emergent technological artifacts and practices take on their more settled and durable forms, arguing that it is these tensions and conflicts, rather than isolated or autonomous acts of design per se, that shape the form and trajectory of technological practice going forward [7, 8].

But a common side effect of this work is to obscure the constitutive interrelations that characterize this emergent moment. Tensions and conflicts tend to be written out of the understanding of objects over time, producing the misleading appearance of inevitability, or a too-simple model of agency that construes technology, now stripped of the social forces and processes by which it was imagined, produced, and enacted, as an actor in its own right [54]. This misreading stems in part from the rearview mirror effect by which established objects and practices become naturalized in the world. Put simply, echoing the principle of 'Whig history' long criticized by professional historians [14], things that come to exist can quickly come to seem inevitable (witness, for example, the effort required to imagine an academic life without email!). Viewed historically, the speed of this ontological adjustment may be breathtaking. Philosophers like Ian Hacking have developed the language of 'historical ontology' to reflect precisely this time-bound quality of our basic categorical understandings of the world [35].

But such effects can also be explained, somewhat more modestly, from the standpoint of the knot metaphor described here. Over time, and with our tendency to overlook the interrelation of these forces, the mutually formative influences of these elements can drop from sight (leaving sometimes strange and inexplicable 'kinks' in the rope – why on earth would they design it that way? why would they make policy like *that*?). The structuring presence of the other strands drops away, and we are left with an image in which objects (or practices, or policies) appear to stand alone. The technology, as concretized in the object, simply *is*. The policy, as concretized in the rule, takes on a life of its own. The practice, now embodied and identified with a determinate set of social actors, becomes what Durkheim would call a 'social fact' [21]. With this distance, we are now able to neglect their common origins – until new controversies emerge to disrupt the presumed settlement, unwinding and revealing what may be the contingent or even arbitrary connections at its core.

In arguing for this model, therefore, we seek to do more than make the simple point that design that fails to take account of policy is likely to be bad design; or that user practices that ignore the policy frameworks around them are likely to prove practically or legally unsustainable (though both these things are true). Rather, we argue that these worlds are *practically speaking* inseparable. Design operates in the shadow of practice and order, whether those figures are represented through the mechanisms of user experience research, or memos from corporate legal departments, or in the hunches and intuitions of the design team. Policymakers may take explicit account of design and practice in their deliberations, or they may not; but in either case, design and practice will muscle in, sometimes in the form of the stories or folk theories that so often shape public decision processes, sometimes in the details of the case being adjudicated or the imagined misuse being prevented. Users can ignore design or policy until they can't, as practices that operate at odds with design or law may be swiftly and forcefully corrected.

We believe that CSCW studies of social computing can benefit from this kind of analytic reframing, and more generally from efforts to bring considerations of policy more centrally into our programs of research and action. In the sections that follow we apply this framework to two separate empirical cases. The first concerns a series of actions and debates around the limits of privacy and the repurposing of publicly available data sparked by 'Girls Around Me,' a mobile application for locating women based on public Foursquare and Facebook profiles that was launched and quickly removed from the Android and Apple app stores in March 2012. The second concerns the launch of the social networking service Google Buzz in February 2010 and the subsequent complaint filed by the Federal Trade Commission (FTC) about its handling of user privacy. In both cases, questions of design get inextricably linked to problems in practice and policy. And in both cases, the precise configuration by which policy, practice, and design get put together proves decisive.

CASE 1: GIRLS AROUND ME

Girls Around Me (GAM)[1] was a mobile application for iOS and Android that integrated data from two widely used social networking platforms, Foursquare[2] and Facebook[3]. Released in December 2011 by SMS Services O.o.o. and its parent company i-Free, GAM re-used and repurposed geo-location data and user profile information made public through individual Foursquare user 'check-ins.' The application's design and supporting online materials suggested its primary use: *"In the mood for love, or just after a one-night stand? ...browse photos of lovely local ladies and tap their thumbnail to find out more about them[4]"*

Figure 3. Girls Around Me website

[1] Girls Around Me. 2012. http://girlsaround.me/.

[2] Foursquare. 2013. https://foursquare.com/.

[3] Facebook, 2013. https://www.facebook.com/.

[4] This is one of several rotating marketing messages for Girls Around Me on its webpage at http://girlsaround.me/.

From a technical perspective, Girls Around Me was a simple tool that gathered data publicly available on other social media sites. By using the application programming interface (API) provided by Foursquare, GAM dynamically queried Foursquare's database to locate users (either gender, though the application defaulted to women) who had recently checked-in near the location of the GAM user. These were displayed as photo icons on a Google Map overlay, with more detailed information just a click away (Figure 4). Foursquare users whose data were being repurposed in this way received no alert that this was happening. And for those with publicly linked Facebook accounts, the GAM app also provided instant connection to the individual's public Facebook profile.

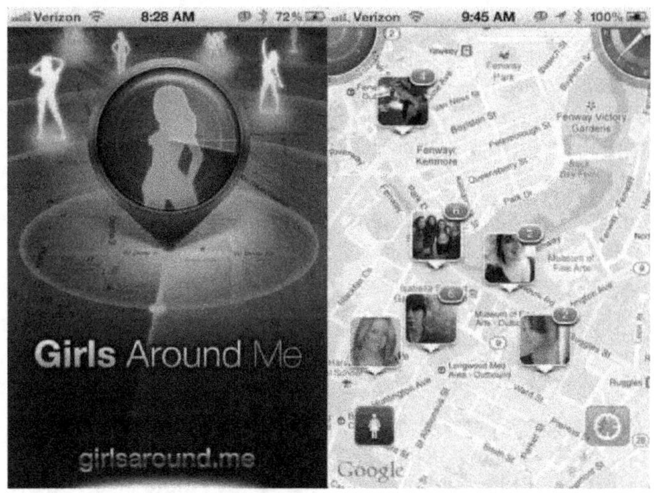

Figure 4. Radar-type view in user interface[5]

Reactions flared in March 2012, after John Brownlee (writing for the news site *Cult of Mac*) decried the application as a "wake up call" for the changing dynamics of online privacy: "It is as innocent as it is insidious; it is just as likely to be reacted to with laughter as it is with tears; it is as much of a novelty as it has the potential to be used a tool for rapists and stalkers" [12] .

In the days following Brownlee's expose, coverage of GAM spread across online technology news sites and blogs, and from there into major newspapers [3,9,19,53]. Critics objected to the presumed relationship the app expressed toward the women it targeted (and women in general), like the writer at TechCrunch who offered, "I submit to evidence that these nice guys present women as shiny metallic objects, targets to be taken down, complete with radar imagery. These nice guys developed an app that made some who first saw it think the women within were prostitutes" [65]. Defenders of the app emphasized that all of the data had already been deliberately made public by the Foursquare users and blasted the patronizing tone of the

[5] This screenshot was captured by John Brownlee, blogger at Cult of Mac.

critique, such as the Forbes staff writer who argued that "[i]n rejecting and banishing the app, we're choosing to ignore the publicity choices these women have made in the name of keeping them safe. And we make the ugly assumption that men who might want to check out women in the area have nefarious intentions" [36].

The public controversy ended just a few days later when Foursquare, bowing to user complaints and online pressure, blocked GAM's access to its API [13] (Foursquare would later go on to alter its API to prevent other app developers from making similar use of their data) [74]. On April 30, 2012, GAM was removed from the Apple iTunes store [62]. The following week, i-Free Innovations, the venture capital foundation that supported the development of GAM, released two public statements. The first was defiant, insisting that the app was not made for stalking and that the GAM developers were fully within their rights to use the data as they had. The second, issued on May 4, was more conciliatory and defensive and signed by the iFree CEO himself:

"[t]he application was developed without any specific gender bias, and its name, as well as the James Bond-style design, were chosen purely for marketing reasons. We now understand that this may have been a misstep, as this has provoked a negative response from some mass media sources and, subsequently, from many people" [38]

On the same day, i-Free announced that funding had been halted for further development of the app, and no further effort would be made to restore it to the Apple iTunes store or regain its Foursquare API privileges. Girls Around Me was effectively dead.

Analysis:

At first glance, the Girls Around Me controversy followed a familiar and increasingly well-worn path. Upstart app designer develops and releases a technology that violates some cultural norm. Bloggers and tech journalists react, and a small but vigorous debate among advocates and critics ensues. When the controversy reaches a certain pitch, actors with larger reputations at stake step in and the app is gutted or removed from circulation.. Days to weeks later, a new upstart developer with a new controversial app appears, and the cycle begins again.

As the controversy developed, the public debate quickly came to occupy one of two positions. The more widely accepted one saw this as an app going too far with public data, transforming the public actions of Foursquare users into a template for stalking. The women identified and represented by the app had not signed up to take part in the service, and did not receive any kind of notification that their Foursquare and Facebook information was being presented in this way [11]. In this account, fault rested with design: it was simply inappropriate to reuse the data in this way. And the designers of GAM certainly made things worse: the unfortunate visual iconography and leering sales pitch made the app easy game for critics who attacked it as a tool catering to and assisting stalkers.

A counter-position (one that the designers of GAM would eventually adopt) saw this as an inevitable and even logical extension of user ignorance around privacy settings in social media: either they *wanted* to be public in which case this is a reasonable extension of that want, or they were unaware of what a public setting meant and had simply screwed up, in which case they should learn to be savvier about their privacy settings. Fault here lay with the users.

Following the contours of this public debate, one could characterize the GAM controversy as a design vs. practice problem. The technology was designed to compile publicly available and location-specific social media data; the practice (as envisioned by critics) was that men would use the information made available to stalk or harass women who didn't know their information was being packaged and recirculated in this way. Or, from another angle: the designers embedded certain ideas and presumptions about appropriate ways of finding and relating to women into their tool, and users found the implied practices reprehensible. So far, this is a recognizable CSCW story, and speaks richly to the problematic (mis)alignments of design and practice that emergent social computing forms often face or produce. But it's also a somewhat limited one, leading primarily to the insight that apps designed to enact, imply, or suggest socially problematic behaviors are likely to fall afoul of the public (so don't do that).

But what happens if we move policy to the center of this story? While not relieving GAM and its developers of responsibility, more proactive attention to the role of policy can highlight the way that policies set by service providers can shape both the design of the tool and its incorporation (problematic or otherwise) into the ongoing flow of practice. It can also open up new questions of agency and responsibility that extend beyond the immediate spheres of practice and design. For example, curiously little of the debate considered the responsibility of Foursquare or Facebook, though both are deeply implicated in the case, having collected the data and devised a way for it to be public. Even less attention was paid to Apple, and none at all to Google Maps, though the two are also obliquely implicated. This is not to imply that they are the responsible parties; the question we have is a different one. Were they in some ways less visible as implicated parties because we focus too little on policy?

Listen carefully, for example, to the way that each of the immediate stakeholders, i-Free Innovations and Foursquare, articulate their positions, both about their responsibilities and obligations and about the app and its cultural harm. The responses read like recitations of policy: either policies that were in place before the controversy broke and thus were constitutive of the GAM app in the first place; or in Foursquare's case, a subsequent change in policy that would let Foursquare distance itself from the embarrassing taint of the offending app.

i-Free's primary defense was that they had simply followed Foursquare's API policy: "Girls Around Me shows to the user only the data that is available to him or her through his or her accounts in Foursquare, and gives the user nothing more than Foursquare app can provide itself" [3]. No other data was being collected from third party providers, and subjects' Facebook profiles could only appear if the subjects had linked them to their Foursquare profiles (meaning that compliance with Foursquare is the only issue in question). In addition, "The Girls Around Me user has to be registered in Foursquare and must be logged in this service to be able to see anything in Girls Around Me. The app Girls Around Me does not have access to user login and password, authentication is carried out on the social network side" [3]. The Girls Around Me user is in fact logging into Foursquare and making a query themselves, merely through a third-party interface. Finally, only users with Foursquare accounts themselves can use Girls Around Me, which both offers an identity assurance mechanism, and lets Girls Around Me serve as a proxy login to Foursquare.

The core of i-Free's defense of Girls Around Me was this: Foursquare established in its API policy a set of allowable uses for data that could be publicly queried, and i-Free complied with those terms. But let's turn this around. Foursquare collects data, and makes it available within a policy-constrained set of terms that extend out categories (like public and private), parameters for how their database can be queried and by whom, and obligations for how the data can and cannot be used subsequently that third party operators (who have contractually accepted these terms when they used Foursquare's API). We might think of Foursquare's API policy not as rules, but as an articulated space of possible practices, some prohibited and others implicitly or explicitly left open. Girls Around Me can only come into existence within the parameters established by those policies; it then can fully occupy the space those policies offer, and can look to them as defense when their own service comes under criticism [67]. This policy-bounded terrain of possible practices is one that Girls Around Me happily filled, but might have been filled by other apps in due time.

Foursquare's terse response to the criticism surrounding Girls Around Me also depended on policy to articulate the appropriate interactions between the app and its service, leaning on the authority of policy to re-frame the controversy and restore its reputation as a responsible and good-faith actor vis-à-vis its user base.

"In a statement given exclusively to Cult of Mac, Foursquare's Laura Covington said: 'This is a violation of our API policy, so we've reached out to the developer and shut off their API access.' Asked to clarify with us the section of their API policy that prohibits apps like Girls Around Me from using their data, Foursquare responded: 'We have a policy against aggregating information across venues using our API, to prevent situations like this where someone would present an inappropriate overview of a series of locations'" [3]

With the advantage of a knot perspective, we might re-order the sequence of events further. Foursquare designed an API policy meant to define the space of possible practices for third-party developers and users. Girls Around Me occupied and took advantage of the space left by Foursquare in that policy, a space either unrecognized by Foursquare, or one that Foursquare was willing to overlook. When hypothetical practices emerged that troubled the design of the app (if you believe the designers), or represented its true intention (if you believe the critics), Foursquare invoked policy, first to exclude GAM from its data through a remarkably open-ended clause in its API platform: "Foursquare may revoke your authentication credentials at any time, for any reason or no reason, with or without notice, and without liability to you or any other person"[30]. Then it redesigned its policy to better constrain the space of possible practices that GAM had exploited. While it would be equally simplistic to say that policy came first and design and practice followed, tracing the strands of controversy by inverting the traditional sequential logic reminds us that policy was a part of the negotiation and constitution of this space from the very start.

Even centering the discussion on GAM and Foursquare may be too limiting however. Facebook also has policies that articulate how user profiles can be linked together, and which aspects of a user profile are made public by decree, by default, or by choice. Apple has policies about the character of the apps it allows, which were either underdeveloped on this issue or were overlooked until the controversy brought the app to public attention. Google Maps has policies about the use of its maps by third parties -- policies designed to fundamentally distance them from any particular use of those maps that might emerge (including presumably, questionable ones like these. When it comes to digital, networked, and social information tools, the engagement between designed artifact and the rights and protections of users and stakeholders is complex and multi-layered. A tiny piece of software may require a mobile platform on which to run, a third-party cloud service on which to store its data, and a partner information service from which to draw information resources. This network of elements means a network of stakeholders, each with its own economic imperatives, legal protections, and contractual obligations.

The implications of a socio-technical ensemble like that are not so easy to anticipate, and responsibility may fall on different stakeholders in different ways. Not only, then, is technical design implicated in policies that may affect how it can be constructed and articulated. It also means that designers and firms must not only craft technologies, they must also craft their firm's legal status, the contractual assurances that partition out responsibility, and their anticipatory defenses in the case that something goes sour. This "symbolic heterogeneous engineering" [5] – or what one of our industry colleagues names more colloquially as "tilling the soil" – is a fundamental and inevitable part of design work writ large, and a powerful reminder of the embedded and 'knotty' character of today's social computing landscape. In this world, policy not only responds to design or practice, it also helps to establish the very terrain on which design and practice can be conceived, articulated, and imagined – and upon which battles of accountability are inevitably waged.

CASE 2: GOOGLE BUZZ

In February 2010, Google introduced a new social networking service known as Google Buzz, promoted as a high-profile competitor to Facebook and Twitter. Like other social networking platforms, Buzz was designed to allow users to "follow" each other and "to be followed." Within Buzz networks, users could post updates, make comments, and share photos, videos, and other information. While described as a new social networking platform, Buzz was deeply integrated into the existing Gmail email platform, and leveraged Gmail's existing personal user data (including first and last names, frequency of contact, and email addresses of people that a user communicates with) to populate and bootstrap the Buzz network.

On the day of the Buzz launch, Gmail users were presented with an announcement that the new service was available, and that with a single click, a pre-populated social network would be automatically established for them. If a user decided to proceed, the user's forty most frequent email contacts were used to pre-fill their Buzz network (with no process of notification or consent). Through this process, Gmail users were configured as "followers" in the Buzz network on the basis of frequency of email or chat interactions [58].

Controversy immediately ensued. Critics charged that Google had in effect publicly exposed private information concerning users' prior communication patterns. Critics noted that email contacts might not represent the kinds of "friends" one wanted made public: one might regularly email a therapist, an ex-spouse, a secret lover, or a political co-conspirator in dangerous situations [56]. They also pointed out that in its initial configuration Google Buzz made it difficult for users to exercise discretion and choice in when and how their patterns of interaction were revealed. For example, if Gmail users later decided to opt out of Buzz, they still appeared as "followers" on the profiles of other users who had once been in their contact list. Google responded by initially defending the service, arguing that its privacy policies and protections matched those of other leading social networking sites (Facebook, Twitter, etc.). But it also apologized and adjusted the service, replacing the automatic, opt-out system with an "auto-suggest," opt-in approach by which frequent email and messaging contacts were *proposed* as followers, but only revealed publicly in the network when approved by the user [41].

In March 2011, in response to a complaint filed by the Electronic Privacy Information Center [23], the U.S. Federal Trade Commission (FTC) opened an official proceeding against Google for privacy violations in the unveiling of Buzz. In its complaint, the FTC argued that Google had violated the FTC Act and engaged in deceptive trade practices when it repurposed email contacts for the purpose of social networking. Most damningly, the FTC argued that Google had violated its own policies with regard to personal data, noting that Google had previously guaranteed: "[i]f we use this information in a manner different than the purpose for which it was collected, then we will ask for your consent prior to such use" [25]. The filing documented numerous instances of harm stemming from the disclosure, including reports of auto-populated Buzz networks that included individuals against whom users had restraining orders, abusive ex-husbands, clients of mental health professionals, clients of attorneys, job recruiters, and children.

In October 2011, the FTC issued its decision and final order on the Google Buzz case, announcing an unprecedented settlement that barred the company from future privacy misrepresentations, ordered it to implement a comprehensive privacy program, and required it to submit to regular, independent privacy audits for a period of 20 years [26]. The watershed nature of this ruling was noted in an FTC press release: "[t]his is the first time an FTC settlement order has required a company to implement a comprehensive privacy program to protect the privacy of consumers' information. In addition, this is the first time the FTC has alleged violations of the substantive privacy requirements of the U.S.-EU Safe Harbor Framework...." [27]. While targeted at Google, the settlement was also widely regarded as a statement and message to the social networking industry as a whole, and was widely hailed as setting an important new standard by privacy advocates around the world. As predicted by Leslie Harris, President of the Center for Democracy and Technology, "the terms of this agreement will have a far reaching effect on how industry develops and implements new technologies and services that make personal information public," setting "new norms" for any company operating services with the potential to make private information public.

Stepping back from the details of the case, it would once again be easy to frame this controversy in terms of a tension between design and practice, with policy following behind to clean up the mess. Google designs Buzz to automatically turn frequent Gmail contacts into Buzz social contacts. The new service stumbles over subtle differences in the nature and meaning of public and private connections on email vs. social media. The results are sufficiently alarming that users and advocacy organizations turn to regulatory bodies like the FTC to sanction Google's actions. Google responds by redesigning its system and accepting a new level of regulatory intervention into its privacy practices going forward. But a policy-centric analysis can go a step further. To begin, as with Foursquare's API policy in the GAM case, Google's Gmail privacy policy set out a space of possible practices – which Google itself subsequently violated. The FTC had the institutional power and legitimacy to turn Google from this endeavor and penalize them for having violated their own terms.

The knot approach also helps us to situate these controversies in an institutional and a temporal framework, recognizing that the stakeholders in controversies like these are (a) not interacting only around this one incident, and (b) exist before and after these dust-ups, in an ongoing relationship. It would be easy to imagine, given the nature of the FTC complaint and the settlement, that Google and the FTC were enemy combatants on opposite sides of this issue. Or, after the model of the arms-length regulator, that the FTC's role was akin to the traffic cop, intervening when clear laws were broken but otherwise staying above and firmly out of the action. But this controversy, and its regulatory conclusion, look different if we think about the ongoing, multi-dimensional, collaborative, and in some ways mutually dependent relationship Google and the FTC have developed over several years.

For instance, even as the Google Buzz controversy was unfolding, the FTC was in the process of developing its own privacy framework through a series of high-profile roundtables and public comment periods designed to source feedback from leading business, trade organizations, legal experts, technology experts, and privacy advocacy organizations. In April 2010 – two months after Google Buzz was launched and almost a year before the FTC issued its formal complaint – Google submitted its letter of commentary to this FTC roundtable, proposing best practices for large platform companies handling significant volumes of personal user data [32]:

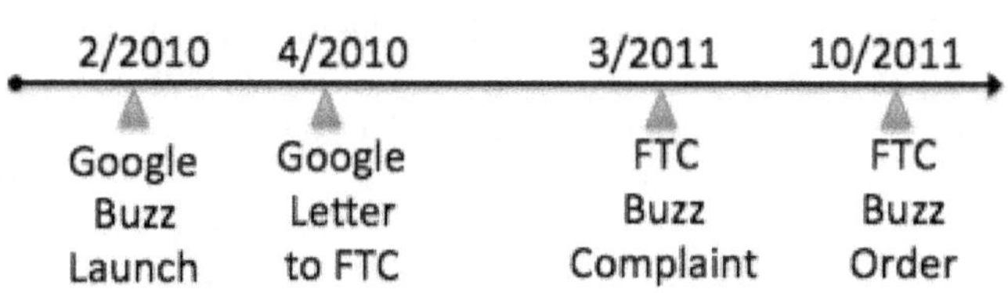

Figure 5: Google and FTC 2010-2011

These two very different interactions, in turn, were part of a much larger and longer set of interactions between Google and the FTC. Turning the clock back three years reveals yet other instances of formal engagement between the company and the FTC.

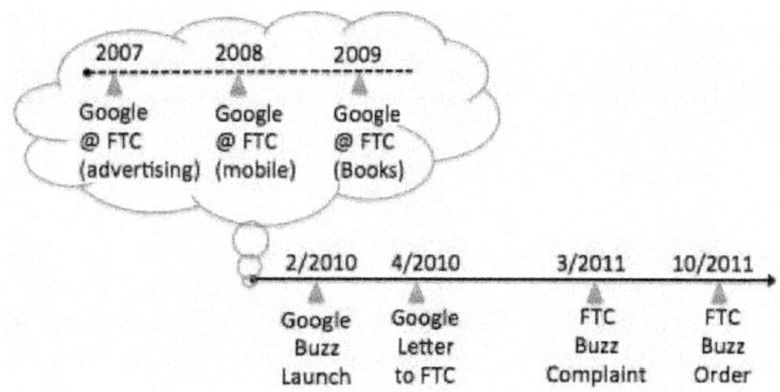

Figure 6. Google and FTC Expanded Timeline

In 2007 Google established a formal policy office in Washington, and contributed comments to an FTC Town Hall meeting on the topic of behavioral advertising – the same year that Google was under scrutiny by the FTC and federal antitrust regulators for its acquisition of rival online ad service DoubleClick [15,20]. In 2008, Google participated in an FTC Town Hall focused on the "mobile marketplace," at which Google's manager for mobile platforms argued that open platforms (such as Google's Android) would result in more innovation and consumer choice [16]. In 2009, Google addressed the FTC regarding appropriate privacy policies for its new Google Books platform, with Google's Global Privacy Counsel acknowledging that the eventual policy was "legally enforceable by the FTC," and that the process of FTC engagement had "helped us clarify our practices and policies" [37]. More generally, over the past half decade – and in contrast to the scrappy start-up image it still sometimes likes to project – Google has established itself as a major policy player in Washington, deeply engaged with Congressional and regulatory authorities around key policy issues including net neutrality, intellectual property, online privacy, security, and freedom of expression [10,33]. In the process, it has joined the rarefied group of telecommunication firms and major equipment manufacturers who maintain an active presence and lobbying effort around the ongoing shape and direction of U.S. technology policy.

In 2012, the FTC issued its landmark "Privacy By Design" report, proposing a new privacy framework designed to "enhance trust and stimulate commerce" [28]. In the report, the FTC urged companies to adopt and implement best practices in accordance with a set of guiding principles that include "considering privacy at every stage of design" (p. 22), "providing simplified choice for customers" (p. 35), and "ensuring greater transparency" (p. 60). While the FTC sanctioned Google in 2011 for Buzz, and launched a nineteen-month antitrust investigation into their mobile and search practices that same year, Google was still engaged with the FTC in a constructive dialog on privacy policy in 2012, and used its letter to highlight its commitment to user empowerment and industry self-regulation.

Our understanding of Google's design choices and the way they intersect with user practices changes if we situate individual design interventions like Buzz amidst the ongoing process of building, maintaining, and negotiating relationships with a complex set of regulatory actors like the FTC, the U.S. Congress, the European Commission, and countless other policy entities. The interactions between companies like Google and the FTC might be viewed as a dance between a regulatory agency and commercial stakeholders. This dance is deeply "knotted" with the tools Google pursues, the design choices they make, the practices they anticipate; the way users respond to or reject these technologies, frame their understanding of them in publicly available terms (like "privacy violation"), and turn to policy actors to counter or challenge them. Whether we should see Google's array of letters, testimonies, lobbying efforts, and policy statements as (a) efforts to ingratiate itself with regulators in anticipation of later inquiries, (b) efforts to frame the debate about current and future policy concerns in ways that will open up future business opportunities, (c) a genuine desire to contribute their expertise to those who are setting important information policy standards, or (d) all of the above, is an empirical question. But it is one that should be within CSCW's intellectual purview to address.

CONCLUSION:

This paper has argued for the importance of new and creative attention to policy as a key third factor alongside CSCW's more traditional orientations to design and practice. It has also advocated a particular framework for conceptualizing this relationship: namely, the understanding of design, practice, and policy as linked in complex knots whose interconnections (rather than any one strand in isolation) constitute new and emerging sociotechnical forms. This general approach goes against both a division of labor argument (in which policy concerns are best left to other fields and scholars), and a priority in time argument, in which policy is regarded as necessarily trailing or chasing after the "true" origin of computational novelty and innovation in design or practice. Such positions we believe misstate the nature of change and innovation in social computing today, which come to us in forms inextricably bound and tangled, with no universal sequencing or priority among them. They also place important questions of policy and governance beyond the reach of CSCW scholarship.

The knot described here functions as a heuristic rather than a simple blueprint, roadmap, or recipe for action. Nor is it primarily oriented to generating the kinds of immediate "implications for design" [18] sometimes looked for in CSCW scholarship. It describes a set of *potential* relations among forces at play in the social computing landscape, but cannot produce global predictions as to how these will play out. In some moments and cases, some factors may be more in dominance than others, with policy driving design, or design determining practice, etc. But these are "effects" of the knot we've described, rather than stable and universal truths that stand outside of it: properties of the particular configurations of design, practice and policy at play in a given circumstance rather than necessary or universal properties of their interrelation. Under such conditions, "structure" is often yet to be established, and the nature of the relationship between various actors or elements in the story (here, design, practice, and policy) is precisely what is to be worked out. An approach that names these elements – but holds their precise nature and the relationship between them open – has important advantages.

Nor do the three elements called out above – design, practice, and policy – exhaust the space of explanatory interest. Implicit in the stories above are different explanatory possibilities: institutional analyses of firms, markets and the state, political economy, and other approaches emphasizing the formative influence of various kinds of structure. We believe the framework proposed here is friendly to these approaches, and may provide other ways of getting at the processes through which such structures are achieved and express themselves. It is also the case that other scholars have pursued a similarly integrative agenda, including recent lines of scholarship in the innovation, intellectual property, and privacy spaces that have shaped and influenced our own analyses [22,59,60,66]. Finally, we are not at the end of the day hung up on knots in particular (though we think the metaphor carries well many of the points of connection and entanglement we wish to make). Other languages and metaphors that point to the constitutive interrelation of the three elements named here may perform broadly similar and equally welcome work.

Such disclaimers aside, we believe that our model has distinct and important affordances, perhaps especially for fields like CSCW that straddle the line between technical and social and in light of the emergent conditions that characterize the social computing landscape today.

First, while the knot cannot definitively settle how design, practice, and policy interact at the local level, it is also emphatically *not* an invitation to throw up our hands and say "well, it's all interconnected." While we cannot (and would not) make a statement about determinism at a meta-level, examining socio-technical controversies with the knot in mind can indeed highlight local determinisms. We know from both research and experience that particular technological forms can have significant consequences for the social and policy arrangements that follow. Likewise, while policy does not always determine what tools are built and how they are used and understood, particular policies can have real ramifications on both. And though the ways users take up a technology does not always determine its ultimate social course, in a specific instances, unanticipated uses can turn both design and policy on their head. These and myriad other examples teach us that while it is certainly true that technology does not always drive practice or policy (or vice versa), it is just as certainly true that, in some instances, it *does*. Calling attention to the ways in which these elements are brought together may help us to understand how these effects are formed, casting much-needed light on the local mechanics of determinism.

Second, taking knots seriously may suggest more immediate tactics of use to CSCW researchers and practitioners. Two stand out here as worth highlighting. The first concerns the powerful temporal assumptions surrounding the relationship between design, practice and policy, and in particular the widespread tendency to place policy at the end of a temporal chain that begins in design and practice. To counter this, we encourage researchers to practice reversing this temporal sequence, if only as an analytical move. What policy frameworks existed before the controversy emerged, before even the technology in question was designed? How did such frameworks limit but also enable the kinds of technologies could be designed and imagined? How did these policy frameworks leave space for, prepare, or otherwise anticipate the design innovations that followed? Such inversions can extend our temporal imagination and help unearth new connections and responsibilities across the intertwined worlds of policy, practice and design.

Another pervasive assumption places policy and innovation in opposition, with policy at best irrelevant to the process of technical invention, and at worst a force that hampers and undercuts it. There are no doubt instances in which this description holds true (and designers and firms may get important mileage out of telling it to discourage forms of regulation they don't want). But try once again inverting this assumption, even if only as analytic tactic. In the case at hand, where has policy been innovative, and technological design constraining? And where have they worked together, producing innovation *through* the interaction rather than despite it? Recognition of the potentially creative and generative interplay of design, practice, and policy can help to correct and rebalance what are too often our single-point stories of change and innovation. It can also help remind us that the nature of work and invention in social computing is complex and multi-faceted, with room for strategic and meaningful action across any and all of the spheres named here.

We have argued that the knot model and more explicit attention to policy have timely and important things to offer CSCW scholarship and practice, especially where it meets the unsettled landscapes of new and emergent computing forms. In such contexts, better understanding of knots can help us go beyond monocausal or deterministic understandings of change by which power and responsibility are mistakenly assigned to one side or element of what is in fact a complex and deeply entangled relationship. It can expand the reach and scope of CSCW analysis, adding sites and processes of policy formation that may turn out to be decisive for the long-term evolution of the social computing field. And it provides one useful way of getting from the particular to the whole without falling back on the shibboleths of structure or scale: the "web of computing," as described by Kling and an earlier generation of CSCW scholars, is nothing more (or less!) than a series of just such knots, progressively wound and rewound through time.

ACKNOWLEDGMENTS

Support for this research was provided by the Intel Science and Technology Center (ISTC) for Social Computing. We wish to thank Phoebe Sengers and our colleagues in the ISTC for their comments on an earlier draft of these ideas, and Alan Grogono at www.animatedknots.com for permission to use Figure 2.

REFERENCES

1. Ackerman, M. The Intellectual Challenge of CSCW: The Gap Between Social Requirements and Technical Feasibility. *Human-Computer Interaction* 15, 2 (2000), 179–203.
2. Aufderheide, P. and Jaszi, P. Reclaiming fair use: How to put balance back in copyright. The University of Chicago Press, Chicago, 2011.
3. Austin, S. and Dowell, A. 'Girls Around Me' Developer Defends App After Foursquare Dismissal. *Wall Street Journal, Digits.*, 2012. http://blogs.wsj.com/digits/2012/03/31/girls-around-me-developer-defends-app-after-foursquare-dismissal/.
4. Barkhuus, L. The Mismeasurement of Privacy: Using Contextual Integrity to Reconsider Privacy in HCI. *Proceedings of the Computer-Human Interaction (CHI)*, (2012).
5. Bazerman, C. *The Language of Edison's Light.* MIT Press, Cambridge Mass., 1999.
6. Bietz, M.J., Paine, D., and Lee, C.P. The work of developing cyberinfrastructure middleware projects. *Proceedings of the 2013 conference on Computer supported cooperative work - CSCW '13*, ACM Press (2013), 1527.
7. Bijker, W.E., Hughes, T.P., and Pinch, T.J. *The Social Construction of Technological Systems: New Directions in the Sociology and History of Technology.* MIT Press, Cambridge Mass., 1987.
8. Bijker, W.E. *Of Bicycles, Bakelites, and Bulbs: Toward a Theory of Sociotechnical Change.* MIT Press, Cambridge, MA, 1997.
9. Bilton, N. Girls Around Me: An App Takes Creepy to a New Level. *New York Times - Bits*, 2012.
10. Birnbaum, J. Learning from microsoft's Error, Google Builds a Lobbying Engine. *Washington Post*, 2007. http://www.washingtonpost.com/wp-

dyn/content/article/2007/06/19/AR2007061902058.html.

11. Blue, V. Stalker app Girls Around Me hunts women via Facebook, Foursquare. *ZDNet*, 2012. http://www.zdnet.com/blog/violetblue/stalker-app-girls-around-me-hunts-women-via-facebook-foursquare/1182.
12. Brownlee, J. This Creepy App Isn't Just Stalking Women Without Their Knowledge, It's a Wake-Up Call About Facebook Privacy. *Cult of Mac*, 2012. http://www.cultofmac.com/157641/this-creepy-app-isnt-just-stalking-women-without-their-knowledge-its-a-wake-up-call-about-facebook-privacy/.
13. Brownlee, J. Our Story Got Foursquare To Kill API Access To Creepy Stalking App Girls Around Me [Update: Facebook Responds]. *Cult of Mac*, 2012.
14. Butterfield, H. *The Whig interpretation of history.* Norton, New York, 1965.
15. Chavez, P. The FTC's close look at online advertising. *Google Public Policy Blog*, 2007. http://googlepublicpolicy.blogspot.com/2007/09/ftcs-close-look-at-online-advertising.html.
16. Chavez, P. Public policy and the new mobile marketplace. *Google Public Policy Blog*, 2008. http://googlepublicpolicy.blogspot.com/2008/05/public-policy-and-new-mobile.html.
17. Chen, Y., Hall, B., and Xu, H. Privacy Management in Dynamic Groups : Understanding Information Privacy in Medical Practices. *Methodology*, (2013), 541–552.
18. Dourish, P. Implications for Design. *Proceedings of the Computer-Human Interaction (CHI) Conference*, 2006., (2006).
19. Dowell, A. 'Girls Around Me' Developer Defends App. 2012. http://live.wsj.com/video/girls-around-me-developer-defends-app/957995EF-52E8-4602-8274-C50D25CED7A0.html.
20. Drummond, D. Analysis: The FTC clears our acquisition of DoubleClick. *Google Public Policy Blog*, 2007. http://googlepublicpolicy.blogspot.com/2007/12/analysis-ftc-clears-our-acquisition-of.html.
21. Durkheim, E. *The elementary forms of the religious life*. Free Press, New York.
22. Edwards, P.N., Jackson, S.J., Chalmers, M.K., et al. *Knowledge Infrastructures: Intellectual Frameworks and Research Challenges*. Ann Arbor, MI, 2013.
23. Electronic Privacy Information Center. In the Matter of Google, Inc., Complaint, Request for Investigation, Injunction, and Other relief". 2010. http://epic.org/privacy/ftc/googlebuzz/GoogleBuzz_Complaint.pdf.
24. Engeström, Y., Miettinen, R., Punamäki-Gitai, R.-L., and International Congress for Research on Activity Theory. *Perspectives on activity theory*. Cambridge University Press., Cambridge, 1999.
25. Federal Trade Commission. File No. 102 3136: Google Complaint. (2011). http://www.ftc.gov/os/caselist/1023136/.
26. Federal Trade Commission. File No. 102 3136: Google Decision and Order. (2011). http://www.ftc.gov/os/caselist/1023136/
27. Federal Trade Commission. File No. 102 3136: Press Release. 2011. http://ftc.gov/opa/2011/03/google.shtm.
28. Federal Trade Commission. Protecting Consumer Privacy in an Era of Rapid Change: Recommendations for Businesses and Policymakers. 2012. www.ftc.gov/os/2012/03/120326privacyreport.pdf
29. Felten, E.W. A Skeptical View of DRM and Fair Use. *Communications of the ACM*, 46, 4 (2003), 56.
30. Foursquare. Foursquare API Platform Policy. 2013. https://foursquare.com/legal/api/platformpolicy.
31. Frederic, S. and Hartzog, W. Boundary regulation in social media. *Proceedings of the ACM 2012 conference on Computer Supported Cooperative Work (CSCW '12)*, ACM (2012).
32. Google Inc. Privay Roundtables - Comment Project No. P095416. 135, 2010. http://www.ftc.gov/os/comments/privacyroundtable/544506-00134.pdf.
33. Google Inc. Google U.S. Public Policy. 2013. http://www.google.com/publicpolicy/.
34. Grudin, J. Why CSCW applications fail: problems in the design and evaluationof organizational interfaces. *Proceedings of the 1988 ACM conference on Computer-supported cooperative work*, ACM (1988).
35. Hacking, I. *Historical Ontology*. Harvard University Press, Cambridge, MA, 2004.
36. Hill, K. The Reaction To 'Girls Around Me' Was Far More Disturbing Than The 'Creepy' App Itself. *Forbes*. http://www.forbes.com/sites/kashmirhill/2012/04/02/the-reaction-to-girls-around-me-was-far-more-disturbing-than-the-creepy-app-itself/.
37. Horvath, J. An update on Google Books and privacy. *Google Public Policy Blog*. http://googlepublicpolicy.blogspot.com/2009/09/update-on-google-books-and-privacy.html.

38. iFree. Statement Concerning the Mobile Application Girls Around Me. *iFree News*, 2012.

39. Jackson, S.J. and Barbrow, S. Infrastructure and Vocation: Field, Calling, and Computation in Ecology. *Proceedings of the 2013 Computer-Human Interaction (CHI) Conference,* (2013).

40. Jackson, S.J., Steinhardt, S.B., and Buyuktur, A. Why CSCW needs science policy (and vice versa). *Proceedings of the 2013 Conference on Computer supported cooperative work - CSCW '13*, (2013), 1113.

41. Jackson, T. A New Buzz Start-up Experience Based on Your Feedback. *Official GMail Blog*, 2010. http://gmailblog.blogspot.com/2010/02/new-buzz-start-up-experience-based-on.html.

42. Jasanoff, S. *States of Knowledge: The Co-Production of Science and the Social Order*. Routledge, 2006.

43. Kervin, K. and Hedstrom, M. How research funding affects data sharing. *Proceedings of the ACM 2012 conference on Computer Supported Cooperative Work Companion (CSCW '12)*, ACM.

44. King, J.L. Rob Kling and the Irvine School. *The Information Society* 20, 2 (2004), 97–99.

45. Kling, R., Hopper, A., and Katz, J. Controversies about privacy and open information in CSCW. *Proceedings of the 1992 ACM conference on Computer-supported cooperative work (CSCW '92)*. ACM, New, ACM (1992).

46. Kling, R. and Scacchi, W. The Web of Computing: Computer Technology as Social Organization. *Advances in Computers* 21, (1982).

47. Kling, R. Computerization and Social Transformations. *Science Technology & Human Values* 16, 3 (1991), 342–367.

48. Kling, R. Social Informatics: A New Perspective on Social Research About Information and Communication Technologies. *Prometheus* 18, 3 (2000), 245–264.

49. Krasner, S.D. Structural Causes and Regime Consequences: Regimes as Intervening Variables. *International Organization* 36, 2 (Spring) (1982).

50. Lampe, C., Arbor, A., Vitak, J., Bldg, H., Wing, S., and Ellison, N. Users and Nonusers : Interactions between Levels of Facebook Adoption and Social Capital. *Proceedings of the 2013 conference on Computer supported cooperative work - CSCW '13*, ACM (2013).

51. Leigh Star, S. and Ruhleder, K. Steps towards an ecology of infrastructure: complex problems in design and access for large-scale collaborative systems. *Proceedings of the 1994 ACM conference on Computer supported cooperative work*, (1994), 253–264.

52. Lipford, H.R., Wisniewski, P.J., Lampe, C., Kisselburgh, L., and Caine, K. Reconciling privacy with social media. *Proceedings of the ACM 2012 conference on Computer Supported Cooperative Work Companion (CSCW '12)*, ACM (2012).

53. Madrigal, A.C. Deconstructing the Creepiness of the 'Girls Around Me' App—and What Facebook Could Do About It. *The Atlantic*, 2012. http://www.theatlantic.com/technology/archive/2012/04/deconstructing-the-creepiness-of-the-girls-around-me-app-151-and-what-facebook-could-do-about-it/255351/.

54. Marvin, C. *When Old Technologies Were New: Thinking About Electric Communication in the Late Nineteenth Century*. Oxford University Press, USA, 1990.

55. Marx, L. and Roe Smith, M. *Does Technology Drive History?: The Dilemma of Technological Determinism*. MIT Press, Cambridge, MA, 1994.

56. Morozov, E. Wrong Kind of Buzz around Google Buzz" Foreign. *Foreign Policy*, 2010. http://neteffect.foreignpolicy.com/posts/2010/02/11/wrong_kind_of_buzz_around_google_buzz.

57. Nardi, B.A. and O'Day, V. *Information ecologies: Using technology with heart*. MIT Press., Cambridge, Mass, 1999.

58. Newman, J. Google Buzz: Then and Now. *PC World*, 2010. http://www.pcworld.com/article/189607/google_buzz_then_and_now.html.

59. Nissenbaum, H. Privacy as Contextual Integrity. *Washington Law Review* 79, 1 (2004), 119–159.

60. Nissenbaum, H. *Privacy in Context: Technology, Policy, and the Integrity of Social Life* (Stanford Law Books). Stanford Law Books, 2009.

61. O'Kane, A.A., Mentis, H.M., and Thereska, E. Non-static nature of patient consent: shifting privacy perspectives in health information sharing. *Proceedings of the 2013 conference on Computer supported cooperative work*, ACM (2013).

62. Paul, I. Girls Around Me App Voluntarily Pulled After Privacy Backlash. *PCWorld*, 2012. http://www.pcworld.com/article/252996/girls_around_me_app_voluntarily_pulled_after_privacy_backlash.html.

63. Pinch, T.J. and Bijker, W.E. The Social Construction of Facts and Artifacts: Or How the Sociology of Science and the Sociology of Technology Might Benefit Each Other. In W. Bijker, T. Hughes and T.

Pinch, eds., *The Social Construction of Technological Systems: New Directions in the Sociology and History* of Technology. MIT Press, Cambridge, MA, 1987.

64. Post, D. Law in cyberspace (tutorial session). *Proceedings of the 1996 ACM conference on Computer supported cooperative work (CSCW '96)*, ACM (1996).
65. Runchal, A. Creating Victims and then Blaming them. *Techcrunch*, 2012. http://techcrunch.com/2012/03/31/creating-victims-and-then-blaming-them/.
66. Solove, D.J. A Taxonomy of Privacy. *University of Pennsylvania Law Review* 154, 3 (2006), 477–564.
67. Streeter, T. *Selling the Air: A Critique of the Policy of Commercial Broadcasting in the United States.* University of Chicago Press, Chicago, 1996.
68. Suchman, L.A. *Human-machine reconfigurations: Plans and situated actions.* Cambridge University Press, Cambridge, 2007.
69. Supreme Court of the United States. Katz v. United States, 389 U.S. 347. 1967. http://www.law.cornell.edu/supct/search/display.html?terms=katz&url=/supct/html/historics/USSC_CR_0389_0347_ZO.html.
70. Velden, T. Explaining Field Differences in Openness and Sharing in Scientific Communities. *Proceedings of the 2013 conference on Computer supported cooperative work (CSCW '13).*, ACM (2013), 445–457.
71. Vertesi, J., Dourish, P., and Ca, I. The Value of Data : Considering the Context of Production in Data Economies. *Proceedings of the ACM 2011 conference on Computer supported cooperative work (CSCW '11).*, ACM (2011), 533–542.
72. Wang, N. and Grossklags, J. An Online Experiment of Privacy Authorization Dialogues for Social Applications. *Proceedings of the 2013 conference on Computer supported cooperative work*, (2013), 261–272.
73. Wyatt, S. Technological Determinism Is Dead; Long Live Technological Determinism. In I. Hackett, O. Amsterdamska, M. Lynch and J. Wajcman, eds., The *Handbook of Science and Technology Studies.* MIT Press, Cambridge Mass., 2008.
74. Foursquare alters API to eliminate apps like Girls Around Me. *About Foursquare,* 2012. http://aboutfoursquare.com/foursquare-api-change-girls-around-me/

Can Plans and Situated Actions be Replicated?

John Rooksby
School of Computing Science,
University of Glasgow, UK.
john.rooksby@glasgow.ac.uk

ABSTRACT

This paper discusses a repetition of a study presented in Suchman's book Plans and Situated Actions. There have been complaints about the lack of replication studies in disciplines related to CSCW (particularly Software Engineering and HCI). However, these complaints often become embedded in wider attempts to install a principled scientific method within these disciplines. Plans and Situated Actions was not a scientific text but drew upon naturalistic analysis. This paper shows there is value in recreating Plans and Situated Actions, and argues it would be helpful to recreate other studies. However, such repetition does not and need not constitute a scientific replication. The paper argues that while repetition and reanalysis may improve rigour in computing research, this need not be with a view to making it more scientific.

Author Keywords

Replication; Qualitative Methods

ACM Classification Keywords

H.5.m. Information interfaces and presentation (e.g., HCI): Miscellaneous.

INTRODUCTION

This paper addresses an argument often made in Human Computer Interaction (HCI), Software Engineering, and related disciplines: *there ought to be more replication studies* [11, 12, 17, 18, 20, 22, 37, 38, 39]. Replication studies are not unheard of in these disciplines, but according to John [17], they are too often seen as a second-class form of research: researchers do not think their time is best spent conducting or writing up replications, and reviewers do not receive replication studies positively. There are also complaints (e.g. [12, 22]) that authors do not adequately facilitate replications; they do not routinely supply code, data, or more than a cursory overview of their research methods and instruments. In Software Engineering, Gomez et al [11] have proposed several forms of replication study that they believe the discipline would benefit from. Replication studies can, they say: 1) follow the same method as the original study to see if the results can be reproduced; 2) follow a different method to see if the results can be reproduced; and/or 3) reanalyse existing data. In HCI, Wilson et al [37] have produced a broadly similar typology of replication. They argue there can and should be: 1) direct replications, attempting to confirm results of a study; 2) conceptual replications, attempting to replicate findings via alternative studies; 3) 'replicate and extend' studies, which reproduce a study and then build upon results; and 4) applied case studies, that attempt to reproduce results from a study in a real world setting.

The calls for replication studies are often embedded in a broader idea: *HCI and Software Engineering ought to be more scientific*. This idea is usually met with resistance (e.g. [13][35]), largely on the grounds that these disciplines address not technical, but sociotechnical issues. Such resistance is rooted in longstanding doubts about the applicability of scientific methods to social life [1, 16, 23]; it is a mistake to believe scientific methods are universally applicable and are the only valid source of knowledge (a belief that is often described, pejoratively, as scientism). To resist this is not to resist the idea that the quality of research in HCI and Software Engineering can be improved, but to resist the assumption that quality is only achievable through the application of methods from the sciences. Naturalistic and discursive methods offer an alternative of at least equal importance [13, 15, 36]. On these grounds, Greiffenhagen and Reeves [13] are critical of programmatic attempts to introduce replication. They fear such attempts will lead to qualitative approaches being devalued, pointing in particular to ethnography. The issue is not that ethnography is ignored, but that it gets evaluated and potentially transformed according to a positivist or falsificationist agenda with which it does not fit.

This paper revisits a classic book, Suchman's Plans and Situated Actions [35, 36]. The book is critical of cognitive science and presents a naturalistic alternative rooted in conversation analysis and ethnomethodology. The book reports a study in which pairs of participants were videoed using a photocopier. This paper reports a recreation of Suchman's study, arguing it is not possible to replicate Suchman's study (in the scientific sense of the word), but contending that: 1) this does not give reason to dismiss Suchman's findings; and, 2) it is possible and helpful to recreate Suchman's study. The paper concludes that while a scientific-replication agenda can and ought to be resisted from the standpoint of naturalistic research, prescient issues

CSCW'14, February 15–19, 2014, Baltimore, Maryland, USA.
Copyright © 2014 ACM 978-1-4503-2540-0/14/02...$15.00.
http://dx.doi.org/10.1145/2531602.2531627.

are subsumed within it. If we chose to throw out replication, we should not throw out the possibility of recreating studies.

PLANS AND SITUATED ACTIONS

Plans and Situated Actions is seen by many as a key text on how people interact with technology. The book argues that approaches to HCI that draw from cognitive science (approaches that were dominant in the 1980s when the book was written, what Rogers [29] refers to as "*classical cognitive approaches*") overlook the practical, embodied and organised ways in which people work with and make sense of technology. Suchman argues it is through human action that machines are imbued with sense, and therefore human action and interaction need to be taken into view. To do so we need to look beyond the specific points at which detectable actions (e.g. button presses) occur and at just what it is the users are doing when they operate technology. Suchman argues usability is not a case of building self-explanatory technologies, but technologies that are explainable, comprehensible and amenable within the uses they are put to. She calls for attention to be paid to what she terms the *accountability* of technology.

Plans and Situated Actions was inspired by the problem that Xerox customers were complaining that their photocopiers were difficult to use. Something was wrong with usability design at Xerox. The majority of the book is discursive, focusing on the problems of cognitive science based approaches to HCI and the alternative supplied by naturalistic analysis rooted in ethnomethodology and conversation analysis. The final chapters of the book report a study of how people use a photocopier. This study demonstrates Suchman's arguments, providing not the basis for them but evidence and application. The study does not drive the book as such, but appears at the end, tying together what was written earlier and making explicit the claims she had made. Neither does it use the specific photocopiers the customers were complaining about. Suchman's ideas are not derived from the study, but the study presents a case of them.

For the study, Suchman invited participants to use a photocopier installed at Xerox PARC that had an experimental expert system connected to it. The expert system would lead users through the process of making photocopies. The users would begin by selecting their objective, and the machine would then display text and diagrams to guide them through an appropriate process. The participants were invited to work together in pairs so that they spoke aloud as they were copying. Four pairs were videoed for the study, in sessions that lasted around an hour and a half each. The study showed that the kinds of trouble users were having in making photocopies were not solved by, and in some ways were exacerbated by, the ostensibly intelligent expert system. The users had to make sense of the photocopier and the instructions in ways other than they would have when interacting with a person.

Recreating Plans and Situated Actions

This paper recreates the study reported in Plans and Situated Actions. The study was recreated out of interest in the original text and in order to pursue issues related to the fact the original was a qualitative study done in the laboratory rather than the field. Recreating the study was not straightforward. The specific details of the study are not always clearly presented in the book, and had to be pieced together from various comments and footnotes as well as later works. There are actually three versions of the text: Suchman's thesis [33]; the book (which had minor changes from the thesis) [36]; and a second, revised edition of the book [35]. There is also a transcript of a speech about the study [34]. An edited video that mixes scenes from a film with footage from Suchman's study is also in circulation (although to my knowledge remains unpublished). The study also had to be interpreted in a way appropriate for a new context. In particular, a modern, 'ordinary' photocopier had to be used instead of the experimental system used by Suchman.

THE STUDY

The study was recreated in the computer science department of a university in Scotland. Suchman's book does not summarise the tasks given to the participants, although her transcripts do contain information about them. Most of Suchman's examples are of making a double-sided copy from a bound document, this being a two-step procedure where a single sided copy is made first and then transformed into a double-sided copy. Similar tasks were devised for this study, including one where the participants were instructed by the machine in how to resolve a paper jam. However, as will be discussed, this paper focuses on a simple task involving copying and stapling A4 paper.

The machine used for the study was an Océ 3145 Multifunctional Printer. This machine functions as a photocopier, printer and scanner. For photocopying, it enables the user to place an original directly onto the glass, or to place documents into an automatic document feeder on top. The machine is controlled via a graphical user interface with buttons above and below. Figure 1 shows the interface with the default menu (the basic menu), and the initial instructions displayed when a paper jam is detected. Unlike the machine used in Suchman's study, the Océ 3145 does not lead users through the process of making their photocopies. Only in the event of a paper jam is the user instructed through a process to resolve this. For the most part, the interface enables users to select options as they wish, and press the green start button when ready. Some written instructions are provided on the machine itself, including on the automatic document feeder. Error messages are also displayed on screen in the event that invalid options are selected.

In the book, Suchman states she feared proficient users of the photocopier would mask the phenomena she was looking for and therefore she invited novice users to participate. She

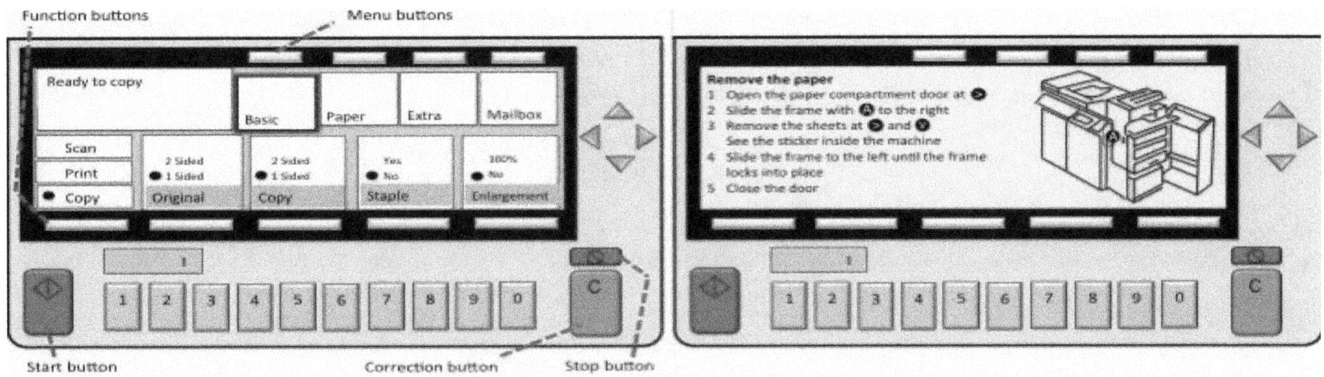

Figure 1: Sketches of the Interface, Showing (1) The "Basic" Menu (2) The Initial Instruction Screen for Paper Jam

invited people to work in pairs so they would talk aloud as they worked. The new study was run with nine pairs of participants. The study was run five times with postgraduate students and then four times with pairs of academics (at UK-professor, lecturer and post-doctoral level). This paper uses examples from the sessions run with academics. The academics were invited given Suchman's study was revealed to have used academic and research staff associated with Xerox [34]. By coincidence, not design, each of the academic pairs had one person that was experienced with the photocopier used for the study, and one that could be described as a novice.

FINDINGS

This paper will concentrate on how the four pairs of academic staff worked on the first and most simple task they were set: "Make a one-sided copy of Document A with a staple at the top left" (document A being an academic article printed single-sided on A4 paper, in a portrait orientation). The transcripts below detail how the pairs completed this task. The transcripts are presented using a simplified version of the format used by Suchman: (( )) – Double brackets contain an action or comment; ((**bold**)) – Writing in bold denotes an action available to the machine; CAPITALS – capitalisation denotes words said in a loud voice; Heh – denotes laughter.

Pair 1

Pair 1 consisted of a senior lecturer (C) and a postdoctoral researcher (D). They spent around 90 seconds on the task. This pair, as can be seen in the transcript below, engaged in some guesswork but completed the task on their first attempt. Interestingly, after making a successful copy, they stepped back over their actions as if to repeat for their own benefit the successful process. Another interesting aspect, which I will return to later in a discussion of the artificialities of laboratory studies, is that D spoke to the camera twice.

Transcript 1: Pair 1, Task 1

C Are you experienced with this machine?

D I am. Are you?

C Not at all. Perhaps you should start then.

D Alright ((*C hands D the task sheet and document A*)), I'll do the first one then. Right, so this is how I would do it. ((*looks up at camera*)) HELLO ((*looks at machine*)).

C Heh

D ((**places document A in feeder**)) Stick it in the feeder. Copy ((*points at option*)). Original is one sided. Copy is one sided ((*points at option*)). Ah staple. ((*steps back to look at task sheet behind them on table*)) It needs a staple in the top left.

C Do we know what's going to be top left?

D It doesn't ((*shakes head and smiles*)). Yeah, so, we're just gonna see what happens ((**selects staple option**)). We may have to do more than one. I shall attempt to staple. If we can't there's a stapler there ((*points to manual stapler*)). Heh ((**presses start**)) So, we can definitely do a one sided copy.

C And it will put a staple somewhere ((*leans in to watch original coming out into output tray*))

D That's the original coming out ((*C steps back*))

C ((*Copy moves into output tray,* **removed** *by C*)) Genius.

D Aha ((*glances at camera*)) CHECK THAT OUT.

C You put that in ((*points at document feeder*))

D Yeah, that way ((*places document over feeder*))

C Ok, so the staple goes there, yeah ((*aligns copy with original and pinches at staple*)). Ok.

D ((*removes document A from machine*))

Pair 2

Pair 2 consisted of two lecturers (E and F). They completed the task on their second attempt, taking about 160 seconds in total. Their first attempt had a staple at the bottom corner, leading them to reject the copy and try again. Interestingly, after placing document A on the document feeder for the first time, they picked it up again and replayed their actions prior to actually pressing the start button. This was in anticipation of an error – they wanted to remember their moves so as not to make the same mistake twice. When the error was made, they carefully stepped through what they did, rotating both the original and copy to work out the correct orientation. I will also return later in this paper to the fact that F referred jokingly to the task sheet as a "specification document".

Transcript 2: Pair 2, Task 1

E I've never used a photocopier before like this. So this will be interesting heh heh heh

F Ok

E I didn't even know you could staple things in a photocopier

F Yeah

E But apparently you can

F You can, so eh, ((*leafs through document A*)) this is a one sided document. So I suppose, image side face down ((*points at instruction on document feeder*))

E Right

F And then we need to position it so that if this thing staples it at the end, the staple is over here right? ((*points to lower left corner of document feeder*)

E In the top left, what does that mean? Top left. Right. Ok, err I have to turn on stapler first I guess.

F Ok so, put this in ((**slides document A into document feeder**)), this bit I know

E Right

F And you've got under basic ((*points at menu*)). Original one sided ((*points at menu*)). Stapler yes ((**selects staple option**)).

E Ok

F That's all you need. And then we could just go and do a run ((*points at start button*)) and see if it staples it, on the correct side.

E Ok

F And then work out from what we're getting from which way around we need to turn it. Ok so we've got it ((**removes document from document feeder** and holds up)) so that we're facing and it tilts in towards us ((**places document back into feeder**))

E Ok

F OK ((**presses start**)) with a bit of luck its going to do the right thing. Although I suspect not heh heh

E Heh heh heh

F ((*leans across in anticipation of output*))

E ((**takes copy from output tray** when it emerges))

F Where's the staple

E Err

F Its at the bottom, ok

E Other way round

F So, ((*holds up document A in same orientation as previously, E holds up copy and pinches staple*)) I had this in front of me and was tilting it towards me ((*rotates paper into opposite position and* **places into document feeder**)).

E Yep So it ended up in that corner ((*rotates copy to align with original, and pinches where staple ought to be*))

F Would that be right?

E I don't know heh

F Heh heh ((**presses start**))

E I didn't see the first way you put it, but yeah, ok

F Yeah you can either spend brain cycles or you can waste paper.

E Yeah you could waste paper.

F I'm sure you could do both as well ((*leans over to output tray*))

E ((**Removes** *output when it emerges and shows to A*)) Dah dah dah

F That complies with the spec. A one sided copy of document A with a staple in the top left.

E Ok ok next one.

Pair 3

Pair 3 consisted of a professor (G) and post-doctoral researcher (H). The pair spent around 180 seconds on the task. The session was somewhat error prone and chaotic. H made several mistakes such as thinking the photocopier had a touchscreen and pressing the wrong buttons. Their first attempt produced a copy with no staple. This was because, after correctly selecting the necessary options, H mistakenly pressed the correction button before pressing the start button, undoing their earlier selections. Their second attempt was successful. Interesting aspects include H's difficulties in understanding the machine, and G's comments to and about the video camera.

Transcript 3: Pair 3, Task 1

G I foolishly consider myself actually quite skilled with photocopiers

H Ok great

G In terms of being able to kind of dig through menus and having a,

H Alright

G Having a, having a silly ability to, try

H To work it?

G Well, to try at least, to kind of, theoretically, ok. make it, so I say we'll

H Document A

G Document A. Make a one sided copy of document A with a staple in the top left. Ok. Document A. Top left. So. Automatic feeder says image side face down, maximum 50 originals to start with, use only undamaged originals. Looks pretty good, so it's a single sided. Do we have to make it single sided?

H Yeah err it doesn't, one sided copy

G A one sided copy

H Yeah

G So it's a one sided document

H Staple, on the top left yeah

G Image side face down ((**places document in feeder**)) happy with that?

H Yep

G ((*Moves finger over options*)) Now this is where we have to pick the staple, so that's with staple ((**selects staple**))

H Oh I didn't even know it. A4 paper. ((*presses screen where it says paper*))

G Yep

H So, no no these are the menus

H Oh, there's no touchscreen?

G No, there's no touchscreen

H Is this the right button ((**selects original**))

G Yep so its two sided now ((H **selects original**)) that's one sided

H Ok, so we're going, I guess ((**selects paper**))

G Oh

H Because we want A4 paper

G Yeah we want A4 paper. Uhu

H Ok

G Looks good

H ((**Presses correction button**))

G And again probably, oh, no, that's that's clear.

H Oh

G That's ok

Heh ok. ((**selects paper**)) So this is all good.

G Uhuh, just cancel that

H ((**Presses start button**))

G Here we go. So if we've got it set up incorrectly you know, it will pop out with all candles printed on it or something

H ((removes original)) It looks good though

G No that's the original, copies gonna come out there

H ((**removes copy**)) yeah.

G But, it didn't staple it, for some reason.

H Oh it can staple it automatically?

G Yeah it can staple it automatically, so I think I know what happened. So I'm just going to cancel that. ((**presses cancel, presses correction**)) Ok so I think it's the staple. ((**selects staple**)) So if you pick this one and then clear it, it wipes all the settings.

H Right, right

G So I think if we do this. ((**presses start**)) It should now work.

H So this is the menu the first row of the settings?

G So these buttons control these menus, and these buttons control these menus

H Right right right right

G And once you've actually got it in the state press copy, and its that one to copy ((*points at start button*))

H Its kind of like

G Yeah I don't quite know. Its just a basic one.

H ((**removes copy**)) Oh yeah, its stapled

G So that is right, its top left. ((reads task sheet)) Make a one sided copy of document A, with a staple on the top left.

H Yeah

G Lets have a look

H That's right

G ((*Turns To camera*)) HELLO, YOU SEE THIS? ((*Turns back*)) This is us using the screen, I think that's what they want. Is that a copy of it?

H Yeah

G Is that the final paper, 969, no I mean the last page. I wanna make sure we've got all the copies.

H Yep

G 969

H Thank you

G Ok, perfect, I'll put the original back into the. Uhuh.

H Oh this is the.

G Original

H No this is the bad one.

G Oh, throw that away. The original's here.

Pair 4

Pair 4 consisted of a lecturer (J) and a postdoctoral researcher (K). They spent about 120 seconds on the task and were successful on their first attempt. This pair were less cooperative. They spoke less and almost fought over the machine. For example, an attempt by K to open the photocopier lid rather than place document A on the feeder was intercepted by J. J held the lid down, and waited for K to infer his preference to use the feeder. This episode differed to the others in that there was no discussion at the outset about respective skills and experience with the copier, and no decision about who would lead.

Transcript 4: Pair 4, Task 1

J Ok, so lets do this.

K So the first one.

J ((*Holds task sheet in hands and reads*)) A one-sided copy of document A ((*puts hand out, and K gives him document A*)). With staple at the top left.

K ((**Opens lid**))

J ((*Places hand on top of lid, restricting further opening*)) Wait wait, wait a second. ((*moves hand over autofeeder*)) So err.

K ((**Closes lid**)) ok

J Soo

K ((*Points to autofeeder*)) face, down

J Yeah. So it can staple them. Erm I think you put it this way ((*places* **document on autofeeder**)). Erm. Face down. And one sided. And with a staple at the top left. So,

K Ah, this document's ((*lifts top sheet of document*)) already one sided

J Yes ((*puts hand over documents, and K moves hers away*)) So the original is one sided ((*points to one sided original option on copier*)). The copy is one sided ((*points to one sided copy option*)). And ((**selects staple**)) we say, staple.

J ((*Pats down document on feeder then* **presses start**))

((*J and K look at screen, then J moves to output tray causing K to step back*))

J ((**Takes output** from machine)) Ok, top left. Right.

K ((*Lifts top page of original*)) ah, ok ((*Takes original from output tray*))

J So, one is done. ((*hands copy to K*)) OK.

K Yeah. This is done.

ANALYSIS: THEMES FROM SUCHMAN

Suchman's analysis covers what she refers to as "*the adept completion of photocopying*", "*responding to the machine*", and "*repair*". This section will demonstrate that even though the current study differs to the one in the original text (i.e. an ordinary photocopier is used, the tasks are somewhat different, and the pairs of participants each had one experienced and one inexperienced person) it is possible to connect transcripts from task one of the current study to Suchman's themes.

The Adept Completion of Photocopying

A key point in Plans and Situated Actions is that plans are resources for actions. So even when someone has a plan or goal, the actions necessary to reach it will need to be worked out (and often reformulated) in ways that cannot be entirely pre-specified. Suchman showed that even where people making photocopies have a goal and are led through a process, reaching that goal is more than blindly following pre-specified steps. The participants had to adeptly make the process work.

Although each pair had a goal (as specified on the task sheet), none of the transcripts above show a plan or process being articulated in advance of the participants' actions. Rather, planning and acting were mutually articulated. Pairs 1, 2 and 3 first established which member was the more experienced, and then the experienced member decided and explained what they should do. The explanation came as a talking-through of the process, starting with the selection of the document feeder and then through the available options.

The first three pairs each anticipated that something might go wrong, in particular that the staple might appear in the wrong place. D, in pair 1, said "this is how I would do it" when explaining what to do (rather than this is how to do it), seemingly orienting to there being alternative ways for completing the task, and probably to limit his accountability for potential failures. Similarly, F in pair 2 began the process with "I suppose" and "this bit I know", and when ready to press start he said "I suppose we could just go and do a run", limiting his accountability for a potential failure. G, in pair 3, was confident in his instructions but as the machine was making the first copy he warned there would be problems "if we've got it set up incorrectly". So, in the first three pairs, one person instructed the other on how to complete the task, but in a way covering more than the specific actions and the button presses required, and in a way that oriented to and limited accountability for potential failure. Two pairs also replayed or re-enacted their actions. F in pair 2, anticipating a potential problem with the orientation of the paper, did not press start when first ready to do so. F placed the document on the feeder and selected 'staple', but then picked the document up again to memorise how he placed it. Pair 1, upon completing the task, replayed and discussed their actions, confirming what it was they did that achieved the successful copy.

In pair 4 there was no initial discussion of competence. K moved to open the photocopier lid, and J physically intervened, signalling but not announcing an alternative course of action. The conflict between these two occurred not because of an absence of a plan, but because the participants had alternative ideas about where to start. The trouble was not resolved by articulating a plan, but simply by signalling or strong-arming a preferred route.

In the examples we have seen that where the task proceeded without error, or where the task proceeded prior to the establishment of an error having occurred, the participants reasoned and narrated through what they were doing, orienting to possible errors, and occasionally replaying their actions. Planning may have been involved, but a comprehensive plan was never formed or relied upon.

Responding to the Machine

Suchman discusses at length the ways in which the users respond to the photocopier, doing this in order to draw out the point that the machine and the people are not interacting on a symmetrical basis. The users are not taking turns with the machine as they do when taking turns in talking to each other. Given the examples are not of users being guided through a process, there is less to say about this here, only that the users account for and anticipate what the machine is doing as much as they react to it. For example, in pair 1, when the original was taken into the feeder after D had pressed the start button, D commented "so we can definitely do a one sided copy". This described what was happening, but in a way that was open to possible problems with the staple. Next, C leaned in to watch the original coming out, and D remarked "that's the original coming out". This was another narration of what was happening, done in a way to give sense to the output and head off any possible confusion by C. Similarly, in pairs 2 and 4, the person who pressed start stepped across to the copy output tray in anticipation of the copy coming out. F in pair 2 placed his arm across the original when doing so. In pair 3, H picked up the original thinking it was the copy, and G had to comment "no that's the original, copies gonna come out there".

Certain other things could only be established once the machine had run. In particular, the output supplied answers to whether the copy would be correctly stapled. Other reactions to the machine were more surprise ridden, for example pair 3 were surprised when the copy had no staple at all.

The interaction with the machine was asymmetrical. The participants did not take turns with the machine but can be seen to: orient to and anticipate what it will do; narrate, work over, and work out what it is doing; and try to figure out what it has just done. The machine was not self-explaining but was explained – it was in Suchman's terms "*accountable*".

Repair

Suchman also focuses heavily upon the ways in which people diagnose and repair actual or potential problems and errors. Several errors can be seen being repaired in the transcripts. In pair 3 the screen was mistaken for a touchscreen. This was immediately recognisable to the participants as an error and could be corrected for immediately. A misidentification of the correction button as the start button also appeared, at first, to be immediately repairable. However, the full effect of this error only became apparent later when the output had no staple. At that point, G realised the mistake "I think I know what happened". Here, it can be seen that the sense of prior events and their status as erroneous or correct can be formed through subsequent events. At the point where the unstapled copy was output, the easiest thing to do would simply have been to staple it using the stapler on the side of the machine, but it is not the intention of this paper (or Suchman's book) to consider errors as being deviations from the best or quickest ways to proceed, but to treat these in terms of how these are anticipated, recognised and made sense of by the users.

The most prominent form of error (and repair) in the transcripts is that of not getting the desired result from the output. The participants heavily oriented to the potential for this, even where ultimately the error was not made. It was only the arrival of a document with the staple at the top left that supplied the participants with evidence that their actions were correct. For pair 3, even the arrival of a stapled copy was not evidence enough of correctness, and they went on to compare the page numbers between the original and copy. For the two pairs that did get the staple in the wrong corner, they went on to repeat the process. In terms of the way they operated the machine, their actions were exactly the same on the first and second attempt. The only change was the orientation by which they placed the document in the feeder. For the participants themselves, this was not a repetition but iteration, where producing the copy was done not just with reference to the possibility of a further error, but also with reference to what was done last time.

ANALYSIS: THE LABORATORY SETTING

One thing that is troubling about the CSCW and HCI literature is that Plans and Situated Actions is discussed in several textbooks and papers as if it were an ethnographic field study [32]. For example, Bentley et al [2] refer to Plans and Situated Actions as the prime example of:

"...ethnographic studies [that] have involved a sociologist observing workers in their environment over a period of several months and hence gaining a deep understanding of the actual rather than the formal working practices."

The study Plans and Situated Actions reports is more akin to a laboratory study than a field study. The book differs to cognitive science not through heading out into the workers' environment, but by taking a naturalistic rather than experimental approach to analysis. The book [36] is critical of laboratory methods insofar as such methods introduce controls and predefined coding schemes that "*presuppose the characterization of the phenomenon studied*". As an alternative, the book draws upon "*sort of uncontrolled experimentation*" in which study participants are videoed as they try to achieve particular tasks with a photocopier. The study is certainly not a laboratory *experiment*, and is perhaps better characterised as a simulation. Suchman does not address this laboratory context in the book. In the light of recent arguments that interaction ought to be studied "*in the wild*" (e.g. [30]), it seems timely to ask: how does the laboratory context feature in the participants' work?

Laboratory factors emerged in the study, and are apparent in the transcripts. Perhaps most obviously, one of the members of pair 1, and one member of pair 3 looked and spoke directly to the cameras. In pair 1, C said to D "this is how I would do it" and then looked at a camera and said in a raised voice "HELLO". In pair 3, G showed the correctly stapled copy to the camera and said in a raised voice "HELLO, SEE THIS?" So, not only did the participants address the camera, they did so with a greeting. The greeting appeared as a marker that something was about to happen that (the participant thought) would be of note to the researcher. In pair 3, the greeting preceded the showing of the copy and the question "SEE THIS?" In pair 1 the greeting seems to demark the beginning of the actual use of the machine. In pair 1, what Francis [9] calls the double-setting of a simulation became particularly apparent; that C was both showing D "how I would do it" but knowingly also demonstrating to the camera how he would do it. The turn to the camera in pair 3 was more of an aside that, once completed, was explained to H as what the researcher wanted (note – they were not actually asked to do this, in the example G is inferring this for himself). Later in pair 1, when they got the correctly stapled copy, F said in a raised voice "CHECK THAT OUT". Similarly to the turn to the camera in pair 3, there is something victorious about this. All of these turns to the camera are done with a special 'camera voice', are accompanied by a look and appear at the beginnings and conclusions of copying rather than in their midst. So, the camera is very obviously not forgotten by the participants in the study. However, in knowing that the camera is there, this just seems to be something to turn to on occasion rather than something that is pervasively obtrusive on the action. The participants also seem to demark when they are engaging with the camera, and spend the rest of the time interacting and working with their partner.

Clearly, the participants are working in a researcher-provoked manner. The participants treated the task almost like a test. In the words of F (pair 2) they were trying to do something that "complies with the spec". That the participants were trying to fulfil a task is obvious at the start of each session where the task is read out. Also, at the end, not only was the production of a successful copy announced but this copy was double checked against the task sheet. The task sheet itself is a physical object. It was not just read out, but handed and moved around, put down, picked up and so on. One of the problems with the task sheet was that it could be mixed up with the other documents, or simply be in the way as the participants do things with the copier. The original documents were also kept organised by the participants during the session. At the end, of each task, the originals were not placed together with the copy but kept separated and treated with the sort of respect often reserved for other people's property. The participants were asked to work together so that they would verbalise their working. This happened, but with a number of side effects. In each transcript the participants not only talked but collaboratively engaged in the activity of copying. Working together required the participants to occupy a physical space at the copier. This meant the person who placed the original into the feeder was not necessarily the person who collected it from the other end, creating a division of labour. The collaborative nature of the tasks also gave them an air of learning or training. Three of the transcripts involve one participant explaining to the other what they would do. A certain level of humour also pervaded the sessions. This humour was part of how the participants managed their interactions with each other, and how they managed their identity on camera.

The participants' actions, however, were not disconnected from ordinary life. The participants can be seen to think about and discuss their experience with the machine, what they ordinarily do, and, to some extent, to think about how using it on this occasion might benefit them for future occasions. Working collaboratively, working with a task sheet, and worrying about what it is someone else wants is also something that plausibly happens in ordinary life. While the laboratory aspects of the task are in some ways a pervasive influence, in most respects the participants orient to the lab context in regular but often fleeting ways. For example, turns to the camera or to the task sheet occurred at the beginning and completion of a task. That the task is researcher-provoked does not mean the participants somehow do photocopying in some strange or new way, but instead makes them orient to what they have been asked and the perceived reasons for being asked as they operate the machine. It does not seem that the participants act in unnatural ways, but in ways that are natural for a laboratory. As long as we don't pretend that a researcher-provoked study is anything other than that, then there does not seem to be any overwhelming reason for saying that interaction is less natural here than in the field.

There are interesting issues here, and room for further debate – not just concerning Suchman's work, but other laboratory simulations (see [31] for another example). In terms of theory, naturalism does not claim there are particular natural environments but that naturalistic work attempts to stay true to the observations [1][31]. This chimes with Suchman's critique of cognitive science, which was a critique of analytical methods and suggests there is no reason from the point of view of interaction analysis to claim that interaction is different in the lab.

DISCUSSION: WAS THIS A REPLICATION?

This work has recreated the study in Plans and Situated Actions. It was not recreated precisely: a modern, ordinary photocopier was used; the tasks were somewhat different; and pairs with one experienced person were used. But it has been argued that the analytical themes from the original text can still be drawn out (which, given the original was designed to throw light on why Xerox customers were having trouble with their machines, should not be entirely surprising). It has also been argued that recreating the study can throw light on concerns about the influence of the laboratory setting in these themes.

But, was this recreation of Plans and Situated Actions a replication? Does this study bolster arguments that there ought to be more replication? I will argue *no*.

What is Replication?

Calls for replication studies are often embedded in programmatic attempts to make computing research more scientific. In 1992 Greenberg and Thimbleby [12] bemoaned "*the pragmatic difficulty of substantiating experiments through replication*" in HCI, criticizing the field as "*weak science*". Their complaint was not just with the lack of replication, but the lack of studies even worth replicating. HCI as a "*weak science*" did not propose and test *falsifiable* theories. More recently, Wilson et al [38] have stated replication is "*a cornerstone of science ... [yet] we have almost no drive and barely any reason to consider replicating the work of other HCI researchers.*" The term "*science*" here could be taken in a general sense indicative of any research (all papers in HCI, CSCW and Software Engineering can be loosely referred to as scientific papers, and all researchers as research scientists) but, in the light of Greenberg and Thimbleby, might equally be taken in a "*strong*", positivist or falsificationist sense: *computing research can be improved if researchers adhere to a scientific method.*

Replication is often said to be a cornerstone of the scientific method. As Popper [28] put it:

"*We do not take even our own observations quite seriously, or accept them as scientific observations, until we have repeated and tested them. Only by such repetitions can we convince ourselves that we are not dealing with a mere isolated coincidence, but with events which, on account of their regularity and reproducibility, are in principle inter-subjectively testable*".

Popper's work is widely read in computing, particularly in Software Engineering where his concept of falsification is foundational to theories of Software Testing (see e.g. [25]). Falsificationism was developed by Popper in the mid 20th century, contradicting the positivist ideas that had dominated to then. The positivists saw science as progressing through the accumulation of empirically observed facts. With falsificationism, Popper contended that nothing can be shown with certainty to be correct or true, but only shown (or not shown) to be incorrect or false. Falsificationism provided a radical critique of positivism but held on to a foundational premise: Popper believed it was the work of philosophy (indeed a moral obligation for philosophy) to articulate the principles for scientists to follow.

There are competing ideas in the philosophy of science, and Popper's work sits among these. Alternative ideas are apparent in the replication literature. Greenberg and Thimbleby's [12] argument was that replications are significant contributions if they falsify a result, whereas Gomez et al [11] and Wilson et al [38, 39] hold a positivistic line in which replications are to confirm (and perhaps extend) prior work. So, if we were to follow a scientific agenda, what is good scientific practice is not a settled issue. It can also be seen that ideas about the scientific method are not necessarily descriptions of how science is practiced but of how science ought to be. Popper's efforts set out, through logic, the principles by which we can learn and know things about the world. For their part, Gomez et al and Wilson et al outline a framework for a more scientifically sound programme of research, one that envisages new practices rather than characterises existing or emerging practices.

New ideas have emerged in the philosophy of science since Popper [5]. In particular, the rise of the sociology of scientific knowledge has led many to question whether there is or can be an ideal method, and to question what value or use defining such an ideal can have for guiding science as it is practiced. Many sociologists have studied scientists in action. Knorr Cetina [19], for example, studied high-energy physics and molecular biology, pointing out that these sciences are practiced in distinct ways. Several sociologists have considered replication in practice (see [3, 6, 7]), finding that replication studies are less common than might be imagined, and that when scientists do try to replicate others' work they do so with reference to their own programmatic interests and usually with alternative equipment and procedures [7]. Therefore, it is doubtful that Poppers' ideals have been fully implemented in science. The successes of science should not be readily taken as evidence for the correctness of Popper's views, and the progress and discoveries made in science should not be readily attributed to replication. As Greiffenhagen and Reeves [13] have previously argued: to embed replication in a broader programme of transforming HCI into a science misunderstands science. It may be possible to contend that Popper's ideas are not invalidated by the sociology of science because sociologists have only studied "*weak science*". But if this is the case, it seems the replication literature in HCI and Software Engineering ought to be working on a much broader vision applicable to all sciences. To make HCI more scientific becomes not a problem of making it more like the sciences but of creating a trans-disciplinary movement from "*weak*" to "*strong*" science.

Replication and Naturalistic Research

Atkinson and Hammersley [1], Lynch [23] and others point out that the social sciences attempt to ensure validity through the specification and strict adherence to defined methods. They explain this contrasts with naturalistic forms of research, which typically seek rigour not through the methods by which data is collected, but through the ways in which the data can be kept true to during the analysis. Claims are often made in ethnography, for example, that the researcher must be immersed over a period of time in a culture. Alternative claims are made in other areas of naturalistic research. Claims are made in ethnomethodology and conversation analysis, for example, that the researcher is dealing in a recognizable social order.

One example that brings to light some of the issues of replication in the humanities is the controversy that surrounded Mead's book Coming of Age in Samoa [24]. Several years after Mead's death, Freedman [10] alleged that her work was misrepresentative and misinformed. Freedman had interviewed one of Mead's original informants, who told him that Mead was tricked. The informant said she and her contemporaries had not been as sexually active in their youth as Mead had described. However, Freedman's critique has not been upheld in Anthropology. Critics of his work pointed out that even if he had located the original interviewees, they were now old women with a different status in society. Samoan society itself had undergone radical change. Of particular note, the interviewee had converted to Christianity. Was it not more likely that the interviewee would lie to Freedman (an older man on a brief visit) than to Mead (a woman of a similar age to the informants, and who had spent time living with them)? A major aspect of the defensibility of Mead's work was that she kept very detailed notes. These notes are publically available and have enabled others to point out, for example, that Mead was well aware of the kinds of joking, hoaxing and lying that went on in Samoa (see [26]). It is also possible to show with reference to her notes where the interpretive elements of her work come in – her book was not simply a record, but a comparative discussion of two cultures.

The Mead controversy shows that while it is unusual to discuss anthropology in terms of replication, forms of study analogous to the types outlined by Gomez et al [11] and Wilson et al [37, 38, 39] exist therein: 1) field sites are returned to and are discussed with reference to previous studies (Freedman was not the only person to visit Mead's fieldsite, although he was the only one to directly attack her work); 2) ideas and theories of culture are developed and discussed with reference to cases (in Mead's case Samoa and America); 3) data can be systematically recorded, made public, and is used for secondary analysis. Importantly, the controversy also shows that revisiting and reanalysis can feature significantly in a dispute yet not settle it. When studying people, applying the same methods (e.g. interview methods) will not necessarily elicit the same responses. Orans [26] has claimed that Mead's work would have been better if her theories were falsifiable; if the book were of scientific quality then the 'replications' could potentially have come to definite conclusions. But to say this is not to suggest Mead's methods should have been tweaked or tightened but that they should have been radically different. In fact to treat the revisits and reanalyses as replications at all might be said to misunderstand why and how these were done. They were not naïve exercises in replication that were dashed with the realisation that the original was not falsifiable.

Wilson et al [37, 38, 39] say that qualitative work, particularly ethnography, is difficult to replicate. They are right to say there are practical problems to do with time, access and so on in replicating ethnographic work, but the Mead example shows these issues are not insurmountable. The crucial problem is that nothing can be scientifically proved or falsified in a qualitative study. If someone answers questions differently or fieldsites have different features, then what can be said about prior findings? If something is interpreted differently then what does that say about prior interpretations? It seems that arguments and questions can be forwarded about the quality of prior research but that nothing can be proved or disproved by consideration of cause and effect. This does not mean that ethnographers can never be wrong, but that it is perfectly legitimate for different ethnographers to find different things. Quality arises in ethnography not from being able to find provably correct data, but through undertaking research in ways in which appropriate bonds can be formed, through a reflexive consideration of such bonds, and through writing in coherent and (preferably) transparent ways. The situation in anthropology is discursive, but in several respects the Mead controversy is remarkably similar to controversies described by the sociologists of scientific knowledge. For example, Collins' [6,7] studies of replication in physics show that controversies are not settled though a crucial test, but by revisiting, repeating and a lot of arguing.

Replication and Plans and Situated Actions

Ideas from Anthropology have been extensively discussed in CSCW and HCI (and to an extent Software Engineering). One of the key texts to do so is Suchman's Plans and Situated Actions [35, 36]. It should be clear that Suchman's book was not of the same intellectual tradition as Mead's. In fact, Suchman was highly critical of comparative anthropology. She singled out Gladwin's comparative accounts of navigation, criticising them for simplistically portraying western navigation as plan driven and Micronesian navigation as situated. Instead of examining just how navigation was achieved, Suchman found anthropologists to be seeking overly simplistic ways for differentiating one culture from another.

An aspect of ethnography that Suchman was critical of was the use of fieldnotes. Suchman was troubled by these: firstly on the grounds that notes cannot go into sufficient detail, and, secondly, on the grounds that fieldnotes are not adequately verifiable. The alternative Suchman advocated was video analysis. Video could capture just what it was that people did with technology. It could be viewed repeatedly, and by people other than the original observer. In Suchman's advocacy of video is an advocacy, of sorts, for repeatable analysis. With video, observation is not a one-off affair, and is not something done by the lone ethnographer whose notes must then be trusted. Observations become something to be seen by others. Such ideas have come in for debate and criticisms (see [14]) but suffice to say, the methods Suchman advocated offer an alternative to Mead's.

In criticising ethnography, Suchman was not attempting to introduce something more scientific. On the contrary, her book contains a lengthy attack on scientific approaches to the study of human action. Suchman was particularly critical of cognitive science. The methods that cognitive science relied on, she complained, erased or obscured the very phenomena she believed HCI ought to address. Suchman's work was not anti-scientific; ethnomethodology and conversation analysis, the area drawn upon by Suchman in her book, has approached science (including replication) in a somewhat idiosyncratic but often supportive way. For example Livingston [21] and Bjelic and Lynch [3] have published accounts of their own replications of classic scientific studies. The points they draw out concern the orderly and embodied ways in which experiments are made to work through the know-how of scientists. Scientific experiments do not and cannot report exactly how that experiment was conducted, but rely on certain competencies of the replicator. For example experiments with prisms cannot specify just how it is one positions the prism and their body to find the light in order to see a spectrum of colours [3]. Ethnomethodology does not criticise or offer an alternative to science but argues that human practices are a constituent and indispensible part of the way science is done. This is problematic only for the human sciences: the scientific study of people requires orderly embodied practice but then erases that in favour of an 'ironic' account of what people do. A social science study of how scientists do replication may itself be replicable, but would give an ironic version of what replication actually involves.

So, while the replication literature in HCI gives the impression that ethnographers have not even begun to think about how qualitative work can be scientifically-replicated, the fact is that replication has long been discussed, and activities that resemble those advocated in the replication literature have long been engaged in. It is well known that in naturalistic research that work cannot be replicated and it is widely understood that this does not invalidate the claims made. There are also longstanding debates about appropriate forms of data gathering and to what extent the documentation of a site or practice needs to stand in and of themselves as representative of that site or practice and therefore analysable by others.

CONCLUSION

Can Plans and Situated Actions be replicated? No, at least not in the scientific sense of that term. But this is not to say Suchman's study was not worth repeating. Doing so has:

- Aided understanding - Although the book is often cited as if it were about instruction following (e.g. [4][27]) it has implications beyond this. The study presented in her book *demonstrated* a widely applicable argument. The book is not about the experimental machine used in the study, but how *any* machine is operated: machines are rendered accountable through the work of the operator. Suchman's study was, after all, inspired by problems real customers were having with mass manufactured machines.
- Aided exploration of further issues - Repeating the study has aided exploration of situated action in a laboratory context. Suchman's arguments were not about studying people in the wild, but about the use of naturalistic methods. There are issues for further debate here, but turning the methods used by Suchman to examine how participants orient to the laboratory aspects of a study does not immediately undermine findings made in a (naturalistic) laboratory study.

Plans and Situated Actions is widely cited, but not always in ways that acknowledge the full implications of the book. It seems that the book needs to be more carefully read and discussed. This can likely be said of many other books and studies too. Recreating studies could play a helpful role in this. This should not be confounded with scientific-replication. Repeating studies will not make computing research more scientific, but may help with increasing rigour. Increased rigour, in this sense, does not mean proving or disproving existing results but having more discussion and debate about existing work.

ACKNOWLEDGEMENTS

I would like to thank the study participants, the anonymous reviewers of this paper, and Fan Zhang (for reading the book with me and helping develop the tasks). I began this study while funded by the LSCITS Initiative. I would like to thank Matthew Chalmers and the Populations Programme for allowing me to continue this work at Glasgow.

REFERENCES

1. Atkinson, P. and Hammersley, M. *Ethnography. Principles and Practice* (3rd Edition). Routledge. (2007).
2. Bentley, R. Hughes, J. A. Randall, D. Rodden, T. Sawyer, P. Shapiro, D. and Sommerville, I. Ethnographically-informed systems design for air traffic control. *In Proc CSCW 92*. New York : ACM, (1992). 123-129.
3. Bjelic, D, and Lynch, M. The work of a scientific demonstration: respecifying Newton's and Goethe's theories of color. In G. Watson and R. Seiler (eds.), *Text in Context: Contributions to Ethnomethodology*. London: Sage Publications. (1992) 52-78.
4. Brown, B., Laurier, E. The normal natural troubles of driving with GPS. *In Proc CHI'12* (2012). 1621-1630.
5. Chalmers, A. *What is this Thing Called Science?* Open University Press. (1976).
6. Collins, H. M. The seven sexes: A study in the sociology of a phenomenon, or the replication of experiments in physics. *Sociology*, 9(2) (1975) 205-224.
7. Collins, H. M., *Changing Order: Replication and Induction in Scientific Practice*. Beverley Hills & London: Sage, (1985).
8. Crabtree, A., Rouncefield, M., and Tolmie, P. *Doing Design Ethnography*. Springer. (2012).
9. Francis, D. Game identities and activities: Some ethnomethodological observations. In Crookall D and Saunders D (eds.) *Communication and simulation. Multilingual Matters*. (1989). 53-68.
10. Freeman, D. *Margaret Mead and Samoa*. Cambridge: Harvard University Press. (1983).
11. Gómez, O., Juristo, N., and Vegas, S. Replication, Reproduction and Re-analysis: Three ways for verifying experimental Findings. *In Proc of RESER International Symposium on Replication in Empirical Software Engineering Research*. (2010).
12. Greenberg, S. and Thimbleby, H. The weak science of human-computer interaction. *In Proc CHI '92*(1992).
13. Greiffenhagen, C., and Reeves, S.. Is replication important for HCI? In *Workshop on replication in HCI (RepliCHI), SIGCHI Conference on Human Factors in Computing Systems (CHI)*, April (2013).
14. Heath, C., Hindmarsh, J., Luff, P. *Video in Qualitative Research*. Sage. (2010).
15. Hutchins, E. *Cognition in the Wild*. Cambridge MA: MIT Press. (1995).
16. Hutchinson, P., Read, R., and Sharrock, W. *There is No Such Thing as a Social Science: In Defence of Peter Winch*. Ashgate. (2008).

17. John, B. Avoiding "It's Just Replication". In *Workshop on replication in HCI (RepliCHI), SIGCHI Conference on Human Factors in Computing Systems (CHI)*, April (2013).

18. Juristo Juzgado, N., and Vegas, S. The role of non-exact replications in software engineering experiments. *Empirical Software Engineering,* 16(3),(2011), 295-324.

19. Knorr Cetina, K. *Epistemic cultures: how the sciences make knowledge.* Harvard University Press. 1999.

20. Krein, J., Knutson, C., Prechelt, L., and Juristo Juzgado, N. Report from the 2nd international workshop on replication in empirical software engineering research. *ACM SIGSOFT Software Engineering Notes 37(1).* (2012), 27-30.

21. Livingston, E. *Ethnographies of Reason.* Ashgate Publishing, Ltd. (2008).

22. Lung, J., Aranda, J., Easterbrook, S., and Wilson, G. On the difficulty of replicating human subjects studies in software engineering. *In Proc ICSE '08*, (2008), 191-201.

23. Lynch, M. *Scientific Practice and Ordinary Action: Ethnomethodology and Social Studies of Science.* Cambridge: Cambridge University Press. (1993).

24. Mead, M. *Coming of Age in Samoa: A Psychological Study of Primitive Youth for Western Civilisation.* New York: William Morrow and Co. (1928).

25. Myers, G., Sandler C, and Badgett T. *The Art of Software Testing*. John Wiley and Sons (2011).

26. Orans, M. *Not Even Wrong: Margaret Mead, Derek Freeman, and the Samoans*. Chandler & Sharp. (1996).

27. Orlikowski, W. The Duality of Technology. *Organization Science* 3(3) (1992). 398-427.

28. Popper, K. *The Logic of Scientific Discovery*. Hutchinson & Co. (1959).

29. Rogers, Y. *HCI Theory: Classical, Modern, and Contemporary*. Morgan & Claypool Publishers. (2012).

30. Rogers, Y. Interaction Design Gone Wild: Striving for Wild Theory. *Interactions* 18,4. (2011). 58–62.

31. Rooksby, J. Does Professional Work Need to be Studied in a Natural Setting? A Secondary Analysis of a Laboratory Study of Software Developers. In Petre M and van der Hoek (eds.) *Software Designers in Action. A Human Centric Look at Design Work.* Chapman Hall/CRC Press. (2013).

32. Rooksby, J. Wild in the Laboratory: A Discussion of Plans and Situated Actions. *TOCHI*, forthcoming.

33. Suchman L. Plans and Situated Actions. The Problem of Human Machine Communication. *Xerox PARC Technical Report ISL-6.* (1985).

34. Suchman, L. Work Practice and Technology: A Retrospective. In Szymanski, M and Whalen, J. (eds.) *Making Work Visible. Ethnographically Grounded Case Studies of Work Practice*, Cambridge: Cambridge University Press. (2011). 21-33.

35. Suchman, L.. *Human-Machine Reconfigurations. Plans and Situated Actions, 2nd Edition.* Cambridge: Cambridge University Press (2007).

36. Suchman, L.. *Plans and Situated Actions: The Problem of Human Machine Communication.* Cambridge: Cambridge University Press (1987).

37. Wilson, M. L., Resnick, P., Coyle, D., and Chi, E. RepliCHI—The Workshop. In *Extended Abstracts. CHI '13* (2013).

38. Wilson, M., Mackay, W., Chi, E., Bernstein, M. and Nichols, J., RepliCHI SIG: from a panel to a new submission venue for replication. *In Ext. Abstracts CHI'12* (2012). 1185-1188.

39. Wilson, M.L., Mackay, W., Chi, E., Bernstein, M., Russell, D. and Thimbleby, H. RepliCHI - CHI should be replicating and validating results more: discuss. *In Ext. Abstracts CHI'11,* (2011). 463-466.

Social Structure and Depression in TrevorSpace

Christopher M. Homan
Department of Computer Science
Rochester Institute of Technology
cmh@cs.rit.edu

Naiji Lu
Department of Biostatistics
University of Rochester
Naiji_Lu@URMC.Rochester.edu

Xin Tu
Department of Biostatistics
University of Rochester
Xin_Tu@URMC.Rochester.edu

Megan C. Lytle
Department of Psychiatry
University of Rochester
Megan_Lytle@URMC.Rochester.edu

Vincent M.B. Silenzio
Department of Psychiatry
University of Rochester
Vincent_Silenzio@URMC.Rochester.edu

ABSTRACT

We discover patterns related to depression in the social graph of an online community of approximately 20,000 lesbian, gay, and bisexual, transgender, and questioning youth. With survey data on fewer than two hundred community members and the network graph of the entire community (which is completely anonymous except for the survey responses), we detected statistically significant correlations between a number of graph properties and those TrevorSpace users showing a higher likelihood of depression, according to the Patient Healthcare Questionnaire-9, a standard instrument for estimating depression. Our results suggest that those who are less depressed are more deeply integrated into the social fabric of TrevorSpace than those who are more depressed. Our techniques may apply to other hard-to-reach online communities, like gay men on Facebook, where obtaining detailed information about individuals is difficult or expensive, but obtaining the social graph is not.

Author Keywords

LGBT youth; social network analysis; social media.

ACM Classification Keywords

H.5.m. Information Interfaces and Presentation (e.g. HCI): Group and Organization Interfaces

INTRODUCTION

Though the relationship between depression and social factors has been the subject of scientific inquiry since at least the late 19th century [15], our understanding of this relationship at a predictive level remains vague [21]. Prior to the explosion in popularity of online social networking it was difficult even to gather large amounts of data on social ties. Social networking sites, by contrast, are designed around the management friends lists, and thus make collecting such data much easier.

However, social support systems are complex, heterogeneous structures in which different social ties perform different roles [48]. Even though many popular social networking sites, such as Facebook and Google+, provide members some capability to organize their social ties, these capabilities are limited and there are no standard practices for using them, certainly not with respect to clarifying social support roles for the benefit of scientific research. Thus, uniform data on the *quality* or *nature* of the social ties present—what role they serve or functions they perform—are not directly available.

Nonetheless, Cohen and Wills, while calling for a better understanding of the diverse functional roles ties may play, acknowledge that viewing social ties as the undifferentiated building blocks of social structure may nonetheless capture factors that promote general psychological health [10]. In this paper, we combine network science and traditional survey methods to discover patterns in the global structural properties of a social networking site that are related to depression. We are motivated by the potential of this line of inquiry to inform the development of intelligent systems for detecting signs of depression in a social network dedicated to reducing self-harm among lesbian, gay, bisexual, transgender, and questioning (LGBTQ) youth. We effectively ask ourselves what the social ties can tell us, even when we regard them as completely homogenous. Doing so brings the global structure of the ties into high relief.

We compare two groups of users of TrevorSpace with respect to six network features indicative of social integration. TrevorSpace a social networking site run by The Trevor Project, the largest nonprofit organization dedicated to preventing suicide among LGBTQ youth. We relied on the social dynamics of the site to recruit the respondents. One group contains those respondents who are screened as depressed according to a standard diagnostic instrument and the other contains those who screen as nondepressed. Our results show that the nondepressed group tends to be better integrated into the Trevorspace social graph than the depressed group, and that the differences between the groups are significant.

Suicide occurs twice as frequently in LGB adolescents and young adults as in their non-LGB peers [1, 35, 38]. Stresses specific to this population (e.g., coming out, sexual orientation stigma) and lack of support (e.g., diminished social and familial support), among other factors contribute to this increased frequency [9]. Moreover, social discord is associated with more suicidal ideation among LGBT youth [27].

Compared to middle age and older LGB adults, sexual minority youth (18-29 years in age) had lower levels of perceived social support (i.e., fit and integration with their social environment) [23]. Perceived social support, connection to the LGB community, and salience with identity have all been correlated with psychological well-being [23]. As a hidden minority, LGBT individuals often compare the benefits of coming out (e.g., increased psychological well-being and improved relationships) with such risks as depression, social isolation, victimization, and giving up privilege (i.e., heterosexual and cisgender privilege) [11, 19, 31, 40].

The Internet offers individuals the capability to connect with a broader community, and facilitate identity development [19, 23, 29, 41]. For instance, online social networks provide LGBT youth with the opportunity to share coming out experiences, discuss stigma, receive support, and get involved with activism [24, 29]. More recently, LGBT youth have been using the Internet as a way to practice disclosing their sexual orientation and/or gender identity before coming out to their friends and family [24, 29].

Online communities may thus play a larger social role for LGBTQ youth than for the general population. We believe that the relative social importance of online social networks to LGBTQ youth, along with the increased prevalence of mental health issues in this population, make online communities for this population, such a TrevorSpace, ideal settings for studying the relationship between social structure and depression.

Contributions

This paper has two main contributions. First, we show how to use the entire social graph of an online community to test the bias and confidence of a sample of the community members. Network statistics are seldom independent and identically distributed (iid), even when the population sample used to recover the network is, and so traditional statistical methods often do not apply. Much social network analysis is thus descriptive, and avoids hypothesis testing. Methods that are more statistically rigorous need to be carefully tailored to the data available and the questions asked, and it requires some explanation so that the procedures involved can be reproduced. Our tests use well established subsampling methods but are designed specifically to the data that social networking sites provide. TrevorSpace is ideal for exploring such methods as it is large enough ($\sim$20,000 users) that scale becomes an issue, but not too large as to be unmanageable. Many online social networks are much larger than this. It would seem that our methods could be used to study subcommunities of any social networking site (note in particular that variations of snowball sampling such as respondent driven sampling are specifically designed to discover hidden communities within larger social environments [18, 20]).

The second contribution is translational [51]. To our knowledge, this is the first study to relate network structure to depression in LGB youth in an online social network. Social networking sites can be regarded as natural systems of collaborative emotional support. We use the collaborative dynamics of the site, in the form of snowball sampling, to obtain a survey that is rich in network structure, more so than what a random sample would provide.

TrevorSpace and a sister message board are monitored by a single counselor for users who show signs of emotional distress. It is very difficult for this person to keep up with the traffic on the site. We hope that our findings may ultimately lead to intelligent systems that help actively identify individuals who may be poorly socially integrated into a social environment and thus may benefit from direct intervention and thus provide assistance in situations like TrevorSpace where expert human resources are limited.

RELATED WORK

A rather substantial body of work exists on the use of social networking systems (SNS) to study emotion (see [5, 14, 43, 32, 24, 4, 32, 7] among many others), though comparatively little of it considers network properties. For instance, Golder and Macy study aggregate global trends in "mood," and show, for example, that people wake up in a relatively good mood that decays as the day progresses [17]. Bollen et al. [7] show that emotionally-charged tweets are often tied to current events, such as elections and holidays. However, most of this data is, from an experimental perspective, unstructured and secondary. Obtaining data in a scientifically rigorous manner often requires interactive data collection, especially when the persons of interest may not wish to make themselves publicly known, as is the case with many LGBT youth.

A large body of literature exists on social support, and a great deal of this work depends on a much more nuanced understanding of the various, conflicting, and changing roles that social ties play [48, 39]. Such an understanding is believed to be especially important to the stress buffering functions social support can provide [10]. Obtaining such detailed information is still challenging because it usually requires the active participation of the respondents to recall detailed information on a potentially large number ties. The purpose of our work is to look precisely at what a completely unnuanced view of the social tie structure says about depression. Such views, while limited, are nevertheless believed to shed light on the degree to which individuals benefit from social integration factors [10].

De Choudhury and colleagues look at depressive disorders using a combination of SNS data and interactive surveys [12, 13]. They use Amazon Mechanical Turk to recruit and screen for depression a number of Twitter users. They then analyze a full year of Twitter posts (tweets) from before the onset of depression by those who screened positive for major depression or reported a diagnosis at some point during the previous year. In addition, they collect a full year of tweets by non-depressed participants of the crowdsourcing activity. We, by contrast, target LGBT youth on TrevorSpace and are working with much less data (to some degree our research is about patterns we can discover with a relatively small amount of sampled data paired with a complete social graph). We also look at global network properties of the complete social graph underlying our sample, while they focus on ego networks of the sampled population and on unstructured Twitter data.

Distribution-free methods such as subsampling are a well-established part of the statistics canon [33, 44]. What is novel in our work is the application of these methods to a complete social graph of the underlying population paired with traditional survey data.

METHODS

The Location

TrevorSpace has all the salient features of a social networking site [8]: user profiles, public (to other TrevorSpace members) testimonials and comments, and publicly (again, only to other TrevorSpace members) articulated, traversable lists of friends. Additionally it provides support for members that are at risk for self

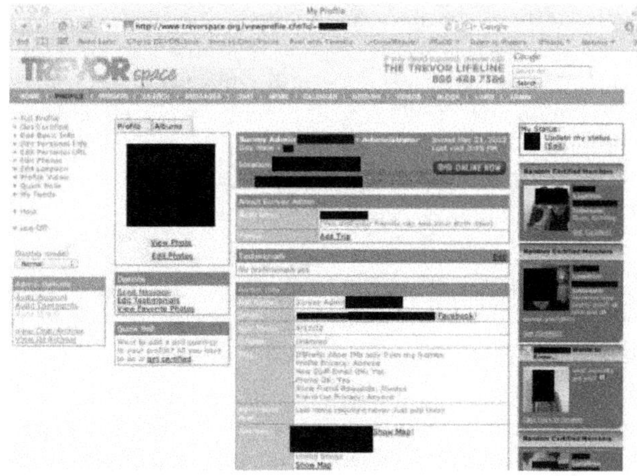

Figure 1. Screenshot of a TrevorSpace user's homepage.

harm: the site is monitored by Trevor Project administrators and links to the Trevor Helpline (a suicide prevention hotline) are posted at the top of the screen. See Figure 1. More information about the Trevor Project is available online at `http://www.thetrevorproject.org/`.

The Data

The sample consisted of LGBT youth and their allies between the ages of 18 and 24 with a TrevorSpace user account that was active during the data collection period. Participation was limited to TrevorSpace users who reported suicidal ideation or a suicide attempt in the past year. Participants were excluded if they endorsed suicide ideation, did not speak English, were unable to read or complete survey materials, or had already participated in this study. Individuals who reported active suicidal ideation were referred to The Trevor Project's Lifeline for immediate care. Trevorspace users who did not complete responses to the inclusion criteria items were also excluded.

The administrative staff of TrevorSpace helped with recruitment by sending an invitation to all TrevorSpace users who were 18–24 years old. During the active recruitment phase, TrevorSpace administrators placed an advertisement on the personal homepages of TrevorSpace users. Individuals who accessed the survey site were prompted to review an information letter before they were screened for eligibility. Participants were paid $25 in an iTunes gift card for their help. This was done to help reduce sentiments of volunteerism or coercion. Once participants completed the survey, they were given the option to forward the recruitment information to their TrevorSpace friends. Thus, data was obtained via a combination of direct marketing and snowball sampling. The survey reached saturation in eight hours and was closed. Out of 270 responses, 75 individuals were excluded for not completing the PHQ9 questions in the survey or submitting duplicate responses. This resulted in a sample of 195 respondents.

Additionally, working with The Trevor Project administrators, we obtained as secondary data two snapshots of the TrevorSpace social graph, one taken March 21, the other April 20, 2012. The survey was conducted on March 31st, so it falls between the two snapshots. The March graph has 18570 and the April graph 20716 actors.

Each of these graphs was anonymized, except that we were told which survey respondent corresponds to which graph actor. This allowed us to observe the structural role of each respondent within the graph.

We performed our analysis on the union of the March and April graphs, which we call the *TrevorSpace social graph*. It has 21306 actors. Ten of the remaining 195 survey respondents do not show up in this graph (we believe they joined, then left, TrevorSpace between when the snapshots were taken), so we excluded them, leaving 185 respondents in total.

Study Design

We based most of the survey questions (i.e., demographics, help-seeking readiness, mental health symptom history, sexual orientation stigma, and mental health stigma) on a web-based survey created by Whitlock, Knox and colleagues [49, 50]. Additional items addressing internet and online social media use were modified from The Pew Internet and American Life Questionnaire [26].

We also embedded into the survey the PHQ9, a widely used instrument for measuring depression [34]. It has 9 questions, each of which is worth up to three points. The total score thus ranges from 0 to 27, with 0 indicating little and 27 indicating strong support for depression.

Our survey website, which was developed on Ruby on Rails with the Surveyor gem, supports complex skip patterns in the survey items [37]. Taking these into account, the average participant required between 10 and 15 minutes to complete the survey.

Experiment Design

We create comparison groups by partitioning the respondent population into those scoring below the median PHQ9 score and those scoring no less than the median. We then compare the difference between the two groups on six different network features (described below).

96 participants have a PHQ9 score greater than or equal to the median value of 9; 89 have a lower score. A score of 9 is often taken as a cutoff for mild depression [22]. Moreover, a meta-analysis of optimal cut-off scores for depression varies; however scores between 8-11 (inclusive) tend to have similar sensitivity and specificity confidence intervals [28]. Sixteen respondents had a PHQ9 score of exactly 9. We had a choice about which group to place them in or whether to include them at all and ran our experiments each way. We only show results for the case where they are grouped with the high PHQ9 respondents; the results in the other cases were comparable if not slightly stronger. We chose to err on the conservative side.

Network Properties

For this study, we look at six primary network features: degree, triangles, clustering coefficient, core number, and the sizes of the largest (singly) connected and biconnected component. For an overview of basic network theoretic terms, many good textbooks are available, e.g. [30, 46, 16].

A *connected component* of a graph is a maximal set of actors such that each pair is connected by a path of ties (though the actors in the pair need not themselves share a tie). A *biconnected component* is a maximal set of actors where each pair is connected by a at least two disjoint paths of ties (disjoint in the sense that neither path shares any actors, except at the endpoints). In many natural and abstract graphs there is a *giant (bi)connected component* that contains most of the nodes in the graph.

The *degree* of an actor is the number of ties the actor has. This is sometimes called the *neighborhood size* and the set of actors with which the ties are formed is the *neighborhood*. We denote the neighborhood of a actor v in a network G as $N_G(v)$. Thus the degree is $|N_G(v)|$.

A *clique* is a set of actors such that any pair of them share a tie. It is also known as a *complete graph* or an *n-clique*, where n is the number of actors. A *triangle* is a 3-clique. The *triangle number* of an actor is the number of triangles the actor is a member of. We denote the triangle number of actor v as $| \bigtriangledown_G (v)|$

The *clustering coefficient* [47] of an actor v is

$$| \bigtriangledown_G (v)| / \binom{|N_G(v)|}{2}.$$

That is, it is the number of triangles to which the actor belongs divided by the total number of triangles the actor *could* belong to, given the number of neighbors the actor has.

An *n-core* is a subgraph relative to which each member actor has a degree at least n [36]. The *core number* of an actor is v is

$$\max\{n \mid v \text{ is a member of some } n\text{-core}\}.$$

An important virtue of n-cores is that they can be computed in linear time. Most other clustering techniques require higher-order polynomial or even exponential time to compute [2].

Bias Tests

Given the previously-discussed lack of iid sampling frames for our network statistics, we adopt a non-parametric (i.e., "distribution-free" [45]), subsampling-based approach to test the significance of our results.

We run two levels of tests. First, since our survey encouraged respondents to recruit their friends into the survey, we expect it to be highly unlikely that a random sample from the social graph would be more tightly interconnected, in terms of the graph features we study, than our pool of survey respondents. To test this, we take as a null hypothesis that our sample was from an independent and uniform sample without replacement from the TrevorSpace population. We simulate this by drawing without replacement a uniform random sample of 185 nodes from the TrevorSpace social graph and, for each of the six network features of interest, testing whether the the value of that feature in the sampled subgraph exceeds that of the same feature in the 185 survey respondents. We repeat this process 100,000 times and for each network feature count the number of times the comparision test is positive for that feature. This gives us an estimate of the likelihood that our survey was drawn from a random sample of the social graph. Table 1 and Figure 2 summarize these results.

Significance Testing

Second, to test the significance our results, we take as a null hypothesis that the level of depression in each of our respondents is independent the network. Then we randomly permute the respondents in the social graph (i.e., "randomly shuffle" their tie lists), keeping all other actors in the social graph fixed, and test, for each of the six network features of interest, whether the difference in that feature between the high and low groups of the permuted nodes exceeds the difference in that same feature between the high and low groups of the 185 survey respondents. We repeat this 100,000 times and for each feature count the number of times the comparison test is positive. By restricting our shuffling of actors to just the surveyed respondents, we effectively control for the effect of selection bias. Table 3 and Figure 3 summarize these results.

RESULTS

Figure 2 shows the results of the bias tests on the medians of degree, triangles, clustering coefficient and core number, and on the largest (bi)connected component. Table 1 summarizes these results. Table 2 shows the median values on each of these statistics for the high and low PHQ9 groups. Figure 3 and Table 3 show the significance tests on the difference between the high and low PHQ9 groups of each network feature value. In all cases the median statistics are taken from the underlying values in the social graph. The largest (bi)connected component is taken from the social graph, restricted to the group(s) of interest.

DISCUSSION

Figures 2 and 3 illustrate nicely the principal that network statistics do not satisfy iid assumptions, even when the population samples underlying the network samples may. By running each of the null hypothesis tests 100,000 times each, we gain fairly accurate distributions

Feature	Value	P-value
Size	185	n/a
Giant Con. Comp.	162	$< 10^{-5}$
Giant Bicon. Comp.	126	$< 10^{-5}$
Med. Degree	66	$< 10^{-5}$
Med. Triangles	700	$< 10^{-5}$
Med. Clustering	0.3485	0.45
Med. Core Number	57	$< 10^{-5}$

Table 1. The size of the medians of degree, triangle number, clustering coefficient and core number, calculated from the social graph, and of the giant (bi)connected component of the subgraph of respondents, along the results of the bias test.

Feature	PHQ9 < 9	PHQ9 ≥ 9
Size	89	96
Giant Con. Comp.	68	49
Giant Bicon. Comp.	52	30
Med. Degree	78	55
Med. Triangles	967	547.5
Med. Clustering	0.316722	0.3709409
Med. Core Number	66	48.5

Table 2. The sizes of the giant connected, and biconnected components, and the median degree, triangle number, clustering coefficient and core number, calculated from the social graph, of the low and high PHQ9 respondent group significance tests.

Feature	Δ	P-value
Giant Con. Comp.	19	0.15
Giant Bicon. Comp.	22	0.086
Med. Degree	23	0.059
Med. Triangles	419.5	0.049
Med. Clustering	-0.05	0.059
Med. Core Number	17.5	0.039

Table 3. The significance tests ("p-value") of the differences ("Δ") of the statistics from Table 2, calculated in the social graph, of the low and high PHQ9 respondents.

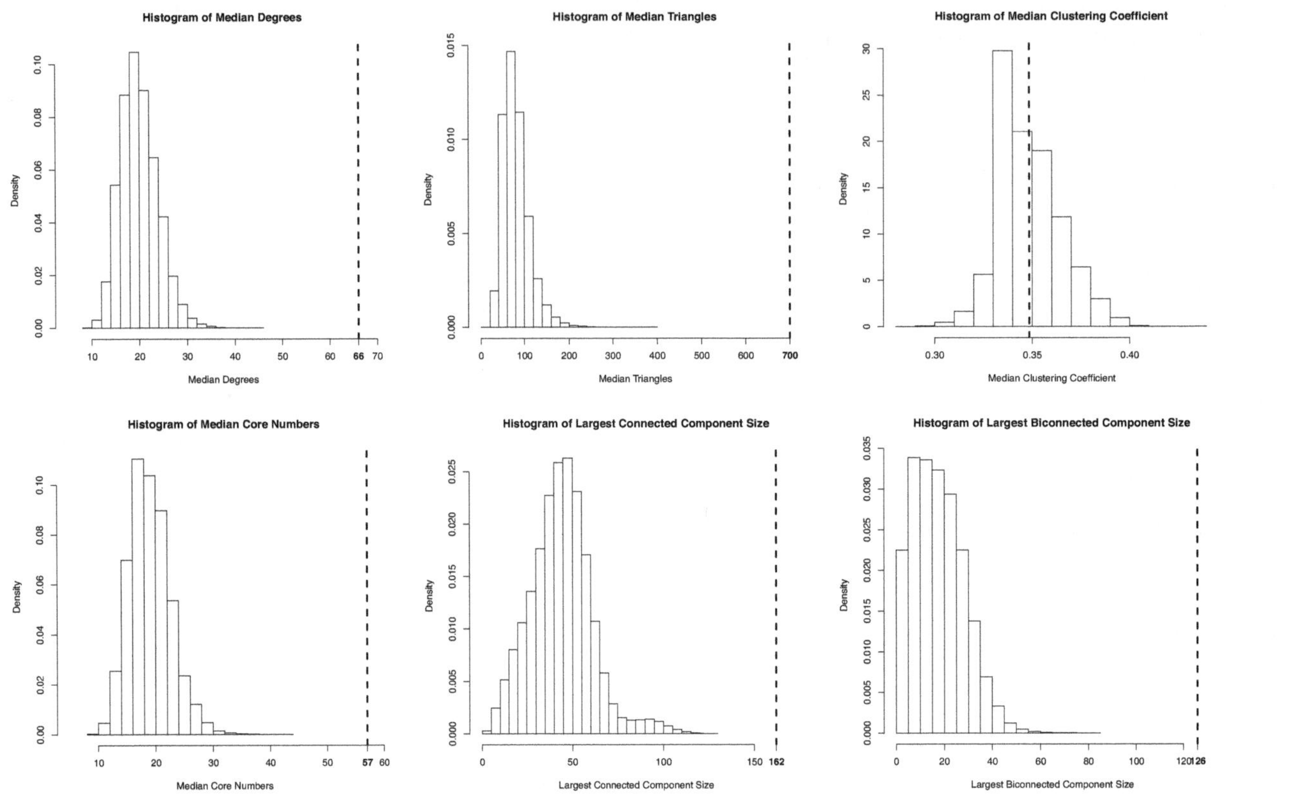

Figure 2. Histograms of the subsampling-based bias tests. The actual values from the survey are indicated by dotted lines. Except for clustering coefficient, the survey data appears at the right end of each histogram, indicating that the likelihood the survey data comes from a uniform random sample of the social graph is negligible.

of the network statistics under uniform sampling of the actors. While some of them look normal, many do not.

The results of the bias test (Table 2) show that all of the statistics observed on the respondent data, except clustering coefficient, are extremely unlikely under the null hypothesis. It thus seems that our mixed snowball/targeted sampling process is highly biased toward samples that are much more socially integrated than a random sample. One explanation for this is that the collective dynamics of the snowball process yield a region of the social network that is structured more like a functioning community than a random sample would be. Another is that most social networking services have a large number of inactive users, and we would expect that such users would be less likely to respond to the survey (and that this would be exacerbated by the narrow time window within which the survey was conducted) and also less integrated into the network, than active users would be. There is maybe some support for both explanations.

Moving on to the high and low PHQ9 groups, Table 3 shows that all differences in network features between these groups, except for the largest connected component, are significant at the 0.1 level and triangle and core numbers are significant at the 0.05 level. Each difference statistic is significant in the direction we expect, i.e., that the low PHQ9 group appears more tightly integrated into the social network than the high PHQ9 group, except for clustering coefficient, which was significant in the opposite direction.

This would seem to indicate that although nondepressed individuals (due to their significantly higher median triangle number) have more friends who know each other than do depressed individuals, they also have proportionally more "isolated" friends who do not know each other. One interpretation is that those who are not depressed are more likely to develop friendships with people outside of their normal social circles—and are thus more socially adventurous—than those who are depressed. Related work on this matter is mixed. Like us, DeChoudhury et al. discover that depressed individuals have a higher clustering coefficient in the Twitter social graph than nondepressed people [13]. Bearman and Moody found that women who have more friends that are not friends with each other are more likely to think about suicide than those who have fewer [3].

The results of the social network analysis are consistent with previous suicide prevention research and have clinical implications. For instance, the lack of connectivity and social belongingness are associated with suicidal behaviors [42], and at times there are social costs when LGBT youth decide to come out to their friends

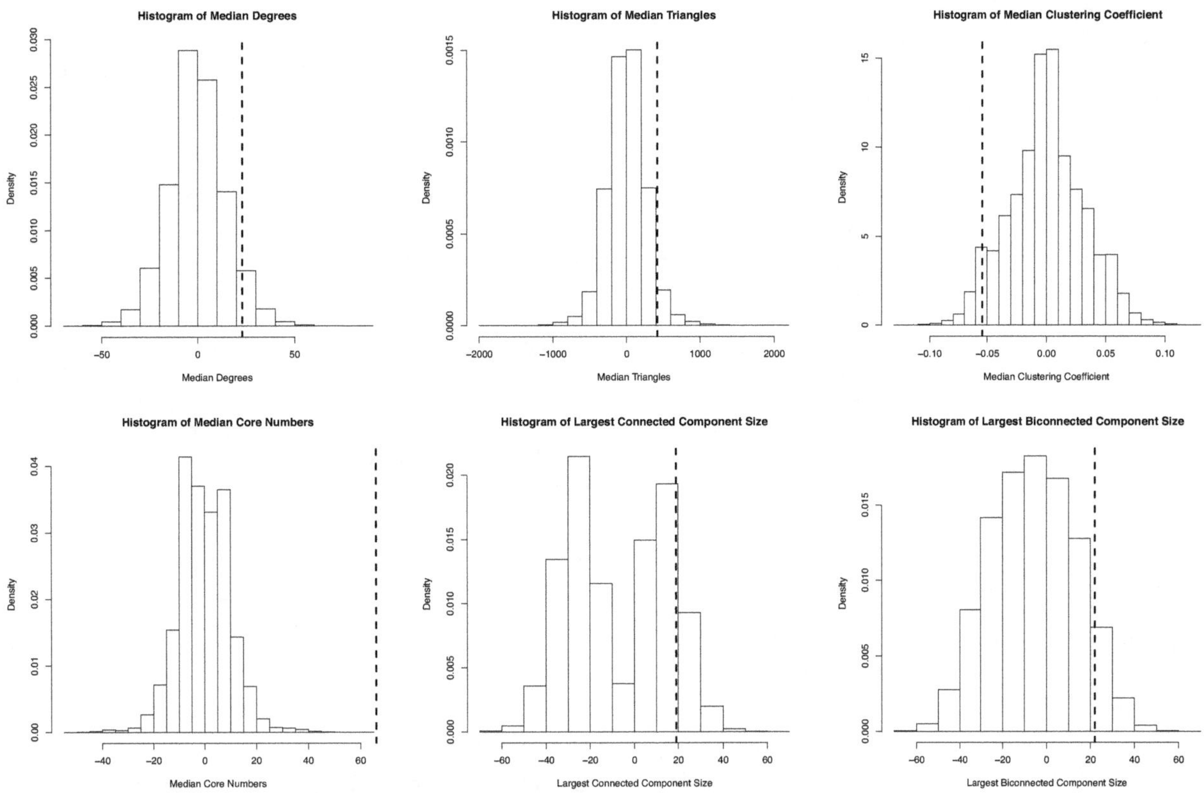

Figure 3. Histograms of the permutation-based significance tests of the differences between the low and high PHQ9 groups for various graph features. The actual values from the survey are indicated by dotted lines. Except for clustering coefficient, the survey results appear at the right end of each histogram, indicating that the likelihood that PHQ9 is independent of network structure is low. Clustering coefficient also appears unlikely to be independent, although in a different direction.

and families. LGBT individuals may experience rejection and victimization when they disclose their sexual orientation and gender identities [11].

Ethics and Broader Issues

This study was approved by our institutional review board (IRB). Respondents were required to read an information letter that discusses the risks and benefits of the research. Consent to participate in the study was indicated by completing the online survey and respondents could withdraw at anytime by closing their browser. Unlike secondary analysis research, we had to consider such ethical issues as privacy and potential risks. As previously mentioned, participants who endorsed suicidal ideation were excluded from this study and received immediate care from the Trevor Project.

As mentioned earlier, we are motivated by the potential of this line of inquiry to inform the development of intelligent systems for detecting signs of depression in a social network dedicated to reducing self harm among LGBT youth. It seems that our approach could also apply to other social networking sites to study similar problems. We are aware of several organizations that are on the cusp of bringing self harm reduction systems into the social networking domain. For instance, the Veterans Crisis Line[1] provides online chat and text messaging and 911 is starting to develop the capability to accept text messages.[2] Facebook has devoted resources and a webpage to detecting suicidal behavior among its users.[3]

The potential for the broader adoption of this approach raises a number of issues about privacy and coercion in the data gathering process, especially given the sensitive nature of both the target audience—LGBT youth—and the behavioral domain—mental health.

One way to ensure privacy in the snowball process, which we practice, is to not ask respondents to name names; rather, they find and contact all new recruits to the survey site. This is an explicit part of respondent-driven sampling (RDS), a widely-used variant of snowball sampling [18]. Only those who choose to step forward and be surveyed are thus known to us. Our IRB was especially careful about how we did this; we were not allowed to observe who recruited whom, even after the data was anonymized. TrevorSpace is particularly

[1] http://www.veteranscrisisline.net

[2] http://www.fcc.gov/text-to-911

[3] https://www.facebook.com/help/contact/305410456169423

careful about protecting the identities of its users. In general, however, a social networking site can monitor any such survey activity in the site, and thus gain information about membership in a hidden community or other sensitive information. Ways to minimize such privacy risks include using site resources, such as APIs, as little as possible and informing participants of the risks.

These methods also raise concerns about coercion, by both the administrators of the site and the snowball process. A related, though less nefarious, worry is that volunteerism can bias the sample in undesirable ways. We did not receive any complaints of coercion. By paying participants we hoped to help mitigate these effects by providing a clear reward for participating. Also, site administrators remained detached and impersonal in targeting site members.

Limitations

Given our desire to obtain a relatively well-connected sample, we did not randomly select participants. Moreover, the sample was collected over a very short period of time (one day). Thus it must be regarded as a convenience sample. There are few if any fully random surveys on LGBT youth.

The population of interest—recently suicidal LGBT youth—is very difficult to access and we were not able to obtain a comparison group (with a comparative network structure) via anything resembling a fully experimental design. This is a very specific group, one that is marginalized and relatively unhappy, and they were recruited from a social venue that is tailored to their needs. The degree to which our results apply to other populations is not yet clear.

A basic goal in social network research is to distinguish influence from selection when correlations are observed among closely related actors. For instance, we observed a slight anticorrelation in the PHQ9 scores of TrevorSpace friends. Is this because, say, depressed people have a slight tendency to not select each other as friends, or does having depressed friends cause one to become less depressed? We do not have the data to answer this question. Our primary concern here is to establish correlations between network features and depression, given a rather small population sample and the complete social graph of the underlying population.

Changes over time

It is known that levels of depression can fluctuate over time and even vary throughout the day [6, 16]. Social networks also change; for instance, in the month-long window between the two network snapshots of Trevorspace we used to construct the social graph, the network lost 590 users and gained 2,736. Kumar, Novak and Tomkins show that the edge density of online social networks fluctuates dramatically over time [25].

It is unclear whether one's level of social integration fluctuates dynamically with mood. We currently have survey data from one point in time only. We do have multiple snapshots of the social graph, and we did some exploration into whether depression in the survey data relates to changes in the social graph, but have yet to discover any convincing evidence.

CONCLUSION AND FUTURE WORK

This paper discovered network signatures for depression in an social networking service. We partitioned the participants of a survey on TrevorSpace, an SNS dedicated to reducing suicide and self harm among LGBTQ, youth into two groups, based on their score on a standard instrument for diagnosing depression. We believe our techniques of combining detailed, respondent-driven survey data with easy-to-obtain but low fidelity social tie data may apply to other hard-to-reach online communities on social networking sites.

The are a number of future directions to go with this work. An obvious goal is to build and assess models that use network structure to assess or predict who in a social network is or might become depressed, and then use this information to stage successful interventions. The techniques we develop here have shed important light on which network features may be most useful in this regard.

In obtaining network data, there seems to be a fundamental tradeoff between samples that are unbiased and those, such as from peer referral processes, that provide rich network structure. Is it possible to control snowball dynamics in a way that balances this tradeoff? For instance, RDS purports to provide a less biased sample than other peer referral methods, through a combination of limiting the number of people any one respondent can recruit and sophisticated estimators [18]. Could the features of a social networking site be used to somehow interactively and differentially regulate the recruitment process to make it more representative of, alternately, the population or the network?

Another next step would be to monitor the level of connectivity and depression LGBT youth have from when they first engage in a supportive network until they choose to leave. This information would help determine whether or not users were reaching out for support when they are depressed and exiting when they have improved psychological well-being. These results could then inform the monitoring of crisis and suicide prevention networks and the training of expert monitors. Such a study also could help tease apart the cause/effect dynamics between social structure and suicide.

Finally, we hope to combine the methods described here with those that uncover more detailed information about the functions and roles specific social ties play. Can the features of social networking sites help with this? We would expect that, at a minimum, the friends lists most sites provide would help the recall process, e.g., by carefully prompting the respondent with information gleaned from the site.

ACKNOWLEDGMENTS

We thank CSCW volunteers and all publications support and staff, who wrote and provided helpful comments on previous versions of this document. We also thank the staff and leadership of the Trevor Project, whose cooperation was essential for performing the work described in this document. This material is based in part upon work supported by the National Science Foundation under Grant Number SoCS-1111016. Any opinions, findings, and conclusions or recommendations expressed in this material are those of the author(s) and do not necessarily reflect the views of the National Science Foundation.

REFERENCES

1. Almeida, J., Johnson, R. M., Corliss, H. L., Molnar, B. E., and Azrael, D. Emotional distress among lgbt youth: The influence of perceived discrimination based on sexual orientation. *Journal of Youth and Adolescence 38*, 7 (2009), 1001–1014.
2. Batagelj, V., and Zaversnik, M. An O(m) algorithm for cores decomposition of networks. *arXiv preprint cs/0310049* (2003).
3. Bearman, P. S., and Moody, J. Suicide and friendships among american adolescents. *Journal Information 94*, 1 (2004).
4. Bollen, J., Gonçalves, B., Ruan, G., and Mao, H. Happiness is assortative in online social networks. *Artificial life 17*, 3 (2011), 237–251.
5. Bollen, J., Mao, H., and Zeng, X. Twitter mood predicts the stock market. *Journal of Computational Science 2*, 1 (2011), 1–8.
6. Bollen, J., Pepe, A., and Mao, H. Modeling public mood and emotion: Twitter sentiment and socio-economic phenomena. *CoRR abs/0911.1583* (2009).
7. Bollen, J., Pepe, A., and Mao, H. Modeling public mood and emotion: Twitter sentiment and socio-economic phenomena. In *Proceedings of the Fifth International AAAI Conference on Weblogs and Social Media* (2011), 450–453.
8. boyd, d. Why youth (heart) social network sites: The role of networked publics in teenage social life.
9. Chu, J. P., Goldblum, P., Floyd, R., and Bongar, B. The cultural theory and model of suicide. *Applied and Preventive Psychology 14*, 1 (2010), 25–40.
10. Cohen, S., and Wills, T. A. Stress, social support, and the buffering hypothesis. *Psychological bulletin 98*, 2 (1985), 310.
11. Corrigan, P., and Matthews, A. Stigma and disclosure: Implications for coming out of the closet. *Journal of Mental Health* (2003).
12. De Choudhury, M., Counts, S., and Horvitz, E. Social Media as a Measurement Tool of Depression in Populations . In *5th ACM International Conference on Web Science (WebSci 2013)* (2013).
13. De Choudhury, M., Gamon, M., Counts, S., and Horvitz, E. Predicting Depression via Social Media . In *7th International AAAI Conference on Weblogs and Social Media (ICWSM 2013)* (2013).
14. Dodds, P. S., Harris, K. D., Kloumann, I. M., Bliss, C. A., and Danforth, C. M. Temporal patterns of happiness and information in a global social network: Hedonometrics and twitter. *PloS one 6*, 12 (2011), e26752.
15. Durkheim, E. Suicide: A study in sociology, 1951.
16. Easley, D., and Kleinberg, J. *Networks, crowds, and markets*, vol. 8. Cambridge Univ Press, 2010.
17. Golder, S., and Macy, M. Diurnal and seasonal mood vary with work, sleep, and daylength across diverse cultures. *Science 333*, 6051 (2011), 1878–1881.
18. Heckathorn, D. D. Respondent-driven sampling: a new approach to the study of hidden populations. *Social problems* (1997), 174–199.
19. Hillier, L., and Harrison, L. Building realities less limited than their own: Young people practising same-sex attraction on the internet. *Sexualities 10*, 1 (2007), 82–100.
20. Homan, C. M., Silenzio, V., and Sell, R. Respondent-driven sampling in online social networks. In *Social Computing, Behavioral-Cultural Modeling and Prediction*. Springer, 2013, 403–411.
21. Kawachi, I., and Berkman, L. F. Social ties and mental health. *Journal of Urban health 78*, 3 (2001), 458–467.
22. Kendrick, T., Dowrick, C., McBride, A., Howe, A., Clarke, P., Maisey, S., Moore, M., and Smith, P. W. Management of depression in uk general practice in relation to scores on depression severity questionnaires: analysis of medical record data. *Bmj 338* (2009).
23. Kertzner, R. M., Meyer, I. H., Frost, D. M., and Stirratt, M. J. Social and psychological weil-being in lesbians, gay men, and bisexuals: The effects of race, gender, age, and sexual identity. *American Journal of Orthopsychiatry 79*, 4 (2009), 500–510.
24. Kim, S., Bak, J., and Oh, A. Do you feel what i feel? social aspects of emotions in twitter conversations. In *Proceedings of the AAAI International Conference on Weblogs and Social Media* (2012).

25. Kumar, R., Novak, J., and Tomkins, A. Structure and evolution of online social networks. In *Link Mining: Models, Algorithms, and Applications*. Springer, 2010, 337–357.

26. Lenhart, A., Maddenn, M., and Hitlin, P. Teens and technology: Youth are leading the transition to a fully wired and mobile nation. Washington, DC: Pew Internet and American Life Project.

27. Liu, R. T., and Mustanski, B. Suicidal ideation and self-harm in lesbian, gay, bisexual, and transgender youth. *American journal of preventive medicine 42*, 3 (2012), 221–228.

28. Manea, L., Gilbody, S., and McMillan, D. Optimal cut-off score for diagnosing depression with the patient health questionnaire (phq-9): a meta-analysis. *Canadian Medical Association Journal 184*, 3 (2012), E191–E196.

29. Mehra, B., Merkel, C., and Bishop, A. P. The internet for empowerment of minority and marginalized users. *New media & society 6*, 6 (2004), 781–802.

30. Newman, M. *Networks: an introduction*. OUP Oxford, 2009.

31. Pachankis, J. E. The psychological implications of concealing a stigma: a cognitive-affective-behavioral model. *Psychological bulletin 133*, 2 (2007), 328.

32. Pfitzner, R., Garas, A., and Schweitzer, F. Emotional divergence influences information spreading in twitter. *AAAI ICWSM 2012* (2012), 2–5.

33. Pitman, E. J. G. Significance tests which may be applied to samples from any populations. *Supplement to the Journal of the Royal Statistical Society 4*, 1 (1937), 119–130.

34. Richardson, L. P., McCauley, E., Grossman, D. C., McCarty, C. A., Richards, J., Russo, J. E., Rockhill, C., and Katon, W. Evaluation of the Patient Health Questionnaire-9 Item for Detecting Major Depression Among Adolescents. *PEDIATRICS 126*, 6 (Nov. 2010), 1117–1123.

35. Russell, S. T., and Joyner, K. Adolescent sexual orientation and suicide risk: Evidence from a national study. *Journal Information 91*, 8 (2001).

36. Seidman, S. B. Network structure and minimum degree. *Social networks 5*, 3 (1983), 269–287.

37. Silenzio, V., Cross, W., Caine, E., Prosser, T., and Cartwright, J. Freds: A novel adaptation of peer-driven sampling methods in online social media, June 2010.

38. Silenzio, V. M., Pena, J. B., Duberstein, P. R., Cerel, J., and Knox, K. L. Sexual orientation and risk factors for suicidal ideation and suicide attempts among adolescents and young adults. *Journal Information 97*, 11 (2007).

39. Stroebe, W., and Stroebe, M. *The social psychology of social support*. Guilford Press, 1996, 597–621.

40. Ullrich, P. M., Lutgendorf, S. K., and Stapleton, J. T. Concealment of homosexual identity, social support and cd4 cell count among hiv-seropositive gay men. *Journal of Psychosomatic Research 54* (2003), 205–212.

41. Valkenburg, P. M., and Peter., J. Online communication among adolescents: An integrated model of its attraction, opportunities, and risks.". *Journal of Adolescent Health 48*, 2 (2011), 121–127.

42. Van Orden, K. A., Witte, T. K., Cukrowicz, K. C., Braithwaite, S. R., Selby, E. A., and Joiner Jr, T. E. The interpersonal theory of suicide. *Psychological review 117*, 2 (2010), 575.

43. Wang, W., Chen, L., Thirunarayan, K., and Sheth, A. P. Harnessing twitter 'big data' for automatic emotion identification. In *Privacy, Security, Risk and Trust (PASSAT), 2012 International Conference on and 2012 International Confernece on Social Computing (SocialCom)*, IEEE (2012), 587–592.

44. Wasserman, L. *All of statistics: a concise course in statistical inference*. Springer Verlag, 2004.

45. Wasserman, L. *All of nonparametric statistics*. Springer Science+ Business Media, 2006.

46. Wasserman, S., and Faust, K. *Social network analysis: Methods and applications*, vol. 8. Cambridge university press, 1994.

47. Watts, D. J., and Strogatz, S. H. Collective dynamics of small-worldnetworks. *nature 393*, 6684 (1998), 440–442.

48. Wellman, B., and Wortley, S. Different strokes from different folks: Community ties and social support. *American journal of Sociology* (1990), 558–588.

49. Whitlock, J., Eckenrode, J., and Silverman, D. Self-injurious behaviors in a college population. *Pediatrics 117*, 6 (2006), 1939–1948.

50. Whitlock, J., and Knox, K. L. The relationship between self-injurious behavior and suicide in a young adult population. *Archives of pediatrics & adolescent medicine 161*, 7 (2007), 634.

51. Zerhouni, E. A. Translational and clinical sciencetime for a new vision. *New England Journal of Medicine 353*, 15 (2005), 1621–1623.

Characterizing and Predicting Postpartum Depression from Shared Facebook Data

Munmun De Choudhury **Scott Counts** **Eric J. Horvitz** **Aaron Hoff**
Microsoft Research, Redmond WA 98052
{munmund, counts, horvitz, aaron.hoff}@microsoft.com

ABSTRACT

The birth of a child is a major milestone in the life of parents. We leverage Facebook data shared voluntarily by 165 new mothers as streams of evidence for characterizing their postnatal experiences. We consider multiple measures including activity, social capital, emotion, and linguistic style in participants' Facebook data in pre- and postnatal periods. Our study includes detecting and predicting onset of post-partum depression (PPD). The work complements recent work on detecting and predicting significant postpartum changes in behavior, language, and affect from Twitter data. In contrast to prior studies, we gain access to ground truth on postpartum experiences via self-reports and a common psychometric instrument used to evaluate PPD. We develop a series of statistical models to predict, from data available before childbirth, a mother's likelihood of PPD. We corroborate our quantitative findings through interviews with mothers experiencing PPD. We find that increased social isolation and lowered availability of social capital on Facebook, are the best predictors of PPD in mothers.

Author Keywords

childbirth; emotion; health; language; postpartum; social media; Twitter; wellness

ACM Classification Keywords

H.3.4; H.5.2; H.5.3

INTRODUCTION

Childbirth is a major life event that changes the lives of parents. Beyond the joy and happiness of childbirth, a significant portion of new mothers experience changes in mood. Such postpartum changes include the "baby blues," lasting about 2-4 weeks after childbirth, and consisting of mild mood instability and anxiety. However, according to estimates from the CDC, about 12 to 20% of new mothers experience a mood disorder of greater severity and duration called *postpartum depression* (http://www.cdc.gov/reproductivehealth/Depression/). PPD is marked by symptoms such as sadness, fatigue, changes in sleeping and eating patterns, reduced libido, crying episodes, anxiety, and irritability [2]. Beyond negative influence on mothers, there is evidence that PPD can bear short and long-term negative effects on the child's behavior, emotional, and social wellbeing [16].

Despite these ramifications, PPD is underreported, with estimates that as many as 50% of cases of PPD go undetected [29]. Underreporting is believed to be due to factors such as the fear of the social stigma of depression, lack of social support, or assumptions that the mood changes are a normal part of the overwhelming nature of new motherhood [7]. Additional barriers to help-seeking include lack of knowledge about predisposition symptoms, the availability of appropriate remedial/prevention services, or even privacy concerns [7].

What makes this form of medical condition even more challenging is that there are no adequate ways for prevention or early detection [39], unless a woman has had a history of depression in the past. Clinical diagnosis of PPD is based on the mother's self-reported experiences (e.g., DSM-IV criteria based on the mood module from the PRIME-MD—Primary Care Evaluation of Mental Disorders: the Diagnostic and Statistical Manual of Mental Disorders (DSM) published by the American Psychiatric Association provides a common language and widely relied upon standard criteria for the classification of mental disorders), prior depression history, life stress, behaviors reported by relatives or friends, and a mental status examination. Naturally, treatment efforts, that typically comprise medication, therapy, or both, are also more successful with early intervention; in fact, the likelihood of achieving full recovery declines as the illness lengthens [7].

Hence, there is value in innovative methods that can identify women at risk, even perhaps in the early stages of PPD, and provide them access to appropriate services and support. To the extent these methods can provide lower cost complements to traditional PPD assessments, they may help reach a larger portion of the population. Prevention efforts could alter women's lifetime trajectory of problems arising from mental illness, and avoid the serious social and medical ramifications associated with psychopathology.

CSCW'14, February 15–19, 2014, Baltimore, Maryland, USA.

http://dx.doi.org/10.1145/2531602.2531675

A Digital Safety Net

We explore the use of online social networks as a lens on mood and behavior to glean insights about the postpartum experience of new mothers. Individuals are increasingly using online social networks and social media such as Facebook and Twitter to share updates about their daily ordeals, but also often to make announcements of major life milestones, including childbirth and parental milestones [4,13]. Data captured from social media can span new mothers' social activity, interactions with friends and other audiences, and emotional and linguistic expression. Consequently, it can provide a natural laboratory for researchers to study their behavior and experience of motherhood in general [4,5]. In fact, a body of work has emerged that has looked at whether the material posted on social networking site profiles accurately portrays someone's mental and physical state [5; 32]. For example, references to depression or drinking on Facebook are concurrently associated with self-reported depression rating scores [25], and postings of displayed risk behavior were found to be related to injuries as well as substance use or violence among college undergraduates [23].

Motivated along those lines, we consider the use of social media data to detect and predict PPD. The work complements earlier efforts to detect and predict postpartum changes in behavior, language, and affect from Twitter data. However, rather than rely on observed changes, in this work we gain access to ground truth on postpartum levels of depression and PPD diagnoses via both self-reports and use of a common psychometric instrument used to evaluate PPD.

Our main contributions include:

(1) We conduct an online survey to collect gold-standard labels of depression on 165 new mothers who use Facebook (scores on the PHQ-9 depression screening tool). We note here that the PHQ9 depression scores are critical as they allow us to distinguish new moms actually suffering from depression versus those that have changed behavior (e.g., posting less on Facebook) for more benign reasons like they simply are too busy with their new baby. Thereafter we characterize participants' Facebook behaviors over 50 weeks of prenatal period and 10 weeks of postnatal, totaling 600K postings on Facebook. We propose 49 different measures of mothers' activity on Facebook, including their available social capital, emotion, and linguistic style.

(2) We develop several statistical models to predict whether or not a mother will have PPD. A model that uses only prenatal data is found to explain as much as 31% of variance in the data, and improves upon a baseline model based on demographic and childbirth history data by 77%. Including a short time horizon (~1 month) after childbirth, we achieve better performance, where our model is found to explain up to 48% of variance in the data.

(3) We corroborate our quantitative findings through semi-structured interviews conducted with a sample of the mothers with PPD. We find that experiences of PPD are best predicted by increased social isolation as manifested in reduced social activity and interaction on Facebook, and decreased access to social capital. We find that emotional measures as captured through Facebook posts are not effective predictors of PPD, perhaps due to the stigma associated with depression.

We believe that this research can bring to the fore variables related to the exacerbation of PPD, thereby enabling new mechanisms to identify at-risk mothers, and provide guidance on valuable interventions. In general it could lay the groundwork for a future digital safety net to scaffold new mothers following an important phase transition in life.

BACKGROUND AND RELATED WORK

Clinical/Psychiatry Literature on PPD

A considerable body of work in psychiatry and the clinical literature is devoted to understanding PPD. Much of this work is survey-driven and relies on self-reported data. Surveys such as the Postpartum Depression Predictors Inventory (PPDI) [1] reflect meta-analyses of risk factors for PPD [2], including lack of social support, socioeconomic status, and infant temperament, among others (see [30] for more on risks and influencers of PPD). Lack of social support and social isolation in particular, along with psychological stress have been shown to influence the attitudes, emotions, and behaviors of new mothers [10,48]. In another study [46], Scott et al. found that the strongest predictors of PPD were past history of psychopathology and psychological disturbance during pregnancy, poor marital relationship, low social support, and stressful life events. Finally, Fleming et al. [11] observed that depressed mothers exhibited fewer affectionate contact behaviors (and in general lower maternal responsiveness) towards their infants postpartum, compared to non-depressed mothers.

Although not exhaustive, proxies for several risk factors of PPD, like the ones studied in prior literature, might be monitored via mothers' activities on social media like Facebook and Twitter. Social support and access to social capital might be inferred from a mother's degree of interaction with her contacts on social media. Further, infant temperament and maternal responsiveness might be measured through posts, photos, and videos the mother shares about her baby on Facebook, while stressful events in the past may have cues manifested in an individual's social media postings.

We note that little prior work has focused on *predicting* PPD. This is likely because collecting longitudinal data is difficult given the resources and invasiveness required to observe mothers behavior over months and years. Online social platforms like Facebook show promise in this regard: As numerous people have been using these tools for years, there are opportunities to track behavioral patterns over time in fine granularity—in this case, before and after childbirth of the mothers to understand and identify predictive factors behind PPD.

New Mothers' Use of Social Media/Networks

Mothers are a growing demographic on the Internet—per NielsenWire polls in 2012, 72% mothers in the US use Facebook [28]. Over the years, several studies have focused on studying mothers' use of social technologies, such as blogging [22], motherhood and parenting forums [45,36], and Facebook [13]. McDaniel et al. [22] observed that new mothers' frequency of blogging was predictive of feelings of social connection to extended family and friends, of social support, and of maternal wellbeing. Based on ethnographic studies, Gibson and Hanson [13] observed that Facebook was perceived as a valuable platform by new mothers in being able to remain socially connected with others postpartum, to construct a new identity, or to seek information and reassurance on their choices and concerns around rearing a newborn. Schoenebeck [45] found that postings made on the anonymous message board YouBeMom.com define new types of social norms and expectations shaping online mom culture.

The prior work suggests that online social technologies may be providing new mothers with mechanisms to utilize their social capital and to find a disinhibiting outlet for communication, venting, and sharing baby tips. We pursue the use of streams of online social activity to understand the role of online social support or its lack in PPD.

In related work, De Choudhury et al. analyzed Twitter postings of new mothers to detect [4] and to predict [5] extreme behavioral changes postpartum. The studies did not gain access to ground truth data on PPD outcomes, but rather relied on the sensing of extreme changes in Twitter. To the best of our knowledge, this paper presents the first of its kind study identifying predictors of postpartum depression based on new mothers' use of Facebook.

Social Media/Networks in Health and Wellness

Beyond PPD, researchers have been increasingly interested in understanding how social media activities can be used to infer the wellbeing of people, and conditions and symptoms related to diseases [36] and disease contagion, e.g., flu [48]. Facebook use has been shown to help those with lower self-esteem to attain higher social capital [47]. Moreno et al., [24] demonstrated that status updates on Facebook could reveal symptoms of major depressive episodes, while Park et al. [32] found differences in the perception of Twitter use between depressed and non-depressed users—the former found value in Twitter due to the ability to garner social awareness and engage in emotional interaction. On similar lines, De Choudhury et al. [6] examined year-long Twitter postings of individuals suffering from major depressive disorder to build statistical models that predict the future occurrence of depression.

A common thread in this research is how computational techniques may be applied to naturalistic data that people share on today's online social platforms to infer their health condition. These techniques are rooted in findings in the social science literature, where computerized analysis of language and social network analysis has revealed markers of depression [42], anxiety, and other psychological disorders [31,43]. Weaving together these ideas, we conjecture that linguistic and activity analyses, and notions of social capital manifested in online social platforms can offer a novel methodology for augmenting traditional approaches to measuring and predicting risk for PPD.

FACEBOOK DATA COLLECTION

We conducted an online survey to collect information about PPD experiences of new mothers, and to gain access to their Facebook data for our analyses, with their consent. The survey website was active between mid-July and mid-September, 2012. It was advertised through multiple channels so as to reach a diverse population of new mothers in the US—mailing lists of new mothers within our organization and the broader community in our metropolitan area (e.g., neighborhood based mommy blogs), postings from our organization's official Twitter and Facebook accounts as well as the authors' personal Twitter, Facebook and Google+ accounts, paid Facebook ads targeting mothers in the age group 20-39 years, and finally sponsored posts on BabyCenter (babycenter.com), a popular website aimed at mothers that hosts discussion forums and parenting articles.

We recruited mothers who were owners of a Facebook account and who gave birth to a child within the last nine months or less, so that we could capture their experiences with postpartum depression while they were possibly still persistent. To incentivize participation and to acknowledge the mothers for their time and effort, they were entered into the random drawing of four $500 Amazon gift cards.

PPD Survey

In the survey of participants, we collected demographic data of the mothers (age, family income, occupation), and data related to the child/childbirth experience, including the child's birthdate, whether the child is the first-born, and whether the mother had been diagnosed with PPD by a clinician at some point following childbirth. The survey also inquired about the different ways the mothers used Facebook—for status updates, photo-sharing, and so on.

In addition to the survey we gave participants a PHQ-9 (Patient Health Questionnaire) depression screening tool [20] to detect whether mothers were currently depressed. Specifically, the questionnaire seeks responses over the past two week period, on the frequency of experiences like "*little interest or pleasure in doing things*"; "*feeling tired or having little energy*". Scores on the PHQ-9 range from zero to 27, where higher scores indicate the presence of more symptomology. Per psychiatric literature [20], individuals with scores greater than or equal to 15 are considered to be moderately severe to severely depressed.

Following the PHQ-9 questionnaire, mothers were asked to optionally authorize a Facebook application, with the goal of allowing us a one-time crawl of their Facebook timeline data. For each of the mothers who opted-in, we archived a data dump of the following timeline data: status updates that they both shared and were tagged in (both content and time), captions associated with photos, videos, and links they shared or were tagged in, and *like* and comment counts on all these items (statuses, photos, videos, links, check-ins). Note that actual photos and videos were not crawled, in the interest of the participants' privacy.

		PHQ-9 Score	
		no	*yes*
Self-report	*no*	137	9
	yes	13	15
		No PPD	137
		PPD	28
		Total	165

Table 1. Mothers with PPD based on self-report and PHQ-9 depression severity scoring.

Constructing PPD Ground Truth

Running this online survey gave us 292 responses. After dismissal of incomplete surveys we obtained 267, out of which 174 also opted-in to grant us access to use their Facebook data for our research (59.58% of total responses). We wished to focus on the subset of the mothers for whom we could validate their self-reported PPD condition, as well as their PHQ-9 questionnaire scores. That is, the set of mothers who reported to have never been diagnosed with PPD, as well as scored negatively on the questionnaire; and those who reported to have had PPD following childbirth, with current PHQ-9 score to be either in the positive PPD range (persistent PPD), or in the negative PPD range (receded PPD).

Using the standard depression severity scoring of PHQ-9 as mentioned above, we present a confusion matrix of the number of mothers with self-reported PPD (yes/no) and PHQ-9 diagnosed PPD (yes/no) in Table 1. Note that per the reasoning presented earlier, we obtain 28 mothers with experiences of PPD following childbirth, while 137 with no PPD experience at any point in time. We also note here that mothers who self-reported to have no PPD, but scored positively in PPD severity in the questionnaire were ignored, since we could not be sure of their actual/true PPD experience, or the possibility that responses on the PHQ-9 questionnaire could simply be noisy. The number of mothers (28, or 16.7% of the sample population) who were detected to have had PPD is toward the higher end of the CDC estimate of mothers suffering from PPD in the United States. We acknowledge here that it might reflect a bias in our recruitment strategy—some of the ads, especially ones on babycenter.com were posted on a forum around PPD—our goal was to ensure we are able to recruit sufficient number of mothers with PPD for reliable statistical analyses. However this number still aligns with most studies conducted around depression and mental illness [6].

Dataset Statistics

We now discuss some statistics of our dataset of mothers. First, in Table 2, we present some demographic information such as age, income, ethnicity, and top five occupation types of the mothers with and without PPD. We do not see any statistically significant differences between no PPD and PPD groups for age (based on an independent sample *t*-test); however we do observe that mothers with PPD tend to be of lower income levels ($p<0.01$) and more likely to be "stay-at-home moms" (24%). For ethnicity, we observe that the majority of the mothers in our dataset are "Caucasian" which may indicate a bias in the respondent-driven sampling method we adopted in our survey.

Age	**all**	**no PPD**	**PPD**
Median age	31	31	30
Average age	30.36875	30.582	29.645
Income			
Median income	80,000	85,500	55,000
Average income	96,127.48	102,040.9	72,724.14
Ethnicity			
African-American	3	3	0
Asian	17	17	0
Caucasian	127	98	29
Latino/Hispanic	9	6	3
Native American	2	2	0
Other	3	2	1
Occupation			
Stay at Home Mom	50	38	12
Computer & Mathematical	21	20	1
Education, Training, & Lib.	14	12	2
Business & Financial Op.	9	9	0
Healthcare Practitioner	8	4	4

Table 2. Demographics of mothers with and without PPD.

We observe that mothers giving birth to a second or later child have considerably higher chances of having PPD (67.12%), compared to those giving birth to their first kid (37.78%). We also observe that premature childbirth had little association with PPD—among the mothers who had PPD, only 13.33% reported having given birth to a premature child, while it was 10.2% for those without PPD.

Facebook Data

We now present some characteristics of the Facebook data dump that we collected for the set of 165 mothers. For each mother, we created two separate data files—one spanning the prenatal period, and the other the postnatal period. In Figure 1, we show cumulative distributions of the duration span of prenatal and postnatal data we could collect from the Facebook dumps of the mothers. We notice that for the set of 165 mothers, we have up to 50 weeks of prenatal data, while for postnatal data, for the same set of mothers we have access to up to 10 weeks of data. Note that 50 weeks is almost close to a year, which gives us ample data to observe manifestations of prenatal depression, or even early signs of PPD. Focusing on 10 weeks of postnatal data consistently for all mothers gives us sufficient time to observe PPD related changes following childbirth. Several studies on PPD in the clinical literature has focused on similar timeframes (e.g., O'Hara et al. [29] identified predictors of PPD at the 2nd trimester of pregnancy, while Fleming et al. in [11] studied PPD at 3 months postpartum).

Based on the above time frames, combining the prenatal and postpartum periods, we obtained 578,220 items that were posted by the 165 mothers (combining wall posts, photos, videos, links, check-ins), which had 534,123 likes and 487,072 comments. In terms of the posts received on the timelines (i.e., posts in which the mothers were tagged in by friends), there were 21,078 posts in all, with 24,259 likes and 23,830 comments.

MEASURING BEHAVIORAL CHARACTERISTICS

We now present a number of measures that we used to characterize the behavior of the mothers. Unless otherwise mentioned, we use *posts* to refer to any item shared/received on a mother's timeline that can be a wall post, a photo, video, link or a check-in.

User Characteristics

We define seven different *user characteristics* that measure a user's nature of activity on Facebook. The first three measures include: the *number of status updates* made by a mother; the *number of media items* (photos/videos) uploaded by a mother; and *number of wall posts she made to specific friends* on Facebook.

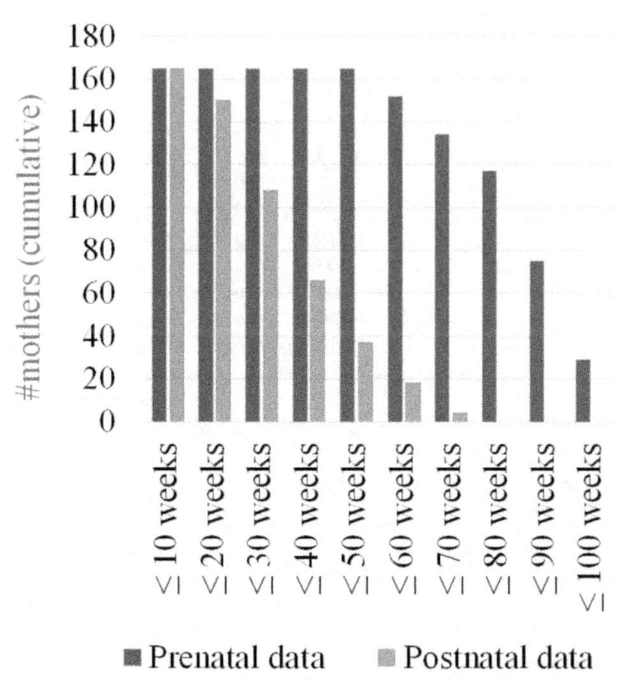

Figure 1. Cumulative distributions of durations of prenatal and postnatal Facebook data for the mothers in our dataset.

The remaining measures capture overall Facebook usage patterns of the mothers. We consider all postings made by a mother on her timeline per day (including status updates, media uploaded) as a time-series signal during the entire duration of the analysis. Based on this data, we define the remaining measures in the user-characteristics category as the different properties of this time-series signal.

A fourth measure captures the *rate of change of posting activity* over time, and is given as the normalized difference between the number of posts made on a certain day and the mean number of posts over a time window before (we consider week-long windows). A fifth measure captures the degree to which a mother's Facebook *activity shows a negative trend*. This measure is computed from the rate of change measure as the fraction of weeks during which the rate of change is negative [17]. A sixth measure captures the entropy or *variation in the number of posts* per week over the entire prenatal period—high entropy would indicate high volatility of activity. A seventh measure is the *mean power of the number of posts per week*, in essence capturing the degree of periodicity in the frequency domain of a mother's activity over time [17].

Social Capital

Previous research has found an inverse relationship between an individual's access to cognitive social capital (social trust, sense of belonging, mutual aid) and depression [12]. Given Facebook's rich friendship networks, we leveraged the following types of one-to-one social interactions as measures of a mother's social capital, as defined as resources and support embedded within social networks: *likes on status updates* (wall posts / check-ins) made by a mother; *comments on status updates*; *likes on uploaded media* (photos/videos/links); *comments on uploaded media*; *wall posts made by friends* to a mother; *likes on wall posts made by friends* to a mother; *comments on wall posts made by friends* to a mother; *media posted by friends on wall*; *likes on media posted by friends on wall*; *comments on media posted by friends on wall*; *likes on media with specific friends tagged*; *comments on media with specific friends tagged*; *likes on wall posts to friends by a mother*; *comments on wall posts to friends* by a mother; *media in which specific friends were tagged*; and *number of friends in which a mother directed a specific communication to via tagging*.

Content Characteristics

Emotional Expression. We consider two measures of the emotional state of mothers in our dataset: *positive affect* (PA), and *negative affect* (NA), motivated from work in [35]. Measurements of PA and NA per mother are computed using the psycholinguistic resource LIWC (http://www.liwc.net/), whose emotion categories have been scientifically validated to perform well for determining affect in Twitter [14].

Question-centric Statuses. We also define a content characterization measure of the posts shared by mothers that captures their information/advice seeking tendency on Facebook. For the purpose, we infer whether or not a post made by a mother contains a question—that is, if the post contains a "?" marker and has one of the words "what", "why", "how", "when", "where", "who", "whom" etc.

Linguistic Style

We also use measures that characterize behavioral change, based on the use of linguistic styles in posts by mothers, during the prenatal and the postnatal periods. Linguistic styles capture how language is used by individuals and provide information about their behavioral characteristics subject to their social and psychological environment [35]. We again use LIWC for determining 22 specific linguistic styles, e.g.: *articles, verbs, conjunctions, adverbs, personal pronouns, prepositions, functional words, assent, negation, certainty* and *quantifiers*.

PPD VERSUS NON-PPD BEHAVIOR

We now present statistics characterizing and distinguishing the behavior of the mothers during prenatal and postpartum periods (combined). Table 3 presents the per-day mean, median, and standard deviation of the measures we use to characterize behavior of the mothers, combining the 50 week prenatal and 10 week postnatal periods. We also show which measures statistically distinguish the two cohorts based on independent sample *t*-tests (after adopting Bonferroni correction).

Our observations indicate that most of the user characteristics can distinguish well the behavior of the two cohorts. Specifically, for the PPD experiencing mothers, Facebook activity as measured by status updates and media items shared is lower (difference of means between prenatal and postnatal periods: 14.8% and 8.4% respectively). They also appear to be less socially interactive in reaching out to friends by tagging them in wall posts (30% lower than non-PPD mothers).

The trends and temporal characteristics of activity of these mothers also has cues attributing the differences in their experiences from those without experiences of PPD. Notably, they show a less periodic (39% lower), highly volatile (note, higher entropy: 15% higher), and raised levels of rate of change of activity over time. We note here that while periodic behavior of social media use often indicates routine nature of lifestyle [14], it is also known that lifestyle irregularities such as sleep disruption often are associated with the psychopathology of depression [37]. Our measures of high volatility and low periodicity in the case of the PPD group attempt to capture such irregularities in Facebook activity. Additionally, we observe that greater fraction of their time on Facebook, the PPD experiencing mothers tend to show a decreasing trend in their levels of activity, a finding in line with prior literature that indicates depression to be associated with social and psychological impairment [34]. Putting these together, we conjecture that PPD experiencing

	No PPD			PPD			
	Mean	Med.	SD	Mean	Med.	SD	*p*
User Characteristics							
Status updates posted	2.106	1.577	2.036	1.794	1.088	2.009	**
Media uploaded	2.822	1.901	3.338	2.585	1.822	2.484	***
Wall posts to specific friends	1.386	0.580	2.375	0.969	0.443	1.547	***
Rate of change of activity	-0.429	-0.299	0.479	-0.445	-0.240	0.639	**
Frac. time w/ -ve activity trend	0.557	0.595	0.173	0.572	0.605	0.139	*
Entropy of activity	0.710	0.818	0.310	0.817	0.877	0.214	**
Mean power of activity signal	37.274	0.702	164.3	22.381	0.463	109.0	**
Social Capital							
Likes on status updates	2.132	1.101	3.517	1.753	0.932	2.138	***
Comments on status updates	3.825	2.365	3.874	3.484	2.328	3.678	***
Likes on uploaded media	1.184	0.940	1.170	0.921	0.720	0.816	***
Comments on uploaded media	0.336	0.255	0.286	0.301	0.211	0.312	**
Likes on wall posts to friends	1.382	0.427	3.453	0.839	0.374	1.239	**
Comments on posts to friends	1.591	0.381	3.237	1.139	0.341	2.085	
Media with friends tagged	0.674	0.264	1.190	0.585	0.206	0.756	**
Likes on media w/ friends	0.270	0.132	0.503	0.274	0.113	0.492	*
Comments on media w/ friends	0.072	0.012	0.148	0.041	0.006	0.083	
Wall posts made by friends	0.213	0.009	0.538	0.166	0.000	0.457	*
Likes on wall posts by friends	0.259	0.006	0.935	0.117	0.000	0.332	
Comments on posts by friends	0.298	0.016	0.816	0.127	0.000	0.528	
Media by friends	0.141	0.000	0.325	0.108	0.000	0.466	**
Likes on media by friends	0.050	0.000	0.146	0.042	0.000	0.179	*
Comments on media by friends	0.013	0.000	0.035	0.006	0.000	0.042	
Friends with directed comm.	1.760	1.071	2.031	1.680	1.071	1.911	***
Content Characteristics							
Positive Affect	0.578	0.579	0.135	0.536	0.535	0.139	*
Negative Affect	0.408	0.416	0.134	0.435	0.451	0.112	
Question-centric Statuses	0.014	0.000	0.071	0.025	0.000	0.094	***
Linguistic Style							
1stPersonPronoun Singular	0.028	0.000	0.096	0.039	0.000	0.154	***
1stPersonPronoun Plural	0.010	0.000	0.047	0.003	0.000	0.013	***
2ndPersonPronoun	0.014	0.000	0.067	0.013	0.000	0.087	**
3rdPersonPronoun	0.017	0.000	0.046	0.010	0.000	0.058	***
Adverbs	0.030	0.004	0.106	0.031	0.002	0.091	
Article	0.032	0.003	0.102	0.020	0.005	0.041	***
Assent	0.013	0.000	0.066	0.005	0.000	0.048	**
AuxVerbs	0.044	0.010	0.110	0.086	0.012	0.224	
Certain	0.018	0.000	0.069	0.012	0.000	0.054	**
Conjunction	0.029	0.004	0.094	0.045	0.004	0.134	
Exclusive	0.007	0.000	0.022	0.017	0.000	0.056	*
Filler	0.004	0.000	0.046	0.001	0.000	0.007	**
FunctionalWords	0.300	0.092	0.730	0.325	0.056	0.883	
Inclusive	0.031	0.006	0.095	0.046	0.004	0.131	*
IndefinitePronoun	0.043	0.001	0.252	0.076	0.001	0.283	*
Inhibition	0.004	0.000	0.015	0.018	0.000	0.148	**
Negate	0.007	0.000	0.020	0.008	0.000	0.052	**
NonFluency	0.000	0.000	0.002	0.004	0.000	0.026	**
Preposition	0.082	0.018	0.273	0.068	0.012	0.167	
Quantifier	0.017	0.000	0.066	0.016	0.000	0.062	
Swear	0.007	0.000	0.036	0.012	0.000	0.134	**
Tentative	0.008	0.000	0.031	0.009	0.000	0.033	
Verbs	0.078	0.020	0.175	0.092	0.016	0.224	
N	137			28			

*** $p<0.001/k$; ** $p<0.01/k$; * $p<0.05/k$ (after Bonferroni correction)
k=49 (number of behavioral measures)

Table 3. Per-day values of the measures characterizing PPD experiencing and non-PPD mothers (combined prenatal and postpartum periods). Results of statistical significance tests (independent sample *t*-tests) comparing the two cohorts are indicated by asterisks.

mothers are posting less, suggesting a possible loss of social connectedness.

Next, PPD experiencing mothers were significantly lower than their non-PPD experiencing counterparts on our measures of social capital. For instance, PPD experiencing mothers seem to receive lower numbers of likes and comments on their status updates as well as uploaded media (17.7% and 22% respectively). They also have fewer wall posts and media made by friends. From prior literature, we know that use of social platforms online, like Facebook, likely supplements people's physical world communication and thereby helps generate and maintain their social capital [3,9]. However, in the case of individuals suffering from major depression, perceptions of levels of cognitive social capital (trust of neighbors) are considerably lower [12], potentially explaining our observation in the data.

We further observe that the PPD experiencing mothers exhibit higher expression of NA (and lower PA) compared to non-PPD mothers, consistent with depression symptoms such as mental instability and helplessness, loneliness, restlessness, exhaustion, lack of energy, and sleep deprivation [38]. However in contrast to previous work on understanding postpartum changes in new mothers using Twitter [4], we do not find these distinctions to be highly statistically significant. This may indicate a reporting bias on Facebook compared to Twitter: Since Facebook is often a platform used to connect to physical world contacts (personal and professional), individuals may be more conscious about their self-presentation, and might be less comfortable discussing emotions related to their depression in their wall posts [27]. There may also be an awkwardness factor or social stigma associated with depression, due to its sensitive nature [41] that prevents them from explicit emotional expression on Facebook.

Apart from emotion measures, the PPD experiencing mothers seem to post considerably greater content that is question-centric (78% higher), reflecting an attempt to use Facebook as a mechanism for information and advice seeking, or perhaps leveraging their available social capital to tackle the challenges of PPD [15,26]. We conjecture this could also be a manifestation of their attempt to seek social and emotional support from contacts they trust.

Finally, among the linguistic style features, we find that the presence of the first-person singular pronoun is considerably high (41.8% higher), while that of 1st person plural, 2nd and 3rd person pronouns is low in posts of the PPD-experiencing mothers (66%, 4.4%, and 43.4% respectively), reflecting their high attention to self, self-preoccupation, and psychological distancing from others [43]. PPD experiencing mothers also show lower use of articles (37% lower), indicating less attribution to things around them in their environment, another correlate of mental illness [43]. Negation, inhibition, non-fluency, and swear words also seem to be higher for this cohort compared to the other, which align with observations in prior work where negative cognitive styles and biases have been found to be associated with depression [40].

PPD PREDICTION

Comparison of Predictive Models

Given the observed differences between the behaviors of the PPD and non-PPD experiencing mothers, we turned to predicting the onset of PPD. To start, we use the behavioral measures collected only from the prenatal period to predict whether or not a mother will have PPD during the postpartum period. We fitted a number of regression models to understand the relative value of considering different behavioral measures: user characteristics alone, social capital, content characteristics, and linguistic style, and finally a model using all of these measures. We also fitted a null model that uses all of the available demographic and self-reported attributes relating to childbirth. Prior literature shows that there is correlation between these attributes and PPD experience [2]; we sought to evaluate the additional contributions of Facebook-derived measures to the literature-identified models.

Measure	β		SE	t-Statistic
Intercept	2.4196	***	0.036	6.709
Age[1]	0.0142	*	0.025	0.174
Ethnicity[1]	0.0079		0.025	0.031
Occupation[1]	-0.174	**	0.023	-0.756
Income	-0.046	***	0.112	-2.691
First child[1]	-0.636	**	0.025	-2.519
Premature child[1]	0.2711		0.023	1.133
Deviance				115.218
Log likelihood				-57.609
pseudo-R^2				0.1398
Estimated dispersion parameter				0.919
Number of observations				156
Error degrees of freedom				149

[1] binary variable coded as 1/0
age: $\leq$ 30years → 0; >30years → 1
ethnicity: Caucasian → 1; Other → 0
occupation: Stay-at-home mom → 1; working mom → 0

Table 4. Performance of demographics model.

For all of our models in this section, we use stepwise logistic regression models, in which the independent variables are the different behavioral measures, and the response variable is whether or not a particular mother reported the onset of PPD following the birth as well as scored in the depression range on the PHQ-9 questionnaire. Particularly, we make use of the "forward selection" approach of stepwise regression—we start with a (modified) simple null model, and then incrementally test the addition of variables spanning various categories based on appropriate model comparison criteria (e.g., deviance/log likelihood in this case). The advantage of such a descriptive model as this is that, it allows us to determine the relative importance of each measure in predicting PPD, although we acknowledge that it would not support higher-order interaction between variables without considerably more data than is available through our dataset. Note that we use a measure called deviance[2] to evaluate goodness of fit, since this model has no direct analog of the proportion of variance explained by the predictors (R^2) in OLS. However we do provide, for each model, a competing analogous index: pseudo R^2 [21]. Because this statistic does not mean what R^2 means in OLS regression (the proportion of variance explained by the predictors), we suggest interpreting this statistic with caution.

Performance of Demographics Model

We begin with a discussion of a modified null model, which we call the demographics model, in order to help us make a stronger claim about the predictive utility of the behavioral measures. The demographics model uses the variables: age, ethnicity, occupation, income, whether or not the childbirth in context of our survey was the first child of the mother, and if it was a premature child. The results of this model are given in Table 4. We notice that the variables occupation, household income, and whether or not it was a mother's first child were significant, with small to moderate beta coefficients. Overall this model explains about 14% of variance in the data (per the value of pseudo R^2).

Measures	β		SE	t-Stat
+ User characteristics (Model 1)				
Intercept	1.303	***	0.084	17.497
status updates	-0.428	**	0.031	-11.86
media uploaded	-0.622	***	0.029	-16.66
income	-0.165	*	0.052	-3.2044
wall posts to friends	-0.468	**	0.031	-9.235
Entropy of activity	0.639	***	0.142	15.48
first child	-0.284	**	0.204	7.3729
occupation	-0.176	*	0.196	-2.2193
Mean power of activity	-0.283	**	0.125	-4.4306
age	0.096	*	0.138	-2.385
Deviance				100.784
Log likelihood				-50.392
pseudo-R^2				0.183
Estimated dispersion parameter				0.87
Error degrees of freedom				142
+ Social capital (Model 2)				
Intercept	0.208	**	0.107	2.4132
likes on status updates	-0.328	*	0.041	-9.8713
likes on uploaded media	-1.405	***	2.306	-0.6124
Media uploaded	-0.639	***	0.032	-10.395
commt. on stat. updates	-1.209	***	0.094	-13.798
comments on media	-0.473	**	0.391	-3.866
wall posts by friends	-0.435	**	0.495	-4.873
status updates	-0.592	**	0.029	-7.953
first child	-0.184	*	0.183	1.3308
#frnds in directed comm.	-1.261	***	1.143	-14.782
Deviance				84.588
Log likelihood				-42.294
pseudo-R^2				0.242
Estimated dispersion parameter				0.81
Error degrees of freedom				126
+ Content Characteristics (Model 3)				
Intercept	0.249	**	0.052	5.1092
media uploaded	-0.635	***	0.149	-9.394
comnt. on stat. updates	-1.038	***	0.583	-14.248
Question-centric status	0.493	**	0.204	2.7366
status updates	-0.441	**	0.352	-10.395
first child	-0.146	*	0.738	1.284
Positive Affect	-0.076	*	0.218	-0.3827
wall posts by friends	-0.483	**	0.193	-6.253
entropy of activity	0.459	**	0.314	8.948
Negative Affect	0.037		0.459	0.0814
Deviance				79.644
Log likelihood				-39.822
pseudo-R^2				0.279
Estimated dispersion parameter				0.79
Error degrees of freedom				123
+ Linguistic style (Model 4)				
Intercept	-0.032	*	0.058	-0.127
1st Person Singular	1.924	***	7.179	0.472
1st Person Plural	-0.392	**	2.224	-0.287
2nd Person Pronoun	-4.824	***	5.262	-0.744
3rd Person Pronoun	-3.209	***	2.933	-0.899
Article	-4.085	***	9.368	-0.405
Certain	-1.771	**	4.303	-0.329
Question-centric status	0.364	**	0.251	1.560
#frnds in directed comm.	2.534	***	6.034	0.748
comnt. on stat. updates	1.783	**	1.686	0.435
Swear words	2.029	**	3.161	0.2067
Deviance				61.32
Log likelihood				-30.668
pseudo-R^2				0.355
Estimated dispersion parameter				0.72
Error degrees of freedom				100

*** $p<0.001$; ** $p<0.01$; * $p<0.05$

Table 5. Performances of different stepwise logistic regression models. We incrementally add variables spanning the four categories: user characteristics, social capital, content characteristics, and linguistic style, to the demographics model. E.g., Model 3 includes variables of content characteristics, along with those of the demographics, user characteristics, and social capital models. Top 10 terms per model according to their β values are shown.

Performance of Stepwise Regression Models

Next we explore the performance of a number of models that are incrementally added to the variables in the demographics model: user characteristics, social capital, content characteristics, and linguistic style. In Table 5, we report the results. On adding the user characteristics variables to the demographics model, it performs slightly better than the demographics model, explaining about 18% of the variance in the data. The deviance[1] of this model is 100.784 compared to 115.218 by the demographics model. Lower number of wall posts made to friends, acting as a proxy of the degree of the mothers' social interactions, was found to be a better predictor of PPD experience. As also found in the previous

[1] In logistic regression analysis, deviance is used instead of sum of squares calculations, like in linear regression [21]. It is a measure of the lack of fit to the data in a logistic regression model—lower numbers are better. Deviance is calculated by comparing a given model with the saturated model – a model with a theoretically perfect fit (the intercept only model in this case).

section, high volatility (entropy) and low periodicity of activity indicated greater likelihood of PPD.

Next we discuss performance of the model that adds the social capital variables to the above model. This model shows considerable improvement in performance over the previous ones, explaining 24% of the variance in the data, as well as showing greater model fit through reduction in deviance (84.58). Reduced number of comments on status updates and uploaded media, as well as fewer likes and less commentary on media posted by friends on wall increased a mother's likelihood of PPD. Aside from this form of direct feedback and acknowledgment from one's social network, we also observe that lower degrees of communication initiated by friends, such as fewer wall posts made by friends was predictive of having PPD.

Our third model that added the content characteristics to the previous model yielded only marginal boost in performance explaining about 27% variance in the data—the deviance reduced to 79.64. We did not observe much effect from the two affect measures, especially negative affect, confirming our findings in the previous section that Facebook affective expression is not characteristically different in the two cohorts.

Our fourth model utilizes the different markers of linguistic style as additional variables in the regression model, explaining more than 35% of the variance in the data, as well as improving on the demographics variable only model (null model) by 153% per the value of pseudo R^2 with the lowest deviance so far: 61.32. Interpersonal pronouns are good predictors as observed in the previous section: higher use of 1st person singular pronouns indicated greater likelihood of PPD, along with lower usage of 2nd, 3rd person pronouns, and articles. Note that this model combines all of the 49 behavioral measures for regression.

	$\chi 2$	*p*-value
Model 1 vs. demographics model	14.434	*3.4e-004*
Model 2 vs. Model 1	16.286	*6.3e-004*
Model 3 vs. Model 2	4.944	7.6e-002
Model 4 vs. Model 3	18.324	*8.2e-006*

Table 6. Model deviance of the different stepwise logistic regression models from Table 5. Significance is judged at α=.001 confidence level. On being assessed upon a chi-square distribution, significant values (in italics) indicate that the addition of variables in a certain model (e.g., Model 2) considerably improved fit to our data compared to the previous model (e.g., Model 1).

Specifically, in this model we note that increased levels of both 1st person singular pronoun use and the frequency of question-centric statuses indicate vulnerability to PPD. One explanation could be that certain mothers might be turning to Facebook to pose questions and inquiries about concerns they might be experiencing themselves, which in turn hints at high self-attentional focus, and a known attribute of depression [43]. Furthermore, lowered usage of 2nd person pronouns in statuses probably indicate less desire for social interaction: hence likely garner fewer comments from friends, thereby leading to decreased access to social capital.

Finally, we briefly discuss the correlations between pairs of predictors in this final model (Model 4). We find that the mean correlation is 0.09 which indicates that there is minimal collinearity in the variables. We also present results of model deviance of the various models (Models 1 to 4), assuming that the difference in deviances across models approximately follows a χ^2 distribution. In Table 6, we report the results of comparison and boost in explanatory power of the incremental addition of variables in the models. The model utilizing all measures (i.e., Model 4, in Table 5) is found to provide considerable (and the most) explanatory power. Compared to the demographics model (null model), it gives $\chi^2(149–49, N=156) = 115.218 – 61.32 = 53.89; p < 10^{-7}$.

Postnatal Time Horizon and Best Model

So far we have investigated predicting new mothers' likelihood of PPD using data from the prenatal period alone. However, clinical literature on PPD marks the typical onset of PPD at about *one month following childbirth* [2,30]. Hence a few weeks of Facebook activity data in the early postnatal phase may contain valuable clues about future PPD experience that can be additionally leveraged to boost prediction performance.

	Prenatal	+10d	+20d	+30d	Postnatal
Dev.	61.32	57.39	52.58	46.61	58.15
LL	-30.668	-26.3	-20.34	-17.24	-28.84
psd. R^2	0.355	0.383	0.439	0.484	0.372
S_{fit}	0.72	0.68	0.62	0.57	0.703
N	156	156	156	156	156
Error df	100	100	100	100	100

Table 7. Performance of models with varying postnatal time horizon. Last column corresponds to a model with month-long postnatal period data only.

Thus we now consider harnessing evidence, incrementally, for an additional period of up to a month following childbirth for each mother (apart from prenatal period). We do not report the details of the models here; however performance is summarized in Table 7. We find that as more information derived from the postnatal period, our model improves in performance monotonically. Best performance is given by the prenatal period + 30 days model, where our predictive power increases considerably, explaining about 48% of variance in the data, and improving over our prenatal only model (Model 4) by 36% and by 246% over the null model, in terms of variance explained. This is also explained in terms of model deviance: $\chi^2(100, N=156) = 61.32 – 46.61 = 14.71; p < 10^{-4}$. We additionally tested a model that uses simply the month-long postnatal period data—yielding a pseudo R^2 of 0.37. This model appears to be marginally better (not statistically significant) compared to the prenatal only model (Model 4) with model deviance: $\chi^2(100, N=156) = 61.32 – 58.15 = 3.17; p < 0.08$.

In essence we conclude that the prenatal period *does* provide PPD-predictive information that together with a brief period of postnatal observations, improves our predictions considerably. This aligns with findings in the clinical literature where typically prepartum depression is known to be a good indicator of PPD, along with post-childbirth anxiety and stress [2].

VALIDATION INTERVIEWS

To corroborate our findings with a qualitative sense of Facebook use by PPD experiencing mothers, we conducted six semi-structured interviews with a random sample drawn from our dataset of 28 PPD experiencing mothers. The interviewee mothers were asked generally about their diagnosis of PPD, timeline of the persistence of the condition, coping strategies they adopted, availability of social and emotional support during the experience, prior mental illness history, and the role of Facebook during the entire experience.

We coded the data into various themes, and overall the mothers indicated numerous instances where our findings were validated. First, in terms of Facebook use, a participant reported how she was not using Facebook during her PPD experience to upload media (photos and videos) related to her newborn daughter—a culture typical of new mothers otherwise:

> *You know, I exclusively stayed away from using Facebook during the [PPD] time; it was only when I really needed to, maybe sometimes to find out about a specific friend. I wasn't even doing the whole "OMG look at my cute baby" pictures thing, like you know, a lot of the new mommies do. I didn't feel as much connection with my baby, actually it was almost like I was angry, that she came in my life, and suddenly everything changed, I was a different person. (Mom B)*

Another mother suffering from PPD indicated a similar experience about how the ill effects of PPD were obstructing her normal lifestyle, and thereby lowering her tendency to be active on Facebook:

> *[PPD] was a terrible time: I would feel exhausted the whole day—I would wake up in the morning after a whole night's sleep, and still not feel fresh and feel like I lack energy to do anything, even stuff about the baby. Posting on Facebook was naturally less during the whole time, until I was on meds and started to feel better. (Mom D)*

Secondly, almost all mothers (5 out of 6) indicated that they refrained from reporting their emotion or their mental state in general during the PPD experience, naturally due to its sensitive nature, and to avoid the risk of facing judgment, scrutiny or stigma—an aspect also revealed by our analyses:

> *When I was first diagnosed, no one except my immediate family knew. Yes I would post less [on Facebook], but when I did, it would never be about how I was feeling, or the bad times I was going through. I actually made sure no one knew about my feelings or thoughts. Doesn't mean I didn't do the occasional posting, but it was hardly anything which would engage my friends, like, I was trying to be less interactive purposefully, and just posting rather objectively. (Mom C)*

Some mothers even reported that the social stigma associated with mental illness was precluding them from expressing their emotionality on Facebook (3 out of 6):

> *It is not like I want privacy in a crazy way or something, but I just thought PPD is such a terrible thing: how could I let my friends know about it? What would they think? Maybe I was lacking something—something was wrong with me? That I was not normal? All those thoughts came to me—and obviously I made a decision: I don't want people who I actually know in real life, to know about it. (Mom E)*

Finally, we found evidence of a variety of negative experiences from mothers with PPD around receiving social and emotional support from Facebook (4 out of 6):

> *I initially thought: oh great! Facebook will be a nice place to connect with my mommy friends and get some help maybe? Turns out I was so wrong. In some sense, several of these mommies I connected with, I mean not all, but they were so inconsiderate and judgmental about me and my condition. I wanted help, not how they thought I was. Clearly I started feeling that maybe I wouldn't be able to get as much help from them as I thought I would. Those Facebook pages around motherhood were slightly better—though kinda same story continued. (Mom C)*

On similar lines, another participant reported on using Facebook as a means of seeking information on issues and concerns at hand; however they felt those postings garnered relatively lesser social support and feedback, especially because of mismatch of their particular PPD context or the maternity experience in general:

> *[I] wasn't really doing the "oh shit I am feeling terrible" thing on Facebook. But I did used to post quite a few questions as and when they popped up, maybe sometimes about what I am going through, or whether I should do X over Y—stuff like that—though I made it a point it was sort of obscure, like I didn't want folks to know that "hey this is what is happening to me". But I felt people were still a little surprised by that—not many people were responding on those, like they would on say, the baby pictures. It was like they weren't really expecting me to ask those questions, or maybe just trying to stay away from the whole thing. (Mom B)*

These interviews, together with our empirical findings, i.e., the Facebook predictors of PPD, indicate three important characteristic aspects of PPD-suffering mothers—(1) their degree of social activity on Facebook is lower, and Facebook posts are often objective in nature or geared toward seeking feedback on concerns and questions; (2) due to the fact that many Facebook contacts are also physical world friends and acquaintances, mothers preferred not to disclose emotionality around their depressive state or feelings relating to helplessness and insecurity; and (3) that they received little social and emotional support (note the *negative* beta weights in the social capital model in Table 5) and were less able to leverage social capital from Facebook. In essence, through the lens of Facebook use, we also observe how social disapproval as well as hardship and stigma related to mental illness weigh on PPD suffering mothers.

IMPLICATIONS

Technology Design

The ability to identify characteristic and predictive factors of PPD presents technology design opportunities for new and expectant mothers. Like other technologies designed for motherhood in general, including systems that enable pregnant women to share baby activity levels with their intimate social groups [18], "smart baby monitors" [19] that help mothers document milestones of their child's development, we envision tools that leverage mothers' activity on online social platforms for the purpose of estimating their risk to PPD. Such tools, including software/ smartphone applications and services, can serve as early warning systems. They can provide pregnant women and new mothers with personalized information on their risk of encountering significant behavioral changes, in the form of PPD, per their Facebook or other social network/media activity.

To be clear, we do not envision these tools as standalone diagnostic tools, but instead as part of a broader awareness, detection, and support system. For instance, this technology could be part of diary-centric systems that capture a self-narrative about postpartum life. Such an application is loosely akin to affective computing systems for depression treatment, which have been shown to be engaging and effective [8]. As part of this mix of this PPD detection and support system, predictions made from Facebook data could assign a personalized "PPD risk score" to mothers. In operation, if inferred likelihoods of forthcoming extreme changes surpass a threshold, mothers could be warned or otherwise engaged in order to reach out for social support or medical attention. In short, we hope analytic approaches based on social media data can play a role in helping PPD suffering women find timely and appropriate support from health care professionals and other mothers.

Ethics and Policy

We envision the systems described above to be designed as privacy preserving applications that are deployed by and for individuals, thereby honoring the sensitive aspect of revealing mental health related information to them. Closely intertwined with this privacy issue is the challenge of interventions. Can we design effective interventions for people, whom we have inferred to be vulnerable to a certain mental illness (PPD in this case), in a way that is private, while raising awareness of this vulnerability to themselves and trusted others (doctors, family, friends)? In extreme situations, when an individual's inferred vulnerability to a mental illness is alarmingly high (e.g., if the individual is suicide-prone), what should be our responsibility as a research community? For instance, should there be other kinds of special interventions where appropriate counseling communities or organizations are engaged?

In short, finding the *right* types of interventions that can actually make a positive impact on people's behavioral state as well as abide by adequate privacy and ethical norms is a research question on its own. We hope this work triggers conversations and involvement with the ethics and clinician community to investigate opportunities and caution in this regard.

Furthermore, there are several other ethical and policy related dimensions to research that utilizes social network activities to make inferences about their mental and behavioral health. Up to what point can such inferences about illness or disability be deemed to be safe for an individual's professional and societal identity? How do we ensure that such measurements do not introduce new means of discrimination or inequality in society given that we now have a mechanism to infer such traditionally stigmatic conditions which are otherwise chosen to be kept private? These and other potential consequences such as revealing nuanced aspects of behavior and mental health conditions to insurance companies or employers make resolution of these ethical questions critical to the successful use of these new data sources.

To summarize, we believe that it is important to bring the possibilities to the fore, so as to leverage the benefits of these methods and ideas to enhance the quality of life for people, as well as to stimulate discussion and awareness of the potential role that policies could play in supporting the identities and practices that individuals suffering mental illness develop in the face of social disadvantage.

CONCLUSION

In this paper, we examined the feasibility of using Facebook as a tool to detect, characterize, and predict postpartum depression in new mothers. First we conducted an online study to gather self-reported diagnoses of PPD, along with scores on a common depression screening instrument (PHQ-9 questionnaire) to evaluate 165 mothers on their PPD experience. Thereafter, based on their activity, interactions, emotional and linguistic expression on Facebook over more than a year, we characterized differences between mothers with PPD and without PPD. Finally, we adopted a mixed methods approach in which first we developed a series of statistical models leveraging these measures, to predict PPD in our dataset, and then corroborated our findings through six semi-structured interviews with our participants.

We found that experiences of PPD were best predicted (best model explained 48% variance in the data) by increased social isolation as manifested in reduced social activity and interaction on Facebook, and decreased access to social capital. Since Facebook friend networks typically include offline social ties spanning friends and coworkers, and due to the stigma associated with mental illness in general, we find that emotional measures were less effective predictors.

Our work is of course not free from limitations. Analyses focused on data from online social platforms may suffer due to challenges of selective self-presentation. In other words, Facebook or Twitter alone may not represent with high fidelity the complex realm and circumstances that define the

PPD experience. Moreover, this work has focused on a somewhat limited set of mothers who are active on Facebook and are concentrated in a particular ethnic community with upper middle class lifestyle. It remains to be seen in future work how we can generalize our findings to a larger population for whom we online data is less available and therefore manifests less of the PPD experience. We also note here that the diagnosis of PPD itself may change Facebook behavior, something we saw some evidence of in the qualitative findings. While we cannot test this broadly here, understanding how medical diagnoses impact social media behavior is an interesting possibility for future work. Further, although we characterized online social capital of the mothers in this paper through their Facebook use, and found that it was a good predictor of PPD, quantifying offline social capital could provide valuable inputs to our findings as well.

Finally, we emphasize here that, like any statistical model, our model is likely to yield false positives. Because we used a descriptive approach in this paper, the exact false positive rate is not known, but we note that the findings of this research should be interpreted with caution, especially in terms of what the medical community could do leveraging them. In particular we recommend against focusing on a single measure such as the amount of Facebook activity, as there could be alternative explanations (e.g., mothers could post less simply because they are now dealing with new time constraints or simply have changed their priorities and are less interested in Facebook). Instead we recommend triangulating with a variety of measures and validating with known diagnostic instruments, like the PHQ9, so as to distinguish between those changing their behavior for benign versus worrisome reasons. Finally, we again stress that this research is intended not as a standalone diagnostic tool, but as a mechanism to complement current diagnoses by giving psychiatrists and caregivers access to a novel and rich non-intrusive data source about people's behavior.

REFERENCES

1. Beck, C.T. (1998). A checklist to identify women at risk for developing postpartum depression. *Journal of Obstetric, Gynecologic, & Neonatal Nursing, 27*, 39-46.
2. Beck, C.T. (2001). Predictors of Postpartum Depression: An Update. *Nursing Research*, 50 (5), 275-285.
3. Burke, M., Kraut, R., & Marlow, C. (2011). Social capital on Facebook: Differentiating uses and users. In *Proc. CHI 2011*. 571-580.
4. De Choudhury, M., Counts, S., & Horvitz, E. (2013). Major Life Changes and Behavioral Markers in Social Media: Case of Childbirth. In *Proc. CSCW 2013*.
5. De Choudhury, M., Counts, S., & Horvitz, E. (2013). Predicting Postpartum Changes in Emotion and Behavior via Social Media. In *Proc. CHI 2013*.
6. De Choudhury, M., Gamon, M., Counts, S., & Horvitz, E. (2013). Predicting Depression via Social Media. In *Proc. ICWSM 2013*.
7. Dennis, C., and Chung-Lee, L. Postpartum Depression Help-Seeking Barriers and Maternal Treatment Preferences: A Qualitative Systematic Review. *Birth*, (2006), 33(4), 323-331.
8. Doherty, G., Coyle, D., & Sharry, J. (2012). Engagement with Online Mental Health Interventions: An Exploratory Clinical Study of a Treatment for Depression. In *Proc. CHI 2012*.
9. Ellison, N. B., Steinfield, C., & Lampe, C. (2011). Connection strategies: Social capital implications of Facebook-enabled communication practices. *New Media & Society*, 13(6), 873-892.
10. Fleming, A. S., Klein, E. and Corter, C. (1992). The Effects of a Social Support Group on Depression, Maternal Attitudes and Behavior in New Mothers. *J. Child Psychology and Psychiatry*, 33: 685–698.
11. Fleming, Alison S.; Ruble, Diane N.; Flett, Gordon L.; Shaul, David L. (1988). Postpartum adjustment in first-time mothers: Relations between mood, maternal attitudes, and mother-infant interactions. *Developmental Psychology*, vol 24(1), pp. 71-81.
12. Fujiwara, T., & Kawachi, I. (2008). A prospective study of individual-level social capital and major depression in the United States. *Journal of Epidemiology and Community Health*, 62(7), 627-633.
13. Gibson, L. & Hanson, V.L. "Digital Motherhood": How Does Technology Support New Mothers? In *Proc. CHI 2013*.
14. Golder, S. A., & Macy, M. W. (2011). Diurnal and Seasonal Mood Vary with Work, Sleep and Daylength Across Diverse Cultures. *Science*. 30 Sep 2011.
15. Gray, R., Ellison, N. B., Vitak, J., & Lampe, C. (2013, February). Who wants to know?: question-asking and answering practices among Facebook users. In *Proc. CSCW 2013*. 1213-1224.
16. Halligan, S.L., Murray, L., Martins, C., and Cooper, P.J. Maternal depression and psychiatric outcomes in adolescent offsprint: A 13-year longitudinal study. *Journal of Affective Disorders* 97 (2007), 145-154.
17. Hamilton, J. D. (1994). Time Series Analysis (Vol. 2). Princeton: Princeton University Press.
18. Hui, M., Ly, C., and Neustaedter, C. MammiBelli: Sharing Baby Activity Levels Between Expectant Mothers and Their Intimate Social Groups. In *Proc. EA CHI 2012*, 1649--1654.
19. Kientz, J. A., Arriaga, R. I., & Abowd, G. D. (2009). Baby Steps : Evaluation Of A System To Support Record- Keeping For Parents Of Young Children. In *Proc. CHI 2009*. 1713–1722.
20. Kroenke K, Spitzer RL, Williams JB (2001). The PHQ-9: validity of a brief depression severity measure. *J Gen Intern Med.* 16(9):606.
21. McCullagh, P., and J. A. Nelder. Generalized Linear Models. New York: Chapman & Hall, 1990.
22. McDaniel, B.T., Coyne, S.M., and Holmes, E.K. (2012) New Mothers and Media Use: Associations between Blogging, Social Networking, and Maternal Well-Being. *Maternal and Child Health Journal*, 16(7), 1509-17.
23. Moreno MA, Parks MR, & Zimmerman FJ, et al. (2009). Display of health risk behaviors on MySpace by

adolescents: Prevalence and associations. *Archives of Pediatrics and Adolescent Medicine*.163(1):35–41.

24. Moreno MA, Jelenchick LA, & Egan KG, et al. (2011). Feeling bad on Facebook: Depression disclosures by college students on a social networking site. *Depressions and Anxiety*. 28(6):447–455.
25. Moreno, M. A., Christakis, D. A., Egan, K. G., Brockman, L. N., & Becker, T. (2011). Associations between displayed alcohol references on Facebook and problem drinking among college students. *Archives of Pediatrics & Adolescent Medicine*. 166(2):157-63.
26. Morris, M. R., Teevan, J., & Panovich, K. (2010). What do people ask their social networks, and why?: a survey study of status message Q&A behavior. In *Proc. CHI 2012*.
27. Newman M, Lauterbach D, Munson SA, Resnick P., Morris, M. (2011). It's not that I don't have problems, I'm just not putting them on Facebook: Challenges and Opportunities in Using Online Social Networks for Health. In *Proc. CSCW 2011*.
28. NielsenWire. Infographic: The Digital Lives of American Moms. http://www.nielsen.com/us/en/newswire/2012/digital-lives-of-american-moms.html May 11, 2012.
29. O'Hara, M. W., Neunaber, D. J., &Zekoski, E. M. (1984). Prospective study of postpartum depression: prevalence, course, and predictive factors. *Journal of abnormal psychology*, 93(2), 158.
30. O'Hara, M.W. (1995). Postpartum Depression: Causes and Consequences. *New York: Springer-Verlag*.
31. Oxman T.E., Rosenberg S.D., & Tucker G.J. (1982). The language of paranoia. *American J. Psychiatry* 139:275–82.
32. Park, M., McDonald D., & Cha, M. (2013). Perception Differences between the Depressed and Non-depressed Users in Twitter. In *Proc. ICWSM 2013*.
33. Paul, M., &Dredze, M. (2011). You are what you tweet: Analyzing Twitter for public health. In *Proc. ICWSM 2011*.
34. Paykel, E. S., &Weissman, M. M. (1973). Social adjustment and depression: a longitudinal study. *Archives of General Psychiatry*, 28(5), 659.
35. Pennebaker, J.W., Mehl, M.R., and Niederhoffer, K.G. (2002). Pychological aspects of natural language use: Our words, ourselves. *Annual Review of Psychology* 54: 547-477.
36. Plantin, Lars, and Kristian Daneback. 2009. "Parenthood, information and support on the internet. A literature review of research on parents and professionals online." *BMC Family Practice* 10(1):34.
37. Prigerson, H. G., Monk, T. H., Reynolds, C. F., Begley, A., Houck, P. R., Bierhals, A. J., & Kupfer, D. J. (1995). Lifestyle regularity and activity level as protective factors against bereavement-related depression in later life. *Depression*, 3(6), 297-302.
38. Rabkin, J. G.; & Struening, E. L. 1976. Life events, stress, and illness. *Science*, 194(4268), 1013-1020.
39. Righetti-Veltema, M., Conne-Perréard, E., Bousquet, A., & Manzano, J. (1998). Risk factors and predictive signs of postpartum depression. Journal of affective disorders, 49(3), 167-180.
40. Robinson, M. S.; & Alloy, L. B. 2003. Negative cognitive styles and stress-reactive rumination interact to predict depression: A prospective study. *Cognitive Therapy and Research*, 27(3), 275-291.
41. Roeloffs, C., Sherbourne, C., Unützer, J., Fink, A., Tang, L., & Wells, K. B. (2003). Stigma and depression among primary care patients. *General hospital psychiatry*, 25(5), 311-315.
42. Rosenquist, J. N., Fowler, J. H., & Christakis, N. A. (2010). Social network determinants of depression. *Molecular psychiatry*, 16(3), 273-281.
43. Rude, S.; Gortner, E.; & Pennebaker, J. 2004. Language use of depressed and depression-vulnerable college students. *Cognition and Emotion*, 1121-1133.
44. Sadilek, A., Kautz, H., & Silenzio, V. (2012). Modeling Spread of Disease from Social Interactions. In *Proc. ICSWM 2011*.
45. Schoenebeck, S.Y. The Secret Life of Online Moms: Anonymity and Disinhibition on YouBeMom.com. In *Proc. ICWSM 2013*.
46. Scott KD, Klaus PH, Klaus MH.(1999). The obstetrical and postpartum benefits of continuous support during childbirth. *J Womens Health Gend Based Med.* vol 8(10):1257-64.
47. Steinfeld, C., Ellison, N., Lampe, C. (2008). Social capital, self-esteem, and use of online social network sites: A longitudinal study. *J. of Applied Developmental Psychology, 29*, 434-445.
48. Tarkka, M.-T. &Paunonen, M. (1996). Social support and its impact on mothers'experiences of childbirth. *Journal of Advanced Nursing*, 23: 70–75.

Books as a Social Technology

Annika Hupfeld
School of Computer Science
University of Nottingham
Nottingham NG8 1BB, UK
psxah4@nottingham.ac.uk

Tom Rodden
School of Computer Science
University of Nottingham
Nottingham NG8 1BB, UK
tar@cs.nott.ac.uk

ABSTRACT
E-books are becoming ubiquitous. Whether or not they will eventually replace books or merely complement them, there is a concern that something important might be lost in moving from print to digital books. While there is a wealth of research into the challenges and opportunities of e-reading, there is little research aiming to understand the broader role of books in everyday life. Rather than speculating on what books *are* in the digital age, in this paper, we wish to ask what books *do*. To do so, we conducted a series of in-depth interviews with ten UK households to understand everyday uses of books. Our findings suggest that books are not merely reading technologies but a resource for everyday social and personal engagements. We discuss re-framing books as social technologies and implications for the design of e-books.

Author Keywords
Books; home; field study; design; e-books.

ACM Classification Keywords
H.5.2 [Information Interfaces and Presentation]: Miscellaneous.

INTRODUCTION
The electronic book has long been looming on the horizon before it finally seems to be becoming an everyday technology. Both its possibility and actuality have sparked a wealth of discourse on how it will change our uses and relationships to print books. Commentators have gone as far as predicting the end of the print book and mourned [2] and celebrated [11] its demise in equal measure. Despite a recent gain in popularity [27], at this stage, e-books seem to be complementing rather than replacing books, the depth and intensity of this discourse suggests that there is a concern that something might be lost in moving from print to digital reading technologies.

CSCW'14, February 15 - 19 2014, Baltimore, MD, USA.
Copyright 2014 ACM 978-1-4503-2540-0/14/02...$15.00.
http://dx.doi.org/10.1145/2531602.2531647

The prominence of the print book suggests that it is clearly cherished and there is a wealth of theoretical, speculative, and journalistic writing underpinning the value of books in the digital age [e.g. 7, 35]. However, there is surprisingly little empirical research investigating how these values might be manifest in everyday practices around books. Empirical studies have predominantly focused on books as they are read, saying little of the broader set of social practices in which they are implicated. Only Rouncefield and Tolmie's study [32] of bedtime reading touch upon some of the broader uses of books and e-books in the home.

The focus of this paper is therefore not on book reading, but on uncovering *the rich life of the book beyond its role as a reading technology*. We are interested in the various ways in which people engage with books in everyday life - socially, materially, and spatially. In other words, rather than asking *what a book is* or is becoming in this digital age, we wish to ask: *what does a book do*? To answer this question we conducted an exploratory field study into people's everyday uses of books. We conducted a series of in-situ interviews as we were given a tour around peoples' homes. By discussing books where they are commonly kept and used, we sought to unpack the social and material practices and relationships people have with books. Based on our findings we argue that books are more than reading technologies, but a part of an ecology of everyday domestic artefacts that are fundamental to people's experience as agents of their own lives.

Our intention here is not to simply argue that books are meaningful and cherished (we know that from other literature), but to document how these values are manifest in everyday practice. As a consequence of books being such a mundane technology, the findings might appear at first blush unremarkable. What makes them remarkable nevertheless is that the rich interactions books afford beyond reading are not reflected in the design of current e-reading technologies. As such, the paper should be understood as a critique of how e-books and their associated ecosystem (of e-readers, applications, etc.) are conceptualised, designed, and marketed today. It further aims to be relevant to designers of e-reading technologies by proposing a set of sensitizing concepts to inspire e-books to become more broadly valued in a way books continue to be today.

In sum, the paper makes the following contributions:

- A detailed account of peoples' socially and materially situated practices and values surrounding books
- An explication of how books are drawn upon as a resource for social and personal engagement beyond reading
- A re-framing of books as a social technology and its implications for the design of e-reading technologies

We start by reviewing the existing literature in the social sciences, human-computer interaction (HCI) and the humanities. After introducing our methodology, we discuss our findings along four themes, including the acquisition and ownership of books, their organization and use, as well as our participants' material and social engagements with books. We conclude with a discussion of our findings, suggesting that, by focusing on the ways in which people draw on books as social, material, temporal and spatial resources, we can start to re-consider existing designs of e-reading technologies, and identify design opportunities.

RELATED WORK

Everyday Things in the Home

There is a range of work that considers artefacts in their entire lifecycle. Since Appadurai's call for a 'methodological fetishism' [1], there has been a range of work taking a biographical approach to studying artefacts as a lens for understanding social relationships [e.g. 14]. Others studied particular practices or stages in the life of artefacts, such as collecting [8], gifting [20], or divesting [12], etc. In addition, there is a wealth of literature aiming to understand the material culture of the home [e.g. 21, 22]. HCI, too, has had a long-standing interest in the home often highlighting the mundane and routine nature of the home [e.g. 5]. A range of work has studied particular domestic practices, such as the archiving [18], reacquisition [28], and modification [36] of everyday artefacts, as well interactions surrounding particular artefacts, including photos [34], tableware [15], and mementos [26]. Interestingly, none of this work has looked at practices surrounding books.

Books in Everyday Life

Work particularly concerned with books can be found in cultural studies, literature, and the history of the book. Miller [23] highlights the tension between culture and commerce in bookselling and consumption and the book's framing as a 'sacred product'. Littau [19] points out the socially and material nature of reading books. Keeping and displaying books at home is also discussed as part of the home decoration literature [e.g. 8, 10]. Pearson [25] presents an analysis of books as historical artefacts in terms of their design, production, and provenance. In addition, much attention has been given to the potential implications of e-reading technologies on the use of print books [e.g. 3, 33]. Much of this work adopts a theoretical rather than an empirical approach to studying books.

There is a set of empirical work from the social sciences looking at the experience of fiction reading, such as romance novel reading [29], ludic reading [24], canonical reading [4], or the phenomenology of novel reading [30]. None of this work moves beyond reading to understand the broader material interactions with books as everyday artefacts. The exception here is Csikszentmihalyi et al's [6] study of domestic objects, arguing books serve 'to embody ideals and to express religious and professional values'. In HCI, Rosner et al [31] considered how we might draw on book restoration practices to design for longevity and authenticity, thereby focusing on production rather than everyday consumption. Rouncefield et al's [32] study on bedtime reading highlights the socially and materially situated nature of reading, but is less concerned with the broader set of practices surrounding books.

METHODOLOGY

We took an in situ approach in form of a 'guided tour' through participants' homes, which allowed the observation of placements of books, as well as the opportunity to discuss core themes, including the acquisition, ownership, use, organization, and sharing of books inside and outside the home. We recruited eleven members (6 female, 5 male) of ten households (Eva and Sid shared the same household) ranging in age between 24 and 72 years old (see Table 1). Household types included: three married without children, three shared, two co-habiting without children, one married with children, and one single household. In addition to reading books, all participants had experience using e-readers (all Kindles), except three (May, Ole, Tia). Among those using e-readers five (Zoe, Ben, Una, Lyn, Eva, Sid) used them frequently at the time of our study. Our sample was chosen for diversity to inform our exploratory study rather than to represent a particular class of use.

P	G	A	H	E
Gus	m	20-29	Co-habiting w/o children	Yes
Zoe	f	40-49	Married with 2 children	Yes
May	f	20-29	Shared	No
Ben	m	20-29	Shared	Yes
Ole	m	20-29	Shared	No
Una	f	30-39	Married w/o children	Yes
Tia	f	50-59	Married w/o children	No
Lyn	f	50-59	Co-habiting w/o children	Yes
Eva	f	70-80	Married w/o children	Yes
Sid	m	70-80	Married w/o children	Yes
Jay	m	50-59	Single	Yes

Table 1. Participant demographics: (P) participant number, **(G)** gender (male/female), **(A)** age range, **(H)** household type and **(E)** experience with e-books.

Our domestic book tours were documented using photographs and audio recording. The audio data was transcribed and coded for motivations and values underlying people's practices. Photographs were used as memory prompts during analysis. Our approach reflects our interest in elaborating the everyday detail of specific instances of book use and the practice surrounding them rather than seek to make broader claims of representation or support or refute particularly theoretical positions.

FINDINGS

In the following we discuss the pathways books took into, through, and out of our participants' households and their lives. Our findings are presented in terms of four themes:

- **Temporal practices** which foregrounds the lifecycle of books as they moved through the home and indexed into the past, present and future of their owners
- **Spatial practices** which highlights the ways in which people placed and organised books inside their homes
- **Material practices** which emphasizes the various ways in which people materially engaged with books for making and re-making
- **Social practices** which presents the ways in which books are embedded in social relationships

The themes are intended to aid legibility but should not be misunderstood as mutually exclusive. In fact, book-related practices are very much interlinked both with each other and with everyday domestic practices more generally. For instance, the acquisition, use, maintenance, and sharing of a cookery book is interlinked with the household's social organization of cooking as an everyday practice. Further, in the presentation of our findings we aim to let participants speak wherever possible. As a result, formal classifications of books (e.g. fiction, art, cookery, etc.) only appear to the extent that they are part of member classifications, such as 'books to read', 'books I got from my grandmother', 'books to return to my colleague', etc. Finally, while reading was not the focus of this study, it inevitably forms part of what makes the ecology of the home and is discussed as such.

Temporal Practices

Here we discuss how *acquiring* used books helped judge a book's potential social value, how *owning* books allowed projecting into one's future, reflecting on the present, and holding on to one's past, how books were *used* for aesthetic and emotional engagement, and *divesting* to extend the life of a book.

Acquiring

Books would be acquired from a range of sources, including bookshops (all), charity shops (May, Tia, Lyn), secondhand bookstores (May, Ole, Tia, Lyn), libraries (Tia, Jay), and online (all, except Jay). Although most participants regularly bought new books, several stated a preference for second-hand books. To Ben and Tia signs of wear indicated that the book had a long reading history, and as a result, was worth reading. Tia: A *book is for not just reading once. If it's pristine it means only one person has read it and it'd not be particularly (good).* Ben: *I actually quite like it when they are a bit worn, cause it shows it has been used as well. I think I'd rather know what loads of people think rather than wasting my time on a bad book.* Buying used books also allowed Ben disconnect his consumption from production: *It means people don't have to produce another book which obviously is a good thing.* Ole felt used books were 'prettier and odder'. Tia bought used books because she took pity with them: *The second hand ones they're like, they can sit on a shelf for ages and no one in particular wants them. I don't know. I just, I'm making them into people now, aren't I.* Buying a used book through a website had allowed Una to get something 'more than just a book': *He wrote me an email and he said 'look after this book'. He gave me an instruction manual on how to use the book. It's not just handing over a book, it's handing over this entire world of knowledge.*

Owning

Participants owned an estimated number of 1 (Jay), 2 (May, Ben, Lyn), 3 (Una), 4 (Gus, Zoe, Ole), 6 (Tia) and 8 (Eva, Sid) bookcases of books (sized approx. 2x1 metres). Several participants relied on their books as a way of projecting into their own futures. Lyn imagined her future as a mother through books: *When we settle down, have our own house and a library or something similar, even if the living room has to be the library, that's fine, my kids are going to have books, actual books, and not just laptops and things, cause they're great.* More specifically, she had particular books in mind she wanted to read to her children: *I want to read that Peter Rabbit book to my kids when we have them. So I keep it up and yeah, I've got a kind of mental list that I remember from childhood that I definitely going to go in the children's library when we have kids.* The persistence of some books led Ole to project even further into the future and to reflect on his existence within the grander scheme of things: *It reminds me that a hundred years is not a long time. You know, these organ manuals they're a hundred and eleven years old and some of these books are older than that, and suddenly it confronts me sort of with the realization that probably nothing I do will last a hundred years, and nothing digital will last a hundred years, because it'll all, it won't even be dust.*

Similarly, books were used to maintain a certain sense of self in the present. Una had an arts background but now worked in a commercial context 'answering emails all day'. Her arts and crafts book collection allowed her to keep alive the 'maker' in herself: *I have this fantasy that I will do things like this myself. It is a fantasy because I'm far too busy but I like to have these kinds of things around me to see what other people have hacked together and just things that people have made, like craft. You see, I don't actually ever look at these books. I just have them. I'm like it's got to be me trying to hold desperately on to what I want to be.*

At the same time, she maintains a collection of work-related books, such as on programming and graphic design, that remind her of who she ought to be: *This is kind of my anxiety wall. Like this is I'd love to be good at that so I buy loads of books in the attempt to make me better.* Her collection of fiction, on the other hand, she dismissed as 'frivolous', possibly because reading for pleasure was at odds with the aspirations she had for herself.

Figure 1. Owning: new and original copy of a book owned since childhood (Ben). **Divesting**: children's books to be given to the charity shop (Zoe).

Books also enabled participants to keep alive certain aspects of their pasts. Books owned since childhood held particular significance in this respect. Gus, for instance, had a 'more sentimental' relationship to one the first books he remembered reading on his own. Ole, too, felt 'massively emotionally connected' to his children's bible. Lyn was clearly moved by a book she had received from a family friend for her 18th birthday: *I don't know if I'd read this. I think it's the only book of poetry I actually got, but I would never get rid of it. Aww, there we go, I've had this my entire life. Aww.* Some participants, who had lost some of their childhood books, even went out to buy new copies in a 'nostalgic' move. 'The nostalgia hit' Lyn when she wanted to share with her fiancé the Winnie the Pooh books she had when she was two years old, but discovered she had given them away 'in a fit of' *I don't know why, I can't even think why I would have given those away.* So she went out to buy new copies. Similarly, 'in a nostalgic turn' Ben bought another Paddington book in addition to one that had been read to him as a child (see Fig. 1). Beyond childhood, books could also be evocative of later stages in life. May's collection of plays let her to hold on to her first studies. They were: *almost like souvenirs of my old degree, because I don't do English anymore, I do Business. They have like a sentimental value.* Una had bought a book as a memento of her honeymoon trip to Paris, and '*instead of like buying an object I bring back a book whenever we go on holidays'*.

Using

Obviously, books were generally kept to be read. Whereas in most cases, unread books were in the minority, in one case as much as an estimated two thirds were unread. In addition to reading books, visible signs of wear enabled participants to engage with a book's social biography. Ben: *The story behind I think. I love how old it is. I love that it belonged to somebody else, that it visibly belonged to somebody else. I don't know why but it's interesting.* To Ole it was these traces of use that gave a book individuality: *It is an old thing which has the humanity in it and it is a human thing, it's one of a kind in a lot of ways and books are to an extent one of a kind, especially ones that have been inscripted.* Tia suggested her preference for books that are 'a bit tatty' was because it made them more like people. Ole assigned books the agency *to trace out their own story. I feel very much that books have a life of their own and quite apart from the story they obviously have inside them they also trace out another story that you only see in tiny clues on or in the books themselves like the inscription on that book.* The connection to one's own or another person's past was also enacted through reading. Eva, for instance, associated reading Jane Eyre with the copy she had read as a teenager. Her grand-daughter, too liked 'thinking that she's reading a book that Daddy read or [her daughter] had read'. To Jay, re-reading a book was an 'emotional thing' which was 'tied into the physical article'.

Books too were cherished for their aesthetics and the sensory engagement they enabled. This engagement was sometimes independent from their use as a reading technology. Tia, for example, thought books should be used to have value 'except for the ones that look pretty'. Una kept a German book not for reading, but because it was 'a beautiful piece of work'. Keeping books as objects was also something she had seen at her grandmother's house who had *a full set of Britannica encyclopaedias behind a glass frame, it was books almost like objects, almost like an ornament would be.* The material of a book was particularly important in this respect as it could produce. Ole appreciated some of his book's 'lovely tactile feel'. Tia said the 'feel' of one of her hand-printed books sometimes made her 'want to stroke it'. Ole suggested it was 'good paper' and 'good binding' that allowed books to 'age gracefully' and so over time *all the crappy ones have fallen to bits and what I've got left are the ones which age gracefully.* Apart from the choice of a particular material, several participants valued the amount of human labour and craftsmanship that had gone into the design and fabrication of a book. Tia was impressed by 'the amount of time and effort' somebody had spent typesetting one of her books. Ole thought someone having handwritten one of his books was 'gorgeous' and 'a complete labour of love'. Una valued the attention to detail a designer had given to 'the differences between colour' used in the book and the 'effort in choosing the layout': *All that is lost in the e- book, and if you go back to like book as object, as beautiful thing, that's all lost.*

Divesting

All participants on occasion divested of books, some rarely (Gus, Zoe, Ole, Una, Jay), others more regularly (May, Ben, Tia, Lyn, Eva, Sid), despite a general reluctance to do so. It was often spatial circumstances, such as running out of storage space (May, Tia), moving house (May, Lyn), de-cluttering (Tia), rearranging furniture (Zoe, Eva), or major life changes, such as children leaving home (Tia) that led participants to divest. Zoe, in particular, was 'being quite ruthless with the books at that point' which was followed by delayed regret: *God, I've been ruthless, I've given so many away. Oh gosh, I've given away a lot more than I thought, basically everything. I didn't realize, aww, I wish I hadn't now, oh no, oh well.* Several participants got rid of books on a more regular basis. May, for instance, had a constant flow of books coming in and out her house because *I buy a lot and give away a lot.*

When it was necessary to divest of books, participants agreed that they had to be passed on rather than thrown away. Una: *I'd never put them in the bin because somebody else might use them.* Before making them more widely available, however, divested books would often be offered to the personal network. Like most participants, Lyn offered her books to friends and family to for 'first dibs' before giving them to the charity shop. Zoe once left a box of books outside their house on the pavement for people to take. Lyn had a habit of buying books from and returning them to a library book sale, so *it just all goes round in circles.* Tia had given books to a local farm that ran a book swapping scheme: *They may end up around the world or something. It just seems a nice [idea], I mean you can be on a train or something and pick a book up, and somebody's left it for you.* Conversely, Ole noted their concerns about passing on certain books: *Depends on how repulsive they are. The thing is if they are unpleasant enough for me to want to get rid of them, generally I cannot think of their being in the world at all is a terribly good thing. And so in extreme cases I have dug very deep holes and buried them.* Selling books was unattractive and only two participants had done so. One of them, Tia, had tried selling some of the books from her mother's house clearing on ebay, but because it was 'quite time consuming' *it'd have to be something where you think there's a good chance of selling and a good chance of getting a reasonable price for it. I mean we sold one or two but not many.*

Books to be divested commonly included books participants had read, but weren't going to read again, books they hadn't enjoyed, or books that had remained unread. Lyn, for instance, thought books she hadn't liked were 'completely disposable'. She had also got rid of books she thought could be easily replaced if she needed to. In the process of divestment, participants inevitably had to make decisions about what to keep and why. Here, apart from books they had liked and intended to re-read, participants kept books that were considered 'beautiful' (e.g. Zoe, Lyn), owned by partners (Lyn), meant to be shared (Lyn), or part of a collection (May). Eva, for instance, 'couldn't throw away' her son's children's books and May kept a book that was part of a collection and had 'special meaning' because her 'mom had it when she was at college'. Tia had a similar attachment to her collection of local history books: *I mean you might not open it for years, you know but it's still there isn't it.* In addition, presents (Zoe, Tia) or passed on books (May) would also commonly kept. Zoe intended to keep a book she had been given by her mother in law: *I would never look at that book, I might flick through it for two minutes, but that type of book would go up on the shelf and then to the charity shop, but because [mother in law] has written in it that will stay for a lot longer than it should, really. And eventually, I might just keep a book like that forever because I wouldn't have the heart to throw it away. I feel it's like a dedication, isn't it.*

Spatial Practices

In this section we discuss how *storing* books maintained stability during times of mobility, how *organizing* books supported their use of them, as well as manage participants' relationships with members of the household, how *placing* books around the house helped settling into a new place, manage the reading process, and issue calls for action, and finally, how *displaying* books in the home facilitated social interaction with visitors.

Storing

While all participants kept the majority of their books on shelves, some would be stored away in lofts (Tia) or outside the home with friends or family (Ben, Ole, Una, Lyn). Tia who kept books in her loft: *We haven't looked at them for years. We'll get them down at some time and go 'oh remember this one?'.* Storing books allowed participants to maintain ownership over their unused books while managing spatial constraints, such as lack shelf space or temporary accommodation. Gus and May who had lacked space while they were students, for instance, had managed using their books by swapping read with unread books. Gus, however, had eventually been 'forced to take their stuff', and May finally 'amalgamated everything in one place'. Storing books could often involve tensions between the keepers and owners of the books (Gus, May, Ben). While Ben's mother, for instance, was 'trying to push them out the door', he was 'trying to evade taking them as long as possible'. He didn't want to take his books until he had a house and children of his own, *because at that point they might have some function or get some use.* Una also had left books she didn't use at her parent's house while she was "*in a state of not living in a home that's going to be mine forever".* May was hoping to keep a former housemate's 'sizeable amount' of books he had left *because he's very generous, and then, four years later, he suddenly remembers, so I'll have to try and find them, but I mean there pretty safe here.*

Organizing

About half of our participants said they organized their books in some way (Gus, May, Ole, Una, Lyn). Actual organization schemes included 'bookshop style' (May), by size (Ben), read and unread (Lyn), topic (Una), recency of use (Zoe, Tia), and ISBN number (Ole). The latter Ole agreed upon with his friend when re-ordering his books and 'settled on something that would allow him to obsess over order and me to enjoy chaos at the same time'. For other, spatial constraints, such as lack of shelf space (Ben) or storage space (Eva), or the way books could be placed on shelves (Gus, Una) would often enforce a certain organization. Those who claimed not to organize their books, said they 'had quite a good memory' (Tia) and 'knew where every book was'. Realizing 'they might now buy a house anytime soon', Una finally re-organized her books after not having been able to find 'anything' 'drove her nuts'. Ole regularly re-ordered books to *generate new ideas. To play with ideas. To go actually this can comment on this, I need to remember this so I put it up here. These are my memory in a lot of ways.*

Organizing books, too, helped mark ownership over space and books, thereby helping participants manage relationships with other household members. While most shared households kept their books separate, it was particularly partners who had recently moved together or were planning to do so that, tensions over the organization of books came to the fore. Una described their negotiation process: *Oh god, it was lots of fighting over it, like shouting at each other. Not only books but with the like the leatherwork stuff. I like very carefully placed them in places and look after them because they're precious items, whereas he is like, they're very rarely used, so put them in behind other things. I was like 'how could you move my things?'* Lyn on the other hand had had a few years to 'amalgamate all our stuff' and for her partner 'to get annoyed with all my hoarding'. May who was planning to move in with her boyfriend anticipated tensions over the organization of their book collections: *I don't want to merge them, but I don't want them to be organized separately either, cause that makes me feel strange. He has his own system as well. He has them in like height order. I hate that.*

Placing

Apart from bookshelves, books would be most commonly placed on bedside tables (all), kitchen counters (cookery books) (9 out of 11), and floors (Zoe, Ole, Una, Tia), as well as on coffee and side tables (May, Una, Tia, Lyn, Eva, Sid), pianos (Ole), mantelpieces (Eva, Sid) stairs (Zoe), and in boxes and baskets (Zoe, Tia). Placing books supported people in settling into a place after moving house. For several participants to 'get your books out and you can put them all out again', was the first thing they did when moving into a new home (Gus, May, Ben) because *they're just something that makes me me. I don't feel like I've moved into somewhere until my books are there.* (May) and Lyn likes having her books around her because it *makes me feel like it's my house, like it's my home, like this is my place, this is my stuff. That's the other thing I don't like about getting rid of things, because I like kind of places to show off the personality and things like that, and books is kind of, 'So what's your hobby? – Reading', so books is pretty much the only hobby I admit to. I love them, and if they're out, I look at them and think 'oh yeah, I fancy reading that'. I like having them about. It makes me feel comfortable.* Gaining a sense of comfort and security through the placement of books is also something Una had experienced. Una had 'given in to there being' an assortment of mediation guides on her bedside table 'almost as a security rather than necessity' in order 'to calm her mind and to bring herself away from work to sleep.'

Figure 2. Organization: making use of the smalls to accommodate books (Eva and Sid). **Placing:** book placed on the steps for any household member to take upstairs (Zoe). **Display:** series of books with two different cover styles (Gus). **Hiding:** disliked books on a shelf behind the door (May).

The placement of books also helped participants manage their reading process. Both unread and currently read books would be placed in rooms where they were intended to be read (Ben), in prominent places, such as bedside tables or coffee tables, 'to encourage me to read it' (May) because on shelves they 'tend to lose them' (Tia). In Una's case, when books remained unread, they would make 'a progression away from the bedroom', via her study, onto her shelf in the living room. Gus kept all his unread books on the shelf, but maintained 'a catalogue of it all on librarything[.com]', where he also kept track of his unread books. On the bedside table, Zoe kept a pile of books on her bedside table that reflected her current priorities in reading, with the Kindle on top of the pile and her book underneath, as she was 'avoiding that one'. Tia typically read several books concurrently, which she left in her 'little nests' around the house, including her bedroom, living room and guest room, so she could 'sit and pick up a book when she wanted to'. Zoe, similarly, had some books, including her laptop and notes, around the kitchen area where she worked. Placing books in prominent places not only helped participants to start books but also to finish them. To several participants finishing a book was a 'matter of pride' (Ben) and even if they didn't like a book they 'would push themselves to the end of it' (Zoe). Jay, who had enjoyed, but recently abandoned Moby Dick on the Kindle, was certain he would have finished it had it been a book *[because] it'll be on here [table], it is viewable, calling to me, whereas here [Kindle] it's not. This is not a book. It's a device and somewhere inside there are books but it's less demanding, I'm not sort of seeing the book and thinking, ah God, I've only read (), and there's the rest of it.*

Books would also be placed as a call for household members to act on. May kept borrowed books separate from her own as otherwise she 'might not remember it's there'. Eva kept a pile of books 'to go back to people, if we they remembered to give them back'. Tia had a book 'sticking out' of her shelf to remind her to give it to one of her grandchildren 'when they came round'. Zoe placed books to be put away*: When the house gets too messy we'll have a clean up, and [husband] would say 'oh, they're all your books here, I'll just put them there on the steps to do something with them, and then they'll end up in the bookcase in the office.*

Displaying

With the exception of two, all participants kept their books visible on shelves in the living room or worktops in the kitchen, as well as in dining rooms (Zoe, Tia, Lyn, Eva, Sid) and bedrooms (Gus, May, Eva, Sid, Jay). Displaying books helped participants engage with other members of the household and visitors as *some people come into your house and always look at your books* (Sid). Eva whose friend had a table with her latest books out thought it was 'interesting to see what she's bought, she's reading'. Lyn felt there was 'no point in having stuff if you're not going to interact with it, be around it, immersed in it' and would like visitors to 'look through the interesting things on her shelves'. Tia remembered her children's school friends being surprised by their 'library' from which they ended up borrowing books. Before her husband acquired a Kindle, they also used to have 'books on the coffee table' *and I was like, 'ooh what's he reading?', and you can perhaps read a chapter of it, and go 'ooh no, it's perhaps not my kind of thing. With the Kindle [] you can't have that summary of what somebody is reading at all.*

The display of books as collections could also be important to some participants. May 'felt stupid' that she liked keeping her collection of poetry books together 'to the point where the same covers are together'. Gus thought it was 'irritating' that halfway through a long running series of books the cover design had changed and the originals become unavailable, so that he considered 're-buying the three books that are not in that style'. He had already re-bought the complete adult edition of Harry Potter because he preferred the cover design to that of the children's edition.

Books that were kept less visible would occasionally be forgotten about. For example, Gus forgot to show us his cookery books as they had been 'tucked behind the door'. Una had her knitting books 'hidden in all these nuts and crooks' from her husband because 'he hates stuff out'. She was dreaming about 'an empty room with the books and an easy chair' so her husband 'could close the door and wouldn't have to see it'. In the meantime e-books allowed her to 'hide her hoarding in the digital'. May kept her 'work stuff', such as textbooks for teach, 'hidden behind her door where you don't have to look at it' and which she 'hadn't put much love and care into' because she found it 'quite boring'. At the same time, placing books in more hidden places could help to ensure that precious books could be kept safe from visitors. Whereas May's 'the transient stuff that just comes and goes' was kept in the living room she had 'some of her old and torn Penguins' in her bedroom to keep them safe from people 'getting a bit drunk and rummaging through them'. Similarly, Tia kept books she wanted to keep in her study and ones she'd get rid of in the living room.

Material Practices

We discuss how *creating* books was a way of making information worth reading and learning new skills, how *modifying*, *replicating*, and *appropriating* books helped create a new life for abandoned books, how *augmenting* changed a book's perceived value, and how *preserving* books could help defy the passing of time.

Creating

Two participants had made books themselves. Eva 'didn't like looking at photos on the computer screen' and so intended to make photo books for their holiday pictures as that way she was 'more likely to look at them', but 'hadn't got round to it. Una was inspired by a handmade book she owned to make one herself, but said it was a 'fantasy' because she was 'far too busy'. In her past, however, she had made sketchbooks and a portfolio. Tia had put together two books in her spare time which were 'not her own ideas' but she was clearly pleased with: *And that's quite nice, tidying it all up and making it available. It was interesting. I had a look at it, and it had my name on it, in [bookstore], yes I did that one, and it's got an ISBN number and everything, so it's a proper book with my name in it.*

Modifying, Replicating, and Appropriating

Three participants had engaged in the modification of books by turning old covers into prints and cards, replication through digitization and copying, or their appropriation as tools. May had modified old books by turning their covers into prints and cards: *Also sometimes I really like book covers. I like the way they look that is why I don't really like e-books. The bookshop I worked in was a [charity] bookshop. Sometimes you'd get beautiful old books in, but you couldn't sell them because they were coming apart, so I'd rescue the covers that I've framed or made into cards.* Ole had produced prints of illustrations out of a book which he 'had to do himself because he couldn't find anywhere that would do a legal one'. Una had photographed and put together as a PDF a library copy of an out of print book which 'you pay a hundred pounds for' so she could 'go back to it if she needed to' but thought she 'never will'. She had also scanned in a set of knitting patterns she had bought to use on her phone when she was 'knitting on the move'. Jay had appropriated a book his mother had given him but not read, to support his webcam whose clip was too small to attach to his monitor. So whenever he was speaking to his son via Skype, his 'the book comes out on the front and it's just the right height'.

Figure 3. Appropriating book used as webcam stand (Jay). **Augmenting:** Annotated poetry book with translations of the text (Ole). **Modifying:** book covers removed from old books (May). **Preserving:** keeping an exhibition catalogue safe in a plastic bag (Una).

Augmenting

Only four of our participants augmented books with annotations or inscriptions (Zoe, May, Ben, Lyn), but all owned or used books that had been augmented. The latter were interpreted in a range of ways between increasing and diminishing the value of a book. May had been 'really cheeky' and annotated a copy from the library which she then used to 'copy notes from the book into her computer' in the process of which the material 'goes in a little bit more and makes some sense'. She also thought other people's annotations in books could be 'useful' because it showed 'what other people thought are the important bits'. To Ole, an annotated poetry book helped him 'see how other people also struggled with translating things that I've struggled with'. At the same time, he was reluctant to annotate books himself because he 'didn't like writing in books'. Ben strongly objected to annotating books and w*hen I see it, I generally think what horrible person, why have you been doing that to this book, but I don't know why it's any better than writing your name in it, that's somehow adds character to it.* He tried working with an annotated copy of a library book that was fundamental to his work, but decided that the 'highlighting ruined the book' and bought his own copy. He conceded it 'might be beneficial to see what they were', he 'couldn't have the thoughts of somebody else around the text' as he 'didn't know who they were'. Rather than annotating a book he would put post-it notes in it 'if you have to do it'. Tia, too, 'didn't like' writing in books and felt other people shouldn't. She found it particularly 'annoying' when somebody had 'corrected a type mistake' because to her it was part of the book, with an error in it'. An annotation she discovered in a cookery book she thought 'made it more personal' on the other hand.

Books containing inscriptions were often presents. Lyn would keep these because 'it 'showed more thoughtfulness'. To May, the ability to inscribe books was key to their suitability as presents because *books are more than just the words inside them, they're also the physical thing, people can put things inside them, write things inside them and I don't really get that- how can you give something in a PDF? It's weird to me.* Apart from presents, several participants owned second-hand books that had inscriptions in them. May had a collection of plays with someone's dedication reading '*To Louise: you are the light of my life, we're going to be married', and I'm like well this book ended up in a charity shop so obviously she didn't think that much of you otherwise she would have kept this.* Ole had found 'the saddest inscriptions in poetry books' that 'made him wonder', such as 'confessions of undying love': *you get these little hints of sadness and of things lost and it's sort of reinforced by the fact that you're never going to know what would have happened, or might have happened.* Still he wouldn't want to know the actual story because 'what he constructed in his head is always going to be more important' and 'because 'things being forgotten was important': *If the story has died then it's gone and it's not my place to want to resurrect it, but it's the footprint of a story that's past, and I feel sadness that this story has ended because stories almost always are alive to me.*

A few participants had books that had been augmented with notes or prints. Una left shopping lists for her husband in his cookery book. *I write this because he's so lazy, he'd rather go and have toast, so I put the page down and I tell him that the ingredients are there. And these are the things that we make regularly.* Similarly, Zoe had found printouts in her baking book: These are, yeah so, this is my eldest daughter, she used this book, but what she's done is used a recipe that she's downloaded off the internet I think.

Preserving

Three participants applied several strategies to preserve cherished books from aging and decay, such as wrapping, replacing, and re-binding books. 'To protect the book' Una kept an exhibition catalogue 'in plastic wrapping', something 'that she had picked up from her mother'. She was also 'compelled to keep' her sewing machine booklet 'precious inside a plastic thing' which 'annoyed her because she 'had to look after it' when 'she should really be throwing it out' whereas in digital form she wouldn't have to because then 'she didn't really have it'. She had also made a pouch for her Kindle but felt it 'was only a prototype because it's too thin, it's tearing really'. Rather than wrapping his books, Gus kept 'two copies of the 'Lord of the Rings'. He bought a new copy a few years ago to replace the 'original copy that he had when he was about 10' and was 'falling apart' and 'becoming all creased and tattered'. Doing so allowed him not to 'risk that one any further', but still 'be able to read it and take it to places'. A few books had been re-bound for preservation. Una's grandfather 'used to go to secondhand bookshops and buy books he felt were of value' or 'he felt the story was a proper story, a story of worth' and 'he would bring them home and re-bind them' and gave to her because 'they were beautiful books'. Tia had received a book from her father of old London maps he had rebound which was 'quite pricey', but at the same time some books were 'worth having them rebound'.

Social Practices

In this section we show how *discussing and recommending* books was used for social engagement inside and outside the home, how *sharing* books was a way of sharing reading experiences and keeping books in use, how *gifting* and *passing on* books helped maintain present and past social relationships.

Discussing and Recommending

All participants engaged in discussing and recommending books, either informally and/or as part of a reading group (May, Una, Jay). Books allowed participants to create 'a talking point'. Before her husband acquired an e-reader, Tia said she 'knew what he was reading' and could recommend books to him, with the Kindle she didn't know, because 'there's no cover on it' and 'you can't read the back'. Since she had 'made it a point to him' that she found his use of the Kindle 'isolating' he agreed 'to make an effort' to let her know what he was reading on the Kindle. *But it's not sharing. Whereas a book is sharing. You know what somebody would like and you can hand it over whereas with an e-reader I believe you can share them between Kindles but I haven't got one. It's me being awkward, I just don't want the Kindle, you know.* To Eva sharing books was 'a way of communicating' with her daughter and sister.

Sharing

Sharing books was a common practice for all participants, particularly among partners and family (all but one), but also friends (all but three) and colleagues (Ben, Una) Nevertheless, several participants were reluctant to lend their books to others. A major concern was the condition in which the book might be returned. Gus 'tended to look after his books' and so 'hesitated' to lend them as 'people tended to take slightly less better care of them than he did'. He found 'spines came back a lot more creased' and 'pages might be more dog-eared'. He could *tell which of the Sci-fi my dad has read, because if he's read it the spine is more cracked whereas the ones that only I've read tend to have a more pristine ((laugh)) spine.* Una, too, felt that *most of the time people don't have that sense of importance with books that I have. They don't put them in plastic bags to keep them safe for example.* Lyn on the other hand would 'be a bit more careful' with borrowed books whereas with her own she didn't mind if she 'battered' them, because *it means it's been read, that's good.* Also, whereas her books 'could sit on the shelf for years' she would give priority to borrowed books. Una felt 'really, really bad' she had damaged a book she had borrowed from a friend. She also *bought my own one, but rather cheeky, I didn't give him the new one, cause I wanted the nice one for myself. So there's something about owning and keeping them safe for myself.*

Not getting lent books back was an additional concern. Zoe recommended but didn't like sharing books because it were typically ones she had 'an attachment to' and didn't want to lose them. Eva, on the other hand, wouldn't mind not getting back books like 'current novels, that weren't really important' but thought it was 'polite' to give them back. Ben considered sharing 'lending in inverted commas', and losing book part of a give and take: *I'm not particular bothered. I'd rather give them away because likewise they would give me them. I don't mind as long as they are (being read). In fact, I'd encourage that rather than building up an anti-library (of unused books).* Part of the problem of losing books was failing to remember whom books had been lent to. Una's 'anxiety from sharing books' was that 'her memory was really bad' and while she didn't 'blame them for not remembering' she didn't want to lose books. As a result, she 'would never give away a book without her name in it'. While Gus replaced lost books, Ben 'wasn't too bothered', but kept track of any read books on goodreads.com so he could *look back and try to remember the books and see what I thought about it and see whether it's worth reading again.* Conversely, May had 'appropriated' a book she had given her boyfriend, and some of Gus's father's books had 'sort of migrated onto his bookcase and never really left again'.

Gifting

Books were commonly given and received as presents by all participants, typically for Christmases and birthdays. Apart from newly bought books, several participants would give used books. May gave secondhand books 'all the time' either for birthdays and Christmas or 'just for random presents' *because I do like shopping in second hand shops and if I see something that so-and-so would love and especially when I've seen books that I read and really loved and want to share them with then I'll just buy them and give them. They're not worth much but I think they're quite nice, thoughtful presents.* Ole added: *Normally doing that is either financially inadmissible or inadvisable or it makes people feel awkward because if you buy (brand new) things people get all awkward about it but if it's a secondhand book it's not very much money so don't get awkward and everyone wins really.* Some participants gave away their own books. Lyn: *I love giving books. I do buy books for people, but mine that I give away are just anytime if anyone takes an interest in it and I don't particularly want that I'll just, 'yeah, take it'.* Ben had already bought a favourite book twice and given it away twice: *I bought it, read it, thought it was fantastic and gave it away and then thought aww I'd really like to read that again so bought it again.* To Ole, on the other hand, giving away books that 'had a history with him' was 'a very important thing for him to do' and 'a fairly special thing'.

Receiving book presents were often perceived as affirming or disconfirming the receiver's sense of self and intimacy of the relationship. May, for instance, felt it was 'reaffirming' when she got books she was interested in by people who knew her well. Ben particularly like *when some people buy me a book I would have never thought I would have read.* Equally, book presents could contradict a person's sense of self. Una: *My friend bought me that and it's something I would never buy cause she has me down as the arty person, but it's there because my friend gave it to me. It's bloody enormous as well.* May would re-gift any disliked books: *I have a friend in [city] who buys me books that I rarely like and I tend to like re-gift them to other people. ((laughs)).* Most of the time, however, presents would be understood as a sign of someone caring. Una, for instance, had received a cookery book from her brother and his wife who had 'thought about the fact' that she and her husband were too busy to 'feed themselves properly: *they're trying to look after us.* May had received a collection of poems by her boyfriend who had *copied out loads of the poems for me and a card that he gave me with it, so it means a lot to me that he bought me that and he doesn't really read poetry, so it's nice that he's gone to the effort.*

Passing On

Many participants owned books that had been informally passed on to them (May, Ben, Ole, Una, Tia, Eva, Jay) and several had the intention of passing on books in the future (May, Ole, Tia). Passing on and passed on books were often cherished for the connection with distant or lost family members they enabled. Tia wanted to pass on her collection of local history books to one of her sons: *I don't know (what to do with them), I mean some of them cost me quite a bit of money and stuff, I mean if they sold them, fair enough, but I wouldn't just get rid of them. I would find that very difficult when it's something that I've been collecting for a long time.* She also wanted to pass on a book of old London maps that had been given to her father by a neighbour: *So I've got it now, it's something worth handing down to the next generation, especially London doesn't look like that anymore.* May wanted to pass on her collection of poetry books and a collection of children's books she had 'all read like so many times' that it had become 'a battered thing', 'all faded from the sun': *It's not worth any money, you can get them really cheap, but I'll just never get rid of it, I love it, I want to give it to my kids.* Ole wanted to pass on a book that had been passed on to him: *Somehow because it's prophecy and because it's very much a message that was meant to be passed on I like the idea of passing the book on as well. And that is one I certainly hope goes to someone else after I've dropped my perch.* His collection of books on the other he felt was too personal to be passed on: *Because these are my memory and as a collection they are intensely subjective. Anybody who took them over as a collection would either have to think very much like me which is very unlikely or they'd be faking it. But at some point it will cease to be my problem and then each of them will have to (trace out) its own story again.*

Figure 4. Bequeathing: re-bound book with old maps of London to be passed on to the next generation (Tia). **Inheriting:** one of several boxes of books taken on from a parent's houseclearing (Tia).

Books were used in a range of ways to pass on particular values, practices or knowledge. Una had been given books by her grandparents and parents that would be left on her bedside table 'in the hope that I would pick up reading because I'm dyslexic'. Ole had received 'businessy' books by a former employer to 'do him proud and actually start making some money'. Una lent books to her colleagues at work *because they're driving me mad because they're not doing it right. Yeah, I need people to think the way I think in order to do my job so I'm trying to give them the same knowledge that I have.* Zoe tried to pass on her own appreciation for books by sharing books with her rather than her Kindle: *I don't want her to use the Kindle. I want her to develop to love the books. It's not really fair. I say I can read the Kindle because I've already read physical books, it's like I've earned the privilege, and I don't want her to go straight to the Kindle. It's weird, I love the fact that she's got her little book at the side of the bed, so she can just touch and feel them.* Giving books rather than 'fluffy toys' to her friend's children was a way for Una to pass on her values through books *because it feels like for my family it's this big thing that things must have use and merit and be useful and these kinds of things.*

WHAT BOOKS DO

Our findings demonstrate the ways in which books are much more than reading devices. They also allow people to engage with their personal and social pasts, presents, and futures. We have seen how people act and draw on books socially, materially, spatially and temporally, and how books in turn are being transformed in the process. In the following we discuss what books *do* for the people in terms of experiencing the self and connecting with others.

Making the Self

Books are drawn on to establish and reflect on a person's social self[1] through:

- Acquiring books in physical places helped people evoke associated experiences (e.g. their honeymoon)
- Owning, collecting, and displaying books allowed people to project forward into their future, maintain a certain sense of self in the present, and re-create their past
- Storing books outside the home enabled people holding on to their past and possible futures while managing the present
- Placing of books around the home helped people manage their reading and sharing activities, as well as to comfort and make a home for themselves
- Making and re-making books served to prolong the life of the book and the experiences associated with it, both for oneself and others

Connecting with People

Books are drawn on to connect with close and distant others through:

- Divesting rather than disposing of books allowed them to be able to be re-valued by others
- Placing books around the home served to manage and maintain relationships among household members
- Displaying books around the home allowed people to present oneself to others and create 'talking points'
- Augmenting and sharing books allowed people to encounter and connect with past and future owners through the creation and interpretation of traces of use and ownership (e.g. wear, inscriptions, etc.)
- Sharing and gifting books helped people establish and maintain close and distant relationships through sharing experiences and values associated with particular books; giving used books made it possible for people to give without producing an obligation to reciprocate
- Passing on books over generations enabled people to connect with distant and deceased family members and pass on the values, knowledge and experiences associated with particular books

BOOKS AS RESOURCE FOR DESIGN

No, I was thinking about ahem, the Kindle versus the paper books and I love having my paper books around me, I really do. I love having my bookcases, and I'd love having a library like I said before, but the Kindle is so convenient and it stops my eyes from hurting and things like that, and there is so much other stuff on it that's free which is nice, so it's really really good but I don't think I'd ever get rid of all my books, I love my books. (Lyn)

What was striking about our findings, and neatly summarized in the above quote, is how our participants' relationship with books seemed intensely emotional. This stands in contrast to people's relationship with e-books, which prior research has shown [16] seems much more functionalist in nature, centering on features like mobility, instantaneity, or the availability of free and low cost content. In other words, e-readers are primarily *valued as reading technologies*. They are designed for individual reading, thereby not only ignoring the socially embedded nature of *reading*, but also their role as a *social technology* that is enacted through various everyday practices, such as placing, sharing, and passing on books.

There is a range of ways in which e-reading could become more social. These might include the move from closed to open formats, from personal to social media, and from business models based on ownership to subscription services [16]. It needs to be emphasized, however, that the shortcomings of current e-reading technologies in this respect are not a result of their being digital. In fact, e-reading technologies are unsocial *by design*. Thus, in addition to improving on e-readers, we might want to consider of ways in which e-reading technologies could be *re-thought as a social technology*. As has been demonstrated in the field of electronic literature [13], e-reading technologies do not have to take the book as their precedent for design. Instead, electronic literature attempts to make use of the unique affordances offered by digital

[1] The self here is very much understood as a social self as discussed in [17] as 'an individual's reflexive sense of her or his own particular identity, constituted *vis-a-vis* others in terms of similarity and difference without which she or he wouldn't know who they are and hence wouldn't be able to act'.

technologies as 'networked and programmable media'. By focusing our attention on what books *do* rather than what books *are* then, we can start designing e-reading technologies that are meaningful to people's lives beyond supporting activities of reading. For instance, how can we design e-reading technologies that:

- Can reflect personal histories of use and ownership to be passed on to others?
- Make uses of and relationships to e-books visible to facilitate social relationships and personal reflection?
- Support the management of social relationships among members of a household?
- Support processes of homemaking and settling in through connecting e-books with places of use and ownership?

We would also like to suggest that our findings have relevance beyond the design of e-reading technologies. Despite e-books being marketed as electronic books, books have an equal if not stronger affinity to other everyday domestic artefacts. What we mean by this is that books exist as part of the material ecosystem the home, often operating in similar ways to other everyday domestic artefacts. It is therefore not by accident that our research is very much in conversation with research in material culture studies in that some of the social and material practices around books are not unlike those observed around other everyday artefacts [e.g. see 22]. Thus, our findings can also be read as a more general roadmap to designing technologies that are meaningful to people's everyday lives.

CONCLUSION

In this paper we presented findings from a field study into people's everyday uses of books. Based on our observations we argued for a re-framing of books, not as reading technologies, but as social technologies. Moreover, we suggested ways in which this framing could be used as a resource for design. Assuming the worst fears and hopes of e-book critics came true, and what we currently observe is just an intermediary step on the way to a future without printed books, our findings not only addressed the questions whether printed books mattered, but why they mattered to those using them. While our participants' relationships to books could be dismissed as mere bibliomania, we suggested people's engagements with books could be interpreted as a more general strategy for personal and social engagements through everyday artefacts.

ACKNOWLEDGMENTS

Thank you to Andy Crabtree for his comments and support. This work is supported by the Horizon Doctoral Training Centre at the University of Nottingham (RCUK Grant No. EP/G037574/1) and by the RCUK's Horizon Digital Economy Research Institute (RCUK Grant No. EP/G065802/1).

REFERENCES

1. Appadurai, A. 'Introduction: Commodities and the Politics of Value'. In Appadurai, A. (ed) *The Social Life of Things: Commodities in Cultural Perspective.* Cambridge University Press, 1986.
2. Birkerts, S. *The Gutenberg Elegies*. Faber and Faber, 2006.
3. Bolter, J.D.: *Writing Space*. Routledge, 2001
4. Boyarin, J. *The Ethnography of Reading*. University of California Press, 1993.
5. Crabtree, A. and Rodden, T. 'Domestic Routines and Design for the Home'. In *CSCW*, 13, 2, 191–220, 2004, Springer (2004).
6. Csikszentmihalyi, M.: *The Meaning of Things: Domestic Symbols and the Self.* Cambridge University Press, 1981.
7. Darnton, R. *The Case for Books*. PublicAffairs, 2010.
8. Dupuich, D. and Beaufre, R. *Living with Books*. Thames and Hudson, 2010.
9. Elsner, J. and Cardinal, R. *The Cultures of Collecting*. Reaktion Books, 1994.
10. Geddes-Brown, L. *Books Do Furnish a Room*. Merrell Publishers, 2009.
11. Gomez, J. *Print is Dead: Books in our Digital Age*. Palgrave Macmillan, 2007.
12. Gregson, N. and Crewe, L. *Second-Hand Cultures*. Berg, 2003.
13. Hayles, K. *Electronic Literature: New Horizons for the Literary*. University of Notre Dame Press, 2008.
14. Hopkins, J.: *Autobiographical Objects: How Things Tell the Stories of People's Lives*. Routledge, 1998.
15. Hupfeld, A., Rodden, T. 'Laying the table for HCI: Uncovering Ecologies of Domestic Food Consumption'. In *Proc. CHI 2012*, ACM Press (2012), 119-128.
16. Hupfeld, A., Sellen, A., O'Hara, K., Rodden, T. 'Leisure-based Reading and the Place of E-books in Everyday Life'. In *Interact 2013*, LNCS, Vol. 8118, Springer (2013), 1-18.
17. Jenkins, R. *Social Identity*. Routledge, 2008 (3rd ed).
18. Kirk, D. and Sellen, A.: 'On Human Remains: Values and Practice in the Home Archiving of Cherished Objects'. *ACM Transactions on Computer-Human Interaction*, 17, 3, 10, 2010, ACM Press (2010).
19. Littau, K. *Theories of Reading*. Polity, 2006.
20. Mauss: *The Gift*. Routledge, 2002 [1954].
21. Miller, D. (ed) *Home Possessions*. Berg, 2001.
22. Miller, D. *The Comfort of Things*. Polity, 2008.

23. Miller, L. *Reluctant Capitalists: Bookselling and the Culture of Consumption*. The University of Chicago Press, 2007.

24. Nell, V. *Lost in a Book: The Psychology of Reading for Pleasure*. Yale University Press, 1990.

25. Pearson, D. *Books as History: The Importance of Books beyond their Texts*. The British Library Publishing Division, 2012.

26. Petrelli, D., Whittaker, S., Brockmeier, J. 'AutoTopography: What Can Physical Mementos Tell us about Digital Memories?' In *Proc. CHI 2008*, ACM Press (2008), 53-62.

27. Pew Internet Center, 2012. http://libraries.pewinternet.org/subjects/e-readers/

28. Pierce, J., Paulos, E. Second-Hand Interactions: Investigating Reacquisition and Dispossession Practices around Domestic Objects. In *Proc. CHI 2011*, ACM Press (2011), 2385-2394.

29. Radway, J. *Reading the Romance: Women, Patriarchy, and Popular Literature*. The University of North Carolina Press, 1991.

30. Rogers, M. *Novels, Novelists, and Readers: Toward a Phenomenological Sociology of Literature*. State University of New York Press, 1991.

31. Rosner, D., Taylor, A. 'Antiquarian Answers: Book Restoration as a Resource for Design'. In *Proc. CHI 2011*, ACM Press (2011), 2665-2668.

32. Rouncefield, M. and Tolmie, P. 'Digtial Words: Reading and the 21st Century Home'. In Harper, R. (ed) *The Connected Home: The Future of Domestic Life*. Springer, 2011.

33. Striphas, T. *The Late Age of Print: Everyday Book Culture from Consumerism to Control*. Columbia University Press, 2011.

34. Swan, L, Taylor, A. 'Photo Displays in the Home'. In *Proc. DIS* 2008, ACM Press (2008), 261-270.

35. Ulin, D. *The Lost Art of Reading: Why Books Matter in a Distracted Time*. Sasquatch Books, 2010.

36. Wakkary, R. and Maestri, L. 'Aspects of Everyday Design: Resourcefulness, Adaptation, and Emergence'. In *Int. Journal of Human-Computer Interaction*, 24, 4, 1-14, 2008, Taylor & Francis (2008).

Framing the Conversation: The Role of Facebook Conversations in Shopping for Eyeglasses

Karim Said, Michele A. Williams, Amy Hurst, Shaun K. Kane
UMBC
1000 Hilltop Circle
Baltimore, MD 21250
{ksaid1, mawilliams, amyhurst, skane}@umbc.edu

ABSTRACT
Individuals often leverage their social network to receive feedback from their peers about various decisions. Capitalizing on this trend, fashion retailers, such as the eyeglass frame retailer Warby Parker, have created "home try-on" programs and encourage customers to solicit feedback from their friends before making a purchasing decision. In this paper, we investigate Warby Parker's Facebook page and explore the ways customers formulate questions and conversations as they shop for new eyeglass frames. Our research presents insights derived from a dataset of over 10,000 Facebook posts, consisting of photos, comments, and "likes". Using statistical analyses and qualitative coding techniques, we examine trends and patterns of conversation on the Warby Parker Facebook page. We find that contributors produce a broad range of content, and use the Warby Parker Facebook page as a platform for creative self-expression, and socially driven decision-making.

Author Keywords
Social Networking; Decision Making; Facebook; Warby Parker; Eyeglasses; Fashion

ACM Classification Keywords
H.5.3 [Group and Organization Interfaces]: Web-Based Interaction.

INTRODUCTION
Social networks provide a platform for large numbers of people to communicate about diverse topics and share personal experiences. Seeing opportunities to better connect with their customers, many businesses are now embracing social network technology. One industry in particular that has rapidly embraced these new technologies is the fashion industry. As individuals often seek personalized feedback from their peers on fashion decisions, some fashion companies are beginning to build and nurture online communities where customers can share their interests and tastes, and discuss potential purchases.

CSCW'14, February 15 - 19 2014, Baltimore, MD, USA

Figure 1 – A Warby Parker home try-on customer shares a collage of self-portraits, solicits advice, and receives a series of comments and "likes" in response.

Warby Parker[1], an online retailer of boutique-inspired eyeglass frames, has embraced social networking sites as customer community-building tools. The company maintains a presence on most currently popular social networks, including Facebook, Twitter, and Pinterest. A collective of Warby Parker stylists (referred to throughout this paper as "Warby Parker") maintain these social network accounts, and actively post status updates and media content, host events both offline and online, and correspond with fans. Warby Parker further engages customers through a "home try-on" program, which allows shoppers to select up to five frames to be mailed to them, free of charge, try them out at home for a week, and encourages them to share pictures of the experience through the company's various social networks. Warby Parker's Facebook page, in particular, has fostered a community of home try-on customers. These customers post their pictures to solicit feedback from friends, family, Warby Parker's stylists, and other Warby Parker fans, as well as offer opinions on other contributors' choices, through Facebook

[1] http://www.warbyparker.com

comments and "likes"[2] (Figure 1). As of May 2013, the Warby Parker Facebook page[3] has become an active community, with over 100,000 followers.

We present a case study of the Warby Parker Facebook page and the patterns of use evident among its contributors. Specifically, we explore how contributors formulate subjective questions and conversations through an examined set of over 10,000 Facebook interactions, including photographs, comments, and "likes". Our analysis of user interactions on the Warby Parker Facebook page includes the composition of the user community, the content of comments and photo posts, patterns of interaction with the site, and the influence of community feedback on purchasing decisions. We also provide implications for designing social networking tools that can further support the solicitation and sharing of peer feedback. Our data show that most contributors are interested primarily in receiving feedback about their own purchasing decisions; however, a small number of users seem primarily interested in contributing advice. Additionally, we find that users of the Warby Parker Facebook page are motivated to use the platform not just for decision support, but also as an outlet for creative self-expression.

RELATED WORK

While there are many competing needs that define the ideal shopping experience, one of the main motivators for shoppers may be the opportunity for social experiences while shopping. Arnold et al. [2] explored six hedonic motivations for shopping, including "the enjoyment of [...] bonding with others while shopping". The authors coined the term "entertailing," arguing that brick-and-mortar retailers must add a level of entertainment and fun to the shopping experience in order to compete with online retailers. Hillman et al. [5] further explored the motivations for use of online group shopping sites (such as Groupon) and found that shoppers tend to predominently use such sites to support social activities, and not necessarily to search for deals. Capitalizing on such "social commerce" trends through the integration of social media has been of primary focus to the business community, especially since the explosion of Facebook's user population [17]. Warby Parker, the retailer of principal focus in our work, appears at the forefront of a new socially networked marketplace, which embeds itself in social media, supports and engages in fan community dialogues, and provides ready access to staffs of experts.

While Facebook is not primarily designed for question answering, many customers visit the Warby Parker page to seek advice about potential purchases. Previous research has investigated the use of mainstream social networking sites to ask and answer questions. Naaman et al. [12] analyzed Twitter status updates from over 350 users, and found that individuals used status updates for numerous purposes, including question asking. Brady et al. [4] found that users frequently ask questions of their friends using status messages on mainstream social networks, such as Facebook, including questions about shopping and personal recommendations for products and services. A recent web survey of 167 web users conducted by Morris [9] found that 50% of Facebook users, and 33% of Twitter users, had used these services at least once to ask a question from their social network. Coining the term "friendsourcing", Bernstein et al. [3] suggested that the use of close-tie social networks to answer questions could provide information and feedback with a dimension of personalization that isn't possible in other forums. Panovich et al. [14] and Morris et al. [10, 11] confirmed that questions answered by close social contacts were perceived to have a higher value than those answered by weak ties. However, despite tendencies among users to leverage social networks and social ties of varying closeness for asking factual and subjective types of questions, research has shown a tendency among social networks to be sparing when providing answers [15], despite the best of intentions. The Warby Parker Facebook page benefits from the high-value conversations that emerge among its socially networked fans, and additionally offers customers access to, and ready responses, from a staff of professional stylists.

Prior research has also explored the types of questions asked on dedicated Q&A social networks as Yahoo Answers [1, 5, 6], Google Answers [6], Naver [13], and Aardvark [8]. This work has demonstrated that people use Q&A forums to ask and answer questions regarding everything from dating advice to computer tech support. Unfortunately, these systems focus primarily on interactions with strangers (or distant social network ties), dictate the roles of their contributors (i.e., either question asker or answer giver), and tend to be highly text-centric, limiting the types of contributions offered. Presenting one's question to a person with the most requisite expertise was the primary focus of the social search engine Aardvark [8]. While several recommender systems and search engines attempt to model expertise algorithmically, we are not aware of any systems since Aardvark that have explored direct contact with experts through the use of social media. Through its Facebook page, Warby Parker overcomes some of the challenges associated with use of a traditional Q&A system, while still allowing customers to engage in informative, as well as entertaining, exchanges.

The present work investigates a previously unexplored and thriving community, the Warby Parker Facebook page, which has uniquely evolved to support an improved shopping experience among its socially networked customers. Conversations analyzed in this paper are an

[2] Facebook "likes" operate as static posts, which users can invoke (usually by clicking a small icon) in order to show interest in any given piece of Facebook-linked content.

[3] https://www.facebook.com/warbyparker

example of the types of distant-tie and friendsourced interactions highlighted by previous research. Specifically, our data reflect a hybrid audience that includes a contributor's immediate social network (i.e., "friends"), as well as professional stylists and a large fan community. These contributors are diverse, creative, and the content they generate reflects a high level of engagement in the Warby Parker Facebook community. Moreover, the present research focuses on how subjective questions and conversations regarding personal fashion are formulated, which is an area that has not been deeply investigated.

DATA AND METHODS

In order to understand the patterns of use evident among Warby Parker Facebook page contributors, our data collection and analysis techniques consisted of both automated and manual techniques. In adopting these techniques, we were able to explore the overall statistical nature of a large dataset, as well as the more nuanced qualitative characteristics of individual posts and users.

Data Collection

We developed a Java application to collect activity data from the Warby Parker Facebook page through the Facebook Graph API[4]. Our application captured all posts, photos, comments, and "likes" posted to Warby Parker's public page, along with related metadata (e.g., date and time stamps, user IDs, content URLs). Our tool also collected data from the profile pages of contributors to the Warby Parker page, although we were only able to collect data that users had declared public. Textual data was stored in both a tab-delimited format and an SQLite database for simpler querying. Pictures were stored as JPEG images.

In total, we collected 29,094 records, spanning from creation of the Warby Parker Facebook page in February 2010 until our data collection date on May 22, 2013. All collected content was publically accessible to anyone with a Facebook account.

Data Pre-Processing and Coding Strategies

Since we were most interested in photos and conversations as a part of the home try-on shopping experience, we used database queries to filter users' photo posts and the resulting comment threads and "likes". In doing so, we reduced our dataset to 10,453 records[5]. In total, our dataset represented 4,373 unique Facebook users.

From our final collection we began an iterative process of sorting and searching our records, and generating summary statistics to guide further analysis. In addition to our quantitative deconstruction of the records, we also performed a manual open coding of the photos and textual content, which consisted of browsing and sorting photos and comments into descriptive categories and continuing the process as patterns emerged. We wrote scripts to categorize text content (e.g., based on keyword searches and grammatical marks), whenever possible, and manually reviewed and recoded results as necessary. Two researchers independently coded the entire dataset, and discrepancies were collaboratively resolved as necessary.

FINDINGS

Our final dataset consists mainly of customers posting photos (or series of photos) of the eyeglasses they received as part of the Warby Parker home try-on program, and the ensuing dialogue of comments and "likes" (see Figure 1). Other interactions included customers showing off their purchases, advertisements from Warby Parker, and customer service dialogs. We categorized our findings around community demographics and themes of motivation. The following sections summarize the findings from our analysis of the collected Warby Parker Facebook page data.

Engagement in the Contributor Community

Our data show that of the 4,373 unique Warby Parker Facebook page users in our dataset, 62% (N=2,670) self-identified in their Facebook profile as female, 33% (N=1,410) self-identified as male, and 293 did not publicly share their gender, χ^2 (1, N=4,080)=389, $p < 10^{-5}$.

Generally, contributor interactions with the Warby Parker Facebook page were short and short-lived. Contributors who posted more than one photo and/or comment (N=1,017 when trimmed for outliers) did so over the course of an average of 36 hours (SD=72). Among the 237 outliers, the average number of contributions was 6 posts (SD=9), over an average period of 142 days (SD=169). Twenty-seven of the outliers remained active within the community for well over a year, with one individual posting 139 times over the course of two years. Conversations resulting from initial photo posts typically spanned 30 hours (SD=20; data trimmed for outliers). There were 151 outlier conversations, which spanned for over 138 hours, and 27 conversations spanned over 1,000 hours. These conversations did not diverge from the overall average for comment count; they were simply temporally more spaced out.

Characteristics of Photo Posts

Women posted more than half of the photos in our dataset. Of the 2,632 photos in our dataset, contributors identifying as female posted 55% (N=1,451) of the photos, while males contributed 35% (N=928). Users who did not publicly report their gender posted the remaining 253 photos.

---

[4] https://developers.facebook.com/docs/reference/api

[5] Our final analyzed dataset contained 2,632 photos, 6,234 comments, and 1,587 "likes".

Figure 2 – Posters to the Warby Parker Facebook page frequently contributed self-portraits (N=1,621), collages of self-portraits (N=748), group photographs (N=77), photos prominently featuring pets and children (N=49), and "unboxing shots" (N=137).

Photo posters' contributions on the Warby Parker Facebook page fell primarily into five distinct categories: self-portraits (N=1,621), collages of self-portraits (N=748), group photographs (N=77), photos prominently featuring pets, children, or inanimate objects posed in eyeglass frames (N=49), and photos of unboxing shots and Warby Parker products or events (N=137) (Figure 2). The average photo poster contributed a total of 1.4 photos (SD=1.1); however seven contributors posted 10 or more photos.

Contributors tended to post photos in the late morning and afternoon, with tapering activity into the late evening. Contributors usually posted a single self-portrait photo; however approximately 180 users posted a series of several photographs, each featuring a different set of frames. Most of these posters demonstrated significant creative thoughtfulness (e.g., wardrobe changes, varied posing, creative background/foreground compositions, and Instagram-style photo filters). Among photos featuring collages and groups of individuals (Figure 2), there was similar creative regard, with approximately 100 posters creatively cropping and arranging images, as well as adding text and other embellishments.

Nearly all photos (N=2,465) posts included captions or text messages. These messages usually provided information about the eyeglass frame the poster was modeling, solicited advice, or recounted an experience with Warby Parker (Figure 3). The average length of these photo messages was approximately 14 words (SD=17). Of all photo messages, 4% (N=101) contained over 50 words, and 10 messages were 100 words or more in length. Of all photos, only 7% (N=167) contained no caption or message, and 16% (N=401) contained only a simple one-to-three word description of the frames being worn (e.g., "Fillmores", or "Tenley in blue").

As photo posts reflected contributors in various stages of the home try-on program, messages conveyed different intents. Specifically, 59% (N=1,460) of messages asked for help, and advice on a photographed pair of frames, or set of frames from a home try-on. Only 1% (N=31) of photo messages simply announced a decision about which frames a contributor liked best and was considering purchasing, while 23% (N=574) were showing off a recently purchased new pair. Finally, 8% (N=199) of messages conveyed positive feedback to Warby Parker following a home try-on or recent order, and five contributors provided negative or critical feedback (Figure 3).

Responses to Photo Posts

By far the largest source of text content from the collected dataset was comments on the photo posts (N=6,234). Overall, across 2,632 photo posts, the average number of comments was 2.4 (SD=2.8). A group of 2,558 unique commenters contributed 4,214 comments (Warby Parker contributed the remainder of comments, as discussed later). On average, these users contributed approximately 1.6 comments (SD=3.0) each. Comments tended to be slightly shorter than photo messages, averaging approximately 13 words (SD=13). Simple one-to-three word comments made

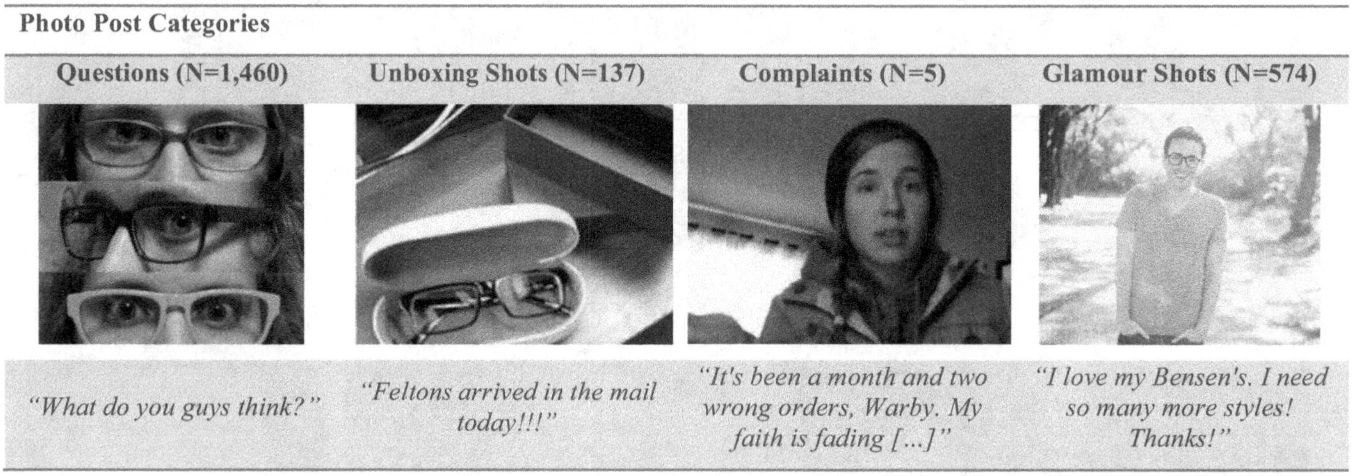

Figure 3 – Photos with messages reflected multiple intentions across the home try-on experience. Contributors asked questions, shared product information, praised and criticized Warby Parker, and highlighted glamour shots.

up 38% (N=1,598) of general user comment posts, usually casting a vote for a favorite frame (e.g. "[frame] 4", "[frame] A", or "I vote Tenleys!").

Contributors identifying as female posted 43% (N=2,769) of all comments, and males posted 20% (N=1,257). On average, photos posted by females garnered slightly more comments than those posted by males (2.5 and 2.3 comments per photo, respectively). Additionally, across gender, commenters most often posted on photos posted by those of the same gender: males commented on male photos 53% (N=671) of the time, and females commented on female photos 69% (N=1,915) of the time.

As with messages attached to photo contributions, the intent of comments was also varied in nature (Figure 4). Specifically, 61% (N=2,564) of users' comments simply offered advice or opinions about a posted photo. Comments asking for clarifying information regarding a photo made up 4% (N=177) of all comments. Users contributed 32 comments to compliment Warby Parker's products and services, and 28 provided critical feedback. Another 32% (N=1,331) of comments were coded as "miscellaneous" and included posts where contributors were simply thanking one another, or were conducting tangential conversations.

Only 17% (N=450) of all photo posts did not receive any comments in response, while 21% (N=556) received four or more comments. Photo contributors commented on the conversation threads they inspired 39% of the time (N=1,024). Of those comments, 49% (N=505) thanked Warby Parker or fellow members of the Warby Parker Facebook page community for their advice and/or compliments.

Among all commenters Warby Parker was by far the most prolific, posting 2,020 comments, usually either the first or last in a conversation thread. Warby Parker's comments were, on average, 21-words in length (SD=2.8), nearly double the length of other comments. These comments consisted mostly of advice on frame styles and colors (N=1,126), miscellaneous customer service messages (N=120), and congratulatory messages or compliments about customers' recent purchases (N=776) (Figure 4). Warby Parker was the only comment contributor on 820 photos posts; however, on average, photos with comments by Warby Parker had a total of 2.8 comments (SD=2.9), which is slightly higher than the gross average.

"Likes" also represented a good portion of the conversations occurring around photo posts. In total, 1,094 unique users "liked" 1,588 photo posts and comments. The average user "liked" 1.5 posts (SD=2.2). One-time "like" contributors made up 86% of all "likes", while only 34 users "liked" five or more posts, with one particular user posting 42 "likes". "Likes" represented the only form of contribution to the Warby Parker Facebook page for 713 users (i.e., 16% of all users in our dataset), with the remainder of "likes" coming from users that also contributed photos and comments.

Across gender, contributors identifying as female posted 67% (N=1,071) of all "likes", with 61% of those posted to photos of other females. Males, who posted only 28% (N=442) of all "likes", tended to do so on female photo posts 60% of the time. This trend among males is opposite of their commenting tendencies, where they seemed to favor other males' photos.

Overall, contributors were divided into three main groups: those that contributed only photos posts (N=1,061), those that contributed only comments (N=1,536), and those that contributed only "likes" (N=713). Only 89 users contributed photos, comments, and likes.

Effects on Purchasing Decisions

To explore the influence of community feedback on purchasing decision, we identified 70 users who asked for advice in their messages and later indicated in their

General Comment Categories

Advice (N=2,564)	Questions (N=177)	Compliments (N=32)	Criticisms (N=28)
"I think the Nedwin or Langston fit your face the best. Like the darker frames on you too!" *"My votes on Bensen!"*	*"Which style is this? =)"* *"Hi Christine, What color are your roosevelts? Thanks!"*	*"You guys rock! Fast shipping, although I did almost run over the UPS guy bolting out of my house to grab these. [...]"*	*"Cheap, Chinese-made frames? Way to support domestic manufacturing."* *"Warby Parkers are such garbage."*

Warby Parker Comments

Advice (N=1,126)	Customer Service and Engagement (N=120)	Compliments and Congratulations (N=776)
"Oh man, really tough decision! Both are definitely a unique look for you. For something a bit less traditional, we say hit up the Preston. If you are looking to make a statement through size, then go with the Winston. Thanks for sharing!" *"Get used to compliments, Sarah, they look great on you!"*	*"Thanks for getting in touch, Richard! We're so sorry to hear about the issues you've been having with your sunglasses. [...] We'd be happy to get this sorted out for you right away. Looking forward to getting you into a perfect pair of shades soon!"* *"You can do as many Home Try-On orders as you need, all for free!"*	*"We love that you are head over heels in love with your Roosevelts! You selected such a stylish frame, it's no wonder you get so many compliments. Thanks for telling others all about us!"* *"Fierce is right! We love the Roosevelt's on you!*

Figure 4 – Contributor comments provided advice and opinions on glasses, asked clarifying questions about Warby Parker products and services, and offered complimentary and critical feedback to the company. Warby Parker was also an active commenter providing stylistic advice, congratulations on new glasses, and miscellaneous customer service.

comments that they had selected a frame and a purchasing decision had been made.

Overwhelmingly, customers purchased glasses recommended by Warby Parker's stylists (this outcome occurred in 67 out of our 70 conversations). In one instance Warby Parker did not comment and the customer chose what the majority of other commenters suggested. In two cases, customers chose a frame contrary to Warby Parker's suggestion. Otherwise, even in cases where the majority of other votes were for other frames or when the decision went against what the customer indicated they would usually choose, Warby Parker's suggestion was the influencing one for customers' purchases.

As noted earlier, most commenters were Warby Parker Facebook page fans, and were not necessarily close social ties. Despite this, comments appeared to be well received and appreciated by the users as they welcomed more opinions and often thanked comment contributors. Users also occasionally indicated that they were posting to the Warby Parker page to break a tie among their friends and family. We believe, users were posting messages on their personal Facebook pages or through other communication channels (e.g., one user mentioned a Skype video chat with two of her family members), and then posting to Warby Parker when consensus among closer social ties was not clear or contrary to the individual's preference. Thus, people were not only gaining opinions from the Warby Parker Facebook community, but also aggregating those opinions with those from other personal networks and interactions.

DISCUSSION

Our analysis of the collected data revealed several trends about the conversations occurring on the Warby Parker Facebook page. Reflecting on the types of photos and messages posted by users along with Warby Parker's responses, we find two main uses for this page: purchasing decision support, and creative self-expression and fun. Both contribution types highlight the general enhancement of the online shopping experience provided by socially networked forums for communication. Here we discuss these trends, and the ramifications of merging social networks with business operations and shopping, and how Warby Parker has successfully managed to do so.

Contributing for Decision Support

The Warby Parker Facebook page exists primarily as a communication tool for Warby Parker to interact with its potential customers, and to provide support throughout the shopping process. However, by incorporating a public social network in collaboration with its home try-on program, Warby Parker has enabled an opportunity for socially driven decision support.

The 4,373 users of the Warby Parker Facebook page from our dataset utilize the forum for both requesting and providing decision support. By posting photos, messages, comments, and "likes", users are able to build up a community of people asking for and providing advice. In addition to fellow fans of Warby Parker, and a staff of expert stylists, users also have access to their trusted network of Facebook friends, all through a platform that allows enjoyable, creative, and socially driven discourse. This access benefits the subjective aspects of the shopping experience, and supports the Bernstein et al. observation that the quality of Q&A interactions is increased by the personalized nature of close-tie social network interactions [3]. Our data show that users post photos and messages that prompt useful information and advice from Warby Parker, display Warby Parker products, and tout the home try-on program and other services. Commenters, in turn, provide content ranging from in-depth stylistic advice, to feedback on Warby Parker services, to simple votes and "likes" on the frames they find most appealing on different individuals. This wide range of contribution types suggests there is a large population of people who want to contribute to the Warby Parker community at a level that doesn't involve posting photos, or formulating complex feedback (i.e., via short comments and likes). This diversity of contributions supports previous work, such as Adamic et al. [1], which found that question asking and answering interactions on social networks are in fact motivated by contributor needs to share expertise, offer personal advice and support, and just for the pleasure of discussion.

Contributing for Creative Self-Expression and Fun

One of the most interesting patterns to emerge from the analysis of our data was the diversity of photo content. Apart from the self-expression inherently offered by selecting and wearing a certain pair of eyeglass frames, contributors to the Warby Parker Facebook page demonstrated a great deal of creativity in their photos including a wide range of subject matter, background/foreground compositions, wardrobe changes, varying poses, and a good deal of editing and photo manipulation.

In addition to contributions that demonstrate a desire to be creative or to give and receive decision support, our data indicate that Warby Parker Facebook page users also contribute content simply for fun and leisure. The consummate examples of these playful contributions are the posted photos of pets, groups of friends, and babies. Such posts seem to indicate that posters just want to share cute or humorous content for others to enjoy, or to share the fun they had with friends or family while posing for group photos. While these posts may be motivated by a desire for feedback, this would seem to be an ancillary goal. Another example of contributions made potentially just for fun and leisure would be comments posted well after the initial photo post. Our data show a number of comments that appeared weeks and months following the initial photo post. While these comments sometimes offered feedback on a pair of pictured frames, they seemed more likely to be just idling contributions made by casual browsers of the Warby Parker Facebook page. These interactions seem closer to the reasons people use social networks in general, including a desire to advertise current interests and activities, and to add to the fun and pleasurable experience of visiting a social network, as seen in [12].

Notably, there were very few negative comments posted in our dataset. The atmosphere provided by contributors' compliments and entertaining content support the use of the Warby Parker Facebook page as a place to enjoy oneself and be at ease. We conjectured that the subjective nature of the questions posed along with the use of a social networking site would promote social support as seen in other research (such as in [10]), and our data confirm this scenario. One contributor, for example posted a comment referring to the Warby Parker community as a "family":

> *"i love how Warby Parker has created this online family; we're all offering sexy and stylish advice whenever someone posts a pic!"*

Through its Facebook page, Warby Parker provides a fun and entertaining, as well as familiar, platform for its customers. Moreover, by using the Warby Parker Facebook page as more than just a tool for selecting eyeglass frames, through the investment of time and creative energy, contributors change the community into a creative medium supportive of rich identity and community building, and self-expression. These themes are reflective of the "entertailing" shopping experience that online retailers are capable of providing to satisfy their customers' hedonic shopping motives, and may offer a distinct advantage over brick-and-mortar retailers [2]. Extending a shopping experience into a positive, communal activity involving close and distant ties, experts, and even strangers is a powerful example of the potential of social commerce and motivations to integrate it into one's retail experience.

Social Networks and the Shopping Experience

In considering the eyeglass purchasing experience at traditional brick-and-mortar stores, the interaction starts with an eye exam. This exam is similar to a doctor's appointment, not a collaborative event to which friends and extended family are typically invited. After the exam, customers are then presented with a plethora of options for which they can often only receive a limited amount of feedback (i.e., if they happen to bring along a friend or two, or find a salesperson's advice useful).

The Warby Parker Facebook page enables consumers to focus on the shopping experience (rather than the medical one). Moreover, users have access to their trusted network of friends as well as expert stylists, and a platform that allows enjoyable, creative, and socially driven discourse. This represents a marked improvement in the subjective aspects of the shopping experience, and benefits from the Bernstein et al. observation that the quality of question-asking and answering interactions is increased by the personalization made possible through close-tie social networks [3].

The use of social networking forums as a means for enhancing the shopping experience has the potential to entice new customers who are primarily drawn to opportunities for interaction with their networks and then seek to extend those interactions through commercial participation (i.e., doing a home try-on of their own). This pattern would support the Hillman et al. view of shopping sites that benefit primarily from their use as a social platform among social ties, which peripherally leads to sales and increased awareness of the shopping platform [7]. Warby Parker has seemingly successfully integrated a trusted and highly populated social network site, Facebook, into their online retail shopping experience. Their users have organically and willfully contributed content that promotes their product and encourages their customers to remain engaged with the company.

IMPLICATIONS FOR DESIGN

Based on our analysis, several implications for the design of social network communication tools emerge. Implementation of these designs could potentially occur at the generic social network level (i.e., Facebook), at the community level (i.e., the Warby Parker Facebook page), or a combination of the two (i.e., through a Warby Parker web application that uses the Facebook API to share content).

Improve Tools for Contribution

The use of the Warby Parker Facebook page as a creative platform suggests that social networks, and the communities that embrace them, should consider providing richer options for the manipulation and editing of multimedia content. Social networks such as Instagram capitalize on a desire to communicate with media beyond text, and provided users a way to interact using digitally editable photographs; networks like Twitter and Facebook have since followed suit, and have augmented their interfaces to support multimedia more fluidly. Social networks like Vine, and Instagram's recent inclusion of video sharing, continue to evidence the demand among users for even more dynamic multimedia sharing. By providing richer post types in the form of media beyond text (e.g., photo and video responses), community contributors, especially the creatively inclined and deeply invested, may benefit a great deal.

Warby Parker, and other similar companies, could take advantage of Apps on Facebook[6] and develop interactive software to support customers that want to share their home try-on experiences with a social network. Features of such an application could include virtual try-ons (i.e., superimposing various frame styles and colors on an existing photo), and rapid generation of interactive photos and animated GIF images.

On the other side of investment in the contributor spectrum, we observed that short comments and "likes" are a popular contribution type to the Warby Parker Facebook page. As "likes" and other low-bandwidth contributions can sometimes be a vague indicator of interest – whether positive, negative, or neutral – providing simple voting and rating interfaces (e.g., a Likert-scale "like" feature) could enhance the expressiveness of contributions without increasing the amount of effort needed to invoke them. Designers taking note of this trend could entice casual contributors into making more meaningful posts without exerting any additional effort. Such rating tools may also serve to improve the overall effectiveness of a social network as a decision-support tool, by providing a quantitative component to the already richly qualitative one evidenced by our data.

Increase Interactivity of Browsing Interfaces

Content contributors on social networks are driven partially by the entertainment that engaging in such communities provides. This trend is evident in our data as well as in previous work [7], and indicates that designers must focus on providing engaging interfaces that users will find fun to use. As our data also show that users rely on their networks as socially driven decision support tools, designers could focus on more interactive displays of information that support such tasks. Using the more robust voting options discussed earlier, such interfaces might include results visualizations for individual users or condense information from across an entire community. Such data could also drive a more tailored browsing experience for contributors by guiding them towards content that matches popular trends or personal preferences. In offering such interfaces, designers stand to engage users in a more dynamic and engaging way.

Relax Company and Customer Roles

The general goal of companies adopting social network technology is to bring their businesses "closer" to customers; however, the exact mechanics of such gap bridging is not obvious, and may involve rethinking (and even reversing) the roles of companies and customers.

Our data suggest the potential for companies' use of social network platforms as semi-autonomous, customer-driven advertising tools that involve customers in a way that is not typical of traditional businesses. Specifically, rather than static catalogs featuring professional models on staged sets, Warby Parker has real customers trying on real products in real environments nearly all day every day). Such a shift in roles encourages conversations among socially networked customers that can significantly benefit word-of-mouth marketing, and engage customers by making them "the face" of the company.

[6] https://developers.facebook.com/docs/guides/canvas/

In addition to social network platforms like the Warby Parker Facebook page bringing customers closer to what are traditionally business operations (i.e., marketing and advertising), they also position companies as members of a community rather than as strictly commercial entities.

The design objective in allowing businesses to operate as members of a community hinges on the rapid adoption of community platforms and active engagement in them. Rather than building its own social networks (i.e., complete with their own logins and passwords), Warby Parker has successfully integrated popular networks like Facebook and Twitter into their operations. Such a strategy democratizes the act of contributing content, and reinforces the view of Warby Parker as a community member. Moreover, our data show that Warby Parker is highly involved in the conversations that occur on its Facebook page, further demonstrating its commitment to its customers and positioning the company as an active community member, and not just the owner of a digital billboard.

The use of a corporate identity page as a platform for other Facebook users to communicate avoids the pitfalls highlighted by Bernstein et al. [3] regarding Facebook App user adoption hurdles, including incentivizing new users and reluctance of existing users to recruit their close ties. Rather, Warby Parker makes the app real, in a sense, through its home try-on program, and further benefits from a self-motivated user community that interacts in support of its own interests as well as for the satisfaction of interacting with others. Moreover, the overhead of "adoption" in this case is lowered through reliance on standard mechanisms of contribution on Facebook (i.e., content posting, commenting, and "liking").

LIMITATIONS

Large datasets of freeform text and photographs, such as those collected in this study, are time-consuming to analyze manually. We have discussed several important characteristics of the posts and comments made on the Warby Parker Facebook page, but there are likely many other aspects of the data, such as the aesthetic characteristics of shared photographs, that could be more deeply explored in future work.

The data presented in this paper was collected from Warby Parker's public Facebook page and the public portions of its contributors' profiles. As such, our analysis did not include posts that users attached to their own Facebook profile, or onto the profiles of friends or private groups. Additionally, we were also unable to collect data about the characteristics of our user group that were not shared publicly, including the age and gender of some of our participants. However, even the public data posted on Warby Parker's own Facebook page has revealed interesting patterns about how customers interact with Warby Parker staff and with one another. In the future, this data could be supplemented through surveys, interviews, and focus group sessions with individuals who have sought out fashion advice online.

FUTURE WORK

Moving forward, we hope to expand our research by investigating other communities, similar to Warby Parker (e.g., Zappos.com, Bonobos, Lookmatic, and Fetch Eyewear), that leverage social networks, including and beyond Facebook, to support decision-making among customers. In doing so, we hope to explore how the merging of business operations, at-home-shopping experiences, and social networks can mutually benefit both customers and companies.

Additionally, we hope to reach out and conduct interviews and focus group sessions with content contributors, to more closely examine their motivations, and patterns of use, especially with regards to final purchasing decisions. Closer examination of Warby Parker as an organizational contributor to social network conversations might also provide insight into decision making processes. Specifically, as our work primarily treated Warby Parker's social media presence as a single user (i.e., despite Warby Parker's account technically consisting of multiple staff members), experiments to compare the decision making outcomes, and subsequent interaction dynamics, between a single stylist and organization of such experts might provide further insights into areas such as trust in regards to social media and Q&A systems.

Finally, for all of the benefits of "friendsourcing" information through a social network, Brady et al. found that people with vision impairments did not always want to use social media for question asking for many reasons including privacy and fear of seeming dependent [4]. Technically people needing prescription eyeglasses are purchasing an assistive device to correct a medical problem, but there is no such stigma on this Warby Parker page because glasses are now considered fashionable. As in Pullin's *Design Meets Disability* [16], thoughtful and creative design can lessen stigmas associated with assistive devices. Thus, an interesting direction for future work would be to explore encouraging this same level of enthusiasm in helping social ties select other assistive devices such as wheelchairs or canes.

CONCLUSION

Our research has shown Warby Parker to be an informative case study for the recent hybrid of online retail coupled with social media interaction. Contributors to the Warby Parker Facebook page have a number of motivations and techniques for formulating and participating in conversations, posting a broad range of photographic and textual content. In doing so, contributors use the Warby Parker Facebook page as a platform for generic customer service concerns, creative self-expression, socially driven decision support, and simply as a source of fun. These emergent patterns of use by thousands of contributors provide cues to designers of social networks as well as the companies and communities that embrace them. Specifically, designers should be mindful of supporting the artistic manipulation and editing of content, lowering the barriers to contribution for casual community members, and allowing the roles of customers and companies on social network platforms to develop naturally and without rigid structure.

ACKNOWLEDGMENTS

We would like to extend special thanks to Quintanna Moody, Jeffrey Boyd, and Mansi Shukla for their help gathering and coding our datasets.

We thank the users of the Warby Parker Facebook page who agreed to share their photographs for this publication.

REFERENCES

1. Adamic, L.A., Zhang, J., Bakshy, E., Ackerman, M.S. Knowledge sharing and Yahoo Answers: Everyone knows something. *Proc. WWW 2008*, (Bejing, China), IW3C2, 665-674.
2. Arnold, M. J., Reynolds, K. E. Hedonic shopping motivations. *Journal of Retailing*, 79(2), 77-95.
3. Bernstein, M.S., Tan, D., Smith, G., Czerwinski, M., Horvitz, E. Personalization via friendsourcing. *ACM Transactions on Computer-Human Interaction*, 17(2),1–28.
4. Brady, E.L., Zhong, Y., Morris, M.R., Bigham, J.P. Investigating the appropriateness of social network question asking as a resource for blind users. *Proc. CSCW 2013*, (San Antonio, TX, US), ACM, 1225-1236.
5. Harper, F.M., Moy, D., Konstan, J.A. Facts or friends? Distinguishing informational and conversational questions in social Q&A sites. *Proc. CHI 2009*, (Boston, MA, US), ACM, 759-768.
6. Harper, F.M., Raban, D., Rafaeli, S., Konstan, J.A. Predictors of answer quality in online Q&A sites. *Proc. CHI 2008*, (Florence, Italy), ACM, 865-874.
7. Hillman, S., Neustaedter, C., Pang, C., Oduor, E. Shared joy is double joy: The social practices of user networks within group shopping sites. *Proc. CHI 2013*, (Paris, France), ACM, 2417-2426.
8. Horowitz, D., Kamvar, S.D. The anatomy of a large-scale social search engine. *Proc. WWW 2010*, (Raleigh, NC, US), IW3C2, 431-440.
9. Morris, M.R. Collaborative search revisited. *Proc. CSCW 2013*, (Paris, France), ACM, 1181-1192.
10. Morris, M.R., Teevan, J., Panovich, K. A. Comparison of information seeking using search engines and social networks. *Proc. ICWSM 2010*, (Washington D.C., US), ICWSM, 23-26.
11. Morris, M.R., Teevan, J., Panovich, K. What do people ask their social networks, and why? A survey study of status message Q&A behavior. *Proc. CHI 2010*, (Atlanta, GA, US), ACM, 1739-1748.
12. Naaman, M., Boase, J., Lai, C.H. Is it really about me? Message content in social awareness streams. *Proc. CSCW 2010*, (Savannah, GA, US), ACM, 189-192.
13. Nam, K.K., Ackerman, M.S., Adamic, L.A. Questions in, knowledge in? A study of naver's question answering community. *Proc. CHI 2009*, (Boston, MA, US), ACM, 779-788.
14. Panovich, K., Miller, R., Krager, D. Tie strength in question & answer on social network sites. *Proc. CSCW 2012*, (Seattle, WA, US), ACM, 1057-1066.
15. Paul, S.A., Hong, L., Chi, E.H. Is Twitter a good place for asking questions? A characterization study. *Proc. AAAI 2011*. (San Francisco, CA, US), AAAI, 578-581.
16. Pullin, G. *Design meets disability*. MIT Press, Cambridge, 2009.
17. Turban, E., Bolloju, N., and Liang, T.P. Social commerce: An e-commerce perspective. *Proc. ICEC 2010*, (Valencia, Spain), INSTICC, 33-42.

Remote Shopping Advice: Enhancing In-Store Shopping with Social Technologies

Meredith Ringel Morris, Kori Inkpen, and Gina Venolia
Microsoft Research
Redmond, WA, USA
{merrie, kori, ginav}@microsoft.com

ABSTRACT
Consumers shopping in "brick-and-mortar" (non-virtual) stores often use their mobile phones to consult with others about potential purchases. Via a survey (n = 200), we detail current practices in seeking remote shopping advice. We then consider how emerging social platforms, such as social networking sites and crowd labor markets, could offer rich next-generation remote shopping advice experiences. We conducted a field experiment in which shoppers shared photographs of potential purchases via MMS, Facebook, and Mechanical Turk. Paid crowdsourcing, in particular, proved surprisingly useful and influential as a means of augmenting in-store shopping. Based on our findings, we offer design suggestions for next-generation remote shopping advice systems.

Author Keywords
shopping; social information seeking; friendsourcing; crowdsourcing;

ACM Classification Keywords
H.5.3 [Group and Organization Interfaces]

INTRODUCTION
Shopping in brick-and-mortar (non-virtual) stores is an everyday occurrence for many people. While sometimes done solo, it is often an activity done in pairs or small groups. We call two or more people shopping together *social shopping*. Motivations for social shopping range from task-related reasons, such as getting assistance with decision-making, to relationship reasons, such as companionship and reinforcing social bonds.

Mobile phones, especially smartphones, make it possible to get some of the benefit of social shopping at a distance. The increasing capabilities of mobile phones and of social platforms further the possibilities for remote collaboration while shopping, an activity we henceforth refer to as seeking *remote shopping advice*. A recent Pew survey suggests that using mobile phones to seek remote shopping advice is an emerging trend – 38% of U.S. shoppers with cell phones made phone calls seeking shopping advice during the 2011 Christmas holiday shopping season, rising to 46% during the 2012 holiday season [21].

We wanted to explore the potential of using smartphones' expanding capabilities for seeking remote shopping advice, in order to discover opportunities for technological innovation in this space. We used a mixed-methods approach to understand current practices and to explore the potential of emerging social platforms (such as online social networks and paid crowd labor markets) to provide remote shopping advice.

We first report findings from a survey of 200 people, detailing their current and desired remote shopping advice habits. Next, we present the results of a field experiment in which people shopping for clothing shared photos of purchase options to (a) a small set of close contacts via MMS (Multimedia Messaging Service, the multimedia version of SMS), (b) their online social network via Facebook, and (c) a set of paid crowd workers on Amazon's Mechanical Turk [mturk.com]. We report on the performance characteristics of these alternatives, including response speed, volume, quality, utility, and influence, as well as participants' comfort level with each experience. Lastly, we synthesize design guidelines for technologies to support seeking remote shopping advice.

RELATED WORK
Our research was informed by related work on shopping habits and technologies and by work on friend- and crowd-sourced information seeking.

Shopping Habits and Technologies
Shopping is an activity that can have important social components [16, 24], although joint shopping trips can pose challenges (e.g., the case of a teenager embarrassed to be seen shopping with a parent) [16]. This paper contributes to the literature on social shopping experiences by presenting survey data on situations in which solo shoppers use mobile technologies to reach out to others, and experimental data on shoppers' reactions to using various social technologies to receive feedback on purchasing decisions.

Hillman et al. have studied how social technologies impact online commerce, such as when making purchases via mobile phones [9] and when sharing deals from social coupon sites (e.g., groupon.com) [6]. Online product reviews (from friends, or even from strangers exhibiting

CSCW'14, February 15 – 19, 2014, Baltimore, MD, USA.

ACM 978-1-4503-2540-0/14/02…$15.00.
http://dx.doi.org/10.1145/2531602.2531707

agreement in large numbers) [9] and product-related discussions on message boards and other shopping-focused digital forums [19] have been shown to influence consumer decisions. Rather than focusing on online commerce, our study complements these by investigating how social technologies can enhance in-store shopping.

Recent survey results indicate that consumers often use mobile phones to take photos of products in stores (often as a memory aid, though sometimes to share with others) [26]; in this work, we consider how the practice of photo-taking while shopping can support novel social interactions.

A few prior systems have prototyped novel social experiences surrounding fashion. Tsujita et al. [27] created the Complete Fashion Coordinator, a system to automatically catalogue the contents of a user's closet, and let them select possible outfit combinations and share their choices with close friends and family for comment. Burton et al. [4] used a variant of the VizWiz [2] system to provide fashion consulting to blind women; the women took photos of their outfits with the VizWiz iPhone app and sent the photos to a dedicated fashion "expert" (a volunteer with a fashion-sense profile similar to the target user), who then sent an opinion about the clothing back to the user. In our research, we examine the potential of several social communications technologies (MMS for receiving feedback from specific close ties, Facebook for receiving feedback from one's broad social network, and crowdsourcing for receiving feedback from strangers) to create a socially-enhanced shopping experience for general users.

There are also several commercial forays into this space, though most seem to have had limited success thus far. For example fashism.com and gotryiton.com are two websites that allow users to post photos of contemplated fashion purchases and receive feedback from other site users. More general purpose apps, like See/Saw [seesaw.com] allow users to friendsource general opinion-seeking questions (about items they have taken photos of), and could potentially be applied to shopping. Some retailers have also begun to integrate social technologies into their stores as a differentiator – for example, Sears stores in Canada have experimented with allowing shoppers to engage in Skype video chat with friends about potential purchases [22]. Our research is one of the first to formally study and report on how social technologies impact in-store shopping experiences, including data on the relative performance of various social resources, how users perceive such experiences, and the extent to which they influence users' preferences. Based on these findings, we suggest guidelines for designing remote shopping advice technologies.

Friendsourced and Crowdsourced Information Seeking

Friendsourced information seeking (asking questions of one's personal contacts) and *crowdsourced information seeking* (asking questions of paid crowd workers) are increasingly common phenomena, due to the availability of enabling platforms (e.g., social networking sites such as Facebook for the former and crowd labor platforms such as Amazon's Mechanical Turk for the latter).

Morris et al. [17] found that, as of 2009, about half of the people they surveyed had engaged in friendsourced information seeking using Facebook or Twitter. They also found that questions seeking opinions and recommendations were predominant. Subsequent work by Lampe et al. [14] revealed that not all people view Facebook as an appropriate venue for information seeking; women, younger people, and those with larger online networks were more likely to engage in this behavior.

Many factors influence the effectiveness of friendsourced information seeking on Facebook, including network size (larger networks reduce answer latency) [25], question phrasing (posts that include question-mark punctuation increase response probability) [25], and having social capital (which increases response probability) [11]. These studies considered text-only inquiries; our study adds to the understanding of friendsourced information seeking by studying the performance of a multi-media information seeking task, in which users posted a photo and accompanying question to Facebook.

Jeong et al. [10] studied the characteristics of naturally occurring (i.e., friendsourced) answers to questions on Twitter and of crowdsourced answers generated for those same questions, and found the overall quality of the two information sources to be similar; Twitter users' reactions to receiving serendipitous crowdsourced replies to their public questions from their system were generally positive [10]. VizWiz Social [3] is an iPhone app that lets blind people take photos of objects in their environment, record audio questions, and post them to a combination of crowd- and friend-sourced answering platforms; however, due to their relatively small online social network sizes and their concerns about appearing dependent to friends, the friendsourcing features of VizWiz Social were rarely used, and crowdsourcing was greatly preferred [3]. Our study adds to this growing body of knowledge about the relative performance of crowd- and friend-sourced information seeking by gauging users' reactions to each for decision making during shopping tasks, and compares the performance of the crowd to that of friends for this task.

Panovich et al. [18] studied the impact of tie strength [6] on Q&A exchanges on Facebook, and found that users found more value in answers from stronger ties; our study allows us to examine the value of subjective information received from "non-ties" (strangers on Mechanical Turk) in contrast to that given by personal connections.

SHOPPING SURVEY

We surveyed U.S.-based teens and adults, aged 15 - 60, on their experience with, and desired use of, mobile phones to connect with others while shopping. Respondents were recruited via Cint Link, a professional recruiting service (they paid participants about $4 per survey completion), and we received 215 responses. Fifteen responses were discarded because of poor-quality answers to the free-text recent-critical-incident description question (e.g., typing random character sequences), which left 200 valid surveys that were analyzed. The survey was conducted over a one week period in March 2013.

Most of our respondents fell into three main age groups: 35-54 (57.5%), 18-24 (15.5%) and 25-34 (15.5%). The breakdown of gender was roughly balanced (48% female and 52% male). Additionally, 60% of those surveyed owned a smartphone (a 2012 Pew survey [20] found that 45% of American adults own smartphones, rising to 68% for those in households earning at least $75,000/yr).

45% of our participants reported that they shop in a traditional "brick-and-mortar" store at least once a week (excepting grocery shopping, which was more common). When asked whether they enjoy shopping in these stores, 58.8% responded positively ("slightly enjoy", "moderately enjoy", "strongly enjoy") on a 7 point scale, 14.5% responded negatively ("slightly dislike", "moderately dislike", "strongly dislike") and 26.6% responded neutral. When asked about shopping with a friend, these percentages were very similar (positive – 59.3%, negative – 17%, neutral – 23.6%).

We asked respondents about the perceived value of receiving feedback from several sources while shopping for clothing. Responses were given on a five-point scale, ranging from 1 = "not at all valuable" to 5 = "very valuable." "A specific close contact" was perceived as the feedback source most likely to be valuable (median = 4). "A specific small group of your contacts" was considered a neutral value proposition (median = 3), and a "topical expert/professional" received a slightly lower-than-neutral rating of 2.5. Receiving feedback from "your entire social network" or from "a group of strangers" were both judged to be not at all likely to be valuable, both receiving a median rating of 1.

Contacting Others While Shopping: Current Practices

We asked respondents about their experience with contacting others while shopping: "Have you ever been shopping in a store and contacted another person about your shopping activity using your mobile phone?" 54% (107 people) reported engaging in this behavior. Mann-Whitney U tests were conducted to evaluate the statistical significance of reported differences in engaging in this activity among different demographic groups. Women were more likely to have engaged in this behavior than men (63% vs. 45%; $z = 2.38$, $p = .017$); younger people were also more likely to engage in this behavior (73% of those under 35, vs. 45% of people 35 and over; $z = 3.55$, $p < .001$), as were smartphone owners (69% of smartphone owners had done this, vs. 31% of non-smartphone owners; $z = 5.21$, $p < .001$).

The 107 people who reported having contacted others while shopping were then asked several follow-on questions, using a recent critical incident approach [5], in which they were asked to provide a free-text response describing the most recent time they had contacted someone while shopping. They were then asked several follow-up questions about this specific incident. Analyses and percentages in the remainder of this section refer to these 107 respondents.

Examples of the incidents participants described included:

- "*I was in Moe's Books, and called my husband to see if he wanted a particular book they had available.*"
- "*I was in Target looking for a shirt, and I couldn't decide between two. I had to call my friend to help me decide.*"
- "*I was in one of the local book/clothing stores on campus and texted my sister pictures of shirts I thought she would like.*"
- *"called mom about which dress looked better for me to wear to daughter's wedding, [at] jc penny"*
- *"I contacted my mom on which set of speakers (Logitech or BOSE) to buy at Walmart."*
- *"I called my girlfriend from Buckle to ask if I should buy a pair of jeans."*

The most common items involved in the described shopping situations were food (37%), followed by clothing (24%) and electronics (10%). 53% of the situations were cases where the respondent was shopping for an item for him/herself, whereas 33% were shopping for an item on behalf of the person they contacted (the remainder were shopping on behalf of a third party).

The person contacted was typically a spouse/partner (31%), a close friend (24%), parent (20%), sibling (11%), or child (8%) of the shopper; 6% responded with other relationships. Typically, the contacted person was not present on the shopping trip because they were busy with other tasks (53%); 24% were too far away to join in the shopping trip (i.e., because they lived in a different geographic region), 15% were not asked to join the shopping experience because the respondent didn't realize they would need their input ahead of time, and 8% didn't accompany the participant for other reasons.

The purpose of the contact was most often to get an opinion about a particular item (in 55% of cases), to inform the other person of an item, sale, or store they might enjoy (32%), or to ask if the person needed anything from the store (19%). In most cases, the shopper needed a response immediately (46%) or within a few minutes (42%). Most received the desired quick replies (70% immediately, 25% within a few minutes).

Phone calls were the most common method of contact (72%), followed by MMS/SMS (47%). Some participants

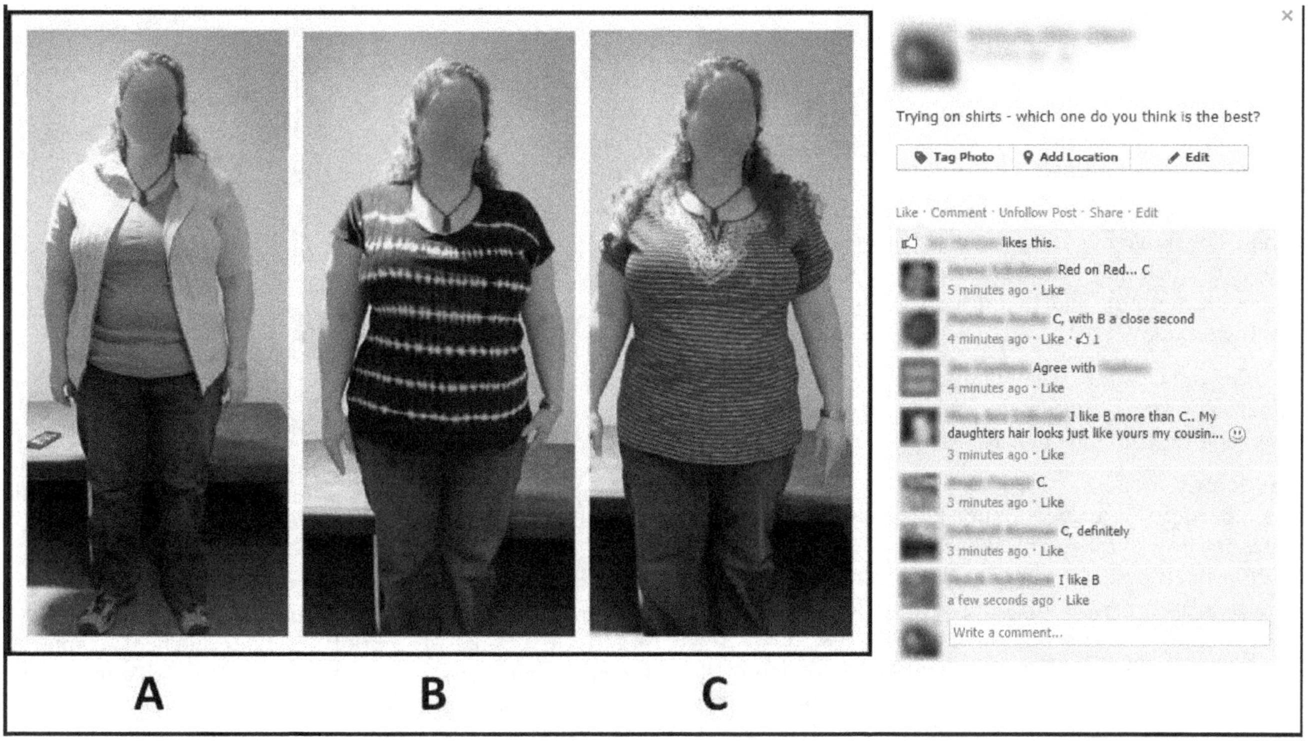

Figure 1. We generated a composite image showing the user's shopping choices, with labels ("A, B, C") to allow easy reference/voting by recipients. In this example, a participant is considering which of three shirts to purchase. Note that facial features are blurred for privacy in the paper, but were not blurred during the study itself. This screenshot shows a participant's Facebook post and the responses received. The participant added a caption to the photo: "*Trying on shirts – which one do you think is the best?*" and received opinions from seven friends within 10 minutes (with a delay of five minutes before receiving the first response). In this instance, the majority (five friends) indicate a preference for item C. Note how the third user's response builds on that of the second user: "*Agree with <name>.*"

used multiple methods to reach out, e.g., MMSing a photo and then calling the person to discuss it. 38% of respondents shared a photo as part of this experience, and an additional 10% mentioned that they would have liked to share a photo but were unable to. Video was less popular, with only 14% having used it and another 12% indicating they did not use video, but would have liked to.

FIELD EXPERIMENT

Inspired by how common our survey revealed contacting others while shopping to be, particularly the most common scenario of seeking an opinion about an item (often with photographic support), we designed an experiment to explore the potential of emerging social platforms (social networking sites and crowd labor markets) to enhance in-store shopping. Our goal was to better understand the potential of, and differences between, targeted friendsourcing, broad friendsourcing, and crowdsourcing as enabling platforms for remote shopping advice.

We conducted the experiment in May 2013, at a Seattle-area branch of the U.S. clothing chain Eddie Bauer, which sells casual men's and women's apparel. In order to participate, participants needed to own a smartphone, have a Facebook account, and be willing to share a photo of themselves on both Facebook and Amazon's Mechanical Turk service as part of the study. Participants received a $50 Eddie Bauer gift card as a gratuity.

Participant Demographics

Participants were recruited from the local community via a recruiting service, and consisted of 14 adults[1] (6 men and 8 women), ranging in age from 20 to 55 years (mean = 32), with diverse occupations such as massage therapist, network consultant, lawyer, personal trainer, stay-at-home mother, and information technology project manager.

Participants were generally familiar with MMS/SMS as a means of communication, with 12 reporting sending basic text messages every day, one sending them a few times a week, and only one indicating they used text messaging rarely (less than once a month). Five participants reported that they typically send photo MMS messages every day,

[1] Data from a fifteenth participant (P_3) was discarded due to poor network connectivity that prevented her from using the MMS feature on her phone.

four others said they did so a few times a week, four a few times a month or less often, and one not at all.

All participants reported viewing Facebook to read others' posts at least a few times per week (with 9 doing so every day). All had prior experience posting photos as Facebook status messages; half reported doing so at least a few times a week, with the other half doing so more rarely. Four reported never having used their status message to ask a question of their networks, eight did so only rarely (less than once a month), and two did so often (a few times a week or every day).

10 participants (71%) were familiar with the concept of paid crowdsourcing prior to their experience in the experiment, though none had used such a service.

Methodology

When a participant arrived at the store, they were given 10 minutes to browse for merchandise to find three items they would be interested in trying on. Participants then tried on each article in a private dressing area. After trying on the first item, we instructed participants to use their own smartphone to take a photo of themselves modeling the item of clothing, in order to understand potential usability difficulties in having solo shoppers capture this type of data. One of the experimenters then used her own phone to capture an image of the participant, and also took photos of the participant modeling the subsequent two items. The experimenter than created a single composite image of the three fashion choices using the PhotoGrid app [photogrid.org], which she then manually modified to add the labels "A, B, C" below the three respective components of the image (left panel of Figure 1). The experimenter then emailed this composite image to the participant, who downloaded it onto his or her phone.

The participant next sent the composite image along with a message to one or more people by MMS, and posted the image and a (possibly different) message on their Facebook Wall (visible to all friends). Meanwhile, the experimenter posted a survey to Mechanical Turk, in a human intelligence task (HIT) that paid U.S.-based workers 25 cents to answer a four question poll giving fashion advice; the HIT had a lifespan of 10 minutes and was set to accept a maximum of 20 workers[2] (25 cents for a two-minute poll translates to $7.50 an hour, an attempt to give an ethical wage in accordance with the proposal of Kittur et al. [12]). Workers completing the HIT were redirected to a survey on surveygizmo.com showing them the composite image and asking them to (1) recommend either A, B, or C (in response to the question "Which outfit should this [man / woman] buy?", where the term "outfit" was sometimes

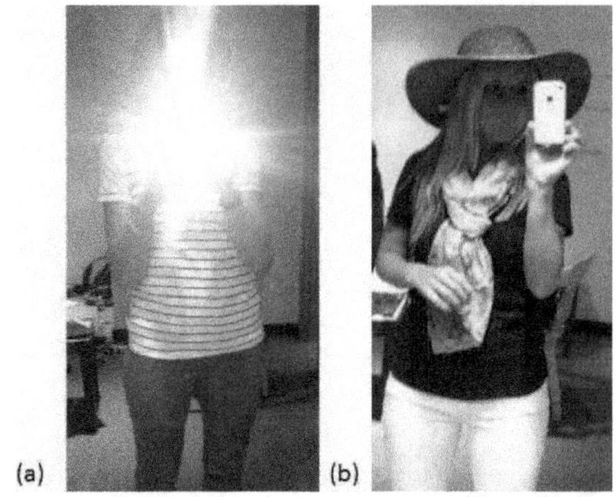

Figure 2. Common self-portrait problems: (a) flash reflections in mirror, (b) eyes gazing at phone rather than directly ahead, and phone partially obscuring face.

substituted with more specific items such as "shirt" or "sunglasses" depending on what the participant chose to try on), (2) enter a brief (single-sentence) explanation explaining their recommendation, (3) specify their gender, and (4) specify their age bracket.

Meanwhile, the participant filled out a questionnaire similar to the survey about using a mobile phone while shopping described earlier in this paper. The survey was augmented with additional questions about which of the three items the participant preferred, their level of confidence in their choice, and the expected value of feedback from MMS, Facebook, and Mechanical Turk platforms. The survey took approximately 10 minutes to complete (if fewer than 10 minutes had passed, the experimenter engaged the participant in conversation to allow each medium to have 10 minutes to gather responses). 10 minutes was chosen based on the initial survey, which found that 88% of people need responses to their shopping questions either "immediately" or "within a few minutes" – we inferred from this that responses beyond a 10 minute window would therefore be of less value in many common shopping scenarios.

The participant next reviewed the responses from the three sources, by checking their phone for any MMS replies, checking their Facebook account for any comments on their post, and viewing a report generated via the Survey Gizmo service that displayed all the results from the Mechanical Turk survey, including breakdowns of the favorite item among different ages and genders of workers, and the comments supporting those choices. We recorded the number of responses from each source and the time (in minutes) to receive the first response (if any was received). Only unique people's comments were counted (i.e., if a person sent multiple MMS replies, or made multiple Facebook posts, that only counted as a single response; Facebook "likes" were not counted as responses).

[2] In one instance 21 workers completed the survey due to a race condition in which some workers began the task before others had submitted their results to Amazon.

The participant then completed a final questionnaire, which asked them again to choose their favorite item, as well as to rate the value and influence of the feedback from the three sources, and to identify positive and negative aspects of their experiences with each. The entire experimental session lasted about 45 minutes. Participants were not obligated to purchase any of the items (though four chose to do so).

RESULTS

Self-Portrait

Participants used two strategies to obtain the self-portrait. 10 participants used the dressing room's mirrors to take a photo of themselves, and 4 held the phone out in front of themselves to snap a portrait. This latter method was used primarily to capture headshot-only portraits (for two men trying on sunglasses and one woman trying on hats), or head-and-torso (for one man trying on T-shirts). P_{14} noted, "*I don't do the mirror picture thing, I hate when people do that.*" Indeed, the mirror portraits suffered from many challenges, including flash artifacts in the final photo due to reflections (Figure 2a), the camera blocking part of the user's face or body in the reflected image (P_4 noted with dismay, "*it blocked out my face!*", Figure 2b), and the user's facial expression being unusual (eyes looking at the phone rather than straight ahead, as in Figure 2b, which was concerning particularly to P_6 who noted, "*normally if I take a picture of myself in an outfit, I don't smile or anything, but if it's going to go on Facebook then I want to look cute.*"). P_9 noted, "*I've never done this before, pictures of myself in the mirror.*"

Number and Speed of Responses

MMS

Seven participants sent an MMS message to exactly one person, with the rest sending to between two and six recipients. Recipients were described as close friends (7), spouses/partners (5), parents (4), siblings (4), and other relatives (2). The number of recipients was negatively correlated with time to receive an MMS reply ($r = -.2$), and the total number of replies was positively correlated with the number of recipients ($r = 0.5$).

Five of the 14 participants (36%) did not receive a reply to their text message within 10 minutes. For those who did receive MMS replies, the mean time to first response was two minutes. The average number of MMS responses received was 0.8 (rising to 1.2 when only considering people who received at least one response); nobody received MMS responses from more than two people.

Facebook

Three participants (21%) did not receive any Facebook replies within 10 minutes while another 2 participants received Facebook responses that did not offer guidance on the shopping task. These responses either sought clarification or were humorous (e.g., "*no swimwear option?*" (P_{10}), "*where are you going?*" (P_{12})).

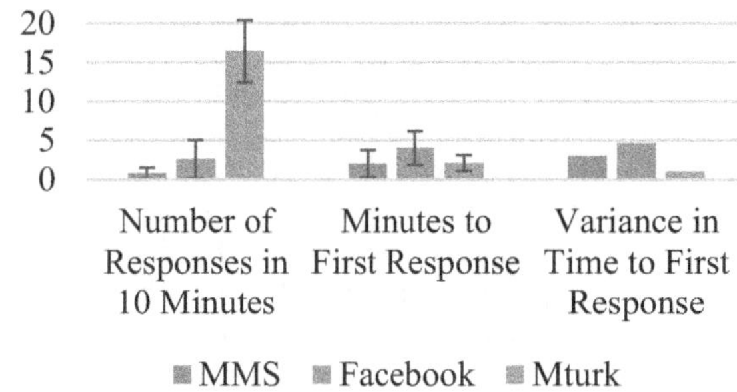

Figure 3. Relative performance of the three social feedback mechanisms used in our field experiment (error bars reflect standard deviation). Crowdsourcing via Mechanical Turk quickly and consistently provided the most responses. MMS performed more quickly than Facebook on average, but was less consistent in producing a response. Time to first response reflects only those participants who received responses in a given medium.

An average of 2.6 Facebook responses were received (3.3 among those who received at least one answer, min = 1, max = 8), with an average of 4 minutes to receive the first response. Figure 1 depicts an example of a Facebook post and the responses obtained during the experiment.

Participants had between 179 and 1559 Facebook friends (median 340, mean 512). As expected, larger network sizes increased Facebook's responsiveness, with the number of responses positively correlated with network size ($r = 0.2$) and time to first response negatively correlated ($r = -0.6$). Factors beyond network size may also have had an impact, such as time of day – for instance, P_8 had immigrated to the United States from India a few years prior, and noted that over half of his Facebook friends still lived in India; due to time zone differences, those friends were likely asleep and therefore not available to see his post (he received no replies). Facebook use habits also impacted performance, with participants' self-reported frequency of posting a status update correlating positively with the number of responses received ($r = .4$) and negatively with time to first response ($r = -.5$).

Crowdsourcing

All participants received feedback from Mechanical Turk within the allotted time period. An average of 16.4 Mechanical Turk workers provided feedback within 10 minutes (min = 8, max = 21), with an average of 2.1 minutes to the first completed response (the four-item survey took between one and two minutes to complete).

Comparisons

Figure 3 illustrates the responsiveness of all three communications platforms used. A one-way repeated measures ANOVA found a significant difference in the number of responses received from each source ($F_{2,12} = 99.9$, $p < .001$); follow-up pairwise comparisons between each feedback source were all significant ($p \leq .01$) with

Mechanical Turk receiving the most responses (a mean of 16.4), followed by Facebook (2.6), and MMS (0.8).

Time to first response was not significantly different across feedback sources when considering only those cases where feedback was received from all three sources, $F(2,5) = 1.28$, $p = .36$. However, using 11 minutes as a generous estimate of the time to first response for people who did not receive a response from a given medium within 10 minutes, a one-way repeated measures ANOVA found a significant difference in the time to first response: $F(2, 12) = 5.34$, $p = .02$. Follow-up pairwise comparisons between time to first response for each feedback source showed no significant difference in response time between MMS and Facebook ($p = .84$), but a significant speed advantage for Mechanical Turk as compared to MMS ($p = .037$) and Facebook ($p = .008$). Furthermore, the speed of response from Mechanical Turk was more consistent, having the least variance in time to first response (1.0), followed by MMS (3.0) and then Facebook (4.6).

Response Quality

MMS replies tended to be quite short (which is understandable, due to the character limits imposed on MMS messages, the difficulty of typing on smartphones, and the social conventions surrounding texting). Examples of typical, brief MMS replies included: "*B*"; "*C. The watch.*"; "*The first one.*" Only two participants received detailed replies via MMS: "*C seems to stand out, A, too, and I could see you choose B (I know, no help)*"; "*Yes, black suits you. And I like the first one also. A or C. A seems very summery.*" The average length of MMS responses was 27.9 characters.

Facebook responses included a roughly equal mix of very brief (e.g., "*A,*" "*I like B,*" "*C, definitely*"), and those elaborating on the reasoning behind the choice ("*... I always love more color... C is my choice*"; "*I like either A or B because they would work better through all the seasons.*"; "*C! Lights up your face!*"). Responses were generally positive, though three male participants (P1, P9, P12) and one female (P10) each received a response that employed sarcastic humor ("*That hat is freaking terrible. Burn it.*"; "*I would kiss the guy in A*"; "*No swimwear option?*"). Facebook responses averaged 23.4 characters

All of the crowd-workers were required to complete a free-response question that asked them to "explain the reasoning behind your recommendation" (of item A, B, or C in the prior survey question). Crowdsourced responses averaged 63.1 characters.

A repeated-measures ANOVA indicates a significant difference in response length: $F(2,5) = 25.7$, $p = .002$; follow-up pairwise comparisons indicate no significant difference in length of response from MMS and Facebook ($p = .61$), but the crowdsourced responses were significantly longer than either MMS responses ($p = .037$) or Facebook responses ($p = .001$). Longer length has been found to be a positive indicator of answer quality in other social media, such as online Q&A forums [7].

We counted the number of generic, low-quality responses from Mechanical Turk (e.g., responses that simply stated that one choice looked best, without offering any specific rationale, such as "*looks best*" or "*It's the most pretty*"). The proportion of such responses ranged from 0% to 26%, averaging 10.6% of all responses. The overwhelming majority of crowd workers offered specific tidbits of thoughtful advice, such as: "*I think the floral pattern is very pretty and adds a bit of flair*"; "*It's sophisticated but casual, and fits her the best.*"; "*I like that it is plain but a good fit.*"; "*It's simple and clean and well [sic] work for any occasion [sic].*"; "*The colors go good with her hair.*"

Unlike MMS and Facebook feedback, which only offered positive comments (with the exception of the few humorous responses), the responses from the crowd workers also gave feedback about which items were not flattering, and why. For example, "*The green shirt does not look good at all, doesn't go well with her face and eyes...*"; "*The white V-neck is kinda cheesy with the flower print.*"; "*...A makes his arms look super short*"; "*the other colors are boring*"; "*It is more for his age.*" Many participants valued this honesty (P_4 noted this contrast with Facebook – "*sometimes your friends lie to you* [by not telling you what looked bad]").

Participants found the ability to see breakdowns of crowd workers' votes by age and gender "*very cool... very interesting*" (P_7). For example, male participant P_{12} found it revealing that men's votes were distributed equally across the three shirts, whereas none of the women liked the shirt that was less tight-fitting, and people aged 35 and over preferred a more conservative, collared shirt, whereas younger people preferred the other options.

For the 11 participants who received responses expressing a fashion preference from at least one of the personalized social sources (MMS or Facebook), in 9 cases (82%) the majority choice of the Mechanical Turk workers agreed with the majority choice from at least one of the personal social sources (in the 7 cases where all three sources returned an opinion, the MMS and Facebook majority opinion matched for 4 (57%) of the cases, and the Turk opinion agreed in all four of these cases). The majority recommendation of the Mechanical Turk workers was the only one to be significantly correlated with participants' own final item preference (Pearson's $R = .53$, $p = .05$).

Impact on Participants' Choice

Recommendations Match Participant's Initial Choice

For five participants (P_5, P_6, P_7, P_{11}, P_{13}) their initial favorite item matched the recommendations from at least one of the feedback sources and they maintained this choice after receiving all of the feedback. Two participants (P_6 and P_{13}), however, did not align with the majority feedback. P_6 commented that "*I usually end up going with my own opinion*" and P_{13} emphasized her personal preference, "*I*

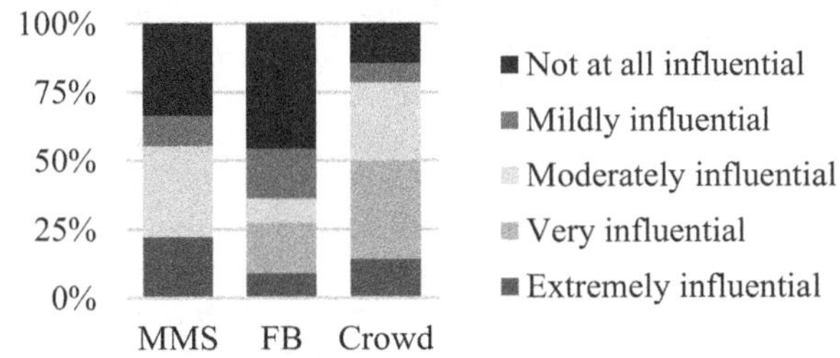

Figure 4. Participants reported that the feedback crowdsourced from strangers was influential.

like the wider spacing on the stripes." In all cases, these participants were initially very confident with their choice (4 or 5 ratings on a five-point scale) and their confidence either stayed the same, or increased.

Participant P_4 was interesting because the recommended feedback from all three sources matched her initial choice, but after the feedback, she changed her choice. When asked what she was looking for from the feedback sources she commented, "*I wouldn't take anyone's feedback.*" Initially, she was very confident in her choice (5 rating) but after she changed her choice (against the recommendations) her confidence in her new choice was low (2 rating).

Recommendations Do Not Match Participant's Initial Choice

For four participants (P_2, P_9, P_{12}, P_{15}), their favorite items did not match the recommendations from the feedback sources, but they maintained their initial choices. Their comments indicated that they primarily stayed with their choice because of personal preference, but did consider the recommendations ("*I still like the white, but the comment that it looks like a undershirt may have some merit. Most women say that A looks better, so I would strongly consider A if B was not available*" P_{15}, "*the age group/gender that I would be most interested in looking attractive to seemed drawn to B or C, and personal preference combined with the crowdsourcing feedback convinced me to choose B*" P_9). P_9 and P_{12} were very confident in their initial choice (ratings of 4 or 5), but after getting feedback P_9's confidence went down and P_{12}'s stayed the same. P_2 and P_{15} were not confident both before and after the feedback (ratings of 1 or 2) and P_2 commented that she didn't like any of the items.

For four participants (P_1, P_8, P_{10}, P_{14}), their initial favorite item was not recommended by any of the feedback sources, and all these participants subsequently changed their choice to match the majority recommendations received. In all four cases, their new choice matched the crowd workers' modal recommendation. Three of the participants (P_1, P_8, P_{14}) were initially very confident with their choices (4 or 5 ratings) but P_{10} was not confident with her choice (1 rating). After the feedback, all four participants were very comfortable with their new choice (4 or 5 ratings). Three of the participants explicitly commented that the crowdsourced feedback caused them to change their rating ("*The crowdsource* [sic] *& MMS responses were different than what I picked and I will go with what looks best to everyone*" P_{14}, and "*The watch seemed to get a lot of good feedback that was well reasoned via crowdsourcing. I find that surprisingly compelling*" P_1).

Usefulness of the Different Feedback Sources

When asked what kind of feedback would be most valuable in helping them decide among the items, eight participants mentioned feedback about whether the items looked good or not ("*opinions of whether they look good or not, fashionable, etc.*" P_5, "*what looks best*" P_{14}) and four participants mentioned feedback from a friend, boyfriend, or girlfriend ("*would want one of my girlfriends to give me a yay or nay*" P_2).

After receiving their feedback, participants ranked how influential the feedback from each source was in determining their preferred choice (on a five-point scale from "not at all influential" to "extremely influential," Figure 4). Participants rated the feedback from the crowdsourcing platform (median = 3.5) as more influential than both MMS (3) and Facebook (2), though this trend is not a statistically significant difference according to the results of a Friedman test, $\chi^2(2, N=7) = 3.7$, $p = .156$ (note that the test excludes cases where participants did not receive feedback from all three sources).

Before receiving feedback, the participants rated how useful they felt each source would be (on a five-point scale from "not at all useful" to "extremely useful") and after receiving feedback they rated the actual usefulness of each source (for those sources from which they received feedback). For MMS, the median rating was 3 ("moderately influential") at both the start and end of the study. A Wilcoxon test indicates that there was no significant difference in participants' opinions of the expected utility of MMS feedback at the beginning of the study with their opinions of its actual utility at the end of the study, $z = 1.5$, $p = 1.0$. A similar trend was found for Facebook, which also had a median rating of 3 in both instances, $z = -1.12$, $p = .27$. (Note that these median ratings likely reflect an overestimate of the perceived utility of MMS and Facebook, as only participants who actually received feedback from these sources rated them – participants who received no feedback at all presumably received a much lower utility from such sources.) The results for the crowdsourced condition however, were significantly different, with the median rating for the perceived utility rising from 3 ("moderately useful") before the experience to 4 ("very useful") after having received feedback, $z = 2.49$, $p = .013$.

Advantages & Disadvantages of the Feedback Sources

MMS

When asked what they liked best about MMS, the main reasons given were the ability to ask specific people (P_1, P_5, P_6, P_9, P_{14}, P_{15}) ("*trusted individual, so the opinion matters more*" P_5, "*exactly the people I want to hear from*" P_6) and that it was quick and easy (P_2, P_7, P_9, P_{13}) ("*a convenient way for me to contact people and receive their responses*" P_7). The main disadvantages expressed for MMS was the potential delay in response time (P_1, P_6, P_7, P_8, P_9) ("*No idea if you'll get feedback from any given person within the timeframe you need*" P_1). Other reasons included not being able to get a large number of opinions (P_{15}), and getting terse responses (P_5).

Facebook

When asked what they liked best about Facebook, the main reasons given were that it was a close community of friends (P_5, P_8, P_9, P_{11}) ("*feedback from my closer community of friends*" P_8) and that they could get feedback from lots of people (P_6, P_9, P_{14}, P_{15}) ("*feedback from a large group of people*" P_{15}). Others commented on the benefit of getting insightful, interesting, or humorous comments (P_1, P_2, P_{10}). The main disadvantages expressed were replies that weren't very useful (P_1, P_4, P_5, P_7, P_{12}, P_{13}), and that it can take time to get responses (P_9, P_{11}, P_{15}) ("*it could take too much time*" P_9, "*they would have to be online at the time and view my picture which they may not see because their newsfeed may be too large and my status and pics may be hidden from them*" P_{15}).

Several participants expressed varying degrees of discomfort with posting the photo-question to Facebook (note that during the study's recruiting phase, participants were forewarned that they would be asked to post a photo to both Facebook and Mechanical Turk if they chose to participate). P_3 (the participant whose data was not used due to a network connectivity issue that prevented MMS messages from being sent) was so uncomfortable with posting to her Facebook Wall that she instead constructed a private Facebook message and sent the photo to only a few close friends. P_4 deleted her Facebook post immediately after the 10 minute response-gathering period was complete. P_8 mentioned that he intended to immediately delete his post (explaining that his manager was on Facebook). P_6 noted that she typically doesn't post photos (although she used to), noting that, "*I decided to be more selective in the last year*" after realizing how large and diverse the audience of her Facebook friends was. P_9 phrased the caption on his photo in a facetious manner ("*Hello friends, I need to know which of these shirts makes me look most attractive/radiant.*"), and when asked about this revealed that the humorous phrasing was due to his discomfort, "*it's not something I would normally do, I don't know when the last time is I actually posted a picture, it's been a while.*" P_{10} commented in the post-study questionnaire that a drawback of using Facebook was that "*everybody sees it.*"

Crowdsourcing

When asked what they liked best about crowdsourcing, the main comments given (by seven participants) were that the feedback came from strangers who could be objective and give a wide variety of responses ("*different people's opinions*" P_{12}, "*representation of the sorts of opinions people on the street would have*" P_7, "*honest opinion*" P_{15}). Five participants liked that they could get many responses quickly ("*lot of feedback in a very short amount of time*" P_9), and four favorably noted that they could get the breakdown of age and gender ("*Breakdown by age and gender. I can make decisions based on what demographics things do well with*" P_1). The main disadvantages expressed were the fact that the respondent do not know them or their style (three participants) ("*Lack of familiarity with what my general style would be like*" P_1, "*Hard to trust opinion of people I don't know*" P_6) and that sometimes there were too many differing opinions (two participants) ("*Opinions were all over the map*" P_5). While some people appreciated the feedback they received ("*responses were very positive and many of the people gave very specific reasons for their choice*" P_{11}), others were uncomfortable with the bluntness of some of the comments. For example, after a crowd worker wrote, "*she [P_{14}] is a bigger woman and the bigger hat kinda hides the bigness,*" P_{14} expressed that she disliked "*[the] comment about my size.*"

DISCUSSION

Our initial survey revealed that many people engage in remote shopping advice experiences via mobile phones, typically via traditional voice-based phone calls, though occasionally employing multi-media including text, photos, and video. These experiences always involved known contacts (friends and family), and survey respondents did not think that social shopping feedback from strangers would be valuable (except perhaps topical experts). However, when exposed to rich, multimedia remote shopping advice experiences in our field experiment (posting photos via MMS, Facebook, and Mechanical Turk), participants reacted favorably, finding feedback from all sources useful and influential. Participants were often surprised by the usefulness of feedback from strangers; their attitudes about this novel social experience changed significantly during the course of the session.

Friends vs. Strangers

The main strengths of receiving feedback from crowds of strangers, rather than from friends (via MMS or Facebook), included:

Independent judgments: Crowd workers did not see others' votes, and were not influenced by them (a prerequisite to effectively harnessing the "wisdom of crowds" [23]); in contrast, Facebook users were sometimes perceived as amplifying the opinions of those who replied earliest (in some cases this echo-chamber effect was explicit, e.g. the third response in Figure 1, which notes "Agree with [name of prior commenter]").

Honesty: While personal contacts told users what items they recommended, the crowd workers also told users what items they *didn't* recommend, and why. Most users found these critical opinions refreshing, though a few were insulted (e.g., the woman whose size was referred to in a blunt manner). Granovetter [6] identified the benefit of "weak ties" for providing novel information; our findings indicate that "non-ties" also provide novel information (critical/negative feedback) not offered by either their strong or weak personal ties.

Speed and consistency: Both personal contacts (via MMS and Facebook) and strangers (via Mechanical Turk) responded within a few minutes of receiving the user's inquiry. Our initial survey study found that feedback within a few minutes would be satisfactory to most people seeking remote shopping advice, suggesting that this level of latency is acceptable for creating a working system. Crowd workers' response latency (and likelihood) was much more consistent than personal contacts, though, who were not always immediately available. However, the performance of Facebook was much faster than in studies from only a few years ago (e.g., [25], which found latencies of nearly an hour to be typical). We attribute this improvement in Facebook's performance to several causes: the increasing penetration of Facebook (since larger networks result in faster response times), the increasing penetration of smartphones (since these allow people to be connected to social media in a larger number of settings, and therefore available to respond to posts), and the use of a photo, rather than a text-only post (although Facebook's Newsfeed algorithm is a proprietary secret, informal observations suggest that posts containing photos seem to be given more prominence).

The main drawbacks of using crowds rather than personal contacts were:

Context: As found in prior studies of social network question asking (e.g., [17]), users appreciate that their personal contacts are often aware of relevant context (in this case, a user's personal style). Additionally, other types of context (such as the price of the items being considered) might be relevant to provide, regardless of whether the answerers are personal contacts or strangers.

Cost: In this experiment, we absorbed the cost of crowdsourcing, but presumably this would be paid by end users in a deployed system. We paid a relatively high cost (25 cents per response) in order to both provide a fair wage [12] and encourage speedy responses. Other mechanisms could be used to facilitate fast replies (e.g., techniques proposed by Bernstein et al. [1] and Bigham et al. [2] for real-time crowdsourcing), but the cost of crowd opinions is still likely to be higher than the free price of responses from personal contacts. However, such responses come with a social cost [3]; for frequent inquiries, many users may prefer a financial cost rather than a social one. Discovering how much participants are willing to pay for such a service in practice is an open question; it may be that participants' enthusiasm for the service would wane if they bore the cost of crowdsourcing rather than our research team.

Privacy did not appear to be a drawback of crowdsourcing, though participants did express concern about sharing images of themselves to their personal networks on Facebook (though perhaps that is a an artifact of the type of participant willing to volunteer for our study; it is possible that people who would have had concerns about sharing images of themselves on Mechanical Turk chose not to participate). Blurring or other techniques such as [15] could be used to mitigate potential privacy issues on Mechanical Turk, although facial features, skin tone, hair, etc. were a factor that influenced many crowd workers' choices, as revealed through their comments (e.g., "*doesn't go well with her face and eyes*"; "*The jacket matches well with her skin complexion and hair*"). The EmailValet project [13], where paid crowd workers triaged a users' email inboxes, is another example of end-users finding value in sharing potentially private information with paid crowd workers. Assessing the risks, benefits, and tradeoffs involved in sharing various types of information with members of the crowd is an important area for additional research. The use of mechanisms like Facebook's Lists or Google Plus's Circles to restrict sharing to a subset of one's social network is a possible mechanism for mitigating users' concerns regarding sharing in that medium, where issues regarding curating a particular type of public image drive many users' decisions about what to post [28].

Towards Remote Shopping Advice Systems

Our survey's findings indicate that seeking input from remote people while shopping is a relatively commonplace occurrence, but that most people currently rely on simple voice or text-based interactions to accomplish this. Our experiment demonstrated that users found value in using richer media (photos) as well as using emerging social platforms (social networking sites and crowd labor markets) to meet these needs, and that such platforms' performance characteristics (particularly Mechanical Turk) were generally suitable for such interactions.

Based on these findings, we suspect that consumers would find value in a smartphone app designed specifically to support seeking remote shopping advice. Our results suggest that key capabilities of (and challenges that must be overcome by) such an app would include:

Image capture: Facilitating a user's ability to capture an image, particularly for clothing, which requires self-portraits, is a challenge. One approach, such as that used by the app "Headshot" [aka.ms/headshot] is to provide visual feedback to help the user better position the camera. Using video and perhaps letting crowd workers choose the best frame for inclusion in an image [1] may be an alternate approach. Crowd labor or automatic techniques could also be used to automate the manual image compositing/labeling we did for our study (we recommend using a single, composite image, due to users' reluctance to bombard their social networks with too many posts). Beyond technical issues, capturing such images or video may be challenging due to evolving societal norms about the use of such technologies – other patrons in dressing rooms may have privacy concerns about being inadvertently included, or shop owners may assume patrons are recording images of merchandise as a reminder to later seek better deals in online shops.

Audience targeting: Providing the ability for users to target their query to one or more audience types would enable users to (if desired) harness both the consistent speed and "blunt" responses from sources like Mechanical Turk as well as the personalized and trusted responses from friends and family. Such a system could show users predictions of the likely response time from each source, based on factors like the price they are willing to pay for crowd labor, the time of day, and the size of their online social networks. Of course, users' choices of which platforms to employ might be influenced by characteristics beyond answer speed and type – privacy preferences, and/or differential preferences for the "informational" versus "social" aspects of the remote shopping advice experience may also influence their selection of medium. Users choosing to engage crowd laborers could potentially specify worker characteristics that were relevant to their task, such as age, gender, geographic region, expertise with certain types of products, personal taste profiles, etc.

Decision support: Finally, an ideal remote shopping advice application would provide interactive support (perhaps through information visualization techniques) to allow users to explore, compare, and contrast feedback from different audiences (participants in our study found the differences and similarities between personal contacts' and strangers' recommendations informative, as well as differences between sub-audiences, such as male versus female workers). Such an interface might also allow users to factor in other sources of information, such as online reviews and pricing.

CONCLUSION

In this paper, we presented a formal study of *remote shopping advice*, in which people use their mobile phone to contact others in support of in-store shopping tasks. We presented results from our multi-method study, comprising (1) survey results about users' status quo practices, and (2) experimental results comparing and contrasting the use of different social technologies to support seeking remote shopping advice (MMS for small groups of close ties, Facebook for extended personal networks, and Mechanical Turk for paid crowd workers). We also presented design guidelines for remote shopping advice systems synthesized from the findings of our survey and experiment. Our key finding was that the crowdsourced feedback was surprisingly useful to our participants – participants were influenced by the high-quality and honest nature of crowd workers' comments, despite the lack of context and potential for privacy concerns. In fact, they were more reticent to share their photos on Facebook than Mechanical Turk. Our findings illustrate how smart mobile devices connected to powerful communications platforms have the potential to transform even mundane daily tasks into experiences that can inform, connect, and delight.

ACKNOWLEDGEMENTS

We would like to thank the staff at Eddie Bauer's Redmond Town Center location for their help in accommodating our study. We would also like to thank John Tang for his insights during the planning stages of this project.

REFERENCES

1. Bernstein, M., Brandt, J., Miller, R., and Karger, D. Crowds in Two Seconds: Enabling Realtime Crowd-Powered Interfaces. *Proceedings of UIST 2011.*
2. Bigham, J.P., Jayant, C., Ji, H., Little, G., Miller, A., Miller, R.C., Miller, R., Tatarowicz, A., White, B., White, S., and Yeh, T. VizWiz: Nearly real-time answers to visual questions. *Proceedings of UIST 2010.*
3. Brady, E., Zhong, Y., Morris, M.R., and Bigham, J. Investigating the Appropriateness of Social Network Question Asking as a Resource for Blind Users. *Proceedings of CSCW 2013.*
4. Burton, M.A., Brady, E., Brewer, R., Neylan, C., Bigham, J.P., and Hurst, A. Crowdsourcing subjective fashion advice using VizWiz: Challenges and opportunities. *Proceedings of ASSETS 2012.*
5. Flanagan,J. The critical incident technique. *Psychological Bulletin*, 51:327-358, 1954.
6. Granovetter, M. The Strength of Weak Ties. *The American Journal of Sociology*, 78(6), 1973, 1360-1380.
7. Harper, F.M., Raban, D., Rafaeli, S., and Konstan, J.A. Predictors of Answer Quality in Online Q&A Sites. *Proceedings of CHI 2008.*
8. Hillman, S., Neustaedter, C., Pang, C., and Oduor, E. "Shared Joy is Double Joy": The Social Practices of User Networks within Group Shopping Sites. *Proceedings of CHI 2013.*
9. Hillman, S., Neustaedter, C., Bowes, J., and Antle, A. Soft Trust and mCommerce Shopping Behaviors. *Proceedings of MobileHCI 2012.*
10. Jeong, J-W., Morris, M.R., Teevan, J., and Liebling, D. A Crowd-Powered Socially Embedded Search Engine. *Proceedings of ICWSM 2013.*
11. Jung, Y., Gray, R., Lampe, C., and Ellison, N.B. Favors from Facebook Friends: Unpacking Dimensions of Social Capital. *Proceedings of CHI 2013.*
12. Kittur, A., Nickerson, J.V., Bernstein, M.S., Gerber, E.M., Shaw, A., Zimmerman, J., Lease, M., and Horton, J.J. The Future of Crowd Work. *Proceedings of CSCW 2013.*
13. Kokkalis, N., Köhn, T., Pfeiffer, C., Chornyi, D., Bernstein, M.S., and Klemmer, S.R. EmailValet:

Managing e-mail overload through private, accountable crowdsourcing. *Proceedings of CSCW 2013.*

14. Lampe, C., Vitak, J., Gray, R., and Ellison, N.B. Perceptions of Facebook's Value as an Information Source. *Proceedings of CHI 2012.*

15. Lasecki, W.S., Song, Y., Kautz, H., and Bigham, J.P. Real-Time Crowd Labeling for Deployable Activity Recognition. *Proceedings of CSCW 2013.*

16. Miller, D., Jackson, P., Thrift, N., Holbrook, B., and Rowlands, M. Shopping, Place and Identity. *Routledge Publishing*, New York, NY, 1998.

17. Morris, M.R., Teevan, J., and Panovich, K. What Do People Ask Their Social Networks, and Why? A Survey Study of Status Message Q&A Behavior. *Proceedings of CHI 2010.*

18. Panovich, K., Miller, R., and Karger, D. Tie Strength in Question & Answer on Social Network Sites. *Proceedings of CSCW 2012.*

19. Pentina, I., Prybutok, V., and Zhang, X. The Role of Virtual Communities as Shopping Reference Groups. *J. Electronic Commerce*, 2008.

20. Rainie, L. Smartphone Ownership Update: September 2012. *Pew Internet & American Life Project.*

21. Smith, A. In-store Mobile Commerce During the 2012 Holiday Shopping Season. *Pew Internet & American Life Project.* January 31, 2013.

22. Strauss, M. Sears shoppers make fashion link with Skype. *The Globe and Mail*, April 21, 2011.

23. Surowiecki, J. The Wisdom of Crowds. 2005.

24. Tauber, E., Why Do People Shop? Marketing Notes and Communications, *J. Marketing*, Vol. 36, (1972).

25. Teevan, J., Morris, M.R., and Panovich, K. Factors Affecting Response Quantity, Quality, and Speed for Questions Asked via Social Network Status Messages. *Proceedings of ICWSM 2011.*

26. Tohidi, M. and Warr, A. The Bigger Picture: The Use of Mobile Phones in Shopping. *Proceedings of Interact 2013.*

27. Tsujita, H., Tsukada, K., Kambara, K., and Sijo, I. Complete Fashion Coordinator: A support system for capturing and selecting daily clothes with social network. *Proceedings of AVI 2010.*

28. Zhao, X., Salehi, N., Naranjit, S., Alwaalan, S., Voida, S., and Cosley, D. The Many Faces of Facebook: Experiencing Social Media as Performance, Exhibition, and Personal Archive. *Proceedings of CHI 2013.*

Specialization, Homophily, and Gender in a Social Curation Site: Findings from Pinterest

Shuo Chang[1], Vikas Kumar[1], Eric Gilbert[2], Loren Terveen[1]

[1]GroupLens Research
Dept. of Computer Science and Engineering
University of Minnesota
{schang,vikas,terveen}@cs.umn.edu

[2]School of Interactive Computing
Georgia Institute of Technology
gilbert@cc.gatech.edu

ABSTRACT

Pinterest is a popular *social curation* site where people collect, organize, and share pictures of items. We studied a fundamental issue for such sites: what patterns of activity attract attention (audience and content reposting)? We organized our studies around two key factors: the extent to which users *specialize* in particular topics, and *homophily* among users. We also considered the existence of differences between female and male users. We found: (a) women and men differed in the types of content they collected and the degree to which they specialized; male Pinterest users were not particularly interested in stereotypically male topics; (b) sharing diverse types of content increases your following, but only up to a certain point; (c) homophily drives repinning: people repin content from other users who share their interests; homophily also affects following, but to a lesser extent. Our findings suggest strategies both for users (e.g., strategies to attract an audience) and maintainers (e.g., content recommendation methods) of social curation sites.

Author Keywords

Social Network; Data Analysis; Topic Detection; User Profiling

ACM Classification Keywords

H.1.2. User/Machine Systems

INTRODUCTION

Social network sites have become central to people's lives. They let people connect and stay in touch with family and friends (e.g., Facebook), find and share information on topics in which they are interested (e.g., Twitter), ask and answer specialized questions (e.g., StackOverflow).

Social curation sites are an important type of social network site. They let users collect, organize, and share collections of items. The focus is not creating new content (unlike, say, YouTube), but rather something akin to, "Here are things I found on the web that I think are interesting." Well-known social curation sites include del.icio.us (for web bookmarks), Digg and Reddit (for news items and other types of web content), and newer sites like Storify, Scoop.it!, and Wanelo.

We have been studying Pinterest as a representative social curation site. Pinterest is organized around the metaphor of a pin board. Users (called "pinners") pin pictures of items they find on the web and organize them into boards representing interests like recipes, crafts, children's toys, etc. Like many other sites, users can follow each other: if you follow someone, their new pins show up on your home page's feed. Pinterest has drawn recent research interest [13, 27, 39] for reasons such as its fast growth, the central role found images play, its strong link to e-commerce, and the gendered nature of its use, with women making up around 80% of US users.

We are interested in a key issue for any social curation or social network site: **What attracts attention?** We study two main ways attention manifests: attracting followers and getting one's content reposted.

We consider two main factors in our study of this issue:

- *Specialization*: the extent to which users specialize in a particular type of content (e.g., a user may pin only recipes) vs. diversifying over a range of topics.
- *Homophily*: similarity of topical interests among people who follow one another.

As we detail below, these factors are well-known to drive behavior both online and offline. For example, large bodies of work have shown the role of homophily in the diffusion of information and behaviors through social networks, online and off (e.g., [14, 25]). We also examine how *gender* may mediate these two factors since a growing body of research has uncovered gender differences in behavior on social network sites. Taken together, these factors allow us to study attention on a social curation site through the lenses of individual characteristics (gender), individual behavior (specialization) and community structure (homophily).

Within this frame, we defined three specific research questions to guide our research:

RQ1-Topics. What is the overall topical structure of content on Pinterest? What topics are most popular? How are different topics related? Do men and women differ in the types of content they pin?

CSCW'14, February 15–19, 2014, Baltimore, Maryland, USA.

http://dx.doi.org/10.1145/2531602.2531660

RQ2-Specialization. To what extent do users specialize in particular topics? Do women and men differ in their degree of specialization? What factors, including degree of specialization, attract more followers?

RQ3-Homophily. Are users more similar to users whom they follow than to random users? Are users more likely to repin from users who are similar to them than from random users?

We used quantitative methods to study these questions. We wrote a web crawler to obtain data from Pinterest and then performed statistical analyses on the data. Our results both illuminate the nature of activity on Pinterest and have implications for social network and social curation sites in general. For example, we found that users attract more followers when they share content on a range of topics – but there is a limit beyond which increased diversity is not helpful. Our results also suggest that Pinterest users may be more interested in content on topics they care about than in content from their social connections; this can inform the design of content recommendation algorithms for social curation sites.

In the remainder of the paper, we describe the theoretical background for our research and survey related work, describe the data we obtained and how we obtained it, describe how we produced a representation of topics to use in our analyses, present our results, and then close by discussing the implications of our results for research and design.

THEORETICAL FOUNDATIONS AND RELATED WORK

There is much research on social network sites and their underlying social phenomena. Most relevant to our concerns is work that: (i) examines the types of behaviors that attract attention and an audience, and (ii) studies of the role of gender in social network sites. We also examine several related studies conducted on Pinterest.

Attracting audience and attention

What makes users pay attention to content or fellow users of a social network site? Numerous studies have investigated this fundamental issue in different contexts.

What types of questions attract answers? In a series of studies of Usenet newsgroups, researchers from CMU investigated properties of the post, poster, and the group itself that influenced likelihood of reply. For example, Arguello et al. [5] found that writing explicit requests, including personal "testimonials" relating one's connection to the group, and staying on-topic increased the odds of receiving a reply.

What types of posts attract reposting? Researchers have studied Twitter, using *retweeting – reposting* someone else's tweet – as a measure of interest, and have investigated features of tweets and users that predict retweeting. Suh [33] found that the presence of URLs and hashtags in tweets predicted more retweeting, as did richer connections with other Twitter users, both in followers (a larger audience) and followees (indicating access to more diverse information).

What attracts an audience? Recent research has sought to identify structural and content factors that predict formation of ties in social network sites. Several researchers found correlations between the content of users' tweets – such as the expression of emotions like joy or sadness [18] or positive vs. negative sentiments [11] – and the number of followers Twitter users have. More generally, preferential attachment is a foundational phenomenon in the formation of social ties: people in a social network tend to connect to others in the network who already are popular. This is a common property of real-life social networks [6] and has been useful in predicting the formation of new social ties [21].

Homophily and Specialization

The principle of *homophily* states that the more similar people are, the more likely they are to form social connections [25]. Shared interests are one type of similarity. Prior work has explored the role of homophily in online social interaction: for example, Ren et al. tested theories about community attachment by forming groups on the MovieLens film recommendation site based on similarity of movie tastes [28].

Various researchers have studied topical specialization in online communities. For example, Demartini observed topic specialization in Wikipedia [12], and Priedhorsky et al. [2] and Masli et al. [24] observed a geographic analog (region specialization) in a geographic wiki for bicyclists. Ziegler et al. [40] did pioneering work on the utility of diversity in recommender systems. They developed an algorithm to diversify lists of recommendations—i.e., to include items that reduce the overall inter-item similarity in the list—and showed that this increased user satisfaction with the results.

More directly relevant for our purposes, Wang and Kraut [37] studied how the intial topical focus of a Twitter user's tweets affected the number of followers they attained. Interestingly, they found theoretical justification that both high focus (specialization) and low focus (diversity) could lead to more followers. The high focus argument is based on homophily, and the low focus argument is based on network externalities, i.e., more diverse content will appeal to a broader audience. Wang and Kraut found that more focused initial tweets led to more followers. Hutto et al. [16] also built a theory-based prediction model of following behavior that included a broad range of prediction variables, including topical focus of tweets. In contrast to Wang and Kraut, they did not find that greater topical focus predicted more followers. This indicates that more work is needed to understand the role of focused vs. diverse content in attracting an audience.

This work. We explore some of the same issues as prior work, but in a different context and with different types of data; we study what factors – including types of interests and degree of specialization – result in Pinterest users gaining more followers.

Gender

In "A theoretical agenda for feminist HCI" [29], Rode identified three paradigms for thinking about gender within HCI and introduced several outside perspectives that she argues enable a richer and more nuanced approach to gender. The paradigm relevant to our research is (in our words) *gender as a variable*. This presumes that gender differences *may* be relevant for analysis and design; thus, quantitative studies include participant gender as an independent variable. For example, Beckwith et al. [7] investigated whether there were differences in "tinkering" behavior and self-efficacy among men and women learning to program; if so, these might inform the design of learning support tools. In another example, Tan et al. [34] found through a controlled experiment that women benefit from a wider field of view when navigating on-screen, 3D displays.

Social media studies. Much research has been done on the role of gender in online social interaction; Herring gives an overview of the early literature [1]. More recent work has studied social network sites. Caverlee and Webb found that female MySpace users were more likely than male users to keep their profiles private, and that men and women used very different terms in their profiles [9]. Thelwall also analyzed MySpace data. His findings included gender differences in social connection: women had more friends than men, and both men and women had more female than male friends [35]. Cunha found that male and female Twitter users used different hashtags for common topics [10]. Lam et al. investigated gender disparities on Wikipedia [19]. They found that men comprised about 84% of Wikipedia editors and made over 90% of edits. They also identified various effects possibly related to this disparity, notably that topics of most interest to women received lower quality coverage.

Potential confounds. Rode identified three potential problems surrounding gender: (1) ignoring the social context in which gender issues occur; (2) treating gender as an essential, immutable characteristic, rather than something socially constructed and performed by individuals; (3) a tendency to design "female versions" of technologies, thus risking ghettoizing women and girls.

This work. We take the *gender as a variable* approach, considering gender in several analyses, notably, whether women and men focus on different topics, and whether women and men differ in the degree to which they are specialists or generalists. Here, Pinterest is the social context in which gender is performed, albeit through the interface affordances provided by Pinterest's designers. Rode's other two confounds are largely problems with the interpretation and application of study results, rather than with the studies per se. This is particularly true for an experiment or quantitative study: this sort of study identifies the *what*, but not the *why* of the results. Therefore, we clearly distinguish our emprical findings from any interpretation or drawing of implications, and keep Rode's concerns in mind when we do offer interpretations and implications. Note that since Pinterest is dominated by female users, it serves as a usefully contrasting context to previous work on sites that are male dominated (e.g., Wikipedia) or have relatively equal gender balance (e.g., MySpace, Twitter).

Aside: popular discourse about Pinterest is gendered. The popular impression of Pinterest is highly gendered: it is *seen as* a site for women [23], and this has engendered much dismissive sexist reaction. A vivid illustration is the emergence of a number of "male Pinterest" sites [32]. A lively debate about the gendered view of Pinterest is occurring online, e.g. [26, 36, 38]. Of course, there is nothing "inherently female" about Pinterest: anyone can pin any sort of content. However, the popular impression of Pinterest as a "women's site" has real effects. Recent research identified stereotypes about Wikipedia editors [4]. Since people are less likely to participate in a group when they don't identify with its members [30], these stereotypes may discourage many people from editing Wikipedia. As we discuss below, stereotypical views concerning Pinterest may have similar affects.

Studies of social curation on Pinterest

Several studies of Pinterest have been published recently. Gilbert et al. [13] did a quantitative study. Their central findings were: female users were repinned more often than males, but had a lower mean number of followers than males; and users employed very different language on Pinterest than on Twitter, with Pinterest language characterized by words of consumption and desire: "use", "look", "want", and "need". Ottoni et al. also did a quantitative study [27] . They found that women on Pinterest used social interaction mechanisms more than men, that men and women concentrated on different topics, and that women tended to be content generalists, while men specialized more. They also reported that women had more followers than men[1].

In contrast to the previous two studies, Zarro et al. [39] used qualitative methods to sketch the nature of social curation on Pinterest. Among their many interesting observations, one particularly relevant to our work is that their participants reported that Pinterest was about *what they enjoyed* (i.e., content), rather than social interaction.

We took a similar approach as Gilbert et al., but studied mostly different issues, although we also modeled the factors that predict the number of followers a user will have. Our model extended theirs by including factors for the type and diversity of content pinned by users. We studied some of the same issues as Ottoni et al., but (as detailed below) we used a richer representation of content and applied more rigorous methods. We studied different questions and applied different methods than Zarro et al. However, our analysis of Pinterest topics and the effect of homophily on repinning and following behavior provide quantitative evidence for the rich observations they drew from qualitative data.

DATA

We describe the data we gathered, how we gathered it, and the properties of our sample. To answer our research questions, we needed data about *pins*, *boards*, and *pinners*. For pinners, we were interested in data that indicated their content and social behavior, including:

- *boards* the user has created;
- *pins* the user has added to his or her boards;
- a list of the users this user is *following*;
- the total number of users this user is *following*;
- the total *number of followers* this user has.

Many Pinterest users also include a link to their Facebook profile; when this was available, we followed the link to obtain the user's self-reported *gender*.

[1]This result may appear to conflict with that of Gilbert et al. However, Ottoni et al. only present this result via a graph with no accompanying statistical analysis. Therefore, it is not clear whether there is a real inconsistency here.

	Q_1	Median	Mean	Q_3
Following	55.0	104.0	293.6	199
Followers	54	115	22,410	233

Table 1. Following and followers: basic statistics in our sample

For pins, we collected data that let us trace how users categorized pins and the flow of information via repinning:

- the *board* to which a specific user added this pin;
- (if this was a repin) the *original pinner*, i.e., the user who first pinned this item and thus started the "tree" of repinning events to which this particular pinning act belonged;
- (if this pin is subsequently repinned by other users) the *repinning user and board to which this pin is repinned.*

For boards, we were interested in data we could use to understand topical structure on Pinterest, specifically:

- the pre-defined Pinterest *category* the board's owner associated with this board (if any).

Gathering the data

Our goal was to obtain a random sample of Pinterest data. However, Pinterest does not provide any publically available way to do so. We therefore wrote a web crawler to approximate a random sample. We ran the crawler in two stages, first to collect a set of *pinners*, then to collect a set of *pins*.

Gathering Pinners

Since we wanted to do analyses based around content, i.e., pinning, we wanted a sample of active pinners. We experimented with several methods of obtaining a sample; we settled on a random walk based method [20], which was simple and performed well. We ran the crawler from Nov 26, 2012 to Jan 15, 2013, performing a random walk from Pinterest's "Everything" page, a public timeline of the most recent pins.

We randomly picked a set of about 10 users whose pins appeared on "Everything" to serve as a "seed set" for the crawler; this seeding method satisfied our bias toward sampling active pinners. The crawler then expanded the seed set by randomly choosing a user from the followers or following list of the user, and then repeating the process from the chosen user. We also did a random "jump" after every 1000 steps of walking the network; again randomly selecting a user from the "Everything" page. We collected the data described above for 46,365 users.

We were able to obtain gender information from Facebook for 32,229 of the users, of whom 30,029 were female and 2,200 were male. This means that 93.2% percent of the known-gender users were female, higher than the overall proportion of female Pinterest users, which is estimated to be about 80%[13, 27]. (Again, this likely is because we focused our sampling on active pinners.)

The Pinterest UI poses a challenge to collecting the following or followed lists of a user. These lists are presented in "infinite scrolling" pages with a limit of about 500 users [2].

[2]Javascript embedded in these pages senses when a user has scrolled to the bottom, and then automatically loads more content.

Users	46,365
Female	30,029 (64.8%)
Male	2,200 (4.7%)
Unknown gender	14,136 (30.5%)
$>$ 90% following obtained	42,369
Pins	3,142,941

Table 2. Summary of the data in our sample

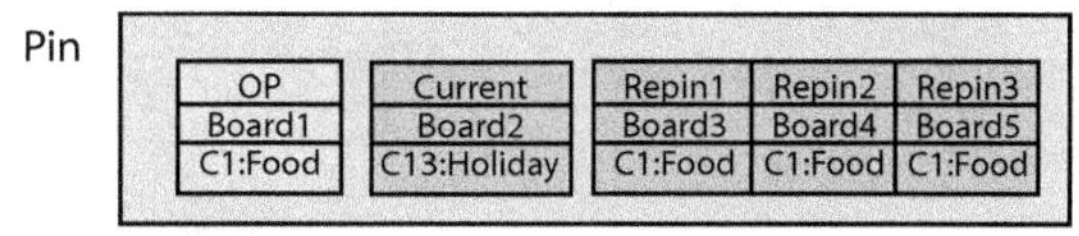

Figure 1. Structure created by different users pinning and repinning the same pin to different boards. OP stands for "Original Pinner".

Thus, in some cases we were not able to obtain all the following users for a user. For reference, Table 1 shows basic data concerning the size of the following and followers lists of users in our sample [3].

In practice, the infinite scrolling / 500-user-limit issue was not a serious obstacle: we were able to obtain at least 90% of the following users for 42,369 of the 46.4K users. We consider this proportion of the data to comprise an adequately complete sample, and so we used this set of 42.4K users for analyses based on social network relationships.

Gathering Pins and Boards and Repin Relationships

We next gathered pins (3.1M in total) for the users from the first step. Again, there was a wrinkle in the access Pinterest provides: only the most recent 10% of all pins from a user can be obtained. For each pin, we also retrieved the original pinner of the pin (if it wasn't the current user), and up to 10 random other users who subsequently repinned this pin[4]; we also obtain the boards which the original pinner and the other users had associated this pin. Finally, for each board, we retrieved its Pinterest category.

Table 2 summarizes the data we collected.

REPRESENTING TOPICS

To perform our analyses, we need a set of topics that represent the content that Pinterest users pin. Pinterest provides a set of 33 categories[5], ranging from "Animals" to "Videos". This set is the first and most obvious candidate for us to consider. However, Pinterest data is richly organized, which offered several other opportunities to consider:

- Co-occurrence relationships between different types of data, e.g. between pins and boards;
- Textual comments users associated with pins and boards.

We explored all these approaches, and experimented with different algorithms as well. However using textual comments was not successful, likely because comments on Pin-

[3]The mean number of followers is so high because a small proprtion of sampled users had huge numbers of followers: the maximum number of followers was over 7 million.

[4]Again, 10 is the limit imposed by Pinterest.

[5]See http://pinterest.com/categories/, downloaded May 2013.

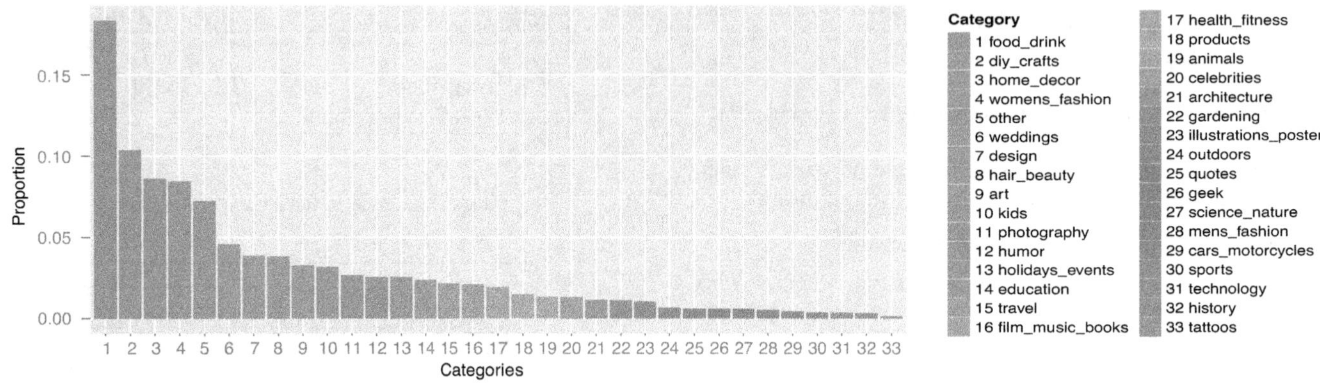

Figure 2. Distribution of content across Pinterest categories. The X axis shows the 33 predefined Pinterest categories, and the Y axis shows the proportion of content in each category.

terest are short and scarce. Both other approaches were successful. We now give more detail on how we applied them and how the results compared.

Categorization 1. Users may assign their boards to one of 33 pre-defined Pinterest categories. Further, pins may appear on multiple boards, which in general will belong to different Pinterest categories. These relationships let us:

- represent the topical structure of pins with a vector over the 33 Pinterest categories;
- aggregate the topic vectors of all a user's pins to derive a topic vector for users;
- represent each pre-defined Pinterest category as a binary vector of length 3,142,941 (the number of pins in our sample), where a 1 indicates the pin appeared in the category and a 0 indicates it did not appear;
- compute similarity relationships between pins, between users, and between the pre-defined Pinterest categories.

Categorization 2. Since the same pin may be added to different boards by different users, we can compute interboard relationships based on the number of pin co-occurrences. We then apply a clustering algorithm to these data to derive another topical structure. This method also reveals more detailed topical information, i.e., sub-category relationships, than the first method.

Comparison. We compared the two topical structures. To the extent they are similar, it gives us confidence in the reliability of results we obtain using either of the structures.

Categorization 1 details

Users may categorize their boards using one of the 33 predefined Pinterest categories. For example, a user might create a board called "Desserts" and categorize it under "Food & Drink". Users can browse pins by category: pins that were added to a board for a given category may be found under that category. For example, if a user pins a recipe for strawberry shortcake to "Desserts", then the pin for that recipe could be found by browsing the "Food & Drink" category.

Of course, this categorization structure is not perfect: some users don't assign categories to their boards (or use the default "Other" which consists about 7% of pins in the data set), and different users may categorize the same item differently. For example, one might pin a reference to a learning toy to a board categorized as "Education", while another may pin it to a board categorized as "Kids".

Therefore, we take the user defined categorization structure as a starting point to represent pins and users.

1. **Representing pins.** When users repin a pin they find interesting, they are indirectly assigning that pin to multiple Pinterest categories. For example, the pin in Figure 1 has been pinned by five users to five boards: four of these boards were categorized as "Food & Drink", and one was categorized as "Holidays & Events". We define the topic vector of a pin as a normalized count of the categories of the pin:

$$\vec{p_i} = < p_{i,1}, p_{i,2}, ..., p_{i,33} > \quad (1)$$

where $p_{i,j}$ is the fraction of appearance of jth category on pin p_i. Therefore, the topic vector for the pin from Figure 1 is $< 0.8, 0, .., 0, 0.2, 0, .., 0 >$ where the nonzero entries are the first and the thirteenth.

2. **Representing users.** We represent each user by aggregating and normalizing the topic vectors of all the user's pins:

$$\hat{u} = \frac{\vec{u}}{||\vec{u}||_1}, \quad where \ \vec{u} = \sum_{\vec{p_i} \in \mathbf{P_u}} \vec{p_i} \quad (2)$$

and $\mathbf{P_u}$ is the set of pins that belongs to user u.

We emphasize that this representation of topics for pins and users is *community-based*. For example, if one user added a pin to a board categorized as "Geek", and another repinned that pin to a board categorized as "Technology", we would consider that pin to be associated with both topics equally; and from the perspective of the two users, we would say that each had pinned content on "Geek" and "Technology". This approach is fundamentally different than that of Ottoni et al. [27]. Their approach does not aggregate beyond the individual, simply using whatever categories an individual user had assigned to her boards in analyzing the categories of the user and her pins. In our example, the first user's pin would be categorized only as "Geek", and that user's categories would include only "Geek". Similarly, the second user's (re)pin would be categorized only as "Technology", and her categories would include only "Technology". We believe the community-based categorization approach makes more sense; in any case, this difference means that even when we seem to be studying the same questions as Ottoni et al., our results are not directly comparable.

Categorization 2 details

In the previous approach, boards played only an intermediary role, linking pins to pre-defined categories. However, in the second approach, boards played a primary role, analogous to tags in a folksonomy [22]. That is, adding a pin **P** to a board **B** is analogous to applying the tag **B** to the object **P**. Many board names are used by multiple users, such as "Recipes", "Kids", "Style", and "Sewing". We constructed an undirected weighted graph whose nodes represent (stemmed[6]) board names and whose edges represent a pin appearing on both boards; the edge weight indicates the number of pins that appeared on both boards. Next, we applied the METIS graph partitioning algorithm [17] to the graph, parameterizing it to produce 33 clusters, which enables us to compare its results to the results obtained using the pre-defined Pinterest categories.

We wanted to verify that these clusters were reasonable. A standard way to do this is to measure how distinct the clusters are: the more distinct, the better the clustering. We measured similarity between clusters using cosine similarity. The average cosine similarity of the 33 clusters was 0.25, which indicates that the categories were acceptably distinct.

Comparing the two categorizations

We needed to select a categorization to use for our analysis. Ideally, the two categorizations would be similar, so we could select one for reasons of convenience. To determine similarity, we represent each cluster as a vector over the 33 Pinterest categories. We assigned each stemmed board name in the cluster to one Pinterest category[7]. The entries in the vector then represent the proportion of boards from the cluster in each Pinterest category. The key observation we made is that most of the plots show a single dominant peak: this indicates that the cluster corresponds closely to one pre-defined Pinterest category. For example, one cluster mapped wholly to the category "DIY & Crafts". In a few other cases, a cluster was an interesting mix of intuitively related categories: for example, one cluster had 75% of its content in "Weddings" and 25% of its content in "Holidays & Events".

The automatically derived clusters reveal more fine-grained topical structure. For example, four clusters had a peak for the category "Food & Drink". We examined these clusters and saw that each had a different focus, for example: baking and cakes vs. breakfast vs. salads, soups, and healthy recipes.

[6]Meaning that "bicycles" and "bicycling" are equated, for example.

[7]Since we stem board names, it is possible that a single stemmed board name may belong to multiple categories. In this case, we assign the stemmed board name to the most frequently occurring category. If there is a tie, we pick a tied category at random.

Since the comparison between the two topic representations showed that they were quite similar, we decide to use the first one for our analysis. We favored it because (a) it is based directly on pre-defined Pinterest categories, which makes the analyses more comprehensible, and (b) our analyses did not need the more detailed topical structure that the second categorization offers.

RESULTS AND DISCUSSION

We organize the presentation of our results around our three research questions, *RQ1-Topics*, *RQ2-Specialization*, and *RQ3-Homophily*.

RQ1-Topics

In this section, we give a descriptive overview of the content on Pinterest based on the topic representation we produced. We show how popular the various topics are, illustrate relationships between topics, and investigate whether men and women (collectively) differ in the categories of their pins.

Which topics are most popular?

To reveal the amount of content in each of the 33 Pinterest categories, we summed and normalized the topic vectors of the 3.143M pins in our dataset. Each entry in this vector represents the proportion of content in one category. Figure 2 shows the result.

Content is distributed unequally across the categories. In fact, topic popularity follows a power law ($p < 0.05$, using the Kolmogorov-Smirnov test): "Food & Drink", "DIY & Craft", "Home Decor" and "Women's Fashion" together account for over 45% of the content, while "History", "Tattoos", "Technology", and "Sports" together account for just over 1%. Note also that 7% of content falls into the default "Other" category, meaning it not categorized by users.

How are topics related?

We also wanted to investigate how topics were related. We use the fact that a single pin can appear on boards belonging to different categories as the basis for computing relationships between categories. For example, some users might pin a recipe for the Christmas drink eggnog to boards in the "Food & Drink" category, while others might pin it to "Holiday & Event" boards. We use the frequency of co-appearance of two categories on all pins as a measure of the relatedness of the categories. For each category i, we define C_i as a binary vector of length 3.143M, where each 1 in the vector denotes that the relevant pin was categorized under category i. We compute the similarity of two categories using Jaccard Similarity, where a 1 indicates perfect similarity and a 0 total dissimilarity.

$$sim(C_i, C_j) = \frac{|C_i \cap C_j|}{|C_i \cup C_j|} \quad (3)$$

Jaccard Similarity is suitable for our purposes since it works well for vectors with many 0 entries, which we have.

We computed the pairwise similarity of all 33 Pinterest categories. This revealed interesting relationships. (1) "Other" is most similar to the rest of the categories. This makes sense:

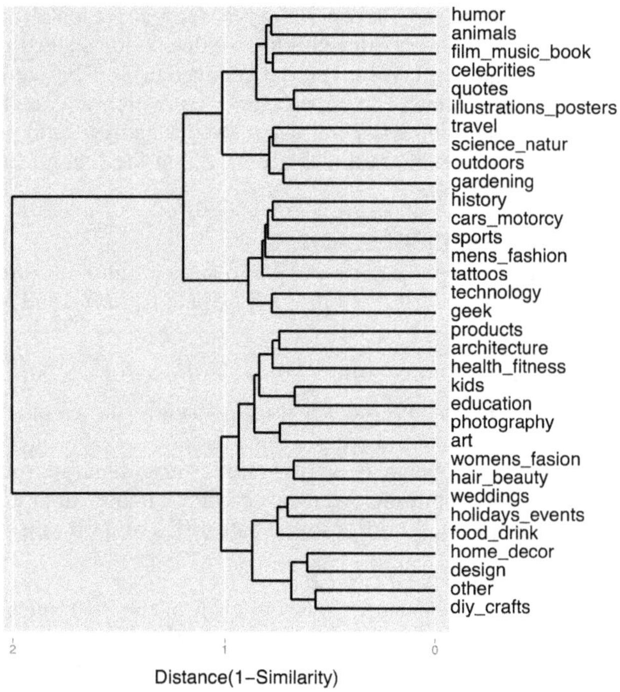

Figure 3. Clustering result of categories

since "Other" is the default category for boards that users did not categorize, the content of these boards will overlap with content in all the other categories. (2) After "Other", "Art", "Photography", and "Design" are most similar to the remaining categories. This may be due to the fact that most pins on Pinterest indicate visually attractive pictures, which naturally could fit under these broad, almost syntactic categories. (3) "Tattoos", "Sports" and "Cars & Motorcycles" are most distinct from other categories. Two factors might play a role here: first, these categories may be better defined and more narrow; second, these categories may be less likely to co-appear with other categories due to their unpopularity.

To understand inter-topic relationships more deeply, we clustered the topics (using Ward Hierarchical Clustering). The results, shown in Figure 3, help paint a picture of activity on Pinterest. They confirm intuitions about how topics are related: for example "DIY & Crafts", "Home Decor", "Design", "Food & Drink", and "Holiday & Events" cluster together, as do "Outdoors", "Gardening", and "Science & Nature", and "Geek" and "Technology". Some of the topics that cluster closely suggest different purposes of categorization applied by different users. For instance, "Kids" and "Education" may be closely related because some users categorize pins according to the content itself, ("Education"), while others categorize according to the usage of the content, (for "Kids"). In addition, to preview an issue we study in detail next, categories that are proportionally more popular among women such as "Weddings" and "Holidays & Events" tend to cluster together, as do categories proportionally more popular among men, such as "Geek" and "Technology".

While these results may seem intuitive, we think it always is helpful to provide empirical evidence that intuitions are true, since sometimes they aren't.

Do men and women differ in the content they pin?

We based our analysis on the subset of 32.2K users whose gender we knew from their Facebook profiles. As we mentioned, women constitute a larger proportion of our sample than in the general Pinterest population. However, we are not comparing the total amount of content contributed by men and women. Instead, we examine the relative proportion of content men and women pin across the Pinterest categories.

Figure 4 shows the distribution of topics for male and female users. There are noticeable differences in the topics which men (in general) and women (in general) pin. For example, roughly 10% of all pins from men, but only about 3% of pins from women were categorized as "Design". And for men, "Design" was the second most popular category, while for women, it was the 9th most popular category (omitting "Other" in both cases). There are many categories that received differing degrees of interest from men and from women, including "Geek", "History", and "Sports" (more popular among men), and "Kids", "Wedding", and "Holiday & Events" (more popular among women). Indeed, men's and women's pinning activity was significantly different for all categories (at the 0.01 level) except for "Humor", "Tattoos", "Animals", "Quotes", and "Gardening". But "Food & Drink" is the most popular category for both women and men.

In addition, women in general concentrate their pinning activity on fewer categories: their top 5 categories account for just over 56% of all their activity, while the top 5 categories for men account for just under 40% of their activity.

Further, stereotypical men's topics are not even that popular among men! While men devote more attention than women to "Sports", "Technology" and "Cars & Motorcycle", these topics are not even among the 10 most popular categories for men. Instead, male Pinterest users pin more content about "Photography", "Art", "Design", and "Home Decor". We offer several conjectures concerning these results in the *Implications for Research and Design* section below.

RQ2-Specialization

The previous investigations painted a picture of global activity on Pinterest. We now zoom in to the individual level, asking: to what extent do users specialize in particular content topics? Do women and men differ in degree of specialization? What factors, including the degree of specialization, attract more followers?

To what extent do users specialize in particular topics?

Building on the previous research covered above, we investigated the extent to which users concentrate their pinning in a few categories vs. distributing it across many categories.

We measure the diversity of users' interests (the opposite of specialization) by computing the entropy of users' topic vectors. Entropy is the state of the art measure of variety, which is the composition of differences in categories [15]. The entropy of a user topic vector reaches a maximum[8] if a user

[8]Given by $ln(x)$, where $x = 33$ in our case; $ln(33) \sim 3.5$

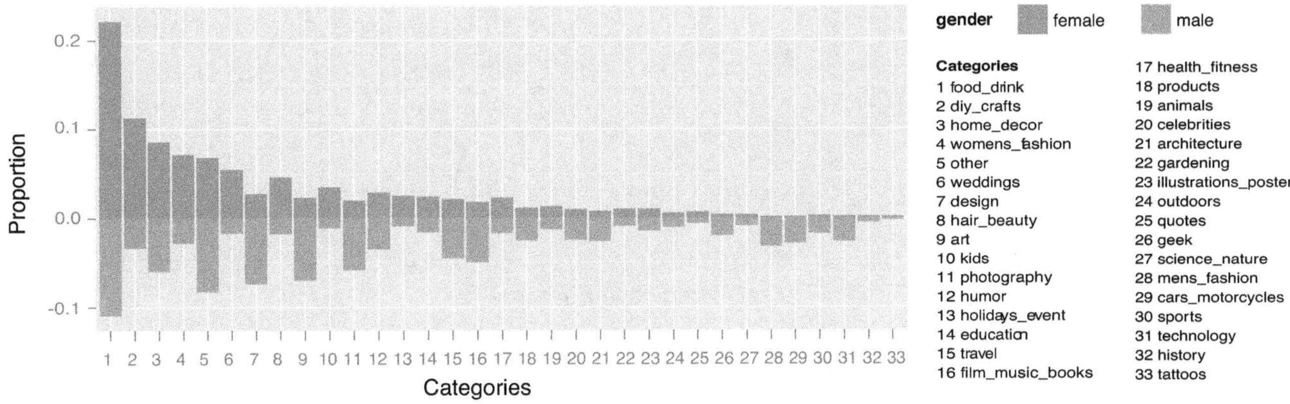

Figure 4. How women's and men's overall pinning activity is distributed across categories. The X axis shows the 33 Pinterest categories, and the Y axis shows the relative proportion of each topic within gender.

pinned the same amount of content from all 33 categories and is equal to zero if all the content is from one category. Entropy is defined as:

$$Entropy(\hat{u}) = -\sum_{j=1}^{33} u_j \log_e u_j \quad (4)$$

where u_j is the jth entry in user vector $\hat{u}$, denoting the fraction of content in jth category.

Intuitively, one would expect users with more pins to cover a wider spectrum of categories; therefore, we group users based on the number of their pins for the topic diversity analysis. Specifically, we divided users into three equal sized groups based on their total number of pins. Figure 5 shows the group intervals and the distributions of the diversity of the groups. Our intuition was borne out: users with larger number of pins do tend to have more diverse interests (differences were significant, $p < .001$). [9] However, there are specialists even among prolific pinners. To take two contrasting examples, one specialist had 1015 pins, with over 90% in "Food & Drink", while a generalist had 1078 pins, with 18% in "Film & Music & Books", 15% in "Food & Drink", 9% in "Other", 8% in "Photography", 6% in "Home Decor", 5% in "Celebrities" etc, spanning 32 categories.

Do women and men differ in degree of specialization?

We next tested whether men and women differed in the diversity of their interests. To handle the greatly differing numbers of men and women in our dataset, we randomly sampled 300 male and 300 female users from each of the three activity-level groups from the previous section.

Table 3 shows the result of comparing the topic diversity of male and female users. In all groups, women pinned significantly more diverse content than men ($p < 0.001$). [10] These

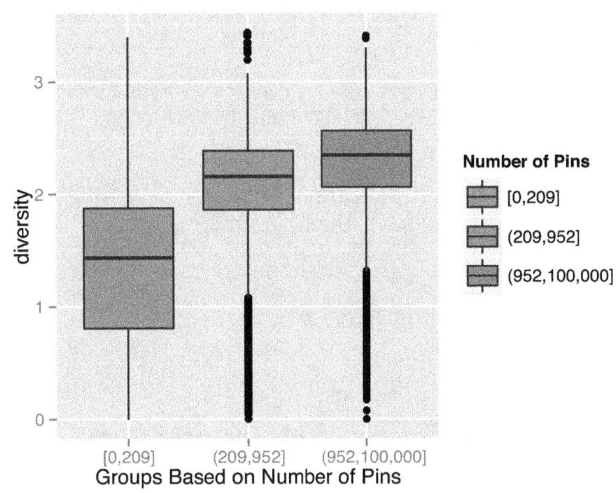

Figure 5. Diversity of 3 equal sized group of users, based on the number of their pins.

results may seem inconsistent with those of Figure 4. However, those results were for the male and the female populations as a whole, while the results of Table 3 aggregate based on individual users. Thus, while men *collectively* have more diverse interests (than women collectively), each *individual* male user is more likely to specialize in specific categories than individual female users.

Recall that Ottoni et al. [27] found that female Pinterest users were content generalists to a greater extent than males. As we explained above, their results are not directly comparable to ours. However, their analysis was done at the individual level, like our analysis in this section. Thus, in this respect our findings are similar to theirs.

What factors, including the degree of specialization, attract more followers?

The data we gathered and the previous analyses we have done let us investigate what makes a Pinterest user "popular". We use *number of followers* as our popularity metric: since the default home page for a logged in Pinterest user

[9] To ensure that these results were not due to outliers, we did the same analysis with 10 groups of users. The pattern of results was the same, with the exception that the two most active groups were indistinguishable.

[10] We did the same analysis using 10 equal sized groups, and the pattern was the same: women pinned more diverse content for all groups except the least and most active.

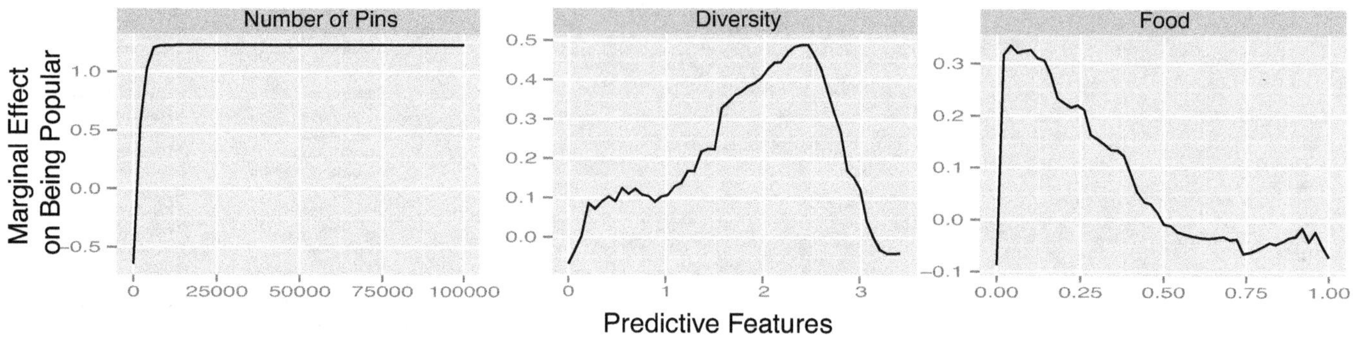

Figure 6. Marginal effect of diversity, food and number of pins on popularity

Group	Group Mean	Gender	Sample Mean
Low	1.327	Male	1.040
		Female	1.42
Medium	2.078	Male	1.82
		Female	2.089
High	2.261	Male	2.13
		Female	2.241

Table 3. Comparison of topic diversity between male and female users. For all three activity levels (Low, Medium, and High), men are significantly less diverse than women.

shows a feed of new pins from the users they follow, the more followers users have, the larger their audience.

We used the following features to model user popularity:

- *gender*: gender of the user;
- *nPins*: number of pins;
- *nBoards*: number of boards;
- *nFollowing*: number of users that the user follows;
- *topics*: the user's normalized topic vector;
- *diversity*: diversity of the user's interest, measured by the entropy of the topic vector.

We use a binary classification model to study the effect of these features on number of followers. We created two classes to predict: the top quartile and the botom quartile of users based on number of followers. We choose a classification model over a regression model because regression models put too much emphasis on predicting the exact number of followers instead of modeling general trends and relationships [3]. Previous work [13] used linear regression to model the effect of several factors on number of followers. However, the model suffers from poor fit (low R^2) and used only basic data from user profiles (like the first four features above) but did not have access to the two features that characterize the content a user pins, *topics* and *diversity*.

In selecting a classification model, our goal was not only high prediction accuracy but also simplicity of model interpretation. We experimented with logistic regression and Random Forest models. The Random Forest model [8] is a widely used and accurate statistical ensemble method that combines multiple simple decision trees, each of which is trained on a bootstrap sample from the entire training data. The Random Forest model performed better and was effective in illuminating the effect of the predictive features. Therefore, we report our findings using this model.

We experimented with models using different number of trees, measuring the error each time. With 25 trees, the error rate was about 0.15, with 100 trees it approached 0.14, and by the time we reached 500 trees, it had converged to 0.136[11]. These low error rates give us confidence in our model.

The Random Forest model provides a robust and accurate way to measure the importance of each predictive feature: the algorithm drops each feature, and then computes the reduction in prediction accuracy using the rest of the features. Figure 7 illustrates the importance of the features. The most important feature is the number of users a user follows: that is, users who follow a lot of users also get followed a lot. The next two features, number of pins and number of boards, measure quantity of contribution: the more you pin, the more followers you earn. After this, the model mostly ranks the relative importance of pinning to various categories: pinning to "Food & Drink" and "Design" will attract the most followers, and more generally, pinning to popular categories attracts more followers.

Note that gender did not play a critical role in popularity. *Diversity*, on the other hand, was about as important as pinning to the most popular categories. To sum up, the model suggests that to attract lots of followers, you should: follow lots of other pinners, create lots of boards and pin a lot, post on popular topics, and don't concentrate on too few topics.

We also can find the *marginal effect* of predictive features on popularity; this is the effect one feature has on the prediction result when all other features have fixed values. For example, the marginal effect of number of pins is shown in Figure 6: the popularity of a user increases steeply as the number of pins increases to 4000, staying steady thereafter.

The marginal effect of diversity shows a more interesting pattern. When the diversity (measured by entropy) is around 2.4, the probability of being popular reaches a peak. In other words, increasing the diversity of the content you pin is good up to a certain point and thereafter, it becomes a disadvantage to be too diverse. Moreover, when we look at the marginal effect graphs for specific content categories, we see

[11] The error rate is the Out-Of-Bag (OOB) error, which is equivalent to errors of cross validation. [8]

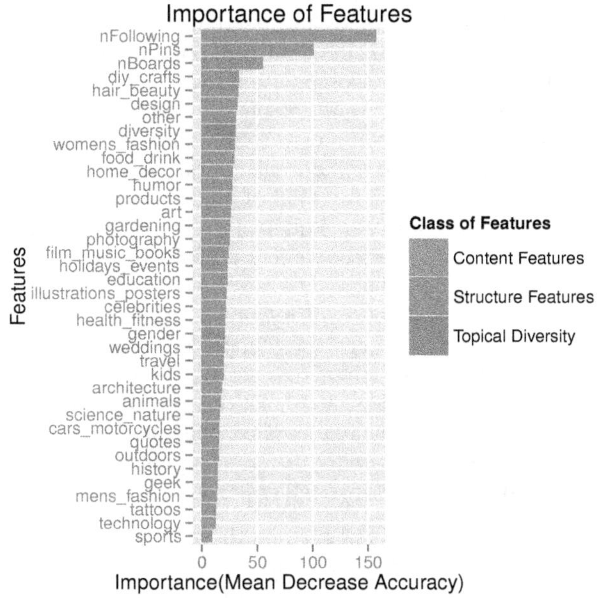

Figure 7. Importance of predictive features

a similar pattern: as the third part of Figure 6 shows, concentrating on "Food & Drink" will gain you more followers until you're devoting about 35% of your pins to that topic; further specialization does no good.

RQ3-Homophily

We were inspired by the observation by Zarro et al. that Pinterest is less of a social network than a *social curation* site [39]; one of their participants reported that "you can like stuff of random people, and you don't have to make a further connection." This suggests that shared interests may be a stronger driver of activity on Pinterest than social connections and interaction.

Based on this suggestion, we studied how homophily of interests influenced the two key Pinterest activities *following* and *repinning*. Specifically, were users more similar in their interests to those they followed than to random Pinterest users? And were users were more likely to repin from users who are similar to them than from random users?

We used the cosine similarity of users' topic vectors as our homophily measure:

$$homophily(\hat{u_1}, \hat{u_2}) = cosine(\hat{u_1}, \hat{u_2}) = \frac{\hat{u_1} \cdot \hat{u_2}}{|\hat{u_1}| \cdot |\hat{u_2}|} \quad (5)$$

We define several terms to facilitate the statement of hypotheses to test our research questions. For each user u, U_{repin} represents the set of users u has repinned, U_{no_repin} represents the set of users u has not repinned, U_{follow} represents the set of users u follows, and U_{no_follow} represents the set of users u does not follow. We then define $S_{repin,u}$ to represent the average cosine similarity between u and U_{repin} and define $S_{no\_repin,u}$, $S_{follow,u}$, and $S_{no\_follow,u}$ correspondingly. Finally, to test our hypotheses, all we need to do is test whether S_{follow} and S_{no_follow} have the same means and whether S_{repin} and S_{no_repin} have the same means, which we can do with a one-sided T-test.

However, while conceptually simple, testing these hypotheses is computationally expensive since S_{no_repin} and S_{no_follow} are very large sets for all the 46.4K users in our sample. We therefore made several simplifications to come up with a feasible computation. *Simplification 1.* We investigated whether we could use a smaller set of users as a "stand-in" for S_{no_repin} and S_{no_follow}. Experimentation showed that sets of size 5000 sufficed. *Simplification 2.* However, a problem remains: we still would have to perform 5000 cosine similarity computations for every user in our sample. To avoid this, we clustered users based on their topic vectors to form groups of users with similar interests. We then used the cluster centroid as the representative of all users in that cluster in the computation of S_{no_repin} and S_{no_follow}, which meant we only had to carry out one statistical test per cluster.

Testing the hypotheses. Different values of the clustering parameter K (the number of clusters the algorithm will create) result in clusters of different size and composition. Therefore, we tested our hypotheses for different values of K. The process we followed to test our hypotheses was:

- For each user, compute the similarity to those users they follow S_{follow} and those users from whom they repin S_{repin} (these are exact values, not approximations).
- For $K = (5, 10, 30, 50, 80, 100)$
  - Obtain a set of K clusters of users.
  - For each cluster C in the set of K clusters:
    * Approximate U_{no_follow} / U_{no_repin} with 5000 randomly selected users whom no user in C follows / repinned.
    * Approximate S_{no_follow} / S_{no_repin} as the similarity of the centroid of C to each of the users in U_{no_follow} / U_{no_repin}.
    * $S_{follows}$ / S_{repin} is the set of similarities of all the users in C to all the users whom they follow / repinned.
    * Run a t-test to compare S_{repin} and S_{no_repin} / S_{follow} and S_{no_follow}.

Table 4 shows the results. The results for repinning behavior were unequivocal: for every case we tested (a total of 275 clusters), users were more similar to those from whom they repinned than they were to random Pinterest users. This is consistent with the conjecture, based on Zarro et al., that content plays a bigger role than social interaction in driving Pinterest activity. The trend was the same for following behavior, but there were many exceptions: in 63 of the 275 clusters, users were not significantly more similar to those they followed than they were to random users. One factor that could contribute to this is if people follow those whom they know – family and friends – but they do not necessarily share many interests with these people. Indeed, we found that people often repin from users whom they do not follow, over 50% of the repin events in our sample.

K	Repin	Follow
5	5	3
10	10	7
30	30	26
50	50	41
80	80	64
100	100	71

Table 4. Result of homophily test. Repin: # of clusters where users are more similar to users from whom they repin than random users. Follow: # of clusters where users are more similar to users whom they follow than random users.

IMPLICATIONS FOR RESEARCH AND DESIGN

Using Pinterest as a research context, we set out to investigate how two factors, *specialization* and *homophily*, influence the attraction of audience. We also considered how gender might mediate the effects of these factors. We articulated specific research questions and carried out a quantitative study to answer these questions.

We built on a set of content categories provided by Pinterest to create a community-based representation of Pinterest content. This let us characterize the content on the site, including quantifying relationships between categories. We then used our representation of topics as the basis for a number of statistical analyses. Our key findings included:

- Women and men differed both in the types of content they collected, and the degree to which they specialized in certain types of content; interestingly, despite these gender differences, men were not particularly interested in stereotypically male topics.
- Sharing diverse types of content is correlated with a larger number of followers, but only up to a certain point; after that, more diversity is not helpful. This result helps refine researchers' understanding of the role of content diversity in attracting an audience, particularly in light of the differing findings of prior work (compare [16] to [37]).
- Homophily of interests is a major driver of repinning: people repin from other users who share their interests; people also share the interests of those they follow, but there are more exceptions to this rule.

Our results raise a number of issues deserving additional research and design attention.

Most generally, our quantitative results illuminate *what* Pinterest users do, but not *why* they behave this way or how they understand their own behaviors. Followup work, particularly using qualitative methods, is needed to answer the latter questions. Some of the most compelling questions concern gender; for example, why are male Pinterest users not particularly interested in stereotypically male content?

Before attempting to answer this question, we should be careful in making assumptions about "stereotypical male" content. A useful guide here is work by Lam et al. [19], which investigated gender differences among editors on Wikipedia. Rather than taking it for granted which topics were of interest to men or women, they found an external data source that allowed them to compute this objectively within a specific domain (movies). We recommend following this approach in future studies of Pinterest. Once this is done, and assuming our results hold, there are several possible conjectures worth investigating. (i) As we discussed in *Theoretical Foundations and Related Work*, the dominant popular portrayal of Pinterest is as a site for women's interests. Therefore, perhaps men who choose to join Pinterestare disproportionately more interested in steroetypically female topics than most men. This is a *selection effect* explanation; some men may perceive Pinterest as "not my kind of place" [4]. (ii) Women make up a large majority of Pinterest users and pin content they find interesting. This content is visually prominent for all users, female and male, and thus influences repinning behavior by all users. This *social influence* has been observed in tagging systems: the tags users apply are strongly influenced by the community tags that are visible to them [31]. Notice that neither of these explanations presumes that the differences between male and female Pinterest users' behavior are due to *inherent* gender differences; instead, they are based on different types of social context.

Second, more research is needed on the utility of topic specialization vs. diversity. For example, are users aware of being topic specialists or generalists? If so, how do they think about this dichotomy (or is it a spectrum?): do they consciously seek a particular level of specialization, and are their self perceptions of their degree of specialization consistent with quantitative measures? Interviews would an appropriate way to study these questions.

Third, we explored two different ways to represent topics on Pinterest, one based on pre-defined Pinterest categories and one consisting of algorithmically derived clusters. While we did not use the second representation of topics for this research, it has the intriquing property that it reveals more fine grained topical structure. In-depth explorations with this representation would illuminate Pinterest users' own emergent categorizations of content, particularly distinctions (of meaning and use) within the pre-defined categories.

Finally, nearly all social network sites provide mechanisms to recommend or filter content and potential social connections. Our results highlight the importance of effective methods for early personalization of site content; if new users perceive a site as "not my kind of place", they are likely to abandon it. While improved personalization methods might make Pinterest "more friendly" to (some) men, the effect is more general and gender neutral: if done well, all users would experience content that matches their interests. We suggest several specific personalization techniques worth exploring:

- Focus more on recommending content from users with similar interests, rather than those whom the user is socially close to.
- Maintain an appropriate amount of diversity in content recommendations.
- Promote the ability of users to follow single *boards*, rather than users.
- Use the category of items as a more prominent visual organizing principle. Even better, try using an automatically derived, more detailed categorization like we described in the *Representing Topics* section: for example, woodwork-

ing and jewelry projects both may be included under "DIY and Crafts", yet may appeal to different audiences.

REFERENCES

1. *Gender and Power in On-line Communication.* Blackwell Publishing Ltd, 2008.
2. Eliciting and Focusing Geographic Volunteer Work. *CSCW* (2010).
3. Anderson, A., Huttenlocher, D., Kleinberg, J., and Leskovec, J. Discovering value from community activity on focused question answering sites. In *KDD*, ACM (2012).
4. Antin, J. My kind of people?: perceptions about wikipedia contributors and their motivations. In *CHI*, ACM (2011).
5. Arguello, J., Butler, B. S., Joyce, E., Kraut, R., Ling, K. S., Rosé, C., and Wang, X. Talk to me: foundations for successful individual-group interactions in online communities. ACM (2006).
6. Barabási, A. Emergence of scaling in random networks. *Science* (1999).
7. Beckwith, L., Kissinger, C., Burnett, M., Wiedenbeck, S., Lawrance, J., Blackwell, A., and Cook, C. Tinkering and gender in end-user programmers' debugging. In *CHI*, ACM (2006).
8. Breiman, L. Random Forests. *Machine Learning 45*, 1 (Oct. 2001), 5–32.
9. Caverlee, J., and Webb, S. The Social Honeypot Project: Protecting Online Communities from Spammers. In *WWW* (2010).
10. Cunha, E., Magno, G., Almeida, V., Gonçalves, M. A., and Benevenuto, F. A gender based study of tagging behavior in twitter. In *HT*, ACM (2012).
11. Daniele Quercia, Jonathan Ellis, Licia Capra, J. C. In the mood for being influential on twitter, 2011.
12. Demartini, G. Finding experts using wikipedia. *ISWC/ASWC2007* (2007).
13. Gilbert, E., Bakhshi, S., Chang, S., and Terveen, L. I Need to Try This!: A Statistical Overview of Pinterest. *CHI* (2013).
14. Goel, S., and Mason, W. Real and perceived attitude agreement in social networks. *Journal of Personality and Social Psychology 99*, 4 (2010), 611–621.
15. Harrison, D., and Klein, K. What's the difference? Diversity constructs as separation, variety, or disparity in organizations. *Academy of Management Review* (2007).
16. Hutto, C., Yardi, S., and Gilbert, E. A longitudinal study of follow predictors on twitter. In *CHI* (2013).
17. Karypis, G., and Kumar, V. A fast and high quality multilevel scheme for partitioning irregular graphs. *SIAM Journal on scientific Computing* (1998).
18. Kivran-Swaine, F., and Naaman, M. Network properties and social sharing of emotions in social awareness streams. In *CSCW* (2011).
19. Lam, S. T. K., Uduwage, A., Dong, Z., Sen, S., Musicant, D. R., Terveen, L., and Riedl, J. WP:clubhouse?: an exploration of Wikipedia's gender imbalance. In *WikiSym*, ACM (2011).
20. Leskovec, J., and Faloutsos, C. Sampling from large graphs. *KDD* (2006).
21. Liben-Nowell, D., and Kleinberg, J. The link prediction problem for social networks. In *CIKM* (2003).
22. Macgregor, G., and McCulloch, E. Collaborative tagging as a knowledge organisation and resource discovery tool. *Library review* (2006).
23. Marcotte, A. A social network of one's own. *The American Prospect* (March 2 2012). `http://prospect.org/article/social-network-ones-own`.
24. Masli, M., Priedhorsky, R., and Terveen, L. Task specialization in social production communities: The case of geographic volunteer work. *ICWSM* (2011).
25. McPherson, M., L. S.-L., and Cook, J. Birds of a feather: Homophily in social networks. *Annual review of sociology* (2001), 415–444.
26. nathanjurgenson. Pinterest and feminism. *thesocietypages.org* (March 5 2012). `http://thesocietypages.org/cyborgology/2012/03/05/pinterest-and-feminism/`.
27. Ottoni, R., Pesce, J., and Casas, D. L. Ladies First: Analyzing Gender Roles and Behaviors in Pinterest. *ICWSM* (2013).
28. Ren, Y., Harper, F. M., Drenner, S., Terveen, L. G., Kiesler, S. B., Riedl, J., and Kraut, R. E. Building member attachment in online communities: Applying theories of group identity and interpersonal bonds. *MIS Quarterly* (2012).
29. Rode, J. A. A theoretical agenda for feminist hci. *Interacting with Computers* (2011).
30. Selwyn, N. Whats in the box? exploring learners rejection of educational computing. *Educational Research and Evaluation* (1998).
31. Sen, S., Lam, S. K., Rashid, A. M., Cosley, D., Frankowski, D., Osterhouse, J., Harper, F. M., and Riedl, J. Tagging, communities, vocabulary, evolution. *CSCW* (2006).
32. Stevenson, S. Pinterest for dudes. *slate.com* (April 1 2013). `http://www.slate.com/articles/technology/technology/2013/04/gentlemint_manteresting_tapiture_is_it_sexist_to_create_a_pinterest_for.single.html`.
33. Suh, B., Hong, L., Pirolli, P., and Chi, E. H. Want to be Retweeted? Large Scale Analytics on Factors Impacting Retweet in Twitter Network. In *SocialCom* (2010).
34. Tan, D. S., Czerwinski, M., and Robertson, G. Women go with the (optical) flow. In *CHI*, ACM (2003).
35. Thelwall, M. Social networks, gender, and friending: An analysis of MySpace member profiles. *Journal of the American Society for Information Science and Technology 59*, 8 (2008), 1321–1330.

36. Wanenchak, S. Pinterest and playing gender. *thesocietypages.org* (April 5 2013). `http://thesocietypages.org/cyborgology/2013/04/05/pinterest-and-playing-gender/`.
37. Wang, Y.-C., and Kraut, R. Twitter and the development of an audience. In *CHI* (2012).
38. Williams, M. E. Pinterests gender trouble. *salon.com* (May 2 2012). `http://www.salon.com/2012/05/02/pinterests_gender_trouble/`.
39. Zarro, M., Hall, C., and Forte, A. Wedding dresses and wanted criminals: Pinterest. com as an infrastructure for repository building. *ICWSM* (2013).
40. Ziegler, C.-N., McNee, S. M., Konstan, J. A., and Lausen, G. Improving recommendation lists through topic diversification. In *WWW* (2005).

Making IT "Pay a Bit Better"- Design Challenges for Micro Rural Enterprise

Andy Crabtree and Alan Chamberlain
School of Computer Science
University of Nottingham
{First name.Last name}@nottingham.ac.uk

ABSTRACT

This paper reports on a field study of small market in Wales undertaken as part of broader research project aimed at developing IT solutions to support rural enterprise. The project is predicated on the assumption that the primary challenge facing rural enterprise is that of scale and that IT solutions could and should add value by enabling growth. The study suggests that many rural enterprises are micro in character, that they are not driven by the need to grow, and that value is and can be added in different ways that reflect the social values oriented to and employed by micro businesses and their consumers. The paper elaborates vernacular understandings of supply chains and their coordination, along with business and consumer motivations to consider alternative possibilities for design that place emphasis on making micro rural enterprise 'pay a bit better' rather than scaling it up.

Author Keywords

Micro rural enterprise; fieldwork; design challenges.

ACM Classification Keywords

H.5.3 [Group and Organisation Interfaces]: Computer-supported cooperative work.

INTRODUCTION

Interest in the rural as a site for computing research and development is growing and a wide range of research initiatives are now seeking to bridge the urban-rural divide. These include infrastructure initiatives to address problems of digital access and inclusion [e.g., 1, 24]; initiatives to design technology around available infrastructures and user characteristics [e.g., 4, 30]; and an increasing array of substantive applications supporting e-Governance [19], mobile enterprise [10], finance [21], healthcare [3], indigenous knowledge [26], community interaction [28], interaction between women [22], games for children [17], and more. Running alongside these developments are an increasing array of studies of technology adoption and use in rural contexts in both developing and developed nations [e.g., 13, 16, 18].

This paper focuses on the challenges involved in developing computer support for micro rural enterprise *in the UK*. We emphasize *in the UK* because context is important. It always is, but it is particularly salient in this case as a great deal of the research conducted in rural settings to date (enterprise-oriented or not) focuses on developing nations and Africa and India in particular. The UK is not a developing nation. On the contrary, it is one the wealthiest economies in the world, ranking 6th in the IMF's 2012 GDP listing. We state the obvious because the context of research frames the kinds of assumptions, expectations, and understandings of the design challenges that are associated with the rural [e.g., 6, 15, 29].

Design-oriented research in the UK and other developed nations is not framed by the kinds assumptions, expectations, and understandings that frame HCI4D and postcolonial computing. The context is different, the challenges are different, and the ways in which we might understand and respond to them are different. Research initiatives and studies in this space are also rather thinner on the ground than they are in developing nations. Those that focus on small and micro rural enterprise focus on the generic infrastructure issues that impact the rural per se, social networking between businesses, and micro logistics [8]. Micro enterprises – or businesses with 9 or fewer employees - represent over 90% of all enterprises within the UK and the broader trading zone in which the country primarily operates: Europe. There are over 18 million micro enterprises across Europe employing over 37 million people with an annual turnover in excess of one trillion euros [11]. The sector is, then, a significant contributor to EU nation state economies.

The design challenges we report here are based on an ongoing field study of (and design intervention in) a small market town in Wales. Findings from the study *challenge the assumptions* framing and motivating the research and reframe understanding of the nature of technical solutions required by micro rural enterprise in an already developed context. The research was based on the assumption that technological support should enable micro businesses to *scale up*, and that augmenting the *consumer-producer* relationship is the primary means of adding value and

CSCW'14, February 15–19, 2014, Baltimore, Maryland, USA.

http://dx.doi.org/10.1145/2531602.2531618

achieving this. This assumption may pay dividends in developing nations. However, our study findings suggest that scale is *not* the problem confronting micro rural enterprise in a developed context, and that the primary means to add value is by augmenting the *consumer-seller* relationship.

These findings are supported by cross-cultural research in Japan (another developed nation). Okamoto [20] reports on "success factors for rural B to C [Business to Consumer] implementations" in revitalizing rural enterprise. These factors include using technology to establish a local brand, coordinating collectives of rural businesses under the auspices of that brand, exploiting the digital to enhance collective advertising, and enhancing the collective bargaining power of rural enterprises. These issues preface the need for enhanced micro logistics and are manifest in various ways in our field study of the various enterprises involved in a small weekly market. We take a closer look at the market below, after explaining our methodological approach. We draw on the findings to elaborate the local character of Okamato's 'success factors' and the implications these have for the design of support for micro rural enterprise. Key among these is the need to connect local rural enterprises *and* consumers together. We consider particular design challenges involved in this, including those occasioned by potential online and situated solutions.

METHODOLOGY

Our study of the market was framed by a sociological rather than an economic perspective on enterprise. It uses fieldwork [23] as an ecological approach enabling the elaboration of the "actor's point of view" [2], rather than adopting rational perspectives on "homo economicus" - i.e., the economic human, a self-interested actor who seeks to create value by maximising utility as a consumer and economic profit as a producer [25].

> *"The value of the ecological approach is that it places "the actor's point of view" at the centre of analysis ... This does not mean (and this is a fallacy that many critics fall into) the incorporation of first person experience into sociological depictions ... We are not concerned with particular people's experience, but with the organisation of experience as that is encountered in the social world as readily available, known and shared schemes of interpretation. We propose to analyse these as aspects of consociation, that is the sharing of social experience. The character which this consociation takes is, of course, a reflection of the environment in which it occurs."* [2]

That 'environment' is a social not a physical one: a lively social milieu in other words, populated by social actors going about their business together. Adopting an ecological approach subsequently supplants home economicus with "homo reciprocans" – i.e., the reciprocal human, a cooperative actor who adds value by explicitly seeking to improve the social milieu.

Our study elaborates the 'shared schemes of interpretation' that drive homo reciprocans and shape micro enterprise in a developed context. It was conducted over a four-month period in 2012 and involved 15 stallholders, 20 customers, and 2 market organisers, along with the collection of audio/visual materials and field notes. Our initial focus when conducting fieldwork was to understand the supply chains implicated in the provision of goods and services provided by the market stallholders. We did not seek to explicate supply chains through the analytic practices of business analysis, however, but as *vernacular* 'naturally accountable' [12] constructs – i.e., as constructs created, articulated and understood by the stallholders.

The motivation for this analytic focus was to explore one of the key assumptions framing the research, which was predicated on the notion of value chains and that supply chain improvements can add value to enterprise [see, for example, 27]. We wanted to understand supply chains from a members' perspective then, rather than from a business analysts' perspective: to understand where the value was perceived to come from and go to from the point of view of those who *do* business in a rural context. Our observations and analysis were not restricted to unpacking vernacular understandings of supply chains. We also looked at the motivations driving the market stall businesses and consumer motivations. We elaborate the findings to emerge from our field study below, key among which was the reframing of where *value* is understood to reside in rural enterprise or at least in rural enterprise in this context. The nature of the findings also suggest that there may be some generality built into the results insofar as they reflect *shared* schemes of interpretation that may be observed in other micro enterprise environments beyond the immediate confines of this market.

THE MARKET FIELD STUDY

The market is situated in a small Welsh town with a population of around 4500 people. This is complemented by a large seasonal influx of tourists, primarily between April and October, across the 180,000 hectare administrative area or 'county' in which the town is located. The county council's annual STEAM report [5] estimates that over 2 million people visited the area in 2011, contributing some £300 million to the economy. The market was set up by a social enterprise created in 2010, which exploits community share schemes to purchase and redevelop disused and derelict sites in an effort to foster business ventures that add value to the town's local economy. The directors and shareholders are concerned to create and retain as much local wealth as possible, especially to stop it being "leached away" by national retailers and global outlets.[1]

[1] It is probably worth making the distinction between 'leech' and 'leach'. The former refers to a blood-sucking parasite. The latter to the draining away of something. It is also probably for the best not to confuse the two.

The market site also houses a car park, crèche, eco shop and agricultural museum. The market itself is currently located in a former agricultural building and houses between 10 and 15 stalls once a week and more at Christmas. Many of the stallholders attend different markets in different towns on different days of the week, and those that don't have other business ventures such as bed and breakfast for tourists, farming, fishing, forestry, etc. There are a variety of stalls as well, some are 'one-man bands' or husband and wife teams, some are small collectives involving a handful of individuals, others are run by larger commercial enterprises. The market stalls sell a variety of locally produced or sourced goods: fresh vegetables, milk and cheese, meat, fish, bread, cakes and pastries, chutneys and sauces, deli foods, plants, garden furniture, and second hand musical instruments and equipment. The seasonal nature of the county economy means that many stallholders stop trading after Christmas until Easter, when the tourist season starts again.

Figure 1. The market.

Market Stall Supply Chains and Coordination

Our initial analytic focus was on the supply chains that stood behind the various market stalls. Seen and understood from a members' perspective – from the point of view of the stallholders when we asked them to explicate their supply chains - this was understood to refer to the various *resources* that they needed to acquire and make use of, and *actors* they needed to engage with, to get their products to market. We mapped supply chains across 10 stalls and, like the stalls themselves, found a range of resources and actors involved in each along with a variety of *coordination* mechanisms pulling those resources and actors together. We present 3 of these by way of example and elaboration.

The cake and pastry stall

The cake and pastry stall only appears at this market and only does so once a week. Unlike some of the other traders at the market, the cake stall is not the primary business of the stallholder. The stallholder runs a bed and breakfast (B&B) as their main business, which occasionally opens in the evening as a restaurant as well. The stall utilises some of its table-space to display leaflets promoting the B&B and restaurant. The produce on the stall consists of a range of handmade cakes and pastries, some of which are gluten-free or vegan. Warm pies and pasties containing local ingredients (Welsh lamb, calon wen - a local cheese – and locally grown vegetables) are also made and sold by the stallholder. The stall's products are often packaged in boxes for people to take home with them, though pies and cakes along with hot soup for the lunchtime trade are also packaged and served for immediate consumption.

The stall has been trading for around a year and in that time has managed to gather a steady client base, some of who predominantly buy the more specialist, gluten-free and vegan produce. Customers are also able to order cakes for special occasions and pre-order for the following week. The stall itself is run by one person who sources and collects ingredients, and bakes and sells the produce. The baking takes place in a semi-domestic kitchen at the B&B. Figure 2 shows the different resources and actors implicated in the cake stall supply chain. The resources consist of various ingredients and packaging. The actors, various wholesalers and retailers who supply the ingredients and packaging.

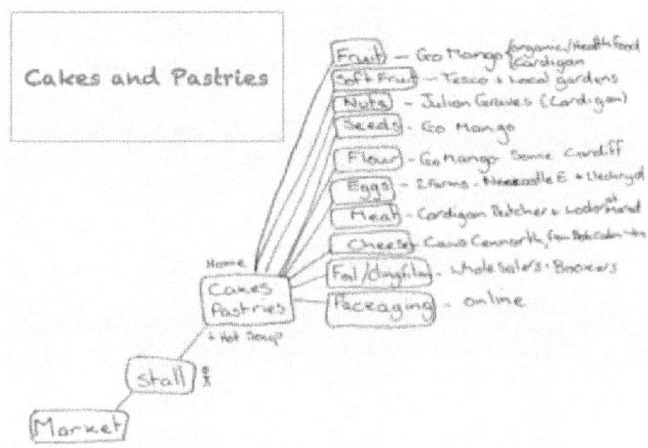

Figure 2. The cake and pastry stall supply chain.

The stallholder is concerned to provide a high quality product and the supply chain mirrors this, with many items being handpicked, fair-trade and organic. Meat is bought from local butchers, eggs are sourced from two local farms, cheese is bought from a local producer who also has a stall in the market and, when in season, fruit is purchased from local growers. More generally fruit, along with seeds, herbs and nuts, are purchased from local 'health' stores and supermarkets. Flour comes from the supermarket. Packaging is bought online. Clingfilm for wrapping and transporting the produce is sourced from a local wholesaler.

Most of these resources are purchased locally, but they are not all produced locally, and their purchase is largely coordinated through face-to-face transactions. All of the ingredients are purchased face-to-face from other local suppliers and physically collected by the stallholder by car. The telephone may occasionally be implicated in coordination, as in the supply of seasonal fruit by local growers. The Internet played a small role in coordination, being used solely to source and arrange the delivery of packaging.

The local growers' stall

The local growers' stall is small cooperative of unaccredited organic fruit and veg producers. The stall consists of 7 people who have small 'allotments' or pieces of land in the local area that are not insufficient in themselves to underpin a business but collectively generate sufficient produce to do so. The produce consists of seasonal fruit, vegetables, fresh flowers, and plants (e.g., fruit bushes). The stall also sells fruit vinegars, eggs, and hot soup. It is often staffed by three people who are themselves part of the producers' collective. The stall is, again, a one-off occurring only once a week at this market. Figure 3 shows that while the underlying supply chain consists of multiple actors, the resources implicated in it are rather more scant: the bulk of them being grown by the producers, who may occasionally buy seed though just as often harvest and swap it. Packing is the only notable resource that the producers purchase online (plant pots, bottles for the vinegar and cartons for the soup). The growers' are also keen recyclers, reusing pots, carrier bags, boxes, etc., behind the scenes and at the stall itself.

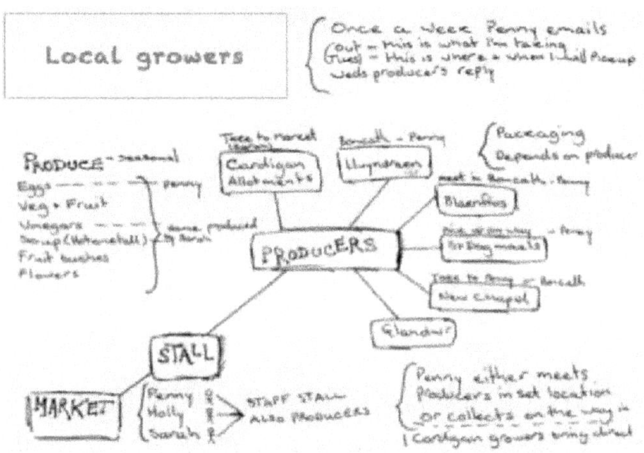

Figure 3. The local growers supply chain.

Coordination in this supply chain centres on the collection and delivery of stock to the stall. This is done by email. Two days before the market an email is sent out by one of the growers who always stands the stall (there are usually 3 of them on hand) to the others telling them what she is taking and where she will be picking the other's produce up from. The other producers usually respond by email the night before the market, saying what they are sending, product prices, and at what pick up point it will be. Growers who live very close to the market drop their produce directly there. Coordination also extends to the sale of goods. The stall's products are not all of apiece but derive from 7 separate producers and sales have therefore to be divided appropriately. Thus, behind the stall alongside the "float" (moneybox) is a price list on which the seller writes down how much of what product they have sold. This enables them to see what has been sold and to "divvy up" or apportion the day's takings.

The milk and cheese stall

The milk and cheese stall is a much larger cooperative, representing 25 accredited organic diary farmers who collectively supply many well-known British supermarkets. The stall sells a range of organic diary products (cheese, milk, yoghurt, butter). It is staffed by one person who works part-time for the cooperative, manning the stall at several different markets per week. Other stallholders buy cheese and milk from the stall and some customers buy their weekly milk supply from the stall. Figure 4 represents the supply chain. It is as interesting for what it doesn't say as for what it does. It tells us that raw milk is collected by tanker from the collective's farms and is taken to a central processing plant. It tells us that bottles are sourced from a large national wholesaler. It tells us that a chap called 'Bob' packs a small van and takes the product to market. The supply chain diagram is remarkably uninformative. There are several reasons for this.

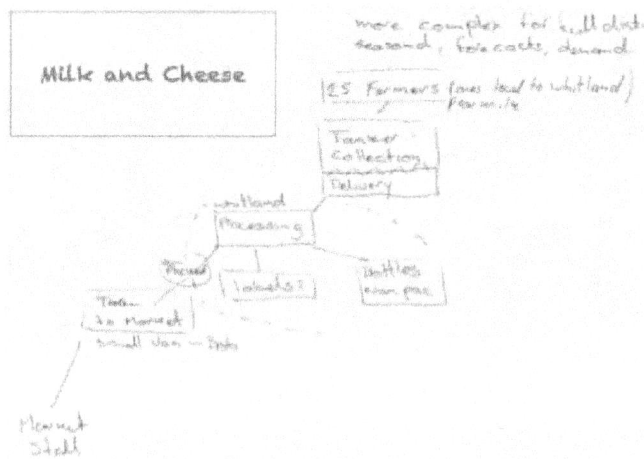

Figure 4. The milk and cheese supply chain.

One is that 'Bob', the chap who stands the stall, isn't privy to the ins and outs of this large commercial supply chain, so no surprise that he couldn't elaborate the resources and actors implicated in it. Two, while we did manage to find out a little more about the supply chain by talking directly to the processing plant (e.g., that the collection of milk and associated routing of tankers is largely coordinated through a rota and phone calls), there was a reluctance to reveal the full details of the supply chain due to commercial sensitivities. Three, the stall is not and nor is it intended to be the cooperative's primary outlet. Rather, it acts to promote the cooperative's brand in the local area.

The promotion works in two key ways. On the hand, the diary products if offers are sold at lower cost than the same ones that are on the shelves in the local outlets of national supermarkets in the area; and on the other hand, in being a part of this particular market, the cooperative demonstrates its support for the social enterprise that owns the market site, in which some of the dairy farmers have invested and nominally 'own' shares. This stall is as much a political statement as it is a business venture, and while it needs to cover cost it nevertheless reflects a commitment on the part of local business to the local community.

The nature of supply chains

Each of the supply chains we mapped reflected the unique character of the individual businesses making up 'the market'. All but the milk and cheese stall elaborated the key resources and actors involved in their production. It became apparent through these vernacular mappings that, as with the cake stall, many of the resources and actors, while being locally available, are essentially external to the town's economy. In short, they take more money out than they put in. When we look at packaging, for example, which was by far and away the most common resource that stallholders purchased (ranging from boxes and jars, bottles and cartons to labels and wrappings), it became apparent that whether bought online or from local outlets, most of the companies that supplied these things were national (UK wide) or international operations.

The same applied when we looked at the purchase of other resources. Indeed, as a rough guide - this is not a quantitative study by the way, the following numbers are merely illustrative – some 65% of the companies that stallholders sourced resources from were not based in Wales, the bulk of them (40%) being UK operations, the remainder international operations. The result, and this rather than statistics is what we really want to draw attention to here, is that when you strip away all the external resources and actors from the supply chains what we are left with is small set of local products of economic value. Specifically meat and fish, diary, fruit and veg, plants and wood products, all natural resources of Wales. What the supply chains show us – regardless of their vernacular nature - is that a significant proportion of the economic value of these resources to the local area is being 'leached away' by external actors.

The vernacular rendering of supply chains also reveals the role of technology in the coordination of resources and actors and the kinds of tools the stallholders used to organise their businesses. One thing the supply chains make painfully visible – at least painful for those of us who want to develop some kind of technological fix - is that there is *very little use* of digital technology in the coordination of micro enterprise. It's not that the stallholders can't afford digital technology or that they are luddites. Most of them have smartphones, which they use to call people and do business with, to leave and pick up messages, and maybe send the occasional text, but that's about it as far enterprise goes for such devices. Most have computers at home as well but their use in business is largely limited to sending, receiving and answering emails and buying resources online.

The supply chains revealed the stark reality of technology use in the micro enterprise, where business is largely conducted face-to-face or by phone, with email usually playing a supporting role. The coordination of micro enterprise largely turns upon *talk* then, more often than not supported by paper resources (notes, lists, rotas, etc.) rather than by digital resources. Out the 10 stalls that mapped their supply chains for us, only 4 had websites. One listed the services provided by the business and enabled online payment via PayPal for one product provided by the business. One listed its products and suppliers where people could buy them from. The other listed products and prices. One listed products and prices and enabled online ordering. The use of websites was, then, largely confined to *marketing* the business. This was complemented in another case by the use of Facebook to do the job of marketing. Nonetheless, most of the stalls – even those with an online presence - relied on physical resources to do marketing (banners, leaflets, information sheets, etc.).

While vernacular renderings of supply chains are never going to satisfy a business analyst or economist, they do convey something of importance to the developers of technology. They tell us that designing technology to support micro rural enterprise is going to be challenging because this class of business doesn't rely on technology for its coordination. While there may be opportunities for collective buying and marketing, micro enterprise is not primarily organised through technology but through the face-to-face interactions and conversations of the parties to it. This seems to work well and (if ain't broke) we might ponder the wisdom of trying to fix it. The situation is further compounded when we turn to consider what motivates micro enterprise

Business Motivations

In order to gain an understanding of what appropriate technological intervention could be about, we also examined the motivations that underpinned the different businesses at the market. We found that many of the stallholders were not motivated by business alone. We have already seen how the milk and cheese stall – the largest business at the market – was politically motivated, for example. This may seem like an over statement of the facts but the company itself recognised the potential negative consequences of not hosting a stall, especially the potential for members of the cooperative to take their business elsewhere, if the cooperative was not seen to support the local community.

Concerns with the local community shot through many of the stallholders business motivations. This was largely reflected in their role as shareholders in the social enterprise which owns the market site, not that this over-rode their or its interest in making money. As a member of the local growers stall put it,

"It would be nice to actually get it to the point where we had a selection of all the local veg and could actually make it pay a bit better than it does at the moment."

Having an interest in the local community doesn't negate business motivations, but it does reshape them and the notion of 'value' along with it.

Perhaps the most obvious example is that of the "life styler" represented by a stall that sells wood products sourced from the holders own woodland which was bought courtesy of an inheritance in an attempt to be self-sufficient and "live off grid". Not all the stallholders share such values. Indeed, the values that motivated most of the businesses operating at the market, particularly the non-shareholding businesses, were much more subtle and nuanced. Others have set up their own businesses as a life style option, but not one based on social or ecological values. The owner of a grocery business and stall, who used to work in a solicitors and started out selling eggs in her spare time (extending her portfolio as customers asked for more) found that she "couldn't do both. I chose this because I have a bit more freedom." That and the time that comes with it to build up the family business on her husband's farm and at her son's farm shop.

Working for yourself and your family is key motivator in micro enterprise, and quite often an end in itself. As a local plant grower put it,

"I don't want to get big. I don't want to get to the stage where I'm employing lots of people. I want to just carry on enjoying it really - make a reasonable amount of money just to live on."

The value placed in being one's own boss and doing enough to get by was expressed by many of the market stallholders.

Wrapped up with this more mundane (less political and politicised) kind of self-sufficiency is a sense of enjoyment that scaling up (the core value entertained by most economists and business analysts) puts at risk and potentially destroys. As the maker of jams and preserves put it,

"I don't want to get really big because I wouldn't enjoy it then I don't think. I did think it would be nice to get really much bigger, but I don't have the energy to do it and I'd just rather do it like this."

Time and again we heard people say similar things when we asked them about growing their businesses. They wanted sustainability – "a few more customers", "more footfall" to "make it pay a bit better", and maybe "a bit better than it does at the moment" in some cases – but "I don't want to get big" was a constant refrain for a host of reasons largely to do with personal effort and responsibility but occasionally to do with the bureaucratic demands placed on business.

Alongside hearing the various ways in which the stallholders "enjoy" working for themselves – the places they go, the people they work with, the people they meet, the conversations they have - we also heard them speak about "quality", not only of life but also of product. Many of the stallholders are artisans, and the things they make and sell are of a different order to those you usually find on supermarket shelves. As the cake and pastry maker puts it,

"For me its about coming out and selling my produce with like minded people ... It's a lovely thing to do and, you know, I feel you're adding to the community ... I feel that it's far nicer to have the contact and for the customer to be able to come in and ask you about something, whereas if I went into Tesco's and wanted to know about a product, nobody could tell me what was in it, you'd have to look at a long list of E numbers and everything, and it's just not the same is it as having it produced freshly yourself."

We walked away from the market with a very different set of values ringing in our ears than those we might have expected. Of course there was a concern with money, but it was tempered by the values that people placed on working for themselves and their families, on enjoying life in the round, on making quality products which are often locally sourced, and on having a relationship with the customer.

Only one stallholder, who was selling his own chilli sauce as a sideline on his Dad's cheese stall, wanted to make it big and become "as successful as the Reggae Reggae Sauce Company." For him, the market was an incubator for a future corporate success story. Other stallholders valued the market as an incubator too, though their visions of the future were rather more modest. The market provided a testing ground for new businesses, product lines, and the opportunity to build up a customer base. It also provided a site where stallholders could promote their other businesses too, many of them relevant to the seasonal influx of tourists.

What we see when we turn our attention to what motivates and drives micro enterprise we find a host of local concerns that respecify 'value' as it is usually understood in economic and business discourse. The respecification is consequential. It replaces the standard economic concern with scale or 'growth', and the mechanisms whereby that might be affected, and puts concern with such things as community, family, sustainability, self-determinacy and self-sufficiency, quality of life and quality of product in its place. Getting bigger is rarely the point whereas earning an enjoyable and, as archaic as this may sound, honourable living often is. This situation again raises real challenges for systems design, not least because it negates the need for enterprise systems in this area of business. Not only is there no use for them as there is nothing (no business, no information, no knowledge management processes, etc.) to scale, trying to apply them would be like using a hammer to crack open a nut (and would probably produce similar results).

Consumer Motivations

Our efforts to understand the potential for making design interventions in rural micro enterprises has also been informed by studies of what motivates consumer engagement. Twenty customers of the market stalls were informally interviewed during the fieldwork whilst the market was running. A key concern that rapidly emerged in our conversations with customers was their manifold interest in "the local" - "I like local food", "I like to keep local traders going when I can", "I like to buy local produce", "I want local things if I can possibly have local things". These and a host of other comments elaborated a number of thematic concerns that motivated customer engagement with the market. We expand on each of these below.

Local Business and Community

A key motivation driving consumer engagement was the perceived need to support local business. This motivated most customers, including the tourists we talked to. They responded to questions probing their reasons for shopping in the market with statements such as, "It's local and I like to support local businesses", "I like to support local producers and suppliers as well", or "I want to support local people". For many customers there is a direct link between spending money at the market and in other local shops and the health and well being of the local community. They consciously operate a local agenda when shopping, even if it means "paying that bit extra", as doing so is understood to accrue tangible benefits for the community at large.

Quality

A key motivation for customer engagement with micro enterprises, and one that makes it worthwhile to pay that bit extra, is encapsulated in the view that they deliver better quality goods and services. Everyone we talked to spoke of the quality of products at the market in one way or another. "I come every week because its locally grown, and I die for the fresh vegetables which are locally grown", "I like the fresh fruit and veg and food", "I like good food – I bought bread and eggs and beans because I just like the look of them", "I come here for the homemade pies and cakes". Sourcing "fantastic produce" was a key driver of customer engagement with the market.

Home-grown/Home-made

The value that consumers place on quality is further reflected in their orientation to the home-grown and home-made. This is a particular feature of the market stalls and the kinds of products they make and sell: fresh foods and foodstuffs. That these are "locally grown" or "made by the people who sell it" is strong motivation for buying such products. It's not labelling these kinds of products as home-grown or home-made that counts however, but in being home-grown or home-made that customers associate this with quality. Home-grown / home-made adds value to a product and warrants paying out that bit more.

Customer service

The value placed on home-grown / home-made reveals another motivation driving customer engagement more generally and this is the value people place on customer service. This plays out in different ways. In the market, for example, customers talked about "Vicky's bread", or "Jen's quiche" and in doing this displayed themselves as 'regulars' having a 'routine' relationship with stallholders. As we watched them go about their routine business we listened their conversations. Some were related to the products on sale and both customer and stallholder reported on the value of "being be able to come and ask about something". However, much of the talk that we witnessed was entirely unrelated to bread or quiche or any other product. Instead, their conversations ranged across community life events, shared friends, family, etc. In turn this leads, as one customer put it, to "building up friendships, you know".

Enjoyment

Good customer service, including the friendships that may get forged through it, is part and parcel of the enjoyment that also motivates customer engagement with the market, though the enjoyment extends far beyond this: "I like the ambience, the relaxedness." "It's my routine. I come here at nine. I put the dogs into the car before I leave. Then I go down to the beach. Today I'm back for a second hit." "I like the atmosphere, I like talking to people. It's an enjoyable occasion." "You bump into your friends while you're here shopping". "I usually come at nine - my friend also comes at nine; by the time we've been through it's almost like, you know, locusts!" These and other comments made it perspicuous that the market is not only a site of economic exchange whose wheels are oiled through good customer service, but also a place enjoyed in its own right for its aesthetic qualities, a place routinely factored into an enjoyable day out, and a place where people meet incidentally and intentionally. In short, a site where both personal and social pleasures play out and can play out.

Alternatives

The sense of enjoyment provided by the market contrasts with customers' orientation to mainstream supermarkets and brings another commonly held value into view. "I can't stand X", where X stands for the brand name of several large supermarkets, was not an infrequent comment. This isn't to say that customers of the market didn't use mainstream supermarkets. They did, whether it was because "you don't have to pay to park" or because they provide "things I can't get anywhere else". Nonetheless many customers thought it "nicer" at the market. Nicer not only aesthetically and socially but also politically. The stance taken by many of the market customers was one where the supermarkets were seen as selling goods and services that don't support the local economy. Given the opportunity they would prefer to support "local businesses". We come full circle then, back to the values that people place in supporting local enterprise and investing modestly but routinely through shopping in the local economy.

The preference exhibited by market customers for alternatives manifests the relevance of consumer politics to micro enterprise. Consumer motivations emphasise the value placed on supporting local business, buying quality products sourced or made locally, good customer service, and enjoyable consumer experiences that offer an alternative to the mainstream. Some of these values are unique and tied to the kind of enterprise that the market is. Others are, we think, more generic. The value placed on supporting local business, on quality and hand-crafting or bespoke design as it were, and on customer service strike us as issues that extend far beyond the market. With them too goes something of the mundane political impetus to invest in the local economy. There are, to put it simply, a great many goods and services that in our capacity as consumers we source and buy locally and that we do so is no accident. It happens because many of us value the local too.

RURAL MICRO ENTERPRISE AND DESIGN

Studies based on fieldwork or 'ethnography' are typically expected to furnish 'implications for design' – i.e., recommendations or requirements for systems development. As Dourish [9] notes,

> *"A common lament to be found in reviews of ethnographic work is, 'yes, it's all very interesting, but I don't understand its implications for design'."*

Dourish also contests the appeal to implications for design as the primary criteria for *assessing* the worth of field studies.

> *"First ... the focus on implications for design is misplaced, misconstruing the nature of the ethnographic enterprise; and second ... ironically, in so doing, it misses where ethnographic inquiry can provide major insight and benefit ... to focus on ... recommendations as the 'outcomes' of ethnography at best distracts from, and often completely obscures, the analytic and conceptual work that lies behind, which is often where the substantive intellectual achievement is to be found ... they typically go beyond specific instances of design."*

One the key virtues of fieldwork lies not in 'telling designers what to build' – i.e., in specifying system requirements - but in telling designers what *not* to build [7]. It provides, in other words, for **'assumptions testing'** (ibid.).

In this case, it has served to disabuse us of two core assumptions that *framed* and *motivated* the research:

- One, that scale is the problem confronting micro rural enterprise.
- Two, that adding value is about adding financial value to goods and services.

Our studies suggest that scale is not the problem that confronts micro rural enterprise and that adding value is not always about adding financial value. Our investigation of business motivations throw both of these assumptions into serious doubt, and elaborate a range of alternative ways in which value is understood in micro rural enterprise.

Thus, the emphasis placed on personal freedom, quality of life, and the sense of satisfaction or 'enjoyment' involved in working for yourself and your family situates the making of money within a constellation of social values that cut across the demands of scaling up or 'growth'. This constellation of social values is constitutive of a shared scheme of interpretation and is reflected and extended by consumer motivations. The two combine to suggest that the design challenges that are assumed to be operative in this context need to be reframed. If not anathema, scale and growth is actively avoided and set aside by many micro rural enterprises, being seen and treated as something that will involve a great deal of effort that undermines the very reasons that people create their own businesses in the first place and the values that underpin and drive it forwards.

Reframing the design challenges

Another key virtue of fieldwork lies in its ability to help designers understand **'what the problem is'** that they are seeking to address [14] and, concomitant to that, identifying **'opportunities'** or areas of activity in which design might usefully intervene [7] So, if scale is not the problem here, what is, and what tangible opportunities are there for design in this context?

Our initial exploration of vernacular supply chains identified two potential areas for design intervention: marketing and collective buying to reduce the cost of packaging in particular in a bid to help micro rural enterprises retain more of the value they create. Both of these possibilities for intervention are problematic, however, and largely because the tools and solutions to support them already exist. Indeed, marketing and collective buying solutions are commonplace: tools and services for creating websites and promoting businesses abound, and solutions such as Groupon are readily available. So where does that leave us?

As Okamoto [20] points out, an important part of the mix here is *community identity* and *branding* and the ways in which this can be supported digitally. The issue of identity permeated our study of the market, running through the market itself as social enterprise created within, by and for the local community, and the motivations that drove many of the stalls and consumer engagement, manifest in various interests and concerns with 'the local'. Okamoto suggests that the digital may usefully be leveraged to "add the special flavour of locality" and "uniqueness" through the creation of collective brands. The retort to this might well be that there is no design challenge here. It is simply a matter of creating branded websites.

The problem with this kind of response is that it assumes that a local brand will be constructed and maintained centrally by a particular service provider. However, most of the micro enterprises in our study didn't have websites and no single party was in control of service provision. What we have here – and what design needs to respond to – are *ad hoc connections* between *independent* actors. Solutions are required then that enable the bespoke construction and management of local brands by independent actors through contingent association rather than central provisioning. This isn't to say that there won't be a central body of some kind involved in branding – e.g., the social enterprise that organises the market in our study – insofar as some body has to control a brand, but that a commercial service provider is not needed to create and sustain it, as each party to the brand can and does (or does not) commission web provisioning as they see fit.

This kind of intervention also requires that we seek to support branding in manifold ways. A business might use social media to promote itself instead of a website, for example, which means that mechanisms for building local brands will have to cut across *a range of existing tools and services*. What initially sounds like a straightforward challenge that is easily solved by currently available solutions begins to open up and mushroom as a broad range of digital tools and services are contingently drawn upon by micro rural enterprises: not only bespoke websites and social media, but in some cases online ordering and online payment as well, along with other potentially relevant services (e.g. collective buying, online advertising, analytics, etc.). In light of *contingency* it starts to make sense then to think about developing a micro enterprise toolkit that *glues together* a range of existing digital services, and enables them to be contingently exploited, to foster and support the construction and management of local brands.

The glue extends, again contingently, to the use of *physical media* to promote micro enterprise. Each of the businesses involved on our study exploited physical media in one way or another – banners, posters, leaflets, flyers, etc. – to promote itself and the products it sells. This suggests that physical artefacts may be used to embed the digital in the world (e.g., via QR codes) and add what Okamoto calls the "rich information" about goods and services (e.g., provenance, history, culture) that enables micro enterprise to differentiate itself and create the kind of competitive advantage that motivates consumers. The possibility also exists to *extend the physical-digital mix*, through (for example) the judicious placement of situated displays, to enable the physical discovery of local brands and connect consumers to local enterprise.

Reframing the design challenges leads us to consider potential design interventions that enable business users to *mash together* a portfolio of digital services and digitally augmented physical resources, which they can use to coordinate themselves as a group having a distinct identity and advertise "a local image" [20] supporting the differentiated values that enable them to earn a living. In place of scale and growth the goal of such a toolkit is, to borrow from the bread maker and local growers cooperative in our study, simply (!) to **attract** a bit more footfall and thereby make it pay a bit better.

CONCLUSION

The rural is attracting growing interest as a site for IT research and systems development. Much of this interest is centred on developing nations such as Africa and India and this *developing context* shapes our expectations about design problems and the nature of solutions. Here IT research is all about enabling development, by redefining the *consumer-producer relationship* for example. Thus, the 'middlemen' might be taken out of the picture and the producer generate more profit, which in turn enables the producer to scale up and society to reap the social and economic benefits that accrue with it.

We do not dispute these ambitions, indeed they are part and parcel of the broader project in which our own research operates, but we do think it important to appreciate that the 'rural' is not a ubiquitous phenomenon. Yes, a large part of the world may not be densely populated and urban in nature, but the rural is not all of apiece, not all the same – rural India is not at all like rural Wales, for example - and that means that the expectations at work in one rural context are not necessarily operative in another.

Our field study is a point in case. Wales is part of the UK, one the richest nations in the world, which is itself a member of the world's most powerful trading bloc: the EU. The rural here exists in a *developed context*, and this raises a different set of design challenges. In the developed world, living and working in a rural context is often a matter of choice, something imbued - as we have glimpsed in our studies - with a distinctive set of values that are seen as desirable and even something to aspire too. This same orientation is not reflected in rural India, or Africa, or China, etc., where people are decamping en masse to cities, mimicking the rise of the industrial revolution in the West in pursuit of the tangible economic benefits that scaling up brings with it.

The design challenges in a developed context are different. Adding value by scaling up is not an appropriate solution as scale itself is not the problem that confronts many rural enterprises. In a developed context many rural businesses are micro enterprises employing 9 or less people. Our studies suggest that growth is not the problem here: what is at stake is making enough money to live on. They also suggest that augmenting the *customer-seller relationship* is a primary area for design intervention. Our study of the market suggests that the augmentation might initially focus on developing tools that enable micro enterprises to mash together and contingently exploit a portfolio of existing digital services and digital-physical resources to create the 'local' brands and promote the 'local' businesses that customers are motivated to engage with. We recognise in saying this that there is nothing to restrict such a toolkit to the rural. The services it provides may be exploited in urban settings too and in doing so it may help build a new bridge spanning the urban-rural divide between micro enterprise in developed contexts. There may be some scale in IT then.

ACKNOWLEDGEMENT

The research on which this article is based was funded by RCUK research grants EP/J000604/1, EP/J000604/2, and EP/G065802/1.

REFERENCES

1. Anand, A., Pejovic, V., Johnson, D. and Belding, E. (2012) "VillageCell: cost effective cellular connectivity in rural areas", *Proceedings of ICTD 2012*, pp. 180-189, Atlanta, ACM.
2. Anderson, R., Hughes, J. and Sharrock, W. (1989) *Working for Profit*, Avebury, Gower Publishing Co. Ltd.
3. Ansari, B., Shaikh, A., Khan, R. and Hamirani, N. (2012) "Telemedicine enlightenment: A smart heath care system for rural areas", *Journal of Emerging Trends in Computing and Information Systems*, vol. 3 (2), pp. 145-149.
4. Agarwal, A., Jian, A., Kumar, A., Amit A., Nanavati, A. and Rajput. N (2010) "The spoken web: a web for the underprivileged", *ACM SIGWEB News,* Summer 2010, Article No.1.
5. Ceredigion County Council STEAM Report 2011, http://www.ceredigion.gov.uk/public-it/tourism/stats/steam/CerRepRR11.pdf
6. Chetty, M. and Grinter, R. (2007) "HCI4D: HCI challenges in the Global South", *Proceedings of CHI 2007*, pp. 2327-2332, San Jose, ACM.
7. Crabtree, A., Rouncefield, M. and Tolmie, P. (2012) *Doing Design Ethnography*, Springer.
8. dot.rural, http://www.dotrural.ac.uk/node/321
9. Dourish, P. (2006) "Implications for design", *Proceedings of CHI 2006*, pp. 541-550, Quebec, ACM.
10. Emmanuel, E and Hippolyte, M. (2010) "A mobile commerce application for rural economy development: a case study for Dwesa", *Proceedings of SAICSIT 2010*, pp. 58-66, Bela Bela, ACM.
11. European Commission (2008) *Enterprise by Size Class*, http://epp.eurostat.ec.europa.eu/cache/ITY_OFFPUB/KS-SF-08-031/EN/KS-SF-08-031-EN.PDF
12. Garfinkel, H. (1967) *Studies in Ethnomethodology*, Prentice-Hall.
13. Gilbert, E., Karahalios, K. and Sandvig, E. (2008) "The network in the garden: an empirical analysis of social media in rural life*", Proceedings of CHI 2008*, pp. 1603-1612, Florence, ACM.
14. Hughes, J., Randall, D. and Shapiro, D. (1992) "Faltering from ethnography to design", Proceedings of CSCW 1992, pp. 115-122, Toronto, ACM.
15. Irani, L. Vertesi, J., Dourish, P., Philip, K. and Grinter, R. (2010) "Postcolonial computing", *Proceedings of CHI 2010*, pp. 1311-1320, Atlanta, ACM.
16. Johnson, D., Pejovic, V., Belding, E. and van Stam (2011) "Traffic characterisation and internet usage in rural Africa", *Proceedings of WWW 2011*, pp. 493-502, Hyderabad, ACM.
17. Kam, M., Mathur, A., Kumar, A. and Canny, J. (2009) "Designing digital games for rural children: a study of traditional village games in India", *Proceedings of CHI 2009*, pp. 31-40 Boston, ACM.
18. Melvin, R. and Bunt, A. (2012) "Designed for work, but not from here: rural and remote perspectives on networked technology", *Proceedings of DIS 2012*, pp. 176-185, Newcastle, ACM.
19. Misra, H. (2009) "Managing rural citizens interfaces in e-Governance systems: a study in Indian context", *Proceedings of ICGOV 2009*, pp. 155-162, Bogata, ACM.
20. Okamoto, T. (2008) "B to C for revitalizing rural economy", *Proceedings of SAINT 2008*, pp. 425-428, Turku, IEEE.
21. Parikh, T. Gosh, K. and Chavan, A. (2003) "Design studies for a financial management system for micro-credit groups in rural India", *Proceedings of CUU 2003*, pp. 15-22, Vancouver, ACM.
22. Parmar, V., Groeneveld, G., Jalote-Parmar, A. and Keyson, D. (2009) "Tangible user interface for increasing social interaction among rural women", *Proceedings of TEI 2009*, pp. 139-145, Cambridge, ACM.
23. Randall, D., Harper, R. and Rouncefield, M. (2007) *Fieldwork for Design: Theory and Practice*, Springer.
24. Rey-Moreno, C., Tucker, W., Bidwell, N., Roro, Z, Siya, M. and Sim0-Reigadas, J. (2013) "Experiences and lessons from rolling out a rural WiFi mesh network", *Proceedings of DEV 2013*, Article No.11, Bangalore, ACM.
25. Rittenberg, L. and Tregarthen, T. (2009) *Principles of Microeconomics*, New York, Flat World Knowledge Inc.
26. Rodil, K., Winschiers-Theophilus, H., Bidwell, N., Eskildsen, S., Rehm, M. and Kapuire, G. (2011) "A new visualisation approach to re-contextualise indigenous knowledge in rural Africa", *Proceedings of INTERACT 2011*, pp. 297-314, Lisbon, Springer.
27. Taylor, D. (2005) "Value chain analysis: an approach to supply chain improvement in agri-food chains", *International Journal of Physical Distribution and Logistics Management*, vol. 35 (10), pp. 744-761.
28. Taylor, N. and Cheverst, K. (2008) " 'This might be stupid, but ...' – participatory design with community displays and postcards", *Proceedings of OzCHI 2008*, pp. 41-48, Cairns, ACM.
29. Wyche, S. (2011) "Designing for everyday interactions in HCI4D", *Interactions*, vol. 18 (2), pp. 52-56.
30. Wyche, S. and Murphy, L. (2012) " 'Dead China-make' phones off the grid: investigating and designing for mobile phone use in rural Africa", *Proceedings of DIS 2012*, pp. 186-195, Newcastle, ACM.

The Role of Data in Aligning the 'Unique Identity' Infrastructure in India

Aditya Johri
George Mason University
Fairfax, VA, USA.
ajohri3@gmu.edu

Janaki Srinivasan
Virginia Tech
Blacksburg, VA, USA.
janaki3@vt.edu

ABSTRACT
We present findings from a qualitative field study of a national e-infrastructure project currently underway in India. We study how this large and complex infrastructure for issuing unique biometric-based identification numbers to the 1.2 billion residents of India was aligned across various stakeholders engaged in the project. We find that the focus on 'data' kept the entire infrastructure together and working. However, this narrow focus also made the design team view the people applying for IDs as numbers whose management could be standardized. In reality, the infrastructure encountered people with differing experiences and expectations of state-issued IDs, expectations that had to be managed by agents on the ground. With our focus on the nation state as a site for studying e-infrastructure, we extend the domains in which CSCW research takes place and contribute to the theory of infrastructure building in a context where state-citizen relations are at stake.

Author Keywords
Infrastructure; Alignment; Qualitative Field Study; ICTD.

ACM Classification Keywords
K.4.0 Computers and Society; general

General Terms
Human Factors; Design; Management.

INTRODUCTION
Developing infrastructure is a complex undertaking that involves multiple stakeholders, relationships, geographical dispersion, and interactions among diverse actors, organizations, and institutions [1]. This complexity prevails whether the infrastructure is a large-scale physical structure, such as a rail or road network built of brick and steel, or an information and communication technology (ICT) infrastructure. In fact, CSCW scholars who have examined ICT-based infrastructure, including Cyberinfrastructure (CI) and e-infrastructure, have demonstrated the complexity of creating such infrastructure [1, 5].

ACM 978-1-4503-2540-0/14/02...$15.00.
http://dx.doi.org/10.1145/2531602.2531687

In this paper, we present findings from a case study of an e-infrastructure project undertaken by a nation state – the Indian Unique Identity (UID) project. The UID project was started in 2009 and has a goal of assigning all Indians a biometric-based unique identification number that can be used to avail of government and private services. Targeting the Indian population of over 1.2 billion people, the project has an equally ambitious timeline, having issued over 300 million identification numbers since 2010. The project consists of three primary steps (Figure 1) that function concurrently: (1) enrollment of individuals, (2) issuance of their IDs, and, (3) use of the IDs to avail government and private services through authentication.

Figure 1: Three Steps of UID -- Enrollment, Issuance of Number, and Authentication (Use) [23]

In this paper, we focus exclusively on the first stage of the process – enrollment. The enrolment stage of the UID project has required the creation of large-scale infrastructure. It provides us a rare opportunity to examine how complex infrastructure is created and held together at this scale. Within the enrolment process, we study two distinct groups of people that work towards the goal of enrolling individuals into the UID system: the designers of the project and the 'enrolment agents' who 'enroll' individuals on the ground in centers across the country. We argue that both designers and enrolment agents focused on 'data' and that is what kept the entire UID infrastructure together and working in the enrolment phase. We also find that this narrow focus on data made it possible for the design team to view the people applying for IDs as numbers to be managed through standardized techniques. However, in reality, the infrastructure encountered people who had differing experiences and expectations of government IDs. These varied expectations too had to be managed by the enrolment agents on the ground.

This paper makes several contributions to CSCW literature. CSCW literature so far has not focused on the role of the state in infrastructure creation. While e-government researchers have studied digitization projects involving government services, they have typically focused on small-scale projects [3, 9, 16]. Their analysis has also not addressed the issue of centralized infrastructure building. Since infrastructure is perceived to be the building block for other activities, the development of infrastructure is among the most important areas of a state's responsibilities. State-backed, ICT-based infrastructure initiatives are, thus, an important site to test the limits of ideas on infrastructure creation in the CSCW literature. A case study of national infrastructure creation also expands the field's scholarship to domains beyond specialized user groups such as scientists or academics to a population that is more heterogeneous. Additionally, in keeping with the call for CSCW scholars to engage with public policy [11], such studies can help inform policy on international development.

We begin the paper with a brief introduction to the UID project. Following that, we review literature on infrastructure creation, including projects sponsored by the state, and lay out concepts that frame our subsequent analysis of the UID project. Next, we describe our methods and sites, explaining the design of the UID system and its implementation. Finally, we discuss our findings and their implications for the literature on the creation of infrastructure.

CREATING A UNIQUE IDENTITY INFRASTRUCTURE

Simply put, the UID project collects demographic and biometric details of residents, ensures these details are not already present in the UID database ('de-duplication'), allots a UID number to that resident (who is now 'enrolled') and later, sends them a document confirming their number.[1] Subsequently, when residents need to use that number, they present their number or ID card and provide their biometrics to the institution requiring 'authentication.' The request is checked against the UID database, which returns a 'yes' or 'no' answer to confirm or reject that the UID number and biometrics match. Our primary goal here is to understand how the designers of the UID system and the agents who actually collect details from individuals in centers across India, work together on enrolling people into this UID infrastructure.

As we study the designers and enrolment agents of the UID infrastructure, we take seriously Star's observation that infrastructure is never a single monolithic 'thing' that can be "changed from above." It is inherently complex and holds multiple meanings for the different people who engage with it [21: 382]. Further, changes in infrastructure happen only through a process of negotiation. Star also claims, "Nobody is really in charge of infrastructure." This focus on the malleability of infrastructure, while true, undervalues the fact that, to a great extent, infrastructure is designed [1: 246]. How, then, are design intentions translated into infrastructure on the ground? This question has long engaged scholars and entailed the study of the day-to-day work of infrastructure building. Unfortunately such 'infrastructure work' continues to be mostly invisible in the case of government infrastructures such as UID.

The UID infrastructure too was built by design. It required bringing on board many actors for its inception, design and implementation. As we will examine in the rest of the paper, designers and enrolment agents were critical to the process of building the UID enrolment infrastructure. While both these groups have the same goal – enrolling individuals into the UID system – the UID infrastructure holds different meanings for each. The two groups also work in contrasting locations and everyday contexts to accomplish the same goal. The daily interaction between UID designers and agents is minimal, but the work they perform is highly interconnected. In fact, the quality of work done by enrolment agents decides how well the design team (rather, the product it designed) can do its work. The interaction between UID designers and enrolment agents is largely regulated by standards and rules. The design team issues strict guidelines to ensure uniformity in operations and goals in geographic locations spread across India. However, it also has to ensure some flexibility at the local level to take into consideration regional variations. This is where 'synergizing' and 'articulation work,' as described in the following section, play an important role in how designers and enrolment agents work together in the UID project's enrolment phase.

Synergizing – Aligning and Leveraging

Bietz et al. argue that the "active, strategic work of managing multiple relationships for infrastructure development" [1: 251] helps embed infrastructures – particularly CIs – in other systems and infrastructures. This complex "process of creating and maintaining productive socio-technical relationships" is referred to as synergizing. (p. 252). The "socio-technical relationships" that are referred to above are interconnections between people and artifacts, or any combination thereof. Synergizing consists of two sub-processes – aligning and leveraging. Aligning is the process of enacting relationships for creating infrastructure while the infrastructure is nascent. Leveraging refers to the use of an existing relationship to build or strengthen a productive relationship.

Synergizing was pivotal to the UID project at every stage, but became more challenging in the enrolment phase as the project evolved and its infrastructure required frequent adjustments. Additionally, as is often the case with CI, it is easy to forget the material form of digital infrastructure and of the data using that infrastructure. As we analyze the work involved in managing socio-technical relationships in the UID project, we pay particular attention to how

[1] Initially, the document was just a letter. It was later replaced by a UID card [14].

seemingly immaterial 'data' helped with the process of aligning as required to keep the infrastructure working.

Metawork and Local Articulation

A second pertinent lens in this study of UID infrastructure is that of 'articulation work' [22]. Gerson distinguishes between two kinds of articulation work, 'metawork' and 'local articulation' [8]. Gerson defines metawork as "putting together, tasks, tasks sequences, task clusters – even aligning larger units such as lines of work and subprojects in the service of work flow."[8: 196] On the other hand, local articulation is concerned with "making sure all the various resources needed to accomplish something are in place and functioning where and when they're needed in the local situation." Thus, metawork is focused on ensuring that different "activities function together well," and not on "the specifics of local situations." Meanwhile, the focus of local articulation is on "bringing together everything needed to accomplish a task at a particular time and place." Within an organization, for instance, local articulation might mean ensuring that administrative and support functions, as well as equipment maintenance, are in place. Furthermore, its emphasis is "on particular situations rather than classes of activity" (p. 196). Gerson points out that these two senses of articulation work can overlap heavily in cases where tasks are "part of the same organization and are carried out in the same place" (p. 196) But in our case, the distinction between 'metawork' and 'local articulation' is important since we are studying UID designers and enrolment agents who are part of the same project but operate from different places.

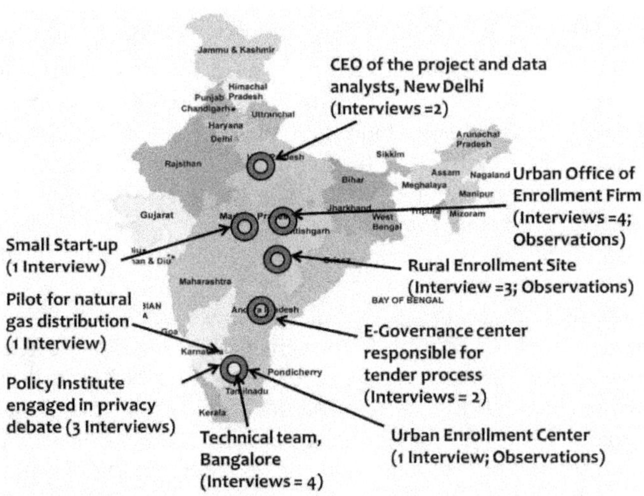

Figure 2: Data Collection Sites

FIELD STUDY

To understand how UID designers and enrolment agents worked together to enroll people into the UID infrastructure, we conducted a qualitative field study [31]. We conducted interviews and observations with designers and enrolment agents in project offices and enrolment centers across India as depicted in the map (Figure 2).

Given the scale and geographical extent of the UID project and the numerous stakeholders involved, our field study was necessarily selective. Besides the main project offices in Delhi and Bangalore where the designers worked, our goal was to study the enrolment process in enrolment centers distributed in different states and across urban and rural locations. Here, we mainly discuss one case study from a rural enrollment center in Madhya Pradesh in central India [33]. We do not disclose city or town names to protect the identity of our study participants. Since a limited number of agencies are involved with the project at the local level, identification of city or town names might compromise the identity of our participants.

Data Collection

Overall, we conducted 21 interviews and more than a week of observations. We recorded these interviews in most instances (with the interviewees' permission). In other cases, we took notes by hand and expanded them later. A few interviews followed a semi-structured protocol, while others took place as informal conversations [29]. We also made video recordings of a few procedures with permission. All field study data was collected by the first author. Since our field study was open-ended, we relied on snowball sampling to collect data. Initial contact with a start-up company engaged in biometrics development led us to an enrollment agency. The manager of the enrollment process at that agency suggested sites for data collection. Since this was one of the few firms conducting enrolment in rural regions, he particularly recommended a rural center that was an overnight train ride from the state capital, which he considered representative of enrollment in rural India.

In addition to interviews and field observations, we also made extensive use of materials on the UID website, including reports, bills, tenders, MOUs, lists of bidders and empanelled firms, and a portal designed by the UID project team that provided counters of IDs issued (Figure 3) [24]. That we could find all these details on the working of the project without undertaking traditional library research reflects the UID team's approach to data transparency and utility. It also indicates the unique nature of this project, particularly in the context of development-related infrastructure projects.

Data Analysis

Our research and analysis followed the interpretive tradition [28, 32]. The two authors analyzed the data independently, discussed their findings and reached concurrence on their interpretations. Data analysis was iterative and, in accordance with interpretive analysis, we collected and introduced new primary and secondary data at different stages of our analysis. We do not directly use all the data we collected in this paper but our interpretations are based on the entirety of what we collected. Both authors have significant experience with similar research in the rural Indian context and this too played a critical role in their analysis. The writing of the paper was done collaboratively, consistent with the interpretive tradition [30].

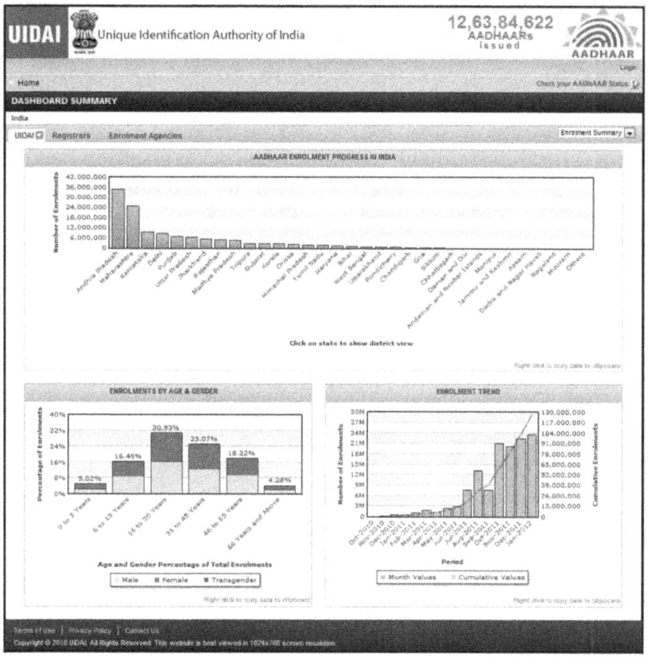

Figure 3: Data Dashboard on UIDAI Web Portal

Following this description of our framework, case and methods, we now come to the details of the UID project, its inception and overall organization, and its working in the enrolment phase in an enrolment center in central India.

DESIGNING UID

Inception

In 2006, an Empowered Group of Ministers under the auspices of the Prime Minister's Office started meeting to put together a strategy to assign unique identification to every resident of India. This group recommended setting up an executive authority called the Unique ID Authority of India (UIDAI). UIDAI was formally constituted on January 28, 2009 and Nandan N. Nilekani was appointed its chairman later that year. Nilekani retired from his position as the CEO of one of India's largest software firms, Infosys, to take this position. In 2010, the project was officially christened 'Aadhaar' (which translates to Foundation) and the first UID number was issued later that year. Since then over 300 million IDs have been issued following the steps outlined in the previous section.

While the UID project has not been modeled on any single e-governance or other project, the project's technical team often invokes Google, Facebook and other systems that deal with datasets of similar magnitudes, as their 'model.' Following the system architecture model used by these firms, UIDAI extensively uses open source software such as MySQL, MongoDB, Hadoop, and Solr.

Organization

UIDAI is the overall regulator and overseer of the UID authentication system. It owns and manages the Central Identities Data Repository (CIDR), which contains the personal identity data of all UID-holders. UIDAI is organized as two primary units: a Technology Development Unit (TDU) and a Project Management Unit (PMU). TDU consists of fulltime technical staff as well as volunteers and individuals on 'loan' to UIDAI from technology firms and academic institutions. The core technology team that designed the system consisted of about a dozen individuals. Team members had several years of work experience with designing and managing software product development and services in small IT start-ups as well as in more established large-scale multinational companies (Intel, Google). PMU provides assistance with the tender process, testing concepts, and communication and awareness efforts.

Beyond these two primary functional units, UIDAI is an 'outsourced ecosystem' of various organizations, which ensure that the enrollment and authentication of individuals for UID is uniform across the country. Public and private sector organizations, including banks, state government agencies and other organization that interact with residents regularly, are made 'registrars.' These registrars then work with empanelled 'enrolment agencies' to enroll residents (for details, see [12:156]). All processes are controlled by UIDAI through published guidelines on how to train and certify enrollment agents, what devices to purchase and how to use them, how to conduct the actual enrollment, and so on. Drafts of all these documents, as well as lists of empaneled and contracted organizations, are available on the UIDAI website [24].

The scale of the project can be gauged from the following statistics. There are currently 25,000-30,000 enrollment centers across the country. An enrollment center is equipped with at least a biometric device, an iris scanner, a webcam, a computer with two monitors (one for the enroller and one for the resident to see the details) and numerous cables. Many enrollment centers have two such 'stations' for enrollment and some have up to four. Thus, hundreds of thousands of each of these devices is being used across the country for enrolment. The CIDR processes over a million UIDs a day, which translates to 200+trillion matches to ensure de-duplication. The system also does around 100+ authentications a day. With a data packet of about 5 MB per resident, that adds up to about 10-15 PB of raw data. Further, the data is mapped across at least two sites for redundancy and security [13].

ENROLLMENT AS DESIGNED BY TECHNICAL TEAM

The core UIDAI technical team works from a nondescript building in Bangalore. Mirroring the previous working environments of a majority of its occupants, the office is arranged like an IT firm, with cubicles occupying the center, while larger offices and conference rooms line the sides. The technological and organizational infrastructure of the UID project was primarily designed from this space. We now examine the priorities and decisions of the core team that shaped this process of design, particularly as it relates to enrollments and to 'data.'

Design Motivations

The overarching goal of the UID project, as laid out in UIDAI Chairperson Nandan Nilekani's book, was to provide every Indian resident the 'unique identity' that many lacked [18]. Other members of the project team shared Nilekani's idea about the benefits of having a unique identity. They also brought up their own particular experiences that reinforced the need for associating a unique number with residents. One team member, for example, mentioned that the American Social Security Number system had first made him realize the advantages of such a number. Another mentioned that his experience living in the US (an experience common to most in the team) had helped him realize the benefits and problems with an identity system. Similarly, the working of government services in the US (issue of birth certificates), and the design of IT systems in US IT companies, had also shaped team members' ideas of what was required of government services in India, as well as how IT systems were best and most efficiently designed.

For the most part, the design priorities and decisions of the UID system were framed relative to the existing system in India. A team member contrasted the potential efficiency of UIDs with the inefficiency of currently prevalent systems of registering for public or private services in India. Using the example of registering for mobile phone SIM cards, he expressed concern that the system allowed paper copies of supporting documents (required for registration) lying around, ripe for misuse and identity theft. Once the UID started being used as the primary proof of identity, he argued, there would be no such danger of sensitive documents lying around. The idea that the UID would provide an identity too was presented as a contrast to prevalent systems where the poor lacked an identity.

Thus, while the members of the core team approached the UID from different perspectives, they agreed that it was required and that it would be useful. For the most part, they seemed to agree with the official explanation for a UID. A public UIDAI presentation summarizes the team's goals and priorities thus (Figure 4).

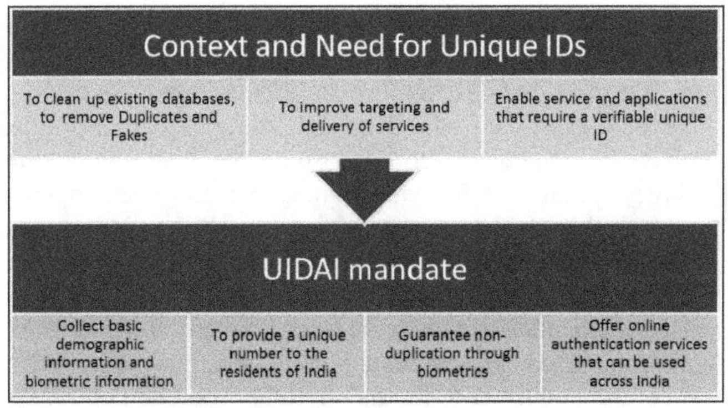

Figure 4: Official Slide from UIDAI Presentation [23]

Design Decisions – The Data Imperative

Given the scale of the UID project, it is not surprising that the technical team's focus and goals were mostly defined, measured and evaluated using technical metrics. Most team members acknowledged that their reasons for joining the UID project included its unprecedented scale and the consequent technological challenges related to the quantity and quality of data that were also unmatched by any project they could work on in the industry. Each described how their own particular professional experience helped them deal with what they had to design. One member pointed to the fact that having encountered unstructured Indian addresses while working on maps for India had helped him recognize and design for unstructured data in UID. He also emphasized that the UID project was "all about the interfaces and what they would look like," and stressed the importance of standards in their work. Another team member emphasized the importance of data quality, and how the idea of having three companies do the de-duplication process was critical to the goal of achieving good data quality in the project. Yet another team member pointed to the incredible number of biometric matches the system would have to undertake in a day (200 trillion), and how that made it imperative that the basic system was built to be simple, and did not have too many "moving parts." Commenting on another e-government system that was dealing with massive amounts of data, he pointed to it as an example where there was lots of data but it was not presented in a form that made it easy to analyze. He added that data accessibility and presentation were key concerns they were addressing in their project and referred to the different data portals they had developed as part of the project. Data was, thus, central to the design of the UID system.

Designed Enrollment: Imagined Users and Beneficiaries

While the UID project team was focused on technological design and standardized systems at all levels of operation, team members worked throughout this process with implicit assumptions about the likely workers and users of the enrolment process. One team member described users as "people who were not in the formal system." A representative of a biometric company that was helping design the biometric specifications for the project mentioned that they would be "doing good" for "people in the rural parts" who didn't have an identity, and would now have one. Nor were these images only of end users. A biometric company representative working with the technical team had formed opinions on enrolment agents based on his deployment experiences. He saw agents as likely to cheat on their work by getting other untrained people to do their work, or by using their own fingerprints where an enrollee's prints could not be read by the system. Impressions of government data collectors were also frequently contrasted to the UID's approach to data collection: "[A government agency] says it's been doing it for 50 years, we have to do it and we will do it. The problem with these guys is that they do it at their own pace. They take 10 years for the census. This is more specialized and should be left to specialized people, that's what we have been telling people." It was also in keeping with these impressions and in reaction to such reports from the field that incentives and systems for reporting and auditing were designed, and then fine-tuned, for enrolment companies and agents. A team member pointed out, for example, that the costs for enrolment agencies had come down from three to one lakh rupees (from $6,000 to $2,000), making it attractive for more entities to consider being an enrolment agency. In another case, to avoid accepting applications that would not result in a UID because of inaccurate or bad data, a system was set in place whereby enrollees were handed acknowledgement slips only when authorization went through.

Meanwhile, the design team's diagrams, such as the ones below (Figure 5), also provide an idea of how the enrolment process, enrolment agents and users were being thought about. The process, documents and other artifacts are neatly laid out. Enrolment is standardized and depicted under ideal conditions, with steps including "Prep Enrolments" and "Setup Enrolment". End users, and their varied reactions to the systems, are mostly absent in this workflow

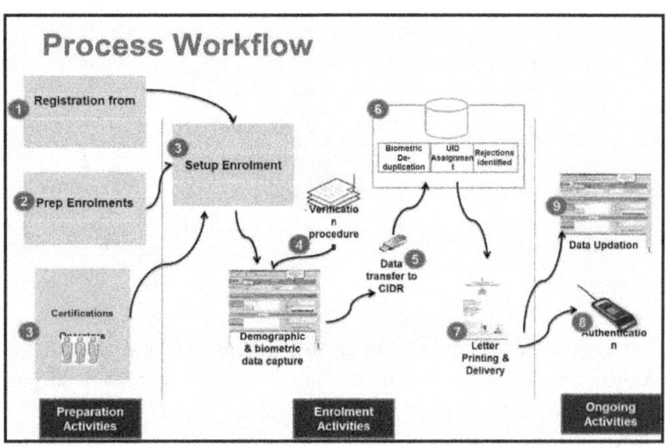

Figure 5: Official Process Workflow from UIDAI [23]

Overall, the UID project team presented and promoted an idealized scenario of how enrollment should take place. It prescribed a suitable location for enrolment centers, a list of required equipment and their placement within the center, and standardized interactions with a generic user, towards the goals envisioned by the project team. The team used a consultancy firm to put in place the required infrastructure, including training documentation and device standardization. Even though the design team tried to account for many factors that could play a role in the field in their design, the idealized version of the enrollment process came face-to-face with reality only during the actual implementation. Without the inventiveness of the enrollment agents in the field, as we now discuss, the infrastructure creation that the project aspired and designed for would have failed.

ENROLLMENT ON THE GROUND

In this section, we move from examining enrolment as envisaged in the designers' plans to enrollment in the field. Since the population for enrollment is the entire Indian population and enrollments take place across the country, there is no one 'representative' site to study. Therefore, our strategy was to select a site and explore it in depth. We focus on the enrolment process at an enrolment center in a rural part of Madhya Pradesh. To highlight the multiple layers of infrastructure present in the process, we first describe the enrolment firm in the state capital that oversaw the enrolment center we chose to study. Following that, we describe the enrolment procedure at the rural center itself.

Enrollment Firm in a Large City in *Madhya Pradesh*

Enrollment agencies had to bid to get a contract to conduct enrollments. Several enrolment firms bid for specific states, especially where they were locally based and already had similar projects underway. In the site we studied, the firm that had won the bid had already been working on other government projects for a while. For one of these projects, it managed the issue of smartcards for driving licenses. Seemingly innocuous, this relationship with the government was nevertheless a significant reason this firm had bid to be an enrolment agency for UID enrolments. The firm was already familiar with the enrollment process and since it worked with offices across the state, it also had a network it could leverage. Especially since it was located in the state capital, the firm knew important people in the government there, who could help get things done in all over the state. For instance, this firm was able to use state buildings as enrollment centers, which would not have been possible without contacts. Even access to electricity for the center was managed through the firm's pre-existing networks.

The enrolment firm headquarters dictated how the rural centers were to function – they determined how many people had to be enrolled in a day, how much could be spent on the operation, and how long the enrollment would last at each of the centers. Here again, the focus was on an imagined user and on their count. Each enrolment center was allotted a manager and 2-4 operators. Operators were not necessarily assigned to a specific center and could move on to other enrollment centers as needed. Furthermore, not all staff was hired solely for this project, with many managers having been transferred from other projects on a temporary basis. However, there was a limit to how many personnel the firm could assign to multiple projects since UID personnel had to undergo training and register themselves with UIDAI, which involved a significant investment of time and resources. Personnel from rural centers also had to do quality control and auditing work, but they shared this work with the headquarters. People from the HQ accompanied the auditors sent by UIDAI, and traveled across the state to oversee the enrollment process at various centers.

Enrolment firms spent significant effort in recruiting 'operators' to conduct enrolments at these centers. Operators underwent extensive training that had been standardized by UIDAI, learning to use equipment that complied with UIDAI standards. The operator, and others working in the firm, had to be adept at using computers and other devices such as the biometric and iris scanners. They were also expected to be able to troubleshoot technical problems with their equipment in the field. We found that it was experience, rather than the standardized training modules, that taught operators to manage such situations. Further, technical skills alone were not sufficient to being an operator: they also had to be fluent in the local dialect and norms because of the need for frequent interactions between the operators and residents during the enrollment process. Given the diversity of languages, and dialects in a region, operators were hired from among local people to satisfy these conditions. The managers, who oversaw the entire process, could also work as operators when needed.

We see how the decision to engage with UID was not an easy one for enrollment firms. They had to make significant upfront investments of both time and money. Firms had to invest in training operators and enrollment managers, and also on equipment. The firm we studied worked on very small margins, making the number of enrollments very important given the paid-per-enrolment structure of their income. There was also intense competition among enrollment agencies, especially in highly populated areas, where several firms could operate. Poaching of employees was common. Given the short timeline of the project, and the need to enroll as many individuals as possible in the shortest time possible, enrolment agencies wanted to avoid spending time hiring and training operators, which slowed them down. As a result, one of the primary duties of the enrolment manager was to maintain the morale of the operators and to reward them sufficiently to retain them.

Enrollment Center in Rural *Madhya Pradesh*

We observed an enrollment center in a rural mining district about 250 miles from the firm HQ. The enrollment center had been set up in a small warehouse, built as an annexure to government offices for the district headquarters. The office was primarily used for storing files and space had been cleared for four enrollment stations. The enrolment manager described how he had leveraged existing personal and professional networks to land a central location for the enrolment center. He also emphasized the possibility of building new contacts because of his newfound stature as manager for an important project. Especially since all government employees were required to enroll for a UID, he was able to ask for help from these individuals and also to extend his networks. In return, government officials found a convenient place to get their enrollments done and also received preferential treatment in being scheduled for enrolment. In the manager's estimation, this kind of 'social capital' was essential for getting work done.

Enrollment happened on all days of the week except Monday and officially, the center functioned between 8 am and 5 pm. In practice, enrollment went on till much later in the evening, depending on the number of people who showed up on a given day. By the time the enrollment agents finished with the verification, and data was transferred to a USB drive or a DVD that could be sent to the firm's central office and from there to CIDR, it was often 8 or 9 pm.

Figure 6: Enrollees Lined Up Outside an Enrollment Center

Figure 7: Enrollment Center Gate Partially Closed to Manage Crowds (on the walls are several notices that list documents required and other information about the enrollment process)

Each of the four enrollment stations consisted of two computer screens, a CPU, a biometric device, an iris scanner, a webcam, keyboard and mouse, and desk and chairs. As mentioned earlier, all this equipment had to satisfy quality standards and the setup too was a standard created by the design team. The enrollee sat by the enroller. The enrollee and the operator had separate screens – arranged perpendicular to each other – on which they could see the applicant's details as they were entered. White cloth screens were used to ensure privacy across stations. The first enrollment station was marked as being for those with disabilities or for pregnant women. Female enrollment agents were present for cases where female enrollees expressed a preference for a female agent (we did not see them making this request).

Many of the artifacts and processes that we observed at the enrollment center were prescribed or required. For instance, the center was required to post notices on center timings, a list of acceptable documents for verification, and so on (seen in the photograph). Similarly, having two monitors was a requirement to enable users to see what details were being entered. What made these artifacts interesting was that while they fulfilled the letter of UIDAI rules, they seldom achieved their goals in spirit. For example, where many enrollees were not literate, the notices and monitors did not automatically make the process more transparent to them. This is where the enrolment managers and operators proved crucial, by making the process of enrolment easier or harder, and more or less intelligible, for enrollees.

Enrollment Process in Rural Center

Much before the enrollment center officially opened in the morning, enrollees lined up outside the building. They held several documents in their hands- the enrolment procedure had a 'proof of identity' requirement that could be satisfied with any document from a prescribed list. At the start of the day, the manager of the enrollment center went around and looked at each enrollee's documentation to determine if it was adequate for the enrollment process. He also assigned a number to each and wrote that down in Roman numerals on the enrollee's documents. On the day we observed the center, many more people showed up to be enrolled than could possibly be enrolled that given day at the four stations in the center.

Figure 8: Managing the Crowd at the Enrollment Center

The manager marked documents with numbers till 350 and asked the rest of the applicants standing in line to return another day. He often gave a single number to a family, especially if there were children to be enrolled as well. He said that he tried to enroll as many people as possible every day, but had to draw the line somewhere. Besides the visibly long line of enrollees, he also had to take into account extra enrollees, such as government officials, who he could not turn down (both for political reasons and because the card was mandatory for government officials, giving them precedence in enrollment).

The manager explained how he had arrived at his specific system of crowd control and numbering. He narrated an incident where he had tried using tokens. He had given five tokens to a woman standing in line with four children early in the day. He found her in line again the next day, and found that she had sold her tokens for Rs. 50 ($1) each. Once he realized that others too were selling their tokens, he decided to discontinue the practice. Furthermore, many enrollees traveled long distances from their villages on buses. Assigning them tokens or appointments for other days or times simply did not work since they preferred to reach the center as early as possible and leave before the last bus at 5 PM. The manager decided that the best mechanism to ensure that only the person who was in line got preference was to assign a number written in his handwriting on the enrollee's document. He claimed his handwriting ensured no one could duplicate numbers and get in line out of turn. Meanwhile, the number also alerted the enroller that the manager had already verified documents for that enrollee, thus saving time and effort in the enrollment process.

Figure 9: Enrollment in Progress

Once enrollees reached the enrolment stations, their interaction with the operators began. As we mentioned earlier, operators too were fluent in the local dialect and also familiar with the local geography, which helped them figure out which village the enrollees were from and simplified the process of data entry. An interesting incident illustrates the challenges of being an operator doing enrollment in this region. Many of the enrollees had never written their name and were unaware of the spelling of their names. Their names, and other details such as gender and address, were different on the different documents they brought with them. Since this was fairly common, the operators had figured out how to do this quickly, using the spellings common in the region. In another instance, a woman did not know her last name and would not say the first name of her husband. In this case, the operators had to fill in the details by talking to a neighbor of the woman's who happened to be present that day.

The inventiveness of operators was at display on several other occasions such as their use of Google transliteration. Google transliteration was integrated in the enrollment software to enable data capture in two languages. As is common with most transliteration software, this one did not have a good success rate with proper nouns. Over time, operators perfected the art of typing words in a way that ensured that the correct spelling in English would be generated. Not all the innovations and workarounds of operators though were in the interests of enrollees. Since speed was of the essence, enrollers also often sidestepped processes or hurried through them. For instance, the enrollment software was designed to force enrollers to go through the enrollment step four times in order to ensure that if biometrics were not well-captured on the first try, the process was repeated before being abandoned. The multiple attempts obviously increased the time spent on enrollment. This was especially true of rural areas where fingerprints were not clear for enrollees who engaged in hard manual labor. To dispense with the multiple trials operators found workarounds that they used when they felt an enrollee's prints would not pass muster. They claimed to draw on their experience looking at hundreds of fingerprints a day in making these estimations about prints. When the CIDR and design team became aware of these issues in the field, they tried to counter them through another design feature – by asking operators to authenticate every enrollment using their own prints. Initially, this authentication was saved offsite on the machine with other enrollment data before the entire packet was sent to the UIDAI office. When some operators provided false data in order to do more enrollments, operator authentication was moved to their machine and was verified after each enrollment rather than at the end of the day. Even though the operators were penalized, the enrollees whose data was lost paid a higher price, as they falsely believed they had undergone the process correctly and would be issued a UID. At the time of this field study, UIDAI had not built a mechanism to re-enroll where enrolment had failed the first time.

The work involved in keeping the system working on the ground, even though all its components were standardized, proved exhausting especially for the manager. He was half serious when he said that he had ramped up his cigarette and alcohol intake to deal with the emotional and psychological stress of being on his feet for hours on end. He seemed especially concerned about turning away people who had traveled a long distance for enrollment. He also commented that it was not entirely clear to him why so many people were coming in for enrolment at the same time. Many of the enrollees said that they had 'heard' that enrollment would stop at the end of the month and therefore, they wanted to make sure they enrolled before the deadline. Others had heard that they would be charged for enrolments starting the next month, and wanted to avoid those charges by enrolling early. Yet others had come to the enrolment center having misunderstood where they had to enroll. There were at least two instances of enrollees trying to bribe the manager to allow them to enroll that day. The manager refused the bribe and alerted the enrollees to read the notice outside the center, which said enrollment was free. This episode illustrates both a general lack of clarity about the procedure involved in the enrolment process, and enrollees' expectations of procedure based on past interactions with the issue of government IDs. It was the enrollment manager and operators who had to deal with both.

The purpose of the UID card or the need to enroll for UID was even harder to explain. Interestingly, this did not seem to be a question that enrollees approached the manager with. When we asked the manager, he said he himself understood the reasons for the card – such as ending corruption – but found it hard to explain it concretely to enrollees. But judging from the numbers enrolling, they saw a benefit to enrolling. We asked a 100 enrollees for their reasons and received a range of answers, including "I don't know," "My neighbor or someone in the village was getting it," and the more prescient "We always get something free from the government every time we get a card." This last statement merits an explanation. Having a government-issued document, such as a voter ID, a Below Poverty Line card, or a ration card, has historically been a means to avail of some privilege or service from the government particularly in rural India. As important, not having such a document can be used as a reason to keep people from availing of certain schemes. Given the level of familiarity with such schemes and enrolments, it is therefore not surprising that the reason for applying for a card was the question that was least asked of the manager.

In summary, there was a prescribed process for enrolment that had been laid out by the design team. Although the tasks and mechanisms for enrollment were designed and carefully structured to ensure uniform quality, many adjustments had to be made in the field. On the ground, the resourcefulness of the operators was critical in keeping the process going. Such resourcefulness did not always align with the benefits of enrollees, with the case of fraudulent entries making the process more difficult for enrollees. The motivations of the design team and the enrollers too did not always overlap. While data quality was paramount for the design team, the enrollment team was motivated by quantity since they were paid based on the number of people they enrolled for whom an ID could be generated. Finally, the enrollees' reasons to apply for a UID, as well as their procedures for going about doing this, were shaped by their own past experiences with the state, and these had to be managed by the enrolment staff on the ground.

DISCUSSION AND IMPLICATIONS

The enrollment process as seen through the eyes of two distinct groups of stakeholders – the designers who conceptualized the overall infrastructure and the enrolment personnel who helped build it on the ground by enrolling individuals– highlights the complex and multifaceted nature of building infrastructure and holding it together. The design team thought of standards and rules for the many components and stages of the enrolment process that they then supplied to enrollment agencies. But on the field, and in practice, the enrollers had to make adjustments all the time. Following Star, we would say that many of these adjustments were unsurprising since infrastructures always emerge only in practice. What is interesting to us, however, is how these two groups managed their socio-technical relationships with each other and with others. The designers and enrolment personnel differed along many facets. Their reasons for undertaking this project, their influences and their social positions were all dramatically different, as were the resources at their disposal and their capacity to wield them. How then did was such a scale of enrolment achieved in spite of the differences between the groups?

Both the design team and the enrollers were engaged in "creating and maintaining productive socio-technical relationships." One part of this was leveraging. The design team leveraged many of its networks and relationships to gain support for the project and in formulating its design. It also leveraged its expertise with artifacts, especially on developing large-scale software systems. The enrolment firm and manager, meanwhile, leveraged their relationships with the local state to arrange for office premises and other amenities, and their understanding of the local context to use available artifacts productively. In addition to leveraging, the need for alignment in the process of maintaining socio-technical relations is fairly established in CSCW literature. In our case, we saw how the designers of the project – with international start-up experiences and trained in the most reputed schools in India and elsewhere – had a particular vision and ways to make that vision come true. The enrollment personnel, on the other hand, were focused on making sure that data was captured accurately and for as many people as possible in a day. These personnel were college-educated, but they had trained primarily on the job. These enrollers did not have to draw up plans and standards, but they had to manage crises on the ground and manage the needs of a diverse population face-to-face.

In implementing the designers' plans on the ground, the enrollers also had to undertake articulation work, ensuring both that "all the various resources needed to accomplish something are in place and functioning where and when they're needed in the local situation" (local articulation) and that "different activities function well together" (metawork). Ensuring that operators could speak the local dialect or of putting in place a system to control crowds and ease the work of operators by marking documents are examples of the former; while ensuring data quality and that data packets travel smoothly between the enrollers and UIDAI are examples of the latter.

Finally, enrollers on the ground also had to pay attention to the material nature of digital data and infrastructure, which are often treated as immaterial in e-infrastructure projects such as UID. Since the project's inception, the data to be collected, its authentication and use were all designed to work in a seamless digital ecosystem. Yet, as is usually the case with e-infrastructure, all of these processes were embedded in different physical forms. Whether it was the biometric data capture machines, iris scanners, computers, or the USB sticks on which data was transferred by the enrollers for uploading to the CIDR, the materiality of 'things' pervaded the project. Much like the standardization of procedures, equipment standardization ensured that the equipment in use was of good quality. Yet, its use is localized and in locations that this equipment was not originally designed for. Issues such as access to regular power supply, extreme temperatures and dust, and fingerprints shaped by excessive manual work, come to mind, all factors that decide how enrolment progresses in practice (an issue that has been dealt with extensively in the ICTD literature; see [2]). There was also the ergonomics of enrolling people for 8-10 hours a day, an issue that enrollment agents felt designers had not given much thought to. Not only did the enrollers have to sit for hours at a stretch, they also had to lean over and help the enrollees with biometrics or camera placement frequently. All of this made enrolling physically taxing, and enrolment agents complained about this. In all fairness, some of the responsibility for this rested with the enrollment firms and not with the UIDAI. The poor ergonomics were often a result of cost saving decisions by the enrollment firm, which felt justified in making the decision given the low profitability of the venture.

Alignment through Data

We argue that at the end of the day, what kept the entire social and material infrastructure of UID together was 'data.' Accurate data was what the UIDAI cared about and monitored constantly through interfaces such as that in Figure 10.

Figure 10: Enrollment Monitoring Interface at CIDR [26]

Making sure such data reached CIDR and was accurate enough to result in a UID was all the enrollment agencies cared about. For UIDAI, accurate data meant easier de-duplication and authentication. For enrollment agencies, payment was based on each UID generated and therefore transferring accurate data was important. Where there were challenges such as with fraudulent data, the design team dealt with the challenge by suggesting and implementing solutions that involved more data (the enroller's prints authenticate the enrollee's).

A slightly different way in which the focus on data facilitated alignment was through the data analytics and visualization capabilities built by the UID team. Details of the enrolment process were uploaded and updated regularly, and were available for monitoring. The companies working on the project, particularly the enrollment agencies, could access significant details about their performance. Companies had their own portal (similar to Figure 3), built by the UID team, separate from the public website, through which they could monitor what was happening on the ground, such as the number of enrollments done, their quality, and the number of IDs had been issued based on their data. This monitoring helped enrollment agencies audit both the quantity and quality of their work continuously, allowing them to respond, if necessary, and to ensure faster and more accurate enrollments. In addition to their own data, enrollment agencies could also view data about other enrolment agencies. From the UID design team's perspective, this was an effective way to maintain competition, keep the different agencies on their toes and ensure that the enrolment process was fast without compromising on data quality.

Viewing Citizens as Numbers

An important point that emerges from our case is the relative invisibility of the end user, especially for the design team. If 'data' was made visible by the project, the user was in some sense invisible, except as a generic category or as a number adding to the project's enrollee count. Even though the UID project is targeted at these users, and project documents as well as interviews with the design team mention the people "without an identity" who will benefit from the project, we notice that these users appear mainly as reified entities with assumed needs in these discussions and documents (see [27] and several other training documents on the UIDAI website for examples).

But enrolment agents, who interacted with individual users all the time, found that unlike the 'users' in their training material, enrollees could not be characterized simply in terms of their age or the proof of identity document they used (the attributes most commonly mentioned in project documents to distinguish between different classes of residents). They found that users had varied experiences of past encounters with the state and equally varied ideas of how their UIDs would mediate their relations with the state. This matter of experiences and expectations brings up the importance of analyzing UID enrolment against the backdrop of the state-citizen relations in which the process was embedded.

While our focus in this paper has been the relationship between UID designers and enrolment agents, we realize that what makes the UID infrastructure unique is that it is attempting to reshape the relationship between a state and its population. It is, therefore, impossible to proceed without considering this second relationship – between state and citizens - in order to understand the building of the UID infrastructure. As a final point for discussion, we examine the UID enrolments in light of this relationship and the role of data in this relationship. We pointed earlier to the focus on enrollee data, and on enrollees as numbers. This is reflected in conversations with the UID design team as well as in project documents. In this, the UID project followed a long tradition of state-sponsored efforts to make a population 'legible' i.e. "to arrange the population in ways that simplified the classic state functions of taxation, conscription, and prevention of rebellion" [20: 2] and more recently, in the administration of welfare schemes. The collection or collation of data about a population is the first step towards achieving such legibility. What modern day states can 'see' of their population in this way has only increased over time, since they intervene in the administration of welfare programs for their population to a much larger extent than ever before [7]. The introduction of cheaper digital tools has also simplified the process of data collection and seeing. As one such infrastructure that changes what a state is able to see of its population, the UID has naturally attracted much criticism [10, 15, 17, 19]. These critiques prompt us to ask who is being made legible, to whom and for what reasons. Meanwhile, the designers of the UID project point to the large number of people who have not yet been 'seen' by the state and leverage their project as enabling such populations to be seen by the state by giving them a unique identity. Scott points out that a state 'sees' its population solely along dimensions it finds important (such as their age or in this case, their biometrics), in the process reducing that population to a few details and representing them as statistics. Is the UID similarly reducing members of a population to numbers, albeit unique ones? If so, what is being lost in the process?

One of the things we believe is being lost, and that merits further exploration, is how different members of a targeted population react to being seen thus by the state. Studying the UID enrolment process offered us an opportunity to understand how these reactions shape enrolment and the enrolment infrastructure. Unfortunately, due to the designers' (to a lesser extent, the enrollment personnel's) focus on data and on the state's enhanced ability to 'see' members of its population,[2] little is said about how the population 'sees' the state. Corbridge et al. argue that a population sees and understands the state through its

[2] Activists across the world have pointed to the dangers of state surveillance with the arrival of a biometric database of the scale of the UID [6, 10, 17, 18].

encounters with it [4, also16]. Whether in the offer to bribe the manager to receive the UID, or in the expectation that it would lead to direct benefits from the state, we saw how such past experiences with government services and schemes also shaped the encounters between enrollees in the UID project and enrolment agents. In fact, for many enrollees, it was these past experiences with government schemes that made them even apply for a UID. Delving into the nature and range of these experiences, we suggest, can open up opportunities to understand enrollees as more than people in need of an identity, as a number or as passive victims of state neglect. This forms an important avenue for future research on the UID project. The difference between the UID enrollee on paper and on the ground also highlights the need to involve potential enrollees as participants at some level of the design process. These questions are especially important in a project such as the one we have been discussing, given that it is a publicly funded governance project and seeks to improve access to government services.

Limitations

Our field study was limited in scope, especially relative to the scale of the project itself. Our conversations and interviews were also limited to people who spoke English or Hindi. The use of a single case to understand e-infrastructure in governance is also limiting. However, given the unique nature of the case and the very small probability of other projects of such scale being implemented, it is important to learn from this experience.

CONCLUSION

In this paper, we presented a case study of an e-infrastructuring project in the domain of governance. Our work makes several contributions. First, we extend the scope of CSCW scholarship to look at a nation state as a canvas for examining e-infrastructure. Second, we show how several concepts of infrastructuring from the CSCW literature are applicable to the UID project. We show how synergizing and articulation work proved critical in keeping the infrastructure working. We saw that the materiality of 'e'-infrastructure mattered. We also found that the focus on 'data' allowed those who designed the project conceptually and the enrolment agents who implemented it on the ground to work together. But we also found that a narrow focus on data had other consequences, which alerted us to think more broadly and inclusively about the consequences of e-infrastructure in our case. As a key goal of nation states, the increased legibility that is offered by an e-infrastructure project such as the UID might well simplify administration, including of welfare schemes. But we need to pause to consider how this increased legibility might affect the rights of a population that is understood as numbers.

ACKNOWLEDGMENTS

We thank our informants and gratefully acknowledge the grant from NSF CAREER Award#EEC-0954034.

REFERENCES

1. Bietz, M., C.P. Lee & E.P.S. Baumer. Synergizing in cyberinfrastructure development. *Computer Supported Cooperative Work* (2010).
2. Brewer, E., Demmer, M., Du, B., Ho, M., Kam, M., Nedevschi, S.,..and Fall, K. The case for technology in developing regions. *Computer*, 38(6) (2005), 25-38.
3. Ciborra, C. Interpreting e-government and Development: Efficiency, Transparency or Governance at a Distance?" *Information Technology and People* 18 (3) (2005), 260-279.
4. Corbridge, S., G. Williams, M. Srivastava, & R. Véron. *Seeing the State: Governance and Governmentality in India*. Cambridge: Cambridge University Press (2005).
5. Edwards, P. N., G.C. Bowker, S. J. Jackson, and R. Williams. Introduction: An Agenda for Infrastructure Studies. *Journal of the Association for Information Systems, Special Issue on e-Infrastructure,* Vol. 10 (5) (2009), 155-173.
6. Electronic Frontier Foundation. Growing mistrust of India's biometric scheme. https://www.eff.org/deeplinks/2012/05/growing-mistrust-india-biometric-id-scheme
7. Foucault, Michel. Governmentality. Republished in *The Anthropology of the State: A Reader,* ed. A. Sharma & A. Gupta, Wiley-Blackwell (2006), 131-143.
8. Gerson, E. M. Reach, bracket, and the limits of rationalized coordination: Some challenges for CSCW. In *Resources, Co-Evolution and Artifacts.* Springer London (2008), 193-220.
9. Heeks, Richard and, Savita Bailur, Analyzing e-government research: Perspectives, philosophies, theories, methods, and practice. *Government Information Quarterly*, 24 (2) (2007).
10. Hindu, The. Aadhaar Bound to Fail: Aruna Roy. *The Hindu*, Kochi edition, (Sep 5, 2011).
11. Jackson, Steven J., Stephanie B. Steinhardt, Ayse G. Buyuktur. Why CSCW needs science policy (and vice versa). *CSCW* (2013), 1113-1124.
12. Jain, Gagan. Understanding the 'Aadhaar'. *The Chartered Accountant* (November 2011).
13. Jayadevan, P.K. UID: Due to the technology challenges of speed and scale, Aadhaar is an object of attention. *The Economic Times*, (Feb. 7, 2012).
14. Julka, Harsimran. Govt Has Decided to Deliver the UID/Aadhaar Number in the Form of Better, Polyvinyl Aadhaars. *The Economic Times*, (Oct 10, 2011).
15. Khera, Reetika. The UID Project and Welfare Schemes. *Economic and Political Weekly* XLVI (9) (2011).
16. Kuriyan, Renee, and Isha Ray. E for express: 'Seeing' the Indian State through ICTD. In *Proceedings of the*

3rd IEEE/ACM International Conference ICTD (2009), 66-73.

17. Mukherjee, Arindam. Aadhar, A Few Basic Issues. *Outlook*, (Dec 5, 2011).

18. Nilekani, Nandan. *Imagining India: Ideas for the New Century* (Revised and Updated Edition). Penguin Books (2009).

19. Ramakumar, R. Aadhaar: on a platform of myths. *The Hindu,* (Jul 17, 2011).

20. Scott, James C. *Seeing Like a State: How Certain Schemes to Improve the Human Condition Have Failed.* Yale University Press (1998).

21. Star, Susan Leigh. The ethnography of infrastructure. *American behavioral scientist* 43(3) (1999): 377-391.

22. Strauss, A. The articulation of project work: An organizational process. *The Sociological Quarterly,* 29(1988): 163–178.

23. UIDAI, "Aadhaar- A Journey" Presentation: http://www.slideshare.net/balucol/aadhaar-9662801

24. UIDAI, Aadhaar enrolments data: http://uidai.gov.in/registrar-link-2.html

25. UIDAI registrar data on "data.gov.in": http://data.gov.in/dataset/aadhaar-generated-registrar-enrollment-agency-ea

26. UIDAI presentation by R.G. Sharma: http://www.biometrics.org/bc2012/presentations/UIDAI/Technology_Tampa_v1040.pdf

27. UIDAI, "Approach Document for Aadhaar Seeding In Service Delivery Databases Version 1.0," http://uidai.gov.in/images/aadhaar_seeding_v_10_280312.pdf

28. Wagenaar, H. (2011). *Meaning in action: Interpretation and dialogue in policy analysis*. M.E. Sharpe, Armonk, NY.

29. Weiss, Robert S., *Learning From Strangers: The Art and Method of Qualitative Interview Studies*, (New York: The Free Press, 1994).

30. Wolcott, Harry. *Writing Up Qualitative Research*, 2nd ed., (Thousand Oaks, CA: Sage, 2001).

31. Wolcott, H. F. (1995). *The Art of Fieldwork.* Walnut Creek, CA: Altamire Press.

32. Yanow, D. Thinking interpretively. In Yanow, D. and Schwartz-Shea, P. (Eds). *Interpretation and Method: Empirical Research Methods and the Interpretive Turn.* (2006), pp. 5-27. M.E. Sharpe, Armonk, NY.

33. Yin, R. K. *Case Study Research: Design and Methods.* (1994).Thousand Oaks, CA: Sage.

Enriching the Distressing Reality: Social Media Use by Chinese Migrant Workers

Jingjing Liu[1], Alexander Boden[2], David Randall[1], Volker Wulf[1,2]

[1]Information Systems and New Media
University of Siegen,
57068 Siegen, Germany
jingjing.liu1002@googlemail.com,
[volker.wulf, dave.randall]@uni-siegen.de

[2]Fraunhofer Institute für Applied
Information Technology FIT
Schloss Birlinghoven
53754 Sankt Augustin, Germany
alexander.boden@fit.fraunhofer.de

ABSTRACT
Based on a field study in Guangdong Province, this paper describes the social media use of Chinese migrant workers in the manufacturing sector. It was found that social media plays a significant role in the lives of young workers who have left their rural hometowns in early adulthood and struggle to survive in the urban centers. They buy expensive IT devices to gain a social reputation, as social media provides opportunities for self-expression; strengthens their self-consciousness; and to a certain extent, influences their world view. For most of the workers in our study, social media has become a very important part of leisure time and entertainment. Moreover, the life in virtual worlds provides them a psychological compensation mechanism to temporarily avoid the pressure of their daily lives.

Author Keywords
China; social media; virtual identity; migrant worker; field study

ACM Classification Keywords
H5.m. Information interfaces and presentation (e.g., HCI): Miscellaneous.

INTRODUCTION
Our interest in this paper is to describe the online activities of a small number of migrant workers in China. We endeavor to show that their practices are best understood as the outcome of a set of relationships between material circumstance, cultural tradition, individual identity and various other constraints. In doing so, we contribute a developing ICT4D literature which describes specific patterns of use among marginalized or poor communities.

The transfer of rural labor to urban centers has been a major feature of historical modernization processes in the West for at least four centuries [12]. More recently, attention has been paid to the distinctive features of this process in the contemporary world, particularly as it pertains to rapidly modernizing societies like China (see for instance in [6, 42, 10]) and deals with important issues such as migration, land management, architectural policy, population studies and resource management. Nevertheless, we should not imagine that these processes are complete. As Yu argues [59], "Modernity is yet to happen in China, in comparison with developed countries whose modernity has already happened." In China, this process is ongoing, and is institutionally framed in a specific manner.

CSCW'14, February 15–19, 2014, Baltimore, Maryland, USA.

http://dx.doi.org/10.1145/2531602.2531632

Due to the Chinese household registration system, called *Hukou*, Chinese people are divided into two groups. Persons with a rural *Hukou* are defined as 'farmers', no matter what kind of work they really do. In contrast, others have a registration with an urban *Hukou* which means higher social status and provides them with privileges, such as better housing and medical care, as well as better education and job opportunities. Under these institutional conditions, migrant workers are defined in the following way [1]:

"The Chinese migrant workers [...], are actually those who have rural registered permanent residence but engage in a non-agricultural activity in the city."

Currently, it is estimated that there are some 163 million migrant workers with rural *Hukou* in China [58]. Since the late 1970s', with rapid economic development, a huge amount of rural manpower has transferred from countryside to the urban centers. The first generation of Chinese migrant workers was characterized by a relatively low level of education and 'fitted' a demand for heavy physical work which the urban population was less willing to do. Over the past three decades, they have been replaced by a 'second' generation of migrant workers, known as the 'post-eighties', having been born under the one-child policy during the 1980s. Compared to the first generation, the 'post eighties' did not suffer under radical internal struggles or political mass mobilization, and live under better economic conditions, in a freer social environment and have access to a more advanced education system [43]. They have grown up with digital media, which in turn greatly affects their world view. Compared with the elders, this generation of migrant workers is more pragmatic [15], more materialistic

[40], and more individualistic [46] in their attitudes. They are also arguably members of a unique generation, one which continues to be located in the cultural traditions of Chinese society, but has experienced the modernizing processes of industrialization and urbanization at exactly the same time as they experience 'cybernization'.

Since the early 1990s, more and more high-tech manufacturing companies have moved their facilities to the Pearl River Delta (PRD) of Guangdong province in the Southern part of China. Young workers with a relatively high educational background and with a basic knowledge of computerized production equipment are preferred by employers nowadays. Guangdong Province is also rather attractive for young people because of its favorable climate, open social atmosphere, and developed economic condition. This mix of demand- and supply- factors meant that second generation migrant workers came in large numbers to the PRD. Compared with the first generation, it is suggested that this second generation is more competitive and more open towards consumerism. They have multidimensional social interactions and more awareness of independence [38]. This young generation prefers to work in manufacturing industries [7], not only because of higher wage levels, but also because of the better career prospects and the more comfortable working environment.

We have conducted an in-depth study of seven migrant workers to obtain a deeper understanding of the role of the Internet and social media for the migration workers of the second generation, in particular with regard to their appropriation. Our study indicates that social media plays an increasingly important role in their daily lives. We will suggest that, in some ways, online experiences are very similar to those of the young in the West, but in others are quite distinct. Like the young in the West, they consider social media an important source of information and amusement. They save money to buy Internet devices (PC, laptop, smartphone etc.) and install a broadband connection. Nevertheless, living in a restrictive social environment, the young migrant workers experience the online world, in our opinion, in some quite distinct ways. These, we argue, are a function of some stark differences between a 'real' world of harsh physical conditions and social isolation versus the colorful world of the virtual space.

STATE OF THE ART

In 2011, a survey on new media use of second generation migrant workers was conducted in Shanghai, the result shows that the popularity of new media (mobile 96%, Internet 75.4%) has already reached a higher level than traditional mass media (television 73.1%, newspapers 34.8%, radio 24.6%) in this group. Most of the participants access the Internet either in Internet cafes/bars or through broadband connections at home. The main activities on the Internet are centered on communication, relaxation, and amusement [60]. In the same year, Wallis [46] emphasizes the connection between the new media use of young people and Chinese social change processes. Damm [15] analyzed the usage and content of the Chinese Internet with focus on consumerism and lifestyle; the study showed that the social and commercial usage of Internet is much more important than the political one. Some researchers have sought to show how internet use in China has specific cultural elements. It has been suggested that, since the state owns and controls all internet access (though it rents bandwidth to private companies) there is no 'internet' in China, only an 'intranet'. There is some controversy as to whether the rich variety of internet use is evidence of the failure of the Chinese government to control access, or whether it is evidence of an intelligent and nuanced approach to control (see [22] for a summary). Certainly, there is clear evidence that access to the internet has on occasion been completely shut off, for instance in Xinjiang province in 2009, after civil unrest there. More commonly, however, the policy has been to make access difficult rather than impossible, by managing bandwidth, blacklisting search terms, censorship and so on (ibid). In addition, the temporary ban of Western websites has contributed to the emergence of a distinct internet ecology consisting of search engines (such as *Baidu*) or microblogging applications (such as *Weibo*).

One consequence of this careful management is that internet use in China needs to be understood as a negotiated order in which government, material circumstance, the individual, and expressions of Chinese 'cultural tradition' interact with each other. Indeed, the phrase, "internet with Chinese characteristics" or "Chinese internet" ([56], [11]) are frequently used in opposition to the more generalized idea of 'the internet in China'. Further, and it is perhaps unsurprising in a vast country, cultural and geographical differences frame the relationship between online and offline behavior. Herold [4] argues that internet use in China has aspects of 'carnival', creating and maintaining a divide between the offline ("normal") world and the online ("carnivalistic") world. Carnival here reflects a world 'turned upside down' in which ordinary social identities (gender, status, etc) are counterposed with fluid online identities, where polyphonous voices rather than univocal hierarchy are in play, and where "normal" standards of behavior are constantly challenged by a new playful, sensual set of interactions. Li [30] has argued that these tensions create a particular use of parody (called 'egao' or 'evil joking') in Chinese internet use. Wu and Wang [52] have demonstrated the popularity of complex forms of in-game marriage in MMogs and MUDs, to the extent that all of the top ten MMogs in China carry these features. They argue that this online behavior can best be understood as a form of playful nostalgia for ethnic folk culture. The point here is that confronted with a historically rigidly organized social structure, with strict hierarchies of status and respect, online modes of behavior may be more starkly contrasted with the 'normal' than in the West. The tension between a historically closed, totalitarian society and a more open capitalistic one simultaneously with the development of a "cyber culture" is relatively unique and has some unique consequences [3].

Recently, Chinese social scientists have become interested in a more 'field research' oriented approach to internet study. Peng [34] has analyzed the conditions of Internet use of migrant workers in PRD by means of a field study and found that most of them utilize Internet cafes/bars despite their low income. Huang [24] focused on the young migrant workers of an automobile company in Huizhou, Guangdong province. He reports that workers used the Internet as their main source of information and amusement, to a much greater degree than any other mass medium. By using qualitative research methods Yang and Zhu [57] also studied migrant workers in the PRD. In spite of their low income, the workers were very willing to purchase mobile phones from famous international brands (Motorola, Nokia etc.), whose prices equal three or four times their monthly salaries. To them, mobile phones are not only a convenient communication tool, but also a symbol of "fashion" and "social status".

Hsu explains the cultural and social reasons for the sensibility around the concept of 'face'. Chinese people traditionally grow up in a culture with very strong mechanisms of social control. Therefore, they pay much attention to their behavior when other people are around (cited by [32]). Referring to this discourse conceptually, Luo and Peng [32] describe the use habits of mobile phones and find a corresponding relationship between the mobile phone migrant workers own and their 'face' expressing dignity, social status and prestige. The study was also conducted in Guandong province.

Mobile phones were also investigated with regard to the mobilization of migrant workers. Ding and Tian [16] carried out case studies with taxi drivers who came from the rural area of the Hunan province and worked in the modern city of Shenzhen. With the usage of in-car communication systems and instant messaging software (IM software), such as QQ, the taxi drivers were able to build a network of new social relationships which included family members and local acquaintances as well. In another highly industrialized city, Shanghai, female part-time servants use their cell phones for adapting to the modern urban daily life and career. For example, the use of mobile phone could help them to meet the needs of flexible work time better. The housekeeping company could contact the part-time servants on time when there is a temporary job. In addition to all of the above, mobile phones are also known to help migrant workers in confronting discrimination; overcome the boredom of working time, and to avoid loneliness and homesickness [8].

Lang et al. [28], in an ethnographic study, argued that the reason why so many young migrant workers purchase mobile phones is because they need them to support their specific social practices, to "give them relief, a sense of belonging, as sense of fun, as well as information related to life and work" (ibid: 60). Now, in and of itself, this is a truism, but is revealing in a context where migrant workers have moved a long way from existing family networks and have no stable networks of social relations to replace them. In the context of a wider culture in which fixed and hierarchical social relationships play a major role, this is hugely problematic for the young migrant worker. The two main categories of interactive social groups of migrant workers are summarized as "local tribes" (current workmates) and "home tribes" (family, friends, classmates from back home etc.), and in online environment, the communication behaviors with the first type happens more frequently than the second. In order to make mobile phones more supportive for young migrant workers' activities, the research group identified five design directions for special network services from a CSCW perspective.

Researchers from Tsinghua University ([48], [31]) also presented an ethnographic study on the use of mobile phones by Chinese migrant workers whose demands have always been neglected by ICT-producers. Based on this study, the researchers offered more conceptual design blueprints for people who received a relatively low education.

Given that there is very little published work on migrant labor and their online behavior, and even less in the specific context of China, our review of the literature has necessarily come from other sources. In this paper, we contribute to the existing literature by focusing on the second generation of migrant workers employed by the manufacturing industry in Guangdong province. Compared to other migrant workers, our informants have rather stable job positions and are relatively well paid. They nevertheless experience discrimination and social isolation. This, as we have tried to show above, is a function of a society in which social roles in the offline world are still substantially dominated by family, community network and tradition. In this paper, we are specifically interested in the appropriation of social media applications as a coping strategy, given their economic and social circumstances.

RESEARCH METHODS

Conducting qualitative research with migrant workers in China is challenging. Being a migrant worker creates a life full of uncertainty, risk and disrespect. There is an understandable level of distrust and suspicion (akin to what is reported by [53]). In the Chinese context, this is compounded by formality. Chinese academics, such as the first author, experienced the social and cultural gap between them and the migrant workers first hand: while the workers consider themselves to be at the "*bottom of society*" (Chen, Respondent), academics appear to be from a "*higher social class"*, who have a better life and hence are entitled to deference and respect. Migrant workers will, for instance, put on their proper clothes when being interviewed by 'researchers (fact-finders)' as a means to preserve 'face'.

The work presented here was preceded by a study which resulted in rather limited results. The study took place in Xiamen, a coastal city located in Fujian province in South-Eastern China. Introduced by the owner of the company, the first author got in contact with young migrant workers in a textile factory. However, the interviews turned out to be difficult for two reasons: (1) the migrant workers came from the regional countryside and spoke only the local language, which the first author did not master; (2) they basically declined to talk with "the boss's friend" about their lives in sufficient depth – indicative again of the sheer importance of social hierarchy. Even so, it was found that these young migrant workers used their phones mainly to contact their families and friends, while very few of them owned computers at that time.

Learning from this experience, we looked for another way to set up this research. A relative of the first author from Hubei province belongs to the new generation of migrant workers. Thanks to his support, the first author managed to do a pre-study in Guangdong in May and June 2011. We partly followed a snow ball sampling approach which was based on personal recommendations by the relative and early informants. Moreover, the first author participated in activities of the Hubei Club in Guangzhou. This club provides a platform for migrant workers from the same region to meet. We were able to acquire additional informants there.

More than 50 young migrant workers were invited separately to teahouses or small restaurants for informal interviews. The topics of these interviews were family and educational background, the use of mobile phones or other IT devices, and their willingness to continue participating in this research. The personal introduction by the relative and the informal settings of the first round of interviews let them overcome their initial distrust and the first author was able to get to know the interviewees to a certain degree. Still, it was not easy to get in-depth data. Facing an 'outsider' some of them talked in very brief statements or merely nodded or shook their heads.

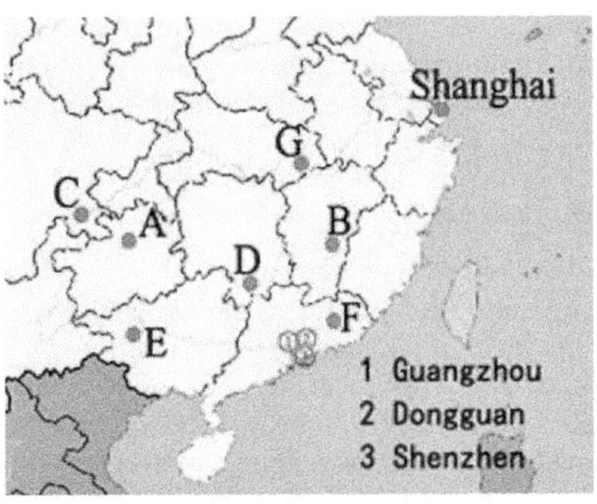

Figure 1. The hometowns of seven respondents and their work place in Guangdong

In order to get deeper insights, we decided to continue working with a smaller subset of migrant workers. Based on the principle of 'maximization of divergence', we asked seven to become part of an in-depth study [33]. The seven participants (four males and three females) are working in three different cities: Guangzhou (2 of them) Shenzhen (4 of them) and Dongguan (1 of them) (see Table 1, Figure 1). To protect their privacy, we use pseudonyms.

A: Chen, male, 26, comes from Zunyi, Guizhou province. He has a technical college background, works as a technician in a cell phone company in Shenzhen, lives in a rented apartment with two colleagues and uses a laptop for surfing on the Internet. *Number of interviews: 4*
B: Deng, female, 26, comes from Donggu, Jiangxi province. She was trained as tour guide by a tourist secondary school from 2000 to 2003. Now she works as QC in a cell phone company in Shenzhen. She uses a laptop purchased in 2006 and shares the DSL fee with three other roommates. *Number of interviews: 3*
C: Wang, female, 21, comes from Yibin, Sichuan province. Because of poverty she didn't finish junior school and followed her sister to Guangdong province at the age of 15. Currently she is employed by a clothing company in Dongguan as a QC. She lives with her sister and her sister's boyfriend in a two-room apartment, the young couple let her use their PC and Internet for free. *Number of interviews: 2*
D: Qi, male, 28, married, comes from Ningyuan, Hunan province. He has a bachelor degree in computer science and now works as a team leader in an electronic components company in Guangzhou. He uses laptop for surfing online. *Number of interviews: 3*
E: Shao, male, 19, comes from Lingyun, Guangxi province. He is Qi's subordinate and works as a machine operator. After graduating from senior high school, he failed the college entrance examination. He now lives with two colleagues in a dormitory equipped by the employer and shares a PC and Internet access with them. *Number of interviews: 3*
F: Lu, female, 20, comes from Dongyuan, Guangdong province. She is a pipeline operator in a molding press company in Shenzhen, lives with her parents and a younger brother in a rented three-room apartment. She has her own PC. *Number of interviews: 4*
G: Wei, male, 24, comes from Huangshi, Hubei province. He is the only child in his family and works as a machine operator at a cell phone company in Shenzhen. During his study at junior college, he bought his first PC. Currently he uses a laptop bought in 2011 to go online and lives with two colleagues in a three-room apartment. *Number of interviews: 4*

Table 1. The migrant workers: some background information

In order to seek heterogeneity, participants with different educational backgrounds had been chosen. One participant, for instance, had not completed the Chinese nine year compulsory education, the others graduated from senior middle school, technical secondary school, junior college or even university. Their professions include technician, quality control (QC), machine operator, pipeline operator and team leader. However, there were some commonalities among our chosen group of migration workers:

- Age: All of them were born after 1980; ages ranged between 19 and 28.
- *Hukou*: All of them come from rural areas and have a rural registered permanent residence, but no one has any agriculture work experience.
- Housing condition: All of them live in rented dwellings.
- Mobile Internet: Besides PC or laptop, all of them use a mobile device for Internet access. The most popular programs are QQ (an IM tool developed by the Chinese company Tencent; the originally design followed MSNICQ; now it includes a combination of the functionality of MSN, Facebook, Twitter and Skype) and WeiChat (an voice IM tool).

Our study is based on qualitative field research methods including in-depth interviews, participatory observation, and focus group interviews. From August 2011 to March 2012, a total of 23 semi-structured interviews were conducted to collect narrative data from the seven selected participants (two to four interviews per person, see Table 1). In January 2012, two focus group interviews were held in Shenzhen and Guangzhou. One was attended by the respondents Chen, Deng, Lu and Wei, the other by Wang, Qi and Shao. Due to their strong aversion to recording equipment, tape recorders or cameras were not utilized during the interviews. All the interviews were transcribed by the first author and a local assistant. A particular problem here was how to deal with gesture, facial expression and body movement and a protocol was developed to record, as far as was possible, such matters at the same time as transcription.

Following their first encounter, the first author remained in steady contact with all of the interviewees via the QQ social media platform. This way she had a large number of informal conversations and could observe parts of their online activities. These contact helped particularly to refine our findings and fill blind spots of the initial rounds of interviews. All data were analyzed following a grounded-theory approach including several iterations of open coding and concept-building. We developed several categories during this process, including almost all functions of internet for migrant workers, such as informational, educational, commercial, recreational and emotional. Two of them, which reflect the great differences between the stressful real life of Chinese migrant workers and their enriching online life, led to the structure of the next section: challenges of being a migrant worker, and building a virtual self.

EMPIRICAL FINDINGS

As already mentioned our research was undertaken in Guangdong province. Due to the highly developed production and service industries, Guangdong is celebrated as the 'window of the opening policy'. It has experienced a very substantial influx of migrant workers over the past twenty years.

Being a migrant worker: a challenging life

The nature of the lives of migrant workers in China has been well-attested [61]. It involves a number of features that are not typically shared by workers in the West. They include forced geographical distance from family and community; long working hours; residential separation and isolation from local social networks.

The awakening of self-consciousness (individual consciousness)

Most members of the new generation of Chinese migrant workers come from a large family with several siblings and cousins (in some rural regions, the one child policy is not strongly enforced). Family members are expected to help each other in many ways. As a rule, elders support and protect the youth. As a result, they develop a strong collective identity which provides them with a sense of security and belonging and, for the most part, attitudes tend not to be individualistic. Conversely, and as we have intimated above, this close network of support obligations is accompanied by a strong sense of 'place', such that status is rigidly ascribed to individuals along family and community lines.

Shao explained how he became a migrant worker: *"After I failed the university entrance examination, I very much wanted to go back to the senior middle school and prepare for the exam next year. But [short pause]… I should think more about the whole family, my younger brother was still in school, [there was] not enough money. I had to go to Guangdong, I had no choice."* Lu complained about the partiality of her parents: *"In my family, I felt like an unnecessary person. Dad and mum prefer my younger brother. I am nobody. […] In primary school I got my first computer as a birthday gift, since then I think I probably spend more time with it than with my family."*

Most of the young migrant workers of our sample began their geographically mobile career directly after school. They left their poor, undeveloped hometown for the modern, developed urban centre. For them, this meant not only a physical relief from the stresses of local living, but also meant a certain psychological freedom: "*When I bought my first laptop, I had no idea how to maintain the machine. It's the most expensive thing that I have purchased with my OWN money.*" said Chen. Deng recalled: "*The transmigration to Guangdong gave me the best chance to escape the cage*".

The Lubricant of work

This narrative of escape and freedom soon comes up against the realities of the working environment. Working conditions are so stressful that the opportunities for social contacts are severely restricted. In the case of our informants, the factory and office places are quite modern. However, they are surrounded by iron railings and fences. Moreover, there are identity card scanners and security controls at the entrances. Everybody has to wear the blue or gray work suits. The day shift and night shift switch every 2 or 4 months, and the average working time per day is about 10 hours. Figure 2 shows the work place of Wei, where accessories for mobile phones are produced. Workers are in this factory daily for 12 hours, 10 hours working time with 2 hours breaks. Chatting with each other or using phones is forbidden during work time. Nevertheless, some workers surreptitiously manage to glance at the news or to chat via QQ from time to time.

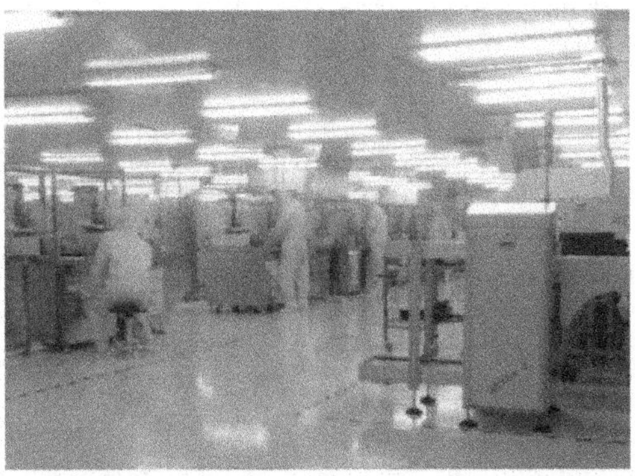

Figure 2. Work place in a factory producing accessories for mobile phones (photo taken by Wei)

Figure 3. A female migrant worker secretly using mobile phone during work hours (photo taken by Wei)

All the seven respondents do simple, repetitive tasks in their daily work. The noisy work environment also increases the mental stress. Meals have to be finished in prescribed break times.

When asked what she does in her breaks, Deng said: *"I read online novels on my mobile phone during lunch break. [Q: Is that not forbidden?] No, only in working time [...]. The job is so intense and hectic that I sometimes feel like I am part of the mechanics of the assembly line. [...] it seems to be the only way to pull me out from the monotonous work".*

Chen still remembers the first day of work: *"As a new recruit, you will be surprised by the rules: no casual conversations, no mobile phones, and very strict requirements for the task [...]. But after the internship, if you get along well with the colleagues, they teach you tricks on how to relax during the intensive production process and how to secretly send SMS, listen to music or chat on QQ."*

High dependence on the Internet

All seven respondents in this study surf the Internet almost every day and estimate that they accumulate a weekly average online time of about 9 hours. It is less than the average cumulative use time of Chinese 'netizens' (19.9 hours/week) because of their long work hours. During the interviews, all respondents were asked to grade their dependence on the Internet (on a scale from 1 to 10, low to high dependence). Six respondents selected more than 6 points, 3 of them more than 8 points. By another request of listing the top three most important types of online services or applications which were 'absolutely essential' (see Table 2). All seven participants considered a search engine (but only the Chinese domestic one: *Baidu*) as their primary information source. Five of them emphasized the importance of the IM software QQ which helps them keep in touch with family and friends. QQ creates a new contact form in the virtual space that promotes the emotional bond between young migrant workers and their relatives and maintains the 'strong relationships'. Despite the relatively low frequency of contacts, migrant workers look forward to getting news or messages from their relatives. Qi describes his feeling when video chatting with his little nephew on his first birthday: "*I was so excited to see the baby that I discussed with my wife about having our own child*".

Chen	search engine, IM software, online cinema
Deng	search engine, EC platform, online cinema
Wang	online cinema, search engine, IM software
Qi	search engine, IM software, online forum
Shao	IM software, MMogs, search engine
Lu	online cinema, IM software, search engine
Wei	MMogs, search engine, IM software

Table 2. The most important network service for the seven migrant workers

Family relationships are the basic social structure in rural China. Since most of their families own neither computer nor internet, young migrant workers often seek help from their relatives of their similar age who convey their greetings from far away. Video chat via IM software can help developing a sense of "absent presence" [18] and increases the opportunity of face-to-face communication. Following Chen's recommendation, the two elder sisters also bought laptops, so that the younger brother could 'participate' in family party-dinner. "*Last year in the Mid-*

Autumn-Day the whole family member were staying together, except me. But we chatted via video on QQ [...]. Although I could not be there, I saw my family, especially my parents, still very happy".

The choices of our respondents also show an obvious bias towards entertainment. Wei, who has been playing online games for almost 10 years, said: "*Without Internet, I wouldn't know what to do*", for him, the Internet is an indispensable part of life. Being asked what he would do if he was cut off from the Internet at home, Wei answered without thinking: *"then I would go to an Internet bar."* Asked what if there were no more bars, he answered: (shrugged*) "Then I'd keep looking. I'll certainly find one somewhere."* For Deng, the network is the biggest shopping mall*: "Without the Internet? How could I live then? I buy almost everything online."*

For Lu, the Internet is the best home theater with thousands of domestic and foreign films as well as television series: *"If someone supplies me a bed and enough food, I would stay there (stay online) all the time"*. She said*: "I always turn the computer on as soon as I get home. And link to the UUSee. It's amazing that it records TV programs I watched earlier and recommends new TV series."* UUSee is one of the largest online TV platforms in China. It provides free Chinese TV shows and movies. Not only Lu, but also all the other respondents consider the entertainment function of the Internet to be the most important function in their lives.

The disappearance of the hardware digital divide

Four of the seven respondents had a laptop, one had his own PC. Wang and Shao shared a computer with others, but both of them display a high willingness to buy their own personal PC or laptop.

Wang complained: *"The computer is in my sister's room. Her boyfriend uses it constantly when he is home from work. What should I do? I can only wait. Or if they want to go to sleep, I have to leave the room. [...] For a long time I've wanted my own computer so much. [...] A computer is much cheaper, but a laptop seems to be more convenient if I should move. And, you know, a laptop is much more modern, many of my colleagues have bought one. It looks very modern!"*

Shao prefers a mobile phone rather than a PC: *"Compared to the PC, I prefer the mobile Internet. The biggest advantage is that you don't have to worry about your privacy. No one can spy on your daily life"*.

Wang and Shao articulated their dissatisfaction and discomfort with sharing a computer with others, as they felt it affected their freedom and privacy. A private computer symbolized independence, security and modern life for the two respondents. For the young migrant workers, the practical functions and the price are unsurprisingly considered as the most important factors in the purchase process. Meanwhile, as in Wang's case, the purchase can also be a result of group action and thereby shared. Colleagues and roommates (colleagues or family members) are the main interactive groups, while life is spent time either in the work place or in their rooms. Due to their limited social circle, colleagues often influence each other strongly. These young people buy new media devices not only for their functions but also for the traditional Chinese 'face culture'. Despite their low income, Shao insisted that he needed to save enough money for a laptop:

Shao explained: *"The PC is so bulky and uncomfortable, and you can take the laptop anywhere. [...] [If I] dressed in a nice suit, sat in a McDonald's with a laptop, no one will see and can judge me as a migrant worker"*.

Qi also expressed this desire*: "I used to use the cheapest mobile phone only for calls and SMS. One day a colleague sent me a MMS that I couldn't read with my old phone, so I got myself a smartphone with a wide screen. [It is] not expensive, but pretty good. [...] I don't like to pursue fashion, but I don't want others judge me as a bumpkin either"*.

Chen reminisced about the pride brought on by ownership of his laptop*: "The time I bought my laptop, most of my colleagues had to go to an Internet bar. One day I brought the laptop to the factory [...]. Aha! How were my colleagues looking at me! In their eyes there was envy, jealousy and hatred! [Laughing for more than 5 seconds] It's true! [Laughing] But now, they all have their own [laptop]"*.

Unlike most existing empirical research on Internet usage of the new generation of Chinese migrant workers which reports that Internet bars would be the most popular way to access the Internet, all seven respondents showed a certain rejection of Internet bars. Wang emphasized that she had never been in an Internet bar, because "*they are far away from home"* and "*it is too dirty there and stinks*". Shao went to an Internet bar only when he and his friends or colleagues played online games there all night long: "*since work always has me so tired, I don't have enough time and energy for such sprees*".

The virtual self: Dressing Up on social media platforms

For the new generation of migrant workers, virtual network environments offer an ideal platform for self-expression, where they can temporarily escape the real world and become anyone they want. All respondents, without exception, paid a very strong attention to his or her image on social media platforms. For example, all respondents used the avatar system of the IM software, QQ (the so called QQ-show), whereby some of them regularly spent money on new, beautiful avatar characters to build a better visual self-image. For example, in Wang's QQ-show, she "dressed" herself as a cute girl with a black silky blouse, a black and white skirt with pantyhose and high heels, and a pair of angel wings on the back. The figure looks very different from her in real life (Figure 4). Not only Wang, but also other respondents admitted that they spent time and money on a "suitable" avatar image. Sometimes it took hours to make the decision. In this way, a "*beautiful and modern*" (Wang) graphical self-representation can be constructed. For Shao, it is an "*eye catcher*" that visualizes the virtual Self. Deng chose a blonde female avatar in a bikini and sunglasses on the beach, "*It would be super cool if you could relax on the beach instead of working in the boring factory*".

It's worth mentioning that four of the seven respondents put down the name of the current city of residence as "hometown" in their personal information on QQ, while the other three chose neither the name of the current resident city nor that of their actual hometown. By answering the question why she used "Irish castle" as the name of her hometown, Wang smiled, "*it's so literary and romantic, though it is just a game, not real*".

Figure 4. A photo of Wang and her virtual self being an avatar in QQ-show- used with permission

In our study, six respondents used Q-zone (a blog service provided by Tencent) for self-representation in form of transmitting articles or expressing their moods and experiences in short sentences. The 19-year-old Shao provided the following information about himself in his Q-zone profile:

Name of Qzone: *Let your soul fly freely*
Current residence: *Solomen Islands, Makira*
Hometown: *Italy*
Occupation: *Student*
Favorite music: *Classical music, Jazz*
Favorite book: *The Unbearable Lightness of Being*

Shao retained his identity as "student" in Q-zone, and provided no information about his current work situation. The self-description reflects Shao's ideal self, which is reconstructed in the virtual space: he strives to portray himself as a modern student with a free spirit, who has a taste for literature and music. In contrast, Shao admitted frankly that he is not fond of classical music or jazz at all: "*the only piano music I know is 'Für Elise', because it's my ringtone*". Similarly, Chen spent a lot of time on his Q-zone picking out the nicest web templates for his blog. The appearance of his blog pages change regularly, popular songs are added or proverbs full of philosophical metaphors and aphorisms as "*can form an impression of the intelligentsia on other people*".

Qi is a regular guest of a forum which is specially built for the national master entrance examination of computer science students, where he can exchange experiences and information with other similar minded young people. He constructed himself in the forum as "*graduate from a computer science college*", "*works as a communication engineer in a high-tech company in Guangzhou*". He doesn't see this "*little embellishment*" of his real identity as a big problem, because "*no one online knows the truth and nobody cares about who you really are*". But when asked, why he made up such a background if nobody was interested, Qi replied with an embarrassed smile:
"*It isn't totally illusory. There is great deal of facts! I am an undergraduate and I do have opportunities to work in big companies [...]. In the forum there are little kids everywhere. If I introduce myself as a professional computer engineer, it certainly would be better than as a team leader in a factory [...]. The judgment standards of those kids [in the forum] are simple: they focus on where did you graduate, what companies are you working at and what your professional position is. I do not want to be discriminated by those kids.*"

Qi compared his real ego with his virtual ego in the interview: „*It's really not easy for a rural child to get a foothold in Guangzhou. In the factory there is only one colleague and I that want to go back to school. The others, frankly, they are just living and muddling along, though they admire my stamina and determination. You may say it's just my craving for recognition or even egotism. [...] It definitely wins me 'face' both online and offline*".

Deng (26-year-old) is the only one in this study who registered herself on a dating website. Working in the factory makes it difficult to get to know people other than colleagues. In the dating web profile, Deng described herself only with the word "*employee*", she admitted that she did not want to reveal her present job because "*the others could probably exclude me because of my job position. Men are interested in women with white-collar jobs*". She now contacts with a few men through QQ and SMS. In explaining why she tries to find a relationship online, she said: "*In rural areas, an unmarried 26-year-old girl would be regarded as a freak. I do not expect to find a husband by a dating site especially when so many people dress up their profiles with fake information. I just hope to enlarge my social interaction. Besides, I don't have any better choice.*"

DISCUSSION

The concept of 'migration workers' covers a wide variety of different phenomena in China. Moreover, the lives of migrant workers and their social practices have changed drastically over the last 35 years as well. Research has demonstrated that the 'Chinese internet' has some features which are distinct from the internet at large. These include the interplay between a very traditional culture in which social status and hierarchy are rigidly ascribed and tightly bound up with family, community and network, and the modernizing, 'cybernization' process. As such, the character of Chinese society is not that of Riesman's "Lonely Crowd" or the so-called "mass society" of C. Wright Mills and others, characterized by an undifferentiated mass of anonymous interactions. Although such depictions were always something of a caricature, they nevertheless point to disjuncture rather than continuity. What characterizes contemporary Chinese society, in contrast (and for the present), is the continued importance of traditional forms and new, more playful interactions with them.

The presentation of self in such a society takes on as much, and arguably a great deal more, importance in Chinese life than in the West. The preservation of 'face' is a vital ingredient in this. It is not surprising that, faced with rigid status ascriptions, workers who see themselves as low in status and who, in virtue of an online presence, have a chance to negotiate this reality, will do so. There are similarities here to what has been reported elsewhere in the context of ICT4D ([37], [5], [55]). Rangaswamy and Cutrell [37], for instance, refer to the way in which identity construction online is compensatory for the teenage urban poor in India; Wyche [55] to the way Facebook is used in rural Kenya, and Bidwell [5] to design which reflects cultural traditions of storytelling in South Africa. All point to the way in which harsh living conditions and material constraints condition the way in which social media are used. They also indicate in some cases the way in which specific cultural conditions as well as material constraints impact on usage. What is of particular interest to us is the intersection of material circumstance and cultural background to produce distinctive patterns of use.

A second element of this, and again arguably a function of the tension between these traditional elements and the irruptive power of the internet, is the 'parodic' form that interaction on the Chinese internet can take. We suggest that the radically different images portrayed by our sample on the Web can be thought of as approaching the parodic - as containing elements of Bakhtin's "carnival". The identities that our respondents construct are celebrations of ambition - playful reinventions of the self - as specific reactions to 'outsider' status. Now, we are not suggesting here that such a finding is unique to Chinese life. Internet studies by researchers such as Mary Chayko [9] and Pierre Levy [29] have pointed to the transformative power of the internet in relation to the formation of community. Others have argued that new social networks or cybercultures are enabled by online behavior ([39], [4]) that identities can be transformed in a playful fashion [45], that new forms of organization are possible ([41], [26]). What is striking here, however, is that *all* of the members of our small sample represented themselves in this playful, re-invented, way. They *all* constructed online identities which, to a varying degree, were distinct from their real life situations. *All* used the internet explicitly to find solace and shelter from a world which demanded a great deal from them in terms of effort, material conditions and low status. That is, the contrast between the realities of work and domestic life and online identity is much more pronounced in the case of migrant labor.

It is worth saying a little about the notions of 'identity' and the 'self' at this point. A great deal of heat, and very little light, is generated in discussions about how these terms should be treated and the degree to which they are distinct. There is, for instance, a substantial difference between the concept of identity as a mental construct - as existing in the mind - and as a social construct.

We have little to say about the distinct categories into which our respondents may or may not place themselves, although there are indications that social status is a significant part of their displays. Rather, we sidestep these problems by dealing with the self in the way that Erving Goffman ([19], [20]) does - as performance. Goffman is adamant that no mental structures need be envisaged when we speak of the self. Selfhood is evident in the way people present themselves in the world. This performativity and the way it is embedded in cultural background is our theme. It is a happy coincidence that Goffman is concerned with what he terms, 'facework' to describe how we engage in both verbal and non- verbal activities in specific settings in order to maintain a positive social image.

Buying modern devices like smartphones, laptops, and tablet PCs gives the migrant workers the feeling of belonging to the city and being on equal grounds with the urban population. They can reap a "large face" by buying expensive digital goods among their urban peers [31], especially when the purchased products are better than those owned by others. Smartphones which represented modernity and wealth in the early 2010s ([47], [50], [57], [32]), have been replaced by laptops, which are now considered to be more advanced. In other words, laptops have become the new icons of "fashion" and "achievement" among migrant workers. Compared to young citizens from the cities, migrants perceive themselves to be in a disadvantage, which stimulates a compensation strategy by emulating the appearance, behavior and manners of their urban peers. In this way they try to urbanize themselves.

In the virtual world, young migrant workers actively appropriate various online services and applications. How they try to hide their real identity by creating a virtual identity online, the extent to which they do so, and the natures of the identities they construct are all afforded by anonymity and an "opportunity for negotiating identity" [46]. It is an ideal space, where the young migrant worker can rebuild his, for himself unsatisfying, real ego as he wishes. According to Peng and Xu [35], the term "network dual personality" refers to the dual existence of a person in real life and in cyberspace. The two dimensions appear to be fully independent personalities that are distinguishable by attitude and behavior. Our data indicates that the fictitious ego typically marks a stark contrast.

Higgins' [23] self-discrepancy theory offers some interesting concepts to discuss this phenomenon. He suggests that the 'self' is divided into three basic domains of self-images: the 'actual' self (representation of one's own attribute), the 'ideal' self (representation of the attributes that other people would hope an individual to possess) and the 'ought' self (representation of the attributes that other people want an individual to have). The migrant workers' virtual self is a mix of these three dimensions and expressed by the individuals' performative behavior as well as his/her attitude to interpersonal communications. The self-image construed by young migrant workers online differs greatly from their actual self. They reinvent themselves in the virtual space as their 'ideal' self or their 'ought' self and this can be thought of as a strategy for image management.

Our findings are interesting because the concept of the individual has always been neglected in Chinese history. It has usually replaced by collective concepts such as 'people', 'population' or 'mass' [27]. By using social media, migrant workers try to escape the closed connections of their current work and social environment whilst continuing to interact with their cultural origins and the cultural controls they have historically contended with. The online world, in sum, affords them an opportunity to negotiate individual identity against the more collectivist or community- oriented traditions embedded in Chinese culture.

CONCLUSION

With the gradual development of "urbanization, marketization, globalization, informatization, and liberalization" in China [46], the second generation of migrant worker faces the challenge of identity transition from 'farmer' to 'city dweller', or even further to 'citizen' in a modern sense. In this process, the ownership of IT devices and the daily use of social media play an important role. To better understand these phenomena detailed empirical studies are necessary to represent not only the landscape of social media use but also their strategies of identity transformation from a micro perspective.

Our study has revealed social practices which are highly relevant for understanding the use to which of IT devices and social media might be put for the large population of Chinese migrant workers and, ultimately (through processes of comparison) cross- culturally. Our research was carried out in Guangdong province, where the high-tech industry is well developed. It confirms that the ownership of IT devices, such as PCs and laptops, is nowadays trickling down to the migrant workers, at least in the manufacturing industry. However, Dourish [17], Pipek and Wulf [36] emphasize that the appropriation of the new refers not only to the physical purchase or the installation of an infrastructure, but also to organizational learning and practical acquisitions of new skills and capabilities. In this sense, social media platforms are appropriated by young migrant workers in order to build their individual self and broaden their access to information. Parallel to that, it also provides the migrant workers with a variety of entertainment functions, on which the new generation of migrant workers is highly dependent given the fact that they have very limited time away from work and few offline social networks.

Our study tried to open a highly relevant research field for the CSCW community, in which comparative approaches to online use in developing societies might reveal more about the complex interrelationship between material circumstance, cultural tradition and the practices of everyday life [54]. We have only made a start here. More in depth studies are required to better understand the diversity of the Chinese migrant worker population, existing as they do in higher numbers than the whole population of Germany, France, Sweden, and the Netherlands together.

REFERENCES

1. Ai, J. Nongmingong wenti de genyuan zaiyu huji zhidu [The root of the problem of migrant workers is the household registration system]. *A New of Labour Unions* 2005, No.23, 4-5.
2. Bakhtin, M. M. *The Dialogic Imagination: Four essays*. 1981, Austing: University of Texas Press.
3. Bakken, G. *The exemplary Society: Human Improvement, social control and the dangers of modernity in China*. 2000, Oxford: OUP.
4. Bell, D. *Introduction to Cybercultures*. 2001, London: Routledge.
5. Bidwell, N., Reitmaeir, T, Marsden, G. and Hansen, S. Designing with Mobile Digital Storytelling in Rural Africa. In: *CHI '10 Proceedings of the SIGCHI Conference on Human Factors in Computing Systems*, 1593-1602.
6. Bracken, G. *Aspects of Urbanization in China: Shanghai, Hong Kong, Guangzhou*. 2012, Amsterdam: Amsterdam University Press.
7. Cai, F. (Ed.). *Renkou yu laodong lüpishu. Zhongguo renkou yu laodong wenti baodao* [Reen Book of Population and Labor (2011). Reports on China's Population and Labor No.12]. 2012, Beijing: Social Sciences Academic Press.
8. Cao, J. Chuanbo jishu yu shehui xingbie: yi liuyi Shanghai de jiazheng zhongdian nügong de shouji shiyong fenxi wei li [Communication Technology and Gender: a Case Study of the Use of Cell-Phone by Migrating Domestic Women in Shanghai]. *Journalism & Communication* 2009, No.1, 71-77.

9. Chayko, M. *Portable Communities: The Social Dynamics of Online and Mobile Connectedness*. 2008, New York: State University of New York Press.

10. Chen, A., Liu, G. and Zhang, K. *Urbanization and Social Welfare in China*. 2004, Aldershot: Ashgate.

11. Chu, R. W. and Cheng, C. Cultural Convulsions: examining the Chinese of Cyber China. In Herold, David and Marolt, Peter (Ed.). *Online Society in China: Creating, celebrating and Instrumentalising the Online Carival*. 2011, London: Routledge.

12. Clarke, P. *The Oxford Handbook of Cities in World History*. 2013, Oxford: OUP.

13. CNNIC. *2007nian zhongguo nongcun hulianwang diaocha baogao* [Statistical Survey Report on Internet in rural China 2007]. Retrieved Feb.7.2013. http://www.cnnic.cn/hlwfzyj/hlwxzbg/ncbg/201206/t20120612_27435.htm.

14. CNNIC. *Di sanshi ci zhongguo hulian wangluo fazhan zhuangkuang diaochabaogao 2012/6)* [30. Statistical Survey Report on The Internet Development in China 2012/6]. Retrieved Feb.7.2013. http://www.cnnic.cn/hlwfzyj/hlwxzbg/hlwtjbg/201207/t20120723_32497.htm.

15. Damm, J. The Internet and the Fragmentation of Chinese Society. *Critical Asian Studies*, 2007, 39(2) , 273-294.

16. Ding, W. and Tian, Q. Liudong de jiayuan – xinmeijie jishu yu nongmingong shehui guanxi geanzanjiu [The Mobile homes: A case study of the new media Usage and Migrant Workers' social Relationship. *Journalism & Communication*, 2009, No.1, 61-70.

17. Dourish, P. The appropriation of interactive technologies. *Computer Supported Cooperative Work*, 2003, Volume 12 Issue 4, 465-490.

18. Gergen, Kenneth J. Self and Community in the New Floating Worlds. In Nyiri, Kristof (Ed.): Mobile Democracy: Essays on Society, Self and Politics. 2002, Vienna: Passagen Verlag.

19. Goffman, E. *Interaction Ritual*. 1955, Garden City, NY: Anchor Books.

20. Goffman, E. *The Presentation of Self in Everyday Life*. 1969, London: Allen Lane.

21. Herold, D. and Marolt, P. (Ed.). *Online Society in China: Creating, celebrating and Instrumentalising the Online Carival*. 2011, London: Routledge.

22. Herold, D. Noise, Spectacle, Politics: carnival in Chinese Cyberspace. In Herold, D. and Marolt, P. (Ed.). *Online Society in China: Creating, celebrating and Instrumentalising the Online Carival*. 2011, London: Routledge.

23. Higgins, E. T. Self-discrepancy: A theory relating self and affect. *Psychological Review*, 1987, 94(3), 319-340.

24. Huang, W. *Meijie yu xinshengdai nongmingong de liudong shenghuo – jiyu guangdongsheng huizhoushi xiangshuihe gongyeyuan de minzuzhi diaocha* [Media and a Migrating New Generation of Peasant Workers – an Ethnological Study on Xiangshuihe Industrial Park in Huizhou, Guangdong]. Master's Thesis, University Anhui, 2011.

25. Jenkins, R. *Social Identity*. 2004, London: Routledge

26. Jordan, T and Taylor, P. *Hacktivism and Cyberwars: Rebels with a cause?* 2013, London: Routledge.

27. Karchow, R. *Das chinesische Urheberrecht. Überblick und Vergleich mit dem Deutschen Urheberrecht*. 2006, Saarbrücken: VDM Verlag Dr. Müller.

28. Lang, X., Oreglia, E. and Thomas, S. Social Practices and Mobile Phone Use of Young Migrant Workers. In De Sá, M. et al. (Ed.): *Proceedings of the 12th Conference on Human-Computer Interaction with Mobile Devices and Services*. Mobile HCI (2010), New York: ACM Press, 59-62.

29. Levy, P. *Cyberculture*. 2001, Minneapolis: University of Minnesota press.

30. Li, H. Parody and Resistance on the Chinese Internet. In Herold, D. and Marolt, P. (Ed). *Online Society in China: Creating, celebrating and Instrumentalising the Online Carival*. 2011, London: Routledge.

31. Liu, X., Liu, J., Cai, J., Liu, Y. and Wang, X. Design for China Migrant Workers: A Case of User Research and Mobile Product Concepts Development. In Kurosu, M.(Ed.): *Human Centered Design, HCII 2009*, 482–491. 2009, Berlin, Heidelberg: Springer-Verlag.

32. Luo, P. and Peng, Y. Guanyu zhongguo nanbu nongmingong de shehui shenghuo yu shouji de yanjiu [Research of the social life and mobile phone use of migrant worker in south China]. In Yang, S. (ed.): *Chengxiang richang shenghuo: yizhong shehuixue fenxi* [Daily Life in urban and rural China – a perspective of sociology], 83-101. 2008, Beijing: Social Sciences Documentation Publishing House.

33. Neuman, W. L. *Social Research Methods. Qualitative and Quantitative Approaches*, fifth edition, übersetzt von Hao, D. 2007, Beijing: China Renmin Universitz Press.

34. Peng, Y. Internet Use of Migrant Worker in the Pearl River Delta. *Knowledge, Technology and Policy*, 2008, 21(2), 47-54.

35. Peng, W. and Xu, T. Qingshaoniang wangluo shuangchong renge fenxi [Analysis of the network dual personality of the youth]. *Contemporary Youth Research*, 2002, No.4, 13-15.

36. Pipek, V. and Wulf, V. Infrastructuring: Toward an Integrated Perspective on the Design and Use of Information Technology. *J. AIS*, 2009, 10(5), 447-473.

37. Rangaswamy, N. and Cutrell, E. Anthropology, Development and ICTs: Slums, Youth and the Mobile Internet in Urban India. In: *Proceedings of ICTD'12, ACM, 2012*, pp 85-93.

38. *Report on China's Migrant Population development 2011*. 2012, Beijing: China Population Publishing House.

39. Rheingold, H. *The Virtual Community: homesteading on the electronic frontier*. 2000, Cambridge Mass.: MIT Press.

40. Rosen, S. Contemporary Chinese youth and the state. *Journal of Asian Studies*, 2009, 68(2), 359–369.

41. Shirky, C. Here Comes Everybody: The power of organizing without organization. 2008, the Penguin Press.

42. Song, Y. and Ding, C. *Urbanization in China: Critical Issues in an Era of Rapid Growth*. 2007, Lincoln Institute of land Policy.

43. Stanat, M. *China's Generation Y: Understanding the Future Leaders of the World's Next Superpower*. 2005, New York: Paramus: Homa & Sekey.

44. Thomas, M.; Lim, S.S. Walled-In, Reaching Out: Benefits and Challenges of Migrant Workers' Use of ICTs for Interpersonal Communication. *Matters of Communication: 2010 Annual Conference of the International Communication Association*.

45. Turkle, S. Life on the screen. 2011, New York: Simon & Schuster.

46. Wallis, C. New Media in China: Youth Patterns, Processes, and Politics. *International Journal of Communication*, 2011, No.5, 406–436.

47. Wang, J. Youth culture, music, and cell phone branding in China. *Global Media and Communication*, 2005, 1(2), 185–201.

48. Wang, J., Wang, W., Liu, Y., Wang, X. and Chen, Q. Ethnographic User Study and Concept Design for Chinese Migrant Workers' Social Networks. In Ozok, A.A. et.al. (Ed.): *Online Communities*, 710–718. 2009, Berlin, Heidelberg: Springer-Verlag.

49. Waskul, D. and Douglass, M. Cyberself: The emergence of self in online chat. *Information society*, 1997, 13(4), 375-396.

50. Wei, R. Lifestyles and new media: Adoption and use of wireless communication technologies in China. *New Media & Society*, 2006, No.8, 991–1008.

51. Wei, R. The state of new media technology research in China: a review and critique. *Asian Journal of Communication*, 2009, 19:1, 116-127.

52. Wu, W., Wang, X.. Lost in virtual carnival and masquerade: In-game marriage on the Chinese Internet. In Herold, D. and Marolt, P. (Ed.). *Online Society in China: Creating, Celebrating and Instrumentalising the Online Carival*. 2011, London: Routledge.

53. Wulf, V., Misaki, K., Atam, M., Randall, D. and Rohde, M. 'On the Ground' in Sidi Bouzid: Investigating Social Media Use during the Tunisian Revolution. In: *Proceedings of ACM Conference on Computer Supported Cooperative Work (CSCW 2013)*, 2013, New York: ACM-Press, 1409-1418.

54. Wulf, V., Rohde, M., Pipek, V. and Stevens, G. Engaging with Practices: Design Case Studies as a Research Framework in CSCW. In: *Proceedings of ACM Conference on Computer Supported Cooperative Work (CSCW 2011)*, 2011, New York: ACM-Press, 505-512.

55. Wyche, S., Forte, A. and Schoenbeck, S. Hustling Online: Understanding Consolidated Facebook Use in an Informal Settlement in Nairobi. Proceedings of CHI'13, 2013 Paris, France.

56. Yang, G. A Chinese Internet? History, Practice and Globalization. *Chinese Journal of Communication*. 2012, 5(1), 49-54.

57. Yang, S. and Zhu, W. Mobile phone: an "active select" in the context globalization – Interpretation of the consume culture and mentality of the migrant workers in the Pearl River Delta. *Social Sciences in Guangdong*, 2006, No.2, 168-173.

58. Yao, K. *China's migrant worker pay growth nearly halved in 2012*, May 27. 2013. Retrieved Feb.7.2013. http://www.reuters.com/article/2013/05/27/us-china-economy-migrants-idUSBRE94Q03A20130527.

59. Yu, H. *Media and Cultural Transformation in China*. 2009, London: Routledge.

60. Zhou, B. and Lü, S. Shanghaishi xinshengdai nongmingong xinmeiti shiyong yu pingjia de shizheng yanjiu [An empirical research of new media use and evaluation of the new Generation of migrant workers in Shanghai]. *Journalism Quarterly*, 2011, No.2, 145-150.

61. Zhou, M. and Cai, G. Trapped in neglected Corners of a Booming metropolis: residential Patterns and Marginalization of Migrant Workers in Guangzhou. In John R. Logan (Ed.): *Urban China in Transition*. 2008, Oxford: Blackwell, 226-249.

The Role of Founders in Building Online Groups

Robert E. Kraut
Carnegie Mellon University
Pittsburgh PA 15213
robert.kraut@cmu.edu

Andrew T. Fiore
Facebook
Menlo Park, CA 94025
atfiore@fb.com

ABSTRACT
As a class, online groups are popular, but many die before they become successful. This research traced the fate of 472,231 new online groups. By the end of a 3-month observation period, 57% of the groups had died, ceasing to post new content. Founders' human and social capital before the group was formed, the decisions they made when they created the group and their behavior in the group during its first week all predicted group survival. Many of the results suggest that founders create more successful groups if they have more resources (e.g., more online friends) and opportunities for acquiring relevant skills (e.g., more experience with online groups) and are more active in their group. However, founders who are too controlling seem to present a threat their groups. Their groups are more likely to fail if they are the only group administrator, if they have ties to all group members and if they were responsible for adding all group members.

Author Keywords
Online groups, Facebook, founder, birth, death

ACM Classification Keywords
H.3.3

INTRODUCTION
Collectively online groups and communities are among the most popular destinations on the Internet. However, many individual groups and communities never get off the ground or peter out after they are established. On SourceForge, which offers free tools to open source projects, thousands of projects have been created, but 90% have fewer than four members [15]. Among guilds (i.e., teams of players) in the online game World of Warcraft, 54% die within any 6-month period. One study of the growth of Ning groups excluded more than 50% of their potential sample as "failed attempts" because they never recruited more than 10 members [11]. Indeed, the median size of a Ning community is only one member. Among email-based discussion groups selected as active, over 11 percent stopped functioning and sending messages during a three-month observation period [6]. As we'll show later in this paper, on Facebook, where members worldwide create over 100,000 new groups a day, 13% produce no content after the first day they were created and 57% have stopped all activity within three months of creation. Although some of these "failures" may result from mistakes, testing or time-limited groups accomplishing their purpose, many others are true failures in the sense that the founders' goals for the group were not accomplished and members' need were not satisfied.

These failures can occur even if founders care passionately about their group's success. For example, in an effort to test the effects of peer support to help people quit smoking, researchers gave volunteers access to an online community plus an informational website, but so few people participated in the community that researchers were not able to report on its effectiveness [21]. While Wikipedia has been highly successful, its precursor organization, Nupedia, failed dramatically, producing only 24 encyclopedia articles [18].

Failure of new social enterprises is not limited to online groups. Many scholars have documented the high probability of death for many types of offline groups and organizations, ranging from new restaurants, to manufacturing firms, labor unions, high tech start-ups and social movements. Indeed early death in these various organizational forms is so common it has been labeled the "liability of newness" [9], and scholars have debated whether newness per se or associated phenomena like small organization size accounts for this liability [see 3 for a recent review].

Previous research predicting the success of offline firms has demonstrated the importance of the founders and their personal endowments, like experience and social networks ties, in predicting the success of their firms [8]. Psychological research on small groups demonstrates the importance of group leaders and their actions in predicting their groups' success [5]. In contrast, research on the survival and growth of online groups and communities has focused on their size and network externalities [11].

The current paper examines whether founders' characteristics and behavior early in a group's history predict how long it will survive or, alternatively, how quickly it will cease functioning. We show that founders' human and social capital, such as their age, experience with Facebook in general and with other groups on Facebook, early decisions they made like allowing multiple group administrators or ornamenting their groups with a description or logo,

CSCW'14, February 15 – 19, 2014, Baltimore, MD, USA.
Copyright 2014 ACM 978-1-4503-2540-0/14/02…$15.00.
http://dx.doi.org/10.1145/2531602.2531648

and the early actions they took in the group, in particular visiting it frequently, positively predicted group survival. Surprisingly, when they had more pre-existing ties in the group and when they added more of its members, their groups died more quickly. These finding suggest that the resources founders bring to the group are important, but they can also be a bottleneck if the group depends on them too much.

Liability of newness and critical mass. Stinchombe [20] and Freedman [9] used the phrase "liability of newness" to hypothesize that newness per se is responsible for the high risk of failure firms experience when they are young. In the beginning the firms don't yet have effective linkages with key stakeholders like funders, future employees, or customers, haven't yet mastered the roles and routines to run their organizations, and don't yet have the resources that allow them to compete with more established organizations in their niche. Substantial controversy exists as to whether newness per se or some other factors correlated with age, like organizational size, account for the higher death rate of new organizations [3].

Research on the founding of organizations shows that larger initial organizational size, whether measured in terms of employees, financial assets, production facilities or customers, predicts longer organization survival, and once initial size is controlled for, newness per se becomes less important and consistent a predictor of organizational survival [see 3, table 2 and page 63].

Theories of network externalities demonstrate how this phenomenon might work in the case of online groups [12]. Because participation in online groups is voluntary, new groups are often caught in a startup paradox: they need content to attract members and members to produce the content [15]. In their early stages, when they don't have many members or much content, they must resort to stratagems such as restricting membership to a small, homogeneous community that is already communicating, as Facebook did in its start-up stage with membership limited to specific universities [2], franchising content from other established groups as Epinions did, or using shills or staff members to produce content [16]. Because initial group size is likely to be an important predictor of group success, we control for it when examining the role of founders in predicting survival of online groups.

The role of founders in offline firms. While research on network externalities and the liability of newness emphases inherent weaknesses in new organizations, they fail to sufficiently account for individual responsibility in making new organizations succeed. In new offline organizations, the resources that founders bring to the organization, the early decisions they make and their actions in the organization all influence its success. For example, in one of the earliest demonstrations of the power of founders, Cooper and colleagues showed that new firms were more likely to thrive if the founders had more human capital – e.g., were better educated, had parents who had previously owned a business, or had previously worked in their firm's industry [7]. An important extension of this research examines the impact of founders' social capital, arguing that entrepreneurs mobilize and capitalize on resources embedded in their social network ties [4, 8]. For example, their network ties connect them to others who can provide financing, knowledge, employees or customers. Comparable processes can occur in online groups as well. For example, open source development projects find it easier to recruit members who had prior ties with the project's founders [10].

Social networks within online groups. Research in online groups demonstrates that social network ties among members of online groups have strong implications for their success. Several studies have shown that online groups often grow through social diffusion processes, in which individuals are more likely to join an online group if they have prior social ties with existing group members [1, 10, 11]. Not only do social network ties promote group growth, they also seem to keep group dissolution at bay. World of Warcraft guilds, for example, are more likely to survive over a 6-month period when they are larger, when subgroups in the guild are smaller and when there are more ties among members (i.e., higher group density). However, except for research on open source software previously cited [10], research on online groups hasn't distinguished the social ties that founders have with other group members from overall tie density. Nor does it focus on the early stages of group formation, when groups are at the greatest risk of failure.

HYPOTHESES: THE ROLE OF FOUNDERS IN ONLINE GROUPS

The goal of the current research is to integrate and extend the prior research on the role of founders' human and social capital in making their firms successful and on the benefits of social ties within groups to explain the survival of online groups. We will test hypotheses in the context of the survival of groups hosted at Facebook, the large social networking site. The literature just reviewed focused on founders' endowment – the human and social capital they possess that gives them access to resources and helps them make decisions that improve their firm's chances of survival. We will extend this literature to also examine the decisions that founders make and the actions they take during the early phases of their groups that may shape expectations in the group and its chances of survival.

By analogy to the literature on business entrepreneurs, we expect that the characteristics, decisions and behavior of founders listed below will improve the survival of their groups.

Founders' human capital. People with more experience and savvy should found groups that are more likely to survive. Thus older founders should establish more successful groups than younger ones. Generalizing the finding that founders with experience in a relevant industry start more successful firms, we expect that founders with more experience in the online domain (in this case Facebook) and more experience with Facebook groups will found more successful groups. They should be able to leverage their knowledge of Facebook technology and user population, the purposes for which people use Facebook groups and the behavioral norms within Facebook and its groups to inform decisions they make about their groups and how to run them. Therefore, we expect founders who have used Facebook for a longer period and who have participated in more Facebook groups will start more successful groups. To summarize:

H1: Groups will survive longer when their founders are older

H2: Groups will survive longer when their founders have participated longer in the online environment that hosts their group

H3: Groups will survive longer when founders have experience in more online groups

Founders' social capital. Nahapiet and Ghoshal define social capital as "the sum of the actual and potential resources embedded within, available through, and derived from the network of relationships possessed by an individual [...]. Social capital thus comprises both the network and the assets that may be mobilized through that network" [13, p. 243]. People with more social ties should be able to recruit more people with desirable resources to their groups.

Those with more social ties in the groups they are starting should be able to engender loyalty and participation from their ties and encourage them to provide the contributions the groups need. Therefore, founders with more ties in general and in their groups should start more successful groups.

H4: Groups will survive longer when their founders have more social ties (friends) prior to founding their groups.

H5: Groups will survive longer when their founders have more social ties within the groups they found

Decisions founders make. The preceding hypotheses assume that human and social capital allows founders to make decisions and perform actions that improve their group's fate. The current research extends prior research on entrepreneurship by focusing on these substantive decisions and actions. In this section we examine how one-time decisions that founders make when starting the group can have longer-term consequences for group survival, and in the next section, we will focus on how their active participation in the group may influence its survival.

While the hypothesis that more social ties should lead to more successful groups follows from the definition of social capital, there may be limits to the value of founders' ties. As Kairam and colleagues note, even though many online groups grow through an interpersonal diffusion process based on social network ties, reliance on social ties for growth can constrain a group's final size, because it prevents people from joining unless they know someone who is already a member [11]. Similar constraints on group success may result if growth and administration of the group depends primarily on the founders. For example, even if people become group members primarily through their ties to the founder, the group size is constrained by the size of the founder's pre-existing social network. Thus, one would expect that:

H6: Groups will survive longer when members join the group spontaneously or are invited by non-founder members, and will survive for less time if founders were responsible for recruiting all its members.

The same logic suggests that groups will be more successful if founders allow others to share the burden of administering the group. Even though founders' leadership and administrative activities are likely to be important to the group, founders can easily be overwhelmed with the chores that they need to accomplish or may make poor administrative decisions. Therefore, it should be helpful for group success if founders could rely upon discussions with and contributions from other administrators.

H7: Groups will survive longer if others augment the founders in administering the group.

Online groups differ on how open they are to non-members. Some hide membership information and content from those who are not members and only allow new members if they are approved by an administrator or other group member. Others, like Wikipedia, allow anyone to see membership, content, and communication, and place no barriers on joining. When groups are more open, membership need not be funneled through the founders or other group members. Moreover, the prior research on recruitment in conventional organizations indicates that if people are more informed about the firm they are joining, they are more likely to make decisions that fit with their goals and skills, will be more satisfied with the organization they join and will stay in it longer [17]. In contrast to more secretive groups, open online groups allow potential members to sample group content and learn about characteristics of existing members before they decide to join. Thus openness should increase group success.

H8: Groups will survive longer if founders set them to be open, allowing outsiders to learn about members, content and interaction in the group before they join.

Following the same logic, groups are more likely to survive if the founders post a description of the group that indicates the group's purpose and what it is about. This information provides another way for potential members to find groups that provide a good match with their needs. Furthermore, the literature on social identity processes in groups suggests that merely providing descriptions and decorations that differentiate one group from another increases members' commitment to the group and helps them succeed [see 14 for an overview of relevant theories of the influence of identity signals on commitment to online groups].

H9: Groups will survive longer if founders decorate their groups with descriptions, logos and similar material that define a group identity and allow potential members to learn more about the group before joining.

Founders' early activity in the group. How founders behave early in a group's history can have longer-term consequences for its survival. The content the founders produce provides some initial material that may engage other group members, causing them to return and to contribute themselves. In addition, the content they produce may shape group norms about the amount and type of content that is appropriate for the group.

H10: Groups will survive longer if founders post more content themselves early in the group's history.

In addition to producing content that may influence others' behavior, merely visiting a group frequently during its early days can enhance group survival. Visiting the group and reading its content allows founders to monitor the early health of the group. Seeing a group in trouble or a new member who needs help could cause the founders to intervene; in contrast, if the group is gaining momentum and working well without their intervention, the founders may reduce their public behavior.

H11: Groups will survive longer if founders visit their group more frequently during its early history and read more of its content.

METHODS

Facebook as a research site

The social networking site Facebook hosts millions of user-created groups ranging in size from a handful of friends to thousands of members, with more than 100,000 new groups created every day. Facebook groups serve a variety of purposes; in a subset of new groups examined in the current study (N=75,311), a group member categorized the purpose of their group. The two most common purposes were running a group associated with "an organization, team or club" (29%) and for "keeping in touch with family or friends" (25%). Other common purposes were groups "working on a project, goal or event" (15%), having a "shared interest or hobby" (11%), having "common identity, beliefs or experiences" (6%) and groups for "networking and professional development" (4%).

The diversity of purposes and discussion topics makes Facebook groups a fruitful research site for examining the characteristics of successful groups across a variety of social contexts. Moreover, Facebook's server logs allow researchers to examine founders' and members' behavior from the moment of a group's inception or even before, facilitating longitudinal analysis of the early development of a group. By adopting a sampling frame of all newly created groups, even those that die quickly, we avoid the survivorship bias that affects even longitudinal research that begins with a sample of successful groups [e.g., 11].

The nature of Facebook groups. The home page of a Facebook group displays the stream of posts, photos, events, files, and other content shared with the group as well as the associated comments and likes, which constitute feedback on the more substantive content (see Figure 1). Navigation tabs at the top of the home page allow users to view the membership roster as well as events, photos, and files posted to the group. Some Facebook groups are public, with their content and membership rosters visible to anyone with a Facebook account ("open" groups), while others have their rosters visible but content hidden from non-members ("closed" groups). A third class of groups is completely invisible to non-members ("secret" groups); because these groups are not discoverable by non-members, the only way to join them is to be added by an existing member.

When a group is created, its founder chooses its name, privacy settings and, optionally, provides additional metadata and decoration to represent the group. For example, the CSCW 2014 Program Committee group shown in Figure 1 is closed and includes a description that reads in part, "Informal discussion/notices for members of the 2014 PC." The founder also selects friends to add to the group; at least one friend must be selected, so all groups have at least two members when they are created. Subsequently, new members may request to join and receive approval from an existing member or be added by friends who are existing members. Some groups (fewer than 8%) have a setting

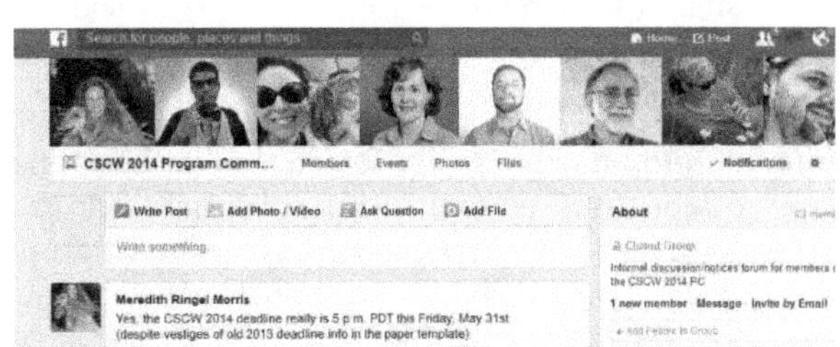

Figure 1. Home page of a Facebook group

enabled that requires administrators, not ordinary members, to initiate or approve new memberships. Potential members may discover a group through search or by browsing a friend's group memberships.

Groups on Facebook cannot be deleted directly. However, they delete themselves if all members leave the group or are removed by an administrator. Thus, we adopt a definition of group survival (defined below) that focuses on the presence of activity over time rather than group deletion.

Sample

The sample for the present work comprises 472,231 English-language groups created over eight days in February 2013. We obtained data from Facebook's server logs on group-level characteristics (e.g., membership, privacy setting, average tie density) and founders' characteristics and behavior (e.g., number of friends, ties to other group member, visits to the group) either before the group was created or seven days after its creation. To ensure that we were considering groups and not merely dyads, we limited the sample to groups with at least three members at the end of their first week of existence. To make network density calculations tractable, we also excluded groups with more than 500 members at the end of their first week.

About 19% of groups had no activity after their creation day. Although some of these "stillborn" groups were created out of curiosity or by mistake, others were groups that failed very rapidly, and excluding them biases the analysis. To test the robustness of our results, we conducted survival analysis both including and excluding these very short-lived groups, and present both sets of analyses in Table 2. Because the results from both analyses are substantively the same, in this paper we primarily discuss results from analysis including these short-lived groups. When results differ we note and discuss the discrepancies.

Explanatory variables

Founders: Facebook records timestamps for most events on the site, including the time and date when people join each group. We define the group founder as the group member with the earliest timestamp for joining the group (typically simultaneous with the group's creation time). Table 1 shows descriptive statistics for the variables used in the analysis.

Initial group size is the number of members who belonged to the group seven days from its creation. Groups tended to start out small (median size = 10; mean = 34.8) and grew only modestly by the end of the 3-month observation period (median size = 11; mean = 55.8).

Founders' human capital: The founders of groups bring a number of forms of personal and social capital to bear when they create a new group. In terms of personal capital, their experience on Facebook and with Facebook groups specifically may be important for the group's success. We measure these forms of experience in several ways:

Facebook tenure: Founders' tenure on Facebook, measured in days since account creation. The median founder was a member of Facebook for 2.7 years, only 4 days more than the median non-founding member.

Facebook group experience: The number of existing Facebook groups founders belonged to at the time of creating the new group. The median founder belonged to 13 other groups versus 16.3 for other group members.

Recent activity: The number of days in the four weeks before they created the group on which founders visited Facebook. Founders were more active (median = 27 days) than other group members (median = 21.9 days).

Founders' social capital: In terms of social capital, the number of founders' Facebook friends at the time of group creation represents a cap on how many members they could recruit by adding them to the group, and the founders' friendship ties with other users who join the group subsequently could help drive group cohesion. In Facebook, friendship ties are reciprocal, and an explicit friend tie exists between two subscribers if one has sent a friend request to the other and the other has accepted it. We measured these types of social capital as follows:

Friend count: The total number of friendship ties founders had before they started the group. Founders had fewer friends (median = 334) than other members of their groups (median = 455).

Tie Density: The number of friends founders had in the group at the end of week 1 divided by the total group size minus 1. Founders were friends with all group members in 51.2% of groups, and typically had more friends in the group (median = 7) than did other members (median = 4.6).

Founders' decisions: In initially setting up the group, founders make a number of decisions as follows:

Number of decorations: In addition to choosing a name, which all groups must have, founders can optionally write a description that elaborates on the nature and purpose of the group, and 19.4% did so. They can upload a cover photo that appears prominently at the top of the group's home page, and 7.9% did so. They can also select an icon that will appear with the group's name on its home page and in the bookmarks section of Facebook's navigation bar; this selection step was on the main script for creating a group, and 64.5% did so. We treat the description, photo and icon as "decorations," since all are optional, and construct a variable ranging from 0 and 3 to indicate how many of the three decorations are present.

Number of administrators: Founders can optionally designate others besides themselves as administrators. In 91% of groups, the founder was the only administrator. We coded this variable as 1 if the founder was the only administrator and 2 if the group contained more than one administrator.

Privacy settings: Founders chose their group's privacy setting. We coded group's privacy as 1 if it was open, with its membership list and content public, 2 if it was closed, with content visible only to group members but with the membership public, and 3 if it was secret, in which case the group could not be discovered through search, its content and membership was visible only to members and new members had to be added by existing ones. Twenty-four percent of groups were open, 42% were closed and 33% were secret.

Percent of members founders added: Although 7.7% of groups require administrative approval to add new members, in most groups any member can add another member. In addition, any outsider can request to join an open or closed (but not secret) group without an invitation. Any member may approve the request in groups without administrative approval required. To assess founders' role in adding new members, we calculated the percentage of new members in its first week that the founders added. On average, they added 78% of members to their groups (median = 86%), and they added all members in 23% of groups.

Founders' activities: Once a group has been created, founders may invest in its ongoing activities to varying degrees.

Founders' actions. The number of posts and comments, the character count in posts and comments, and the number of likes the administrator produces in the first 7 days of the group's existence, and likes of an existing post or comment, standardized and averaged.

Founders' days active. How many days in the first seven of the group's life the admin viewed the group's home page, made a post or comment, and liked an existing post or comment, standardized and averaged. During the first week, founders visited their groups more frequently than other members, viewing content on an average of 3.2 days (versus 1.3 for other members) and creating content on 1.8 days (versus .44 days for other members).

Group survival: This paper analyzes the extent to which the explanatory variables just described predict how long groups survive. Since most Facebook groups are never deleted, but many become inactive, we define a group as surviving as long as it is continuing to produce new posts, comments, photographs and likes, and conversely as failed when it is no longer generating content. Survival analysis is the appropriate statistical technique for analyzing time-to-an-event data, because it appropriately deals with cases in which the event of interest has not occurred during the observation period (i.e., when groups have not died during the three-month data collection period) [19].

Variable	Median	Mean	Std.Dev.
Membership size week 1	10.0	34.76	1048.61
Founder age	21.8	25.40	11.72
Founder's Facebook tenure (years)	2.7	2.76	1.84
Days founder was active in the 28 days before group creation	26.0	22.00	6.79
Other groups in which founder was member	13.0	22.77	30.89
Founder's FB friend count	334.0	507.69	584.23
Founder's tie density within group	1.0	0.81	0.33
Privacy (1 = public, 2= private, 3=secret)	2.0	2.09	0.75
Number of decorations	1.0	0.97	0.74
Number of administrators	1.0	1.19	1.13
% of members added by founder	0.9	0.78	0.24
Founder's days visits in first week	-0.2	0.10	0.90
Founder's content creation	-0.1	0.03	0.71
Days from creation to last content	42.0	44.27	37.22
Note: N = 472,231 groups			

Table 1. Descriptive statistics

Because group failure is right-censored and depends on how far into the future one looks for content, we assume that a group has failed if it has stopped producing content for at least 30 consecutive days before the end of the 89-day observation period. The average time between two content-creation events was 3.45 days (std=7.47), and 30 days represents four times the standard deviation of the time between consecutive posts.

RESULTS

Group demographics and descriptive statistics

Table 1 shows descriptive statistics for all the variables included in the analysis. In this table, we also included days the group was active (the number of days from group creation to its last content production) as a surrogate for group survival. The median group in the sample lasted 42 days.

Survival analysis

The main outcome variable is the length of time from a group's creation date until it stops producing content. As discussed previously, we consider a group to have died if it has no new content during the last 30 days of the observation period.

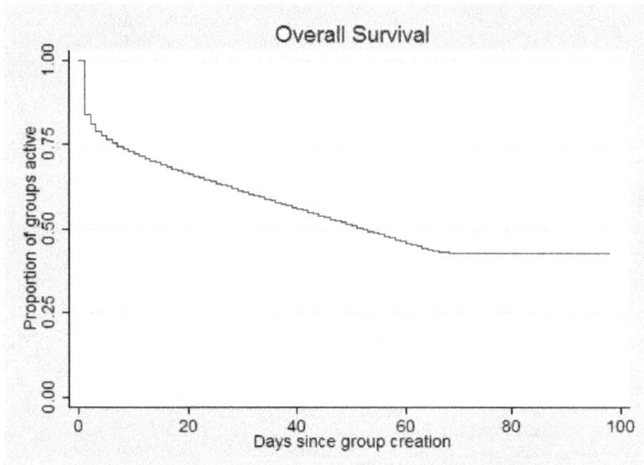

Figure 2. Overall group survival

Figure 2 shows the baseline survival curve for groups in the sample. In this plot, we've dropped groups with any missing values in any of the explanatory variables presented above. The survival curve shows that 13.5% of groups have stopped producing content within one day of creation and almost 57% have died by the end of the observation period.

Figure 3 shows the relative importance of group size and the variables measuring founders' resources, decisions and actions. It is based on the results of the multivariate Cox regression analysis on group survival presented in Model 1 in Table 2. Cox regression calculates a hazard ratio, the relative risk of an event occurring (i.e., group death) for levels of an explanatory variable, controlling for other variables in the model. Because the explanatory variables were not normally distributed and were measured on different scales, we normalized them by calculating a hazard ratio comparing groups in the top third of the distribution on an explanatory variable with groups in the bottom third. For number of administrators, the hazard ratio compares groups

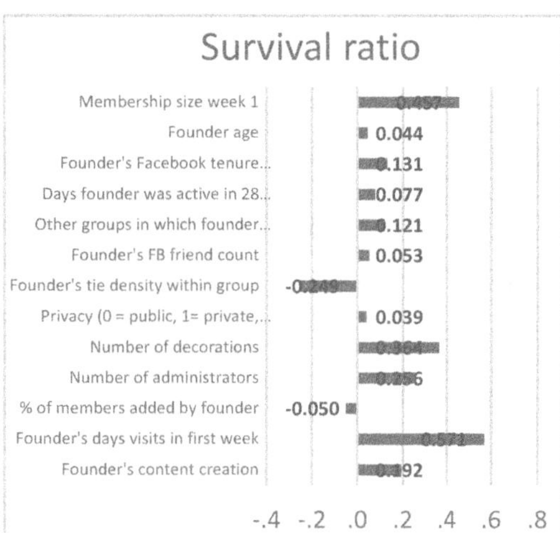

Figure 3. Survival ratios, comparing the probability of groups surviving when they are in the top versus bottom of a distribution

with more than one administrator to groups with a single administrator. For number of decorations, it compares groups with three decorations to groups with none. For group openness, it compares secret groups to open ones. To make interpretation of results easier, we then transformed the hazard ratio (HR) into a survival ratio (SR) by subtracting it from one (SR = 1-HR). These survival ratios are plotted in Figure 3. To examine whether short-lived groups were qualitatively different from other groups, we also conducted a robustness check, which excluded the 19% of groups that lasted only a single day. These results are presented in Model 2 in Table 2 and mentioned in the text when results differ from those from Model 1.

Given the large sample size, all survival ratios were reliably different from zero at $p <= .0004$. Results of a survival analysis based on log-transformed raw scores as independent variables were substantively the same as the results in Figure 3, which used quantized variables. The only exception was that founders' age, which had a small but significant relationship with survival in the analysis using quantized variables, was no longer a statistically significant predictor of group survival using logged age.

Founders' characteristics, decisions and behavior predicted group survival quite well. An ordinary least squares regression analysis predicting the number of days a group continued to generate content from the variables in Figure 3 explained 25.1% of the variance in a regression using the quantized explanatory variables and 29% in a regression using log-transformed variables.

Figure 4 visually represents the survival ratios by comparing survival curves when groups are at the top and bottom quantile (typically thirds) of each explanatory variable, holding all other variables constant at their mean. Because of the large sample size, all the explanatory variables were statistically related to survival at greater than chance levels. We consider important explanatory variables to be ones where the survival increases by at least 10% when contrasting groups at the top quantile to those at the bottom.

By this criterion, the control variable, initial group size, was a very important predictor of group success. Groups that started out large (14 or more members) were 46% more likely to survive than groups that started out small (fewer than 5 members).

Founders' human capital. Most of the measures of founders' pre-existing human capital predicted survival in a manner consistent with hypotheses 1-4, with the number of other Facebook groups they belong to and their tenure on Facebook being the most important. These are the two human capital attributes that are most reflective of founders' experience in this online platform and are most likely to give them knowledge and skills that allow them to create a successful group. Groups were 12% more likely to survive if the founders were members of more than 21 groups than if they belonged to fewer than 8.

Predictor variable	Change in probablity of dealth comparing top vs bottom quantile								
	Model 1: All groups			Model 2: Excluding single-day groups			Model 3: . All groups with non-founder variables		
	Haz. Ratio	Std. Err.	z	Haz. Ratio	Std. Err.	z	Haz. Ratio	Std. Err.	z
Membership size week 1	.543	.003	-99.6	.531	.003	-101.1	.527	.004	-81.45
Founder's age	.956	.005	-8.14	.775	.004	-45.45	.881	.005	-20.83
Founder's Facebook tenure (years)	.869	.006	-21.27	1.025	.007	3.62	.955	.007	-6.62
Days founder was active in 28 days before group start date	.923	.005	-14.61	1.054	.006	8.97	.984	.005	-2.92
Number of other groups in which founder was a member	.879	.005	-21.39	.919	.006	-13.91	.944	.006	-9.49
Founder's FB friend count	.947	.006	-8.33	1.052	.007	7.67	.939	.006	-9.7
Founder's tie density within group	1.249	.012	22.58	1.143	.006	23.92	1.156	.007	25.66
Privacy (1 = public, 2= private, 3=secret)	.961	.006	-6.83	1.112	.007	17.39	1.091	.006	15.71
Number of decorations	.636	.012	-24.58	.631	.010	-28.6	.639	.010	-28.47
Number of administrators	.744	.008	-28.58	.763	.007	-28.99	.738	.007	-32.73
% of members added by founder	1.050	.006	8.03	1.050	.006	8.01	1.004	.006	0.67
Members days visits in first week (mean)	.429	.003	-109.44	.639	.005	-55.48	.556	.004	-78.36
Member's content creation (mean)	.808	.006	-27.09	.977	.008	-2.9	.939	.007	-8.62
Members mean age (mean)							.916	.006	-14.55
Members'Facebook tenure (mean years)							1.043	.008	5.75
Days members were active in 28 days before group start date							1.263	.008	36.12
Other groups in which member were member (mean)							1.263	.008	36.12
Members' FB friend count (mean)							1.196	.007	30.39
Members' tie density within group (mean)							1.082	.009	9.55
Members' days visits in first week (mean)							.743	.006	-34.39
Members' content creation (mean)							.772	.006	-34.28
Number of groups	441633			378479			441633		
df	26			26			42		
Log likelihood	-3822872			-3024828			-3794885		
AIC	7645797			6049707			7589855		
BIC	7646083			6049989			7590317		
ChiSq to test improvement over model 1							55974		
ChiSq df							16		
ChiSq p-value							.000		

Note: The hazard ratio is the ratio of the probability of group death when a explanatory variables is in the highest quantile versus bottom quantile. For most explanatory variables, this compares groups in the top third versus bottom third of the distribution on an explanatory variable

Table 2. Cox regression models predicting group survival

Groups were 13% more likely to survive if founders had more than 3.4 years of experience with Facebook than if they had less than 1.8 years. The robustness check presented in Model 2, however, casts doubt on the importance of Facebook tenure: Among groups that lasted longer than one day, founders' Facebook tenure predicted a small reduction in group survival.

Other measures of human capital were less predictive of their group's survival, including founders' age and how actively they participated in Facebook. Moreover, the robustness check in Model 2 suggests that among groups lasting at least one day, groups founded by more active founders were less likely to survive.

Founders' social capital. Founders' social capital measures had mixed relationships with group survival, confirming Hypothesis 4 and disconfirming Hypothesis 5.

Founders' Facebook friend count, representing one source of potential group members, positively predicted group survival, although the effect was small (a 5% increase comparing founders with more than 512 friends with those with fewer than 189). Moreover, the robustness check in Model 2 shows this effect is reversed among groups that lasted at least one day. In contrast, founders' social network ties within the group negatively predicted survival. When founders were Facebook friends with everyone else in the group, the group was 25% less likely to survive than if founders had ties with fewer than 70% of group members.

Founders' decisions. The decisions founders made in creating their groups were also powerful predictors of group survival in ways consistent with Hypotheses 6-9. Groups were 36% more likely to survive if the group home page was decorated with a description, logo and cover photo

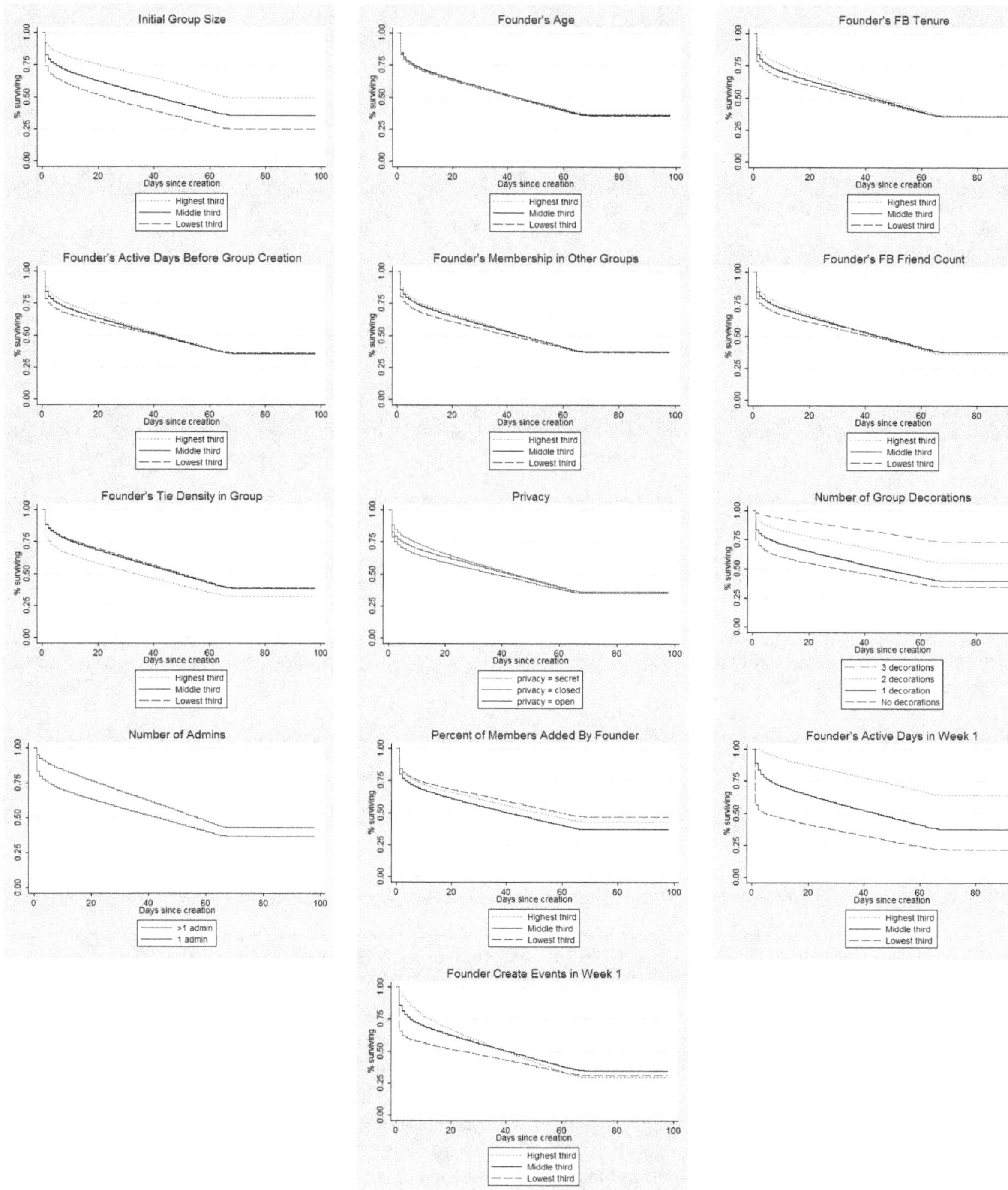

Figure 4. Survival plots comparing groups in the top versus bottom quantiles of the explanatory variables

than if it had none of these. Groups with more than one administrator were 25% more likely to survive than groups in which the founder was the only administrator. Groups in which the founders invited at least 90% of the members were 5% less likely to survive than groups in which they invited less than 67% of them.

Hypothesis 8, that openness would promote group survival, was disconfirmed in the analysis involving all groups: open groups were 4% less likely to survive than secret groups. However, this result was reversed in groups that lasted at least one day (see Model 2). Among these groups, open groups were 11% more likely to survive than secret ones.

Founders' activities. Founders' activities during the first week of a group's existence were strong predictors of group survival. Groups where founders created new content most frequently were 19% more likely to survive, compare to groups where they posted content least frequently. Besides providing content to engage other group members, they provided models of behavior for others to emulate. The correlation between founder content production during the first week and content production by other members was .40.

Frequency of participation was more important than the amount of content the founders produced. Groups in which the founders visited most frequently were 57% more likely to survive than groups where founders visited least frequently, even holding constant the amount they posted. By visiting and posting more frequently, founders could ensure that there would be fresh content to engage members whenever they visited during the first week. In addition, their frequent visits allowed them to assess the health of the group in its early days and respond appropriately, depending on how the group was faring.

DISCUSSION

This research traced the fate of almost half a million Facebook groups that were created in an 8-day period in 2013. The majority of these groups (57%) ceased to create new content by the end of the 3-month observation period. Some of these group "deaths" were spurious, reflecting groups that were never intended to be real or that had completed their functions. In other cases, the individuals involved continued to meet and communicate in person or using other electronic methods, but abandoned the Facebook groups as the mechanism. Despite these caveats, true failure of Facebook groups occurred very frequently.

Founders' human and social capital before the group was formed, the decisions they made when they created the group and their behavior in the group during its first week all predicted group survival. Many of the results are consistent with the literature on the role of entrepreneurs in starting firms, suggesting that the more human and social capital founders bring to the group and the more they engage in it, the more the group will succeed.

However, there were important exceptions to this more-resources-lead-to-longer-survival summarization. In particular, groups were less likely to survive whenthe founders had more ties to group members, when the founders invited more of the members and when the founders served as the exclusive administrator of the group. These results suggest that founders can be a bottleneck and potential point of failure if they concentrate too much responsibility in themselves. This interpretation is consistent with and generalizes research by Kairam and colleagues, who show that most people join online groups through direct ties with existing members, but that recruiting through personal ties limits the group's ultimate size [11]. However, another interpretation is that when founders know all potential group members and invite them all to join, this collection of people does not need the institution of a Facebook group to support its purposes. A tight-knit collection of people with common ties to the founder may have other methods to support the communication and information exchange that Facebook groups could afford.

Limitations: This research used longitudinal methods to predict the longer-term success of new groups from founders' human and social capital, decisions and behavior before their group was formed or in its first week. Results are consistent with hypotheses that founders can have a causal influence on the success of the groups they create. Yet because the research uses correlational methods, we cannot make strong causal claims about the role of the founders.

We highlight three methodological limitations that undercut our ability to make causal claims. First, founders' attributes and behavior are correlated with those of the non-founding group members. For example, the correlation between the founders' age and the average age of non-founding members is r=.68, between content creation by founders and other members is r=.40, between founders' friend count and other members' friend count is r=.40, and between founders' tie density and the tie density of other group members is r=.27. To assess whether founders' characteristics, decisions and behavior predict group success beyond what can be predicted by non-founders' behavior, we compared a survival analysis that included the attributes and behavior of non-founders to the analysis that included only the control and founder variables (see Model 3 in Table 2). A comparison of the Akaike Information Criterion (AIC) and Bayesian Information Criterion (BIC) of the two models shows that the addition of the founder variables improved model fit (ChiSq = 55974, df = 16, $p < .0001$). Moreover, all the predictor variables listed in Figure 3 predicted group survival even when the comparable non-founder variables are included.

Second, some of the predictor variables, including initial membership size and founders' activities in the group, may be indicators of a group's early success rather than causes of it. Groups that were larger and engaged founders more vigorously in week one may already be more successful than smaller and less engaging groups, and this initial success may endure. This alternative explanation does not apply to behavior measured before the group's creation, however.

Third, some of the decisions founders make when setting up their group may reflect their predictions about ultimate group success, rather than cause it. For example, they may decide to appoint more administrators or invest the time to write a group description only for groups that they expect will be successful.

Design and management implications: Because the conclusions from this research are based on correlational data, they will need experimental verification to establish causation. However, if founders' resources, decisions and actions indeed have causal impact on group survival, then some managerial and design implications are clear.

Starting with a large group seems to increase the group's chances of survival. Social media sites could offer group administrators better tools for recruiting members, including tools to identify those who have ties with current members. They could also recommend nascent groups to people looking for a new group to join or a new place to interact. It is important that these recommendations be appropriate to the interests of the potential members and the topic of the group; tie-based recommendations alone do not guarantee this, as friends may have heterogeneous interests. Software could also suggest non-connected potential members if founders seem to be recruiting only members with whom they have pre-existing ties.

Group descriptions and cover graphics or logos are strongly associated with group success. Yet 26% of founders provide none of these decorations. The group creation process could require a group description and make the creation of group logos or graphics easier.

ACKNOWLEDGMENTS.

This research was supported by Facebook, Google and NSF grants IIS-0808711 and OCI -09-43159. We thank Dean Eckles and Haiyi Zhu for helpful comments.

REFERENCES

[1] Backstrom, L., Huttenlocher, D., Kleinberg, J. and Lan, X. 2006. Group formation in large social networks: membership, growth, and evolution. *Proceedings of the 12th ACM SIGKDD international conference on knowledge discovery and data mining*, 44-54.

[2] Barnett, W. P., Leslie, M. and Harke, M. 2006. *Facebook (Case e-220)*. Harvard Business Publishing, Cambridge, MA.

[3] Baum, J. A. and Shipilov, A. V. 2006 Ecological Approaches to Organizations. In (Eds). *The Sage Handbook of Organization Studies* Sage, Thousand Oaks, CA.

[4] Brüderl, J. and Preisendörfer, P. 1998. Network support and the success of newly founded business. *Small business economics*, 10, 3, 213-225.

[5] Burke, C., Stagl, K., Klein, C., Goodwin, G., Salas, E. and Halpin, S. 2006. What type of leadership behaviors are functional in teams? A meta-analysis. *The Leadership Quarterly*, 17, 3, 288-307.

[6] Butler, B. 2001. Membership size, communication activity, and sustainability: A resource-based model of online social structures. *Information Systems Research*, 12, 4, 346–362.

[7] Cooper, A. C., Gimeno-Gascon, F. J. and Woo, C. Y. 1994. Initial human and financial capital as predictors of new venture performance. *Journal of Business Venturing*, 9, 5, 371-395.

[8] Davidsson, P. and Honig, B. 2003. The role of social and human capital among nascent entrepreneurs. *Journal of Business Venturing*, 18, 3, 301-331.

[9] Freeman, J., Carroll, G. R. and Hannan, M. T. 1983. The liability of newness: Age dependence in organizational death rates. *American sociological review*, 692-710.

[10] Hahn, J., Moon, J. Y. and Zhang, C. 2008. Emergence of new project teams from open source software developer networks: Impact of prior collaboration ties. *Information Systems Research*, 19, 3, 369-391.

[11] Kairam, S., Wang, D. J. and Leskovec, J. 2012. Life and death of online groups: Predicting group growth and longevity. In (Eds). *WSDM'12: Proceedings of the ACM conference on web search and data mining.* ACM, NY.

[12] Katz, M. L. and Shapiro, C. 1994. Systems competition and network effects. *Journal of Economic Perspectives*, 8, 2, 93-115.

[13] Nahapiet, J. and Ghoshal, S. 1998. Social capital, intellectual capital, and the organizational advantage. *Academy of management review*, 242-266.

[14] Ren, Y., Kraut, R. E. and Kiesler, S. 2007. Applying Common Identity and Bond Theory to Design of Online Communities. *Organization Studies*, 28, 3, 377-408.

[15] Resnick, P., Konstan, J., Chen, Y. and Kraut, R. E. 2012. Starting a community. In R. E. Kraut and P. Resnick (Eds). *Building successful online communities: Evidence-based social design* MIT Press, Cambridge MA.

[16] Resnick, P., Janney, A., Buis, L. R. and Richardson, C. R. In press. Starting an Online Community on Demand: A Case Study of Adding Forums to a Physical Activity Promotion Program. *Journal of Medical Internet Research.*

[17] Rynes, S. L. and Barber, A. E. 1990. Applicant attraction strategies: An organizational perspective. *Academy of Management Review*, 15, 2, 286-310.

[18] Sanger, L. 2005. The Early History of Nupedia and Wikipedia: A Memoir. In C. DiBona, D. Cooper and M. Stone (Eds). *Open Sources 2.0: The Continuing Evolution* O'Reilly Media, Inc., Sebastopol, CA.

[19] Singer, J. D. and Willett, J. B. 2003. *Applied longitudinal data analysis*. Oxford University Press, New York.

[20] Stinchcombe, A. 1965. *Social structure and organizations*. Rand McNally, City.

[21] Stoddard, J. L., Augustson, E. M. and Moser, R. P. 2008. Effect of adding a virtual community (bulletin board) to smokefree. gov: randomized controlled trial. *Journal of medical Internet research*, 10, 5.

The Communication Patterns of Technical Leaders: Impact on Product Development Team Performance

Kate Ehrlich
IBM Research
Cambridge, MA 02142
katee@us.ibm.com

Marcelo Cataldo
ConnReperio, LLC
New York, NY 11101
mcataldo@connreperio.com

ABSTRACT

Leaders are important for the smooth functioning of teams but their effect on team performance is less well established. Based on a sample of 55 software development teams from two companies we examined the association between technical leaders' communication structure and the team's performance. Consistent with past research, we found that a team's productivity and quality improve when the team communication follows hierarchical and small-world patterns, respectively. However, there was significant additional improvement in both productivity and quality when technical leaders shared more information than they gathered, and when they were more central in the communication network. Surprisingly they were not necessarily the most "central" individuals in the team's communication structure. We discuss the implication of these results for new tools that provide feedback to leaders and the team.

Author Keywords

Communication; Technical Leadership; Hierarchy; Centrality; Social Network Analysis; Teams

ACM Classification Keywords

H.5.3 [Group and Organization Interfaces]: Asynchronous Communication, Computer-supported Cooperative Work;

General Terms

Human Factors, Management, Measurement, Performance.

INTRODUCTION

Product development teams face the challenge of delivering high quality work on time and within budget while navigating uncertainty, conflicting goals and distributed work (e.g. [2]). It is not surprising that products are frequently delivered late, over budget and with poor quality [35]. It is generally acknowledged that the success of product development is dependent on informal communication for building the shared knowledge that is necessary for coordination especially in distributed teams [13, 23]. However, responsibility for keeping teams on track falls to technical team leaders who define and design the core technical elements and direct the team. These leaders help members identify and leverage expertise that is distributed across the team members to apply the knowledge to the tasks at hand [19]. They must coordinate separate, but inter-dependent, tasks [9] while also allowing individuals to pursue their own work with minimal distractions (e.g. [10]). They also must support collaboration despite differing opinions, backgrounds and perspectives amongst team members [6, 17].

Yet despite their important role, there has been scant research on the effect of technical leaders on team performance. Research in other settings suggests that leadership can influence the flow of information and consequently impact project performance [1, 18, 37]. In product development teams, technical leaders have an important role in coordination of work within and across teams [9]. However, that research did not look at the implications for team performance. Investigations of sales and other types of teams suggest that teams perform better when leaders are central within a social network [3, 28]. However, this research has not shed light on how leaders are positioned within the flow of communication and how their position may be associated with team performance.

This paper reports the results of a study that examined the communication structure of technical leaders, and whether their position in the flow of information is associated with delivery and quality product performance. We performed our analyses using archival data from 55 teams working on large-scale development projects from two companies.

PREVIOUS RESEARCH

Product Development Tasks

Product development is highly complex and the impact of leadership styles and communication patterns is dependent on the kind of task being performed. Cataldo and Ehrlich [8] distinguished between tasks such as iteration planning which contributes to the **delivery performance** of a project, and core development which contributes to the number of defects and hence the **quality** of the software.

Delivery performance involves planning and executing development activities. Communication within the team needs to be sufficient to keep team members informed and

CSCW'14, February 15–19, 2014, Baltimore, Maryland, USA.
Copyright © 2014 ACM 978-1-4503-2540-0/14/02...$15.00.

aligned with the current set of goals without distracting them from the tasks. Cataldo and Ehrlich [8] argued, and found, that a team benefitted when there was a hierarchical communication structure in which information flows out from a core person without flowing back (see also [26])

Quality performance, on the other hand, emphasizes the identification and integration of the right knowledge to make wise design or implementation decisions that minimize defects [10, 16]. Project members might struggle to make sense of new knowledge and effectively integrate it into the relevant context because of differences in perspectives, lack of common understandings and lack of familiarity working together [6]. Failure to adequately make sense of the knowledge and information can result, for instance, in unidentified dependencies, which lead to coordination breakdowns and ultimately, lower product quality [10]. Cataldo and Ehrlich [8] found that a hierarchical communication structure, which benefitted delivery performance, was detrimental to quality performance. Rather, quality outcomes benefitted from a small-world communication structure, which is characterized by small dense clusters of people who communicate frequently and few connections among those clusters. This communication structure brings about higher shared knowledge and greater trust amongst team members which makes it easier to integrate knowledge and access information more rapidly [7, 36].

The present study builds on this research to examine whether the position of the technical leader within the flow of communication has any additional contribution to the performance of the team over and above the effect of the team's communication structure. Specifically, we examine the effect on the team's delivery performance and quality performance, of technical leaders who are (a) centrally positioned, overall, within the team's communication network, (b) positioned to receive information from team members (focus on in-flow communication), and (c) positioned to share information with team members (focused on out-flow communication).

Leadership and Network Centrality

Research on the social network of team leaders in organizations found that leaders' centrality is associated with better team performance [3, 4, 28]. For instance, Mehra and colleagues [28] found that sales teams, where leaders were located within the center of the network, had higher sales and higher customer loyalty.

It is not clear whether we should expect similar results for product development teams, which typically have a much flatter organizational structure than other teams. Moreover, product team members are engaged in tasks with a high degree of inter-dependency that are generally resolved at the individual rather than the team level [10] and therefore may not benefit from any additional direction that comes from the technical leaders. According to this argument, technical leaders may not be more central in the network of successful teams than other team members.

On the other hand, technical leaders are crucial for coordination both internally and externally in product development projects, especially large-scale projects (e.g. [1, 9]). Technical leaders who are centrally located within a communication network are better positioned to collect and disperse the information necessary for coordination [24] and therefore in a better position to help mobilize the resources in the team.

RQ1a: Will the centrality of technical leaders be positively associated with team performance in delivery outcomes?

RQ1b: Will the centrality of technical leaders be positively associated with team performance in quality outcomes?

Leaders as Receivers of Information

There are further insights to be gained by studying the directionality associated with network position. In a communication network, leaders can be positioned as receivers of information (in-flow) when team members send information to them. Alternatively, they can be positioned as providers of information to the team (out-flow).

Technical leaders may be centrally positioned within the in-flow of communication because of their technical reputation. Research suggests that teams perform better when the leader is perceived as having a stronger and more positive reputation [28, 40]. Additionally, technical leaders who receive information from more team members are better informed about the on-going work and better positioned to integrate diverse information. This argument suggests that teams will benefit when the technical leaders are positioned within the incoming flow of information.

On the other hand, product development is an information intensive activity involving a high degree of interdependence between tasks. Developers may resolve these dependencies locally without the need for additional intervention by technical leaders [10]. This argument suggests that the team's performance is not associated with the position of the leader in the in-flow of information.

RQ2a: Will in-degree centrality of technical leaders be positively associated with team performance in delivery outcomes?

RQ2b: Will in-degree centrality of technical leaders be positively associated with team performance in quality outcomes?

Leaders as Providers of Information

A different model of technical leadership borrows from research on leader-member exchange theory (LMX). Recent research on the antecedents of LMX demonstrated that relational behaviors such as supporting, recognizing, consulting and delegating, produce higher quality leader-member relationships, and, by extension, higher group performance [40]. Similarly, others have found evidence that leaders have better team outcomes when they sustain strong personal relationships by integrating and combining contributions from team members [39].

Research with software development teams find that these teams perform better with empowering leaders who encourage self-development, better teamwork and who participate in individual goal setting [18]. Further, performance is improved when leaders are able to share information that is relevant to the context of each team and their needs [37]. This result is consistent with a perspective in which product development teams benefit from having leaders who are centrally positioned within the out-flow of information.

On the other hand, an overly directive leadership may stifle an individual's ability to coordinate directly with others.

> *RQ3a: Will out-degree centrality of technical leaders be positively associated with team performance in delivery outcomes?*

> *RQ3b: Will out-degree centrality of technical leaders be positively associated with team performance in quality outcomes?*

RESEARCH SETTING

We examined the proposed hypotheses using data collected from two product development endeavors from two different companies. We collected data from the development of the first release of the Jazz software development environment on which the IBM[R] Rational[R] Team Concert[TM] (RTC) products are based[1]. We will refer to this dataset as Project A. The second dataset corresponds to the development effort associated with the 9th release of a complex embedded system produced by a company operating in the automotive industry. We will refer to this dataset as Project B. The following paragraphs describe both projects in more detail.

Project A

Our analysis of the RTC project focused on the 13 months prior to the release of the product's first version, which was the period of time between July 2007 and August of 2008. The time period was chosen because prior to July 2007 the amount of development activity was minimal and on that month the project underwent a significant change in process opening up the development process to the Jazz community. A total of 161 developers, worked on the project during the period analyzed. There were 26 functional teams distributed in 21 different sites across the U.S., Canada and Europe. Teams were responsible for one or more components of the system. Project members belonged to one or more of these teams. In addition, individuals have roles within each team and those roles were made transparent to all project members via the role definition capabilities of the RTC tool. The defined roles were "component lead", "contributor", "part-time contributor", "project admin", "connector admin", "dashboard admin", "integration stream admin" and 10 more roles, which were specialized variants of the "contributor" role. .

The project organized its development effort using iterations, which are short-lived (e.g. 6 to 8 weeks) units of development activities. The tasks to be performed in each iteration and by each development team were planned at the beginning of each iteration. However, the amount of development work varied across teams. In order to focus on the main development effort, we used 20 work items as a cutoff to determine which teams to include in our analysis. This resulted in data for 16 out of the 26 teams. The 16 teams were distributed across 15 development sites. One of the teams had 3 technical leaders, 9 teams had 2 technical leaders and the remaining 6 teams had one technical leader. The 10 excluded teams had just a few members and represented a very small fraction of the overall development effort (7.2%) and communication activity (0.9%).

Project B

We collected data from a multi-national development organization responsible for producing a complex embedded system for the automotive industry. The collected data covered the 27 months of development activities associated with the 9th version of the product from the beginning of the project in the beginning of 2009 until mid of 2011. Four hundred and seventeen developers located in four development sites distributed across Europe and India participated in the project. Those developers were organized in 39 development teams ranging from 7 and 21 members. Most project members belonged to just one of the teams. In addition, individuals have roles within each team and those roles were formalized in the process manual of the project. The defined roles were "project manager", "sub-project manager", "architect", "component owner", "developer", "tester", "system integrator" and "component integrator". Each team had a person with the "component owner" role and the project had 12 members with the role of "architect". Two of the people had both roles "component owner" and "architect". One team had two people with the "component owner" role. Our analyses used the data from all 39 teams.

The project organized its development effort using quarterly deliveries to the customer. The first 8 quarters constituted preliminary versions of the system while the last quarter corresponded to the production release. The tasks to be performed for each quarter and by each development team were planned at the beginning of each quarter. This development process shares some similarities with the agile approach used in Project A. However, the development organization of Project B did not consider itself as using an agile development process but rather an iterative version of more traditional sequential (or V-model) process.

Identification of Technical Leaders

We define technical leaders are those individuals that have strong technical competence and are responsible for the defining, architecting and/or designing the core technical

[1] IBM, the IBM logo, ibm.com, and Rational are trademarks or registered trademarks of International Business Machines Corporation in the United States, other countries, or both

properties of part of a complex system. In addition, those individual, typically, have in-depth knowledge of various parts of a system that represent valuable resources for the rest of the development organization. After performing an initial analysis of the datasets and confirming our understanding of the projects' context via interviews, we consider technical leaders in Project A as those individuals with the "component lead" role and in Project B those individuals with the roles of "component owner" and/or "architect". The people with those roles match the characteristics of a technical leader presented in our definition.

Comparison across Projects

The two studied projects were chosen because they represent two very distinct points across two key dimensions of maturity: product maturity and process maturity. Differences across those dimensions are important aspects to consider because they have been found to influence communication and organizational processes in product development endeavors [22]. Table 1 highlights the key differences where Project A represents the less mature development context while Project B exhibited high levels of product and process maturity. It is worth pointing out that the two dimensions of maturity are not completely orthogonal. In fact, they might be confounded. Such a limitation can be addressed from an experimental design point of view. If the impact of the communication patterns of technical leaders, our main focus, is the same across the two projects, then the confounding effect between product maturity and process maturity does not represent a problem.

Table 1: Comparison between Projects along Product and Process Dimensions of Maturity

	Project A	Project B
Process Maturity	Agile process. Highly geographically distributed. No CMM assessment.	Well-established use of V-model approach. Very mature org. with more than 23 years developing the product.
Product Maturity	Novel Product, first in class. First release of product.	Market-leader. 9th generation of the product.

Description of Measures

We used 4 sources of data for our analyses. First, we collected the software repositories from both projects including version control activity, task and defect tracking reports as well as a wide range of technical properties of the software systems being developed. Second, we also collected information about the project member's location from personnel records and corporate directories. In project B, we also collected 13 months worth of communication activity from the project's instant messaging system. Finally, we conducted semi-structured interviews with individuals who were members of the projects throughout the development, to validate our assumptions about the interpretation of the measures (4 in Project A and 16 in Project B).

As discussed earlier, both projects produced a particular outcome in predefined time periods. In Project A, those time periods were called iterations as it is traditional in agile development processes and lasted 6 to 8 weeks. In Project B, those time periods were called delivery periods and they lasted 3 months. We will refer to these time periods as iterations throughout the rest of paper.

Measuring Delivery Performance

Our unit of analysis is the pair (iteration, team). We measured *Delivery Performance* of an iteration as the number of tasks that were planned for the (iteration, team) pair but were rescheduled to the following iteration because they were not completed. This measure focuses on how well the team members that participated in the iteration were able to execute the planned set of activities as well as capturing aspects of the development process such as adequate planning and adequate handling of unexpected situations. Interviews in both projects confirmed that rescheduling was an adequate measure since it was an integral part of the development process.

Measuring Quality

The quality outcomes of an iteration were assessed following the procedure proposed by Cataldo and Ehrlich [8]. For a given iteration i_t, we first selected all the defects reported in the following iteration i_{t+1}. Our measure of *Quality* captured the number of defects that either impacted components changed during iteration i_t and took 1 or more days to get resolved or impacted components not changed in iteration i_t nor in iteration i_{t+1}. Following the guidelines of [8], we validated this measure by analyzing a random sample of defects corresponding to 10% of all the defects reported across all the iterations (527 defects in Project A and 891 in Project B) and found our measure to be reliable.

Construction of the Communication Network

Both projects used development environments that had features that provide project members with contextualized interaction for work items. These interactions took the form of comments in a work item report and were stored in the software repositories of both projects. Those data allowed us to identify the work items, the individuals that made the comment(s) as well as the content of the comment. We constructed iteration-level communication networks following the procedure proposed by Ehrlich and Cataldo [8, 16]. Since tasks could span multiple iterations, we considered only those comments made in the work item reports that were within the time frame of the focal iteration. The first comment in the work item linked the person that made the comment with the owner of the task at the time the comment was made. If the owner and the commenter were the same person, the link was ignored. For the subsequent comments in the work item report, a link in the communication network between two project members was made if the comments were adjacent in the sequence of comments and they were associated with the task at hand. These comments also resulted in a link between the commenter and the owner of the work item at the time it was made.

We also have instance messaging logs for Project B. In this case, we had 3 raters examine the logs and identify the context of the discussions to link them to specific work item. The linkages between individuals were time-stamped so we only included in a focal interaction those interactions that were time-stamped during the time period covered by the iteration. Due to the volume of the data, we divided the data among the 3 raters, however, they had a 15% overlap in the content coded by them. The raters agreed in the interaction linkages as well as in the linkage of comments to work items in 99.2% of the cases.

Communication Patterns of Technical Leaders

We measured the *Technical Leader Centrality* in the communication networks using the traditional degree centrality network measure. We also measured the directionality of the technical leader communication patterns using in-flow and out-flow degree centrality measures. More specifically, we measured *Ratio Leader's In-Flow vs. Rest of Team* and *Ratio of Leader's Out-Flow vs. Rest of Team* as the ratio between the leader's in- or out-degree centrality in the communication network and the average in- or out-degree centrality of all the other team members. In the case the team had more than one technical leader, we averaged the in-flow/out-flow degree centrality of the leaders. We also computed the *Ratio Leader's Out-Flow/In-Flow* measure that captures the proportion of the technical leader's communication that was out-going. More specifically, the measure was computed as out-flow degree centrality / (out-flow degree centrality + in-flow degree centrality).

Additional Control Factors

Past research work suggests a wide range of factors that may impact outcomes such as performance and quality in software development (e.g. [5, 8, 10, 11, 16, 20]). We organized our control variables into six groups:

Team-level Communication Structure: Cataldo and Ehrlich [8] found that two particular team-level communication structures, hierarchical and small-world patterns, impacted product development team outcomes differently. Given those results, we computed the *Hierarchical Communication Pattern* measure based on the hierarchy metric proposed by Krackhardt [26] and *Small World Communication Pattern* measure as proposed in Uzzi and Spiro [36], following the procedure described in Cataldo and Ehrlich [8].

Controls for Volume of Communication-related factors: Since our independent measures focus on patterns of communication, it is important to control for factors related to the propensity of the team members and, in particular, technical leaders to communicate. We computed the *Amount of Intra-Team Communication* as the number of dyads from the communication networks where both members belonged to the same team. On the other hand, *Amount of Inter-Team Communication* captured the number of dyads where at least one of the persons in the pair also belonged to a different team. We also computed the *Leader-to-out-team Communication* measure as the amount of times the technical leaders interacted with members from other teams. Finally, the technical leaders in both projects were active in the development effort so we measured the propensity of the individuals to comment in work items not owned by them (*Leader Involvement in non-Owned Work Items*) as the number of work items not owned by the technical leader normalized by the total number of work items in the team and team size.

Controls for product-related factors: Technical dependencies that exist among the components of a system are an important driver of work dependencies and consequently, of interaction among interdependent project members (e.g. [12, 33]). Building on the work of Cataldo and Nambiar [11], we computed the *Internal Technical Coupling* measure as the density of the sub-matrix based on the set of relationships defined in the technical dependencies matrix that are contained within a team's area of responsibility. We also computed the *External Technical Coupling* measure as the number of components not under the responsibility of the focal team that had technical dependencies with those components changed by the focal team.

Controls for task-related factors: Since iterations vary in the amount of work they generate and in the importance of the work, we measured the *Ratio of High Priority Work Items* that each team faced in each iteration as well as the *Average Size of Work Items* as the average number of files modified in the commits associated with the work items.

Controls for team-related factors: We computed several measures that capture attributes of the teams we studied. Since comments on work items could also come from people outside the team, we computed two measures: *Number of Project Members Involved* captures the total of team and non-team members that participated in the work associated with each pair (iteration, team) and *Number of Multi-Team Project Members* captures the subset of those individuals that were part of more than one formal team. Both projects involved members across multiple geographical locations in different countries. Therefore, we assessed the geographical dispersion of the teams, *GSD*, as a dichotomous variable where 1 indicates that the project members involved in the work associated with a pair (iteration, team) were geographically distributed; otherwise it was set to 0. We collected measures of experience based on the work by Boh and colleagues [6]. We measured: *Average Level of Technical Experience* as the average number of work items that the team member worked on prior to the focal iteration, *Average Level of Shared-work Experience* measures the average number of times that team members worked together in work items prior to the beginning of the focal iteration, and *Average Level of Team Workload* as the average number of work items owned per team member during the iteration.

Controls for unobserved effects: Finally, we included additional controls for unobserved, team- and iteration-specific factors. These were recorded as Dummy A through F for the teams (16 teams in Project A and 39 in Project B) and Dummy Iteration A through D for the iterations (14 iterations in Project A and 9 in Project B).

Finally, it is worth pointing out that we computed and evaluated other network measures such as density, which did not have any impact in our models. Therefore, we did not include them in the final results reported in the paper.

Description of the Model

In our analyses, we used a multi-level Negative Binomial regression model because our two dependent variables, *Delivery Performance* and *Quality*, are count variables. We examined our research questions by creating several models, which included the different control variables as well as our independent measures as fixed effects. We also added iteration and team as random effects. In order to assess the fit of each model, we report the log-likelihood of each model as well as the percentage of deviance explained by the model. The percentage of the deviance explained is a ratio of the deviance of the null model (containing only the intercept) and the deviance of the final model. Although coefficients are often reported as part of the results, we opted for reporting the incidence rate ratios (IRRs) associated with the fixed effect factors of the regression models because they simplify the interpretation of the results. IRRs indicate the rate at which the dependent variable would change for one unit change in one independent variable keeping the other factors constant.

RESULTS

We report the results of the various analyses performed. We started our analyses with an examination of issues of collinearity. Secondly, we replicated the results from Cataldo and Ehrlich [8] using new data from Project B. This is an important step because we are examining whether effects of leader position occur even when we account for effects of communication structure in the teams. We conclude with results related to our research questions.

Initial Analyses

As discussed earlier, in Project A we only considered data from 16 out of the 26 teams. The 14 iterations and 16 teams resulted in 197 pairs <iteration, team>. We did not have 224 pairs because not all the teams had development activity planned in all iterations. In the case of Project B, the 39 teams and 9 iterations resulted in 324 pairs <iteration, team>. Again, we did not have 351 pairs because not all teams had planned development activity in all iterations.

Testing for Collinearity

We computed descriptive statistics of the measures described in the previous section and log-transformed all those variables that exhibited skewed distributions. We also performed various collinearity diagnostics. A variance inflation factors (VIF) analysis identified collinearity problems with *Technical Leader Centrality* and *Amount of Intra-Team Communication* measures. We kept the latter measure out of our regression analyses. We only included *Technical Leader Centrality* in a subset of the models. All the other measures included in our models did not exhibit collinearity problems since they had VIFs below 5 as recommended guidelines suggest [21]. A pair-wise correlation analysis among those measures also showed levels of correlation that were not problematic (all below 0.40).

Replication Analyses

The first step in our analyses consisted in replicating the results of Cataldo and Ehrlich [8] using new data from Project B. Overall, our analyses showed that project B exhibited results consistent with those reported by Cataldo and Ehrlich [8] in terms of higher levels of hierarchical communication patterns being associated with higher levels of delivery performance (IRR: 0.247, $p < 0.01$, log-likelihood = -395.47, deviance explained = 59.3%). In fact, the effect size of *Hierarchical Communication Pattern* is significantly higher in Project B as suggested by the difference in the deviance explained between the full model (59.3%) and the model without the factor (32.6%). On the other hand, we did not find evidence in Project B for an impact of *Small-World Communication Pattern* on delivery performance. It is worth pointing out that Cataldo and Ehrlich [8] found a marginal effect in Project A. We also found that hierarchical communication structures have a significant detrimental effect on quality (IRR: 1.322, $p < 0.01$, log-likelihood = -759.41, deviance explained = 46.5%) while small-world communication structures improved the quality outcomes of an iteration (IRR: 0.393, $p < 0.01$, log-likelihood = -619.14, deviance explained = 56.4%). These results confirm the previous findings and provide the foundation for examining additional effects associated with leader communication.

Technical Leaders and their Centrality in the Communication Patterns of Teams

Our first set of research questions (RQ1a and 1b) concerned the role of centrality of the technical leader. As Table 2 shows, *Technical Leader Centrality* has statistically significant IRRs and those values are between 0 and 1 in all cases. Those results indicate that the more central the technical leader is in the communication network of the team, the more likely the team is to exhibit higher levels of delivery and quality performance. Due to space constraints, we only show a subset of the regression models that we constructed. The impact of *Technical Leader Centrality* was consistent across both datasets and across all models. For instance, the same significance and directionality of impact was found when *Hierarchical Comm. Pattern* was included in the quality performance models or *Small-World Comm. Pattern* was included in the delivery performance models.

Certainly this result is not novel. Numerous studies have highlighted the team-level benefits of centrally positioned leaders (e.g. [3]). Interestingly and despite finding an impact of centrality, further analysis revealed that the leaders were not the most central individuals in their teams suggesting that technical leaders need to be engaged in the flow of communication but do not need to dominate or control the flow. Figure 1 shows aggregate average values of degree centrality (DC) across both projects for those teams that were in the lower quarter in both outcome measures as well as those teams in the upper quarter on both measures. We observe that level of centrality of the technical leaders was marginally above the average centrality level across the other team members. Furthermore, an examination of each pair (iteration, team) from both projects revealed that in only 7 out of the 521 pairs, the technical leader was the team member with the highest degree centrality level. In 378 pairs technical leaders were in the third quartile (considering the forth quartile as the highest). In the remaining pairs (136), the leaders were positioned in the lowest 2 quartiles.

Figure 1: Aggregate Average Levels of Centrality

Delivery \ Quality	Low	High
Low	Leader DC=0.032 (0.077) Rest DC=0.027 (0.069)	
High		Leader DC=0.137 (0.248) Rest DC=0.107 (0.221)

Technical Leaders and the Impact of the Directionality of their Communication Patterns

The next step in our analysis was to examine how the directionality of the communication of technical leaders impacts the teams' performance (Research questions 2a, 2b, 3a an3b). Tables 3a, 3b and 3c report the results of our regression analyses. It is important to point out that in those three tables, we only report the odds ratio of our independent measures *Ratio Leader's Out-Flow/In-Flow*, *Ratio Leader's In-Flow vs. Rest of Team* and *Ratio of Leader's Out-Flow vs. Rest of Team*, respectively, and the fit of the various models. The *Ratio Leader's Out-Flow/In-Flow* measure has a consistent positive effect on performance across both projects. The higher the amount of out-flow degree centrality the technical leader exhibits in his/her communication patterns relative to the in-flow degree centrality, the better the delivery performance (the number of rescheduled tasks are reduced) and quality performance (the number of defects is reduced) of the teams as shown by the statistically significant odds ratios below 1 in Table 3a. Comparing the fit of the models in Table 2 and Table 3a, we observe that considering the ratio of the out-/in-degree centrality has a significantly large size effect in the models, averaging about 5% more deviance explained in Project B, about 14% more in project A in the delivery performance models and about 7% more in Project A in the quality performance models. Combined, these results suggest that teams benefits when leaders provide more information than they receive.

Arguably, the impact of out-flow communication could suggest that the benefits stem from leaders being directive rather than sharing information. However, an examination of a random sample of interactions in both projects provided some valuable insights. Overall, technical leaders tended to engage mostly in interactions that answer questions, provide suggestions about technical challenges, provide advice about the best course of action and provide pros/cons analysis of proposed ways to tackle a technical problem. For example, we identified a pair of technical leaders with similar communication network metrics (Leader #1, In-degree Centrality = 0.0309, Out-degree Centrality = 0.0451 – Leader #2, In-degree Centrality = 0.0287, Out-degree Centrality = 0.0575) but from two different teams to explore whether there might be additional effects of communication style that could be explored in future work.. We identified very distinct styles between those leaders. Leader #1 tends to be directive in their interactions as this typical example shows: "*...The problem here is the XUL runner which tweaks the selection. Have to investigate how we deal with links in the edit mode anyway...*". On the other hand, leader #2 seems to be more constructive in their interactions "*...My reading of the material suggests that it should be: it's a secondary command (a peripheral action that, while helpful, isn't essential to the purpose of the window); it navigates to another page, window, or Help topic; and it's label is plenty more than recommended four word limit. I ask not ... to see whether we end up at the same point after reading the same material. If you and I can't agree - with all the additional background material we have available - it's going to be tough to get the regular developer on board (when they're not going to have the time or inclination to wade through the pages of content that we've waded through)...*".

In Tables 3b and 3c, we report the results of our analyses of directionality of communication patterns addressing research questions 2a and 2b (in-flow of communication). We compare the amount of in-flow (Table 3b) or out-flow (Table 3c) communication from the technical leaders relative to the rest of the team. Our analyses do not provide evidence that *Ratio Leader's In-Flow vs. Rest of Team* influences either performance outcome in the teams (see Table 3b). On the other hand, Table 3c shows that the *Ratio Leader's Out-Flow vs. Rest of Team* has a consistent positive impact across both projects and across both performance outcomes.

These results further suggest that the directionality of the communication of technical leaders is an important factor to consider in terms of two key product development outcomes: delivery and quality performance.

DISCUSSION

Formal leaders play an important role in the functioning and well-being of teams [3, 4, 28]. However, the increasing prevalence of self-organized teams [15], emergent leaders [39] and shared leadership [41], raises the question of whether formal leaders' have a significant effect on a team's performance. We addressed this question by studying the pattern of communication between leaders and team members in 55 product development teams from two companies. Specifically, we examined whether the leader's position in the team's communication network and the direction of their communication was associated with team

Table 2: The Impact of "*Technical Leaders Centrality*" in the Team Communication Network

	Delivery Performance				Quality Performance			
	Project A		Project B		Project A		Project B	
	Model I	Model II	Model III	Model IV	Model V	Model VI	Model VII	Model VIII
Controls for Unobserved Effects								
Team Dummy A	1.171*	1.402*	1.403**	1.305**	1.079*	1.102*	1.109**	1.141**
Team Dummy B	0.723**	0.899**	0.991	1.092	0.872**	0.798**	1.011	0.929
Team Dummy C	1.011	0.941	0.801**	1.089**	0.589	0.945	1.201**	1.011
Team Dummy D	1.429**	0.899**	1.195*	0.901*	0.621**	0.749**	0.848*	0.851*
Team Dummy E	-	-	1.178*	0.937*	-	-	0.561*	0.374*
Team Dummy F	-	-	0.684*	1.099*	-	-	1.071*	0.927*
Iteration Dummy A	0.601**	0.602**	0.402	0.389	0.903**	1.202**	1.017	1.189
Iteration Dummy B	0.257**	0.478**	0.501	1.745	0.486**	0.382**	0.809	0.486
Iteration Dummy C	0.071**	0.079**	0.152*	0.392*	0.078**	0.092**	0.121*	0.091*
Iteration Dummy D	1.191*	1.414*	1.892**	1.451**	1.109*	1.203*	1.055**	1.203*
Controls for Team-related factors								
Num. of Members	6.249**	8.194**	9.204**	4.244**	1.893**	1.943**	2.422**	2.892**
Num. of Multi-team Members	0.392*	0.674*	0.902*	0.934*	1.023	1.294	1.349	1.195
GSD	1.485**	1.568**	2.044**	1.605**	1.478**	1.345**	1.882**	1.922**
Avg. of Tech. Experience	0.795*	0.985*	0.678**	0.895**	0.899*	0.892**	0.809**	0.985**
Avg. of Shared-work Exp.	0.506	0.793	0.793*	0.673*	1.102	1.185	0.692	0.902
Avg. of Team Workload	1.356**	1.545**	1.935**	1.932**	2.119**	1.902**	1.242**	1.155**
Controls for Task-related factors								
Ratio of High Priority Tasks	0.342**	0.842**	0.724*	0.799*	0.702**	0.678**	0.289**	0.678**
Average Size of Tasks	1.055	1.002	0.899	0.994	1.894**	1.792**	0.992	0.995
Controls for Product-related factors								
Internal Tech. Coupling	1.485*	1.593*	3.842**	4.522**	2.195**	1.953**	3.092**	2.827**
External Tech. Coupling	1.249**	1.345**	1.784**	1.902**	1.154**	1.274**	1.986**	1.752**
Controls for Volume of Comm.								
Intra-team Comm.	0.895*	0.951*	0.824*	0.842*	0.930*	0.917*	0.792*	0.801*
Leader-to-out-team Comm.	1.795**	2.294**	2.224**	4.002**	1.701**	1.643**	1.195**	1.442**
Leader in not-Owned Tasks	1.143**	1.687**	2.394**	2.032**	1.762**	1.985**	2.249**	1.942**
Comm. Network Structure								
Hierarchical Comm. Pattern	0.394**		0.304**		1.302**		1.509**	
Small World Comm. Pattern		1.785**		1.013		0.892**		0.455**
Leader Comm. Pattern								
Technical Leader Centrality	0.875**	0.911**	0.567**	0.703**	0.689**	0.621**	0.263**	0.301**
Log-Likelihood	-401.87	-404.59	-380.01	-609.74	-468.17	-472.73	-659.89	-561.54
Deviance Explained	40.6%	40.2%	60.9%	37.2%	54.0%	53.5%	53.5%	60.4%

(+ $p < 0.10$, * $p < 0.05$, ** $p < 0.01$)

performance measures of productivity and quality. Previous research demonstrated that product development teams are more productive when they have a hierarchical communication structure, and, they produce higher quality products when they have a small-world communication structure [8]. This finding, replicated in the present study, says that the team's own communication contributes to performance. The present study examined whether the leader's pattern of communication has any additional effect on team performance. Several important results emerged.

First, we found that teams performed better when the leader was central in the network (RQ 1a,b) confirming previous research [3, 28]. Surprisingly, the leader was not always <u>the most</u> central in the network, implying that leader centrality may not be as simple as previously thought [29, 34]. One interpretation is that we are tapping into a model in which people who emerge as central in a network [14] come to share responsibilities with formal leaders [32, 41].

Second, we established that teams had higher productivity and higher quality when leaders communicated out to the team (RQ 3a,b) even after accounting for the significant effects of hierarchical and small-world communication structures. This is an important finding because it provides strong empirical evidence that leaders not only contribute to the general well-being of a team but their position in the communication network has a measurable effect on the team's performance. This result is consistent with leader-member exchange theory, which emphasizes the importance of relational behaviors between leaders and members [4, 39]. The present study contributes to and extends that line of research by demonstrating the importance of leader centrality within the out-flow communication.

Third, we did not find any benefit for either productivity or quality for teams whose leaders were receivers of information (RQ 2a,b). Leaders who are centrally positioned within the in-flow of communication are often perceived as more important or having higher expertise [28, 40]. In a technical environment, expertise is highly valued so it is surprising that we did not find effects of perceived expertise on team performance. Perhaps leader expertise is less important than the perceived expertise of team members.

Even though product development teams can succeed without leaders [15], a key contribution of this study is to demonstrate that technical leaders are important to the team's performance even after accounting for the team's communication. Moreover, the replication of our results across two distinct companies speaks to the generality of our findings.

Limitations

Our study has some limitations worth pointing out. We relied on archival data from asynchronous communication which under-reports any face-to-face communication that might have occurred between collocated team members. Interviews with some of the members of Project A confirmed that developers, even those who were collocated, were encouraged to discuss technical issues in the comments field that we used as our data source, so that issues could be tracked and be visible to all developers regardless of their location. A similar finding was obtained through interviews in Project B. While we obtained strong results with respect to the structure and flow of communication in product development teams, there is value in studying the content of the communication. A complete analysis of the content is beyond the scope of this paper. However, a very preliminary comparison between leaders with similar network metrics revealed marked differences with one leader having a directive style and the other leader adopting a more constructive and conversational style. Future research using content analysis could shed light on additional aspects of the communication of technical leaders.

Implications for New Tools

The results of the present study suggest that leaders might benefit from tools to adjust their communication. First, there is a direct implication from the growing body of work in the area of communication, coordination and awareness tools. For example, tools that support task-centric interactions such as task or defect tracking systems (e.g. Bugzilla) or integrated development environments (e.g. IBM RTC) could be enhanced to provide concrete guidance to technical leaders regarding their in/out flow communication patterns. Furthermore, tools such as Worldview [31] or Ensemble [38] could be enhanced to support the identification of dependencies where technical leaders could play a role in working with those most directly affected.

A different breed of tools comes from research, which used visual feedback to improve team performance [25, 30]. Kim and Pentland [25] used sociometric badges to capture group dynamics in real-time and display the results to each team member. They obtained a significant change in behavior for both collocated and distributed groups who received visual feedback on group dynamics, In particular, there were fewer overlapping conversations, greater interactivity, less dominance and distributed teams became more like collocated teams. A similar approach could be developed to provide feedback to leaders.

A third approach can be found in recent research on leaders of online communities. Matthews and colleagues [27] developed a set of metrics reflecting the participation and engagement of community members over time that leaders could use to intervene in the community. What was especially valuable to leaders were metrics that helped them identify critical contributors and content. A similar approach in product development teams could help leaders identify which people to communicate with to have the greatest impact on the team.

CONCLUSION

The contributions of our study are two-fold. First, our analyses and results linked the leader position in the team's communication network and in the flow of communication to measurable performance outcomes of product development teams. Finally, our results were obtained after controlling for other structural effects of communication on team performance and replicated in two companies with very distinct product and process maturity.

ACKNOWLEDGMENTS

This research was partially sponsored by the Army Research Laboratory and was accomplished under Cooperative Agreement Number W911NF-09-2-0053. The views and conclusions contained in this document are those of the authors and should not be interpreted as representing the official policies, either expressed or implied, of the Army Research Laboratory or the U.S. Government. The U.S. Government is authorized to reproduce and distribute reprints for Government purposes notwithstanding any copyright notation here on.

Table 3a: The Impact of the "*Ratio Leader's Out-Flow/In-Flow*" Communication Patterns

	Delivery Performance				Quality Performance			
	Project A		Project B		Project A		Project B	
	Model I	Model II	Model III	Model IV	Model V	Model VI	Model VII	Model VIII
Comm. Network Structure								
Hierarchical Comm. Pattern	0.436**		0.281**		1.411**		1.497**	
Small World Comm. Pattern		1.993**		1.001		0.879**		0.478**
Leader Comm. Pattern								
Ratio Leader's Out-Flow/In-Flow	0.899**	0.878**	0.886**	0.871**	0.272**	0.257**	0.271***	0.326**
Log-Likelihood	-306.27	-309.35	-335.36	-564.98	-422.37	-383.92	-593.7	-495.26
Deviance Explained	54.8%	54.3%	65.5%	41.8%	58.5%	62.3%	58.2%	65.1%

(+ p < 0.10, * p < 0.05, ** p < 0.01)

Table 3b: The Impact of the "*Ratio Leader's In-Flow vs. Rest of Team*" Communication Patterns

	Delivery Performance				Quality Performance			
	Project A		Project B		Project A		Project B	
	Model I	Model II	Model III	Model IV	Model V	Model VI	Model VII	Model VIII
Comm. Network Structure								
Hierarchical Comm. Pattern	0.427**		0.249**		1.219**		1.392**	
Small World Comm. Pattern		1.916**		1.003		0.929**		0.401**
Leader Comm. Pattern								
Ratio Leader's In-Flow vs. Rest of Team	0.948	0.923	0.945	0.927	0.967	0.929	0.792+	0.825+
Log-Likelihood	-414.19	-420.07	-394.69	-645.91	-489.71	-498.01	-747.09	-607.99
Deviance Explained	38.8%	37.9%	59.3%	33.5%	51.9%	51.1%	47.4%	57.2%

(+ p < 0.10, * p < 0.05, ** p < 0.01)

Table 3c: The Impact of the "*Ratio Leader's Out-Flow vs. Rest of Team*" Communication Patterns

	Delivery Performance				Quality Performance			
	Project A		Project B		Project A		Project B	
	Model I	Model II	Model III	Model IV	Model V	Model VI	Model VII	Model VIII
Comm. Network Structure								
Hierarchical Comm. Pattern	0.507**		0.465**		1.989**		1.983**	
Small World Comm. Pattern		1.804**		0.999		0.906**		0.298**
Leader Comm. Pattern								
Ratio Leader's Out-Flow vs. Rest of Team	0.901**	0.793*	0.833*	0.901*	0.985	0.755*	0.704**	0.561*
Log-Likelihood	-349.19	-397.72	-378.52	-618.13	-495.25	-483.41	-698.17	-597.69
Deviance Explained	48.4%	41.2%	61.0%	36.3%	51.3%	52.5%	50.8%	57.9%

(+ p < 0.10, * p < 0.05, ** p < 0.01)

REFERENCES

1. Ancona, D. and Caldwell, D. Bridging the boundary: External activity and performance in organizational teams. *Administrative Science Quarterly,* 37 (1992), 634-665.
2. Ancona, D. G. and Bresman, H., *X-teams: How to build teams that lead, innovate, and succeed*: Harvard Business Press, 2007.
3. Balkundi, P. and Harrison, D. A.. Ties, Leaders, and Time in Teams: Strong inference about network structure's effects on team viability and performance. *Academy of Management Journal,* 49 (2006), 49-68.

4. Balkundi, P. and Kilduff, M.. The ties that lead: A social network approach to leadership. *The Leadership Quarterly,* 17 (2006), 419-439.
5. Bass, M., *et al.*. Architectural Misalignment: An Experience Report. In *Proceedings of the Sixth Working IEEE/IFIP Conference on Software Architecture* (2007).
6. Boh, W. F., *et al.*. Learning from Experience in Software Development: A Multilevel Analysis. *Management Science,* 53 (2007), 1315-1331.
7. Burt, R. *Brokerage and closure: An introduction to social capital*. Oxford University Press, USA, 2005.
8. Cataldo, M. and Ehrlich, K. The impact of communication structure on new product development outcomes. In *Proc. CHI 2012*, ACM Press (2012).
9. Cataldo, M. and Herbsleb, J. D. Communication networks in geographically distributed software development. In *Proc. CSCW 2008*, ACM Press (2008).
10. Cataldo, M. and Herbsleb, J. D. Coordination Breakdowns and Their Impact on Development Productivity and Software Failures.,*IEEE Transactions on Software Engineering,* 39 (2013), 343-360.
11. Cataldo, M. and Nambiar, S. The impact of geographic distribution and the nature of technical coupling on the quality of global software development projects. *Journal of Software Maintenance and Evolution: Research and Practice,* 24 (2012), 153-168.
12. Cataldo, M., *et al.* Identification of coordination requirements: implications for the Design of collaboration and awareness tools. In *Proc. CSCW 2006*, ACM Press (2006).
13. Cramton, C. The mutual knowledge problem and its consequences for dispersed collaboration. *Organization Science,* 12 (2001), 346-371.
14. Cross, R., *et al.* Supporting knowledge creation and sharing in social networks. *Organizational Dynamics,* 30 (2001), 100-120.
15. Crowston, K., *et al.* Self-organization of teams for free/libre open source software development. *Information and Software Technology,* 49 (2007), 564-575.
16. Ehrlich, K. and Cataldo, M. All-for-one and one-for-all?: a multi-level analysis of communication patterns and individual performance in geographically distributed software development. In *Proc. CSCW 2012*, ACM Press (2012), 945-954.
17. Espinosa, J. A., *et al.* Familiarity, Complexity, and Team Performance in Geographically Distributed Software Development. *Organization Science,* 18 (2007), 613-630.
18. Faraj, S. and Sambamurthy, V. Leadership of information systems development projects. *IEEE Transactions on Engineering Management,* 53 (2006), 238-249.
19. Faraj, S. and Sproull, L. Coordinating Expertise in Software Development Teams. *Management Science,* 46 (2000), 1554-1568.
20. Graves, T. L., *et al.* Predicting fault incidence using software change history. *IEEE Transactions on Software Engineering, ,* 26 (2000), 653-661.
21. Hair, J. F., *et al.* *Multivariate data analysis 5th Edition*. Upper Saddle River, NJ: Prentice Hall, 1998.
22. Henderson, R. M. and Clark, K. B. Architectural Innovation: The Reconfiguration of Existing Product Technologies and the Failure of Established Firms. *Administrative Science Quarterly,* 35 (1990), 9-30.
23. Herbsleb, J. D. and Mockus, A. An Empirical Study of Speed and Communication in Globally Distributed Software Development. *IEEE Trans. Softw. Eng.,* 29 (2003), 481-494.
24. Hossain, L., *et al.* Actor centrality correlates to project based coordination. In *Proc. CSCW 2006,* ACM Press (2006), 363-372.
25. Kim, T., *et al.* Meeting mediator: enhancing group collaborationusing sociometric feedback. In *Proc. CSCW 2008*, ACM Press (2008), 457-466.
26. Krackhardt, D. Graph theoretical dimensions of informal organizations. In *Computational Organization Theory,* Psychology Press (1994), 89-111.
27. Matthews, T., *et al.* Community insights: helping community leaders enhance the value of enterprise online communities. In *Proc. CHI 2013*, ACM Press 2013, 513-522.
28. Mehra, A., *et al.* The social network ties of group leaders: Implications for group performance and leader reputation. *Organization Science,* 17 (2006), 64-79.
29. Mehra, A., *et al.* The social networks of high and low self-monitors: Implications for workplace performance. *Administrative Science Quarterly,* 46 (2001), 121-146.
30. Pentland, A. S., *et al.*, Awareness as an antidote to distance: Making distributed groups cooperative and consistent. In *Proc. CSCW 2012*, ACM Press 2012, 1237-1246.
31. Ripley, R. M., *et al.* A Visualization for Software Project Awareness and Evolution. In *Proc. VISSOFT 2007.* IEEE Press 2007, 137-144.
32. Robert, L. P. A multi-level analysis of the impact of shared leadership in diverse virtual teams. In *Proc. CSCW 2013*, ACM Press 2013, 363-374.
33. Sosa, M. E., *et al.* The Misalignment of Product Architecture and Organizational Structure in Complex Product Development. *Management Science,* 50 (2004), 1674-1689.

34. Sparrowe, R., *et al.* Social networks and the performance of individuals and groups. *Academy of Management Journal,* 44 (2001), 316-325.

35. Ulrich, K. T. and Eppinger, S. *Product Design and Development 4th Edition*. New York, NY: McGraw-Hill (2007).

36. Uzzi, B. and Spiro, J. Collaboration and creativity: The small world problem. *American Journal of Sociology,* 111 (2005), 447-504.

37. Weisband, S. P. *Leadership at a distance: research in technologically-supported work.* Psychology Press (2008).

38. Xiang, P. F., *et al.* Ensemble: a recommendation tool for promoting communication in software teams,. In *Proceedings of the Int'l Workshop on Recommendation Systems for Software Engineering*, IEEE Press 2008.

39. Yoo, Y. and Alavi, M. Emergent leadership in virtual teams: what do emergent leaders do? *Information and Organization,* 14 (2004), 27-58.

40. Yukl, G., *et al.* Influence of leader behaviors on the leader-member exchange relationship. *Journal of Managerial Psychology,* 24 (2009), 289-299.

41. Zhu, H., *et al.* Effectiveness of shared leadership in online communities. in *Proc. CSCW 2012*, ACM Press 2012, 407-416.

Ensemble: Exploring Complementary Strengths of Leaders and Crowds in Creative Collaboration

Joy Kim, Justin Cheng, Michael S. Bernstein
Stanford University HCI Group
{jojo0808, jcccf, msb}@cs.stanford.edu

ABSTRACT
In story writing, the diverse perspectives of the crowd could support an author's search for the perfect character, setting, or plot. However, structuring crowd collaboration is challenging. Too little structure leads to unfocused, sprawling narratives, and too much structure stifles creativity. Motivated by the idea that individual creative leaders and the crowd have complementary creative strengths, we present an approach where a leader directs the high-level vision for a story and articulates creative constraints for the crowd. This approach is embodied in Ensemble, a novel collaborative story-writing platform. In a month-long short story competition, over one hundred volunteer users on the web started over fifty short stories using Ensemble. Leaders used the platform to direct collaborator work by establishing creative goals, and collaborators contributed meaningful, high-level ideas to stories through specific suggestions. This work suggests that asymmetric creative contributions may support a broad new class of creative collaborations.

Author Keywords
Social computing; online creative collaboration; storytelling.

ACM Classification Keywords
H.5.3 Group and Organization Interfaces: Collaborative computing

INTRODUCTION
Peer production has proven itself a powerful lever for coordinating *knowledge* [3]; now, crowds are demonstrating their ability to empower *creativity*. Creative collaboration has drawn together diverse viewpoints [22] to support goals such as songwriting [5], animation [17] and remixing [10]. Storytelling, too, can be collaborative: if the author's role is to provide an authentic emotional experience for their story's audience [19], then the diverse perspectives and expertise of the crowd could support an author's search for the perfect character, setting, or plot.

Though the Web has produced the great collaborative encyclopedia, it has not yet been able to produce a collaborative novel of similar scale and impact. Peer production often splits collaborative work into independent, discrete parts, but stories are not so easily untangled. Unstructured attempts at collaborative creative writing, such as the experimental wikinovel A Million Penguins [18], resulted in rampant vandalism and uncertainty about the direction the story should pursue. On the other hand, highly structured approaches, such as sentence-level round-robin writing in FoldingStory [29], constrained participant contributions and resulted in patchwork, incoherent stories. In other words, while constraints may allow a story to follow a consistent creative trajectory, too many restrictions may prevent collaboration at the level of an overall plot.

In this paper, we explore the potential of *structuring collaborative roles to reflect the complementary creative strengths of the crowd and the individual.* Many successful storytelling collaborations already separate creative leadership from more general participation [15]. In television screenwriting, for example, collaborating writers do not create a script in piecemeal and glue together the pieces at the end; instead, a leader and supporting writers each take on complementary creative powers and responsibilities [30]. By adapting these strategies for the Web, we may enable the creation of stories that draw on the unique experiences of hundreds of people.

Based on these patterns, we propose a model for collaborative storytelling where a leader maintains the high-level vision and articulates creative constraints for the crowd, while the crowd generates text and contributions within those constraints. We embody this idea in a collaborative writing system called *Ensemble*[1] (Figure 1).

Lone writers view the writing process as solving a series of rhetorical problems [8]; similarly, in Ensemble, a lead author can use *prompts* to guide overall creative direction and focus collaborative work around provided goals. For example, a leader may create a prompt that asks contributors to write a short amount of text that describes how two characters meet. Collaborators can write text for any prompt, as well as vote or comment on text contributed by others. By explicitly assigning the responsibility of maintaining creative direction to a leader, collaborators can concentrate on creating contributions beneficial to the creative work.

CSCW'14, February 15–19, 2014, Baltimore, Maryland, USA.

ACM 978-1-4503-2540-0/14/02...$15.00.
http://dx.doi.org/10.1145/2531602.2531638

[1] http://ensemble.stanford.edu

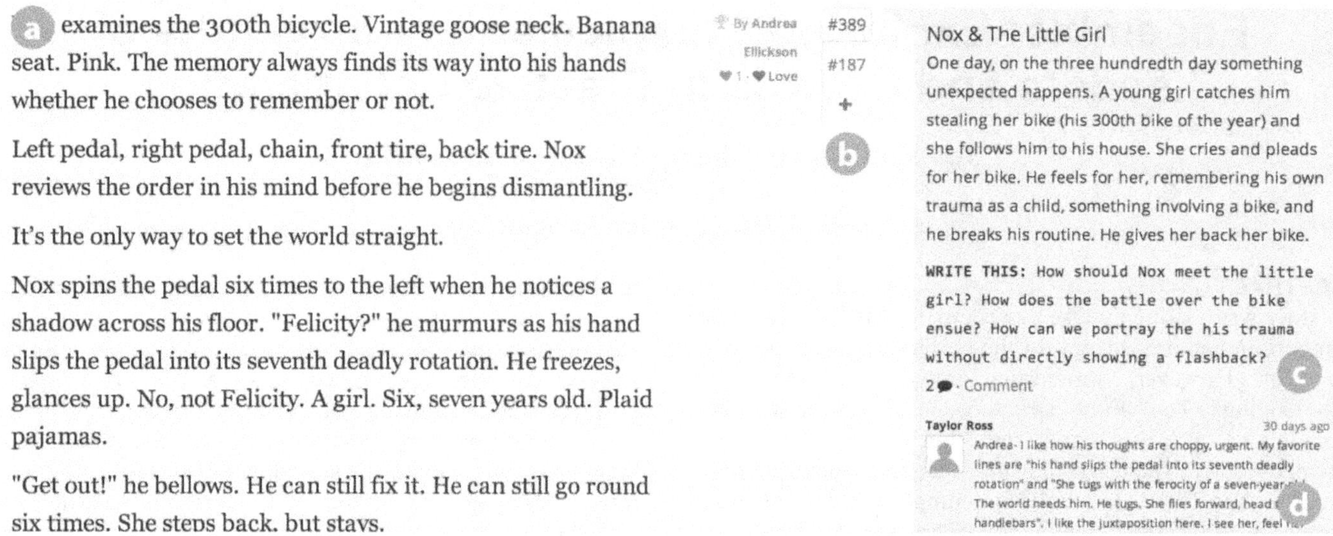

Figure 1. A story scene showing (a) the winning draft for a scene. (b) Tabs can be used to switch to different drafts, with the winning draft being shown by default. (c) The scene prompt helps focus contributors on specific writing goals. (d) Contributors can make comments discussing the scene at a high level.

In an initial small-scale public deployment via a month-long short story competition, over one hundred volunteer writers started over fifty short stories using Ensemble. Through analysis of user activity and interviews with competition participants, we observed that both leaders and collaborators used leader-created constraints to coordinate work and explore the space of ideas for a story, with leaders even using rejected collaborator contributions to look at the story from different perspectives. Furthermore, leaders and collaborators had complementary motivations for collaboration; while leaders sought feedback, collaborators viewed their expertise as valuable input useful for leaders. Ensemble focuses specifically on writing short stories, but by framing writing as a form of problem solving, its model may apply to many modes of creative collaboration including journalism, film, and animation. In this paper, we focus on observing in a realistic context *how* leaders and collaborators work together to complete stories; the question of whether this approach results in *better* stories is left as future work.

RELATED WORK

This paper distinguishes between *creative collaboration* and other instances of peer production. Here, creative collaboration aims to produce pieces of art such as film, music, and stories that may not have predetermined goals. A Wikipedia page, for example, has implicit but commonly understood goals that guide contributor work: contributors understand that a Wikipedia page about apples should present information about apples in a holistic way expected from an encyclopedia. However, the goals of story writing are less clear because creators must come up with their own constraints.

Writing as a cognitive process

Most previous writing process research is done in the context of pedagogy, but understanding the writing process also has implications for the design of writing tools. Early research challenged the traditional model of teaching writing as linear, irreversible stages that moved from prewriting to writing to revision [23]. However, more recent models suggest that skilled writers create and continually revise goals to develop purpose for the work overall [8]. Ensemble adopts this more recent perspective as a theoretical base for its design, framing collaborative work around rhetorical problems defined by a leader and making it possible for writing work to progress in a non-linear, evolutionary fashion.

Collaborative creativity

Effective strategies for creative collaboration exist in many offline contexts such as television screenwriting or execution of stage plays. A primary inspiration for Ensemble is the storytelling system seen in role-playing games [31]. In many role-playing games, a single player acts as the narrator while the remaining players take on the roles of characters interacting with the world laid out by the narrator. Despite the presence of a power imbalance where the narrator ultimately decides what happens, all the players contribute ideas to the progression of the story by working within constraints agreed upon by the group (i.e., what their characters would do in the situations presented by the narrator). Luther *et al.* [16] examined how this strategy of separating a leader's role from general collaborative work is used in online animation collaborations and observed a similar distribution of power. In Ensemble, we generalize this idea of working together within agreed-upon creative constraints and apply it as a general strategy for collaborative writing.

There have been many successes in mobilizing strangers to complete complex creative projects in non-writing domains. Aaron Koblin created a number of projects where the crowd contributes to interactive artwork using a predefined

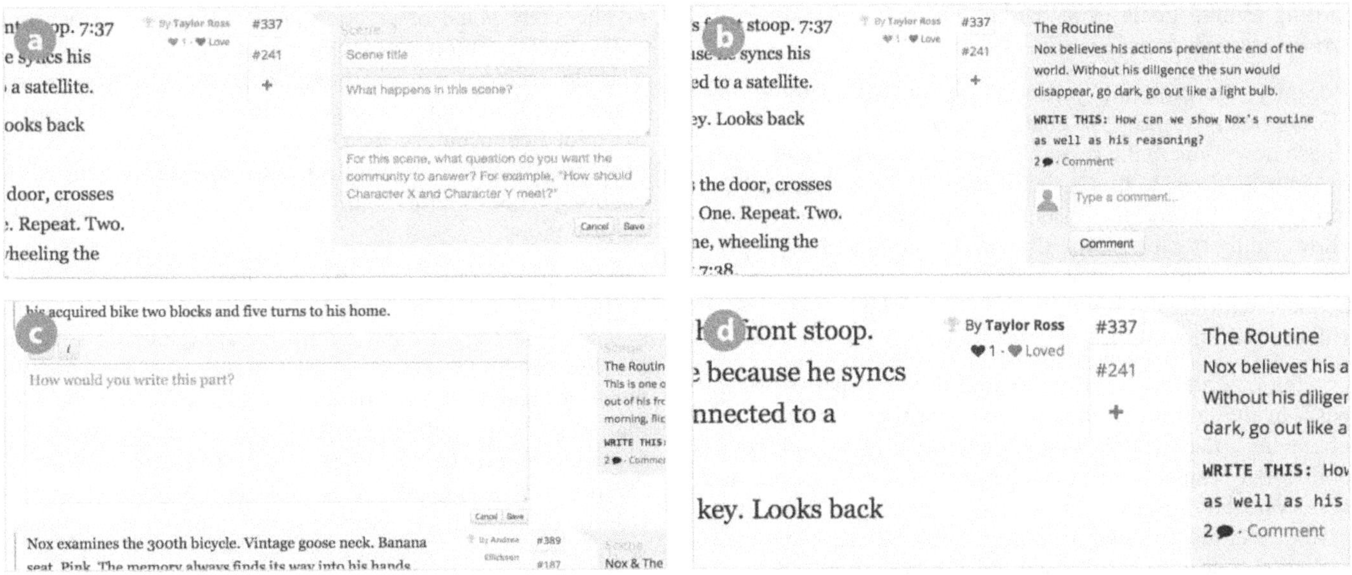

Figure 2. The collaboration process between lead authors and contributors on Ensemble. (a) The author creates a scene with a prompt to ask for specific help on a section of the story. (b) Contributors can make comments discussing the scene and possible solutions for the prompt. (c) Contributors can also submit alternative versions of the scene as solutions for the prompt. (d) Contributors can vote for alternatives they like. The author can declare a winning solution.

structure. In the Johnny Cash Project [32], for example, contributors redraw frames from a provided music video which are compiled into a redrawn version of the video. In this case, Koblin determined the project's goals and vision before opening the project up to others; participants were not involved in the formation of the idea behind the project itself but needed only to execute the piece of work they volunteered for. While the visible uniqueness of frames in a crowdsourced video may be desired in the Johnny Cash project, a story needs a cohesive narrative arc to be understood. By structuring contributor work around high-level goals to achieve rather than low-level instructions to follow, Ensemble allows contributors the space to contribute in a way that complements work done by others.

Collaborative writing on the web

Communities surrounding the creation of fan fiction and forum-based role-playing games which attest to online writers' desires to build off of existing work, share their own work, and seek the help of others for ideas and feedback. However, existing collaborative storytelling platforms online tend to be simply implementations of round-robin storytelling games [29,33]. Ensemble, in contrast, attempts to support a larger part of the story writing process, including idea generation, revision, and discussion with others.

Our work builds on previous tools for collaborative writing online [7,21] by extending previous work's findings concerning task-based writing to creative writing. People tend to divide collaborative writing work by identifying sections of text that are independent from each other, and then working in parallel on a single document or writing in turn [12]. This behavior often occurs through document exchange over email or through a shared workspace such as Google Docs or a wiki. However, when collaborators all manipulate a common product, the potential for conflict and need for coordination grow [13]. In contrast to non-fiction collaborative products such as Wikipedia articles or academic papers [26], a story is not a modular presentation of ideas but a multi-layered work consisting of interdependent characters, plot elements, and settings; it is extremely difficult to divide the work of story writing into independent, parallel pieces. Furthermore, creative works measure success in terms of emotional engagement of readers and viewers [19] rather than through objective metrics people can individually assess and agree on (such as whether a piece of open-source software "works"). To manage coordination and monitor progress towards creative goals, Ensemble uses an explicitly appointed creative leader.

Hypermedia approaches, where stories are built up using links or through branching paths rather than linearly, can allow groups to exchange new ideas; in the case of groups of young children [11,24], this strategy can assist in social and emotional development. Liu *et al.* [14] compared how elementary school children create a picture book with their peers when using a branching story editing system and when using a linear story editing system. Students who used the branching story editing system reported a higher sense of appreciation for their peers' contributions and a higher sense of authorship over the stories they contributed to. However, while a branching editing system leaves previous content intact, creates a stronger sense of ownership over work, and prevents creative conflict, it leaves unclear how one would build a cohesive, finished story out of all the generated options. In contrast, Ensemble structures story writing around goals from the beginning in order to direct writers towards creating a final story.

Recently, the blogging platform Medium added tools that allow readers to propose changes to an author's post [34]. These new tools make it easy for others to propose changes or contributions to the original blog post written by an individual. Unlike in Ensemble, this platform does not allow authors to explicitly direct collaborator work; however, it indicates that enabling an online audience to connect with creators over ideas is viewed as a potentially valuable addition to the creative process.

For the exploratory study presented in this paper, we echo past evaluations of collaborative writing [1] by first observing the collaborative behavior of small non-collocated teams rather than large crowds. However, we focus on studying whether we can enable a certain outcome given a new collaborative *approach* rather than new technology designed to support existing behavior.

ENSEMBLE

Ensemble supports creative writing collaboration by empowering a *lead author* to guide overall creative direction, while recruiting the crowd to focus on specific writing tasks. In this section, we introduce Ensemble and its techniques for structuring asymmetric collaboration.

Scenario

Kim, a writer, has an idea for a short story. She drafts the introduction and the general framing text for the story, then posts the incomplete draft on Ensemble. Kim isn't sure how to manage some of the character encounters in the plot, so she creates *scenes* with prompts for incomplete sections, indicating that she wants feedback or even alternative rewrites to improve what she already has (Figure 2a). She posts a link to the incomplete story to her favorite writing community, hoping to attract a few contributors.

A while later, one of these prompts catches Laura's eye as she is skimming through Kim's story. She adds a quick comment with an idea for one of the scenes (Figure 2b). Miles, another Ensemble user, builds on Kim's idea by writing an alternate telling of that scene. He submits the draft text as an alternative for Kim's original (Figure 2c). Other visitors find Miles's contribution interesting, and it receives several upvotes (Figure 2d).

Having received email notifications about the new additions, Kim returns to Ensemble and looks at the newly-added contributions. She particularly likes Miles's, and marks it as a winner so that it appears by default for that scene in the story. She looks at the additions made to other parts of the story, marking some contributions as winners for a few of the scenes, and building on the ideas to write her own alternatives for others.

Contributions with constraints

The scenario above exemplifies Ensemble's approach to creative collaboration: rather than placing all participants on the same plane of creative power, Ensemble structures online collaboration by putting a crowd of *contributors* and a single *lead author* in charge of different aspects of a story. Where the lead author is responsible for the overall creative direction, contributors focus work around leader-provided prompts. The aim is to keep the story coherent while enabling contributors to make meaningful creative contributions.

Lead authors frame contributions using scenes

Rather than allowing contributors to edit any part of the story, *scenes* direct contributors towards specific sections the lead author has chosen. In Ensemble, scenes are the basic collaborative unit of each story, reflecting the idea that a scene roughly corresponds to a turning point that reveals character development, new information, and a goal for the next scene [19]. Ensemble scenes consist of raw story text, as well as a short description and a short prompt written by the lead author. Scenes help the lead author coordinate with contributors on the intended vision for the story by providing both an outline of a story's overall frame and direction towards specific tasks to complete.

As Kim did in the scenario above, a lead author can convert any section of the story into a scene by writing a description or prompt (Figure 1c). *Prompts* allow the lead author to suggest problems that need to be solved within the bounds of the scene (e.g., "I need Character X to meet Character Y. How do they meet?"). A story may have as many or as little scenes as the lead author likes, and a scene can only have one prompt at a time. Prompts do not need to be created in any particular order — leaders may choose to create a prompt for the end of the story, then later create a separate prompt for the beginning of the story, and still later delete or modify already existing prompts. Lead authors have the flexibility to direct collaborator work to any part of the text according to the story's changing needs.

By localizing contributor participation, scenes allow contributors to focus on small sections of the story at a time [2]. In addition, descriptions of other scenes can help contributors better frame their contributions in the context of the overall story. Finally, scenes provide a quick way for contributors to identify the contribution opportunities a story contains.

Contributors participate via drafts, comments and votes

Ensemble allows for different levels of contributor involvement, an important consideration in designing successful peer production systems [3]. While contributors primarily participate in a story by writing alternative paragraphs, or *drafts* (Figure 1a), for a scene, they can also comment on scenes or vote on drafts that they like. Authors and contributors can use scene *comments* (Figure 1d) to discuss specific scenes, or discuss more general topics in a discussion forum specific to that story.

Each scene can thus have multiple drafts written by many contributors, each representing a different interpretation of that scene (Figure 1b). In editing interfaces like wikis or Google Docs where the goal is a single final version of the text, conflicts can arise through others unilaterally editing that text, which discourages further contribution [4,9]. We minimize conflict in Ensemble by asking collaborators to submit draft alternatives instead of directly editing each other's work. Collaborators receive credit for the drafts they write, supporting ownership and potentially reducing social loafing [25].

The most highly-voted draft for each scene is shown by default as part of the story, with the other drafts accessible through the use of scene-specific tabs (Figure 1b). Although contributors can communicate their vision for a story by voting for drafts, the lead author ultimately maintains creative control by choosing a winning draft for each scene. These winning contributions become part of the story text, signaling that they are aligned with the lead author's overall vision. Alternatively, the lead author can simply take inspiration from the contributed drafts and write their own.

For stories with many contributors, lead authors can optionally appoint *moderators* who can edit scene descriptions, prompts, others' drafts, and also mark drafts as winners, supporting the distribution of leadership [16].

Through these feedback channels of contributed drafts, voting, and comments, a lead author can work with contributors to continuously refine their creative vision and revise a story's text. Ensemble leverages the crowd for creativity and diversity by constraining and specifying the nature of contributions, and maintains narrative flow by granting creative control to a single author.

Limitations
Ensemble was primarily designed for an unequal power distribution, which is advantageous when there is high variance in contributor quality or motivation; alternative approaches may better suit scenarios where equitable contribution is desirable. Furthermore, because a lead author dictates the creative direction of the story, especially prolific contributors may find it difficult to make suggestions or changes beyond the bounds of a scene.

EVALUATION
Ensemble embodies the design hypothesis that the crowd can support the creative process for an author. In this section, we report on an evaluation of Ensemble that explored how users adopted Ensemble's division of creative responsibility to create short stories.

Method
We evaluated Ensemble through a public short story writing competition where teams of users were invited to write stories using the platform. Because we wanted users to behave as naturally as possible, we framed our study around a real competition so that users would focus on writing a good story rather than on the system itself. Rather than doing a controlled comparative study framed around story quality, our aim was to determine how teams would adapt to the asymmetric structure of Ensemble and whether Ensemble allowed teams to write coherent stories. This approach allowed us to trace the ramifications of Ensemble's design on collaborative writing patterns.

The writing prompt provided to users was the following:

> There are over 15,000 bikes used by students, staff, and faculty to get around campus. Over 300 bikes are stolen each year. Where do they go?

Teams were allowed to interpret the prompt in broad and unexpected ways, and stories were limited to 1,000 words. The prizes for the competition were $500 in Amazon.com gift cards to be split among the team and publication in a major arts review publication on campus. The editor-in-chief of the arts review publication selected the grand prize and runner-up winners.

We advertised the writing challenge to several writing communities on the web, including FanFiction.net, FictionPress, and Reddit's writing communities. We also solicited a few well-known writing blogs to advertise the competition. Lastly, on-campus student arts publications and creative writing classes promoted the competition.

During the competition, Ensemble logged all participant activity, including the creation of stories, scenes, and drafts. After the competition, we emailed a survey to all Ensemble users asking for their motivations for starting stories, contributing to stories, and editing work written by others. We also asked how their experiences writing collaborative stories on other platforms compared with their experience using Ensemble.

We conducted semi-structured interviews with the seven of the most active Ensemble users (five male, two female). These participants were between the ages of 19 and 32, and most were amateur writers; their jobs ranged from student to manufacturing manager to humor columnist. We focused the interviews on how they used and adapted Ensemble to their story writing process, whether or not they perceived personal benefits of the platform on themselves as a writer, power dynamics between the head and supporting author, attitudes toward the resulting stories they participated in, and whether or not they would use Ensemble to work with others on stories again. Two interviews were conducted via Skype voice call, and five interviews were conducted via chat.

We then consolidated interview and survey responses and analyzed them according to the following predetermined themes framed by our research questions: prior experiences with collaboration on story writing, contributor activity and motivation, lead author activity and motivation, the interaction between contributors and leaders, organization of team workflow, system design feedback, and participant perceptions of the resulting story and their experiences using Ensemble. The themes that emerged from responses allowed us to form the following initial inferences about the

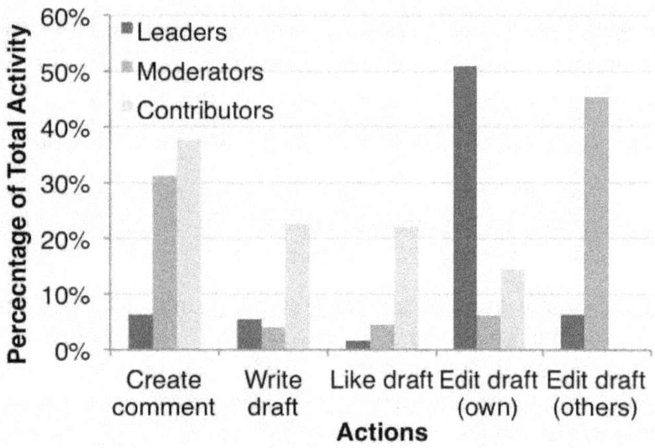

Figure 3. Percentage of total activity across Ensemble, by user role. Users in different roles contributed to stories in different ways.

relationship between leaders and their collaborators in online creative collaborations.

Results

The stories submitted to the short story competition displayed collaborative effort while demonstrating both coherency and creativity. Figure 1 shows one such story — this particular story was one of the runner-up winners of the competition. The team behind this story made liberal use of prompts and comments to frame the type of feedback they gave on each other's work.

During the competition, 106 total users started 55 Ensemble stories, and 20 of these stories were submitted as entries into the competition by a total of 52 users. Over the course of the competition, 1067 unique visitors made a total of 2081 visits to the site (12165 pageviews), with stories receiving a median of 37.5 pageviews.

Visitors came from over 45 different countries, with most visitors coming from the USA (1376 visits), India (285 visits), and Canada (123 visits). Users made, in aggregate, a median of 552 comments, drafts, edits, and likes per day, with the most activity happening the day of the competition deadline (10848 actions).

Equal work despite asymmetric roles

Among the 20 submitted stories, there was a median of two members per story team, with only two stories by single authors. Team sizes ranged from one to seven people. We counted the number of comments, drafts, and edits to drafts made by each team member involved in a story and used the Gini coefficient of inequality to quantify the distribution of work across these users. The Gini coefficient ranges from 0 (work was done equally by everyone involved) to 1 (a single contributor did all of the work). The mean Gini coefficient across the 20 stories submitted to the competition was 0.286 (SD = 0.194), meaning that despite the asymmetric division of creative *responsibility* in Ensemble, the spread of work *quantity* was fairly balanced. That is, both story leaders and contributors contributed fairly equal amounts of work, but in different ways. We describe this division of labor next.

Lead authors maintained creative authority

Lead authors worked to maintain creative ownership over the story, often by managing privileges and permissions. In Ensemble, anyone can participate in a story as a *contributor* (only able to comment and write alternatives for scene prompts), and lead authors can designate some users as *moderators* (able to edit anybody's work). Of the 34 stories that had multiple team members, 25 stories had teams with a leader and contributors only: that is, only the leader was able to directly edit the work done by others. The remaining nine stories had all-moderator teams, where all members had the power to edit work by anybody else. There were no teams with a mix of contributors and moderators, perhaps due to small team sizes.

50% of lead authors' activity was spent revising drafts they wrote themselves (Figure 3). In practice, this means they manually integrated ideas from others' contributions, rather than directly including contributions as written. Lead authors would interpret the contributed draft for the high-level idea being suggested by the contributor, then manually tweak their existing work while keeping the suggestion in mind:

> *Participant 3: for the one that another person submitted for the story i submitted, i didn't end up using [their contribution], but it helped me pinpoint things that i liked and didn't like in both my version and theirs.*

Interestingly, moderators did not add many new drafts to the story even though they had the power to do so: instead, they directly edited drafts created by the lead author, with this making up 45% of their activity on Ensemble (Figure 3). Moderators reported making edits mainly for the purpose of fixing typos, grammatical errors, and adjusting sentence structure, engaging in behavior similar to wiki-gardening [28].

Though they tended to reserve creative control for themselves, lead authors went through pains to portray themselves as benevolent dictators. Instead of simply accepting or rejecting contributions, lead authors would use comments to express their rationale and give the contributor the chance to respond:

> *Participant 1: Actually she did make quite a few changes at one point, but at that point in the story I had already plotted it out... And I let her know in the comments that, 'Look, I like the suggestions, but at this point I kind of know what I'm doing with the prose, so I would rather get suggestions with the plot elements, character motivations, things like that.'*

Prompts reflected the variety of issues leaders thought about during the high-level writing process. Two researchers independently coded all prompts according to

Prompt Type	Count	Percentage
Story problems	29	32%
Outline	25	28%
Writing problems	11	12%
Request for review	11	12%
Placeholder	7	8%
Call for ideas	6	7%
Commentary	1	1%

Table 1. The types of prompts created by lead authors.

the categories in Table 1, and disagreements were resolved through discussion. We ignored 41 prompts that either had not been changed from the default text or were spam.

We found that 32% of all prompts created presented story-related problems that needed to be solved ("Is this the first time the bully and the main character have met?" or "When do Dean and Melanie let the others know the truth?"). 12% of prompts asked about writing technique or stylistic decisions ("How thorough should the descriptions of the character's research be?" or "Is the ending too ambiguous?"). A smaller percentage of prompts called for brainstorming of ideas, sometimes while giving broad constraints ("Some kind of snappy ending here." or "Any suggestions?"), or asked readers to review the written text ("Is there a certain imagery invoked when reading?" or "Does it sound alright?"). 28% of prompts did not present questions at all, and instead acted as points in an outline representing the overall story structure ("In which our protagonist borrows something of ours." or "Intro! The first clue is found, and our narrator is intrigued."). 8% of prompts simply marked the existence of a scene, but did not contain meaningful information about the type of scene the author was envisioning ("Bike #1"). One prompt was not related to collaboration, but rather served as a comment on the author's creative choice for a scene ("yay for jokes"). In other words, prompts reflected how story writing goals ranged from very specific to very broad at different points in the story at different times.

Contributors offered high-level ideas through low-level work

Unsurprisingly, creating comments and drafts made up 60% of contributor activity on Ensemble (Figure 3). Limiting contributors to these actions resulted in collaborative work that was directed and detailed, facilitating discussion between leader authors and their collaborators. Furthermore, because new drafts never overwrote work written by others, contributors felt free to express ideas.

Contributor efforts were directed by scenes. Contributors used scenes provided by the leader to make comments and write story text. The number of comments per story ranged widely, with some stories getting as many as 33 comments. Out of the 20 submitted stories, the median number of comments was 5.5 (Q1 = 1.75, Q3 = 14). There was no correlation between comment count and team size (Pearson's $r(18) = 0.268$, $p = 0.2537$). Comment areas essentially served as localized discussion boards surrounding individual scenes, and served three main purposes in Ensemble stories. First, contributors would make comments directly answering the prompts posed by lead authors in scene descriptions. Second, contributors would make unsolicited comments concerning grammar, sentence structure, and other technical issues within the scene, as opposed to unsolicited ideas for plot and character. Lastly, in the case of moderators, comments served as a place to notify others about direct changes that had been made to drafts for that scene (e.g., "I just edited the opening paragraph").

Because they created drafts in the context of scenes rather than the story as a whole, contributors felt that they were able to make focused and substantial contributions to the story. Drafts were not so small as to feel incremental, as with the sentence-sized contributions one would make in a round-robin game such as FoldingStory; neither were they so big as to be daunting, as with a single document shared by all team members.

> *Participant 3: it still was really rewarding... because the way the website's set up helps that whole first draft, peer critiques, second draft process go smoothly and in little, manageable sections.*

Scene descriptions acted as planning notes that kept track of overall story composition so that contributors did not have to. By structuring the story into scenes, contributors were able to focus on local creative issues without worrying about how their work would affect the story as a whole.

Contributors used drafts to safely share ideas. Users wrote an average of 1.2 drafts per scene (SD = 0.48). Without the ability to edit work by others, contributors used drafts (Figure 4) for two separate purposes. First, contributors would copy and paste existing drafts, make desired changes, then save the revised text as a new draft. Second, contributors and leaders alike would use drafts as a form of version control, creating drafts as true alternatives for writing a particular scene. Users viewed these alternative drafts as a safe way to show rather than describe ideas without changing existing work:

> *Participant 6: It's harder to describe what you want to do than just do it. So you could do it and have them look at it and say, that's what I was intending, [instead of them saying] I think we should go here, and I think that's maybe what should happen, and then they start criticizing their picture of what it is rather than your picture, because it's impossible to talk around it.*

In other words, drafts were used as a way to clearly communicate ideas among team members rather than as a way to merge work written by multiple people. This fork-

and-merge behavior was unexpected; future versions of Ensemble could help leaders explicit give credit where due when merging ideas into the story's text.

Prior relationships affected creative process

An unexpected difference in collaboration workflows emerged depending on whether or not the lead author knew contributors previously. Through interviews, we asked participants whether they knew their teammates prior to collaborating with them. We later sent out a survey to gather this information from authors we did not interview. Out of the 20 submitted stories, seven stories were written by teams made up of friends, four stories were written by teams made up of strangers, and two stories were written by single authors. For the remaining seven submitted stories, we were unable to gather information about the relationships among team members from the authors involved. Though we cannot quantitatively test this difference through the current study, we present observed trends regarding this difference.

Friends preferred an equal division of power. Teams that knew each other seemed to prefer a balanced power dynamic. In these cases, the entire team was often made moderators so that they could freely edit text written by anyone else; team members sometimes saw restrictions on editing ability as frustrating. Scene descriptions acted as notes from an earlier story planning session, usually carried out by the team in real-time over phone, email, or in person. The lead author would then create an outline for the story using Ensemble scenes based on the planning session. Team members would assign themselves to scenes, after which the team would begin loops of feedback and iteration.

Though this type of dynamic was not the core design scenario for Ensemble, participants explained that the system facilitated collaboration in a way that wikis and Google docs could not; scene descriptions provided a structure that aided in completing the collaboration. As one participant said, "*It was kind of nice just to have an explicit place to work on collaborative stories. I wouldn't have gone and emailed [my partners] and said, 'Hey, want to start a Google Doc and write a collaborative story?*" (Participant 6)

Lead authors preferred creative authority over strangers. In teams made up of strangers, lead authors often took on a much more central and active role during story writing. After outlining a new story through scene descriptions and skeleton paragraphs, the lead author would then leave the door open for input before returning to the story. Surprisingly, contributions made by strangers, in part because of how out of sync they sometimes were with the leader's vision, ended up being serendipitous and influential in guiding a story to its finished state. As an example, one lead author reported that a contributor wrote a draft about how the bikes in the story could talk — an idea he had not considered, but eventually chose to include as a central element in the story. Leaders viewed limiting the direct editing ability of collaborators as desirable, and felt that alternative drafts were sufficient for enabling collaborators' creativity.

Quality of submitted stories

Though this study focused on the relationship between leaders and collaborators, we wanted to conduct a preliminary investigation into whether or not Ensemble's collaboration strategy demonstrated an effect on creative outcomes. Did Ensemble's leader-directed collaboration strategy at least not worsen creative outcomes?

Two researchers independently rated the 20 submitted stories based on creativity, flow, and technical merit based on 7-point Likert scales, where 1 was worst and 7 was best for each category. Highly divergent ratings were discussed and re-scored by the researchers. The final rating for each story was the sum of the points linearly converted to a 1 to 7 scale to represent overall quality. The measured weighted Cohen's Kappa (squared weights) for the ratings by the two raters was 0.8, indicating substantial agreement.

Though we would need a controlled experiment to determine whether these factors truly affect story quality, it seems that for this initial study there is no relationship between quality and how work was split (Gini coefficient) amongst team members (Pearson's $r(18) = 0.385$, $p = 0.093$) or the number of collaborators per story (Pearson's $r(18) = 0.069$, $p = 0.7715$).

From the perspective of the competition participants, the written stories seemed to be of adequate quality. All seven interviewees expressed satisfaction with the story they had participated in, with some of the interviewees further stating that they had read through a few stories by other teams and "liked what they saw".

Expectations for collaboration

Lead authors and contributors had complementary motivations for participating in Ensemble stories. When asked what they had expected from collaboration through Ensemble, lead authors overwhelmingly cited that they hoped for outside perspectives on their work. Notably,

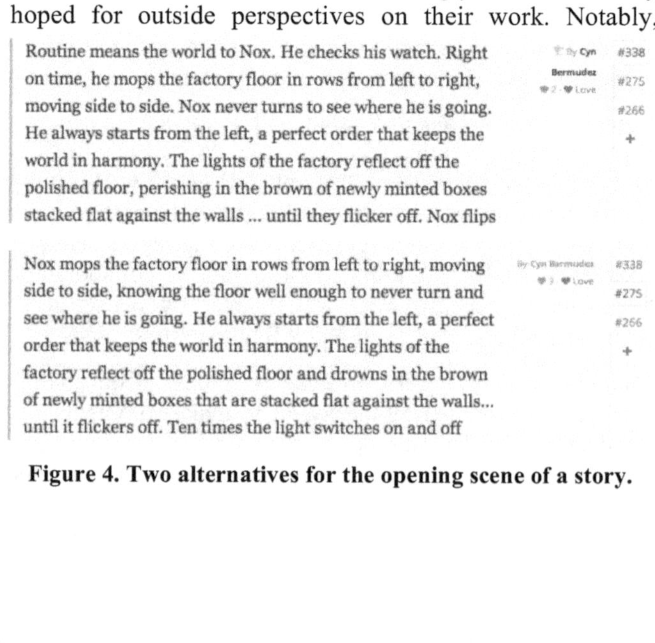

Figure 4. Two alternatives for the opening scene of a story.

contributors reported that they *wanted* to give input to others' work, describing the collaboration process as a way to hone their feedback skills as a method for improving their own writing. In turn, leaders felt more motivated to actively work on their stories because others were paying attention to their work.

Overall, the asymmetric structure of Ensemble did not just sync the complementary creative strengths of leaders and more general collaborators; it also revealed complementary motivations that served to spur work from both sides.

DISCUSSION

Through Ensemble, lead authors were able to successfully direct contributors' work through the use of scene descriptions and specific prompts, and contributors were able to offer high-level ideas by writing drafts and comments within provided constraints. Contributors did not feel creatively restricted, and the stories that were written were coherent and readable by non-writer audiences. In this section, we discuss what we might see in a large-scale deployment of Ensemble and propose a framework for collaboration by division of creative responsibility.

Scale

Many people participated in the story competition, but most stories had a small number of contributors. Likewise, in many crowdsourcing systems such as open-source software, a small number of dedicated contributors do most of the work [20]. What would happen if an Ensemble story had tens or hundreds of contributors?

As we saw in Ensemble, lead authors often take it upon themselves to manually integrate contributions done made by others when producing a collaborative work. However, coordinating creative work can overburden the leader [16], especially as the *number of contributors increases*. In Ensemble, collaborative writing was effective when the story leader was able to concentrate on their role of providing creative direction for the story. Introducing a leadership hierarchy could help lead authors integrate a large number of contributions.

In this study, teams wrote short stories. As *length of a creative work* increases, it may become harder for collaborators to contribute meaningfully. Changing details about a character or setting in one section, for example, may invalidate earlier or later parts of the story. As another example, contributors may need to take the time to become familiar with what has been written so far to even be in a position to add new content. However, this may reveal other opportunities to utilize the strength of the crowd; much like in Wikipedia [27], the crowd may be able to quickly and accurately identify inconsistencies in the story as they appear, or even manually maintain summaries of story sections through scene descriptions.

Designing power balance

Lead authors were bottlenecks for the writing process. While contributors were able to contribute to prompts that already existed, they had to request additional scenes or structural changes through comments and wait for the leader to act on their requests.

What does this imply for whether Ensemble's design strikes the right balance between lead authors and contributors? Ensemble may be able to borrow from the theory of distributed leadership [16] and shift more organizational power to contributors. For example, Ensemble could structure collaboration similarly to open source software engineering, where contributors first identify their *own* problems to solve before submitting their work for acceptance into the main project. However, this may introduce more contention over the direction of the story and further increase what the lead author must moderate. Moreover, lead authors in our study valued having strong control over the story; giving too much power to contributors may cause lead authors to feel threatened.

Framework for dividing creative responsibility

In Ensemble, lead authors controlled creative direction and merged work, moderators made detailed edits to work already present, and contributors generated ideas by contributing paragraphs. Table 2 maps how the major creative behaviors seen in Ensemble are split among different roles in other online collaborative systems. In this first attempt at mapping the space for designing collaboration systems around creative roles, we can see that there are unexplored combinations that may generate further insight into where leaders, moderators, and crowds best fit in the creative process. One possible direction for further research is to examine the types of collaborative work these unexplored combinations best support. For example, a collaboration structure where the crowd is in charge of providing story goals and an individual is in charge of merging together input from the crowd through detailed writing and editing may result in different kinds of stories than the ones created through Ensemble.

This design space may be extended to include new roles and thus generate new ideas for collaborative processes. One might imagine adding rows for the support roles discussed earlier, including "filter out spam or off-topic

Task	Folding Story	A Million Penguins	Pipeline [16]	Ensemble
Providing goals	–	–	Leader/ Mods	Leader
Merging work	Crowd	Crowd	Leader/ Mods	Leader
Generating ideas	Crowd	Crowd	Crowd	Crowd
Detailed edits	–	Crowd	Crowd	Leader/ Mods
Doing work	Crowd	Crowd	Crowd	Crowd

Table 2. A selection of online creative collaboration systems and how each system splits creative work.

contributions". A possible collaboration system, then, could center around a story fully generated by the crowd, with a leader simply pruning contributions as they come in to keep the story following a single creative direction. Another possible collaboration system could take advantage of the fact Ensemble enables alternative drafts for each scene in a story to create a story (or several stories) that branch in several possible directions. A "navigator" support role could help readers find story paths that make sense.

Future research could also examine how the motivations of users to participate in collaborative work changes as they fulfill different types of roles. What combinations of roles are most effective at encouraging people to take part in massively participatory stories? In Ensemble, leaders were in charge of providing creative direction, and were motivated to take part in collaboration because they felt perspectives from others would benefit the writing of a story they owned. If the leader was instead responsible for generating high-level ideas according to direction provided by the crowd, they might instead view collaboration as a helpful creative exercise. How might responsibility change users' perception of the benefits and expectations of collaboration?

Limitations

The study in this paper was not controlled; we did not compare Ensemble and other collaborative story writing platforms through metrics such as writing quality and time to completion. While we were able to provide insight on the nature of asymmetric collaboration, we cannot claim anything about the quality the stories that emerged out of collaboration. We leave this as future work: some possibilities for measures of quality may be ratings by writing experts, comparative analysis of lexical quality of Ensemble stories, or measures of reader engagement.

Another limitation is that our user evaluation was framed around a competition. It is unclear to what extent the competition affected users' motivations for using Ensemble. Participants described round-robin storytelling games such as FoldingStory as frameworks for supporting play, but tended to describe Ensemble as a platform with the potential to support production of serious stories or to support peer learning. It may be the case that the presence of a competition prompt and a deadline impacts users' perceptions of whether a collaborative storytelling platform is for creative play or for creative work.

CONCLUSION & FUTURE WORK

In this paper, we explored the complementary creative strengths of the crowd and an individual by framing collaborative creativity as a process where collaborator activity can be guided by leader-generated constraints. Ensemble enabled small teams of both strangers and friends to collectively write short stories by channeling the complementary creative strengths of the crowd and the individual. In a creative writing competition, leaders directed collaborator work by establishing creative goals while collaborators assisted leaders in exploring the space of ideas for a story. Collaborators did not feel creatively restricted by a lack of edit privileges and were able to contribute meaningful, high-level ideas to the story through detailed contributions. Furthermore, leaders and collaborators encouraged work from each other through complementary motivations for collaboration; leaders sought feedback from collaborators, and collaborators felt their input would be valuable to leaders.

In future work, we would like to see if Ensemble's asymmetric strategy results in similar behavior at large scale. Much like Neil Gaiman mobilized his fans to help write A Calendar of Tales [35], we envision a system that enables authors to engage their tens of thousands of fans or fellow writers in a collective creative endeavor, using participation as the medium through which story, creator and audience experience each other.

We plan to explore this dynamic through a larger scale story called Arrowhead. Tom Kealey, a lecturer in the creative writing department at Stanford University, and Chris Baty, the founder of NaNoWriMo (National Novel Writing Month), will take turns using Ensemble to write chapters of the story, using scenes and prompts to gather contributions from the NaNoWriMo community after each chapter. This may reveal to what extent the crowd can help support authors who already have significant writing experience compared to the amateur writers that participated in our earlier evaluation; at the same time, working with such well-established authors may result in a story where the crowd becomes more of a vocal audience rather than a deeply involved group of participants.

We would also like to explore how Ensemble's asymmetric creative strategy can be applied to mediums and contexts beyond creative writing. Could we, for example, crowdsource a painting that doesn't look crowdsourced, or create collaboratively authored newspapers? Does Ensemble have the potential to enable new ways of teaching writing in K–12 schools? The Web is a rich space for sharing experiences through many media, not just through writing; through the right collaborative strategies, we can further empower its creative potential.

ACKNOWLEDGMENTS

We would like to thank the Stanford Arts Review and the Stanford Creative Writing Department for helping make the Ensemble Story Slam possible, as well as everyone who participated in the competition and interviews. We also thank Tom Kealey, Chris Baty, and the NaNoWriMo community. This project was supported by the Brown Institute Magic Grant.

REFERENCES

1. Baecker, R.M., Nastos, D., Posner, I.R., and Mawby, K.L. The user-centered iterative design of collaborative writing software. In *Proc. CHI* (1993).

2. Beenen, G., Ling, K., Wang, X., et al. Using social psychology to motivate contributions to online communities. In *Proc. CSCW* (2004).
3. Benkler, Y. *The wealth of networks: How social production transforms markets and freedom*. 2006.
4. Birnholtz, J. and Ibara, S. Tracking changes in collaborative writing: edits, visibility and group maintenance. In *Proc. CSCW* (2012).
5. Burke, M. and Settles, B. Plugged in to the community: Social motivators in online goal-setting groups. In *Proc. ICCT* (2011).
6. Cranshaw, J. and Kittur, A. The polymath project. In *Proc. CHI* (2011).
7. Dourish, P. and Bellotti, V. Awareness and coordination in shared workspaces. In *Proc. CSCW* (1992).
8. Flower, L. and Hayes, J.R. A cognitive process theory of writing. *College composition and communication* (1981).
9. Halfaker, A., Kittur, A., and Riedl, J. Don't bite the newbies: how reverts affect the quantity and quality of Wikipedia work. In *Proc. WikiSym* (2011).
10. Hill, B.M., Monroy-Hernández, A., and Olson, K. Responses to remixing on a social media sharing website. In *Proc. ICWSM*, (2010).
11. Hourcade, J.P., Bederson, B.B., Druin, A., and Taxén, G. KidPad: collaborative storytelling for children. In *Proc. CHI Extended Abstracts* (2002).
12. Kim, H.-C.E. and Eklundh, K.S. Reviewing practices in collaborative writing. In *Proc. CSCW* (2001).
13. Kittur, A., Suh, B., Pendleton, B.A., and Chi, E.H. He says, she says: conflict and coordination in Wikipedia. In *Proc. CHI* (2007).
14. Liu, C.-C., Liu, K.-P., Chen, W.-H., Lin, C.-P., and Chen, G.-D. Collaborative storytelling experiences in social media: Influence of peer-assistance mechanisms. *Computers & Education* (2011).
15. Luther, K. and Bruckman, A. Leadership in online creative collaboration. In *Proc. CSCW* (2008).
16. Luther, K., Fiesler, C., and Bruckman, A. Redistributing leadership in online creative collaboration. In *Proc. CSCW* (2013).
17. Luther, K., Ziegler, K., Caine, K.E., and Bruckman, A. Predicting successful completion of online collaborative animation projects. In *Proc. CC* (2009).
18. Mason, B. and Thomas, S. A million penguins research report. *Institute of Creative Technologies* (2008).
19. McKee, R. *Story: Style, Structure, Substance, and the Principles of Screenwriting*. 1997.
20. Mockus, A., Fielding, R.T., and Herbsleb, J.D. Two case studies of open source software development: Apache and Mozilla. *ACM TOSEM* (2002).
21. Noël, S. and Robert, J.-M. Empirical study on collaborative writing: What do co-authors do, use, and like? In *Proc. CSCW* (2004).
22. Paulus, P.B. and Nijstad, B.A. *Group creativity: Innovation through collaboration*. 2003.
23. Perl, S. The composing processes of unskilled college writers. *Research in the Teaching of English* (1979).
24. Ryokai, K. and Cassell, J. Computer support for children's collaborative fantasy play and storytelling. In *Proc. CSCL* (1999).
25. Thom-Santelli, J., Cosley, D.R., and Gay, G. What's mine is mine: territoriality in collaborative authoring. In *Proc. CHI* (2009).
26. Tomlinson, B., Ross, J., Andre, P., et al. Massively distributed authorship of academic papers. In *Proc. CHI Extended Abstracts* (2012).
27. Viégas, F.B., Wattenberg, M., and Dave, K. Studying cooperation and conflict between authors with history flow visualizations. In *Proc. CHI* (2004).
28. Welser, H.T., Cosley, D., Kossinets, G., et al. Finding social roles in Wikipedia. In *Proc. iConference* (2011).
29. FoldingStory. http://foldingstory.com/.
30. Who really runs things - Los Angeles Times. http://articles.latimes.com/2007/nov/23/entertainment/et-channel23.
31. Dungeons & Dragons. http://www.wizards.com/dnd/.
32. The Johnny Cash Project. http://www.thejohnnycashproject.com/.
33. The Collabowriters. http://www.thecollabowriters.com/.
34. Why Medium Notes Are Different and How to Use Them Well. https://medium.com/about/5972c72b18f2.
35. A Calendar of Tales. http://keepmoving.blackberry.com/desktop/en/us/ambassador/neil-gaiman.html

The Perception of Others: Inferring Reputation from Social Media in the Enterprise

Michal Jacovi, Ido Guy, Shiri Kremer-Davidson, Sara Porat, Netta Aizenbud-Reshef
IBM Research – Haifa
Mt. Carmel, Haifa – 31905
jacovi@il.ibm.com

ABSTRACT
The emergence of social media allows people to interact with others all over the world. During interaction, people leave many traces behind that can reveal things about themselves, or about how they perceive others: having many followers may indicate that one is an influencer; forum answers that gain high ranking, are likely to testify for expertise; people who gain high ranking in eCommerce sites are likely to be trustworthy. In this paper, we examine whether public online traces can be used for inferring the reputation of a person as perceived by others in relation to trustworthiness, influence, expertise, and impact. We describe a study performed on indicators of reputation that employees leave in a rich organizational social media platform. We compare different indicators, and report the results of an extensive user study with over 500 participants who provided their perception of thousands of others through a set of hypothetical scenarios.

Author Keywords
Reputation; social media; enterprise; workplace; trust; influence; expertise.

ACM Classification Keywords
H.5.3 Group and Organizational Interfaces: Computer-supported cooperative work.

INTRODUCTION
Reputation is defined in the literature as an expectation about an entity's behavior, based on information about or observations of its past behavior. Social media provides access to information and observations about people's past behavior from their past public interactions. As users of social media, we leave public traces of our online interactions in the form of tweets, talkbacks, forum questions and answers, wiki edits, and more. These traces may serve as indicators, telling others about us. Other people's reaction during interaction with us, e.g., comments, re-shares, or "likes", form special types of indicators – they may testify to how we are perceived in the eyes of others. The sociologist Steven Nock [29] defines reputation as "*shared or collective perception about a person*". That is, the traces other people leave during interaction with us may serve as indicators to our reputation.

In this paper we propose a framework for inferring reputation from such indicators. We harvest social network information – people's interaction with other people and with their content, such as blogs, forum, files, and more – and suggest that this data may serve for inferring reputation.

Our research is conducted in IBM – a global IT company, with over 400,000 employees world-wide, in which the use of social media is well established for several years. This gives us the unique opportunity to examine a very rich set of indicators. While the majority of our findings are easily extensible outside the enterprise, our focus in this work is on *reputation in the enterprise*. This study is part of a larger research where we investigate the potential value in enterprise social media. In a related study, we examine the role of network size in the enterprise as well as different user roles in terms of contributions [24].

In a series of interviews we conducted with employees – managers and regular staff members – we discovered that people have a hard time referring to the term "reputable person". Our interviewees kept asking about the specific type of reputation we referred to, offering various scenarios that would yield, in their minds, different answers. Examples covered cases such as "*if you ask me whom I would like to work with, the answer would be different than if you ask me who made the greatest impact*" or "*I might pick the person who most people turn to for assistance – you know, the 'know it all', but then that would be different from, say, the person people look up to – the best 'mentor'*".

Analyzing the responses we received, we identified four principle characteristics that employees refer to as different types of reputation: the *influential*, the *expert*, the most *trustworthy*, and the person who made the largest business *impact*. Studying the literature, we realized that most works focus on one specific reputation type – with the vast majority studying *trust*, and a substantial body of research studying *influence*. *Impact* does not seem to have been studied in the context of reputation; while *expertise* has its own research domain that is not necessarily paralleled with reputation and is often evaluated by the users' presentation of self, as reflected in their email, files, or self assessments.

CSCW'14, February 15 - 19 2014, Baltimore, MD, USA
Copyright 2014 ACM 978-1-4503-2540-0/14/02…$15.00.
http://dx.doi.org/10.1145/2531602.2531667.

In this paper we suggest that reputation has various types, and that examining them together may shed new light on the ability to infer reputation. We set out to examine the four reputation types that we identify as relevant in the enterprise: *Trust*, *Influence*, *Expertise*, and *Impact*.

Trustworthiness is the quality that makes other people feel that they can rely on a person and feel confident during interaction and collaboration. *Influence* is the characteristic that allows a person to reach a wide audience and affect the behavior of many people, be that by changing their way of thinking, or by introducing a new technology. While *expertise* is usually examined as an objective characteristic, implying extensive experience with a domain, in this paper we refer to the subjective quality that sets a person high above others as a good source for information or knowledge. Finally, by *impact* we refer to the footprint a person leaves on the business, or in our terms, the perception of this footprint in other people's mind.

Our research sets out to address the following questions: Can implicit traces in social media be used for inferring these reputation types? Are some types more easily inferable than others? Are different indicators more useful for inferring certain types? We examine the ability of inferring each type from individual indicators out of the rich set of social indicators at our disposal. We further continue to comparing the different types with each other, so as to determine which types have better potential to be inferred, and which indicators better serve for inferring each type. It should be noted that this is a preliminary study to examine the power of individual indicators. Future research sets out to examine aggregates of indicators.

The literature does not define a standard way for evaluating reputation. Evaluation often relies on the selection of one suggested algorithm or indicator as a 'ground truth', or on the comparison of different algorithms to each other. In this work, we looked for a direct way to "unlock" how people perceive their peers. In order to do that, we suggest an innovative evaluation method, by which we define a 'ground truth' of how people are perceived by others through a survey. In our survey employees are presented with hypothetical scenarios that reflect the need for specific types of reputation, and asked to point out the most suitable from a list of employees they are familiar with.

The design of our survey takes into consideration various difficulties, such as avoiding the need to single out any one specific person – for better or for worse; and engaging participants in an enjoyable and non-time-consuming process so as to ensure a large amount of responses. By gathering responses from over 500 employees about how they perceive tens of peers they are familiar with, we were able to calculate the public perception of a set of thousands of employees under different circumstances, requiring one of the four types of reputation. We then used this public perception as the ground truth for assessing the ability of our indicators to infer reputation.

The contribution of this paper is threefold: 1) Understanding how social media can be used for inferring reputation from **other people's** interaction with a person, 2) wrapping **several reputation types** in one study and crossing them over with a rich set of individual social indicators, 3) presenting an **innovative evaluation method**.

RELATED WORK

Reputation types and terminology. It is worth pointing that while the use of reputation systems is widely studied, there is still a lack of common terminology and means to exchange reputation information. This led to attempts to define and analyze reputation ontologies [1,4]. The term "reputation" is used in many works interchangeably with terms such as "*trust*" [19], or "*influence*" (as done by Klout.com). These models do not refer to the same notion, yet they all use the term "reputation", as indeed they study certain types of reputation. In this work we set out to compare, for the first time, how the same rich set of data may contribute to the inference of different types of reputation: *trust*, *influence*, *expertise*, and *impact*.

Works on *trust* were done by [8,20,21,38], encouraging trustworthiness, studying with whom to interact, and motivating users to enhance the quantity and quality of their contributions. In our study we present participants with a hypothetical scenario that pinpoints the people they would most *trust* with confidential information.

Influence is measured by commercial tools such as Klout.com, providing scores of users by capturing activities made on their posts, such as retweets, mentions, comments, posts, likes, and shares. Works on *influence* were also done by [30,33,37], examining various aspects of influencing other users, showing that popularity is not necessarily an indication of *influence*. In our study we aim to identify the people who are perceived to have the strongest *influence* on others in terms of reaching out to a wide audience for the dissemination of new technology.

Expertise location is highly correlated with identifying reputable individuals, and is at the core of many works (e.g., [25,27].]). In this work, we examine the notion of *expertise* from the viewpoint of other's perception. Rather than analyzing the users' own created content (e.g., emails, blogs, file system documents), we examine if they are perceived by others as experts.

Impact is the footprint a person leaves on the business, and this is how we present it in our survey. Steinfield et al. [32] refer to it as "social capital", providing a link between the internal use of corporate social networking and social capital.

Social Media in the Enterprise. Internal use of social media in the enterprise has been widely studied in recent years, covering information-centric tools such as blogging, wikis, social bookmarking [6,13,15,26], and even investigating the use of a corporate social network site to enable a more social-centric employee communication [7].

The work by Steinfield et al. [32] takes the study of corporate social networking further ahead by providing an empirical analysis of the link between the internal use of corporate social networking and social capital.

A body of research examines the mining of different relationship types from social media in the enterprise, including familiarity [9], similarity [11], and interest [16]. In all of these works, relationships are inferred based on the user's own activity, while in this work we use others' activities that relate to the user to infer reputation. Using graph terminology, this work is concerned with examining and comparing the "in-degrees", while previous works focused on "out-degrees" in social graphs.

While there is a significant body of research on the benefits of using corporate social information, there is no prior work, to the best of our knowledge, on the link between corporate social information and reputation. Our work thus lays the foundation for future work on social media as a base to assess the reputation of employees.

Evaluating Reputation. The literature does not define a standard way to evaluate reputation as it does, for example, for evaluating search engine results. A common evaluation method relies on comparing the outcomes of various algorithms – e.g., Kuter & Golbeck [21] evaluate their trust values by comparing them against the performance of TIDALTRUST, an algorithm they studied before; while other studies suggest several forms of calculating reputation and report the comparison between these calculations [3,14,18,31]. Another evaluation method suggests splitting the data set into a training set and a testing set, examining whether the algorithm can predict reputation values of the testing set based on the training set [2,8]. Finally, another evaluation method relies on one of the reputation indicators as the 'ground truth' [34]. Some studies do not provide any evaluation [14,27]. We suggest a method for tapping into the perceptions of real users, in order to establish a ground truth for evaluating reputation.

Characteristics of reputation systems. Some reputation systems are based on collecting *explicit feedback* on users – directly asking users about other users [8,19,30,38]. As stated by McNally et al. [28], systems based on explicit feedback are vulnerable, as in many cases the information given is false, for various sociological reasons. This is even more acute in the enterprise, where accountability inhibits people from providing negative testimony. Other systems use *implicit indicators* such as number of followers, retweets and mentions in Twitter [3,18], or number of comments made on content authored by the user. Our work examines a wide variety of implicit indicators, which are side-effects of people's interaction over social media inside IBM. Our focus on implicit indicators ensures feedback that is less vulnerable, while also minimizing the effort of the users.

Resnick et al. [30] explore the principles of *external reputation systems*, where reputation scores are made public and revealed to users. In eBay, for example, the buyer and seller can rate each other after a transaction [20]. Users have feedback points visibly attached to their screen names. In contrast, *internal reputation systems* do not reveal scores to users, but use them under the scenes to support in assessing content quality or user reputation in applications such as community question answering or news forums [2,5,14]. Our work focuses on studying the quality of reputation indicators (referred to as "criteria" by Kardara et al. [18], "features" by Bian et al. [2], or "metrics" by Maresch [23]), with no references to the application that uses them. Our contribution is thus expected to be valuable for both external and internal reputation systems.

RESEARCH SETTINGS AND METHODOLOGY

We conducted our research inside IBM – a large global corporation that employs a rich social media platform – IBM Connection[1] – for internal use. The platform is deployed for over five years, and individual components of it were deployed for years before that. It is therefore well disseminated within the company.

IBM Connections supports the following social applications: a **blogging** system that allows users to write blog posts, comment, or 'like' others' posts; a **board** application that allows posting messages on other individuals' boards (sometimes called "walls" in social media) and comment on existing posts; a **file sharing** system that allows users to upload files they authored. Users can share a file with other users (even if they are not the authors), download, comment on, or like files; a **forum** system that allows users to create new topics for discussion, or to comment on others' topics; a **people tagging** application where users can tag each other with descriptive tags; and a system that allows users to create **wikis** where pages can be co-edited by multiple users. In addition, IBM Connections allows one user to **follow** all public activities of another user, and two users to reciprocally connect (or "**friend**") with each other.

We claim that many activities in these applications, either through direct interaction of people with each other or through interaction of people over artifacts, can serve as indicators of how people perceive each other – indicators of reputation. We set out to examine the potential of the in-degree of the interaction graph of the various indicators to infer various types of reputation.

For each of the eight social applications listed above, we selected activities that may serve as such indicators. For example, an activity of liking a blog post is a positive indication about the author. Similarly, downloading a person's file, following one's activities, or writing on one's

[1] http://www-03.ibm.com/software/products/us/en/conn/

board, may all serve as indications about how one is perceived. We used the applications' APIs to harvest all public activities of these types over the past two years.

An outcome of a single indicator is a list of employees with a value assigned to them by the indicator (e.g., a list of all employees who have followers, along with the number of followers per each; or a list of all employees whose blog posts were liked, along with the number of people who liked one or more of their posts). The returned values may be used for calculating reputation scores; and the returned lists, when sorted, may be paralleled to the results returned by a search engine – a list of results, ranked and scored by their relevance. Our goal is to evaluate the returned lists in comparison to a ground-truth, much as search engine results are evaluated in comparison to ground-truth results, typically annotated by a small group of individuals [22], thus examining the potential value of the returned lists for inferring people's reputation of the various types.

Table I details the indicators we inspect, along with the number of people for whom information could be extracted (i.e., the number of individuals each indicator covers) in the past two years. The coverage range is high: from around 1,000 people whose files were liked, to over 100,000 with friends. Our goal is to examine the potential accuracy of the indicators, regardless of their current coverage; our analysis is thus oblivious to the number of people covered by the indicators and examines their potential to reflect reputation.

App	Indicator Semantics	#People
Blogs	Comments on one's blog posts	4,205
	"Likes" of one's blog posts	3,884
Profiles	Posts on one's board	27,027
	Replies on one's board	4,312
Files	Comments on one's files	1,439
	"Likes" of one's files	1,010
	Downloads of one's files	6,923
	Shares of one's files	2,924
	Sharing (others') files with one	10,193
Followers	People following one's activities	24,113
Forums	Replies on one's posted topics	5,935
Friends	Friends (reciprocated)	100,942
Tags	Person tags associated with one	35,048
Wikis	Edits of pages of wikis one owns	10,854

Table I. Indicators examined in our study

We observe that our indicators could be classified into two classes that may have a different interpretation to how other people are perceived. One class of indicators deals with activities done directly between **people** and thus directly reflects on how a person is perceived. These are: friending and following which are direct relations between two people; board, which allows people to communicate with a person directly through a "wall"-like page; and tagging, in which a person assigns a tag directly to another person. The other class of indicators refers to activities in which people interact over **content** artifacts. These are blogs, files, forums, and wikis, in which other people interact with a person's artifacts (blog posts, files, forum topics, and wiki pages) and this interaction indirectly reflects on how the person is perceived in their eyes.

In order to evaluate the potential of our data to serve for reputation inference, we conducted two types of analysis: on the one hand, we compared the outcome lists of the different indicators with each other, to understand the differences in their potential. The method we used in order to compare the lists is *match@k* [10], which measures the percentage of common people between the top *k* individuals in each of the lists.

On the other hand, we studied the potential of indicators to reflect a person's reputation. To this end, we defined a "ground truth" through a broad user study in which hundreds of employees provided us with their perception of thousands of other employees they are familiar with. Given a list of people returned by an indicator (e.g., the 10,854 people whose wikis were edited, ranked by the number of people who edited them), we examined the relationship of this list with the "ground truth" using the popular *normalized Discounted Cumulative Gain* (NDCG) measure [17], typically used to evaluate the results of search engines against a given ground truth.

For the user survey, we focused on employees for whom we had information from at least three of the eight applications (i.e., they were "covered" by at least one type of indicator from at least three applications) in order to ensure we had a good base to assess their reputation. Our aim was to understand how the peers of these subjects perceive them.

In order to locate peers to participate in our survey, we used the SONAR *familiarity* list, which is based on aggregated data stemming from social media applications and has been shown to produce accurate results for social media users [9]. We identified 2,474 employees who had at least 10 of our subjects in their familiarity list, covering 5,695 subjects. We chose to focus on these 2,474 as survey participants since they could provide us explicit feedback on at least 10 people they know and for whom we have substantial information from the inspected indicators.

Our goal in the survey was to understand how participants perceive their peers in the four reputation types that we set out to study: *trust*, *influence*, *expertise*, and *impact*, as well as in a general *reputation* notion. Asking a direct question about how people are perceived is a delicate matter. In order to avoid being so direct, we developed a unique type of a survey: we provided our participants with the list of their 10 peers, and asked them to choose up-to-three of them who best match a certain hypothetical scenario. The option of choosing up-to-three, freed participants from the difficulty of picking just one person, and from the need to "put down" too small a group of peers (as would have been the case, for example, in one-on-one comparisons).

The hypothetical scenarios we presented to our participants were focused around the types of reputation. Each participant was first introduced with a scenario about the general notion of reputation, followed by four other scenarios representing the four types of reputation that we study. The latter four were presented in random order.

While a more elaborated method would employ multiple scenarios per reputation type, our goal to reach out to hundreds of respondents and thus the need to simplify the survey led us to stick to a single scenario per type. In order to establish the validity of the scenarios in representing the reputation type we intended for it, we conducted a preliminary survey in which 19 participants were presented by the scenarios in random order and asked to match them to a set of eight reputation types (our five along with "leader", "visionary", and "meticulous"; choice of multiple types per scenario was enabled). The 19 validators originated from a group of 30 individuals invited to take part. They come from four different countries. 9 were females, 10 males. The results over all scenarios indicated that our intended type is indeed the highest one selected – with a consensus of 14 to 19 out of 19 participants (*"reputable"* reached a consensus of 14; *"influence"* and *"impact"*, 16; and *"trust"* and *"expertise"* a straight 19 of 19 consensus). These are the scenarios:

Reputation: CNN is making a new documentary series about reputable people. Gamma[2] was asked to identify a group of the most reputable Gamma employees in various fields, to be included in a chapter about IT companies. Imagine you are sitting on the selection committee, and that the list below contains the 10 finalists. Who would you nominate?

Trust: You just got some really exciting news, but were asked to keep it under wraps until the formal announcement. You were given permission to share this news with up to three people. Suppose these people you were going to tell are ones from the list below. Who would you tell?

Influence: A group at Gamma Research has developed a new tool for internal use. The group is looking for early adopters who would be willing to use the tool and later spread it across Gamma. Imagine you are sitting on the committee responsible for picking these early adopters. The list below contains the 10 finalists. Who would you pick?

Expertise: Gamma has created a new forum of experts, and is looking for people who are experts in their field to act as the core team of the forum. Imagine you are sitting on the committee responsible for picking this core team. The list below contains 10 finalists. Who would you pick?

Impact: To celebrate its second centennial, Gamma is announcing an award for people whose work had the most impact on the company. Imagine you are sitting on the committee responsible for picking these people. The list below contains the 10 finalists. Who would you nominate for the award?

[2] A pseudonym is used

The reason we opened each set of questions with the general *reputation* scenario is that we aimed to capture people's natural interpretation of reputation without being "contaminated" with the different types. The hypothetical scenarios help focus on a specific question, sparing the need to interpret abstract terms such as *"trust"* or *"influence"* which are typically hard to define.

Each survey participant received a different set of 10 people to select from, based on their computed top familiarity list. In order to collect more data, those of the 2,474 participants who happened to be familiar with more than 10 of our subjects, were presented with more than one set of 10 people. Those who were familiar with over 20 subjects, were presented with two sets – one set with their 10 most familiar subjects, and another with the next 10 familiar subjects. Those who were familiar with over 30, were presented with three sets – with the third set including subjects in positions 21-30 on their familiarity list. No one was presented with more than three sets. Participants could quit the survey at any time.

In all scenarios, we asked participants to mark those on the list who are unfamiliar to them, in order to exclude these from our analysis. We use the notation "presented" to denote the 10 subjects given in a set. Of these, the participant would mark "unfamiliar" people that we remove from the analysis. The rest of the people – those presented and found to be familiar, are denoted as "mentioned". Of these, the user would mark up-to-three "selected" subjects.

The outcomes of the survey provided us with data about people's perception of their peers in five different types. We aggregated all votes of a type into a "ground truth" ranking based on a simple measure denoted ***s/m*** – the number of participants who "selected" a subject divided by the number of participants to whom this subject was "mentioned". In our ground-truth ranking, we included only individuals who were mentioned to at least three survey participants, to make sure our ***s/m*** measure is robust.

To measure the quality of lists of people stemming from the indicators, we set out to assess the ranking (weak ordering) of people by the various indicators, in comparison to the ground-truth. We focused on the ranking of people in the lists rather than on the scoring, since different indicators use different scoring measures (e.g., number of followers vs. number of files shared). For this reason, we used the *normalized Discount Cumulative Gain* (NDCG) measure [17], which is commonly used in the Information Retrieval domain to evaluate the ranking of a search engine's results. In our case, we considered the ***s/m*** score as the graded relevance score of the person, and the lists extracted from the indicators as the search engine results. For a given p, NDCG(p) considers both the graded scores of the top p results and their relative order as retuned by the indicator.

For each indicator, we considered only people for whom we had a graded score from the survey (i.e., they were mentioned to at least three participants), relying on the fact that the survey provided over 1,000 scored individuals for each type, thus having a high coverage of the lists returned by the different indicators.

RESULTS

We sent invitations to 2,474 employees to take part in our survey. 554 people responded, going through 1,073 sets. 237 (42.78%) of the participants responded on one set, 115 (20.76%) on two sets, and 202 (36.46%) on three.

The distribution of the 1,073x10=10,730 responses between the various sets may be seen on Table II. 1,445 (13.46%) of the presented subjects were marked as unfamiliar – a rather low percentage, indicating that our chosen mechanism for locating familiar people is effective. Naturally, the percentage of unfamiliar people grows from the first set to the second and third, as familiarity with the respective individuals is weaker. For the remaining 9,285 responses (3,320 unique subjects), whose distribution among the sets may be seen on the "mentioned" row, we examined the percentage they were selected by participants for the various scenarios. The result is at the bottom of Table II.

	Set 1	Set 2	Set 3
Presented	5540	3170	2020
Unfamiliar	419 (8%)	541 (17%)	485 (24%)
Mentioned	5121	2629	1535
Selected (% out of Mentioned)			
Reputation	23%	22%	22%
Trust	23%	19%	18%
Influence	23%	23%	23%
Expertise	24%	24%	23%
Impact	18%	19%	19%

Table II. Number of people presented, unfamiliar, selected

The percentage of selected people on the first set was about 23% for almost all types, indicating a slight inclination to choose two or three people over just one. The exception is *impact* for which the average is only 18%, indicating people preferred to choose just one or two people in this scenario. These percentages remain steady in the second and third sets, with the exception of a drop in *trust* to 18%, which can be explained by a stronger tie between familiarity and *trust*, leading to fewer people being selected as the familiarity with people in these sets is weaker.

Calculating the ***s/m*** score for those who were mentioned to at least three participants resulted in 1,132 unique subjects with ***s/m*** score for *reputation* and 1,065-1,072 subjects with ***s/m*** score for the other types. We believe this is a rich basis for comparison between the indicators.

Comparison across the types. Realizing that the percentage of selected subjects is quite similar in all types, we wanted to get an indication of how similar the selections are – are the same people being chosen as top results of all types, or do participants indeed convey different semantics to different types. We were especially interested in the *reputation* type, to see which other types are close to it.

The method we used in order to compare the lists returned by the different types is *match*@100 [10], where we compare the top 100 people receiving the highest score in each type with the top 100 of all other types. The results are presented in Table III.

	Reputation	Trust	Influence	Expertise	Impact
Reputation	-	29	18	35	39
Trust		-	44	29	53
Influence			-	27	48
Expertise				-	41
Impact					-

Table III. *match@100* across the types

Overall, results are distinct: *match@100* does not surpass 53%, showing that participants selected differently across types and that there are no redundant types we can ignore – this supports our suggestion to distinguish between types, and our choice of types to be examined. *Impact* has the highest overlap with *reputation*, followed by *expertise*. *Influence* has the lowest overlap with *reputation*.

Inspecting Content Indicators. For content indicators (blogs, forums, files, wikis), we experimented with several methods for calculating a person's reputation. The differences between the methods stemmed from two factors: (1) Calculating based on counting **content** artifacts vs. **people**. E.g., for wiki editing, counting the number of edits to the person's wikis, vs. counting the number of unique people who edited them. (2) Calculating **numbers** vs. **averages**. E.g., for wiki editing, counting the overall number of edits on the person's wikis, vs. the average number of edits over them.

We first set out to examine our raw data – using *match@100* for comparing the lists of people stemming from our indicators, examining the above two factors. The results were quite similar across all indicators and we depict three representative examples in Table IV.

	Num Artifacts to Avg Artifacts	Num Artifacts to Num People	Num Artifacts to Avg People	Avg Artifacts to Num People	Avg Artifacts to Avg People	Num People to Avg People
Blog Comments	19	75	18	21	81	21
Forum Replies	46	67	36	48	75	50
Wiki Edits	11	27	7	13	40	27

Table IV. Artifact-people and num-avg *match@100*

It can be seen that typically there is a higher match between lists based on number of unique people and lists based on number of artifacts as well as between those based on average number of unique people and on average number of artifacts. This gives an indication that counting people or counting artifacts typically leads to similar results. For wikis the match is lower, possibly since the same people make many multiple edits. The match between number and average is lower in general, indicating that averaging yields quite different results, motivating the comparison of the two approaches.

Equipped with these observations, we experimented with four score calculation methods per each content indicator, using our survey results as the ground truth. We observed similar patterns for all content indicators. Figure 1 demonstrates them for blog commenting and wiki editing, across all types, for NDCG(30).

As was already hinted by the match of the people lists, number of people and number of artifacts produce similar results (two top lines in the figure); similarly, the average of people and average artifacts produce similar results as well. It seems that in all cases but *trust*, using the number (of either people or artifacts) is closer to the ground truth than using the average. We conclude that taking the number of people or artifacts rather than their average, typically improves the reputation inference capability.

The differences between considering the number of people vs. number of artifacts were minor, giving a slight preference to one or the other for different types. Based on these outcomes, we report on results stemming from counting the number of people as a unified basis for comparison.

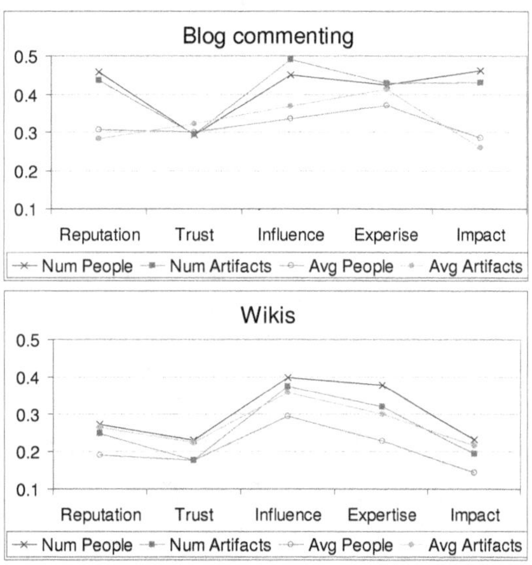

Figure 1. Four calculation methods for blog commenting and wikis

Comparing Indicator semantics in the same application. Some applications contributed more than one type of indicator, with different semantics. Blogs contributed two indicators: commenting, and liking. Similarly, boards also contributed two indicators: posting on one's board (creating a thread), and adding a comment (to a thread) on one's board. Files contributed as many as five indicators: commenting, liking, downloading, sharing (one's file with others), and being shared with (when a person shares a file with one, indicating a certain care for the one). We set out to examine the differences between the indicators of the same application.

For blogs, *match@100* between comments and likes was rather low at 32%. For board, the *match@100* between number of people who posted on one's board and number of people who commented was a high 68%. The *match@100* comparison of the file indicators are shown on Table V.

	Comm.	Like.	Down.	Share.	being Shared
Commenters		73	9	10	7
Likers			10	11	7
Downloaders				38	9
Sharers					12
being Shared					

Table V. Comparing Five Files Indicator semantics using *match@100*

As could be expected, being-shared-files has the lowest match with the rest since it represents a different semantic that is more person-centric, while the rest refer to different forms of feedback on the user's content (files). Commenters and likers have high match (i.e., people who have high number of commeners are also likely to have high number of likers and vice versa), and to some degree downloaders and sharers are also matched. Still, the match between all feedback forms is low, motivating the comparison between them using the ground truth.

Table VI compares the NDCG(30) of the different indicators within each of the source applications that had more than one indicator type. For both blogs and boards, commenting consistently performs slightly better, implying it's a slightly stronger feedback form for inferring reputation types. For files, as expected, being-shared behaves differently than the rest across the types. It has a clear edge in *reputation* and *impact*, but is very weak for *influence* and *expertise*, where downloading is the best. Liking is strongest for *trust*.

App	Indicator Type	Rep	Tru	Inf	Exp	Imp
Blogs	Commenting	**0.46**	**0.29**	**0.45**	**0.42**	**0.46**
	Liking	0.40	0.26	0.43	0.37	0.42
Board	Posting	**0.44**	**0.21**	0.36	0.34	0.36
	Commenting	0.43	**0.21**	**0.41**	**0.37**	**0.39**
Files	Commenting	0.34	0.28	0.38	0.32	0.33
	Liking	0.37	**0.34**	0.39	0.34	0.31
	Downloading	0.36	0.28	**0.42**	**0.40**	0.34
	Sharing	0.26	0.19	0.33	0.32	0.31
	Being shared	**0.44**	0.28	0.24	0.29	**0.38**

Table VI. NDCG(30) Comparison of same-application indicators

Comparing eight indicators representing eight apps. For the cross-application comparison, aiming to understand if any one application is a better indicator for any type of reputation, we chose the indicators that perform better from each application that has more than one indicator. These are the indicators we compared: board commenting, following, tagging, friending, blog commenting, file downloading, forum replying, and wiki editing. As before, we start by examining the raw data stemming from the indicators – matching the lists of people they produce. Table VII shows the results for all eight representing indicators.

	Board	Followers	Taggers	Friends	Blogs	Files	Forums	Wikis
Board	.	47	41	36	22	24	9	0
Followers		.	37	29	27	18	7	0
Taggers			.	29	18	22	6	0
Friends				.	17	21	4	1
Blogs					.	15	9	0
Files						.	3	
Forums							.	0
Wikis								.

Table VII. Comparing eight indicators representing eight apps using *match@100*

The match among the eight indicators is generally low, all under 50%, indicating that the different applications produce different lists and motivating the comparison between them. There is clearly a higher match across the four people-indicators (left side of the table), probably since they reflect a perception of the person as a whole rather than with regards to a specific content. Overall, the low match motivates comparing all to the ground truth.

We examine the eight representative indicators in light of each of our five types. For each type we present below (in Figures 2-6) the comparison of each indicator with the ground truth as defined by the survey outcomes (using NDCG(p)). For saving space, each graph is depicted in its optimal scale.

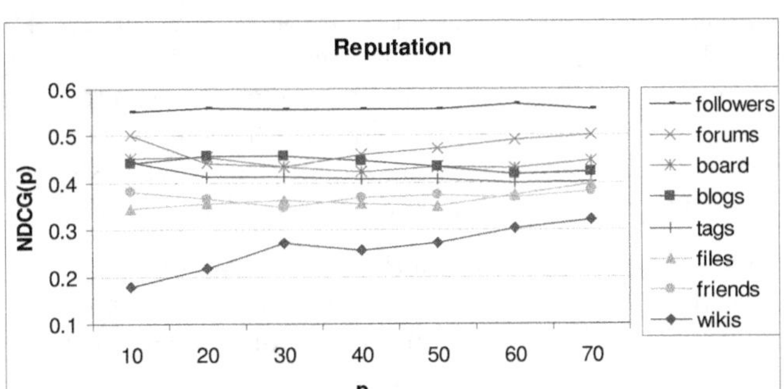

Figure 2. Comparison of the eight sources as indicators for reputation

For inferring the general notion of *reputation* (Figure 2), the followers indicator is clearly best – a person with many followers is likely to be perceived as *reputable*. Forums and the boards are also quite high – receiving responses from many people on a forum, or comments from many people on the board, are indications of being *reputable*. It seems that having many friends is not a good indicator for *reputation* and neither is having many people who edit your wikis.

The NDCG results for *trust* (Figure 3) are much lower across all indicators, suggesting that *trust* is more difficult to infer. This is an expected result as *trust* is a more personal type. Surprisingly, the friends indicator fails to be useful for inference here, too. Forums and followers seem to be the most useful for *trust* inference.

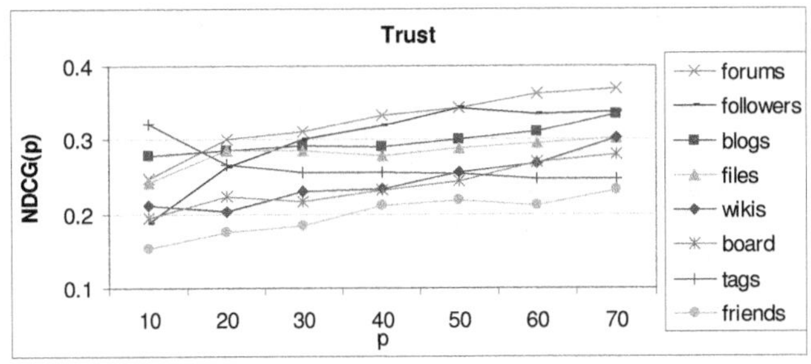

Figure 3. Comparison of the eight sources as indicators for trust

The picture for *influence* (Figure 4) is different than for *reputation* and *trust*. Followers, does not seem to be strongest for *influence*. Previous research on Twitter [3], showed that the number of followers is not a very strong indicator for likelihood of retweet (a form of *influence*), which is in line with our result. Here, content indicators such as blogs, forums, and wikis seem to be stronger.

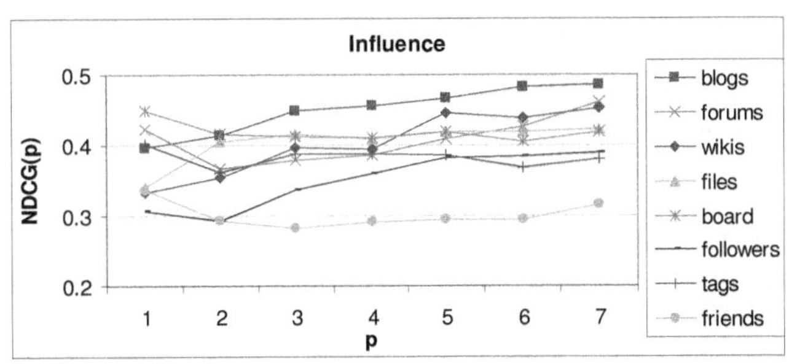

Figure 4. Comparison of the eight sources as indicators for influence

The graph for *expertise* (Figure 5) is similar to that of *influence*. Content indicators are strong here, too, as may be expected since *expertise* is associated with content. Friends are clearly last here, as in the previous three graphs, rendering it a rather insufficient indicator for inferring any type of reputation.

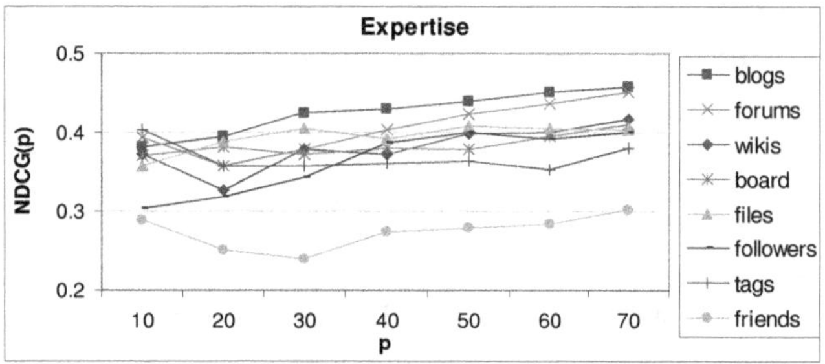

Figure 5. Comparison of the eight sources as indicators for expertise

As was already noted when examining the raw data (Table III), *impact* has the highest match to the *general reputation* type. The NDCG results are also quite similar between *impact* (Figure 6) and *reputation* (Figure 2), with the followers indicator even more dominant for *impact.*

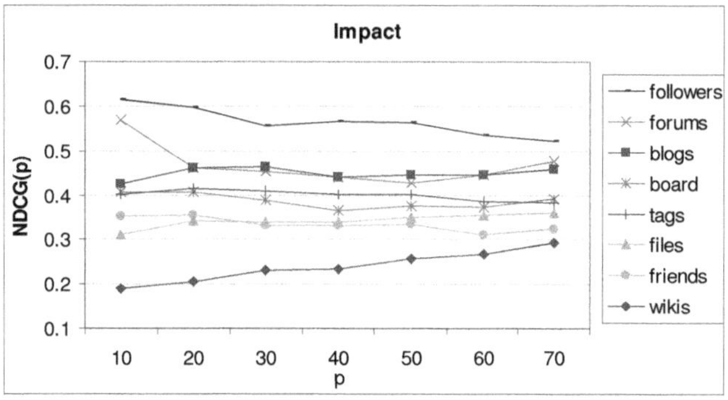

Figure 6. Comparison of the eight sources as indicators for impact

In the next section we list some limitations of our study. We then turn to discuss our method and results and present a few directions for future work.

LIMITATIONS

For assigning reputation scores to our subjects based on the survey's results we used a basic *selected/mentioned (s/m)* measure. The advantage of this measure lies in its simplicity and intuitiveness, however it has two main shortcomings: (1) it ignores the actual number of familiar people out of the 10 presented, and gives the same weight to selecting one or two or three subjects; and (2) it does not take into account the other individuals who appear next to a mentioned person and their own scores – e.g., one who always appear next to the CEO may never get selected despite having strong reputation. Our attempt to apply a liner programming approach did not go well since too many constraints were left unsatisfied. However, given the scale of our survey, the ***s/m*** measure gives a reliable picture of the ground truth as reflected in participants' input.

Our study was conducted inside an enterprise. As such, it may have characteristics that are specific to enterprises, as well specific to this one enterprise. However, as we used popular social media applications and rich and mature social media settings, we believe the study is suitable to serve as a first example. Generalizing may require additional future work.

Our paper encompasses a range of reputation types. Each type is typically measured with complex, multi-faceted questionnaires; while our survey dedicates a single question per type and may thus be sensitive to other factors. As our goal was to reach large participation, complex questionnaires were unsuitable. However, there is no obvious bias towards any of the indicators we examine, and we believe that the large participation we indeed achieved (554 participants, providing 10,730 responses) and the 14-19 out of 19 consensuses reached when validating the scenarios, help assure noise effects are reduced.

Finally, it should be noted that our ground truth is based on hypothetical scenarios. Although such scenarios may tell us what people think they would do in each situation, it does not necessarily shed light on their actual behavior.

DISCUSSION AND FUTURE WORK

One of the main contributions of this paper is that is refers to four different types of reputation under one umbrella. Most of these types were studied separately in the past, often being referred to simply as "reputation". Our results show that participants indeed regard different scenarios with different semantics, and that various indicators contribute differently to the inference of different reputation types. We believe this lays the ground for extensive future research, fine-tuning the terminology, identifying additional types, and studying their inference from social media.

The survey we developed is unique and deserves addressing. People are better able to formulate their preferences in a relative way, thus we opted to present a list of people to pick from, rather than directly ask for the most suitable person. Similarly, to avoid abstract terms like "reputable" or "trustworthy", we used hypothetical scenarios. The results reinforce our choice. Among the 554 who accepted our invitation and started the survey, 458 (82.67%) completed it in full, with 199 of them going through three full sets of scenarios, out of 253 who received three sets (78.66%). This suggests that the survey was clear and even enjoyable. The high familiarity level (86.54%) proves the mechanism we used was effective.

Another important contribution of our study is the distinction between people-related and content-related indicators, and the multiple types of measurements of content-related indicators (number vs. average, people vs. artifacts). Using number (of people or artifacts) seems to be closer to ground truth than using average.

In addition to the four types we examined, we included a scenario for general *reputation*, in order to understand how people interpret this concept. Results tell us that the type closest to general *reputation* is *impact*, followed by *expertise*. Trust and to a larger extent influence, the two types most associated with reputation in the literature, are found to have lower overlap with general *reputation*.

General *reputation* and *impact* seem to be the easiest to infer – their NDCG values (showing proximity to the ground truth) were highest for most examined indicators. For both, the followers indicator is strongest. Followers does not seem to be useful for the inference of the other reputation types, though, not even for *influence*.

Expertise is best inferred through content indicators, which is expected. The blogs indicators were the strongest, and were prominent for all types but *trust*. Of all types, *trust* is the hardest to infer. Getting forums responses from many people was the best indicator for *trust*.

The friends indicator turned out to be a weak indicator for all types, even for *trust*, although one might assume that friendship implies a sense of *trust*. This is not surprising, however, as social media "friending", being a reciprocated action, does not correlate well with real-world friendship – especially in the enterprise. Wikis were the weakest indicator for *reputation* and *impact*, but were stronger for the other types, especially *expertise* and *influence*.

Inspecting the different semantics of activities within the eight applications, we learn that commenting is a better indicator than both liking (in blogs) and posting (in boards). Sentiment analysis may help fine tune the commenting indicator, by referring not only to the fact that people respond to a post, but actually inferring whether their response is positive or negative.

An interesting finding came up in the files application, where we learned that to be on the receiving end of a file sharing activity is a good indication for *impact*. This indicator is very different from the other files indicators, where liking one's files turned out to be best for indicating *trust* and downloading is best for *expertise* and *influence*

Our scenarios reflect reputation in an overall sense. In contrast, Hennis [12] introduces a method for evaluating scores per context or topic. While this is beyond the scope of our work, our findings can still be incorporated in systems that seek for contextual reputation: as social media data can be used to associate people with terms, global reputation measures can be combined with IR methods that rank people with respect to a given topic. Alternatively, for indicators with textual elements (all content indicators plus boards and tags), a topic-based reputation can be inferred by narrowing the graph to include edges that are associated with the topic. We leave these ideas for future work.

Previous studies applied link analysis algorithms, such as PageRank or HITS, to measure reputation [14,28,35,36]. In this work, we used the simpler in-degree measure as the basis for comparison across indicators. Link analysis may improve the ability to infer reputation by assigning higher weight to an incoming edge from a node whose own reputation is higher. Future studies should examine how link analysis can be effectively applied over the enterprise social graph and whether it can improve the inference capabilities for the different reputation types.

There are several other directions to pursue for further enhancement of reputation inference: while our paper focuses on reputation indicators largely from the perspective of employees. It is of interest to search for evidence of whether employers consider different indicators to be predictive of employee reputation. This would require a different definition of ground truth, focusing on employers' perspective.

We examine a wide set of indicators. As social media continues to evolve there are more opportunities to infer reputation. For example, retweet data on Twitter has been commonly used for influence analysis [3] and an analogous feature in the enterprise can be interesting to examine; applications that apply voting mechanisms, such as for ideas or for answers, can also serve as fertile ground for deriving reputation.

On the other hand, it would be interesting to study how our work is extended to the web outside the workplace. Social media applications have different usage patterns on the web, and it is interesting to understand where the differences apply. Aggregation of various reputation indicators is also a subject we leave for future work. Our results indicate that different indicators are stronger for different types and it would be interesting to examine aggregation methods for reputation indicators and to what extent they can improve reputation inference from social media.

ACKNOWLEDGEMENTS

This work has been partially funded in the 7th framework of the European scientific targeted research projects +Spaces and SocIoS which are co-financed by the European Commission. +Spaces is co-financed through theme ICT-2009.7.3 ICT for Governance and Policy Modelling under contract no. 248726 (see http://www.positivespaces.eu). SocIoS is co-financed under contract no. 257774 through theme ICT 2009.1.2: Internet of Services (for more details see http://www.sociosproject.eu).

We are grateful to the IBM employees who participated in our survey.

REFERENCES

1. Alnemr, R. & Meinel, C. From reputation models and systems to reputation ontologies. Proc. IFIPTM'11, 99-116.
2. Bian, J., Liu, Y., Zhou, D., Agichtein, E., & Zha, H. Learning to recognize reliable users and content in social media with coupled mutual reinforcement. Proc. WWW'09, 51-60.
3. Cha, M., Haddadi, H., Benevenuto, F. & Gummadi, K.P. Measuring User Influence in Twitter: The Million Follower Fallacy. Proc. ICWSM'10, 10-17

4. Chang, E., Hussain, F.K. & Dillon, T.: Reputation ontology for reputation systems. OTM Workshops. LNCS, 4278, 2006, 1724–1733.

5. Chen, B.C., Guo J., Tseng, B., & Yang, J. User reputation in a comment rating environment. Proc. KDD'11, 159-167.

6. Dencheva, S., Prause, C.R., & Prinz, W. 2011. Dynamic Self-moderation in a Corporate Wiki to Improve Participation and Contribution Quality. Proc. ECSCW'11, 24-28.

7. DiMicco, J.M., Millen, D.R., Geyer, W., Dugan, C., Brownholtz, B. & Muller, M. Motivations for social networking at work. Proc. CSCW'08, 711-720

8. DuBois, T., Golbeck, J., and Srinivasan, A. Predicting Trust and Distrust in Social Networks. Proc. IEEE 3rd SocialCom'11, 418-424

9. Guy, I., Jacovi, M., Shahar, E., Meshulam, N., Soroka, V., Farrel. S. Harvesting with SONAR – The Value of Aggregating Social Network Information. CHI'08: 1017-1026

10. Guy, I., Jacovi, M., Meshulam, N., Ronen, I., Shahr, E. Public vs. private: comparing public social network information with email. CSCW 2008: 393-402

11. Guy, I., Jacovi, M., Perer, A., Ronen, I., Uziel, E. Same places, Same Things, Same People?: mining user similarity on social media. CSCW'10: 41-50

12. Hennis, T. Monitoring contributions online: a reputation system to model expertise in online communities. Proc. UMAP'11, 422-425

13. Hasan, H. & Pfaff, C.C. The Wiki: an environment to revolutionise employees' interaction with corporate knowledge. Proc OZCHI'06, 377-380

14. Hong, L., Yang, Z., & Davison, B.D. Incorporating Participant Reputation in Community-Driven Question Answering Systems. Proc. CSE'09, 475-480.

15. Jackson, A., Yates, J. & Orlikowski, W. Corporate Blogging: Building community through persistent digital talk. Proc HICSS'07, 80

16. Jacovi, M., Guy, I., Ronen, I., Perer, A., Uziel, E., & Maslenko, M. 2011. Digital Traces of Interest: Deriving Interest Relationships from Social Media Interactions. Proc ECSCW'11, 21-40

17. Jarvelin, K. & Kakalainen, J. Cumulated gain-based evaluation of IR techniques. ACM Trans. Inf. Syst. 20, 4, 2002, 422-446.

18. Kardara, M., Papadakis, G., Papaoikonomou, T., Tserpes, K., & Varvarigou, T. Influence Patterns in Topic Communities of Social Media. Proc. WIMS'12.

19. Kiefhaber, R., Hammer, S., Savs, B., Schmitt, J., Roth, M., Kluge, F., Andre, E., & Ungerer, T. The Neighbor-Trust Metric to Measure Reputation in Organic Computing Systems. Proc. SASOW'11. 41-46.

20. Kollock, P. The production of trust in online markets. Advances in Group Processes, vol. 16, 1999.

21. Kuter, U., & Golbeck, J. SUNNY: a new algorithm for trust inference in social networks using probabilistic confidence models. Proc. AAAI'07, 1377-1382

22. Manning, C., Raghavan, P., & Schtze, H. 2008. Introduction to information retrieval. Cambridge University Press.

23. Maresch, O.M. Reputationsbasierte Trust Metriken im Kontext des Semantic Web. Master's thesis, Technische Universit at Berlin, 2005.

24. Mark, G., Guy, I., Kremer-Davidson S., Jacovi, M. Most Liked, Fewest Friends: Patterns of Enterprise Social Media Use. Proc. CSCW'2014.

25. Martín-Vicente, M.I., Gil-Solla, A., Ramos-Cabrer, M., Blanco-Fernández, Y. & López-Nores, M. Semantic inference of user's reputation and expertise to improve collaborative recommendations. Expert Syst. Appl. 39, 9, 2012, 8248-8258

26. Millen, D.R., Feinberg, J. & Kerr, B. Dogear: Social bookmarking in the enterprise. Proc CHI'06, 111-120.

27. McDonald, D.W. & Ackerman, M.S., Expertise Recommender: A Flexible Recommendation System and Architecture. Proc. CSCW'00, 231-240.

28. McNally, K., O'Mahony, M.P., Smyth, B., Coyle, M., & Briggs, P. Towards a reputation-based model of social web search. Proc. IUI'10. 179-188.

29. Nock, S.L. The Costs of Privacy: Surveillance and Reputation in America. Aldine, New York (1993)

30. Resnick, P., Kuwabara, K., Zeckhauser, R. & Friedman. E. 2000. Reputation systems. Com. ACM 43, 12, 2000, 45-48.

31. Romero, D.M., Galuba, W., Asur, S. & Huberman, B.A.Influence and Passivity in Social Media. Proc. WWW'11.

32. Steinfield, C., DiMicco, J.M., Ellison, N.B. & Lampe, C. Bowling online: social networking and social capital within the organization. Proc. C&T'09, 245-254

33. Sun, J. & Tang, J. A survey of models and algorithms for social influence analysis. Charu C. Aggarwal, editor, Social Network Data Analytics, chapter 7, 2011, 177-214.

34. Tausczik, Y.R. & Pennebaker, J.W. Predicting the perceived quality of online mathematics contributions from users' reputations. Proc. CHI'11, 1885-1888.

35. Weng, J., Lim, E., Jiang, J. & He, Q. 2010. TwitterRank: finding topic-sensitive influential twitterers. Proc. WSDM'10, 261-270

36. Zhang, J., Ackerman, M., & Adamic, L. Expertise networks in online communities: structure and algorithms. Proc. WWW'07.

37. Zhu, H., Huberman, B. & Luon, Y. 2012. To switch or not to switch: understanding social influence in online choices. Proc. CHI'12.

38. Ziegler, C.N. & Lausen G. Spreading Activation Models for Trust Propagation. Proc. IEEE International Conference on e-Technology, e-Commerce, and e-Service, 2004.

Supporting Task Resumption Using Visual Feedback

Yikun Liu, Yuan Jia, Wei Pan, Mark Pfaff
School of Informatics and Computing
Indiana University, Indianapolis
Indianapolis, IN 46202
{yikliu, jiayuan, panwei, mpfaff}@iupui.edu

ABSTRACT

For information workers, maintaining high productivity relies on timely task resumption after interruptions, which are frequent. However, people's task resumption ability is compromised by disruptive environments and human cognitive limitations. We propose that a helpful intervention is to provide visual feedback about the duration of a suspended task. Results from a controlled study show significantly shorter average off-task time by adding visual feedback. Further, using emotionally attachable visual objects in the visualization has the additional benefit of decreasing off-task time without increasing stress. Punishment-oriented persuasion strategies produced faster resumption, but also caused higher stress levels. Combined with other related results, we discuss the implications for design as well directions for future study.

Author Keywords

Interruptions; task resumption; visual feedback; persuasive computing;

ACM Classification Keywords

H.4.1. [Information Systems Applications]: Office Automation - Time Management; H.5.2. [Information Interfaces and Presentation]: User Interfaces — Theory and Methods

General Terms

Human Factor; Design

INTRODUCTION

Information exchange and task coordination are often achieved by group members interrupting each other through face-to-face or computer-mediated communication. At any moment of work, among all the tasks a person is involved in, there typically is a set of primary tasks that are of higher priority and demand more cognitive control and attentiveness to produce meaningful results. To maintain workflow, workers need to resume primary tasks in a timely fashion after an interruption, whether from a team member or self-initiated.

CSCW'14, February 15 - 19 2014, Baltimore, MD, USA
Copyright 2014 ACM 978-1-4503-2540-0/14/02…$15.00.
http://dx.doi.org/10.1145/2531602.2531710

However, task resumption is becoming increasingly difficult given the fragmentation of work [19]. For example, O'Connaill and Frohlich [39] found that 41% of the time interrupted workers failed to resume their original tasks. For group work, failure to resume tasks is not only directly attributed to unmanaged group interruptions, but also in turn impedes the completion of cooperative work. After all, it is these individuals who need to manage his/her own share of work and keep up with schedules in order to collectively advance the group's work. Thus, a successful and efficient cooperative environment should also incorporate assistive techniques that maintain personal working efficiency within the inevitable interruptions associated with group work.

To study potential interventions, the purpose of this study is to test whether providing visual feedback regarding the duration of task suspension can improve primary task resumption. Providing dynamic visual cues indicating the length of the task suspension helps a worker become more aware of it and its implications. The visual feedback serves two primary purposes: 1) reminding the worker of the existence of the suspended task and its status and 2) motivating an immediate resumption of the suspended task.

RELATED WORK

Interruption at workplaces

Researchers of communication and workplace interruptions have been studying their negative effects for many years [12, 36]. Not only do interruptions create difficulties for maintaining task flow, they also cause stress and frustration [36]. Constant interruptions often lead to discontinuity of primary tasks [39] and procrastination [27]. Existing intervention methods in group work contexts include minimizing occurrences of interruptions by either controlling notifications [24] or broadcasting the individual's availability in order to regulate mutual interruptions between group members [13]. However, filtering or delaying the arrival of interruptions could result in missing important messages and losing the optimal timing for dealing with the interruptions.

In addition, researchers also identify an equally if not more significant type of interruption: self-initiated interruptions [14]. Self-interruptions are initiated by internal causes rather than explicit external sources. A previous study indicates that self-interruptions are more disruptive than external ones [14]. Since self-interruptions do not have explicit sources, it becomes very difficult to suppress them by managing the sources, which are inside the human mind.

Thus it is proposed that an alternative approach is to help task resumption regardless of its source. Previous designs in supporting task resumption focus on preserving and resuming context of the original task to enhance goal retrieval from memory [15, 18]. These attempts try to ease the transition by providing some kind of memory aid. Though it is important to support goal retrieval, it neglects to address other relevant problems behind failed resumption: missing the resumption cues and the lack of motivation for resumption. These issues apply equally to external and self-interruptions.

Failure to resume at the right time

Common to both external and self-interruptions, a critical moment in an interruption cycle is when the interrupting task is completed, or its urgency has been contained, and thus the person is supposed to return to primary tasks. However, numerous factors influence a worker's decision making at this moment, including environmental characteristics and individuals' cognitive limitations.

Subtle Cues

Firstly, the opportune timing for resumption is usually not well defined. For example, a person browsing Facebook feeds often does not have a clear cue signaling the proper end of the activity. On the other hand, ending a conversation and hanging-up the phone clearly signals the end of a phone call interruption. In cases like Facebook browsing, it often depends on the person to be aware of the time to end that task. Different people have different ways of defining how much time is too much for deferring task resumption. In other cases, interruptions are cascaded in such a way that resumption cues for previous interruptions are shadowed by new interruptions and old interruptions are never returned to [35].

Ego Depletion

Secondly, people need to be sufficiently alert to cues and fully motivated to control their behaviors to complete the resumption. Research in self-control indicates that this critical cognitive resource for self-regulation diminishes over time, which is coined as "Ego Depletion" by Baumeister and colleagues [1]. Inzlicht and Schmeichel [23] further reveals that lack of motivation and dampening of attention are the culprits for the failure of self-control. When people are less motivated to exert self-control, they pay more attention to cues that meet their predominant response tendencies. With low motivation and divided attention, especially at later stages of task execution, information workers become more susceptible to impulsive tendencies to go off-task.

Disruptive Environment

Thirdly, working environments nowadays increasingly enable self-indulgence, which does a disservice to self-regulation. Part of the reason why resumption cues are too subtle to catch can be attributed to the principles of modern information system design, which emphasize capturing user attention and indulging continuous browsing [38]. Techniques like push notifications, shortcuts, and related links all try to encourage frequent visits and extended stays on these information services, which in many cases are entirely off-task. Group working environments such as open cubicles also result in a higher interruption rate [14].

Visual Feedback

Based on these previous findings, a feedback mechanism is needed to boost self-regulation when self-control strength is low. Visual feedback works as a "discrepancy-reducer" in self-control by decreasing the gap between one's self-control goals and actual behaviors [5]. In order to detect such discrepancies, a monitoring process is key to successful control [7]. Similar to the Cybernetic model in engineering [42], this monitoring process operates on a negative feedback loop in which feedback is given in proportion to the discrepancy. A monitoring lapse of neglecting a goal often leads to failure in self-control [29]. Thus it is predicted that using visual feedback that highlights the goal and discrepancy could enhance this monitoring process and improve self-control behaviors.

Emotionally-Attachable Objects as Motivators

Many persuasive devices or applications implement an emotional motivator, referred to as an *emotionally-attachable object*. For example, UbiGarden [11] presents an aesthetically pleasing display of a growing garden to represent the amount and variety of the user's exercise activities. Fish'n'Steps [34] encourages physical activity using an animated visualization of a fish in a tank, which also includes other players' fish. Designs in persuasive computing use similar objects as a way of encouraging target behaviors [8, 32]. To mitigate motivation loss, amiable visual feedback encourages users to respond to an unfavorable state of the object with the motivation to return it to a favorable state, hence serving as a motivation for immediate task resumption.

Persuasion Strategies

Another factor concerns the persuasion strategy for motivation. Operant Conditioning theory in behavioral change uses the general category of punishment" and "reward" as two basic persuasion strategies [41]. Punishment emphasizes negative feedback for unfavorable behaviors while reward emphasizes giving positive feedback for favorable behaviors. This study tests which of the two general strategies could have a larger effect on task resumption.

METHODOLOGY

Experiment Setting

To test the effect of visual feedback on task resumption, we implemented two forms of computer animations as visual stimuli: a dynamically changing flower (rose) and a traditional horizontal progress bar (See Figure 1). With a total of 1024 frames, the flower animation changed from being fully bloomed to withered and dying. To establish direct comparison, the progress bar also updated in 1/1024 increments. Both flower and progress bar start at 2/3 of full scale. Both visualizations occupied the full screen on an extended display attached to the primary working display. For the control group, the extended display showed an empty black screen. Participants were told to only operate on the primary display, leaving the extended display unoccupied. We enforced the display to be full screen on the extended monitor in order be consistent across groups.

Figure 1. Sample Flower Frames and Progress Bar

Our choice of using a blooming/withering flower is inspired by and partly in accordance with design strategies put forward by Consolvo et al [10]. A blooming/withering flower satisfies most of their design strategies such as Aesthetic, Unobtrusive, Abstract/Reflective and Controllable. The principle of Positive is tested as an independent variable (Persuasion Strategy) while Trending/Historical and Comprehensive are not fully implemented. The deviation from some of these principles is due to the lab-based nature of this study. Moreover, Consolvo et al's design strategies are drawn from projects targeted at changing long-time lifestyles, e.g. physical activity, while the goal of our tool is more interested in correcting short-time task management behaviors.

Using the Windows API, we developed a logging tool that constantly monitored the topmost window in the participant's primary display. This was used as an indication of what the participant was looking at any moment and determined whether the participant was on or off task at that moment.

With two visualizations (Flower and Progress Bar) and two persuasion strategies (Punishment and Reward), this experiment has 2x2 factorial design plus the Empty condition as a control group, receiving no visual feedback and consequently no persuasion strategies. In the "Punishment" condition, the longer a person was deviating from the windows that were related to primary tasks (such as a Microsoft Word document), the more withered the flower appeared, or the less full the progress bar became, depending on the visualization condition. In the reward condition, the longer a user stayed on windows that are related to primary tasks, the more the flower blossomed or the more the progress bar became full. The transition of direction in both visualizations was instantaneous: the moment a user changed the topmost window from primary tasks to work-unrelated task, or vice versa, the direction changed to reflect this.

The punishment and reward strategies were manipulated by adjusting the change rate of the visualizations, as described in Table 1. Fast animation changed at the rate of 4 frames per second while slow animation changed at the rate of 2 frames per second.

Visualization	Punishment	Reward
Flower	Slowly blossom/ Fast decay	Fast blossom/ Slowly decay
Progress Bar	Slowly grow/ Fast reduce	Fast grow/ Slowly reduce

Table 1. Implementation of Persuasion Strategies

Calibration on the Flower Frames

The actual difference between two neighboring frames in the flower visualization is almost undetectable from a human eye. However, given the change rate described earlier, over 2~3 seconds the difference should be obvious to participants.

To have at least a roughly linear representation of flower florescence, we calibrated the flower image frames based on florescence ratings from a pilot study. We selected nine equally-spaced frames from the flower visualization with each representing 10% increment for the whole range of florescence from 10% blossomed to 90% blossomed. We put these images on Amazon Mechanical Turk (AMT) along with images representing the two extreme states of flowering: the fully withered and the fully blossomed, labeled with a score of 0 and 10 respectively. We asked the participants on AMT to rate the 9 randomly presented frames in terms of their level of florescence in comparison with the two extremes. In return, 52 participants from AMT responded with their ratings. The mean values are shown in Table 2. Though the perceived florescence did not follow the spacing of the frames perfectly, only the midpoint (5/10) was substantially higher than anticipated.

Actual Frame	**1/10**	**2/10**	**3/10**	**4/10**	**5/10**
Mean Ratings	1.87	2.85	3.04	4.62	6.23
Actual Frame	**6/10**	**7/10**	**8/10**	**9/10**	
Mean Ratings	6.65	7.58	7.88	8.56	

Table 2. Florescence Ratings from AMT Study

Hypotheses

Our first set of hypotheses was focused on studying differences caused by visualizations and persuasion strategies on time spent on off-task activities:

- H1: Participants with visual feedback (Flower or Progress Bar) will spend shorter off-task time than participants without visualization.

- H2: Participants with the Flower will spend shorter off-task time than participants with the Progress Bar visualization.

We were also interested in whether participants would perform more voluntary switching behaviors without visual feedback. Voluntary switching activities are task switching that are driven by their own volition, including self-interruptions and subsequent voluntary switching after the initial interruption.

- H3: Participants with visual feedback (Flower or Progress Bar) will have less voluntary switching than participants without visual feedback.

We also wanted to observe depletion effects in this study as predicted by Ego Depletion theory, thus:

- H4: Participants will have slower task resumption in later stages of the experimental session.

Finally, we were also interested in whether different visualizations or persuasion strategies would cause more psychological effects such as stress, thus:

- H5: Participants with visual feedback (Flower or Progress Bar) will have a higher subjective stress level than participants without visual feedback.
- H6: Participants receiving Punishment feedback will have higher subjective stress levels than participants receiving Reward feedback.

Participants
30 participants were recruited from a Midwestern university campus via online and in-person solicitation. Participants were randomly assigned into three visualization groups with ten in each group. Each participant in the intervention groups (Flower or Progress Bar) was randomly assigned to either the Punishment or Reward persuasion strategy, resulting in five Punishment recipients and five Reward recipients in each of the intervention groups. This allowed us to compare between five independent groups: Empty, Flower/Punishment, Flower/Reward, Progress Bar/Punishment and Progress Bar/Reward. Each participant was compensated with a $10 Amazon gift card at the end of the study.

Procedure

Framing
It is known that people will behave differently when they know they are being tested [6]. To increase our chances of capturing the behaviors of interest, despite the inherent limitations of a laboratory setting, and to cover our true intent of studying interruption behaviors, we framed our study as an evaluation of new office working environments, in which the participant would perform a typical office task: editing Microsoft Word documents.

After reading and signing the consent form, participants were asked to fill out a questionnaire collecting their demographic information and social media/computer usage. The facilitator then introduced several "new office setting elements" to the participant, including green plants, a new type of office chair, some newly designed lamps, and a seat beside a large window in order to provide an outdoor view and natural light (Figure 2). Participants in the intervention groups were also introduced to the visualization intervention (flower or progress bar). The facilitator introduced each of these office setting elements with equal emphasis and in random order. This design intended to minimize participants' suspicion toward the visualization as the tool under evaluation.

The monitoring application detects inputs from the mouse and keyboard and considers any input as legitimate as long as the Microsoft Word windows stay on the topmost position. This knowledge, if shared with participants beforehand, could result in participants abusing the system by just randomly using the keyboard/mouse to fake productivity. Therefore we did not tell them these operational details beforehand, but only told them that the visualization changes based on their progress on the primary task.

Figure 2. Experiment Setting

Task
The primary task was editing a Word document continuously for 40 minutes. The document was ill-formatted with inconsistent fonts, unaligned paragraphs, messy tables and other features requiring editing. They were given four such documents and asked to fill the time by performing the editing task, but not to be concerned about making a specific amount of progress. Participants were told that this task is of low importance and has no deadline. Each document was at least 20 pages long and they were not expected to finish any of four documents. They were reminded that neither editing quality nor speed was important to the study. They were encouraged to relax and perform the task at the rate and in the way they feel comfortable. They were told that no audio or video recording devices were implemented in the room and that they were allowed to perform any habit they may have when doing computer-based tasks, e.g. listening to music, checking emails, etc. All these instructions aimed to lower

participants' awareness of being in an experiment and encourage spontaneous behaviors. Participants were still reminded that the editing task is the primary goal during the experiment and relinquishing the editing task is not appreciated.

Interruptions

Mimicking a group work environment, distracting interruptions were sent over Google Chat in the form of task requests. These external interruptions forced a baseline level of interruptions in the task in addition to participants' voluntary interruption behaviors such as self-interruptions and delayed resumptions. Typical requests included "Please go check your Facebook feeds and follow any links or stories for as long as you like" and "Please go check new uploads in your YouTube subscription and watch any video you like." All these interruption destinations (e.g. Facebook and YouTube) were drawn randomly from the participants' answers to the question regarding their most frequently visited websites in the pre-study survey. Participants were told that they did not have to reply to the facilitator upon completing the requests. All subsequent actions were of their own volition. This was to eliminate the possibility that replying in the chat box would constitute an additional resumption cue for the participants.

The logging program continuously broadcasts the participant's window changing activities to a web service by sending out the window titles (not the actual content of the windows). The facilitator in another room then was able to monitor participants' window-switching activities via a browser-based client. Based on moment-by-moment updates, the facilitator decided when to send the next request according to the following rules: 1) if the participant is on the editing task, wait for five minutes and send a request; 2) if the participant is off task, do not send requests; 3) when the participant resumes the editing task, reset the timer and wait for another five minutes to send the next interruption; 4) if the participant self-interrupts and goes off task before the five minute timer is up, stop the timer and wait for the participant to resume on his/her own.

Both the logging and monitoring program were not revealed to the participant until the end of the study. At the end of the study we had signed consent from participants to allow us to use the log file after the file was reviewed by the participants. No participants requested any deletion of entries from the log files.

Pre- and post-tests

Before the editing task, each participant went through a five-minute digit-span test. A digit-span test asks subjects to repeat a sequence of digits immediately after seeing the sequence. The digit-span tests were used to deliberately deplete participants' cognitive resources before entering the actual experiment. As adopted in Ego Depletion studies [31], this technique is used to make the depletion effect more detectable.

After the editing task, participants were asked to fill out a modified NASA TLX [20], with one additional question about self-reported stress level, as used by Mark and colleagues [36]. Participants also rated how much they liked the visualization after the study. The study concluded with a semi-structured interview about the participant's experience using the tool, their motivations behind interruption behaviors, and their general impression toward the visualizations.

DATA COLLECTION

The logging tool captures all the window-switching activities and writes all activities into a file. Each entry contains the timestamp of the switching as well as the title of the current topmost window. This log file provides the ability to determine if a participant is on or off of the editing task at any moment of the study. Two measures were extracted from the log files as dependent variables:

Average Off-task Time (AOT): For each participant, we computed the average duration of off-task time as a measure of primary task resumption speed. This quantity was calculated by dividing their total off-task time by the number of window-switches away from Microsoft Word to other windows. Incidents where the participant peeked at other windows and switched right back to the editing task within 10 seconds were excluded. This is based on the observation from the data that a task deviation that lasts shorter than 10 seconds usually ends at the Google Chat window. This suggested that such deviations were intended at checking for new requests, rather than leaving the editing task. AOT is preferable to using total off-task time as a measure of resumption speed because the total duration of the experiment varied from participant to participant due to the off-task time being open-ended. The five minute limit for on-task time before an interruption created a floor effect where even the most efficient workers suffered a baseline penalty without being rewarded for remaining on-task for the full duration.

Voluntary Switching (VS): For each participant, we counted the incidents of window switching that were driven by their own volition. Specifically, we counted the number of different webpages a participant visited other than the websites requested by the facilitator. This includes all the subsequent visited websites after an initial interruption as well as all the target websites visited by self-initiated interruptions.

RESULTS

Task Switching:

Overall, participants spent on average 45.0% ($M = 0.45$, $SD = 0.15$) of time off tasks which amounts to about 18 minutes of off task time if we normalize total experiment time to 40 minutes. The mean AOT across all groups was 169 ($M = 169.46$, $SD = 111.50$) seconds. On average, participants made 114 ($M = 114.0$, $SD = 82.37$) window switches. Participants made 8.53 ($M = 8.53$, $SD = 3.55$)

switches away from the editing task. Of those switches, a mean of 4.86 ($M = 4.86$, $SD = 2.23$) were self-initiated.

Average Off-task Time (AOT)

One-way ANOVA on five between-subject groups revealed significant differences of AOT[1] across the groups ($F(4, 20) = 3.21$, $p < 0.05$). Planned contrasts showed the Empty group ($M = 249.60$, $SE = 43.81$) had significant higher AOT than the rest of the groups ($t(20) = -2.72$, $p < 0.05$), confirming H1 that providing the visualization significant shortens average off-task time compared to the control. Further, Flower group's AOT ($M = 119.03$, $SE = 15.35$) was also significantly shorter than that of Empty group ($t(20) = -2.64$, $p < 0.05$). Progress Bar ($M = 139.76$, $SE = 27.51$) also produced a significantly shorter AOT than the Empty group ($t(20) = -2.32$, $p < 0.05$), but the Flower and Progress Bar did not have a significantly different AOT ($t(20) = 0.40$, *ns*). This rejects H2 and indicates that the Progress Bar and Flower are not significantly different in term of resumption effectiveness. Figure 3 illustrates AOT among the three groups. The fact that having a visualization produced lower AOT is partially supported in interview data. For example, P24 mentioned: "As soon as I see the petals get a little brown edge, I jump back to the Word. I want to keep it normal!"

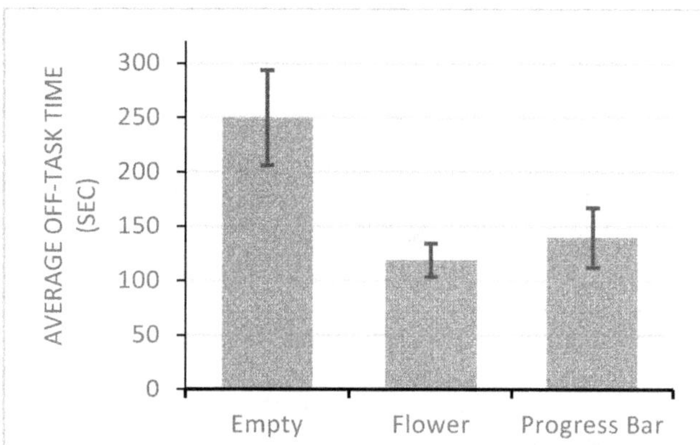

Figure 3. AOT across Visualization Groups

For persuasion strategies in the intervention groups, a two-way Factorial (2x2) ANOVA of both visualizations (excluding Empty) and persuasion strategy revealed a significant main effect of persuasion strategy ($F(2, 16) = 11.04$, $p < 0.05$), but no significant main effect of visualization and no significant interaction effect between the two. Regardless of visualization, Reward ($M = 170.23$, $SE = 21.07$) produced significantly longer AOT than Punishment ($M = 88.56$, $SE = 14.20$). Figure 4 shows the AOT between two strategies.

[1] AOT was log10 transformed for a normal distribution.

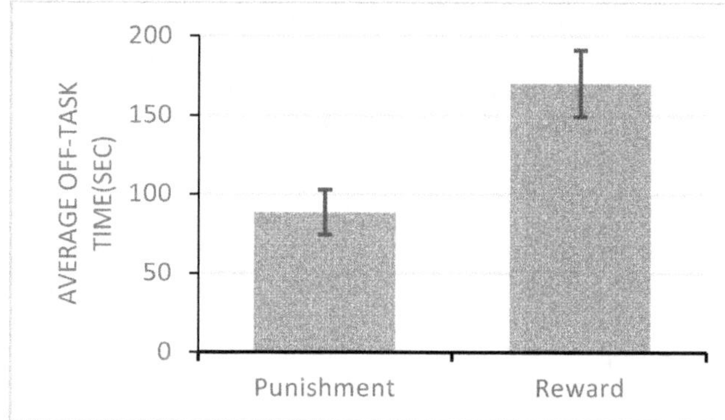

Figure 4. AOT between Persuasion Strategies

Even though there was no significant interaction effect between visualization and persuasion strategy, Figure 5 shows that the Progress Bar is marginally more sensitive to persuasion strategies.

Figure 5. Interaction between Visualization and Persuasion Strategy on AOT

Factorial ANOVA on gender and visualization failed to find a significant main effect of gender or interaction effect of gender and visualizations in terms of average off-task time.

Depletion Effect

To investigate the depletion effect over time, we extracted all off-task time (OT) from log files. We also calculated the time into the study for each entry based on the timestamps. A multiple regression was run to predict OT from time and visualization type. Both variables significantly predicted OT, $F(2, 253) = 5.89$, $p < .005$, and both added significantly to the prediction, $p < .05$. Time's $\beta = 0.26$, meaning that regardless of the visualization type, OT increases over time. There was no significant interaction between visualization and time into the study.

Voluntary Switching (VS)

The mean number of voluntary switches was 34.7 ($SE = 4.06$) for the Flower group, 30.5 ($SE = 3.52$) for the Progress Bar group, and 42.0 ($SE = 4.60$) for the Empty Group. In terms of persuasion strategy, the mean VS was 31.3 ($SE = 3.61$) for the Punishment group and 33.9 ($SE = 4.05$) for the Reward group. The number of voluntary switches was not significant across the five groups based on one-way ANOVA ($F(4, 20) = 1.86$, *ns*). Excluding the Empty group, a two-way factorial ANOVA of visualization and persuasion strategy also failed to find significant results ($F(3,16) = 0.516$, *ns*). This result rejects H3 and concludes that there is no significant difference in terms of voluntary switching across visualization groups.

Subjective Workload

Subjective Stress

In answering the stress related question in the NASA TLX questionnaire ("How stressed do you feel throughout the task?"), the Flower group produced the lowest subjective stress level ($M = 2.40$, $SE = 0.50$), followed by the Empty group ($M = 2.70$, $SE = 0.63$), and the Progress Bar group with highest subjective stress level ($M = 9.20$, $SE = 1.78$). Non-normal distribution of subjective stress level required nonparametric analysis (Kruskal-Wallis), which indicated there was a significant subjective stress level difference across the three visualization groups ($H(2) = 11.23$, $p < 0.05$). Mann-Whitney tests were used to perform pair-wise comparisons using a Bonferroni corrected significance level of .0167 (3 comparisons). The Flower group's subjective stress level was significantly lower than the Progress Bar group ($U = 12.00$, $p < .0167$). The Empty group's subjective stress was also significantly lower than Progress Bar group ($U = 13.50$, $p < .0167$). The difference of subjective stress levels between the Flower group and Empty group was not significant. This rejected H5 but also shows that the Progress Bar elicited higher stress levels than other two visualizations. Figure 7 shows subjective stress across the three visualization groups.

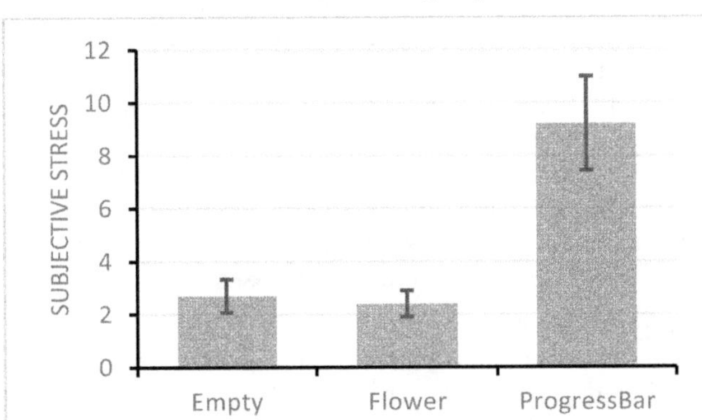

Figure 7. Subjective Stress across Visualization groups

A Mann-Whitney test also revealed that within the intervention groups, the Punishment strategy produced significant higher subjective stress levels ($M = 8.20$, $SE = 1.96$) than the Reward strategy ($M = 3.40$, $SE = 0.92$; Mann-Whitney's $U = 23.50$, $p < 0.05$). This result confirms H6 that Punishment recipients have higher stress levels than Reward recipients. Figure 8 shows the subjective stress level between persuasion strategies. In our interview, P18 confirmed the result that Punishment produced higher stress level by saying: "I feel like the flower's speed of decaying is faster than recovering and it made me more nervous".

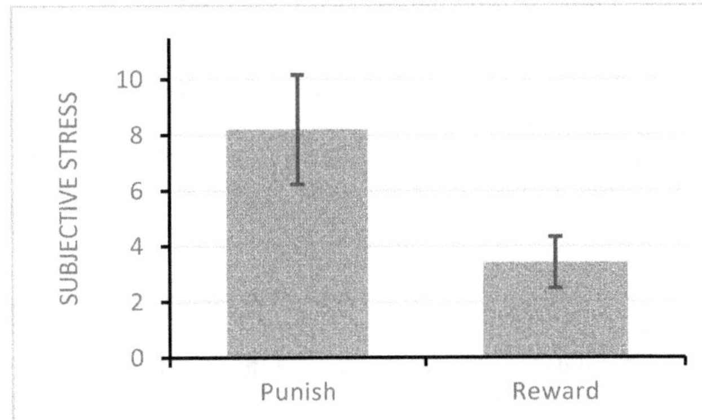

Figure 8. Subjective Stress between Persuasion Strategies

Subjective Time Pressure

For the survey question regarding time pressure ("How hurried were you while doing the task?"), visualization types did not have a significant effect on subjective time pressure. However, persuasion strategy did: Punishment produced a significantly higher self-reported time pressure ($M = 9.30$, $SE = 1.71$) than the Reward strategy ($M = 2.80$, $SE = 0.65$; Mann-Whitney's $U = 13.50$, $p < 0.05$).

Subjective Likability and Gender

Even though gender and visualization did not have a significant interaction effect on AOT performance, they did have significant interaction effect on self-reported liking of the visualization in post-test survey. Factorial ANOVA revealed a significant interaction effect between visualization and gender ($F(3,16) = 17.74$, $p < 0.05$). Specifically, male participants rated both the Progress Bar ($M = 3.14$, $SE = 0.55$) and Flower ($M = 3.00$, $SE = 0.649$) similarly, while female participants liked the Flower visualization significantly higher ($M = 5.80$, $SE = 0.65$) than the Progress Bar ($M = 2.00$, $SE = 0.84$). Participant 19 (Male) confirmed his preference toward the progress bar by saying that "it gives direct feedback and I can see where I am clearly."

DISCUSSION

On Visualization

The significant difference of AOT across visualization groups indicates that providing visual feedback helps participants return to tasks faster. Even though the Flower group produced a somewhat lower mean AOT than the Progress Bar group, the effect of adding an emotionally attachable element like the flower does not significantly help. On the other hand, the Progress Bar elicited a significantly higher level of subjective stress than the Flower intervention, indicating that in the long run, immediate and direct feedback such as a progress bar could wear people out. It is thus recommended that amiable and emotionally attachable visualizations could achieve a similar level of effectiveness in boosting task resumption while creating less stress on users. However, due to the limitations of a lab-based study, how well these visualizations could support long-term use needs to be further studied in a real workplace environment.

On Persuasion Strategy

The punishment strategy produced significantly faster resumption while also inducing significantly higher subjective stress levels and subjective time pressure. This result shows the double-bladed effect of using the punishment method: it has higher effectiveness but also creates higher pressure on users. The Reward group's lower stress level and time pressure as well as longer off-task time may be explained by some information gathered in the post-test interview. Many Reward recipients mentioned the opportunities of "taking a breath" granted by the Reward intervention. Once they attained a high level with the visualization (almost fully blossomed flower or almost full progress bar), they gave themselves a license to take a break by visiting non-work related websites. Since the reduction of the progress bar or flower is much faster in the Punishment condition, those participants did not perceive themselves as having this license. This "self-licensing" behavior is often seen as a motivation deficit or justification for immediate gratification and over-indulgence [16]. Designing for a relaxing condition like Reward requires vigilance for excessive self-licensing behaviors and must balance the manipulation between encouraging high concentration and allowing mental and physical relaxation. The result from this study also gives evidence as to why the reward strategy could help persuasive technology's continuous use, as predicted by Consolvo et al [10].

On Depletion Effect

As predicted by Ego Depletion theory [1], a depletion effect on AOT was observed over time for all groups. Thus H4 is confirmed. However, no significant interaction was found between the time into the study and the visualization type. Further study is still needed to investigate how visual feedback could influence the depletion effect.

On Voluntary Switching

The analysis on voluntary switching did not yield significant results. This is probably due to the relatively small sample size and limited study time (40 minutes on average). It might also have to do with the fact that some websites are better at grasping user attention and making users stay (e.g. YouTube) than others and that is why the significant results in AOT is not reflected on the number of webpages visited.

On Taking Breaks

It is worth noting that tools such as these that continuously encourage people to get back to work should not prohibit taking breaks during working hours. Numerous studies indicate the benefits of taking breaks at workplaces [21, 26]. Research in attention restoration advocates taking breaks as a way of replenishing attention resources [2]. However, for more and more information workers, taking breaks often means visiting non-work-related websites, which tend not to replenish cognitive resources, compared to restorative activities such as taking a stroll in the park [4].

As predicted by previous research, visiting these websites as a way of taking breaks is counterproductive in replenishing cognitive resource. Firstly, these websites are what Kaplan and colleagues refer to as *hard fascinations* that fixate one's attention and disallow any reflection about anything else. Thus they are less effective in attention restoration [30]. On the contrary, *soft fascinations* are natural objects such as flowers, plants, or woods that promote reflection on other things and are validated ways of attention restoration. Secondly, Zeigarnik shows that unfinished issues could persist in memory [44]. These *attention residues* [33] create interferences with normal task execution by disrupting cognitive functioning [3, 28]. It is recommended that visual feedback be integrated with scheduled breaks to produce a sustainable working flow.

On Multitasking Tendencies

Ophir et al [40] aims to debunk the myth of multitasking efficiency in the digital age. Their work recognizes that people are not as good at multitasking as they think they are, especially given the saturation of information in today's world. Their results indicate that heavy media multitaskers are habituated to "explorative" rather than "exploitative" ways of information processing and they are more attracted to off-task stimuli. This means they are more likely to be disrupted by the external environment and more likely to interrupt themselves to explore novel stimuli.

Therefore, based on Ophir et al's results and those learned from this study, an intervention for heavy media multitaskers could aim to limit the extent of this "explorative" way of information processing by providing visual feedback reminding them about the extent and duration of off-task behaviors. This will narrow their attention allocation to more important tasks. In other words, for multitaskers, tools like those in this study serve as a container that prevents irrational time and attention allocation to secondary or irrelevant tasks.

Design Implications

The effectiveness of providing visual feedback is confirmed in this study. The insignificant AOT differences between the Flower and Progress Bar shows that either dynamic cue can effectively remind and motivate task resumption. In addition, rewarding strategies are potentially more suitable for long time use since they produced lower stress level, as recommended by [10].

Confirming the visualization likability results, our interview data identified a theme of male participants reacting rather lukewarm toward the Flower visualizations. This indicates potential individual differences in terms of acceptance of different visualizations. Previous studies confirmed that in persuasive computing, designers should consider gender as a factor in persuasive design [43]. For long-term use in real-life work environments, different people will respond differently to visualizations as motivators [10]. It is important to match individual differences to maximize the motivation effect, or offer customizations that improve effectiveness.

A higher-level design suggestion is to recognize the differences between two modes of operating a computer: recreational and serious working. System designers should take into account the human cognition characteristics under the two modes and provide support accordingly.

LIMITATION AND FUTURE WORK

Task Urgency

One of the side-effects of this framing was misrepresenting real-life behaviors. 13 out of the 30 participants mentioned in their interview that if they knew the task was urgent, they would have spent much less time on irrelevant tasks and focus more on the editing task. Indeed, task urgency can increase rate of task completion [9]. Thus the results of this study do not directly apply to contexts with high task urgency, whose effects on motivation for task completion could be large enough such that visual feedback is unnecessary. Further studies are needed to explore how external factors such as task urgency would enhance or diminish the effect of visual feedback on the rate of task resumption.

On the other side, because of the large effect of task urgency on task resumption and in order to prevent task urgency from masking the effect caused by visual feedback, we had to bring every participant down to a similar low-level task urgency in order to observe how visual feedback alone could influence the resumption efficiency.

Moreover, the results of this study still have validity in certain circumstances. First, workers whose tasks are not deadline-driven depend more on self-regulation capacity than task characteristics to manage interruptions and resumptions. Second, claiming that situational differences would alter their behaviors does not stand as an excuse for self-control failure in general non-urgent scenarios, which characterizes much of routine office work. Lastly, delaying a task to the last minute to increase its urgency is a common type of procrastination behavior identified by researchers as *Arousal Procrastination* [17], which is an extreme example of over-dependence on deadlines.

Complex Real-life Interruptions

We recognize the complexity of real-life interruptions and their formation [35]. In particular, interruptions are often interleaved and the setting of primary tasks often changes over time. This study demonstrated the efficacy of visual feedback in a simplified context and may not be fully replicable when faced with the complexity in real-scenarios.

However, we can still see the potential even with this complexity: as long as there is some relative difference of importance among tasks, more sophisticated tools can be built which intelligently learn about the environment and adjust the settings to accommodate this complexity. Examples include dynamically detecting the primary tasks or pausing the feedback upon important immediate interruptions. Other projects demonstrate the potential of systems that are able to learn about working environments such as [22] and [25].

Sources of Interruptions

Real-life interruptions are not always coming from chat-based communication like this study. As described earlier, some interruptions have explicit cues for resumption while others do not. Thus some interruptions are inherently easier to conclude, e.g. phone call vs. visiting Facebook. Thus the effect of visual feedback should be more pronounced for wrapping up interruptions that are more open-ended.

Limited Sample Size

The limited number of participants prevented us from arriving at other interesting conclusions such as gender differences, voluntary switching behaviors, and the effect on mental workload. These factors remain to be investigated in future studies with larger sample sizes.

Future Work

Follow-up studies are applying field research methods and investigating the usage of such tools in real-life settings. A diary-based study recording daily use of the tool will enable a deeper understanding of the problems of interruptions in collaborative work settings and produce robust designs for addressing them. Natural settings give us opportunities to investigate contextual influences on task resumptions. Such context variables could be: task urgency, task completion level, time of day, nature of the task, and others.

In regard to supporting group motivation, this tool also could be extended to involve multiple group members competing with each other by sharing each other's visualizations. Such effort in gamifying working spaces has seen positive results [37].

CONCLUSION

Disruptive environments and cognition limitations delay timely task resumption after interruptions. The results of this study suggest that the use of visual feedback on task suspension can function as an effective intervention to help people resume tasks more gracefully and efficiently. Results also show the efficacy of using emotionally attachable objects of both reducing off-task time and controlling stress level. However, further studies are needed to address individual differences on responsiveness to visual persuasion to maximize its effectiveness. Lastly, future work must investigate the effectiveness of this intervention on long-term use and whether it is best used on an ongoing basis, or if it may function most effectively as a tool to train more productive behaviors, and then be discontinued.

ACKNOWLEDGEMENT

The authors thank Michael Durham (www. durmphoto.com) for allowing the use of his time-lapse rose photography in this study.

REFERENCES

1. Baumeister, R. F., et al. Ego depletion: is the active self a limited resource? *Journal of personality and social psychology, 74*, 5 (1998), 1252.
2. Berman, M. G., et al. The cognitive benefits of interacting with nature. *Psychological science, 19*, 12 (2008), 1207-1212.
3. Berman, M. G., et al. In search of decay in verbal short-term memory. *Journal of experimental psychology. Learning, memory, and cognition, 35*, 2 (2009), 317.
4. Bock, G. W. and Ho, S. L. Non-work related computing (NWRC). *Communications of the ACM, 52*, 4 (2009), 124-128.
5. Botvinick, M. M., et al. Conflict monitoring and cognitive control. *Psychological review, 108*, 3 (2001), 624.
6. Carlopio, J. *The Hawthorne effect awareness of experimental participation or experimental demands?* , National Library of Canada, Ottawa, 1983.
7. Carver, C. S. and Scheier, M. *Attention and self-regulation: A control-theory approach to human behavior*. Springer-Verlag New York, 1981.
8. Chiu, M.-C., et al. Playful bottle: a mobile social persuasion system to motivate healthy water intake. In *Proc. Proceedings of the 11th international conference on Ubiquitous computing*, ACM (2009), 185-194.
9. Claessens, B. J. C., et al. Things to Do Today . . . : A Daily Diary Study on Task Completion at Work. *Applied Psychology, 59*, 2 (2010), 273-295.
10. Consolvo, S., et al. Theory-driven design strategies for technologies that support behavior change in everyday life. In *Proc. Proceedings of the SIGCHI Conference on Human Factors in Computing Systems*, ACM (2009), 405-414.
11. Consolvo, S., et al. Activity sensing in the wild: a field trial of ubifit garden. In *Proc. Proceedings of the SIGCHI Conference on Human Factors in Computing Systems*, ACM (2008), 1797-1806.
12. Czerwinski, M., et al. A diary study of task switching and interruptions. In *Proc. Proceedings of the SIGCHI conference on Human factors in computing systems*, ACM (2004), 175-182.
13. Dabbish, L. and Kraut, R. Coordinating communication: Awareness displays and interruption. In *Proc. CHI'03 extended abstracts on Human factors in computing systems*, ACM (2003), 786-787.
14. Dabbish, L., et al. Why do I keep interrupting myself?: Environment, habit and self-interruption. In *Proc. Proceedings of the SIGCHI Conference on Human Factors in Computing Systems*, ACM (2011), 3127-3130.
15. Daniels, J. J., et al. Support for intelligent interruption and augmented context recovery. In *Proc. Proceedings of the 2002 IEEE 7th Conference on Human Factors and Power Plants.*, IEEE (2002), 7-15-17-21.
16. De Witt Huberts, J. C., et al. License to sin: Self-licensing as a mechanism underlying hedonic consumption. *European Journal of Social Psychology, 42*, 4 (2012), 490-496.
17. Ferrari, J. R. Psychometric validation of two procrastination inventories for adults: Arousal and avoidance measures. *J Psychopathol Behav, 14*, 2 (1992), 97-110.
18. Franke, J. L., et al. Recovering context after interruption. In *Proc. Proceedings 24th Annual Meeting of the Cognitive Science Society* (2002), 310-315.
19. González, V. M. and Mark, G. *"Constant, constant, multi-tasking craziness": managing multiple working spheres.* ACM, City, 2004.
20. Hart, S. G. and Staveland, L. E. Development of NASA-TLX (Task Load Index): Results of empirical and theoretical research. *Human mental workload, 1* (1988), 139-183.
21. Henning, R. A., et al. Frequent short rest breaks from computer work: effects on productivity and well-being at two field sites. *Ergonomics, 40*, 1 (1997/01/01 1997), 78-91.
22. Horvitz, E., et al. Attention-sensitive alerting. In *Proc. Proceedings of the 15th conference on Uncertainty in artificial intelligence.* (1999), 305-313.
23. Inzlicht, M. and Schmeichel, B. J. What is ego depletion? Toward a mechanistic revision of the resource model of self-control. *Perspectives on Psychological Science, 7*, 5 (2012), 450-463.
24. Iqbal, S. T. and Bailey, B. P. Investigating the effectiveness of mental workload as a predictor of opportune moments for interruption. In *Proc. CHI '05 extended abstracts on Human factors in computing systems*, ACM (2005), 1489-1492.
25. Iqbal, S. T. and Bailey, B. P. Oasis: A framework for linking notification delivery to the perceptual structure of goal-directed tasks. *ACM Transactions on Computer-Human Interaction (TOCHI), 17*, 4 (2010), 15.
26. Jett, Q. R. and George, J. M. Work interrupted: A closer look at the role of interruptions in organizational life. *Academy of Management Review, 28*, 3 (2003), 494-509.
27. Jin, J. and Dabbish, L. A. Self-interruption on the computer: a typology of discretionary task interleaving. In *Proc. Proceedings of the 27th international*

conference on Human factors in computing systems, ACM (2009), 1799-1808.

28. Jonides, J., et al. The Mind and Brain of Short-Term Memory. *Annual Review of Psychology*, *59*, 1 (2008), 193-224.
29. Kane, M. J. and Engle, R. W. Working-memory capacity and the control of attention: The contributions of goal neglect, response competition, and task set to Stroop interference. *Journal of Experimental Psychology-General*, *132*, 1 (2003), 47-70.
30. Kaplan, S. The restorative benefits of nature: Toward an integrative framework. *Journal of environmental psychology*, *15*, 3 (1995), 169-182.
31. Kaplan, S. and Berman, M. G. Directed attention as a common resource for executive functioning and self-regulation. *Perspectives on Psychological Science*, *5*, 1 (2010), 43-57.
32. Kim, T., et al. Coralog: use-aware visualization connecting human micro-activities to environmental change. In *Proc. CHI'09 Extended Abstracts on Human Factors in Computing Systems*, ACM (2009), 4303-4308.
33. Leroy, S. Why is it so hard to do my work? The challenge of attention residue when switching between work tasks. *Organizational Behavior and Human Decision Processes*, *109*, 2 (2009), 168-181.
34. Lin, J. J., et al. Fish'n'Steps: Encouraging physical activity with an interactive computer game. In *Proc. UbiComp 2006: Ubiquitous Computing*, Springer (2006), 261-278.
35. Mark, G., et al. No task left behind?: Examining the nature of fragmented work. In *Proc. Proceedings of the SIGCHI conference on Human factors in computing systems*, ACM (2005), 321-330.
36. Mark, G., et al. The cost of interrupted work: more speed and stress. In *Proc. Proceedings of the twenty-sixth annual SIGCHI conference on Human factors in computing systems*, ACM (2008), 107–110.
37. Neil, D., et al. Limber: exploring motivation in a workplace exergame. In *Proc. Proceedings of the 2013 conference on Computer supported cooperative work companion*, ACM (2013), 239-242.
38. Nieson, J. Scrolling and Attention.(2010), http://www.nngroup.com/articles/scrolling-and-attention/
39. O'Conaill, B. and Frohlich, D. Timespace in the workplace: Dealing with interruptions. In *Proc. Conference companion on Human factors in computing systems*, ACM (1995), 262-263.
40. Ophir, E., et al. Cognitive control in media multitaskers. *Proceedings of the National Academy of Sciences of the United States of America*, *106*, 37 (Sep 15 2009), 15583-15587.
41. Skinner, B. F. Two types of conditioned reflex: a reply to Konorski and Miller. *J. Gen. Psychology*, *17*, 272 (1937), 79.
42. Wiener, N. Cybernetics: or Control and Communication in the Animal and the Machine (1948).
43. Zanbaka, C., et al. Can a virtual cat persuade you?: the role of gender and realism in speaker persuasiveness. In *Proc. Proceedings of the SIGCHI conference on Human Factors in computing systems*, ACM (2006), 1153-1162.
44. Zeigarnik, B. Über das Behalten von erledigten und unerledigten Handlungen. [Remembering completed and uncompleted tasks]. *Psychologische Forschung*, *9*, 1 (1927), 1-85.

Geographical and Organizational Commonalities in Enterprise Crowdfunding

Michael Muller*, Werner Geyer*, Todd Soule*, and John Wafer**
* IBM Research and ** IBM
* IBM Research, One Rogers Street, Cambridge, MA, USA 02142
** IBM, Shelbourne Road, Ballsbridge, Dublin 4 Ireland
{michael_muller, werner.geyer, tssoule}@us.ibm.com, waferjon@ie.ibm.com

ABSTRACT
Enterprise crowdfunding offers a series of opportunities for voluntary or unplanned collaborations within organizations. In an enterprise crowdfunding experiment, we study the influence of interpersonal attributes-in-common on collaborations. Using ideas from Homophily Theory and Social Identity Theory, we analyze attributes-in-common in terms of multiple *identity facets*: of geography, of formal corporate structure, and of working groups/teams. We combine quantitative and self-report data to show how each identity facet has an influence on the likelihood of voluntary collaborations, and we show their "superadditive" combination. We propose new questions for theory, and we consider how our results can lead to new features and technologies to enhance voluntary collaborations in organizations.

Author Keywords
Crowdfunding; Enterprise; Organization; CSCW; Voluntary collaboration; Homophily Theory; Social identity theory.

ACM Classification Keywords
H.5.3 [Group and organizational interfaces]: CSCW.

INTRODUCTION
"Distance matters," as Olson and Olson concluded in a landmark paper fourteen years ago [42]. Their analysis was primarily focused on geographical limits to collaboration via simultaneous or synchronous collaborations amongst members of structured teams. While their work has led to additional foundational studies of synchronous team collaboration [5, 45, 47], their treatment invoked a decades-long investigation into the impacts of geographical distance on various forms and configurations of collaborative work (e.g., [30]) that continues to be relevant for contemporary social technologies [45].

CSCW'14, February 15–19, 2014, Baltimore, Maryland, USA.

http://dx.doi.org/10.1145/2531602.2531716

Among other contributions, the Olson and Olson paper served as a major update to research that explored the influence of distance on collaboration *before* the recent explosion in synchronous technologies and real-time collaborations. Earlier work showed that distance could impact collaboration over spans as small as 30 meters [2; 27]. As in the analysis of Olson and Olson, Espinosa and colleagues theorized the effects in terms of decreased communication quality and increased timezone stress [15]. In contrast with formal work assignments, these issues can be particularly important for voluntary collaborations in many settings and applications [37], in which the potential collaboration partners could choose whether to engage in a particular project, and could choose between projects based on factors such as ease of communication, as well as serendipitous discovery of shared interests – e.g., "watercooler" collaborations [8].

Research programmes in social psychology and sociology offer alternative explanations. *Homophily theory* proposes that people tend to associate with people who are similar to themselves [9,49]. Early research examined people's statements and actions regarding others; more recent work has shown similar patterns of homophilous association in social media [37,51], with impact upon group performance [10]. Within this view, geographic location may serve as a cue to *similarity*, rather than *physical* constraint.

Another approach, *social identity theory*, proposes that people form part of their identities in terms of what they perceive they have in common with specified others (e.g., [24,48]; for a recent summary of social identity theory, see [50]). These perceptions can influence choices in whom to prefer to engage in certain activities [48]. Again, for social identity theory, geographic location may serve as a similarity cue.

Considered in those terms, the influence of distance may reflect fewer opportunities for the discovery of shared attributes among distant partners, rather than a problem of communication richness or effort [31,42,54] or convenience factors, such as timezone stress [15]. In this analysis, the "distance penalty" [28] might be reduced by the perception of attributes-in-common with remote potential collaborators.

Large global enterprises may offer an opportunity to re-examine the effects of geographical distance (or commonalities based on geography) – for both the synchronous focus of [7, 42] and the asynchronous focus of [2, 31]. Potential collaboration partners can be analyzed in terms of the fractional identities that they carry, such as their geographical location or national identity. Through people's roles in organizations, we can also consider the fractions of their identities that are derived from organizational position and/or matrixed teams or groups. We examine the influences of these different fractional identities in an experiment based on enterprise crowdfunding in a 5500-person globally distributed IT organization inside IBM, a large global corporation that conducts business in software and services.

Enterprise crowdfunding provides an interesting test of fractional identity effects in an asynchronous application. In enterprise crowdfunding, employees may create project proposals, and other employees may invest the organization's funds in those proposals [39]. There is no formal requirement to participate. Collaboration "partners" (i.e., proposer-and-investor or proposer-and-volunteer) need to find one another, and must determine whether they have sufficient motivation to collaborate – i.e., for the investor to decide to make an investment in the proposer's project. The enterprise crowdfunding Intranet site becomes a kind of connection-making site, where employees can engage not only in resource exchange [21], but also in serendipitous discovery of shared interests and collaborative relationships. The two published studies of crowdfunding inside academic [44] or industrial [39] organizations, suggest that members of the organization view their funding capabilities *not* as "their money," but rather as a shared resource to be allocated for the benefit of other members of the organization.

The remainder of this paper is organized as follows. We provide background information related to geographical issues in collaboration, and our intention to re-analyze those issues in terms of homophily theory and social identity theory. Based on these theories, we propose three "facets" of people's identities for our study. We then provide a brief orientation to Internet crowdfunding, and greater detail on our particular experiment with Intranet or "enterprise" crowdfunding. We describe our methodology, including diverse data sources that we used for a convergent analysis. Our results section describes the treatment of quantitative and qualitative data, showing how the three distinct facets of social identity have both independent and interactive influences on the likelihood of collaborating through crowdfunding. Our discussion applies these learnings to theory and design concepts. We conclude with a review of the contributions of this paper.

BACKGROUND

Geographical Obstacles to Collaboration

Earlier research into asynchronous collaboration found that distance could disrupt collaborative work [2, 31, 32, 54]. Variously called the "distance penalty" [28] or the "'distance matters' problem" [51], these issues continue to challenge organizations and researchers. O'Leary and Mortensen describe both communication and performance problems in virtual teams whose members are in remote locations [41].

Gittelman provides a nuanced view of both advantages and disadvantages in citation outcomes (not processes) for biotechnology teams in different spatial configurations [19], suggesting that some of the issues with geographical distance may be concerned with awareness of the work of others. Gittelman's theme of differential effects of distance was pursued by Birnholtz and colleagues, who dimensionalized some of the distance and difference effects and showed comparative advantages and disadvantages [5]. Other complexities were introduced by Jovanović, who examined the contributions of *local* proximity to *global* competitiveness [28].

In a more analytic vein, Espinosa and colleagues proposed five types of team boundaries: geographical, functional, temporal (see also [15]), identity, and organizational [16]. We examine three of those boundary concepts in this paper – geographical, identity, and organizational boundaries – as they affect the asynchronous collaboration practice of crowdfunding.

Homophily

To pursue the concept of identity that was introduced by Espinosa and colleagues [16], we consider two social theories: homophily theory and social identity theory.

Homophily theory has a long history stretching (in the West) back to Greek philosophers of antiquity [37]. The core of the idea is that people prefer people who are similar to themselves – "birds of a feather flock together" (e.g., [35]). Different causal mechanisms have been proposed, such as Byrne's attraction paradigm [9] and Turner's theory of self-categorization [49]. Applications of these core theories have led to predictions of collaboration based on similarity, including online collaborations. Chang et al. examined how work-related similarity and familiarity affected wiki-based collaborations [10], and Weinberg et al. studied similar phenomena in weblog usage [52]. For more examples, see the detailed review by McPherson et al. [37].

Social Identity Theory

A second, convergent explanation comes from social identity theory. This theory was proposed to explore the balance between individual characteristics and social context (or memberships) in influencing an individual's behavior [48]. Applications of the theory have been broad.

In this paper, we are concerned with how the theory can inform the likelihood to collaborate.

The concept of *ingroup favoritism* describes preferential treatment that an individual or a group may give to people perceived as similar to them – i.e., people who share common identity attributes [48]. In this paper, we consider the three dimensions as being reflections of shared (low-difference) or unshared (high-difference) attributes, specifically regarding location, organizational structure, and group or team membership. We soften the concept of favoritism a bit, to focus on how shared attributes may or may not increase the likelihood of providing support to a colleague's project.

The most common treatments of social identity theory have emphasized conflicts of identities. Lampinen and colleagues described issues of the co-presence of multiple social groups within the experience of one user in social networking environments [34]. They recommended better tools for managing (i.e., selectively separating) these different social identities. Ding et al. advocated the use of social context displays to help to manage membership in multiple groups [13].

In-group vs. out-group phenomena may be thought of as two aspects of the same underlying phenomenon – described in these cases by social identity theory. In-group favoritism is, as it were, the "positive", collaborative aspect of "negative," conflictual out-group bias. Bradner and Mark examined in-group favoritism within the context of social identity theory, finding an initial advantage for people who share geography; however, that advantage rapidly faded with increased familiarity [7]. Farnham and Churchill examined social identity as a determinant of sharing personal information online [17]. For a detailed review and theorizing about social identity and social capital, see Jiang and Carroll [27].

Faceted Homophily and/or Identity

To work with derived predictions of these theories, we need a vocabulary to consider the components of homophily or identity in organizations. From a more critical perspective, Farnham and Churchill explicitly questioned concepts of unitary identity, and documented the everyday practices through which people "facet" their identities for different social groups [17]. Similarly, in studies of homophily, several researchers have proposed a dimensionalized or multiplex [37] approach, conceiving of additive types of homophily such as "network ties" [51], "features" [12], or "dimensions" [37] of homophily (see also earlier studies of Blau [6] and Fischer [18]). Again within the context of homophily studies, Chang et al. combined theoretical vocabularies in their "social identity dimensions" of homophily [10].

Thus, both theory traditions have involved, in part, an analytic approach in which different influences of homophily or social identity have been identified, analyzed, and compared. For this paper, we adopt Farnham's and Churchill's concept of "facets" [17] and we apply the "team boundaries" concept of Espinosa et al. [16] (described above) in terms of a "geographical facet," a "structural (i.e., working-group) facet," and an "organizational facet" of employees' homophilous tendencies or social identities in organizations. For simplicity, we will refer to these as "identity facets" in this paper.

Examining Identity Facets in Crowdfunding

Internet Crowdfunding

We will use these concepts based on homophily theory and social identity theory, to predict collaborations in crowdfunding. Crowdfunding on the Internet has become a driving force for innovation. Among more than 200 crowdfunding sites [33], some sites have in excess of half a billion US dollars in play [29].

At sites like Kickstarter [29] and Indiegogo [26], the high-level sequence of activity is as follows (see [37] for a more detailed analysis):

- A *proposer* creates a description of a project for which s/he is requesting funding. The project description includes a "pitch" or assertion-of-value/likelihood-of-success, optional rewards (benefits) offered to investors, and (crucially) the target amount of funds and the timetable for receiving those funds.
- An *investor* may read the project description and decide to pledge money to the project.
- If the project receives the specified amount of funding from investors, within the specified amount of time, then the project is considered "successful" (in raising funds), and the investors' pledged money is committed to the project. The proposer is then responsible for managing and completing the project – including delivering the rewards to investors.

Researchers in economics and business have studied the crowdfunding phenomenon, attributing three main motivations for people to invest: return on investment, access to new resources or products, and/or charitable giving [19,33, 43], as well as recognition of the utility of the project [23]. Several researchers mention additional social aspects, such as enhanced self-esteem and public recognition [43], and informal collaborations among proposers []. However, there is general agreement that research into crowdfunding is in the very early stages [4,38]. It is not yet clear, for example, how important are factors such as shared location [1,38] or active social ties [38]. Some of these active research questions mirror the CSCW and CHI concerns about whether "distance matters" [42].

Enterprise Crowdfunding and iFundIT

Researchers have begun to explore crowdfunding as an *Intranet* phenomenon, conducted inside a company's firewall [39]. We adopted a similar strategy for a campaign

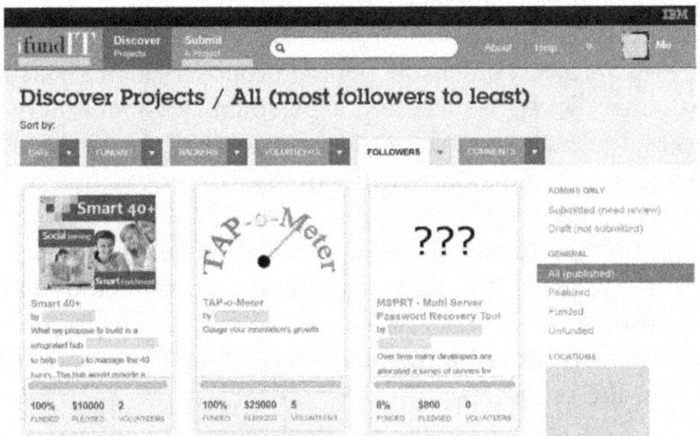

Figure 1. The page for browsing projects that had been submitted to iFundIT. Names and certain other details have been obscured for employee anonymity.

called iFundIT, which organized a crowdfunding trial for a 5500-person IT organization within IBM. The IT department in this company is strongly virtualized, with employees in more than 25 countries. Some employees work entirely from home, seeing co-workers on a face-to-face basis only once or twice a year.

As is true for all crowdfunding initiatives [4,19,22,25, 39,43], participation in iFundIT was voluntary and opt-in. Any member of the IT organization could propose a project at the iFundIT Intranet site (Figure 1). 302 members of the IT organization volunteered to act in the role of investor. Each investor received a personal budget of $US2000 to spend on other employees' proposals. The rules for managing this personal budget were as follows:

- The money could be spent only within iFundIT.
- Any unspent money would be forfeit at the conclusion of the trial.
- If an investor took on the dual role of proposing a project, s/he was prevented from pledging any funds to her/his own project.
- Unlike the Internet crowdfunding models, investments were limited to the target amount of funding. (The motivation for this restriction was to fund as many projects as possible.)

All employees of IBM had access to the iFundIT site. Possible actions included volunteering, commenting, sharing/recommending, liking, following, and viewing (see Table 1 for definitions). Two additional actions were restricted to members of the IT organization:

- Proposing a project – Could be done by any member of the IT organization.
- Investing in a project – Could be done only by members of the IT organization who had registered as investors.

The iFundIT site was run for a one-month period during early 2013, with a total budget of $US150,000. The campaign was closed when that budget was exhausted on successful projects.

Unlike the two published studies of organizational crowdfunding in co-located groups [39,44], nearly all promotional activities were conducted online. The IT organization publicized the entire trial vigorously through email campaigns. Some of the proposers sent email to potential investors, with mixed results: Some investors were interested, while other investors complained about "spam messages." See [19,21,33,39] for other reports on proposal-promotion in crowdfunding.

The relationship of the researchers to the IT organization was that of provider and client. We created the software to run iFundIT. Promotion of the iFundIT Intranet site and program was performed by project management staff within the IT organization. As researchers, we were free to request information from iFundIT participants. We made such requests, for the email surveys reported in this paper. However, members of the IT organization were free to decline our requests. Our data are therefore less complete than some industry studies that operate within Research departments, because many participants were spending their limited time on submitting their idea and the funding process.

Action	Definition	Events	Participants
Propose	Create project proposal and "publish" it for action(s) by others*	55	43
Invest	Pledge money to a project**	572	178
Volunteer	Offer to help on a project	70	58
Comment	Comment on a project	165	81
Share	Tell other people about a project	59	23
Like	Indicate preference for a project	251	193
Follow	Register to receive notifications about a project	684	262
View	Navigate to a description of a project	9616	521
Total		11472	521

Table 1. Number of events and of participants for each major type of action. * Proposing was limited to members of the IT organization. ** Investing was limited to members of the IT organization who had registered as investors. All other actions were available to any employee of IBM.

Research Hypotheses

We propose three research hypotheses that are directly derived from the preceding discussion of identity facets [17] and team boundaries [15]:

RH1: Collaborations (investments) will be associated with geographical similarities (proposer and supporter from the same country).

RH2: Collaborations (investments) will be associated with working-group similarities (proposer and supporter from the same group).

RH3: Collaborations (investments) will be associated with company-division similarities (proposer and support from the same company division).

Research has also shown the importance of prior social relationships (strong and weak ties) as the basis for collaborations, both in HCI in general [5,8,10,27,34,36,53] and also in Internet crowdfunding [1]. That is, people are more likely to help friends than strangers (see [37] for review). We therefore propose a fourth research hypothesis:

RH4: Collaborations (investments) will be associated with prior relationships among proposers and supporters.

METHOD

Participants

The primary participants were members of the larger, 5500-person IT organization. Participants worked in diverse job titles, from tester to vice president, in a total of 29 countries. Users spanned a range of hierarchical levels in the organization's hierarchy.

Datasets

Data for our analyses came from two major sources, and one supplementary source. Quantitative analyses are based on action logs recorded in the iFundIT server, and on social-network surveys sent to project proposers. Qualitative analyses are based on email surveys to iFundIT participants. Quantitative analyses were further clarified with data from the IBM's internal employee profile service, which provided information about each employee's country, division (formal organizational structure), and working group.

Action Logs

The iFundIT website recorded each user action on the site, including proposing, investing, volunteering, commenting, sharing, liking, following, and viewing. The log contained a total of 11,472 of these events that were performed by 572 employees.[1]

Social-Network Surveys to Proposers

A total of 43 employees proposed projects; most proposed only one project, but a few people proposed as many as five distinct projects. We created a personalized social-network survey for each proposer (and for each project, as needed), asking about the relationship of the proposer to each of her/his supporters (investors or volunteers). We asked proposers to indicate one or more relationship categories for each supporter. Of the 43 proposers, 28 provided complete responses to the survey (covering a total of 36 proposals). Our effective return rate was thus 65% of the proposers or 84% of the proposals.

Investor/Volunteer Surveys

We emailed brief questions to all of the users who had engaged in certain classes of actions. For this paper, we report on the email surveys that we sent to investors and volunteers (148 investors, 40 volunteers, and 30 employees who had both invested and volunteered).

In the email survey, we asked employees to describe their motivations to invest or volunteer, and their relationship to the project proposers. Responses were in free-form text. We received responses from 63 employees (36% response rate).

Profiles Service

We supplemented the above records with data from IBM's employee-profile service. This service allowed us to extract, for each employee:

- **Country**
- **Division**: Division was the formal, hierarchical organization structure in which the employee was recorded by IBM.
- **Group**: Group or team was the active, collaborative body in which the employee did much of her his work. Groups and teams were typically medium-to-large structures that spanned countries and divisions.
- **Reporting structure**: The hierarchical path or "org chart" that provided the official "chain of management" from the employee to the Chief Executive Officer (CEO) of IBM.

RESULTS

We begin by describing how we analyzed each of the datasets. We proceed with a high-level introduction to the patterns of investing, derived from the action logs. We then perform χ^2 analyses of several factors that could influence

[1] An additional 853 events were excluded from the analysis. These events took place "invisibly" from the perspective most employees – e.g., editing a proposal before it was "published" for view, noting that a proposal had achieved its target funding level, and various administrative tasks, such as approving a project for view by employees. We hope to report on the process of creating and editing proposals, and negotiating for their acceptance, in a future paper.

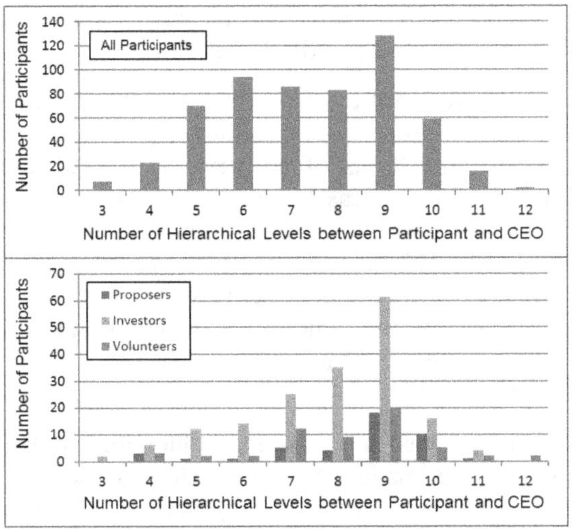

Figure 2. Frequency distribution of number of hierarchical steps (distance) between each participant and the head of the company. Top: All participants. Bottom: Principal participants (Proposers, Investors, and Volunteers).

those patterns (RH1, RH2, and RH3), and we supplement those statistical analyses with employees' statements from the email surveys.

Action Logs

As noted above, Table 1 contains information about the eight core actions in iFundIT, along with a count of the number of times each action occurred, and the number of employees who engaged in each action. Each employee could engage in multiple instances and multiple types of actions. Most actions were available to any employee in IBM. The exceptions were proposing and investing. Proposing was restricted to members of the IT organization. Investing was restricted to the 302 members of the IT organization who had registered as investors.

Social-Network Surveys to Proposers

We counted the number of types of relationships to supporters, as reported by proposers.

Email Surveys to Investors and Volunteers

We performed a limited grounded theory analysis [11] on the free-text responses to the email surveys from investors and volunteers, summarized in Table 2. For these limited purposes, a single analyst iteratively assigned open codes, axial codes, and some dimensional codes (note that, because of the amount of labor involved, coding by a single analyst is the norm in grounded theory method [11,40]). Four categories emerged initially – *interest* in the project, *value* of the project, *relationship* to the proposer, and *awareness* of other stakeholders.

A core aspect of grounded theory method is constant comparison of data with the emerging theory, and the evolution of both coding categories and theory as a result of these comparisons [11]. Over successive iterations of coding and theorizing, the simple *value* category became a dimension with its own subcategories, and the *awareness* category also became a dimension with sub-categories (Table 2). Because participants indicated a very nuanced view of who would be helped by each project, we combined earlier tentative sub-categories into a new top-level category of *beneficiary* as a combination of an organization-oriented sub-category of *value* and an advocacy-oriented sub-category of *awareness*.

Categories and subcategories
Value of the proposal. Why was this proposal interesting? Why was it worth funding? * **Indicators of probable success.** Why does the investor or volunteer have confidence in this project? **Personal value.** What is the direct personal benefit of the project to the investor/volunteer? **Neglected areas.** What is the promise of the proposal to solve long-standing problems that have not achieved a sufficient priority level for formal organizational funding?
* **Beneficiaries.** Who is likely to benefit from this proposal? * **Clients/customers** * **Teams** * **Company divisions** * **Entire company**
* **Relationship with proposer.** Did the investor/volunteer have a **personal or organizational relationship** with the proposer? (no subcategories)
* **Awareness of other stakeholders / interested parties.** Who else would be interested in the project? Why? How should s/he be **notified**? Is s/he a potential **supporter**? (no subcategories)

Table 2. Categories and subcategories from the grounded theory method analysis of email surveys. In this paper, we make selective use of categories marked with asterisks.

Table 2 provides a summary of the coding categories and subcategories. For this paper, we do not report a full grounded theory analysis. Rather, we use these categories in combination with the quantitative results, to address the Research Hypotheses developed above. This limited use of grounded theory method, for interpretation of qualitative data as part of a convergent analysis with other types of data, is an established approach in CSCW and HCI [40].

Patterns of Action across Organizational Levels

Who was performing the actions? The company directory supported a programmatic look-up of each employee's reporting relationships. For a standardized metric of comparison, we followed the example of [3], and calculated the number of hierarchical levels between each employee and the chief executive officer of IBM. The range was 3-12 hierarchical levels away from the CEO, with the majority of

Outcome	Countries	Working Groups	Divisions
Success	8.30	6.6	6.40
Failure	4.63	4.11	4.14
All	5.44	4.67	4.64

Table 3. Per-project results for mean number of countries, of working groups, and of divisions. All success-failure differences were significant at p<.001, using t-tests.

Facet	Number (%) Same	Number (%) Different
Country	202 (35%)	370 (65%)
Group	158 (28%)	414 (72%)
Division	227 (40%)	345 (60%)

Table 4.Counts and (percentages) of investors who pledged to proposers from the same and different facets (country, working group, or division).

participants between 5 and 9 levels from the CEO (see Figure 2, Top). Participation was well-spread across levels in the organizational hierarchy.

We also looked at the "principal" actions – the ones that directly impact the success of each project, namely proposing, investing, and volunteering (Figure 2, Bottom). There was a tendency for those principal actions to occur at lower levels in the organizational hierarchy, as contrasted with all actions. This pattern of results is similar to the "grassroots" concept in other employee innovation reports [3, 39]. However, this tendency could not be tested statistically, because of a lack of independence – i.e., each individual might engage in zero, one, two… or all of these actions.

Social Patterns of Investing

RH1, RH2, and RH3 address commonalities in the social relationships among proposers and their supporters (investors, volunteers, and so on), as predicted from homophily theory and social identity theory. From the log data, we used each project as a connection-point between proposers and supporters. In the next step, we removed the project from the representation, leaving simple person-to-person ties. We could then analyze in terms of persons, and in terms of the type of action that connected those persons (e.g., investment relationships as contrasted with volunteer relationships).

First, we note that investment support for each project was relatively wide-spread. In Table 3, we aggregate the identity facets of investors on a per-project basis. The mean number of countries per project was 5.44; the mean number of working groups per project was 4.67; and the mean number of organizational divisions per project was 4.64. These figures were higher for successful projects, in part because more people invested in those projects. Differences between successful vs. unsuccessful projects were highly significant for all three identity facets (country, working group, and organizational division).

Next, we examined whether projects were supported by investors from the same country as their proposer, or the same working group, or the same division. Table 4 summarizes these results, showing that investors supported project proposed by people with the same identity facets, and also with different identity facets.

For further insight, we turned to formal statistical analyses. For each pair of proposer-and-supporter, we coded the pair along the identity-facets of country, group, and division. Each coded attribute was binary – i.e., the proposer and supporter were from the *same* or *different* country, *same* or *different* group, and *same* or *different* division. Across these three binary dimensions, there were eight possible configurations (same-same-same, same-same-different, etc.). We conducted χ^2 analyses to assess the effects of the three identity facets.

First, we established the expected values for the analysis. To do this, we made pairs of each proposer with all investors (7654 pairs from 43 proposers *x* 178 investors). We performed the *same-different* analysis on each of the three identity facets, and used the percentages from this summary of all the data as the expected values. Our second step was to perform the *same-different* analysis on each pair of proposers with their actual investors (572 pairs). Our χ^2 analyses were based on a comparison of the expected-value percentages (from the 7654 pairs) vs. the obtained percentages (from the 572 actual pairs).

For all three identity facets, there were more actual proposer-investor pairs, than expected by chance (Country: $\chi^2(1)$= 190.45, p<.001; Group $\chi^2(1)$= 236.27, p<.001; Division: $\chi^2(1)$= 71.33, p<.001).[2] Figure 3A-C shows these effects graphically. Because the expected values were different, depending on the 7654 pairs, we plot the *percentage of expected value* for each bar in Figure 3. Bars that are greater than 100% show unexpectedly *high* counts investments among the 572 proposer-investor pairs. All of these bars are for the *same* pairs (same Country, same Group, or same Division, respectively).

All two-way interactions were also significant (Country*Group: $\chi^2(3)$= 424.13, p<.001; Country* Division: $\chi^2(3)$= 210.57, p<.001; Group*Division: $\chi^2(3)$= 236.27, p<.001).[3] As shown in Figure 3D-F, all of these

[2] The stated p values for all χ^2 analyses include a Bonferroni correction for repeated testing, because the same people were involved in multiple analyses.

[3] In a conventional χ^2 analysis, expected values are derived from the primary data table (for our analysis, that would be the 572 actual pairs of proposer-investor). The degrees of freedom for an interaction term would be 1. However, in our case, the test of the significance of the interaction term is based on the comparison of expected values from the 7654 pairs, vs. the observed values from the 572 pairs. For this reason, the degrees of freedom for testing each of the two-way interactions is 3, and the degrees of freedom for testing the threeway interaction is 7.

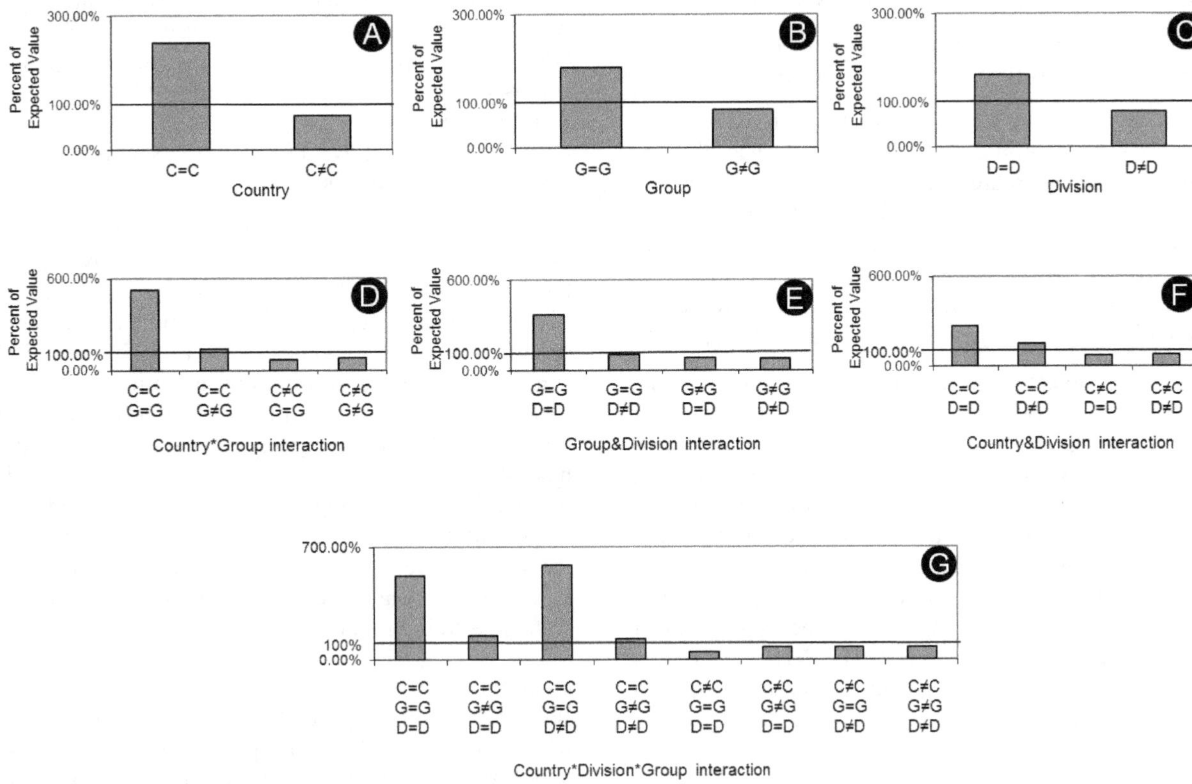

Figure 3. *Same-different* analyses by Country, Group, and Division. Each graph shows deviations from the expected value (100%). "C=C" is same country; "G=G" is same group; "D≠D" is different Division; and so on. A-C: Main effects. D-F: Two-way interactions. G: Three-way interactions. All results are significantly different from expected values at p<.001 or better.

interactions suggest a "super-additive" effect – i.e., having *two* attributes in common is significantly more powerful than the simple additive effects of one factor plus the other factor. The significant triple interaction ($\chi^2(7)$= 426.02, $p<.001$) shows a similar super-additive effect, but in this case the core of the phenomenon appears to involve Country and Group more than Division (Figure 3G).

The main effects support RH1 (Country), RH2 (Group), and RH3 (Division). In each case, having an attribute in common is associated with greater tendency for an investor to contribute to a proposer's project. The interactions confirm these core phenomena, and suggest that one attribute of similarity may potentiate the effects of another attribute of similarity.

Responses from the email surveys were partially supportive of RH2 (Group):

> *My decision was based on... value/usefulness to IBM... ex team-membership* (client services, Slovakia)

> *supporting my team was initially what dragged me in the process* (transformation specialist, Slovakia)

There was also evidence of intended support for the user's organization (RH3):

> *I finally decided to look at my work area / business unit, use the issues and gaps that I see in either directly in my work or in the area around me.* (IT architect, Germany)

However, we found no remarks specifically about locality in the email surveys, and thus there was an absence of qualitative support for RH1 (geography).

We now consider the last research hypothesis. The research literature on the importance of social ties, leads us to our hypothesis that people will be more likely to support proposers whom they know (RH4):

> *If I know the people in the project* (IT architect, Mexico)

One volunteer noted that s/he decided to participate based on the skills of the people involved, again reflecting knowledge of other participants:

> *I knew I could act as a contributing member* (consultant, US)

However, many investors reported that they did not have *personal* knowledge of the proposer:

> *I did not know anyone who had submitted a project* (operations director, US)

Not advertisement or friendship (manager, China)

I did not look at 'friends/team members' as criterion for investment decisions (project support, Nederland)

These qualitative results suggest a weakness in RH4 (prior relationships should promote collaborations). The absence of a direct personal relationship between proposer and investor was confirmed quantitatively in the social network survey that we sent to proposers. In describing their relationships to their supporters (investors and/or volunteers), proposers reported that 70% of their supporters were people they did not know at the time of investing or volunteering.

As noted above, investors were also able to access personal profiles of the proposers, through direct links from their names to the profiles server. (Unfortunately, these access events took place outside of the scope of our server, and we were therefore unable to record them.) In this way, an investor was only two clicks away from rich information about a proposer, which could tell the investor about they shared an identity facet such as country, division, and/or group with the proposer. It may be that the perception of one or more shared identity-facets (RH1, RH2, RH3) was sufficient to overcome any deficit due to an absence of a personal relationship (RH4).

DISCUSSION

We began with the problem of *distance* articulated by Olson and Olson [42], Kraut [31], and others [2,5,7,15,16, 28,30, 41,51]. We proposed to reframe that problem in terms of *difference*, as a reflection of homophily theory [9,35,37,49] and social identity theory [17,48], inspired by the use of social identity theory by Bradner and Mark [7]. In this reframing, we conceived of several types of difference, each of which corresponded to one identity facet [17] of a person's role or identity in a workplace: a geographical identity facet (RH1), a group or team identity facet (RH2), and an organizational identity facet based on an organization's hierarchical "org-chart" (RH3). Using data from an experiment in enterprise crowdfunding, we showed that each type of difference performed as predicted in RH1, RH2, and RH3 – i.e., each identity facet was associated with increased collaboration (investment) in the crowdfunding paradigm.

We also considered a fourth Research Hypothesis, based on theories of social ties, that pre-existing social relationships should be associated with increased collaboration. To our surprise, there was little support for this prediction (RH4).

The remainder of this section considers the implications of these findings for theory and for design.

Implications for Theory

The "distance matters" hypothesis (based on [30,42,45]) would have predicted the results that we found for RH1 (geography). However, that hypothesis would not predict any influence of working group (RH2) or organizational division (RH3). We found that all three research hypotheses were supported at $p<.001$ (Figure 3). Similarly, the "distance matters" hypothesis would not have predicted the super-additive interactions of Country*Group or Country*Division (Figure 3). In contrast with the distance-based explanation, we think there is a broader principle operating in our results.

According to both homophily theory and social identity theory, each shared identity facet should have strengthened the likelihood of collaboration (investment). The results in Figure 3 strongly support this prediction, as well as its more specific research hypotheses RH1, RH2, and RH3. We suggest that, in our results, consideration of *distance* as a contributing factor, should be reconsidered as one of multiple *differences* or *facets* in people's identities. The next steps in this research should examine mechanisms for these effects, including users' experiences and interpretations. Additional studies should explore when and how *distance* can be reduced to *difference*, and when *distance* is indeed the crucial determinant. This subsection considers some research directions.

Mechanisms

Jiang & Carroll proposed a model of social networking in which shared social identity gives rise to social ties, and in which both factors contribute to social capital [27]. In our case, we seem to have evidence of social capital (investments) without any antecedent social ties – at least for the 70% of investors who were unknown to their project proposers. It may be that social ties come after social capital (the act of investing).

However, it is also possible that investing takes place without any increase in reciprocated sociality. We will need to ask directly about how much investors have perceived about proposers, prior to investing. Would enhanced social awareness [13] be useful? We hope to clarify these relationship topics in future research.

Faceted Identities, Homophily, and Social Identity

In our analysis, we used three facets of workplace identity – country, working group, and organization (division), motivated in terms of homophily theory and social identity theory. Further work will be needed to find differentiating hypotheses and tests between these two theories.

A better understanding of these two theories may help us to discover additional personal attributes for studies of collaboration. We do not know whether these three identity facets are the most compelling social attributes for employees in the organization that we studied. Also, it is not clear whether these facets would be as compelling in other organizational cultures. The IT organization in IBM is highly distributed, and much of the work (and the managerial reporting) is both matrixed and virtualized. Would members of other entities, in other organizational cultures, experience their identities in the same ways?

More broadly, we do not yet know how "identity" and "identity facet" are experienced by the employees. For example, do employees perceive any aspect of shared identity facets as a generalized kind of "familiarity?" Or (in a different scenario) do employees strategize different types of shared identities? Prior work has focused (a) on boundaries and potential conflicts among facets of identity [17,34] and/or features of homophily [12,37,48], but also (b) on ways that commonalities can bring people together [7,27,37]. Crowdfunding tends to strengthen collaboration [19,39], so we hope to learn more about how homophily and shared identity can help people work together..

Comparing Sources of Identities

In this paper, we used a quasi-experimental design, analyzing the country, group, and division identity facets "as given" – i.e., as they occurred in the non-controlled voluntary participation of employees into our data sample. In this kind of setting, it is not meaningful to ask if group-identity is "more powerful" than geographical identity, because we have no apriori notion that we are comparing the same extent of diversity in each of those identity facets. It would be helpful to run more controlled studies (e.g., as in [41]), in which "measured" amounts of diversity in each identity facet could be formally compared.

Balancing Similarity and Diversity

The results in this paper have discussed identity in terms of the benefits of *similarity* i.e., people are more likely to collaborate if they have more identity-facets in common. However, other research has shown powerful benefits from combining diverse perspectives and knowledges into a single group or team to solve difficult problems [23,36] – theorized as heterophily [46]. How can we think about balancing these two necessary attributes that emerge when individuals join to collaborate?

Investors in Multiple Projects

The quantitative analyses in this paper were structured around individual projects. We examined links between a project proposer and all of her/his supporters. However, we also noted that 62% of the investors pledged money to two or more projects. These "poly-investors" may help to discover projects with conceptual overlap, or projects that can be combined into stronger configurations. Future studies should focus on how people choose multiple investments, and whether they consider each investment separately, or in some form of constructive or strategic combination.

Implications for Design

For Individuals: From Serendipity to Recommendation

Enterprise systems (including crowdfunding) are often embedded in a richer ecosystem of social media, including profile information about potential collaborators. For people to discover their commonalities, they may consult an online profile of a potential collaborator. How can we design richer profiles with information that encourages the discovery of commonalities among potential collaboration partners? How can we structure these profiles to support ego-centric search – e.g., finding people who have (a) needed expertise and also (b) *identity facets in common with the searcher?* Previous research suggests ways to increase the richness of an individual's online profile [14]. It might be useful to recommend collaboration partners, based on shared identity facets. We hope to move from serendipity to discovery to search to recommendation.

For Organizations: "Trending Commonalities?"

Subject to privacy protections, organizations want to know how their members are building connections and collaborations with one another. It may be worthwhile to perform privacy-preserving *aggregate* analyses to understand which forms of connection and shared identity show promise to support new collaborations.

For Internet Crowdfunding Sites

Our results show the importance of knowledge about other people on crowdfunding sites. Shared identity facets can help people to find collaborators – but only if they can discover those attributes in common. In our enterprise setting, employees could easily consult the internal profile service to explore one another's' attributes. We suggest that Internet crowdfunding sites explore profile capabilities, such as profiles that are internal to the crowdfunding site, but also links to existing social network services.

The ego-centric search capabilities (discussed in the preceding subsection) could be useful here, but there might be a need to search across multiple social network sites for relevant attributes. Recommendations would be similarly complex in an Internet setting, because of the need to aggregate data about individuals across social networking sites. Because people may not use the same ID at each Internet site, the crowdfunding site might need to ask proposers and investors to opt-in to an omnibus search/recommendation feature.

CONCLUSION AND CONTRIBUTION

In this paper, we followed the lead of [5,17] in applying homophily theory and social identity theory to CSCW – specifically to collaboration patterns in crowdfunding. Our work joins other CSCW/HCI reports in the "nascent" [4] study of crowdfunding [19,25,33,44]. As has happened with other major developments in social media, we hope to see HCI and CSCW research lead to major improvements for the broad public that is engaged in crowdfunding.

This paper makes several contributions. We join [7] in expanding our understanding of why "distance matters" through the analytic lens of homophily theory and social identity theory. We propose that distance may be reconsidered as one of several identity facets that can divide [7,17,34] but can also unite [10,12,52,53] people.

We show how shared identity facets are associated with increased collaboration (investments), even in the absence of prior social relationships. We also join others [7,17] in showing that faceted identities are important in CSCW and HCI – not only in the domain of social networking, but also in the performance of consequential work in organizations. Finally, we have proposed areas for further development of theory and method, and we have suggested how our research could lead to new features and technologies to enhance the experience and effectiveness of crowdfunding.

ACKNOWLEDGMENTS

We thank Kate Ehrlich and Elizabeth Gerber for insightful discussions on results and plans.

REFERENCES[4]

1. Agrawal, A., Catalini, C., & Goldfarb, A. (2011). The geography of crowdfunding. Agrawal, A.; Catalini, C.; and Goldfarb, A. 2011. The geography of crowdfunding. NBER Working Paper #16820, http://www.nber.org/ papers/ w16820
2. Allen, T.J. (1977). *Managing the flow of technology*. Cambridge, MA, USA: MIT Press.
3. Bailey, B.P., & Horvitz, E. (2010). What's *your* idea? A case study of a grassroots innovation pipeline within a large software company. *Proc. CHI 2010*, 2065-2074.
4. Belleflamme, P., Lambert, T., & Schwienbecker, A. (2012). Crowdfunding: Tapping the right crowd. Tech. Rep. 1578175, Social Science Research Network, http:// papers.ssrn.com/sol3/papers.cfm?abstract_id=1578175.
5. Birnholtz, J., Dixon, G., & Hancock, J. (2012). Distance, ambiguity and appropriation: Structures affording impression management in a collocated organization. *Comp. Hum. Beh. 28*, 3, 1028-1035.
6. Blau, P. M. (1984). *Crosscutting social circles: Testing a macro-structural theory of intergroup relations*. Orlando, FL, USA: Academic Press.
7. Bradner, E., & Mark, G. (2002). Why distance matters: Effects on cooperation, persuasion, and deception. *Proc. CSCW 2002*, 226-235.
8. Brzozowski, M. (2009). Watercooler: Exploring an organization through enterprise social media. *Proc. GROUP 2009*, 219-228.
9. Byrne, D. E. (1971). *The attraction paradigm*. New York, NY, USA: Academic Press.
10. Chang, K., Chang, A., & Sha, X. (2009). Work role similarity and familiarity between members: A tripartite view of social identity towards knowledge construction. *Proc. PACIS 2009*.
11. Charmaz, K. (2006). *Constructing grounded theory: A practical guide through qualitative analysis*. Thousand Oaks, CA, USA: Sage.
12. Chin, A., Xu, B., & Wang, H. (2013). Who should I add as a "friend"? A study of friend recommendations using proximity and homophily. *Proc. MSM 2013*.
13. Ding, X., Erickson, T., Kellogg, W.A, & Patterson, D.J. (2012). Informing and performing: Investigating how mediated sociality becomes visible. *Pers. Ubiq. Comp. 16*, 1095-1117.
14. Dugan, C., Geyer, W., Muller, M., DiMicco, J., Brownholtz, B., & Millen, D.R. (2008). It's all 'about you': Diversity in online profiles. *Proc. CSCW 2008*, 703-706.
15. Espinosa, J.A., Cummings, J.N., & Pickering, C. (2012). Time separation, coordination, and performance in technical teams. *IEEE Trans. Eng. Mgmt. 59*, 1, 91-103.
16. Espinosa, J.A., Cummings, J.N., Wilson, J.M., & Pearce, B.M. (2003). Team boundary issues across multiple global firms. *J. Mgmt. Info. Sys.19*, 4, 157-190.
17. Farnham, S.D., & Churchill, E.F. (2011). Faceted identity, faceted lives: Social and technical issues with being yourself online. *Proc. CSCW 2011*, 359-368.
18. Fischer, C. S. (1982). *To dwell among friends*. Chicago: Chicago, IL, USA: University of Chicago Press.
19. Gerber, E.M., Hui, J.S., & Kuo, P.-Y. (2014 in press). Crowdfunding: Why people are motivated to post and fund projects on crowdfunding platforms. To appear in *Proc. CSCW 2014*.
20. Gittelman, M. (2007). Does geography matter for science-based firms? Epistemic communities and the geography of research and patenting in biotechnology. *Org. Sci. 18*, 4, 724-741.
21. Greenberg, M.D., Hui, J., & Gerber, E.M. (2013). Crowdfunding: A resource exchange perspective. *CHI 2013 EA*, 883-888.
22. Harms, M. (2007). *What drives motivation to participate financially in a crowdfunding community?* Master's thesis, Vrije Universiteit Amsterdam.
23. Heckathorn, D.D. (1993). Collective action and group heterogeneity: Voluntary provision versus selective incentives. *Am. Soc. Rev. 58*, 329-350.
24. Hogg, M.A.; Turner, J.C. (1987). Intergroup behaviour, self-stereotyping and the salience of social categories. *B. J. Soc. Psych. 26,* 325–340.
25. Hui, J.S., Greenberg, M.B., & Gerber, E.M (2014 in press). Understanding the role of community in crowdfunding work. To appear in *Proc. CSCW 2014*.
26. Indiegogo (n.d.). http://www.indiegogo.com.
27. Jiang, H., & Carroll, J.M. (2009). Social capital, social network and identity bonds: A reconceptualization. *Proc. C&T 2009*, 51-60.

[4] All URLs were verified on 25 July 2013.

28. Jovanović, M.N. (2003). Local vs. global location of firms and industries. *J. Econ. Integ. 18*, 1, 60-104.

29. Kickstarter (n.d.). http://www.kickstarter.com/help/stats

30. Kiesler, S., & Cummings, J. N. (2002). What do we know about proximity in work groups? A legacy of research on physical distance. In P. Hinds & S. Kiesler (eds.) *Distributed Work*. Cambridge, MA, USA: MIT Press, 57-80.

31. Kraut, R.E., Egido, C., & Galegher, J. (1990). Patterns of contact and communication in scientific research. In J. Galegher, R.E. Kraut, & C. Egido (eds.), *Intellectual teamwork: Social and technological foundations of cooperative work*. Hillsdale, NJ, USA: Earlbaum, 149-171.

32. Kraut, R.E., Fussel, S.R., Brennan, S.E., & Siegel, J. (2002). Understanding effects of proximity on collaboration: Implications for technologies to support remote collaborative work. In P. Hinds and S. Kiesler, (eds), *Distributed Work*, pages 137–162. Cambridge, MA, USA: MIT Press.

33. Kuo, P.-Y., & Gerber, L. (2012). Design principles: Crowd-funding as a creativity support tool. *CHI 2012 EA*, 1601-1606.

34. Lampinen, A., Tamminen, S., & Oulasvirta, A. (2009). "All my people right here, right now": Management of group co-presence on a social networking site. *Proc. GROUP 2009*, 281-290.

35. Lazarsfeld, P.F., & Merton, R.K. (1954). Friendship as a social process: A substantive and methodological analysis. In M. Berger (ed.), *Freedom and control in modern society*. New York, NY, USA: Van Nostrand.

36. Ludford, P., Cosley, D., Frankowski, D., & Terveen, L. (2004). Think different: Increasing online community participation using uniqueness and group dissimilarity. *Proc. CHI 2004*, 631-638.

37. McPherson, M., Smith-Lovin, L., & Cook, J. M. (2001). Birds of a feather: Homophily in social networks. *Ann. Rev. Soc. 27*, 415-444.

38. Mollich, E. (2013). The dynamics of crowdfunding: Determinants of success and failure. http://papers.ssrn.com/sol3/papers.cfm?abstract_id=2088298.

39. Muller, M., Geyer, W., Soule, T., Daniels, S., Cheng, L.-T. (2013). Crowdfunding inside the enterprise: Employee-initiatives for innovation and collaboration. *Proc. CHI 2013*, 503-512.

40. Muller, M., & Kogan, S. (2012). Grounded theory method in HCI and CSCW. In J. Jacko (ed.), *Human-Computer Interaction Handbook*, Minneapolis MN: CRC Press.

41. O'Leary, M. B., & Mortensen, M. (2009). "Go (con) figure: Subgroups, imbalance, and isolates in geographically dispersed teams." *Org. Sci. 21*. 1, 115-131.

42. Olson, G.M., & Olson, J.S. (2000). Distance matters. *Human-Computer Interaction 15*, 139-178.

43. Ordanini, A., Miceli, L., Pizzetti, M., & Parasuraman, A. (2011). Crowdfunding: Transforming customers into investors through innovative service platforms. *J. Serv. Mgnt. 22*(4), 443-470.

44. Sakamoto, M., Nakajima, T., Liu, Y., & Alexandrova, T. (2013). Achieving sustainable society through micro-level crowdfunding. *CHI 2013 EA*, 1443-1448.

45. Scellato, S., Mascolo, C., Musolesi, M., & Latora, V. (2010). Distance matters: Geo-social metrics for online social networks. *Proc. WOSN 2010*, 8.

46. Simmel, G. 1950. *The sociology of Georg Simmel.* Glencoe, IL, USA: Free Press.

47. Smite, D., & Wohlin, C. (2011). A whisper of evidence in global software engineering. *J. IEEE SW 28*, 4, 15-18.

48. Tajfel, H., & Turner, J. C. (1979). An integrative theory of intergroup conflict. In W. G. Austin & S. Worchel (Eds.), *The social psychology of intergroup relations* (pp. 33–47). Monterey, CA: Brooks/Cole

49. Turner, J. C. (1987). *Rediscovering the social group: A self-categorization theory*. Oxford, UK: Basil Blackwell.

50. Turner, J. C. & Reynolds, K. J. (2010). The story of social identity. In T. Postmes & N. Branscombe (eds). *Rediscovering Social Identity: Core Sources*. London, UK: Psychology Press..

51. Wallis, J.C., & Buyuktur, A. (2010). Information challenges in collaboration science. *Proc ASIS&T 2010*.

52. Weinberg, C., Roemmele, M., & Gordon, A.S. (2013). Content-based similarity measures of weblog authors. *Proc. WebSci 2013*.

53. Yuan, Y.C., & Gay, G. (2006). Homophily of network ties and bonding and bridging social capital in computer-mediated distributed teams. *JCMC 11*(4), article 9. http://jcmc.indiana.edu/vol11/issue4/yuan.html

54. Zipf, G.K. (1949). *Human behavior and the principal of least effort*. Menlo Park, CA, USA: Addison-Wesley.

Author Index

Abowd, Gregory D. 84
Agosto, Denise E. 28
Ahmed, Osman Hassan 1491
Aizenbud-Reshef, Netta 756
Ames, Morgan G. 319
Anderson, Kenneth M. 866
André, Paul 967, 989
Aschoff, Felix-Robinson 171
Assogba, Yannick 379
Agustina 519
Backstrom, Lars 831
Badenes, Hernan 900
Bailey, Brian P. 1433
Bayyapunedi, Mydhili 1167
Beck, Stephan 1388
Bederson, Benjamin B. 1456
Bender, Jackie L. 1491
Benford, Steve 1049
Bennett, Peter D. 1366
Bernstein, Michael S. 745, 1211
Bertot, John C. 1308
Bharadwaj, Ankitha 888
Bhattacharya, Parantapa 197
Birk, Max 1333
Birnholtz, Jeremy 449
Bjørn, Pernille 1107
Blair, Lynne 1060
Boden, Alexander 710, 1120
Bonnar, Caitlin 1188
Borning, Alan 1188
Bossen, Claus 257
Bove, Michael R. 999
boyd, danah 1502
Brown, Chloë 1072
Brown, Michelle 1344
Bruckman, Amy 1023
Capra, Licia 934
Carroll, John M. 1144, 1258
Castillo, Carlos 211
Cataldo, Marcelo 733
Chamberlain, Alan 687
Chang, Shuo 674
Cheliotis, Giorgos 1011
Chen, Jilin 405
Chen, Lu 415
Cheng, Justin 745, 1211
Chrysanthi, Angeliki 1366
Clawson, James 1467
Cobb, Camille 888
Coetzee, Derrick 1176
Comis, Jared 888
Cosley, Dan 1549
Counts, Scott 625
Coyle, David 1222
Crabtree, Andy 687
Cramer, Henriette 945
Crist, Emily Anne 1479
Cross, Andrew 1167
Crowston, Kevin 109
Culotta, Aron 1523
Cutrell, Edward 1167
Czerwinski, Mary 1082
Dabbish, Laura A. 146, 922
Davies, Nigel 1060
De Choudhury, Munmun ...368, 625
Del Valle, Sara Y. 1523
Desjardins, Audrey 877
Devanbu, Prem 342
Dickard, Michael 28
Dillahunt, Tawanna R. 1246
Ding, Xianghua 530
Diriye, Abdigani 999
Do, Brian 888
Dougal, Michael C. 1297
Douglas, Sara 1409, 1422
Dow, Steven P. 989, 1445
Dugan, Casey 379
Duysburgh, Pieter 1537
Earl, Graeme 1366
Efstratiou, Christos 1072
Ehrlich, Kate 733
El-Haddad, Mohammed 211
Ellison, Nicole B. 3
Elprama, Shirley A. 1537
Faucett, Heather 1422
Ferguson, Robert Douglas 1479
Ferrar, Jonathan 379
Fiesler, Casey 1023
Filkov, Vladimir 342
Fiore, Andrew T. 3, 722
Fitzpatrick, Geraldine 911
Flanagan, Mary 1
Fleischmann, Kenneth R. 426
Forte, Andrea 28, 475
Fox, Armando 1176
Fraser, Mike 1366
Froehlich, Bernd 1388
Fu, Wai-Tat 184
Fussell, Susan R. 1549
Ganglbauer, Eva 911
Ganguly, Niloy 197
Gao, Ge 1549
García-Gavilanes, Ruth 1511
Garimella, Venkata RK 1297
Gazan, Rich 1033
Gerber, Elizabeth M. 62, 1043
Gergle, Darren 16
Geyer, Werner 379, 778
Ghosh, Saptarshi 197
Gilbert, Eric 49, 674, 1043, 1400
Gilbert, Michael 550
Gill, Brian 1188
Gillespie, Tarleton 588
Graham, Nicholas 1344
Gray, Rebecca 3
Greenberg, Michael D. 62
Greenberg, Saul 877
Greenhalgh, Chris 1049
Grevet, Catherine 1400
Groth Jensen, Lotte 257
Grudin, Jonathan 368
Gu, Ning 530
Güldenpfennig, Florian 911
Gummadi, Krishna P. 197
Gupta, Neha 224
Gutwin, Carl 1333, 1344, 1377
Guy, Ido 379, 393, 756
Håkansson, Maria 487
Han, Kyungsik 1144
Han, Shuguang 820
Hancock, Jeff 449
Hannon, James 1060
Hanrahan, Benjamin V. 224
Hansen, Derek L. 1308
Harding, Mike 1060
Harper, Richard 854, 1131
Hartmann, Björn 1176
Hasler, Béatrice S. 564
Hassman, Katie DeVries 109
He, Daqing 820
He, Yilin 1356
Hearst, Marti A. 1176
Hecht, Brent 16
Heinrich, Peter 171
Hemphill, Libby 1200
Hirose, Michitaka 75
Hoff, Aaron 625
Homan, Christopher M. 615
Horvitz, Eric J. 625
Hsieh, Gary 405
Hu, Nan 1011
Huang, Ai-Ju 436
Huang, Jianhui 1011

Huang, Shih-Wen 1433
Huang, Yun 979
Hui, Julie S. 62
Hupfeld, Annika 639
Hurst, Amy 652
Hwang, Chanyou 1283
Hwang, Inseok 1283
Inkpen, Kori 662
Iqbal, Shamsi 1082
Izadi; Shahram 1366
Jackson, Corey Brian 109
Jackson, Steven J. 134, 588
Jacobs, An 1537
Jacobs, Maia 1467
Jacovi, Michal 393, 756
Jaeger, Paul T. 1308
Jia, Yuan 767
Johns, Paul 1082
Johri, Aditya 332, 697
Jones, Rachel 120
Kamar, Ece 248
Kane, Aimée 797
Kane, Shaun K. 652
Kang, Ruogu 797
Kaye, Joseph 'Jofish' 487
Kelly, Ryan 807
Kervin, Karina 542
Kiesler, Sara 797
Kilic, Mehmet 171
Kim, Jinyoung 461
Kim, John 1283
Kim, Joy 745
Kinney, Bo 1188
Kittur, Aniket 355, 967, 989, 999, 1445
Kleinberg, Jon 831
Knibbe, Jarrod 1366
Knowles, Bran 1060
Koepfler, Jes A. 426, 1308
Kraut, Robert E. 146
Kraut, Robert E. 355, 722, 1445, 967, 1356
Kremer-Davidson, Shiri 393, 756
Kriplean, Travis 1188
Kulik, Alexander 1388
Kulshrestha, Juhi 197
Kumar, Vikas 674
Kunert, André 1388
Lampe, Cliff 3
Lampinen, Airi 499
Lasecki, Walter S. 248
Lee, Joon-Suk 1561
Lee, Youngki 1283
Leontiadis, Ilias 1072
Leshed, Gilly 487
Li, Guo 530
Li, Mo 505
Liao, Q. Vera 184
Lindqvist, Janne 236
Lingel, Jessa 295, 1502
Litt, Eden 449
Liu, Jingjing 710
Liu, Yikun 767
Livingston, Ian J. 1333
Lu, Naiji 615
Lu, Tun 530
Lupushor, Stela 379
Lutters, Wayne 0
Lytle, Megan C. 615
Magee, Rachel 28
Mahmud, Jalal U. 405
Mandryk, Regan L. 1333
Mankoff, Jennifer 1246
Mark, Gloria 393, 1082
Markopoulos, Panos 84
Marlow, Jennifer 922
Marshall, Mark T. 1366
Martin, David 224
Maruyama, Misa 1409, 1422
Mascolo, Cecilia 1072
Mashhadi, Afra 934
Masli, Mikhil 956
Mason, Winter 236
Massimi, Michael 854, 1131, 1479,1491
Massung, Elaine 1222
Matthews, Tara 900
Matthiesen, Stina 1107
Mazmanian, Melissa 283
McCarthy, Ted 888
McDonald, David W. 550
Meier, Patrick 1573
Mejova, Yelena 1297, 1511
Milic-Frayling, Natasa 120
Miller, Lisa J. 1033
Miller, Robert C. 1043
Min, Chulhong 1283
Mitra, Tanushree 49
Moffatt, Karyn 1479
Mondal, Mainack 197
Morgan, Jonathan T. 550
Morris, Jessica 1131
Morris, Meredith Ringel 16, 662, 1272
Mugar, Gabriel 109
Muller, Michael 778
Müller, Jörg 1323
Munson, Sean A. 542
Murphy, Alison R. 269
Murphy-Hill, Emerson 1095
Mutlu, Bilge 97
Mynatt, Elizabeth D. 1467
Naaman, Mor 236, 1502
Nakazato, Naoto 75
Narumi, Takuji 75
Neustaedter, Carman 877, 1156
Nichols, Jeffrey 405
Oeldorf-Hirsch, Anne 16
O'Hara, Kenton P. 1366, 1131
O'Hare, Neil 945
Oleksik, Gerard 120
O'Neill, Jacki 224
Østerlund, Carsten 109
Ozturk, Pinar 236
Palen, Leysia 866
Pan, Wei 767
Panc, Laura 379
Payette, Sandy 588
Payne, Stephen J. 807
Perkins, Annuska 888
Peters, Andrew M. 999
Petersen, Lise Møller 1107
Pfaff, Mark 767
Pfeffer, Jürgen 211
Pine, Kathleen 283
Porat, Sara 756
Preist, Chris 1222
Priedhorsky, Reid 1523
Procyk, Jason 1156
Quattrone, Giovanni 934
Quercia, Daniele ... 945, 1072, 1511
Quinn, Alexander J. 1456
Quiñones, Pablo-Alejandro 305
Randall, David William 710
Rasmussen, Jamie 379
Ratan, Rabindra 564
Ratchford, Tristan 379
Ravindran, Dilip 1167
Reddy, Madhu C. 269
Reeves, Stuart 1049
Regan, Tim 295
Reynolds, Lindsay 449
Ribes, David 158, 574
Riedl, John 1356
Roback, Andrew 1200
Robert, Lionel P. 542

Robertson, Scott P. 1409, 1422
Rodden, Tom 639, 1049
Rooksby, John 603
Rosner, Daniela K. 319
Rosson, Mary Beth 1144, 1258
Rosswog, Frank 1120
Rouncefield, Mark 1060
Rubens, Simon 1131
Said, Karim 652
Sakurai, Sho 75
Sauppé, Allison 97
Savery, Cheryl 1344
Schwabe, Gerhard 171
Sellen, Abigail 854
Semaan, Bryan 1409, 1422
Serebrenik, Alexander 342
Shami, N. Sadat 379
Shao, Bin 530
Sheppard, S. Andrew 1234
Sheth, Amit P. 415
Shih, Patrick C. 1144
Shilton, Katie 426
Shores, Kenneth 1356
Silenzio, Vincent M. B. 615
Smith, Barton A. 900
Smith, Madeline E. 449
Solomon, Jacob 38
Song, Junehwa 1283
Soule, Todd 379, 778
Spottswood, Erin 449
Srinivasan, Janaki 697
Starbird, Kate 888
Steier, Tal 379
Steinfeld, Aaron 979
Steinhardt, Stephanie B. 134
Stempeck, Matt 211
Stevens, Gunnar 1120
Still, Susanne 1033
Subasi, Özge 911
Sun, Chengzheng 505, 519
Swanenburg, Kristina L. 1356
Tanikawa, Tomohiro 75
Tatar, Deborah 1561
Tausczik, Yla R. 146, 355
Teevan, Jaime 16, 248
Teo, Hon Jie 332
Teodoro, Rannie 236
Terveen, Loren 674, 956, 1234, 1400
Thies, William 1167
Thirunarayan, Krishnaprasad 415
Tolmie, Peter 1049
Tomasic, Anthony 979
Tu, Xin 615
Valkanova, Nina 1323
Vande Moere, Andrew 1323
Vasilescu, Bogdan 342
Venolia, Gina 662
Viselli, Tracy 1308
Vitak, Jessica 461, 842
Wafer, John 778
Wakkary, Ron 877
Walden, John 1060
Walter, Robert 1323
Wang, Hao-Chuan 436
Wang, Wenbo 415
Wash, Rick 38
Weber, Ingmar 1297
White, Joanne I. 866
Whittaker, Steve 900
Wiggins, Andrea 1234
Willever-Farr, Heather 475
Williams, Michele A. 652
Wisniewski, Pamela 1258
Witschey, Jim 1095
Witteman, Holly O. 1491
Wong, Nelson 1377
Wulf, Volker 710, 1120
Xia, Huanhuan 530
Xiao, Shundan 1095
Xu, Anbang 1433
Xu, Bin 1549
Xu, Heng 269, 1258
Xu, Yi 505, 519
Yang, Jiang 379
Yarosh, Svetlana 84
Yew, Jude 1011
Yim, Dongsun 1283
Yoo, Chungkuk 1283
Yoshida, Shigeo 75
Yu, Lixiu 967
Yuan, Chien Wen 436
Yue, Zhen 820
Zachry, Mark 550
Zafar, Muhammad Bilal 197
Zhang, Haoqi 1043
Zhang, Hui 368
Zhu, Haiyi 1445
Zimmerman, John 979

www.ingramcontent.com/pod-product-compliance
Lightning Source LLC
LaVergne TN
LVHW080102011026
849160LV00013B/1019